ISBN 978-0-260-02215-8
PIBN 10922849

FB &c Ltd, Dalton House, 60 Windsor Avenue, London, SW19 2RR.
Company number 08720141. Registered in England and Wales.

For support please visit www.forgottenbooks.com

Economics and Statistics Administration
Lee Price, Acting Under Secretary for Economic Affairs

BUREAU OF THE CENSUS
Martha Farnsworth Riche, Director
Bradford R. Huther, Deputy Director
Nancy A. Potok, Principal Associate Director and Chief Financial Officer
Michael S. McKay, Acting Associate Director for Administration/Controller

ADMINISTRATIVE AND CUSTOMER SERVICES DIVISION
Walter C. Odom, Chief

Acknowledgments

Lars B. Johanson was responsible for the technical supervision and coordination of this volume under the general direction of **Glenn W. King,** Chief, Statistical Compendia Branch. Assisting in the research and analytical phases of assigned sections and in the developmental aspects of new tables were **Rosemary E. Clark, Edward C. Jegers,** and **David J. Fleck. Geraldine W. Blackburn** provided primary editorial assistance. Other editorial assistance was rendered by **Catherine Cruaan, Patricia S. Lancaster, Catherine Lavender,** and **Joyce Mori.**

The staff of the Administrative and Customer Services Division, under the general supervision of **Walter C. Odom,** Chief, and direct supervision of **Michael G. Garland,** Assistant Chief, performed publication planning, editorial review, design, composition, and printing planning and procurement. **Patricia Helston,** assisted by **Gloria Davis,** provided publication coordination and editing. **Janet Sweeney** provided design and graphics services, and **Arlene Duckett** provided printing services.

The cooperation of many contributors to this volume is gratefully acknowledged. The source note below each table credits the various government and private agencies which have collaborated in furnishing information for the *Statistical Abstract.* In a few instances, contributors have requested that their data be designated as subject to copyright restrictions, as indicated in the source notes to the tables affected. Permission to use copyright material should be obtained directly from the copyright owner.

Library of Congress Card No. 4-18089

SUGGESTED CITATION

U.S. Bureau of the Census, *Statistical Abstract of the United States: 1997* (117th edition.) Washington, DC, 1997

For sale by the U.S. Government Printing Office
Superintendent of Documents, Mail Stop: SSOP, Washington, DC 20402-9328
ISBN 0-16-049280-7

Preface

The *Statistical Abstract of the United States,* published since 1878, is the standard summary of statistics on the social, political, and economic organization of the United States. It is designed to serve as a convenient volume for statistical reference and as a guide to other statistical publications and sources. The latter function is served by the introductory text to each section, the source note appearing below each table, and Appendix I, which comprises the Guide to Sources of Statistics, the Guide to State Statistical Abstracts, and the Guide to Foreign Statistical Abstracts.

This volume includes a selection of data from many statistical publications, both government and private. Publications cited as sources usually contain additional statistical detail and more comprehensive discussions of definitions and concepts than can be presented here. Data not available in publications issued by the contributing agency but obtained from unpublished records are identified in the source notes as "unpublished data." More information on the subjects covered in the tables so noted may generally be obtained from the source.

Except as indicated, figures are for the United States as presently constituted. Although emphasis in the *Statistical Abstract* is primarily given to national data, many tables present data for regions and individual States and a smaller number for metropolitan areas and cities. Appendix II, Metropolitan Area Concepts and Components, presents explanatory text, a complete current listing and population data for metropolitan statistical areas (MSA's), the primary metropolitan statistical areas (PMSA's), and the consolidated metropolitan statistical areas (CMSA's) defined as of July 1, 1996. Table 43 in section 1 presents selected population characteristics for MSA's with population of 250,000 or more. Statistics for the Commonwealth of Puerto Rico and for outlying areas of the United States are included in many State tables and are supplemented by information in section 29. Additional information for States, cities, counties, metropolitan areas, and other small units, as well as more historical data, are available in various supplements to the *Abstract* (see inside back cover).

Changes in this edition—We are continuing to increase the number of source citations which provide Internet addresses, either as the sole citation or a supplement to a printed or electronic product. In addition, our Telephone Contact Guide now provides Internet addresses where appropriate, as does our Guide to State Statistical Abstracts.

This year we have introduced 97 new tables covering a wide range of subject matter. They cover such topics as ambulatory surgery, mammography, overweight persons, schools with Internet access, college remedial coursework, hate crimes, weather disasters, pet ownership, employer tenure, work disabilities, workplace drug testing, family net worth, family debt payments, minority-owned businesses, traffic fatalities, supply and use of various foods, coal production and reserves, housing indicators, and international statistics for continuing education and tourism receipts. See Appendix V, pp. 968 for a complete list of new tables.

Statistics in this edition are generally for the most recent year or period available by spring 1997. Each year almost 1,500 tables and charts are reviewed and evaluated; new tables and charts of current interest are added, continuing series are updated, and less timely data are condensed or eliminated. Text notes and appendices are revised as appropriate.

USA Statistics in Brief, a pocket-size pamphlet highlighting many statistical series in the *Abstract,* is available separately. Single copies can be obtained free from U.S. Bureau of the Census, Customer Services, Washington, DC 20233 (telephone 301-457-4100).

Statistics for States and metropolitan areas—Data for States and metro areas may also be found in the *State and Metropolitan Area Data Book, 1991* and its forthcoming 1997-98 edition.

Statistical reliability and responsibility—The contents of this volume were taken from many sources. All data from either censuses and surveys or from administrative records are subject to error arising from a number of factors: Sampling variability (for statistics based on samples), reporting errors in the data for individual units, incomplete coverage, nonresponse, imputations, and processing error. (See also Appendix III, pp. 948-964.) The Bureau of the Census cannot accept the responsibility for the accuracy or limitations of the data presented here, other than those for which it collects. The responsibility for selection of the material and for proper presentation, however, rests with the Bureau.

For additional information on data presented—Please consult the source publications available in local libraries or write to the agency indicated in the source notes. Write to the Bureau of the Census only if it is cited as the source.

Suggestions and comments—Users of the *Statistical Abstract* and its supplements (see inside back cover) are urged to make their data needs known for consideration in planning future editions. Suggestions and comments for improving coverage and presentation of data should be sent to the Director, U.S. Bureau of the Census, Washington, DC 20233.

Contents

[Numbers following subjects are page numbers]

APPROXIMATE CONVERSION MEASURES

[For assistance on metric usage, call or write the Office of Metric Programs, U.S. Department of Commerce, Washington, DC 20230 (301-975-3690) Internet site <http://www.nist.gov/metric>]

Symbol	When you know conventional	Multiply by	To find metric	Symbol
in	inch	2.54	centimeter	cm
ft	foot	30.48	centimeter	cm
yd	yard	0.91	meter	m
mi	mile	1.61	kilometer	km
in^2	square inch	6.45	square centimeter	cm^2
ft^2	square foot	0.09	square meter	m^2
yd^2	square yard	0.84	square meter	m^2
mi^2	square mile	2.59	square kilometer	km^2
	acre	0.41	hectare	ha
oz	ounce [1]	28.35	gram	g
lb	pound [1]	.45	kilograms	kg
oz (troy)	ounce [2]	31.10	gram	g
	short ton (2,000 lbs)	0.91	metric ton	t
	long ton (2,240 lbs)	1.02	metric ton	t
fl oz	fluid ounce	29.57	milliliter	mL
c	cup	0.24	liter	L
pt	pint	0.47	liter	L
qt	quart	0.95	liter	L
gal	gallon	3.78	liter	L
ft^3	cubic foot	0.03	cubic meter	m^3
yd^3	cubic yard	0.76	cubic meter	m^3
F	degrees Fahrenheit (subtract 32)	0.55	degrees Celsius	C

Symbol	When you know metric	Multiply by	To find conventional	Symbol
cm	centimeter	0.39	inch	in
cm	centimeter	0.33	foot	ft
m	meter	1.09	yard	yd
km	kilometer	0.62	mile	mi
cm^2	square centimeter	0.15	square inch	in^2
m^2	square meter	10.76	square foot	ft^2
m^2	square meter	1.20	square yard	yd^2
km^2	square kilometer	0.39	square mile	mi^2
ha	hectare	2.47	acre	
g	gram	.035	ounce [1]	oz
kg	kilogram	2.21	pounds [1]	lb
g	gram	.032	ounce [2]	oz (troy)
t	metric ton	1.10	short ton (2,000 lbs)	
t	metric ton	0.98	long ton (2,240 lbs)	
mL	milliliter	0.03	fluid ounce	fl oz
L	liter	4.24	cup	c
L	liter	2.13	pint (liquid)	pt
L	liter	1.06	quart (liquid)	qt
L	liter	0.26	gallon	gal
m^3	cubic meter	35.32	cubic foot	ft^3
m^3	cubic meter	1.32	cubic yard	yd^3
C	degrees Celsius	1.80	degrees Fahrenheit (after subtracting 32)	F

[1] For weighing ordinary commodities. [2] For weighing precious metals, jewels, etc.

Example of table structure:

**State and Local Government Retirement Systems—
Beneficiaries and Finances: 1980 to 1991**

[In millions of dollars, except as indicated. For fiscal years closed during the 12 months ending June 30]

YEAR AND LEVEL OF GOVERNMENT	Number of beneficiaries (1,000)	RECEIPTS					BENEFITS AND WITHDRAWALS			Cash and security holdings
		Total	Employee contributions	Government contributions		Earnings on investments	Total	Benefits	Withdrawals	
				State	Local					
1980: All systems	(NA)	37,313	6,466	7,581	9,951	13,315	14,008	12,207	1,801	185,226
State-administered	(NA)	28,603	5,285	7,399	5,611	10,308	10,257	8,809	1,448	144,682
Locally administered	(NA)	8,710	1,180	181	4,340	3,008	3,752	3,399	353	40,544
1985: All systems	3,378	71,411	9,468	12,227	15,170	34,546	24,413	21,999	2,414	374,433
State-administered	2,661	55,960	7,901	11,976	8,944	27,139	18,230	16,183	2,047	296,951
Locally administered	716	15,451	1,567	251	6,226	7,407	6,183	5,816	367	77,481
1990: All systems	4,026	111,339	13,853	13,994	18,583	64,907	38,396	35,966	2,430	703,772
State-administered	3,232	89,162	11,648	13,964	11,538	52,012	29,603	27,562	2,041	565,641
Locally administered	794	22,177	2,205	32	7,045	12,895	8,793	8,404	389	138,131
1991: All systems	4,179	108,240	16,268	14,473	18,691	58,808	42,028	39,421	2,607	783,405
State-administered	3,357	85,576	12,563	14,455	11,553	47,006	32,323	30,167	2,156	630,551
Locally administered	822	22,664	3,705	18	7,138	11,803	9,706	9,255	451	152,854

NA Not available.
Source: U.S. Bureau of the Census, *Finances of Employee-Retirement Systems of State and Local Governments*, series GF, No. 2, annual.

Headnotes immediately below table titles provide information important for correct interpretation or evaluation of the table as a whole or for a major segment of it.

Footnotes below the bottom rule of tables give information relating to specific items or figures within the table.

Unit indicators show the *specified quantities* in which data items are presented. They are used for two primary reasons. Sometimes data are not available in absolute form and are estimates (as in the case of many surveys). In other cases we round the numbers in order to save space to show more data, as in the case above.

EXAMPLES OF UNIT INDICATOR INTERPRETATION FROM TABLE

Year	Item	Unit indicator	Number shown	Multiplier
1991	Beneficiaries	Thousands	4,179	1,000
1991	Receipts	$ Millions	108,240	1,000,000

To Determine the Figure It Is Necessary to Multiply the Number Shown by the Unit Indicator:

Beneficiaries = 4,179 * 1,000 or 4,179,000 (over 4 million).
Receipts = 108,240 * 1,000,000 or 108,240,000,000 (over 108 billion).

When a table presents data with more than one unit indicator, they are found in the headnotes and column headings (shown above), spanner (table 53), stub (table 39), or unit column (table 79). When the data in a table are shown in the same unit indicator, it is shown in boldface as the first part of the headnote (table 2). If no unit indicator is shown, data presented are in absolute form (table 1).

Heavy vertical rules are used to separate independent sections of a table, as shown above, or in tables where the stub is continued into one or more additional columns (table 4).

Averages. An average is a single number or value that is often used to represent the "typical value" of a group of numbers. It is regarded as a measure of "location" or "central tendency" of a group of numbers.

The *arithmetic mean* is the type of average used most frequently. It is derived by summing the individual item values of a particular group and dividing the total by the number of items. The arithmetic mean is often referred to as simply the "mean" or "average."

The *median* of a group of numbers is the middle number or value when each item in the group is arranged according to size (lowest to highest or visa versa); it generally has the same number of items above it as well as below it. If there is an even number if items in the group, the median is taken to be the average of the two middle numbers.

Per capita (or per person) quantities. A per capita figure represents an average computed for every person in a specified group (or population). It is derived by taking the total for an item (such as income, taxes, or retail sales) and dividing it by the number of persons in the specified population.

Index numbers. An index number is the measure of difference or change, usually expressed as a percent, relating one quantity (the variable) of a specified kind to another quantity of the same kind. Index numbers are widely used to express changes in prices over periods of time but may also be used to express differences between related subjects for a single point in time.

To compute a price index, a base year or period is selected. The base year price (of the commodity or service) is then designated as the base or reference price to which the prices for other years or periods are related. Many price indexes use the year 1982 as the base year; in tables this is shown as "1982=100". A method of expressing the price relationship is: The price of a set of one or more items for a related year (e.g. 1990) **divided by** the price of the same set of items for the base year (e.g. 1982). The result multiplied by 100 provides the index number. When 100 is subtracted from the index number, the result equals the percent change in price from the base year.

Average annual percent change. Unless otherwise stated in the *Abstract* (as in Section 1, Population), average annual percent change is computed by use of a *compound interest formula*. This formula assumes that the rate of change is constant throughout a specified compounding period (one year for average annual rates of change). The formula is similar to that used to compute the balance of a savings account which receives compound interest. According to this formula, at the end of a compounding period the amount of accrued change (e.g. school enrollment or bank interest) is added to the amount which existed at the beginning the period. As a result, over time (e.g., with each year or quarter), the same rate of change is applied to a larger and larger figure.

The *exponential formula*, which is based on continuous compounding, is often used to measure population change. It is preferred by population experts because they view population and population-related subjects as changing without interruption, ever ongoing. Both exponential and compound interest formulas assume a constant rate of change. The former, however, applies the amount of change continuously to the base rather than at the end of each compounding period. When the average annual rates are small (e.g., less than 5 percent) both formulas give virtually the same results. For an explanation of these two formulas as they relate to population, see U.S. Bureau of the Census, *The Methods and Materials of Demography*, vol. 2, 3d printing (rev.), 1975, pp. 372-381.

Current and constant dollars. Statistics in some tables in a number of sections are expressed in both current and constant dollars (see, for example, table 706 in section 14). Current dollar figures reflect actual prices or costs prevailing during the specified year(s). Constant dollar figures are estimates representing an effort to remove the effects of price changes from statistical series reported in dollar terms. In general, constant dollar series are derived by dividing current dollar estimates by the appropriate price index for the appropriate period (for example, the Consumer Price Index). The result is a series as it would presumably exist if prices were the same throughout, as in the base year—in other words as if the dollar had constant purchasing power. Any changes in this constant dollar series would reflect only changes in real volume of output, income, expenditures, or other measure.

Explanation of Symbols:

The following symbols, used in the tables throughout this book, are explained in condensed form in footnotes to the tables where they appear:

- Represents zero or rounds to less than half the unit of measurement shown.

B Base figure too small to meet statistical standards for reliability of a derived figure.

D Figure withheld to avoid disclosure pertaining to a specific organization or individual.

NA Data not enumerated, tabulated, or otherwise available separately.

NS Percent change irrelevant or insignificant.

S Figure does not meet publication standards for reasons other than that covered by symbol B, above.

X Figure not applicable because column heading and stub line make entry impossible, absurd, or meaningless.

Z Entry would amount to less than half the unit of measurement shown.

In many tables, details will not add to the totals shown because of rounding.

Telephone Contacts List

To help *Abstract* users find more data and information about statistical publications, we are issuing this list of contacts for Federal agencies with major statistical programs. The intent is to give a single, first-contact point-of-entry for users of statistics. These agencies will provide general information on their statistical programs and publications, as well as specific information on how to order their publications. For the first time, we are also including the Internet (World Wide Web) addresses for many of these agencies.

Executive Office of the President

Office of Management and Budget

Administrator
Office of Information and Regulatory Affairs
Office of Management and Budget
Washington, DC 20503
Information: 202-395-3080
Publications: 202-395-7332
Internet address: http://www.whitehouse.gov/WH/EOP/omb

Department of Agriculture

Economic Research Service

Reading Information Center
U.S. Department of Agriculture
Room 3098
1800 M St. N.W.
Washington, DC 20036-5831
Information and Publications: 202-694-5050
Internet address: http://www.econ.ag.gov/

National Agricultural Statistics Service

National Agricultural Statistics Service
U.S. Department of Agriculture
1400 Independence Ave., S.W.
Washington, DC 20250
Information hotline: 1-800-727-9540
Internet address: http://www.usda.gov/nass/

Department of Commerce

Bureau of the Census

Customer Services Branch
Bureau of the Census
U.S. Department of Commerce
Washington, DC 20233
Information and Publications: 301-457-4100
Internet address: http://www.census.gov/

Bureau of Economic Analysis

Current Business Analysis Division, BE-53
Bureau of Economic Analysis
U.S. Department of Commerce
Washington, DC 20230
Information and Publications: 202-606-9900
Internet address: http://www.bea.doc.gov/

Department of Commerce —Con.

International Trade Administration

Trade Statistics Division
Office of Trade and Investment Analysis
International Trade Administration
Room 2814 B
U.S. Department of Commerce
Washington, DC 20230
Information and Publications: 202-482-2185
Internet address: http://ita.doc.gov/tradestats/

National Oceanic and Atmospheric Administration

National Oceanic and Atmospheric Administration Library
U.S. Department of Commerce
1315 East-West Highway 2nd Floor
Silver Spring MD 20910
Library: 301-713-2600
Internet address: http://www.noaa.gov/

Department of Defense

Department of Defense

Office of the Assistant Secretary of Defense (Public Affairs)
Room 1E794
Attention: Directorate for Communications
1400 Defense Pentagon
Washington, DC 20301-1400
Information: 703-697-5737
Internet address: http://web1.whs.osd.mil/mmid/mmidhome.htm

Department of Education

Office of Information Services

Statistical Information Office
U.S. Department of Education
555 New Jersey Ave., N.W.
Washington, DC 20208-5641
Information and Publications: 1-800-424-1616
Internet address: http://www.ed.gov/NCES/

Department of Energy

Energy Information Administration

National Energy Information Center
U.S. Department of Energy
1000 Independence Ave., SW
1F048, EI-30
Washington, DC 20585
Information and Publications: 202-586-8800
Internet address: http://www.eia.doe.gov/

Department of Health and Human Services

Health Resources and Services Administration

HRSA Office of Communications

5600 Fishers Lane, Room 14-45

Rockville, MD 20857

Publications: 301-443-3376

Internet address: http://www.hrsa.dhhs.gov/

Substance Abuse Mental Health Services Administration

U.S. Department of Health and Human Services
5600 Fishers Lane
Room 12C105
Rockville, MD 20857
Information: 301-443-4795
Publications: 1-800-729-6686
Internet address: http://www.samhsa.gov/

Centers for Disease Control and Prevention

Office of Information
Centers for Disease Control
21600 Clifton Road, N.E.
Atlanta, GA 30333
Public Inquiries: 404-639-3534
Internet address: http://www.cdc.gov/cdc.html

Health Care Financing Administration

Office of Public Affairs
Health Care Financing Administration
U.S. Department of Health and Human Services
Room 403B, Humphrey Building
200 Independence Ave., S.W.
Washington, DC 20201
Media Relations: 202-690-6145
Internet address: http://www.hcfa.gov/

National Center for Health Statistics

Scientific and Technical Information Branch
National Center for Health Statistics
U.S. Department of Health and Human Services
6525 Belcrest Rd. Rm. 1064
Hyattsville, MD 20782
Information and Publications: 301-436-8500
Internet address: http://www.cdc.gov/nchswww/nchshome.htm

Social Security Administration

Office of Research Evaluation and Statistics
Social Security Administration
Division of Publications
Intl. Trade Commission Bldg.
500 E St. S.W.
Washington, DC 20254
Information and Publications: 202-282-7138
Internet address: http://www.ssa.gov/statistics/ores_home. html

Department of Housing and Urban Development

Assistant Secretary for Community Planning and Development

Office of the Assistant Secretary for Community Planning and Development
U.S. Department of Housing and Urban Development
451 7th St., S.W.
Washington, DC 20410-0555
Information: 202-708-2690
Publications: 1-800-245-2691
Internet address: http://www.huduser.org/

Department of the Interior

Geological Survey

Earth Science Information Center
Geological Survey
U.S. Department of the Interior
507 National Center
Reston, VA 20192
Information and Publications: 703-648-6045
Internet address for minerals: http://minerals.er.usgs.gov:80/minerals/
Internet address for other USGS materials: http://www.usgs.gov/

Department of Justice

Bureau of Justice Statistics

Statistics Division
Bureau of Justice Statistics
U.S. Department of Justice
1110 Vermont Ave., NW, 10th Floor
Washington, DC 20005
Information and Publications: 202-307-0765
Internet address: http://www.ojp.usdoj.gov/bjs/

National Criminal Justice Reference Service

Box 6000
Rockville, MD 20850
Information and Publications: 301-251-5500
Publications: 1-800-732-3277
Internet address: http://www.ncjrs.org/

Federal Bureau of Investigation

National Crime Information Center
Federal Bureau of Investigation
U.S. Department of Justice
935 Pennsylvania Ave., N.W.
Washington, DC 20535
Information and Publications: 202-324-3691
Publications: 202-324-5611
Internet address: http://www.fbi.gov/

artment of Justice —Con.

Immigration and Naturalization Service

Statistics Branch
Immigration and Naturalization Service
U.S. Department of Justice
425 I St., NW, Rm. 5309
Washington, DC 20536
Information and Publications: 202-305-1613
Internet address: *http://www.usdoj.gov/ins/index.html*

artment of Labor

Bureau of Labor Statistics

Office of Publications and Information Services
Bureau of Labor Statistics
U.S. Department of Labor
2 Mass. Ave. N.E., Room 2860
Washington, DC 20212
Information and Publications: 202-606-5886
Internet address: http://stats.bls.gov/

Employment and Training Administration

Office of Public Affairs
Employment and Training Administration
U.S. Department of Labor
200 Constitution Ave., N.W., Room S4206
Washington, DC 20210
Information and Publications: 202-219-6871
Internet address: http://www.doleta.gov/

artment of Transportation

Federal Aviation Administration

Public Inquiry Center
APA 200
Federal Aviation Administration
U.S. Department of Transportation
800 Independence Ave., S.W.
Washington, DC 20591
Information and Publications: 202-267-3484
Internet address: http://www.faa.gov/

Bureau of Transportation Statistics
Internet address: http://www.bts.gov/

Federal Highway Administration

Office of Public Affairs
Federal Highway Administration
U.S. Department of Transportation
400 7th St. S.W.
Washington, DC 20590
Information: 202-366-0660
Internet address: *http://fhwa.dot.gov/*

Department of Transportation —Con.

National Highway Traffic Safety Administration

Office of Public Affairs
National Highway Traffic Safety Administration
U.S. Department of Transportation
400 7th St., S.W.
Washington, DC 20590
Information: 202-366-9550
Publications: 202-366-2587
Internet address: http://www.nhtsa.dot.gov/

Department of the Treasury

Internal Revenue Service

Statistics of Income Division
Internal Revenue Service
Attn: Beth Kilss
P.O. Box 2608
Washington, DC 20013-2608
Information and Publications: 202-874-0410
Internet address: *http://www.irs.ustreas.gov/cover.html*

Department of Veterans Affairs

Department of Veterans Affairs

Office of Public Affairs
Department of Veterans Affairs
810 Vermont Ave., N.W.
Washington, DC 20420
Information: 202-273-5400
Internet address: *http://www.va.gov/*

Independent Agencies

Environmental Protection Agency

Information Resource Center, Rm. MC3404
Environmental Protection Agency
401 M St., S.W.
Washington, DC 20460
Information: 202-260-5922
Internet address: http://www.epa.gov/

Federal Reserve Board

Division of Research and Statistics
Federal Reserve Board
Washington, DC 20551
Information: 202-452-3301
Publications: 202-452-3245
Internet address: http://www.bog.frb.fed.us/

National Science Foundation

Office of Legislative and Public Affairs
National Science Foundation
4201 Wilson Boulevard.
Arlington Virginia 22230
Information: 703-306-1234
Publications: 703-306-1134
Internet address: *http://www.nsf.gov:80/sbe/srs/stats.htm*

Securities and Exchange Commission

Office of Public Affairs
Securities and Exchange Commission
450 5th St. N.W.
Washington, DC 20549
Information: 202-942-0020
Publications: 202-942-4040
Internet address: http://www.sec.gov/

Section 1

Population

This section presents statistics on the growth, distribution, and characteristics of the U.S. population. The principal source of these data is the Bureau of the Census, which conducts a decennial census of population, a monthly population survey, a program of population estimates and projections, and a number of other periodic surveys relating to population characteristics. For a list of relevant publications, see the Guide to Sources of Statistics in Appendix I.

In Brief

Total population, 1996	265 million
Northeast	*19%*
Midwest	*23%*
South	*35%*
West	*22%*
Total households, 1996	100 million
One-person households	*25%*

Decennial censuses—The U.S. Constitution provides for a census of the population every 10 years, primarily to establish a basis for apportionment of members of the House of Representatives among the States. For over a century after the first census in 1790, the census organization was a temporary one, created only for each decennial census. In 1902, the Bureau of the Census was established as a permanent Federal agency, responsible for enumerating the population and also for compiling statistics on other subjects.

Historically the census of population has been a complete count. That is, an attempt is made to account for every person, for each person's residence, and for other characteristics (sex, age, family relationships, etc.). Since the 1940 census, in addition to the complete count information, some data have been obtained from representative samples of the population. In the 1990 census, variable sampling rates were employed. For most of the country, 1 in every 6 households (about 17 percent) received the long form or sample questionnaire; in governmental units estimated to have fewer than 2,500 inhabitants, every other household (50 percent) received the sample questionnaire to enhance the reliability of sample data for small areas. Exact agreement is not to be expected between sample data and the complete census count. Sample data may be used with confidence where large numbers are involved and assumed to indicate trends and relationships where small numbers are involved.

Census data presented here have not been adjusted for underenumeration. Results from the evaluation program for the 1990 census indicate that the overall national undercount was between 1 and 2 percent - the estimate from the Post Enumeration Survey (PES) was 1.6 percent and the estimate from Demographic Analysis (DA) was 1.8 percent. Both the PES and DA estimates show disproportionately high undercounts for some demographic groups. For example, the PES estimates of percent net undercount for Blacks (4.4 percent), Hispanics (5.0 percent), and American Indians (4.5 percent) were higher than the estimated undercount of non-Hispanic whites (0.7 percent). Historical DA estimates demonstrate that the overall undercount rate in the census has declined significantly over the past 50 years (from an estimated 5.4 percent in 1940 to 1.8 percent in 1990), yet the undercount of Blacks has remained disproportionately high.

Current Population Survey (CPS)—This is a monthly nationwide survey of a scientifically selected sample representing the noninstitutional civilian population. The sample is located in 754 areas comprising 2,121 counties, independent cities, and minor civil divisions with coverage in every State and the District of Columbia and is subject to sampling error. At the present time, about 50,000 occupied households are eligible for interview every month; of these between 4 and 5 percent are, for various reasons, unavailable for interview.

While the primary purpose of the CPS is to obtain monthly statistics on the labor force, it also serves as a vehicle for inquiries on other subjects. Using CPS data, the Bureau issues a series of publications under the general title of *Current Population Reports*, which cover population characteristics (P20), consumer income (P60), special studies (P23), and other topics.

Estimates of population characteristics based on the CPS will not agree with the counts from the census because the CPS and the census use different procedures for collecting and processing the data for racial groups, the Hispanic population, and other topics. Caution should also be used when comparing estimates for various years because of the periodic introduction of changes into the CPS. Beginning in January 1994, a number of changes were introduced into the CPS that effect all data comparisons with prior years. These changes include the results of a major redesign of the survey questionnaire and collection methodology and the introduction of 1990 census population controls, adjusted for the estimated undercount. This change in population controls had relatively little impact on derived measures such as means, medians, and percent distribution, but did have a significant impact on levels.

Population estimates and projections—National population estimates start with decennial census data as benchmarks and add annual population component of change data. Component of change data comes from various agencies, as follows: National Center for Health Statistics (births and deaths), Immigration and Naturalization Service (legal immigrants), Office of Refugee Resettlement (refugees), U.S. Census Bureau's International Programs Center (net movement between Puerto Rico and the U.S. mainland), Armed Forces, Department of Defense, and Office of Personnel Management (movement of military and civilian citizens abroad). Estimated population components of change included emigration - 222,000 people per year - and net undocumented immigration - 225,000 people per year. Estimates for states and smaller areas are based on data series such as births and deaths, ...ol statistics from state departments of education and parochial school systems, and federal income tax returns.

Data for the population by age for April 1, 1990, (shown in tables 14, 21, and 23) are modified counts. The review of detailed 1990 information indicated that respondents tended to provide their age as of the date of completion of the questionnaire, not their age as of April 1, 1990. In addition, there may have been a tendency for respondents to round up their age if they were close to having a birthday. A detailed explanation of the age modification procedure appears in 1990 Census of Population and Housing Data Paper Listing (CPH-L-74).

Population estimates and projections are published in the P25 series of *Current Population Reports* and *Population Paper Listings (PPL's)*. These estimates and projections are generally consistent with official decennial census figures and do not reflect the amount of estimated census underenumeration. However, these estimates and projections by race have been modified and are not comparable to the census race categories (see section below under "race"). For details on methodology, see the sources cited below the individual tables.

The state population projections, by single year of age, sex, race, and Hispanic origin, prepared for 1995 to 2025 use a cohort-component methodology to generate the projected populations. This method requires separate assumptions for each population component of change: births, deaths, internal migration, and international migration. Data for population components of change derive from various governmental administrative records and census distributions. The 1994 state population estimates serve as the starting point for these projections, which are consistent with the national population projections listed in Current Population Reports, series P25-1130. The two series of projections (see table 35) are based on different internal migration assumptions: Series A, the preferred series model, which uses state-to-state migration observed from 1975-76 through 1993-94; and Series B, the economic model, which uses the Bureau of Economic Analysis employment projections.

Immigration—The principal source of immigration data is the *Statistical Yearbook of the Immigration and Naturalization Service*, published annually by the Immigration and Naturalization Service (INS), a unit of the Department of Justice. Immigration statistics are prepared from entry visas and change of immigration status forms. Immigrants are aliens admitted for legal permanent residence in the United States. The procedures for admission depend on whether the alien is residing inside or outside the United States at the time of application for permanent residence. Eligible aliens residing outside the United States are issued immigrant visas by the U.S. Department of State. Eligible aliens residing in the United States are allowed to change their status from temporary to permanent residence at INS district offices. The category, immigrant, includes persons who may have entered the United States as nonimmigrants or refugees, but who subsequently changed their status to that of a permanent resident. Nonresident aliens admitted to the United States for a temporary period are nonimmigrants (tables 7 and 436). Refugees are considered nonimmigrants when initially admitted into the United States, but are not included in nonimmigrant admission data. A refugee is any person who is outside his or her country of nationality who is unable or unwilling to return to that country because of persecution or a well-founded fear of persecution.

U.S. immigration law gives preferential immigration status to aliens who are related to certain U.S. citizens or legal permanent residents, aliens with needed job skills, or aliens who qualify as refugees. Immigration to the United States can be divided into two general categories: (1) those subject to the annual worldwide limitation, and (2) those exempt from it. The Immigration Act of 1990 established major revisions in the numerical limits and preference system regulating legal immigration. The numerical limits are imposed on visas issued and not on admissions. The maximum number of visas allowed to be issued under the preference categories in 1995 was 400,224—253,721 for family-sponsored immigrants and 146,503 for employment-based immigrants. There are nine categories among which the family-sponsored and employment-based immigrant visas are distributed, beginning in fiscal year 1992. The family-sponsored preferences are based on the alien's relationship with a U.S. citizen or legal permanent resident (see table 6). The employment-based preferences are 1) priority workers (persons of extraordinary ability, outstanding professors and researchers, and certain multinational executives and managers); 2) professionals with advanced degrees or aliens with exceptional ability; 3) skilled workers, professionals without advanced degrees, and needed unskilled workers; 4) special immigrants; and 5) employment creation immigrants (investors). Within the overall limitations the per-country limit for independent countries is set to 7 percent of the total family-sponsored and employment-based limits, while dependent areas are limited to two percent of the total. The 1995 limit allowed no more than 28,016 preference visas for any independent country and 8,004 for any dependency. Those exempt from the worldwide limitation include immediate relatives of U.S. citizens, refugees and asylees adjusting to permanent residence, and other various classes of special immigrants (see table 6).

The Refugee Act of 1980, effective April 1, 1980, provides for a uniform admission procedure for refugees of all countries, based on the United Nations' definition of refugees. Authorized admission ceilings are set annually by the President in consultation with Congress. After one year of residence in the United States, refugees are eligible for immigrant status.

The Immigration Reform and Control Act of 1986 (IRCA) allows two groups of illegal aliens to become temporary and then permanent residents of the United States: aliens who have been in the United States unlawfully since January 1, 1982, (legalization applicants), and aliens who were employed in seasonal agricultural work for a minimum period of time (Special Agricultural Worker (SAW) applicants). The application period for temporary residency for legalization applicants began on May 5, 1987, and ended on May 4, 1988, while the application period for SAW applicants began on June 1, 1987, and ended on November 30, 1988. Legalization applicants became eligible for permanent residence beginning in fiscal year 1989. Beginning 1989 immigrant data include temporary residents who were granted permanent residence under the legalization program of IRCA.

Metropolitan Areas (MA's)—The general concept of a metropolitan area is one of a core area containing a large population nucleus, together with adjacent communities that have a high degree of social and economic integration with that core. Metropolitan statistical areas (MSA's), consolidated metropolitan statistical areas (CMSA's), and primary metropolitan statistical areas (PMSA's) are defined by the Office of Management and Budget (OMB) as a standard for Federal agencies in the preparation and publication of statistics relating to metropolitan areas. The entire territory of the United States is classified as metropolitan (inside MSA's or CMSA's—PMSA's are components of CMSA's) or nonmetropolitan (outside MSA's or CMSA's). MSA's, CMSA's, and PMSA's are defined in terms of entire counties except in New England, where the definitions are in terms of cities and towns. The OMB also defines New England County Metropolitan Areas (NECMA's) which are county-based alternatives to the MSA's and CMSA's in the six New England States. From time to time, new MA's are created and the boundaries of others change. As a result, data for MA's over time may not be comparable and the analysis of historical trends must be made cautiously. For descriptive details and a listing of titles and components of MA's, see Appendix II.

Urban and rural—According to the 1990 census definition, the urban population comprises all persons living in (a) places of 2,500 or more inhabitants incorporated as cities, villages, boroughs (except in Alaska and New York), and towns (except in the New England States, New York, and Wisconsin), but excluding those persons living in the rural portions of extended cities (places with low population density in one or more large parts of their area); (b) census designated places (previously termed unincorporated) of 2,500 or more inhabitants; and (c) other territory, incorporated or unincorporated, included in urbanized areas. An urbanized area comprises one or more places and the adjacent densely settled surrounding territory that together have a minimum population of 50,000 persons. In all definitions, the population not classified as urban constitutes the rural population

Residence—In determining residence, the Bureau of the Census counts each person as an inhabitant of a usual place of residence (i.e., the place where one usually lives and sleeps). While this place is not necessarily a person's legal residence or voting residence, the use of these different bases of classification would produce the same results in the vast majority of cases.

Race—The Bureau of the Census collects and publishes racial statistics as outlined in Statistical Policy Directive No. 15 issued by the U.S. Office of Management and Budget. This directive provides standards on ethnic and racial categories for statistical reporting to be used by all Federal agencies. According to the directive, the basic racial categories are American Indian or Alaska Native, Asian or Pacific Islander, Black, and White. (The directive identifies Hispanic origin as an ethnicity.) The concept of race the Bureau of the Census uses reflects self-identification by respondents; that is the individual's perception of his/her racial identity. The concept is not intended to reflect any biological or anthropological definition. Although the Bureau of the Census adheres to the overall guidelines of Directive No. 15, it recognizes that there are persons who do not identify with a specific racial group. The 1990 census race question includes an "Other race" category with provisions for a write-in entry. Furthermore, the Bureau of the Census recognizes that the categories of the race item include both racial and national origin or socio-cultural groups.

Differences between the 1990 census and earlier censuses affect the comparability of data for certain racial groups and American Indian tribes. The lack of comparability is due to changes in the way some respondents reported their race as well as changes in 1990 census procedures related to the racial classification. (For a fuller explanation, see *1990 Census of Population, Volume I,*

General Population Characteristics (1990 CP-1).)

Data for the population by race for April 1, 1990, (shown in tables 12, 13, 18, 19, 21, and 23) are modified counts and are not comparable to the 1990 census race categories. These numbers were computed using 1990 census data by race which had been modified to be consistent with the guidelines in Federal Statistical Directive No. 15 issued by the Office of Management and Budget. A detailed explanation of the race modification procedure appears in 1990 Census of Population and Housing Data Paper Listing (CPH-L-74).

In the CPS and other household sample surveys in which data are obtained through personal interview, respondents are asked to classify their race as: (1) White, (2) Black, (3) American Indian, Aleut, or Eskimo, or (4) Asian or Pacific Islander. The procedures for classifying persons of mixed races who could not provide a single response to the race question are generally similar to those used in the census.

Hispanic population—In the 1990 census, the Bureau of the Census collected data on the Hispanic origin population in the United States by using a self-identification question. Persons of Spanish/Hispanic origin are those who classified themselves in one of the specific Hispanic origin categories listed on the questionnaire—Mexican, Puerto Rican, Cuban, or Other Spanish/Hispanic origin. Both in 1980 and 1990, the Hispanic origin question contained prelisted categories for the largest Hispanic origin groups—Mexican, Puerto Rican, and Cuban as well as for the residual category Other Spanish/Hispanic. The 1990 Hispanic origin question differed from the 1980 question in that in 1990, unlike in 1980, the question contained a write-in line for the subgroups. Another difference between the 1980 and 1990 Hispanic origin question is that in 1980 the wording of the Hispanic origin question read: "Is this person of Spanish/Hispanic origin or descent?" while in 1990 the word "descent" was dropped from the question. Persons of Hispanic origin may be of any race.

In the CPS information on Hispanic persons is gathered by using a self-identification question. Persons classify themselves in one of the Hispanic categories in response to the question: "What is the origin or descent of each person in this household?" Hispanic persons in the CPS are persons who report themselves as Mexican-American, Chicano, Mexican, Puerto Rican, Cuban, Central or South American (Spanish countries), or other Hispanic origin.

Nativity—The native population consists of all persons born in the United States, Puerto Rico, or an outlying area of the United States. It also includes persons born in a foreign country who had at least one parent who was a U.S. citizen. All other persons are classified as "foreign born."

Mobility status—The U.S. population is classified according to mobility status on the basis of a comparison between the place of residence of each individual at the time of the survey or census and the place of residence at a specified earlier date. Nonmovers are all persons who were living in the same house or apartment at the end of the period as at the beginning of the period. Movers are all persons who were living in a different house at the end of the period from that in which they were living at the beginning of the period. Movers from abroad include all persons, either U.S. citizens or noncitizens, whose place of residence was outside the United States at the beginning of the period; that is, in Puerto Rico, an outlying area under the jurisdiction of the United States, or a foreign country.

Living arrangements—Living arrangements refer to residency in households or in group quarters. A "household" comprises all persons who occupy a "housing unit," that is, a house, an apartment or other group of rooms, or a single room that constitutes "separate living quarters." A household includes the related family members and all the unrelated persons, if any, such as lodgers, foster children, wards, or employees who share the housing unit. A person living alone or a group of unrelated persons sharing the same housing unit is also counted as a household. See text, section 25,

Construction and Housing, for definition of housing unit.

All persons not living in households are classified as living in group quarters. These individuals may be institutionalized, e.g., under care or custody in juvenile facilities, jails, correctional facilities, hospitals, or nursing homes; or they may be residents in noninstitutional group quarters such as college dormitories, military barracks, or rooming houses.

Householder—The householder is the first adult household member listed on the questionnaire. The instructions call for listing first the person (or one of the persons) in whose name the home is owned or rented. If a home is owned or rented jointly by a married couple, either the husband or the wife may be listed first. Prior to 1980, the husband was always considered the household head (householder) in married-couple households.

Family—The term "family" refers to a group of two or more persons related by birth, marriage, or adoption and residing together in a household. A family includes among its members the householder.

Subfamily—A subfamily consists of a married couple and their children, if any, or one parent with one or more never-married children under 18 years old living in a household. Subfamilies are divided into "related" and "unrelated" subfamilies. A related subfamily is related to, but does not include, the householder. Members of a related subfamily are also members of the family with whom they live. The number of related subfamilies, therefore, is not included in the count of families. An unrelated subfamily may include persons such as guests, lodgers, or resident employees and their spouses and/or children; none of whom is related to the householder.

Married couple—A "married couple" is defined as a husband and wife living together in the same household, with or without children and other relatives.

Unrelated individuals—"Unrelated individuals" are persons (other than inmates of institutions) who are not members of families or subfamilies.

Secondary individuals—Secondary individuals are persons of any age who reside in a household, but are not related to the householder (except unrelated subfamily members). Persons who reside in group quarters are also secondary individuals. Examples of a secondary individual include (1) a guest, partner, roommate, or resident employee; (2) a foster child; or (3) a person residing in a rooming house, a halfway house, staff quarters at a hospital, or other type of group quarters.

Statistical reliability—For a discussion of statistical collection and estimation, sampling procedures, and measures of statistical reliability applicable to Census Bureau data, see Appendix III.

Figure 1.1
Ten Fastest Growing States, Percent Population Change: 1990 to 1996

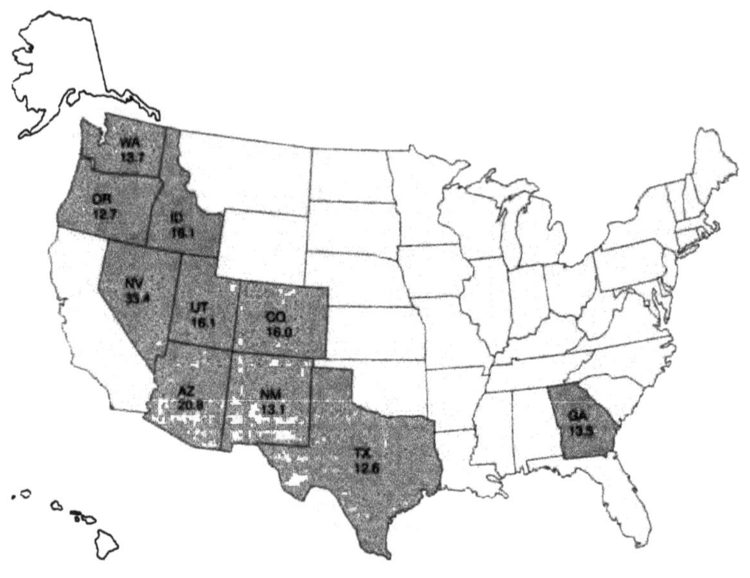

Source: Charts prepared by U.S. Bureau of the Census. For data, see table 26.

Figure 1.2
Household Composition— Percent Change: 1980 to 1996

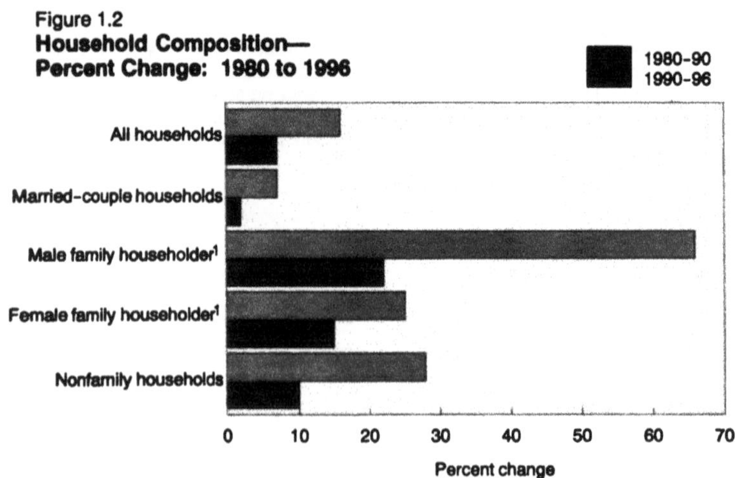

[1] No spouse present.
Source: Charts prepared by U.S. Bureau of the Census. For data, see table 66.

No. 1. Population and Area: 1790 to 1990

[Area figures represent area on indicated date including in some cases considerable areas not then organized or settled, and not covered by the census. Total area figures for 1790 to 1970 have been recalculated on the basis of the remeasurement of States and counties for the 1980 census, but not on the basis of the 1990 census. The land and water area figures for past censuses have not been adjusted and are not strictly comparable with the total area data for comparable dates because the land areas were derived from different base data, and these values are known to have changed with the construction of reservoirs, draining of lakes, etc. Density figures are based on land area measurements as reported in earlier censuses]

CENSUS DATE	RESIDENT POPULATION				AREA (square miles)		
	Number	Per square mile of land area	Increase over preceding census		Total	Land	Water
			Number	Percent			
CONTERMINOUS U.S. [1]							
1790 (Aug. 2)	3,929,214	4.5	(X)	(X)	891,364	864,746	24,065
1800 (Aug. 4)	5,308,483	6.1	1,379,269	35.1	891,364	864,746	24,065
1810 (Aug. 6)	7,239,881	4.3	1,931,398	36.4	1,722,685	1,681,828	34,175
1820 (Aug. 7)	9,638,453	5.5	2,398,572	33.1	1,792,552	1,749,462	38,544
1830 (June 1)	12,866,020	7.4	3,227,567	33.5	1,792,552	1,749,462	38,544
1840 (June 1)	17,069,453	9.8	4,203,433	32.7	1,792,552	1,749,462	38,544
1850 (June 1)	23,191,876	7.9	6,122,423	35.9	2,991,655	2,940,042	52,705
1860 (June 1)	31,443,321	10.6	8,251,445	35.6	3,021,295	2,969,640	52,747
1870 (June 1)	[2]39,818,449	[2]13.4	8,375,128	26.6	3,021,295	2,969,640	52,747
1880 (June 1)	50,155,783	16.9	10,337,334	26.0	3,021,295	2,969,640	52,747
1890 (June 1)	62,947,714	21.2	12,791,931	25.5	3,021,295	2,969,640	52,747
1900 (June 1)	75,994,575	25.6	13,046,861	20.7	3,021,295	2,969,834	52,553
1910 (Apr. 15)	91,972,266	31.0	15,977,691	21.0	3,021,295	2,969,565	52,822
1920 (Jan. 1)	105,710,620	35.6	13,738,354	14.9	3,021,295	2,969,451	52,936
1930 (Apr. 1)	122,775,046	41.2	17,064,426	16.1	3,021,295	2,977,128	45,259
1940 (Apr. 1)	131,669,275	44.2	8,894,229	7.2	3,021,295	2,977,128	45,259
1950 (Apr. 1)	150,697,361	50.7	19,028,086	14.5	3,021,295	2,974,726	47,661
1960 (Apr. 1)	178,464,236	60.1	27,766,875	18.4	3,021,295	2,968,054	54,207
UNITED STATES							
1950 (Apr. 1)	151,325,798	42.6	19,161,229	14.5	3,618,770	3,552,206	63,005
1960 (Apr. 1)	179,323,175	50.6	27,997,377	18.5	3,618,770	3,540,911	74,212
1970 (Apr. 1)	[3]203,302,031	[3]57.4	23,978,856	13.4	3,618,770	[3]3,540,023	[3]78,444
1980 (Apr. 1)	[4]226,542,199	64.0	23,240,168	11.4	3,618,770	3,539,289	79,481
1990 (Apr. 1)	[5]248,718,301	70.3	22,176,102	9.8	[6]3,717,796	[6]3,536,278	[6,7]181,518

X Not applicable. [1] Excludes Alaska and Hawaii. [2] Revised to include adjustments for underenumeration in southern States; unrevised number is 38,558,371 (13.0 per square mile). [3] Figures corrected after 1970 final reports were issued. [4] Total population count has been revised since the 1980 census publications. Numbers by age, race, Hispanic origin, and sex have not been corrected. [5] The April 1, 1990, census count includes count question resolution corrections processed through December 1994, and does not include adjustments for census coverage errors. [6] Data reflect corrections made after publication of the results. [7] Comprises Great Lakes, inland, and coastal water. Data for prior years cover inland water only. For further explanation, see table 367.

Source: U.S. Bureau of the Census, *1990 Census of Population and Housing, Population and Housing Unit Counts* (CPH-2); 1990 Census of Population and Housing Listing (1990 CPH-L-157); and unpublished data.

No. 2. Population: 1950 to 1996

[In thousands, except percent. Estimates as of July 1. Total population includes Armed Forces abroad; civilian population excludes Armed Forces. For basis of estimates, see text, section 1]

YEAR	TOTAL		Resident population	Civilian population	YEAR	TOTAL		Resident population	Civilian population
	Population	Percent change				Population	Percent change		
1950	152,271	(X)	151,868	150,790	1974	213,854	0.92	213,342	211,636
1951	154,878	1.71	153,982	151,599	1975	215,973	0.99	215,465	213,789
1952	157,553	1.73	156,393	153,892	1976	218,035	0.95	217,563	215,894
1953	160,184	1.67	158,956	156,595	1977	220,239	1.01	219,760	218,106
1954	163,026	1.77	161,884	159,695	1978	222,585	1.06	222,095	220,467
1955	165,931	1.78	165,069	162,967	1979	225,055	1.11	224,567	222,969
1956	168,903	1.79	168,088	166,055	1980	227,726	1.19	227,225	225,621
1957	171,984	1.82	171,187	169,110	1981	229,966	0.98	229,466	227,818
1958	174,882	1.68	174,149	172,226	1982	232,188	0.97	231,664	229,995
1959	177,830	1.69	177,135	175,277	1983	234,307	0.91	233,792	232,097
1960	180,671	1.60	179,979	178,140	1984	236,348	0.87	235,825	234,110
1961	183,691	1.67	182,992	181,143	1985	238,466	0.90	237,924	236,219
1962	186,538	1.55	185,771	183,677	1986	240,651	0.92	240,133	238,412
1963	189,242	1.45	188,483	186,493	1987	242,804	0.89	242,289	240,550
1964	191,889	1.40	191,141	189,141	1988	245,021	0.91	244,499	242,817
1965	194,303	1.26	193,526	191,605	1989	247,342	0.95	246,819	245,131
1966	196,560	1.16	195,576	193,420	1990	249,907	1.04	249,398	247,758
1967	198,712	1.09	197,457	195,264	1991	252,618	1.08	252,106	250,496
1968	200,706	1.00	199,399	197,113	1992	255,391	1.10	255,011	253,426
1969	202,677	0.98	201,385	199,145	1993	258,132	1.07	257,795	256,323
1970	205,052	1.17	203,984	201,895	1994	260,682	0.99	260,372	258,960
1971	207,661	1.27	206,827	204,866	1995	263,168	0.95	262,890	261,538
1972	209,896	1.08	209,284	207,511	1996	265,557	0.91	265,284	263,998
1973	211,909	0.96	211,357	209,600					

X Not applicable.

Source: U.S. Bureau of the Census, *Current Population Reports*, P25-1045 and P25-1126 and Population Paper Listings PPL-57.

No. 3. Resident Population Projections: 1997 to 2050

[In thousands. As of July 1. Each series shown assumes middle levels of fertility, life expectancy, and net immigration unless otherwise specified. Middle level components are shown in footnote 1]

YEAR	Middle series[1]	Lowest series[2]	Highest series[3]	FERTILITY		LIFE EXPECTANCY		NET IMMIGRATION	
				Low	High	Low	High	Low	High
1997	267,645	266,733	268,577	267,389	267,872	267,512	267,796	267,122	268,196
1998	270,002	268,396	271,647	269,565	270,392	269,783	270,250	269,050	271,006
1999	272,330	269,861	274,865	271,678	272,915	272,006	272,697	270,835	273,910
2000	274,634	271,237	278,129	273,731	275,448	274,185	275,141	272,581	276,802
2005	285,981	276,990	295,318	283,299	288,471	284,647	287,467	280,949	291,287
2010	297,716	281,468	314,571	292,303	302,893	294,966	300,482	289,423	306,444
2015	310,134	285,472	335,597	301,444	318,595	305,539	314,376	298,356	322,506
2020	322,742	288,807	357,702	310,429	334,889	315,865	328,698	307,290	338,955
2025	335,050	290,789	380,781	318,575	351,554	325,530	343,023	315,709	355,318
2030	346,899	291,070	405,089	325,517	368,732	334,331	357,227	323,414	371,480
2040	369,980	287,685	458,444	336,407	405,660	350,592	385,898	337,416	403,966
2050	393,931	282,524	518,903	345,352	447,502	367,913	415,908	351,354	438,299

[1] Ultimate total fertility rate = 2,245; life expectancy in 2050 = 82.0 years; and annual net immigration = 820,000. These are middle level assumptions. For explanation of total fertility rate; see headnote, table 93. [2] Ultimate total fertility rate = 1,910; life expectancy in 2050 = 74.8 years; and annual net immigration = 300,000. These are lowest level assumptions. [3] Ultimate total fertility rate = 2,580; life expectancy in 2050 = 89.4 years; and annual net immigration = 1,370,000. These are highest level assumptions.

Source: U.S. Bureau of the Census, *Current Population Reports*, P25-1130.

No. 4. Components of Population Change, 1980 to 1996, and Projections, 1997 to 2050

[Resident population. The estimates prior to 1990 are consistent with the original 1990 census count of 248,709,873. Starting with 1990, estimates reflect the revised April 1, 1990, census count of 248,718,291 which includes count question resolution corrections processed through March 1994, and does not include adjustments for coverage errors]

YEAR	TOTAL (Jan. 1-Dec. 31)						RATE PER 1,000 MIDYEAR POPULATION			
	Population at start of period (1,000)	Net increase[1]		Natural increase		Net migration[3] (1,000)	Net growth rate[1]	Natural increase		Net migration[3]
		Total (1,000)	Percent[2]	Births (1,000)	Deaths (1,000)			Birth rate	Death rate	
1980[4]	226,546	1,900	0.8	2,743	1,463	724	11.1	16.0	8.6	4.2
1981	228,446	2,200	1.0	3,629	1,978	690	9.6	15.8	8.6	3.0
1982	230,645	2,157	0.9	3,681	1,975	595	9.3	15.9	8.5	2.6
1983	232,803	2,066	0.9	3,639	2,019	592	8.8	15.6	8.6	2.5
1984	234,868	2,070	0.9	3,669	2,039	589	8.8	15.6	8.6	2.5
1985	236,938	2,171	0.9	3,761	2,086	649	9.1	15.8	8.8	2.7
1986	239,109	2,158	0.9	3,757	2,105	661	9.0	15.6	8.8	2.8
1987	241,267	2,195	0.9	3,809	2,123	666	9.1	15.7	8.8	2.7
1988	243,462	2,243	0.9	3,910	2,168	662	9.2	16.0	8.9	2.7
1989	245,705	2,438	1.0	4,041	2,150	712	9.9	16.4	8.7	2.9
1990[5]	248,143	2,549	1.0	4,148	2,155	[6]556	10.2	16.6	8.6	[6]2.2
1991	250,660	2,929	1.2	4,111	2,170	[6]988	11.6	16.3	8.6	[6]3.9
1992	253,589	2,923	1.2	4,065	2,176	1,034	11.5	15.9	8.5	4.1
1993	256,512	2,647	1.0	4,000	2,269	916	10.3	15.5	8.8	3.6
1994	259,159	2,528	1.0	3,953	2,279	854	9.7	15.2	8.8	3.3
1995	261,687	2,475	0.9	3,900	2,312	888	9.4	14.8	8.8	3.4
1996	264,162	2,330	0.9	3,850	2,349	829	8.8	14.5	8.9	3.1
PROJECTIONS[7]										
1997	266,449	2,374	0.9	3,907	2,353	820	8.9	14.6	8.8	3.1
1998	268,823	2,342	0.9	3,899	2,377	820	8.7	14.4	8.8	3.0
1999	271,166	2,316	0.9	3,896	2,401	820	8.5	14.3	8.8	3.0
2000	273,482	2,294	0.8	3,899	2,425	820	8.4	14.2	8.8	3.0
2005	284,847	2,276	0.8	4,001	2,543	820	8.0	14.0	8.9	2.9
2010	296,511	2,426	0.8	4,243	2,638	820	8.1	14.3	8.9	2.8
2015	308,675	2,521	0.8	4,450	2,749	820	8.1	14.3	8.9	2.6
2020	321,487	2,504	0.8	4,579	2,895	820	7.8	14.2	9.0	2.5
2025	333,638	2,414	0.7	4,679	3,085	820	7.2	14.0	9.2	2.4
2030	345,730	2,333	0.7	4,822	3,309	820	6.7	13.9	9.5	2.4
2040	368,823	2,319	0.6	5,248	3,749	820	6.3	14.2	10.1	2.2
2050	392,681	2,517	0.6	5,672	3,975	820	6.4	14.4	10.1	2.1

[1] Prior to April 1, 1990, includes "error of closure" (the amount necessary to make the components of change add to the net change between censuses), for which figures are not shown separately. [2] Percent of population at beginning of period. [3] Covers net international migration and movement of Armed Forces, federally affiliated civilian citizens, and their dependents. [4] Data are for period April 1 to December 31. [5] Net change for 1990 excludes "error of closure" for the three months prior to the April 1 census date. Therefore, it may not equal the difference between the populations at the beginning of 1990 and 1991. [6] Data reflect movement of Armed Forces due to the Gulf War. [7] Based on middle series of assumptions. See footnote 1, table 3.

Source: U.S. Bureau of the Census, *Current Population Reports*, P25-1095 and P25-1130; and Population Paper Listings PPL-57.

No. 5. Immigration: 1901 to 1995

[In thousands, except rate. For fiscal years ending in year shown ; see text, section 9. For definition of immigrants, see text, section 1. Data represent immigrants admitted. Rates based on Bureau of the Census estimates as of July 1 for resident population through 1929, and for total population thereafter (excluding Alaska and Hawaii prior to 1959)]

PERIOD	Number	Rate [1]	YEAR	Number	Rate [1]
1901 to 1910	8,795	10.4	1980	531	2.3
1911 to 1920	5,736	5.7	1985	570	2.4
1921 to 1930	4,107	3.5	1988	643	2.6
1931 to 1940	528	0.4	1989	1,091	4.4
1941 to 1950	1,035	0.7	1990	1,536	6.1
1951 to 1960	2,515	1.5	1991	1,827	7.2
1961 to 1970	3,322	1.7	1992	974	3.8
1971 to 1980	4,493	2.1	1993	904	3.5
1981 to 1990	7,338	3.1	1994	804	3.1
1991 to 1995	5,230	4.1	1995	720	2.7

[1] Annual rate per 1,000 U.S. population. Rate computed by dividing sum of annual immigration totals by sum of annual U.S. population totals for same number of years.

Source: U.S. Immigration and Naturalization Service, *Statistical Yearbook*, annual.

No. 6. Immigrants Admitted, by Class of Admission: 1990 to 1995

[For fiscal year ending September 30. For definition of immigrants, see text, section 1]

CLASS OF ADMISSION	1990	1991	1992	1993	1994	1995
Immigrants, total	1,536,483	1,827,167	973,977	904,292	804,416	720,461
New arrivals	435,729	443,107	511,769	536,294	490,429	380,291
Adjustments	1,100,754	1,384,060	462,208	367,998	313,987	340,170
Preference immigrants, total	272,742	275,613	329,321	373,788	335,252	323,458
Family-sponsored immigrants, total	214,550	216,088	213,123	226,776	211,961	238,122
Unmarried sons/daughters of U.S. citizens and their children	15,861	15,385	12,486	12,819	13,181	15,182
Spouses, unmarried sons/daughters of alien residents, and their children	107,686	110,126	118,247	128,308	115,000	144,535
Married sons/daughters of U.S. citizens [1]	26,751	27,115	22,195	23,385	22,191	20,876
Brothers or sisters of U.S. citizens [1]	64,252	63,462	60,195	62,264	61,589	57,529
Employment-based immigrants, total	58,192	59,525	116,198	147,012	123,291	85,336
Priority workers [1]	(X)	(X)	5,456	21,114	21,053	17,339
Professionals with advanced degrees [1]	(X)	(X)	58,401	29,468	14,432	10,475
Skilled workers, professionals, unskilled workers [1]	(X)	(X)	47,568	87,689	76,956	50,245
Special immigrants [1]	4,463	4,576	4,063	8,158	10,406	6,737
Employment creation [1]	(X)	(X)	59	583	444	540
Professional or highly skilled immigrants [1] [2]	26,546	27,748	340	(X)	(X)	(X)
Needed skilled or unskilled workers [1] [2]	27,183	27,201	311	(X)	(X)	(X)
Immediate relatives	231,680	237,103	235,484	255,059	249,764	220,360
Spouses of U.S. citizens	125,426	125,397	128,396	145,843	145,247	123,238
Children of U.S. citizens	46,065	48,130	42,324	46,788	48,147	48,740
Orphans	7,088	9,008	6,536	7,348	8,200	9,384
Parents of U.S. citizens	60,189	63,576	64,764	62,428	56,370	48,382
Refugees and asylees	97,364	139,079	117,037	127,343	121,434	114,664
Cuban Refugee Act, Nov. 1966	5,730	5,486	5,365	6,976	8,316	9,579
Indochinese Refugee Act, Oct. 1977	33	22	29	24	11	10
Refugee-Parolee Act, Oct. 1978	153	69	82	53	20	22
Asylees, Refugee Act of 1980	4,937	22,664	10,658	11,804	5,983	7,837
Refugees, Refugee Act of 1980	86,511	110,838	100,902	108,486	107,104	97,169
Other refugees	-	-	1	-	-	47
Other immigrants	934,697	1,175,372	292,135	148,102	97,966	61,979
Children born abroad to resident aliens or subsequent to issuance of visa	2,630	2,516	2,116	2,359	2,109	2,062
Diversity Programs [3]	29,161	22,070	36,348	33,480	41,056	47,245
Amerasians (P.L. 100-202) [4]	13,059	16,010	17,253	11,116	2,822	939
Immigration Reform and Control Act of 1986 legalization adjustments	880,372	1,123,162	163,342	24,278	6,022	4,267
Legalization dependents [5]	(X)	(X)	52,272	55,344	34,074	277
Other	9,475	11,614	20,804	21,525	11,883	7,189

- Represents zero. X Not applicable. [1] Includes spouses and children. [2] Category was eliminated in 1992 by the Immigration Act of 1990. [3] Includes categories of immigrants admitted under three laws intended to diversify immigration: P.L. 99-603, P.L. 100-658, and P.L. 101-649. [4] Under Public Law 100-202, Amerasians are aliens born in Vietnam between January 1, 1962, and January 1, 1976, who were fathered by U.S. citizens. [5] Spouses and children of persons granted permanent resident status under provisions of the Immigration Reform and Control Act of 1986.

Source: U.S. Immigration and Naturalization Service, *Statistical Yearbook*, annual.

No. 7. Nonimmigrants Admitted, by Class of Admission: 1985 to 1995

[In thousands, except as noted. For fiscal years ending Sept. 30; see text, section 9. Nonimmigrants are nonresident aliens (non-U.S. citizens) admitted to the United States for a temporary period. Excluded are border crossers, crewmen, and insular travelers]

CLASS OF ADMISSION	1985	1988	1990	1991	1992	1993	1994	1995
Nonimmigrants [1]	9,540	16,145	17,574	18,963	20,794	21,566	22,119	22,641
Temporary visitors, total	8,405	14,667	16,080	17,386	19,238	19,879	20,319	20,887
For pleasure	6,609	12,115	13,418	14,734	16,450	16,918	17,155	17,612
For business	1,797	2,553	2,661	2,652	2,788	2,961	3,164	3,275
Transit aliens [2]	237	293	306	364	346	331	331	320
Foreign government officials [3]	90	102	97	96	103	102	105	104
Treaty traders and investors [3]	97	140	148	155	152	145	141	132
Students [3]	286	361	355	314	275	403	428	395
Representatives to international organizations [3]	57	61	61	64	70	73	75	72
Temporary workers and trainees [4]	75	139	140	161	163	163	186	197
Registered nurses [5]	(X)	(X)	(X)	1	7	7	6	7
Specialty occupations [6]	(X)	(X)	(X)	117	110	93	108	118
Workers of distinguished merit or ability [7]	47	90	100	(X)	(X)	(X)	(X)	(X)
Performing services unavailable in U.S.	25	47	36	40	34	29	29	26
North America Free-Trade Agreement [8]	(X)	3	5	8	13	17	25	24
Spouses and children of workers and trainees [9]	13	24	29	35	41	42	49	54
Representatives of foreign information media [3]	17	21	20	21	22	21	26	24
Exchange visitors [3]	141	217	215	224	232	239	259	240
NATO officials [3]	8	9	6	9	9	9	9	9
Fiance(ees) of U.S. citizens [10]	8	7	7	8	9	9	9	9
Intracompany transferees [3]	107	101	103	113	121	132	154	174
Parolees [11]	64	107	90	127	137	124	111	114
Refugees	68	101	110	100	123	113	114	96

X Not applicable. [1] Includes nonimmigrants whose class of admission is unknown. [2] Includes foreign government officials and their spouses and (unmarried minor or dependent) children, in transit. [3] Includes spouses and children. [4] Includes other classes of admission, not shown separately. [5] Entries began October 1, 1990 (fiscal year 1991). Data for fiscal year 1991 are underreported; an unknown number of H1A entries were counted as H1B entries. [6] Prior to October 1, 1991 (fiscal year 1992), H1B entries were termed "Distinguished merit or ability." Data for fiscal year 1991 are overreported; an unknown number of H1A entries were counted as H1B entries. [7] Beginning 1992, as a result of the Immigration Act of 1990, the existing temporary worker and trainee classes of admission have been revised and new worker classes have been created. [8] Entries under the U.S.-Canada Free Trade Agreement began in January 1989 and under the North American Free Trade Agreement (NAFTA) in January 1994. [9] Includes spouses and children under NAFTA. [10] Includes children of fiances(ees) of U.S. citizens. [11] Aliens allowed to enter the United States for a temporary period of time on emergency conditions or when the entry is determined to be in the public interest (e.g., witness in court).

No. 8. Immigrants, by Country of Birth: 1981 to 1995

[In thousands. For fiscal years ending in year shown; see text, section 9. For definition of immigrants, see text, section 1]

COUNTRY OF BIRTH	1981-90, total	1991-93, total	1994	1995
All countries	7,338.1	3,705.4	804.4	720.5
Europe [1]	705.6	438.9	160.9	128.2
France	23.1	8.6	2.7	2.5
Germany	70.1	23.7	7.0	6.2
Greece	29.1	5.8	1.4	1.3
Ireland	32.8	30.6	17.3	5.3
Italy	32.9	7.7	2.3	2.2
Poland	97.4	72.5	28.0	13.8
Portugal	40.0	9.4	2.2	2.6
Romania	38.9	20.2	3.4	4.9
Soviet Union, former [2]	84.0	159.2	63.4	54.5
Armenia	(NA)	(NA)	4.0	2.0
Azerbaijan	(NA)	(NA)	3.8	1.9
Belarus	(NA)	(NA)	5.4	3.8
Moldova	(NA)	(NA)	2.3	1.9
Russia	(NA)	(NA)	15.2	14.6
Ukraine	(NA)	(NA)	21.0	17.4
Uzbekistan	(NA)	(NA)	3.4	3.6
United Kingdom	142.1	52.7	16.3	12.4
Yugoslavia	19.2	8.1	3.4	8.3
Asia [1]	2,817.4	1,073.5	292.6	267.9
Afghanistan	26.6	8.5	2.3	1.4
Bangladesh	15.2	17.7	3.4	6.1
Cambodia	116.6	7.5	1.4	1.5
China	[3]388.8	137.5	54.0	35.5
Hong Kong	63.0	30.0	7.7	7.2
India	261.9	121.9	34.9	34.7
Iran	154.8	47.6	11.4	9.2
Iraq	19.6	9.7	6.0	5.6
Israel	36.3	13.8	3.4	2.5
Japan	43.2	23.0	6.1	4.8
Jordan	32.6	13.0	4.0	3.6
Korea	338.8	63.9	16.0	16.0
Laos	145.6	25.9	5.1	3.9
Lebanon	41.6	17.3	4.3	3.9
Pakistan	61.3	39.5	8.7	9.8
Philippines	495.3	188.1	53.5	51.0
Syria	20.6	8.7	2.4	2.4
Taiwan	(3)	43.9	10.0	9.4
Thailand	64.4	21.1	5.5	5.1
Turkey	20.9	7.2	1.8	2.9
Vietnam	401.4	192.7	41.3	41.8
North America [1]	3,125.0	1,896.4	272.2	231.5
Canada	119.2	45.9	16.1	12.9
Mexico	1,653.3	1,286.5	111.4	89.9
Caribbean [1]	892.7	337.0	104.8	96.8
Cuba	159.2	35.8	14.7	17.9
Dominican Republic	251.8	128.8	51.2	38.5
Haiti	140.2	68.6	13.3	14.0
Jamaica	213.8	60.0	14.3	16.4
Trinidad and Tobago	39.5	22.0	6.3	5.4
Central America [1]	458.7	226.8	39.9	31.8
El Salvador	214.6	100.4	17.6	11.7
Guatemala	87.9	47.9	7.4	6.2
Honduras	49.5	25.3	5.3	5.5
Nicaragua	44.1	33.9	5.3	4.4
Panama	29.0	9.7	2.4	2.2
South America [1]	455.9	189.2	47.4	45.7
Argentina	25.7	10.6	2.3	1.8
Brazil	23.7	17.5	4.5	4.6
Chile	23.4	6.6	1.6	1.5
Colombia	124.4	45.7	10.8	10.8
Ecuador	56.0	24.6	5.9	6.4
Guyana	95.4	29.1	7.7	7.4
Peru	64.4	36.6	9.2	8.1
Venezuela	17.9	7.7	2.4	2.6
Africa [1]	192.3	91.0	26.7	42.5
Egypt	31.4	12.7	3.4	5.6
Ethiopia	27.2	15.0	3.9	7.0
Nigeria	35.3	16.9	4.0	6.8
South Africa	15.7	6.6	2.1	2.6
Other countries [4]	41.9	16.4	4.6	4.7

NA Not available. [1] Includes countries not shown separately. [2] Includes other republics and unknown republics, not shown separately. [3] Data for Taiwan included with China. [4] Includes Australia, New Zealand, and unknown countries.

Source of tables 7 and 8: U.S. Immigration and Naturalization Service, *Statistical Yearbook*, annual; and releases.

No. 9. Immigrants Admitted as Permanent Residents Under Refugee Acts, by Country of Birth: 1981 to 1995

[For fiscal years ending in year shown; see text, section 9. Covers immigrants who were allowed to enter the United States under 1953 Refugee Relief Act and later acts; Hungarian parolees under July 1958 Act; refugee-escapee parolees under July 1960 Act; conditional entries by refugees under Oct. 1965 Act; Cuban parolees under Nov. 1966 Act; Indochina refugees under Act of Oct. 1977; refugee-parolees under the Act of Oct. 1978, and asylees under the Act of March 1980; and refugees under the Act of March 1980]

COUNTRY OF BIRTH	1981-90, total	1991-93, total	1994	1995	COUNTRY OF BIRTH	1981-90, total	1991-93, total	1994	1995
Total	1,013,620	383,459	121,434	114,664	China [3]	7,926	2,673	774	806
Europe [1]	155,512	158,862	54,978	46,998	Hong Kong	1,916	358	82	48
Albania	353	1,812	733	314	Iran	46,773	15,483	2,186	1,245
Bulgaria	1,197	1,176	138	105	Iraq	7,540	2,414	4,400	3,848
Czechoslovakia	8,204	1,097	41	38	Laos	142,964	23,700	4,482	3,364
Hungary	4,942	1,126	37	28	Philippines	3,403	592	103	80
Poland	33,889	6,448	334	245	Syria	2,145	463	34	258
Romania	29,798	12,901	1,199	592	Thailand	30,259	11,375	3,076	2,932
Soviet Union,					Turkey	1,896	204	156	58
former [2]	72,306	130,955	50,756	40,120	Vietnam	324,453	83,947	27,318	28,595
Armenia	(NA)	(NA)	342	214	**North America** [1]	121,840	53,205	14,204	16,265
Azerbaijan	(NA)	(NA)	2,668	1,594	Cuba	113,367	29,475	11,998	12,355
Belarus	(NA)	(NA)	5,156	3,421	El Salvador	1,383	2,803	275	283
Moldova	(NA)	(NA)	2,154	1,597	Guatemala	(NA)	(NA)	131	158
Russia	(NA)	(NA)	10,359	8,176	Nicaragua	5,590	18,793	986	727
Ukraine	(NA)	(NA)	19,366	14,937	**South America**	1,976	1,223	383	497
Uzbekistan	(NA)	(NA)	3,211	3,258	**Africa** [1]	22,149	15,155	6,078	7,527
Yugoslavia	324	201	506	4,744	Ethiopia	18,542	10,532	2,530	2,006
Asia [1]	712,092	154,967	45,768	43,314	Sudan	(NA)	(NA)	402	935
Afghanistan	22,946	6,415	1,665	616					
Cambodia	114,064	5,053	557	268	**Other**	51	47	23	63

NA Not available. [1] Includes other countries, not shown separately. [2] Includes other republics and unknown republics, not shown separately. [3] Includes Taiwan.

Source: U.S. Immigration and Naturalization Service, *Statistical Yearbook*, annual; and releases.

No. 10. Estimated Undocumented Immigrants, by Selected States and Countries of Origin: 1994 and 1996

[In thousands. The ranges of estimates supplied by the Bureau of the Census represent indicators of magnitude which the Bureau believes is responsive to the inherent uncertainty in the assumptions underlying these estimates. The Census indicators are the results of applying three calculated percent distributions to two national estimates of the undocumented population. The three percent distributions by State are based on: (1) an average between the number of undocumented immigrants by State included in the 1980 census and of the number of legalization applicants by State produced by the Immigration Reform and Control Act (IRCA) of 1986; (2) the number of undocumented immigrants by State estimated by the Immigration and Naturalization Service (INS); and (3) the number of foreign born non-citizens by State counted in the 1990 census. The figures supplied by INS are based on estimates of illegal immigrant population who established residence in the United States before 1982 and did not legalize under IRCA and annual estimates of the number of persons who enter surreptitiously across land borders and nonimmigrant overstays who established residence here during the 1982 to 1996 period. The estimates for each country were distributed to States by INS based on U.S. residence pattern of each country's total number of applicants for legalization under IRCA]

STATE	BUREAU OF THE CENSUS ESTIMATES, 1994		INS estimates, Oct. 1996	COUNTRY	INS estimates, Oct. 1996
	Low	High			
United States, total [1]	3,500	4,000	5,000	**Total** [1]	5,000
California	1,321	1,784	2,000	Mexico	2,700
New York	462	539	540	El Salvador	335
Texas	300	427	700	Guatemala	165
Florida	243	385	350	Canada	120
Illinois	157	225	290	Haiti	105
New Jersey	98	168	135	Philippines	95
Massachusetts	42	108	85	Honduras	90
Arizona	50	68	115	Bahamas, The	70
Maryland	29	63	44	Nicaragua	70
Virginia	37	63	55	Poland	70
Washington	32	59	52	Colombia	65
Michigan	10	53	37	Ecuador	55
Pennsylvania	15	51	37	Jamaica	50
Connecticut	13	46	29	Dominican Republic	50
Georgia	29	36	32	Trinidad & Tobago	50
Ohio	7	36	23	Pakistan	41
Colorado	22	29	45	India	33
Oregon	21	27	33	Ireland	30
Hawaii	4	25	9	Portugal	27
New Mexico	14	25	37	Italy	25

[1] Includes other States and countries not shown separately.

Source: U.S. Bureau of the Census, *"Illustrative Ranges of the Distribution of Undocumented Immigrants by State"* by Edward W. Fernandez and J. Gregory Robinson, *Technical Working Paper No. 8, October 1994*; and U.S. Immigration and Naturalization Service, unpublished data.

No. 11. Immigrants Admitted, by Leading Country of Birth and State: 1995

[For year ending September 30. For definition of immigrants, see text, section 1]

REGION, DIVISION, AND STATE	Total [1]	Mexico	Soviet Union, former	Philippines	Vietnam	Dominican Republic	China	India	Cuba
U.S. [2]	720,461	89,932	54,494	50,984	41,752	38,512	35,463	34,748	17,937
Northeast	218,107	2,221	26,692	6,780	4,151	28,712	15,079	11,657	1,261
N.E.	34,907	263	3,249	576	1,725	2,801	1,820	1,490	88
ME	814	20	62	31	60	6	48	27	1
NH	1,186	27	66	44	129	23	58	61	1
VT	535	6	35	14	17	-	30	19	-
MA	20,523	89	2,253	229	1,247	1,970	1,287	873	54
RI	2,609	24	158	50	30	553	93	22	3
CT	9,240	97	675	208	242	249	304	488	29
M.A	183,200	1,958	23,443	6,204	2,426	25,911	13,259	10,167	1,173
NY	128,406	848	19,227	3,216	963	21,471	11,254	4,859	331
NJ	39,729	375	1,631	2,626	435	4,136	1,134	3,958	805
PA	15,065	735	2,585	362	1,028	304	871	1,350	37
Midwest	84,731	10,214	8,071	4,415	4,383	228	3,057	6,528	187
E.N.C	65,127	8,193	6,386	3,839	1,753	207	2,355	5,638	140
OH	8,585	212	1,481	300	350	44	525	806	8
IN	3,590	471	203	208	198	12	221	292	3
IL	33,898	6,500	3,384	2,690	583	102	986	3,051	96
MI	14,135	507	881	499	541	44	447	1,247	24
WI	4,919	503	437	144	81	5	176	242	9
W.N.C	19,604	2,021	1,685	576	2,630	21	702	890	47
MN	8,111	348	800	169	853	11	212	266	13
IA	2,260	337	94	65	430	-	52	140	1
MO	3,990	270	406	167	449	5	266	248	23
ND	483	12	28	15	15	-	10	28	-
SD	495	12	73	13	9	-	12	13	-
NE	1,831	495	119	49	454	2	52	47	3
KS	2,434	547	165	98	420	3	98	148	7
South	182,793	28,683	5,664	7,464	11,753	2,685	4,339	8,503	15,502
S.A.	118,199	4,645	4,313	4,802	5,828	2,522	2,626	4,810	15,283
DE	1,051	91	42	48	11	13	48	84	3
MD	15,055	133	1,576	823	722	179	633	1,029	34
DC	3,047	24	99	83	217	96	117	38	16
VA	16,319	318	575	1,219	1,236	69	455	931	36
WV	540	7	17	50	5	1	29	83	-
NC	5,617	407	241	262	623	27	235	423	19
SC	2,165	122	64	169	162	6	108	194	2
GA	12,381	1,621	678	342	1,658	39	362	887	61
FL	62,023	1,922	1,021	1,806	1,194	2,090	639	1,141	15,112
E.S.C	7,906	328	426	343	651	26	401	787	11
KY	1,857	80	197	90	185	4	84	155	1
TN	3,392	88	147	119	354	9	135	310	3
AL	1,900	134	66	85	80	5	107	237	4
MS	757	26	15	49	32	8	75	85	3
W.S.C	56,689	23,710	926	2,319	5,274	137	1,312	2,906	208
AR	934	167	17	83	123	2	35	41	5
LA	3,000	91	43	134	386	32	171	197	70
OK	2,792	660	42	105	514	2	104	268	2
TX	49,963	22,792	824	1,997	4,251	101	1,002	2,400	131
West	228,434	48,773	14,059	30,123	21,445	186	12,859	8,035	778
Mountain	27,581	10,601	1,422	1,358	1,534	60	934	719	330
MT	409	11	18	40	2	1	20	16	-
ID	1,612	841	69	53	90	2	46	29	3
WY	252	85	13	12	1	-	14	5	-
CO	7,713	2,677	782	151	600	6	276	177	1
NM	2,758	1,655	68	62	92	10	55	85	92
AZ	7,700	3,640	215	294	396	15	270	218	13
UT	2,831	565	174	59	255	15	105	74	1
NV	4,306	1,127	83	687	98	11	148	115	220
Pacific	196,853	38,172	12,637	28,765	19,911	126	11,925	7,316	448
WA	15,862	2,489	2,186	1,381	2,101	15	776	437	17
OR	4,923	1,166	313	224	695	2	371	188	1
CA	166,482	34,416	10,045	22,584	16,755	71	10,256	6,646	428
AK	1,049	56	77	268	28	37	42	9	2
HI	7,537	45	16	4,306	332	1	480	36	-

- Represents zero. [1] Includes other countries, not shown separately. [2] Includes Guam, Puerto Rico, Northern Mariana Islands, Virgin Islands, and other or unknown areas not shown separately.

Source: U.S. Immigration and Naturalization Service, *Statistical Yearbook*, annual.

[illegible] Population—Selected Characteristics, 1790 to 1996, and Projections, 2000 to 2050

[In thousands]

[illegible]	[illegible] Male	[illegible] Female	RACE White	RACE Black	RACE Other Total	RACE Other American Indian, Eskimo, Aleut	RACE Other Asian and Pacific Islanders	Hispanic origin [1]
[illegible]	NA	NA	3,172	757	(NA)	(NA)	(NA)	(NA)
[illegible]	NA	NA	4,306	1,002	(NA)	(NA)	(NA)	(NA)
[illegible]	[illegible]	[illegible]	19,553	3,639	(NA)	(NA)	(NA)	(NA)
[illegible]	[illegible]	[illegible]	66,809	8,834	351	(NA)	(NA)	(NA)
[illegible]	[illegible]	[illegible]	81,732	9,828	413	(NA)	(NA)	(NA)
[illegible]	[illegible]	[illegible]	94,821	10,463	427	(NA)	(NA)	(NA)
[illegible]	[illegible]	[illegible]	110,287	11,891	597	(NA)	(NA)	(NA)
[illegible]	[illegible]	[illegible]	118,215	12,866	589	(NA)	(NA)	(NA)
[illegible]	[illegible]	[illegible]	134,942	15,042	713	(NA)	(NA)	(NA)
[illegible]	[illegible]	[illegible]	135,150	15,045	1,131	(NA)	(NA)	(NA)
[illegible]	[illegible]	[illegible]	158,832	18,872	1,620	(NA)	(NA)	(NA)
[illegible]	[illegible]	[illegible]	178,098	22,581	2,557	(NA)	(NA)	(NA)
[illegible]	[illegible]	[illegible]	194,713	26,683	5,150	1,420	3,729	14,609
[illegible]	[illegible]	127,474	208,710	30,486	9,523	2,065	7,458	22,354
[illegible]	[illegible]	128,122	210,979	31,107	10,020	2,110	7,911	23,416
[illegible]	[illegible]	130,500	212,910	31,654	10,448	2,147	8,300	24,349
[illegible]	[illegible]	[illegible]	214,760	32,168	10,867	2,184	8,683	25,326
[illegible]	[illegible]	133,111	216,480	32,647	11,245	2,220	9,025	26,300
[illegible]	[illegible]	134,321	218,149	33,095	11,646	2,254	9,392	27,277
[illegible]	[illegible]	135,474	219,749	33,503	12,032	2,288	9,743	28,269
[illegible]	[illegible]	140,453	225,532	35,454	13,647	2,402	11,245	31,366
[illegible]	[illegible]	146,198	232,463	37,734	15,784	2,572	13,212	36,057
[illegible]	[illegible]	152,132	239,588	40,109	18,019	2,754	15,265	41,139
[illegible]	[illegible]	158,383	247,193	42,588	20,355	2,941	17,413	46,705
[illegible]	[illegible]	164,721	254,887	45,075	22,780	3,129	19,651	52,652
[illegible]	[illegible]	170,931	262,227	47,539	25,284	3,319	21,965	58,930
[illegible]	[illegible]	200,696	294,615	60,592	38,724	4,371	34,352	96,508

[illegible] [1] Persons of Hispanic origin may be of any race. [2] Excludes Alaska and Hawaii. [3] The revised 1970 [illegible] count is 203,302,031; which incorporates changes due to errors found after tabulations were completed. The [illegible] shown here reflect the official 1970 census count. [4] The race data shown have been modified; see text, section [illegible]. [5] See footnote 4, table 1. [6] The April 1, 1990, census count (248,718,291) includes count question [illegible] processed through March 1994 and does not include adjustments for census coverage errors. [illegible] [7] Middle series projection; see table 3.

No. 13. Resident Population Characteristics—Percent Distribution and Median Age, 1850 to 1996, and Projections, 2000 to 2050

[In percent, except as indicated. For definition of median, see Guide to Tabular Presentation]

DATE	SEX Male	SEX Female	RACE White	RACE Black	RACE Other	Hispanic origin [1]	Median age (years)
[illegible]	51.0	49.0	84.3	15.7	(NA)	(NA)	18.9
[illegible]	51.1	48.9	87.9	11.6	0.5	(NA)	22.9
[illegible]	51.5	48.5	88.9	10.7	0.4	(NA)	24.1
[illegible]	51.0	49.0	89.7	9.9	0.4	(NA)	25.3
[illegible]	50.6	49.4	89.8	9.7	0.5	(NA)	26.4
[illegible]	50.2	49.8	89.8	9.8	0.4	(NA)	29.0
[illegible]	49.7	50.3	89.5	10.0	0.5	(NA)	30.2
[illegible]	49.7	50.3	89.3	9.9	0.7	(NA)	30.2
[illegible]	49.3	50.7	88.6	10.5	0.9	(NA)	29.5
[illegible]	48.7	51.3	87.6	11.1	1.3	(NA)	28.0
[illegible]	48.6	51.4	85.9	11.8	2.3	6.4	30.0
[illegible]	48.7	51.3	83.9	12.3	3.8	9.0	32.8
[illegible]	48.9	51.1	83.0	12.6	4.4	10.4	34.3
[illegible]	48.9	51.1	82.8	12.6	4.5	10.7	34.6
[illegible]	48.9	51.1	82.1	12.9	5.0	11.4	35.7
[illegible]	49.0	51.0	78.3	14.2	7.5	17.6	38.0
[illegible]	49.1	50.9	74.8	15.4	9.8	24.5	38.1

NA Not available. [1] Persons of Hispanic origin may be of any race. [2] Excludes Alaska and Hawaii. [3] The race data shown have been modified; see text, section 1 for explanation. [4] See footnote 4, table 1. [5] See footnote 6, table 12. [6] Estimated. [7] Middle series projection; see table 3.

Source of tables 12 and 13: U.S. Bureau of the Census, *U.S. Census of Population: 1940*, vol. II, part 1, and vol IV, part 1; [illegible] vol II, part 1; *1960*, vol. I, part 1; *1970*, vol. I, part B; *Current Population Reports*, P25-1095 and P25-1130; Population Paper [illegible] PPL-57, and unpublished data.

No. 14. Resident Population, by Age and Sex: 1980 to 1996

[In thousands, except as indicated. 1980 and 1990 data are enumerated population as of April 1; data for other years are estimated population as of July 1. Excludes Armed Forces overseas. For definition of median, see Guide to Tabular Presentation]

YEAR AND SEX	Total, all years	Under 5 years	5-9 years	10-14 years	15-19 years	20-24 years	25-29 years	30-34 years	35-39 years	40-44 years	45-49 years	50-54 years	55-59 years	60-64 years	65-74 years	75-84 years	85 years and over	5-13 years	14-17 years	18-24 years	Median age (yr.)
1980, total [1]	226,546	16,348	16,700	18,242	21,168	21,319	19,521	17,561	13,965	11,669	11,090	11,710	11,615	10,088	15,581	7,729	2,240	31,159	16,247	30,022	30.0
Male	110,053	8,362	8,539	9,316	10,755	10,663	9,705	8,677	6,862	5,708	5,388	5,621	5,482	4,670	6,757	2,867	682	15,923	8,298	15,054	28.8
Female	116,493	7,986	8,161	8,926	10,413	10,655	9,816	8,884	7,104	5,961	5,702	6,089	6,133	5,418	8,824	4,862	1,559	15,237	7,950	14,969	31.3
1981, total	229,466	16,893	16,060	18,300	20,541	21,663	20,169	18,731	14,366	12,028	10,985	11,595	11,554	10,359	15,890	7,982	2,349	30,711	15,609	30,245	30.3
1982, total	231,664	17,228	15,958	18,145	19,962	21,682	20,704	18,714	15,566	12,464	11,011	11,414	11,463	10,567	16,147	8,203	2,437	30,528	15,057	30,162	30.5
1983, total	233,792	17,547	16,053	17,869	19,388	21,632	21,141	19,067	16,117	13,150	11,201	11,155	11,457	10,655	16,414	8,429	2,518	30,279	14,740	29,922	30.8
1984, total	235,825	17,695	16,338	17,450	18,931	21,529	21,459	19,503	16,867	13,636	11,429	10,957	11,352	10,803	16,626	8,656	2,595	30,062	14,725	29,461	31.1
1985, total	237,924	17,842	16,665	17,027	18,727	21,265	21,671	20,025	17,604	14,087	11,606	10,854	11,229	10,906	16,858	8,890	2,667	29,893	14,888	28,902	31.4
1986, total	240,133	17,963	17,098	16,474	18,813	20,744	21,893	20,479	18,611	14,398	11,878	10,781	11,135	10,859	17,137	9,129	2,742	30,078	14,824	28,227	31.7
1987, total	242,289	18,052	17,430	16,377	18,698	20,192	21,857	20,984	18,619	15,606	12,294	10,802	10,968	10,783	17,426	9,376	2,823	30,502	14,502	27,694	32.0
1988, total	244,499	18,195	17,759	16,496	18,496	19,655	21,739	21,391	18,993	16,188	12,954	10,995	10,722	10,791	17,626	9,612	2,885	31,028	14,023	27,356	32.3
1989, total	246,819	18,508	17,917	16,797	18,133	19,258	21,560	21,676	19,455	16,960	13,421	11,212	10,534	10,707	17,864	9,850	2,968	31,413	13,536	27,156	32.6
1990, total [2]	248,718	18,757	18,035	17,060	17,886	19,135	21,328	21,833	19,846	17,589	13,744	11,313	10,487	10,625	18,046	10,012	3,022	31,826	13,340	26,950	32.8
Male	121,244	9,599	9,232	8,739	9,175	9,744	10,703	10,862	9,834	8,677	6,739	5,493	5,008	4,947	7,907	3,745	841	16,295	6,857	13,738	31.6
Female	127,474	9,158	8,803	8,322	8,711	9,391	10,625	10,971	10,012	8,912	7,004	5,820	5,479	5,679	10,139	6,267	2,180	15,532	6,482	13,212	34.0
1991, total	252,106	19,185	18,200	17,654	17,230	19,174	20,714	22,153	20,522	18,758	14,098	11,650	10,423	10,581	18,268	10,311	3,185	32,446	13,439	26,374	33.1
1992, total	255,011	19,488	18,292	18,071	17,170	19,084	20,153	22,243	21,093	18,803	15,359	12,058	10,486	10,439	18,439	10,526	3,306	32,920	13,680	26,018	33.4
1993, total	257,795	19,670	18,446	18,476	17,358	18,839	19,598	22,239	21,604	19,205	15,933	12,732	10,681	10,237	18,624	10,722	3,431	33,364	13,958	25,797	33.7
1994, total	260,372	19,696	18,760	18,686	17,717	18,455	19,150	22,156	21,982	19,713	16,682	13,199	10,937	10,079	18,696	10,925	3,541	33,702	14,453	25,463	34.0
1995, total	262,890	19,535	19,107	18,826	18,169	18,055	18,972	21,863	22,310	20,260	17,462	13,647	11,092	10,049	18,743	11,149	3,652	34,189	14,786	25,181	34.3
1996, total	265,284	19,286	19,441	18,981	18,662	17,560	19,007	21,361	22,577	20,816	18,436	13,934	11,362	9,999	18,669	11,430	3,762	34,592	15,170	24,882	34.6
Male	129,810	9,868	9,954	9,727	9,619	8,999	9,538	10,653	11,259	10,310	9,060	6,776	5,455	4,711	8,325	4,486	1,070	17,716	7,817	12,766	33.5
Female	135,474	9,418	9,487	9,254	9,043	8,561	9,469	10,708	11,318	10,506	9,376	7,157	5,907	5,288	10,345	6,944	2,692	16,876	7,353	12,116	35.8
Percent:																					
1980 [1]	100.0	7.2	7.4	8.1	9.3	9.4	8.6	7.8	6.2	5.2	4.9	5.2	5.1	4.5	6.9	3.4	1.0	13.8	7.2	13.3	(X)
1990 [2]	100.0	7.5	7.3	6.9	7.2	7.7	8.6	8.8	8.0	7.1	5.5	4.5	4.2	4.3	7.3	4.0	1.2	12.8	5.4	10.8	(X)
1996	100.0	7.3	7.3	7.2	7.0	6.6	7.2	8.1	8.5	7.8	6.9	5.3	4.3	3.8	7.0	4.3	1.4	13.0	5.7	9.4	(X)
Male	100.0	7.6	7.7	7.5	7.4	6.9	7.3	8.2	8.7	7.9	7.0	5.2	4.2	3.6	6.4	3.5	0.8	13.6	6.0	9.8	(X)
Female	100.0	7.0	7.0	6.8	6.7	6.3	7.0	7.9	8.4	7.8	6.9	5.3	4.4	3.9	7.6	5.1	2.0	12.5	5.4	8.9	(X)

X Not applicable. [1] Total population count has been revised since the 1980 census publications. Numbers by age, race, Hispanic origin, and sex have not been corrected. [2] The data shown have been modified from the official 1990 census counts. See text, section 1, for explanation. The April 1, 1990, census count (248,718,291) includes count question resolution corrections processed through March 1994 and does not include adjustments for census coverage errors.

Source: U.S. Bureau of the Census, *Current Population Reports*, P25-1095; and Population Paper Listings 57.

No. 15. Ratio of Males to Females, by Age Group, 1980 to 1996, and Projections, 2000 and 2025

[Number of males per 100 females. Total resident population]

AGE	1980 (Apr. 1)	1990 [1] (Apr. 1)	1994 (July 1)	1995 (July 1)	1996 (July 1)	PROJECTIONS [2]	
						2000 (July 1)	2025 (July 1)
All ages	94.5	95.1	95.6	95.7	95.8	95.5	96.0
Under 14 years	104.6	104.9	104.9	104.9	104.9	104.8	105.1
14 to 24 years	101.9	104.6	105.3	105.5	105.7	104.1	104.2
25 to 44 years	97.4	98.9	99.3	99.4	99.4	98.9	97.7
45 to 64 years	90.7	92.5	93.5	93.6	93.8	93.8	93.5
65 years and over	67.6	67.2	68.6	69.1	69.5	70.4	82.9

[1] The April 1, 1990, census count (248,718,291) includes count question resolution corrections processed through March 1994, and does not include adjustments for census coverage errors. [2] Middle series projections; see table 3.

Source: U.S. Bureau of the Census, *Current Population Reports*, P25-1095 and P25-1130; and Population Paper Listings PPL-57.

No. 16. Resident Population, by Sex and Age: 1996

[In thousands, except as indicated. As of July For derivation of estimates, see text, section 1]

AGE	Total	Male	Female
Total	265,284	129,810	135,474
Under 5 yrs. old	19,286	9,868	9,418
Under 1 yr. old	3,769	1,928	1,841
1 yr. old	3,785	1,934	1,850
2 yrs. old	3,828	1,961	1,868
3 yrs. old	3,885	1,990	1,894
4 yrs. old	4,019	2,054	1,964
5 to 9 yrs. old	19,441	9,954	9,487
5 yrs. old	4,046	2,072	1,974
6 yrs. old	4,020	2,058	1,962
7 yrs. old	3,876	1,984	1,892
8 yrs. old	3,645	1,865	1,780
9 yrs. old	3,853	1,975	1,878
10 to 14 yrs. old	18,981	9,727	9,254
10 yrs. old	3,862	1,982	1,880
11 yrs. old	3,798	1,946	1,853
12 yrs. old	3,688	1,887	1,800
13 yrs. old	3,803	1,947	1,856
14 yrs. old	3,830	1,965	1,865
15 to 19 yrs. old	18,662	9,619	9,043
15 yrs. old	3,789	1,948	1,841
16 yrs. old	3,822	1,973	1,849
17 yrs. old	3,729	1,932	1,798
18 yrs. old	3,570	1,838	1,732
19 yrs. old	3,752	1,929	1,823
20 to 24 yrs. old	17,560	8,999	8,561
20 yrs. old	3,571	1,840	1,731
21 yrs. old	3,545	1,827	1,719
22 yrs. old	3,369	1,730	1,640
23 yrs. old	3,403	1,738	1,666
24 yrs. old	3,671	1,865	1,806
25 to 29 yrs. old	19,007	9,538	9,469
25 yrs. old	3,893	1,963	1,930
26 yrs. old	3,860	1,937	1,923
27 yrs. old	3,772	1,895	1,878
28 yrs. old	3,521	1,762	1,759
29 yrs. old	3,961	1,982	1,980
30 to 34 yrs. old	21,361	10,653	10,708
30 yrs. old	3,980	1,984	1,996
31 yrs. old	4,124	2,055	2,069
32 yrs. old	4,295	2,140	2,155
33 yrs. old	4,357	2,166	2,191
34 yrs. old	4,605	2,307	2,298
35 to 39 yrs. old	22,577	11,259	11,318
35 yrs. old	4,585	2,288	2,296
36 yrs. old	4,518	2,253	2,265
37 yrs. old	4,502	2,241	2,260
38 yrs. old	4,255	2,116	2,139
39 yrs. old	4,718	2,360	2,358
40 to 44 yrs. old	20,816	10,310	10,506
40 yrs. old	4,402	2,185	2,217
41 yrs. old	4,264	2,114	2,150
42 yrs. old	4,136	2,046	2,090
43 yrs. old	3,977	1,958	2,018
44 yrs. old	4,038	2,007	2,032
45 to 49 yrs. old	18,436	9,060	9,376
45 yrs. old	3,778	1,864	1,915
46 yrs. old	3,641	1,792	1,849
47 yrs. old	3,599	1,763	1,837
48 yrs. old	3,413	1,669	1,744
49 yrs. old	4,005	1,973	2,032
50 to 54 yrs. old	13,934	6,776	7,157
50 yrs. old	2,830	1,381	1,449
51 yrs. old	2,789	1,359	1,430
52 yrs. old	2,770	1,346	1,424
53 yrs. old	2,937	1,427	1,510
54 yrs. old	2,608	1,262	1,345
55 to 59 yrs. old	11,362	5,455	5,907
55 yrs. old	2,407	1,159	1,248
56 yrs. old	2,346	1,127	1,218
57 yrs. old	2,327	1,117	1,210
58 yrs. old	2,135	1,022	1,112
59 yrs. old	2,148	1,029	1,119
60 to 64 yrs. old	9,999	4,711	5,288
60 yrs. old	2,078	980	1,098
61 yrs. old	2,061	978	1,083
62 yrs. old	1,921	907	1,014
63 yrs. old	1,942	916	1,025
64 yrs. old	1,997	929	1,068
65 to 69 yrs. old	9,892	4,507	5,384
65 yrs. old	2,044	944	1,100
66 yrs. old	2,017	933	1,084
67 yrs. old	1,978	905	1,073
68 yrs. old	1,944	879	1,066
69 yrs. old	1,909	847	1,062
70 to 74 yrs. old	8,778	3,818	4,960
70 yrs. old	1,839	811	1,028
71 yrs. old	1,827	800	1,027
72 yrs. old	1,780	780	1,000
73 yrs. old	1,664	715	949
74 yrs. old	1,668	711	956
75 to 79 yrs. old	6,873	2,821	4,052
75 yrs. old	1,603	679	924
76 yrs. old	1,442	603	839
77 yrs. old	1,347	552	795
78 yrs. old	1,282	512	770
79 yrs. old	1,198	474	724
80 to 84 yrs. old	4,557	1,666	2,892
80 yrs. old	1,081	415	665
81 yrs. old	1,003	376	627
82 yrs. old	904	329	575
83 yrs. old	838	295	544
84 yrs. old	731	251	481
85 to 89 yrs. old	2,394	739	1,655
90 to 94 yrs. old	1,024	261	763
95 to 99 yrs. old	286	60	226
100 yrs. old and over	57	10	47
Median age (yr.)	34.6	33.5	35.8

Source: U S. Bureau of the Census, Population Paper Listings PPL-57

No. 17. Resident Population Projections, by Age and Sex: 1997 to 2050

[In thousands. As of July. See headnote, table 3]

YEAR	Total	Under 5 years	5 to 13 years	14 to 17 years	18 to 24 years	25 to 34 years	35 to 44 years	45 to 54 years	55 to 64 years	65 to 74 years	75 to 84 years	85 years and over
TOTAL												
Lowest series:												
1997	266,733	18,945	35,138	15,420	24,584	39,500	43,858	33,542	21,772	18,465	11,680	3,831
1998	268,396	18,626	35,487	15,428	24,972	38,530	44,257	34,432	22,585	18,286	11,851	3,943
1999	269,861	18,295	35,658	15,547	25,423	37,518	44,450	35,580	23,260	18,068	12,019	4,044
2000	271,237	17,943	35,790	15,602	25,876	36,740	44,364	36,840	23,798	17,974	12,162	4,148
2005	276,990	16,896	34,366	16,667	27,491	35,095	41,365	40,992	29,145	17,943	12,465	4,566
2010	281,468	16,563	31,950	16,319	29,050	36,393	37,049	42,589	34,393	20,245	11,912	5,005
2015	285,472	16,941	30,832	15,026	28,899	38,644	35,351	39,630	38,217	24,843	11,962	5,128
2020	288,807	17,168	30,998	14,331	26,671	40,067	36,640	35,487	39,642	29,219	13,598	4,987
2025	290,789	16,901	31,576	14,234	25,368	38,969	38,834	33,847	36,821	32,395	16,748	5,094
2030	291,070	16,450	31,454	14,631	25,111	36,312	40,222	35,075	32,948	33,483	19,610	5,776
2040	287,885	16,200	30,164	14,405	25,849	35,018	36,489	36,475	32,631	27,827	22,376	8,250
2050	282,524	16,330	30,124	13,925	24,810	35,604	35,185	34,868	35,747	27,700	18,588	9,642
Middle series:												
1997	267,645	19,229	35,206	15,463	24,690	39,624	43,930	33,591	21,816	18,511	11,723	3,862
1998	270,002	19,117	35,609	15,503	25,160	38,757	44,389	34,520	22,662	18,365	11,925	3,996
1999	272,330	19,041	35,848	15,661	25,710	37,876	44,661	35,717	23,378	18,186	12,129	4,124
2000	274,634	18,987	36,043	15,752	26,258	37,233	44,659	37,030	23,962	18,136	12,315	4,259
2005	285,981	19,127	35,850	16,986	28,268	36,306	42,165	41,507	29,606	18,369	12,898	4,899
2010	297,716	20,012	35,605	16,894	30,138	38,292	38,521	43,564	35,283	21,057	12,680	5,671
2015	310,134	21,174	36,698	16,651	30,516	41,084	37,598	41,196	39,650	26,243	13,130	6,193
2020	322,742	21,979	38,660	16,965	29,919	42,934	39,612	37,740	41,714	31,385	15,375	6,460
2025	335,050	22,498	40,413	17,872	30,372	43,119	42,391	36,890	39,542	35,425	19,481	7,046
2030	346,899	23,066	41,569	18,788	31,826	42,744	44,263	38,897	36,348	37,406	23,517	8,455
2040	369,980	24,980	43,993	19,844	34,570	45,932	44,159	43,530	37,739	33,013	28,668	13,552
2050	393,931	27,106	47,804	21,207	36,333	49,365	47,393	43,494	42,368	34,731	25,905	18,223
Highest series:												
1997	268,577	19,483	35,277	15,507	24,798	39,761	44,024	33,644	21,853	18,552	11,775	3,902
1998	271,647	19,563	35,735	15,581	25,352	39,004	44,561	34,615	22,728	18,434	12,011	4,063
1999	274,865	19,726	36,039	15,780	26,004	38,264	44,932	35,868	23,482	18,290	12,257	4,225
2000	278,129	19,955	36,300	15,909	26,651	37,766	45,038	37,241	24,105	18,276	12,490	4,399
2005	295,318	21,350	37,266	17,318	29,064	37,599	43,197	42,119	29,997	18,723	13,367	5,317
2010	314,571	23,649	39,195	17,467	31,248	40,275	40,302	44,738	36,018	21,696	13,465	6,518
2015	335,597	25,757	42,763	18,228	32,120	43,587	40,161	43,020	40,839	27,278	14,260	7,583
2020	357,702	27,273	46,855	19,641	33,084	45,836	42,878	40,263	43,473	32,937	17,007	8,456
2025	380,781	28,828	50,036	21,737	35,428	47,204	46,208	40,172	41,925	37,593	21,882	9,768
2030	405,089	30,818	52,876	23,276	38,886	49,091	48,519	42,895	39,398	40,270	26,861	12,198
2040	458,444	35,901	60,446	26,000	44,069	57,362	51,925	48,560	42,258	37,096	33,907	20,920
2050	518,903	41,213	70,000	30,005	49,683	64,279	60,324	51,967	47,950	40,319	32,070	31,093
MALE (middle series)												
1997	130,712	9,839	18,024	7,941	12,550	19,774	21,808	16,409	10,390	8,266	4,621	1,089
1998	131,883	9,780	18,232	7,961	12,787	19,325	22,044	16,860	10,805	8,224	4,730	1,134
1999	133,039	9,740	18,355	8,042	13,063	18,869	22,184	17,446	11,150	8,171	4,839	1,179
2000	134,181	9,712	18,454	8,090	13,338	18,535	22,181	18,092	11,433	8,180	4,937	1,228
2005	139,785	9,786	18,353	8,724	14,359	18,014	20,891	20,304	14,166	8,408	5,306	1,473
2010	145,584	10,243	18,232	8,679	15,313	18,990	18,993	21,325	16,922	9,752	5,363	1,771
2015	151,750	10,844	18,801	8,554	15,505	20,393	18,479	20,119	19,077	12,273	5,711	1,995
2020	158,021	11,259	19,813	8,718	15,201	21,319	19,466	18,347	20,120	14,791	6,845	2,141
2025	164,119	11,525	20,712	9,184	15,432	21,405	20,848	17,878	19,048	16,826	8,839	2,422
2030	169,950	11,813	21,311	9,653	16,171	21,214	21,775	18,854	17,441	17,878	10,819	3,021
2040	181,261	12,788	22,534	10,192	17,563	22,808	21,723	21,139	18,093	15,796	13,522	5,103
2050	193,234	13,877	24,488	10,893	18,462	24,533	23,352	21,150	20,403	16,699	12,342	7,036
FEMALE (middle series)												
1997	136,933	9,389	17,182	7,522	12,139	19,850	22,122	17,182	11,426	10,246	7,102	2,773
1998	138,119	9,336	17,377	7,542	12,373	19,432	22,345	17,659	11,857	10,141	7,194	2,862
1999	139,291	9,302	17,492	7,619	12,647	19,007	22,476	18,271	12,228	10,015	7,290	2,945
2000	140,453	9,274	17,589	7,662	12,920	18,699	22,478	18,938	12,529	9,956	7,377	3,031
2005	146,196	9,341	17,498	8,262	13,909	18,291	21,273	21,203	15,440	9,961	7,592	3,426
2010	152,132	9,768	17,373	8,215	14,824	19,301	19,527	22,240	18,362	11,305	7,317	3,899
2015	158,383	10,330	17,897	8,097	15,010	20,691	19,119	21,078	20,572	13,971	7,419	4,199
2020	164,721	10,719	18,847	8,247	14,717	21,615	20,146	19,393	21,594	16,594	8,530	4,319
2025	170,931	10,973	19,701	8,688	14,939	21,715	21,543	19,011	20,495	18,599	10,643	4,624
2030	176,949	11,253	20,278	9,135	15,655	21,529	22,488	20,044	18,907	19,529	12,699	5,433
2040	188,719	12,192	21,459	9,652	17,006	23,125	22,436	22,391	19,646	17,216	15,146	8,449
2050	200,696	13,229	23,316	10,314	17,871	24,832	24,041	22,344	21,965	18,032	13,563	11,188

Source: U.S. Bureau of the Census, *Current Population Reports*, P25-1130.

No. 18. Resident Population, by Race, 1980 to 1996, and Projections, 1997 to 2050

[In thousands, except as indicated. As of July, except as indicated. These data are consistent with the 1980 and 1990 decennial enumerations and have been modified from the official census counts; see text, section 1, for explanation. See headnote, table 3]

YEAR	Total	White	Black	American Indian, Eskimo, Aleut	Asian, Pacific Islander
1980 (April) [1]	226,546	194,713	26,683	1,420	3,729
1981	229,466	196,635	27,133	1,483	4,214
1982	231,664	198,037	27,508	1,537	4,581
1983	233,792	199,420	27,867	1,596	4,909
1984	235,825	200,708	28,212	1,656	5,249
1985	237,924	202,031	28,569	1,718	5,606
1986	240,133	203,430	28,942	1,783	5,978
1987	242,289	204,770	29,325	1,851	6,343
1988	244,499	206,129	29,723	1,923	6,724
1989	246,819	207,540	30,143	2,001	7,134
1990 (April) [2]	248,718	208,710	30,486	2,065	7,458
1991	252,106	210,979	31,107	2,110	7,911
1992	255,011	212,910	31,654	2,147	8,300
1993	257,795	214,760	32,168	2,184	8,683
1994	260,372	216,480	32,647	2,220	9,025
1995	262,890	218,149	33,095	2,254	9,392
1996	265,284	219,749	33,503	2,288	9,743
PROJECTIONS					
Lowest series:					
1997	266,733	220,507	33,973	2,300	9,953
1998	268,396	221,501	34,357	2,328	10,211
1999	269,861	222,346	34,721	2,355	10,440
2000	271,237	223,114	35,074	2,382	10,667
2005	276,990	226,006	36,695	2,514	11,774
2010	281,468	227,841	38,139	2,642	12,845
2015	285,472	229,295	39,491	2,766	13,920
2020	288,807	230,202	40,709	2,881	15,015
2030	291,070	228,310	42,519	3,060	17,161
2040	287,685	221,671	43,674	3,247	19,092
2050	282,524	213,782	44,477	3,383	20,882
Middle series:					
1997	267,645	221,163	34,075	2,305	10,102
1998	270,002	222,648	34,537	2,337	10,480
1999	272,330	224,103	34,997	2,369	10,861
2000	274,634	225,532	35,454	2,402	11,245
2005	285,981	232,463	37,734	2,572	13,212
2010	297,716	239,588	40,109	2,754	15,265
2015	310,134	247,193	42,586	2,941	17,413
2020	322,742	254,887	45,075	3,129	19,651
2030	346,899	269,046	50,001	3,515	24,337
2040	369,980	281,720	55,094	3,932	29,235
2050	393,931	294,615	60,592	4,371	34,352
Highest series:					
1997	268,577	221,809	34,200	2,310	10,257
1998	271,647	223,785	34,755	2,346	10,761
1999	274,865	225,848	35,332	2,383	11,302
2000	278,129	227,937	35,919	2,421	11,851
2005	295,318	238,906	39,050	2,627	14,735
2010	314,571	251,262	42,590	2,860	17,859
2015	335,597	264,859	46,435	3,108	21,195
2020	357,702	279,139	50,490	3,365	24,709
2030	405,089	309,404	59,449	3,934	32,302
2040	458,444	343,201	69,844	4,609	40,790
2050	518,903	381,505	81,815	5,384	50,199
PERCENT DISTRIBUTION					
Middle series:					
2000	100.0	82.1	12.9	0.9	4.1
2010	100.0	80.5	13.5	0.9	5.1
2020	100.0	79.0	14.0	1.0	6.1
2030	100.0	77.6	14.4	1.0	7.0
2040	100.0	76.1	14.9	1.1	7.9
2050	100.0	74.8	15.4	1.1	8.7
PERCENT CHANGE (middle series)					
2000-2010	8.4	6.2	13.1	14.6	35.8
2010-2020	8.4	6.4	12.4	13.6	28.7
2020-2030	7.5	5.6	10.9	12.3	23.8
2030-2040	6.7	4.7	10.2	11.8	20.1
2040-2050	6.5	4.6	10.0	11.2	17.5

[1] See footnote 4, table 1. [2] The April 1, 1990, census count (248,718,291) includes count question resolution corrections processed through March 1994 and does not include adjustments for census coverage errors.

Source: U.S. Bureau of the Census, *Current Population Reports*, P25-1095 and P25-1130; and Population Paper Listing PPL-57.

No. 19. Resident Population, by Hispanic Origin Status, 1980 to 1996, and Projections, 1997 to 2050

[In thousands, except as indicated. As of July, except as indicated. These data are consistent with the 1980 and 1990 decennial enumerations and have been modified from the official census counts; see text, section 1, for explanation. See headnote, table 3. Minus sign (-) indicates decrease]

YEAR	Total	Hispanic origin [1]	NOT OF HISPANIC ORIGIN			
			White	Black	American Indian, Eskimo, Aleut	Asian, Pacific Islander
1980 (April) [2]	226,546	14,609	180,906	26,142	1,326	3,563
1981	229,466	15,560	181,974	26,532	1,377	4,022
1982	231,664	16,240	182,782	26,856	1,420	4,367
1983	233,792	16,935	183,561	27,159	1,466	4,671
1984	235,825	17,640	184,243	27,444	1,512	4,986
1985	237,924	18,368	184,945	27,738	1,558	5,315
1986	240,133	19,154	185,678	28,040	1,606	5,655
1987	242,289	19,946	186,353	28,351	1,654	5,985
1988	244,499	20,786	187,012	28,669	1,703	6,329
1989	246,819	21,648	187,713	29,005	1,755	6,698
1990 (April) [3]	248,718	22,354	188,306	29,275	1,798	6,988
1991	252,106	23,416	189,610	29,829	1,829	7,422
1992	255,011	24,349	190,693	30,317	1,856	7,796
1993	257,795	25,326	191,658	30,767	1,882	8,161
1994	260,372	26,300	192,496	31,183	1,907	8,486
1995	262,890	27,277	193,281	31,565	1,931	8,836
1996	265,284	28,269	193,978	31,912	1,954	9,171
PROJECTIONS						
Lowest series:						
1997	266,733	28,431	194,657	32,314	1,977	9,354
1998	268,396	29,115	195,037	32,647	1,999	9,598
1999	269,861	29,757	195,307	32,962	2,020	9,815
2000	271,237	30,393	195,505	33,267	2,041	10,030
2005	276,990	33,527	195,589	34,652	2,145	11,077
2010	281,468	36,652	194,628	35,856	2,243	12,088
2015	285,472	39,927	193,150	36,956	2,337	13,102
2020	288,807	43,287	191,047	37,913	2,424	14,136
2030	291,070	49,834	183,295	39,202	2,573	16,166
2040	287,685	56,104	171,054	39,841	2,695	17,991
2050	282,524	62,230	157,701	40,118	2,793	19,683
Middle series:						
1997	267,645	28,680	195,091	32,396	1,980	9,497
1998	270,002	29,566	195,786	32,789	2,005	9,856
1999	272,330	30,461	196,441	33,180	2,029	10,219
2000	274,634	31,366	197,061	33,568	2,054	10,584
2005	285,981	36,057	199,802	35,465	2,183	12,454
2010	297,716	41,139	202,390	37,466	2,320	14,402
2015	310,134	46,705	205,019	39,512	2,461	16,437
2020	322,742	52,652	207,393	41,538	2,601	18,557
2030	346,899	65,570	209,998	45,448	2,891	22,993
2040	369,980	80,164	209,621	49,379	3,203	27,614
2050	393,931	96,508	207,901	53,555	3,534	32,432
Highest series:						
1997	238,577	28,931	195,516	32,501	1,963	9,646
1998	271,647	30,019	196,521	32,971	2,010	10,127
1999	274,885	31,172	197,556	33,457	2,038	10,642
2000	278,129	32,350	198,594	33,952	2,066	11,166
2005	295,318	38,648	203,949	36,589	2,218	13,914
2010	314,571	45,760	209,963	39,572	2,391	16,885
2015	335,597	53,686	216,482	42,800	2,575	20,055
2020	357,702	62,279	223,082	46,183	2,765	23,392
2030	405,089	81,803	235,898	53,604	3,192	30,593
2040	458,444	105,274	248,715	62,132	3,703	38,620
2050	518,903	133,106	262,140	71,863	4,295	47,498
PERCENT DISTRIBUTION						
Middle series:						
2000	100.0	11.4	71.8	12.2	0.7	3.9
2010	100.0	13.8	68.0	12.6	0.8	4.8
2020	100.0	16.3	64.3	12.9	0.8	5.7
2030	100.0	18.9	60.5	13.1	0.8	6.6
2040	100.0	21.7	56.7	13.3	0.9	7.5
2050	100.0	24.5	52.8	13.6	0.9	8.2
PERCENT CHANGE (middle series)						
2000-2010	8.4	31.2	2.7	11.6	12.9	36.1
2010-2020	8.4	28.0	2.5	10.9	12.1	28.9
2020-2030	7.5	24.5	1.3	9.4	11.1	23.9
2030-2040	6.7	22.3	-0.2	8.6	10.8	20.1
2040-2050	6.5	20.4	-0.8	8.5	10.3	17.4

[1] Persons of Hispanic origin may be of any race. [2] See footnote 4, table 1. [3] The April 1, 1990, census count (248,718,291) includes count question resolution corrections processed through March 1994 and does not include adjustments for census coverage errors.

Source: U.S. Bureau of the Census, *Current Population Reports*, P25-1095 and P25-1130; and Population Paper Listing PPL-57.

No. 20. Components of Population Change, by Race and Hispanic Origin, 1990 to 1996, and Projections, 2000

[The April 1, 1990, census count (248,718,291) includes count question resolution corrections processed through March 1994 and does not include adjustments for census coverage errors]

YEAR	TOTAL (Jan. 1-Dec. 31)						RATE PER 1,000 MIDYEAR POPULATION			
	Population at start of period (1,000)	Net increase [1]		Natural increase		Net migration [3] (1,000)	Net growth rate [1]	Natural increase		Net migration rate [3]
		Total (1,000)	Percent [2]	Births (1,000)	Deaths (1,000)			Birth rate	Death rate	
WHITE										
1990	208,376	1,711	0.8	3,285	1,860	[4]306	8.2	15.6	8.9	[4]1.5
1992	211,969	1,950	0.9	3,202	1,874	622	9.2	15.0	8.8	2.9
1993	213,919	1,751	0.8	3,150	1,951	553	8.2	14.7	9.1	2.6
1994	215,670	1,691	0.8	3,121	1,960	530	7.8	14.4	9.1	2.4
1995	217,361	1,653	0.8	3,105	1,991	538	7.6	14.2	9.1	2.5
1996	219,014	1,520	0.7	3,043	2,023	500	6.9	13.8	9.2	2.3
2000, proj. [5]	224,818	1,419	0.6	2,986	2,058	491	6.3	13.2	9.1	2.2
BLACK										
1990	30,377	453	1.5	692	266	[4]27	14.8	22.6	8.7	[4]0.9
1992	31,394	540	1.7	674	269	135	17.0	21.3	8.5	4.3
1993	31,934	489	1.5	659	282	113	15.2	20.5	8.8	3.5
1994	32,423	461	1.4	636	282	107	14.1	19.5	8.6	3.3
1995	32,884	425	1.3	599	284	110	12.8	18.1	8.6	3.3
1996	33,309	427	1.3	605	288	111	12.8	18.1	8.6	3.3
2000, proj. [5]	35,225	457	1.3	685	319	90	12.9	19.3	9.0	2.6
AMERICAN INDIAN, ESKIMO, ALEUT										
1990	2,044	35	1.7	42	8	[4]1	16.7	20.1	4.1	[4]0.6
1992	2,128	38	1.8	39	9	8	17.7	18.4	4.2	3.5
1993	2,166	36	1.7	39	10	7	16.6	17.7	4.4	3.3
1994	2,203	34	1.5	38	10	6	15.5	17.0	4.3	2.8
1995	2,237	34	1.5	38	10	6	15.2	16.8	4.4	2.8
1996	2,271	35	1.5	38	10	6	15.1	16.5	4.2	2.8
2000, proj. [5]	2,386	33	1.4	42	13	4	13.7	17.3	5.2	1.6
ASIAN, PACIFIC ISLANDER										
1990	7,345	372	5.1	149	21	[4]244	49.3	19.8	2.7	[4]32.3
1992	8,097	395	4.9	150	24	269	47.6	18.1	2.9	32.4
1993	8,493	371	4.4	153	25	243	42.7	17.6	2.9	28.0
1994	8,863	342	3.9	158	27	211	37.9	17.5	3.0	23.4
1995	9,205	363	3.9	158	28	232	38.7	16.9	3.0	24.8
1996	9,568	347	3.6	164	28	212	35.7	16.8	2.9	21.7
2000, proj. [5]	11,053	386	3.5	186	36	235	34.3	16.6	3.2	20.9
HISPANIC ORIGIN [6]										
1990	22,122	803	3.6	595	84	[4]292	35.6	26.4	3.7	[4]12.9
1992	23,867	965	4.0	649	87	403	39.6	26.6	3.6	16.5
1993	24,832	975	3.9	661	93	407	38.5	26.1	3.7	16.1
1994	25,807	968	3.8	672	97	393	36.8	25.6	3.7	14.9
1995	26,775	1,013	3.8	679	101	434	37.1	24.9	3.7	15.9
1996	27,787	969	3.5	688	105	386	34.3	24.4	3.7	13.7
2000, proj. [5]	30,913	910	2.9	683	123	350	29.0	21.8	3.9	11.2
WHITE, NON-HISPANIC										
1990	188,160	969	0.5	2,720	1,782	[4]52	5.2	14.4	9.4	[4]0.3
1992	190,188	1,076	0.6	2,609	1,794	261	5.6	13.7	9.4	1.4
1993	191,265	868	0.5	2,546	1,865	187	4.5	13.3	9.7	1.0
1994	192,132	816	0.4	2,508	1,871	179	4.2	13.0	9.7	0.9
1995	192,948	732	0.4	2,486	1,898	144	3.8	12.9	9.8	0.7
1996	193,681	639	0.3	2,413	1,925	151	3.3	12.4	9.9	0.8
2000, proj. [5]	196,751	605	0.3	2,365	1,946	186	3.1	12.0	9.9	0.9
BLACK, NON-HISPANIC										
1990	29,191	397	1.4	659	262	[4]-	13.5	22.4	8.9	[4]-
1992	30,069	476	1.6	636	265	105	15.7	21.0	8.7	3.5
1993	30,566	426	1.4	620	277	83	13.8	20.2	9.0	2.7
1994	30,992	395	1.3	597	277	76	12.7	19.1	8.9	2.4
1995	31,386	361	1.2	558	279	82	11.4	17.7	8.8	2.6
1996	31,748	366	1.2	565	283	84	11.5	17.7	8.9	2.6
2000, proj. [5]	33,374	387	1.2	641	312	57	11.5	19.1	9.3	1.7

- Represents or rounds to zero. [1] Net change for 1990 excludes "error of closure" for the three months prior to the April 1 census date. [2] Percent of population at beginning of period. [3] Covers net international migration and movement of Armed Forces, federally affiliated civilian citizens, and their dependents. [4] Data reflect movement of Armed Forces due to the Gulf War. [5] Based on middle series of assumptions. See footnote 1, table 3. [6] Persons of Hispanic origin may be of any race.

Source: U.S. Bureau of the Census, *Current Population Reports*, P25-1130; and Population Paper Listing 57.

No. 21. Resident Population, by Age and Race: 1990 to 1996

[In thousands, except percent. As of July, except 1990 as of April. See headnote, table 18]

YEAR, SEX, AND RACE	Total, all years	Under 5 years	5-9 years	10-14 years	15-19 years	20-24 years	25-29 years	30-34 years	35-39 years	40-44 years	45-49 years	50-54 years	55-59 years	60-64 years	65-74 years	75-84 years	85 years and over	5-13 years	14-17 years	18-24 years
ALL RACES																				
1990 [1]	248,718	18,757	18,036	17,060	17,886	19,135	21,328	21,833	19,846	17,589	13,744	11,313	10,487	10,625	18,046	10,012	3,022	31,826	13,340	26,950
1995	262,890	19,535	19,107	18,826	18,169	18,055	18,972	21,863	22,310	20,260	17,462	13,647	11,092	10,049	18,743	11,149	3,652	34,189	14,786	25,181
1996	265,284	19,286	19,441	18,981	18,662	17,560	19,007	21,361	22,577	20,816	18,436	13,934	11,362	9,999	18,669	11,430	3,762	34,592	15,170	24,882
Male	129,810	9,868	9,954	9,727	9,619	8,999	9,538	10,653	11,259	10,310	9,060	6,776	5,455	4,711	8,325	4,486	1,070	17,716	7,817	12,766
Female	135,474	9,418	9,487	9,254	9,043	8,561	9,469	10,708	11,318	10,506	9,376	7,157	5,907	5,288	10,345	6,944	2,692	16,876	7,353	12,116
WHITE																				
1990 [1]	208,710	14,960	14,502	13,670	14,354	15,640	17,638	18,190	16,652	15,001	11,826	9,744	9,131	9,381	16,175	9,085	2,761	25,557	10,664	21,946
1995	218,149	15,458	15,142	14,978	14,464	14,429	15,356	17,980	18,502	16,956	14,862	11,730	9,539	8,720	16,622	10,098	3,312	27,147	11,744	20,123
1996	219,749	15,289	15,361	15,077	14,838	14,010	15,340	17,477	18,697	17,384	15,643	11,952	9,763	8,652	16,512	10,348	3,406	27,401	12,030	19,855
Male	108,052	7,839	7,879	7,744	7,677	7,233	7,775	8,812	9,422	8,706	7,776	5,873	4,738	4,126	7,419	4,076	959	14,060	6,216	10,257
Female	111,696	7,450	7,482	7,334	7,161	6,776	7,565	8,665	9,275	8,678	7,867	6,079	5,025	4,526	9,093	6,273	2,447	13,341	5,814	9,599
BLACK																				
1990 [1]	30,486	2,939	2,711	2,629	2,715	2,656	2,780	2,718	2,360	1,882	1,413	1,178	1,041	972	1,498	772	223	4,838	2,056	3,818
1995	33,095	3,037	3,019	2,873	2,827	2,648	2,592	2,825	2,792	2,393	1,854	1,382	1,138	990	1,618	831	277	5,318	2,303	3,745
1996	33,503	2,948	3,093	2,906	2,904	2,593	2,601	2,810	2,834	2,481	1,997	1,413	1,163	995	1,634	846	286	5,407	2,362	3,725
Male	15,903	1,494	1,569	1,475	1,475	1,281	1,244	1,320	1,331	1,154	912	633	510	427	682	311	83	2,744	1,205	1,851
Female	17,600	1,454	1,524	1,430	1,429	1,311	1,357	1,490	1,503	1,327	1,085	780	653	568	951	535	203	2,663	1,157	1,874
AMERICAN INDIAN, ESKIMO, ALEUT																				
1990 [1]	2,065	220	209	197	191	179	188	181	157	132	99	79	64	53	73	34	9	388	151	257
1995	2,254	205	228	234	203	189	183	188	178	156	125	94	72	58	84	42	15	414	176	263
1996	2,288	203	227	237	212	188	188	186	181	161	131	97	74	59	86	44	17	416	182	263
Male	1,136	102	115	120	107	95	98	94	90	78	64	47	35	28	39	18	5	212	92	134
Female	1,152	100	111	117	105	91	90	92	92	83	67	51	39	31	47	26	11	205	90	129
ASIAN, PACIFIC ISLANDER																				
1990 [1]	7,458	638	612	564	626	661	722	745	678	574	405	312	252	220	300	122	29	1,063	469	930
1995	9,392	836	718	742	674	789	841	870	837	755	620	441	342	281	419	178	47	1,310	563	1,051
1996	9,743	846	761	761	708	771	878	888	865	791	666	471	361	293	438	192	52	1,368	596	1,038
Male	4,719	432	391	388	360	389	422	427	416	372	309	223	171	131	185	82	22	701	304	524
Female	5,024	414	370	373	349	382	457	461	449	419	357	248	190	162	254	110	31	667	292	514
PERCENT																				
Total, 1996	100.0	7.3	7.3	7.2	7.0	6.6	7.2	8.1	8.5	7.8	6.9	5.3	4.3	3.8	7.0	4.3	1.4	13.0	5.7	9.4
White	100.0	7.0	7.0	6.9	6.8	6.4	7.0	8.0	8.5	7.9	7.1	5.4	4.4	3.9	7.5	4.7	1.5	12.5	5.5	9.0
Black	100.0	8.8	9.2	8.7	8.7	7.7	7.8	8.4	8.5	7.4	6.0	4.2	3.5	3.0	4.9	2.5	0.9	16.1	7.1	11.1
American Indian, Eskimo, Aleut	100.0	8.9	9.9	10.4	9.3	8.1	8.2	8.1	7.9	7.0	5.7	4.2	3.2	2.6	3.8	1.9	0.7	18.2	8.0	11.5
Asian, Pacific Islander	100.0	8.7	7.8	7.8	7.3	7.9	9.0	9.1	8.9	8.1	6.8	4.8	3.7	3.0	4.5	2.0	0.5	14.0	6.1	10.7

[1] The April 1, 1990, census count (248,718,291) includes count question resolution corrections processed through March 1994, and does not include adjustments for census coverage errors.

Source: U.S. Bureau of the Census, *Current Population Reports*, P25-1095; and Population Paper Listing 57.

No. 22. Resident Population, by Race, Hispanic Origin, and Single Years of Age: 1996

[In thousands, except as indicated. As of July 1. Resident population. For derivation of estimates, see text, section 1]

AGE	Total	RACE: White	RACE: Black	RACE: American Indian, Eskimo, Aleut	RACE: Asian, Pacific Islander	Hispanic origin [1]	NOT OF HISPANIC ORIGIN: White	NOT OF HISPANIC ORIGIN: Black	NOT OF HISPANIC ORIGIN: American Indian, Eskimo, Aleut	NOT OF HISPANIC ORIGIN: Asian, Pacific Islander
Total	**265,284**	**219,749**	**33,503**	**2,288**	**9,743**	**28,269**	**193,978**	**31,912**	**1,964**	**9,171**
Under 5 yrs. old	19,286	15,289	2,948	203	846	3,273	12,300	2,762	169	781
Under 1 yr. old	3,769	3,015	546	40	168	670	2,403	508	33	155
1 yr. old	3,785	3,013	566	39	167	659	2,412	528	32	154
2 yrs. old	3,828	3,028	591	40	169	651	2,433	554	33	156
3 yrs. old	3,865	3,065	609	41	168	643	2,478	573	35	156
4 yrs. old	4,019	3,168	636	42	173	650	2,573	599	36	160
5-9 yrs. old	19,441	15,361	3,093	227	761	2,743	12,875	2,929	191	704
5 yrs. old	4,046	3,193	638	43	172	618	2,628	603	36	160
6 yrs. old	4,020	3,186	633	47	154	577	2,862	599	39	142
7 yrs. old	3,876	3,052	630	47	147	535	2,569	598	39	136
8 yrs. old	3,645	2,881	578	44	142	501	2,429	548	37	131
9 yrs. old	3,853	3,060	612	46	145	512	2,588	581	39	134
10-14 yrs. old	18,981	15,077	2,905	237	761	2,449	12,861	2,784	200	707
10 yrs. old	3,862	3,070	595	47	149	509	2,610	565	40	138
11 yrs. old	3,796	3,027	578	46	147	488	2,585	550	39	137
12 yrs. old	3,688	2,922	567	47	152	475	2,492	540	40	141
13 yrs. old	3,803	3,020	575	49	158	490	2,577	547	42	147
14 yrs. old	3,830	3,036	591	47	155	487	2,597	563	40	144
15-19 yrs. old	18,662	14,838	2,904	212	708	2,483	12,575	2,766	179	659
15 yrs. old	3,789	3,000	588	47	154	495	2,551	559	40	144
16 yrs. old	3,822	3,032	600	45	145	493	2,583	573	38	135
17 yrs. old	3,729	2,961	584	43	142	491	2,514	556	36	132
18 yrs. old	3,570	2,853	551	38	128	487	2,408	524	32	119
19 yrs. old	3,752	2,992	582	39	139	518	2,518	554	33	130
20-24 yrs. old	17,560	14,010	2,593	186	771	2,492	11,723	2,465	156	725
20 yrs. old	3,571	2,855	537	37	142	513	2,384	510	31	133
21 yrs. old	3,545	2,831	528	37	150	506	2,367	501	31	141
22 yrs. old	3,369	2,689	493	36	151	484	2,244	469	30	142
23 yrs. old	3,403	2,704	505	37	157	491	2,254	480	31	148
24 yrs. old	3,671	2,930	530	39	172	498	2,474	505	33	162
25-29 yrs. old	19,007	15,340	2,601	188	878	2,539	13,027	2,462	155	824
25 yrs. old	3,893	3,122	547	41	183	513	2,653	520	34	172
26 yrs. old	3,860	3,118	523	39	180	505	2,658	496	32	169
27 yrs. old	3,772	3,058	501	37	177	507	2,596	473	30	166
28 yrs. old	3,521	2,849	478	33	160	479	2,412	452	27	150
29 yrs. old	3,961	3,193	551	38	179	534	2,708	521	31	168
30-34 yrs. old	21,361	17,477	2,810	186	888	2,613	15,097	2,660	155	836
30 yrs. old	3,980	3,220	549	36	175	533	2,734	518	30	164
31 yrs. old	4,124	3,360	552	37	176	525	2,882	522	30	165
32 yrs. old	4,295	3,519	560	37	179	523	3,042	530	31	169
33 yrs. old	4,357	3,586	556	37	178	520	3,113	526	31	168
34 yrs. old	4,605	3,792	594	39	180	512	3,327	564	33	170
35-39 yrs. old	22,577	18,697	2,834	181	865	2,316	16,593	2,698	154	817
35 yrs. old	4,585	3,787	576	38	183	513	3,320	547	32	172
36 yrs. old	4,518	3,741	568	37	173	479	3,305	541	31	163
37 yrs. old	4,502	3,723	570	36	173	456	3,309	542	31	164
38 yrs. old	4,255	3,541	521	33	159	422	3,158	496	28	150
39 yrs. old	4,718	3,905	599	37	177	446	3,501	572	32	168
40-44 yrs. old	20,816	17,384	2,481	161	791	1,864	15,693	2,370	139	750
40 yrs. old	4,402	3,651	544	35	172	423	3,268	519	30	163
41 yrs. old	4,264	3,549	516	34	165	394	3,191	493	29	157
42 yrs. old	4,136	3,461	489	32	154	365	3,130	467	28	146
43 yrs. old	3,977	3,322	463	32	160	347	3,007	442	28	152
44 yrs. old	4,038	3,402	469	29	139	336	3,097	449	25	132

See footnotes at end of table.

No. 22. Resident Population, by Race, Hispanic Origin, and Single Years of Age: 1996—Continued

[See headnote, page 22]

AGE	Total	RACE				Hispanic origin [1]	NOT OF HISPANIC ORIGIN			
		White	Black	American Indian, Eskimo, Aleut	Asian, Pacific Islander		White	Black	American Indian, Eskimo, Aleut	Asian, Pacific Islander
45-49 yrs. old	18,436	15,643	1,997	131	666	1,426	14,345	1,914	116	635
45 yrs. old	3,778	3,168	439	28	143	322	2,875	421	24	136
46 yrs. old	3,641	3,066	413	26	137	296	2,797	395	23	130
47 yrs. old	3,599	3,027	406	27	139	279	2,774	391	23	132
48 yrs. old	3,413	2,924	346	24	119	255	2,691	332	21	113
49 yrs. old	4,005	3,458	392	27	129	275	3,208	376	24	123
50-54 yrs. old	13,934	11,952	1,413	97	471	1,028	11,014	1,355	87	449
50 yrs. old	2,830	2,406	293	22	109	232	2,194	280	19	104
51 yrs. old	2,789	2,381	289	20	99	214	2,186	277	18	95
52 yrs. old	2,770	2,384	277	19	90	200	2,201	266	17	86
53 yrs. old	2,937	2,553	279	19	86	200	2,370	268	17	83
54 yrs. old	2,608	2,229	276	18	85	182	2,063	265	16	81
55-59 yrs. old	11,362	9,763	1,163	74	361	799	9,032	1,118	67	346
55 yrs. old	2,407	2,052	256	17	81	173	1,895	246	15	78
56 yrs. old	2,346	2,013	244	15	74	168	1,858	234	14	71
57 yrs. old	2,327	1,998	241	15	73	163	1,849	231	14	69
58 yrs. old	2,135	1,850	208	13	64	147	1,714	200	12	61
59 yrs. old	2,148	1,850	214	14	69	147	1,715	206	13	66
60-64 yrs. old	9,999	8,652	995	59	293	652	8,054	959	54	281
60 yrs. old	2,078	1,792	209	13	64	143	1,661	201	12	61
61 yrs. old	2,061	1,792	198	12	59	139	1,664	191	11	57
62 yrs. old	1,921	1,656	195	12	58	125	1,541	188	11	56
63 yrs. old	1,942	1,684	191	11	56	123	1,570	185	10	54
64 yrs. old	1,997	1,729	202	11	56	121	1,618	195	10	53
65-69 yrs. old	9,892	8,667	929	48	247	564	8,148	899	43	237
65 yrs. old	2,044	1,771	207	11	55	125	1,657	200	10	53
66 yrs. old	2,017	1,761	194	10	51	119	1,651	188	9	49
67 yrs. old	1,978	1,732	188	9	49	114	1,628	181	8	47
68 yrs. old	1,944	1,715	173	9	47	107	1,617	168	8	45
69 yrs. old	1,909	1,687	167	9	45	100	1,595	162	8	44
70-74 yrs. old	8,778	7,844	704	38	191	424	7,451	684	35	184
70 yrs. old	1,839	1,624	163	8	43	95	1,536	158	8	42
71 yrs. old	1,827	1,633	147	8	40	91	1,548	142	7	38
72 yrs. old	1,780	1,597	135	8	40	86	1,517	131	7	38
73 yrs. old	1,664	1,491	130	7	36	78	1,418	127	6	34
74 yrs. old	1,668	1,499	129	7	33	73	1,431	126	6	31
75-79 yrs. old	6,873	6,198	526	26	122	278	5,940	512	24	118
75 yrs. old	1,603	1,442	124	6	30	69	1,377	121	6	29
76 yrs. old	1,442	1,300	110	5	27	61	1,244	107	5	26
77 yrs. old	1,347	1,215	102	5	24	54	1,166	99	5	23
78 yrs. old	1,282	1,161	96	5	21	49	1,115	93	4	20
79 yrs. old	1,198	1,079	94	5	20	45	1,038	91	4	20
80-84 yrs. old	4,557	4,150	320	17	70	176	3,986	313	16	67
80 yrs. old	1,081	984	75	4	17	41	946	73	4	17
81 yrs. old	1,003	914	70	4	15	39	878	68	3	15
82 yrs. old	904	824	63	3	13	35	792	62	3	13
83 yrs. old	838	763	60	3	12	33	732	59	3	12
84 yrs. old	731	664	53	3	11	28	636	51	3	11
85-89 yrs. old	2,394	2,182	170	9	33	95	2,093	167	9	31
90-94 yrs. old	1,024	923	82	5	14	42	883	81	5	13
95-99 yrs. old	286	254	27	2	4	11	243	26	2	4
100 yrs. old and over	57	47	8	1	1	3	45	7	1	1
Median age (yr.)	34.6	35.7	29.5	27.0	30.8	26.4	37.0	29.6	27.6	31.1

[1] Persons of Hispanic origin may be of any race.

Source: U.S. Bureau of the Census, Population Paper Listing 57.

No. 23. Resident Population, by Age and Hispanic Origin: 1990 to 1996

[In thousands, except percent. As of July, except 1990 as of April. See headnote, table 18. Hispanic persons may be of any race]

YEAR AND SEX	Total, all years	Under 5 years	5-9 years	10-14 years	15-19 years	20-24 years	25-29 years	30-34 years	35-39 years	40-44 years	45-49 years	50-54 years	55-59 years	60-64 years	65-74 years	75-84 years	85 years and over	5-13 years	14-17 years	18-24 years
HISPANIC ORIGIN																				
1990 [1]	22,354	2,467	2,178	1,989	2,065	2,320	2,337	2,045	1,642	1,276	936	750	633	550	715	340	91	3,782	1,574	3,215
1995	27,277	3,205	2,595	2,387	2,387	2,465	2,508	2,560	2,202	1,757	1,326	971	766	634	947	428	139	4,503	1,893	3,438
1996	28,269	3,273	2,743	2,449	2,483	2,492	2,539	2,613	2,316	1,864	1,426	1,028	799	652	988	454	151	4,705	1,986	3,496
Male	14,519	1,677	1,403	1,255	1,316	1,361	1,386	1,392	1,212	952	712	500	380	302	439	179	51	2,406	1,029	1,899
Female	13,750	1,596	1,340	1,194	1,168	1,130	1,152	1,221	1,104	912	715	527	419	350	549	275	99	2,298	937	1,597
NON-HISPANIC WHITE																				
1990 [1]	188,308	12,721	12,516	11,854	12,450	13,524	15,508	16,331	15,182	13,839	10,971	9,057	8,548	8,872	15,511	8,767	2,675	22,106	9,224	19,014
1995	193,281	12,531	12,794	12,814	12,287	12,170	13,072	15,649	16,503	15,362	13,654	10,843	8,838	8,137	15,747	9,700	3,182	23,069	10,023	16,973
1996	193,978	12,300	12,875	12,861	12,575	11,723	13,027	15,097	16,593	15,683	14,345	11,014	9,032	8,054	15,599	9,926	3,264	23,139	10,246	16,649
Male	94,799	6,308	6,608	6,608	6,476	5,979	6,508	7,541	8,319	7,841	7,127	5,415	4,390	3,847	7,012	3,909	911	11,881	5,281	8,509
Female	99,179	5,993	6,267	6,254	6,099	5,744	6,519	7,557	8,274	7,852	7,218	5,599	4,642	4,206	8,587	6,017	2,353	11,259	4,964	8,140
BLACK																				
1990 [1]	29,275	2,798	2,596	2,525	2,605	2,528	2,650	2,601	2,265	1,811	1,362	1,138	1,008	945	1,465	758	219	4,638	1,975	3,642
1995	31,565	2,856	2,865	2,738	2,696	2,520	2,452	2,679	2,661	2,289	1,779	1,328	1,096	955	1,570	811	272	5,056	2,198	3,585
1996	31,912	2,762	2,929	2,764	2,766	2,465	2,462	2,660	2,698	2,370	1,914	1,355	1,118	959	1,582	825	281	5,131	2,251	3,543
Male	15,098	1,399	1,485	1,403	1,403	1,215	1,172	1,242	1,260	1,098	872	606	489	411	661	303	82	2,602	1,147	1,757
Female	16,814	1,364	1,444	1,361	1,363	1,250	1,291	1,418	1,438	1,273	1,043	750	629	548	922	522	199	2,529	1,104	1,786
AMERICAN INDIAN, ESKIMO, ALEUT																				
1990 [1]	1,796	185	179	170	165	151	160	156	138	117	90	72	58	48	68	31	9	316	131	217
1995	1,931	172	191	198	172	158	151	157	152	136	111	84	65	53	77	39	14	349	149	221
1996	1,954	169	191	200	179	156	155	155	154	139	116	87	67	54	78	41	16	351	154	220
Male	961	85	97	101	90	79	79	77	75	67	56	42	32	25	35	17	5	178	78	111
Female	993	84	94	99	89	77	76	78	79	72	60	45	35	29	43	24	11	173	76	109
ASIAN, PACIFIC ISLANDER																				
1990 [1]	6,988	586	566	522	581	612	673	700	640	545	384	297	240	210	287	116	27	983	436	862
1995	8,836	772	663	689	627	741	788	818	791	717	592	421	327	270	403	171	45	1,213	523	986
1996	9,171	781	704	707	659	725	824	836	817	750	635	449	346	281	421	185	50	1,267	554	973
Male	4,433	399	362	360	335	365	393	401	392	352	295	213	164	125	178	79	20	649	282	490
Female	4,738	383	342	347	325	360	431	435	425	398	341	236	182	156	244	106	30	618	272	483
1990, PERCENT																				
Hispanic origin	100.0	11.6	9.7	8.7	8.8	8.8	9.0	9.2	8.2	6.6	5.0	3.6	2.8	2.3	3.5	1.6	0.5	16.6	7.0	12.4
Non-Hispanic:																				
White	100.0	6.3	6.6	6.6	6.5	6.0	6.7	7.8	8.6	8.1	7.4	5.7	4.7	4.2	8.0	5.1	1.7	11.9	5.3	8.6
Black	100.0	8.7	9.2	8.7	8.7	7.7	7.7	8.3	8.5	7.4	6.0	4.2	3.5	3.0	5.0	2.6	0.9	16.1	7.1	11.1
American Indian, Aleut	100.0	8.8	9.5	10.0	8.9	7.7	7.5	7.8	7.8	7.2	5.9	4.5	3.5	2.9	4.3	2.4	1.1	17.4	7.6	11.0
Asian, Pacific Islander	100.0	9.2	8.4	8.5	7.8	7.7	8.8	9.2	8.8	7.8	6.6	4.7	3.7	2.8	4.0	1.7	0.3	15.2	6.6	10.6

[1] The April 1, 1990, census count (248,718,291) includes count question resolution corrections processed through March 1994 and does not include adjustments for census coverage errors.

Source: U.S. Bureau of the Census, *Current Population Reports*, P25-1095; and Population Paper Listing 57.

No. 24. Projections of Resident Population, by Age, Sex, and Race: 2000 to 2025

[As of July 1. Data are for middle series; for assumptions, see table 3]

AGE, SEX, AND RACE	POPULATION (1,000)				PERCENT DISTRIBUTION			
	2000	2005	2010	2025	2000	2005	2010	2025
Total	274,634	285,981	297,716	335,050	100.0	100.0	100.0	100.0
Under 5 years old	18,987	19,127	20,012	22,498	6.9	6.7	6.7	6.7
5 to 13 years old	36,043	35,850	35,605	40,413	13.1	12.5	12.0	12.1
14 to 17 years old	15,752	16,986	16,894	17,872	5.7	5.9	5.7	5.3
18 to 24 years old	26,258	28,268	30,138	30,372	9.6	9.9	10.1	9.1
25 to 34 years old	37,233	36,306	38,292	43,119	13.6	12.7	12.9	12.9
35 to 44 years old	44,659	42,165	38,521	42,391	16.3	14.7	12.9	12.7
45 to 54 years old	37,030	41,507	43,564	36,890	13.5	14.5	14.6	11.0
55 to 64 years old	23,962	29,806	35,283	39,542	8.7	10.4	11.9	11.8
65 to 74 years old	18,136	18,369	21,057	35,425	6.6	6.4	7.1	10.6
75 to 84 years old	12,315	12,898	12,680	19,481	4.5	4.5	4.3	5.8
85 years old and over	4,259	4,899	5,671	7,046	1.6	1.7	1.9	2.1
Male	134,181	139,785	145,584	164,119	48.9	48.9	48.9	49.0
Female	140,453	146,196	152,132	170,931	51.1	51.1	51.1	51.0
White, total	225,532	232,463	239,588	262,227	100.0	100.0	100.0	100.0
Under 5 years old	14,724	14,618	15,142	16,630	6.5	6.3	6.3	6.3
5 to 13 years old	28,254	27,716	27,087	29,949	12.5	11.9	11.3	11.4
14 to 17 years old	12,412	13,177	12,951	13,166	5.5	5.7	5.4	5.0
18 to 24 years old	20,852	22,306	23,489	22,702	9.2	9.6	9.8	8.7
25 to 34 years old	29,837	28,705	30,099	32,831	13.2	12.3	12.6	12.5
35 to 44 years old	36,762	34,201	30,646	32,869	16.3	14.7	12.8	12.5
45 to 54 years old	31,247	34,574	35,911	29,010	13.9	14.9	15.0	11.1
55 to 64 years old	20,600	25,334	29,845	32,246	9.1	10.9	12.5	12.3
65 to 74 years old	15,846	15,844	18,101	29,733	7.0	6.8	7.6	11.3
75 to 84 years old	11,131	11,553	11,208	16,969	4.9	5.0	4.7	6.5
85 years old and over	3,866	4,434	5,106	6,122	1.7	1.9	2.1	2.3
Male	110,799	114,350	118,000	129,596	49.1	49.2	49.3	49.4
Female	114,734	118,113	121,588	132,631	50.9	50.8	50.7	50.6
Black, total	35,454	37,734	40,109	47,539	100.0	100.0	100.0	100.0
Under 5 years old	3,127	3,244	3,454	3,964	8.8	8.6	8.6	8.3
5 to 13 years old	5,727	5,813	5,962	6,990	16.2	15.4	14.9	14.7
14 to 17 years old	2,414	2,735	2,737	3,104	6.8	7.2	6.8	6.5
18 to 24 years old	3,966	4,233	4,674	5,053	11.2	11.2	11.7	10.6
25 to 34 years old	5,172	5,212	5,489	6,514	14.6	13.8	13.7	13.7
35 to 44 years old	5,649	5,499	5,236	6,017	15.9	14.6	13.1	12.7
45 to 54 years old	4,111	4,909	5,326	5,007	11.6	13.0	13.3	10.5
55 to 64 years old	2,406	2,995	3,801	4,865	6.8	7.9	9.5	10.2
65 to 74 years old	1,675	1,781	2,033	3,901	4.7	4.7	5.1	8.2
75 to 84 years old	890	959	1,002	1,582	2.5	2.5	2.5	3.3
85 years old and over	317	354	396	541	0.9	0.9	1.0	1.1
Male	16,811	17,874	18,981	22,473	47.4	47.4	47.3	47.3
Female	18,643	19,860	21,129	25,066	52.6	52.6	52.7	52.7
American Indian, Eskimo, Aleut, total	2,402	2,572	2,754	3,319	100.0	100.0	100.0	100.0
Under 5 years old	210	226	245	275	8.7	8.8	8.9	8.3
5 to 13 years old	418	409	429	516	17.4	15.9	15.6	15.5
14 to 17 years old	196	210	197	240	8.2	8.2	7.2	7.2
18 to 24 years old	283	323	342	368	11.8	12.6	12.4	11.1
25 to 34 years old	361	376	421	475	15.0	14.6	15.3	14.3
35 to 44 years old	354	351	349	459	14.7	13.6	12.7	13.8
45 to 54 years old	263	300	321	333	10.9	11.7	11.7	10.0
55 to 64 years old	152	186	225	276	6.3	7.2	8.2	8.3
65 to 74 years old	93	104	122	210	3.9	4.0	4.4	6.3
75 to 84 years old	51	59	65	109	2.1	2.3	2.4	3.3
85 years old and over	22	28	36	59	0.9	1.1	1.3	1.8
Male	1,185	1,266	1,354	1,629	49.3	49.2	49.2	49.1
Female	1,217	1,306	1,400	1,690	50.7	50.8	50.8	50.9
Asian, Pacific Islander, total	11,245	13,212	15,265	21,965	100.0	100.0	100.0	100.0
Under 5 years old	926	1,040	1,170	1,628	8.2	7.9	7.7	7.4
5 to 13 years old	1,644	1,912	2,126	2,958	14.6	14.5	13.9	13.5
14 to 17 years old	729	864	1,006	1,362	6.5	6.5	6.6	6.2
18 to 24 years old	1,158	1,405	1,633	2,250	10.3	10.6	10.7	10.2
25 to 34 years old	1,863	2,012	2,283	3,300	16.6	15.2	15.0	15.0
35 to 44 years old	1,894	2,114	2,290	3,046	16.8	16.0	15.0	13.9
45 to 54 years old	1,409	1,724	2,006	2,539	12.5	13.0	13.1	11.6
55 to 64 years old	804	1,091	1,412	2,155	7.1	8.3	9.2	9.8
65 to 74 years old	522	640	802	1,581	4.6	4.8	5.3	7.2
75 to 84 years old	242	327	406	821	2.2	2.5	2.7	3.7
85 years old and over	55	83	130	324	0.5	0.6	0.9	1.5
Male	5,386	6,295	7,250	10,421	47.9	47.6	47.5	47.4
Female	5,859	6,918	8,015	11,543	52.1	52.4	52.5	52.6

Source: U.S. Bureau of the Census, *Current Population Reports*, P25-1130.

No. 25. Projections of Hispanic and Non-Hispanic Populations, by Age and Sex: 2000 to 2025

[As of July 1. Resident population. Data are for middle series; for assumptions, see table 3]

AGE AND SEX	POPULATION (1,000)				PERCENT DISTRIBUTION			
	2000	2005	2010	2025	2000	2005	2010	2025
Hispanic origin, total [1]	31,366	36,057	41,139	58,930	100.0	100.0	100.0	100.0
Under 5 years old	3,203	3,580	4,080	5,662	10.2	9.9	9.9	9.6
5 to 13 years old	5,651	6,215	6,654	9,479	18.0	17.2	16.2	16.1
14 to 17 years old	2,179	2,672	3,007	3,944	6.9	7.4	7.3	6.7
18 to 24 years old	3,679	4,270	5,101	6,560	11.7	11.8	12.4	11.1
25 to 34 years old	5,181	5,414	6,059	8,748	16.5	15.0	14.7	14.8
35 to 44 years old	4,836	5,421	5,562	7,345	15.4	15.0	13.5	12.5
45 to 54 years old	3,049	3,927	4,833	5,791	9.7	10.9	11.7	9.8
55 to 64 years old	1,717	2,260	2,997	5,272	5.5	6.3	7.3	8.9
65 to 74 years old	1,120	1,308	1,606	3,595	3.6	3.6	3.9	6.1
75 to 84 years old	568	748	896	1,771	1.8	2.1	2.2	3.0
85 years old and over	183	242	345	763	0.6	0.7	0.8	1.3
Male	15,799	18,082	20,557	29,276	50.4	50.1	50.0	49.7
Female	15,568	17,975	20,582	29,654	49.6	49.9	50.0	50.3
Non-Hispanic White, total	197,061	199,802	202,390	209,117	100.0	100.0	100.0	100.0
Under 5 years old	11,807	11,367	11,445	11,510	6.0	5.7	5.7	5.5
5 to 13 years old	23,125	22,072	21,063	21,396	11.7	11.0	10.4	10.2
14 to 17 years old	10,444	10,769	10,230	9,622	5.3	5.4	5.1	4.6
18 to 24 years old	17,510	18,443	18,880	16,785	8.9	9.2	9.3	8.0
25 to 34 years old	25,144	23,606	24,631	24,935	12.8	11.9	12.2	11.9
35 to 44 years old	32,382	29,299	25,628	26,278	16.4	14.7	12.7	12.6
45 to 54 years old	28,485	31,024	31,541	23,797	14.5	15.5	15.6	11.4
55 to 64 years old	19,039	23,285	27,137	27,490	9.7	11.7	13.4	13.1
65 to 74 years old	14,825	14,660	16,653	26,504	7.5	7.3	8.2	12.7
75 to 84 years old	10,607	10,868	10,394	15,373	5.4	5.4	5.1	7.4
85 years old and over	3,694	4,209	4,788	5,428	1.9	2.1	2.4	2.6
Male	96,438	97,946	99,381	103,169	48.9	49.0	49.1	49.3
Female	100,624	101,856	103,009	105,948	51.1	51.0	50.9	50.7
Non-Hispanic Black, total	33,568	35,485	37,466	43,511	100.0	100.0	100.0	100.0
Under 5 years old	2,929	3,016	3,187	3,571	8.7	8.5	8.5	8.2
5 to 13 years old	5,391	5,430	5,531	6,339	16.1	15.3	14.8	14.6
14 to 17 years old	2,285	2,568	2,547	2,831	6.8	7.2	6.8	6.5
18 to 24 years old	3,751	3,975	4,354	4,609	11.2	11.2	11.6	10.6
25 to 34 years old	4,863	4,883	5,111	5,942	14.5	13.8	13.6	13.7
35 to 44 years old	5,347	5,154	4,877	5,521	15.9	14.5	13.0	12.7
45 to 54 years old	3,922	4,654	5,008	4,613	11.7	13.1	13.4	10.6
55 to 64 years old	2,301	2,850	3,601	4,498	6.9	8.0	9.6	10.3
65 to 74 years old	1,608	1,695	1,921	3,634	4.8	4.8	5.1	8.4
75 to 84 years old	862	919	947	1,457	2.6	2.6	2.5	3.3
85 years old and over	310	344	381	496	0.9	1.0	1.0	1.1
Male	15,871	16,760	17,676	20,494	47.3	47.2	47.2	47.1
Female	17,697	18,725	19,790	23,017	52.7	52.8	52.8	52.9
Non-Hispanic American Indian, Eskimo, Aleut, total	2,054	2,183	2,320	2,744	100.0	100.0	100.0	100.0
Under 5 years old	180	192	206	229	8.8	8.8	8.9	8.4
5 to 13 years old	352	347	364	429	17.1	15.9	15.7	15.6
14 to 17 years old	165	175	166	198	8.0	8.0	7.1	7.2
18 to 24 years old	239	268	282	304	11.6	12.3	12.1	11.1
25 to 34 years old	303	316	349	390	14.7	14.5	15.0	14.2
35 to 44 years old	301	293	290	372	14.7	13.4	12.5	13.6
45 to 54 years old	231	259	272	275	11.2	11.8	11.7	10.0
55 to 64 years old	136	164	195	227	6.6	7.5	8.4	8.3
65 to 74 years old	82	91	106	176	4.0	4.2	4.6	6.4
75 to 84 years old	46	52	57	92	2.2	2.4	2.4	3.4
85 years old and over	21	27	34	52	1.0	1.2	1.4	1.9
Male	1,008	1,070	1,136	1,342	49.1	49.0	48.9	48.9
Female	1,046	1,113	1,184	1,401	50.9	51.0	51.1	51.1
Non-Hispanic Asian, Pacific Islander, total	10,584	12,454	14,402	20,748	100.0	100.0	100.0	100.0
Under 5 years old	867	973	1,093	1,526	8.2	7.8	7.6	7.4
5 to 13 years old	1,524	1,787	1,993	2,770	14.4	14.4	13.8	13.4
14 to 17 years old	680	803	944	1,277	6.4	6.4	6.6	6.2
18 to 24 years old	1,080	1,311	1,521	2,114	10.2	10.5	10.6	10.2
25 to 34 years old	1,744	1,887	2,141	3,104	16.5	15.2	14.9	15.0
35 to 44 years old	1,793	1,998	2,165	2,876	16.9	16.0	15.0	13.9
45 to 54 years old	1,344	1,644	1,910	2,415	12.7	13.2	13.3	11.6
55 to 64 years old	770	1,046	1,354	2,055	7.3	8.4	9.4	9.9
65 to 74 years old	500	615	771	1,516	4.7	4.9	5.4	7.3
75 to 84 years old	231	311	387	787	2.2	2.5	2.7	3.8
85 years old and over	51	78	123	306	0.5	0.6	0.9	1.5
Male	5,065	5,928	6,835	9,838	47.9	47.6	47.5	47.4
Female	5,520	6,526	7,567	10,910	52.1	52.4	52.5	52.6

[1] Persons of Hispanic origin may be of any race.

Source: U.S. Bureau of the Census, *Current Population Reports*, P25-1130.

Figure 1.3
Centers of Population: 1790 to 1990

[Prior to 1960, excludes Alaska and Hawaii. The median center is located at the intersection of two median lines, a north-south line constructed so that half of the nation's population lives east and half lives west of it, and an east-west line selected so that half of the Nation's population lives north and half lives south of it. The mean center of population is that point at which an imaginary, flat, weightless, and rigid map of the United States would balance if weights of identical value were placed on it so that each weight represented the location of one person on the date of the census]

YEAR	MEDIAN CENTER		MEAN CENTER		
	Latitude-N	Longitude-W	Latitude-N	Longitude-W	Approximate location
1790 (August 2)	(NA)	(NA)	39 16 30	76 11 12	In Kent County, MD, 23 miles E of Baltimore, MD
1850 (June 1) ..	(NA)	(NA)	38 59 00	81 19 00	In Wirt County, WV, 23 miles SE of Parkersburg, WV[1]
1900 (June 1) ..	40 03 32	84 49 01	39 09 36	85 48 54	In Bartholomew County, IN, 6 miles SE of Columbus, IN
1950 (April 1) ..	40 00 12	84 56 51	38 50 21	88 09 33	In Richland County, IL, 8 miles NNW of Olney, IL
1960 (April 1) ..	39 56 25	85 16 60	38 35 58	89 12 35	In Clinton County, IL, 6.5 miles NW of Centralia, IL
1970 (April 1) ..	39 47 43	85 31 43	38 27 47	89 42 22	In St. Clair Country, IL, 5.3 miles ESE of Mascoutah, IL
1980 (April 1) ..	39 18 60	86 08 15	38 08 13	90 34 26	In Jefferson Country, MO, .25 mile W of DeSoto, MO
1990 (April 1) ..	38 57 55	86 31 53	37 52 20	91 12 55	In Crawford Country, MO, 10 miles SE of Steelville, MO

NA Not available. [1] West Virginia was set off from Virginia, Dec. 31, 1862, and admitted as a State, June 19, 1863.

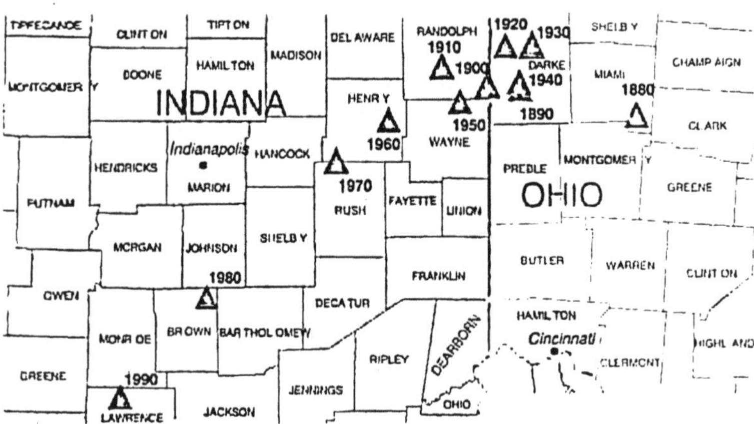

No. 26. Resident Population—States: 1970 to 1996

[In thousands. As of July 1; except 1970, 1980, and 1990, as of April 1. Insofar as possible, population shown for all years is that of present area of State]

REGION, DIVISION, AND STATE	1970	1980 [1]	1985	1989	1990 [2]	1991	1992	1993	1994	1995	1996
U.S.	203,302	226,546	237,924	246,819	248,718	252,106	255,011	257,795	260,372	262,890	265,284
Northeast	49,061	49,135	49,869	50,757	50,811	50,954	51,097	51,293	51,426	51,506	51,580
N.E.	11,848	12,348	12,741	13,182	13,207	13,204	13,196	13,230	13,265	13,306	13,361
ME	994	1,125	1,163	1,220	1,228	1,236	1,236	1,239	1,238	1,239	1,243
NH	738	921	997	1,105	1,109	1,108	1,114	1,123	1,135	1,148	1,162
VT	445	511	530	558	563	568	571	575	581	585	589
MA	5,689	5,737	5,881	6,015	6,016	5,999	5,998	6,017	6,042	6,071	6,092
RI	950	947	969	1,001	1,003	1,005	1,002	1,000	996	992	990
CT	3,032	3,108	3,201	3,283	3,287	3,289	3,276	3,276	3,273	3,271	3,274
M.A.	37,213	36,787	37,128	37,575	37,604	37,750	37,899	38,063	38,161	38,200	38,229
NY	18,241	17,558	17,792	17,983	17,991	18,037	18,099	18,170	18,197	18,191	18,185
NJ	7,171	7,365	7,566	7,726	7,730	7,767	7,811	7,860	7,906	7,950	7,988
PA	11,801	11,864	11,771	11,866	11,883	11,946	11,989	12,033	12,058	12,060	12,056
Midwest	56,589	58,866	58,820	59,468	59,669	60,160	60,597	61,016	61,371	61,732	62,082
E.N.C	40,262	41,682	41,418	41,873	42,009	42,363	42,663	42,934	43,152	43,381	43,614
OH	10,657	10,798	10,735	10,829	10,847	10,929	11,000	11,059	11,097	11,134	11,173
IN	5,195	5,490	5,459	5,524	5,544	5,603	5,652	5,707	5,750	5,797	5,841
IL	11,110	11,427	11,400	11,410	11,431	11,516	11,596	11,670	11,734	11,790	11,847
MI	8,882	9,262	9,076	9,253	9,295	9,366	9,418	9,453	9,486	9,538	9,594
WI	4,418	4,706	4,748	4,857	4,892	4,948	4,996	5,045	5,084	5,122	5,160
W.N.C	16,327	17,183	17,402	17,595	17,660	17,797	17,934	18,082	18,219	18,351	18,468
MN	3,806	4,076	4,184	4,338	4,376	4,429	4,475	4,526	4,572	4,615	4,658
IA	2,825	2,914	2,830	2,771	2,777	2,792	2,808	2,822	2,832	2,843	2,852
MO	4,678	4,917	5,000	5,096	5,117	5,157	5,189	5,233	5,275	5,319	5,359
ND	618	653	677	646	639	634	635	637	640	642	644
SD	666	691	698	697	696	702	710	717	724	730	732
NE	1,485	1,570	1,586	1,575	1,578	1,592	1,604	1,615	1,626	1,639	1,652
KS	2,249	2,364	2,427	2,473	2,478	2,492	2,514	2,532	2,550	2,564	2,572
South	62,812	75,372	81,409	84,700	85,454	86,934	88,186	89,457	90,738	91,968	93,098
S.A.	30,678	36,959	40,159	43,006	43,571	44,444	45,097	45,733	46,397	47,013	47,616
DE	548	594	618	658	666	680	690	699	708	717	725
MD	3,924	4,217	4,413	4,727	4,781	4,859	4,909	4,953	5,000	5,039	5,072
DC	757	638	635	624	607	595	586	579	568	555	543
VA	4,651	5,347	5,715	6,120	6,189	6,286	6,388	6,475	6,550	6,615	6,675
WV	1,744	1,950	1,907	1,807	1,793	1,799	1,807	1,819	1,822	1,825	1,826
NC	5,084	5,882	6,254	6,565	6,632	6,754	6,841	6,960	7,079	7,202	7,323
SC	2,591	3,122	3,303	3,457	3,486	3,556	3,595	3,629	3,643	3,667	3,699
GA	4,588	5,463	5,963	6,411	6,478	6,625	6,767	6,906	7,063	7,209	7,353
FL	6,791	9,746	11,351	12,638	12,938	13,291	13,513	13,714	13,965	14,184	14,400
E.S.C	12,808	14,666	14,971	15,136	15,180	15,343	15,516	15,708	15,884	16,046	16,193
KY	3,221	3,661	3,695	3,677	3,687	3,715	3,753	3,794	3,826	3,857	3,884
TN	3,926	4,591	4,715	4,854	4,877	4,949	5,020	5,094	5,175	5,247	5,320
AL	3,444	3,894	3,973	4,030	4,040	4,067	4,131	4,182	4,215	4,246	4,273
MS	2,217	2,521	2,588	2,574	2,575	2,592	2,612	2,639	2,668	2,696	2,716
W.S.C	19,326	23,747	26,279	26,556	26,703	27,147	27,574	28,016	28,457	28,909	29,290
AR	1,923	2,286	2,327	2,346	2,351	2,371	2,396	2,427	2,455	2,485	2,510
LA	3,645	4,206	4,408	4,253	4,220	4,241	4,274	4,290	4,315	4,338	4,351
OK	2,559	3,025	3,271	3,150	3,146	3,168	3,207	3,234	3,254	3,275	3,301
TX	11,199	14,229	16,273	16,807	16,986	17,367	17,697	18,065	18,434	18,801	19,128
West	34,838	43,172	47,827	51,894	52,784	54,058	55,131	56,029	56,837	57,694	58,523
Mountain	8,289	11,373	12,741	13,496	13,659	14,025	14,388	14,800	15,256	15,750	16,118
MT	694	787	822	800	799	806	823	841	857	870	879
ID	713	944	994	994	1,007	1,039	1,067	1,102	1,136	1,166	1,189
WY	332	470	500	458	454	458	464	470	476	479	481
CO	2,210	2,890	3,209	3,276	3,294	3,369	3,464	3,566	3,663	3,748	3,823
NM	1,017	1,303	1,438	1,504	1,515	1,548	1,583	1,619	1,659	1,690	1,713
AZ	1,775	2,718	3,184	3,622	3,665	3,750	3,841	3,953	4,092	4,306	4,428
UT	1,059	1,461	1,643	1,706	1,723	1,767	1,812	1,861	1,910	1,958	2,000
NV	489	800	951	1,137	1,202	1,286	1,334	1,386	1,464	1,533	1,603
Pacific	26,549	31,800	35,086	38,397	39,125	40,033	40,743	41,230	41,581	41,944	42,406
WA	3,413	4,132	4,400	4,746	4,867	5,018	5,147	5,260	5,351	5,448	5,533
OR	2,092	2,633	2,673	2,791	2,842	2,921	2,978	3,040	3,094	3,149	3,204
CA	19,971	23,668	26,441	29,218	29,758	30,396	30,863	31,172	31,362	31,565	31,878
AK	303	402	532	547	550	569	587	596	601	603	607
HI	770	965	1,040	1,095	1,108	1,130	1,148	1,160	1,173	1,179	1,184

[1] See footnote 4, table [2] The April 1, 1990, census counts include count question resolution corrections processed through December 1994 and do not include adjustments for census coverage errors.

Source: U.S. Bureau of the Census, *1990 Census of Population and Housing, Population and Housing Unit Counts* (CPH-2); *Current Population Reports*, P25-1106; and "ST-96-1 Estimates of the Population of States: Annual Time Series, July 1, 1990 to July 1, 1996"; release date: December 30, 1996; <http://www.census.gov/population/estimates/state/ST9096T1.txt>.

No. 27. State Population—Rank, Percent Change, and Population Density: 1980 to 1996

[As of April 1, except 1996, as of July 1. For area figures of States, see table 367. Minus sign (-) indicates decrease]

REGION, DIVISION, AND STATE	RANK			PERCENT CHANGE			POPULATION PER SQ. MILE OF LAND AREA [1]		
	1980	1990	1996	1980-90	1990-95	1995-96	1980	1990	1996
U.S.	(X)	(X)	(X)	**9.8**	**5.7**	**0.9**	**64.1**	**70.3**	**75.0**
Northeast	(X)	(X)	(X)	**3.4**	**1.4**	**0.1**	**302.8**	**313.1**	**317.9**
N.E.	(X)	(X)	(X)	**6.9**	**0.7**	**0.3**	**196.8**	**210.3**	**212.6**
ME	38	38	39	9.1	0.9	0.4	36.5	39.8	40.3
NH	42	40	42	20.5	3.5	1.2	102.6	123.7	129.6
VT	48	48	49	10.0	3.9	0.7	55.3	60.8	63.6
MA	11	13	13	4.9	0.9	0.4	732.0	767.6	777.3
RI	40	43	43	5.9	-1.2	-0.1	906.4	960.3	947.6
CT	25	27	28	5.8	-0.5	0.1	641.4	678.5	675.8
M.A.	(X)	(X)	(X)	**2.2**	**1.6**	**0.1**	**369.9**	**378.1**	**384.4**
NY	2	2	3	2.5	1.1	(-Z)	371.8	381.0	385.1
NJ	9	9	9	5.0	2.8	0.5	992.7	1,041.9	1,076.7
PA	4	5	5	0.2	1.5	(-Z)	264.7	265.1	269.0
Midwest	(X)	(X)	(X)	**1.4**	**3.5**	**0.6**	**78.3**	**79.4**	**82.6**
E.N.C.	(X)	(X)	(X)	**0.8**	**3.3**	**0.5**	**171.2**	**172.5**	**179.1**
OH	6	7	7	0.5	2.6	0.3	263.7	264.9	272.8
IN	12	14	14	1.0	4.6	0.8	153.1	154.6	162.8
IL	5	6	6	(Z)	3.1	0.5	205.6	205.6	213.1
MI	8	8	8	0.4	2.6	0.6	163.0	163.6	168.9
WI	16	16	18	4.0	4.7	0.7	86.6	90.1	95.0
W.N.C.	(X)	(X)	(X)	**2.8**	**3.9**	**0.8**	**33.8**	**34.8**	**36.4**
MN	21	20	20	7.4	5.5	0.9	51.2	55.0	58.5
IA	27	30	30	-4.7	2.4	0.3	52.1	49.7	51.0
MO	15	15	16	4.1	4.0	0.7	71.4	74.3	77.8
ND	46	47	47	-2.1	0.4	0.3	9.5	9.3	9.3
SD	45	45	45	0.8	4.8	0.4	9.1	9.2	9.7
NE	35	36	37	0.5	3.9	0.8	20.4	20.5	21.5
KS	32	32	32	4.8	3.5	0.3	28.9	30.3	31.4
South	(X)	(X)	(X)	**13.4**	**7.6**	**1.2**	**86.5**	**98.1**	**106.9**
S.A.	(X)	(X)	(X)	**17.9**	**7.9**	**1.3**	**138.8**	**163.6**	**178.9**
DE	47	46	46	12.1	7.6	1.1	304.0	340.8	370.8
MD	18	19	19	13.4	5.4	0.6	431.4	489.2	518.8
DC	(X)	(X)	(X)	-4.9	-8.6	-2.0	10,397.9	9,949.2	8,847.1
VA	14	12	12	15.8	6.9	0.9	135.0	156.3	168.6
WV	34	34	35	-8.0	1.8	(Z)	81.0	74.5	75.8
NC	10	10	11	12.8	8.6	1.7	120.7	136.1	150.3
SC	24	25	26	11.7	5.2	0.9	103.6	115.8	122.8
GA	13	11	10	18.6	11.3	2.0	94.3	111.8	127.0
FL	7	4	4	32.7	9.6	1.5	180.5	239.6	266.7
E.S.C.	(X)	(X)	(X)	**3.5**	**5.7**	**0.9**	**82.1**	**86.0**	**90.7**
KY	23	23	24	0.7	4.6	0.7	92.1	92.8	97.7
TN	17	17	17	6.2	7.6	1.4	111.4	118.3	129.1
AL	22	22	23	3.8	5.1	0.6	76.7	79.6	84.2
MS	31	31	31	2.2	4.7	0.7	53.7	54.8	57.9
W.S.C.	(X)	(X)	(X)	**12.5**	**8.2**	**1.4**	**55.7**	**62.6**	**66.7**
AR	33	33	33	2.8	5.7	1.0	43.9	45.1	48.2
LA	19	21	22	0.3	2.8	0.3	96.5	96.9	99.9
OK	26	28	27	4.0	4.1	0.8	44.1	45.8	48.1
TX	3	3	2	19.4	10.7	1.7	54.3	64.9	73.0
West	(X)	(X)	(X)	**22.3**	**9.3**	**1.4**	**24.6**	**30.1**	**33.4**
Mountain	(X)	(X)	(X)	**20.1**	**15.3**	**2.3**	**13.3**	**16.0**	**18.6**
MT	44	44	44	1.6	8.9	1.0	5.4	5.5	6.0
ID	41	42	40	6.6	15.8	2.0	11.4	12.2	14.4
WY	49	50	50	-3.4	5.6	0.5	4.8	4.7	5.0
CO	28	26	25	14.0	13.8	2.0	27.9	31.8	36.9
NM	37	37	36	16.2	11.5	1.4	10.7	12.5	14.1
AZ	29	24	21	34.9	17.5	2.9	23.9	32.3	39.0
UT	36	35	34	17.9	13.7	2.2	17.8	21.0	24.3
NV	43	39	38	50.1	27.6	4.5	7.3	10.9	14.6
Pacific	(X)	(X)	(X)	**23.0**	**7.2**	**1.1**	**35.5**	**43.7**	**47.4**
WA	20	18	15	17.8	11.9	1.6	62.1	73.1	83.1
OR	30	29	29	7.9	10.8	1.7	27.4	29.6	33.4
CA	1	1	1	25.7	6.1	1.0	151.7	190.8	204.4
AK	50	49	48	36.9	9.5	0.7	0.7	1.0	1.1
HI	39	41	41	14.9	6.4	0.4	150.2	172.5	184.3

X Not applicable. Z Less than 0.05 percent. [1] Persons per square mile were calculated on the basis of land area data from the 1990 census.

Source: U.S. Bureau of the Census, *1990 Census of Population and Housing, Population and Housing Unit Counts* (CPH-2); and "ST-96-1 Estimates of the Population of States: Annual Time Series, July 1, 1990 to July 1, 1996"; release date: December 30, 1996; <http://www.census.gov/population/estimates/state/ST9096T1.txt>.

No. 28. Components of Population Change—States: 1995 to 1996

[In thousands, except percent. Covers period July 1, 1995 to July 1, 1996]

REGION, DIVISION, AND STATE	NET CHANGE [1]		Births	Deaths	NET MOVEMENT FROM ABROAD		Net domestic migration
	Number	Percent			International migration	Federal U.S. citizen	
United States	2,394.1	0.9	3,879.8	2,330.9	855.6	-10.4	-
Northeast	72.6	0.1	697.5	499.0	205.3	-0.5	-326.4
New England	46.2	0.3	168.5	122.0	31.7	-0.2	-30.2
Maine	4.7	0.4	14.0	11.9	0.5	(-Z)	2.3
New Hampshire	14.2	1.2	15.0	9.4	0.9	(-Z)	7.7
Vermont	3.9	0.7	6.8	5.0	0.5	-	1.5
Massachusetts	21.3	0.4	75.0	56.4	19.1	(-Z)	-15.3
Rhode Island	-1.5	-0.1	12.4	9.8	2.0	(-Z)	-6.0
Connecticut	3.5	0.1	45.3	29.4	8.7	-0.1	-20.5
Middle Atlantic	26.4	0.1	529.0	377.0	173.6	-0.3	-296.2
New York	-5.8	(-Z)	264.1	172.1	118.5	-0.2	-216.6
New Jersey	36.4	0.5	113.8	76.6	40.6	-0.1	-39.3
Pennsylvania	-4.2	(-Z)	151.1	128.3	14.4	(-Z)	-40.0
Midwest	350.2	0.6	877.6	575.5	84.9	-0.8	-34.5
East North Central	232.6	0.5	624.7	400.9	65.8	-0.3	-55.1
Ohio	38.8	0.3	153.9	106.7	7.4	-0.1	-14.8
Indiana	43.6	0.8	83.2	53.9	3.8	(-Z)	10.7
Illinois	56.2	0.5	185.7	109.9	38.7	-0.2	-58.4
Michigan	56.4	0.6	134.2	84.4	12.9	(-Z)	-5.8
Wisconsin	37.7	0.7	67.7	46.0	3.0	(-Z)	13.1
West North Central	117.6	0.6	252.9	174.6	19.1	-0.4	20.6
Minnesota	43.1	0.9	63.5	38.2	6.2	(-Z)	11.6
Iowa	8.7	0.3	37.0	28.5	2.5	(-Z)	-2.0
Missouri	39.4	0.7	72.9	54.9	4.4	-0.1	16.9
North Dakota	2.0	0.3	8.5	6.1	0.7	-0.1	-0.9
South Dakota	2.9	0.4	10.5	7.1	0.6	(-Z)	-1.1
Nebraska	12.9	0.8	23.3	15.5	1.8	-0.1	3.3
Kansas	8.5	0.3	37.2	24.2	2.9	-0.1	-7.2
South	1,139.6	1.2	1,349.6	835.7	247.7	-5.8	381.9
South Atlantic	602.6	1.3	654.4	440.3	147.7	-3.8	244.3
Delaware	7.8	1.1	10.2	6.4	1.1	(-Z)	2.8
Maryland	32.7	0.6	71.9	42.7	15.5	-0.3	-11.7
District of Columbia	-11.3	-2.0	7.9	6.0	3.8	(-Z)	-17.2
Virginia	60.2	0.9	91.1	52.4	19.6	-1.2	2.4
West Virginia	0.5	(Z)	21.2	20.5	0.5	(-Z)	-0.6
North Carolina	120.5	1.7	101.3	65.2	7.0	-0.8	77.9
South Carolina	31.7	0.9	50.6	33.6	2.5	-0.3	12.4
Georgia	144.5	2.0	111.7	58.9	14.4	-0.5	76.6
Florida	215.8	1.5	188.3	154.7	83.3	-0.6	101.5
East South Central	146.6	0.9	226.2	157.8	7.9	-0.6	70.7
Kentucky	26.8	0.7	52.1	37.3	1.9	-0.2	10.4
Tennessee	72.9	1.4	73.1	51.5	3.0	-0.1	48.2
Alabama	26.9	0.6	60.0	42.3	2.1	-0.1	7.2
Mississippi	19.9	0.7	41.0	26.8	0.8	-0.1	4.9
West South Central	390.5	1.4	469.0	237.6	92.1	-1.4	66.9
Arkansas	25.0	1.0	35.1	26.8	1.0	(-Z)	15.6
Louisiana	12.5	0.3	65.1	39.8	3.1	-0.2	-15.9
Oklahoma	26.0	0.8	45.4	32.7	3.6	-0.2	10.2
Texas	326.9	1.7	323.4	138.3	84.4	-0.9	57.0
West	829.8	1.4	955.1	420.7	317.6	-3.4	-21.0
Mountain	368.0	2.3	254.6	117.5	40.3	-0.7	188.8
Montana	9.0	1.0	11.2	7.8	0.3	(-Z)	5.2
Idaho	23.1	2.0	18.1	8.6	2.4	(-Z)	11.0
Wyoming	2.2	0.5	6.3	3.8	0.3	(-Z)	-0.6
Colorado	75.1	2.0	54.5	25.2	9.4	-0.2	36.0
New Mexico	23.6	1.4	26.9	12.7	4.7	-0.1	4.7
Arizona	123.1	2.9	72.6	35.9	13.2	-0.2	72.5
Utah	42.2	2.2	39.8	11.0	3.5	(-Z)	9.9
Nevada	69.7	4.5	25.1	12.6	6.4	-0.1	50.1
Pacific	461.8	1.1	700.5	303.2	277.4	-2.7	-209.8
Washington	85.2	1.6	77.5	41.3	16.3	-0.5	33.1
Oregon	54.9	1.7	42.9	28.6	7.1	(-Z)	33.4
California	312.8	1.0	551.7	224.0	246.4	-1.7	-258.9
Alaska	4.5	0.7	10.2	2.6	1.1	-0.2	-4.2
Hawaii	4.5	0.4	18.2	6.8	6.6	-0.4	-13.2

- Represents zero. Z Less than 50 or .05 percent. [1] Includes residual change, not shown separately. The residual is the effect of national controls on subnational estimates. It is the difference between the implementation of the national estimates model and the county/State estimates model.

Source: U.S. Bureau of the Census, "ST-96-3 Estimates of the Population of States: Annual Time Series, July 1, 1990 to July 1, 1996, and Demographic Components of Population Change, Annual Time Series, July 1, 1990 to July 1, 1996"; release date: December 30, 1996; <http://www.census.gov/population/estimates/state/STCOM96.txt>.

No. 29. U.S. Resident Population, by Region and Division: 1970 to 1996

[As of April 1; except 1985, 1995 and 1996, as of July 1. For composition of divisions, see table 26]

REGION AND DIVISION	POPULATION (millions)						PERCENT DISTRIBUTION					
	1970	1980	1985	1990	1995	1996	1970	1980	1985	1990	1995	1996
United States	203.3	226.5	237.9	248.7	262.9	265.3	100.0	100.0	100.0	100.0	100.0	100.0
Northeast	49.1	49.1	49.9	50.8	51.5	51.6	24.1	21.7	21.0	20.4	19.6	19.4
New England	11.8	12.3	12.7	13.2	13.3	13.4	5.8	5.5	5.4	5.3	5.1	5.0
Middle Atlantic	37.2	36.8	37.1	37.6	38.2	38.2	18.3	16.2	15.6	15.1	14.5	14.4
Midwest	56.6	58.9	58.8	59.7	61.7	62.1	27.8	26.0	24.7	24.0	23.5	23.4
East North Central	40.3	41.7	41.4	42.0	43.4	43.6	19.8	18.4	17.4	16.9	16.5	16.4
West North Central	16.3	17.2	17.4	17.7	18.4	18.5	8.0	7.6	7.3	7.1	7.0	7.0
South	62.8	75.4	81.4	85.5	92.0	93.1	30.9	33.3	34.2	34.4	35.0	35.1
South Atlantic	30.7	37.0	40.2	43.6	47.0	47.6	15.1	16.3	16.9	17.5	17.9	17.9
East South Central	12.8	14.7	15.0	15.2	16.0	16.2	6.3	6.5	6.3	6.1	6.1	6.1
West South Central	19.3	23.7	26.3	26.7	28.9	29.3	9.5	10.5	11.0	10.7	11.0	11.0
West	34.8	43.2	47.8	52.8	57.7	58.5	17.1	19.1	20.1	21.2	21.9	22.1
Mountain	8.3	11.4	12.7	13.7	15.7	16.1	4.1	5.0	5.4	5.5	6.0	6.1
Pacific	26.5	31.8	35.1	39.1	41.9	42.4	13.1	14.0	14.7	15.7	16.0	16.0

Source: U.S. Bureau of the Census, *1990 Census of Population and Housing, Population and Housing Unit Counts* (CPH-2); and "ST-96-1 Estimates of the Population of States: Annual Time Series, July 1, 1990 to July 1, 1996"; release date: December 30, 1996; <http://www.census.gov/population/estimates/state/ST9096T1.txt>.

No. 30. Resident Population, by Region, Race, and Hispanic Origin: 1990

[As of April 1. For composition of regions, see table 26]

RACE AND HISPANIC ORIGIN	POPULATION (1,000)					PERCENT DISTRIBUTION				
	United States	North-east	Midwest	South	West	United States	North-east	Midwest	South	West
Total	248,710	50,809	59,669	85,446	52,786	100.0	20.4	24.0	34.4	21.2
White	199,686	42,069	52,018	65,582	40,017	100.0	21.1	26.0	32.8	20.0
Black	29,986	5,613	5,716	15,829	2,828	100.0	18.7	19.1	52.8	9.4
American Indian, Eskimo, Aleut	1,959	125	338	563	933	100.0	6.4	17.2	28.7	47.6
American Indian	1,878	122	334	557	866	100.0	6.5	17.8	29.7	46.1
Eskimo	57	2	2	3	51	100.0	2.9	3.5	4.9	88.8
Aleut	24	2	2	3	17	100.0	8.1	8.1	11.5	72.3
Asian or Pacific Islander	7,274	1,335	768	1,122	4,048	100.0	18.4	10.6	15.4	55.7
Chinese	1,645	445	133	204	863	100.0	27.0	8.1	12.4	52.4
Filipino	1,407	143	113	159	991	100.0	10.2	8.1	11.3	70.5
Japanese	848	74	63	67	643	100.0	8.8	7.5	7.9	75.9
Asian Indian	815	285	146	196	189	100.0	35.0	17.9	24.0	23.1
Korean	799	182	109	153	355	100.0	22.8	13.7	19.2	44.4
Vietnamese	615	61	52	169	334	100.0	9.8	8.5	27.4	54.3
Laotian	149	16	28	29	76	100.0	10.7	18.6	19.6	51.0
Cambodian	147	30	13	19	85	100.0	20.5	8.8	13.1	57.7
Thai	91	12	13	24	43	100.0	12.9	14.2	26.0	46.8
Hmong	90	2	37	2	50	100.0	1.9	41.3	1.8	55.0
Pakistani	81	28	15	22	17	100.0	34.3	18.9	26.5	20.4
Hawaiian	211	4	6	12	189	100.0	2.0	2.6	5.8	89.6
Samoan	63	2	2	4	55	100.0	2.4	3.6	6.4	87.6
Guamanian	49	4	3	8	34	100.0	7.3	6.4	16.8	69.5
Other Asian or Pacific Islander	263	49	34	54	126	100.0	18.6	12.9	20.5	48.0
Other races	9,805	1,667	829	2,350	4,960	100.0	17.0	8.5	24.0	50.6
Hispanic origin [1]	22,354	3,754	1,727	6,767	10,106	100.0	16.8	7.7	30.3	45.2
Mexican	13,496	175	1,153	4,344	7,824	100.0	1.3	8.5	32.2	58.0
Puerto Rican	2,728	1,872	258	406	192	100.0	68.6	9.4	14.9	7.0
Cuban	1,044	184	37	735	88	100.0	17.6	3.5	70.5	8.5
Other Hispanic	5,086	1,524	279	1,282	2,002	100.0	30.0	5.5	25.2	39.4
Not of Hispanic origin	226,356	47,055	57,942	78,679	42,680	100.0	20.8	25.6	34.8	18.9

[1] Persons of Hispanic origin may be of any race.

Source: U.S. Bureau of the Census, *1990 Census of Population, General Population Characteristics, United States* (CP-1-1).

No. 23. Resident Population, by Age and Hispanic Origin: 1990 to 1996

[In thousands, except percent. As of July, except 1990 as of April. See headnote, table 18. Hispanic persons may be of any race]

YEAR AND SEX	Total, all years	Under 5 years	5-9 years	10-14 years	15-19 years	20-24 years	25-29 years	30-34 years	35-39 years	40-44 years	45-49 years	50-54 years	55-59 years	60-64 years	65-74 years	75-84 years	85 years and over	5-13 years	14-17 years	18-24 years
HISPANIC ORIGIN																				
1990 [1]	22,354	2,467	2,178	1,989	2,085	2,320	2,337	2,045	1,642	1,276	936	750	633	550	715	340	91	3,782	1,574	3,215
1995	27,277	3,205	2,595	2,387	2,387	2,465	2,508	2,560	2,202	1,757	1,326	971	766	634	947	428	139	4,503	1,893	[illegible]
1996	28,269	3,273	2,743	2,449	2,483	2,492	2,539	2,613	2,316	1,864	1,426	1,028	799	652	988	454	151	4,705	1,966	[illegible]
Male	14,519	1,677	1,403	1,255	1,316	1,361	1,386	1,392	1,212	952	712	500	380	302	439	179	51	2,406	1,029	[illegible]
Female	13,750	1,596	1,340	1,194	1,168	1,130	1,152	1,221	1,104	912	715	527	419	350	549	275	99	2,298	937	[illegible]
NON-HISPANIC WHITE																				
1990 [1]	188,306	12,721	12,516	11,854	12,450	13,524	15,508	16,331	15,162	13,839	10,971	9,057	8,548	8,872	15,511	8,767	2,675	22,106	9,224	19,014
1995	193,281	12,531	12,794	12,814	12,287	12,170	13,072	15,649	16,503	15,362	13,654	10,843	8,838	8,137	15,747	9,700	3,182	23,069	10,023	16,973
1996	193,978	12,300	12,875	12,861	12,575	11,723	13,027	15,097	16,593	15,693	14,345	11,014	9,032	8,054	15,599	9,926	3,264	23,139	10,246	16,649
Male	94,799	6,308	6,608	6,608	6,476	5,979	6,508	7,541	8,319	7,841	7,127	5,415	4,390	3,847	7,012	3,909	911	11,881	5,281	8,509
Female	99,179	5,993	6,267	6,254	6,099	5,744	6,519	7,557	8,274	7,852	7,218	5,599	4,642	4,206	8,587	6,017	2,353	11,259	4,964	8,140
BLACK																				
1990 [1]	29,275	2,798	2,596	2,525	2,605	2,528	2,650	2,601	2,265	1,811	1,362	1,138	1,008	945	1,465	758	219	4,638	1,975	3,642
1995	31,565	2,856	2,865	2,738	2,695	2,520	2,452	2,679	2,661	2,289	1,779	1,328	1,096	955	1,570	811	272	5,056	2,198	3,585
1996	31,912	2,762	2,929	2,764	2,766	2,465	2,462	2,660	2,698	2,370	1,914	1,355	1,118	959	1,582	825	281	5,131	2,251	3,643
Male	15,098	1,399	1,485	1,403	1,403	1,215	1,172	1,242	1,260	1,098	872	606	489	411	661	303	82	2,602	1,147	1,757
Female	16,814	1,364	1,444	1,361	1,363	1,250	1,291	1,418	1,438	1,273	1,043	750	629	548	922	522	199	2,529	1,104	1,786
AMERICAN ''DIAN, O, ALEUT																				
	1,796	185	179	170	165	151	160	156	138	117	90	72	58	48	68	31	9	316	131	217
	1,931	172	191	198	172	158	151	157	152	136	111	84	65	53	77	39	14	349	149	221
	1,954	169	191	200	179	156	155	155	154	139	116	87	67	54	78	41	16	351	154	220
	961	85	97	101	90	79	79	77	75	67	56	42	32	25	35	17	5	178	78	111
	993	84	94	99	89	77	76	78	79	72	60	45	35	29	43	24	11	173	76	109
	6,988	586	566	522	581	612	673	700	640	545	384	297	240	210	287	116	27	983	436	882
	8,836	772	663	689	627	741	788	818	791	717	592	421	327	270	403	171	45	1,213	523	985
	9,171	781	704	707	659	725	824	836	817	750	635	449	346	281	421	185	50	1,267	554	973
	4,433	399	362	360	335	365	393	401	392	352	295	213	164	125	178	79	20	649	282	490
	4,738	383	342	347	325	360	431	435	425	398	341	236	182	156	244	106	30	618	272	483
	[illegible]	11.6	9.7	8.7	8.8	8.8	9.0	9.2	8.2	6.6	5.0	3.8	2.8	2.3	3.5	1.6	0.5	16.6	7.0	12.4
			6.6	6.6	6.5	6.0	6.7	7.8	8.6	8.1	7.4	5.7	4.7	4.2	8.0	5.1	1.7	11.9	5.3	8.6
			9.2	8.7	8.7	7.7	7.7	8.3	8.5	7.4	6.0	4.2	3.5	3.0	5.0	2.6	0.9	16.1	7.1	11.1
				10.0	8.9	7.7	7.5	7.8	7.8	7.2	5.9	4.5	3.5	2.9	4.3	2.4	1.1	17.4	7.6	11.0
				8.5	7.8	7.7	8.8	9.2	8.8	7.8	6.6	4.7	3.7	2.8	4.0	1.7	0.3	15.2	6.6	10.6

cludes count question resolution corrections processed
ulation Reports, P25-1095; Paper Listing

No. 33. Resident Population, by Age and State: 1996

[In thousands, except percent. As of July 1. Includes Armed Forces stationed in area. See text, section 1, for basis of estimates]

REGION, DIVISION, AND STATE	Total	Under 5 years	5 to 17 years	18 to 24 years	25 to 34 years	35 to 44 years	45 to 54 years	55 to 64 years	65 to 74 years	75 to 84 years	85 years and over	Percent 65 years and over
U.S.	265,284	19,286	49,762	24,862	40,368	43,393	32,370	21,361	18,669	11,430	3,762	12.8
Northeast	51,580	3,514	9,106	4,431	7,929	8,520	6,470	4,295	3,966	2,510	839	14.2
N.E.	13,351	859	2,338	1,120	2,164	2,271	1,684	1,046	989	652	229	14.0
ME	1,243	71	228	111	177	216	163	103	94	58	21	13.9
NH	1,162	76	220	94	189	215	146	84	76	47	16	12.0
VT	589	35	111	52	88	105	80	46	39	24	9	12.1
MA	6,092	391	1,031	515	1,046	1,017	759	474	452	301	106	14.1
RI	990	63	172	85	160	162	117	75	82	55	19	15.8
CT	3,274	223	575	262	504	556	419	265	246	166	57	14.3
M.A	38,229	2,655	6,767	3,311	5,766	6,249	4,786	3,248	2,977	1,858	611	14.2
NY	18,185	1,322	3,219	1,605	2,862	2,939	2,267	1,537	1,335	815	284	13.4
NJ	7,988	572	1,415	665	1,195	1,352	1,021	666	604	376	119	13.8
PA	12,056	761	2,133	1,041	1,710	1,958	1,497	1,044	1,037	667	208	15.9
Midwest	62,082	4,344	11,901	5,841	9,105	10,149	7,546	5,070	4,384	2,773	970	13.1
E.N.C	43,614	3,092	8,290	4,107	6,482	7,148	5,341	3,557	3,071	1,896	629	12.8
OH	11,173	759	2,089	1,051	1,634	1,823	1,379	942	834	502	161	13.4
IN	5,841	410	1,089	573	871	952	723	488	406	246	82	12.6
IL	11,847	915	2,241	1,096	1,806	1,930	1,424	947	803	510	172	12.5
MI	9,594	672	1,865	904	1,423	1,587	1,188	763	666	400	126	12.4
WI	5,160	337	1,006	482	749	856	627	417	361	238	87	13.3
W.N.C	18,468	1,252	3,611	1,734	2,622	3,001	2,205	1,513	1,313	877	341	13.7
MN	4,658	316	931	420	695	797	562	359	298	202	78	12.4
IA	2,852	182	537	271	386	448	345	250	219	153	61	15.2
MO	5,359	367	1,027	495	771	858	644	454	398	251	93	13.8
ND	644	41	127	66	88	102	73	53	46	34	13	14.5
SD	732	51	153	73	94	114	82	59	54	37	15	14.4
NE	1,652	113	329	162	225	265	195	134	117	79	33	13.8
KS	2,572	180	507	246	364	417	302	203	182	122	48	13.7
South	93,098	6,716	17,408	9,009	14,091	14,995	11,361	7,696	6,638	3,929	1,257	12.7
S.A.	47,616	3,279	8,493	4,355	7,369	7,749	5,880	3,969	3,662	2,186	672	13.7
DE	725	50	126	65	122	123	88	59	54	30	9	12.8
MD	5,072	360	927	427	837	897	653	393	329	190	59	11.4
DC	543	34	75	46	110	89	67	46	41	25	9	13.9
VA	6,675	455	1,177	649	1,116	1,141	860	530	428	243	76	11.2
WV	1,826	107	315	187	233	284	244	178	156	93	29	15.2
NC	7,323	513	1,321	703	1,157	1,180	911	621	527	298	92	12.5
SC	3,699	254	684	378	569	593	464	310	261	144	42	12.1
GA	7,353	552	1,401	733	1,224	1,243	916	555	414	240	75	9.9
FL	14,400	956	2,467	1,167	2,001	2,199	1,675	1,277	1,452	925	281	18.5
E.S.C	16,193	1,123	3,000	1,646	2,386	2,564	2,015	1,410	1,144	677	226	12.6
KY	3,884	259	710	396	568	625	492	342	274	161	54	12.6
TN	5,320	364	958	511	804	862	666	488	375	220	73	12.5
AL	4,273	296	780	438	629	670	528	376	312	185	60	13.0
MS	2,716	204	552	300	385	407	310	224	184	111	39	12.3
W.S.C	29,290	2,313	5,913	3,008	4,336	4,682	3,466	2,317	1,832	1,063	360	11.1
AR	2,510	175	464	249	340	369	304	226	195	125	42	14.4
LA	4,351	328	906	460	615	677	514	354	283	161	52	11.4
OK	3,301	228	653	330	445	506	401	293	242	149	54	13.5
TX	19,128	1,583	3,869	1,970	2,935	3,129	2,247	1,444	1,112	627	212	10.2
West	58,523	4,712	11,350	5,601	9,243	9,729	6,994	4,301	3,681	2,218	695	11.3
Mountain	16,118	1,238	3,221	1,619	2,321	2,633	1,975	1,286	1,035	606	182	11.3
MT	879	56	177	86	102	146	118	79	61	41	14	13.2
ID	1,189	90	258	130	150	186	143	96	72	47	15	11.4
WY	481	31	102	51	56	82	63	41	31	17	6	11.2
CO	3,823	270	728	355	561	695	521	308	218	125	42	10.1
NM	1,713	136	365	171	230	277	206	138	109	61	19	11.0
AZ	4,428	343	807	429	677	704	524	358	332	199	56	13.2
UT	2,000	188	490	262	289	276	194	125	97	60	19	8.8
NV	1,603	124	293	134	256	267	206	141	115	56	13	11.4
Pacific	42,406	3,474	8,128	3,982	6,922	7,096	5,018	3,014	2,646	1,613	513	11.3
WA	5,533	386	1,051	509	835	973	719	419	346	223	72	11.6
OR	3,204	212	597	289	439	541	434	263	226	152	50	13.4
CA	31,878	2,736	6,131	3,003	5,394	5,266	3,634	2,198	1,961	1,180	375	11.0
AK	607	50	135	65	86	117	83	41	21	9	2	5.2
HI	1,184	91	215	116	168	198	149	93	89	49	14	12.9

Source: U.S. Bureau of the Census, press release CB97-64 and unpublished data.

No. 34. Resident Population by Race, Hispanic Origin, and State: 1994

[In thousands. As of July 1. These estimates are consistent with data released in PE-47, PE-48, PPL-49, and PPL-50 released August 20, 1996. Consequently the estimates shown in this table are not consistent with subsequently released national and State estimates. These estimates are developed using a cohort-component method whereby each component of population change - births, deaths, domestic migration, and international migration is estimated separately for each birth cohort by sex and race]

REGION, DIVISION, AND STATE	Total	RACE						Hispanic origin [1]
		White			Black	American Indian, Eskimo, Aleut	Asian, Pacific Islander	
		Total	Hispanic	Non-Hispanic				
U.S.	**260,341**	216,477	**23,742**	**192,736**	**32,670**	**2,209**	**8,966**	**26,073**
Northeast	**51,400**	**43,422**	**3,406**	**40,016**	**6,191**	**140**	**1,647**	**4,296**
N.E	**13,271**	**12,230**	**541**	**11,689**	**721**	**35**	**285**	**660**
ME	1,240	1,222	7	1,215	5	6	8	7
NH	1,137	1,117	12	1,105	7	2	11	13
VT	580	572	4	568	2	2	4	4
MA	6,041	5,485	263	5,222	364	14	178	339
RI	997	924	45	879	47	4	21	58
CT	3,275	2,910	211	2,699	295	8	63	239
M.A	**38,129**	**31,192**	2,865	**28,327**	**5,471**	**104**	**1,362**	**3,636**
NY	18,173	14,086	1,894	12,192	3,179	69	839	2,499
NJ	7,904	6,398	744	5,654	1,134	19	353	868
PA	12,052	10,709	226	10,482	1,157	16	171	270
Midwest	**61,396**	**53,982**	1,847	**52,135**	**6,114**	**363**	**969**	**2,018**
E.N.C	**43,184**	**37,197**	1,530	**35,667**	**5,133**	**182**	**693**	**1,661**
OH	11,102	9,738	140	9,599	1,235	21	108	157
IN	5,752	5,229	106	5,123	464	13	46	115
IL	11,752	9,588	984	8,604	1,795	25	344	1,051
MI	9,497	7,949	201	7,748	1,364	58	126	227
WI	5,082	4,693	100	4,594	276	44	69	112
W.N.C.	**18,214**	**16,786**	**316**	**16,468**	**981**	**201**	247	**355**
MN	4,567	4,290	61	4,229	122	55	100	72
IA	2,829	2,736	39	2,697	54	8	31	43
MO	5,278	4,624	63	4,561	582	20	52	71
ND	638	603	4	598	4	27	5	5
SD	724	662	5	657	4	54	4	6
NE	1,623	1,532	44	1,487	62	13	16	48
KS	2,554	2,338	99	2,239	154	23	39	109
South	**90,685**	**71,404**	**7,486**	**63,917**	**17,197**	**612**	**1,472**	**7,942**
S.A	**46,391**	**35,557**	**2,326**	33,231	**9,810**	**194**	829	**2,571**
DE	709	566	16	549	129	2	12	19
MD	5,002	3,490	131	3,358	1,320	14	178	163
DC	567	184	27	157	364	2	17	39
VA	6,551	5,055	171	4,884	1,277	18	202	196
WV	1,823	1,754	8	1,745	58	2	9	9
NC	7,069	5,344	80	5,263	1,568	87	70	96
SC	3,664	2,526	29	2,496	1,102	9	27	36
GA	7,055	4,968	121	4,848	1,966	15	105	140
FL	13,951	11,671	1,742	9,930	2,025	45	209	1,872
E.S.C	**15,890**	**12,596**	**101**	12,494	**3,148**	**42**	106	**119**
KY	3,827	3,527	23	3,505	272	6	22	26
TN	5,175	4,284	37	4,247	839	11	41	43
AL	4,219	3,096	26	3,070	1,079	17	27	31
MS	2,669	1,687	15	1,672	958	9	15	19
W.S.C.	**28,404**	**23,252**	**5,059**	**18,193**	**4,239**	**376**	537	**5,252**
AR	2,453	2,035	23	2,011	389	14	16	27
LA	4,315	2,882	87	2,795	1,364	19	50	101
OK	3,258	2,703	84	2,619	251	263	41	102
TX	18,378	15,632	4,864	10,767	2,235	81	430	5,022
West	**56,869**	**47,669**	**11,063**	**36,606**	**3,167**	**1,094**	4,929	**11,819**
Mountain	**15,214**	**13,906**	**2,209**	11,697	**467**	**561**	**291**	**2,350**
MT	856	797	12	785	3	51	5	15
ID	1,133	1,101	61	1,040	5	16	12	66
WY	476	459	25	433	4	10	3	27
CO	3,656	3,387	462	2,925	158	34	77	492
NM	1,654	1,446	621	824	40	148	20	646
AZ	4,075	3,623	770	2,853	139	238	75	824
UT	1,908	1,820	97	1,724	15	29	44	105
NV	1,457	1,273	160	1,113	103	26	55	176
Pacific	**41,644**	**33,763**	**8,793**	**24,970**	**2,700**	**543**	4,638	**9,469**
WA	5,343	4,796	235	4,560	176	98	274	269
OR	3,086	2,900	129	2,771	55	44	88	142
CA	31,431	25,211	8,371	16,840	2,415	302	3,504	8,939
AK	605	462	18	445	25	94	24	22
HI	1,179	395	40	354	29	7	749	97

[1] Persons of Hispanic origin may be of any race.

Source: U.S. Bureau of the Census, "Estimates of the population of States by race and Hispanic origin: July 1, 1994;" <http://www.census.gov/population/estimate-extract/state/sasr/sasr94.txt>; (accessed: 9 April 1997).

No. 35. State Population Projections: 2000 to 2025

[In thousands. As of July 1. The two series of projections are based on different internal migration assumptions: 1) Series A, is the preferred series model and uses State-to-State migration observed from 1975-76 through 1993-94; and 2) Series B, the economic model, uses the Bureau of Economic Analysis employment projections. For explanation of methodology, see text, section 1]

REGION, DIVISION, AND STATE	Series A						Series B					
	2000	2005	2010	2015	2020	2025	2000	2005	2010	2015	2020	2025
U.S.	274,634	285,981	297,716	310,133	322,742	335,050	274,634	285,981	297,716	310,134	322,742	335,069
Northeast	52,107	52,767	53,692	54,836	56,103	57,392	52,152	52,731	53,399	54,270	55,304	56,400
N.E.	13,581	13,843	14,172	14,546	14,938	15,321	13,573	13,786	13,969	14,242	14,511	14,781
ME	1,259	1,285	1,323	1,362	1,396	1,423	1,250	1,259	1,268	1,276	1,282	1,282
NH	1,224	1,281	1,329	1,372	1,410	1,439	1,217	1,267	1,307	1,344	1,377	1,402
VT	617	638	651	662	671	678	607	623	636	646	655	661
MA	6,199	6,310	6,431	6,574	6,734	6,902	6,224	6,361	6,498	6,653	6,824	7,001
RI	998	1,012	1,038	1,070	1,105	1,141	989	986	986	989	998	1,007
CT	3,284	3,317	3,400	3,506	3,621	3,739	3,286	3,291	3,303	3,332	3,376	3,428
M.A.	38,526	38,923	39,520	40,289	41,164	42,071	38,579	38,943	39,400	40,028	40,792	41,619
NY	18,146	18,250	18,530	18,916	19,359	19,830	18,174	18,227	18,363	18,616	18,969	19,396
NJ	8,178	8,392	8,638	8,924	9,238	9,558	8,185	8,387	8,594	8,832	9,096	9,369
PA	12,202	12,281	12,352	12,449	12,567	12,683	12,220	12,329	12,443	12,580	12,727	12,854
Midwest	63,502	64,825	65,915	67,024	68,114	69,109	63,579	65,230	66,963	68,800	70,609	72,293
E.N.C.	44,419	45,151	45,764	46,410	47,063	47,675	44,517	45,486	46,507	47,619	48,746	49,826
OH	11,319	11,428	11,505	11,588	11,671	11,744	11,352	11,534	11,726	11,937	12,148	12,343
IN	6,045	6,215	6,318	6,404	6,481	6,546	6,060	6,301	6,532	6,758	6,969	7,158
IL	12,051	12,266	12,515	12,808	13,121	13,440	12,069	12,314	12,601	12,945	13,323	13,717
MI	9,679	9,763	9,836	9,917	10,002	10,078	9,711	9,835	9,966	10,115	10,272	10,423
WI	5,326	5,479	5,590	5,693	5,788	5,867	5,324	5,502	5,682	5,864	6,035	6,185
W.N.C.	19,082	19,673	20,151	20,615	21,051	21,434	19,063	19,745	20,456	21,181	21,863	22,467
MN	4,830	5,005	5,147	5,283	5,406	5,510	4,822	5,014	5,212	5,414	5,606	5,778
IA	2,900	2,941	2,968	2,994	3,019	3,040	2,891	2,939	2,992	3,047	3,095	3,133
MO	5,540	5,718	5,864	6,005	6,137	6,250	5,547	5,750	5,953	6,153	6,336	6,492
ND	662	677	690	704	717	729	657	677	701	727	754	778
SD	777	810	826	840	853	866	770	811	853	893	930	962
NE	1,705	1,761	1,806	1,850	1,892	1,930	1,700	1,766	1,837	1,912	1,984	2,050
KS	2,668	2,761	2,849	2,939	3,026	3,108	2,675	2,788	2,908	3,034	3,158	3,273
South	97,613	102,788	107,597	112,384	117,060	121,448	97,667	103,112	108,500	113,900	119,130	124,018
S.A.	50,147	52,921	55,457	57,966	60,411	62,675	50,132	52,976	55,712	58,394	60,931	63,220
DE	768	800	817	832	847	861	758	793	823	851	877	899
MD	5,275	5,467	5,657	5,862	6,071	6,274	5,261	5,426	5,577	5,736	5,904	6,072
DC	523	529	560	594	625	655	530	542	572	611	654	702
VA	6,997	7,324	7,627	7,921	8,204	8,466	6,965	7,234	7,474	7,708	7,939	8,165
WV	1,841	1,849	1,851	1,851	1,850	1,845	1,833	1,842	1,852	1,861	1,866	1,864
NC	7,777	8,227	8,552	8,840	9,111	9,349	7,789	8,312	8,780	9,206	9,588	9,916
SC	3,858	4,033	4,205	4,369	4,517	4,645	3,852	4,015	4,169	4,318	4,455	4,574
GA	7,875	8,413	8,824	9,200	9,552	9,869	7,893	8,540	9,167	9,785	10,386	10,962
FL	15,233	16,279	17,363	18,497	19,634	20,710	15,250	16,273	17,299	18,318	19,262	20,066
E.S.C.	16,918	17,604	18,122	18,586	19,002	19,345	16,920	17,714	18,478	19,211	19,881	20,461
KY	3,995	4,098	4,170	4,231	4,281	4,314	3,990	4,109	4,220	4,322	4,411	4,480
TN	5,657	5,966	6,180	6,365	6,529	6,665	5,668	6,039	6,385	6,707	6,998	7,249
AL	4,451	4,631	4,798	4,956	5,100	5,224	4,436	4,617	4,802	4,986	5,162	5,319
MS	2,816	2,908	2,974	3,035	3,093	3,142	2,826	2,949	3,072	3,195	3,310	3,413
W.S.C.	30,548	32,263	34,019	35,832	37,647	39,427	30,616	32,422	34,310	36,296	38,318	40,337
AR	2,631	2,750	2,840	2,922	2,997	3,055	2,623	2,757	2,887	3,008	3,109	3,184
LA	4,425	4,535	4,683	4,840	4,991	5,133	4,445	4,558	4,687	4,828	4,972	5,111
OK	3,373	3,491	3,639	3,789	3,930	4,057	3,370	3,471	3,578	3,684	3,784	3,871
TX	20,119	21,487	22,857	24,280	25,729	27,183	20,178	21,635	23,158	24,775	26,453	28,170
West	61,413	65,603	70,512	75,889	81,465	87,101	61,236	64,907	68,854	73,164	77,700	82,338
Mountain	17,725	19,249	20,221	21,122	22,049	22,962	17,717	19,631	21,469	23,258	24,963	26,559
MT	950	1,006	1,040	1,069	1,097	1,121	937	998	1,056	1,108	1,152	1,187
ID	1,347	1,480	1,557	1,622	1,683	1,739	1,332	1,489	1,637	1,775	1,900	2,008
WY	525	568	607	641	670	694	519	559	598	636	671	702
CO	4,168	4,468	4,658	4,833	5,012	5,188	4,154	4,510	4,837	5,152	5,454	5,743
NM	1,860	2,016	2,155	2,300	2,454	2,612	1,858	2,035	2,223	2,425	2,636	2,850
AZ	4,798	5,230	5,522	5,808	6,111	6,412	4,838	5,432	6,025	6,620	7,193	7,729
UT	2,207	2,411	2,551	2,670	2,781	2,883	2,216	2,477	2,738	2,995	3,246	3,487
NV	1,871	2,070	2,131	2,179	2,241	2,312	1,863	2,130	2,355	2,547	2,712	2,854
Pacific	43,686	46,354	50,291	54,767	59,416	64,139	43,519	45,276	47,385	49,906	52,736	55,780
WA	5,858	6,258	6,658	7,058	7,446	7,808	5,829	6,184	6,524	6,857	7,179	7,480
OR	3,397	3,613	3,803	3,992	4,177	4,349	3,397	3,625	3,837	4,036	4,213	4,361
CA	32,521	34,441	37,644	41,373	45,278	49,285	32,423	33,511	34,968	36,838	39,034	41,480
AK	653	700	745	791	838	885	632	659	690	728	773	825
HI	1,257	1,342	1,440	1,553	1,677	1,812	1,238	1,297	1,367	1,447	1,537	1,634

Source: U.S. Bureau of the Census, Population Paper Listings PPL-47.

No. 36. Population Projections, by Age—States: 2000 to 2010

[In thousands. As of July 1. The projections shown here are based on certain internal migration assumptions: Series A, is the preferred series model and uses State-to-State migration observed from 1975-76 through 1993-94]

REGION, DIVISION, AND STATE	UNDER 18 YEARS			18 TO 44 YEARS			45 TO 64 YEARS			65 YEARS AND OVER		
	2000	2005	2010	2000	2005	2010	2000	2005	2010	2000	2005	2010
U.S.	70,782	71,994	72,510	108,151	106,738	106,951	60,991	71,113	78,847	34,710	36,166	39,408
Northeast	12,808	12,725	12,493	20,300	19,550	19,293	11,810	13,367	14,529	7,188	7,104	7,377
N.E	3,281	3,246	3,187	5,405	5,233	5,165	3,055	3,541	3,900	1,840	1,823	1,920
ME	293	284	281	485	462	449	309	366	407	172	173	186
NH	304	303	300	503	494	486	275	336	380	142	148	163
VT	152	150	145	245	238	232	147	173	188	73	77	86
MA	1,496	1,468	1,452	2,499	2,429	2,393	1,361	1,566	1,723	843	827	863
RI	245	244	242	390	374	374	215	251	276	148	143	146
CT	791	777	767	1,283	1,234	1,232	749	850	924	461	456	477
M.A	9,527	9,479	9,306	14,896	14,317	14,128	8,755	9,846	10,629	5,348	5,281	5,457
NY	4,620	4,610	4,535	7,101	6,817	6,763	4,067	4,502	4,833	2,358	2,321	2,399
NJ	2,004	2,024	2,009	3,216	3,136	3,131	1,868	2,139	2,348	1,090	1,093	1,150
PA	2,902	2,845	2,762	4,582	4,363	4,236	2,819	3,206	3,448	1,899	1,867	1,908
Midwest	16,167	16,034	15,840	24,933	24,160	23,591	14,129	16,163	17,504	8,273	8,468	8,990
E.N.C	11,313	11,219	11,051	17,522	16,891	16,482	9,910	11,257	12,131	5,674	5,784	6,100
OH	2,817	2,766	2,702	4,411	4,214	4,082	2,566	2,894	3,097	1,525	1,554	1,624
IN	1,518	1,524	1,499	2,398	2,330	2,270	1,368	1,567	1,697	763	794	852
IL	3,141	3,151	3,142	4,807	4,665	4,604	2,619	2,956	3,204	1,464	1,494	1,565
MI	2,495	2,455	2,400	3,817	3,641	3,540	2,170	2,456	2,620	1,197	1,211	1,276
WI	1,344	1,322	1,308	2,090	2,045	1,987	1,187	1,382	1,512	705	730	783
W.N.C.	4,853	4,814	4,789	7,411	7,267	7,109	4,219	4,907	5,373	2,599	2,685	2,880
MN	1,236	1,216	1,212	1,935	1,906	1,858	1,063	1,256	1,391	596	627	686
IA	706	691	678	1,091	1,052	1,018	661	746	796	442	452	476
MO	1,392	1,390	1,378	2,146	2,099	2,053	1,247	1,455	1,603	755	774	830
ND	168	163	163	253	249	243	142	162	173	99	103	111
SD	210	211	210	293	292	283	164	193	212	110	114	121
NE	443	442	443	654	646	636	369	425	462	239	248	265
KS	698	700	704	1,036	1,026	1,018	575	669	736	359	366	391
South	24,836	25,341	25,428	38,345	38,109	38,094	21,984	26,029	29,243	12,446	13,309	14,832
S.A	12,189	12,409	12,346	19,618	19,477	19,400	11,507	13,758	15,802	6,833	7,277	8,109
DE	191	191	185	311	307	298	169	201	225	97	101	109
MD	1,319	1,333	1,330	2,174	2,131	2,106	1,193	1,392	1,557	589	611	664
DC	125	130	136	215	212	226	114	122	133	69	65	65
VA	1,697	1,728	1,725	2,912	2,876	2,861	1,600	1,875	2,096	788	845	945
WV	404	394	379	679	636	607	471	523	549	287	296	316
NC	1,908	1,934	1,885	3,083	3,065	3,029	1,795	2,147	2,420	991	1,061	1,218
SC	970	980	968	1,513	1,479	1,470	897	1,057	1,183	478	517	584
GA	2,070	2,155	2,164	3,301	3,326	3,318	1,725	2,080	2,368	779	852	974
FL	3,507	3,563	3,573	5,425	5,443	5,483	3,546	4,362	5,072	2,755	2,911	3,235
E.S.C	4,210	4,248	4,174	6,643	6,504	6,375	3,924	4,578	5,072	2,141	2,274	2,501
KY	963	951	923	1,577	1,516	1,461	946	1,093	1,197	509	538	589
TN	1,376	1,408	1,390	2,238	2,225	2,191	1,336	1,573	1,755	707	760	844
AL	1,105	1,119	1,110	1,731	1,696	1,676	1,033	1,203	1,338	582	613	674
MS	767	769	751	1,096	1,068	1,048	609	708	782	344	363	393
W.S.C.	8,438	8,683	8,909	12,084	12,129	12,318	6,553	7,693	8,568	3,473	3,758	4,224
AR	653	651	636	977	958	929	624	739	824	377	402	451
LA	1,214	1,204	1,207	1,722	1,678	1,676	966	1,098	1,190	523	555	610
OK	861	852	856	1,265	1,242	1,242	775	893	960	472	504	561
TX	5,708	5,976	6,210	8,122	8,251	8,471	4,188	4,963	5,575	2,101	2,297	2,601
West	16,971	17,865	18,749	24,574	24,920	25,972	13,068	15,532	17,573	6,800	7,286	8,218
Mountain	4,822	5,035	5,094	6,919	7,094	7,088	3,923	4,777	5,332	2,061	2,343	2,707
MT	240	242	242	348	345	337	234	276	297	128	143	164
ID	378	400	404	516	537	538	296	361	402	157	182	213
WY	139	146	153	201	205	212	123	146	160	62	71	82
CO	1,049	1,078	1,080	1,694	1,714	1,707	973	1,153	1,260	452	523	611
NM	534	568	594	717	737	757	403	483	545	206	228	259
AZ	1,313	1,375	1,387	1,812	1,859	1,863	1,038	1,289	1,465	635	707	807
UT	719	759	776	896	941	958	390	477	541	202	234	276
NV	450	468	456	738	754	718	464	591	662	219	257	295
Pacific	12,148	12,830	13,655	17,654	17,825	18,884	9,145	10,756	12,241	4,739	4,943	5,511
WA	1,459	1,496	1,534	2,346	2,351	2,378	1,368	1,654	1,866	685	757	880
OR	810	821	828	1,277	1,273	1,270	839	997	1,100	471	522	605
CA	9,350	9,946	10,689	13,260	13,412	14,407	6,524	7,629	8,759	3,387	3,454	3,789
AK	200	213	225	278	286	301	137	155	164	38	46	55
HI	328	354	379	495	505	528	277	319	351	157	164	182

Source: U.S. Bureau of the Census, Population Paper Listings PPL-47.

No. 37. Population Projections, by Race—States: 2000 to 2010

[In thousands. As of July 1. Data shown are for series A, the preferred series model; for explanation of methodology, see text, section 1]

REGION, DIVISION, AND STATE	WHITE			BLACK			AMERICAN INDIAN, ESKIMO, ALEUT			ASIAN, PACIFIC ISLANDER		
	2000	2005	2010	2000	2005	2010	2000	2005	2010	2000	2005	2010
U.S	225,533	232,462	239,588	35,466	37,735	40,110	2,402	2,573	2,754	11,246	13,212	15,265
Northeast	43,279	43,201	43,330	6,575	6,913	7,300	149	157	168	2,104	2,497	2,894
N.E	12,348	12,444	12,590	811	889	982	37	38	43	384	471	558
ME	1,238	1,261	1,296	5	5	7	6	6	6	9	11	13
NH	1,199	1,251	1,293	9	10	10	2	2	2	14	17	21
VT	606	625	638	2	4	4	2	2	2	6	7	8
MA	5,523	5,534	5,549	417	461	508	14	14	15	246	303	361
RI	911	911	922	54	60	68	4	6	8	28	35	41
CT	2,873	2,882	2,893	324	350	384	8	8	8	80	96	115
M.A	30,931	30,757	30,740	5,764	6,021	6,316	111	118	128	1,721	2,026	2,337
NY	13,747	13,567	13,529	3,299	3,416	3,563	73	76	79	1,026	1,191	1,359
NJ	6,442	6,465	6,512	1,239	1,328	1,422	20	23	23	475	578	681
PA	10,741	10,725	10,700	1,224	1,279	1,334	18	22	22	218	258	296
Midwest	55,327	56,077	56,626	6,553	6,879	7,199	406	440	474	1,215	1,429	1,614
E.N.C	37,910	38,251	38,467	5,449	5,681	5,914	174	184	193	906	1,036	1,172
OH	9,835	9,852	9,842	1,320	1,386	1,452	22	24	24	140	166	186
IN	5,486	5,599	5,671	502	530	551	16	16	17	80	72	78
IL	9,736	9,839	9,968	1,865	1,914	1,971	26	28	31	423	484	543
MI	8,021	8,024	8,016	1,435	1,486	1,539	61	63	65	163	190	215
WI	4,853	4,937	4,968	326	366	400	49	52	55	100	126	147
W.N.C.	17,416	17,826	18,142	1,103	1,198	1,286	231	257	282	330	393	443
MN	4,469	4,580	4,662	158	185	210	64	71	80	139	170	196
IA	2,786	2,810	2,825	62	69	76	9	11	12	43	52	58
MO	4,825	4,957	5,061	628	662	696	24	26	28	63	72	80
ND	617	628	635	5	5	5	32	37	43	6	6	7
SD	706	730	739	5	5	6	60	66	72	5	6	7
NE	1,595	1,636	1,668	72	82	88	16	18	20	23	29	31
KS	2,419	2,467	2,550	173	188	203	27	29	30	50	59	64
South	76,069	79,429	82,496	18,963	20,399	21,779	669	715	765	1,902	2,244	2,556
S.A	37,933	39,613	41,099	10,931	11,818	12,675	212	225	238	1,070	1,266	1,448
DE	603	621	626	147	158	169	2	2	2	15	17	19
MD	3,546	3,580	3,621	1,489	1,609	1,724	16	16	16	223	260	296
DC	184	194	209	321	316	329	-	-	-	15	18	21
VA	5,295	5,457	5,599	1,416	1,526	1,637	19	19	21	267	320	370
WV	1,769	1,774	1,772	58	60	60	2	2	2	11	13	15
NC	5,851	6,160	6,367	1,738	1,857	1,957	94	98	101	96	113	128
SC	2,660	2,781	2,898	1,156	1,205	1,255	8	8	9	33	38	42
GA	5,438	5,713	5,893	2,279	2,515	2,724	17	18	18	142	168	187
FL	12,588	13,332	14,113	2,326	2,573	2,820	51	58	64	267	316	366
E.S.C	13,365	13,863	14,221	3,367	3,529	3,673	46	50	52	138	161	178
KY	3,671	3,760	3,817	287	298	310	6	6	8	29	33	37
TN	4,658	4,887	5,036	929	999	1,057	12	14	14	57	66	72
AL	3,262	3,391	3,509	1,137	1,183	1,227	18	18	20	34	40	44
MS	1,774	1,826	1,861	1,012	1,049	1,078	8	8	8	19	23	25
W.S.C.	24,788	25,951	27,176	4,685	5,061	5,432	411	442	475	692	819	934
AR	2,186	2,286	2,363	409	423	434	15	16	18	19	22	24
LA	2,895	2,923	2,979	1,448	1,521	1,600	20	20	22	62	72	83
OK	2,759	2,825	2,917	282	311	341	281	295	315	51	58	65
TX	16,920	17,916	18,917	2,543	2,797	3,058	95	107	120	562	667	762
West	50,868	53,755	57,134	3,343	3,545	3,831	1,179	1,259	1,347	6,022	7,043	8,202
Mountain	16,074	17,361	18,153	601	690	756	632	692	745	418	506	566
MT	879	926	952	3	6	6	61	67	72	7	9	9
ID	1,300	1,425	1,497	8	11	12	21	25	27	17	19	22
WY	501	539	573	6	7	8	13	16	19	4	6	7
CO	3,823	4,068	4,216	196	224	246	41	46	51	108	129	147
NM	1,615	1,737	1,843	48	56	63	169	186	209	29	35	41
AZ	4,252	4,623	4,867	177	203	222	262	277	290	107	129	143
UT	2,067	2,267	2,390	22	27	29	37	43	47	62	75	85
NV	1,619	1,777	1,817	138	159	171	31	32	32	85	103	111
Pacific	34,794	36,394	38,979	2,742	2,856	3,075	547	567	602	5,604	6,537	7,634
WA	5,200	5,506	5,811	192	208	224	107	115	126	358	427	496
OR	3,167	3,350	3,508	65	74	80	51	55	59	116	135	155
CA	25,517	26,583	28,655	2,425	2,511	2,702	292	296	318	4,289	5,051	5,969
AK	486	508	524	29	31	33	93	92	91	46	69	96
HI	423	449	478	31	33	35	6	6	7	796	853	920

- Represents or rounds to zero.

Source: U.S. Bureau of the Census, Population Paper Listings PPL-47.

No. 38. Population Projections, by Hispanic Origin Status—States: 2000 to 2010

[In thousands. As of July 1. Data shown are for series A, the preferred series model; for explanation of methodology, see text, section 1. Persons of Hispanic origin may be of any race]

REGION, DIVISION, AND STATE	HISPANIC ORIGIN			NOT OF HISPANIC ORIGIN								
	2000	2005	2010	WHITE			BLACK		AMERICAN INDIAN, ESKIMO, ALEUT		ASIAN, PACIFIC ISLANDER	
				2000	2005	2010	2000	2010	2000	2010	2000	2010
U.S	31,366	36,057	41,139	197,062	199,802	202,390	33,569	37,466	2,055	2,321	10,585	14,402
Northeast	5,016	5,644	6,314	39,327	38,769	38,379	5,934	6,092	113	123	2,017	2,784
N.E	633	969	1,164	11,566	11,638	11,944	679	794	30	33	370	538
ME	8	10	14	1,230	1,251	1,284	5	5	6	6	9	13
NH	17	20	22	1,184	1,233	1,273	7	8	2	2	14	21
VT	6	6	8	600	619	630	2	4	2	2	6	8
MA	437	524	619	5,182	5,123	5,063	332	391	10	10	239	350
RI	76	92	112	851	838	834	40	48	4	6	26	39
CT	286	332	386	2,622	2,574	2,561	293	336	6	6	76	109
M.A	4,185	4,655	5,151	27,669	27,131	26,735	4,964	5,298	82	91	1,647	2,246
NY	2,805	3,071	3,357	11,640	11,271	11,023	2,668	2,790	53	56	981	1,304
NJ	1,044	1,196	1,348	5,558	5,462	5,387	1,104	1,232	14	15	456	656
PA	334	391	448	10,460	10,396	10,325	1,161	1,276	16	18	210	285
Midwest	2,438	2,797	3,155	53,096	53,521	53,746	6,430	7,031	372	436	1,164	1,547
E.N.C	1,987	2,261	2,543	36,084	36,175	36,157	5,349	5,779	152	167	846	1,120
OH	183	206	230	9,672	9,689	9,638	1,306	1,433	20	22	136	181
IN	140	162	179	5,336	5,453	5,509	494	540	14	15	58	74
IL	1,267	1,450	1,637	8,553	8,487	8,445	1,813	1,900	18	19	399	512
MI	261	289	319	7,790	7,767	7,732	1,417	1,517	55	59	157	208
WI	136	156	173	4,732	4,799	4,833	318	390	45	51	97	143
W.N.C.	452	536	614	17,012	17,346	17,589	1,080	1,252	220	270	318	427
MN	95	114	132	4,387	4,480	4,546	152	202	61	76	135	192
IA	54	61	71	2,737	2,755	2,762	60	72	8	10	41	56
MO	90	105	121	4,745	4,863	4,953	622	689	22	26	61	76
ND	6	8	10	611	620	625	5	5	32	43	6	7
SD	8	9	10	696	721	729	5	6	60	72	5	7
NE	61	72	80	1,540	1,572	1,596	70	84	14	18	21	29
KS	138	166	191	2,293	2,337	2,377	167	193	23	26	48	60
South	9,610	11,049	12,547	67,060	69,168	70,966	16,553	21,111	599	667	1,771	2,365
S.A	3,306	3,932	4,564	34,971	36,114	37,058	10,672	12,271	169	205	1,009	1,359
DE	25	29	33	582	596	597	143	165	2	2	15	19
MD	214	258	300	3,371	3,368	3,372	1,462	1,687	14	14	213	284
DC	40	46	55	152	156	163	315	322	-	-	13	19
VA	269	322	376	5,061	5,175	5,270	1,394	1,606	16	17	257	358
WV	11	15	17	1,756	1,761	1,757	58	58	2	2	11	15
NC	121	139	154	5,746	6,040	6,233	1,726	1,943	92	99	92	124
SC	42	50	58	2,624	2,738	2,848	1,152	1,249	8	9	31	40
GA	189	226	252	5,270	5,515	5,671	2,262	2,702	15	16	138	181
FL	2,390	2,845	3,319	10,405	10,764	11,145	2,159	2,536	39	44	239	319
E.S.C	149	171	192	13,236	13,713	14,053	3,353	3,657	44	60	134	172
KY	32	38	42	3,643	3,727	3,781	285	306	6	8	27	35
TN	57	67	75	4,607	4,828	4,969	925	1,051	12	14	55	70
AL	37	42	47	3,231	3,355	3,468	1,133	1,223	18	20	32	42
MS	21	24	27	1,755	1,804	1,836	1,010	1,076	8	8	19	25
W.S.C.	6,152	6,946	7,792	18,871	19,340	19,795	4,528	5,184	366	412	629	833
AR	33	40	46	2,155	2,249	2,320	407	432	15	18	19	23
LA	119	138	156	2,792	2,803	2,841	1,438	1,568	18	20	58	79
OK	124	143	167	2,653	2,700	2,769	276	332	273	309	47	61
TX	5,875	6,624	7,421	11,273	11,587	11,866	2,406	2,833	60	66	506	671
West	14,300	16,566	19,123	37,558	38,344	39,359	2,952	3,231	971	1,094	5,631	7,707
Mountain	2,965	3,471	3,936	13,300	14,125	14,493	522	628	566	668	373	496
MT	20	26	28	861	904	926	3	4	59	72	7	9
ID	96	121	140	1,211	1,314	1,368	6	8	18	23	15	19
WY	35	42	48	469	501	529	4	6	12	17	4	7
CO	594	682	770	3,268	3,434	3,505	178	216	30	37	98	132
NM	736	821	912	912	958	984	34	37	157	195	22	28
AZ	1,071	1,269	1,450	3,254	3,441	3,518	150	179	232	256	91	119
UT	138	164	185	1,961	2,117	2,219	18	23	33	43	58	81
NV	277	350	403	1,366	1,456	1,445	128	156	25	26	77	101
Pacific	11,337	13,097	15,187	24,256	24,219	24,864	2,429	2,602	406	426	5,258	7,211
WA	360	437	519	4,881	5,115	5,346	179	203	95	112	342	477
OR	195	237	278	2,990	3,133	3,253	59	71	45	53	110	147
CA	10,647	12,268	14,214	15,562	15,123	15,394	2,138	2,268	170	165	4,006	5,603
AK	31	37	41	461	476	487	27	31	91	91	44	94
HI	107	119	132	363	372	383	27	29	4	5	755	891

Source: U.S. Bureau of the Census, Population Paper Listings PPL-47.

No. 39. Population in Coastal Counties: 1970 to 1996

[Enumerated population as of April 1, except as indicated. Areas as defined by U.S. National Oceanic and Atmospheric Agency, 1992. Covers 672 counties and equivalent areas with at least 15 percent of their land area either in a coastal watershed (drainage area) or in a coastal cataloging unit (a coastal area between watersheds)]

YEAR	Total	COUNTIES IN COASTAL REGIONS					Balance of United States
		Total	Atlantic	Gulf of Mexico	Great Lakes	Pacific	
Land area, 1990 (1,000 sq. mi.)	3,536	888	148	114	115	510	2,649
POPULATION							
1970 (mil.)	203.3	110.0	51.1	10.0	26.0	22.8	93.3
1980 (mil.)	226.5	119.8	53.7	13.1	26.0	27.0	106.7
1990 (mil.)	248.7	133.4	59.0	15.2	25.9	33.2	115.3
1995 (July 1) (mil.)	262.9	139.3	61.1	16.5	26.4	35.3	123.6
1996 (July 1) (mil.)	265.3	140.3	61.4	16.7	26.5	35.6	125.0
1970 (percent)	100	54	25	5	13	11	46
1980 (percent)	100	53	24	6	11	12	47
1990 (percent)	100	54	24	6	10	13	46
1995 (July 1) (percent)	100	53	23	6	10	13	47
1996 (July 1) (percent)	100	53	23	6	10	13	47

Source: U.S. Bureau of the Census, *U.S. Census of Population: 1970; 1980 Census of Population*, vol. 1, chapter A (PC80-1-A-1), *U.S. Summary; 1990 Census of Population and Housing* (CPH1); and unpublished data.

No. 40. Metropolitan and Nonmetropolitan Area Population: 1970 to 1994

[As of April 1, except 1994, as of July 1. Data exclude Puerto Rico. Metropolitan areas are as defined by U.S. Office of Management and Budget as of year shown, except as noted]

ITEM	1970	1980 [1] (SMSA's)	MSA's AND CMSA's [2]		
			1980	1990	1994
Metropolitan areas: Number of areas	243	318	271	271	271
Population (1,000)	139,480	169,431	177,143	198,023	207,654
Percent change over previous year shown	[3]23.6	21.5	(X)	11.8	4.9
Percent of total U.S. population	68.6	74.8	78.2	79.6	79.8
Land area, percent of U.S. land area	10.9	16.0	19.8	19.8	19.8
Nonmetropolitan areas, population (1,000)	63,822	57,115	49,399	50,696	52,687

X Not applicable. [1] SMSA=standard metropolitan statistical area. Areas are as defined June 30, 1981. [2] Areas are as defined June 30, 1995. [3] Percent change from 1960.

Source: U.S. Bureau of the Census, *U.S. Census of Population: 1970; 1990 Census of Population and Housing, Supplementary Reports, Metropolitan Areas as Defined by the Office of Management and Budget, June 30, 1993* (1990 CPH-S-1-1); *1990 Census of Population and Housing, Population and Housing Unit Counts* (CPH-2-1); Population Paper Listings PPL-27; and unpublished data.

No. 41. Number and Population of Metropolitan Areas, by Population Size of Area in 1990: 1990 and 1994

[As of April 1 for 1990 and as of July for 1994. Data exclude Puerto Rico. CMSA=consolidated metropolitan statistical area. MSA=metropolitan statistical area. PMSA=primary metropolitan statistical area. Areas are as defined by U.S. Office of Management and Budget, June 30, 1995. For area definitions, see Appendix II]

LEVEL AND POPULATION SIZE-CLASS OF METROPOLITAN AREA IN 1990	CMSA's AND MSA's				MSA's AND PMSA's		
	Number	Population, 1990 (mil.)	Population, 1994		Number	Population, 1994	
			Total (mil.)	Percent in each class		Total (mil.)	Percent in each class
Total, all metropolitan areas	271	198.0	207.7	100	326	207.7	100
Level A (1,000,000 or more)	40	132.9	138.7	67	51	123.9	60
2,500,000 or more	15	94.1	97.9	47	13	60.5	29
1,000,000 to 2,499,999	25	38.8	40.8	20	38	63.4	31
Level B (250,000 to 999,999)	96	46.4	49.2	24	119	60.2	29
500,000 to 999,999	33	24.3	25.9	12	41	31.2	15
250,000 to 499,999	63	22.0	23.3	11	78	29.0	14
Level C (100,000 to 249,999)	111	16.6	17.6	8	131	21.3	10
Level D (less than 100,000)	24	2.1	2.1	1	25	2.2	1

Source: U.S. Bureau of the Census, *1990 Census of Population and Housing, Supplementary Reports, Metropolitan Areas as Defined by the Office of Management and Budget, June 30, 1993*, (1990 CPH-S-1-1); and *1990 Census of Population and Housing, Population and Housing Unit Counts* (CPH-2-1); and Population Paper Listings PPL-27.

No. 42. Metropolitan and Nonmetropolitan Area Population by State: 1980 to 1994

[As of April 1, except 1994, as of July. Metropolitan refers to 253 metropolitan statistical areas and 18 consolidated metropolitan statistical areas as defined by U.S. Office of Management and Budget, June 30, 1995; nonmetropolitan is the area outside metropolitan areas; see Appendix II. Minus sign (-) indicates decrease]

REGION, DIVISION, AND STATE	METROPOLITAN POPULATION						NONMETROPOLITAN POPULATION					
	Total (1,000)			Percent change, 1990-94	Percent of State		Total (1,000)			Percent change, 1990-94	Percent of State	
	1980	1990	1994		1990	1994	1980	1990	1994		1990	1994
U.S.	177,143	198,023	207,654	4.9	79.6	79.8	49,399	50,686	52,667	3.9	20.4	20.2
Northeast	44,047	45,457	45,931	1.0	89.5	89.4	5,090	5,354	5,464	2.1	10.5	10.6
N.E.	10,470	11,127	11,155	0.3	84.2	84.1	1,878	2,090	2,116	1.7	15.8	15.9
ME	405	443	445	0.5	36.1	35.9	721	785	795	1.3	63.9	64.1
NH	535	659	677	2.8	59.4	59.6	386	450	460	2.0	40.6	40.4
VT	133	152	158	4.3	26.9	27.2	378	411	422	2.6	73.1	72.8
MA	5,530	5,788	5,807	0.3	96.2	96.1	207	229	234	2.4	3.8	3.9
RI	886	938	935	-0.4	93.5	93.8	61	65	62	-5.1	6.5	6.2
CT	2,982	3,148	3,133	-0.5	95.8	95.7	126	140	142	2.0	4.2	4.3
M.A.	33,576	34,330	34,777	1.3	91.3	91.2	3,212	3,274	3,349	2.3	8.7	8.8
NY	16,144	16,516	16,666	0.9	91.8	91.7	1,414	1,475	1,503	1.9	8.2	8.3
NJ	7,365	7,730	7,904	2.2	100.0	100.0	(X)	(X)	(X)	(X)	(X)	(X)
PA	10,067	10,084	10,206	1.2	84.9	84.7	1,798	1,799	1,846	2.6	15.1	15.3
Midwest	42,557	43,691	45,049	3.1	73.2	73.4	16,310	15,978	16,345	2.3	26.8	26.6
E.N.C.	33,031	33,391	34,308	2.7	79.5	79.4	8,652	8,618	8,876	3.0	20.5	20.6
OH	8,791	8,826	9,016	2.2	81.4	81.2	2,007	2,021	2,086	3.2	18.6	18.8
IN	3,885	3,962	4,124	4.1	71.5	71.7	1,605	1,582	1,628	2.9	28.5	28.3
IL	9,461	9,574	9,879	3.2	83.8	84.1	1,967	1,857	1,873	0.9	16.2	15.9
MI	7,719	7,698	7,837	1.8	82.8	82.5	1,543	1,598	1,659	3.9	17.2	17.5
WI	3,176	3,331	3,452	3.6	68.1	67.9	1,530	1,561	1,630	4.4	31.9	32.1
W.N.C.	9,526	10,300	10,741	4.3	58.3	59.0	7,658	7,360	7,470	1.5	41.7	41.0
MN	2,674	3,011	3,172	5.3	68.8	69.4	1,402	1,364	1,395	2.3	31.2	30.6
IA	1,198	1,200	1,246	3.8	43.2	44.0	1,716	1,577	1,584	0.4	56.8	56.0
MO	3,314	3,491	3,591	2.9	68.2	68.1	1,603	1,626	1,686	3.7	31.8	31.9
ND	234	257	269	4.5	40.3	42.1	418	381	369	-3.2	59.7	57.9
SD	194	221	238	8.0	31.7	33.0	497	475	483	1.6	68.3	67.0
NE	728	787	823	4.5	49.9	50.7	842	791	800	1.1	50.1	49.3
KS	1,184	1,333	1,402	5.2	53.8	54.9	1,180	1,145	1,152	0.7	46.2	45.1
South	53,724	63,194	67,581	6.9	74.0	74.5	21,643	22,260	23,111	3.8	26.0	25.5
S.A.	28,226	34,296	36,694	7.0	78.7	79.1	6,732	9,274	9,715	4.8	21.3	20.9
DE	496	553	584	5.7	83.0	82.7	98	113	122	7.9	17.0	17.3
MD	3,920	4,438	4,641	4.6	92.8	92.7	297	343	366	6.6	7.2	7.3
DC	638	607	570	-6.6	100.0	100.0	(X)	(X)	(X)	(X)	(X)	(X)
VA	3,966	4,775	5,091	6.6	77.2	77.7	1,381	1,414	1,461	3.3	22.8	22.3
WV	796	748	762	1.9	41.7	41.8	1,155	1,045	1,060	1.4	58.3	58.2
NC	3,749	4,380	4,708	7.5	66.0	66.6	2,131	2,253	2,362	4.9	34.0	33.4
SC	2,114	2,422	2,555	5.5	69.5	69.7	1,006	1,064	1,109	4.2	30.5	30.3
GA	3,507	4,351	4,804	10.4	67.2	68.1	1,956	2,127	2,251	5.8	32.8	31.9
FL	9,039	12,024	12,970	7.9	92.9	93.0	708	915	982	7.4	7.1	7.0
E.S.C.	8,147	8,662	9,139	5.5	57.1	57.5	6,519	6,518	6,751	3.6	42.9	42.5
KY	1,735	1,780	1,848	3.8	48.3	48.3	1,925	1,907	1,979	3.8	51.7	51.7
TN	3,045	3,298	3,509	6.4	67.6	67.8	1,546	1,579	1,666	5.5	32.4	32.2
AL	2,560	2,710	2,847	5.1	67.1	67.5	1,334	1,331	1,371	3.1	32.9	32.5
MS	806	874	935	6.9	34.0	35.0	1,715	1,701	1,734	2.0	66.0	65.0
W.S.C.	17,351	20,235	21,758	7.5	75.8	76.6	6,392	6,468	6,646	2.8	24.2	23.4
AR	963	1,040	1,103	6.1	44.2	45.0	1,323	1,311	1,350	3.0	55.8	55.0
LA	3,125	3,160	3,240	2.6	74.9	75.1	1,082	1,061	1,075	1.3	25.1	24.9
OK	1,724	1,870	1,960	4.8	59.4	60.2	1,301	1,276	1,298	1.7	40.6	39.8
TX	11,539	14,166	15,455	9.1	83.4	84.1	2,686	2,821	2,923	3.6	16.6	15.9
West	36,816	45,680	49,093	7.5	86.5	86.3	6,356	7,104	7,766	9.3	13.5	13.7
Mountain	7,806	9,800	10,967	12.1	71.7	72.2	3,566	3,858	4,226	9.5	28.3	27.8
MT	189	191	204	6.7	23.9	23.8	598	606	652	7.3	76.1	76.2
ID	257	296	348	17.6	29.4	30.7	687	711	785	10.5	70.6	69.3
WY	141	134	142	5.8	29.6	29.8	329	319	334	4.6	70.4	70.2
CO	2,408	2,779	3,086	11.0	84.4	84.4	482	515	570	10.6	15.6	15.6
NM	675	842	932	10.7	55.6	56.4	628	673	722	7.2	44.4	43.6
AZ	2,339	3,202	3,557	11.1	87.4	87.3	378	463	518	11.9	12.6	12.7
UT	1,132	1,341	1,475	10.0	77.8	77.3	329	382	433	13.3	22.2	22.7
NV	666	1,014	1,243	22.6	84.4	85.3	135	188	214	13.9	15.6	14.7
Pacific	29,010	35,881	38,106	6.2	91.7	91.5	2,790	3,245	3,539	9.0	8.3	8.5
WA	3,366	4,036	4,428	9.7	82.9	82.9	766	830	915	10.2	17.1	17.1
OR	1,799	1,985	2,162	8.9	69.8	70.1	834	858	924	7.8	30.2	29.9
CA	22,907	28,797	30,388	5.5	96.8	96.7	760	961	1,043	8.4	3.2	3.3
AK	174	226	254	12.1	41.1	41.8	227	324	353	8.9	58.9	58.2
HI	763	836	874	4.6	75.5	74.2	202	272	304	11.9	24.5	25.8

X Not applicable.

Source: U.S. Bureau of the Census, *1990 Census of Population and Housing, Supplementary Reports, Metropolitan Areas as Defined by the Office of Management and Budget, June 30, 1993,* (1990 CPH-S-1-1); *1990 Census of Population and Housing, Population and Housing Unit Counts* (CPH-2-1); *Current Population Reports,* P25-1127; and Population Paper Listings PPL-27.

No. 43. Large Metropolitan Areas—Population: 1980 to 1994

[In thousands, except percent. As of April 1, except as noted. Covers 18 consolidated metropolitan statistical areas (CMSA's), their 73 component primary metropolitan statistical areas (PMSA's), and the remaining 121 MSA's with 250,000 and over population in 1994 as defined by the U.S. Office of Management and Budget as of June 30, 1995. For definitions and components of all metropolitan areas and population of NECMA's (New England County Metropolitan Areas), see Appendix II. Minus sign (-) indicates decrease]

METROPOLITAN AREA	1980	1990 [1]	1991 (July)	1992 (July)	1993 (July)	1994 (July)	PERCENT CHANGE 1980-90	PERCENT CHANGE 1990-94
Albany-Schenectady-Troy, NY MSA	825	862	869	872	874	875	4.5	1.6
Albuquerque, NM MSA	485	589	602	616	630	646	21.4	9.6
Allentown-Bethlehem-Easton, PA MSA	551	595	602	606	609	612	8.0	2.8
Anchorage, AK MSA	174	226	235	246	250	254	29.8	12.1
Appleton-Oshkosh-Neenah, WI MSA	291	315	320	324	329	332	8.2	5.4
Atlanta, GA MSA	2,233	2,960	3,054	3,135	3,229	3,331	32.5	12.6
Augusta-Aiken, GA-SC MSA	363	415	430	443	444	448	14.2	8.0
Austin-San Marcos, TX MSA	585	846	873	900	932	964	44.6	13.9
Bakersfield, CA MSA	403	545	571	588	600	609	35.2	11.8
Baton Rouge, LA MSA	494	528	537	546	553	558	6.9	5.7
Beaumont-Port Arthur, TX MSA	373	361	366	369	372	373	-3.2	3.2
Biloxi-Gulfport-Pascagoula, MS MSA	300	312	316	323	330	339	4.1	8.6
Binghamton, NY MSA	263	264	265	266	264	262	0.4	-1.0
Birmingham, AL MSA	815	840	849	856	865	872	3.0	3.8
Boise City, ID MSA	257	296	310	320	334	348	15.2	17.6
Boston-Worcester-Lawrence, MA-NH-ME-CT CMSA	5,122	5,455	5,439	5,443	5,468	5,497	6.5	0.8
Boston, MA-NH PMSA	3,149	3,228	3,216	3,215	3,226	3,240	2.5	0.4
Brockton, MA PMSA	225	236	236	236	238	239	5.1	1.1
Fitchburg-Leominster, MA PMSA	125	138	137	137	136	136	10.5	-1.6
Lawrence, MA-NH PMSA	298	353	356	358	361	364	18.4	3.2
Lowell, MA-NH PMSA	249	281	281	282	284	285	12.5	1.6
Manchester, NH PMSA	146	174	174	175	176	177	18.9	2.1
Nashua, NH PMSA	134	168	169	171	173	176	25.4	4.5
New Bedford, MA PMSA	167	176	175	173	173	172	5.4	-1.9
Portsmouth-Rochester, NH-ME PMSA	189	223	217	218	220	222	18.0	-0.6
Worcester, MA-CT PMSA	439	478	477	478	482	485	8.9	1.4
Brownsville-Harlingen-San Benito, TX MSA	210	260	270	279	291	300	24.0	15.2
Buffalo-Niagara Falls, NY MSA	1,243	1,189	1,192	1,193	1,192	1,189	-4.3	-
Canton-Massillon, OH MSA	404	394	397	399	401	402	-2.6	2.1
Charleston-North Charleston, SC MSA	430	507	523	527	526	522	17.8	3.0
Charleston, WV MSA	270	250	251	253	254	255	-7.1	1.7
Charlotte-Gastonia-Rock Hill, NC-SC MSA	971	1,162	1,192	1,210	1,234	1,260	19.6	8.5
Chattanooga, TN-GA MSA	418	424	428	430	435	439	1.6	3.5
Chicago-Gary-Kenosha, IL-IN-WI CMSA	8,115	8,240	8,326	8,400	8,466	8,527	1.5	3.5
Chicago, IL PMSA	7,246	7,411	7,486	7,553	7,612	7,668	2.3	3.5
Gary, IN PMSA	643	605	611	614	617	620	-5.9	2.5
Kankakee, IL PMSA	103	96	98	99	100	101	-6.5	5.2
Kenosha, WI PMSA	123	128	132	134	136	138	4.1	7.5
Cincinnati-Hamilton, OH-KY-IN CMSA	1,726	1,818	1,843	1,862	1,881	1,894	5.3	4.2
Cincinnati, OH-KY-IN PMSA	1,468	1,526	1,544	1,558	1,572	1,581	4.0	3.6
Hamilton-Middletown, OH PMSA	259	291	299	304	309	313	12.6	7.3
Cleveland-Akron, OH CMSA	2,938	2,860	2,874	2,887	2,894	2,899	-2.7	1.4
Akron, OH PMSA	660	658	664	668	673	677	-0.4	2.9
Cleveland-Lorain-Elyria, OH PMSA	2,278	2,202	2,211	2,219	2,221	2,222	-3.3	0.9
Colorado Springs, CO MSA	309	397	404	421	435	452	28.3	14.0
Columbia, SC MSA	410	454	465	471	480	486	10.7	7.1
Columbus, GA-AL MSA	255	261	260	270	271	274	2.4	5.1
Columbus, OH MSA	1,214	1,345	1,371	1,391	1,409	1,423	10.8	5.8
Corpus Christi, TX MSA	326	350	356	361	369	376	7.3	7.4
Dallas-Fort Worth, TX CMSA	3,046	4,037	4,139	4,207	4,279	4,362	32.5	8.1
Dallas, TX PMSA	2,055	2,676	2,742	2,790	2,844	2,898	30.2	8.3
Fort Worth-Arlington, TX PMSA	991	1,361	1,397	1,417	1,435	1,464	37.4	7.6
Davenport-Moline-Rock Island, IA-IL MSA	385	351	354	357	357	358	-8.8	2.0
Dayton-Springfield, OH MSA	942	951	956	959	959	956	1.0	0.5
Daytona Beach, FL MSA	270	399	414	423	432	440	48.1	10.3
Denver-Boulder-Greeley, CO CMSA	1,742	1,980	2,029	2,088	2,146	2,190	13.7	10.6
Boulder-Longmont, CO PMSA	190	225	231	238	244	250	18.8	10.8
Denver, CO PMSA	1,429	1,623	1,664	1,714	1,762	1,796	13.6	10.7
Greeley, CO PMSA	123	132	134	136	140	144	6.8	9.3
Des Moines, IA MSA	368	393	400	406	412	416	6.9	6.0
Detroit-Ann Arbor-Flint, MI CMSA	5,293	5,187	5,215	5,236	5,246	5,256	-2.0	1.3
Ann Arbor, MI PMSA	455	490	498	504	509	515	7.7	5.1
Detroit, MI PMSA	4,388	4,267	4,285	4,299	4,304	4,307	-2.8	0.9
Flint, MI PMSA	450	430	432	432	433	433	-4.4	0.7
El Paso, TX MSA	480	592	613	628	647	665	23.3	12.4
Erie, PA MSA	280	276	278	279	280	280	-1.5	1.7
Eugene-Springfield, OR MSA	275	283	288	291	295	299	2.8	5.7
Evansville-Henderson, IN-KY MSA	276	279	281	283	285	287	1.0	2.7
Fayetteville, NC MSA	247	275	278	277	284	286	11.1	4.2
Fort Myers-Cape Coral, FL MSA	205	335	347	353	359	367	63.3	9.6
Fort Pierce-Port St. Lucie, FL MSA	151	251	261	266	272	278	66.1	10.8
Fort Wayne, IN MSA	445	456	460	463	466	469	2.6	2.8
Fresno, CA MSA	578	756	785	805	823	835	30.8	10.5

See footnotes at end of table.

No. 43. Metropolitan Areas—Population: 1980 to 1994—Continued

[See headnote, page 41]

METROPOLITAN AREA	1980	1990 [1]	1991 (July)	1992 (July)	1993 (July)	1994 (July)	PERCENT CHANGE	
							1980-90	1990-94
Grand Rapids-Muskegon-Holland, MI MSA	841	938	954	964	974	985	11.5	5.0
Greensboro—Winston-Salem—High Point, NC MSA	951	1,050	1,066	1,078	1,092	1,107	10.5	5.4
Greenville-Spartanburg-Anderson, SC MSA	744	831	843	852	862	873	11.6	5.2
Harrisburg-Lebanon-Carlisle, PA MSA	556	588	596	601	605	610	5.7	3.7
Hartford, CT MSA	1,081	1,158	1,159	1,156	1,154	1,151	7.1	-0.5
Hickory-Morganton, NC MSA	270	292	296	298	302	306	8.1	4.6
Honolulu, HI MSA	763	836	849	861	867	874	9.7	4.6
Houston-Galveston-Brazoria, TX CMSA	3,118	3,731	3,854	3,950	4,028	4,099	19.6	9.9
Brazoria, TX PMSA	170	192	199	203	207	212	13.0	10.3
Galveston-Texas City, TX PMSA	196	217	223	227	232	235	11.1	8.0
Houston, TX PMSA	2,753	3,322	3,433	3,520	3,589	3,653	20.7	10.0
Huntington-Ashland, WV-KY-OH MSA	336	313	314	315	316	316	-7.1	1.3
Huntsville, AL MSA	243	293	300	307	314	'6	20.6	7.9
Indianapolis, IN MSA	1,306	1,380	1,406	1,424	1,443	1,462	5.7	5.9
Jackson, MS MSA	362	395	399	404	407	412	9.2	4.2
Jacksonville, FL MSA	722	907	931	950	962	972	25.5	7.2
Johnson City-Kingsport-Bristol, TN-VA MSA	434	436	440	444	448	451	0.6	3.3
Kalamazoo-Battle Creek, MI MSA	421	429	433	436	440	443	2.1	3.1
Kansas City, MO-KS MSA	1,449	1,583	1,601	1,614	1,631	1,647	9.2	4.1
Killeen-Temple, TX MSA	215	255	251	255	269	287	19.0	12.5
Knoxville, TN MSA	546	586	598	610	620	631	7.2	7.7
Lafayette, LA MSA	331	345	349	353	358	361	4.3	4.7
Lakeland-Winter Haven, FL MSA	322	405	413	419	423	430	26.0	6.0
Lancaster, PA MSA	362	423	430	434	439	443	16.7	4.7
Lansing-East Lansing, MI MSA	420	433	436	436	436	436	3.1	0.8
Las Vegas, NV-AZ MSA	528	853	927	967	1,010	1,076	61.5	26.2
Lexington, KY MSA	371	406	413	419	426	431	9.4	6.1
Little Rock-North Little Rock, AR MSA	474	513	519	525	533	538	8.1	4.8
Los Angeles-Riverside-Orange County, CA CMSA	11,498	14,532	14,823	15,063	15,210	15,302	26.4	5.3
Los Angeles-Long Beach, CA PMSA	7,477	8,863	8,960	9,068	9,134	9,150	18.5	3.2
Orange County, CA PMSA	1,933	2,411	2,447	2,486	2,515	2,543	24.7	5.5
Riverside-San Bernardino, CA PMSA	1,558	2,589	2,739	2,823	2,867	2,907	66.1	12.3
Ventura, CA PMSA	529	669	677	687	694	703	26.4	5.0
Louisville, KY-IN MSA	954	949	958	966	974	981	-0.5	3.4
Macon, GA MSA	273	291	295	298	303	307	6.6	5.6
Madison, WI MSA	324	367	375	380	386	390	13.5	6.3
McAllen-Edinburg-Mission, TX MSA	283	384	402	421	443	461	35.4	20.2
Melbourne-Titusville-Palm Bay, FL MSA	273	399	415	425	436	443	46.2	11.2
Memphis, TN-AR-MS MSA	939	1,007	1,021	1,032	1,042	1,056	7.3	4.8
Miami-Fort Lauderdale, FL CMSA	2,644	3,193	3,266	3,317	3,354	3,408	20.8	6.7
Fort Lauderdale, FL PMSA	1,018	1,256	1,288	1,311	1,351	1,383	23.3	10.2
Miami, FL PMSA	1,626	1,937	1,978	2,006	2,003	2,025	19.2	4.5
Milwaukee-Racine, WI CMSA	1,570	1,607	1,620	1,629	1,634	1,637	2.4	1.9
Milwaukee-Waukesha, WI PMSA	1,397	1,432	1,443	1,450	1,454	1,456	2.5	1.6
Racine, WI PMSA	173	175	178	179	180	182	1.1	3.8
Minneapolis-St. Paul, MN-WI MSA	2,198	2,539	2,582	2,617	2,655	2,688	15.5	5.9
Mobile, AL MSA	444	477	485	494	505	512	7.5	7.4
Modesto, CA MSA	266	371	386	395	402	407	39.3	9.8
Montgomery, AL MSA	273	293	298	302	307	312	7.3	6.7
Nashville, TN MSA	851	985	1,003	1,022	1,045	1,070	15.8	8.6
New London-Norwich, CT-RI MSA	273	291	290	284	284	285	6.5	-2.0
New Orleans, LA MSA	1,304	1,285	1,290	1,299	1,304	1,309	-1.5	1.8
New York-Northern New Jersey-Long Island, NY-NJ-CT-PA CMSA	18,906	19,550	19,586	19,652	19,738	19,796	3.4	1.3
Bergen-Passaic, NJ PMSA	1,293	1,279	1,282	1,290	1,298	1,304	-1.1	2.0
Bridgeport, CT PMSA	439	444	444	443	443	443	1.2	-0.2
Danbury, CT PMSA	175	194	195	196	198	199	10.3	2.7
Dutchess County, NY PMSA	245	259	261	263	263	261	5.9	0.8
Jersey City, NJ PMSA	557	553	553	553	553	552	-0.7	-0.1
Middlesex-Somerset-Hunterdon, NJ PMSA	886	1,020	1,031	1,044	1,057	1,069	15.1	4.8
Monmouth-Ocean, NJ PMSA	849	986	998	1,010	1,023	1,035	16.1	4.9
Nassau-Suffolk, NY PMSA	2,606	2,609	2,617	2,631	2,643	2,652	0.1	1.6
New Haven-Meriden, CT PMSA	500	530	529	527	525	523	5.9	-1.4
New York, NY PMSA	8,275	8,547	8,538	8,546	8,574	8,586	3.3	0.5
Newark, NJ PMSA	1,964	1,916	1,915	1,921	1,929	1,934	-2.4	0.9
Newburgh, NY-PA PMSA	278	336	343	348	353	356	20.8	6.1
Stamford-Norwalk, CT PMSA	326	330	331	330	331	332	1.3	0.6
Trenton, NJ PMSA	308	326	327	327	329	329	5.8	1.1
Waterbury, CT PMSA	205	222	223	222	222	221	8.1	-0.2
Norfolk-Virginia Beach-Newport News, VA-NC MSA	1,201	1,445	1,463	1,496	1,514	1,529	20.3	5.8
Oklahoma City, OK MSA	861	959	969	982	996	1,007	11.4	5.1
Omaha, NE-IA MSA	605	640	649	656	658	663	5.6	3.6
Orlando, FL MSA	805	1,225	1,275	1,303	1,334	1,361	52.2	11.2
Pensacola, FL MSA	290	344	352	360	365	371	18.9	7.7
Peoria-Pekin, IL MSA	366	339	342	343	343	344	-7.3	1.3

See footnotes at end of table.

No. 43. Metropolitan Areas—Population: 1980 to 1994—Continued

[See headnote, page 41]

METROPOLITAN AREA	1980	1990 [1]	1991 (July)	1992 (July)	1993 (July)	1994 (July)	PERCENT CHANGE 1980-90	PERCENT CHANGE 1990-94
Philadelphia-Wilmington-Atlantic City, PA-NJ-DE-MD CMSA	5,649	5,893	5,916	5,926	5,942	5,959	4.3	1.1
Atlantic-Cape May, NJ PMSA	276	319	324	327	328	330	15.6	3.3
Philadelphia, PA-NJ PMSA	4,781	4,922	4,930	4,933	4,940	4,949	2.9	0.5
Vineland-Millville-Bridgeton, NJ PMSA	133	138	139	139	139	139	3.9	0.5
Wilmington-Newark, DE-MD PMSA	459	513	523	529	535	541	11.9	5.5
Phoenix-Mesa, AZ MSA	1,600	2,238	2,285	2,333	2,392	2,473	39.9	10.5
Pittsburgh, PA MSA	2,571	2,395	2,399	2,405	2,407	2,402	-6.9	0.3
Portland-Salem, OR-WA CMSA	1,584	1,793	1,857	1,899	1,944	1,982	13.3	10.5
Portland-Vancouver, OR-WA PMSA	1,334	1,515	1,571	1,607	1,645	1,676	13.6	10.6
Salem, OR PMSA	250	278	286	293	300	306	11.3	10.0
Providence-Fall River-Warwick, RI-MA MSA	1,077	1,134	1,134	1,132	1,131	1,129	5.4	-0.5
Provo-Orem, UT MSA	218	264	269	276	283	291	20.9	10.4
Raleigh-Durham-Chapel Hill, NC MSA	665	858	888	911	938	965	29.1	12.4
Reading, PA MSA	313	337	341	343	346	348	7.7	3.3
Reno, NV MSA	194	255	262	268	275	283	31.5	11.1
Richmond-Petersburg, VA MSA	761	866	880	894	906	917	13.7	5.9
Rochester, NY MSA	1,031	1,062	1,072	1,082	1,089	1,091	3.1	2.6
Rockford, IL MSA	326	330	336	340	343	347	1.2	5.2
Sacramento-Yolo, CA CMSA	1,100	1,481	1,538	1,561	1,576	1,588	34.7	7.2
Sacramento, CA PMSA	986	1,340	1,395	1,416	1,431	1,441	35.8	7.6
Yolo, CA PMSA	113	141	143	145	146	146	24.6	3.7
Saginaw-Bay City-Midland, MI MSA	422	399	401	402	403	402	-5.3	0.7
St. Louis, MO-IL MSA	2,414	2,492	2,508	2,516	2,528	2,536	3.2	1.8
Salinas, CA MSA	290	356	363	369	366	352	22.5	-1.0
Salt Lake City-Ogden, UT MSA	910	1,072	1,100	1,127	1,154	1,178	17.8	9.9
San Antonio, TX MSA	1,089	1,325	1,349	1,377	1,407	1,437	21.7	8.5
San Diego, CA MSA	1,862	2,498	2,556	2,602	2,612	2,632	34.2	5.4
San Francisco-Oakland-San Jose, CA CMSA	5,368	6,250	6,335	6,410	6,469	6,513	16.4	4.2
Oakland, CA PMSA	1,762	2,080	2,117	2,148	2,169	2,182	18.1	4.9
San Francisco, CA PMSA	1,489	1,604	1,614	1,626	1,638	1,646	7.7	2.6
San Jose, CA PMSA	1,295	1,498	1,511	1,528	1,544	1,557	15.6	4.0
Santa Cruz-Watsonville, CA PMSA	188	230	229	231	233	235	22.1	2.3
Santa Rosa, CA PMSA	300	388	397	403	406	410	29.5	5.7
Vallejo-Fairfield-Napa, CA PMSA	334	450	467	474	479	483	34.6	7.2
Santa Barbara-Santa Maria-Lompoc, CA MSA	299	370	374	377	378	380	23.7	2.9
Sarasota-Bradenton, FL MSA	351	489	501	504	510	518	39.6	5.8
Savannah, GA MSA	231	258	262	267	272	276	11.8	6.9
Scranton—Wilkes-Barre—Hazleton, PA MSA	659	639	640	640	639	637	-3.2	-0.2
Seattle-Tacoma-Bremerton, WA CMSA	2,409	2,970	3,057	3,132	3,189	3,226	23.3	8.6
Bremerton, WA PMSA	147	190	200	211	215	220	28.9	16.2
Olympia, WA PMSA	124	161	170	177	183	187	29.8	16.1
Seattle-Bellevue-Everett, WA PMSA	1,652	2,033	2,082	2,125	2,159	2,180	23.1	7.2
Tacoma, WA PMSA	486	586	605	620	632	638	20.7	8.9
Shreveport-Bossier City, LA MSA	377	376	373	374	377	378	-0.1	0.5
South Bend, IN MSA	242	247	249	251	253	255	2.2	3.4
Spokane, WA MSA	342	361	372	382	391	396	5.7	9.6
Springfield, MO MSA	228	264	270	276	282	289	15.9	9.3
Springfield, MA MSA	570	588	585	583	582	580	3.2	-1.4
Stockton-Lodi, CA MSA	347	481	495	504	511	518	38.4	7.8
Syracuse, NY MSA	723	742	749	752	755	754	2.7	1.6
Tallahassee, FL MSA	190	234	240	245	250	253	22.7	8.5
Tampa-St. Petersburg-Clearwater, FL MSA	1,614	2,068	2,101	2,117	2,137	2,157	28.2	4.3
Toledo, OH MSA	617	614	614	614	614	614	-0.4	-
Tucson, AZ MSA	531	667	676	692	710	732	25.5	9.7
Tulsa, OK MSA	657	709	721	730	738	743	7.9	4.8
Utica-Rome, NY MSA	320	317	319	319	318	316	-1.1	-0.1
Visalia-Tulare-Porterville, CA MSA	246	312	323	331	336	343	26.9	10.0
Washington-Baltimore, DC-MD-VA-WV CMSA	5,791	6,726	6,829	6,906	6,980	7,051	16.2	4.8
Baltimore, MD PMSA	2,199	2,382	2,412	2,430	2,444	2,458	8.3	3.2
Hagerstown, MD PMSA	113	121	124	125	126	127	7.3	4.3
Washington, DC-MD-VA-WV PMSA	3,478	4,223	4,293	4,353	4,410	4,466	21.4	5.8
West Palm Beach-Boca Raton, FL MSA	577	864	890	909	932	955	49.7	10.5
Wichita, KS MSA	442	485	492	500	505	507	9.7	4.4
York, PA MSA	313	340	345	350	354	358	8.5	5.4
Youngstown-Warren, OH MSA	645	601	603	605	605	604	-6.8	0.5

\- Represents or rounds to zero. [1] The April 1, 1990, census count includes count question resolution corrections processed through March 1994, and does not include adjustments for census coverage errors.

Source: U.S. Bureau of the Census, *1990 Census of Population and Housing, Supplementary Reports, Metropolitan Areas as Defined by the Office of Management and Budget, June 30, 1993* (CPH-S-1-1); *1990 Census of Population and Housing, Population and Housing Unit Counts* (CPH-2-1); computer diskette PE-23; and unpublished data.

No. 44. Urban and Rural Population, 1960 to 1990, and by State, 1990

[In thousands, except percent. As of April 1. Resident population]

REGION, DIVISION, AND STATE	Total	URBAN		Rural
		Number	Percent	
1960	179,323	125,269	69.9	54,054
1970	[1]203,212	149,647	73.6	53,565
1980	[2]226,546	167,051	73.7	59,495
1990, total	[2]248,710	187,053	75.2	61,656
Northeast	50,809	40,092	78.9	10,717
N.E	13,207	9,829	74.4	3,378
ME	1,228	548	44.6	680
NH	1,109	565	51.0	544
VT	563	181	32.2	382
MA	6,016	5,070	84.3	947
RI	1,003	863	86.0	140
CT	3,287	2,602	79.1	686
M.A	37,602	30,263	80.5	7,340
NY	17,990	15,164	84.3	2,826
NJ	7,730	6,910	89.4	820
PA	11,882	8,188	68.9	3,693
Midwest	59,669	42,774	71.7	16,894
E.N.C	42,009	31,074	74.0	10,935
OH	10,847	8,039	74.1	2,808
IN	5,544	3,598	64.9	1,946
IL	11,431	9,669	84.6	1,762
MI	9,295	6,556	70.5	2,739
WI	4,892	3,212	65.7	1,680
W.N.C.	17,660	11,700	66.3	5,959
MN	4,375	3,056	69.9	1,319
IA	2,777	1,683	60.6	1,094
MO	5,117	3,516	68.7	1,601
ND	639	340	53.3	298
SD	696	348	50.0	348
NE	1,578	1,044	66.1	534
KS	2,478	1,713	69.1	765
South	85,446	58,656	68.6	26,790
S.A	43,567	30,231	69.4	13,336
DE	666	487	73.0	180
MD	4,781	3,888	81.3	893
DC	607	607	100.0	-
VA	6,187	4,293	69.4	1,894
WV	1,793	648	36.1	1,145
NC	6,629	3,338	50.4	3,291
SC	3,487	1,905	54.6	1,581
GA	6,478	4,097	63.2	2,381
FL	12,938	10,967	84.8	1,971
E.S.C	15,176	8,531	56.2	6,646
KY	3,685	1,910	51.8	1,775
TN	4,877	2,970	60.9	1,907
AL	4,041	2,440	60.4	1,601
MS	2,573	1,211	47.1	1,362
W.S.C.	26,703	19,894	74.5	6,808
AR	2,351	1,258	53.5	1,093
LA	4,220	2,872	68.1	1,348
OK	3,146	2,130	67.7	1,015
TX	16,987	13,635	80.3	3,352
West	52,786	45,531	86.3	7,255
Mountain	13,659	10,881	79.7	2,777
MT	799	420	52.5	379
ID	1,007	578	57.4	429
WY	454	295	65.0	159
CO	3,294	2,716	82.4	579
NM	1,515	1,106	73.0	409
AZ	3,665	3,207	87.5	458
UT	1,723	1,499	87.0	224
NV	1,202	1,061	88.3	140
Pacific	39,127	34,650	88.6	4,477
WA	4,867	3,718	76.4	1,149
OR	2,842	2,003	70.5	839
CA	29,760	27,571	92.6	2,189
AK	550	371	67.5	179
HI	1,108	986	89.0	122

- Represents zero. [1] The revised 1970 resident population count is 203,302,031; which incorporates changes due to errors found after tabulations were completed. [2] Total population count has been revised since the 1980 and 1990 censuses publications to 226,542,199 and 248,718,301, respectively.

Source: U.S. Bureau of the Census, *1990 Census of Population and Housing, Population and Housing Unit Counts* (1990 CPH-2).

No. 45. Incorporated Places, by Population Size: 1970 to 1994

POPULATION SIZE	NUMBER OF INCORPORATED PLACES				POPULATION (mil.)				PERCENT OF TOTAL			
	1970	1980	1990	1994	1970	1980	1990	1994	1970	1980	1990	1994
Total	18,666	19,097	19,262	19,314	131.9	140.3	152.9	160.7	100.0	100.0	100.0	100.0
1,000,000 or more	6	6	8	8	18.8	17.5	20.0	20.0	14.2	12.5	13.0	12.4
500,000 to 999,999	20	16	15	16	13.0	10.9	10.1	10.8	9.8	7.8	6.6	6.7
250,000 to 499,999	30	33	41	41	10.5	11.8	14.2	14.8	7.9	8.4	9.3	9.2
100,000 to 249,999	97	114	131	144	13.9	16.6	19.1	21.1	10.5	11.8	12.5	13.1
50,000 to 99,999	232	250	309	343	16.2	17.6	21.2	23.4	12.2	12.3	13.9	14.6
25,000 to 49,999	455	526	567	588	15.7	18.4	20.0	20.6	11.9	13.1	13.0	12.8
10,000 to 24,999	1,127	1,260	1,290	1,372	17.6	19.8	20.3	21.5	13.3	14.1	13.3	13.4
Under 10,000	16,699	16,892	16,901	16,802	26.4	28.0	28.2	28.6	20.0	20.0	18.4	17.8

Source: U..S. Bureau of the Census, *Census of Population: 1970* and *1980*, vol. I, *1990 Census of Population and Housing, Population and Housing Unit Counts* (CPH-2-1); computer diskette PE-28; and unpublished data.

No. 46. Cities With 100,000 or More Inhabitants in 1994—Population, 1980 to 1994, and Land Area, 1990

[Population: As of April 1; except 1994, as of July 1. Data refer to boundaries in effect on January 1, 1990. Minus sign (-) indicates decrease]

CITY	POPULATION									Land area, 1990 (square miles)
	1980, total (1,000)	1990					1994			
		Total (1,000)	Percent—				Total (1,000)	Rank	Percent change, 1990-94	
			Black	American Indian, Eskimo, Aleut	Asian, Pacific Islander	Hispanic [1]				
Abilene, TX	98	107	7.0	0.4	1.3	15.5	110	182	3.1	103.1
Akron, OH	237	223	24.5	0.3	1.2	0.7	222	75	-0.5	62.2
Albany, NY	102	100	20.6	0.3	2.3	3.1	105	195	4.8	21.4
Albuquerque, NM	332	385	3.0	3.0	1.7	34.5	412	36	7.1	132.2
Alexandria, VA	103	111	21.9	0.3	4.2	9.7	113	174	1.5	15.3
Allentown, PA	104	105	5.0	0.2	1.3	11.7	105	193	(Z)	17.7
Amarillo, TX	149	158	6.0	0.8	1.9	14.7	165	110	4.7	87.9
Anaheim, CA	219	266	2.5	0.5	9.4	31.4	282	58	5.9	44.3
Anchorage, AK	174	226	6.4	6.4	4.8	4.1	254	64	12.1	1,697.6
Ann Arbor, MI	108	110	9.0	0.4	7.7	2.6	109	186	-0.7	25.9
Arlington, TX	160	262	8.4	0.5	3.9	8.9	287	56	9.6	93.0
Arlington, VA [2]	153	171	10.5	0.3	6.8	13.5	175	105	2.2	25.9
Atlanta, GA	425	394	67.1	0.1	0.9	1.9	396	37	0.5	131.8
Aurora, CO	159	222	11.4	0.6	3.8	6.6	251	65	12.9	132.5
Aurora, IL	81	100	11.9	0.2	1.3	23.0	112	176	12.8	33.5
Austin, TX	346	466	12.4	0.4	3.0	23.0	514	23	10.4	217.8
Bakersfield, CA	106	175	9.4	1.1	3.6	20.5	191	89	9.2	91.8
Baltimore, MD	787	736	59.2	0.3	1.1	1.0	703	14	-4.5	80.8
Baton Rouge, LA	220	220	43.9	0.1	1.7	1.6	227	72	3.6	73.9
Beaumont, TX	118	114	41.3	0.2	1.7	4.3	115	168	0.6	80.1
Birmingham, AL	284	265	63.3	0.1	0.6	(Z)	265	61	-0.3	148.5
Boise City, ID	102	126	0.6	0.6	1.6	2.7	146	126	16.3	46.1
Boston, MA	563	574	25.6	0.3	5.3	10.8	548	21	-4.6	48.4
Bridgeport, CT	143	142	26.6	0.3	2.3	26.5	133	144	-6.2	16.0
Brownsville, TX	85	99	0.2	0.1	0.3	90.1	113	173	14.1	27.9
Buffalo, NY	358	328	30.7	0.8	1.0	4.9	313	53	-4.6	40.6
Cedar Rapids, IA	110	109	2.9	0.2	1.0	1.1	113	172	4.3	53.5
Chandler, AZ	30	90	2.6	1.2	2.4	17.3	119	159	32.7	47.6
Charlotte, NC	315	396	31.8	0.4	1.8	1.4	438	32	10.6	174.3
Chattanooga, TN	170	152	33.7	0.2	1.0	0.6	152	118	-0.1	118.4
Chesapeake, VA	114	152	27.4	0.3	1.2	1.3	181	98	18.8	340.7
Chicago, IL	3,005	2,784	39.1	0.3	3.7	19.6	2,732	3	-1.9	227.2
Chula Vista, CA	84	135	4.6	0.6	8.9	37.3	149	122	10.4	29.0
Cincinnati, OH	385	364	37.9	0.2	1.1	0.7	358	46	-1.6	77.2
Cleveland, OH	574	506	46.6	0.3	1.0	4.6	493	26	-2.5	77.0
Colorado Springs, CO	215	280	7.0	0.8	2.4	9.1	316	51	12.9	183.2
Columbia, SC	101	103	43.7	0.3	1.4	2.0	104	197	0.6	117.1
Columbus, GA [3]	169	179	38.1	0.3	1.4	3.0	186	92	4.4	216.1
Columbus, OH	565	633	22.6	0.2	2.4	1.1	636	16	0.5	190.9
Concord, CA	104	111	2.4	0.7	8.7	11.5	112	177	0.5	29.5
Corpus Christi, TX	232	257	4.8	0.4	0.9	50.4	275	59	7.0	135.0
Dallas, TX	905	1,006	29.5	0.5	2.2	20.9	1,023	8	1.5	342.4
Dayton, OH	194	182	40.4	0.2	0.6	0.7	179	100	-1.9	55.0
Denver, CO	493	468	12.8	1.2	2.4	23.0	494	25	5.5	153.3
Des Moines, IA	191	193	7.1	0.4	2.4	2.4	194	86	0.4	75.3
Detroit, MI	1,203	1,028	75.7	0.4	0.8	2.8	992	10	-3.5	138.7
Durham, NC	101	137	45.7	0.2	2.0	1.2	143	131	5.0	69.3
Elizabeth, NJ	106	110	19.8	0.3	2.7	39.1	106	190	-3.4	12.3
El Monte, CA	79	106	1.0	0.6	11.8	72.5	105	196	-1.4	9.5
El Paso, TX	425	515	3.4	0.4	1.2	69.0	579	19	12.4	245.4
Erie, PA	119	109	12.0	0.2	0.5	2.4	108	187	-0.3	22.0
Escondido, CA	64	109	1.5	0.8	3.7	23.4	116	165	7.1	36.6
Eugene, OR	106	113	1.3	0.9	3.5	2.7	118	161	4.8	38.0
Evansville, IN	130	126	9.5	0.2	0.6	0.6	129	145	2.5	40.7
Flint, MI	160	141	47.9	0.7	0.5	2.9	138	140	-2.0	33.8
Fontana, CA	37	88	8.7	0.9	4.5	36.1	104	198	18.5	36.6
Fort Lauderdale, FL	153	149	28.1	0.2	0.9	7.2	163	112	9.1	31.4
Fort Wayne, IN	172	184	16.7	0.3	1.0	2.7	183	95	-0.5	62.7
Fort Worth, TX	385	448	22.0	0.4	2.0	19.5	452	29	0.9	281.1
Fremont, CA	132	173	3.8	0.7	19.4	13.3	184	93	5.9	77.0
Fresno, CA	217	354	8.3	1.1	12.5	29.9	387	38	9.2	99.1
Fullerton, CA	102	114	2.2	0.5	12.2	21.3	117	163	2.4	22.1
Garden Grove, CA	123	143	1.5	0.6	20.5	23.5	148	124	3.5	17.9
Garland, TX	139	181	8.9	0.5	4.5	11.6	194	84	7.5	57.3
Gary, IN	152	117	80.6	0.2	0.2	5.7	114	170	-2.0	50.2
Glendale, AZ	97	148	3.0	0.9	2.1	15.5	168	108	13.9	52.2
Glendale, CA	139	180	1.3	0.3	14.1	21.0	178	101	-0.9	30.6
Grand Prairie, TX	71	100	9.7	0.8	3.0	20.5	109	185	9.3	68.5
Grand Rapids, MI	182	189	18.5	0.8	1.1	5.0	190	90	0.7	44.3
Green Bay, WI	88	96	0.5	2.5	2.3	1.1	103	203	6.5	43.8
Greensboro, NC	156	184	33.9	0.5	1.4	1.0	196	80	6.7	79.8

See footnotes at end of table.

No. 46. Cities With 100,000 or More Inhabitants in 1994—Population, 1980 to 1994, and Land Area, 1990—Continued

[See headnote, p. 45]

CITY	POPULATION: 1980, total (1,000)	1990: Total (1,000)	1990: Percent— Black	1990: Percent— American Indian, Eskimo, Aleut	1990: Percent— Asian, Pacific Islander	1990: Percent— Hispanic [1]	1994: Total (1,000)	1994: Rank	1994: Percent change, 1990-94	Land area, 1990 (square miles)
Hampton, VA	123	134	38.9	0.3	1.7	2.0	140	136	4.3	51.8
Hartford, CT	136	140	38.9	0.3	1.4	31.6	124	151	-11.1	17.3
Hayward, CA	94	111	9.8	1.0	15.5	23.9	116	167	3.8	43.5
Henderson, NV	24	65	2.7	1.0	2.0	8.1	102	205	57.0	71.5
Hialeah, FL	145	188	1.9	0.1	0.5	87.6	194	85	3.3	19.2
Hollywood, FL	121	122	8.5	0.2	1.3	11.9	125	150	2.7	27.3
Honolulu, HI [4]	365	377	1.3	0.3	70.5	4.6	386	39	2.3	85.7
Houston, TX	1,595	1,631	28.1	0.3	4.1	27.6	1,702	4	4.4	539.9
Huntington Beach, CA	171	182	0.9	0.6	8.3	11.2	189	91	4.2	26.4
Huntsville, AL	143	160	24.4	0.5	2.1	1.2	160	113	0.3	164.4
Independence, MO	112	112	1.4	0.6	1.0	2.0	112	178	-0.6	78.2
Indianapolis, IN [3]	701	731	22.6	0.2	0.9	1.1	752	12	2.9	361.7
Inglewood, CA	94	110	51.9	0.4	2.5	38.5	110	181	0.4	9.2
Irvine, CA	62	110	1.8	0.2	18.1	6.3	126	148	13.9	42.3
Irving, TX	110	155	7.5	0.6	4.6	16.3	165	111	6.4	67.6
Jackson, MS	203	197	55.7	0.1	0.5	0.4	193	87	-1.8	109.0
Jacksonville, FL [3]	541	635	25.2	0.3	1.9	2.6	665	15	4.7	758.7
Jersey City, NJ	224	229	29.7	0.3	11.4	24.2	226	73	-1.1	14.9
Kansas City, KS	161	150	29.3	0.7	1.2	7.1	143	133	-4.8	107.8
Kansas City, MO	448	435	29.6	0.5	1.2	3.9	444	31	2.1	311.5
Knoxville, TN	175	165	15.8	0.2	1.0	0.7	169	107	2.6	77.2
Lafayette, LA	81	97	27.2	0.2	1.3	1.7	102	204	5.0	40.9
Lakewood, CO	114	126	1.0	0.7	1.9	9.1	126	147	-0.4	40.8
Lancaster, CA	48	97	7.4	0.9	3.7	15.2	119	160	22.5	88.8
Lansing, MI	130	127	18.6	1.0	1.8	7.9	120	156	-6.1	33.9
Laredo, TX	91	123	0.1	0.2	0.4	93.9	150	120	22.0	32.9
Las Vegas, NV	165	258	11.4	0.9	3.6	12.5	328	49	27.0	83.3
Lexington-Fayette, KY	204	225	13.4	0.2	1.6	1.1	238	69	5.4	284.5
Lincoln, NE	172	192	2.4	0.6	1.7	2.0	203	77	5.8	63.3
Little Rock, AR	159	176	34.0	0.3	0.9	0.8	178	102	1.4	102.9
Livonia, MI	105	101	0.3	0.2	1.3	1.3	100	209	-0.4	35.7
Long Beach, CA	361	429	13.7	0.6	13.6	23.6	434	34	1.1	50.0
Los Angeles, CA	2,969	3,486	14.0	0.5	9.8	39.9	3,449	2	-1.1	469.3
Louisville, KY	299	270	29.7	0.2	0.7	0.7	270	60	0.3	62.1
Lubbock, TX	174	186	8.6	0.3	1.4	22.5	194	83	4.4	104.1
Macon, GA	117	107	52.2	0.1	0.4	0.6	109	183	1.7	47.9
Madison, WI	171	191	4.2	0.4	3.9	2.0	195	82	2.0	57.8
Memphis, TN	646	619	54.8	0.2	0.8	0.7	614	18	-0.7	256.0
Mesa, AZ	152	289	1.9	1.0	1.5	10.9	314	52	8.5	108.6
Mesquite, TX	67	101	5.8	0.5	2.6	8.8	114	171	12.0	42.8
Miami, FL	347	359	27.4	0.2	0.6	62.5	373	42	4.0	35.6
Milwaukee, WI	636	628	30.5	0.9	1.9	6.3	617	17	-1.8	96.1
Minneapolis, MN	371	368	13.0	3.3	4.3	2.1	355	47	-3.7	54.9
Mobile, AL	200	196	38.9	0.2	1.0	1.0	204	76	4.2	118.0
Modesto, CA	107	165	2.7	1.0	7.9	16.3	176	104	7.0	30.2
Montgomery, AL	178	188	42.3	0.2	0.7	0.8	195	81	4.2	136.0
Moreno Valley, CA	(5)	119	13.8	0.7	6.6	22.9	139	137	17.3	49.1
Naperville, IL	43	86	2.1	0.1	4.8	1.8	101	206	17.9	27.9
Nashville-Davidson, TN [3]	456	488	24.3	0.2	1.4	0.9	505	24	3.3	473.3
Newark, NJ	329	275	58.5	0.2	1.2	26.1	259	63	-6.0	23.8
New Haven, CT	126	130	36.1	0.3	2.4	13.2	120	155	-6.3	18.9
New Orleans, LA	558	497	61.9	0.2	1.9	3.5	484	27	-2.6	180.6
Newport News, VA	145	171	33.6	0.3	2.3	2.8	179	99	4.5	68.3
New York, NY	7,072	7,323	28.7	0.4	7.0	24.4	7,333	1	0.1	308.9
Norfolk, VA	267	261	39.1	0.4	2.6	2.9	241	67	-7.6	53.8
Norwalk, CA	85	94	3.2	0.9	12.4	47.9	101	207	6.9	9.8
Oakland, CA	339	372	43.9	0.6	14.8	13.9	367	44	-1.4	56.1
Oceanside, CA	77	128	7.9	0.7	6.1	22.6	146	125	14.2	40.7
Oklahoma City, OK	404	445	16.0	4.2	2.4	5.0	463	28	4.2	608.2
Omaha, NE	314	336	13.1	0.7	1.0	3.1	345	48	2.8	100.6
Ontario, CA	89	133	7.3	0.7	3.9	41.7	135	141	1.2	36.7
Orange, CA	91	111	1.4	0.5	7.9	22.8	117	164	5.5	23.3
Orlando, FL	128	165	26.9	0.3	1.6	8.7	177	103	7.5	67.3
Overland Park, KS	82	112	1.8	0.3	1.9	2.0	125	149	12.0	55.7
Oxnard, CA	108	143	5.2	0.8	8.6	54.4	146	127	2.3	24.4
Palmdale, CA	12	70	6.4	0.9	4.4	22.0	103	201	47.2	77.6
Pasadena, CA	118	132	19.0	0.4	8.1	27.3	134	142	2.0	23.0
Pasadena, TX	113	120	1.0	0.5	1.6	28.8	129	146	8.1	43.8
Paterson, NJ	138	141	36.0	0.3	1.4	41.0	138	138	-1.8	8.4
Peoria, IL	124	114	20.9	0.2	1.7	1.6	113	175	-0.6	40.9
Philadelphia, PA	1,688	1,586	39.9	0.2	2.7	5.6	1,524	5	-3.9	135.1
Phoenix, AZ	790	984	5.2	1.9	1.7	20.0	1,049	7	6.6	419.9
Pittsburgh, PA	424	370	25.8	0.2	1.6	0.9	359	45	-3.0	55.6

See footnotes at end of table.

No. 46. Cities With 100,000 or More Inhabitants in 1994—Population, 1980 to 1994, and Land Area, 1990—Continued

[See headnote, p. 45]

CITY	POPULATION: 1980, total (1,000)	1990: Total (1,000)	1990: Percent—Black	1990: Percent—American Indian, Eskimo, Aleut	1990: Percent—Asian, Pacific Islander	1990: Percent—Hispanic [1]	1994: Total (1,000)	1994: Rank	1994: Percent change, 1990-94	Land area, 1990 (square miles)
Plano, TX	72	128	4.1	0.3	4.0	6.2	157	115	23.1	66.2
Pomona, CA	93	132	14.4	0.6	6.7	51.3	144	130	9.2	22.8
Portland, OR	368	439	7.7	1.2	5.3	3.2	451	30	2.7	124.7
Portsmouth, VA	105	104	47.3	0.3	0.8	1.3	103	200	-0.4	33.1
Providence, RI	157	161	14.8	0.9	5.9	15.5	151	119	-6.3	18.5
Pueblo, CO	102	99	2.2	0.8	0.6	39.5	100	208	1.9	36.9
Raleigh, NC	150	212	27.6	0.3	2.5	1.4	237	70	11.6	88.1
Rancho Cucamonga, CA	55	101	5.9	0.6	5.4	20.0	115	169	13.2	37.8
Reno, NV	101	134	2.9	1.4	4.9	11.1	145	128	8.4	57.5
Richmond, VA	219	203	55.2	0.2	0.9	0.9	201	78	-0.8	60.1
Riverside, CA	171	227	7.4	0.8	5.2	26.0	242	66	6.7	77.7
Rochester, NY	242	230	31.5	0.5	1.8	8.7	231	71	0.4	35.8
Rockford, IL	140	140	15.0	0.3	1.5	4.2	143	132	2.3	45.0
Sacramento, CA	276	369	15.3	1.2	15.0	16.2	374	41	1.2	96.3
St. Louis, MO	453	397	47.5	0.2	0.9	1.3	368	43	-7.2	61.9
St. Paul, MN	270	272	7.4	1.4	7.1	4.2	262	62	-3.7	52.8
St. Petersburg, FL	239	240	19.6	0.2	1.7	2.6	239	68	-0.7	59.2
Salem, OR	89	108	1.5	1.6	2.4	6.1	116	166	7.5	41.5
Salinas, CA	80	109	3.0	0.9	8.1	50.6	120	154	10.1	18.6
Salt Lake City, UT	163	160	1.7	1.6	4.7	9.7	172	106	7.5	109.0
San Antonio, TX	786	935	7.0	0.4	1.1	55.6	999	9	6.8	333.0
San Bernardino, CA	119	164	16.0	1.0	4.0	34.6	182	97	10.7	55.1
San Diego, CA	876	1,111	9.4	0.6	11.8	20.7	1,152	6	3.7	324.0
San Francisco, CA	679	724	10.9	0.5	29.1	13.9	735	13	1.5	46.7
San Jose, CA	629	782	4.7	0.7	19.5	26.6	817	11	4.4	171.3
Santa Ana, CA	204	294	2.6	0.5	9.7	65.2	291	55	-1.0	27.1
Santa Clarita, CA	(5)	118	1.5	0.6	4.2	13.4	124	152	4.7	40.5
Santa Rosa, CA	83	113	1.8	1.2	3.4	9.5	117	162	3.3	33.7
Savannah, GA	142	138	51.3	0.2	1.1	1.4	141	135	2.0	62.6
Scottsdale, AZ	89	130	0.8	0.6	1.2	4.8	152	117	17.2	184.4
Seattle, WA	494	516	10.1	1.4	11.8	3.6	521	22	0.9	83.9
Shreveport, LA	206	199	44.8	0.2	0.5	1.1	197	79	-0.8	98.6
Simi Valley, CA	78	100	1.5	0.6	5.5	12.7	107	189	6.7	33.0
Sioux Falls, SD	81	101	0.7	1.6	0.7	0.6	109	184	8.3	45.1
South Bend, IN	110	106	20.9	0.4	0.9	3.4	105	194	-0.4	36.4
Spokane, WA	171	177	1.9	2.0	2.1	2.1	193	88	8.8	55.9
Springfield, IL	100	105	13.0	0.2	1.0	0.8	106	191	0.5	42.5
Springfield, MA	152	157	19.2	0.2	1.0	16.9	149	123	-5.0	32.1
Springfield, MO	133	140	2.5	0.7	0.9	1.0	150	121	6.6	68.0
Stamford, CT	102	108	17.8	0.1	2.6	9.8	107	188	-0.8	37.7
Sterling Heights, MI	109	118	0.4	0.2	2.9	1.1	120	158	1.4	36.6
Stockton, CA	150	211	9.6	1.0	22.8	25.0	223	74	5.5	52.6
Sunnyvale, CA	107	117	3.4	0.5	19.3	13.2	120	157	1.9	21.9
Syracuse, NY	170	164	20.3	1.3	2.2	2.9	160	114	-2.4	25.1
Tacoma, WA	159	177	11.4	2.0	6.9	3.8	183	96	3.6	48.0
Tallahassee, FL	82	125	29.1	0.2	1.8	3.0	134	143	7.2	63.3
Tampa, FL	272	280	25.0	0.3	1.4	15.0	286	57	2.0	108.7
Tempe, AZ	107	142	3.2	1.3	4.1	10.9	144	129	1.6	39.5
Thousand Oaks, CA	77	104	1.2	0.4	4.8	9.6	111	180	6.3	49.6
Toledo, OH	355	333	19.7	0.3	1.0	4.0	323	50	-3.1	80.6
Topeka, KS	119	120	10.6	1.3	0.8	5.8	121	153	0.6	55.2
Torrance, CA	130	133	1.5	0.4	21.9	10.1	138	139	3.8	20.5
Tucson, AZ	331	409	4.3	1.6	2.2	29.3	435	33	6.4	156.3
Tulsa, OK	361	367	13.6	4.7	1.4	2.6	375	40	2.1	183.5
Vallejo, CA	80	109	21.2	0.7	23.0	10.8	111	179	2.1	30.2
Virginia Beach, VA	262	393	13.9	0.4	4.3	3.1	430	35	9.5	248.3
Waco, TX	101	104	23.1	0.3	0.9	16.3	106	192	2.2	75.8
Warren, MI	161	145	0.7	0.5	1.3	1.1	143	134	-1.5	34.3
Washington, DC	638	607	65.8	0.2	1.8	5.4	567	20	-6.6	61.4
Waterbury, CT	103	109	13.0	0.3	0.7	13.4	104	199	-5.0	28.6
West Covina, CA	80	96	8.5	0.5	17.2	34.6	103	202	7.3	16.2
Wichita, KS	280	304	11.3	1.2	2.6	5.0	310	54	2.0	115.1
Winston-Salem, NC	132	151	39.3	0.2	0.8	0.9	155	116	2.8	71.1
Worcester, MA	162	170	4.5	0.3	2.8	9.6	165	109	-2.6	37.6
Yonkers, NY	195	188	14.1	0.2	3.0	16.7	183	94	-2.4	18.1

Z Less than .05 percent. [1] Hispanic persons may be of any race. [2] Data are for Arlington CDP (census designated place) which is not incorporated as a city but is recognized for census purposes as a large urban place. Arlington CDP is coextensive with Arlington County. [3] Represents the portion of a consolidated city that is not within one or more separately incorporated places. [4] The population shown in this table is for the CDP; the 1990 census population for the City and County of Honolulu is 836,231. [5] Not incorporated.

Source: U.S. Bureau of the Census, *1980 Census of Population*, vol. 1, chapters A and B; *1990 Census of Population and Housing, Population and Housing Unit Counts*, (CPH-2) and *General Population Characteristics*, (CP-1); and "City/Place Population Estimates," <http://www.census.gov/ftp/pub/population/www/estimates/citypop.html>; (accessed; 15 March 1996).

pulation 65 Years Old and Over, by Age Group and Sex, 1980 to 1996, and Projections, 2000

f April, except 1996 and 2000, as of July. Projection based on middle series, see table 3]

AND SEX	NUMBER (1,000)				PERCENT DISTRIBUTION			
	1980	1990 [1]	1996	2000, proj.	1980	1990 [1]	1996	2000, proj.
rs. and over	25,549	31,080	33,861	34,709	100	100	100	100
	8,782	10,066	9,892	9,410	34	32	29	27
	6,798	7,980	8,778	8,726	27	26	26	25
	4,794	6,103	6,873	7,415	19	20	20	21
	2,935	3,909	4,557	4,900	12	13	14	14
er	2,240	3,022	3,762	4,259	9	10	11	12
ver	10,305	12,493	13,881	14,346	100	100	100	100
1	3,903	4,508	4,507	4,321	38	36	33	30
1	2,854	3,399	3,818	3,859	28	27	28	27
1	1,848	2,389	2,821	3,092	18	19	20	22
1	1,019	1,356	1,666	1,846	10	11	12	13
over	682	841	1,070	1,228	7	7	8	9
d over	15,245	18,587	19,980	20,364	100	100	100	100
1	4,880	5,558	5,384	5,089	32	30	27	25
1	3,945	4,580	4,960	4,867	26	25	25	24
1	2,946	3,714	4,052	4,323	19	20	20	21
1	1,916	2,553	2,892	3,055	13	14	15	15
over	1,559	2,180	2,892	3,031	10	12	14	15

990, census count (248,718,291) includes count question resolution corrections processed through March include adjustments for census coverage errors.

ureau of the Census, *Current Population Reports*, P25-1095 and P25-1130; and Population Paper Listing 57.

'ersons 65 Years Old and Over—Characteristics, by Sex: 1980 to 1996

March, except as noted. Covers civilian noninstitutional population. See headnote, table 49]

TERISTIC	TOTAL				MALE				FEMALE			
	1980	1990	1995	1996	1980	1990	1995	1996	1980	1990	1995	1996
)	24.2	29.6	31.7	32.0	9.9	12.3	13.2	13.4	14.2	17.2	18.5	18.7
	21.9	26.5	28.4	28.6	9.0	11.0	11.9	12.0	12.9	15.4	16.6	16.6
	2.0	2.5	2.6	2.6	0.8	1.0	1.0	1.0	1.2	1.5	1.6	1.6
rty level [2]	15.2	11.4	11.7	10.5	11.1	7.8	7.2	6.2	17.9	13.9	14.9	13.6
STRIBUTION												
	5.5	4.6	4.2	4.0	4.9	4.2	4.2	4.0	5.9	4.9	4.2	4.1
	55.4	56.1	56.9	56.3	78.0	76.5	77.0	75.6	39.5	41.4	42.5	42.6
t.	53.6	54.1	54.7	54.1	76.1	74.2	74.5	73.2	37.9	39.7	40.6	40.4
	1.8	2.0	2.2	2.2	1.9	2.3	2.5	2.4	1.7	1.7	1.9	2.0
	35.7	34.2	33.2	33.3	13.5	14.2	13.5	14.7	51.2	48.6	47.3	46.8
	3.5	5.0	5.7	6.4	3.6	5.0	5.2	5.8	3.4	5.1	6.0	6.7
	67.6	66.7	66.6	66.6	83.0	81.9	80.6	79.9	56.8	55.8	56.7	57.0
holders	31.2	31.9	32.4	32.2	15.7	16.6	18.4	18.5	42.0	42.8	42.4	42.0
luals	1.2	1.4	1.0	1.2	1.3	1.5	1.0	1.6	1.1	1.4	0.9	0.9
:												
ld	99.8	99.7	99.9	100.0	99.9	99.9	100.0	100.0	99.7	99.5	99.9	100.0
	30.3	31.0	31.5	31.1	14.9	15.7	17.3	17.4	41.0	42.0	41.7	40.9
t.	53.6	54.1	54.7	54.1	76.1	74.3	74.5	73.2	37.9	39.7	40.6	40.4
eone else	15.9	14.6	13.7	14.8	8.9	9.9	8.1	9.4	20.8	17.8	17.6	18.7
[4]	0.2	0.3	0.1	-	0.1	0.1	-	-	0.3	0.5	0.1	-
pleted:												
	43.1	28.5	21.0	19.4	45.3	30.0	22.0	20.3	41.6	27.5	20.3	18.8
gh school	16.2	16.1	[5] 15.2	[5] 15.7	15.5	15.7	[5] 14.5	[5] 14.3	16.7	16.4	[5] 15.6	[5] 16.7
chool	24.0	32.9	[6] 33.8	[6] 33.9	21.4	29.0	[6] 29.2	[6] 29.4	25.8	35.6	[6] 37.1	[6] 37.2
llege	8.2	10.9	[7] 17.1	[7] 17.0	7.5	10.8	[7] 17.1	[7] 17.1	8.6	11.0	[7] 17.0	[7] 16.9
f college	8.6	11.6	[8] 13.0	[8] 13.9	10.3	14.5	[8] 17.2	[8] 18.9	7.4	9.5	[8] 9.9	[8] 10.4
ation: [9]												
	12.2	11.5	11.7	11.6	16.4	15.9	16.1	16.3	7.8	8.4	8.5	8.2
	0.4	0.4	0.5	0.4	0.6	0.5	0.7	0.6	0.3	0.3	0.3	0.3
	87.5	88.1	87.9	87.9	81.0	83.6	83.2	83.1	91.9	91.3	91.2	91.4

ero. [1] Includes other races, not shown separately. [2] Poverty status based on income in preceding year. ng in unrelated subfamilies. [4] In group quarters other than institutions. [5] Represents those who completed de, but have no high school diploma. [6] High school graduate. [7] Some college or associate degree. nced degree. [8] Annual averages of monthly figures. Source: U.S. Bureau of Labor Statistics, *Employment* ry issues. Data beginning 1994 not directly comparable with earlier years. See text, section 13, and February 96 issues of *Employment and Earnings*.

as noted, U.S. Bureau of the Census, *Current Population Reports*, P20-488, and earlier reports; P60-194; and

No. 49. Social and Economic Characteristics of the White and Black Populations: 1990 to 1996

[As of March, except labor force status, annual average. Excludes members of Armed Forces except those living off post or with their families on post. Data for 1990 are based on 1980 census population controls; 1995 and 1996 data based on 1990 census population controls. Based on Current Population Survey; see text, section 1, and Appendix III]

CHARACTERISTIC	NUMBER (1,000)						PERCENT DISTRIBUTION			
	White			Black			White		Black	
	1990	1995	1996	1990	1995	1996	1990	1996	1990	1996
Total persons	208,963	216,751	218,442	30,392	33,531	33,889	100.0	100.0	100.0	100.0
Under 5 years old	15,161	15,915	15,736	2,932	3,342	3,243	7.3	7.2	9.6	9.6
5 to 14 years old	28,405	30,786	31,110	5,546	6,266	6,432	13.7	14.2	18.2	19.0
15 to 44 years old	96,656	97,876	96,146	14,660	16,101	16,154	46.6	44.9	48.2	47.7
45 to 64 years old	40,282	44,189	45,016	4,766	5,264	5,582	19.5	20.6	15.7	16.5
65 years old and over	26,479	27,985	28,436	2,487	2,557	2,478	12.8	13.0	8.2	7.3
EDUCATIONAL ATTAINMENT										
Persons 25 years old and over	134,687	141,113	142,733	16,751	18,457	18,715	100.0	100.0	100.0	100.0
Elementary: 0 to 8 years	14,131	11,101	11,141	2,701	1,800	1,734	10.5	7.8	16.1	9.3
High school: 1 to 3 years	14,080	[1]12,882	[1]13,461	2,969	[1]3,041	[1]3,065	10.5	[1]9.4	17.7	[1]16.5
4 years	52,449	[2]47,986	[2]48,356	6,239	[2]6,686	[2]6,576	38.9	[2]33.9	37.2	[2]35.1
College: 1 to 3 years	24,350	[3]35,321	[3]35,161	2,952	[3]4,486	[3]4,769	18.1	[3]24.6	17.6	[3]25.5
4 years or more	29,677	[4]33,824	[4]34,614	1,890	[4]2,444	[4]2,551	22.0	[4]24.3	11.3	[4]13.6
LABOR FORCE STATUS [5]										
Civilians 16 years old and over	160,625	166,914	168,317	21,477	23,246	23,604	100.0	100.0	100.0	100.0
Civilian labor force	107,447	111,950	113,108	13,740	14,817	15,134	66.9	67.2	64.0	64.1
Employed	102,261	106,490	107,808	12,175	13,279	13,542	63.7	64.1	56.7	57.4
Unemployed	5,186	5,459	5,300	1,565	1,538	1,592	3.2	3.1	7.3	6.7
Unemployment rate [6]	4.8	4.9	4.7	11.4	10.4	10.5	(X)	(X)	(X)	(X)
Not in labor force	53,178	54,965	55,209	7,737	8,429	8,470	33.1	32.8	36.0	35.9
FAMILY TYPE										
Total families	56,590	58,437	58,869	7,470	8,093	8,055	100.0	100.0	100.0	100.0
With own children [7]	26,718	27,951	28,066	4,378	4,682	4,583	47.2	47.7	58.6	56.9
Married couple	46,981	47,899	47,873	3,750	3,842	3,713	83.0	81.3	50.2	46.1
With own children [7]	21,579	22,005	21,835	1,972	1,926	1,901	38.1	37.1	26.4	23.6
Female householder, no spouse present	7,306	8,031	8,284	3,275	3,716	3,769	12.9	14.1	43.8	46.8
With own children [7]	4,199	4,841	4,975	2,232	2,489	2,404	7.4	8.5	29.9	29.8
Male householder, no spouse present	2,303	2,507	2,712	446	536	573	4.1	4.6	6.0	7.1
With own children [7]	939	1,105	1,276	173	267	278	1.7	2.2	2.3	3.4
FAMILY INCOME IN PREVIOUS YEAR IN CONSTANT (1996) DOLLARS										
Total families	56,590	58,437	58,869	7,470	8,093	8,055	100.0	100.0	100.0	100.0
Less than $5,000	1,132	1,286	1,163	627	647	632	2.0	2.0	8.4	7.9
$5,000 to $9,999	2,037	2,572	2,228	934	1,028	926	3.6	3.8	12.5	11.5
$10,000 to $14,999	3,056	3,507	3,425	837	862	881	5.4	5.8	11.2	10.9
$15,000 to $24,999	7,413	8,299	8,204	1,374	1,449	1,478	13.1	13.9	18.4	18.3
$25,000 to $34,999	7,696	8,299	8,372	956	1,117	1,149	13.6	14.2	12.8	14.3
$35,000-$49,999	11,148	10,754	11,095	1,173	1,198	1,279	19.7	18.8	15.7	15.9
$50,000 or more	24,051	23,728	24,385	1,569	1,772	1,710	42.5	41.4	21.0	21.3
Median income (dol.) [8]	44,214	42,043	42,646	24,838	25,398	25,970	(X)	(X)	(X)	(X)
Families below poverty level [9]	4,409	5,312	4,994	2,077	2,212	2,127	7.8	8.5	27.8	26.4
Persons below poverty level [9]	20,785	25,379	24,423	9,302	10,196	9,872	10.0	11.2	30.7	29.3
HOUSING TENURE										
Total occupied units	80,163	83,737	84,511	10,486	11,655	11,577	100.0	100.0	100.0	100.0
Owner-occupied	54,094	57,449	58,282	4,445	4,888	5,085	67.5	69.0	42.4	43.9
Renter-occupied	24,685	24,793	24,798	5,862	6,547	6,290	30.8	29.3	55.9	54.3
No cash rent	1,384	1,494	1,430	178	220	201	1.7	1.7	1.7	1.7

X Not applicable. [1] Represents those who completed ninth to twelfth grade, but have no high school diploma. [2] High school graduate. [3] Some college or associate degree. [4] Bachelor's or advanced degree. [5] Source: U.S. Bureau of Labor Statistics, *Employment and Earnings*, January issues. [6] Total unemployment as percent of civilian labor force. [7] Children under 18 years old. [8] For definition of median, see Guide to Tabular Presentation. [9] For explanation of poverty level, see text, section 14.

Source: Except as noted, U.S. Bureau of the Census, *Current Population Reports*, P20-448, and earlier reports; P60-193; and unpublished data.

No. 50. Social and Economic Characteristics of the Asian and Pacific Islander Population: 1990 and 1996

[As of March. Excludes members of Armed Forces except those living off post or with their families on post. Data for 1990 are based on 1980 census population controls; 1996 data are based on 1990 census population controls. Based on Current Population Survey; see text, section 1, and Appendix III]

CHARACTERISTIC	NUMBER (1,000)		PERCENT DISTRIBUTION	
	1990	1996	1990	1990
Total persons	6,679	9,653	100.0	100.0
Under 5 years old	602	867	9.0	9.0
5 to 14 years old	1,112	1,565	16.6	16.2
15 to 44 years old	3,345	4,906	50.1	50.8
45 to 64 years old	1,155	1,692	17.3	17.5
65 years old and over	465	622	7.0	6.4
EDUCATIONAL ATTAINMENT				
Persons 25 years old and over	3,961	5,677	100.0	100.0
Elementary: 0 to 8 years	543	582	13.7	10.2
High school: 1 to 3 years	234	[1]370	5.9	[1]6.5
4 years	1,038	[2]1,233	26.2	[2]21.7
College: 1 to 3 years	568	[3]1,123	14.3	[3]19.8
4 years or more	1,578	[4]2,369	39.9	[4]41.7
LABOR FORCE STATUS [5]				
Civilians 18 years old and over	4,849	7,044	100.0	100.0
Civilian labor force	3,216	4,641	66.3	65.9
Employed	3,079	4,408	63.5	62.6
Unemployed	136	233	2.8	3.3
Unemployment rate [6]	4.2	5.0	(X)	(X)
Not in labor force	1,634	2,402	33.7	34.1
FAMILY TYPE				
Total families	1,531	2,125	100.0	100.0
Married couple	1,256	1,692	82.1	79.6
Female householder, no spouse present	188	260	12.3	12.2
Male householder, no spouse present	86	173	5.6	8.2
FAMILY INCOME IN PREVIOUS YEAR IN CONSTANT (1995) DOLLARS				
Total families	1,531	2,125	100.0	100.0
Less than $5,000	(NA)	59	(NA)	2.8
$5,000 to $9,999	(NA)	106	(NA)	5.0
$10,000 to $14,999	(NA)	131	(NA)	6.2
$15,000 to $24,999	(NA)	245	(NA)	11.6
$25,000 to $34,999	(NA)	224	(NA)	10.5
$35,000 to $49,999	(NA)	382	(NA)	18.0
$50,000 or more	(NA)	978	(NA)	46.0
Median income [7]	49,593	46,356	(NA)	(NA)
Families below poverty level [8]	182	264	11.9	12.4
Persons below poverty level [8]	938	1,411	14.1	14.6
HOUSING TENURE				
Total occupied units	1,990	2,777	100.0	100.0
Owner-occupied	977	1,411	49.1	50.8
Renter-occupied	982	1,313	49.4	47.3
No cash rent	30	53	1.5	1.9

NA Not available. X Not applicable. [1] Represents those who completed ninth to twelfth grade, but have no high school diploma. [2] High school graduate. [3] Some college or associate degree. [4] Bachelor's or advanced degree. [5] Data beginning 1994 not directly comparable with earlier years. See text, section 13. [6] Total unemployment as percent of civilian labor force. [7] For definition of median, see Guide to Tabular Presentation. [8] For explanation of poverty level, see text, section 14.

Source: U.S. Bureau of the Census, *Current Population Reports*, P20-459; and unpublished data.

No. 51. Population Living on Selected Reservations and Trust Lands and American Indian Tribes With 10,000 or More American Indians: 1990

[As of April]

RESERVATION AND TRUST LANDS WITH 5,000 OR MORE AMERICAN INDIANS, ESKIMOS, AND ALEUTS	Total population	AMERICAN INDIANS, ESKIMOS, ALEUTS		AMERICAN INDIAN TRIBE	Number	Percent distribution
		Number	Percent of total			
All reservation and trust lands	**808,163**	**437,431**	**54.1**	**American Indian population, total[2]**	**1,878,285**	**100.0**
				Cherokee	308,132	16.4
Navajo and Trust Lands, AZ-NM-UT	148,451	143,405	96.6	Navajo	219,198	11.7
				Chippewa	103,826	5.5
Pine Ridge and Trust Lands, NE-SD	12,215	11,182	91.5	Sioux[3]	103,255	5.5
Fort Apache, AZ	10,394	9,825	94.5	Choctaw	82,299	4.4
Gila River, AZ	9,540	9,116	95.6	Pueblo	52,939	2.8
Papago, AZ	8,730	8,480	97.1	Apache	50,051	2.7
				Iroquois[4]	49,038	2.6
Rosebud and Trust Lands, SD	9,696	8,043	83.0	Lumbee	48,444	2.6
San Carlos, AZ	7,294	7,110	97.5	Creek	43,550	2.3
Zuni Pueblo, AZ-NM	7,412	7,073	95.4	Blackfoot	32,234	1.7
Hopi and Trust Lands, AZ	7,360	7,061	95.9	Canadian and Latin American	22,379	1.2
Blackfeet, MT	8,549	7,025	82.2	Chickasaw	20,631	1.1
				Potawatomi[4]	16,763	0.9
Turtle Mountain and Trust Lands, ND-SD	7,106	6,772	95.3	Tohono O'Odham	16,041	0.9
Yakima and Trust Lands, WA	27,668	6,307	22.8	Pima	14,431	0.8
				Tlingit	13,925	0.7
Osage, OK[1]	41,645	6,161	14.8	Seminole	13,797	0.7
Fort Peck, MT	10,595	5,782	54.6	Alaskan Athabaskans	13,738	0.7
Wind River, WY	21,851	5,676	26.0	Cheyenne	11,456	0.6
Eastern Cherokee, NC	6,527	5,388	82.5	Comanche	11,322	0.6
Flathead, MT	21,259	5,130	24.1	Paiute	11,142	0.6
Cheyenne River, SD	7,743	5,100	65.9	Puget Sound Salish	10,246	0.5

[1] The Osage Reservation is coextensive with Osage County. Data shown for the reservation are for the entire reservation. [2] Includes other American Indian tribes, not shown separately. [3] Any entry with the spelling "Siouan" was miscoded to Sioux in North Carolina. [4] Reporting and/or processing problems have affected the data for this tribe.

Source: U.S. Bureau of the Census, *1990 Census of Population, General Population Characteristics, American Indian and Alaska Native Areas* (CP-1-1A); and press releases CB91-232 and CB92-244.

No. 52. Social and Economic Characteristics of the American Indian Population: 1990

[As of April. Based on a sample and subject to sampling variability]

CHARACTERISTIC	American Indian, total[1]	Cherokee	Navajo	Sioux[2]	Chippewa	Choctaw	Pueblo	Apache	Iroquois[3]	Lumbee
Total persons	**1,937,391**	**369,035**	**225,298**	**107,321**	**105,988**	**86,231**	**55,330**	**53,330**	**52,557**	**50,888**
Percent under 5 years old	9.7	6.3	13.6	12.3	10.3	8.2	10.3	10.2	8.1	8.3
Percent 18 years old and over	65.8	73.3	57.7	60.0	64.0	68.8	64.2	64.7	71.1	66.2
Percent 65 years old and over	5.9	7.2	4.6	4.4	4.7	8.0	5.8	3.4	6.7	5.6
EDUCATIONAL ATTAINMENT										
Persons 25 years old and over	1,040,955	229,231	100,594	51,014	54,804	49,128	28,597	27,717	30,882	27,343
Percent high school graduates or higher	65.6	68.2	51.0	69.7	69.7	70.3	71.5	63.8	71.9	51.6
Percent bachelor's degree or higher	9.4	11.1	4.5	8.9	8.2	13.3	7.3	6.9	11.3	9.4
FAMILY TYPE										
Total families	449,281	96,610	44,845	22,669	25,077	21,858	11,825	12,314	12,988	12,650
Percent distribution:										
Married couple	65.8	73.1	61.1	54.2	58.4	75.2	61.2	66.9	67.5	68.5
Female householder, no spouse present	26.2	20.8	28.6	36.0	33.1	20.0	29.2	24.7	25.5	23.9
Male householder, no spouse present	8.0	6.1	10.3	9.8	8.5	4.8	9.6	8.4	7.0	7.6
INCOME IN 1989										
Median family (dol.)[4]	21,619	24,907	13,940	16,525	20,249	24,467	19,845	19,690	27,025	23,934
Median household (dol.)[4]	19,900	21,922	12,817	15,611	18,801	21,640	19,097	18,484	23,460	21,708
Per capita (dol.)	8,284	10,469	4,788	6,508	7,777	9,463	6,679	7,271	10,568	8,625
Families below poverty level[5]	122,237	19,100	21,204	8,939	7,814	4,347	3,691	3,913	2,249	2,554
Percent below poverty level	27.2	19.4	47.3	39.4	31.2	19.9	31.2	31.8	17.3	20.2
Persons below poverty level[5]	585,273	79,271	107,526	45,658	35,231	19,453	17,981	19,246	10,253	10,966
Percent below poverty level	31.2	22.0	48.8	44.4	34.3	23.0	33.2	37.5	20.1	22.1

[1] Includes other American Indian tribes not shown separately. [2] Any entry with the spelling "Siouan" was miscoded to Sioux in North Carolina. [3] Reporting and/or processing problems have affected the data for this tribe. [4] For definition of median, see Guide to Tabular Presentation. [5] For explanation of poverty level, see text, section 14.

Source: U.S. Bureau of the Census, *1990 Census of Population, Characteristics of American Indians by Tribe and Language*, 1990 CP-3-7.

No. 53. Social and Economic Characteristics of the Hispanic Population: 1995

[As of March, except labor force status, annual average. Excludes members of the Armed Forces except those living off post or with their families on post. Based on Current Population Survey; see text, section 1, and Appendix III]

CHARACTERISTIC	NUMBER (1,000)						PERCENT DISTRIBUTION					
	Hispanic, total	Mexican	Puerto Rican	Cuban	Central and South American	Other Hispanic	Hispanic, total	Mexican	Puerto Rican	Cuban	Central and South American	Other Hispanic
Total persons	27,521	17,982	2,730	1,156	3,686	1,967	100.0	100.0	100.0	100.0	100.0	100.0
Under 5 years old	3,318	2,413	272	68	360	205	12.1	13.4	10.0	5.9	9.8	10.4
5 to 14 years old	5,215	3,611	539	131	577	356	18.9	20.1	19.7	11.3	15.7	18.1
15 to 44 years old	13,894	9,049	1,323	486	2,102	933	50.5	50.3	48.5	42.0	57.0	47.4
45 to 64 years old	3,666	2,127	466	265	469	320	13.3	11.8	17.1	22.9	13.3	16.3
65 years old and over	1,428	781	130	207	159	154	5.2	4.3	4.8	17.9	4.3	7.8
EDUCATIONAL ATTAINMENT												
Persons 25 years old and over	14,171	8,737	1,437	820	2,082	1,096	100.0	100.0	100.0	100.0	100.0	100.0
High school graduate or higher	7,563	4,067	880	531	1,337	749	53.4	46.5	61.3	64.7	64.2	68.4
Bachelor's degree or higher	1,312	572	153	158	272	156	9.3	6.5	10.7	19.3	13.1	14.2
LABOR FORCE STATUS [1]												
Civilians 16 years old and over	18,629	11,889	1,898	1,019	2,686	1,419	100.0	100.0	100.0	100.0	100.0	100.0
Civilian labor force	12,267	7,765	1,098	613	1,885	906	65.8	66.9	57.9	60.2	70.2	63.8
Employed	11,127	7,016	974	588	1,734	835	59.7	60.4	51.4	55.7	64.6	58.8
Unemployed	1,140	750	123	45	150	72	6.1	6.5	6.5	4.4	5.6	5.1
Unemployment rate [2]	9.3	9.7	11.2	7.4	8.0	7.9	(X)	(X)	(X)	(X)	(X)	(X)
Not in labor force	6,362	3,844	796	406	802	512	34.2	33.1	42.1	39.8	29.9	36.1
FAMILY TYPE												
Total families	6,200	3,847	729	315	817	491	100.0	100.0	100.0	100.0	100.0	100.0
Married couple	4,235	2,745	386	235	541	328	68.3	71.4	52.9	74.6	66.1	66.8
Female householder, no spouse present	1,485	766	300	67	206	145	24.0	19.9	41.2	21.3	25.4	29.5
Male householder, no spouse present	479	336	43	13	69	18	7.7	8.7	5.9	4.0	8.5	3.7
FAMILY INCOME IN 1994												
Total families	6,200	3,847	729	315	817	491	100.0	100.0	100.0	100.0	100.0	100.0
Less than $5,000	375	232	54	14	45	30	6.0	6.0	7.4	4.4	5.6	6.0
$5,000 to $9,999	730	448	136	27	73	49	11.8	11.6	18.6	8.5	8.9	9.9
$10,000 to $14,999	779	517	97	24	92	50	12.6	13.4	13.3	7.5	11.3	10.1
$15,000 to $24,999	1,301	844	122	68	180	88	21.0	21.9	16.7	21.5	22.0	17.9
$25,000 to $34,999	923	583	92	46	133	68	14.9	15.2	12.6	14.5	16.3	13.9
$35,000 to $49,999	924	575	80	38	139	92	14.9	14.9	10.9	12.0	17.1	18.7
$50,000 or more	1,168	650	149	100	154	115	18.8	16.9	20.4	31.7	18.8	23.4
Median income (dol.) [3]	24,313	23,609	20,929	30,584	26,558	28,658	(X)	(X)	(X)	(X)	(X)	(X)
Families below poverty level [4]	1,724	1,138	242	43	196	105	27.8	29.6	33.2	13.6	23.9	21.4
Persons below poverty level [4]	8,416	5,781	981	205	949	500	30.7	32.3	36.0	17.8	25.8	25.5
HOUSING TENURE												
Total occupied units	7,735	4,653	935	451	1,040	656	100.0	100.0	100.0	100.0	100.0	100.0
Owner-occupied	3,278	2,145	268	236	304	325	42.4	46.1	28.7	52.3	29.2	49.6
Renter-occupied [5]	4,457	2,508	667	215	736	331	57.6	53.9	71.3	47.7	70.8	50.4

X Not applicable. [1] Source: U.S. Bureau of Labor Statistics, *Employment and Earnings*, January 1996. [2] Total unemployment as percent of civilian labor force. [3] For definition of median, see Guide to Tabular Presentation. [4] For explanation of poverty level, see text, section 14. [5] Includes no cash rent.

Source: Except as noted, U.S. Bureau of the Census, unpublished data.

No. 54. Native and Foreign-Born Population, by Place of Birth: 1950 to 1990

[In thousands, except percent. Data are based on a sample from the census; for details, see text, section 1. See source for sampling variability]

YEAR	Total population	NATIVE POPULATION						FOREIGN-BORN	
		Total	Born in State of residence	Born in other States	State of birth not reported	Born in outlying areas [1]	Born abroad or at sea of American parents	Number	Percent of total population
1950	150,216	139,869	102,788	35,284	1,370	330	96	10,347	6.9
1960	178,467	168,806	118,802	44,264	4,526	817	397	9,661	5.4
1970	203,194	193,454	131,296	51,659	8,882	873	744	9,740	4.8
1980	226,546	212,466	144,871	65,452	(NA)	1,088	1,055	14,080	6.2
1990	248,710	228,943	153,685	72,011	(NA)	1,382	1,864	19,767	7.9

NA Not available. [1] 1950, includes Alaska and Hawaii. Includes Puerto Rico.

Source: U.S. Bureau of the Census, *1970 Census of Population*, vol. II, PC(2)-2A; and *1990 Census of Population Listing* (1990CPH-L-121).

No. 55. Native and Foreign-Born Populations by Selected Characteristics: 1996

[In thousands, except as indicated. The foreign-born population includes some undocumented immigrants, refugees, and temporary residents such as students and temporary workers as well as legally-admitted immigrants. Based on Current Population Survey; see text, section 1 and Appendix III]

CHARACTERISTIC	Native population	FOREIGN-BORN POPULATION						
		Total [1]	Year of entry				Country of birth	
			Before 1970	1970 to 1979	1980 to 1989	1990 to 1996	Mexico	Philippines
Total	**239,757**	**24,557**	**4,806**	**4,756**	**8,416**	**6,579**	**6,679**	**1,164**
Under 5 years old	19,777	292	(X)	(X)	2	290	85	5
5 to 17 years old	48,636	2,443	(X)	26	1,036	1,381	635	113
18 to 24 years old	22,109	2,734	(X)	422	997	1,314	1,116	72
25 to 29 years old	16,817	2,645	56	364	1,217	1,008	1,017	114
30 to 34 years old	18,498	2,959	189	515	1,448	808	944	118
35 to 44 years old	37,978	5,100	562	1,637	2,041	860	1,314	297
45 to 64 years old	47,045	5,624	2,112	1,462	1,347	701	1,024	308
65 years old and over	28,897	2,761	1,888	327	330	217	343	136
Male	117,118	12,025	2,070	2,293	4,357	3,304	3,650	534
Female	122,639	12,532	2,735	2,463	4,059	3,275	3,029	630
White	201,814	16,629	4,124	3,177	5,242	4,087	6,573	35
Black	31,906	1,961	200	463	741	575	55	-
Asian or Pacific Islander	3,799	5,855	453	1,108	2,411	1,883	5	1,129
Hispanic origin [2]	17,652	10,786	1,549	2,254	4,155	2,829	6,624	37
EDUCATIONAL ATTAINMENT								
Persons 25 years old and over	149,234	19,088	4,806	4,307	6,382	3,595	4,642	973
Not high school graduate	23,924	6,800	1,476	1,541	2,460	1,322	3,262	127
High school grad/some college	90,131	7,800	2,403	1,750	2,413	1,234	1,232	427
Bachelor's degree	23,695	2,845	560	668	997	621	120	353
Graduate or professional degree	11,485	1,643	366	348	512	418	29	67
LABOR FORCE STATUS								
Persons 16 years old and over [3]	178,343	22,378	4,806	4,752	7,668	5,153	5,909	1,076
In the civilian labor force	118,025	14,298	2,296	3,513	5,440	3,051	3,876	809
Employed	111,309	13,203	2,182	3,289	5,032	2,701	3,449	777
Unemployed	6,716	1,095	113	224	408	350	427	32
Not in the labor force	59,562	8,039	2,504	1,211	2,224	2,101	2,032	249
INCOME IN 1995								
Persons 16 years old and over	178,343	22,378	4,806	4,752	7,668	5,153	5,909	1,076
Without income	10,712	3,308	280	421	1,202	1,401	1,215	116
With income	167,631	19,070	4,526	4,331	6,466	3,752	4,694	960
$1 to $9,999 or loss	52,571	6,962	1,563	1,349	2,269	1,782	2,047	219
$10,000 to $19,999	39,878	5,392	1,206	1,103	2,008	1,074	1,711	228
$20,000 to $34,999	38,394	3,646	837	949	1,330	531	696	261
$35,000 to $49,999	18,726	1,555	398	494	470	194	176	149
$50,000 or more	18,062	1,515	520	436	389	171	64	102
Median income (dollars)	$17,635	$14,772	$15,795	$17,403	$14,801	$10,875	$11,753	$21,897
POVERTY STATUS [4]								
In poverty	30,972	5,452	478	800	1,989	2,186	2,312	61
Not in poverty	208,233	19,075	4,328	3,957	6,417	4,373	4,353	1,103
HOMEOWNERSHIP								
In owner-occupied unit	167,379	11,487	3,631	2,898	3,506	1,451	2,331	777
In renter-occupied unit	72,378	13,070	1,175	1,858	4,910	5,128	4,348	387

- Represents or rounds to zero. X Not applicable. [1] Includes other countries, not shown separately. [2] Persons of Hispanic origin may be of any race. [3] Includes persons in Armed Forces, not shown separately. [4] Persons for whom poverty status is determined.

Source: U.S. Bureau of the Census, *Current Population Reports*, P20-494 and Population Paper Listing PPL-59.

No. 56. Population, by Selected Ancestry Group and Region: 1990

[As of April 1. Covers persons who reported single and multiple ancestry groups. Persons who reported a multiple ancestry group may be included in more than one category. Major classifications of ancestry groups do not represent strict geographic or cultural definitions. Based on a sample and subject to sampling variability; see text, section 1]

ANCESTRY GROUP	Total (1,000)	PERCENT DISTRIBUTION, BY REGION			
		Northeast	Midwest	South	West
European: [1]					
Austrian	865	38	21	19	22
British	1,119	17	18	39	26
Croatian	544	21	43	20	16
Czech	1,296	10	52	22	16
Danish	1,635	9	34	12	45
Dutch	6,227	16	34	29	21
English	32,652	18	22	35	25
European	467	14	17	31	39
Finnish	659	14	47	11	27
French [2]	10,321	26	26	29	20
German	57,947	17	39	25	19
Greek	1,110	37	23	21	19
Hungarian	1,582	36	32	17	16
Irish	38,736	24	25	33	17
Italian	14,665	51	17	17	15
Lithuanian	812	43	28	16	13
Norwegian	3,869	6	52	10	33
Polish	9,366	37	37	15	11
Portuguese	1,153	49	3	8	41
Russian	2,953	44	16	18	22
Scandinavian	679	8	33	15	45
Scotch-Irish	5,618	14	19	47	20
Scottish	5,394	20	21	33	26
Slovak	1,883	40	34	14	11
Swedish	4,681	14	40	14	32
Swiss	1,045	16	36	17	30
Ukrainian	741	51	22	14	13
Welsh	2,034	22	24	27	27
Yugoslavian	258	23	28	12	37
Central & South America [3] and Spain:					
Cuban	860	18	3	69	9
Dominican	506	86	1	10	2
Hispanic [4]	1,113	13	6	31	50
Mexican	11,587	1	9	33	57
Puerto Rican	1,955	66	11	15	8
Salvadoran	499	13	2	23	62
Spanish	2,024	16	8	30	45
West Indian: [1]					
Jamaican	435	59	5	31	6
Asia:					
Asian Indian	570	32	19	26	24
Chinese	1,505	25	8	12	55
Filipino	1,451	10	9	13	68
Japanese	1,005	9	8	11	72
Korean	837	22	14	20	44
Vietnamese	536	9	8	28	54
North America:					
Acadian/Cajun	668	1	2	91	5
Afro-American	23,777	15	21	54	10
American Indian	8,706	9	22	47	23
American	12,396	10	18	61	11
Canadian	550	34	18	21	28
French Canadian	2,167	45	20	20	15
United States	844	16	18	53	13
White	1,800	7	13	53	28

[1] Non-Hispanic groups. [2] Excludes French Basque. [3] Hispanic groups. [4] A general type of response which may encompass several ancestry groups.

Source: U.S. Bureau of the Census, *1990 Census of Population, Supplementary Reports, Detailed Ancestry Groups for States* (1990 CP-S-1-2).

No. 57. Persons Speaking a Language Other Than English at Home, by Age and Language: 1990

[As of April. Based on a sample and subject to sampling variability]

AGE GROUP AND LANGUAGE SPOKEN AT HOME	Persons who speak language (1,000)	Percent who speak English less than "very well"
Persons 5 years old and over	230,446	(X)
Speak only English	198,601	(X)
Speak other language	31,845	43.9
Speak Spanish or Spanish Creole	17,345	47.9
Speak Asian or Pacific Island language	4,472	54.1
Speak other language	10,028	32.4
Persons 5 to 17 years old	45,342	(X)
Speak only English	39,020	(X)
Speak other language	6,323	37.8
Speak Spanish or Spanish Creole	4,168	39.3
Speak Asian or Pacific Island language	816	44.2
Speak other language	1,340	29.2
Persons 18 to 64 years old	153,908	(X)
Speak only English	132,200	(X)
Speak other language	21,708	45.1
Speak Spanish or Spanish Creole	12,121	49.6
Speak Asian or Pacific Island language	3,301	54.7
Speak other language	6,286	31.4
Persons 65 years old and over	31,195	(X)
Speak only English	27,381	(X)
Speak other language	3,814	47.2
Speak Spanish or Spanish Creole	1,057	62.3
Speak Asian or Pacific Island language	355	72.0
Speak other language	2,402	36.9

LANGUAGE	Persons, 5 years old and over who speak language (1,000)
Speak only English	198,601
Spanish	17,339
French	1,702
German	1,547
Italian	1,309
Chinese	1,249
Tagalog	843
Polish	723
Korean	626
Vietnamese	507
Portuguese	430
Japanese	428
Greek	388
Arabic	355
Hindi (Urdu)	331
Russian	242
Yiddish	213
Thai (Laotian)	206
Persian	202
French Creole	188
Armenian	150
Navaho	149
Hungarian	148
Hebrew	144
Dutch	143
Mon-Khmer (Cambodian)	127
Gujarathi	102

X Not applicable.

Source: U.S. Bureau of the Census, *1990 Census of Population and Housing Data Paper Listing* (CPH-L-133); and Summary Tape File 3C.

No. 58. Marital Status of the Population, by Sex, Race, and Hispanic Origin: 1980 to 1996

[In millions, except percent. As of March. Persons 18 years old and over. Excludes members of Armed Forces except those living off post or with their families on post. Based on Current Population Survey, see text, section 1, and Appendix III]

MARITAL STATUS, RACE, AND HISPANIC ORIGIN	TOTAL				MALE				FEMALE			
	1980	1990	1995	1996	1980	1990	1995	1996	1980	1990	1995	1996
Total [1]	**159.5**	**181.8**	**191.6**	**193.2**	**75.7**	**86.9**	**92.0**	**92.7**	**83.8**	**95.0**	**99.6**	**100.4**
Never married	32.3	40.4	43.9	44.9	18.0	22.4	24.6	24.9	14.3	17.9	19.3	20.0
Married	104.6	112.6	116.7	116.4	51.8	55.8	57.7	57.6	52.8	56.7	58.9	58.8
Widowed	12.7	13.8	13.4	13.5	2.0	2.3	2.3	2.5	10.8	11.5	11.1	11.1
Divorced	9.9	15.1	17.6	18.2	3.9	6.3	7.4	7.8	6.0	8.8	10.3	10.5
Percent of total	100.0	100.0	100.0	100.0	100.0	100.0	100.0	100.0	100.0	100.0	100.0	100.0
Never married	20.3	22.2	22.9	23.3	23.8	25.8	26.8	26.8	17.1	18.9	19.4	19.9
Married	65.5	61.9	60.9	60.3	68.4	64.3	62.7	62.1	63.0	59.7	59.2	58.6
Widowed	8.0	7.6	7.0	7.0	2.6	2.7	2.5	2.7	12.8	12.1	11.1	11.0
Divorced	6.2	8.3	9.2	9.5	5.2	7.2	8.0	8.4	7.1	9.3	10.3	10.5
White, total	**139.5**	**155.5**	**161.3**	**162.6**	**66.7**	**74.8**	**78.1**	**78.8**	**72.8**	**80.6**	**83.2**	**83.8**
Never married	26.4	31.6	33.2	33.7	15.0	18.0	19.2	19.3	11.4	13.6	14.0	14.4
Married	93.8	99.5	102.0	102.2	46.7	49.5	50.6	50.9	47.1	49.9	51.3	51.3
Widowed	10.9	11.7	11.3	11.5	1.6	1.9	1.9	2.1	9.3	9.8	9.4	9.4
Divorced	8.3	12.6	14.8	15.2	3.4	5.4	6.3	6.5	5.0	7.3	8.4	8.7
Percent of total	100.0	100.0	100.0	100.0	100.0	100.0	100.0	100.0	100.0	100.0	100.0	100.0
Never married	18.9	20.3	20.6	20.7	22.5	24.1	24.6	24.5	15.7	16.9	16.9	17.2
Married	67.2	64.0	63.2	62.8	70.0	66.2	64.9	64.5	64.7	61.9	61.7	61.3
Widowed	7.8	7.5	7.0	7.1	2.5	2.6	2.5	2.7	12.8	12.2	11.3	11.2
Divorced	6.0	8.1	9.1	9.3	5.0	7.2	8.1	8.3	6.8	9.0	10.1	10.3
Black, total	**16.6**	**20.3**	**22.1**	**22.3**	**7.4**	**9.1**	**9.9**	**10.0**	**9.2**	**11.2**	**12.2**	**12.4**
Never married	5.1	7.1	8.5	8.8	2.5	3.5	4.1	4.2	2.5	3.6	4.4	4.6
Married	8.5	9.3	9.6	9.4	4.1	4.5	4.6	4.5	4.5	4.8	4.9	4.9
Widowed	1.6	1.7	1.7	1.6	0.3	0.3	0.3	0.3	1.3	1.4	1.4	1.3
Divorced	1.4	2.1	2.4	2.6	0.5	0.8	0.8	1.0	0.9	1.3	1.5	1.6
Percent of total	100.0	100.0	100.0	100.0	100.0	100.0	100.0	100.0	100.0	100.0	100.0	100.0
Never married	30.5	35.1	38.4	39.2	34.3	38.4	41.7	42.1	27.4	32.5	35.8	36.8
Married	51.4	45.8	43.2	42.2	54.6	49.2	46.7	45.0	48.7	43.0	40.4	39.9
Widowed	9.8	8.5	7.6	7.2	4.2	3.7	3.1	2.8	14.3	12.4	11.3	10.7
Divorced	8.4	10.6	10.7	11.5	7.0	8.8	8.5	10.2	9.5	12.0	12.5	12.6
Hispanic, [2] **total**	**7.9**	**13.6**	**17.6**	**18.1**	**3.8**	**6.7**	**8.8**	**9.1**	**4.1**	**6.8**	**8.8**	**9.0**
Never married	1.9	3.7	5.0	5.5	1.0	2.2	3.0	3.3	0.9	1.5	2.1	2.2
Married	5.2	8.4	10.4	10.6	2.5	4.1	5.1	5.1	2.6	4.3	5.3	5.5
Widowed	0.4	0.5	0.7	0.7	0.1	0.1	0.2	0.1	0.3	0.4	0.6	0.6
Divorced	0.5	1.0	1.4	1.4	0.2	0.4	0.6	0.6	0.3	0.6	0.8	0.8
Percent of total	100.0	100.0	100.0	100.0	100.0	100.0	100.0	100.0	100.0	100.0	100.0	100.0
Never married	24.1	27.2	28.6	30.2	27.3	32.1	33.8	36.0	21.1	22.5	23.5	24.3
Married	65.6	61.7	59.3	58.3	67.1	60.9	57.9	56.3	64.3	62.4	60.7	60.3
Widowed	4.4	4.0	4.2	3.9	1.6	1.5	1.8	1.4	7.1	6.5	6.6	6.4
Divorced	5.8	7.0	7.9	7.7	4.0	5.5	6.6	6.3	7.6	8.5	9.2	9.0

[1] Includes persons of other races, not shown separately. [2] Hispanic persons may be of any race.

Source: U.S. Bureau of the Census, *Current Population Reports*, P20-491, and earlier reports; and unpublished data.

No. 59. Marital Status of the Population, by Sex and Age: 1996

[As of March. Persons 18 years old and over. Excludes members of Armed Forces except those living off post or with their families on post. Based on Current Population Survey; see text, section 1, and Appendix III]

SEX AND AGE	NUMBER OF PERSONS (1,000)					PERCENT DISTRIBUTION				
	Total	Never married	Married	Widowed	Divorced	Total	Never married	Married	Widowed	Divorced
Male	92,741	24,893	57,817	2,476	7,755	100.0	26.8	62.1	2.7	8.4
18 to 19 years old	3,610	3,525	77	-	8	100.0	97.6	2.1	-	0.2
20 to 24 years old	8,792	7,126	1,561	-	106	100.0	81.0	17.8	-	1.2
25 to 29 years old	9,752	5,075	4,264	12	402	100.0	52.0	43.7	0.1	4.1
30 to 34 years old	10,638	3,147	6,565	32	895	100.0	29.6	61.7	0.3	8.4
35 to 39 years old	11,091	2,303	7,611	19	1,159	100.0	20.8	68.6	0.2	10.4
40 to 44 years old	10,182	1,443	7,320	47	1,372	100.0	14.2	71.9	0.5	13.5
45 to 54 years old	15,324	1,247	11,889	124	2,064	100.0	8.1	77.6	0.8	13.5
55 to 64 years old	10,092	501	8,315	299	976	100.0	5.0	82.4	3.0	9.7
65 to 74 years old	8,213	359	6,494	788	571	100.0	4.4	79.1	9.6	7.0
75 years old and over	5,048	167	3,521	1,156	203	100.0	3.3	69.8	22.9	4.0
Female	100,425	20,023	58,822	11,070	10,611	100.0	19.9	58.6	11.0	10.6
18 to 19 years old	3,580	3,300	273	1	6	100.0	92.2	7.6	-	0.1
20 to 24 years old	8,861	6,070	2,529	10	252	100.0	68.5	28.5	0.1	2.8
25 to 29 years old	9,709	3,650	5,426	26	607	100.0	37.6	55.9	0.2	6.3
30 to 34 years old	10,819	2,215	7,481	58	1,066	100.0	20.5	69.1	0.5	9.9
35 to 39 years old	11,388	1,487	8,262	122	1,518	100.0	13.1	72.6	1.0	13.3
40 to 44 years old	10,417	1,009	7,566	157	1,685	100.0	9.7	72.6	1.5	16.2
45 to 54 years old	16,260	1,025	11,869	699	2,667	100.0	6.3	73.0	4.3	16.4
55 to 64 years old	10,992	512	7,617	1,390	1,474	100.0	4.7	69.3	12.6	13.4
65 to 74 years old	10,057	384	5,514	3,301	858	100.0	3.8	54.8	32.8	8.5
75 years old and over	8,341	370	2,285	5,306	379	100.0	4.4	27.4	63.6	4.5

- Represents or rounds to zero.

Source: U.S. Bureau of the Census, unpublished data.

No. 60. Marital Status of the Population—Projections, by Age and Sex: 2000 and 2010

[These numbers are based on the 1990 census, as enumerated, with modifications for age and race, and household estimates from 1991 to 1994, and are projected forward using alternative marital status and household-type proportions. Series 1, shown here, is based on a time series model and is the preferred projection. For series 1, assumptions about future changes in family and household situation extend trends of the past 30 years]

CHARACTERISTIC	NUMBER (1,000)		PERCENT DISTRIBUTION	
	2000	2010	2000	2010
Population 18 years and over	203,852	225,206	100.0	100.0
Never married (single)	44,459	50,747	21.8	22.5
Ever married	159,393	174,459	78.2	77.5
Married, spouse present	111,408	119,016	54.7	52.8
Other	47,985	55,443	23.5	24.6
18 to 24 years old	26,258	30,138	100.0	100.0
Never married (single)	20,917	24,429	79.7	81.1
Ever married	5,341	5,708	20.3	18.9
Married, spouse present	3,750	4,003	14.3	13.3
Other	1,591	1,705	6.1	5.7
25 to 34 years old	37,233	38,292	100.0	100.0
Never married (single)	12,288	14,006	33.0	36.6
Ever married	24,946	24,286	67.0	63.4
Married, spouse present	18,967	18,115	50.9	47.3
Other	5,979	6,171	16.1	16.1
35 to 44 years old	44,659	38,521	100.0	100.0
Never married (single)	5,886	5,660	13.2	14.7
Ever married	38,774	32,860	86.8	85.3
Married, spouse present	28,930	23,628	64.8	61.3
Other	9,844	9,233	22.0	24.0
45 to 54 years old	37,030	43,564	100.0	100.0
Never married (single)	2,346	2,836	6.3	6.5
Ever married	34,684	40,729	93.7	93.5
Married, spouse present	25,736	29,212	69.5	67.1
Other	8,948	11,517	24.2	26.4
55 to 64 years old	23,962	35,283	100.0	100.0
Never married (single)	1,254	1,905	5.2	5.4
Ever married	22,707	33,379	94.8	94.6
Married, spouse present	16,424	23,360	68.5	66.2
Other	6,283	10,019	26.2	28.4
65 to 74 years old	18,136	21,057	100.0	100.0
Never married (single)	825	899	4.5	4.3
Ever married	17,311	20,159	95.5	95.7
Married, spouse present	11,309	13,305	62.4	63.2
Other	6,002	6,854	33.1	32.5
75 years and over	16,574	18,351	100.0	100.0
Never married (single)	943	1,012	5.7	5.5
Ever married	15,631	17,339	94.3	94.5
Married, spouse present	6,293	7,394	38.0	40.3
Other	9,338	9,944	56.3	54.2
Females, 18 years and over	105,927	116,776	100.0	100.0
Never married (single)	19,955	22,904	18.8	19.6
Ever married	85,972	93,872	81.2	80.4
Married, spouse present	55,682	59,485	52.6	50.9
Other	30,290	34,387	28.6	29.4
Males, 18 years and over	97,925	108,430	100.0	100.0
Never married (single)	24,504	27,843	25.0	25.7
Ever married	73,421	80,587	75.0	74.3
Married, spouse present	55,726	59,531	56.9	54.9
Other	17,695	21,056	18.1	19.4

Source: U.S Bureau of the Census, *Current Population Reports*, P25-1129.

No. 61. Unmarried Couples, by Selected Characteristics: 1980 to 1996

[In thousands. As of March. An "unmarried couple" is two unrelated adults of the opposite sex sharing the same household. See headnote, table 66]

PRESENCE OF CHILDREN AND AGE OF HOUSEHOLDER	1980	1985	1990	1995	1996
Unmarried couples, total	**1,589**	**1,983**	**2,856**	**3,668**	**3,958**
No children under 15 years old	1,159	1,380	1,966	2,349	2,516
Some children under 15 years old	431	603	891	1,319	1,442
Under 25 years old	411	425	596	742	816
25 to 44 years old	837	1,203	1,775	2,188	2,315
45 to 64 years old	221	239	358	558	606
65 years old and over	119	116	127	180	221

Source: U.S. Bureau of the Census, *Current Population Reports*, P20-491 and earlier reports; and unpublished data.

No. 62. Married Couples of Same or Mixed Races and Origins: 1980 to 1996

[In thousands. As of March. Persons 15 years old and over. Persons of Hispanic origin may be of any race. Except as noted, based on Current Population Survey; see headnote, table 66]

RACE AND ORIGIN OF SPOUSES	1980	1990	1995	1996
Married couples, total	**49,714**	**53,256**	**54,937**	**54,664**
RACE				
Same race couples	48,264	50,889	51,733	51,616
White/White	44,910	47,202	48,030	48,056
Black/Black	3,354	3,687	3,703	3,560
Interracial couples	651	964	1,392	1,260
Black/White	167	211	328	337
Black husband/White wife	122	150	206	220
White husband/Black wife	45	61	122	117
White/other race [1]	450	720	988	884
Black/other race [1]	34	33	76	39
All other couples [1]	799	1,401	1,811	1,789
HISPANIC ORIGIN				
Hispanic/Hispanic	1,906	3,085	3,857	3,888
Hispanic/other origin (not Hispanic)	891	1,193	1,434	1,464
All other couples (not of Hispanic origin)	46,917	48,979	49,646	49,312

[1] Excluding White and Black.

Source: U.S. Bureau of the Census, *Current Population Reports*, P20-488, and earlier reports; and unpublished data.

No. 63. Householder and Marital Status of Population, 15 Years Old and Over: 1996

[In thousands. As of March. See headnote, table 66]

HOUSEHOLDER AND MARITAL STATUS	Total, 15 yrs. and over	MALE					FEMALE				
		Total [1]	20 to 24 years	25 to 44 years	45 to 64 years	65 yr. and over	Total [1]	20 to 24 years	25 to 44 years	45 to 64 years	65 yr. and over
Total persons	**204,625**	**98,593**	**8,792**	**41,663**	**26,416**	**13,260**	**106,031**	**8,861**	**42,333**	**27,252**	**18,396**
Householder	99,627	60,760	2,362	26,921	20,244	11,007	38,868	2,322	15,530	10,165	10,479
Never married	16,132	7,842	1,254	4,893	1,095	413	8,289	1,585	4,721	1,082	590
Married, spouse present	53,567	43,899	1,000	18,757	15,939	8,165	9,668	444	5,100	2,963	1,116
Married, spouse absent	4,825	1,754	61	863	596	234	3,071	165	1,703	897	307
Widowed	11,527	2,011	-	74	365	1,573	9,515	9	305	1,807	7,395
Divorced	13,577	5,253	47	2,335	2,248	621	8,324	128	3,704	3,418	1,071
Not householder	104,997	37,833	6,430	14,743	5,172	2,253	67,164	6,539	26,803	17,087	7,919
Never married	40,087	22,849	5,872	7,075	653	113	17,239	4,485	3,643	456	164
Married, spouse present	55,767	10,768	406	5,372	3,420	1,537	44,999	1,748	21,337	15,373	6,310
Married, spouse absent	2,403	1,236	94	768	248	81	1,167	182	596	252	67
Widowed	2,029	466	-	36	58	370	1,562	1	58	282	1,212
Divorced	4,711	2,514	59	1,493	792	153	2,197	123	1,169	723	166

- Represents or rounds to zero. [1] Includes 15 to 19 year olds.

Source: U.S. Bureau of the Census, unpublished data.

No. 64. Living Arrangements of Persons 15 Years Old and Over, by Selected Characteristics: 1995

[In thousands. As of March. Based on Current Population Survey which includes members of Armed Forces living off post or with families on post, but excludes other Armed Forces; see text, section 1, and Appendix III]

LIVING ARRANGEMENT	Total	15 to 19 years old	20 to 24 years old	25 to 34 years old	35 to 44 years old	45 to 54 years old	55 to 64 years old	65 to 74 years old	75 years old and over
Total [1]	204,825	16,648	17,653	40,919	43,077	31,584	21,084	18,270	13,388
Alone	24,900	80	992	3,736	3,803	3,506	2,941	4,377	5,464
With spouse	109,335	349	3,598	21,888	28,678	22,423	15,272	11,600	5,526
With other persons	70,390	16,219	13,063	15,295	10,596	5,655	2,871	2,293	2,398
White	171,597	14,769	14,094	33,487	35,794	26,820	18,196	16,306	12,129
Alone	21,194	67	821	2,991	3,149	2,877	2,434	3,844	5,011
With spouse	97,338	317	3,221	19,371	25,065	19,795	13,664	10,754	5,152
With other persons	53,065	14,385	10,052	11,125	7,580	4,148	2,098	1,708	1,966
Black	24,214	2,959	2,540	5,354	5,303	3,457	2,125	1,482	997
Alone	3,055	11	131	536	525	568	431	449	405
With spouse	7,496	24	240	1,510	2,200	1,619	1,061	585	257
With other persons	13,663	2,924	2,169	3,308	2,578	1,270	633	448	335
Hispanic origin [2]	19,580	2,433	2,606	5,355	4,065	2,171	1,492	983	475
Alone	1,280	10	69	205	236	191	181	222	146
With spouse	9,240	92	768	2,862	2,501	1,385	939	543	151
With other persons	9,060	2,331	1,769	2,288	1,328	595	372	218	178

[1] Includes other races and persons not of Hispanic origin, not shown separately. [2] Persons of Hispanic origin may be of any race.

Source: U.S. Bureau of the Census, unpublished data.

No. 65. Living Arrangements of Young Adults: 1980 to 1995

[1980 as of April. Beginning 1985, as of March and based on Current Population Survey, see headnote, table 64]

LIVING ARRANGEMENTS AND SEX	PERSONS 18 TO 24 YEARS OLD				PERSONS 25 TO 34 YEARS OLD			
	1980	1985	1990	1995	1980	1985	1990	1995
Total (1,000)	29,122	27,844	25,310	25,158	36,796	40,857	43,240	41,389
Percent distribution:								
Child of householder [1]	48	54	53	53	9	11	12	12
Family householder or spouse	29	24	22	21	72	68	65	63
Nonfamily householder	10	8	9	9	12	13	13	13
Other	13	14	16	17	7	9	11	13
Male (1,000)	14,278	13,695	12,450	12,545	18,107	20,184	21,462	20,589
Percent distribution:								
Child of householder [1]	54	60	58	58	11	13	15	15
Family householder or spouse	21	16	15	13	66	60	56	53
Nonfamily householder	11	10	10	10	15	16	16	16
Other	13	14	17	18	8	11	13	15
Female (1,000)	14,844	14,149	12,860	12,613	18,689	20,673	21,779	20,800
Percent distribution:								
Child of householder [1]	43	48	48	47	7	8	8	8
Family householder or spouse	36	32	30	28	78	76	73	72
Nonfamily householder	8	7	8	9	9	10	10	10
Other	13	13	15	16	6	7	9	10

[1] Includes unmarried college students living in dormitories.

Source: U.S. Bureau of the Census, *1980 Census of Population*, PC(2)-4B and *Current Population Reports*, P20-491 and prior reports.

No. 66. Households, Families, Subfamilies, Married Couples, and Unrelated Individuals: 1970 to 1996

[In thousands, except as indicated. As of March. Based on Current Population Survey; includes members of Armed Forces living off post or with their families on post, but excludes all other members of Armed Forces; see text, section 1, and Appendix III. For definition of terms, see text, section 1. Minus sign (-) indicates decrease]

TYPE OF UNIT	1970	1975	1980	1985	1990	1994	1995	1996	PERCENT CHANGE		
									1970-80	1980-90	1990-96
Households	**63,401**	**71,120**	**80,776**	**86,789**	**93,347**	**97,107**	**98,990**	**99,627**	27	16	7
Average size	3.14	2.94	2.76	2.69	2.63	2.67	2.65	2.65	(X)	(X)	(X)
Family households	51,456	55,563	59,550	62,706	66,090	68,490	69,305	69,594	16	11	5
Married couple	44,728	46,951	49,112	50,350	52,317	53,171	53,858	53,567	10	7	2
Male householder [1]	1,228	1,485	1,733	2,228	2,884	2,913	3,226	3,513	41	66	22
Female householder [1]	5,500	7,127	8,705	10,129	10,890	12,406	12,220	12,514	58	25	15
Nonfamily households	11,945	15,557	21,226	24,082	27,257	28,617	29,686	30,033	78	28	10
Male householder	4,063	5,912	8,807	10,114	11,606	12,462	13,190	13,348	117	32	15
Female householder	7,882	9,645	12,419	13,968	15,651	16,155	16,496	16,685	58	26	7
One person	10,851	13,939	18,296	20,602	22,999	23,611	24,732	24,900	69	26	8
Families	**51,586**	**55,712**	**59,550**	**62,796**	**66,090**	**68,490**	**69,305**	**69,594**	15	11	5
Average size	3.58	3.42	3.29	3.23	3.17	3.20	3.19	3.20	(X)	(X)	(X)
Married couple	44,755	46,971	49,112	50,350	52,317	53,171	53,858	53,567	10	7	2
Male householder [1]	1,239	1,499	1,733	2,228	2,884	2,913	3,226	3,513	40	66	22
Female householder [1]	5,591	7,242	8,705	10,129	10,890	12,406	12,220	12,514	56	25	15
Unrelated subfamilies	130	149	360	526	534	716	674	588	177	48	10
Married couple	27	20	20	46	68	66	64	51	(B)	(B)	(B)
Male reference persons [1]	11	14	36	85	45	78	59	45	(B)	(B)	(B)
Female reference persons [1]	91	115	304	395	421	571	550	493	234	39	17
Related subfamilies	1,150	1,349	1,150	2,228	2,403	2,813	2,878	2,942	-	109	22
Married couple	617	576	582	719	871	1,014	1,015	1,046	-6	50	20
Father-child [1]	48	69	54	116	153	164	195	189	(B)	(B)	24
Mother-child [1]	484	705	512	1,392	1,378	1,636	1,668	1,706	6	169	24
Married couples	**45,373**	**47,547**	**49,714**	**51,114**	**53,256**	**54,251**	**54,937**	**54,664**	10	7	3
With own household	44,728	46,951	49,112	50,350	52,317	53,171	53,858	53,567	10	7	2
Without own household	645	596	602	764	939	1,080	1,079	1,097	-7	56	17
Percent without	1.4	1.3	1.2	1.5	1.8	2.0	2.0	2.0	(X)	(X)	(X)
Unrelated individuals	**14,988**	**19,100**	**26,426**	**30,518**	**35,384**	**38,469**	**39,048**	**40,077**	76	34	13
Nonfamily householders	11,945	15,557	21,226	24,082	27,257	28,617	29,686	30,033	78	28	10
Secondary individuals	3,043	3,543	5,200	6,436	8,127	9,852	9,362	10,044	71	56	24
Male	1,631	2,087	3,006	3,743	4,711	5,892	5,442	5,739	84	57	22
Female	1,412	1,456	2,194	2,693	3,416	3,961	3,920	4,305	55	56	26

- Represents or rounds to zero. B Not shown; base less than 75,000. X Not applicable. [1] No spouse present.

Source: U.S. Bureau of the Census, *Current Population Reports*, P20-488 and unpublished data.

No. 67. Households—Projections, by Type of Household: 1997 to 2010

[In thousands. These numbers are based on the 1990 census, as enumerated, with modifications for age and race, and household estimates from 1991 to 1994, and are projected forward using alternative marital status and household-type proportions. Series 2 reflects the consequences of projected changes in the age/sex structure of the population only assuming no change from the composition in 1990 of the proportion maintaining households for specific types by age and sex. For details of assumptions for series 1 and 3, see tables 71 and 72]

TYPE OF HOUSEHOLD	1997	1998	1999	2000	2005	2010
TOTAL HOUSEHOLDS						
Series 1	99,965	101,043	102,119	103,246	108,819	114,825
Series 2	99,880	100,924	101,966	103,058	108,426	114,200
Series 3	99,680	100,684	101,683	102,734	107,892	113,426
TYPE OF HOUSEHOLD (Series 1)						
Total	99,965	101,043	102,119	103,246	108,819	114,825
Family households	69,761	70,387	71,015	71,669	74,733	77,895
Married couple	54,319	54,707	55,092	55,496	57,371	59,306
Female householder, no spouse present	11,774	11,935	12,101	12,272	13,084	13,927
Male householder, no spouse present	3,668	3,745	3,822	3,901	4,278	4,660
With children under 18	32,951	33,001	33,058	33,117	32,699	32,203
Married couple	24,770	24,740	24,713	24,686	23,958	23,126
Female householder, no spouse present	6,571	6,624	6,679	6,737	6,944	7,189
Male householder, no spouse present	1,610	1,638	1,666	1,694	1,797	1,888
Without children under 18	36,810	37,386	37,957	38,552	42,034	45,692
Married couple	29,549	29,968	30,378	30,810	33,413	36,182
Female householder, no spouse present	5,202	5,311	5,422	5,535	6,140	6,738
Male householder, no spouse present	2,058	2,107	2,157	2,208	2,481	2,772
Nonfamily households	30,204	30,656	31,104	31,577	34,086	36,931
Female householder, total	16,464	16,671	16,875	17,095	18,301	19,702
Living alone [1]	14,480	14,684	14,844	15,035	16,093	17,327
Male householder, total	13,741	13,985	14,228	14,482	15,784	17,229
Living alone [1]	10,587	10,789	10,969	11,195	12,244	13,400

[1] These counts cover individuals 15 years of age or older.

Source: U.S. Bureau of the Census, *Current Population Reports*, P25-1129.

No. 68. Households, 1980 to 1996, and Persons in Households, 1996, by Type of Household and Presence of Children

[As of March. Based on Current Population Survey; see headnote, table 66]

TYPE OF HOUSEHOLD AND PRESENCE OF CHILDREN	HOUSEHOLDS: Number (1,000) 1980	HOUSEHOLDS: Number (1,000) 1990	HOUSEHOLDS: Number (1,000) 1996	HOUSEHOLDS: Percent distribution 1990	HOUSEHOLDS: Percent distribution 1996	PERSONS IN HOUSEHOLDS, 1996: Number (1,000)	PERSONS IN HOUSEHOLDS, 1996: Percent distribution	Persons per household, 1996
Total households	80,776	93,347	99,627	100	100	264,234	100	2.65
Family households	59,550	66,090	69,594	71	70	226,811	86	3.26
With own children under 18	31,022	32,289	34,203	35	34	136,001	51	3.98
Without own children under 18	28,528	33,801	35,391	36	36	90,810	34	2.57
Married couple family	49,112	52,317	53,567	56	54	174,985	66	3.27
With own children under 18	24,961	24,537	24,920	26	25	104,667	40	4.20
Without own children under 18	24,151	27,780	28,647	30	29	70,318	26	2.44
Male householder, no spouse present	1,733	2,884	3,513	3	4	11,168	4	3.18
With own children under 18	616	1,153	1,628	1	2	5,522	2	3.39
Without own children under 18	1,117	1,731	1,885	2	2	5,646	2	3.00
Female householder, no spouse present	8,705	10,890	12,514	12	13	40,658	15	3.25
With own children under 18	5,445	6,599	7,656	7	8	25,812	10	3.37
Without own children under 18	3,261	4,290	4,859	5	5	14,846	6	3.06
Nonfamily households	21,226	27,257	30,033	29	30	37,424	14	1.25
Living alone	18,296	22,999	24,900	25	25	24,900	9	1.00
Male householder	8,807	11,606	13,348	12	13	18,072	7	1.35
Living alone	6,966	9,049	10,288	10	10	10,288	4	1.00
Female householder	12,419	15,651	16,685	17	17	19,352	7	1.16
Living alone	11,330	13,950	14,612	15	15	14,612	6	1.00

Source: U.S. Bureau of the Census, *Current Population Reports*, P20-488, and earlier reports; and unpublished data.

No. 69. Household Characteristics, by Type of Household: 1995

[As of March. Based on Current Population Survey; see headnote, table 66. For composition of regions, see table 26]

CHARACTERISTIC	NUMBER OF HOUSEHOLDS (1,000): Total	Family households: Total [1]	Family households: Married couple	Family households: Female householder [2]	Nonfamily households	PERCENT DISTRIBUTION: Total	Family households: Total [1]	Family households: Married couple	Family households: Female householder [2]	Nonfamily households
Total	98,990	69,305	53,858	12,220	29,686	100	100	100	100	100
Age of householder:										
15 to 24 years old	5,444	3,079	1,632	1,124	2,365	5	4	3	9	8
25 to 29 years old	8,400	5,575	3,959	1,234	2,825	8	8	7	10	10
30 to 34 years old	11,052	8,502	6,357	1,731	2,551	11	12	12	14	9
35 to 44 years old	22,914	18,273	13,919	3,502	4,641	23	26	26	29	16
45 to 54 years old	17,590	13,746	11,163	2,037	3,845	18	20	21	17	13
55 to 64 years old	12,224	8,894	7,552	1,056	3,330	12	13	14	9	11
65 to 74 years old	11,803	7,268	6,169	853	4,535	12	10	11	7	15
75 years old and over	9,562	3,969	3,117	683	5,593	10	6	6	6	19
Region:										
Northeast	19,593	13,482	10,336	2,515	6,111	20	19	19	21	21
Midwest	23,683	16,264	12,836	2,754	7,418	24	23	24	23	25
South	34,766	24,871	19,201	4,590	9,895	35	36	36	38	33
West	20,948	14,687	11,485	2,363	6,261	21	21	21	19	21
Size of household:										
One person	24,732	(X)	(X)	(X)	24,732	25	(X)	(X)	(X)	83
Two persons	31,834	27,875	21,366	5,065	3,959	32	40	40	41	13
Three persons	16,827	16,212	11,485	3,809	614	17	23	21	31	2
Four persons	15,321	15,056	12,741	1,837	265	15	22	24	15	1
Five persons	6,616	6,530	5,433	904	86	7	9	10	7	(Z)
Six persons	2,279	2,260	1,823	337	19	2	3	3	3	(Z)
Seven persons or more	1,382	1,372	1,010	269	10	1	2	2	2	(Z)
Marital status of householder:										
Never married (single)	15,802	4,421	(X)	3,240	11,381	16	6	(X)	27	38
Married, spouse present	53,858	53,858	53,858	(X)	(X)	54	78	100	(X)	(X)
Married, spouse absent	4,708	2,645	(X)	2,160	2,063	5	4	(X)	18	7
Widowed	11,450	2,715	(X)	2,283	8,734	12	4	(X)	19	29
Divorced	13,174	5,666	(X)	4,537	7,508	13	8	(X)	37	25
Tenure:										
Owner occupied	64,045	49,970	42,780	5,440	14,075	65	72	79	45	47
Renter occupied	34,946	19,335	11,078	6,781	15,611	35	28	21	55	53

X Not applicable. Z Less than 0.5 percent. [1] Includes male householder, no spouse present. [2] No spouse present.

Source: U.S. Bureau of the Census, unpublished data.

No. 70. Households, by Age of Householder and Size of Household: 1980 to 1996

[In millions. As of March. Based on Current Population Survey; see headnote, table 66]

AGE OF HOUSEHOLDER AND SIZE OF HOUSEHOLD	1980	1985	1990	1994	1995	1996			
						Total [1]	White	Black	Hispanic [2]
Total	80.8	86.8	93.3	97.1	99.0	99.6	84.5	11.6	7.9
Age of householder:									
15 to 24 years old	6.6	5.4	5.1	5.3	5.4	5.3	4.3	0.8	0.7
25 to 29 years old	9.3	9.6	9.4	8.5	8.4	8.4	6.8	1.2	1.0
30 to 34 years old	9.3	10.4	11.0	11.2	11.1	10.9	9.0	1.5	1.2
35 to 44 years old	14.0	17.5	20.6	22.3	22.9	23.2	19.4	2.9	2.1
45 to 54 years old	12.7	12.6	14.5	16.8	17.6	18.0	15.2	2.1	1.2
55 to 64 years old	12.5	13.1	12.5	12.2	12.2	12.4	10.6	1.4	0.8
65 to 74 years old	10.1	10.9	11.7	11.6	11.8	11.9	10.6	1.1	0.6
75 years old and over	6.4	7.3	8.4	9.2	9.6	9.6	8.7	0.7	0.3
One person	18.3	20.6	23.0	23.6	24.7	24.9	21.2	3.1	1.3
Male	7.0	7.9	9.0	9.4	10.1	10.3	8.7	1.2	0.6
Female	11.3	12.7	14.0	14.2	14.6	14.6	12.5	1.8	0.7
Two persons	25.3	27.4	30.1	31.2	31.8	32.5	28.6	3.0	1.8
Three persons	14.1	15.5	16.1	16.9	16.8	16.7	13.9	2.2	1.5
Four persons	12.7	13.6	14.5	15.1	15.3	15.1	12.7	1.7	1.5
Five persons	6.1	8.1	6.2	6.7	6.6	6.6	5.4	0.9	1.0
Six persons	2.5	2.3	2.1	2.2	2.3	2.4	1.9	0.4	0.5
Seven persons or more	1.8	1.3	1.3	1.4	1.4	1.4	1.0	0.3	0.4

[1] Includes other races, not shown separately. [2] Hispanic persons may be of any race.

Source: U.S. Bureau of the Census, *Current Population Reports*, P20-488, and earlier reports; and unpublished data.

No. 71. Households—Projections, by Age of Householder: 1997 to 2010

[In thousands. These numbers are based on the 1990 census, as enumerated, with modifications for age and race, and household estimates from 1991 to 1994, and are projected forward using alternative marital status and household-type proportions. Series 1, shown here, is based on a time series model and is the preferred projection. For series 1, assumptions about future changes in family and household situation extend trends of the past 30 years]

AGE OF HOUSEHOLDER	1997	1998	1999	2000	2005	2010
Households, total	99,985	101,043	102,119	103,246	108,819	114,825
Under 25 years old	4,700	4,758	4,854	4,966	5,399	5,724
25 to 34 years old	18,159	17,746	17,336	17,045	16,547	17,426
35 to 44 years old	23,517	23,767	23,916	23,914	22,560	20,581
45 to 54 years old	19,179	19,727	20,434	21,210	23,924	25,283
55 to 64 years old	12,735	13,237	13,658	14,002	17,331	20,693
65 to 74 years old	11,682	11,588	11,475	11,446	11,597	13,298
75 years and over	9,993	10,221	10,447	10,663	11,462	11,821

Source: U.S. Bureau of the Census, *Current Population Reports*, P25-1129.

No. 72. Households—Projections, by Race and Hispanic Origin of Householder: 1997 to 2010

[In thousands. These numbers are based on the 1990 census, as enumerated, with modifications for age and race, and household estimates from 1991 to 1994, and are projected forward using alternative marital status and household-type proportions. Race and Hispanic origin of householders were not tabulated for either series 1 or series 2. Series 3, shown here, reflects the consequences of projected change in both the age/sex structure and race/origin composition of the population. Current patterns of family and householdership are assumed to remain at their 1990 proportions]

CHARACTERISTIC OF HOUSEHOLDER	1997	1998	1999	2000	2005	2010
Households, total	99,680	100,684	101,683	102,734	107,892	113,426
White	84,586	85,271	85,952	86,676	90,204	94,010
Black	11,556	11,753	11,948	12,149	13,137	14,185
American Indian, Eskimo, Aleut	713	727	740	754	827	906
Asian, Pacific Islander	2,824	2,933	3,043	3,155	3,724	4,324
Hispanic origin [1]	7,917	8,195	8,474	8,761	10,236	11,866

[1] Persons of Hispanic origin may be of any race.

Source: U.S. Bureau of the Census, *Current Population Reports*, P25-1129.

No. 73. Households—States: 1980 to 1996

[As of April 1, except beginning 1993, as of July 1. Minus sign (-) indicates decrease]

REGION, DIVISION, AND STATE	NUMBER (1,000)							PERCENT CHANGE		PERSONS PER HOUSEHOLD		
	1980	1990	1993	1994	1995	1996		1980-90	1990-96	1980	1990	1996
						Total	Householder 65 yrs. and over					
U.S.	**80,390**	**91,946**	**95,358**	**95,968**	**97,386**	**98,751**	**21,381**	**14.4**	**7.4**	**2.76**	**2.63**	**2.62**
Northeast	**17,471**	**18,873**	**19,080**	**19,058**	**19,180**	**19,296**	**4,567**	**8.0**	**2.3**	**2.74**	**2.61**	**2.64**
N.E.	**4,362**	**4,943**	**4,980**	**4,962**	**5,030**	**5,078**	**1,158**	**13.3**	**2.7**	**2.74**	**2.58**	**2.61**
ME	395	465	474	473	477	483	109	17.7	3.8	2.75	2.56	2.54
NH	323	411	419	423	431	439	85	27.1	6.7	2.75	2.62	2.62
VT	178	211	218	220	223	227	45	18.1	7.5	2.75	2.57	2.57
MA	2,033	2,247	2,264	2,269	2,297	2,322	536	10.5	3.3	2.72	2.58	2.61
RI	339	378	378	376	376	378	96	11.6	-0.1	2.70	2.55	2.56
CT	1,094	1,230	1,227	1,222	1,225	1,231	287	12.5	-	2.76	2.59	2.65
M.A.	**13,109**	**13,930**	**14,100**	**14,077**	**14,150**	**14,219**	**3,409**	**6.3**	**2.1**	**2.74**	**2.62**	**2.66**
NY	6,340	6,639	6,702	6,684	6,709	6,737	1,524	4.7	1.5	2.70	2.63	2.65
NJ	2,549	2,795	2,839	2,841	2,866	2,889	674	9.7	3.4	2.84	2.70	2.75
PA	4,220	4,496	4,559	4,552	4,575	4,594	1,211	6.6	2.2	2.74	2.57	2.58
Midwest	**20,859**	**22,317**	**22,876**	**22,928**	**23,156**	**23,390**	**5,184**	**7.0**	**4.8**	**2.75**	**2.60**	**2.59**
E.N.C	**14,654**	**15,597**	**16,006**	**16,029**	**16,178**	**16,339**	**3,567**	**6.4**	**4.8**	**2.78**	**2.63**	**2.61**
OH	3,834	4,088	4,187	4,187	4,223	4,260	956	6.6	4.2	2.76	2.59	2.54
IN	1,927	2,065	2,149	2,156	2,182	2,209	472	7.2	6.9	2.77	2.61	2.57
IL	4,045	4,202	4,294	4,295	4,322	4,352	942	3.9	3.6	2.76	2.65	2.65
MI	3,195	3,419	3,494	3,500	3,534	3,576	765	7.0	4.6	2.84	2.66	2.66
WI	1,652	1,822	1,883	1,891	1,917	1,943	432	10.3	6.6	2.77	2.61	2.61
W.N.C	**6,206**	**6,720**	**6,870**	**6,899**	**6,978**	**7,051**	**1,617**	**8.3**	**4.9**	**2.68**	**2.55**	**2.54**
MN	1,445	1,648	1,702	1,716	1,740	1,763	366	14.0	7.0	2.74	2.58	2.58
IA	1,053	1,064	1,064	1,084	1,093	1,103	275	1.1	3.6	2.68	2.52	2.51
MO	1,793	1,961	2,001	2,009	2,031	2,052	478	9.4	4.6	2.67	2.53	2.51
ND	228	241	242	242	244	247	60	5.8	2.4	2.75	2.55	2.51
SD	243	259	265	267	270	273	68	6.8	5.4	2.74	2.59	2.56
NE	571	602	615	616	624	631	147	5.4	4.8	2.66	2.54	2.54
KS	872	945	962	965	975	982	224	8.3	3.9	2.62	2.53	2.54
South	**26,486**	**31,821**	**33,363**	**33,733**	**34,351**	**34,949**	**7,535**	**20.1**	**9.8**	**2.77**	**2.61**	**2.58**
S.A.	**13,160**	**16,502**	**17,325**	**17,525**	**17,837**	**18,146**	**4,102**	**25.4**	**10.0**	**2.73**	**2.56**	**2.56**
DE	207	247	262	264	270	276	58	19.5	11.4	2.79	2.61	2.62
MD	1,461	1,749	1,816	1,830	1,853	1,871	356	19.7	7.0	2.82	2.67	2.70
DC	253	250	243	238	233	231	50	-1.4	-7.3	2.40	2.26	2.24
VA	1,863	2,292	2,414	2,439	2,476	2,511	469	23.0	9.6	2.77	2.61	2.61
WV	686	689	705	705	709	714	187	0.3	3.7	2.79	2.55	2.50
NC	2,043	2,517	2,646	2,680	2,738	2,796	589	23.2	11.1	2.78	2.54	2.53
SC	1,030	1,258	1,328	1,331	1,352	1,376	289	22.1	9.4	2.93	2.68	2.64
GA	1,872	2,366	2,533	2,567	2,654	2,723	465	26.4	15.1	2.84	2.66	2.65
FL	3,744	5,135	5,379	5,451	5,551	5,648	1,640	37.1	10.0	2.55	2.46	2.45
E.S.C	**5,051**	**5,652**	**5,866**	**5,933**	**6,026**	**6,122**	**1,342**	**11.9**	**8.3**	**2.83**	**2.62**	**2.56**
KY	1,263	1,380	1,430	1,437	1,457	1,478	322	9.2	7.1	2.82	2.60	2.55
TN	1,619	1,854	1,941	1,965	2,002	2,041	431	14.5	10.1	2.77	2.56	2.52
AL	1,342	1,507	1,574	1,582	1,603	1,624	367	12.3	7.8	2.84	2.62	2.56
MS	827	911	941	948	964	979	222	10.2	7.4	2.97	2.75	2.66
W.S.C	**8,276**	**9,667**	**10,152**	**10,276**	**10,466**	**10,681**	**2,091**	**16.8**	**10.5**	**2.80**	**2.69**	**2.65**
AR	816	891	919	925	938	951	236	9.2	6.7	2.74	2.57	2.51
LA	1,412	1,499	1,539	1,543	1,559	1,572	324	6.2	4.8	2.91	2.74	2.67
OK	1,119	1,206	1,235	1,238	1,250	1,265	291	7.8	4.9	2.62	2.53	2.50
TX	4,929	6,071	6,458	6,570	6,741	6,894	1,240	23.2	13.6	2.82	2.73	2.69
West	**15,574**	**18,935**	**20,036**	**20,269**	**20,699**	**21,113**	**4,096**	**21.6**	**11.5**	**2.71**	**2.72**	**2.70**
Mountain	**3,986**	**5,033**	**5,444**	**5,607**	**5,844**	**6,022**	**1,157**	**26.3**	**19.8**	**2.79**	**2.65**	**2.61**
MT	284	306	321	326	335	341	75	7.9	11.3	2.70	2.53	2.50
ID	324	361	395	405	419	430	86	11.3	19.1	2.85	2.73	2.68
WY	166	169	176	178	181	184	35	1.9	8.8	2.78	2.63	2.55
CO	1,061	1,282	1,388	1,424	1,466	1,502	246	20.8	17.1	2.65	2.51	2.47
NM	441	543	578	592	607	619	122	22.9	14.1	2.90	2.74	2.64
AZ	957	1,369	1,466	1,518	1,624	1,687	366	43.0	23.3	2.79	2.62	2.59
UT	449	537	586	600	621	639	112	19.8	19.0	3.20	3.15	3.06
NV	304	466	535	562	591	619	115	53.2	32.8	2.59	2.53	2.53
Pacific	**11,587**	**13,902**	**14,593**	**14,662**	**14,855**	**15,092**	**2,939**	**20.0**	**8.6**	**2.68**	**2.74**	**2.73**
WA	1,541	1,872	2,019	2,049	2,097	2,139	406	21.5	14.2	2.61	2.53	2.53
OR	992	1,103	1,160	1,197	1,223	1,249	273	11.3	13.2	2.60	2.52	2.51
CA	8,630	10,381	10,812	10,829	10,941	11,101	2,153	20.3	6.9	2.68	2.79	2.79
AK	131	189	206	207	210	214	20	43.7	13.4	2.93	2.80	2.76
HI	294	356	376	380	384	389	87	21.2	9.0	3.15	3.01	2.97

- Represents or rounds to zero.

Source: U.S. Bureau of the Census, *1980 Census of Population*, vol. 1, chapter B; *1990 Census of Population, General Population Characteristics, United States* (1990 CP-1-1); and unpublished data.

No. 74. Family and Nonfamily Households, by Race, Hispanic Origin, and Type: 1980 to 1996

[As of March, except as noted. Based on Current Population Survey, except as noted; see headnote, table 66]

RACE, HISPANIC ORIGIN, AND TYPE	NUMBER (1,000)					PERCENT DISTRIBUTION				
	1980	1985	1990	1995	1996	1980	1985	1990	1995	1996
TOTAL HOUSEHOLDS										
Total [1]	**80,776**	**86,789**	**93,347**	**98,990**	**99,627**	100	100	100	100	100
White	70,766	75,328	80,163	83,737	84,511	88	87	86	85	85
Black	8,586	9,480	10,486	11,655	11,577	11	11	11	12	12
Hispanic [2]	3,684	4,883	5,933	7,735	7,939	5	6	6	8	8
FAMILY HOUSEHOLDS										
White, total	**52,243**	**54,400**	**56,590**	**58,437**	**58,869**	100	100	100	100	100
Married couple	44,751	45,643	46,981	47,899	47,873	86	84	83	82	81
Male householder [3]	1,441	1,816	2,303	2,507	2,712	3	3	4	4	5
Female householder [3]	6,052	6,941	7,306	8,031	8,284	12	13	13	14	14
Black, total	**6,184**	**6,778**	**7,470**	**8,093**	**8,055**	100	100	100	100	100
Married couple	3,433	3,469	3,750	3,842	3,713	56	51	50	47	46
Male householder [3]	256	344	446	536	573	4	5	6	7	7
Female householder [3]	2,495	2,964	3,275	3,716	3,769	40	44	44	46	47
Asian or Pacific Islander, total [4]	**818**	(NA)	**1,531**	**1,588**	**2,125**	100	(NA)	100	100	100
Married couple	691	(NA)	1,256	1,290	1,692	84	(NA)	82	81	80
Male householder [3]	39	(NA)	86	98	173	5	(NA)	6	6	8
Female householder [3]	88	(NA)	188	200	260	11	(NA)	12	13	12
Hispanic, total [2]	**3,029**	**3,939**	**4,840**	**6,200**	**6,287**	100	100	100	100	100
Married couple	2,282	2,824	3,395	4,235	4,247	75	72	70	68	68
Male householder [3]	138	210	329	479	436	5	5	7	8	7
Female householder [3]	610	905	1,116	1,485	1,604	20	23	23	24	26
NONFAMILY HOUSEHOLDS										
White, total	**18,522**	**20,928**	**23,573**	**25,300**	**25,642**	100	100	100	100	100
Male householder	7,499	8,608	9,951	11,093	11,367	40	41	42	44	44
Female householder	11,023	12,320	13,622	14,207	14,275	60	59	58	56	56
Black, total	**2,402**	**2,703**	**3,015**	**3,582**	**3,521**	100	100	100	100	100
Male householder	1,146	1,244	1,313	1,653	1,532	48	46	44	46	44
Female householder	1,256	1,459	1,702	1,909	1,989	52	54	56	54	56
Hispanic, total [2]	**654**	**944**	**1,093**	**1,535**	**1,652**	100	100	100	100	100
Male householder	365	509	587	790	865	56	54	54	51	52
Female householder	289	435	506	745	787	44	46	46	49	48

NA Not available. [1] Includes other races not shown separately. [2] Hispanic persons may be of any race. [3] No spouse present. [4] 1980 data as of April and are from 1980 Census of Population. When comparing 1995 estimates of number of households with other years, caution should be used.

Source: U.S. Bureau of the Census, *Current Population Reports*, P20-488, and earlier reports; and unpublished data.

No. 75. Family Groups with Children Under 18 Years Old, by Race and Hispanic Origin: 1980 to 1996

[As of March. Family groups comprise family households, related subfamilies, and unrelated subfamilies. Excludes members of Armed Forces except those living off post or with their families on post. Based on Current Population Survey; see text, section 1, and Appendix III]

RACE AND HISPANIC ORIGIN OF HOUSEHOLDER OR REFERENCE PERSON	NUMBER (1,000)				PERCENT DISTRIBUTION			
	1980	1990	1995	1996	1980	1990	1995	1996
All races, total [1]	**32,150**	**34,670**	**37,168**	**37,077**	100	100	100	100
Two-parent family groups	25,231	24,921	25,640	25,361	79	72	69	68
One-parent family groups	6,920	9,749	11,528	11,717	22	28	31	32
Maintained by mother	6,230	8,398	9,834	9,855	19	24	26	27
Maintained by father	690	1,351	1,694	1,862	2	4	5	5
White, total	**27,294**	**28,294**	**29,846**	**29,947**	100	100	100	100
Two-parent family groups	22,628	21,905	22,320	22,178	83	77	75	74
One-parent family groups	4,664	6,389	7,525	7,769	17	23	25	26
Maintained by mother	4,122	5,310	6,239	6,329	15	19	21	21
Maintained by father	542	1,079	1,286	1,440	2	4	4	5
Black, total	**4,074**	**5,087**	**5,491**	**5,434**	100	100	100	100
Two-parent family groups	1,961	2,006	1,962	1,942	48	39	36	36
One-parent family groups	2,114	3,081	3,529	3,493	52	61	64	64
Maintained by mother	1,984	2,860	3,197	3,171	49	56	58	58
Maintained by father	129	221	332	322	3	4	6	6
Hispanic, total [2]	**2,194**	**3,429**	**4,527**	**4,560**	100	100	100	100
Two-parent family groups	1,626	2,289	2,879	2,858	74	67	64	63
One-parent family groups	568	1,140	1,647	1,702	26	33	36	37
Maintained by mother	526	1,003	1,404	1,483	24	29	31	33
Maintained by father	42	138	243	219	2	4	5	5

[1] Includes other races, not shown separately. [2] Hispanic persons may be of any race.

Source: U.S. Bureau of the Census, *Current Population Reports*, P20-488, and earlier reports; and unpublished data.

No. 76. Family Groups With Children Under 18 Years Old, by Type, Race and Hispanic Origin: 1995

[As of March. Excludes members of Armed Forces except those living off post or with their families on post. Based on Current Population Survey; see text, section 1, and Appendix III]

RACE AND HISPANIC ORIGIN OF HOUSEHOLDER OR REFERENCE PERSON	NUMBER (1,000)					PERCENT DISTRIBUTION				
	Total	Family households	Subfamilies			Total	Family households	Subfamilies		
			Total	Related	Unrelated			Total	Related	Unrelated
All races, total [1]	37,168	34,296	2,872	2,241	631	100	100	100	100	100
Two-parent family groups	25,640	25,241	399	377	22	69	74	14	17	3
One-parent family groups	11,528	9,055	2,473	1,863	609	31	26	86	83	97
Maintained by mother	9,834	7,615	2,219	1,668	550	26	22	77	74	87
Maintained by father	1,694	1,440	254	195	59	5	4	9	9	9
White, total	29,846	27,951	1,895	1,371	524	100	100	100	100	100
Two-parent family groups	22,320	22,005	315	295	20	75	79	17	22	4
One-parent family groups	7,525	5,946	1,579	1,075	504	25	21	83	78	96
Maintained by mother	6,239	4,841	1,398	940	458	21	17	74	69	87
Maintained by father	1,286	1,105	181	135	46	4	4	10	10	9
Black, total	5,481	4,682	809	729	80	100	100	100	100	100
Two-parent family groups	1,952	1,926	36	34	2	36	41	4	5	3
One-parent family groups	3,529	2,756	773	694	79	64	59	96	95	99
Maintained by mother	3,197	2,489	708	642	66	58	53	88	88	83
Maintained by father	332	267	65	52	13	6	6	8	7	16
Hispanic, total [2]	4,527	3,984	543	448	95	100	100	100	100	100
Two-parent family groups	2,879	2,743	136	123	13	64	69	25	27	14
One-parent family groups	1,647	1,240	407	325	82	36	31	75	73	86
Maintained by mother	1,404	1,048	356	277	79	31	26	66	62	83
Maintained by father	243	192	51	48	3	5	5	9	11	3

[1] Includes other races, not shown separately. [2] Hispanic persons may be of any race.

Source: U.S. Bureau of the Census, unpublished data.

No. 77. Families, by Size and Presence of Children: 1980 to 1996

[In thousands, except as indicated. As of March. Excludes members of Armed Forces except those living off post or with their families on post. Based on Current Population Survey; see text, section 1, and Appendix III. For definition of families, see text, section 1]

CHARACTERISTIC	NUMBER					PERCENT DISTRIBUTION				
	1980	1985	1990	1995	1996	1980	1985	1990	1995	1996
Total	59,550	62,706	66,090	69,305	69,594	100	100	100	100	100
Size of family:										
Two persons	23,461	25,349	27,606	29,176	29,765	39	40	42	42	43
Three persons	13,603	14,804	15,353	15,903	15,771	23	24	23	23	23
Four persons	12,372	13,259	14,026	14,624	14,421	21	21	21	21	21
Five persons	5,930	5,894	5,938	6,283	6,234	10	9	9	9	9
Six persons	2,461	2,175	1,997	2,106	2,182	4	4	3	3	3
Seven or more persons	1,723	1,225	1,170	1,213	1,221	3	2	2	2	2
Average per family	3.29	3.23	3.17	3.19	3.20	(X)	(X)	(X)	(X)	(X)
Own children under age 18:										
None	28,528	31,594	33,801	35,009	35,391	48	50	51	51	51
One	12,443	13,108	13,530	14,066	14,041	21	21	20	20	20
Two	11,470	11,645	12,263	13,213	13,206	19	19	19	19	19
Three	4,674	4,486	4,650	5,044	4,913	8	7	7	7	7
Four or more	2,435	1,873	1,846	1,951	2,044	4	3	3	3	3
Own children under age 6:										
None	46,063	48,505	50,905	53,696	54,145	77	77	77	77	78
One	9,441	9,677	10,304	10,733	10,672	16	15	16	15	15
Two or more	4,047	4,525	4,882	4,876	4,778	7	7	7	7	7

X Not applicable.

Source. U.S. Bureau of the Census, *Current Population Reports*, P20-488, and earlier reports; and unpublished data.

No. 78. Families, by Number of Own Children Under 18 Years Old: 1980 to 1996

[As of March and based on Current Population Survey; see headnote, table 77]

CE, HISPANIC ORIGIN, AND YEAR	NUMBER OF FAMILIES (1,000)					PERCENT DISTRIBUTION				
	Total	No children	One child	Two children	Three or more children	Total	No children	One child	Two children	Three or more children
ALL FAMILIES [1]										
	59,550	28,528	12,443	11,470	7,109	100	48	21	19	12
	62,706	31,594	13,108	11,645	6,359	100	50	21	19	10
	66,090	33,801	13,530	12,263	6,496	100	51	20	19	10
	69,305	35,009	14,088	13,213	6,995	100	51	20	19	10
	69,594	35,391	14,041	13,206	6,957	100	51	20	19	10
ied couple	53,567	28,647	9,352	10,278	5,290	100	53	17	19	10
householder [2]	3,513	1,885	1,005	471	152	100	54	29	13	4
ale householder [2]	12,514	4,859	3,683	2,457	1,514	100	39	29	20	12
WHITE FAMILIES										
	52,243	25,769	10,727	9,977	5,769	100	49	21	19	11
	54,400	28,169	11,174	9,937	5,120	100	52	21	18	9
	56,590	29,872	11,186	10,342	5,191	100	53	20	18	9
	58,437	30,486	11,491	10,983	5,478	100	52	20	19	9
	58,869	30,783	11,455	11,110	5,521	100	52	19	19	9
BLACK FAMILIES										
	6,184	2,364	1,449	1,235	1,136	100	38	23	20	18
	6,778	2,887	1,579	1,330	982	100	43	23	20	15
	7,470	3,093	1,894	1,433	1,049	100	41	25	19	14
	8,093	3,411	1,971	1,593	1,117	100	42	24	20	14
	8,055	3,472	1,958	1,485	1,140	100	43	24	18	14
HISPANIC FAMILIES [3]										
	3,029	946	680	696	708	100	31	22	23	23
	3,939	1,337	904	865	833	100	34	23	22	21
	4,840	1,790	1,095	1,036	919	100	37	23	21	19
	6,200	2,216	1,408	1,408	1,171	100	36	23	23	19
	6,287	2,238	1,450	1,437	1,160	100	36	23	23	18

ncludes other races, not shown separately. [2] No spouse present. [3] Hispanic persons may be of any race.

urce: U.S. Bureau of the Census, *Current Population Reports*, P20-488, and earlier reports; and unpublished data.

No. 79. Female Family Householders With No Spouse Present—Characteristics, by Race and Hispanic Origin: 1980 to 1995

s of March. Covers persons 15 years old and over. Based on Current Population Survey; see headnote, table 77]

CHARACTERISTIC	Unit	WHITE			BLACK			HISPANIC ORIGIN [1]		
		1980	1990	1995	1980	1990	1995	1980	1990	1995
male family householder	1,000	6,052	7,306	8,031	2,495	3,275	3,716	610	1,116	1,486
status:										
r married (single)	Percent	11	15	19	27	39	42	23	27	31
ied, spouse absent	Percent	17	16	17	29	21	19	32	29	26
wed	Percent	33	26	21	22	17	14	15	16	14
rced	Percent	40	43	43	22	23	25	30	29	29
ce of children under 8:										
wn children	Percent	41	43	40	28	32	33	25	33	29
own children	Percent	59	58	60	72	68	67	75	67	71
ne child	Percent	28	30	31	26	30	28	28	25	28
o children	Percent	20	19	20	23	22	21	23	22	22
ree children	Percent	7	7	7	11	9	11	15	13	13
ur or more children	Percent	3	2	3	11	7	7	9	6	8
n per family	Number	1.03	0.95	1.02	1.51	1.26	1.27	1.56	1.37	1.50

ersons of Hispanic origin may be of any race.

urce: U.S. Bureau of the Census, *Current Population Reports*, P20-491, and earlier reports; and unpublished data.

No. 80. Family Households With Own Children Under Age 18, by Type of Family, 1980 to 1995, and by Age of Householder, 1995

[As of March. Excludes members of Armed Forces except those living off post or with their families on post. Based on Current Population Survey; see text, section 1, and Appendix III]

FAMILY TYPE	1980	1990	1995: Total	1995: 15 to 24 years old	1995: 25 to 34 years old	1995: 35 to 44 years old	1995: 45 to 54 years old	1995: 55 to 64 years old	1995: 65 years old and over
NUMBER (1,000)									
Family households with children	31,022	32,289	34,296	1,969	10,763	14,922	5,752	743	147
Married couple	24,961	24,537	25,241	899	7,526	11,383	4,712	602	118
Male householder [1]	616	1,153	1,440	106	486	556	243	53	16
Female householder [1]	5,445	6,599	7,615	963	2,769	2,983	796	88	13
PERCENT DISTRIBUTION									
Family households with children	100	100	100	100	100	100	100	100	100
Married couple	81	76	74	46	70	76	82	81	80
Male householder [1]	2	4	4	5	4	4	4	7	11
Female householder [1]	18	20	22	49	26	20	14	12	9
HOUSEHOLDS WITH CHILDREN, AS A PERCENT OF ALL FAMILY HOUSEHOLDS, BY TYPE									
Family households with children, total	52	49	49	64	76	82	42	8	1
Married couple	51	47	47	55	73	82	42	8	1
Male householder [1]	36	40	45	33	59	65	44	19	4
Female householder [1]	63	61	62	86	93	85	39	8	1

[1] No spouse present.

Source: U.S. Bureau of the Census, *Current Population Reports*, P20-488, and earlier reports.

No. 81. Children Under 18 Years Old, by Presence of Parents: 1980 to 1996

[As of March. Excludes persons under 18 years old who maintained households or family groups. Based on Current Population Survey; see headnote, table 77]

RACE, HISPANIC ORIGIN, AND YEAR	Number (1,000)	PERCENT LIVING WITH— Both parents	Mother only: Total	Mother only: Divorced	Mother only: Married, spouse absent	Mother only: Never married	Mother only: Widowed	Father only	Neither parent
ALL RACES [1]									
1980	63,427	77	18	8	6	3	2	2	4
1985	62,475	74	21	9	5	6	2	3	3
1990	64,137	73	22	8	5	7	2	3	3
1995	70,254	69	23	9	6	8	1	4	4
1996	70,908	68	24	9	6	9	1	4	4
WHITE									
1980	52,242	83	14	7	4	1	2	2	2
1985	50,836	80	16	8	4	2	1	2	2
1990	51,390	79	16	8	4	3	1	3	2
1995	55,327	76	18	8	5	4	1	3	3
1996	55,714	75	18	8	5	5	1	4	3
BLACK									
1980	9,375	42	44	11	16	13	4	2	12
1985	9,479	40	51	11	12	25	3	3	7
1990	10,018	38	51	10	12	27	2	4	8
1995	11,301	33	52	11	11	29	2	4	11
1996	11,434	33	53	9	11	31	2	4	9
HISPANIC [2]									
1980	5,459	75	20	6	8	4	2	2	4
1985	6,057	68	27	7	11	7	2	2	3
1990	7,174	67	27	7	10	8	2	3	3
1995	9,843	63	28	8	9	10	1	4	4
1996	10,251	62	29	7	9	11	1	4	5

[1] Includes other races not shown separately. [2] Hispanic persons may be of any race.

Source: U.S. Bureau of the Census, *Current Population Reports*, P20-491, and earlier reports; and unpublished data.

No. 82. Living Arrangements of Children Under 18 Years Old Living With One or Both Parents: 1996

[In thousands. As of March. Covers only those persons under 18 years old who are living with one or both parents. Characteristics are shown for the householder or reference person in married-couple situations. See also headnote, table 77]

CHARACTERISTIC OF PARENT	ALL RACES [1]				WHITE				BLACK				HISPANIC [2]			
	Total	Living with—			Total	Living with—			Total	Living with—			Total	Living with—		
		Both parents	Mother only	Father only		Both parents	Mother only	Father only		Both parents	Mother only	Father only		Both parents	Mother only	Father only
Children under 18 years old	**67,976**	**48,224**	**16,993**	**2,759**	**53,944**	**41,609**	**10,239**	**2,096**	**10,376**	**3,816**	**6,056**	**504**	**9,702**	**6,381**	**2,937**	**384**
Age:																
15 to 24 years old	4,317	1,468	2,604	247	2,829	1,289	1,359	181	1,307	128	1,127	51	989	388	539	62
25 to 29 years old	7,474	4,146	2,967	361	5,623	3,731	1,631	261	1,602	289	1,240	72	1,496	911	536	49
30 to 34 years old	14,132	9,813	3,795	524	11,200	8,574	2,235	390	2,275	708	1,454	113	2,347	1,626	620	101
35 to 39 years old	17,227	12,904	3,735	589	13,848	11,126	2,256	465	2,481	1,069	1,328	83	2,330	1,631	650	49
40 to 44 years old	13,794	10,910	2,388	496	11,573	9,507	1,694	371	1,449	795	569	85	1,423	994	362	67
45 to 54 years old	9,760	7,933	1,373	452	7,918	6,584	967	367	1,097	723	305	69	919	690	190	40
55 to 64 years old	1,045	879	95	72	806	694	66	45	142	89	26	26	166	123	28	15
65 years old and over	227	171	38	18	148	104	28	15	23	14	7	3	30	19	11	-
Educational attainment:																
Less than 9th grade	4,537	3,174	1,199	165	3,633	2,672	850	112	454	162	251	41	2,874	2,114	695	64
9th to 12th grade, no diploma	7,734	3,842	3,403	489	5,322	3,239	1,733	350	2,122	417	1,589	115	2,127	1,136	884	108
High school graduate [3]	21,715	14,610	6,001	1,104	17,046	12,616	3,598	832	3,838	1,421	2,198	219	2,427	1,556	744	127
Some college, no degree or associate degree	18,485	12,937	4,867	681	14,716	11,253	2,917	545	2,938	1,104	1,732	102	1,634	1,036	519	78
Bachelor's degree	9,891	8,529	1,139	223	8,438	7,410	849	179	752	505	229	18	444	372	65	7
Graduate or professional degree	5,615	5,132	385	98	4,789	4,419	293	78	272	207	57	8	196	166	30	-
Employment status: [4]																
In the civilian labor force	56,272	42,590	11,280	2,402	46,186	37,124	7,171	1,891	7,290	3,242	3,653	395	7,223	5,326	1,557	340
Employed	53,097	40,917	9,991	2,189	44,012	35,694	6,575	1,742	6,475	3,090	3,033	351	6,474	4,844	1,328	303
Both parents employed	28,298	28,298	(X)	(X)	24,472	24,472	(X)	(X)	2,332	2,332	(X)	(X)	2,512	2,512	(X)	(X)
Unemployed	3,175	1,673	1,289	213	2,175	1,429	596	149	815	152	619	44	749	482	229	38
Not in the labor force	10,843	4,809	5,707	328	7,119	3,857	3,067	195	2,968	470	2,398	100	2,421	1,002	1,380	40
Family income:																
Under $5,000	2,886	467	2,268	151	1,622	392	1,135	95	1,140	40	1,072	29	676	149	509	19
$5,000 to $9,999	4,633	1,075	3,314	245	2,767	820	1,761	186	1,579	135	1,396	48	1,269	428	795	46
$10,000 to $14,999	4,804	1,850	2,664	290	3,222	1,502	1,518	202	1,271	174	1,024	73	1,200	626	514	60
$15,000 to $24,999	9,272	5,149	3,533	588	6,874	4,300	2,168	407	1,894	515	1,226	152	2,194	1,510	581	104
$25,000 to $29,999	4,650	3,205	1,196	249	3,656	2,711	757	188	753	306	399	48	948	770	147	30
$30,000 to $39,999	8,713	6,574	1,733	406	7,277	5,713	1,249	316	1,052	557	423	73	1,263	1,002	209	52
$40,000 to $49,999	7,928	6,686	946	296	6,735	5,791	695	249	819	573	204	42	709	612	66	31
$50,000 and over	25,091	23,217	1,341	533	21,792	20,381	957	454	1,868	1,515	313	40	1,443	1,285	115	43
Tenure: [5]																
Owned	43,012	35,807	5,782	1,423	37,165	31,837	4,183	1,146	3,918	2,324	1,398	196	3,802	3,099	556	148
Rented	24,964	12,417	11,211	1,336	16,779	9,773	6,056	951	6,458	1,492	4,658	308	5,900	3,282	2,381	236

- Represents or rounds to zero. X Not applicable. [1] Includes other races, not shown separately. [2] Persons of Hispanic origin may be of any race. [3] Includes equivalency. [4] Excludes children whose parent is in the Armed Forces. [5] Refers to the tenure of the householder (who may or may not be the child's parent).

Source: U.S. Bureau of the Census, unpublished data.

No. 83. Nonfamily Households, by Sex and Age of Householder: 1980 to 1996

[In thousands. As of March. See headnote, table 77]

ITEM	MALE HOUSEHOLDER					FEMALE HOUSEHOLDER				
	Total	15 to 24 yr. old	25 to 44 yr. old	45 to 64 yr. old	65 yr. old and over	Total	15 to 24 yr. old	25 to 44 yr. old	45 to 64 yr. old	65 yr. old and over
1980, total	**8,807**	**1,567**	**3,854**	**1,822**	**1,565**	**12,419**	**1,189**	**2,198**	**3,048**	**5,983**
One person (living alone)	6,966	947	2,920	1,613	1,486	11,330	779	1,809	2,901	5,842
Nonrelatives present	1,841	620	934	209	79	1,089	410	389	147	141
1990, total	**11,606**	**1,236**	**5,780**	**2,536**	**2,053**	**15,651**	**1,032**	**3,697**	**3,545**	**7,377**
One person (living alone)	9,049	674	4,231	2,203	1,943	13,950	536	2,881	3,300	7,233
Nonrelatives present	2,557	560	1,551	334	112	1,701	497	817	245	143
Never married	5,844	1,175	3,689	696	285	4,382	976	2,406	510	491
Married [1]	1,117	28	513	391	187	794	15	261	320	198
Widowed	1,417	-	29	221	1,166	7,426	4	52	1,333	6,036
Divorced	3,228	33	1,550	1,229	416	3,048	37	977	1,382	649
1996, total	**13,348**	**1,156**	**6,355**	**3,390**	**2,448**	**16,685**	**1,110**	**3,865**	**3,976**	**7,733**
One person (living alone)	10,288	573	4,568	2,839	2,307	14,612	499	2,972	3,606	7,534
Nonrelatives present	3,061	581	1,788	551	140	2,073	612	893	368	198
Single (Never married)	6,563	1,088	4,135	967	375	4,898	1,037	2,639	720	502
Married [1]	1,210	35	583	395	197	843	30	234	341	239
Widowed	1,578	-	29	229	1,321	7,154	5	75	961	6,093
Divorced	3,996	33	1,609	1,799	555	3,789	38	918	1,935	898

- Represents or rounds to zero. [1] No spouse present.

Source: U.S. Bureau of the Census, *Current Population Reports*, P20-450, and earlier reports; and unpublished data.

No. 84. Persons Living Alone, by Sex and Age: 1980 to 1996

[As of March. Based on Current Population Survey; see headnote, table 77]

SEX AND AGE	NUMBER OF PERSONS (1,000)					PERCENT DISTRIBUTION				
	1980	1985	1990	1995	1996	1980	1985	1990	1995	1996
Both sexes	**18,296**	**20,902**	**22,999**	**24,732**	**24,900**	**100**	**100**	**100**	**100**	**100**
15 to 24 years old	1,726	1,324	1,210	1,196	1,072	9	6	5	5	4
25 to 34 years old	[1]4,729	3,905	3,972	3,653	3,736	[1]26	19	17	15	15
35 to 44 years old	([1])	2,322	3,138	3,663	3,803	([1])	11	14	15	15
45 to 64 years old	4,514	4,939	5,502	6,377	6,447	25	24	24	26	26
65 to 74 years old	3,851	4,130	4,350	4,374	4,377	21	20	19	18	18
75 years old and over	3,477	3,962	4,825	5,470	5,464	19	19	21	22	22
Male	**6,966**	**7,922**	**9,049**	**10,140**	**10,288**	**38**	**38**	**39**	**41**	**41**
15 to 24 years old	947	750	674	623	573	5	4	3	3	2
25 to 34 years old	[1]2,920	2,307	2,395	2,213	2,250	[1]16	11	10	9	9
35 to 44 years old	([1])	1,406	1,836	2,263	2,318	([1])	7	8	9	9
45 to 64 years old	1,613	1,845	2,203	2,787	2,839	9	9	10	11	11
65 to 74 years old	775	868	1,042	1,134	1,240	4	4	5	5	5
75 years old and over	711	746	901	1,120	1,067	4	4	4	5	4
Female	**11,330**	**12,980**	**13,950**	**14,592**	**14,612**	**62**	**62**	**61**	**59**	**59**
15 to 24 years old	779	573	536	572	499	4	3	2	2	2
25 to 34 years old	[1]1,809	1,598	1,578	1,440	1,487	[1]10	8	7	6	6
35 to 44 years old	([1])	916	1,303	1,399	1,485	([1])	4	6	6	6
45 to 64 years old	2,901	3,095	3,300	3,589	3,608	16	15	14	15	14
65 to 74 years old	3,076	3,262	3,309	3,240	3,137	17	16	14	13	13
75 years old and over	2,766	3,236	3,924	4,351	4,398	15	16	17	18	18

[1] Data for persons 35 to 44 years old included with persons 25 to 34 years old.

Source: U.S. Bureau of the Census, *Current Population Reports*, P20-491, and earlier reports; and unpublished data.

No. 85. Religious Bodies—Selected Data

[Includes the self-reported membership of religious bodies with 60,000 or more as reported to the Yearbook of American and Canadian Churches. Groups may be excluded if they do not supply information. The data are not standardized so comparisons between groups are difficult. The definition of "church member" is determined by the religious body]

RELIGIOUS BODY	Year reported	Churches reported	Membership (1,000)	Pastors serving parishes [1]
African Methodist Episcopal Church [2]	1991	8,000	3,500	(NA)
African Methodist Episcopal Zion Church	1996	3,098	1,231	2,571
American Baptist Association	1986	1,705	250	1,740
American Baptist Churches in the U.S.A.	1995	5,823	1,517	4,974
Antiochian Orthodox Christian Archdiocese of North America, The	1995	184	300	200
Armenian Apostolic Church of America	1995	28	180	23
Assemblies of God	1995	11,823	2,388	17,893
Baptist Bible Fellowship International, The	1995	3,600	1,560	(NA)
Baptist General Conference	1995	857	135	(NA)
Baptist Missionary Association of America	1995	1,355	231	1,300
Buddhist [3]	1990	(NA)	401	(NA)
Christian and Missionary Alliance, The	1995	1,957	307	1,578
Christian Brethren (a.k.a. Plymouth Brethren)	1994	1,150	98	500
Christian Church (Disciples of Christ)	1995	4,036	930	4,010
Christian Churches and Churches of Christ	1988	5,579	1,071	5,525
Christian Congregation, Inc., The	1995	1,431	113	1,427
Christian Methodist Episcopal Church	1983	2,340	719	2,340
Christian Reformed Church in North America	1996	718	207	666
Church of God (Anderson, IN)	1995	2,307	224	3,011
Church of God (Cleveland, TN)	1995	6,060	753	3,121
Church of God in Christ, The	1991	15,300	5,500	28,988
Church of God of Prophecy, The	1995	1,961	73	8,636
Church of Jesus Christ of Latter-day Saints, The	1995	10,417	4,712	31,251
Church of the Brethren	1995	1,114	143	844
Church of the Nazarene	1995	5,135	602	5,111
Churches of Christ	1988	13,020	1,655	10,000
Conservative Baptist Association of America	1992	1,084	200	(NA)
Coptic Orthodox Church	1992	85	180	65
Cumberland Presbyterian Church	1995	783	88	(NA)
Diocese of the Armenian Church of America	1991	72	414	49
Episcopal Church, The	1995	7,415	2,537	8,037
Evangelical Covenant Church, The	1995	(NA)	91	(NA)
Evangelical Free Church of America	1996	1,224	243	1,936
Evangelical Lutheran Church in America	1995	10,955	5,190	9,819
Free Methodist Church of North America	1995	1,068	75	(NA)
Full Gospel Fellowship of Churches & Ministers International	1995	650	195	725
General Association of Regular Baptist Churches	1994	1,458	136	(NA)
General Baptists (General Association of)	1990	876	74	1,384
Grace Gospel Fellowship	1992	128	60	160
Greek Orthodox Archdiocese of North and South America	1977	532	1,950	610
Hindu [3]	1990	(NA)	227	(NA)
Independent Fundamental Churches of America	1995	670	70	(NA)
International Church of the Foursquare Gospel	1995	1,742	227	(NA)
International Council of Community Churches	1995	517	250	491
International Pentecostal Holiness Church	1995	1,653	157	(NA)
Jehovah's Witnesses	1995	10,541	966	(NA)
Jewish [3]	1990	(NA)	3,137	(NA)
Lutheran Church - Missouri Synod, The	1995	6,154	2,595	5,287
Mennonite Church	1995	966	91	1,350
Muslim / Islamic [3]	1990	(NA)	527	(NA)
National Association of Congregational Christian Churches	1995	426	70	600
National Association of Free Will Baptists	1995	2,491	214	2,800
National Baptist Convention of America, Inc.	1987	2,500	3,500	8,000
National Baptist Convention, U.S.A., Inc.	1992	33,000	8,200	32,832
National Missionary Baptist Convention of America	1992	(NA)	2,500	(NA)
Old Order Amish Church	1993	898	81	3,592
Orthodox Church in America	1995	600	2,000	650
Pentecostal Assemblies of the World	1994	1,760	1,000	4,262
Pentecostal Church of God, Inc.	1995	1,224	119	(NA)
Polish National Catholic Church of North America	1960	162	282	141
Presbyterian Church in America	1995	1,299	268	1,522
Presbyterian Church (U.S.A.)	1995	11,361	3,669	9,588
Progressive National Baptist Convention, Inc.	1995	2,000	2,500	(NA)
Reformed Church in America	1995	908	306	855
Reorganized Church of Jesus Christ of Latter-day Saints	1995	1,160	178	16,671
Roman Catholic Church, The	1995	19,726	60,280	(NA)
Romanian Orthodox Episcopate of America	1995	37	65	37
Salvation Army, The	1995	1,264	453	3,645
Serbian Orthodox Church in the U.S.A. and Canada	1986	68	67	60
Seventh-day Adventist Church	1995	4,297	791	2,307
Southern Baptist Convention	1995	40,039	15,663	38,123
Unitarian Universalist [3]	1990	(NA)	502	(NA)
United Church of Christ	1995	6,145	1,472	4,439
United Methodist Church, The	1995	36,361	8,539	19,560
Wesleyan Church (USA), The	1996	1,624	116	1,785
Wisconsin Evangelical Lutheran Synod	1995	1,252	412	1,196

NA Not available. [1] Does not include retired clergy or clergy not working with congregations. [2] Figures obtained from the *Directory of African American Religious Bodies, 1991*. [3] Figures obtained from the National Survey of Religious Identification, a survey conducted by the City University of New York in 1990 and published in *One Nation Under God: Religion in Contemporary American Society*, by Barry Kosmin and Seymour Lachman (1993).

Source: Kenneth B. Bedell, editor, *Yearbook of American and Canadian Churches*, annual (copyright).

No. 86. Religious Preference, Church Membership, and Attendance: 1980 to 1995

[In percent. Covers civilian noninstitutional population, 18 years old and over. Data represent averages of the combined results of several surveys during year or period indicated. Data are subject to sampling variability, see source]

YEAR	RELIGIOUS PREFERENCE					Church/ synagogue members	Persons attending church/ synagogue [1]	AGE AND REGION	Church/ synagogue members, 1995
	Protestant	Catholic	Jewish	Other	None				
1980	61	28	2	2	7	69	40	18-29 years old	61
1985	57	28	2	4	9	71	42	30-49 years old	65
1989	56	28	2	4	10	69	43	50-64 years old	74
1990	56	25	2	6	11	65	40	65 years and over	80
1991	56	25	2	6	11	68	42	East [4]	69
1992	56	26	2	7	9	69	40	Midwest [5]	72
1993	57	26	1	8	[2] 8	68	40	South [6]	77
1995 [3]	58	25	2	(NA)	(NA)	69	43	West [7]	53

NA Not available. [1] Persons who attended a church or synagogue in the last seven days. [2] Includes those respondents who did not designate. [3] Preference data are for the period 1994-95. [4] ME, NH, RI, NY, CT, VT, MA, NJ, PA, WV, DE, MD, and DC. [5] OH, IN, IL, MI, MN, WI, IA, ND, SD, KS, NE, and MO. [6] KY, TN, VA, NC, SC, GA, FL, AL, MS, TX, AR, OK, and LA. [7] AZ, NM, CO, NV, MT, ID, WY, UT, CA, WA, OR, AK, and HI.

Source: Princeton Religion Research Center, Princeton, NJ, *Religion in America*, 1996. Based on surveys conducted by The Gallup Organization, Inc.

No. 87. Christian Church Adherents, 1990, and Jewish Population, 1995—States

[Christian church adherents were defined as "all members, including full members, their children and the estimated number of other regular participants who are not considered as communicant, confirmed or full members." Data on Christian church adherents are based on reports of 133 church groupings and exclude 34 church bodies that reported more than 100,000 members to the *Yearbook of American and Canadian Churches*. The Jewish population includes Jews who define themselves as Jewish by religion as well as those who define themselves as Jewish in cultural terms. Data on Jewish population are based primarily on a compilation of individual estimates made by local Jewish federations. Additionally, most large communities have completed Jewish demographic surveys from which the Jewish population can be determined]

REGION, DIVISION, AND STATE	CHRISTIAN ADHERENTS, 1990		JEWISH POPULATION, 1995	
	Number (1,000)	Percent of population [1]	Number (1,000)	Percent of population [1]
U.S.	**131,084**	**52.7**	**5,900**	**2.3**
Northeast	**28,691**	**56.5**	**2,824**	**5.5**
N.E.	**7,456**	**56.5**	**404**	**3.0**
ME	439	36.1	8	0.6
NH	431	38.9	10	0.8
VT	233	40.4	6	1.0
MA	3,666	60.9	268	4.4
RI	754	75.1	16	1.6
CT	1,933	58.9	97	3.0
M.A	**21,235**	**56.5**	**2,420**	**6.3**
NY	9,970	55.5	1,654	9.1
NJ	4,305	55.7	436	5.5
PA	6,960	58.6	330	2.7
Midwest	**32,890**	**55.1**	**989**	**1.1**
E.N.C	**22,212**	**52.9**	**858**	**1.3**
OH	5,313	48.9	129	1.2
IN	2,615	47.1	18	0.3
IL	6,579	57.5	268	2.3
MI	4,580	49.2	107	1.1
WI	3,125	63.9	35	0.7
W.N.C	**10,678**	**60.5**	**132**	**0.7**
MN	2,807	64.2	42	0.9
IA	1,674	60.3	6	0.2
MO	2,892	56.6	62	1.2
ND	485	75.9	1	0.1
SD	474	68.1	(Z)	0.1
NE	1,000	63.4	7	0.4
KS	1,346	54.3	14	0.6
South	**48,358**	**56.8**	**1,244**	**1.4**
S.A.	**21,248**	**48.8**	**1,070**	**2.3**
DE	297	44.6	9	1.3
MD	2,101	43.9	211	4.2
DC	349	57.5	26	4.5
VA	2,896	46.8	73	1.1
WV	740	41.3	2	0.1
NC	3,949	59.6	22	0.3
SC	2,149	61.7	9	0.2
GA	3,659	56.5	77	1.1
FL	5,106	39.5	641	4.6
E.S.C	**9,843**	**64.8**	**39**	**0.2**
KY	2,213	60.1	11	0.3
TN	2,968	60.8	18	0.3
AL	2,858	70.7	9	0.2
MS	1,804	70.1	1	0.1
W.S.C	**17,267**	**64.7**	**134**	**0.5**
AR	1,423	60.5	2	0.1
LA	2,959	70.1	17	0.4
OK	2,097	66.5	5	0.2
TX	10,788	63.5	110	0.6
West	**21,147**	**40.1**	**1,145**	**2.0**
Mt	**6,433**	**47.1**	**169**	**1.0**
MT	341	42.7	1	0.1
ID	507	50.4	(Z)	0.1
WY	216	47.6	(Z)	0.1
CO	1,244	37.8	52	1.4
NM	863	56.3	9	0.5
AZ	1,505	41.1	72	1.8
UT	1,371	79.6	4	0.2
NV	366	29.6	21	1.4
Pac	**14,714**	**37.8**	**986**	**2.4**
WA	1,579	32.4	34	0.6
OR	904	31.8	20	0.6
CA	11,665	39.2	922	2.9
AK	175	31.8	3	0.5
HI	391	35.3	7	0.6

Z Fewer than 500. [1] Based on U.S. Bureau of the Census data for resident population enumerated as of April 1, 1990, and estimated as of July 1, 1995.

Source: Christian church adherents—M. Bradley; N. Green, Jr.; D. Jones; M. Lynn; and L. McNeil; *Churches and Church Membership in the United States 1990*, Glenmary Research Center, Atlanta, GA, 1992 (copyright); Jewish population—American Jewish Committee, New York, NY, *American Jewish Year Book, 1995* (copyright).

Vital Statistics

This section presents vital statistics data on births, deaths, abortions, fetal deaths, fertility, life expectancy, marriages, and divorces. Vital statistics are compiled for the country as a whole by the National Center for Health Statistics (NCHS) and published in its annual report, *Vital Statistics of the United States,* in certain reports of the *Vital and Health Statistics* series, and in the *Monthly Vital Statistics Report.* Reports in this field are also issued by the various State bureaus of vital statistics. Data on fertility, on age of persons at first marriage, and on marital status and marital history are compiled by the Bureau of the Census from its Current Population Survey (CPS; see text, section 1) and published in *Current Population Reports,* P20 series. Data on abortions are published by the Alan Guttmacher Institute, New York, NY, in selected issues of *Family Planning Perspectives.*

Registration of vital events—The registration of births, deaths, fetal deaths, and other vital events in the United States is primarily a State and local function. The civil laws of every State provide for a continuous and permanent birth- and death-registration system. Many States also provide for marriage- and divorce-registration systems. Vital events occurring to U.S. residents outside the United States are not included in the data.

Births and deaths—The live-birth, death, and fetal-death statistics prepared by NCHS are based on vital records filed in the registration offices of all States, of New York City, and of the District of Columbia. The annual collection of death statistics on a national basis began in 1900 with a national death-registration area of 10 States and the District of Columbia; a similar annual collection of birth statistics for a national birth-registration area began in 1915, also with 10 reporting States and the District of Columbia. Since 1933, the birth- and death-registration areas have comprised the entire United States, including Alaska (beginning 1959) and Hawaii (beginning 1960). National statistics on fetal deaths were first compiled for 1918 and annually since 1922.

In Brief

	1995
Births	*3,244,000*
Deaths	*1,926,000*
Marriages	*1,954,000*
Divorces	*973,000*

Prior to 1951, birth statistics came from a complete count of records received in the Public Health Service (now received in NCHS). From 1951 through 1971, they were based on a 50-percent sample of all registered births (except for a complete count in 1955 and a 20- to 50-percent sample in 1967). Beginning in 1972, they have been based on a complete count for States participating in the Vital Statistics Cooperative Program (VSCP) (for details, see the technical appendix in *Vital Statistics of the United States*) and on a 50-percent sample of all other areas. Beginning 1986 all reporting areas participated in the VSCP. Mortality data have been based on a complete count of records for each area (except for a 50-percent sample in 1972). Beginning in 1970, births to, and deaths of nonresident aliens of the United States and U.S. citizens outside the United States have been excluded from the data. Fetal deaths and deaths among Armed Forces abroad are excluded. Data based on samples are subject to sampling error; for details, see annual issues of *Vital Statistics of the United States.*

Mortality statistics by cause of death are compiled in accordance with World Health Organization regulations according to the *International Classification of Diseases* (ICD). The ICD is revised approximately every 10 years. The ninth revision of the ICD was employed beginning in 1979. Deaths for prior years were classified according to the revision of the ICD in use at the time. Each revision of the ICD introduces a number of discontinuities in mortality statistics; for a discussion of those between the eighth and ninth revisions of the ICD, see

Monthly Vital Statistics Report, vol. 28, No. 11, supplement.

Some of the tables present age-adjusted death rates in addition to crude death rates. Age-adjusted death rates shown in this section were prepared using the direct method, in which age-specific death rates for a population of interest are applied to a standard population distributed by age. Age adjustment eliminates the differences in observed rates between points in time or among compared population groups that result from age differences in population composition.

Fertility and life expectancy—The total fertility rate, defined as the number of births that 1,000 women would have in their lifetime if, at each year of age, they experienced the birth rates occurring in the specified year, is compiled and published by NCHS. Other data relating to social and medical factors which affect fertility rates, such as contraceptive use and birth expectations, are collected and made available by both NCHS and the Bureau of the Census. NCHS figures are based on information in birth and fetal death certificates and on the periodic National Surveys of Family Growth; Bureau of the Census data are based on decennial censuses and the CPS.

Data on life expectancy, the average remaining lifetime in years for persons who attain a given age, are computed and published by NCHS. For details, see the technical appendix in *Vital Statistics of the United States*.

Marriage and divorce—The compilation of nationwide statistics on marriages and divorces in the United States began in 1887-88 when the National Office of Vital Statistics prepared estimates for the years 1867-86. Although periodic updates took place after 1888, marriage and divorce statistics were not collected and published annually until 1944 by that Office. In 1957 and 1958, respectively, the same Office established marriage- and divorce-registration areas. Beginning in 1957, the marriage-registration area comprised 30 States, plus Alaska, Hawaii, Puerto Rico, and the Virgin · It currentl includes 42 States

divorce-registration area, starting in 1958 with 14 States, Alaska, Hawaii, and the Virgin Islands, currently includes a total of 31 States and the Virgin Islands. Procedures for estimating the number of marriages and divorces in the registration States are discussed in *Vital Statistics of the United States*, vol. III—*Marriage and Divorce*. Total counts of events for registration and nonregistration States are gathered by collecting already summarized data on marriages and divorces reported by State offices of vital statistics and by county offices of registration.

Another important source of data on marriage and divorce trends in the United States is the March supplement to the Current Population Survey conducted by the Bureau of the Census. For information on marital status, see section 1.

Vital statistics rates—Except as noted, vital statistics rates computed by NCHS are based on decennial census population figures as of April 1 for 1940, 1950, 1960, 1970, 1980, and 1990; and on midyear population figures for other years, as estimated by the Bureau of the Census (see text, section 1).

Race—Data by race for births, deaths, marriages, and divorces from NCHS are based on information contained in the certificates of registration. The Census Bureau's Current Population Survey obtains information on race by asking respondents to classify their race as: (1) White, (2) Black, (3) American Indian, Eskimo, or Aleut, or (4) Asian or Pacific Islander.

Beginning with the 1989 data year, NCHS is tabulating its birth data primarily by race of the mother. In 1988 and prior years, births were tabulated by the race of the child, which was determined from the race of the parents as entered on the birth certificate.

Trend data by race shown in this section are by race of mother beginning with the 1980 data. Hispanic origin of the mother is reported and tabulated, independently of race. Thus persons of Hispanic origin may be or any race. In 1994, 91 percent of women of His in were re-

2.1
…ution of AIDS Deaths, by Age: 1982 Through 1995

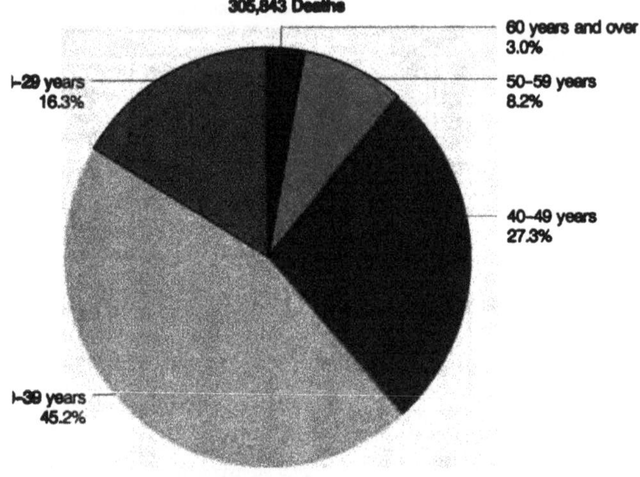

…art prepared by U.S. Bureau of the Census. For data, see table 133.

Figure 2.2
Births to Teenage Mothers as a Percent of Total Births, by Race: 1994

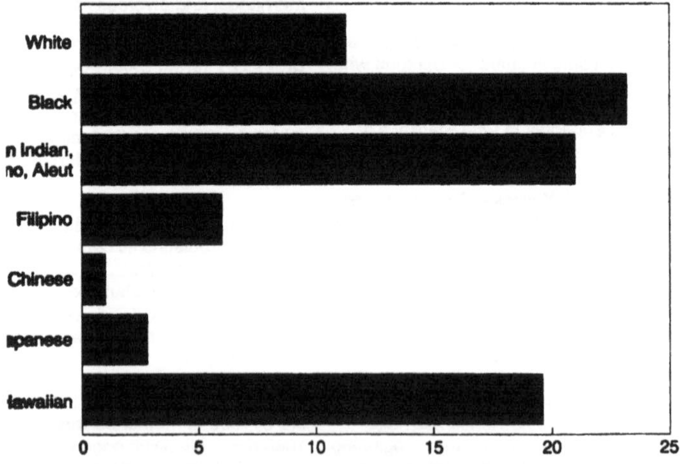

Source: Chart prepared by U.S. Bureau of the Census. For data, see table 89.

No. 88. Live Births, Deaths, Marriages, and Divorces: 1950 to 1995

[Prior to 1960, excludes Alaska and Hawaii. Beginning 1970, excludes births to, and deaths of nonresidents of the United States. See Appendix III]

YEAR	NUMBER (1,000)					RATE PER 1,000 POPULATION				
	Births [1]	Deaths		Marriages [3]	Divorces [4]	Births [1]	Deaths		Marriages [3]	Divorces [4]
		Total	Infant [2]				Total	Infant [2]		
1950	3,632	1,452	104	1,667	385	24.1	9.6	29.2	11.1	2.6
1955	4,097	1,529	107	1,531	377	25.0	9.3	26.4	9.3	2.3
1957	4,300	1,633	112	1,518	381	25.3	9.6	26.3	8.9	2.2
1960	4,258	1,712	111	1,523	393	23.7	9.5	26.0	8.5	2.2
1965	3,760	1,828	93	1,800	479	19.4	9.4	24.7	9.3	2.5
1970	3,731	1,921	75	2,159	708	18.4	9.5	20.0	10.6	3.5
1971	3,556	1,928	68	2,190	773	17.2	9.3	19.1	10.6	3.7
1972	3,258	1,964	60	2,282	845	15.6	9.4	18.5	10.9	4.0
1973	3,137	1,973	56	2,284	915	14.8	9.3	17.7	10.8	4.3
1974	3,160	1,934	53	2,230	977	14.8	9.1	16.7	10.5	4.6
1975	3,144	1,893	51	2,153	1,036	14.6	8.8	16.1	10.0	4.8
1976	3,168	1,909	48	2,155	1,083	14.6	8.8	15.2	9.9	5.0
1977	3,327	1,900	47	2,178	1,091	15.1	8.6	14.1	9.9	5.0
1978	3,333	1,928	46	2,282	1,130	15.0	8.7	13.8	10.3	5.1
1979	3,494	1,914	46	2,331	1,181	15.6	8.5	13.1	10.4	5.3
1980	3,612	1,990	46	2,390	1,189	15.9	8.8	12.6	10.6	5.2
1981	3,629	1,978	43	2,422	1,213	15.8	8.6	11.9	10.6	5.3
1982	3,681	1,975	42	2,456	1,170	15.9	8.5	11.5	10.6	5.1
1983	3,639	2,019	41	2,446	1,158	15.6	8.6	11.2	10.5	5.0
1984	3,669	2,039	40	2,477	1,169	15.6	8.6	10.8	10.5	5.0
1985	3,761	2,086	40	2,413	1,190	15.8	8.8	10.6	10.1	5.0
1986	3,757	2,105	39	2,407	1,178	15.6	8.8	10.4	10.0	4.9
1987	3,809	2,123	38	2,403	1,166	15.7	8.8	10.1	9.9	4.8
1988	3,910	2,168	39	2,396	1,167	16.0	8.9	10.0	9.8	4.8
1989	4,041	2,150	40	2,403	1,157	16.4	8.7	9.8	9.7	4.7
1990	4,158	2,148	38	2,443	1,182	16.7	8.6	9.2	9.8	4.7
1991	4,111	2,170	37	2,371	1,187	16.3	8.6	8.9	9.4	4.7
1992	4,065	2,176	35	2,362	1,215	15.9	8.5	8.5	9.3	4.8
1993	4,000	2,269	33	2,334	1,187	15.5	8.8	8.4	9.0	4.6
1994 prel.	3,979	2,286	31	2,362	1,191	15.0	8.8	7.9	9.1	4.6
1995 prel. [5]	3,244	1,926	24	1,954	973	13.4	8.8	7.7	7.6	4.1

[1] Prior to 1960, data adjusted for underregistration. [2] Infants under 1 year, excluding fetal deaths; rates per 1,000 registered live births. [3] Includes estimates for some States through 1965 and also for 1976 and 1977 and marriage licenses for some States for all years except 1973 and 1975. Beginning 1978, includes nonlicensed marriages in California. [4] Includes reported annulments and some estimated State figures for all years. [5] Rates are for the month of December 1995 only.

Source: U.S. National Center for Health Statistics, *Vital Statistics of the United States*, annual, *Monthly Vital Statistics Report*; and unpublished data.

No. 89. Live Births, by Race and Type of Hispanic Origin—Selected Characteristics: 1990 and 1994

[Represents registered births. Excludes births to nonresidents of the United States. Data are based on race of mother]

RACE AND HISPANIC ORIGIN	NUMBER OF BIRTHS (1,000)		BIRTHS TO TEENAGE MOTHERS, PERCENT OF TOTAL		BIRTHS TO UNMARRIED MOTHERS, PERCENT OF TOTAL		PERCENT OF MOTHERS BEGINNING PRENATAL CARE DURING—				PERCENT OF BIRTHS WITH LOW BIRTH WEIGHT [1]	
							First trimester		Third trimester or no care			
	1990	1994	1990	1994	1990	1994	1990	1994	1990	1994	1990	1994
Total	**4,158**	**3,953**	**12.8**	**13.1**	**28.6**	**32.6**	**74.2**	**80.2**	**6.0**	**4.4**	**7.0**	**7.3**
White	3,290	3,121	10.9	11.3	16.9	25.4	77.7	82.8	4.9	3.6	5.7	6.1
Black	684	636	23.1	23.2	66.7	70.4	60.7	68.3	10.9	8.2	13.3	13.2
American Indian, Eskimo, Aleut	39	38	19.5	21.0	53.6	57.0	57.9	65.2	12.9	9.8	6.1	6.4
Asian and Pacific Islander [2]	142	158	5.7	5.7	(NA)	16.2	(NA)	79.7	(NA)	4.1	(NA)	6.8
Filipino	26	30	6.1	6.0	15.9	18.5	77.1	81.3	4.5	3.6	7.3	7.8
Chinese	23	27	1.2	1.0	5.0	7.2	81.3	86.2	3.4	2.7	4.7	4.8
Japanese	9	9	2.9	2.8	9.6	11.2	87.0	89.2	2.9	1.9	6.2	6.9
Hawaiian	6	6	18.4	19.6	45.0	48.6	65.8	77.0	8.7	4.7	7.2	7.2
Hispanic origin [3]	595	665	16.8	17.8	36.7	43.1	60.2	68.9	12.0	7.6	6.1	6.2
Mexican	386	455	17.7	18.6	33.3	40.8	57.8	67.3	13.2	8.3	5.5	5.8
Puerto Rican	59	57	21.7	23.2	55.9	60.2	63.5	71.7	10.6	6.5	9.0	9.1
Cuban	11	12	7.7	7.3	18.2	22.9	84.8	90.1	2.8	1.6	5.7	6.3
Central and South American	83	93	9.0	10.4	41.2	45.9	61.5	71.2	10.9	6.5	5.8	6.0
Other and unknown Hispanic	(NA)	48	(NA)	20.8	(NA)	43.5	(NA)	72.1	(NA)	6.2	(NA)	7.5

NA Not available. [1] Births less than 2,500 grams (5 lb.-8 oz.). [2] Includes other races not shown separately. [3] Hispanic persons may be of any race. Includes other types, not shown separately.

Source: U.S. National Center for Health Statistics, *Vital Statistics of the United States*, annual, *Monthly Vital Statistics Report*; and unpublished data.

No. 90. Births and Birth Rates: 1980 to 1994

[Births in thousands. Births by race of child. Excludes births to nonresidents of the United States. For population bases used to derive these data, see text, section 2, and Appendix III]

ITEM	1980	1985	1986	1987	1988	1989	1990	1991	1992	1993	1994
Live births [1]	3,612	3,761	3,757	3,809	3,910	4,041	4,158	4,111	4,065	4,000	3,953
White	2,936	3,038	3,019	3,044	3,102	3,192	3,290	3,241	3,202	3,150	3,121
Black	568	582	593	611	639	673	684	683	674	659	636
American Indian	29	34	34	35	37	39	39	39	39	39	38
Asian or Pacific Islander	74	105	108	117	129	133	142	145	150	153	158
Male	1,853	1,928	1,925	1,951	2,002	2,069	2,129	2,102	2,082	2,049	2,023
Female	1,760	1,833	1,832	1,858	1,907	1,971	2,029	2,009	1,983	1,951	1,930
Males per 100 females	105	105	105	105	105	105	105	105	105	105	105
Age of mother:											
Under 20 years old	562	478	472	473	489	518	533	532	518	501	518
20 to 24 years old	1,226	1,141	1,102	1,076	1,067	1,078	1,094	1,090	1,070	1,038	1,001
25 to 29 years old	1,108	1,201	1,200	1,216	1,239	1,263	1,277	1,220	1,179	1,129	1,089
30 to 34 years old	550	696	721	761	804	842	886	885	895	901	906
35 to 39 years old	141	214	230	248	270	294	318	331	345	357	372
40 years old or more	24	29	31	36	41	46	50	54	58	61	66
Birth rate per 1,000 population	15.9	15.8	15.6	15.7	16.0	16.4	16.7	16.3	15.9	15.5	15.2
White	15.1	15.0	14.8	14.9	15.0	15.4	15.8	15.4	15.0	14.7	14.4
Black	21.3	20.4	20.5	20.8	21.5	22.3	22.4	21.9	21.3	20.5	19.5
American Indian	20.7	19.8	19.2	19.1	19.3	19.7	18.9	18.3	18.4	17.8	17.1
Asian or Pacific Islander	19.9	18.7	18.0	18.4	19.2	18.7	19.0	18.2	18.0	17.7	17.5
Male	16.8	16.7	16.5	16.5	16.8	17.2	17.6	17.1	16.7	(NA)	(NA)
Female	15.1	15.0	14.9	14.9	15.2	15.6	15.9	15.6	15.2	(NA)	(NA)
Plural birth ratio [2]	19.3	21.0	21.6	22.0	22.4	23.0	23.3	23.9	24.4	25.2	25.7
White	18.5	20.4	21.2	21.6	22.0	22.5	22.9	23.4	24.0	24.9	25.5
Black	24.1	25.3	24.9	25.4	25.8	26.9	27.0	27.8	28.2	28.7	29.4
Fertility rate per 1,000 women [3]	68.4	66.2	65.4	65.7	67.2	69.2	70.9	69.6	68.9	67.6	66.7
White [3]	64.8	64.1	63.1	63.3	64.5	66.4	68.3	67.0	66.5	65.4	64.9
Black [3]	84.7	78.8	78.9	80.1	82.6	86.2	86.8	85.2	83.2	80.5	76.9
American Indian [3]	82.7	78.6	75.9	75.6	76.8	79.0	76.2	75.1	75.4	73.4	70.9
Asian or Pacific Islander [3]	73.2	68.4	66.0	67.1	70.2	68.2	69.6	67.6	67.2	66.7	66.8
Age of mother:											
10 to 14 years old	1.1	1.2	1.3	1.3	1.3	1.4	1.4	1.4	1.4	1.4	1.4
15 to 19 years old	53.0	51.0	50.2	50.6	53.0	57.3	59.9	62.1	60.7	59.6	58.9
20 to 24 years old	115.1	108.3	107.4	107.9	110.2	113.8	116.5	115.7	114.6	112.6	111.1
25 to 29 years old	112.9	111.0	109.8	111.6	114.4	117.6	120.2	118.2	117.4	115.5	113.9
30 to 34 years old	61.9	69.1	70.1	72.1	74.8	77.4	80.8	79.5	80.2	80.8	81.5
35 to 39 years old	19.8	24.0	24.4	26.3	28.1	29.9	31.7	32.0	32.5	32.9	33.7
40 to 44 years old	3.9	4.0	4.1	4.4	4.8	5.2	5.5	5.5	5.9	6.1	6.4
45 to 49 years old	0.2	0.2	0.2	0.2	0.2	0.2	0.2	0.2	0.3	0.3	0.3

NA Not available. [1] Includes other races not shown separately. [2] Number of multiple births per 1,000 live births. [3] Per 1,000 women, 15 to 44 years old in specified group. The rate for *age of mother 45 to 49 years old* computed by relating births to mothers 45 years old and over to women 45 to 49 years old.

Source: U.S. National Center for Health Statistics, *Vital Statistics of the United States*, annual; *Monthly Vital Statistics Report;* and unpublished data.

No. 91. Teenagers—Births and Birth Rates, by Race , Age, and Sex: 1980 to 1994

[Birth rates per 1,000 women in specified group, see text, section 2]

ITEM	1980	1985	1986	1987	1988	1989	1990	1991	1992	1993	1994
NUMBER OF BIRTHS											
All races, total [1]	552,161	467,485	461,905	462,312	478,353	506,503	521,826	519,577	505,415	501,093	505,488
15-17 years	198,222	167,789	168,572	172,591	176,624	181,044	183,327	188,226	187,549	190,535	195,169
18-19 years	353,939	299,696	293,333	289,721	301,729	325,459	338,499	331,351	317,866	310,558	310,319
White	393,564	324,590	317,970	315,464	323,830	340,472	354,482	352,359	342,739	341,817	348,081
15-17 years	129,341	107,993	107,177	108,592	109,739	111,736	114,934	118,809	118,786	121,309	126,388
18-19 years	264,223	216,597	210,793	206,872	214,091	228,736	239,548	233,550	223,953	220,508	221,693
Black	147,378	130,857	131,594	134,050	140,608	150,699	151,613	150,956	146,800	143,153	140,968
15-17 years	65,069	55,656	57,003	59,361	61,856	63,832	62,881	63,571	63,002	63,156	62,563
18-19 years	82,309	75,201	74,591	74,689	78,752	86,867	88,732	87,385	83,798	79,997	78,405
BIRTH RATE											
All races, total [1]	53.0	51.0	50.2	50.6	53.0	57.3	59.9	62.1	60.7	59.6	58.9
15-17 years	32.5	31.0	30.5	31.7	33.6	36.4	37.5	38.7	37.8	37.8	37.6
18-19 years	82.1	79.6	79.6	78.5	79.9	84.2	88.6	94.4	94.5	92.1	91.5
White	45.4	43.3	42.3	42.5	44.4	47.9	50.8	52.8	51.8	51.1	51.1
15-17 years	25.5	24.4	23.8	24.6	26.0	28.1	29.5	30.7	30.1	30.3	30.7
18-19 years	73.2	70.4	70.1	68.9	69.6	72.9	78.0	83.5	83.8	82.1	82.1
Black	97.8	95.4	95.8	97.6	102.7	111.5	112.8	115.5	112.4	108.6	104.5
15-17 years	72.5	69.3	69.3	72.1	75.7	81.9	82.3	84.1	81.3	79.8	76.3
18-19 years	135.1	132.4	135.1	135.8	142.7	151.9	152.9	158.6	157.9	151.9	148.3

[1] Includes races other than white and black.

Source: U.S. National Center for Health Statistics, *Monthly Vital Statistics Report*, Vol. 45, No. 5, Supplement.

No. 92. Live Births, by State: 1994

[Number of births, except rate. Registered births. Excludes births to nonresidents of the United States. By race of mother. See Appendix III]

DIVISION AND STATE	All races [1]	WHITE		BLACK		Hispanic [2]	Birth rate [3]	Fertility rate [4]
		Total	Non-Hispanic	Total	Non-Hispanic			
United States	3,952,767	3,121,004	3,245,115	636,391	619,198	665,026	15.2	66.7
Northeast	732,796	581,627	620,498	120,632	110,287	93,274	(NA)	(NA)
New England	179,832	158,687	158,544	15,149	12,630	15,687	(NA)	(NA)
Maine	14,441	14,118	14,124	77	69	107	11.6	51.4
New Hampshire	15,106	14,840	14,090	104	87	187	13.3	56.2
Vermont	7,377	7,263	6,864	27	25	38	12.7	54.6
Massachusetts	83,787	72,107	75,033	8,121	6,667	8,435	13.9	59.3
Rhode Island	13,466	11,839	10,682	1,085	946	1,623	13.5	59.6
Connecticut	45,655	38,520	37,751	5,735	4,836	5,297	13.9	62.1
Middle Atlantic	552,964	422,940	461,954	105,483	97,657	77,587	43.2	182.3
New York	278,392	204,271	212,247	58,901	53,155	53,216	15.3	66.8
New Jersey	117,501	88,343	99,215	23,185	21,546	18,083	14.9	65.9
Pennsylvania	157,071	130,326	150,492	23,397	22,956	6,288	13.0	59.6
Midwest	888,659	736,071	825,305	128,086	126,858	50,507	(NA)	(NA)
East North Central	634,106	511,934	584,800	107,582	106,994	42,246	(NA)	(NA)
Ohio	155,944	130,279	152,952	23,615	23,505	2,717	14.0	61.8
Indiana	82,595	72,711	80,004	8,978	8,941	2,324	14.4	62.4
Illinois	189,257	142,348	158,799	40,971	40,798	30,350	16.1	70.5
Michigan	138,028	107,783	127,222	27,175	26,876	4,454	14.5	63.1
Wisconsin	68,282	58,813	65,823	6,843	6,814	2,401	13.4	59.9
West North Central	254,553	224,137	240,505	20,504	19,924	8,261	(NA)	(NA)
Minnesota	64,305	57,617	57,784	3,015	2,554	1,661	14.1	61.9
Iowa	37,079	35,226	35,985	1,055	1,047	1,060	13.1	60.8
Missouri	73,543	60,489	72,253	11,875	11,813	1,224	13.9	62.6
North Dakota	8,584	7,700	8,392	68	67	116	13.5	62.6
South Dakota	10,507	8,777	10,377	76	76	124	14.6	66.6
Nebraska	23,156	21,148	21,393	1,273	1,265	1,382	14.3	64.9
Kansas	37,379	33,180	34,321	3,142	3,102	2,694	14.6	66.7
South	1,364,273	967,827	1,172,373	331,428	327,781	189,869	(NA)	(NA)
South Atlantic	665,854	480,919	614,469	187,800	184,882	50,217	(NA)	(NA)
Delaware	10,411	7,774	9,870	2,396	2,315	526	14.7	62.7
Maryland	73,971	46,497	70,319	24,615	23,641	3,090	14.8	61.9
Dist. of Columbia	9,930	1,481	9,040	8,032	7,618	850	17.4	66.5
Virginia	95,039	69,315	90,323	22,331	22,176	4,609	14.5	60.5
West Virginia	21,375	20,451	21,260	796	794	106	11.7	53.3
North Carolina	101,420	70,295	98,260	27,882	27,807	3,135	14.3	62.1
South Carolina	52,043	32,016	51,357	19,409	19,380	643	14.2	60.6
Georgia	111,011	69,641	106,400	39,070	38,852	4,363	15.7	64.9
Florida	190,654	143,449	157,640	43,267	42,299	32,895	13.7	65.8
East South Central	229,067	164,486	226,875	62,102	62,020	2,072	(NA)	(NA)
Kentucky	52,983	47,641	52,479	4,895	4,876	466	13.8	60.1
Tennessee	73,191	55,613	72,319	16,603	16,576	845	14.1	61.4
Alabama	60,939	39,690	60,320	20,649	20,615	579	14.4	62.9
Mississippi	41,954	21,541	41,757	19,955	19,953	182	15.7	68.2
West South Central	469,352	372,428	331,029	81,526	80,879	137,580	(NA)	(NA)
Arkansas	34,718	26,378	33,893	7,836	7,806	782	14.2	64.9
Louisiana	67,817	37,925	66,340	28,645	28,432	1,413	15.7	67.6
Oklahoma	45,703	35,812	43,381	4,769	4,734	2,260	14.0	64.6
Texas	321,114	272,306	187,415	40,276	39,907	133,125	17.5	75.0
West	967,039	805,479	626,939	56,245	54,272	331,376	(NA)	(NA)
Mountain	249,719	223,466	189,216	8,300	7,889	58,405	(NA)	(NA)
Montana	11,067	9,733	10,457	32	24	250	12.9	60.9
Idaho	17,526	16,952	15,512	62	59	1,978	15.5	70.3
Wyoming	6,428	6,104	5,963	61	57	460	13.5	61.2
Colorado	54,071	49,292	43,391	2,773	2,679	10,667	14.8	63.3
New Mexico	27,591	23,053	14,601	521	505	12,964	16.7	74.8
Arizona	70,846	61,570	45,135	2,485	2,322	24,135	17.4	79.7
Utah	38,279	36,333	35,538	287	201	2,704	20.1	85.9
Nevada	23,911	20,429	18,619	2,079	2,042	5,227	16.4	74.5
Pacific	717,320	582,013	437,723	47,945	46,383	272,971	(NA)	(NA)
Washington	77,358	67,600	66,599	3,065	2,880	8,108	14.5	62.9
Oregon	41,837	38,819	37,450	947	931	4,357	13.6	61.3
California	567,930	462,719	306,435	42,807	41,510	257,750	18.1	78.3
Alaska	10,678	7,440	9,905	499	461	580	17.6	75.2
Hawaii	19,517	5,435	17,334	627	601	2,176	16.6	74.7

NA Not available. [1] Includes other races not shown separately. [2] Persons of Hispanic origin may be of any race. Births by Hispanic origin of mother. [3] Per 1,000 estimated population. [4] Per 1,000 women aged 15-44 years estimated.

Source: U.S. National Center for Health Statistics, *Vital Statistics of the United States*, annual, and *Monthly Vital Statistics Report*.

No. 93. Total Fertility Rate and Intrinsic Rate of Natural Increase: 1960 to 1994

[Based on race of child and registered births only, thru 1979. Beginning 1980, based on race of mother. Beginning 1970, excludes births to nonresidents of United States. The *total fertility rate* is the number of births that 1,000 women would have in their lifetime if, at each year of age, they experienced the birth rates occurring in the specified year. A total fertility rate of 2,110 represents "replacement level" fertility for the total population under current mortality conditions (assuming no net immigration). The *intrinsic rate of natural increase* is the rate that would eventually prevail if a population were to experience, at each year of age, the birth rates and death rates occurring in the specified year and if those rates remained unchanged over a long period of time. Minus sign (-) indicates decrease. See also Appendix III]

ANNUAL AVERAGE AND YEAR	TOTAL FERTILITY RATE			INTRINSIC RATE OF NATURAL INCREASE			ANNUAL AVERAGE AND YEAR	TOTAL FERTILITY RATE			INTRINSIC RATE OF NATURAL INCREASE		
	Total	White	Black and other	Total	White	Black and other		Total	White	Black and other	Total	White	Black and other
1960-64 . . .	3,449	3,326	4,326	18.6	17.1	27.7	1979	1,808	1,716	2,310	-5.7	-7.7	3.8
1965-69 . . .	2,622	2,512	3,362	8.2	6.4	18.6	1980	1,840	1,773	2,177	-5.1	-7.0	4.0
1970-74 . . .	2,094	1,997	2,680	-0.7	-2.5	9.1	1981	1,812	1,748	2,118	-5.6	-7.4	3.0
1975-79 . . .	1,774	1,685	2,270	-6.6	-8.5	3.0	1982	1,828	1,767	2,107	-5.2	-7.0	3.0
1980-84 . . .	1,819	1,731	2,262	-5.4	-7.3	3.0	1983	1,799	1,741	2,066	-5.8	-7.5	2.2
1985-88 . . .	1,870	1,769	2,339	-4.2	-6.3	4.3	1984	1,807	1,749	2,071	-5.6	-7.3	2.1
							1985	1,844	1,787	2,109	-4.8	-6.6	2.7
1970	2,480	2,385	3,067	6.0	4.5	14.4	1986	1,838	1,776	2,136	-4.9	-6.7	2.8
1971	2,267	2,161	2,920	2.6	0.8	12.6	1987	1,872	1,805	2,198	-4.1	-6.1	4.0
1972	2,010	1,907	2,628	-2.0	-3.9	8.6	1988	1,934	1,857	2,298	-2.9	-5.1	5.7
1973	1,879	1,783	2,443	-4.5	-6.5	5.7	1989	2,014	1,931	2,433	-1.4	-3.6	7.4
1974	1,835	1,749	2,339	-5.4	-7.2	4.0	1990	2,081	2,003	2,480	-0.1	-2.3	8.3
1975	1,774	1,686	2,276	-6.7	-8.6	3.0	1991	2,073	1,996	2,480	-0.2	-2.4	8.2
1976	1,738	1,652	2,223	-7.4	-9.3	2.1	1992	2,065	1,994	2,442	-0.4	-2.5	7.5
1977	1,790	1,703	2,279	-6.2	-8.1	3.2	1993	2,046	1,982	2,385	-0.7	-1.9	3.7
1978	1,760	1,668	2,265	-6.8	-8.8	2.9	1994	2,036	1,985	2,300	(NA)	(NA)	(NA)

NA Not available.

Source: U.S. National Center for Health Statistics, *Vital Statistics of the United States*, annual; and unpublished data.

No. 94. Projected Fertility Rates, by Race and Age Group: 1996 and 2010

[For definition of total fertility rate, see headnote, table 93. Birth rates represent live births per 1,000 women in age group indicated. Projections are based on middle fertility assumptions. For explanations of methodology, see text, section 1]

AGE GROUP	ALL RACES [1]		WHITE		BLACK		AMERICAN INDIAN, ESKIMO, ALEUT		ASIAN AND PACIFIC ISLANDERS		HISPANIC [2]	
	1996	2010	1996	2010	1996	2010	1996	2010	1996	2010	1996	2010
Total fertility rate . .	2,059	2,106	1,988	2,046	2,428	2,438	2,152	2,159	1,952	1,954	2,977	2,977
Birth rates:												
10 to 14 years old. . . .	1.4	1.6	0.8	0.9	4.8	4.8	1.7	1.7	0.9	0.8	2.6	2.6
15 to 19 years old. . . .	59.4	63.6	50.7	56.0	109.7	111.5	78.2	81.8	28.2	28.7	103.7	103.7
20 to 24 years old. . . .	115.7	118.2	109.2	112.6	157.4	158.7	143.3	143.7	80.3	79.5	184.1	184.1
25 to 29 years old. . . .	117.9	119.5	118.8	120.7	112.4	113.1	108.7	109.0	121.5	121.7	152.4	152.4
30 to 34 years old. . . .	78.8	81.0	79.9	82.0	66.6	67.8	61.7	62.9	100.8	101.1	96.7	96.7
35 to 39 years old. . . .	31.6	32.1	31.5	31.7	27.8	27.7	27.4	27.4	48.0	47.3	45.3	45.3
40 to 44 years old. . . .	5.6	5.9	5.4	5.6	5.4	5.3	6.0	6.0	10.4	10.3	10.8	10.8
45 to 49 years old. . . .	0.3	0.3	0.2	0.2	0.3	0.2	0.3	0.3	1.0	1.0	0.6	0.6

[1] Includes other races not shown separately. [2] Persons of Hispanic origin may be of any race.

Source: U.S. Bureau of the Census, *Current Population Reports*, P25-1130.

No. 95. Birth Rates, by Live-Birth Order and Race: 1980 to 1995

[Births per 1,000 women 15 to 44 years old in specified racial group. Live-birth order refers to number of children born alive. Figures for births of order not stated are distributed. See also headnote, table 90]

LIVE-BIRTH ORDER	ALL RACES [1]					WHITE					BLACK				
	1980	1990	1993	1994	1995	1980	1990	1993	1994	1995	1980	1990	1993	1994	1995
Total.	68.4	70.9	67.6	66.7	65.6	65.6	68.3	65.4	64.9	64.5	84.9	86.8	80.5	76.9	71.7
First birth	29.5	29.0	27.5	27.5	27.3	28.8	28.4	27.0	27.0	27.0	33.7	32.4	30.2	29.8	28.5
Second birth	21.8	22.8	21.9	21.5	21.1	21.3	22.4	21.7	21.4	21.2	24.7	25.6	23.4	22.2	20.6
Third birth.	10.3	11.7	11.0	10.7	10.5	9.6	11.1	10.5	10.4	10.3	14.0	15.6	14.1	13.1	11.9
Fourth birth [2].	3.9	4.5	4.3	4.2	6.8	3.4	4.0	3.9	3.8	6.0	6.5	7.4	6.9	6.3	10.7
Fifth birth	1.5	1.7	1.6	1.6	(NA)	1.3	1.4	1.4	1.3	(NA)	2.9	3.2	3.1	2.9	(NA)
Sixth and seventh	1.0	1.0	1.0	1.0	(NA)	0.8	0.8	0.8	0.8	(NA)	2.1	2.0	2.2	2.0	(NA)
Eighth and over	0.4	0.3	0.3	0.3	(NA)	0.3	0.2	0.2	0.2	(NA)	0.9	0.5	0.7	0.6	(NA)

NA Not available. [1] Includes other races not shown separately. [2] 1995 data represents 'forth child and over'.

Source: U.S. National Center for Health Statistics, *Vital Statistics of the United States*, annual; and *Monthly Vital Statistics Reports*.

No. 96. Births to Teens, Unmarried Mothers, and Prenatal Care: 1985 to 1994

[In percents. Represents registered births. See headnote, table 89]

CHARACTERISTIC	1985	1989	1990	1991	1992	1993	1994
Births to teenage mothers, total	12.7	12.8	12.8	12.9	12.7	12.8	13.1
White	10.8	10.7	10.9	11.0	10.9	11.0	11.3
Black	23.0	23.1	23.1	23.1	22.7	22.7	23.2
American Indian, Eskimo, Aleut	19.1	18.8	19.5	20.3	20.0	20.3	21.0
Asian and Pacific Islander [1]	5.5	6.1	5.7	5.8	5.6	5.7	5.7
Filipino	5.8	6.4	6.1	6.1	5.6	5.8	6.0
Chinese	1.1	1.2	1.2	1.1	1.0	1.0	1.0
Japanese	2.9	2.9	2.9	2.7	2.6	2.7	2.8
Hawaiian	15.9	16.4	18.4	18.1	18.4	18.5	19.6
Other	(NA)	(NA)	(NA)	(NA)	(NA)	6.5	6.4
Hispanic origin [2]	16.5	16.7	16.8	17.2	17.1	17.4	17.8
Mexican	17.5	17.4	17.7	18.1	18.0	18.2	16.6
Puerto Rican	20.9	21.9	21.7	21.7	21.4	22.3	23.2
Cuban	7.1	7.0	7.7	7.1	7.1	6.8	7.3
Central and South American	8.2	8.6	9.0	9.4	9.6	9.9	10.4
Other and unknown Hispanic	(NA)	(NA)	(NA)	(NA)	(NA)	21.0	20.8
Percent births to unmarried mothers	22.0	27.1	26.6	28.0	30.1	31.0	32.6
White	14.5	19.0	16.9	18.0	22.6	23.6	25.4
Black	60.1	64.5	66.7	68.2	68.1	68.7	70.4
American Indian, Eskimo, Aleut	40.7	NA	53.6	55.3	55.3	55.8	57.0
Asian and Pacific Islander [1]	10.1	NA	(NA)	(NA)	14.7	15.7	16.2
Filipino	12.1	NA	15.9	16.8	16.8	17.7	18.5
Chinese	3.7	NA	5.0	5.5	6.1	6.7	7.2
Japanese	7.9	NA	9.6	9.8	9.8	10.0	11.2
Hawaiian	(NA)	NA	45.0	45.0	45.7	47.8	48.6
Hispanic origin [2]	29.5	35.5	36.7	38.5	39.1	40.0	43.1
Mexican	25.7	31.7	33.3	35.3	36.3	37.0	40.8
Puerto Rican	51.1	55.2	55.9	57.5	57.5	59.4	60.2
Cuban	16.1	17.5	18.2	19.5	20.2	21.0	22.9
Central and South American	34.9	38.9	41.2	43.1	43.9	45.2	45.9
Percent of mothers beginning prenatal care 1st trimester	76.2	75.5	74.2	76.2	77.7	78.9	80.2
White	79.4	79.0	77.7	79.5	80.8	81.8	82.8
Black	61.8	60.4	60.7	61.9	63.9	66.0	68.3
American Indian, Eskimo, Aleut	60.3	60.5	57.9	59.9	62.1	63.4	65.2
Asian and Pacific Islander [1]	75.0	75.6	(NA)	(NA)	76.6	77.6	79.7
Filipino	77.2	78.0	77.1	77.1	78.7	79.3	81.3
Chinese	82.4	81.9	81.3	82.3	83.8	84.6	86.2
Japanese	85.8	86.7	87.0	87.7	88.2	87.2	89.2
Hawaiian	(NA)	69.7	65.8	68.1	69.9	70.6	77.0
Hispanic origin [2]	61.2	59.5	60.2	61.0	64.2	66.6	68.9
Mexican	59.9	56.7	57.8	58.7	62.1	64.8	67.3
Puerto Rican	58.3	62.7	63.5	65.0	67.8	70.0	71.7
Cuban	82.5	83.2	84.8	85.4	86.8	88.9	90.1
Central and South American	60.6	60.8	61.5	63.4	66.8	68.7	71.2
Percent of mothers beginning prenatal care 3d trimester or no care	5.7	6.4	6.0	5.8	5.2	4.8	4.4
White	4.7	5.2	4.9	4.7	4.2	3.9	3.6
Black	10.0	11.7	10.9	10.7	9.9	9.0	8.2
American Indian, Eskimo, Aleut	11.5	11.9	12.9	12.2	11.0	10.3	9.8
Asian and Pacific Islander [1]	6.1	5.8	(NA)	(NA)	4.9	4.6	4.1
Filipino	4.6	4.6	4.5	5.0	4.3	4.0	3.6
Chinese	4.2	3.5	3.4	3.4	2.9	2.9	2.7
Japanese	2.6	2.6	2.9	2.5	2.4	2.8	1.9
Hawaiian	(NA)	7.6	8.7	7.5	7.0	6.7	4.7
Hispanic origin [2]	12.5	13.0	12.0	11.0	9.5	8.8	7.6
Mexican	12.9	14.6	13.2	12.2	10.5	9.7	8.3
Puerto Rican	15.5	11.3	10.6	9.1	8.0	7.1	6.5
Cuban	3.7	4.0	2.8	2.4	2.1	1.8	1.6
Central and South American	12.5	11.9	10.9	9.5	7.9	7.3	6.5
Percent of births with low birth weight [3]	6.8	7.0	7.0	7.1	7.1	7.2	7.3
White	5.6	5.7	5.7	5.8	5.8	6.0	6.1
Black	12.4	13.2	13.3	13.6	13.3	13.3	13.2
American Indian, Eskimo, Aleut	5.9	6.4	6.1	6.2	6.2	6.4	6.4
Asian and Pacific Islander [1]	6.1	6.9	(NA)	(NA)	6.6	6.6	6.8
Filipino	6.9	7.3	7.3	7.3	7.4	7.0	7.8
Chinese	5.0	5.0	4.7	5.1	5.0	4.9	4.8
Japanese	5.9	6.4	6.2	5.9	7.0	6.5	6.9
Hawaiian	6.4	7.2	7.2	6.7	6.9	6.8	7.2
Hispanic origin [2]	6.2	6.2	6.1	6.1	6.1	6.2	6.2
Mexican	5.8	5.6	5.5	5.6	5.6	5.8	5.8
Puerto Rican	8.7	9.5	9.0	9.4	9.2	9.2	9.1
Cuban	6.0	5.8	5.7	5.6	6.1	6.2	6.3
Central and South American	5.7	5.8	5.8	5.9	5.8	5.9	6.0

NA Not available. [1] Includes other races not shown separately. [2] Hispanic persons may be of any race. Includes other types, not shown separately. [3] Births less than 2,500 grams (5 lb.-8 oz.).

Source: U.S. National Center for Health Statistics, *Vital Statistics of the United States*, annual, *Monthly Vital Statistics Report*, and unpublished data.

No. 97. Births to Unmarried Women, by Race of Child and Age of Mother: 1980 to 1994

[Excludes births to nonresidents of United States. Marital status is inferred from a comparison of the child's and parents' surnames on the birth certificate for those States that do not report on marital status. No estimates included for misstatements on birth records or failures to register births. See also Appendix III]

RACE OF CHILD AND AGE OF MOTHER	1980	1990	1992	1993	1994
NUMBER (1,000)					
Total live births [1]	666	1,165	1,225	1,240	1,290
White	320	647	722	742	794
Black	326	473	459	452	448
Under 15 years old	9	11	11	11	12
15 to 19 years old	263	350	354	357	361
20 to 24 years old	237	404	436	439	449
25 to 29 years old	100	230	233	234	238
30 to 34 years old	41	118	128	132	137
35 years old and over	16	53	63	67	72
PERCENT DISTRIBUTION					
Total [1]	100.0	100.0	100.0	100.0	100.0
White	48.1	55.6	58.9	59.8	61.6
Black	48.9	40.6	37.5	36.5	34.8
Under 15 years	1.4	0.9	0.9	0.9	0.9
15 to 19 years	39.5	30.0	28.9	28.8	29.6
20 to 24 years	35.6	34.7	35.6	35.4	34.8
25 to 29 years	15.0	19.7	19.1	18.9	18.4
30 to 34 years	6.2	10.1	10.4	10.7	10.6
35 years and over	2.4	4.5	5.1	5.4	5.6
AS PERCENT OF ALL BIRTHS IN RACIAL GROUPS					
Total [1]	18.4	28.0	30.1	31.0	32.6
White	11.0	20.1	22.6	23.6	25.4
Black	55.2	65.2	68.1	68.7	70.4
BIRTH RATE [2]					
Total [1, 3]	29.4	43.8	45.2	45.3	46.9
White [3]	17.6	31.8	35.2	35.9	38.3
Black [3]	82.9	93.9	86.5	84.0	82.1
15 to 19 years	27.6	42.5	44.6	44.5	46.4
20 to 24 years	40.9	65.1	68.5	69.2	72.2
25 to 29 years	34.0	56.0	56.5	57.1	59.0
30 to 34 years	21.1	37.6	37.9	38.5	40.1

[1] Includes other races not shown separately. [2] Rate per 1,000 unmarried women (never-married, widowed, and divorced) estimated as of July 1. [3] Covers women aged 15 to 44 years.

Source: U.S. National Center for Health Statistics, *Vital Statistics of the United States*, annual; *Monthly Vital Statistics Report;* and unpublished data.

No. 98. Low Birth Weight and Births to Teenage Mothers and to Unmarried Women—States: 1990 and 1995

[Represents registered births. Excludes births to nonresidents of the United States. Based on 100 percent of births in all States and the District of Columbia. See Appendix III]

DIVISION AND STATE	PERCENT OF BIRTHS WITH LOW BIRTH WEIGHT[1]		BIRTHS TO TEENAGE MOTHERS, PERCENT OF TOTAL		BIRTHS TO UNMARRIED WOMEN, PERCENT OF TOTAL	
	1990	1995	1990	1995	1990	1995
U.S.	7.0	7.3	12.8	13.2	28.0	32.0
N.E.	5.9	(NA)	8.4	(NA)	24.2	(NA)
ME	5.1	6.3	10.8	10.6	22.6	27.8
NH	4.9	5.3	7.2	7.6	16.9	22.4
VT	5.3	5.4	8.5	8.1	20.1	24.8
MA	5.9	6.0	8.0	7.5	24.7	25.6
RI	6.2	6.7	10.5	9.7	26.3	29.2
CT	6.6	6.9	8.2	8.5	[2]26.6	29.9
M.A.	7.3	(NA)	9.5	(NA)	29.9	(NA)
NY	7.6	7.6	9.1	9.3	[2]33.0	37.9
NJ	7.0	7.4	8.4	8.0	24.3	27.0
PA	7.1	7.4	10.9	10.8	28.6	32.3
E.N.C.	7.1	(NA)	13.2	(NA)	28.3	(NA)
OH	7.1	7.5	13.8	13.7	[2]28.9	32.9
IN	6.6	7.5	14.5	14.6	26.2	31.7
IL	7.6	7.8	13.1	12.8	31.7	33.6
MI	7.6	7.5	13.5	12.4	[2]26.2	0.0
WI	5.9	6.0	10.2	10.5	24.2	27.3
W.N.C.	5.9	(NA)	11.1	(NA)	23.2	(NA)
MN	5.1	5.7	8.0	8.4	20.9	23.7
IA	5.4	6.0	10.2	11.0	21.0	25.2
MO	7.1	7.6	14.4	14.4	28.6	32.0
ND	5.5	5.2	8.6	9.6	18.4	23.5
SD	5.1	5.5	10.8	11.9	22.9	28.4
NE	5.3	6.4	9.8	10.0	20.7	24.3
KS	6.2	6.4	12.3	13.3	21.5	26.4
S.A.	7.9	(NA)	14.4	(NA)	30.9	(NA)
DE	7.6	8.4	11.9	13.2	29.0	35.0
MD	7.8	8.5	10.5	10.3	[2]29.6	33.4
DC	15.1	13.2	17.8	16.2	64.9	66.0
VA	7.2	7.6	11.7	11.4	26.0	29.2
WV	7.1	7.9	17.8	17.2	25.4	30.5
NC	8.0	8.7	16.2	15.2	29.4	31.4
SC	8.7	9.3	17.1	17.3	32.7	37.3
GA	8.7	8.7	16.7	16.3	32.8	35.2
FL	7.4	7.7	13.9	13.7	31.7	35.8
E.S.C.	8.2	(NA)	18.4	(NA)	30.6	(NA)
KY	7.1	7.6	17.5	17.1	23.6	28.6
TN	8.2	8.6	17.6	16.9	30.2	32.8
AL	8.4	9.0	18.2	18.5	30.1	34.5
MS	9.6	9.8	21.3	22.2	40.5	45.3
W.S.C.	7.3	(NA)	16.3	(NA)	22.2	(NA)
AR	8.2	8.2	19.7	19.6	29.4	32.9
LA	9.2	9.5	17.6	19.2	36.8	42.6
OK	6.6	6.9	16.2	17.0	25.2	30.4
TX	6.9	7.1	15.6	16.6	[2]17.5	30.0
Mountain	6.8	(NA)	12.8	(NA)	25.1	(NA)
MT	6.2	5.8	11.5	12.6	[2]23.7	26.3
ID	5.7	5.9	12.3	14.1	16.7	19.9
WY	7.4	7.4	13.6	15.2	19.8	26.5
CO	8.0	8.4	11.3	12.2	21.2	24.9
NM	7.4	7.5	16.3	18.4	35.4	42.6
AZ	6.4	6.8	14.2	15.2	32.7	38.2
UT	5.7	6.3	10.3	10.8	13.5	15.7
NV	7.2	7.4	12.6	13.7	[2]25.4	42.0
Pacific	5.7	(NA)	11.5	(NA)	30.2	(NA)
WA	5.3	5.5	10.8	11.5	23.7	26.7
OR	5.0	5.5	12.0	13.0	25.7	28.9
CA	5.8	6.0	11.6	12.4	[2]31.6	31.9
AK	4.8	5.4	9.7	11.2	26.2	29.9
HI	7.1	7.0	10.5	10.1	24.8	29.2

NA Not available. [1] Less than 2,500 grams (5 pounds-8 ounces). [2] Marital status of mother is inferred.

Source: U.S. National Center for Health Statistics, *Vital Statistics of the United States*, annual; and *Monthly Vital Statistics Report.*

No. 99. Live Births, by Place of Delivery, Median and Low Birth Weight, and Prenatal Care: 1980 to 1995

[Represents registered births. Excludes births to nonresidents of the United States. For total number of births, see table 90. See Appendix III]

ITEM	1980	1985	1990	1992	1993	1994	1995, prel.
Births attended (1,000):							
In hospital [1]	3,576	3,722	4,110	4,022	3,959	3,912	(NA)
By physician, not in hospital	12	10	14	10	8	7	(NA)
By midwife and other, not in hospital [2]	24	29	21	21	20	21	(NA)
Median birth weight [3 4]	7 lb.-7 oz.	7 lb.-7 oz.	7 lb.-7 oz.	7 lb.-7 oz.	7 lb.-7 oz.	(NA)	(NA)
Percent of births with low birth weight	6.8	6.8	7.0	7.1	7.2	7.3	7.3
White	5.7	5.6	5.7	5.8	6.0	6.1	6.2
Black	12.5	12.4	13.3	13.3	13.3	13.2	13.0
Percent of births by period in which prenatal care began:							
1st trimester	76.3	76.2	74.2	77.7	78.9	80.2	81.2
3d trimester or no prenatal care	5.1	5.7	6.0	5.2	4.8	4.4	(NA)

NA Not available. [1] Includes all births in hospitals or institutions and in clinics. [2] Includes births with attendant not specified. [3] Beginning 1990, median birth weight based on race of mother; prior to 1990, based on race of child. [4] Includes other races not shown separately.

No. 100. Cesarean Section Deliveries, by Age of Mother: 1990 to 1994

[In thousands, except rate. 1990 excludes data for Oklahoma, which did not report method of delivery on the birth certificate]

AGE OF MOTHER	1990	1993	1994	AGE OF MOTHER	1990	1993	1994
Births by method of delivery	4,111	4,000	3,953	Black births by method of delivery	679	659	636
Vaginal	3,111	3,099	3,068	Vaginal	517	510	494
After previous cesarean	84	104	110	Cesarean deliveries	146	143	136
Cesarean deliveries	914	862	831	Rate			
Primary	575	539	521				
Repeat	339	323	310	Cesarean delivery rate [1]	23	22	21
White births by method of delivery	3,252	3,150	3,121	Primary [2]	16	15	15
Vaginal	2,454	2,435	2,436	Rate of vaginal cesarean birth			
Cesarean deliveries	733	682	656	after previous cesarean [3]	19	24	26

[1] Percent of all live births by cesarean delivery. [2] Number of primary cesareans per 100 live births to women who have not had a previous cesarean. [3] Number of vaginal births after previous cesarean delivery per 100 live births to women with a previous cesarean delivery.

No. 101. Live Births and Births to Teen Mothers—20 Largest Metro. Areas: 1993

[Excludes births to nonresidents of the United States. Data are by place of residence. Metropolitan statistical areas (MSA's), consolidated metropolitan statistical areas (CMSA's), and New England County Metropolitan Areas (NECMA's) are defined by the U.S. Office of Management and Budget as of June 30,1990. See Appendix II for definitions and components]

METROPOLITAN AREA	ALL BIRTHS		BIRTHS TO TEENS	
	Number	Rate per 1,000 population	Number of teen births	Percent of total births
New York-Northern New Jersey-Long Island, NY-NJ-CT-PA CMSA/NECMA	290,532	16	22,950	8
Los Angeles-Anaheim-Riverside, CA CMSA	310,792	20	36,390	12
Chicago-Gary-Lake County, IL-IN-WI CMSA	146,678	18	17,688	12
Washington, DC-MD-VA MSA	66,625	16	5,262	8
San Francisco-Oakland-San Jose, CA CMSA	101,011	16	8,753	9
Philadelphia-Wilmington-Trenton, PA-NJ-DE-MD CMSA	89,732	15	9,609	11
Boston-Lawrence-Salem-Lowell-Brockton, MA NECMA	54,291	14	3,402	6
Detroit-Ann Arbor, MI CMSA	72,354	15	8,347	12
Dallas-Fort Worth, TX CMSA	73,645	18	9,788	13
Houston-Galveston-Brazoria, TX CMSA	74,277	19	10,226	14
Miami-Fort Lauderdale, FL CMSA	52,393	16	5,476	10
Seattle-Tacoma, WA CMSA	40,565	15	3,458	9
Atlanta, GA MSA	51,280	17	5,955	12
Cleveland-Akron-Lorain, OH CMSA	40,822	15	4,891	12
Minneapolis-St.Paul, MN-WI MSA	40,314	16	2,972	7
San Diego, CA MSA	48,935	19	5,207	11
St. Louis, MO-IL MSA	38,042	15	4,953	13
Pittsburgh-Beaver Valley, PA CMSA	27,177	12	2,548	9
Phoenix, AZ MSA	40,406	18	5,643	14
Tampa-St. Petersburg-Clearwater, FL MSA	27,658	13	3,653	13
Baltimore, MD MSA	36,237	15	4,028	11
Denver-Boulder, CO CMSA	31,139	16	3,330	11
Cinncinati-Hamilton, OH-KY-IN CMSA	27,104	15	3,611	13
Milwaukee-Racine, WI CMSA	25,099	15	3,235	13
Kansas City, MO-KS MSA	24,787	15	3,011	12

Source of tables 99-101: U.S. National Center for Health Statistics, *Vital Statistics of the United States*, annual; and unpublished data.

No. 102. Women Who Have Had a Child in the Last Year, by Age: 1980 to 1994

[See headnote, table 103]

AGE OF MOTHER	WOMEN WHO HAD A CHILD IN LAST YEAR (1,000)			TOTAL BIRTHS PER 1,000 WOMEN			FIRST BIRTHS PER 1,000 WOMEN		
	1980	1990	1994	1980	1990	1994	1980	1990	1994
Total	3,247	3,913	3,890	71.1	67.0	64.7	28.5	26.4	27.4
15 to 29 years old [1]	2,476	2,568	2,389	103.7	90.8	85.6	48.6	43.2	46.3
15 to 19 years old	(NA)	338	397	(NA)	39.8	45.2	(NA)	30.1	36.3
20 to 24 years old [2]	1,396	1,038	938	96.6	113.4	100.7	(NA)	51.8	58.4
25 to 29 years old	1,081	1,192	1,054	114.8	112.1	107.7	(NA)	46.2	43.9
30 to 44 years old	770	1,346	1,501	35.4	44.7	46.6	6.3	10.6	11.0
30 to 34 years old	519	892	1,006	60.0	80.4	90.4	(NA)	21.9	23.0
35 to 39 years old	192	377	399	26.9	37.3	36.0	(NA)	6.5	7.3
40 to 44 years old	59	77	95	9.9	8.6	9.6	(NA)	1.2	1.8

NA Not available. [1] For 1980-88, 18 to 29 years old. [2] For 1980-88, 18 to 24 years old.

Source: U.S. Bureau of the Census, *Current Population Reports*, P20-375, P20-454 and P20-482.

No. 103. Characteristics of Women Who Have Had a Child in the Last Year: 1995

[As of June. Covers civilian noninstitutional population. Since the number of women who had a birth during the 12-month period was tabulated and not the actual numbers of births, some small underestimation of fertility for this period may exist due to the omission of: (1) Multiple births, (2) Two or more live births spaced within the 12-month period (the woman is counted only once), (3) Women who had births in the period and who did not survive to the survey date, (4) Women who were in institutions and therefore not in the survey universe. These losses may be somewhat offset by the inclusion in the CPS of births to immigrants who did not have their children born in the United States and births to nonresident women. These births would not have been recorded in the vital registration system. Based on Current Population Survey (CPS); see text, section 1, and Appendix III]

CHARACTERISTIC	TOTAL, 15 TO 44 YEARS OLD			15 TO 29 YEARS OLD			30 TO 44 YEARS OLD		
	Number of women (1,000)	Women who have had a child in the last year: Total births per 1,000 women	Women who have had a child in the last year: First births per 1,000 women	Number of women (1,000)	Women who have had a child in the last year: Total births per 1,000 women	Women who have had a child in the last year: First births per 1,000 women	Number of women (1,000)	Women who have had a child in the last year: Total births per 1,000 women	Women who have had a child in the last year: First births per 1,000 women
Total [1]	60,225	61.4	23.2	27,742	81.2	38.1	32,483	44.4	10.4
White	48,603	59.2	22.6	22,001	76.6	36.5	26,602	44.8	11.1
Black	8,617	70.6	26.4	4,276	109.0	49.6	4,342	32.7	3.7
Hispanic [2]	6,632	79.6	25.0	3,511	99.9	40.6	3,120	56.8	7.5
Currently married	31,616	85.5	30.3	8,445	168.2	76.1	23,171	55.3	13.6
Married, spouse present	29,202	87.2	31.4	7,720	172.4	78.9	21,482	56.6	14.3
Married, spouse absent [3]	2,414	64.5	17.4	725	123.4	46.6	1,689	39.3	4.9
Widowed or divorced	5,762	28.4	4.1	1,015	65.2	11.8	4,748	20.6	2.5
Never married	22,846	36.3	18.0	18,282	41.9	22.0	4,564	14.0	2.1
Educational attainment:									
Less than high school	12,629	57.3	19.6	9,005	65.6	26.2	3,624	36.9	3.1
High school, 4 years	18,404	67.4	25.5	7,050	119.6	56.6	11,354	35.0	6.2
College: 1 or more years	29,192	59.3	23.2	11,687	70.0	36.2	17,505	52.2	14.6
No degree	12,724	56.1	21.2	6,578	71.1	34.3	6,147	40.0	7.2
Associate degree	4,663	56.9	19.2	1,451	102.6	47.1	3,213	36.2	6.7
Bachelor's degree	8,884	65.3	27.0	3,149	56.2	34.2	5,735	70.2	23.1
Grad. or prof. degree	2,921	59.2	26.8	510	48.8	41.7	2,411	61.4	23.7
Labor force status:									
Employed	39,989	46.5	20.9	16,596	61.8	35.4	23,393	35.6	10.6
Unemployed	3,287	53.5	22.8	2,086	59.8	30.4	1,202	42.6	9.6
Not in labor force	16,949	96.1	28.5	9,060	121.7	44.8	7,889	71.0	9.8
Occupation of employed women:									
Managerial-professional	11,059	46.2	22.3	3,148	65.3	40.2	7,911	38.6	15.2
Tech., sales, admin. support	16,997	48.6	21.5	7,754	63.8	36.6	9,243	35.9	8.8
Service workers	7,612	44.0	16.6	4,001	53.0	25.6	3,611	34.0	6.6
Farming, forestry, and fishing	501	41.0	27.9	235	40.7	40.7	266	41.3	16.5
Precision prod., craft, repair	813	56.6	37.5	272	87.4	70.4	541	41.1	21.0
Operators, fabricators, laborers	3,007	39.5	17.8	1,186	67.3	39.1	1,821	21.5	3.6
Family income: Under $10,000	6,957	91.0	32.8	4,081	124.1	49.7	2,875	44.1	8.8
$10,000 to $19,999	8,159	64.3	25.8	4,358	93.1	44.5	3,801	31.4	4.3
$20,000 to $24,999	4,542	60.6	20.3	2,355	83.5	37.6	2,188	36.0	1.7
$25,000 to $29,999	4,364	57.0	18.9	2,104	77.8	34.1	2,259	37.7	4.7
$30,000 to $34,999	4,076	60.6	24.3	1,840	75.6	43.4	2,236	48.2	8.6
$35,000 to $49,999	9,949	59.1	20.8	4,160	80.8	32.9	5,789	43.5	12.2
$50,000 to $74,999	9,720	52.5	23.3	3,735	62.8	41.0	5,985	46.0	12.3
$75,000 and over	7,088	53.1	19.2	2,765	34.8	13.6	4,323	64.8	22.8

[1] Includes women of other races and women with family income not reported, not shown separately. [2] Persons of Hispanic origin may be of any race. [3] Includes separated women.

Source: U.S. Bureau of the Census, *Current Population Reports*, P20-375, P20-454 and P20-482.

No. 104. Women Who Have Had a Child in the Last Year, by Age and Labor Force Status: 1980 to 1995

[See headnote, table 103]

YEAR	TOTAL, 18 TO 44 YEARS OLD			18 TO 29 YEARS OLD			30 TO 44 YEARS OLD		
	Number (1,000)	In the labor force		Number (1,000)	In the labor force		Number (1,000)	In the labor force	
		Number (1,000)	Percent		Number (1,000)	Percent		Number (1,000)	Percent
1980	3,247	1,233	38	2,476	947	38	770	287	37
1981	3,381	1,411	42	2,499	1,004	40	881	407	46
1982	3,433	1,508	44	2,445	1,040	43	988	469	48
1983	3,625	1,563	43	2,682	1,138	42	942	425	45
1984	3,311	1,547	47	2,375	1,058	45	936	489	52
1985	3,497	1,691	48	2,512	1,204	48	984	488	50
1986	3,625	1,805	50	2,452	1,185	48	1,174	620	53
1987	3,701	1,881	51	2,521	1,258	50	1,180	623	53
1988	3,667	1,866	51	2,384	1,177	49	1,283	688	54
1990 [1]	3,913	2,068	53	2,568	1,275	50	1,346	793	59
1992 [1]	3,688	1,985	54	2,346	1,182	50	1,342	802	60
1994 [1]	3,890	2,066	53	2,389	1,209	51	1,501	857	57
1995 [1]	3,696	2,034	55	2,252	1,150	51	1,444	884	61

[1] Lower age limit is 15 years old.

Source: U.S. Bureau of the Census, *Current Population Reports*, P20-482; and unpublished data from the June 1995 Current Population Survey.

No. 105. Childless Women and Children Ever Born, by Race, Age, and Marital Status: 1995

[See headnote, table 103]

CHARACTERISTIC	Total number of women (1,000)	WOMEN BY NUMBER OF CHILDREN EVER BORN (percent)				CHILDREN EVER BORN	
		Total	None	One	Two or more	Total number (1,000)	Per 1,000 women
ALL RACES [1]							
Women ever married	37,378	100	19.0	22.3	58.7	65,946	1,764
15 to 19 years old	319	100	43.9	45.5	10.6	218	684
20 to 24 years old	3,036	100	36.7	34.4	28.9	3,098	1,020
25 to 29 years old	6,105	100	28.8	29.2	42.0	8,112	1,329
30 to 34 years old	9,006	100	18.7	23.0	58.4	15,634	1,736
35 to 39 years old	9,660	100	13.2	16.9	69.8	19,578	2,027
40 to 44 years old	9,252	100	12.3	17.9	69.8	19,310	2,087
Women never married	22,846	100	79.1	10.8	10.2	8,886	389
15 to 19 years old	8,701	100	92.4	6.3	1.3	826	95
20 to 24 years old	6,018	100	78.3	12.6	9.1	2,106	350
25 to 29 years old	3,564	100	69.6	13.4	17.0	2,181	612
30 to 34 years old	2,050	100	61.7	14.9	23.4	1,684	821
35 to 39 years old	1,523	100	60.5	15.4	24.1	1,315	863
40 to 44 years old	992	100	65.9	14.6	19.5	775	782
WHITE							
Women ever married	31,819	100	19.6	22.3	58.1	55,113	1,732
15 to 19 years old	269	100	40.1	48.6	11.3	197	732
20 to 24 years old	2,651	100	37.5	34.3	28.3	2,636	994
25 to 29 years old	5,243	100	29.7	29.6	40.7	6,758	1,289
30 to 34 years old	7,652	100	19.3	22.8	58.1	12,958	1,693
35 to 39 years old	8,233	100	13.6	16.6	69.9	16,519	2,006
40 to 44 years old	7,771	100	12.5	17.9	69.6	16,045	2,065
Women never married	16,784	100	87.0	8.0	5.0	3,597	214
15 to 19 years old	6,606	100	94.6	4.5	0.9	456	67
20 to 24 years old	4,516	100	84.1	10.2	6.7	1,075	238
25 to 29 years old	2,517	100	80.5	10.6	8.8	872	346
30 to 34 years old	1,306	100	77.0	9.9	13.0	605	463
35 to 39 years old	946	100	81.3	10.9	7.8	312	329
40 to 44 years old	693	100	80.4	11.8	7.9	277	400
BLACK							
Women ever married	3,746	100	14.1	22.8	63.1	7,417	1,980
15 to 19 years old	23	(B)	(B)	(B)	(B)	13	(B)
20 to 24 years old	235	100	29.4	36.7	33.9	297	1,263
25 to 29 years old	568	100	16.4	29.1	54.9	951	1,676
30 to 34 years old	888	100	13.9	24.3	61.7	1,841	2,073
35 to 39 years old	986	100	10.7	18.0	71.4	2,079	2,109
40 to 44 years old	1,046	100	11.7	19.4	69.0	2,236	2,137
Women never married	4,872	100	52.1	20.6	27.4	4,773	980
15 to 19 years old	1,439	100	82.9	14.6	2.5	302	210
20 to 24 years old	1,160	100	54.7	22.3	23.0	933	804
25 to 29 years old	851	100	37.4	22.2	40.4	1,166	1,370
30 to 34 years old	641	100	30.9	26.0	43.1	974	1,519
35 to 39 years old	521	100	22.9	23.1	54.0	953	1,831
40 to 44 years old	260	100	28.8	22.5	48.8	444	1,711

B Base figure too small to meet statistical standards for reliability. [1] Includes other races, not shown separately.

Source: U.S. Bureau of the Census, *Current Population Reports*, series P20-482.

No. 106. Lifetime Births Expected per 1,000 Wives: 1971 to 1992

[See headnote, table 103]

YEAR	LIFETIME BIRTHS TO ALL WIVES [1] AGED—			LIFETIME BIRTHS TO WHITE WIVES AGED—			LIFETIME BIRTHS TO BLACK WIVES AGED—			LIFETIME BIRTHS TO HISPANIC [2] WIVES AGED—		
	18 to 24 yrs. old	25 to 29 yrs. old	30 to 34 yrs. old	18 to 24 yrs. old	25 to 29 yrs. old	30 to 34 yrs. old	18 to 24 yrs. old	25 to 29 yrs. old	30 to 34 yrs. old	18 to 24 yrs. old	25 to 29 yrs. old	30 to 34 yrs. old
1971	2,375	2,619	2,989	2,353	2,577	2,936	2,623	3,112	3,714	(NA)	(NA)	(NA)
1975	2,173	2,260	2,610	2,147	2,233	2,564	2,489	2,587	3,212	2,223	2,607	3,236
1980	2,134	2,166	2,248	2,130	2,146	2,223	2,155	2,426	2,522	2,428	2,495	2,909
1985	2,183	2,236	2,167	2,177	2,227	2,139	2,242	2,259	2,521	2,367	2,628	2,712
1990	2,244	2,285	2,277	2,218	2,272	2,257	2,509	2,443	2,579	2,404	2,482	2,824
1992	2,279	2,271	2,218	2,274	2,259	2,208	2,353	2,389	2,362	2,511	2,437	2,600

NA Not available. [1] Includes other races not shown separately. [2] Persons of Hispanic origin may be of any race.

No. 107. Lifetime Births Expected by Women, 18 to 34 Years Old, by Selected Characteristics: 1992

[As of June. Covers women in the civilian noninstitutional population. Based on Current Population Survey; see text, section 1, and Appendix III]

CHARACTERISTIC	Women reporting on birth expectations (1,000)	RATE PER 1,000 WOMEN			PERCENTAGE EXPECTING—	
		Births to date	Future births expected	Lifetime births expected	No lifetime births	No future births
Total [1]	24,223	1,135	963	2,098	9.3	48.3
White	20,141	1,077	1,014	2,091	9.3	46.1
Black	3,217	1,508	628	2,136	9.3	63.4
Hispanic [2]	2,357	1,493	838	2,331	5.7	51.4
Not a high school graduate	3,599	1,776	616	2,393	7.6	63.8
High school, 4 years	8,760	1,325	718	2,043	9.0	57.9
College: 1 or more years	11,864	800	1,249	2,049	10.0	36.5
Some college, no degree	5,871	848	1,216	2,064	10.0	39.2
Associate degree	1,731	1,020	1,018	2,038	8.9	43.4
Bachelor's degree	3,466	663	1,380	2,043	10.3	31.0
Graduate or professional degree	795	563	1,427	1,990	12.0	26.0
In labor force	17,834	929	1,069	1,998	10.5	44.1
Employed	16,130	903	1,077	1,980	10.7	43.6
Unemployed	1,705	1,176	991	2,167	8.4	49.3
Not in labor force	6,389	1,710	667	2,377	6.0	60.1
Managerial and professional	3,760	725	1,232	1,957	11.3	36.8
Technical, sales, and admin. support	7,511	835	1,126	1,962	10.2	41.0
Service workers	3,127	1,097	974	2,071	9.5	48.2
Farming, forestry, and fishing	198	1,426	972	2,398	14.1	55.5
Precision production, craft, and repair	299	1,135	714	1,849	12.7	59.5
Operators, fabricators, and laborers	1,235	1,223	675	1,897	13.5	62.4

[1] Includes other races not shown separately. [2] Persons of Hispanic origin may be of any race.
Source of tables 106 and 107: U.S. Bureau of the Census, *Current Population Reports*, series P20-470.

No. 108. Pregnancies, Number and Outcome: 1976 to 1992

[**Live births:** source of data is statistics of registered births published annually by National Center for Health Statistics (NCHS). **Induced abortions:** derived from published reports by the Alan Guttmacher Institute. **Fetal losses:** based on the National Survey of Family Growth conducted by NCHS]

YEAR	NUMBER (1,000)				RATE PER 1,000 WOMEN, 15 TO 44 YEARS OLD			
	Total	Live births	Induced abortions	Fetal losses	Total	Live births	Induced abortions	Fetal losses
1976	5,002	3,168	1.179	655	102.7	65.0	24.2	13.4
1977	5,331	3,327	1,317	687	107.0	66.8	26.4	13.8
1978	5,433	3,333	1,410	690	106.7	65.5	27.7	13.5
1979	5,714	3,494	1,498	722	109.9	67.2	28.8	13.9
1980	5,912	3,612	1,554	746	111.9	68.4	29.4	14.1
1981	5,958	3,629	1,577	751	110.5	67.3	29.3	13.9
1982	6,024	3,681	1,574	769	110.1	67.3	28.8	14.1
1983	5,977	3,639	1,575	763	108.0	65.7	28.5	13.8
1984	6,019	3,669	1,577	773	107.4	65.5	28.1	13.8
1985	6,144	3,761	1,589	795	108.3	66.3	28.0	14.0
1986	6,129	3,757	1,574	798	106.7	65.4	27.4	13.9
1987	6,183	3,809	1,559	815	106.8	65.8	26.9	14.1
1988	6,341	3,910	1,591	840	109.1	67.3	27.4	14.5
1989	6,480	4,041	1,567	873	111.0	69.2	26.8	15.0
1990	6,668	4,158	1,609	902	113.8	70.9	27.4	15.4
1991	6,563	4,111	1,557	896	111.1	69.6	26.3	15.2
1992	6,484	4,065	1,529	890	109.9	68.9	25.9	15.1

Source: U.S. National Center for Health Statistics, *Monthly Vital Statistics Report*, vol. 41, No. 6, Supplement.

No. 109. Pregnancies, by Outcome, Age of Woman, and Race: 1991

[See headnote, table 108]

ITEM	Total	Under 15 years old	15 to 19 years old	20 to 24 years old	25 to 29 years old	30 to 34 years old	35 to 39 years old	40 years old and over
PREGNANCIES								
Non-Hispanic:								
White, pregnancies	3,964	8	489	1,007	1,145	684	368	63
Live births	2,636	3	250	637	834	640	235	36
Induced abortions	774	4	164	264	163	106	58	16
Fetal losses	556	1	75	107	148	136	76	11
Black, pregnancies	1,344	14	272	439	320	202	81	15
Live births	673	6	149	216	160	98	37	6
Induced abortions	507	7	101	178	119	67	29	7
Fetal losses	164	1	22	45	41	37	15	3
Hispanic:								
Pregnancies	965	5	177	306	250	149	64	14
Live births	623	2	105	199	170	100	39	8
Induced abortions	208	1	40	73	60	28	13	4
Fetal losses	134	1	32	33	30	22	12	2
RATE PER 1,000 WOMEN								
Non-Hispanic:								
White, pregnancies	91.8	1.3	84.7	151.4	154.7	107.6	47.3	8.6
Live births	61.0	0.5	43.4	95.7	112.7	77.9	30.2	4.8
Induced abortions	17.9	0.7	28.4	39.6	22.0	12.9	7.4	2.2
Fetal losses	12.9	0.2	13.0	16.0	20.0	16.8	9.7	1.6
Black, pregnancies	174.8	11.0	216.7	337.2	232.3	142.7	63.9	14.4
Live births	87.6	4.9	118.9	166.1	116.3	69.3	28.9	5.7
Induced abortions	65.9	5.1	80.5	136.4	86.3	47.1	23.0	6.2
Fetal losses	21.3	0.9	17.2	34.7	29.7	26.3	12.1	2.4
Hispanic:								
Pregnancies	167.4	4.8	180.2	285.6	224.3	143.9	74.8	19.8
Live births	108.1	2.4	106.7	186.3	152.8	96.1	44.9	11.1
Induced abortions	36.2	1.4	40.4	68.1	44.4	27.1	15.5	5.2
Fetal losses	23.2	1.0	33.1	31.2	27.1	20.7	14.4	3.6

Source: U.S. National Center for Health Statistics, *Monthly Vital Statistics Report*, vol. 43, No. 12.

No. 110. Contraceptive Use by Women, 15 to 44 Years Old: 1995

[Based on samples of the female population of of the United States; see source for details. See Appendix III]

CONTRACEPTIVE STATUS AND METHOD	All women [1]	AGE			RACE			MARITAL STATUS		
		15-24 years	25-34 years	35-44 years	Non-Hispanic		His-panic	Never married	Cur-rently married	For-merly married
					White	Black				
All women (1,000)	60,201	18,002	20,758	21,440	42,522	8,210	6,702	22,679	29,673	7,849
PERCENT DISTRIBUTION										
Sterile [2]	29.7	2.6	25.0	57.0	30.2	31.5	28.4	6.9	43.2	45.1
Surgically sterile	27.9	1.8	23.6	54.0	28.5	29.7	26.3	5.7	41.1	42.5
Noncontraceptively sterile [3]	3.1	0.1	1.2	7.4	3.2	3.7	2.3	0.9	4.1	5.8
Contraceptively sterile [4]	24.8	1.7	22.4	46.6	25.3	26.0	24.0	4.8	37.0	36.7
Nonsurgically sterile [5]	1.7	0.7	1.3	2.8	1.6	1.8	2.0	1.1	2.0	2.2
Pregnant, postpartum	4.6	5.9	6.9	1.3	4.3	4.5	6.3	3.1	6.4	1.9
Seeking pregnancy	4.0	2.1	6.2	3.5	3.7	4.6	4.0	1.5	6.4	2.1
Other nonusers	22.3	44.4	13.3	12.6	21.1	23.1	26.3	46.8	4.7	18.4
Never had intercourse	10.9	30.8	3.4	1.4	10.4	8.9	12.1	28.9	-	0.0
No intercourse in last month [6]	6.2	7.0	5.3	6.5	5.7	7.2	8.6	11.5	0.5	12.7
Had intercourse in last month [6]	5.2	6.6	4.6	4.7	5.0	7.0	5.6	6.4	4.2	5.7
Nonsurgical contraceptors	39.7	45.0	49.1	26.1	41.2	36.1	35.1	41.8	39.7	32.4
Pill	17.3	23.1	23.7	6.3	18.8	14.8	13.6	20.4	15.6	14.6
IUD	0.5	0.1	0.6	0.8	0.5	0.5	0.9	0.3	0.7	0.4
Diaphragm	1.2	0.2	1.2	2.0	1.5	0.5	0.4	0.5	1.8	0.9
Condom	13.1	13.9	15.0	10.7	13.0	12.5	12.1	13.9	13.3	10.1
Periodic abstinence	1.5	0.5	1.8	2.0	1.6	0.7	1.3	0.6	2.3	0.7
Natural family planning	0.2	-	0.3	0.3	0.3	-	0.1	-	0.4	-
Withdrawal	2.0	1.6	2.3	1.9	2.1	0.9	2.0	1.5	2.3	1.8
Other methods [7]	3.9	5.6	4.2	2.1	3.4	6.2	4.7	4.6	3.3	3.9

- Represents or rounds to zero. [1] Includes other races, not shown separately. [2] Total sterile includes male sterile for unknown reasons. [3] Persons who had sterilizing operation and who gave as one reason that they had medical problems with their female organs. [4] Includes all other sterilization operations, and sterilization of the husband or current partner. [5] Persons sterile from illness, accident, or congenital conditions. [6] Data refer to no intercourse in the 3 months prior to interview. [7] Includes implants, injectables, morning-after-pill, suppository, Today(TM) sponge and less frequently used methods.

Source: U.S. National Center for Health Statistics, *Advance Data from Vital and Health Statistics*, No. 182.

No. 111. Live Births—Mothers Who Smoked During Pregnancy: 1994

[In thousands, except percents. Excludes California, Indiana, New York, and South Dakota, which did not require reporting of tobacco use during pregnancy]

SMOKING MEASURE AND RACE OF MOTHER	Total	YEARS OF SCHOOL COMPLETED BY MOTHER					
		0-8 years	9-11 years	12 years	13-15 years	16 years or more	Not stated
All races [1]	3,141	150	508	1,111	682	641	49
White	2,446	121	345	844	543	561	34
Black	569	21	146	226	116	48	11
Percent:							
Smoker [1]	14.6	13.6	27.0	18.2	10.7	2.8	13.9
White	15.6	14.7	31.8	20.4	11.5	2.9	13.8
Black	11.4	9.5	16.7	11.3	7.9	3.4	16.4
PERCENT DISTRIBUTION							
All races smoker	100.0	100.0	100.0	100.0	100.0	100.0	100.0
10 cigarettes or less	63.9	58.7	62.9	63.5	66.4	71.7	66.5
11-20 cigarettes	31.3	33.2	31.6	32.0	29.7	25.4	28.8
21 cigarettes or more	4.8	8.1	5.5	4.5	3.9	2.9	4.7
White smoker	100.0	100.0	100.0	100.0	100.0	100.0	100.0
10 cigarettes or less	61	56	59	61	64	71	63
11-20 cigarettes	34	35	35	34	32	27	32
21 cigarettes or more	5	9	6	5	4	3	5
Black smoker	100.0	100.0	100.0	100.0	100.0	100.0	100.0
10 cigarettes or less	79.3	76.3	78.5	80.1	80.3	81.8	72.7
11-20 cigarettes	18.3	20.2	18.8	17.7	17.9	16.5	23.4
21 cigarettes or more	2.4	3.5	2.8	2.2	1.8	1.7	3.9

[1] Includes races other than White and Black.

No. 112. Percent Low Birthweight, by Smoking Status, Age, and Race of Mother: 1994

[Low birthweight is defined as weight of less than 2,500 grams (5 lb. 8 oz.). Excludes California, Indiana, New York, and South Dakota, which did not require reporting of tobacco use during pregnancy]

SMOKING STATUS AND RACE OF MOTHER	All ages	AGE OF MOTHER								
		Under 15 years	15-19 years			20-24 years	25-29 years	30-34 years	35-39 years	40-49 years
			Total	15-17 years	18-19 years					
All races [1]	7.6	14.3	9.7	10.5	9.1	7.6	6.6	6.9	8.2	9.7
Smoker	12.3	17.1	11.4	12.0	11.1	10.6	11.9	13.9	17.0	19.0
Nonsmoker	6.7	14.1	9.3	10.2	8.7	6.9	5.8	5.9	7.0	8.5
White	6.2	11.6	8.1	8.8	7.7	6.2	5.5	5.8	6.9	8.3
Smoker	10.6	16.3	10.9	11.5	10.6	9.6	9.9	11.2	13.9	16.1
Nonsmoker	5.4	10.8	7.2	8.0	6.8	5.3	4.8	5.0	6.0	7.3
Black	13.3	16.5	13.2	13.7	12.9	12.2	12.9	14.6	16.4	18.0
Smoker	22.8	20.6	16.8	17.3	16.6	18.3	23.1	26.5	29.3	30.6
Nonsmoker	12.1	16.4	13.0	13.5	12.6	11.5	11.1	12.0	13.3	15.4

[1] Includes races other than White and Black.

No. 113. Live Births—Drinking Status of Mother: 1994

[In absolutes, except percents. Excludes California, New York, and South Dakota, which did not require reporting of alcohol abuse during pregnancy]

DRINKING STATUS, DRINKING MEASURE, AND RACE OF MOTHER	All ages	AGE OF MOTHER								
		Under 15 years	15-19 years			20-24 years	25-29 years	30-34 years	35-39 years	40-49 years
			Total	15-17 years	18-19 years					
All races [1]	3,374,330	11,201	435,964	168,354	267,610	858,177	930,843	773,920	311,080	53,145
Drinker	57,056	70	3,964	1,387	2,577	11,329	14,941	17,100	8,256	1,396
Nondrinker	3,262,567	10,992	425,544	164,523	261,021	833,989	900,859	743,413	297,164	50,626
White	2,649,508	4,677	290,536	104,365	186,171	643,812	760,370	649,069	257,828	43,196
Drinker	40,163	44	2,809	974	1,835	7,547	9,936	12,596	6,177	1,054
Nondrinker	2,566,617	4,556	283,210	101,771	181,439	626,553	738,483	625,565	247,006	41,244
Black	593,508	6,208	133,280	59,446	73,834	185,799	131,707	91,098	38,459	6,957
Drinker	14,808	17	871	290	581	3,186	4,490	4,066	1,881	297
Nondrinker	569,512	6,133	130,784	58,456	72,328	180,098	124,896	85,231	35,867	6,505
Percent:										
Drinker [1]	1.7	0.6	0.9	0.8	1.0	1.3	1.6	2.2	2.7	2.7
White	1.5	1.0	1.0	0.9	1.0	1.2	1.3	2.0	2.4	2.5
Black	2.5	(Z)	0.7	0.5	0.8	1.7	3.5	4.6	5.0	4.4

Z Less than 50. [1] Includes races other than White or Black.

Source of tables 111-113: U.S. National Center for Health Statistics, *Monthly Vital Statistics Reports*.

No. 114. Abortions—Number, Rate, and Ratio, by Race: 1975 to 1992

YEAR	ALL RACES				WHITE				BLACK AND OTHER			
	Women 15-44 years old (1,000)	Abortions			Women 15-44 years old (1,000)	Abortions			Women 15-44 years old (1,000)	Abortions		
		Number (1,000)	Rate per 1,000 women	Ratio per 1,000 live births [1]		Number (1,000)	Rate per 1,000 women	Ratio per 1,000 live births [1]		Number (1,000)	Rate per 1,000 women	Ratio per 1,000 live births [1]
1975	47,606	1,034	21.7	331	40,857	701	17.2	276	6,749	333	49.3	565
1979	52,016	1,498	28.8	420	44,266	1,062	24.0	373	7,750	436	56.2	625
1980	53,048	1,554	29.3	428	44,942	1,094	24.3	376	8,106	460	56.5	642
1981	53,901	1,577	29.3	430	45,494	1,108	24.3	377	8,407	470	55.9	645
1982	54,679	1,574	28.8	428	46,049	1,095	23.8	373	8,630	479	55.5	646
1983 [2]	55,340	1,575	28.5	436	46,506	1,084	23.3	376	8,834	491	55.5	670
1984	56,061	1,577	28.1	423	47,023	1,087	23.1	366	9,038	491	54.3	646
1985	56,754	1,589	28.0	422	47,512	1,076	22.6	360	9,242	513	55.5	659
1986 [2]	57,483	1,574	27.4	416	48,010	1,045	21.8	350	9,473	529	55.9	661
1987	57,964	1,559	27.1	405	48,288	1,017	21.1	338	9,676	542	56.0	648
1988	58,192	1,591	27.3	401	48,325	1,026	21.2	333	9,867	565	57.3	638
1989 [2]	58,365	1,567	26.8	380	48,104	1,006	20.9	309	10,261	561	54.7	650
1990 [2]	58,700	1,609	27.4	389	48,224	1,039	21.5	318	10,476	570	54.4	655
1991	59,080	1,557	26.3	379	48,406	982	20.3	303	10,674	574	53.8	661
1992	59,020	1,529	25.9	379	48,161	944	19.6	298	10859	585	53.9	681

[1] Live births are those which occurred from July 1 of year shown through June 30 of the following year (to match time of conception with abortions). Births are classified by race of child 1972-1988, and by race of mother after 1988. [2] Total numbers of abortions in 1983 and 1986 have been estimated by interpolation; 1989 and 1990 have been estimated using trends in CDC data.

No. 115. Abortions, by Selected Characteristics: 1985 to 1992

[Number of abortions from surveys conducted by source; characteristics from the U.S. Centers for Disease Control's (CDC) annual abortion surveillance summaries, with adjustments for changes in States reporting data to the CDC each year]

CHARACTERISTIC	NUMBER (1,000)			PERCENT DISTRIBUTION			ABORTION RATIO [1]		
	1985	1990 [1]	1992	1985	1990 [1]	1992	1985	1990 [1]	1992
Total abortions	1,589	1,609	1529	100	100	100	297	280	275
Age of woman:									
Less than 15 years old	17	13	13	1	1	1	624	515	511
15 to 19 years old	399	351	295	25	22	19	462	403	370
20 to 24 years old	548	532	526	35	33	34	328	328	333
25 to 29 years old	338	360	341	21	22	22	219	224	228
30 to 34 years old	181	216	213	11	13	14	203	196	192
35 to 39 years old	87	108	110	5	7	7	280	249	239
40 years old and over	21	29	31	1	2	2	409	354	338
Race of woman:									
White	1,076	1,039	944	68	65	62	265	241	229
Black and other	513	570	585	32	35	38	397	396	405
Marital status of woman: [2]									
Married	281	284	257	18	18	17	88	88	84
Unmarried	1,307	1,325	1272	82	82	83	605	527	506
Number of prior live births:									
None	872	780	691	55	49	45	358	316	298
One	349	396	396	22	25	26	219	230	233
Two	240	280	281	15	17	18	288	292	299
Three	85	102	105	5	6	7	281	279	290
Four or more	43	50	57	3	3	4	230	223	244
Number of prior induced abortions:									
None	944	891	810	60	55	53	(NA)	(NA)	(NA)
One	416	443	431	26	28	28	(NA)	(NA)	(NA)
Two or more	228	275	288	14	17	19	(NA)	(NA)	(NA)
Weeks of gestation: [3]									
Less than 9 weeks	779	817	799	49	51	52	(NA)	(NA)	(NA)
9 to 10 weeks	425	418	378	27	26	25	(NA)	(NA)	(NA)
11 to 12 weeks	211	199	182	13	12	12	(NA)	(NA)	(NA)
13 weeks or more	173	175	171	11	11	11	(NA)	(NA)	(NA)

NA Not available. [1] Number of abortions per 1,000 abortions and live births. Live births are those which occurred from July 1 of year shown through June 30 of the following year (to match time of conception with abortions). [2] Separated women included with unmarried women. [3] Data not exactly comparable with prior years because of a change in the method of calculation.

Source of tables 114 and 115: S.K. Henshaw and J. Van Vort, eds., *Abortion Factbook, 1992 Edition: Readings, Trends, and State and Local Data to 1988*, The Alan Guttmacher Institute, New York, NY, 1992 (copyright); S.K. Henshaw and J. Van Vort, *Abortion Services in the United States, 1991 and 1992; Family Perspectives, 26:100, 1994;* and unpublished data.

No. 116. Abortions—Number, Rate, and Abortion/Live Birth Ratio, by State: 1980 to 1992

[Number of abortions from surveys of hospitals, clinics, and physicians identified as providers of abortion services conducted by The Alan Guttmacher Institute. Abortion rates are computed per 1,000 women 15 to 44 years of age on July 1 of specified year; abortion ratios are computed as the number of abortions per 1,000 live births from July 1 of year shown to June 30 of following year, by State of occurrence]

DIVISION, REGION, AND STATE	NUMBER OF ABORTIONS (1,000)			RATE PER 1,000 WOMEN, 15 TO 44 YEARS OLD			RATIO: ABORTIONS PER 1,000 LIVE BIRTHS		
	1980	1985	1992	1980	1985	1992	1980	1985	1992
United States	1,554	1,589	1,529	29.3	28.0	25.9	428	422	379
Northeast	396	407	379	34.9	(NA)	32.1	604	(NA)	506
New England	84	86	78	28.9	28.6	25.2	530	504	429
Maine	5	5	4	18.6	18.6	14.7	289	308	282
New Hampshire	5	7	4	21.1	29.0	14.6	347	419	289
Vermont	4	3	3	30.4	26.2	21.2	466	448	393
Massachusetts	46	40	41	33.5	29.3	28.4	609	533	472
Rhode Island	7	8	7	30.7	35.5	30.0	529	572	461
Connecticut	19	22	20	25.6	29.3	26.2	561	550	444
Middle Atlantic	312	322	300	37.0	37.6	34.6	627	607	530
New York	186	195	195	45.8	47.4	46.2	780	746	694
New Jersey	56	69	55	32.8	39.6	31.0	591	672	460
Pennsylvania	69	57	50	26.1	21.3	18.6	423	348	302
Midwest	318	289	262	23.3	(NA)	18.9	336	(NA)	297
East North Central	243	221	206	24.9	22.1	20.7	369	366	313
Ohio	67	57	50	26.8	22.4	19.5	397	357	294
Indiana	20	16	16	15.3	12.2	12.0	227	202	185
Illinois	69	65	68	25.9	23.8	25.4	374	372	361
Michigan	65	64	56	29.7	26.7	25.2	457	466	393
Wisconsin	22	18	15	20.1	15.7	13.6	292	246	223
West North Central	75	68	57	19.2	16.7	14.3	260	252	221
Minnesota	20	17	16	20.7	16.6	15.6	288	257	251
Iowa	9	10	7	14.3	15.0	11.4	195	248	185
Missouri	22	20	14	19.4	17.3	11.6	273	261	175
North Dakota	3	3	1	21.5	18.5	10.7	235	230	149
South Dakota	1	2	1	9.0	10.6	6.8	103	140	92
Nebraska	6	7	6	17.9	18.2	15.7	227	268	246
Kansas	14	10	13	25.6	18.2	22.4	343	264	353
South	457	463	450	25.9	(NA)	22.0	369	(NA)	323
South Atlantic	255	257	269	29.4	27.1	25.9	462	429	397
Delaware	4	5	6	25.9	30.9	35.2	395	451	502
Maryland	31	30	31	29.2	26.9	26.4	571	480	454
District of Columbia	29	24	21	168.3	145.9	138.4	1,569	1,186	1,104
Virginia	32	34	35	24.2	24.0	22.7	417	412	373
West Virginia	3	5	3	6.9	10.1	7.7	104	165	134
North Carolina	32	34	36	22.8	22.6	22.4	377	379	357
South Carolina	14	11	12	18.2	13.7	14.2	274	228	229
Georgia	38	38	40	28.4	26.1	24.0	395	397	350
Florida	74	77	85	35.5	31.8	30.0	547	465	436
East South Central	66	57	54	19.2	15.8	14.9	271	258	228
Kentucky	13	10	10	15.1	11.0	11.4	215	189	191
Tennessee	26	22	19	23.6	19.1	16.2	352	315	243
Alabama	21	19	17	23.1	20.2	18.2	331	333	277
Mississippi	6	6	8	10.6	9.7	12.4	132	142	176
West South Central	137	139	127	24.5	21.8	19.6	308	290	266
Arkansas	6	5	7	12.3	10.1	13.5	173	159	213
Louisiana	18	19	14	17.6	17.4	13.4	218	240	195
Oklahoma	11	13	9	16.4	17.1	12.5	221	269	193
Texas	102	101	97	30.0	25.5	23.1	367	320	297
West	383	440	486	36.8	(NA)	34.1	486	(NA)	446
Mountain	68	75	70	25.0	23.6	21.0	302	316	280
Montana	4	4	3	20.1	19.0	18.2	265	288	298
Idaho	3	3	2	12.7	11.1	7.2	141	155	97
Wyoming	1	1	-	9.5	7.9	4.3	107	125	74
Colorado	23	24	20	31.4	28.8	23.6	447	438	362
New Mexico	8	6	6	27.0	17.4	17.7	358	219	228
Arizona	16	22	21	25.0	29.9	24.1	310	373	295
Utah	4	4	4	12.3	11.1	9.3	97	116	104
Nevada	9	10	13	46.6	40.5	44.2	697	641	591
Pacific	315	365	368	41.0	42.8	38.7	561	594	501
Washington	37	31	33	37.5	28.0	27.7	522	458	447
Oregon	18	15	16	28.3	22.3	23.9	396	374	372
California	250	304	304	43.7	47.9	42.1	598	640	519
Alaska	2	4	2	17.9	27.7	16.5	196	283	222
Hawaii	8	11	12	34.4	43.7	46.0	441	611	617

- Represents or rounds to zero. NA Not available.

Source: S.K. Henshaw and J. Van Vort, eds., *Abortion Factbook, 1992 Edition: Readings, Trends, and State and Local Data to 1988*, The Alan Guttmacher Institute, New York, NY, 1992 (copyright); S.K. Henshaw and J. Van Vort, *Abortion Services in the United States, 1991 and 1992, Family Planning Perspectives, 26:100, 1994;* and unpublished data.

No. 117. Expectation of Life at Birth, 1970 to 1995, and Projections: 1995 to 2010

[In years. Excludes deaths of nonresidents of the United States]

YEAR	TOTAL			WHITE			BLACK AND OTHER			BLACK		
	Total	Male	Female	Total	Male	Female	Total	Male	Female	Total	Male	Female
1970	70.8	67.1	74.7	71.7	68.0	75.6	65.3	61.3	69.4	64.1	60.0	68.3
1975	72.6	68.8	76.6	73.4	69.5	77.3	68.0	63.7	72.4	66.8	62.4	71.3
1980	73.7	70.0	77.4	74.4	70.7	78.1	69.5	65.3	73.6	68.1	63.8	72.5
1982	74.5	70.8	78.1	75.1	71.5	78.7	70.9	66.8	74.9	69.4	65.1	73.6
1983	74.6	71.0	78.1	75.2	71.6	78.7	70.9	67.0	74.7	69.4	65.2	73.5
1984	74.7	71.1	78.2	75.3	71.8	78.7	71.1	67.2	74.9	69.5	65.3	73.6
1985	74.7	71.1	78.2	75.3	71.8	78.7	71.0	67.0	74.8	69.3	65.0	73.4
1986	74.7	71.2	78.2	75.4	71.9	78.8	70.9	66.8	74.9	69.1	64.8	73.4
1987	74.9	71.4	78.3	75.6	72.1	78.9	71.0	66.9	75.0	69.1	64.7	73.4
1988	74.9	71.4	78.3	75.6	72.2	78.9	70.8	66.7	74.8	68.9	64.4	73.2
1989	75.1	71.7	78.5	75.9	72.5	79.2	70.9	66.7	74.9	68.8	64.3	73.3
1990	75.4	71.8	78.8	76.1	72.7	79.4	71.2	67.0	75.2	69.1	64.5	73.6
1991	75.5	72.0	78.9	76.3	72.9	79.6	71.5	67.3	75.5	69.3	64.6	73.8
1992	75.8	72.3	79.1	76.5	73.2	79.8	71.8	67.7	75.7	69.6	65.0	73.9
1993	75.5	72.2	78.8	76.3	73.1	79.5	71.5	67.3	75.5	69.2	64.6	73.7
1994	75.7	72.3	79.0	76.4	73.2	79.6	71.7	67.5	75.8	69.6	64.9	74.1
1995	75.8	72.6	78.9	76.5	73.4	79.6	(NA)	(NA)	(NA)	69.8	65.4	74.0
Projections: [1] 1995	(NA)	72.5	79.3	(NA)	73.6	80.1	(NA)	(NA)	(NA)	(NA)	64.8	74.5
2000	(NA)	73.0	79.7	(NA)	74.2	80.5	(NA)	(NA)	(NA)	(NA)	64.6	74.7
2005	(NA)	73.5	80.2	(NA)	74.7	81.0	(NA)	(NA)	(NA)	(NA)	64.5	75.0
2010	(NA)	74.1	80.6	(NA)	75.5	81.6	(NA)	(NA)	(NA)	(NA)	65.1	75.5

NA Not available. [1] Based on middle mortality assumptions; for details, see source. Source: U.S. Bureau of the Census, *Current Population Reports*, P25-1104.

Source: Except as noted, U.S. National Center for Health Statistics, *Vital Statistics of the United States*, annual, and *Monthly Vital Statistics Reports*.

No. 118. Selected Life Table Values: 1979 to 1994

AGE AND SEX	TOTAL [1]			WHITE			BLACK		
	1979-1981	1990	1994	1979-1981	1990	1994	1979-1981	1990	1994
AVERAGE EXPECTATION OF LIFE IN YEARS									
At birth: Male	70.1	71.8	72.4	70.8	72.7	73.3	64.1	64.5	64.9
Female	77.6	78.8	79.0	78.2	79.4	79.6	72.9	73.6	73.9
Age 20: Male	51.9	53.3	53.6	52.5	54.0	54.4	46.4	46.7	47.1
Female	59.0	59.8	59.9	59.4	60.3	60.4	54.9	55.3	55.5
Age 40: Male	33.6	35.1	35.5	34.0	35.6	36.0	29.5	30.1	30.5
Female	39.8	40.6	40.7	40.2	41.0	41.1	36.3	36.8	37.0
Age 50: Male	25.0	26.4	26.9	25.3	26.7	27.2	22.0	22.5	23.1
Female	30.7	31.3	31.5	31.0	31.6	31.7	27.8	28.2	28.5
Age 65: Male	14.2	15.1	15.5	14.3	15.2	15.6	13.3	13.2	13.6
Female	18.4	18.9	19.0	18.6	19.1	19.1	17.1	17.2	17.2
EXPECTED DEATHS PER 1,000 ALIVE AT SPECIFIED AGE [2]									
At birth: Male	13.9	10.3	8.7	12.3	8.6	(NA)	23.0	19.7	(NA)
Female	11.2	8.2	7.1	9.7	6.6	(NA)	19.3	16.3	(NA)
Age 20: Male	1.8	1.6	1.5	1.8	1.4	(NA)	2.2	2.7	(NA)
Female	0.6	0.5	0.4	0.6	0.5	(NA)	0.7	0.7	(NA)
Age 40: Male	3.0	3.1	3.4	2.6	2.7	(NA)	6.9	7.1	(NA)
Female	1.6	1.4	1.4	1.4	1.2	(NA)	3.2	3.1	(NA)
Age 50: Male	7.8	6.2	6.1	7.1	5.6	(NA)	14.9	12.8	(NA)
Female	4.2	3.5	3.4	3.8	3.2	(NA)	7.7	6.6	(NA)
Age 65: Male	28.2	12.9	22.8	27.4	23.0	(NA)	38.5	36.8	(NA)
Female	14.3	13.5	(NA)	13.6	12.8	(NA)	21.6	21.4	(NA)
NUMBER SURVIVING TO SPECIFIED AGE PER 1,000 BORN ALIVE									
Age 20: Male	973	979	980	975	981	(NA)	961	963	(NA)
Female	982	986	987	984	988	(NA)	972	976	(NA)
Age 40: Male	933	938	939	940	946	(NA)	885	880	(NA)
Female	965	971	971	969	975	(NA)	941	944	(NA)
Age 50: Male	890	899	899	901	912	(NA)	801	801	(NA)
Female	941	950	950	947	957	(NA)	896	904	(NA)
Age 65: Male	706	741	748	724	760	(NA)	551	571	(NA)
Female	835	851	855	848	864	(NA)	733	751	(NA)

NA Not available. [1] Includes other races not shown separately. [2] See footnote 1, table 119.

Source: U.S. National Center for Health Statistics, *U.S. Life Tables and Actuarial Tables, 1959-61, 1969-71, and 1979-81*; *Vital Statistics of the United States*, annual; and unpublished data.

No. 119. Expectation of Life and Expected Deaths, by Race, Sex, and Age: 1994

AGE IN 1990 (years)	EXPECTATION OF LIFE IN YEARS					EXPECTED DEATHS PER 1,000 ALIVE AT SPECIFIED AGE[1]				
	Total	White		Black		Total	White		Black	
		Male	Female	Male	Female		Male	Female	Male	Female
At birth	75.7	73.3	79.6	64.9	73.9	8.01	7.21	5.88	17.42	14.05
1	75.3	72.8	79.1	65.1	73.9	0.62	0.60	0.45	1.22	0.90
2	74.4	71.8	78.1	64.1	73.0	0.45	0.43	0.34	0.86	0.73
3	73.4	70.9	77.1	63.2	72.0	0.35	0.32	0.27	0.63	0.58
4	72.4	69.9	76.1	62.2	71.1	0.28	0.26	0.22	0.51	0.46
5	71.4	68.9	75.2	61.3	70.1	0.24	0.23	0.18	0.45	0.37
6	70.5	67.9	74.2	60.3	69.1	0.22	0.22	0.16	0.42	0.30
7	69.5	67.0	73.2	59.3	68.2	0.20	0.21	0.15	0.39	0.25
8	68.5	66.0	72.2	58.3	67.2	0.18	0.19	0.14	0.33	0.22
9	67.5	65.0	71.2	57.3	66.2	0.16	0.16	0.12	0.25	0.21
10	66.5	64.0	70.2	56.4	65.2	0.14	0.14	0.12	0.18	0.21
11	65.5	63.0	69.5	55.4	64.2	0.14	0.15	0.12	0.17	0.23
12	64.5	62.0	68.2	54.4	63.2	0.20	0.21	0.15	0.31	0.27
13	63.5	61.0	67.2	53.4	62.3	0.31	0.36	0.20	0.63	0.31
14	62.6	60.0	66.3	52.4	61.3	0.46	0.55	0.26	1.07	0.36
15	61.6	59.1	65.3	51.5	60.3	0.63	0.77	0.34	1.57	0.43
16	60.6	58.1	64.3	50.6	59.3	0.79	0.97	0.41	2.04	0.50
17	59.7	57.2	63.3	49.7	58.4	0.91	1.13	0.46	2.43	0.56
18	58.7	56.2	62.3	48.8	57.4	0.96	1.23	0.47	2.70	0.62
19	57.8	55.3	61.4	47.9	56.4	1.01	1.28	0.47	2.86	0.68
20	56.8	54.4	60.4	47.1	55.5	1.04	1.32	0.45	3.02	0.74
21	55.9	53.4	59.4	46.2	54.5	1.07	1.38	0.44	3.19	0.81
22	55.0	52.5	58.5	45.3	53.5	1.10	1.41	0.44	3.32	0.88
23	54.0	51.6	57.5	44.5	52.6	1.12	1.43	0.45	3.40	0.96
24	53.1	50.7	56.5	43.6	51.6	1.13	1.43	0.47	3.45	1.04
25	52.1	49.7	55.5	42.8	50.7	1.14	1.43	0.50	3.47	1.12
26	51.2	48.8	54.6	41.9	49.8	1.16	1.43	0.52	3.51	1.21
27	50.3	47.9	53.6	41.1	48.8	1.19	1.47	0.54	3.61	1.31
28	49.3	47.0	52.6	40.2	47.9	1.26	1.55	0.57	3.82	1.43
29	48.4	46.0	51.7	39.4	46.9	1.34	1.67	0.60	4.09	1.57
30	47.4	45.1	50.7	38.5	46.0	1.44	1.81	0.63	4.41	1.72
31	46.5	44.2	49.7	37.7	45.1	1.53	1.94	0.66	4.72	1.87
32	45.6	43.3	48.7	36.9	44.2	1.62	2.06	0.71	5.00	2.03
33	44.6	42.4	47.8	36.1	43.3	1.71	2.16	0.76	5.23	2.18
34	43.7	41.4	46.8	35.3	42.4	1.80	2.24	0.82	5.44	2.33
35	42.8	40.5	45.9	34.5	41.5	1.89	2.33	0.89	5.64	2.50
36	41.9	39.6	44.9	33.6	40.6	1.99	2.44	0.96	5.87	2.67
37	41.0	38.7	43.9	32.8	39.7	2.10	2.55	1.03	6.19	2.84
38	40.1	37.8	43.0	32.0	38.8	2.20	2.66	1.10	6.60	3.01
39	39.1	36.9	42.0	31.2	37.9	2.32	2.79	1.15	7.09	3.18
40	38.2	36.0	41.1	30.5	37.0	2.44	2.94	1.22	7.63	3.36
41	37.3	35.1	40.1	29.7	36.1	2.58	3.10	1.31	8.17	3.56
42	36.4	34.2	39.2	28.9	35.3	2.73	3.25	1.41	8.66	3.78
43	35.5	33.3	38.2	28.2	34.4	2.88	3.41	1.54	9.08	4.04
44	34.6	32.5	37.3	27.4	33.5	3.04	3.57	1.70	9.45	4.33
45	33.7	31.6	36.4	26.7	32.7	3.22	3.74	1.87	9.82	4.66
46	32.8	30.7	35.4	26.0	31.8	3.44	3.96	2.07	10.26	5.00
47	31.9	29.8	34.5	25.2	31.0	3.69	4.24	2.28	10.79	5.35
48	31.1	28.9	33.6	24.5	30.1	4.00	4.60	2.52	11.45	5.69
49	30.2	28.1	32.7	23.8	29.3	4.36	5.02	2.79	12.22	6.05
50	29.3	27.2	31.7	23.1	28.5	4.76	5.51	3.08	13.06	6.42
51	28.4	26.4	30.8	22.4	27.7	5.20	6.04	3.41	13.94	6.84
52	27.6	25.5	29.9	21.7	26.9	5.67	6.61	3.76	14.84	7.35
53	26.7	24.7	29.1	21.0	26.1	6.16	7.19	4.12	15.76	7.97
54	25.9	23.8	28.2	20.3	25.3	6.68	7.82	4.50	16.70	8.69
55	25.1	23.0	27.3	19.6	24.5	7.25	8.49	4.91	17.68	9.48
56	24.3	22.2	26.4	19.0	23.7	7.87	9.25	5.38	18.74	10.29
57	23.4	21.4	25.6	18.3	22.9	8.62	10.17	5.93	19.97	11.13
58	22.6	20.6	24.7	17.7	22.2	9.50	11.31	6.58	21.43	11.95
59	21.9	19.9	23.9	17.1	21.5	10.51	13.62	7.33	23.06	12.80
60	21.1	19.1	23.1	16.5	20.7	11.62	14.05	8.15	24.88	13.69
61	20.3	18.4	22.2	15.9	20.0	12.77	15.56	9.01	26.77	14.68
62	19.6	17.7	21.4	15.3	19.3	13.96	17.11	9.90	28.57	15.75
63	18.9	17.0	20.6	14.7	18.6	15.14	18.69	10.79	30.19	16.93
64	18.1	16.3	19.9	14.2	17.9	16.36	20.32	11.70	31.70	18.22
65	17.4	15.6	19.1	13.6	17.2	17.64	22.05	12.68	33.11	19.56
70	14.1	12.5	15.4	11.0	14.1	26.44	33.19	19.66	48.61	29.36
75	11.0	9.6	12.0	8.9	11.2	39.29	49.61	30.62	65.60	40.79
80	8.3	7.2	9.0	6.8	8.6	60.17	76.21	49.38	89.75	58.95
85 and over	6.1	5.2	6.4	5.3	6.3	1,000.0	1,000.0	1,000.0	1,000.0	1,000.0

[1] Based on the proportion of the cohort who are alive at the beginning of an indicated age interval who will die before reaching the end of that interval. For example, out of every 1,000 people alive and exactly 50 years old at the beginning of the period, between 4 and 5 (4.76) will die before reaching their 51st birthdays.

Source: U.S. National Center for Health Statistics, *Vital Statistics of the United States*, annual; and unpublished data.

No. 120. Deaths and Death Rates, by Sex and Race: 1980 to 1995

[Rates are per 1,000 population for specified groups. Excludes deaths of nonresidents of the United States and fetal deaths. For explanation of age-adjustment, see text, section 2. The standard population for this table is the total population of the United States enumerated in 1940. See Appendix III]

SEX AND RACE	1980	1985	1986	1987	1988	1989	1990	1991	1992	1993	1994	1995
Deaths [1] (1,000)	1,990	2,086	2,105	2,123	2,168	2,150	2,148	2,170	2,176	2,268	2,279	2,312
Male [1] (1,000)	1,075	1,098	1,104	1,108	1,126	1,114	1,113	1,122	1,122	1,162	1,163	1,173
Female [1] (1,000)	915	989	1,001	1,015	1,042	1,036	1,035	1,048	1,053	1,107	1,116	1,140
White (1,000)	1,739	1,819	1,831	1,843	1,877	1,854	1,853	1,869	1,874	1,951	1,980	1,991
Male (1,000)	934	950	953	953	965	951	951	956	957	988	989	999
Female (1,000)	805	869	879	890	911	903	902	912	917	963	971	992
Black (1,000)	233	244	250	255	264	268	266	270	269	282	282	284
Male (1,000)	130	134	137	140	144	146	145	147	147	154	153	153
Female (1,000)	103	111	113	115	120	121	120	122	123	129	129	131
Death rates [1]	8.8	8.8	8.8	8.8	8.8	8.7	8.6	8.6	8.5	8.8	8.8	8.8
Male [1]	9.8	9.5	9.4	9.4	9.5	9.3	9.2	9.1	9.0	9.2	9.2	9.1
Female [1]	7.9	8.1	8.1	8.2	8.3	8.2	8.1	8.1	8.1	8.4	8.4	8.5
White	8.9	9.0	9.0	9.0	9.1	8.9	8.9	8.9	8.8	9.1	9.1	9.1
Male	9.8	9.6	9.6	9.5	9.6	9.4	9.3	9.3	9.2	9.4	9.3	9.3
Female	8.1	8.4	8.4	8.5	8.7	8.5	8.5	8.5	8.4	8.8	8.8	8.9
Black	8.8	8.5	8.6	8.7	8.9	8.9	8.8	8.6	8.5	8.8	8.6	8.6
Male	10.3	9.9	10.0	10.1	10.3	10.3	10.1	10.0	9.8	10.1	9.9	9.7
Female	7.3	7.3	7.4	7.5	7.6	7.6	7.5	7.4	7.4	7.6	7.5	7.5
Age-adjusted death rates [1]	5.9	5.5	5.4	5.4	5.4	5.3	5.2	5.1	5.0	5.1	5.1	5.0
Male [1]	7.8	7.2	7.2	7.1	7.1	6.9	6.8	6.7	6.6	6.6	6.5	6.5
Female [1]	4.3	4.1	4.1	4.0	4.1	4.0	3.9	3.9	3.8	3.9	3.9	3.9
White	5.6	5.2	5.2	5.1	5.1	5.0	4.9	4.9	4.8	4.9	4.8	4.8
Male	7.5	6.9	6.8	6.7	6.7	6.5	6.4	6.3	6.2	6.3	6.2	6.1
Female	4.1	3.9	3.9	3.8	3.9	3.8	3.7	3.7	3.6	3.7	3.6	3.7
Black	8.4	7.9	8.0	8.0	8.1	8.1	7.9	7.8	7.7	7.9	7.7	7.6
Male	11.1	10.5	10.6	10.6	10.8	10.8	10.6	10.5	10.3	10.5	10.3	10.1
Female	6.3	5.9	5.9	5.9	6.0	5.9	5.8	5.8	5.7	5.8	5.7	5.7

[1] Includes other races, not shown separately.

Source: U.S. National Center for Health Statistics, *Vital Statistics of the United States*, annual; and *Monthly Vital Statistics Report*.

No. 121. Death Rates, by Age, Sex, and Race: 1970 to 1995

[Number of deaths per 100,000 population in specified group. See headnote, table 120]

SEX, YEAR, AND RACE	All ages [1]	Under 1 yr. old	1-4 yr. old	5-14 yr. old	15-24 yr. old	25-34 yr. old	35-44 yr. old	45-54 yr. old	55-64 yr. old	65-74 yr. old	75-84 yr. old	85 yr. old and over
MALE [2]												
1970	1,090	2,410	93	51	189	215	403	959	2,283	4,874	10,010	17,822
1980	977	1,429	73	37	172	196	299	767	1,815	4,105	8,817	18,801
1990	918	1,083	52	29	147	204	310	610	1,553	3,492	7,889	18,057
1994	915	899	47	27	146	209	333	599	1,444	3,332	7,441	17,972
1995	914	836	45	27	139	204	332	596	1,418	3,293	7,385	17,950
White: 1970	1,087	2,113	84	48	171	177	344	883	2,203	4,810	10,099	18,552
1980	983	1,230	66	35	167	171	257	699	1,729	4,036	8,830	19,097
1990	931	896	46	26	131	176	268	549	1,467	3,396	7,845	18,268
1994	932	740	41	24	124	180	287	536	1,365	3,247	7,366	18,196
1995	933	716	39	24	121	178	288	533	1,334	3,212	7,336	18,143
Black: 1970	1,187	4,299	151	67	321	560	957	1,778	3,257	5,803	9,455	12,222
1980	1,034	2,587	111	47	209	407	690	1,480	2,873	5,131	9,232	16,099
1990	1,008	2,112	86	41	252	431	700	1,261	2,618	4,946	9,130	16,955
1994	966	1,797	64	42	276	434	732	1,268	2,423	4,654	8,830	16,267
1995	971	1,551	77	41	247	412	714	1,254	2,420	4,577	8,706	16,512
FEMALE [2]												
1970	808	1,864	75	32	68	102	231	517	1,099	2,580	6,678	15,518
1980	785	1,142	55	24	58	76	159	413	934	2,145	5,440	14,747
1990	812	856	41	19	49	74	138	343	879	1,991	4,883	14,274
1994	838	736	38	18	48	78	146	330	842	1,990	4,871	14,265
1995	848	685	36	18	48	77	150	326	842	1,991	4,888	14,492
White: 1970	813	1,615	66	30	62	84	193	463	1,015	2,471	6,699	15,980
1980	806	963	49	23	56	65	138	373	876	2,067	5,402	14,980
1990	847	690	36	18	46	62	117	309	823	1,924	4,839	14,401
1994	880	605	32	16	44	64	122	297	792	1,930	4,822	14,416
1995	893	571	31	17	44	64	126	294	791	1,933	4,842	14,652
Black: 1970	829	3,369	129	44	112	231	533	1,044	1,986	3,861	6,692	10,707
1980	733	2,124	84	31	71	150	324	768	1,561	3,057	6,212	12,367
1990	748	1,736	68	28	69	160	299	639	1,453	2,866	5,888	13,310
1994	753	1,453	70	27	72	168	327	629	1,342	2,816	5,779	13,166
1995	753	1,317	63	26	71	165	325	612	1,342	2,797	5,793	13,352

[1] Includes unknown age. [2] Includes other races not shown separately.

Source: U.S. National Center for Health Statistics, *Vital Statistics of the United States*, annual; *Monthly Vital Statistics Report*; and unpublished data.

No. 122. Deaths and Death Rates, by State: 1980 to 1995

[By State of residence. Excludes deaths of nonresidents of the United States, except as noted. Caution should be used in comparing death rates by State; rates are affected by the population composition of the area. See also Appendix III]

DIVISION AND STATE	NUMBER OF DEATHS (1,000)							RATE PER 1,000 POPULATION [1]						
	1980	1985	1990	1992	1993	1994	1995, prel.	1980	1985	1990	1992	1993	1994	1995, prel.
United States	**1,990**	**2,086**	**2,148**	**2,176**	**2,269**	**2,279**	**2,312**	**8.8**	**8.8**	**8.6**	**8.5**	**8.8**	**8.8**	**8.8**
New England	**115**	**118**	**115**	**116**	**120**	**119**	**121**	**9.3**	**9.3**	**8.7**	**8.8**	**9.1**	**9.0**	**9.1**
Maine	11	11	11	11	12	12	12	9.6	9.8	9.0	9.0	9.3	9.4	9.4
New Hampshire	8	8	8	9	9	9	9	8.3	8.5	7.7	7.7	7.9	7.8	8.1
Vermont	5	5	5	5	5	5	5	9.0	8.8	8.2	8.4	8.5	8.2	8.6
Massachusetts	55	56	53	54	56	55	56	9.6	9.5	8.8	9.0	9.4	9.1	9.2
Rhode Island	9	10	10	9	10	9	10	9.8	10.0	9.5	9.5	9.7	9.4	9.7
Connecticut	27	28	28	28	29	29	29	8.8	8.8	8.4	8.6	8.9	8.9	8.8
Middle Atlantic	**366**	**367**	**361**	**361**	**370**	**369**	**370**	**9.9**	**9.9**	**9.6**	**9.5**	**9.7**	**9.7**	**9.7**
New York	173	172	169	166	171	169	168	9.8	9.7	9.4	9.2	9.4	9.3	9.3
New Jersey	69	71	70	71	73	72	74	9.4	9.4	9.1	9.1	9.2	9.1	9.3
Pennsylvania	124	124	122	124	126	128	128	10.4	10.5	10.3	10.3	10.5	10.6	10.6
East North Central	**366**	**370**	**373**	**373**	**389**	**390**	**396**	**8.8**	**8.9**	**8.9**	**8.7**	**9.0**	**9.0**	**9.1**
Ohio	98	99	99	99	103	103	106	9.1	9.2	9.1	9.0	9.1	9.3	9.5
Indiana	47	48	50	50	52	52	52	8.6	8.8	8.9	8.8	9.1	9.1	9.0
Illinois	103	102	103	102	107	107	109	9.0	9.0	9.0	8.8	9.2	9.1	9.2
Michigan	75	79	79	79	83	83	84	8.1	8.7	8.5	8.4	8.7	8.7	8.7
Wisconsin	41	41	43	42	45	44	45	8.7	8.7	8.7	8.5	8.7	8.7	8.8
West North Central	**159**	**162**	**161**	**162**	**169**	**169**	**174**	**9.2**	**9.3**	**9.1**	**9.0**	**9.6**	**9.3**	**9.5**
Minnesota	33	35	35	35	36	37	37	8.2	8.3	7.9	7.8	8.0	8.0	8.1
Iowa	27	28	27	27	28	28	26	9.3	9.8	9.7	9.5	9.9	9.8	9.1
Missouri	50	50	50	51	54	54	59	10.1	10.1	9.8	9.8	10.8	10.2	11.0
North Dakota	6	6	6	6	6	6	6	8.6	8.3	8.9	9.0	9.3	9.2	9.5
South Dakota	7	7	6	7	7	7	7	9.5	9.5	9.1	9.5	9.6	9.4	9.4
Nebraska	14	15	15	15	15	15	15	9.2	9.4	9.4	9.2	9.6	9.3	9.4
Kansas	22	22	22	22	24	23	24	9.3	9.1	9.0	8.8	9.2	9.1	9.3
South Atlantic	**336**	**364**	**392**	**404**	**423**	**428**	**437**	**8.9**	**9.1**	**9.0**	**9.0**	**9.3**	**9.2**	**9.3**
Delaware	5	5	6	6	6	6	6	8.5	8.9	8.7	8.6	8.7	9.0	8.8
Maryland	34	37	38	39	40	41	42	8.1	8.3	8.0	7.9	8.7	8.2	8.3
Dist. of Col.	7	7	7	7	7	7	7	11.1	11.0	12.0	12.1	11.6	12.6	12.4
Virginia	43	45	48	49	52	52	53	8.0	7.9	7.8	7.7	8.0	8.0	8.0
West Virginia	19	19	19	20	20	20	20	9.9	10.2	10.8	10.9	11.0	11.1	11.1
North Carolina	48	53	57	60	62	63	65	8.2	8.5	8.6	8.7	9.0	8.9	9.0
South Carolina	25	27	30	31	32	32	33	8.1	8.2	8.5	8.5	8.6	8.8	8.9
Georgia	44	49	52	53	56	57	58	8.1	8.2	8.0	7.8	8.1	8.0	8.1
Florida	105	121	134	140	147	149	154	10.7	10.7	10.4	10.4	10.7	10.7	10.8
East South Central	**134**	**140**	**146**	**146**	**154**	**156**	**158**	**9.1**	**9.4**	**9.6**	**9.4**	**9.8**	**9.8**	**9.9**
Kentucky	34	35	35	35	37	37	38	9.2	9.4	9.5	9.3	9.7	9.7	9.9
Tennessee	41	43	46	47	49	51	51	8.9	9.2	9.5	9.3	9.7	9.8	9.7
Alabama	36	38	39	39	41	42	42	9.1	9.5	9.7	9.5	9.9	9.9	10.0
Mississippi	24	25	25	25	26	27	27	9.4	9.5	9.8	9.7	10.1	10.0	10.0
West South Central	**195**	**209**	**218**	**222**	**233**	**234**	**236**	**8.2**	**8.0**	**8.2**	**8.1**	**8.4**	**8.2**	**8.3**
Arkansas	23	24	25	25	27	26	27	9.9	10.4	10.5	10.4	10.9	10.7	10.7
Louisiana	36	37	38	38	40	39	40	8.5	8.4	8.9	8.8	9.3	9.0	9.1
Oklahoma	28	30	30	31	32	32	33	9.3	9.1	9.7	9.5	10.1	9.9	10.0
Texas	108	118	125	129	135	136	139	7.6	7.3	7.4	7.3	7.5	7.4	7.4
Mountain	**80**	**86**	**97**	**103**	**110**	**112**	**116**	**7.0**	**6.9**	**7.1**	**7.2**	**7.3**	**7.4**	**7.4**
Montana	7	7	7	7	7	7	8	8.5	8.2	8.6	8.6	8.9	8.6	8.7
Idaho	7	7	7	8	8	8	8	7.2	7.2	7.4	7.4	7.6	7.5	7.3
Wyoming	3	3	3	3	3	3	4	6.9	6.6	7.1	7.1	7.5	7.3	7.8
Colorado	19	20	22	22	24	24	25	6.6	6.3	6.6	6.5	6.7	6.6	6.7
New Mexico	9	10	11	11	12	12	13	7.0	6.8	7.0	7.1	7.3	7.3	7.4
Arizona	21	25	29	31	33	34	35	7.9	7.7	7.9	8.1	8.2	8.4	8.4
Utah	8	9	9	10	10	10	11	5.6	5.5	5.3	5.4	5.5	5.5	5.5
Nevada	6	7	9	10	11	12	13	7.4	7.6	7.8	7.7	7.8	8.2	8.2
Pacific	**247**	**268**	**286**	**289**	**300**	**301**	**302**	**7.8**	**7.6**	**7.3**	**7.1**	**7.2**	**7.2**	**7.2**
Washington	32	35	37	38	40	40	41	7.7	7.8	7.6	7.4	8.0	7.5	7.5
Oregon	22	24	25	26	28	27	28	8.3	8.9	8.8	8.7	9.0	8.9	9.0
California	187	202	214	216	222	224	223	7.9	7.6	7.2	7.0	7.0	7.1	7.1
Alaska	2	2	2	2	2	2	3	4.3	3.9	4.0	3.9	3.8	4.0	4.2
Hawaii	5	6	7	7	7	7	8	5.2	5.6	6.1	6.0	6.2	6.2	6.4

[1] Rates based on enumerated resident population as of April 1 for 1980; and 1990; estimated resident population as of July 1 for all other years.

Source: U.S. National Center for Health Statistics, *Vital Statistics of the United States*, annual; and *Monthly Vital Statistics Report*.

No. 123. Infant, Maternal, and Neonatal Mortality Rates and Fetal Mortality Ratios, by Race: 1980 to 1994

[Deaths per 1,000 live births, except as noted. Excludes deaths of nonresidents of U.S. Race for live births tabulated according to race of mother, for infant and neonatal mortality rates. Beginning 1989, race for live births tabulated according to race of mother, for maternal mortality rates and mortality rates. See also Appendix III]

ITEM	1980	1983	1984	1985	1986	1987	1988	1989	1990	1991	1992	1993	1994
Infant deaths [1]	12.6	11.2	10.8	10.6	10.4	10.1	10.0	9.8	9.2	8.9	8.5	8.4	8.0
White	10.9	9.6	9.3	9.2	8.8	8.5	8.4	8.1	7.6	7.3	6.9	6.8	6.6
Black and other	20.2	17.8	17.1	16.8	16.7	16.5	16.1	16.3	15.5	15.1	14.4	14.1	13.5
Black	22.2	20.0	19.2	19.0	18.9	18.8	18.5	18.6	18.0	17.6	16.8	16.5	15.8
Maternal deaths [2]	9.2	8.0	7.8	7.8	7.2	6.6	8.4	7.9	8.2	7.9	7.8	(NA)	(NA)
White	6.7	5.9	5.4	5.2	4.9	5.1	5.9	5.6	5.4	5.8	5.0	(NA)	(NA)
Black and other	19.8	16.3	16.9	18.1	16.0	12.0	17.4	16.5	19.1	15.6	18.2	(NA)	(NA)
Black	21.5	18.3	19.7	20.4	18.8	14.2	19.5	18.4	22.4	18.3	20.8	(NA)	(NA)
Fetal deaths [3]	9.2	8.5	8.2	7.9	7.7	7.7	7.5	7.5	7.5	7.3	7.4	(NA)	(NA)
White	8.2	7.5	7.4	7.0	6.8	6.7	6.4	6.4	6.4	6.2	6.3	(NA)	(NA)
Black and other	13.4	12.4	11.5	11.3	11.2	11.5	11.4	11.7	11.9	11.4	11.7	(NA)	(NA)
Neonatal deaths [4]	8.5	7.3	7.0	7.0	6.7	6.5	6.3	6.2	5.8	5.6	5.4	5.3	5.1
White	7.4	6.3	6.1	6.0	5.7	5.4	5.3	5.1	4.8	4.5	4.3	4.3	4.2
Black and other	13.2	11.4	10.9	11.0	10.8	10.7	10.3	10.3	9.9	9.5	9.2	9.0	8.6
Black	14.6	12.9	12.3	12.6	12.3	12.3	12.1	11.9	11.6	11.2	10.8	10.7	10.2

NA Not available. [1] Represents deaths of infants under 1 year old, exclusive of fetal deaths. [2] Per 100,000 live births from deliveries and complications of pregnancy, childbirth, and the puerperium. Beginning 1979, deaths are classified according to the ninth revision of the *International Classification of Diseases;* earlier years classified according to the revision in use at the time; see text, section 2. [3] Includes only those deaths with stated or presumed period of gestation of 20 weeks or more. [4] Represents deaths of infants under 28 days old, exclusive of fetal deaths.

No. 124. Fetal and Infant Deaths—Number and Percent Distribution: 1970 to 1993

[State requirements for reporting of fetal deaths vary. Most States require reporting of fetal deaths of gestations of 20 weeks or more. There is substantial evidence that not all fetal deaths for which reporting is required are reported. For details of methodology, see Appendix III and source]

YEAR	NUMBER						PERCENT DISTRIBUTION					
	Total	Fetal deaths		Infant deaths			Total	Fetal deaths		Infant deaths		
		Early [1]	Late [2]	Neonatal		Post-neonatal [5]		Early [1]	Late [2]	Neonatal		Post-neonatal [5]
				Early [3]	Late [4]					Early [3]	Late [4]	
1970	127,628	17,170	35,791	50,821	5,458	18,388	100.0	13.5	28.0	39.8	4.3	14.4
1980	78,879	10,754	22,599	25,492	5,126	14,908	100.0	13.6	28.7	32.3	6.5	18.9
1982	75,095	11,028	21,666	23,706	4,629	14,066	100.0	14.7	28.9	31.6	6.2	18.7
1983	71,379	10,933	19,819	22,315	4,192	14,120	100.0	15.3	27.8	31.3	5.9	19.8
1984	69,679	10,963	19,136	21,566	4,125	13,869	100.0	15.7	27.5	31.0	5.9	19.9
1985	69,691	10,958	18,703	21,865	4,314	13,851	100.0	15.7	26.8	31.4	6.2	19.9
1986	67,863	11,100	17,872	21,053	4,159	13,679	100.0	16.4	26.3	31.0	6.1	20.2
1987	67,757	11,656	17,693	20,471	4,156	13,781	100.0	17.2	26.1	30.2	6.1	20.3
1988	68,352	11,833	17,609	20,471	4,219	14,220	100.0	17.3	25.8	29.9	6.2	20.8
1989	70,124	12,397	18,072	20,796	4,372	14,487	100.0	17.7	25.8	29.7	6.2	20.7
1990	67,696	12,554	16,791	20,020	4,289	14,042	100.0	18.5	24.8	29.6	6.3	20.7
1991	65,000	12,310	15,924	18,916	4,062	13,788	100.0	18.9	24.5	29.1	6.2	21.2
1992	63,153	12,704	15,821	17,798	4,051	12,779	100.0	20.1	25.1	28.2	6.4	21.8
1993	55,387	12,588	14,243	(NA)	(NA)	(NA)	(NA)	(NA)	(NA)	(NA)	(NA)	(NA)

NA Not available. [1] 20-27 weeks gestation. [2] 28 weeks or more gestation. [3] Less than 7 days. [4] 7-27 days. [5] 28 days-11 months.

No. 125. Infant Deaths and Infant Mortality Rates, by Cause of Death: 1980 to 1994

[Excludes deaths of nonresidents of the United States. Deaths classified according to ninth revision of *International Classification of Diseases*. See also Appendix III]

CAUSE OF DEATH	NUMBER			PERCENT DISTRIBUTION			INFANT MORTALITY RATE [1]		
	1980	1990	1994	1980	1990	1994	1980	1990	1994
Total	45,526	38,351	31,710	100	100	100	12.6	9.2	8.0
Congenital anomalies	9,220	8,239	6,854	20	21	22	2.6	2.0	1.7
Disorders relating to short gestation and unspecified low birth weight	3,648	4,013	4,254	8	10	13	1.0	1.0	1.1
Sudden infant death syndrome	5,510	5,417	4,073	12	14	13	1.5	1.3	1.0
Respiratory distress syndrome	4,989	2,850	1,567	11	7	5	1.4	0.7	0.4
Newborn affected by maternal complications of pregnancy	1,572	1,655	1,296	4	4	4	0.4	0.4	0.3
Newborn affected by complications of placenta, cord, and membranes	985	975	948	2	3	3	0.3	0.2	0.2
Accidents and adverse effects	1,166	930	889	3	2	3	0.3	0.2	0.2
Infections specific to the perinatal period	971	875	828	2	2	3	0.3	0.2	0.2
Pneumonia and influenza	1,012	634	559	2	2	2	0.3	0.2	0.1
Intrauterine hypoxia and birth asphyxia	1,497	762	537	3	2	2	0.4	0.2	0.1
All other causes	14,956	12,001	9,905	33	31	30	4.1	2.9	2.5

[1] Deaths of infants under 1 year old per 1,000 live births.

Sources of tables 123-125: U.S. National Center for Health Statistics, *Vital Statistics of the United States*, annual, and *Monthly Vital Statistics Report;* and unpublished data.

No. 126. Infant Mortality Rates, by Race—States: 1980 to 1994

[Deaths per 1,000 live births, by place of residence. Represents deaths of infants under 1 year old, exclusive of fetal deaths. Excludes deaths of nonresidents of the United States. See Appendix III]

DIVISION AND STATE	TOTAL [1]				WHITE				BLACK			
	1980	1985	1990	1994	1980	1985	1990	1994	1980	1985	1990	1994
U.S.	12.6	10.6	9.2	8.0	11.0	9.3	7.7	6.6	21.4	18.2	18.0	15.8
N.E.	10.5	9.2	7.2	6.5	10.1	8.5	6.8	5.9	17.7	20.1	14.0	13.9
ME	9.2	9.1	6.2	6.2	9.4	9.2	6.2	6.0	(S)	12.0	(S)	(S)
NH	9.9	9.3	7.1	6.2	9.9	9.2	7.2	6.1	22.5	29.9	(S)	(S)
VT	10.7	8.5	6.4	7.5	10.7	8.5	6.5	7.6	(S)	(NA)	(S)	(S)
MA	10.5	9.1	7.0	6.0	10.1	8.2	6.7	5.6	16.8	20.8	11.9	11.0
RI	11.0	8.2	8.1	5.0	10.9	8.1	8.3	4.1	(S)	(S)	(S)	(S)
CT	11.2	10.0	7.9	7.9	10.2	8.5	6.6	6.5	19.1	20.9	17.6	18.3
M.A.	12.8	10.6	9.5	7.9	11.1	9.3	7.5	6.1	21.1	17.6	18.7	16.8
NY	12.5	10.8	9.6	7.8	10.8	9.4	7.7	6.0	20.0	16.1	18.1	14.4
NJ	12.5	10.6	9.0	7.7	10.3	8.8	6.8	5.8	21.9	18.8	18.4	16.3
PA	13.2	11.0	9.6	8.2	11.9	9.5	7.8	6.4	23.1	20.4	20.5	18.6
E.N.C.	13.0	10.9	10.1	8.8	10.9	9.3	8.0	6.8	24.4	20.2	21.0	18.5
OH	12.8	10.3	9.8	8.7	11.2	9.3	8.2	7.2	23.0	16.9	19.5	17.7
IN	11.9	10.9	9.6	8.8	10.5	10.0	8.9	7.6	23.4	19.5	17.4	19.5
IL	14.8	11.7	10.7	9.3	11.7	9.3	7.7	6.8	26.3	21.4	22.4	18.7
MI	12.8	11.4	10.7	8.6	10.6	9.3	7.9	6.3	24.2	22.4	21.6	18.3
WI	10.3	9.1	8.2	7.9	9.7	8.5	7.2	6.5	18.5	17.4	19.0	20.2
W.N.C.	11.3	9.5	8.4	7.7	10.5	9.0	7.5	6.7	21.3	16.0	18.9	16.9
MN	10.0	8.8	7.3	7.0	9.6	8.8	6.7	6.2	20.0	15.5	23.7	18.6
IA	11.8	9.5	8.1	7.5	11.5	9.4	7.8	7.0	27.2	12.3	21.9	22.7
MO	12.4	10.2	9.4	8.1	11.1	9.0	7.8	6.6	20.7	17.0	18.2	16.3
ND	12.1	8.5	8.0	7.2	11.7	8.4	7.9	6.5	27.5	6.9	(S)	(S)
SD	10.9	9.9	10.1	9.6	9.0	8.9	8.6	7.6	(NA)	(NA)	(S)	(S)
NE	11.5	9.6	8.3	7.7	10.7	9.0	7.2	7.2	25.2	17.7	18.9	15.7
KS	10.4	9.3	8.4	7.7	9.5	9.0	7.7	6.9	20.6	14.4	17.7	15.9
S.A.	14.5	12.1	10.7	9.1	11.6	9.4	8.0	6.7	21.6	19.2	17.9	15.3
DE	13.9	14.8	10.1	6.8	9.8	11.6	7.3	5.1	27.9	25.8	20.1	11.7
MD	14.0	11.9	9.5	9.0	11.6	9.1	6.5	6.2	20.4	18.9	17.1	14.7
DC	25.0	20.8	20.7	18.2	17.8	10.8	12.1	(S)	26.7	23.7	24.6	20.9
VA	13.6	11.5	10.2	8.3	11.9	9.3	7.5	6.4	19.8	19.2	19.5	15.1
WV	11.8	10.7	9.9	6.7	11.4	10.4	9.6	6.6	21.5	20.6	(S)	(S)
NC	14.5	11.8	10.6	10.0	12.1	9.4	8.3	7.5	20.0	17.8	16.5	16.6
SC	15.6	14.2	11.7	9.3	10.8	9.6	8.3	6.6	22.9	21.8	17.3	14.1
GA	14.5	12.7	12.4	10.2	10.8	9.5	9.1	7.1	21.0	19.0	18.3	16.1
FL	14.6	11.3	9.6	8.1	11.8	9.2	7.6	6.5	22.8	17.8	16.8	13.9
E.S.C.	14.5	12.1	10.4	9.4	11.8	9.7	8.1	6.8	21.8	18.7	16.4	16.2
KY	12.9	11.2	8.5	7.8	12.0	10.3	8.0	7.1	22.0	20.5	14.3	14.7
TN	13.5	11.4	10.3	8.9	11.9	8.9	8.0	6.3	19.3	20.2	17.9	18.0
AL	15.1	12.6	10.8	10.1	11.6	10.4	8.3	7.0	21.6	17.0	16.0	16.4
MS	17.0	13.7	12.1	11.0	11.1	9.3	8.5	7.3	23.7	18.9	16.2	14.7
W.S.C.	12.7	10.4	8.7	7.9	11.1	9.3	7.4	6.8	19.8	16.2	15.3	13.7
AR	12.7	11.6	9.2	9.2	10.3	10.9	8.0	8.2	20.0	14.2	13.9	13.0
LA	14.3	11.9	11.1	10.6	10.5	8.6	7.3	6.8	20.6	17.2	16.7	16.0
OK	12.7	10.9	9.2	8.5	12.1	10.8	9.4	8.3	21.8	18.5	14.3	11.3
TX	12.2	9.8	8.1	7.1	11.2	9.0	7.1	6.4	18.8	15.5	14.7	12.6
Mountain	11.0	9.8	8.6	7.2	10.7	9.7	8.3	6.8	19.5	13.1	18.6	16.4
MT	12.4	10.3	9.0	7.4	11.8	9.8	8.6	7.1	(NA)	13.2	(S)	(S)
ID	10.7	10.4	8.7	6.9	10.7	10.5	8.7	6.7	(NA)	(NA)	(S)	(S)
WY	9.8	12.2	8.6	6.7	9.3	12.2	8.8	6.6	25.9	9.9	(S)	(S)
CO	10.1	9.4	8.8	7.0	9.8	9.1	8.4	6.4	19.1	15.9	19.4	20.2
NM	11.5	10.6	9.0	8.3	11.3	10.6	9.3	7.9	23.1	14.4	(S)	(S)
AZ	12.4	9.7	8.8	7.8	11.8	9.4	8.2	7.4	18.4	12.4	20.6	16.5
UT	10.4	9.6	7.5	6.2	10.5	9.7	7.4	5.8	27.3	3.3	(S)	(S)
NV	10.7	8.5	8.4	6.5	10.0	8.7	8.1	6.2	20.6	11.7	14.2	12.0
Pacific	11.2	9.7	7.9	6.9	10.9	9.4	7.6	6.4	17.8	16.2	17.1	15.1
WA	11.8	10.7	7.8	6.2	11.5	10.9	7.6	6.0	16.4	12.6	20.6	14.7
OR	12.2	9.9	8.3	7.1	12.2	9.7	8.1	6.9	15.9	17.3	(S)	(S)
CA	11.1	9.5	7.9	7.0	10.6	9.2	7.6	6.5	18.0	16.3	16.8	15.2
AK	12.3	10.8	10.5	7.6	9.4	9.6	8.5	6.9	19.5	20.5	(S)	(S)
HI	10.3	8.8	6.7	6.7	11.6	7.5	5.1	4.4	11.8	20.0	(S)	(S)

NA Not available. S Figure does not meet publication standards. [1] Includes other races, not shown separately.

Source: U.S. National Center for Health Statistics, *Vital Statistics of the United States*, annual; and unpublished data.

No. 127. Deaths and Death Rates, by Selected Causes: 1980 to 1995

hs of nonresidents of the United States, except as noted. Beginning 1980, deaths classified according to ninth *rnational Classification of Diseases;* for earlier years, classified according to revision in use at that time. See also

SE OF DEATH	DEATHS (1,000				CRUDE DEATH RATE PER 100,000 POPULATION [2]			
	1980	1990	1994 [1]	1995	1980	1990	1994 [1]	1995
s	1,989.8	2,148.5	2,286.0	2,312.2	878.3	863.8	876.9	880.0
scular diseases	988.5	916.0	945.2	952.5	436.4	368.3	362.6	362.5
heart	761.1	720.1	734.1	738.8	336.0	289.5	281.6	281.2
of total	38.3	33.5	32.1	32.0	38.3	33.5	32.1	32.0
: fever and rheumatic ease	7.8	6.0	5.5	5.2	3.5	2.4	2.1	2.0
ive heart disease [3]	24.8	23.4	23.8	24.4	10.9	9.5	9.1	9.3
heart disease	565.8	489.2	487.5	482.2	249.7	196.7	187.0	183.5
ases of endocardium	7.2	13.0	14.5	16.3	3.2	5.2	5.6	6.2
orms of heart disease	155.5	188.4	200.1	208.2	68.7	75.8	76.8	79.2
1 [3]	7.8	9.2	11.7	12.5	3.5	3.7	4.5	4.7
ular diseases	170.2	144.1	154.4	158.1	75.1	57.9	59.2	60.2
els	29.4	18.0	18.0	16.8	13.0	7.3	6.9	6.4
	20.0	24.6	27.1	26.4	8.8	9.9	10.4	10.1
	416.5	505.3	534.3	538.0	183.9	203.2	205.2	204.7
f total	20.9	23.5	23.4	23.3	20.9	23.5	23.4	23.3
y and intrathoracic	108.5	146.4	154.3	156.1	47.9	58.9	59.2	59.4
organs and	110.6	120.8	127.2	126.4	48.8	48.6	48.8	48.1
gans	46.4	57.5	62.1	60.3	20.5	23.1	23.8	23.0
	35.9	43.7	43.3	44.3	15.8	17.6	16.6	16.9
gans	17.8	20.7	22.0	22.5	7.9	8.3	8.4	8.6
	16.5	18.6	20.1	20.0	7.3	7.5	7.7	7.6
adverse effects	105.7	92.0	90.1	89.7	46.7	37.0	34.6	34.1
e	53.2	46.8	42.2	41.8	23.5	18.8	16.2	15.9
	52.5	45.2	48.0	47.9	23.3	18.2	18.4	18.2
ctive pulmonary allied conditions	56.1	86.7	101.9	104.8	24.7	34.9	39.1	39.9
hronic and unspecified	3.7	3.6	3.6	3.4	1.6	1.4	1.4	1.3
	13.9	15.7	17.3	17.3	6.1	6.3	6.6	6.6
	2.9	4.8	5.7	5.6	1.3	1.9	2.2	2.1
	35.6	62.6	75.3	78.4	15.7	25.2	28.9	29.9
d influenza	54.6	79.5	82.1	83.5	24.1	32.0	31.5	31.8
	51.9	77.4	80.8	82.9	22.9	31.1	31.0	31.6
	2.7	2.1	1.3	0.6	1.2	0.8	0.5	0.2
us	34.9	47.7	55.4	59.1	15.4	19.2	21.2	22.5
	26.9	30.9	32.4	30.9	11.9	12.4	12.4	11.8
isease and cirrhosis	30.6	25.8	25.7	24.8	13.5	10.4	9.9	9.5
s and parasitic diseases	5.1	32.2	48.5	49.6	2.2	13.0	18.6	18.9
legal intervention	24.3	24.9	23.7	21.6	10.7	10.0	9.1	8.2
rotic syndrome, and	16.8	20.8	23.6	23.8	7.4	8.3	9.1	9.1
	9.4	19.2	19.9	21.1	4.2	7.7	7.6	8.0
ons originating in the od	22.9	17.7	14.1	13.2	10.1	7.1	5.4	5.0
malies	13.9	13.1	11.9	11.9	6.2	5.3	4.6	4.5
sms [5]	6.2	6.8	7.0	7.8	2.7	2.7	2.7	3.0
ch and duodenum	6.1	6.2	6.0	5.4	0.0	2.5	2.3	2.1
minal cavity and ruction [6]	5.4	5.8	6.0	6.2	2.4	2.3	2.3	2.4
	3.2	4.1	4.2	4.5	1.4	1.8	1.8	1.7
nd other disorders of	3.3	3.0	2.6	2.7	1.5	1.2	1.0	1.0
ciencies	2.4	3.0	3.2	3.5	1.0	1.2	1.2	1.3
	2.0	1.8	1.6	1.3	0.9	0.7	0.6	0.5
dney	2.7	1.3	1.0	0.9	1.2	0.5	0.4	0.3
	0.8	1.6	2.8	3.4	0.4	0.6	1.1	1.3
	1.4	1.0	0.9	0.8	0.6	0.4	0.4	0.3
s and bronchiolitis	0.6	0.6	0.5	0.6	0.3	0.3	0.2	0.2
prostate	0.8	0.5	0.5	0.4	0.3	0.2	0.2	0.2
ns, and ill-defined	28.8	24.1	26.6	33.0	12.7	9.7	10.2	12.6
s.	120.0	172.9	206.1	212.3	53.0	69.5	79.1	80.8

a 10-percent sample of deaths. Includes deaths of nonresidents. [2] 1980 and 1990 based on resident population of April 1. Other years based on resident population estimated as of July 1. [3] With or without renal disease. r types of malignancies not shown separately. [5] Includes neoplasms of unspecified nature; beginning 1980 also oma in situ. [6] Without mention of hernia.

S. National Center for Health Statistics, *Vital Statistics of the United States*, annual; *Monthly Vital Statistics Report;* d data.

No. 128. Age-Adjusted Death Rates, by Selected Causes: 1980 to 1995

[Rates per 100,000 population. For explanation of age-adjustment, see text, section 2. The standard population for this table is the total population of the United States enumerated in 1940. See also headnote, table 127]

CAUSE OF DEATH	1980	1985	1988	1989	1990	1991	1992	1993	1994	1995
All causes	585.8	548.9	539.9	528.0	520.2	513.7	504.5	513.3	507.4	502.9
Major cardiovascular diseases	256.0	225.1	208.3	196.1	189.8	185.0	180.4	181.8	176.8	174.7
Diseases of heart	202.0	181.4	167.7	157.5	152.0	148.2	144.3	145.3	140.4	138.2
Rheumatic fever and rheumatic heart disease	2.6	1.9	1.7	1.5	1.5	1.4	1.3	1.3	1.2	1.2
Hypertensive heart disease [1]	5.9	5.3	5.0	4.9	4.8	4.7	4.8	4.9	5.0	4.9
Hypertensive heart and renal disease	0.9	0.6	0.5	0.5	0.5	0.5	0.5	0.5	0.5	0.4
Ischemic heart disease	149.8	126.1	111.1	106.2	102.6	99.1	95.7	94.9	91.4	89.6
Other diseases of endocardium	2.0	2.2	2.4	2.4	2.5	2.5	2.6	2.6	2.6	2.8
Acute mycocardial infraction	85.9	69.6	58.3	56.5	53.7	51.5	49.1	47.5	45.6	44.0
Old myocardial infraction and other	62.3	55.2	51.8	48.7	47.8	46.6	45.7	46.5	45.0	44.9
Hypertension [1]	2.0	1.8	1.8	1.9	1.9	1.9	2.0	2.2	2.2	2.3
Cerebrovascular diseases	40.8	32.5	29.9	28.3	27.7	26.8	26.2	26.5	26.5	26.7
Atherosclerosis	5.7	4.0	3.5	3.0	2.7	2.6	2.4	2.4	2.3	2.3
Intracerebral/intracranial hemorage	6.2	5.6	5.5	5.2	5.2	5.1	5.1	5.1	5.0	5.0
Cerebral thrombosis	7.6	4.8	4.0	3.6	3.3	2.9	2.7	2.5	2.4	2.3
Cerebral embolism	0.2	0.2	0.2	0.1	0.1	0.1	0.1	0.1	0.1	0.1
Malignancies [2]	132.8	134.4	134.0	134.5	135.0	134.5	133.1	132.6	131.5	129.8
Of respiratory and intrathoracic organs	36.4	39.1	40.3	40.8	41.4	41.1	40.8	40.8	40.1	39.6
Of digestive organs and peritoneum	33.0	31.7	30.3	30.3	30.2	29.9	29.6	29.5	29.3	29.0
Of genital organs	13.6	13.1	13.2	13.2	13.6	13.6	13.5	13.2	13.2	12.7
Of breast	12.5	12.8	12.7	12.7	12.7	12.4	12.0	11.8	11.8	11.5
Of urinary organs	5.2	5.1	4.9	5.1	5.1	5.1	5.1	5.0	5.1	5.0
Leukemia	5.4	5.1	4.9	5.0	5.0	5.0	4.9	4.9	4.9	4.8
Of lip,oral cavity, and pharynx	2.9	2.6	2.5	2.4	2.4	2.4	2.3	2.3	2.1	2.1
Accidents and adverse effects	42.3	34.8	35.0	33.9	32.5	31.0	29.4	30.3	30.3	29.2
Motor vehicle	22.9	18.8	19.7	18.9	18.5	17.0	15.8	16.0	16.1	15.7
All other	19.5	16.0	15.4	15.0	14.0	13.9	13.7	14.4	14.2	13.5
Chronic obstructive pulmonary diseases and allied conditions [3]	15.9	18.8	19.6	19.6	19.7	20.1	19.9	21.4	21.0	21.2
Bronchitis, chronic and unspecified	1.0	0.9	0.8	0.8	0.8	0.8	0.8	0.8	0.7	0.7
Emphysema	4.0	3.7	3.8	3.7	3.7	3.8	3.7	3.9	3.7	3.7
Asthma	1.0	1.2	1.4	1.4	1.4	1.5	1.4	1.4	1.5	1.5
Other	9.9	13.0	13.6	13.6	13.7	14.1	14.0	15.2	15.1	15.3
Pneumonia and influenza	12.9	13.5	14.3	13.8	14.0	13.4	12.7	13.5	13.0	13.0
Pneumonia	12.4	13.1	14.0	13.5	13.7	13.2	12.5	13.3	12.8	12.9
Influenza	0.5	0.3	0.3	0.3	0.3	0.2	0.2	0.2	0.2	0.1
Diabetes mellitus	10.1	9.7	10.2	11.6	11.7	11.8	11.9	12.4	12.9	13.2
Suicide	11.4	11.5	11.5	11.3	11.5	11.4	11.1	11.3	11.2	11.0
Chronic liver disease and cirrhosis	12.2	9.7	9.1	9.0	8.6	8.3	8.0	7.9	7.9	7.5
Homicide and legal intervention	10.8	8.3	9.0	9.4	10.2	10.9	10.5	10.7	10.3	8.8
Nephritis, nephrotic syndrome, and Renal failure	3.8	4.5	4.4	4.0	3.9	3.9	4.0	4.1	3.9	4.0
Acute glomerulonephritis/nephrotic syndrome	0.1	0.1	0.1	0.1	0.1	0.1	0.1	(NA)	0.1	(NA)
Septicemia	2.6	4.1	4.6	4.2	4.1	4.1	4.0	4.1	4.0	4.1
Other infectious and parasitic diseases	1.4	2.6	8.7	10.9	12.0	13.3	14.7	15.9	17.5	17.4
Benign neoplasms [4]	2.0	1.9	1.7	1.7	1.7	1.7	1.7	1.7	1.7	1.8
Ulcer of stomach and duodenum	1.7	1.5	1.4	1.4	1.3	1.2	1.2	1.2	1.2	1.0
Hernia of abdominal cavity and intestinal obstruction [5]	1.4	1.1	1.1	1.1	1.1	1.1	1.1	1.0	1.1	1.1
Anemias	0.9	0.9	0.9	0.9	0.9	0.9	0.9	0.9	0.9	0.9
Cholelithiasis and other disorders of gallbladder	0.8	0.6	0.6	0.6	0.6	0.5	0.5	0.5	0.5	0.5
Nutritional deficiencies	0.5	0.5	0.5	0.5	0.5	0.5	0.5	0.5	0.5	0.5
Tuberculosis	0.6	0.5	0.5	0.6	0.5	0.5	0.4	0.4	0.4	0.3
Tuberculosis of respiratory system	0.5	0.4	0.4	0.4	0.4	0.4	0.3	0.3	0.3	0.3
Other tuberculosis	0.1	0.1	0.1	0.1	0.1	0.1	0.1	0.1	0.1	0.1
Infections of kidney	0.7	0.4	0.3	0.3	0.2	0.2	0.2	0.2	0.2	0.2
Viral hepatitis	0.3	0.3	0.4	0.5	0.5	0.6	0.6	0.8	0.9	1.0
Meningitis	0.6	0.4	0.4	0.4	0.3	0.3	0.2	0.3	0.3	0.3
Acute bronchitis and bronchiolitis	0.2	0.1	0.1	0.1	0.1	0.1	0.1	0.1	0.1	0.1
Hyperplasia of prostate	0.2	0.1	0.1	0.1	0.1	0.1	0.1	0.1	0.1	0.1
Symptoms, signs, and ill-defined conditions	9.8	9.4	9.3	8.2	7.3	7.2	6.7	7.4	6.8	9.2
Meningococcal infection	0.2	0.1	0.1	0.1	0.1	0.1	0.1	0.1	0.1	0.1
Angina pectoris	0.2	0.2	0.2	0.2	0.2	0.2	0.2	0.2	0.2	0.1
Appendicitis	0.2	0.1	0.1	0.1	0.1	0.1	0.1	0.1	0.1	0.1
Complications of pregnancy, childbirth	0.1	0.1	0.1	0.1	0.1	0.1	0.1	0.1	0.1	0.1
Congenital anomalies	6.0	5.3	5.1	5.0	5.0	4.7	4.6	4.6	4.5	4.4
Perinatal period conditions	9.9	8.0	7.4	7.5	6.9	6.4	6.0	5.9	4.8	4.4
Birth trauma, intrauterine hypoxia, etc.	3.3	2.2	1.7	1.8	1.5	1.3	1.1	1.0	0.9	0.9

NA Not available. [1] With or without renal disease. [2] Includes other types of malignancies not shown separately. [3] Prior to 1980, data are shown for bronchitis, emphysema, and asthma. [4] Includes neoplasms of unspecified nature; also includes carcinoma in situ. [5] Without mention of hernia.

Source: U.S. National Center for Health Statistics, *Vital Statistics of the United States*, annual; *Monthly Vital Statistics Reports*; and unpublished data.

No. 129. Deaths, by Selected Causes and Selected Characteristics: 1994

[In thousands. Excludes deaths of nonresidents of the U.S. Deaths classified according to ninth revision of *International Classification of Diseases*. See also Appendix III]

AGE, SEX, AND RACE	Total [1]	Heart disease	Cancer	Accidents and adverse effects	Cerebrovascular diseases	Chronic obstructive pulmonary diseases [2]	Pneumonia, flu	Suicide	Chronic liver disease, cirrhosis	Diabetes mellitus	Homicide and legal intervention
ALL RACES [3]											
Both sexes, total [4]	2,279.0	732.4	534.3	91.4	153.3	101.6	80.2	31.1	25.4	56.7	24.9
1 to 4 years old	6.8	0.3	0.5	2.5	0.1	0.4	0.2	-	(Z)	(Z)	0.5
5 to 14 years old	8.5	0.3	1.1	3.5	0.1	0.1	0.1	0.3	(Z)	(Z)	0.6
15 to 24 years old	35.2	1.0	1.7	13.9	0.2	0.2	0.2	5.0	(Z)	0.1	8.1
25 to 44 years old	158.8	16.8	21.9	27.0	3.5	1.1	2.2	12.7	4.4	2.5	11.4
45 to 64 years old	375.0	103.0	132.8	15.2	14.9	13.0	5.5	7.1	10.6	11.5	-
65 years old and over	1,662.6	610.3	376.2	28.3	134.3	87.0	72.8	6.0	10.3	42.6	-
Male, total [4]	1,162.7	361.3	280.5	60.5	60.2	53.7	37.3	25.2	16.5	24.8	19.7
1 to 4 years old	3.8	0.1	0.3	1.5	-	-	0.1	-	-	-	0.3
5 to 14 years old	5.2	0.2	0.6	2.3	-	0.1	0.1	0.2	-	-	0.4
15 to 24 years old	26.8	0.6	1.1	10.4	0.1	0.1	0.1	4.3	-	-	7.0
25 to 44 years old	111.9	11.9	10.1	20.7	1.8	-	1.3	10.3	3.2	1.5	9.0
45 to 64 years old	231.6	72.6	71.2	10.8	8.2	6.9	3.4	5.4	7.5	6.0	-
65 years old and over	765.3	275.4	197.2	14.2	49.9	45.9	32.0	-	-	17.2	-
Female, total [4]	1,116.2	371.1	253.8	30.9	93.1	47.9	44.1	6.0	8.9	31.9	5.2
1 to 4 years old	3.0	0.1	0.2	1.0	-	-	0.1	-	-	-	0.2
5 to 14 years old	3.3	0.2	0.4	1.2	-	(Z)	(Z)	-	-	-	0.2
15 to 24 years old	8.5	0.4	0.7	3.5	-	0.1	0.1	0.7	-	-	1.1
25 to 44 years old	46.9	4.9	11.8	6.3	1.7	-	0.8	2.5	1.3	1.0	2.4
45 to 64 years old	143.4	30.3	61.7	4.4	6.8	6.1	2.1	1.7	3.1	5.5	-
65 years old and over	897.3	334.9	179.0	14.2	84.4	41.1	40.7	-	-	25.4	-
WHITE											
Both sexes, total [4]	1,959.9	646.1	465.8	75.9	132.5	94.1	72.6	28.0	21.5	45.7	12.0
1 to 4 years old	4.6	0.2	0.4	1.7	-	-	0.1	-	-	-	0.3
5 to 14 years old	6.1	0.2	0.8	2.6	-	0.1	0.1	0.3	-	-	0.3
15 to 24 years old	24.5	0.6	1.4	11.5	0.1	0.1	0.2	4.1	-	-	3.1
25 to 44 years old	112.5	11.8	17.2	21.8	2.2	-	1.4	11.2	3.4	1.8	5.5
45 to 64 years old	300.5	82.7	110.8	12.2	10.6	11.4	4.2	6.7	8.6	8.4	-
65 years old and over	1,490.8	550.1	335.1	25.4	119.4	81.7	66.3	-	-	35.4	-
White male, total [4]	988.8	318.5	243.0	49.8	51.0	49.2	32.7	22.6	14.0	20.4	-
1 to 4 years old	2.6	0.1	0.2	1.1	-	-	0.1	-	-	-	0.1
5 to 14 years old	3.7	0.1	0.5	1.7	-	-	-	0.2	-	-	0.2
15 to 24 years old	18.3	0.4	0.9	8.6	0.1	0.1	0.1	3.6	-	-	2.6
25 to 44 years old	80.7	8.8	8.0	16.9	1.2	-	0.9	9.0	2.5	1.1	4.3
45 to 64 years old	187.0	60.0	59.0	8.6	5.8	6.1	2.5	5.1	6.2	4.6	-
65 years old and over	684.6	248.8	174.4	12.5	43.8	42.7	28.9	-	-	14.7	-
White females, total [4]	971.1	327.5	222.8	26.1	81.5	44.8	39.9	-	-	25.3	-
1 to 4 years old	2.0	0.1	0.2	0.7	-	-	0.1	-	-	-	0.1
5 to 14 years old	2.4	0.1	0.4	0.9	-	-	-	0.1	-	-	0.1
15 to 24 years old	6.2	0.2	0.5	2.9	0.1	-	0.1	0.5	-	-	0.6
25 to 44 years old	31.8	3.0	9.2	4.9	1.0	-	0.5	2.2	0.9	0.7	1.3
45 to 64 years old	113.5	22.6	51.8	3.6	4.8	5.4	1.7	1.6	2.4	3.8	-
65 years old and over	808.2	301.2	160.7	12.9	75.5	39.1	37.5	-	-	20.7	-
BLACK											
Both sexes, total [4]	282.4	76.9	59.9	12.8	18.0	6.5	7.5	2.3	3.2	9.8	-
1 to 4 years old	1.9	0.1	0.1	0.7	-	-	-	-	-	-	-
5 to 14 years old	2.0	0.1	0.2	0.8	-	-	-	-	-	-	-
15 to 24 years old	9.4	0.3	0.3	1.8	-	0.1	-	0.6	-	-	-
25 to 44 years old	42.0	4.6	4.0	4.3	1.2	-	0.7	1.1	0.8	0.6	-
45 to 64 years old	66.2	18.3	19.3	2.5	3.9	1.4	1.2	-	1.6	2.7	-
65 years old and over	150.6	53.3	36.2	2.4	12.8	4.5	5.3	-	4.5	6.4	-
Black male, total [4]	153.0	37.2	32.9	8.8	7.8	3.9	3.9	-	-	3.8	10.1
1 to 4 years old	1.1	0.1	-	0.4	-	-	-	-	-	-	-
5 to 14 years old	1.2	-	0.1	0.5	-	-	-	-	-	-	0.2
15 to 24 years old	7.5	0.2	0.1	1.4	-	0.1	-	0.6	-	(Z)	4.3
25 to 44 years old	28.4	2.8	1.7	3.2	0.6	-	0.4	0.9	0.5	0.4	4.5
45 to 64 years old	39.8	11.2	10.8	1.8	2.1	0.8	0.8	-	1.1	1.3	0.8
65 years old and over	69.4	22.8	20.0	1.3	5.0	2.7	2.5	-	-	2.2	-
Black females, total [4]	124.0	39.6	27.1	3.9	10.2	2.7	3.6	-	-	-	-
1 to 4 years old	0.9	0.1	-	0.3	-	-	-	-	-	-	0.1
5 to 14 years old	0.8	-	0.1	0.3	-	-	-	-	-	-	0.1
15 to 24 years old	2.0	0.1	0.1	0.4	-	-	-	0.1	-	-	0.5
25 to 44 years old	13.7	1.7	2.2	1.1	0.6	0.2	0.3	-	0.3	0.3	1.1
45 to 64 years old	26.5	7.1	8.5	0.7	1.7	0.7	0.4	-	0.5	1.5	-
65 years old and over	81.2	30.5	16.1	1.1	7.8	1.7	2.7	-	-	4.2	-

- Represents zero. Z Fewer than 50. [1] Includes other causes, not shown separately [2] Includes allied conditions. [3] Includes other races, not shown separately. [4] Includes those deaths with age not stated.

Source: U.S. National Center for Health Statistics, Vital Statistics of the United States, annual.

No. 130. Deaths, by Age and Leading Cause: 1994

[Excludes deaths of nonresidents of the United States. Deaths classified according to ninth revision of *International Classification of Diseases*. See also Appendix III]

AGE AND LEADING CAUSE OF DEATH	NUMBER OF DEATHS			DEATH RATE PER 100,000 POPULATION		
	Total	Male	Female	Total	Male	Female
All ages [1]	**2,278,994**	**1,162,747**	**1,116,247**	**875.4**	**916.0**	**837.6**
Leading causes of death:						
Heart disease	732,409	361,276	371,133	281.3	284.3	278.5
Malignant neoplasms (cancer)	534,310	280,465	253,845	205.2	220.7	190.5
Cerebrovascular disease (stroke)	153,306	60,225	93,081	58.9	47.4	69.8
Chronic obstructive pulmonary disease	101,628	53,729	47,899	39.0	42.3	35.9
Accidents	91,437	60,509	30,928	35.1	47.6	23.2
Pneumonia	81,473	37,339	44,134	31.3	29.4	33.1
Diabetes	56,692	24,758	31,934	21.8	19.5	24.0
HIV infection [2]	42,114	35,641	(NA)	16.2	28.0	(NA)
Suicide	31,142	25,174	(NA)	12.0	19.8	(NA)
Homicide and legal intervention	(NA)	19,707	(NA)	(NA)	15.5	(NA)
1 TO 4 YEARS OLD						
All causes	**6,800**	**3,841**	**2,959**	**42.9**	**47.3**	**38.2**
Leading causes of death:						
Accidents	2,517	1,518	999	15.9	18.7	12.9
Congenital anomalies	714	354	360	4.5	4.4	4.6
Malignant neoplasms (cancer)	518	287	231	3.3	3.5	3.0
Homicide and legal intervention	473	265	208	3.0	3.3	2.7
Heart disease	285	146	139	1.8	1.8	1.8
Pneumonia and influenza	178	98	80	1.1	1.2	1.0
HIV infection [2]	199	98	101	1.3	1.2	1.3
5 TO 14 YEARS OLD						
All causes	**8,464**	**5,182**	**3,282**	**22.5**	**26.9**	**17.9**
Leading causes of death:						
Accidents	3,508	2,305	1,203	9.3	12.0	6.6
Malignant neoplasms (cancer)	1,053	604	449	2.8	3.1	2.4
Congenital anomalies	434	232	202	1.2	1.2	1.1
Suicide	322	234	88	0.9	1.2	0.5
Homicide and legal intervention	572	357	215	1.5	1.9	1.2
Heart disease	327	174	153	0.9	0.9	0.8
Pneumonia and influenza	103	58	45	0.3	0.3	0.2
HIV infections [2]	182	96	86	0.5	0.5	0.5
15 TO 24 YEARS OLD						
All causes	**35,241**	**26,758**	**8,483**	**96.0**	**146.8**	**46.2**
Leading causes of death:						
Accidents	13,898	10,417	3,481	38.7	56.8	19.8
Homicide and legal intervention	8,116	7,024	1,092	22.6	38.3	6.2
Suicide	4,956	4,302	654	13.8	23.4	3.7
Malignant neoplasms (cancer)	1,740	1,059	681	4.8	5.8	3.9
Cerebrovascular disease (stroke)	183	98	(NA)	0.5	0.5	(NA)
Chronic obstructive pulmonary disease	232	143	89	0.6	0.8	0.5
Congenital anomalies	463	272	191	1.3	1.5	1.1
Heart disease	992	631	361	2.8	3.4	2.1
Pneumonia and influenza	221	115	106	0.6	0.6	0.6
HIV infection [2]	641	420	221	1.8	2.3	1.3
25 TO 44 YEARS OLD						
All causes	**158,776**	**111,924**	**46,852**	**191.3**	**270.8**	**112.4**
Leading causes of death:						
Accidents	27,012	20,729	6,283	32.5	50.2	15.1
Malignant neoplasms (cancer)	21,899	10,091	11,808	26.4	24.4	28.3
Cerebrovascular disease (stroke)	3,519	1,845	1,674	4.2	4.5	4.0
HIV infection [2]	30,476	25,773	4,703	36.7	62.4	11.3
Heart disease	16,763	11,903	4,860	20.2	28.8	11.7
Pneumonia and influenza	2,155	1,341	814	2.6	3.2	2.0
Diabetes	2,467	1,480	987	3.0	3.6	2.4
Homicide and legal intervention	11,419	8,987	2,432	13.8	21.7	5.8
Suicide	12,729	10,265	2,464	15.3	24.8	5.9
45 TO 64 YEARS OLD						
All causes	**375,016**	**231,647**	**143,369**	**736.9**	**942.6**	**544.8**
Leading causes of death:						
Malignant neoplasms (cancer)	132,839	71,165	61,674	261.0	289.6	234.4
Heart disease	102,956	72,623	30,333	202.3	295.5	115.3
Pneumonia and influenza	5,490	3,369	2,121	10.8	13.7	8.1
HIV infection [2]	9,822	8,659	1,163	19.3	35.2	4.4
Cerebrovascular (stroke)	14,932	8,179	6,753	29.3	33.3	25.7
Accidents	15,200	10,794	4,406	29.9	43.9	16.7
Chronic obstructive pulmonary disease	13,011	6,930	6,081	25.6	28.2	23.1
Chronic liver disease and cirrhosis	10,573	7,501	3,072	20.8	30.5	11.7
Diabetes	11,473	5,998	5,475	22.5	24.4	20.8
Suicide	7,108	5,427	1,681	14.0	22.1	6.4
65 YEARS OLD AND OVER						
All causes	**1,662,573**	**765,270**	**897,303**	**5,014.1**	**5,679.2**	**4,558.8**
Leading causes of death:						
Heart disease	610,330	275,383	334,947	1,840.7	2,043.6	1,701.7
Malignant neoplasms (cancer)	376,186	197,220	178,966	1,134.5	1,463.6	909.2
Cerebrovascular (stroke)	134,340	49,910	84,430	405.2	370.4	429.0
Chronic obstructive pulmonary disease	87,048	45,945	41,103	262.5	341.0	208.8
Pneumonia and influenza	72,762	32,018	40,744	219.4	237.6	207.0
Diabetes	42,600	17,198	25,402	128.5	127.6	129.1
Accidents	28,314	14,152	14,162	85.4	105.0	72.0

NA Not available. [1] Includes those deaths with age not stated. [2] Human immunodeficiency virus.

Source: U.S. National Center for Health Statistics, *Vital Statistics of the United States*, annual; and unpublished data.

No. 131. Death Rates, by Leading Causes and Age: 1980 to 1994

[Deaths per 100,000 population in specified group. Except as noted, excludes deaths of nonresidents of the United States. See text, section 2]

YEAR, RACE, AND AGE	Heart disease	Malignant neoplasms	Accidents and adverse effects	Cerebrovascular diseases	Chronic obstructive pulmonary diseases [1]	Pneumonia, flu	Suicide	Chronic liver disease, cirrhosis	Diabetes mellitus	Homicide and legal intervention
All races, both sexes: [2]										
1980	336.0	183.9	46.7	75.1	24.7	24.1	11.9	13.5	15.4	10.7
1990	289.5	203.2	37.0	57.9	34.9	32.0	12.4	10.4	19.2	10.0
1993	288.4	205.6	35.1	58.2	39.2	32.1	12.1	9.8	20.9	10.1
1994	281.3	205.2	35.1	58.9	39.0	31.3	12.0	9.8	21.8	(NA)
1 to 4 years old	1.8	3.3	15.9	(NA)	(NA)	1.1	(NA)	(NA)	(NA)	3.0
5 to 14 years old	0.9	2.8	9.3	(NA)	0.3	0.3	0.9	(NA)	(NA)	1.5
15 to 24 years old	2.8	4.8	38.7	0.5	0.6	0.6	13.8	(NA)	(NA)	22.6
25 to 44 years old	20.2	26.4	32.5	4.2	(NA)	2.8	15.3	5.3	3.0	13.8
45 to 64 years old	202.3	261.0	29.9	29.3	25.6	10.8	14.0	20.8	22.5	(NA)
65 years old and over	1,840.7	1,134.5	85.4	405.2	262.5	219.4	(NA)	(NA)	128.5	(NA)
All races, males:										
1994	284.3	220.7	47.6	47.4	42.3	29.4	19.8	(NA)	19.5	15.5
1 to 4 years old	1.8	3.5	18.7	(NA)	(NA)	1.2	(NA)	(NA)	(NA)	3.3
5 to 4 years old	0.9	3.1	12.0	(NA)	0.4	0.3	1.2	(NA)	(NA)	1.9
15 to 24 years old	3.4	5.8	56.8	0.5	0.8	0.6	23.4	(NA)	(NA)	38.3
25 to 44 years old	28.8	24.4	50.2	4.5	(NA)	3.2	24.8	7.7	3.8	21.7
45 to 64 years old	295.5	289.6	43.9	33.3	28.2	13.7	22.1	30.5	24.4	(NA)
65 years old and over	2,043.6	1,463.6	106.0	370.4	341.0	237.6	(NA)	(NA)	127.6	(NA)
All races, females:										
1994	278.5	190.5	23.2	69.8	35.9	33.1	(NA)	(NA)	24.0	(NA)
1 to 4 years old	1.8	3.0	12.9	(NA)	(NA)	1.0	(NA)	(NA)	(NA)	2.7
5 to 4 years old	0.8	2.4	6.6	(NA)	0.2	0.2	0.5	(NA)	(NA)	1.2
15 to 24 years old	2.1	3.9	19.8	(NA)	0.5	0.6	3.7	(NA)	(NA)	6.2
25 to 44 years old	11.7	28.3	15.1	4.0	(NA)	2.0	5.9	3.0	2.4	5.8
45 to 64 years old	115.3	234.4	16.7	25.7	23.1	8.1	6.4	11.7	20.8	(NA)
65 years old and over	1,701.7	909.2	72.0	429.0	206.8	207.0	(NA)	(NA)	129.1	(NA)
White, both sexes:										
1994	296.5	215.2	35.1	61.2	43.5	33.5	12.9	9.9	21.1	(NA)
1 to 4 years old	1.4	3.3	13.9	(NA)	(NA)	0.9	(NA)	(NA)	(NA)	2.1
5 to 14 years old	0.8	2.8	8.5	(NA)	0.2	0.2	0.9	(NA)	(NA)	1.0
15 to 24 years old	2.2	4.9	40.1	0.5	0.5	0.6	14.2	(NA)	(NA)	10.9
25 to 44 years old	17.2	25.1	31.7	3.2	(NA)	2.0	16.3	5.0	2.6	8.1
45 to 64 years old	188.7	252.8	27.9	24.1	26.0	9.6	15.2	19.7	19.2	(NA)
65 years old and over	1,848.9	6,126.3	85.4	401.3	274.7	223.0	(NA)	(NA)	118.8	(NA)
White, males:										
1994	300.1	228.9	46.9	48.1	46.4	30.8	21.3	13.2	19.2	(NA)
1 to 4 years old	1.4	3.7	16.5	0.4	(NA)	1.0	(NA)	(NA)	(NA)	2.3
5 to 4 years old	0.8	3.1	10.9	(NA)	0.3	0.2	1.3	(NA)	(NA)	1.1
15 to 24 years old	2.8	5.9	58.3	0.5	0.5	0.6	24.1	(NA)	(NA)	17.4
25 to 44 years old	25.4	23.2	48.8	3.4	(NA)	2.5	26.1	7.4	3.2	12.3
45 to 64 years old	280.8	275.7	40.4	27.1	28.3	11.9	23.8	28.8	21.4	(NA)
65 years old and over	2,051.4	1,437.8	103.4	361.4	351.8	237.9	(NA)	(NA)	120.9	(NA)
White females:										
1994	296.8	201.9	23.6	73.9	40.6	36.2	(NA)	(NA)	22.9	(NA)
1 to 4 years old	1.4	2.9	11.2	(NA)	(NA)	0.9	(NA)	(NA)	(NA)	1.9
5 to 4 years old	0.8	2.5	6.0	0.2	(NA)	0.2	0.5	(NA)	(NA)	0.8
15 to 24 years old	1.6	3.9	21.0	0.4	(NA)	0.5	3.8	(NA)	(NA)	3.9
25 to 44 years old	8.9	27.0	14.3	2.9	(NA)	1.5	6.5	2.6	2.0	3.7
45 to 64 years old	100.9	231.0	15.9	21.4	23.9	7.4	7.0	10.9	17.1	(NA)
65 years old and over	1,709.5	911.9	73.1	428.7	221.6	212.7	(NA)	(NA)	117.4	(NA)
Black, both sexes:										
1994	235.2	183.5	39.1	55.2	19.9	22.9	(NA)	(NA)	30.1	37.4
1 to 4 years old	4.2	3.3	26.3	(NA)	(NA)	1.9	(NA)	(NA)	(NA)	7.4
5 to 14 years old	1.3	2.9	13.8	(NA)	1.1	0.4	0.7	(NA)	(NA)	4.3
15 to 24 years old	5.7	4.8	23.4	(NA)	1.7	(NA)	11.6	(NA)	(NA)	88.1
25 to 44 years old	43.5	37.6	41.3	11.6	(NA)	6.8	10.5	7.8	6.0	53.0
45 to 64 years old	353.4	373.2	47.9	74.5	27.8	22.7	(NA)	31.8	52.8	18.5
65 years old and over	1,986.3	1,349.2	89.0	478.4	167.3	196.7	(NA)	(NA)	240.1	(NA)
Black males:										
1994	240.4	212.1	57.0	50.5	24.9	25.2	(NA)	(NA)	24.7	65.1
1 to 4 years old	3.9	3.2	30.8	(NA)	(NA)	2.1	(NA)	(NA)	(NA)	8.4
5 to 4 years old	1.5	3.3	18.0	(NA)	1.3	(S)	1.1	(NA)	(NA)	5.6
15 to 24 years old	6.8	5.4	52.6	(NA)	2.1	(NA)	20.6	(NA)	1.0	157.6
25 to 44 years old	57.6	35.4	65.3	12.3	(NA)	8.5	18.9	10.7	7.1	90.9
45 to 64 years old	484.7	468.2	78.4	92.1	34.1	32.9	(NA)	49.0	54.9	33.4
65 years old and over	2,203.6	1,933.5	126.4	485.2	264.5	244.6	(NA)	(NA)	211.1	(NA)
Black females:										
1994	230.6	157.6	22.9	59.3	15.4	20.8	(NA)	(NA)	35.0	(NA)
1 to 4 years old	4.4	3.4	21.7	(NA)	(NA)	1.8	(NA)	(NA)	(NA)	6.4
5 to 4 years old	1.2	2.5	9.5	(NA)	0.8	(NA)	(S)	(NA)	(NA)	3.0
15 to 24 years old	4.7	4.2	15.0	(NA)	1.2	(NA)	2.7	(NA)	(NA)	18.7
25 to 44 years old	31.0	39.6	9.7	11.0	3.5	5.3	(NA)	5.3	5.0	19.5
45 to 64 years old	247.8	298.8	23.3	60.3	22.7	14.5	(NA)	18.0	51.2	(NA)
65 years old and over	1,852.6	981.0	65.5	474.1	106.0	166.5	(NA)	(NA)	258.4	(NA)

NA Not available. S Figure does not meet publication standards. [1] Includes allied conditions. [2] Includes other races not shown separately.

Source: U.S. National Center for Health Statistics, *Vital Statistics of the United States*, annual; and *Monthly Vital Statistics Report*.

No. 132. Death Rates, by Leading Cause—States: 1994

[Deaths per 100,000 resident population enumerated as of April 1. By place of residence. Excludes nonresidents of the United States. Causes of death classified according to ninth revisions of International Classification of Diseases]

DIVISION AND STATE	Total [1]	Heart disease	Cancer	Cerebrovascular diseases [2]	Accidents and adverse effects	Motor vehicle accidents	Chronic obstructive pulmonary diseases [2]	Diabetes mellitus	HIV [3]	Suicide	Homicide
U.S.	875.4	281.3	206.2	58.9	35.1	16.3	39.0	21.8	16.2	12.0	9.6
Northeast:											
N.E.	897.1	284.6	224.9	56.2	25.7	9.7	39.9	22.1	13.4	9.7	4.2
ME	941.3	288.4	240.0	61.4	33.5	16.6	50.9	25.6	5.9	13.5	2.7
NH	784.6	248.3	199.6	51.5	23.8	10.4	42.5	22.5	3.8	12.1	1.9
VT	824.5	262.3	199.4	60.0	29.8	12.4	46.0	23.4	6.2	10.0	-
MA	909.5	280.1	230.0	55.3	21.8	8.0	39.0	22.4	15.6	8.5	3.9
RI	943.9	319.0	243.7	59.6	22.2	7.5	38.1	24.3	11.5	8.2	4.9
CT	893.8	297.4	217.6	55.9	30.8	10.0	36.1	19.1	17.2	9.9	6.4
M.A.	968.4	343.5	230.6	54.5	30.5	10.9	36.7	23.9	30.7	8.9	8.5
NY	928.9	347.9	215.6	45.3	27.4	10.1	33.7	20.1	44.5	8.2	11.3
NJ	914.8	299.4	232.5	51.9	26.8	9.8	33.5	27.6	29.5	7.3	5.4
PA	1,062.4	365.8	251.9	70.1	36.1	12.9	43.5	27.3	10.7	11.0	6.3
Midwest:											
E.N.C.	904.0	301.4	213.2	62.4	32.4	14.8	39.2	24.2	8.1	10.5	8.7
OH	930.1	313.0	224.7	57.8	29.5	12.6	43.4	28.3	7.1	9.9	5.1
IN	911.9	302.2	210.4	69.9	34.1	17.2	42.2	24.3	5.5	12.5	7.9
IL	913.4	301.1	213.9	62.0	34.4	15.0	36.6	22.0	12.0	9.1	12.4
MI	873.4	297.5	205.0	60.0	31.5	15.6	36.4	23.5	8.0	10.9	10.9
WI	874.5	282.8	205.0	69.2	34.1	14.7	38.1	21.3	4.0	11.6	4.4
W.N.C.	927.9	299.2	212.2	70.0	39.0	18.4	42.5	20.9	5.5	12.1	6.0
MN	800.0	225.7	187.7	63.5	35.6	15.8	34.3	18.7	5.6	10.8	3.3
IA	979.1	326.8	233.6	74.5	39.9	18.5	46.5	21.9	2.9	11.4	2.3
MO	1,019.1	345.7	227.2	72.5	43.3	20.9	46.8	22.6	8.6	13.8	11.6
ND	924.0	302.7	212.9	79.8	36.4	13.5	36.5	27.0	-	12.5	-
SD	935.0	316.8	204.1	68.8	41.9	22.0	41.6	24.0	-	13.5	3.3
NE	925.0	310.1	202.0	70.2	35.4	16.9	46.3	17.4	5.1	11.6	3.3
KS	913.8	291.0	210.1	68.9	37.6	18.7	43.3	19.9	4.2	11.4	7.3
South:											
S.A.	922.3	287.7	219.2	63.3	37.1	18.6	40.6	22.4	21.3	12.9	11.0
DE	897.4	281.7	230.2	49.3	39.9	17.3	37.9	23.5	19.4	11.3	4.2
MD	819.7	240.5	201.2	50.3	27.6	13.2	33.0	26.4	24.2	10.5	13.0
DC	1,264.2	306.9	274.0	66.5	28.8	11.6	30.0	34.2	116.8	5.1	61.4
VA	796.6	243.3	192.7	55.8	33.5	14.0	33.3	17.2	11.1	12.5	8.9
WV	1,106.0	377.2	259.8	67.2	41.2	20.6	58.6	34.1	3.3	14.2	6.3
NC	894.5	272.6	206.4	73.3	41.3	20.7	36.3	22.6	13.8	12.7	11.6
SC	860.8	270.8	202.3	69.4	44.2	22.6	35.8	25.4	14.3	12.8	10.8
GA	801.8	241.4	175.0	55.2	40.0	21.1	34.7	15.4	20.4	11.8	11.6
FL	1,106.0	348.7	263.3	68.8	36.5	19.4	51.4	24.1	29.8	14.9	9.5
E.S.C.	962.5	322.6	222.1	68.3	49.0	25.5	42.9	22.4	8.2	12.7	11.6
KY	970.9	320.0	232.5	64.9	44.3	20.7	49.4	24.6	4.9	13.5	6.1
TN	976.3	312.9	219.8	76.9	46.4	24.6	42.0	20.5	8.8	12.8	10.6
AL	988.6	312.2	223.0	62.0	51.3	26.8	42.7	25.3	9.4	12.6	14.2
MS	1,003.3	361.8	210.5	66.7	57.2	31.8	35.6	18.7	10.1	11.8	17.2
W.S.C.	821.7	257.4	187.9	56.2	37.9	19.7	36.8	24.6	13.4	13.0	12.9
AR	1,072.5	340.6	241.1	88.9	46.5	26.7	47.9	21.9	6.2	14.8	13.1
LA	904.2	277.4	207.6	55.1	41.9	20.2	33.9	33.5	14.9	12.8	21.1
OK	991.4	342.5	216.9	65.9	45.0	22.6	47.8	19.5	7.9	13.8	8.6
TX	740.4	226.5	171.0	50.3	34.5	18.1	34.0	23.8	14.9	12.7	11.7
West:											
Mt.	737.6	203.5	167.1	47.6	41.8	20.8	42.9	17.5	8.7	18.3	7.7
MT	860.0	224.5	204.0	67.1	46.1	22.7	56.9	25.1	3.0	18.5	4.1
ID	745.5	214.0	163.1	56.6	46.1	22.5	43.7	17.8	2.7	17.7	3.4
WY	731.3	202.7	163.2	46.0	47.3	25.0	56.7	16.4	-	22.5	5.5
CO	663.4	173.2	148.5	42.2	37.2	17.7	41.5	12.6	10.5	16.8	5.7
NM	733.5	185.2	157.2	46.8	51.2	25.5	39.5	25.2	8.3	18.3	11.1
AZ	841.7	245.0	195.5	52.3	44.9	21.6	46.0	18.8	10.6	18.8	11.2
UT	548.9	148.0	109.6	37.6	33.9	19.0	23.7	17.8	4.2	15.3	3.3
NV	817.6	236.6	203.6	44.3	36.2	19.4	53.2	13.1	15.3	23.4	11.3
Pac.	724.4	216.7	168.2	52.8	31.8	14.2	36.1	16.2	18.8	12.6	10.9
WA	747.9	209.7	181.6	58.2	33.2	13.4	41.6	18.3	11.3	14.2	6.0
OR	888.1	240.8	211.9	77.3	40.9	15.8	46.3	20.6	9.8	16.6	5.8
CA	713.6	218.9	163.7	50.2	30.1	14.3	35.2	15.7	21.5	11.8	12.5
AK	403.3	88.4	93.7	20.3	53.8	13.9	16.5	7.9	3.3	20.0	5.9
HI	622.5	192.9	149.8	49.6	28.5	10.8	17.8	13.2	11.0	11.7	3.8

- Represents zero. [1] Includes other causes not shown separately. [2] Includes allied conditions. [3] Human immunodeficiency virus.

Source: U.S. National Center for Health Statistics, *Monthly Vital Statistics Report;* and unpublished data.

No. 133. Acquired Immunodeficiency Syndrome (AIDS) Deaths, by Selected Characteristics: Thru 1995

[Data are shown by year of death and are subject to substantial retrospective changes. For data on AIDS cases reported, see table 215. Based on reporting by State health departments]

CHARACTERISTIC	NUMBER									PERCENT DISTRIBUTION	
	Total cases	1988 and before [1]	1989	1990	1991	1992	1993	1994	1995	1995	1982-1995
Total [2]	305,843	12,493	26,365	29,934	34,651	38,813	41,077	43,975	31,256	100.0	100.0
Age:											
13 to 29 years old	53,632	2,558	4,924	5,427	6,059	6,481	6,615	6,930	5,105	16.3	16.2
30 to 39 years old	138,660	5,714	12,056	13,695	15,582	17,437	18,548	20,037	14,063	45.1	45.3
40 to 49 years old	77,425	2,726	6,205	7,329	8,943	10,339	10,975	11,921	8,543	27.3	27.0
50 to 59 years old	25,383	1,104	2,218	2,433	2,822	3,175	3,389	3,721	2,572	8.2	8.3
60 years old and over	10,743	391	952	1,050	1,245	1,381	1,350	1,366	953	3.0	3.2
Sex:											
Male	268,987	11553	23,742	26,752	30,725	34,072	35,551	37,360	26,375	84.4	85.4
Female	36,856	940	2,613	3,182	3,926	4,741	5,526	6,615	4,881	15.6	14.6
Race/ethnicity:											
White	159,292	7,267	14,481	16,517	18,693	19,982	20,376	20,733	14,389	46.0	47.7
Black	100,167	3,424	7,950	9,010	10,722	12,839	14,420	16,294	11,879	38.0	36.6
Hispanic	43,154	1,719	3,656	4,120	4,851	5,578	5,820	6,421	4,574	14.6	14.5
Other/unknown	3,230	83	268	287	385	414	461	527	414	1.3	1.2

[1] Includes deaths prior to 1982. [2] Includes other race/ethnicity groups not shown separately.

Source: U.S. Centers for Disease Control, Surveillance Report, annual.

No. 134. Death Rates From Heart Disease, by Sex and Age: 1980 to 1994

[Deaths per 100,000 population in specified age groups. Excludes deaths of nonresidents of the United States. Deaths classified according to the ninth revision of the *International Classification of Diseases*. See text, section 2. See Appendix III]

AGE AT DEATH AND SELECTED TYPE OF HEART DISEASE	MALE					FEMALE				
	1980	1990	1992	1993	1994	1980	1990	1992	1993	1994
Total U.S. rate [1]	365	286	287	292	284	305	282	276	286	276
25 to 34 years old	11	10	11	11	11	5	5	5	6	6
35 to 44 years old	69	48	48	47	47	21	15	16	17	17
45 to 54 years old	283	183	174	173	171	85	61	58	58	57
55 to 64 years old	747	537	504	499	478	272	216	205	205	196
65 to 74 years old	1,728	1,250	1,179	1,175	1,133	829	617	588	589	566
75 to 84 years old	3,834	2,968	2,754	2,754	2,655	2,497	1,894	1,776	1,808	1,741
85 years old and over	8,753	7,418	7,157	7,332	7,123	7,351	6,478	6,263	6,415	6,253
Persons 45 to 54 years old:										
Ischemic heart	217.3	123.8	114.9	112.0	109.2	52.2	33.6	31.6	30.8	30.6
Rheumatic heart	3.1	1.1	1.2	0.9	1.0	4.3	1.9	1.6	1.7	1.4
Hypertensive heart [2]	8.3	7.6	7.6	(NA)	8.7	5.5	4.3	4.1	(NA)	4.1
Persons 55 to 64 years old:										
Ischemic heart	581.1	375.4	345.1	337.9	323.4	189.0	135.4	126.7	124.5	120.4
Rheumatic heart	6.2	3.4	2.6	2.7	2.4	9.2	4.7	4.3	3.9	3.7
Hypertensive heart [2]	21.8	18.1	18.9	(NA)	17.3	13.3	10.9	11.4	(NA)	9.5
Persons 65 to 74 years old:										
Ischemic heart	1,355.5	896.5	837.5	823.7	794.0	605.3	415.2	387.9	383.6	368.1
Rheumatic heart	11.8	7.1	5.7	6.0	5.9	18.6	10.5	9.9	9.7	9.1
Hypertensive heart [2]	44.3	33.2	32.5	(NA)	29.4	36.2	25.9	24.5	(NA)	21.4
Persons 75 to 84 years old:										
Ischemic heart	2,953.7	2,129.6	1,961.2	1,962.7	1,863.9	1,842.7	1,287.6	1,186.1	1,188.3	1,142.9
Rheumatic heart	16.7	12.3	12.1	12.4	11.1	25.4	22.5	20.7	19.6	18.5
Hypertensive heart [2]	90.7	67.9	64.8	(NA)	59.3	101.1	69.7	66.9	(NA)	61.7
Persons 85 years old and over:										
Ischemic heart	6,501.6	5,120.7	4,878.3	4,920.7	4,771.9	5,280.6	4,257.8	4,056.4	4,097.6	3,960.8
Rheumatic heart	19.5	18.7	19.9	24.6	19.2	25.8	33.3	30.0	31.3	28.1
Hypertensive heart [2]	180.3	154.3	157.8	(NA)	143.0	250.8	212.1	216.4	(NA)	216.3

NA Not available. [1] Includes persons under 25 years old not shown separately. [2] With or without renal disease.

Source: U.S. National Center for Health Statistics, *Vital Statistics of the United States*, annual; and unpublished data.

No. 135. Death Rates From Cancer, by Sex and Age: 1980 to 1994

[Deaths per 100,000 population in the specified age groups. See headnote, table 134]

AGE AT DEATH AND SELECTED TYPE OF CANCER	MALE					FEMALE				
	1980	1990	1992	1993	1994	1980	1990	1992	1993	1994
Total [1]	206.3	221.3	220.8	222.1	220.7	163.6	186.0	188.2	189.8	190.5
25 to 34 years	13.4	12.6	12.1	11.9	(NA)	14.0	12.6	12.9	12.3	(NA)
35 to 44 years	44.0	38.5	38.1	38.0	(NA)	53.1	48.1	46.5	44.1	(NA)
45 to 54 years	188.7	162.5	153.8	150.7	(NA)	171.8	155.5	147.0	145.2	(NA)
55 to 64 years	520.8	532.9	513.4	507.4	(NA)	361.7	375.2	369.7	366.7	(NA)
65 to 74 years	1,093.2	1,122.2	1,111.1	1,113.3	(NA)	607.1	677.4	686.5	688.4	(NA)
75 to 84 years	1,790.5	1,914.4	1,882.7	1,885.4	(NA)	903.1	1,010.3	1,025.6	1,046.1	(NA)
85 years old and over	2,369.5	2,739.9	2,802.3	2,830.7	(NA)	1,255.7	1,372.1	1,393.9	1,415.3	(NA)
Persons, 35 to 44 years old:										
Respiratory, intrathoracic	12.6	9.1	8.6	8.3	8.0	6.8	5.4	5.6	5.0	4.9
Digestive organs, peritoneum	9.5	8.9	9.1	9.1	8.9	6.5	5.5	5.7	5.5	5.4
Breast	-	(B)	-	(B)	(B)	17.9	17.8	16.1	15.2	15.2
Genital organs	0.7	0.6	0.6	0.6	0.6	8.3	7.3	7.3	6.8	6.6
Lymphatic and hematopoietic tissues, excl. leukemia	4.3	4.5	4.9	4.7	(NA)	2.4	2.1	2.2	2.0	(NA)
Urinary organs	1.4	1.5	1.4	1.5	1.3	0.6	0.6	0.7	0.7	0.7
Lip, oral cavity, and pharynx	1.8	1.3	1.2	1.3	1.1	0.5	0.3	0.4	0.4	0.4
Leukemia	3.2	2.5	2.5	2.5	2.2	2.6	2.2	1.8	2.0	1.8
Persons, 45 to 54 years old:										
Respiratory, intrathoracic	79.8	63.0	57.7	54.6	51.9	34.8	35.3	32.5	31.6	30.4
Digestive organs, peritoneum	44.3	40.4	37.6	37.6	38.7	27.8	23.3	21.6	21.5	21.3
Breast	0.2	0.3	0.2	0.3	0.2	48.1	45.4	42.8	42.0	41.6
Genital organs	3.4	2.9	2.7	2.7	2.9	24.1	19.4	18.2	17.9	18.1
Lymphatic and hematopoietic tissues, excl. leukemia	10.2	10.9	10.8	10.3	(NA)	6.6	6.0	6.1	6.0	(NA)
Urinary organs	7.4	7.2	7.4	7.4	7.1	3.3	2.9	2.8	3.0	2.8
Lip, oral cavity, and pharynx	8.2	5.9	5.5	6.0	5.6	2.6	1.6	1.6	1.7	1.3
Leukemia	6.2	5.6	5.2	5.2	5.2	4.4	4.1	4.0	3.9	3.8
Persons, 55 to 64 years old:										
Respiratory, intrathoracic	223.8	232.6	217.0	216.0	206.8	74.5	107.6	108.4	107.3	105.3
Digestive organs, peritoneum	129.3	124.0	122.0	122.0	120.0	79.1	69.3	67.8	67.9	66.4
Breast	0.7	0.6	0.5	0.7	0.7	80.5	78.6	73.6	72.2	69.8
Genital organs	23.5	27.9	26.6	24.9	24.0	46.8	40.1	39.2	38.1	39.0
Lymphatic and hematopoietic tissues, excl. leukemia	24.4	27.2	26.5	26.1	(NA)	16.8	16.7	17.3	18.4	(NA)
Urinary organs	22.9	23.5	23.1	22.3	22.5	8.9	8.8	9.1	8.4	8.8
Lip, oral cavity, and pharynx	17.9	16.2	14.8	14.2	13.5	6.0	4.7	4.4	4.3	4.0
Leukemia	14.7	14.7	14.9	14.7	14.8	9.3	8.8	9.0	8.7	8.5
Persons, 65 to 74 years old:										
Respiratory, intrathoracic	422.0	447.3	439.8	441.2	434.5	106.1	181.7	195.3	199.2	203.6
Digestive organs, peritoneum	284.1	267.4	263.6	259.6	260.8	173.6	153.0	148.4	151.8	149.7
Breast	1.1	1.1	1.1	1.2	1.4	101.1	111.7	109.3	105.7	105.6
Genital organs	107.6	123.5	122.0	117.9	115.1	73.6	71.0	70.5	67.0	69.2
Lymphatic and hematopoietic tissues, excl. leukemia	48.1	56.8	58.7	59.0	(NA)	34.4	39.5	41.0	42.5	(NA)
Urinary organs	56.9	50.7	51.2	53.3	52.1	19.7	19.8	19.8	19.5	20.9
Lip, oral cavity, and pharynx	25.4	21.5	20.3	20.1	18.0	8.8	8.3	7.8	7.5	7.9
Leukemia	35.3	36.0	36.1	36.7	35.6	18.7	18.8	19.0	19.1	19.1
Persons, 75 to 84 years old:										
Respiratory, intrathoracic	511.5	594.4	587.5	384.8	576.7	98.0	194.5	216.0	226.3	236.4
Digestive organs, peritoneum	496.6	466.0	444.0	441.7	437.2	326.3	293.3	288.7	287.7	284.0
Breast	2.1	1.6	2.0	2.3	2.0	126.4	146.3	140.8	146.4	145.9
Genital organs	315.4	358.5	365.7	366.6	350.7	95.7	95.3	97.2	97.4	96.7
Lymphatic and hematopoietic tissues, excl. leukemia	80.0	104.5	106.5	107.8	(NA)	57.8	71.2	74.6	78.4	(NA)
Urinary organs	112.4	107.5	104.5	103.4	105.3	37.4	38.5	40.0	38.0	39.9
Lip, oral cavity, and pharynx	31.4	26.1	23.3	24.6	23.5	10.9	11.6	10.9	10.4	10.6
Leukemia	71.5	71.9	72.3	71.4	71.5	38.5	38.8	38.0	37.8	38.3
Persons, 85 years old and over:										
Respiratory, intrathoracic	386.3	538.0	545.4	559.7	556.1	96.3	142.8	160.8	173.9	171.8
Digestive organs, peritoneum	705.8	699.5	683.8	668.5	661.4	504.3	497.6	495.7	487.0	477.2
Breast	2.6	2.4	4.4	5.1	3.9	169.3	196.8	195.5	206.0	197.5
Genital organs	612.3	750.0	806.3	842.2	822.5	115.9	115.6	115.8	114.4	115.3
Lymphatic and hematopoietic tissues, excl. leukemia	93.2	140.5	138.9	145.6	(NA)	63.0	90.0	92.5	95.5	(NA)
Urinary organs	177.0	186.3	192.9	190.3	189.6	63.8	68.5	69.6	64.5	67.3
Lip, oral cavity, and pharynx	40.2	37.4	32.8	31.1	30.0	16.0	17.5	16.9	16.8	16.0
Leukemia	117.1	116.0	116.8	115.6	118.5	61.1	65.0	67.7	68.2	68.1

- Represents zero. B Base figure too small to meet statistical standards for reliability of a derived figure. NA Not available. [1] Includes persons under 25 years of age and malignant neoplasms of other and unspecified sites, not shown separately.

Source: U.S. National Center for Health Statistics, *Vital Statistics of the United States*, annual; and unpublished data.

No. 136. Death Rates From Accidents and Violence, by Race and Sex: 1980 to 1994

[Rates are per 100,000 population. Excludes deaths of nonresidents of the United States. Deaths classified according to the ninth revision of the *International Classification of Diseases*. See text, section 2. See Appendix III]

CAUSE OF DEATH AND AGE	WHITE						BLACK					
	Male			Female			Male			Female		
	1980	1990	1994	1980	1990	1994	1980	1990	1994	1980	1990	1994
Total [1]	97.1	81.2	(NA)	36.3	32.1	(NA)	154.0	142.0	(NA)	42.6	38.8	(NA)
Motor vehicle accidents	35.9	26.1	22.5	12.8	11.4	10.6	31.1	28.1	23.9	8.3	9.4	9.5
All other accidents	30.4	23.6	24.4	14.4	12.4	13.0	46.0	32.7	33.1	18.6	13.4	13.4
Suicide	19.9	22.0	21.3	5.9	5.3	4.9	10.3	12.0	12.4	2.2	2.3	2.0
Homicide	10.9	9.0	8.5	3.2	2.8	2.6	66.6	69.2	65.1	13.5	13.5	12.4
15 to 24 years old	138.6	107.3	(NA)	37.3	30.6	(NA)	162.0	206.0	(NA)	35.0	34.9	(NA)
25 to 34 years old	118.4	97.4	(NA)	29.0	26.0	(NA)	256.9	218.1	(NA)	49.4	48.1	(NA)
35 to 44 years old	94.1	82.3	(NA)	29.2	24.4	(NA)	218.1	176.6	(NA)	43.2	38.5	(NA)
45 to 54 years old	90.8	73.6	(NA)	31.8	25.3	(NA)	207.3	138.5	(NA)	40.2	30.7	(NA)
55 to 64 years old	92.3	79.5	(NA)	33.8	29.4	(NA)	188.5	129.9	(NA)	47.3	36.1	(NA)
65 years old and over	163.9	150.7	(NA)	87.2	80.1	(NA)	215.8	175.5	(NA)	102.9	81.6	(NA)

NA Not available. [1] Includes persons under 15 years old, not shown separately.

No. 137. Deaths and Death Rates From Accidents, by Type: 1980 to 1994

[See headnote, table 136 and Appendix III]

TYPE OF ACCIDENT	DEATHS (number)					RATE PER 100,000 POPULATION				
	1980	1990	1992	1993	1994	1980	1990	1992	1992	1994
Total	105,718	91,983	86,777	90,523	(NA)	46.7	37.0	34.0	35.1	(NA)
Motor vehicle accidents	53,172	46,814	40,982	41,893	42,524	23.5	18.8	16.1	16.3	16.3
Traffic	51,930	45,827	39,985	40,899	41,507	22.9	18.4	15.7	15.9	15.9
Nontraffic	1,242	987	997	994	1,017	0.5	0.4	0.4	0.4	0.4
Water-transport accidents	1,429	923	837	763	723	0.6	0.4	0.3	0.3	0.3
Air and space transport accidents	1,494	941	1,094	859	1,075	0.7	0.4	0.4	0.3	0.4
Railway accidents	632	663	642	670	635	0.3	0.3	0.3	0.3	0.2
Accidental falls	13,294	12,313	12,646	13,141	13,450	5.9	5.0	5.0	5.1	5.2
Accidental drowning	6,043	3,979	3,524	3,807	3,404	2.7	1.6	1.4	1.5	1.3
Accidents caused by—										
Fires and flames	5,822	4,175	3,958	3,900	3,986	2.6	1.7	1.6	1.5	1.5
Firearms, unspecified and other	1,667	1,175	1,176	1,261	1,123	0.7	0.5	0.5	0.5	0.4
Handguns	288	241	233	260	233	0.1	0.1	0.1	0.1	0.1
Electric current	1,095	670	525	548	561	0.5	0.3	0.2	0.2	0.2
Accidental poisoning by—										
Drugs and medicines	2,492	4,506	5,951	7,382	7,828	1.1	1.8	2.3	2.9	3.0
Other solid and liquid substances	597	549	496	495	481	0.3	0.2	0.2	0.2	0.2
Gases and vapors	1,242	748	633	660	685	0.5	0.3	0.2	0.3	0.3
Complications due to medical procedures	2437	2,669	2,669	2,724	(NA)	1.1	1.1	1.0	1.1	(NA)
Inhalation and ingestion of objects	3,249	3,303	3,128	3,160	3,065	1.5	1.3	1.2	1.2	1.2

NA Not available.

Source of tables 136-137: U.S. National Center for Health Statistics, *Vital Statistics of the United States*, annual; and unpublished data.

No. 138. Death Rates for Injury by Firearms, Sex, Race, and Age: 1994

[Death rate per 100,000 population. Deaths classified according to the ninth revision of the *International Classification of Diseases*]

ITEM	5-14 yrs old	15-24 yrs old	25-34 yrs old	35-44 yrs old	45-54 yrs old	55-64 yrs old	65-74 yrs old	75-84 yrs old	85 yrs and over
MALE									
Firearms: White	2.3	34.2	27.6	22.3	20.5	20.8	25.1	42.1	53.2
Black	6.5	169.6	109.0	57.7	33.6	22.2	25.0	20.0	(NA)
Accidents: White	0.6	2.2	0.9	0.6	0.5	0.4	0.5	0.8	(NA)
Black	1.1	5.5	1.7	(NA)	(NA)	(NA)	(NA)	(NA)	(NA)
Suicide: White	0.8	16.7	15.4	14.0	15.1	17.1	22.9	39.9	51.3
Black	0.7	15.6	11.9	8.4	6.4	6.6	12.0	12.6	(NA)
Homicide: White	0.9	14.5	10.8	7.3	4.6	3.0	1.5	1.1	(NA)
Black	4.4	146.3	94.6	47.8	26.4	14.8	12.3	7.5	(NA)
FEMALE									
Firearms: White	0.9	4.9	5.3	5.1	4.6	3.3	3.0	2.6	1.9
Black	2.1	15.5	14.3	9.3	5.7	3.0	3.5	(NA)	(NA)
Accidents: White	(NA)	0.2	0.2	0.1	(NA)	(NA)	(NA)	(NA)	(NA)
Black	(NA)	(NA)	(NA)	(NA)	(NA)	(NA)	(NA)	(NA)	(NA)
Suicide: White	0.3	2.1	2.6	3.0	3.1	2.3	2.2	1.8	1.2
Black	(NA)	1.7	1.5	1.2	(NA)	(NA)	(NA)	(NA)	(NA)
Homicide: White	0.4	2.5	2.5	1.9	1.3	0.9	0.7	0.7	(NA)
Black	2.0	13.4	12.4	8.0	4.1	2.4	(NA)	(NA)	(NA)

NA Not available.

Source: U.S. National Center for Health Statistics, *Advance Data from Vital and Health Statistics*, No. 231.

No. 139. Suicides, by Race, Age, and Method: 1980 to 1994

[Death rates per 100,000 population in specified group]

SEX, AGE, AND METHOD	1980	1985	1986	1987	1988	1989	1990	1991	1992	1993	1994
All races, both sexes	26,869	29,453	30,904	30,796	30,407	30,232	30,906	30,810	30,484	31,102	31,142
5 to 9 years old	3	3	5	1	6	4	6	1	10	6	4
10 to 14 years old	139	275	250	250	237	236	258	265	304	315	318
15 to 19 years old	1,797	1,849	1,896	1,902	2,059	2,009	1,979	1,899	1,847	1,884	1,948
20 to 24 years old	3,442	3,272	3,224	3,022	2,870	2,861	2,890	2,852	2,846	2,965	3,008
25 to 29 years old	3,228	3,364	3,429	3,372	3,355	3,299	3,192	3,086	2,864	2,979	3,026
30 to 34 years old	2,692	3,012	3,282	3,283	3,355	3,266	3,358	3,428	3,308	3,328	3,328
35 to 39 years old	2,150	2,528	2,852	2,799	2,909	2,937	3,098	3,089	3,177	3,248	3,397
40 to 44 years old	1,785	2,098	2,161	2,333	2,296	2,394	2,619	2,678	2,832	2,922	2,978
White, both sexes	24,829	27,087	28,437	28,217	27,790	27,424	28,086	27,996	27,611	28,035	27,976
5 to 9 years old	2	3	2	1	6	2	4	-	6	4	2
10 to 14 years old	130	243	212	218	195	196	219	228	265	258	269
15 to 19 years old	1,635	1,643	1,716	1,679	1,819	1,743	1,701	1,628	1,531	1,594	1,588
20 to 24 years old	3,057	2,866	2,875	2,649	2,489	2,399	2,481	2,450	2,404	2,443	2,490
25 to 29 years old	2,876	2,985	3,004	2,940	2,940	2,847	2,731	2,629	2,484	2,504	2,557
30 to 34 years old	2,391	2,674	2,915	2,910	2,904	2,850	2,952	3,045	2,895	2,940	2,933
35 to 39 years old	1,979	2,316	2,572	2,517	2,626	2,628	2,779	2,799	2,845	2,902	3,003
40 to 44 years old	1,639	1,948	2,012	2,157	2,124	2,189	2,404	2,470	2,582	2,665	2,719
Black, both sexes	1,607	1,795	1,892	1,963	2,022	2,153	2,111	2,097	2,143	2,259	2,271
5 to 9 years old	1	-	2	-	-	2	2	1	1	2	2
10 to 14 years old	9	22	25	25	29	32	29	31	33	39	39
15 to 19 years old	108	135	128	162	167	175	183	183	223	213	263
20 to 24 years old	307	289	252	263	298	350	282	298	313	395	366
25 to 29 years old	278	294	332	341	325	340	357	344	303	353	325
30 to 34 years old	245	262	303	311	360	349	318	301	331	296	282
35 to 39 years old	133	175	218	225	226	244	252	237	257	265	296
40 to 44 years old	128	115	113	129	131	168	171	153	194	183	201
Method total, both sexes:											
Drugs, medicaments, and biologicals	2,761	2,668	2,796	2,891	2,910	2,989	2,920	3,096	3,216	2,976	3,022
Other solid or liquid substances	274	269	274	215	223	227	223	219	223	204	207
Gases and vapors	2,418	2,767	2,966	3,215	2,692	2,228	2,281	2,230	2,057	2,092	2,044
Suicide by hanging [1]	3,691	4,264	4,606	4,235	4,375	4,484	4,444	4,561	4,678	4,627	4,745
Handgun	169	179	202	228	235	216	246	271	261	282	302
Other and unspecified firearms	13,287	14,382	14,834	14,841	14,972	15,058	15,421	14,907	14,714	15,354	15,059
All other	2,329	2,122	2,109	2,104	2,038	2,127	2,153	2,179	2,142	2,264	2,359
Method, White:											
Drugs, medicaments, and biologicals	2,620	2,503	2,633	2,676	2,694	2,774	2,703	2,894	2,979	2,742	2,756
Other solid or liquid substances	246	234	232	187	200	195	190	195	194	180	171
Gases and vapors	2,375	2,713	2,891	3,122	2,623	2,154	2,227	2,172	1,994	2,017	1,987
Handgun	1,940	2,802	3,117	3,067	2,962	2,904	3,218	3,348	3,194	3,304	3,404
Other and unspecified firearms	12,346	13,318	13,719	13,686	13,763	13,767	14,126	13,626	13,412	13,967	13,603
All other	2,014	1,805	1,786	1,812	1,741	1,777	1,810	1,816	1,788	1,882	1,992
Method, Black:											
Drugs, medicaments, and biologicals	106	120	123	158	167	164	159	144	160	164	188
Other solid or liquid substances	17	26	27	20	15	23	22	14	12	14	24
Gases and vapors	29	39	58	67	52	53	30	44	46	49	33
Handgun	151	146	156	184	176	171	178	191	185	205	201
Other and unspecified firearms	795	886	925	959	1,006	1,070	1,085	1,062	1,096	1,160	1,192
All other	246	244	253	225	230	264	263	267	265	249	239

- Represents or rounds to zero. [1] Includes strangulation and suffocation.

Source: U.S. National Center for Health Statistics, *Vital Statistics of the United States*, annual, and unpublished data.

No.140. Homicide Rates by Race, Sex, and Age: 1990 and 1994

AGE	WHITE				BLACK			
	Male		Female		Male		Female	
	1990	1994	1990	1994	1990	1994	1990	1994
Total [1]	9.0	8.5	2.8	2.6	69.2	65.1	13.5	12.4
15-24 yrs. old	15.4	17.4	4.0	3.9	138.3	157.6	18.9	18.7
25-34 yrs. old	15.1	14.3	4.3	4.2	125.4	112.1	25.3	23.1
35-44 yrs. old	11.4	10.4	3.2	3.3	82.3	67.6	15.6	15.6
45-54 yrs. old	8.3	7.1	2.6	2.2	47.7	39.5	7.3	7.9
55-64 yrs. old	5.5	5.1	1.8	1.6	34.0	24.0	5.6	4.7
65-74 yrs. old	4.1	3.5	1.8	1.6	24.3	22.4	6.8	6.8
75-84 yrs. old	3.9	3.7	2.8	2.3	29.2	21.7	11.3	8.3
65 yrs. old and over	4.1	(NA)	2.2	(NA)	25.9	(NA)	9.5	(NA)
85 yrs. old and over	4.9	4.3	2.5	2.2	(B)	(B)	19.2	(B)

B Base figure to small to meet statistical standards for reliability of a derived figure. NA Not available. [1] Includes persons under 15 years old, not shown separately.

Source: U.S. National Center for Health Statistics, *Vital Statistics of the United States*, annual.

No. 141. Deaths and Death Rates for Injury by Firearms, by Race and Sex: 1980 to 1994

[Age-adjusted rates per 100,000]

YEAR	ALL RACES			WHITE			ALL OTHER					
							Total			Black		
	Both sexes	Male	Female	Both sexes	Male	Female	Both sexes	Male	Female	Both sexes	Male	Female
NUMBER												
1980	33,780	28,322	5,458	24,849	20,714	4,135	8,931	7,608	1,323	8,505	7,265	1,240
1985	31,566	26,382	5,184	24,507	20,389	4,118	7,059	5,993	1,066	6,565	5,584	981
1990	37,155	31,736	5,419	26,299	22,249	4,050	10,856	9,487	1,369	10,175	8,922	1,253
1992	37,776	32,425	5,351	26,120	22,208	3,912	11,656	10,217	1,439	10,906	9,581	1,325
1993	39,595	33,711	5,884	26,948	22,606	4,268	12,647	11,031	1,616	11,763	10,310	1,453
1994	38,505	33,021	5,484	26,403	22,408	3,995	12,102	10,613	1,489	11,223	9,880	1,343
RATE [1]												
1980	14.8	25.3	4.8	12.4	21.1	4.2	29.1	53.0	8.1	33.5	61.8	9.1
1985	12.7	21.8	4.2	11.4	19.4	3.9	19.7	35.4	5.7	23.2	42.2	6.5
1990	14.6	25.4	4.2	11.9	20.5	3.7	26.9	48.9	6.5	33.4	61.5	7.8
1992	14.9	25.9	4.1	11.8	20.4	3.6	28.0	50.9	6.6	35.1	64.5	8.0
1993	15.6	26.9	4.6	12.2	20.7	3.9	30.1	54.4	7.3	37.6	68.8	8.8
1994	15.1	26.2	4.2	11.9	20.4	3.6	28.4	51.6	6.6	35.5	65.1	8.0

[1] Age-adjusted death rate. For method of computation see source.

No. 142. Deaths and Death Rates for Drug-Induced Causes, by Race and Sex: 1980 to 1994

[Age-adjusted rates per 100,000]

YEAR	ALL RACES			WHITE			ALL OTHER					
							Total			Black		
	Both sexes	Male	Female	Both sexes	Male	Female	Both sexes	Male	Female	Both sexes	Male	Female
NUMBER												
1980	6,900	3,771	3,129	5,814	3,088	2,726	1,086	683	403	1,006	648	358
1985	8,663	5,342	3,321	6,946	4,172	2,774	1,717	1,170	547	1,600	1,107	493
1990	9,463	5,897	3,566	7,603	4,646	2,957	1,860	1,251	609	1,703	1,155	548
1992	11,703	7,766	3,937	9,360	6,124	3,236	2,343	1,642	701	2,148	1,533	615
1993	13,275	9,052	4,223	10,394	7,005	3,389	2,881	2,047	834	2,688	1,924	764
1994	13,923	9,491	4,432	10,895	7,339	3,556	3,028	2,152	876	2,780	1,995	785
RATE [1]												
1980	3.0	3.4	2.6	2.9	3.2	2.6	3.7	4.9	2.5	4.1	5.8	2.7
1985	3.5	4.5	2.6	3.3	4.0	2.5	4.9	7.2	2.9	5.9	8.9	3.3
1990	3.6	4.6	2.6	3.3	4.2	2.5	4.6	6.7	2.8	5.7	8.4	3.4
1992	4.3	5.9	2.8	4.1	5.5	2.7	5.5	8.3	3.1	6.8	10.6	3.6
1993	4.8	6.8	3.0	4.5	6.2	2.8	6.6	10.0	3.6	8.3	13.0	4.4
1994	5.0	7.0	3.0	4.7	6.5	2.9	6.8	10.5	3.7	8.6	13.4	4.4

[1] Age-adjusted death rate. For method of computation see source.

No. 143. Deaths and Death Rates for Alcohol-Induced Causes, by Race and Sex: 1980 to 1994

[Age-adjusted rates per 100,000]

YEAR	ALL RACES			WHITE			ALL OTHER					
							Total			Black		
	Both sexes	Male	Female	Both sexes	Male	Female	Both sexes	Male	Female	Both sexes	Male	Female
NUMBER												
1980	19,765	14,447	5,318	14,815	10,936	3,879	4,950	3,511	1,439	4,451	3,170	1,281
1985	17,741	13,216	4,525	13,216	9,922	3,294	4,525	3,294	1,231	4,114	3,030	1,084
1990	19,757	14,842	4,915	14,904	11,334	3,570	4,853	3,508	1,345	4,337	3,172	1,165
1992	19,568	14,926	4,642	15,143	11,701	3,442	4,425	3,225	1,200	3,809	2,800	1,009
1993	19,557	14,873	4,684	15,293	11,716	3,577	4,264	3,157	1,107	3,663	2,759	904
1994	20,163	15,293	4,870	15,853	12,154	3,699	4,310	3,139	1,171	3,648	2,700	948
RATE [1]												
1980	8.4	13.0	4.3	6.9	10.8	3.5	18.8	29.5	10.0	20.4	32.4	10.6
1985	7.0	11.0	3.4	5.8	9.2	2.8	14.6	23.5	7.2	16.8	27.7	8.0
1990	7.2	11.4	3.4	6.2	9.9	2.8	13.6	22.0	6.8	16.1	26.6	7.7
1992	6.8	11.0	3.1	6.1	9.9	2.6	11.6	18.9	5.6	13.4	22.3	6.3
1993	6.7	10.8	3.0	6.1	9.7	2.7	10.8	17.8	5.0	12.5	21.3	5.5
1994	6.8	10.9	3.1	6.2	9.9	2.7	10.6	17.3	5.2	12.2	20.4	5.6

[1] Age-adjusted death rate. For method of computation see source.

Source of tables 141-143: U.S. National Center for Health Statistics, *Monthly Vital Statistics Reports*.

No. 144. Deaths—Life Years Lost and Mortality Costs, by Age, Sex, and Cause: 1994

[Life years lost: Number of years person would have lived in absence of death. Mortality cost: value of lifetime earnings lost by persons who die prematurely, discounted at 6 percent]

CHARACTERISTIC	Number of deaths (1,000)	LIFE YEARS LOST[1]		MORTALITY COST[2]	
		Total (1,000)	Per death	Total (mil.)	Per death
Total	2,279	38,450	17	356,632	156,487
Under 5 yrs.	39	2,897	75	20,868	541,885
5-14 yrs.	8	575	68	6,127	723,930
15-24 yrs.	35	2,018	57	33,116	939,713
25-44 yrs.	159	6,749	43	136,819	861,709
45-64 yrs.	375	9,461	25	120,314	320,823
65 yrs. and over	1,663	16,751	10	39,388	23,691
Heart disease	732	9,216	13	60,786	82,994
Cancer	534	8,811	16	71,070	133,013
Cerebrovascular diseases	153	1,800	12	10,091	65,824
Injuries	91	3,164	35	48,774	533,418
Other	768	15,459	20	165,911	216,162
Male	1,163	20,807	18	253,024	217,609
Under 5 yrs.	22	1,565	72	12,739	588,288
5-14 yrs.	5	338	65	4,045	780,602
15-24 yrs.	27	1,490	56	26,463	988,976
25-44 yrs.	112	4,585	41	105,507	942,669
45-64 yrs.	232	5,465	24	83,357	359,846
65 yrs. and over	765	7,365	10	20,912	27,326
Heart disease	361	4,829	13	44,032	121,880
Cancer	280	4,220	15	40,875	145,741
Cerebrovascular diseases	60	721	12	5,844	97,034
Injuries	61	2,167	36	38,567	637,384
Other	400	8,870	22	123,705	309,053
Female	1,116	17,643	16	103,608	92,818
Under 5 yrs.	17	1,332	79	8,129	482,267
5-14 yrs.	3	237	72	2,082	634,449
15-24 yrs.	8	529	62	6,653	784,321
25-44 yrs.	47	2,164	46	31,311	668,305
45-64 yrs.	143	3,996	28	36,957	257,772
65 yrs. and over	897	9,366	10	18,476	20,591
Heart disease	371	4,387	12	16,753	45,141
Cancer	254	4,591	18	30,195	118,949
Cerebrovascular diseases	93	1,079	12	4,247	45,631
Injuries	31	997	32	10,207	330,013
Other	367	6,589	18	42,206	114,922

[1] Based on life expectancy at year of death. [2] Cost estimates based on the person's age, sex, life expectancy at the time of death, labor force participation rates, annual earnings, value of homemaking services, and a 4 percent discount rate by which to convert to present worth the potential aggregate earnings lost over the years.

Source: Institute for Health and Aging, University of California, San Francisco, CA, unpublished data.

No. 145. Marriages and Divorces: 1970 to 1995

YEAR	MARRIAGES[1]						DIVORCES AND ANNULMENTS		
	Number (1,000)	Rate per 1,000 population					Number (1,000)	Rate per 1,000 population	
		Total	Men, 15 yrs. old and over[2]	Women, 15 yrs. old and over[2]	Unmarried women			Total[2]	Married women, 15 yrs. old and over
					15 yrs. old and over	15 to 44 yrs. old			
1970	2,159	10.6	31.1	28.4	76.5	140.2	708	3.5	14.9
1975	2,153	10.0	27.9	25.6	66.9	118.5	1,036	4.8	20.3
1980	2,390	10.6	28.5	26.1	61.4	102.6	1,189	5.2	22.6
1983	2,446	10.5	28.0	25.7	59.9	99.3	1,158	5.0	21.3
1984	2,477	10.5	28.0	25.8	59.5	99.0	1,169	5.0	21.5
1985	2,413	10.1	27.0	24.9	57.0	94.9	1,190	5.0	21.7
1986	2,407	10.0	26.6	24.5	56.2	93.9	1,178	4.9	21.2
1987	2,403	9.9	26.3	24.3	55.7	92.4	1,166	4.8	20.8
1988	2,396	9.8	26.0	24.0	54.6	91.0	1,167	4.8	20.7
1989	2,403	9.7	25.8	23.9	54.2	91.2	1,157	4.7	20.4
1990	2,443	9.8	26.0	24.1	54.5	91.3	1,182	4.7	20.9
1991	2,371	9.4	(NA)	(NA)	54.2	86.8	1,189	4.7	20.9
1992	2,362	9.3	(NA)	(NA)	53.3	88.2	1,215	4.8	21.2
1993	2,334	9.0	(NA)	(NA)	52.3	86.8	1,187	4.6	20.5
1994	2,362	9.1	(NA)	(NA)	51.5	84.0	1,191	4.6	20.5
1995 provisional	2,336	8.9	(NA)	(NA)	50.8	83.0	1,169	4.4	19.8

NA Not available. [1] Beginning 1980, includes nonlicensed marriages registered in California. [2] Rates for 1981-88 are revised and may differ from rates published

No. 146. Percent Distribution of Marriages, by Marriage Order: 1970 to 1988

[Excludes marriages with marriage order not stated. See headnote, table 148]

MARRIAGE ORDER	1970	1980	1981	1982	1983	1984	1985	1986	1987	1988
Total	100.0	100.0	100.0	100.0	100.0	100.0	100.0	100.0	100.0	100.0
First marriage of bride and groom	68.6	56.2	54.7	54.8	54.4	54.4	54.3	53.9	53.9	54.1
First marriage of bride, remarriage of groom	7.6	11.3	11.8	11.6	11.6	11.5	11.5	11.3	11.3	11.1
Remarriage of bride, first marriage of groom	7.3	9.8	10.1	10.3	10.5	10.7	10.9	11.2	11.3	11.4
Remarriage of bride and groom	16.5	22.7	23.4	23.3	23.5	23.4	23.4	23.6	23.5	23.4

Source of tables 145 and 146: U.S. National Center for Health Statistics, *Vital Statistics of the United States*, annual; *Monthly Vital Statistics Report*; and unpublished data.

No. 147. Percent Distribution of Marriages, by Age, Sex, and Previous Marital Status: 1980 and 1990

[Data cover marriage registration area; see text, section 2. Based on a sample and subject to sampling variability; for details, see source]

SEX AND PREVIOUS MARITAL STATUS	Total	Under 20 years old	20-24 years old	25-29 years old	30-34 years old	35-44 years old	45-64 years old	65 years old and over
WOMEN								
All marriages: [1]								
1980	100.0	21.1	37.1	18.7	9.3	7.8	5.0	1.0
1990	100.0	10.6	29.3	24.6	14.2	13.9	6.1	1.0
First marriages: [2]								
1980	100.0	30.4	47.3	16.0	4.0	1.6	0.6	0.1
1990	100.0	16.6	40.8	27.2	10.1	4.5	0.7	0.1
Remarriages: [2 3]								
1980	100.0	1.7	15.3	24.4	20.6	20.8	14.3	2.9
1990	100.0	0.6	8.0	19.9	21.7	31.3	16.0	2.7
Previously divorced: [4] 1980	100.0	1.7	16.7	26.7	22.5	21.6	10.0	0.6
1990	100.0	0.6	8.6	20.9	23.0	32.5	13.6	0.6
MEN								
All marriages: [1]								
1980	100.0	8.5	35.7	23.8	12.3	10.5	7.4	1.8
1990	100.0	4.3	24.7	27.1	16.6	16.4	9.1	1.9
First marriages: [2]								
1980	100.0	12.7	50.0	25.7	7.5	2.9	1.1	0.1
1990	100.0	6.6	36.0	34.3	14.8	7.1	1.1	0.1
Remarriages: [2 3]								
1980	100.0	0.2	7.2	20.1	21.9	25.6	20.0	5.1
1990	100.0	0.1	3.6	13.8	19.9	33.8	23.8	5.1
Previously divorced: [4] 1980	100.0	0.2	7.7	21.7	24.1	27.7	17.3	1.4
1990	100.0	0.1	3.8	14.8	21.2	35.8	22.6	1.7

[1] Includes marriage order not stated. [2] Excludes data for Iowa. [3] Includes remarriages of previously widowed. [4] Excludes remarriages in Michigan, Ohio, and South Carolina.

No. 148. Marriage Rates and Median Age of Bride and Groom, by Previous Marital Status: 1970 to 1990

[Data cover marriage registration area; see text, section 2. Figures for previously divorced and previously widowed exclude data for Michigan and Ohio for all years, for South Carolina beginning 1975, and for the District of Columbia for 1970. Based on a sample and subject to sampling variability; for details, see source. For definition of median, see Guide to Tabular Presentation]

YEAR	MARRIAGE RATES [1]						MEDIAN AGE AT MARRIAGE (years)					
	Women			Men			Women			Men		
	Single	Divorced	Widowed	Single	Divorced	Widowed	First marriage	Remarriage: Divorced	Remarriage: Widowed	First marriage	Remarriage: Divorced	Remarriage: Widowed
1970	93.4	123.3	10.2	80.4	204.5	40.6	20.6	30.1	51.2	22.5	34.5	58.7
1975	75.9	117.2	8.3	61.5	189.8	40.4	20.8	30.2	52.4	22.7	33.6	59.4
1980	66.0	91.3	6.7	54.7	142.1	32.2	21.8	31.0	53.6	23.6	34.0	61.2
1985	61.5	81.8	5.7	50.1	121.6	27.7	23.0	32.8	54.6	24.8	36.1	62.7
1986	59.7	79.5	5.5	49.1	117.8	26.8	23.3	33.1	54.3	25.1	36.6	62.9
1987	58.9	80.7	5.4	48.8	115.7	26.1	23.6	33.3	53.9	25.3	36.7	62.8
1988	58.4	78.6	5.3	48.3	109.7	25.1	23.7	33.6	53.9	25.5	37.0	63.0
1989	58.7	75.6	5.1	48.2	105.6	24.5	23.9	34.0	53.8	25.9	37.3	62.9
1990	57.7	76.2	5.2	47.0	105.9	23.8	24.0	34.2	54.0	25.9	37.4	63.1

[1] Rate per 1,000 population 15 years old and over in specified group.

No. 149. Divorces and Annulments—Duration of Marriage, Age at Divorce and Children Involved: 1970 to 1990

[Data cover divorce-registration area; see text, section 2. Based on a sample and subject to sampling variability; for details, see source. Median age computed on data by single years of age]

DURATION OF MARRIAGE, AGE AT DIVORCE, AND CHILDREN INVOLVED	1970	1975	1980	1983	1984	1985	1986	1987	1988	1989	1990
Median duration of marriage (years)	6.7	6.5	6.8	7.0	6.9	6.8	6.9	7.0	7.1	7.2	7.2
Men (years)	32.9	32.2	32.7	34.0	34.3	34.4	34.6	34.9	35.1	35.4	35.6
Women (years)	29.8	29.5	30.3	31.5	31.7	31.9	32.1	32.5	32.6	32.9	33.2
Estimated number of children involved in divorce (1,000)	870	1,123	1,174	1,091	1,081	1,091	1,064	1,038	1,044	1,063	1,075
Avg. number of children per decree	1.22	1.08	0.98	0.94	0.92	0.92	0.90	0.89	0.89	0.91	0.90
Rate per 1,000 children under 18 years of	12.5	16.7	17.3	17.4	17.2	17.3	16.8	16.3	16.4	16.8	16.8

Source of tables 147-149: U.S. National Center for Health Statistics of the United States, *Vital Statistics of the United States*, annual, *Monthly Vital Statistics Report;* and unpublished data.

No. 150. First Marriage Dissolution and Years Until Remarriage for Women, by Race and Hispanic Origin: 1988

[For women 15 to 44 years old. Based on 1988 National Survey of Family Growth; see Appendix III. Marriage dissolution includes death of spouse, separation because of marital discord, and divorce]

ITEM	Number (1,000)	YEARS UNTIL REMARRIAGE (cumulative percent)					
		All	1	2	3	4	5
ALL RACES [1]							
Year of dissolution of first marriage:							
All years	11,577	56.8	20.6	32.8	40.7	46.2	49.7
1980-84	3,504	47.5	16.3	28.1	36.4	[2]41.1	[2]45.4
1975-79	3,235	65.3	21.9	36.0	44.7	52.7	55.4
1970-74	1,887	83.2	24.9	38.6	47.9	56.4	61.2
1965-69	1,013	89.9	32.6	48.7	60.2	65.0	72.8
WHITE							
Year of dissolution of first marriage:							
All years	10,103	59.9	21.9	35.2	43.5	49.4	53.0
1980-84	3,030	51.4	18.2	31.1	40.3	[2]45.2	[2]49.8
1975-79	2,839	69.5	23.2	38.5	46.9	55.6	58.4
1970-74	1,622	87.5	24.9	39.8	49.8	59.3	64.3
1965-69	893	91.0	34.7	52.3	64.9	69.3	76.9
BLACK							
Year of dissolution of first marriage:							
All years	1,166	34.0	10.9	16.5	19.6	22.7	25.0
1980-84	380	19.7	[3]4.7	[3]10.6	[3]12.9	[2]14.8	[2]14.8
1975-79	301	32.3	[3]11.4	[3]15.6	18.5	22.2	24.9
1970-74	227	59.0	22.3	29.4	35.3	38.7	42.3
1965-69	98	81.2	[3]20.9	[3]27.3	[3]31.3	40.8	52.1
Hispanic, [4] all years	942	44.7	12.5	16.6	22.7	27.8	29.9

[1] Includes other races. [2] The percent having remarried is biased downward because the women had not completed the indicated number of years since dissolution of first marriage at the time of the survey. [3] Figure does not meet standard of reliability or precision. [4] Hispanic persons may be of any race.

Source: National Center for Health Statistics, *Advance Data from Vital and Health Statistics*, No. 194.

No. 151. Marriage Experience for Women, by Age and Race: 1980 and 1990

[In percent. As of June. Based on Current Population Survey; see text, section]

MARITAL STATUS AND AGE	ALL RACES		WHITE		BLACK		HISPANIC [1]	
	1980	1990	1980	1990	1980	1990	1980	1990
EVER MARRIED								
20 to 24 years old	49.5	38.5	52.2	41.3	33.3	23.5	55.4	45.8
25 to 29 years old	78.6	69.0	81.0	73.2	62.3	45.0	80.2	69.6
30 to 34 years old	89.9	82.2	91.6	85.6	77.9	61.1	88.3	83.0
35 to 39 years old	94.3	89.4	95.3	91.4	87.4	74.9	91.2	88.9
40 to 44 years old	95.1	92.0	95.8	93.4	89.7	82.1	94.2	92.8
45 to 49 years old	95.9	94.4	96.4	95.1	92.5	89.7	94.4	91.7
50 to 54 years old	95.3	95.5	95.8	96.1	92.1	91.9	95.0	91.8
DIVORCED AFTER FIRST MARRIAGE								
20 to 24 years old	14.2	12.5	14.7	12.8	10.5	9.6	9.4	6.8
25 to 29 years old	20.7	19.2	21.0	19.8	20.2	17.8	13.9	13.5
30 to 34 years old	26.2	28.1	25.8	28.6	31.4	26.6	21.1	19.9
35 to 39 years old	27.2	34.1	26.7	34.6	32.9	35.8	21.9	29.7
40 to 44 years old	26.1	35.8	25.5	35.2	33.7	45.1	19.7	26.6
45 to 49 years old	23.1	35.2	22.7	35.5	29.0	39.8	23.9	24.6
50 to 54 years old	21.8	29.5	21.0	28.5	29.0	39.2	22.5	22.9
REMARRIED AFTER DIVORCE								
20 to 24 years old	45.5	38.1	47.0	39.3	(B)	(B)	(B)	(B)
25 to 29 years old	53.4	51.8	56.4	52.8	27.9	44.4	(B)	49.5
30 to 34 years old	60.9	59.6	63.3	61.4	42.0	42.0	58.3	45.9
35 to 39 years old	64.9	65.0	66.9	66.5	50.6	54.0	45.2	51.2
40 to 44 years old	67.4	67.1	68.6	69.5	58.4	50.3	(B)	53.9
45 to 49 years old	69.2	65.9	70.4	67.2	62.7	55.0	(B)	51.0
50 to 54 years old	72.0	63.0	72.6	65.4	72.7	50.2	(B)	62.2
REDIVORCED AFTER REMARRIAGE								
20 to 24 years old	8.5	13.1	(NA)	(NA)	(NA)	(NA)	(NA)	(NA)
25 to 29 years old	15.6	17.8	(NA)	(NA)	(NA)	(NA)	(NA)	(NA)
30 to 34 years old	19.1	22.7	(NA)	(NA)	(NA)	(NA)	(NA)	(NA)
35 to 39 years old	24.7	28.5	(NA)	(NA)	(NA)	(NA)	(NA)	(NA)
40 to 44 years old	28.4	30.6	(NA)	(NA)	(NA)	(NA)	(NA)	(NA)
45 to 49 years old	25.1	36.4	(NA)	(NA)	(NA)	(NA)	(NA)	(NA)
50 to 54 years old	29.0	34.5	(NA)	(NA)	(NA)	(NA)	(NA)	(NA)

B Base is less than 75,000. NA Not available. [1] Persons of Hispanic origin may be of any race.

Source: U.S. Bureau of the Census, *Current Population Reports*, P23-180.

No. 152. Marriages and Divorces—Number and Rate, by State: 1980 to 1995

[By place of occurrence]

DIVISION AND STATE	MARRIAGES [1]						DIVORCES [3]					
	Number (1,000)			Rate per 1,000 population [2]			Number (1,000)			Rate per 1,000 population [2]		
	1980	1990	1995	1980	1990	1995	1980	1990	1995	1980	1990	1995
U.S.	**2,390.3**	**2,443.0**	**2,336.0**	**10.6**	**9.8**	**8.9**	**1,189.0**	**1,182.0**	**1,169.0**	**5.2**	**4.7**	**4.4**
New England	**106.3**	**112.2**	**99.5**	**8.6**	**8.5**	**7.5**	**49.0**	**44.0**	**39.8**	**4.0**	**3.4**	**3.0**
Maine	12.0	11.8	10.8	10.7	9.7	8.7	6.2	5.3	5.5	5.5	4.3	4.4
New Hampshire	9.3	10.6	9.6	10.0	9.5	8.4	5.3	5.3	4.9	5.7	4.7	4.2
Vermont	5.2	6.1	6.1	10.2	10.9	10.3	2.6	2.6	2.8	5.1	4.5	4.8
Massachusetts	46.3	47.8	43.6	8.1	7.9	7.2	17.9	16.8	13.5	3.1	2.8	2.2
Rhode Island	7.5	8.1	7.4	7.9	8.1	7.5	3.6	3.8	3.7	3.8	3.7	3.7
Connecticut	26.0	27.8	22.0	8.4	7.9	6.7	13.5	10.3	9.6	4.3	3.2	2.9
Middle Atlantic	**294.0**	**314.1**	**276.1**	**8.0**	**8.3**	**7.2**	**124.7**	**121.6**	**119.7**	**3.4**	**3.2**	**3.1**
New York	144.5	169.3	147.4	8.2	8.6	8.1	62.0	57.9	56.0	3.5	3.2	3.1
New Jersey	55.8	58.0	52.9	7.6	7.6	6.7	27.8	23.6	24.3	3.8	3.0	3.1
Pennsylvania	93.7	86.8	75.8	7.9	7.1	6.3	34.9	40.1	39.4	2.9	3.3	3.3
East North Central	**395.5**	**364.5**	**331.0**	**9.5**	**8.6**	**7.6**	**212.4**	**[4]153.3**	**[4]144.9**	**5.1**	**[4]4.2**	**[4]3.3**
Ohio	99.8	95.8	90.1	9.2	9.0	8.1	58.8	51.0	48.7	5.4	4.7	4.4
Indiana	57.9	54.3	50.4	10.5	9.6	8.7	40.0	(NA)	(NA)	7.3	(NA)	(NA)
Illinois	109.8	97.1	83.2	9.6	8.8	7.0	51.0	44.3	38.8	4.5	3.8	3.3
Michigan	86.9	76.1	71.0	9.4	8.2	7.4	45.0	40.2	39.9	4.9	4.3	4.2
Wisconsin	41.1	41.2	36.3	8.7	7.9	7.1	17.5	17.8	17.5	3.7	3.6	3.4
West North Central	**173.7**	**156.1**	**145.8**	**10.1**	**8.7**	**7.9**	**79.6**	**76.9**	**75.3**	**4.6**	**4.3**	**4.1**
Minnesota	37.6	33.7	32.8	9.2	7.7	7.1	15.4	15.4	15.8	3.8	3.5	3.4
Iowa	27.5	24.8	22.0	9.4	9.0	7.8	11.9	11.1	10.5	4.1	3.9	3.7
Missouri	54.6	49.3	44.9	11.1	9.6	8.4	27.6	26.4	26.8	5.6	5.1	5.0
North Dakota	6.1	4.8	4.6	9.3	7.5	7.2	2.1	2.3	2.2	3.3	3.6	3.4
South Dakota	8.8	7.7	7.3	12.7	11.1	10.0	2.8	2.6	2.9	4.1	3.7	4.0
Nebraska	14.2	12.5	12.1	9.1	8.0	7.4	6.4	6.5	6.3	4.1	4.0	3.8
Kansas	24.8	23.4	22.1	10.5	9.2	8.6	13.4	12.6	10.7	5.7	5.0	4.2
South Atlantic	**413.1**	**455.4**	**442.9**	**11.2**	**10.4**	**9.4**	**206.3**	**226.1**	**227.3**	**5.6**	**5.2**	**4.8**
Delaware	4.4	5.6	5.4	7.5	8.4	7.5	2.3	3.0	3.7	3.9	4.4	5.1
Maryland	46.3	46.1	42.8	11.0	9.7	8.5	17.5	16.1	15.0	4.1	3.4	3.0
Dist. of Columbia	5.2	4.7	3.5	8.1	8.2	6.4	4.7	2.7	1.9	7.3	4.5	3.4
Virginia	60.2	71.3	67.9	11.3	11.4	10.3	23.6	27.3	28.9	4.4	4.4	4.4
West Virginia	17.4	13.2	11.2	8.9	7.2	6.1	10.3	9.7	9.4	5.3	5.3	5.1
North Carolina	46.7	52.1	61.6	7.9	7.8	8.6	28.1	34.0	37.0	4.8	5.1	5.1
South Carolina	53.9	55.8	44.6	17.3	15.9	12.1	13.6	16.1	14.8	4.4	4.5	4.0
Georgia	70.6	64.4	61.5	12.9	10.3	8.5	34.7	35.7	37.2	6.4	5.5	5.2
Florida	108.3	142.3	144.3	11.1	10.9	10.2	71.6	81.7	79.5	7.3	6.3	5.6
East South Central	**168.8**	**186.5**	**193.4**	**11.5**	**12.0**	**12.0**	**87.5**	**93.8**	**96.0**	**6.0**	**6.1**	**5.9**
Kentucky	32.7	51.3	47.6	8.9	13.5	12.3	16.7	21.8	22.9	4.6	5.8	5.9
Tennessee	59.2	66.6	82.3	12.9	13.9	15.7	30.2	32.3	33.1	6.6	6.5	6.3
Alabama	49.0	43.3	42.0	12.6	10.6	9.9	26.7	25.3	26.0	6.9	6.1	6.1
Mississippi	27.9	24.3	21.5	11.1	9.4	8.0	13.8	14.4	13.1	5.5	5.5	4.8
West South Central	**296.2**	**292.9**	**294.5**	**12.6**	**10.8**	**10.2**	**156.0**	**[4]135.7**	**[4]136.2**	**6.5**	**[4]6.0**	**[4]4.7**
Arkansas	26.5	35.7	36.6	11.6	15.3	14.7	15.9	16.8	16.0	6.9	6.9	6.5
Louisiana	43.5	41.2	40.8	10.3	9.6	9.4	18.1	(NA)	(NA)	4.3	(NA)	(NA)
Oklahoma	46.5	33.2	28.5	15.4	10.6	8.7	24.2	24.9	21.8	8.0	7.7	6.7
Texas	181.8	182.8	188.5	12.8	10.5	10.1	96.8	94.0	98.4	6.8	5.5	5.3
Mountain	**241.7**	**250.9**	**272.0**	**21.3**	**18.3**	**17.4**	**86.1**	**87.0**	**[4]74.3**	**7.6**	**6.3**	**[4]4.7**
Montana	8.3	7.0	6.6	10.6	8.6	7.6	4.9	4.1	4.2	6.3	5.1	4.8
Idaho	13.4	15.0	15.5	14.2	13.9	13.3	6.6	6.6	6.8	7.0	6.5	5.8
Wyoming	6.9	4.8	5.2	14.6	10.7	10.7	4.0	3.1	3.2	8.5	6.6	6.7
Colorado	34.9	31.5	34.3	12.1	9.8	9.2	18.6	18.4	(NA)	6.4	5.5	(NA)
New Mexico	16.6	13.2	15.1	12.8	8.8	9.0	10.4	7.7	11.3	8.0	4.9	6.7
Arizona	30.2	37.0	38.9	11.1	10.0	9.2	19.9	25.1	27.6	7.3	6.9	6.6
Utah	17.0	19.0	21.6	11.6	11.2	11.1	7.8	8.8	8.9	5.3	5.1	4.6
Nevada	114.3	123.4	134.8	142.8	99.0	88.1	13.8	13.3	12.4	17.3	11.4	8.1
Pacific	**296.8**	**334.4**	**291.5**	**9.4**	**8.5**	**6.9**	**167.9**	**160.7**	**[4]53.2**	**5.9**	**4.6**	**[4]1.3**
Washington	47.7	48.6	42.0	11.6	9.5	7.7	28.6	28.8	29.7	6.9	5.9	5.5
Oregon	23.0	25.2	25.7	8.7	8.9	8.2	17.8	15.9	15.0	6.7	5.5	4.8
California [5]	210.9	236.7	199.6	8.9	7.9	6.3	133.5	128.0	(NA)	5.6	4.3	(NA)
Alaska	5.4	5.7	5.5	13.3	10.2	9.0	3.5	2.9	3.0	8.8	5.5	5.0
Hawaii	11.9	18.1	18.8	12.3	16.4	15.8	4.4	5.2	5.5	4.6	4.6	4.6

NA Not available. [1] Data are counts of marriages performed, except as noted. [2] Based on total population residing in area; population enumerated as of April 1 for 1980; estimated as of July 1 for all other years. [3] Includes annulments. [4] Excludes data for states shown below as not available. [5] Marriage data include nonlicensed marriages registered.

Source: U.S. National Center for Health Statistics, *Vital Statistics of the United States*, annual; and *Monthly Vital Statistics Reports*.

Section 3

Health and Nutrition

ection presents statistics on health
ditures and insurance coverage, in-
g Medicare and Medicaid, medical
nel, hospitals, nursing homes and
care facilities, incidence of acute and
ence of chronic conditions, nutritional
of the population, and food con-
ion. Summary statistics showing re-
ends on health care and discussions
cted health issues are published
lly by the U.S. National Center for
Statistics (NCHS) in *Health, United*
. Data on national health expendi-
medical costs, and insurance cover-
e compiled by the U.S. Health Care
ing Administration (HCFA) and ap-
the quarterly *Health Care Financ-*
view and in the *Annual Medicare*
m Statistics series. Statistics on
insurance are also collected by
and are published in series 10 of
nd Health Statistics. The Census
u also publishes data on insurance
ge. Statistics on health facilities are
ed by NCHS and are published in
14 of *Vital and Health Statistics*. Sta-
on hospitals are published annually
American Hospital Association,
go, IL, in *Hospital Statistics*. Primary
s for data on nutrition are the quar-
lational Food Review and the annual
Consumption, Prices, and Expendi-
both issued by the U.S. Department
iculture. NCHS also conducts period-
veys of nutrient levels in the popula-
ncluding estimates of food and nutri-
take, overweight and obesity, hyper-
sterolemia, hypertension, and clinical
of malnutrition.

nal health expenditures—HCFA
les estimates of national health ex-
tures (NHE) to measure spending for
care in the United States. The NHE
nts are structured to show spending
e of expenditure (i.e., hospital care,
ian care, dental care, and other pro-
nal care; home health; drugs and
medical nondurables;
products and other medical dura-
nursing home care and other
nal health expenditures; plus nonper-
health expenditures for such items
blic health, research, construction of
al facilities, and administration) and

In Brief

In 1995:
41 million with no health insurance.

1994: Persons with—

Chronic sinusitis	*35 million*
Arthritis	*33 million*
Hypertension	*28 million*

Per capita consumption of chicken:

1980	*33 pounds*
1995	*49 pounds*

by source of funding (e.g., private health insurance, out-of-pocket payments, and a range of public programs including Medicare, Medicaid, and those operated by the Department of Veterans Affairs (VA)).

In all cases except private insurance (HCFA conducts its own survey of part of the health insurance industry), data used to estimate health expenditures come from existing sources which are tabulated for other purposes. The type of expenditure estimates rely upon statistics produced by such groups as the American Hospital Association, the Internal Revenue Service, the Department of Commerce, and the Department of Health and Human Services (HHS). Source of funding estimates are constructed using administrative and statistical records from the Medicare and Medicaid programs, the Department of Defense and VA medical programs, the Social Security Administration, Census Bureau's *Governmental Finances*, State and local governments, other HHS agencies, and other nongovernment sources. Detailed descriptions of sources and methods, along with the most recent analysis of health care expenditure estimates, are published in the *Health Care Financing Review's* annual article on national health expenditures.

Medicare and Medicaid—Since July 1966, the Federal Medicare program has provided two coordinated plans for nearly all people age 65 and over: (1) A hospital insurance plan which covers hospital and related services and (2) a voluntary supplementary medical insurance plan, financed partially by monthly premiums paid by participants, which partly covers physicians' and related medical services. Such insurance also applies, since July 1973, to disabled beneficiaries of any age after 24 months of entitlement to cash benefits under the social security or railroad retirement programs and to persons with end stage renal disease.

Under Medicaid, all States offer basic health services to certain very poor people: Individuals who are pregnant, aged, disabled or blind, and families with dependent children. Medicaid eligibility is automatic for almost all cash welfare recipients in these States. Thirty-nine States also extend Medicaid to certain other persons who qualify, except for incomes above regular eligibility levels; those persons include those who have medical expenses which, when subtracted from their income, spend down to a State "medically needy" level or those who meet the higher "medically needy" income restrictions. Within Federal guidelines, each State determines its own Medicaid eligibility criteria and the health services to be provided under Medicaid. The cost of providing Medicaid services is jointly shared by the Federal Government and the States.

Health resources—Hospital statistics based on data from the American Hospital Association's yearly survey are published annually in *Hospital Statistics,* and cover all hospitals accepted for registration by the Association. To be accepted for registration, a hospital must meet certain requirements relating to number of beds, construction, equipment, medical and nursing staff, patient care, clinical records, surgical and obstetrical facilities, diagnostic and treatment facilities, laboratory services, etc. Data obtained from NCHS cover all U.S. hospitals which meet certain criteria for inclusion. The criteria are published in *Vital and Health Statistics* reports, series 13. NCHS defines a hospital as a non-Federal short-term general or special facility with six or more inpatient beds with an average stay of less than 60 days.

Statistics on the demographic characteristics of persons employed in the health occupations are compiled by the U.S. (see table 645, section 13). Data based on surveys of health personnel and utilization of health facilities providing long-term care, ambulatory care, and hospital care are presented in NCHS series 13 and series 14, *Data on Health Resources Utilization* and *Data on Health Resources: Manpower and Facilities.* Statistics on patient visits to health care providers, as reported in health interviews, appear in NCHS series 10, *National Health Interview Survey Data.*

The HCFA's *Health Care Financing Review* and *Health Care Financing Program Statistics* present data for hospitals and nursing homes as well as extended care facilities and home health agencies. These data are based on records of the Medicare program and differ from those of other sources because they are limited to facilities meeting Federal eligibility standards for participation in Medicare.

Data on patients in hospitals for the mentally ill and on mental health facilities are collected by the National Institute of Mental Health (NIMH) and appear in *Mental Health, U.S.*, the *Mental Health Statistics* reports, (series CN), and the Mental Health Statistical Note series.

Disability and illness—General health statistics, including morbidity, disability, injuries, preventive care, and findings from physiological testing are collected by NCHS in its National Health Interview Survey and its National Health and Nutrition Examination Surveys and appear in *Vital and Health Statistics,* series 10 and 11, respectively. The Department of Labor compiles statistics on occupational injuries (see section 13). Annual incidence data on notifiable diseases are compiled by the Public Health Service (PHS) at its Centers for Disease Control and Prevention in Atlanta, Georgia, and are published as a supplement to its *Morbidity and Mortality Weekly Report.* The list of diseases is revised annually and includes those which, by mutual agreement of the States and PHS, are communicable diseases of national importance.

Nutrition—Statistics on annual per capita consumption of food and its nutrient value are estimated by the U.S. Department of

be found in *Food Consumption, Prices, and Expenditures*, issued annually.

Statistics on food insufficiency and food and nutrient intake are collected by NCHS to estimate the diet of the nation's population. NCHS also collects physical examination data to assess the population's nutritional status, including growth, overweight/obesity, nutritional deficiencies, and prevalence of nutrition-related conditions, such as hypertension, hypercholesterolemia, and diabetes.

Statistical reliability—For discussion of statistical collection, estimation, and sampling procedures and measures of reliability applicable to data from NCHS and HCFA, see Appendix III.

Figure 3.1
Percent of Population Overweight: 1988 - 1991

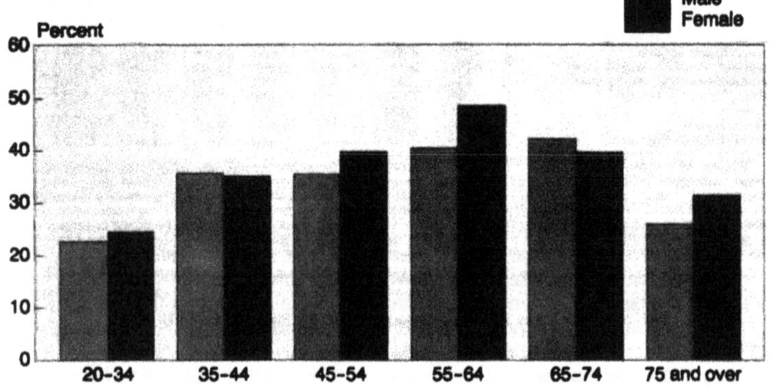

Age group

Source: Charts prepared by U.S. Bureau of the Census. For data, see table 225.

Figure 3.2
Per Capita Food Consumption, by Selected Products: 1970 to 1995

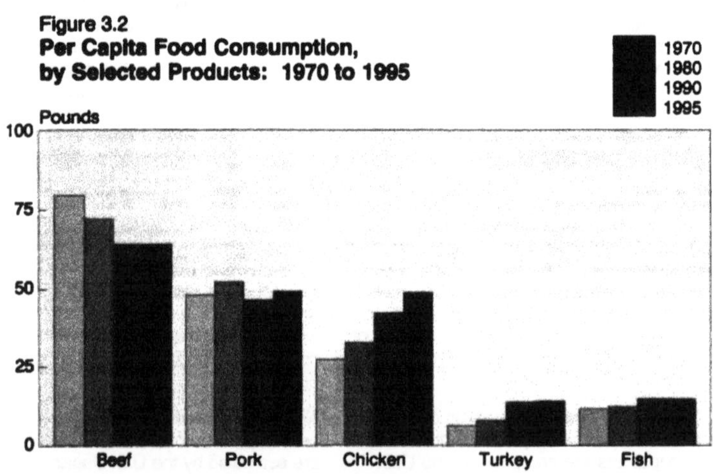

No. 153. National Health Expenditures, by Type: 1980 to 1995

[In millions of dollars, except percent. Includes Puerto Rico and outlying areas]

TYPE OF EXPENDITURE	1980	1985	1990	1991	1992	1993	1994	1995
Total	**247,245**	**428,204**	**697,453**	761,704	**834,226**	**892,074**	**937,139**	**988,489**
Annual percent change [1]	14.9	9.5	12.1	9.2	9.5	6.9	5.1	5.5
Private expenditures	**142,463**	**253,906**	**413,145**	441,409	**478,780**	**505,548**	**517,250**	**532,089**
Health services and supplies	138,010	247,403	402,896	431,286	467,774	493,651	505,478	521,152
Out-of-pocket payments	60,254	100,595	148,390	154,984	165,763	171,590	175,972	182,563
Insurance premiums [2]	69,728	132,254	232,436	252,312	277,015	295,413	302,691	310,616
Other	8,028	14,554	22,071	23,990	24,996	26,647	26,815	27,972
Medical research	292	538	960	1,090	1,183	1,215	1,276	1,372
Medical facilities construction	4,161	5,962	9,288	9,033	9,824	10,682	10,496	9,566
Public expenditures	**104,782**	**174,301**	**284,309**	**320,295**	**355,446**	**386,526**	**419,889**	**456,400**
Percent Federal of public	68.7	70.7	68.9	70.1	71.4	71.8	71.9	72.0
Health services and supplies	97,599	164,430	270,033	305,486	338,910	369,415	401,234	436,678
Medicare [3]	37,519	72,186	112,091	123,017	138,280	150,927	167,602	187,024
Public assistance medical payments [4]	28,033	44,439	80,396	99,235	111,917	124,833	136,440	146,411
Temporary disability insurance [5]	52	51	62	66	70	52	51	50
Workers' compensation (medical) [5]	5,141	7,971	16,067	17,163	18,984	18,909	19,147	19,787
Defense Dept. hospital, medical	4,350	7,498	11,579	12,849	12,964	13,315	13,170	13,488
Maternal, child health programs	892	1,262	1,892	2,014	2,129	2,204	2,293	2,362
Public health activities	6,732	11,618	19,613	21,422	23,416	25,275	28,204	31,402
Veterans' hospital, medical care	5,934	8,713	11,424	12,367	13,208	14,299	15,291	15,618
Medical vocational rehabilitation	298	401	555	595	638	629	705	703
State and local hospitals [6]	5,589	7,030	11,346	11,049	11,114	12,440	12,329	12,322
Other [7]	3,059	3,263	5,009	5,710	6,192	6,532	7,002	7,511
Medical research	5,169	7,302	11,254	11,827	12,995	13,271	14,555	15,246
Medical facilities construction	2,014	2,569	3,022	2,981	3,541	3,840	4,100	4,476

[1] Change from immediate prior year. For explanation of average annual percent change, see Guide to Tabular Presentation. [2] Covers insurance benefits and amount retained by insurance companies for expenses, additions to reserves, and profits (net cost of insurance). [3] Represents expenditures for benefits and administrative cost from Federal hospital and medical insurance trust funds under old-age, survivors, disability, and health insurance programs; see text, section 12. [4] Payments made directly to suppliers of medical care (primarily Medicaid). [5] Includes medical benefits paid under public law by private insurance carriers, state governments, and self-insurers. [6] Expenditures not offset by other revenues. [7] Covers expenditures for Substance Abuse and Mental Health Services Administration, Indian Health Service; school health and other programs.

Source: U.S. Health Care Financing Administration, *Health Care Financing Review*, fall 1996.

No. 154. National Health Expenditures, by Object: 1980 to 1995

[In billions of dollars. Includes Puerto Rico and outlying areas]

OBJECT OF EXPENDITURE	1980	1985	1990	1991	1992	1993	1994	1995
Total	**247.2**	**428.2**	**697.5**	**761.7**	**834.2**	**892.1**	**937.1**	**988.5**
Spent by—								
Consumers	130.0	232.8	380.8	407.3	442.8	467.0	478.7	493.2
Government	104.8	174.3	284.3	320.3	355.4	386.5	419.9	456.4
Other [1]	12.5	21.1	32.3	34.1	36.0	38.5	38.6	38.9
Spent for—								
Health services and supplies	235.6	411.8	672.9	736.8	806.7	863.1	906.7	957.8
Personal health care expenses	217.0	376.4	614.7	676.6	740.5	786.9	827.9	878.8
Hospital care	102.7	168.3	256.4	282.3	305.4	323.3	335.0	350.1
Physician services	45.2	83.6	146.3	159.2	175.7	182.7	190.6	201.6
Dental services	13.3	21.7	31.6	33.3	37.0	39.2	42.1	45.8
Other professional services [2]	6.4	16.6	34.7	38.3	42.1	46.3	49.1	52.6
Home health care	2.4	5.6	13.1	16.1	19.6	23.0	26.3	28.6
Drugs/other medical nondurables	21.6	37.1	59.9	65.6	71.2	75.0	77.7	83.4
Vision products/other med. durables [3]	3.8	6.7	10.5	11.2	11.9	12.5	12.9	13.8
Nursing home care	17.6	30.7	50.9	57.2	62.3	67.0	72.4	77.9
Other health services	4.0	6.1	11.2	13.6	15.4	17.9	21.7	25.0
Net cost of insurance and admin. [4]	11.8	23.8	38.6	38.8	42.7	50.9	50.6	47.7
Government public health activities	6.7	11.6	19.6	21.4	23.4	25.3	28.2	31.4
Medical research	5.5	7.8	12.2	12.9	14.2	14.5	15.8	16.6
Medical facilities construction	6.2	8.5	12.3	12.0	13.4	14.5	14.6	14.0

[1] Includes nonpatient revenues, privately funded construction, and industrial inplant. [2] Includes services of registered and practical nurses in private duty, podiatrists, optometrists, physical therapists, clinical psychologists, chiropractors, naturopaths, and Christian Science practitioners. [3] Includes expenditures for eyeglasses, hearing aids, orthopedic appliances, artificial limbs, crutches, wheelchairs, etc. [4] Includes administrative expenses of federally financed health programs.

Source: U.S. Health Care Financing Administration, *Health Care Financing Review*, fall 1996.

No. 155. Health Services and Supplies—Per Capita Consumer Expenditures, by Object: 1980 to 1995

[In dollars, except percent. Based on Social Security Administration estimates of total U.S. population as of July 1, including Armed Forces and Federal employees abroad and civilian population of outlying areas. Excludes research and construction]

OBJECT OF EXPENDITURE	1980	1985	1989	1990	1991	1992	1993	1994	1995
Total, national	1,002	1,660	2,331	2,588	2,806	3,041	3,222	3,353	3,509
Annual percent change [1]	13.9	9.3	10.3	11.0	8.4	8.4	5.9	4.1	4.7
Hospital care	437	681	900	986	1,075	1,151	1,207	1,239	1,283
Physicians' services	192	338	510	563	606	663	682	705	739
Dentists' services	57	88	115	121	127	140	146	156	168
Other professional services [2]	27	67	116	133	146	159	173	182	193
Home health care	10	23	40	50	61	74	86	97	105
Drugs and other medical nondurables	92	150	209	230	250	266	280	287	306
Vision products and other medical durables [2]	16	27	37	40	43	45	47	48	50
Nursing home care	75	124	175	196	218	236	250	266	285
Other health services	17	25	37	43	52	58	67	80	92
Net cost of insurance and administration [2]	50	96	123	149	148	161	190	187	175
Government public health activities	29	47	70	75	82	88	94	104	115
Total, private consumer [3]	553	942	1,321	1,466	1,551	1,669	1,743	1,770	1,807
Hospital care	178	273	370	401	425	443	457	454	456
Physicians' services	135	234	345	380	409	454	463	475	490
Dentists' services	54	85	111	118	122	134	139	148	161
Other professional services [2]	19	50	86	98	105	114	123	127	132
Home health care	4	8	19	23	26	30	33	35	34
Drugs and other medical nondurables	85	137	188	206	221	238	246	250	264
Vision products and other medical durables [2]	14	21	28	30	30	31	31	31	32
Nursing home care	32	58	80	93	97	100	102	108	114
Net cost of insurance	33	75	94	118	117	127	150	141	124

[1] Change from immediate prior year. [2] See footnotes for corresponding objects in table 154. [3] Represents out-of-pocket payments and private health insurance.

Source: U.S. Health Care Financing Administration, *Health Care Financing Review*, fall 1996.

No. 156. Government Expenditures for Health Services and Supplies: 1995

[In millions of dollars. Includes Puerto Rico and outlying areas. Excludes medical research and construction]

TYPE OF SERVICE	Total [1]	Federal	State and local	Medicare [2] (OASDHI)	Public assistance [3]	OTHER HEALTH SERVICES		
						Veterans	Defense Dept. [4]	Workers' compensation [5]
Total [1]	436,678	314,440	122,238	187,024	146,411	15,618	13,488	19,787
Hospital care	214,303	175,350	38,953	112,848	55,043	12,912	10,537	8,778
Physician services	64,005	50,914	13,091	39,963	14,703	137	1,640	6,703
Nursing home care	45,273	29,291	15,982	7,344	36,305	1,624	-	-
Drugs and other medical nondurables	11,438	5,883	5,556	-	10,788	13	230	362
Administration	13,157	7,066	6,091	3,032	7,868	77	195	1,711
Public health activities	31,402	3,797	27,605	-	-	-	-	-

- Represents zero. [1] Includes other items not shown separately. [2] Covers hospital and medical insurance payments and administrative costs under old-age, survivors, disability, and health insurance program. [3] Covers Medicaid and other medical public assistance. Excludes funds paid into Medicare trust fund by states to cover premiums for public assistance recipients and medically indigent persons. [4] Includes care for retirees and military dependents. [5] Medical benefits.

Source: U.S. Health Care Financing Administration, *Health Care Financing Review*, fall 1996.

No. 157. Expenditures for Health Services and Supplies, by Type of Payer: 1980 to 1994

[In billions of dollars. Beginning 1991 data are not consistent with later revisions shown in table 154]

TYPE OF PAYER	1980	1985	1987	1988	1989	1990	1991	1992	1993	1994
Total expenditures	235.6	411.8	481.8	538.3	599.8	672.9	736.3	806.0	863.1	919.2
Private	158.4	282.2	330.3	371.5	411.0	450.8	481.9	520.1	544.2	577.3
Business	61.7	106.6	129.4	144.0	165.4	185.8	198.2	215.9	226.8	241.3
Share of private health insurance premiums	45.3	79.1	92.8	104.1	121.4	138.4	146.6	160.4	170.0	179.5
Households [1]	89.5	160.5	185.0	209.2	226.8	245.3	262.2	281.9	292.9	310.1
Share of private health insurance premiums	14.6	30.7	33.5	40.1	45.8	51.3	57.4	63.6	68.2	70.6
Out-of-pocket spending	60.3	100.6	116.0	129.2	136.2	148.4	155.1	164.4	169.4	174.9
Nonpatient revenues [2]	7.2	13.1	15.9	18.3	18.8	19.8	21.5	22.3	24.4	25.9
Public	77.3	129.6	151.5	166.8	188.9	222.1	254.4	285.9	318.9	342.0
Federal government	42.4	68.4	75.3	84.1	96.3	115.1	136.2	159.7	181.1	190.6
State/local government	34.8	61.2	76.2	82.7	92.5	107.0	118.2	126.2	137.8	151.3

[1] Includes other items not shown separately. [2] Includes philanthropy.

Source: U.S. Health Care Financing Administration, *Health Care Financing Review*, spring 1996.

No. 158. Personal Health Care—Third Party Payments and Private Consumer Expenditures: 1980 to 1995

[In billions of dollars, except percent. See headnote, table 159]

ITEM	1980	1988	1989	1990	1991	1992	1993	1994	1995
Personal health care expenditures	217.0	376.4	550.1	614.7	676.6	740.5	786.9	827.9	878.8
Third party payments, total	156.8	275.8	413.9	466.3	521.6	574.8	615.3	651.9	696.2
Percent of personal health care	72.2	73.3	75.2	75.9	77.1	77.6	78.2	78.7	79.2
Private insurance payments	62.0	113.8	179.5	201.8	221.6	243.2	255.4	264.5	276.8
Government expenditures	87.0	148.0	214.1	243.0	276.6	307.1	333.9	361.2	392.1
Other [1]	7.8	14.1	20.3	21.5	23.4	24.4	26.1	26.2	27.3
Private consumer expenditures [2]	122.2	214.4	315.7	360.2	376.6	409.0	428.9	440.5	469.3
Percent met by private insurance	50.7	53.1	56.9	57.6	58.8	59.5	59.6	60.0	60.3
Hospital care	41.8	67.5	95.1	104.3	111.6	117.4	122.4	122.8	124.5
Percent met by private insurance	87.2	87.0	89.8	90.1	90.0	90.0	90.3	90.8	90.8
Physicians' services	31.8	57.8	86.7	96.7	107.3	120.3	124.0	128.4	133.9
Percent met by private insurance	53.9	57.8	62.1	64.1	66.8	68.2	69.7	70.9	72.5

[1] Includes nonpatient revenues and industrial inplant health services. [2] Includes expenditures not shown separately. Represents out-of-pocket payments and private health insurance benefits. Excludes net cost of insurance.

Source: U.S. Health Care Financing Administration, *Health Care Financing Review*, fall 1996.

No. 159. Personal Health Care Expenditures, by Object and Source of Payment: 1995

[In millions of dollars, except as indicated. Includes Puerto Rico and outlying areas. Covers all expenditures for health services and supplies, except net cost of insurance and administration, government public health activities, and expenditures of philanthropic agencies for fund raising activities]

OBJECT OF PAYMENT	Total	Out of pocket payments	THIRD PARTY PAYMENTS				Private payments [2]
			Total	Private health insurance	Government	Other [1]	
Total	878,777	182,563	696,214	276,756	392,119	27,339	486,658
Hospital care	350,120	11,414	338,706	113,074	214,303	11,329	135,817
Physicians' services	201,614	36,858	164,756	97,019	64,005	3,732	137,609
Dentists' services	45,833	21,848	23,985	21,986	1,829	169	44,004
Other professional services [3]	52,590	20,204	32,386	15,813	12,663	3,910	39,927
Home health care	28,573	6,004	22,569	3,340	15,792	3,437	12,781
Drugs/other medical nondurables	83,406	49,837	33,569	22,131	11,438	-	71,968
Vision products/other med. durables [3]	13,783	7,799	5,984	860	5,124	-	8,659
Nursing home care	77,877	28,599	49,278	2,532	45,273	1,472	32,604
Other health services	24,981	-	24,981	-	21,692	3,289	3,289
PERCENT DISTRIBUTION							
Total	100	21	79	31	45	3	55
Hospital care	100	3	97	32	61	3	39
Physicians' services	100	18	82	48	32	2	68
Dentists' services	100	48	52	48	4	-	96
Other professional services [3]	100	38	62	30	24	7	76
Home health care	100	21	79	12	55	12	45
Drugs/other medical nondurables	100	60	40	27	14	-	86
Vision products/other med. durables [3]	100	57	43	6	37	-	63
Nursing home care	100	37	63	3	58	2	42
Other health services	100	-	100	-	87	13	13

- Represents zero. [1] Includes nonpatient revenues and industrial plant. [2] Covers out-of-pocket payments, private health insurance, and other. [3] See footnotes for corresponding items on table 154.

Source: U.S. Health Care Financing Administration, *Health Care Financing Review*, fall 1996.

No. 160. Health Care Expenditures, by Type and State: 1993

[In millions of dollars. Expenditures are distributed by state where services are provided. These estimates differ from national health expenditures estimates shown in table 154]

STATE	Hospital care	Physician services	Purchases of prescription drugs [1]	STATE	Hospital care	Physician services	Purchases of prescription drugs [1]
U.S.	323,919	171,226	48,840	VA	7,031	3,769	1,343
				WV	2,346	968	412
N.E.	19,668	9,260	2,710	NC	7,801	3,717	1,392
ME	1,376	601	213	SC	4,221	1,665	665
NH	1,368	780	197	GA	8,704	4,543	1,397
VT	562	265	108	FL	17,131	10,496	2,832
MA	10,034	4,442	1,337	E.S.C.	19,921	8,913	3,402
RI	1,314	575	206	KY	4,515	2,036	846
CT	4,360	2,567	650	TN	7,206	3,137	1,153
M.A.	57,854	25,236	7,219	AL	5,301	2,631	904
NY	28,001	12,003	3,232	MS	2,897	1,107	499
NJ	10,312	5,776	1,601	W.S.C.	33,601	15,947	5,039
PA	19,540	7,460	2,386	AR	2,723	1,244	484
E.N.C.	54,172	26,275	8,360	LA	5,956	2,537	832
OH	14,305	7,118	2,095	OK	3,329	1,640	569
IN	6,998	3,263	1,106	TX	21,592	10,526	3,153
IL	15,621	6,970	2,206	Mt.	16,095	8,897	2,436
MI	11,711	5,562	2,054	MT	894	392	120
WI	5,537	3,362	899	ID	900	488	182
W.N.C.	22,252	10,967	3,196	WY	417	160	64
MN	4,796	3,617	739	CO	3,932	2,452	534
IA	3,111	1,376	516	NM	1,846	716	259
MO	7,652	2,958	975	AZ	3,999	2,799	728
ND	903	445	103	UT	1,743	864	302
SD	920	342	104	NV	1,362	1,029	246
NE	2,003	825	293	Pac.	45,259	36,677	7,067
KS	2,868	1,425	465	WA	5,305	3,720	853
S.A.	56,711	30,041	9,412	OR	2,966	1,904	431
DE	937	466	129	CA	34,827	28,981	5,501
MD	5,926	3,704	1,140	AK	701	301	85
DC	2,612	672	103	HI	1,460	771	197

[1] Covers spending for products purchased in retail outlets. The value of drugs and other products provided by hospitals, nursing homes, or other health professionals is included in estimates of spending for these providers' services.

Source: U.S. National Center for Health Statistics, *Health, United States, 1995.*

No. 161. Medicare Enrollees and Expenditures: 1980 to 1995

[Enrollment as of July 1. Includes Puerto Rico and outlying areas and enrollees in foreign countries and unknown place of residence]

ITEM	1980	1985	1990	1991	1992	1993	1994	1995
ENROLLEES (mil.)								
Total	28.5	31.1	34.2	34.9	35.6	36.3	36.9	37.5
Hospital insurance	28.1	30.6	33.7	34.4	35.2	35.9	36.5	37.1
Supplementary medical insurance	27.4	30.0	32.6	33.2	33.9	34.6	35.2	35.7
EXPENDITURES (mil. dol.)								
Total	36,802	72,294	110,984	121,447	135,845	150,370	163,087	181,483
Hospital insurance [1]	25,557	48,414	66,997	72,570	85,015	94,391	102,770	114,883
Inpatient hospital	24,116	44,940	59,451	62,777	71,147	76,402	80,786	87,503
Skilled nursing facility	395	548	2,575	2,652	4,119	5,780	7,056	9,142
Home health agency	540	1,913	3,666	5,327	7,579	10,049	12,136	14,895
Hospice	-	43	358	561	846	1,059	1,363	1,854
Supplementary medical insurance [1]	11,245	23,880	43,987	48,877	50,830	55,979	60,317	66,600
Physician	8,187	17,312	29,609	32,313	32,473	35,282	36,900	40,457
Outpatient hospital	1,897	4,319	8,482	9,783	10,894	11,539	14,034	15,405
Home health agency	234	38	74	65	79	112	154	182
Group practice prepayment	203	720	2,827	3,531	3,942	5,002	5,480	6,883
Independent laboratory	114	558	1,476	1,644	1,876	2,044	2,050	2,046

- Represents zero. [1] Includes administrative expenses and, for hospital insurance, peer review activity, not shown separately.

Source: U.S. Health Care Financing Administration, Office of the Actuary.

No. 162. Medicare—Persons Served and Reimbursements: 1990 to 1995

[Persons served are enrollees who use covered services, incurred expenses greater than the applicable deductible amounts and for whom Medicare paid benefits. Reimbursements are amounts paid to providers for covered services. Excluded are retroactive adjustments resulting from end of fiscal year cost settlements and certain lump-sum interim payments. Also excluded are beneficiary (or third party payor) liabilities for applicable deductibles, coinsurance amounts, and charges for noncovered services. Includes data for enrollees living in outlying territories and foreign countries]

TYPE OF COVERAGE AND SERVICE	Unit	PERSONS 65 YEARS OLD AND OVER			DISABLED PERSONS [1]		
		1990	1994	1995	1990	1994	1995
Persons served, total [2]	1,000	24,809	27,223	27,379	2,390	3,126	3,333
Hospital insurance [2]	1,000	6,367	7,043	7,147	680	879	933
Inpatient hospital	1,000	5,906	6,157	6,148	644	803	844
Skilled-nursing services	1,000	615	1,026	1,186	23	42	54
Home health services	1,000	1,818	2,938	3,165	122	237	272
Supplementary medical insurance [2]	1,000	24,687	27,075	27,234	2,365	3,094	3,299
Physicians' and other medical services	1,000	24,193	26,476	26,621	2,249	2,986	3,184
Outpatient services	1,000	14,055	16,969	17,597	1,496	2,097	2,281
Home health services	1,000	38	37	42	-	-	-
Persons served per 1,000 enrollees, total [2]	Rate	802	830	826	734	755	759
Hospital insurance [2]	Rate	209	217	218	209	213	212
Inpatient hospital	Rate	194	190	188	198	194	192
Skilled-nursing services	Rate	20	32	36	7	10	12
Home health services	Rate	60	91	97	38	57	62
Supplementary medical insurance [2]	Rate	832	861	858	804	831	837
Physicians' and other medical services	Rate	815	842	839	764	803	808
Outpatient services	Rate	474	540	554	506	564	579
Home health services	Rate	1	1	1	-	-	-
Reimbursements, total	Mil. dol	88,778	129,033	138,948	11,239	18,818	21,024
Per person served	Dollars	3,578	4,740	5,075	4,703	6,021	6,308
Hospital insurance	Mil. dol	54,244	83,072	89,631	6,694	11,501	12,752
Inpatient hospital	Mil. dol	48,952	65,722	68,213	6,346	10,230	11,079
Skilled-nursing services	Mil. dol	1,886	5,735	7,504	85	258	374
Home health services	Mil. dol	3,406	11,614	13,914	264	1,013	1,300
Supplementary medical insurance	Mil. dol	34,533	45,961	49,317	4,545	7,317	8,272
Physicians' and other medical services	Mil. dol	27,379	34,408	37,069	2,831	4,321	4,888
Outpatient services	Mil. dol	7,077	11,395	12,045	1,714	2,996	3,384
Home health services	Mil. dol	78	158	203	-	-	-

- Represents or rounds to zero. [1] Age under 65; includes persons enrolled because of end-stage renal disease (ESRD) only. [2] Persons are counted once for each type of covered service used, but are not double counted in totals.

Source: U.S. Health Care Financing Administration, *Medicare Program Statistics*, annual; and unpublished data.

No. 163. Medicare—Utilization and Charges: 1980 to 1995

[Fiscal year data, except as indicated. Data reflect date expense was incurred based on bills submitted for payment and recorded in Health Care Financing Administration central records through September 1996. Includes Puerto Rico, Virgin Islands, Guam, other outlying areas, and enrollees in foreign countries]

ITEM	Unit	PERSONS 65 YEARS OLD AND OVER				DISABLED PERSONS [1]			
		1980	1990	1994	1995	1980	1990	1994	1995
Hospital inpatient care:									
Admissions [2]	1,000	9,258	9,216	10,399	10,574	1,271	1,257	1,418	1,442
Per 1,000 enrollees [3]	Rate	369	309	317	323	429	396	343	328
Covered days of care	Millions	98	82	79	76	13	11	11	10
Per 1,000 enrollees [3]	Rate	3,885	2,702	2,408	2,313	4,549	3,464	2,680	2,351
Per admission	Days	10.5	8.9	7.6	7.2	10.6	8.8	7.8	7.2
Hospital covered charges	Mil. dol.	26,615	90,846	133,591	138,469	4,087	11,910	18,217	18,885
Per covered day	Dollars	293	1,104	1,691	1,828	303	1,083	1,656	1,828
Percent of covered charges reimbursed [4]	Percent	70.0	47.5	48.9	47.5	68.6	46.5	48.9	47.5
Physician allowed charges [5]	Mil. dol.	9,011	30,447	38,151	41,409	1,112	2,907	5,202	5,647
Percent reimbursed	Percent	78.0	77.0	76.2	76.2	78.7	75.7	76.2	76.2

[1] Disabled persons under age 65 and persons enrolled solely because of end-stage renal disease. [2] Beginning 1990, represents number of discharges and includes pass-through amounts, except for kidney acquisition. [3] Based on Hospital Insurance (HI) enrollment as of July 1. [4] Prior to 1990, billing reimbursements exclude: (1) PPS pass-through amounts for capital, direct medical education, kidney acquisitions, and bad debts by Medicare patients; (2) certain lump-sum interim payments. All years exclude retroactive adjustments resulting from end-of-fiscal year cost reports. [5] Calendar year data.

Source: U.S. Health Care Financing Administration, unpublished data.

No. 164. Medicare—Summary, by State and Other Areas: 1995 and 1996

STATE AND AREA	ENROLLMENT [1] (1,000)		PAYMENTS [2] (mil. dol)		STATE AND AREA	ENROLLMENT [1] (1,000)		PAYMENTS [2] (mil. dol)	
	1995	1996	1995	1996		1995	1996	1995	1996
All areas	**37,496**	**37,980**	**176,884**	**191,178**	MO	832	838	3,821	4,122
U.S.	**36,703**	**37,169**	**175,976**	**190,187**	MT	130	132	489	470
					NE	249	250	840	934
AL	641	651	3,042	3,349	NV	192	202	894	1,004
AK	34	35	133	156	NH	156	159	597	653
AZ	597	614	2,717	2,950	NJ	1,169	1,177	5,603	5,958
AR	422	427	1,638	1,749	NM	211	216	710	799
CA	3,633	3,690	20,406	21,688	NY	2,639	2,653	13,904	14,660
CO	421	432	1,835	2,022	NC	1,025	1,049	4,276	4,689
CT	502	506	2,584	2,811	ND	103	103	412	438
DE	100	103	445	474	OH	1,666	1,676	7,262	7,870
DC	78	77	1,164	1,207	OK	487	492	2,178	2,472
FL	2,610	2,655	14,828	16,046	OR	467	472	1,685	1,801
GA	832	849	4,090	4,444	PA	2,069	2,078	10,796	11,468
HI	149	153	580	612	RI	168	169	772	867
ID	150	153	463	523	SC	508	520	1,926	2,144
IL	1,617	1,623	7,276	7,792	SD	117	117	563	447
IN	823	830	3,491	3,770	TN	770	783	4,063	4,487
IA	474	475	1,527	1,642	TX	2,076	2,117	11,504	12,733
KS	383	385	1,545	1,631	UT	187	191	708	813
KY	586	596	2,401	2,610	VT	83	84	284	306
LA	580	586	3,448	3,938	VA	817	833	2,979	3,277
ME	202	205	707	791	WA	687	699	2,603	2,826
MD	601	610	2,868	3,005	WV	329	331	1,208	1,373
MA	933	942	5,496	5,884	WI	761	767	2,673	2,909
MI	1,348	1,361	6,237	6,566	WY	60	61	180	198
MN	631	636	2,378	2,593	PR	477	490	875	953
MS	397	402	1,723	2,016	Other areas	317	321	33	36

[1] Hospital and/or medical insurance enrollment as of September. [2] Benefit payments for all areas represent 100% fee for service experience and actual HMO expenditures through the fiscal year and relate to the State of the provider.

Source: U.S. Health Care Financing Administration, unpublished data.

No. 165. Medicaid—Summary, by State and Other Areas: 1994 and 1995

[Data are for fiscal years]

STATE AND AREA	RECIPIENTS [1] (1,000)		PAYMENTS [2] (mil. dol)		STATE AND AREA	RECIPIENTS [1] (1,000)		PAYMENTS [2] (mil. dol)	
	1994	1995	1994	1995		1994	1995	1994	1995
All areas	**35,053**	**36,282**	**108,270**	**120,141**	MO	669	695	1,809	2,039
U.S.	**34,110**	**35,210**	**108,029**	**119,885**	MT	96	99	303	326
					NE	164	168	593	608
AL	544	539	1,312	1,455	NV	95	105	307	350
AK	69	68	243	252	NH	86	97	389	473
AZ	510	494	199	218	NJ	790	790	3,612	3,813
AR	340	353	1,253	1,376	NM	268	287	638	714
CA	5,008	5,017	9,988	10,521	NY	2,908	3,035	18,731	22,086
CO	289	294	952	1,063	NC	965	1,084	2,685	3,175
CT	354	380	1,943	2,125	ND	63	61	284	297
DE	75	79	277	324	OH	1,523	1,533	4,995	5,585
DC	127	138	550	532	OK	391	394	974	1,056
FL	1,727	1,735	4,266	4,802	OR	411	452	1,036	1,327
GA	1,085	1,147	2,845	3,076	PA	1,255	1,230	4,224	4,633
HI	121	52	336	258	RI	115	135	685	673
ID	110	115	331	360	SC	486	496	1,396	1,438
IL	1,441	1,552	4,826	5,600	SD	72	74	284	305
IN	605	559	2,250	1,878	TN	939	1,466	1,965	2,772
IA	303	304	982	1,036	TX	2,514	2,562	6,141	6,565
KS	252	256	782	831	UT	157	160	451	464
KY	638	641	1,779	1,945	VT	94	100	259	320
LA	778	785	2,684	2,708	VA	643	681	1,723	1,833
ME	177	153	807	760	WA	668	639	1,574	1,461
MD	415	414	1,875	2,019	WV	367	389	1,107	1,169
MA	710	728	3,052	3,972	WI	474	460	1,830	1,894
MI	1,187	1,168	3,274	3,409	WY	51	51	157	171
MN	426	473	1,982	2,550	PR	927	1,055	233	244
MS	537	520	1,090	1,266	Virgin Islands	16	17	8	12

[1] Persons who had payments made on their behalf at any time during the fiscal year. [2] Payments are for fiscal year and reflect Federal and state contribution payments. Data exclude disproportionate hospital share payments.

Source: U.S. Health Care Financing Administration, unpublished data.

No. 166. Medicaid—Selected Utilization Measures: 1980 to 1995

[In thousands. For fiscal years ending in year shown. Includes Virgin Islands. See text, section 3]

MEASURE	1980	1985	1990	1991	1992	1993	1994	1995
General hospitals:								
Recipients discharged	2,255	2,390	3,261	3,638	3,866	4,050	3,890	3,743
Total days of care	24,089	29,562	27,471	28,998	29,921	31,095	28,941	25,711
Nursing facilities: [1]								
Total recipients	1,395	1,375	1,461	1,500	1,573	1,610	1,639	1,667
Total days of care	273,497	277,996	360,044	367,621	406,191	422,965	400,785	400,123
Intermediate care facilities: [2]								
Total recipients	121	147	146	146	151	149	159	151
Total days of care	250,124	47,324	49,730	50,223	53,538	44,952	54,105	56,876

[1] Includes skilled nursing facilities and intermediate care facilities for all other than the mentally retarded. [2] Mentally retarded.

Source: U.S. Health Care Financing Administration, Bureau of Data Management and Strategy, Division of Program Systems, *Statistical Report on Medical Care: Eligibles, Recipients, Payments, and Services.*

No. 167. Medicaid—Selected Characteristics of Persons Covered: 1990 to 1995

[In thousands, except percent. Represents number of persons as of March of following year who were enrolled at any time in year shown. Person did not have to receive medical care paid for by Medicaid in order to be counted. See headnote, table 563]

POVERTY STATUS	1990	1994	1995							
			Total [1]	White	Black	Hispanic [2]	Under 18 years old	18-44 years old	45-64 years old	65 years and over
Persons covered, total	24,160	31,401	31,621	20,385	9,083	6,442	16,268	9,362	3,172	2,820
Below poverty level	15,175	17,578	16,900	9,788	5,983	4,088	9,522	4,845	1,534	998
Above poverty level	8,985	13,823	14,721	10,597	3,100	2,354	6,746	4,517	1,638	1,822
Percent of population covered	9.7	12.0	12.0	9.3	28.9	22.7	23.1	8.6	6.0	8.9
Below poverty level	45.2	46.2	46.4	40.1	60.6	47.7	64.9	35.1	33.1	30.1
Above poverty level	4.2	8.2	6.5	5.5	13.0	11.9	12.1	4.8	3.4	6.4

[1] Includes other races not shown separately. [2] Persons of Hispanic origin may be of any race.

Source: U.S. Bureau of the Census, *Current Population Reports*, P60-195, earlier reports; and unpublished data.

No. 168. Medicaid—Recipients and Payments: 1980 to 1995

[For fiscal year ending in year shown; see text, section 10. Includes Puerto Rico and outlying areas. Medical vendor payments are those made directly to suppliers of medical care]

BASIS OF ELIGIBILITY AND TYPE OF SERVICE	RECIPIENTS (1,000)					PAYMENTS (mil. dol.)				
	1980	1985	1990	1994	1995	1980	1985	1990	1994	1995
Total [1]	21,605	21,814	25,255	35,053	36,282	23,311	37,508	64,859	108,270	120,141
Age 65 and over	3,440	3,061	3,202	4,035	4,119	8,739	14,096	21,508	33,618	36,527
Blindness	92	80	83	86	92	124	249	434	644	848
Disabled [2]	2,819	2,937	3,635	5,372	5,767	7,497	13,203	23,969	41,654	48,570
AFDC [3] program	14,210	15,275	17,230	24,780	24,767	6,354	9,160	17,690	30,887	31,487
Other and unknown	1,499	1,214	1,105	779	1,537	596	798	1,257	1,467	2,708
Inpatient services in—										
General hospital	3,680	3,434	4,593	5,866	5,561	6,412	9,453	16,674	26,180	26,331
Mental hospital	66	60	92	85	84	775	1,192	1,714	2,057	2,511
Intermediate care facilities:										
Mentally retarded	121	147	147	159	151	1,989	4,731	7,354	8,347	10,383
Nursing facility services [4]	1,396	1,375	1,461	1,639	1,667	7,887	11,587	17,693	27,095	29,052
Physicians	13,765	14,387	17,078	24,267	23,789	1,875	2,346	4,018	7,189	7,360
Dental	4,652	4,672	4,552	6,352	6,383	462	458	593	969	1,019
Other practitioner	3,234	3,357	3,873	5,409	5,528	198	251	372	1,040	986
Outpatient hospital	9,705	10,072	12,370	16,567	16,712	1,101	1,789	3,324	6,342	6,627
Clinic	1,531	2,121	2,804	5,258	5,322	320	714	1,688	3,747	4,280
Laboratory [5]	3,212	6,354	8,959	13,412	13,064	121	337	721	1,176	1,180
Home health	392	535	719	1,293	1,639	332	1,120	3,404	7,042	9,406
Prescribed drugs	13,707	13,921	17,294	24,470	23,723	1,318	2,315	4,420	8,875	9,791
Family planning	1,129	1,636	1,752	2,566	2,501	81	195	265	516	514

[1] Recipient data do not add due to small number of recipients that are reported in more than one category. Includes recipients of, and payments for, other care not shown separately. [2] Permanently and totally. [3] Aid to families with dependent children. [4] Nursing facility services includes skilled nursing facility services and intermediate care facility services for all other than the mentally retarded. [5] Includes radiological services.

Source: U.S. Health Care Financing Administration, *Health Care Financing Review*, quarterly.

No. 169. Consumer Price Indexes of Medical Care Prices: 1980 to 1996

[1982-1984=100. Indexes are annual averages of monthly data based on components of consumer price index for all urban consumers; for explanation, see text, section 15]

YEAR	Medical care	MEDICAL CARE SERVICES: Total [1]	Professional services: Total [1]	Professional services: Physicians	Professional services: Dental	Hospital room	Medical care commodities	ANNUAL PERCENT CHANGE [2]: Medical care	Medical care services: Total [1]	Medical care services: Physicians	Medical care services: Dental	Medical care services: Hospital room	Medical care commodities
1980	74.9	74.8	77.9	76.5	78.9	68.0	75.4	11.0	11.3	10.5	11.9	13.1	9.3
1985	113.5	113.2	113.5	113.3	114.2	115.4	115.2	6.3	6.1	5.9	6.2	5.9	7.2
1988	138.6	138.3	137.5	139.8	137.5	143.3	139.9	6.5	6.4	7.2	6.8	9.3	6.8
1989	149.3	148.9	146.4	150.1	146.1	158.1	150.8	7.7	7.7	7.4	6.3	10.3	7.8
1990	162.8	162.7	156.1	160.8	155.8	175.4	163.4	9.0	9.3	7.1	6.6	10.9	8.4
1991	177.0	177.1	165.7	170.5	167.4	191.9	176.8	8.7	8.9	6.0	7.4	9.4	8.2
1992	190.1	190.5	175.8	181.2	178.7	208.7	188.1	7.4	7.6	6.3	6.8	8.8	6.4
1993	201.4	202.9	184.7	191.3	188.1	226.4	195.0	5.9	6.5	5.6	5.3	8.5	3.7
1994	211.0	213.4	192.5	199.8	197.1	239.2	200.7	4.8	5.2	4.4	4.8	5.7	2.9
1995	220.5	224.2	201.0	208.8	208.8	251.2	204.5	4.5	5.1	4.5	4.9	5.0	1.9
1996	228.2	232.4	208.3	216.4	216.5	261.0	210.4	3.5	3.7	3.6	4.7	3.9	2.9

[1] Includes other services not shown separately. [2] Percent change from the immediate prior year.

Source: U.S. Bureau of Labor Statistics, *CPI Detailed Report,* January 1997.

No. 170. Average Annual Expenditures per Consumer Unit for Health Care: 1985 to 1995

[In dollars, except percent. See text, section 14, and headnote, table 712. For composition of regions, see table 26]

ITEM	HEALTH CARE, TOTAL: Amount	HEALTH CARE, TOTAL: Percent of total expenditures	Health insurance	Medical services	Drugs and medical supplies [1]	PERCENT DISTRIBUTION: Health insurance	Medical services	Drugs and medical supplies [1]
1985	1,108	4.7	375	496	238	33.8	44.8	21.5
1988	1,298	5.0	474	529	294	36.5	40.8	22.7
1989	1,407	5.1	537	542	327	38.2	38.5	23.2
1990	1,480	5.2	581	562	337	39.3	38.0	22.8
1991	1,554	5.2	656	555	344	42.2	35.7	22.1
1992	1,634	5.5	725	533	375	44.4	32.6	22.9
1993	1,776	5.8	800	574	402	45.0	32.3	22.6
1994	1,755	5.5	815	571	369	46.4	32.5	21.0
1995	1,732	5.4	860	511	360	49.7	29.5	20.8
Age of reference person:								
Under 25 years old	465	2.5	209	157	99	44.9	33.8	21.3
25 to 34 years old	1,096	3.5	517	380	199	47.2	34.7	18.2
35 to 44 years old	1,609	4.2	726	596	286	45.1	37.0	17.8
45 to 54 years old	1,850	4.4	817	664	369	44.2	35.9	19.9
55 to 64 years old	1,909	5.9	896	587	427	46.9	30.7	22.4
65 to 74 years old	2,617	10.3	1,528	471	618	58.4	18.0	23.6
75 years old and over	2,683	14.4	1,557	487	639	58.0	18.2	23.8
Origin of reference person: Hispanic	1,055	3.9	477	394	184	45.2	37.3	17.4
Non-Hispanic	1,790	5.5	893	521	375	49.9	29.1	20.9
Black	1,057	4.5	572	223	262	54.1	21.1	24.8
Other	1,878	5.5	932	557	389	49.6	29.7	20.7
Region of residence:								
Northeast	1,757	5.3	890	541	325	50.7	30.8	18.5
Midwest	1,759	5.5	890	479	390	50.6	27.2	22.2
South	1,790	5.9	907	483	399	50.7	27.0	22.3
West	1,584	4.5	720	567	296	45.5	35.8	18.7
Size of consumer unit:								
One person	1,109	5.7	560	308	241	50.5	27.8	21.7
Two or more persons	1,977	5.3	979	591	407	49.5	29.9	20.6
Two persons	2,126	6.4	1,132	511	482	53.2	24.0	22.7
Three persons	1,775	4.7	826	588	361	46.5	33.1	20.3
Four persons	1,969	4.6	924	701	345	46.9	35.6	17.5
Five persons or more	1,856	4.5	828	686	342	44.6	37.0	18.4
Income before taxes:								
Complete income reporters [2]	1,747	5.2	864	502	380	49.5	28.7	21.8
Quintiles of income:								
Lowest 20 percent	1,111	7.6	565	259	288	50.9	23.3	25.9
Second 20 percent	1,603	7.2	851	358	395	53.1	22.3	24.6
Third 20 percent	1,687	5.8	871	441	374	51.6	26.1	22.2
Fourth 20 percent	1,912	4.9	971	568	373	50.8	29.7	19.5
Highest 20 percent	2,417	3.9	1,063	881	473	44.0	36.5	19.6
Incomplete reporters of income	1,683	6.2	644	552	286	50.1	32.8	17.0

[1] Includes prescription and nonprescription drugs. [2] A complete reporter is a consumer unit providing values for at least one of the major sources of income.

Source: Bureau of Labor Statistics, *Consumer Expenditure Survey,* annual.

No. 171. Health Insurance Coverage Status, by Selected Characteristics: 1987 to 1995

[Persons as of following year for coverage in the year shown. Government health insurance includes Medicare, Medicaid, and military plans. Based on Current Population Survey; see text, section 1, and Appendix III]

CHARACTERISTIC	NUMBER (mil.)							PERCENT			
	Total persons	Covered by private or Government health insurance					Not covered by health insurance	Covered by private or Government health insurance			Not covered by health insurance
		Total [1]	Private		Government						
			Total	Group health [2]	Medicare	Medicaid		Total [1]	Private	Medicaid	
1987	241.2	210.2	182.2	149.7	30.5	20.2	31.0	87.1	75.5	8.4	12.9
1988	243.7	211.0	182.0	150.9	30.9	20.7	32.7	86.6	74.7	8.5	13.4
1989	246.2	212.8	183.6	151.6	31.5	21.2	33.4	86.4	74.6	8.6	13.6
1990	248.9	214.2	182.1	150.2	32.3	24.3	34.7	86.1	73.2	9.7	13.9
1991	251.4	216.0	181.4	150.1	32.9	26.9	35.4	85.9	72.1	10.7	14.1
1992 [3]	256.8	218.2	181.5	148.8	33.2	29.4	38.6	85.0	70.7	11.5	15.0
1993 [3]	259.8	220.0	182.4	148.3	33.1	31.7	39.7	84.7	70.2	12.2	15.3
1994 [3]	262.1	222.4	184.3	159.6	33.9	31.6	39.7	84.8	70.3	12.1	15.2
1995, total [3] [4]	**264.3**	**223.7**	**185.9**	**161.5**	**34.7**	**31.9**	**40.6**	**84.6**	**70.3**	**12.1**	**15.4**
Age: Under 18 years	71.1	61.4	47.0	43.8	0.3	16.5	9.8	86.2	66.1	23.2	13.8
18 to 24 years	24.8	17.8	15.0	12.5	0.1	3.0	7.0	71.8	60.2	12.1	28.2
25 to 34 years	40.9	31.6	27.9	26.0	0.4	3.5	9.4	77.1	68.3	8.5	22.9
35 to 44 years	43.1	35.9	32.8	30.6	0.8	2.9	7.1	83.4	76.2	6.6	16.6
45 to 54 years	31.6	27.4	25.3	23.3	0.9	1.8	4.2	86.7	80.0	5.6	13.3
55 to 64 years	21.1	18.3	16.1	14.1	1.7	1.4	2.8	86.7	76.5	6.7	13.3
65 years and over	31.7	31.4	21.8	11.1	30.5	2.8	0.3	99.1	68.7	8.9	0.9
Sex: Male	129.1	107.5	91.3	80.7	14.9	13.4	21.6	83.2	70.7	10.4	16.8
Female	135.2	116.2	94.6	80.7	19.8	18.5	18.9	86.0	70.0	13.7	14.0
Race: White	218.4	187.3	161.3	139.2	30.6	20.5	31.1	85.8	73.8	9.4	14.2
Black	33.9	26.8	17.1	15.7	3.3	9.2	7.1	79.0	50.5	27.1	21.0
Hispanic origin [5]	28.4	19.0	12.2	11.3	1.7	6.5	9.5	66.7	42.9	22.8	33.3

[1] Includes other Government insurance, not shown separately. Persons with coverage counted only once in total, even though they may have been covered by more that one type of policy. [2] Related to employment of self or other family members. [3] Beginning 1992, data based on 1990 census adjusted population controls. [4] Includes other races not shown separately. [5] Persons of Hispanic origin may be of any race.

Source: U.S. Bureau of the Census; "Health Insurance Coverage: 1995 - Table B;" published 26 September 1996; <http://www.census.gov/hhes/hlthins/cover95/c95tabb.html>; and unpublished data.

No. 172. Persons With and Without Health Insurance Coverage, by State: 1995

[Based on the Current Population Survey and subject to sampling error; see text, section 1, and Appendix III]

STATE	Persons covered (1,000)	PERSONS NOT COVERED		STATE	Persons covered (1,000)	PERSONS NOT COVERED	
		Number (1,000)	Percent of total			Number (1,000)	Percent of total
United States	**223,733**	**40,582**	**15.4**	Missouri	4,416	756	14.6
Alabama	3,804	595	13.5	Montana	762	111	12.7
Alaska	552	79	12.5	Nebraska	1,504	149	9.0
Arizona	3,461	885	20.4	Nevada	1,271	292	18.7
Arkansas	2,079	454	17.9	New Hampshire	1,027	114	10.0
California	25,517	6,601	20.6	New Jersey	6,782	1,121	14.2
Colorado	3,246	564	14.8	New Mexico	1,344	463	25.6
Connecticut	2,996	289	8.8	New York	15,522	2,779	15.2
Delaware	602	112	15.7	North Carolina	5,951	996	14.3
District of Columbia	459	96	17.3	North Dakota	585	53	8.3
Florida	11,724	2,628	18.3	Ohio	9,894	1,336	11.9
Georgia	5,966	1,301	17.9	Oklahoma	2,591	615	19.2
Hawaii	1,082	106	8.9	Oregon	2,817	403	12.5
Idaho	993	161	14.0	Pennsylvania	10,849	1,195	9.9
Illinois	10,504	1,294	11.0	Rhode Island	839	124	12.9
Indiana	4,972	716	12.6	South Carolina	3,205	546	14.6
Iowa	2,569	327	11.3	South Dakota	649	67	9.4
Kansas	2,223	316	12.4	Tennessee	4,669	814	14.8
Kentucky	3,327	567	14.6	Texas	14,190	4,615	24.5
Louisiana	3,428	885	20.5	Utah	1,767	235	11.7
Maine	1,060	166	13.5	Vermont	519	79	13.2
Maryland	4,350	783	15.3	Virginia	5,521	862	13.5
Massachusetts	5,400	671	11.1	Washington	4,759	676	12.4
Michigan	8,706	938	9.7	West Virginia	1,523	276	15.3
Minnesota	4,260	370	8.0	Wisconsin	4,930	391	7.3
Mississippi	2,159	531	19.7	Wyoming	406	77	15.9

Source: U.S. Bureau of the Census; "Health Insurance Coverage: 1995 - Table 2;" published 26 September 1996; <http://www.census.gov/hhes/hlthins/cover95/c95tab2.html>.

No. 173. Health Maintenance Organizations (HMO's): 1980 to 1995

[As of January 1, except as noted. An HMO is a prepaid health plan delivering comprehensive care to members through designated providers, having a fixed periodic payment for health care services, and requiring members to be in a plan for a specified period of time (usually 1 year). A group HMO delivers health services through a physician group that is controlled by the HMO unit or contracts with one or more independent group practices to provide health services. An individual practice association (IPA) HMO contracts directly with physicians in independent practice, and/or contracts with one or more associations of physicians in independent practice, and/or contracts with one or more multispecialty group practices. Data are based on a census of HMO's. For composition of regions, see table 26]

TYPE OF PRACTICE AND SIZE	1980 (June 30)	1985 (Dec. 31)	1989	1990	1991	1992	1993	1994	1995
NUMBER OF PLANS									
Total	**235**	**478**	**604**	**572**	**553**	**555**	**551**	**540**	**550**
Model type:									
I.P.A	97	244	385	360	346	340	332	319	323
Network	138	234	219	212	168	166	150	117	107
Mixed	(NA)	(NA)	(NA)	(NA)	39	49	69	104	120
Region:									
Northeast	55	81	118	115	116	111	102	101	99
Midwest	72	157	183	160	157	165	169	159	154
South	45	141	172	176	163	161	167	173	190
West	63	99	131	121	117	118	113	107	107
ENROLLMENT [1] (mil.)									
Total	**9.1**	**21.0**	**31.9**	**33.0**	**34.0**	**36.1**	**38.4**	**42.2**	**46.2**
Model type:									
I.P.A	1.7	6.4	13.5	13.7	13.6	14.7	15.3	16.1	17.4
Group	7.4	14.6	18.3	19.3	17.1	16.5	15.4	13.6	12.9
Mixed	(NA)	(NA)	(NA)	(NA)	3.3	4.9	7.7	12.5	15.9
Federal program: [2]									
Medicaid [3]	0.3	0.6	1.0	1.2	1.4	1.7	1.7	2.6	3.5
Medicare	0.4	1.1	1.8	1.8	2.0	2.2	2.2	2.5	2.9

NA Not available. [1] Excludes enrollees participating in open-ended plans. [2] Refers to enrollment by Medicaid or Medicare beneficiaries, where the program contracts directly with the HMO to pay the appropriate annual premium. [3] Data for 1989 and later include enrollment in managed care health insuring organizations. Enrollment for 1989 and 1990 as of June 30.

Source: Interstudy, Minneapolis, MN, *The InterStudy Competitive Edge, 1995*, vol. 5, No. 2, and earlier publications (copyright); and U.S. National Center for Health Statistics, *Health United States, 1995*, 1996.

No. 174. Annual Receipts/Revenue for the Health Service Industries: 1990 to 1995

[In millions of dollars. Unless otherwise noted, receipts estimates are obtained from a sample of employer and nonemployer firms. Revenue estimates are obtained from a sample of employer firms only]

INDUSTRY	1987 SIC code [1]	1990	1991	1992	1993	1994	1995
TAXABLE FIRMS—RECEIPTS							
Health services [2]	80	271,212	293,907	321,653	337,233	355,189	382,553
Offices and clinics of MD's	801	128,871	138,576	151,824	154,826	160,809	170,327
Offices and clinics of dentists	802	31,502	33,279	36,939	39,145	42,084	45,617
Offices and clinics of doctors of osteopathy	803	3,254	3,584	4,008	4,088	4,209	4,496
Offices and clinics of other practitioners [2]	804	20,139	21,449	23,893	25,184	25,450	26,630
Offices and clinics of chiropractors	8041	5,467	5,647	6,555	7,118	7,151	7,315
Offices and clinics of optometrists	8042	4,799	5,028	5,333	5,696	5,979	6,053
Offices and clinics of podiatrists	8043	1,811	1,957	2,102	2,188	2,258	2,499
Nursing and personal care facilities	805	30,162	32,862	34,743	37,422	39,570	44,175
Hospitals [3]	806	26,487	28,807	31,083	32,894	34,103	36,694
General medical and surgical hospitals [3]	8062	20,442	22,220	24,162	26,070	26,658	28,565
Psychiatric hospitals [3]	8063	4,129	4,402	4,396	3,935	4,126	4,378
Specialty hospitals, except psychiatric [3]	8069	1,916	2,185	2,525	2,889	3,319	3,751
Medical and dental laboratories	807	12,033	13,567	15,172	16,186	17,757	19,246
Medical laboratories	8071	9,996	11,458	12,882	13,886	15,401	16,718
Dental laboratories	8072	2,037	2,109	2,290	2,300	2,356	2,528
Home health care services	808	7,556	9,129	11,208	13,026	15,042	17,523
Miscellaneous allied services, n.e.c. [2] [4]	809	11,208	12,654	12,783	14,462	16,165	17,843
Kidney dialysis centers	8092	1,451	1,717	2,140	2,483	2,932	3,326
Specialty outpatient facilities, n.e.c. [4]	8093	5,326	6,508	6,476	7,022	8,013	8,825
TAX EXEMPT FIRMS—REVENUE [3]							
Selected health services [2]	80 pt.	267,858	298,168	324,416	343,916	360,492	380,680
Offices and clinics of doctors of medicine	801	12,888	14,744	16,548	19,126	20,662	22,810
Nursing and personal care facilities	805	12,132	13,628	15,221	16,618	17,951	19,801
Hospitals	806	233,615	259,188	279,736	293,255	304,809	319,664
General medical and surgical hospitals	8062	210,503	234,056	254,391	266,997	277,468	291,179
Psychiatric hospitals	8063	11,008	11,461	10,933	11,141	11,605	11,815
Specialty hospitals, exc. psychiatric	8069	12,104	13,671	14,412	15,117	15,736	16,670
Home health care services	808	3,874	4,624	5,714	6,827	7,944	8,822
Miscellaneous allied services, n.e.c. [2] [4]	809	5,285	5,915	7,123	8,010	9,040	9,695
Kidney dialysis centers	8092	305	357	400	455	510	592
Specialty outpatient facilities, n.e.c. [4]	8093	3,519	3,834	4,437	4,720	5,285	5,804

[1] Based on the 1987 Standard Industrial Classification code; see text, section 13. [2] Includes other industries not shown separately. [3] Estimates are obtained from a sample of employer firms only. [4] N.e.c. means not elsewhere classified.

Source: U.S. Bureau of the Census, *Current Business Reports, Service Annual Survey: 1995*, BS/95.

No. 175. Employment in the Health Service Industries: 1980 to 1996

[In thousands. See headnote table 662]

INDUSTRY	1987 SIC code [1]	1980	1985	1990	1994	1995	1996
Health services [2]	80	5,278	6,293	7,814	8,992	9,257	9,566
Offices and clinics of MD's	801	802	1,028	1,338	1,545	1,606	1,672
Offices and clinics of dentists	802	(NA)	439	513	574	597	625
Offices and clinics of other practitioners	804	96	165	277	378	407	446
Nursing and personal care facilities	805	997	1,198	1,415	1,649	1,693	1,742
Skilled nursing care facilities	8051	(NA)	791	989	1,221	1,252	1,287
Intermediate care facilities	8052	(NA)	(NA)	200	206	213	219
Other, n.e.c. [3]	8059	(NA)	(NA)	227	222	229	235
Hospitals	806	2,750	2,997	3,549	3,763	3,784	3,852
General medical and surgical hospitals	8062	(NA)	2,811	3,268	3,459	3,484	3,551
Psychiatric hospitals	8063	(NA)	59	104	97	91	89
Specialty hospitals, exc. psychiatric	8069	(NA)	126	176	207	208	211
Medical and dental laboratories	807	(NA)	119	166	189	193	209
Home health care services	808	(NA)	(NA)	291	559	626	656

NA Not available. [1] Based on the 1987 Standard Industrial Classification code; see text, section 13. [2] Includes other industries not shown separately. [3] N.e.c. means not elsewhere classified.

Source: U.S. Bureau of Labor Statistics, Bulletins 2445 and 2481, and *Employment and Earnings*, monthly, March and June issues.

No. 176. Physicians, by Selected Activity: 1980 to 1995

[In thousands. 1980, 1985, and 1990, as of Dec. 31; other years as of Jan. 1, except as noted. Includes Puerto Rico and outlying areas]

ACTIVITY	1980	1985	1990	1992	1993	1994	1995
Doctors of medicine, total	**467.7**	**552.7**	**615.4**	**653.1**	**670.3**	**684.4**	**720.3**
Professionally active	435.5	511.1	560.0	594.7	605.7	619.8	646.0
Place of medical education:							
U.S. medical graduates	343.6	398.4	437.2	460.4	466.6	475.0	492.2
Foreign medical graduates [1]	91.8	112.7	122.8	134.3	139.1	144.8	153.8
Sex: Male	386.7	436.3	463.9	484.6	488.5	494.9	505.9
Female	48.7	74.8	96.1	110.1	117.2	124.9	140.1
Active Non-Federal	417.7	489.5	539.5	575.5	584.0	597.3	624.9
Patient care	361.9	431.5	487.8	520.2	531.7	543.2	564.1
Office-based practice	271.3	329.0	359.9	387.9	398.8	407.0	427.3
General and family practice	47.8	53.9	57.6	58.6	58.1	58.2	59.9
Cardiovascular diseases	6.7	9.1	10.7	11.4	12.1	12.9	13.7
Dermatology	4.4	5.3	6.0	6.3	6.5	6.7	7.0
Gastroenterology	2.7	4.1	5.2	5.7	6.3	6.7	7.3
Internal medicine	40.5	52.7	57.8	65.1	67.3	67.9	72.6
Pediatrics	17.4	22.4	26.5	29.0	30.8	31.5	33.9
Pulmonary diseases	2.0	3.0	3.7	4.0	4.4	4.6	5.0
General surgery	22.4	24.7	24.5	24.9	24.3	24.2	24.1
Obstetrics and gynecology	19.5	23.5	25.5	27.1	27.6	28.2	29.1
Ophthalmology	10.6	12.2	13.1	13.7	13.9	14.3	14.6
Orthopedic surgery	10.7	13.0	14.2	15.8	16.3	16.6	17.1
Otolaryngology	5.3	5.8	6.4	6.6	6.7	6.9	7.1
Plastic surgery	2.4	3.3	3.8	4.0	4.1	4.3	4.6
Urological surgery	6.2	7.1	7.4	7.7	7.8	7.8	8.0
Anesthesiology	11.3	15.3	17.8	20.0	20.6	22.0	23.8
Diagnostic radiology	4.2	7.7	9.8	10.9	11.9	12.1	12.8
Emergency medicine	(NA)	(NA)	8.4	9.4	9.8	10.6	11.7
Neurology	3.2	4.7	5.6	6.3	6.8	7.1	7.6
Pathology, anatomical/clinical	6.0	6.9	7.3	7.9	8.5	8.7	9.0
Psychiatry	15.9	18.5	20.0	21.8	22.3	22.6	23.3
Other specialty	31.9	35.8	26.8	31.7	32.4	33.2	36.0
Hospital-based practice	90.6	102.5	127.9	132.3	132.9	136.1	136.8
Residents and interns [2]	59.6	72.2	89.9	92.2	89.0	91.5	93.7
Full-time hospital staff	31.0	30.3	38.0	40.1	43.9	44.6	43.1
Other professional activity [3]	35.2	44.0	39.0	38.7	37.7	39.9	40.3
Not classified	20.6	14.0	12.7	16.6	14.7	14.3	20.6
Federal	17.8	21.6	20.5	19.2	21.7	22.5	21.1
Patient care	14.6	17.3	16.1	15.0	18.8	19.3	18.1
Office-based practice	0.7	1.2	1.1	1.5	0.1	-	-
Hospital-based practice	13.9	16.1	15.0	13.5	18.7	19.3	18.1
Other professional activity [3]	3.2	4.3	4.4	4.2	2.9	3.2	3.0
Inactive/unknown address	32.1	41.6	55.4	58.4	64.7	64.7	74.3
Doctors of osteopathy [4]	**18.8**	**24.0**	**30.9**	**33.5**	**33.4**	**35.0**	**36.7**

- Represents zero. NA Not available. [1] Foreign medical graduates received their medical education in schools outside the United States and Canada. [2] Includes clinical fellows. [3] Includes medical teaching, administration, research, and other. [4] As of July. Total DO's. Source: American Osteopathic Association, Chicago, IL.

Source: Except as noted, American Medical Association, Chicago, IL, *Physician Characteristics and Distribution in the U.S.*, annual (copyright).

No. 177. Dentists and Nurses: 1980 to 1995

[As of end of year. Excludes Puerto Rico and outlying areas]

ITEM	Unit	1980	1985	1989	1990	1991	1992	1993	1994	1995
Dentists, number [1]	1,000	141	156	168	[2]173	179	183	187	190	(NA)
Active (exc. in Federal service) [3]	1,000	121	136	144	147	149	152	154	157	(NA)
Rate per 100,000 population [4]	Rate	53	57	58	59	59	60	60	60	(NA)
Nurses, number (active registered)	1,000	1,273	1,538	1,731	1,790	1,853	1,907	1,976	2,044	2,116
Rate per 100,000 population [4]	Rate	560	644	696	713	730	755	774	793	796

NA Not available. [1] Includes current year's graduates. [2] Revised since originally published. [3] Source: American Dental Association, Bureau of Economic and Behavioral Research, Master Membership file and periodic censuses. [4] Based on Bureau of Census estimated resident population as of July 1. Estimates reflect revisions based on the 1990 Census of Population.

Source: Except as noted, U.S. Dept. of Health and Human Services, Health Resources and Services Administration, unpublished data.

No. 178. Health Professions Schools—Number, Enrollment, and Graduates: 1980 to 1995

[Data on the number of schools are reported as of the beginning of the academic year; all other data are reported as of the end of the academic year. Data are based on reporting by health professions schools]

YEAR	Medicine	Osteopathy	REGISTERED NURSING				Licensed practical nursing	Dentistry	Optometry	Pharmacy
			Total	Baccalaureate	Associate degree	Diploma				
NUMBER OF SCHOOLS [1]										
1980	126	14	1,385	377	697	311	1,299	60	16	72
1985	127	15	1,473	441	776	256	1,165	60	17	72
1986	127	15	1,469	455	776	238	1,087	59	17	73
1987	127	15	1,465	467	789	209	1,068	58	17	74
1988	127	15	1,442	479	792	171	1,095	58	17	74
1989	127	15	1,457	488	812	157	1,171	58	17	74
1990	126	15	1,470	489	829	152	1,154	56	17	74
1991	126	15	1,484	501	838	145	1,125	55	17	74
1992	126	15	1,484	501	848	135	1,154	55	17	74
1993	126	16	1,493	507	857	129	1,159	54	17	74
1994	126	16	1,501	509	868	124	(NA)	54	17	74
1995	126	16	1,516	521	876	119	(NA)	54	17	74
FIRST-YEAR ENROLLMENT										
1980	16,930	1,426	105,952	35,414	53,633	16,905	55,316	6,132	1,202	8,035
1985	16,997	1,750	118,224	39,573	63,776	14,875	47,034	5,047	1,187	6,986
1986	16,963	1,737	100,791	34,310	56,635	9,846	44,477	4,843	1,251	7,091
1987	16,819	1,724	90,693	28,026	54,330	8,337	42,452	4,554	1,234	7,554
1988	16,713	1,692	94,269	28,505	57,375	8,389	43,774	4,370	1,268	7,751
1989	16,868	1,780	103,025	29,042	63,973	10,010	47,602	4,196	1,271	7,990
1990	16,756	1,844	108,580	29,858	68,634	10,088	52,969	3,979	1,258	8,033
1991	16,876	1,950	113,526	33,437	69,869	10,220	56,176	4,001	1,239	8,267
1992	17,071	1,974	122,656	37,886	74,079	10,691	58,245	4,047	1,355	8,343
1993	17,079	2,035	126,837	41,290	75,382	10,165	60,749	4,072	1,395	8,664
1994	17,121	2,162	129,897	42,953	77,343	9,601	(NA)	4,100	1,351	8,970
1995	17,085	2,217	127,184	43,451	76,016	7,717	(NA)	4,121	1,390	9,157
1996	17,058	2,274	(NA)	(NA)	(NA)	(NA)	(NA)	4,237	1,438	8,740
TOTAL ENROLLMENT										
1980	63,800	4,571	234,659	98,939	92,069	43,651	52,202	22,482	4,517	23,074
1985	67,016	6,547	237,232	95,008	104,968	37,256	48,840	20,588	4,569	18,646
1986	66,585	6,608	217,955	91,020	96,756	30,179	39,345	19,563	4,562	19,098
1987	66,125	6,640	193,712	81,602	89,469	22,641	38,510	18,673	4,636	20,073
1988	65,735	6,586	182,947	73,621	90,399	18,927	40,035	17,885	4,646	21,424
1989	65,300	6,614	184,924	70,078	95,986	18,860	42,808	17,094	4,708	22,447
1990	65,016	6,615	201,458	74,865	106,175	20,418	46,720	16,412	4,723	23,013
1991	65,163	6,792	221,170	81,788	117,413	21,969	52,749	15,951	4,760	23,238
1992	65,602	7,012	237,598	90,877	123,816	22,905	56,762	15,882	4,864	23,482
1993	66,142	7,375	257,983	102,128	132,603	23,252	59,095	15,980	5,078	26,287
1994	66,629	7,822	270,228	110,693	137,300	22,235	61,007	16,250	(NA)	27,143
1995	67,072	8,146	268,350	112,659	135,895	19,796	(NA)	16,353	5,201	27,667
1996	66,970	8,475	261,219	109,505	135,235	16,479	(NA)	16,552	5,312	28,060
GRADUATES										
1980	15,113	1,059	75,523	24,994	36,034	14,495	41,892	5,256	1,073	7,432
1985	16,318	1,474	82,075	24,975	45,208	11,892	36,955	5,353	1,114	5,735
1986	16,117	1,560	77,027	25,170	41,333	10,524	29,599	4,957	1,065	5,800
1987	15,830	1,587	70,561	23,761	38,528	8,272	27,285	4,717	1,061	5,854
1988	15,919	1,572	64,839	21,504	37,397	5,938	26,912	4,581	1,106	6,184
1989	15,630	1,609	61,660	18,997	37,837	4,826	30,368	4,312	1,143	6,560
1990	15,398	1,529	66,088	18,571	42,318	5,199	35,417	4,233	1,115	6,956
1991	15,427	1,534	72,230	19,264	46,794	6,172	38,100	3,995	1,224	7,122
1992	15,365	1,532	80,839	21,415	52,896	6,528	41,951	3,918	1,150	7,113
1993	15,466	1,606	88,149	24,442	56,770	6,932	44,822	3,778	1,167	7,360
1994	15,555	1,775	94,870	28,912	58,839	7,119	(NA)	3,875	1,125	7,504
1995	15,888	1,843	97,052	31,254	58,749	7,049	(NA)	3,908	1,219	7,837
1996	15,907	1,877	(NA)	(NA)	(NA)	(NA)	(NA)	(NA)	(NA)	(NA)
2000, proj.	16,112	1,934	79,660	26,490	47,790	5,360	(NA)	3,242	1,200	7,120

NA Not available. [1] Some nursing schools offer more than one type of program. Numbers shown for nursing are number of nursing programs.

Source: U.S. National Center for Health Statistics, *Health United States*, annual.

No. 179. Active Non-Federal Physicians and Nurses, by State: 1995

[As of December. Excludes doctors of osteopathy, federally-employed persons, and physicians with addresses unknown. Includes all physicians not classified according to activity status]

STATE	PHYSICIANS		NURSES	
	Total	Rate [1]	Total	Rate [1]
United States	617,362	235	2,115,800	809
Alabama	7,814	184	32,300	763
Alaska	890	153	5,900	1,011
Arizona	8,315	198	31,900	760
Arkansas	4,246	171	17,100	690
California	75,496	241	180,300	574
Colorado	8,425	227	30,800	830
Connecticut	10,919	334	33,700	1,032
Delaware	1,546	217	7,800	1,067
District of Columbia	3,823	682	9,300	1,699
Florida	31,053	220	115,200	818
Georgia	13,964	196	52,300	733
Hawaii	2,812	248	8,700	766
Idaho	1,583	137	6,900	595
Illinois	28,765	244	102,200	866
Indiana	10,428	180	45,500	784
Iowa	4,703	166	28,200	992
Kansas	4,961	195	20,700	814
Kentucky	7,416	193	29,000	756
Louisiana	9,804	222	31,300	724
Maine	2,449	198	13,100	1,059
Maryland	17,463	349	42,700	854
Massachusetts	23,471	387	72,500	1,195
Michigan	20,061	210	78,300	820
Minnesota	11,007	239	44,000	955
Mississippi	3,703	138	19,000	709
Missouri	11,594	218	49,900	940
Montana	1,589	181	6,500	751
Nebraska	3,236	199	15,300	940
Nevada	2,391	157	9,300	611
New Hampshire	2,451	214	11,400	993
New Jersey	21,895	276	67,400	850
New Mexico	3,320	199	11,400	683
New York	65,299	361	165,700	915
North Carolina	15,159	214	58,200	820
North Dakota	1,291	204	6,900	1,090
Ohio	24,402	219	99,800	896
Oklahoma	5,203	160	19,200	591
Oregon	6,648	212	25,300	808
Pennsylvania	32,919	273	122,800	1,018
Rhode Island	2,942	298	11,200	1,136
South Carolina	6,904	190	25,700	707
South Dakota	1,206	166	7,800	1,077
Tennessee	11,846	226	45,500	869
Texas	35,100	189	120,400	647
Utah	3,766	194	12,600	647
Vermont	1,577	270	5,400	924
Virginia	14,676	227	52,700	816
Washington	12,032	224	42,900	798
West Virginia	3,582	196	14,500	793
Wisconsin	10,903	213	45,200	882
Wyoming	716	150	3,800	798

[1] Per 100,000 civilian population. Based on U.S. Bureau of the Census estimates as of July 1, 1995.

Source: Physicians: American Medical Association, Chicago, IL, *Physician Characteristics and Distribution in the U.S.*, annual (copyright); Nurses: U.S. Dept. of Health and Human Services, Health Resources and Services Administration, unpublished data.

No. 180. Physician Contacts, by Patient Characteristics: 1980 to 1994

[See headnote, table 206. Based on National Health Interview Survey; see Appendix III]

YEAR	TOTAL VISITS (mil.)				VISITS PER PERSON PER YEAR									
	Sex		Race		Sex		Race		Age (years)					
	Male	Female	White	Black	Male	Female	White	Black	Under 5	5 to 17	18 to 24	25 to 44	45 to 64	65 and over
1980	426	610	903	115	4.0	5.4	4.8	4.5	[1] 6.7	[2] 3.2	[3] 4.0	4.6	5.1	6.4
1985	498	733	1,074	132	4.4	6.1	5.4	4.7	[1] 6.3	[2] 3.1	[3] 4.2	4.9	6.1	8.3
1986	515	756	1,110	131	4.5	6.2	5.5	4.6	6.3	3.3	4.2	4.7	6.6	9.1
1987	523	765	1,118	140	4.5	6.2	5.5	4.9	6.7	3.3	4.4	4.8	6.4	8.9
1988	530	774	1,139	136	4.5	6.2	5.6	4.6	7.0	3.4	3.8	5.1	6.1	8.7
1989	552	771	1,148	140	4.7	6.1	5.6	4.7	6.7	3.5	3.9	5.1	6.1	8.9
1990	558	806	1,178	148	4.7	6.4	5.7	4.9	6.9	3.2	4.3	5.1	6.4	9.2
1991	589	842	1,243	152	4.9	6.6	6.0	4.9	7.1	3.4	3.9	5.1	6.6	10.4
1992	624	889	1,286	181	5.1	6.9	6.1	5.8	6.9	3.5	4.1	5.4	7.2	10.6
1993	634	917	1,314	183	5.1	7.0	6.2	5.7	7.2	3.6	4.0	5.4	7.1	10.9
1994	652	930	1,350	179	5.2	7.0	6.3	5.4	6.8	3.5	3.9	5.5	7.3	11.3

[1] Under 6 years. [2] 6 to 16 years. [3] 17 to 24 years.

Source: U.S. National Center for Health Statistics, *Vital and Health Statistics*, series 10, No. 193, and earlier reports; and unpublished data.

No. 181. Visits to Office Based Physicians: 1995

[Based on the 1995 National Ambulatory Medical Care Survey and subject to sampling error; see source for details]

CHARACTERISTIC	Number of visits (1,000)	Percent distribution	Visits per person per year
All visits	697,082	100.0	2.7
Age:			
Under 15 years old	131,548	18.9	2.2
15 to 24 years old	56,278	8.1	1.6
25 to 44 years old	181,590	26.1	2.2
45 to 64 years old	159,531	22.9	3.1
65 to 74 years old	90,544	13.0	4.9
75 years old and over	77,591	11.1	5.9
Sex:			
Male	280,762	40.3	2.2
Female	416,320	59.7	3.1
Race:			
White	608,384	87.3	2.8
Black	59,678	8.6	1.8
Asian/Pacific Islander	26,718	3.8	(NA)
American Indian/Eskimo/Aleut.	2,302	0.3	(NA)
Visit status:			
Old patient	599,537	86.0	(X)
Old problem	457,126	65.6	(X)
New problem	142,411	20.4	(X)
New patient	97,545	14.0	(X)
Expected source of payment: [1]			
Insurance [2]	597,484	85.7	(X)
Blue Cross / Blue Shield	104,082	14.9	(X)
Other private insurance	219,945	31.6	(X)
Medicare	150,472	21.6	(X)
Medicaid	72,952	10.5	(X)
Worker's compensation	16,461	2.4	(X)
Other source of insurance	66,682	9.6	(X)
Unknown source of insurance [3]	44,230	6.3	(X)
Self pay	74,074	10.6	(X)
No charge	7,746	1.1	(X)
Other	9,214	1.3	(X)
Disposition: [1]			
Return at specified time	427,418	61.3	(X)
Return if needed	192,523	27.6	(X)
No follow-up planned	60,570	8.7	(X)
Admit to hospital	5,580	0.8	(X)
Other	26,590	3.8	(X)

NA Not available. X Not applicable. [1] More than one source of payment or disposition may be reported. [2] Equal to all visits minus self pay, no charge, other source, and no answer. [3] Type of payment indicated, expected source was left blank.

Source: U.S. National Center for Health Statistics, *Advance Data*, No. 286, May 8, 1997.

No. 182. Medical Practice Characteristics, by Selected Specialty: 1985 to 1994

[Dollar figures in thousands. Based on a sample telephone survey of 4,000 non-Federal office and hospital based patient care physicians, excluding residents, with a response rate of 69.1% in 1990, 66.7% in 1991, 64.4% in 1992, 64.6% in 1993 and 63.1% in 1994. For details see source. For definition of mean, see Guide to Tabular Presentation]

SPECIALTY	1985	1989	1990	1991	1992	1993	1994
MEAN PATIENT VISITS PER WEEK							
All physicians [1]	117.1	121.6	120.9	118.4	114.8	112.4	109.6
General/Family practice	138.1	143.0	146.0	144.4	138.4	137.0	133.5
Internal medicine	105.2	117.9	112.0	110.7	109.4	105.3	105.4
Surgery	108.2	107.7	107.6	106.9	101.6	98.3	98.8
Pediatrics	130.8	138.1	134.0	133.5	126.9	130.9	125.5
Obstetrics/Gynecology	112.0	115.6	120.0	112.2	110.5	111.0	102.9
MEAN HOURS IN PATIENT CARE PER WEEK							
All physicians [1]	51.3	53.3	53.3	53.3	52.9	52.9	52.1
General/Family practice	53.6	54.4	55.0	54.7	53.1	54.0	51.9
Internal medicine	52.4	56.8	55.7	56.3	55.5	56.0	56.6
Surgery	51.2	53.3	53.1	53.4	53.0	54.3	53.4
Pediatrics	50.6	53.4	52.4	52.4	52.6	53.8	51.6
Obstetrics/Gynecology	56.9	59.0	60.4	59.5	58.8	58.9	58.1
MEAN NET INCOME							
All physicians [1]	112.2	155.8	164.3	170.6	181.7	189.3	182.4
General/Family practice	77.9	95.9	102.7	111.5	114.4	116.8	121.2
Internal medicine	102.0	146.5	152.5	149.6	162.1	180.8	174.9
Surgery	155.0	220.5	236.4	233.8	250.5	262.7	255.2
Pediatrics	76.2	104.7	106.5	119.3	123.9	135.4	126.2
Obstetrics/Gynecology	124.3	194.3	207.3	221.8	220.7	221.9	200.4
MEAN PROFESSIONAL EXPENSES							
All physicians [1]	102.7	148.4	150.0	168.4	183.4	182.2	183.1
General/Family practice	96.5	128.5	134.5	146.4	162.9	162.4	190.5
Internal medicine	90.0	139.1	139.2	159.0	174.1	185.2	186.4
Surgery	135.7	203.2	201.0	215.6	245.1	245.9	249.9
Pediatrics	87.3	132.5	138.0	145.4	173.7	167.4	157.8
Obstetrics/Gynecology	131.9	197.4	212.6	236.2	239.7	238.1	196.8
MEAN LIABILITY PREMIUM							
All physicians [1]	10.5	15.5	14.5	14.9	13.8	14.4	15.1
General/Family practice	6.8	9.0	7.8	8.1	8.2	7.9	10.2
Internal medicine	5.8	8.2	9.2	8.0	8.6	9.0	8.6
Surgery	16.6	25.8	22.8	22.5	20.9	22.7	22.3
Pediatrics	4.7	7.8	7.8	8.4	7.7	8.6	7.6
Obstetrics/Gynecology	23.5	37.0	34.3	34.9	34.4	33.7	37.4

[1] Includes other specialties not shown separately.

Source: American Medical Association, Chicago IL, *Socioeconomic Characteristics of Medical Practice*, annual (copyright).

No. 183. Percent of Adult Persons with a Dental Visit Within Past Year, by Patient Characteristics: 1989 to 1993

[Covers civilian noninstitutional population, 25 years old and over. Data are age-adjusted. Estimates are based on one adult member per sample household. Excludes persons with unknown dental data. Based on National Health Interview Survey; see Appendix III]

CHARACTERISTIC	1989	1990	1991	1993
Total [1]	58.9	62.3	58.2	60.8
25 to 34 years old	60.9	65.1	59.1	60.3
35 to 44 years old	65.9	69.1	64.8	66.9
45 to 64 years old	59.9	62.8	59.2	62.0
65 years old and over	45.8	49.6	47.2	51.7
65 to 74 years old	50.0	53.5	51.1	56.3
75 years old and over	39.0	43.4	41.3	44.9
Male	56.2	58.8	55.5	58.2
Female	61.4	65.6	60.8	63.4
White, non-Hispanic	61.8	64.9	61.5	64.0
Black, non-Hispanic	43.3	49.1	44.3	47.3
Hispanic origin [2]	48.9	53.8	43.1	46.2
Years of school completed:				
Less than 12 years	36.9	41.2	35.2	36.0
12 years	58.2	61.3	56.7	56.7
13 years or more	73.9	75.7	72.2	73.8
Poverty status: [3]				
Below poverty	33.3	38.2	33.0	35.9
At or above poverty	62.1	65.4	61.9	64.3

[1] Includes all other races not shown separately and unknown education level and poverty status. [2] Persons of Hispanic origin may be of any race. [3] For explanation of poverty level, see text, section 14.

Source: U.S. National Center for Health Statistics, *Health, United States, 1995.*

No. 184. Hospitals and Nursing Homes—Summary Characteristics: 1980 to 1993

[Except as indicated, based on National Master Facility Inventory]

YEAR AND TYPE OF FACILITY	Total	FACILITIES UNDER—			FACILITIES WITH—			Residents [2] (1,000)	Full-time employees (1,000)
		Gov't. control	Proprietary control	Nonprofit control	Fewer than 25 beds [1]	25-74 beds	75 or more beds		
1980: All facilities	30,116	3,496	19,611	7,007	8,852	8,573	12,691	2,427	3,919
Nursing homes [3] [4]	23,065	936	18,669	3,460	8,496	6,362	8,205	1,396	[5] 798
Hospitals	7,051	2,562	942	3,547	354	2,211	4,486	1,031	3,121
1986: All facilities	32,800	3,275	21,399	7,926	9,903	8,755	13,942	2,427	(NA)
All hospitals [6]	6,954	2,230	1,176	3,548	290	2,150	4,514	874	3,241
General	5,956	1,871	829	3,256	259	1,849	3,848	690	2,871
Psychiatric	564	267	218	99	12	140	432	139	248
Chronic	44	30	4	10	-	6	38	13	21
Tuberculosis	4	3	-	1	-	1	3	(Z)	1
Nursing homes [3]	25,646	1,045	20,223	4,378	9,613	6,605	9,428	1,553	(NA)
1990: All hospitals [6]	6,779	2,145	1,203	3,431	326	2,077	4,376	840	3,562
General	5,611	1,788	711	3,112	290	1,890	3,631	673	3,168
Psychiatric	734	272	350	112	17	211	506	128	262
Chronic	34	27	2	5	-	6	28	10	18
Tuberculosis	4	3	-	1	-	1	3	(Z)	1
1993: All hospitals [6]	6,580	2,046	1,167	3,367	310	2,010	4,260	781	3,783
General	5,403	1,697	660	3,046	260	1,586	3,557	634	3,401
Psychiatric	737	266	358	113	24	242	471	107	231
Chronic	26	21	1	4	1	3	22	9	16
Tuberculosis	4	3	-	1	-	2	2	(Z)	1

- Represents zero. NA Not available. Z Fewer that 500. [1] For hospitals, minimum of six beds; for nursing homes, minimum of three beds. [2] Number of residents as of date of interview. [3] See footnote 1, table 202. [4] Includes 1978 data for Alaska and South Dakota. [5] Estimated. [6] Includes types not shown separately. Based on data from the American Hospital Association.

Source: U.S. National Center for Health Statistics, unpublished data.

No. 185. Hospitals—Summary Characteristics: 1980 to 1995

[Covers hospitals accepted for registration by the American Hospital Association; see text, section 3. Short-term hospitals have an average patient stay of less than 30 days; long-term, an average stay of longer duration. Special hospitals include obstetrics and gynecology; eye, ear, nose, and throat; rehabilitation; orthopedic; and chronic and other special hospitals except psychiatric, tuberculosis, alcoholism, and chemical dependency hospitals]

ITEM	1980	1985	1989	1990	1991	1992	1993	1994	1995
Number:									
All hospitals	6,965	6,872	6,720	6,649	6,634	6,539	6,467	6,374	6,291
With 100 beds or more	3,755	3,805	3,650	3,620	3,611	3,572	3,558	3,492	3,376
Non-Federal [1]	6,606	6,529	6,380	6,312	6,300	6,214	6,151	6,067	5,992
Community hospitals [2]	5,830	5,732	5,455	5,384	5,342	5,292	5,261	5,229	5,194
Nongovernmental nonprofit	3,322	3,349	3,220	3,191	3,175	3,173	3,154	3,139	3,092
For profit	730	805	769	749	738	723	717	719	752
State and local government	1,778	1,578	1,466	1,444	1,429	1,396	1,390	1,371	1,350
Long-term general and special	157	128	138	131	126	115	117	110	112
Psychiatric	534	610	741	757	800	774	741	696	657
Tuberculosis	11	7	4	4	4	4	4	5	3
Federal	359	343	340	337	334	325	316	307	299
Beds (1,000):									
All hospitals [3]	1,365	1,309	1,224	1,211	1,197	1,174	1,158	1,128	1,081
Rate per 1,000 population [4]	6.0	5.5	5.0	4.9	4.7	4.6	4.5	4.3	4.1
Beds per hospital	196	190	182	182	180	180	179	177	172
Non-Federal [1]	1,248	1,197	1,124	1,113	1,101	1,085	1,071	1,044	1,004
Community hospitals [2]	988	1,001	933	928	924	921	918	902	873
Rate per 1,000 population [4]	4.3	4.2	3.8	3.7	3.7	3.6	3.6	3.6	3.3
Nongovernmental nonprofit	692	707	660	657	656	656	649	637	610
For profit	87	104	103	102	100	99	99	101	106
State and local government	209	189	170	169	168	167	169	164	157
Long-term general and special	39	31	27	25	25	23	21	19	19
Psychiatric	215	169	160	158	150	139	131	121	110
Tuberculosis	2	1	(Z)	(Z)	(Z)	(Z)	(Z)	1	(Z)
Federal	117	112	100	98	95	89	87	84	78
Expenses (bil. dol.): [5]									
All hospitals	91.9	153.3	214.9	234.9	258.5	282.5	301.5	310.8	320.3
Non-Federal [1]	84.0	141.0	199.8	219.6	241.7	264.3	281.9	290.8	300.0
Community hospitals [2]	76.9	130.5	184.9	203.7	225.0	248.1	266.1	275.8	285.6
Nongovernmental nonprofit	55.8	96.1	136.9	150.7	166.8	183.8	197.2	204.2	209.6
For profit	5.8	11.5	17.2	18.8	20.5	22.5	23.1	23.4	26.7
State and local government	15.2	22.9	30.8	34.2	37.7	41.8	45.8	48.1	49.3
Long-term general and special	1.2	1.9	2.5	2.7	2.9	2.7	2.7	2.3	2.2
Psychiatric	5.8	8.3	12.0	12.9	13.5	13.2	12.7	12.3	11.7
Tuberculosis	0.1	0.1	(Z)	0.1	(Z)	(Z)	0.1	0.7	0.4
Federal	7.9	12.3	15.1	15.2	16.8	18.2	19.6	20.0	20.2
Personnel (1,000): [6]									
All hospitals	3,492	3,625	3,937	4,063	4,165	4,236	4,289	4,270	4,273
Non-Federal [1]	3,213	3,326	3,648	3,760	3,864	3,929	3,970	3,969	3,971
Community hospitals [2]	2,873	2,997	3,303	3,420	3,535	3,620	3,677	3,692	3,714
Nongovernmental nonprofit	2,086	2,216	2,454	2,533	2,624	2,692	2,711	2,719	2,702
For profit	189	221	261	273	281	285	289	301	343
State and local government	598	561	589	614	630	643	676	672	670
Long-term general and special	56	58	56	55	55	49	45	38	38
Psychiatric	275	263	284	280	269	256	242	233	215
Tuberculosis	3	2	1	1	1	1	1	1	1
Federal	279	299	288	303	301	306	320	301	301
Personnel per 100 patients [6]	329	398	482	482	504	525	548	573	602
Outpatient visits (mil.)	263.0	282.1	352.2	368.2	387.7	417.9	435.7	453.6	483.2
Emergency	82.0	80.1	89.9	92.8	93.5	95.8	97.4	96.0	99.9
Closures	73	59	80	63	67	60	83	40	43

Z Less than 500 beds or $50 million. [1] Short term (average length of stay less than 30 days) general and special (e.g., obstetrics and gynecology; eye, ear, nose and throat; rehabilitation etc. except psychiatric, tuberculosis, alcoholism and chemical dependency). Includes hospital units of institutions. [2] Excludes hospital units of institutions. [3] Beginning 1989, number of beds at end of reporting period; prior years, average number in 12 month period. [4] Based on Bureau of the Census estimated resident population as of July 1. Estimates reflect revisions based on the 1990 Census of Population. [5] Excludes new construction. [6] Includes full-time equivalents of part-time personnel.

Source: American Hospital Association, Chicago, IL, *Hospital Statistics*, annual (copyright).

No. 187. Hospital Use Rates, by Type of Hospital: 1980 to 1995

TYPE OF HOSPITAL	1980	1985	1990	1991	1992	1993	1994	1995
Community hospitals: [1]								
Admissions per 1,000 population [2]	159	141	125	123	122	119	118	118
Admissions per bed	37	33	34	34	34	33	34	35
Average length of stay [3] (days)	7.6	7.1	7.2	7.2	7.1	7.0	6.7	6.5
Outpatient visits per admission	5.6	6.5	9.7	10.4	11.2	11.9	12.5	13.4
Outpatient visits per 1,000 population [2]	890	919	1,208	1,277	1,367	1,423	1,471	1,577
Surgical operations (million)	18.8	20.1	21.9	22.4	22.9	22.8	23.0	23.2
Number per admission	0.5	0.6	0.7	0.7	0.7	0.7	0.7	0.7
Non-Federal psychiatric:								
Admissions per 1,000 population [2]	2.5	2.5	2.9	2.9	2.9	2.9	2.9	2.7
Days in hospital per 1,000 population [2]	295	224	190	179	162	149	136	124

[1] For definition of community hospitals, see footnotes 1 and 2, table 185. [2] Based on Bureau of the Census estimated resident population as of July 1. Estimates reflect revisions based on the 1990 Census of Population. [3] Number of inpatient days divided by number of admissions.

Source: American Hospital Association, Chicago, IL, *Hospital Statistics*, annual (copyright).

No. 188. Average Cost to Community Hospitals per Patient: 1980 to 1995

[In dollars, except percent. Covers non-Federal short-term general or special hospitals (excluding psychiatric or tuberculosis hospitals and hospital units of institutions). Total cost per patient based on total hospital expenses (payroll, employee benefits, professional fees, supplies, etc.). Data have been adjusted for outpatient visits]

TYPE OF EXPENSE AND HOSPITAL	1980	1985	1988	1989	1990	1991	1992	1993	1994	1995
Average cost per day, total	245	460	586	637	687	752	820	881	931	968
Annual percent change [1]	12.9	11.9	8.7	8.7	7.8	9.5	9.0	7.4	5.7	4.0
Nongovernmental nonprofit	246	463	591	642	692	758	828	898	950	994
For profit	257	500	649	706	752	820	889	914	924	947
State and local government	239	433	539	582	634	696	754	800	859	878
Average cost per stay, total	1,851	3,245	4,207	4,588	4,947	5,360	5,794	6,132	6,230	6,216
Nongovernmental nonprofit	1,902	3,307	4,273	4,649	5,001	5,393	5,809	6,178	6,257	6,279
For profit	1,676	3,033	4,023	4,406	4,727	5,134	5,546	5,643	5,529	5,426
State and local government	1,750	3,106	4,034	4,430	4,838	5,340	5,871	6,206	6,513	6,445

[1] Change from immediate prior year.

Source: American Hospital Association, Chicago, IL, *Hospital Statistics*, annual (copyright).

No. 189. Average Cost to Community Hospitals per Patient, by State: 1990 to 1995

[In dollars. See headnote, table 188]

STATE	AVERAGE COST PER DAY			AVERAGE COST PER STAY			STATE	AVERAGE COST PER DAY			AVERAGE COST PER STAY		
	1990	1994	1995	1990	1994	1995		1990	1994	1995	1990	1994	1995
U.S.	687	931	968	4,947	6,230	6,216	MO	679	915	967	5,022	6,249	6,228
AL	586	781	819	4,175	4,895	5,028	MT	405	470	493	3,973	4,965	5,184
AK	1,070	1,263	1,341	6,249	8,168	8,282	NE	490	606	661	4,675	6,006	5,880
AZ	867	1,091	1,191	4,877	5,375	5,613	NV	854	1,016	1,072	5,511	6,526	6,014
AR	534	724	704	3,730	4,514	4,459	NH	671	825	915	4,544	5,978	6,188
CA	939	1,301	1,316	5,709	7,252	7,111	NJ	613	934	962	4,573	6,933	7,007
CO	725	993	1,069	5,209	6,241	6,289	NM	734	1,047	1,073	4,172	5,564	5,358
CT	825	1,121	1,264	6,238	7,835	7,358	NY	641	854	909	6,397	8,127	8,077
DE	771	1,042	1,058	5,112	7,303	7,298	NC	595	806	832	4,408	5,701	5,631
DC	995	1,304	1,346	7,876	9,021	8,632	ND	427	515	521	4,468	5,547	5,589
FL	769	975	1,004	5,312	6,106	6,040	OH	720	1,008	1,061	4,801	6,103	6,141
GA	630	797	836	4,303	5,621	5,618	OK	632	848	861	4,302	5,291	5,188
HI	638	958	956	6,048	8,428	8,445	OR	800	1,077	1,141	4,432	5,492	5,325
ID	547	679	719	3,701	4,448	4,686	PA	662	892	963	5,120	6,332	6,482
IL	717	968	1,050	5,253	6,372	6,584	RI	663	970	1,092	4,839	5,984	6,202
IN	667	955	963	4,390	5,715	5,610	SC	590	876	923	4,168	6,056	5,936
IA	495	672	702	4,135	5,077	5,049	SD	391	470	476	3,905	4,797	5,494
KS	532	715	732	4,161	5,240	5,308	TN	633	870	871	4,340	5,621	5,355
KY	563	748	795	3,762	4,873	4,838	TX	752	1,055	1,063	4,663	6,051	5,879
LA	701	929	902	4,575	5,916	5,612	UT	832	1,115	1,213	4,409	5,378	5,676
ME	574	802	916	4,604	5,685	6,083	VT	598	651	714	4,343	5,400	5,863
MD	678	981	1,064	4,640	5,833	5,899	VA	635	885	901	4,408	5,518	5,423
MA	788	1,131	1,157	5,709	7,018	7,099	WA	817	1,206	1,318	4,519	5,909	6,180
MI	716	929	994	5,358	6,169	6,218	WV	565	727	763	3,918	4,839	4,974
MN	536	695	736	4,782	6,029	6,241	WI	554	802	794	4,083	5,536	5,679
MS	439	584	584	3,116	4,235	4,265	WY	462	504	545	3,990	4,639	4,817

Source: American Hospital Association, Chicago, IL, *Hospital Statistics*, annual (copyright).

No. 190. Hospital Utilization Rates: 1980 to 1994

[Represents estimates of inpatients discharged from noninstitutional, short-stay hospitals, exclusive of Federal hospitals. Excludes newborn infants. Based on sample data collected from the National Hospital Discharge Survey, a sample survey of hospital records of patients discharged in year shown; subject to sampling variability. For composition of regions, see table 26]

SELECTED CHARACTERISTIC	Patients discharged (1,000)	PATIENTS DISCHARGED PER 1,000 PERSONS [1]			DAYS OF CARE PER 1,000 PERSONS [1]			AVERAGE STAY (days)		
		Total	Male	Female	Total	Male	Female	Total	Male	Female
1980	37,832	168	139	194	1,217	1,068	1,356	7.3	7.7	7.0
1985	35,056	148	124	171	954	849	1,053	6.5	6.9	6.2
1986	34,256	143	121	164	913	817	1,003	6.4	6.8	6.1
1987	33,387	138	116	159	889	806	966	6.4	6.9	6.1
1988 [2]	31,146	128	107	147	834	757	907	6.5	7.1	6.2
1989 [2]	30,947	126	105	145	815	741	884	6.5	7.0	6.1
1990 [2]	30,788	124	102	144	792	704	875	6.4	6.9	6.1
1991 [2]	31,098	124	103	144	796	715	869	6.4	7.0	6.0
1992 [2]	30,951	122	101	142	751	680	818	6.2	6.7	5.8
1993 [2]	30,825	120	98	141	720	644	792	6.0	6.5	5.6
1994, [2] total	30,843	119	96	139	664	610	755	5.7	6.2	5.4
Age:										
Under 1 year old	730	189	214	162	1,069	1,195	977	5.8	5.6	6.0
1 to 4 years old	683	43	48	38	149	164	132	3.4	3.4	3.5
5 to 14 years old	836	22	24	21	114	130	96	5.1	5.5	4.7
15 to 24 years old	3,154	89	39	140	323	212	436	3.6	5.4	3.1
25 to 34 years old	4,377	107	51	163	413	293	530	3.8	5.8	3.3
35 to 44 years old	3,425	83	70	96	426	422	430	5.1	6.1	4.5
45 to 64 years old	6,311	124	127	121	727	741	715	5.9	5.8	5.9
65 to 74 years old	4,894	262	281	246	1,799	1,879	1,735	6.9	6.7	7.0
75 years old and over	6,433	445	468	432	3,446	3,561	3,381	7.7	7.6	7.8
Region:										
Northeast	7,128	139	122	155	930	854	1,000	6.7	7.0	6.5
Midwest	7,133	116	97	135	648	586	705	5.6	6.0	5.2
South	11,310	126	101	149	716	623	804	5.7	6.2	5.4
West	5,271	93	72	115	450	400	498	4.8	5.6	4.3

[1] Based on Bureau of the Census estimated civilian population as of July 1. Estimates for 1980-90 do not reflect revisions based on the 1990 Census of Population. [2] Comparisons beginning 1988 with data for earlier years should be made with caution as estimates of change may reflect improvements in the design rather than true changes in hospital use.

Source: U.S. National Center for Health Statistics, *Vital and Health Statistics*, series 13; and unpublished data.

No. 191. Procedures for Inpatients Discharged From Short-Stay Hospitals: 1980 to 1994

[Excludes newborn infants and discharges from Federal hospitals. See headnote, table 190]

SEX AND TYPE OF PROCEDURE	NUMBER OF PROCEDURES (1,000)				RATE PER 1,000 POPULATION [2]			
	1980	1990 [1]	1993 [1]	1994 [1]	1980	1990 [1]	1993 [1]	1994 [1]
Surgical procedures, total [3] [4]	24,494	23,051	22,767	22,629	106.6	92.4	88.8	87.4
MALE								
Total [3] [4]	8,505	8,538	8,355	8,369	78.1	70.6	67.1	66.5
Cardiac catheterization	228	620	613	633	2.1	5.1	4.9	5.0
Prostatectomy	335	364	317	263	3.1	3.0	2.5	2.1
Reduction of fracture [5]	325	300	294	261	3.0	2.5	2.4	2.1
Repair of inguinal hernia	483	181	96	82	4.4	1.5	0.8	0.7
FEMALE								
Total [3] [4]	15,989	14,513	14,411	14,260	137.1	113.0	109.3	107.1
Procedures to assist delivery [4]	2,391	2,491	2,428	2,410	20.5	19.4	18.4	18.1
Cesarean section	619	945	917	858	5.3	7.4	7.0	6.5
Repair of current obstetric laceration	355	795	860	910	3.0	6.2	6.5	6.8
Hysterectomy	649	591	562	556	5.6	4.6	4.3	4.2
Diagnostic and other nonsurgical procedures [4] [6]	6,918	17,455	18,842	18,081	30.7	70.0	73.5	69.8
MALE								
Total [4] [6]	3,386	7,378	7,767	7,501	31.1	61.0	62.5	59.6
Angiocardiography and arteriography [7]	355	1,051	1,024	1,058	3.3	8.7	8.2	8.4
CAT scan [8]	152	736	565	500	1.4	6.1	4.5	4.0
FEMALE								
Total [4] [6]	3,532	10,077	11,055	10,580	30.3	78.5	83.8	78.5
Diagnostic ultrasound	204	941	848	771	1.7	7.3	6.4	5.8
CAT scan [8]	154	770	594	528	1.3	6.0	4.5	4.0

[1] Comparisons beginning 1990 with data for earlier years should be made with caution as estimates of change may reflect improvements in the design rather than true changes in hospital use. [2] Based on Bureau of the Census estimated civilian population as of July 1. Population estimates for the 1980's do not reflect revised estimates based on the 1990 Census Population. [3] Includes other types of surgical procedures not shown separately. [4] Beginning in 1990, the definition of some surgical and diagnostic and other nonsurgical procedures was revised, causing a discontinuity in the trends for some totals. [5] Excluding skull, nose, and jaw. [6] Includes other nonsurgical procedures not shown separately. [7] Using contrast material. [8] Computerized axial tomography.

Source: U.S. National Center for Health Statistics, *Vital and Health Statistics*, series 13; and unpublished data.

No. 192. Hospital Discharges and Days of Care: 1994

[See headnote, table 190]

AGE AND FIRST-LISTED DIAGNOSIS	DISCHARGES: Number (1,000)	DISCHARGES: Per 1,000 persons [1]	Days of care per 1,000 persons [1]	Average stay (days)	AGE AND FIRST-LISTED DIAGNOSIS	DISCHARGES: Number (1,000)	DISCHARGES: Per 1,000 persons [1]	Days of care per 1,000 persons [1]	Average stay (days)
MALE					FEMALE				
All ages [2]	12,293	94.2	580.8	6.2	All ages [2]	18,550	119.1	609.5	5.1
Under 15 years [3]	1,272	43.3	211.5	4.9	Under 15 years [3]	978	34.9	165.7	4.7
Pneumonia	195	6.7	25.7	3.9	Pneumonia	127	4.5	18.3	4.0
Injuries and poisoning	150	5.1	20.2	3.9	Injuries and poisoning	95	3.4	12.4	3.6
Asthma	107	3.6	9.1	2.5	Asthma	63	2.2	5.8	2.6
15 to 44 years [3]	3,146	53.8	313.3	5.8	15 to 44 years [3]	7,810	132.1	466.7	3.5
Injuries and poisoning	584	10.0	46.6	4.7	Delivery	3,885	65.7	157.3	2.4
Psychoses	325	5.6	63.9	11.5	Injuries and poisoning	356	6.0	26.4	4.4
Diseases of heart	170	2.9	12.2	4.2	Psychoses	318	5.4	56.9	10.6
Intervertebral disk disorders	103	1.8	7.3	4.1					
45 to 64 years [3]	3,120	127.1	740.9	5.8	45 to 64 years [3]	3,191	121.3	715.0	5.9
Diseases of heart	721	29.4	148.0	5.0	Diseases of heart	458	17.4	96.8	5.6
Injuries and poisoning	268	10.9	63.8	5.8	Malignant neoplasms	246	9.4	63.1	6.7
Malignant neoplasms	199	8.1	66.1	8.2	Injuries and poisoning	236	9.0	54.1	6.0
Pneumonia	109	4.4	31.9	7.2	Pneumonia	96	3.6	26.4	7.3
					Diabetes	87	3.3	20.2	6.1
65 to 74 years [3]	2,328	280.9	1,878.8	6.7	65 to 74 years [3]	2,566	246.2	1,735.1	7.0
Diseases of heart	612	73.8	443.0	6.0	Diseases of heart	529	50.8	311.0	6.1
Malignant neoplasms	235	28.3	231.7	8.2	Injuries and poisoning	187	18.0	130.3	7.2
Injuries and poisoning	148	17.9	124.2	6.9	Malignant neoplasms	201	19.2	153.7	8.0
Cerebrovascular diseases	130	15.7	108.2	6.9	Cerebrovascular diseases	126	12.1	87.3	7.2
Pneumonia	100	12.1	88.5	7.3	Pneumonia	102	9.8	76.3	7.8
75 years old and older [3]	2,428	466.2	3,562.1	7.6	75 years old and older [3]	4,005	432.4	3,380.7	7.8
Diseases of heart	587	113.2	736.4	6.5	Diseases of heart	879	94.9	661.6	7.0
Pneumonia	197	38.0	309.2	8.1	Injuries and poisoning	422	45.6	359.5	7.9
Malignant neoplasms	153	29.4	253.0	8.6	Cerebrovascular diseases	258	27.9	218.5	7.8
Injuries and poisoning	158	30.4	247.8	8.1	Pneumonia	237	25.6	225.7	8.8
Cerebrovascular diseases	163	31.5	219.3	7.0	Malignant neoplasms	192	20.8	194.3	9.4

[1] Based on Bureau of the Census estimated civilian population as of July 1. [2] Average length of stay and rates per 1,000 population are age-adjusted. [3] Includes other first-listed diagnoses not shown separately.

No. 193. Hospital Discharges—Principal Source of Expected Payment: 1994

[See headnote, table 190]

CHARACTERISTIC	Total discharges [1] (1,000)	PRINCIPAL SOURCE OF EXPECTED PAYMENT—PERCENT DISTRIBUTION: Private insurance	Government: Medicare	Government: Medicaid	Government: Worker's compensation	Government: Other	Self-pay	No charge	Other [2]
All ages	30,843	34.1	37.6	14.9	1.0	1.7	4.7	0.5	2.0
Under 15 years old	2,249	41.6	1.5	39.2	(X)	2.8	5.4	1.1	2.4
15 to 44 years old	10,956	47.5	5.3	25.9	1.6	2.6	8.0	0.7	2.9
45 to 64 years old	6,311	55.7	15.6	11.2	1.7	2.2	5.8	0.6	2.3
65 years old and over	11,327	7.6	88.3	1.4	0.2	0.3	0.7	([3])	0.8
SEX									
Male, all ages	12,293	32.4	40.9	11.2	1.8	1.8	5.6	0.6	2.1
Under 15 years old	1,272	41.9	1.4	38.9	(X)	2.8	5.5	1.1	2.3
15 to 44 years old	3,146	42.1	10.4	16.8	4.1	3.4	12.6	1.5	3.9
45 to 64 years old	3,120	54.5	17.8	9.4	2.4	2.2	6.0	0.5	2.5
65 years old and over	4,756	9.0	86.7	1.3	0.2	0.3	0.7	([3])	0.7
Female, all ages	18,550	35.2	35.5	17.3	0.4	1.6	4.1	0.4	1.8
Under 15 years old	978	41.1	1.7	39.7	(X)	2.8	5.2	1.1	2.6
15 to 44 years old	7,810	49.7	3.3	29.5	0.6	2.3	6.2	0.4	2.5
45 to 64 years old	3,191	56.9	13.4	13.0	1.0	2.3	5.7	0.6	2.2
65 years old and over	6,571	6.6	89.5	1.5	0.1	0.2	0.7	([3])	0.8
RACE									
White	20,003	35.2	42.1	10.1	1.1	1.4	4.1	0.4	1.9
All other	5,063	26.3	25.7	30.3	0.6	3.2	6.5	1.2	2.5
Not stated	5,777	37.2	32.6	17.9	0.8	1.5	5.2	([3])	1.6
REGION									
Northeast	7,128	33.5	38.7	14.5	1.1	0.8	4.8	0.5	2.2
Midwest	7,133	37.4	38.1	12.3	0.7	1.5	4.4	0.3	0.9
South	11,310	32.2	39.7	14.4	1.1	2.4	5.3	0.7	2.5
West	5,271	34.5	31.1	19.8	0.8	1.6	3.6	([3])	1.9

X Not applicable. [1] Includes discharges for whom expected source of payment was unknown. [2] Includes all other nonprofit source of payment such as church, welfare, or United Way. [3] Figure does not meet standards of reliability or precision.

Source of tables 192 and 193: U.S. National Center for Health Statistics, unpublished data.

No. 194. Outpatient Surgery Performed in Hospitals: 1980 to 1995

TYPE OF HOSPITAL	1980	1985	1989	1990	1991	1992	1993	1994	1995
OUTPATIENT SURGERIES (1,000)									
All hospitals	**3,198**	**7,309**	**10,953**	**11,678**	**12,209**	**12,849**	**13,096**	**13,612**	**13,836**
Ownership:									
Non-Federal hospitals	3,063	6,984	10,362	11,085	11,724	12,316	12,641	13,167	13,470
Community hospitals [1]	3,054	6,951	10,351	11,070	11,712	12,308	12,624	13,155	13,462
Nongovernmental nonprofit	2,416	5,392	7,834	8,389	8,969	9,500	9,686	10,045	10,166
Federal hospitals	135	325	591	593	486	533	457	445	366
Size of hospital: 6 to 99 beds	354	752	1,241	1,303	1,366	1,464	1,473	1,588	1,740
100 to 199 beds	571	1,502	2,360	2,498	2,636	2,824	2,927	3,042	3,191
200 to 299 beds	630	1,521	2,383	2,543	2,696	2,790	2,906	3,072	3,050
300 to 499 beds	977	2,069	2,920	3,172	3,293	3,340	3,424	3,421	3,425
500 beds or more	666	1,465	2,049	2,162	2,220	2,431	2,368	2,489	2,433
OUTPATIENT SURGERIES AS PERCENT OF TOTAL									
All hospitals	**16.4**	**34.5**	**48.7**	**50.6**	**52.1**	**53.6**	**54.9**	**56.9**	**57.6**
Ownership:									
Non-Federal hospitals	16.3	34.5	48.5	50.5	52.3	53.8	55.4	57.2	58.1
Community hospitals [1]	16.3	34.6	48.5	50.5	52.3	53.8	55.4	57.2	58.1
Nongovernmental nonprofit	17.1	35.5	48.6	50.7	52.5	54.0	55.7	57.4	58.4
Federal hospitals	18.6	33.9	51.5	51.8	47.8	49.3	45.4	48.7	42.5
Size of hospital: 6 to 99 beds	17.9	36.5	54.1	56.2	58.7	61.1	62.5	65.0	65.6
100 to 199 beds	15.4	36.3	52.3	55.0	56.3	58.3	59.4	61.7	61.8
200 to 299 beds	16.7	36.4	50.7	52.9	54.6	55.3	57.2	58.8	59.0
300 to 499 beds	17.2	34.4	48.0	48.8	50.6	51.9	53.2	54.2	55.1
500 beds or more	15.1	30.4	41.6	43.9	44.4	46.5	46.9	49.7	50.2

[1] For definition of community hospital, see footnotes 1 and 2, table 185.

Source: American Hospital Association, Chicago, IL, *Hospital Statistics*, annual (copyright); and unpublished data from the Annual Survey of Hospitals.

No. 195. Ambulatory Surgery Procedures, by Sex and Age: 1994

[In thousands. Covers procedures done on an ambulatory (outpatient) basis in hospitals and freestanding ambulatory surgery centers. Excluded specialties include dentistry, podiatry, abortion, family planning, birthing, pain block, and small procedures. Based on sample data collected from the National Survey of Ambulatory Surgery, a sample survey of medical records in hospitals and free- standing ambulatory surgery centers; subject to sampling variability]

TYPE OF PROCEDURE	Total	SEX		AGE			
		Male	Female	Under 15 years	15-44 years	45-64 years	65 years and over
Total [1]	**28,278**	**12,331**	**15,947**	**2,446**	**9,006**	**7,497**	**9,330**
Injection of agent into spinal canal	339	145	194	(B)	113	114	110
Release of carpal tunnel	348	118	230	(B)	159	123	66
Extraction of lens	1,989	738	1,251	(B)	45	271	1,658
Insertion of prosthetic lens (pseudophakos)	1,575	588	986	(B)	32	229	1,306
Myringotomy with insertion of tube	579	340	239	556	14	(B)	(B)
Operations on nasal sinuses	409	208	201	48	181	142	39
Tonsillectomy with or without adenoidectomy	378	163	215	263	106	(B)	(B)
Cardiac catheterization	323	198	125	(B)	37	150	131
Endoscopy of small intestine [2]	1,242	543	699	20	315	418	488
Endoscopy of large intestine [2]	1,836	837	1,000	12	349	661	815
Endoscopic polypectomy of large intestine	462	257	206	(B)	36	175	250
Repair of inguinal hernia	501	452	49	87	158	118	138
Laparoscopy	392	31	361	(B)	321	55	11
Cystoscopy with or without biopsy	784	473	311	31	160	232	361
Bilateral destruction or occlusion of fallopian tubes	319	(X)	319	-	314	(B)	-
Dilation and curettage of uterus	597	(X)	597	(B)	386	167	43
Arthroscopy of knee	569	340	228	10	326	163	70
Excision of semilunar cartilage of knee	387	244	143	(B)	193	127	62
Operations on muscle, tendon, fascia and bursa	580	280	299	28	269	194	90
Biopsy of breast	369	(B)	364	(B)	131	148	87
Local excision of lesion of breast (lumpectomy)	355	(B)	343	(B)	146	131	76
Excision or destruction of lesion or tissue of skin and subcutaneous tissue	900	440	460	69	342	249	240
Arteriography and angiocardiography using contrast material	553	322	230	(B)	58	249	243

- Represents zero. B Figure too small to meet statistical standard for reliability. X Not applicable [1] Includes other procedures not shown separately. [2] With or without biopsy.

Source: U.S. National Center for Health Statistics, *Advance Data*, No. 283, March 14, 1997.

No. 196. Visits to Hospital Outpatient and Emergency Departments: 1994 and 1995

[In thousands. An outpatient department is a hospital facility where nonurgent ambulatory care is provided under the supervision of a physician. Data for outpatient departments exclude clinics where only ancillary services, such as radiology, are provided. An emergency room is a hospital facility staffed by physicians for the provision of providing outpatient services to patients whose conditions require immediate attention and is staffed 24 hours a day. Data are for non-Federal short stay, or general hospitals. Based on the National Hospital Ambulatory Care Surveys and subject to sampling error; see source for details]

CHARACTERISTIC	OUTPATIENT DEPARTMENT		EMERGENCY DEPARTMENT	
	1994	1995	1994	1995
All visits	66,345	67,232	93,402	96,545
Age:				
Under 15 years old	13,516	15,039	23,751	22,709
15 to 24 years old	7,834	8,307	15,411	15,681
25 to 44 years old	19,815	18,568	28,219	30,086
45 to 64 years old	14,306	14,811	13,011	13,978
65 to 74 years old	5,955	6,004	5,797	6,057
75 years old and over	4,920	4,482	7,214	8,033
Sex:				
Male	25,746	26,221	44,666	46,501
Female	40,599	41,011	48,736	50,044
Race:				
White	49,701	50,110	72,337	74,593
Black	15,132	15,022	18,603	19,284
Asian/Pacific islander	1,283	1,926	1,489	1,963
American Indian/Eskimo/Aleut	228	[1]174	972	705
Visit status:				
Old patient	52,180	54,741	(NA)	(NA)
Old problem	42,258	44,305	(NA)	(NA)
New problem	9,922	10,436	(NA)	(NA)
New patient	14,165	12,491	(NA)	(NA)
Expected source of payment: [2]				
Insurance [3]	(NA)	53,921	(NA)	75,656
Blue Cross/Blue Shield	(NA)	8,269	(NA)	10,987
Other private insurance	(NA)	14,489	(NA)	25,056
Medicare	11,867	10,876	13,933	14,949
Medicaid	20,029	19,333	23,054	22,041
Worker's compensation	(NA)	834	(NA)	3,776
Other source of insurance	(NA)	4,594	(NA)	4,544
Unknown source of insurance	(NA)	2,002	(NA)	3,474
Self pay	7,323	7,113	12,523	16,113
No charge	923	990	227	519
Other/unknown source of payment	(NA)	2,930	(NA)	4,023
Disposition: [2]				
Return to clinic:				
By appointment	42,821	43,352	4,123	(NA)
As needed	13,136	16,154	25,843	26,826
Refer to other clinic/physician	5,045	4,825	34,760	38,765
No followup	4,122	3,817	6,652	8,573
Telephone followup	2,044	2,082	(NA)	(NA)
Return to referring physician	2,004	2,075	23,526	18,874
Admit to hospital	936	670	11,315	10,626
Left before being seen	(NA)	(NA)	(NA)	1,110
Admit to ICU/CCU [4]	(NA)	(NA)	(NA)	1,822
Transfer to other facility	(NA)	(NA)	(NA)	1,751
Dead on arrival, died in emergency dept.	(NA)	(NA)	(NA)	301
Other	1,659	1,657	(NA)	2,547

NA Not available. [1] Figure does not meet standard of reliability or precision. [2] More than one reported source of payment or disposition may be reported. [3] Equal to all visits minus self pay, no charge, other source, and no answer. [4] Intensive/critical care unit.

Source: U.S. National Center for Health Statistics, *Advance Data*, Nos. 284 and 285, May 7, 1997 and April 15, 1997 and prior issues.

No. 197. Use of Mammography for Women 40 Years Old and Over by Patient Characteristics: 1987 to 1993

[Percent of women having a mammogram within the past two years. Covers civilian noninstitutional population. Based on National Health Interview Survey; see Appendix III]

CHARACTERISTIC	1987	1990	1991	1993
Women 40 years old and over, total [1]	**28.7**	**51.4**	**54.6**	**59.7**
40 to 49 years old	31.9	55.1	55.6	59.9
50 years old and over	27.4	49.7	54.1	59.7
50 to 64 years old	31.7	56.0	60.3	65.1
65 years old and over	22.8	43.4	48.1	54.2
White, non-Hispanic	30.3	52.7	56.0	60.6
Black, non-Hispanic	23.8	46.0	47.7	59.2
Hispanic origin [2]	18.3	45.2	49.2	50.9
Years of school completed:				
Less than 12 years	17.8	36.4	40.0	46.4
12 years	31.3	52.7	55.8	59.0
13 years or more	37.7	62.8	65.2	69.5
Poverty status: [3]				
Below poverty	15.0	28.7	36.5	41.6
At or above poverty	31.0	54.8	58.4	62.8

[1] Includes all other races not shown separately and unknown education level and poverty status. [2] Persons of Hispanic origin may be of any race. [3] For explanation of poverty level, see text, section 14.

Source: U.S. National Center for Health Statistics, *Health, United States, 1995*.

No. 198. Organ Transplants and Grafts: 1985 to 1996

[As of end of year. Based on reports of procurement programs and transplant centers in the United States, except as noted]

PROCEDURE	NUMBER OF PROCEDURES							NUMBER OF CENTERS		Number of people waiting, 1996	1-year patient survival rates, 1995 (percent)
	1985	1990	1991	1992	1993	1994	1995	1990	1996		
Transplant: [1]											
Heart	719	2,108	2,125	2,171	2,297	2,340	2,361	148	166	3,698	84.3
Liver	602	2,690	2,953	3,064	3,441	3,652	3,924	85	120	7,467	83.8
Kidney	7,695	9,878	10,122	10,230	11,020	11,390	11,816	232	253	34,550	97.5
Heart-lung	30	52	51	48	60	71	68	79	99	237	(NA)
Lung	2	203	405	535	667	723	871	70	93	2,309	76.2
Pancreas/islet cell	130	528	531	557	774	842	1,027	84	121	323	94.7
Cornea grafts [2]	26,300	40,631	41,393	42,337	40,215	43,743	44,652	[3]107	(NA)	(NA)	(NA)
Bone grafts	(NA)	350,000	350,000	350,000	(NA)	(NA)	450,000	30	(NA)	(NA)	(NA)
Skin grafts	(NA)	5,500	5,500	5,500	(NA)	(NA)	5,500	25	(NA)	(NA)	(NA)

NA Not available. [1] Simultaneous kidney-pancreas transplants are counted twice, both in kidney transplants and in pancreas transplants. Double kidney, double lung, and heart-lung transplants are counted as one transplant. [2] 1985 through 1992, number of procedures and eye banks include Canada. [3] Eye banks.

Source: Transplants: through 1992, U.S. Department of Health and Human Services, Public Health Service, Division of Organ Transplantation; beginning 1993, United Network for Organ Sharing, Richmond, VA; American Association of Tissue Banks, McLean, VA; and Eye Bank Association of America, Washington, DC; and unpublished data.

No. 199. Home Health and Hospice Care Patients, by Selected Characteristics: 1994

[See headnote, table 201]

ITEM	CURRENT PATIENTS [1]			DISCHARGES [2]		
	Total	Home health agency	Hospice	Total	Home health agency	Hospice
Total (1,000)	**1,950.3**	**1,889.4**	**61.0**	**5,600.2**	**5,272.2**	**328.0**
PERCENT DISTRIBUTION						
Age: [3]						
Under 45 years old	12.4	12.5	8.6	12.3	12.7	5.7
45-54 years old	4.6	4.6	6.8	7.4	7.4	7.4
55-64 years old	10.1	9.9	15.6	7.8	7.4	13.9
65 years old and over	72.3	72.4	68.8	71.7	71.7	72.9
65-69 years old	9.3	9.3	9.5	9.4	9.2	11.6
70-74 years old	12.6	12.6	13.8	14.6	14.5	16.2
75-79 years old	14.9	15.0	12.3	16.4	16.5	15.5
80-84 years old	15.9	15.9	16.5	18.1	18.5	12.4
85 years old and over	19.5	19.6	16.6	13.2	13.0	17.2
Sex:						
Male	32.8	32.5	44.7	41.0	40.3	52.3
Female	67.2	67.5	55.3	59.0	59.7	47.7
Race:						
White	63.8	63.3	80.8	66.8	66.0	79.4
Black	15.6	15.9	7.2	8.6	8.6	7.3
Other or unknown	20.6	20.8	12.0	24.7	25.4	13.3
Marital status: [4]						
Married	31.2	30.6	48.4	38.3	37.7	48.9
Widowed	36.0	36.2	30.6	30.6	30.7	29.7
Divorced or separated	4.8	4.7	6.0	4.7	4.6	5.5
Never married	16.5	16.7	11.4	14.9	15.2	9.2
Unknown	11.5	11.7	3.7	11.5	11.8	6.8
Primary admission diagnosis:						
Neoplasms	7.7	6.1	58.7	(NA)	(NA)	(NA)
Endocrine, nutritional and metabolic and immunity disorders	9.2	9.4	(NA)	(NA)	(NA)	(NA)
Diseases of the nervous system and sense organs	7.8	7.8	6.7	(NA)	(NA)	(NA)
Diseases of the circulatory system	26.2	26.6	12.8	(NA)	(NA)	(NA)
Diseases of the musculoskeletal system and connective tissue	8.0	8.2	(NA)	(NA)	(NA)	(NA)
Injuries and poisoning	7.7	8.0	(NA)	(NA)	(NA)	(NA)

NA Not available. [1] Patients on the rolls of the agency as of midnight the day prior to the survey. [2] Patients removed from the rolls of the agency during the 12 months prior to the day of the survey. A patient could be included more than once if the individual had more than one episode of care during the year. [3] Excludes unknown. [4] For current patients, marital status at admission; for discharged patients, status at time of discharge.

Source: U.S. National Center for Health Statistics, *Advance Data*, No. 274, April 24, 1996.

No. 200. Elderly Home Health Patients: 1994

[Covers the civilian noninstitutionalized population 65 years old and over who are home health care patients. Home health care is provided to individuals and families in their place of residence. Based on the 1994 National Home and Hospice Care Survey]

ITEM	CURRENT PATIENTS [1]		DISCHARGES [2]	
	Number (1,000)	Percent	Number (1,000)	Percent
Total 65 years old and over	1,379.8	100.0	3,826.5	100.0
Received help with—				
Bathing or showering	746.6	54.1	1,580.1	41.3
Dressing	632.4	45.8	1,307.7	34.2
Eating	127.1	9.2	223.3	5.8
Transferring in/out of a bed or chair	436.3	31.6	1,048.0	27.4
Using the toilet	336.6	24.4	759.7	19.9
Doing light housework	564.4	40.9	918.4	24.0
Managing money	27.4	2.0	40.4	1.1
Shopping for groceries or clothes	252.5	18.3	454.1	11.9
Using the telephone	47.0	3.4	40.6	1.1
Preparing meals	351.4	25.5	728.8	19.0
Taking medications	340.4	24.7	755.6	19.7
Primary source of payment of last billing:				
Private insurance	26.2	1.9	315.5	8.2
Own income	63.1	4.6	116.1	3.0
Medicare	1,004.6	72.8	3,068.5	80.2
Medicaid	120.5	8.7	108.9	2.8
Services rendered last billing period:				
Skilled nursing	1,122.4	81.3	3,302.8	86.3
Personal care	585.5	42.4	1,176.7	30.8
Social services	124.6	9.0	368.4	9.6
Counseling	48.3	3.5	165.7	4.3
Medications	74.3	5.4	190.2	5.0
Physical therapy	232.3	16.8	933.9	24.4
Homemaker/companion services	322.2	23.4	612.4	16.0
Referral services	20.8	1.5	66.4	1.7
Dietary and nutrition services	44.1	3.2	76.0	2.0
Physician services	16.2	1.2	48.9	1.3
High tech care	13.9	1.0	39.8	1.0
Occupational/vocational therapy	39.0	2.8	164.2	4.3
Speech therapy/audiology	17.0	1.2	46.9	1.2

[1] Patients on the rolls of the agency as of midnight the day prior to the survey. [2] Patients removed from the rolls of the agency during the 12 months prior to the day of the survey. A patient could be included more than once if the individual had more than one episode of care during the year.

Source: U.S. National Center for Health Statistics, *Advance Data*, No. 279, September 26, 1996.

No. 201. Home Health and Hospice Care Agencies, by Selected Characteristics: 1994

[In percent, except as indicated. Based on the 1994 National Home and Hospice Care Survey. Home health care is provided to individuals and families in their place of residence. Hospice care is available in both the home and inpatient settings. Agencies which provide both types of care are classified according to how the majority of their patients are cared for. See source for details. For composition of regions, see table 26]

ITEM	AGENCIES			CURRENT PATIENTS [1]			DISCHARGES [2]		
	Total	Home health agency	Hospice	Total	Home health agency	Hospice	Total	Home health agency	Hospice
Total (1,000)	10.9	9.8	1.1	1,950.3	1,889.4	61.0	5,600.2	5,272.2	328.0
PERCENT DISTRIBUTION									
Ownership:									
Proprietary	40.2	43.8	7.3	29.7	30.3	11.0	26.9	28.0	10.2
Voluntary nonprofit	42.0	36.8	90.4	59.8	59.0	86.3	66.6	65.4	87.0
Government and other	17.8	19.5	2.3	10.5	10.7	2.7	6.4	6.7	2.8
Certification:									
Medicare	79.9	80.6	73.7	88.1	88.0	92.8	95.0	95.1	92.9
Medicaid	79.5	81.0	65.5	88.2	88.1	90.0	91.6	91.7	90.9
Region:									
Northeast	18.0	18.1	16.9	33.4	33.7	25.2	36.9	37.1	33.5
Midwest	26.8	26.8	27.0	19.5	19.4	23.4	20.4	20.2	22.4
South	41.1	41.7	35.9	34.0	34.0	34.2	26.8	26.7	29.8
West	14.0	13.3	20.3	13.1	12.9	17.2	15.9	16.0	14.3

[1] Patients on the rolls of the agency as of midnight the day prior to the survey. [2] Patients removed from the rolls of the agency during the 12 months prior to the day of the survey. A patient could be included more than once if the individual had more than one episode of care during the year.

Source: U.S. National Center for Health Statistics, *Advance Data*, No. 274, April 24, 1996.

No. 202. Nursing and Related Care Facilities: 1960 to 1995

ITEM	Unit	1960	1986	1989	1991	1992	1993	1994	1995
Nursing and related care: [1]									
Facilities	Number	[2]23,085	25,646	(NA)	33,006	(NA)	(NA)	(NA)	(NA)
Beds	1,000	[2]1,537	1,707	(NA)	1,921	(NA)	(NA)	(NA)	(NA)
Resident patients	1,000	[2]1,396	1,553	(NA)	1,729	(NA)	(NA)	(NA)	(NA)
Employees, full-time	1,000	[2]798	(NA)	(NA)	(NA)	(NA)	(NA)	(NA)	(NA)
Per 1,000 patients	Rate	[2]571	(NA)	(NA)	(NA)	(NA)	(NA)	(NA)	(NA)
Skilled nursing facilities [3]	Number	5,052	6,897	8,198	9,674	10,589	11,309	12,265	13,122
Beds	1,000	436	(NA)	491	567	597	617	639	652
Per 1,000 Medicare enrollees [4]	Rate	17.7	(NA)	16.8	15.3	16.2	18.3	17.4	15.9

NA Not available. [1] Covers nursing homes with three beds or more and all other places providing some form of nursing, personal, or domiciliary care; standards vary widely among States. Excludes hospital-based nursing homes. Includes skilled nursing facilities. 1960 based on National Master Facility Inventory. 1986 data based on the 1986 Inventory of Long Term Care Places. Data may not be strictly comparable with previous years. 1991 based on National Health Provider Inventory; excludes board and care homes for the mentally retarded. [2] Includes 1978 data for Alaska and South Dakota. [3] Source: U.S. Health Care Financing Administration, *Medicare Participating Providers and Suppliers of Health Services, 1980;* and unpublished data. Covers facilities and beds certified for participation under Medicare as of midyear. Includes facilities which have transfer agreements with one or more participating hospitals, and are engaged primarily in providing skilled nursing care and related services for the rehabilitation of injured, disabled, or sick persons. [4] Based on number of aged persons residing in United States who were enrolled in the Medicare hospital insurance program as of July 1 of year stated.

Source: Except as noted, U.S. National Center for Health Statistics, *Advance Data from Vital and Health Statistics,* Nos. 147 and 244; and unpublished data.

No. 203. Nursing Homes—Selected Characteristics: 1985 and 1995

[Covers nursing and related care homes in the conterminous United States that had three or more beds, were staffed for use by residents, and routinely provided nursing and personal care services. Excludes places providing only room and board and places serving specific health problems. Based on the 1995 National Nursing Home Survey, a two-stage survey sample of nursing homes and their residents. Subject to sampling variability. For composition of regions, see table 26]

CHARACTERISTIC	Nursing homes	BEDS		CURRENT RESIDENTS		FULL-TIME EQUIVALENT EMPLOYMENT			
						Administrative, medical, and therapeutic		Nursing	
		Number (1,000)	Per nursing home	Number (1,000)	Occupancy rate [1]	Number (1,000)	Rate per 100 beds	Number (1,000)	Rate per 100 beds
1985	19,100	1,624	85	1,491	91.8	(NA)	(NA)	(NA)	(NA)
1995, total	16,700	1,771	106	1,549	87.4	20.1	1.1	914	51.6
OWNERSHIP									
Proprietary	11,000	1,152	105	990	85.9	13.6	1.2	574	49.8
Voluntary nonprofit	4,300	468	109	421	89.9	4.9	1.0	254	54.3
Government and other	1,400	151	108	138	91.5	1.6	1.1	85	56.3
CERTIFICATION									
Medicare and Medicaid certified	11,600	1,378	118	1,214	88.0	15.0	1.1	728	52.8
Medicare only	[2]1,000	60	60	50	83.9	1.9	3.2	36	60.0
Medicaid only	3,400	280	82	241	85.8	2.8	1.0	128	45.5
Not certified	[2]700	53	75	44	84.2	0.4	0.8	22	42.4
BED SIZE									
Less than 50 beds	2,800	87	31	71	81.4	4.7	5.4	50	56.8
50-99 beds	5,900	430	73	378	87.9	5.2	1.2	221	51.4
100-199 beds	6,700	903	135	794	88.0	8.4	0.9	469	51.9
200 beds or more	1,300	351	270	305	86.9	1.8	0.5	174	49.6
REGION									
Northeast	2,900	379	131	347	91.5	4.2	1.1	215	56.6
Midwest	5,600	564	101	495	87.7	4.8	0.9	264	46.8
South	5,500	573	104	495	86.4	6.3	1.1	300	52.3
West	2,600	255	91	212	83.2	4.8	1.9	135	52.9
AFFILIATION [3]									
Chain	9,100	978	108	857	87.7	(NA)	(NA)	(NA)	(NA)
Independent	7,600	788	91	689	87.4	(NA)	(NA)	(NA)	(NA)

NA Not available. [1] Number of residents divided by number of available beds multiplied by 100. [2] Figure does not meet standards of reliability or precision. [3] Excludes a small number of homes, beds, and residents with unknown affiliation

Source: U.S. National Center for Health Statistics, *Advance Data,* No. 280, January 23, 1997.

No. 204. Residential Facilities for Persons with Mental Retardation: 1980 to 1993

[For years ending June 30. Persons with mental retardation refers to those who have been so designated by State governments in the process of placing them into residential facilities]

ITEM	STATE OPERATED FACILITIES [1]					PRIVATE FACILITIES [2]			
	1980	1985	1990	1992	1993	1982	1990	1992	1993
Number of facilities [3]	394	881	1,321	1,681	1,765	14,605	41,588	47,922	58,790
Residents beginning of year	148,734	117,101	94,625	86,498	73,856	(NA)	(NA)	(NA)	(NA)
Admissions [4]	14,084	7,713	5,548	5,691	4,700	22,431	(NA)	(NA)	(NA)
Deaths in institutions	2,142	1,537	1,100	1,075	1,167	920	(NA)	(NA)	(NA)
Live releases, total	16,225	10,310	7,620	7,666	7,258	12,999	(NA)	(NA)	(NA)
Residents end of year	140,230	112,183	91,640	84,007	69,760	115,032	188,902	210,132	229,279
Rate per 100,000 population [5]	62.2	47.5	34.7	33.3	31.9	50.0	76.0	82.7	89.6
Average daily residents	136,304	111,791	92,729	84,580	71,477	(NA)	(NA)	(NA)	(NA)
Maintenance expenditures per day per average daily resident (dollars) [6]	66	122	196	211	225	[7]37	(NA)	(NA)	(NA)

NA Not available. [1] Data as submitted by many State agencies; figures reflect some estimates. Resident patients at the end of a year do not equal the number at the beginning of a succeeding year. Includes estimates for underreporting. Includes data for 142 facilities in 1980, 121 facilities in 1985, 108 in 1990, 124 in 1992, and 110 in 1993 operated as mental hospitals or other facilities and which have residents with mental retardation. The average daily number of residents with mental retardation in these facilities was 8,240 in 1980, 5,602 in 1985, 1,487 in 1990, 1,561 in 1992, and 1,515 in 1993. [2] A privately-operated living quarter which provides 24-hour, 7-days-a-week responsibility for room, board, and supervision of mentally retarded persons. Excludes single-family homes providing services to a relative; and nursing homes, boarding homes, and foster homes not formally licensed or contracted as mental retardation service providers. [3] Beginning 1985, reflects the development of a large number of community based State-operated facilities which were developed in the early 1980's. [4] Includes readmissions and excludes transfers. Excludes people entering newly opened facilities. [5] Based on Bureau of the Census estimated civilian population as of July 1. Estimates reflect revisions based on 1990 Census of Population. [6] Reporting facilities only; includes salaries and wages, purchased provisions, fuel, light, water, etc. [7] Represents average daily reimbursement rate per resident.

Source: Center for Residential Services and Community Living (CRSCL), Institute on Community Integration, UAP, University of Minnesota, Minneapolis, MN, Magan, Blake, Prouty, and Larkin, Report No. 40, and earlier reports and unpublished data.

No. 205. Mental Health Facilities—Summary, by Type of Facility: 1992

[Facilities, beds and inpatients as of year-end; other data are for calendar year or fiscal year ending in a month other than December since facilities are permitted to report on either a calendar or fiscal year basis. Excludes private psychiatric office practice and psychiatric service modes of all types in hospitals or outpatient clinics of Federal agencies other than U.S. Dept. of Veterans Affairs. Excludes data from Puerto Rico, Virgin Islands, Guam, and other territories]

TYPE OF FACILITY	Number of facilities	INPATIENT BEDS		INPATIENTS		Average daily inpatients (1,000)	Inpatient care episodes [2] (1,000)	EXPENDITURES		Patient care staff [4] (1,000)
		Total (1,000)	Rate [1]	Total (1,000)	Rate [1]			Total (mil. dol.)	Per capita [3] (dol.)	
Total	**5,498**	**271.1**	**108.0**	**214.9**	**85.8**	**216.9**	**2,039**	**29,765**	**117.0**	**432.2**
Mental hospitals:										
State and county	273	93.1	36.7	83.4	32.9	83.9	93.8	7,970	31.3	110.9
Private [5]	972	73.8	29.1	51.8	20.4	52.7	555.8	7,469	29.5	99.7
General hospitals [6]	1,616	52.1	21.3	35.6	14.6	36.3	987.6	5,193	20.4	72.9
Veterans Administration [7]	162	22.5	9.2	18.5	7.6	18.1	198.9	1,530	6.0	20.8
Free-standing psychiatric outpatient clinics [8]	862	(X)	(X)	(X)	(X)	(X)	(X)	821	3.2	13.2
Other [9]	1,613	29.6	11.7	25.6	10.3	25.9	202.5	6,782	26.6	114.7

X Not applicable. [1] Rate per 100,000 population. Based on Bureau of the Census estimated civilian population as of July 1. [2] "Inpatient care episodes" is defined as the number of residents in inpatient facilities at the beginning of the year plus the total additions to inpatient facilities during the year. [3] Based on Bureau of the Census estimated civilian population as of July 1. [4] Full-time equivalent. [5] Includes residential treatment centers for emotionally disturbed children. [6] Non-Federal hospitals with separate psychiatric services. [7] Includes U.S. Department of Veterans Affairs (VA) neuropsychiatric hospitals, VA general hospitals with separate psychiatric settings and VA freestanding psychiatric outpatient clinics. [8] Includes mental health facilities which provide only psychiatric outpatient services. [9] Includes other multiservice mental health facilities with two or more settings, which are not elsewhere classified, as well as freestanding partial care facilities which only provide psychiatric partial care services. Number of facilities, expenditures, and staff data also include freestanding psychiatric partial care facilities.

Source: U.S. Substance Abuse and Mental Health Services Administration, Center for Mental Health Services, unpublished data.

No. 206. Days of Disability, by Type and Selected Characteristics: 1980 to 1994

[Covers civilian noninstitutional population. Beginning 1985, the levels of estimates may not be comparable to estimates for 1980 because the later data are based on a revised questionnaire and field procedures; for further information, see source. Based on National Health Interview Survey; see Appendix III. For composition of regions, see table 26]

ITEM	TOTAL DAYS OF DISABILITY (millions)						DAYS PER PERSON					
	1980	1985	1990	1992	1993	1994	1980	1985	1990	1992	1993	1994
Restricted-activity days [1]	4,165	3,453	3,669	4,096	4,346	4,143	19.1	14.8	14.9	16.3	17.1	16.0
Male	1,802	1,442	1,558	1,739	1,844	1,723	17.1	12.8	13.1	14.2	14.9	13.6
Female	2,363	2,011	2,111	2,357	2,502	2,420	21.0	16.6	16.7	18.2	19.2	18.2
White	3,518	2,899	3,057	3,384	3,598	3,375	18.7	14.5	14.8	16.2	17.0	15.7
Black	580	489	536	586	616	608	22.7	17.4	17.7	18.6	19.2	18.4
Under 65 years	3,228	2,557	2,734	3,005	3,289	3,070	16.6	12.4	12.6	13.6	14.7	13.4
65 years and over	937	895	938	1,091	1,057	1,073	39.2	33.1	31.4	35.4	33.8	34.6
Northeast	862	689	656	684	798	803	17.9	13.8	13.2	13.7	15.9	15.9
Midwest	989	744	836	946	978	879	17.2	12.7	14.0	15.4	15.8	13.9
South	1,415	1,308	1,404	1,518	1,564	1,443	19.8	16.3	16.7	18.0	18.3	16.4
West	899	712	773	948	1,006	1,017	22.0	15.7	14.8	17.1	17.7	17.6
Family income:												
Under $10,000	(NA)	893	862	712	741	681	(NA)	25.8	27.3	29.0	30.2	29.1
$10,000 to $19,999	(NA)	781	758	847	857	801	(NA)	16.7	19.1	22.1	22.3	21.5
$20,000 to $34,999	(NA)	791	715	750	849	825	(NA)	12.1	13.5	14.6	15.7	15.2
$35,000 or more	(NA)	568	912	940	1,086	1,051	(NA)	9.9	10.3	10.3	11.2	10.6
Bed-disability days [2]	1,520	1,438	1,521	1,586	1,708	1,603	7.0	6.1	6.2	6.3	6.7	6.2
Male	616	583	625	648	688	623	5.9	5.2	5.2	5.3	5.6	4.9
Female	904	852	896	938	1,020	980	8.0	7.1	7.1	7.3	7.8	7.4
Under 65 years	1,190	1,084	1,115	1,130	1,286	1,155	6.1	5.1	5.2	5.1	5.8	5.1
65 years and over	330	371	406	455	422	448	13.8	13.7	13.6	14.8	13.5	14.4
Work-loss days [3]	485	575	621	597	666	642	5.0	5.3	5.3	5.1	5.6	5.2
Male	271	287	303	280	315	311	4.9	4.8	4.7	4.4	4.8	4.6
Female	215	288	319	317	351	332	5.1	6.0	5.9	5.9	6.4	5.9
School-loss days [4]	204	217	212	215	250	225	5.3	4.8	4.6	4.6	5.3	4.5
Male	95	100	100	101	121	104	4.8	4.4	4.3	4.2	5.0	4.1
Female	109	117	112	114	129	121	5.7	5.3	5.0	5.0	5.5	5.0

NA Not available. [1] A day when a person cuts down on his activities for more than half a day because of illness or injury. Includes bed-disability, work-loss, and school-loss days. Total includes other races and unknown income, not shown separately. [2] A day when a person stayed in bed more than half a day because of illness or injury. Includes those work-loss and school-loss days actually spent in bed. [3] A day when a person lost more than half a workday because of illness or injury. Computed for persons 17 years of age and over (beginning 1985, 18 years of age and over) in the currently employed population, defined as those who were working or had a job or business from which they were not on layoff during the 2-week period preceding the week of interview. [4] Child's loss of more than half a school day because of illness or injury. Computed for children 6-16 years of age. Beginning 1985, children 5-17 years old.

Source: U.S. National Center for Health Statistics, *Vital and Health Statistics*, series 10, No. 193; and earlier reports and unpublished data.

No. 207. Injuries, by Sex, Age and Type: 1980 to 1993

[Covers civilian noninstitutional population and comprises incidents leading to restricted activity and/or medical attention. Beginning 1985, data not strictly comparable with other years. See headnote, table 206. Based on National Health Interview Survey; see Appendix III]

YEAR	INJURIES (mil.)			RATE PER 100 POPULATION		
	Total	Male	Female	Total	Male	Female
1980	68.1	39.0	29.1	31.2	37.1	25.8
1985	62.6	34.6	28.0	26.8	30.6	23.1
1990	60.1	33.6	26.6	24.4	28.1	21.0
1991	59.7	32.2	27.5	24.0	26.7	21.5
1992	59.6	32.8	26.8	23.7	26.8	20.7
1993, total [1]	62.1	33.4	28.7	24.4	27.0	22.0
Under 5 years	5.0	2.7	2.2	24.9	26.6	23.1
5 to 17 years	12.5	7.6	4.9	26.2	31.0	21.2
18 to 44 years	29.1	16.7	12.4	27.5	32.0	23.2
45 years and over	15.6	6.5	9.1	19.2	17.4	20.7
Fractures [2]	7.9	4.3	3.6	3.1	3.5	2.8
Sprains and strains	14.2	7.4	6.8	5.6	6.0	5.2
Open wounds and lacerations	12.5	8.6	3.9	4.9	7.0	3.0
Contusions [3]	12.1	6.2	5.9	4.8	5.0	4.5
Other	15.4	6.8	8.5	6.1	5.5	6.5

[1] Includes unknown place of accident not shown separately. [2] Includes dislocations. [3] Includes superficial injuries.

Source: U.S. National Center for Health Statistics, *Vital and Health Statistics*, series 10, No. 190, and earlier reports; and unpublished data.

No. 208. Injuries Associated With Consumer Products: 1990 and 1994

[For products associated with more than 18,000 injuries in 1994. Estimates calculated from a representative sample of hospitals with emergency treatment departments in the United States. Data are estimates of the number of emergency room treated cases nationwide associated with various products. Product involvement does not necessarily mean the product caused the accident. Products were selected from the U.S. Consumer Product Safety Commission's National Electronic Injury Surveillance System]

PRODUCT	1990	1994
Home maintenance:		
Noncaustic cleaning equip. [1]	24,452	27,697
Cleaning agents (except soap)	40,475	40,284
Paints, solvents, lubricants	21,712	21,659
Home workshop equipment:		
Power home tools, except saws	29,825	35,455
Power home workshop saws	93,722	87,875
Welding, soldering, cutting tools	19,359	18,663
Workshop manual tools	118,068	122,871
Household packaging and containers:		
Cans, other containers	216,726	238,476
Glass bottles, jars	75,510	60,159
Housewares:		
Cookware, pots, pans	32,971	28,218
Cutlery, knives, unpowered	446,318	472,085
Drinking glasses	133,084	122,464
Scissors	26,966	30,684
Small kitchen appliances	43,571	38,708
Tableware and accessories	111,413	108,242
Home furnishing: [2]		
Bathroom structures, fixtures	204,859	233,079
Beds, mattresses, pillows	352,113	408,049
Carpets, rugs	92,950	128,463
Chairs, sofas, sofa beds	369,403	410,878
Desks, cabinets, shelves, racks	206,689	221,475
Electric fixtures, lamps, equipment	49,833	56,274
Ladders, stools	171,230	189,715
Mirrors, mirror glass	21,595	25,010
Tables	316,531	325,975
Misc. covers, fabrics	(NA)	23,665
Other misc. accessories	47,267	64,038
Home structures, construction: [3]		
Cabinets or door hardware	21,987	23,749
Ceilings, walls, inside panels	219,571	253,991
Counters, counter tops	29,651	39,638
Fences	120,866	122,551
Garage doors and openers	(NA)	19,656
Glass doors, windows, panels	227,321	209,884
Handrails, railings, banisters	42,225	46,422
Nails, carpet tacks, etc	253,874	227,666
Nonglass doors, panels	345,458	329,801
Outside attached structures [3]	(NA)	26,693
Porches, open side floors, etc	119,234	133,918
Stairs, ramps, landings, floors	1,711,966	1,946,802
Window, door sills, frames	52,057	66,264
General household appliances:		
Cooking ranges, ovens, etc	48,378	49,555
Refrigerators, freezers	35,227	35,096
Washers, dryers	21,406	19,888
Heating, cooling equipment: [4]		
Chimneys, fireplaces	18,957	23,680
Fans (except stove)	19,240	19,229
Heating stoves, space heaters	33,306	30,227
Pipes, heating and plumbing	23,272	29,596
Home entertainment equipment:		
Sound recording equipment [5]	44,211	43,470
Television sets, stands	37,881	43,313
Personal use items:		
Cigarettes, lighters, fuels	19,509	19,771
Clothing	118,735	144,910
Grooming devices	28,853	35,371
Jewelry	49,004	54,689
Paper money, coins	29,613	27,422
Pencils, pens, other desk supplies	46,224	46,939
Razors, shavers, razor blades	46,765	38,162
Yard and garden equipment:		
Chains and saws	39,331	41,474
Hand garden tools	35,327	49,349
Lawn, garden care equipment	49,501	64,778
Lawn mowers	77,373	80,712
Other power lawn equipment	22,967	24,652
Sports and recreation equipment:		
Beach, picnic, camping equipment	(NA)	20,313
Bicycles, accessories	580,119	604,455
Exercise equipment	78,814	89,864
Horseback riding	(NA)	71,162
Mopeds, minibikes, ATV's [6]	124,345	125,136
Nonpowder guns, BB's, pellets	24,216	27,156
Playground equipment	253,030	266,810
Skateboards	82,428	25,486
Toboggans, sleds, snow disks, etc	26,510	53,870
Trampolines	32,554	52,892
Miscellaneous products:		
Gasoline and diesel fuels	20,408	20,124
Nursery equipment	96,746	108,217
Toys	164,532	160,302

NA Not available. [1] Includes detergent. [2] Includes accessories. [3] Includes materials. [4] Includes ventilating equipment. [5] Includes reproducing equipment. [6] All-terrain vehicles.

Source: National Safety Council, Itasca, IL, *Accident Facts*, annual (copyright).

No. 209. Costs of Unintentional Injuries: 1995

[Covers costs of deaths or disabling injuries together with vehicle accidents and fires]

COST	AMOUNT (bil. dol.)					PERCENT DISTRIBUTION				
	Total [1]	Motor vehicle	Work	Home	Other	Total [1]	Motor vehicle	Work	Home	Other
Total	**434.8**	**170.6**	**119.4**	**95.1**	**63.3**	**100.0**	**100.0**	**100.0**	**100.0**	**100.0**
Wage and productivity losses [2]	222.4	63.5	59.8	59.5	42.9	51.1	37.2	50.1	62.6	67.8
Medical expense	75.1	21.5	19.2	22.8	12.8	17.3	12.6	16.1	24.0	20.2
Administrative expenses [3]	73.6	47.8	25.5	4.4	3.3	16.9	28.0	21.4	4.6	5.2
Motor vehicle damage	36.2	36.2	1.4	(NA)	(NA)	8.3	21.2	1.2	(NA)	(NA)
Employer cost [4]	19.3	1.6	11.0	3.9	3.1	4.4	1.0	9.2	4.1	4.9
Fire loss	8.2	(NA)	2.5	4.5	1.2	1.9	(NA)	2.1	4.7	1.9

NA Not available. [1] Excludes duplication between work and motor vehicle ($13.6 billion in 1995). [2] Actual loss of wages and household production, and the present value of future earnings lost. [3] Includes the administrative cost of public and private insurance, and police and legal costs. [4] Estimate of the uninsured costs incurred by employers, representing the money value of time lost by noninjured workers.

Source: National Safety Council, Itasca, IL, *Accident Facts, 1996* (copyright).

No. 210. Disability Status of Persons 21 to 64 Years Old: 1991 to 1994

[For period September through December of year shown. Covers civilian noninstitutional population and members of the Armed Forces living off post or with their families on post. The criteria for presence of disability varied by age. In general, a disability is considered a reduced ability to perform tasks one would normally do at a given stage in life. Based on the Survey of Income and Program Participation; for details, see source]

DISABILITY STATUS	1991		1993		1994	
	Number (1,000)	Percent employed	Number (1,000)	Percent employed	Number (1,000)	Percent employed
Persons 21 to 64 years old, total	144,075	75.1	148,244	75.1	149,369	76.2
With no disability	116,641	80.5	119,414	80.6	119,960	82.1
With a disability	27,434	52.0	28,830	52.4	29,409	52.3
Severe	12,494	23.3	13,819	25.0	14,219	26.1
Not severe	14,940	76.0	15,011	77.7	15,190	76.9
With a functional limitation	18,012	48.6	19,400	49.7	17,797	48.6
Severe	6,352	27.6	7,232	29.7	6,841	32.2
With difficulty—						
Seeing words and letters	4,567	45.5	5,155	45.5	4,002	43.7
Hearing normal conversation	5,222	63.7	5,650	65.4	4,489	64.4
Lifting and carrying	7,548	32.1	8,149	34.5	8,026	34.8
Climbing stairs	7,803	30.1	8,584	31.6	8,517	33.9
Walking three city blocks	7,672	31.5	8,600	31.9	8,697	33.5
With an ADL [1] limitation	3,313	25.3	3,820	26.8	3,640	27.2
With an IADL [2] limitation	4,811	22.9	5,375	25.4	5,434	27.1
Needs personal assistance with an ADL or IADL	3,704	21.2	4,021	23.1	4,065	24.6
Uses a wheelchair	495	18.4	582	20.9	685	22.0
Does not use a wheelchair but uses a cane, crutches, or a walker	1,464	25.2	1,841	29.2	1,609	27.5

[1] ADL's are activities of daily living and include getting around inside the home, getting in or out of a bed or chair, taking a bath or shower, dressing, eating, and using the toilet. [2] IADL's are instrumental activities of daily living and include going outside the home, keeping track of money and bills, preparing meals, doing light housework, and using the telephone.

Source: U.S. Bureau of the Census, "Disability-Employment Rate of Persons with Disabilities;" published 30 October 1996; <http://www.census.gov/hhes/www/disable/sipp/emprate.html>.

No. 211. Osteoporosis—Prevalence Among Women 50 Years Old and Over: 1988-91

[In percent. Osteopenia is defined as a bone mineral density 1-2.5 standard deviations below the mean of white, non-Hispanic women 20-29 years of age as measured in the National Health and Nutrition Examination Survey III (NHANES) (Phase I). Osteoporosis is defined as a bone mineral density value of more than 2.5 standard deviations below the mean of young white, non-Hispanic women. Osteoporosis is an important cause of hip fractures among older women, with decreased bone mass density predicting future hip fracture risk. Based on sample data collected from NHANES III (Phase I)]

DEGREE OF BONE LOSS	50 to 59 years old	60 to 69 years old	70 to 79 years old	80 years old and over
Total	55	69	88	95
Osteopenia	51	50	57	45
Osteoporosis	4	19	31	50

Source: U.S. National Center for Health Statistics, *Health, United States, 1995.*

No. 212. Children Immunized Against Specified Diseases: 1991 to 1994

[In percent. Covers civilian noninstitutionalized population ages 19 months to 35 months. Based on estimates from the National Health Interview Survey. Excludes respondents with unknown or missing information. See Appendix III]

VACCINATION	1991, total	1992, total	1993, total	1994			
				Total	White	Black	Other
Diphtheria-tetanus-pertussis (DPT)/ diphtheria-tetanus:							
3+ doses	68.8	83.1	88.2	89.5	90.6	84.4	87.9
4+ doses	43.3	59.0	72.1	70.1	70.8	64.4	77.3
Polio: 3+ doses	53.1	72.4	78.9	79.2	80.3	73.2	81.7
Hib [1]: 3+ doses	1.7	28.2	55.0	75.0	76.6	67.2	72.3
Hepatitis B: 3+ doses	(NA)	(NA)	16.3	34.4	33.7	36.2	39.7
Measles containing	82.0	82.5	84.1	90.3	91.7	86.0	81.1
3 DPT/3 polio/1 MMR [2]	50.0	68.7	74.5	77.3	78.7	70.5	76.3
4 DPT/3 polio/1 MMR [2 3]	37.0	55.3	67.1	67.5	68.4	61.2	72.4

NA Not available. [1] Haemophilus B. [2] Measles, measles/rubella, measles/mumps, and measles/mumps/rubella. [3] Up-to-date for age.

Source: U.S. Centers for Disease Control and Prevention, Atlanta, GA, unpublished data.

No. 213. Specified Reportable Diseases—Cases Reported: 1980 to 1995

[Figures should be interpreted with caution. Although reporting of some of these diseases is incomplete, the figures are of value in indicating trends of disease incidence. Includes cases imported from outside the United States]

DISEASE	1980	1985	1989	1990	1991	1992	1993	1994	1995
AIDS [1]	(NA)	8,249	33,722	41,595	43,672	45,472	103,533	78,279	71,547
Amebiasis	5,271	4,433	3,217	3,328	2,989	2,942	2,970	2,983	(2)
Aseptic meningitis	8,028	10,619	10,274	11,852	14,526	12,223	12,848	8,932	(2)
Botulism [3]	89	122	89	92	114	91	97	143	97
Brucellosis (undulant fever)	183	153	95	85	104	105	120	119	98
Chickenpox [4] (1,000)	190.9	178.2	185.4	173.1	147.1	158.4	134.7	151.2	120.6
Diphtheria	3	3	3	4	5	4	-	2	-
Encephalitis:									
Primary infectious	1,362	1,376	981	1,341	1,021	774	919	717	(2)
Post infectious	40	161	88	105	82	129	170	143	(2)
Escherichia coli 0157:H7	(2)	(2)	(2)	(2)	(2)	(2)	(2)	1,420	2,139
Haemophilius influenza	(2)	(2)	(2)	(2)	2,764	1,412	1,419	1,174	1,180
Hepatitis: B (serum) (1,000)	19.0	26.6	23.4	21.1	18.0	16.1	13.4	12.5	10.8
A (infectious) (1,000)	29.1	23.2	35.8	31.4	24.4	23.1	24.2	29.8	31.6
Unspecified (1,000)	11.9	5.5	2.3	1.7	1.3	0.9	0.6	0.4	(2)
C/Non-A, non-B (1,000) [5]	(2)	4.2	2.5	2.6	3.6	6.0	4.8	4.4	4.6
Legionellosis	(2)	830	1,190	1,370	1,317	1,339	1,280	1,615	1,241
Leprosy (Hansen disease)	223	361	163	198	154	172	187	136	144
Leptospirosis	85	57	93	77	58	54	51	38	(2)
Lyme disease	(2)	(2)	(2)	(2)	9,465	9,895	8,257	13,043	11,700
Malaria	2,062	1,049	1,277	1,292	1,278	1,087	1,411	1,229	1,419
Measles (1,000)	13.5	2.8	18.2	27.8	9.6	2.2	0.3	1.0	0.3
Meningococcal infections	2,840	2,479	2,727	2,451	2,130	2,134	2,637	2,688	3,243
Mumps (1,000)	8.6	3.0	5.7	5.3	4.3	2.6	1.7	1.5	0.9
Pertussis [6] (1,000)	1.7	3.6	4.2	4.6	2.7	4.1	6.6	4.6	5.1
Plague	18	17	4	2	11	13	10	17	9
Poliomyelitis, acute [7]	9	7	9	6	10	6	4	5	2
Psittacosis	124	119	116	113	94	92	60	38	64
Rabies, animal	6,421	5,565	4,724	4,826	6,910	8,589	9,377	8,147	7,811
Rabies, human	-	1	1	1	3	1	3	6	5
Rheumatic fever, acute [8]	432	90	144	108	127	75	112	112	(2)
Rubella [9] (1,000)	3.9	0.6	0.4	1.1	1.4	0.2	0.2	0.2	0.1
Salmonellosis [10] (1,000)	33.7	65.3	47.8	48.6	48.2	40.9	41.6	43.3	46.0
Shigellosis [11] (1,000)	19.0	17.1	25.0	27.1	23.5	23.9	32.2	29.8	32.1
Tetanus	95	83	53	64	57	45	48	51	41
Toxic-shock syndrome	(2)	384	400	322	280	244	212	192	191
Trichinosis	131	61	30	129	62	41	16	32	29
Tuberculosis [12] (1,000)	27.7	22.2	23.5	25.7	26.3	26.7	25.3	24.4	22.9
Tularemia	234	177	152	152	193	159	132	96	(2)
Typhoid fever	510	402	460	552	501	414	440	441	369
Typhus fever:									
Flea-borne (endemic-murine)	81	37	41	50	43	28	25	(2)	(2)
Tick-borne (Rocky Mt. spotted fever)	1,163	714	623	651	628	502	456	465	590
Sexually transmitted diseases:									
Gonorrhea (1,000)	1,004	911	733	690	620	501	440	418	393
Syphilis (1,000)	69	68	111	134	129	113	101	82	69
Chlamydia (1,000)	(2)	(2)	(2)	(2)	(2)	(2)	(2)	(2)	478
Chancroid (1,000)	0.8	2.1	4.7	4.2	3.5	1.9	1.4	0.8	0.6

- Represents zero. NA Not available. [1] Acquired immunodeficiency syndrome was not a notifiable disease until 1984. Figures are shown for years in which cases were reported to the CDC. Beginning 1993, based on revised classification system and expanded surveillance case definition. [2] Disease was not notifiable. [3] Includes foodborne, infant, wound, and unspecified cases. [4] Chickenpox was taken off the nationally notifiable list in 1991 but many states continue to report. [5] Includes some persons positive for antibody to hepatitis C virus who do not have hepatitis. [6] Whooping cough. [7] Revised. Data subject to annual revisions. [8] Based on reports from States: 37 in 1980, 31 in 1985, 28 in 1989, 30 in 1990, 23 in 1991, 26 in 1992 and 1993, and 27 in 1994. [9] German measles. [10] Excludes typhoid fever. [11] Bacillary dysentery. [12] Newly reported active cases.

Source: U.S. Centers for Disease Control and Prevention, Atlanta, GA, *Summary of Notifiable Diseases, United States, 1995, Morbidity and Mortality Weekly Report*, vol. 44, No. 53, October 25, 1996.

No. 214. Selected Measures of Hospital Utilization for Patients Discharged With the Diagnosis of Human Immunodeficiency Virus (HIV): 1985 to 1994

[See headnote, table 190]

MEASURE OF UTILIZATION	Unit	1985	1990	1991	1992	1993	1994
Number of patients discharged [1]	1,000	23	146	165	194	225	234
Rate of patient discharges [2]	Rate	1.0	5.9	6.6	7.6	8.8	9.0
Number of days of care	1,000	387	2,188	2,108	2,136	2,561	2,317
Rate of days of care [2]	Rate	16.3	87.7	84.1	84.3	99.9	89.5
Average length of stay [3]	Days	17.1	14.9	12.8	11.0	11.4	9.9

[1] Comparisons beginning 1990 with data for earlier years should be made with caution as estimates of change may reflect improvements in the 1988 sample design rather than true changes in hospital use. [2] Per 10,000 population. Based on Bureau of the Census estimated civilian population as of July 1. Population estimates for the 1980's do not reflect revised estimates based on the 1990 Census of Population. [3] For similar data on all patients, see table 190.

Source: National Center for Health Statistics, *Vital and Health Statistics*, series 13.

No. 215. AIDS Cases Reported, by Patient Characteristic: 1981 to 1996

[Provisional. For cases reported in the year shown. For data on AIDS deaths, see table 133. Data are subject to retrospective changes and may differ from those data in table 213]

CHARACTERISTIC	1981-1996, total	1990	1992	1993	1994	1995	1996
Total	562,549	41,595	45,789	102,287	77,268	71,180	66,886
Age:							
Under 5 years old	5,743	585	610	673	750	556	486
5 to 12 years old	1,521	139	139	196	220	193	175
13 to 19 years old	2,633	173	148	561	399	386	381
20 to 29 years old	99,137	8,077	7,888	18,391	12,636	11,114	9,778
30 to 39 years old	255,260	18,815	20,615	46,509	35,006	31,925	29,990
40 to 49 years old	140,718	9,651	11,540	26,137	20,359	19,470	18,891
50 to 59 years old	41,761	2,926	3,405	7,284	5,848	5,586	5,321
Over 60 years old	15,776	1,229	1,444	2,534	2,049	1,920	1,865
Sex:							
Male	477,518	36,726	39,457	85,881	63,447	57,666	53,293
Female	85,031	4,869	6,332	16,406	13,821	13,464	13,593
Race/ethnic group:							
Non-Hispanic White	268,746	22,302	22,446	47,597	32,808	29,500	26,324
Non-Hispanic Black	203,025	13,205	16,052	38,025	30,972	29,195	28,764
Hispanic	84,443	5,672	6,766	15,443	12,577	11,569	10,865
Other/unknown	6,335	416	525	1,222	911	666	933
Transmission category:							
Males, 13 years and over	473,770	36,335	39,082	85,452	62,972	57,323	52,966
Men who have sex with men	284,410	23,843	24,482	49,651	35,296	30,857	26,937
Injecting drug use	99,696	6,956	8,040	20,077	15,145	13,250	11,491
Men who have sex with men and injecting drug use	35,825	2,793	3,144	7,116	4,328	3,648	2,874
Hemophilia/coagulation disorder	4,220	332	324	1,047	478	418	297
Heterosexual contact [1]	9,279	260	611	1,806	1,854	1,840	2,168
Heterosexual contact with injecting drug user	6,121	460	627	1,180	919	889	792
Transfusion [2]	4,435	452	347	806	384	347	275
Undetermined [3]	29,782	1,239	1,507	3,969	4,568	6,074	8,124
Females, 13 years and over	81,515	4,536	5,958	15,964	13,325	13,078	13,268
Injecting drug use	37,027	2,325	2,966	7,996	5,853	5,209	4,534
Hemophilia/coagulation disorder	170	15	10	32	27	23	16
Heterosexual contact [1]	16,539	503	963	3,289	3,381	3,434	3,401
Heterosexual contact with injecting drug user	13,916	1,037	1,320	2,774	2,014	1,873	1,744
Transfusion [2]	3,234	336	258	494	316	279	263
Undetermined [3]	10,629	320	441	1,379	1,734	2,260	3,310

[1] Includes persons who have had heterosexual contact with a person with human immunodeficiency virus (HIV) infection or at risk of HIV infection. [2] Receipt of blood transfusion, blood components, or tissue. [3] Includes persons for whom risk information is incomplete (because of death, refusal to be interviewed, or loss to followup), persons still under investigation, men reported only to have had heterosexual contact with prostitutes, and interviewed persons for whom no specific risk is identified.

Source: U.S. Centers for Disease Control and Prevention, Atlanta, GA, *HIV/AIDS Surveillance Reports*, semiannual.

No. 216. AIDS, Syphilis, Tuberculosis, and Measles Cases Reported, by State: 1996

[Diseases selected are those included in the Healthy People 2000 Indicators series]

STATE	AIDS	Syphilis [1]	Tuber-culosis	Measles	STATE	AIDS	Syphilis [1]	Tuber-culosis	Measles
U.S.	66,816	11,110	19,096	488	MO	858	214	196	3
AL	607	854	425	-	MT	34	-	14	-
AK	36	-	70	63	NE	100	12	21	-
AZ	594	94	259	8	NV	427	19	128	5
AR	269	234	197	-	NH	93	1	21	-
CA	9,610	496	4,097	46	NJ	3,613	144	753	3
CO	522	23	78	7	NM	205	1	83	17
CT	1,112	96	132	1	NY	12,379	192	2,318	12
DE	285	35	30	1	NC	895	1,070	558	4
DC	1,262	130	130	1	ND	12	-	6	-
FL	7,330	366	1,160	1	OH	1,161	530	303	6
GA	2,411	679	607	2	OK	272	177	174	-
HI	198	4	191	35	OR	463	12	173	11
ID	39	4	12	1	PA	2,348	118	543	13
IL	2,199	388	990	3	RI	178	4	39	-
IN	596	206	184	-	SC	869	384	329	-
IA	112	21	68	1	SD	14	-	17	-
KS	239	36	65	1	TN	826	837	349	2
KY	401	154	256	-	TX	4,830	751	1,879	28
LA	1,470	493	235	-	UT	196	3	51	119
ME	50	1	16	-	VT	25	-	4	2
MD	2,253	675	296	2	VA	1,195	386	293	3
MA	1,307	85	234	12	WA	804	6	231	51
MI	965	183	373	3	WV	121	3	57	-
MN	304	51	112	18	WI	270	164	102	2
MS	450	772	227	-	WY	7	2	6	1

- Represents zero. [1] Primary and Secondary.

Source: U.S. Centers for Disease Control and Prevention, Atlanta, GA, *Morbidity and Mortality Weekly Report*, vol. 45, Nos. 51 and 52, January 3, 1997 and unpublished data.

No. 217. Acute Conditions, by Type: 1980 to 1994

[Covers civilian noninstitutional population. Estimates include only acute conditions which were medically attended or caused at least 1 day of restricted activity. Based on National Health Interview Survey; see Appendix III. See headnote, table 206. For composition of regions, see table 26]

YEAR AND CHARACTERISTIC	NUMBER OF CONDITIONS (mil.)					RATE PER 100 POPULATION				
	Infective and parasitic	Respiratory		Digestive system	Injuries	Infective and parasitic	Respiratory		Digestive system	Injuries
		Common cold	Influenza				Common cold	Influenza		
1980	53.6	(NA)	(NA)	24.9	72.7	24.6	(NA)	(NA)	11.4	33.4
1985	47.8	(NA)	(NA)	16.3	64.0	20.5	(NA)	(NA)	7.0	27.4
1990	51.7	61.5	106.8	13.0	60.1	21.0	25.0	43.4	5.3	24.4
1992	56.2	64.6	107.3	17.6	59.6	22.4	25.7	42.7	7.0	23.7
1993	54.3	68.2	132.6	16.1	62.1	21.3	26.8	52.2	6.3	24.4
1994, total [1]	54.2	66.0	90.4	15.9	61.9	20.9	25.4	34.8	6.1	23.8
Under 5 years old	11.2	14.0	7.6	2.2	5.2	54.7	68.5	37.3	10.5	25.6
5 to 17 years old	20.8	14.6	22.9	4.1	12.9	41.9	29.4	46.3	8.3	26.0
18 to 24 years old	4.7	6.6	9.8	1.9	8.3	18.5	26.1	38.7	7.4	32.7
25 to 44 years old	12.1	18.6	31.4	3.9	20.7	14.6	22.4	37.8	4.7	25.0
45 to 64 years old	3.9	8.4	13.1	2.1	8.7	7.7	16.6	25.9	4.1	17.2
65 years old and over	1.6	3.8	5.7	1.7	6.1	5.2	12.3	18.3	5.6	19.6
Male	23.8	30.3	43.2	6.9	32.6	18.8	24.0	34.1	5.5	25.8
Female	30.4	35.7	47.3	9.0	29.2	22.8	26.8	35.5	6.7	22.0
White	46.4	52.2	78.3	12.1	53.1	21.6	24.3	36.5	5.7	24.8
Black	6.7	9.7	7.7	2.9	6.8	20.2	29.3	23.2	8.9	20.6
Northeast	12.4	14.9	13.2	2.6	10.2	24.5	29.4	26.0	5.2	20.2
Midwest	10.5	14.8	26.9	3.3	15.9	16.6	23.3	42.5	5.2	25.2
South	21.5	17.1	22.0	5.9	20.8	24.4	19.4	25.0	6.7	23.6
West	9.8	19.2	28.3	4.1	14.9	17.0	33.3	49.1	7.0	25.8
Family income:										
Under $10,000	3.8	8.0	8.9	2.4	7.9	16.2	34.4	38.0	10.1	33.9
$10,000 to $19,999	6.9	9.7	11.7	3.0	9.3	18.4	26.0	31.3	8.0	25.1
$20,000 to $34,999	11.2	13.6	20.8	3.1	12.5	20.7	25.1	38.5	5.7	23.0
$35,000 or more	24.6	25.5	38.1	5.1	22.1	24.6	25.4	38.0	5.1	22.0

NA Not available. [1] Includes other races and unknown income not shown separately.

No. 218. Prevalence of Selected Chronic Conditions, by Age and Sex: 1994

[Covers civilian noninstitutional population. Conditions classified according to ninth revision of International Classification of Diseases. Based on National Health Interview Survey; see Appendix III. See headnote, table 206]

CHRONIC CONDITION	Conditions (1,000)	RATE [1]							
		Male				Female			
		Under 45 years old	45 to 64 years old	65 to 74 years old	75 years old and over	Under 45 years old	45 to 64 years old	65 to 74 years old	75 years old and over
Arthritis	33,446	27.4	176.8	430.8	424.9	38.2	297.0	513.6	604.4
Dermatitis, including eczema	9,192	29.3	21.8	25.3	[2]17.6	43.6	44.6	38.6	40.2
Trouble with—									
Dry (itching) skin	6,166	17.1	29.6	36.6	46.7	20.5	36.1	30.8	40.5
Ingrown nails	5,967	16.0	32.1	40.9	38.8	16.4	29.7	52.9	61.4
Corns and calluses	4,356	6.9	25.3	21.0	[2]17.8	12.2	32.5	46.5	58.1
Visual impairments	8,601	29.5	52.7	78.4	113.7	12.9	38.0	48.0	110.7
Cataracts	6,473	2.5	12.3	79.0	214.7	2.5	21.9	140.0	259.2
Hearing impairments	22,400	43.2	191.9	298.8	447.1	30.4	87.5	183.3	307.8
Tinnitus	7,033	11.6	60.4	118.1	106.6	9.8	33.2	67.7	79.9
Deformities or orthopedic impairments	31,068	93.5	166.7	144.4	169.3	101.3	173.2	161.8	189.9
Ulcer	4,447	11.3	27.4	27.1	[2]30.9	13.3	23.3	42.8	22.3
Hernia of abdominal cavity	4,778	7.8	31.2	54.7	55.6	5.8	31.3	70.0	72.3
Frequent indigestion	6,957	20.5	42.8	44.6	51.5	18.9	39.0	41.0	45.3
Frequent constipation	4,040	4.3	6.8	[2]13.8	60.2	15.1	17.3	47.3	102.2
Diabetes	7,766	7.3	63.3	102.4	115.6	8.9	63.0	101.0	91.8
Migraine	11,256	22.0	24.2	[2]17.1	[2]5.2	67.1	78.9	29.9	26.2
Heart conditions	22,279	27.0	162.0	319.3	429.9	33.1	111.0	250.8	361.4
High blood pressure (Hypertension)	28,236	31.9	220.0	307.7	339.2	32.4	224.5	378.7	417.5
Varicose veins of lower extremities	7,260	3.7	17.8	32.5	58.5	23.3	81.0	109.0	83.8
Hemorrhoids	9,321	19.1	68.7	51.0	66.6	29.0	55.8	70.2	58.6
Chronic bronchitis	14,021	43.6	43.8	41.7	68.0	56.5	82.7	79.0	51.7
Asthma	14,562	57.1	32.3	39.3	70.3	60.0	68.0	62.8	34.1
Hay fever, allergic rhinitis without asthma	26,146	98.0	107.3	79.6	56.6	99.2	133.4	92.2	78.8
Chronic sinusitis	34,902	101.9	147.5	118.2	113.9	135.5	210.2	175.5	176.1

[1] Conditions per 1,000 persons. [2] Figure does not meet standards of reliability or precision.

Source of tables 217 and 218: U.S. National Center for Health Statistics, *Vital and Health Statistics*, series 10, No. 193, and earlier reports; and unpublished data.

No. 219. Substance Abuse Treatment Services: 1995

[As of October 2. Preliminary. Based on the Uniform Facility Data Set Survey (UFDS), a census of all known drug abuse and alcoholism treatment providers in the United States and associated jurisdictions. Data collected in cooperation with State agencies which defined what constitutes a provider for reporting purposes]

TYPE OF CARE AND LOCATION	Service locations reporting	All clients	Drug abuse clients only	Alcoholism clients only	Clients with both problems	Clients with a drug problem [1]	Clients with an alcohol problem [2]
Total	[3]10,738	1,008,626	236,048	307,838	464,740	700,788	772,578
TYPE OF CARE							
Detoxification: [4]							
Hospital inpatient	970	9,893	1,579	3,206	5,108	6,687	8,314
Free-standing residential	695	12,881	2,391	3,297	7,193	9,584	10,490
Rehab/residential: [5]							
Hospital inpatient	748	13,998	1,713	3,963	8,322	10,035	12,285
Short-term—30 days or less	966	21,392	3,144	5,615	12,633	15,777	18,248
Long-term—over 30 days	2,435	86,638	15,459	13,476	57,703	73,162	71,179
Ambulatory: [6]							
Outpatient	7,129	729,164	182,497	242,468	304,199	486,696	546,667
Intensive outpatient [7]	3,483	115,153	19,397	31,407	64,349	83,746	95,756
Detoxification	638	19,507	9,868	4,406	5,233	15,101	9,639
INSTITUTIONAL SETTING							
Hospital [8]	1,546	140,355	31,357	36,213	72,785	104,142	108,998
Correctional facility	357	48,804	5,868	9,878	33,058	38,926	42,936
School	74	10,052	683	7,085	2,284	2,967	9,369
Solo or group practice	520	23,014	3,198	11,343	8,473	11,671	19,816
Other freestanding [3 9]	8,235	784,375	194,877	241,403	348,095	542,972	589,498
Multi-service mental health	2,024	213,560	42,757	74,660	96,143	138,900	170,803
Community health center	444	50,222	11,864	16,806	21,552	33,416	38,358
Other community facility	164	8,644	1,404	3,066	4,174	5,578	7,240
Specialty substance abuse center	4,822	506,566	145,395	136,649	226,522	371,917	363,171
Halfway house	989	49,816	9,034	14,481	26,301	35,335	40,782
A therapeutic community	775	59,248	15,873	13,695	29,680	45,553	43,375
A social model	748	52,725	8,984	16,753	26,988	35,972	43,741
HMO/MCE/MCO [10]	114	9,708	1,763	3,575	4,370	6,133	7,945
Other	934	96,597	18,697	44,629	33,271	51,968	77,900
Unknown	6	2,026	65	1,916	45	110	1,961

[1] Sum of clients with a drug problem and clients with both diagnoses. [2] Sum of clients with an alcohol problem and clients with both diagnoses. [3] Some units provide more than one type of care or report more than one setting, but are counted only once in the total. [4] 24 hour care for the withdrawal and transition to ongoing treatment. [5] Other than detoxification. Provides treatment services for dependency. [6] Ambulatory care provides care in a nonresidential setting. [7] "Intensive" outpatient involves at least 2 hours of treatment a day for 3 or more days a week. [8] Includes general hospitals, alcoholism hospitals, mental/psychiatric hospitals, and other specialized hospitals. [9] Each of these facilities is described by 1 or more of the categories below. [10] HMO: Health maintenance organization; MCE: Managed care entity; MCO: Managed care organization.

Source: U.S. Substance Abuse and Mental Health Services Administration, unpublished data.

No. 220. Drug Use, by Type of Drug and Age Group: 1979 to 1995

[In percent. Current users are those who used drugs at least once within month prior to this study. Based on national samples of respondents residing in households. Subject to sampling variability; see source]

AGE AND TYPE OF DRUG	EVER USED					CURRENT USER				
	1979	1985	1990	1994	1995	1979	1985	1990	1994	1995
12 YEARS OLD AND OVER										
Marijuana and hashish	27.9	29.4	30.5	31.1	31.0	13.2	9.7	5.4	4.8	4.7
Cocaine	8.6	11.2	11.2	10.4	10.3	2.6	3.0	0.9	0.7	0.7
Inhalants	(NA)	7.9	5.7	5.8	5.7	(NA)	0.6	0.4	0.4	0.4
Hallucinogens	8.9	6.9	7.9	8.7	9.5	1.9	1.2	0.4	0.5	0.7
Heroin	1.3	0.9	0.8	1.0	1.2	0.1	0.1	-	0.1	0.1
Stimulants [1]	(NA)	7.3	5.5	4.6	4.9	(NA)	1.8	0.6	0.3	0.4
Sedatives [1]	(NA)	4.8	2.8	2.6	2.7	(NA)	0.5	0.2	0.1	0.2
Tranquilizers [1]	(NA)	7.6	4.0	4.0	3.9	(NA)	2.2	0.6	0.5	0.4
Analgesics [1]	(NA)	7.6	6.3	6.0	6.1	(NA)	1.4	0.9	0.7	0.6
Alcohol	88.5	84.9	82.2	84.2	82.3	63.2	60.2	52.6	53.9	52.2
12 to 17 YEARS OLD										
Marijuana and hashish	26.7	20.1	12.7	13.6	16.2	14.2	10.2	4.4	6.0	8.2
Cocaine	5.5	4.7	2.6	1.7	2.0	1.5	1.5	0.6	0.3	0.8
Alcohol	70.8	56.1	48.8	41.7	40.6	49.6	41.2	32.5	21.6	21.1
Cigarettes	(NA)	50.7	45.1	37.6	38.1	(NA)	29.4	22.4	18.9	20.2
18 TO 25 YEARS OLD										
Marijuana and hashish	68.1	57.6	50.4	41.9	41.4	35.6	21.7	12.7	12.1	12.0
Cocaine	27.2	24.3	19.3	12.1	9.8	9.9	8.1	2.3	1.2	1.3
Alcohol	(NA)	(NA)	87.6	86.3	84.4	75.1	70.1	62.8	63.1	61.3
26 TO 34 YEARS OLD										
Marijuana and hashish	45.0	54.1	58.5	52.7	51.8	19.7	19.0	9.5	6.9	6.7
Cocaine	13.4	23.6	25.4	23.0	21.6	3.0	6.3	1.9	1.3	1.2
Alcohol	(NA)	(NA)	(NA)	91.8	90.1	71.6	70.6	64.4	65.3	63.0
35 YEARS OLD AND OVER										
Marijuana and hashish	9.0	13.9	19.6	25.4	25.3	2.9	2.6	2.4	2.3	1.8
Cocaine	1.3	4.1	5.9	7.9	8.6	0.2	0.5	0.2	0.4	0.4
Alcohol	(NA)	(NA)	83.5	89.0	87.1	59.7	57.5	49.5	54.1	52.6

- Represents or rounds to zero. NA Not available. [1] Nonmedical use; does not include over-the-counter drugs.

Source: U.S. Substance Abuse and Mental Health Services Administration, *National Household Survey on Drug Abuse*, annual.

No. 221. Current Cigarette Smoking: 1979 to 1993

[In percent. Prior to 1992, a current smoker is a person who has smoked at least 100 cigarettes and who now smokes. Beginning 1992, definition includes persons who smoke only "some days". Excludes unknown smoking status. Based on the National Health Interview Survey; for details, see Appendix III]

SEX, AGE, AND RACE	1979	1985	1987	1988	1990	1991	1992	1993
Total smokers, 18 years old and over	33.5	30.1	28.8	28.1	25.5	25.6	26.5	25.0
Male, total	37.5	32.6	31.2	30.8	28.4	28.1	28.6	27.7
18 to 24 years	35.0	28.0	28.2	25.5	26.6	23.5	28.0	28.8
25 to 34 years	43.9	38.2	34.8	36.2	31.6	32.8	32.8	30.2
35 to 44 years	41.8	37.6	36.6	36.5	34.5	33.1	32.9	32.0
45 to 64 years	39.3	33.4	33.5	31.3	29.3	29.3	28.6	29.2
65 years and over	20.9	19.6	17.2	18.0	14.6	15.1	16.1	13.5
White, total	36.8	31.7	30.5	30.1	28.0	27.4	28.2	27.0
18 to 24 years	34.3	28.4	29.2	26.7	27.4	25.1	30.0	30.4
25 to 34 years	43.6	37.3	33.8	35.4	31.6	32.1	33.5	29.9
35 to 44 years	41.3	36.6	36.2	35.8	33.5	32.1	30.9	31.2
45 to 64 years	38.3	32.1	32.4	30.0	28.7	28.0	28.1	27.8
65 years and over	20.5	18.9	16.0	16.9	13.7	13.7	14.9	12.5
Black, total	44.1	39.9	39.0	36.5	32.5	35.0	32.2	32.7
18 to 24 years	40.2	27.2	24.9	18.6	21.3	15.0	16.2	19.9
25 to 34 years	47.5	45.6	44.9	41.6	33.8	39.4	29.5	30.7
35 to 44 years	48.6	45.0	44.0	42.5	42.0	44.4	47.5	38.9
45 to 64 years	50.0	46.1	44.3	43.2	36.7	42.0	35.4	42.4
65 years and over	26.2	27.7	30.3	29.8	21.5	24.3	28.3	27.9
Female, total	29.9	27.9	26.5	25.7	22.8	23.5	24.6	22.5
18 to 24 years	33.8	30.4	26.1	26.3	22.5	22.4	24.9	22.9
25 to 34 years	33.7	32.0	31.8	31.3	28.2	28.4	30.1	27.3
35 to 44 years	37.0	31.5	29.6	27.8	24.8	27.6	27.3	27.4
45 to 64 years	30.7	29.9	28.6	27.7	24.8	24.6	26.1	23.0
65 years and over	13.2	13.5	13.7	12.8	11.5	12.0	12.4	10.5
White, total	30.1	27.7	26.7	25.7	23.4	23.7	25.1	23.1
18 to 24 years	34.5	31.8	27.8	27.5	25.4	25.1	28.5	26.8
25 to 34 years	34.1	32.0	31.9	31.0	28.5	28.4	31.5	28.4
35 to 44 years	37.2	31.0	29.2	28.3	25.0	27.0	27.6	27.3
45 to 64 years	30.6	29.7	29.0	27.7	25.4	25.3	25.8	23.4
65 years and over	13.8	13.3	13.9	12.6	11.5	12.1	12.6	10.5
Black, total	31.1	31.0	28.0	27.8	21.2	24.4	24.2	20.8
18 to 24 years	31.8	23.7	20.4	21.8	10.0	11.8	10.3	8.2
25 to 34 years	35.2	36.2	35.8	37.2	29.1	32.4	26.9	24.7
35 to 44 years	37.7	40.2	35.3	27.6	25.5	35.3	32.4	31.5
45 to 64 years	34.2	33.4	28.4	29.5	22.6	23.4	30.9	21.3
65 years and over	8.5	14.5	11.7	14.8	11.1	9.6	11.1	10.2

Source: U.S. National Center for Health Statistics, *Health, United States, 1994.*

No. 222. Cancer—Estimated New Cases, 1997, and Survival Rates, 1974-78 to 1989-92

[The 5-year relative survival rate, which is derived by adjusting the observed survival rate for expected mortality, represents the likelihood that a person will not die from causes directly related to their cancer within 5 years. Survival data shown are based on those patients diagnosed while residents of an area listed below during the time periods shown. Data are based on information collected as part of the National Cancer Institute's Surveillance, Epidemiology and End Results (SEER) program, a collection of population-based registries in Connecticut, New Mexico, Utah, Iowa, Hawaii, Atlanta, Detroit, Seattle-Puget Sound, and San Francisco-Oakland]

SITE	ESTIMATED NEW CASES,[1] 1997 (1,000)			5-YEAR RELATIVE SURVIVAL RATES (percent)							
				White				Black			
	Total	Male	Female	1974-78	1979-83	1984-88	1989-92	1974-78	1979-83	1984-88	1989-92
All sites[2]	1,382	785	597	52.6	53.8	57.9	62.7	40.4	40.6	42.5	46.7
Lung	178	98	80	13.7	14.4	14.3	15.1	11.2	12.5	11.6	10.7
Breast[3]	182	1	180	76.1	77.7	83.5	86.9	63.6	65.1	67.9	71.2
Colon and rectum	131	66	65	52.5	56.3	62.0	63.8	45.7	48.7	51.5	53.2
Prostate	335	335	(X)	71.0	76.2	83.6	94.6	62.8	63.4	68.7	79.6
Bladder	55	40	15	74.8	78.6	81.5	83.0	50.5	58.7	60.1	63.5
Corpus uteri	35	(X)	35	88.7	84.3	85.9	87.6	60.8	54.3	57.7	56.2
Non-Hodgkin's lymphoma[4]	54	30	23	47.8	52.0	54.1	52.3	48.2	51.1	47.1	42.0
Oral cavity and pharynx	31	21	10	55.2	55.4	56.4	55.5	36.6	32.9	35.0	32.9
Leukemia[4]	28	16	12	36.3	38.5	42.5	43.1	31.6	31.5	34.5	29.1
Melanoma of skin	40	23	17	81.0	83.1	87.1	87.6	57.9	64.2	66.0	69.5
Pancreas	28	13	14	1.9	2.7	2.7	4.1	1.8	4.3	4.8	3.5
Kidney	29	17	12	54.9	56.1	61.6	64.3	53.4	56.4	57.4	59.3
Stomach	22	14	8	15.6	16.8	18.6	19.3	16.3	17.5	19.7	21.6
Ovary	27	(X)	27	37.6	39.8	41.7	51.0	41.6	39.2	40.8	45.0
Cervix uteri[5]	15	(X)	15	69.9	68.8	71.5	71.2	63.6	61.4	56.5	60.6

X Not applicable. [1] Estimates provided by American Cancer Society are based on rates from the National Cancer Institute's SEER program. [2] Includes other sites not shown separately. [3] Survival rates for female only. [4] All types combined. [5] Invasive cancer only.

Source: U.S. National Institutes of Health, National Cancer Institute, *Cancer Statistics Review*, annual.

No. 223. Cumulative Percent Distribution of Population, by Height and Sex: 1988-94

[For persons 20 to 79 years old. Height was measured without shoes. Based on sample and subject to sampling variability; see source]

HEIGHT	MALES						FEMALES					
	20-29 years	30-39 years	40-49 years	50-59 years	60-69 years	70-79 years	20-29 years	30-39 years	40-49 years	50-59 years	60-69 years	70-79 years
Percent under—												
4'8"	-	-	-	-	-	-	0.6	0.1	-	-	0.2	1.7
4'9"	-	-	-	-	-	-	0.7	0.2	0.3	0.1	0.7	3.3
4'10"	-	-	-	-	0.1	-	1.2	0.7	0.7	1.9	1.7	4.9
4'11"	-	-	-	-	0.1	0.1	3.1	2.6	1.7	3.1	4.4	9.8
5'	0.1	-	0.2	-	0.4	0.1	6.0	5.5	5.3	6.6	9.9	15.4
5'1"	0.1	-	0.4	0.1	0.5	0.6	11.5	10.4	9.9	11.9	19.0	28.9
5'2"	0.5	0.8	0.7	0.2	0.7	1.9	21.8	18.5	18.8	24.4	34.3	45.6
5'3"	1.3	1.4	0.9	1.0	2.2	2.7	34.3	30.7	31.9	38.6	48.3	61.2
5'4"	3.4	2.2	1.7	2.5	5.8	7.8	48.9	42.9	49.2	52.6	65.5	74.5
5'5"	6.9	5.1	5.6	6.0	9.4	16.5	62.7	59.1	64.3	69.9	76.5	86.9
5'6"	11.7	10.1	12.1	11.7	15.8	27.3	74.0	71.8	77.0	81.6	87.8	93.9
5'7"	20.8	18.9	19.6	20.5	27.4	39.5	84.7	84.1	87.0	89.3	92.5	97.3
5'8"	32.0	26.3	28.0	32.6	38.6	53.4	92.4	91.6	94.5	95.6	96.7	99.2
5'9"	46.3	44.3	42.1	43.9	55.1	68.7	96.2	95.6	97.3	99.0	99.3	99.9
5'10"	58.7	58.0	58.1	60.6	68.8	79.5	98.6	98.1	98.9	99.6	99.8	100.0
5'11"	70.1	70.4	71.1	75.2	81.4	89.2	99.5	99.5	99.4	100.0	100.0	100.0
6'	81.2	79.7	81.5	85.4	90.0	94.1	100.0	100.0	100.0	100.0	100.0	100.0
6'1"	87.4	86.2	89.0	92.4	95.2	97.2	100.0	100.0	100.0	100.0	100.0	100.0
6'2"	94.7	92.4	94.4	96.4	98.2	99.3	100.0	100.0	100.0	100.0	100.0	100.0
6'3"	97.9	98.1	97.2	98.2	99.5	99.9	100.0	100.0	100.0	100.0	100.0	100.0

- Represents or rounds to zero.

Source: U.S. National Center for Health Statistics, unpublished data.

No. 224. Cumulative Percent Distribution of Population, by Weight and Sex: 1988-94

[For persons 20 to 79 years old. Weight measured includes clothes weight, estimated as ranging from .20 pounds to .62 pounds. Based on sample and subject to sampling variability; see source]

WEIGHT	MALES						FEMALES					
	20-29 years	30-39 years	40-49 years	50-59 years	60-69 years	70-79 years	20-29 years	30-39 years	40-49 years	50-59 years	60-69 years	70-79 years
Percent under—												
90 pounds	-	-	-	-	-	-	0.5	0.5	-	0.3	0.2	1.8
100 pounds	-	-	-	-	0.2	0.2	3.8	2.0	1.6	1.3	1.7	4.7
110 pounds	0.5	0.1	0.2	0.1	0.8	0.4	13.3	7.7	5.5	3.7	5.6	9.2
120 pounds	1.8	1.0	0.7	0.6	1.5	1.7	27.0	17.8	12.6	9.5	13.8	19.0
130 pounds	6.7	3.4	3.3	2.2	3.1	5.8	46.1	31.4	25.1	19.7	24.3	31.6
140 pounds	15.8	7.8	6.7	5.4	7.5	13.2	58.7	44.3	37.4	30.0	36.2	46.6
150 pounds	29.0	17.0	14.1	9.9	15.5	23.3	70.4	55.5	49.4	42.0	48.8	57.3
160 pounds	42.1	27.6	23.0	16.2	24.5	36.2	76.5	65.3	59.3	52.7	61.3	67.9
170 pounds	54.9	42.0	32.4	28.9	36.1	48.4	82.6	72.6	70.0	61.5	71.3	77.6
180 pounds	66.7	54.9	48.6	41.5	48.2	59.5	87.6	78.3	78.6	70.9	79.0	84.6
190 pounds	76.2	66.4	61.0	55.2	60.5	73.1	90.1	82.2	82.6	77.0	84.3	90.2
200 pounds	82.1	74.8	70.1	66.5	72.5	82.6	92.5	86.2	87.4	83.8	89.1	92.8
210 pounds	86.8	81.2	78.0	77.4	81.0	87.8	94.5	89.3	90.5	89.0	92.6	94.6
220 pounds	90.4	86.3	83.8	84.4	87.1	93.2	96.0	92.1	93.2	92.1	94.7	95.7
230 pounds	92.9	91.6	88.8	89.3	92.6	95.7	97.7	94.2	94.9	93.7	96.4	96.3
240 pounds	95.4	94.3	92.6	92.6	95.7	96.7	98.7	96.0	97.3	95.1	97.3	97.5
250 pounds	96.2	95.5	94.1	94.5	97.2	97.4	99.0	96.7	97.6	96.7	97.6	98.8
260 pounds	97.2	96.6	95.7	96.3	98.0	98.5	99.4	97.5	98.1	97.9	98.8	99.3
270 pounds	97.9	97.4	96.5	97.3	98.6	99.4	99.7	98.7	98.4	98.1	99.2	99.5
280 pounds	98.7	97.6	97.5	98.1	98.9	99.8	99.8	98.7	98.7	98.7	99.4	99.8
290 pounds	99.0	98.0	97.8	98.6	99.5	100.0	99.9	99.1	99.0	98.8	99.6	99.9
300 pounds	99.3	98.2	98.7	99.0	99.5	100.0	100.0	99.4	99.2	99.5	99.8	99.9
310 pounds	99.3	98.5	98.9	99.2	100.0	100.0	100.0	99.7	99.4	99.9	99.8	100.0
320 pounds	99.5	98.6	99.2	99.5	100.0	100.0	100.0	99.9	99.5	99.9	99.8	100.0
330 pounds	99.5	98.8	99.3	99.6	100.0	100.0	100.0	99.9	99.5	100.0	99.8	100.0
340 pounds	99.5	99.3	99.3	99.9	100.0	100.0	100.0	99.9	99.6	100.0	99.9	100.0
350 pounds	99.6	99.7	99.3	100.0	100.0	100.0	100.0	99.9	100.0	100.0	99.9	100.0
360 pounds	99.6	99.8	99.3	100.0	100.0	100.0	100.0	99.9	100.0	100.0	100.0	100.0
370 pounds	99.6	98.8	99.3	100.0	100.0	100.0	100.0	99.9	100.0	100.0	100.0	100.0
380 pounds	99.6	99.8	99.4	100.0	100.0	100.0	100.0	99.9	100.0	100.0	100.0	100.0

- Represents or rounds to zero.

Source: U.S. National Center for Health Statistics, unpublished data.

No. 225. Percent of Population Overweight, by Age, Sex, and Race: 1976 to 1991

[In percent. Overweight is defined for men as body mass index greater than or equal to 27.8 kilograms/meter squared, and for women as body mass index greater than or equal to 27.3 kilograms/meter squared. These points were used because they represent the sex-specific 85th percentiles for persons 20-29 years of age in the 1976-80 National Health and Nutrition Examination Survey (NHANES). Data are based on physical examinations of a sample of the civilian noninstitutional population in the NHANES]

SEX, AGE, AND RACE	1976-80	1988-91	SEX, AGE, AND RACE	1976-80	1988-91	SEX, AGE, AND RACE	1976-80	1988-91
Persons 20 to 74 years old [1]	25.4	33.0	MALE			FEMALE [2]		
Male	24.0	31.9	20 to 34 years old	17.3	22.8	20 to 34 years old	16.8	24.5
Female [2]	26.5	34.1	35 to 44 years old	28.9	35.7	35 to 44 years old	27.0	36.1
White male	24.2	32.3	45 to 54 years old	31.0	35.5	45 to 54 years old	32.5	39.8
White female [2]	24.4	32.6	55 to 64 years old	28.1	40.5	55 to 64 years old	37.0	48.7
Black male	25.7	32.9	65 to 74 years old	25.2	42.2	65 to 74 years old	38.4	39.7
Black female [2]	44.3	49.6	75 years old and over	(NA)	26.0	75 years old and over	(NA)	31.5

NA Not available. [1] Age-adjusted. Includes other races not shown separately. [2] Excludes pregnant women.

Source: U.S. National Center for Health Statistics, *Health, United States, 1995.*

No. 226. Self-Perception of Being Overweight: 1988-1991

[In percent. See headnote, table 225]

AGE	PERCENT OF OVERWEIGHT PEOPLE WHO THINK THEY ARE OVERWEIGHT						PERCENT OF POPULATION NOT OVERWEIGHT WHO THINK THEY ARE OVERWEIGHT					
	Total [1]		Non-Hispanic White		Non-Hispanic Black		Total [1]		Non-Hispanic White		Non-Hispanic Black	
	Male	Female	Male	Female	Male	Female	Male	Female	Male	Female	Male	Female
Total	83.4	91.8	86.2	94.2	71.9	87.4	25.3	47.9	28.1	50.2	13.1	37.5
20 to 39 years old	84.5	94.5	88.8	97.4	73.4	90.9	24.8	49.5	28.1	51.4	10.1	41.1
40 to 59 years old	89.0	95.4	92.1	96.0	74.0	93.4	27.6	56.5	30.7	59.6	19.6	46.5
60 years old and over	73.0	83.6	74.6	86.5	63.7	71.7	23.2	35.3	24.7	38.6	12.6	13.5

[1] Includes other races and persons of Hispanic origin not shown separately.

Source: Federation of American Societies for Experimental Biology, Life Sciences Research Office, *Third Report on Nutrition Monitoring in the United States, 1995.*

No. 227. Healthy Eating Indexes, by Selected Food Groups and Dietary Guidelines: 1994

[Healthy Eating Index is comprised of the sum of 10 dietary component indices for a maximum possible score of 100. A score of 80 or above was judged to reflect a "good" diet. Each of the dietary components has a scoring range of zero to 10. Individuals with an intake at the recommended level received a maximum score of 10 points. A score of zero was assigned when no foods in a particular group were eaten. Intermediate scores were calculated proportionately. The indexes for grains, vegetables, fruits, milk, and meat groups measure the degree to which a person's diet conforms to the U.S. Department of Agriculture's (USDA) "Food Guide Pyramid" serving recommendations. The index was applied to USDA one-day food and nutrient intake data from the Continuing Survey of Food Intakes by Individuals. The data are based on a representative sample of 5,169 individuals two years old and over excluding women who were pregnant or lactating at the time of the survey]

FOOD GROUP AND DIETARY GUIDELINE	Average score on one day	Percent receiving score of 10	Perfect score of 10 [1]	Score of zero
Healthy Eating Index	62.8	[2]11.9	(X)	(X)
Grains [3]	6.6	21.8	6-11 servings	0 servings
Vegetables [4]	5.9	26.7	3-5 servings	0 servings
Fruits [4]	3.9	19.5	2-4 servings	0 servings
Milk [5]	6.1	31.5	2-3 servings	0 servings
Meat [6]	6.8	33.1	2-3 servings	0 servings
Total fat [7]	6.7	35.9	30% or less energy from fat	45% or more energy from fat
Saturated fat [7]	6.3	39.9	Less than 10% energy from saturated fat	15% or more energy from saturated fat
Cholesterol	7.9	71.2	300 mg. or less	450 mg. or more
Sodium	6.3	35.6	2,400 mg. or less	4,800 mg or more
Variety [8]	6.3	34.4	8 different food items over 1 day	Fewer than 4 items over 1 day

X Not applicable. [1] Depends on recommended energy intake. All amounts listed are based on a per day basis. [2] Percent receiving a score of 80 or higher. [3] One serving: a slice of bread, one-half cup of cooked pasta or one-half cup of cooked cereal grains. [4] One serving: one-half cup of cooked vegetables, 1 cup of raw leafy vegetables, or one-half cup of raw nonleafy chopped vegetables. Fruits are similar. [5] One serving: one cup of milk or equivalent. [6] Includes eggs, nuts, and some legumes. One serving: 2.5 ounces of lean meat or equivalent. [7] Consumption of specified fat as a percentage of total food energy intake. [8] Amount of variety in a person's diet over a 1-day period.

Source: U.S. Department of Agriculture, Center for Nutrition Policy and Promotion, unpublished data.

No. 228. Personal Health Practices, by Selected Characteristic: 1990

[In percent, except total persons. For persons 18 years of age and over. Based on the National Health Interview Survey and subject to sampling error; for details see source and Appendix III]

CHARACTERISTIC	Total persons (1,000)	Eats breakfast [1]	Rarely snacks	Exercised regularly [2]	Had two or more drinks on any day [3]	Current smoker	20 percent or more above weight [4]
All persons [5]	181,447	56.4	25.5	40.7	5.5	25.5	27.5
Sex: Male	86,278	54.6	25.6	44.0	9.7	28.4	29.6
Female	95,169	58.0	25.4	37.7	1.7	22.8	25.6
Race: White	155,301	57.8	25.8	41.5	5.8	25.6	26.7
Black	20,248	46.9	22.7	34.3	4.3	26.2	38.0
Hispanic origin: Hispanic	14,314	52.5	29.3	34.9	4.6	23.0	27.6
Non-Hispanic	166,599	56.7	25.2	41.2	5.6	25.7	27.5
Marital status:							
Currently married	117,413	57.8	25.3	39.4	5.3	24.6	29.2
Formerly married	30,439	61.5	31.2	34.3	5.3	30.3	29.1
Never married	33,413	46.9	20.9	51.3	6.6	24.3	19.8
Education level:							
Less than 12 years	38,367	58.6	27.8	25.9	5.1	31.8	32.7
12 years	69,405	52.6	24.3	37.0	5.9	29.6	28.6
More than 12 years	73,244	58.8	25.5	52.1	5.4	18.3	23.8
Income: Less than $10,000	18,469	54.1	27.8	32.9	4.8	31.6	29.3
$10,000 to $19,999	30,452	56.6	25.9	32.3	4.9	29.8	28.5
$20,000 to $34,999	40,216	55.2	25.1	40.5	5.8	26.9	28.2
$35,000 to $49,999	29,795	53.7	23.8	46.1	5.6	23.4	27.8
$50,000 or more	36,199	57.2	25.8	51.7	6.7	19.3	24.9

[1] Almost every day. [2] Or played sports regularly. [3] On average per day in the past 2 weeks. [4] Above desirable weight. Based on 1983 Metropolitan Life Insurance Company standards. Height and weight data are self-reported. [5] Includes persons whose characteristics are unknown.

Source: U.S. National Center for Health Statistics, *Health Promotion and Disease Prevention: United States, 1990, Vital and Health Statistics*, series 10, No. 185.

No. 229. Nutrition—Nutrients in Foods Available for Civilian Consumption per Capita per Day: 1970 to 1994

[Computed by the Center for Nutrition Policy and Promotion (CNPP). Based on Economic Research Service (ERS) estimates of per capita quantities of food available for consumption from "Food Consumption, Prices, and, Expenditures," on imputed consumption data for foods no longer reported by ERS, and on CNPP estimates of quantities of produce from home gardens. Food supply estimates do not reflect loss of food or nutrients from further marketing or home processing. Enrichment and fortification levels of iron, thiamin, riboflavin, niacin, vitamin A, vitamin B_6, vitamin B_{12}, and ascorbic acid are included]

NUTRIENT	Unit	1970-79	1980-89	1990	1993	1994
Food energy	Calories	3,300	3,400	3,600	3,700	3,800
Carbohydrate	Grams	391	417	458	482	491
Protein	Grams	95	100	105	108	110
Total fat [1]	Grams	151	157	156	161	159
Saturated	Grams	52	53	51	52	52
Monounsaturated	Grams	61	63	63	66	65
Polyunsaturated	Grams	28	31	32	32	31
Cholesterol	Milligrams	440	420	400	410	410
Vitamin A	Micrograms RE [2]	1,530	1,510	1,530	1,530	1,520
Carotenes	Micrograms RE [2]	580	620	670	670	660
Vitamin E	Milligrams α-TE [3]	14.2	15.7	16.6	17.6	16.9
Vitamin C	Milligrams	109	114	111	122	124
Thiamin	Milligrams	2.1	2.4	2.6	2.7	2.7
Riboflavin	Milligrams	2.4	2.5	2.6	2.6	2.6
Niacin	Milligrams	23.6	26.4	28.0	29.0	29.0
Vitamin B_6	Milligrams	2.0	2.1	2.2	2.3	2.3
Folacin	Micrograms	289	303	311	329	331
Vitamin B_{12}	Micrograms	9.1	8.4	8.2	8.0	8.1
Calcium	Milligrams	880	900	940	950	960
Phosphorus	Milligrams	1,460	1,530	1,620	1,650	1,680
Magnesium	Milligrams	320	340	370	380	380
Iron	Milligrams	18.7	18.2	20.2	20.9	21.2
Zinc	Milligrams	12.1	12.3	12.7	13.0	13.2
Copper	Milligrams	1.6	1.7	1.8	1.9	1.9
Potassium	Milligrams	3,470	3,530	3,650	3,750	3,780

[1] Includes other types of fat not shown separately. [2] Retinol equivalents. [3] Alpha-Tocopherol equivalents.

Source: U.S. Dept. of Agriculture, Center for Nutrition Policy and Promotion. Data published by Economic Research Service in *Food Consumption, Prices, and Expenditures*, annual.

No. 230. Per Capita Consumption of Major Food Commodities: 1980 to 1995

[In pounds, retail weight except as indicated. Consumption represents the residual after exports, nonfood use and ending stocks are subtracted from the sum of beginning stocks, domestic production, and imports. Based on Bureau of the Census estimated population. Estimates reflect revisions based on the 1990 Census of Population]

COMMODITY	1980	1985	1990	1991	1992	1993	1994	1995
Red meat, total (boneless, trimmed weight) [1 2]	126.4	124.9	112.3	111.9	114.1	112.1	114.8	114.7
Beef	72.1	74.6	64.0	63.1	62.8	61.5	63.6	64.0
Veal	1.3	1.5	0.9	0.8	0.8	0.8	0.8	0.8
Lamb and mutton	1.0	1.1	1.0	1.0	1.0	1.0	0.9	0.9
Pork (excluding lard)	52.1	47.7	46.4	46.9	49.5	48.9	49.5	49.0
Fish and shellfish (edible weight) [3]	12.4	15.0	15.0	14.8	14.7	14.9	15.1	14.9
Fresh and frozen	7.8	9.7	9.6	9.6	9.8	10.1	10.3	9.9
Canned	4.3	5.0	5.1	4.9	4.6	4.5	4.5	4.7
Tuna	3.0	3.3	3.7	3.6	3.5	3.5	3.3	3.4
Cured	0.3	0.3	0.3	0.3	0.3	0.3	0.3	0.3
Poultry products: (boneless weight) [2 4]	40.8	45.5	56.3	58.3	60.8	62.5	63.3	62.9
Chicken	32.7	36.4	42.5	44.3	46.7	48.5	49.3	48.8
Turkey	8.1	9.1	13.8	14.1	14.1	14.0	14.1	14.1
Eggs (number)	271.1	254.7	234.3	233.7	236.0	235.6	237.6	233.4
Dairy products:								
Total (milk equivalent, milkfat basis) [5]	543.2	593.7	568.5	565.7	565.9	574.0	585.8	584.8
Fluid milk and cream [6]	245.5	240.8	233.4	233.0	230.5	225.7	225.4	223.8
Beverage milks	237.4	229.7	221.8	221.2	218.3	213.4	212.7	210.1
Plain whole milk	141.7	119.7	87.7	84.7	81.2	77.4	75.8	72.7
Plain reduced-fat milk (2%)	54.7	68.5	78.4	78.9	78.1	76.0	74.6	70.7
Plain light and skim milks	26.9	27.4	42.8	44.7	46.2	47.3	49.5	53.8
Flavored whole milk	4.7	3.7	2.8	2.7	2.7	2.7	2.7	2.7
Flavored reduced-fat, light, and skim milk	5.3	6.0	6.6	6.8	6.9	6.9	7.1	7.3
Buttermilk	4.1	4.4	3.5	3.4	3.2	3.0	2.9	2.8
Yogurt (excl. frozen)	2.5	4.0	4.0	4.2	4.2	4.3	4.7	5.2
Cream [7]	3.4	4.4	4.6	4.6	4.8	4.9	4.9	5.1
Sour cream and dips	1.8	2.3	2.5	2.6	2.7	2.7	2.7	2.7
Condensed and evaporated milks:								
Whole milk	3.8	3.6	3.2	3.2	3.2	3.0	2.6	2.2
Skim milk	3.3	3.8	4.8	5.0	5.2	5.2	4.8	4.7
Cheese [8]	17.5	22.5	24.6	25.0	26.0	26.2	26.8	27.4
American	9.6	12.2	11.1	11.1	11.3	11.4	11.5	11.8
Cheddar	6.9	9.8	9.0	9.1	9.2	9.1	9.1	9.1
Italian	4.4	6.5	9.0	9.4	10.0	9.8	10.3	10.3
Mozzarella	3.0	4.6	6.9	7.2	7.7	7.6	7.9	8.0
Other [9]	3.4	3.9	4.5	4.6	4.7	5.0	5.0	5.3
Swiss	1.3	1.3	1.4	1.2	1.2	1.2	1.2	1.1
Cream and Neufchatel	1.0	1.2	1.7	1.8	2.0	2.1	2.2	2.3
Cottage cheese	4.5	4.1	3.4	3.3	3.1	2.9	2.8	2.7
Ice cream	17.5	18.1	15.8	16.3	16.3	16.1	16.1	15.6
Ice milk	7.1	6.9	7.7	7.4	7.1	6.9	7.6	7.3
Frozen yogurt	(NA)	(NA)	2.8	3.5	3.1	3.5	3.5	3.5
Fats and oils:								
Total, fat content only [10]	57.2	64.3	62.2	63.9	65.7	68.3	66.0	64.1
Butter (product weight)	4.5	4.9	4.4	4.4	4.4	4.7	4.8	4.5
Margarine (product weight)	11.3	10.8	10.9	10.6	11.0	11.1	9.9	9.2
Lard (direct use)	2.6	1.8	1.9	1.7	1.7	1.6	1.7	1.7
Edible tallow (direct use)	1.1	1.9	0.6	1.4	2.4	2.2	2.4	2.7
Shortening	18.2	22.9	22.2	22.4	22.4	25.1	24.1	22.5
Salad and cooking oils	21.2	23.5	24.2	25.2	25.6	25.1	24.3	24.6
Other edible fats and oils	1.5	1.6	1.2	1.3	1.4	1.7	1.6	1.6
Flour and cereal products	144.7	156.4	181.6	183.6	186.2	191.0	194.1	192.4
Wheat flour [11]	116.9	124.6	135.6	136.9	138.8	143.3	144.5	141.7
Rye flour	0.7	0.7	0.6	0.6	0.6	0.6	0.6	0.6
Rice, milled	9.4	9.0	16.3	16.8	17.5	17.6	19.3	20.1
Corn products	12.9	17.2	21.9	22.0	22.1	22.3	22.5	22.7
Oat products	3.9	4.0	6.5	6.5	6.5	6.5	6.5	6.5
Barley products	1.0	1.0	0.8	0.7	0.7	0.7	0.7	0.7
Caloric sweeteners, total [12]	123.0	126.8	137.0	138.0	141.2	144.4	147.3	150.0
Sugar, refined cane and beet	83.6	62.7	64.4	63.8	64.6	64.3	65.0	65.5
Corn sweeteners (dry weight)	38.2	64.8	71.1	72.8	75.2	78.7	81.0	83.2
Other:								
Cocoa beans	3.4	4.6	5.4	5.7	5.7	5.4	4.8	4.6
Coffee (green beans)	10.3	10.5	10.3	10.3	10.0	9.1	8.2	8.0
Peanuts (shelled)	4.8	6.3	6.0	6.5	6.2	6.0	5.8	5.7
Tree nuts (shelled)	1.8	2.5	2.4	2.2	2.2	2.2	2.3	2.1

NA Not available. [1] Excludes edible offals. [2] Excludes shipments to Puerto Rico and the other U.S. possessions. [3] Excludes game fish consumption. [4] Includes skin, neck meat, and giblets. [5] Includes other products, not shown separately. [6] Fluid milk figures are aggregates of commercial sales and milk produced and consumed on farms. [7] Heavy cream, light cream, and half and half. [8] Excludes cottage, pot, and baker's cheese. [9] Includes other cheeses not shown separately. [10] The fat content of butter and margarine is 80 percent of product weight. [11] White, whole wheat, semolina, and durum flour. [12] Dry weight. Includes edible syrups (maple, molasses, etc.) and honey not shown separately.

Source: U.S. Department of Agriculture, Economic Research Service, *Food Consumption, Prices, and Expenditures, 1997: Annual Data, 1970-1995*; and *Agricultural Outlook*, monthly.

No. 231. Per Capita Utilization of Selected Commercially Produced Fruits and Vegetables: 1980 to 1995

[In pounds, farm weight. Domestic food use of fresh fruits and vegetables reflects the fresh-market share of commodity production plus imports and minus exports. All data are on a calendar year basis except for citrus fruits, October or November; apples, August; grapes and pears, July. See headnote, table 230]

COMMODITY	1980	1985	1989	1990	1991	1992	1993	1994	1995
Fresh fruits	104.8	110.6	123.0	116.5	113.2	123.6	124.9	126.5	126.1
Noncitrus	78.8	89.2	99.4	95.2	94.1	99.3	99.0	101.6	101.7
Bananas	20.8	23.5	24.7	24.4	25.1	27.3	26.8	28.1	27.4
Apples	19.2	17.3	21.2	19.6	18.2	19.2	19.2	19.6	18.9
Grapes	4.0	6.8	7.9	7.9	7.3	7.2	7.0	7.3	7.6
Nectarines and peaches	7.1	5.5	5.9	5.5	6.4	6.0	6.0	5.5	5.4
Pears	2.6	2.8	3.2	3.2	3.2	3.1	3.4	3.5	3.4
Strawberries	2.0	3.0	3.3	3.2	3.6	3.6	3.6	4.1	3.8
Pineapples	1.5	1.5	2.0	2.1	1.9	2.0	2.1	2.0	1.9
Plums and prunes	1.5	1.4	1.4	1.5	1.4	1.8	1.3	1.6	0.9
Watermelons	10.7	13.5	13.6	13.3	12.8	14.8	14.6	15.4	15.9
Cantaloups	5.8	8.5	10.4	9.2	8.7	8.5	8.7	8.6	9.9
Honeydews	1.4	2.1	2.5	2.1	1.9	2.1	1.7	1.8	2.4
Other [1]	2.2	3.3	3.3	3.2	3.6	3.7	4.6	4.1	4.2
Citrus	26.1	21.5	23.5	21.4	19.1	24.4	26.0	25.0	24.4
Oranges	14.3	11.6	12.2	12.4	8.5	12.9	14.3	13.1	12.2
Grapefruit	7.3	5.5	6.6	4.4	5.9	5.9	6.2	6.1	6.1
Other [2]	4.5	4.4	4.7	4.6	4.7	5.6	5.6	5.8	6.1
Processed fruits	153.1	153.0	141.4	144.1	151.6	138.7	153.4	153.9	154.8
Noncitrus	55.6	58.0	60.2	64.1	62.0	63.8	64.8	63.7	61.3
Apples	20.6	26.0	25.3	28.5	25.7	27.4	29.5	30.1	27.4
Grapes	11.8	12.0	12.5	12.5	13.4	12.2	13.0	11.8	14.1
Pineapples	10.6	10.7	12.2	12.7	12.8	13.3	11.8	10.7	10.6
Other [3]	12.7	9.3	10.1	10.4	10.1	10.9	10.5	11.1	9.2
Citrus	97.6	95.0	81.2	80.0	89.7	74.9	88.6	90.2	93.5
Oranges	81.0	78.4	67.0	64.9	77.4	64.0	73.3	75.0	78.0
Other [4]	16.6	16.6	14.3	15.1	12.3	10.9	15.3	15.3	15.5
Selected fresh vegetables	149.3	156.1	172.3	166.2	163.3	171.3	172.3	175.9	173.5
Asparagus	0.3	0.5	0.6	0.6	0.6	0.6	0.6	0.6	0.6
Broccoli	1.4	2.6	3.8	3.4	3.1	3.4	2.9	3.4	3.2
Cabbage	8.1	8.8	8.7	8.8	8.5	8.9	9.7	9.7	9.1
Carrots	6.2	6.5	8.1	8.3	7.7	8.3	8.2	9.6	10.1
Cauliflower	1.1	1.8	2.3	2.2	2.0	1.8	1.7	1.6	1.3
Celery	7.4	6.9	7.5	7.2	6.8	7.4	7.1	6.8	6.4
Corn	6.5	6.4	6.5	6.7	5.9	6.9	7.0	7.9	7.8
Cucumbers	3.9	4.4	4.8	4.7	4.6	5.0	5.3	5.4	5.6
Head lettuce	25.6	23.7	28.8	27.8	26.1	25.9	24.6	24.3	21.6
Mushrooms	1.2	1.8	2.0	2.0	1.9	2.0	2.0	2.0	2.0
Onions	11.4	13.6	14.8	15.1	15.7	16.2	16.5	16.5	17.7
Snap beans	1.3	1.3	1.2	1.1	1.1	1.5	1.5	1.6	1.6
Bell peppers	2.9	3.8	4.7	4.5	5.1	5.7	6.2	6.5	5.8
Potatoes	51.1	46.3	50.1	45.8	46.4	48.9	49.7	49.1	49.2
Sweet potatoes [5]	4.4	5.4	4.1	4.6	4.0	4.3	3.9	4.7	4.5
Tomatoes	12.8	14.9	16.8	15.5	15.4	15.5	16.0	16.1	16.6
Other fresh vegetables [6]	3.7	7.4	7.5	7.9	8.4	9.0	9.4	10.1	10.4
Selected vegetables for freezing	51.6	64.5	67.6	70.5	72.8	71.6	76.7	81.3	81.8
Selected vegetables for canning	102.7	99.4	102.4	110.9	113.3	111.6	111.5	106.9	109.8
Potatoes for chips	16.5	17.6	17.5	17.0	17.3	17.5	17.6	17.1	17.1
Pulses [7]	5.8	7.6	6.3	7.1	7.8	8.2	7.7	7.9	8.6

[1] Includes apricots, avocados, cherries, cranberries, kiwi fruit, mangos, and papayas. [2] Includes tangerines, tangelos, lemons, and limes. [3] Includes peaches, pears, and strawberries. [4] Includes grapefruit, lemons, limes, tangelos, and tangerines. [5] Fresh and processed. [6] Includes artichokes, brussels sprouts, eggplant, escarole/endive, garlic, romaine and leaf lettuce (after 1984), radishes, and spinach. [7] Dry edible beans, dry field peas, and lentils.

No. 232. Per Capita Consumption of Selected Beverages, by Type: 1980 to 1995

[In gallons. See headnote, table 230]

COMMODITY	1980	1985	1989	1990	1991	1992	1993	1994	1995
Nonalcoholic	(NA)	(NA)	126.4	127.8	131.0	130.3	132.3	133.1	133.2
Milk (plain and flavored)	27.6	26.7	26.0	25.7	25.7	25.3	24.7	24.7	24.4
Whole	17.0	14.3	11.3	10.5	10.2	9.8	9.3	9.1	8.8
Reduced-fat, light, and skim	10.5	12.3	14.7	15.2	15.5	15.6	15.4	15.5	15.6
Tea	7.3	7.1	6.9	6.9	7.4	8.1	8.4	8.2	8.0
Coffee	26.7	27.4	26.2	26.9	26.8	25.9	23.4	21.1	20.5
Bottled water	2.4	4.5	7.4	8.0	8.0	8.2	9.4	10.7	11.6
Soft drinks	35.1	35.7	45.4	46.3	47.9	48.5	50.2	51.4	51.2
Diet	5.1	7.1	10.7	10.7	11.7	11.6	11.9	12.3	12.3
Regular	29.9	28.7	34.7	35.6	36.3	36.9	38.2	39.1	39.0
Selected fruit juices	7.2	7.7	8.2	7.3	7.8	7.3	8.5	8.7	8.7
Fruit drinks, cocktails, and ades	(NA)	(NA)	5.9	6.3	6.9	6.5	7.0	7.4	7.8
Canned iced tea	(NA)	(NA)	0.1	0.1	0.2	0.2	0.4	0.6	0.7
Vegetable juices	(NA)	(NA)	0.3	0.3	0.3	0.3	0.3	0.3	0.3
Alcoholic (adult population)	42.8	40.7	39.1	40.0	37.8	37.3	36.7	36.6	35.9
Beer	36.6	34.6	33.9	34.9	33.2	32.7	32.4	32.2	31.6
Wine [1]	3.2	3.5	3.1	2.9	2.7	2.7	2.5	2.5	2.6
Distilled spirits	3.0	2.6	2.2	2.2	2.0	2.0	1.9	1.8	1.8

NA Not available [1] Beginning 1985, includes wine coolers.

Source of tables 231 and 232: U.S. Department of Agriculture, Economic Research Service, *Food Consumption, Prices, and Expenditures, 1997: Annual Data, 1970-1995.*

Section 4

Education

This section presents data primarily concerning formal education as a whole, at various levels, and for public and private schools. Data shown relate to the school-age population and school enrollment, educational attainment, education personnel, and financial aspects of education. In addition, data are shown for libraries, computer usage in schools, and adult education. The chief sources are the decennial census of population and the Current Population Survey (CPS), both conducted by the Bureau of the Census (see text, section 1); annual, biennial, and other periodic surveys conducted by the National Center for Education Statistics, a part of the U.S. Department of Education; and surveys conducted by the National Education Association.

The censuses of population have included data on school enrollment since 1840 and on educational attainment since 1940. The CPS has reported on school enrollment annually since 1945 and on educational attainment periodically since 1947.

The National Center for Education Statistics is continuing the pattern of statistical studies and surveys conducted by the U.S. Office of Education since 1870. The annual *Digest of Education Statistics* provides summary data on pupils, staff, finances, including government expenditures, and organization at the elementary, secondary, and higher education levels. It is also a primary source for detailed information on Federal funds for education, projections of enrollment, graduates, and teachers. *The Condition of Education,* issued annually, presents a summary of information on education of particular interest to policymakers.

Other sources of data include special studies by the National Center for Education Statistics and annual or biennial reports of education agencies in individual States. The census of governments, conducted by the Bureau of the Census every 5 years (for the years ending in "2" and "7"), provides data on school district finances and State and local government expenditures for education. Reports published by the Bureau of Labor Statistics contain data relating civilian labor force experience to educational attainment (see also tables 622, 623, 648, 656, and 657 in section 13).

In Brief

The enrollment rate of 3 to 5 year olds in preprimary school:

1970	*37 percent*
1995	*62 percent*

Persons 25 years old and over completing college:

1970	*11 percent*
1996	*24 percent*

Public elementary and secondary schools with Internet access:

1994	*35 percent*
1996	*65 percent*

Types and sources of data—The statistics in this section are of two general types. One type, exemplified by data from the Bureau of the Census, is based on direct interviews with individuals to obtain information about their own and their family members' education. Data of this type relate to school enrollment and level of education attained, classified by age, sex, and other characteristics of the population. The school enrollment statistics reflect attendance or enrollment in any regular school within a given period; educational attainment statistics reflect the highest grade completed by an individual or, beginning in 1992, the highest diploma or degree received.

For enrollment data starting in October 1994, the CPS used 1990 census population controls plus adjustments for undercount. Also the survey changed from paper to computer assisted technology; for years 1981 through 1993, 1980 population controls were used; 1971 through 1980, 1970 census population controls had been used. These changes had little impact on summary measures (e.g., medians) and proportional measures (e.g., enrollment rates); however, use of the controls may have significant impact on absolute numbers.

Beginning with data for 1986, a new edit and tabulation package for school enrollment has been introduced. In 1988, a new edit and tabulation package was introduced for educational attainment data.

The second type, generally exemplified by data from the National Center for Education Statistics and the National Education Association, is based on reports from administrators of educational institutions and of State and local agencies having jurisdiction over education. Data of this type relate to enrollment, attendance, staff, and finances for the Nation, individual States, and local areas.

Unlike the National Center for Education Statistics, the Census Bureau does not regularly include specialized vocational, trade, business, or correspondence schools in its surveys. The National Center for Education Statistics includes nursery schools and kindergartens that are part of regular grade schools in their enrollment figures. The Census Bureau includes all nursery schools and kindergartens. At the higher education level, the statistics of both agencies are concerned with institutions granting degrees or offering work acceptable for degree-credit, such as junior colleges.

School attendance—All States require that children attend school. While State laws vary as to the ages and circumstances of compulsory attendance, generally they require that formal schooling begin by age 6 and continue to age 16.

Schools—The National Center for Education Statistics defines a *school* as "a division of the school system consisting of students composing one or more grade groups or other identifiable groups, organized as one unit with one or more teachers to give instruction of a defined type, and housed in a school plant of one or more buildings. More than one school may be housed in one school plant, as is the case when the elementary and secondary programs are housed in the same school plant."

Regular schools are those which advance a person toward a diploma or degree. They include public and private nursery schools, kindergartens, graded schools, colleges, universities, and professional schools.

Public schools are schools controlled and supported by local, State, or Federal governmental agencies; *private* schools are those controlled and supported mainly by religious organizations or by private persons or organizations.

The Bureau of the Census defines *elementary* schools as including grades 1 through 8; *high* schools as including grades 9 through 12; and *colleges* as including junior or community colleges, regular 4-year colleges, and universities and graduate or professional schools. Statistics reported by the National Center for Education Statistics and the National Education Association by type of organization, such as elementary level and secondary level, may not be strictly comparable with those from the Bureau of the Census because the grades included at the two levels vary, depending on the level assigned to the middle or junior high school by the local school systems.

School year—Except as otherwise indicated in the tables, data refer to the school year which, for elementary and secondary schools, generally begins in September of the preceding year and ends in June of the year stated. For the most part, statistics concerning school finances are for a 12-month period, usually July 1 to June 30. Enrollment data generally refer to a specific point in time, such as fall, as indicated in the tables.

Statistical reliability—For a discussion of statistical collection, estimation, and sampling procedures and measures of statistical reliability applicable to Census Bureau and the National Center for Education Statistics data, see Appendix III.

No. 233. School Enrollment: 1965 to 2006

[In thousands. As of fall]

YEAR	TOTAL	ALL LEVELS		K THROUGH GRADE 8		GRADES 9 THROUGH 12		COLLEGE	
		Public	Private	Public	Private	Public	Private	Public	Private
1965	54,394	46,143	8,251	30,563	4,900	11,610	1,400	3,970	1,951
1970	59,838	52,322	7,516	32,558	4,052	13,336	1,311	6,428	2,153
1975	61,004	53,654	7,350	30,515	3,700	14,304	1,300	8,835	2,350
1980	58,305	50,335	7,971	27,647	3,992	13,231	1,339	9,457	2,640
1981	57,916	49,691	8,225	27,280	4,100	12,764	1,400	9,647	2,725
1982	57,591	49,262	8,330	27,161	4,200	12,405	1,400	9,696	2,730
1983	57,432	48,935	8,497	26,981	4,315	12,271	1,400	9,683	2,782
1984	57,150	48,686	8,465	26,905	4,300	12,304	1,400	9,477	2,765
1985	57,226	48,901	8,325	27,034	4,195	12,388	1,362	9,479	2,768
1986	57,709	49,467	8,242	27,420	4,116	12,333	1,336	9,714	2,790
1987	58,254	49,982	8,272	27,933	4,232	12,076	1,247	9,973	2,793
1988	58,485	50,349	8,136	28,501	4,036	11,687	1,206	10,161	2,894
1989	59,436	51,120	8,316	29,152	4,162	11,390	1,193	10,578	2,961
1990	60,267	52,061	8,206	29,878	4,095	11,338	1,137	10,845	2,974
1991	61,605	53,357	8,248	30,506	4,074	11,541	1,125	11,310	3,049
1992	62,686	54,208	8,478	31,088	4,212	11,735	1,163	11,385	3,103
1993	63,241	54,654	8,587	31,504	4,280	11,961	1,191	11,189	3,116
1994, prel.	63,984	55,242	8,741	31,894	4,360	12,214	1,236	11,134	3,145
1995, est. [1]	64,623	55,753	8,869	32,085	4,431	12,576	1,269	11,092	3,169
1996, proj.	66,081	57,140	8,942	32,837	4,493	13,049	1,304	11,254	3,145
1997, proj.	66,996	57,930	9,067	33,226	4,547	13,299	1,329	11,405	3,191
1998, proj.	67,807	58,615	9,192	33,522	4,587	13,466	1,346	11,627	3,259
1999, proj.	68,570	59,251	9,319	33,692	4,610	13,673	1,367	11,686	3,342
2000, proj.	69,165	59,747	9,418	33,852	4,632	13,804	1,380	12,091	3,405
2001, proj.	69,604	60,116	9,488	34,029	4,656	13,862	1,386	12,225	3,446
2002, proj.	69,966	60,421	9,545	34,098	4,666	14,004	1,400	12,319	3,479
2003, proj.	70,244	60,654	9,589	34,065	4,661	14,169	1,416	12,420	3,512
2004, proj.	70,527	60,896	9,631	33,882	4,636	14,483	1,446	12,531	3,547
2005, proj.	70,816	61,144	9,672	33,680	4,609	14,818	1,481	12,646	3,582
2006, proj.	71,004	61,296	9,707	33,507	4,585	15,021	1,501	12,768	3,621

[1] College data are preliminary.

Source: U.S. National Center for Education Statistics, *Digest of Education Statistics*, annual, and *Projections of Education Statistics*, annual.

No. 234. School Expenditures, by Type of Control and Level of Instruction in Constant (1994-95) Dollars: 1960 to 1996

[In millions of dollars. For school years ending in year shown. Total expenditures for public elementary and secondary schools include current expenditures, interest on school debt and capital outlay. Data deflated by the Consumer Price Index, wage earners, and clerical workers through 1975; thereafter, all urban consumers, on a school year basis (supplied by the National Center for Education Statistics). See also Appendix III]

YEAR	Total	ELEMENTARY AND SECONDARY SCHOOLS			COLLEGES AND UNIVERSITIES		
		Total	Public	Private [1]	Total	Public	Private [1]
1960	122,139	85,553	79,922	5,631	36,585	19,982	16,603
1970	272,582	171,943	161,988	9,954	100,640	64,639	36,000
1975	315,569	199,934	188,317	11,616	115,635	78,313	37,322
1980	320,889	199,868	185,918	13,949	121,021	80,275	40,746
1983	325,000	197,262	181,478	15,784	127,738	83,269	44,469
1984	337,806	205,405	188,411	16,994	132,401	85,892	46,509
1985	352,187	212,457	194,823	17,634	139,730	90,593	49,137
1986	372,485	223,642	205,396	18,245	148,843	96,850	51,993
1987	394,604	236,903	217,567	19,336	157,900	100,808	57,092
1988	406,881	244,096	224,230	19,865	162,786	103,688	59,097
1989	430,506	259,853	239,499	20,354	170,654	108,106	62,548
1990	451,583	273,243	251,685	21,559	178,340	114,175	64,166
1991	463,466	279,584	257,682	21,901	183,882	117,293	66,589
1992	472,422	284,325	262,342	21,983	188,097	118,650	69,447
1993, prel.	482,308	289,614	266,925	22,689	192,695	121,757	70,938
1994, est	492,801	295,726	272,889	22,836	197,075	124,160	72,916
1995, est.	504,500	302,900	279,400	23,500	201,600	126,700	74,900
1996, est.	514,691	309,533	285,432	24,102	205,157	128,964	76,193

[1] Estimated.

Source: U.S. National Center for Education Statistics, *Digest Education Statistics*, annual.

No. 235. School Enrollment, Faculty, Graduates, and Finances, With Projections: 1985 to 2006

[As of fall, except as indicated]

ITEM	Unit	1985	1990	1995, est.	1996, proj.	2000, proj.	2003, proj.	2006, proj.
ELEMENTARY AND SECONDARY SCHOOLS								
School enrollment, total	1,000	44,979	46,446	50,362	51,683	53,668	54,312	54,615
Kindergarten through grade 8	1,000	31,229	33,973	36,516	37,330	38,484	38,726	38,092
Grades 9 through 12	1,000	13,750	12,475	13,845	14,353	15,184	15,586	16,523
Public, total	1,000	39,422	41,217	44,662	45,885	47,656	48,234	48,528
Kindergarten through grade 8	1,000	27,034	29,878	32,085	32,837	33,852	34,065	33,507
Grades 9 through 12	1,000	12,388	11,338	12,576	13,049	13,804	14,169	15,021
Private, total	1,000	5,557	5,232	5,700	5,798	6,012	6,078	6,086
Kindergarten through grade 8	1,000	4,195	4,095	4,431	4,493	4,632	4,661	4,585
Grades 9 through 12	1,000	1,362	1,137	1,269	1,304	1,380	1,416	1,501
Enrollment rate:								
5 and 6 year olds	Percent	96.1	96.5	96.0	(NA)	(NA)	(NA)	(NA)
7 to 13 year olds	Percent	99.2	99.6	98.9	(NA)	(NA)	(NA)	(NA)
14 to 17 year olds	Percent	94.9	95.8	96.3	(NA)	(NA)	(NA)	(NA)
Classroom teachers, total [1]	1,000	2,549	2,753	2,972	3,071	3,239	3,334	3,431
Public, total	1,000	2,206	2,398	2,586	2,679	2,826	2,910	2,996
Private, total	1,000	343	355	386	392	413	424	435
High school graduates, total [2]	1,000	2,643	2,503	2,572	2,612	2,873	2,981	3,022
Public	1,000	2,383	2,235	2,305	2,343	2,631	2,739	2,710
Public schools: [2]								
Average daily attendance (ADA)	1,000	36,523	38,427	41,819	42,570	44,213	44,749	(NA)
Constant (1993-94) dollars:								
Teachers' average salary	Dol.	33,867	36,126	35,756	36,698	37,717	37,982	(NA)
Current school expenditures	Bil. dol.	184	221	253	262	293	310	(NA)
HIGHER EDUCATION								
Enrollment, total	1,000	12,247	13,819	14,262	14,398	15,497	15,932	16,389
Male	1,000	5,818	6,284	6,343	6,470	6,985	7,194	7,375
Full time	1,000	3,606	3,808	3,807	3,989	4,458	4,654	4,825
Part time	1,000	2,211	2,476	2,535	2,481	2,526	2,540	2,549
Female	1,000	6,429	7,535	7,919	7,929	8,512	8,738	9,014
Full time	1,000	3,468	4,013	4,321	4,235	4,713	4,901	5,117
Part time	1,000	2,961	3,521	3,598	3,694	3,799	3,837	3,897
Public	1,000	9,479	10,845	11,092	11,254	12,091	12,420	12,768
Four-year institutions	1,000	5,210	5,848	5,815	5,960	6,458	6,671	6,867
Two-year institutions	1,000	4,270	4,996	5,278	5,294	5,635	5,749	5,882
Private	1,000	2,768	2,974	3,169	3,145	3,406	3,512	3,621
Four-year institutions	1,000	2,506	2,730	2,955	2,899	3,137	3,236	3,336
Two-year institutions	1,000	261	244	215	245	269	276	285
Undergraduate	1,000	10,597	11,959	12,232	12,336	13,336	13,757	14,189
Graduate	1,000	1,376	1,586	1,732	1,754	1,826	1,834	1,861
First-time professional	1,000	274	273	298	308	335	341	349
Full-time equivalent	1,000	8,943	9,983	10,335	10,457	11,457	11,860	12,272
Public	1,000	6,668	7,558	7,752	7,890	8,636	8,936	9,243
Private	1,000	2,276	2,425	2,583	2,586	2,819	2,924	3,029
Faculty, total	1,000	715	817	910	922	894	(NA)	(NA)
Public	1,000	503	574	648	654	626	(NA)	(NA)
Private	1,000	212	244	264	268	268	(NA)	(NA)
Degrees conferred, total [2]	1,000	1,830	2,025	2,259	2,253	2,325	2,451	(NA)
Associate's	1,000	446	482	534	519	549	576	(NA)
Bachelor's	1,000	988	1,095	1,195	1,188	1,211	1,288	(NA)
Master's	1,000	289	337	409	421	435	452	(NA)
Doctorate's	1,000	34	39	43	44	46	44	(NA)
First-professional	1,000	74	72	78	81	84	90	(NA)

NA Not available. [1] Full-time equivalents. [2] For school year ending June the following year.

Source: U.S. National Center for Education Statistics, *Digest of Education Statistics*, annual, and *Projections of Educational Statistics*, annual.

No. 236. Federal Funds for Education and Related Programs: 1994 to 1996

[In millions of dollars, except percent. For fiscal years ending in September. Figures represent on-budget funds]

LEVEL, AGENCY, AND PROGRAM	1994	1995	1996 [1]
Total, all programs	68,811.5	71,718.8	70,867.0
Percent of Federal budget outlays	4.7	4.7	4.5
Elementary/secondary education programs	32,304.4	33,623.8	35,202.8
Department of Education [2]	13,769.2	14,029.0	15,416.0
Grants for the disadvantaged	6,845.7	6,808.0	7,113.0
School improvement programs	1,470.0	1,397.0	1,594.0
Indian education	79.1	71.0	78.0
Education for the handicapped	2,980.3	3,177.0	3,511.0
Vocational and adult education	1,340.8	1,482.0	1,513.0
Department of Agriculture [2]	7,604.4	8,201.3	8,192.6
Child nutrition programs	[3]7,043.7	[3]7,644.8	[3]7,644.8
Agricultural Marketing Service—commodities [4]	400.0	400.0	400.0
Department of Defense [2]	1,210.2	1,295.5	1,322.3
Overseas dependents schools	849.6	855.8	816.6
Section VI schools [5]	265.0	284.2	332.8
Department of Energy	11.6	12.6	7.7
Department of Health and Human Services	4,669.2	5,116.6	5,119.3
Head Start	3,215.9	3,534.0	3,534.0
Social security student benefits	839.0	953.0	959.0
Department of the Interior [2]	485.8	493.1	481.8
Mineral Leasing Act and other funds	61.5	56.2	27.3
Indian Education	423.6	435.9	433.5
Department of Justice	112.4	128.9	151.6
Inmate programs	111.2	125.9	147.6
Department of Labor	4,011.2	3,957.8	4,096.0
Job Corps	964.2	1,029.0	1,096.0
Department of Veterans Affairs	335.9	311.8	354.2
Vocational rehab for disabled veterans	265.6	298.1	348.8
Other agencies and programs	94.5	77.2	81.3
Higher education programs	16,734.4	17,623.9	14,802.3
Department of Education [2]	13,432.0	14,243.0	11,419.0
Student financial assistance	7,118.0	7,047.0	7,395.0
Federal Family Education Loans	5,070.3	5,190.0	2,371.0
Department of Agriculture	25.5	33.4	32.9
Department of Defense	679.0	729.5	746.0
Tuition assistance for military personnel	130.2	127.0	131.0
Service academies [6]	141.5	163.3	174.9
Senior ROTC	195.3	219.4	236.7
Professional development education	212.0	219.8	203.4
Department of Energy [2]	18.0	28.0	15.0
Department of Health and Human Services [2]	795.9	796.0	783.4
Health professions training programs	305.5	298.3	276.6
National Health Service Corps scholarships	79.3	78.2	78.0
National Institutes of Health training grants [7]	372.7	380.5	390.9
Department of the Interior	156.7	159.1	151.0
Shared revenues, Mineral Leasing Act and other receipts—estimated education share	79.8	82.8	76.3
Indian programs	76.9	76.2	74.7
Department of Transportation	56.6	56.1	56.1
Department of Veterans Affairs [2]	1,043.7	1,010.1	1,069.0
Other agencies and programs [2]	526.9	568.8	509.9
Post-Vietnam veterans	48.1	33.6	24.9
All-volunteer-force educational assistance	887.0	868.4	957.4
National Endowment for the Humanities	58.4	56.5	34.0
National Science Foundation	225.2	211.8	208.4
United States Information Agency	200.4	260.8	231.2
Other education programs	4,483.7	4,721.7	4,941.4
Department of Education [2]	2,798.0	2,863.0	3,234.0
Administration	403.9	405.0	464.0
Libraries	142.2	117.0	169.0
Rehabilitative services and handicapped research	2,244.2	2,334.0	2,594.0
Department of Agriculture	426.3	422.9	413.5
Department of Health and Human Services	107.9	138.0	153.0
Department of Justice	34.1	36.3	39.1
Department of State	46.6	51.6	51.2
Department of the Treasury	62.0	48.0	49.0
Other agencies and programs [2]	1,010.9	1,161.8	1,001.5
Agency for International Development	241.9	260.4	247.2
Library of Congress	312.7	241.0	243.0
National Endowment for the Arts	2.2	2.3	1.9
National Endowment for the Humanities	96.8	94.2	57.0
Research programs at universities and related institutions [2]	15,289.1	15,749.4	15,910.6
Department of Agriculture	438.5	432.1	434.2
Department of Defense	2,010.4	1,922.1	1,654.1
Department of Energy	2,642.1	2,888.5	2,697.6
Department of Health and Human Services	6,348.7	6,514.1	6,766.1
National Aeronautics and Space Administration	1,412.7	1,636.1	1,617.0
National Science Foundation	1,805.9	1,894.6	2,036.2

[1] Estimated. [2] Includes other programs and agencies, not shown separately. [3] The Special Milk Program is included in the Child Nutrition Program. [4] Purchased under Section 32 of the Act of August 1935 for use in child nutrition programs. [5] Program provides for the education of dependents of federal employees residing on federal property where free public education is unavailable in the nearby community. [6] Instructional costs only including academics, audiovisual, academic computer center, faculty training, military training, physical education, and libraries. [7] Includes alcohol, drug abuse, and mental health training programs.

Source: U.S. National Center for Education Statistics, *Digest of Education Statistics*, 1996.

No. 237. School Expenditures, by Source of Funds in Constant (1993-94) Dollars: 1980 to 1994

[In billions of dollars. For school years ending in year shown. Includes nursery, kindergarten, and special programs when provided by school system. Data are deflated by the Consumer Price Index for all urban consumers, on a school year basis (supplied by the U.S. National Center for Education Statistics). Distribution by source of funds is estimated]

SOURCE OF FUNDS AND CONTROL OF SCHOOL	1980	1985	1987	1988	1989	1990	1991	1992	1993	1994
Total	**311.9**	**342.4**	**383.6**	**395.5**	**418.6**	**439.0**	**450.6**	**439.4**	**439.0**	**479.1**
Federal	35.6	29.5	33.1	33.7	35.0	36.3	37.2	39.4	41.1	42.3
State	121.2	132.9	149.1	153.1	157.1	163.5	165.5	164.1	164.0	164.6
Local	81.5	87.5	96.5	100.1	111.2	112.6	115.2	117.9	120.4	125.1
All other	73.7	92.5	104.9	108.7	115.3	126.5	132.7	138.1	143.4	147.1
Public	258.8	277.5	310.1	319.6	337.9	355.7	364.5	370.4	377.9	386.0
Federal	27.9	21.9	23.8	24.3	25.2	26.4	27.2	29.0	30.8	32.0
State	120.4	132.0	147.9	151.6	155.5	162.0	164.1	162.4	162.4	163.1
Local	81.1	87.2	96.2	99.7	110.7	112.2	114.7	117.4	120.0	124.8
All other	29.3	36.4	42.3	44.0	46.4	55.1	58.6	61.6	64.7	66.3
Private	53.2	64.9	73.5	76.0	80.6	83.3	86.0	89.0	91.0	93.1
Federal	7.7	7.6	9.3	9.4	9.8	9.9	10.0	10.4	10.3	10.3
State and local	1.1	1.2	1.6	1.8	2.0	2.1	1.9	2.1	2.0	2.0
All other	44.3	56.1	62.6	64.8	68.8	71.3	74.1	76.5	78.7	80.8
Elementary and secondary	**194.3**	**206.5**	**230.3**	**237.3**	**252.7**	**265.6**	**271.8**	**276.4**	**281.5**	**287.5**
Federal	17.7	12.6	13.5	13.8	14.5	15.0	15.5	16.8	18.1	18.7
State	84.2	92.3	104.8	107.6	110.8	115.7	118.1	118.3	118.8	119.8
Local	78.3	84.0	92.6	96.0	106.9	108.1	110.4	113.2	115.5	119.7
All other	14.1	17.7	19.4	20.0	20.5	26.9	27.8	28.1	29.1	29.3
Public	180.7	189.4	211.5	218.0	232.8	244.7	250.5	255.1	259.5	265.3
Federal	17.7	12.6	13.5	13.8	14.5	15.0	15.5	16.8	18.1	18.7
State	84.2	92.3	104.8	107.6	110.8	115.7	118.1	118.3	118.8	119.8
Local	78.3	84.0	92.6	96.0	106.9	108.1	110.4	113.2	115.5	119.7
All other [1]	0.5	0.6	0.6	0.7	0.7	5.9	6.5	6.8	7.0	7.1
Private	13.6	17.1	18.8	19.3	19.8	21.0	21.3	21.4	22.1	22.2
Higher education	**117.6**	**135.8**	**153.3**	**158.2**	**165.9**	**173.4**	**178.8**	**182.9**	**187.4**	**191.6**
Federal	17.9	16.9	19.6	19.9	20.6	21.4	21.7	22.5	23.1	23.6
State	37.0	40.6	44.3	45.5	46.2	47.8	47.4	45.8	45.2	44.8
Local	3.2	3.5	4.0	4.1	4.3	4.5	4.7	4.7	4.9	5.3
All other	59.6	74.8	85.5	88.8	94.8	99.6	104.9	109.9	114.3	117.9
Public	78.0	88.1	98.6	101.6	105.1	111.0	114.0	115.3	118.5	120.7
Federal	10.2	9.3	10.2	10.5	10.8	11.4	11.7	12.2	12.8	13.3
State	36.1	39.7	43.1	44.1	44.7	46.3	45.9	44.1	43.6	43.3
Local	2.9	3.2	3.6	3.7	3.9	4.1	4.2	4.2	4.4	4.8
All other	28.8	35.8	41.7	43.3	45.7	49.2	52.1	54.8	57.7	59.3
Private	39.6	47.8	54.7	56.6	60.8	62.4	64.7	67.6	69.0	70.9
Federal	7.7	7.6	9.3	9.4	9.8	9.9	10.0	10.4	10.3	10.3
State and local	1.1	1.2	1.6	1.8	2.0	2.1	1.9	2.1	2.0	2.0
All other	30.8	39.0	43.8	45.4	49.0	50.4	52.8	55.1	56.6	58.6

[1] Beginning in 1989-90, includes all fees for transportation, books, and food services.

Source: U.S. National Center for Education Statistics, *Digest of Education Statistics*, annual.

No. 238. Enrollment in Public and Private Schools, by Control and Level, With Projections: 1970 to 2006

[In thousands. As of fall. Data are for regular day schools and exclude independent nursery schools and kindergartens, residential schools for exceptional children, subcollegiate departments of colleges, Federal schools for Indians, and federally operated schools on Federal installations. College data include degree-credit and nondegree-credit enrollment]

CONTROL OF SCHOOL AND LEVEL	1970	1980	1985	1990	1994, prel.	1995, est. [1]	2000, proj.	2003, proj.	2004, proj.	2005, proj.	2006, proj.
Total	**59,838**	**58,305**	**57,226**	**60,267**	**63,994**	**64,623**	**69,165**	**70,244**	**70,527**	**70,816**	**71,004**
Public	52,322	50,335	48,901	52,061	55,242	55,753	59,747	60,654	60,896	61,144	61,296
Private	7,516	7,971	8,325	8,206	8,741	8,869	9,418	9,589	9,631	9,672	9,707
Kindergarten through 8	36,610	31,639	31,229	33,973	36,254	36,516	38,484	38,726	38,518	38,289	38,092
Public	32,558	27,647	27,034	29,878	31,894	32,085	33,852	34,065	33,882	33,680	33,507
Private	4,052	3,992	4,195	4,095	4,360	4,431	4,632	4,661	4,636	4,609	4,585
Grades 9 through 12	14,647	14,570	13,750	12,475	13,450	13,845	15,184	15,585	15,931	16,299	16,522
Public	13,336	13,231	12,388	11,338	12,214	12,576	13,804	14,169	14,483	14,818	15,021
Private	1,311	1,339	1,362	1,137	1,236	1,269	1,380	1,416	1,448	1,481	1,501
College	8,581	12,097	12,247	13,819	14,279	14,262	15,497	15,932	16,078	16,229	16,389
Public	6,428	9,457	9,479	10,845	11,134	11,092	12,091	12,420	12,531	12,646	12,768
Private	2,153	2,640	2,768	2,974	3,145	3,169	3,406	3,512	3,547	3,582	3,621

[1] College data are preliminary.

Source: U.S. National Center for Education Statistics, *Digest of Education Statistics*, annual; *Projections of Education Statistics*, annual; and unpublished data.

No. 239. School Enrollment, by Age: 1970 to 1995

[As of October. Covers civilian noninstitutional population enrolled in nursery school and above. Based on Current Population Survey, see text, section 1]

AGE	1970	1980	1985	1988	1990	1991	1992	1993	1994	1995
ENROLLMENT										
Total 3 to 34 years old	60,357	57,348	58,013	59,236	60,588	61,276	62,084	62,730	66,427	66,939
3 and 4 years old	1,461	2,280	2,801	2,898	3,292	3,068	3,063	3,275	3,917	4,042
5 and 6 years old	7,000	5,853	6,697	6,990	7,207	7,178	7,252	7,298	7,752	7,901
7 to 13 years old	28,943	23,751	22,849	24,431	25,016	25,445	25,768	26,110	26,768	27,003
14 and 15 years old	7,869	7,282	7,362	6,493	6,555	6,634	6,861	7,011	7,519	7,651
16 and 17 years old	6,927	7,129	6,654	6,254	6,098	6,155	6,272	6,339	6,895	6,997
18 and 19 years old	3,322	3,788	3,716	4,125	4,044	3,969	4,012	4,063	4,180	4,274
20 and 21 years old	1,949	2,515	2,708	2,630	2,852	3,041	3,027	2,810	3,133	3,025
22 to 24 years old	1,410	1,931	2,068	2,207	2,231	2,365	2,577	2,579	2,724	2,545
25 to 29 years old	1,011	1,714	1,942	1,960	2,013	2,045	1,907	1,942	2,070	2,216
30 to 34 years old	466	1,105	1,218	1,248	1,281	1,377	1,344	1,303	1,468	1,284
35 years old and over	(NA)	1,290	1.766	2,230	2,439	2,620	2,473	2,634	2,845	2,830
ENROLLMENT RATE										
Total 3 to 34 years old	56.4	49.7	48.3	49.1	50.2	50.7	51.4	51.8	53.3	53.7
3 and 4 years old	20.5	36.7	38.9	39.1	44.4	40.5	39.7	40.4	47.3	48.7
5 and 6 years old	89.5	95.7	96.1	95.2	96.5	95.4	95.5	95.4	96.7	96.0
7 to 13 years old	99.2	99.3	99.2	99.3	99.6	99.7	99.4	99.5	99.3	98.9
14 and 15 years old	98.1	98.2	98.1	98.8	99.0	98.8	99.1	98.9	98.8	98.9
16 and 17 years old	90.0	89.0	91.7	92.7	92.5	93.3	94.1	94.0	94.4	93.6
18 and 19 years old	47.7	46.4	51.6	56.0	57.3	59.6	61.4	61.6	60.2	59.4
20 and 21 years old	31.9	31.0	35.3	38.5	39.7	42.0	44.0	42.7	44.9	44.9
22 to 24 years old	14.9	16.3	16.9	19.9	21.0	22.2	23.7	23.6	24.1	23.2
25 to 29 years old	7.5	9.3	9.2	9.3	9.7	10.2	9.8	10.2	10.8	11.6
30 to 34 years old	4.2	6.4	6.1	5.7	5.8	6.2	6.1	5.9	6.7	6.0
35 years old and over	(NA)	1.4	1.6	2.0	2.1	2.2	2.1	2.2	2.3	2.2

NA Not available.

Source: U.S. Bureau of the Census, *Current Population Reports*, P20-492; and earlier reports.

No. 240. School Enrollment, by Race, Hispanic Origin, and Age: 1980 to 1995

[See headnote, table 239]

AGE	WHITE			BLACK			HISPANIC ORIGIN [1]		
	1980	1990	1995	1980	1990	1995	1980	1990	1995
ENROLLMENT									
Total 3 to 34 years old	47,673	48,899	52,982	8,251	8,854	10,396	4,263	6,073	8,313
3 and 4 years old	1,844	2,700	3,205	371	452	657	172	249	503
5 and 6 years old	4,781	5,750	6,211	904	1,129	1,305	491	835	1,159
7 to 13 years old	19,585	20,076	21,296	3,598	3,832	4,308	2,009	2,794	3,620
14 and 15 years old	6,038	5,265	6,008	1,088	1,023	1,223	568	739	977
16 and 17 years old	5,937	4,858	5,484	1,047	982	1,127	454	592	778
18 and 19 years old	3,199	3,271	3,379	494	596	631	226	329	467
20 and 21 years old	2,206	2,402	2,483	242	305	363	111	213	288
22 to 24 years old	1,669	1,781	2,033	196	274	309	93	121	250
25 to 29 years old	1,473	1,706	1,783	187	162	254	84	130	172
30 to 34 years old	942	1,090	979	124	119	217	54	72	120
35 years old and over	1,104	2,096	2,324	186	238	359	(NA)	145	250
ENROLLMENT RATE									
Total 3 to 34 years old	48.9	49.5	53.2	53.9	51.9	56.1	49.8	47.4	49.7
3 and 4 years old	36.3	44.9	49.6	38.2	41.6	47.5	28.5	29.8	36.9
5 and 6 years old	95.8	96.5	96.2	95.4	96.3	95.5	94.5	94.8	93.9
7 to 13 years old	99.2	99.6	99.0	99.4	99.8	98.5	99.2	99.4	98.9
14 and 15 years old	98.3	99.1	98.8	97.9	99.2	99.0	94.3	99.0	98.9
16 and 17 years old	88.6	92.5	93.7	90.6	91.7	92.9	81.8	85.4	88.2
18 and 19 years old	46.3	57.1	59.3	45.7	55.2	57.4	37.8	44.1	46.1
20 and 21 years old	31.9	41.0	46.2	23.4	28.4	37.4	19.5	27.2	27.1
22 to 24 years old	16.4	20.2	23.1	13.6	20.0	19.9	11.7	9.9	15.6
25 to 29 years old	9.2	9.9	11.5	8.8	6.1	10.0	6.9	6.3	7.1
30 to 34 years old	6.3	5.9	5.5	6.8	4.4	7.8	5.1	3.6	4.7
35 years old and over	1.3	2.1	2.1	1.8	2.1	2.7	(NA)	2.1	2.7

NA Not available. [1] Persons of Hispanic origin may be of any race.

Source: U.S. Bureau of the Census, *Current Population Reports*, P20-492; and earlier reports.

No. 241. Enrollment in Public and Private Schools: 1960 to 1995

[In millions, except percent. As of October. For civilian noninstitutional population. For 1960, 5 to 34 years old; for 1970 to 1985, 3 to 34 years old; beginning 1986, for 3 years old and over]

YEAR	PUBLIC						PRIVATE					
	Total	Nursery	Kindergarten	Elementary	High School	College	Total	Nursery	Kindergarten	Elementary	High School	College
1960	39.0	(NA)	([1])	27.5	9.2	2.3	7.2	(NA)	([1])	4.9	1.0	1.3
1970	52.2	0.3	2.6	30.0	13.5	5.7	8.1	0.8	0.5	3.9	1.2	1.7
1975	52.8	0.6	2.9	27.2	14.5	7.7	8.2	1.2	0.5	3.3	1.2	2.0
1978	50.0	0.6	2.5	25.3	14.2	7.4	8.6	1.2	0.5	3.2	1.2	2.4
1979	50.0	0.6	2.6	24.8	14.0	7.7	8.2	1.2	0.4	3.1	1.1	2.3
1980	(NA)	0.6	2.7	24.4	(NA)	(NA)	(NA)	1.4	0.5	3.1	(NA)	(NA)
1981	49.7	0.7	2.6	24.8	13.5	8.2	8.7	1.4	0.5	3.0	1.1	2.6
1982	49.2	0.7	2.7	24.4	13.0	8.4	8.2	1.4	0.6	3.0	1.1	2.6
1983	48.7	0.8	2.7	24.2	12.8	8.2	9.0	1.5	0.7	3.0	1.2	2.6
1984	49.0	0.8	3.0	24.1	12.7	8.5	8.3	1.6	0.5	2.7	1.1	2.4
1985	49.0	0.9	3.2	23.8	12.8	8.4	9.0	1.6	0.6	3.1	1.2	2.5
1986 [2]	51.2	0.8	3.4	24.2	13.0	9.8	9.4	1.7	0.6	3.0	1.2	2.9
1987 [2]	51.7	0.8	3.4	24.8	12.7	10.0	8.9	1.7	0.6	2.8	1.1	2.8
1988 [2]	52.2	0.9	3.4	25.5	12.2	10.3	8.9	1.8	0.5	2.8	1.0	2.8
1989 [2]	52.5	0.9	3.3	25.9	12.1	10.3	8.9	1.9	0.6	2.7	0.8	2.9
1990 [2]	53.8	1.2	3.3	26.6	11.9	10.7	9.2	2.2	0.6	2.7	0.9	2.9
1991 [2]	54.5	1.1	3.5	26.6	12.2	11.1	9.4	1.8	0.6	3.0	1.0	3.0
1992 [2]	55.0	1.1	3.5	27.1	12.3	11.1	9.4	1.8	0.6	3.1	1.0	3.0
1993 [2]	56.0	1.2	3.5	27.7	12.6	10.9	9.4	1.8	0.7	2.9	1.0	3.0
1994 [2]	58.6	1.9	3.3	28.1	13.5	11.7	10.7	2.3	0.6	3.4	1.1	3.3
1995 [2]	58.7	2.0	3.2	28.4	13.7	11.4	11.1	2.4	0.7	3.4	1.2	3.3
Percent White:												
1960	85.7	(NA)	([1])	84.3	88.2	92.2	95.7	(NA)	([1])	95.3	96.7	96.3
1970	84.5	59.5	84.4	83.1	85.6	90.7	93.4	91.1	88.2	94.1	96.1	92.8
1980	(NA)	68.2	80.7	80.9	(NA)	(NA)	(NA)	89.0	87.0	90.7	(NA)	(NA)
1990	79.8	71.7	78.3	78.9	79.2	84.1	87.4	89.6	83.2	88.2	89.4	85.0
1993	78.9	68.5	78.6	78.4	78.3	82.5	85.3	89.7	86.9	87.0	83.1	81.4
1994	77.9	68.6	76.4	77.4	77.8	80.4	85.4	88.2	86.2	85.3	85.2	80.4
1995	78.0	71.3	76.9	77.5	76.9	81.9	85.0	88.7	84.1	86.1	86.0	81.1

NA Not available. [1] Included in elementary school. [2] See table 286 for college enrollment 35 years old and over. Also data beginning 1986 based on a revised edit and tabulation package.

Source: U.S. Bureau of the Census, *Current Population Reports*, P20-492; and earlier reports.

No. 242. School Enrollment, by Sex and Level: 1960 to 1995

[In millions. As of Oct. For the civilian noninstitutional population. For 1960, persons 5 to 34 years old; 1970-1979, 3 to 34 years old; beginning 1980, 3 years old and over. Elementary includes kindergarten and grades 1-8; high school, grades 9-12; and college, 2-year and 4-year colleges, universities, and graduate and professional schools. Data for college represent degree-credit enrollment]

YEAR	ALL LEVELS [1]			ELEMENTARY			HIGH SCHOOL			COLLEGE		
	Total	Male	Female	Total	Male	Female	Total	Male	Female	Total	Male	Female
1960	46.3	24.2	22.0	32.4	16.7	15.7	10.2	5.2	5.1	3.6	2.3	1.2
1970	60.4	31.4	28.9	37.1	19.0	18.1	14.7	7.4	7.3	7.4	4.4	3.0
1975	61.0	31.6	29.4	33.8	17.3	16.5	15.7	8.0	7.7	9.7	5.3	4.4
1978	58.6	30.1	28.6	31.5	16.1	15.3	15.5	7.8	7.6	9.8	5.1	4.7
1979	57.9	29.5	28.3	30.9	15.9	15.0	15.1	7.7	7.4	10.0	5.0	5.0
1980	58.6	29.6	29.1	30.6	15.8	14.9	14.6	7.3	7.3	11.4	5.4	6.0
1981 [2]	58.4	29.5	28.9	30.1	15.5	14.7	14.4	7.3	7.1	11.8	5.6	6.2
1981 [3]	59.9	30.3	29.6	31.0	15.9	15.0	14.7	7.5	7.3	12.1	5.8	6.3
1982	59.4	30.0	29.4	30.7	15.8	14.9	14.2	7.2	7.0	12.3	5.9	6.4
1983	59.3	30.1	29.2	30.6	15.7	14.8	14.1	7.1	7.0	12.4	6.0	6.3
1984	58.9	29.9	29.0	30.3	15.6	14.7	13.9	7.1	6.8	12.3	6.0	6.3
1985	59.8	30.0	29.7	30.7	15.7	15.0	14.1	7.2	6.9	12.5	5.9	6.6
1986	60.1	30.4	29.7	31.1	16.1	15.0	14.0	7.1	6.9	12.4	5.8	6.6
1986 [4]	60.5	30.6	30.0	31.1	16.1	15.0	14.2	7.2	7.0	12.7	6.0	6.7
1987	60.6	30.7	29.9	31.6	16.3	15.3	13.8	7.0	6.8	12.7	6.0	6.7
1988	61.1	30.7	30.5	32.2	16.6	15.6	13.2	6.7	6.4	13.1	5.9	7.2
1989	61.5	30.8	30.7	32.5	16.7	15.8	12.9	6.6	6.3	13.2	6.0	7.2
1990	63.0	31.5	31.5	33.2	17.1	16.0	12.8	6.5	6.4	13.6	6.2	7.4
1991	63.9	32.1	31.8	33.8	17.3	16.4	13.1	6.8	6.4	14.1	6.4	7.6
1992	64.6	32.2	32.3	34.3	17.7	16.6	13.3	6.8	6.5	14.0	6.2	7.8
1993	65.4	32.9	32.5	34.8	17.9	16.9	13.6	7.0	6.6	13.9	6.3	7.6
1994	69.3	34.6	34.6	35.4	18.2	17.2	14.6	7.4	7.2	15.0	6.8	8.2
1995	69.8	35.0	34.8	35.7	18.3	17.4	15.0	7.7	7.3	14.7	6.7	8.0

[1] Beginning 1970, includes nursery schools, not shown separately. [2] Based on 1970 population controls. [3] Based on 1980 population controls. [4] Revised. Data beginning 1986, based on a revised edit and tabulation package.

Source: U.S. Bureau of the Census, *Current Population Reports*, P20-492; and earlier reports.

No. 243. Educational Attainment, by Race and Hispanic Origin: 1960 to 1996

[In percent. For persons 25 years old and over. 1960, 1970, and 1990 as of April 1 and based on sample data from the censuses of population. Other years as of March and based on the Current Population Survey; see text, section 1, and Appendix III. See table 244 for data by sex]

YEAR	Total [1]	White	Black	Asian and Pacific Islander	HISPANIC [2] Total [3]	HISPANIC [2] Mexican	HISPANIC [2] Puerto Rican	HISPANIC [2] Cuban
COMPLETED 4 YEARS OF HIGH SCHOOL OR MORE								
1960	41.1	43.2	20.1	(NA)	(NA)	(NA)	(NA)	(NA)
1965	49.0	51.3	27.2	(NA)	(NA)	(NA)	(NA)	(NA)
1970	52.3	54.5	31.4	(NA)	32.1	24.2	23.4	43.9
1975	62.5	64.5	42.5	(NA)	37.9	31.0	28.7	51.7
1980	66.5	68.8	51.2	(NA)	44.0	37.6	40.1	55.3
1985	73.9	75.5	59.8	(NA)	47.9	41.9	46.3	51.1
1990	77.6	79.1	66.2	80.4	50.8	44.1	55.5	63.5
1993 [4]	80.2	81.5	70.4	(NA)	53.1	46.2	59.8	62.1
1994 [4]	80.9	82.0	72.9	(NA)	53.3	46.7	59.4	64.1
1995 [4]	81.7	83.0	73.8	(NA)	53.4	46.5	61.3	64.7
1996 [4]	81.7	82.8	74.3	(NA)	53.1	46.9	60.4	63.8
COMPLETED 4 YEARS OF COLLEGE OR MORE								
1960	7.7	8.1	3.1	(NA)	(NA)	(NA)	(NA)	(NA)
1965	9.4	9.9	4.7	(NA)	(NA)	(NA)	(NA)	(NA)
1970	10.7	11.3	4.4	(NA)	4.5	2.5	2.2	11.1
1975	13.9	14.5	6.4	(NA)	(NA)	(NA)	(NA)	(NA)
1980	16.2	17.1	8.4	(NA)	7.6	4.9	5.6	16.2
1985	19.4	20.0	11.1	(NA)	8.5	5.5	7.0	13.7
1990	21.3	22.0	11.3	39.9	9.2	5.4	9.7	20.2
1993 [4]	21.9	22.6	12.2	(NA)	9.0	5.9	8.0	16.5
1994 [4]	22.2	22.9	12.9	(NA)	9.1	6.3	9.7	16.2
1995 [4]	23.0	24.0	13.2	(NA)	9.3	6.5	10.7	19.4
1996 [4]	23.6	24.3	13.6	(NA)	9.3	6.5	11.0	18.8

NA Not available. [1] Includes other races, not shown separately. [2] Persons of Hispanic origin may be of any race. [3] Includes persons of other Hispanic origin, not shown separately. [4] Beginning 1993, persons high school graduates and those with a BA degree or higher.

Source: U.S. Bureau of the Census, *U.S. Census of Population, U.S. Summary*, PC80-1-C1 and *Current Population Reports* P20-455, P20-459, P20-462, P20-465RV, P20-475,P20-489, P20-493; and unpublished data.

No. 244. Educational Attainment, by Race, Hispanic Origin, and Sex: 1960 to 1996

[See headnote, table 243. See table 243 for totals for both sexes]

YEAR	ALL RACES [1] Male	ALL RACES [1] Female	WHITE Male	WHITE Female	BLACK Male	BLACK Female	ASIAN AND PACIFIC ISLANDER Male	ASIAN AND PACIFIC ISLANDER Female	HISPANIC [2] Male	HISPANIC [2] Female
COMPLETED 4 YEARS OF HIGH SCHOOL OR MORE										
1960	39.5	42.5	41.6	44.7	18.2	21.8	(NA)	(NA)	(NA)	(NA)
1965	48.0	49.9	50.2	52.2	25.8	28.4	(NA)	(NA)	(NA)	(NA)
1970	51.9	52.8	54.0	55.0	30.1	32.5	(NA)	(NA)	37.9	34.2
1975	63.1	62.1	65.0	64.1	41.6	43.3	(NA)	(NA)	39.5	36.7
1980	67.3	65.8	69.6	68.1	50.8	51.5	(NA)	(NA)	67.3	65.8
1985	74.4	73.5	76.0	75.1	58.4	60.8	(NA)	(NA)	48.5	47.4
1990	77.7	77.5	79.1	79.0	65.8	66.5	84.0	77.2	50.3	51.3
1993 [3]	80.5	80.0	81.8	81.3	69.6	71.1	(NA)	(NA)	52.9	53.2
1994 [3]	81.0	80.7	82.1	81.9	71.7	73.8	(NA)	(NA)	53.4	53.2
1995 [3]	81.7	81.6	83.0	83.0	73.4	74.1	(NA)	(NA)	52.9	53.8
1996 [3]	81.9	81.6	82.7	82.8	74.3	74.2	(NA)	(NA)	53.0	53.3
COMPLETED 4 YEARS OF COLLEGE OR MORE										
1960	9.7	5.8	10.3	6.0	2.8	3.3	(NA)	(NA)	(NA)	(NA)
1965	12.0	7.1	12.7	7.3	4.9	4.5	(NA)	(NA)	(NA)	(NA)
1970	13.5	8.1	14.4	8.4	4.2	4.6	(NA)	(NA)	7.8	4.3
1975	17.6	10.6	18.4	11.0	6.7	6.2	(NA)	(NA)	8.3	4.6
1980	20.1	12.8	21.3	13.3	8.4	8.3	(NA)	(NA)	9.4	6.0
1985	23.1	16.0	24.0	16.3	11.2	11.0	(NA)	(NA)	9.7	7.3
1990	24.4	18.4	25.3	19.0	11.9	10.8	44.9	35.4	9.8	8.7
1993 [3]	24.8	19.2	25.7	19.7	11.9	12.4	(NA)	(NA)	9.5	8.5
1994 [3]	25.1	19.6	26.1	20.0	12.8	13.0	(NA)	(NA)	9.6	8.6
1995 [3]	26.0	20.2	27.2	21.0	13.6	12.9	(NA)	(NA)	10.1	8.4
1996 [3]	26.0	21.4	26.9	21.8	12.4	14.6	(NA)	(NA)	10.3	8.3

NA Not available. [1] Includes other races, not shown separately. [2] Persons of Hispanic origin may be of any race. [3] Beginning 1993, persons high school graduates and those with a BA degree or higher.

Source: U.S. Bureau of the Census, *U.S. Census of Population, 1960, 1970, and 1980, vol.1;* and *Current Population Reports* P20-459, P20-493, P20-475, P20-489, P20-493; and unpublished data.

No. 245. Educational Attainment, by Selected Characteristic: 1996

[For persons 25 years old and over. As of March. Based on Current Population Survey; see text, section 1, and Appendix III. For composition of regions, see table 26]

CHARACTERISTIC	Population (1,000)	PERCENT OF POPULATION—HIGHEST LEVEL					
		Not a high school graduate	High school graduate	Some college, but no degree	Associate's degree [1]	Bachelor's degree	Advanced degree
Total persons	168,323	18.3	33.6	17.3	7.2	15.8	7.6
Age:							
25 to 34 years old	40,919	13.1	32.0	19.7	8.7	20.5	6.0
35 to 44 years old	43,077	12.1	33.9	18.9	8.9	17.7	8.5
45 to 54 years old	31,584	13.5	32.7	17.6	8.1	16.4	11.6
55 to 64 years old	21,064	22.5	37.0	14.8	5.4	11.8	8.4
65 to 74 years old	18,270	30.7	36.3	14.6	3.6	9.3	5.6
75 years old or over	13,388	41.2	30.8	12.2	3.1	8.3	4.3
Sex: Male	80,339	18.1	31.9	17.4	6.6	16.4	9.5
Female	87,964	18.4	35.1	17.3	7.8	15.1	6.2
Race: White	142,733	17.2	33.9	17.3	7.3	16.1	8.1
Black	18,715	25.7	35.1	18.8	6.7	10.0	3.6
Other	6,878	18.9	23.7	13.7	7.3	23.7	12.7
Hispanic origin: Hispanic	14,541	46.9	26.0	13.2	3.6	6.6	2.6
Non-Hispanic	153,782	15.5	34.3	17.7	7.5	16.6	8.3
Region: Northeast	33,889	17.1	36.4	13.4	6.7	16.9	9.5
Midwest	39,245	15.0	37.3	17.2	7.8	15.3	7.4
South	59,105	21.8	33.0	17.5	6.3	14.3	7.0
West	36,084	17.0	27.9	21.0	8.5	17.7	7.9
Marital status:							
Never married	24,895	16.7	29.7	17.7	7.4	20.4	8.1
Married spouse present	105,388	15.3	34.3	17.1	7.5	16.8	8.9
Married spouse absent	6,611	29.3	33.5	18.2	5.6	9.6	3.8
Separated	4,717	28.3	35.6	18.9	6.1	8.4	2.8
Widowed	13,535	40.7	32.7	12.6	3.9	7.1	2.9
Divorced	17,895	16.9	35.4	21.3	8.5	12.0	5.8
Civilian labor force status:							
Employed	106,662	10.6	32.6	18.9	8.8	19.4	10.0
Unemployed	5,257	25.2	37.6	18.3	5.7	9.5	3.7
Not in the labor force	55,741	32.4	36.2	14.1	4.4	9.9	3.9

[1] Includes vocational degrees.
Source: U.S. Bureau of the Census, *Current Population Reports*, P20-493; and unpublished data.

No. 246. Earnings, by Highest Degree Earned: 1996

[For persons 18 years old and over with earnings. Persons as of March. Earnings for prior year. Based on Current Population Survey; see Appendix III. For definition of mean, see Guide to Tabular Presentation]

CHARACTERISTIC	Total persons	LEVEL OF HIGHEST DEGREE							
		Not a high school graduate	High school graduate only	Some college, no degree	Associate's	Bachelor's	Master's	Professional	Doctorate
MEAN EARNINGS (dol.)									
All persons [1]	26,792	14,013	21,431	22,392	27,780	36,980	47,609	85,322	64,550
Age: 18 to 24 years old	10,173	6,837	11,378	8,852	13,774	16,145	22,770	20,262	19,563
25 to 34 years old	23,956	13,742	20,243	21,422	24,288	31,658	37,033	50,019	40,366
35 to 44 years old	31,949	17,313	23,926	28,347	31,230	42,056	51,184	111,026	62,806
45 to 54 years old	34,914	17,197	25,661	32,761	32,238	44,115	54,506	93,517	75,070
55 to 64 years old	30,949	18,692	24,766	29,065	33,474	45,055	44,443	89,158	68,293
65 years old and over	19,612	10,603	16,443	17,528	16,004	26,442	31,258	58,844	60,885
Sex: Male	33,251	16,748	26,333	28,458	33,881	46,111	58,302	101,730	71,016
Female	19,414	9,790	15,970	16,152	22,429	26,841	34,911	47,959	47,733
White	27,556	14,234	22,154	22,896	28,137	37,711	48,029	85,229	64,606
Male	34,276	17,032	27,467	29,206	34,286	47,016	58,817	100,856	72,542
Female	19,647	9,582	16,196	16,125	22,547	26,916	35,125	48,562	45,202
Black	20,537	12,956	17,072	20,275	26,818	29,666	38,294	(B)	(B)
Male	23,876	14,877	19,514	24,694	33,674	36,026	41,777	(B)	(B)
Female	17,485	10,739	14,473	16,627	22,113	25,577	35,222	(B)	(B)
Hispanic [2]	18,262	13,065	18,333	18,903	23,406	30,602	36,633	(B)	(B)
Male	20,312	14,774	20,882	21,705	24,021	35,109	38,539	(B)	(B)
Female	15,310	9,809	14,960	15,899	22,883	25,336	33,390	(B)	(B)

B Base figure too small to meet statistical standards for reliability of a derived figure. [1] Includes other races, not shown separately. [2] Persons of Hispanic origin may be of any race.
Source: U.S. Bureau of the Census, unpublished data.

No. 247. Educational Attainment—States: 1990

[As of April 1. For persons 25 years old and over, except as indicated. Based on the 1990 Census of Population; see text, section 1, and Appendix III]

STATE	Population (1,000)	PERCENT OF POPULATION—HIGHEST LEVEL						Drop-outs[1] (percent)
		Not a high school graduate	High school graduate	Some college, but no degree	Associate's degree	Bachelor's degree	Advanced degree	
United States	156,868	24.8	30.0	18.7	6.2	13.1	7.2	11.2
Alabama	2,546	33.1	29.4	16.8	5.0	10.1	5.5	12.6
Alaska	323	13.4	28.7	27.6	7.2	15.0	8.0	10.9
Arizona	2,301	21.3	26.1	25.4	6.6	13.3	7.0	14.4
Arkansas	1,496	33.7	32.7	16.6	3.7	8.9	4.5	11.4
California	18,695	23.8	22.3	22.6	7.9	15.3	8.1	14.2
Colorado	2,107	15.6	26.5	24.0	6.9	18.0	9.0	9.8
Connecticut	2,199	20.8	29.5	15.9	6.6	16.2	11.0	9.0
Delaware	428	22.5	32.7	16.9	6.5	13.7	7.7	10.4
District of Columbia	409	26.9	21.2	15.8	3.1	16.1	17.2	13.9
Florida	8,887	25.6	30.1	19.4	6.6	12.0	6.3	14.3
Georgia	4,023	29.1	29.6	17.0	5.0	12.9	6.4	14.1
Hawaii	710	19.9	28.7	20.1	8.3	15.8	7.1	7.5
Idaho	601	20.3	30.4	24.2	7.5	12.4	5.3	10.4
Illinois	7,294	23.8	30.0	19.4	5.8	13.6	7.5	10.8
Indiana	3,489	24.4	38.2	16.6	5.3	9.2	6.4	11.4
Iowa	1,777	19.9	38.5	17.0	7.7	11.7	5.2	6.6
Kansas	1,566	18.7	32.8	21.9	5.4	14.1	7.0	8.7
Kentucky	2,334	35.4	31.8	15.2	4.1	8.1	5.5	13.3
Louisiana	2,537	31.7	31.7	17.2	3.3	10.5	5.6	12.5
Maine	796	21.2	37.1	16.1	6.9	12.7	6.1	8.3
Maryland	3,123	21.6	28.1	18.6	5.2	15.6	10.9	10.9
Massachusetts	3,962	20.0	29.7	15.8	7.2	16.6	10.6	8.5
Michigan	5,843	23.2	32.3	20.4	6.7	10.9	6.4	10.0
Minnesota	2,771	17.6	33.0	19.0	8.6	15.6	6.3	6.4
Mississippi	1,539	35.7	27.5	16.9	5.2	9.7	5.1	11.8
Missouri	3,292	26.1	33.1	18.4	4.5	11.7	6.1	11.4
Montana	506	19.0	33.5	22.1	5.6	14.1	5.7	8.1
Nebraska	996	18.2	34.7	21.1	7.1	13.1	5.9	7.0
Nevada	790	21.2	31.5	25.8	6.2	10.1	5.2	15.2
New Hampshire	714	17.8	31.7	18.0	8.1	16.4	7.9	9.4
New Jersey	5,166	23.3	31.1	15.5	5.2	16.0	8.8	9.6
New Mexico	923	24.9	28.7	20.9	5.0	12.1	8.3	11.7
New York	11,819	25.2	29.5	15.7	6.5	13.2	9.9	9.9
North Carolina	4,253	30.0	29.0	16.8	6.8	12.0	5.4	12.5
North Dakota	397	23.3	28.0	20.5	10.0	13.5	4.5	4.6
Ohio	6,925	24.3	36.3	17.0	5.3	11.1	5.9	8.9
Oklahoma	1,995	25.4	30.5	21.3	5.0	11.8	6.0	10.4
Oregon	1,855	18.5	28.9	25.0	6.9	13.6	7.0	11.8
Pennsylvania	7,873	25.3	38.6	12.9	5.2	11.3	6.6	9.1
Rhode Island	659	28.0	29.5	15.0	6.3	13.5	7.8	11.1
South Carolina	2,166	31.7	29.5	15.8	6.3	11.2	5.4	11.7
South Dakota	431	22.9	33.7	18.8	7.4	12.3	4.9	7.7
Tennessee	3,139	32.9	30.0	16.9	4.2	10.5	5.4	13.4
Texas	10,311	27.9	25.6	21.1	5.2	13.9	6.5	12.9
Utah	897	14.9	27.2	27.9	7.8	15.4	6.8	8.7
Vermont	357	19.2	34.6	14.7	7.2	15.4	8.9	8.0
Virginia	3,975	24.8	26.6	18.5	5.5	15.4	9.1	10.0
Washington	3,126	16.2	27.9	25.0	7.9	15.9	7.0	10.6
West Virginia	1,172	34.0	36.6	13.2	3.8	7.5	4.8	10.9
Wisconsin	3,094	21.4	37.1	16.7	7.1	12.1	5.6	7.1
Wyoming	278	17.0	33.2	24.2	6.9	13.1	5.7	6.9

[1] For persons 16 to 19 years old. A dropout is a person who is not in regular school and who has not completed the 12th grade or received a general equivalency degree.

Source: U.S. Bureau of the Census, *1990 Census of Population*, CPH-L-96.

No. 248. Preprimary School Enrollment—Summary: 1970 to 1995

[As of October. Civilian noninstitutional population. Includes public and nonpublic nursery school and kindergarten programs. Excludes 5 year olds enrolled in elementary school. Based on Current Population Survey; see text, section 1]

ITEM	1970	1975	1980	1985	1990	1992	1993	1994	1995
NUMBER OF CHILDREN (1,000)									
Population, 3 to 5 years old	10,949	10,183	9,284	10,733	11,207	11,544	11,954	12,328	12,518
Total enrolled [1]	4,104	4,954	4,878	5,865	6,659	6,403	6,581	7,514	7,739
Nursery	1,094	1,745	1,981	2,477	3,378	2,857	2,984	4,162	4,331
Public	332	570	628	846	1,202	1,074	1,204	1,848	1,950
Private	762	1,174	1,353	1,631	2,177	1,784	1,779	2,314	2,381
Kindergarten	3,010	3,211	2,897	3,388	3,281	3,546	3,597	3,352	3,408
Public	2,498	2,682	2,438	2,847	2,767	2,996	3,020	2,819	2,799
Private	511	528	459	541	513	550	577	534	608
White	3,443	4,105	3,994	4,757	5,389	5,137	5,224	5,869	6,144
Black	586	731	725	919	964	966	1,011	1,269	1,236
Hispanic [2]	(NA)	(NA)	370	496	642	728	657	851	1,040
3 years old	454	683	857	1,035	1,205	1,081	1,097	1,385	1,489
4 years old	1,007	1,418	1,423	1,765	2,086	1,982	2,179	2,532	2,553
5 years old	2,643	2,852	2,598	3,065	3,367	3,340	3,306	3,597	3,697
ENROLLMENT RATE									
Total enrolled [1]	37.5	48.6	52.5	54.6	59.4	55.5	55.1	61.0	61.8
White	37.8	48.6	52.7	54.7	59.7	55.8	55.7	60.9	63.0
Black	34.9	48.1	51.8	55.8	57.8	55.1	52.7	64.2	58.9
Hispanic [2]	(NA)	(NA)	43.3	43.3	49.0	48.4	43.9	47.7	51.1
3 years old	12.9	21.5	27.3	28.8	32.6	27.7	27.1	33.9	36.9
4 years old	27.8	40.5	46.3	49.1	56.0	52.1	53.9	60.3	61.6
5 years old	69.3	81.3	84.7	86.5	88.8	87.2	85.7	88.9	87.5

NA Not available. [1] Includes races not shown separately. [2] Persons of Hispanic origin may be of any race. The method of identifying Hispanic children was changed in 1980 from allocation based on status of mother to status reported for each child. The number of Hispanic children using the new method is larger.

Source: U.S. Bureau of the Census, *Current Population Reports*, P20-492.

No. 249. School Enrollment of 3- to 5-Year-Olds, by Education and Labor Force Status of Mother and Family Income: 1995

[In thousands. As of October. Civilian noninstitutional population. Based on Current Population Survey; see text, section 1]

CHARACTERISTIC	Total population [1]	ENROLLED IN NURSERY SCHOOL			ENROLLED IN KINDERGARTEN			Enrolled in elementary school
		Total	Public	Private	Total	Public	Private	
NUMBER (1,000)								
Total children 3 to 5 years old	12,518	4,331	1,952	2,381	3,408	2,799	608	268
3- and 4-year-olds	8,294	3,720	1,565	2,155	322	221	101	-
5 year olds	4,224	611	385	226	3,086	2,578	507	268
Education of mother:								
Children living with mother	11,711	4,062	1,772	2,289	3,196	2,622	575	249
Elementary: 0 to 8 years	607	115	110	5	162	156	7	24
High school: 1-3 years	1,310	323	268	56	334	324	10	26
High school graduate	3,878	1,178	616	562	1,056	909	146	73
College: Less than a BA degree	3,492	1,346	550	796	966	772	194	67
BA degree or higher	2,425	1,099	229	871	679	461	219	59
Labor force status of mother:								
Children living with mother	11,711	4,062	1,772	2,289	3,196	2,622	575	249
Mother in the labor force	7,404	2,683	1,103	1,580	2,096	1,686	413	165
Employed	6,829	2,533	992	1,541	1,921	1,522	398	147
Full time	4,607	1,681	687	993	1,237	987	249	115
Part time	2,221	853	305	548	683	535	150	32
Unemployed	576	149	111	39	177	162	14	18
Mother not in the labor force	4,306	1,379	669	710	1,101	937	164	83
Children not living with mother	807	271	178	92	210	177	33	19
Family income:								
Less than $10,000	1,915	564	477	87	470	450	21	73
$10,000 to 14,999	1,002	269	219	50	245	223	22	25
$15,000 to 19,999	793	209	151	58	196	183	14	13
$20,000 to 24,999	937	261	148	113	262	229	34	12
$25,000 to 29,999	896	290	154	136	225	208	17	34
$30,000 to 34,999	869	289	117	172	219	194	25	11
$35,000 to 39,999	861	284	107	177	256	189	67	18
$40,000 to 49,999	1,199	421	148	272	372	283	88	17
$50,000 to 74,999	1,778	804	180	624	471	346	126	24
$75,000 and over	1,276	633	91	542	370	235	135	24
Not reported	993	306	158	149	319	261	59	15

- Represents zero. [1] Includes those not enrolled, not shown separately.

Source: U.S. Bureau of the Census, *Current Population Reports*, P20-492.

No. 250. Public Elementary and Secondary Schools—Summary: 1980 to 1996

[For school year ending in year shown, except as indicated. Data are estimates]

ITEM	Unit	1980	1985	1990	1992	1994	1995	1996
School districts, total	Number	16,044	15,812	15,552	15,217	15,056	14,947	14,906
ENROLLMENT								
Population 5-17 years old [1]	1,000	48,041	44,787	44,949	46,600	47,322	48,155	48,975
Percent of resident population	Percent	21.4	19.0	18.2	18.3	18.4	18.5	18.6
Fall enrollment [2]	1,000	41,778	39,354	40,527	42,661	43,308	43,932	44,676
Percent of population 5-17 years old	Percent	87.0	87.9	90.2	91.5	91.5	91.2	91.2
Elementary [3]	1,000	24,397	23,830	26,253	27,854	28,182	28,177	28,901
Secondary [4]	1,000	17,381	15,524	14,274	14,807	15,126	15,755	15,775
Average daily:								
Attendance (ADA)	1,000	38,411	36,530	37,573	39,605	40,142	40,808	41,375
High school graduates	1,000	2,762	2,424	2,327	2,250	2,227	2,276	2,289
INSTRUCTIONAL STAFF								
Total [5]	1,000	2,521	2,473	2,685	2,811	2,862	2,906	2,972
Classroom teachers	1,000	2,211	2,175	2,362	2,466	2,511	2,549	2,611
Average salaries:								
Instructional staff	Dollar	16,715	24,666	32,638	36,460	37,441	38,442	39,461
Classroom teachers	Dollar	15,970	23,600	31,367	35,030	35,741	36,605	37,685
REVENUES								
Revenue receipts	Mil. dol.	97,635	141,013	208,656	247,773	259,422	272,837	283,526
Federal	Mil. dol.	9,020	9,533	13,184	17,392	18,466	18,774	20,054
State	Mil. dol.	47,929	69,107	100,787	115,904	119,389	129,880	135,845
Local	Mil. dol.	40,686	62,373	94,685	114,478	121,567	124,183	127,628
Percent of total:								
Federal	Percent	9.2	6.8	6.3	7.0	7.1	6.9	7.1
State	Percent	49.1	49.0	48.3	46.8	46.0	47.6	47.9
Local	Percent	41.7	44.2	45.4	46.2	46.9	45.5	45.0
EXPENDITURES								
Total	Mil. dol.	96,105	139,382	209,698	248,786	262,723	276,594	289,091
Current expenditures (day schools)	Mil. dol.	85,661	127,230	186,583	219,233	230,979	242,768	252,494
Other current expenditures [6]	Mil. dol.	1,859	2,109	3,341	5,057	5,331	5,457	5,979
Capital outlay	Mil. dol.	6,504	7,529	16,012	18,788	20,452	21,970	23,667
Interest on school debt	Mil. dol.	2,081	2,514	3,762	5,708	5,961	6,398	6,951
Percent of total:								
Current expenditures (day schools)	Percent	89.1	91.3	89.0	88.1	87.9	87.8	87.3
Other current expenditures [6]	Percent	1.9	1.5	1.6	2.0	2.0	2.0	2.1
Capital outlay	Percent	6.8	5.4	7.6	7.6	7.8	7.9	8.2
Interest on school debt	Percent	2.2	1.8	1.8	2.3	2.3	2.3	2.4
In current dollars:								
Revenue receipts per pupil enrolled	Dollar	2,337	3,583	5,149	5,808	5,990	6,210	6,346
Current expenditures per pupil enrolled	Dollar	2,050	3,233	4,604	5,139	5,333	5,526	5,652
In constant (1996) dollars: [7]								
Revenue receipts per pupil enrolled	Dollar	4,653	5,233	6,263	6,297	6,330	6,380	6,346
Current expenditures per pupil enrolled	Dollar	4,082	4,721	5,601	5,572	5,636	5,677	5,652

[1] Estimated resident population as of July 1 of the previous year. Estimates reflect revisions based on the 1990 Census of Population. [2] Fall enrollment of the previous year. [3] Kindergarten through grade 6. [4] Grades 7 through 12. [5] Full-time equivalent. [6] Current expenses for summer schools, adult education, post-high school vocational education, personnel retraining, etc., when operated by local school districts and not part of regular public elementary and secondary day-school program. [7] Compiled by U.S. Bureau of the Census. Deflated by the Consumer Price Index, all urban consumers (for school year) supplied by U.S. National Center for Education Statistics.

Source: Except as noted, National Education Association, Washington, DC, Estimates of School Statistics Database (copyright).

No. 251. Elementary and Secondary Schools—Teachers and Pupil-Teacher Ratios With Projections: 1960 to 1996

[In thousands, except ratios. As of fall. Data are for full-time equivalents. Schools are classified by type of organization, rather than by grade group; elementary includes kindergarten and secondary includes junior high]

ITEM	TOTAL			PUBLIC			PRIVATE		
	Total	Elementary	Secondary	Total	Elementary	Secondary	Total	Elementary	Secondary
Number of teachers:									
1960	1,600	991	609	1,408	858	550	192	133	59
1970	2,292	1,283	1,009	2,059	1,130	929	233	153	80
1975	2,453	1,353	1,100	2,198	1,181	1,017	255	172	83
1980	2,485	1,401	1,084	2,184	1,189	995	301	212	89
1985	2,549	1,483	1,066	2,206	1,237	969	343	246	97
1986	2,592	1,521	1,071	2,244	1,271	973	348	250	98
1987	2,632	1,564	1,068	2,279	1,307	973	353	257	95
1988	2,668	1,604	1,064	2,323	1,353	970	345	251	94
1989	2,679	1,622	1,057	2,357	1,387	970	322	235	87
1990	2,753	1,680	1,073	2,398	1,426	972	355	254	101
1991	2,787	1,713	1,074	2,432	1,459	973	355	254	101
1992	2,822	1,746	1,075	2,459	1,486	972	363	260	103
1993	2,870	1,777	1,093	2,504	1,515	989	366	262	104
1994	2,931	1,777	1,153	2,552	1,510	1,041	379	267	112
1995, prel.	2,972	1,800	1,172	2,586	1,529	1,058	386	272	114
1996, proj.	3,071	1,851	1,220	2,679	1,576	1,103	392	276	117
Pupil-teacher ratio:									
1960	26.4	29.4	21.4	25.8	28.4	21.7	30.7	36.1	18.6
1970	22.4	24.6	19.5	22.3	24.3	19.8	23.0	26.5	16.4
1975	20.3	21.7	18.6	20.4	21.7	18.8	19.6	21.5	15.7
1980	18.6	20.1	16.6	18.7	20.4	16.8	17.7	18.8	15.0
1985	17.8	19.1	15.6	17.9	19.5	15.8	16.2	17.1	14.0
1986	17.4	18.8	15.5	17.7	19.3	15.7	15.7	16.5	13.6
1987	17.3	18.8	15.0	17.6	19.3	15.2	15.5	16.4	13.1
1988	17.0	18.6	14.7	17.3	19.0	14.9	15.2	16.1	12.8
1989	17.1	18.8	14.5	17.2	19.0	14.6	16.6	17.7	13.7
1990	16.9	18.5	14.3	17.2	19.0	14.6	14.7	16.1	11.3
1991	17.0	18.6	14.3	17.3	19.0	14.7	14.6	16.0	11.1
1992	17.1	18.5	14.8	17.4	18.9	15.1	14.8	16.2	11.3
1993	17.1	18.4	14.8	17.4	18.8	15.2	14.9	16.3	11.5
1994	17.0	18.7	14.5	17.3	19.0	14.9	15.2	16.8	11.2
1995, prel.	17.1	18.7	14.6	17.4	19.1	14.9	15.1	16.7	11.3
1996, proj.	17.1	18.7	14.6	17.4	19.1	14.9	15.1	16.7	11.3

Source: U.S. National Center for Education Statistics, *Digest of Education Statistics*, annual.

No. 252. Public Elementary and Secondary Schools, by Type and Size of School: 1994-95

[Data reported by schools, rather than school districts]

ENROLLMENT SIZE OF SCHOOL	NUMBER OF SCHOOLS					ENROLLMENT (1,000) [1]				
	Total	Elementary [1]	Secondary [2]	Combined [3]	Other [4]	Total	Elementary [1]	Secondary [2]	Combined [3]	Other [4]
Total	86,221	60,808	20,282	2,764	2,367	44,031	28,620	14,139	1,140	133
PERCENT DISTRIBUTION										
Total	100.0	100.0	100.0	100.0	100.0	100.0	100.0	100.0	100.0	100.0
Under 100 students	9.0	5.9	13.1	29.4	59.3	0.8	0.6	0.9	3.2	16.0
100 to 199 students	9.7	9.1	10.6	14.2	15.5	2.8	2.9	2.2	5.1	14.2
200 to 299 students	11.4	12.4	8.7	10.4	10.2	5.5	6.6	3.1	6.3	15.9
300 to 399 students	13.6	16.0	7.6	8.1	6.1	9.2	11.9	3.8	6.8	13.5
400 to 499 students	13.4	15.9	7.3	7.0	2.9	11.6	15.2	4.7	7.6	8.4
500 to 599 students	11.8	13.8	6.9	6.7	1.7	12.4	16.0	5.5	8.9	5.6
600 to 699 students	8.7	9.8	6.4	5.6	1.3	10.8	13.4	5.9	8.7	5.3
700 to 799 students	6.1	6.4	5.5	3.9	0.6	8.7	10.1	6.0	7.1	2.7
800 to 999 students	7.3	6.6	9.2	5.6	0.9	12.4	12.7	11.6	12.2	5.4
1,000 to 1,499 students	6.1	3.7	13.8	5.6	1.1	14.1	9.0	24.1	16.9	7.7
1,500 to 1,999 students	1.9	0.3	6.7	2.1	0.2	6.3	1.2	16.4	8.8	2.7
2,000 to 2,999 students	1.0	0.1	3.8	0.8	-	4.4	0.3	12.8	4.5	(Z)
3,000 or more students	0.2	(Z)	0.6	0.4	0.1	1.1	(Z)	3.0	4.0	(Z)
Average enrollment	(X)	(X)	(X)	(X)	(X)	520	471	697	412	156

- Represents zero. X Not applicable. Z Less than .05 percent. [1] Data for those schools reporting enrollment. [2] Includes schools beginning with grade 6 or below and with no grade higher than 8. [3] Includes schools with no grade lower than 7. [4] Includes schools with both elementary and secondary grades. [5] Includes special education, alternative, and other schools not classified by grade span.

Source: U.S. National Center for Education Statistics, *Digest of Education Statistics*, annual.

No. 253. Public Elementary and Secondary School Enrollment, by State: 1980 to 1995

[In thousands, except rate. As of fall. Includes unclassified students]

STATE	ENROLLMENT								ENROLLMENT RATE [2]				
	K through grade 8 [1]				Grades 9 through 12								
	1980	1985	1990	1994, prel.	1980	1985	1990	1994, prel.	1980	1985	1990	1994, prel.	1995, est.
U.S.	27,647	27,034	29,878	31,898	13,231	12,388	11,338	12,214	86.2	87.7	91.3	91.3	90.9
AL	528	517	527	536	231	213	195	201	87.6	89.6	93.3	94.7	94.4
AK	60	77	85	94	26	30	29	33	94.0	99.4	97.4	93.6	91.9
AZ	357	366	479	543	157	162	161	195	88.9	90.8	93.3	92.8	91.5
AR	310	304	314	319	138	130	123	128	90.3	91.8	95.9	95.6	96.3
CA	2,730	2,927	3,615	3,955	1,347	1,329	1,336	1,452	87.1	89.5	92.8	92.5	91.0
CO	374	379	420	470	172	172	154	171	92.2	92.7	94.6	91.5	92.1
CT	364	321	347	376	168	141	122	131	83.3	83.4	90.2	91.0	90.3
DE	62	63	73	77	37	30	27	30	79.5	80.1	87.4	86.3	85.3
DC	71	62	61	62	29	25	19	18	91.6	96.6	100.9	106.1	106.6
FL	1,042	1,086	1,370	1,567	466	476	492	542	84.4	86.7	92.6	91.7	90.4
GA	742	757	849	936	327	323	303	336	86.8	86.2	93.6	94.6	95.5
HI	110	113	123	134	55	51	49	50	83.4	84.2	87.6	87.9	87.4
ID	144	149	160	169	59	59	61	72	95.4	93.6	96.9	95.5	94.0
IL	1,335	1,246	1,310	1,368	649	580	512	548	82.6	83.3	86.9	88.4	87.4
IN	708	654	676	679	347	312	279	290	88.0	88.4	90.4	90.9	90.8
IA	351	324	345	345	183	161	139	155	88.4	89.1	92.1	92.3	92.9
KS	283	286	320	329	133	125	117	132	88.7	91.0	92.6	91.0	91.0
KY	464	449	459	467	206	195	177	191	83.7	85.8	90.5	92.8	89.7
LA	544	573	586	584	234	215	199	214	80.2	83.9	88.2	88.9	86.5
ME	153	142	155	156	70	64	60	57	91.6	93.3	96.5	93.2	95.2
MD	493	446	527	581	258	225	188	210	83.9	84.9	89.1	89.5	89.1
MA	676	559	604	659	346	285	230	235	88.6	86.3	88.8	89.3	89.3
MI	1,227	1,086	1,145	1,170	570	517	440	445	86.9	87.8	90.3	88.5	89.5
MN	482	468	546	581	272	237	211	240	87.2	89.4	91.2	89.9	90.3
MS	330	330	372	367	147	141	131	139	79.6	81.0	91.3	92.2	91.0
MO	567	544	588	628	277	251	228	250	83.8	84.9	86.5	87.6	86.3
MT	106	108	111	117	50	46	42	48	92.9	93.8	93.8	92.0	92.4
NE	189	184	198	203	91	82	76	84	86.6	87.7	88.7	88.1	88.0
NV	101	107	150	185	49	48	51	65	93.4	93.3	98.7	96.0	94.9
NH	112	107	126	139	55	54	46	50	85.3	87.5	89.1	89.5	87.1
NJ	820	740	784	862	426	376	306	312	81.5	82.9	86.1	86.9	86.4
NM	186	187	208	229	85	90	94	96	89.5	91.6	94.3	91.5	90.8
NY	1,838	1,703	1,828	1,949	1,033	918	770	817	80.8	82.3	86.6	88.4	89.1
NC	786	749	783	847	343	337	304	309	90.1	91.2	94.8	92.8	90.7
ND	77	84	85	83	40	35	33	36	85.9	89.2	92.8	92.6	92.6
OH	1,312	1,206	1,258	1,295	645	586	514	519	84.8	85.6	88.0	87.6	88.1
OK	399	414	425	443	179	178	154	167	92.9	94.3	95.1	94.9	95.2
OR	319	305	340	372	145	142	132	150	88.5	89.7	90.7	91.0	89.9
PA	1,231	1,093	1,172	1,244	678	591	496	522	80.4	80.3	83.6	84.1	84.8
RI	98	90	102	108	51	44	37	40	80.1	81.2	87.3	87.4	87.6
SC	426	424	452	469	193	183	170	180	88.1	89.6	94.0	95.6	93.5
SD	86	88	95	102	42	37	34	42	87.4	90.7	89.7	93.0	93.5
TN	602	575	598	641	252	239	226	241	87.8	88.3	93.5	94.7	93.2
TX	2,049	2,261	2,511	2,721	851	871	872	957	92.4	93.2	96.4	96.3	97.9
UT	250	299	325	328	93	105	122	146	98.2	96.3	97.7	96.8	96.5
VT	66	63	71	76	29	27	25	29	87.9	89.3	93.9	97.2	96.6
VA	703	665	728	774	307	303	270	286	90.7	94.0	94.2	93.6	94.0
WA	515	507	613	673	242	243	227	265	91.7	92.2	94.0	92.6	92.2
WV	270	249	224	213	113	109	98	98	92.6	92.2	95.7	96.7	97.2
WI	528	501	566	601	303	267	232	259	82.1	83.8	86.0	86.4	86.1
WY	70	74	71	70	28	29	27	30	97.3	97.0	97.3	96.2	96.0

[1] Data include a small number of pre-kindergarten students. [2] Percent of persons 5-17 years old. Based on enumerated resident population as of April 1, 1980, and 1990, and estimated resident population as of July 1 for other years. Data not adjusted for revisions based on the 1990 Census of Population.

Source: U.S. National Center for Education Statistics, *Digest of Education Statistics*, annual.

No. 254. Public Elementary and Secondary School Enrollment, by Grade: 1980 to 1994

[In thousands. As of fall of year. Kindergarten includes nursery schools]

GRADE	1980	1985	1986	1987	1988	1989	1990	1991	1992	1993	1994, prel.
Pupils enrolled	40,877	39,422	39,753	40,008	40,189	40,543	41,217	42,047	42,823	43,465	44,109
Kindergarten and grades 1 to 8	27,647	27,034	27,420	27,933	28,501	29,152	29,878	30,506	31,088	31,504	31,894
Kindergarten	2,689	3,192	3,310	3,388	3,433	3,486	3,610	3,686	3,817	3,922	4,043
First	2,894	3,239	3,358	3,407	3,460	3,485	3,499	3,556	3,542	3,529	3,593
Second	2,800	2,941	3,054	3,173	3,223	3,289	3,327	3,360	3,431	3,429	3,440
Third	2,893	2,895	2,933	3,046	3,167	3,235	3,297	3,334	3,361	3,437	3,439
Fourth	3,107	2,771	2,896	2,938	3,051	3,182	3,248	3,315	3,342	3,361	3,426
Fifth	3,130	2,776	2,775	2,901	2,945	3,067	3,197	3,268	3,325	3,350	3,372
Sixth	3,038	2,789	2,806	2,811	2,937	2,987	3,110	3,239	3,303	3,356	3,381
Seventh	3,085	2,938	2,899	2,910	2,905	3,027	3,067	3,181	3,299	3,355	3,404
Eighth	3,086	2,982	2,870	2,839	2,853	2,853	2,979	3,020	3,129	3,249	3,302
Unclassified [1]	924	511	520	520	527	540	543	545	539	515	494
Grades 9 to 12	13,231	12,388	12,333	12,076	11,687	11,390	11,338	11,541	11,735	11,961	12,214
Ninth	3,377	3,439	3,256	3,143	3,106	3,141	3,169	3,313	3,352	3,487	3,604
Tenth	3,368	3,230	3,215	3,020	2,895	2,868	2,896	2,915	3,027	3,050	3,131
Eleventh	3,195	2,866	2,954	2,936	2,749	2,629	2,612	2,645	2,656	2,751	2,749
Twelfth	2,925	2,550	2,601	2,681	2,650	2,473	2,381	2,392	2,431	2,424	2,488
Unclassified [1]	366	303	308	296	288	279	282	275	269	248	242

[1] Includes ungraded and special education.

Source: U.S. National Center for Education Statistics, *Digest of Education Statistics*, annual.

No. 255. Public Elementary and Secondary School Teachers—Selected Characteristics: 1993-94

[For school year. Based on survey and subject to sampling error; for details, see source. Excludes prekindergarten teachers. See table 270 for similar data on private school teachers]

CHARACTERISTIC	Unit	AGE				SEX		RACE/ETHNICITY		
		Under 30 years old	30 to 39 years old	40 to 49 years old	Over 50 years old	Male	Female	White [1]	Black [1]	Hispanic
Total teachers [2]	1,000	479	782	981	339	894	1,867	2,217	188	109
Highest degree held:										
Bachelor's	Percent	76.3	52.8	43.1	41.4	46.2	54.1	51.8	48.4	62.8
Master's	Percent	21.5	42.0	49.6	48.8	45.7	40.6	42.5	44.6	29.8
Education specialist	Percent	1.5	4.0	5.8	6.7	5.1	4.4	4.4	5.4	4.6
Doctorate	Percent	0.1	0.5	0.8	1.9	1.3	0.5	0.7	0.9	1.4
Full-time teaching experience:										
Less than 3 years	Percent	33.9	7.0	3.0	1.0	8.9	10.0	9.4	8.5	16.7
3 to 9 years	Percent	61.8	28.5	12.2	5.8	21.6	26.9	25.5	20.9	32.1
10 to 20 years	Percent	4.3	62.3	33.5	21.8	29.9	37.0	35.2	35.6	34.1
20 years or more	Percent	(X)	2.2	51.3	71.5	39.6	26.1	30.0	35.3	17.1
Full-time teachers	1,000	440	685	902	314	643	1,697	2,012	182	103
Earned income	Dol.	27,974	33,448	39,586	41,951	39,591	34,536	36,000	35,548	34,837
Salary	Dol.	25,966	31,737	37,803	40,414	36,162	33,384	34,221	33,869	32,996
Supplemental contract during school year:										
Teachers receiving	1,000	193	242	301	79	349	467	723	49	32
Salary	Dol.	1,930	2,146	2,115	2,064	2,922	1,442	2,067	2,325	1,930
Supplemental contract during summer:										
Teachers receiving	1,000	92	121	151	38	147	254	328	41	24
Salary	Dol.	1,860	1,891	2,273	2,290	2,530	1,803	2,015	2,221	2,477
Teachers with nonschool employment:										
Teaching/tutoring	1,000	20	33	49	16	37	81	100	11	8
Education related	1,000	15	25	31	9	39	41	69	5	4
Not education related	1,000	46	67	97	28	124	113	208	16	7

X Not applicable. [1] Non-Hispanic. [2] Includes teachers with no degrees and associates degrees, not shown separately.

Source: U.S. National Center for Education Statistics, *Digest of Education Statistics*, 1995.

No. 256. Newly Hired Teachers, by Selected Characteristics: 1988 to 1994

[In percent. Based on sample and subject to sampling error; see source for details]

CHARACTERISTIC	PUBLIC SCHOOLS			PRIVATE SCHOOLS		
	1988	1991	1994	1988	1991	1994
Total newly hired teachers	100.0	100.0	100.0	100.0	100.0	100.0
First-time teachers	30.6	41.7	45.8	25.2	34.0	42.4
Transfers	36.6	34.3	31.4	38.1	36.1	34.3
Within State and sector	20.8	21.6	20.2	19.0	18.1	14.6
Across State	8.3	7.1	7.1	8.3	7.0	11.5
Across sector	7.5	5.6	4.1	10.9	11.0	8.1
Reentrants	32.8	24.0	22.9	36.7	30.0	23.3
Main previous year activity:						
First-time teachers	100.0	100.0	100.0	100.0	100.0	100.0
Work in education (non-teaching)	5.7	5.2	10.7	4.8	7.5	13.6
Work outside education	11.0	10.0	11.6	24.5	20.6	19.9
College	66.5	58.4	56.7	51.8	48.7	43.1
Homemaking and childrearing	3.6	4.4	2.1	7.7	5.8	5.8
Other	13.3	22.0	18.9	11.3	17.4	17.6
Substitute teaching	(NA)	18.0	17.2	(NA)	12.0	15.2
Reentrants	100.0	100.0	100.0	100.0	100.0	100.0
Work in education (non-teaching)	10.3	19.1	15.0	8.9	11.7	19.9
Work outside education	17.4	17.9	19.2	21.2	26.1	26.0
College	18.0	10.4	18.1	20.0	5.6	11.9
Homemaking and childrearing	27.8	19.3	14.6	28.6	23.1	21.4
Other	26.5	33.3	33.1	21.3	33.6	20.9
Substitute teaching	(NA)	23.8	29.6	(NA)	18.7	18.1

NA Not available.

Source: U.S. Department of Education, National Center for Education Statistics, *Condition of Education, 1996.*

No. 257. Public Elementary and Secondary Schools—Number and Average Salary of Classroom Teachers, 1970 to 1996, and by State, 1996

[Estimates for school year ending in June of year shown. Schools classified by type of organization rather than by grade-group; elementary includes kindergarten]

YEAR AND STATE	TEACHERS [1] (1,000)			AVG. SALARY ($1,000)			YEAR AND STATE	TEACHERS [1] (1,000)			AVG. SALARY ($1,000)		
	Total	Elementary	Secondary	All teachers	Elementary	Secondary		Total	Elementary	Secondary	All teachers	Elementary	Secondary
1970	2,006	1,109	899	8.6	8.4	8.9	LA	48.9	34.3	14.6	26.8	26.8	26.8
1975	2,171	1,169	1,001	11.7	11.3	12.0	ME	15.3	9.4	6.0	32.9	32.4	33.9
1980	2,211	1,206	1,005	16.0	15.6	16.5	MD	46.2	26.0	20.2	41.2	40.2	42.3
1985	2,175	1,212	963	23.6	23.2	24.2	MA	62.7	27.0	35.7	42.9	42.9	42.9
1986	2,215	1,242	973	25.2	24.7	25.8	MI	72.7	51.9	20.8	44.8	44.8	44.8
1987	2,249	1,274	975	26.6	26.1	27.2	MN	48.4	24.3	24.1	36.9	36.8	37.1
1988	2,282	1,308	974	28.0	27.5	28.8	MS	29.2	16.0	13.2	27.7	27.3	28.2
1989	2,324	1,354	970	29.6	29.0	30.2	MO	57.7	29.8	27.8	33.3	31.8	33.4
1990	2,362	1,390	972	31.4	30.8	32.0	MT	10.1	7.0	3.1	29.4	29.0	30.1
1991	2,409	1,435	974	33.1	32.5	33.9	NE	19.9	11.4	8.5	31.5	31.5	31.5
1992	2,429	1,466	963	34.1	33.5	34.8	NV	13.7	7.9	5.8	36.2	35.8	36.7
1993	2,466	1,496	970	35.0	34.3	35.9	NH	12.4	8.5	3.9	35.8	35.8	35.8
1994	2,511	1,517	994	35.7	35.2	36.6	NJ	86.9	56.0	30.9	47.9	46.9	49.8
1995	2,549	1,523	1,025.9	36.6	36.1	37.4	NM	18.8	13.5	5.3	29.6	29.3	29.3
1996, U.S.	2,611	1,535	1,077	37.7	37.1	38.5	NY	196.6	100.9	95.7	48.1	47.0	49.3
AL	44.3	26.6	17.6	31.3	31.3	31.3	NC	72.2	44.8	27.3	30.4	30.3	30.7
AK	7.7	4.9	2.8	49.6	49.6	49.6	ND	7.8	5.0	2.8	27.0	27.1	26.8
AZ	39.6	30.5	9.1	32.5	32.5	32.2	OH	105.3	70.0	35.3	37.8	37.4	38.7
AR	26.9	13.2	13.7	29.3	28.5	30.1	OK	39.4	20.7	18.7	28.4	27.8	29.1
CA	226.8	132.2	94.6	43.1	42.6	44.8	OR	27.2	17.8	9.5	39.6	39.1	40.3
CO	35.4	18.0	17.4	35.4	35.1	35.7	PA	104.9	54.2	50.7	46.1	45.4	46.8
CT	36.3	26.0	10.3	50.3	49.8	51.8	RI	10.2	5.7	4.5	42.2	42.1	42.2
DE	6.5	3.2	3.3	40.5	40.2	40.8	SC	39.0	26.8	12.3	31.6	31.3	32.3
DC	5.6	3.4	2.2	43.7	44.2	45.0	SD	8.9	6.4	2.5	26.3	26.2	26.5
FL	131.4	74.1	57.4	33.3	33.3	33.3	TN	50.7	36.1	14.6	33.1	32.8	34.1
GA	80.6	44.2	36.4	34.1	33.3	34.6	TX	240.4	126.6	113.7	32.0	31.3	32.8
HI	10.8	6.0	4.8	35.8	35.8	35.8	UT	19.9	10.7	9.2	30.6	30.7	30.5
ID	12.8	6.6	6.2	30.9	30.8	31.0	VT	7.5	3.8	3.7	36.3	37.0	35.6
IL	115.4	80.8	34.6	40.9	39.1	45.1	VA	74.2	45.3	28.9	35.0	33.6	36.2
IN	55.8	29.9	25.9	37.7	37.7	37.6	WA	46.6	27.3	19.4	38.0	37.9	38.2
IA	32.4	15.1	17.3	32.4	31.4	33.2	WV	20.9	12.4	8.6	32.2	31.9	32.6
KS	30.7	16.4	14.3	35.1	35.1	35.1	WI	53.6	36.6	17.0	38.2	37.7	39.1
KY	37.4	26.4	11.0	33.1	32.6	34.3	WY	6.7	3.4	3.4	31.6	31.6	31.5

[1] Full-time equivalent.

Source: National Education Association, Washington, DC, Estimates of School Statistics Database (copyright).

No. 258. Average Salary and Wages Paid in Public School Systems: 1980 to 1997

[In dollars. For school year ending in year shown. Data reported by a stratified sample of school systems enrolling 300 or more pupils. Data represent unweighted means of average salaries paid school personnel reported by each school system]

POSITION	1980	1985	1990	1992	1993	1994	1995	1996	1997
ANNUAL SALARY									
Central office administrators:									
Superintendent (contract salary)	39,344	56,954	75,425	83,342	85,120	87,717	90,198	94,229	98,106
Deputy/assoc. superintendent	37,440	52,877	69,623	76,796	77,057	78,672	81,266	84,077	86,564
Assistant superintendent	33,452	48,003	62,698	69,315	70,525	72,701	75,236	77,007	80,176
Administrators for—									
Finance and business	27,147	40,344	52,354	57,036	57,854	59,997	61,323	63,840	65,797
Instructional services	29,790	43,452	56,359	62,102	62,508	64,676	66,767	68,463	70,788
Public relations/information	24,021	35,287	44,926	50,625	50,622	52,368	53,263	53,860	55,928
Staff personnel services	29,623	44,182	56,344	62,269	62,162	63,690	65,819	67,760	70,088
Subject area supervisors	23,974	34,422	45,929	50,580	51,407	52,837	54,534	56,145	58,776
School building administrators:									
Principals:									
Elementary	25,165	36,452	48,431	53,856	54,905	56,906	58,589	60,922	62,903
Junior high/middle	27,625	39,650	52,163	57,504	58,620	60,651	62,311	64,452	66,859
Senior high	29,207	42,094	55,722	61,768	63,054	64,993	66,596	69,277	72,410
Assistant principals:									
Elementary	20,708	30,496	40,916	45,558	45,377	47,067	48,491	50,537	52,284
Junior high/middle	23,507	33,793	44,570	48,956	49,925	51,518	52,942	54,365	56,451
Senior high	24,816	35,491	46,486	51,318	52,348	54,170	55,556	57,555	59,739
Classroom teachers	15,913	23,587	31,278	34,565	35,291	36,531	37,264	38,708	39,580
Auxiliary professional personnel:									
Counselors	18,847	27,593	35,979	39,563	40,413	41,355	42,486	44,073	45,365
Librarians	16,764	24,981	33,469	37,227	37,945	39,319	40,418	41,761	43,315
School nurses	13,788	19,944	26,090	28,721	29,555	30,830	31,086	32,786	33,720
Secretarial/clerical personnel:									
Central office:									
Secretaries	10,331	15,343	20,238	22,309	22,770	23,495	23,935	24,809	25,709
Accounting/payroll clerks	10,479	15,421	20,086	22,215	22,605	23,275	24,042	25,009	25,861
Typists/data entry clerks	8,359	12,481	16,125	17,646	17,772	18,296	18,674	19,447	20,726
School building level:									
Secretaries	8,346	12,504	16,184	17,784	18,104	18,692	19,170	20,076	20,709
Library clerks	6,778	9,911	12,151	13,347	13,311	13,809	14,381	14,791	15,349
HOURLY WAGE RATE									
Other support personnel:									
Teacher aides:									
Instructional	4.06	5.89	7.43	8.15	8.31	8.50	8.77	9.04	9.25
Noninstructional	3.89	5.60	7.08	7.70	7.82	8.14	8.29	8.52	8.88
Custodians	4.88	6.90	8.54	9.35	9.51	9.76	10.05	10.35	10.66
Cafeteria workers	3.78	5.42	6.77	7.39	7.56	7.72	7.89	8.15	8.30
Bus drivers	5.21	7.27	9.21	10.04	10.15	10.35	10.69	11.04	11.50

Source: Educational Research Service, Arlington, VA, *National Survey of Salaries and Wages in Public Schools*, annual, vols. 2 and 3.

No. 259. Public School Employment: 1982 and 1994

[In thousands. Covers full-time employment. Excludes Hawaii. 1982 also excludes District of Columbia and New Jersey. 1982 based on sample survey of school districts with 250 or more students. 1994 based on sample survey of school districts with 100 or more employees; see source for sampling variability]

OCCUPATION	1982					1994				
	Total	Male	Female	White [1]	Black [1]	Total	Male	Female	White [1]	Black [1]
All occupations	**3,082**	**1,063**	**2,019**	**2,496**	**432**	**3,518**	**967**	**2,551**	**2,740**	**606**
Officials, administrators	41	31	10	36	3	45	27	18	38	5
Principals and assistant principals	90	72	19	76	11	97	55	42	75	15
Classroom teachers [2]	1,680	534	1,146	1,435	186	1,948	500	1,448	1,637	205
Elementary schools	798	129	669	667	98	947	119	828	783	105
Secondary schools	706	363	343	619	67	753	327	425	645	73
Other professional staff	235	91	144	193	35	258	61	197	213	31
Teachers aides [3]	215	14	200	146	45	371	62	309	235	80
Clerical, secretarial staff	210	4	206	177	19	240	6	234	186	28
Service workers [4]	611	316	295	434	132	558	256	302	364	141

[1] Excludes individuals of Hispanic origin. [2] Includes other classroom teachers, not shown separately. [3] Includes technicians. [4] Includes craftworkers and laborers.

Source: U.S. Equal Employment Opportunity Commission, *Elementary-Secondary Staff Information (EEO-5)*, biennial.

No. 260. Public Elementary and Secondary School Price Indexes: 1975 to 1995

[1983=100. For years ending June 30. Reflects prices paid by public elementary-secondary schools. For explanation of average annual percent change, see Guide to Tabular Presentation]

YEAR	Index, total	PERSONNEL COMPENSATION				CONTRACTED SERVICES, SUPPLIES AND EQUIPMENT						
		Total	Professional salaries	Nonprofessional salaries	Fringe benefits	Total	Services	Supplies and materials	Equipment replacement	Library materials and textbooks	Utilities	Fixed costs
1975 . .	52.7	53.4	56.0	55.6	40.9	50.4	56.7	58.0	53.7	53.8	34.5	45.2
1980 . .	76.6	75.9	76.7	77.8	71.0	79.2	77.4	85.9	79.6	82.1	71.1	77.9
1982 . .	93.7	92.6	92.8	94.4	90.3	97.8	94.6	101.1	95.5	91.6	102.3	94.1
1983 . .	100.0	100.0	100.0	100.0	100.0	100.0	100.0	100.0	100.0	100.0	100.0	100.0
1984 . .	105.0	106.0	105.7	104.5	106.3	101.7	105.6	99.8	103.4	107.8	94.5	105.4
1985 . .	112.0	113.7	113.4	111.3	117.1	105.5	112.4	103.2	107.2	111.0	93.1	110.8
1986 . .	118.5	121.1	121.4	117.8	123.3	106.3	117.4	103.0	109.3	120.8	93.9	116.2
1987 . .	123.3	127.4	128.4	121.9	128.8	107.5	123.7	101.5	112.9	128.5	75.6	122.7
1988 . .	129.8	134.5	135.5	127.5	137.0	111.8	128.1	105.9	113.4	140.0	78.5	128.4
1989 . .	136.3	141.6	142.2	133.3	147.0	116.2	131.8	112.0	116.0	149.4	75.4	134.6
1990 . .	144.3	150.0	150.1	139.4	159.3	122.6	137.7	119.2	121.2	171.7	77.6	140.3
1991 . .	152.3	158.3	158.1	146.5	169.8	129.7	142.5	122.7	125.7	189.4	93.1	144.9
1992 . .	158.5	165.4	165.8	152.4	175.8	132.0	148.0	122.5	128.5	199.0	91.3	148.9
1993 . .	162.2	169.6	169.2	156.1	184.4	133.9	151.5	121.9	131.8	205.6	90.8	153.8
1994 . .	167.1	175.1	175.1	159.3	189.9	136.5	154.0	122.7	136.4	218.4	90.9	158.7
1995 . .	170.6	179.2	178.8	163.7	194.8	138.1	157.2	124.4	138.7	230.7	83.1	163.9

Source: Research Associates of Washington, Washington, DC, *Inflation Measures for Schools, Colleges, and Libraries*, annual (copyright).

No. 261. Finances of Public Elementary and Secondary School Systems, by Enrollment-Size Group: 1993-94

[In millions of dollars, except as indicated. Data are estimates subject to sampling variability. For details, see source. See also Appendix III]

ITEM	All school systems	SCHOOL SYSTEMS WITH ENROLLMENT OF—						
		50,000 or more	25,000 to 49,999	15,000 to 24,999	7,500 to 14,999	5,000 to 7,499	3,000 to 4,999	Under 3,000
Fall enrollment (1,000)	40,880	8,182	4,720	3,872	6,723	3,720	4,707	8,957
General revenue	249,576	50,788	27,152	21,377	39,172	22,527	28,831	59,730
From Federal sources	16,686	4,531	1,961	1,341	2,297	1,245	1,499	3,814
Through State	15,336	4,302	1,797	1,232	2,124	1,157	1,374	3,350
Compensatory programs	6,029	1,817	677	456	799	448	549	1,282
Handicapped programs	1,799	306	203	156	274	158	177	525
Child nutrition programs	4,600	1,302	604	396	676	355	428	837
Direct	1,352	229	164	109	173	88	126	464
From State sources [1]	115,020	23,323	13,811	10,967	18,494	9,734	12,000	26,689
General formula assistance	78,105	14,871	8,851	7,682	12,744	6,667	8,440	18,852
Handicapped programs	7,625	1,464	1,093	796	1,152	628	679	1,793
From local sources	117,869	22,934	11,380	9,070	18,381	11,548	15,331	29,227
Taxes	78,761	11,372	7,498	6,040	12,959	8,309	11,448	21,135
Contributions from parent government	20,878	8,355	1,670	1,334	2,445	1,681	2,042	3,352
From other local governments	4,829	996	696	521	758	312	365	1,182
Current charges	6,701	1,004	746	587	1,073	630	833	1,829
School lunch	3,806	525	404	346	666	388	510	966
Other	6,701	1,208	771	589	1,144	616	644	1,729
General expenditure	248,537	50,751	26,948	21,276	39,413	22,520	28,856	58,773
Current spending	222,660	45,641	24,010	18,845	34,773	20,320	25,866	53,203
By function:								
Instruction	133,930	27,440	14,100	11,268	21,083	12,339	15,779	31,921
Support services	75,322	15,131	8,427	6,420	11,635	6,823	8,645	18,241
Other current spending	13,409	3,070	1,483	1,158	2,055	1,158	1,442	3,042
By object:								
Total salaries and wages	144,052	29,511	15,837	12,510	22,772	13,283	16,759	33,380
Total employee benefits	34,420	7,954	3,616	2,775	5,430	2,979	3,822	7,844
Other	44,188	8,177	4,557	3,560	6,571	4,058	5,285	11,980
Capital outlay	20,612	4,197	2,436	1,911	3,766	1,730	2,277	4,294
Interest on debt	4,517	867	471	463	744	385	584	1,006
Payments to other governments	747	46	31	57	130	85	128	271
Debt outstanding	84,751	15,543	8,667	8,495	13,852	7,567	11,211	19,415
Long-term	81,879	15,526	8,340	8,325	13,321	7,292	10,723	18,353
Short-term	2,871	17	328	170	531	275	488	1,063
Long-term debt issued	18,464	3,813	2,046	1,837	3,005	1,632	2,097	4,035
Long-term debt retired	9,565	1,544	1,070	757	1,594	886	1,275	2,459

[1] Includes other sources, not shown separately.

Source: U.S. Bureau of the Census, *Public Education Finances: 1993-94*, GF/94-10.

No. 262. Public Elementary and Secondary Estimated Finances, 1980 to 1996, and by State, 1996

[In millions of dollars, except as noted. For school years ending in June of year shown]

YEAR AND STATE	RECEIPTS						EXPENDITURES				
	Total	Revenue receipts				Non-revenue receipts [1]	Total [2]	Per capita [3] (dol.)	Current expenditures		
		Total	Source						Elementary and secondary day schools	Average per pupil in ADA [4]	
			Federal	State	Local					Amount (dol.)	Rank
1980	101,724	97,635	9,020	47,929	40,686	4,089	96,105	428	85,661	2,230	(X)
1985	146,976	141,013	9,533	69,107	62,373	5,963	139,382	591	127,230	3,483	(X)
1990	218,126	208,656	13,184	100,787	94,685	9,469	209,698	850	186,583	4,966	(X)
1991	243,817	223,896	14,178	108,021	101,697	19,921	227,459	915	200,911	5,262	(X)
1992	248,958	235,122	15,707	111,530	107,885	13,836	236,786	939	208,512	5,357	(X)
1993	263,063	247,773	17,392	115,904	114,478	15,289	248,786	976	219,233	5,536	(X)
1994	274,942	259,422	18,468	119,369	121,567	15,520	262,723	1,019	230,979	5,754	(X)
1995	287,563	272,837	18,774	129,880	124,183	14,726	276,594	1,062	242,768	5,949	(X)
1996, total	299,236	283,526	20,054	135,846	127,628	15,710	289,091	1,100	252,494	6,103	(X)
Alabama	3,521	3,395	338	2,407	650	126	3,695	870	3,161	4,479	47
Alaska	1,227	1,097	138	698	262	130	1,205	1,999	1,106	10,156	1
Arizona	4,406	3,905	341	1,640	1,925	501	4,098	952	3,056	4,332	49
Arkansas	2,290	2,174	184	1,423	567	116	2,118	853	1,834	4,353	48
California	31,599	30,734	2,697	17,533	10,504	865	30,966	982	26,769	4,977	41
Colorado	4,270	3,832	211	1,693	1,928	438	4,030	1,075	3,315	5,447	35
Connecticut	4,658	4,656	207	1,820	2,629	3	4,658	1,424	4,272	8,716	4
Delaware	871	823	67	536	219	48	829	1,156	753	7,549	7
District of Columbia	517	476	70	-	406	41	603	1,067	564	7,944	5
Florida	14,193	13,493	971	6,685	5,837	700	14,666	1,034	11,653	5,983	26
Georgia	8,610	7,749	521	4,075	3,153	860	8,412	1,167	7,013	5,852	27
Hawaii	1,274	1,274	107	1,141	26	-	1,269	1,076	1,068	6,335	18
Idaho	1,205	1,117	86	683	348	88	1,158	993	1,030	4,511	46
Illinois	13,513	12,301	1,062	3,682	7,537	1,212	11,469	973	9,820	5,530	33
Indiana	6,602	6,374	333	3,332	2,710	228	6,550	1,130	5,569	6,222	19
Iowa	3,071	2,960	151	1,466	1,343	111	2,987	1,051	2,719	5,742	30
Kansas	3,215	2,950	156	1,695	1,100	265	2,800	1,092	2,516	6,059	25
Kentucky	3,844	3,582	320	2,407	856	262	3,787	982	3,461	6,075	23
Louisiana	4,315	3,874	510	2,106	1,258	441	3,844	886	3,560	4,844	42
Maine	1,413	1,363	95	648	620	50	1,413	1,141	1,310	6,478	15
Maryland	5,806	5,536	320	2,177	3,039	270	5,788	1,149	5,161	6,930	13
Massachusetts	6,861	6,856	362	2,433	4,061	5	6,633	1,092	6,261	7,385	10
Michigan	12,965	12,317	799	7,133	4,386	648	12,331	1,293	10,801	7,090	12
Minnesota	6,652	5,914	264	3,059	2,591	738	6,088	1,319	4,788	6,203	20
Mississippi	2,377	2,203	338	1,224	641	174	2,222	824	1,970	4,185	50
Missouri	5,224	4,954	339	1,849	2,766	271	4,732	890	4,044	5,078	39
Montana	950	934	94	463	377	16	951	1,092	861	5,774	28
Nebraska	1,570	1,560	66	600	894	10	1,703	1,039	1,491	5,513	34
Nevada	1,931	1,492	70	513	909	440	1,676	1,093	1,280	5,256	36
New Hampshire	1,327	1,264	38	88	1,138	63	1,259	1,096	1,144	6,458	16
New Jersey	12,168	12,071	440	4,867	6,764	98	11,612	1,461	11,115	9,967	2
New Mexico	1,956	1,801	193	1,339	269	155	2,080	1,231	1,546	5,655	31
New York	27,614	25,711	1,568	10,114	14,029	1,903	26,187	1,440	23,748	9,535	3
North Carolina	6,315	6,155	530	4,094	1,531	160	6,086	845	5,640	5,147	37
North Dakota	646	628	69	267	292	18	601	936	545	4,785	43
Ohio	11,798	10,748	679	4,483	5,586	1,050	11,595	1,041	9,728	5,749	29
Oklahoma	3,211	2,971	265	1,887	820	240	3,059	934	2,595	4,523	45
Oregon	3,545	3,082	219	1,741	1,122	464	3,581	1,137	3,080	6,390	17
Pennsylvania	14,287	14,255	798	5,958	7,499	31	12,863	1,067	12,153	7,411	9
Rhode Island	1,125	1,125	45	461	619	-	1,096	1,108	1,082	7,733	6
South Carolina	3,818	3,656	317	1,687	1,652	162	3,552	969	3,113	5,140	38
South Dakota	761	729	74	190	464	33	731	1,002	651	5,070	40
Tennessee	4,109	4,026	352	2,026	1,648	82	4,028	768	3,864	4,717	44
Texas	22,375	21,208	1,858	9,233	10,117	1,168	21,958	1,168	19,330	5,593	32
Utah	2,102	2,001	126	1,168	704	101	2,129	1,087	1,738	3,909	51
Vermont	781	757	39	225	493	24	752	1,285	687	7,474	8
Virginia	6,179	6,109	326	2,218	3,565	70	6,810	1,029	6,106	6,072	24
Washington	6,477	6,209	391	4,311	1,508	268	7,352	1,349	5,468	6,114	22
West Virginia	2,210	2,165	168	1,267	731	45	2,182	1,195	1,958	6,902	14
Wisconsin	6,785	6,297	278	2,777	3,242	489	6,243	1,219	5,633	7,231	11
Wyoming	698	663	43	325	295	35	634	1,323	571	6,129	21

- Represents or rounds to zero. X Not applicable. [1] Amount received by local education agencies from the sales of bonds and real property and equipment, loans, and proceeds from insurance adjustments. [2] Includes interest on school debt and other current expenditures not shown separately. [3] Based on Bureau of the Census estimated resident population, as of July 1, the previous year. Estimates reflect revisions based on the 1990 Census of Population. [4] Average daily attendance.

Source: National Education Association, Washington, DC, Estimates of School Statistics Database (copyright).

No. 263. Computers for Student Instruction in Elementary and Secondary Schools: 1985 and 1997

[Market Data Retrieval collects student use computer information in elementary and secondary schools nationwide through a comprehensive annual technology survey that utilizes both mail and telephone methods]

LEVEL	1984-85				1996-97			
	Total schools	Total enrollment (1,000)	Number of computers [1]	Students per computer [2]	Total schools	Total enrollment (1,000)	Number of computers [1]	Students per computer
U.S. total	**105,509**	**44,091**	**631,983**	**62.7**	**107,716**	**51,022**	**6,854,026**	**7.4**
Public schools, total	81,100	39,186	569,825	63.5	85,514	45,959	6,281,544	7.3
Elementary	50,967	19,373	215,393	79.3	50,717	23,177	2,896,090	8.0
Middle/junior high	9,791	6,662	100,331	61.2	12,648	8,409	1,136,834	7.4
Senior high	15,152	11,191	228,726	51.5	15,156	11,931	1,855,261	6.4
K-12/other	5,190	1,959	25,375	45.8	6,795	2,443	393,358	6.2
Catholic schools, total	9,483	2,813	28,427	73.5	8,269	2,640	279,546	9.4
Elementary	7,831	2,065	15,863	85.1	6,868	1,967	199,580	9.9
Secondary	1,481	700	12,147	57.8	1,254	627	73,724	8.5
K-12/other	151	48	417	(NA)	147	46	6,243	7.3
Other private schools, total	14,946	2,093	33,731	40.5	13,933	2,423	292,933	8.3
Elementary	8,226	1,049	13,400	42.7	6,920	1,055	116,536	9.1
Secondary	950	79	6,266	40.1	1,065	218	41,650	5.2
K-12/other	5,770	965	14,065	(NA)	5,946	1,149	134,746	6.5

NA Not available. [1] Includes estimates for schools not reporting number of computers. [2] Excludes schools with no computers.

Source: Market Data Retrieval, Shelton, CT, unpublished data (copyright).

No. 264. Public Schools with Access or Planned Access to the Internet: 1994 to 1996

[In percent. As of fall. Excludes special education, vocational education, and alternative based on sample and subject to sampling error; see source for details]

SCHOOL CHARACTERISTIC	PERCENT OF SCHOOLS WITH INTERNET ACCESS			PERCENT OF INSTRUCTIONAL ROOMS WITH INTERNET ACCESS			Percent of schools without Internet access in 1996 which plan for access by the year 2000
	1994	1995	1996	1994	1995	1996	
Total [1]	35	50	65	3	8	14	87
Instructional level:							
Elementary	30	46	61	3	8	13	85
Secondary	49	65	77	4	8	16	93
Size of enrollment:							
Less than 300	30	39	57	3	9	15	83
300 to 999	35	52	66	3	8	13	88
1,000 or more	58	69	80	3	4	16	87
Percent minority enrollment:							
Less than 6 percent	(NA)	52	65	(NA)	9	18	86
6 to 20 percent	(NA)	58	72	(NA)	10	18	88
21 to 49 percent	(NA)	54	65	(NA)	9	12	95
50 percent or more	(NA)	40	56	(NA)	3	5	78
Percent of students eligible for free or reduced-price school lunch:							
Less than 11 percent	(NA)	62	78	(NA)	9	18	88
11 to 30 percent	(NA)	59	72	(NA)	10	16	92
31 to 70 percent	(NA)	47	58	(NA)	7	14	84
71 percent or more	(NA)	31	53	(NA)	3	7	85

NA Not available. [1] Includes combined schools.

Source: U.S. National Center for Education Statistics, "Advanced Telecommunications in U.S. Public Elementary and Secondary Schools, Fall 1996", NCES 97-944.

No. 265. Student Use of Computers: 1984 and 1993

[In percent. As of October. Based on the Current Population Survey and subject to sampling error; see Appendix III and source]

CHARACTERISTIC	1984, total	1993					
		Total	Prekindergarten and kindergarden	Grades 1-8	Grades 9-12	1st to 4th year of college	5th or later year of college
USING COMPUTERS AT SCHOOL							
Total	27.3	59.0	26.2	68.9	58.2	55.2	52.1
Sex:							
Male	29.0	59.4	25.9	69.5	56.5	57.5	56.7
Female	25.5	58.7	26.5	68.4	60.0	53.3	47.6
Race/ethnicity:							
White [1]	30.0	61.6	29.4	73.7	59.9	54.9	49.8
Black [1]	16.8	51.5	16.5	56.5	54.5	56.9	57.9
Hispanic	18.6	52.3	19.2	58.4	54.1	51.9	53.7
Other	28.6	59.0	23.5	65.7	57.3	60.9	69.4
Household income:							
Less than $5,000	18.7	51.2	19.6	55.0	50.6	61.7	66.7
$5,000 to $9,999	21.0	53.3	24.4	60.3	51.9	53.9	56.2
$10,000 to $14,999	22.4	56.4	20.1	64.7	56.7	50.7	76.1
$15,000 to $19,999	25.9	58.1	23.8	67.5	57.4	51.2	68.5
$20,000 to $24,999	26.7	56.4	23.7	64.3	53.0	57.4	52.4
$25,000 to $29,999	30.5	60.0	28.0	70.1	60.3	51.5	58.0
$30,000 to $34,999	30.5	59.1	23.7	69.6	59.7	51.7	45.3
$35,000 to $39,999	32.3	60.7	27.1	72.1	61.7	49.2	47.9
$40,000 to $49,999	32.8	59.3	28.5	70.3	57.2	53.9	46.6
$50,000 to $74,999	35.5	62.6	28.6	75.6	61.5	57.4	44.2
$75,000 or more	36.0	64.6	33.5	78.7	62.5	60.9	47.7
Control of school:							
Public	27.4	60.2	30.1	68.6	58.1	53.9	54.1
Private	28.5	52.1	18.7	72.5	60.7	60.7	48.0
USING COMPUTERS AT HOME							
Total	11.5	27.0	15.6	24.7	28.7	32.8	52.6
Sex:							
Male	14.0	27.4	15.1	24.8	28.2	36.6	56.1
Female	9.0	26.6	16.1	24.6	29.2	29.7	49.5
Race/ethnicity:							
White [1]	13.7	32.8	19.4	31.4	35.9	36.0	53.6
Black [1]	4.9	10.9	4.2	9.0	10.4	19.4	48.1
Hispanic	3.6	10.4	5.7	7.5	9.8	22.0	52.2
Other	9.0	28.7	17.0	23.2	37.0	33.0	47.1
Household income:							
Less than $5,000	2.9	9.7	1.1	4.1	6.8	25.6	45.2
$5,000 to $9,999	3.2	8.0	0.9	4.5	5.3	21.3	45.6
$10,000 to $14,999	5.0	11.4	4.6	6.4	8.7	29.8	50.0
$15,000 to $19,999	7.5	15.1	6.9	10.9	14.1	28.9	43.0
$20,000 to $24,999	9.9	16.8	7.4	13.1	17.9	27.7	49.6
$25,000 to $29,999	12.8	21.1	12.3	19.3	22.0	28.1	47.0
$30,000 to $34,999	15.8	24.1	18.7	20.5	29.1	26.4	44.4
$35,000 to $39,999	19.4	27.1	13.0	26.3	28.1	32.7	52.7
$40,000 to $49,999	20.4	32.2	21.6	32.9	33.9	32.5	45.9
$50,000 to $74,999	24.2	43.0	25.5	45.3	46.4	40.1	58.2
$75,000 or more	22.1	56.1	38.2	62.3	61.0	47.0	64.7
Control of school:							
Public	11.2	25.3	12.1	23.0	27.2	31.9	50.0
Private	13.8	37.4	22.4	41.5	47.2	36.9	57.7
USING COMPUTERS AT HOME FOR SCHOOL WORK							
Total	4.6	14.9	0.6	10.8	20.9	23.1	36.6
Sex:							
Male	5.9	14.8	0.9	10.1	20.5	26.3	40.3
Female	3.3	15.0	0.4	11.5	21.4	20.5	33.2
Race/ethnicity:							
White [1]	5.4	18.2	0.8	13.8	26.5	25.7	37.8
Black [1]	2.3	5.7	(NA)	4.0	6.9	11.5	30.1
Hispanic	1.4	5.6	(NA)	2.9	6.7	15.9	36.8
Other	3.8	16.0	1.1	9.3	27.0	23.7	29.2
Household income:							
Less than $5,000	1.0	6.7	(NA)	2.5	4.0	18.7	36.0
$5,000 to $9,999	1.5	4.8	(NA)	1.1	3.6	16.1	36.5
$10,000 to $14,999	1.9	7.3	(NA)	2.6	5.6	25.9	34.6
$15,000 to $19,999	3.0	8.6	0.4	4.7	10.8	18.7	31.0
$20,000 to $24,999	3.1	9.8	0.7	5.1	12.6	22.9	36.0
$25,000 to $29,999	5.1	10.4	1.1	6.3	13.4	19.5	34.9
$30,000 to $34,999	4.9	13.0	0.8	8.1	21.9	18.0	36.1
$35,000 to $39,999	7.1	15.4	0.8	12.4	21.0	22.6	37.2
$40,000 to $49,999	9.2	17.1	1.1	14.7	24.2	22.2	32.1
$50,000 to $74,999	11.5	23.2	1.0	19.7	35.0	27.0	38.2
$75,000 or more	9.8	30.4	0.8	29.4	45.2	30.6	41.5
Control of school:							
Public	4.5	14.2	0.5	10.1	19.8	22.7	34.7
Private	5.4	18.8	1.0	17.8	35.4	24.8	40.1

NA Not available. [1] Non-Hispanic.

Source: U.S. National Center for Education Statistics, *Digest of Education Statistics*, 1994.

No. 266. Technology in Public Schools: 1992 to 1996

school year ending in year shown. Based on surveys of school districts conducted in the spring and summer of the school year. For details, see source]

TECHNOLOGY	NUMBER					PERCENT OF TOTAL	
	1992	1993	1994	1995	1996	1992	1996
with interactive videodisk							
... [1]	6,502	11,729	19,189	27,059	29,759	8	35
ntary [2]	2,921	5,966	10,043	14,594	16,200	6	31
high [3]	1,258	2,386	3,844	5,460	6,009	10	43
r high [4]	2,106	3,129	5,026	6,661	7,196	14	42
nts represented (1,000)	5,781	9,064	13,434	18,552	20,258	14	46
with modems [1]	13,597	18,471	24,277	35,696	40,147	16	47
ntary [2]	5,831	8,492	11,679	18,858	21,733	11	42
high [3]	2,608	3,431	4,531	6,546	7,266	20	52
r high [4]	5,001	6,371	7,853	9,930	10,682	30	62
nts represented (1,000)	10,717	13,382	18,476	22,372	24,688	25	56
with networks [1]	4,184	11,657	19,272	27,805	31,966	5	38
ntary [2]	1,583	4,663	8,477	13,582	16,189	3	31
high [3]	778	2,030	3,611	5,194	5,971	6	43
r high [4]	1,736	4,895	7,104	8,839	9,562	10	56
nts represented (1,000)	3,754	8,043	12,713	17,540	19,997	9	45
with CD-ROM's [1]	5,706	11,021	24,526	40,509	45,918	7	54
ntary [2]	1,897	4,457	11,794	22,305	25,965	4	50
high [3]	1,231	2,326	4,874	7,501	8,341	9	60
r high [4]	2,543	4,188	7,724	10,354	11,150	15	65
nts represented (1,000)	5,296	8,534	15,576	24,121	27,070	12	61
with satellite dishes [1]	1,129	8,812	12,580	15,400	16,298	1	19
ntary [2]	351	2,968	4,269	5,565	6,014	1	12
high [3]	166	1,503	2,497	3,214	3,409	1	24
r high [4]	606	4,292	5,770	6,550	6,782	4	40
nts represented (1,000)	1,906	4,666	6,740	8,963	9,270	4	21
with cable [1]	(NA)	47,745	58,652	63,639	64,310	(NA)	76
ntary [2]	(NA)	27,923	35,325	38,336	38,714	(NA)	75
high [3]	(NA)	9,266	10,696	11,518	11,575	(NA)	83
r high [4]	(NA)	10,296	12,196	13,114	13,262	(NA)	78
nts represented (1,000)	(NA)	27,324	33,510	36,284	36,950	(NA)	83

Not available. [1] Includes schools for special education and adult education, not shown separately. [2] Includes K-12, l, preschool through 3, K-6, and K-8. [3] Includes schools with grade spans of 4-6, 7-8, and 7-9. [4] Includes 7-12, 9-12, ocational technical, and alternative high schools.

rce: Quality Education Data, Inc., Denver, CO, *Technology in Public Schools*, annual.

7. Children and Youth with Disabilities Served by Selected Programs: 1989 to 1995

ool year ending in year shown. Excludes outlying areas. For persons age 6 to 21 years old served under IDEA als with Disabilities Act), Part B and Chapter 1 of ESEA (Elementary and Secondary Education Act), SOP (State Operated)]

ITEM	1989	1990	1991	1992	1993	1994	1995
lions (1,000)	4,173.5	4,219.5	4,320.3	4,459.2	4,586.2	4,730.4	4,859.1
PERCENT DISTRIBUTION							
disabilities	47.8	48.6	49.3	50.1	51.3	50.9	51.2
impairments	23.1	23.1	22.8	22.3	21.7	21.4	20.9
tardation	13.8	13.0	12.4	12.0	11.3	11.3	11.4
l disturbance	8.9	9.0	9.0	8.9	8.7	8.7	8.8
impairments	1.4	1.3	1.3	1.3	1.3	1.3	1.3
lically impairments	1.1	1.1	1.1	1.1	1.1	1.2	1.2
alth impairments	1.2	1.2	1.3	1.3	1.4	1.7	2.2
mpaired	0.5	0.5	0.5	0.5	0.5	0.5	0.5
disabilities	2.0	2.0	2.2	2.2	2.2	2.3	1.8
d	(Z)	(Z)	(Z)	(Z)	(Z)	(Z)	(Z)
...	(NA)	(NA)	(NA)	0.1	0.3	0.4	0.5
c brain injury	(NA)	(NA)	(NA)	(Z)	0.1	0.1	0.1

s than .05 percent. NA Not available.

ce: U.S. Department of Education, Office of Special Education Programs, Data Analysis System (DANS).

No. 268. Children and Youth With Disabilities, by Age and Educational Environment: 1993

[For school year ending in year shown. Covers children 3 to 21 served under IDEA, Part B and Chapter 1 of ESEA (SOP); see headnote, table 267]

ENVIRONMENT	NUMBER (1,000)					PERCENT DISTRIBUTION			
	Total	3-5 years old	6-11 years old	12-17 years old	18-21 years old	3-5 years old	6-11 years old	12-17 years old	18-21 years old
Total	5,016.6	466.9	2,324.0	1,997.8	237.9	100.0	100.0	100.0	100.0
Regular class [1]	2,042.1	217.1	1,160.9	607.6	56.4	47.5	50.0	30.4	23.7
Resource room [2]	1,493.9	56.4	609.5	750.2	77.9	12.3	26.2	37.5	32.7
Separate class [3]	1,206.2	139.1	474.2	523.8	69.0	30.4	20.4	26.2	29.0
Separate school facility:									
Public	133.5	22.1	37.7	53.8	19.7	4.8	1.6	2.7	8.3
Private	70.0	13.2	25.4	25.7	5.8	2.9	1.1	1.3	2.4
Separate residential facility:									
Public	28.3	1.5	7.2	15.1	4.5	0.3	0.3	0.8	1.9
Private	11.9	0.3	2.2	7.5	1.8	0.1	0.1	0.4	0.7
Correctional facility [4]	12.5	(NA)	(NA)	(NA)	(NA)	(NA)	(NA)	(NA)	(NA)
Home/hospital	30.8	7.1	6.9	14.0	2.7	1.6	0.3	0.7	1.2

NA Not available. [1] Receives special education and related services outside the regular classroom for less than 21 percent of the school day. [2] Receives special education and related services outside the regular classroom between 21 and 60 percent of the school day. [3] Receives special education and related services outside the regular classroom for more than 60 percent of the school day. [4] Students in correctional facilities are also distributed by type environment, but not duplicated in the total.

Source: U.S. Department of Education, Office of Special Education Programs, Data Analysis System (DANS).

No. 269. Catholic Elementary and Secondary Schools: 1960 to 1995

[As of October 1. Regular sessions only]

ITEM	Unit	1960	1970	1980	1985	1990	1991	1992	1993	1994	1995
Elementary schools	Number	10,501	9,362	8,043	7,806	7,291	7,239	7,174	7,114	7,055	7,022
Pupils enrolled	1,000	4,373	3,359	2,269	2,057	1,884	1,964	1,964	1,992	2,004	2,011
Teachers, total [1]	1,000	108	112	97	97	91	109	110	112	118	119
Religious	1,000	79	52	25	18	11	12	11	12	11	10
Lay	1,000	29	60	72	79	80	96	98	100	107	109
Secondary schools	Number	2,392	1,981	1,516	1,430	1,296	1,269	1,249	1,231	1,238	1,228
Pupils enrolled	1,000	880	1,008	837	762	592	587	584	585	615	624
Teachers, total [1]	1,000	44	54	49	50	40	44	45	45	47	48
Religious	1,000	33	28	14	11	6	6	6	7	6	6
Lay	1,000	11	26	35	39	34	37	38	38	40	42

[1] Beginning 1991, includes part-time teachers.

Source: National Catholic Educational Association, (NCEA) Washington, DC; from the NCEA Data Bank—*U.S. Catholic Schools 1967-1968*, (copyright) and *U.S. Catholic Elementary and Secondary Schools 1995-1996 Annual Statistical Report on Schools, Enrollment & Staffing*, NCEA, annual (copyright); and NCEA/Ganley's *Catholic Schools in America*, 1996 edition, annual (copyright).

No. 270. Private Elementary and Secondary School Teachers—Selected Characteristics: 1993-94

[For school year. Based on survey and subject to sampling error; for details, see source. See table 253 for similar data on public school teachers]

CHARACTERISTIC	Unit	AGE				SEX		RACE/ETHNICITY		
		Under 30 years old	30 to 39 years old	40 to 49 years old	Over 50 years old	Male	Female	White [1]	Black [1]	Hispanic
Total teachers [2]	1,000	102	109	116	52	93	285	348	12	12
Highest degree held:										
Bachelor's	Percent	74.5	57.7	53.1	44.0	47.3	62.8	59.4	55.6	57.4
Master's	Percent	14.9	31.0	35.9	43.3	40.6	26.3	30.2	26.4	19.9
Education specialist	Percent	1.7	3.1	3.4	3.7	2.6	3.0	2.6	4.8	4.4
Doctorate	Percent	0.5	1.6	2.2	3.0	4.3	0.8	1.6	1.0	2.3
Full-time teaching experience:										
Less than 3 years	Percent	42.9	19.1	9.5	6.6	21.7	20.6	20.4	26.9	25.5
3 to 9 years	Percent	54.3	35.3	25.2	10.2	28.2	35.8	33.6	34.9	41.8
10 to 20 years	Percent	2.7	44.6	42.1	22.9	28.7	29.9	30.0	27.9	21.6
20 years or more	Percent	(Z)	1.0	23.2	60.3	21.4	13.7	16.0	10.3	11.1
Full-time teachers	1,000	87	83	92	40	72	230	278	9	10
Earned income	Dol.	19,776	23,700	25,225	26,437	28,948	21,657	23,415	22,532	22,013
Salary	Dol.	18,052	22,193	23,999	25,362	26,120	20,669	22,000	20,796	20,672

Z Less than .05 percent. [1] Non-Hispanic. [2] Includes teachers with no degrees and associates degrees, not shown separately.

Source: U.S. National Center for Education Statistics, *Digest of Education Statistics*, 1995.

No. 271. Private Elementary and Secondary Schools—Enrollment and Tuition, by Orientation: 1993-94

[For school year ending in year shown. Based on survey and subject to sampling error; for details see source]

CHARACTERISTIC	ENROLLMENT (1,000)				SCHOOLS			
	Total	Catholic	Other religious	Non-sectarian	Total	Catholic	Other religious	Non-sectarian
Total	**4,970.6**	**2,516.1**	**1,686.1**	**768.5**	**26,093**	**8,351**	**12,180**	**5,563**
School enrollment:								
Less than 150 students	890.3	168.2	509.0	213.1	14,155	1,572	8,499	4,084
150 to 299 students	1,482.2	853.1	467.7	161.3	6,820	3,815	2,232	773
300 to 499 students	1,243.6	719.0	359.3	165.3	3,272	1,885	973	414
500 to 749 students	736.1	432.6	196.8	106.7	1,228	729	327	172
750 or more students	618.5	343.2	153.3	122.0	619	350	149	120
Percent minority students:								
Less than 5 percent	1,855.4	876.6	774.1	204.7	10,750	3,152	6,137	1,461
5 percent, less than 20 percent	1,620.4	761.7	502.8	355.8	7,482	2,376	3,070	2,036
20 percent, less than 50 percent	704.4	375.8	189.6	139.0	3,785	1,096	1,395	1,295
50 percent or more	790.5	502.0	219.6	68.9	4,076	1,727	1,578	771
Average annual tuition (dol.):								
Total	(X)	(X)	(X)	(X)	3,116	2,178	2,915	6,631
Elementary	(X)	(X)	(X)	(X)	2,138	1,628	2,606	4,693
Secondary	(X)	(X)	(X)	(X)	4,578	3,643	5,261	9,525
Combined	(X)	(X)	(X)	(X)	4,266	4,153	2,831	7,056

X Not applicable.

Source: U.S. National Center for Education Statistics, *Digest of Education Statistics*, 1995.

No. 272. High School Dropouts, by Race and Hispanic Origin: 1975 to 1995

[In percent. As of October]

ITEM	1975	1980	1985	1987 [1]	1988	1989	1990	1991	1992	1993	1994	1995
EVENT DROPOUTS [2]												
Total [3]	**5.8**	**6.0**	**5.2**	**4.1**	**4.8**	**4.5**	**4.0**	**4.0**	**4.3**	**4.2**	**5.0**	**5.4**
White	5.4	5.6	4.8	3.7	4.7	3.9	3.8	3.7	4.1	4.1	4.7	5.1
Male	5.0	6.4	4.9	4.1	5.1	4.1	4.1	3.6	3.8	4.1	4.6	5.4
Female	5.8	4.9	4.7	3.4	4.3	3.8	3.5	3.8	4.4	4.1	4.9	4.8
Black	8.7	8.3	7.7	6.4	6.3	7.7	5.1	6.2	4.9	5.4	6.2	6.1
Male	8.3	8.0	8.3	6.2	6.7	6.9	4.1	5.5	3.3	5.7	6.5	7.9
Female	9.0	8.5	7.2	6.4	6.0	8.6	6.0	7.0	6.7	5.0	5.7	4.4
Hispanic [4]	10.9	11.5	9.7	5.6	10.5	7.7	8.0	7.3	7.9	5.4	9.2	11.6
Male	10.1	16.9	9.3	5.0	12.3	7.6	8.7	10.4	5.8	5.7	8.4	10.9
Female	11.6	6.9	9.8	6.2	8.4	7.7	7.2	4.8	8.6	5.0	10.1	12.5
STATUS DROPOUTS [5]												
Total [3]	**15.6**	**15.6**	**13.9**	**14.5**	**14.6**	**14.4**	**13.6**	**14.2**	**12.7**	**12.7**	**13.3**	**13.9**
White	13.9	14.4	13.5	14.2	14.2	14.1	13.5	14.2	12.2	12.2	12.7	13.6
Male	13.5	15.7	14.7	15.1	15.4	15.4	14.2	15.4	13.3	13.0	13.6	14.3
Female	14.2	13.2	12.3	13.2	13.0	12.8	12.8	13.1	11.1	11.5	11.7	13.0
Black	27.3	23.5	17.6	17.0	17.7	16.4	15.1	15.6	16.3	16.4	15.5	14.4
Male	27.8	26.0	18.8	18.7	18.9	18.6	13.6	15.4	15.5	15.6	17.5	14.2
Female	26.9	21.5	16.6	15.4	16.6	14.5	16.2	15.8	17.1	17.2	13.7	14.6
Hispanic [4]	34.9	40.3	31.5	32.8	39.6	37.7	37.3	39.6	33.9	32.7	34.7	34.7
Male	32.6	42.6	35.8	34.5	40.2	40.3	39.8	44.4	38.4	34.7	36.1	34.2
Female	36.8	38.1	27.0	30.8	38.8	35.0	34.5	34.5	29.6	31.0	33.1	35.4

[1] Beginning 1987 reflects new editing procedures for cases with missing data on school enrollment. [2] Percent of students who drop out in a single year without completing high school. For grades 10 to 12. [3] Includes other races, not shown separately. [4] Persons of Hispanic origin may be of any race. [5] Percent of the population who have not completed high school and are not enrolled, regardless of when they dropped out. For persons 18 to 24 years old.

Source: U.S. Bureau of the Census, *Current Population Reports*, P20-492.

No. 273. High School Dropouts by Age, Race, and Hispanic Origin: 1970 to 1995

[As of October. For persons 14 to 24 years old. See table 275 for definition of dropouts]

AGE AND RACE	NUMBER OF DROPOUTS (1,000)					PERCENT OF POPULATION				
	1970	1980	1985	1990	1995	1970	1980	1985	1990	1995
Total dropouts [1 2]	4,670	5,212	4,456	3,854	3,963	12.2	12.0	10.6	10.1	9.9
16 to 17 years	617	709	505	418	406	8.0	8.8	7.0	6.3	5.4
18 to 21 years	2,138	2,578	2,095	1,921	1,960	16.4	15.8	14.1	13.4	14.2
22 to 24 years	1,770	1,798	1,724	1,458	1,491	18.7	15.2	14.1	13.8	13.6
White [2]	3,577	4,169	3,583	3,127	3,098	10.8	11.3	10.3	10.1	9.7
16 to 17 years	485	619	424	334	314	7.3	9.2	7.1	6.4	5.4
18 to 21 years	1,618	2,032	1,678	1,516	1,530	14.3	14.7	13.6	13.1	13.6
22 to 24 years	1,356	1,416	1,372	1,235	1,181	16.3	14.0	13.3	14.0	13.4
Black [2]	1,047	934	748	611	605	22.2	16.0	12.6	10.9	10.0
16 to 17 years	125	80	70	73	70	12.8	6.9	6.5	6.9	5.8
18 to 21 years	500	486	376	345	328	30.5	23.0	17.5	16.0	15.8
22 to 24 years	397	346	279	185	194	37.8	24.0	17.8	13.5	12.5
Hispanic [2 3]	(NA)	919	820	1,122	1,355	(NA)	29.5	23.3	26.8	24.7
16 to 17 years	(NA)	92	97	89	94	(NA)	16.6	14.6	12.9	10.7
18 to 21 years	(NA)	470	335	502	652	(NA)	40.3	29.3	32.9	29.9
22 to 24 years	(NA)	323	365	523	598	(NA)	40.6	33.9	42.8	37.4

NA Not available. [1] Includes other groups not shown separately. [2] Includes persons 14 to 15 years, not shown separately. [3] Persons of Hispanic origin may be of any race.

Source: U.S. Bureau of the Census, *Current Population Reports*, P20-492; and earlier reports.

No. 274. Enrollment Status, by Race, Hispanic Origin, and Sex: 1975 and 1995

[As of October. For persons 18 to 21 years old. For the civilian noninstitutional population. Based on the Current Population Survey; see text, section 1 and Appendix III]

CHARACTERISTIC	TOTAL PERSONS 18 TO 21 YEARS OLD (1,000)		PERCENT DISTRIBUTION							
			Enrolled in high school		High school graduates				Not high school graduates	
					Total		In college			
	1975	1995	1975	1995	1975	1995	1975	1995	1975	1995
Total [1]	15,693	13,934	5.7	8.9	78.0	76.8	33.5	43.3	16.3	14.2
White	13,448	11,075	4.7	7.6	80.6	78.5	34.6	45.3	14.7	13.8
Black	1,997	2,070	12.5	14.9	60.4	69.0	24.9	33.0	27.0	15.8
Hispanic [2]	899	2,001	12.0	11.3	57.2	56.1	24.4	25.4	30.8	32.6
Male [1]	7,584	6,895	7.4	11.0	76.6	74.7	35.4	41.4	15.9	14.2
White	6,545	5,530	6.2	9.7	79.7	76.6	36.9	43.3	14.1	13.5
Black	911	955	15.9	18.6	55.0	63.8	23.9	30.0	29.0	17.6
Hispanic [2]	416	1,020	17.3	13.9	54.6	56.1	25.2	22.7	27.9	30.1
Female [1]	8,109	7,039	4.2	6.9	79.2	78.8	31.8	45.3	16.6	14.2
White	6,903	5,545	3.2	5.5	81.4	80.4	32.4	47.2	15.3	14.1
Black	1,085	1,115	9.7	11.7	65.0	76.6	25.8	35.5	25.4	14.3
Hispanic [2]	484	982	7.6	8.4	59.3	56.2	23.6	28.2	33.1	35.2

[1] Includes other races not shown separately. [2] Persons of Hispanic origin may be of any race.

Source: U.S. Bureau of the Census, *Current Population Reports*, P20-492; and earlier reports.

No. 275. Employment Status of High School Graduates and School Dropouts: 1980 to 1995

[In thousands, except percent. As of October. For civilian noninstitutional population 16 to 24 years old. Based on Current Population Survey; see text, section 1, and Appendix III]

EMPLOYMENT STATUS, SEX, AND RACE	GRADUATES [1]				DROPOUTS [2]			
	1980	1985	1990	1995 [3]	1980	1985	1990	1995 [3]
Civilian population	11,622	10,381	8,370	6,627	5,254	4,323	3,800	3,876
In labor force	9,795	8,825	7,107	5,530	3,549	2,920	2,506	2,443
Percent of population	84.3	85.0	84.9	83.4	67.5	67.5	66.0	63.0
Employed	8,567	7,707	6,279	4,863	2,651	2,165	1,993	1,894
Percent of labor force	87.5	87.3	88.3	87.9	74.7	74.1	79.5	77.5
Unemployed	1,228	1,118	828	667	898	755	513	549
Unemployment rate, total [4]	12.5	12.7	11.7	12.1	25.3	25.9	20.5	22.5
Male	13.5	12.5	11.1	11.7	23.5	23.9	18.8	19.2
Female	11.5	12.9	12.3	12.5	28.7	29.8	23.5	26.8
White	10.8	9.8	9.0	10.5	21.6	23.6	17.0	19.1
Black	26.1	29.4	26.0	20.3	43.9	41.5	43.3	48.0
Not in labor force	1,827	1,556	1,262	1,097	1,705	1,403	1,294	1,433
Percent of population	15.7	15.0	15.1	16.6	32.5	32.5	34.1	37.0

[1] For persons not enrolled in college who have completed 4 years of high school only. [2] For persons not in regular school and who have not completed the 12th grade nor received a general equivalency degree. [3] See footnote 3, table 631. [4] Includes other races not shown separately.

Source: U.S. Bureau of Labor Statistics, Bulletin 2307; *News*, USDL 96-152, April 25, 1996; and unpublished data.

No. 276. Scholastic Assessment Test (SAT) Scores and Characteristics of College-Bound Seniors: 1967 to 1996

[For school year ending in year shown. Data are for the SAT I: Reasoning Tests. Scores between the two tests have been equated to the same 200-800 scale and are thus comparable. Scores for 1995 and prior years have been recentered and revised. SAT I: Reasoning Test replaced the SAT in March 1994]

TYPE OF TEST AND CHARACTERISTIC	Unit	1967	1970	1975	1980	1985	1990	1993	1994	1995	1996
AVERAGE TEST SCORES [1]											
Verbal, total [2]	Point	543	537	512	502	509	500	500	499	504	505
Male	Point	540	536	515	506	514	505	504	501	505	507
Female	Point	545	538	509	498	503	496	497	497	502	503
Math, total [2]	Point	516	512	498	492	500	501	503	504	506	508
Male	Point	535	531	518	515	522	521	524	523	525	527
Female	Point	495	493	479	473	480	483	484	487	490	492
PARTICIPANTS											
Total	1,000	(NA)	(NA)	996	922	977	1,026	1,044	1,050	1,068	1,085
Male	Percent	(NA)	(NA)	49.9	48.2	48.3	47.8	47.4	46.9	46.4	46.5
White	Percent	(NA)	(NA)	86.0	82.1	81.0	73.0	70.4	69.4	69.2	68.7
Black	Percent	(NA)	(NA)	7.9	9.1	7.5	10.0	10.8	10.8	10.7	10.8
Obtaining scores [1] of—											
600 or above:											
Verbal	Percent	(NA)	(NA)	(NA)	(NA)	(NA)	20.3	20.9	21.1	21.9	21.1
Math	Percent	(NA)	(NA)	(NA)	(NA)	(NA)	20.4	20.7	22.0	23.4	22.7
Below 400:											
Verbal	Percent	(NA)	(NA)	(NA)	(NA)	(NA)	17.3	17.7	21.0	16.4	15.9
Math	Percent	(NA)	(NA)	(NA)	(NA)	(NA)	15.8	15.7	15.5	16.0	16.0
Selected intended area of study:											
Business and commerce	Percent	(NA)	(NA)	11.5	18.6	21.0	20.9	15.0	13.8	13.3	12.8
Engineering	Percent	(NA)	(NA)	6.7	11.1	11.7	10.2	10.2	9.4	8.8	8.5
Social science	Percent	(NA)	(NA)	7.7	7.8	7.5	12.6	12.2	12.1	11.6	11.3
Education	Percent	(NA)	(NA)	9.1	6.1	4.7	7.5	8.0	8.0	8.1	8.2

NA Not available. [1] Minimum score 200; maximum score, 800. [2] 1967 and 1970 are estimates based on total number of persons taking SAT.

Source: College Entrance Examination Board, New York, NY, *National College-Bound Senior*, annual (copyright).

No. 277. American College Testing (ACT) Program Scores and Characteristics of College-Bound Students: 1967 to 1996

[For academic year ending in year shown. Except as indicated, test scores and characteristics of college-bound students. Through 1985, data based on 10 percent sample; thereafter, based on all ACT tested seniors]

TYPE OF TEST AND CHARACTERISTIC	Unit	1967	1970	1975	1980	1985	1990 [1]	1993 [1]	1994 [1]	1995 [1]	1996 [1]
TEST SCORES [2]											
Composite	Point	19.9	18.6	18.5	18.5	18.6	20.6	20.7	20.8	20.8	20.9
Male	Point	20.3	19.5	19.3	19.3	19.4	21.0	21.0	20.9	21.0	21.0
Female	Point	19.4	17.8	17.9	17.8	17.9	20.3	20.5	20.7	20.7	20.8
English	Point	18.5	17.7	17.9	17.8	18.1	20.5	20.3	20.3	20.2	20.3
Male	Point	17.6	17.1	17.3	17.3	17.6	20.1	19.8	19.8	19.8	19.8
Female	Point	19.4	18.3	18.3	18.2	18.6	20.9	20.6	20.7	20.6	20.7
Math	Point	20.0	17.6	17.4	17.3	17.2	19.9	20.1	20.2	20.2	20.2
Male	Point	21.1	19.3	18.9	18.9	18.6	20.7	20.8	20.8	20.9	20.9
Female	Point	18.8	16.2	16.2	16.0	16.0	19.3	19.6	19.6	19.7	19.7
Reading [3]	Point	19.7	17.4	17.2	17.2	17.4	(NA)	21.2	21.2	21.3	21.3
Male	Point	20.3	18.7	18.2	18.3	18.3	(NA)	21.2	21.1	21.1	21.0
Female	Point	19.0	16.4	16.4	16.4	16.6	(NA)	21.2	21.4	21.4	21.6
Science reasoning [4]	Point	20.8	21.1	21.1	21.0	21.2	(NA)	20.8	20.9	21.0	21.1
Male	Point	21.6	22.4	22.4	22.3	22.6	(NA)	21.5	21.6	21.6	21.7
Female	Point	20.0	20.0	20.0	20.0	20.0	(NA)	20.3	20.4	20.5	20.5
PARTICIPANTS [5]											
Total	1,000	788	714	822	836	739	817	876	892	945	925
Male	Percent	52	46	45	45	46	46	45	45	44	44
White	Percent	(NA)	77	83	83	82	79	80	79	80	80
Black	Percent	4	7	8	8	8	9	9	9	9	9
Obtaining composite scores [6]											
of— 27 or above	Percent	14	14	13	13	14	12	12	13	13	13
18 or below	Percent	21	33	33	33	32	35	35	34	34	34
Planned educational major:											
Business [7]	Percent	16	21	20	19	21	20	15	14	14	13
Engineering	Percent	8	6	8	10	9	9	10	9	9	9
Social science [8]	Percent	10	9	6	6	7	10	10	9	9	9
Education	Percent	16	12	9	7	6	8	9	10	9	9

NA Not available. [1] Beginning 1990, not comparable with previous years because a new version of the ACT was introduced. Estimated average composite scores for prior years: 1989, 20.6; 1988, 1987, and 1986, 20.8. [2] Minimum score, 1; maximum score, 36. [3] Prior to 1990, social studies; data not comparable with previous years. [4] Prior to 1990, natural sciences; data not comparable with previous years. [5] Beginning 1985, data are for seniors who graduated in year shown and had taken the ACT in their junior or senior years. [6] Prior to 1990, 26 or above and 15 or below. [7] Includes political and persuasive (e.g. sales) fields through 1975; thereafter, business and commerce. [8] Includes religion through 1975.

Source: The American College Testing Program, Iowa City, IA, *High School Profile Report*, annual.

No. 278. Proficiency Test Scores for Selected Subjects, by Characteristic: 1977 to 19

[Based on The National Assessment of Educational Progress Tests which are administered to a representative sample of students in public and private schools. Test scores can range from 0 to 500. For details, see source]

TEST AND YEAR	Total	SEX: Male	SEX: Female	RACE: White [1]	RACE: Black [1]	Hispanic origin	PARENTAL EDUCATION: Less than high school	PARENTAL EDUCATION: High school	More than high sch: Total	More than high sch: Some college
READING										
9 year olds:										
1979-80	215	210	220	221	189	190	194	213	226	(NA)
1987-88	212	208	216	218	189	194	193	211	220	(NA)
1989-90	209	204	215	217	182	189	193	209	218	(NA)
1993-94	211	207	215	218	185	186	189	207	221	(NA)
13 year olds:										
1979-80	259	254	263	264	233	237	239	254	271	(NA)
1987-88	258	252	263	261	243	240	247	253	265	(NA)
1989-90	257	251	263	262	242	238	241	251	267	(NA)
1993-94	258	251	266	265	234	235	237	251	269	(NA)
17 year olds:										
1979-80	286	282	289	293	243	261	262	278	290	(NA)
1987-88	290	286	294	295	274	271	267	282	300	(NA)
1989-90	290	284	297	297	267	275	270	283	300	(NA)
1993-94	288	282	295	296	266	263	268	276	299	(NA)
WRITING [2]										
4th graders:										
1983-84	204	201	208	211	182	189	179	192	217	208
1987-88	206	199	213	215	173	190	194	199	212	211
1989-90	202	195	209	211	171	184	186	197	210	214
1991-92	207	198	216	217	175	189	191	202	212	201
8th graders:										
1983-84	267	258	276	272	247	247	258	261	276	271
1987-88	264	254	274	269	246	250	254	258	271	275
1989-90	257	246	266	262	239	246	246	253	265	267
1991-92	274	264	285	279	258	265	258	268	283	280
11th graders:										
1983-84	290	281	299	297	270	259	274	284	299	296
1987-88	291	282	299	296	275	274	276	285	298	296
1989-90	287	276	298	293	268	277	266	278	296	292
1991-92	287	279	296	294	263	274	271	278	295	292
MATHEMATICS										
9 year olds:										
1977-78	219	217	220	224	192	203	200	219	231	230
1985-86	222	222	222	227	202	205	201	218	231	229
1989-90	230	229	230	235	208	214	210	226	237	236
1993-94	231	232	230	237	212	210	210	225	(NA)	239
13 year olds:										
1977-78	264	264	265	272	230	238	245	263	280	273
1985-86	269	270	268	274	249	254	252	263	278	274
1989-90	270	271	270	276	249	255	253	263	279	277
1993-94	274	276	273	281	252	256	255	266	(NA)	277
17 year olds:										
1977-78	300	304	297	306	268	276	280	294	313	305
1985-86	302	305	299	308	279	283	279	293	310	305
1989-90	305	306	303	310	289	284	285	294	313	308
1993-94	306	309	304	312	286	291	284	295	(NA)	305
SCIENCE										
9 year olds:										
1976-77	220	221	218	230	175	192	199	223	233	237
1985-86	224	230	221	232	196	199	204	220	235	236
1989-90	229	235	227	238	196	206	210	226	236	238
1993-94	231	232	230	240	201	201	211	225	(NA)	239
13 year olds:										
1976-77	247	251	244	256	208	213	224	245	264	260
1985-86	251	256	247	259	222	226	229	245	262	258
1989-90	255	259	252	264	226	232	233	247	266	263
1993-94	257	259	254	267	224	232	234	247	(NA)	260
17 year olds:										
1976-77	290	297	282	298	240	262	265	284	304	296
1985-86	289	295	282	298	253	259	258	277	300	295
1989-90	290	296	285	301	253	262	261	276	302	297
1993-94	294	300	289	306	257	261	256	279	(NA)	295
HISTORY, 1993-94										
4th graders	205	203	206	215	177	180	177	197	(NA)	214
8th graders:	259	259	259	267	239	243	241	251	(NA)	264
12th graders	286	288	285	292	265	267	263	276	(NA)	287
GEOGRAPHY, 1993-94										
4th graders	206	208	203	218	168	183	186	197	(NA)	216
8th graders	260	262	258	270	229	239	238	250	(NA)	265
12th graders	285	288	281	291	258	268	263	274	(NA)	286

NA Not available. [1] Non-Hispanic. [2] Writing scores revised from previous years; previous writing scores were records a 0 to 400 rather than 0 to 500 scale.

Source: U.S. National Center for Education Statistics, *Digest of Education Statistics*, annual.

No. 279. Foreign Language Enrollment in Public High Schools: 1970 to 1994

[In thousands, except percent. As of fall, for grades 9 through 12]

LANGUAGE	1970	1974	1976	1978	1982	1985	1990	1994
Total enrollment	13,301.9	13,648.9	13,952.1	13,941.4	12,879.3	12,466.5	11,099.6	11,847.5
Enrolled in all foreign languages	3,779.3	3,294.5	3,174.0	3,200.1	2,909.8	4,028.9	4,256.9	5,001.9
Percent of all students	28.4	24.1	22.7	23.0	22.6	32.3	38.4	42.2
Enrolled in modern foreign languages [1]	3,514.1	3,127.3	3,023.5	3,048.3	2,740.2	3,852.0	4,093.0	4,813.0
Spanish	1,810.8	1,678.1	1,717.0	1,631.4	1,562.8	2,334.4	2,611.4	3,219.8
French	1,230.7	977.9	888.4	856.0	858.0	1,133.7	1,089.4	1,105.9
German	410.5	393.0	352.7	330.6	266.9	312.2	295.4	326.0
Italian	27.3	40.2	45.6	45.5	44.1	47.3	40.4	43.8
Japanese	(NA)	(NA)	(NA)	(NA)	6.2	8.6	25.1	42.3
Russian	20.2	15.1	11.3	8.8	5.7	6.4	16.5	16.4
Percent of all students [1]	26.4	22.9	21.7	21.9	21.3	30.9	36.9	40.6
Spanish	13.6	12.3	12.3	11.7	12.1	18.7	23.5	27.2
French	9.3	7.2	6.4	6.1	6.7	9.1	9.8	9.3
German	3.1	2.9	2.5	2.4	2.1	2.5	2.7	2.8
Italian	0.2	0.3	0.3	0.3	0.3	0.4	0.4	0.4
Japanese	(NA)	(NA)	(NA)	(NA)	0.1	0.1	0.2	0.4
Russian	0.2	0.1	0.1	0.1	(Z)	0.1	0.2	0.1

NA Not available. Z Less than .05 percent. [1] Includes other foreign languages, not shown separately.

Source: The American Council on the Teaching of Foreign Languages, Yonkers, NY, *Foreign Language Enrollments in Public Secondary Schools, Fall 1994.*

No. 280. Public High School Graduates, by State: 1980 to 1996

[In thousands. For school year ending in year shown]

STATE	1980	1985	1989	1990	1991	1992	1993	1994	1995	1996, est.
U.S.	2,747.7	2,414.0	2,458.8	2,320.3	2,234.9	2,226.0	2,233.2	2,221.1	2,287.7	2,304.7
AL	45.2	40.0	43.4	40.5	39.0	38.7	36.0	34.4	36.3	36.4
AK	5.2	5.2	5.6	5.4	5.5	5.5	5.5	5.7	5.8	6.3
AZ	28.6	27.9	31.9	32.1	31.3	31.3	31.7	31.8	29.5	30.4
AR	29.1	26.3	27.9	26.5	25.7	25.8	25.7	25.0	26.0	26.4
CA	249.2	225.4	244.6	236.3	234.2	244.6	249.3	253.1	257.4	261.8
CO	36.8	32.3	35.5	33.0	31.3	31.1	31.8	31.9	32.4	33.4
CT	37.7	32.1	30.9	27.9	27.3	27.1	26.8	26.3	26.3	26.4
DE	7.6	5.9	6.1	5.6	5.2	5.3	5.5	5.2	5.2	5.5
DC	5.0	3.9	3.6	3.6	3.4	3.4	3.1	3.2	3.0	2.7
FL	87.3	81.1	90.8	88.9	87.4	93.7	89.4	88.0	89.8	90.6
GA	61.6	58.7	61.9	56.6	60.1	57.7	57.6	56.4	59.7	59.4
HI	11.5	10.1	10.4	10.3	9.0	9.2	8.9	9.4	10.0	10.0
ID	13.2	12.1	12.5	12.0	12.0	12.7	13.0	13.3	14.2	14.5
IL	135.6	117.0	116.7	108.1	103.3	102.7	103.6	102.1	105.2	105.1
IN	73.1	63.3	63.6	60.0	57.9	56.6	57.6	54.7	56.6	57.7
IA	43.4	36.1	34.3	31.8	28.6	29.2	30.7	30.2	31.2	31.8
KS	30.9	26.0	26.8	25.4	24.4	24.1	24.7	25.3	26.4	26.0
KY	41.2	38.0	38.9	38.0	35.8	33.9	36.4	38.5	36.7	36.2
LA	46.3	39.7	37.2	36.1	33.5	32.2	33.7	34.8	36.7	35.6
ME	15.4	13.9	13.9	13.8	13.2	13.2	12.1	11.6	13.0	11.3
MD	54.3	48.3	45.8	41.6	39.0	39.7	39.5	39.1	41.8	41.6
MA	73.8	63.4	57.3	55.9	50.2	50.3	48.3	47.5	49.1	49.7
MI	124.3	105.9	101.8	93.8	88.2	87.8	85.3	83.4	84.1	87.4
MN	64.9	53.4	53.1	49.1	46.5	46.2	48.0	47.5	49.7	51.6
MS	27.6	25.3	24.2	25.2	23.7	22.9	23.6	23.4	23.7	23.1
MO	62.3	51.3	52.0	49.0	46.9	46.6	46.9	46.6	48.9	49.2
MT	12.1	10.0	10.5	9.4	9.0	9.0	9.4	9.6	10.0	10.3
NE	22.4	18.0	18.7	17.7	16.5	17.1	17.6	17.1	18.0	16.2
NV	8.5	8.6	9.5	9.5	9.4	8.8	9.0	9.5	10.0	10.6
NH	11.7	11.1	11.3	10.8	10.1	10.3	10.1	9.9	9.1	8.8
NJ	94.6	81.5	76.3	69.8	67.0	66.7	67.1	66.1	68.6	69.5
NM	18.4	15.6	15.5	14.9	15.2	14.8	15.2	14.9	14.9	15.0
NY	204.1	166.8	154.6	143.3	133.6	134.6	133.0	132.7	135.5	137.2
NC	70.9	67.2	70.0	64.8	62.8	61.2	60.5	57.7	59.3	56.4
ND	9.9	8.1	8.1	7.7	7.6	7.4	7.3	7.5	7.8	7.9
OH	144.2	122.3	125.0	114.5	107.5	104.5	109.2	107.7	109.4	110.2
OK	39.3	34.6	36.8	35.6	33.0	32.7	30.5	31.9	33.4	32.9
OR	29.9	26.9	26.9	25.5	24.6	25.3	26.3	26.3	26.9	27.1
PA	146.5	127.2	118.9	110.5	104.8	103.9	103.7	102.0	105.4	106.5
RI	10.9	9.2	8.6	7.8	7.7	7.9	7.6	7.5	7.8	7.6
SC	38.7	34.5	37.0	32.5	33.0	30.7	31.3	30.6	33.3	32.5
SD	10.7	8.2	8.2	7.7	7.1	7.3	8.0	8.4	8.4	8.7
TN	49.8	43.3	48.6	46.1	44.8	45.1	44.2	40.6	40.6	43.5
TX	171.4	159.2	177.0	172.5	174.3	162.3	160.5	163.2	169.1	166.5
UT	20.0	19.9	22.9	21.2	22.2	23.5	24.2	26.4	29.1	27.9
VT	6.7	5.8	6.0	6.1	5.2	5.2	5.2	5.4	5.6	5.3
VA	66.6	61.0	65.0	60.6	58.4	57.3	56.9	56.1	59.6	59.6
WA	50.4	45.4	48.9	45.9	42.5	44.4	45.3	47.2	48.8	50.8
WV	23.4	22.3	22.9	21.9	21.1	20.1	20.2	19.9	20.6	20.7
WI	69.3	58.9	55.0	52.0	49.3	48.6	50.0	48.4	51.8	52.8
WY	6.1	5.7	6.1	5.8	5.7	5.8	6.2	6.0	5.9	6.1

Source: U.S. National Center for Education Statistics, *Digest of Education Statistics*, annual.

No. 281. General Educational Development (GED) Credentials Issued: 1974 to 1994

[Includes outlying areas]

YEAR	GED's issued (1,000)	PERCENT DISTRIBUTION BY AGE OF TEST TAKER				
		Under 19 years old	20 to 24 years old	25 to 29 years old	30 to 34 years old	35 years old or over
1974	295	35	27	13	9	17
1975	342	33	28	14	9	18
1980	488	37	27	13	8	15
1985	427	33	28	15	10	16
1990	419	35	25	14	10	17
1991	471	33	27	14	10	17
1992	465	32	28	13	11	16
1993	476	33	27	14	11	16
1994	496	35	26	13	10	16

Source: U.S. National Center for Education Statistics, *Digest of Education Statistics*, 1996.

282. College Enrollment of Recent High School Graduates: 1960 to 1995

[For persons 16 to 24 who graduated from high school in the preceding 12 months. Includes persons receiving GED's. Based on surveys and subject to sampling error]

YEAR	NUMBER OF HIGH SCHOOL GRADUATES (1,000)					PERCENT ENROLLED IN COLLEGE [2]				
	Total [1]	Male	Female	White	Black	Total [1]	Male	Female	White	Black
1960	1,679	756	923	1,565	(NA)	45.1	54.0	37.9	45.8	(NA)
1965	2,659	1,254	1,405	2,417	(NA)	50.9	57.3	45.3	51.7	(NA)
1970	2,757	1,343	1,414	2,461	(NA)	51.8	55.2	48.5	52.0	(NA)
1975	3,186	1,513	1,673	2,825	(NA)	50.7	52.6	49.0	51.2	(NA)
1980	3,089	1,500	1,589	2,682	361	49.3	46.7	51.8	49.9	41.8
1981	3,053	1,490	1,563	2,626	359	53.9	54.8	53.1	54.6	42.9
1982	3,100	1,508	1,592	2,644	384	50.6	49.0	52.1	52.0	36.5
1983	2,964	1,390	1,574	2,496	392	52.7	51.9	53.4	55.0	38.5
1984	3,012	1,429	1,583	2,514	438	55.2	56.0	54.5	57.9	40.2
1985	2,668	1,286	1,380	2,241	333	57.7	58.6	56.9	59.4	42.3
1986	2,786	1,331	1,455	2,307	386	53.8	55.9	51.9	56.0	36.5
1987	2,647	1,278	1,369	2,207	337	56.8	58.4	55.3	56.6	51.9
1988	2,673	1,334	1,339	2,187	382	58.9	57.0	60.8	60.7	45.0
1989	2,454	1,208	1,245	2,051	337	59.6	57.6	61.6	60.4	52.8
1990	2,355	1,169	1,185	1,921	341	59.9	57.8	62.0	61.5	46.3
1991	2,276	1,139	1,137	1,867	320	62.4	57.6	67.1	64.6	45.6
1992	2,398	1,216	1,182	1,900	353	61.7	59.6	63.8	63.4	47.9
1993	2,338	1,118	1,219	1,910	302	62.6	59.7	65.4	62.8	55.6
1994	2,517	1,244	1,273	2,065	318	61.9	60.6	63.2	63.6	50.9
1995	2,599	1,238	1,361	2,066	356	61.9	62.6	61.4	62.6	51.4

NA Not available. [1] Includes other races, not shown separately. [2] As of October.

Source: U.S. Department of Education Statistics, *Digest of Education Statistics*, 1996.

No. 283. College Enrollment, by Sex and Attendance Status: 1983 to 1994

[As of fall. In thousands]

SEX AND AGE	1983		1985		1991		1993		1994, prel.	
	Total	Part time	Total	Part time	Total	Part time	Total	Part time	Total	Part time
Total	12,465	5,204	13,539	5,878	14,359	6,244	14,305	6,177	14,279	6,141
Male	6,024	2,264	6,190	2,450	6,502	2,572	6,427	2,537	6,372	2,517
14 to 17 years old	102	16	71	12	46	6	83	10	66	13
18 to 19 years old	1,256	158	1,342	113	1,217	121	1,224	138	1,251	153
20 to 21 years old	1,241	205	1,189	196	1,306	230	1,294	209	1,185	221
22 to 24 years old	1,158	382	1,090	367	1,214	378	1,260	392	1,280	413
25 to 29 years old	1,115	624	1,036	639	1,082	587	950	564	890	483
30 to 34 years old	570	384	603	439	664	475	661	484	606	430
35 years old and over	583	494	857	682	972	775	955	739	1,092	806
Female	6,441	2,940	7,349	3,428	7,857	3,671	7,877	3,640	7,907	3,624
14 to 17 years old	142	16	101	12	76	-	93	6	96	9
18 to 19 years old	1,496	179	1,515	184	1,498	186	1,416	172	1,504	185
20 to 21 years old	1,125	204	1,253	213	1,462	240	1,414	279	1,353	231
22 to 24 years old	884	378	1,104	470	1,072	411	1,263	493	1,204	473
25 to 29 years old	947	658	1,052	732	1,053	679	1,058	689	1,045	670
30 to 34 years old	721	553	750	583	804	591	811	575	801	583
35 years old and over	1,126	953	1,574	1,253	1,896	1,563	1,824	1,427	1,903	1,504

Source: U.S. National Center for Education Statistics, *Digest of Education Statistics*, annual.

No. 284. College Enrollment, by Selected Characteristics: 1980 to 1995

[In thousands. As of fall. Totals may differ from other tables because of adjustments to underreported and nonreported racial/ethnic data. Nonresident alien students are not distributed among racial/ethnic groups]

CHARACTERISTIC	1980	1988	1990	1991	1992	1993	1994	1995, prel.
Total	**12,086.8**	**13,043.1**	**13,819.5**	**14,359.0**	**14,487.4**	**14,304.8**	**14,278.8**	**14,261.8**
Male	5,868.1	5,998.2	6,284.4	6,501.8	6,524.0	6,427.5	6,371.9	6,342.5
Female	6,218.7	7,044.9	7,535.1	7,857.1	7,963.4	7,877.4	7,906.9	7,919.2
Public	9,456.4	10,156.4	10,844.7	11,309.6	11,384.6	11,189.1	11,133.7	11,092.4
Private	2,630.4	2,886.7	2,974.8	3,049.4	3,101.7	3,115.7	3,145.1	3,169.4
2-year	4,521.4	4,868.1	5,240.1	5,651.9	5,722.4	5,565.9	5,529.7	5,492.5
4-year	7,565.4	8,175.0	8,579.4	8,707.1	8,765.0	8,738.9	8,749.1	8,769.3
Undergraduate	10,469.1	11,304.2	11,959.2	12,439.3	12,537.7	12,324.0	12,262.6	12,232.0
Graduate	1,340.9	1,471.9	1,586.2	1,639.1	1,688.7	1,688.4	1,721.5	1,732.0
First professional	276.8	267.1	274.1	280.5	280.9	292.4	294.7	297.6
White [1]	9,833.0	10,283.2	10,723.0	10,989.8	10,875.4	10,600.0	10,427.0	10,311.2
Male	4,772.9	4,711.6	4,861.3	4,962.2	4,884.6	4,755.0	4,650.7	4,594.1
Female	5,060.1	5,571.6	5,861.7	6,027.6	5,990.8	5,845.1	5,776.3	5,717.2
Public	7,656.1	7,963.8	8,385.4	8,622.2	8,492.8	8,226.6	8,056.3	7,945.4
Private	2,176.9	2,319.4	2,337.6	2,367.5	2,382.6	2,373.4	2,370.6	2,365.9
2-year	3,558.5	3,701.5	3,954.3	4,198.8	4,131.2	3,960.6	3,861.7	3,794.0
4-year	6,274.5	6,581.6	6,768.7	6,791.0	6,744.3	6,639.5	6,565.3	6,517.2
Undergraduate	8,480.7	8,906.7	9,272.6	9,507.7	9,387.6	9,100.4	8,916.0	8,805.6
Graduate	1,104.7	1,153.2	1,228.4	1,258.0	1,267.2	1,273.6	1,286.8	1,282.3
First professional	247.7	223.2	222.0	224.0	220.6	225.9	224.2	223.3
Black [1]	1,106.8	1,129.6	1,247.1	1,335.4	1,392.9	1,412.8	1,448.6	1,473.7
Male	463.7	442.7	484.7	517.0	536.9	543.7	549.7	555.9
Female	643.0	686.9	762.4	818.4	856.0	869.1	898.9	917.8
Public	876.1	881.1	976.5	1,053.4	1,100.5	1,114.3	1,144.6	1,160.7
Private	230.7	248.5	270.6	281.9	292.3	298.5	304.1	313.0
2-year	472.5	473.3	524.3	577.6	601.6	599.0	615.0	621.5
4-year	634.3	656.3	722.8	757.7	791.2	813.7	833.6	852.2
Undergraduate	1,018.8	1,038.8	1,147.2	1,229.3	1,280.6	1,290.4	1,317.3	1,333.6
Graduate	75.1	76.5	83.9	88.9	94.1	102.2	110.6	118.6
First professional	12.8	14.3	16.0	17.2	18.2	20.2	20.7	21.4
Hispanic	471.7	680.0	782.6	866.6	955.0	988.8	1,045.6	1,093.8
Male	231.6	310.3	354.0	390.5	427.7	441.2	464.0	480.2
Female	240.1	369.6	428.6	476.0	527.3	547.6	581.6	613.7
Public	406.2	586.9	671.4	742.1	822.3	851.3	898.7	937.1
Private	65.5	93.1	111.1	124.5	132.7	137.5	146.8	156.6
2-year	255.1	383.9	424.2	483.7	545.0	556.8	582.9	608.4
4-year	216.6	296.0	358.3	382.9	409.9	432.0	462.7	485.5
Undergraduate	433.1	631.2	724.6	804.2	887.8	918.1	968.3	1,012.0
Graduate	32.1	39.5	47.2	50.9	55.3	57.9	63.9	68.0
First professional	6.5	9.3	10.9	11.4	12.0	12.8	13.4	13.8
American Indian [1]	83.9	92.5	102.8	113.7	119.3	121.7	127.4	131.3
Male	37.8	39.1	43.1	47.6	50.2	51.2	53.0	54.8
Female	46.1	53.4	59.7	66.1	69.1	70.5	74.4	76.5
Public	74.2	81.1	90.4	100.2	103.3	106.4	110.7	113.8
Private	9.7	11.5	12.4	13.6	15.9	15.3	16.6	17.5
2-year	47.0	50.4	54.9	62.6	64.4	63.2	66.2	65.6
4-year	36.9	42.1	47.9	51.2	54.9	58.5	61.2	65.7
Undergraduate	77.9	85.9	95.5	105.8	110.9	112.7	117.4	120.7
Graduate	5.2	5.6	6.2	6.6	7.0	7.3	8.1	8.5
First professional	0.8	1.1	1.1	1.3	1.5	1.7	1.8	2.1
Asian [1]	286.4	496.7	572.5	637.2	697.0	724.4	774.3	797.4
Male	151.3	259.2	294.9	325.1	351.5	363.1	385.0	393.3
Female	135.2	237.5	277.6	312.0	345.6	361.3	389.3	404.1
Public	239.7	405.7	461.0	516.3	565.9	586.3	622.1	638.0
Private	46.7	91.0	111.6	120.9	131.1	138.2	152.2	159.4
2-year	124.3	199.3	215.2	255.7	289.5	295.0	312.5	314.9
4-year	162.1	297.4	357.3	381.5	407.5	429.4	461.8	482.4
Undergraduate	248.7	436.6	500.5	558.7	613.0	634.2	674.1	692.2
Graduate	31.6	45.7	53.2	57.6	61.5	65.2	72.6	75.6
First professional	6.1	14.4	18.8	20.8	22.5	25.0	27.6	29.6
Nonresident alien	305.0	361.2	391.5	416.4	447.7	457.1	455.9	454.4
Male	210.8	235.3	246.3	259.4	273.1	273.4	269.5	264.3
Female	94.2	125.9	145.2	157.0	174.6	183.7	186.4	190.1
Public	204.1	237.8	260.0	275.3	299.5	304.3	301.2	297.5
Private	100.8	123.3	131.5	141.0	148.1	152.7	154.7	156.9
2-year	64.1	59.6	67.1	73.5	90.6	91.2	91.4	88.1
4-year	240.9	301.5	324.4	342.8	357.0	365.9	364.5	366.2
Undergraduate	209.9	205.0	218.7	233.6	257.9	268.2	269.4	267.6
Graduate	92.2	151.4	167.3	177.0	183.6	182.0	179.5	179.5
First professional	2.9	4.7	5.4	5.8	6.2	6.9	7.0	7.3

[1] Non-Hispanic.

Source: U.S. National Center for Education Statistics, *Digest of Education Statistics*, annual.

No. 285. Foreign (Nonimmigrant) Student Enrollment in College: 1976 to 1996

[For fall of the previous year]

REGION OF ORIGIN	ENROLLMENT (1,000)									PERCENT ENROLLED IN—					
	1976	1980	1985	1990	1992	1993	1994	1995	1996	Engineering		Science[1]		Business	
										1980	1994	1980	1994	1980	1994
All regions	179	286	342	387	420	439	449	453	454	25	18	8	9	16	20
Africa	25	36	40	25	22	21	21	21	21	20	15	9	8	19	19
Nigeria	11	16	18	4	3	2	2	2	2	19	10	9	7	22	19
Asia[2]	97	165	200	245	277	291	294	292	290	32	21	8	10	16	20
China: Taiwan	11	18	23	31	36	37	37	36	33	17	21	15	7	17	23
Hong Kong	12	10	10	11	13	14	14	13	12	22	16	9	5	26	31
India	10	9	15	26	23	36	35	34	32	31	39	16	9	21	13
Indonesia	1	2	7	9	10	11	11	12	13	27	20	7	4	21	41
Iran	20	51	17	7	5	4	4	3	3	45	28	7	21	11	6
Japan	7	12	13	30	42	43	44	45	46	7	4	5	3	19	21
Malaysia	2	4	22	14	13	13	14	14	14	13	30	14	3	22	32
Saudi Arabia	3	10	8	4	4	4	4	4	4	30	32	4	5	14	12
South Korea	3	5	16	22	26	29	31	34	36	17	13	11	9	15	16
Thailand	7	7	7	7	8	9	9	11	12	17	14	6	3	26	42
Europe	14	23	33	46	54	58	62	65	67	15	11	9	9	14	22
Latin America[3]	30	42	49	48	43	43	45	47	47	20	15	8	7	14	23
Mexico	5	6	6	7	7	8	8	9	9	16	14	7	6	11	20
Venezuela	5	10	10	3	3	3	4	4	4	30	17	8	6	11	24
North America	10	16	16	19	20	22	23	23	24	8	6	6	6	13	11
Canada	10	15	15	18	19	21	22	23	23	8	6	6	6	12	11
Oceania	3	4	4	4	4	4	4	4	4	5	5	7	6	16	16

[1] Physical and life sciences. [2] Includes countries not shown separately. [3] Includes Central America, Caribbean, and South America.

Source: Institute of International Education, New York, NY, *Open Doors*, annual (copyright).

No. 286. College Enrollment, by Sex, Age, Race, and Hispanic Origin: 1975 to 1995

[In thousands. As of October for the civilian noninstitutional population, 14 years old and over. Based on the Current Population Survey; see text, section 1, and Appendix III]

CHARACTERISTIC	1975	1980	1985	1988[1]	1989	1990	1991	1992	1993	1994	1995
Total[2]	10,880	11,387	12,524	13,116	13,180	13,621	14,057	14,035	13,898	15,022	14,715
Male[3]	5,911	5,430	5,906	5,950	5,950	6,192	6,439	6,192	6,324	6,764	6,703
18 to 24 years	3,693	3,604	3,749	3,770	3,717	3,922	3,954	3,912	3,994	4,152	4,089
25 to 34 years	1,521	1,325	1,464	1,395	1,443	1,412	1,605	1,392	1,406	1,589	1,561
35 years old and over	569	405	561	727	716	772	832	789	873	958	985
Female[3]	4,969	5,957	6,618	7,166	7,231	7,429	7,618	7,844	7,574	8,258	8,013
18 to 24 years	3,243	3,625	3,788	4,021	4,065	4,042	4,218	4,429	4,199	4,576	4,452
25 to 34 years	947	1,378	1,599	1,568	1,639	1,749	1,680	1,732	1,688	1,830	1,788
35 years old and over	614	802	1,100	1,452	1,396	1,546	1,636	1,575	1,616	1,786	1,684
White[3]	9,546	9,925	10,781	11,140	11,243	11,488	11,686	11,710	11,434	12,222	12,021
18 to 24 years	6,116	6,334	6,500	6,659	6,631	6,635	6,813	6,916	6,763	7,118	7,011
25 to 34 years	2,147	2,328	2,604	2,448	2,597	2,698	2,661	2,582	2,505	2,735	2,686
35 years old and over	1,031	1,051	1,448	1,896	1,868	2,023	2,107	2,053	2,068	2,267	2,208
Male	5,263	4,804	5,103	5,078	5,136	5,235	5,304	5,210	5,222	5,524	5,535
Female	4,284	5,121	5,679	6,063	6,107	6,253	6,382	6,499	6,212	6,698	6,486
Black[3]	1,099	1,163	1,263	1,321	1,287	1,393	1,477	1,424	1,545	1,800	1,772
18 to 24 years	665	688	734	752	835	894	828	886	861	1,001	988
25 to 34 years	248	269	295	330	275	258	373	302	386	440	426
35 years old and over	152	156	213	206	146	207	257	208	284	323	334
Male	523	476	552	494	480	587	629	527	636	745	710
Female	577	686	712	827	807	807	848	897	909	1,054	1,062
Hispanic origin[3,4]	411	443	580	747	754	748	830	918	995	1,187	1,207
18 to 24 years	295	315	375	450	453	435	516	586	602	662	745
25 to 34 years	103	118	189	191	170	168	196	214	249	312	250
35 years old and over	(NA)	(NA)	(NA)	93	114	130	109	102	129	205	193
Male	218	222	279	355	353	364	347	388	442	529	568
Female	193	221	299	391	401	384	483	530	553	659	639

NA Not available. [1] Beginning 1988, based on a revised edit and tabulation package. [2] Includes other races not shown separately. [3] Includes persons 14 to 17 years old, not shown separately. [4] Persons of Hispanic origin may be of any race.

Source: U.S. Bureau of the Census, *Current Population Reports*, P20-492; and earlier reports.

No. 287. Higher Education—Summary: 1970 to 1995

ions, staff, and enrollment as of fall. Finances for fiscal year ending in the following year. Covers universities, col- ofessional schools, junior and teachers colleges, both publicly and privately controlled, regular session. Includes estimates utions not reporting. See also Appendix III]

ITEM	Unit	1970	1980	1985	1990	1991	1992	1993	1994, est.	1995, est.
L INSTITUTIONS										
of institutions [1]	Number	2,556	3,231	3,340	3,559	3,601	3,638	3,632	3,688	3,706
r	Number	1,665	1,957	2,029	2,141	2,157	2,169	2,190	2,215	2,244
r	Number	891	1,274	1,311	1,418	1,444	1,469	1,442	1,473	1,462
ional staff—										
ter or above) [2]	1,000	474	686	715	817	826	877	915	918	910
nt full-time	Percent	78	66	64	61	65	(NA)	60	(NA)	(NA)
rollment [3]	1,000	8,581	12,097	12,247	13,819	14,359	14,486	14,305	14,279	14,262
	1,000	5,044	5,874	5,818	6,284	6,502	6,524	6,427	6,372	6,343
le	1,000	3,537	6,223	6,429	7,535	7,857	7,963	7,877	7,907	7,919
r institutions	1,000	6,262	7,571	7,716	8,579	8,707	8,765	8,739	8,749	8,769
r institutions	1,000	2,319	4,526	4,531	5,240	5,652	5,722	5,566	5,530	5,493
me	1,000	5,816	7,098	7,075	7,821	8,115	8,162	8,128	8,138	8,129
ime	1,000	2,765	4,999	5,172	5,998	6,244	6,325	6,177	6,141	6,133
	1,000	6,428	9,457	9,479	10,845	11,310	11,385	11,189	11,134	11,092
e	1,000	2,153	2,640	2,768	2,974	3,049	3,102	3,116	3,145	3,169
rgraduate [4]	1,000	7,376	10,475	10,597	11,959	12,439	12,538	12,324	12,263	12,232
n	1,000	4,254	5,000	4,962	5,380	5,571	5,583	5,484	5,422	5,401
men	1,000	3,122	5,475	5,635	6,579	6,868	6,955	6,840	6,840	6,831
ll-time freshmen	1,000	2,063	2,588	2,292	2,257	2,278	2,184	2,161	2,133	2,169
professional	1,000	173	278	274	273	281	281	292	295	298
n	1,000	159	199	180	167	170	169	173	174	174
men	1,000	15	78	94	107	111	112	120	121	124
uate [4]	1,000	1,031	1,343	1,376	1,586	1,639	1,669	1,688	1,721	1,732
n	1,000	630	675	677	737	761	772	771	776	768
men	1,000	400	670	700	849	878	896	917	946	965
funds revenues [5]	Mil. dol	23,879	65,585	100,438	149,766	161,396	170,881	179,227	(NA)	(NA)
n and fees	Mil. dol	5,021	13,773	23,117	37,434	41,559	45,346	48,647	(NA)	(NA)
al government	Mil. dol	4,190	9,748	12,705	18,236	19,833	21,015	22,076	(NA)	(NA)
government	Mil. dol	6,503	20,106	29,912	39,481	40,587	41,248	41,910	(NA)	(NA)
ary enterprises	Mil. dol	3,125	7,287	10,674	14,903	15,759	16,663	17,538	(NA)	(NA)
nds [6]	Mil. dol	(NA)	4,774	7,713	(NA)	(NA)	(NA)	(NA)	(NA)	(NA)
in fund balance [7]	Mil. dol	498	2,793	7,239	(NA)	(NA)	(NA)	(NA)	(NA)	(NA)
funds expenditures [5]	Mil. dol	23,375	64,053	97,536	146,088	156,189	165,241	173,351	(NA)	(NA)
tional and general [8]	Mil. dol	17,616	50,074	76,128	114,140	121,567	128,978	136,024	(NA)	(NA)
ary enterprises [9]	Mil. dol	2,988	7,286	10,528	14,272	14,966	15,562	16,429	(NA)	(NA)
ddition to plant value	Mil. dol	4,165	6,471	10,149	19,672	(NA)	(NA)	(NA)	(NA)	(NA)
plant	Mil. dol	46,054	88,761	122,261	190,355	(NA)	(NA)	(NA)	(NA)	(NA)
ent (market value)	Mil. dol	13,714	23,465	50,281	72,049	(NA)	(NA)	(NA)	(NA)	(NA)
EAR INSTITUTIONS										
of institutions [1, 10]	Number	891	1,274	1,311	1,418	1,444	1,469	1,442	1,473	1,462
	Number	654	945	932	972	999	1,024	1,021	1,036	1,047
e	Number	237	329	379	446	445	445	421	437	415
ional staff—										
ter or above) [2]	1,000	92	192	211	(NA)	236	(NA)	290	(NA)	(NA)
ent [3, 4]	1,000	2,319	4,526	4,531	5,240	5,652	5,722	5,566	5,530	5,493
	1,000	2,195	4,329	4,270	4,996	5,405	5,485	5,337	5,308	5,278
e	1,000	124	198	261	244	247	238	229	221	215
	1,000	1,375	2,047	2,002	2,233	2,402	2,413	2,345	2,323	2,329
le	1,000	945	2,479	2,529	3,007	3,250	3,309	3,220	3,207	3,164
funds revenue [5]	Mil. dol	2,504	8,505	12,293	18,021	19,585	20,805	21,961	(NA)	(NA)
n and fees	Mil. dol	413	1,618	2,618	4,029	4,649	5,218	5,594	(NA)	(NA)
government	Mil. dol	926	3,961	5,659	8,001	8,537	8,647	8,730	(NA)	(NA)
government	Mil. dol	701	1,623	2,027	3,044	3,259	3,524	3,936	(NA)	(NA)
funds expenditures	Mil. dol	2,327	8,212	11,976	17,494	18,814	19,941	21,187	(NA)	(NA)
tion and general [8]	Mil. dol	2,073	7,608	11,118	16,270	17,462	18,578	19,763	(NA)	(NA)
truction	Mil. dol	1,205	3,764	5,398	7,903	8,547	9,018	9,476	(NA)	(NA)

Not available. [1] Beginning 1980, number of institutions includes count of branch campuses. Due to revised survey res, data beginning 1990 are not comparable with previous years. [2] Due to revised survey methods, data beginning t comparable with previous years. [3] Beginning 1980, branch campuses counted according to actual status, e.g., 2-year n 2-year category; previously a 2-year branch included in university category. [4] Includes unclassified students. (Students ourses for credit, but are not candidates for degrees.) [5] Includes items not shown separately. [6] Annual net increase funds. [7] Includes endowment, and, beginning 1980, annuity and student loans. [8] Data for 1970 are not strictly ble with later years. [9] Includes activities. [10] Beginning 1980, includes schools accredited by the National Association and Technical Schools.

rce: U.S. National Center for Education Statistics, *Digest of Education Statistics*, annual; *Projections of Education* , annual; and unpublished data.

No. 288. Colleges—Number and Enrollment, by State: 1995

[Number of institutions beginning in academic year. Opening fall enrollment of resident and extension students attending full-time or part-time. Excludes students taking courses for credit by mail, radio, or TV, and students in branches of U.S. institutions operated in foreign countries. See Appendix III]

STATE	Number of institutions [1]	ENROLLMENT, prel. (1,000)										
		Total	Male	Female	Public	Private	Full time	White [2]	Minority enrollment			Nonresident alien
									Total [3]	Black [2]	Hispanic	
United States	3,706	14,262	6,343	7,919	11,092	3,169	8,129	10,311	3,496	1,474	1,094	464
Alabama	82	226	100	126	203	22	152	163	58	52	2	5
Alaska	9	29	12	17	28	1	12	23	6	1	1	1
Arizona	45	274	123	151	255	19	126	200	67	9	39	7
Arkansas	38	98	42	56	87	11	67	79	17	14	1	2
California	348	1,817	819	998	1,564	253	867	905	832	138	368	80
Colorado	59	243	111	132	210	32	129	196	42	8	22	6
Connecticut	42	158	69	89	101	57	82	126	26	12	8	6
Delaware	9	44	19	25	36	8	26	35	8	6	1	1
District of Columbia	19	78	35	43	10	68	51	38	32	24	3	8
Florida	114	637	278	360	531	107	305	426	191	83	86	20
Georgia	120	315	135	180	249	66	210	216	91	77	5	8
Hawaii	17	63	28	35	50	13	35	17	41	1	1	6
Idaho	12	60	27	33	49	11	40	55	4	(Z)	2	1
Illinois	169	718	316	402	530	188	368	509	191	91	58	18
Indiana	78	290	132	157	225	65	190	250	31	18	6	9
Iowa	59	174	78	96	122	51	121	154	12	5	3	7
Kansas	54	178	79	99	160	17	98	150	22	9	6	6
Kentucky	61	179	74	105	149	30	118	160	18	12	1	3
Louisiana	36	204	86	118	175	29	144	135	63	53	5	6
Maine	33	57	23	34	38	18	32	53	3	1	(Z)	1
Maryland	57	266	112	154	223	43	127	178	79	58	6	9
Massachusetts	118	414	181	233	177	237	262	322	67	23	18	24
Michigan	109	548	241	307	462	86	274	440	91	60	12	17
Minnesota	107	281	126	155	217	64	158	250	24	8	4	6
Mississippi	46	123	53	70	111	12	92	83	38	36	1	2
Missouri	101	292	127	164	190	102	166	246	38	25	5	7
Montana	26	43	20	23	37	5	33	37	5	(Z)	(Z)	1
Nebraska	35	116	52	63	96	20	67	104	9	3	2	3
Nevada	10	68	30	38	67	1	22	52	14	4	5	2
New Hampshire	30	64	27	37	36	28	40	60	3	1	1	1
New Jersey	61	334	146	188	271	63	175	230	92	39	31	11
New Mexico	35	102	43	59	97	5	52	57	43	3	32	2
New York	311	1,042	444	597	588	453	665	691	306	136	100	45
North Carolina	121	372	160	212	303	69	238	278	88	73	4	6
North Dakota	20	40	20	20	37	4	32	36	3	(Z)	(Z)	2
Ohio	156	540	242	298	410	130	338	453	72	51	8	16
Oklahoma	45	181	82	96	158	23	108	137	35	13	4	8
Oregon	45	167	77	90	144	24	89	139	22	3	8	6
Pennsylvania	217	618	278	340	340	278	388	517	84	51	11	17
Rhode Island	12	74	33	41	39	35	47	63	9	3	3	3
South Carolina	59	174	73	101	149	25	109	128	43	39	2	3
South Dakota	21	37	16	20	30	7	27	33	3	(Z)	(Z)	1
Tennessee	76	246	108	138	193	53	160	196	43	36	2	5
Texas	179	953	436	514	837	116	516	590	336	94	195	26
Utah	17	147	74	73	111	37	96	133	9	1	4	5
Vermont	22	35	15	20	20	15	24	32	2	(Z)	(Z)	1
Virginia	89	356	155	201	293	63	200	284	64	57	8	8
Washington	64	286	126	159	247	39	176	228	48	11	10	9
West Virginia	28	86	38	48	75	11	60	79	5	3	(Z)	2
Wisconsin	66	300	132	168	246	54	182	265	28	13	6	7
Wyoming	9	30	13	17	29	1	18	28	2	(Z)	1	(Z)
U.S. military [4]	10	88	74	14	88	-	19	70	17	12	3	1

- Represents zero. Z Fewer than 500. [1] Branch campuses counted as separate institutions. [2] Non-Hispanic. [3] Includes other races not shown separately. [4] Service schools.

Source: U.S. National Center for Education Statistics, *Digest of Education Statistics*, annual.

No. 289. Higher Education Price Indexes: 1965 to 1995

[1983=100. For years ending June 30. Reflects prices paid by colleges and universities]

YEAR	Index, total	PERSONNEL COMPENSATION: Total	Professional salaries	Nonprofessional salaries	Fringe benefits	CONTRACTED SERVICES, SUPPLIES, AND EQUIPMENT: Total	Services	Supplies and materials	Equipment	Library acquisitions	Utilities
965 . .	29.8	30.5	34.9	31.0	13.0	27.6	35.6	33.8	36.0	19.3	15.7
970 . .	39.5	42.1	47.7	38.8	24.7	31.9	42.8	37.6	41.9	25.7	16.3
971 . .	42.1	44.8	50.1	41.8	28.0	34.1	45.1	39.0	43.5	30.8	18.0
972 . .	44.3	47.1	52.0	44.9	31.1	36.0	47.8	39.8	45.1	34.9	19.2
973 . .	46.7	49.8	54.3	47.6	34.7	37.6	49.9	41.1	46.5	37.7	20.2
974 . .	49.9	52.8	57.2	50.6	38.6	41.4	52.2	46.5	49.4	41.6	24.8
975 . .	54.3	56.3	60.3	54.6	42.9	48.5	56.8	58.0	58.3	46.7	31.8
976 . .	57.8	60.0	63.5	59.0	47.8	51.3	59.1	60.7	61.7	52.1	34.4
977 . .	61.5	63.5	66.4	63.1	52.8	55.7	62.6	63.8	64.8	56.8	40.5
978 . .	65.7	67.6	69.9	68.1	58.4	60.2	66.6	66.6	69.3	63.2	45.9
979 . .	70.5	72.4	74.1	73.4	64.5	65.1	71.2	71.7	74.7	70.0	50.3
980 . .	77.5	78.4	79.4	80.2	72.6	75.0	77.0	84.6	81.6	77.8	64.1
981 . .	85.8	85.8	86.3	87.7	81.8	85.9	86.2	95.6	89.6	85.9	79.7
982 . .	93.9	93.5	93.7	94.6	91.5	94.9	94.2	100.4	96.4	93.5	92.4
983 . .	100.0	100.0	100.0	100.0	100.0	100.0	100.0	100.0	100.0	100.0	100.0
984 . .	104.8	105.4	104.7	105.1	108.3	103.0	104.9	99.7	102.3	105.3	102.5
985 . .	110.8	112.0	111.4	109.2	117.7	107.1	110.8	103.0	104.8	111.3	105.3
986 . .	116.3	118.8	118.2	112.8	127.7	109.0	115.1	102.6	107.2	121.2	103.1
987 . .	120.9	125.4	125.0	116.3	137.4	107.4	119.7	99.0	108.9	132.9	91.0
988 . .	126.1	131.7	130.9	120.6	147.1	109.8	123.0	101.1	120.5	140.5	87.7
989 . .	132.8	139.5	138.8	125.3	158.7	112.8	128.8	106.3	115.1	153.5	85.3
990 . .	140.8	148.3	147.6	130.3	171.3	118.7	134.0	114.3	119.6	167.0	90.1
991 . .	148.2	156.5	155.6	135.4	184.4	123.2	139.8	116.4	123.3	179.8	92.2
992 . .	153.4	162.4	160.8	140.2	193.8	126.9	145.7	115.2	126.3	193.9	93.3
993 . .	157.9	167.6	165.0	144.2	204.2	129.4	149.5	113.2	128.6	203.7	94.7
994 . .	163.3	173.4	170.3	148.2	214.1	133.6	154.8	114.3	130.8	213.6	96.7
995 . .	168.2	179.1	176.1	152.5	221.4	135.9	158.0	115.7	133.5	226.6	96.8

Source: Research Associates of Washington, Washington, DC, *Inflation Measures for Schools, Colleges, and Libraries*, nnual (copyright).

No. 290. Institutions of Higher Education—Finances: 1980 to 1994

[In millions of dollars. For fiscal years ending in year shown. For coverage, see headnote, table 287. See also Appendix III]

ITEM	1980	1985	1990	1991	1992	1993	1994: Total	1994: Public	1994: Private
urrent funds revenues	58,520	92,473	139,635	149,766	161,396	170,861	179,227	112,968	66,259
Tuition and fees	11,930	21,283	33,926	37,434	41,559	45,346	48,647	20,825	27,821
Federal government	8,902	11,509	17,255	18,236	19,833	21,015	22,076	12,465	9,611
State government	18,378	27,583	38,349	39,481	40,587	41,248	41,910	40,536	1,374
Local government	1,588	2,387	3,640	3,931	4,160	4,445	4,998	4,509	490
Private gifts, grants, and contracts [1]	2,808	4,896	7,781	8,361	8,977	9,660	10,203	4,521	5,682
Endowment earnings	1,177	2,096	3,144	3,269	3,442	3,628	3,670	639	3,030
Educational activities [2]	1,239	2,127	3,632	4,055	4,521	5,038	5,294	3,330	1,964
Auxiliary enterprises	6,481	10,100	13,938	14,903	15,759	16,663	17,536	10,815	6,723
Hospitals	(3)	7,475	13,217	15,150	17,240	18,124	18,960	12,260	6,700
Other funds revenues [4]	6,015	3,015	4,753	4,946	5,318	5,715	5,931	3,068	2,864
urrent funds expenditures [5]	56,914	89,951	134,656	146,088	156,189	165,241	173,351	109,310	64,041
Educational and general	44,543	70,061	105,585	114,140	121,567	128,978	136,023	87,139	48,885
Instruction	18,497	28,777	42,146	45,496	47,997	50,341	52,776	35,688	17,087
Institutional support	5,054	8,587	12,674	13,726	14,475	15,250	15,926	9,328	6,598
Research	5,099	7,552	12,506	13,444	14,262	15,291	16,118	11,180	4,937
Plant operation [6]	4,700	7,345	9,458	10,063	10,347	10,784	11,368	7,433	3,935
Academic support	3,876	6,074	9,438	10,051	10,577	11,073	11,678	8,036	3,642
Libraries	1,624	2,362	3,254	3,344	3,596	3,685	3,906	2,449	1,459
Student services	2,587	4,178	6,388	7,025	7,509	8,165	8,563	5,315	3,247
Scholarships and fellowships . . .	2,200	3,670	6,656	7,551	9,060	10,148	11,238	4,223	7,015
Unrestricted funds	905	1,962	3,854	4,445	5,206	5,949	6,645	1,935	4,710
Restricted funds	1,296	1,709	2,802	3,106	3,854	4,199	4,593	2,288	2,305
Public service	1,817	2,861	4,690	5,076	5,489	5,935	6,242	4,742	1,501
Mandatory transfers	732	1,016	1,630	1,707	1,851	1,991	2,115	1,193	922
Auxiliary enterprises [5]	6,486	10,012	13,204	14,272	14,966	15,562	16,429	10,638	5,792
Hospitals [5]	4,757	8,010	12,679	14,326	16,104	17,050	17,510	11,318	6,192
Independent operations [5]	1,128	1,868	3,187	3,350	3,552	3,652	3,387	215	3,172

[1] Private grants represent nongovernmental revenue for sponsored research and other sponsored programs; includes private ontracts. [2] Sales and service of educational departments only. [3] Included in other. [4] Includes sales and services of federally unded research and development centers, and others sources. [5] Includes mandatory transfers which are primarily current xpenditures for plant. [6] Includes maintenance.

Source: U.S. National Center for Education Statistics, *Digest of Education Statistics*, annual.

No. 291. Major Federal Student Financial Assistance Programs: 1970 to 1996

[For award years July 1 of year shown to the following June 30, except as indicated. Funds utilized exclude operating costs, etc., and represent funds given to students]

PROGRAM	Unit	1970	1980	1985	1990	1992	1993	1994	1995, est.	1996, est.
Pell Grants:										
Number of recipients	1,000	(X)	2,708	2,813	3,405	4,002	3,756	3,675	3,620	3,601
Funds utilized	Mil. dol.	(X)	2,387	3,597	4,935	6,176	5,654	5,519	5,427	5,642
Average grant	Dollars	(X)	882	1,279	1,449	1,543	1,506	1,502	1,499	1,567
Supplemental Educational Opportunity Grants: [1]										
Number of recipients	1,000	253.4	716.5	686.0	761.2	976.3	1,068	1,056	991	991
Funds utilized	Mil. dol.	134	368	410	503	651	752	755	738	738
Average grant	Dollars	527	513	598	661	667	705	715	745	745
College Work-Study:										
Number of recipients	1,000	425.0	819.1	728.4	687.4	714.4	711	700	713	713
Funds utilized [2]	Mil. dol.	200	660	656	727	780	771	757	760	760
Average annual earnings	Dollars	470	806	901	1,059	1,097	1,084	1,081	1,065	1,065
Perkins Loans: [3]										
Number of recipients	1,000	452.0	813.4	700.9	660.2	669.0	684	663	744	764
Loan funds utilized [2]	Mil. dol.	241	694	703	870	868	918	970	999	1,026
Average loan	Dollars	532	853	1,003	1,318	1,333	1,342	1,464	1,342	1,342
Loans in default [4]	Mil. dol.	(NA)	612.0	690.0	727.5	569.3	733	760	(NA)	(NA)
Default rate	Percent	(NA)	11.6	8.3	6.2	12.2	11.42	10.76	(NA)	(NA)
Federal Family Education Loans [5]										
Number of loans	1,000	1,017	2,905	3,833	4,493	5,130	5,647	6,393	6,541	5,083
Loan funds utilized [6]	Mil. dol.	1,015	6,200	8,913	12,291	14,749	17,863	21,176	22,936	18,756
Average loan	Dollars	998	2,135	2,374	2,734	2,875	3,163	3,312	3,507	3,690
Default rate [7]	Percent	(NA)	10.1	9.0	10.4	11.6	13.4	12.9	12.5	(NA)

NA Not available. X Not applicable. [1] For 1970, data represents Educational Opportunity Grants Program. [2] Includes institutional matching funds. [3] Formerly National Direct Student Loans. [4] Loans in default represents all loans in institutions' portfolio. [5] Formerly Guaranteed Student Loans. Beginning with 1985, data include activity under the Stafford program, the PLUS (Parent Loans for Undergraduate Students), FISL (Federally Insured Student Loans), and SLS (Supplemental Loans Students) programs. [6] Represents dollar amount of commitments. [7] Cumulative dollar amount of default claims to lenders, minus cumulative collections as a percent of all loans that have ever gone into repayment.

Source: U.S. Dept. of Education, Office of Postsecondary Education, unpublished data.

No. 292. Finances of Public Colleges, 1990 to 1994, and by State, 1995

[For academic years ending in year shown. Data provided by the State higher education finance officers, except as noted]

STATE	FTE [1] enrollment (1,000)	Appropriations for current operations [2] (mil. dol.)	Net tuition revenues (mil. dol.)[3]	STATE	FTE [1] enrollment (1,000)	Appropriations for current operations [2] (mil. dol.)	Net tuition revenues (mil. dol.)[3]
Total, 1990	7,883.0	33,857.6	11,310.2	Michigan	340.1	1,580.8	1,265.8
Total, 1991	8,088.1	35,211.9	12,474.5	Minnesota	167.5	835.8	359.8
Total, 1992	8,288.0	35,025.0	14,192.0	Mississippi	100.8	433.1	202.8
Total, 1993	8,359.9	35,272.0	15,764.0	Missouri	130.6	638.6	395.4
Total, 1994	8,296.4	36,619.0	16,664.0	Montana	32.1	114.7	66.4
				Nebraska	68.3	291.4	116.3
Total, 1995	8,288.7	38,636.1	17,671.7	Nevada	35.1	170.9	42.1
Alabama	179.3	732.2	396.4	New Hampshire	26.7	80.7	139.0
Alaska	16.6	157.8	32.8	New Jersey [4]	194.2	1,175.8	450.0
Arizona	160.5	733.9	330.3	New Mexico	68.6	414.5	97.1
Arkansas	74.0	301.5	158.6	New York	443.1	2,505.0	868.2
California	1,257.5	5,535.2	1,382.5	North Carolina	239.3	1,365.4	346.3
Colorado	135.0	444.0	406.4	North Dakota	30.0	115.7	66.0
Connecticut	59.3	405.2	188.5	Ohio	342.9	1,323.5	1,056.3
Delaware	26.5	118.8	155.4	Oklahoma	114.5	488.3	193.4
District of Columbia	7.9	49.9	9.3	Oregon	95.5	422.4	200.5
Florida	362.5	1,807.7	491.2	Pennsylvania	290.4	1,362.5	1,219.8
Georgia	206.2	1,097.1	348.6	Rhode Island	25.7	120.1	108.8
Hawaii	33.4	276.8	32.7	South Carolina	126.5	481.2	312.8
Idaho	40.2	217.2	66.8	South Dakota	22.9	80.6	53.9
Illinois	356.3	1,760.7	449.4	Tennessee	153.1	715.2	286.0
Indiana	172.6	765.0	535.0	Texas	624.3	2,825.7	1,169.6
Iowa	93.6	529.5	274.4	Utah	79.7	360.8	137.9
Kansas	106.3	485.9	203.9	Vermont	15.4	35.6	128.6
Kentucky	117.4	446.4	208.6	Virginia	217.7	782.3	626.8
Louisiana	135.9	420.7	314.7	Washington	187.1	827.1	305.1
Maine	27.9	158.3	93.6	West Virginia	61.5	179.4	140.3
Maryland	160.3	692.8	483.6	Wisconsin	181.5	1,032.1	408.3
Massachusetts	116.8	575.0	312.3	Wyoming	21.5	142.3	34.4

[1] Full-time equivalent (FTE). Credit and noncredit program enrollment including summer session. Excludes medical enrollments. [2] State and local appropriations. Includes aid to students attending in-State public institutions. Excludes sums for research, agriculture stations and cooperative extension, and hospitals and medical schools. [3] Excludes appropriated aid to students attending in-State public institutions. [4] Estimated by source.

Source: Research Associates of Washington, Washington, DC, *State Profiles: Financing Public Higher Education*, annual (copyright).

No. 293. Institutions of Higher Education—Charges: 1985 to 1996

[In dollars. Estimated. For the entire academic year ending in year shown. Figures are average charges per full-time equivalent student. Room and board are based on full-time students]

ACADEMIC CONTROL AND YEAR	TUITION AND REQUIRED FEES [1]				BOARD RATES [2]				DORMITORY CHARGES			
	All institutions	2-yr. colleges	4-yr. colleges	Other 4-yr. schools	All institutions	2-yr. colleges	4-yr. colleges	Other 4-yr. schools	All institutions	2-yr. colleges	4-yr. colleges	Other 4-yr. schools
Public:												
1985	971	584	1,386	1,117	1,241	1,302	1,276	1,201	1,196	921	1,237	1,200
1988	1,218	706	1,726	1,407	1,454	1,417	1,462	1,434	1,378	943	1,410	1,409
1989	1,285	730	1,846	1,515	1,533	1,488	1,576	1,504	1,457	965	1,483	1,506
1990	1,356	756	2,035	1,608	1,635	1,581	1,728	1,561	1,513	962	1,561	1,554
1991	1,454	824	2,159	1,707	1,691	1,594	1,767	1,641	1,612	1,050	1,658	1,655
1992	1,624	937	2,410	1,933	1,780	1,612	1,852	1,745	1,731	1,074	1,789	1,782
1993	1,782	1,025	2,604	2,192	1,841	1,668	1,982	1,761	1,756	1,108	1,856	1,787
1994	1,942	1,125	2,820	2,360	1,880	1,681	1,993	1,828	1,873	1,190	1,897	1,958
1995	2,057	1,192	2,977	2,499	1,949	1,712	2,108	1,866	1,959	1,232	1,992	2,044
1996 [3]	2,176	1,245	3,151	2,661	2,019	1,688	2,193	1,936	2,057	1,303	2,107	2,130
Private:												
1985	5,315	3,485	6,843	5,135	1,462	1,294	1,647	1,405	1,426	1,424	1,753	1,309
1988	6,988	4,161	8,771	6,574	1,775	1,537	2,060	1,667	1,748	1,380	2,244	1,593
1989	7,461	4,817	9,451	7,172	1,880	1,609	2,269	1,762	1,849	1,540	2,353	1,686
1990	8,174	5,196	10,348	7,778	1,948	1,811	2,339	1,823	1,923	1,663	2,411	1,774
1991	8,772	5,570	11,379	8,389	2,074	1,989	2,470	1,943	2,063	1,744	2,654	1,889
1992	9,434	5,752	12,192	9,053	2,252	2,090	2,727	2,098	2,221	1,789	2,860	2,038
1993	9,942	6,059	13,055	9,533	2,344	1,875	2,825	2,197	2,348	1,970	3,018	2,151
1994	10,572	6,370	13,874	10,100	2,434	1,970	2,946	2,278	2,490	2,067	3,277	2,261
1995	11,111	6,914	14,537	10,653	2,509	2,023	3,035	2,362	2,587	2,233	3,469	2,347
1996 [3]	11,858	7,039	15,581	11,294	2,610	2,100	3,216	2,434	2,739	2,363	3,672	2,475

[1] For in-State students. [2] Beginning 1988, rates reflect 20 meals per week, rather than meals served 7 days a week. [3] Preliminary.

Source: U.S. National Center for Education Statistics, *Digest of Education Statistics*, annual.

No. 294. Voluntary Financial Support of Higher Education: 1970 to 1995

[For school years ending in years shown; enrollment as of fall of preceding year. Voluntary support, as defined in Gift Reporting Standards, excludes income from endowment and other invested funds as well as all support received from Federal, State, and local governments and their agencies and contract research]

ITEM	Unit	1970	1980	1985	1990	1992	1993	1994	1995
Estimated support, total [1]	Mil. dol.	1,780	3,800	6,320	9,800	10,706	11,200	12,350	12,750
Individuals	Mil. dol	822	1,757	2,876	4,770	5,340	5,510	6,210	6,540
Alumni	Mil. dol	381	910	1,460	2,540	2,840	2,960	3,410	3,600
Business corporations	Mil. dol	269	696	1,574	2,170	2,260	2,400	2,510	2,560
Foundations	Mil. dol	434	903	1,175	1,920	2,090	2,200	2,540	2,460
Religious organizations	Mil. dol	102	155	208	240	240	250	240	250
Current operations	Mil. dol	960	2,250	3,800	5,440	6,100	6,300	6,710	7,230
Capital purposes	Mil. dol	820	1,550	2,520	4,360	4,600	4,900	5,640	5,520
Enrollment, higher education	1,000	8,094	11,570	12,242	13,539	14,359	14,486	14,306	14,279
Support per student	Dollars	220	328	516	724	745	773	863	893
In 1994-95 dollars	Dollars	875	636	734	857	811	816	889	893
Expenditures, higher education	Bil. dol	24.7	62.5	98.3	150.6	172.8	182.7	191.5	200.8
Expenditures per student	Dollars	3,052	5,402	8,026	11,120	12,037	12,611	13,386	14,063
In 1994-95 dollars	Dollars	12,426	10,457	11,417	13,166	13,097	13,306	13,782	14,063
Institutions reporting support	Number	1,045	1,019	1,114	1,056	1,060	1,106	992	1,086
Total support reported	Mil. dol.	1,472	3,055	5,295	8,214	9,033	9,491	10,326	10,992
Private 4-year institutions	Mil. dol	1,154	2,178	3,522	5,072	5,360	5,767	6,103	6,500
Public 4-year institutions	Mil. dol	292	856	1,728	3,056	3,583	3,610	4,138	4,382
2-year colleges	Mil. dol	26	20	45	85	89	115	84	110

[1] Includes other contributions, not shown separately.

Source: Council for Aid to Education, New York, NY, *Voluntary Support of Education*, annual.

No. 295. Average Salaries for College Faculty Members: 1994 to 1996

[In thousands of dollars. For academic year ending in year shown. Figures are for 9 months teaching for full-time faculty members in 4-year institutions. Fringe benefits averaged in 1994 $12,000 in public institutions and $13,900 in private institutions, in 1995, $12'400 in public institutions and $14,300 in private institutions, and in 1996, $12,600 in public institutions and $14,600 in private institutions]

TYPE OF CONTROL AND ACADEMIC RANK	1994	1995	1996	TYPE OF CONTROL AND ACADEMIC RANK	1994	1995	1996
Public: All ranks	47.3	49.1	50.4	Private: [1] All ranks	53.8	55.4	57.5
Professor	59.8	62.0	63.9	Professor	71.2	73.2	75.6
Associate professor	45.3	47.0	48.2	Associate professor	48.5	50.0	51.5
Assistant professor	38.0	39.2	40.2	Assistant professor	40.1	41.2	42.4
Instructor	28.8	29.8	30.8	Instructor	30.2	31.7	32.9

[1] Excludes church-related colleges and universities.

Source: American Association of University Professors, Washington, DC, *AAUP Annual Report on the Economic Status of the Profession*.

No. 296. Instructional Faculty and Staff, by Selected Characteristics and Field: 1992

[As of fall. For full-time faculty and staff]

CHARACTERISTIC	Total (1,000) [1]	PERCENT DISTRIBUTION, BY FIELD								
		All fields [1]	Business	Education	Engineering	Fine arts	Health	Humanities	Natural sciences	Social sciences
Total	526	100.0	100.0	100.0	100.0	100.0	100.0	100.0	100.0	100.0
Age:										
Under 30 years old	8	1.4	1.2	1.1	1.3	1.3	1.1	1.6	1.5	0.8
30 to 34 years old	35	6.7	6.3	3.5	11.1	6.1	8.5	4.7	6.7	7.3
35 to 39 years old	66	12.6	13.5	7.8	13.2	13.0	16.2	9.5	13.9	12.9
40 to 44 years old	90	17.0	16.4	17.5	16.8	17.7	21.7	13.3	15.9	16.4
45 to 49 years old	97	18.5	20.9	19.6	14.7	18.4	19.3	20.0	17.1	17.8
50 to 54 years old	95	18.0	16.1	21.1	12.2	17.4	13.4	21.6	19.3	19.2
55 to 59 years old	67	12.7	11.9	14.2	15.0	14.1	9.5	14.6	13.3	12.3
60 to 64 years old	45	8.5	8.0	10.6	10.7	7.9	7.6	9.9	7.5	9.2
65 years old and over	24	4.5	5.8	4.7	5.1	4.0	2.7	4.8	4.7	4.2
Sex:										
Male	356	67.5	69.8	49.9	94.1	67.8	50.6	59.1	80.3	73.2
Female	171	32.5	30.2	50.1	5.9	32.2	49.4	40.9	19.7	26.8
Race/ethnicity:										
White [2]	457	86.8	88.9	85.1	76.8	88.7	86.6	88.3	86.3	87.7
Black [2]	26	4.9	3.9	9.0	2.7	5.7	5.2	4.1	3.4	5.9
Hispanic	13	2.5	1.4	3.3	2.9	2.4	2.0	4.0	1.8	2.7
Asian	28	5.2	4.9	1.6	16.9	2.7	6.0	3.2	8.1	3.3
American Indian	3	0.5	1.0	1.0	0.7	0.5	0.2	0.5	0.3	0.5
Highest degree:										
Less than bachelor's	6	1.2	0.5	0.3	2.0	0.7	1.2	(Z)	0.2	0.1
Bachelor's	21	4.0	4.5	2.9	5.1	5.3	5.9	1.2	2.8	0.7
Master's	154	29.4	37.9	30.3	18.4	56.0	29.6	31.6	21.9	18.9
Professional	57	10.9	4.5	3.0	2.3	4.4	43.3	2.4	4.5	3.5
Doctorate	285	54.5	52.6	63.6	72.2	33.6	20.0	64.8	70.7	76.8
Rank:										
Full professor	161	30.6	24.9	24.6	36.9	32.3	21.5	33.3	37.3	37.2
Associate professor	123	23.5	25.7	29.6	28.0	25.5	23.0	22.2	22.6	24.7
Assistant professor	123	23.4	25.5	22.8	22.4	21.4	32.8	19.3	20.6	24.1
Instructor	73	13.9	16.5	13.2	10.4	10.1	16.6	14.8	11.6	7.9
Lecturer	12	2.2	1.3	2.5	0.9	2.9	2.3	3.8	1.8	1.7
Other	17	3.2	2.1	5.5	0.5	3.2	2.4	1.9	2.4	2.0
No rank	17	3.2	4.0	1.9	1.0	4.6	1.4	4.7	3.9	2.5

Z less than .05 percent. [1] Includes other fields, not shown separately. [2] Non-Hispanic.

Source: U.S. National Center for Education Statistics, *Digest of Education Statistics*, 1995.

No. 297. Higher Education Registrations in Foreign Languages: 1970 to 1995

[As of fall]

ITEM	1970	1972	1974	1977	1980	1983	1986	1990	1995
Registrations [1] (1,000)	1,111.5	1,006.9	946.6	933.5	924.8	966.0	1,003.2	1,184.1	1,138.8
Index (1960=100)	171.8	155.9	146.3	144.3	142.9	149.3	155.0	183.0	176.0
By selected language (1,000):									
Spanish	389.2	364.5	362.2	376.7	379.4	386.2	411.3	533.9	606.3
French	359.3	293.1	253.1	246.1	248.4	270.1	275.3	272.5	205.4
German	202.6	177.1	152.1	135.4	126.9	128.2	121.0	133.3	96.3
Italian	34.2	33.3	33.0	33.3	34.8	38.7	40.9	49.7	43.8
Japanese	6.6	8.3	9.6	10.7	11.5	16.1	23.5	45.7	44.7
Russian	36.1	36.4	32.5	27.8	24.0	30.4	34.0	44.6	24.7
Latin	27.6	24.4	25.2	24.4	25.0	24.2	25.0	28.2	25.9
Chinese	6.2	10.0	10.6	9.8	11.4	13.2	16.9	19.5	26.5
Ancient Greek	16.7	20.6	24.4	25.8	22.1	19.4	17.6	16.4	16.3
Hebrew	16.6	21.1	22.4	19.4	19.4	18.2	15.6	13.0	13.1
Portuguese	5.1	4.8	5.1	5.0	4.9	4.4	5.1	6.2	6.5
Arabic	1.3	1.7	2.0	3.1	3.5	3.4	3.4	3.5	4.4
12 languages as percent of total	99.1	98.7	98.5	98.3	98.5	98.6	98.6	98.5	97.8

[1] Includes other foreign languages, not shown separately.

Source: Association of Departments of Foreign Languages, New York, NY, *ADFL Bulletin*, vol. 28, No. 2, and earlier issues (copyright).

No. 298. College Freshmen—Summary Characteristics: 1970 to 1996

[In percent. As of fall for first-time full-time freshmen. Based on sample survey and subject to sampling error; see source]

CHARACTERISTIC	1970	1980	1985	1990	1992	1993	1994	1995	1996
Sex: Male	55	49	48	46	46	45	46	46	46
Female	45	51	52	54	54	55	54	54	54
Applied to three or more colleges	[1]15	26	29	36	33	37	36	36	37
Average grade in high school:									
A- to A+	16	21	21	23	26	27	28	28	32
B- to B+	58	60	59	58	57	57	56	56	54
C to C+	27	19	20	19	17	16	15	15	14
D	1	1	1	-	-	-	-	-	-
Political orientation:									
Liberal	34	20	21	23	24	25	23	21	22
Middle of the road	45	60	57	55	53	50	53	54	53
Conservative	17	17	19	20	19	21	21	20	21
Probable field of study:									
Arts and humanities	16	9	8	9	8	8	8	10	10
Biological sciences	4	4	4	4	5	6	7	7	7
Business	16	24	27	21	16	16	16	16	16
Education	11	7	7	10	10	10	10	10	11
Engineering	9	12	11	8	9	9	8	7	8
Physical science	2	3	2	2	2	3	2	2	2
Social science	14	7	8	10	9	9	10	9	9
Professional	(NA)	15	13	15	20	20	19	18	16
Technical	4	6	5	4	3	3	3	4	2
Data processing/computer programming	(NA)	2	2	1	1	1	1	1	1
Other [2]	(NA)	(NA)	16	16	17	17	17	17	19
Communications	(NA)	2	2	2	2	2	2	2	2
Computer science	(NA)	1	2	2	1	2	2	2	3
Recipient of financial aid:									
Pell grant	(NA)	33	19	23	23	24	23	23	20
Supplemental educational opportunity grant	(NA)	8	5	7	6	6	6	6	6
State scholarship or grant	(NA)	16	14	16	14	14	16	16	17
College grant	(NA)	13	19	22	24	24	26	26	29
Federal guaranteed student loan	(NA)	21	23	23	23	28	29	29	26
Perkins loan [3]	(NA)	9	6	8	8	8	9	9	9
College loan	(NA)	4	4	6	6	6	8	10	9
College work-study grant	(NA)	15	10	10	12	12	13	13	12
Attitudes—agree or strongly agree:									
Activities of married women are best confined to home and family	48	27	22	25	26	24	25	24	24
Capital punishment should be abolished	56	34	27	22	21	22	20	21	22
Legalize marijuana	38	39	22	19	23	28	32	34	33
There is too much concern for the rights of criminals	52	66	(NA)	(NA)	67	68	73	73	72
Abortion should be legalized	(NA)	54	55	65	64	62	60	58	56
Aspires to an advanced degree	49	49	51	61	55	65	64	64	67
Male	57	50	52	60	55	64	62	61	65
Female	41	47	50	62	56	67	66	66	68
Median family income ($1,000)	12	23	34	43	45	46	48	49	53

- Represents or rounds to zero. NA Not available. [1] 1969 data. [2] Includes other fields, not shown separately. [3] National Direct Student Loan prior to 1990.

Source: The Higher Education Research Institute, University of California, Los Angeles, CA, *The American Freshman: National Norms*, annual.

No. 299. Freshmen Enrollment in Remedial Courses, by Institutional Characteristic: 1995

[In percent, except number of freshmen. As of fall. Remedial courses are those developed for students lacking skills necessary to perform college-level work as required by the institution. Based on survey and subject to sampling error; for details, see source]

INSTITUTIONAL CHARACTERISTIC	Number of freshmen (1,000)	INSTITUTIONS OFFERING COURSES				FRESHMEN TAKING COURSES			
		Total	Reading	Writing	Math	Total	Reading	Writing	Math
All institutions	2,128	78	57	71	72	29	13	17	24
Control: Public, 2 year	943	100	99	99	99	41	20	25	34
Private, 2 year	56	63	29	61	62	26	11	18	23
Public, 4 year	726	81	52	71	78	22	8	12	18
Private, 4 year	403	63	34	52	51	13	7	8	9
Minority enrollment:									
High [1]	338	94	87	85	93	43	25	29	35
Low [2]	1,790	76	53	70	70	26	11	15	21

[1] Total enrollment, excluding nonresident aliens, is less than 50% White, Non-Hispanic. [2] Total enrollment, excluding nonresident aliens, is more than 50% White, Non-Hispanic.

Source: U.S. National Center for Education Statistics, "Remedial Education at Higher Education Institutions in Fall of 1995," NCES 97-584.

No. 300. College Population, by Selected Characteristics: 1987 and 1996

[In thousands, except percent. As of October. Based on the Current Population Survey. See text, section 1, and Appendix III]

CHARACTERISTIC	Total population	ENROLLED IN COLLEGE							
		Total	Type of school			Percent enrolled full time	Percent employed		
			2-year	4-year	Graduate school		Total	Full-time	Part-time
Total, 1987 [1]	190,058	12,719	3,648	6,656	2,415	62.6	60.4	31.7	28.7
Male	90,610	6,030	1,522	3,356	1,152	67.2	60.6	31.7	28.9
Female	99,449	6,689	2,127	3,299	1,264	58.4	60.1	31.8	28.5
White	162,757	10,731	3,039	5,617	2,075	61.6	62.2	32.6	29.6
Black	21,520	1,351	422	748	181	66.3	50.5	28.6	21.9
Hispanic origin [2]	13,887	739	307	342	90	57.3	65.5	37.0	28.6
14 to 19 years old	21,410	3,284	1,111	2,172	1	88.1	44.0	7.6	36.4
20 and 21 years old	7,078	2,642	624	1,961	58	84.4	53.3	14.5	38.8
22 to 24 years old	11,712	2,006	457	1,055	494	67.2	62.5	29.8	32.7
25 to 34 years old	42,374	2,985	851	996	1,137	36.4	74.0	55.8	18.2
35 years and older	107,484	1,802	605	471	725	22.3	83.1	62.8	20.3
Total, 1996	203,113	14,715	3,882	8,084	2,749	64.8	61.9	32.4	29.5
Male	97,484	6,703	1,626	3,787	1,290	68.0	62.0	34.9	27.2
Female	105,629	8,013	2,256	4,298	1,459	62.2	61.8	30.3	31.4
White	170,406	12,021	3,067	6,724	2,231	64.7	63.9	32.7	31.2
Black	23,994	1,772	573	902	297	69.1	54.5	35.1	19.4
Hispanic origin [2]	19,291	1,207	484	632	111	58.7	58.1	33.5	24.6
15 to 19 years old	16,599	3,259	1,028	2,223	8	7.4	45.9	9.1	36.8
20 and 21 years old	6,736	2,940	606	2,273	60	5.8	55.8	14.3	41.4
22 to 24 years old	10,966	2,498	593	1,440	465	5.6	60.2	25.3	34.8
25 to 34 years old	40,648	3,349	892	1,258	1,198	3.2	71.6	51.6	20.0
35 years and older	126,165	2,669	761	890	1,018	1.7	77.6	63.1	14.4

[1] Includes other races, not shown separately. [2] Persons of Hispanic origin may be of any race.

Source: U.S. Bureau of the Census, *Current Population Reports*, P20-443 and P20-492.

No. 301. Salary Offers to Candidates for Degrees: 1990 to 1995

[In dollars. Data are average beginning salaries based on offers made by business, industrial, government, and nonprofit and educational employers to graduating students. Data from representative colleges throughout the United States]

FIELD OF STUDY	BACHELOR'S			MASTER'S[1]			DOCTOR'S		
	1990	1994	1995	1990	1994	1995	1990	1994	1995
Accounting	26,391	28,372	27,926	29,647	32,395	31,474	(NA)	(NA)	(NA)
Business, general [2]	23,529	25,102	25,711	36,175	38,792	39,293	(NA)	(NA)	(NA)
Marketing	23,543	24,584	25,400	35,440	45,999	40,899	(NA)	(NA)	(NA)
Engineering:									
Civil	28,136	29,809	30,618	32,336	34,967	34,600	44,481	51,200	42,323
Chemical	35,122	39,204	39,880	37,862	40,457	41,757	50,524	57,803	57,299
Computer	31,490	33,842	34,941	35,748	39,056	40,889	50,526	62,000	59,280
Electrical	31,778	34,840	36,049	37,526	41,924	43,137	53,147	59,184	56,065
Mechanical	32,064	35,051	35,744	36,506	41,450	42,067	49,867	52,678	51,989
Nuclear [3]	31,750	33,603	38,531	36,728	36,500	45,167	(NA)	(NA)	(NA)
Petroleum	35,202	38,286	37,476	38,412	(NA)	43,517	(NA)	(NA)	(NA)
Engineering technology	29,318	30,509	31,663	(NA)	(NA)	(NA)	(NA)	(NA)	(NA)
Chemistry	27,494	28,128	29,340	32,320	36,392	38,000	45,356	49,455	52,907
Mathematics	27,032	28,221	30,271	30,069	30,552	35,570	42,775	49,154	52,057
Physics	28,002	28,117	31,996	31,480	31,800	37,835	41,486	54,469	53,660
Humanities	23,213	23,519	22,811	(NA)	(NA)	(NA)	(NA)	(NA)	(NA)
Social sciences [4]	21,627	23,023	24,010	(NA)	(NA)	(NA)	(NA)	(NA)	(NA)
Computer science	29,804	31,783	33,712	36,849	37,512	42,885	54,788	55,228	48,000

NA Not available. [1] Candidates with 1 year or less of full-time nonmilitary employment. [2] For master's degree, offers are after nontechnical undergraduate degree. [3] Includes engineering physics. [4] Excludes economics.

Source: National Association of Colleges and Employers, Bethlehem, PA, Salary Survey, *A Study of Beginning Offers*, annual (copyright).

No. 302. Time Spent Earning Bachelor's Degree, by Selected Characteristic: 1993

[As of spring. Based on Survey of Income and Program Participation; for details, see source]

CHARACTERISTIC	Total with bachelor's degrees (1,000)	YEARS TO BA DEGREE FROM END OF HIGH SCHOOL						
		Number (1,000)			Percent			Mean duration[1]
		4 years or less	5 years or less	6 years or less	4 years or less	5 years or less	6 years or less	
All persons	36,787	15,624	23,810	27,334	42.5	64.7	74.3	6.29
Male	19,351	7,321	11,695	13,827	37.8	60.4	71.5	6.28
Female	17,436	8,302	12,115	13,506	47.6	69.5	77.5	6.30
White	32,279	14,161	21,201	24,235	43.9	65.7	75.1	6.24
Male	17,258	6,717	10,537	12,411	38.9	61.1	71.9	6.22
Female	15,021	7,444	10,664	11,824	49.6	71.0	78.7	6.26
Black	2,314	713	1,258	1,473	30.8	54.4	63.7	7.19
Male	926	264	493	570	28.5	53.2	61.6	6.96
Female	1,388	448	764	904	32.3	55.0	65.1	7.33
Hispanic origin[2]	1,367	363	689	852	26.6	50.4	62.3	6.79
Male	693	187	306	407	27.0	44.4	58.7	7.06
Female	674	176	381	445	26.1	56.5	66.0	6.50
Field of Bachelor's degree:[3]								
Agriculture/Forestry	395	103	209	293	26.1	52.9	74.2	5.78
Biology	624	241	416	471	38.6	66.7	75.5	6.34
Business/Management	5,282	1,952	3,117	3,628	37.0	59.0	68.7	6.72
Economics	660	321	433	479	48.6	65.6	72.6	6.35
Education	3,613	1,522	2,338	2,658	42.1	64.7	73.6	7.03
Engineering	2,577	729	1,392	1,733	28.3	54.0	67.2	6.66
English/Journalism	1,137	553	743	854	48.6	65.3	75.1	6.28
Home Economics	337	177	262	284	52.5	77.7	84.3	4.71
Law	145	73	96	104	(B)	(B)	(B)	6.33
Liberal Arts/Humanities	2,188	894	1,413	1,592	40.9	64.6	72.8	6.44
Mathematics/Statistics	567	283	412	457	49.9	72.7	80.6	5.28
Medicine/Dentistry	142	39	74	104	(B)	(B)	(B)	6.32
Nursing/Pharmacy/Technical Health	1,626	498	914	1,092	30.6	56.2	67.2	7.10
Physical/Earth Sciences	614	194	362	470	31.6	59.0	76.5	6.25
Police Science/Law Enforcement	326	95	182	240	29.1	55.8	73.6	6.11
Psychology	815	328	555	619	40.2	68.1	76.0	6.02
Religion/Theology	138	52	66	71	(B)	(B)	(B)	7.64
Social Sciences	1,760	683	1,113	1,333	38.8	63.2	75.7	6.44
Vo-tech Studies	181	64	121	135	(B)	(B)	(B)	7.39
Other	1,816	735	1,082	1,302	40.5	59.6	71.7	6.63
Advanced degree	11,843	6,089	8,507	9,417	51.4	71.8	79.5	5.67

B Base is less than 200,000 persons. [1] For definition of mean, see Guide to Tabular Presentation. [2] Persons of Hispanic origin may be of any race. [3] For persons whose highest degree is the BA.

Source: U.S. Bureau of the Census, unpublished data.

No. 303. Earned Degrees Conferred, by Level and Sex, With Projections: 1960 to 2006

[In thousands, except percent. Includes Alaska and Hawaii]

YEAR ENDING	ALL DEGREES		ASSOCIATE'S		BACHELOR'S		MASTER'S		FIRST PROFESSIONAL		DOCTOR'S	
	Total	Percent male	Male	Female	Male	Female	Male	Female	Male	Female	Male	Female
1960[1]	477	65.8	(NA)	(NA)	254	138	51	24	(NA)	(NA)	9	1
1965	660	61.5	(NA)	(NA)	282	212	81	40	27	1	15	2
1970	1,271	59.2	117	89	451	341	126	83	33	2	26	4
1975	1,666	56.0	191	169	505	418	162	131	49	7	27	7
1980	1,731	51.1	184	217	474	456	151	147	53	17	23	10
1985	1,828	49.3	203	252	483	497	143	143	50	25	22	11
1986	1,830	49.0	196	250	486	502	144	145	49	25	22	12
1987	1,823	48.4	191	245	481	510	141	148	47	25	22	12
1988	1,835	48.0	190	245	477	518	145	154	45	25	23	12
1989	1,873	47.3	186	250	483	535	149	161	45	26	23	13
1990	1,940	46.6	191	264	492	560	154	171	44	27	24	14
1991	2,025	45.8	199	283	504	590	156	181	44	28	25	15
1992	2,108	45.6	207	297	521	616	162	191	45	29	26	15
1993	2,167	45.5	212	303	533	632	169	200	45	30	26	16
1994	2,217	45.1	221	321	532	637	176	211	45	31	27	17
1995, proj.	2,247	45.3	216	314	535	657	195	210	45	32	27	16
2000, proj.	2,287	45.3	212	326	539	652	208	220	50	34	26	19
2004, proj.	2,451	44.6	222	354	580	708	212	240	55	36	24	21
2005, proj.	2,473	44.4	223	356	585	717	212	245	55	36	23	21
2006, proj.	2,497	44.2	224	360	591	725	212	250	55	37	22	21

NA Not available. [1] First-professional degrees are included with bachelor's degrees.

Source: U.S. National Center for Education Statistics, *Digest of Education Statistics*, annual; and *Projections of Education Statistics to 2006*, annual.

No. 304. Degrees and Awards Earned Below Bachelor's, by Field: 1994

[Covers associate degrees and other awards based on postsecondary curriculums of less than 4 years in institutions of higher education]

FIELD OF STUDY	LESS THAN 1-YEAR AWARDS		1- TO LESS THAN 4-YEAR AWARDS		ASSOCIATE DEGREES	
	Total	Women	Total	Women	Total	Women
Total	71,748	37,016	152,849	88,963	542,449	321,469
Agriculture and natural resources	1,459	331	4,157	1,867	5,720	1,651
Architecture and related programs	10	10	44	28	353	236
Area, ethnic, and cultural studies	133	101	505	364	92	58
Biological/life sciences	43	9	93	48	1,852	1,108
Business management and administrative services	12,535	8,994	30,908	24,977	103,098	72,529
Communications and communications technologies	508	209	681	354	4,899	2,108
Computer and information sciences	1,793	915	3,938	1,973	9,456	4,716
Construction trades	1,495	102	4,557	246	1,724	80
Consumer and personal services	1,229	933	6,109	4,647	5,212	1,713
Education	499	384	1,294	1,161	10,021	6,872
Engineering and engineering technologies	2,579	348	9,115	1,007	39,676	4,445
English language and literature/letters	92	64	120	81	1,354	861
Foreign languages and literatures	324	192	77	42	517	386
Health professions and related sciences	24,909	17,769	42,569	35,764	96,832	80,356
Home economics and vocational home economics	3,428	2,454	8,570	6,778	7,562	6,919
Law and legal studies	962	795	2,104	1,726	9,008	7,905
Liberal/general studies and humanities	149	92	631	361	164,575	98,696
Library science	97	93	57	52	118	102
Mathematics	17	6	-	-	765	329
Mechanics and repairers	3,505	132	20,526	1,519	11,618	745
Multi/interdisciplinary studies	379	251	119	72	8,461	4,402
Parks, recreation, leisure, and fitness	47	13	129	76	767	302
Physical sciences	38	16	57	24	2,622	1,095
Precision production trades	2,374	378	7,662	1,290	9,661	1,862
Protective services	6,663	1,280	2,396	731	19,416	5,460
Psychology	30	23	6	5	1,756	1,323
Public administration and services	249	177	500	357	3,720	2,958
R.O.T.C. and military technologies	-	-	-	-	265	20
Social sciences and history	40	8	93	68	4,100	2,469
Theological studies, religion and philosophy	179	88	1,104	604	736	336
Transportation and material moving	5,591	633	500	82	1,968	334
Visual and performing arts	329	208	3,913	2,470	13,979	8,152
Undistributed and unclassified	43	28	313	189	1,526	727

- Represents zero.
Source: U.S. National Center for Education Statistics, *Digest of Education Statistics*, 1996.

No. 305. Bachelor's Degrees Earned, by Field: 1971 to 1994

FIELD OF STUDY	1971	1980	1985	1990	1994	PERCENT FEMALE	
						1971	1994
Total	839,730	929,417	979,477	1,051,344	1,169,275	43.4	54.5
Agriculture and natural resources	12,672	22,802	18,107	12,900	18,070	4.2	35.0
Architecture and environmental design	5,570	9,132	9,325	9,364	8,975	11.9	35.8
Area, ethnic and cultural studies	2,582	2,840	2,985	4,613	5,573	52.4	64.9
Biological sciences/life sciences	35,743	46,370	38,445	37,204	51,383	29.1	51.2
Business and management	114,729	184,867	232,636	248,698	246,654	9.1	47.6
Communications [1]	10,802	28,616	42,002	51,308	51,827	35.3	58.6
Computer and information sciences	2,388	11,154	38,878	27,257	24,200	13.6	28.4
Education	176,307	118,038	88,072	105,112	107,600	74.5	77.3
Engineering [1]	50,046	68,893	95,828	81,322	78,225	0.8	14.9
English language and literature/letters	64,342	32,541	33,218	47,519	53,924	65.6	65.8
Foreign languages	20,536	12,089	10,827	12,386	14,378	74.0	70.1
Health sciences	25,226	63,920	64,422	58,302	74,421	77.1	82.4
Home economics	11,167	18,411	15,157	14,491	15,522	97.3	87.5
Law	545	683	1,157	1,592	2,171	5.0	70.2
Liberal/general studies	7,481	23,196	21,818	27,985	33,397	33.6	60.7
Library and archival sciences	1,013	398	197	77	62	92.0	91.9
Mathematics	24,937	11,872	15,861	15,176	14,396	37.9	46.3
Military technologies	357	38	299	196	19	0.3	15.8
Multi/interdisciplinary studies	6,286	11,277	12,978	16,267	25,167	22.8	64.0
Parks and recreation	1,621	5,753	4,725	4,582	11,470	34.7	49.2
Philosophy, religion, and theology	11,890	13,276	12,447	12,068	12,980	25.5	30.9
Physical sciences [1]	21,412	23,410	23,704	16,066	18,400	13.8	33.6
Protective services	2,045	15,015	12,510	15,354	23,009	9.2	38.4
Psychology	38,187	42,093	39,900	53,952	69,259	44.4	73.1
Public affairs	5,466	16,644	11,754	13,908	17,815	68.4	78.0
Social sciences [2]	155,324	103,662	91,570	118,083	133,680	36.8	46.1
Visual and performing arts	30,394	40,892	38,140	39,934	49,053	59.7	60.2
Unclassified	682	1,535	2,515	5,628	7,645	0.9	29.0

[1] Includes technologies. [2] Includes history.
Source: U.S. National Center for Education Statistics, *Digest of Education Statistics*, annual.

No. 308. Master's and Doctorate's Degrees Earned, by Field: 1971 to 1994

LEVEL AND FIELD OF STUDY	1971	1980	1985	1990	1994	PERCENT FEMALE	
						1971	1994
MASTER'S DEGREES							
Total	230,509	298,081	286,251	324,301	387,070	40.1	54.5
Agriculture and natural resources	2,457	3,976	3,928	3,382	4,119	5.9	36.9
Architecture and related programs	1,705	3,139	3,275	3,499	3,943	13.8	36.4
Area, ethnic and cultural studies	1,032	852	904	1,212	1,633	38.3	53.0
Biological sciences/life sciences	5,728	6,510	5,059	4,869	5,198	33.6	52.6
Business management and administrative services	25,977	54,484	66,996	76,676	93,437	3.9	36.5
Communications and technologies	1,856	3,082	3,669	4,362	5,419	34.6	61.3
Computer and information sciences	1,588	3,647	7,101	9,677	10,416	10.3	25.8
Education	87,666	101,819	74,654	84,881	98,938	56.2	76.7
Engineering and engineering technologies	16,443	16,243	21,555	24,772	29,754	1.1	15.5
English language and literature/letters	10,686	6,189	5,187	6,567	7,886	60.6	65.6
Foreign languages	5,217	2,854	2,471	2,760	3,288	64.2	66.9
Health sciences	5,749	15,704	17,365	20,321	28,025	55.3	79.3
Home economics	1,452	2,690	2,375	2,100	2,421	93.9	83.3
Law and legal studies	955	1,817	1,796	1,686	2,432	4.8	33.9
Liberal arts and sciences, general studies and humanities	885	2,646	1,896	1,999	2,496	44.6	63.4
Library science	7,001	5,374	3,870	4,341	5,116	81.3	79.7
Mathematics	5,696	3,382	3,413	4,146	4,100	27.1	38.1
Military technologies	2	46	119	-	124	-	5.6
Multi/interdisciplinary studies	821	2,306	2,583	2,834	2,464	25.0	51.5
Parks and recreation	218	647	596	529	1,625	29.8	48.0
Philosophy, religion, and theology	4,036	5,126	5,802	6,265	6,306	27.1	38.6
Physical sciences and science technologies	6,367	5,219	5,796	5,449	5,679	13.3	29.2
Protective services	194	1,805	1,235	1,151	1,437	10.3	37.2
Psychology	5,717	9,938	9,891	10,730	12,181	40.6	72.1
Public administration and services	7,785	17,560	15,575	17,399	21,833	50.0	70.7
Social sciences [1]	16,539	12,176	10,503	11,634	14,561	28.5	44.0
Visual and performing arts	6,675	8,708	8,718	8,481	9,925	47.4	57.4
Unclassified	63	142	299	2,377	2,317	-	42.2
DOCTORATE'S DEGREES							
Total	32,107	32,615	32,943	38,371	43,185	14.3	38.5
Agriculture and natural resources	1,086	991	1,213	1,295	1,278	2.9	23.2
Architecture and related programs	36	79	89	103	161	8.3	31.1
Area, ethnic and cultural studies	144	151	140	131	156	16.7	51.6
Biological sciences/life sciences	3,645	3,636	3,432	3,844	4,534	16.3	40.7
Business management and administrative services	757	753	831	1,093	1,364	2.8	28.2
Communications and technologies	145	193	234	273	345	13.1	49.6
Computer and information sciences	128	240	248	627	810	2.3	15.4
Education	6,041	7,314	6,612	6,502	6,908	21.0	60.8
Engineering and engineering technology	3,638	2,507	3,230	4,981	5,979	0.6	11.1
English language and literature/letters	1,650	1,294	1,041	1,078	1,344	28.8	57.7
Foreign languages	988	755	635	724	886	34.6	59.9
Health sciences	466	786	1,199	1,536	1,902	16.5	56.5
Home economics	123	192	273	301	365	61.0	74.5
Law and legal studies	20	40	105	111	79	-	20.3
Liberal arts and sciences, general studies and humanities	32	192	112	63	80	31.3	42.5
Library science	39	73	87	42	45	28.2	68.9
Mathematics	1,249	763	734	966	1,157	7.6	21.9
Multi/interdisciplinary studies	59	209	219	272	227	6.8	33.5
Parks and recreation	2	21	36	35	116	50.0	39.7
Philosophy, religion, and theology	866	1,693	1,612	1,756	1,976	5.8	18.1
Physical sciences and science technologies	4,390	3,089	3,403	4,164	4,650	5.6	21.7
Protective services	1	18	33	38	25	-	44.0
Psychology	2,144	3,395	3,447	3,811	3,563	24.0	62.2
Public administration and services	174	342	431	508	519	24.1	54.1
Social sciences [1]	3,660	3,230	2,851	3,010	3,627	13.9	36.1
Visual and performing arts	621	655	696	849	1,054	22.2	44.5
Unclassified	3	4	-	258	38	-	41.7

- Represents zero. [1] Includes history.

Source: U.S. National Center for Education Statistics, *Digest of Education Statistics*, annual.

No. 307. First Professional Degrees Earned in Selected Professions: 1960 to 1994

[First professional degrees include degrees which require at least 6 years of college work for completion (including at least 2 years of preprofessional training). See Appendix III]

TYPE OF DEGREE AND SEX OF RECIPIENT	1960	1970	1975	1980	1985	1990	1991	1992	1993	1994
Medicine (M.D.):										
Institutions conferring degrees	79	86	104	112	120	124	121	120	122	121
Degrees conferred, total	7,032	8,314	12,447	14,902	16,041	15,075	15,043	15,243	15,531	15,368
Percent to women	5.5	8.4	13.1	23.4	30.4	34.2	36.0	35.7	37.7	37.9
Dentistry (D.D.S. or D.M.D.):										
Institutions conferring degrees	45	48	52	58	59	57	55	52	55	53
Degrees conferred, total	3,247	3,718	4,773	5,258	5,339	4,100	3,699	3,593	3,605	3,787
Percent to women	0.8	0.9	3.1	13.3	20.7	30.9	32.1	32.3	33.9	38.5
Law (LL.B. or J.D.):										
Institutions conferring degrees	134	145	154	179	181	182	179	177	184	185
Degrees conferred, total	9,240	14,916	29,296	35,647	37,491	36,485	37,945	38,848	40,302	40,044
Percent to women	2.5	5.4	15.1	30.2	38.5	42.2	43.0	42.7	42.5	43.0
Theological (B.D., M.Div., M.H.L.):										
Institutions conferring degrees	(NA)	(NA)	(NA)	(NA)	(NA)	(NA)	(NA)	(NA)	(NA)	(NA)
Degrees conferred, total	(NA)	5,298	5,095	7,115	7,221	5,851	5,695	5,251	5,447	5,967
Percent to women	(NA)	2.3	6.8	13.8	18.5	24.8	23.4	23.3	24.8	24.8

NA Not available.

Source: U.S. National Center for Education Statistics, *Digest of Education Statistics*, annual.

No. 308. Degrees Earned, by Level and Race/Ethnicity: 1981 to 1994

[For school year ending in year shown. Data exclude some institutions not reporting field of study and are slight undercounts of degrees awarded]

LEVEL OF DEGREE AND RACE/ETHNICITY	TOTAL						PERCENT DISTRIBUTION	
	1981	1985	1990	1992	1993, prel.	1994, prel.	1981	1994, prel.
Associate's degrees, total	410,174	429,815	450,263	494,387	506,154	540,923	100.0	100.0
White, non-Hispanic	339,167	355,343	369,580	400,530	405,883	428,273	82.7	79.2
Black, non-Hispanic	35,330	35,791	35,327	39,411	42,340	46,451	8.6	8.6
Hispanic	17,800	19,407	22,195	26,905	29,991	32,438	4.3	6.0
Asian or Pacific Islander	8,650	9,914	13,482	15,596	16,632	18,659	2.1	3.4
American Indian/Alaskan Native	2,584	2,953	3,530	4,008	4,379	4,975	0.6	0.9
Nonresident alien	6,643	6,407	6,149	7,937	8,929	10,127	1.6	1.9
Bachelor's degrees, total	934,800	968,311	1,048,631	1,129,833	1,159,931	1,165,973	100.0	100.0
White, non-Hispanic	807,319	826,106	884,376	936,771	947,309	936,227	86.4	80.3
Black, non-Hispanic	60,673	57,473	61,063	72,326	77,872	83,576	6.5	7.2
Hispanic	21,832	25,874	32,844	40,761	45,376	50,241	2.3	4.3
Asian or Pacific Islander	18,794	25,395	39,248	46,720	51,463	55,660	2.0	4.8
American Indian/Alaskan Native	3,593	4,246	4,392	5,176	5,671	6,189	0.4	0.5
Nonresident alien	22,589	29,217	26,708	28,079	32,240	34,080	2.4	2.9
Master's degrees, total	294,183	280,421	322,465	348,682	368,701	385,419	100.0	100.0
White, non-Hispanic	241,216	223,628	251,690	268,371	278,829	268,286	82.0	74.8
Black, non-Hispanic	17,133	13,939	15,446	18,116	19,780	21,937	5.8	5.7
Hispanic	6,461	6,864	7,950	9,358	10,665	11,913	2.2	3.1
Asian or Pacific Islander	6,282	7,782	10,577	12,658	13,866	15,267	2.1	4.0
American Indian/Alaskan Native	1,034	1,256	1,101	1,273	1,407	1,697	0.4	0.4
Nonresident alien	22,057	26,952	35,701	38,906	44,154	46,317	7.5	12.0
Doctor's degrees, total	32,839	32,307	38,113	40,090	42,021	43,149	100.0	100.0
White, non-Hispanic	25,908	23,934	25,880	25,813	26,700	27,156	78.9	62.9
Black, non-Hispanic	1,265	1,154	1,153	1,223	1,352	1,393	3.9	3.2
Hispanic	456	677	788	811	827	903	1.4	2.1
Asian or Pacific Islander	877	1,106	1,235	1,559	1,582	2,025	2.7	4.7
American Indian/Alaskan Native	130	119	99	118	106	134	0.4	0.3
Nonresident alien	4,203	5,317	8,958	10,566	11,454	11,538	12.8	26.7
First-professional degrees, total	71,340	71,057	70,744	72,129	74,960	75,418	100.0	100.0
White, non-Hispanic	64,551	63,219	60,240	59,800	60,830	60,140	90.5	79.7
Black, non-Hispanic	2,931	3,029	3,410	3,560	4,100	4,444	4.1	5.9
Hispanic	1,541	1,884	2,427	2,766	2,984	3,134	2.2	4.2
Asian or Pacific Islander	1,456	1,816	3,362	4,455	5,160	5,892	2.0	7.8
American Indian/Alaskan Native	192	248	257	296	368	371	0.3	0.5
Nonresident alien	669	861	1,048	1,252	1,518	1,437	0.9	1.9

Source: U.S. National Center for Education Statistics, *Digest of Education Statistics*, annual.

No. 309. Libraries—Number, by Type: 1980 to 1995

TYPE	1980	1985	1990	1995	TYPE	1980	1985	1990	1995
Total [1]	**31,564**	**32,323**	**34,613**	**36,980**	Junior college	1,191	1,168	1,233	1,261
United States	28,638	29,843	30,761	32,441	Colleges, universities	3,400	3,846	3,360	3,423
Public	8,717	8,849	9,080	9,101	Departmental	1,489	1,824	1,454	1,482
Public branches	5,936	6,330	5,833	6,172	Law, medicine, religious	269	531	501	491
Special [2]	7,649	7,530	9,051	10,192	Government	1,260	1,574	1,735	1,864
Medicine	1,674	1,667	1,861	1,929	Armed Forces	485	526	489	428
Religious	913	839	946	1,032	Outlying areas	113	114	110	(NA)
Law [3]	417	435	647	1,146					
Academic	4,591	5,034	4,593	4,684					

NA Not available. [1] Includes Canadian libraries, and libraries in regions administered by the United States, not shown separately. Data are exclusive of elementary and secondary school libraries. Law libraries with fewer than 10,000 volumes are included only if they specialize in a particular field. [2] Includes other types of special libraries, not shown separately. Increase between 1980 and 1990 is due mainly to revised criteria for identifying special libraries and improved methods of counting. [3] Increase beginning 1995 due to increased effort in identifying special libraries.

Source: R.R. Bowker Co., New York, NY, *The Bowker Annual: Library and Book Trade Almanac* and *American Library Directory,* annual. (Copyright by Reed Publishing (USA) Inc.)

No. 310. Public Libraries, Selected Characteristics: 1994

[Based on survey of public libraries. Data are for public libraries in the 50 States and the District of Columbia. The response rates for these items are between 97 and 100 percent]

POPULATION OF SERVICE AREA	NUMBER OF—		OPERATING INCOME			PAID STAFF [3]		Books and serial volumes (per capita)
				Source (percent)				
	Public libraries	Stationary outlets [1]	Total (mil. dol.) [2]	State government	Local government	Total	Librarians with ALA-MLS [4]	
Total	**8,921**	**15,900**	**5,260**	**12.3**	**78.2**	**112,817**	**25,878**	**2.7**
1,000,000 or more	20	854	720	12.5	73.9	13,567	4,019	2.4
500,000 to 999,000	49	1,069	876	17.6	74.5	16,290	4,317	2.5
250,000 to 499,999	88	1,033	606	10.7	82.6	12,064	3,120	2.4
100,000 to 249,999	304	1,902	843	9.7	82.3	18,226	4,223	2.2
50,000 to 99,999	504	1,580	658	14.0	77.9	14,633	3,304	2.4
25,000 to 49,999	863	1,649	646	11.6	79.8	14,556	3,226	2.8
10,000 to 24,999	1,649	2,129	556	10.0	79.6	13,058	2,622	3.4
5,000 to 9,999	1,494	1,679	213	11.2	75.5	5,620	754	4.1
2,500 to 4,999	1,325	1,361	82	7.0	75.1	2,514	206	5.2
1,000 to 2,499	1,655	1,672	47	5.7	70.1	1,685	73	7.5
Fewer than 1,000	970	972	12	8.3	65.0	605	15	13.2

[1] The sum of central and branches libraries. The total number of central libraries was 8,876; the total of branch libraries was 7,024. [2] Includes income from the Federal Government (1.1%) and other sources (8.4%), not shown separately. [3] Full-time equivalents. [4] Librarians with master's degrees from a graduate library education program accredited by the American Library Association (ALA). Total librarians, including those without ALA-MLS, were 38,045.

Source: U.S. National Center for Education Statistics, *Public Libraries in the United States: 1994.*

No. 311. College and University Libraries—Summary: 1975 to 1992

[For school year ending in year shown, except enrollment as of fall of the prior year. Prior to 1982, includes outlying areas]

ITEM	1975	1979	1982	1985	1988	1990	1992
Number of libraries	2,972	3,122	3,104	3,322	3,438	3,274	3,274
Total enrollment (1,000)	10,322	11,392	12,372	12,242	12,767	13,539	14,359
COLLECTIONS (1,000)							
Number of volumes	447,059	519,895	567,826	631,727	706,504	717,042	749,429
Volumes added during year	23,242	21,608	19,507	20,658	21,907	19,003	20,982
Number of serial subscriptions	4,434	4,775	4,890	6,317	6,416	5,748	6,966
STAFF							
Total	56,836	58,416	58,476	58,476	67,251	69,359	67,166
Librarians and professional	23,530	23,676	23,816	21,822	25,115	26,101	26,341
OPERATING EXPENDITURES ($1,000)							
Total [1]	1,091,784	1,502,158	1,943,769	2,404,524	2,770,075	3,257,813	3,648,654
Salaries	592,568	824,438	1,061,894	1,156,138	1,451,551	1,693,813	1,889,368
Collection	327,904	450,160	561,199	750,282	891,281	1,040,928	1,197,293

[1] Includes other expenditures, not shown separately.

Source: U.S. National Center for Education Statistics, *Digest of Education Statistics*, 1995; and *Academic Libraries: 1990.* 1992.

No. 312. Participation in Adult Education: 1994-95

[For the civilian noninstitutional population 17 years old and over not enrolled full-time in elementary or secondary school at the time of the survey. Adult education is considered any enrollment in any educational activity at any time in the prior 12 months. Based on survey and subject to sampling error; source for details]

CHARACTERISTIC	Adult population (1,000)	PARTICIPANTS IN ADULT EDUCATION					
		Number taking adult ed. courses (1,000)	Percent of total	Reason for taking course (percent) [1]			
				Personal/ social	Advance on the job	Train for a new job	Complete degree or diploma
Total	189,543	76,261	40	44	54	11	10
Age: 17 to 24 years old	22,407	10,539	47	39	33	21	19
25 to 34 years old	40,326	19,506	48	41	56	14	8
35 to 44 years old	42,304	20,814	49	40	64	10	9
45 to 54 years old	31,807	14,592	46	39	65	7	10
55 to 64 years old	21,824	6,117	28	52	54	4	6
65 years old and over	30,876	4,691	15	86	14	1	3
Sex: Male	90,256	34,450	38	34	60	10	10
Female	99,287	41,811	42	51	49	12	9
Race/ethnicity:							
White [2]	144,587	59,962	41	44	57	10	9
Black [2]	20,806	7,704	37	45	48	13	12
Hispanic	15,689	5,281	34	40	37	13	11
Other races [2]	8,461	3,294	39	40	45	16	13
Marital status:							
Never married	38,627	17,094	44	37	44	20	15
Currently married	114,678	48,200	42	45	58	8	8
Other	36,238	10,967	30	48	52	9	8
Children under 18 in household:							
Yes	77,787	36,103	46	43	56	11	9
No	111,756	40,158	36	44	52	11	10
Educational attainment:							
Up to 8th grade	12,806	1,283	10	52	20	8	9
9th to 12th grade	16,511	3,332	20	45	27	10	18
High school diploma or GED	62,956	19,341	31	44	49	10	8
Vocational school after high school	6,327	2,646	42	44	57	8	8
Some college	34,433	16,978	49	45	47	16	13
Associate's degree	9,975	5,601	56	39	64	9	9
Bachelor's or higher	46,535	27,078	58	43	65	9	9
Labor force status:							
Employed	117,826	59,734	51	37	64	10	10
Unemployed	8,155	2,963	37	39	27	25	13
Not in the labor force	63,562	13,544	21	72	15	11	8
Occupation: [3]							
Professional	16,814	12,219	73	37	74	8	10
Executive, administrative and managerial	12,500	7,070	57	37	76	8	10
Technical and related support	4,812	3,300	69	32	73	9	11
Sales workers	15,666	7,131	46	41	53	12	11
Administrative support [4]	20,460	10,727	52	43	62	11	8
Service	17,365	8,238	47	37	51	14	12
Agriculture, forestry, and fishing	1,906	500	26	40	49	6	12
Precision production, craft and repair	11,441	4,977	43	30	62	8	11
Machine operators, assemblers [5]	8,309	2,515	30	28	58	10	9
Transportation and materials moving	4,486	1,296	29	35	60	13	12
Handlers, equipment cleaners, helpers and laborers	1,989	519	26	33	43	24	5
Nonclassifiable, undetermined	2,022	1,194	59	35	71	6	4
Household income:							
Under $10,000	30,198	6,883	23	48	25	20	12
$10,001 to $15,000	13,523	3,610	27	51	32	17	10
$15,001 to $20,000	13,116	4,176	32	45	38	15	12
$20,001 to $25,000	13,812	4,339	31	47	44	13	11
$25,001 to $30,000	16,386	6,208	38	45	46	13	11
$30,001 to $40,000	28,628	12,220	43	45	55	11	9
$40,001 to $50,000	20,446	9,567	47	41	61	10	8
$50,001 to $75,000	29,161	15,169	52	39	67	7	8
More than $75,000	24,274	14,089	58	43	64	7	9

[1] Reason for taking at least one course. Includes duplication. Excludes "to improve basic skills," cited by no more than 6 percent of participants. [2] Non-Hispanic. [3] For those employed in the 12 months prior to the interview. Excludes those participating exclusively in full-time credential programs. [4] Includes clerical. [5] Includes inspectors.

Source: U.S. Department of Education, National Center for Education Statistics, *1995 National Household Education Survey.*

Section 5

Law Enforcement, Courts, and Prisons

ion presents data on crimes com-
:tims of crimes, arrests, and data
criminal violations and the crimi-
system. The major sources of
a are the Bureau of Justice Sta-
IS), the Federal Bureau of Inves-
-BI), and the Administrative Office
S. Courts. BJS issues several re-
luding *Sourcebook of Criminal*
tatistics, Criminal Victimization in
d States, Prisoners in State and
nstitutions, Children in Custody,
Survey of Courts, Census of State
nal Facilities and *Survey of Prison*
Census of Jails and *Survey of*
tes, Parole in the United States,
unishment, and the annual *Ex-*
and Employment Data for the
Justice System. The Federal
f Investigation's major annual re-
ime in the United States, which
data on reported crimes as
from State and local law
ent agencies.

'isdiction and law enforce-
aw enforcement is, for the
t, a function of State and local offi-
agencies. The U.S. Constitution
general police powers to the
y act of Congress, Federal of-
clude only offenses against the
ernment and against or by its em-
while engaged in their official du-
offenses which involve the cross-
ite lines or an interference with
commerce. Excluding the military,
52 separate criminal law jurisdic-
e United States: 1 in each of the
, 1 in the District of Columbia,
Federal jurisdiction. Each of these
vn criminal law and procedure
vn law enforcement agencies.
systems of law enforcement are
lar among the States, there are
stantial differences in the penal-
e offenses.

rcement can be divided into three
estigation of crimes and arrests of
suspected of committing them;
on of those charged with crime;
unishment or treatment of per-
victed of crime.

In Brief

Criminal victimization rates in 1995 for U.S. residents age 12 or older experienced their largest single year decline ever in both personal crimes, 13%, and property crimes, 12.4%.

The Nation's prisons and jails both reached new record highs in 1995 with 1,085,000 and 507,000 inmates, respectively, incarcerated.

Juvenile courts disposed of 1.55 million cases in 1994, an increase of just over 50% from ten years before.

Crime—There are two major approaches taken in determining the extent of crime. One perspective is provided by the FBI through its Uniform Crime Reporting Program (UCR). The FBI receives monthly and annual reports from law enforcement agencies throughout the country, currently representing 98 percent of the national population. Each month, city police, sheriffs, and State police file reports on the number of index offenses that become known to them.

The FBI Crime Index offenses are as follows: *Murder and nonnegligent manslaughter,* is based on police investigations, as opposed to the determination of a medical examiner or judicial body, includes willful felonious homicides, and excludes attempts and assaults to kill, suicides, accidental deaths, justifiable homicides, and deaths caused by negligence; *forcible rape* includes forcible rapes and attempts; *robbery* includes stealing or taking anything of value by force or violence or threat of force or violence and includes attempted robbery; *aggravated assault* includes assault with intent to kill; *burglary* includes any unlawful entry to commit a felony or a theft and includes attempted burglary and burglary followed by larceny; *larceny* includes theft of property or articles of value without use of force and violence or fraud and excludes embezzlement, "con games," forgery, etc.; *motor vehicle theft* includes all cases where vehicles are driven away and abandoned, but excludes vehicles taken for temporary use and returned by the taker. Arson was added as the eighth Index offense in April 1979 following a Congressional mandate. *Arson* includes any willful or malicious burning or attempt to burn with or without intent to defraud, a dwelling house, public building, motor vehicle or aircraft, personal property of another, etc.

The monthly Uniform Crime Reports also contain data on crimes cleared by arrest and on characteristics of persons arrested for all criminal offenses. In summarizing and publishing crime data, the FBI depends primarily on the adherence to the established standards of reporting for statistical accuracy, presenting the data as information useful to persons concerned with the problem of crime and criminal-law enforcement.

National Crime Victimization Survey (NCVS)—A second perspective on crime is provided by this survey (formerly the National Crime Survey until August 1991) of the Bureau of Justice Statistics. Details about the crimes come directly from the victims. No attempt is made to validate the information against police records or any other source.

The NCVS measures rape, robbery, assault, household and personal larceny, burglary, and motor vehicle theft. The NCVS includes offenses reported to the police, as well as those not reported. Police reporting rates (percent of victimizations) varied by type of crime. In 1994, for instance, 32 percent of the rapes/sexual assaults were reported; 55 percent of the robberies; 40 percent of assaults; 33 percent of personal thefts; 51 percent of the household burglaries; and 78 percent of motor vehicle thefts.

Murder and kidnaping are not covered. Commercial burglary and robbery were dropped from the program during 1977. The so-called victimless crimes, such as drunkenness, drug abuse, and prostitution, also are excluded, as are crimes for which it is difficult to identify knowledgeable respondents or to locate data records.

Crimes of which the victim may not be category, as may some instances of embezzlement. Attempted crimes of many types probably are under recorded for this reason. Events in which the victim has shown a willingness to participate in illegal activity also are excluded.

In any encounter involving a personal crime, more than one criminal act can be committed against an individual. For example; a rape may be associated with a robbery; or a household offense, such as a burglary, can escalate into something more serious in the event of a personal confrontation. In classifying the survey-measured crimes, each criminal incident has been counted only once—by the most serious act that took place during the incident and ranked in accordance with the seriousness classification system used by the Federal Bureau of Investigation. The order of seriousness for crimes against persons is as follows: Rape, robbery, assault, and larceny. Consequently, if a person were both robbed and assaulted, the event would be classified as robbery; if the victim suffered physical harm, the crime would be categorized as robbery with injury. Personal crimes take precedence over household offenses.

A *victimization,* basic measure of the occurrence of a crime, is a specific criminal act as it affects a single victim. The number of victimizations is determined by the number of victims of such acts. Victimization counts serve as key elements in computing rates of victimization. For crimes against persons, the rates are based on the total number of individuals age 12 and over or on a portion of that population sharing a particular characteristic or set of traits. As general indicators of the danger of having been victimized during the reference period, the rates are not sufficiently refined to represent true measures of risk for specific individuals or households.

An *incident* is a specific criminal act involving one or more victims; therefore, the number of incidents of personal crimes lower than that of victimizations.

A major redesign of the survey was recently implemented involving such changes as a new screening questionnaire, improved measurement of rape and sexual assault categories, improvements to measurement of domestic violence,

uter-assisted telephone interviewing). The effects of the redesign show e new methods elicit more reports of zations.

s—Statistics on criminal offenses e outcome of prosecutions are in- ete for the country as a whole, al- n data are available for many States ually. The only national compilations h statistics were made by the Bu- f the Census for 1932 to 1945 cov- a maximum of 32 States and by the u of Justice Statistics for 1986, 1988, and 1992 based on a nationally rep- tative sample survey.

ulk of civil and criminal litigation in untry is commenced and determined various State courts. Only when the Constitution and acts of Congress ically confer jurisdiction upon the al courts may civil litigation be heard ecided by them. Generally, the al courts have jurisdiction over the ng types of cases: Suits or proceed- y or against the United States; civil s between private parties arising the Constitution, laws, or treaties of nited States; civil actions between e litigants who are citizens of different ; civil cases involving admiralty, mari- or prize jurisdiction; and all matters kruptcy.

are several types of courts with va- degrees of legal jurisdiction. These ctions include original, appellate, al, and limited or special. A *court of al jurisdiction* is one having the au- initially to try a case and pass judg- on the law and the facts; a *court of ate jurisdiction* is one with the legal ity to review cases and hear ap- a *court of general jurisdiction* is a ourt of unlimited original jurisdiction in nd/or criminal cases, also called a trial court"; a *court of limited or spe- isdiction* is a trial court with legal au- over only a particular class of cases, as probate, juvenile, or traffic cases.

4 Federal courts of original jurisdic- e known as the U.S. district courts. r more of these courts is established in every State and one each in the District of Columbia, Puerto Rico, the Virgin Is- lands, the Northern Mariana Islands, and Guam. Appeals from the district courts are taken to intermediate appellate courts of which there are 13, known as U.S. courts of appeals and the United States Court of Appeals for the Federal Circuit. The Su- preme Court of the United States is the final and highest appellate court in the Federal system of courts.

Juvenile offenders—For statistical pur- poses, the FBI and most States classify as juvenile offenders persons under the age of 18 years who have committed a crime or crimes.

Delinquency cases are all cases of youths referred to a juvenile court for violation of a law or ordinance or for seriously "antiso- cial" conduct. Several types of facilities are available for those adjudicated delinquent, ranging from the short-term physically un- restricted environment to the long-term very restrictive atmosphere.

Prisoners—Data on prisoners in Federal and State prisons and reformatories were collected annually by the Bureau of the Census until 1950, by the Federal Bureau of Prisons until 1971, transferred then to the Law Enforcement Assistance Adminis- tration and, in 1979, to the Bureau of Jus- tice Statistics. Adults convicted of criminal activity may be given a prison or jail sen- tence. A *prison* is a confinement facility having custodial authority over adults sen- tenced to confinement of more than one year. A *jail* is a facility, usually operated by a local law enforcement agency, holding persons detained pending adjudication and/or persons committed after adjudica- tion to 1 year or less. Nearly every State publishes annual data either for its whole prison system or for each separate State institution.

Statistical reliability—For discussion of statistical collection, estimation, and sampling procedures and measures of statistical reliability pertaining to the National Crime Victimization Survey and Uniform Crime Reporting Program, see Appendix III.

Figure 5.1
Criminal Victimization and Federal and State Prisoners

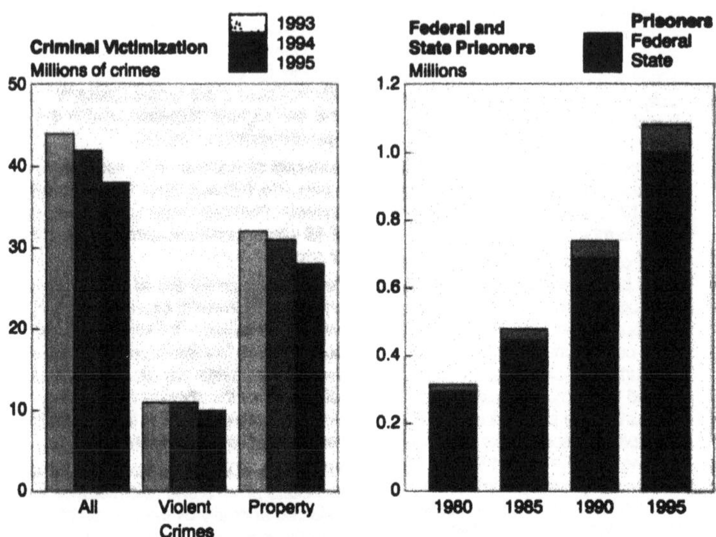

Source: Chart prepared by U.S. Bureau of the Census. For data, see tables 324 and 355.

Figure 5.2
Child Abuse and Neglect Cases: 1995

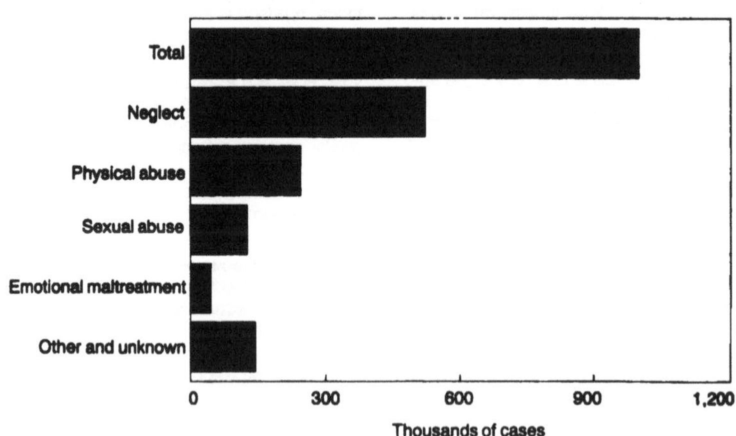

Note: More than one type of maltreatment may be substantiated per child. Therefore, items add up to more than the total shown.
Source: Chart prepared by U.S Bureau of the Census. For data, see table 352.

No. 313. Crimes and Crime Rates, by Type of Offense: 1985 to 1995

[Data refer to offenses known to the police. Rates are based on Bureau of the Census estimated resident population as of July 1, 1990, enumerated as of April 1. See source for details. Minus sign (-) indicates decrease. For definitions of crimes, see text, section 5]

ITEM AND YEAR	Total	VIOLENT CRIME					PROPERTY CRIME			
		Total	Murder [1]	Forcible rape	Robbery	Aggravated assault	Total	Burglary	Larceny—theft	Motor vehicle theft
Number of offenses (1,000):										
1985	12,431	1,329	19.0	88.7	498	723	11,103	3,073	6,926	1,103
1986	13,212	1,489	20.6	91.5	543	834	11,723	3,241	7,257	1,224
1987	13,509	1,484	20.1	91.1	518	855	12,025	3,236	7,500	1,289
1988	13,923	1,566	20.7	92.5	543	910	12,357	3,218	7,706	1,433
1989	14,251	1,646	21.5	94.5	578	952	12,605	3,168	7,872	1,565
1990	14,476	1,820	23.4	102.6	639	1,055	12,656	3,074	7,946	1,636
1991	14,873	1,912	24.7	106.6	688	1,093	12,961	3,157	8,142	1,662
1992	14,438	1,932	23.8	109.1	672	1,127	12,506	2,980	7,915	1,611
1993	14,142	1,926	24.5	106.0	660	1,136	12,219	2,835	7,821	1,563
1994	13,990	1,858	23.3	102.2	619	1,113	12,132	2,713	7,860	1,539
1995	13,867	1,799	21.6	97.5	581	1,099	12,068	2,595	8,001	1,473
Percent change, number of offenses:										
1985 to 1995	11.5	35.4	13.8	10.0	16.7	52.0	8.7	-15.6	15.5	33.6
1992 to 1993	-2.1	-0.3	3.2	-2.8	-1.9	0.8	-2.3	-4.9	-1.2	-3.0
1993 to 1994	-1.1	-3.5	-5.0	-3.6	-6.2	-2.0	-0.7	-4.3	0.8	-1.5
1994 to 1995	-0.9	-3.2	-7.3	-4.6	-6.1	-1.3	-0.5	-4.3	1.5	-4.3
Rate per 100,000 population:										
1985	5,207.1	556.6	7.9	37.1	208.5	302.9	4,650.5	1,287.3	2,901.2	462.0
1986	5,480.4	617.7	8.6	37.9	225.1	346.1	4,862.6	1,344.6	3,010.3	507.8
1987	5,550.0	609.7	8.3	37.4	212.7	351.3	4,940.3	1,329.6	3,081.3	529.4
1988	5,664.2	637.2	8.4	37.6	220.9	370.2	5,027.1	1,309.2	3,134.9	582.9
1989	5,741.0	663.7	8.7	38.1	233.0	383.4	5,077.9	1,276.3	3,171.3	630.4
1990	5,820.3	731.8	9.4	41.2	257.0	424.1	5,088.5	1,235.9	3,194.8	657.8
1991	5,897.8	758.1	9.8	42.3	272.7	433.3	5,139.7	1,252.0	3,228.8	659.0
1992	5,660.2	757.5	9.3	42.8	263.6	441.8	4,902.7	1,168.2	3,103.0	631.5
1993	5,484.4	746.8	9.5	41.1	255.9	440.3	4,737.6	1,099.2	3,032.4	606.1
1994	5,374.4	714.0	9.0	39.3	237.7	428.0	4,660.0	1,041.8	3,027.0	591.2
1995	5,278.0	685.0	8.2	37.1	221.0	418.0	4,593.0	988.0	3,045.0	561.0
Percent change, rate per 100,000 population:										
1985 to 1995	1.4	23.1	3.8	0.0	6.0	38.0	-1.2	-23.3	5.0	21.4
1992 to 1993	-3.1	-1.4	2.2	-4.0	-2.9	-0.3	-3.4	-5.9	-2.3	-4.0
1993 to 1994	-2.0	-4.4	-5.3	-4.4	-7.1	-2.8	-1.6	-5.2	-0.2	-2.5
1994 to 1995	-1.8	-4.1	-8.9	-5.6	-7.0	-2.3	-1.4	-5.2	0.6	-5.1

[1] Includes nonnegligent manslaughter.

Source: U.S. Federal Bureau of Investigation, *Crime in the United States*, annual.

No. 314. Crimes and Crime Rates, by Type and Area: 1995

[In thousands, except rate. Rate per 100,000 population; see headnote, table 313. Estimated totals based on reports from city and rural law enforcement agencies representing 96 percent of the national population. For definitions of crimes, see text, section 5]

TYPE OF CRIME	UNITED STATES		METROPOLITAN AREAS [1]		OTHER CITIES		RURAL AREAS	
	Total	Rate	Total	Rate	Total	Rate	Total	Rate
Total	13,867	5,278	12,046	5,761	1,158	5,315	664	2,083
Violent crime	1,799	685	1,619	774	106	484	75	234
Murder and nonnegligent manslaughter	22	8	19	9	1	5	2	5
Forcible rape	97	37	81	39	8	38	8	25
Robbery	581	221	560	268	16	72	5	17
Aggravated assault	1,099	418	959	459	80	369	60	187
Property crime	12,068	4,593	10,428	4,986	1,053	4,833	590	1,850
Burglary	2,595	988	2,192	1,048	201	924	202	634
Larceny-theft	8,001	3,045	6,853	3,278	799	3,669	348	1,091
Motor vehicle theft	1,473	561	1,381	660	52	240	40	125

[1] For definition, see Appendix II.

Source: U.S. Federal Bureau of Investigation, *Crime in the United States*, annual.

No. 315. Crime Rates, by State, 1993 to 1995, and by Type, 1995

[Offenses known to the police per 100,000 population. Based on Bureau of the Census estimated resident population as of July 1. For definitions of crimes, see text, section 5]

REGION, DIVISION, AND STATE	1993, total	1994, total	1995										
			Total	Violent crime					Property crime				
				Total	Murder[1]	Forcible rape	Robbery	Aggravated assault	Total	Burglary	Larceny—theft	Motor vehicle theft
United States	5,483	5,374	5,278	685	8.2	37.1	221	418	4,593	988	3,045	560
Northeast	4,613	4,346	4,180	611	6.2	24.9	260	319	3,570	758	2,296	516
New England	4,431	4,136	4,091	468	3.4	26.8	121	317	3,623	798	2,352	473
Maine	3,154	3,273	3,285	131	2.0	21.4	27	81	3,153	726	2,292	135
New Hampshire	2,905	2,741	2,655	115	1.8	29.0	27	56	2,541	419	1,977	145
Vermont	3,972	3,250	3,434	118	2.2	28.2	11	77	3,315	761	2,419	135
Massachusetts	4,894	4,441	4,342	687	3.6	29.0	150	504	3,654	818	2,232	605
Rhode Island	4,499	4,119	4,245	368	3.3	27.0	92	245	3,877	933	2,503	441
Connecticut	4,560	4,548	4,503	406	4.6	23.7	163	214	4,097	868	2,689	540
Middle Atlantic	4,676	4,417	4,212	660	7.1	24.3	309	320	3,552	744	2,276	531
New York	5,551	5,071	4,560	842	8.5	23.7	400	410	3,718	808	2,344	566
New Jersey	4,801	4,661	4,704	600	5.1	24.3	283	287	4,104	875	2,597	632
Pennsylvania	3,271	3,272	3,365	427	6.3	25.2	189	207	2,938	562	1,963	413
Midwest	4,806	4,818	4,751	588	6.9	40.1	182	359	4,164	841	2,871	452
East North Central	4,963	4,961	4,831	649	7.6	41.9	208	392	4,182	847	2,839	496
Ohio	4,485	4,461	4,405	483	5.4	43.4	179	255	3,923	839	2,669	415
Indiana	4,465	4,593	4,632	525	8.0	33.3	135	348	4,107	822	2,820	465
Illinois[2]	5,618	5,626	5,456	996	10.3	36.5	331	619	4,460	918	3,019	523
Michigan	5,453	5,445	5,183	688	8.5	62.0	187	430	4,495	910	2,940	645
Wisconsin	4,054	3,944	3,886	281	4.3	23.3	105	148	3,605	613	2,628	364
West North Central	4,454	4,496	4,562	441	5.1	36.1	121	279	4,120	828	2,947	345
Minnesota	4,386	4,341	4,497	356	3.9	56.2	124	172	4,141	797	3,003	342
Iowa	3,846	3,655	4,102	354	1.8	21.8	53	278	3,748	758	2,767	223
Missouri	5,095	5,306	5,121	664	8.8	32.1	204	419	4,457	933	3,051	473
North Dakota	2,820	2,736	2,866	87	0.9	22.8	10	53	2,780	351	2,250	179
South Dakota	2,958	3,102	3,061	208	1.8	41.0	26	139	2,853	541	2,192	121
Nebraska	4,117	4,440	4,545	382	2.9	19.4	65	295	4,163	632	3,179	351
Kansas	4,975	4,894	4,887	421	6.2	36.6	108	270	4,466	1,068	3,074	324
South	5,963	5,848	5,742	738	9.8	40.9	212	474	5,004	1,137	3,337	530
South Atlantic	6,334	6,257	6,134	807	9.1	39.7	246	512	5,327	1,191	3,578	558
Delaware	4,872	4,148	5,159	725	3.5	80.2	199	443	4,434	905	3,114	414
Maryland	6,107	6,123	6,295	987	11.8	42.2	423	510	5,306	1,058	3,533	715
District of Columbia[3]	11,761	11,085	12,174	2,661	65.0	52.7	1,239	1,305	9,512	1,838	5,834	1,840
Virginia	4,116	4,048	3,989	362	7.6	27.2	132	195	3,628	595	2,740	293
West Virginia	2,533	2,528	2,458	210	4.9	21.2	43	141	2,248	565	1,517	166
North Carolina	5,652	5,625	5,640	646	9.4	32.2	179	426	4,993	1,418	3,265	311
South Carolina	5,903	6,001	6,064	982	7.9	47.3	176	751	5,082	1,255	3,442	385
Georgia	6,193	6,010	6,004	657	9.5	35.3	205	407	5,347	1,060	3,678	609
Florida	8,351	8,250	7,702	1,071	7.3	48.6	300	715	6,631	1,522	4,322	787
East South Central	4,528	4,624	4,601	592	10.3	38.0	169	374	4,009	1,012	2,571	427
Kentucky	3,260	3,499	3,352	365	7.2	31.9	104	222	2,987	736	1,992	259
Tennessee	5,240	5,120	5,363	772	10.6	47.1	223	491	4,591	1,143	2,800	648
Alabama	4,879	4,903	4,848	632	11.2	31.7	186	404	4,216	1,025	2,844	347
Mississippi	4,418	4,837	4,515	503	12.9	39.1	131	320	4,012	1,131	2,520	361
West South Central	6,228	5,866	5,738	706	10.7	44.4	181	470	5,032	1,119	3,375	538
Arkansas	4,811	4,799	4,691	553	10.4	37.2	126	380	4,138	997	2,815	326
Louisiana	6,847	6,671	6,676	1,007	17.0	42.7	269	679	5,669	1,232	3,839	598
Oklahoma	5,294	5,570	5,597	664	12.2	44.6	116	492	4,933	1,272	3,164	497
Texas	6,439	5,872	5,684	664	9.0	45.7	180	429	5,021	1,082	3,378	561
West	6,220	6,152	6,083	770	9.0	38.6	242	481	5,312	1,111	3,436	765
Mountain	5,929	6,097	6,357	561	7.2	40.5	131	382	5,796	1,108	4,067	621
Montana	4,790	5,019	5,305	171	3.0	25.9	33	109	5,134	721	4,106	306
Idaho	3,845	4,077	4,402	322	4.1	28.4	24	266	4,079	780	3,058	242
Wyoming	4,163	4,290	4,320	254	2.1	34.4	18	200	4,066	612	3,286	168
Colorado	5,527	5,318	5,396	440	5.8	39.5	96	299	4,956	934	3,635	388
New Mexico	6,266	6,188	6,428	819	8.8	56.6	155	599	5,609	1,447	3,649	513
Arizona	7,432	7,925	8,214	714	10.4	33.6	174	496	7,500	1,417	4,926	1,158
Utah	5,237	5,301	6,091	329	3.9	42.7	67	215	5,762	801	4,572	389
Nevada	6,180	6,677	6,579	945	10.7	61.2	325	549	5,634	1,323	3,566	745
Pacific	6,324	6,172	5,981	849	9.6	37.9	283	518	5,132	1,113	3,199	820
Washington	5,952	6,028	6,270	484	5.1	59.2	133	287	5,786	1,091	4,140	554
Oregon	5,766	6,296	6,564	522	4.1	41.7	138	339	6,042	1,103	4,237	702
California	6,457	6,174	5,831	966	11.2	33.4	331	590	4,865	1,120	2,857	888
Alaska	5,568	5,706	5,754	771	9.1	80.3	155	526	4,983	837	3,624	522
Hawaii	6,277	6,681	7,199	296	4.7	28.3	131	132	6,903	1,165	5,047	691

[1] Includes nonnegligent manslaughter. [2] Forcible rape figures for 1993 to 1995 were estimated using the national rate of forcible rapes when grouped by like agencies as figures submitted were not in accordance with national Uniform Crime Reporting program guidelines. [3] Includes offenses reported by the police at the National Zoo.

Source: U.S. Federal Bureau of Investigation, *Crime in the United States*, annual.

No. 316. Crime Rates, by Type—Selected Large Cities: 1995

to the police per 100,000 population. Based on Bureau of the Census estimated resident population as of July 1. For definitions of crimes, see text, section 5]

) BY SIZE,	Crime index, total	VIOLENT CRIME					PROPERTY CRIME			
		Total	Murder	Forcible rape	Robbery	Aggravated assault	Total	Burglary	Larceny—theft	Motor vehicle theft
......	6,076.3	1,573.2	16.1	32.4	809.9	714.8	4,503.1	1,009.5	2,500.7	992.9
......	7,680.0	2,034.4	24.5	45.9	840.5	1,123.6	5,645.5	1,192.2	3,120.1	1,333.2
......	(NA)	(NA)	30.0	(NA)	1,094.1	1,425.7	7,197.5	1,483.3	4,417.9	1,316.3
......	7,588.0	1,283.5	18.2	48.3	531.7	685.3	6,304.5	1,431.7	3,573.5	1,299.4
......	7,077.7	1,436.2	28.2	50.5	689.8	467.7	5,641.5	1,058.6	3,028.5	1,556.3
......	5,548.2	956.8	7.9	29.9	280.2	638.8	4,591.4	890.6	2,634.8	1,066.0
......	10,880.1	1,067.5	19.7	37.9	340.1	669.8	9,812.6	1,929.9	5,749.4	2,133.3
......	9,464.1	1,532.4	26.5	81.8	566.1	858.1	7,931.7	1,603.0	4,708.6	1,620.0
......	7,993.9	517.9	14.2	65.8	234.5	203.3	7,476.0	1,396.2	5,237.5	842.3
......	11,938.8	2,407.6	47.6	110.7	1,010.3	1,238.9	9,531.2	2,242.7	4,353.3	2,935.2
......	7,627.8	327.4	4.3	24.7	155.7	142.7	7,300.4	1,150.4	5,304.8	845.2
......	4,386.7	808.1	4.6	47.0	146.9	609.5	3,578.7	665.6	2,399.6	513.5
......	7,584.5	1,200.2	14.9	72.0	467.8	645.5	6,364.3	1,540.0	3,837.1	1,007.1
\.....	8,190.2	1,476.6	13.4	41.2	876.1	545.9	6,713.6	965.2	4,625.5	1,122.9
......	13,318.4	3,018.1	45.6	95.9	1,594.1	1,282.5	10,300.3	2,326.4	6,405.3	1,568.6
......	9,000.8	1,412.9	12.7	92.0	430.0	878.3	7,587.9	1,839.2	4,904.1	844.6
......	9,192.5	1,037.1	12.1	99.6	521.2	404.2	8,155.4	2,058.1	4,995.1	1,102.2
......	10,514.0	1,769.3	29.0	125.8	926.3	688.2	8,744.6	2,568.7	3,958.2	2,217.8
......	8,462.9	1,082.3	22.2	59.4	586.4	414.3	7,380.6	1,344.0	4,214.0	1,822.6
......	7,063.9	838.3	6.3	41.0	182.3	608.8	6,225.5	648.6	4,919.2	657.7
......	12,166.4	2,661.6	65.2	52.7	1,239.0	1,304.7	9,504.9	1,838.3	5,826.9	1,839.7
......	9,492.8	1,737.6	17.4	68.8	653.2	998.2	7,755.2	1,211.3	4,721.5	1,822.4
......	9,576.5	1,695.9	16.4	67.3	542.0	1,070.3	7,880.6	1,830.2	5,379.6	670.8
......	10,482.4	926.1	7.7	49.1	417.9	451.3	9,556.3	1,452.1	6,792.9	1,311.4
......	8,131.9	773.4	8.8	58.8	255.1	450.6	7,358.5	1,436.2	5,238.6	683.8
n, TN..	10,710.7	1,790.4	20.1	93.0	510.8	1,166.5	8,920.3	1,572.7	5,798.0	1,549.6
......	6,873.5	861.3	16.0	63.3	279.3	502.7	6,012.1	1,464.9	3,511.2	1,036.1
......	7,809.9	1,646.2	26.1	139.2	853.2	627.8	6,163.7	1,553.9	2,780.2	1,829.6
......	10,960.9	2,232.4	74.5	100.0	1,098.0	960.0	8,728.4	2,101.1	4,609.0	2,018.4
K.....	11,501.8	1,292.7	48.7	101.5	343.8	798.7	10,209.1	2,234.9	6,877.0	1,097.1
......	8,617.2	1,160.9	23.5	72.1	426.9	638.5	7,456.3	1,593.2	4,807.1	1,056.0
......	12,068.3	1,926.0	9.4	92.9	501.1	1,322.7	10,142.3	1,703.6	8,451.7	1,987.0
......	12,157.4	1,206.1	14.4	64.9	264.9	861.8	10,951.4	1,332.3	8,274.8	1,344.3
......	11,800.0	2,184.7	24.0	105.5	751.0	1,304.2	9,615.3	2,187.9	5,903.1	1,524.4
......	7,030.9	1,295.5	18.3	39.2	636.2	601.8	5,735.3	1,279.0	3,213.3	1,243.0
\.....	4,651.8	222.0	3.7	22.7	109.9	85.8	4,429.8	668.6	3,496.7	264.5
......	(NA)	(NA)	12.6	70.5	386.7	658.3	8,772.2	1,992.3	5,589.8	1,190.1
......	17,067.7	3,646.5	45.5	109.1	1,300.9	2,191.0	13,421.2	2,892.1	8,463.5	2,065.6
......	11,909.3	1,456.6	18.3	54.6	557.5	826.3	10,452.6	1,966.0	5,290.2	3,196.4
......	15,623.7	3,413.3	29.0	52.3	1,498.7	1,833.3	12,210.3	2,607.2	7,271.1	2,332.1
......	7,377.4	1,155.8	8.0	67.6	251.1	829.1	6,221.6	1,610.0	3,444.5	1,167.2
......	10,324.2	1,138.8	15.2	42.0	566.5	515.1	9,185.4	2,129.3	4,932.4	2,123.7
......	16,082.9	3,352.5	54.9	73.5	1,382.8	1,841.3	12,730.4	2,878.6	7,696.6	2,155.2
......	7,486.1	1,289.8	13.9	113.4	599.0	563.4	6,196.3	1,491.6	4,172.9	531.8
......	11,545.4	1,978.1	26.8	161.6	992.4	797.3	9,567.3	2,243.2	6,069.2	1,254.9
......	6,130.0	979.2	16.3	68.5	585.4	308.9	5,150.8	1,014.1	3,182.0	954.7
......	8,894.7	812.6	5.2	39.4	156.2	611.7	8,082.1	1,467.4	5,233.6	1,381.2
CO...	6,765.2	482.7	5.5	63.8	128.2	285.1	6,282.5	1,062.1	4,792.6	427.8
......	8,394.6	886.8	10.8	85.8	436.5	353.7	7,507.7	1,944.0	4,574.8	989.0
......	9,205.3	2,027.2	19.8	83.5	907.8	1,016.0	7,178.1	2,270.2	3,560.9	1,347.0
......	8,221.7	701.1	13.2	65.1	287.2	335.6	7,520.7	1,721.0	4,950.3	849.3
......	6,979.9	881.2	3.1	52.7	178.2	647.2	6,098.7	1,102.9	4,209.7	786.1
......	5,196.9	859.8	24.6	22.6	422.2	390.4	4,337.1	746.5	2,530.4	1,060.3
......	14,182.3	3,013.3	16.2	95.6	905.9	1,995.6	11,169.0	2,284.4	6,821.1	2,063.6
......	6,136.1	872.9	8.8	26.8	356.5	480.7	5,263.2	1,107.7	3,090.8	1,064.7
(.....	10,432.5	985.0	11.0	77.0	179.6	717.4	9,447.4	1,348.9	7,580.4	518.2
......	7,149.0	1,195.7	18.3	49.5	583.9	543.9	5,953.3	1,639.9	3,227.7	1,065.7
......	12,203.0	2,456.0	44.7	91.6	797.1	1,522.6	9,747.1	2,363.6	6,024.1	1,359.3
......	7,657.1	958.6	9.5	88.1	351.6	509.6	6,696.4	1,614.9	4,241.0	842.6
......	15,511.9	3,985.3	39.2	83.0	2,105.8	1,757.3	11,526.6	2,831.7	4,904.1	3,790.8
......	6,577.8	762.0	7.0	53.7	213.7	487.6	5,815.8	948.0	4,348.2	519.5
......	7,220.9	990.1	11.4	95.5	306.5	576.7	6,230.8	994.5	4,399.2	837.1
......	8,448.4	981.3	21.7	72.6	530.2	356.8	7,467.1	1,285.2	5,227.2	954.7
......	8,104.7	1,568.4	14.0	48.2	415.9	1,090.3	6,536.3	1,742.6	3,518.5	1,276.2
......	9,453.5	2,136.0	12.4	71.0	585.0	1,467.6	7,317.5	1,740.9	4,985.4	591.2
......	7,274.2	846.4	7.5	43.2	269.0	526.8	6,427.8	1,528.5	4,385.8	513.5
, KY...	6,648.2	875.6	5.8	54.7	265.4	549.9	5,772.3	1,242.6	4,135.9	393.9
......	9,847.1	1,106.4	23.0	65.0	683.0	335.4	8,740.7	2,205.4	5,577.9	957.3
......	13,445.6	2,860.4	28.4	75.5	608.7	2,147.8	10,585.2	2,254.8	6,897.0	1,433.5
......	7,946.0	1,906.3	11.0	40.5	1,015.0	639.8	6,039.7	1,677.0	2,815.6	1,547.1
......	9,288.0	1,424.3	18.8	59.4	548.8	797.3	7,863.6	1,714.4	4,593.5	1,555.7
......	7,134.8	1,017.7	8.1	93.8	392.6	523.2	6,117.2	1,252.8	3,959.4	905.0

ble. [1] Crime data were not available for Indianapolis, IN and Albuquerque, NM in 1994. [2] The rates for nt crime, and crime index are not shown because the forcible rape figures were not in accordance with national porting guidelines.

Federal Bureau of Investigation, *Crime in the United States*, annual.

No. 317. Murder—Circumstances and Weapons Used or Cause of Death: 1980 to 1995

[Based solely on police investigation. For definition of murder, see text, section 5]

CHARACTERISTIC	1980	1990	1994	1995
Murders, total	21,860	20,273	22,084	20,220
Percent distribution	100.0	100.0	100.0	100.0
CIRCUMSTANCES				
Felonies, total	17.7	20.8	18.4	17.7
Robbery	10.8	9.2	9.4	9.3
Narcotics	1.7	6.7	5.6	5.1
Sex offenses	1.5	1.1	0.6	0.6
Other felonies	3.7	3.7	2.8	2.8
Suspected felonies	6.7	0.7	0.6	0.6
Argument, total	39.9	34.4	29.8	29.0
Property or money	2.6	2.5	1.8	1.7
Romantic triangle	2.3	2.0	1.7	1.4
Other arguments	35.0	29.8	26.3	25.9
Other motives	20.6	19.4	23.1	23.9
Unknown	15.1	24.8	28.1	28.9
TYPE OF WEAPON OR CAUSE OF DEATH				
Guns	62.4	64.3	70.0	68.2
Handguns	45.8	49.8	57.8	55.8
Cutting or stabbing	19.3	17.4	12.7	12.6
Blunt objects [1]	5.0	5.4	4.1	4.5
Personal weapons [2]	5.9	5.5	5.3	5.9
Strangulations, asphyxiations	2.3	2.0	1.8	1.9
Fire	1.3	1.4	0.9	0.8
All other [3]	3.8	4.0	5.2	6.1

[1] Refers to club, hammer, etc. [2] Hands, fists, feet, etc. [3] Includes poison, drowning, explosives, narcotics, and unknown.
Source: U.S. Federal Bureau of Investigation, *Crime in the United States*, annual.

No. 318. Murder Victims, by Age, Sex, and Race: 1995

AGE	Total	SEX			RACE			
		Male	Female	Unknown	White	Black	Other	Unknown
Total	20,220	15,487	4,700	33	9,714	9,767	544	195
Percent distribution	100.0	76.6	23.2	0.2	48.0	48.3	2.7	1.0
Under 18 yrs. old	2,455	1,754	701	-	1,156	1,196	86	17
18 yrs. old and over	17,424	13,510	3,912	2	8,425	8,441	447	111
Infant (under 1 yr. old)	256	146	110	-	154	91	7	4
1 to 4 yrs. old	422	231	191	-	232	179	10	1
5 to 9 yrs. old	118	59	59	-	63	47	8	-
10 to 14 yrs. old	319	225	94	-	158	141	19	1
15 to 19 yrs. old	2,858	2,401	456	1	1,163	1,591	83	21
20 to 24 yrs. old	3,586	3,074	512	-	1,455	2,035	79	17
25 to 29 yrs. old	2,836	2,262	574	-	1,237	1,515	68	16
30 to 34 yrs. old	2,546	1,932	613	1	1,183	1,279	66	18
35 to 39 yrs. old	1,987	1,424	563	-	984	936	54	13
40 to 44 yrs. old	1,529	1,125	404	-	855	624	33	17
45 to 49 yrs. old	1,002	770	232	-	561	409	25	7
50 to 54 yrs. old	650	480	170	-	398	217	29	6
55 to 59 yrs. old	473	357	116	-	287	163	22	1
60 to 64 yrs. old	356	269	87	-	220	123	11	2
65 to 69 yrs. old	296	202	94	-	190	98	6	2
70 to 74 yrs. old	228	126	102	-	158	65	4	1
75 yrs. old and over	417	181	236	-	283	124	9	1
Age unknown	341	223	87	31	133	130	11	67

\- Represents zero.
Source: U.S. Federal Bureau of Investigation, *Crime in the United States*, annual.

No. 319. Homicide Victims, by Race and Sex: 1970 to 1995

[Rates per 100,000 resident population in specified group. Excludes deaths to nonresidents of United States. Beginning 1980, deaths classified according to the ninth revision of the *International Classification of Diseases*; for earlier years, classified according to revision in use at the time; see text, section 2]

YEAR	HOMICIDE VICTIMS					HOMICIDE RATE [2]				
	Total [1]	White		Black		Total [1]	White		Black	
		Male	Female	Male	Female		Male	Female	Male	Female
1970	16,848	5,865	1,938	7,265	1,569	8.3	6.8	2.1	67.6	13.3
1980	24,278	10,381	3,177	8,385	1,898	10.7	10.9	3.2	66.6	13.5
1981	23,646	9,941	3,125	8,312	1,825	10.3	10.4	3.1	64.8	12.7
1982	22,358	9,260	3,179	7,730	1,743	9.6	9.6	3.1	59.1	12.0
1983	20,191	8,355	2,880	6,822	1,672	8.6	8.6	2.8	51.4	11.3
1984	19,796	8,171	2,956	6,563	1,677	8.4	8.3	2.9	48.7	11.2
1985	19,893	8,122	3,041	6,616	1,666	8.3	8.2	2.9	48.4	11.0
1986	21,731	8,567	3,123	7,634	1,861	9.0	8.6	3.0	55.0	12.1
1987	21,103	7,979	3,149	7,518	1,969	8.7	7.9	3.0	53.3	12.6
1988	22,032	7,994	3,072	8,314	2,089	9.0	7.9	2.9	58.0	13.2
1989	22,909	8,337	2,971	8,888	2,074	9.2	8.2	2.8	61.1	12.9
1990	24,932	9,147	3,006	9,981	2,163	10.0	9.0	2.8	69.2	13.5
1991	26,513	9,581	3,201	10,628	2,330	10.5	9.3	3.0	72.0	14.2
1992	25,488	9,456	3,012	10,131	2,187	10.0	9.1	2.8	67.5	13.1
1993	26,009	9,054	3,232	10,640	2,297	10.1	8.6	3.0	69.7	13.6
1994	24,926	9,055	2,921	10,083	2,124	9.6	8.5	2.6	65.1	12.4
1995	21,577	(NA)	(NA)	(NA)	(NA)	8.2	(NA)	(NA)	(NA)	(NA)

NA Not available. [1] Includes races not shown separately. [2] Rate based on enumerated population figures as of April 1 for 1970, 1980, and 1990; July 1 estimates for other years.
Source: U.S. National Center for Health Statistics, *Vital Statistics of the United States*, annual, and unpublished data.

No. 320. Forcible Rape—Number and Rate: 1970 to 1995

[For definition of rape, see text, section 5]

ITEM	1970	1980	1985	1989	1990	1991	1992	1993	1994	1995
NUMBER										
Total	37,990	82,990	88,670	94,500	102,560	106,590	109,060	106,010	102,220	97,460
By force	26,888	63,599	71,060	78,411	86,541	91,522	93,825	92,360	89,297	85,249
Attempt	11,102	19,391	17,610	16,089	16,019	15,068	15,235	13,650	12,923	12,211
RATE										
Per 100,000 population	18.7	36.8	37.1	38.1	41.2	42.3	42.8	41.1	39.3	37.1
Per 100,000 females	30.4	71.6	72.3	74.3	80.5	82.5	83.5	80.3	76.7	72.5
Per 100,000 females 12 years old and over	46.3	86.3	86.6	89.3	96.6	100.9	100.5	96.4	92.0	87.1
AVERAGE ANNUAL PERCENT CHANGE IN RATE [1]										
Per 100,000 population	(NA)	6.1	3.9	1.3	8.1	2.7	1.2	-4.0	-4.4	-5.6
Per 100,000 females 12 years old and over	(NA)	6.0	4.3	1.4	8.2	4.5	-0.4	-4.1	-4.6	-5.3

NA Not available. [1] Represents annual average from prior year shown except for 1980, from 1979; for 1985, from 1984; and for 1989, from 1988.

Source: U.S. Federal Bureau of Investigation, *Population-at-Risk Rates and Selected Crime Indicators*, annual.

No. 321. Robbery and Property Crimes, by Type and Selected Characteristic: 1980 to 1995

[For definition of crime, see text, section 5]

ITEM	NUMBER OF OFFENSES (1,000)				RATE PER 100,000 INHABITANTS				AVERAGE VALUE LOST (dol.)	
	1980	1990	1994	1995	1980	1990	1994	1995	1994	1995
Robbery, total [1]	566	639	620	581	251.1	257.0	237.7	220.9	801	873
Type of crime:										
Street or highway	293	359	338	315	130.1	144.2	129.7	120.0	651	645
Commercial house	78	73	76	71	34.6	29.5	29.2	27.2	1,229	1,351
Gas station	23	18	13	13	10.4	7.1	5.2	5.1	450	959
Convenience store	38	39	32	30	17.0	15.6	12.2	11.4	387	400
Residence	60	62	67	63	26.8	25.1	25.9	24.0	1,041	1,082
Bank	8	9	9	9	3.8	3.8	3.4	3.5	3,551	4,015
Weapon used:										
Firearm	228	234	257	238	101.3	94.1	98.8	90.6	(NA)	(NA)
Knife or cutting instrument	73	76	59	53	32.3	30.7	22.5	20.1	(NA)	(NA)
Other dangerous weapon	51	61	60	53	22.8	24.5	22.9	20.2	(NA)	(NA)
Strongarm	214	268	243	236	94.8	107.7	93.5	90.0	(NA)	(NA)
Burglary, total	3,795	3,074	2,712	2,595	1,684.1	1,235.9	1,041.8	987.6	1,311	1,259
Forcible entry	2,789	2,150	1,822	1,737	1,237.5	864.5	700.0	661.2	(NA)	(NA)
Unlawful entry	711	678	677	657	315.6	272.8	260.1	250.1	(NA)	(NA)
Attempted forcible entry	295	245	213	201	131.0	98.7	81.7	76.4	(NA)	(NA)
Residence	2,525	2,033	1,814	1,736	1,120.6	817.4	696.7	660.6	1,296	1,211
Nonresidence	1,270	1,041	898	859	563.5	418.5	345.1	327.0	1,341	1,257
Occurred during the night	1,508	1,135	957	905	669.0	456.4	367.7	344.4	(NA)	(NA)
Occurred during the day	1,263	1,151	1,049	1,000	560.3	462.8	402.7	380.5	(NA)	(NA)
Larceny-theft, total	7,137	7,946	7,876	8,001	3,167.0	3,194.8	3,026.4	3,044.9	505	535
Pocket picking	85	81	64	51	37.9	32.4	24.5	19.4	428	350
Purse snatching	107	82	60	51	47.5	32.8	23.2	19.5	279	279
Shoplifting	773	1,291	1,178	1,205	343.0	519.1	452.4	458.4	133	108
From motor vehicles	1,231	1,744	1,865	1,940	546.4	701.3	716.4	738.5	542	531
Motor vehicle accessories	1,366	1,185	1,014	964	606.2	476.3	389.4	367.0	312	329
Bicycles	715	443	496	501	317.5	178.2	190.7	190.5	252	286
From buildings	1,187	1,118	1,027	1,004	526.9	449.4	394.3	382.1	851	891
From coin-operated machines	58	63	53	50	25.8	25.4	20.4	18.9	228	283
Other	1,613	1,940	2,120	2,235	715.7	780.0	814.2	850.5	680	770
Motor vehicles, total [2]	1,132	1,636	1,539	1,473	502.2	657.8	591.2	560.5	4,940	5,129
Automobiles	845	1,304	1,216	1,154	374.8	524.3	467.2	439.2	(NA)	(NA)
Trucks and buses	149	238	239	240	66.1	95.5	92.0	91.2	(NA)	(NA)

NA Not available. [1] Includes other crimes not shown separately. [2] Includes other types of motor vehicles not shown separately.

Source: U.S. Federal Bureau of Investigation, *Population-at-Risk Rates and Selected Crime Indicators*, annual.

No. 322. Hate Crimes—Number of Incidents, Offenses, Victims, and Offenders, by Bias Motivation: 1995

[The FBI collects statistics on hate crimes from 9,500 law enforcement agencies in forty-five states and Washington, D.C., covering seventy-five percent of the U.S. population. Hate crime offenses cover incidents motivated by race, religion, sexual orientation, and ethnicity/national origin]

BIAS MOTIVATION	Incidents	Offenses	Victims	Known offenders
Total bias motivations	7,947	9,895	10,469	8,433
Race, total	4,831	6,170	6,438	5,751
Anti-White	1,226	1,511	1,554	2,032
Anti-Black	2,988	3,805	3,945	3,089
Anti-American Indian/Alaskan native	41	59	59	38
Anti-Asian/Pacific Islander	355	484	496	390
Anti-multi-racial group	221	311	384	202
Ethnicity/national origin, total	814	1,022	1,044	958
Anti-Hispanic	516	680	698	685
Anti-other ethnicity/national origin	298	342	346	273
Religion, total	1,277	1,414	1,617	437
Anti-Jewish	1,058	1,145	1,236	350
Anti-Catholic	31	35	53	8
Anti-Protestant	36	47	65	12
Anti-Islamic	29	39	41	26
Anti-other religious group	102	122	196	36
Anti-multi-religious group	20	25	25	4
Anti-atheism/agnosticism/etc.	1	1	1	1
Sexual orientation, total	1,019	1,266	1,347	1,273
Anti-male homosexual	735	915	937	1,081
Anti-female homosexual	146	189	191	131
Anti-homosexual	103	125	182	30
Anti-heterosexual	17	19	19	13
Anti-bisexual	18	16	18	18
Multiple bias	6	23	23	14

Source: U.S. Federal Bureau of Investigation, *<http://www.fbi.gov/ucr/hatecm.htm>; (accessed: 11 November 1996).*

No. 323. Hate Crimes Reported, by State: 1995

STATE	Number of participating agencies	Population	Agencies submitting incidents	Incidents reported
United States	9,584	196,011,279	1,560	7,947
Alabama	(1)	(1)	(1)	(1)
Alaska	1	253,500	1	8
Arizona	87	4,095,027	25	220
Arkansas	190	2,476,091	5	7
California	744	31,575,724	215	1,751
Colorado	228	3,740,318	34	149
Connecticut	94	2,866,092	44	87
Delaware	51	716,612	8	45
District of Columbia	1	554,000	1	4
Florida	411	14,214,988	60	164
Georgia	3	404,337	3	49
Hawaii	(1)	(1)	(1)	(1)
Idaho	116	1,154,533	28	114
Illinois	1	2,749,811	1	146
Indiana	164	3,234,261	14	35
Iowa	232	2,832,372	14	29
Kansas	(1)	(1)	(1)	(1)
Kentucky	513	3,839,698	25	81
Louisiana	146	2,681,595	5	7
Maine	130	1,234,660	14	75
Maryland	148	5,041,200	41	353
Massachusetts	202	4,563,851	88	333
Michigan	480	7,471,391	132	405
Minnesota	6	2,222,490	66	285
Mississippi	51	619,465	3	6
Missouri	157	3,440,651	14	135
Montana	6	146,201	4	11
Nebraska	(1)	(1)	(1)	(1)
Nevada	35	1,528,846	3	88
New Hampshire	2	80,401	1	24
New Jersey	566	7,948,721	243	768
New Mexico	70	1,213,889	7	24
New York	520	17,607,895	50	845
North Carolina	59	2,319,606	24	52
North Dakota	74	495,868	3	3
Ohio	321	7,531,175	51	267
Oklahoma	7	924,403	5	37
Oregon	243	3,129,911	25	152
Pennsylvania	1,134	11,842,573	38	282
Rhode Island	45	990,000	8	46
South Carolina	293	3,666,417	15	28
South Dakota	38	301,872	3	5
Tennessee	104	1,401,961	12	25
Texas	914	18,659,819	96	326
Utah	116	1,906,800	28	107
Vermont	19	309,236	8	10
Virginia	175	3,330,876	22	51
Washington	229	5,292,420	54	266
West Virginia	(1)	(1)	(1)	(1)
Wisconsin	337	5,120,215	18	46
Wyoming	59	457,505	3	19

[1] Did not report.

Source: U.S. Federal Bureau of Investigation, *<http://www.fbi.gov/ucr/hatecm.htm>; (accessed: 11 November 1996).*

No. 324. Criminal Victimizations and Victimization Rates: 1993 to 1995

[Based on National Crime Victimization Survey; see text, section 5, and Appendix III. The total population age 12 or older in 1993 was 211,524,770; in 1994 the population was 213,747,400; and in 1995 the population was 215,709,450]

TYPE OF CRIME	NUMBER OF VICTIMIZATIONS (1,000)			VICTIMIZATION RATES [1]		
	1993	1994	1995	1993	1994	1995
All crimes, total	43,547	42,359	38,447	(X)	(X)	(X)
Personal crimes [2]	11,365	11,349	9,966	53.7	53.1	46.2
Crimes of violence	10,848	10,860	9,601	51.3	50.8	44.5
Completed violence	3,213	3,205	2,779	15.2	15.0	12.9
Attempted/threatened violence	7,635	7,654	6,822	36.1	35.8	31.6
Rape/sexual assault	485	433	340	2.3	2.0	1.6
Rape/attempted rape	313	316	234	1.5	1.5	1.1
Rape	160	168	141	0.8	0.8	0.7
Attempted rape	152	149	93	0.7	0.7	0.4
Sexual assault	173	117	106	0.8	0.5	0.5
Robbery	1,291	1,299	1,142	6.1	6.1	5.3
Completed/property taken	815	795	745	3.9	3.7	3.5
With injury	274	288	218	1.3	1.3	1.0
Without injury	541	507	527	2.6	2.4	2.4
Attempted to take property	476	504	397	2.3	2.4	1.8
With injury	96	122	95	0.5	0.6	0.4
Without injury	381	382	302	1.8	1.8	1.4
Assault	9,072	9,128	8,119	42.9	42.7	37.6
Aggravated	2,563	2,478	1,892	12.1	11.6	8.8
With injury	713	679	509	3.4	3.2	2.4
Threatened with weapon	1,850	1,799	1,383	8.7	8.4	6.4
Simple	6,509	6,650	6,227	30.8	31.1	28.9
With minor injury	1,356	1,466	1,291	6.4	6.9	6.0
Without injury	5,153	5,184	4,936	24.4	24.3	22.9
Personal theft [3]	517	489	365	2.4	2.3	1.7
Property crimes	32,182	31,011	28,480	322.1	307.6	279.5
Household burglary	5,984	5,482	4,825	59.9	54.4	47.4
Completed	4,824	4,573	4,072	48.3	45.4	40.0
Attempted forcible entry	1,160	910	752	11.6	9.0	7.4
Motor vehicle theft	1,961	1,764	1,654	19.6	17.5	16.2
Completed	1,291	1,172	1,098	12.9	11.6	10.8
Attempted	670	591	556	6.7	5.9	5.5
Theft	24,238	23,765	22,002	242.6	235.7	215.9
Completed [4]	23,020	22,743	21,149	230.4	225.6	207.6
Attempted	1,218	1,022	583	14.3	10.1	8.4

X Not applicable. [1] Per 1,000 persons age 12 or older or per 1,000 households. [2] The victimization survey cannot measure murder because of the inability to question the victim. [3] Includes pocket picking, purse snatching, and attempted purse snatching. [4] Includes thefts in which the amount taken was not ascertained. In 1993, this category accounted for 1,433,000 victimizations and in 1994, 1,241,000.

Source: U.S. Bureau of Justice Statistics, *Criminal Victimization 1995*, December 1996.

No. 325. Victimization Rates, by Type of Crime and Characteristic of the Victim: 1995

[Rate per 1,000 persons age 12 years or older. Based on National Crime Victimization Survey; see text, section 5, and Appendix III]

CHARACTERISTIC	All crime	CRIMES OF VIOLENCE						Personal theft
		All crimes of violence	Rape/sexual assault	Robbery	Assault			
					Total	Aggravated	Simple	
Total	46.2	44.5	1.6	5.3	37.6	8.8	28.9	1.7
Male	54.4	53.2	0.3	7.5	45.3	11.9	33.5	1.3
Female	38.5	36.4	2.8	3.2	30.4	5.9	24.6	2.1
12 to 15 yrs. old	110.9	107.1	2.2	9.5	95.4	15.4	80.1	3.8
16 to 19 yrs. old	110.3	107.7	5.7	9.0	93.0	24.4	68.6	2.7
20 to 24 yrs. old	79.8	78.8	3.0	10.8	65.0	15.4	49.6	1.1
25 to 34 yrs. old	55.9	54.7	2.0	6.9	45.8	11.7	34.1	1.2
35 to 49 yrs. old	35.6	33.8	1.4	4.7	27.7	6.8	20.9	1.8
50 to 64 yrs. old	15.6	14.0	0.1	1.8	12.1	2.6	9.5	1.6
65 yrs. old and over	6.9	5.9	0.0	1.3	4.6	1.3	3.3	1.0
White	44.6	43.1	1.6	4.2	37.3	8.2	29.1	1.4
Black	58.4	55.4	1.6	12.5	41.3	12.6	28.7	3.1
Other	43.8	40.9	1.2	6.3	33.4	9.2	24.2	2.9
Hispanic	56.1	53.4	1.3	10.6	41.5	13.6	27.9	2.6
Non-Hispanic	45.0	43.4	1.6	4.8	37.0	8.2	28.8	1.6
Household income:								
Less than $7,500	74.6	71.0	3.5	11.8	55.7	16.5	39.2	3.6
$7,500-$14,999	49.7	48.4	1.6	9.1	37.7	10.0	27.7	1.3
$15,000-$24,999	49.2	47.7	1.6	6.5	39.5	9.1	30.4	1.5
$25,000-$34,999	48.1	46.4	1.5	5.1	39.8	8.9	30.8	1.7
$35,000-$49,999	45.8	44.2	1.8	3.6	38.9	8.8	30.1	1.5
$50,000-$74,999	44.1	42.7	1.2	3.1	38.4	8.5	29.9	1.5
$75,000 or more	37.9	36.2	0.8	2.4	33.0	5.5	27.6	1.7

Source: U.S. Bureau of Justice Statistics, *Criminal Victimization 1995*, December 1996.

No. 326. Victim-Offender Relationship in Crimes of Violence, by Characteristics of the Criminal Incident: 1995

[In percent. Covers only crimes of violence. Based on National Crime Victimization Survey; see text, section 5, and Appendix III]

CHARACTERISTICS OF INCIDENT	Total	Rape/sexual assault	Robbery	ASSAULT		
				Total	Aggravated[1]	Simple
Total	100	100	100	100	100	100
Victim/offender relationship:[2]						
Relatives	9	12	5	10	8	10
Well-known	24	34	12	25	23	26
Casual acquaintance	15	25	6	17	13	18
Stranger	51	29	76	48	56	46
Time of day:						
6 a.m. to 6 p.m.	54	34	44	57	50	59
6 p.m. to midnight	33	37	41	32	36	31
Midnight to 6 a.m.	11	25	14	10	13	9
Location of crime:						
At or near victim's home or lodging	26	43	26	26	25	26
Friend's/relative's/neighbor's home	9	24	6	8	12	7
Commercial places	12	4	4	14	10	15
Parking lots/garages	8	5	10	8	7	8
School	14	4	6	16	6	19
Streets other than near victim's home	19	5	39	17	28	14
Other[3]	12	15	11	12	12	12
Victim's activity:						
At work or traveling to or from work	21	13	17	22	19	23
School	13	3	7	14	7	16
Activities at home	21	43	15	21	23	21
Shopping/errands	4	2	10	4	4	4
Leisure activities away from home	23	28	24	22	26	21
Traveling	9	5	18	8	12	7
Other	8	5	9	8	10	8
Distance from victim's home:						
Inside home or lodging	14	40	12	13	13	13
Near victim's home	14	7	15	15	16	14
1 mile or less	21	13	31	20	23	19
5 miles or less	24	12	19	26	21	27
50 miles or less	22	20	16	23	25	23
More than 50 miles	4	7	6	3	3	3
Weapons:						
No weapons present	74	94	42	77	5	100
Weapons present	26	6	58	23	95	-
Firearm	10	3	32	8	31	-
Other type of weapon[4]	16	3	26	15	63	-

- Represents zero. [1] An aggravated assault is any assault in which an offender possesses or uses a weapon or inflicts serious injury. [2] Excludes "don't know" relationships. [3] Includes areas on public transportation or inside station, in apartment yard, park, field, playground, or other areas. [4] Includes knives, other sharp objects, blunt objects, and other types of weapons.

Source: U.S. Bureau of Justice Statistics, *Criminal Victimization 1995*, December 1996.

No. 327. Property Victimization Rates, by Selected Household Characteristic: 1995

[Victimizations per 1,000 households. Based on National Crime Victimization Survey; see text, section 5, and Appendix III]

CHARACTERISTIC	Total	Burglary	Motor vehicle theft	Theft
Total	279.5	47.4	18.2	215.9
Race:				
White	272.9	45.4	14.0	213.6
Black	322.3	61.6	30.4	230.3
Other	292.6	46.4	21.9	224.3
Ethnicity:				
Hispanic	364.1	59.0	27.8	277.3
Non-Hispanic	272.7	46.3	15.3	211.1
Household income:				
Less than $7,500	290.7	71.4	13.9	205.4
$7,500-$14,999	256.1	55.0	15.6	185.5
$15,000-$24,999	286.8	48.7	15.7	222.4
$25,000-$34,999	283.0	42.0	16.5	224.5
$35,000-$49,999	293.6	42.6	18.3	232.8
$50,000-$74,999	317.1	41.8	17.2	258.1
$75,000 or more	336.1	43.3	19.1	273.7
Residence:				
Urban	347.9	59.9	25.7	262.3
Suburban	267.0	39.0	15.0	213.0
Rural	218.4	46.6	6.9	164.8
Form of tenure:				
Home owned	244.2	40.6	12.3	191.3
Home rented	344.4	59.8	23.5	261.1

Source: U.S. Bureau of Justice Statistics, *Criminal Victimization 1995*, December 1996.

No. 328. Persons Arrested, by Charge and Race: 1995

[Represents arrests (not charges) reported by 9,495 agencies with a total 1995 population 196 million as estimated by FBI]

OFFENSE CHARGED	TOTAL ARRESTS (1,000)					PERCENT DISTRIBUTION				
	Total	White	Black	American Indian or Alaskan Native	Asian or Pacific Islander	Total	White	Black	American Indian or Alaskan Native	Asian or Pacific Islander
Total	**11,387**	**7,808**	**3,523**	**130**	**126**	**100.0**	**66.8**	**30.9**	**1.1**	**1.1**
Serious crimes [1]	2,237	1,384	798	23	32	100.0	61.9	35.7	1.0	1.4
Murder and nonnegligent manslaughter	17	7	9	(Z)	(Z)	100.0	43.4	54.4	0.8	1.4
Forcible rape	27	15	11	(Z)	(Z)	100.0	55.8	42.4	1.0	1.1
Robbery	138	53	82	1	2	100.0	38.7	59.5	0.5	1.3
Aggravated assault	436	261	168	4	5	100.0	59.6	38.4	0.9	1.1
Burglary	292	195	90	3	3	100.0	67.0	31.0	0.9	1.1
Larceny/theft	1,163	754	377	13	19	100.0	64.8	32.4	1.1	1.6
Motor vehicle theft	149	87	57	2	3	100.0	58.5	38.3	1.2	2.0
Arson	15	11	4	(Z)	(Z)	100.0	74.2	23.7	1.0	1.0
All other nonserious crimes:										
Other assaults	974	613	338	12	11	100.0	63.0	34.7	1.2	1.1
Forgery and counterfeiting	92	60	30	1	1	100.0	65.0	33.1	0.6	1.4
Fraud	319	204	111	2	2	100.0	64.0	34.7	0.5	0.8
Embezzlement	12	8	4	(Z)	(Z)	100.0	64.9	33.1	0.6	1.4
Stolen property—buying, receiving, possessing	128	75	50	1	2	100.0	58.6	39.4	0.7	1.2
Vandalism	232	171	56	3	3	100.0	73.4	23.9	1.4	1.3
Weapons; carrying, possessing, etc.	187	111	72	1	2	100.0	59.4	38.8	0.7	1.2
Prostitution and commercialized vice	81	49	30	(Z)	1	100.0	60.9	36.8	0.3	1.7
Sex offenses (except forcible rape and prostitution)	72	54	16	1	1	100.0	75.0	22.6	1.1	1.3
Drug abuse violations	1,143	710	421	5	7	100.0	62.1	36.9	0.5	0.6
Gambling	16	8	6	(Z)	1	100.0	53.3	41.3	0.5	4.9
Offenses against family and children	104	68	34	1	2	100.0	65.2	32.2	1.0	1.7
Driving under the influence	1,019	881	111	16	12	100.0	86.4	10.9	1.5	1.2
Liquor laws	434	345	75	10	3	100.0	79.6	17.3	2.4	0.7
Drunkenness	527	426	87	13	2	100.0	80.8	16.4	2.4	0.4
Disorderly conduct	561	353	197	8	3	100.0	62.9	35.1	1.3	0.6
Vagrancy	21	11	9	(Z)	(Z)	100.0	52.4	45.0	2.3	0.4
All other offenses (except traffic)	2,916	1,841	1,013	30	32	100.0	63.1	34.7	1.0	1.1
Suspicion	9	5	4	(Z)	(Z)	100.0	51.9	47.5	0.4	0.2
Curfew and loitering law violations	115	87	24	2	2	100.0	75.8	21.3	1.3	1.6
Runaways	190	146	36	2	6	100.0	76.9	19.0	0.9	3.2

Z Less than 500. [1] Includes arson.
Source: U.S. Federal Bureau of Investigation, *Crime in the United States*, annual.

No. 329. Juvenile Arrests for Selected Offenses: 1980 to 1995

[Juveniles are persons between the ages 10-17]

OFFENSE	1980	1985	1986	1988	1990	1991	1992	1993	1994	1995
Number of contributing agencies	8,178	11,263	10,077	10,502	10,765	10,148	11,058	10,277	10,693	10,033
Population covered (1,000)	169,439	206,269	192,275	199,096	204,543	189,962	217,754	213,705	208,035	205,460
NUMBER										
Violent crime, total	77,220	75,077	71,251	84,551	97,103	95,677	118,358	122,434	125,141	115,160
Murder	1,475	1,384	1,827	2,204	2,661	2,626	3,025	3,473	3,114	2,753
Forcible rape	3,666	5,073	4,278	4,691	4,971	4,766	5,451	5,490	4,873	4,430
Robbery	38,529	31,833	25,459	30,728	34,944	35,632	42,639	44,598	47,046	42,056
Aggravated assault	33,548	36,787	39,687	46,928	54,527	52,653	67,243	68,873	70,108	65,921
Weapon law violations	21,203	27,035	27,473	31,480	33,123	37,575	49,903	54,414	52,278	45,179
Drug abuse, total	86,685	78,660	72,303	86,757	66,300	58,603	73,232	90,618	124,931	143,315
Sale and manufacturing	13,004	14,846	23,174	33,652	24,575	22,929	25,331	27,635	32,746	31,332
Heroin/cocaine	1,318	2,851	14,914	19,760	17,511	16,915	17,881	18,716	20,327	16,790
Marijuana	8,876	8,646	4,811	6,781	4,372	3,579	4,853	6,144	8,812	10,389
Synthetic narcotics	465	414	846	701	346	570	663	455	465	688
Dangerous nonnarcotic drug	2,345	2,935	2,603	6,410	2,346	1,865	1,934	2,320	3,142	3,465
Possession	73,681	63,814	49,129	53,105	41,725	35,674	47,901	62,983	92,185	111,983
Heroin/cocaine	2,614	7,809	15,754	19,745	15,194	13,747	16,855	17,726	21,004	20,405
Marijuana	64,465	50,582	28,885	27,253	20,940	16,490	25,004	37,915	61,003	79,778
Synthetic narcotics	1,524	1,085	1,096	1,115	1,155	885	897	1,008	1,227	2,004
Dangerous nonnarcotic drug	5,078	4,338	3,394	4,992	4,436	4,552	5,145	6,334	8,951	9,796

Source: U.S. Federal Bureau of Investigation, *Crime in the United States*, annual.

No. 330. Persons Arrested, by Charge, Sex, and Age: 1995

[Represents arrests (not charges) reported by 9,498 agencies (reporting 12 months) with a total 1995 population of 196 million as estimated by FBI]

CHARGE	Total (1,000)	PERCENT DISTRIBUTION							
		Male	Under 15 years	Under 18 years	18-24 years	25-44 years	45-54 years	55-64 years	65 yr. and over
Total arrests	11,416	79.6	6.2	18.3	26.1	47.4	5.9	1.6	0.7
Serious crimes [1]	2,240	76.1	12.0	30.2	24.6	39.1	4.3	1.2	0.6
Murder and nonnegligent manslaughter	17	90.5	2.1	15.3	41.1	36.3	4.5	1.9	0.9
Forcible rape	27	98.8	5.8	15.8	25.8	49.4	6.2	2.0	0.9
Robbery	138	90.7	9.1	32.3	31.9	33.7	1.8	0.3	0.1
Aggravated assault	436	82.3	4.7	14.7	25.0	51.5	6.3	1.8	0.8
Burglary [2]	292	88.9	13.7	35.1	26.4	35.5	2.5	0.4	0.1
Larceny—theft	1,164	66.7	14.7	33.4	22.6	37.3	4.6	1.3	0.8
Motor vehicle theft	149	86.9	11.9	42.0	27.9	27.9	1.8	0.3	0.1
Arson	15	84.3	35.2	52.3	15.9	25.5	4.4	1.3	0.6
All other nonserious crimes	9,176	80.4	4.8	15.3	26.5	49.5	6.3	1.8	0.7
Other assaults	975	80.4	6.9	16.7	23.0	52.3	5.8	1.5	0.6
Forgery and counterfeiting	92	64.1	0.9	7.2	31.6	55.5	4.6	0.9	0.3
Fraud	320	59.0	1.5	5.8	26.8	58.2	7.0	1.6	0.7
Embezzlement	12	56.4	0.8	8.2	34.9	49.0	6.4	1.3	0.3
Stolen property [3]	128	85.8	7.1	25.7	32.4	37.9	3.1	0.7	0.2
Vandalism	233	86.4	21.2	44.9	23.4	26.4	2.5	0.6	0.3
Weapons (carrying, etc.)	187	92.1	7.0	23.1	33.3	36.7	4.7	1.5	0.6
Prostitution and commercialized vice	81	38.9	0.2	1.3	19.9	71.0	5.7	1.4	0.7
Sex offenses [4]	72	92.0	8.7	17.0	18.5	49.1	9.3	3.8	2.2
Drug abuse violations	1,144	83.3	2.2	12.9	31.1	50.7	4.4	0.7	0.2
Gambling	16	84.8	1.4	8.3	23.1	45.0	13.3	7.3	3.1
Offenses against family and children	105	79.8	1.5	4.8	20.3	65.5	7.3	1.6	0.6
Driving under the influence	1,033	85.4	(Z)	1.0	21.0	62.1	10.9	3.6	1.4
Liquor laws	435	81.1	2.1	20.2	46.8	26.2	4.8	1.6	0.5
Drunkenness	527	88.2	0.4	2.9	20.4	59.8	11.7	3.9	1.4
Disorderly conduct	562	78.3	8.2	23.2	26.0	41.8	5.1	1.4	0.6
Vagrancy	21	80.6	2.8	13.5	25.9	50.2	7.7	1.9	0.8
Suspicion	9	84.8	4.5	16.9	23.6	52.2	5.8	1.2	0.3
Curfew, loitering (juveniles)	115	70.4	28.8	100.0	(X)	(X)	(X)	(X)	(X)
Runaways (juveniles)	190	42.6	43.8	100.0	(X)	(X)	(X)	(X)	(X)
All other offenses, except traffic	2,920	81.6	3.1	10.9	28.2	52.5	6.2	1.6	0.6

X Not applicable. Z Less than .05 percent. [1] Includes arson arrests, a newly established index offense in 1979. [2] Breaking or entering. [3] Buying, receiving, possessing. [4] Excludes forcible rape and prostitution, shown separately.

Source: U.S. Federal Bureau of Investigation, *Crime in the United States*, annual.

No. 331. Drug Use by Arrestees in Major U.S. Cities, by Type of Drug and Sex: 1995

[Percent testing positive]

CITY	MALE				FEMALE			
	Any drug [1]	Marijuana	Cocaine	Heroin	Any drug [1]	Marijuana	Cocaine	Heroin
Atlanta, GA	74	32	57	3	66	13	62	3
Birmingham, AL	73	36	49	2	57	12	48	3
Chicago, IL	79	41	51	22	(NA)	(NA)	(NA)	(NA)
Cleveland, OH	65	29	42	5	71	11	63	6
Dallas, TX	60	37	31	5	58	21	44	5
Denver, CO	66	33	44	5	66	21	52	6
Detroit, MI	67	42	30	7	78	18	61	15
Fort Lauderdale, FL	58	33	39	2	60	18	50	3
Houston, TX	58	29	40	5	50	18	32	3
Indianapolis, IN	64	38	39	2	72	24	54	7
Los Angeles, CA	62	23	44	7	68	14	49	10
Manhattan, NY	83	26	68	20	84	16	71	19
Miami, FL	57	29	42	3	(NA)	(NA)	(NA)	(NA)
New Orleans, LA	66	32	47	7	50	16	37	4
Omaha, NE	54	42	19	1	56	24	30	2
Philadelphia, PA	76	34	51	12	77	20	59	14
Phoenix, AZ	63	29	27	8	63	19	33	12
Portland, OR	65	29	30	15	68	16	40	18
St. Louis, MO	77	39	51	11	69	18	57	8
San Antonio, TX	51	34	24	10	41	16	24	13
San Diego, CA	72	36	28	8	73	20	28	12
San Jose, CA	52	27	18	5	50	12	16	10
Washington, DC	64	32	35	8	65	18	46	16

NA Not available. [1] Includes other drugs not shown separately.

Source: U.S. National Institute of Justice, *Drug Use Forecasting*, annual.

No. 332. Drug Arrest Rates for Drug Abuse Violations, 1980 to 1995, and by Region, 1995

[Rate per 100,000 inhabitants. Based on Bureau of the Census estimated resident population as of July 1, except 1980 and 1990, enumerated as of April 1. For composition of regions, see table 26]

OFFENSE	1980	1990	1993	1994	1995				
					Total	Region			
						Northeast	Midwest	South	West
Drug arrest rate, total	256.0	435.3	437.2	510.5	536.6	563.3	368.4	509.9	681.5
Sale and/or manufacture	57.9	139.0	129.8	136.5	129.7	178.1	98.5	115.6	136.4
Heroin or cocaine [1]	10.8	93.7	84.1	85.7	74.1	134.9	27.8	73.6	61.3
Marijuana	28.4	26.4	27.1	29.5	31.4	34.7	29.0	28.1	35.8
Synthetic or manufactured drugs	2.8	2.7	2.5	2.7	3.9	3.5	1.5	5.9	2.8
Other dangerous nonnarcotic drugs	15.9	16.2	16.1	18.6	20.2	4.9	40.2	8.0	36.5
Possession	198.1	296.3	307.4	374.0	407.0	385.3	269.9	394.3	545.0
Heroin or cocaine [1]	22.2	144.4	136.1	154.6	145.6	179.8	55.1	136.4	199.9
Marijuana	146.2	104.9	120.6	152.1	187.9	186.9	162.9	223.1	152.9
Synthetic or manufactured drugs	6.7	6.6	5.2	6.2	8.4	5.5	5.1	10.0	10.7
Other dangerous nonnarcotic drugs	23.0	40.4	45.6	61.1	65.0	13.1	46.8	24.8	181.5

[1] Includes other derivatives such as morphine, heroin, and codeine.

Source: U.S. Federal Bureau of Investigation, *Crime in the United States*, annual.

No. 333. Federal Drug Seizures, by Type of Drug: 1989 to 1995

[For fiscal years ending in year shown. Reflects the combined drug seizure effort of the Drug Enforcement Administration, the Federal Bureau of Investigation, the U.S. Customs Services within the jurisdiction of the United States as well as maritime seizures by the U.S. Coast Guard. Based on reports to the Federal-wide Drug Seizure System, which eliminates duplicate reporting of a seizure involving more than one Federal agency]

DRUG	1989	1990	1991	1992	1993	1994	1995, prel.
AMOUNTS (lbs.)							
Total	1,343,204	737,318	926,636	1,093,334	1,046,203	1,084,964	1,259,560
Heroin	2,414	1,794	3,030	2,551	3,514	2,801	2,527
Cocaine	218,695	235,214	246,324	303,260	244,302	286,498	221,549
Marijuana	1,070,514	483,248	499,070	783,475	772,307	794,051	1,003,454
Hashish	51,581	17,062	178,211	4,048	26,060	1,616	32,020
PERCENT CHANGE							
Heroin	(NA)	-25.7	68.9	-15.8	37.7	-20.3	-9.8
Cocaine	(NA)	7.6	4.7	23.1	-19.4	17.3	-22.7
Marijuana	(NA)	-54.9	3.3	57.0	-1.4	2.8	26.4
Hashish	(NA)	-66.9	944.5	-97.7	544.3	-93.8	1881.4

NA Not available.

Source: U.S. Bureau of Justice Statistics, *Fact Sheet: Drug Data Summary*, July 1994, series NCJ-148213; and unpublished data.

No. 334. Drug Removals, Laboratory Seizures, and Persons Indicted, by DEA: 1985 to 1995

[Represents domestic drug removals. 1 kg=.454 lbs; du=dosage unit]

ITEM	Unit	1985	1990	1991	1992	1993	1994	1995
Domestic drug removals:								
Heroin	kg	447	637	1,124	698	722	475	539
Cocaine	kg	18,129	73,636	57,060	78,211	60,571	66,112	52,013
Cannabis (Marijuana)	1,000 kg	745	149	108	202	143	153	232
Dangerous drugs	mil. du	26	148	532	49	86	157	166
Clandestine laboratory seizures	Number	338	549	408	335	286	272	319
Narcotic Title III intercepts	Number	136	235	256	291	308	367	330
Asset removals:								
Total seizures	$1,000	246,344	1,106,827	956,960	879,058	688,288	650,842	644,604
DEA seizures	$1,000	171,888	886,184	705,003	669,581	560,674	501,159	500,772
Seizures through interagency cooperation	$1,000	74,456	220,643	251,957	209,478	127,615	149,683	143,831
Arrests	Number	15,727	23,082	23,025	24,386	21,710	21,641	23,791
Convictions	Number	10,519	15,662	15,962	17,476	18,309	14,837	14,101

Source: Drug Enforcement Administration (DEA), *Annual Report*.

No. 335. Authorized Intercepts of Communication—Summary: 1980 to 1995

[Data for jurisdictions with statutes authorizing or approving interception of wire or oral communication]

ITEM	1980	1985	1986	1987	1988	1989	1990	1991	1992	1993	1994	1995
Jurisdictions: [1]												
With wiretap statutes	28	32	32	33	34	37	40	41	41	41	41	41
Reporting interceptions	22	22	24	22	23	25	25	23	23	23	18	19
Intercept applications authorized	564	784	754	673	738	763	872	856	919	976	1,154	1,058
Intercept installations	524	722	676	634	678	720	812	802	846	938	1,100	1,024
Federal	79	235	247	233	286	305	321	349	332	444	549	527
State	445	487	429	401	392	415	491	453	514	494	551	497
Intercepted communications, average [2]	1,058	1,320	1,328	1,299	1,251	1,656	1,487	1,584	1,861	1,801	2,139	2,028
Incriminating	315	275	253	230	316	337	321	290	347	364	373	459
Persons arrested [3]	1,871	2,469	2,410	2,226	2,486	2,804	2,057	2,364	2,685	2,428	2,852	2,577
Convictions [3]	259	660	761	506	543	706	420	605	607	413	772	494
Major offense specified:												
Gambling	199	206	189	135	126	111	116	98	66	96	86	95
Drugs	282	434	348	379	435	471	520	536	634	679	876	732
Homicide and assault	13	25	34	18	14	20	21	21	35	28	19	30
Other	70	119	183	141	163	161	204	201	184	173	173	201

[1] Jurisdictions include Federal Government, States, and District of Columbia. [2] Average per authorized installation. [3] Based on information received from intercepts installed in year shown; additional arrests/convictions will occur in subsequent years but are not shown here.

Source: Administrative Office of the U.S. Courts, *Report on Applications for Orders Authorizing or Approving the Interception of Wire, Oral or Electronic Communications* (Wiretap Report), annual.

No. 336. Aliens Expelled and Immigration Violations: 1980 to 1995

[For fiscal years ending in year shown. See text, section 9]

ITEM	Unit	1985	1988	1989	1990	1991	1992	1993	1994	1995
Aliens expelled	1,000	737	1,062	860	1,046	1,091	1,144	1,280	1,074	1,363
Deported	1,000	17	21	30	26	28	38	37	40	42
Other [1]	1,000	719	1,041	830	1,019	1,063	1,106	1,243	1,035	1,321
Prosecutions disposed of	Number	14,863	17,688	18,580	20,079	18,882	14,655	19,650	15,348	17,273
Immigration violations	Number	14,498	16,976	17,992	19,351	18,297	14,138	18,958	14,842	16,947
Nationality violations	Number	365	712	588	728	585	517	692	506	326
Convictions	Number	12,935	9,833	12,561	12,719	11,509	9,865	12,538	10,646	12,294
Immigration violations	Number	12,678	9,635	12,379	12,515	11,392	9,766	12,252	10,496	12,182
Nationality violations	Number	257	198	182	204	117	99	286	160	112

[1] Through 1993, covers required departures; beginning 1994, covers required departures, exclusions, and voluntary departures.

No. 337. Immigration Border Patrol and Investigation Activities: 1980 to 1995

[In thousands, except where indicated. For fiscal years ending in year shown. See text, section 9]

ITEM	Unit	1980	1985	1989	1990	1991	1992	1993	1994	1995
BORDER PATROL										
Border patrol agents:										
Authorized number	Number	2,484	3,228	4,804	4,852	4,968	4,948	4,143	4,559	5,259
On duty	Number	2,329	3,023	3,857	4,360	4,312	4,759	3,991	4,226	4,881
Border patrol obligations	Mil. dol.	82.5	141.9	246.4	261.1	295.5	325.8	354.5	376.8	457.2
Persons apprehended [1]	1,000	766.6	1,272.4	906.5	1,123.2	1,152.7	1,221.9	1,281.7	1,046.6	1,336.5
Deportable aliens located [2]	1,000	759.4	1,262.4	893.0	1,103.4	1,132.9	1,199.6	1,263.5	1,031.7	1,324.2
Mexican	1,000	734.2	1,218.7	832.2	1,054.8	1,095.1	1,168.9	1,230.1	999.9	1,293.5
Canadian	1,000	5.3	5.9	5.3	5.7	6.7	6.2	5.2	3.4	3.5
Other	1,000	19.9	37.8	55.5	42.8	31.1	24.4	28.1	28.4	27.2
Number of seizures	Number	1,920	7,827	10,789	17,275	14,261	11,391	10,995	9,134	9,327
Value of seizures	Mil. dol.	116.1	122.0	1,212.7	843.6	950.2	1,247.9	1,363	1,598	733.0
Narcotics	Mil. dol.	110.3	119.8	1,191.5	797.8	910.1	1,216.8	1,338	1,566	695.6
INVESTIGATIONS										
Deportable aliens located	1,000	150.9	83.9	61.1	64.1	63.6	57.4	60.4	61.6	68.9
Mexican	1,000	83.3	48.3	33.1	35.6	35.5	36.2	38.6	40.1	46.3
Canadian	1,000	1.5	1.1	0.5	0.4	0.5	0.4	0.4	0.5	0.5
Other	1,000	66.1	34.5	28.5	30.0	29.7	20.8	21.1	21.1	22.0

[1] Covers deportable aliens located and U.S. citizens engaged in smuggling or other immigration violations. [2] Beginning 1988, includes apprehension by the antismuggling unit.

Source of tables 336 and 337: U.S. Immigration and Naturalization Service, *Statistical Yearbook*, annual; and unpublished data.

No. 338. Criminal Justice System—Direct and Intergovernment Expenditures and Employment, by Type of Activity and Level of Government: 1982 to 1992

ITEM	DIRECT AND INTERGOVERNMENTAL EXPENDITURES (mil. dol.)				EMPLOYMENT (1,000)			
	Total	Police protection	Judicial and legal	Corrections	Total	Police protection	Judicial and legal	Corrections
All governments:								
1982	35,841.9	19,022.2	7,770.8	9,048.9	1,270.3	723.9	247.7	298.7
1983	39,680.2	20,648.2	8,620.6	10,411.4	1,313.8	733.1	261.4	319.3
1984	43,942.7	22,685.8	9,463.2	11,793.7	1,373.4	747.0	277.6	348.8
1985	48,563.1	24,399.4	10,628.8	13,534.9	1,422.7	757.0	293.0	372.7
1986	53,499.8	26,255.0	11,485.4	15,759.4	1,464.1	771.9	300.1	392.0
1987	58,871.3	28,767.6	12,555.0	17,548.8	1,525.0	792.8	312.3	419.8
1988	65,230.5	30,960.8	13,970.6	20,299.2	1,583.7	804.7	323.6	455.4
1989	70,949.5	32,794.2	15,588.7	22,566.6	1,636.9	811.5	336.9	488.5
1990	79,434.0	35,923.5	17,356.8	26,153.7	1,710.4	825.4	350.8	534.2
1991	87,566.8	38,971.2	19,298.4	29,297.2	1,760.6	837.0	362.2	561.3
1992	93,776.9	41,326.5	20,988.9	31,461.4	1,797.7	857.6	373.6	566.5
Federal								
1982	4,458.0	2,527.0	1,390.0	541.0	94.6	55.9	28.6	10.0
1983	4,844.0	2,815.0	1,523.0	606.0	103.8	63.9	29.8	10.1
1984	5,868.0	3,396.0	1,785.0	687.0	106.9	65.2	31.2	10.5
1985	6,416.0	3,495.0	2,129.0	792.0	110.7	66.6	33.2	11.5
1986	6,595.0	3,643.0	2,090.0	862.0	112.4	66.7	33.6	12.1
1987	7,496.0	4,231.0	2,271.0	994.0	121.3	72.8	35.7	12.9
1988	8,851.0	4,954.0	2,639.0	1,258.0	130.4	78.8	37.8	13.9
1989	9,674.0	5,307.0	2,949.0	1,418.0	134.5	78.7	39.7	16.1
1990	12,798.0	5,666.0	5,398.0	1,734.0	139.8	77.6	43.3	18.9
1991	15,231.0	6,725.0	6,384.0	2,122.0	150.1	81.8	46.8	21.5
1992	17,423.0	7,400.0	7,377.0	2,646.0	162.2	87.6	50.8	23.8
State and local								
1982	31,572.9	16,656.2	6,380.8	8,535.9	1,175.8	668.0	219.1	288.7
1983	34,836.2	17,903.2	7,097.6	9,835.4	1,210.0	669.2	231.6	309.2
1984	38,155.7	19,330.8	7,678.2	11,146.7	1,266.4	681.8	246.4	338.3
1985	42,284.1	20,969.4	8,499.8	12,814.9	1,312.1	691.0	259.9	361.2
1986	47,069.8	22,713.0	9,395.4	14,961.4	1,351.7	705.2	266.5	380.0
1987	51,640.3	24,731.6	10,284.0	16,624.8	1,403.7	720.0	276.7	407.0
1988	56,766.5	26,303.8	11,331.6	19,131.2	1,453.3	725.9	285.8	441.5
1989	61,745.5	27,842.2	12,639.7	21,263.6	1,502.3	732.8	297.1	472.4
1990	69,215.0	30,579.5	14,075.8	24,559.7	1,570.6	747.8	307.5	515.3
1991	75,460.8	32,801.2	15,303.4	27,356.2	1,610.5	755.2	315.4	539.9
1992	80,247.9	34,623.5	16,573.9	29,050.4	1,635.5	770.0	322.8	542.7

Source: U.S. Bureau of Justice Statistics, *Sourcebook of Criminal Justice Statistics—1994.*

No. 339. Full-Time Sworn Police Officers in State and Local Government—Number and Rate: 1992

[In thousands, except "rate per 10,000 population. Rate based on Bureau of the Census estimated resident population as of July 1]

CHARACTERISTICS OF INCIDENT	Number [1]	Rate	TYPE OF AGENCY			CHARACTERISTICS OF INCIDENT	Number [1]	Rate	TYPE OF AGENCY		
			Local	State	Sheriff				Local	State	Sheriff
United States	604.0	24	373.1	53.0	136.5	Missouri	11.3	22	7.9	0.9	2.1
Alabama	8.8	21	5.6	0.6	1.9	Montana	1.4	17	0.6	0.2	0.6
Alaska	1.1	18	0.7	0.3	-	Nebraska	3.1	19	1.7	0.5	0.8
Arizona	7.9	21	5.2	1.1	1.4	Nevada	3.1	23	1.8	0.3	0.8
Arkansas	4.5	19	2.5	0.5	1.1	New Hampshire	2.1	19	1.7	0.3	0.1
California [2]	65.8	21	33.2	6.1	22.6	New Jersey	26.7	34	19.2	2.6	3.8
Colorado	8.7	25	4.8	0.5	3.0	New Mexico	3.4	22	2.1	0.4	0.8
Connecticut	7.6	23	6.1	0.9	0.4	New York	68.2	38	45.8	4.0	5.0
Delaware	1.6	23	0.9	0.5	-	North Carolina	14.6	21	8.0	1.3	4.6
District of Columbia	5.2	89	4.9	-	-	North Dakota	1.1	17	0.5	0.1	0.3
Florida	32.9	24	18.0	1.6	11.8	Ohio	20.9	19	14.7	1.3	3.9
Georgia	16.8	25	9.4	0.8	5.9	Oklahoma	6.5	20	4.5	0.8	0.8
Hawaii	2.8	24	2.7	-	-	Oregon	5.5	18	2.8	0.9	1.7
Idaho	2.2	20	0.9	0.2	1.0	Pennsylvania	23.7	20	17.3	4.1	1.1
Illinois	35.7	31	25.0	2.0	7.8	Rhode Island	2.4	24	2.0	0.2	0.1
Indiana	10.0	18	6.0	1.1	2.4	South Carolina	7.8	22	3.5	1.2	2.5
Iowa	4.7	17	2.9	0.4	1.2	South Dakota	1.1	16	0.6	0.2	0.3
Kansas	5.6	22	3.2	0.6	1.5	Tennessee	10.4	21	6.2	0.8	2.9
Kentucky	6.1	16	3.8	1.0	1.0	Texas	41.3	23	24.6	2.8	9.9
Louisiana	15.0	35	5.5	0.7	8.2	Utah	3.0	16	1.5	0.4	0.8
Maine	2.3	18	1.4	0.3	0.4	Vermont	1.0	17	0.6	0.3	0.1
Maryland	12.6	26	8.3	1.7	1.3	Virginia	16.4	26	8.2	1.6	5.6
Massachusetts	16.0	27	12.1	2.1	1.3	Washington	8.2	16	4.7	1.0	2.2
Michigan	19.6	21	13.0	2.0	4.0	West Virginia	2.6	14	1.3	0.5	0.7
Minnesota	7.4	16	4.6	0.5	1.9	Wisconsin	11.6	23	7.2	0.5	3.3
Mississippi	4.7	18	2.7	0.5	1.1	Wyoming	1.2	26	0.6	0.2	0.4

[1] Includes special police.

Source: U.S. Bureau of Justice Statistics, *Sourcebook of Criminal Justice Statistics*, 1994.

No. 340. General Purpose Law Enforcement Agencies—Number, Employment, and Expenditures: 1993

[Includes both full-time and part-time employees. State police data are based on the 49 main State police agencies; Hawaii does not have a State police agency. Expenditure data cover fiscal years ending in year stated]

TYPE OF AGENCY	Number of agencies [1]	NUMBER OF EMPLOYEES						Operating expenditures (bil. dol.)
		Full time			Part time			
		Total	Sworn	Civilian	Total	Sworn	Civilian	
NUMBER								
Total	17,120	828,435	622,913	205,522	87,876	42,990	44,986	41.9
Local police	12,361	474,072	373,554	100,518	58,146	28,186	29,960	24.3
Sheriff	3,084	224,236	155,815	68,421	19,680	11,048	8,612	10.7
State police	49	76,972	51,874	25,098	845	228	617	4.2
Special police	1,626	53,156	41,670	11,486	9,224	3,426	5,796	2.8

[1] The number of agencies reported here is the result of a weighted sample and not an exact enumeration.

Source: U.S. Bureau of Justice Statistics, *Local Police Departments, 1993,* April 1995.

No. 341. Federal Agencies Employing 500 or More Full-Time Officers With Authority to Carry Firearms and Make Arrests, by Function: 1993

[As of December]

AGENCY	Total	Police response and patrol	Criminal investigation and enforcement	Other
All agencies [1]	68,825	7,127	40,002	21,696
U.S. Customs Service	10,120	43	10,077	-
Federal Bureau of Investigation	10,075	-	10,000	75
Federal Bureau of Prisons	9,984	-	-	9,984
Immigration and Naturalization Service	9,466	3,920	4,457	1,089
Administrative Office of the U.S. Courts	3,763	-	-	3,763
Internal Revenue Service	3,621	-	3,621	-
U.S. Postal Inspection Service	3,587	-	2,129	1,458
Drug Enforcement Administration	2,813	-	2,813	-
U.S. Secret Service	2,186	-	1,594	592
National Park Service	2,160	439	1,563	158
Ranger Activities Division	1,500	-	1,500	-
U.S. Park Police	660	439	63	158
U.S. Marshals Service	2,153	-	-	2153
Bureau of Alcohol, Tobacco and Firearms	1,959	-	1,832	127
U.S. Capitol Police	1,080	122	41	917
Tennessee Valley Authority	740	357	-	383
U.S. Forest Service	732	527	205	-
GSA - Federal Protective Services	732	505	66	161
U.S. Fish and Wildlife Service	620	397	223	-

- Represents or rounds to zero. [1] Includes agencies not shown separately.

Source: U.S. Bureau of Justice Statistics, *Federal Law Enforcement Officers, 1993.*

No. 342. Law Enforcement Officers Killed and Assaulted: 1980 to 1995

[Covers officers killed feloniously and accidentally in line of duty; includes Federal officers. For composition of regions, see table 27]

ITEM	1980	1985	1989	1990	1991	1992	1993	1994	1995
OFFICERS KILLED									
Total killed	165	148	145	132	123	129	129	140	131
Northeast	31	19	23	13	16	16	12	17	16
Midwest	23	23	22	20	26	15	27	30	19
South	72	64	68	68	55	68	57	50	61
West	32	29	23	23	17	23	22	30	32
Puerto Rico	6	10	8	8	8	7	11	8	2
Outlying areas, foreign countries	1	3	1	-	1	-	-	5	1
ASSAULTS									
Population (1,000) [1]	182,288	196,935	189,641	199,065	191,397	217,997	210,658	260,341	201,111
Number of—									
Agencies represented	9,235	9,906	9,213	9,483	9,263	10,662	9,809	10,626	8,925
Police officers	345,554	369,808	380,232	412,314	405,069	460,430	454,105	480,343	455,804
Total assaulted	57,847	61,724	62,172	71,794	62,852	81,252	66,975	64,912	56,535
Firearm	3,295	2,793	3,154	3,662	3,532	4,455	4,002	3,168	2,277
Knife or cutting instrument	1,653	1,715	1,379	1,641	1,493	2,095	1,574	1,513	1,325
Other dangerous weapon	5,415	5,263	5,778	7,390	7,014	8,604	7,551	7,210	6,299
Hands, fists, feet, etc	47,484	51,953	51,861	59,101	50,813	66,098	53,848	53,021	46,634

- Represents zero. [1] Represents the number of persons covered by agencies shown.

Source: U.S. Federal Bureau of Investigation, *Law Enforcement Officers Killed and Assaulted,* annual.

No. 343. Lawyers—Selected Characteristics: 1960 to 1991

[Data based on editions of Martindale-Hubbell Law Directory. Represents all persons who are members of the bar, including those in industries, educational institutions, etc., and those inactive or retired]

CHARACTERISTIC	1960	1970	1980	1985	1988	1991
All lawyers [1]	285,933	355,242	542,205	655,191	723,189	805,872
Lawyers reporting [2]	252,385	324,818	(X)	(X)	(X)	(X)
Male	245,897	315,715	498,019	569,649	606,768	646,495
Female	6,488	9,103	44,185	85,542	116,421	159,377
Status in practice: [3]						
Government	25,621	35,803	50,490	53,035	57,742	66,227
Federal	13,045	18,710	20,132	19,989	23,042	27,985
State	4,316	9,293	30,358	33,046	34,700	38,242
City or county	8,260	7,800	(4)	(4)	(4)	(4)
Judicial [5]	8,180	10,349	19,160	21,677	19,547	21,536
Federal	599	878	2,611	3,003	2,846	3,119
State and county	5,301	7,548	16,549	18,674	16,701	18,417
City	2,280	1,923	(4)	(4)	(4)	(4)
Private practice	192,353	236,085	370,111	460,206	519,941	587,289
Individual	116,911	118,963	179,923	216,336	240,141	262,822
Partner	60,709	92,442	144,279	177,392	194,976	213,016
Associate [5]	14,733	24,680	45,906	66,478	84,824	111,651
Salaried	25,196	40,486	73,862	83,843	85,671	93,849
Private industry	22,533	33,593	54,626	63,622	66,627	71,022
Educational institutions	1,796	3,732	6,606	7,254	7,575	8,177
Other private employment	867	3,161	12,630	12,967	11,469	14,650
Inactive or retired	10,887	16,812	28,582	36,430	40,288	36,971

X Not applicable. [1] 1960 to 1970 includes lawyers not reporting and an adjustment (subtraction) for duplications; 1980 to 1991, weighted to account for nonreporters and duplicate listings. [2] 1960 and 1970 includes duplications; 1980, 1985, and figures are weighted to adjust for duplication of entries. [3] 1960 and 1970, in cases where more than one subentry was applicable, the individual was tabulated in each. In 1980 and 1985 lawyers who were in both private practice and government service are coded in private practice. [4] Data no longer available separately; included with category above. [5] Associates are lawyers designated as such by their employers.

Source: American Bar Foundation, Chicago, IL, 1960 to 1970, *The 1971 Lawyer Statistical Report*, 1971 (copyright); 1980, *The Lawyer Statistical Report: A Statistical Profile of the U.S. Legal Profession in the 1980's*, 1985 (copyright); 1985 and 1988, *Supplement to The Lawyer Statistical Report: The U.S. Legal Profession in 1988*, 1991 and similar report for 1985; 1991 Lawyer Statistical Report: The U.S. Legal Profession in the 1990's, 1994 (copyright).

No. 344. U.S. Supreme Court—Cases Filed and Disposition: 1980 to 1995

[Statutory term of court begins first Monday in October]

ACTION	1980	1985	1989	1990	1991	1992	1993	1994	1995
Total cases on docket	5,144	5,158	5,746	6,316	6,770	7,245	7,786	8,100	7,565
Appellate cases on docket	2,749	2,571	2,416	2,351	2,451	2,441	2,442	2,515	2,456
From prior term	527	400	384	365	365	379	342	377	361
Docketed during present term	2,222	2,171	2,032	1,986	2,086	2,062	2,100	2,138	2,095
Cases acted upon [1]	2,324	2,185	2,096	2,042	2,125	2,140	2,099	2,185	2,130
Granted review	167	166	103	114	103	83	78	83	92
Denied, dismissed, or withdrawn	1,999	1,863	1,861	1,802	1,914	1,920	1,947	2,016	1,945
Summarily decided	90	78	44	81	52	84	34	52	62
Cases not acted upon	425	386	320	309	326	301	343	330	326
Pauper cases on docket	2,371	2,577	3,316	3,951	4,307	4,792	5,332	5,574	5,098
Cases acted upon	2,027	2,189	2,891	3,436	3,768	4,261	4,621	4,983	4,514
Granted review	17	20	19	27	17	14	21	10	13
Denied, dismissed, or withdrawn	1,968	2,136	2,824	3,369	3,716	4,209	4,568	4,955	4,439
Summarily decided	32	24	35	28	22	25	30	14	55
Cases not acted upon	344	388	425	515	539	531	711	591	584
Original cases on docket	24	10	14	14	12	12	12	11	9
Cases disposed of during term	7	2	2	3	1	1	1	-	5
Total cases available for argument	264	276	204	201	196	166	145	136	145
Cases disposed of	162	175	147	131	130	120	105	97	93
Cases argued	154	171	146	125	127	116	99	94	90
Cases dismissed or remanded without argument	8	4	1	6	3	4	6	3	3
Cases remaining	102	101	57	70	66	46	40	39	52
Cases decided by signed opinion	144	161	143	121	120	111	93	91	87
Cases decided by per curiam opinion	8	10	3	4	3	4	6	3	3
Number of signed opinions	123	146	129	112	107	107	84	82	75

- Represents zero. [1] Includes cases granted review and carried over to next term, not shown separately.

Source: Office of the Clerk, Supreme Court of the United States, unpublished data.

No. 345. U.S. Courts of Appeals—Cases Commenced and Disposition: 1980 to 1996

[For years ending June 30]

ITEM	1980	1985	1990	1991	1992	1993	1994	1995	1996
Cases commenced [1]	23,200	33,360	40,898	42,033	46,032	49,770	48,815	49,671	51,524
Criminal	4,405	4,989	9,493	9,949	10,956	11,885	11,052	10,171	10,653
U.S. civil	4,654	6,744	6,626	6,663	7,113	7,758	7,518	7,761	8,661
Private civil	10,200	16,827	20,490	20,796	22,862	24,030	24,781	25,992	27,188
Administrative appeals	2,950	3,179	2,578	2,764	3,052	3,824	3,560	3,345	2,858
Cases terminated [1]	20,887	31,387	38,520	41,414	42,933	47,466	48,546	50,085	49,359
Criminal	3,993	4,892	7,509	9,198	9,830	11,043	11,519	11,320	9,995
U.S. civil	4,346	6,353	6,379	6,579	6,797	7,462	7,637	7,710	7,831
Private civil	8,942	15,743	20,369	20,698	21,628	23,437	23,943	25,574	25,999
Administrative appeals	2,643	2,760	2,582	3,148	2,801	3,464	3,480	3,254	3,131
Cases disposed of [2]	10,607	16,369	21,006	22,707	23,162	25,567	26,475	28,187	26,988
Affirmed or granted	8,017	12,286	16,629	17,988	18,463	20,604	21,371	22,825	21,696
Reversed or denied	1,845	2,770	2,565	2,503	2,681	2,514	2,636	2,679	2,533
Other	745	1,313	1,812	2,216	2,018	2,449	2,468	2,683	2,759
Median months [3]	8.9	10.3	10.1	10.2	10.5	10.4	10.5	10.5	10.3

[1] Includes original proceedings and bankruptcy appeals not shown separately. [2] Terminated on the merits after hearing or submission. [3] Prior to 1985, the figure is from filing of complete record to final disposition; beginning 1985, figure is from filing notice of appeal to final disposition. For definition of median, see Guide to Tabular Presentation.

No. 346. U.S. District Courts—Civil and Criminal Cases: 1980 to 1996

[In thousands, except percent. For years ending June 30]

ITEM	1980	1985	1990	1991	1992	1993	1994	1995	1996
Civil cases: Commenced	168.8	273.7	217.9	207.7	226.9	228.6	236.0	239.0	272.7
Cases terminated [1]	155.0	268.6	213.4	211.7	239.6	225.2	228.9	226.1	246.4
No court action	68.7	129.4	51.6	44.6	51.4	44.0	40.5	37.0	36.8
Court action, total	86.2	139.2	161.8	166.5	187.6	181.2	188.4	189.1	209.6
Before pretrial	53.8	95.5	127.0	136.9	153.4	152.3	159.6	161.6	183.3
Pretrial	22.4	31.1	25.5	21.1	26.2	21.1	21.0	19.7	18.8
Trials	10.1	12.6	9.2	8.4	8.0	7.9	7.8	7.7	7.5
Percent reaching trial	6.5	4.7	4.3	4.0	3.4	3.5	3.4	3.4	3.1
Criminal cases: Commenced [2]	28.0	38.5	46.5	45.1	47.5	45.7	44.9	44.2	47.1
Defendants disposed of [3]	36.6	47.4	56.5	56.7	58.4	59.5	61.2	55.3	59.5
Not convicted	8.0	8.8	9.8	10.0	10.0	9.2	10.0	9.0	8.5
Convicted	28.6	38.5	46.7	46.8	48.4	50.4	51.1	46.3	51.0
Imprisonment	13.2	18.7	27.8	29.2	31.1	34.2	34.5	31.7	36.5
Probation	11.1	14.4	14.2	13.8	13.1	12.6	12.8	11.5	11.6
Fine and other	4.4	5.4	4.7	3.8	4.3	3.7	3.9	3.2	2.9

[1] Excludes land condemnation cases. [2] Excludes transfers. [3] Includes Guam, Virgin Islands, and Northern Mariana Islands; 1980 includes Canal Zone.

No. 347. U.S. District Courts—Civil Cases Commenced and Pending: 1993 to 1996

[For years ending June 30]

TYPE OF CASE	CASES COMMENCED				CASES PENDING			
	1993	1994	1995	1996	1993	1994	1995	1996
Cases total [1]	**228,562**	**235,996**	**239,013**	**272,661**	**215,574**	**217,963**	**224,378**	**250,233**
Contract actions [1]	38,240	31,988	31,619	33,413	40,525	29,697	27,337	29,934
Recovery of overpayments [2]	7,255	2,591	2,099	3,583	5,995	1,227	1,041	2,379
Real property actions	8,436	7,468	7,282	6,276	7,743	5,855	5,073	4,554
Tort actions	40,939	48,067	44,511	67,029	45,148	47,186	52,334	69,309
Personal injury	37,409	44,734	41,102	63,222	41,324	43,638	48,789	65,527
Personal injury product liability [1]	16,545	23,977	17,631	38,170	15,208	20,694	24,166	37,261
Asbestos	4,900	7,111	6,821	6,760	7,154	3,704	3,524	4,503
Other personal injury	20,864	20,757	23,471	25,052	26,116	22,944	24,623	28,266
Personal property damage	3,530	3,333	3,409	3,807	3,824	3,548	3,545	3,782
Actions under statutes [1]	140,811	148,344	155,495	165,922	121,964	135,020	139,487	146,303
Civil rights [1]	26,483	31,521	35,566	40,476	26,477	33,271	37,512	42,961
Employment	12,221	15,256	18,225	22,150	12,530	17,359	20,375	24,428
Bankruptcy suits	6,192	5,675	5,138	4,737	4,203	4,705	4,541	4,067
Commerce (ICC rates, etc.)	1,475	1,228	613	1,622	1,238	693	446	795
Environmental matters	1,077	1,059	1,136	1,158	1,943	1,864	1,823	1,866
Prisoner petitions	52,454	56,283	62,597	69,352	39,512	45,417	47,382	51,428
Forfeiture and penalty	4,832	3,548	2,670	2,255	4,850	3,359	2,399	2,068
Labor laws	16,174	15,800	15,030	15,068	13,026	12,346	11,829	11,942
Protected property rights [3]	6,202	7,051	6,990	6,800	5,281	5,963	5,998	6,367
Securities commodities and exchanges	1,875	1,742	1,870	1,741	3,983	3,130	2,969	2,861
Social Security laws	11,602	11,142	10,168	8,517	8,304	12,302	11,310	9,226
Tax suits	2,267	2,275	2,144	2,078	2,255	1,884	1,692	1,669
Freedom of information	425	566	481	465	498	502	500	497

[1] Includes other types not shown separately. [2] Includes enforcement of judgments in student loan cases, and overpayments of veterans benefits [3] Includes copyright, patent, and trademark rights

Source of tables 345-347. Administrative Office of the U.S. Courts, *Annual Report of the Director.*

No. 348. U.S. District Courts—Offenders Convicted and Sentenced to Prison, and Length of Sentence: 1995

MOST SERIOUS OFFENSE OF CONVICTION	Offenders convicted	Convicted offenders sentenced to prison	Length of sentence (mo.)	MOST SERIOUS OFFENSE OF CONVICTION	Offenders convicted	Convicted offenders sentenced to prison	Length of sentence (mo.)
Total [1]	47,387	31,767	61.0	Drug offenses [2]	16,043	14,030	82.8
				Possession	1,726	885	34.1
Violent offenses	2,562	2,237	89.9	Trafficking and manufacturing	14,317	13,145	86.1
Property offenses	13,327	6,746	25.1	Public-order offenses	15,424	8,744	46.7
Fraudulent offenses [2]	9,774	5,245	20.3	Regulatory offenses	1,949	746	27.9
Embezzlement	1,170	521	15.5	Other offenses	13,475	7,998	48.4
Fraud [3]	7,548	4,171	21.0	Weapons	3,133	2,816	91.1
Forgery	312	124	16.7	Immigration	3,655	3,174	21.1
Other offenses [2]	3,553	1,501	41.9	Tax law violations [4]	888	304	17.5
Larceny	2,435	783	21.0				

[1] Total may include offenders for whom offense category could not be determined. [2] Includes offenses not shown separately. [3] Excludes tax fraud. [4] Includes tax fraud.

Source: U.S. Bureau of Justice Statistics, *Federal Criminal Case Processing*, annual.

No. 349. Federal Prosecutions of Public Corruption: 1980 to 1995

[As of Dec. 31. Prosecution of persons who have corrupted public office in violation of Federal Criminal Statutes]

PROSECUTION STATUS	1980	1985	1986	1987	1988	1989	1990	1991	1992	1993	1994	1995
Total: [1] Indicted	727	1,157	1,208	1,276	1,274	1,348	1,176	1,452	1,189	1,371	1,165	1,051
Convicted	602	997	1,026	1,081	1,067	1,149	1,084	1,194	1,081	1,362	969	878
Awaiting trial	213	256	246	368	288	375	300	346	380	403	332	323
Federal officials: Indicted	123	563	596	651	629	695	615	803	624	627	571	527
Convicted	131	470	523	545	529	610	583	665	532	595	488	438
Awaiting trial	16	90	83	118	86	126	103	149	139	133	124	120
State officials: Indicted	72	79	88	102	66	71	96	115	84	113	99	61
Convicted	51	66	71	76	69	64	79	77	92	133	97	61
Awaiting trial	28	20	24	26	14	18	28	42	24	39	17	23
Local officials: Indicted	247	248	232	246	276	269	257	242	232	309	248	236
Convicted	168	221	207	204	229	201	225	180	211	272	202	191
Awaiting trial	82	49	55	89	79	122	98	88	91	132	96	89

[1] Includes individuals who are neither public officials nor employees but who were involved with public officials or employees in violating the law, not shown separately.

Source: U.S. Department of Justice, *Federal Prosecutions of Corrupt Public Officials, 1970-1980* and *Report to Congress on the Activities and Operations of the Public Integrity Section*, annual.

No. 350. Delinquency Cases Disposed by Juvenile Courts, by Reason for Referral: 1984 to 1994

[In thousands. A delinquency offense is an act committed by a juvenile for which an adult could be prosecuted in a criminal court. Disposition of a case involves taking a definite action such as transferring the case to criminal court, dismissing the case, placing the youth on probation, placing the youth in a facility for delinquents, or such actions as fines, restitution, and community service]

REASON FOR REFERRAL	1984	1985	1986	1987	1988	1989	1990	1991	1992	1993	1994
All delinquency offenses	1,034	1,112	1,150	1,155	1,170	1,212	1,299	1,407	1,482	1,482	1,555
Case rate [1]	38.7	42.2	43.9	44.5	45.7	47.8	51.0	53.9	54.7	54.6	56.1
Violent offenses	61	67	73	67	71	78	95	111	124	122	131
Criminal homicide	1	1	2	1	2	2	3	3	3	3	3
Forcible rape	3	4	5	4	4	4	4	5	5	6	5
Robbery	22	26	26	22	22	23	28	34	37	36	37
Aggravated assault	35	36	40	39	43	49	60	69	78	77	85
Property offenses	442	489	496	498	501	525	546	599	602	570	567
Burglary	129	139	140	131	129	131	142	156	161	149	142
Larceny	276	307	308	314	311	319	326	362	360	352	356
Motor vehicle theft	31	36	42	47	55	68	71	73	74	61	59
Arson	6	7	6	6	7	7	7	8	8	8	10
Delinquency offenses	530	555	583	590	599	610	658	697	756	791	858
Simple assault	73	92	95	100	104	110	125	136	153	166	178
Vandalism	69	84	84	83	81	83	97	112	119	117	119
Drug law violations	65	76	73	73	82	78	71	66	74	89	120
Obstruction of justice	63	68	76	79	79	82	86	81	86	96	108
Other [2]	260	235	255	256	253	256	279	301	324	324	333

[1] Number of cases disposed per 1,000 youth (ages 10 to 17) at risk. [2] Includes such offenses as stolen property offenses, trespassing, weapons offenses, other sex offenses, liquor law violations, disorderly conduct, and miscellaneous offenses.

Source: National Center for Juvenile Justice, Pittsburgh, PA, *Juvenile Court Statistics*, annual.

No. 351. Delinquency Cases and Case Rates: 1985 to 1994

[A delinquency offense is an act committed by a juvenile for which an adult could be prosecuted in a criminal court. Disposition of a case involves taking a definite action such as transferring the case to criminal court, dismissing the case, placing the youth on probation, placing the youth in a facility for delinquents, or such actions as fines, restitution, and community service. Offenses may not add to toal sex and race categories due to rounding]

SEX, RACE, AND OFFENSE	NUMBER OF CASES			CASE RATE [1]		
	1985	1990	1994	1985	1990	1994
Male, total	**893,200**	**1,054,800**	**1,230,800**	**66.4**	**80.3**	**86.5**
Person	139,700	194,500	258,300	10.4	14.8	18.2
Property	538,500	610,900	635,100	40.0	46.5	44.7
Drugs	61,100	61,400	103,900	4.5	4.7	7.3
Public order	153,800	187,900	233,400	11.4	14.3	16.4
Female, total	**210,800**	**244,500**	**324,800**	**16.4**	**19.6**	**24.0**
Person	34,700	48,900	77,800	2.7	3.9	5.8
Property	120,000	140,600	168,300	9.4	11.3	12.5
Drugs	13,000	9,600	16,400	1.0	0.8	1.2
Public order	43,000	45,300	62,200	3.4	3.6	4.6
White, total	**793,700**	**857,600**	**995,900**	**37.0**	**41.7**	**45.2**
Person	100,300	135,300	190,200	4.7	6.6	8.6
Property	483,700	526,400	548,100	22.6	25.6	24.8
Drugs	58,900	38,500	72,600	2.7	1.9	3.3
Public order	150,800	157,800	186,700	7.0	7.7	8.5
Black, total	**281,000**	**397,400**	**498,700**	**72.5**	**103.0**	**119.4**
Person	69,700	100,800	135,300	18.0	26.1	32.4
Property	156,900	198,100	222,000	40.5	51.3	53.1
Drugs	13,200	31,200	44,900	3.4	8.1	10.7
Public order	41,200	67,300	96,600	10.6	17.4	23.1
Other races, total	**29,200**	**44,100**	**56,700**	**30.3**	**37.0**	**39.6**
Person	4,400	7,400	10,800	4.5	6.2	7.4
Property	18,000	27,000	33,300	18.6	22.7	23.2
Drugs	2,000	1,400	2,500	2.1	1.2	1.7
Public order	4,800	8,300	10,300	5.0	6.9	7.2

[1] Cases per 1,000 youth at risk.

Source: National Center for Juvenile Justice, Pittsburgh, PA, *Juvenile Court Statistics*, annual.

No. 352. Child Abuse and Neglect Cases Substantiated and Indicated—Victim Characteristics: 1990 to 1995

[Based on reports alleging child abuse and neglect that were referred for investigation by the respective child protective services agency in each State. The reporting period may be either calendar or fiscal year. The majority of States provided duplicated counts. Also, varying number of States reported the various characteristics presented below. A substantiated case represents a type of investigation disposition that determines that there is sufficient evidence under State law to conclude that maltreatment occurred or that the child is at risk of maltreatment. An indicated case represents a type of disposition that concludes that there was a reason to suspect maltreatment had occurred]

ITEM	1990		1993		1994		1995	
	Number	Percent	Number	Percent	Number	Percent	Number	Percent
TYPES OF SUBSTANTIATED MALTREATMENT								
Victims, total [1]	690,658	(X)	966,163	(X)	1,011,595	(X)	1,000,502	(X)
Neglect	338,770	49.1	472,170	48.9	520,550	51.5	523,049	52.3
Physical abuse	186,801	27.0	231,111	23.9	241,338	23.9	244,903	24.5
Sexual abuse	119,506	17.3	137,265	14.2	136,362	13.5	126,095	12.6
Emotional maltreatment	45,621	6.6	47,643	4.9	47,337	4.7	44,648	4.5
Medical Neglect	(NA)	(NA)	23,009	2.4	24,593	2.4	29,454	2.9
Other and unknown	61,477	8.9	145,096	15.0	153,894	15.2	144,733	14.5
SEX OF VICTIM								
Victims, total	794,101	100.0	926,322	100.0	903,195	100.0	834,174	100.0
Male	357,367	45.0	413,277	44.6	420,817	46.6	393,227	47.1
Female	405,409	51.1	470,658	50.8	472,535	52.3	437,407	52.4
Unknown	31,325	3.9	42,387	4.6	9,843	1.1	3,540	0.4
AGE OF VICTIM								
Victims, total	807,965	100.0	926,674	100.0	901,573	100.0	833,115	100.0
1 year and younger	106,507	13.2	121,700	13.1	119,203	13.2	105,375	12.6
2 to 5 years old	192,018	23.8	236,997	25.6	240,925	26.7	222,243	26.7
6 to 9 years old	175,609	21.7	209,292	22.6	210,334	23.3	202,315	24.3
10 to 13 years old	150,507	18.6	177,561	19.2	172,800	19.2	160,107	19.2
14 to 17 years old	118,015	14.4	133,866	14.4	132,566	14.7	125,221	15.0
18 and over	5,464	0.7	6,799	0.7	6,821	0.8	8,029	1.0
Unknown	61,845	7.7	40,439	4.4	18,924	2.1	9,825	1.2
RACE/ETHNIC GROUP OF VICTIM [2]								
Victims, total	793,773	100.0	926,924	100.0	895,831	100.0	822,609	100.0
White	428,506	54.0	497,924	53.7	499,465	55.8	456,163	55.5
Black	198,365	25.0	229,724	24.8	239,798	26.8	222,638	27.1
Asian and Pacific Islander	6,479	0.8	7,775	0.8	7,961	0.9	8,098	1.0
American Indian, Eskimo, and Aleut	10,323	1.3	13,657	1.5	15,098	1.7	14,819	1.8
Other races	11,088	1.4	13,659	1.5	13,678	1.5	15,412	1.9
Hispanic origin	73,590	9.3	85,067	9.2	85,332	9.5	84,754	10.3
Unknown	65,422	8.2	79,118	8.5	34,459	3.8	20,725	2.5

X Not applicable. [1] More than one type of maltreatment may be substantiated per child. Therefore, totals for this category will add up to more than 100%. Victim totals and maltreatment types are based on subset of states which reported both the number of child victims and maltreatment incidences by type for that year. [2] Some States were unable to report on the number of Hispanic victims, thus it is probable that nationwide the percentage of Hispanic victims is higher.

Source: U.S. Department of Health and Human Services, National Center on Child Abuse and Neglect, National Child Abuse *and Neglect Data System, Child Maltreatment - 1995; and previous reports.*

No. 353. Child Abuse and Neglect Cases Reported and Investigated, by State: 1994 and 1995

[Based on reports alleging child abuse and neglect that were referred for investigation by the respective child protective services agency in each State. The reporting period may be either calendar or fiscal year. The majority of States were unable to provide unduplicated counts. Only nine jurisdictions (Alaska, Hawaii, Michigan, Montana, Ohio, Oregon, South Carolina, Vermont, and Washington) provided unduplicated counts of children subject of report. Excludes the Armed Forces]

STATE	1994				1995			
	Population under 18 years old	Reports		Investigation disposition, number of children substantiated [2]	Population under 18 years old	Reports		Investigation disposition, number of children substantiated [2]
		Number of reports [1]	Number of children subject of a report			Number of reports [1]	Number of children subject of a report	
United States	**68,024,000**	**1,979,797**	**2,939,170**	**1,011,595**	**68,739,952**	**1,986,514**	**2,959,237**	**1,000,502**
Alabama	1,080,000	26,515	40,164	21,591	1,080,145	25,704	38,559	18,120
Alaska	192,000	[3]10,071	10,071	6,774	189,253	9,898	9,696	8,142
Arizona	1,139,000	28,275	48,722	29,531	1,193,270	[3]26,180	43,762	25,154
Arkansas	640,000	18,429	18,429	7,915	649,521	17,612	28,563	8,169
California	8,677,000	352,059	449,177	159,031	8,793,616	364,432	458,262	166,418
Colorado	970,000	27,797	44,390	(NA)	981,200	32,382	52,517	7,602
Connecticut	788,000	24,036	37,043	27,618	797,733	24,669	38,701	23,762
Delaware	175,000	5,275	9,441	2,542	178,826	5,448	9,659	2,300
District of Columbia	119,000	5,612	13,369	5,636	114,652	5,185	12,341	5,916
Florida	3,262,000	108,943	164,945	77,101	3,371,328	115,108	170,727	77,976
Georgia	1,893,000	55,578	89,958	63,721	1,923,594	57,118	95,925	57,250
Hawaii	304,000	[3]5,944	5,944	2,380	309,262	[3]5,601	5,601	2,635
Idaho	339,000	13,592	34,313	9,461	347,924	13,406	35,968	10,743
Illinois	3,083,000	77,289	140,651	53,056	3,125,894	73,904	132,570	49,217
Indiana	1,473,000	41,725	62,553	25,343	1,487,359	43,429	67,390	22,493
Iowa	729,000	21,210	31,240	9,172	724,511	22,131	32,801	9,967
Kansas	690,000	[3]33,928	33,928	3,644	692,761	[3]30,552	30,552	3,264
Kentucky	970,000	37,911	59,540	25,940	972,708	40,470	63,313	28,630
Louisiana	1,235,000	28,094	44,901	15,015	1,239,214	27,587	45,326	14,194
Maine	306,000	4,010	8,902	4,769	304,895	4,106	8,291	4,628
Maryland	1,263,000	26,906	41,373	(NA)	1,271,966	26,114	42,352	(NA)
Massachusetts	1,424,000	33,844	56,178	23,964	1,431,854	33,522	56,175	25,375
Michigan	2,525,000	57,394	136,969	21,951	2,519,455	57,914	139,289	21,165
Minnesota	1,241,000	17,967	28,286	10,436	1,245,492	16,991	26,213	10,142
Mississippi	756,000	17,322	27,123	7,982	761,909	16,786	27,224	5,586
Missouri	1,379,000	52,754	86,007	15,842	1,381,552	52,931	85,927	17,764
Montana	238,000	8,905	13,528	4,194	236,134	8,905	13,528	4,194
Nebraska	442,000	8,405	17,508	4,514	443,297	7,858	16,109	3,510
Nevada	376,000	13,329	21,286	8,037	396,586	12,716	20,623	7,791
New Hampshire	292,000	6,118	9,770	1,043	294,969	5,639	7,778	1,059
New Jersey	1,931,000	[3]65,954	65,954	9,519	1,963,523	[3]63,684	63,684	9,279
New Mexico	496,000	[3]24,933	24,933	7,356	500,099	[3]26,034	26,034	8,842
New York	4,511,000	128,111	210,997	54,993	4,536,862	128,896	211,445	57,699
North Carolina	1,756,000	59,136	95,144	30,013	1,799,119	59,968	96,690	30,935
North Dakota	172,000	4,518	7,753	3,617	170,445	4,642	7,673	3,340
Ohio	2,854,000	96,747	156,635	61,806	2,859,848	95,001	156,975	58,416
Oklahoma	880,000	[3]34,846	34,846	10,891	878,039	[3]39,831	39,831	11,700
Oregon	783,000	26,436	42,216	7,946	797,040	26,765	43,407	8,991
Pennsylvania	2,898,000	[3]23,722	23,722	7,038	2,909,302	[3]24,109	24,109	6,891
Rhode Island	240,000	8,862	14,303	3,207	237,611	8,951	14,492	4,437
South Carolina	952,000	21,656	40,461	11,628	944,384	22,756	43,503	11,439
South Dakota	208,000	[3]10,156	10,156	1,923	206,436	[4]8,821	9,063	2,526
Tennessee	1,297,000	[3]34,714	34,714	12,175	1,310,297	[3]36,286	36,286	12,166
Texas	5,301,000	110,742	173,644	55,266	5,400,417	103,029	158,352	46,768
Utah	672,000	17,125	29,112	10,430	674,618	16,114	26,447	8,848
Vermont	146,000	2,579	3,025	1,234	146,760	2,197	2,618	1,122
Virginia	1,603,000	36,431	56,331	10,264	1,612,527	35,992	55,553	10,416
Washington	1,408,000	41,050	57,100	44,197	1,418,404	42,109	56,926	44,893
West Virginia	429,000	12,370	19,754	(NA)	421,868	12,370	19,544	(NA)
Wisconsin	1,347,000	[3]47,561	47,561	18,185	1,353,205	[3]44,661	44,661	17,118
Wyoming	138,000	3,906	5,080	1,702	136,268	(NA)	(NA)	1,506

NA Not available. [1] Except as noted, reports are on incident/family based basis or based on number of reported incidents regardless of the number of children involved in the incidents. [2] Type of investigation disposition that determines that there is sufficient evidence under State law to conclude that maltreatment occurred or that the child is at risk of maltreatment. [3] Child-based report that enumerates each child who is a subject of a report. [4] South Dakota has both child and incident based reports.

Source: U.S. Department of Health and Human Services, National Center on Child Abuse and Neglect, National Child Abuse and Neglect Data System, *Child Maltreatment - 1995*.

No. 354. Jail Inmates, by Race and Detention Status: 1985 to 1995

[Excludes Federal and State prisons or other correctional institutions; institutions exclusively for juveniles; State-operated jails in Alaska, Connecticut, Delaware, Hawaii, Rhode Island, and Vermont; and other facilities which retain persons for less than 48 hours. As of June 30. Data for 1988 based on National Jail Census; for other years, based on sample survey and subject to sampling variability]

CHARACTERISTIC	1985	1988	1989	1990	1991	1992	1993	1994	1995
Total inmates [1]	**256,615**	**343,569**	**395,553**	**405,320**	**426,479**	**444,584**	**459,804**	**486,474**	**507,044**
Percent of rated capacity	94	101	108	104	101	99	97	96	93
Male	235,909	313,158	356,050	368,002	386,865	403,768	415,576	437,600	455,400
Female	19,077	30,411	37,253	37,318	39,614	40,816	44,228	48,800	51,600
White [2]	151,403	166,302	201,732	186,989	190,333	191,362	180,914	253,500	266,200
Black [2]	102,646	141,979	185,910	174,335	187,618	195,156	203,483	224,900	232,000
Other races [2]	2,566	3,932	7,911	5,321	5,391	5,831	6,178	8,100	8,800
Hispanic [3]	35,926	51,455	55,377	57,449	60,129	62,961	69,200	74,900	74,400
Non-Hispanic	220,689	292,114	340,176	347,871	366,350	381,623	390,600	411,600	432,700
Adult [4]	254,986	341,893	393,303	403,019	424,129	441,781	455,500	479,800	499,300
Juvenile [5]	1,629	1,676	2,250	2,301	2,350	2,804	4,300	6,700	7,800

[1] For 1985, 1989-1994, includes juveniles not shown separately by sex, and for 1988 and 1990-1994 includes 31,356, 36,675, 43,138, 52,235, 66,249, and 93,058 persons, respectively, of unknown race not shown separately. [2] Beginning 1993, data represent White, non-hispanic and Black, non-hispanic and rounded to nearest 100. [3] Hispanic persons may be of any race. Data for 1993 and 1994 are estimated and rounded to nearest 100. [4] Includes inmates not classified by conviction status. [5] Juveniles are persons whose age makes them initially subject to juvenile court authority although they are sometimes tried as adults in criminal court. In 1993, includes juveniles who were tried as adults. In 1994, includes all persons under age 18.

Source: U.S. Bureau of Justice Statistics, *Profile of Jail Inmates, 1978 and 1989; Jail Inmates*, annual; and *1988 Census of Local Jails.*

No. 355. Federal and State Prisoners: 1970 to 1995

[Based on Bureau of the Census estimated resident population, as of July 1. Prior to 1970, excludes State institutions in Alaska. Beginning 1980, includes all persons under jurisdiction of Federal and State authorities rather than those in the custody of such authorities. Represents inmates sentenced to maximum term of more than a year]

YEAR	PRESENT AT END OF YEAR						RECEIVED FROM COURTS					
	All institutions		Federal		State		All institutions		Federal		State	
	Number	Rate [1]	Number	Rate [1]	Number	Rate [1]	Number	Rate [1]	Number	Rate [1]	Number	Rate [1]
1970	196,429	96.7	20,038	9.8	176,391	86.8	79,351	39.1	12,047	5.9	67,304	33.1
1975	240,593	113.3	24,131	11.4	216,462	102.0	129,573	61.0	16,770	7.9	112,803	53.1
1980	315,974	139.2	20,611	9.1	295,363	130.1	142,122	62.7	10,907	4.8	131,215	57.9
1985	480,568	216.5	32,695	13.6	447,873	187.6	198,499	82.7	15,368	6.4	183,131	76.3
1987	560,812	229.0	39,523	16.0	521,289	214.2	241,887	99.0	16,260	7.0	225,627	92.0
1988	603,732	244.0	42,738	17.0	560,994	227.0	261,242	106.0	15,932	6.4	245,310	99.3
1989	680,907	274.3	47,168	19.0	633,739	255.3	316,215	127.4	18,388	7.4	297,827	120.0
1990	739,980	295.0	50,403	20.1	689,577	274.9	(NA)	(NA)	(NA)	(NA)	323,069	128.8
1991	789,610	309.6	56,696	22.2	732,914	287.3	(NA)	(NA)	(NA)	(NA)	317,237	124.4
1992	846,277	331.8	65,706	25.8	780,571	306.0	(NA)	(NA)	(NA)	(NA)	334,301	130.3
1993	932,074	359.4	74,399	28.8	857,675	330.7	(NA)	(NA)	(NA)	(NA)	(NA)	(NA)
1994	1,016,691	388.6	79,795	30.5	936,896	358.1	345,035	131.9	23,956	9.2	321,079	122.7
1995	1,085,363	411.1	83,663	31.7	1,001,700	379.4	361,464	136.9	23,972	9.1	337,492	127.8

NA Not available. [1] Rate per 100,000 estimated population.

Source: U.S. Bureau of Justice Statistics, *Prisoners in State and Federal Institutions on December 31*, annual, and *Correctional Populations in the United States*, annual.

No. 356. State Prison Inmates—Selected Characteristics: 1986 and 1991

[Based on a sample survey of about 13,986 inmates in 1991 and 13,711 inmates in 1986; subject to sampling variability]

CHARACTERISTIC	NUMBER		PERCENT OF PRISON INMATES	
	1986	1991	1986	1991
Total [1]	**450,416**	**711,643**	**100.0**	**100.0**
Under 18 years old	2,057	4,552	0.5	0.6
18 to 24 years old	120,384	151,328	26.7	21.3
25 to 34 years old	205,817	325,429	45.7	45.7
35 to 44 years old	87,502	161,651	19.4	22.7
45 to 54 years old	23,524	46,475	5.2	6.5
55 to 64 years old	8,267	16,997	1.8	2.4
65 years old and over	2,808	5,210	0.6	0.7
Male	430,604	672,847	95.6	94.5
Female	19,812	38,796	4.4	5.5
White	223,648	349,628	49.7	49.1
Black	211,021	336,920	46.9	47.3
Other races	15,412	25,094	3.4	3.5

CHARACTERISTIC	NUMBER		PERCENT OF PRISON INMATES	
	1986	1991	1986	1991
Never married	241,707	369,302	53.7	56.3
Married	91,492	127,369	20.3	16.1
Widowed	8,343	13,038	1.9	1.9
Divorced	81,264	129,913	18.1	18.5
Separated	26,965	44,096	6.0	6.3
Years of school:				
Less than 12 years	276,309	[2]290,722	61.6	[2]41.2
12 years or more	172,386	415,451	38.4	58.8
Pre-arrest employment status:				
Employed	309,364	476,068	69.0	67.3
Not employed	139,097	230,876	31.0	32.7
Looking for work	80,750	115,590	18.0	16.4
Not looking for work	58,347	115,286	13.0	16.3

[1] For 1986, includes data not reported for all characteristics except sex. For 1991, includes data not reported for marital status, re-arrest, employment status, and years of school. [2] In 1991, the survey question was revised; therefore, the response may not be entirely comparable with 1986 and before.

Source: U.S. Bureau of Justice Statistics, *Profile of State Prison Inmates, 1986*, and *Survey of State Prison Inmates, 1991*.

No. 357. State Prison Inmates Who Committed Crimes Against Children: 1991

[Based on a sample survey of about 13,986 inmates of State correctional facilities, subject to sampling variability]

OFFENSE	ALL PRISONERS		PRISONERS SERVING TIME FOR CRIMES AGAINST CHILDREN					
						Violent child victimizers		
	Total	Percent distribution	Child victimizers, total	Percent of all prisoners	Percent distribution	Total Total	Victims age 12 or younger	Victims age 13 to 17
All offenses	711,643	100.0	65,163	9.2	100.0	(NA)	(NA)	(NA)
Violent offenses	327,958	46.1	61,037	18.6	93.7	60,285	33,287	26,998
Homicide	87,479	12.3	5,792	6.6	8.9	5,792	3,006	2,787
Murder	74,693	10.5	4,677	6.3	7.2	4,677	2,279	2,399
Negligent manslaughter	12,786	1.8	1,115	8.7	1.7	1,115	727	388
Kidnaping	8,369	1.2	1,508	18.0	2.3	1,508	682	826
Rape and sexual assault	66,482	9.3	43,552	65.5	66.8	42,993	25,102	17,892
Forcible rape	22,797	3.2	8,908	39.1	13.7	8,908	3,893	5,015
Forcible sodomy	2,036	0.3	1,741	85.5	2.7	1,729	1,039	690
Statutory rape	1,162	0.2	1,102	94.8	1.7	984	611	373
Lewd acts with children	10,799	1.5	10,799	100.0	16.6	10,370	7,175	3,195
Other sexual assault	29,688	4.2	21,002	70.7	32.2	21,002	12,384	8,619
Robbery	104,136	14.6	3,772	3.6	5.8	3,656	1,051	2,605
Assault	59,275	8.3	6,058	10.2	9.3	6,035	3,215	2,818
Aggravated assault	55,549	7.8	3,933	7.1	6.0	3,933	1,623	2,309
Child abuse	1,717	0.2	1,717	100.0	2.6	1,694	1,513	181
Simple assault	2,009	0.3	408	20.3	0.6	408	79	328
Other violent	2,217	0.3	355	16.0	0.5	301	231	70
Nonviolent offenses	383,685	53.9	4,126	1.1	6.3	(NA)	(NA)	(NA)

NA Not available.

Source: U.S. Bureau of Justice Statistics, *Child Victimizers: Violent Offenders and Their Victims*, March 1996.

No. 358. Prisoners Under Jurisdiction of State and Federal Correctional Authorities—Summary, by State: 1980 to 1995

[For years ending December 31]

SEX, REGION, DIVISION, AND STATE	1980	1990	1994	1995	
				Total	Percent change, 1994-1995
U.S.	329,821	773,919	1,054,702	1,126,287	6.8
Male	316,401	729,840	990,306	1,057,810	6.8
Female	13,420	44,079	64,396	68,477	6.3
Federal	24,363	65,526	95,034	100,250	5.5
State	305,458	708,393	959,668	1,026,037	6.9
Northeast	45,796	123,464	153,072	162,044	5.9
N.E.	9,926	25,151	33,388	34,079	2.1
ME	814	1,523	1,474	1,396	-5.3
NH	326	1,342	2,021	2,014	-0.3
VT[1]	480	1,049	1,301	1,279	-1.7
MA[2,3]	3,185	8,345	11,293	11,687	3.5
RI	813	2,392	2,919	2,902	-0.6
CT[1]	4,308	10,500	14,380	14,801	2.9
M.A.	35,870	98,313	119,684	127,965	6.9
NY	21,815	54,895	66,750	68,489	2.6
NJ	5,884	21,128	24,632	27,066	9.9
PA	8,171	22,290	28,302	32,410	14.5
Midwest	66,211	145,894	183,342	193,220	5.4
E.N.C.	51,175	113,806	144,106	150,757	4.6
OH	13,489	31,822	41,908	44,663	6.6
IN	6,683	12,736	15,014	16,125	7.4
IL[2]	11,899	27,516	36,531	37,658	3.1
MI[2,3]	15,124	34,267	40,631	41,112	1.2
WI	3,980	7,465	10,022	11,199	11.7
W.N.C.	15,036	32,088	39,236	42,463	8.2
MN	2,001	3,176	4,575	4,846	5.9
IA[2]	2,481	3,967	5,437	5,906	8.6
MO	5,726	14,943	17,898	19,134	6.9
ND	253	483	536	608	13.4
SD	635	1,341	1,708	1,841	7.8
NE	1,446	2,403	2,711	3,074	13.4
KS	2,494	5,775	6,371	7,054	10.7
South	148,358	284,651	422,764	454,182	7.4
S.A.	78,815	152,952	198,948	212,991	7.1

SEX, REGION, DIVISION, AND STATE	1980	1990	1994	1995	
				Total	Percent change, 1994-1995
DE[1]	1,474	3,471	4,466	4,802	7.5
MD	7,731	17,848	20,998	21,453	2.2
DC[1]	3,145	9,947	10,949	9,800	-10.5
VA	8,920	17,593	26,968	27,415	1.7
WV	1,257	1,565	2,332	2,512	7.7
NC	15,513	18,411	23,648	29,253	23.7
SC	7,862	17,319	18,999	19,611	3.2
GA[2]	12,178	22,411	33,425	34,266	2.5
FL[2]	20,735	44,387	57,163	63,879	11.7
E.S.C.	21,065	43,451	55,970	60,668	8.4
KY	3,588	9,023	11,066	12,060	9.0
TN	7,022	10,388	14,401	15,206	5.6
AL	6,543	15,665	19,573	20,718	5.8
MS	3,902	8,375	10,930	12,684	16.0
W.S.C.	46,488	88,248	167,846	180,523	7.6
AR	2,911	7,322	8,957	9,411	5.1
LA	8,889	18,599	24,063	25,195	4.7
OK[3]	4,796	12,285	16,631	18,151	9.1
TX	29,892	50,042	118,195	127,766	8.1
West	47,093	154,384	200,490	216,591	8.0
Mt	13,141	37,433	50,006	54,369	8.7
MT	739	1,425	1,764	1,999	13.3
ID	817	1,961	2,811	3,328	18.4
WY	534	1,110	1,217	1,395	14.6
CO	2,629	7,671	10,717	11,063	3.2
NM	1,279	3,187	3,712	4,078	9.9
AZ[2]	4,372	14,261	19,746	21,341	8.1
UT	932	2,496	3,045	3,452	13.4
NV	1,839	5,322	6,993	7,713	10.3
Pac	33,952	116,951	150,485	162,222	7.8
WA	4,399	7,995	10,833	11,608	7.2
OR	3,177	6,492	6,936	7,886	13.7
CA	24,569	97,309	126,091	135,646	7.6
AK[1]	822	2,622	3,292	3,522	7.0
HI[1]	985	2,533	3,333	3,560	6.8

[1] Includes both jail and prison inmates (State has combined jail and prison system). [2] Numbers are for custody rather than jurisdiction counts. [3] Data are for custody counts until 1994 when jurisdiction counts are reported.

Source: U.S. Bureau of Justice Statistics, *Prisoners in 1995*, and earlier reports.

No. 359. Adults on Probation, in Jail or Prison, or on Parole: 1980 to 1994

[As of December 31, except jail counts as June 30]

ITEM	Total [1]	Probation	Jail	Prison	Parole
1980	1,840,400	1,118,097	[2] 182,288	319,598	220,438
1981	2,006,600	1,225,934	[2] 195,085	360,029	225,539
1982	2,192,600	1,357,264	207,853	402,914	224,604
1983	2,475,100	1,582,947	221,815	423,898	246,440
1984	2,689,200	1,740,948	233,018	448,264	266,992
1985	3,011,400	1,968,712	254,986	487,593	300,203
1986	3,239,400	2,114,621	272,735	526,436	325,638
1987	3,459,600	2,247,158	294,092	562,814	355,505
1988	3,714,100	2,356,483	341,893	607,766	407,977
1989	4,055,600	2,522,125	393,303	683,367	456,803
1990	4,348,100	2,670,234	403,019	743,382	531,407
1991	4,536,200	2,729,322	424,129	792,535	590,198
1992	4,762,600	2,811,611	441,781	850,566	658,601
1993	4,944,000	2,903,061	[2] 455,500	909,381	676,100
1994	5,129,700	2,964,171	483,717	991,612	690,159
Sex:					
Male	4,367,500	2,375,600	434,800	934,700	622,400
Female	762,200	588,600	48,900	56,900	67,800
Race:					
White	3,061,100	1,966,500	252,300	469,300	363,000
Black	2,013,400	982,700	223,900	507,000	319,600
Other	65,200	34,900	7,600	15,300	7,400

[1] Totals may not add due to individuals having multiple correctional statuses. [2] Estimated. [3] Totals may not add due to rounding.

Source: U.S. Bureau of Justice Statistics, *Correctional Populations in the United States*, annual.

No. 360. Prisoners Under Sentence of Death: 1980 to 1995

[As of December 31. Excludes prisoners under sentence of death who remained within local correctional systems pending exhaustion of appellate process or who had not been committed to prison]

CHARACTERISTIC	1980	1985	1986	1987	1988	1989	1990	1991	1992	1993	1994	1995
Total [1]	**688**	**1,575**	**1,800**	**1,967**	**2,117**	**2,243**	**2,346**	**2,466**	**2,575**	**2,727**	**2,890**	**3,054**
White	418	896	1,013	1,128	1,235	1,308	1,368	1,450	1,508	1,575	1,645	1,730
Black and other	270	679	787	839	882	935	978	1,016	1,067	1,152	1,245	1,324
Under 20 years	11	13	19	10	11	6	8	14	12	13	19	20
20 to 24 years	173	212	217	222	195	191	168	179	188	211	231	264
25 to 34 years	334	804	872	969	1,048	1,080	1,110	1,067	1,078	1,066	1,088	1,068
35 to 54 years	186	531	639	744	823	917	1,006	1,129	1,212	1,330	1,449	1,583
55 years and over	10	31	34	39	47	56	64	73	85	96	103	119
Years of school completed:												
7 years or less	68	147	164	181	180	183	178	173	181	185	186	191
8 years	74	159	174	183	184	178	186	181	180	183	196	195
9 to 11 years	204	483	577	650	692	739	775	810	836	885	930	979
12 years	162	440	515	591	657	695	729	783	831	887	939	995
More than 12 years	43	127	143	168	180	192	209	222	232	244	255	272
Unknown	163	235	208	211	231	263	279	313	315	332	382	422
Marital status:												
Never married	268	655	772	856	896	956	998	1,071	1,132	1,222	1,320	1,412
Married	229	487	525	571	594	610	632	663	663	671	707	718
Divorced [2]	217	449	484	557	632	684	726	746	780	823	863	924
Time elapsed since sentencing:												
Less than 12 months	185	273	293	295	293	231	231	252	265	262	280	287
12 to 47 months	389	739	757	804	812	809	753	718	720	716	755	784
48 to 71 months	102	303	376	412	409	408	438	441	444	422	379	423
72 months and over	38	276	355	473	610	802	934	1,071	1,146	1,316	1,476	1,560
Legal status at arrest:												
Not under sentence	384	861	992	1,123	1,207	1,301	1,345	1,415	1,476	1,562	1,662	1,764
Parole or probation [3]	115	350	409	480	545	585	578	615	702	754	800	866
Prison or escaped	45	81	82	91	93	94	128	102	101	102	103	110
Unknown	170	299	298	290	279	270	305	321	296	298	325	314

[1] For 1980 to 1993, revisions to the total number of prisoners were not carried to the characteristics except for race. [2] Includes persons married but separated, widows, widowers, and unknown. [3] Includes prisoners on mandatory conditional release, work release, leave, AWOL, or bail. Covers 24 prisoners in 1989, 28 in 1990, and 29 in 1991 and 1992, 33 in 1993 and 1995, and 31 in 1994.

Source: U.S. Bureau of Justice Statistics, *Capital Punishment*, annual.

No. 361. Movement of Prisoners Under Sentence of Death: 1980 to 1995

[Prisoners reported under sentence of death by civil authorities. The term "under sentence of death" begins when the court pronounces the first sentence of death for a capital offense]

STATUS	1980	1985	1987	1988	1989	1990	1991	1992	1993	1994	1995
Under sentence of death, Jan. 1	595	1,420	1,800	1,967	2,117	2,243	2,348	2,465	2,580	2,727	2,905
Received death sentence [1] [2]	203	281	299	296	251	244	268	265	282	306	310
White	125	165	190	196	133	147	163	147	146	162	168
Black	77	114	106	91	114	94	101	114	130	136	138
Dispositions other than executions	101	108	90	128	102	108	116	124	108	112	105
Executions	-	18	25	11	16	23	14	31	38	31	56
Under sentence of death, Dec. 31 [1] [2]	688	1,575	1,967	2,117	2,243	2,348	2,466	2,575	2,727	2,890	3,054
White	425	896	1,128	1,238	1,306	1,368	1,450	1,508	1,575	1,645	1,730
Black	268	664	813	853	898	940	1,016	1,029	1,111	1,197	1,275

- Represents zero. [1] Includes races other than White or Black. [2] Revisions to total number of prisoners under death sentence not carried to this category.

Source: U.S. Bureau of Justice Statistics, *Capital Punishment*, annual.

No. 362. Prisoners Executed Under Civil Authority: 1930 to 1995

[Excludes executions by military authorities. The Army (including the Air Force) carried out 160 (148 between 1942 and 1950; 3 each in 1954, 1955, and 1957; and 1 each in 1958, 1959, and 1961). Of the total, 106 were executed for murder (including 21 involving rape), 53 for rape, and 1 for desertion. The Navy carried out no executions during the period]

YEAR OR PERIOD	Total [1]	White	Black	EXECUTED FOR MURDER			EXECUTED FOR RAPE			EXECUTED, OTHER OFFENSES [2]		
				Total [1]	White	Black	Total [1]	White	Black	Total [1]	White	Black
All years	**4,172**	**1,940**	**2,187**	**3,647**	**1,863**	**1,756**	**455**	**48**	**466**	**70**	**39**	**31**
1930 to 1939	1,667	827	816	1,514	803	687	125	10	115	28	14	14
1940 to 1949	1,284	490	781	1,064	458	595	200	19	179	20	13	7
1950 to 1959	717	336	376	601	316	280	102	13	89	14	7	7
1960 to 1967	191	98	93	155	87	68	28	6	22	8	5	3
1968 to 1976	-	-	-	-	-	-	-	-	-	-	-	-
1977 to 1982	6	5	1	6	5	6	-	-	-	-	-	-
1983	5	4	1	5	4	1	-	-	-	-	-	-
1984	21	13	8	21	13	8	-	-	-	-	-	-
1985	18	11	7	18	11	7	-	-	-	-	-	-
1986	18	11	7	18	11	7	-	-	-	-	-	-
1987	25	13	12	25	13	12	-	-	-	-	-	-
1988	11	6	5	11	6	5	-	-	-	-	-	-
1989	16	8	8	16	8	8	-	-	-	-	-	-
1990	23	16	7	23	16	7	-	-	-	-	-	-
1991	14	7	7	14	7	7	-	-	-	-	-	-
1992	31	19	11	31	19	11	-	-	-	-	-	-
1993	38	23	14	38	23	14	-	-	-	-	-	-
1994	31	20	11	31	20	11	-	-	-	-	-	-
1995	56	33	22	56	33	22	-	-	-	-	-	-

- Represents zero. [1] Includes races other than White or Black. [2] Includes 25 armed robbery, 20 kidnapping, 11 burglary, 8 espionage (6 in 1942 and 2 in 1953), and 6 aggravated assault.

Source: Through 1978, U.S. Law Enforcement Assistance Administration; thereafter, U.S. Bureau of Justice Statistics, *Correctional Populations in the United States*, annual.

No. 363. Prisoners Under Sentence of Death and Executed Under Civil Authority, by States: 1977 to 1995

[Alaska, District of Columbia, Hawaii, Iowa, Maine, Massachusetts, Michigan, Minnesota, New York, North Dakota, Rhode Island, Vermont, West Virginia, and Wisconsin are jurisdictions without a death penalty]

STATE	1977 to 1995	1992	1993	1994	1995	STATE	1977 to 1995	1992	1993	1994	1995	STATE	1977 to 1995	1992	1993	1994	1995
U.S.	**313**	**31**	**38**	**31**	**56**	ID	1	-	-	1	-	NC	8	1	-	1	2
						IL	7	-	-	1	5	OK	6	2	-	-	3
AL	12	2	-	-	2	IN	3	-	-	1	-	SC	5	-	-	-	1
AZ	4	1	2	-	1	LA	22	-	1	-	1	TX	104	12	17	14	19
AR	11	2	-	5	2	MD	1	-	-	1	-	UT	4	1	-	-	-
CA	2	1	1	-	-	MS	4	-	-	-	-	VA	29	4	5	2	5
DE	5	1	2	1	1	MO	17	1	4	-	6	WA	2	-	1	1	-
FL	36	2	3	1	3	NE	1	-	-	1	-	WY	1	1	-	-	-
GA	20	-	2	1	2	NV	5	-	-	-	-						

- Represents zero.

Source: Through 1978, U.S. Law Enforcement Assistance Administration; thereafter, U.S. Bureau of Justice Statistics, *Capital Punishment*, annual.

No. 364. Fire Losses—Total and Per Capita: 1970 to 1995

[Includes allowance for uninsured and unreported losses but excludes losses to government property and forests. Represents incurred losses]

YEAR	Total (mil. dol.)	Per capita [1]	YEAR	Total (mil. dol.)	Per capita [1]	YEAR	Total (mil. dol.)	Per capita [1]
1970	2,328	11.41	1979	4,851	21.60	1988	9,626	39.11
1971	2,316	11.20	1980	5,579	24.56	1989	9,514	38.33
1972	2,304	11.01	1981	5,625	24.53	1990	9,495	38.26
1973	2,639	12.49	1982	5,894	25.61	1991	11,302	44.83
1974	3,190	14.95	1983	6,320	27.20	1992	13,588	48.24
1975	3,190	14.81	1984	7,602	32.35	1993	11,331	43.96
1976	3,558	16.35	1985	7,753	32.70	1994	12,778	49.06
1977	3,764	17.13	1986	8,488	35.21	1995	11,856	45.12
1978	4,008	18.05	1987	8,504	34.96			

[1] Based on Bureau of the Census estimated resident population as of July 1.
Source: Insurance Information Institute, New York, NY, *Insurance Facts*, annual.

No. 365. Fires—Number and Loss, by Type and Property Use: 1992 to 1995

[Based on annual sample survey of fire departments. No adjustments were made for unreported fires and losses. Property loss includes direct property loss only]

TYPE AND PROPERTY USE	NUMBER (1,000)				PROPERTY LOSS (mil. dol.)			
	1992	1993	1994	1995	1992	1993	1994	1995
Fires, total	1,965	1,953	2,054	1,966	8,295	8,546	8,151	8,918
Structure	636	621	614	574	6,957	7,408	6,867	7,620
Outside of structure [1]	50	52	66	61	318	63	120	77
Brush and rubbish	743	732	795	778	-	-	-	-
Vehicle	405	421	422	406	965	1,030	1,111	1,152
Other	129	127	157	147	55	47	53	69
Structure by property use:								
Public assembly	17	16	17	15	361	298	334	336
Educational	10	9	9	9	68	64	91	84
Institutional	12	10	11	9	35	30	20	31
Stores and offices	33	29	30	29	[2]1,105	741	596	[3]681
Residential	472	470	451	426	3,880	4,843	4,317	4,363
1-2 family units [4]	358	358	341	320	3,178	[5]4,111	3,537	3,615
Apartments	101	100	97	94	597	653	678	649
Other residential [6]	13	12	13	12	105	79	102	99
Storage [7]	42	39	43	39	734	651	568	710
Industry, utility, defense [7]	19	19	19	18	597	623	758	[8]1,248
Special structures	33	29	34	29	177	156	181	167

- Represents zero. [1] Includes outside storage, crops, timber, etc. [2] Includes estimated loss of $567 involving 862 structures from the April 1992 civil disturbance in Los Angeles, CA. [3] Includes an estimated $135 million in property loss that occurred in the explosion and fire in the federal office building in Oklahoma City on April 19, 1995. [4] Includes mobile homes. [5] Reflects wildfires that occurred in southern California in 1993 that resulted in $809 million in property damage. [6] Includes hotels and motels, college dormitories, boarding houses, etc. [7] Data underreported as some incidents were handled by private fire brigades or fixed suppression systems which do not report. [8] Includes estimated losses of $500 million in an industrial complex fire in Massachusetts and $200 million in a manufacturing plant in Georgia in 1995.

Source: National Fire Protection Association, Quincy, MA, " NFPA Reports on U.S. Fire Loss — 1995", *NFPA Journal*, September 1996, and prior issues (copyright 1996).

No. 366. Fires and Property Loss for Incendiary and Suspicious Fires and Civilian Fire Deaths and Injuries, by Selected Property Type: 1992 to 1995

[Based on sample survey of fire departments]

ITEM	1992	1993	1994	1995	ITEM	1992	1993	1994	1995
NUMBER (1,000)					CIVILIAN FIRE DEATHS				
Structure fires, total	636	621	614	574	Deaths, total [2]	4,730	4,635	4,275	4,585
Structure fires of incendiary or suspicious origin	94	85	86	91	Residential property	3,765	3,825	3,465	3,695
					One- and two-family dwellings	3,160	3,035	2,785	3,035
Fires of incendiary origin	58	54	53	58	Apartments	545	685	640	605
Fires of suspicious origin	36	31	33	33	Vehicles	730	595	630	535
PROPERTY LOSS [1] (mil. dol.)					CIVILIAN FIRE INJURIES				
					Injuries, total [2]	28,700	30,475	27,250	25,775
Structure fires, total	6,957	7,406	6,867	7,620	Residential property	21,600	22,600	20,025	19,125
Structure fires of incendiary or suspicious origin	1,999	2,351	1,447	1,647	One- and two-family dwellings	15,275	15,700	14,000	13,450
					Apartments	5,825	6,300	5,475	5,200
Fires of incendiary origin	[3]1,493	[4]1,901	964	[5]1,116	Vehicles	3,000	2,675	2,625	2,525
Fires of suspicious origin	506	450	483	531					

[1] Direct property loss only. [2] Includes other not shown separately. [3] Includes estimated loss of $567 million from the April 1992 civil disturbance in Los Angeles, CA. [4] Includes fire losses that occurred during the wildfires in California and the World Trade Center bombing in New York city, which resulted in combined estimated losses of $1.039 billion. [5] Includes $135 million in property loss that occurred in the explosion and fire in the federal office building in Oklahoma City on April 19, 1995.

Source: National Fire Protection Association, Quincy, MA, "NFPA Reports on U.S. Fire Loss — 1995", *NFPA Journal*, September 1996, and prior issues (copyright 1996).

Section 6

Geography and Environment

This section presents a variety of information on the physical environment of the United States, starting with basic area measurement data and ending with climatic data for selected weather stations around the country. The subjects covered between those points are mostly concerned with environmental trends, but include such related subjects as land use, water consumption, air pollutant emissions, toxic releases, oil spills, hazardous waste sites, threatened and endangered wildlife, and expenditures for pollution abatement and control.

The information in this section is selected from a wide range of Federal agencies that compile the data for various administrative or regulatory purposes, such as the Environmental Protection Agency, U.S. Geological Survey, National Oceanic and Atmospheric Administration, Soil Conservation Service, and General Services Administration. Other agencies include the Bureau of the Census, which presents nationwide area measurement information and the Bureau of Economic Analysis, which compiles data on pollution abatement and control expenditures.

Area—For the 1990 census, area measurements were calculated by computer based on the information contained in a single, consistent geographic data base, the TIGER™ File (described below), rather than relying on historical, local, and manually calculated information. This especially affects water area figures reported in 1990; these had only included those bodies of water of least 40 acres and those streams with a width of at least one-eighth of a statute mile from 1940 to 1980. Water area figures for 1990 increased because the data reflected all water recorded in the Census Bureau's geographic data base including coastal, Great Lakes, and territorial waters.

Geography—The U.S. Geological Survey conducts investigations, surveys, and research in the fields of geography, geology, topography, geographic information systems, mineralogy, hydrology, and geothermal energy resources as well as natural hazards. In cooperation with State and local agencies, the U.S. Geological Survey prepares and publishes topographic, land use/land cover, geologic, and hydrologic maps and digital data compilations. The U.S. Geological Survey provides United States cartographic data through the Earth Sciences Information Center, water resources data through the National Water Data Exchange (NAWDEX), and a variety of research and Open-File reports which are announced monthly in New Publications of the U.S. Geological Survey. In a joint project with the Census Bureau, the U.S. Geological Survey provided the basic information on geographic features for input into a national geographic and cartographic data base prepared by the Census Bureau, called the TIGER™ (Topologically Integrated Geographic Encoding and Referencing) System.

Maps prepared by the Bureau of the Census show the names and boundaries of various types of legal and statistical entities, such as places, county subdivisions, and larger areas and are available as of the specific decennial census. An inventory is available for the 1990 census, both on computer tape and CD-ROM as the 1990 TIGER/GICS (Geographic Identification Code Scheme)

In Brief

Municipal solid waste generated grew only 5.5% between 1990 and 1995 while waste recovery and recycling grew almost 66%. Twenty-seven percent of waste is now recovered compared with 17% in 1990.

Toxic chemical releases into the environment declined for the fourth consecutive year since 1990 to just under 2 billion pounds in 1994, a 29% drop since 1990.

The environmental industry employed just over 1.3 million workers in 1996, an increase of 11% since 1990.

and for the 1992 economic censuses in the *Geographic Reference Manual* (EC92-R-1). The Census Bureau maintains a current inventory of governmental units and their legal boundaries through its Boundary and Annexation Survey. The TIGER™ System contains information on the legal and statistical entities used by the Census Bureau, as well as on both manmade and natural features, such as streets, roads, railroads, rivers, and lakes; information is available to the public in the form of machine-readable TIGER™ extract files.

An inventory of the Nation's land resources by type of use/cover was conducted by the Soil Conservation Service in 1982, 1987, and 1992. The results, published in the *1992 National Inventory of Land Resources*, cover all non-Federal land in Puerto Rico, the Virgin Islands, and the United States except Alaska.

Environment—The principal Federal agency responsible for pollution abatement and control activities is the Environmental Protection Agency (EPA). It is responsible for establishing and monitoring national air quality standards, water quality activities, solid and hazardous waste disposal, and control of toxic substances.

National Ambient Air Quality Standards (NAAQS) for suspended particulate matter, sulfur dioxide, photochemical oxidants, carbon monoxide, and nitrogen dioxide were originally set by the EPA in April 1971. Every 5 years, each of the NAAQS is reviewed and revised if new health or welfare data indicates that a change is necessary. The standard for photochemical oxidants, now called ozone, was revised in February 1979. Also, a new NAAQS for lead was promulgated in October 1978 and for suspended particulate matter in 1987. Table 378 gives some of the health-related standards for the six air pollutants having NAAQS. Responsibility for demonstrating compliance with or progress toward achieving these standards lies with the State agencies. In 1995, there were 1,737 non-Federal sampling stations for particulates, 695 for sulfur dioxide, 542 for carbon monoxide, 972 for ozone, 406 for nitrogen dioxide, and 448 for lead. Data from these State networks are periodically submitted to EPA's National Aerometric Information Retrieval System (AIRS) for summarization in annual reports on the nationwide status and trends in air quality; for details, see *National Air Quality and Emissions Trends Report, 1995.*

Pollution abatement and control expenditures—Data on expenditures for pollution abatement and control were compiled and published by the Bureau of Economic Analysis (BEA) and the U.S. Bureau of the Census through 1994 data. The BEA conducts surveys on national expenditures for pollution abatement and control and presents the data in its *Survey of Current Business*. The Bureau of the Census still collects data on expenditures for pollution control activities for State and local governments and industry. Data on government expenditures are reported in an annual series of publications, *Government Finances*, which covers expenditures on sewage and sanitation outlays. Industry data were reported annually in *Current Industrial Reports* series MA-200 until the final report in 1996. The Council on Environmental Quality published some expenditure data in *Environmental Quality* along with other environmental indicator.

Climate—NOAA, through the National Weather Service and the National Environmental Satellite, Data and Information Service, is responsible for data on climate. NOAA maintains about 11,600 weather stations, of which over 3,000 produce autographic precipitation records, about 600 take hourly readings of a series of weather elements, and the remainder record data once a day. These data are reported monthly in the *Climatological Data* (published by State), and monthly and annually in the *Local Climatological Data* (published by location for major cities).

The normal climatological temperatures, precipitation, and degree days listed in this publication are derived for comparative purposes and are averages for the 30-year period, 1961-90. For stations that did not have continuous records for the entire 30 years from the same instrument site, the normals have been adjusted to provide representative values for the current location. The information in all other tables is based on data from the beginning of the record at that location through 1995, except as noted.

No. 367. Land and Water Area of States and Other Entities: 1990

[One square mile=2.59 square kilometers. Excludes territorial water, which was included in the 1993 edition of the *Statistical Abstract*]

REGION, DIVISION, STATE, AND OTHER AREA	TOTAL AREA		LAND AREA		WATER AREA				
	Sq. mi.	Sq. km.	Sq. mi.	Sq. km.	Total Sq. mi.	Total Sq. km.	Inland sq. mi.	Coastal sq. mi.	Great Lakes sq. mi.
United States	3,717,796	9,629,091	3,536,278	9,158,960	181,518	470,131	78,937	42,528	60,052
Northeast	176,917	458,215	162,274	420,289	14,643	37,926	6,444	3,549	4,650
New England	68,656	177,815	62,812	162,682	5,843	15,133	3,696	2,148	-
Maine	33,741	87,388	30,865	79,939	2,876	7,449	2,263	613	-
New Hampshire	9,283	24,044	8,969	23,231	314	813	314	-	-
Vermont	9,615	24,903	9,249	23,956	366	947	366	-	-
Massachusetts	9,241	23,934	7,838	20,300	1,403	3,634	424	979	-
Rhode Island	1,231	3,189	1,045	2,707	186	482	168	18	-
Connecticut	5,544	14,358	4,845	12,550	698	1,808	161	538	-
Middle Atlantic	108,263	280,400	99,462	257,607	8,800	22,793	2,749	1,401	4,650
New York	53,989	139,833	47,224	122,310	6,766	17,523	1,888	976	3,901
New Jersey	8,215	21,277	7,419	19,215	796	2,062	371	425	-
Pennsylvania	46,058	119,291	44,820	116,083	1,239	3,208	490	-	749
Midwest	821,792	2,128,384	751,519	1,946,435	70,243	181,929	14,841	-	55,402
East North Central	301,369	780,547	243,539	630,766	57,830	149,781	4,974	-	52,856
Ohio	44,828	116,103	40,953	106,067	3,875	10,036	376	-	3,499
Indiana	36,420	94,328	35,870	92,904	550	1,424	315	-	235
Illinois	57,918	150,007	55,593	143,987	2,325	6,021	750	-	1,575
Michigan	96,705	250,465	56,809	147,136	39,895	103,329	1,704	-	38,192
Wisconsin	65,499	169,643	54,314	140,672	11,186	28,971	1,831	-	9,355
West North Central	520,393	1,347,817	507,980	1,315,669	12,412	32,148	9,866	-	2,546
Minnesota	86,943	225,182	79,617	206,207	7,326	18,975	4,780	-	2,546
Iowa	56,276	145,754	55,875	144,716	401	1,038	401	-	-
Missouri	69,709	180,546	68,898	178,446	811	2,100	811	-	-
North Dakota	70,704	183,123	68,994	178,695	1,710	4,428	1,710	-	-
South Dakota	77,121	199,744	75,896	196,571	1,225	3,174	1,225	-	-
Nebraska	77,358	200,358	76,878	199,113	481	1,245	481	-	-
Kansas	82,282	213,110	81,823	211,922	459	1,189	459	-	-
South	907,178	2,349,591	871,010	2,255,916	36,168	93,674	27,355	8,813	-
South Atlantic	284,085	735,780	266,160	689,355	17,925	46,426	12,557	5,368	-
Delaware	2,396	6,206	1,955	5,062	442	1,144	71	371	-
Maryland	12,297	31,849	9,775	25,316	2,522	6,533	680	1,842	-
District of Columbia	68	177	61	159	7	18	7	-	-
Virginia	42,326	109,625	39,598	102,558	2,729	7,067	1,000	1,728	-
West Virginia	24,231	62,759	24,087	62,384	145	375	145	-	-
North Carolina	52,672	136,421	48,718	126,180	3,954	10,241	3,954	-	-
South Carolina	31,189	80,779	30,111	77,988	1,078	2,791	1,006	72	-
Georgia	58,977	152,750	57,919	150,010	1,058	2,740	1,011	47	-
Florida	59,928	155,214	53,937	139,697	5,991	15,517	4,683	1,308	-
East South Central	183,080	474,176	178,616	462,615	4,464	11,561	3,355	1,109	-
Kentucky	40,411	104,665	39,732	102,907	679	1,759	679	-	-
Tennessee	42,146	109,158	41,219	106,758	926	2,400	926	-	-
Alabama	52,237	135,293	50,750	131,443	1,486	3,850	968	519	-
Mississippi	48,286	125,060	46,914	121,506	1,372	3,553	781	591	-
West South Central	440,013	1,139,634	426,234	1,103,947	13,779	35,687	11,444	2,335	-
Arkansas	53,182	137,742	52,075	134,875	1,107	2,867	1,107	-	-
Louisiana	49,651	128,595	43,566	112,836	6,085	15,759	4,153	1,931	-
Oklahoma	69,903	181,048	68,679	177,877	1,224	3,171	1,224	-	-
Texas	267,277	692,248	261,914	678,358	5,363	13,890	4,959	404	-
West	1,811,939	4,692,921	1,751,475	4,536,320	60,464	156,601	30,297	30,167	-
Mountain	863,613	2,236,757	856,121	2,217,354	7,492	19,404	7,492	-	-
Montana	147,046	380,849	145,556	376,991	1,490	3,859	1,490	-	-
Idaho	83,574	216,456	82,751	214,325	823	2,131	823	-	-
Wyoming	97,818	253,349	97,105	251,501	714	1,848	714	-	-
Colorado	104,100	269,618	103,729	268,658	371	960	371	-	-
New Mexico	121,598	314,939	121,364	314,334	234	605	234	-	-
Arizona	114,006	295,276	113,642	294,333	364	943	364	-	-
Utah	84,904	219,902	82,168	212,815	2,736	7,086	2,736	-	-
Nevada	110,567	286,367	109,806	284,396	761	1,971	761	-	-
Pacific	948,326	2,456,164	895,354	2,318,967	52,972	137,197	22,805	30,167	-
Washington	70,637	182,949	66,581	172,445	4,055	10,503	1,545	2,511	-
Oregon	97,132	251,571	96,002	248,646	1,129	2,925	1,050	80	-
California	158,869	411,470	155,973	403,971	2,895	7,499	2,674	222	-
Alaska	615,230	1,593,444	570,374	1,477,268	44,856	116,177	17,501	27,355	-
Hawaii	6,459	16,729	6,423	16,636	36	93	36	-	-
Other areas:									
Puerto Rico	3,508	9,085	3,427	8,875	81	210	65	16	-
American Samoa	90	233	77	200	13	33	7	6	-
Guam	217	561	210	543	7	18	7	-	-
No. Mariana Islands	189	490	179	464	10	26	2	8	-
Palau	241	624	177	458	64	165	40	24	-
Virgin Islands of the U.S.	171	443	134	346	37	96	17	20	-

- Represents or rounds to zero.

Source: U.S. Bureau of the Census, *1990 Census of Population and Housing*, series CPH-2; and unpublished data from the TIGER/Geographic Information Control System (TIGER/GICS)computer file. Corrections have been made subsequent to the 1990 Census reports.

No. 368. Area and Acquisition of the Federal Public Domain: 1781 to 1994

[In millions of acres. Areas of acquisitions are as computed in 1912, and do not agree with figures in square miles shown in table 367 which include later adjustments and reflect subsequent remeasurement. Excludes outlying areas of the United States amounting to 645,949 acres in 1978]

YEAR	Land area, total[1]	YEAR	LAND AREA[1]			YEAR AND ACQUISITION	ACREAGE		
			Total	Public domain	Acquired		Total	Land	Inland water
1802 . . .	200.0	1980 . . .	719.5	648.0	71.5	**Aggregate**	1,840.7	1,807.5	33.2
1850 . . .	1,200.0	1981 . . .	730.8	668.7	62.2				
1880 . . .	900.0	1982 . . .	729.8	670.0	59.8	1781-1802 (State Cessions)	236.8	233.4	3.4
1912 . . .	600.0	1983 . . .	732.0	672.4	59.6	1803, Louisiana Purchase[2]	529.9	523.4	6.5
1946 . . .	413.0	1984 . . .	726.6	658.9	67.7	1819, Cession from Spain	46.1	43.3	2.8
1950 . . .	412.0	1985 . . .	726.7	656.2	70.5	Red River Basin[3]	29.6	29.1	0.5
1955 . . .	407.9	1986 . . .	727.1	662.7	64.4				
1959 . . .	768.6	1987 . . .	724.3	661.0	63.3	1846, Oregon Compromise	183.4	180.6	2.7
1960 . . .	771.5	1988 . . .	688.2	623.2	65.0	1848, Mexican Cession[2]	338.7	334.5	4.2
1965 . . .	765.8	1989 . . .	662.2	597.9	64.3	1850, Purchase from Texas	78.9	78.8	0.1
1970 . . .	761.3	1990 . . .	649.8	587.4	62.4	1853, Gadsden Purchase	19.0	19.0	(Z)
1975 . . .	760.4	1991 . . .	649.3	587.6	61.8	1867, Alaska Purchase	378.3	365.3	12.9
1976 . . .	762.2	1992 . . .	651.1	590.9	60.2				
1977 . . .	741.5	1993 . . .	650.3	590.5	59.9				
1978 . . .	775.2	1994 . . .	657.3	573.2	84.1				
1979 . . .	744.1								

Z Less than 50,000. [1] Owned by Federal Government. Comprises original public domain plus acquired lands. Estimated from imperfect data available for indicated years. Prior to 1959, excludes Alaska, and 1960, Hawaii. Source: Beginning 1955, U.S. General Services Administration, *Inventory Report on Real Property Owned by the United States Throughout the World*, annual. [2] Data for Louisiana Purchase exclude areas eliminated by Treaty of 1819 with Spain. Such areas are included in figures for Mexican Cession. [3] Represents drainage basin of Red River of the North, south of 49th parallel. Authorities differ as to method and date of its acquisition. Some hold it as part of the Louisiana Purchase; others, as acquired from Great Britain.

Source: Except as noted, U.S. Dept. of the Interior, Estimated area, Bureau of Land Management; all other data, Office of the Secretary, *Areas of Acquisitions to the Territory of the U.S.*, 1922.

No. 369. Total and Federally Owned Land, 1960 to 1994, and by State, 1994

[As of end of fiscal year; see text, section 9. Total land area figures are not comparable with those in table 367]

REGION, DIVISION, AND STATE	Total (1,000 acres)	Not owned by Federal Government (1,000 acres)	OWNED BY FEDERAL GOVERNMENT[1]		REGION, DIVISION, AND STATE	Total (1,000 acres)	Not owned by Federal Government (1,000 acres)	OWNED BY FEDERAL GOVERNMENT[1]	
			Acres (1,000)	Percent				Acres (1,000)	Percent
1960	2,273,407	1,501,894	771,512	33.9	**South**	561,238	536,565	24,674	4.4
1965	2,271,343	1,505,546	765,797	33.7	**S.A.**	171,325	158,798	12,527	7.3
1970	2,271,343	1,510,042	761,301	33.5	DE	1,266	1,024	242	19.1
1975	2,271,343	1,510,929	760,414	33.5	MD	6,319	5,789	530	8.4
1980	2,271,343	1,551,822	719,522	31.7	DC	39	30	9	23.4
1985	2,271,343	1,544,658	726,686	32.0	VA	25,496	22,478	3,018	11.8
1990	2,271,343	1,621,541	649,802	28.6	WV	15,411	14,318	1,092	7.1
1993	2,271,343	1,621,021	650,322	28.6	NC	31,403	28,955	2,448	7.8
					SC	19,374	18,583	791	4.1
1994, total	2,271,343	1,609,446	661,896	29.1	GA	37,295	35,618	1,677	4.5
Northeast	104,700	101,156	3,543	3.4	FL	34,721	32,002	2,719	7.8
N.E.	40,401	38,644	1,756	4.3	**E.S.C**	116,141	110,064	5,077	4.4
ME	19,848	19,518	329	1.7	KY	25,512	24,439	1,074	4.2
NH	5,769	5,006	763	13.2	TN	26,728	25,164	1,564	5.9
VT	5,937	5,504	432	7.3	AL	32,678	31,597	1,081	3.3
MA	5,035	4,833	202	4.0	MS	30,223	28,865	1,358	4.5
RI	677	659	18	2.6	**W.S.C**	274,772	267,703	7,070	2.6
CT	3,135	3,123	12	0.4	AR	33,599	30,667	2,933	8.7
M.A	64,299	62,512	1,787	2.8	LA	28,868	27,857	1,011	3.5
NY	30,681	30,258	423	1.4	OK	44,088	43,318	770	1.7
NJ	4,813	4,175	638	13.3	TX	168,218	165,861	2,356	1.4
PA	28,804	28,079	725	2.5	**West**	1,122,535	513,848	608,687	54.2
Midwest	482,870	457,877	24,993	5.2	**Mt**	548,449	278,597	269,851	49.2
E.N.C	156,679	147,138	9,541	6.1	MT	93,271	67,312	25,959	27.8
OH	26,222	25,872	350	1.3	ID	52,933	19,987	32,946	62.2
IN	23,158	22,688	470	2.0	WY	62,343	31,319	31,024	49.8
IL	35,795	34,717	1,078	3.0	CO	66,486	42,346	24,140	36.3
MI	36,492	31,779	4,713	12.9	NM	77,766	51,217	26,550	34.1
WI	35,011	32,082	2,929	8.4	AZ	72,688	40,200	32,488	44.7
W.N.C	326,191	310,739	15,453	4.7	UT	52,697	18,859	33,838	64.2
MN	51,206	43,902	7,304	14.3	NV[2]	70,264	7,359	62,905	89.5
IA	35,860	35,443	418	1.2	**Pac**	574,086	235,251	338,836	59.0
MO	44,248	42,140	2,108	4.8	WA	42,694	31,237	11,456	26.8
ND	44,452	42,604	1,849	4.2	OR	61,599	24,660	36,939	60.0
SD	48,882	46,184	2,698	5.5	CA	100,207	53,250	46,956	46.9
NE	49,032	48,331	700	1.4	AK	365,482	122,686	242,796	66.4
KS	52,511	52,134	377	0.7	HI	4,106	3,417	688	16.8

[1] Excludes trust properties. [2] Data revised after publication of the report.

Source: U.S. General Services Administration, *Inventory Report on Real Property Owned by the United States Throughout the World*, annual.

No. 370. Land Cover/Use, by State: 1992

[In thousands of acres. Excludes Alaska and District of Columbia]

STATE	Total surface area[1]	Federal land	NONFEDERAL LAND							
			Total	Developed[2]	Rural					
					Total	Cropland	Pasture land	Rangeland	Forest land	Minor cover/use
Total	**1,940,011**	**407,989**	**1,483,126**	**92,352**	**1,390,774**	**382,317**	**125,927**	**396,948**	**394,958**	**88,624**
United States	1,937,678	407,899	1,480,916	91,946	1,388,970	381,950	125,215	396,803	394,437	88,565
Alabama	33,091	921	31,192	2,046	29,147	3,147	3,760	67	20,966	1,205
Arizona	72,960	30,280	42,408	1,404	41,004	1,196	76	32,227	4,718	2,785
Arkansas	34,040	3,207	29,803	1,322	28,480	7,730	5,727	159	14,267	598
California	101,572	46,792	52,892	5,001	47,892	10,052	1,161	17,140	14,794	4,746
Colorado	66,618	23,923	42,240	1,694	40,547	8,940	1,256	23,537	3,755	3,059
Connecticut	3,212	15	3,054	816	2,238	229	110	-	1,760	140
Delaware	1,309	33	1,213	205	1,008	499	26	-	353	130
Florida	37,545	3,791	30,406	4,645	25,761	2,997	4,373	3,487	12,378	2,545
Georgia	37,702	2,087	34,599	3,077	31,523	5,173	3,075	-	21,714	1,560
Hawaii	4,093	432	3,621	170	3,451	274	88	925	1,483	680
Idaho	53,481	33,296	19,521	587	18,934	5,600	1,243	6,668	4,024	1,399
Illinois	36,061	521	34,766	3,094	31,672	24,100	2,764	-	3,419	1,390
Indiana	23,159	487	22,287	2,095	20,193	13,513	1,866	-	3,626	1,188
Iowa	36,016	184	35,363	1,779	33,584	24,988	3,712	-	1,931	2,953
Kansas	52,658	606	51,488	1,997	49,491	26,565	2,306	15,723	1,331	3,565
Kentucky	25,862	1,201	23,985	1,653	22,332	5,092	5,859	-	10,312	1,069
Louisiana	30,561	1,264	26,373	1,764	24,609	5,972	2,269	227	12,961	3,181
Maine	21,290	164	19,517	697	18,820	448	111	-	17,557	705
Maryland	6,695	167	6,034	1,095	4,939	1,673	545	-	2,364	356
Massachusetts	5,302	89	4,839	1,309	3,530	272	170	-	2,778	310
Michigan	37,457	3,166	33,040	3,686	29,354	8,985	2,353	-	15,608	2,408
Minnesota	54,017	3,383	47,092	2,418	44,674	21,356	3,282	-	13,815	6,222
Mississippi	30,521	1,726	27,992	1,337	26,655	5,726	4,047	-	15,765	1,117
Missouri	44,606	2,017	41,710	2,336	39,374	13,347	11,911	126	11,656	2,332
Montana	94,109	27,122	65,656	1,096	64,561	15,035	3,370	36,835	5,156	4,165
Nebraska	49,507	739	48,137	1,252	46,885	19,239	2,066	22,669	777	2,135
Nevada	70,759	60,290	10,025	394	9,631	762	297	7,854	353	364
New Hampshire	5,938	747	4,952	563	4,389	142	98	-	3,932	217
New Jersey	4,984	159	4,549	1,588	2,961	650	159	-	1,766	386
New Mexico	77,819	27,394	50,196	866	49,330	1,892	212	39,792	4,600	2,835
New York	31,429	231	29,788	3,005	26,783	5,616	3,001	-	17,178	987
North Carolina	33,708	2,448	28,476	3,542	24,933	5,960	2,019	-	15,979	975
North Dakota	45,250	1,951	42,187	1,344	40,843	24,743	1,168	10,325	426	4,181
Ohio	26,451	375	25,654	3,558	22,096	11,929	2,269	-	6,624	1,275
Oklahoma	44,772	1,202	42,395	1,875	40,520	10,081	7,720	14,061	6,988	1,672
Oregon	62,127	32,291	29,155	1,125	28,030	3,776	1,900	9,375	11,839	1,142
Pennsylvania	28,997	682	27,813	3,432	24,381	5,598	2,326	-	15,316	1,143
Rhode Island	776	4	661	190	472	25	24	-	393	30
South Carolina	19,912	1,156	17,961	1,856	16,105	2,983	1,190	-	10,922	1,010
South Dakota	49,354	2,907	45,459	1,135	44,324	16,436	2,158	21,933	540	3,257
Tennessee	26,972	1,379	24,740	2,161	22,579	4,857	5,165	-	11,580	977
Texas	170,756	3,203	163,687	8,231	155,456	28,261	16,710	94,155	9,960	6,369
Utah	54,336	35,582	16,866	561	16,305	1,815	665	10,050	1,626	2,148
Vermont	6,153	366	5,521	324	5,197	635	349	-	4,138	75
Virginia	26,091	2,389	22,774	2,183	20,591	2,901	3,444	-	13,539	707
Washington	43,606	12,479	29,931	1,851	28,081	6,745	1,352	5,476	12,547	1,960
West Virginia	15,508	1,201	14,138	689	13,449	915	1,609	-	10,534	391
Wisconsin	35,938	1,829	32,747	2,357	30,390	10,813	2,954	-	13,410	3,212
Wyoming	62,596	30,020	32,012	541	31,471	2,272	901	26,015	975	1,309
Caribbean	2,334	90	2,211	407	1,804	367	712	145	521	59

- Represents zero. [1] Includes water area not shown separately. [2] Includes urban and built-up areas in units of 10 acres or greater, and rural transportation.

Source: U.S. Dept. of Agriculture, Soil Conservation Service, and Iowa State University, Statistical Laboratory; *Summary Report, 1992 National Resources Inventory.*

No. 371. Extreme and Mean Elevations States and Other Areas

[One foot=.305 meter]

STATE OR OTHER AREA	HIGHEST POINT			LOWEST POINT			APPROXIMATE MEAN ELEVATION	
	Name	Elevation		Name	Elevation			
		Feet	Meters		Feet	Meters	Feet	Meters
U.S.	**Mt. McKinley (AK)**	**20,320**	**6,198**	**Death Valley (CA)**	**-282**	**-86**	**2,500**	**763**
AL	Cheaha Mountain	2,405	733	Gulf of Mexico	([1])	([1])	500	153
AK	Mount McKinley	20,320	6,198	Pacific Ocean	([1])	([1])	1,900	580
AZ	Humphreys Peak	12,633	3,853	Colorado River	70	21	4,100	1,251
AR	Magazine Mountain	2,753	840	Ouachita River	55	17	650	198
CA	Mount Whitney	14,494	4,419	Death Valley	-282	-86	2,900	885
CO	Mt. Elbert	14,433	4,402	Arkansas River	3,350	1,022	6,800	2,074
CT	Mt. Frissell on South slope	2,380	726	Long Island Sound	([1])	([1])	500	153
DE	Ebright Road,[2] New Castle County	448	137	Atlantic Ocean	([1])	([1])	60	18
DC	Tenleytown at Reno Reservoir	410	125	Potomac River	1	(Z)	150	46
FL	Sec. 30, T6N, R20W, Walton County	345	105	Atlantic Ocean	([1])	([1])	100	31
GA	Brasstown Bald	4,784	1,459	Atlantic Ocean	([1])	([1])	600	183
HI	Puu Weldu	13,796	4,208	Pacific Ocean	([1])	([1])	3,030	924
ID	Borah Peak	12,662	3,862	Snake River	710	217	5,000	1,525
IL	Charles Mound	1,235	377	Mississippi River	279	85	600	183
IN	Franklin Twp., Wayne Co	1,257	383	Ohio River	320	98	700	214
IA	Sec. 29, T100N, R41W, Osceola County[3]	1,670	509	Mississippi River	480	146	1,100	336
KS	Mount Sunflower	4,039	1,232	Verdigris River	679	207	2,000	610
KY	Black Mountain	4,139	2,162	Mississippi River	257	78	750	229
LA	Driskill Mountain	535	163	New Orleans	-8	-2	100	31
ME	Mount Katahdin	5,267	1,606	Atlantic Ocean	([1])	([1])	600	183
MD	Backbone Mountain	3,360	1,025	Atlantic Ocean	([1])	([1])	350	107
MA	Mount Greylock	3,487	1,064	Atlantic Ocean	([1])	([1])	500	153
MI	Mount Arvon	1,979	604	Lake Erie	571	174	900	275
MN	Eagle Mountain, Cook Co	2,301	702	Lake Superior	600	183	1,200	366
MS	Woodall Mountain	806	246	Gulf of Mexico	([1])	([1])	300	92
MO	Taum Sauk Mountain	1,772	540	St. Francis River	230	70	800	244
MT	Granite Peak	12,799	3,904	Kootenai River	1,800	549	3,400	1,037
NE	Johnson Twp., Kimball Co	5,424	1,654	Missouri River	840	256	2,600	793
NV	Boundary Peak	13,140	4,007	Colorado River	479	146	5,500	1,678
NH	Mount Washington	6,288	1,918	Atlantic Ocean	([1])	([1])	1,000	305
NJ	High Point	1,803	550	Atlantic Ocean	([1])	([1])	250	76
NM	Wheeler Peak	13,161	4,014	Red Bluff Reservoir	2,842	867	5,700	1,739
NY	Mount Marcy	5,344	1,630	Atlantic Ocean	([1])	([1])	1,000	305
NC	Mount Mitchell	6,684	2,039	Atlantic Ocean	([1])	([1])	700	214
ND	White Butte, Slope Co	3,506	1,069	Red River	750	229	1,900	580
OH	Campbell Hill	1,549	472	Ohio River	455	139	850	259
OK	Black Mesa	4,973	1,517	Little River	289	88	1,300	397
OR	Mount Hood	11,239	3,428	Pacific Ocean	([1])	([1])	3,300	1,007
PA	Mount Davis	3,213	980	Delaware River	([1])	([1])	1,100	336
RI	Jerimoth Hill	812	248	Atlantic Ocean	([1])	([1])	200	61
SC	Sassafras Mountain	3,560	1,086	Atlantic Ocean	([1])	([1])	350	107
SD	Harney Peak	7,242	2,209	Big Stone Lake	966	295	2,200	671
TN	Clingmans Dome	6,643	2,026	Mississippi River	178	54	900	275
TX	Guadalupe Peak	8,749	2,668	Gulf of Mexico	([1])	([1])	1,700	519
UT	Kings Peak	13,528	4,126	Beaverdam Wash	2,000	610	6,100	1,861
VT	Mount Mansfield	4,393	1,340	Lake Champlain	95	29	1,000	305
VA	Mount Rogers	5,729	1,747	Atlantic Ocean	([1])	([1])	950	290
WA	Mount Rainier	14,410	4,395	Pacific Ocean	([1])	([1])	1,700	519
WV	Spruce Knob	4,861	1,483	Potomac River	240	73	1,500	458
WI	Timms Hill	1,951	595	Lake Michigan	579	177	1,050	320
WY	Gannett Peak	13,804	4,210	Belle Fourche River	3,099	945	6,700	2,044
Other areas:								
Puerto Rico	Cerro de Punta	4,390	1,339	Atlantic Ocean	([1])	([1])	1,800	549
American Samoa	Lata Mountain	3,160	964	Pacific Ocean	([1])	([1])	1,300	397
Guam	Mount Lamlam	1,332	406	Pacific Ocean	([1])	([1])	330	101
Virgin Is.	Crown Mountain	1,556	475	Atlantic Ocean	([1])	([1])	750	229

Z Less than 0.5 meter. [1] Sea level. [2] At DE-PA State line. [3] "Sec." denotes section; "T," township; "R," range; "N," north; and "W," west.

Source: U.S. Geological Survey, for highest and lowest points, *Elevations and Distances in the United States, 1990*; for mean elevations, 1983 edition.

No. 372. Water Areas for Selected Major Bodies of Water: 1990

[Includes only that portion of body of water under the jurisdiction of the United States, excluding Hawaii. One square mile=2.59 square kilometers]

BODY OF WATER AND STATE	AREA	
	Sq. mi.	Sq. km.
Atlantic Coast water bodies:		
Chesapeake Bay (MD-VA)	2,747	7,115
Pamlico Sound (NC)	1,622	4,200
Long Island Sound (CT-NY)	914	2,368
Delaware Bay (DE-NJ)	614	1,591
Cape Cod Bay (MA)	598	1,548
Albemarle Sound (NC)	492	1,274
Biscayne Bay (FL)	218	565
Buzzards Bay (MA)	215	558
Tangier Sound (MD-VA)	172	445
Currituck Sound (NC)	116	301
Pocomoke Sound (MD-VA)	111	286
Chincoteague Bay (MD-VA)	105	272
Great South Bay (NY)	94	243
Core Sound (NC)	88	229
Gulf Coast water bodies:		
Mississippi Sound (AL-LA-MS)	813	2,106
Laguna Madre (TX)	733	1,897
Lake Pontchartrain (LA)	631	1,635
Florida Bay (FL)	616	1,596
Breton Sound (LA)	511	1,323
Mobile Bay (AL)	310	802
Lake Borgne (LA-MS)	271	702
Matagorda Bay (TX)	253	656
Atchafalaya Bay (LA)	245	635
Galveston Bay (TX)	236	611
Tampa Bay (FL)	212	549
Vermilion Bay (LA)	189	489
Corpus Christi Bay (TX)	151	392
West Cote Blanche Bay (LA)	146	378
Trinity Bay (TX)	129	335
Choctawhatchee Bay (FL)	122	315
San Antonio Bay (TX)	118	306
Timbalier Bay (LA)	112	291
Charlotte Harbor (FL)	112	291
Aransas Bay (TX)	104	268
Apalachicola Bay (FL)	101	262
Terrebonne Bay (LA)	99	256
East Cote Blanche Bay (LA)	94	243
St. George Sound (FL)	93	240
Sabine Lake (LA-TX)	89	229
White Lake (LA)	85	221
Old Tampa Bay (FL)	83	214
Bon Secour Bay (AL)	79	204
Pine Island Sound (FL)	75	194
Pacific Coast water bodies:		
Puget Sound (WA)	808	2,092
San Francisco Bay (CA)	264	684
Willapa Bay (WA)	125	325
Hood Canal (WA)	117	303
Interior water bodies:		
Lake Michigan (IL-IN-MI-WI)	22,342	57,866
Lake Superior (MI-MN-WI) [1]	20,557	53,243
Lake Huron (MI) [1]	8,800	22,792
Lake Erie (MI-NY-OH-PA) [1]	5,033	13,036
Lake Ontario (NY) [1]	3,446	8,926
Great Salt Lake (UT)	1,836	4,756
Green Bay (MI-WI)	1,396	3,617
Lake Okeechobee (FL)	663	1,717
Lake Sakakawea (ND)	563	1,459
Lake Oahe (ND-SD)	538	1,394
Lake of the Woods (MN) [1]	462	1,196
Lake Champlain (NY-VT) [1]	414	1,072
Fort Peck Lake (MT)	379	981
Salton Sea (CA)	364	944
Toledo Bend Reservoir (LA-TX)	268	694
Lower Red Lake (MN)	257	666
Lake Powell (AZ-UT)	250	649
Kentucky Lake (KY-TN)	234	605
Lake Mead (AZ-NV)	233	603
Lake Winnebago (WI)	206	535
Mille Lacs Lake (MN)	200	518
Flathead Lake (MT)	191	495
Lake Tahoe (CA-NV)	187	486
Upper Red Lake (MN)	186	483
Pyramid Lake (NV)	170	440
Leech Lake (MN)	162	419
Lake St. Clair (MI) [1]	161	416
Eufaula Lake (OK)	157	407
Sam Rayburn Reservoir (TX)	150	389
Goose Lake (CA-OR)	147	381
Utah Lake (UT)	139	361
Lake Marion (SC)	139	360
Lake Francis Case (SD)	134	346
Lake Pend Oreille (ID)	133	343
Lake Texoma (OK-TX)	132	342
Yellowstone Lake (WY)	131	339
Livingston Reservoir (TX)	127	330
Franklin D. Roosevelt Lake (WA)	124	322
Moosehead Lake (ME)	116	301
Clark Hill Lake (GA-SC)	105	272
Lake Maurepas (LA)	91	235
Lake Moultrie (SC)	89	230
Lake Winnibigoshish (MN)	87	225
Hartwell Lake (GA-SC)	86	224
Upper Klamath Lake (OR)	85	221
Harry S. Truman Reservoir (MO)	84	217
Oneida Lake (NY)	80	207
Malheur Lake (OR)	75	195
Alaska water bodies:		
Chatham Strait	1,559	4,039
Prince William Sound	1,382	3,579
Clarence Strait	1,199	3,107
Iliamna Lake	1,022	2,646
Frederick Sound	792	2,051
Sumner Strait	791	2,048
Stephens Passage	702	1,819
Kvichak Bay	640	1,659
Montague Strait	463	1,198
Becharof Lake	447	1,158
Icy Strait	436	1,130
Hotham Inlet	433	1,120
Selawik Lake	403	1,044
Nushagak Bay	393	1,018
Baird Inlet	348	902
Yakutat Bay	345	894
Teshekpuk Lake	324	839
Behm Canal	324	839
Turnagain Arm	322	834
Kachemak Bay	310	803
Glacier Bay	310	803
Stefansson Sound	301	780
Revillagigedo Channel	295	764
Kasegaluk Lagoon	293	759
Cordova Bay	241	623
Sitka Sound	229	593
Naknek Lake	225	582
Eschscholtz Bay	210	543
Stepovak Bay	206	534
Keku Strait	206	534
Port Clarence	187	486
Orca Bay	184	476
Knik Arm	169	437
Dall Lake	167	433
Knight Island Passage	167	432
Scammon Bay	163	423
Port Moller	159	412
Ernest Sound	158	410
Spafarief Bay	157	405
Pavlov Bay	153	396
Shishmaref Inlet	153	395
Smith Bay	140	363
Seymour Canal	140	361
Sitkalidak Strait	135	349
Tlevak Strait	135	349
Lake Clark	130	336
Lynn Canal	130	336
Chignik Bay	119	309
Elson Lagoon	119	309
Bucareli Bay	119	307
Hinchinbrook Entrance	118	306

[1] Area measurements for Lake Champlain, Lake Erie, Lake Huron, Lake Ontario, Lake St. Clair, Lake Superior, and Lake of the Woods include only those portions under the jurisdiction of the United States.

Source: U. S. Bureau of the Census, unpublished data from the Census TIGER ™ data base.

No. 373. Flows of Largest U.S. Rivers—Length, Discharge, and Drainage Area

RIVER	Location of mouth	Source stream (name and location)	Length (miles) [1]	Average discharge at mouth (1,000 cubic ft. per second)	Drainage area (1,000 sq. mi.)
Missouri	Missouri	Red Rock Creek, MT	2,540	76.2	[5]529
Mississippi	Louisiana	Mississippi River, MN	[2]2,340	[3]593	[4 5]1,150
Yukon	Alaska	McNeil River, Canada	1,980	225	[5]328
St. Lawrence	Canada	North River, MN	1,900	348	[5]396
Rio Grande	Mexico-Texas	Rio Grande, CO	1,900	-	336
Arkansas	Arkansas	East Fork Arkansas River, CO	1,460	41	161
Colorado	Mexico	Colorado River, CO	1,450	-	246
Atchafalaya [6]	Louisiana	Tierra Blanca Creek, NM	1,420	58	95.1
Ohio	Illinois-Kentucky	Allegheny River, PA	1,310	281	203
Red	Louisiana	Tierra Blanca Creek, NM	1,290	56	93.2
Brazos	Texas	Blackwater Draw, NM	1,280	-	45.6
Columbia	Oregon-Washington	Columbia River, Canada	1,240	265	[5]258
Snake	Washington	Snake River, WY	1,040	56.9	108
Platte	Nebraska	Grizzly Creek, CO	990	-	84.9
Pecos	Texas	Pecos River, NM	926	-	44.3
Canadian	Oklahoma	Canadian River, CO	906	-	46.9
Tennessee	Kentucky	Courthouse Creek, NC	886	66	40.9
Colorado (of Texas)	Texas	Colorado River, TX	862	-	42.3
North Canadian	Oklahoma	Corrumpa Creek, NM	800	-	17.6
Mobile	Alabama	Tickanetley Creek, GA	774	67.2	44.6
Kansas	Kansas	Arikaree River, CO	743	-	59.5
Kuskokwim	Alaska	South Fork Kuskokwim River, AK	724	67	48
Yellowstone	North Dakota	North Folk Yellowstone River, WY	692	-	70
Tanana	Alaska	Nabesna River, AK	659	41	44.5
Gila	Arizona	Middle Fork Gila River, NM	649	-	58.2

- Represents zero. [1] From source to mouth. [2] The length from the source of the Missouri River to the Mississippi River and thence to the Gulf of Mexico is about 3,710 miles. [3] Includes about 167,000 cubic ft. per second diverted from the Mississippi into the Atchafalaya River but excludes the flow of the Red River. [4] Excludes the drainage areas of the Red and Atchafalaya Rivers. [5] Drainage area includes both the United States and Canada. [6] In east-central Louisiana, the Red River flows into the Atchafalaya River, a distributary of the Mississippi River. Data on average discharge, length, and drainage area include the Red River, but exclude all water diverted into the Atchafalaya from the Mississippi River.

Source: U.S. Geological Survey, *Largest Rivers in the United States*, Open File Report 87-242, May 1990.

No. 374. Water Withdrawals and Consumptive Use—States and Other Areas: 1990

[In millions of gallons per day, except as noted. Figures may not add due to rounding. Withdrawal signifies water physically withdrawn from a source. Includes fresh and saline water]

STATE OR OTHER AREA	WATER WITHDRAWN: Total	WATER WITHDRAWN: Per capita (gal. per day) fresh	WATER WITHDRAWN: Source: Ground water	WATER WITHDRAWN: Source: Surface water	Consumptive use, [1] fresh water
U.S. [2]	407,900	1,340	80,640	327,280	93,980
Alabama	8,090	2,000	403	7,680	454
Alaska	641	517	112	529	26
Arizona	6,570	1,790	2,740	3,830	4,350
Arkansas	7,840	3,330	4,710	3,130	4,140
California	46,800	1,180	14,900	31,900	20,900
Colorado	12,700	3,850	2,800	9,910	5,250
Connecticut	4,840	325	165	4,680	103
Delaware	1,370	1,540	89	1,280	59
District of Columbia	9	15	1	8	16
Florida	17,900	582	4,680	13,200	3,130
Georgia	5,350	816	996	4,360	822
Hawaii	2,740	1,070	590	2,150	627
Idaho	19,700	19,600	7,590	12,100	6,090
Illinois	18,000	1,570	945	17,100	750
Indiana	9,430	1,700	621	8,810	451
Iowa	2,860	1,030	495	2,370	271
Kansas	6,060	2,460	4,360	1,720	4,410
Kentucky	4,320	1,170	247	4,070	309
Louisiana	9,350	2,200	1,340	8,010	1,590
Maine	1,140	433	85	1,060	51
Maryland	6,420	307	239	6,180	126
Massachusetts	5,520	338	338	5,180	195
Michigan	11,600	1,250	707	10,900	738
Minnesota	3,270	748	797	2,480	872
Mississippi	3,640	1,290	2,670	963	1,800
Missouri	6,930	1,150	728	6,200	529

STATE OR OTHER AREA	WATER WITHDRAWN: Total	WATER WITHDRAWN: Per capita (gal. per day) fresh	WATER WITHDRAWN: Source: Ground water	WATER WITHDRAWN: Source: Surface water	Consumptive use, [1] fresh water
Montana	9,320	11,600	218	9,100	2,090
Nebraska	8,940	5,660	4,800	4,150	4,230
Nevada	3,350	2,780	1,070	2,280	1,690
New Hampshire	1,310	378	64	1,250	26
New Jersey	12,800	287	566	12,200	211
New Mexico	3,480	2,300	1,760	1,720	2,060
New York	19,000	583	840	18,100	562
North Carolina	8,940	1,350	436	8,510	390
North Dakota	2,680	4,190	141	2,540	228
Ohio	11,700	1,080	904	10,800	901
Oklahoma	1,670	452	905	760	659
Oregon	8,430	2,970	767	7,660	3,160
Pennsylvania	9,830	827	1,020	8,810	561
Rhode Island	526	132	25	501	18
South Carolina	6,000	1,720	282	5,720	293
South Dakota	592	851	251	341	345
Tennessee	9,190	1,880	503	8,690	252
Texas	25,200	1,180	7,880	17,300	9,020
Utah	4,480	2,540	971	3,510	2,230
Vermont	632	1,120	45	587	29
Virginia	6,860	762	443	6,420	224
Washington	7,940	1,630	1,450	6,490	2,830
West Virginia	4,580	2,560	726	3,860	509
Wisconsin	6,510	1,330	681	5,830	461
Wyoming	7,600	16,700	403	7,200	2,730
Puerto Rico	3,040	163	157	2,880	199
Virgin Islands	164	91	3	160	2

[1] Water that has been evaporated, transpired, or incorporated into products, plant or animal tissue; and therefore, is not available for immediate reuse. [2] Includes Puerto Rico and Virgin Islands.

Source: U.S. Geological Survey, *Estimated Use of Water in the United States in 1990*, circular 1081.

No. 375. U.S. Water Withdrawals and Consumptive Use Per Day, by End Use: 1940 to 1990

[Includes Puerto Rico. Withdrawal signifies water physically withdrawn from a source. Includes fresh and saline water; excludes water used for hydroelectric power]

YEAR	Total (bil. gal.)	Per capita [1] (gal.)	Irrigation (bil. gal.)	PUBLIC SUPPLY [2] Total (bil. gal.)	PUBLIC SUPPLY [2] Per capita [3] (gal.)	Rural [4] (bil. gal.)	Industrial and misc. [5] (bil. gal.)	Steam electric utilities (bil. gal.)
WITHDRAWALS								
1940	140	1,027	71	10	75	3.1	29	23
1950	180	1,185	89	14	145	3.6	37	40
1955	240	1,454	110	17	148	3.6	39	72
1960	270	1,500	110	21	151	3.6	38	100
1965	310	1,602	120	24	155	4.0	46	130
1970	370	1,815	130	27	166	4.5	47	170
1975	420	1,972	140	29	168	4.9	45	200
1980	440	1,953	150	34	183	5.6	45	210
1985	399	1,650	137	38	189	7.8	31	187
1990	408	1,620	137	41	195	7.9	30	195
CONSUMPTIVE USE								
1960	61	339	52	3.5	25	2.8	3.0	0.2
1965	77	403	66	5.2	34	3.2	3.4	0.4
1970	87	427	73	5.9	36	3.4	4.1	0.8
1975	96	451	80	6.7	38	3.4	4.2	1.9
1980	100	440	83	7.1	38	3.9	6.0	3.2
1985	92	380	74	(6)	(6)	9.2	6.1	6.2
1990	94	370	76	(6)	(6)	8.9	6.7	4.0

[1] Based on Bureau of the Census resident population as of July 1. [2] Includes commercial water withdrawals. [3] Based on population served. [4] Rural farm and nonfarm household and garden use, and water for farm stock and dairies. [5] For 1940 to 1960, includes manufacturing and mineral industries, rural commercial industries, air-conditioning, resorts, hotels, motels, military and other State and Federal agencies, and miscellaneous; thereafter, includes manufacturing, mining and mineral processing, ordnance, construction, and miscellaneous. [6] Public supply consumptive use included in end-use categories.

Source: 1940-1960, U.S. Bureau of Domestic Business Development, based principally on committee prints, *Water Resources Activities in the United States*, for the Senate Committee on National Water Resources, U.S. Senate, thereafter, U.S. Geological Survey, *Estimated Use of Water in the United States in 1990*, circular 1081, and previous quinquennial issues.

No. 376. National Ambient Water Quality in Rivers and Streams—Violation Rate: 1980 to 1995

[In percent. Violation level based on U.S. Environmental Protection Agency water quality criteria. Violation rate represents the proportion of all measurements of a specific water quality pollutant which exceeds the "violation level" for that pollutant. "Violation" does not necessarily imply a legal violation. Data based on U.S. Geological Survey's National Stream Quality Accounting Network (NASQAN) data system; for details, see source. Years refer to water years. A water year begins in Oct. and ends in Sept. µg=micrograms; mg=milligrams. For metric conversion, see page ix]

POLLUTANT	VIOLATION LEVEL	1980	1985	1989	1990	1991	1992	1993	1994	1995
Fecal coliform bacteria	Above 200 cells per 100 ml.	31	28	30	26	15	28	31	28	35
Dissolved oxygen	Below 5 mg per liter	5	3	3	2	2	2	(Z)	2	1
Phosphorus, total, as phosporous	Above 1.0 mg per liter	4	3	2	3	2	2	2	2	4
Lead, dissolved	Above 50 µg per liter	(Z)	(Z)	(Z)	(Z)	(Z)	(Z)	(NA)	(NA)	(NA)
Cadmium, dissolved	Above 10 µg per liter	1	(Z)	(Z)	(Z)	(Z)	(Z)	(NA)	(NA)	(NA)

NA Not available. Z Less than 1.

Source: U.S. Geological Survey, national-level data, unpublished; State-level data, *Water-Data Report*, annual series prepared in cooperation with the State governments.

No. 377. Oil Polluting Incidents Reported in and Around U.S. Waters: 1973 to 1993

YEAR	Incidents	Gallons	YEAR	Incidents	Gallons
1973	11,054	15,289,188	1986	5,818	4,427,544
1974	12,083	15,739,792	1987	5,693	3,759,983
1975	10,998	21,528,444	1988	6,733	10,650,138
1976	11,066	18,517,384	1989	8,562	25,531,292
1977	10,979	8,188,398	1990	10,186	13,907,783
1978	12,174	11,035,890	1991	10,405	2,156,063
1979	11,556	10,051,271	1992	9,131	1,572,341
1980	9,886	12,638,848			
1981	9,589	8,919,789	**1993**	**9,672**	**1,543,578**
1982	9,416	10,404,646	Tankships	185	14,138
1983	10,530	8,378,719	Tank barges	338	295,243
1984	10,089	19,007,332	Other vessels	5,220	412,430
1985	7,740	8,465,055	Non-vessels	3,929	821,767

Source: U.S. Coast Guard. Based on unpublished data from the *Marine Safety Information System*.

No. 378. National Ambient Air Pollutant Concentrations: 1986 to 1995

[Data represent annual composite averages of pollutant based on daily 24-hour averages of monitoring stations, except carbon monoxide is based on the second-highest, non-overlapping, 8-hour average; ozone, average of the second-highest daily maximum 1-hour value; and lead, quarterly average of ambient lead levels. Based on data from the Aerometric Information Retrieval System. µg/m³=micrograms of pollutant per cubic meter of air; ppm=parts per million]

POLLUTANT	Unit	Monitoring stations, number	Air quality standard[1]	1986	1990	1991	1992	1993	1994	1995
Carbon monoxide	ppm	334	[2]9	7.10	5.90	5.60	5.20	4.90	5.00	4.5
Ozone	ppm	573	[3]0.12	0.120	0.113	0.115	0.107	0.109	0.109	0.113
Sulfur dioxide	ppm	473	0.03	0.009	0.008	0.0078	0.0073	0.0071	0.0069	0.0057
Particulates (PM-10)[4]	µg/m³	955	50	(X)	29.4	29.1	26.7	26.0	26.1	25.0
Nitrogen dioxide	ppm	212	0.053	0.022	0.020	0.020	0.019	0.019	0.020	0.019
Lead	µg/m³	189	[5]1.5	0.18	0.08	0.08	0.05	0.05	0.04	0.04

X Not applicable. [1] Refers to the primary National Ambient Air Quality Standard that protects the public health. [2] Based on 8-hour standard of 9 ppm. [3] Based on 1-hour standard of .12 ppm. [4] The particulates (PM-10) standard replaced the previous standard for total suspended particulates in 1987. [5] Based on 3-month standard of 1.5 µg/m³.

Source: U.S. Environmental Protection Agency, *National Air Quality and Emissions Trends Report*, annual.

No. 379. National Air Pollutant Emissions: 1970 to 1995

[In thousands of tons, except as indicated. PM-10=Particulate matter of less than ten microns. Methodologies to estimate data for 1970 to 1984 period and 1985 to present emissions differ. Beginning with 1985, the estimates are based on a modified National Acid Precipitation Assessment Program inventory]

YEAR	PM-10	PM-10, fugitive dust[1]	Sulfur dioxide	Nitrogen dioxides	Volatile organic compounds	Carbon monoxide	Lead (tons)
1970	13,044	(NA)	31,161	20,625	30,646	128,079	219,471
1975	7,617	(NA)	28,011	21,889	25,677	115,110	158,541
1980	7,050	(NA)	25,905	23,281	25,893	115,625	74,956
1984	6,220	(NA)	23,470	23,172	25,572	114,262	42,217
1985	4,094	40,889	23,230	22,860	25,798	114,690	20,124
1986	3,890	46,582	22,442	22,348	24,991	109,199	7,296
1987	3,931	38,041	22,204	22,403	24,778	108,012	6,857
1988	4,750	55,851	22,647	23,618	25,719	115,849	6,513
1989	3,927	48,650	22,785	23,222	23,935	103,144	6,034
1990	3,195	40,142	22,433	23,038	23,599	100,650	5,666
1991	3,170	45,738	22,068	22,672	22,677	97,376	5,280
1992	3,222	40,499	21,836	22,847	22,420	94,043	4,862
1993	3,163	39,389	21,517	23,276	22,575	94,133	4,945
1994	2,371	42,250	21,047	23,661	23,281	98,779	5,028
1995	3,050	39,586	18,319	21,779	22,865	92,099	4,986

NA Not available. [1] Sources such as agricultural tilling, construction, mining and quarrying, paved roads, unpaved roads, and wind erosion.

No. 380. Air Pollutant Emissions, by Pollutant and Source: 1995

[In thousands of tons, except as indicated. See headnote, table 379]

SOURCE	Particulates[1]	Sulfur dioxide	Nitrogen oxides	Volatile organic compounds	Carbon monoxide	Lead (tons)
Total	42,636	18,320	21,777	22,864	92,099	4,986
Fuel combustion, stationary sources	905	15,658	10,077	709	3,960	493
Electric utilites	258	12,013	6,233	35	324	63
Industrial	239	3,046	3,137	135	672	17
Other fuel combustion	408	599	707	539	2,964	413
Residential	374	161	397	523	2,829	6
Industrial processes	630	2,014	781	2,744	5,606	2,072
Chemical and allied product manufacturing	66	471	283	1,617	2,237	80
Metals processing	145	720	84	77	2,223	1,937
Petroleum and related industries	26	385	91	628	379	(NA)
Other	393	438	323	422	767	55
Solvent utilization	2	1	3	6,394	2	(NA)
Storage and transport	60	5	3	1,803	65	(NA)
Waste disposal and recycling	253	37	85	2,411	1,766	842
Highway vehicles	304	305	7,604	6,105	58,624	1,387
Light-duty gas vehicles and motorcycles	62	142	3,611	3,621	35,961	1,036
Light-duty trucks	32	71	1,624	1,783	16,292	332
Heavy-duty gas vehicles	10	12	347	375	4,883	19
Diesels	200	80	2,022	326	1,468	(NA)
Off highway[2]	393	292	2,996	2,252	15,622	191
Miscellaneous[3]	40,088	8	228	446	6,454	(NA)

NA Not available. [1] Represents both PM-10 and PM-10 fugitive dust; see table 379. [2] Includes emissions from farm tractors and other farm machinery, construction equipment, industrial machinery, recreational marine vessels, and small general utility engines such as lawn mowers. [3] Includes emissions such as from forest fires and other kinds of burning, various agricultural activities, fugitive dust from paved and unpaved roads, and other construction and mining activities, and natural sources.

Source of tables 379 and 380: U.S. Environmental Protection Agency, *National Air Pollutant Emission Trends, 1900-1995*.

No. 381. Metropolitan Areas Failing to Meet National Ambient Air Quality for Carbon Monoxide—Number of Days Exceeding Standards: 1994 and 1995

[Areas generally represent the officially defined metropolitan area, but may, in some cases, not have all the counties identified as part of the area; see *Federal Register*, 40 CFR, part 81, *Air Quality Designations: Revised*, July 1994. Nonattainment status was as of December 1996]

METROPOLITAN AREA	1994	1995	METROPOLITAN AREA	1994	1995	METROPOLITAN AREA	1994	1995
Anchorage, AK	2	-	Las Vegas, NV	5	1	Phoenix, AZ	3	3
Chico, CA	-	-	Longmont, CO[1]	-	-	Portland, OR-WA CMSA	1	-
Colorado Springs, CO	-	-	Los Angeles, CA CMSA	24	14	Provo-Orem, UT	1	-
Denver-Boulder, CO CMSA	1	2	Medford, OR	-	-	Reno, NV	-	-
El Paso, TX	-	-	Minneapolis-St. Paul, MN-WI	-	1	Sacramento, CA	-	-
Fairbanks, AK[1]	3	9	Missoula County, MT[1]	-	-	San Diego, CA	-	-
Fort Collins, CO	-	-	Modesto, CA	-	-	San Francisco, CA CMSA	-	-
Fresno, CA	-	-	New York, NY-NJ-CT CMSA	2	1	Spokane, WA	-	4
Grant Pass, OR[1]	-	-	Ogden, UT	-	-	Stockton, CA	-	-
Klamath County, OR[1]	-	-						
Lake Tahoe S. Shore, CA[1]	-	-						

- Represents zero. [1] Not a metropolitan area.

Source: U.S. Environmental Protection Agency. Published in the *1995 Air Quality Update*, December 1996.

No. 382. Metropolitan Areas Failing to Meet National Ambient Air Quality Standards for Ozone—Average Number of Days Exceeding Standards: 1993 to 1995

[See headnote, table 381. Nonattainment status was as of December 1996]

METROPOLITAN AREA	1993-95, avg.	1996[1]	METROPOLITAN AREA	1993-95, avg.	1996[1]
Albany-Schenectady-Troy, NY	0.3	-	Milwaukee-Racine, WI CMSA	1.7	4.0
Allentown-Bethlehem-Easton, PA-NJ	-	-	Monterey Bay, CA[6]	0.7	1.4
Altoona, PA	-	-	Muskegon, MI	2.0	4.0
Atlanta, GA	6.0	3.4	Nashville, TN	1.0	-
Atlantic City, NJ	-	0.0	New York, NY-NJ-CT CMSA[7]	5.7	5.0
Baltimore, MD	3.3	4.0	Norfolk-Virginia Beach-Newport News, VA	1.0	-
Baton Rouge, LA	1.7	4.0	Philadelphia, PA-NJ-DE-MD CMSA	3.5	4.3
Beaumont-Port Arthur, TX	1.8	5.3	Phoenix, AZ	1.3	3.0
Birmingham, AL	1.3	4.0	Pittsburgh-Beaver Valley, PA CMSA	3.0	7.0
Boston-Lawrence-Salem, MA-NH CMSA[2]	2.0	2.0	Portland-Vancouver, OR-WA CMSA	0.3	-
Buffalo-Niagara Falls, NY CMSA	-	-	Portland, ME	2.5	2.5
Chicago-Gary-Lake County, IL-IN-WI CMSA	2.1	2.0	Portsmouth-Dover-Rochester, NH-ME	1.7	3.1
Cincinnati-Hamilton, OH-KY-IN CMSA	1.3	2.0	Poughkeepsie, NY	1.7	2.0
Dallas-Fort Worth, TX CMSA	4.1	6.0	Providence, RI[8]	1.8	3.0
Door County, WI[3]	1.0	1.0	Reading, PA	0.3	-
El Paso, TX	2.3	3.1	Reno, NV	-	-
Erie, PA	-	-	Richmond-Petersburg, VA	0.7	1.0
Essex County, NY[3]	-	-	Sacramento, CA	3.9	7.2
Evansville, IN-KY	-	-	St. Louis, MO-IL	4.5	4.7
Greater Connecticut, CT[4]	4.4	8.3	Salt Lake City-Ogden, UT	0.3	1.0
Hancock and Waldo counties, ME[3]	1.0	1.0	San Diego, CA	9.4	9.0
Harrisburg-Lebanon-Carlisle, PA	-	-	San Joaquin Valley, CA	31.4	34.5
Houston-Galveston-Brazoria, TX CMSA	11.4	19.6	Santa Barbara-Santa Maria-Lompoc, CA	1.7	2.0
Jefferson County, NY[3]	0.3	1.0	Scranton-Wilkes-Barre, PA	-	-
Johnstown, PA	-	-	Seattle-Tacoma, WA	0.7	-
Kent County and Queen Anne's Co., MD[3]	1.0	1.0	Smyth County, VA[3]	(NA)	(NA)
Knox and Lincoln counties, ME[3]	0.8	1.2	Southeast Desert Modified AQMD, CA[9]	53.4	26.4
Lake Charles, LA	1.0	1.0	Springfield, MA	2.4	2.0
Lancaster, PA	0.7	1.0	Sunland Park, NM[3]	3.1	3.1
Lewiston-Auburn, ME	-	-	Sussex County, DE[3]	-	-
Louisville, KY-IN	2.7	2.1	Ventura County, CA	15.6	22.1
Los Angeles South Coast Air, CA[5]	86.2	67.0	Washington, DC-MD-VA	2.7	2.5
Manchester, NH	-	-	York, PA	-	-
Manitowoc Co, WI	1.5	1.0	Youngstown-Warren, OH[10]	-	-

- Represents zero. NA Not available. [1] May represent a different monitoring location than one used to calculate average. [2] Includes also both the Worcester, MA, and New Bedford, MA MSA's. [3] Not a metropolitan area. [4] Primarily represents Hartford-New Haven area. [5] Primarily represents Los Angeles and Orange counties. [6] Primarily represents Monterey, Santa Cruz, and San Benito counties. [7] Excludes the Connecticut portion. [8] Covers entire State of Rhode Island. [9] Represents primarily San Joaquin, Turlock, Merced, Madera, Fresno, Kings, Tulare, and Kern counties. [10] Includes Sharon, PA.

Source: U.S. Environmental Protection Agency, Published in *1995 Air Quality Update*, December 1996.

No. 383. Emissions of Greenhouse Gases, by Type and Source: 1989 to 1995

[Emission estimates were mandated by Congress through Section 1605(a) of the Energy Policy Act of 1992 (title XVI). Gases that contain carbon can be measured either in terms of the full molecular weight of the gas or just in terms of their carbon content]

TYPE AND SOURCE	Unit	1989	1990	1991	1992	1993	1994	1995, prel.
Carbon dioxide:								
Carbon content, total	Mil. metric tons	1,384.3	1,372.0	1,358.8	1,379.5	1,404.8	1,431.4	1,442.3
Energy sources	Mil. metric tons	1,355.8	1,344.2	1,324.6	1,346.3	1,375.0	1,396.5	1,409.4
Cement production	Mil. metric tons	8.7	8.8	8.5	8.6	9.1	9.7	10.5
Gas flaring	Mil. metric tons	1.7	1.8	2.1	2.1	2.9	2.9	1.8
Other industrial	Mil. metric tons	8.3	8.3	8.3	8.3	8.2	8.4	9
Other, adjustments	Mil. metric tons	9.8	8.9	15.3	14.2	9.6	14.0	11.7
Methane:								
Gas, total	Mil. metric tons	30.9	31.3	31.4	31.5	30.5	31.0	(NA)
Energy sources	Mil. metric tons	11.8	12.0	11.9	11.9	11.0	11.4	(NA)
Landfills	Mil. metric tons	10.8	11.0	10.9	10.8	10.6	10.3	(NA)
Agricultural sources	Mil. metric tons	8.2	8.3	8.6	8.8	8.8	9.1	9.2
Industrial sources	Mil. metric tons	0.1	0.1	0.1	0.1	0.1	0.1	0.1
Nitrous oxide, total	1,000 metric tons	444	449	452	452	462	471.0	462
Agriculture	1,000 metric tons	159	164	167	168	176	179	172
Mobile sources	1,000 metric tons	147	150	148	150	146	146	145
Stationary combustion	1,000 metric tons	38	37	37	37	38	39	39
Industrial sources	1,000 metric tons	100	97	100	96	103	107	107
Nitrogen oxide, total	Mil. metric tons	21.1	20.9	20.6	20.7	21.1	21.4	(NA)
Energy related	Mil. metric tons	20.0	19.8	19.5	19.7	20.1	20.3	(NA)
Transportation	Mil. metric tons	9.6	9.4	9.2	9.4	9.5	9.6	(NA)
Industrial processes	Mil. metric tons	0.7	0.7	0.7	0.7	0.7	0.7	(NA)
Stationary source fuel combustion	Mil. metric tons	10.5	10.4	10.3	10.4	10.6	10.6	(NA)
Solid waste disposal	Mil. metric tons	0.1	0.1	0.1	0.1	0.1	0.1	(NA)
Other	Mil. metric tons	0.3	0.3	0.3	0.2	0.2	0.3	(NA)
Nonmethane volatile organic compounds (VOC's), total	Mil. metric tons	21.7	21.4	20.8	20.3	20.5	21.0	(NA)
Energy related	Mil. metric tons	9.7	9.0	8.7	8.4	8.4	8.6	(NA)
Industrial processes	Mil. metric tons	9.4	9.4	9.3	9.5	9.6	9.8	(NA)
Solid waste disposal	Mil. metric tons	2.1	2.1	2.1	2.1	2.1	2.1	(NA)
Other	Mil. metric tons	0.6	1.0	0.7	0.4	0.5	0.6	(NA)
Carbon monoxide, total	Mil. metric tons	93.5	91.2	88.3	85.3	85.3	86.9	(NA)
Energy related	Mil. metric tons	79.8	74.8	74.4	72.6	72.9	74.0	(NA)
Transportation	Mil. metric tons	73.1	70.3	69.5	67.8	68.5	69.6	(NA)
Stationary source fuel combustion	Mil. metric tons	6.7	4.5	4.8	5.0	4.5	4.4	(NA)
Industrial processes	Mil. metric tons	4.8	4.7	4.6	4.7	4.8	4.9	(NA)
Solid waste disposal	Mil. metric tons	1.6	1.5	1.5	1.6	1.6	1.6	(NA)
Other	Mil. metric tons	7.4	10.1	7.7	6.1	6.1	6.4	(NA)
Chlorofluorocarbons (CFCs) gases [1]	1,000 metric tons	272	231	210	187	166	133	87
Hydrofluorocarbons	1,000 metric tons	5	5	5	8	11	18	26
Hydrochlorofluorocarbons (HCFCs) gases [2]	1,000 metric tons	76	84	89	96	107	121	136

NA Not available. [1] Covers principally CFC-11, CFC-12, and CFC-113. [2] Covers principally HCFC-22.

Source: U.S. Energy Information Administration, *Emissions of Greenhouse Gases in the United States, annual.*

No. 384. Municipal Solid Waste Generation, Recovery, and Disposal: 1970 to 1995

[In millions of tons, except as indicated. Covers post-consumer residential and commercial solid wastes which comprise the major portion of typical municipal collections. Excludes mining, agricultural and industrial processing, demolition and construction wastes, sewage sludge, and junked autos and obsolete equipment wastes. Based on material-flows estimating procedure and wet weight as generated]

ITEM AND MATERIAL	1970	1980	1988	1990	1991	1992	1993	1994	1995
Waste generated	121.9	151.5	164.4	197.3	198.9	202.2	205.4	209.6	208.1
Per person per day (lb.)	3.3	3.7	3.8	4.3	4.3	4.3	4.4	4.4	4.3
Materials recovered	8.6	14.5	16.4	33.9	37.7	41.4	44.8	52.0	56.2
Per person per day (lb.)	0.23	0.35	0.36	0.7	0.8	0.9	1.0	1.1	1.2
Combustion for energy recovery	0.4	2.7	7.6	29.7	31.1	30.5	31.3	31.2	32.5
Per person per day (lb.)	0.02	0.06	0.17	0.7	0.7	0.7	0.7	0.7	0.7
Combustion without energy recovery	24.7	11.0	4.1	2.2	2.2	2.2	1.6	1.3	1.0
Per person per day (lb.)	0.66	0.27	0.10	0.05	0.05	0.05	0.03	0.03	0.02
Landfill, other disposal	88.2	123.3	136.4	131.6	125.9	128.1	127.6	125.2	118.4
Per person per day (lb.)	2.37	2.97	3.13	2.9	2.7	2.8	2.7	2.6	2.5
Percent distribution of generation:									
Paper and paperboard	36.3	36.1	37.4	36.9	36.1	36.7	37.7	38.6	39.2
Glass	10.4	9.9	6.0	6.6	6.4	6.5	6.6	6.4	6.2
Metals	11.6	9.6	8.6	8.4	8.4	7.9	7.8	7.7	7.6
Plastics	2.5	5.2	7.1	8.7	9.0	9.1	9.2	9.2	9.1
Rubber and leather	2.6	2.8	2.3	2.9	3.0	2.9	2.8	3.0	2.9
Textiles	1.6	1.7	1.7	2.9	3.1	3.3	3.3	3.5	3.6
Wood	3.3	4.4	5.0	6.0	6.2	6.4	6.6	6.9	7.1
Food wastes	10.5	8.7	8.0	6.7	6.9	6.7	6.7	6.6	6.7
Yard wastes	19.0	18.2	18.2	17.7	17.8	17.3	16.2	15.0	14.3
Other wastes	2.2	3.4	3.6	3.2	3.1	3.2	3.1	3.1	3.3

NA Not available.

Source: Franklin Associates, Ltd., Prairie Village, KS, *Characterization of Municipal Solid Waste in the United States: 1995.* Prepared for the U.S. Environmental Protection Agency.

No. 385. Generation and Recovery of Selected Materials in Municipal Solid Waste: 1970 to 1995

[In millions of tons, except as indicated. Covers post-consumer residential and commercial solid wastes which comprise the major portion of typical municipal collections. Excludes mining, agricultural and industrial processing, demolition and construction wastes, sewage sludge, and junked autos and obsolete equipment wastes. Based on material-flows estimating procedure and wet weight as generated]

ITEM AND MATERIAL	1970	1980	1988	1990	1991	1992	1993	1994	1995
Waste generated, total	121.9	151.5	184.4	197.3	198.9	202.2	205.4	209.8	208.1
Paper and paperboard	44.2	54.7	61.5	72.7	71.0	74.3	77.4	80.8	81.5
Ferrous metals	12.6	11.6	10.9	12.6	12.7	12.1	11.9	11.8	11.6
Aluminum	0.8	1.8	2.3	2.8	2.8	2.9	2.9	3.0	3.0
Other nonferrous metals	0.7	1.1	1.0	1.1	1.1	1.1	1.1	1.4	1.3
Glass	12.7	15.0	13.2	13.1	12.6	13.1	13.6	13.4	12.8
Plastics	3.1	7.9	11.6	17.1	17.7	18.4	19.0	19.3	19.0
Yard waste	23.2	27.5	30.0	35.0	35.0	35.0	33.3	31.5	29.8
Other wastes	24.6	31.9	33.9	42.8	44.0	45.3	46.2	48.5	49.1
Materials recovered, total	8.6	14.5	18.4	33.9	37.7	41.4	44.8	52.0	56.2
Paper and paperboard	7.4	11.9	13.1	20.2	22.5	24.5	25.5	29.5	32.6
Ferrous metals	0.1	0.4	0.4	2.6	3.1	3.4	3.9	4.1	4.2
Aluminum	-	0.3	0.6	1.0	1.0	1.1	1.1	1.2	1.0
Other nonferrous metals	0.3	0.5	0.5	0.7	0.7	0.7	0.7	1.0	0.9
Glass	0.2	0.8	1.0	2.6	2.6	2.9	3.0	3.1	3.1
Plastics	-	-	0.1	0.4	0.5	0.6	0.7	0.9	1.0
Yard waste	-	-	-	4.2	4.8	5.4	6.9	8.0	9.0
Other wastes	0.6	0.6	0.7	2.1	2.6	2.9	3.1	4.2	4.3
Percent of generation recovered, total	7.1	9.6	10.0	17.2	19.1	20.5	21.8	24.8	27.0
Paper and paperboard	16.7	21.8	21.3	27.8	31.7	33.0	32.9	36.5	40.0
Ferrous metals	0.8	3.4	3.7	20.4	24.1	27.7	32.8	35.0	36.5
Aluminum	-	16.7	26.1	35.9	35.6	38.7	35.8	37.8	34.6
Other nonferrous metals	42.9	45.5	50.0	66.4	65.5	63.4	63.1	73.3	69.5
Glass	1.6	5.3	7.6	20.0	20.3	22.0	22.1	23.3	24.5
Plastics	-	-	0.9	2.2	2.5	3.3	3.5	4.9	5.3
Yard waste	-	-	-	12.0	13.7	15.4	20.8	25.4	30.3
Other wastes	2.4	1.9	2.1	4.9	5.8	6.4	6.8	8.6	8.7

- Represents zero.

Source: Franklin Associates, Ltd., Prairie Village, KS, *Characterization of Municipal Solid Waste in the United States: 1995*. Prepared for the U.S. Environmental Protection Agency.

No. 386. Toxic Release Inventory, by Industry and Source: 1990 to 1994

[In millions of pounds. Based on reports from almost 23,000 manufacturing facilities which have 10 or more full-time employees and meet established thresholds for manufacturing, processing, or otherwise using the list of more than 300 chemicals covered. Only chemicals that were reportable in all years shown are compared so that data do not reflect any chemicals added or deleted from the list covered. The inventory was established under the Emergency Planning and Community Right-to-Know Act of 1986 (EPCRA). A release is an on-site discharge of a toxic chemical to the environment]

INDUSTRY	1987 SIC [1] code	1990	1991	1992	1993	1994			
						Total [2]	Air [3], nonpoint	Air [4], point	Water
Total	(X)	2,803.7	2,584.3	2,449.6	2,157.4	1,976.9	350.0	991.0	47.0
Food and kindred products	20	9.9	12.0	11.9	12.0	10.3	2.5	6.3	0.1
Tobacco products	21	1.0	0.6	0.6	0.6	1.0	0.1	0.9	-
Textile mill products	22	23.4	22.2	19.1	17.6	15.9	3.2	12.5	0.1
Apparel and other textile products	23	1.1	1.3	1.3	1.0	1.3	0.3	1.0	-
Lumber and wood products	24	33.6	30.2	30.0	29.8	31.7	3.7	27.9	-
Furniture and fixtures	25	57.8	52.8	53.2	54.0	50.6	6.4	44.1	-
Paper and allied products	26	203.6	207.2	199.1	179.8	218.6	18.4	186.6	8.9
Printing and publishing	27	51.4	46.4	40.4	35.9	34.2	19.9	14.3	-
Chemical and allied products	28	1,007.9	980.5	991.3	874.4	700.7	87.5	220.4	33.5
Petroleum and coal products	29	62.4	56.5	61.7	50.9	43.8	28.4	13.6	0.5
Rubber and misc. plastic products	30	154.5	134.2	121.1	111.0	111.6	30.7	80.6	-
Leather and leather products	31	9.5	7.8	7.2	4.4	3.6	1.0	2.6	-
Stone, clay, glass products	32	20.5	16.4	14.3	14.3	12.4	2.1	8.9	-
Primary metal industries	33	438.6	386.8	341.2	304.6	293.8	21.6	88.7	1.7
Fabricated metals products	34	125.6	109.1	100.6	88.6	86.1	29.5	55.8	0.1
Industrial machinery and equip.	35	48.0	38.8	33.0	26.5	23.5	7.1	16.1	0.1
Electronic, electric equipment	36	73.4	60.2	47.1	32.9	29.0	6.1	22.7	0.1
Transportation equipment	37	157.5	137.5	125.3	123.8	119.7	29.5	89.9	0.1
Instruments and related products	38	38.9	34.9	29.1	22.5	15.7	4.2	11.3	0.3
Misc. manufacturing industries	39	21.6	18.4	16.9	15.2	13.7	3.9	9.8	-
Multiple codes	20-39	251.7	203.6	191.8	137.2	142.9	39.0	70.3	1.3
No codes	20-39	11.9	26.6	13.6	20.1	16.9	5.2	6.4	0.2

- Represents or rounds to zero. X Not applicable. [1] Standard Industrial Classification, see text, section 13. [2] Includes other releases not shown separately. [3] Fugitive. [4] Stack.

Source: U.S. Environmental Protection Agency, *1994 Toxics Release Inventory*, June 1996.

No. 387. Toxic Releases, by State: 1988 to 1994

[In thousands of pounds. See headnote, table 386]

STATE AND OUTLYING AREAS	1988	1992	1993	1994	STATE AND OUTLYING AREAS	1988	1992	1993	1994
Total	**3,536,060**	**2,449,644**	**2,157,355**	1,976,912	MT	35,719	43,331	44,660	46,428
U.S. total	**3,521,835**	**2,436,663**	**2,145,463**	1,966,989	NE	13,889	10,884	9,669	8,148
AL	110,190	101,015	96,337	88,256	NV	2,316	3,422	7,781	3,009
AK	6,203	5,299	2,774	1,667	NH	12,287	5,269	3,205	2,362
AZ	66,057	44,749	11,899	30,482	NJ	36,677	16,340	14,836	12,827
AR	40,676	28,088	28,768	32,123	NM	30,252	19,523	22,957	17,140
CA	97,587	57,347	43,442	35,042	NY	95,609	50,424	39,476	33,387
CO	13,765	4,648	4,113	3,744	NC	125,148	99,431	77,888	79,652
CT	32,538	15,680	12,345	10,148	ND	1,131	1,078	907	926
DE	7,825	4,896	4,400	4,132	OH	166,274	109,711	102,171	98,556
DC	1	(NA)	(NA)	24	OK	34,085	18,823	16,921	15,018
FL	96,972	68,234	56,871	82,452	OR	17,600	16,369	15,630	15,460
GA	81,661	45,447	41,746	45,248	PA	99,845	61,148	47,203	47,589
HI	935	568	497	512	RI	6,351	3,365	3,325	2,879
ID	7,898	3,037	1,838	2,422	SC	61,847	53,632	47,433	44,786
IL	118,263	105,305	88,265	86,493	SD	2,314	2,813	1,870	1,963
IN	169,720	111,618	86,829	70,231	TN	159,647	139,070	140,374	146,696
IA	36,349	25,456	22,005	22,592	TX	310,985	250,576	215,850	213,061
KS	104,567	66,758	28,284	17,656	UT	134,108	94,387	91,141	70,974
KY	82,349	64,658	32,015	30,368	VT	1,598	730	619	610
LA	435,022	254,514	271,665	120,017	VA	115,320	50,806	48,113	46,243
ME	16,017	11,987	9,245	7,472	WA	26,133	21,432	19,210	22,140
MD	19,587	11,463	11,823	12,267	WV	33,152	19,966	19,655	19,324
MA	27,009	13,432	10,108	8,579	WI	50,777	35,033	30,997	30,272
MI	98,792	74,940	74,621	79,026	WY	42,221	12,110	12,189	18,683
MN	54,772	28,729	22,282	19,699	Am. Samoa	-	-	23	-
MS	94,357	97,214	100,714	112,958	Puerto Rico	12,368	11,836	10,313	8,962
MO	87,441	51,907	48,493	45,252	Virgin Island	1,848	1,144	1,580	961

- Represents zero. NA Not available.

Source: U.S. Environmental Protection Agency, Office of Pollution Prevention and Toxics, *1994 Toxics Release Inventory*, June 1996.

No. 388. Hazardous Waste Sites on the National Priority List, by State: 1996

[Includes both proposed and final sites listed on the National Priorities List for the Superfund program as authorized by the Comprehensive Environmental Response, Compensation, and Liability Act of 1980 and the Superfund Amendments and Reauthorization Act of 1986]

STATE	Total sites	Rank	Percent distribution	Federal	Non-Federal	STATE	Total sites	Rank	Percent distribution	Federal	Non-Federal
Total	1,259	(X)	(X)	158	1,101	Montana	9	41	0.72	-	9
						Nebraska	10	38	0.80	1	9
United States	**1,245**	(X)	100.00	**156**	**1,089**	Nevada	1	49	0.08	-	1
						New Hampshire	18	19	1.45	1	17
Alabama	13	30	1.04	3	10	New Jersey	108	1	8.67	6	102
Alaska	7	43	0.56	6	1	New Mexico	11	34	0.88	2	9
Arizona	10	38	0.80	3	7	New York	79	4	6.35	4	75
Arkansas	12	31	0.96	-	12	North Carolina	23	17	1.85	2	21
California	94	3	7.55	23	71	North Dakota	1	49	0.08	-	1
Colorado	18	19	1.45	3	15	Ohio	38	10	3.05	5	33
Connecticut	15	26	1.20	1	14	Oklahoma	11	34	0.88	1	10
Delaware	18	19	1.45	1	17	Oregon	11	34	0.88	2	9
District of Columbia	-	(X)	-	-	-	Pennsylvania	102	2	8.19	6	96
Florida	53	6	4.26	6	47	Rhode Island	12	31	0.96	2	10
Georgia	15	26	1.20	2	13	South Carolina	26	15	2.09	2	24
Hawaii	4	45	0.32	3	1	South Dakota	3	46	0.24	1	2
Idaho	10	38	0.80	2	8	Tennessee	15	26	1.20	4	11
Illinois	40	9	3.21	4	36	Texas	27	14	2.17	4	23
Indiana	31	11	2.49	-	31	Utah	16	24	1.29	4	12
Iowa	17	23	1.37	1	16	Vermont	8	42	0.64	-	8
Kansas	11	34	0.88	2	9	Virginia	25	16	2.01	7	18
Kentucky	16	24	1.29	1	15	Washington	50	7	4.02	14	36
Louisiana	18	19	1.45	1	17	West Virginia	7	43	0.56	2	5
Maine	12	31	0.96	3	9	Wisconsin	41	8	3.29	-	41
Maryland	15	26	1.20	5	10	Wyoming	3	46	0.24	1	2
Massachusetts	30	13	2.41	8	22						
Michigan	75	5	6.02	1	74	Guam	2	(X)	(X)	1	1
Minnesota	31	11	2.49	3	28	Puerto Rico	10	(X)	(X)	1	9
Mississippi	3	46	0.24	-	3	Virgin Islands	2	(X)	(X)	-	2
Missouri	22	18	1.77	3	19						

- Represents zero. X Not applicable.

Source: U.S. Environmental Protection Agency, *Supplementary Materials: National Priorities List, Proposed Rule*, December 1996.

No. 389. Environmental Industry—Revenues and Employment, by Industry Segment: 1980 to 1996

[Covers approximately 59,000 private and public companies engaged in environmental activities]

INDUSTRY SEGMENT	REVENUE (bil. dol.)					EMPLOYMENT (1,000)				
	1980	1990	1994	1995	1996	1980	1990	1994	1995	1996
Industry total	52.0	146.4	172.5	180.0	184.3	462.5	1,174.3	1,274.0	1,299.6	1,306.1
Analytical services [1]	0.4	1.5	1.6	1.5	1.5	6.0	20.2	19.7	17.2	16.5
Water treatment works [2]	9.2	19.8	25.7	27.3	28.6	53.9	95.0	113.7	118.2	120.9
Solid waste management [3]	8.5	26.1	31.0	32.5	33.8	83.2	209.5	227.9	232.1	234.6
Hazardous waste management [4]	0.6	6.3	6.4	6.2	6.0	6.8	56.9	53.3	52.5	51.2
Remediation/industrial services	0.4	8.5	8.6	8.5	8.6	6.9	107.2	100.0	96.6	95.3
Consulting & engineering	1.5	12.5	15.3	15.5	15.6	20.5	144.2	162.8	160.6	159.7
Water equipment & chemicals	6.3	13.5	15.6	16.5	17.4	62.4	97.9	116.4	119.8	123.3
Instrument manufacturing	0.2	2.0	2.9	3.0	3.2	2.5	18.8	24.8	25.9	26.6
Air pollution control equipment [5]	3.0	10.7	11.7	11.9	11.8	28.3	82.7	83.3	84.8	82.6
Waste management equipment [6]	4.0	10.4	11.2	11.7	12.1	41.9	88.8	88.2	93.8	94.9
Process & prevention technology	0.1	0.4	0.8	0.8	0.9	2.1	8.9	17.3	19.5	20.3
Water utilities [7]	11.9	19.8	24.2	25.3	26.3	76.9	104.7	118.0	120.5	122.2
Resource recovery [8]	4.4	13.1	15.4	16.9	16.3	48.7	118.4	124.2	132.0	131.3
Environmental energy sources [9]	1.5	1.8	2.2	2.3	2.4	22.4	21.1	24.4	26.1	26.7

[1] Covers environmental laboratory testing and services. [2] Mostly revenues collected by municipal entities. [3] Covers such activities as collection, transportation, transfer stations, disposal, landfill ownership and management for solid waste. [4] Transportation and disposal of hazardous, medical and nuclear waste. [5] Includes stationery and mobile sources. [6] Includes vehicles, containers, liners, processing and remediation equipment. [7] Revenues generated from the sale of water. [8] Revenues generated from the sale of recovered metals, paper, plastic, etc. [9] Includes solar, wind, geothermal and conservation devices.

Source: Environmental Business International, Inc., San Diego, CA, *Environmental Business Journal*, monthly (copyright).

No. 390. Pollution Abatement and Control Expenditures, in Current and Constant (1987) Dollars, 1973 to 1993, and by Media, 1993

[In millions of dollars]

YEAR	Total expenditures	POLLUTION ABATEMENT								Regulation and monitoring	Research and development
		Total	Personal consumption	Business	Government						
					Total	Federal	State and local	Govt. enterprise [1]			
CURRENT DOLLARS											
1973	19,404	18,011	1,867	12,261	3,883	203	1,433	2,246		490	903
1980	50,399	47,352	6,558	29,706	11,088	494	2,768	7,825		1,296	1,751
1985	71,169	68,268	11,991	42,058	14,220	1,225	4,858	8,137		1,279	1,621
1986	75,389	72,111	12,385	43,954	15,772	1,346	5,515	8,912		1,532	1,746
1987	77,649	74,349	11,075	45,432	17,842	1,237	6,266	10,339		1,519	1,781
1988	83,020	79,453	12,285	48,415	18,752	1,402	7,283	10,067		1,695	1,872
1989	87,622	83,774	10,950	52,429	20,395	1,379	8,705	10,312		1,803	2,044
1990	93,877	90,321	9,241	58,498	22,582	1,391	10,161	11,031		1,784	1,772
1991 [2]	95,893	92,012	7,425	60,594	23,634	1,417	11,417	10,800		1,868	2,013
1992 [2]	101,846	98,134	7,896	65,592	24,646	1,215	12,630	10,801		1,848	1,864
1993	109,044	105,386	8,458	69,983	26,945	1,068	14,583	11,295		1,924	1,734
Air	31,902	30,236	8,458	21,274	506	80	21	404		561	1,104
Water	39,015	37,984	-	25,932	12,052	567	595	10,890		789	243
Solid Waste	38,844	38,326	-	24,202	14,124	250	13,873	-		418	102
CONSTANT (1987) DOLLARS											
1973	49,683	46,166	4,543	31,997	9,626	539	3,723	5,364		1,190	2,327
1980	65,590	61,305	7,297	38,673	15,335	679	4,015	10,641		1,873	2,413
1985	72,813	69,773	11,935	42,833	15,005	1,300	5,200	8,505		1,361	1,678
1986	77,487	74,110	12,831	45,002	16,277	1,402	5,726	9,149		1,589	1,788
1987	77,649	74,349	11,075	45,432	17,842	1,237	6,266	10,339		1,519	1,781
1988	80,698	77,263	12,069	47,131	18,063	1,340	6,953	9,771		1,643	1,792
1989	81,802	78,266	10,445	48,901	18,920	1,271	7,982	9,667		1,657	1,879
1990	84,648	81,453	8,659	52,630	20,165	1,228	8,864	10,073		1,636	1,559
1991 [2]	84,152	80,806	6,783	53,667	20,356	1,220	9,661	9,475		1,654	1,692
1992 [2]	88,083	84,817	7,037	57,028	20,751	1,040	10,437	9,274		1,619	1,648
1993	91,826	88,731	7,356	59,299	22,077	902	11,691	9,484		1,656	1,438
Air	27,964	26,560	7,356	18,764	440	68	18	354		487	918
Water	33,503	32,612	-	22,463	10,150	480	541	9,129		690	201
Solid Waste	31,025	30,594	-	19,326	11,268	213	11,055	-		348	84

- Represents or rounds to zero. [1] Fixed capital. [2] Includes "other and unallocated" expenditures (such as for noise, radiation, and pesticide pollution and business expenditures not assigned to media) which may be either positive or negative; therefore, data may not add.

Source: U. S. Bureau of Economic Analysis, *Survey of Current Business, May 1995.*

No. 391. Threatened and Endangered Wildlife and Plant Species—Number: 1997

[As of March 31. Endangered species: One in danger of becoming extinct throughout all or a significant part of its natural range. Threatened species: One likely to become endangered in the foreseeable future]

ITEM	Mammals	Birds	Reptiles	Amphibians	Fishes	Snails	Clams	Crustaceans	Insects	Arachnids	Plants
Total listings	331	273	111	23	118	23	64	18	37	5	637
Endangered species, total	307	253	79	16	78	16	58	15	28	5	524
United States	55	75	15	8	67	15	56	15	24	5	523
Foreign	252	178	64	8	11	1	2	-	4	-	1
Threatened species, total	24	20	32	7	40	7	6	3	9	-	113
United States	8	14	18	6	40	7	6	3	9	-	111
Foreign	16	6	14	1	-	-	-	-	-	-	2

- Represents zero. [1] Species outside United States and outlying areas as determined by Fish and Wildlife Service.
Source: U.S. Fish and Wildlife Service, *Endangered Species Technical Bulletin*, quarterly.

No. 392. Major U.S. Weather Disasters: 1980 to 1997

[Covers only weather related disasters costing $1 billion or more]

EVENT	Description	Time period	Estimated cost (bil. dol.)	Deaths
West Coast Flooding	Flooding from rains and snowmelt in CA, WA, OR, ID, NV, & MT	Dec. 1996-Jan. 1997	$2-$3	36
Hurricane Fran	Category 3 hurricane in NC and VA	Sept. 1996	$5	36
Southern Plains Severe Drought	Drought in agricultural areas of TX & OK	Fall '95-summer '96	Over $4	(NA)
Pacific Northwest Severe Flooding	Flooding from heavy rain & snowmelt in OR, WA, ID, and MT	Feb. 1996	$1	9
Blizzard of '96 Followed by Flooding	Heavy snowstorm followed by severe flooding in Appalachians, Mid-Atlantic, and Northeast	Jan. 1996	$3	187
Hurricane Opal	Category 3 hurricane in FL, AL, parts of GA, TN, & Carolinas	Oct. 1995	Over $3	27
Hurricane Marilyn	Category 2 hurricane in Virgin Islands	Sept. 1995	$2.1	13
TX/OK/LA/MS Severe Weather and Flooding	Flooding, hail, & tornadoes across TX, OK, parts of LA, MS, Dallas & New Orleans hardest hit	May 1995	$5-$6	32
California Flooding	Flooding from frequent winter storms across much of CA	Jan.-Mar. 1995	$3	27
Texas Flooding	Flooding from torrential rain & thunderstorms across S.E. TX	Oct. 1994	$1	19
Tropical Storm Alberto	Flooding due to 10 to 25 inch rain across GA, AL, part of FL	July 1994	$1	32
Southeast Ice Storm	Intense ice storm in pts of TX, OK, AR, LA, MS, AL, TN, GA, SC, NC, & VA	Feb. 1994	$3	9
California Wildfires	Out-of-control wildfires over southern CA	Fall 1993	$1	4
Midwest Flooding	Extreme flooding across central U.S.	Summer 1993	$15-$20	48
Drought/Heat Wave	Extreme drought/heatwave across southeastern U.S.	Summer 1993	$1	(NA)
Storm/Blizzard	Storm/blizzard over eastern U.S.	Mar. 1993	$3-$6	270
Nor'easter of 1992	Slow-moving storm batters northeast U.S. coast, New England	Dec. 1992	$1-$2	19
Hurricane Iniki	Category 4 hurricane hit Hawaiian island of Kauai	Sept. 1992	$1.8	7
Hurricane Andrew	Category 4 hurricane hit FL & LA	Aug. 1992	$27	58
Oakland Firestorm	Oakland, CA firestorm due to low humidity & high winds	Oct. 1991	$1.5	25
Hurricane Bob	Category 2 hurricane—mainly coastal NC, Long Island, & N. E.	Aug. 1991	$1.5	18
Hurricane Hugo	Category 4 hurricane hit Puerto Rico & Virgin Islands, devastated NC & SC	Sept. 1989	Over $9	86
Drought/Heat Wave	Drought/heatwave over central & eastern U.S.	Summer 1988	$40	5,000-10,000
Hurricane Juan	Category 1 hurricane, flooding most severe problem, hit LA and southeast U.S.	Oct.-Nov. 1985	$1.5	63
Hurricane Elena	Category 3 hurricane across FL to LA	Aug.-Sept.1985	$1.3	4
Florida Freeze	Severe freeze central/northern FL, damage to citrus industry	Dec. 1983	$2	-
Hurricane Alicia	Category 3 hurricane across TX	Aug. 1983	$3	21
Drought/Heat Wave	Drought/heatwave over central & eastern U.S.	June-Sept.1980	$20	10,000

- Represents zero. NA Not available or not reported.

Source: U.S. National Oceanic and Atmospheric Administration, National Climatic Data Center. *"Billion Dollar U.S. Weather Disaster, 1980-1997,"* January 27, 1997. <http://www.ncdc.noaa.gov/publications/billionz.html>.

No. 393. Tornadoes, Floods, and Tropical Storms: 1985 to 1995

ITEM	1985	1986	1987	1988	1989	1990	1991	1992	1993	1994	1995, prel.
Tornadoes, number [1]	684	764	656	702	856	1,133	1,132	1,303	1,173	1,082	1,235
Lives lost, total	94	15	59	32	50	53	39	39	33	69	30
Most in a single tornado	18	3	30	5	21	29	13	10	7	22	6
Property loss of $500,000 and over	69	75	38	48	60	91	64	108	72	63	63
Floods: Lives lost	304	80	82	29	81	147	63	87	101	72	103
Property loss (mil. dol.)	3,000	4,000	1,490	114	415	2,058	1,416	800	16,400	1,224	5,111
North Atlantic tropical storms and hurricanes: [2]											
Number reaching U.S. coast	11	6	7	12	11	14	8	7	8	7	19
Hurricanes only	6	2	1	1	3	-	1	1	1	-	2
Lives lost in U S	30	9	-	6	56	10	17	26	9	38	29
Property loss (mil. (1990) dol.)[3]	4,457	18	8	9	7,840	57	1,500	25,000	57	973	5,000

- Represents zero [1] A violent, rotating column of air descending from a cumulonimbus cloud in the form of a tubular- or funnel-shaped cloud, usually characterized by movements along a narrow path and wind speeds from 100 to over 300 miles per hour. Also known as a "twister" or "waterspout." [2] Source: National Hurricane Center, Coral Gables, FL, unpublished data. Tropical storms have maximum winds of 39 to 73 miles per hour; hurricanes have maximum winds of 74 miles per hour or higher. [3] Source: Hebert, Jarrell, & Mayfield, "The Deadliest, Costliest, and Most Intense U.S. Hurricanes of this Century," NOAA Technical Memo, NHC-31, February 1993

Source: Except as noted, U.S. National Oceanic and Atmospheric Administration, *Storm Data*, monthly.

No. 394. Normal Daily Mean, Maximum, and Minimum Temperatures—Selected Cities

[In Fahrenheit degrees. Airport data except as noted. Based on standard 30-year period, 1961 through 1990]

STATE	STATION	DAILY MEAN TEMPERATURE			DAILY MAXIMUM TEMPERATURE			DAILY MINIMUM TEMPERATURE		
		Jan.	July	Annual average	Jan.	July	Annual average	Jan.	July	Annual average
AL	Mobile	49.9	82.3	67.5	59.7	91.3	77.4	40.0	73.2	57.4
AK	Juneau	24.2	56.0	40.6	29.4	63.9	46.9	19.0	48.1	34.1
AZ	Phoenix	53.6	93.5	72.6	65.9	105.9	85.9	41.2	81.0	59.3
AR	Little Rock	39.1	81.9	61.8	49.0	92.4	72.5	29.1	71.5	51.0
CA	Los Angeles	56.8	69.1	63.0	65.7	75.3	70.4	47.8	62.8	55.5
	Sacramento	45.2	75.7	60.8	52.7	93.2	73.5	37.7	58.1	48.1
	San Diego	57.4	71.0	64.2	65.9	76.2	70.8	48.9	65.7	57.6
	San Francisco	48.7	62.7	57.1	55.6	71.6	65.2	41.8	53.9	49.0
CO	Denver	29.7	73.5	50.3	43.2	88.2	64.2	16.1	58.6	36.2
CT	Hartford	24.6	73.7	49.9	33.2	85.0	60.2	15.8	62.2	39.5
DE	Wilmington	30.6	76.4	54.2	38.7	85.6	63.6	22.4	67.1	44.8
DC	Washington	34.6	80.0	58.0	42.3	88.5	66.9	26.8	71.4	49.2
FL	Jacksonville	52.4	81.6	68.0	64.2	91.4	78.9	40.5	71.9	57.1
	Miami	67.2	82.6	75.9	75.2	89.0	82.8	59.2	76.2	69.0
GA	Atlanta	41.0	78.8	61.3	50.4	88.0	71.2	31.5	69.5	51.3
HI	Honolulu	72.9	80.5	77.2	80.1	87.5	84.4	65.6	73.5	70.0
ID	Boise	29.0	74.0	50.9	36.4	90.2	62.8	21.6	57.7	39.1
IL	Chicago	21.0	73.2	49.0	29.0	83.7	58.6	12.9	62.6	39.5
	Peoria	21.6	75.5	50.7	29.9	85.7	60.4	13.2	65.4	41.0
IN	Indianapolis	25.5	75.4	52.3	33.7	85.5	62.1	17.2	65.2	42.4
IA	Des Moines	19.4	76.6	49.9	28.1	86.7	59.8	10.7	66.5	40.0
KS	Wichita	29.5	81.4	56.2	39.8	92.8	67.4	19.2	69.9	45.0
KY	Louisville	31.7	77.2	56.1	40.3	87.0	66.0	23.2	67.3	46.0
LA	New Orleans	51.3	81.9	68.1	60.8	90.6	77.6	41.8	73.1	58.5
ME	Portland	20.8	68.6	45.4	30.3	78.8	54.9	11.4	58.3	35.8
MD	Baltimore	31.8	77.0	55.1	40.2	87.2	65.0	23.4	66.8	45.2
MA	Boston	28.6	73.5	51.3	35.7	81.8	59.0	21.6	65.1	43.6
MI	Detroit	22.9	72.3	48.6	30.3	83.3	58.1	15.6	61.3	39.0
	Sault Ste. Marie	12.9	63.8	39.7	21.1	76.3	49.6	4.6	51.3	29.8
MN	Duluth	7.0	66.1	38.5	16.2	77.1	47.9	-2.2	55.1	29.0
	Minneapolis-St. Paul	11.8	73.6	44.9	20.7	84.0	54.3	2.8	63.1	35.3
MS	Jackson	44.1	81.5	64.2	55.6	92.4	76.4	32.7	70.5	52.0
MO	Kansas City	25.7	78.5	53.6	34.7	88.7	63.6	16.7	68.2	43.7
	St. Louis	29.3	79.8	56.1	37.7	89.3	65.4	20.8	70.4	46.7
MT	Great Falls	21.2	68.2	44.8	30.6	83.3	56.4	11.6	53.2	33.1
NE	Omaha	21.1	76.9	50.6	31.3	87.9	61.5	10.9	65.9	39.5
NV	Reno	32.9	71.6	50.8	45.1	91.9	66.8	20.7	51.3	34.7
NH	Concord	18.6	69.5	45.1	29.8	82.4	57.0	7.4	56.5	33.1
NJ	Atlantic City	30.9	74.7	53.0	40.4	84.5	63.2	21.4	64.8	42.8
NM	Albuquerque	34.2	78.5	56.2	46.8	92.5	70.1	21.7	64.4	42.2
NY	Albany	20.6	71.8	47.4	30.2	84.0	58.1	11.0	59.6	36.6
	Buffalo	23.6	71.1	47.7	30.2	80.2	55.8	17.0	61.9	39.5
	New York [1]	31.5	76.8	54.7	37.6	85.2	62.3	25.3	68.4	47.1
NC	Charlotte	39.3	79.3	60.1	49.0	88.9	70.4	29.6	69.6	49.7
	Raleigh	38.9	78.1	59.3	48.9	88.0	70.1	28.8	68.1	48.4
ND	Bismarck	9.2	70.4	41.6	20.2	84.4	53.8	-1.7	56.4	29.4
OH	Cincinnati	28.1	75.1	53.2	36.6	85.5	63.2	19.5	64.8	43.2
	Cleveland	24.8	71.9	49.6	31.9	82.4	58.7	17.6	61.4	40.5
	Columbus	26.4	73.2	51.4	34.1	83.7	61.2	18.5	62.7	41.6
OK	Oklahoma City	35.9	82.0	60.0	46.7	93.4	71.1	25.2	70.6	48.8
OR	Portland	39.6	68.2	53.6	45.4	79.9	62.6	33.7	56.5	44.5
PA	Philadelphia	30.4	76.7	54.3	37.9	86.1	63.4	22.8	67.2	45.1
	Pittsburgh	26.1	72.1	50.3	33.7	82.6	59.9	18.5	61.6	40.7
RI	Providence	27.9	72.7	50.4	36.6	82.1	59.8	19.1	63.2	41.0
SC	Columbia	43.8	80.8	63.1	55.3	91.6	75.1	32.1	70.0	50.9
SD	Sioux Falls	13.8	74.3	45.5	24.3	86.3	56.8	3.3	62.3	34.2
TN	Memphis	39.7	82.6	62.3	48.5	92.3	72.1	30.9	72.9	52.4
	Nashville	36.2	79.3	59.1	45.9	89.5	69.8	26.5	68.9	48.4
TX	Dallas-Fort Worth	43.4	85.3	65.4	54.1	96.5	76.3	32.7	74.1	54.6
	El Paso	42.8	82.3	63.2	56.1	96.1	77.5	29.4	68.4	49.0
	Houston	50.4	82.6	67.9	61.0	92.7	78.6	39.7	72.4	57.3
UT	Salt Lake City	27.9	77.9	52.0	36.4	92.2	63.6	19.3	63.7	40.3
VT	Burlington	16.3	70.5	44.6	25.1	81.2	54.0	7.5	59.7	35.2
VA	Norfolk	39.1	78.2	59.2	47.3	86.4	67.8	30.9	70.0	50.6
	Richmond	35.7	78.0	57.7	45.7	88.4	68.8	25.7	67.5	46.6
WA	Seattle-Tacoma	40.1	65.2	52.0	45.0	75.2	59.4	35.2	55.2	44.6
	Spokane	27.1	68.8	47.3	33.2	83.1	57.5	20.8	54.4	36.9
WV	Charleston	32.1	75.1	55.0	41.2	85.7	65.8	23.0	64.4	44.2
WI	Milwaukee	18.9	70.9	46.1	26.1	79.9	54.3	11.6	62.0	37.9
WY	Cheyenne	26.5	68.4	45.6	37.7	82.2	58.0	15.2	54.6	33.2
PR	San Juan	77.0	82.6	80.2	83.2	88.5	86.4	70.8	76.8	74.0

[1] City office data.

Source: U.S. National Oceanic and Atmospheric Administration, *Climatography of the United States*, No. 81.

No. 395. Highest Temperature of Record—Selected Cities

[In Fahrenheit degrees. Airport data, except as noted. For period of record through 1995]

STATE	STATION	Length of record (yr.)	Jan.	Feb.	Mar.	Apr.	May	June	July	Aug.	Sept.	Oct.	Nov.	Dec.	Ann
AL	Mobile	54	84	82	90	94	100	102	104	102	99	93	87	81	
AK	Juneau	51	57	57	59	72	82	86	90	83	72	61	56	54	
AZ	Phoenix	58	88	92	100	105	113	122	121	116	118	107	93	88	
AR	Little Rock	54	83	85	91	95	98	105	112	108	106	97	86	80	
CA	Los Angeles	60	88	92	95	102	97	104	97	98	110	106	101	94	
	Sacramento	45	70	76	88	93	105	115	114	109	108	101	87	72	
	San Diego	55	88	90	93	98	96	101	95	98	111	107	97	88	
	San Francisco	68	72	78	85	92	97	106	105	100	103	99	85	75	
CO	Denver	61	73	76	84	90	96	104	104	101	97	89	79	75	
CT	Hartford	41	65	73	87	96	97	100	102	101	99	91	81	74	
DE	Wilmington	48	75	78	86	94	96	100	102	101	100	91	85	74	
DC	Washington	54	79	82	89	95	99	101	104	103	101	94	86	75	
FL	Jacksonville	54	85	88	91	95	100	103	105	102	100	96	88	84	
	Miami	53	88	89	92	96	96	98	98	98	97	95	89	87	
GA	Atlanta	47	79	80	89	93	95	101	105	102	98	95	84	79	
HI	Honolulu	26	87	88	88	89	93	92	94	93	95	94	93	89	
ID	Boise	56	63	71	81	92	98	109	111	110	102	94	74	65	
IL	Chicago	37	65	71	88	91	93	104	104	101	99	91	78	71	
	Peoria	56	70	72	86	92	93	105	103	103	100	90	81	71	
IN	Indianapolis	56	71	74	85	89	93	102	104	102	100	90	81	74	
IA	Des Moines	56	65	73	91	93	98	103	105	108	101	95	76	69	
KS	Wichita	43	75	84	89	96	100	110	113	110	107	95	85	83	
KY	Louisville	48	77	77	86	91	95	102	105	101	104	92	84	76	
LA	New Orleans	49	83	85	89	92	96	100	101	102	101	92	87	84	
ME	Portland	55	64	64	86	85	94	98	99	103	95	88	74	69	
MD	Baltimore	45	75	79	87	94	98	101	104	105	100	92	83	77	
MA	Boston	44	66	70	81	94	95	100	102	102	100	90	79	73	
MI	Detroit	37	62	65	81	89	93	104	102	100	98	91	77	68	
	Sault Ste. Marie	55	45	47	75	85	89	93	97	98	95	80	67	60	
MN	Duluth	54	52	55	78	88	90	94	97	97	95	86	70	55	
	Minneapolis-St. Paul	57	58	60	83	95	96	102	105	102	98	89	75	63	
MS	Jackson	32	82	85	89	94	99	105	106	102	104	95	88	84	
MO	Kansas City	23	69	77	86	93	92	105	107	109	102	92	82	70	
	St. Louis	50	76	81	87	93	93	101	113	106	104	93	80	77	
MT	Great Falls	58	67	70	78	89	93	101	105	106	98	91	76	69	
NE	Omaha	59	69	78	89	97	99	105	114	110	104	96	80	72	
NV	Reno	54	70	75	83	89	96	103	104	105	101	91	77	70	
NH	Concord	54	68	66	85	95	97	98	102	101	98	90	80	68	
NJ	Atlantic City	52	78	75	87	94	99	106	104	102	99	90	84	75	
NM	Albuquerque	56	69	76	85	89	98	107	105	101	100	91	77	72	
NY	Albany	49	65	67	86	92	94	99	100	99	100	89	82	71	
	Buffalo	52	72	65	81	94	90	96	97	99	98	87	80	74	
	New York [1]	127	72	75	86	96	99	101	106	104	102	94	84	72	
NC	Charlotte	56	78	81	90	93	100	103	103	103	104	98	85	77	
	Raleigh	51	79	84	92	95	97	104	105	105	104	98	88	79	
ND	Bismarck	56	62	69	81	93	98	107	109	109	105	95	75	65	
OH	Cincinnati	34	69	73	84	89	93	102	103	102	98	88	81	75	
	Cleveland	54	73	69	83	88	92	104	103	102	101	90	82	77	
	Columbus	56	74	73	85	89	94	102	100	101	100	90	80	76	
OK	Oklahoma City	42	80	84	93	100	104	105	109	110	102	96	87	86	
OR	Portland	55	63	71	80	87	100	100	107	107	105	92	73	65	
PA	Philadelphia	54	74	74	87	94	97	100	104	101	100	96	81	72	
	Pittsburgh	43	69	69	82	89	91	98	103	100	97	87	82	74	
RI	Providence	42	69	72	80	98	94	97	102	104	100	86	78	70	
SC	Columbia	48	84	84	91	94	101	107	107	107	101	101	90	83	
SD	Sioux Falls	50	66	70	87	94	100	110	108	108	104	94	76	61	
TN	Memphis	54	78	81	85	94	99	104	108	105	103	95	85	81	
	Nashville	56	78	84	86	91	97	106	107	104	105	94	84	79	
TX	Dallas-Fort Worth	42	88	88	96	95	103	113	110	108	106	102	89	88	
	El Paso	56	80	83	89	98	104	114	112	108	104	96	87	80	
	Houston	26	84	91	91	95	97	103	104	107	102	96	89	85	
UT	Salt Lake City	67	62	69	78	86	93	104	107	106	100	89	75	69	
VT	Burlington	52	66	62	84	91	93	100	100	101	94	85	75	65	
VA	Norfolk	47	78	81	88	97	100	101	103	104	99	95	86	80	
	Richmond	66	80	83	93	96	100	104	105	102	103	99	86	80	
WA	Seattle-Tacoma	51	64	70	75	85	93	96	100	99	98	89	74	64	
	Spokane	48	59	63	71	90	96	101	103	108	98	86	67	56	
WV	Charleston	48	79	78	89	94	93	98	104	101	102	92	85	80	
WI	Milwaukee	55	62	65	82	91	93	101	103	103	98	89	77	63	
WY	Cheyenne	60	66	71	74	83	90	100	100	96	95	83	73	69	
PR	San Juan	41	92	96	96	97	96	97	95	97	97	98	96	94	

[1] City office data.

Source: U.S. National Oceanic and Atmospheric Administration, *Comparative Climatic Data*, annual.

No. 396. Lowest Temperature of Record—Selected Cities

[In Fahrenheit degrees. Airport data, except as noted. For period of record through 1995]

STATE	STATION	Length of record (yr.)	Jan.	Feb.	Mar.	Apr.	May	June	July	Aug.	Sept.	Oct.	Nov.	Dec.	Annual
AL	Mobile	54	3	11	21	32	43	49	60	59	42	30	22	8	3
AK	Juneau	51	-22	-22	-15	6	25	31	36	27	23	11	-5	-21	-22
AZ	Phoenix	58	17	22	25	32	40	50	61	60	47	34	25	22	17
AR	Little Rock	54	-4	-5	11	28	40	46	54	52	37	29	17	-1	-5
CA	Los Angeles	60	23	32	34	39	43	48	49	51	47	41	34	32	23
	Sacramento	45	23	23	26	32	36	41	48	49	43	36	26	18	18
	San Diego	55	29	36	39	41	48	51	55	57	51	43	38	34	29
	San Francisco	68	24	25	30	31	36	41	43	42	38	34	25	20	20
CO	Denver	61	-25	-30	-11	-2	22	30	43	41	17	3	-8	-25	-30
CT	Hartford	41	-26	-21	-6	9	28	37	44	36	30	17	1	-14	-26
DE	Wilmington	48	-14	-6	2	18	30	41	48	43	36	24	14	-7	-14
DC	Washington	54	-5	4	11	24	34	47	54	49	39	29	16	1	-5
FL	Jacksonville	54	7	19	23	34	45	47	61	63	48	36	21	11	7
	Miami	53	30	32	32	46	53	60	69	68	68	51	39	30	30
GA	Atlanta	47	-8	5	10	26	37	46	53	55	36	28	3	-	-8
HI	Honolulu	26	53	53	55	57	60	65	66	67	66	61	57	54	53
ID	Boise	56	-17	-15	6	19	22	31	35	34	23	11	-3	-25	-25
IL	Chicago	37	-27	-17	-8	7	24	36	40	41	28	17	1	-25	-27
	Peoria	56	-25	-18	-10	14	25	39	47	41	26	19	-2	-23	-25
IN	Indianapolis	56	-27	-21	-7	16	28	37	44	41	28	17	-2	-23	-27
IA	Des Moines	56	-24	-20	-22	9	30	38	47	40	26	14	-4	-22	-24
KS	Wichita	43	-12	-21	-2	15	31	43	51	48	31	18	1	-16	-21
KY	Louisville	48	-22	-19	-1	22	31	42	50	46	33	23	-1	-15	-22
LA	New Orleans	49	14	19	25	32	41	50	60	60	42	35	24	11	11
ME	Portland	55	-26	-39	-21	8	23	33	40	33	23	15	3	-21	-39
MD	Baltimore	45	-7	-3	6	20	32	40	50	45	35	25	13	-	-7
MA	Boston	44	-12	-4	6	16	34	45	50	47	38	28	15	-7	-12
MI	Detroit	37	-21	-15	-4	10	25	36	41	38	29	17	9	-10	-21
	Sault Ste. Marie	55	-36	-35	-24	-2	18	26	36	29	25	16	-10	-31	-36
MN	Duluth	54	-39	-33	-29	-5	17	27	35	32	22	8	-23	-34	-39
	Minneapolis-St. Paul	57	-34	-28	-32	2	18	34	43	39	26	15	-17	-29	-34
MS	Jackson	32	2	11	15	27	38	47	51	55	35	26	17	4	2
MO	Kansas City	23	-17	-19	-10	12	30	42	52	43	31	17	1	-23	-23
	St. Louis	38	-18	-10	-5	22	31	43	51	47	36	23	1	-16	-18
MT	Great Falls	58	-37	-35	-29	-6	15	31	40	30	20	-11	-25	-43	-43
NE	Omaha	59	-23	-21	-16	5	27	38	44	43	25	13	-9	-23	-23
NV	Reno	54	-16	-16	-2	13	18	25	33	24	20	8	1	-16	-16
NH	Concord	54	-33	-37	-16	8	21	30	35	29	21	10	-5	-22	-37
NJ	Atlantic City	52	-10	-11	5	12	25	37	42	40	32	20	10	-7	-11
NM	Albuquerque	56	-17	-5	8	19	28	40	52	50	37	21	-7	-7	-17
NY	Albany	49	-28	-21	-21	10	26	36	40	34	24	16	5	-22	-28
	Buffalo	52	-16	-20	-7	12	26	35	43	38	32	20	9	-10	-20
	New York [1]	127	-6	-15	3	12	32	44	52	50	39	28	5	-13	-15
NC	Charlotte	56	-5	5	4	24	32	45	53	53	39	24	11	2	-5
	Raleigh	51	-9	5	11	23	31	36	46	46	37	19	11	4	-9
ND	Bismarck	56	-44	-43	-31	-12	15	30	35	33	11	-10	-30	-43	-44
OH	Cincinnati	34	-25	-11	-11	17	27	39	47	43	31	16	1	-20	-25
	Cleveland	54	-20	-15	-5	10	25	31	41	38	32	19	3	-15	-20
	Columbus	56	-22	-13	-6	14	25	35	43	39	31	20	5	-17	-22
OK	Oklahoma City	42	-4	-3	3	20	37	47	53	51	36	16	11	-8	-8
OR	Portland	55	-2	-3	19	29	29	39	43	44	34	26	13	6	-3
PA	Philadelphia	54	-7	-4	7	19	28	44	51	44	35	25	15	1	-7
	Pittsburgh	43	-22	-12	-1	14	26	34	42	39	31	16	-1	-12	-22
RI	Providence	42	-13	-7	1	14	29	41	48	40	33	20	6	-10	-13
SC	Columbia	48	-1	5	4	26	34	44	54	53	40	23	12	4	-1
SD	Sioux Falls	50	-36	-31	-23	5	17	33	38	34	22	9	-17	-28	-36
TN	Memphis	54	-4	-11	12	29	38	48	52	48	36	25	9	-13	-13
	Nashville	56	-17	-13	2	23	34	42	51	47	36	26	-1	-10	-17
TX	Dallas-Fort Worth	42	4	7	15	29	41	51	59	56	43	29	20	-1	-1
	El Paso	56	-8	8	14	23	31	46	57	56	41	25	1	5	-8
	Houston	26	12	20	22	31	44	52	62	60	48	29	19	7	7
UT	Salt Lake City	67	-22	-30	2	14	25	35	40	37	27	16	-14	-21	-30
VT	Burlington	52	-30	-30	-20	2	24	33	39	35	25	15	-2	-26	-30
VA	Norfolk	47	-3	8	18	28	36	45	54	49	45	27	20	7	-3
	Richmond	66	-12	-10	11	23	31	40	51	46	35	21	10	-1	-12
WA	Seattle-Tacoma	51	-	1	11	29	28	38	43	44	35	28	6	6	-
	Spokane	48	-22	-17	-7	17	24	33	37	35	24	10	-21	-25	-25
WV	Charleston	48	-16	-6	-	19	26	33	46	41	34	17	6	-12	-16
WI	Milwaukee	55	-26	-19	-10	12	21	33	40	44	28	18	-5	-20	-26
WY	Cheyenne	60	-29	-34	-21	-8	16	25	38	36	8	-1	-16	-28	-34
PR	San Juan	41	61	62	60	64	66	69	69	70	69	67	66	63	60

\- Represents zero. [1] City office data.

Source: U.S. National Oceanic and Atmospheric Administration, *Comparative Climatic Data*, annual.

No. 397. Normal Monthly and Annual Precipitation—Selected Cities

[In inches. Airport data, except as noted. Based on standard 30-year period, 1961 through 1990]

STATE	STATION	Jan.	Feb.	Mar.	Apr.	May	June	July	Aug.	Sept.	Oct.	Nov.	Dec.	Annual
AL	Mobile	4.76	5.46	6.41	4.48	5.74	5.04	6.85	6.96	5.91	2.94	4.10	5.31	63.96
AK	Juneau	4.54	3.75	3.28	2.77	3.42	3.15	4.16	5.32	6.73	7.84	4.91	4.44	54.31
AZ	Phoenix	0.67	0.68	0.88	0.22	0.12	0.13	0.83	0.96	0.86	0.65	0.66	1.00	7.66
AR	Little Rock	3.42	3.61	4.91	5.49	5.17	3.57	3.60	3.26	4.05	3.75	5.20	4.83	50.86
CA	Los Angeles	2.40	2.51	1.98	0.72	0.14	0.03	0.01	0.15	0.31	0.34	1.76	1.66	12.01
	Sacramento	3.73	2.87	2.57	1.16	0.27	0.12	0.05	0.07	0.37	1.08	2.72	2.51	17.52
	San Diego	1.80	1.53	1.77	0.79	0.19	0.07	0.02	0.10	0.24	0.37	1.45	1.57	9.90
	San Francisco	4.35	3.17	3.06	1.37	0.19	0.11	0.03	0.05	0.20	1.22	2.86	3.09	19.70
CO	Denver	0.50	0.57	1.28	1.71	2.40	1.79	1.91	1.51	1.24	0.98	0.87	0.64	15.40
CT	Hartford	3.41	3.23	3.63	3.85	4.12	3.75	3.19	3.65	3.79	3.57	4.04	3.91	44.14
DE	Wilmington	3.03	2.91	3.43	3.39	3.84	3.55	4.23	3.40	3.43	2.88	3.27	3.48	40.84
DC	Washington	2.72	2.71	3.17	2.71	3.66	3.38	3.80	3.91	3.31	3.02	3.12	3.12	38.63
FL	Jacksonville	3.31	3.93	3.68	2.77	3.55	5.69	5.60	7.93	7.05	2.90	2.19	2.72	51.32
	Miami	2.01	2.08	2.39	2.85	6.21	9.33	5.70	7.58	7.63	5.64	2.66	1.83	55.91
GA	Atlanta	4.75	4.81	5.77	4.26	4.29	3.56	5.01	3.66	3.42	3.05	3.86	4.33	50.77
HI	Honolulu	3.55	2.21	2.20	1.54	1.13	0.50	0.59	0.44	0.78	2.28	3.00	3.80	22.02
ID	Boise	1.45	1.07	1.29	1.24	1.08	0.81	0.35	0.43	0.80	0.75	1.48	1.36	12.11
IL	Chicago	1.53	1.36	2.69	3.64	3.32	3.78	3.66	4.22	3.82	2.41	2.92	2.47	35.82
	Peoria	1.51	1.42	2.91	3.77	3.70	3.99	4.20	3.10	3.87	2.65	2.69	2.44	36.25
IN	Indianapolis	2.32	2.46	3.79	3.70	4.00	3.49	4.47	3.64	2.87	2.63	3.23	3.34	39.94
IA	Des Moines	0.96	1.11	2.33	3.36	3.66	4.46	3.78	4.20	3.53	2.62	1.79	1.32	33.12
KS	Wichita	0.79	0.96	2.43	2.38	3.81	4.31	3.13	3.02	3.49	2.22	1.59	1.20	29.33
KY	Louisville	2.86	3.30	4.66	4.23	4.62	3.46	4.51	3.54	3.16	2.71	3.70	3.64	44.39
LA	New Orleans	5.05	6.01	4.90	4.50	4.56	5.84	6.12	6.17	5.51	3.05	4.42	5.75	61.88
ME	Portland	3.53	3.33	3.67	4.08	3.62	3.44	3.09	2.87	3.09	3.90	5.17	4.55	44.34
MD	Baltimore	3.05	3.12	3.38	3.09	3.72	3.67	3.69	3.92	3.41	2.98	3.32	3.41	40.76
MA	Boston	3.59	3.62	3.69	3.60	3.25	3.09	2.84	3.24	3.06	3.30	4.22	4.01	41.51
MI	Detroit	1.76	1.74	2.55	2.95	2.92	3.61	3.18	3.43	2.89	2.10	2.67	2.82	32.62
	Sault Ste. Marie	2.42	1.74	2.30	2.35	2.71	3.14	2.71	3.61	3.69	3.23	3.45	2.88	34.23
MN	Duluth	1.22	0.80	1.91	2.25	3.03	3.82	3.61	3.99	3.84	2.49	1.80	1.24	30.00
	Minneapolis-St. Paul	0.95	0.88	1.94	2.42	3.39	4.05	3.53	3.62	2.72	2.19	1.55	1.08	28.32
MS	Jackson	5.24	4.70	5.82	5.57	5.05	3.18	4.51	3.77	3.55	3.26	4.81	5.91	55.37
MO	Kansas City	1.09	1.10	2.51	3.12	5.04	4.72	4.38	4.01	4.86	3.29	1.92	1.58	37.62
	St. Louis	1.81	2.12	3.58	3.50	3.97	3.72	3.85	2.85	3.12	2.68	3.28	3.03	37.51
MT	Great Falls	0.91	0.57	1.10	1.41	2.52	2.39	1.24	1.54	1.24	0.78	0.66	0.85	15.21
NE	Omaha	0.74	0.77	2.04	2.66	4.52	3.87	3.51	3.24	3.72	2.28	1.49	1.02	29.86
NV	Reno	1.07	0.99	0.71	0.38	0.69	0.46	0.28	0.32	0.39	0.38	0.87	0.99	7.53
NH	Concord	2.51	2.53	2.72	2.91	3.14	3.15	3.23	3.32	2.81	3.23	3.66	3.16	36.37
NJ	Atlantic City	3.46	3.06	3.62	3.58	3.33	2.64	3.83	4.14	2.93	2.82	3.58	3.32	40.29
NM	Albuquerque	0.44	0.46	0.54	0.52	0.50	0.59	1.37	1.64	1.00	0.89	0.43	0.50	8.88
NY	Albany	2.36	2.27	2.93	2.99	3.41	3.62	3.18	3.47	2.95	2.83	3.23	2.93	36.17
	Buffalo	2.70	2.31	2.68	2.87	3.14	3.55	3.08	4.17	3.49	3.09	3.83	3.67	38.58
	New York [1]	3.42	3.27	4.08	4.20	4.42	3.67	4.35	4.01	3.89	3.56	4.47	3.91	47.25
NC	Charlotte	3.71	3.84	4.43	2.68	3.82	3.39	3.92	3.73	3.50	3.36	3.23	3.48	43.09
	Raleigh	3.48	3.69	3.77	2.59	3.92	3.68	4.01	4.02	3.19	2.86	2.98	3.24	41.43
ND	Bismarck	0.45	0.43	0.77	1.67	2.18	2.72	2.14	1.72	1.49	0.90	0.49	0.51	15.47
OH	Cincinnati	2.59	2.69	4.24	3.75	4.28	3.84	4.24	3.35	2.88	2.86	3.46	3.15	41.33
	Cleveland	2.04	2.19	2.91	3.14	3.49	3.70	3.52	3.40	3.44	2.54	3.17	3.09	36.63
	Columbus	2.18	2.24	3.27	3.21	3.93	4.04	4.31	3.72	2.96	2.15	3.22	2.86	38.09
OK	Oklahoma City	1.13	1.56	2.71	2.77	5.22	4.31	2.61	2.60	3.84	3.23	1.98	1.40	33.36
OR	Portland	5.35	3.85	3.56	2.39	2.06	1.48	0.63	1.09	1.75	2.67	5.34	6.13	36.30
PA	Philadelphia	3.21	2.79	3.46	3.62	3.75	3.74	4.28	3.80	3.42	2.62	3.34	3.38	41.41
	Pittsburgh	2.54	2.39	3.41	3.15	3.59	3.71	3.75	3.21	2.97	2.36	2.86	2.92	36.85
RI	Providence	3.88	3.61	4.06	4.11	3.76	3.33	3.18	3.63	3.48	3.69	4.43	4.38	45.53
SC	Columbia	4.42	4.12	4.82	3.28	3.68	4.80	5.50	6.09	3.67	3.04	2.90	3.59	49.91
SD	Sioux Falls	0.51	0.64	1.64	2.52	3.03	3.40	2.68	2.85	3.02	1.78	1.09	0.70	23.86
TN	Memphis	3.73	4.35	5.41	5.46	4.98	3.57	3.79	3.43	3.53	3.01	5.10	5.74	52.10
	Nashville	3.58	3.81	4.85	4.37	4.88	3.57	3.97	3.46	3.46	2.62	4.12	4.61	47.30
TX	Dallas-Fort Worth	1.83	2.18	2.77	3.50	4.88	2.98	2.31	2.21	3.39	3.52	2.29	1.84	33.70
	El Paso	0.40	0.41	0.29	0.20	0.25	0.67	1.54	1.58	1.70	0.76	0.44	0.57	8.81
	Houston	3.29	2.96	2.92	3.21	5.24	4.96	3.60	3.49	4.89	4.27	3.79	3.45	46.07
UT	Salt Lake City	1.11	1.23	1.91	2.12	1.80	0.93	0.81	0.86	1.28	1.44	1.29	1.40	16.18
VT	Burlington	1.82	1.63	2.23	2.76	3.12	3.47	3.65	4.06	3.30	2.88	3.13	2.42	34.47
VA	Norfolk	3.78	3.47	3.70	3.06	3.81	3.82	5.06	4.81	3.90	3.15	2.85	3.23	44.64
	Richmond	3.24	3.16	3.61	2.96	3.84	3.62	5.03	4.40	3.34	3.53	3.17	3.26	43.16
WA	Seattle-Tacoma	5.38	3.99	3.54	2.33	1.70	1.50	0.76	1.14	1.88	3.23	5.83	5.91	37.19
	Spokane	1.98	1.49	1.49	1.18	1.41	1.26	0.67	0.72	0.73	0.99	2.15	2.42	16.49
WV	Charleston	2.91	3.04	3.63	3.31	3.94	3.59	4.99	4.01	3.24	2.89	3.59	3.39	42.53
WI	Milwaukee	1.60	1.45	2.67	3.50	2.84	3.24	3.47	3.53	3.38	2.41	2.51	2.33	32.93
WY	Cheyenne	0.40	0.39	1.03	1.37	2.39	2.06	2.09	1.69	1.27	0.74	0.53	0.42	14.40
PR	San Juan	2.81	2.15	2.35	3.76	5.93	4.00	4.37	5.32	5.28	5.71	5.94	4.72	52.34

[1] City office data.

Source: U.S. National Oceanic and Atmospheric Administration, *Climatography of the United States*, No. 81.

No. 398. Average Number of Days With Precipitation of .01 Inch or More—Selected Cities

[Airport data, except as noted. For period of record through 1996, except as noted]

STATE	STATION	Length of record (yr.)	Jan.	Feb.	Mar.	Apr.	May	June	July	Aug.	Sept.	Oct.	Nov.	Dec.	Annual
AL	Mobile	54	11	10	10	7	9	11	16	14	10	6	8	10	122
AK	Juneau	51	18	17	18	17	17	15	17	17	20	24	20	21	222
AZ	Phoenix	56	4	4	4	2	1	1	4	5	3	3	3	4	36
AR	Little Rock	53	10	9	10	10	10	8	8	7	7	7	8	9	105
CA	Los Angeles	60	6	6	6	3	1	1	1	(Z)	1	2	3	5	35
	Sacramento	56	10	9	9	5	3	1	(Z)	(Z)	1	3	7	9	58
	San Diego	55	7	6	7	4	2	1	(Z)	1	1	2	4	6	42
	San Francisco	68	11	10	10	6	3	1	(Z)	(Z)	1	4	7	10	62
CO	Denver	61	6	6	9	9	11	9	9	9	6	5	6	5	89
CT	Hartford	41	11	10	12	11	12	11	10	10	9	9	11	12	127
DE	Wilmington	48	11	9	11	11	11	10	9	9	8	8	9	10	116
DC	Washington	54	10	9	11	10	11	9	10	9	8	7	9	9	112
FL	Jacksonville	54	8	8	8	6	8	12	15	14	13	9	7	8	116
	Miami	53	7	6	6	6	10	15	16	17	17	14	9	6	130
GA	Atlanta	61	11	10	11	9	9	10	12	10	8	7	9	10	115
HI	Honolulu	46	9	9	9	9	7	6	7	6	7	9	9	10	98
ID	Boise	56	12	10	10	8	8	6	2	3	4	6	10	11	90
IL	Chicago	37	11	9	12	13	11	10	10	9	9	9	11	11	126
	Peoria	56	9	8	11	12	11	10	9	8	9	8	9	10	114
IN	Indianapolis	56	12	10	13	12	12	10	10	9	8	8	11	12	126
IA	Des Moines	56	8	7	10	11	11	11	9	9	9	8	7	8	106
KS	Wichita	42	6	5	8	8	11	9	8	8	8	6	5	6	86
KY	Louisville	48	11	11	13	12	12	10	10	8	8	8	10	11	124
LA	New Orleans	47	10	9	9	7	8	11	14	13	10	6	7	10	114
ME	Portland	55	11	10	11	12	12	11	10	9	9	9	12	12	129
MD	Baltimore	45	11	9	11	11	11	9	9	9	8	8	9	9	114
MA	Boston	44	12	11	12	11	11	11	9	10	9	9	11	12	127
MI	Detroit	37	13	11	13	13	11	10	10	10	10	10	12	14	136
	Sault Ste. Marie	54	19	15	13	11	11	11	10	11	13	14	17	19	166
MN	Duluth	54	12	10	11	11	12	13	11	11	12	10	11	12	135
	Minneapolis-St. Paul	57	9	7	10	10	11	12	10	10	10	8	8	9	115
MS	Jackson	32	11	9	10	8	9	8	10	10	8	7	8	10	109
MO	Kansas City	23	7	7	10	11	12	10	9	9	8	7	8	8	106
	St. Louis	38	9	8	11	11	11	9	9	8	8	8	9	9	111
MT	Great Falls	58	9	8	9	9	12	12	8	8	7	6	7	8	101
NE	Omaha	59	6	7	9	10	12	11	9	9	8	6	6	7	99
NV	Reno	53	6	6	6	4	4	3	2	2	2	3	5	6	51
NH	Concord	54	11	10	11	12	12	11	10	10	9	9	11	11	126
NJ	Atlantic City	52	11	10	11	11	10	9	9	9	8	7	9	10	112
NM	Albuquerque	56	4	4	5	3	5	4	9	10	6	5	3	4	61
NY	Albany	49	12	11	12	12	13	11	10	10	10	9	12	12	134
	Buffalo	52	20	17	16	14	12	10	10	10	11	12	16	19	169
	New York [1]	126	11	10	11	11	11	10	11	10	8	8	9	10	121
NC	Charlotte	56	10	10	11	9	10	10	11	10	7	7	8	10	111
	Raleigh	51	10	10	10	9	10	9	11	10	8	7	8	9	112
ND	Bismarck	56	8	7	8	8	10	11	9	8	7	6	6	8	96
OH	Cincinnati	48	12	11	13	13	12	11	10	9	8	8	11	12	130
	Cleveland	54	16	14	15	14	13	11	10	10	10	11	14	16	155
	Columbus	56	13	11	14	13	13	11	11	9	8	9	12	13	137
OK	Oklahoma City	56	6	6	7	8	10	9	6	6	7	6	5	6	83
OR	Portland	55	18	16	17	14	12	9	4	5	7	12	18	19	151
PA	Philadelphia	55	11	9	11	11	11	10	9	9	8	8	9	10	116
	Pittsburgh	43	16	14	16	14	13	12	11	10	10	10	13	16	153
RI	Providence	42	11	10	12	11	11	11	9	9	8	9	11	12	124
SC	Columbia	48	10	10	10	8	9	10	12	11	8	6	7	9	110
SD	Sioux Falls	50	6	7	9	10	11	11	10	9	8	6	6	6	98
TN	Memphis	45	10	9	11	10	10	9	9	7	7	6	9	10	107
	Nashville	54	11	11	12	11	11	9	10	9	8	7	9	11	119
TX	Dallas-Fort Worth	42	7	7	7	8	9	6	5	5	7	6	6	7	79
	El Paso	56	4	3	2	2	2	3	8	8	5	4	3	4	49
	Houston	26	11	9	9	7	9	9	9	9	9	7	8	9	106
UT	Salt Lake City	67	10	9	10	10	8	5	5	6	5	6	8	9	91
VT	Burlington	52	14	12	13	12	14	12	12	13	12	12	14	15	154
VA	Norfolk	47	11	10	11	10	10	9	11	10	8	8	8	9	115
	Richmond	58	10	9	11	9	11	9	11	10	8	7	8	9	113
WA	Seattle-Tacoma	51	18	16	17	14	10	9	5	6	9	13	18	19	154
	Spokane	48	14	11	11	9	9	8	5	5	6	7	13	15	112
WV	Charleston	48	15	14	15	14	13	11	13	11	10	10	12	14	151
WI	Milwaukee	55	11	10	12	12	11	11	10	9	9	9	11	11	125
WY	Cheyenne	60	6	6	9	10	12	11	11	10	8	6	6	6	101
PR	San Juan	40	17	13	12	13	16	15	19	18	17	17	18	19	196

Z Less than 1/2 day. [1] City office data.

Source: U.S. National Oceanic and Atmospheric Administration, *Comparative Climatic Data*, annual.

No. 399. Snow and Ice Pellets—Selected Cities

[In inches. Airport data, except as noted. For period of record through 1995. T denotes trace]

STATE	STATION	Length of record (yr)	Jan.	Feb.	Mar.	Apr.	May	June	July	Aug.	Sept.	Oct.	Nov.	Dec.	Annual
AL	Mobile	54	0.1	0.1	0.1	T	T	-	T	-	-	-	T	0.1	0.4
AK	Juneau	51	26.3	19.1	15.3	3.4	-	T	-	-	T	1	12.9	22.7	100.7
AZ	Phoenix	58	T	-	T	T	T	-	-	-	-	T	-	-	T
AR	Little Rock	53	2.4	1.4	0.5	T	-	-	-	-	-	T	0.2	0.6	5.1
CA	Los Angeles	60	T	T	T	-	-	-	-	-	-	-	-	T	T
	Sacramento	47	T	-	T	-	T	-	-	-	-	-	-	T	T
	San Diego	55	T	-	T	-	-	-	-	-	-	-	T	T	T
	San Francisco	68	-	T	T	-	-	-	-	-	-	-	-	-	T
CO	Denver	61	8.1	7.5	12.5	8.9	1.6	-	T	T	1.6	3.7	9.1	7.3	60.3
CT	Hartford	41	12.3	11.8	9.8	1.5	-	T	-	-	-	0.1	2.1	10.3	47.9
DE	Wilmington	48	6.4	6.1	3.3	0.2	T	T	T	-	-	0.1	0.9	3.3	20.3
DC	Washington	52	5.3	5.2	2.1	-	T	-	T	T	-	-	0.8	3	16.4
FL	Jacksonville	54	T	-	-	-	-	-	T	-	-	-	-	-	T
	Miami	53	-	-	-	-	-	-	-	-	-	-	-	-	-
GA	Atlanta	61	0.9	0.5	0.4	T	-	-	-	-	-	T	-	0.2	2.0
HI	Honolulu	49	-	-	-	-	-	-	-	-	-	-	-	-	-
ID	Boise	56	6.6	3.6	1.6	0.6	0.1	T	T	T	-	0.1	2.3	5.6	20.7
IL	Chicago	37	10.8	8.4	6.7	1.6	0.1	T	T	T	T	0.4	1.9	8.3	38.2
	Peoria	52	6.6	5.5	4.0	0.8	-	-	T	-	T	0.1	2.0	5.8	24.6
IN	Indianapolis	64	6.3	5.8	3.3	0.5	-	T	-	T	-	0.2	1.8	5.0	22.9
IA	Des Moines	56	8.1	7.2	6.1	1.8	-	T	T	-	T	0.3	3.1	6.7	33.3
KS	Wichita	42	4.4	4.2	2.5	0.2	T	T	T	T	T	-	1.2	3.2	15.7
KY	Louisville	48	5.2	4.4	3.2	0.1	T	T	T	-	-	0.1	1	2.1	16.1
LA	New Orleans	49	-	0.1	T	T	T	-	-	-	-	-	T	0.1	0.2
ME	Portland	55	19.3	17.3	12.8	3.0	0.2	-	-	-	T	0.2	3.0	15.0	70.8
MD	Baltimore	45	5.7	6.5	3.7	0.1	T	-	T	-	-	-	1.0	3.4	20.4
MA	Boston	60	12.3	11.7	7.9	0.9	-	-	-	T	-	-	1.3	7.6	41.7
MI	Detroit	37	10.5	9.2	6.8	1.7	T	-	-	-	T	0.2	2.9	10.0	41.3
	Sault Ste. Marie	54	28.7	18.4	14.8	5.7	0.5	T	T	T	0.1	2.4	15.7	30.8	117.1
MN	Duluth	52	17.1	11.3	13.4	6.7	0.7	-	T	T	0.1	1.5	12.7	15.4	78.9
	Minneapolis-St. Paul	57	9.9	8.4	10.5	2.8	0.1	T	T	T	-	0.5	7.9	9.4	49.5
MS	Jackson	32	0.5	0.2	0.2	-	-	-	-	-	-	-	-	-	0.9
MO	Kansas City	61	5.6	4.5	3.5	0.8	T	T	T	-	T	-	1.1	4.4	19.9
	St. Louis	59	5.2	4.6	4.1	0.4	-	T	-	-	-	T	1.4	3.8	19.5
MT	Great Falls	56	9.6	8.3	10.3	7.3	1.7	0.3	T	0.1	1.5	3.4	7.5	8.4	58.4
NE	Omaha	60	7.3	6.6	6.3	1	0.1	T	T	-	T	0.3	2.6	5.6	29.8
NV	Reno	53	5.9	5.2	4.3	1.2	0.8	-	-	-	-	0.3	2.4	4.3	24.4
NH	Concord	54	17.9	14.6	11.0	2.3	0.1	T	-	-	T	0.1	3.9	13.6	63.5
NJ	Atlantic City	51	5.0	5.3	2.5	0.3	T	T	T	-	-	T	0.4	2.2	15.7
NM	Albuquerque	56	2.5	2.1	1.8	0.6	-	T	T	T	T	0.1	1.2	2.5	10.8
NY	Albany	49	16.3	14.4	11.1	2.6	0.1	T	T	-	T	0.2	4.2	14.9	63.6
	Buffalo	52	23.5	18.6	11.5	3.2	0.2	T	T	T	T	0.3	11.3	23.2	91.8
	New York [1]	127	7.5	8.6	5.0	0.9	T	-	T	-	-	-	0.9	5.4	28.3
NC	Charlotte	56	2.0	1.6	1.2	-	T	-	-	-	-	T	0.1	0.5	5.4
	Raleigh	51	2.2	2.5	1.3	-	T	-	T	-	-	-	0.1	0.8	6.9
ND	Bismarck	56	7.4	6.8	8.4	3.8	0.9	T	T	T	0.2	1.7	6.5	7.0	42.7
OH	Cincinnati	48	7.0	5.5	4.3	0.5	-	T	T	-	-	0.3	2.0	3.8	23.4
	Cleveland	54	13.0	12.3	10.4	2.3	0.1	T	T	-	T	0.6	5.0	12.0	56.7
	Columbus	48	8.5	6.2	4.5	0.9	-	T	T	-	T	0.1	2.2	5.5	27.9
OK	Oklahoma City	56	3.0	2.4	1.5	-	T	T	-	-	T	-	0.5	1.8	9.2
OR	Portland	55	3.2	1.1	0.4	T	-	T	-	T	T	-	0.4	1.4	6.5
PA	Philadelphia	53	6.2	6.6	3.7	0.3	T	T	-	-	-	-	0.7	3.3	20.8
	Pittsburgh	43	11.6	9.3	8.7	1.7	0.1	T	T	T	T	0.4	3.5	8.2	43.5
RI	Providence	42	9.5	10.0	7.5	0.7	0.2	-	-	-	-	0.1	1.1	6.8	35.9
SC	Columbia	48	0.4	0.8	0.2	T	-	-	-	T	-	-	T	0.3	1.7
SD	Sioux Falls	50	6.5	8.1	9.4	2.7	-	T	T	-	-	0.8	5.5	7.1	40.1
TN	Memphis	45	2.2	1.4	0.8	T	T	T	-	-	-	T	0.1	0.6	5.1
	Nashville	54	3.7	3.0	1.4	-	-	T	-	T	-	-	0.4	1.4	9.9
TX	Dallas-Fort Worth	42	1.1	0.9	0.2	T	T	-	-	-	-	T	0.1	0.2	2.5
	El Paso	56	1.3	0.8	0.4	0.3	T	T	T	-	T	-	0.9	1.6	5.3
	Houston	61	0.2	0.2	0.0	T	T	T	-	-	-	-	T	-	0.4
UT	Salt Lake City	67	13.4	9.5	9.3	4.9	0.6	T	T	T	0.1	1.2	6.9	11.8	57.7
VT	Burlington	52	19.0	17.0	12.7	3.9	0.2	-	T	-	-	0.2	6.6	18.4	78.0
VA	Norfolk	47	2.7	2.8	1.0	-	T	T	-	T	-	-	-	0.9	7.4
	Richmond	58	4.8	4.0	2.4	0.1	T	-	-	-	-	T	0.4	2.0	13.7
WA	Seattle-Tacoma	51	4.8	1.6	1.3	0.1	T	-	T	-	T	-	1.1	2.4	11.3
	Spokane	46	15.6	7.6	3.9	0.6	0.1	T	-	-	T	0.4	6.4	14.9	49.5
WV	Charleston	46	10.6	8.6	5.1	0.9	-	T	T	T	T	0.2	2.4	5.3	33.1
WI	Milwaukee	55	13.1	10.0	8.6	1.7	0.1	T	T	T	T	0.2	3.2	10.3	47.2
WY	Cheyenne	60	6.5	6.4	11.9	9.0	3.3	0.2	-	-	0.9	3.7	7.3	6.2	55.4
PR	San Juan	40	-	-	-	-	-	-	-	-	-	-	-	-	-

- Represents zero or rounds to zero. [1] City office data.

Source: U.S. National Oceanic and Atmospheric Administration, *Comparative Climatic Data*, annual.

No. 400. Sunshine, Average Wind Speed, Heating and Cooling Degree Days, and Average Relative Humidity—Selected Cities

[Airport data, except as noted. For period of record through 1994, except as noted. M=morning. A=afternoon]

STATE	STATION	AVERAGE PERCENTAGE OF POSSIBLE SUNSHINE[1]		AVERAGE WIND SPEED (m.p.h.)				Heating degree days	Cooling degree days	AVERAGE RELATIVE HUMIDITY (percent)						
		Length of record (yr.)	Annual	Length of record (yr.)	Annual	Jan.	July			Length of record (yr.)	Annual M	Annual A	Jan. M	Jan. A	July M	July A
AL	Mobile	46	60	46	8.9	10.3	6.9	1,702	2,627	32	87	57	82	61	90	60
AK	Juneau	44	23	49	8.3	8.2	7.5	8,897	-	28	84	73	81	78	83	70
AZ	Phoenix	57	81	49	6.2	5.3	7.1	1,350	4,162	34	51	23	66	32	44	20
AR	Little Rock	35	60	52	7.8	8.4	6.7	3,155	2,005	34	84	58	80	62	88	56
CA	Los Angeles	59	72	46	7.5	6.7	7.9	1,458	727	35	79	64	70	59	86	68
	Sacramento	46	73	44	7.9	7.2	9.0	2,749	1,237	34	83	46	90	70	77	28
	San Diego	54	72	54	7.0	6.9	7.5	1,256	984	34	77	62	71	56	82	66
	San Francisco	67	72	67	10.6	7.2	13.6	3,016	145	36	84	62	86	66	86	59
CO	Denver	60	67	46	8.6	8.6	8.3	6,020	679	34	68	40	64	49	69	34
CT	Hartford	40	52	40	8.5	9.0	7.3	6,151	677	35	77	52	71	56	79	51
DE	Wilmington	47	55	46	9.0	9.8	7.8	4,937	1,046	47	78	55	75	60	79	54
DC	Washington	46	55	46	9.4	10.0	8.3	4,047	1,549	34	74	53	70	55	76	53
FL	Jacksonville	46	61	45	7.9	8.2	7.0	1,434	2,551	58	88	56	87	58	88	58
	Miami	45	68	45	9.3	9.6	8.0	200	4,198	30	84	61	84	59	84	63
GA	Atlanta	60	59	56	9.1	10.4	7.6	2,991	1,667	34	82	56	78	59	88	60
HI	Honolulu	45	74	45	11.3	9.5	13.1	-	4,474	25	72	56	81	61	67	51
ID	Boise	55	58	55	8.7	8.0	8.4	5,861	754	55	69	43	81	71	54	21
IL	Chicago	36	52	36	10.4	11.7	8.3	6,536	752	36	80	60	77	68	82	57
	Peoria	51	53	51	10.0	11.1	7.8	6,148	982	35	83	62	79	69	87	59
IN	Indianapolis	63	51	46	9.6	10.9	7.5	5,615	1,014	35	84	62	81	70	87	60
IA	Des Moines	45	55	45	10.7	11.5	8.9	6,497	1,036	33	80	60	76	67	82	58
KS	Wichita	39	62	41	12.3	12.1	11.4	4,791	1,628	41	80	56	79	63	79	49
KY	Louisville	47	53	47	8.3	9.5	6.8	4,514	1,288	34	81	58	77	64	85	58
LA	New Orleans	46	60	46	8.2	9.3	6.1	1,513	2,655	46	88	63	85	66	91	66
ME	Portland	54	55	54	8.8	9.1	7.6	7,378	268	54	79	59	76	60	80	59
MD	Baltimore	44	58	44	9.1	9.7	7.9	4,707	1,137	41	77	54	72	57	80	53
MA	Boston	59	55	37	12.5	13.8	10.9	5,641	678	30	72	58	67	57	74	56
MI	Detroit	36	50	36	10.4	12.0	8.6	6,569	626	36	81	60	80	69	82	54
	Sault Ste. Marie	53	43	53	9.2	9.7	7.8	9,316	131	53	85	67	81	74	89	62
MN	Duluth	46	49	45	11.0	11.6	9.4	9,818	180	33	81	63	77	70	85	59
	Minneapolis-St. Paul	56	54	56	10.5	10.5	9.4	7,981	682	35	79	60	74	67	81	54
MS	Jackson	30	59	31	7.3	8.4	5.8	2,467	2,215	31	91	58	87	65	94	60
MO	Kansas City	22	59	22	10.8	11.4	9.4	5,393	1,288	22	81	60	77	64	85	58
	St. Louis	46	55	45	9.7	10.6	8.0	4,758	1,534	34	83	59	81	66	84	56
MT	Great Falls	57	51	53	12.7	15.2	10.0	7,741	388	33	67	45	67	61	67	30
NE	Omaha	49	59	58	10.5	10.9	8.9	6,300	1,072	30	82	59	78	65	85	58
NV	Reno	52	69	52	6.6	5.6	7.1	5,674	508	31	70	31	79	50	62	18
NH	Concord	53	55	52	6.8	7.3	5.7	7,554	328	29	81	54	75	58	84	51
NJ	Atlantic City	36	56	36	9.9	10.9	8.4	5,169	826	30	82	56	78	58	83	57
NM	Albuquerque	55	76	55	8.9	8.0	9.0	4,425	1,244	34	60	29	70	40	60	27
NY	Albany	56	49	56	8.9	9.8	7.5	6,894	507	29	80	57	77	63	81	55
	Buffalo	51	43	55	11.9	14.2	10.3	6,747	477	34	80	62	79	72	78	55
	New York[3]	42	64	58	9.4	10.7	7.6	4,805	1,096	61	72	56	68	60	75	55
NC	Charlotte	46	58	45	7.4	7.8	6.6	3,341	1,582	34	82	53	78	55	86	56
	Raleigh	46	59	45	7.8	8.5	6.7	3,457	1,417	30	85	54	79	55	89	58
ND	Bismarck	55	55	55	10.2	10.0	9.2	8,968	488	35	80	57	75	69	84	47
OH	Cincinnati	43	49	47	9.0	10.6	7.2	5,248	996	32	82	60	79	68	85	57
	Cleveland	53	45	53	10.5	12.2	8.6	6,201	621	34	79	62	78	69	81	57
	Columbus	45	48	45	8.3	9.9	6.6	5,708	797	35	80	59	77	67	84	56
OK	Oklahoma City	44	64	46	12.3	12.6	10.9	3,659	1,859	29	80	55	78	59	80	50
OR	Portland	46	39	46	7.9	9.9	7.6	4,522	371	54	86	59	86	75	82	45
PA	Philadelphia	54	56	54	9.5	10.3	8.2	4,954	1,101	36	76	55	73	59	79	54
	Pittsburgh	42	44	42	9.1	10.6	7.3	5,968	654	34	79	58	76	66	83	54
RI	Providence	41	55	41	10.5	11.1	9.4	5,884	606	31	75	55	71	56	77	56
SC	Columbia	47	60	46	6.9	7.2	6.3	2,649	1,966	28	87	51	82	54	89	54
SD	Sioux Falls	49	57	46	11.1	11.0	9.8	7,809	744	31	82	60	77	68	83	54
TN	Memphis	42	59	46	8.9	10.0	7.5	3,082	2,118	55	81	57	78	63	84	57
	Nashville	53	57	53	8.0	9.1	6.5	3,729	1,616	29	84	57	80	63	89	57
TX	Dallas-Fort Worth	41	64	41	10.7	10.9	9.8	2,407	2,603	31	82	56	80	61	81	49
	El Paso	52	80	52	8.8	8.3	8.3	2,708	2,094	34	57	28	66	35	62	29
	Houston	25	56	25	7.9	8.2	7.0	1,599	2,700	25	90	60	86	64	93	57
UT	Salt Lake City	66	62	65	8.8	7.5	9.5	5,765	1,047	35	67	43	79	69	52	22
VT	Burlington	51	44	51	9.0	9.8	8.0	7,771	388	29	77	59	72	64	79	53
VA	Norfolk	46	58	46	10.6	11.5	8.9	3,495	1,422	46	78	57	75	59	81	59
	Richmond	49	56	46	7.7	8.1	6.9	3,963	1,348	60	83	53	80	57	85	56
WA	Seattle-Tacoma[2]	50	38	46	9.0	9.6	8.3	4,908	190	35	83	62	82	74	82	49
	Spokane	47	47	47	8.9	8.8	8.6	6,842	398	35	78	52	86	79	65	28
WV	Charleston	47	48	47	6.2	7.4	4.9	4,646	1,031	47	83	56	77	63	90	59
WI	Milwaukee	54	52	54	11.5	12.6	9.7	7,324	479	34	80	64	76	68	82	61
WY	Cheyenne	59	64	37	12.9	15.3	10.4	7,326	285	35	65	44	58	50	70	38
PR	San Juan	39	76	39	8.4	8.5	9.7	-	5,558	39	79	65	82	64	79	67

- Represents zero. [1] Percent of days that are either clear or partly cloudy. [2] Does not represent airport data.

Source: U.S. National Oceanic and Atmospheric Administration, *Comparative Climatic Data*, annual.

Figure 7.1
Participation in Sports Activities: 1995

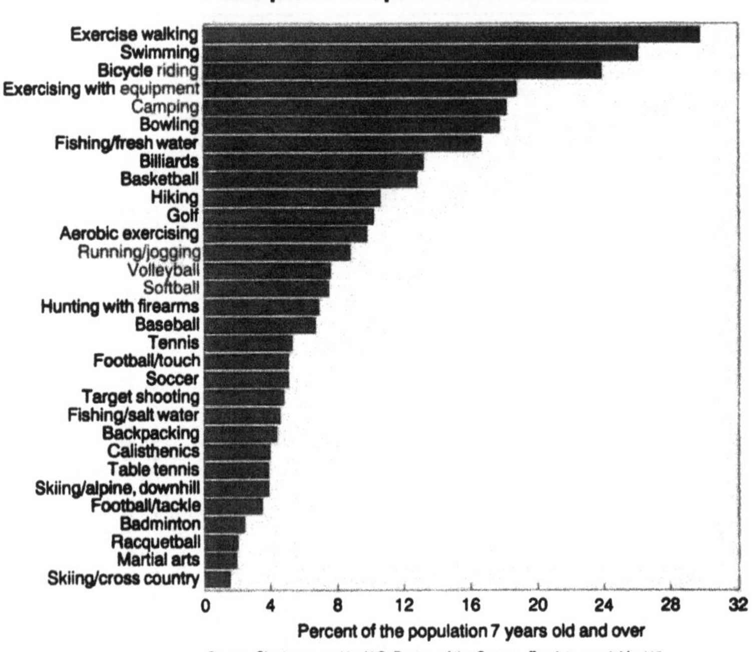

Source: Chart prepared by U.S. Bureau of the Census. For data, see table 419.

Figure 7.2
Attendance for Various Activities: 1992

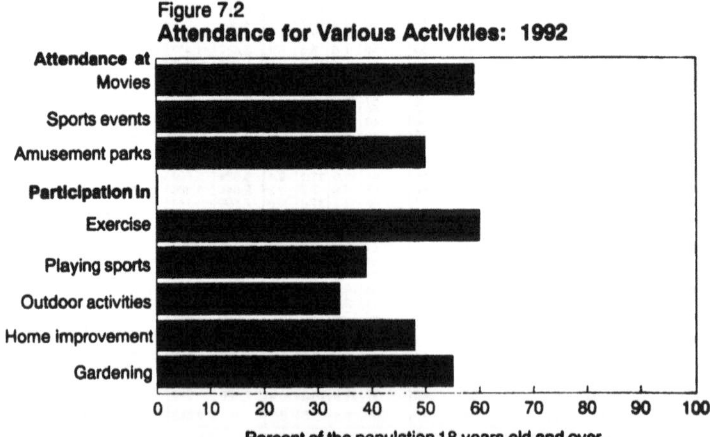

Source: Chart prepared by U.S. Bureau of the Census. For data, see table 416.

Parks, Recreation, and Travel

This section presents data on national parks and forests, State parks, recreational activities, the arts and humanities, and domestic and foreign travel.

Parks and recreation—The Department of the Interior has responsibility for administering the national parks. As part of this function, it issues reports relating to the usage of public parks for recreation purposes. The National Park Service publishes information on visits to national park areas in its annual report, *National Park Statistical Abstract. The National Parks: Index (year)* is a biannual report which has appeared under a variety of *Index* titles prior to 1985. Beginning with the 1985 edition, the report has appeared under the current title. The *Index* contains brief descriptions, with acreages, of each area administered by the Service, plus certain "related" areas. A statistical summary of service-administered areas is also presented. The annual *Federal Recreation Fee Report* summarizes the prior year's recreation fee receipts and recreation visitation statistics for seven Federal land managing agencies.

Statistics for State parks are compiled by the National Association of State Park Directors which issues its annual *Information Exchange*. The Bureau of Land Management, in its *Public Land Statistics*, also issues data on recreational use of its lands. The Department of Agriculture's Forest Service, in its *Report of the Forest Service*, issues data on recreational uses of the national forests.

Visitation—Data on visitation to reporting areas are collected by several different agencies and groups. The methodology used to collect these results may vary accordingly, from visual counts and estimates to the use of electromagnetic traffic counters. In using and comparing these data, one should also be aware of several different definitions that follow: Recreation visit, which is the entry of any person into an area for recreation purposes; nonrecreation visits, which include visits going to and from inholdings, through traffic, tradespeople and personnel with business in the area; and visitor hour, which constitutes the presence of a person in a recreation area or site for recreational purposes for periods of time aggregating 60 minutes.

In Brief

Persons who golf:	
1975	*13 million*
1995	*25 million*
Expenditures for sound recordings:	
1990	*$7.5 billion*
1996	*$12.5 billion*

Recreation and leisure activities—Statistics on the participation in various recreation and leisure time activities are based on several sample surveys. Data on participation in fishing, hunting, and other forms of wildlife-associated recreation are published periodically by the U.S. Department of Interior, Fish and Wildlife Service. The most recent data are from the 1991 survey. Data on participation in various sports recreation activities are published by the National Sporting Goods Association.

Travel—Information on foreign travel and personal expenditures abroad, as well as expenditures by foreign citizens traveling in the United States, is compiled annually by the U.S. Bureau of Economic Analysis and published in selected issues of the monthly *Survey of Current Business.* Statistics on arrivals to the United States had been reported by the U.S. Travel and Tourism Administration (USTTA), in cooperation with the U.S. Immigration and Naturalization Service, and are published in *Summary and Analysis of International Travel to the United States.* Sources of statistics on departures from the United States included USTTA's in-flight survey, the Department of Transportation's *International Air Travel Statistics*, and other sources. Data on domestic travel, business receipts and employment of the travel industry, and travel expenditures are published by the U.S. Travel Data Center, the national nonprofit center for travel and tourism research which is located in Washington, DC. Other data on household transportation characteristics may be found in section 21.

No. 401. Visitation to Federal Recreation Areas: 1980 to 1992

[In millions of visitor hours. For years ending September 30. Covers persons entering and using a recreation area over a specified period of time. For definition of visitor hour, see text, section 7]

ADMINISTERING FEDERAL AGENCY	1980	1985	1986	1987	1988	1989	1990	1991	1992
All areas	6,367	6,403	6,858	7,332	7,419	7,475	7,567	7,829	7,995
Fish and Wildlife Service	17	65	67	72	81	45	(NA)	(NA)	(NA)
Forest Service	2,819	2,705	2,718	2,861	2,908	3,030	3,157	3,346	3,462
U.S. Army Corps of Engineers [1]	1,926	1,721	2,068	2,176	2,290	2,296	2,280	2,306	2,306
National Park Service	1,042	1,298	1,348	1,394	1,376	1,315	1,322	1,344	1,390
Bureau of Land Management [2]	68	246	284	515	461	493	518	540	563
Bureau of Reclamation	407	289	296	306	294	286	280	280	269
Tennessee Valley Authority [3]	87	79	77	8	9	10	10	13	14

NA Not available. [1] Beginning 1986, not comparable with previous years. [2] Data not comparable for all years. [3] Beginning in 1989, the TVA discontinued reporting visitation to nonfee charging areas. Data for 1987 and 1988 have been adjusted to reflect this policy.

Source: 1980, U.S. Heritage Conservation and Recreation Service, *Federal Recreation Fee Report*, annual; thereafter, U.S. National Park Service, unpublished data.

No. 402. National Park System—Summary: 1985 to 1995

[For fiscal years ending in year shown, except as noted; see text, section 10. Includes data for five areas in Puerto Rico and Virgin Islands, one area in American Samoa, and one area in Guam]

ITEM	1985	1989	1990	1991	1992	1993	1994	1995
Finances (mil. dol.): [1]								
Expenditures reported	848.1	1,036.8	986.1	1,104.4	1,268.7	1,429.4	1,404.0	1,445.0
Salaries and wages	369.4	441.4	459.1	495.3	518.1	596.1	627.2	633.0
Improvements, maintenance	127.4	197.5	160.0	179.6	212.1	224.8	222.9	234.0
Construction	84.7	85.2	108.5	134.1	193.3	228.8	205.6	192.0
Other	266.6	312.7	258.5	295.4	345.2	379.7	348.3	386.0
Funds available	1,248.2	1,440.0	1,505.5	1,988.4	2,274.8	2,346.5	2,307.7	2,225.0
Appropriations	821.6	996.7	1,052.5	1,284.7	1,392.8	1,334.0	1,388.8	1,325.0
Other [2]	426.6	443.3	453.0	703.7	882.0	1,012.5	918.9	900.0
Revenue from operations	50.6	86.3	78.6	78.1	88.3	89.5	97.0	106.3
Recreation visits (millions): [3]								
All areas	263.4	269.4	258.7	267.8	274.7	273.1	268.6	269.6
National parks [4]	50.0	57.4	57.7	57.4	58.7	59.8	63.0	64.8
National monuments	15.9	23.7	23.9	25.8	26.6	26.5	23.6	23.5
National historical, commemorative, archaeological [5]	61.9	63.9	57.5	61.0	63.3	61.9	59.5	56.9
National parkways	40.0	31.2	29.1	28.8	30.7	30.4	29.3	31.3
National recreation areas [4]	49.4	49.6	47.2	49.8	50.3	50.8	52.3	53.7
National seashores and lakeshores	25.3	21.9	23.3	24.4	23.9	24.1	24.0	22.5
National Capital Parks	8.3	8.9	7.5	7.5	8.1	9.1	5.4	5.5
Miscellaneous other areas	12.6	12.8	12.5	13.1	13.1	10.5	11.8	11.4
Recreation overnight stays (millions) [3]	15.8	17.4	17.6	17.7	18.3	17.7	18.3	16.8
In commercial lodgings	3.5	3.9	3.9	4.0	4.1	4.0	3.9	3.8
In Park Service campgrounds	7.3	7.8	7.9	7.8	8.1	7.5	7.6	7.1
In tents	3.6	3.9	4.1	4.2	4.4	4.1	4.2	3.9
In recreation vehicles	3.8	3.9	3.8	3.6	3.7	3.4	3.4	3.2
In backcountry	1.7	1.6	1.7	2.0	2.2	2.4	2.4	2.2
Other	3.2	4.1	4.2	3.9	3.9	3.8	4.4	3.7
Land (1,000 acres): [6]								
Total	75,749	76,331	76,362	76,607	76,492	75,515	74,905	77,355
Parks	45,739	46,081	46,089	46,135	46,208	45,521	48,111	49,307
Recreation areas	3,335	3,342	3,344	3,346	3,347	3,349	3,351	3,353
Other	26,675	26,907	26,929	27,126	26,937	26,645	23,443	24,695
Acquisition, gross	34	73	21	66	23	39	32	27
By purchase	29	14	18	15	21	29	29	25
By gift	2	58	2	43	1	10	1	1
By transfer or exchange	3	1	3	8	1	1	(Z)	1
Exclusion	(Z)	1	1	(Z)	(Z)	(Z)	(Z)	(Z)
Acquisition, net	34	71	21	66	23	39	32	27

Z Less than 500 acres. [1] Financial data are those associated with the National Park System. Certain other functions of the National Park Service (principally the activities absorbed from the former Heritage Conservation and Recreation Service in 1981) are excluded. [2] Includes funds carried over from prior years. [3] For calendar year. [4] Through 1990, combined data for North Cascades National Park and two adjacent National Recreation Areas are included in National Parks total. [5] Includes military areas. [6] Federal land only, as of Dec. 31. Federal land acreages, in addition to National Park Service administered lands, also include lands within national park system area boundaries but under the administration of other agencies. Year-to-year changes in the federal lands figures include changes in the acreages of these other lands and hence often differ from "net acquisition."

Source: U.S. National Park Service, Visits, *National Park Statistical Abstract*, annual; and unpublished data. Other data are unpublished.

No. 403. National Forest Recreation Use, Summary: 1980 to 1995

[For year ending September 30. Estimated. Represents recreational use of National Forest land and water in States which have a Forest Service recreation program]

YEAR AND ACTIVITY	Recreation visitor-days [1] (1,000)	Percent	STATE	Recreation visitor-days [1], 1995 (1,000)	STATE OR OTHER AREA	Recreation visitor-days [1], 1995 (1,000)
1980	233,549	100.0	U.S.	345,083	NV	3,742
1981	235,709	100.0			NH	3,352
1982	233,438	100.0	AL	680	NM	9,475
1983	227,708	100.0	AK	5,980	NY	103
1984	227,554	100.0	AZ	33,165	NC	6,756
1985	225,407	100.0	AR	2,206	ND	116
1986	226,533	100.0	CA	80,877	OH	851
1987	238,458	100.0	CO	30,971	OK	389
1988	242,316	100.0	FL	3,157	OR	37,032
1989	252,495	100.0	GA	3,191	PA	3,503
1990	263,051	100.0	ID	14,264	SC	987
1991	278,849	100.0	IL	1,118	SD	3,536
1992	287,891	100.0	IN	618	TN	3,188
1993	295,473	100.0	KS	85	TX	2,440
1994	330,348	100.0				
1995, total	345,083	100.0	KY	2,251	UT	18,880
Mechanized travel and viewing scenery	128,999	37.4	LA	591	VT	1,393
Camping, picnicking, and swimming	85,777	24.9	MA	147	VA	4,702
Hiking, horseback riding, and water travel	32,317	9.4	MI	4,720	WA	24,797
Winter sports	20,348	5.9	MN	5,824	WV	1,461
Hunting	18,945	5.5	MS	1,409	WI	2,531
Resorts, cabins, and organization camps	17,634	5.1	MO	2,230	WY	8,353
Fishing	17,787	5.2	MT	13,602		
Nature studies	3,208	0.9	NE	248	PR	171
Other [2]	20,068	5.8				

[1] One recreation visitor-day is the recreation use of National Forest land or water that aggregates 12 visitor-hours. This may entail 1 person for 12 hours, 12 persons for 1 hour, or any equivalent combination of individual or group use, either continuous or intermittent. [2] Includes team sports, gathering forest products, attending talks and programs, and other uses.

Source: U.S. Forest Service, unpublished data.

No. 404. Recreational Use of Public Lands Administered by Bureau of Land Management: 1985 to 1993

[In thousands. For year ending Sept. 30. Beginning 1987, increase due to an estimated longer length of stay per visit, especially in California. See text, section 7]

YEAR AND STATE	Number of visits	TYPE OF RECREATION USE (visitor hours)										
		Total	Off-highway vehicle travel	Other motorized travel	Non-motorized travel	Camping	Hunting	Misc. site based	Fishing	Boating	Misc. water based	Snow- and ice-based recreational activity, winter sports
1985	51,739	244,612	36,995	24,053	10,047	65,397	51,842	23,098	14,254	11,710	2,193	5,023
1986	54,253	284,142	49,688	25,868	14,397	95,196	35,570	19,331	18,227	15,891	3,951	6,025
1987	56,427	514,716	123,325	34,325	19,172	196,315	57,624	38,412	22,932	15,140	5,212	3,259
1988	57,460	492,756	122,014	35,748	19,761	178,703	55,285	38,340	21,617	13,294	4,979	3,015
1989	60,957	493,214	65,806	74,075	36,676	173,597	46,760	45,871	23,392	18,491	5,425	3,119
1990	71,820	523,753	63,016	83,445	41,316	165,366	47,053	57,958	28,664	20,806	8,313	7,816
1991	72,541	539,779	50,849	85,835	44,398	196,310	49,593	59,928	20,939	19,676	8,353	3,896
1992	69,418	519,429	46,411	93,477	43,845	181,536	44,557	59,857	19,768	18,735	7,586	3,657
1993, total	(NA)	428,825	40,197	61,113	27,780	162,683	47,246	42,800	19,466	17,127	7,009	3,724
AK	(NA)	5,924	152	466	87	3,719	567	201	432	173	5	122
AZ [1]	(NA)	59,022	749	619	2,473	36,351	2,334	8,748	756	4,927	2,061	4
CA	(NA)	132,143	24,969	10,159	7,177	66,606	7,727	9,213	2,745	1,584	1,688	253
CO	(NA)	27,795	1,418	6,122	946	5,692	9,204	1,535	791	1,710	54	323
Eastern States [2]	(NA)	52	-	-	-	-	1	1	6	2	42	-
ID	(NA)	18,199	1,032	1,326	692	5,168	2,568	1,588	2,288	1,433	570	1,534
MT [3]	(NA)	13,004	2,523	967	503	3,187	2,822	418	1,734	476	57	317
NV	(NA)	26,897	1,668	11,309	2,796	4,191	2,192	2,706	1,434	262	172	163
NM	(NA)	20,098	926	5,137	1,721	3,001	5,329	2,917	600	392	71	4
OR [4]	(NA)	60,564	1,828	8,291	5,625	15,759	6,627	9,718	7,232	3,026	1,902	556
UT	(NA)	56,008	4,618	15,988	5,481	17,341	4,868	3,985	465	2,812	336	114
WY	(NA)	9,119	294	729	277	1,646	3,007	1,468	983	330	51	334

- Represents or rounds to zero. NA Not available. [1] Includes concession visitation data. These data relate to Bureau of Land Management concession leases along the Colorado River. The leases consist of boat docks and storage areas, trailer parks, restaurants, etc. The visitation by the recreating public to these areas and facilities is monitored and recorded. [2] States bordering on or east of the Mississippi River. [3] Includes North Dakota and South Dakota. [4] Includes Washington.

Source: U.S. Bureau of Land Management, *Public Land Statistics*, annual.

No. 405. State Parks and Recreation Areas—States: 1995

[For year ending June 30. Data are shown as reported by State park directors. In some States, park agency has under its control forests, fish and wildlife areas, and/or other areas. In other States, agency is responsible for State parks only]

STATE	Acreage (1,000)	Visitors (1,000) [1]	REVENUE: Total ($1,000)	REVENUE: Percent of operating expenditures	STATE	Acreage (1,000)	Visitors (1,000) [1]	REVENUE: Total ($1,000)	REVENUE: Percent of operating expenditures
United States	11,807	745,602	535,685	43.0	Missouri	134	16,058	5,158	22.4
					Montana	52	1,837	1,016	22.4
Alabama	50	6,213	25,105	87.4	Nebraska	133	9,023	10,877	94.3
Alaska	3,242	4,299	1,725	31.5	Nevada	149	2,874	1,096	21.7
Arizona	46	2,180	3,572	30.9	New Hampshire	154	1,178	4,386	108.6
Arkansas	51	7,491	12,647	56.1	New Jersey	321	13,574	6,650	25.7
California	1,334	64,314	58,306	32.3	New Mexico	120	4,649	11,781	97.5
Colorado	337	10,949	8,062	55.1	New York	261	64,406	36,931	28.7
Connecticut	176	7,993	3,345	36.0	North Carolina	140	11,974	2,849	20.0
Delaware	16	3,247	4,862	33.5	North Dakota	20	1,043	718	39.0
Florida	437	11,798	21,024	44.0	Ohio	204	62,284	19,609	36.3
Georgia	66	15,880	15,081	38.9	Oklahoma	72	15,615	19,077	64.8
Hawaii	25	19,000	(NA)	(NA)	Oregon	92	41,265	11,237	47.0
Idaho	42	2,675	2,763	42.8	Pennsylvania	283	36,541	9,033	16.4
Illinois	419	40,027	5,251	16.3	Rhode Island	9	3,372	2,792	46.4
Indiana	59	10,700	9,780	72.4	South Carolina	82	10,565	14,264	69.0
Iowa	62	12,185	2,800	30.4	South Dakota	93	7,712	5,880	81.6
Kansas	324	6,708	2,639	44.7	Tennessee	134	29,656	23,328	55.8
Kentucky	43	8,530	43,835	71.9	Texas	519	24,249	19,522	59.1
Louisiana	39	1,435	2,582	31.9	Utah	98	7,059	4,395	28.1
Maine	92	2,006	1,768	34.4	Vermont	64	828	4,933	102.8
Maryland	247	10,985	11,131	42.4	Virginia	16	4,573	3,625	32.3
Massachusetts	315	18,236	6,306	14.6	Washington	255	47,186	9,128	18.3
Michigan	265	24,292	24,143	(NA)	West Virginia	199	9,082	14,961	61.6
Minnesota	245	8,065	9,190	45.4	Wisconsin	128	13,420	10,943	72.9
Mississippi	23	4,263	5,313	42.1	Wyoming	120	2,108	427	11.4

NA Not available. [1] Includes overnight visitors.

Source: National Association of State Park Directors, Tallahassee, FL, *1996 Annual Information Exchange*.

No. 406. Personal Consumption Expenditures for Recreation: 1985 to 1995

[In billions of dollars, except percent. Represents market value of purchases of goods and services by individuals and nonprofit institutions]

TYPE OF PRODUCT OR SERVICE	1985	1989	1990	1991	1992	1993	1994	1995
Total recreation expenditures	116.3	185.9	281.6	292.0	310.8	339.0	374.8	401.7
Percent of total personal consumption [1]	6.6	6.9	7.3	7.3	7.4	7.6	8.0	8.2
Books and maps	6.5	10.6	16.5	16.9	17.7	19.0	20.1	20.9
Magazines, newspapers, and sheet music	12.0	15.9	21.5	21.9	21.6	22.6	24.0	25.6
Nondurable toys and sport supplies	14.6	21.4	31.6	32.8	34.2	36.5	40.1	42.7
Wheel goods, sports and photographic equipment [2]	15.6	21.2	29.8	29.5	29.9	32.6	39.1	43.8
Video and audio products, computer equipment, and musical instruments	19.9	33.7	53.8	57.3	61.2	68.8	80.0	88.3
Radio and television repair	2.5	3.2	4.2	4.0	4.2	4.6	4.7	5.1
Flowers, seeds, and potted plants	4.7	6.9	11.1	11.3	12.3	12.8	14.0	14.2
Admissions to specified spectator amusements	6.7	9.7	15.1	15.7	16.6	18.2	19.5	19.9
Motion picture theaters	2.6	3.2	5.2	5.3	5.0	5.2	5.5	5.6
Legitimate theaters and opera, and entertainments of nonprofit institutions [3]	1.8	3.2	5.6	6.0	6.8	7.9	8.7	9.0
Spectator sports [4]	2.3	3.3	4.4	4.5	4.8	5.1	5.3	5.3
Clubs and fraternal organizations except insurance [5]	3.1	6.0	8.9	9.6	10.3	11.2	12.1	12.9
Commercial participant amusements [6]	9.1	15.1	23.0	23.8	27.2	31.4	34.9	37.0
Pari-mutuel net receipts	2.3	2.8	3.4	3.3	3.3	3.3	3.3	3.3
Other [7]	19.4	39.2	62.7	65.9	72.4	78.1	83.2	88.2

[1] See table 702. [2] Includes boats and pleasure aircraft. [3] Except athletic. [4] Consists of admissions to professional and amateur athletic events and to racetracks, including horse, dog, and auto. [5] Consists of dues and fees excluding insurance premiums. [6] Consists of billiard parlors; bowling alleys; dancing, riding, shooting, skating, and swimming places; amusement devices and parks; golf courses; sightseeing buses and guides; private flying operations; casino gambling; and other commercial participant amusements. [7] Consists of net receipts of lotteries and expenditures for purchases of pets and pet care services, cable TV, film processing, photographic studios, sporting and recreation camps, video cassette rentals, and recreational services, not elsewhere classified.

Source: U.S. Bureau of Economic Analysis, *The National Income and Product Accounts of the United States, 1929-97*, forthcoming, and *Survey of Current Business*, May, 1997.

No. 407. Expenditures per Consumer Unit for Entertainment and Reading: 1985 to 1995

[Data are annual averages. In dollars, except as indicated. Based on Consumer Expenditure Survey; see text, section 14, for description of survey. See also headnote, table 712. For composition of regions, see table 26]

YEAR AND CHARACTERISTIC	ENTERTAINMENT AND READING		ENTERTAINMENT				Reading
	Total	Percent of total expenditures	Total	Fees and admissions	Television, radios, and sound equipment	Other equipment and services [1]	
1985	1,311	5.6	1,170	320	371	479	141
1986	1,289	5.4	1,149	308	371	470	140
1987	1,335	5.5	1,193	323	379	491	142
1988	1,479	5.7	1,329	353	416	560	150
1989	1,581	5.7	1,424	377	429	618	157
1990	1,575	5.6	1,422	371	454	597	153
1991	1,635	5.5	1,472	378	468	627	163
1992	1,662	5.6	1,500	379	492	629	162
1993	1,792	5.8	1,626	414	590	621	166
1994	1,732	5.5	1,567	439	533	595	165
1995, total	**1,775**	**5.5**	**1,612**	**433**	**542**	**637**	**163**
Age of reference person:							
Under 25 years old	1,152	6.3	1,081	225	456	400	71
25 to 34 years old	1,816	5.8	1,682	394	580	708	134
35 to 44 years old	2,124	5.5	1,951	531	657	763	173
45 to 54 years old	2,337	5.5	2,138	585	664	889	199
55 to 64 years old	1,765	5.4	1,577	418	492	666	188
65 to 74 years old	1,336	5.3	1,156	377	397	382	180
75 years old and over	790	4.3	652	223	260	170	138
Origin of reference person: Hispanic	1,134	4.2	1,060	231	459	369	74
Non-Hispanic	1,829	5.6	1,659	450	549	660	170
Black	1,008	4.3	935	147	516	273	73
Other	1,929	5.7	1,747	487	553	708	182
Region of residence: Northeast	1,730	5.2	1,544	429	520	595	186
Midwest	1,772	5.5	1,602	419	572	612	170
South	1,594	5.3	1,459	373	514	572	135
West	2,116	6.0	1,939	552	570	816	177
Size of consumer unit: One person	1,112	5.7	992	265	367	360	120
Two or more persons	2,035	5.5	1,856	499	611	747	179
Two persons	1,854	5.6	1,667	459	516	693	187
Three persons	2,010	5.3	1,834	452	618	764	176
Four persons	2,376	5.6	2,187	650	739	797	189
Five persons or more	2,132	5.1	1,986	476	701	809	146

[1] Other equipment and services includes pets, toys, and playground equipment; sports, exercise, and photographic equipment; and recreational vehicles.

Source: U.S. Bureau of Labor Statistics, *Consumer Expenditure Survey, annual.*

No. 408. Motion Pictures and Amusement and Recreation Services—Annual Receipts: 1990 to 1995

[In millions of dollars. For taxable employer and nonemployer firms]

KIND OF BUSINESS	1987 SIC code [1]	1990	1991	1992	1993	1994	1995
Motion pictures	78	39,982	42,838	45,662	50,211	54,318	58,113
Production, distribution, and allied services	781, 782	28,888	31,590	34,288	38,096	41,170	44,370
Theaters	783	6,088	6,213	5,879	6,149	6,587	7,032
Video tape rental	784	5,006	5,035	5,495	5,966	6,561	6,711
Amusement and recreation services	79	50,126	51,654	57,699	63,561	68,186	77,384
Dance studios, schools, and halls	791	626	662	784	862	866	870
Theatrical producers (except motion picture), bands, orchestras, and entertainers	792	10,735	11,694	13,054	15,385	15,991	17,467
Bowling centers	793	2,800	2,747	2,915	2,886	3,021	3,150
Commercial sports	794	8,636	8,597	9,010	9,122	9,411	10,184
Professional sports clubs and promoters	7941	3,702	3,719	3,978	4,559	4,924	5,530
Racing, including track operation	7948	4,934	4,878	5,032	4,563	4,487	4,654
Miscellaneous amusement and recreation services [2]	799	27,329	27,954	31,936	35,306	38,897	45,713
Physical fitness facilities	7991	3,623	3,449	4,135	4,087	4,278	4,818
Public golf courses	7992	2,254	2,386	2,609	2,903	3,225	3,913
Coin-operated amusement devices	7993	2,146	2,301	2,566	2,760	2,959	3,295
Amusement parks	7996	4,922	4,820	5,366	5,663	5,905	6,376
Membership sports and recreation clubs	7997	4,825	5,151	5,397	5,974	6,400	6,829

[1] 1987 Standard Industrial Classification code; see text, section 13. [2] Includes kinds of businesses, not shown separately.

Source: U.S. Bureau of the Census, *Current Business Reports, Service Annual Survey: 1995*, BS/95.

No. 409. Quantity of Books Sold and Value of U.S. Domestic Consumer Expenditures: 1982 to 1995

[Includes all titles released by publishers in the United States and imports which appear under the imprints of American publishers. Multi-volume sets, such as encyclopedias, are counted as one unit]

TYPE OF PUBLICATION AND MARKET AREA	UNITS SOLD (mil.)					CONSUMER EXPENDITURES (mil. dol.)				
	1982	1985	1990	1994	1995	1982	1985	1990	1994	1995
Total [1]	1,723	1,788	2,006	2,142	2,153	9,889	12,611	19,043	23,911	25,041
Hardbound, total	646	694	824	830	823	6,190	7,969	11,789	14,588	15,110
Softbound, total	1,077	1,094	1,181	1,312	1,330	3,699	4,642	7,254	9,323	9,931
Trade	459	553	705	821	822	2,484	3,660	6,498	9,271	9,498
Adult	315	360	403	492	466	2,028	2,871	4,777	7,197	7,171
Juvenile	144	193	301	330	355	456	789	1,721	2,074	2,327
Religious	144	134	130	142	146	706	926	1,362	1,693	1,791
Professional	106	110	131	142	146	1,630	2,043	2,957	3,867	4,153
Bookclubs	133	130	106	116	118	510	582	705	850	912
Elhi text	233	234	209	211	237	1,067	1,415	1,948	2,074	2,384
College text	115	110	137	136	142	1,388	1,575	2,319	2,536	2,706
Mail order publications	134	121	138	96	94	581	650	752	576	583
Mass market paperbacks-rack sized	382	362	433	461	432	1,102	1,244	1,775	2,156	2,066
General retailers	756	829	1,010	1,133	1,124	3,743	5,103	8,465	11,524	11,834
College stores	224	225	255	289	271	1,910	2,309	3,403	4,070	4,292
Libraries and institutions [2]	80	80	86	97	97	688	1,090	1,592	2,028	2,120
Schools [2]	262	260	244	247	271	1,313	1,685	2,365	2,569	2,868
Direct to consumers	319	300	304	284	283	1,889	2,214	2,901	3,322	3,501
Other	82	94	104	111	106	146	210	316	397	406

[1] Types of publications include university press publications and subscription reference works, not shown separately. [2] Elhi libraries included in schools.

Source: Book Industry Study Group, Inc., New York, NY, *Book Industry Trends, 1996*, annual, (copyright).

No. 410. Book Purchasing by Adults: 1991 and 1995

[In percent. Excludes books purchased for or by children under 13. Based on a survey of 16,000 households conducted over 12 months ending in December of year shown. For details, see source]

CHARACTERISTIC	TOTAL		MASS MARKET [1]		TRADE [2]		HARDCOVER	
	1991	1995	1991	1995	1991	1995	1991	1995
Total	100.0	100.0	100.0	100.0	100.0	100.0	100.0	100.0
Age of purchaser:								
Under 25 years old	4.3	4.4	3.7	4.6	5.2	4.7	4.4	3.9
25 to 34 years old	18.8	15.2	13.9	12.0	25.4	18.3	19.6	16.0
35 to 44 years old	23.7	26.6	22.8	22.6	25.2	30.5	23.7	27.2
45 to 54 years old	22.4	22.8	26.0	23.3	18.5	22.7	20.5	22.1
55 to 64 years old	15.6	14.3	15.8	15.7	13.9	12.2	17.2	14.7
65 years old and over	15.2	16.7	17.8	21.8	11.8	11.6	14.6	16.1
Household income:								
Under $30,000	37.1	32.3	41.7	40.7	32.6	27.0	34.1	27.9
$30,000 to 49,999	27.2	24.5	27.3	25.0	27.7	24.8	26.5	23.6
$50,000 to 59,999	11.0	9.0	9.8	8.8	12.3	8.9	11.5	9.3
$60,000 to 69,999	6.9	8.2	7.0	6.7	7.2	8.8	6.3	9.3
$70,000 and over	17.8	26.0	14.2	18.8	20.2	30.5	21.6	29.9
Household size:								
Singles	20.8	18.8	17.7	19.6	24.1	18.4	22.8	18.1
Families with no children	40.4	40.9	42.3	40.6	38.0	40.1	39.7	42.0
Families with children	38.8	40.3	40.0	39.8	37.9	41.5	37.5	39.9
Age of reader:								
Under 25 years old	7.3	8.1	5.2	6.3	10.1	10.4	7.7	7.8
25 to 34 years old	18.7	15.9	14.1	12.6	24.7	19.2	20.2	16.5
35 to 44 years old	22.9	24.9	22.3	21.6	24.0	26.0	22.7	25.5
45 to 54 years old	20.8	21.0	24.9	22.3	16.5	20.4	18.4	19.9
55 to 64 years old	14.9	13.4	15.9	15.6	12.7	11.3	15.6	13.2
65 years old and over	15.4	16.7	17.6	21.6	12.0	10.7	15.6	17.1
Category of book:								
Popular fiction	54.9	50.0	93.0	94.2	14.9	12.7	31.8	37.4
General nonfiction	10.3	9.3	3.6	2.5	15.6	12.5	16.5	14.0
Cooking/crafts	10.2	11.3	0.4	0.3	20.6	19.4	18.2	15.8
Other	24.6	29.4	3.0	3.0	48.9	55.4	33.5	32.8
Sales outlet:								
Independent	32.5	19.5	26.5	12.0	44.9	29.4	29.0	17.7
Chain book store	22.0	26.2	17.2	22.8	27.4	29.6	25.2	26.3
Book clubs	16.6	17.9	17.8	17.0	9.5	11.9	22.6	26.2
Other [3]	28.9	36.4	38.5	48.2	18.2	29.1	23.2	29.8

[1] "Pocket size" books sold primarily through magazine and news outlets, supermarkets, variety stores, etc. [2] All paperbound books, except mass market. [3] Includes mail order, price clubs, discount stores, food/drug stores, used book stores, and other outlets.

Source: Book Industry Study Group, Inc., New York, NY, *1995 Consumer Research Study on Book Purchasing*, annual, (copyright).

No. 411. Profile of Consumer Expenditures for Sound Recordings: 1990 to 1996

[In percent, except total value. Based on monthly telephone surveys of the population 10 years old and over]

ITEM	1990	1995	1996	ITEM	1990	1995	1996
Total value (mil. dol.)	7,541.1	12,320.3	12,533.8	Music club	8.9	14.3	14.3
PERCENT DISTRIBUTION [1]				Mail order	2.5	4.0	2.9
Age: 10 to 14 years	7.6	8.0	7.9	Music type: [2]			
15 to 19 years	18.3	17.1	17.2	Rock	36.1	33.5	32.6
20 to 24 years	16.5	15.3	15.0	Country	9.6	16.7	14.7
25 to 29 years	14.6	12.3	12.5	R&B	11.6	11.3	12.1
30 to 34 years	13.2	12.1	11.4	Pop	13.7	10.1	9.3
35 to 39 years	10.2	10.8	11.1	Rap	8.5	6.7	8.9
40 to 44 years	7.8	7.5	9.1	Classical	3.1	2.9	3.4
45 years and over	11.1	16.1	15.1	Jazz	4.8	3.0	3.3
Sex: Male	54.4	53.0	50.9	Gospel	2.5	3.1	4.3
Female	45.6	47.0	49.1	Soundtracks	0.8	0.9	0.8
Sales outlet:				New age	1.1	0.7	0.7
Record store	69.8	52.0	49.9	Children's	0.5	0.5	0.7
Other store	18.5	28.2	31.5	Other	5.6	7.0	5.2

[1] Percent distributions exclude nonresponses and responses of don't know. [2] As classified by respondent.

Source: Recording Industry Association of America, Inc., Washington, DC, *Top Ten Factbook*, 1996.

No. 412. Household Pet Ownership: 1996

[Based on a sample survey of 80,000 households in 1996; for details, see source]

ITEM	Unit	Dog	Cat	Pet bird	Horse
Households owning companion pets [1]	Million	31.2	27.0	4.6	1.5
Percent of all households	Percent	31.6	27.3	4.6	1.5
Average number owned	Number	1.7	2.2	2.7	2.7
Total companion pet population [1]	Million	52.9	59.1	12.6	4.0
Households obtaining veterinary care [2]	Percent	88.7	72.9	15.8	66.3
Average visits per household per year	Number	2.6	1.9	0.2	2.3
Average annual costs per household	Dollars	186.80	112.24	10.95	226.26
Total expenditures	Mil. dol.	5,828	3,030	50	339
PERCENT DISTRIBUTION OF HOUSEHOLDS OWNING PETS					
Annual household income: Under $12,500	Percent	12.7	13.9	17.3	9.5
$12,500 to $24,999	Percent	19.1	19.7	20.9	20.3
$25,000 to $39,999	Percent	21.6	21.5	22.0	21.8
$40,000 to $59,999	Percent	21.5	21.2	17.5	23.1
$60,000 and over	Percent	25.2	23.7	22.3	25.4
Family size: [1] One person	Percent	13.2	16.8	12.7	12.1
Two persons	Percent	31.0	32.6	27.9	29.1
Three persons	Percent	21.4	20.6	20.4	22.0
Four or more persons	Percent	34.5	29.9	38.9	36.7

[1] As of December. [2] During 1996.

Source: American Veterinary Medical Association, Schaumburg, IL, *U.S. Pet Ownership and Demographics Sourcebook, 1997*, (copyright).

No. 413. Household Participation in Lawn and Garden Activities: 1991 to 1995

[For calendar year. Based on national household sample survey conducted by the Gallup Organization. Subject to sampling variability; see source]

ACTIVITY	PERCENT HOUSEHOLDS ENGAGED IN—					RETAIL SALES (mil. dol.)				
	1991	1992	1993	1994	1995	1991	1992	1993	1994	1995
Total	78	75	71	74	72	22,134	22,824	22,410	25,897	22,242
Lawn care	62	54	54	56	53	6,890	7,460	6,446	8,417	7,621
Indoor houseplants	42	34	31	37	30	852	926	689	999	864
Flower gardening	41	39	39	44	38	2,302	2,167	2,396	3,147	2,107
Insect control	35	27	24	28	24	1,260	1,593	1,080	1,127	1,049
Shrub care	32	27	28	30	25	1,030	1,437	1,274	1,133	774
Vegetable gardening	31	31	26	31	28	1,652	1,440	1,063	1,476	1,359
Tree care	27	20	21	22	17	1,443	1,664	2,011	1,408	1,002
Landscaping	26	22	24	26	20	4,828	4,444	5,006	5,797	5,524
Flower bulbs	26	23	22	28	21	520	503	453	635	377
Fruit trees	15	13	13	14	11	371	350	759	389	241
Container gardening	13	9	11	12	12	330	239	441	359	377
Raising transplants [1]	12	8	10	11	8	141	169	201	182	187
Herb gardening	9	7	8	10	8	161	135	175	112	140
Growing berries	7	6	6	6	5	90	62	126	85	55
Ornamental gardening	7	5	6	5	5	264	235	290	264	144
Water gardening	(NA)	(NA)	(NA)	5	5	(NA)	(NA)	(NA)	367	421

NA Not available. [1] Starting plants in advance of planting in ground.

Source: The National Gardening Association, Burlington, VT, *National Gardening Survey*, annual, (copyright).

No. 414. Sport Fishing and Hunting Licenses—Number and Cost: 1980 to 1995

[In millions, except as indicated. For fiscal years ending in year shown; see text, section 9]

ITEM	1980	1985	1988	1989	1990	1991	1992	1993	1994	1995
Fishing licenses: Sales	35.2	35.7	36.8	36.6	37.0	37.0	37.4	37.9	37.9	37.9
Resident	30.1	30.5	31.3	31.0	31.0	31.1	31.4	31.8	31.6	31.4
Nonresident	5.1	5.2	5.5	5.6	6.0	5.9	6.0	6.1	6.3	6.5
Paid license holders [1]	28.0	29.7	31.4	30.3	30.7	30.7	30.6	30.2	30.2	30.3
Cost to anglers (mil. dol.)	196	282	330	341	363	375	396	412	425	449
Hunting licenses: Sales	27.0	27.7	30.0	29.3	30.0	30.7	31.3	31.6	31.6	32.1
Resident	25.6	26.1	27.7	27.3	27.4	28.5	29.1	29.5	29.7	30.0
Nonresident	1.4	1.6	2.0	2.0	2.3	2.2	2.2	2.0	2.0	2.2
Paid license holders [1]	16.3	15.9	15.9	15.9	15.8	15.7	15.7	15.6	15.3	15.2
Cost to hunters (mil. dol.)	222	301	381	400	422	439	481	492	502	533
Federal duck stamps sold (1,000)	2,090	1,914	1,663	1,395	1,401	1,420	1,330	1,401	1,466	1,483

[1] Resident and nonresident. Includes multiple counting of license holders who bought nonresident licenses as well as a home State license. "Licenses" includes licenses, tags, permits, and stamps.

Source: U.S. Fish and Wildlife Service, *Federal Aid in Fish and Wildlife Restoration*, annual.

No. 415. Anglers and Hunters: 1991

[For persons 16 years old and over. An angler or hunter is anyone who has fished or hunted in 1991. Based on the 1991 National Survey of Fishing, Hunting, and Wildlife-Associated Recreation conducted for the U.S. Fish and Wildlife Service by the U.S. Bureau of the Census]

TYPE OF FISHING	ANGLERS		Days of fishing [1] (mil.)	Expenditures [2] (mil. dol.)	TYPE OF HUNTING	HUNTERS		Days of hunting [1] (mil.)	Expenditures [2] (mil. dol.)
	Number (1,000)	Percent of population				Number (1,000)	Percent of population		
All fishing	[3]35,578	19	[3]511	23,990	**All hunting**	[3]14,063	7	[3]236	12,336
All freshwater fishing	[3]31,041	16	[3]440	15,149	Big game	10,745	6	128	5,090
Freshwater, except Great Lakes	30,186	16	431	13,812	Small game	7,642	4	77	1,550
Great Lakes	2,552	1	25	1,337	Migratory birds	3,009	2	22	686
Saltwater	8,885	5	75	4,992	Other animals	1,411	1	19	255

[1] Any part of a day constitutes a day. [2] Totals include expenditures for equipment, trips, magazines, membership dues, contributions, land leasing and ownership, licenses, stamps, tags, and other expenditures. Figures by type of fishing and hunting include only expenditures for trips and equipment. [3] Includes duplication for persons who participate in more than one category.

Source: U.S. Fish and Wildlife Service, *1991 National Survey of Fishing, Hunting, and Wildlife-Associated Recreation.*

No. 416. Participation in Various Leisure Activities: 1992

[In percent, except as indicated. Covers activities engaged in at least once in the prior 12 months. See headnote, table 425. See also table 426]

ITEM	Adult population (mil.)	ATTENDANCE AT—			PARTICIPATION IN—				
		Movies	Sports events	Amusement park	Exercise program	Playing sports	Outdoor activities [1]	Home improvement/ repair	Gardening
Total	185.8	59	37	50	60	39	34	48	55
Sex: Male	89.0	60	44	51	61	50	39	53	46
Female	96.8	59	30	50	59	29	29	42	62
Race: White	158.8	60	38	51	61	40	37	50	57
Black	21.1	54	32	45	51	32	10	32	39
Other	5.9	62	20	46	51	38	28	31	42
Age: 18 to 24 years old	24.1	82	51	68	67	59	43	33	31
25 to 34 years old	42.4	70	47	68	67	52	41	47	51
35 to 44 years old	39.8	66	43	58	62	44	42	58	57
45 to 54 years old	27.7	58	35	44	62	34	36	57	64
55 to 64 years old	21.2	40	23	30	56	21	21	53	63
65 to 74 years old	18.3	34	20	29	50	18	21	42	63
75 to 96 years old	12.3	19	7	14	34	7	5	20	55
Education: Grade school	14.3	16	9	24	24	10	11	24	44
Some high school	18.6	35	19	35	39	18	21	34	50
High school graduate	69.4	54	33	51	55	34	31	47	53
Some college	39.2	21	45	59	71	49	42	53	55
College graduate	26.2	77	51	58	75	55	42	52	61
Graduate school	18.1	81	51	54	79	57	51	65	65

[1] Camping, hiking, and canoeing.

Source: U.S. National Endowment for the Arts, *Arts Participation in America: 1982 to 1992.*

No. 417. Selected Spectator Sports: 1985 to 1995

SPORT	Unit	1985	1987	1990	1991	1992	1993	1994	1995
Baseball, major leagues: [1]									
Attendance	1,000	47,742	53,182	55,512	57,820	56,852	71,237	50,010	51,288
Regular season	1,000	46,824	52,011	54,824	56,814	55,873	70,257	50,010	50,469
National League	1,000	22,292	24,734	24,492	24,696	24,113	36,924	25,808	25,110
American League	1,000	24,532	27,277	30,332	32,118	31,760	33,333	24,202	25,359
Playoffs	1,000	591	784	479	633	668	636	(X)	533
World Series	1,000	327	387	209	373	311	344	(X)	286
Players' salaries: [2]									
Average	$1,000	371	412	598	851	1,029	1,076	1,168	1,111
Basketball: [3 4]									
NCAA—Men's college:									
Teams	Number	753	760	767	796	813	831	858	868
Attendance	1,000	26,584	26,798	28,741	29,250	29,378	28,527	28,390	28,548
NCAA—Women's college:									
Teams	Number	746	756	782	806	815	826	859	864
Attendance	1,000	2,072	2,156	2,777	3,013	3,397	4,193	4,557	4,962
Pro: [5]									
Teams	Number	23	23	27	27	27	27	27	27
Attendance, total [6]	1,000	11,534	13,190	18,586	18,009	18,609	19,120	19,350	19,883
Regular season	1,000	10,506	12,065	17,369	16,876	17,367	17,778	17,984	18,516
Average per game	Number	11,141	12,795	15,690	15,245	15,689	16,060	16,246	16,727
Playoffs	1,000	985	1,091	1,203	1,109	1,228	1,338	1,349	1,347
Players' salaries:									
Average	$1,000	325	440	817	989	1,202	1,348	1,700	(NA)
Football:									
NCAA College: [4]									
Teams	Number	509	507	533	548	552	560	568	565
Attendance	1,000	34,952	35,008	35,330	35,528	35,225	34,871	36,460	35,638
National Football League: [7]									
Teams	Number	28	28	28	28	28	28	(NA)	(NA)
Attendance, total [8]	1,000	14,058	[9]15,180	17,668	17,752	17,784	14,772	(NA)	(NA)
Regular season	1,000	13,345	[9]11,406	13,960	13,841	13,829	13,967	(NA)	(NA)
Average per game	Number	59,567	[9]54,315	62,321	61,792	61,736	62,352	(NA)	(NA)
Postseason games [10]	1,000	711	656	848	813	815	805	(NA)	(NA)
Players' salaries: [11]									
Average	$1,000	194	203	352	415	645	683	637	714
Median base salary	$1,000	140	175	236	250	325	330	325	335
National Hockey league: [12]									
Regular season attendance	1,000	11,621	12,118	12,344	12,770	13,917	15,714	(NA)	15,658
Playoffs attendance	1,000	1,153	1,337	1,442	1,328	1,346	1,440	(NA)	1,447
Horseracing: [13 14]									
Racing days	Number	13,745	14,208	13,841	(NA)	13,644	13,237	13,082	(NA)
Attendance	1,000	73,346	70,105	63,803	(NA)	49,275	45,688	42,065	(NA)
Pari-mutuel turnover	Mil. dol	12,222	13,122	7,162	14,094	14,078	13,718	14,143	(NA)
Revenue to government	Mil. dol	625	608	611	624	491.3	473	453	(NA)
Greyhound: [13]									
Total performances	Number	9,590	11,156	14,915	(NA)	17,528	17,976	17,035	(NA)
Attendance	1,000	23,853	26,215	28,660	(NA)	28,003	(NA)	(NA)	(NA)
Pari-mutuel turnover	Mil. dol	2,702	3,193	3,422	3,422	3,306	3,255	2,948	(NA)
Revenue to government	Mil. dol	201	221	235	(NA)	204.2	194.9	183.0	(NA)
Jai alai: [13]									
Total performances	Number	2,736	2,906	3,620	3,619	3,288	3,200	3,146	(NA)
Games played	Number	32,260	38,476	(NA)	(NA)	45,067	43,056	42,607	(NA)
Attendance	1,000	4,722	6,816	5,329	(NA)	4,634	4,194	3,684	(NA)
Pari-mutuel turnover	Mil. dol	664.0	707.5	545.5	(NA)	425.9	384.2	330.7	(NA)
Revenue to government	Mil. dol	50	51	39	39	30	27	22	(NA)
Professional rodeo: [15]									
Rodeos	Number	617	637	754	796	791	791	782	739
Performances	Number	1,887	1,832	2,159	2,241	2,269	2,269	2,245	2,217
Members	Number	5,239	5,342	5,693	5,748	5,760	5,760	6,415	6,894
Permit-holders (rookies)	Number	2,534	2,746	3,290	3,006	2,888	2,888	3,346	3,835

NA Not available. X Not applicable. [1] Source: The National League of Professional Baseball Clubs, New York, NY, *National League Green Book*; and The American League of Professional Baseball Clubs, New York, NY, *American League Red Book*. [2] Source: Major League Baseball Players Association, New York, NY. [3] Season ending in year shown. [4] Source: National Collegiate Athletic Assn., Overland Park, KS. For women's attendance total, excludes double-headers with men's teams. [5] Source: National Basketball Assn., New York, NY. [6] Includes All-Star game, not shown separately. [7] Source: National Football League, New York, NY. [8] 1987 through 1992 includes preseason attendance, not shown separately. [9] Season was interrupted by a strike. [10] Includes Pro Bowl, a nonchampionship game and Super Bowl. [11] Source: National Football League Players Association, Washington, DC. [12] For season beginning in year shown. Source: National Hockey League, Montreal, Quebec. [13] Source: Association of Racing Commissioners International, Inc., Lexington, KY. [14] Includes thoroughbred, harness, quarter horse, and fairs. [15] Source: Professional Rodeo Cowboys Association, Colorado Springs, CO., *Official Professional Rodeo Media Guide*, annual, (copyright).

Source: Compiled from sources listed in footnotes.

No. 418. Selected Recreational Activities: 1975 to 1995

ACTIVITY	Unit	1975	1980	1985	1990	1992	1993	1994	1995
Softball, amateur: [1]									
Total participants [2]	Million	26	30	41	41	41	42	42	42
Youth participants	1,000	450	650	712	1,100	1,207	1,208	1,209	1,350
Adult teams [3]	1,000	66	110	152	188	202	200	198	187
Youth teams [3]	1,000	9	18	31	46	57	62	68	74
Golfers (one round or more) [4 5]	1,000	13,036	15,112	17,520	27,800	24,800	24,800	24,300	25,000
Golf rounds played [5]	1,000	308,562	357,701	414,777	502,000	505,400	498,600	484,800	490,200
Golf facilities	Number	11,370	12,005	12,346	12,846	13,210	13,439	13,683	14,074
Classification:									
Private	Number	4,770	4,839	4,861	4,810	4,568	4,492	4,367	4,324
Daily fee	Number	5,014	5,372	5,573	6,024	6,552	6,803	7,126	7,491
Municipal	Number	1,586	1,794	1,912	2,012	2,090	2,144	2,190	2,259
Tennis: [6]									
Players	1,000	[7]34,000	(NA)	13,000	21,000	22,630	21,500	16,500	17,820
Courts	1,000	130	(NA)	220	220	230	230	240	240
Indoor	1,000	8	(NA)	14	14	14	14	15	15
Tenpin bowling: [8]									
Participants, total	Million	62.5	72.0	67.0	71.0	82.0	79.0	79.0	79.0
Male	Million	29.9	34.0	32.0	35.4	40.2	36.3	36.3	36.3
Female	Million	32.6	38.0	35.0	35.6	41.8	42.6	42.3	42.3
Establishments	Number	8,577	8,591	8,275	7,611	7,395	7,250	7,183	7,049
Lanes	1,000	141	154	155	148	144	143	142	139
Membership, total [9]	1,000	8,751	9,664	8,064	6,588	5,873	5,599	5,201	4,925
American Bowling Congress	1,000	4,300	4,688	3,657	3,036	2,712	2,576	2,455	2,370
Women's Bowling Congress	1,000	3,692	4,187	3,714	2,859	2,523	2,403	2,191	2,036
Young American Bowling Alliance [10]	1,000	759	789	693	693	638	620	555	519
Motion picture theaters [11]	1,000	15	18	21	24	26	26	26	28
Four-wall	1,000	11	14	18	23	25	25	26	27
Drive-in	1,000	4	4	3	1	1	1	(Z)	1
Receipts, box office	Mil. dol.	2,115	2,749	3,749	5,022	4,871	5,154	5,396	5,494
Admission, average price	Dollars	2.05	2.69	3.55	4.23	4.15	4.14	4.18	4.35
Attendance	Million	1,033	1,022	1,056	1,187	1,173	1,244	1,292	1,263
Boating: [12]									
Recreational boats owned	Million	9.7	11.8	13.8	16.0	16.2	16.2	16.6	17.1
Outboard boats	Million	5.7	6.8	7.4	7.9	7.7	7.7	7.9	7.8
Inboard boats	Million	0.8	1.2	1.4	2.2	2.5	2.7	2.9	2.6
Sailboats	Million	0.8	1.0	1.2	1.3	1.3	1.3	1.3	1.4
Canoes	Million	2.4	1.3	1.8	2.3	2.4	2.4	2.4	2.3
Rowboats and other	Million	([13])	1.5	1.8	2.3	2.3	2.1	2.1	3.0
Expenditures, total [14]	Bil. dol.	4.8	7.4	13.3	13.7	10.3	11.3	14.1	17.2
Outboard motors in use	1,000	7,649	8,241	9,733	11,524	12,000	12,240	12,511	12,819
Motors sold	1,000	435	315	392	352	272	283	317	308
Value, retail	Mil. dol.	411	554	1,319	1,546	1,268	1,364	1,793	1,882
Outboard boats sold	1,000	328	290	305	227	192	205	231	215
Value, retail	Mil. dol.	263	408	759	978	839	914	1,426	1,362
Inboard/outdrive boats sold	1,000	70	56	115	97	75	75	94	95
Value, retail	Mil. dol.	420	616	1,663	1,794	1,239	1,244	1,791	1,925
Inboard cruisers sold	1,000	6.5	5.3	12.2	7.5	3.5	3.4	5.4	5.3
Value, retail	Mil. dol.	256	457	1,341	1,363	621	655	1,170	1,215

NA Not available. Z Fewer than 500. [1] Source: Amateur Softball Association, Oklahoma City, OK. [2] Amateur Softball Association teams and other amateur softball teams. [3] Amateur Softball Association teams only. [4] Source: National Golf Foundation, Jupiter, FL. [5] Prior to 1990, for persons 5 years of age and over; thereafter for persons 12 years of age and over. [6] Source: Tennis Industry Association, White Plains, NY. Players for persons 12 years old and over who played at least once. [7] 1974 data. [8] For season ending in year shown. Persons 5 years old and over. Source: Bowling Headquarters, Greendale, WI. [9] Membership totals are for U.S., Canada and for U.S. military personnel worldwide. [10] Prior to 1985, represents American Jr. Bowling Congress and ABC/WIBC Collegiate Division. [11] Source: Motion Picture Association of America, Inc., Encino, CA. Prior to 1975, figures represent theaters; thereafter, screens. [12] Source: National Marine Manufacturers Association, Chicago, IL. [13] Included in canoes. [14] Represents estimated expenditures for new and used boats, motors, accessories, safety equipment, fuel, insurance, docking, maintenance, storage, repairs, and other expenses.

Source: Compiled from sources listed in footnotes.

No. 419. Participation in Selected Sports Activities: 1995

[In thousands, except rank. For persons 7 years of age or older. Except as indicated, a participant plays a sport more than once in the year. Based on a sampling of 15,000 households]

ACTIVITY	ALL PERSONS		SEX		AGE								HOUSEHOLD INCOME (dol.)					
	Number	Rank	Male	Female	7-11 years	12-17 years	18-24 years	25-34 years	35-44 years	45-54 years	55-64 years	65 years and over	Under 15,000	15,000-24,999	25,000-34,999	35,000-49,999	50,000-74,999	75,000 and over
Total	**235,460**	**(X)**	**114,348**	**121,114**	**18,896**	**22,154**	**25,467**	**41,670**	**42,149**	**30,224**	**21,241**	**33,659**	**46,429**	**36,325**	**34,290**	**41,556**	**47,424**	**29,436**
Number participated in:																		
Aerobic exercising [1]	23,052	12	4,302	18,750	784	1,553	4,120	6,522	4,587	2,872	1,164	1,450	3,043	2,895	2,974	4,159	5,626	4,356
Backpacking [2]	10,244	23	6,413	3,831	980	1,724	1,461	2,627	2,065	914	299	175	1,779	1,389	1,435	2,069	1,997	1,575
Badminton	5,758	28	2,541	3,217	890	1,255	777	1,055	1,137	508	85	51	795	1,027	932	1,224	1,200	581
Baseball	15,728	17	12,087	3,642	5,443	4,547	1,499	1,911	1,474	539	207	107	2,204	2,095	2,453	3,249	3,527	2,199
Basketball	30,098	9	20,918	9,180	6,315	8,720	4,707	5,331	3,389	1,038	413	184	4,594	3,765	4,246	5,569	7,593	4,331
Bicycle riding [1]	56,308	3	29,830	26,478	12,796	10,152	5,018	9,694	8,550	4,455	2,710	2,933	8,763	8,074	8,567	10,362	11,975	8,547
Billiards	31,108	8	19,364	11,744	1,465	3,744	7,547	9,189	5,228	2,426	913	597	5,067	5,086	4,553	6,446	6,112	3,844
Bowling	41,898	6	21,142	20,756	4,951	5,850	7,174	9,492	7,078	3,535	1,776	2,043	5,817	6,494	6,409	8,164	9,891	5,123
Calisthenics [1]	9,339	24	4,042	5,298	1,218	1,578	1,096	1,669	1,397	989	468	924	1,096	1,426	1,549	1,536	2,159	1,572
Camping [3]	42,818	5	22,835	19,983	5,379	5,707	5,482	9,061	8,619	4,337	2,504	1,729	6,218	6,518	6,896	9,360	9,417	4,586
Exercise walking [1]	70,268	1	25,097	45,171	2,176	3,503	6,241	13,294	14,180	11,626	8,266	10,961	12,143	10,543	10,121	12,322	14,906	10,233
Exercising with equipment [1]	44,328	4	20,583	23,745	722	3,357	5,899	10,599	9,773	7,084	3,380	3,515	4,550	5,408	5,693	8,223	11,723	8,732
Fishing—fresh water	39,282	7	26,444	12,838	4,621	4,363	4,430	7,961	7,782	4,919	2,703	2,502	7,051	5,715	6,474	8,186	7,814	4,042
Fishing—salt water	10,717	22	7,685	3,032	687	1,059	1,189	2,152	2,268	1,668	819	874	1,738	1,391	1,367	2,263	2,387	1,571
Football—tackle	8,270	27	7,366	904	1,623	3,579	1,383	1,029	384	137	47	88	1,402	1,147	1,431	1,493	1,824	974
Football—touch	12,095	19	9,796	2,299	2,956	3,803	2,086	1,898	917	255	127	53	1,941	1,855	1,717	2,312	2,720	1,549
Golf	23,959	11	18,016	5,943	866	2,020	2,451	5,697	4,921	3,675	1,823	2,506	1,580	2,020	3,170	4,101	7,106	5,981
Hiking	25,047	10	13,848	11,199	2,696	3,098	2,926	5,704	5,244	3,044	1,354	980	3,702	3,408	3,316	4,784	5,846	4,191
Hunting with firearms	16,253	16	13,968	2,285	555	1,896	2,312	4,246	3,497	1,983	988	775	2,503	2,585	2,828	3,608	3,096	1,630
Martial arts	4,549	30	2,912	1,637	1,317	822	621	786	538	242	152	71	931	718	623	821	792	664
Racquetball	4,699	29	3,343	1,356	150	425	1,135	1,543	791	485	103	66	514	590	643	813	1,299	839
Running/jogging [1]	20,635	13	11,874	8,761	2,037	3,594	3,703	5,008	3,215	1,960	616	503	2,488	2,569	2,650	3,840	5,101	3,989
Skiing—alpine/downhill	9,261	26	5,623	3,638	615	1,558	1,588	2,393	1,638	877	369	203	597	637	786	1,575	2,677	2,990
Skiing—cross country	3,428	31	1,757	1,672	288	438	443	557	801	479	298	125	509	203	374	464	963	914
Soccer	11,976	20	7,691	4,285	5,054	3,487	1,258	946	838	218	85	86	1,384	1,359	1,626	2,190	3,144	2,272
Softball	17,611	15	10,007	7,604	2,513	3,877	2,465	4,615	2,734	907	222	279	2,050	2,390	3,025	3,693	4,279	2,174
Swimming [1]	61,531	2	28,944	32,587	11,255	10,096	6,860	10,809	10,905	5,172	3,110	3,322	8,258	7,763	8,468	11,695	14,492	10,855
Table tennis	9,274	25	5,474	3,799	1,087	2,165	1,341	1,782	1,664	699	255	280	1,012	1,170	1,212	1,986	2,315	1,579
Target shooting	11,193	21	9,019	2,174	720	1,450	1,632	3,084	2,270	1,207	565	267	1,570	1,730	1,964	2,540	2,123	1,267
Tennis	12,571	18	6,813	5,758	1,157	2,250	2,479	2,720	2,102	1,073	512	278	1,414	1,502	1,335	2,045	3,210	3,065
Volleyball	17,957	14	8,772	9,184	2,003	4,290	3,429	4,172	2,728	968	294	73	2,586	2,336	2,622	3,759	4,229	2,425

X Not applicable. [1] Participant engaged in activity at least six times in the year. [2] Includes wilderness camping. [3] Vacation/overnight.

Source: National Sporting Goods Association, Mt. Prospect, IL, *Sports Participation in 1995: Series I* (copyright).

No. 420. Participation in Selected Sports Activities: 1995

[In thousands, except rank. For persons 7 years of age or older. Based on a sampling of 20,000 households]

ACTIVITY	ALL PERSONS		SEX		AGE								HOUSEHOLD INCOME (dol.)					
	Number	Rank	Male	Female	7-11 years	12-17 years	18-24 years	25-34 years	35-44 years	45-54 years	55-64 years	65 years and over	Under 15,000	15,000-24,999	25,000-34,999	35,000-49,999	50,000-74,999	75,000 and over
Total	235,454	(X)	114,344	121,107	18,898	22,154	25,467	41,670	42,149	30,224	21,241	33,649	46,165	36,070	33,687	40,686	46,912	31,933
Number participating in:																		
Archery (target)	4,827	14	3,699	1,129	744	838	697	1,082	912	341	129	84	978	655	526	983	1,083	602
Boating, motor/power	24,999	1	14,354	10,645	1,739	2,188	3,046	6,055	5,217	3,377	1,960	1,417	2,834	3,116	3,397	4,622	6,474	4,557
Canoeing	7,201	8	4,165	3,037	676	1,044	1,087	1,399	1,532	847	371	246	1,006	805	956	1,097	2,061	1,278
Dart throwing	19,374	4	11,702	7,671	1,437	1,576	3,662	6,443	3,793	1,591	540	332	4,178	2,972	3,151	3,605	3,446	2,022
Hunting with bow arrow	5,267	13	4,760	507	117	464	908	1,672	1,205	490	286	126	952	645	772	1,265	1,129	504
Ice hockey	2,473	18	2,029	444	524	708	516	315	312	58	42	-	431	104	220	541	625	553
Ice/figure skating	7,060	9	2,647	4,413	1,946	1,768	978	915	886	313	160	115	895	546	868	1,507	1,936	1,309
Mountain biking-off road	5,717	11	3,732	1,984	526	640	1,225	1,754	1,034	340	134	64	981	653	950	877	1,218	1,037
Mountain biking-on road	10,451	7	6,094	4,357	982	1,311	1,923	3,193	1,925	654	296	167	1,595	1,080	1,671	1,881	2,418	1,805
Roller hockey	3,162	17	2,507	655	1,162	1,142	380	261	138	15	21	43	401	276	433	607	883	561
Roller skating/in-line wheels	23,869	2	11,864	12,005	8,012	6,827	3,013	3,223	1,851	491	164	298	2,959	2,437	3,439	4,751	6,209	4,075
Roller skating/traditional 2x2 wheel	13,645	5	4,925	8,720	4,724	3,535	1,149	1,816	1,506	391	253	270	2,593	1,887	2,345	3,239	2,367	1,214
Sailing	3,692	16	2,017	1,675	197	423	328	748	864	470	340	324	440	385	224	445	980	1,240
Scuba (open water)	2,383	19	1,640	743	29	131	467	732	548	335	91	50	230	201	168	528	619	636
Skate boarding	4,336	15	3,322	1,015	1,500	1,829	445	279	170	46	26	41	785	633	619	756	875	669
Snorkeling	5,714	12	3,044	2,670	371	454	722	1,332	1,274	1,016	358	188	474	327	420	812	1,555	2,126
Snowboarding	2,254	20	1,646	607	409	776	471	351	175	29	35	8	203	351	319	415	465	500
Step aerobics	11,428	6	1,308	10,120	107	677	2,295	3,515	2,580	1,144	548	560	1,875	1,381	1,521	2,109	2,511	2,031
Water skiing	6,935	10	4,035	2,900	505	992	1,554	2,130	1,117	426	181	31	675	727	992	1,217	1,958	1,367
Wind surfing	521	21	330	191	-	59	108	167	52	80	38	17	58	75	50	58	150	130
Work out at club	22,008	3	10,773	11,235	242	1,019	4,368	6,234	5,070	2,623	1,224	1,227	2,388	2,346	2,781	3,905	5,335	5,252

- Represents or rounds to zero. X Not applicable.

Source: National Sporting Goods Association, Mt. Prospect, IL, *Sports Participation in 1995: Series II* (copyright).

No. 421. Sporting Goods Sales, by Product Category: 1987 to 1996

[In millions of dollars, except percent. Based on a sample survey of consumer purchases of 80,000 households, (100,000 beginning 1995), except recreational transport, which was provided by industry associations. Excludes Alaska and Hawaii]

SELECTED PRODUCT CATEGORY	1987	1988	1989	1990	1991	1992	1993	1994	1995	1996, proj.
Sales, all products	36,791	43,937	46,585	48,250	47,104	47,110	48,129	53,453	55,452	57,168
Annual percent change [1]	10.2	19.4	10.6	-0.7	-2.4	(Z)	4.3	8.8	3.7	3.1
Percent of retail sales	2.4	2.7	2.8	2.8	2.5	2.4	2.4	2.4	2.4	2.3
Athletic and sport clothing [2]	4,645	9,555	10,286	10,130	10,731	8,990	9,096	9,521	9,699	10,030
Athletic and sport footwear [3]	6,373	6,797	10,435	11,654	11,767	11,733	11,084	11,120	11,420	11,835
Walking shoes	996	1,471	2,419	2,950	2,669	2,666	2,673	2,543	2,841	2,955
Gym shoes, sneakers	1,537	1,602	2,303	2,536	2,545	2,397	2,016	1,869	1,741	1,758
Jogging and running shoes	1,023	987	1,106	1,110	1,192	1,232	1,231	1,069	1,043	1,106
Tennis shoes	467	448	645	740	759	748	599	556	480	469
Aerobic shoes	634	514	667	611	600	590	500	366	372	380
Basketball shoes	364	493	631	918	974	984	874	867	999	1,049
Golf shoes	186	183	186	226	249	260	275	238	225	234
Athletic and sport equipment [3]	9,900	10,705	11,504	11,964	12,062	12,846	13,880	15,257	15,060	15,691
Firearms and hunting	1,804	1,894	2,139	2,202	2,091	2,533	2,722	3,490	2,955	3,015
Exercise equipment	1,191	1,452	1,748	1,824	2,106	2,050	2,602	2,449	2,857	3,000
Golf	948	1,111	1,167	1,219	1,149	1,338	1,248	1,342	1,366	1,434
Camping	858	945	996	1,072	1,006	903	906	1,017	1,208	1,305
Bicycles (10-12-15-18+ speed)	930	819	906	1,092	(NA)	(NA)	(NA)	(NA)	(NA)	(NA)
Fishing tackle	830	766	769	776	711	678	716	717	737	751
Snow skiing	661	710	608	606	577	627	611	652	607	644
Tennis	238	264	315	287	295	296	267	257	241	248
Archery	224	236	261	265	270	334	265	306	302	296
Baseball and softball	173	174	206	217	214	245	323	295	249	254
Water skis	146	160	96	86	63	56	51	51	54	55
Bowling accessories	129	129	143	155	156	164	159	157	160	165
Recreational transport	15,873	16,880	16,360	14,502	12,524	13,541	15,069	17,555	19,273	19,612
Pleasure boats	8,906	9,637	9,319	7,644	5,862	5,766	6,246	7,679	9,064	9,518
Recreational vehicles	4,507	4,839	4,481	4,113	3,615	4,412	4,775	5,690	5,894	5,766
Bicycles and supplies	2,272	2,131	2,259	2,423	2,686	2,973	3,534	3,470	3,390	3,356
Snowmobiles	188	273	301	322	362	391	515	715	924	970

NA Not available. Z Less than .05 percent. [1] Represents change from immediate prior year. [2] Category expanded in 1988; not comparable with earlier years. [3] Includes other products not shown separately.

Source: National Sporting Goods Association, Mt. Prospect, IL, *The Sporting Goods Market in 1996*; and prior issues (copyright).

No. 422. Consumer Purchases of Sporting Goods, by Consumer Characteristics: 1995

[In percent. Based on sample survey of consumer purchases of 100,000 households. Excludes Alaska and Hawaii]

CHARACTERISTIC	Total households	FOOTWEAR				EQUIPMENT					
		Aerobic shoes	Gym shoes/ sneakers	Jogging/ running shoes	Walking shoes	Fishing tackle	Camping equipment	Exercise equipment	Hunting equipment	Team sports equipment guns	Golf equipment
Total	100	100	100	100	100	100	100	100	100	100	100
Age of user:											
Under 14 years old	21	7	42	13	5	6	15	-	3	48	2
14 to 17 years old	6	4	13	12	3	4	10	2	3	23	6
18 to 24 years old	10	8	6	8	3	4	10	3	5	5	3
25 to 34 years old	16	26	11	18	11	16	23	17	26	11	17
35 to 44 years old	16	28	12	24	18	23	21	28	23	8	21
45 to 64 years old	20	21	12	22	37	33	13	37	33	3	35
65 years old and over	13	4	4	4	23	7	3	9	7	-	16
Multiple ages	-	-	-	-	-	8	9	4	1	1	-
Sex of user:											
Male	49	12	52	58	36	80	62	41	93	81	82
Female	51	88	48	42	64	18	30	52	6	19	18
Both sexes	-	-	-	-	-	4	9	7	1	-	-
Education of household head:											
Less than high school	10	5	6	4	7	10	6	6	7	4	10
High school	26	23	28	16	25	21	19	22	22	17	26
Some college	35	36	35	32	34	40	38	34	44	34	35
College graduate	29	36	31	49	33	29	39	39	27	44	29
Annual household income:											
Under $15,000	22	14	12	9	13	12	9	8	9	7	4
$15,000 to $24,999	18	12	15	11	16	12	14	13	14	9	5
$25,000 to $34,999	15	14	15	12	16	15	15	13	15	12	11
$35,000 to $49,999	18	21	23	21	20	21	22	20	22	23	23
$50,000 to $74,999	17	20	21	25	21	23	24	22	23	28	25
$75,000 and over	11	18	14	22	15	17	18	24	18	21	32

- Represents or rounds to zero.

Source: National Sporting Goods Association, Mt. Prospect, IL, *The Sporting Goods Market in 1996* (copyright).

No. 423. Arts Grants by Major Subject: 1992

[Arts categories are those used in the Foundation Center's grants classification system and are adapted from the National Taxonomy of Exempt Entities. Based on a sample of 802 larger foundations in 1992]

SUBJECT	NUMBER OF GRANTS		VALUE OF GRANTS	
	Number	Percent	Mil. dol.	Percent
Total	9,526	100.0	726.2	100.0
Performing arts	4,119	43.2	275.5	37.9
Centers	374	3.9	32.8	4.5
Dance	525	5.5	31.8	4.4
Ballet	239	2.5	15.6	2.1
Other	274	2.9	15.7	2.2
Choreography	12	0.1	0.6	0.1
Theater	1,065	11.2	52.9	7.3
General	1,033	10.8	52.0	7.2
Playwriting	32	0.3	0.9	0.1
Opera/musical theater	430	4.5	23.0	3.2
Music	1,160	12.2	102.1	14.1
Orchestras	588	6.2	58.7	8.1
Ensembles/groups	129	1.4	4.7	0.6
Choral music	88	0.9	5.6	0.8
Music composition	33	0.3	3.0	0.4
Other	322	3.4	30.1	4.1
Education	311	3.3	20.0	2.8
Multi-media	43	0.5	1.4	0.2
Circus arts	12	0.1	0.4	0.1
Other	199	2.1	11.1	1.5
Museum activities	1,966	20.6	225.4	31.0
Art	827	8.7	94.1	13.0
Children's	121	1.3	9.1	1.2
Ethnic/folk	113	1.2	8.2	1.1
History	184	1.9	19.9	2.7
Natural history	206	2.2	24.6	3.4
Science	194	2.0	27.3	3.8
Specialized	122	1.3	15.2	2.1
Other	199	2.1	27.2	3.7
Media/Communications	922	9.7	57.1	7.9
Film/video	117	1.2	7.9	1.1
Television	296	3.1	21.5	3.0
Publishing/Journalism	293	3.1	15.2	2.1
Radio	94	1.0	5.5	0.8
Other	120	1.3	6.8	0.9
Multidisciplinary arts	874	9.2	50.4	6.9
Centers	267	2.8	23.9	3.3
Ethnic/folk	167	1.8	7.2	1.0
Education	291	3.1	13.3	1.8
Councils	149	1.6	5.9	0.8
Arts-related humanities	350	3.7	39.3	5.4
General	87	0.9	17.8	2.4
Art history	39	0.4	1.2	0.2
History/archeology	108	1.1	6.3	0.9
Literature	116	1.2	14.0	1.9
Historical activities	661	6.9	39.7	5.5
Preservation	559	5.9	34.8	4.8
Societies	26	0.3	1.0	0.1
Other	76	0.8	3.9	0.5
Visual arts	333	3.5	24.6	3.4
General	221	2.3	16.8	2.3
Architecture	25	0.3	1.8	0.3
Photography	23	0.2	1.4	0.2
Sculpture	17	0.2	1.9	0.3
Design	7	0.1	0.2	0.0
Painting	8	0.1	0.3	0.0
Drawing	8	0.1	0.2	0.0
Conservation	24	0.3	2.0	0.3
Other	301	3.2	14.2	2.0
Policy/education	15	0.2	0.6	0.1
Associations/administration	42	0.4	3.4	0.5
Fundraising/management	94	1.0	4.0	0.6
Artist's services	40	0.4	1.2	0.2
Unspecified	110	1.2	4.8	0.7

Source: The Foundation Center, New York, NY, *Arts Funding Revisited: An Update on Foundation Trends in the 1990s*, 1995 (copyright).

No. 424. Arts and Humanities—Selected Federal Aid Programs: 1980 to 1995

[In millions of dollars, except as indicated. For fiscal years ending in year shown, see text, section 9]

TYPE OF FUND AND PROGRAM	1980	1985	1989	1990	1991	1992	1993	1994	1995
National Endowment for the Arts:									
Funds available [1]	188.1	171.7	166.7	170.8	166.5	163.0	159.7	158.1	152.1
Program appropriation	97.0	118.7	123.5	124.3	124.6	123.0	120.0	116.3	109.0
Matching funds [2]	42.9	29.5	23.6	32.4	32.4	30.3	27.4	29.4	28.5
Grants awarded (number)	5,505	4,801	4,604	4,475	4,239	4,229	4,096	3,843	3,581
Funds obligated [3]	166.4	149.4	148.3	157.6	158.0	154.6	148.4	145.2	147.9
Music	13.6	15.3	15.3	16.5	14.1	14.9	12.4	10.9	10.9
State programs	22.1	24.4	25.5	26.1	37.7	37.0	42.0	40.7	39.2
Museums	11.2	11.9	12.7	12.1	11.3	11.1	9.9	9.4	9.0
Theater	8.4	10.6	10.7	10.6	9.4	9.4	8.3	8.8	7.3
Dance	8.0	9.0	9.5	9.6	8.5	8.2	7.9	7.6	7.1
Media arts	8.4	9.9	12.7	13.9	11.8	12.0	10.2	10.9	8.9
Challenge [4]	50.8	20.7	15.4	19.7	19.7	13.8	11.7	9.6	21.1
Visual arts	7.3	6.2	6.1	5.9	5.3	5.6	5.1	4.8	4.4
Other	36.6	41.3	40.2	43.1	40.2	42.7	40.9	42.5	40.0
National Endowment for the Humanities:									
Funds available [1]	186.2	125.6	137.1	140.6	152.1	156.5	158.5	157.9	151.4
Program appropriation	100.3	95.2	108.3	114.2	125.1	131.2	131.9	131.4	125.7
Matching funds [2]	38.4	30.4	28.7	26.3	27.0	25.2	26.5	26.5	25.7
Grants awarded (number)	2,917	2,241	2,285	2,195	2,171	2,199	2,197	1,881	1,871
Funds obligated [3]	185.5	125.7	137.1	141.0	149.8	159.1	160.3	169.0	151.8
Education programs	18.3	17.9	16.5	16.3	18.5	20.0	20.8	19.6	19.2
State programs	26.0	24.4	29.0	29.6	30.8	31.8	32.4	32.2	32.0
Research grants	32.0	24.4	22.1	22.5	24.0	25.3	23.7	23.4	22.2
Fellowship program	18.0	15.3	15.3	15.3	16.2	17.4	18.9	17.7	16.5
Challenge [4]	53.5	19.6	16.7	14.6	15.1	12.4	14.2	14.4	13.8
Public programs	25.1	24.1	25.1	25.4	25.3	27.0	26.7	27.5	25.8
Preservation and access [5]	(X)	(X)	12.3	17.5	19.9	25.1	23.5	24.1	22.2
National Capital Arts and Cultural Affairs Program	(X)	(X)	(X)	(X)	(X)	(X)	(X)	(X)	(X)
Other	12.6	(X)	(X)	(X)	(X)	(X)	(X)	(X)	(X)

X Not applicable. [1] Includes other funds, shown separately. Excludes administrative funds. Gifts are included through 1980; excluded thereafter. [2] Represents Federal funds obligated only upon receipt or certification by Endowment of matching non-Federal gifts. [3] Includes obligations for new grants, supplemental awards on previous years' grants, and program contracts. [4] Program designed to stimulate new sources and higher levels of giving to institutions for the purpose of guaranteeing long-term stability and financial independence. Program requires a match of at least 3 private dollars to each Federal dollar. Funds for challenge grants are not allocated by program area because they are awarded on a grant-by-grant basis. [5] Program designed to support projects which preserve and guarantee access to print and nonprint media in danger of disintegration or deterioration.

Source: U.S. National Endowment for the Arts, *Annual Report;* and U.S. National Endowment for the Humanities, *Annual Report.*

No. 425. Attendance Rates for Various Arts Activities: 1992

nt. For persons 18 years old and over. Excludes elementary and high school performances. Based on 1992 household blic Participation in the Arts conducted January through December 1992. Data are subject to sampling error; see source. tables 416 and 426]

ITEM	ATTENDANCE AT LEAST ONCE IN THE PRIOR 12 MONTHS AT— Jazz performance	Classical music performance	Opera	Musical play	Non-musical play	Ballet	Art museum	Historic park	Reading literature[1]
....	11	13	3	17	14	5	27	36	54
).	12	12	3	15	12	4	27	35	47
).	9	13	4	20	15	6	27	34	60
ite	10	13	3	18	14	5	28	37	56
....	16	7	2	14	12	3	19	18	45
....	6	12	5	11	10	6	29	23	42
o 24 years old ..	11	10	3	16	13	5	29	33	53
4 years old	14	10	3	16	12	5	29	36	54
4 years old	13	12	3	19	14	5	30	40	59
4 years old	11	17	4	22	17	5	29	41	57
4 years old	8	15	4	19	15	5	25	33	53
'4 years old	7	14	4	17	13	4	20	29	50
6 years old	2	8	2	9	7	2	10	12	40
: Grade school ..	1	2	1	3	2	1	4	8	17
high school.	2	3	1	5	4	1	7	15	32
chool graduate ..	6	7	1	12	8	2	16	26	49
college	14	14	3	21	16	6	35	43	65
graduate	20	23	6	30	23	9	46	52	71
ite school.	25	36	12	37	35	12	59	64	79
Jnder $5,000 ...	8	5	2	8	8	2	12	17	37
to $9,999	5	6	1	7	6	3	14	16	40
0 to $14,999. ...	5	6	2	8	7	2	13	20	43
0 to $24,999. ...	9	11	2	14	11	3	23	31	50
0 to $49,999. ...	11	13	3	18	14	5	29	40	58
0 and over	18	23	6	33	24	10	44	51	71
orted	11	13	4	18	15	5	28	33	50

ludes novels, short stories, poetry, or plays.

ce: U.S. National Endowment for the Arts, *Arts Participation in America: 1982 to 1992.*

No. 426. Participation in Various Arts Activities: 1992

percent, except as indicated. Covers activities engaged in at least once in the prior 12 months. See headnote, table 425. See also table 416]

ITEM	Adult population (mil.)	IN THE PAST 12 MONTHS PERCENT ENGAGED AT LEAST ONCE IN— Playing classical music	Modern dancing[1]	Pottery work[2]	Needle-work[3]	Photo-graphy[4]	Paint-ing[5]	Creative writing	Buying art work
....	185.8	4	8	8	25	12	10	7	22
)	89.0	3	8	8	5	13	9	7	22
)	96.8	5	8	9	43	10	10	8	22
ite.	158.8	4	8	9	26	12	10	7	24
....	21.1	3	8	8	15	11	5	6	12
....	5.9	5	9	5	24	9	10	11	8
o 24 years old ...	24.1	6	11	9	18	11	19	14	13
4 years old	42.4	3	10	10	24	15	10	7	19
4 years old	39.8	4	7	10	25	13	10	8	27
4 years old	27.7	5	6	9	26	13	8	7	29
4 years old	21.2	5	6	6	27	10	6	5	26
'4 years old	18.3	4	9	6	29	7	6	5	20
5 years old	12.3	3	5	3	26	2	4	2	17
: Grade school ..	14.3	1	4	2	22	3	1	(Z)	4
high school	18.6	1	4	7	25	5	5	3	11
chool graduate ...	69.4	2	8	8	25	9	9	4	15
college	39.2	6	10	12	26	15	13	11	27
graduate	26.2	8	8	9	26	16	12	12	32
ite school	18.1	9	10	8	21	22	13	16	49
Jnder $5,000	8.6	2	7	7	22	6	8	7	10
to $9,999	15.2	2	7	4	27	7	8	7	10
0 to $14,999	19.2	3	7	8	26	8	8	6	14
0 to $24,999	32.9	4	9	8	26	9	10	7	17
0 to $49,999	62.2	5	8	10	25	13	10	7	22
0 and over.	32.1	6	8	8	23	17	11	9	40
orted	15.6	4	8	8	24	12	11	9	24

ss than .5 percent. [1] Dancing other than ballet (e.g. folk and tap). [2] Includes ceramics, jewelry, leatherwork, and k. [3] Includes weaving, crocheting, quilting, and sewing. [4] Includes making movies or video as an artistic activity. s drawing, sculpture, and printmaking.

ce: U.S. National Endowment for the Arts, *Arts Participation in America: 1982 to 1992.*

No. 427. Performing Arts—Selected Data: 1980 to 1995

[Receipts and expenditures in millions of dollars. For season ending in year shown, except as indicated]

ITEM	1980	1985	1988	1989	1990	1991	1992	1993	1994	1995
Legitimate theater: [1]										
Broadway shows:										
New productions	67	31	31	29	35	28	38	(NA)	(NA)	(NA)
Playing weeks [2] [3]	1,541	1,062	1,114	1,097	1,062	970	901	(NA)	(NA)	(NA)
Number of tickets sold (1,000)	9,380	7,156	8,142	7,968	8,039	7,314	7,365	(NA)	(NA)	(NA)
Gross box office receipts	143.4	208.0	253.4	262.0	283.3	267.2	292.4	(NA)	(NA)	(NA)
Road shows:										
Playing weeks [3]	1,351	993	893	869	944	1,152	1,171	(NA)	(NA)	(NA)
Gross box office receipts	181.2	225.9	222.9	255.5	367.1	450.2	502.7	(NA)	(NA)	(NA)
Nonprofit professional theatres: [4]										
Companies reporting	147	217	189	192	185	184	182	177	231	215
Gross income	113.6	234.7	276.4	349.0	307.6	333.9	359.1	342.5	455.1	444.4
Earned income	67.3	146.1	167.0	224.6	188.4	202.6	222.5	209.7	277.4	281.2
Contributed income	46.3	88.6	109.4	124.4	119.2	131.3	136.6	132.8	177.7	163.1
Gross expenses	113.6	239.3	277.9	349.2	306.3	336.7	365.6	349.3	460.2	444.9
Productions	1,852	2,710	2,369	2,469	2,265	2,277	2,310	2,319	2,929	2,646
Performances	42,109	52,341	46,149	53,263	46,131	48,695	46,184	44,933	59,542	56,608
Total attendance (mil.)	14.2	14.2	13.9	18.7	15.2	16.9	16.0	16.5	20.7	18.6
OPERA America professional member companies: [5]										
Number of companies [6]	79	97	99	101	98	98	100	85	86	88
Expenses [6]	122.4	216.4	294.4	311.7	321.2	348.7	371.8	369.5	404.9	435.0
Performances [7]	1,372	1,909	2,378	2,429	2,336	2,283	2,424	1,945	1,982	2,251
Total attendance (mil.) [7] [8]	5.5	6.7	6.8	7.4	7.5	7.6	7.3	5.5	6.0	6.5
Main season attendance (mil.) [7] [9]	(NA)	3.3	3.9	4.0	4.1	4.3	4.3	3.6	3.7	3.9
Symphony orchestras: [10]										
Concerts	(NA)	19,573	21,306	20,630	18,931	18,074	19,778	18,389	17,796	18,543
Attendance (mil.)	(NA)	24.0	27.4	25.8	24.7	26.7	26.3	24.0	24.4	23.2
Gross revenue	(NA)	252.4	325.3	353.2	377.5	394.5	414.0	430.5	442.5	458.7
Concert income	(NA)	168.6	218.0	231.0	253.3	273.8	284.1	294.1	303.6	316.5
Endowment income	(NA)	(NA)	42.6	46.8	52.1	52.5	55.3	59.7	60.4	64.6
Other earned income	(NA)	83.8	64.7	75.4	72.1	68.2	74.6	76.8	78.5	77.7
Operating expenses	(NA)	426.1	541.2	583.5	621.7	662.2	683.0	689.9	710.0	741.6
Artistic personnel	(NA)	231.9	288.0	310.2	327.3	355.8	396.9	378.8	389.9	400.6
Concert production	(NA)	69.2	85.8	89.0	104.3	110.3	117.2	114.3	129.3	138.7
Advertising and promotion	(NA)	32.5	42.0	47.5	51.3	57.3	58.3	63.1	67.3	64.9
General and administrative	(NA)	51.3	61.5	68.4	73.3	75.6	76.2	73.6	74.4	76.6
Other	(NA)	41.3	63.9	68.4	65.6	63.2	32.4	60.1	49.1	60.8
Support	(NA)	188.1	229.2	249.0	257.8	281.2	279.6	293.0	293.1	304.2
Tax supported grants	(NA)	42.2	52.1	54.5	55.6	58.3	49.1	48.0	46.4	48.0
Private sector support	(NA)	145.9	177.1	194.5	202.1	222.9	230.5	245.0	246.7	256.2

NA Not available. [1] Source: *Variety*, New York, NY, various June issues, (copyright). [2] All shows (new productions and holdovers from previous seasons). [3] Eight performances constitute one playing week. [4] Source: Theatre Communications Group, New York, NY. For years ending on or prior to Aug. 31. [5] Source: OPERA America, Washington, DC. [6] United States companies. [7] Prior to 1993, United States and Canadian companies; beginning 1993, US companies only. [8] Includes educational performances, outreach, etc. [9] For paid performances. [10] Source: American Symphony Orchestra League, Inc., Washington, DC. For years ending Aug. 31. Data represent all United States orchestras, excluding college/university and youth orchestras.

Source: Compiled from sources listed in footnotes.

No. 428. Boy Scouts and Girl Scouts—Membership and Units: 1970 to 1996

[In thousands. Boy Scouts as of Dec. 31; Girl Scouts as of Sept. 30. Includes Puerto Rico and outlying areas]

ITEM	1970	1975	1980	1985	1990	1991	1992	1993	1994	1995	1996
BOY SCOUTS OF AMERICA											
Membership	6,287	5,318	4,318	4,845	5,448	5,319	5,334	5,354	5,378	5,457	5,629
Boys	4,683	3,933	3,207	3,755	4,293	4,150	4,146	4,165	4,188	4,256	4,399
Adults	1,604	1,385	1,110	1,090	1,155	1,168	1,188	1,189	1,190	1,201	1,230
Total units (packs, troops, posts, groups)	157	150	129	134	130	128	128	128	129	132	135
GIRL SCOUTS OF THE U.S.A.											
Membership	3,922	3,234	2,784	2,802	3,269	3,383	3,510	3,438	3,363	3,318	3,390
Girls	3,248	2,723	2,250	2,172	2,480	2,561	2,647	2,612	2,561	2,534	2,584
Adults	674	511	534	630	788	822	863	826	802	784	807
Total units (troops, groups)	164	159	154	166	202	210	219	221	216	215	219

Source: Boy Scouts of America, National Council, Irving, TX, *Annual Report;* and Girl Scouts of the United States of America, New York, NY, *Annual Report.*

No. 429. Travel by U.S. Residents—Summary: 1985 to 1995

[In millions, except party size. See headnote table 430]

TYPE OF TRIP	1985	1988	1989	1990	1991	1992	1993	1994	1995
All travel: Total trips [1]	497.8	584.9	592.2	589.4	592.4	650.7	648.2	665.3	669.7
Person trips	808.3	924.5	945.2	956.0	960.1	1,063.0	1,057.5	1,139.1	1,172.6
Party size	1.6	1.6	1.6	1.6	1.7	1.6	1.6	1.7	1.8
Business travel: Total trips	156.6	182.8	199.3	182.8	176.9	210.8	210.4	193.2	207.8
Person trips	196.1	224.1	245.6	221.8	224.0	278.0	275.4	246.7	275.2
Party size	1.3	1.2	1.2	1.2	1.3	1.3	1.3	1.3	1.3
Pleasure travel: Total trips	301.2	356.7	358.3	361.1	364.3	411.7	413.4	434.3	413.0
Person trips	539.5	620.5	632.5	649.4	666.6	736.4	740.0	781.2	809.5
Party size	1.8	1.7	1.8	1.8	1.8	1.8	1.8	1.8	1.9
Vacation travel: Total trips	264.5	308.4	324.4	328.7	327.7	352.8	352.2	343.4	349.7
Person trips	487.8	556.2	587.9	591.6	605.3	637.1	633.2	664.6	680.4
Party size	1.8	1.8	1.8	1.8	1.9	1.8	1.8	1.9	1.9

[1] Includes other trips, not shown separately.

Source: U.S. Travel Data Center/Travel Industry Association of America, Washington, DC, *National Travel Survey*, annual, (copyright).

No. 430. Characteristics of Business Trips and Pleasure Trips: 1985 to 1995

[Represents trips to places 100 miles or more from home by one or more household members traveling together. Based on a monthly telephone survey of 1,500 U.S. adults. For details, see source]

CHARACTERISTIC	Unit	BUSINESS TRIPS				PLEASURE TRIPS			
		1985	1990	1994	1995	1985	1990	1994	1995
Total trips	Millions	156.6	182.8	193.2	207.8	301.2	361.1	434.3	413.0
Average household members on trip	Number	1.3	1.2	1.3	1.3	1.8	1.8	1.8	1.9
Average nights per trip [1]	Nights	3.6	3.7	2.9	3.1	5.6	4.4	3.6	3.8
Average miles per trip [2]	Miles	1,180	1,020	979	1022	1,010	867	759	781
Traveled primarily by auto/truck/RV [3] rental car	Percent	51	58	62	63	73	77	85	84
Traveled primarily by air	Percent	44	37	36	35	21	18	12	13
Used a rental car while on trip	Percent	20	14	23	22	6	7	9	8
Stayed in a hotel while on trip	Percent	62	71	69	66	39	37	41	39
Used a travel agent	Percent	28	21	24	24	13	12	8	9
Also a vacation trip	Percent	13	17	11	14	80	82	76	74
Male travelers	Percent	67	71	74	74	48	49	52	53
Female travelers	Percent	33	29	26	26	52	51	48	47
Household income:									
Less than $40,000	Percent	58	42	21	25	73	63	49	47
$40,000 or more	Percent	42	56	79	75	27	38	51	53

[1] Includes no overnight stays. [2] United States only. [3] Recreational vehicle.

Source: U.S. Travel Data Center/Travel Industry Association of America, Washington, DC, *National Travel Survey*, annual, (copyright).

No. 431. Arrangement of Passenger Transportation—Receipts and and Expenses, by Source: 1989 to 1995

[In millions of dollars. For taxable employer firms. Data are for SIC 472. Based on the 1987 Standard Industrial Classification code; see text, section 13]

ITEM	1989	1990	1991	1992	1993	1994	1995
RECEIPTS							
Total	9,822	10,921	10,152	10,573	11,073	11,795	12,891
Air carriers	5,401	5,837	5,527	5,881	6,138	6,375	6,846
Water carriers	394	474	520	523	528	584	663
Hotels and motels	693	771	676	744	758	808	867
Motor coaches	343	403	385	379	388	397	413
Railroads	106	127	130	110	125	126	145
Rental cars	157	175	171	187	189	204	242
Packaged tours	1,978	2,250	1,931	1,989	2,158	2,425	2,634
Other	750	884	812	760	789	876	1,081
EXPENSES							
Total	8,799	9,912	9,469	9,705	10,136	10,869	11,565
Annual payroll	3,468	3,891	3,740	3,924	4,031	4,526	4,818
Employer contributions to Social Security and other supplemental benefits	464	519	516	526	558	628	663
Lease and rental payments	825	919	874	873	908	908	1,021
Advertising and promotion	588	722	636	653	713	746	753
Taxes and licenses	148	158	134	135	144	163	181
Utilities	295	352	341	371	386	388	412
Depreciation	371	409	379	326	339	361	381
Purchased office supplies	306	321	295	300	294	325	352
Purchased repair services	124	156	139	124	134	152	168
Other	2,210	2,465	2,415	2,473	2,629	2,692	2,806

Source: U.S. Bureau of the Census, *Current Business Reports, Service Annual Survey: 1995*, BS/95.

No. 432. Domestic Travel Expenditures, by State: 1994

[Represents U.S. spending on domestic overnight trips and day trips of 100 miles or more away from home. Excludes spending by foreign visitors and by U.S. residents in U.S. territories and abroad]

STATE	Total (mil. dol.)	Share of total (percent)	Rank	STATE	Total (mil. dol.)	Share of total (percent)	Rank	STATE	Total (mil. dol.)	Share of total (percent)	Rank
U.S., total	**340,026**	**100.0**	(X)	KY	3,791	1.1	29	OH	9,126	2.7	11
AL	3,845	1.1	28	LA	5,548	1.6	21	OK	2,790	0.8	37
AK	1,164	0.3	45	ME	1,475	0.4	42	OR	3,938	1.2	27
AZ	5,867	1.7	19	MD	5,411	1.6	22	PA	10,589	3.1	8
AR	2,928	0.9	34	MA	7,679	2.3	14	RI	737	0.2	51
CA	43,962	12.9	1	MI	7,943	2.3	13	SC	5,130	1.5	23
CO	6,396	1.9	17	MN	4,639	1.4	24	SD	861	0.3	49
CT	3,472	1.0	30	MS	2,970	0.9	32	TN	7,262	2.1	15
DE	879	0.3	48	MO	6,560	1.9	16	TX	21,157	6.2	3
DC	3,083	0.9	31	MT	1,446	0.4	43	UT	2,846	0.8	35
FL	29,050	8.6	2	NE	1,868	0.6	39	VT	1,041	0.3	47
GA	9,795	2.9	9	NV	14,485	4.3	6	VA	9,479	2.8	10
HI	6,179	1.8	18	NH	1,503	0.4	41	WA	5,590	1.6	20
ID	1,536	0.5	40	NJ	11,187	3.3	7	WV	1,421	0.4	44
IL	14,883	4.4	5	NM	2,837	0.8	36	WI	4,588	1.4	25
IN	4,423	1.3	26	NY	20,713	6.1	4	WY	1,130	0.3	46
IA	2,963	0.9	33	NC	8,512	2.5	12				
KS	2,503	0.7	38	ND	833	0.2	50				

X Not applicable.
Source: U.S. Travel Data Center, Washington, DC, *Impact of Travel on State Economies, 1994* (copyright).

No. 433. International Travelers and Expenditures, With Projections: 1987 to 1997

[For coverage, see table 434. Minus sign (-) indicates deficit]

YEAR	TRAVEL AND PASSENGER FARE (mil. dol.)				U.S. net travel and passenger payments (mil. dol.)	U.S. travelers to foreign countries (1,000)	Foreign visitors to the U.S. (1,000)
	Payments by U.S. travelers		Receipts from foreign visitors				
	Total [1]	Expenditures abroad	Total [1]	Travel receipts			
1987	36,593	29,310	30,566	23,563	-6,027	39,410	27,834
1988	39,843	32,114	38,409	29,434	-1,434	40,669	33,942
1989	41,665	33,416	46,863	36,205	5,198	41,138	36,365
1990	47,880	37,349	58,305	43,007	10,425	44,623	39,363
1991	45,334	35,322	64,237	48,384	18,903	41,566	42,674
1992	49,108	38,552	71,359	54,742	22,251	43,896	47,261
1993	52,026	40,713	74,486	57,875	22,460	44,411	45,779
1994	56,667	43,782	75,500	58,417	18,833	46,450	44,753
1995	60,168	45,855	79,671	61,137	19,503	50,763	43,318
1996, est.	68,976	52,567	84,133	64,373	15,157	52,050	44,791
1997, proj.	75,032	57,183	88,928	68,043	13,896	53,991	46,216

[1] Includes passenger fares not shown separately.
Source: U.S. Dept. of Commerce, International Trade Administration, Internet site <http://www.tinet.ita.doc.gov/free> (Accessed 09 June 1997)

No. 434. Foreign Travel: 1988 to 1995

[Travelers in thousands; expenditures in millions of dollars. U.S. travelers cover residents of the United States, its territories and possessions. Foreign travelers to the U.S. include travelers for business and pleasure, international travelers in transit through the United States, and students; excludes travel by international personnel and international businessmen employed in the United States]

ITEM AND AREA	1988	1989	1990	1991	1992	1993	1994	1995
U.S. travelers to foreign countries	**40,669**	**41,138**	**44,623**	**41,566**	**43,896**	**44,411**	**46,450**	**50,763**
Canada	12,763	12,184	12,252	12,003	11,819	12,024	12,542	12,933
Mexico	13,463	14,163	16,381	15,042	16,114	15,285	15,759	18,771
Total overseas	14,443	14,791	15,990	14,521	15,965	17,102	18,149	19,059
Europe	7,438	7,233	8,043	6,316	7,136	7,491	8,167	8,596
Latin America [1]	4,203	4,392	4,749	5,155	5,285	5,729	5,880	6,003
Japan	793	921	1,103	897	1,017	1,043	871	839
Australia, New Zealand, South Africa	849	730	721	684	639	719	835	801
Other	1,160	1,515	1,374	1,469	1,888	2,120	2,396	2,820
Expenditures abroad	32,114	33,416	37,349	35,322	38,552	40,713	43,782	45,855
Fares to foreign carriers	7,729	8,249	10,531	10,012	10,556	11,313	12,885	14,313
Foreign travelers to the U.S.	**33,942**	**36,365**	**39,363**	**42,674**	**47,261**	**45,779**	**44,753**	**43,318**
Canada	13,700	15,325	17,263	19,113	18,598	17,293	14,974	14,663
Mexico	7,730	7,041	7,041	7,406	10,872	9,824	11,321	8,016
Total overseas	12,512	13,999	15,059	16,155	17,791	18,662	18,458	20,639
Total travel receipts	29,434	36,205	43,007	48,384	54,742	57,875	58,417	61,137
Fares to U.S. carriers	8,976	10,658	15,298	15,854	16,618	16,611	17,083	18,534

[1] Includes Central and South America and the Caribbean.
Source: U.S. Dept. of Commerce, International Trade Administration, Internet site <http://www.tinet.ita.doc.gov/free> (Accessed 09 June 1997)

No. 435. Top States and Cities Visited by Overseas Travelers: 1994 and 1995

[Includes travelers for business and pleasure, international travelers in transit through the United States, and students; excludes travel by international personnel and international businessmen employed in the United States]

STATE	OVERSEAS VISITORS (1,000)		MARKET SHARE (percent)		CITY	OVERSEAS VISITORS (1,000)		MARKET SHARE (percent)	
	1994	1995	1994	1995		1994	1995	1994	1995
Total overseas travelers	18,458	20,639	100.0	100.0					
Florida	4,910	5,346	26.6	25.9	New York City	3,968	4,252	21.5	20.6
California	4,984	5,304	27.0	25.7	Los Angeles	3,175	3,323	17.2	16.1
New York	4,190	4,479	22.7	21.7	Miami	2,732	2,951	14.8	14.3
Hawaii	2,639	2,910	14.3	14.1	San Francisco	2,381	2,539	12.9	12.3
Nevada	1,790	1,858	9.7	9.0	Orlando	2,233	2,621	12.1	12.7
Guam	941	1,238	5.1	6.0	Honolulu	2,178	2,373	11.8	11.5
Illinois	960	1,115	5.2	5.4	Las Vegas	1,696	1,754	9.2	8.5
Massachusetts	960	1,053	5.2	5.1	DC Metro Area	1,218	1,589	6.6	7.7
Arizona	904	887	4.9	4.3	Chicago	904	1,053	4.9	5.1
Texas	923	867	5.0	4.2	Boston	886	970	4.8	4.7
Washington	443	599	2.4	2.9	San Diego	701	722	3.8	3.5
Georgia	572	599	3.1	2.9	Atlanta	498	495	2.7	2.4
Pennsylvania	554	599	3.0	2.9	Anaheim	443	495	2.4	2.4
New Jersey	554	599	3.0	2.9	Houston	332	433	1.8	2.1
Utah	406	433	2.2	2.1	Tampa/St. Petersburg	388	516	2.1	2.5
Colorado	406	433	2.2	2.1	Seattle	406	537	2.2	2.6

Source: U.S. Dept. of Commerce, International Trade Administration, Internet site <http://www.tinet.ita.doc.gov/free> (Accessed 09 June 1997)

No. 436. Foreign Visitors for Pleasure Admitted, by Country of Last Residence: 1985 to 1995

[In thousands. For years ending September 30. See headnote, table 7, section 1]

COUNTRY	1985	1990	1994	1995
Total [1]	6,609	13,418	17,155	17,612
Europe [2]	2,048	5,383	6,944	7,012
Austria	34	87	132	146
Belgium	39	95	153	153
Denmark	36	75	79	78
Finland	24	83	48	47
France	226	566	686	738
Greece	34	43	47	44
Ireland	55	81	126	126
Italy	155	308	457	427
Netherlands	82	214	302	308
Norway	41	80	80	71
Poland	40	55	33	36
Soviet Union	2	53	44	54
Spain	64	183	236	248
Sweden	71	230	154	142
Switzerland	110	236	294	321
United Kingdom	598	1,899	2,461	2,342
Germany [3]	373	969	1,450	1,550
Asia [2]	1,866	3,830	5,023	5,666
China (Mainland China and Taiwan)	83	187	353	378
Hong Kong	64	111	145	162
India	52	75	67	75
Israel	80	128	150	160
Japan	1,277	2,846	3,506	3,986
Korea	26	120	361	427
Philippines	59	76	87	85
Saudi Arabia	31	33	47	45
Singapore	23	32	47	61

COUNTRY	1985	1990	1994	1995
Africa [2]	101	105	138	137
Egypt	16	16	17	16
Nigeria	25	11	10	10
Oceania [2]	282	562	478	478
Australia	195	380	334	327
New Zealand	74	153	103	115
North America	1,664	2,463	2,763	2,240
Canada	79	119	144	127
Mexico	773	1,061	1,324	893
Caribbean [2]	584	963	886	831
Bahamas, The	211	332	269	234
Barbados	17	34	38	36
Cayman Islands	18	31	33	31
Dominican Republic	57	137	150	138
Haiti	56	57	27	43
Jamaica	74	132	129	130
Netherlands Antilles	27	31	39	32
Trinidad and Tobago	71	81	68	64
Central America [2]	228	320	408	387
Costa Rica	41	62	91	91
El Salvador	38	46	63	63
Guatemala	53	91	108	99
Panama	38	43	58	54
South America [2]	606	1,016	1,718	1,978
Argentina	66	136	338	320
Brazil	148	300	507	710
Chile	28	54	96	117
Colombia	123	122	174	174
Ecuador	42	57	78	77
Peru	44	97	99	96
Venezuela	122	199	353	400

[1] Includes countries unknown or not reported. [2] Includes countries not shown separately. [3] Data prior to 1994 for former West Germany.

Source: U.S. Immigration and Naturalization Service, *Statistical Yearbook*, annual.

Figure 8.1
Participation in Elections for President and Representatives—Percent of Voting-Age Population: 1972 to 1996

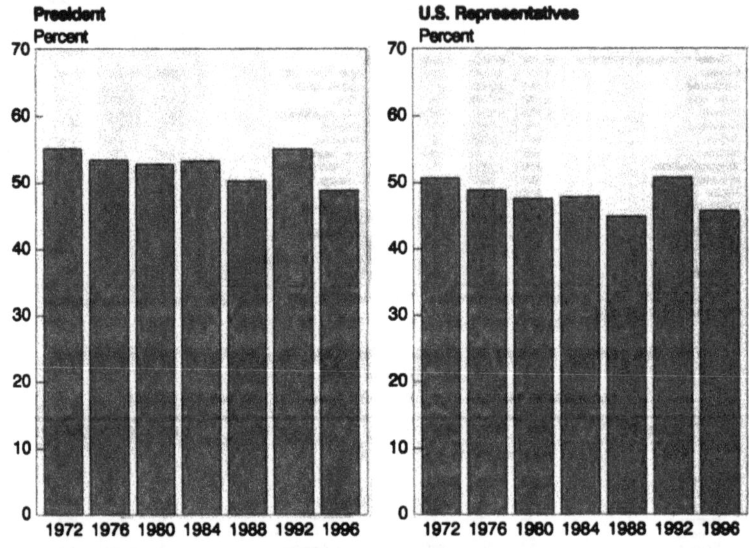

Source: Chart prepared by U.S. Bureau of the Census. For data, see table 464.

Figure 8.2
Political Campaign Receipts: 1981 to 1994

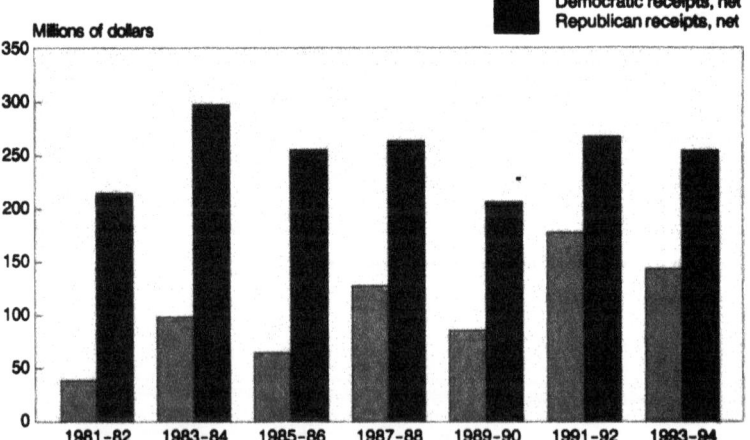

Democratic receipts, net
Republican receipts, net

Millions of dollars
350
300
250
200
150
100
50
0
1981-82 1983-84 1985-86 1987-88 1989-90 1991-92 1993-94

Source: Chart prepared by U.S. Bureau of the Census. For data, see table 466.

Elections

ection relates primarily to Presiden-
ngressional, and gubernatorial elec-
Also presented are summary tables
ngressional legislation; State legisla-
Black, Hispanic, and female office-
's; population of voting age; voter
pation; and campaign finances.

al statistics on Federal elections,
ted by the Clerk of the House, are
hed biennially in *Statistics of the
dential and Congressional Election
Statistics of the Congressional Elec-*
Federal and State elections data
ar also in *America Votes*, a biennial
e published by Congressional
erly, Inc., Washington, D.C. Federal
ons data also appear in the U.S.
ress, *Congressional Directory*, and
cial State documents. Data on re-
d registration and voting for social
conomic groups are obtained by
.S. Bureau of the Census as part of
urrent Population Survey (CPS)
re published in *Current Population
ts*, P20 (see text, section 1).

st all Federal, State, and local gov-
ental units in the United States con-
lections for political offices and oth-
poses. The conduct of elections is
ated by State laws or, in some cities
ounties, by local charter. An excep-
that the U.S. Constitution pre-
es the basis of representation in
ress and the manner of electing the
dent, and grants to Congress the
o regulate the times, places, and
er of electing Federal officers.
dments to the Constitution have
ribed national criteria for voting eli-
y. The 15th Amendment, adopted in
gave all citizens the right to vote
dless of race, color, or previous
tion of servitude. The 19th Amend-
adopted in 1919, further extended
ght to vote to all citizens regardless
. The payment of poll taxes as a
quisite to voting in Federal elections
anned by the 24th Amendment in
In 1971, as a result of the 26th
dment, eligibility to vote in national
ons was extended to all citizens, 18
old and over.

In Brief

Percent of voting-age population voting for Representatives:

1990	*33.1%*
1996	*45.7%*

Members of Congress:

	1981	1995
Black	*17*	*41*
Asian, Pacific Islander	*6*	*6*
Hispanic	*6*	*17*
Female	*21*	*55*

Presidential election—The Constitution specifies how the President and Vice President are selected. Each State elects, by popular vote, a group of electors equal in number to its total of members of Congress. The 23d Amendment, adopted in 1961, grants the District of Columbia three presidential electors, a number equal to that of the least populous State. Subsequent to the election, the electors meet in their respective States to vote for President and Vice President. Usually, each elector votes for the candidate receiving the most popular votes in his or her State. A majority vote of all electors is necessary to elect the President and Vice President. If no candidate receives a majority, the House of Representatives, with each State having one vote, is empowered to elect the President and Vice President, again, with a majority of votes required.

The 22d Amendment to the Constitution, adopted in 1951, limits presidential tenure to two elective terms of 4 years each, or to one elective term for any person who, upon succession to the Presidency, has held the office or acted as President for more than 2 years.

Congressional election—The Constitution provides that Representatives be apportioned among the States according to their population; that a census of population be taken every 10 years as a basis for apportionment; and that each State have at least one Representative. At the time of each apportionment, Congress decides what the total number of Representatives will be. Since 1912, the total has been 435, except during 1960 to 1962 when it increased to 437, adding one Representative each for Alaska and Hawaii. The total reverted to 435 after reapportionment following the 1960 census. Members are elected for 2-year terms, all terms covering the same period. The District of Columbia, American Samoa, Guam, and the Virgin Islands each elect one nonvoting Delegate and Puerto Rico elects a nonvoting Resident Commissioner.

The Senate is composed of 100 members, two from each State, who are elected to serve for a term of 6 years. One-third of the Senate is elected every 2 years. Senators were originally chosen by the State legislatures. The 17th Amendment to the Constitution, adopted in 1913, prescribed that Senators be elected by popular vote.

Voter eligibility and participation—The Census Bureau publishes estimates of the population of voting age and the percent casting votes in each State for Presidential and congressional election years. These voting-age estimates include a number of persons who meet the age requirement but are not eligible to vote, (e.g. aliens and some institutionalized persons). In addition, since 1964, voter participation and voter characteristics data have been collected during November of election years as part of the CPS. These survey data include noncitizens in the voting age population estimates, but exclude members of the Armed Forces and the institutional population.

Statistical reliability—For a discussion of statistical collection and estimation, sampling procedures, and measures of statistical reliability applicable to Census Bureau data, see Appendix III.

Figure 8.3
Popular Vote Cast for President, by Major Political Party: 1972 to 1996

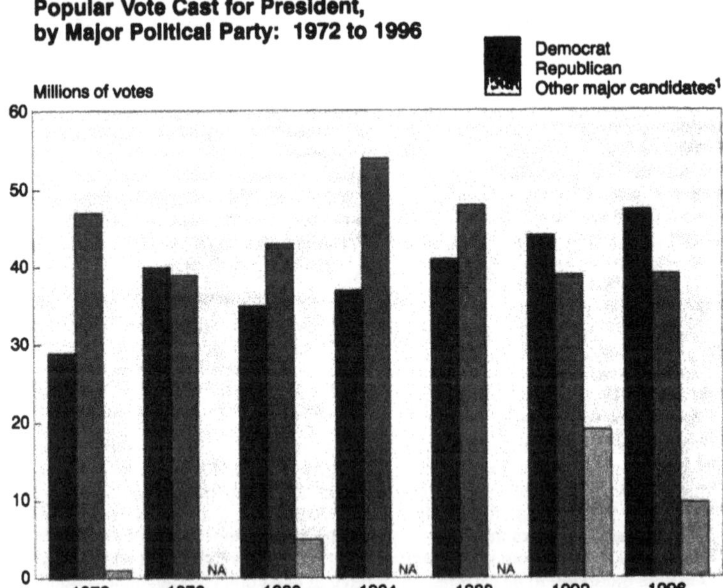

[1] 1972—American, John Schmitz; 1980—Independent, John Anderson; 1992—Independent, Ross Perot; 1996 Reform, Ross Perot, Green, Ralph Nader.

No. 437. Vote Cast for President, by Major Political Party: 1936 to 1996

[Prior to 1960, excludes Alaska and Hawaii; prior to 1964, excludes DC. Vote cast for major party candidates include the votes of minor parties cast for those candidates]

YEAR	Candidates for president: Democratic	Candidates for president: Republican	Total popular vote[1] (1,000)	Democratic: Popular vote: Number (1,000)	Democratic: Popular vote: Percent	Democratic: Electoral vote	Republican: Popular vote: Number (1,000)	Republican: Popular vote: Percent	Republican: Electoral vote
1936	F. D. Roosevelt	Landon	45,655	27,757	60.8	523	16,684	36.5	8
1940	F. D. Roosevelt	Willkie	49,900	27,313	54.7	449	22,348	44.8	82
1944	F. D. Roosevelt	Dewey	47,977	25,613	53.4	432	22,018	45.9	99
1948	Truman	Dewey	48,794	24,179	49.6	303	21,991	45.1	189
1952	Stevenson	Eisenhower	61,551	27,315	44.4	89	33,936	55.1	442
1956	Stevenson	Eisenhower	62,027	26,023	42.0	73	35,590	57.4	457
1960	Kennedy	Nixon	68,838	34,227	49.7	303	34,108	49.5	219
1964	Johnson	Goldwater	70,645	43,130	61.1	486	27,178	38.5	52
1968	Humphrey	Nixon	73,212	31,275	42.7	191	31,785	43.4	301
1972	McGovern	Nixon	77,719	29,170	37.5	17	47,170	60.7	520
1976	Carter	Ford	81,556	40,831	50.1	297	39,148	48.0	240
1980	Carter	Reagan	86,515	35,484	41.0	49	43,904	50.7	489
1984	Mondale	Reagan	92,653	37,577	40.6	13	54,455	58.8	525
1988	Dukakis	Bush	91,595	41,809	45.6	111	48,886	53.4	426
1992	Clinton	Bush	104,425	44,909	43.0	370	39,104	37.4	168
1996	Clinton	Dole	96,273	47,401	49.2	379	39,197	40.7	159

[1] Include votes for minor party candidates, independents, unpledged electors, and scattered write-in votes.

Source: Congressional Quarterly, Inc., Washington, D.C.. *America at the Polls 2*, 1965, and *America Votes*, biennial, (copyright).

No. 438. Vote Cast for Leading Minority Party Candidates for President: 1936 to 1996

[See headnote, table 437]

YEAR	Candidate	Party	Popular vote (1,000)	Candidate	Party	Popular vote (1,000)
1936	William Lemke	Union	892	Norman Thomas	Socialist	188
1940	Norman Thomas	Socialist	116	Roger Babson	Prohibition	59
1944	Norman Thomas	Socialist	79	Claude Watson	Prohibition	75
1948	Strom Thurmond	States' Rights	1,176	Henry Wallace	Progressive	1,157
1952	Vincent Hallinan	Progressive	140	Stuart Hamblen	Prohibition	73
1956	T. Coleman Andrews	States' Rights	111	Eric Hass	Socialist Labor	44
1960	Eric Hass	Socialist Labor	48	Rutherford Decker	Prohibition	46
1964	Eric Hass	Socialist Labor	45	Clifton DeBerry	Socialist Workers	33
1968	George Wallace	American Independent	9,906	Henning Blomen	Socialist Labor	53
1972	John Schmitz	American	1,099	Benjamin Spock	People's	79
1976	Eugene McCarthy	Independent	757	Roger McBride	Libertarian	173
1980	John Anderson	Independent	5,720	Ed Clark	Libertarian	921
1984	David Bergland	Libertarian	228	Lyndon H. LaRouche	Independent	79
1988	Ron Paul	Libertarian	432	Lenora B. Fulani	New Alliance	217
1992	H. Ross Perot	Independent	19,742	Andre Marrou	Libertarian	292
1996	H. Ross Perot	Reform Party	8,085	Ralph Nader	Green	685

Source: Congressional Quarterly, Inc. Washington, D.C., *America at the Polls 1920-1996*, 1997; and *America Votes*, biennial (copyright).

No. 439. Democratic and Republican Percentages of Two-Party Presidential Vote, by Selected Characteristics of Voters: 1988 and 1992

[In percent. Covers citizens of voting age living in private housing units in the contiguous United States. Percentages for Democratic Presidential vote are computed by subtracting the percentage Republican vote from 100 percent; third-party or independent votes are not included as valid data. Data are from the National Election Studies and are based on a sample and subject to sampling variability; for details, see source]

CHARACTERISTIC	1988: Democratic	1988: Republican	1992: Democratic	1992: Republican
Total[1]	47	53	58	42
Year of birth:				
1959 or later	48	52	58	42
1943 to 1958	47	53	58	42
1927 to 1942	49	51	56	44
1911 to 1926	44	56	62	38
1895 to 1910	47	53	58	42
Sex:				
Male	44	56	55	45
Female	50	50	61	39
Race:				
White	41	59	53	47
Black	92	8	94	6
Education:				
Grade school	61	39	70	30
High school	51	49	63	37
College	42	58	55	45
Union household	59	41	68	32
Non-union household	44	56	57	43

[1] Includes other characteristics, not shown separately.

Source: Center for Political Studies, University of Michigan, Ann Arbor, MI, unpublished data (copyright).

No. 440. Electoral Vote Cast for President, by Major Political Party—States: 1956 to 1996

[D=Democratic, R=Republican. For composition of regions, see table 27]

REGION, DIVISION, AND STATE	1956 [1]	1960 [2]	1964	1968 [3]	1972 [4]	1976 [5]	1980	1984	1988 [6]	1992	1996
Democratic	73	303	486	191	17	297	49	13	111	370	379
Republican	457	219	52	301	520	240	489	525	426	168	159
Northeast: Democratic	-	121	126	102	14	86	4	-	53	106	106
Republican	133	12	-	24	108	36	118	113	60	-	-
Midwest: Democratic	13	71	149	31	-	58	10	10	29	100	100
Republican	140	82	-	118	145	67	135	127	108	29	29
South: Democratic	60	101	121	45	3	149	31	3	8	68	80
Republican	105	50	47	77	165	20	138	174	168	116	104
West: Democratic	-	10	90	13	-	4	4	-	21	96	93
Republican	79	75	5	82	102	97	98	111	90	23	26
New England: ME	R-5	R-5	D-4	D-4	R-4	R-4	R-4	R-4	R-4	D-4	D-4
NH	R-4	R-4	D-4	R-4	R-4	R-4	R-4	R-4	R-4	D-4	D-4
VT	R-3	R-3	D-3	R-3	R-3	R-3	R-3	R-3	R-3	D-3	D-3
MA	R-16	D-16	D-14	D-14	D-14	D-14	R-14	R-13	D-13	D-12	D-12
RI	R-4	D-4	D-4	D-4	R-4	D-4	D-4	R-4	D-4	D-4	D-4
CT	R-8	D-8	D-8	D-8	R-8	R-8	R-8	R-8	R-8	D-8	D-8
Middle Atlantic: NY	R-45	D-45	D-43	D-43	R-41	D-41	R-41	R-36	D-36	D-33	D-33
NJ	R-16	D-16	D-17	R-17	R-17	R-17	R-17	R-16	R-16	D-15	D-15
PA	R-32	D-32	D-29	D-29	R-27	D-27	R-27	R-25	R-25	D-23	D-23
East North Central: OH	R-25	R-25	D-26	R-26	R-25	D-25	R-25	R-23	R-23	D-21	D-21
IN	R-13	R-13	D-13	R-13	R-13	R-13	R-13	R-12	R-12	R-12	R-12
IL	R-27	D-27	D-26	R-26	R-26	R-26	R-26	R-24	R-24	D-22	D-22
MI	R-20	D-20	D-21	D-21	R-21	R-21	R-21	R-20	R-20	D-18	D-18
WI	R-12	R-12	D-12	R-12	R-11	D-11	R-11	R-11	D-11	D-11	D-11
West North Central: MN	R-11	D-11	D-10	D-10	R-10	D-10	D-10	D-10	D-10	D-10	D-10
IA	R-10	R-10	D-9	R-9	R-8	R-8	R-8	R-8	D-8	D-7	D-7
MO	D-13	D-13	D-12	R-12	R-12	D-12	R-12	R-11	R-11	D-11	D-11
ND	R-4	R-4	D-4	R-4	R-3	R-3	R-3	R-3	R-3	R-3	R-3
SD	R-4	R-4	D-4	R-4	R-4	R-4	R-4	R-3	R-3	R-3	R-3
NE	R-6	R-6	D-5	R-5	R-5	R-5	R-5	R-5	R-5	R-5	R-5
KS	R-8	R-8	D-7	R-7	R-7	R-7	R-7	R-7	R-7	R-6	R-6
South Atlantic: DE	R-3	D-3	D-3	R-3	R-3	D-3	R-3	R-3	R-3	D-3	D-3
MD	R-9	D-9	D-10	D-10	R-10	D-10	D-10	R-10	R-10	D-10	D-10
DC	(X)	(X)	D-3	D-3	D-3	D-3	D-3	D-3	D-3	D-3	D-3
VA	R-12	R-12	D-12	R-12	[4]R-11	R-12	R-12	R-12	R-12	R-13	R-13
WV	R-8	D-8	D-7	D-7	R-6	D-6	D-6	R-6	[6]D-5	D-5	D-5
NC	D-14	D-14	D-13	[3]R-12	R-13	D-13	R-13	R-13	R-13	R-14	R-14
SC	D-8	D-8	R-8	R-8	R-8	D-8	R-8	R-8	R-8	R-8	R-8
GA	D-12	D-12	R-12	([3])	R-12	D-12	D-12	R-12	R-12	D-13	R-13
FL	R-10	R-10	D-14	R-14	R-17	D-17	R-17	R-21	R-21	R-25	D-25
East South Central: KY	R-10	R-10	D-9	R-9	R-9	D-9	R-9	R-9	R-9	D-8	D-8
TN	R-11	R-11	D-11	R-11	R-10	D-10	R-10	R-11	R-11	D-11	D-11
AL	[1]D-10	[2]D-5	R-10	([3])	R-9	D-9	R-9	R-9	R-9	R-9	R-9
MS	D-8	([2])	R-7	([3])	R-7	D-7	R-7	R-7	R-7	R-7	R-7
West South Central: AR	D-8	D-8	D-6	([3])	R-6	D-6	R-6	R-6	R-6	D-6	D-6
LA	R-10	D-10	R-10	([3])	R-10	D-10	R-10	R-10	R-10	D-9	D-9
OK	R-8	[2]R-7	D-8	R-8	R-8	R-8	R-8	R-8	R-8	R-8	R-8
TX	R-24	D-24	D-25	D-25	R-26	D-26	R-26	R-29	R-29	R-32	R-32
Mountain: MT	R-4	R-4	D-4	R-4	R-4	R-4	R-4	R-4	R-4	D-3	R-3
ID	R-4	R-4	D-4	R-4	R-4	R-4	R-4	R-4	R-4	R-4	R-4
WY	R-3	R-3	D-3	R-3	R-3	R-3	R-3	R-3	R-3	R-3	R-3
CO	R-6	R-6	D-6	R-6	R-7	R-7	R-7	R-8	R-8	D-8	R-8
NM	R-4	D-4	D-4	R-4	R-4	R-4	R-4	R-5	R-5	D-5	D-5
AZ	R-4	R-4	R-5	R-5	R-6	R-6	R-6	R-7	R-7	R-8	D-8
UT	R-4	R-4	D-4	R-4	R-4	R-4	R-4	R-5	R-5	R-5	R-5
NV	R-3	D-3	D-3	R-3	R-3	R-3	R-3	R-4	R-4	D-4	D-4
Pacific: WA	R-9	R-9	D-9	D-9	R-9	[5]R-8	R-9	R-10	D-10	D-11	D-11
OR	R-6	R-6	D-6	R-6	R-6	R-6	R-6	R-7	D-7	D-7	D-7
CA	R-32	R-32	D-40	R-40	R-45	R-45	R-45	R-47	R-47	D-54	D-54
AK	(X)	R-3	D-3	R-3	R-3	R-3	R-3	R-3	R-3	R-3	R-3
HI	(X)	D-3	D-4	D-4	R-4	D-4	D-4	R-4	D-4	D-4	D-4

- Represents zero. X Not applicable. [1] Excludes one electoral vote cast for Walter B. Jones in Alabama. [2] Excludes 15 electoral votes cast for Harry F. Byrd as follows: AL 6, MS 8, and OK 1. [3] Excludes 46 electoral votes cast for American Independent George C. Wallace as follows: AL 10, AR 6, GA 12, LA 10, MS 7, and NC 1. [4] Excludes one electoral vote cast for Libertarian John Hospers in Virginia. [5] Excludes one electoral vote cast for Ronald Reagan in Washington. [6] Excludes one electoral vote cast for Lloyd Bentsen for President in West Virginia.

Source: 952-72, U.S. Congress, Clerk of the House, *Statistics of the Presidential and Congressional Election*, quadrennial; 1976-96, Congressional Quarterly, Inc., Washington D.C. *America Votes*, biennial (copyright).

Popular Vote Cast for President, by Political Party—States: 1992 and 1996

[In thousands, except percent]

ON,	1992				1996						
	Total [1]	Demo-cratic Party	Repub-lican Party	Percent for leading party [2]	Total [1]	Demo-cratic Party	Repub-lican Party	Perot (Inde-pen-dent)	Percent of total vote		
									Demo-cratic Party	Repub-lican Party	Perot (Inde-pen-dent)
ss. .	104,425	44,909	39,104	19,742	96,273	47,401	39,197	8,085	49.2	40.7	8.4
. . .	21,581	9,940	7,507	3,994	19,601	10,862	6,607	1,772	55.4	33.7	9.0
. . .	6,351	2,820	2,012	1,479	5,703	3,237	1,769	576	56.8	31.0	10.1
. . .	679	263	207	207	606	313	186	86	51.6	30.8	14.2
. . .	538	209	202	121	499	246	196	48	49.3	39.4	9.7
. . .	290	134	88	66	258	138	80	31	53.4	31.1	12.0
. . .	2,774	1,319	805	631	2,556	1,572	718	227	61.5	28.1	8.9
. . .	453	213	132	105	390	233	105	44	59.7	26.8	11.2
. . .	1,616	682	578	349	1,393	736	483	140	52.8	34.7	10.0
. . .	15,230	7,120	5,496	2,516	13,898	7,624	4,838	1,196	54.9	34.8	8.6
. . .	6,927	3,444	2,347	1,091	6,316	3,756	1,933	503	59.5	30.6	8.0
. . .	3,344	1,436	1,357	522	3,076	1,652	1,103	262	53.7	35.9	8.5
. . .	4,960	2,239	1,792	903	4,506	2,216	1,801	431	49.2	40.0	9.6
. . .	27,735	11,692	10,234	5,668	24,953	12,076	10,151	2,426	48.4	40.7	9.7
. . .	19,102	8,198	7,104	3,702	17,026	8,439	6,780	1,618	49.6	39.8	9.5
. . .	4,940	1,985	1,894	1,036	4,534	2,148	1,860	483	47.4	41.0	10.7
. . .	2,306	848	989	456	2,135	887	1,007	224	41.6	47.1	10.5
. . .	5,050	2,453	1,734	841	4,311	2,342	1,587	346	54.3	36.8	8.0
. . .	4,275	1,871	1,555	825	3,849	1,990	1,481	337	51.7	38.5	8.7
. . .	2,531	1,041	931	544	2,196	1,072	845	227	48.8	38.5	10.4
. . .	8,633	3,493	3,130	1,966	7,927	3,637	3,371	808	45.9	42.5	10.2
. . .	2,348	1,021	748	563	2,193	1,120	766	258	51.1	35.0	11.8
. . .	1,355	586	505	253	1,234	620	493	105	50.3	39.9	8.5
. . .	2,392	1,054	811	519	2,158	1,026	890	217	47.5	41.2	10.1
. . .	306	99	136	71	266	107	125	33	40.1	46.9	12.2
. . .	336	125	137	73	324	139	151	31	43.0	46.5	9.7
. . .	738	217	344	174	677	237	363	71	35.0	53.7	10.5
. . .	1,157	390	450	312	1,074	388	583	93	36.1	54.3	8.6
. . .	33,625	14,118	14,014	5,325	31,756	14,850	14,346	2,315	46.8	45.2	7.3
. . .	17,196	7,352	7,103	2,667	16,558	7,897	7,294	1,242	47.7	44.1	7.5
. . .	290	126	102	59	271	140	99	29	51.8	36.6	10.6
. . .	1,985	989	707	281	1,781	966	682	116	54.3	38.3	6.5
. . .	228	193	21	10	186	158	17	4	85.2	9.3	1.9
. . .	2,559	1,039	1,151	349	2,417	1,091	1,138	160	45.1	47.1	6.6
. . .	664	331	242	109	636	328	234	72	51.5	36.8	11.3
. . .	2,612	1,114	1,135	358	2,516	1,108	1,226	168	44.0	48.7	6.7
. . .	1,203	480	578	139	1,151	506	573	64	44.0	49.8	5.6
. . .	2,321	1,009	995	310	2,299	1,054	1,081	146	45.8	47.0	6.4
. . .	5,314	2,073	2,173	1,053	5,301	2,546	2,243	484	48.0	42.3	9.1
. . .	6,145	2,689	2,751	673	5,711	2,602	2,696	371	45.6	47.2	6.5
. . .	1,493	665	617	204	1,389	637	623	120	45.8	44.9	8.7
. . .	1,983	934	841	200	1,894	909	864	106	48.0	45.6	5.6
. . .	1,688	690	804	183	1,534	662	769	92	43.2	50.1	6.0
. . .	982	400	488	86	894	394	440	52	44.1	49.2	5.8
. . .	10,285	4,077	4,160	1,985	9,487	4,351	4,356	703	45.9	45.9	7.4
. . .	951	506	337	99	884	475	325	70	53.7	36.8	7.9
. . .	1,790	816	733	211	1,784	928	713	123	52.0	39.9	6.9
. . .	1,390	473	593	320	1,207	488	582	131	40.4	48.3	10.8
. . .	6,154	2,282	2,496	1,355	5,612	2,460	2,736	379	43.8	48.8	6.7
. . .	21,484	9,160	7,349	4,755	19,994	9,613	8,093	1,572	48.2	40.5	7.9
. . .	5,970	2,167	2,272	1,437	5,711	2,435	2,649	498	42.6	46.4	8.7
. . .	411	155	144	107	407	168	180	55	41.3	44.1	13.6
. . .	482	137	203	130	492	165	257	63	33.6	52.2	12.7
. . .	201	68	79	51	212	78	105	26	36.8	49.8	12.3
. . .	1,569	630	563	366	1,511	671	692	100	44.4	45.8	6.6
. . .	570	262	213	92	556	273	233	32	49.2	41.9	5.8
. . .	1,487	543	572	354	1,404	653	622	112	46.5	44.3	8.0
. . .	744	183	323	203	666	222	362	66	33.3	54.4	10.0
. . .	506	189	176	133	464	204	199	44	43.9	42.9	9.5
. . .	15,514	6,993	5,076	3,318	14,253	7,178	5,444	1,074	50.4	38.2	7.5
. . .	2,288	993	731	542	2,254	1,123	841	201	49.8	37.3	8.9
. . .	1,463	621	476	354	1,378	650	538	121	47.2	39.1	8.8
. . .	11,132	5,121	3,631	2,296	10,019	5,120	3,828	698	51.1	38.2	7.0
. . .	259	78	102	73	242	80	123	26	33.3	50.8	10.9
. . .	373	179	137	53	360	205	114	27	56.9	31.6	7.6

ble. [1] Includes other parties. [2] D=Democratic, R=Republican. Leading party vote refers to the party vote r a majority or a plurality for the victorious party in the area shown.

gressional Quarterly, Inc., Washington, DC. *America Votes*, biennial (copyright).

No. 442. Vote Cast for United States Senators, 1994 and 1996, and Incumbent Senators, 1996—States

[D=Democrat; R=Republican]

DIVISION AND STATE	1994 [1]		1996 [1]		INCUMBENT SENATORS AND YEAR TERM EXPIRES	
	Total (1,000)	Percent for leading party	Total (1,000)	Percent for leading party	Name, party, and year	Name, party, and year
N.E.:						
ME	511	R-60.3	607	R-49.2	Susan Collins (R) 2003	Olympia Snowe (R) 2001
NH	(X)	(X)	493	R-49.2	Judd Gregg (R) 1999	Robert C. Smith (R) 2003
VT	212	R-50.3	(X)	(X)	Patrick J. Leahy (D) 1999	James M. Jeffords (R) 2001
MA	2,179	D-58.1	2,556	D-52.2	Edward M. Kennedy (D) 2001	John F. Kerry (D) 2003
RI	345	R-64.5	363	D-63.5	Jack Reed (D) 2003	John H. Chafee (R) 2001
CT	1,080	D-67.0	(X)	(X)	Christopher J. Dodd (D) 1999	Joseph I. Lieberman (D) 2003
M.A.:						
NY	4,790	D-55.2	(X)	(X)	Daniel P. Moynihan (D) 2001	Alfonse M. D'Amato (R) 1999
NJ	2,055	D-50.3	2,884	D-52.5	Robert G. Torricelli (D) 2003	Frank R. Lautenberg (D) 2003
PA	3,513	R-49.4	(X)	(X)	Rick Santorum (R) 2001	Arlen Specter (R) 1999
E.N.C.:						
OH	3,437	R-53.4	(X)	(X)	John Glenn (D) 1999	Mike DeWine (R) 2001
IN	1,544	R-67.4	(X)	(X)	Dan Coats (R) 1999	Richard G. Lugar (R) 2001
IL	(X)	(X)	4,251	D-55.8	Carol Moseley Braun (D) 1999	Richard J. Durbin (D) 2003
MI	3,043	R-51.9	3,763	D-58.4	Carl Levin (D) 2003	Spencer Abraham (R) 2001
WI	1,565	D-58.3	(X)	(X)	Herb Kohl (D) 2001	Russell Feingold (D) 1999
W.N.C.:						
MN	1,773	R-49.1	2,183	D-50.3	Paul David Wellstone (D) 2003	Rod Grams (R) 2001
IA	(X)	(X)	1,224	D-51.8	Tom Harkin (D) 2003	Charles E. Grassley (R) 1999
MO	1,775	R-59.7	(X)	(X)	Christopher S. Bond (R) 1999	John Ashcroft (R) 2001
ND	237	D-58.0	(X)	(X)	Byron L. Dorgan (D) 1999	Kent Conrad (D) 2001
SD	(X)	(X)	325	D-51.3	Thomas A. Daschle (D) 1999	Tim Johnson (D) 2003
NE	579	D-54.8	677	R-56.1	Chuck Hagel (R) 2003	J. Robert Kerrey (D) 2001
KS	(X)	(X)	[2]1,065	R-53.8	Sam Brownback (R) 1999	Pat Roberts (R) 2003
S.A.:						
DE	199	R-55.8	276	D-60.0	Joseph R. Biden Jr. (D) 2003	William V. Roth, Jr. (R) 2003
MD	1,369	D-59.1	(X)	(X)	Barbara A. Mikulski (D) 1999	Paul S. Sarbanes (D) 2001
VA	2,057	D-45.6	2,355	R-52.5	Charles S. Robb (D) 2001	John W. Warner (R) 2003
WV	421	D-69.0	596	D-76.6	Robert C. Byrd (D) 2001	John D. Rockefeller IV (D)
NC	(X)	(X)	2,557	R-52.6	Lauch Faircloth (R) 1999	Jesse Helms (R) 2003
SC	(X)	(X)	1,161	R-53.4	Ernest F. Hollings (D) 1999	Strom Thurmond (R) 2003
GA	(X)	(X)	2,259	D-48.8	Paul Coverdell (R) 1999	Max Cleland (D) 2003
FL	4,105	R-70.5	(X)	(X)	Bob Graham (D) 1999	Connie Mack (R) 2001
E.S.C.:						
KY	(X)	(X)	1,307	R-55.5	Wendell H. Ford (D) 1999	Mitch McConnell (R) 2003
TN	[3]1,480	[3]R-56.4	1,779	R-61.4	Fred Thompson (R) 2003	Bill Frist (R) 2001
AL	(X)	(X)	1,499	R-51.9	Jeff Sessions (R) 2003	Richard C. Shelby (R) 1999
MS	608	R-68.8	879	R-71.0	Thad Cochran (R) 2003	Trent Lott (R) 2001
W.S.C.:						
AR	(X)	(X)	846	R-52.7	Dale Bumpers (D) 1999	Tim Hutchinson (R) 2003
LA	(X)	(X)	[4]1,700	D-50.2	John B. Breaux (D) 1999	Mary Landrieu (D) 2003
OK	962	R-55.2	(X)	(X)	James Inhofe (R) 2001	Don Nickles (R) 1999
TX	4,280	R-60.8	5,527	R-54.8	Kay Bailey Hutchison (R) 2001	Phil Gramm (R) 2003
Mountain:						
MT	350	R-62.4	407	D-49.6	Max Baucus (D) 2003	Conrad Burns (R) 2001
ID	(X)	(X)	497	R-57.0	Larry E. Craig (R) 2003	Dirk Kempthorne (R) 1999
WY	202	R-58.9	211	R-54.1	Mike Enzi (R) 2003	Craig Thomas (R) 2001
CO	(X)	(X)	1,470	R-50.7	Ben N. Campbell (R) 1999	Wayne Allard (R) 2003
NM	463	D-54.0	552	R-64.7	Jeff Bingaman (D) 2001	Pete V. Domenici (R) 2003
AZ	1,119	R-53.7	(X)	(X)	John McCain (R) 1999	Jon Kyl (R) 2001
UT	519	R-68.8	(X)	(X)	Robert F. Bennett (R) 1999	Orrin G. Hatch (R) 2001
NV	368	D-52.7	(X)	(X)	Harry Reid (D) 1999	Richard H. Bryan (D) 2001
Pacific:						
WA	1,700	R-55.7	(X)	(X)	Patty Murray (D) 1999	Slade Gorton (R) 2001
OR	[5]1,190	[5]D-48.4	1,360	R-48.8	Gordon Smith (R) 2003	Ron Wyden (D) 1999
CA	8,503	D-46.8	(X)	(X)	Barbara Boxer (D) 1999	Dianne Feinstein (D) 2001
AK	(X)	(X)	232	R-76.7	Frank H. Murkowski (R) 1999	Ted Stevens (R) 2003
HI	357	D-71.8	(X)	(X)	Daniel K. Akaka (D) 2001	Daniel K. Inouye (D) 1999

X Not applicable. [1] Includes vote cast for minor parties. [2] Kansas had elections to fill two Senate seats in 1996. Pat Roberts was elected to fill the full-term seat vacated by the retiring Nancy Kassenbaum. Sam Brownback was elected to fill the short-term seat vacated by Robert Dole, who resigned in 1996 to run for president. [3] In a special election in 1994 to fill an unexpired term, the Republican candidate received 60.4 percent of 1,465,835 total votes cast. [4] Louisiana holds an open-primary election with candidates from all parties running on the same ballot. Any candidate who receives a majority is elected. [5] Special election in January 1996 to fill the unexpired term of Senator Packwood.

Source: Congressional Quarterly, Inc., Washington, D.C. *America Votes*, biennial (copyright).

No. 443. Vote Cast for U.S. Representatives, by Major Political Party—States: 1990 to 1996

[In thousands, except percent. In each State, totals represent the sum of votes cast in each Congressional District or votes cast for Representative at Large in States where only one member is elected. In all years there are numerous districts within the State where either the Republican or Democratic party had no candidate. In some States the Republican and Democratic vote includes votes cast for the party candidate by endorsing parties]

REGION, DIVISION, AND STATE	1990				1994				1996			
	Total[1]	Democratic	Republican	Percent for leading party	Total[1]	Democratic	Republican	Percent for leading party	Total[1]	Democratic	Republican	Percent for leading party
U.S.[2]	**81,513**	**32,565**	**27,648**	**D-52.9**	**69,770**	**31,896**	**36,590**	**R-52.4**	**89,647**	**43,690**	**43,629**	**D-48.7**
Northeast	**12,792**	**6,483**	**5,868**	**D-50.7**	**14,398**	**7,016**	**6,927**	**D-48.7**	**18,097**	**9,788**	**7,770**	**D-54.1**
ME	517	284	233	D-55.0	503	236	234	D-47.0	600	379	211	D-63.2
NH	291	141	149	R-51.2	309	117	180	R-58.2	491	221	247	R-50.3
VT	210	6	83	[3]I-56.0	211	-	99	[3]I-49.9	255	24	83	[3]I-58.1
MA	2,051	1,420	567	D-69.2	1,976	1,363	593	D-69.0	2,407	1,584	780	D-65.8
RI	347	182	165	D-52.5	342	209	132	D-61.3	360	241	108	[4]D-65.9
CT	1,037	489	546	R-52.6	1,069	506	516	R-48.3	1,294	724	547	D-55.9
M.A.	**8,339**	**3,959**	**4,126**	**R-47.1**	**9,967**	**4,585**	**5,173**	**R-51.8**	**12,690**	**6,616**	**5,794**	**D-52.1**
NY[4]	3,662	1,830	1,662	D-50.0	4,611	2,213	2,251	R-48.8	5,551	3,041	2,358	D-54.8
NJ	1,827	837	911	R-49.9	2,005	880	1,091	R-54.4	2,823	1,352	1,399	R-49.6
PA	2,851	1,293	1,552	R-54.5	3,371	1,492	1,831	R-54.3	4,316	2,223	2,038	D-51.5
E.N.C	**11,899**	**6,202**	**5,363**	**D-53.0**	**12,348**	**5,421**	**6,803**	**R-55.1**	**16,447**	**8,187**	**7,913**	**D-49.8**
OH	3,418	1,807	1,590	D-52.9	3,298	1,328	1,925	R-58.4	4,389	2,031	2,192	R-49.9
IN	1,514	831	683	D-54.9	1,546	667	875	R-56.6	2,082	931	1,109	R-53.3
IL	3,077	1,646	1,349	D-53.5	3,044	1,460	1,577	R-51.8	4,128	2,268	1,813	D-54.9
MI	2,434	1,321	1,089	D-54.3	3,001	1,418	1,532	R-51.0	3,699	1,945	1,679	D-52.6
WI	1,256	597	652	R-51.9	1,459	548	893	R-61.2	2,149	1,013	1,121	R-52.1
W.N.C	**5,786**	**3,168**	**2,607**	**D-54.6**	**6,420**	**2,992**	**3,344**	**R-52.1**	**7,755**	**3,723**	**3,720**	**D-48.0**
MN	1,781	1,042	736	D-58.5	1,748	884	847	D-50.6	2,142	1,180	895	D-55.1
IA	792	401	385	D-50.6	977	407	560	R-57.3	1,200	533	650	R-54.1
MO	1,353	728	625	D-53.8	1,766	894	834	D-50.6	[5]2,116	1,116	833	D-52.8
ND	234	153	81	D-65.2	235	123	108	D-52.3	263	145	114	D-55.1
SD	257	174	83	D-67.6	306	183	112	D-59.8	323	120	186	R-57.7
NE	587	277	309	R-52.7	571	203	365	R-64.0	662	205	450	R-68.0
KS	781	394	387	D-50.4	817	298	519	R-63.5	1,049	425	591	R-56.4
S.A.[2]	**9,409**	**5,222**	**4,063**	**D-55.5**	**10,660**	**4,566**	**6,017**	**R-56.4**	**15,052**	**6,964**	**7,942**	**R-52.8**
DE	177	116	58	D-65.5	195	52	138	R-70.7	267	73	186	R-69.5
MD	1,091	566	517	D-51.9	1,345	662	683	R-50.7	1,639	877	762	D-53.5
DC	160	98	42	D-61.7	(NA)	(NA)	(NA)	(NA)	(NA)	(NA)	(NA)	(NA)
VA	1,153	663	411	D-57.5	1,908	753	1,089	R-57.1	2,199	1,027	1,117	R-50.8
WV	375	251	123	D-67.1	407	269	138	D-66.1	522	459	64	D-87.8
NC	2,011	1,076	935	D-53.5	1,588	681	907	R-57.1	2,514	1,136	1,340	R-53.3
SC	670	383	275	D-57.2	867	313	552	R-63.6	1,057	345	683	R-64.6
GA	1,394	855	539	D-61.3	1,498	681	816	R-54.5	2,163	1,011	1,152	R-53.3
FL[6 7]	2,378	1,213	1,163	D-51.0	2,852	1,156	1,694	R-59.4	4,691	2,037	2,639	R-56.3
E.S.C	**2,866**	**1,712**	**1,070**	**D-59.7**	**3,936**	**1,839**	**2,041**	**R-51.9**	**5,394**	**2,417**	**2,893**	**R-53.6**
KY	784	353	397	R-52.0	784	316	451	R-57.5	1,238	507	731	R-59.0
TN	717	369	289	D-51.5	1,416	615	776	R-54.8	1,783	857	889	R-49.8
AL	1,017	690	315	D-67.9	1,115	554	558	R-50.1	1,469	656	786	R-53.5
MS	369	299	69	D-81.2	620	354	256	D-57.1	904	397	488	R-54.0
W.S.C	**4,906**	**2,758**	**2,132**	**D-56.2**	**5,798**	**2,438**	**3,222**	**R-55.6**	**7,738**	**3,489**	**4,100**	**R-53.0**
AR[6]	665	369	296	D-55.5	709	336	373	R-52.6	863	396	456	R-52.8
LA[8]	106	106	-	D-100.0	(X)	(X)	(X)	(X)	475	339	136	D-71.4
OK	857	519	338	D-60.6	969	368	555	R-57.3	1,180	431	723	R-61.3
TX[9]	3,278	1,763	1,496	D-53.8	4,120	1,734	2,294	R-55.7	5,220	2,323	2,785	R-53.4
Mountain	**3,872**	**1,783**	**2,043**	**R-52.8**	**4,438**	**1,706**	**2,580**	**R-58.1**	**5,588**	**2,280**	**3,147**	**R-56.3**
MT	317	157	160	R-50.5	352	171	149	D-48.7	404	175	212	R-52.4
ID	315	183	131	D-58.2	393	138	255	R-65.0	494	194	290	R-58.7
WY	158	71	87	R-55.1	196	81	104	R-53.2	210	86	116	R-55.2
CO	1,001	504	487	D-50.3	1,056	364	687	R-65.1	1,461	597	833	R-57.0
NM	359	146	214	R-59.5	462	188	263	R-57.1	548	271	261	D-49.4
AZ	966	345	621	R-64.3	1,099	410	653	R-59.4	1,356	521	801	R-59.0
UT	442	234	191	D-52.9	504	216	252	R-50.0	664	264	386	R-58.2
NV	313	144	151	R-48.2	376	138	216	R-57.4	450	173	249	R-55.3
Pacific	**10,185**	**5,239**	**4,502**	**D-51.4**	**11,771**	**5,719**	**5,657**	**D-48.6**	**13,577**	**6,842**	**6,144**	**D-50.4**
WA	1,313	696	596	D-53.0	1,687	827	854	R-50.6	2,174	1,130	1,021	D-52.0
OR	1,053	667	342	D-63.4	1,193	647	499	D-54.2	1,335	725	558	D-54.3
CA	7,287	3,568	3,347	D-49.0	8,328	3,958	4,066	R-48.8	9,481	4,707	4,292	D-49.6
AK	192	92	99	R-51.7	208	68	119	R-56.9	234	85	139	R-59.4
HI	341	216	118	D-63.3	354	219	120	D-61.9	353	196	136	D-55.5

- Represents zero. NA Not available. X Not applicable. [1] Includes vote cast for minor parties. Total for 1996 includes results from 431 districts, including 14 where members were elected without major party opposition. In 4 districts candidates ran unopposed and no vote was recorded. [2] Includes vote cast for nonvoting Delegate at Large in District of Columbia, except for 1994 and 1996. [3] Leading party candidate was Independent. [4] Includes votes cast by other endorsing parties [5] Total vote includes 112,472 votes cast for an Independent candidate This candidate won the election and joined Congress as a Republican. [6] State law does not require tabulation of votes for unopposed candidates. [7] In 1990 Districts 8, 10, 12, 13, and 16 were unopposed; in 1994 Districts 4, 10, 13, 14, 18, and 23 were unopposed; in 1996 District 4 was unopposed. [8] 1990 data are for a general election runoff in one district. In 1994 all Representatives won their seats in the open primary. In 1996, Districts 1, 2, and 3 were unopposed. Districts 4 and 6 were contested in the September primary election but the Republican candidate in both won a majority and did not have to run again in the November general election. In Districts 5 and 7 no candidate in the primary won a majority; as a result the top two finishers in the primary ran in the general election. 1996 data are for general election runoffs in these two districts. 1996 open primary totals-total, 660,000, Democratic 398,000 and Republican, 262,000. [9] Total includes votes from races held on November 5. Court-ordered redistricting in the Houston area, however, required runoff elections in three districts where no candidate received a majority. Those runoffs were held December 5; they are not included in the total vote count reported here.

Source: Congressional Quarterly, Inc., Washington, DC, *America Votes*, biennial (copyright).

No. 444. Vote Cast for United States Representatives, by Major Political Party—Congressional Districts: 1996

[In some States the Democratic and Republican vote includes votes cast for the party candidate by endorsing parties]

STATE AND DISTRICT	DEMOCRATIC CANDIDATE		REPUBLICAN CANDIDATE	
	Name	Percent of total	Name	Percent of total
AL	(X)	(X)	(X)	(X)
1st	Womack	33.9	Callahan	64.5
2d	Gaines	35.5	Everett	63.3
3d	Little	46.9	Riley	50.9
4th	Wilson	48.3	Aderholt	50.0
5th	Cramer	56.1	Parker	41.8
6th	Bates	27.4	Bachus	70.9
7th	Hilliard	71.2	Powell	27.1
AK	Lincoln	37.1	Young	59.1
AZ	(X)	(X)	(X)	(X)
1st	Cox	40.1	Salmon	59.9
2d	Pastor	64.7	Buster	31.1
3d	Schneider	33.6	Stump	66.4
4th	Milton	33.4	Shadegg	66.6
5th	Nelson	26.0	Kolbe	68.7
6th	Owens	46.9	Hayworth	47.2
AR	(X)	(X)	(X)	(X)
1st	Berry	52.8	Dupwe	44.3
2d	Snyder	52.3	Cummins	47.7
3d	Henry	41.9	Hutchinson	55.7
4th	Tolliver	36.5	Dickey	63.5
CA	(X)	(X)	(X)	(X)
1st	Alioto	44.1	Riggs	49.0
2d	Braden	34.0	Herger	60.5
3d	Fazio	53.6	LeFever	41.0
4th	Hirning	36.3	Doolittle	60.2
5th	Matsui	70.5	Dinsmore	26.1
6th	Woolsey	62.0	Hughes	33.8
7th	Miller	71.9	Reece	22.2
8th	Pelosi	84.5	Raimondo	12.2
9th	Dellums	77.2	Wright	18.2
10th	Tauscher	49.0	Baker	46.8
11th	Silva	36.3	Pombo	59.2
12th	Lantos	71.8	Jenkins	23.5
13th	Stark	65.4	Fay	30.2
14th	Eshoo	65.1	Brink	30.8
15th	Lane	35.4	Campbell	57.8
16th	Lofgren	66.1	Wojslaw	29.7
17th	Farr	58.5	Brown	38.1
18th	Condit	65.6	Conrad	31.9
19th	Barile	27.9	Radanovich	67.0
20th	Dooley	55.2	Harvey	40.3
21st	Vollmer	26.7	Thomas	65.7
22d	Capps	49.3	Seastrand	43.3
23d	Unruhe	35.9	Gallegly	58.5
24th	Sherman	50.4	Sybert	42.5
25th	Trautman	33.4	McKeon	62.2
26th	Berman	66.0	Glass	28.5
27th	Kahn	43.4	Rogan	49.9
28th	Levering	37.2	Dreier	60.4
29th	Waxman	68.1	Stepanek	24.1
30th	Becerra	72.7	Parker	18.2
31st	Martinez	67.7	Flores	27.7
32d	Dixon	82.7	Ardito	12.1
33d	Roybal-Allard	82.4	Leonard	13.8
34th	Torres	68.7	Nunez	26.3
35th	Waters	85.8	Carlson	11.8
36th	Harmon	52.8	Brooks	43.6
37th	Millender-McDonald	85.3	Voetee	14.7
38th	Zbur	42.6	Horn	52.6
39th	Davis	32.2	Royce	62.5
40th	Conaway	29.1	Lewis	64.8
41st	Waldron	33.3	Kim	58.1
42d	Brown	50.6	Wilde	49.4
43d	Kimbrough	38.5	Calvert	54.2
44th	Rufus	39.1	Bono	57.2
45th	Alexander	33.4	Rohrabacher	60.7
46th	Sanchez	46.1	Dornan	46.4
47th	Laine	29.1	Cox	65.3
48th	Farrell	27.3	Packard	65.4
49th	Navarro	42.5	Bilbray	52.0
50th	Filner	62.1	Baize	32.1
51st	Tamerius	29.3	Cunningham	64.7
52d	Wesley	30.0	Hunter	65.1
CO	(X)	(X)	(X)	(X)
1st	DeGette	56.9	Rogers	40.2
2d	Skaggs	57.0	Miller	38.3
3d	Gurule	31.1	McInnis	68.9
4th	Kelley	38.1	Schaffer	56.1
5th	Robinson	28.1	Hefley	71.9
6th	Fitz-Gerald	37.8	Schaefer	62.2
CT	(X)	(X)	(X)	(X)
1st	Kennelly	73.8	Steele	24.9
2d	Gejdenson	51.5	Munster	45.0
3d	DeLauro	71.2	Coppola	28.2
4th	Finch	37.5	Shays	60.6
5th	Maloney	52.1	Franks	45.9
6th	Koskoff	48.8	Johnson	49.8
DE	Williams	27.5	Castle	69.5
FL	(X)	(X)	(X)	(X)
1st	Beck	27.4	Scarborough	72.6
2d	Boyd	59.5	Sutton	40.5
3d	Brown [1]	61.2	(2)	(2)
4th	(2)	(2)	Fowler	(NA)
5th	Thurman	61.7	Gentry	38.3
6th	O'Brien	32.8	Stearns	67.2
7th	Stuart	38.0	Mica	62.0
8th	Krulick	32.5	McCollum	67.5
9th	Provenzano	31.3	Bilirakis	68.7
10th	Green	33.4	Young	66.6
11th	Davis	58.0	Sharpe	42.0
12th	Canady	38.4	Canady	61.6
13th	Gordon	35.6	Miller	64.4
14th	Nolan	26.5	Goss	73.5
15th	Byron	42.9	Weldon	51.4
16th	Stuber	35.9	Foley	64.1
17th	Meek	88.8	Rolle	11.2
18th	(2)	(2)	Ros-Lehtinen	(NA)
19th	Wexler	65.6	Kennedy	34.4
20th	Deutsch	65.0	Jacobs	35.0
21st	(2)	(2)	Diaz-Balart	(NA)
22d	Cooper	38.1	Shaw	61.9
23d	Hastings	73.5	Brown	26.5
GA	(X)	(X)	(X)	(X)
1st	Kaazans	31.8	Kingston	68.2
2d	Bishop	53.8	Ealum	46.2
3d	Chafin	38.9	Collins	61.1
4th	McKinney	57.8	Mitnick	42.2
5th	Lewis	(NA)	(2)	(2)
6th	Coles	42.2	Gingrich	57.8
7th	Watts	42.2	Barr	57.8
8th	Wiggins	47.4	Chambliss	52.6
9th	Poston	34.6	Deal	65.4
10th	Bell	48.2	Norwood	51.8
11th	Stephenson	35.7	Linder	64.3
HI	(X)	(X)	(X)	(X)
1st	Abercrombie	50.4	Swindle	46.5
2d	Mink	57.0	Pico	29.1
ID	(X)	(X)	(X)	(X)
1st	Williams	47.5	Chenoweth	50.0
2d	Seidl	29.5	Crapo	68.8

See footnotes at end of table.

No. 444. Vote Cast for United States Representatives, by Major Political Party—Congressional Districts: 1996—Continued

[See headnote, p. 276]

STATE AND DISTRICT	DEMOCRATIC CANDIDATE		REPUBLICAN CANDIDATE	
	Name	Percent of total	Name	Percent of total
IL	(X)	(X)	(X)	(X)
1st	Rush	86.1	Naughton	13.1
2d	Jackson	94.0	(2)	(2)
3d	Lipinski	65.2	Nalepa	32.1
4th	Gutierrez	93.6	(2)	(2)
5th	Blagojevich	64.1	Flanagan	35.9
6th	de la Rosa	33.4	Hyde	64.3
7th	Davis	82.3	Borow	15.3
8th	Hull	36.1	Crane	62.2
9th	Yates	63.3	Walsh	36.7
10th	Torf	30.9	Porter	69.1
11th	Balanoff	48.3	Weller	51.7
12th	Costello	71.6	Hunter	26.6
13th	Hynes	40.1	Fawell	59.9
14th	Mains	35.6	Hastert	64.4
15th	Prussing	42.7	Ewing	57.3
16th	Lee	39.7	Manzullo	60.3
17th	Evans	51.9	Baker	47.3
18th	Curran	40.7	LaHood	59.3
19th	Poshard	66.7	Winters	31.8
20th	Hoffman	49.7	Shimkus	50.3
IN	(X)	(X)	(X)	(X)
1st	Visclosky	69.1	Petyo	29.3
2d	Carmichael	39.7	McIntosh	58.1
3d	Roemer	57.9	Zakas	40.9
4th	Houseman	38.2	Souder	59.4
5th	Clark	32.6	Buyer	64.9
6th	Dillard-Trammell	23.1	Burton	74.9
7th	Hellmann	34.6	Pease	62.0
8th	Weinzapfel	48.3	Hostettler	49.9
9th	Hamilton	56.3	Leising	42.7
10th	Carson	52.6	Blanken-baker	45.1
IA	(X)	(X)	(X)	(X)
1st	Rush	45.7	Leach	52.9
2d	Smith	45.9	Nussle	53.5
3d	Boswell	49.2	Mahaffey	47.8
4th	McBurney	46.8	Ganske	52.1
5th	Smith	33.7	Latham	65.4
KS	(X)	(X)	(X)	(X)
1st	Divine	24.5	Moran	73.5
2d	Frieden	45.5	Ryun	52.2
3d	Hancock	45.4	Snowbarger	49.9
4th	Rathbun	46.6	Tiahrt	50.0
KY	(X)	(X)	(X)	(X)
1st	Null	46.4	Whitfield	53.6
2d	Wright	41.8	Lewis	58.2
3d	Ward	49.7	Northrup	50.3
4th	Bowman	31.7	Bunning	68.3
5th	(2)	(2)	Rogers	(X)
6th	Beesler	55.7	Fletcher	44.3
LA [3]	(X)	(X)	(X)	(X)
1st	(X)	(X)	Livingston [4]	(X)
2d	Jefferson [4]	(X)	(X)	(X)
3d	(X)	(X)	Tauzin [4]	(X)
4th	(X)	(X)	McCrery [4]	(X)
5th	Thompson	41.6	Cooksey	58.4
6th	(X)	(X)	Baker [4]	(X)
7th	Chris John [5]	53.1	(2)	(2)
ME	(X)	(X)	(X)	(X)
1st	Allen	55.4	Longley	44.6
2d	Baldacci	71.8	Young	24.9
MD	(X)	(X)	(X)	(X)
1st	Eastaugh	38.7	Gilchrest	61.3
2d	DeJuliis	38.3	Ehrlich	61.7
3d	Cardin	67.0	McDonough	33.0
4th	Wynn	85.4	Kimble	14.6
5th	Hoyer	57.0	Morgan	43.0
6th	Crawford	43.1	Bartlett	56.9
7th	Cummings	83.2	Kondner	16.8
8th	Mooers	38.7	Morella	61.3
MA	(X)	(X)	(X)	(X)
1st	Olver	52.7	Swift	47.3
2d	Neal	71.7	Steele	22.0
3d	McGovern	53.1	Blute	45.5
4th	Frank	71.6	Raymond	28.4
5th	Meehan	(X)	(X)	(X)
6th	Tierney	48.3	Torkildsen	48.1
7th	Markey	69.8	Long	30.2
8th	Kennedy	84.3	Hyde	15.7
9th	Moakley	72.4	Gryska	27.6
10th	Delahunt	54.5	Teague	41.8
MI	(X)	(X)	(X)	(X)
1st	Stupak	70.6	Carr	27.4
2d	Kruszynski	32.7	Hoekstra	65.5
3d	Flory	29.5	Ehlers	68.8
4th	Donaldson	32.7	Camp	65.5
5th	Barcia	70.0	Sims	28.2
6th	Annen	30.7	Upton	67.7
7th	Tunnicliff	44.5	Smith	53.4
8th	Stabenow	54.2	Chrysler	43.7
9th	Kildee	59.1	Nowak	38.9
10th	Bonior	54.5	Heintz	43.4
11th	Frumin	35.8	Knollenberg	61.3
12th	Levin	58.4	Pappa-george	39.4
13th	Rivers	56.3	Fitzsimmons	41.6
14th	Conyers	84.0	Ashe	13.6
15th	Kilpatrick	87.9	Hume	9.8
16th	Dingell	62.1	DeSana	35.6
MN	(X)	(X)	(X)	(X)
1st	Rieder	47.2	Gutknecht	52.8
2d	Minge	55.0	Revier	41.0
3d	Leino	29.8	Ramstad	70.2
4th	Vento	57.0	Newinski	36.8
5th	Sabo	64.5	Uldrich	28.4
6th	Luther	55.9	Jude	44.1
7th	Peterson	68.1	McKigney	31.9
8th	Oberstar	68.5	Larson	24.0
MS	(X)	(X)	(X)	(X)
1st	Boyd	30.5	Wicker	67.7
2d	Thompson	59.4	Covington	38.1
3d	Eaves	36.5	Pickering	61.4
4th	Antoine	36.0	Parker	61.6
5th	Taylor	58.3	Dollar	40.1
MO	(X)	(X)	(X)	(X)
1st	Clay	70.0	O'Sullivan	27.8
2d	Horn	37.1	Talent	61.3
3d	Gephardt	59.0	Wheelehan	38.8
4th	Skelton	63.8	Phelps	33.9
5th	McCarthy	67.4	Bennett	28.9
6th	Danner	68.6	Bailey	29.3
7th	Bamberger	31.6	Blunt	64.9
8th	Firebaugh	37.3	Emerson	50.5
9th	Volkmer	47.0	Hulshof	49.4
MT	Yellowtail	43.2	Hill	52.4
NE	(X)	(X)	(X)	(X)
1st	Combs	29.9	Bereuter	70.1
2d	Davis	40.4	Christensen	56.8
3d	Webster	22.6	Barrett	77.4
NV	(X)	(X)	(X)	(X)
1st	Coffin	43.6	Ensign	50.1
2d	Wilson	35.2	Gibbons	58.6
NH	(X)	(X)	(X)	(X)
1st	Keefe	46.6	Sununu	50.2
2d	Arnesen	43.5	Bass	50.6
NJ	(X)	(X)	(X)	(X)
1st	Andrews	76.2	Suplee	21.0
2d	Katz	38.2	LoBiondo	60.4
3d	Leonardi	33.3	Saxton	64.1
4th	Mears	33.7	Smith	63.7
5th	Auer	24.6	Roukema	71.3
6th	Pallone	61.6	Corodemus	35.8
7th	Lerner	42.1	Franks	55.1
8th	Pascrell	51.0	Martini	48.1
9th	Rothman	54.6	Donovan	43.4
10th	Payne	83.8	Williams	14.9
11th	Evangel	31.1	Freling-huysen	66.0
12th	Del Vecchio	46.5	Pappas	49.9
13th	Menendez	78.9	Munoz	17.7

See footnotes at end of table.

No. 444. Vote Cast for United States Representatives, by Major Political Party—Congressional Districts: 1996—Continued

[See headnote, p. 276]

STATE AND DISTRICT	DEMOCRATIC CANDIDATE		REPUBLICAN CANDIDATE	
	Name	Percent of total	Name	Percent of total
NM	(X)	(X)	(X)	(X)
1st	Wertheim	38.4	Schiff	54.9
2d	Baca	44.0	Skeen	56.0
3d	Richardson	67.4	Redmond	30.4
NY	(X)	(X)	(X)	(X)
1st	Bredes	46.0	Forbes	55.0
2d	Herman	33.4	Lazio	63.9
3d	LaMagna	41.9	King	55.6
4th	McCarthy	57.2	Frisa	40.7
5th	Ackerman	63.4	Lally	35.2
6th	Flake	85.0	Mier	15.0
7th	Manton	70.6	Birtley	29.4
8th	Nadler	81.8	Benjamin	16.5
9th	Schumer	74.0	Verga	21.9
10th	Towns	90.7	Parker	8.0
11th	Owens	91.5	Hayle	8.5
12th	Velazquez	84.0	Prado	14.1
13th	Butler	34.6	Molinari	61.6
14th	Maloney	72.4	Livingston	23.6
15th	Rangel	90.9	Adams	4.9
16th	Serrano	96.4	Torres	2.9
17th	Engel	84.7	McCarthy	13.6
18th	Lowey	63.3	Katsorhis	32.3
19th	Klein	39.5	Kelly	46.2
20th	Aggarwal	37.7	Gilman	56.9
21st	McNulty	66.3	Norman	26.8
22d	James	36.8	Solomon	61.2
23d	Hapanowicz	26.1	Boehlert	64.2
24th	Ravenscroft	24.8	McHugh	71.2
25th	Mack	44.7	Walsh	55.3
26th	Hinchey	54.9	Wittig	42.4
27th	Fricano	40.0	Paxon	60.0
28th	Slaughter	57.0	Rosen-berger	43.0
29th	LaFalce	61.9	Callard	38.1
30th	Pordum	45.1	Quinn	54.9
31st	MacBain	25.5	Houghton	71.5
NC	(X)	(X)	(X)	(X)
1st	Clayton	65.7	Tyler	33.3
2d	Etheridge	52.6	Funderburk	45.6
3d	Parrott	36.2	Jones	63.0
4th	Price	54.4	Heineman	43.8
5th	Cashion	36.4	Burr	62.1
6th	Costley	25.4	Coble	73.4
7th	McIntyre	52.9	Caster	45.8
8th	Hefner	54.9	Blackwood	44.0
9th	Daisley	35.7	Myrick	62.7
10th	Neill	28.8	Ballenger	69.9
11th	Ferguson	40.0	Taylor	58.3
12th	Watt	71.5	Martino	26.8
ND	Pomeroy	55.1	Cramer	43.2
OH	(X)	(X)	(X)	(X)
1st	Longabaugh	43.2	Chabot	54.3
2d	Chandler	22.6	Portman	72.1
3d	Hall	59.1	Westbrock	31.0
4th	McClain	30.5	Oxley	64.6
5th	Saunders	34.0	Gillmor	61.1
6th	Strickland	51.2	Cremeans	48.8
7th	Blain	26.4	Hobson	67.9
8th	Kitchen	26.1	Boehner	70.3
9th	Kaptur	77.1	Whitman	20.7
10th	Kucinich	49.0	Hoke	46.4
11th	Stokes	81.1	Sykora	15.4
12th	Ruccia	30.5	Kasich	66.5
13th	Brown	60.5	Blair	36.0
14th	Sawyer	54.3	George	41.8
15th	Arnebeck	26.9	Pryce	71.1
16th	Burkhart	28.0	Regula	68.7
17th	Traficant	91.0	(2)	(2)
18th	Burch	46.4	Ney	50.1
19th	Coyne	40.8	LaTourette	54.8
OK	(X)	(X)	(X)	(X)
1st	Amen	27.6	Largent	68.2
2d	Johnson	44.5	Coburn	55.5
3d	Roberts	45.2	Watkins	51.4
4th	Crocker	39.9	Watts	57.7
5th	Forsythe	27.1	Istook	69.7
6th	Barby	36.1	Lucas	63.9
OR	(X)	(X)	(X)	(X)
1st	Furse	54.6	Witt	42.2
2d	Dugan	39.0	Smith	59.1
3d	Blumenauer	68.2	Bruun	24.9
4th	DeFazio	66.6	Newkirk	26.6
5th	Hooley	51.6	Bunn	45.0
PA	(X)	(X)	(X)	(X)
1st	Foglietta	87.4	Cella	12.6
2d	Fattah	88.1	Murphy	11.9
3d	Borski	68.9	McColgan	31.1
4th	Klink	64.2	Adametz	35.8
5th	Rudy	39.8	Peterson	60.2
6th	Holden	58.6	Leinbach	40.6
7th	Innelli	32.3	Weldon	67.0
8th	Murray	35.3	Greenwood	59.1
9th	Kemmler	26.3	Shuster	73.7
10th	Cullen	36.6	McDade	59.4
11th	Kanjorski	68.5	Urban	31.5
12th	Murtha	69.9	Choby	30.1
13th	Hoeffel	48.9	Fox	48.9
14th	Coyne	60.6	Ravotti	39.0
15th	McHale	55.3	Kilbanks	40.8
16th	Blaine	37.5	Pitts	59.4
17th	Kettl	27.8	Gekas	72.2
18th	Doyle	56.0	Fawcett	40.5
19th	Chronister	35.9	Goodling	62.6
20th	Mascara	53.9	McCormick	46.1
21st	DiNicola	49.3	English	50.7
RI	(X)	(X)	(X)	(X)
1st	Kennedy	69.1	Cicione	28.3
2d	Weygand	64.5	Wild	31.6
SC	(X)	(X)	(X)	(X)
1st	(2)	(2)	Sanford	96.5
2d	(2)	(2)	Spence	89.9
3d	Dorn	38.4	Graham	60.6
4th	Curry	27.8	Inglis	70.9
5th	Spratt	54.0	Bigham	45.4
6th	Clyburn	68.4	McLeod	29.7
SD	Weiland	37.0	Thune	57.7
TN	(X)	(X)	(X)	(X)
1st	Smith	33.2	Jenkins	63.9
2d	Smith	28.6	Duncan	70.7
3d	Jolly	42.6	Wamp	56.4
4th	Stewart	41.1	Hilleary	58.0
5th	Clement	72.4	Ed-mondson	23.8
6th	Gordon	54.4	Gill	41.6
7th	Trotter	34.6	Bryant	64.1
8th	Tanner	67.3	Watson	30.1
9th	Ford	61.1	DeBerry	37.3

See footnotes at end of table.

No. 444. Vote Cast for United States Representatives, by Major Political Party—Congressional Districts: 1996—Continued

[See headnote, p. 276]

STATE AND DISTRICT	DEMOCRATIC CANDIDATE		REPUBLICAN CANDIDATE	
	Name	Percent of total	Name	Percent of total
TX	(X)	(X)	(X)	(X)
1st	Sandlin	51.6	Merritt	46.7
2d	Turner	52.2	Babin	45.6
3d	Cole	24.4	Johnson	73.0
4th	Hall	63.8	Hall	34.3
5th	Pouland	46.9	Sessions	53.1
6th	(2)	(2)	Barton	77.1
7th	Siegmund	15.1	Archer	81.4
8th	Newman [6]	13.6	Brady [7]	41.5
9th	Lampson [8]	44.1	Stockman	46.4
10th	Doggett	56.2	Doggett	41.4
11th	Edwards	56.8	Mathis	42.4
12th	Parmer	41.0	Granger	57.8
13th	Silverman	32.2	Thornberry	67.0
14th	Morris	47.7	Paul	51.0
15th	Hinojosa	62.2	Haughey	36.8
16th	Reyes	70.6	Ledesma	27.6
17th	Stenholm	51.7	Izzard	47.4
18th	Jackson-Lee	77.1	White	10.1
19th	Sawyer	19.6	Combest	80.4
20th	Gonzalez	63.7	Walker	34.4
21st	Wharton	22.4	Smith	76.4
22d	Cunningham	31.9	DeLay	68.1
23d	Jones	36.4	Bonilla	61.9
24th	Frost	55.8	Harrison	39.1
25th	Bentsen [9]	34.0	McKenna [10]	17.1
26th	Frankel	26.4	Armey	73.6
27th	Ortiz	64.7	Gardner	33.9
28th	Tejeda	75.4	Cude	23.4
29th	Green	67.4	Rodriguez	31.1
30th	Johnson [11]	54.6	Hendry [12]	18.3
UT	(X)	(X)	(X)	(X)
1st	Sanders	30.0	Hansen	68.3
2d	Anderson	42.4	Cook	55.0
3d	Orton	47.3	(2)	(2)
VT [13]	(2)	(2)	Sweetser	32.5
VA	(X)	(X)	(X)	(X)
1st	(2)	(2)	Bateman	(X)
2d	Pickett	65.2	Tate	34.8
3d	Scott	82.2	Holland	17.8
4th	Sisisky	78.5	Zevgolis	21.5
5th	Goode	60.1	Landrith	36.4
6th	(2)	(2)	Goodlatte	66.9
7th	Slayton	20.3	Bliley	75.2
8th	Moran	66.5	Otey	28.4
9th	Boucher	65.1	Muldoon	30.7
10th	Weinberg	25.4	Wolf	71.8
11th	Horton	34.6	Davis	64.2
WA	(X)	(X)	(X)	(X)
1st	Coopersmith	47.9	White	52.1
2d	Quigley	48.7	Metcalf	47.5
3d	Baird	50.7	Smith	49.3
4th	Locke	48.0	Hastings	52.0
5th	Olson	45.1	Nethercutt	54.9
6th	Dicks	66.3	Tinsley	28.2
7th	McDermott	82.3	Kleschen	17.7
8th	Little	36.5	Dunn	63.5
9th	Smith	51.4	Tate	45.9
WV	(X)	(X)	(X)	(X)
1st	Mollohan	(X)	(2)	(2)
2d	Wise	68.9	Morris	31.1
3d	Rahall	(X)	(2)	(2)
WI	(X)	(X)	(X)	(X)
1st	Spottswood	49.0	Neumann	51.0
2d	Soglin	41.0	Klug	57.4
3d	Kind	52.1	Harsdorf	47.9
4th	Kleczka	57.7	Reynolds	42.3
5th	Barrett	73.3	Melotik	24.6
6th	Lindskoog	23.8	Petri	73.1
7th	Obey	57.0	West	43.0
8th	Johnson	52.0	Prosser	48.0
9th	Brenhold	25.5	Sensen-brenner	74.5
WY	Maxfield	40.9	Cubin	55.2

NA Not available. X Not applicable. [1] There were 2 Democratic candidates; Preston Fields received 36.8 percent of Democratic votes. [2] No candidate. [3] Louisiana holds an open-primary election with candidates from all parties running on the same ballot. Any candidate who receives a majority is elected; if no candidate receives 50 percent, there is a run-off election in November between the top two finishers. [4] Candidate listed won seat in open-primary. [5] There were 2 Democratic candidates; Hunter Lundy received 46.9 percent of Democratic votes. [6] There were 2 Democratic candidates; Robert Musemeche received 6.0 percent of Democratic votes. [7] There were 2 Republican candidates; Gene Fontenot received 36.9 percent of Republican votes. [8] There were 2 Democratic candidates; Geraldine Sam received 9.4 percent of Democratic votes. [9] There were 2 Democratic candidates; Beverly Clark received 16.9 percent of Democratic votes. [10] There were 7 additional Republican candidates who received a total of 31.7 percent of Republican votes. [11] There were 2 additional Democratic candidates who received a total of 15.7 percent of Democratic candidates. [12] There were 2 Republican candidates; Lisa Kitterman received 6.9 percent of Republican votes. [13] The winning candidate was Sanders, an Independent, who received 49.9 percent of the vote.

Source: Congressional Quarterly Inc., *Congressional Quarterly Weekly Report*, (copyright).

No. 445. Composition of Congress, by Political Party: 1971 to 1996

[D=Democratic, R=Republican. Data for beginning of first session of each Congress (as of January 3), except as noted. Excludes vacancies at beginning of session]

YEAR	Party and President	Congress	HOUSE			SENATE		
			Majority party	Minority party	Other	Majority party	Minority party	Other
1971 [1]	R (Nixon)	92d	D-254	R-180	-	D-54	R-44	2
1973 [1 2]	R (Nixon)	93d	D-239	R-192	1	D-56	R-42	2
1975 [3]	R (Ford)	94th	D-291	R-144	-	D-60	R-37	2
1977 [4]	D (Carter)	95th	D-292	R-143	-	D-61	R-38	1
1979 [4]	D (Carter)	96th	D-276	R-157	-	D-58	R-41	1
1981 [4]	R (Reagan)	97th	D-243	R-192	-	R-53	D-46	1
1983	R (Reagan)	98th	D-269	R-165	-	R-54	D-46	-
1985	R (Reagan)	99th	D-252	R-182	-	R-53	D-47	-
1987	R (Reagan)	100th	D-258	R-177	-	D-55	R-45	-
1989	R (Bush)	101st	D-259	R-174	-	D-55	R-45	-
1991 [5]	R (Bush)	102d	D-267	R-167	1	D-56	R-44	-
1993 [5]	D (Clinton)	103d	D-258	R-176	1	D-57	R-43	-
1995 [5]	D (Clinton)	104th	R-230	D-204	1	R-52	D-48	-
1996 [5 6]	D (Clinton)	104th	R-236	D-197	1	R-53	D-46	-

- Represents zero. [1] Senate had one Independent and one Conservative-Republican. [2] House had one Independent-Democrat. [3] Senate had one Independent, one Conservative-Republican, and one undecided (New Hampshire). [4] Senate had one Independent. [5] House had one Independent-Socialist. [6] As of beginning of second session.

Source: U.S. Congress, Joint Committee on Printing, *Congressional Directory*, annual; beginning 1977, biennial.

No. 446. Composition of Congress, by Political Party Affiliation—States: 1989 to 1996

[Figures are for the beginning of the first session (as of January 3), except as noted. Dem.=Democratic; Rep.=Republican]

REGION, DIVISION, AND STATE	REPRESENTATIVES								SENATORS							
	101st Cong.,[1] 1989		102d Cong.,[2] 1991		103rd Cong.,[2] 1993		104th Cong.,[2 3 4] 1996		101st Cong., 1989		102d Cong., 1991		103rd Cong., 1993		104th Cong.,[3 5] 1996	
	Dem.	Rep.	Dem.	Rep.	Dem.	Rep.	Dem.	Rep.	Dem.	Rep.	Dem.	Rep.	Dem.	Rep.	Dem.	Rep.
U.S.	267	167	258	176	204	230	197	236	56	44	57	43	48	52	46	53
Northeast	56	38	50	37	47	40	47	40	10	8	11	7	9	9	9	9
N.E.	16	7	14	8	14	8	14	8	7	5	7	5	6	6	6	6
ME	1	1	1	1	1	1	1	1	1	1	1	1	-	2	-	2
NH	1	1	1	1	-	2	-	2	-	2	-	2	-	2	-	2
VT	-	-	-	-	-	-	-	-	1	1	1	1	1	1	1	1
MA	10	1	8	2	8	2	8	2	2	-	2	-	2	-	2	-
RI	1	1	1	1	2	-	2	-	1	1	1	1	1	1	1	1
CT	3	3	3	3	3	3	3	3	2	-	2	-	2	-	2	-
M.A.	40	31	36	29	33	32	33	32	3	3	4	2	3	3	3	3
NY	21	13	18	13	17	14	17	14	1	1	1	1	1	1	1	1
NJ	8	6	7	6	5	8	5	8	2	-	2	-	2	-	2	-
PA	11	12	11	10	11	10	11	10	-	2	1	1	-	2	-	2
Midwest	66	45	61	44	46	59	46	59	14	10	15	9	13	11	13	11
E.N.C.	49	31	43	31	32	42	32	42	7	3	8	2	6	4	6	4
OH	11	10	10	9	6	13	6	13	2	-	2	-	1	1	1	1
IN	8	2	7	3	4	6	4	6	-	2	-	2	-	2	-	2
IL	15	7	12	8	10	10	10	10	2	-	2	-	2	-	2	-
MI	11	7	10	6	9	7	9	7	2	-	2	-	1	1	1	1
WI	4	5	4	5	3	6	3	6	1	1	2	-	2	-	2	-
W.N.C.	19	14	18	13	14	17	14	17	7	7	7	7	7	7	7	7
MN	6	2	6	2	6	2	6	2	1	1	1	1	1	1	1	1
IA	2	4	1	4	-	5	-	5	1	1	1	1	1	1	1	1
MO	6	3	6	3	6	3	6	3	-	2	-	2	-	2	-	2
ND	1	-	1	-	1	-	1	-	2	-	2	-	2	-	2	-
SD	1	-	1	-	1	-	1	-	1	1	1	1	1	1	1	1
NE	1	2	1	2	-	3	-	3	2	-	2	-	2	-	2	-
KS	2	3	2	2	-	4	-	4	-	2	-	2	-	2	-	2
South	96	47	92	57	71	78	66	83	22	10	20	12	16	16	15	17
S.A.	45	24	42	33	31	44	30	45	11	5	9	7	9	7	9	7
DE	1	-	-	1	-	1	-	1	1	1	1	1	1	1	1	1
MD	5	3	4	4	4	4	4	4	2	-	2	-	2	-	2	-
VA	6	4	7	4	6	5	6	5	1	1	1	1	1	1	1	1
WV	4	-	3	-	3	-	3	-	2	-	2	-	2	-	2	-
NC	7	4	8	4	4	8	4	8	1	1	-	2	-	2	-	2
SC	4	2	3	3	2	4	2	4	1	1	1	1	1	1	1	1
GA	9	1	7	4	4	7	3	8	2	-	1	1	1	1	1	1
FL	9	10	10	13	8	15	8	15	1	1	1	1	1	1	1	1
E.S.C.	20	8	19	8	14	13	13	14	5	3	5	3	3	5	2	6
KY	4	3	4	2	2	4	2	4	1	1	1	1	1	1	1	1
TN	6	3	6	3	4	5	4	5	2	-	2	-	-	2	-	2
AL	5	2	4	3	4	3	4	3	2	-	2	-	2	-	1	1
MS	5	-	5	-	4	1	3	2	-	2	-	2	-	2	-	2
W.S.C.	30	15	31	16	28	21	23	24	6	2	6	2	4	4	4	4
AR	3	1	2	2	2	2	2	2	2	-	2	-	2	-	2	-
LA	4	4	4	3	4	3	2	5	2	-	2	-	2	-	2	-
OK	4	2	4	2	1	5	1	5	1	1	1	1	-	2	-	2
TX	19	8	21	9	19	11	18	12	1	1	1	1	-	2	-	2
West	46	37	55	38	40	53	38	54	10	16	11	15	10	16	9	16
Mountain	11	13	11	13	6	18	6	18	6	10	6	10	5	11	4	12
MT	1	1	1	-	1	-	1	-	1	1	1	1	1	1	1	1
ID	2	-	1	1	-	2	-	2	-	2	-	2	-	2	-	2
WY	-	1	-	1	-	1	-	1	-	2	-	2	-	2	-	2
CO	3	3	2	4	2	4	2	4	1	1	1	1	1	1	-	2
NM	1	2	1	2	1	2	1	2	1	1	1	1	1	1	1	1
AZ	1	4	3	3	1	5	1	5	1	1	1	1	-	2	-	2
UT	2	1	2	1	1	2	1	2	-	2	-	2	-	2	-	2
NV	1	1	1	1	-	2	-	2	2	-	2	-	2	-	2	-
Pacific	37	24	44	25	34	35	32	36	4	6	5	5	5	5	5	4
WA	5	3	8	1	2	7	2	7	1	1	1	1	1	1	1	1
OR	4	1	4	1	3	2	3	2	-	2	-	2	-	2	-	1
CA	26	19	30	22	27	25	25	26	1	1	2	-	2	-	2	-
AK	-	1	-	1	-	1	-	1	-	2	-	2	-	2	-	2
HI	2	-	2	-	2	-	2	-	2	-	2	-	2	-	2	-

- Represents zero. [1] Alabama and Indiana had one vacancy each. [2] Vermont had one Independent-Socialist Representative. [3] As of beginning of second session. [4] California had one vacancy. [5] Oregon had one vacancy.

Source: U.S. Congress, Joint Committee on Printing, *Congressional Directory*, biennial; and unpublished data.

No. 447. Members of Congress—Incumbents Re-elected: 1964 to 1996

YEAR	REPRESENTATIVES						SENATORS					
	Retirements [1]	Incumbent candidates					Retirements [1]	Incumbent candidates				
		Total	Re-elected		Defeated in—			Total	Re-elected		Defeated in—	
			Number	Percent of candidates	Primary	General election			Number	Percent of candidates	Primary	General election
PRESIDENTIAL-YEAR ELECTIONS												
1964	33	397	344	86.6	8	45	2	33	28	84.8	1	4
1968	23	409	396	96.8	4	9	6	28	20	71.4	4	4
1972	40	390	365	93.6	12	13	6	27	20	74.1	2	5
1976	47	384	368	95.8	3	13	8	25	16	64.0	-	9
1980	34	398	361	90.7	6	31	5	29	16	55.2	4	9
1984	22	411	392	95.4	3	16	4	29	26	89.7	-	3
1988	23	409	402	98.3	1	6	6	27	23	85.2	-	4
1992	65	368	325	88.3	[2]19	[3]24	7	28	23	82.1	1	4
1996	50	384	361	94.0	2	21	13	21	19	90.5	1	1
MIDTERM ELECTIONS												
1966	22	411	362	88.1	8	41	3	32	28	87.5	3	1
1970	29	401	379	94.5	10	12	4	31	24	77.4	1	6
1974	43	391	343	87.7	8	40	7	27	23	85.2	2	2
1978	49	382	358	93.7	5	19	10	25	15	60.0	3	7
1982	40	393	354	90.1	[2]10	29	3	30	28	93.3	-	2
1986	40	394	385	97.7	3	6	6	28	21	75.0	-	7
1990	27	406	390	96.1	1	15	3	32	31	96.9	-	1
1994	48	387	349	90.2	4	34	9	26	24	92.3	-	2

- Represents zero. [1] Does not include persons who died or resigned before the election. [2] Number of incumbents defeated in primaries by other incumbents due to redistricting: six in 1982 and four in 1992. [3] Five incumbents defeated in general election by other incumbents due to redistricting.

Source: Ornstein, Norman J., Thomas E. Mann, and Michael J. Malbin, *Vital Statistics on Congress, 1993-1994*, Congressional Quarterly, Inc., Washington, DC, 1995; Congressional Quarterly, Inc., Washington, DC, *America Votes, biennial (copyright)*.

No. 448. Members of Congress—Selected Characteristics: 1981 to 1995

[As of beginning of first session of each Congress, (January 3). Figures for Representatives exclude vacancies]

MEMBERS OF CONGRESS AND YEAR	Male	Female	Black [1]	Asian, Pacific Islander [2]	Hispanic [3]	AGE [4] (in years)					SENIORITY [5]				
						Under 40	40 to 49	50 to 59	60 to 69	70 and over	Less than 2 yrs.	2 to 9 yrs.	10 to 19 yrs.	20 to 29 yrs.	30 yrs. or more
REPRESENTATIVES															
97th Cong., 1981	416	19	17	3	6	94	142	132	54	13	77	231	96	23	8
98th Cong., 1983	413	21	21	3	8	86	145	132	57	14	83	224	88	28	11
99th Cong., 1985	412	22	20	3	10	71	154	131	59	19	49	237	104	34	10
100th Cong., 1987	412	23	23	4	11	63	153	137	56	26	51	221	114	37	12
101st Cong., 1989	408	25	24	5	10	41	163	133	74	22	39	207	139	35	13
102d Cong., 1991	407	28	25	3	11	39	152	134	86	24	55	178	147	44	11
103d Cong., 1993 [6]	388	47	38	4	17	47	151	128	89	15	118	141	132	32	12
104th Cong., 1995	388	47	40	4	17	53	155	135	79	13	92	188	110	36	9
SENATORS															
97th Cong., 1981	98	2	-	3	-	9	35	36	14	6	19	51	17	11	2
98th Cong., 1983	98	2	-	2	-	7	28	39	20	6	5	61	21	10	3
99th Cong., 1985	98	2	-	2	-	4	27	38	25	6	8	56	27	7	2
100th Cong., 1987	98	2	-	2	-	5	30	36	22	7	14	41	36	7	2
101st Cong., 1989	98	2	-	2	-	-	30	40	22	8	23	22	43	10	2
102d Cong., 1991	98	2	-	2	-	-	23	46	24	7	5	34	47	10	4
103d Cong., 1993 [6]	93	7	1	2	-	1	16	48	22	12	15	30	39	11	5
104th Cong., 1995	92	8	1	2	-	1	14	41	27	17	12	38	30	15	5

- Represents zero. [1] Source: Joint Center for Political and Economic Studies, Washington, DC, Black Elected Officials: A National Roster, annual, (copyright). [2] Source: Library of Congress, Congressional Research Service, "Asian Pacific Americans in the United States Congress", Report 94-767 GOV. [3] Source: National Association of Latino Elected and Appointed Officials, Washington, DC, *National Roster of Hispanic Elected Officials*, annual. [4] Some members do not provide date of birth. [5] Represents consecutive years of service. [6] Includes members elected to fill vacant seats through June 14, 1993.

Source: Except as noted, compiled by U.S. Bureau of the Census from data published in *Congressional Directory*, biennial.

No. 449. U.S. Congress—Measures Introduced and Enacted and Time in Session: 1979 to 1996

[Excludes simple and concurrent resolutions]

ITEM	96th Cong., 1979-80	97th Cong., 1981-82	98th Cong., 1983-84	99th Cong., 1985-86	100th Cong., 1987-88	101st Cong., 1989-90	102d Cong., 1991-92	103d Cong., 1993-94	104th Cong., 1995-96
Measures introduced	12,583	11,490	11,156	9,885	9,588	6,664	6,775	8,544	6,808
Bills	11,722	10,582	10,134	8,697	8,515	5,977	6,212	7,883	6,545
Joint resolutions	861	908	1,022	1,188	1,073	687	563	661	263
Measures enacted	736	529	677	483	761	666	609	473	337
Public	613	473	623	466	713	650	589	465	333
Private	123	56	54	17	48	16	20	8	4
HOUSE OF REPRESENTATIVES									
Number of days	326	303	266	281	298	281	280	265	290
Number of hours	1,876	1,420	1,705	1,794	1,659	1,688	1,796	1,887	2,445
Number of hours per day	5.8	4.7	6.4	6.4	5.6	6.0	6.4	7.1	8.4
SENATE									
Number of days	333	312	281	313	307	274	287	291	343
Number of hours	2,324	2,158	1,951	2,531	2,341	2,254	2,292	2,514	2,876
Number of hours per day	7.0	6.9	6.9	8.1	7.6	8.2	8.0	8.6	8.4

Source: U.S. Congress, *Congressional Record* and *Daily Calendar*, selected issues.

No. 450. Congressional Bills Vetoed: 1961 to 1996

PERIOD	President	Total vetoes	Regular vetoes	Pocket vetoes	Vetoes sustained	Bills passed over veto
1961-63	Kennedy	21	12	9	21	-
1963-69	Johnson	30	16	14	30	-
1969-74	Nixon	43	26	17	36	7
1974-77	Ford	66	48	18	54	12
1977-81	Carter	31	13	18	29	2
1981-89	Reagan	78	39	39	69	9
1989-93	Bush	44	29	15	43	1
1993-96	Clinton	17	17	-	16	1

- Represents zero.

Source: U.S. Congress, Senate Library, *Presidential Vetoes ... 1789-1968*; U.S. Congress, *Calendars of the U.S. House of Representatives and History of Legislation*, annual.

No. 451. Congressional Staff, by Location of Employment: 1972 to 1995

[Excludes those persons employed in Congressional support agencies such as the U.S. General Accounting Office, the Library of Congress, and the Congressional Budget Office]

YEAR	PERSONAL STAFF		YEAR	STANDING COMMITTEE STAFF		LOCATION OF EMPLOYMENT	1985	1990	1991	1993	1995
	House	Senate		House	Senate						
1972	5,280	2,426	1970	702	635	**Total**	18,136	17,625	17,851	(NA)	16,184
1980	7,371	3,746	1980	1,917	1,191						
1981	7,487	3,945	1981	1,843	1,022	House of Representatives	11,636	11,064	11,041	10,791	9,913
1982	7,511	4,041	1982	1,839	1,047	Committee staff [2]	2,146	2,173	2,321	2,070	1,266
1983	7,606	4,059	1983	1,970	1,075	Personal staff	7,528	7,496	7,278	7,390	7,186
1984	7,385	3,949	1984	1,944	1,095	Leadership staff	144	156	149	137	134
1985	7,528	4,097	1985	2,009	1,080	Officers of House, staff	1,818	1,239	1,293	1,194	1,327
1986	[1]7,920	[1]3,774	1986	1,954	1,075						
1987	7,584	4,075	1987	2,024	1,074	Senate	6,369	6,425	6,665	6,529	6,163
			1988	1,976	970	Committee staff [2]	1,178	1,207	1,154	1,032	796
1989	7,569	3,837	1989	1,986	1,013	Personal staff	4,097	4,162	4,294	4,200	4,247
1990	7,496	4,162	1990	1,993	1,090	Leadership staff	118	94	125	132	126
1991	7,278	4,294	1991	2,201	1,030	Officers of Senate, staff	976	962	1,092	1,165	994
1992	7,597	4,249	1992	2,178	1,008						
1993	7,400	4,138	1993	2,118	897						
1994	7,390	4,200	1994	2,046	958						
1995	7,186	4,247	1995	1,246	732	Joint committee staff	131	136	145	(NA)	108

NA Not available. [1] House figure is average for year, and Senate figure only covers period following implementation of Gramm-Rudman budget reductions. [2] Covers standing, select, and special committees.

Source: Ornstein, Norman J., Thomas E. Mann, and Michael J. Malbin, *Vital Statistics on Congress, 1993-1994*, Congressional Quarterly, Inc., Washington, DC, 1994, and unpublished data (copyright).

No. 452. Number of Governors, by Political Party Affiliation: 1970 to 1997

[Reflects figures after inaugurations for each year]

YEAR	Demo-cratic	Re-pub-lican	Inde-pen-dent	YEAR	Demo-cratic	Re-pub-lican	Inde-pen-dent	YEAR	Demo-cratic	Re-pub-lican	Inde-pen-dent
1970	18	32	-	1988	27	23	-	1993	30	18	2
1975	36	13	1	1989	28	22	-	1994	29	19	2
1980	31	19	-	1990	29	21	-	1995	19	30	1
1985	34	16	-	1991 [1]	29	19	2	1996	18	31	1
1987	26	24	-	1992	28	20	2	1997	17	32	1

- Represents zero. [1] Reflects result of runoff election in Arizona in February 1991.

Source: National Governors' Association, Washington, DC, 1970-87 and 1991-97, *Directory of Governors of the American States, Commonwealths & Territories,* annual; and 1988-90, *Directory of Governors,* annual. (Copyright.)

No. 453. Vote Cast for and Governor Elected, by State: 1990 to 1996

[In thousands, except percent. D=Democratic, R=Republican, I=Independent]

DIVISION AND STATE	1990		1992		1994		1996		Candidate elected at most recent election
	Total vote [1]	Percent leading party	Total vote [1]	Percent leading party	Total vote [1]	Percent leading party	Total vote [1]	Percent leading party	
N.E.:									
ME	522	R-46.7	(X)	(X)	511	I-35.4	(X)	(X)	Angus King
NH	295	R-60.3	516	R-56.0	312	R-69.9	497	D-57.2	Jeanne Shaheen
VT	211	R-51.8	286	D-74.7	212	D-68.7	255	D-70.6	Howard Dean
MA	2,343	R-50.2	(X)	(X)	2,164	R-70.9	(X)	(X)	William Weld
RI	357	D-74.1	425	D-61.5	361	R-47.4	(X)	(X)	Lincoln Almond
CT	1,141	I-40.4	(X)	(X)	1,147	R-36.2	(X)	(X)	John Rowland
M.A.:									
NY	4,057	D-53.2	(X)	(X)	5,204	R-48.8	(X)	(X)	George Pataki
NJ [2]	2,254	D-61.2	2,506	R-49.3	(X)	(X)	(X)	(X)	Christine T. Whitman
PA	3,053	D-67.7	(X)	(X)	3,585	R-45.4	(X)	(X)	Thomas Ridge
E.N.C.:									
OH	3,478	R-55.7	(X)	(X)	3,346	R-71.8	(X)	(X)	George Voinovich
IN	(X)	(X)	2,229	D-62.0	(X)	(X)	2,110	D-51.5	Frank L. O'Brien
IL	3,257	R-50.7	(X)	(X)	3,107	R-63.9	(X)	(X)	Jim Edgar
MI	2,565	R-49.8	(X)	(X)	3,088	R-61.5	(X)	(X)	John Engler
WI	1,380	R-58.2	(X)	(X)	1,563	R-67.3	(X)	(X)	Tommy Thompson
W.N.C.:									
MN	1,807	R-49.6	(X)	(X)	1,766	R-62.0	(X)	(X)	Arne Carlson
IA	976	R-60.6	(X)	(X)	997	R-56.8	(X)	(X)	Terry Branstad
MO	(X)	(X)	2,344	D-58.7	(X)	(X)	2,143	D-57.2	Mel Carnahan
ND	(X)	(X)	305	R-57.9	(X)	(X)	264	R-66.2	Edward T. Schafer
SD	257	R-58.9	(X)	(X)	312	R-55.4	(X)	(X)	William Janklow
NE	587	D-49.9	(X)	(X)	580	D-73.0	(X)	(X)	Ben Nelson
KS	783	D-48.6	(X)	(X)	821	R-64.1	(X)	(X)	Bill Graves
S.A.:									
DE	(X)	(X)	277	D-64.7	(X)	(X)	271	D-69.5	Thomas R. Carper
MD	1,111	D-59.8	(X)	(X)	1,410	D-50.2	(X)	(X)	Parris Glendening
VA [2]	1,789	D-50.1	1,794	R-58.3	(X)	(X)	(X)	(X)	George F. Allen
WV	(X)	(X)	657	D-56.0	(X)	(X)	629	R-51.6	Cecil H. Underwood
NC	(X)	(X)	2,595	D-52.7	(X)	(X)	2,566	D-56.0	James B. Hunt
SC	761	R-69.5	(X)	(X)	934	R-50.4	(X)	(X)	David Beasley
GA	1,450	D-52.9	(X)	(X)	1,545	D-51.1	(X)	(X)	Zell Miller
FL	3,531	D-56.5	(X)	(X)	4,206	D-50.8	(X)	(X)	Lawton Chiles
E.S.C.:									
KY [3]	835	D-64.7	(X)	(X)	984	D-50.9	(X)	(X)	Paul Patton
TN	790	D-60.8	(X)	(X)	1,487	R-54.3	(X)	(X)	Don Sundquist
AL	1,216	R-52.1	(X)	(X)	1,202	R-50.3	(X)	(X)	Fob James, Jr.
MS [3]	711	R-50.8	(X)	(X)	819	R-55.6	(X)	(X)	Kirk Fordice
W.S.C.:									
AR	696	D-57.5	(X)	(X)	717	D-59.8	(X)	(X)	Jim Guy Tucker
LA	[4] 1,728	[4] D-61.2	(X)	(X)	[5] 1,550	[5] R-63.5	(X)	(X)	Mike Foster
OK	911	D-57.4	(X)	(X)	995	R-46.9	(X)	(X)	Frank Keating
TX	3,893	D-49.5	(X)	(X)	4,396	R-53.5	(X)	(X)	George W. Bush
Mountain:									
MT	(X)	(X)	406	R-51.3	(X)	(X)	405	R-79.6	Marc Racicot
ID	321	D-68.2	(X)	(X)	413	R-52.3	(X)	(X)	Phil Batt
WY	160	D-65.4	(X)	(X)	201	R-58.7	(X)	(X)	Jim Geringer
CO	1,011	D-61.9	(X)	(X)	1,116	D-55.5	(X)	(X)	Roy Romer
NM	411	D-54.6	(X)	(X)	468	R-49.8	(X)	(X)	Gary Johnson
AZ	[6] 941	[6] R-52.4	(X)	(X)	1,129	R-52.5	(X)	(X)	Fife Symington
UT	(X)	(X)	763	R-42.2	(X)	(X)	672	R-75.0	Mike Leavitt
NV	321	D-64.8	(X)	(X)	371	D-53.9	(X)	(X)	Bob Miller
Pacific:									
WA	(X)	(X)	2,271	D-52.2	(X)	(X)	2,237	D-58.0	Gary Locke
OR	1,113	D-45.7	(X)	(X)	1,221	D-50.9	(X)	(X)	John Kitzhaber
CA	7,699	R-49.2	(X)	(X)	8,659	R-55.2	(X)	(X)	Pete Wilson
AK	195	I-38.9	(X)	(X)	213	D-41.1	(X)	(X)	James Campbell
HI	340	D-59.8	(X)	(X)	369	D-36.6	(X)	(X)	Ben Cayetano

X Not applicable. [1] Includes minor party and scattered votes. [2] Voting years 1989 and 1993. [3] Voting years 1987, 1991, and 1995. [4] Result of runoff election in 1991. [5] Result of runoff election in November 1995. [6] Result of runoff election in February 1991.

Source: Congressional Quarterly, Inc., Washington, DC. *America Votes,* biennial; and unpublished data, (copyright) and Congressional Quarterly, Inc., Washington, DC, *Congressional Quarterly Weekly Report,* vol. 53, No. 15, April 15, 1995, and unpublished data (copyright).

No. 454. Composition of State Legislatures, by Political Party Affiliation: 1990 to 1996

[Data reflect election results in year shown for most States; and except as noted, results in previous year for other States. Figures reflect immediate results of elections, including holdover members in State houses which do not have all of their members running for re-election. Dem.=Democrat, Rep.=Republican. In general, Lower House refers to body consisting of State Representatives; Upper House, of State Senators]

STATE	LOWER HOUSE								UPPER HOUSE							
	1990 [1,2]		1992 [3,4]		1994 [5,6]		1996		1990 [1,7]		1992 [3,8]		1994 [9]		1996 [5,9]	
	Dem.	Rep.	Dem.	Rep.	Dem.	Rep.	Dem.	Rep.	Dem.	Rep.	Dem.	Rep.	Dem.	Rep.	Dem.	Rep.
U.S.	3,242	2,202	3,186	2,223	2,817	2,803	2,886	2,539	1,186	757	1,132	799	1,021	905	996	931
AL [10]	82	23	82	23	74	31	72	33	28	7	27	8	23	12	22	12
AK [11]	23	17	20	18	17	22	16	24	10	10	10	10	8	12	7	13
AZ [12]	27	33	25	35	22	38	22	38	17	13	12	18	11	19	12	18
AR [11]	90	9	88	11	88	12	86	13	31	4	30	5	28	7	28	6
CA [11]	47	33	47	33	39	40	43	37	25	13	21	16	21	17	25	15
CO [11]	27	38	31	34	24	41	24	41	12	23	16	19	16	19	15	20
CT [12]	87	64	85	64	90	61	97	54	20	16	19	17	17	19	19	17
DE [11]	17	24	18	23	14	27	14	27	15	6	15	6	12	9	13	8
FL [11]	74	46	71	49	63	57	59	61	22	18	20	20	19	21	17	23
GA [12]	145	35	128	51	114	65	106	74	45	11	41	15	35	20	34	22
HI [11]	45	6	47	4	44	7	39	12	22	3	22	3	23	2	23	2
ID [12]	28	56	20	50	13	57	11	59	21	21	12	23	8	27	5	30
IL [11]	72	46	67	51	54	64	60	58	31	28	27	32	26	33	28	31
IN [11]	52	48	55	45	44	56	50	50	24	26	22	28	20	30	19	31
IA [11]	55	45	49	51	36	64	46	54	29	21	27	23	27	23	21	29
KS [11]	63	62	59	66	45	80	48	77	18	22	13	27	13	27	13	27
KY [11]	68	32	71	29	64	36	64	36	27	11	25	13	21	17	20	18
LA [10]	89	16	88	16	86	17	76	28	34	5	33	6	33	6	25	14
ME [12]	97	54	93	58	77	74	81	69	21	14	20	15	16	18	19	15
MD [10]	116	25	116	25	100	41	100	41	38	9	38	9	32	15	32	15
MA [12]	118	37	123	34	125	34	134	25	25	15	31	9	30	10	34	6
MI [11]	61	49	55	55	53	56	58	52	18	20	16	22	16	22	16	22
MN [11]	78	56	85	49	71	63	70	64	46	21	45	22	43	21	42	24
MS [10]	98	23	91	29	89	31	86	33	43	9	37	15	36	14	34	18
MO [11]	99	64	98	65	87	76	88	75	23	11	20	14	19	15	19	15
MT [11]	61	39	47	53	33	67	35	65	29	21	30	20	19	31	16	34
NE	(13)	(13)	(13)	(13)	(13)	(13)	(13)	(13)	(13)	(13)	(13)	(13)	(13)	(13)	(13)	(13)
NV [11]	22	19	27	12	21	21	25	17	10	10	10	11	8	13	9	12
NH [12]	125	268	136	258	112	286	143	255	11	13	11	13	6	18	9	15
NJ [11]	22	58	27	53	28	52	30	50	13	27	16	24	16	24	16	24
NM [11]	49	21	53	17	46	24	42	28	26	16	27	15	27	15	25	17
NY [12]	95	55	100	50	94	56	96	54	26	35	26	35	25	36	26	35
NC [12]	81	39	78	42	52	68	59	61	36	14	39	11	26	24	30	20
ND [11]	48	58	33	65	23	75	26	72	27	26	25	24	20	29	19	30
OH [11]	61	38	53	46	43	56	39	60	12	21	13	20	13	20	12	21
OK [11]	68	33	70	31	65	36	65	36	37	11	37	11	35	13	33	15
OR [11]	28	32	28	32	26	34	29	31	20	10	16	14	11	19	10	20
PA [11]	107	94	105	98	101	102	99	104	24	26	24	25	21	29	20	30
RI [12]	89	11	85	15	84	16	84	16	45	5	39	11	40	10	41	9
SC [11]	79	43	71	52	56	62	53	70	33	13	30	16	29	17	26	20
SD [12]	25	45	28	42	24	46	23	47	17	18	20	15	16	19	13	22
TN [11]	57	42	63	36	59	40	61	38	20	13	19	14	18	15	18	15
TX [11]	93	57	91	58	89	61	82	68	22	9	18	13	17	14	14	16
UT [11]	31	44	26	49	20	55	20	55	10	19	11	18	10	19	9	20
VT [12]	73	75	87	57	86	61	89	57	15	15	14	16	12	18	17	13
VA [11]	56	41	52	47	52	47	53	46	22	18	22	18	22	18	20	20
WA [11]	58	40	65	33	38	60	45	53	24	25	28	21	25	24	23	26
WV [11]	74	26	79	21	69	30	74	25	33	1	32	2	26	8	25	9
WI [11]	58	41	51	47	48	51	47	52	19	14	16	17	16	17	17	16
WY [11]	22	42	19	41	13	47	17	43	10	20	10	20	10	20	9	21

[1] Status as of May 1992; reflects results of elections held in LA, KY, MS, and NJ in 1991. [2] Excludes one Independent each for MA, MS, NH, SC, and VA; one Independent Democrat for NH; two Independents for VT; one vacancy each for AR, NV, and SC; two vacancies for PA; four vacancies for MA; and five vacancies for NH. [3] Status as of November 11, 1993. [4] Excludes one Independent each for AR, LA, NH, SC, and VA; two Independents each for AK and MS; four Independents for VT; members of political parties other than Democratic, Republican, or Independent (one in MA, two in VT, and four in NH); one vacancy each for GA, NH, TX, and WI; two vacancies each for CT and MA; and three vacancies for NV. [5] Status as of December 7, 1994. [6] Excludes one Independent each for AK, CA, LA, and VA; two Independents each for MS and VT; four Independents for SC; members of political parties other than Democratic, Republican, or Independent (one each in MA and VT and two in NH); one undecided in GA; and one vacancy each in LA, MI, and WV. [7] Excludes two Independents for CA; and one vacancy for NV. [8] Excludes two Independents for CA; and one vacancy each for CA and PA. [9] Excludes one Independent in ME, two Independents in CA, one vacancy in GA, two vacancies in MS, and three vacancies in MN. [10] Members of both houses serve 4-year terms. [11] Upper House members serve 4-year terms and Lower House members serve 2-year terms. [12] Members of both houses serve 2-year terms. [13] Single chamber (unicameral body) of 49 members, elected without party designation.

Source: 1990, The Council of State Governments, Lexington, KY, *State Elective Officials and the Legislatures*, biennial (copyright); 1992, 1994, and 1996, National Conference of State Legislatures, Denver, CO, unpublished data (copyright).

No. 455. Political Party Control of State Legislatures, by Party: 1975 to 1997

[As of beginning of year. Until 1972 there were two nonpartisan legislatures in Minnesota and Nebraska. Since then only Nebraska has had a nonpartisan legislature]

YEAR	LEGISLATURES UNDER—			YEAR	LEGISLATURES UNDER—			YEAR	LEGISLATURES UNDER—		
	Democratic control	Split control or tie	Republican control		Democratic control	Split control or tie	Republican control		Democratic control	Split control or tie	Republican control
1975	37	7	5	1985	27	11	11	1993	25	16	8
1977	36	8	5	1987	28	12	9	1994	24	17	8
1979	30	7	12	1989 [2]	28	13	8	1995	18	12	19
1981	28	6	15	1990	29	11	9	1996	18	15	16
1983 [1]	34	4	11	1992	29	14	6	1997	20	11	18

[1] Two 1984 midterm recall elections resulted in a change in control of the Michigan State Senate. At the time of the 1984 election, therefore, Democrats controlled 33 legislatures. [2] A party change during the year by a Democratic representative broke the tie in the Indiana House of Representatives, giving the Republicans control of both chambers.

Source: National Conference of State Legislatures, Denver, CO, *State Legislatures*, periodic.

No. 456. Local Elected Officials, by Sex, Race, Hispanic Origin, and Type of Government: 1992

SEX, RACE, AND HISPANIC ORIGIN	Total	GENERAL PURPOSE			SPECIAL PURPOSE	
		County	Municipal	Town, township	School district	Special district
Total	493,830	58,818	135,531	126,958	88,434	84,089
Male	324,255	43,563	94,808	76,213	54,443	55,228
Female	100,531	12,525	26,825	27,702	24,730	8,749
Sex not reported	69,044	2,730	13,898	23,043	9,261	20,112
White	405,905	52,706	114,880	102,676	73,894	61,750
Black	11,542	1,715	4,566	369	4,222	670
American Indian, Eskimo, Aleut	1,800	147	776	86	564	227
Asian, Pacific Islander	514	80	97	16	184	137
Hispanic	5,859	906	1,701	216	2,466	570
Non-Hispanic	413,902	53,741	118,618	102,931	76,398	62,214
Race, Hispanic origin not reported	74,069	4,171	15,212	23,811	9,570	21,305

Source: U.S. Bureau of the Census, *1992 Census of Governments, Popularly Elected Officials*, (GC92(1)-2).

No. 457. Women Holding State Public Offices, by Office and State: 1996

[As of January. For data on women in U.S. Congress, see table 448]

STATE	Statewide elective executive office [1]	State legislature	STATE	Statewide elective executive office [1]	State legislature	STATE	Statewide elective executive office [1]	State legislature
United States	80	1,539	Kentucky	-	11	North Dakota	5	21
Alabama	3	5	Louisiana	1	16	Ohio	2	31
Alaska	1	14	Maine	-	49	Oklahoma	3	18
Arizona	3	27	Maryland	1	54	Oregon	1	27
Arkansas	2	17	Massachusetts	-	47	Pennsylvania	2	29
California	2	24	Michigan	2	33	Rhode Island	1	36
Colorado	3	33	Minnesota	3	51	South Carolina	1	21
Connecticut	2	50	Mississippi	-	20	South Dakota	3	20
Delaware	4	13	Missouri	[2]2	39	Tennessee	1	18
Florida	1	31	Montana	1	36	Texas	1	32
Georgia	1	42	Nebraska	1	11	Utah	2	15
Hawaii	1	15	Nevada	1	22	Vermont	1	55
Idaho	2	30	New Hampshire	-	125	Virginia	-	21
Illinois	2	41	New Jersey	1	18	Washington	4	59
Indiana	4	33	New Mexico	2	23	West Virginia	-	21
Iowa	1	27	New York	1	37	Wisconsin	-	31
Kansas	3	46	North Carolina	-	28	Wyoming	2	18

- Represents zero. [1] Excludes women elected to the judiciary, women appointed to State cabinet-level positions, women elected to executive posts by the legislature, and elected members of university Board of Trustees or board of education. [2] Includes one official who was appointed to an elective position.

Source: Center for the American Woman and Politics, Eagleton Institute of Politics, Rutgers University, New Brunswick, NJ, information releases, (copyright).

No. 458. Black Elected Officials, by Office, 1970 to 1993, and by Region and State, 1993

[As of January 1993, no Black elected officials had been identified in Hawaii, Idaho, Montana, North Dakota, or Utah]

REGION, DIVISION, AND STATE	Total	U.S. and State legislatures[1]	City and county offices[2]	Law enforcement[3]	Education[4]	REGION, DIVISION, AND STATE	Total	U.S. and State legislatures[1]	City and county offices[2]	Law enforcement[3]	Education[4]
1970 (Feb.)	1,469	179	715	213	362	**South**	5,492	328	3,676	516	971
1980 (July)	4,890	326	2,832	526	1,206	S.A	2,200	173	1,522	147	358
1985 (Jan.)	6,016	407	3,517	661	1,431	DE	23	3	14	-	6
1990 (Jan.)	7,335	436	4,485	769	1,645	MD	140	32	79	23	6
1991 (Jan.)	7,445	473	4,496	847	1,629	DC	198	[5]4	185	-	9
1992 (Jan.)	7,517	499	4,557	847	1,614	VA	155	14	126	15	-
1993 (Jan.)	7,984	561	4,819	922	1,682	WV	21	1	17	3	-
Northeast	777	96	291	126	264	NC	468	28	328	31	81
N.E	109	35	60	4	10	SC	450	26	269	15	140
ME	1	-	1	-	-	GA	545	43	371	32	99
NH	2	2	-	-	-	FL	200	22	133	28	17
VT	2	2	-	-	-	E.S.C	1,681	85	1,175	175	246
MA	30	8	18	2	2	KY	63	4	47	5	7
RI	12	9	3	-	-	TN	168	16	104	24	24
CT	62	14	38	2	8	AL	699	23	529	58	89
M.A	668	61	231	122	254	MS	751	42	495	88	126
NY	299	30	63	70	136	W.S.C	1,611	70	978	196	367
NJ	211	13	113	-	85	AR	380	13	214	51	102
PA	158	18	55	52	33	LA	636	33	346	104	153
Midwest	1,361	106	757	171	327	OK	123	6	95	1	21
E.N.C	1,119	78	604	143	294	TX	472	18	323	40	91
OH	219	16	124	30	49	**West**	364	31	96	107	120
IN	72	12	50	4	6	Mountain	49	11	11	16	11
IL	465	25	282	37	121	WY	1	-	-	-	1
MI	333	17	133	68	115	CO	20	4	4	10	2
WI	30	8	15	4	3	NM	3	-	-	2	1
W.N.C	242	28	153	28	33	AZ	15	4	3	3	5
MN	16	1	2	10	3	NV	10	3	4	1	2
IA	11	1	6	1	3	Pacific	305	20	85	91	109
MO	185	18	134	14	19	WA	19	2	9	5	3
SD	3	1	2	-	-	OR	10	4	2	4	-
NE	6	1	2	-	3	CA	273	13	72	82	106
KS	21	6	7	3	5	AK	3	1	2	-	-

- Represents zero. [1] Includes elected State administrators. [2] County commissioners and councilmen, mayors, vice mayors, aldermen, regional officials, and other. [3] Judges, magistrates, constables, marshals, sheriffs, justices of the peace, and other. [4] Members of State education agencies, college boards, school boards, and other. [5] Includes two shadow senators and one shadow representative.

Source: Joint Center for Political and Economic Studies, Washington, DC, *Black Elected Officials: A National Roster*, annual, (copyright).

No. 459. Hispanic Public Officials, by Office, 1985 to 1994, and by State, 1994

[As of September. For States not shown, no Hispanic public officials had been identified]

REGION, DIVISION, AND STATE	Total	State executives and legislators[1]	County and municipal officials	Judicial and law enforcement	Education and school boards	REGION, DIVISION, AND STATE	Total	State executives and legislators[1]	County and municipal officials	Judicial and law enforcement	Education and school boards
1985	3,147	129	1,316	517	1,185	**South**	2,298	61	1,059	410	768
1990	4,004	144	1,819	583	1,458	S.A	68	16	35	13	4
1991	4,202	151	1,867	596	1,588	DE	1	-	1	-	-
1992	4,994	150	1,908	628	2,308	MD	2	-	1	-	1
1993	5,170	182	2,023	633	2,332	DC	1	-	-	1	-
1994	5,459	199	2,197	651	2,412	FL	64	16	33	12	3
Northeast	156	28	42	13	73	W.S.C	2,230	45	1,024	397	764
N.E	28	13	9	-	6	AR	2	1	-	-	1
MA	1	-	-	-	1	LA	12	3	1	8	-
RI	1	1	-	-	-	OK	1	-	1	-	-
CT	26	12	9	-	5	TX	2,215	41	1,022	389	763
M.A	128	15	33	13	67	**West**	2,089	95	1,053	220	720
NY	83	12	13	11	47	Mountain	1,270	74	697	167	332
NJ	37	2	17	1	17	MT	2	-	-	1	1
PA	8	1	3	1	3	ID	2	1	1	-	-
Midwest	917	15	43	8	851	WY	3	1	2	-	-
E.N.C	903	8	39	7	849	CO	201	9	140	10	42
OH	4	-	1	2	1	NM	716	50	410	105	151
IN	8	1	5	1	1	AZ	341	11	144	50	136
IL	881	7	26	3	[2]845	UT	1	1	-	-	-
MI	8	-	5	1	2	NV	4	1	-	1	2
WI	2	-	2	-	-	Pacific	818	21	356	53	388
W.N.C	14	7	4	1	2	WA	14	2	4	2	6
MN	3	2	-	1	-	OR	5	-	3	1	1
MO	1	-	1	-	-	CA	796	16	349	50	381
NE	3	-	2	-	1	AK	1	1	-	-	-
KS	7	5	1	-	1	HI	2	2	-	-	-

- Represents zero. [1] Includes U.S. Representatives. [2] Includes local school council members in the Chicago area.

Source: National Association of Latino Elected and Appointed Officials, Washington, DC, *National Roster of Hispanic Elected Officials*, annual.

No. 460. Public Confidence Levels in Selected Public and Private Institutions: 1996

[Based on a sample survey of 1,509 persons 18 years old and over conducted during the spring and subject to sampling variability; see source]

INSTITUTION	LEVEL OF CONFIDENCE				
	A great deal	Quite a lot	Some	Very little	Can't say/ no answer
Religious organizations	23.6	31.1	31.3	12.3	1.7
Higher education (colleges or univ.)	18.3	38.7	28.3	7.5	7.1
Private elementary or secondary education	15.1	35.3	33.4	9.7	6.5
Youth development and recreation organizations	14.8	35.2	32.7	11.6	5.7
Federated charitable appeals	12.6	26.3	34.9	21.6	4.5
Health organizations	10.8	28.2	42.0	15.9	3.1
Environmental organizations	9.4	23.1	41.0	20.3	6.2
Human service organizations	9.1	28.1	42.6	15.1	5.0
Recreational organizations (adult)	7.8	27.5	41.9	13.4	9.4
Arts, culture, & humanities organizations	9.3	26.7	39.8	14.3	9.9
Private and community foundations	7.6	24.0	42.3	13.5	12.6
Public /society benefit organizations [1]	7.5	22.7	43.4	20.8	5.6
International/foreign organizations [2]	6.3	19.1	37.5	24.2	12.8
Small businesses	15.3	40.8	32.6	7.6	3.6
Military	16.9	37.0	31.0	12.1	3.1
Public higher educ. (colleges or univ.)	15.0	36.4	34.2	11.6	2.8
Public elementary or secondary education	13.3	31.7	37.2	15.3	2.4
Organized labor	6.6	17.7	40.9	29.3	5.6
Media (e.g. newspapers, TV, radio)	6.3	22.7	39.5	29.7	1.8
Work-related organizations	6.1	21.5	47.2	17.4	7.9
Major corporations	4.9	16.7	44.2	27.4	4.8
State government	4.1	22.2	44.9	26.4	2.5
Organizations that lobby for a particular cause	4.0	15.7	42.7	29.5	8.1
Political organizations, parties	3.8	10.8	39.2	42.6	3.7
Local government	5.4	25.9	43.3	23.1	2.3
Federal government	5.2	17.5	43.9	31.1	2.2
Congress	3.4	12.4	41.7	39.0	3.5

[1] Civil rights, social justice, or community improvement organizations. [2] Culture exchange or relief organizations.

Source: Hodgkinson, Virginia, Murray Weitzman, and the Gallup Organization, Inc., *Giving & Volunteering in the United States: 1994 Edition*. (Copyright and published by INDEPENDENT SECTOR, Washington, DC, 1996.)

No. 461. Political Party Identification of the Adult Population, by Degree of Attachment, 1972 to 1994, and by Selected Characteristics, 1994

[In percent. Covers citizens of voting-age living in private housing units in the contiguous United States. Data are from the National Election Studies and are based on a sample and subject to sampling variability; for details, see source]

YEAR AND SELECTED CHARACTERISTIC	Total	Strong Democrat	Weak Democrat	Independent Democrat	Independent	Independent Republican	Weak Republican	Strong Republican	Apolitical
1972	100	15	26	11	13	11	13	10	1
1980	100	18	23	11	13	10	14	9	2
1984	100	17	20	11	11	12	15	12	2
1986	100	18	22	10	12	11	15	11	2
1988	100	18	18	12	11	13	14	14	2
1990	100	20	19	12	11	12	15	10	2
1992	100	18	18	14	12	12	14	11	1
1994, total [1]	**100**	**15**	**19**	**13**	**10**	**12**	**15**	**16**	**1**
Age:									
17 to 24 years old	100	9	20	22	10	8	19	10	1
25 to 34 years old	100	11	19	14	12	11	16	16	1
35 to 44 years old	100	13	18	14	12	11	14	18	-
45 to 54 years old	100	15	16	15	7	16	12	17	1
55 to 64 years old	100	18	22	8	8	16	12	15	-
65 to 74 years old	100	28	17	6	8	13	14	15	-
75 to 99 years old	100	19	26	9	9	5	17	13	2
Sex:									
Male	100	13	17	12	11	14	14	18	1
Female	100	18	21	13	10	9	15	13	1
Race:									
White	100	12	19	12	10	13	16	17	1
Black	100	38	23	20	8	4	2	3	1
Education:									
Grade school	100	26	26	7	13	7	11	6	4
High school	100	15	22	14	13	10	13	11	1
College	100	14	16	13	7	13	16	21	-

- Represents zero. [1] Includes other characteristics, not shown separately.

Source: Center for Political Studies, University of Michigan, Ann Arbor, MI, unpublished data. Data prior to 1988 published in Warren E. Miller and Santa A. Traugott, *American National Election Studies Data Sourcebook, 1952-1986*, Harvard University Press, Cambridge, MA, 1989 (copyright).

No. 462. Voting-Age Population, Percent Reporting Registered, and Voted: 1980 to 1996

[As of November. Covers civilian noninstitutional population 18 years old and over. Includes aliens. Figures are based on Current Population Survey (see text, section 1, and Appendix III) and differ from those in table 464 based on population estimates and official vote counts]

CHARACTERISTIC	VOTING-AGE POPULATION (mil.)								PERCENT REPORTING THEY REGISTERED								PERCENT REPORTING THEY VOTED							
									Presidential election years				Congressional election years				Presidential election years				Congressional election years			
	1980	1984	1986	1988	1990	1992	1994	1996	1980	1988	1992	1996	1982	1986	1990	1994	1980	1988	1992	1996	1982	1986	1990	1994
Total [1]	157.1	170.0	173.9	178.1	182.1	185.7	190.3	193.7	66.9	66.6	68.2	65.9	64.1	64.3	62.2	62.0	59.2	57.4	61.3	54.2	48.5	46.0	45.0	44.6
18 to 20 years old	12.3	11.2	10.7	10.7	10.8	9.7	10.3	10.8	44.7	44.9	48.3	45.6	35.0	35.4	35.4	37.2	35.7	33.2	38.5	31.2	19.8	18.6	18.4	16.5
21 to 24 years old	15.9	16.7	15.7	14.8	14.0	14.6	14.9	13.9	52.7	50.6	55.3	51.2	47.8	46.6	43.3	45.5	43.1	38.3	45.7	33.4	28.4	24.2	22.0	22.3
25 to 34 years old	35.7	40.3	41.9	42.7	42.7	41.6	41.1	40.1	62.0	57.8	60.6	56.9	57.1	55.8	52.0	51.5	54.6	48.0	53.2	43.1	40.4	35.1	33.8	32.2
35 to 44 years old	25.6	30.7	33.0	35.2	37.9	39.7	41.9	43.3	70.6	69.3	69.2	66.5	67.5	67.9	65.5	63.3	64.4	61.3	63.6	54.9	52.2	49.3	48.4	46.0
45 to 64 years old	43.6	44.3	44.8	45.9	46.9	49.1	50.9	53.7	75.8	75.5	75.3	73.5	75.6	74.8	71.4	71.0	69.3	67.9	70.0	(NA)	62.2	58.7	55.8	56.0
65 years old and over	24.1	26.7	27.7	28.8	29.9	30.8	31.1	31.9	74.6	78.4	78.0	77.0	75.2	76.9	76.5	75.6	65.1	68.8	70.1	(NA)	59.9	60.9	60.3	60.7
Male	74.1	80.3	82.4	84.5	86.6	88.6	91.0	92.6	66.6	65.2	66.9	64.4	63.7	63.4	61.2	60.8	59.1	56.4	60.2	52.8	48.7	45.8	44.6	44.4
Female	83.0	89.6	91.5	93.6	95.5	97.1	99.3	101.0	67.1	67.8	69.3	67.3	64.4	65.0	63.1	63.2	59.4	58.3	62.3	55.5	48.4	46.1	45.4	44.9
White	137.7	146.8	149.9	152.9	155.6	157.8	160.3	162.8	68.4	67.9	70.1	67.7	65.6	65.3	63.8	64.2	60.9	59.1	63.6	56.0	49.9	47.0	46.7	46.9
Black	16.4	18.4	19.0	19.7	20.4	21.0	21.8	22.5	60.0	64.5	63.9	63.5	59.1	64.0	58.8	58.3	50.5	51.5	54.0	50.6	43.0	43.2	39.2	37.0
Hispanic [2]	8.2	9.5	11.8	12.9	13.8	14.7	17.5	18.4	36.3	35.5	35.0	35.7	35.3	35.9	32.3	30.0	29.9	28.8	28.9	26.7	25.3	24.2	21.0	19.1
Region: [3]																								
Northeast	35.5	36.9	37.3	37.9	38.1	38.3	38.4	38.3	64.8	64.8	67.0	64.7	62.5	62.0	61.0	60.9	58.5	57.4	61.2	54.5	49.8	44.4	45.2	45.2
Midwest	41.5	42.1	42.8	43.3	43.9	44.4	44.5	45.2	73.8	72.5	74.6	71.6	71.1	70.7	68.2	68.7	65.8	62.9	67.2	59.3	54.7	49.5	48.6	48.8
South	50.6	57.6	59.2	60.7	62.4	63.7	66.4	68.1	64.8	65.6	67.2	65.9	61.7	63.0	61.3	60.7	55.6	54.5	59.0	52.2	41.8	43.0	42.4	40.5
West	29.5	33.4	34.8	36.2	37.7	39.3	41.0	42.1	63.3	63.0	63.6	60.8	60.6	60.8	57.7	58.1	57.2	55.6	58.5	51.8	50.7	48.4	45.0	46.4
School years completed:																								
8 years or less	22.7	20.6	19.6	19.1	17.7	15.4	14.7	14.1	53.0	47.5	43.9	40.7	52.3	50.5	44.0	40.1	42.6	36.7	35.1	28.1	35.7	32.7	27.7	23.2
High school:																								
1 to 3 years	22.5	22.1	21.4	21.1	21.0	[4]21.0	[4]20.7	21.0	54.6	52.8	[4]50.4	47.9	53.3	52.4	47.9	[4]44.7	45.6	41.3	[4]41.2	33.8	37.7	33.8	30.9	[4]27.0
4 years	61.2	67.8	68.6	70.0	71.5	[5]65.3	[5]64.9	65.2	66.4	64.6	[5]64.9	62.2	62.9	62.9	60.0	[5]58.9	58.9	54.7	[5]57.5	49.1	47.1	44.1	42.2	[5]40.5
College:																								
1 to 3 years	26.7	30.9	33.0	34.3	36.3	[6]46.7	[6]50.4	50.9	74.4	73.5	[6]75.4	72.9	70.0	70.0	68.7	[6]68.4	67.2	64.5	[6]68.7	60.5	53.3	49.9	50.0	[6]49.1
4 years or more	24.0	28.6	31.3	33.6	35.6	[7]37.4	[7]39.4	42.5	84.3	83.1	[7]84.8	80.4	79.4	77.8	77.3	[7]76.3	79.9	77.6	[7]81.0	73.0	66.5	62.5	62.5	[7]63.1
Employed	95.0	104.2	108.5	113.8	115.5	116.3	122.6	125.6	68.7	67.1	69.9	67.0	65.5	64.4	62.6	62.9	61.8	58.4	63.8	55.2	50.0	45.7	45.1	45.2
Unemployed	6.9	7.4	6.6	5.8	6.7	8.3	6.5	6.4	50.3	50.4	53.7	52.5	49.8	50.6	44.6	46.4	41.2	38.6	46.2	37.2	34.1	31.2	27.9	28.3
Not in labor force	55.2	58.4	58.8	58.5	59.9	61.1	61.2	61.6	65.8	67.2	66.8	65.1	64.3	65.4	63.4	61.9	57.0	57.3	58.7	54.1	48.7	48.2	46.7	45.3

NA Not available. [1] Includes other races not shown separately. [2] Hispanic persons may be of any race. [3] For composition of regions, see table 27. [4] Represents those who completed 9th to 12th grade, but have no high school diploma. [5] High school graduate. [6] Some college or associate degree. [7] Bachelor's or advanced degree.

Source: U.S. Bureau of the Census, *Current Population Reports*, P20-453 and P20-466; and unpublished data.

No. 463. Persons Reported Registered and Voted, by State: 1994

[See headnote, table 462]

STATE	Voting-age population (1,000)	PERCENT OF VOTING-AGE POPULATION		STATE	Voting-age population (1,000)	PERCENT OF VOTING-AGE POPULATION	
		Registered	Voted			Registered	Voted
U.S.	190,267	62.0	44.6	DC	440	66.9	55.6
				VA	4,760	60.0	45.7
Northeast	38,386	60.9	45.2	WV	1,396	60.8	33.9
N.E.	9,865	67.8	51.0	NC	5,211	60.8	36.7
ME	909	81.6	58.2	SC	2,681	60.8	45.2
NH	832	64.3	41.2	GA	5,105	54.9	35.4
VT	432	70.7	48.8	FL	10,582	55.5	42.3
MA	4,532	65.6	51.6	E.S.C	11,662	66.7	41.9
RI	729	64.2	50.6	KY	2,807	62.5	34.5
CT	2,431	68.4	51.3	TN	3,856	63.7	43.0
M.A	28,521	58.5	43.1	AL	3,136	70.6	45.8
NY	13,599	56.8	44.6	MS	1,863	72.6	44.3
NJ	5,918	61.6	40.3	W.S.C	20,273	61.0	38.5
PA	9,004	58.9	42.7	AR	1,801	60.0	41.6
Midwest	44,505	68.7	48.7	LA	3,013	70.6	34.2
E.N.C	31,463	66.4	46.1	OK	2,325	65.8	46.8
OH	8,152	64.6	46.6	TX	13,134	58.2	37.6
IN	4,191	55.6	38.7	West	41,009	58.1	46.4
IL	8,561	63.0	42.8	Mountain	10,911	60.0	45.9
MI	6,921	73.7	52.2	MT	619	73.2	60.7
WI	3,638	77.2	49.6	ID	796	63.0	50.7
W.N.C	13,042	74.3	55.2	WY	333	69.0	63.5
MN	3,296	80.9	58.4	CO	2,703	64.3	46.4
IA	2,059	71.7	52.5	NM	1,175	58.8	46.8
MO	3,797	72.3	54.5	AZ	2,971	56.0	41.6
ND	441	93.3	61.1	UT	1,231	59.4	44.1
SD	495	75.4	63.9	NV	1,081	49.5	40.1
NE	1,156	72.6	54.3	Pacific	30,098	57.4	46.6
KS	1,796	65.3	50.5	WA	3,924	66.8	46.3
South	68,364	60.7	40.5	OR	2,309	72.7	60.9
S.A.	34,429	58.4	41.2	CA	22,639	54.2	45.0
DE	528	58.7	41.2	AK	393	71.7	59.1
MD	3,726	62.6	46.2	HI	833	51.5	46.0

Source: U.S. Bureau of the Census, unpublished data.

No. 464. Participation in Elections for President and U.S. Representatives: 1932 to 1996

[As of November. Estimated resident population 21 years old and over, 1932-70, except as noted, and 18 years old and over thereafter; includes Armed Forces. Prior to 1960, excludes Alaska and Hawaii. District of Columbia is included in votes cast for President beginning 1964 and in votes cast for Representative from 1972 to 1992]

YEAR	Resident population (incl. aliens) of voting age [1] (1,000)	VOTES CAST: For President [2] (1,000)	VOTES CAST: Percent of voting-age population	VOTES CAST: For U.S. Representatives (1,000)	VOTES CAST: Percent of voting-age population	YEAR	Resident population (incl. aliens) of voting age [1] (1,000)	VOTES CAST: For President [2] (1,000)	VOTES CAST: Percent of voting-age population	VOTES CAST: For U.S. Representatives (1,000)	VOTES CAST: Percent of voting-age population
1932	75,768	39,758	52.5	37,657	49.7	1966	116,638	(X)	(X)	52,908	45.4
1934	77,997	(X)	(X)	32,256	41.4	1968	120,285	73,212	60.9	66,288	55.1
1936	80,174	45,654	56.9	42,886	53.5	1970	124,498	(X)	(X)	54,173	43.5
1938	82,354	(X)	(X)	36,236	44.0	1972	140,777	77,719	55.2	71,430	50.7
1940	84,728	49,900	58.9	46,951	55.4	1974	146,338	(X)	(X)	52,495	35.9
1942	86,465	(X)	(X)	28,074	32.5	1976	152,308	81,556	53.5	74,422	48.9
1944	85,654	47,977	56.0	45,103	52.7	1978	158,369	(X)	(X)	55,332	34.9
1946	92,659	(X)	(X)	34,398	37.1	1980	163,945	86,515	52.8	77,995	47.6
1948	95,573	48,794	51.1	45,933	48.1	1982	169,643	(X)	(X)	64,514	38.0
1950	98,134	(X)	(X)	40,342	41.1	1984	173,995	92,653	53.3	83,231	47.8
1952	99,929	61,551	61.6	57,571	57.6	1986	177,922	(X)	(X)	59,619	33.5
1954	102,075	(X)	(X)	42,580	41.7	1988	181,956	91,595	50.3	81,786	44.9
1956	104,515	62,027	59.3	58,426	55.9	1990	185,812	(X)	(X)	61,513	33.1
1958	106,447	(X)	(X)	45,818	43.0	1992	189,524	104,425	55.1	96,239	50.8
1960	109,672	68,838	62.8	64,133	58.5	1994	193,650	(X)	(X)	70,780	37.4
1962	112,952	(X)	(X)	51,267	45.4	1996	196,509	96,273	48.9	89,832	45.7
1964	114,090	70,645	61.9	65,895	57.8						

X Not applicable. [1] Population 18 and over in Georgia, 1944-70, and in Kentucky, 1956-70; 19 and over in Alaska and 20 and over in Hawaii, 1960-70. [2] Source: 1932-58, U.S. Congress, Clerk of the House, *Statistics of the Presidential and Congressional Election*, biennial.

Source: Except as noted, U.S. Bureau of the Census, *Current Population Reports*, P25-1085; Congressional Quarterly Inc., Washington, DC. *America Votes*, biennial, (copyright).

No. 465. Resident Population of Voting Age and Percent Casting Votes—States: 1988 to 1996

[As of November. Estimated population, 18 years old and over. Includes Armed Forces stationed in each State, aliens, and institutional population]

REGION, DIVISION, AND STATE	VOTING-AGE POPULATION							PERCENT CASTING VOTES FOR—				
	1988 (1,000)	1990 (1,000)	1992 (1,000)	1994 (1,000)	1996, proj. (1,000)			Presidential electors		U.S. Representatives		
					Total	Black	Hispanic [1]	1992	1996	1992	1994	1996
U.S.	181,955	185,812	189,524	193,650	196,509	22,857	18,609	55.1	49.0	50.8	36.0	45.6
Northeast	38,670	38,836	38,920	38,849	38,861	4,396	2,903	55.4	50.4	49.9	37.1	46.6
N.E.	10,069	10,137	10,091	10,017	10,081	473	459	62.9	56.6	58.6	44.0	53.6
ME	902	924	932	931	939	4	6	72.9	64.5	71.8	54.0	63.9
NH	817	835	838	843	860	5	9	64.2	58.0	61.0	36.7	57.1
VT	411	422	429	429	441	2	3	67.5	58.6	65.6	49.3	57.8
MA	4,642	4,646	4,616	4,564	4,623	234	229	60.1	55.3	56.6	43.3	52.1
RI	772	776	768	764	750	29	39	59.0	52.0	51.9	44.8	48.0
CT	2,525	2,534	2,506	2,486	2,468	199	173	64.4	56.4	57.2	43.0	52.4
M.A.	28,601	28,701	28,829	28,832	28,780	3,925	2,444	52.8	48.3	46.9	34.6	44.1
NY	13,659	13,683	13,705	13,646	13,579	2,292	1,616	50.5	46.5	43.2	33.8	40.9
NJ	5,905	5,927	5,964	5,974	6,005	819	632	56.1	51.2	50.2	33.6	47.0
PA	9,037	9,091	9,161	9,212	9,196	814	196	54.1	49.0	50.1	36.6	46.9
Midwest	43,684	44,160	44,803	45,529	46,021	4,248	1,394	61.9	54.2	58.5	41.2	52.6
E.N.C.	30,775	31,133	31,636	32,083	32,382	3,594	1,156	60.4	52.6	56.6	38.5	50.8
OH	7,986	8,066	8,207	8,313	8,356	866	112	60.2	54.3	55.8	39.7	52.5
IN	4,046	4,105	4,209	4,298	4,369	331	81	54.8	48.9	52.7	36.0	47.7
IL	8,411	8,495	8,596	8,712	8,764	1,245	728	58.7	49.2	56.2	34.9	47.1
MI	6,774	6,851	6,947	6,983	7,067	972	159	61.5	54.5	55.9	43.0	52.3
WI	3,559	3,616	3,675	3,777	3,824	180	76	68.9	57.4	65.0	38.6	56.2
W.N.C.	12,910	13,027	13,167	13,446	13,638	654	238	65.6	58.1	63.3	47.7	56.9
MN	3,167	3,222	3,272	3,362	3,412	65	44	71.8	64.3	69.5	52.0	62.8
IA	2,053	2,061	2,073	2,112	2,138	38	30	65.3	57.7	59.9	46.3	56.1
MO	3,770	3,813	3,851	3,902	3,960	397	47	62.1	54.2	61.0	45.2	53.2
ND	470	462	462	467	473	3	3	66.7	56.3	64.5	50.4	55.6
SD	498	498	505	522	530	3	4	66.6	61.1	65.9	58.6	60.9
NE	1,145	1,152	1,164	1,192	1,208	41	35	63.4	56.1	61.1	47.9	54.8
KS	1,809	1,819	1,840	1,889	1,898	107	75	62.9	56.6	61.1	43.3	55.3
South	62,134	63,821	65,609	67,501	69,173	11,986	5,859	51.3	45.9	45.9	30.2	40.7
S.A.	32,148	33,312	34,210	35,211	36,011	6,947	1,891	50.3	46.0	46.7	30.3	41.8
DE	490	507	521	534	547	92	15	55.6	49.5	53.0	36.5	48.8
MD	3,536	3,640	3,705	3,750	3,811	982	110	53.6	46.7	48.8	35.9	43.0
DC	503	481	467	452	435	269	20	48.7	42.7	42.1	(NA)	(NA)
VA	4,572	4,716	4,855	4,967	5,069	924	133	52.7	47.5	48.8	38.4	43.2
WV	1,358	1,349	1,376	1,389	1,414	40	7	49.7	45.0	40.9	29.3	36.9
NC	4,903	5,061	5,190	5,364	5,499	1,126	69	50.3	45.8	48.7	29.6	45.7
SC	2,505	2,587	2,669	2,740	2,777	771	27	45.1	41.5	41.8	31.7	38.1
GA	4,631	4,791	5,006	5,159	5,396	1,368	101	46.4	42.6	44.2	29.0	40.1
FL	9,651	10,180	10,422	10,856	11,043	1,375	1,409	51.0	48.0	[2] 47.2	[2] 26.3	42.5
E.S.C.	11,095	11,252	11,547	11,813	12,124	2,166	76	53.2	47.1	49.0	33.3	44.5
KY	2,710	2,740	2,798	2,857	2,924	201	15	53.4	47.5	48.6	27.5	42.3
TN	3,609	3,685	3,796	3,913	4,021	589	29	52.2	47.1	45.5	36.2	44.3
AL	2,950	2,995	3,060	3,138	3,218	744	20	54.8	47.7	52.0	35.5	45.6
MS	1,816	1,832	1,873	1,905	1,961	632	12	52.4	45.6	51.5	32.6	46.1
W.S.C.	18,901	19,257	19,852	20,477	21,038	2,883	3,892	51.8	45.1	42.7	28.3	36.8
AR	1,717	1,737	1,774	1,817	1,860	253	18	53.6	47.5	50.1	39.0	46.4
LA	3,006	2,968	3,045	3,100	3,137	902	75	58.8	56.9	[3] 22.4	[3] (X)	15.1
OK	2,300	2,310	2,352	2,394	2,419	164	69	59.1	49.9	54.2	40.5	48.8
TX	11,878	12,222	12,681	13,166	13,622	1,564	3,730	48.5	41.2	44.3	31.3	38.3
West	37,468	38,993	40,194	41,771	42,452	2,216	8,450	53.5	47.0	51.0	38.8	45.1
Mountain	9,524	9,856	10,370	10,906	11,494	311	1,750	57.6	49.7	56.3	40.7	48.6
MT	574	579	600	623	647	2	9	68.4	62.9	67.3	56.5	62.4
ID	683	707	750	803	845	4	49	64.3	58.2	63.0	49.0	58.5
WY	321	319	329	343	352	3	20	61.0	60.1	59.9	57.2	59.7
CO	2,397	2,447	2,579	2,713	2,843	113	351	60.8	53.1	57.4	38.9	51.4
NM	1,047	1,075	1,121	1,167	1,210	22	505	50.8	46.0	49.6	39.6	45.3
AZ	2,610	2,696	2,812	2,923	3,094	85	602	52.9	45.4	50.1	37.6	43.8
UT	1,070	1,104	1,169	1,246	1,323	10	69	63.6	50.3	62.2	40.5	50.2
NV	824	929	1,011	1,088	1,180	72	145	50.1	39.3	48.7	34.6	38.1
Pacific	27,943	29,137	29,824	30,865	30,958	1,905	6,700	52.0	46.0	49.4	38.1	43.9
WA	3,465	3,650	3,812	4,000	4,122	111	193	60.0	54.7	58.3	42.2	52.7
OR	2,055	2,140	2,220	2,311	2,396	37	101	65.9	57.5	62.6	51.6	55.7
CA	21,250	22,124	22,521	23,225	23,133	1,716	6,323	49.4	43.3	46.8	35.9	41.0
AK	369	382	405	429	425	17	14	63.8	56.9	59.0	48.5	55.1
HI	804	841	866	900	882	24	69	43.1	40.8	41.4	39.3	40.0

NA Not available. X Not applicable. [1] Persons of Hispanic origin may be of any race. [2] State law does not require tabulation of votes for unopposed candidates. [3] See footnote 6, table 443.

Source: Compiled by U.S. Bureau of the Census. Population data from U.S. Bureau of the Census, *Current Population Reports*, P25-1117 and Statistical Brief (SB/96-2); votes cast from Elections Research Center, Chevy Chase, MD, *America Votes*, biennial, (copyright); and 1994, Congressional Quarterly Inc., *Congressional Quarterly Weekly Report*, vol. 53, No. 15, April 15, 1995, (copyright).

No. 466. Political Party Financial Activity, by Major Political Party: 1981 to 1994

[In millions of dollars. Covers financial activity during 2-year calendar period indicated. Some political party financial activities, such as building funds and State and local election spending, are not reported to the source. Also excludes contributions earmarked to Federal candidates through the party organizations, since some of those funds never passed through the committees' accounts]

YEAR AND TYPE OF COMMITTEE	DEMOCRATIC				REPUBLICAN			
	Receipts, net [1]	Disbursements, net [1]	Contributions to candidates	Monies spent on behalf of party's nominees [2]	Receipts, net [1]	Disbursements, net [1]	Contributions to candidates	Monies spent on behalf of party's nominees [2]
1981-82	39.3	40.1	1.7	3.3	215.0	214.0	5.6	14.3
1983-84	98.5	97.4	2.6	9.0	297.9	300.8	4.9	20.1
1985-86	64.8	65.9	1.7	9.0	255.2	258.9	3.4	14.3
1987-88	127.9	121.9	1.8	17.9	263.3	257.0	3.4	22.7
1989-90	85.8	90.9	1.5	8.7	206.3	213.5	2.9	10.7
1991-92, total	**177.7**	**171.9**	**1.9**	**28.1**	**267.3**	**256.1**	**3.0**	**33.9**
National committee	65.8	65.0	-	11.3	85.4	81.9	0.8	11.3
Senatorial committee	25.5	25.5	0.6	11.2	73.8	71.3	0.7	16.5
Congressional committee	12.8	12.7	0.8	4.1	35.3	34.3	0.7	5.2
Other national	9.8	8.6	-	-	-	-	-	-
State and local	63.9	60.2	0.5	1.4	72.8	68.6	0.8	0.9
1993-94, total	**143.3**	**141.8**	**2.2**	**21.2**	**254.4**	**243.7**	**3.0**	**20.6**
National committee	41.8	44.0	0.1	-0.3	87.4	85.3	0.5	4.7
Senatorial committee	26.4	26.4	0.5	12.3	65.3	65.4	0.6	10.9
Congressional committee	19.4	19.4	1.0	7.7	26.7	26.3	0.8	3.9
Other national	7.8	8.1	-	-	-	-	-	-
State and local	47.8	44.0	0.6	1.5	75.0	66.7	1.0	1.1

- Represents zero. [1] Excludes monies transferred between affiliated committees. [2] Monies spent in the general election. Minus sign (-) indicates refunds for expenditures.

Source: U.S. Federal Election Commission, *FEC Reports on Financial Activity, Final Report, Party and Non-Party Political Committees*, biennial.

No. 467. Independent Expenditures for Presidential and Congressional Campaigns: 1985 to 1994

[In thousands of dollars. Covers campaign finance activity during 2-year calendar period indicated. An "independent expenditure" is money spent to support or defeat a clearly identified candidate. According to Federal election law, such an expenditure must be made without cooperation or consultation with the candidate or his/her campaign. Independent expenditures are not limited, as are contributions]

TYPE OF OFFICE AND YEAR	ALL PARTIES			DEMOCRATS		REPUBLICANS		OTHERS	
	Total	For	Against	For	Against	For	Against	For	Against
TOTAL									
1985-86	10,205	8,832	1,373	3,450	888	5,376	485	6	-
1987-88	21,341	16,654	4,687	2,865	4,248	13,784	439	6	-
1989-90	5,774	4,177	1,597	1,530	735	2,645	862	2	-
1991-92	11,052	8,710	2,342	3,044	1,483	5,548	847	118	12
1993-94	4,980	3,256	1,724	672	1,119	2,571	590	13	15
PRESIDENTIAL									
1985-86	841	795	45	76	28	719	17	-	-
1987-88	14,127	10,628	3,499	568	3,352	10,054	146	6	-
1989-90	497	322	174	5	169	318	5	-	-
1991-92	4,431	3,695	736	583	561	3,052	163	60	12
1993-94	112	27	85	12	84	15	(Z)	-	1
SENATE									
1985-86	5,312	4,331	980	988	632	3,343	348	-	-
1987-88	4,401	3,641	761	831	617	2,810	143	(Z)	-
1989-90	3,506	2,362	1,144	756	428	1,604	716	2	-
1991-92	2,604	1,912	692	1,025	462	886	230	1	-
1993-94	2,627	1,612	1,015	261	476	1,351	539	(Z)	-
HOUSE OF REPRESENTATIVES									
1985-86	4,053	3,706	347	2,386	227	1,314	120	6	-
1987-88	2,813	2,385	427	1,466	279	920	149	(Z)	-
1989-90	1,772	1,493	279	770	138	723	141	-	-
1991-92	4,017	3,103	914	1,436	460	1,610	454	57	-
1993-94	2,241	1,617	624	399	559	1,205	51	13	14

- Represents zero. Z Less than $500.

Source: U.S. Federal Election Commission, *FEC Index of Independent Expenditures, 1987-88*, May 1989; press release of May 19, 1989; and unpublished data.

No. 468. Political Action Committees—Number, by Committee Type: 1980 to 1995

[As of December 31]

COMMITTEE TYPE	1980	1985	1990	1991	1992	1993	1994	1995
Total	2,551	3,992	4,172	4,094	4,195	4,210	3,954	4,016
Corporate	1,206	1,710	1,795	1,738	1,735	1,789	1,660	1,674
Labor	297	388	346	338	347	337	333	334
Trade/membership/health	576	695	774	742	770	761	792	815
Nonconnected	374	1,003	1,062	1,083	1,145	1,121	980	1,020
Cooperative	42	54	59	57	56	56	53	44
Corporation without stock	56	142	136	136	142	146	136	129

Source: U.S. Federal Election Commission, press release of January 23, 1996.

No. 469. Political Action Committees—Financial Activity Summary, by Committee Type: 1989 to 1994

[In millions of dollars. Covers financial activity during 2-year calendar period indicated. Data have not been adjusted for transfers between affiliated committees]

COMMITTEE TYPE	RECEIPTS			DISBURSEMENTS [1]			CONTRIBUTIONS TO CANDIDATES		
	1989-90	1991-92	1993-94	1989-90	1991-92	1993-94	1989-90	1991-92	1993-94
Total	372.1	385.5	391.9	357.6	394.8	388.1	159.1	188.9	189.6
Corporate	106.5	112.5	116.0	101.1	112.4	116.6	58.1	68.4	69.6
Labor	88.9	89.9	90.3	84.6	94.6	88.4	34.7	41.4	41.9
Trade/membership/health	92.5	95.7	96.4	88.1	97.5	94.1	44.8	53.9	52.9
Nonconnected	71.6	73.8	76.9	71.4	78.2	75.1	15.1	18.3	18.2
Cooperative	5.0	4.8	4.4	4.8	4.9	4.5	2.9	3.0	3.0
Corporation without stock	7.6	8.7	8.9	7.7	9.2	9.2	3.4	4.0	4.1

[1] Comprises contributions to candidates, independent expenditures, and other disbursements.

Source: U.S. Federal Election Commission, *FEC Reports on Financial Activity, Final Report, Party and Non-Party Political Committees*, biennial.

No. 470. Presidential Campaign Finances—Federal Funds for General Election: 1980 to 1992

[In millions of dollars. Based on FEC certifications, audit reports, and Dept. of Treasury reports]

1980		1984		1988		1992	
Candidate	Amount	Candidate	Amount	Candidate	Amount	Candidate	Amount
Total	62.7	Total	80.3	Total	92.2	Total	110.4
Anderson [1]	4.2	Mondale	40.2	Bush	46.1	Bush	55.2
Carter	29.4	Reagan	40.1	Dukakis	46.1	Clinton	55.2
Reagan	29.2					Perot	-

- Represents zero. [1] John Anderson, as the candidate of a new party, was permitted to raise funds privately. Total receipts for the Anderson campaign, including Federal funds, were $17.6 million, and total expenditures were $15.6 million.

Source: U.S. Federal Election Commission, periodic press releases.

No. 471. Presidential Campaign Finances—Primary Campaign Receipts and Disbursements: 1983 to 1992

[In millions of dollars. Covers campaign finance activity during 2-year calendar period indicated. Covers candidates who received Federal matching funds or who had significant financial activity]

ITEM	TOTAL			DEMOCRATIC			REPUBLICAN		
	1983-84 [1]	1987-88 [2]	1991-92 [3]	1983-84	1987-88	1991-92	1983-84	1987-88	1991-92
Receipts, total [4]	105.0	213.8	125.2	77.5	91.9	70.0	27.1	116.0	49.7
Individual contributions	62.8	141.1	82.4	46.2	59.4	44.7	16.4	76.8	34.4
Federal matching funds	34.9	65.7	41.5	24.6	30.1	24.4	10.1	34.7	15.0
Disbursements	103.6	210.7	118.7	77.4	90.2	64.4	25.9	114.6	46.6

[1] Includes Citizens Party candidate, not shown separately. [2] Includes a minor party candidate who sought several party nominations and a Democratic candidate who did not receive Federal matching funds, but who had significant financial activity. [3] Includes other parties, not shown separately. [4] Includes other types of receipts, not shown separately.

Source: U.S. Federal Election Commission, *FEC Reports on Financial Activity, Final Report, Presidential Pre-Nomination Campaigns*, quadrennial.

No. 472. Congressional Campaign Finances—Receipts and Disbursements: 1989 to 1994

[Covers all campaign finance activity during 2-year calendar period indicated for primary, general, run-off, and special elections. for 1989-90 to 1,580 House of Representatives candidates and 179 Senate candidates; for 1991-92 to 2,585 House of Representatives candidates and 365 Senate candidates. for 1993-94 to 2,045 House of Representatives candidates and 331 Senate candidates; Data have been adjusted to eliminate transfers between all committees within a campaign. For further information on legal limits of contributions, see Federal Election Campaign Act of 1971, as amended]

ITEM	HOUSE OF REPRESENTATIVES						SENATE					
	Amount (mil. dol.)			Percent distribution			Amount (mil. dol.)			Percent distribution		
	1989-90	1991-92	1993-94	1989-90	1991-92	1993-94	1989-90	1991-92	1993-94	1989-90	1991-92	1993-94
Total receipts [1]	**285.4**	**395.9**	**421.3**	**100**	**100**	**100**	**186.3**	**263.4**	**319.1**	**100**	**100**	**100**
Individual contributions	129.9	192.4	216.1	46	49	51	119.6	162.8	186.4	64	62	58
Other committees	106.5	127.4	132.4	38	32	31	41.2	51.2	47.2	22	19	15
Candidate loans	20.9	43.0	43.9	7	11	10	10.0	28.7	43.5	5	11	14
Candidate contributions	4.8	11.4	10.3	2	3	2	2.4	6.5	24.9	1	2	8
Democrats	163.4	217.7	216.7	57	56	51	89.5	143.8	133.6	48	55	42
Republicans	120.9	174.3	201.8	42	44	48	96.8	118.3	183.6	52	45	58
Others	1.1	3.9	2.8	(Z)	1	1	(Z)	1.3	2.0	(Z)	(Z)	1
Incumbents	181.9	203.5	224.1	64	51	53	118.7	99.7	113.3	64	38	36
Challengers	47.7	91.3	100.6	17	23	24	54.8	95.6	119.2	29	36	37
Open seats [2]	55.9	101.1	96.6	20	26	23	12.8	68.2	86.6	7	26	27
Total disbursements	**265.8**	**407.6**	**407.2**	**100**	**100**	**100**	**180.4**	**272.1**	**318.8**	**100**	**100**	**100**
Democrats	151.0	228.3	213.4	57	56	52	87.6	147.6	136.3	49	54	43
Republicans	113.7	176.0	191.0	43	43	47	92.9	123.2	180.6	52	45	57
Others	1.1	3.3	2.8	(Z)	1	1	(Z)	1.2	2.0	(Z)	(Z)	1
Incumbents	163.4	217.9	213.5	62	53	52	113.5	107.2	115.1	63	39	36
Challengers	47.0	90.0	99.1	18	22	24	54.9	95.3	118.3	30	35	37
Open seats [2]	55.4	99.7	94.6	21	24	23	12.1	69.6	85.5	7	26	27

Z Less than $50,000 or 0.5 percent. [1] Includes other types of receipts, not shown separately. [2] Elections in which an incumbent did not seek re-election.

Source: U.S. Federal Election Commission, *FEC Reports on Financial Activity, Final Report, U.S. Senate and House Campaigns*, biennial.

No. 473. Contributions to Congressional Campaigns by Political Action Committees (PAC), by Type of Committee: 1981 to 1994

[In millions of dollars. Covers amounts given to candidates in primary, general, run-off, and special elections during the 2-year calendar period indicated. For number of political action committees, see table 468]

TYPE OF COMMITTEE	Total [1]	Democrats	Republicans	Incumbents	Challengers	Open seats [2]
HOUSE OF REPRESENTATIVES						
1981-82	61.1	34.2	26.8	40.8	10.9	9.4
1983-84	75.7	46.3	29.3	57.2	11.3	7.2
1985-86	87.4	54.7	32.6	65.9	9.1	12.4
1987-88	102.2	67.4	34.7	82.2	10.0	10.0
1989-90	108.5	72.2	36.2	87.5	7.3	13.6
1991-92	127.4	85.4	41.7	94.4	12.2	20.8
1993-94, total [3]	**132.4**	**88.2**	**43.9**	**101.4**	**12.7**	**18.3**
Corporate	43.5	23.6	19.9	36.3	2.9	4.3
Trade association [4]	38.8	22.1	16.6	30.0	3.3	5.5
Labor	33.4	31.9	1.4	23.6	4.1	5.6
Nonconnected [5]	11.8	7.4	4.4	7.4	2.0	2.4
SENATE						
1981-82	22.6	11.2	11.4	14.3	5.2	3.0
1983-84	29.7	14.0	15.6	17.9	6.3	5.4
1985-86	45.3	20.2	25.1	23.7	10.2	11.4
1987-88	45.7	24.2	21.5	28.7	8.0	9.0
1989-90	41.2	20.2	21.0	29.5	8.2	3.5
1991-92	51.2	29.0	22.2	31.9	9.4	10.0
1993-94, total [3]	**47.2**	**24.0**	**23.2**	**26.3**	**5.7**	**15.1**
Corporate	20.8	7.8	13.0	11.7	2.0	7.2
Trade association [4]	11.5	4.9	6.6	6.8	1.1	3.6
Labor	7.3	7.1	0.2	3.6	1.7	2.0
Nonconnected [5]	5.7	3.1	2.6	3.1	0.8	1.8

[1] Includes other parties, not shown separately. [2] Elections in which an incumbent did not seek re-election. [3] Includes other types of political action committees not shown separately. [4] Includes membership organizations and health organizations. [5] Represents "ideological" groups as well as other issue groups not necessarily ideological in nature.

Source: U.S. Federal Election Commission, *FEC Reports on Financial Activity, Party and Non-Party Political Committees, Final Report*, biennial.

Figure 9.1
Per Capita State Tax Collections: 1996

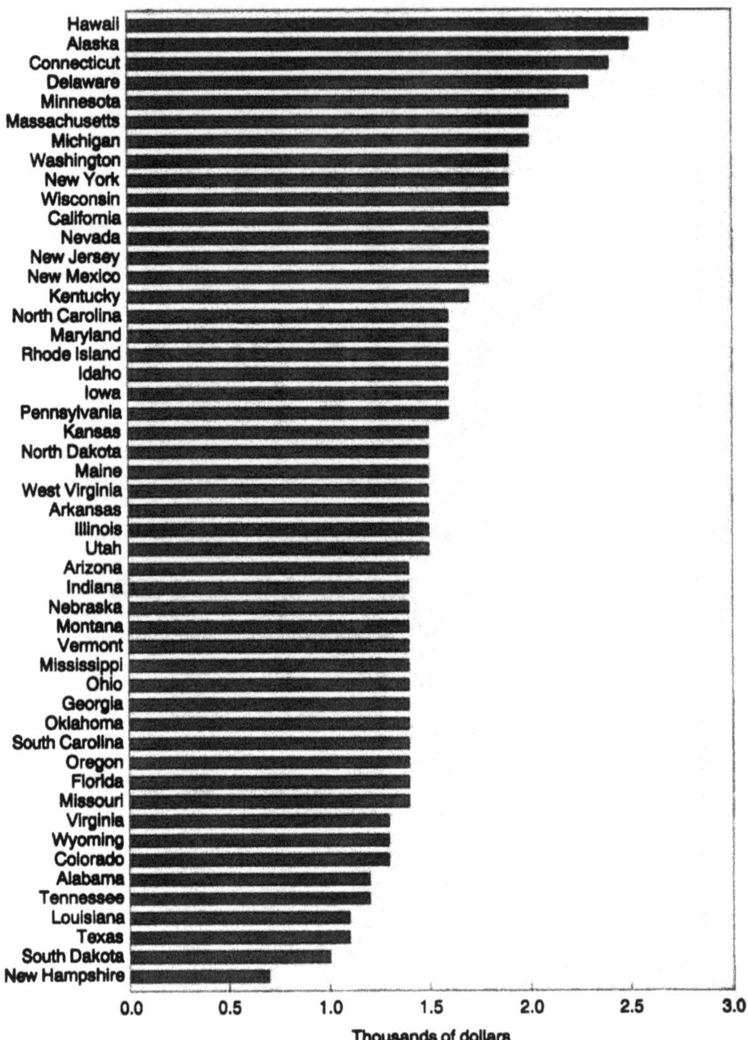

Source: Chart prepared by U.S. Bureau of the Census. For data, see table 495.

State and Local Government Finances and Employment

This section presents data on revenues, expenditures, debt, and employment of State and local governments. Nationwide statistics relating to State and local governments, their numbers, finances, and employment, are compiled primarily by the Bureau of the Census through a program of censuses and surveys. Every fifth year (for years ending in "2" and "7") the Bureau conducts a census of governments involving collection of data for all governmental units in the United States. In addition, the Bureau conducts annual surveys which cover all the State governments and a sample of local governments.

Annually, the Bureau of the Census releases information on the Internet which present financial data for the Federal Government, nationwide totals for State and local governments, and State-local data by States. Also released annually is a series on State, city, county, and school finances, and on State and local public employment. There is also a series of quarterly data releases covering tax revenue and finances of major public employee retirement systems.

Basic information for Census Bureau statistics on governments is obtained by mail canvass from State and local officials; however, financial data for each of the State governments and for many of the large local governments are compiled from their official records and reports by Census Bureau personnel. In over two thirds of the States, all or part of local government financial data are obtained through central collection arrangements with State governments. Financial data on the Federal Government is primarily based on the *Budget* published by the Office of Management and Budget (see text, section 10).

Governmental units—The governmental structure of the United States includes, in addition to the Federal Government and the States, thousands of local governments—counties, municipalities, townships, school districts, and numerous kinds of "special districts." In 1992, 84,955 local governments were identified by the census of governments. As defined by the census, governmental units include all agencies or bodies having an organized existence, governmental character, and substantial autonomy. While most of these governments can impose taxes, many of the special districts—such as independent public housing authorities, and numerous local irrigation, power, and other types of districts—are financed from rentals, charges for services, benefit assessments, grants from other governments, and other nontax sources. The count of governments excludes semi-autonomous agencies through which States, cities, and counties sometimes provide for certain functions—for example, "dependent" school systems, State institutions of higher education, and certain other "authorities" and special agencies which are under the administrative or fiscal control of an established governmental unit.

In Brief

State government revenue (from own sources) in 1995: $688,198 million

Taxes	58%
Insurance trust funds	23%
Charges	9%
Interest earnings	4%
Utility and liquor stores	1%

State government direct expenditures in 1995: $595,916 million

Public welfare	27%
Education	17%
Insurance trust funds	16%
Health and hospitals	8%
Highways	8%

Finances—The financial statistics relate to government fiscal years ending June 30, or at some date within the 12 previous months. The following governments are exceptions and are included as though they were part of the June 30 group; ending September 30, the State governments of Alabama and Michigan, the District of Columbia, and Alabama school districts; and ending August 31, the State government of Texas and Texas school districts. New York State ends its fiscal year on March 31. The Federal Government ended the fiscal year June 30 until 1976 when its fiscal year, by an act of Congress, was revised to extend from Oct. 1 to Sept. 30. A 3-month quarter (July 1 to Sept. 30, 1976) bridged the transition.

Nationwide government finance statistics have been classified and presented in terms of uniform concepts and categories, rather than according to the highly diverse terminology, organization, and fund structure utilized by individual governments. Accordingly, financial statistics which appear here for the Federal Government and for individual States or local governments have been standardized and may not agree directly with figures appearing in the original sources.

Statistics on governmental finances distinguish among general government, utilities, liquor stores, and insurance trusts. *General government* comprises all activities except utilities, liquor stores, and insurance trusts. Utilities include government water supply, electric light and power, gas supply, and transit systems. Liquor stores are operated by 17 States and by local governments in 6 States. Insurance trusts relate to employee retirement, unemployment compensation, and other social insurance systems administered by the Federal, State, and local governments.

Data for cities or counties relate only to municipal or county governments and their dependent agencies and do not include amounts for other local governments in the same geographic location. Therefore, expenditure figures for "education" do not include spending by the separate school districts which administer public schools within most municipal or county areas. Variations in the assignment of governmental responsibility for public assistance, health, hospitals, public housing, and other functions to a lesser degree also have an important effect upon reported amounts of city or county expenditure, revenue, and debt. Therefore, any comparisons based upon these figures should be made with caution and with due recognition of variations that exist among areas.

Employment and payrolls—These data are based mainly on mail canvassing of State and local governments. Payroll includes all salaries, wages, and individual fee payments for the month specified, and employment relates to all persons on governmental payrolls during a pay period of the month covered—including paid officials, temporary help, and (unless otherwise specified) part-time as well as full-time personnel. Beginning 1986, statistics for full-time equivalent employment have been computed with a formula using hours worked by part-time employees. A payroll based formula was used prior to 1985. Full-time equivalent employment statistics were not computed for 1985. Figures shown for individual governments cover major dependent agencies such as institutions of higher education, as well as the basic central departments and agencies of the government.

Statistical reliability—For a discussion of statistical collection and estimation, sampling procedures, and measures of statistical reliability applicable to Census Bureau data, see Appendix III.

No. 474. Number of Governmental Units, by Type: 1942 to 1992

TYPE OF GOVERNMENT	1942	1952 [1]	1957 [1]	1962	1967	1972	1977	1982	1987	1992
Total	155,116	116,807	102,392	91,237	81,299	78,269	79,913	81,831	83,237	86,006
U.S. Government	1	1	1	1	1	1	1	1	1	1
State government	48	50	50	50	50	50	50	50	50	50
Local governments	155,067	116,756	102,341	91,186	81,248	78,218	79,862	81,780	83,186	84,955
County	3,050	3,052	3,050	3,043	3,049	3,044	3,042	3,041	3,042	3,043
Municipal	16,220	16,807	17,215	18,000	18,048	18,517	18,862	19,076	19,200	19,279
Township and town	18,919	17,202	17,198	17,142	17,105	16,991	16,822	16,734	16,691	16,656
School district	108,579	67,355	50,454	34,678	21,782	15,781	15,174	14,851	14,721	14,422
Special district	8,299	12,340	14,424	18,323	21,264	23,885	25,962	28,078	29,532	31,555

[1] Adjusted to include units in Alaska and Hawaii which adopted statehood in 1959.

No. 475. Number of Governments, by Type—States: 1992

[Governments in existence in January. Limited to governments actually in existence. Excludes, therefore, a few counties and numerous townships and "incorporated places" existing as areas for which statistics can be presented as to population and other subjects, but lacking any separate organized county, township, or municipal government]

STATE	All governmental units [1]	County	Municipal	Township [2]	School district	SPECIAL DISTRICT: Total [3]	Natural resources	Fire protection	Housing and community development
U.S.	86,006	3,043	19,279	16,656	14,422	31,555	6,228	5,260	3,470
Alabama	1,122	67	438	-	129	487	68	4	152
Alaska	175	12	148	-	-	14	-	-	13
Arizona	591	15	86	-	228	261	69	130	-
Arkansas	1,447	75	489	-	321	561	226	48	125
California	4,393	57	460	-	1,078	2,797	480	369	84
Colorado	1,761	62	266	-	180	1,252	167	239	91
Connecticut	584	-	29	149	17	388	1	59	94
Delaware	276	3	57	-	19	196	187	-	4
District of Columbia	2	-	1	-	-	1	-	-	-
Florida	1,014	66	390	-	95	462	135	53	105
Georgia	1,298	157	536	-	183	421	36	6	203
Hawaii	21	3	1	-	-	16	16	-	-
Idaho	1,087	44	199	-	115	728	165	129	12
Illinois	6,723	102	1,282	1,433	985	2,920	903	804	114
Indiana	2,899	91	566	1,008	294	939	132	-	61
Iowa	1,881	99	952	-	441	388	239	67	19
Kansas	3,892	105	627	1,363	324	1,482	258	-	203
Kentucky	1,321	119	435	-	176	590	128	92	22
Louisiana	459	61	301	-	66	30	2	-	-
Maine	797	16	22	468	91	199	13	-	26
Maryland	402	23	155	-	-	223	151	-	21
Massachusetts	844	12	39	312	84	396	14	15	253
Michigan	2,722	83	534	1,242	585	277	82	2	-
Minnesota	3,580	87	854	1,803	458	377	109	-	163
Mississippi	870	82	294	-	173	320	235	-	56
Missouri	3,310	114	933	324	552	1,386	168	204	142
Montana	1,276	54	128	-	537	556	125	145	17
Nebraska	2,924	93	534	452	797	1,047	93	418	133
Nevada	208	16	18	-	17	156	32	14	16
New Hampshire	528	10	13	221	167	116	10	15	22
New Jersey	1,513	21	320	247	550	374	17	169	2
New Mexico	342	33	98	-	94	116	71	-	5
New York	3,299	57	619	929	713	980	2	900	-
North Carolina	938	100	516	-	-	321	148	-	98
North Dakota	2,765	53	364	1,350	275	722	78	269	36
Ohio	3,524	88	942	1,314	666	513	98	40	59
Oklahoma	1,795	77	588	-	605	524	100	18	122
Oregon	1,451	36	239	-	340	835	188	263	22
Pennsylvania	5,159	66	1,022	1,548	516	2,006	8	1	88
Rhode Island	126	-	8	31	3	83	3	38	26
South Carolina	698	46	269	-	91	291	48	84	45
South Dakota	1,786	64	310	969	180	262	103	51	42
Tennessee	924	93	339	-	14	477	112	-	89
Texas	4,792	254	1,171	-	1,100	2,266	413	95	398
Utah	627	29	228	-	40	329	77	20	16
Vermont	682	14	50	237	276	104	14	21	9
Virginia	455	95	230	-	-	129	44	-	-
Washington	1,761	39	268	-	296	1,157	154	404	51
West Virginia	692	55	231	-	55	350	15	-	36
Wisconsin	2,739	72	583	1,266	440	377	168	-	177
Wyoming	550	23	97	-	56	373	123	54	-

- Represents zero. [1] Includes the Federal Government and the 50 State governments not shown separately. [2] Includes "town" governments in the six New England States and in Minnesota, New York, and Wisconsin. [3] Includes other special districts not shown separately.

Source of tables 474 and 475: U.S. Bureau of the Census, *1992 Census of Governments, Government Organization.*

No. 476. County, Municipal, and Township Governments: 1992

[Number of governments as of January 1992. Population enumerated as of April 1, 1990. Consolidated city-county governments are classified as municipal rather than county governments. Township governments include "towns" in the six New England States, Minnesota, New York, and Wisconsin]

POPULATION-SIZE GROUP	COUNTY GOVERNMENTS			MUNICIPAL GOVERNMENTS			TOWNSHIP GOVERNMENTS		
	Number, 1992	Population, 1990		Number, 1992	Population, 1990		Number, 1992	Population, 1990	
		Number (1,000)	Percent		Number (1,000)	Percent		Number (1,000)	Percent
Total	3,043	224,924	100	19,279	153,819	100	16,656	53,061	100
200,000 or more	[1]174	[1]120,551	[1]54	76	47,809	31	6	2,140	4
100,000 to 199,999	[2]244	[2]37,336	[2]17	119	16,390	11	27	3,554	7
50,000 to 99,999	377	26,555	12	310	21,282	14	77	5,214	10
25,000 to 49,999	612	21,510	10	566	19,877	13	249	8,461	16
10,000 to 24,999	908	14,851	7	1,290	20,324	13	728	11,225	21
5,000 to 9,999	[3]728	[3]4,121	[3]2	1,566	11,136	7	1,019	7,112	13
2,500 to 4,999	(NA)	(NA)	(NA)	2,036	7,238	5	1,800	6,301	12
1,000 to 2,499	(NA)	(NA)	(NA)	3,670	5,894	4	3,626	5,796	11
Less than 1,000	(NA)	(NA)	(NA)	9,646	3,874	3	9,124	3,251	6

NA Not available. [1] For population-size group of 250,000 or more. [2] 100,000 to 249,999. [3] Less than 10,000.

Source: U.S. Bureau of the Census, *Census of Governments: 1992*, vol. 1, No. 1, *Government Organization*.

Figure 9.2
Lottery Sales—Type of Game and Use of Proceeds: 1996

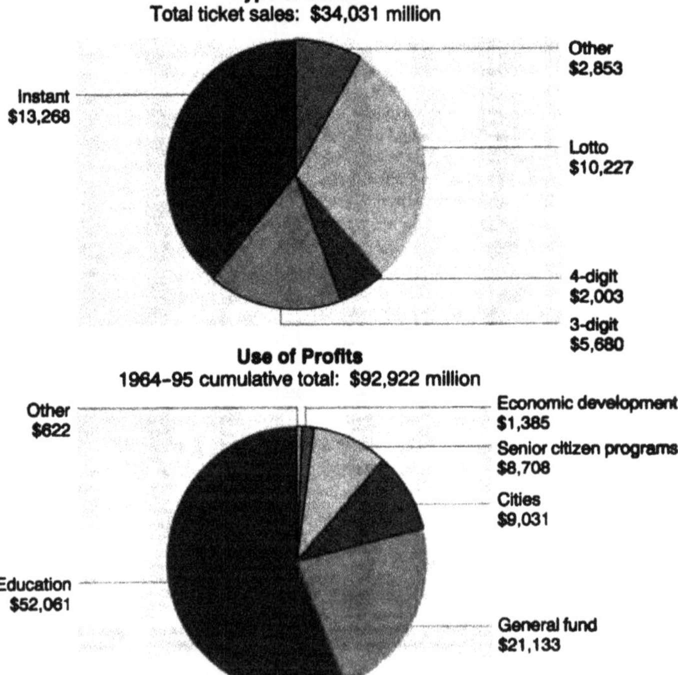

Source: Chart prepared by U.S. Bureau of the Census. For data, see table 499.

No. 477. All Governments—Revenue, Expenditure, and Debt: 1980 to 1994

[For fiscal year ending in year shown; see text, section 9. Local government amounts are estimates subject to sampling variation; see Appendix III and source]

ITEM	All govern-ments (bil. dol.)	FEDERAL [1]		STATE AND LOCAL (bil. dol.)			PER CAPITA [2] (dollars)		
		Total (bil. dol.)	Percent of total	Total	State	Local	Total	Federal	State and local
Revenue: [3] 1980	[4]932	565	60.7	[4]452	277	258	[4]4,115	2,496	1,993
1990	[4]2,047	1,155	56.4	[4]1,032	632	580	[4]8,230	4,642	4,150
1993	[4]2,374	1,306	55.0	[4]1,271	805	662	[4]9,210	5,068	4,918
1994	[4]2,513	1,401	55.7	[4]1,331	842	721	[4]9,654	5,380	5,114
Intergovernmental: 1980	(X)	2	(X)	[4]83	64	102	(X)	8	367
1990	(X)	3	(X)	[4]137	126	191	(X)	12	550
1993	(X)	3	(X)	[4]199	188	227	(X)	12	771
1994	(X)	3	(X)	[4]215	205	242	(X)	12	828
General, own sources:									
1980	717	417	58.2	299	169	130	3,163	1,842	1,321
1990	1,493	780	52.2	713	391	322	6,004	3,138	2,866
1993	1,730	887	51.4	843	465	378	6,699	3,441	3,258
1994	1,831	946	51.7	885	488	397	7,031	3,632	3,399
Taxes: [3] 1980	574	351	61.1	223	137	86	2,535	1,548	986
1990	1,134	632	55.7	502	301	201	4,559	2,542	2,017
1993	1,307	713	54.6	594	354	240	5,065	2,765	2,300
1994	1,406	780	55.5	626	373	252	5,400	2,997	2,403
Property: 1980	68	(X)	(X)	68	3	66	302	(X)	302
1990	156	(X)	(X)	156	6	150	626	(X)	626
1993	190	(X)	(X)	190	8	182	731	(X)	731
1994	197	(X)	(X)	197	8	189	757	(X)	757
Individual income:									
1980	286	244	85.3	42	37	5	1,263	1,077	186
1990	573	467	81.6	106	96	10	2,302	1,877	425
1993	633	510	80.5	123	112	11	2,455	1,977	478
1994	672	543	80.8	129	117	12	2,581	2,086	495
Corporate income:									
1980	78	65	82.9	13	13	-	344	286	59
1990	117	94	80.3	24	22	2	471	376	95
1993	144	118	81.6	26	24	2	558	456	103
1994	169	140	83.2	28	26	3	648	539	109
Sales or gross receipts:									
1980	112	[5]32	28.6	80	68	12	494	[5]141	353
1990	232	[5]54	23.3	178	147	31	932	[5]217	715
1993	277	[5]67	24.3	210	175	35	1,074	[5]262	813
1994	298	[5]75	25.0	224	186	38	1,146	[5]287	859
Current charges and miscellaneous: 1980	142	67	46.7	76	32	44	629	294	335
1990	359	148	41.3	211	91	120	1,445	596	849
1993	423	174	41.4	249	111	137	1,634	676	958
1994	425	165	38.9	259	114	145	1,632	635	997
Expenditures: [3] 1980	[4]959	617	64.4	[4]434	258	261	[4]4,232	2,724	1,916
1990	[4]2,219	1,393	62.8	[4]976	572	561	[4]8,921	5,601	3,924
1993	[4]2,089	1,570	75.1	[4]1,214	743	688	[4]8,102	6,088	4,697
1994	[4]2,150	1,630	75.8	[4]1,264	775	719	[4]8,259	6,262	4,856
Intergovernmental: 1980	(X)	91	(X)	[4]2	85	2	(X)	401	8
1990	(X)	147	(X)	[4]3	175	6	(X)	591	13
1993	(X)	205	(X)	[4]3	214	7	(X)	794	14
1994	(X)	218	(X)	[4]4	225	9	(X)	837	14
Direct: [3] 1980	959	526	54.9	432	173	259	4,232	2,323	1,908
1990	2,219	1,246	56.2	973	397	575	8,921	5,010	3,911
1993	2,089	879	42.1	1,210	529	681	8,091	3,408	4,682
1994	2,150	890	41.4	1,261	550	710	8,259	3,417	4,842
Current operation: 1980	517	209	40.5	308	108	200	2,282	923	1,359
1990	1,190	490	41.2	700	258	442	4,785	1,970	2,815
1993	1,367	491	36.0	876	345	531	5,290	1,904	3,386
1994	1,422	494	34.8	928	368	560	5,462	1,898	3,564
Capital outlay: 1980	99	36	36.7	63	23	40	439	161	278
1990	221	98	44.3	123	46	78	888	394	495
1993	221	85	38.6	136	50	86	858	331	527
1994	217	80	36.7	138	53	85	835	307	528
Debt outstanding: [6] 1980	1,250	914	73.2	336	122	214	5,522	4,036	1,486
1990	4,127	3,266	79.2	861	318	542	16,592	13,132	3,460
1993	5,454	4,436	81.4	1,018	390	628	21,156	17,208	3,948
1994	5,796	4,721	81.5	1,075	411	664	22,263	18,135	4,128

- Represents or rounds to zero. X Not applicable. [1] Data adjusted to system for reporting State and local data, and therefore; differ from figures in section 10 tables. [2] 1980 and 1990 based on enumerated resident population as of April 1; all other years based on estimated resident population as of July 1. [3] Includes amounts not shown separately. [4] Excludes duplicate transactions between levels of government; see source. [5] Includes customs. [6] End of fiscal year.

Source: U.S. Bureau of the Census; *"Government Finances"*, GF, No. 5, annual; <http://www.census.gov/ftp/pub/govs/www/index.html>; (released June 24,1997).

No. 478. All Governments—Detailed Finances: 1994

[For fiscal year ending in year shown, see text, section 9. Local government amounts are estimates subject to sampling variation; see Appendix III and source]

ITEM	All govern-ments (mil. dol.)	Federal (mil. dol.)	STATE AND LOCAL (mil. dol.)			PER CAPITA[1] (dol.)	
			Total	State	Local	Fed-eral	State and local
Revenue	2,513,442	1,400,664	1,331,442	841,702	720,840	5,380	5,114
Intergovernmental revenue	(2)	3,219	215,445	204,518	242,027	12	828
Revenue from own sources	2,513,442	1,397,445	1,115,998	637,184	478,812	5,368	4,286
General revenue from own sources	1,830,634	945,638	884,996	487,780	397,215	3,632	3,399
Taxes [3]	1,405,796	780,269	625,527	373,319	252,207	2,997	2,403
Property	197,140	(X)	197,140	8,386	188,754	(X)	757
Individual income	671,865	543,055	128,810	117,128	11,682	2,086	495
Corporation income	168,705	140,385	28,320	25,692	2,627	539	109
Sales and gross receipts	298,276	74,648	223,628	185,871	37,757	287	859
Customs duties	20,264	20,264	(X)	(X)	(X)	78	(X)
General	149,039	(X)	149,039	123,006	26,034	(X)	572
Selective [3]	128,972	54,384	74,588	62,865	11,723	209	287
Motor fuel	51,644	26,441	25,203	24,490	713	102	97
Alcoholic beverages	11,504	7,600	3,904	3,610	293	29	15
Tobacco products	12,647	5,744	6,903	6,717	186	22	27
Public utilities	23,987	8,924	15,063	8,490	6,572	34	58
Motor vehicle and operators' licenses	12,762	(X)	12,762	11,835	927	(X)	49
Death and gift	50,093	15,225	34,868	24,407	10,461	58	134
Charges and miscellaneous [3]	424,838	165,369	259,469	114,461	145,008	635	997
Current charges [3]	257,836	96,670	161,166	61,018	100,148	371	619
National defense and international relations	10,075	10,075	(X)	(X)	(X)	39	(X)
Postal service	48,412	48,412	(X)	(X)	(X)	186	(X)
Education [3]	44,493	(X)	44,493	33,185	11,308	(X)	171
School lunch sales	4,003	(X)	4,003	16	3,987	(X)	15
Higher education	37,059	(X)	37,059	32,729	4,330	(X)	142
Natural resources	15,256	13,150	2,106	1,616	491	51	8
Hospitals	55,562	11,351	44,211	14,930	29,281	44	170
Sewerage	18,321	(X)	18,321	32	18,289	(X)	70
Solid waste management	8,189	3	8,189	375	7,814	-	31
Parks and recreation	4,470	168	4,302	884	3,418	1	17
Housing and community development	6,363	3,006	3,357	300	3,058	12	13
Airports	7,099	25	7,074	652	6,422	-	27
Sea and inland port facilities	3,202	1,417	1,785	434	1,351	5	7
Highways	5,900	691	5,209	3,174	2,034	3	20
Interest earnings	59,159	10,482	48,677	24,280	24,396	40	187
Special assessments	2,989	(X)	2,989	158	2,832	(X)	11
Sale of property	4,436	3,670	766	216	549	14	3
Utility and liquor store revenue	70,075	(X)	70,075	6,836	63,238	(X)	269
Insurance trust revenue	612,734	451,807	160,927	142,568	18,359	1,736	618
Expenditure	2,150,224	1,630,283	1,264,289	775,040	719,136	6,262	4,866
Intergovernmental expenditure	(2)	217,919	[2]3,648	224,764	8,770	837	14
Direct expenditure	2,150,224	889,582	1,260,642	550,276	710,366	3,417	4,842
General expenditure [3]	2,181,518	1,107,501	1,074,017	457,880	616,137	4,254	4,125
Education [3]	376,526	23,239	353,287	94,896	258,391	89	1,357
Elementary and secondary education	246,981	(X)	246,981	2,334	244,647	(X)	949
Higher education	90,871	(X)	90,871	77,128	13,743	(X)	349
Public welfare	236,033	56,204	179,829	148,244	31,585	216	691
Hospitals	76,452	11,351	65,101	28,064	37,037	44	250
Health	49,145	13,816	35,329	18,932	16,397	53	136
Highways	72,758	691	72,067	43,812	28,255	3	277
Police protection	45,973	7,328	38,645	5,325	33,320	28	148
Fire protection	16,123	(X)	16,123	(X)	16,123	(X)	62
Corrections	34,857	2,587	32,270	21,266	11,004	10	124
Natural resources	64,624	50,637	13,987	11,151	2,837	195	54
Sewerage	21,624	(X)	21,624	1,318	20,305	(X)	83
Solid waste management	16,873	2,832	14,041	1,370	12,671	11	54
Housing and community development	35,716	15,817	19,899	2,045	17,854	61	76
Governmental administration	67,504	11,788	55,716	22,201	33,515	45	214
Parks and recreation	18,830	2,154	16,676	2,799	13,876	8	64
Interest on general debt	257,623	202,663	54,960	23,719	31,241	778	211
Utility and liquor store expenditure	91,163	(X)	91,163	9,709	81,453	(X)	350
Insurance trust expenditure	618,244	522,782	95,462	82,687	12,775	2,008	367
By character and object:							
Current operation	1,422,154	494,255	927,899	368,009	559,890	1,898	3,564
Capital outlay	217,328	79,827	137,501	52,895	84,606	307	528
Construction	111,638	9,646	101,992	41,649	60,343	37	392
Equip., land, and existing structures	105,690	70,181	35,509	11,246	24,263	270	136
Assistance and subsidies	148,132	112,837	35,295	22,192	13,103	433	136
Interest on debt (general and utility)	267,147	202,663	64,484	24,494	39,991	778	248
Insurance benefits and repayments	618,244	522,782	95,462	82,687	12,775	2,008	367
Expenditure for salaries and wages [4]	*573,268*	*162,658*	*410,610*	*120,332*	*290,278*	*625*	*1,577*

- Represents or rounds to zero. X Not applicable. [1] Based on estimated resident population as of July 1. See table 2. [2] Excludes duplicate transactions between level of government. [3] Includes amounts not shown separately. [4] Included in items shown above.

Source: U.S. Bureau of the Census; <http://www.census.gov/pub/govs/www/index.html>; (Released June 1997); and unpublished data.

No. 479. All Governments—Capital Outlays: 1970 to 1994

[In millions of dollars, except percent. For fiscal year ending in year shown; see text, section 9. Local government amounts are subject to sampling variation; see Appendix III and source]

LEVEL AND FUNCTION	1970	1980	1985	1989	1990	1991	1992	1993	1994
Total	47,519	99,386	156,912	211,734	220,960	227,225	227,798	221,304	217,305
Federal Government:									
Total	17,869	36,492	77,014	99,790	97,891	95,575	93,095	85,326	79,804
Annual percent change [1]	-6	11	6	7	-2	-2	-3	-7	-7
Percent of direct expenditure	10	7	8	9	8	6	7	6	6
By function:									
National defense [2]	14,027	28,161	64,154	78,891	75,624	72,775	69,061	61,754	59,160
Education	9	97	39	9	41	97	90	86	146
Highways	9	132	121	165	181	143	310	210	203
Health and hospitals	166	673	916	1,403	1,096	1,367	1,594	1,703	1,508
Natural resources	1,691	4,046	4,092	3,786	4,696	4,721	5,466	6,122	2,990
Housing [3]	853	317	1,935	5,032	4,343	4,147	4,017	3,942	3,557
Air transportation	234	151	785	658	664	778	879	916	909
Water transportation [4]	285	1,003	583	306	385	459	506	739	495
Other	595	1,912	4,389	9,540	10,859	10,068	11,172	10,856	10,664
State and local governments:									
Total	29,650	62,894	79,898	111,944	123,069	131,650	134,703	135,899	137,501
Annual percent change [1]	5	7	13	7	10	7	2	-	1
Percent of direct expenditure	20	15	12	13	13	12	12	11	11
By function:									
Education [5]	7,621	10,737	13,477	21,854	25,997	27,251	30,845	31,359	29,012
Higher education	2,705	2,972	4,629	6,851	7,441	7,064	9,180	8,949	8,959
Elementary and secondary	4,658	7,362	8,358	14,584	18,057	19,852	21,319	22,102	19,693
Highways	10,762	19,133	23,900	32,754	33,867	36,409	37,031	36,980	39,503
Health and hospitals	790	2,443	2,709	3,445	3,848	4,142	4,331	5,291	4,464
Natural resources	789	1,052	1,736	2,019	2,545	2,474	2,266	2,137	2,349
Housing [3]	1,319	2,248	3,217	3,765	3,997	4,369	4,182	4,890	4,066
Air transportation	691	1,391	1,875	2,965	3,434	3,941	4,605	5,413	5,170
Water transportation [4]	258	623	717	943	924	984	778	996	1,483
Sewerage	1,385	6,272	5,926	8,343	8,356	9,104	8,926	10,261	7,989
Parks and recreation	684	2,023	2,196	3,350	3,677	4,702	3,934	3,849	3,919
Utilities	2,437	9,933	13,435	15,371	16,601	17,028	17,785	15,931	18,180
Water	1,201	3,335	4,160	6,372	6,873	7,499	7,567	6,490	6,893
Electric	820	4,572	5,247	4,291	3,976	3,579	3,950	3,760	4,030
Transit	366	1,921	3,830	4,430	5,443	5,636	5,836	5,253	6,966
Gas	50	105	198	279	310	314	432	428	290
Other	2,915	7,039	10,711	17,135	19,623	21,226	20,020	18,727	21,366

- Represents or rounds to zero. [1] Change from prior year shown except 1970, change from 1969 and 1980, change from 1975. [2] Includes international relations and U.S. service schools. [3] Includes community development. [4] Includes terminals. [5] Includes other education.

Source: U.S. Bureau of the Census, *Historical Statistics on Governmental Finances and Employment*; and *Government Finances*, series GF, No. 5, annual; <http://www.census.gov/govs/www/estimate.html> (Released June 1997).

No. 480. All Governments—Direct Expenditures for Public Works: 1980 to 1994

[In millions of dollars. Public works include expenditures on highways, airports, water transport and terminals, sewerage, solid waste management, water supply, and mass transit systems. Represents direct expenditures excluding intergovernmental grants]

ITEM	Total	Highways	Airport transportation	Water transport and terminals	Sewerage	Solid waste management	Water supply	Mass transit
1980: Total	72,177	33,745	5,071	3,278	9,892	3,322	9,228	7,641
Federal	5,114	434	2,570	2,110	-	-	-	-
State	22,832	20,661	360	360	334	-	91	1,026
Local	44,231	12,650	2,141	808	9,558	3,322	9,137	6,615
Capital expenditures (percent)	48	57	30	50	63	11	38	25
1990: Total	146,762	61,913	10,963	4,524	18,309	10,144	22,101	18,788
Federal	7,911	856	4,499	2,556	-	-	-	-
State	43,787	36,464	635	504	636	891	136	4,521
Local	95,064	24,593	5,848	1,464	17,673	9,253	21,966	14,267
Capital expenditures (percent)	42	55	37	29	46	18	31	29
1993: Total	167,075	68,989	15,504	5,121	22,785	12,829	24,621	17,226
Federal	9,786	619	6,214	2,953	-	-	-	-
State	46,136	42,056	915	572	1,097	1,304	188	4
Local	111,153	26,314	8,375	1,596	21,688	11,525	24,433	17,222
Capital expenditures (percent)	41	54	41	34	45	11	27	25
1994: Total	180,634	72,758	15,896	5,476	21,624	14,041	26,617	24,221
Federal	10,021	691	6,482	2,848	-	-	-	-
State	52,534	43,812	788	635	1,318	1,370	176	4,434
Local	118,079	28,255	8,626	1,993	20,305	12,671	26,441	19,786
Capital expenditures (percent)	40	55	38	36	37	13	26	29

- Represents or rounds to zero.

Source: U.S. Bureau of the Census, *Government Finances*, series GF, No. 5, annual; <http://www.census.gov/govs/www/estimate/html> (revised 27 May 1997); and unpublished data.

No. 481. Federal Grants-in-Aid Summary: 1970 to 1997

[For fiscal year ending in year shown; see text, section 9. Minus sign (-) indicates decrease]

YEAR	CURRENT DOLLARS							CONSTANT (1982) DOLLARS	
	Total grants (mil. dol.)	Annual percent change [1]	Grants to individuals		Grants as percent of—			Total grants (bil. dol.)	Annual percent change [1]
			Total (mil. dol.)	Percent of total grants	State-local govt. outlays [2]	Federal outlays	Gross domestic product		
1970	24,065	19.3	8,727	36.3	19.0	12.3	2.4	86.9	11.8
1975	49,791	14.8	16,762	33.7	23.5	15.0	3.2	126.6	3.3
1980	91,385	9.7	32,652	35.7	26.3	15.5	3.4	155.7	-1.1
1985	105,852	8.5	49,352	46.6	21.3	11.2	2.6	135.6	4.7
1989	121,928	5.7	67,353	55.2	18.6	10.7	2.3	136.2	1.7
1990	135,325	11.0	77,132	57.0	18.7	10.8	2.4	144.7	6.2
1991	154,519	14.2	92,497	59.9	19.5	11.7	2.6	158.6	9.6
1992	178,065	15.2	112,185	63.0	20.8	12.9	2.9	178.1	12.3
1993	193,612	8.7	124,289	64.2	21.2	13.7	3.0	188.7	6.0
1994	210,596	8.8	135,232	64.2	21.8	14.4	3.1	201.3	6.7
1995	224,991	6.8	145,793	64.8	22.2	14.8	3.1	209.7	4.2
1996	227,811	1.3	147,598	64.8	(NA)	14.6	3.0	207.5	-1.0
1997 est.	244,794	7.5	156,862	64.1	(NA)	15.0	3.1	217.1	4.6

NA Not available. [1] Average annual percent change from prior year shown. For explanation, see Guide to Tabular Presentation. 1970, change from 1969. [2] Outlays as defined in the national income and product accounts.

Source: Office of Management and Budget, based on *Historical Tables, Budget of the United States Government*, FY 98.

No. 482. Federal Aid to State and Local Governments: 1970 to 1997

[In millions of dollars. For fiscal year ending in year shown; see text, section 9. Includes trust funds]

PROGRAM	1970	1980	1990	1993	1994	1995	1996	1997, est.
Grant-in-aid shared revenue	[1]24,065	91,385	135,325	193,612	210,596	224,991	227,811	244,794
National defense	37	93	241	152	169	68	38	9
Energy	25	499	461	460	466	492	481	435
Natural resources and environment	411	5,363	3,745	3,796	3,765	4,148	3,900	4,118
Environmental Protection Agency	194	4,603	2,874	2,852	2,700	2,912	2,779	2,689
Agriculture	604	569	1,285	1,117	937	780	641	661
Transportation [2]	4,599	13,022	19,174	22,292	23,633	25,787	25,957	25,877
Airports	83	590	1,220	1,931	1,620	1,826	1,826	1,655
Highways	4,395	9,208	14,171	16,409	18,667	19,475	19,366	19,370
Urban mass transit	104	3,129	3,730	3,885	3,267	4,353	4,291	4,384
Community and regional development [2]	1,780	6,486	4,965	5,666	7,789	7,230	7,850	9,344
Appalachian development	184	335	124	138	181	182	230	191
Community development block grants	(X)	3,902	2,818	3,198	3,651	4,333	4,545	4,837
Education, employment, training, social services	6,417	21,862	23,359	30,160	32,744	34,125	34,034	35,926
Compensatory education for the disadvantaged	1,470	3,370	4,437	6,582	6,819	6,785	7,006	7,219
School improvement programs	86	523	1,080	1,903	1,358	1,288	1,140	1,414
Bilingual and immigrant education	-	166	152	101	176	189	160	212
Federally affected areas impact aid	622	622	799	468	797	803	945	895
Vocational and adult education	285	854	1,287	1,133	1,292	1,449	1,323	1,573
Libraries	105	158	127	159	125	109	156	160
Payments to States for Family Support Activities	81	383	265	736	839	953	953	931
Social services-block grants to States	574	2,763	2,749	2,785	2,728	2,797	2,484	2,694
Human development services	390	1,548	2,618	3,614	3,998	4,463	4,494	4,781
Training and employment assistance	954	6,191	3,042	3,245	3,310	3,620	3,231	3,459
Health [2]	3,849	15,758	43,890	79,665	86,265	93,587	97,650	103,407
Alcohol, drug abuse, and mental health [3]	146	679	1,241	1,994	2,132	2,444	2,083	1,905
Medicaid [3]	2,727	13,957	41,103	75,774	82,034	89,070	91,990	98,542
Income security [2]	5,795	18,495	35,189	46,991	51,532	55,122	53,375	59,868
Family support payments to States [3]	4,142	6,888	12,246	15,628	16,508	17,133	16,670	6,426
Food stamps-administration	559	412	2,130	2,611	2,688	2,740	3,030	3,662
Child nutrition and special milk programs [3]	380	3,388	4,871	6,589	6,938	7,387	7,757	8,140
Housing assistance [3]	436	3,435	9,516	14,100	15,791	18,416	16,762	18,222
Veterans benefits and services	18	90	134	189	199	253	266	279
Administration of justice	42	529	574	987	992	1,222	1,547	2,644
General government [4]	479	8,616	2,309	2,131	2,098	2,172	2,064	2,191

- Represents or rounds to zero. X Not applicable. [1] Includes $5 million for international affairs subsequently provided to a private institution. [2] Includes items not shown separately. [3] Includes grants for payments to individuals. [4] Includes general purpose fiscal assistance.

Source: U.S. Office of Management and Budget, *Historical Tables, Budget of the United States Government*, FY 98.

No. 483. Federal Aid to State and Local Governments—Selected Programs, by State: 1996

[In millions of dollars, except per capita. For fiscal year ending September 30]

STATE	FEDERAL AID [1]		OE [3]	EPA [5]	HHS [6]		HUD [8]		ETA [10]	DOT [11]
	Total	Per capita [2] (dol.)	OE compensatory education [4]	waste treatment facilities construction	Administration for Children and Families [7]	Medicaid	Lower income housing assistance [9]	Community development	employment/training	highway trust fund
United States [12]	227,872	858	6,379	3,165	10,046	91,844	12,273	4,394	6,366	19,427
Alabama	3,325	778	125	24	167	1,455	131	59	86	257
Alaska	1,051	1,731	22	24	43	199	43	7	43	231
Arizona	3,095	699	97	31	171	1,174	120	50	97	230
Arkansas	2,131	849	71	20	96	956	112	36	53	204
California	26,415	829	824	391	1,139	9,021	1,416	650	1,084	1,523
Colorado	2,410	631	69	27	128	777	203	38	79	275
Connecticut	3,080	941	51	29	115	1,429	165	52	106	311
Delaware	600	828	15	20	25	215	14	8	18	74
District of Columbia	2,578	4,746	-	66	166	390	177	26	47	63
Florida	8,442	586	266	78	440	3,382	363	193	288	610
Georgia	5,359	729	186	35	272	2,276	319	96	124	406
Hawaii	1,126	951	20	18	42	357	77	15	33	177
Idaho	887	746	27	23	45	268	57	10	34	122
Illinois	9,232	779	324	97	531	3,280	846	249	289	601
Indiana	3,657	626	107	51	192	1,654	181	77	93	325
Iowa	2,030	712	32	39	103	771	123	69	48	230
Kansas	1,700	661	61	30	87	588	96	42	42	208
Kentucky	3,355	864	130	47	182	1,541	162	55	74	192
Louisiana	4,735	1,088	186	48	185	2,588	169	88	99	256
Maine	1,359	1,117	31	19	59	642	124	23	37	86
Maryland	3,545	699	90	63	185	1,303	249	79	104	315
Massachusetts	6,814	1,118	124	216	227	2,546	689	113	159	1,005
Michigan	7,196	750	297	152	351	3,119	283	149	234	441
Minnesota	3,536	759	80	39	165	1,580	177	70	90	242
Mississippi	2,754	1,014	119	29	193	1,264	139	45	60	182
Missouri	4,091	763	-	72	197	1,822	282	111	114	324
Montana	964	1,096	26	16	49	291	27	12	26	178
Nebraska	1,232	746	30	26	61	449	63	31	27	143
Nevada	876	547	20	13	47	264	71	15	43	106
New Hampshire	890	766	16	11	39	391	90	15	25	78
New Jersey	6,507	815	147	97	253	2,782	460	115	210	514
New Mexico	1,942	1,133	59	19	83	709	77	24	41	167
New York	24,563	1,351	550	324	701	12,875	1,243	441	461	960
North Carolina	5,227	714	131	59	253	2,591	189	75	121	265
North Dakota	734	1,141	18	13	42	220	41	16	22	94
Ohio	8,778	786	317	159	404	3,971	362	190	236	667
Oklahoma	2,435	738	85	34	143	882	132	60	72	211
Oregon	2,797	873	88	22	109	987	152	37	86	214
Pennsylvania	10,118	839	322	120	435	4,333	642	268	307	686
Rhode Island	1,176	1,187	19	17	39	469	156	18	37	117
South Carolina	3,033	820	99	28	153	1,482	153	41	79	207
South Dakota	867	1,184	19	15	51	227	45	12	18	138
Tennessee	4,477	842	120	39	194	2,202	190	52	81	348
Texas	13,299	695	509	138	642	6,031	630	279	386	1,074
Utah	1,446	723	36	61	72	470	66	24	49	143
Vermont	641	1,089	18	13	33	236	46	7	18	81
Virginia	3,404	510	95	62	223	1,137	221	78	116	340
Washington	4,152	750	96	60	180	1,640	182	54	165	332
West Virginia	2,089	1,144	69	36	77	941	114	28	63	156
Wisconsin	3,679	713	119	51	190	1,545	184	84	104	283
Wyoming	706	1,471	15	14	23	114	21	6	18	123
Outlying areas	3,995	7,371	40	40	348	146	210	158	155	117

- Represents or rounds to zero. [1] Includes programs not shown separately. [2] Based on estimated resident population as of July 1, 1996. [3] Department of Education, Office of Elementary and Secondary Education. [4] For the disadvantaged. [5] Environmental Protection Agency. [6] Department of Health and Human Services. [7] Includes family support payments (Aid to Families with Dependent Children), social services block grants, children and family services, foster care and adoption assistance, low-income home energy assistance, community services block grants, refugee assistance, and assistance for legalized aliens. [8] Department of Housing and Urban Development. [9] Includes public housing, housing payments (section 8) to public agencies, and college housing. [10] Department of Labor, Employment and Training Administration, Insurance and Employment Service Operations; and Community Service. [11] Department of Transportation, Highway Trust Fund. [12] Includes undistributed amounts not shown separately.

Source: U.S. Bureau of the Census, *Federal Expenditures by State for Fiscal Year 1996.*

No. 484. State and Local Governments—Summary of Finances: 1980 to 1994

[For fiscal year ending in year shown; see text, section 9. Local government amounts are estimates subject to sampling variation; see Appendix III and source]

ITEM	TOTAL (mil. dol.)				PER CAPITA [1] (dol.)			
	1980	1990	1993	1994	1980	1990	1993	1994
Revenue [2]	451,537	1,032,115	1,270,748	1,331,442	1,993	4,150	4,927	5,114
From Federal Government	83,029	136,802	198,591	215,445	367	550	770	826
Public welfare	24,921	59,961	102,587	111,315	110	241	398	428
Highways	8,980	14,368	16,948	18,259	40	58	66	70
Education	14,435	23,233	30,380	30,413	-	93	118	117
Health and hospitals	2,513	5,904	8,332	9,364	11	24	32	36
Housing and community development	3,905	9,655	11,828	13,106	17	39	46	50
Other and unallocable	28,275	23,683	28,515	32,987	125	95	111	127
From State and local sources	368,509	895,313	1,072,157	1,115,998	1,627	3,600	4,158	4,286
General, net intergovernmental	299,293	712,700	842,977	884,996	1,321	2,865	3,269	3,399
Taxes	223,463	501,619	594,300	625,527	986	2,017	2,304	2,403
Property	68,499	155,613	189,743	197,140	302	626	736	757
Sales and gross receipts	79,927	177,885	209,649	223,628	353	715	813	859
Individual income	42,080	105,640	123,235	128,810	186	425	478	495
Corporation income	13,321	23,566	26,417	28,320	59	95	102	109
Other	19,636	38,915	45,255	47,630	87	156	175	183
Charges and miscellaneous	75,830	211,081	248,677	259,469	335	849	964	997
Utility and liquor stores	25,560	58,642	65,243	70,075	113	236	253	269
Water supply system	6,766	17,674	20,449	22,692	30	71	79	87
Electric power system	11,387	29,268	31,984	33,808	50	118	124	130
Transit system	2,397	5,216	3,334	3,713	11	21	13	14
Gas supply system	1,809	3,043	5,835	6,256	8	12	23	24
Liquor stores	3,201	3,441	3,641	3,607	14	14	14	14
Insurance trust revenue [3]	43,656	123,970	163,937	160,927	193	498	636	618
Employee retirement	25,441	94,268	113,054	114,304	112	379	438	439
Unemployment compensation	13,529	18,441	34,649	29,901	60	74	134	115
Direct expenditure	432,328	972,662	1,210,096	1,260,842	1,908	3,911	4,692	4,842
By function:								
Direct general expenditure [3]	367,340	834,786	1,026,806	1,074,017	1,622	3,356	3,981	4,125
Education [3]	133,211	288,148	342,287	353,287	588	1,159	1,327	1,357
Elementary and secondary	92,930	202,009	240,310	246,981	410	812	932	949
Higher education	33,919	73,418	88,109	90,871	150	295	342	349
Highways	33,311	61,057	68,370	72,067	147	245	265	277
Public welfare	45,552	110,518	167,098	179,829	201	444	648	691
Health	8,387	24,223	32,291	35,329	37	97	125	136
Hospitals	23,787	50,412	62,563	65,101	105	203	243	250
Police protection	13,494	30,577	36,407	38,645	60	123	141	148
Fire protection	5,718	13,186	15,373	16,123	25	53	60	62
Natural resources	5,509	12,330	13,236	13,967	24	50	51	54
Sanitation and sewerage	13,214	28,453	35,614	35,665	58	114	138	137
Housing and community development	6,062	15,479	18,775	19,899	27	62	73	76
Parks and recreation	6,520	14,326	16,177	16,676	29	58	63	64
Financial administration	6,719	16,217	19,324	20,577	30	65	75	79
Interest on general debt [4]	14,747	49,739	55,100	54,960	65	200	214	211
Utility and liquor stores [4]	36,191	77,801	84,483	91,163	160	313	328	350
Water supply system	9,228	22,101	24,621	26,617	41	89	95	102
Electric power system	15,016	30,997	32,231	33,829	66	125	125	130
Gas supply system	1,715	2,989	3,273	3,510	8	12	13	13
Transit system	7,641	18,788	21,296	24,221	34	76	83	93
Liquor stores	2,591	2,926	3,062	2,985	11	12	12	11
Insurance trust expenditure [3]	28,797	63,321	98,807	95,462	127	255	383	367
Employee retirement	14,008	38,355	51,662	51,662	55,665	154	200	196
Unemployment compensation	12,070	16,499	35,409	28,624	53	66	137	110
By character and object:								
Current operation	307,811	700,131	875,924	927,899	1,359	2,815	3,396	3,564
Capital outlay	62,894	123,069	135,899	137,501	278	495	527	528
Construction	51,492	89,114	100,153	101,992	227	358	388	392
Equipment, land, and existing structures	11,402	33,955	35,745	35,509	50	137	139	136
Assistance and subsidies	15,222	27,227	34,664	35,295	67	109	134	136
Interest on debt (general and utility)	17,604	58,914	64,802	64,484	78	237	251	248
Insurance benefits and repayments	28,797	63,321	98,807	95,462	127	255	383	367
Expenditure for salaries and wages	*163,896*	*341,158*	*396,336*	*410,610*	*723*	*1,372*	*1,537*	*1,577*
Debt outstanding, year end	335,603	860,584	1,017,686	1,074,660	1,481	3,460	3,946	4,126
Long-term	322,456	841,278	994,968	1,047,994	1,423	3,382	3,858	4,025
Short-term	13,147	19,306	22,718	26,666	58	78	88	102
Long-term debt:								
Issued	42,364	108,468	195,564	207,807	187	436	758	798
Retired	17,404	64,831	146,977	166,552	77	261	570	640

- Represents zero. NA Not available. [1] 1980 and 1990 based on enumerated resident population as of April 1. Other years based on estimated resident population as of July 1; see table 2. [2] Aggregates exclude duplicative transactions between State and local governments; see source. [3] Includes amounts not shown separately. [4] Interest on utility debt included in "utility expenditure." For total interest on debt, see "Interest on debt (general and utility)."

Source: U.S. Bureau of the Census, *Historical Statistics on Governmental Finances and Employment*; <http://www.census.gov/ftp/pub/govs/estimate.html>; (released May 1997).

No. 485. State and Local Government Receipts and Current Expenditures in the National Income and Product Accounts: 1980 to 1995

[In billions of dollars. For explanation of national income, see text, section 14]

ITEM	1980	1985	1988	1989	1990	1991	1992	1993	1994	1995
Receipts	**361.4**	**528.7**	**631.4**	**681.0**	**728.9**	**784.2**	**844.3**	**897.1**	**946.4**	**998.1**
Personal tax and nontax receipts	56.2	94.0	117.6	131.4	139.1	147.8	159.7	166.2	170.0	179.4
Income taxes	42.6	72.1	89.9	101.4	106.3	110.4	118.1	123.4	125.7	133.5
Nontaxes	5.0	9.9	12.7	14.1	15.6	19.2	22.5	22.9	23.4	23.9
Other	8.6	11.9	15.0	15.9	17.3	18.2	19.1	19.9	20.9	22.0
Corporate profits tax accruals	14.5	20.2	26.0	24.2	22.5	23.6	24.4	26.3	30.9	34.4
Indirect business tax and nontax accruals [1]	172.3	271.4	324.6	353.0	377.6	396.4	423.7	451.8	479.9	504.3
Sales taxes	82.9	131.1	161.5	172.7	183.2	190.0	202.2	212.9	227.4	236.3
Property taxes	68.6	107.0	127.8	143.3	155.5	167.6	177.5	194.2	205.1	216.3
Contributions for social insurance	29.7	42.8	51.9	54.1	57.4	60.9	64.3	66.9	69.7	71.9
Federal grants-in-aid	88.7	100.3	111.2	118.2	132.4	153.4	172.2	185.7	195.9	208.1
Current expenditures	**307.0**	**437.8**	**545.6**	**585.9**	**648.8**	**708.4**	**758.0**	**802.2**	**846.8**	**901.1**
Consumption expenditures	261.3	382.6	471.3	507.2	550.1	579.4	603.6	627.9	651.7	682.6
Transfer payments to persons	65.7	101.9	131.0	144.5	166.5	199.0	227.2	246.8	267.4	291.6
Net interest paid	-19.3	-38.9	-44.6	-51.2	-51.7	-53.3	-54.7	-51.9	-49.8	-47.4
Interest received by government	38.7	81.0	99.0	106.8	112.1	116.8	119.4	116.3	114.0	111.4
Less: Dividends received	1.9	4.5	6.9	8.1	9.0	9.5	10.1	10.5	11.4	12.6
Subsidies	0.4	0.3	0.4	0.4	0.4	0.4	0.4	0.3	0.4	0.4
Less: Current surplus of government enterprises	-0.9	3.7	5.7	7.0	7.5	7.8	8.4	10.5	11.6	13.5
Current surplus or deficit	**54.4**	**91.0**	**85.9**	**95.1**	**80.1**	**75.8**	**86.3**	**94.9**	**99.7**	**95.0**
Social insurance funds	26.9	47.0	56.7	60.2	59.9	64.3	68.0	66.9	62.9	58.2
Other	27.5	44.0	29.2	34.9	20.2	11.5	18.3	28.0	36.9	36.8

[1] Includes other items not shown separately.

Source: U.S. Bureau of Economic Analysis, *National Income and Product Accounts of the United States, 1929-94* and *Survey of Current Business*, May 1997.

No. 486. State and Local Government Consumption Expenditures and Transfers in the National Income and Product Accounts: 1980 to 1995

[In billions of dollars. For explanation of national income, see text, section 14]

EXPENDITURE	1980	1985	1988	1989	1990	1991	1992	1993	1994	1995
Consumption expenditures and gross investment [1]	**324.4**	**464.9**	**574.7**	**617.9**	**672.6**	**703.4**	**735.8**	**767.8**	**798.4**	**841.7**
Consumption expenditures	261.3	382.6	471.3	507.2	550.1	579.4	603.6	627.9	651.7	682.6
Durable goods [2]	4.7	7.4	9.4	10.2	10.9	11.7	12.4	13.1	13.8	14.7
Nondurable goods	28.8	38.7	44.4	50.4	56.5	58.4	60.9	63.8	66.8	72.8
Services	227.8	336.5	417.5	446.6	482.8	509.4	530.3	551.0	571.2	595.1
Gross investment	63.1	82.3	103.4	110.6	122.5	123.9	132.2	139.9	146.6	159.1
Structures	55.1	67.6	84.8	88.7	98.5	100.5	108.1	113.9	119.0	130.0
Equipment	8.1	14.8	18.6	21.9	23.9	23.4	24.0	25.9	27.7	29.1
Transfers	**65.7**	**101.9**	**131.0**	**144.5**	**166.5**	**199.0**	**227.2**	**246.8**	**267.4**	**(NA)**
Benefits from social insurance funds	17.8	30.4	41.1	44.7	49.6	55.1	61.0	65.7	73.1	(NA)
State and local employee retirement	15.1	25.5	34.1	37.0	40.6	44.7	49.6	54.3	61.4	(NA)
Temporary disability insurance	0.8	1.4	1.8	1.9	2.2	2.8	3.0	2.3	2.3	(NA)
Workers' compensation	2.0	3.5	5.3	5.8	6.9	7.6	8.4	9.0	9.5	(NA)
Public assistance	42.8	65.7	82.9	92.1	108.1	134.4	156.0	170.1	182.4	(NA)
Medical care	24.6	41.8	55.9	63.8	76.7	100.2	119.7	132.5	143.5	(NA)
Aid to Families with Dependent Children	12.4	15.4	17.3	18.0	19.8	22.0	23.3	23.9	24.2	(NA)
Supplemental Security Income [3]	2.0	2.3	3.1	3.4	3.8	3.8	4.1	3.9	3.8	(NA)
General assistance	1.4	2.4	2.7	2.8	3.0	2.9	3.3	3.3	3.4	(NA)
Energy assistance	1.3	2.1	1.8	1.4	1.6	1.6	1.6	1.6	1.9	(NA)
Other [4]	1.0	1.6	2.3	2.7	3.2	3.8	4.0	4.8	5.7	(NA)
Education	2.4	3.5	4.2	4.6	5.3	5.7	6.0	6.6	7.2	(NA)
Employment and training	1.7	0.9	0.9	0.9	0.9	0.9	1.1	1.1	1.1	(NA)
Other [5]	0.8	1.3	1.9	2.2	2.5	2.9	3.1	3.4	3.6	(NA)

NA Not available. [1] Gross government investment consists of general government and government enterprise expenditures for fixed assets; inventory investment is included in government consumption expenditures. [2] Consumption expenditures for durable goods excludes expenditures classified as investment, except for goods transferred to foreign countries by the Federal Government. [3] Prior to 1974, consists of old-age assistance, aid to the blind, and aid to the permanently and totally disabled, which were partly federally funded. [4] Consists of emergency assistance and medical insurance premium payments paid on behalf of indigents. [5] Consists largely of foster care, veterans benefits, Alaska dividends, and crime victim payments.

Source: U.S. Bureau of Economic Analysis, *National Income and Product Accounts of the United States 1929-94*, to be published in late 1997, and *Survey of Current Business*, May 1997.

No. 487. Long Term Municipal New Issues For State and Local Governments: 1980 to 1996

[In billions of dollars]

ITEM	1980	1985	1989	1990	1991	1992	1993	1994	1995	1996
Total [1]	45.6	202.4	121.8	125.7	169.5	231.7	289.6	162.1	156.4	181.6
General obligation	13.7	39.6	37.6	40.2	57.0	80.3	91.4	55.6	60.5	64.1
Revenue	31.9	162.8	84.2	85.5	112.5	151.4	198.2	106.5	95.9	117.5
Competitive	19.3	27.8	29.7	30.2	40.2	44.4	55.6	49.5	41.0	47.0
Negotiated	26.3	174.6	92.1	95.5	129.3	187.3	234.0	112.6	115.4	134.6
States with largest issuance:[2]										
California	3.6	25.3	16.0	15.7	23.4	25.9	38.2	25.4	20.2	24.9
New York	2.9	12.7	13.8	16.8	20.9	22.2	30.6	18.8	18.8	21.1
Texas	3.8	21.2	7.8	6.5	11.3	17.1	16.3	10.3	10.4	11.8
Florida	2.2	13.2	8.3	5.9	8.7	13.3	17.7	7.7	9.1	10.0
Illinois	2.3	9.2	5.4	6.3	6.5	10.8	11.7	7.9	6.6	8.7
All others	30.8	120.8	70.5	74.5	98.7	142.4	175.1	92.0	91.3	105.1
Type of issuer:[3]										
City, town	8.5	36.5	23.4	22.7	31.2	44.6	51.3	26.6	27.9	30.3
College or university	0.2	2.9	2.0	1.5	3.7	3.7	4.9	2.6	2.5	4.5
County/parish	4.6	15.8	10.0	10.0	14.8	20.1	24.4	17.2	13.3	16.8
District	3.9	15.6	13.4	15.2	23.3	31.8	38.2	21.7	22.4	27.5
Local authority	9.2	51.2	23.6	20.8	27.8	41.1	56.9	26.4	27.9	34.1
State authority	14.1	68.3	37.5	40.5	49.2	65.2	85.7	47.8	47.6	54.1
State	5.1	12.1	11.9	15.0	19.5	25.2	28.2	19.8	14.8	14.3
Refunding	1.6	70.4	35.0	25.1	53.6	122.3	194.5	49.8	47.4	60.3
New capital	44.0	132.0	86.8	100.6	115.9	109.4	95.1	112.3	109.0	121.3
Use of proceeds:										
Airports	0.4	2.6	1.4	4.7	3.5	5.1	1.7	3.0	3.2	4.1
Combined utilities	0.2	0.5	0.9	0.5	0.7	0.4	0.4	0.2	0.3	0.3
Economic development	0.2	1.8	1.6	1.7	2.2	2.0	2.2	3.1	1.5	1.1
Education	3.9	10.8	14.0	16.5	17.9	18.2	14.6	20.1	21.7	25.2
Electric & public power	3.7	8.9	2.6	1.8	3.6	2.8	3.2	2.4	1.5	1.2
General purpose/public improvement	10.8	23.8	29.2	32.4	41.7	35.3	31.7	38.9	32.7	36.8
Health care	3.0	17.0	8.7	9.0	11.7	9.1	8.7	8.5	6.8	10.3
Industrial development	1.0	2.5	2.2	1.7	1.5	1.5	1.2	1.4	2.6	2.4
Multi family housing	2.5	20.1	1.8	1.0	1.8	2.2	2.0	2.8	3.7	4.4
Nursing homes/life care retirement	0.3	0.9	1.3	1.3	1.2	1.8	1.4	1.4	1.4	2.0
Pollution control	2.3	8.3	1.0	1.4	2.6	1.9	2.3	2.0	2.1	2.2
Seaports & marine terminals	0.5	0.9	0.4	0.2	0.1	0.3	0.4	0.4	0.6	1.0
Single family housing	10.6	15.7	6.4	10.7	6.9	5.5	3.6	8.0	8.5	8.7
Solid waste/resource recovery	0.4	3.3	1.9	2.3	2.4	2.0	3.1	2.9	2.5	1.7
Student loans	0.2	2.7	1.3	0.9	1.6	3.0	3.0	2.4	4.0	3.9
Transportation	1.3	6.8	5.2	6.9	6.3	9.3	7.3	7.8	8.1	7.5
Water, sewer, and gas facilities	2.7	5.4	6.9	7.6	10.2	9.0	8.3	7.0	7.8	8.5

[1] Excludes issues with a final maturity of less than 13 months, private placements, and not-for-profit cooperative utilities. [2] Ranked by 1996 long term municipal new issue volume. [3] Includes outlying areas.

Source: Securities Data Company, Newark, NJ, Municipal New Issues Database (copyright).

No. 488. State and Local Governments—Indebtedness: 1980 to 1994

[In billions of dollars, except per capita. For fiscal year ending in year shown; see text, section 9. Local government amounts are estimates subject to sampling variation; see Appendix III and source]

ITEM	DEBT OUTSTANDING						LONG-TERM		
	Total	Per capita [1] (dol.)	Long-term: Local schools [2]	Long-term: Utilities	Long-term: All other	Short-term	Net long-term	Debt issued	Debt retired
1980: Total	335.6	1,481	32.3	55.2	236.0	13.1	262.9	42.4	17.4
State	122.0	540	3.8	4.6	111.5	2.1	79.8	16.4	5.7
Local	213.6	943	28.5	50.6	123.5	11.0	183.1	25.9	11.7
1985: Total	568.6	2,390	43.8	90.8	414.5	19.6	430.5	101.2	43.5
State	211.9	893	6.7	8.6	193.8	2.8	110.4	41.7	16.4
Local	356.7	1,499	37.1	82.2	220.6	16.8	320.1	59.5	27.2
1990: Total	860.6	3,460	60.4	134.8	646.1	19.3	477.0	108.5	64.8
State	318.3	1,283	4.4	12.3	298.8	2.8	125.5	43.5	22.9
Local	542.3	2,181	56.0	122.4	347.4	16.5	351.5	65.0	42.0
1991: Total	915.8	3,641	71.0	141.2	681.8	21.7	509.9	118.1	65.7
State	345.6	1,371	5.9	12.5	323.7	3.4	139.9	50.5	25.4
Local	570.2	2,262	65.1	128.7	358.1	18.3	369.9	67.6	40.3
1992: Total	970.5	3,814	78.4	150.4	720.4	21.3	561.6	155.1	99.2
State	372.3	1,460	7.6	13.7	348.1	2.9	125.4	70.2	45.0
Local	598.1	2,345	70.9	136.7	373.1	18.4	409.1	85.0	54.3
1993: Total	1,017.7	3,942	89.2	157.5	746.9	22.7	617.1	195.6	147.0
State	389.8	1,515	9.4	14.8	361.7	3.9	176.9	77.2	60.7
Local	626.4	2,430	79.8	142.7	385.2	18.7	440.2	117.8	85.6
1994: Total	1,074.7	4,127	96.6	164.9	659.9	26.7	672.8	207.8	166.6
State	411.0	1,582	10.4	16.7	383.9	4.9	200.8	78.5	61.3
Local	663.7	2,549	86.2	148.2	276.0	21.8	472.0	129.3	105.3

[1] 1980 and 1990 based on enumerated resident population as of April 1; other years based on estimated resident population as of July 1; see table 2. [2] Includes debt for education activities other than higher education.

Source: U.S. Bureau of the Census, <http://www.census.gov/ftp/pub/govs/www/state.html> (released June 1997).

No. 489. Bond Ratings for State Governments, by State: 1995

[As of fourth quarter. Key to investment grade ratings are in declining order of quality. The ratings from AA to CCC may be modified by the addition of a plus or minus sign to show relative standing within the major rating categories. S&P:AAA,AA,A,BBB,BB,B,CCC,CC,C;Moody's:Aaa,Aa1,Aa,A1,A,Baa1,Baa,Ba1,Ba,B1,B; Fitch:AAA,AA,A,BBB,BB,B,CCC,CC,C]

STATE	Standard & Poor's	Moody's	Fitch	STATE	Standard & Poor's	Moody's	Fitch
Alabama	AA	Aa	AA	Montana	AA-	Aa	(1)
Alaska	AA	Aa	AA	Nebraska	(1)	(1)	(1)
Arizona	(1)	(1)	(1)	Nevada	AA	Aa	(1)
Arkansas	AA	Aa	(1)	New Hampshire	AA+	Aa	AA+
California	A+	A1	A+	New Jersey	AA+	Aa1	AA+
Colorado	(1)	(1)	(1)	New Mexico	AA+	Aa1	(1)
Connecticut	AA-	Aa	AA	New York	A-	A	A+
Delaware	AA+	Aa1	(1)	North Carolina	AAA	Aaa	AAA
Florida	AA	Aa	AA	North Dakota	AA-	Aa	(1)
Georgia	AA+	Aaa	AAA	Ohio	AA+	Aa1	(1)
Hawaii	AA	Aa	(1)	Oklahoma	AA	Aa1	AA
Idaho	(1)	(1)	(1)	Oregon	AA	Aa	AA
Illinois	AA-	A1	(2)	Pennsylvania	AA-	A1	AA-
Indiana	(1)	(1)	(1)	Rhode Island	AA-	A1	AA-
Iowa	(1)	(1)	(1)	South Carolina	AAA	Aaa	AAA
Kansas	(1)	(1)	(1)	South Dakota	(1)	(1)	(1)
Kentucky	(1)	Aa	(1)	Tennessee	AA+	Aaa	AAA
Louisiana	A-	Baa1	(1)	Texas	AA	Aa+	AA+
Maine	AA+	Aa	(1)	Utah	AAA	Aaa	AAA
Maryland	AAA	Aaa	AAA	Vermont	AA-	Aa	AA
Massachusetts	A+	A1	A+	Virginia	AAA	Aaa	AAA
Michigan	AA	Aa	AA	Washington	AA	Aa	AA
Minnesota	AA+	Aaa	AAA	West Virginia	AA-	A1	A+
Mississippi	AA	Aa	(1)	Wisconsin	AA	Aa	(2)
Missouri	AAA	Aaa	AAA	Wyoming	(1)	(1)	(1)

[1] Not reviewed. [2] Under general review.

Source: Congressional Quarterly Inc., Washington, DC, *Governing Magazine* (copyright).

No. 490 Bond Ratings for City Governments, by Largest Cities: 1996

[As of fourth quarter. For key to ratings, see headnote in table above]

CITIES RANKED BY 1994 POPULATION	Standard & Poors	Moody's	Fitch	CITIES RANKED BY 1994 POPULATION	Standard & Poors	Moody's	Fitch
New York, NY	BBB+	Baa1	A-	Tulsa, OK	AA	Aa	(1)
Los Angeles, CA	AA	Aa	(1)	Sacramento, CA	AA	Aa	(1)
Chicago, IL	A	A	(1)	Miami, FL	B	Baa	(1)
Houston, TX	AA-	Aa	AA	St. Louis, MO	A-	Baa	BBB
Philadelphia, PA	BBB	Ba	BBB-	Oakland, CA	AA-	A1	(1)
San Diego, CA	AA	Aa1	(1)	Pittsburgh, PA	BBB	Baa1	BBB+
Phoenix, AZ	AA+	Aa1	(1)	Cincinnati, OH	AA+	Aa	(1)
Dallas, TX	AAA	Aaa	(1)	Minneapolis, MN	AAA	Aaa	(1)
San Antonio, TX	AA	Aa	AA	Omaha, NE	AAA	Aaa	(1)
Detroit, MI	BBB	Baa	BBB	Toledo, OH	A	Baa1	(1)
San Jose, CA	(1)	Aa	(1)	Colorado Springs, CO	AA-	Aa	(1)
Indianapolis, IN	(1)	Aaa	AAA	Mesa, AZ	AA-	A1	(1)
San Francisco, CA	AA-	A1	AA	Buffalo, NY	BBB	Baa	(1)
Baltimore, MD	A	A1	AAA	Wichita, KS	AA	Aa	(1)
Jacksonville, FL	AA	A1	AA	Santa Ana, CA	(1)	(1)	(1)
Columbus, OH	AAA	Aaa	(1)	Arlington, TX	AA	Aa	(1)
Milwaukee, WI	AA+	Aa	AA+	Tampa, FL	(1)	(1)	(1)
Memphis, TN	AA	Aa	(1)	Anaheim, CA	AA	Aa1	(1)
El Paso, TX	AA	Aa	(1)	Corpus Christi, TX	AA-	A	(1)
Washington, DC	B	Ba	BB	Louisville, KY	AA-	A1	(1)
Boston, MA	A+	A1	(1)	Birmingham, AL	AA	*A1	(1)
Seattle, WA	AA+	Aa1	(1)	St. Paul, MN	AA+	Aa	(1)
Austin, TX	AA	Aa	AA	Newark, NJ	A	Baa1	(1)
Nashville-Davidson, TN	AA	Aa	(1)	Anchorage, AK	A	A1	(1)
Denver, CO	AA	Aa	AA	Aurora, CO	AA-	A1	(1)
Cleveland, OH	A	A	A-	Riverside, CA	(1)	(1)	(1)
New Orleans, LA	BBB+	Baa	(1)	Norfolk, VA	AA	Aa	(1)
Oklahoma City, OK	AA	Aa	(1)	St Petersburg, FL	(1)	A1	(1)
Fort Worth, TX	AA	Aa	AA	Lexington-Fayette, KY	AAA	(1)	(1)
Portland, OR	AA+	Aaa	(1)	Raleigh, NC	AAA	Aaa	(1)
Kansas City, MO	AA	Aa	(1)	Rochester, NY	AA	A1	(1)
Charlotte, NC	AAA	Aaa	(1)	Baton Rouge, LA	(1)	(1)	(1)
Tucson, AZ	AA	A1	(1)	Jersey City, NJ	BBB	Baa	(1)
Long Beach, CA	(1)	(1)	(1)	Stockton CA	(1)	(1)	(1)
Virginia Beach, VA	AA	Aa	(1)	Akron, OH	AA-	A	(1)
Albuquerque, NM	AA	Aa	(1)	Mobile, AL	(1)	A	(1)
Atlanta, GA	AA	Aa	(1)	Richmond, VA	AA	A1	(1)
Fresno, CA	(1)	(1)	(1)				
Honolulu, HI	AA	Aa	(1)				

[1] Not rated.

Source: Congressional Quarterly Inc., Washington, DC , *Governing Magazine* (copyright).

No. 491. State Resources, Expenditures, and Balances: 1995 and 1996

[For fiscal year ending in year shown; see text; section 9. General funds exclude special funds earmarked for particular purposes, such as highway trust funds and federal funds; they support most on-going broad-based State services and are available for appropriation to support any governmental activity. Minus sign (-) indicates deficit]

STATE	EXPENDITURES BY FUND SOURCE					STATE GENERAL FUND					
	Total, 1995 (mil. dol.)	1996 [1]				Resources [3] [4]		Expenditures [4]		Balance [5]	
		Total [2] (mil. dol.)	General fund (percent)	Federal funds (percent)	Other State funds (percent)	1995 (mil. dol.)	1996 [1] (mil. dol.)	1995 (mil. dol.)	1996 [1] (mil. dol.)	1995 (mil. dol.)	1996 [1] (mil. dol.)
United States	719,357	746,191	48	26	25	366,754	388,960	352,275	371,574	13,109	16,440
Alabama	11,419	11,664	36	29	34	4,206	4,298	4,151	4,240	54	58
Alaska	4,594	-	-	-	-	2,572	2,506	2,572	2,506	-	-
Arizona	9,923	12,763	35	25	39	4,695	4,934	4,425	4,533	270	400
Arkansas	7,073	7,609	33	26	41	2,453	2,632	2,453	2,632	-	-
California	88,497	94,082	47	34	18	42,644	46,078	41,961	45,393	[6]683	[6]685
Colorado	8,082	8,775	48	22	30	4,401	4,757	3,913	4,411	[6]489	[6]369
Connecticut	12,825	13,104	68	15	11	8,480	9,111	8,399	8,861	81	250
Delaware	3,331	3,743	44	15	37	1,915	2,030	1,541	1,651	[6]374	[6]379
Florida	37,559	39,441	37	22	37	14,377	14,997	14,248	14,710	129	287
Georgia	18,372	18,825	56	26	13	9,745	10,928	9,500	10,439	224	469
Hawaii	6,167	6,310	50	15	30	3,259	3,284	3,169	3,124	90	161
Idaho	2,748	2,870	47	29	25	1,271	1,349	1,268	1,337	3	12
Illinois	26,486	27,131	48	23	27	17,232	18,267	17,201	18,041	331	426
Indiana	12,778	13,220	54	26	19	7,367	8,249	7,019	7,202	679	1,025
Iowa	8,465	8,762	44	24	32	3,907	4,095	3,616	3,781	292	253
Kansas	7,218	7,905	44	21	34	3,677	3,818	3,310	3,439	367	379
Kentucky	11,413	12,589	42	23	35	5,411	5,789	5,006	5,266	261	223
Louisiana	14,883	14,089	34	33	33	5,007	5,311	4,729	5,090	146	318
Maine	3,825	4,086	42	30	26	1,712	1,723	1,687	1,682	4	13
Maryland	13,951	14,556	51	21	25	7,133	7,401	7,000	7,387	133	13
Massachusetts	19,014	19,837	70	22	3	15,923	18,054	15,705	16,881	[6]179	[6]1,172
Michigan	26,226	27,698	30	27	43	7,842	8,442	7,842	8,422	[6]-	[6]-
Minnesota	14,172	14,622	63	20	15	9,624	10,421	8,603	9,078	[6]1,021	[6]1,343
Mississippi	6,477	7,307	36	34	30	2,786	2,816	2,602	2,731	[6]115	[6]86
Missouri	11,607	12,492	47	23	30	5,734	6,286	5,261	5,622	473	464
Montana	2,334	2,306	43	34	23	995	1,016	948	986	47	30
Nebraska	4,058	4,247	41	25	34	1,858	2,005	1,683	1,758	176	248
Nevada	3,747	(X)	(X)	(X)	(X)	1,500	1,393	1,317	1,259	102	159
New Hampshire	2,306	2,312	39	35	23	859	830	854	874	4	-44
New Jersey	22,725	23,872	66	20	13	15,878	16,234	14,947	15,532	[6]952	[6]867
New Mexico	5,524	6,161	45	30	24	2,788	2,937	2,714	2,773	-	144
New York	66,676	68,688	45	31	21	33,557	33,331	33,399	33,044	158	287
North Carolina	18,577	18,194	54	25	21	10,123	10,411	9,510	9,685	[6]293	[6]291
North Dakota	1,769	1,789	36	33	30	660	699	629	651	31	48
Ohio	29,401	30,515	52	13	32	16,011	16,645	14,979	15,858	70	251
Oklahoma	7,741	8,175	38	27	34	3,631	3,838	3,436	3,549	195	289
Oregon	9,937	11,067	32	22	45	3,830	4,027	3,333	3,531	496	496
Pennsylvania	30,754	32,771	49	30	19	16,215	16,347	15,732	16,279	429	156
Rhode Island	3,525	3,487	48	26	24	1,646	1,729	1,641	1,702	5	27
South Carolina	10,133	10,912	40	28	30	4,641	4,935	4,051	4,336	[6]589	[6]599
South Dakota	1,650	1,657	36	39	25	622	631	589	616	-	-
Tennessee	11,534	12,534	44	33	21	5,339	5,471	5,174	5,326	[6]136	[6]125
Texas	37,005	39,987	62	28	10	22,492	26,682	20,640	24,636	1,852	2,046
Utah	4,718	5,080	51	22	25	2,402	2,793	2,341	2,595	61	197
Vermont	1,635	1,609	42	34	20	675	707	690	702	15	-
Virginia	16,825	17,181	44	17	38	7,507	7,759	7,490	7,655	17	104
Washington	16,566	16,689	53	23	21	9,043	9,175	8,484	8,619	559	556
West Virginia	5,237	4,915	38	38	21	2,380	2,496	2,210	2,338	127	124
Wisconsin	16,075	16,678	49	23	28	8,228	8,785	7,827	8,132	[6]401	[6]582
Wyoming	1,801	1,885	24	23	53	502	512	476	459	26	53

- Represents zero. X Not applicable. [1] Estimated. [2] Includes bonds not shown separately. [3] Includes funds budgeted, adjustments, and balances from previous year. [4] May or may not include budget stabilization fund transfers, depending on State accounting practices. [5] Resources less expenditures. [6] Ending balance is held in a budget stabilization fund.

Source: National Association of State Budget Officers, Washington, DC, *1996 State Expenditure Report*, and National Governors' Association and NASBO, *Fiscal Survey of the States*, semi-annual (copyright).

No. 492. State Governments—Summary of Finances: 1980 to 1995

[For fiscal year ending in year shown; see text; section 9]

ITEM	TOTAL (mil. dol.)				PER CAPITA[1] (dol.)			
	1980	1990	1994	1995	1980	1990	1994	1995
Borrowing and revenue	**293,356**	**672,994**	**925,473**	**957,452**	**1,299**	**2,712**	**3,562**	**3,650**
Borrowing	16,394	40,532	79,585	53,697	126	185	306	205
Revenue	276,962	632,462	845,887	903,756	2,222	2,629	3,256	3,445
General revenue	233,592	517,720	693,187	739,016	1,827	2,194	2,666	2,817
Taxes	137,075	300,779	373,827	399,148	1,063	1,236	1,439	1,522
Sales and gross receipts	67,855	147,404	185,853	196,851	534	610	715	750
General	43,168	99,929	123,298	132,236	357	410	475	504
Motor fuels	9,722	19,379	24,520	25,440	71	82	94	97
Alcoholic beverages	2,478	3,191	3,615	3,597	13	14	14	14
Tobacco products	3,738	5,541	6,605	7,348	20	24	25	28
Other	8,750	19,365	27,815	28,230	74	81	107	108
Licenses	8,690	18,849	24,203	26,063	70	77	93	99
Motor vehicles	4,936	9,850	11,946	12,433	36	40	46	47
Corporations in general	1,388	3,096	4,505	5,018	13	12	17	19
Other	2,366	5,903	7,752	8,632	20	25	30	33
Individual income	37,089	96,076	117,729	125,610	329	395	453	479
Corporation net income	13,321	21,751	25,500	29,075	89	81	98	111
Property	2,892	5,775	8,386	9,518	21	25	32	36
Other	7,227	10,922	12,158	12,014	41	47	47	46
Charges and miscellaneous	32,190	90,612	114,466	124,310	304	388	441	474
Intergovernmental revenue	64,326	126,329	204,897	215,558	440	571	789	822
From Federal Government	61,892	118,353	191,829	202,485	412	536	738	772
Public welfare	24,680	59,397	110,522	114,945	196	266	425	436
Education	12,765	21,271	30,186	31,944	74	93	116	122
Highways	8,860	13,931	17,767	19,419	55	56	68	74
Other	15,587	23,754	33,354	25,834	87	102	128	98
From local governments	2,434	7,976	13,067	13,073	28	34	50	50
Utility revenue	1,304	3,305	3,784	3,845	12	14	15	15
Liquor store revenue	2,765	2,907	3,052	3,073	11	12	12	12
Insurance trust revenue[2]	39,301	106,530	145,864	157,821	371	410	561	602
Employee retirement	21,146	78,896	98,550	104,451	261	288	379	398
Unemployment compensation	13,468	18,370	29,707	37,041	70	71	114	141
Expenditure and debt redemption	**263,494**	**592,213**	**824,804**	**874,366**	**2,076**	**2,586**	**3,175**	**3,333**
Expenditure	257,812	572,318	779,459	836,894	1,989	2,500	3,000	3,190
General expenditure	228,223	508,284	686,300	733,504	1,772	2,206	2,642	2,796
Education	87,939	184,935	230,791	249,670	654	782	888	952
Public welfare	44,219	104,971	185,186	194,854	345	495	713	743
Health and hospitals	17,855	42,666	56,577	60,003	143	182	218	229
Highways	25,044	44,249	53,849	57,374	167	187	207	219
Police protection	2,263	5,166	6,000	6,451	18	22	23	25
Correction	4,449	17,266	23,135	26,069	55	76	89	99
Natural resources	4,346	9,909	11,878	12,534	34	41	46	48
Housing and community development	601	2,856	([3])	3,466	10	11	([3])	13
Other and unallocable	41,507	96,266	118,882	97,003	345	410	458	370
Utility expenditure	2,401	7,131	7,214	7,586	26	29	28	29
Liquor store expenditure	2,206	2,452	2,495	2,522	10	10	10	10
Insurance trust expenditure[2]	24,981	54,452	83,450	93,282	181	255	321	356
Employee retirement	10,256	29,562	40,045	47,541	99	128	154	181
Unemployment compensation	12,006	16,423	35,197	35,032	53	86	135	134
By character and object:								
Intergovernmental expenditure	84,504	175,028	225,166	240,978	622	742	867	919
Direct expenditure	173,307	397,291	554,293	595,916	1,367	1,758	2,134	2,272
Current operation	108,131	258,046	370,409	396,035	874	1,141	1,426	1,510
Capital outlay	23,325	45,524	52,929	57,829	167	191	204	220
Construction	19,736	34,803	39,604	46,113	129	150	152	176
Land and existing structure	1,345	3,471	5,020	(NA)	13	14	19	(NA)
Equipment	2,243	7,250	8,305	(NA)	25	27	32	(NA)
Assistance and subsidies	9,818	16,902	23,012	23,511	62	75	89	90
Interest on debt	7,052	22,367	24,494	25,259	83	96	94	96
Insurance benefits[4]	24,981	54,452	83,450	93,282	181	255	321	356
Debt redemption	5,682	19,895	45,345	37,471	88	86	175	143
Debt outstanding, year end	**121,958**	**318,254**	**410,996**	**427,239**	**540**	**1,283**	**1,582**	**1,629**
Long-term	119,821	315,490	406,086	421,139	1,129	1,360	1,563	1,605
Full-faith and credit	49,364	74,972	112,475	116,195	279	337	433	443
Nonguaranteed	70,457	240,518	293,611	304,944	850	1,023	1,130	1,162
Short-term	2,137	2,764	4,912	6,100	5	13	19	23
Net long-term	79,810	125,524	200,785	205,348	446	558	773	783
Full-faith and credit only	39,357	63,481	103,007	106,571	222	291	396	406

NA Not available. [1] 1980 and 1990 based on enumerated resident population as of April 1; other years based on estimated resident population as of July 1. [2] Includes other items not shown separately. [3] Included in other and unallocable. [4] Includes repayments.

Source: U.S. Bureau of the Census, *State Government Finances*, series GF, No. 3, annual; <http://www.census.gov/ftp/pub/govs/www/state.html>; (Released February 1997).

No. 493. State Governments—Revenue, by State: 1995

[In millions of dollars, except as noted. For fiscal year ending in year shown; see text, section 9]

STATE	Total revenue [1]	GENERAL REVENUE								
		Total	Per capita [2]		Intergovernmental revenue			Charges and miscellaneous		
			Total (dol.)	Rank	Total	From Federal Government	From local governments	Total	Current charges	Miscellaneous general revenue
United States	**903,756**	**739,016**	**2,817**	**(X)**	**215,558**	**202,485**	**13,073**	**124,310**	**64,774**	**59,536**
Alabama	12,280	10,583	2,492	38	3,240	3,194	46	2,265	1,621	643
Alaska	8,288	7,358	12,212	1	980	975	5	4,456	279	4,177
Arizona	12,593	10,510	2,441	42	3,027	2,681	346	1,260	619	640
Arkansas	7,368	6,467	2,603	32	2,078	2,068	10	997	688	309
California	118,303	94,252	2,986	20	29,982	27,527	2,455	11,001	6,472	4,529
Colorado	11,555	9,191	2,453	41	2,683	2,666	17	1,977	1,043	934
Connecticut	13,718	12,060	3,687	6	2,761	2,755	5	1,825	851	974
Delaware	3,441	3,114	4,343	2	563	554	9	956	454	502
Florida	37,359	31,013	2,186	49	7,973	7,642	331	4,475	1,697	2,778
Georgia	20,284	17,123	2,375	44	5,224	5,162	62	2,413	1,330	1,083
Hawaii	5,778	5,099	4,324	3	1,138	1,120	19	1,086	715	371
Idaho	3,845	3,151	2,702	28	810	781	29	608	280	328
Illinois	34,689	29,064	2,465	39	8,166	7,770	396	4,308	1,828	2,480
Indiana	16,261	14,848	2,561	33	3,438	3,313	125	3,364	2,033	1,331
Iowa	9,268	8,087	2,845	23	2,189	2,093	96	1,496	967	528
Kansas	7,374	6,495	2,533	37	1,599	1,570	29	1,130	706	424
Kentucky	12,846	11,085	2,874	22	3,048	3,039	9	1,751	1,023	729
Louisiana	13,956	12,066	2,781	24	4,670	4,642	28	2,719	1,637	1,081
Maine	4,208	3,673	2,966	21	1,173	1,169	4	687	280	407
Maryland	16,430	13,696	2,718	25	3,111	3,013	98	2,525	1,282	1,242
Massachusetts	24,101	21,545	3,549	7	5,758	5,297	461	4,186	1,622	2,564
Michigan	35,328	30,217	3,168	14	7,518	7,130	388	4,976	3,076	1,900
Minnesota	18,329	15,210	3,296	11	3,569	3,394	175	2,313	1,362	952
Mississippi	8,301	7,056	2,617	31	2,556	2,448	108	900	652	248
Missouri	15,586	12,516	2,353	46	3,802	3,758	44	1,962	1,039	922
Montana	3,293	2,644	3,038	17	877	861	16	553	233	321
Nebraska	4,615	4,195	2,559	34	1,114	1,091	23	861	540	321
Nevada	5,478	3,896	2,540	35	782	736	45	415	242	174
New Hampshire	3,270	2,674	2,329	47	925	791	134	830	351	479
New Jersey	32,675	25,343	3,188	13	6,051	5,781	271	5,685	2,467	3,217
New Mexico	6,634	5,660	3,350	9	1,377	1,334	43	1,438	596	843
New York	90,997	69,875	3,841	5	26,918	21,683	5,235	8,662	3,649	5,013
North Carolina	22,091	19,170	2,662	29	5,475	5,045	430	2,269	1,474	795
North Dakota	2,448	2,143	3,340	10	692	660	32	492	369	123
Ohio	41,306	28,263	2,538	36	8,172	7,945	227	4,905	2,971	1,934
Oklahoma	9,160	7,724	2,359	45	2,051	1,982	69	1,257	874	383
Oregon	12,986	9,438	2,997	18	3,065	3,002	63	2,087	1,090	997
Pennsylvania	40,015	32,772	2,717	26	9,184	9,117	68	5,326	3,146	2,180
Rhode Island	4,156	3,386	3,414	8	1,193	1,141	52	703	277	425
South Carolina	12,068	9,609	2,621	30	3,069	2,953	116	1,777	1,288	490
South Dakota	2,090	1,766	2,421	43	665	658	7	407	177	229
Tennessee	12,900	11,522	2,196	48	4,045	3,992	53	1,569	1,094	475
Texas	49,422	40,352	2,146	50	12,681	12,322	359	7,382	3,271	4,111
Utah	6,325	5,304	2,708	27	1,498	1,453	46	1,130	812	318
Vermont	2,074	1,869	3,197	12	633	631	2	435	243	192
Virginia	18,993	16,251	2,457	40	3,474	3,296	179	3,992	2,387	1,605
Washington	23,576	16,765	3,077	16	3,977	3,923	53	2,593	1,590	1,002
West Virginia	6,629	5,628	3,083	15	2,001	1,987	14	895	528	367
Wisconsin	16,826	15,337	2,994	19	3,766	3,545	221	2,542	1,480	1,062
Wyoming	2,240	1,952	4,073	4	814	796	18	471	89	382

See footnote at end of table.

No. 493. State Governments—Revenue, by State: 1995—Continued

[See headnote, page 310]

STATE	GENERAL REVENUE							Utility revenue	Liquor store revenue	Insurance trust revenue
	Taxes									
	Total	General sales	Selective sales	License taxes	Individual income	Corporation net income	Other taxes			
United States	**398,148**	**132,236**	**64,615**	**26,083**	**125,810**	**29,075**	**21,528**	**3,846**	**3,073**	**157,821**
Alabama	5,078	1,365	1,260	481	1,483	236	233	(X)	130	1,567
Alaska	1,922	(X)	101	75	(X)	528	1,218	24	(X)	906
Arizona	6,223	2,772	828	344	1,483	417	380	19	(X)	2,064
Arkansas	3,392	1,302	587	197	1,047	192	67	(X)	(X)	901
California	53,269	17,687	4,933	2,871	18,344	5,748	3,685	137	(X)	23,915
Colorado	4,531	1,231	682	268	2,102	190	59	(X)	(X)	2,364
Connecticut	7,474	2,368	1,341	317	2,474	699	276	21	(X)	1,637
Delaware	1,595	(X)	246	525	562	194	68	6	(X)	321
Florida	18,565	10,657	3,670	1,300	(X)	945	1,993	5	(X)	6,342
Georgia	9,487	3,539	921	402	3,842	653	129	(X)	(X)	3,161
Hawaii	2,874	1,363	432	84	926	47	23	(X)	(X)	679
Idaho	1,733	576	236	149	600	129	40	(X)	46	649
Illinois	16,590	4,959	3,471	949	5,312	1,481	417	(X)	(X)	5,626
Indiana	8,046	2,710	866	228	3,257	874	110	(X)	(X)	1,412
Iowa	4,403	1,463	604	402	1,617	221	96	(X)	84	1,097
Kansas	3,765	1,379	516	199	1,233	261	177	(X)	(X)	860
Kentucky	6,285	1,681	1,246	373	1,965	341	679	(X)	(X)	1,761
Louisiana	4,677	1,490	917	445	1,062	283	480	(X)	(X)	1,890
Maine	1,813	650	275	115	640	63	69	(X)	68	467
Maryland	8,061	1,951	1,547	357	3,400	366	440	89	(X)	2,645
Massachusetts	11,601	2,481	1,255	429	5,974	1,206	256	65	(X)	2,490
Michigan	17,723	5,866	1,801	853	5,473	2,130	1,599	(X)	458	4,853
Minnesota	9,328	2,742	1,428	711	3,664	666	117	(X)	(X)	3,119
Mississippi	3,599	1,692	731	226	683	203	64	(X)	131	1,114
Missouri	6,752	2,348	928	481	2,535	369	90	(X)	(X)	3,071
Montana	1,214	(X)	249	141	372	76	377	(X)	37	611
Nebraska	2,220	781	406	151	741	124	17	(X)	(X)	420
Nevada	2,698	1,438	823	306	(X)	(X)	130	81	(X)	1,501
New Hampshire	918	(X)	541	112	38	166	62	-	211	385
New Jersey	13,607	4,133	2,842	721	4,540	1,029	342	428	(X)	6,904
New Mexico	2,844	1,219	397	156	592	150	331	(X)	(X)	974
New York	34,294	6,845	4,929	1,014	17,589	2,815	1,103	2,108	(X)	19,014
North Carolina	11,426	2,794	2,067	710	4,699	906	249	(X)	(X)	2,921
North Dakota	959	283	265	76	143	70	122	(X)	(X)	306
Ohio	15,186	4,752	2,730	1,333	5,553	713	106	(X)	370	12,673
Oklahoma	4,416	1,144	707	575	1,417	167	407	248	(X)	1,188
Oregon	4,286	(X)	547	504	2,798	312	126	(X)	176	3,372
Pennsylvania	18,262	5,550	3,103	1,873	4,930	1,785	1,022	(X)	676	6,567
Rhode Island	1,490	457	312	85	530	82	24	8	(X)	763
South Carolina	4,763	1,794	676	327	1,656	250	60	606	(X)	1,853
South Dakota	694	359	179	88	(X)	40	29	(X)	(X)	324
Tennessee	5,908	3,361	1,204	603	102	493	146	(X)	(X)	1,378
Texas	20,289	10,275	6,162	2,791	(X)	(X)	1,062	(X)	(X)	9,070
Utah	2,676	1,067	292	99	1,024	147	46	(X)	80	941
Vermont	801	174	221	65	250	48	44	(X)	28	176
Virginia	8,784	1,921	1,525	430	4,316	368	226	(X)	248	2,494
Washington	10,196	6,048	1,588	482	(X)	(X)	2,078	(X)	253	6,558
West Virginia	2,732	793	667	151	710	219	192	-	45	956
Wisconsin	9,029	2,572	1,276	436	3,933	671	141	(X)	(X)	1,489
Wyoming	667	206	64	72	(X)	(X)	323	(X)	33	255

- Represents or rounds to zero. X Not applicable. [1] Includes items not shown separately. [2] Based on estimated resident population as of July 1.

Source: U.S. Bureau of the Census; <http://www.census.gov/govs/www/state.html>; (Released: February 1997).

No. 494. State Governments—Expenditures and Debt, by State: 1995

[In millions of dollars, except as indicated. For fiscal year ending in year shown; see text, section 9]

STATE	Total expenditure [1]	GENERAL EXPENDITURE: Total: Amount	GENERAL EXPENDITURE: Total: Per capita [2] (dol.)	GENERAL EXPENDITURE: Intergovernmental	GENERAL EXPENDITURE: Direct expenditures	Selected functions: Education	Selected functions: Public welfare	Selected functions: Health and hospitals	Selected functions: Highways	Selected functions: Police protection
United States	836,894	733,503	2,796	240,978	492,525	249,670	194,854	60,003	57,374	6,451
Alabama	11,542	10,490	2,470	2,620	7,870	4,401	2,291	1,303	924	83
Alaska	5,599	5,047	8,377	1,096	3,952	1,258	643	176	579	55
Arizona	11,162	10,072	2,340	3,992	6,080	3,601	2,468	545	925	110
Arkansas	6,616	6,071	2,443	1,586	4,485	2,352	1,519	579	613	51
California	109,231	94,007	2,978	44,893	49,114	30,027	28,513	7,782	4,821	899
Colorado	9,802	8,434	2,250	2,703	5,731	3,691	2,135	371	780	49
Connecticut	13,576	11,603	3,548	2,409	9,194	2,815	2,910	1,287	750	108
Delaware	2,980	2,709	3,778	510	2,199	920	414	201	246	47
Florida	34,750	32,168	2,268	10,950	21,219	10,846	7,046	2,451	2,995	261
Georgia	19,154	17,771	2,485	4,850	12,921	7,341	4,590	1,241	1,325	137
Hawaii	6,015	5,372	4,555	144	5,227	1,645	894	522	282	20
Idaho	3,360	2,941	2,522	944	1,998	1,251	467	130	366	29
Illinois	32,991	28,845	2,446	7,989	20,856	8,505	8,824	2,015	2,651	272
Indiana	15,284	14,326	2,471	5,115	9,211	5,840	3,207	870	1,398	119
Iowa	8,586	7,916	2,784	2,587	5,329	3,167	1,650	713	979	54
Kansas	7,116	6,460	2,520	2,206	4,254	2,876	1,212	514	828	41
Kentucky	11,395	10,191	2,642	2,790	7,401	4,082	2,776	592	922	113
Louisiana	14,461	13,135	3,028	2,981	10,154	4,245	3,876	1,576	796	139
Maine	4,179	3,664	2,958	750	2,914	1,046	1,257	218	307	29
Maryland	15,069	12,902	2,561	3,074	9,829	3,818	2,956	1,045	1,175	229
Massachusetts	24,282	21,870	3,602	4,740	17,130	4,102	6,178	2,006	1,703	247
Michigan	34,669	30,875	3,237	13,590	17,285	13,889	6,179	3,346	1,832	220
Minnesota	16,360	14,808	3,209	5,829	9,179	5,556	3,923	1,026	1,036	115
Mississippi	7,414	6,708	2,488	2,279	4,429	2,495	1,631	542	585	60
Missouri	12,482	11,400	2,143	3,462	7,938	4,285	2,888	929	1,160	126
Montana	2,988	2,565	2,947	685	1,880	981	463	154	298	28
Nebraska	4,250	4,094	2,497	1,144	2,950	1,440	916	444	545	41
Nevada	4,581	3,718	2,425	1,425	2,294	1,351	612	128	415	33
New Hampshire	3,096	2,718	2,367	374	2,344	557	943	160	205	27
New Jersey	32,605	26,436	3,326	7,901	18,537	7,406	6,773	1,693	2,119	296
New Mexico	6,363	5,867	3,472	1,906	3,901	2,363	879	570	698	49
New York	81,372	68,308	3,755	25,190	43,118	17,494	25,785	6,024	3,047	348
North Carolina	20,437	18,735	2,601	6,665	12,069	7,761	4,020	1,584	1,818	193
North Dakota	2,213	2,048	3,193	437	1,611	737	438	103	270	7
Ohio	34,990	28,129	2,526	9,534	18,595	9,891	7,593	2,322	2,288	189
Oklahoma	8,990	7,566	2,310	2,449	5,118	3,371	1,656	578	726	48
Oregon	11,030	9,509	3,020	2,960	6,530	3,066	2,076	837	962	115
Pennsylvania	39,394	33,633	2,789	9,031	24,602	9,677	11,111	2,916	2,506	363
Rhode Island	4,265	3,544	3,574	504	3,041	885	902	335	266	29
South Carolina	11,623	9,889	2,697	2,367	7,522	3,537	2,447	1,206	594	122
South Dakota	1,880	1,774	2,432	337	1,438	515	375	107	258	16
Tennessee	13,432	12,578	2,397	3,263	9,316	4,303	3,805	1,060	1,220	85
Texas	44,643	40,475	2,153	11,797	28,677	16,286	10,635	3,106	3,038	240
Utah	5,780	5,289	2,701	1,447	3,843	2,463	924	422	354	37
Vermont	2,014	1,854	3,171	309	1,546	611	511	58	157	27
Virginia	17,040	15,664	2,368	4,297	11,367	5,979	2,804	1,586	1,983	289
Washington	21,200	17,555	3,222	5,340	12,215	7,273	3,730	1,368	1,537	157
West Virginia	6,262	5,418	2,968	1,255	4,164	1,994	1,576	215	663	37
Wisconsin	16,302	14,546	2,840	5,723	8,823	5,030	3,160	938	1,115	56
Wyoming	2,045	1,803	3,763	676	1,127	626	252	108	287	12

See footnote at end of table.

No. 494. State Governments—Expenditures and Debt, by State: 1995—Continued

[In millions of dollars, except as indicated. For fiscal year ending in year shown; see text, section 9]

STATE	GENERAL EXPENDITURE					Utility expen-ditures	Liquor stores expen-ditures	Insur-ance trust expen-ditures	Cash and security holdings	DEBT OUTSTANDING	
	Selected functions										
	Cor-rection	Natural resources	Parks and recre-ation	Govern-mental adminis-tration	Interest on general debt					Total	Per capita [2] (dol.)
United States	**26,069**	**12,534**	**3,403**	**26,078**	**24,486**	**7,586**	**2,522**	**93,282**	**1,368,527**	**427,239**	**1,629**
Alabama	231	186	11	299	194	(X)	140	913	17,373	3,759	885
Alaska	147	242	15	356	276	48	(X)	504	28,233	3,232	5,364
Arizona	437	159	26	333	180	24	(X)	1,067	18,431	3,037	705
Arkansas	161	134	36	173	117	(X)	(X)	545	9,240	1,963	796
California	3,676	1,791	258	3,194	2,666	97	(X)	15,126	182,653	46,197	1,527
Colorado	320	159	36	290	233	4	(X)	1,364	18,295	3,368	899
Connecticut	481	70	57	575	846	235	(X)	1,737	17,189	15,456	4,726
Delaware	110	37	42	207	219	27	(X)	244	6,279	3,524	4,915
Florida	1,599	1,092	106	1,224	673	34	(X)	2,547	52,464	15,370	1,084
Georgia	765	359	185	397	310	(X)	(X)	1,383	28,648	5,622	780
Hawaii	110	95	127	280	299	1	(X)	643	8,949	5,196	4,406
Idaho	76	115	22	97	93	(X)	36	384	6,193	1,303	1,117
Illinois	816	311	225	763	1,381	(X)	(X)	4,146	45,334	21,950	1,862
Indiana	351	154	36	333	285	(X)	(X)	958	19,550	5,457	941
Iowa	177	203	19	286	116	(X)	58	612	11,582	2,111	742
Kansas	191	149	9	233	71	(X)	(X)	657	7,435	1,145	447
Kentucky	221	252	83	402	358	8	(X)	1,196	16,637	7,097	1,840
Louisiana	353	311	95	322	600	(X)	(X)	1,326	24,226	8,520	1,984
Maine	63	85	14	141	175	(X)	47	468	6,841	3,041	2,456
Maryland	747	313	72	653	503	352	(X)	1,815	25,478	9,438	1,873
Massachusetts	660	182	99	1,079	1,573	97	(X)	2,315	29,475	27,734	4,586
Michigan	1,185	306	60	734	715	(X)	356	3,437	39,872	12,535	1,314
Minnesota	246	333	78	495	275	(X)	(X)	1,572	26,655	4,494	974
Mississippi	139	164	90	180	116	(X)	106	601	12,548	1,924	714
Missouri	265	238	27	400	350	(X)	(X)	1,062	27,125	6,714	1,262
Montana	50	128	5	120	118	(X)	33	390	6,642	2,210	2,539
Nebraska	85	128	19	119	83	(X)	(X)	157	5,521	1,368	834
Nevada	136	48	14	156	99	78	(X)	785	8,839	1,996	1,302
New Hampshire	59	37	13	134	373	-	167	210	8,228	5,781	5,036
New Jersey	825	273	332	891	1,168	1,400	(X)	4,767	51,886	24,358	3,084
New Mexico	161	87	30	229	96	(X)	(X)	496	15,252	1,824	1,079
New York	2,273	322	261	2,799	3,393	4,170	(X)	8,895	129,845	68,466	3,784
North Carolina	820	393	59	601	258	(X)	(X)	1,702	35,306	4,548	631
North Dakota	18	87	7	65	54	(X)	(X)	165	3,183	855	1,333
Ohio	1,052	263	77	948	816	(X)	263	6,598	100,480	12,295	1,104
Oklahoma	247	128	48	312	162	243	(X)	1,180	12,762	3,736	1,141
Oregon	281	251	27	677	367	8	106	1,408	17,286	5,482	1,741
Pennsylvania	955	437	96	1,104	1,234	(X)	634	5,128	54,869	14,294	1,186
Rhode Island	114	35	29	182	304	39	(X)	682	7,192	5,516	5,562
South Carolina	348	157	41	262	180	704	(X)	1,030	16,213	5,020	1,369
South Dakota	41	78	16	83	106	(X)	(X)	105	4,706	1,663	2,280
Tennessee	424	169	92	397	186	4	(X)	850	14,605	2,822	538
Texas	2,590	614	60	1,294	752	(X)	(X)	4,169	80,650	9,922	528
Utah	144	113	40	252	119	(X)	60	431	10,798	2,061	1,053
Vermont	41	54	9	112	100	1	26	132	2,585	1,668	2,852
Virginia	778	138	65	736	511	4	207	1,166	28,745	8,716	1,318
Washington	483	512	100	435	492	(X)	216	3,429	35,502	8,820	1,619
West Virginia	77	151	37	237	147	9	39	798	6,864	2,586	1,417
Wisconsin	510	401	61	410	492	(X)	(X)	1,755	37,784	8,236	1,606
Wyoming	30	90	14	75	48	(X)	29	213	6,058	788	1,645

- represents zero. X Not applicable. [1] Includes items not shown separately. [2] Based on estimated resident population as of July 1.

Source: U.S. Bureau of the Census; <http://www.census.gov/govs/www/state.html>; (Released: February 1997).

No. 495. State Government Tax Collections, by State: 1996

[In millions of dollars, except as indicated. For fiscal year ending in year shown; see text, section 9. Includes local shares of State-imposed taxes N.e.c.=Not elsewhere classified]

STATE	ALL TAXES			Total property taxes	SALES AND GROSS RECEIPTS TAXES						
	Total [1]	Per capita			Total [1]	Total general sales taxes	Selective sales taxes				
		Total (dol.)	Rank				Total [1]	Alcoholic beverages and tobacco sales	Insurance premiums	Motor fuels sales	Public utilities
United States . . .	**418,808**	**1,581**	**(X)**	**9,973**	**206,581**	**139,307**	**66,274**	**11,004**	**9,053**	**25,998**	**8,881**
Alabama	5,258	1,230	45	134	2,774	1,439	1,335	185	160	462	404
Alaska	1,519	2,503	2	56	99	(X)	99	29	26	38	3
Arizona	6,409	1,447	29	363	3,658	2,720	938	215	132	498	83
Arkansas	3,709	1,478	26	7	1,940	1,376	564	122	61	330	(X)
California	57,747	1,811	11	3,375	24,093	18,980	5,113	927	1,251	2,722	41
Colorado	4,820	1,261	44	-	2,037	1,322	716	91	113	445	7
Connecticut	7,830	2,392	3	-	3,932	2,445	1,487	165	163	498	192
Delaware	1,688	2,329	4	-	253	(X)	253	34	51	94	25
Florida	19,699	1,368	40	754	15,241	11,429	3,812	1,000	482	1,338	543
Georgia	10,292	1,400	36	36	4,786	3,824	962	209	205	548	(X)
Hawaii	3,069	2,592	1	-	1,895	1,432	463	77	86	77	104
Idaho	1,857	1,562	19	-	912	600	311	36	52	159	3
Illinois	17,277	1,458	27	212	8,486	5,057	3,428	480	144	1,191	849
Indiana	8,437	1,444	30	3	3,761	2,868	894	120	135	613	5
Iowa	4,441	1,557	20	-	2,148	1,456	691	112	104	367	(X)
Kansas	3,979	1,547	22	40	1,931	1,401	530	116	97	298	1
Kentucky	6,489	1,671	15	412	3,066	1,784	1,282	79	267	401	(X)
Louisiana	4,906	1,128	47	20	2,559	1,622	937	141	238	502	20
Maine	1,897	1,526	24	43	936	658	278	79	39	156	1
Maryland	8,167	1,610	17	227	3,555	2,000	1,555	156	166	606	137
Massachusetts	12,453	2,044	6	-	3,888	2,610	1,278	293	294	599	(X)
Michigan	19,129	1,994	7	1,640	8,324	6,587	1,738	710	210	783	(X)
Minnesota	10,056	2,159	5	8	4,407	2,900	1,507	236	164	520	-
Mississippi	3,863	1,422	34	24	2,602	1,832	770	95	105	355	(X)
Missouri	7,300	1,362	41	15	3,353	2,454	899	139	179	581	-
Montana	1,256	1,429	32	230	269	(X)	269	33	36	176	13
Nebraska	2,369	1,434	31	4	1,225	815	410	64	38	269	3
Nevada	2,889	1,802	12	55	2,435	1,572	863	67	95	196	6
New Hampshire	837	720	50	-	429	(X)	429	55	47	107	53
New Jersey	14,365	1,801	13	3	7,364	4,318	3,045	327	300	461	1,435
New Mexico	3,061	1,787	14	37	1,736	1,284	452	61	59	226	10
New York	34,150	1,878	9	-	11,914	6,963	4,950	866	736	504	1,667
North Carolina	11,862	1,623	16	11	5,144	2,971	2,173	212	231	952	299
North Dakota	985	1,530	23	2	560	282	278	30	20	95	28
Ohio	16,649	1,401	35	17	7,604	4,991	2,613	377	338	1,202	660
Oklahoma	4,618	1,399	37	-	1,870	1,210	660	136	141	342	14
Oregon	4,416	1,378	39	-	591	(X)	591	131	70	380	8
Pennsylvania	18,725	1,553	21	221	8,816	5,741	3,075	491	396	761	665
Rhode Island	1,549	1,565	18	9	778	465	313	62	34	126	65
South Carolina	5,113	1,382	38	12	2,604	1,919	684	142	76	322	31
South Dakota	730	998	49	-	572	383	189	32	31	90	2
Tennessee	6,165	1,163	46	-	4,744	3,537	1,207	150	222	715	6
Texas	21,259	1,111	48	-	17,224	10,811	6,412	965	590	2,323	337
Utah	2,914	1,457	28	-	1,471	1,170	300	51	42	207	(X)
Vermont	841	1,428	33	11	404	183	221	27	18	59	6
Virginia	8,900	1,333	42	19	3,589	1,996	1,593	125	218	707	115
Washington	10,586	1,913	8	1,800	7,868	6,182	1,685	414	203	677	239
West Virginia	2,771	1,517	25	2	1,452	797	655	41	71	206	203
Wisconsin	9,617	1,864	10	84	4,010	2,708	1,302	245	99	674	279
Wyoming	626	1,301	43	84	274	211	63	7	13	43	(X)

See footnotes at end of table.

No. 495. State Government Tax Collections, by State: 1996—Continued

[See headnote, page 314]

STATE	LICENSE TAXES: Total[1]	LICENSE TAXES: Corporation license	LICENSE TAXES: Hunting and fishing license	LICENSE TAXES: Motor vehicle and operators license	LICENSE TAXES: Occupancy and business license, n.e.c.	OTHER TAXES: Total[1]	OTHER TAXES: Individual income	OTHER TAXES: Corporation net income	OTHER TAXES: Death and gift	OTHER TAXES: Severance
d States	26,968	5,196	990	13,838	5,624	176,065	134,309	29,425	5,306	4,434
a	423	111	18	188	96	1,927	1,578	218	32	79
	79	1	18	30	27	1,285	(X)	326	2	957
	391	5	16	300	45	1,997	1,494	448	54	(X)
s	216	10	19	113	60	1,545	1,162	229	117	13
a	3,035	23	74	1,629	1,190	27,244	20,760	5,831	614	38
o	256	4	55	144	40	2,527	2,274	206	32	15
icut	331	12	3	232	73	3,567	2,614	641	246	(X)
e	533	360	1	33	145	902	632	166	22	(X)
	1,315	123	14	880	223	2,389	(X)	1,008	407	66
	420	31	20	242	63	5,051	4,244	719	67	(X)
	85	2	-	61	15	1,089	1,000	66	18	6
	96	28	24	6	35	849	655	153	6	3
	962	102	22	758	61	7,627	5,781	1,621	187	(X)
	202	4	14	124	47	4,471	3,478	894	98	1
	414	27	17	286	62	1,879	1,588	203	80	(X)
	203	20	11	135	29	1,804	1,377	255	99	74
y	381	91	17	177	86	2,631	2,075	285	81	186
a	418	237	17	106	49	1,909	1,160	328	58	363
	114	3	11	66	31	803	709	71	12	10
d	358	15	11	214	115	4,027	3,485	331	109	(X)
usetts	396	19	5	275	57	8,170	6,707	1,228	188	(X)
n	982	10	41	665	212	8,182	5,868	2,190	87	37
ta	636	-	37	499	81	5,002	4,136	703	43	32
pi	249	68	11	126	37	987	742	202	15	28
	596	82	23	252	215	3,334	2,896	375	57	-
	148	1	30	52	27	609	383	78	15	88
a	158	6	10	78	48	963	840	127	9	1
	313	14	-	103	115	86	(X)	(X)	38	47
mpshire	108	4	6	60	28	300	52	180	38	(X)
sey	753	129	12	423	123	6,266	4,734	1,155	311	66
xico	165	2	14	125	19	1,123	643	163	10	307
k	974	31	46	713	91	21,263	17,399	2,730	799	(X)
arolina	733	198	16	408	97	5,994	4,929	939	124	2
akota	78	(X)	7	41	29	346	152	74	4	115
	1,219	372	30	544	241	6,609	5,903	807	90	9
a	659	38	11	526	74	2,089	1,512	184	68	320
	581	5	26	358	180	3,244	2,823	300	41	64
vania	1,820	906	44	545	282	7,869	5,389	1,706	538	211
sland	80	10	1	54	15	681	581	87	9	(X)
arolina	389	34	13	114	94	2,108	1,813	251	21	(X)
akota	90	1	13	32	38	68	(X)	38	22	7
ee	610	273	18	240	70	831	114	534	70	1
	3,048	1,668	48	848	418	988	(X)	(X)	160	827
	99	3	13	56	15	1,345	1,139	177	8	20
	72	1	5	48	15	355	281	45	6	(X)
	419	26	18	282	82	4,874	4,301	363	69	2
ton	493	11	29	261	142	426	(X)	(X)	61	88
ginia	156	6	14	93	20	1,160	751	235	10	159
n	664	71	50	252	282	4,858	4,151	579	46	3
g	74	5	19	45	3	194	(X)	(X)	5	189

presents or rounds to zero. X Not applicable. [1] Includes amounts not shown separately.

rce: U.S. Bureau of the Census, <http://www.census.gov/govs/www/sttax96.html>; (Revised May 22, 1997).

No. 496. Estimated State and Local Taxes Paid by a Family of Four in Selected Cities: 1995

[Data based on average family of four (two wage earners and two school age children) owning their own home and living in a city where taxes apply. Comprises State and local sales, income, auto, and real estate taxes. For definition of median, see Guide to Tabular Presentation]

CITY	TOTAL TAXES PAID, BY GROSS FAMILY INCOME LEVEL (dollars)				TOTAL TAXES PAID AS PERCENT OF INCOME			
	$25,000	$50,000	$75,000	$100,000	$25,000	$50,000	$75,000	$100,000
Albuquerque, NM	1,652	3,723	6,414	9,048	6.6	7.4	8.6	9.0
Atlanta, GA	1,556	4,027	7,061	9,702	6.2	8.1	9.4	9.7
Baltimore, MD	2,437	5,446	8,558	11,324	9.7	10.9	11.4	11.3
Boston, MA	2,387	5,211	8,817	11,545	9.5	10.4	11.8	11.5
Charlotte, NC	2,027	4,395	7,288	9,822	8.1	8.8	9.7	9.8
Chicago, IL	2,041	4,017	6,357	8,354	8.2	8.0	8.5	8.4
Columbus, OH	2,176	4,594	7,535	10,434	8.7	9.2	10.0	10.4
Denver, CO	1,699	3,727	5,942	7,918	6.8	7.5	7.9	7.9
Detroit, MI	2,461	5,205	8,234	10,915	9.8	10.4	11.0	10.9
Honolulu, HI	2,023	4,525	7,643	10,427	8.1	9.1	10.2	10.4
Houston, TX	1,553	2,758	4,366	5,553	6.2	5.5	5.8	5.6
Indianapolis, IN	2,241	4,070	6,871	8,867	9.0	8.1	9.2	8.9
Jacksonville, FL	1,114	2,409	4,009	5,287	4.5	4.8	5.3	5.3
Kansas City, MO	1,775	3,822	6,254	8,433	7.1	7.6	8.3	8.4
Las Vegas, NV	1,433	2,301	3,766	4,732	5.7	4.6	5.0	4.7
Los Angeles, CA	1,659	3,942	7,440	10,842	6.6	7.9	9.9	10.8
Memphis, TN	1,575	2,529	4,148	5,384	6.3	5.1	5.5	5.4
Milwaukee, WI	2,786	6,075	9,730	12,905	11.1	12.2	13.0	12.9
Minneapolis, MN	1,605	4,226	7,795	10,784	6.4	8.5	10.4	10.8
New Orleans, LA	1,560	3,514	6,116	8,462	6.2	7.0	8.2	8.5
New York City, NY	2,564	6,514	11,243	15,245	10.3	13.0	15.0	15.2
Oklahoma City, OK	1,926	4,038	6,889	9,457	7.7	8.1	9.2	9.5
Omaha, NE	2,354	4,816	8,239	11,242	9.4	9.6	11.0	11.2
Philadelphia, PA	3,114	5,924	8,906	11,582	12.5	11.8	11.9	11.6
Phoenix, AZ	1,995	4,048	6,712	8,960	8.0	8.1	8.9	9.0
Portland, ME	2,756	6,252	10,537	14,308	11.0	12.5	14.0	14.3
Seattle, WA	1,735	2,978	4,746	6,046	6.9	6.0	6.3	6.0
Virginia Beach, VA	2,176	4,256	7,167	9,571	8.7	8.5	9.6	9.6
Washington, DC	2,101	4,592	7,876	10,947	8.4	9.2	10.5	10.9
Wichita, KS	1,942	3,805	6,826	9,368	7.8	7.6	9.1	9.4
Average	[1]2,043	4,305	7,195	9,676	8.2	8.6	9.6	9.7
Median	[1]1,985	4,048	7,030	9,490	7.9	8.1	9.4	9.5

[1] Based on the largest city in each state and District of Columbia. For complete list of cities, see table 497.

Source: Government of the District of Columbia, Department of Finance and Revenue, *Tax Rates and Tax Burdens in the District of Columbia: A Nationwide Comparison*, annual.

No. 497. Residential Property Tax Rates in Selected Cities: 1995

[Effective tax rate is amount each jurisdiction considers based upon assessment level used. Assessment level is ratio of assessed value to assumed market value. Nominal rate is announced rates it levied at taxable value of house]

CITY	EFFECTIVE TAX RATE PER $100		Assessment level (percent)	Nominal rate per $100	CITY	EFFECTIVE TAX RATE PER $100		Assessment level (percent)	Nominal rate per $100
	Rank	Rate				Rank	Rate		
Bridgeport, CT	1	4.75	70.0	6.78	Memphis, TN	28	1.53	24.1	6.34
Newark, NJ	2	3.68	17.0	21.64	Columbia, SC	29	1.42	4.0	35.46
Milwaukee, WI	3	3.58	98.2	3.65	Anchorage, AK	30	1.40	100.0	1.40
Manchester, NH	4	3.43	116.0	2.96	Boston, MA	31	1.39	100.0	1.39
Des Moines, IA	5	2.98	68.0	4.38	Louisville, KY	32	1.38	100.0	1.38
Detroit, MI	6	2.89	50.0	5.77	Wichita, KS	33	1.38	12.0	11.47
Providence, RI	7	2.82	100.0	2.82	Albuquerque, NM	34	1.34	33.3	4.02
Houston, TX	8	2.67	100.0	2.67	Minneapolis, MN	35	1.34	91.6	1.46
Philadelphia, PA	9	2.64	32.0	8.26	Little Rock, AR	36	1.27	18.9	6.72
Sioux Falls, SD	10	2.55	100.0	2.55	Charlotte, NC	37	1.14	92.6	1.23
Omaha, NE	11	2.49	90.0	2.77	Virginia Beach, VA	38	1.12	100.0	1.12
Portland, ME	12	2.46	100.0	2.46	Oklahoma City, OK	39	1.10	11.0	10.00
Baltimore, MD	13	2.42	40.0	6.06	Wilmington, DE	40	1.09	100.0	1.09
Jacksonville, FL	14	2.20	100.0	2.20	Kansas City, MO	41	1.08	19.0	5.67
Fargo, ND	15	2.06	4.4	46.85	Las Vegas, NV	42	1.05	35.0	3.00
Atlanta, GA	16	2.00	40.0	4.99	Seattle, WA	43	0.98	88.1	1.11
Burlington, VT	17	1.96	100.0	1.96	Charleston, WV	44	0.94	60.0	1.56
Boise City, ID	18	1.82	97.3	1.87	Washington, DC	45	0.94	97.5	0.96
Phoenix, AZ	19	1.82	10.0	18.19	New York City, NY	46	0.86	8.0	10.69
Portland, OR	20	1.80	100.0	1.80	Denver, CO	47	0.84	10.4	8.12
Chicago, IL	21	1.79	19.0	9.44	Cheyenne, WY	48	0.76	9.5	8.01
Columbus, OH	22	1.73	35.0	4.94	Los Angeles, CA	49	0.74	70.0	1.06
Billings, MT	23	1.66	3.9	42.67	Birmingham, AL	50	0.70	10.0	6.95
New Orleans, LA	24	1.61	10.0	16.13	Honolulu, HI	51	0.33	93.4	0.36
Jackson, MS	25	1.61	10.0	16.06					
Indianapolis, IN	26	1.59	15.0	10.60	Unweighted average	(X)	1.78	56.8	7.51
Salt Lake City, UT	27	1.55	80.3	1.93	Median	(X)	1.59	(X)	(X)

X Not applicable.

Source: Government of the District of Columbia, Department of Finance and Revenue, *Tax Rates and Tax Burdens in the District of Columbia: A Nationwide Comparison*, annual.

o. 498. Gross Revenue From Parimutuel and Amusement Taxes and Lotteries, by State: 1995

[In millions of dollars. For fiscal years; see text, section 9]

STATE	Gross revenue	Amusement taxes [1]	Parimutuel taxes	LOTTERY REVENUE			
				Total [2]	Apportionment of funds		
					Prizes	Administration	Proceeds available from ticket sales
ited States	31,924	1,620	506	29,799	17,368	1,880	11,241
l.	5	-	5	(X)	(X)	(X)	(X)
	2	2	(X)	(X)	(X)	(X)	(X)
	278	1	8	269	151	27	91
s	12	1	11	(X)	(X)	(X)	(X)
a	2,134	-	109	2,025	1,061	182	762
o.	339	1	8	330	201	28	101
icut.	798	145	17	636	386	26	224
e	109	-	(Z)	109	56	9	44
	2,214	(Z)	87	2,126	1,128	122	876
	1,292	-	-	1,292	694	97	1,001
	(X)	(X)	(X)	(X)	(X)	(X)	(X)
	90	-	2	88	53	16	19
	1,784	272	44	1,466	859	59	549
	565	-	2	563	350	30	183
	215	26	2	186	113	25	49
	170	1	6	163	92	19	51
y	501	-	21	480	303	30	147
a	286	2	5	279	152	19	108
	156	-	3	153	89	17	48
d	991	4	3	984	545	42	397
usetts.	2,649	8	13	2,629	1,938	72	619
n.	1,286	-	15	1,272	699	50	523
ta.	383	64	1	318	196	59	63
ppi	191	191	-	(X)	(X)	(X)	(X)
	449	62	-	387	222	35	131
	31	-	(Z)	31	16	6	8
a	91	11	1	79	39	16	24
	449	449	-	(X)	(X)	(X)	(X)
mpshire	141	3	6	132	85	6	42
sey.	1,795	302	2	1,491	799	47	645
xico	2	1	1	(X)	(X)	(X)	(X)
k	2,832	1	57	2,774	1,471	68	1,235
arolina	(X)	(X)	(X)	(X)	(X)	(X)	(X)
akota	11	11	-	(X)	(X)	(X)	(X)
	2,063	-	14	2,049	1,237	86	726
a.	16	13	3	(X)	(X)	(X)	(X)
	888	-	2	885	560	190	135
vania	1,508	-	20	1,488	813	55	620
sland	294	-	7	287	207	5	75
arolina	27	27	-	(X)	(X)	(X)	(X)
akota	84	-	(Z)	84	19	9	56
ee	(X)	(X)	(X)	(X)	(X)	(X)	(X)
	2,778	21	13	2,743	1,694	53	996
	(X)	(X)	(X)	(X)	(X)	(X)	(X)
	72	(X)	-	72	42	5	25
	880	-	-	880	487	79	314
ton.	404	-	3	401	208	55	139
ginia	162	(X)	7	155	85	16	54
in.	499	1	7	492	299	32	162
g	(Z)	-	(Z)	-	-	-	-

presents or rounds to zero. X Not applicable. Z Less than $500,000. [1] Represents nonlicense taxes. [2] Excludes ions.

rce: U.S. Bureau of the Census, <http://www.census.gov/govs/www/state.html>; (Released June 1997), and unpublished

. 499. Lottery Sales—Type of Game, 1980 to 1996 and Use of Proceeds, 1964-95

[In millions of dollars. For fiscal years]

GAME	1980	1985	1990	1994	1995	1996	USE OF PROFITS 1964-95	Cumulative [1]
plet sales	2,393	9,035	20,017	28,514	31,931	34,031	Total	92,922
	206	88	(NA)	(NA)	(NA)	(NA)	Education	52,061
	527	1,296	5,204	9,681	11,511	13,268	General fund	21,133
[4]	1,554	3,376	4,572	5,294	5,737	5,680	Cities	9,013
	55	693	1,302	1,872	1,941	2,003	Senior citizen programs	8,708
	52	3,583	8,563	10,024	10,594	10,227	Economic development	1,385
	(NA)	(NA)	409	1,642	2,148	2,853	Environment	485
proceeds (net income) [7]	978	3,735	7,703	9,977	11,100	11,576	Other	137

Not available. [1] Cumulative profits tracks lottery revenue to government from March 12, 1964 - June 30, 1995. [2] Also s draw game or ticket. Player must match his ticket to winning numbers drawn by lottery. Players cannot choose their . [3] Player scratches a latex section on ticket which reveals instantly whether ticket is a winner. [4] Players choose and hree or four digits, depending on game, with various payoffs for different straight order or mixed combination bets. typically select six digits out of a large field of numbers. Varying prizes are offered for matching three through six numbers lottery. [6] Includes breakopen tickets, spiel, keno, video lottery, etc. [7] Sales minus prizes and expenses equal net ent income.

rce: TLF Publications, Inc., Boyds, MD, *1997 World Lottery Almanac* annual; *LaFleur's Fiscal 1996 Lottery Special Report*; *leur's Lottery World Government Profits Report* (copyright).

No. 500. City Governments—Total and Per Capita Finances for Largest Cities: 1994

[For fiscal year ending in year shown; see text, section 9. Cities ranked by size of population enumerated as of April 1, 1990, except Honolulu ranked by county population. Data reflect inclusion of fiscal activity of dependent school systems where applicable. Intercity comparisons should be made with caution due to variations in responsibilities among urban areas; for details see text, section 9, and source]

CITIES RANKED BY 1990 POPULATION	REVENUE		GENERAL REVENUE		TAXES		GENERAL EXPENDITURE		DEBT OUTSTANDING	
	Total (mil. dol.)	Per capita [1] (dol.)	Total (mil. dol.)	Per capita [1] (dol.)	Total (mil. dol.)	Per capita [1] (dol.)	Total (mil. dol.)	Per capita [1] (dol.)	Total (mil. dol.)	Per capita [1] (dol.)
New York City, NY [2]	44,930	6,136	39,497	5,394	18,090	2,470	40,850	5,579	40,295	5,503
Los Angeles, CA	7,467	2,142	4,077	1,170	1,813	520	3,682	1,056	8,461	2,428
Chicago, IL	4,384	1,575	3,436	1,234	1,562	561	3,491	1,254	6,966	2,502
Houston, TX	2,022	1,240	1,486	911	796	488	1,696	1,041	3,822	2,344
Philadelphia, PA [2]	3,980	2,510	3,146	1,984	1,564	986	2,956	1,864	3,673	2,317
San Diego, CA	1,477	1,330	1,210	1,089	399	359	1,114	1,003	1,807	1,627
Detroit, MI	2,138	2,080	1,624	1,580	588	572	1,506	1,465	2,016	1,961
Dallas, TX	1,562	1,551	1,145	1,137	501	498	1,260	1,252	3,876	3,849
Phoenix, AZ	1,279	1,300	1,106	1,125	375	382	1,088	1,106	2,789	2,836
San Antonio, TX	1,677	1,792	669	715	254	271	763	815	4,274	4,567
Honolulu, HI [2]	1,079	1,290	973	1,163	530	634	1,094	1,308	1,556	1,860
San Jose, CA	885	1,132	743	950	352	451	766	979	1,513	1,934
Baltimore, MD [2]	2,135	2,901	1,855	2,520	697	947	1,560	2,120	1,232	1,674
Indianapolis, IN [2]	1,069	1,461	1,036	1,416	501	686	1,257	1,719	1,560	2,133
San Francisco, CA [2]	3,746	5,174	2,963	4,092	945	1,305	2,762	3,815	3,523	4,866
Jacksonville, FL [2]	1,691	2,662	806	1,268	325	512	864	1,361	4,798	7,553
Columbus, OH	704	1,112	605	956	295	467	647	1,023	1,367	2,160
Milwaukee, WI	895	1,425	641	1,020	169	270	644	1,026	559	891
Memphis, TN	2,103	3,446	997	1,634	220	360	986	1,615	840	1,376
Washington, DC [2]	4,991	8,224	4,706	7,755	2,498	4,117	4,904	8,080	4,110	6,772
Boston, MA [2]	2,049	3,568	1,805	3,142	701	1,221	1,682	2,930	1,115	1,942
Seattle, WA	1,266	2,453	817	1,582	406	786	784	1,518	1,319	2,556
El Paso, TX	421	817	312	605	156	304	298	577	545	1,057
Cleveland, OH	797	1,576	593	1,172	288	570	643	1,272	1,100	2,177

[1] Based on enumerated population as of April 1, 1990. [2] Represents, in effect, city-county consolidated government.

Source: U.S. Bureau of the Census, <http://www.census.gov/ftp/pub/govs/www/city94.html>; (Released June 1997).

No. 501. City Governments—Revenue for Largest Cities: 1994

[In millions of dollars. For fiscal year ending in year shown; see text, section 9. See headnote, table 500]

CITIES RANKED BY 1990 POPULATION	Total revenue [1]	GENERAL REVENUE									Utility and liquor store
		Total [1]	Intergovernmental				Taxes				
			Total	From State Government	From Federal Government	From local government	Total [1]	Property	Sales and gross receipts	
New York City, NY [2]	44,930	39,497	15,812	14,194	1,477	142	18,090	7,870	3,647	2,166
Los Angeles, CA	7,467	4,077	737	346	312	79	1,813	642	779	2,340
Chicago, IL	4,384	3,436	950	708	242	-	1,562	624	774	280
Houston, TX	2,022	1,486	96	20	66	10	796	406	367	253
Philadelphia, PA [2]	3,980	3,146	1,071	773	215	84	1,564	343	131	675
San Diego, CA	1,477	1,210	272	106	111	54	399	138	204	156
Detroit, MI	2,138	1,624	693	510	151	33	586	226	53	170
Dallas, TX	1,562	1,145	73	12	56	5	501	285	207	140
Phoenix, AZ	1,279	1,106	372	243	97	32	375	117	233	119
San Antonio, TX	1,677	669	151	74	25	52	254	131	114	975
Honolulu, HI [2]	1,079	973	140	58	82	1	530	427	63	106
San Jose, CA	885	743	98	54	15	29	352	124	154	10
Baltimore, MD [2]	2,135	1,855	938	833	58	48	697	483	46	60
Indianapolis, IN [2]	1,069	1,036	304	251	52	1	501	413	22	7
San Francisco, CA [2]	3,746	2,963	1,129	978	137	14	945	474	226	255
Jacksonville, FL [2]	1,691	806	134	64	70	-	325	207	108	752
Columbus, OH	704	605	108	68	34	6	295	24	7	99
Milwaukee, WI	895	641	339	278	60	1	169	158	5	47
Memphis, TN	2,103	997	629	339	31	259	220	179	30	932
Washington, DC [2]	4,991	4,706	1,696	-	1,624	73	2,498	811	780	53
Boston, MA [2]	2,049	1,805	812	753	56	2	701	655	27	89
Seattle, WA	1,266	817	129	98	26	6	406	137	171	378
El Paso, TX	421	312	36	14	18	4	156	82	70	46
Cleveland, OH	797	593	148	74	73	1	288	51	5	204

- Represents or rounds to zero. [1] Includes items not shown separately. [2] Represents, in effect, city-county consolidated government.

Source: U.S. Bureau of the Census, <http://www.census.gov/ftp/pub/govs/www/city94.html>; (Released June 1997).

No. 502. City Governments—Expenditures for Largest Cities: 1994

[In millions of dollars. For fiscal year ending in year shown; see text, section 9. See headnote, table 500]

ES RANKED BY 0 POPULATION	Total expenditure [1]	GENERAL EXPENDITURE								Utility and liquor store
		Total [1]	Education	Housing and community development	Public welfare	Health and hospitals	Police protection	Fire protection	Highways	
rk City, NY [2]	49,002	40,650	9,022	2,557	7,724	4,063	2,055	784	917	4,421
geles, CA	6,695	3,682	12	259	-	19	692	263	159	2,301
o, IL	4,201	3,491	1	141	127	108	731	252	277	210
n, TX	2,055	1,698	-	37	-	69	321	167	180	274
lphia, PA [2]	3,998	2,956	16	108	256	373	334	120	86	712
ego, CA	1,360	1,114	-	96	-	1	174	70	79	207
MI	2,070	1,506	4	67	-	102	287	89	76	261
TX	1,538	1,260	-	17	-	18	170	79	65	171
x, AZ	1,336	1,088	2	62	-	1	168	94	71	220
tonio, TX	1,685	763	14	12	24	22	113	76	64	906
lu, HI [2]	1,315	1,094	-	119	-	12	119	50	29	221
se, CA	846	766	-	92	-	2	119	60	46	26
re, MD [2]	1,729	1,560	599	76	-	67	168	85	87	60
polis, IN [2]	1,317	1,257	1	117	89	198	93	43	69	24
ncisco, CA [2]	3,585	2,762	63	86	356	631	194	128	59	551
nville, FL [2]	1,596	864	-	64	11	39	90	62	40	686
bus, OH	770	647	-	13	-	25	125	61	53	123
kee, WI	761	644	-	56	-	14	133	62	48	30
is, TN	1,915	966	511	19	-	7	86	68	33	854
gton, DC [2]	5,286	4,904	741	221	1,060	527	281	101	158	102
, MA [2]	1,927	1,682	483	60	94	226	147	86	61	54
, WA	1,330	784	-	28	-	17	112	72	71	483
, TX	396	296	-	6	-	20	53	30	28	77
nd, OH	950	643	-	50	-	23	135	73	58	307

epresents or rounds to zero. Z Less than $500,000. [1] Includes items not shown separately. [2] Represents, in effect, nty consolidated government.

urce: U.S. Bureau of the Census, <http://www.census.gov/ftp/pub/govs/www/city94.html>; (Released June 1997).

. 503. County Governments—Total and Per Capita Finances for Largest Counties: 1994

cal year ending in year shown; see text, section 9. Counties ranked by size of population enumerated as of April 1, 1990. late only to county governments and their dependent agencies and do not includes amounts for other local governments ame geographic location such as separate school districts; for details see text, section 9, and source]

NTIES RANKED BY 1990 POPULATION	REVENUE		GENERAL REVENUE		TAXES		GENERAL EXPENDITURE		DEBT OUTSTANDING	
	Total (mil. dol.)	Per capita [1] (dol.)	Total (mil. dol.)	Per capita [1] (dol.)	Total (mil. dol.)	Per capita [1] (dol.)	Total (mil. dol.)	Per capita [1] (dol.)	Total (mil. dol.)	Per capita [1] (dol.)
geles, CA	13,162	1,485	11,747	1,325	1,902	215	13,944	1,573	4,016	453
L	2,096	410	1,807	354	1,128	221	1,750	343	1,754	343
TX	1,517	538	1,517	538	689	245	1,606	570	4,378	1,554
ego, CA	2,383	954	2,187	876	411	165	2,607	1,043	358	143
, CA	2,572	1,067	2,370	983	420	174	2,351	975	6,721	2,788
a, AZ	1,256	592	1,256	592	273	128	1,246	587	1,453	685
MI	1,162	550	1,067	505	223	106	1,132	536	974	461
L	3,680	1,900	3,502	1,808	1,023	528	3,687	1,903	5,219	2,694
TX	791	427	780	421	346	187	763	412	839	453
/A	815	541	815	541	388	257	815	541	766	506
Clara, CA	1,830	1,222	1,810	1,209	426	285	1,893	1,264	629	420
rnadino, CA	1,777	1,253	1,692	1,193	225	159	2,141	1,509	1,784	1,258
ga, OH	1,109	786	1,109	786	337	239	1,133	802	1,050	743
sex, MA	106	76	69	49	3	2	71	51	10	7
ny, PA	937	701	897	672	279	209	1,056	790	1,576	1,179
NY	1,600	1,210	1,517	1,148	907	686	1,697	1,284	1,768	1,337
, NY	2,027	1,575	2,027	1,575	1,219	947	2,213	1,719	2,212	1,718
e, CA	1,568	1,226	1,403	1,097	240	188	1,636	1,279	560	437
d, FL	1,013	807	984	784	436	347	914	728	2,442	1,945
TX	544	459	543	458	204	172	561	474	1,193	1,007
de, CA	1,515	1,295	1,515	1,295	323	276	1,650	1,409	1,457	1,245
, TX	505	432	505	432	230	197	463	396	850	726
d, CA	669	617	582	537	158	146	542	500	333	307
ento, CA	1,674	1,608	1,565	1,503	334	321	1,970	1,892	1,547	1,485
in, MN	1,109	1,075	1,109	1,075	322	312	1,093	1,058	758	734

ased on enumerated population as of April 1, 1990.

urce: U.S. Bureau of the Census, <http://www.census.gov/ftp/pub/govs/www/cou94.html>; (Released June 1997).

No. 504. County Governments—Revenue for Largest Counties: 1994

[In millions of dollars. For fiscal year ending in year shown; see text, section 9. See headnote, table 503]

COUNTIES RANKED BY 1990 POPULATION	Total revenue [1]	General revenue									Utility and liquor store
		Total [1]	Intergovernmental				Taxes				
			Total	From State government	From Federal government	From local government	Total [1]	Property	Sales and gross receipts		
Los Angeles, CA	13,162	11,747	8,532	8,079	187	268	1,902	1,753	94		28
Cook, IL	2,096	1,807	325	310	14	1	1,128	750	366		-
Harris, TX	1,517	1,517	357	291	13	53	689	635	20		-
San Diego, CA	2,383	2,187	1,501	1,372	55	74	411	372	14		1
Orange, CA	2,572	2,370	1,094	998	19	77	420	394	8		-
Maricopa, AZ	1,256	1,256	657	602	31	24	273	260	-		-
Wayne, MI	1,162	1,067	577	498	57	21	223	219	-		-
Dade, FL	3,680	3,502	689	343	343	3	1,023	710	242		178
Dallas, TX	791	780	307	284	2	21	346	314	2		-
King, WA	815	815	208	150	14	44	388	270	99		-
Santa Clara, CA	1,830	1,810	1,171	1,078	58	37	426	309	99		20
San Bernadino, CA	1,777	1,692	1,195	1,080	59	55	225	202	15		3
Cuyahoga, OH	1,109	1,109	415	402	9	5	337	199	111		-
Middlesex, MA	106	69	36	33	-	3	3	-	-		-
Allegheny, PA	937	897	407	386	19	2	279	268	9		-
Suffolk, NY	1,600	1,517	455	408	23	24	907	407	487		83
Nassau, NY	2,027	2,027	452	415	37	-	1,219	617	598		-
Alameda, CA	1,568	1,403	942	905	11	26	240	210	20		-
Broward, FL	1,013	984	133	109	23	1	436	376	39		29
Bexar, TX	544	543	110	98	2	11	204	186	4		-
Riverside, CA	1,515	1,515	919	825	23	71	323	286	20		-
Tarrant, TX	505	505	164	149	7	9	230	211	-		-
Oakland, CA	669	882	346	211	7	128	158	149	-		14
Sacramento, CA	1,674	1,565	806	780	17	11	334	192	109		4
Hennepin, MN	1,109	1,109	452	401	37	13	322	320	-		-

- Represents or rounds to zero. [1] Includes items not shown separately. [2] Represents, in effect, city-county consolidated government.

Source: U.S. Bureau of the Census, <http://www.census.gov/ftp/pub/govs/www/cou94.html>; (Released June 1997).

No. 505. County Governments—Expenditures for Largest Counties: 1994

[In millions of dollars. For fiscal year ending in year shown; see text, section 9. See headnote, table 503]

COUNTIES RANKED BY 1990 POPULATION	Total expenditure [1]	GENERAL EXPENDITURE								Utility and liquor store
		Total [1]	Education	Housing and community development	Public welfare	Health and hospitals	Police protection	Fire protection	Highways	
Los Angeles, CA	14,712	13,944	334	162	4,537	2,461	673	316	206	39
Cook, IL	1,867	1,750	3	13	2	648	39	-	75	-
Harris, TX	1,608	1,608	-	6	16	458	96	1	125	-
San Diego, CA	2,693	2,607	80	44	872	253	83	-	73	7
Orange, CA	2,414	2,351	70	21	553	163	110	66	142	-
Maricopa, AZ	1,246	1,246	14	15	377	264	51	-	65	-
Wayne, MI	1,209	1,132	-	3	89	338	27	-	100	-
Dade, FL	4,040	3,687	-	92	51	680	290	121	69	353
Dallas, TX	766	763	-	1	15	396	19	-	21	-
King, WA	815	815	1	12	1	194	58	5	75	-
Santa Clara, CA	2,113	1,893	90	3	552	364	38	28	33	220
San Bernadino, CA	2,211	2,141	61	10	683	316	97	21	42	5
Cuyahoga, OH	1,133	1,133	-	5	201	542	14	-	40	-
Middlesex, MA	109	71	-	-	-	21	-	-	-	-
Allegheny, PA	1,091	1,056	24	21	87	230	20	1	38	-
Suffolk, NY	1,806	1,697	204	7	361	120	271	4	26	111
Nassau, NY	2,234	2,213	215	26	348	361	338	9	99	21
Alameda, CA	1,702	1,636	17	5	506	340	27	12	83	-
Broward, FL	1,004	914	-	11	19	67	115	14	43	91
Bexar, TX	562	561	-	2	24	235	21	-	16	-
Riverside, CA	1,650	1,650	75	25	470	185	91	1	59	-
Tarrant, TX	463	463	-	6	9	201	11	-	13	-
Oakland, CA	569	542	4	5	2	131	26	-	64	14
Sacramento, CA	2,024	1,970	47	100	568	88	53	1	71	5
Hennepin, MN	1,093	1,093	-	3	194	472	37	-	60	-

- Represents or rounds to zero. [1] Includes items not shown separately. [2] Represents, in effect, city-county consolidated government.

Source: U.S. Bureau of the Census, <http://www.census.gov/ftp/pub/govs/www/cou94.html>; (Released June 1997).

No. 506. Governmental Employment and Payrolls: 1980 to 1995

[For October. Covers both full-time and part-time employees. Local government data are estimates subject to sampling variation; see Appendix III and source]

TYPE OF GOVERNMENT	1980	1985	1988	1989	1990	1991	1992	1993	1994	1995
EMPLOYEES (1,000)										
Total	16,213	16,690	17,588	17,879	18,369	18,554	18,745	18,823	19,420	19,521
Federal (civilian) [1]	2,898	3,021	3,112	3,114	3,105	3,103	3,047	2,999	2,952	2,895
State and local	13,315	13,669	14,476	14,765	15,263	15,452	15,698	15,824	16,468	16,626
Percent of total	82	82	82	83	83	83	84	84	85	85
State	3,753	3,984	4,236	4,365	4,503	4,521	4,595	4,673	4,694	4,719
Local	9,562	9,685	10,240	10,400	10,760	10,930	11,103	11,151	11,775	11,906
Counties	1,853	1,891	2,024	2,085	2,167	2,196	2,253	2,270	(NA)	(NA)
Municipalities	2,561	2,467	2,570	2,569	2,642	2,662	2,665	2,644	(NA)	(NA)
School districts	4,270	4,416	4,679	4,774	4,950	5,045	5,134	(NA)	(NA)	(NA)
Townships	394	392	415	405	418	415	424	(NA)	(NA)	(NA)
Special districts	484	519	552	568	585	612	627	(NA)	(NA)	(NA)
OCTOBER PAYROLLS (mil. dol.)										
Total	19,935	28,945	34,203	36,763	39,228	41,237	43,120	(NA)	(NA)	(NA)
Federal (civilian) [1]	5,205	7,580	7,976	8,636	8,999	9,687	9,937	(NA)	(NA)	(NA)
State and local	14,730	21,365	26,227	28,127	30,229	31,551	33,183	34,540	36,545	37,714
Percent of total	74	74	77	77	77	77	77	(NA)	(NA)	(NA)
State	4,285	6,329	7,842	8,443	9,083	9,437	9,828	10,288	10,666	10,927
Local	10,445	15,036	18,385	19,684	21,146	22,113	23,355	24,252	25,878	26,787
Counties	1,936	2,819	3,532	3,855	4,192	4,404	4,696	4,839	(NA)	(NA)
Municipalities	2,951	4,191	4,979	5,274	5,564	5,784	6,207	6,328	(NA)	(NA)
School districts	4,683	6,746	8,298	8,852	9,551	9,975	10,394	(NA)	(NA)	(NA)
Townships	330	446	556	599	642	664	685	(NA)	(NA)	(NA)
Special districts	546	834	1,020	1,104	1,197	1,287	1,370	(NA)	(NA)	(NA)

NA Not available. [1] Includes employees outside the United States.

Source: U.S. Bureau of the Census, *Historical Statistics on Governmental Finances and Employment*, and *Public Employment*, series GE, No. 1, annual; <http://www.census.gov/pub/govs/www/apes.html>; (released August 1997).

No. 507. All Governments—Employment and Payroll, by Function: 1995

[For October. Covers both full-time and part-time employees. Local government amounts are estimates subject to sampling variation; see Appendix III and source]

FUNCTION	EMPLOYEES (1,000)					OCTOBER PAYROLLS (mil. dol.)				
	Total	Federal (civilian) [1]	State and local			Total	Federal (civilian) [1]	State and local		
			Total	State	Local			Total	State	Local
Total	19,521	2,895	16,626	4,719	11,906	(NA)	(NA)	37,714	10,927	26,787
National defense [2]	831	831	(X)	(X)	(X)	(NA)	(NA)	(X)	(X)	(X)
Postal Service	849	849	(X)	(X)	(X)	(NA)	(NA)	(X)	(X)	(X)
Space research and technology	22	22	(X)	(X)	(X)	(NA)	(NA)	(X)	(X)	(X)
Elem and secondary educ	6,252	(X)	6,252	50	6,202	13,939	(NA)	13,939	119	13,820
Higher education	2,414	(X)	2,414	1,954	461	4,591	(NA)	4,591	3,794	797
Other education	129	12	117	117	(X)	260	(NA)	260	260	(X)
Health	544	141	403	166	238	(NA)	(NA)	977	431	546
Hospitals	1,303	174	1,129	522	608	(NA)	(NA)	2,658	1,258	1,399
Public welfare	526	10	516	230	286	(NA)	(NA)	1,145	549	597
Social insurance administration	167	68	98	98	-	(NA)	(NA)	254	254	(X)
Police protection	926	86	840	91	749	(NA)	(NA)	2,477	287	2,190
Fire protection	360	(X)	360	(X)	360	950	(NA)	950	(X)	950
Correction	655	28	627	413	213	(NA)	(NA)	1,620	1,062	559
Streets & highways	564	4	560	257	303	(NA)	(NA)	1,357	667	690
Air transportation	86	49	37	3	35	(NA)	(NA)	104	8	96
Water transport/Terminals	27	15	12	5	7	(NA)	(NA)	37	14	23
Solid waste management	115	(X)	115	2	114	263	(NA)	263	6	258
Sewerage	130	(X)	130	1	128	345	(NA)	345	4	341
Parks & recreation	387	26	361	47	314	(NA)	(NA)	502	81	421
Natural resources	421	210	211	168	43	(NA)	(NA)	475	395	80
Housing & community dev.	151	20	131	(X)	131	(NA)	(NA)	315	(X)	315
Water supply	165	(X)	165	1	164	410	(NA)	410	3	407
Electric power	82	(X)	82	6	76	296	(NA)	296	26	270
Gas supply	11	(X)	11	(X)	11	28	(NA)	28	(X)	28
Transit	210	(X)	210	20	190	676	(NA)	676	80	595
Libraries	152	5	147	1	147	(NA)	(NA)	207	1	206
State liquor stores	10	(X)	10	10	(X)	18	(NA)	18	18	(X)
Financial administration	520	131	388	168	220	(NA)	(NA)	916	444	472
Other government administration	436	24	413	53	359	(NA)	(NA)	644	137	507
Judicial and legal	401	53	349	130	219	(NA)	(NA)	994	428	565
Other & unallocable	673	138	535	208	329	(NA)	(NA)	1,258	603	653

X Not applicable. NA Not available. [1] Includes employees outside the United States. [2] Includes international relations.

Source: U.S. Bureau of the Census; <http://www.census.gov/pub/govs/www/apes.html>; (released August 1997).

No. 508. State and Local Government—Full-Time Employment and Salary, by Sex and Race/Ethnic Group: 1973 to 1995

[As of June 30. Excludes school systems and educational institutions. Based on reports from State governments (44 in 1973, 46 in 1975, 1976, and 1979, 47 in 1977 and 1983, 45 in 1978, 42 in 1980, 49 in 1981 and 1984 through 1987, and 50 in 1989 through 1991) and a sample of county, municipal, township, and special district jurisdictions employing 15 or more nonelected, nonappointed full-time employees. Data for 1993 and 1995 only for State and Local Governments with 100 or more employees. Data for 1974, 1982, 1988, 1992, and 1994 not available. For definition of median, see Guide to Tabular Presentation]

YEAR AND OCCUPATION	EMPLOYMENT (1,000)							MEDIAN ANNUAL SALARY ($1,000)					
	Total	Male	Female	White [1]	Minority			Male	Female	White [1]	Minority		
					Total [2]	Black [1]	Hispanic [3]				Total [2]	Black [1]	Hispanic [3]
1973	3,809	2,486	1,322	3,115	693	523	125	9.6	7.0	8.8	7.5	7.4	7.4
1975	3,899	2,436	1,464	3,102	797	602	147	11.3	8.2	10.2	8.8	8.6	8.9
1976	4,369	2,724	1,645	3,490	880	664	165	11.8	8.6	10.7	9.2	9.1	9.4
1977	4,415	2,737	1,678	3,480	935	705	175	12.4	9.1	11.3	9.7	9.5	9.9
1978	4,447	2,711	1,736	3,481	966	723	181	13.3	9.7	12.0	10.4	10.1	10.7
1979	4,576	2,761	1,816	3,568	1,008	751	192	14.1	10.4	12.8	10.9	10.6	11.4
1980	3,987	2,350	1,637	3,146	842	619	163	15.2	11.4	13.8	11.8	11.5	12.3
1981	4,665	2,740	1,925	3,591	1,074	780	205	17.7	13.1	16.1	13.5	13.3	14.7
1983	4,492	2,674	1,818	3,423	1,069	768	219	20.1	15.3	18.5	15.9	15.6	17.3
1984	4,580	2,700	1,880	3,458	1,121	799	233	21.4	16.2	19.6	17.4	16.5	18.4
1985	4,742	2,789	1,952	3,563	1,179	835	248	22.3	17.3	20.6	18.4	17.5	19.2
1986	4,779	2,797	1,982	3,549	1,230	865	259	23.4	18.1	21.5	19.6	18.7	20.2
1987	4,849	2,818	2,031	3,600	1,249	872	268	24.2	18.9	22.4	20.9	19.3	21.1
1989	5,257	3,030	2,227	3,863	1,394	961	308	26.1	20.6	24.1	22.1	20.7	22.7
1990	5,374	3,071	2,302	3,918	1,456	994	327	27.3	21.8	25.2	23.3	22.0	23.8
1991	5,459	3,110	2,349	3,965	1,494	1,011	340	28.4	22.7	26.4	23.8	22.7	24.5
1993	5,024	2,820	2,204	3,588	1,436	948	341	30.6	24.3	28.5	25.9	24.2	26.8
1995, total	5,315	**2,960**	**2,355**	**3,781**	**1,534**	**993**	**379**	**33.5**	**27.0**	**31.4**	**28.3**	26.8	**28.6**
Officials/administrators	299	201	98	250	48	31	12	52.7	45.2	50.6	44.9	47.7	49.0
Professionals	1,313	624	689	999	314	183	68	41.4	36.1	38.9	35.8	35.0	36.3
Technicians	481	280	202	359	122	71	34	33.3	27.4	31.1	29.6	27.8	29.2
Protective service	931	788	142	687	244	160	69	34.1	28.9	33.7	32.3	30.5	35.5
Paraprofessionals	380	105	275	231	149	114	26	23.8	21.9	23.1	22.3	21.0	22.2
Admin. support	926	123	803	627	299	187	82	24.6	22.9	23.0	23.1	23.0	23.0
Skilled craft	408	389	19	306	102	62	30	31.1	25.6	30.8	30.7	30.3	31.1
Service/maintenance	578	450	128	321	258	186	59	25.0	19.9	24.1	25.6	22.9	24.5

NA Not available. [1] Non-Hispanic. [2] Includes other minority groups not shown separately. [3] Persons of Hispanic origin may be of any race.

Source: U.S. Equal Employment Opportunity Commission, *State and Local Government Information Report*, biennially.

No. 509. State and Local Government—Employer Costs per Hour Worked: 1995

[In dollars. As of March. Based on a sample; see source for details. For additional data, see table 676]

ITEM	Total compensation	Wages and salaries	BENEFITS						
			Total	Paid leave	Supplemental pay	Insurance	Retirement and savings	Legally required benefits	Other [1]
All State & local government	**25.73**	**17.96**	**7.77**	**1.99**	**0.22**	**2.07**	**1.90**	**1.56**	**0.03**
Occupational group:									
White-collar occupations	28.56	20.43	8.13	2.08	0.14	2.19	2.02	1.67	0.03
Professional specialty and technical	33.81	24.86	8.95	2.07	0.16	2.32	2.44	1.92	0.04
Teachers	37.56	28.14	9.43	1.92	0.06	2.52	2.84	2.05	0.05
Executive, admin., & managerial	32.81	22.72	10.09	3.29	0.18	2.25	2.40	1.96	(Z)
Admin. support including clerical	16.55	10.93	5.61	1.51	0.09	1.92	1.04	1.05	(Z)
Blue-collar occupations	20.88	13.56	7.32	1.95	0.36	1.97	1.51	1.50	0.03
Service occupations	18.92	12.09	6.83	1.72	0.42	1.73	1.71	1.22	0.03
Industry group:									
Services	26.98	19.43	7.55	1.83	0.15	2.09	1.88	1.58	0.03
Health services	21.86	14.49	7.37	2.26	0.57	1.79	1.18	1.56	0.02
Hospitals	22.29	14.88	7.41	2.32	0.55	1.74	1.21	1.56	0.03
Educational services	28.21	20.59	7.62	1.74	0.09	2.13	2.03	1.60	0.03
Elementary and secondary education	28.04	20.58	7.45	1.59	0.06	2.23	1.99	1.55	0.04
Higher education	29.25	21.08	8.17	2.16	0.17	1.89	2.17	1.77	(Z)
Public administration	23.39	15.24	8.15	2.31	0.31	2.01	2.03	1.46	0.03

Z Cost per hour worked is less than one cent. [1] Includes severance pay and supplemental unemployment benefits.

Source: U.S. Bureau of Labor Statistics, *News, Employer Costs for Employee Compensation*, USDL 96-424.

No. 510. State and Local Government—Employee Benefits: 1994

[For January through July. Covers full-time employees in State and local governments. Covers only benefits for ployer pays part or all of the premium or expenses involved, except unpaid maternity and paternity leave, and e insurance. Based on sample. For data on employee benefits in businesses, see table 678]

BENEFIT	All employees	White collar employees [1]	Teachers [2]	Blue collar employees [3]
ons.	66	84	9	91
	73	86	33	91
leave	94	94	94	93
ave	62	59	58	70
ve	4	4	3	6
ave.	75	80	61	82
i.	94	93	96	94
eave	38	30	58	31
ve	93	93	96	90
ans:				
	87	89	84	86
	62	62	59	66
d care facility	81	83	81	78
ealth care	84	84	86	84
/room & board	100	100	100	100
r's	30	34	24	28
t surgery	100	100	100	100
health care:				
ient	99	99	100	99
atient	97	98	97	97
	35	36	30	37
abuse treatment:				
ient detox	99	99	99	99
ient rehab	77	76	78	76
atient	83	83	83	82
use treatment:				
ient detox	98	98	99	99
ient rehab	74	73	76	74
atient	80	79	82	80

BENEFIT	All employees	White collar employees [1]	Teachers [2]	Blue collar employees [3]
Life	87	87	85	87
Noncontributory	86	85	85	88
Accident/sickness	21	24	11	26
Noncontributory	76	72	86	79
Long-term disability	30	31	37	23
Noncontributory	77	77	77	79
Retirement and savings plans:				
Defined benefit pension	91	90	93	91
Noncontributory	28	30	20	31
Defined contribution	9	10	7	9
Money purchase pension [4]	7	7	5	7
Additional benefits:				
Child care	9	11	5	9
Educational assistance:				
Job related	64	69	51	66
Not job related	20	22	15	20
Sabbatical leave	27	19	59	9
Employee assistance program	68	73	55	74
Flexible benefits plans	5	5	7	3
Financial councilling	6	7	6	4
Long-term care insurance	4	5	2	3
Nonproduction bonuses, cash	34	40	17	41
Subsidized commuting	7	8	4	9
Recreation facilities	14	13	19	13
Reimbursement accounts [5]	64	68	59	61
Severance pay	29	26	32	32
Travel accident insurance	13	13	14	12
Wellness programs	34	38	29	32

s all professional, administrative, technical, and clerical employees except teachers. [2] Includes all personnel in secondary schools, junior colleges, and universities whose primary duty is teaching or closely related activities. lice, firefighters, and all production and service employees. [4] Fixed contributions are periodically placed in an ccount and benefits are based on how much money has accumulated at retirement. [5] Account which is used e year to pay for plan premiums or to reimburse the employee for benefit related expenses. Account may be financed employee, or both.

J.S. Bureau of Labor Statistics, *Employee Benefits in State and Local Governments, 1994.*

511. State and Local Government Major Collective Bargaining Agreements— Percent Changes in Wage and Compensation Rates Negotiated: 1985 to 1995

cent, except as indicated. Averages presented are means; for definition, see Guide to Tabular Presentation]

ITEM	1985	1988	1989	1990	1991	1992	1993	1994	1995[1]
n rate changes, [2] all									
r	4.2	5.4	5.1	5.1	1.8	0.6	0.9	2.8	1.8
of contract [3]	5.1	5.3	4.9	5.1	2.9	1.9	1.8	3.1	2.0
mment: First year	4.8	5.3	4.9	4.4	1.9	0.2	1.2	2.8	2.0
of contract [3]	4.8	4.9	4.6	3.9	2.8	2.0	2.1	2.9	2.4
mment: First year	3.7	5.5	5.6	5.4	1.6	1.2	0.7	2.8	1.5
of contract [3]	5.5	5.8	5.5	5.8	2.9	1.5	1.6	3.3	1.4
anges, [4] all settlements:									
r	4.6	5.1	5.1	4.9	2.3	1.1	1.1	2.7	2.0
of contract [3]	5.4	5.3	5.1	5.0	2.8	2.1	2.1	3.0	2.3
mment: First year	4.8	5.3	5.0	4.7	2.0	0.5	1.3	3.0	2.3
of contract [3]	4.9	5.0	4.7	4.2	3.0	2.0	2.4	3.2	2.7
mment: First year	4.4	5.0	5.2	5.0	2.5	1.7	1.0	2.5	1.9
of contract [3]	5.7	5.5	5.4	5.2	2.7	2.1	1.9	3.0	2.2
workers affected (mil.) [5]	1.5	1.1	1.1	0.9	0.8	1.2	1.7	1.2	0.4
vernment	0.5	0.4	0.5	0.2	0.4	0.6	0.6	0.4	0.1
vernment	0.9	0.7	0.6	0.7	0.4	0.6	1.1	0.8	0.2
anges, all agreements [6]	5.7	4.7	5.1	4.6	2.6	1.9	2.8	3.3	0.5
rrent settlements	4.1	2.3	2.5	2.0	0.6	0.8	1.6	1.4	(Z)
lements	1.6	2.4	2.6	2.6	1.8	1.1	1.1	1.9	(Z)
iving adjustments	(Z)	(Z)	(Z)	(Z)	0.1	(Z)	(Z)	(Z)	(Z)
mment	4.5	4.1	4.0	4.7	2.5	1.6	3.4	3.5	0.3
mment	6.5	5.1	5.9	4.6	2.6	2.1	2.2	3.2	0.7

an .05 percent. [1] 1st 6 months. [2] Data relate to settlements of 5,000 workers or more in each calendar year, s and benefits were changed or not. [3] Average annual rate of change. [4] Data relate to settlements covering or more in each calendar year but exclude possible changes in wages under cost-of-living adjustment (COLA) pt increases guaranteed by the contract. Includes all settlements, whether wages were changed or not. [5] Number vered by settlements reached in each calendar year. [6] Data relate to all wage changes implemented in the year n settlements reached in the year, deferred from prior-year agreements, and cost-of-living clauses.

J.S. Bureau of Labor Statistics, *Current Wage Developments*, quarterly.

No. 512. State and Local Government Full-Time Equivalent Employment, by Selected Function and State: 1995

[In thousands, for October. Local government amounts are estimates subject to sampling variation; see Appendix III and source]

STATE	EDUCATION						PUBLIC WELFARE		HEALTH		HOSPITALS	
	Total		Elem. & secondary		Higher education							
	State	Local	State	Local	State	Local	State	Local	State	Local	State	Local
United States	**1,468.7**	**5,619.2**	**41.4**	**5,341.2**	**1,330.8**	**278.0**	**226.8**	**285.1**	**160.1**	**208.6**	**496.2**	**551.4**
Alabama	34.2	86.7	-	86.7	30.3	-	4.3	1.1	6.8	3.9	12.2	20.1
Alaska	7.3	11.4	2.9	11.4	3.9	-	1.8	0.1	0.5	0.6	0.3	0.2
Arizona	24.8	90.8	-	83.6	22.4	7.2	5.3	4.0	2.1	2.7	0.7	4.6
Arkansas	18.6	58.2	-	58.2	15.3	-	3.7	0.2	4.0	0.3	4.9	3.8
California	117.2	553.1	-	490.9	112.6	62.1	3.7	52.0	10.1	33.3	34.5	75.4
Colorado	32.7	77.4	-	76.0	31.5	1.4	1.0	4.4	1.2	2.4	4.6	7.9
Connecticut	18.0	67.0	-	67.0	15.2	-	4.8	1.8	2.6	1.4	12.3	-
Delaware	6.8	13.7	-	13.7	6.5	-	2.0	-	1.8	0.2	2.3	-
District of Columbia	(X)	10.0	(X)	8.8	(X)	1.1	(X)	1.8	(X)	2.1	(X)	3.8
Florida	42.2	274.4	-	253.0	39.6	21.4	11.2	5.8	14.7	5.8	16.4	36.8
Georgia	40.7	181.4	-	180.7	35.0	0.7	7.7	1.4	4.4	8.2	14.4	42.0
Hawaii	30.4	-	23.2	-	7.1	-	1.1	0.1	2.8	0.2	3.2	-
Idaho	7.6	27.1	-	26.2	7.1	0.9	1.8	0.2	1.2	0.9	1.0	4.3
Illinois	55.3	232.1	-	212.6	52.4	19.5	13.4	7.1	3.2	6.7	15.2	15.2
Indiana	46.6	123.0	-	123.0	41.8	-	5.2	1.6	1.7	2.7	11.1	23.0
Iowa	26.9	72.8	-	66.6	24.7	6.2	2.7	1.5	0.3	2.0	8.1	8.9
Kansas	21.0	70.6	-	64.9	20.3	5.7	1.7	0.8	0.9	3.2	6.6	7.3
Kentucky	30.3	90.7	-	90.7	26.2	-	4.6	0.5	2.0	4.5	5.5	3.2
Louisiana	34.1	102.0	-	102.0	30.2	-	6.0	0.7	5.3	0.9	18.7	13.3
Maine	6.8	31.1	-	31.1	5.6	-	1.9	0.2	1.1	0.2	1.5	1.1
Maryland	19.7	104.9	-	96.0	17.7	8.9	7.9	2.3	6.0	3.6	6.9	-
Massachusetts	23.7	129.5	-	129.5	23.0	-	6.6	2.7	3.9	2.1	11.8	6.1
Michigan	63.4	196.2	-	184.2	62.8	12.0	14.6	2.6	2.1	9.7	15.6	13.2
Minnesota	36.7	109.8	-	106.1	37.2	3.7	2.2	11.0	2.1	3.7	7.2	13.3
Mississippi	16.8	69.5	-	63.9	15.3	5.7	3.4	0.3	3.3	0.3	9.0	18.0
Missouri	26.3	118.1	-	113.0	24.4	5.1	7.5	2.1	3.3	3.5	12.4	7.8
Montana	7.1	26.7	-	26.5	6.4	0.1	1.3	0.9	0.4	0.6	1.3	0.8
Nebraska	10.8	43.7	-	41.2	10.1	2.5	2.9	1.1	0.7	0.4	4.4	4.3
Nevada	6.1	27.3	-	27.3	6.0	-	1.0	0.4	0.7	0.8	1.7	3.6
New Hampshire	5.7	24.7	-	24.7	5.3	-	1.3	2.5	0.6	0.1	1.0	-
New Jersey	45.6	178.9	14.6	169.2	27.6	9.8	5.4	11.5	2.5	4.0	17.1	6.4
New Mexico	16.9	43.3	-	40.9	15.9	2.4	1.4	0.5	2.9	0.4	5.4	2.6
New York	49.0	400.8	-	375.3	43.9	25.5	7.5	51.8	8.9	17.2	55.6	61.4
North Carolina	45.6	162.5	-	149.0	42.6	13.5	1.3	13.4	2.0	13.9	15.6	17.6
North Dakota	7.8	13.6	-	13.6	7.3	-	0.3	0.9	1.3	0.3	1.4	-
Ohio	68.0	212.7	-	207.5	65.6	5.2	2.2	22.3	3.8	17.5	17.7	15.1
Oklahoma	25.5	80.0	-	79.6	23.5	0.4	5.8	0.4	3.8	1.0	6.1	9.5
Oregon	16.2	68.2	-	61.0	15.2	7.2	4.6	0.8	1.5	3.5	7.3	2.3
Pennsylvania	50.6	208.4	-	200.1	47.6	8.3	11.6	21.7	1.7	5.2	21.0	2.8
Rhode Island	7.0	18.1	0.4	18.1	5.8	-	1.8	0.1	1.3	0.1	1.5	-
South Carolina	27.2	80.4	-	80.4	24.3	-	4.9	0.2	8.1	2.0	9.8	14.3
South Dakota	5.6	16.8	-	16.8	5.1	-	1.0	0.2	0.6	0.2	1.4	0.4
Tennessee	38.6	100.7	-	100.7	36.5	-	4.6	3.7	3.6	3.3	10.6	12.3
Texas	91.5	547.9	-	517.3	86.8	30.7	24.0	3.7	10.4	16.1	40.3	43.7
Utah	22.0	39.0	-	39.0	21.1	-	3.0	0.4	1.4	1.1	3.9	1.0
Vermont	4.6	16.6	-	16.6	4.2	-	1.1	-	0.5	-	0.3	-
Virginia	44.9	149.2	-	149.2	42.2	-	2.3	7.5	5.8	5.3	18.0	3.5
Washington	36.8	87.0	-	87.0	36.1	-	7.3	1.2	7.0	4.1	8.1	8.9
West Virginia	13.6	41.0	-	41.0	12.1	-	2.6	-	0.7	1.5	1.5	3.3
Wisconsin	29.8	114.1	-	105.2	28.5	8.9	1.2	13.3	1.7	4.7	7.6	3.9
Wyoming	3.3	16.1	-	14.4	3.2	1.7	0.3	-	0.5	0.2	1.4	4.1

See footnote at end of table.

512. State and Local Government Full-Time Equivalent Employment, by Selected Function and State: 1995—Continued

[In thousands, for October. Local government amounts are estimates subject to sampling variation; see Appendix III and source]

TATE	HIGHWAYS		POLICE PROTECTION		FIRE PROTECTION		CORRECTION		PARKS AND RECREATION		GOVERNMENT ADMINISTRATION[1]	
	State	Local	State	Local	State	Local	State	Local	State	Local	State	Local
ed States. .	253.3	286.9	89.6	689.2	(X)	274.3	408.2	205.8	38.6	207.3	339.6	586.1
	4.3	6.6	1.0	9.9	(X)	4.5	4.3	2.4	0.8	2.9	5.4	6.8
	2.8	0.9	0.4	1.4	(X)	0.7	1.3	-	0.1	0.6	2.5	1.9
	2.9	4.0	1.7	11.1	(X)	3.9	7.6	4.8	0.7	3.5	5.5	13.0
	3.6	3.6	0.9	5.4	(X)	2.3	3.4	1.2	0.8	0.8	2.6	5.8
	17.3	21.6	11.0	79.5	(X)	30.0	43.1	27.8	3.7	32.2	23.6	78.4
	3.1	5.3	1.1	9.5	(X)	3.7	4.2	2.9	0.3	5.8	5.3	9.4
ut.	4.0	3.8	1.6	8.0	(X)	4.1	7.4	-	0.4	2.2	7.0	4.4
	1.5	0.7	0.8	1.2	(X)	0.3	1.8	-	0.3	0.3	2.3	0.9
Columbia .	(X)	0.8	(X)	4.5	(X)	1.6	(X)	4.2	(X)	0.4	(X)	3.3
	10.6	13.6	3.8	44.9	(X)	18.2	31.1	13.3	1.1	15.6	21.2	35.6
	6.1	7.8	2.3	18.8	(X)	12.2	19.1	6.2	2.9	4.3	5.0	16.4
	0.6	1.0	-	3.3	(X)	1.6	2.1	-	0.3	1.9	3.6	2.2
	1.8	1.6	0.4	2.9	(X)	0.9	1.5	0.8	0.2	0.7	1.8	3.4
	8.4	11.5	3.7	39.4	(X)	14.6	13.6	8.1	0.8	17.5	11.8	29.0
	4.6	6.4	2.0	12.5	(X)	5.8	6.3	3.8	0.1	3.9	4.1	14.3
	2.7	5.5	0.9	5.7	(X)	1.7	2.3	0.9	0.2	2.2	4.0	5.4
	3.8	5.6	1.0	6.6	(X)	2.5	3.6	1.9	0.5	2.4	4.6	6.7
	5.4	3.0	1.7	6.0	(X)	2.8	5.3	2.2	2.2	1.5	8.1	4.8
	5.7	4.9	1.1	12.4	(X)	4.1	6.8	2.6	0.9	2.8	5.3	10.6
	2.8	1.5	0.5	2.4	(X)	1.6	1.2	0.6	0.2	0.6	2.0	2.3
	5.0	4.6	2.3	13.4	(X)	6.1	10.6	2.5	0.7	6.4	8.2	7.5
setts.	4.6	5.9	1.9	16.4	(X)	12.8	6.1	5.0	1.1	2.1	12.6	9.1
	3.8	10.1	3.0	20.3	(X)	7.7	16.5	4.8	0.8	5.8	7.1	21.1
a.	4.9	7.5	0.9	9.0	(X)	2.3	3.4	3.8	0.6	4.3	5.3	12.5
pi	3.4	5.3	1.0	6.6	(X)	2.6	3.7	1.0	0.4	0.8	2.0	6.5
	6.7	5.3	2.2	14.1	(X)	5.0	6.7	2.3	0.7	3.5	5.9	9.5
	1.8	1.3	0.4	1.7	(X)	0.5	0.8	0.3	0.1	0.4	1.4	2.1
	2.4	3.1	0.7	3.5	(X)	1.1	2.0	0.8	0.4	1.1	1.6	4.0
	1.5	1.3	0.6	4.1	(X)	1.6	2.9	1.3	0.2	2.2	1.9	4.8
pshire	2.0	1.3	0.4	2.6	(X)	1.4	1.0	0.5	0.2	0.3	1.5	1.7
ey.	8.0	10.7	3.7	28.5	(X)	7.7	9.0	7.1	2.4	5.6	18.0	20.9
ico	2.7	1.6	0.6	4.4	(X)	1.6	3.9	1.3	0.7	1.6	4.2	4.0
	14.1	30.1	5.4	71.1	(X)	19.7	33.9	24.2	2.6	10.7	40.5	39.6
rolina.	12.6	3.3	3.3	16.5	(X)	5.4	12.4	3.6	0.7	4.0	10.0	10.4
kota.	1.0	1.1	0.2	1.1	(X)	0.3	0.5	0.2	0.1	0.7	1.1	1.5
	6.6	13.3	2.5	27.2	(X)	16.5	14.7	7.5	0.9	7.8	11.7	30.6
a.	4.1	5.6	1.7	7.9	(X)	3.9	7.6	1.1	1.8	2.2	5.1	6.1
	3.4	4.0	1.2	6.2	(X)	3.2	2.9	2.8	0.5	2.2	6.5	6.1
nia.	13.7	10.6	6.4	25.1	(X)	5.7	12.8	10.7	1.0	4.2	13.6	26.6
land.	0.9	1.0	0.3	2.6	(X)	2.0	1.7	-	0.1	0.8	2.5	1.6
rolina.	5.1	2.4	2.3	8.5	(X)	3.2	8.1	2.0	0.6	2.3	4.3	7.6
kota	1.2	1.6	0.3	1.3	(X)	0.4	0.7	0.3	0.1	0.7	1.4	1.7
e	4.7	6.7	1.6	12.0	(X)	5.9	7.0	4.3	1.1	3.7	4.9	9.8
	14.0	18.9	3.4	53.4	(X)	18.5	43.0	20.9	1.2	13.4	16.3	39.4
	1.8	1.5	0.7	4.0	(X)	1.6	2.5	0.7	0.3	2.3	2.9	3.4
	1.1	1.0	0.5	0.8	(X)	0.3	0.9	-	0.2	0.2	1.3	1.0
	12.0	3.9	2.5	14.2	(X)	7.0	12.7	6.2	0.9	6.0	7.4	13.2
on.	6.2	6.7	1.8	10.6	(X)	5.4	7.4	3.5	0.5	4.9	5.2	13.9
inia.	6.1	0.8	0.9	2.4	(X)	0.9	0.8	0.4	1.0	0.9	3.0	3.2
n.	2.0	9.1	0.9	13.3	(X)	4.8	6.5	2.4	0.3	3.8	5.5	10.7
	1.7	0.7	0.2	1.4	(X)	0.3	0.5	0.3	0.1	0.6	0.9	1.5

resents or rounds to zero. X Not applicable.
des Financial Administration, Central Administration, and Judicial and Legal.

e: U.S. Bureau of the Census; <http://www.census.gov/ftp/pub/govs/www/apes/95html>; (released June 97).

No. 513. State and Local Government Employment and Average Earnings, by State: 1990 and 1995

[For October]

STATE	FULL-TIME EQUIVALENT EMPLOYMENT (1,000)				FULL-TIME EQUIVALENT EMPLOYMENT PER 10,000 POPULATION [2]				AVERAGE OCTOBER EARNINGS [3] (dol.)			
	State		Local [1]		State		Local [1]		State		Local [1]	
	1990	1995	19890	1995	1990	1995	1990	1995	1990	1995	1990	1995
United States	**3,840**	**3,971**	**9,239**	**10,119**	**154**	**151**	**371**	**386**	**2,472**	**2,864**	**2,364**	**2,763**
Alabama	79	81	148	165	196	191	367	389	2,196	2,421	1,749	2,017
Alaska	22	22	21	24	401	366	385	391	3,543	3,727	3,491	4,051
Arizona	50	58	136	161	137	135	370	373	2,334	2,570	2,540	2,689
Arkansas	43	48	78	90	182	192	330	364	1,922	2,353	1,545	1,823
California	325	338	1,091	1,141	109	107	367	362	3,209	3,664	3,073	3,523
Colorado	54	57	130	148	165	153	395	394	2,765	3,234	2,292	2,612
Connecticut	58	63	98	102	178	193	299	311	3,018	3,321	2,854	3,491
Delaware	21	22	17	19	314	307	250	269	2,245	2,743	2,458	2,755
District of Columbia	(X)	(X)	57	47	(X)	(X)	939	927	(X)	(X)	3,024	3,425
Florida	160	175	497	534	123	123	384	377	2,095	2,488	2,247	2,485
Georgia	112	115	270	333	173	159	418	462	2,037	2,456	1,872	2,164
Hawaii	49	51	13	14	445	436	120	119	2,317	2,624	2,536	3,013
Idaho	19	21	37	46	186	179	372	396	2,100	2,476	1,772	2,165
Illinois	145	141	416	444	127	119	364	377	2,520	3,027	2,463	2,985
Indiana	89	89	196	217	161	153	354	375	2,496	2,583	2,036	2,375
Iowa	57	53	107	116	207	187	387	408	2,936	3,126	2,024	2,367
Kansas	50	48	104	118	200	187	421	461	2,077	2,325	1,979	2,315
Kentucky	75	73	114	133	204	190	310	344	2,141	2,488	1,823	2,523
Louisiana	85	93	155	171	200	214	368	394	2,047	2,359	1,713	1,860
Maine	22	21	42	45	179	172	345	364	2,352	2,618	1,978	2,349
Maryland	89	81	159	172	186	161	333	341	2,609	2,835	2,776	3,159
Massachusetts	93	82	196	220	155	135	325	362	2,541	3,068	2,554	2,961
Michigan	144	141	316	324	155	148	340	339	2,858	3,342	2,646	3,256
Minnesota	70	73	163	196	160	157	374	425	2,936	3,266	2,552	2,830
Mississippi	47	50	105	122	183	186	407	453	1,824	2,394	1,543	1,798
Missouri	74	79	171	192	145	149	334	361	1,965	2,232	2,052	2,297
Montana	17	18	35	36	211	208	434	439	2,072	2,534	1,959	2,347
Nebraska	29	30	68	76	186	181	430	465	2,075	2,290	2,089	2,413
Nevada	19	21	42	53	160	134	348	345	2,502	2,864	2,574	3,085
New Hampshire	16	17	33	36	145	147	301	335	2,352	2,669	2,215	2,641
New Jersey	112	125	304	312	145	157	393	393	2,859	3,563	2,698	3,553
New Mexico	40	42	57	68	262	251	379	404	2,100	2,390	1,783	2,119
New York	285	257	866	856	158	142	482	471	2,997	3,423	2,795	3,479
North Carolina	107	115	244	281	161	159	368	389	2,372	2,570	2,065	2,287
North Dakota	15	16	20	22	234	257	314	340	2,057	2,440	2,138	2,450
Ohio	139	143	385	425	128	128	355	381	2,510	3,083	2,236	2,696
Oklahoma	65	68	116	129	208	206	369	393	1,975	2,018	1,761	2,113
Oregon	52	52	100	114	184	166	353	362	2,302	2,848	2,322	2,896
Pennsylvania	127	152	361	369	107	126	304	306	2,437	3,025	2,403	2,911
Rhode Island	21	20	27	29	205	203	266	288	2,586	3,240	2,656	3,169
South Carolina	79	78	116	136	227	213	333	370	1,956	2,318	1,848	2,141
South Dakota	13	14	24	27	192	194	349	364	1,979	2,365	1,733	2,004
Tennessee	79	84	175	188	163	161	358	359	2,065	2,389	1,863	2,196
Texas	223	268	706	858	131	143	415	456	2,192	2,492	1,952	2,229
Utah	37	42	51	63	216	214	294	321	2,000	2,524	2,092	2,460
Vermont	13	13	18	21	233	216	312	363	2,302	2,471	2,090	2,455
Virginia	117	116	221	247	188	175	356	373	2,267	2,553	2,248	2,505
Washington	91	96	164	188	187	175	336	344	2,459	3,094	2,515	3,338
West Virginia	34	35	59	60	188	189	326	327	1,919	2,212	1,862	2,203
Wisconsin	67	64	183	201	136	126	375	393	2,503	3,153	2,372	2,900
Wyoming	11	11	24	27	239	227	539	565	2,045	2,203	2,110	2,309

X Not applicable. [1] Estimates subject to sampling variation; see Appendix III and source. [2] Based on estimated resident population as of July 1. [3] For full-time employees.

Source: U.S. Bureau of the Census, *Public Employment*, series GE-90-1, No.1, and <http://www.census.gov/pub/govs/www/apes.html>; (released August 1997).

14. City Government Employment and Payroll—Largest Cities: 1990 and 1995

r October. See footnote 2, table 500, for those areas representing city-county consolidated governments]

RANKED BY 1994 OPULATION	TOTAL EMPLOYMENT (1,000)		FULL-TIME EQUIVALENT EMPLOYMENT: Total (1,000)		FULL-TIME EQUIVALENT EMPLOYMENT: Per 10,000 population[1]		OCTOBER PAYROLL (mil. dol.)		AVERAGE EARNINGS IN OCTOBER, FULL-TIME EMPLOYEES (dol.)	
	1990	1995	1990	1995	1990	1995	1990	1995	1990	1995
Y[2,3]	456	425	395	388	539	529	1,092	1,306	2,783	3,454
, CA	51	48	51	47	146	136	177	191	3,488	4,133
	42	41	42	41	149	152	125	156	3,002	3,757
	20	23	20	23	120	135	40	57	2,061	2,459
, PA	32	30	32	29	201	190	89	92	2,843	3,220
CA	10	12	10	10	88	88	29	34	3,019	3,472
	12	12	11	12	116	112	32	36	2,876	3,281
	15	15	15	14	144	140	28	41	1,945	2,876
, TX	13	16	13	15	137	148	28	37	2,227	2,539
	22	18	21	17	206	173	50	50	2,390	2,908
A	6	7	5	6	62	74	16	27	3,453	4,700
IN	13	12	12	12	171	155	23	33	1,910	2,490
co, CA	26	26	26	26	356	361	94	98	3,648	3,710
FL[2]	11	10	10	9	154	132	24	28	2,582	3,064
D[2]	30	28	29	27	395	391	73	81	2,540	3,010
OH	8	8	7	8	118	125	18	26	2,416	3,324
WI	9	9	9	9	137	138	21	23	2,431	2,793
[2]	22	22	21	21	341	336	48	54	2,287	2,679
	5	6	5	6	94	102	9	13	1,973	2,302
DC[2,3]	50	40	48	39	789	679	139	124	2,930	3,269
[2]	21	22	21	22	363	393	50	49	2,391	2,279
	11	11	10	11	198	202	32	40	3,274	3,985
	10	13	10	12	205	224	21	28	2,186	2,512
vidson, TN[2]	18	21	17	19	347	386	42	41	2,510	2,135
	13	16	12	14	254	292	31	45	2,649	3,126
OH	9	10	8	9	163	178	21	24	2,521	2,805
, LA	10	9	10	9	194	178	16	19	1,623	2,226
ty, OK	5	5	4	5	101	106	11	14	2,430	3,084
TX	5	6	5	5	117	117	11	12	2,171	2,403
	5	6	5	5	103	113	15	19	3,305	3,950
MO	6	7	6	7	145	147	15	17	2,390	2,685
C	5	5	5	5	122	106	11	13	2,399	2,847
	5	6	5	5	115	121	12	14	2,528	2,882
, CA	6	6	5	5	126	125	18	21	3,413	3,947
ch, VA[2]	14	17	13	15	334	354	28	35	2,232	2,385
, NM	7	8	6	6	161	150	12	15	2,040	2,432
	8	8	8	8	205	199	18	20	2,286	2,541
	3	3	3	3	77	70	8	10	2,944	3,652
	10	10	9	9	245	105	24	28	2,600	3,083
	4	4	4	4	115	111	11	11	2,555	2,734
, CA	4	4	4	4	105	107	11	14	3,021	3,713
	4	4	4	3	113	92	15	12	3,771	3,503
O	8	8	7	8	186	209	17	20	2,363	2,606
	5	5	4	5	111	128	15	19	3,948	4,482
A	6	6	6	5	152	145	12	16	2,240	3,221
OH	7	8	6	7	173	206	16	23	2,634	3,480
MN	6	7	6	6	154	179	15	23	2,815	3,921
	3	3	3	3	81	83	8	10	3,051	3,533
NV	2	2	(NA)	2	(NA)	63	5	7	2,563	3,570
	3	3	3	3	91	96	9	10	2,847	3,191
rings, CO	6	6	5	6	188	187	13	19	2,618	3,242
	2	3	2	3	81	87	7	9	2,898	3,307
	13	12	12	12	379	370	31	40	2,596	3,733
	3	4	3	3	87	102	5	8	2,083	2,617
CA	2	2	2	2	58	68	7	8	4,144	4,813
	2	2	2	2	66	74	5	6	2,538	2,991
	4	4	4	4	151	146	10	13	2,505	3,176
	4	4	3	2	99	81	9	10	3,728	4,635
ti, TX	3	3	3	3	116	118	6	8	2,009	2,384
Y	5	5	4	4	159	163	9	9	2,180	2,224
AL	4	4	4	4	142	151	8	9	2,243	2,354
	4	4	3	3	124	126	10	11	3,265	3,601
	5	6	5	5	177	206	8	18	1,698	3,544
AK	9	(NA)	8	9	351	343	28	39	3,706	4,682
	2	(NA)	2	2	84	84	5	6	2,586	2,971
	10	(NA)	10	(NA)	376	(NA)	22	(NA)	2,268	(NA)

vailable. [1] 1990 based on enumerated resident population as of April 1, 1990. 1995 based on enumerated resident s of April 1, 1994. [2] Includes city-operated elementary and secondary schools. [3] Includes city-operated university

U.S. Bureau of the Census, *City Employment*, GE-90-2; and unpublished data.

Figure 10.1
The Government of the United States
(As of July 1, 1993)

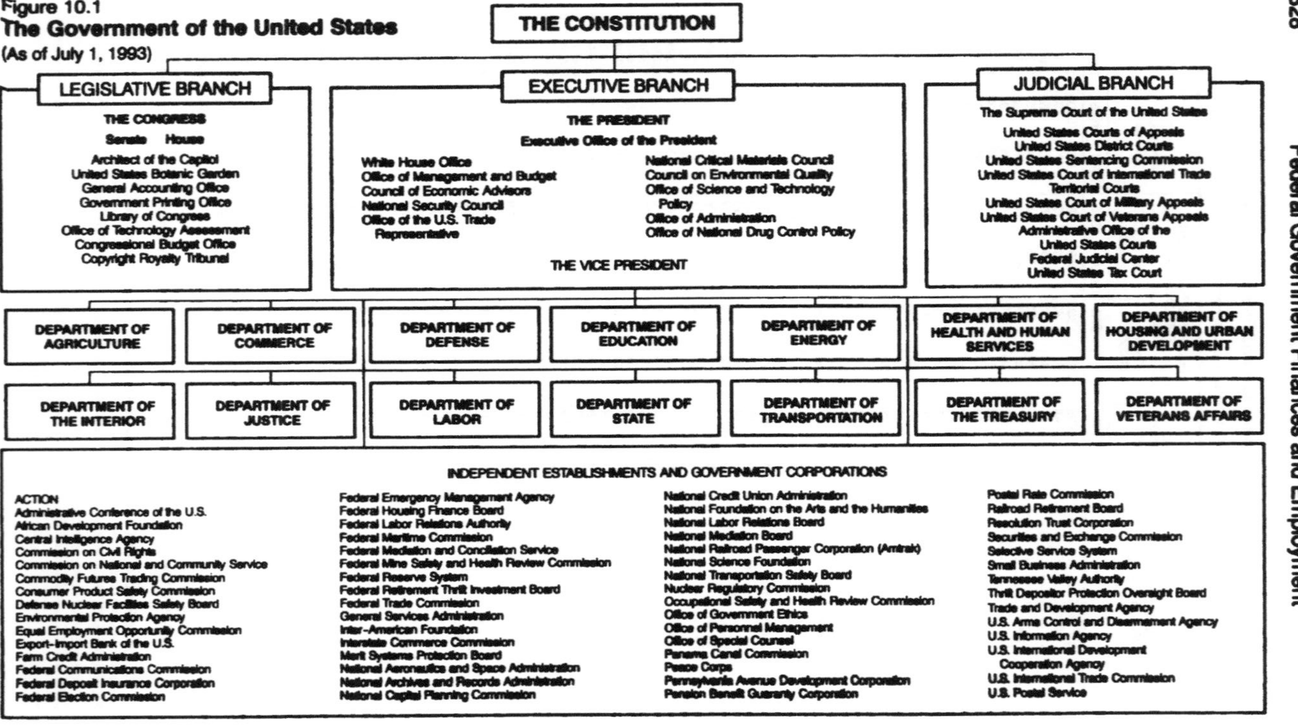

Source: Chart prepared by U.S. Bureau of the Census.

Section 10

Federal Government Finances and Employment

ion presents statistics relating to ial structure and the civilian ent of the Federal Government. l data cover taxes, other re- ıtlays, and debt. The principal of fiscal data are *The Budget of d States Government* and re- uments, published annually by of Management and Budget nd the Department of the Trea- *ited States Government Annual* nd its *Appendix.* Detailed data turns and collections are pub- nually by the Internal Revenue Personnel data relating to staf- payrolls for the various public and agencies, to employee ristics, and to civil service sta- ublished by the Office of Per- lanagement and the Bureau of atistics. The primary source for ublic lands is *Public Land Sta-* blished annually by the Bureau Management, Department of the Data on federally-owned land property are collected by the Services Administration and d in its annual *Inventory Report Property Owned by the United hroughout the World.*

concept—Under the unified oncept, all Federal monies are in one comprehensive budget. onies comprise both Federal d trust funds. Federal funds are nainly from taxes and borrowing not restricted by law to any spe- ernment purpose. Trust funds, the Unemployment Trust Fund, ertain taxes and other receipts n carrying out specific purposes ams in accordance with the the trust agreement or statute. lances include both cash bal- ith Treasury and investments in urities. Part of the balance is ob- part unobligated. Prior to 1985, get totals, under provisions of luded some Federal activities— the Federal Financing Bank, al Service, the Synthetic Fuels tion, and the lending activities of the Rural Electrification Administration. The Balanced Budget and Emergency Deficit Control Act of 1985 (P.L.99-177) repealed the off-budget status of these entities and placed social security (Federal old-age and survivors insurance and the Federal disability insurance trust funds) off-budget. Though social security is now off-budget and, by law, excluded from coverage of the congressional budget resolutions, it continues to be a Federal program.

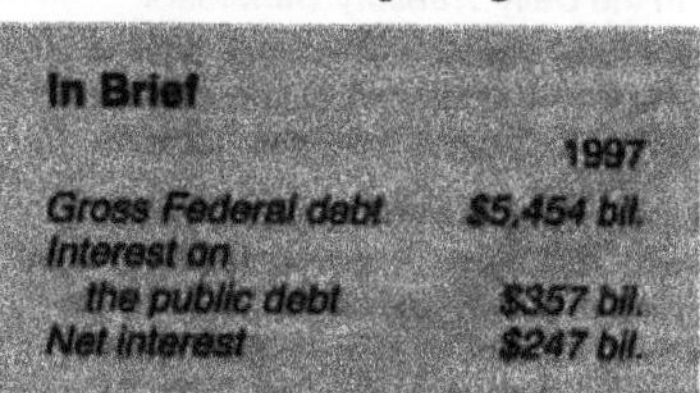

In Brief

	1997
Gross Federal debt	*$5,454 bil.*
Interest on the public debt	*$357 bil.*
Net interest	*$247 bil.*

Receipts arising from the Government's sovereign powers are reported as governmental receipts; all other receipts, i.e., from business-type or market-oriented activities, are offset against outlays. Outlays are reported on a checks-issued (net) basis (i.e., outlays are recorded at the time the checks to pay bills are issued).

Debt concept—For most of U.S. history, the total debt consisted of debt borrowed by the Treasury (i.e., public debt). The present debt series includes both public debt and agency debt. The *gross Federal debt* includes money borrowed by the Treasury and by various Federal agencies; it is the broadest generally used measure of the Federal debt. *Total public debt* is covered by a statutory debt limitation and includes only borrowing by the Treasury.

Treasury receipts and outlays—All receipts of the Government, with a few exceptions, are deposited to the credit of the U.S. Treasury regardless of ultimate disposition. Under the Constitution, no money may be withdrawn from the Treasury unless appropriated by the Congress.

The day-to-day cash operations of the Federal Government clearing through the accounts of the U.S. Treasury are reported in the *Daily Treasury Statement*. Extensive detail on the public debt is published in the *Monthly Statement of the Public Debt of the United States*.

Budget receipts such as taxes, customs duties, and outlays represented by checks issued and cash payments made by disbursing officers as well as government agencies are reported in the *Daily Treasury Statement of Receipts and Outlays of the United States Government* and in the Treasury's *United States Government Annual Report* and its *Appendix*. These deposits in and payments from accounts maintained by Government agencies are on the same basis as the unified budget.

The quarterly *Treasury Bulletin* contains data on fiscal operations and related Treasury activities, including financial statements of Government corporations and other business-type activities.

Income tax returns and tax collections—Tax data are compiled by the Internal Revenue Service of the Treasury Department. The *Annual Report of the Commissioner and Chief Counsel of the Internal Revenue Service Data Book* gives a detailed account of tax collections by kind of tax and by regions, districts, and States. The agency's annual *Statistics of Income* reports present detailed data from individual income tax returns and corporation income tax returns. The quarterly *Statistics of Income Bulletin* has, in general, replaced the supplemental *Statistics of Income* publications which presented data on such diverse subjects as tax-exempt organizations, unincorporated businesses, fiduciary income tax and estate tax returns, sales of capital assets by individuals, international income and taxes reported by corporations and individuals, and estate tax wealth.

Employment and payrolls—The Office of Personnel Management collects employment and payroll data from all departments and agencies of the Federal Government, except the Central Intelligence Agency, the National Security Agency, and the Defense Intelligence Agency. Employment figures represent the number of persons who occupied civilian positions at the end of the report month shown and who are paid for personal services rendered for the Federal Government, regardless of the nature of appointment or method of payment.

Federal payrolls include all payments for personal services rendered during the report month and payments for accumulated annual leave of employees who separate from the service. Since most Federal employees are paid on a biweekly basis, the calendar month earnings are partially estimated on the basis of the number of work days in each month where payroll periods overlap.

Federal employment and payroll figures are published by the Office of Personnel Management in its *Federal Civilian Workforce Statistics—Employment and Trends*. It also publishes biennial employment data for minority groups, data on occupations of white- and blue-collar workers, and data on employment by geographic area; reports on salary and wage distribution of Federal employees are published annually. General schedule is primarily white-collar; wage system primarily blue-collar. Data on Federal employment are also issued by the Bureau of Labor Statistics in its *Monthly Labor Review* and in *Employment and Earnings* and by the Bureau of the Census in its annual *Public Employment*.

Public lands—These data refer to transactions which involve the disposal, under public land laws, of Federal public lands to non-Federal owners. In general, original entries and selections are applications to secure title to public lands which have been accepted as properly filed (i.e., allowed). Some types of applications, however, are not reported until issuance of the final certificate, which passes equitable title to the land to the applicant. Applications are approved when full compliance with the requirements of the laws is shown and become final entries (perfected entries) upon issuance of a final certificate. Patents are Government deeds which pass legal title to the land to the applicant. Certifications are issued in lieu of patents in connection with certain State selections.

Figure 10.2
Federal Budget Summary: 1945 to 1997

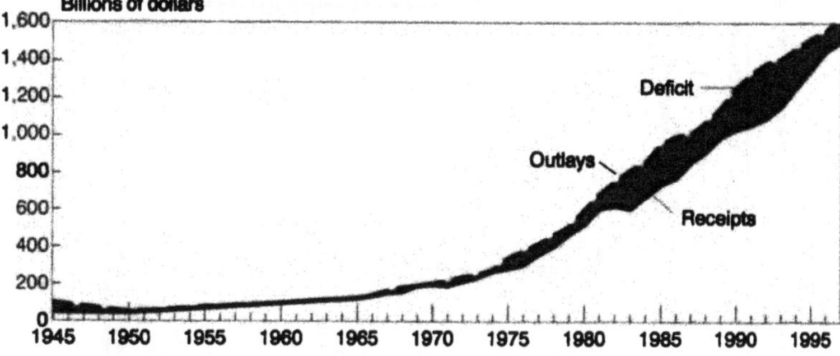

Outlays and debt as a percent of Gross Domestic Product

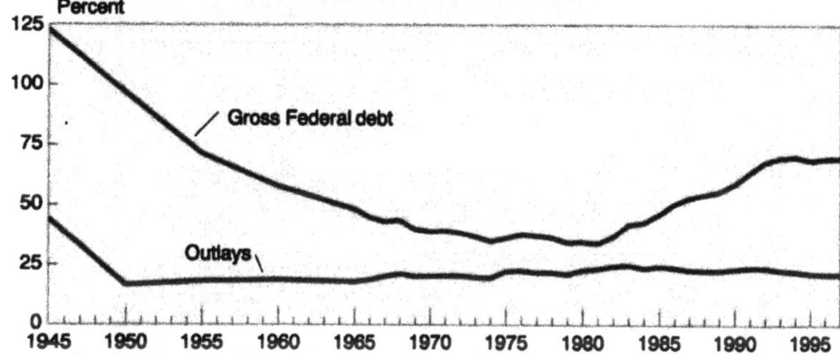

Gross Federal debt
Billions of dollars

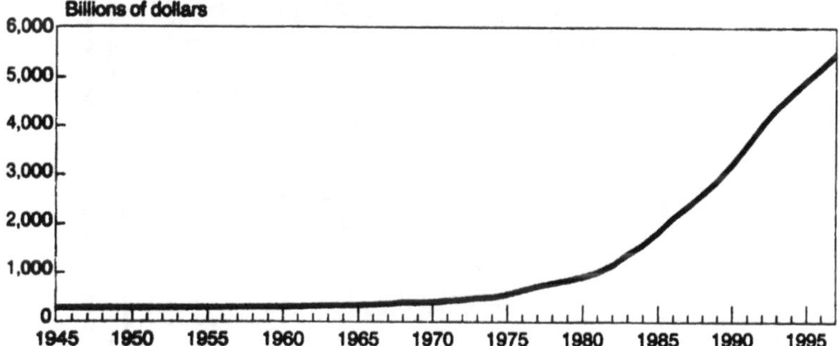

Source: Charts prepared by U.S. Bureau of the Census. For data, see table 515.

No. 515. Federal Budget—Summary: 1945 to 1997

[In millions of dollars, except percent. For fiscal years ending in year shown; see text, section 9. The Balanced Budget and Emergency Deficit Control Act of 1985 put all the previously off-budget Federal entities into the budget and moved Social Security off-budget. Minus sign (-) indicates deficit or decrease]

YEAR	Receipts [1]	OUTLAYS [1]				Surplus or deficit (-)	GROSS FEDERAL DEBT [3]					ANNUAL PERCENT CHANGE [4]			Outlays, off-budget
		Total	Human resources	National defense	Percent of GDP [2]		Total	Held by— Federal Gov't Account	The public: Total	The public: Federal Reserve System	As percent of GDP [2]	Receipts	Outlays	Gross Federal debt [3]	
1945	45,159	92,712	1,859	82,965	42.6	-47553	260,123	24,941	235,182	21,792	119.7	3.2	1.5	27.5	143
1950	39,443	42,562	14,221	13,724	15.6	-3119	256,853	37,830	219,023	18,331	94.2	0.1	9.6	1.7	524
1955	65,451	68,444	14,908	42,729	17.3	-2993	274,366	47,751	226,616	23,607	69.4	-6.0	-3.4	1.3	3,963
1960	92,492	92,191	26,184	48,130	17.8	301	290,525	53,686	236,840	26,523	56.1	16.7	0.1	1.1	10,850
1965	116,817	118,228	36,576	50,620	17.2	-1411	322,318	61,540	260,778	39,100	46.9	3.7	-0.3	2.0	16,529
1970	192,807	195,649	75,349	81,692	19.4	-2842	380,921	97,723	283,198	57,714	37.7	3.2	6.5	4.1	27,607
1973	230,799	245,707	119,522	76,681	18.8	-14908	466,291	125,381	340,910	75,181	35.7	11.3	6.5	7.0	45,589
1974	263,224	269,359	135,783	79,347	18.7	-6135	483,893	140,194	343,699	80,648	33.6	14.0	9.6	3.8	52,089
1975	279,090	332,332	173,245	86,509	21.4	-53242	541,925	147,225	394,700	84,993	34.9	6.0	23.4	12.0	60,440
1976	298,060	371,792	203,594	89,619	21.5	-73732	628,970	151,566	477,404	94,714	36.3	6.8	11.9	16.1	69,609
1976 [5]	81,232	95,975	52,065	22,269	21.1	-14744	643,561	148,052	495,509	96,702	35.4	(X)	(X)	(X)	19,421
1977	355,559	409,218	221,895	97,241	20.8	-53659	706,398	157,295	549,103	105,004	35.8	19.3	10.1	12.3	80,716
1978	399,561	458,746	242,329	104,495	20.7	-59186	776,602	169,477	607,125	115,480	35.1	12.4	12.1	9.9	89,657
1979	463,302	504,032	267,574	116,342	20.2	-40729	829,470	189,162	640,308	115,594	33.2	16.0	9.8	6.8	99,978
1980	517,112	590,947	313,374	133,995	21.7	-73835	909,050	199,212	709,838	120,846	33.4	11.6	17.2	9.6	114,329
1981	599,272	678,249	362,022	157,513	22.2	-78976	994,845	209,507	785,338	124,466	32.6	15.9	14.8	9.4	135,196
1982	617,766	745,755	388,681	185,309	23.2	-127989	1,137,345	217,560	919,785	134,497	35.4	3.1	10.0	14.3	151,404
1983	600,562	808,380	426,003	209,903	23.6	-207818	1,371,710	240,114	1,131,596	155,527	40.4	-2.8	8.4	20.6	147,108
1984	666,499	851,888	432,042	227,413	22.3	-185388	1,564,657	264,159	1,300,498	155,122	41.0	11.0	5.4	14.1	165,813
1985	734,165	946,499	471,822	252,748	23.1	-212334	1,817,521	317,612	1,499,908	169,806	44.3	10.1	11.1	16.2	176,807
1986	769,260	990,505	481,594	273,375	22.6	-221245	2,120,629	383,919	1,736,709	190,855	48.5	4.8	4.6	16.7	183,498
1987	854,396	1,004,164	502,196	281,999	21.8	-149769	2,346,125	457,444	1,888,680	212,040	50.9	11.1	1.4	10.6	193,832
1988	909,303	1,064,489	533,404	290,361	21.5	-155187	2,601,307	550,507	2,050,799	229,218	52.5	6.4	6.0	10.9	202,691
1989	991,190	1,143,671	568,668	303,559	21.4	-152481	2,868,039	678,157	2,189,882	220,088	53.6	9.0	7.4	10.3	210,911
1990	1,031,969	1,253,163	619,329	299,331	22.0	-221194	3,206,564	795,841	2,410,722	234,410	56.4	4.1	9.6	11.8	225,065
1991	1,055,041	1,324,400	689,668	273,292	22.6	-269359	3,598,498	910,362	2,688,137	258,591	61.4	2.2	5.7	12.2	241,687
1992	1,091,279	1,381,681	772,440	298,350	22.5	-290402	4,002,136	1,003,302	2,998,834	296,397	65.1	3.4	4.3	11.2	252,339
1993	1,154,401	1,409,414	827,535	291,086	21.8	-255013	4,351,416	1,103,945	3,247,471	325,653	67.2	5.8	2.0	8.7	266,587
1994	1,258,627	1,461,731	869,414	281,642	21.4	-203104	4,643,705	1,211,588	3,432,117	355,150	68.0	9.0	3.7	6.7	279,372
1995	1,351,830	1,515,729	923,765	272,066	21.1	-163899	4,921,018	1,317,645	3,603,373	374,114	68.5	7.4	3.7	6.0	288,664
1996	1,426,775	1,572,411	969,942	265,556	21.4	-145636	5,207,298	1,438,614	3,768,684	(NA)	71.0	5.5	3.7	5.8	302,119
1997, est.	1,505,425	1,631,016	1,019,395	267,176	20.8	-125591	5,453,677	1,577,902	3,875,775	(NA)	69.4	5.5	3.7	4.7	315,002

NA Not available. X Not applicable. [1] Includes off-budget receipts and outlays. [2] Gross domestic product as of fiscal year; for calendar year GDP, see section 14. [3] See text, section 10, for discussion of debt concept. [4] Change from previous year. For explanation of average annual percent see Guide to Tabular Presentation. [5] Represents transition quarter, July-Sept.

Source: U.S. Office of Management and Budget, *Historical Tables*, annual.

No. 516. Federal Receipts, by Source: 1980 to 1997

[In millions of dollars. For fiscal years ending in year shown; see text, section 9. Receipts reflect collections. Covers both Federal funds and trust funds; see text, section 10. Excludes government-sponsored but privately-owned corporations, Federal Reserve System, District of Columbia government, and money held in suspense as deposit funds]

SOURCE	1980	1985	1990	1994	1995	1996	1997, est.
Total receipts [1]	517,112	734,165	1,031,969	1,258,627	1,351,830	1,453,062	1,505,425
Individual income taxes	244,069	334,531	466,884	543,055	590,244	656,417	672,683
Corporation income taxes	64,600	61,331	93,507	140,385	157,004	171,824	176,199
Social insurance	157,803	265,163	380,047	461,475	484,473	509,414	535,766
Employment taxes and contributions	138,748	234,646	353,891	428,810	451,045	476,361	501,963
Old-age and survivors insurance (Off-udget)	96,581	169,822	255,031	302,607	284,091	311,869	334,139
Disability insurance (Off-Budget)	16,628	16,348	26,625	32,419	66,988	55,623	54,764
Hospital insurance	23,217	44,871	68,556	90,062	96,024	104,997	109,180
Railroad retirement/ pension fund	2,323	2,213	2,292	2,323	2,424	2,362	2,384
Railroad social security equivalent account	(X)	1,391	1,387	1,399	1,518	1,510	1,496
Unemployment insurance	15,336	25,758	21,635	28,004	28,878	28,584	29,465
Other retirement contributions	3,719	4,759	4,522	4,661	4,550	4,469	4,338
Excise taxes [1]	24,329	35,992	35,345	55,225	57,484	54,014	57,247
Federal funds	15,563	19,097	15,591	31,226	26,941	25,447	26,168
Alcohol	5,601	5,562	5,695	7,539	7,216	7,220	7,171
Tobacco	2,443	4,779	4,081	5,691	5,878	5,795	5,694
Crude oil windfall profit	6,934	6,348	(X)	(X)	(X)	(X)	(X)
Telephone	(X)	2,147	2,995	3,526	3,794	4,234	4,485
Ozone depleting chemicals/products	(X)	(X)	360	761	616	320	113
Transportation fuels	(X)	(X)	(X)	9,407	8,491	7,488	7,669
Aviation user fees	(X)	(X)	(X)	(X)	(X)	(X)	(X)
Trust funds [1]	8,766	16,894	19,754	23,999	30,543	28,567	31,079
Highways	6,620	13,015	13,867	16,668	22,611	24,651	24,882
Airport and airway	1,874	2,851	3,700	5,189	5,534	2,369	4,823
Black lung disability	272	581	665	567	608	614	604
Inland waterway	(X)	40	63	88	103	108	117
Hazardous substance superfund	(X)	273	818	807	867	313	147
Post closure liability (hazardous waste	(X)	7	-1	(X)	(X)	(X)	(X)
Oil spill liability	(X)	(X)	143	48	211	34	34
Aquatic resources	(X)	126	218	301	306	315	324
Leaking underground storage tank	(X)	(X)	122	152	165	48	23
Vaccine injury compensations	(X)	(X)	159	179	138	115	125
Estate and gift taxes	6,389	6,422	11,500	15,225	14,763	17,189	17,588
Customs duties	7,174	12,079	16,707	20,099	19,301	18,670	17,328
Federal Reserve deposits	11,767	17,059	24,319	18,023	23,378	20,477	23,184

(X) Not applicable. [1] Totals reflect interfund and intragovernmental transactions and/or other functions, not shown separately.

Source: U.S. Office of Management and Budget, *Historical Tables*, annual.

No. 517. Federal Trust Fund Receipts, Outlays, and Balances: 1993 to 1996

[In billions of dollars. For fiscal years ending in year shown; see text section 9. Receipts deposited. Outlays on a checks-issued basis less refunds collected. Balances: That which have not been spent. See text, section 10, for discussion of the budget concept and trust funds]

DESCRIPTION	INCOME			OUTLAYS			BALANCES [1]		
	1994	1995	1996	1994	1995	1996	1994	1995	1996
Total [2]	749	786	835	653	687	720	1,161	1,282	1,391
Airport and airway trust fund	6	6	3	7	7	7	12	12	8
Federal employees retirement funds	65	67	68	37	39	40	346	374	402
Federal old-age, survivors and disability insurance trust funds	378	399	418	321	338	352	423	483	550
Foreign military sales trust fund	13	13	15	13	13	14	6	6	6
Health insurance trust funds	164	173	206	163	180	197	151	144	152
Medicare: Hospital insurance	106	115	124	103	115	128	130	130	125
Supplemental medical insurance	57	58	82	60	65	69	21	14	27
Transportation	24	(NA)	(NA)	29	(NA)	(NA)	30	(NA)	(NA)
Surface transportation	18	24	26	22	23	23	18	19	22
Federal employees health benefits	16	16	16	16	16	16	8	8	7
Military retirement trust funds	35	35	33	27	28	29	120	127	131
Railroad retirement trust funds	11	12	9	11	11	8	12	14	14
Unemployment trust funds	34	33	32	31	25	26	40	48	54
Veterans life insurance trust funds	2	2	2	2	2	2	14	14	14
Other trust funds [3]	10	11	10	8	9	9	32	35	31

NA Not available. [1] Balances available on a cash basis (rather than an authorization basis) at the end of the year. Balances are primarily invested in Federal debt securities. [2] Includes funds not shown separately. [3] Effective August 9, 1989, the permanent insurance fund of the FDIC was classified under law as a Federal fund.

Source: U.S. Office of Management and Budget, *Analytical Perspectives*, annual.

No. 518. Federal Budget Outlays—Defense, Human and Physical Resources, and Net Interest Payments: 1940 to 1997

[In millions of dollars. For fiscal year ending in year shown. Minus sign (-) indicates offsets]

YEAR	Outlays, total	National defense	HUMAN RESOURCES							PHYSICAL RESOURCES			Net interest	Other	Undistributed offsets
			Total	Social Security	Income security	Medicare	Health	Education [1]	Veterans benefits	Total [2]	Transportation	Commerce and housing			
1940	9,468	1,660	4,139	28	1,514	(NA)	55	1,972	570	2,312	392	550	899	775	-317
1945	92,712	82,965	1,859	267	1,137	(NA)	211	134	110	1,747	3,654	-2630	3,112	4,418	-1,389
1950	42,562	13,724	14,221	781	4,097	(NA)	268	241	8,834	3,667	967	1,035	4,812	7,955	-1,817
1955	68,444	42,729	14,908	4,427	5,071	(NA)	291	445	4,675	2,732	1,246	92	4,850	6,718	-3,493
1960	92,191	48,130	26,184	11,602	7,378	(NA)	795	968	5,441	7,991	4,126	1,618	6,947	7,760	-4,820
1965	118,228	50,620	36,576	17,460	9,462	(NA)	1,791	2,140	5,716	11,264	5,763	1,157	8,591	17,066	-5,908
1966	134,532	58,111	43,257	20,694	9,671	64	2,543	4,363	5,916	13,410	5,730	3,245	9,386	16,911	-6,542
1967	157,464	71,417	51,272	21,725	10,253	2,748	3,351	6,453	6,735	14,674	5,936	3,979	10,268	17,126	-7,294
1968	178,134	81,926	59,375	23,854	11,806	4,649	4,390	7,634	7,043	16,002	6,316	4,280	11,090	17,786	-8,045
1969	183,640	82,497	66,410	27,298	13,066	5,695	5,162	7,548	7,631	11,869	6,526	-119	12,699	18,151	-7,986
1970	195,649	81,692	75,349	30,270	15,645	6,213	5,907	8,634	8,669	15,574	7,008	2,112	14,380	17,286	-8,632
1971	210,172	78,872	91,901	35,872	22,936	6,622	6,843	9,849	9,768	18,286	8,052	2,366	14,841	16,379	-10,107
1972	230,681	79,174	107,211	40,157	27,638	7,479	8,674	12,529	10,720	19,574	8,392	2,222	15,478	18,828	-9,583
1973	245,707	76,681	119,522	49,090	28,264	8,052	9,356	12,745	12,003	20,614	9,066	931	17,349	24,950	-13,409
1974	269,359	79,347	135,783	55,867	33,699	9,639	10,733	12,457	13,374	25,106	9,172	4,705	21,449	24,423	-16,749
1975	332,332	86,509	173,245	64,658	50,160	12,875	12,930	16,022	16,584	35,449	10,918	9,947	23,244	27,487	-13,602
1976	371,792	89,619	203,594	73,899	60,784	15,834	15,734	18,910	18,419	39,188	13,739	7,619	26,727	27,050	-14,386
1976 [3]	95,975	22,269	52,065	19,763	14,981	4,264	3,924	5,169	3,960	9,512	3,358	931	6,949	9,388	-4,206
1977	409,218	97,241	221,895	85,061	61,044	19,345	17,302	21,104	18,022	40,746	14,829	3,093	29,901	34,315	-14,879
1978	458,746	104,495	242,329	93,861	61,488	22,768	18,524	26,710	18,961	52,591	15,521	6,254	35,458	39,594	-15,720
1979	504,032	116,342	267,574	104,073	66,359	26,495	20,494	30,223	19,914	54,559	17,532	4,686	42,636	40,396	-17,476
1980	590,947	133,995	313,374	118,547	86,540	32,090	23,169	31,843	21,169	65,985	21,329	9,390	52,538	44,996	-19,942
1981	678,249	157,513	362,022	139,584	99,723	39,149	26,866	33,709	22,973	70,886	23,379	8,206	68,774	47,095	-28,041
1982	745,755	185,309	388,681	155,964	107,717	46,567	27,445	27,029	23,938	61,752	20,625	6,256	85,044	51,069	-26,099
1983	808,380	209,903	426,003	170,724	122,598	52,588	28,641	26,606	24,824	57,600	21,334	6,681	89,828	59,023	-33,976
1984	851,888	227,413	432,042	178,223	112,668	57,540	30,417	27,579	25,588	57,980	23,669	6,959	111,123	55,267	-31,957
1985	946,499	252,748	471,822	188,623	128,200	65,822	33,542	29,342	26,262	56,897	25,838	4,337	129,504	68,227	-32,698
1986	990,505	273,375	481,594	198,757	119,796	70,164	35,936	30,585	26,327	58,783	28,117	5,059	136,047	73,713	-33,007
1987	1,004,164	281,999	502,196	207,353	123,250	75,120	39,967	29,724	26,750	55,185	26,222	6,435	138,652	62,588	-36,455
1988	1,064,489	290,361	533,404	219,341	129,332	78,878	44,487	31,938	29,386	68,632	27,272	19,164	151,838	57,222	-36,967
1989	1,143,671	303,559	568,668	232,542	136,031	84,964	48,390	36,674	30,031	81,568	27,608	29,710	169,266	57,822	-37,212
1990	1,253,163	299,331	619,329	248,623	147,022	98,102	57,716	38,755	29,058	126,004	29,485	67,600	184,221	60,893	-36,615
1991	1,324,400	273,292	689,666	269,015	170,276	104,489	71,183	43,354	31,305	135,176	31,099	76,271	194,541	71,061	-39,356
1992	1,381,681	298,350	772,440	287,585	196,948	119,024	89,497	45,248	34,069	75,613	33,333	10,919	199,421	75,136	-39,280
1993	1,409,414	291,086	827,535	304,585	207,250	130,552	99,415	50,012	35,671	46,762	35,004	-21,853	198,811	82,606	-37,386
1994	1,461,731	281,642	869,414	319,565	214,031	144,747	107,122	46,307	37,585	70,575	38,066	-4,228	202,957	74,914	-37,772
1995	1,515,729	272,066	923,765	335,846	220,493	159,855	115,418	54,263	37,890	59,197	39,350	-17,808	232,169	72,967	-44,455
1996	1,560,330	265,748	958,254	349,676	225,989	174,225	119,378	52,001	36,985	64,054	39,565	-10,646	241,090	68,404	-37,620
1997, est.	1,631,016	267,176	1,019,395	367,713	238,855	194,256	127,630	51,291	39,650	68,032	39,262	-8,806	247,382	75,518	-46,487

NA Not available. [1] Also includes training, employment, and social services. [2] Includes outlays not shown separately. [3] Transition quarter, July to September.

Source: U. S. Office of Management and Budget, *Historical Tables*, annual.

No. 519. Federal Budget Outlays in Constant (1987) Dollars: 1980 to 1997

[Dollar amounts in billions of dollars. For fiscal years ending in year shown; see text, section 9. Given the inherent imprecision in deflating outlays, the data shown in constant dollars present a reasonable perspective—not precision. The deflators and the categories that are deflated are as comparable over time as feasible. See headnote, table 515. Minus sign (-) indicates offset]

OUTLAYS	1980	1985	1987	1988	1989	1990	1991	1992	1993	1994	1995	1996	1997, est.
Outlays, total	1,016.5	1,209.0	1,213.8	1,245.6	1,284.7	1,353.7	1,366.1	1,381.7	1,374.8	1,393.2	1,410.6	1,419.6	1,445.6
National defense	229.3	306.2	330.0	333.9	338.3	324.6	283.3	298.4	286.2	270.9	255.5	242.1	237.4
Nondefense outlays	786.2	902.7	883.8	911.7	946.4	1,029.1	1,082.8	1,083.3	1,088.5	1,122.4	1,155.2	1,177.5	1,208.1
Payments for individuals	484.5	564.3	583.7	595.5	608.0	632.3	671.8	727.6	761.1	781.2	810.9	826.4	851.3
Direct payments	-427.7	-499.1	-512.2	-521.2	-531.6	-548.9	-576.2	-615.5	-640.3	-652.6	-675.7	-692.3	-712.6
Grants to State and local govt's	-56.8	-65.2	-71.5	-74.2	-76.4	-83.4	-95.5	-112.2	-120.9	-128.5	-135.2	-134.1	-138.7
Other grants	98.8	70.2	58.7	59.5	59.6	61.1	62.9	65.6	67.6	72.5	74.3	73.3	76.4
Net interest	88.6	165.4	167.2	176.9	189.2	197.8	200.3	199.4	193.7	193.3	215.7	219.4	219.6
All other	149.4	145.4	119.2	123.6	131.7	177.9	188.3	130.0	101.6	109.9	93.3	89.9	96.8
Undistributed offsetting receipts	-35.0	-42.6	-44.9	-43.8	-42.1	-40.1	-40.4	-39.3	-35.7	-34.5	-39.1	-31.5	-37.9
PERCENT OF GDP													
Outlays, total	21.7	23.1	21.8	21.5	21.4	22.0	22.6	22.5	21.8	21.4	21.1	20.8	20.8
National defense	4.9	6.2	6.1	5.9	5.7	5.3	4.7	4.9	4.5	4.1	3.8	3.6	3.4
Nondefense outlays	16.8	16.9	15.7	15.6	15.7	16.8	17.9	17.6	17.3	17.3	17.3	17.3	17.4
Payments for individuals	10.2	10.4	10.2	10.1	10.0	10.3	11.1	11.8	12.1	12.0	12.2	12.2	12.3
Direct payments	-9.0	-9.2	-9.0	-8.8	-8.8	-8.9	-9.5	-10.0	-10.2	-10.1	-10.1	-10.2	-10.3
Grants to State and local govt's	-1.2	-1.2	-1.3	-1.3	-1.3	-1.4	-1.6	-1.8	-1.9	-2.0	-2.0	-2.0	-2.0
Other grants	2.2	1.4	1.1	1.1	1.0	1.0	1.1	1.1	1.1	1.1	1.1	1.1	1.1
Net interest	1.9	3.2	3.0	3.1	3.2	3.2	3.3	3.2	3.1	3.0	3.2	3.2	3.1
All other	3.2	2.8	2.1	2.1	2.2	2.9	3.1	2.1	1.6	1.7	1.4	1.4	1.4
Undistributed offsetting receipts	-0.7	-0.8	-0.8	-0.7	-0.7	-0.6	-0.7	-0.6	-0.6	-0.6	-0.6	-0.5	-0.6
PERCENT OF OUTLAYS													
Outlays, total	100.0	100.0	100.0	100.0	100.0	100.0	100.0	100.0	100.0	100.0	100.0	100.0	100.0
National defense	22.7	26.7	28.1	27.3	26.5	23.9	20.6	21.6	20.7	19.3	17.9	17.0	16.4
Nondefense outlays	77.3	73.3	71.9	72.7	73.5	76.1	79.4	78.4	79.3	80.7	82.1	83.0	83.6
Payments for individuals	47.1	45.1	46.9	47.0	46.9	46.6	49.1	52.7	55.5	56.2	57.7	58.3	59.0
Direct payments	-41.6	-39.9	-41.2	-41.2	-41.0	-40.5	-42.1	-44.5	-46.7	-47.0	-48.1	48.8	49.4
Grants to State and local govt's	-5.5	-5.2	-5.8	-5.9	-5.9	-6.2	-7.0	-8.1	-8.8	-9.3	-9.6	-9.5	-9.6
Other grants	9.9	6.0	5.0	5.0	4.7	4.6	4.7	4.7	4.9	5.1	5.2	5.1	5.4
Net interest	8.9	13.7	13.8	14.3	14.8	14.7	14.7	14.4	14.1	13.9	15.3	15.5	15.2
All other	14.8	12.0	9.8	9.9	10.3	13.1	13.9	9.4	7.5	8.0	6.7	6.5	6.9
Undistributed offsetting receipts	-3.4	-3.5	-3.6	-3.5	-3.3	-2.9	-3.0	-2.8	-2.7	-2.6	-2.9	-2.4	-2.9

Source: U.S. Office of Management and Budget, *Historical Tables*, annual.

No. 520. Federal Outlays, by Detailed Function: 1990 to 1997

[In millions of dollars. For fiscal years ending in year shown; outlays stated in terms of checks issued or cash payments. See headnote, table 519]

FUNCTION	1990	1993	1994	1995	1996	1997, est.
Total outlays	1,253,163	1,409,414	1,461,731	1,515,729	1,560,330	1,631,016
Legislative branch	2,241	2,406	2,552	2,625	2,273	2,531
The Judiciary	1,646	2,628	2,677	2,910	3,059	3,617
Funds appropriated to President [1]	10,087	11,526	10,511	11,161	9,713	9,736
Departments:						
Agriculture	46,012	63,144	60,753	56,665	54,344	56,954
Commerce	3,734	2,798	2,915	3,401	3,702	3,808
Defense-Military	289,755	278,574	268,646	259,556	253,253	254,284
Defense-Civil	24,975	29,266	30,407	31,669	32,536	33,873
Education	22,972	30,109	24,577	31,205	29,727	28,340
Energy	12,084	16,942	17,839	17,617	16,203	15,423
Health and Human Services	175,531	253,835	278,901	303,081	319,803	351,088
Housing and Urban Development	20,167	25,181	25,845	29,044	25,508	29,928
Interior	5,790	6,784	6,900	7,405	6,725	7,404
Justice	6,507	10,170	10,005	10,788	11,954	14,520
Labor [2]	25,215	44,651	37,047	32,090	32,492	32,874
State	3,979	5,384	5,718	5,344	4,951	5,487
Transportation	28,650	34,457	37,228	38,777	38,780	38,398
Treasury	255,172	298,804	307,577	348,579	364,629	380,569
Veterans Affairs	28,998	35,487	37,401	37,771	36,920	39,619
Independent agencies:						
Environmental Protection Agenc.	5,108	5,930	5,855	6,351	6,046	6,272
General Services Administration	-93	825	448	831	732	1,243
NASA [3]	12,429	14,305	13,695	13,378	13,881	13,687
Office of Personnel Management	31,949	36,794	38,596	41,276	42,870	44,838
Small Business Administration	692	785	779	677	873	460
Other independent agencies	72,608	-11,428	10,281	4,199	9,543	8,489
Undistributed offsetting receipts	-98,930	-119,711	-123,469	-137,628	-134,997	-150,537
Outlays, by function	1,253,163	1,409,414	1,461,731	1,515,729	1,560,330	1,631,016
National defense	299,331	291,086	281,642	272,066	265,748	267,176
Dept. of Defense—Military	289,755	278,561	268,622	259,442	253,187	254,272
Military personnel	75,622	75,904	73,137	70,809	66,669	70,063
Operation and maintenance	88,340	94,094	87,929	91,078	88,759	92,143
Procurement	80,972	69,936	61,769	54,982	48,913	45,575
R and D, test, and evaluation	37,458	36,968	34,762	34,594	36,494	36,034
Military construction	5,080	4,831	4,979	6,823	6,683	6,568
Family housing	3,501	3,255	3,316	3,571	3,828	4,352
Other	-1,218	-6,428	2,729	-2,415	1,841	-453
Atomic energy defense activities	8,988	11,017	11,892	11,777	11,639	11,939
Defense related activities	587	1,508	1,128	847	922	965
International affairs	13,764	17,248	17,083	16,434	13,496	14,822
International development and humanitarian assistance	5,498	5,827	7,049	7,599	6,180	6,498
Conduct of foreign affairs	3,050	4,325	4,557	4,192	3,761	4,080
Income security	147,076	207,299	214,069	220,493	225,989	236,865
General retirement and disability insurance	5,148	4,347	5,720	5,106	5,234	4,631
Federal employee retirement and disability	52,037	60,095	62,544	65,882	68,093	71,214
Housing assistance	15,891	21,542	23,884	27,520	26,754	29,046
Food and nutrition assistance	23,964	35,148	36,773	37,594	37,933	37,985
Other income security	31,146	48,366	56,439	60,753	63,077	70,862
Unemployment compensation	18,889	37,802	28,729	23,638	24,898	25,117
Health	57,716	99,415	107,122	115,418	119,378	127,630
Health care services	47,642	86,860	94,259	101,931	106,822	112,822
Health research	8,611	10,794	11,000	11,569	10,827	12,741
Consumer and occupational health and safety	1,462	1,762	1,863	1,918	1,929	2,067
Medicare	98,102	130,552	144,747	159,855	174,225	194,256
Social Security	248,623	304,585	319,565	335,846	349,676	367,713
Veterans benefits and services	29,058	35,671	37,585	37,890	36,985	39,650
Income security for veterans	15,241	17,758	19,613	18,966	18,201	20,540
Educ., training, and rehab.	278	826	1,115	1,124	1,114	1,079
Hospital and medical care	12,134	14,812	15,678	16,428	16,586	17,487
Housing for veterans	517	1,299	197	329	66	-517
Other	888	976	982	1,043	1,018	1,081

See footnotes at end of table.

. 520. Federal Outlays, by Detailed Function: 1990 to 1997—Continued

[In millions of dollars. See headnote, table 516]

FUNCTION	1990	1993	1994	1995	1996	1997, est.
ing, employment, services	38,755	50,012	46,307	54,263	52,001	51,291
secondary, and education	9,918	13,481	14,258	14,694	14,871	16,215
ion	11,107	14,483	7,876	14,172	12,191	9,154
d general educ. aids	1,577	2,040	2,086	2,120	2,215	2,283
employment	5,619	6,700	7,097	7,430	7,030	6,836
services	810	948	958	965	925	1,004
es	9,723	12,380	14,031	14,862	14,769	15,800
l housing credit	67,600	-21,853	-4,228	-17,808	-10,646	-8,808
edit	3,845	1,554	-501	-1,038	-4,753	-3,220
e	2,116	1,602	1,233	-1,839	-504	2,097
rance	57,891	-27,957	-7,570	-17,827	-8,394	-12,056
erce	3,748	2,949	2,609	2,896	3,005	4,371
	29,485	35,004	38,066	39,350	39,565	39,262
sportation	18,954	21,251	23,940	25,297	25,650	25,591
tion	7,234	10,049	10,146	10,020	10,135	9,929
ortation	3,151	3,423	3,648	3,732	3,460	3,418
ortation	146	281	333	301	320	324
es and environment	17,080	20,239	21,064	22,078	21,614	22,773
ces	4,401	4,258	4,528	4,791	4,617	5,008
and land management	3,553	4,777	5,161	5,318	5,396	5,920
resources	1,876	2,820	2,619	2,801	2,673	2,746
trol and abatement	5,170	6,061	6,050	6,512	6,180	6,448
l resources	2,080	2,522	2,706	2,656	2,746	2,651
	3,341	4,319	5,219	4,936	2,836	2,063
	1,976	3,286	3,899	3,584	1,646	1,220
	365	521	582	671	624	565
preparedness	442	336	275	223	141	31
policy, and regs	559	176	462	456	425	237
ional develop	8,498	9,052	10,454	10,641	10,685	12,752
development	3,530	3,681	4,133	4,744	4,860	5,611
gional development	2,868	2,443	2,166	2,615	2,667	2,966
f and insurance	2,100	2,928	4,156	3,282	3,158	4,173
	11,958	20,363	15,046	9,778	9,159	10,252
stabilization	9,761	17,720	12,350	7,020	6,477	7,474
d services	2,197	2,643	2,695	2,758	2,682	2,778
	184,221	198,811	202,957	232,169	241,090	247,362
	-200,212	*-225,599*	*-232,160*	*-265,474*	*-277,597*	*-288,620*
	-15,991	*-26,788*	*-29,203*	*-33,305*	*-36,507*	*-41,238*
e public debt	264,724	292,502	296,278	332,414	343,955	368,740
ived by on-budget	-46,321	-55,537	-56,494	-59,871	-60,869	-62,812
ived by off-budget	-15,991	-26,788	-29,203	-33,305	-36,507	-41,236
t	-18,191	-11,367	-7,623	-7,069	-5,489	-5,308
e/space/technology	14,444	17,030	16,227	16,724	16,709	16,551
and basic research	2,835	3,936	3,863	4,131	4,016	4,203
ment	10,734	13,009	11,303	13,835	11,892	13,109
nctions	1,763	2,124	2,042	1,995	1,965	2,032
on and management	160	197	244	248	252	299
l operations	6,004	6,976	7,417	7,936	7,459	7,543
perty and records ent	31	1,005	590	920	820	1,094
ose fiscal assistance	2,161	1,935	1,899	2,057	1,981	2,090
l government	792	1,321	987	1,622	1,006	1,082
offsetting receipts	-361	-739	-2,067	-1,077	1,694	-1,184
of justice	9,993	14,955	15,256	16,216	17,548	20,764
enforcement	4,848	6,674	6,624	6,384	7,022	8,520
tive and judicial	3,577	5,336	5,470	6,116	6,067	6,674
ectional activities	1,291	2,124	2,315	2,749	3,013	3,104
ce assistance	477	822	847	967	1,446	2,488
ffsetting receipts	*-36,615*	*-37,386*	*-37,772*	*-44,455*	*-37,620*	*-46,487*

ts international affairs funds mainly. [2] Includes Pension Benefit Guaranty Corporation. [3] National Aeronautics ministration.

S. Office of Management and Budget, *Budget of the United States Government*, annual.

No. 521. Tax Expenditures Estimates, by Function: 1996 to 1999

[In millions of dollars. For years ending, Sept. 30, except as noted. Tax expenditures are defined as *revenue losses* attributable to provisions of the Federal tax laws which allow a special exclusion, exemption, or deduction from gross income or which provide a special credit, a preferential rate of tax, or a deferral of liability. Represents tax expenditures of $2 billion or more in 1998]

PROVISION	1996	1997	1998	1999
National defense:				
Exclusion of benefits and allowances to Armed Forces personnel	2,060	2,080	2,095	2,120
International affairs:				
Exclusion of income earned abroad by United States citizens	1,520	1,680	1,865	2,065
Deferral of income from controlled foreign corps [1]	2,100	2,200	2,400	2,600
	10,525	11,210	11,940	12,715
Housing:				
Deductibility of mortgage interest on owner-occupied homes	47,525	49,820	52,115	54,440
Deductibility of state and local property tax on owner-occupied homes	15,900	16,670	17,435	18,215
Deferral of capital gains on home sales	14,410	14,845	15,290	15,745
Exclusion of capital gains on home sales for persons age 55 and over	5,225	5,230	5,095	5,515
Exception from passive loss rules for $25,000 of rental loss	3,950	3,700	3,470	3,280
Credit for low-income housing investments	2,600	2,840	3,270	3,500
Commerce:				
Capital gains (other than agriculture, timber, iron ore and coal) [1]	7,990	8,230	8,480	8,730
Step-up basis of capital gains at death	29,530	30,715	31,945	33,225
Accelerated depreciation of buildings other than rental housing [1]	6,800	5,800	4,660	3,420
Accelerated depreciation of machinery and equipment [1]	25,430	27,280	29,285	32,500
Graduated corporation income tax rate [1]	4,435	4,695	4,940	5,125
Education, training, employment, and social services:				
Education:				
Deductibility of charitable contributions (education)	1,865	1,960	2,060	2,165
Training, employment, and social services:				
Credit for child and dependent care expenses	2,580	2,705	2,840	2,985
Deductibility of charitable contributions, other than education and health	16,045	16,845	17,680	18,560
Health:				
Exclusion of employer contributions for medical insurance premiums and medical care	64,450	70,460	75,750	81,285
Deductibility of medical expenses	3,675	4,060	4,535	4,895
Deductibility of charitable contributions (health)	2,360	2,460	2,600	2,735
Income security:				
Exclusion of workmen's compensation benefits	4,695	4,970	5,305	5,550
Net exclusion of pension contributions and earnings:				
Employer plans	55,410	55,810	56,245	56,665
Individual Retirement Accounts	8,025	8,345	8,600	8,880
Keogh plans	3,030	3,200	3,325	3,500
Exclusion of other employee benefits:				
Premiums on group term life insurance	2,495	2,615	2,745	2,880
Earned income credit [2]	5,097	5,653	5,814	6,112
Social Security:				
Exclusion of social security benefits:				
OASI benefits for retired workers	17,005	17,810	18,495	19,290
Disability insurance benefits	2,090	2,375	2,615	2,820
Benefits for dependents and survivors	3,795	3,965	4,175	4,355
Veterans benefits and services:				
Exclusion of veterans disability compensation	2,615	2,770	2,930	3,100
General purpose fiscal assistance:				
Exclusion of interest on public purpose state and local debt	15,720	15,600	15,735	15,595
Deductibility of nonbusiness state and local taxes other than on owner-occupied homes	28,265	29,630	30,995	32,375
Tax credit for corporations receiving income from doing business in US possessions	2,760	2,700	2,770	2,800
Addendum—Aid to state and local governments:				
Deductibility of—				
Property taxes on owner-occupied homes	15,900	16,670	17,435	18,215
Nonbusiness state and local taxes other than on owner-occupied homes	28,265	29,630	30,995	32,375
Exclusion of interest on—				
Public purpose state and local debt	15,720	15,800	15,735	15,595

[1] Normal Tax method. [2] Indicates the effect of the earned income tax credit on receipts.

Source: U.S. Office of Management and Budget, *Analytical Perspectives*, annual.

No. 522. United States Government—Balance Sheet: 1985 to 1996

[In millions of dollars. For fiscal year ending in year shown]

ITEM	1985	1990	1994	1995	1996
Assets, total	**55,204**	**70,415**	**72,914**	**89,349**	**103,159**
Cash and monetary assets, total	39,839	60,839	71,379	84,090	86,056
U.S. Treasury operating cash:					
Federal Reserve account	4,174	7,638	6,848	8,620	7,700
Tax and loan note accounts	12,886	32,517	29,094	29,329	36,525
Special drawing rights (SDR):					
Total holdings	6,847	10,666	9,971	11,036	10,177
SDR's certificates issued to Federal Reserve banks	-4,618	-8,518	-8,018	-10,168	-9,718
Monetary assets with IMF [1]	11,678	8,883	12,069	14,682	15,428
Other cash and monetary assets:					
U.S. Treasury monetary assets	1,310	1,572	415	356	87
Cash and other assets held outside the Treasury Account	7,558	8,079	20,638	29,697	21,133
U.S. Treasury time deposits	(NA)	(NA)	362	528	4,724
Loan financing accounts:					
Guaranteed loans	(NA)	(NA)	-9,806	-12,714	-14,022
Direct loans	(NA)	(NA)	12,726	19,732	32,780
Miscellaneous asset accounts	(NA)	9,576	-1,385	-1,748	-1,655
Total assets and excess of liabilities over assets	1,567,780	2,479,165	3,494,792	3,674,266	3,794,738
Excess of liabilities over assets at beginning of fiscal year	1,301,228	2,188,926	3,219,491	3,421,723	3,584,917
Add: Total deficit for fiscal year	211,931	220,388	203,102	163,916	107,277
Subtotal	(NA)	(NA)	(NA)	3,585,639	3,692,194
Deduct: Other transactions not applied to surplus or deficit	582	564	722	722	615
Excess of liabilities over assets at close of fiscal year	1,512,576	2,408,750	3,421,878	3,584,917	3,691,579
Liabilities, total	**1,567,780**	**2,479,165**	**3,494,792**	**3,674,266**	**3,794,738**
Borrowing from the public, total	1,509,857	2,470,166	3,432,050	3,603,299	3,732,957
Public debt securities outstanding	1,623,103	3,233,313	4,692,752	4,973,985	5,224,812
Premium and discount on public debt securities	(NA)	59,811	-77,298	-79,996	-77,932
Total public debt securities	(NA)	(NA)	4,615,453	4,893,989	5,146,880
Agency securities outstanding	4,366	32,758	28,185	26,955	35,043
Federal securities, total	(NA)	3,266,073	4,643,638	4,920,944	5,181,923
Deduct: Net Federal securities held as investments by Government accounts	(NA)	795,907	1,211,588	1,317,645	1,448,967
Accrued interest payable	26,709	43,799	43,287	50,611	45,605
Special drawing rights allocated by IMF [1]	5,191	6,823	7,189	7,380	7,052
Deposit fund liabilities	14,385	8,306	7,327	8,186	7,218
Miscellaneous liability accounts (checks outstanding, etc.)	11,639	9,882	4,813	4,790	1,906

NA Not available. [1] IMF = International Monetary Funds.

Source: U.S. Dept of Treasury, *United States Government Annual Report.*

No. 523. Direct Loan Transactions and Primary Guaranteed Loans: 1994 to 1996

DIRECT LOAN TRANSACTIONS	1994	1995	1996	PRIMARY GUARANTEED LOANS [1]	1994	1995	1996
Obligations	22,702	30,901	23,387	Commitments	204,142	138,272	174,430
Loan disbursements	19,281	21,982	23,566	New guaranteed loans	194,221	117,875	143,885
Change in outstandings	-800	1,626	3,978	Change in outstandings	38,678	26,170	89,887
Outstandings	**159,211**	**163,323**	**166,534**	**Outstandings**	**696,813**	**726,770**	**806,104**

[1] When guaranteed loans result in loans receivable, they are shown in direct loans.

Source: U.S. Office of Management and Budget, *Budget of the United States Government*, annual.

No. 524. Summary of Federal Debt: 1985 to 1995

[In millions of dollars. Based on end of fiscal year]

ITEM	1985	1990	1993	1994	1995
Debt outstanding, total	**1,827,470**	**3,266,073**	**4,436,171**	**4,721,293**	**5,000,945**
Public debt securities	1,823,103	3,233,313	4,411,489	4,692,750	4,973,983
Agency securities	4,366	32,758	24,682	28,543	26,962
Securities held by—					
Government accounts, total	317,612	795,907	1,116,713	1,213,115	1,320,800
Public debt securities	316,545	795,762	1,116,693	1,213,098	1,320,784
Agency securities	1,067	145	21	17	16
The public, total	1,509,857	2,470,166	3,319,458	3,508,178	3,680,145
Public debt securities	1,506,558	2,437,551	3,294,796	3,479,652	3,653,199
Agency securities	3,299	32,613	24,661	28,526	26,946
Interest-bearing public debt, total	**1,821,010**	**3,210,943**	**4,408,567**	**4,669,524**	**4,950,644**
Marketable, total	1,360,179	2,092,759	2,904,910	3,091,602	3,260,447
Treasury bills	384,220	482,454	658,381	697,295	742,462
Treasury notes	776,449	1,218,081	1,734,161	1,867,507	1,980,343
Treasury bonds	199,510	377,224	497,367	511,800	522,643
Nonmarketable, total	460,831	1,118,184	1,503,657	1,597,922	1,690,197
U.S. savings bonds	77,011	122,152	167,024	176,413	181,181
Foreign series: Government	6,638	36,041	42,459	41,996	40,950
Government account series, total	313,928	779,412	1,114,289	1,211,689	1,324,270
Airport and airway trust fund	7,410	14,312	12,672	12,206	11,145
Bank insurance fund	16,130	8,438	4,325	13,972	20,117
Employees life insurance fund	6,312	9,561	13,576	14,929	15,839
Exchange stabilization fund	2,073	1,863	5,637	7,326	2,399
Federal disability insurance trust fund	5,443	11,254	10,162	6,025	35,150
Federal employees retirement funds	127,253	223,229	301,711	329,602	357,539
Federal hospital insurance trust fund	20,721	96,249	126,078	128,716	129,864
Federal Housing Administration	3,485	6,678	5,360	5,933	6,277
Fed. old-age & survivors insurance trust fund	30,968	203,717	355,510	413,425	447,947
Fed. S&L Corp., resolution fund	4,953	929	828	1,649	528
Fed. supplementary medical insur. trust fund	10,736	14,286	23,269	21,489	13,513
Government life insurance fund	269	184	125	114	106
Highway trust fund	9,422	9,530	11,475	7,751	8,954
National service life insurance fund	9,296	10,917	11,666	11,852	11,954
Postal Service fund	2,362	3,063	3,826	1,270	1,249
Railroad retirement account	4,232	8,356	10,457	10,596	12,129
Treasury deposit funds	681	304	147	130	130
Unemployment trust fund	16,454	50,186	36,563	39,745	47,098
Other	35,728	106,376	180,883	184,959	202,332
State and local government series	62,778	161,248	149,449	137,386	113,368
Domestic series	(X)	18,886	29,995	29,995	29,995
Other	477	447	442	445	432
MATURITY DISTRIBUTION					
Amount outstanding, priva	**1,185,675**	**1,841,903**	**2,562,336**	**2,719,861**	**2,870,781**
Maturity class:					
Within 1 year	472,661	626,297	858,135	877,932	1,002,875
1-5 years	402,766	630,144	978,714	1,128,322	1,157,492
5-10 years	159,383	267,573	306,663	289,998	290,111
10-20 years	62,853	82,713	94,345	88,208	87,297
20 years and over	88,012	235,176	324,479	335,401	333,006

X Not applicable.

Source: U.S. Department of the Treasury, *Treasury Bulletin*, quarterly.

No. 525. U.S. Savings Bonds: 1980 to 1995

[In billions of dollars, except percent. As of end of fiscal year, see text, section 9]

ITEM	1980	1985	1987	1988	1989	1990	1991	1992	1993	1994	1995
Amounts outstanding, total [1]	73	77	97	107	114	123	134	149	167	177	182
Funds from sales	5	5	10	7	8	8	9	14	17	9	7
Accrued discounts	4	5	6	8	8	8	10	9	9	9	9
Redemptions [2]	17	6	5	6	7	8	8	7	8	9	12
Percent of total outstanding	23.0	7.4	5.1	5.6	6.3	6.1	5.6	5.0	4.7	5.3	6.5

[1] Interest-bearing debt only for amounts end of year. [2] Matured and unmatured bonds.

Source: U.S. Dept. of the Treasury, *Treasury Bulletin*, quarterly.

No. 528. Federal Funds—Summary Distribution, by State: 1996

[In millions of dollars. For year ending Sept. 30. Data for grants, salaries and wages and direct payments to individuals are on an expenditures basis; procurement is on obligation basis]

REGION, DIVISION, AND STATE	FEDERAL FUNDS		Defense	Non-defense	Direct payments to individuals	Procure-ment	Grants to State and local govern-ments	Salaries and wages
	Total [1]	Per capita [2] (dol.)						
U.S. [3]	1,394,057	5,180	232,297	1,161,759	749,273	200,843	227,572	169,731
Northeast	271,792	5,269	28,070	243,722	158,566	27,101	55,178	22,687
New England	74,613	5,588	12,295	62,317	39,670	11,500	13,990	6,348
Maine	6,808	5,477	1,328	5,480	3,654	907	1,389	722
New Hampshire	5,001	4,304	836	4,165	2,842	672	890	448
Vermont	2,775	4,711	324	2,451	1,486	295	641	270
Massachusetts	36,456	5,984	5,686	30,770	18,731	6,081	6,814	2,857
Rhode Island	5,658	5,715	776	4,881	3,266	423	1,176	634
Connecticut	17,915	5,472	3,345	14,570	9,692	3,123	3,080	1,418
Middle Atlantic	197,179	5,158	15,775	181,405	118,896	15,601	41,188	16,338
New York	94,667	5,206	5,342	89,325	54,035	6,320	24,563	7,157
New Jersey	38,346	4,800	4,154	34,193	23,869	3,750	6,507	3,556
Pennsylvania	64,166	5,322	6,279	57,887	40,973	5,531	10,118	5,625
Midwest	279,574	4,603	31,014	248,559	166,059	28,248	46,732	25,871
East North Central	184,831	4,238	14,222	170,608	117,114	13,189	32,542	16,178
Ohio	50,143	4,488	5,171	44,971	31,166	4,583	8,778	4,612
Indiana	24,215	4,146	2,573	21,642	15,096	2,090	3,657	1,970
Illinois	51,229	4,324	3,281	47,948	31,744	3,165	9,232	5,440
Michigan	39,286	4,095	2,185	37,101	26,183	2,189	7,196	2,778
Wisconsin	19,958	3,868	1,012	18,948	12,925	1,162	3,679	1,377
West North Central	94,743	5,130	16,792	77,951	48,945	15,059	14,190	9,693
Minnesota	18,857	4,048	1,437	17,420	10,694	1,535	3,536	1,655
Iowa	13,408	4,701	646	12,762	7,687	778	2,030	944
Missouri	35,094	6,549	10,828	24,266	15,667	10,594	4,091	3,185
North Dakota	3,570	5,544	554	3,016	1,656	210	734	644
South Dakota	3,872	5,290	375	3,497	1,971	249	867	534
Nebraska	7,595	4,596	1,088	6,507	4,216	585	1,232	1,031
Kansas	12,347	4,800	1,864	10,483	7,054	1,110	1,700	1,700
South	511,446	5,494	99,080	412,366	269,977	78,132	70,788	79,546
South Atlantic	288,307	6,055	62,947	225,361	145,223	45,962	34,276	52,842
Delaware	3,363	4,639	442	2,922	2,096	154	800	411
Maryland	37,040	7,303	7,463	29,578	14,491	8,522	3,545	7,324
District of Columbia	22,475	41,391	2,493	19,982	2,596	4,580	2,578	11,304
Virginia	50,301	7,536	21,796	28,504	18,562	14,529	3,404	12,322
West Virginia	10,059	5,509	476	9,583	6,407	514	2,089	815
North Carolina	32,771	4,475	5,911	26,860	19,453	2,293	5,227	4,896
South Carolina	18,401	4,975	3,300	15,101	10,336	2,505	3,033	2,203
Georgia	34,731	4,723	8,400	26,331	17,933	4,741	5,359	5,904
Florida	79,166	5,496	12,666	66,500	53,349	8,126	8,442	7,660
East South Central	85,768	5,297	12,216	73,552	48,593	11,585	13,911	9,613
Kentucky	19,618	5,051	2,544	17,074	11,289	2,005	3,365	2,442
Tennessee	27,557	5,180	2,271	25,286	15,497	4,317	4,477	2,702
Alabama	23,409	5,478	4,083	19,326	13,616	2,937	3,325	2,896
Mississippi	15,184	5,591	3,318	11,866	8,191	2,326	2,754	1,571
West South Central	137,371	4,690	23,917	113,453	76,161	17,585	22,800	17,090
Arkansas	12,076	4,811	996	11,077	7,984	453	2,131	1,037
Louisiana	22,117	5,083	2,421	19,696	12,575	2,066	4,735	2,084
Oklahoma	16,685	5,055	2,957	13,728	9,880	1,205	2,435	2,721
Texas	86,493	4,522	17,541	68,952	45,723	13,840	13,299	11,249
West	295,708	5,083	60,239	235,469	148,436	50,427	47,871	39,187
Mountain	82,486	5,118	15,445	67,040	40,108	15,658	12,330	11,429
Montana	4,973	5,658	397	4,576	2,416	263	964	632
Idaho	5,476	4,606	482	4,994	2,865	945	887	630
Wyoming	2,515	5,228	328	2,187	1,195	153	708	395
Colorado	20,009	5,234	5,112	14,897	8,814	4,656	2,410	3,235
New Mexico	12,073	7,048	1,879	10,194	4,429	3,676	1,942	1,686
Arizona	21,819	4,927	4,837	16,981	12,269	3,485	3,095	2,523
Utah	8,193	4,097	1,344	6,849	3,919	1,072	1,446	1,478
Nevada	7,428	4,634	1,066	6,362	4,201	1,407	876	850
Pacific	213,222	5,028	44,794	168,428	108,327	34,768	35,541	27,758
Washington	29,246	5,286	6,246	23,000	14,838	4,603	4,152	4,574
Oregon	14,173	4,423	736	13,437	8,798	610	2,797	1,410
California	157,446	4,939	33,091	124,355	80,432	27,724	26,415	18,038
Alaska	4,341	7,151	1,462	2,878	1,021	804	1,051	1,327
Hawaii	8,016	6,771	3,259	4,758	3,238	1,027	1,126	2,409

[1] Includes other programs not shown separately. [2] Based on 1996 population estimates. [3] Includes Outlying Areas, not shown separately.

Source: U.S. Bureau of the Census, *Federal Expenditures by State for Fiscal Year*, annual.

No. 527. Tax Returns Filed—Examination Coverage: 1988 to 1995

[In thousands, except as indicated. Return classification as Schedule C or C-EZ (nonfarm sole proprietorships) or Schedule F (farm proprietorships) for audit examination purposes was based on the largest source of income on the return and certain other characteristics. Therefore, some returns with business activity are reflected in the nonbusiness individual income tax return statistics in the table below (and vise versa), so that the statistics for the number of returns with Schedule C is not comparable to the number of nonfarm sole proprietorship returns in table 836. Series completely revised starting with fiscal year 1988; data not comparable to earlier years]

YEAR AND ITEM	Returns filed [1]	RETURNS EXAMINED					AVERAGE TAX AND PENALTY PER RETURN (Dollars)		
		Total	Percent coverage	By— Revenue agents	By— Tax auditors	By— Service centers [2]	Revenue agents [3]	Tax auditors	Service centers
INDIVIDUAL RETURNS									
1988	103,251	1,621	1.57	353	532	736	997,696	2,188	1,950
1989	107,029	1,385	1.29	243	543	599	246,371	1,827	1,649
1990	109,868	1,145	1.04	202	517	426	309,566	1,962	2,432
1991 [4]	112,305	1,313	1.17	200	500	613	864,440	2,398	2,738
1992 [4]	113,829	1,206	1.06	210	537	459	1,365,896	2,280	2,539
1993 [4]	114,719	1,059	0.92	251	506	303	103,250	2,825	2,974
1994 [4]	113,754	1,226	1.08	364	456	406	246,785	3,113	1,983
1995 [4]									
Individual, Total	114,683	1,919	1.67	339	459	1,122	204,616	3,497	1,404
1040A, TPI under $25,000 [5]	46,617	913	1.96	84	151	678	17,776	3,491	1,408
Non 1040, TPI under $25,000 [5]	12,997	170	1.3	28	55	86	21,702	1,921	1,419
TPI $25,000 under $50,000 [5]	27,096	245	0.9	33	88	123	5,304	2,061	525
TPI $50,000 under $100,000 [5]	15,862	166	1.05	25	54	87	7,616	2,581	579
TPI $100,000 and over [5]	4,082	114	2.79	37	26	52	247,520	5,854	3,269
Sch C—TGR under $25,000 [6]	2,505	147	5.85	50	45	52	5,388	4,509	2,320
Sch C—TGR $25,000 under $100,000	3,026	93	3.08	40	27	26	1,155,872	6,663	1,866
Sch C—TGR $100,000 and over [6]	1,699	59	3.47	37	10	12	183,636	10,938	3,195
Sch F—TGR under $100,000 [6]	523	6	1.23	2	2	2	24,356	1,836	714
Sch F—TGR $100,000 and over [6]	278	7	2.51	3	1	3	99,248	4,463	1,651
Corporation (except S Corporation)	2,530	52	2.05	50	(NA)	2	4,943,935	(NA)	14,952
Fiduciary	3,088	4	0.14	1	(NA)	3	155,227	(NA)	503
Estate	80	11	14.2	11	(NA)	0.2	79,373	(NA)	12,657
Gift	216	2	0.88	2	(NA)	0.001	5,084,067	(NA)	(NA)
Employment	29,298	54	0.18	49	5	0.2	163,831	1,829	625
Excise	823	31	3.72	29	2	0.005	101,164	829	419
Windfall Profit	(NA)	0.04	(NA)	0.03	(NA)	0.003	136,843	(NA)	303
Misc. Taxable	(NA)	0.5	(NA)	0.5	(NA)	0.06	502,856	(NA)	1,148
Partnerships	1,539	7	0.46	5	(NA)	2	(NA)	(NA)	(NA)
S Corporations (nontaxable)	2,037	19	0.92	18	(NA)	1	(NA)	(NA)	(NA)
Miscellaneous Nontaxable [7]	(NA)	0.7	(NA)	0.07	(NA)	(NA)	(NA)	(NA)	(NA)

NA Not available. [1] Returns filed in previous calender year. [2] Includes taxpayer contacts by correspondence. [3] Mostly reflects coordinated examination of large corporations and related returns. [4] Includes activities to protect release of funds in Treasury in response to taxpayer efforts to recoup tax previously assessed and paid with penalty. [5] Total positive income, i.e., excludes losses. [6] Total gross receipts. [7] Includes Domestic International Sales Corporations, Interest-Charge Domestic International Sales Corporations, Real Estate Investment Morgage Conduits, and other.

Source: U.S. Internal Revenue Service, *IRS Data Book, 1995* Publication 55B

No. 528. Internal Revenue Gross Collections, by Source: 1980 to 1995

[For fiscal year ending in year shown; see text, section 9]

SOURCE OF REVENUE	COLLECTIONS (bil. dol.) 1980	1985	1990	1994	1995	PERCENT OF TOTAL 1980	1985	1990	1994	1995
All taxes	519	743	1,066	1,276	1,389	100.0	100.0	100.0	100.0	100.0
Individual income taxes	288	397	540	620	676	54.9	53.4	51.1	48.9	48.7
Withheld by employers	224	299	388	460	534	43.1	40.2	36.8	36.1	38.5
Employment taxes [1]	128	225	367	444	465	24.7	30.2	34.8	34.8	33.5
Old-age and disability insurance	123	216	358	434	455	23.6	29.0	33.8	34.0	32.8
Unemployment insurance	3	6	6	6	6	0.6	0.8	0.5	0.5	0.4
Corporation income taxes	72	77	110	154	174	13.9	10.4	10.4	12.1	12.5
Estate and gift taxes	7	7	12	16	15	1.3	0.9	1.1	1.3	1.1
Excise taxes	25	37	27	43	57	4.7	5.0	2.6	3.4	4.1

[1] Includes railroad retirement, not shown separately.

Source: U.S. Internal Revenue Service, *Annual Report*, and Bureau of Alcohol, Tobacco, and Firearms, *Alcohol and Tobacco Tax Collections*.

No. 529. Federal Individual Income Tax Returns With Adjusted Gross Income (AGI)—Summary: 1980 to 1994

[Includes Puerto Rico and Virgin Islands. Includes returns of resident aliens, based on a sample of unaudited returns as filed. Data are not comparable for all years because of tax changes and other changes, as indicated. See *Statistics of Income, Individual Income Tax Returns* publications for a detailed explanation. See Appendix III]

ITEM	NUMBER OF RETURNS (1,000)				AMOUNT (mil. dol.)				AVERAGE AMOUNT (dollars)			
	1980	1985	1990	1994	1980	1985	1990	1994	1980	1985	1990	1994
Total returns	93,902	101,660	113,717	115,943	1,613,731	2,305,951	3,405,427	3,907,518	17,185	22,683	29,947	33,702
Form 1040	57,123	67,006	69,270	66,391	1,310,068	1,938,263	2,772,625	3,056,958	22,935	28,927	40,026	46,045
Salaries and wages	83,802	87,198	96,730	99,356	1,349,843	1,928,201	2,599,401	3,026,778	16,108	22,113	26,873	30,464
Interest received	49,020	64,526	70,370	65,340	102,009	182,109	227,084	126,169	2,081	2,822	3,227	1,931
Dividends in AGI	10,739	15,528	22,904	25,236	38,761	55,046	80,169	82,410	3,609	3,545	3,500	3,266
Business or profession profit less loss	8,881	11,900	11,222	15,944	55,129	78,773	141,430	166,204	6,207	6,620	12,603	10,424
Sales of capital assets, net gain less loss, in AGI	9,971	11,126	14,288	18,823	30,029	67,694	114,231	142,288	3,012	6,084	7,995	7,559
Pensions and annuities in AGI	7,374	13,133	17,041	17,894	43,340	95,096	159,294	205,423	5,878	7,241	9,348	11,480
Rents and royalties, net income less loss	8,208	9,964	10,317	10,126	4,105	-10946	-3156	15,967	500	-1099	-306	1,577
Partnerships and S Corporations [1], profit less loss	3,910	5,488	5,977	5,590	10,099	-2527	67,022	114,386	2,583	-460	11,213	20,464
Farm profit less loss	2,608	2,621	2,321	2,242	-1792	-12005	-434	-7378	-687	-4580	-187	-3290
Statutory adjustments, total	13,149	37,763	16,648	17,859	28,614	95,082	33,974	39,103	2,176	2,518	2,041	2,190
Individual Retirement Arrangements	2,564	16,206	5,224	4,319	3,431	38,212	9,858	8,389	1,338	2,358	1,887	1,942
Self-employed retirement (Keogh) plan	569	676	824	996	2,008	5,182	6,778	8,195	3,529	7,666	8,226	8,229
Married couples who both work	(NA)	24,835	(NA)	(NA)	(NA)	24,615	(NA)	(NA)	(NA)	991	(NA)	(NA)
Exemptions, total [2]	227,925	244,180	227,549	232,716	227,569	253,720	485,985	562,559	998	1,039	2,135	2,417
Age 65 or older	11,847	16,749	(NA)	(NA)	(NA)	(NA)	(NA)	(NA)	(NA)	(NA)	(NA)	(NA)
Blind	185	327	(NA)	(NA)	(NA)	(NA)	(NA)	(NA)	(NA)	(NA)	(NA)	(NA)
Standard and itemized deductions, total [3]	88,105	96,849	112,796	114,965	362,776	554,734	789,942	890,760	4,118	5,728	7,003	7,748
Itemized deductions, total [3]	28,950	39,848	32,175	33,018	218,028	405,024	458,485	493,654	7,531	10,164	14,250	14,951
Medical and dental expenses	19,458	10,777	5,091	5,229	14,972	22,926	21,457	26,378	769	2,127	4,215	5,044
Taxes paid	28,749	39,548	31,594	32,569	69,404	128,065	140,011	175,848	2,414	3,239	4,432	5,399
Interest paid	26,677	36,287	29,395	27,873	91,187	180,095	208,354	197,240	3,418	4,963	7,088	7,076
Contributions	26,601	36,162	29,230	29,849	25,810	47,963	57,243	70,545	970	1,326	1,958	2,363
Taxable income [4]	88,105	96,124	93,148	92,793	1,279,985	1,820,741	2,263,661	2,597,960	14,528	18,942	24,302	27,998
Income tax before credits	76,136	85,994	93,089	92,702	256,294	332,165	453,128	541,571	3,366	3,863	4,868	5,842
Tax credits, total [2] [5]	19,674	20,995	12,484	15,042	7,216	10,248	6,831	8,927	367	488	547	594
Child care	4,231	8,418	6,144	6,012	956	3,128	2,549	2,526	226	372	415	420
Elderly and disabled	562	463	339	222	135	109	61	47	240	235	180	210
Residential energy	4,670	2,979	(NA)	(NA)	562	812	(NA)	(NA)	120	273	(NA)	(NA)
Foreign tax	393	454	772	1,546	1,342	783	1,682	2,309	3,415	1,725	2,179	1,494
General business credit [6]	(NA)	4,614	263	301	(NA)	4,791	616	690	(NA)	1,038	2,342	2,291
Income tax, total [7]	73,906	82,846	89,862	87,619	250,341	325,710	447,127	534,856	3,387	3,932	4,976	6,104

NA Not available. [1] S Corporations are certain small corporations with up to 35 shareholders (25 for 1982; 15 for 1980-81; 10 for 1970-75), mostly individuals, electing to be taxed at the shareholder level. [2] Includes items not shown separately. Beginning 1991, total exemptions amount is after limitation. [3] For 1985, includes charitable deduction for nonitemizers. Starting 1989, includes additional standard deductions for age 65 or older for blindness. Beginning 1991, total itemized deductions are after limitation. [4] For 1980 and 1985, includes amounts "taxed" at zero percent. [5] For 1981, includes tax reduction credit. [6] Investment credit was included in the more-inclusive general business tax credit starting with 1984. With exceptions, investment credit was repealed effective 1986. [7] Includes minimum tax or alternative minimum tax.

Source: U.S. Internal Revenue Service, *Statistics of Income Bulletin*, and *Statistics of Income, Individual Income Tax Returns*, annual.

No. 530. Individual Income Tax Returns—Number, Income Tax, and Average Tax, by Size of Adjusted Gross Income: 1993 and 1994

[Number in thousands; money amounts in billions of dollars, except as indicated]

SIZE OF ADJUSTED GROSS INCOME	NUMBER OF RETURNS		ADJUSTED GROSS INCOME (AGI)		TAXABLE INCOME		INCOME TAX TOTAL [1]		TAX AS PERCENT OF AGI [2]		AVERAGE TAX ($1,000) [2]	
	1993	1994, prel.	1993	1994, prel.	1993	1994, prel.	1993	1994, prel.	1993	1994, prel.	1993	1994, prel.
Total	114,602	115,943	3,723.3	3,907.5	2,453.5	2,598.0	502.8	534.9	13.5	14.3	5.8	6.1
Less than $1,000 [3]	3,550	3,342	-50.7	-52.2	0.1	0.1	0.1	0.1	-0.2	-2.9	0.2	0.2
$1,000-$2,999	6,472	6,389	12.8	12.8	0.7	0.7	0.1	0.1	0.9	4.7	0.1	0.1
$3,000-$4,999	5,748	5,854	22.9	23.5	1.3	1.3	0.2	0.2	1.0	2.9	0.2	0.1
$5,000-$6,999	5,826	5,577	35.0	33.5	2.9	2.9	0.4	0.4	1.3	4.3	0.2	0.3
$7,000-$8,999	5,964	5,840	47.6	46.8	7.2	7.1	1.1	1.0	2.4	3.7	0.3	0.3
$9,000-$10,999	5,701	5,496	56.9	54.9	12.5	11.3	1.8	1.7	3.3	5.4	0.6	0.5
$11,000-$12,999	5,496	5,401	65.9	64.8	18.4	17.3	2.6	2.4	4.0	6.2	0.8	0.7
$13,000-$14,999	5,210	5,385	72.7	75.2	24.4	24.2	3.2	3.2	4.4	6.5	0.9	0.9
$15,000-$16,999	4,860	4,955	77.7	79.1	29.6	30.4	3.8	4.0	4.9	7.5	1.1	1.2
$17,000-$18,999	4,306	4,318	77.5	77.7	34.3	33.7	4.4	4.3	5.7	7.4	1.3	1.3
$19,000-$21,999	6,253	6,281	127.9	128.7	64.4	63.9	8.9	8.7	7.0	7.6	1.5	1.6
$22,000-$24,999	5,427	5,521	127.4	129.5	70.4	70.0	10.4	10.1	8.1	8.1	2.0	1.9
$25,000-$29,999	7,784	8,121	212.8	222.5	124.5	130.4	18.5	19.4	8.7	8.8	2.4	2.4
$30,000-$39,999	12,358	12,014	429.4	418.1	272.8	265.1	43.3	41.9	10.1	10.1	3.5	3.5
$40,000-$49,999	9,072	9,024	405.4	403.8	269.8	269.1	43.5	43.6	10.7	10.8	4.8	4.9
$50,000-$74,999	12,248	13,127	741.5	794.7	516.9	555.5	91.1	96.8	12.3	12.2	7.5	7.4
$75,000-$99,999	4,225	4,784	359.9	409.0	262.8	300.3	54.1	61.5	15.0	15.1	12.8	12.9
$100,000-$199,999	3,108	3,405	408.0	446.5	313.4	346.3	75.3	82.7	18.5	18.5	24.3	24.3
$200,000-$499,999	786	890	228.0	256.2	193.4	218.0	58.3	65.6	25.6	25.6	74.2	73.7
$500,000-$999,999	141	149	94.4	100.7	82.9	88.9	28.3	30.4	30.0	30.2	201.5	203.7
$1,000,000 or more	66	70	170.6	181.8	150.9	161.5	53.2	56.6	31.2	31.2	801.6	810.7

[1] Consists of income after credits, and alternative minimum tax. [2] Computed using taxable returns only. [3] In addition to low income taxpayers, this size class (and others) includes taxpayers with "tax preferences," not reflected in adjusted gross income or taxable income which are subject to the "alternative minimum tax" (included in total income tax).

Source: U.S. Internal Revenue Service, *Statistics of Income Bulletin*, quarterly and *Statistics of Income, Individual Income Tax Returns*, annual.

No. 531. Individual Income Tax Returns—Itemized Deductions and Statutory Adjustments, by Size of Adjusted Gross Income: 1994

[Preliminary]

ITEM	Unit	ADJUSTED GROSS INCOME CLASS							
		Total	Under $10,000	$10,000 to $19,999	$20,000 to $29,999	$30,000 to $39,999	$40,000 to $49,999	$50,000 to $99,999	$100,000 and over
Returns with itemized deductions:									
Number [1]	1,000	33,018	745	2,123	3,438	4,132	4,662	13,663	4,234
Amount	Mil. dol	493,654	7,179	21,442	32,596	42,012	51,661	195,111	143,652
Medical and dental expenses:									
Returns	1,000	5,229	485	1,146	1,072	837	628	932	130
Amount	Mil. dol	26,378	2,774	6,448	3,933	3,276	2,612	5,767	1,570
Taxes paid: Returns, total	1,000	32,569	656	2,013	3,366	4,065	4,643	13,608	4,217
State, local income taxes	1,000	27,815	371	1,341	2,785	3,486	4,061	12,046	3,725
Real estate taxes	1,000	29,294	517	1,665	2,840	3,530	4,155	12,604	3,962
Amount, total	Mil. dol	175,848	1,236	3,893	7,738	11,393	15,638	67,992	67,956
State, local income taxes	Mil. dol	106,403	241	813	2,944	5,340	8,021	39,113	48,930
Real estate taxes	Mil. dol	63,122	916	2,783	4,341	5,302	6,814	25,724	17,242
Interest paid: Returns	1,000	27,873	448	1,421	2,707	3,496	4,015	12,151	3,635
Amount	Mil. dol	197,240	2,399	7,069	13,691	18,135	22,780	83,009	50,156
Home mortgages interest:									
Returns	1,000	27,518	441	1,382	2,673	3,474	4,004	12,041	3,503
Amount	Mil. dol	185,709	2,312	6,867	13,371	17,827	22,417	81,023	41,892
Contributions: Returns	1,000	29,849	503	1,708	2,948	3,610	4,193	12,827	4,059
Amount	Mil. dol	70,545	476	2,206	3,690	5,031	6,495	24,651	27,993
Employee business expense:									
Returns	1,000	10,021	69	355	965	1,334	1,513	4,716	1,079
Amount	Mil. dol	29,679	113	889	2,785	3,544	3,769	13,064	5,515
Returns with statutory adjus'mts: [2]									
Returns	1,000	17,859	2,821	3,050	2,730	2,277	1,708	3,572	1,702
Amount of adjustments	Mil. dol	39,103	1,779	3,371	4,052	4,042	2,884	9,615	13,361
Payments to IRA's: [3] Returns	1,000	4,319	294	597	1,025	829	594	677	304
Amount	Mil. dol	8,389	457	1,077	1,753	1,588	881	1,725	907
Payments to Keogh plans:									
Returns	1,000	996	10	32	55	81	69	336	413
Amount	Mil. dol	8,195	12	81	143	223	249	1,797	5,689
Alimony paid: Returns	1,000	639	41	64	70	89	59	203	113
Amount	Mil. dol	5,514	216	350	436	457	267	1,497	2,289

[1] After limitations. [2] Includes disability income exclusion, employee business expenses, moving expenses, forfeited interest penalty, alimony paid, deduction for expense of living abroad, and other data not shown separately. [3] Individual Retirement Account.

Source: U.S. Internal Revenue Service, *Statistics of Income, Individual Income Tax Returns*, annual.

No. 532. Federal Individual Income Tax Returns—Adjusted Gross Income (AGI), by Source of Income and Income Class for Taxable Returns: 1994

[In millions of dollars, except as indicated. Minus sign (-) indicates net loss was greater than net income. See headnote, table 529]

ITEM	Total [1]	Under $10,000	$10,000 to $19,999	$20,000 to $29,999	$30,000 to $39,999	$40,000 to $49,999	$50,000 to $99,999	$100,000 and over
Number of returns(1,000)	87,619	10,547	16,699	17,065	11,931	8,992	17,878	4,506
Source of income:								
Adjusted gross income (AGI)	3,736,645	59,214	251,511	422,768	415,295	402,378	1,201,511	983,967
Salaries and wages	2,845,867	49,552	182,872	349,758	350,035	339,321	1,002,788	571,540
Percent of AGI for taxable returns	76.2	83.7	72.7	82.7	84.3	84.3	83.5	58.1
Interest received	113,776	4,942	14,362	11,599	8,916	8,945	24,602	40,412
Dividends in AGI	76,832	1,948	5,505	5,536	4,857	4,935	17,066	36,984
Business; profession, net profit less loss	152,548	1,546	7,593	12,668	12,812	11,681	42,499	63,750
Pensions and annuities in AGI	191,142	4,174	31,913	31,795	24,343	21,747	54,503	22,667
Sales of property, [2] net gain less loss	136,775	2,096	2,177	2,847	3,129	3,755	18,425	104,345
Rents and royalties, net income less loss	17,728	202	1,222	838	45	160	960	14,281
Other sources, [3] net	201,975	-5,247	5,867	7,728	11,157	11,834	40,628	130,008
Percent of all returns [4]:								
Number of returns	75.6	25.7	21.5	15.3	10.4	7.8	15.4	3.9
Adjusted gross income	95.6	1.6	6.7	11.3	11.1	10.8	32.2	26.3
Salaries and wages	94.0	11.0	17.2	19.7	14.3	10.8	21.7	5.2
Interest received	90.2	9.7	14.3	15.8	13.5	12.0	27.2	7.7
Dividends in AGI	93.2	8.1	12.0	12.6	11.4	11.0	31.3	13.7
Business; profession, net profit less loss	91.8	5.2	13.8	17.4	15.1	10.5	26.3	11.7
Pensions and annuities in AGI	93.0	5.6	24.6	18.9	12.8	10.3	21.8	6.0
Sales of property [2] net gain less loss	87.7	6.6	10.9	12.3	11.0	10.2	31.4	17.6

[1] Includes a small number of taxable returns with no adjusted gross income. [2] Includes sales of capital assets and other property; net gain less loss. [3] Excludes rental passive losses disallowed in the computation of AGI; net income less loss. [4] Without regard to taxability.

Source: U.S. Internal Revenue Service, *Statistics of Income*, annual.

No. 533. Federal Individual Income Tax Returns, by State, 1994

DIVISION, AND STATE	Number of returns [1] (1,000)	Adjusted gross income (AGI) [2]	INCOME TAX: Total [3] (mil. dol.)	INCOME TAX: Per capita [4] (dol.)	DIVISION, AND STATE	Number of returns [1] (1,000)	Adjusted gross income (AGI) [2]	INCOME TAX: Total [3] (mil. dol.)	INCOME TAX: Per capita [4] (dol.)
U.S.	116,466	3,898,340	584,526	2,168	VA	2,960	107,026	15,016	2,292
Northeast	23,219	868,346	132,313	2,574	WV	705	19,407	2,460	1,350
N.E.	6,184	233,826	36,065	2,718	NC	3,225	99,061	13,074	1,849
ME	553	15,840	2,020	1,629	SC	1,604	45,973	5,767	1,574
NH	549	19,230	2,814	2,475	GA	3,100	100,656	13,959	1,979
VT	268	7,958	1,041	1,795	FL	6,361	203,882	31,427	2,252
MA	2,812	106,961	16,598	2,748	**E.S.C**	6,755	195,485	26,481	1,667
RI	449	14,747	2,014	2,020	KY	1,579	45,360	5,927	1,549
CT	1,553	69,090	11,576	3,535	TN	2,313	70,225	10,124	1,956
M.A.	17,035	634,520	96,248	2,525	AL	1,763	52,309	7,004	1,660
NY	7,851	299,876	46,297	2,548	MS	1,080	27,591	3,426	1,284
NJ	3,777	156,825	24,555	3,107	**W.S.C**	11,927	359,360	52,225	1,839
PA	5,407	177,817	25,396	2,107	AR	1,016	27,470	3,560	1,451
Midwest	27,881	923,611	132,243	2,154	LA	1,723	49,056	6,778	1,571
E.N.C	19,696	666,732	96,792	2,241	OK	1,342	37,690	4,951	1,520
OH	5,189	161,120	22,273	2,006	TX	7,846	245,144	36,936	2,010
IN	2,603	83,987	11,824	2,056	**West**	24,690	838,704	120,000	2,110
IL	5,351	197,016	30,674	2,610	**Mt.**	6,810	215,974	30,256	1,969
MI	4,216	147,739	21,610	2,276	MT	386	10,152	1,319	1,541
WI	2,337	76,870	10,411	2,049	ID	483	14,204	1,855	1,637
W.N.C	8,185	257,879	35,451	1,947	WY	218	6,762	1,010	2,122
MN	2,103	72,982	10,206	2,235	CO	1,738	59,976	8,866	2,426
IA	1,270	37,343	4,895	1,730	NM	719	19,553	2,500	1,511
MO	2,323	72,284	10,145	1,922	AZ	1,766	55,045	7,507	1,842
ND	289	7,837	1,052	1,649	UT	782	24,595	3,118	1,634
SD	328	8,773	1,228	1,703	NV	718	25,687	4,079	2,800
NE	753	22,060	2,965	1,827	**Pac**	17,880	622,730	89,744	2,155
KS	1,119	35,800	4,960	1,942	WA	2,444	86,382	12,909	2,416
South	38,827	1,243,327	176,452	1,946	OR	1,392	44,462	6,080	1,970
S.A	20,945	668,482	97,746	2,107	CA	13,132	462,967	66,661	2,121
DE	337	11,945	1,656	2,346	AK	358	10,411	1,624	2,680
MD	2,332	90,026	12,658	2,529	HI	554	18,506	2,470	2,095
DC	281	10,506	1,729	3,033	*Other* [5]	*1,049*	*24,155*	*3,517*	*(NA)*

NA Not available. [1] Includes returns constructed by Internal Revenue Service for certain self-employment tax returns. [2] Less deficit. [3] Includes additional tax for tax preferences, self-employment tax, tax from investment credit recapture and other income-related taxes. Total is before earned income credit. [4] Based on resident population as of July 1. [5] Includes returns filed from Army Post Office and Fleet Post Office addresses by members of the armed forces stationed overseas; returns by other U.S. citizens abroad; and returns filed by residents of Puerto Rico with income from sources outside of Puerto Rico or with income earned as U.S. Government employees.

Source: U.S. Internal Revenue Service, *Statistics of Income Bulletin*. Quarterly.

No. 534. Federal Individual Income Tax—Tax Liability, Effective and Marginal Tax Rates, for Selected Income Groups: 1985 to 1996

[Refers to income after exclusions. Effective rate represents tax liability divided by stated income. The marginal tax rate is the percentage of the first additional dollar of income which would be paid in income tax. Computations assume the low income allowance, standard deduction, zero bracket amount, or itemized deductions equal to 10 percent of adjusted gross income, whichever is greatest. Excludes self employment tax]

ADJUSTED GROSS INCOME	1985	1990	1992	1993	1994	1995	1996
TAX LIABILITY							
Single person, no dependents:							
$5,000	177	-	-	-	-306	-314	-323
$10,000	888	705	615	593	563	540	518
$20,000	2,854	2,206	2,115	2,093	2,063	2,040	2,018
$25,000	4,125	2,988	2,865	2,843	2,813	2,790	2,766
$35,000	6,916	5,718	5,360	5,233	5,093	4,973	4,846
$50,000	12,067	9,498	9,168	9,069	8,957	8,865	8,766
$75,000	22,195	16,718	15,867	15,719	15,555	15,418	15,270
Married couple, 2 dependents: [1]							
$5,000	-550	-700	-920	-975	-1500	-1800	-1800
$10,000	132	-953	-1384	-1511	-2528	-3110	-3200
$20,000	1682	926	409	235	-359	-832	-1039
$25,000	2,566	1,703	1,470	1,410	1,275	929	722
$35,000	4,916	3,203	2,970	2,910	2,828	2,768	2,715
$50,000	9,086	5,980	5,220	5,160	5,078	5,018	4,965
$75,000	17,649	12,386	11,670	11,471	11,216	11,030	10,831
EFFECTIVE RATE							
Single person, no dependents:							
$5,000 [2]	3.5	-	-	-	-6.1	-6.3	-6.5
$10,000	8.9	7.1	6.2	5.9	5.6	5.4	5.2
$20,000	14.3	11.0	10.6	10.5	10.3	10.2	10.1
$25,000	16.5	12.0	11.5	11.4	11.3	11.2	11.1
$35,000	19.8	16.3	15.3	15.0	14.6	14.2	13.8
$50,000	24.1	19.0	18.3	18.1	17.9	17.7	17.5
$75,000	29.6	22.3	21.2	21.0	20.7	20.6	20.4
Married couple, 2 dependents: [1]							
$5,000 [3]	-11.0	-14.0	-18.4	-19.5	-30.0	-36.0	-36
$10,000 [3]	1.3	-9.5	-13.8	-15.1	-25.3	-31.1	-32
$20,000 [4]	8.4	4.6	2.0	1.2	-1.8	-4.2	-5.2
$25,000	10.3	6.8	5.9	5.6	5.1	3.7	2.9
$35,000	14.0	9.2	8.5	8.3	8.1	7.9	7.8
$50,000	18.2	11.9	10.4	10.3	10.2	10.0	9.9
$75,000	23.5	16.5	15.6	15.3	15.0	14.7	14.4
MARGINAL TAX RATE							
Single person, no dependents:							
$5,000 [1]	12	-	-	-	7.7	-	-
$10,000	16	15	15	15	15	15	15
$20,000	26	15	15	15	15	15	15
$25,000	26	28	15	15	15	15	15
$35,000	34	28	28	28	28	28	28
$50,000	42	28	28	28	28	28	28
$75,000	48	33	31	31	31	31	31
Married couple, 2 dependents: [1]							
$5,000 [3]	-	-14	-18.4	-19.5	-30	-36	-36
$10,000 [3]	24.2	-	-	-	-	-	-
$20,000 [4]	16	25	28.1	28.9	32.7	36.2	36.2
$25,000	18	15	15	15	32.7	36.2	36.2
$35,000	25	15	15	15	15	15	15
$50,000	33	28	15	15	15	15	15
$75,000	42	28	28	28	28	28	28

- Represents zero. [1] Only one spouse is assumed to work. [2] 1994, refundable earned income credit. [3] Refundable earned income credit. [4] Beginning 1990, refundable earned income credit.

Source: U.S. Dept. of the Treasury, Office of Tax Analysis, unpublished data.

No. 535. Federal Individual Income Tax—Current Income Equivalent to 1995 Constant Income for Selected Income Groups: 1985 to 1996

[Constant 1995 dollar incomes calculated by using the NIPA Personal Consumption Expenditure (PCE) Implicit Price Deflator (1992=100): 1970, 29.5; 1985, 75.8; 1988, 84.3; 1990, 92.9; 1991, 96.8; 1992, 100.0; 1993 ,102.6; and 1994, 105.1; 1995, 107.6; and 1996, 109.8]

ADJUSTED GROSS INCOME	1985	1990	1992	1993	1994	1995	1996
REAL INCOME EQUIVALENT							
Single person, no dependents:							
$5,000	3,300	4,320	4,650	4,770	4,880	5,000	5,100
$10,000	6,600	8,630	9,290	9,540	9,770	10,000	10,200
$20,000	13,190	17,270	18,590	19,070	19,540	20,000	20,410
$25,000	16,490	21,580	23,230	23,840	24,420	25,000	25,510
$35,000	23,090	30,220	32,630	33,370	34,190	35,000	35,720
$50,000	32,990	43,170	46,470	47,680	48,840	50,000	51,020
$75,000	49,480	64,750	69,700	71,510	73,260	75,000	76,530
Married couple, 2 dependents: [1]							
$5,000	3,300	4,320	4,650	4,770	4,880	5,000	5,100
$10,000	6,600	8,630	9,290	9,540	9,770	10,000	10,200
$20,000	13,190	17,270	18,590	19,070	19,540	20,000	20,410
$25,000	16,490	21,580	23,230	23,840	24,420	25,000	25,510
$35,000	23,090	30,220	32,630	33,370	34,190	35,000	35,720
$50,000	32,990	43,170	46,470	47,680	48,840	50,000	51,020
$75,000	49,480	64,750	69,700	71,510	73,260	75,000	76,530
EFFECTIVE RATE (percent)							
Single person, no dependents.							
$5,000 [2]	-	-	-	-	-6.3	-6.3	-6.3
$10,000	5.9	5.8	5.5	5.5	5.4	5.4	5.4
$20,000	10.7	10.4	10.2	10.2	10.2	10.2	10.2
$25,000	12.4	11.3	11.2	11.2	11.2	11.2	11.1
$35,000	15.8	14.7	14.3	14.3	14.2	14.2	14.1
$50,000	19.1	18.0	17.8	17.8	17.7	17.7	17.7
$75,000	24.0	21.1	20.6	20.6	20.6	20.6	20.5
Married couple, 2 dependents: [1]							
$5,000 [3]	-11.0	-14.0	-18.4	-19.5	-30.0	-36.0	-36.0
$10,000 [3]	8.1	-11.0	-14.9	-15.8	-25.9	-31.1	-31.4
$20,000 [4]	5.0	1.4	0.1	-0.2	-2.6	-4.2	-4.4
$25,000	6.8	5.5	5.2	5.2	4.4	3.7	3.5
$35,000	9.6	8.2	8.0	8.0	7.9	7.9	7.9
$50,000	13.4	10.3	10.1	10.1	10.0	10.0	10.0
$75,000	18.1	15.1	14.8	14.8	14.7	14.7	14.7
MARGINAL TAX RATE (percent)							
Single person, no dependents:							
$5,000 [2]	-	-	-	-	-	-	-
$10,000	14	15	15	15	15	15	15
$20,000	18	15	15	15	15	15	15
$25,000	20	15	15	15	15	15	15
$35,000	26	28	28	28	28	28	28
$50,000	34	28	28	28	28	28	28
$75,000	42	33	31	31	31	31	31
Married couple, 2 dependents: [1]							
$5,000 [3]	-11	-14	-18.4	-19.5	-30	-36	-36
$10,000 [3]	12.2	-	-	-	-	-	-
$20,000 [4]	14	25	28.1	28.9	32.7	35.2	35.2
$25,000	14	15	15	15	32.7	35.2	35.2
$35,000	18	15	15	15	15	15	15
$50,000	25	15	15	28	15	15	15
$75,000	33	28	28	28	28	28	28

- Represents zero. [1] Only one spouse is assumed to work. [2] 1994, refundable earned income credit. [3] Refundable earned income credit. [4] Beginning 1990, refundable earned income credit.

Source: U.S. Dept. of the Treasury, Office of Tax Analysis, unpublished data.

No. 536. Federal Civilian Employment, by Branch and Agency: 1990 to 1996

[As of September 30]

AGENCY	1990	1994	1995	1996	PERCENT CHANGE 1990-95	PERCENT CHANGE 1995-96
Total, all agencies	3,128,267	2,971,584	2,920,277	2,847,284	-6.6	-2.5
Legislative Branch, total[1]	37,495	35,357	33,367	31,547	-11.0	-5.5
Judicial Branch	23,605	28,035	28,993	29,581	22.8	2.0
Executive Branch, total	3,067,167	2,908,192	2,857,917	2,786,156	-6.8	-2.5
Executive Departments	2,065,542	1,907,895	[4] 1,782,834	1,714,352	-13.7	-3.8
State	25,288	25,596	24,859	24,489	-1.7	-1.5
Treasury	158,655	156,373	155,951	146,137	-1.7	-6.3
Defense	1,034,152	879,878	832,352	795,813	-19.5	-4.4
Justice	83,932	97,910	103,262	109,794	23.0	6.3
Interior	77,679	80,704	76,439	71,028	-1.6	-7.1
Agriculture	122,594	119,558	113,321	109,586	-7.6	-3.3
Commerce	69,920	37,642	36,803	35,156	-47.4	-4.5
Labor	17,727	16,732	16,204	15,230	-8.6	-6.0
Health & Human Services	123,959	128,244	[4] 59,788	58,491	-51.8	-2.2
Housing & Urban Development	13,596	13,218	11,822	11,462	-13.0	-3.0
Transportation	67,364	64,896	63,552	63,309	-5.7	-0.4
Energy	17,731	19,899	19,589	18,237	10.5	-6.9
Education	4,771	4,813	4,988	4,721	4.5	-5.4
Veterans Affairs[2]	248,174	262,432	263,904	250,899	6.3	-4.9
Independent agencies[1]	999,894	998,729	[4] 1,073,510	1,070,245	7.4	-0.3
American Battle Monuments Comm	396	380	375	371	-5.3	-1.1
Armed Forces Retirement Home	986	1,056	960	908	(X)	-5.4
Arms Control & Disarmament Agency	216	233	266	244	23.1	-8.3
Board of Gov Fed Reserve System	1,525	1,669	1,704	1,740	11.7	2.1
Commodity Futures Trading Comm	542	551	544	553	0.4	1.7
Consumer Product Safety Comm	520	484	486	468	-6.5	-3.7
Corp Natl & Community Service	(X)	607	574	516	(X)	-10.1
Defense Nuclear Facilities Safety Bd	25	102	106	106	324.0	-
Environmental Protection Agency	17,123	18,092	17,910	17,160	4.6	-4.2
Equal Employment Opportunity Comm	2,880	2,914	2,796	2,655	-2.9	-5.0
Export-Import Bank of US	343	462	443	426	29.2	-3.8
Farm Credit Administration	515	412	380	332	-26.2	-12.6
Federal Communications Commission	1,778	2,015	2,116	2,069	19.0	-2.2
Federal Deposit Insurance Corporation	17,641	18,775	14,765	10,006	-16.3	-32.2
Federal Election Commission	250	316	327	294	30.8	-10.1
Fed. Emergency Managmt Agency	3,137	5,221	5,256	6,569	67.5	25.0
Federal Housing Finance Board[5]	65	104	113	119	73.8	5.3
Federal Labor Relations Auth	251	229	221	232	-12.0	5.0
Federal Maritime Commission	230	200	169	150	-26.5	-11.2
Federal Med & Concil Svc	316	309	297	293	-6.0	-1.3
Fed Ret Thrift Invest Board	93	105	110	110	18.3	-
Federal Trade Commission	988	969	996	941	0.8	-5.5
General Services Administration[3]	20,277	19,257	16,500	15,654	-18.6	-5.1
Holocaust Memorial Council	26	188	207	217	696.2	4.8
Int Boun & Wat Comm (US & Mex)	260	248	236	246	-9.2	4.2
International Trade Commission	491	464	442	391	-10.0	-11.5
Interstate Commerce Comm	656	553	397	-	-39.5	(X)
Merit Sys Protection Board	310	296	271	265	-12.6	-2.2
National Archives & Recds Admin	3,120	3,073	2,833	3,061	-9.2	8.0
National Aeronautics & Space Admin	24,872	23,338	21,635	21,006	-13.0	-2.9
Natl Credit Union Admin	900	921	912	935	1.3	2.5
Natl Fnd Arts & Humanities	547	584	493	337	-9.9	-31.6
Natl Labor Relations Board	2,263	2,077	2,050	1,970	-9.4	-3.9
Natl Science Foundation	1,318	1,252	1,292	1,249	-2.0	-3.3
Natl Trans Safety Board	366	358	368	370	0.5	0.5
Nuclear Regulatory Commission	3,353	3,336	3,212	3,148	-4.2	-2.0
Office of Personnel Management	6,636	5,340	4,354	3,524	-34.4	-19.1
Panama Canal Commission	8,240	8,562	9,060	9,335	10.0	3.0
Peace Corps	1,178	1,223	1,179	1,122	0.1	-4.8
Pension Benefit Guar Corp	574	697	716	763	24.7	6.6
Railroad Retirement Board	1,772	1,683	1,544	1,440	-12.9	-6.7
Securities & Exchange Comm	2,302	2,689	2,852	2,838	23.9	-0.5
Selective Service System	288	230	218	221	-24.3	1.4
Small Business Administration	5,128	6,824	5,085	4,839	-0.8	-4.8
Smithsonian Institution, Summary	5,092	5,527	5,444	5,188	6.9	-4.7
Social Security Admin	(X)	(X)	[4] 66,850	66,314	(X)	-0.8
Tennessee Valley Authority	28,392	18,846	16,545	16,022	-41.7	-3.2
U.S. Information Agency	8,555	7,888	7,480	6,850	-12.6	-8.4
U.S. International Development Cooperation Agency	4,698	4,059	3,755	3,267	-20.1	-13.0
U.S. Postal Service	816,886	822,699	845,393	852,285	3.5	0.8

- Represents zero. X Not applicable. [1] Includes branches, or agencies, not shown separately. [2] Formerly Veterans Administration. [3] 1980 figure includes the National Archives and Records Administration which became an independent agency in 1985. [4] Sizable changes due to the Social Security Administration which was separated from the Department of Health and Human Services to become an independent agency effective April 1995. [5] Formerly Federal Home Loan Bank Board.

Source: U.S. Office of Personnel Management, *Federal Civilian Workforce Statistics— Employment and Trends*, bimonthly.

No. 537. Federal Civilian Employment and Annual Payroll, by Branch: 1970 to 1996

[Average Annual employment: For fiscal year ending in year shown; see text, section 9. Includes employees in U.S. territories and foreign countries. Data represent employees in active-duty status, including intermittent employees. Annual employment figures are averages of monthly figures. Excludes Central Intelligence Agency, National Security Agency, and, as of November 1984, the Defense Intelligence Agency, National Security Agency, and, as of November 1984, the Defense Intelligence Agency]

YEAR	EMPLOYMENT						PAYROLL (mil. dol.)				
	Total (1,000)	Percent of U.S. employed [1]	Executive		Legislative (1,000)	Judicial (1,000)	Total	Executive		Legislative	Judicial
			Total (1,000)	Defense				Total	Defense		
1970	[2]2,997	3.8	2,961	1,263	29	7	27,322	26,894	11,264	338	89
1971	2,899	3.7	2,861	1,162	31	7	29,475	29,007	11,579	369	98
1972	2,882	3.5	2,842	1,128	32	8	31,626	31,102	12,181	411	112
1973	2,822	3.3	2,780	1,076	33	9	33,240	32,671	12,414	447	121
1974	2,825	3.3	2,781	1,041	35	9	35,661	35,035	12,789	494	132
1975	2,877	3.4	2,830	1,044	37	10	39,126	38,423	13,418	549	154
1976	2,879	3.2	2,831	1,025	38	11	42,259	41,450	14,699	631	179
1977	2,855	3.1	2,803	997	39	12	45,895	44,975	15,696	700	219
1978	2,875	3.0	2,822	987	40	13	49,921	48,899	16,995	771	251
1979	2,897	2.9	2,844	974	40	13	53,590	52,513	18,065	817	260
1980	[3]2,987	3.0	2,933	971	40	14	58,012	56,841	18,795	883	288
1981	2,909	2.9	2,855	986	40	15	63,793	62,510	21,227	922	360
1982	2,871	2.9	2,816	1,019	39	16	65,503	64,125	22,226	980	398
1983	2,878	2.9	2,823	1,033	39	16	69,878	68,420	23,406	1,013	445
1984	2,935	2.8	2,879	1,052	40	17	74,616	73,084	25,253	1,081	451
1985	3,001	2.8	2,944	1,080	39	18	80,599	78,992	28,330	1,098	509
1986	3,047	2.8	2,991	1,089	38	19	82,598	80,941	29,272	1,112	545
1987	3,075	2.7	3,018	1,084	38	19	85,543	83,797	29,786	1,153	593
1988	3,113	2.7	3,054	1,073	38	21	88,841	86,960	29,609	1,226	656
1989	3,133	2.7	3,074	1,067	38	22	92,847	90,870	30,301	1,266	711
1990	[4]3,233	2.7	3,173	1,060	38	23	99,138	97,022	31,990	1,329	787
1991	3,101	2.7	3,038	1,015	38	25	104,273	101,965	32,956	1,434	874
1992	3,106	2.6	3,040	1,004	39	27	108,054	105,402	31,486	1,569	1,083
1993	3,043	2.5	2,976	952	39	28	114,323	111,523	32,755	1,609	1,191
1994	2,993	2.4	2,928	900	37	28	116,138	113,264	32,144	1,613	1,260
1995	2,943	2.4	2,880	852	34	28	118,304	115,328	31,753	1,598	1,379
1996	2,881	2.3	2,819	811	32	29	119,322	116,386	31,569	1,519	1,417

[1] Civilian only. See table 621. [2] Includes 33,000 temporary census workers. [3] Includes 81,116 temporary census workers. [4] Includes 111,020 temporary census workers.

Source: U.S. Office of Personnel Management, *Federal Civilian Workforce Statistics—Employment and Trends*, bimonthly; and unpublished data.

No. 538. Federal Executive Branch (Non-Postal) Employment, by Race and National Origin: 1990 to 1995

[As of Sept. 30. Covers total employment for only Executive branch agencies participating in OPM's Central Personnel Data File (CPDF)]

PAY SYSTEM	1990	1992	1993	1994	1995
All personnel	2,150,359	2,175,715	2,110,510	2,043,449	1,960,577
White, non-Hispanic	1,562,646	1,570,812	1,515,700	1,462,185	1,394,690
General schedule and related	1,218,188	1,228,834	1,190,705	1,146,990	1,101,108
Grades 1-4 ($12,141 - $21,734)	132,028	112,948	99,008	90,029	79,195
Grades 5-8 ($18,707 - $33,357)	337,453	338,182	320,410	303,999	288,755
Grades 9-12 ($28,345 - $53,434)	510,261	509,978	500,616	484,681	465,908
Grades 13-15 ($48,878 - $88,326)	238,448	267,526	270,673	268,281	267,250
Total Executives/Senior Pay Levels [1]	9,337	13,661	13,162	13,114	13,307
Wage pay system	244,220	232,753	215,122	202,440	186,184
Other pay systems	91,101	95,764	96,711	99,641	94,091
Black	356,867	360,725	351,879	340,512	327,302
General schedule and related	272,657	277,264	272,393	265,926	258,586
Grades 1-4 ($12,141 - $21,734)	65,077	56,650	51,142	46,189	41,381
Grades 5-8 ($18,707 - $33,357)	114,993	120,259	118,438	115,966	112,962
Grades 9-12 ($28,345 - $53,434)	74,985	78,970	80,130	80,284	79,795
Grades 13-15 ($48,878 - $88,326)	17,602	21,385	22,683	23,487	24,448
Total Executives/Senior Pay Levels [1]	479	662	716	865	942
Wage pay system	72,755	69,976	65,422	60,335	55,637
Other pay systems	10,976	12,823	13,348	13,386	12,137
Hispanic	115,170	120,298	117,935	116,863	115,964
General schedule and related	83,218	87,947	87,200	86,816	86,762
Grades 1-4 ($12,141 - $21,734)	15,738	14,240	13,027	12,033	11,081
Grades 5-8 ($18,707 - $33,357)	28,727	31,708	30,985	30,749	31,152
Grades 9-12 ($28,345 - $53,434)	31,615	33,121	33,758	34,104	34,056
Grades 13-15 ($48,878 - $88,326)	7,138	8,878	9,430	9,930	10,473
Total Executives/Senior Pay Levels [1]	154	281	274	323	382
Wage pay system	26,947	26,151	24,515	23,122	22,128
Other pay systems	4,851	5,917	5,946	6,602	6,692
American Indian, Alaska Natives, Asians, and Pacific	115,476	123,882	124,996	123,889	122,621

[1] General schedule pay rates as of January 1993. Senior Pay Levels effective as of October 1, 1991.

Source: Office of Personnel Management, Central Personnel Data File.

No. 539. Paid Civilian Employment in the Federal Government: 1994

[As of December 31. Excludes Central Intelligence Agency, Defense Intelligence Agency, seasonal and on-call employees, and National Security Agency]

DIVISION AND STATE	Total (1,000)	Percent Defense	DIVISION AND STATE	Total (1,000)	Percent Defense
United States	2,903	27.8	Virginia	160	61.0
			West Virginia	18	10.0
Northeast	467	21.6	North Carolina	54	32.6
New England	123	20.8	South Carolina	30	46.0
Maine	14	43.3	Georgia	92	37.9
New Hampshire	9	15.8	Florida	114	26.4
Vermont	6	10.5	**East South Central**	169	31.6
Massachusetts	60	16.1	Kentucky	36	34.2
Rhode Island	11	36.7	Tennessee	53	11.3
Connecticut	25	17.1	Alabama	55	43.4
Middle Atlantic	344	22.2	Mississippi	25	40.9
New York	145	10.6	**West South Central**	273	31.2
New Jersey	72	29.8	Arkansas	20	20.2
Pennsylvania	127	31.1	Louisiana	35	25.0
North Central	511	21.4	Oklahoma	42	44.9
East North Central	330	22.8	Texas	176	30.4
Ohio	92	34.2	**West**	629	32.1
Indiana	42	33.7	**Mountain**	198	25.8
Illinois	106	15.9	Montana	13	9.5
Michigan	60	16.1	Idaho	11	11.3
Wisconsin	30	10.9	Wyoming	7	14.5
West North Central	180	18.7	Colorado	57	23.0
Minnesota	34	7.9	New Mexico	27	31.6
Iowa	21	6.8	Arizona	40	22.4
Missouri	64	25.5	Utah	31	47.7
North Dakota	8	23.6	Nevada	12	17.8
South Dakota	10	13.5	**Pacific**	430	34.9
Nebraska	16	22.7	Washington	66	40.2
Kansas	26	23.3	Oregon	30	9.9
South	1,253	31.0	California	295	33.3
South Atlantic	811	30.9	Alaska	15	32.1
Delaware	6	26.9	Hawaii	25	72.2
Maryland	133	28.4	Unspecified State	44	0.5
District of Columbia	204	7.6			

Source: U.S. Office of Personnel Management, *Biennial Report of Employment by Geographic Area.*

No. 540. Paid Full-Time Federal Civilian Employment, All Areas: 1990 to 1996

[As of March 31. Excludes employees of Congress and Federal courts, maritime seamen of Dept. of Commerce, and small number for whom rates were not reported. See text, section 10, for explanation of general schedule and wage system]

COMPENSATION AUTHORITY	EMPLOYEES (1,000)				AVERAGE PAY			
	1990	1994	1995	1996	1990	1994	1995	1996
Total	2,697	2,681	1,867	1,803	31,174	39,129	(NA)	42,195
General Schedule	1,506	1,479	1,417	1,381	31,239	39,070	40,568	42,139
Wage System	369	290	269	252	26,565	31,299	32,084	32,976
Postal pay system [1]	661	729	(NA)	(NA)	29,264	33,592	(NA)	(NA)
Other	161	183	181	170	41,149	51,996	53,839	56,296

NA Not available. [1] Source: Employees—U.S. Postal Service, *Annual Report of the Postmaster General.* Average pay—U.S. Postal Service, *Comprehensive Statement of Postal Operations,* annual.

Source: Except as noted, U.S. Office of Personnel Management, *Pay Structure of the Federal Civil Service,* annual.

No. 541. Federal General Schedule Employee Pay Increases: 1965 to 1996

[Percent change from prior year shown, except 1965, change from 1964. Represents legislated pay increases. For some years data based on range for details see source]

DATE	Pay increase	DATE	Pay increase	DATE	Pay increase
1965	3.6	1975	5.0	1987	3.0
1966	2.9	1976	5.2	1988	2.0
1967	4.5	1977	7.0	1989	4.1
1968	4.9	1978	5.5	1990	3.6
1969	9.1	1979	7.0	1991	4.1
1970	6.0	1980	9.1	1992	4.2
1971	6.0	1981	4.8	1993	3.7
1972	5.5	1982	4.0	1994	-
1972	5.1	1984	4.0	1995	2.0
1973	4.8	1985	3.5	1996	2.0
1974	5.5	1986	-		

- Represents zero.

Source of tables: U.S. Office of Personnel Management, *Pay Structure of the Federal Civil Service,* annual.

No. 542. Accessions to and Separations From Employment in the Federal Government: 1995 and 1996

[As of September 30]

AGENCY	ACCESSIONS				SEPARATIONS			
	Number		Rate		Number		Rate	
	1995	1996	1995	1996	1995	1996	1995	1996
Total, all agencies	556,695	481,523	19.2	17.0	638,733	546,444	22.1	19.3
Legislative Branch, total [1]	1,074	767	6.6	5.2	1,985	2,320	12.2	15.6
General Accounting Office	39	15	0.9	0.4	392	827	8.9	22.2
Government Printing Office	77	113	1.8	2.9	318	400	7.6	10.4
Library of Congress	540	382	11.6	8.4	642	491	13.8	10.8
Judicial Branch	-	-	-	-	-	-	-	-
Executive Branch, total	555,621	480,756	19.3	17.1	636,748	544,124	22.1	19.3
Executive Office of the President	384	342	24.3	21.9	373	338	23.6	21.6
Executive Departments	257,125	245,483	14.0	14.1	422,606	327,910	23.0	18.9
State	3,336	3,158	13.3	12.8	3,919	3,433	15.6	14.0
Treasury	24,532	25,116	15.0	16.0	52,634	56,983	32.2	36.4
Defense	104,066	107,505	12.2	13.3	155,722	144,082	18.3	17.8
Justice	14,958	16,609	14.9	15.8	7,496	8,579	7.5	8.2
Interior	12,936	12,700	17.1	18.0	16,147	14,353	21.4	20.4
Agriculture	25,365	29,944	23.3	28.5	41,384	34,704	37.9	33.0
Commerce	5,900	4,272	15.8	11.9	6,460	5,274	17.3	14.7
Labor	1,436	517	8.7	3.3	2,003	1,496	12.2	9.6
Health & Human Services	8,774	7,457	9.3	12.7	78,780	8,136	83.7	13.8
Housing & Urban Development	489	451	4.0	3.9	1,952	853	15.8	7.4
Transportation	2,673	3,028	4.2	4.8	4,740	3,990	7.4	6.3
Energy	2,087	621	10.5	3.3	2,671	93	13.4	10.9
Education	683	253	13.8	5.3	354	300	7.2	6.3
Veterans Affairs [2]	49,864	33,853	19.0	13.2	48,344	45,685	18.5	17.8
Independent agencies [1]	298,112	234,931	28.6	21.8	213,769	215,876	20.5	20.0
Board of Governors, Fed RSRV System	231	192	13.7	11.1	199	205	11.8	11.8
Environmental Protection Agency	2,232	736	12.3	4.3	2,078	1,403	11.5	8.1
Equal Employment Opportunity Comm	129	62	4.5	2.3	156	114	5.4	4.2
Federal Deposit Insurance Corporation	360	269	2.2	2.3	4,404	5,060	26.8	43.1
Fed Emergency Management Agency	3,165	3,492	60.2	65.7	3,059	2,702	58.2	50.8
General Services Administration	292	331	1.7	2.1	2,562	576	14.8	3.6
National Aeronautics & Space Admin	2,004	1,225	8.9	5.7	3,673	1,896	16.2	8.9
National Archives & Records Admin	583	612	20.0	20.7	307	144	10.5	4.9
Nuclear Regulatory Commission	96	158	3.0	5.0	263	187	8.0	5.9
Office of Personnel Management	506	563	10.3	13.8	1,407	1,231	28.6	30.2
Panama Canal Comm	1,744	1,499	19.6	16.5	1,246	1,225	14.0	13.5
Railroad Retirement Board	46	36	2.9	2.5	185	142	11.6	9.5
Securities and Exchange Commission	584	415	21.1	14.7	356	351	12.8	12.5
Small Business Administration	1,065	1,488	18.1	30.8	2,799	1,715	47.6	35.5
Smithsonian Institution	707	350	13.1	6.6	980	615	18.2	11.6
Tennessee Valley Authority	674	281	4.1	1.7	2,873	625	17.3	3.2
US Information Agency	356	175	4.7	2.5	836	952	11.0	13.4
US International Dev Coop Agency	333	193	8.6	5.3	665	674	17.2	18.7
US Postal Service	210,447	214,281	25.0	25.0	179,494	187,546	21.3	21.8

- Represents zero. [1] Includes other branches, or other agencies, not shown separately. [2] Formerly Veterans Administration.

Source: U.S. Office of Personnel Management, *Federal Civilian Workforce Statistics— Employment and Trends*, bimonthly.

No. 543. Federal Land and Buildings Owned and Leased, and Predominant Land Usage: 1980 to 1994

[For fiscal years ending in years shown; see text, section 9. Covers Federal real property throughout the world, except as noted. Cost of land figures represent total cost of property owned in year shown. For further details see source. For data on Federal land by State, see table 369]

ITEM AND AGENCY	Unit	1980	1985	1989	1990	1991	1992	1993	1994
Federally owned: Land	Mil. acres	720	727	662	650	650	651	651	678
Buildings, number [1]	1,000	403	454	451	446	441	453	444	452
Cost of land, buildings, etc.[2]	Bil. dol.	107	148	164	180	181	193	194	209
Federally leased: Land	Mil. acres	1.4	1.3	1.5	0.9	(NA)	(NA)	(NA)	(NA)
Buildings, floor area [1]	Mil. sq/ft	214	237	254	234	242	(NA)	(NA)	(NA)
Rental property, cost	Mil. dol	1,054	1,681	2,127	2,125	(NA)	(NA)	(NA)	(NA)
Predominant usage (U.S. only)	Mil. acres	720	727	662	650	650	651	650	677
Forest and wildlife	Mil. acres	422	431	375	368	(NA)	368	366	396
Grazing	Mil. acres	162	155	151	154	(NA)	154	154	154
Parks and historic sites	Mil. acres	93	94	98	98	(NA)	98	98	99
Other	Mil. acres	43	48	39	33	(NA)	(NA)	(NA)	(NA)

NA Not available. [1] Excludes data for Dept. of Defense military functions outside United States. [2] Includes other uses not shown separately.

Source: U.S. General Services Administration, *Inventory Report on Real Property Owned by the United States Throughout the World*, annual.

Figure 11.1
Military and Civilian Personnel: 1985 to 1996

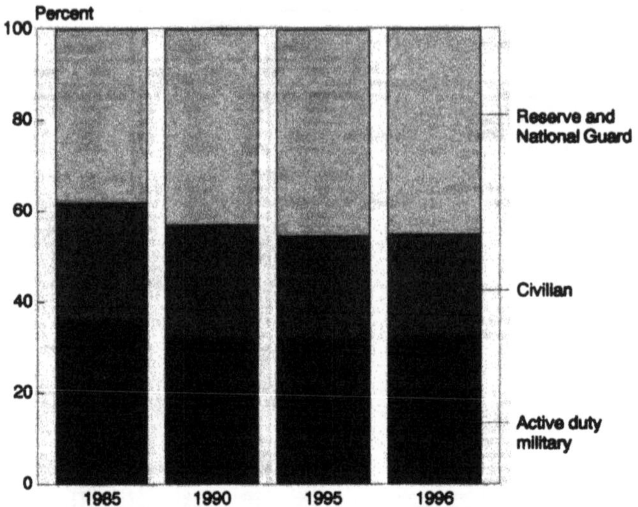

Source: Chart prepared by U.S. Bureau of the Census. For data, see table 546.

Figure 11.2
Military and Civilian Expenditures, by Major Location: 1996

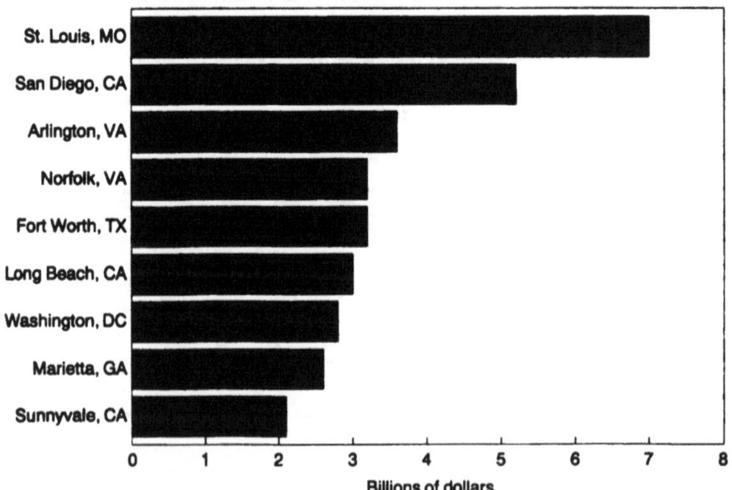

Source: Chart prepared by U.S. Bureau of the Census. For data, see table 548.

Section 11

National Defense and Veterans Affairs

This section presents data on national defense and its human and financial costs; active and reserve military personnel; ships, equipment and aircraft; and federally sponsored programs and benefits for veterans. The principal sources of these data are the annual *Selected Manpower Statistics* and the *Atlas/Data Abstract for the United States and Selected Areas* issued by the Office of the Secretary of Defense; *Annual Report of Secretary of Veterans Affairs, Department of Veterans Affairs,* and *The Budget of the United States Government,* Office of Management and Budget. For more data on expenditures, personnel, and ships, see section 31.

Department of Defense (DOD)—DOD is responsible for providing military forces of the United States. The President serves as Commander in Chief of the Armed Forces; from him, the authority flows to the Secretary of Defense and through the Joint Chiefs of Staff to the commanders of unified and specified commands (e.g., United States European Command).

Reserve components—Reserve personnel of the Armed Forces consist of the Army National Guard, Army Reserve, Naval Reserve, Marine Corps Reserve, Air National Guard, Air Force Reserve, and Coast Guard Reserve. They provide trained personnel available for active duty in the Armed Forces in time of war or national emergency and at such other times as authorized by law. The National Guard has dual Federal-State responsibilities and uses jointly provided equipment, facilities, and budget support. The President is empowered to mobilize the National Guard and to use such of the Armed Forces as he considers necessary to enforce Federal authority in any State.

The ready reserve includes selected reservists who are intended to assist active forces in a war and the individual ready reserve who, in a major war, would be used to fill out active and reserve units and later would be a source of combat replacements; a portion of the ready reserve serves in an active status. The standby reserve cannot be called to active duty unless the Congress gives explicit approval. The retired reserve represents a low potential for mobilization.

In Brief

	1997
U.S. military expenditures	*$267 bil.*
Defense outlays as percent of gross domestic product	*3.4%*

Department of Veterans Affairs—The Department of Veterans Affairs administers laws authorizing benefits for eligible former and present members of the Armed Forces and for the beneficiaries of deceased members. Veterans benefits available under various acts of Congress include compensation for service-connected disability or death; pensions for nonservice-connected disability or death; vocational rehabilitation, education, and training; home loan insurance; life insurance; health care; special housing and automobiles or other conveyances for certain disabled veterans; burial and plot allowances; and educational assistance to families of deceased or totally disabled veterans, servicemen missing in action, or prisoners of war. Since these benefits are legislated by Congress, the dates they were enacted and the dates they apply to veterans may be different from the actual dates the conflicts occurred.

VA estimates of veterans cover all persons with active duty service during periods of war or armed conflict and until 1982 include those living outside the United States. Veteran population estimates for September 1982 are for the 50 States, the District of Columbia and Puerto Rico. Veterans whose active duty service was entirely during periods of peacetime are eligible for some veterans benefits and, where appropriate, are included in VA estimates.

No. 544. National Defense Outlays and Veterans Benefits: 1960 to 1997

[For fiscal year ending in year shown; see text, section 9. Includes outlays of Department of Defense, Department of Veterans Affairs, and other agencies for activities primarily related to national defense and veterans programs. For explanation of average annual percent change, see Guide to Tabular Presentation. Minus sign (-) indicates decline]

YEAR	NATIONAL DEFENSE AND VETERANS OUTLAYS				ANNUAL PERCENT CHANGE [1]			DEFENSE OUTLAYS, PERCENT OF—	
	Total outlays (bil. dol.)	Defense outlays: Current dollars (bil. dol.)	Defense outlays: Constant (1987) dollars (bil. dol.)	Veterans outlays (bil. dol.)	Total outlays	Defense outlays	Veterans outlays	Federal outlays	Gross domestic product [2]
1960	53.5	48.1	257.2	5.4	2.5	2.4	3.1	52.2	9.3
1965	56.3	50.6	245.6	5.7	-6.8	-7.6	0.7	42.8	7.4
1966	64.0	58.1	270.8	5.9	13.7	14.8	3.5	43.2	7.7
1967	78.1	71.4	320.0	6.7	22.1	22.9	13.8	45.4	8.8
1968	88.9	81.9	349.2	7.0	13.8	14.7	4.4	46.0	9.4
1969	90.1	82.5	333.5	7.6	1.3	0.7	8.5	44.9	8.7
1970	90.4	81.7	310.7	8.7	0.3	-1.0	13.6	41.8	8.1
1971	88.7	78.9	283.0	9.8	-1.9	-3.5	12.7	37.5	7.3
1972	89.9	79.2	262.3	10.7	1.4	0.4	9.8	34.3	6.7
1973	88.7	76.7	239.6	12.0	1.3	-3.1	12.0	31.2	5.9
1974	92.7	79.3	228.3	13.4	4.6	3.5	11.4	29.5	5.5
1975	103.1	86.5	224.1	16.6	11.2	9.0	24.0	26.0	5.6
1976	108.1	89.6	216.8	18.4	4.8	3.6	11.0	24.1	5.2
1976, TQ [3]	26.2	22.3	52.1	4.0	(X)	(X)	(X)	23.2	4.9
1977	115.2	97.2	216.4	18.0	6.7	8.5	-2.1	23.8	4.9
1978	123.5	104.5	217.4	19.0	7.1	7.5	5.2	22.8	4.7
1979	136.2	116.3	221.8	19.9	10.4	11.3	5.0	23.1	4.7
1980	155.2	134.0	229.3	21.2	13.9	15.2	6.3	22.7	4.9
1981	180.5	157.5	241.8	23.0	16.3	17.6	8.5	23.2	5.2
1982	209.3	185.3	263.7	24.0	15.9	17.6	4.2	24.8	5.8
1983	234.7	209.9	284.0	24.8	12.1	13.3	3.3	26.0	6.1
1984	253.0	227.4	287.4	25.6	7.8	8.3	3.2	26.7	6.0
1985	279.0	252.7	306.2	26.3	10.3	11.1	2.7	26.7	6.2
1986	299.8	273.4	324.8	26.4	7.4	8.2	0.4	27.6	6.2
1987	308.8	282.0	330.0	26.8	3.0	3.1	1.5	28.1	6.1
1988	319.8	290.4	333.9	29.4	3.6	3.0	9.7	27.3	5.9
1989	333.7	303.6	338.3	30.1	4.3	4.5	2.4	26.5	5.7
1990	328.4	299.3	324.6	29.1	-1.6	-1.4	-3.3	23.9	5.3
1991	304.6	273.3	283.3	31.3	-7.2	-8.7	7.6	20.6	4.7
1992	332.5	298.4	298.4	34.1	12.0	12.4	8.0	21.6	4.9
1993	326.1	291.1	286.2	35.7	-1.9	-2.4	4.6	20.7	4.5
1994	319.2	281.6	270.9	37.6	-2.3	-3.3	5.3	19.3	4.1
1995	310.0	272.1	255.5	37.9	-2.9	-3.4	0.8	17.9	3.8
1996	302.7	265.7	242.1	37.0	-2.4	-2.3	-2.4	17.0	3.6
1997, est.	306.8	267.2	237.4	39.7	1.4	0.5	7.2	16.4	3.4

X Not applicable. [1] Change from prior year shown; for 1960, change from 1955. [2] Represents fiscal year GDP; for definition, see text, section 14. [3] Transition quarter, July-Sept.

Source: U.S. Office of Management and Budget, *Historical Tables*, annual.

No. 545. Federal Budget Outlays for National Defense Functions: 1980 to 1997

[In billions of dollars, except percent. For fiscal year ending in year shown; see text, section 9. Minus sign (-) indicates decline]

DEFENSE FUNCTION	1980	1985	1988	1989	1990	1991	1992	1993	1994	1995	1996	1997, est.
Total	134.0	252.7	290.4	303.6	299.3	273.3	298.4	291.1	281.6	272.1	265.7	267.2
Percent change [1]	15.2	11.1	3.0	4.5	-1.4	-8.7	9.2	-2.4	0.6	-3.4	-2.3	0.5
Defense Dept., military	130.9	245.2	281.9	294.9	289.8	262.4	286.9	278.6	268.6	259.4	253.2	254.3
Military personnel	40.9	67.8	76.3	80.7	75.6	83.4	81.2	75.9	73.1	70.8	66.7	70.1
Percent of military	31.2	27.7	27.1	27.0	26.1	31.8	28.3	27.2	27.2	27.3	26.3	27.6
Operation, maintenance	44.8	72.4	84.5	87.0	88.3	101.8	92.0	94.1	87.9	91.1	88.8	92.1
Procurement	29.0	70.4	77.2	81.6	81.0	82.0	74.9	69.9	61.8	55.0	48.9	45.6
Research and development	13.1	27.1	34.8	37.0	37.5	34.6	34.6	37.0	34.8	34.6	36.5	36.0
Military construction	2.5	4.3	5.9	5.3	5.1	3.5	4.3	4.8	5.0	6.8	6.7	6.6
Family housing	1.7	2.6	3.1	3.3	3.5	3.3	3.3	3.3	3.3	3.6	3.8	4.4
Other [2]	-1.1	0.6	0.2	0.1	-1.2	-46.2	-3.3	-6.4	2.7	-2.4	1.8	-0.5
Atomic energy activities [3]	2.9	7.1	7.9	8.1	9.0	10.0	10.6	11.0	11.9	11.8	11.6	11.9
Defense-related activities [4]	0.2	0.5	0.5	0.6	0.6	0.9	0.8	1.5	1.1	0.8	0.9	1.0

[1] Change from immediate prior year; for 1970, change from 1965. [2] Revolving and management funds, trust funds, special foreign currency program, allowances, and offsetting receipts. [3] Defense activities only. [4] Includes civil defense activities.

Source: U.S. Office of Management and Budget, *Historical Tables*, annual.

No. 546. National Defense—Budget Authority and Outlays: 1980 to 1997

[In billions of dollars, except percent. For fiscal year ending in year shown, except as noted; see text, section 9]

ITEM	1980	1985	1989	1990	1991	1992	1993	1994	1995	1996	1997, est.
Budget authority [1]	143.9	294.7	299.6	303.3	288.9	295.1	281.1	263.3	266.3	266.0	262.3
Department of Defense-Military [2]	140.6	286.8	290.8	293.0	276.2	282.1	267.2	251.4	255.7	254.4	250.0
Atomic energy [1] [3]	3.2	7.3	8.1	9.7	11.6	12.0	12.1	10.9	10.1	10.7	11.3
Outlays (Defense) [1]	134.0	252.7	303.6	299.3	273.3	298.4	291.1	281.6	272.1	265.7	267.2
Department of Defense-Military	130.9	245.2	294.9	289.8	262.4	266.9	278.6	268.6	259.4	253.2	254.3
Atomic energy [1] [3]	3.1	7.6	8.7	9.6	10.0	10.6	11.0	11.9	11.8	11.6	11.9

[1] Includes defense budget authority, balances, and outlays by other departments. [2] Excluding accruals. [3] Includes other defense related activities.

Source: U.S. Office of Management and Budget, *Historical Tables*, annual.

No. 547. Defense-Related Agencies: 1980 to 1995

[In thousands, except percent. Annual averages]

EMPLOYMENT	1980	1985	1989	1990	1991	1992	1993	1994	1995
Total U.S. employment [1]	100,907	108,856	119,030	120,430	119,282	120,058	121,744	123,060	124,900
Federal	4,386	4,608	4,662	4,577	4,541	4,549	4,403	(NA)	(NA)
Resident Armed Forces	1,604	1,706	1,688	1,637	1,564	1,566	1,485	(NA)	(NA)
Civilian personnel [2]	2,987	3,001	3,133	3,233	3,101	2,983	2,918	2,993	2,943
DOD-Civilian employment [3]	948	1,073	1,067	1,024	1,083	1,044	973	926	874
Percent of Federal civilian personnel	31.7	35.8	34.1	31.7	34.9	35.0	33.3	30.9	(NA)
DOD-Military and civilian employment	2,552	2,779	2,755	2,661	2,647	2,610	2,458	(NA)	(NA)
Percent of total Federal	58.2	60.3	59.1	58.1	58.3	57.4	55.8	(NA)	(NA)
Percent of total U.S.	2.5	2.6	2.3	2.2	2.2	2.2	2.0	(NA)	(NA)

NA Not available. [1] Includes resident Armed Forces. [2] See table 537. [3] Source: Beginning 1980, U.S. Dept. of Defense, *Civilian Manpower Statistics*, annual (Sept. issues).

Source: Except as noted, U.S. Bureau of Labor Statistics, *Employment and Earnings*, monthly.

No. 548. Military and Civilian Personnel and Expenditures: 1990 to 1996

ITEM	1990	1992	1993	1994	1995	1996
Personnel, total [1] (1,000)	3,693	3,889	3,762	3,623	3,391	3,252
Active duty military	1,185	1,214	1,171	1,131	1,085	1,056
Civilian	931	899	847	810	768	732
Reserve and National Guard	1,577	1,777	1,744	1,682	1,538	1,464
Expenditures, total (mil. dol.)	209,904	211,534	214,655	210,138	209,695	211,740
Payroll outlays	88,650	99,250	100,510	99,822	98,396	99,794
Active duty military pay	33,705	39,447	38,782	37,694	35,188	38,389
Civilian pay	28,230	31,205	31,619	30,587	29,932	29,230
Retired military pay	21,159	23,936	25,658	26,386	27,595	27,817
Reserve and National Guard pay	5,556	4,661	4,451	5,154	5,681	4,357
Prime contract awards [2] (mil. dol.)	121,254	112,285	114,145	110,316	109,005	109,408
Supply contracts	66,895	54,880	54,856	48,642	46,471	47,725
Service contracts	28,540	30,503	32,163	33,040	34,981	35,366
R and D contracts	21,955	21,508	22,076	21,513	21,266	20,033
Construction contracts	2,066	2,894	2,829	4,786	3,646	3,974
Civil function contracts	1,775	2,500	2,222	2,335	2,440	2,309
Major area of work (mil. dol.):						
Aircraft, fixed wing	6,329	8,197	6,926	6,277	7,543	6,521
Research, devel'mt, testing and evaluation (RDTE)	(NA)	1,266	1,422	3,256	(NA)	(NA)
RDTE/Aircraft-Engineering development	(NA)	1,266	1,422	1,769	(NA)	(NA)
RDTE/Missile and space systems-op systems	(NA)	(NA)	(NA)	1,487	(NA)	(NA)
Gas turbines and jet engines	1,856	974	(NA)	(NA)	(NA)	(NA)
Guided missiles	928	(NA)	793	494	495	625
Guided missile handling and servicing equip.	448	(NA)	757	(NA)	(NA)	(NA)
Major location of expenditures (mil. dol.):						
San Diego, CA	4,820	5,289	6,405	4,748	5,280	5,245
Pico Rivera, CA	(NA)	4,284	2,428	3,272	(NA)	(NA)
St. Louis, MO	5,616	3,462	5,442	6,087	5,770	7,049
Norfolk, VA	2,741	3,257	3,265	3,228	3,399	3,170
Arlington, VA	2,527	2,974	3,246	3,284	3,483	3,573
Fort Worth, TX	3,594	2,948	3,136	2,492	3,343	3,239
Washington, DC	2,771	2,828	3,045	2,347	2,347	2,759
Marietta, GA	(NA)	2,573	2,734	2,828	2,349	2,612
Long Beach, CA	(NA)	(NA)	2,236	3,550	2,563	3,030
Sunnyvale, CA	(NA)	(NA)	2,625	3,088	2,222	2,061

NA Not available. [1] Includes those based ashore and excludes those temporarily shore-based, in a transient status, or afloat. [2] Represents contract awards over $25,000.

Source: U.S. Dept. of Defense, *Atlas/Data Abstract for the United States and Selected Areas*, annual.

No. 549. Military Prime Contract Awards to All Businesses, by Program: 1980 to 1994

[In billions of dollars. Net values for fiscal year ending in year shown; see text, section 9. Includes all new prime contracts; debit or credit changes in contracts are also included. Actions cover official awards, amendments, or other changes in prime contracts to obtain military supplies, services, or construction. Excludes term contracts and contracts which do not obligate a firm total dollar amount or fixed quantity, but includes job orders, task orders, and delivery orders against such contracts]

DOD PROCUREMENT PROGRAM	1980	1985	1986	1989	1990	1991	1992	1993	1994
Total	83.7	163.7	151.4	139.3	144.7	150.9	136.3	132.2	131.4
Intragovernmental [1]	10.2	12.4	8.9	9.6	10.0	11.9	9.6	11.1	12.3
For work outside the U.S.	5.4	8.6	8.2	6.4	7.1	9.2	5.9	5.6	5.6
Educ. and nonprofit institutions	1.5	3.1	3.5	3.3	3.5	3.6	3.4	3.3	3.3
With business firms for work in the U.S. [2]	66.7	139.6	130.8	120.0	123.8	125.9	117.2	112.0	110.0
Major hard goods	41.0	98.1	85.9	79.9	79.1	74.1	67.1	59.2	56.0
Aircraft	12.5	34.6	25.0	24.2	24.0	23.6	24.1	23.5	18.8
Electronics and communication equip.	9.6	22.0	17.8	18.1	18.5	15.2	14.2	12.4	12.3
Missiles and space systems	7.9	18.7	19.7	18.7	17.1	16.4	13.1	11.6	10.6
Ships	6.0	10.4	13.7	9.6	10.3	9.3	8.3	6.8	9.1
Tanks, ammo. and weapons	5.1	12.5	9.7	9.2	9.2	9.6	7.4	4.9	5.3
Services	5.9	9.1	12.0	11.7	14.6	16.9	17.3	17.7	18.6

[1] Covers only purchases from other Federal agencies and reimbursable purchases on behalf of foreign governments. [2] Includes Department of Defense. Includes other business not shown separately. Contracts awarded for work in U.S. possessions, and other areas subject to complete sovereignty of United States; contracts in a classified location; and any intragovernmental contracts entered into overseas.

Source: U.S. Dept. of Defense, *Prime Contract Awards*, semiannual.

No. 550. Department of Defense Contract Awards, Payroll, and Civilian and Military Personnel—States: 1996

[For years ending Sept. 30. **Contracts** refer to awards made in year specified; expenditures relating to awards may extend over several years. **Civilian employees** include United States citizen and foreign national direct hire civilians subject to Office of Management and Budget (OMB) ceiling controls and civilian personnel involved in civil functions in the United States. Excludes indirect hire civilians and those direct hire civilian not subject to OMB ceiling controls. **Military personnel** include active duty personnel based ashore. Excludes personnel temporarily shore-based in a transient status, or afloat. **Payroll outlays** include the gross earnings of civilian and active duty military personnel for services rendered to the government and for cash allowances for benefits. Excludes employer's share of employee benefits, accrued military retirement benefits and most permanent change of station costs]

STATE	Contract awards [1] (mil. dol.)	Payroll (mil. dol.)	PERSONNEL (1,000)		STATE	Contract awards [1] (mil. dol.)	Payroll (mil. dol.)	PERSONNEL (1,000)	
			Civilian	Military				Civilian	Military
U.S.	109,406	99,794	732.0	1,056.1	MO	7,093	1,630	15.8	14.6
AL	1,838	2,183	22.0	14.6	MT	91	298	1.1	3.7
AK	565	879	4.4	16.6	NE	322	711	3.7	9.4
AZ	2,911	1,865	8.8	21.8	NV	285	777	2.2	7.8
AR	249	730	3.9	5.0	NH	568	240	1.3	0.4
CA	18,230	12,332	84.7	118.8	NJ.	2,564	1,419	19.4	7.6
CO	2,045	2,157	12.5	29.4	NM	676	1,168	8.5	14.4
CT	2,638	613	3.4	5.8	NY	3,501	1,688	12.8	20.4
DE	102	332	1.6	4.0	NC	1,421	4,259	17.5	96.3
DC	1,483	1,237	14.0	14.5	ND	106	439	1.7	9.5
FL.	5,863	6,670	29.0	56.1	OH	2,733	2,337	28.4	8.4
GA	3,966	4,332	32.9	63.0	OK	771	2,172	19.7	28.1
HI	928	2,331	16.8	34.4	OR	203	481	2.9	0.9
ID	133	346	1.4	4.0	PA	3,687	2,218	30.9	3.3
IL	1,256	1,988	15.3	29.0	RI	334	437	4.3	3.0
IN	1,552	1,022	12.3	1.2	SC	1,012	2,263	10.4	33.8
IA	371	244	1.4	0.4	SD	110	258	1.2	3.3
KS	763	1,079	5.6	17.2	TN	1,137	1,072	5.1	5.8
KY	874	1,723	10.1	33.4	TX	8,819	8,383	51.7	115.2
LA	1,078	1,333	8.4	16.3	UT	395	916	12.7	5.0
ME	797	525	5.5	1.8	VT	225	90	0.5	0.1
MD	4,137	3,265	35.6	29.9	VA	9,563	11,356	89.4	89.0
MA	4,675	843	8.6	3.0	WA	2,382	3,813	25.2	36.4
MI.	1,241	764	8.4	1.2	WV	199	242	1.7	0.5
MN	960	393	2.5	0.9	WI.	551	413	3.3	0.4
MS	1,912	1,301	10.3	12.5	WY	92	233	1.0	3.6

[1] Military awards for supplies, services, and construction. Net value of contracts of over $25,000 for work in each State and DC. Figures reflect impact of prime contracting on State distribution of defense work. Often the State in which a prime contractor is located in is not the State where the subcontracted work is done. See also headnote, table 549. Undistributed civilians and military personnel, their payrolls, and prime contract awards for performance in classified locations are excluded.

Source: U.S. Dept. of Defense, *Atlas/Data Abstract for the United States and Selected Areas*, annual.

No. 551. Worldwide Military Expenditures: 1986 to 1994

[In billions of dollars. For military expenditures and Armed Forces by country, see section 30. GNP=Gross national product]

COUNTRY GROUP	1986	1987	1988	1989	1990	1991	1992	1993	1994
Current dollars, total [1]	**997**	**1,030**	**1,059**	**1,069**	**1,081**	**1,027**	**932**	**867**	**840**
United States	281	288	293	304	306	280	305	298	288
Percent of total	28.2	28.0	27.7	28.4	28.3	27.3	32.8	34.3	34.3
Developed countries [2]	825	860	890	900	889	829	731	698	677
Developing countries [2]	172	170	169	169	193	198	200	169	164
NATO countries [3]	433	448	456	475	486	469	490	480	469
Constant (1994) dollars, total [1]	**1,297**	**1,298**	**1,285**	**1,241**	**1,203**	**1,101**	**971**	**885**	**840**
United States	365	363	356	353	341	300	318	304	288
Percent of total	28.2	28.0	27.7	28.4	28.3	27.3	32.8	34.3	34.3
Developed countries [2]	1,073	1,083	1,080	1,045	989	889	762	712	677
Developing countries [2]	224	214	205	196	214	213	209	173	164
NATO countries [3]	563	564	553	552	540	502	511	490	469
Percent of GNP	**5.4**	**5.2**	**4.9**	**4.6**	**4.4**	**4.0**	**3.6**	**3.2**	**3.0**
United States	6.6	6.3	6.0	5.8	5.5	4.9	5.1	4.7	4.3
Developed countries [2]	5.4	5.2	5.0	4.7	4.4	3.9	3.6	3.3	3.1
Developing countries [2]	5.4	4.9	4.5	4.2	4.5	4.3	3.6	2.8	2.6
NATO countries [3]	4.9	4.7	4.5	4.3	4.2	3.7	3.6	3.6	3.3

[1] Includes countries not shown separately. [2] Twenty-eight developed countries; see table 552 for selected countries; for complete list, see source. [3] North Atlantic Treaty Organization.

No. 552. Arms Trade in Constant (1994) Dollars—Selected Countries: 1992 to 1994

[In millions of dollars, except percent. Because some countries exclude arms imports or exports from their trade statistics and their "total" imports and exports are therefore understated, and because arms transfers may be estimated independently of trade data, the ratio of arms to total imports or exports may be overstated and may even exceed 100 percent]

COUNTRY	1992	1993	1994: Total	1994: Arms imports as percent of total imports	COUNTRY	1992	1993	1994: Total	1994: Arms imports as percent of total imports
World total [1]	29,740	28,590	22,120	0.5	Iran	375	1,021	390	3.2
Exporters: [1]					Iraq	-	-	-	-
Canada	1,251	791	230	0.1	Israel	886	1,123	1,000	4.1
China: Mainland	965	1,123	800	0.1	Italy	115	92	110	0.1
Czechoslovakia	146	(NA)	(NA)	(NA)	Japan	860	536	650	0.2
France	1,564	842	800	0.1	Jordan	21	31	40	1.2
Poland	21	10	30	-	Kuwait	1,043	765	250	1.2
United Kingdom	4,797	4,491	3,400	0.1	Libya	83	-	-	-
United States	14,080	14,080	12,400	0.2	Morocco	94	71	130	1.8
Germany	1,356	1,735	700	0.1	Nicaragua	5	5	-	-
Importers: [1]					North Korea	10	5	50	(NA)
Afghanistan	-	-	20	(NA)	Oman	10	122	50	1.3
Algeria	5	20	140	1.5	Pakistan	469	536	260	2.9
Angola	42	245	600	30.0	Peru	63	10	20	0.3
Argentina	10	20	10	-	Poland	-	-	5	-
Australia	240	337	430	0.8	Romania	31	-	-	-
Canada	428	194	170	0.1	Saudi Arabia	8,864	6,940	5,200	22.3
Cuba	104	102	-	-	South Korea	730	1,327	1,000	1.0
Czechoslovakia	-	(NA)	(NA)	(NA)	Spain	282	306	525	0.6
Egypt	1,147	1,429	1,500	14.7	Syria	396	225	10	0.2
El Salvador	52	41	30	1.3	Turkey	1,043	1,225	950	4.1
Ethiopia	-	5	-	-	United Kingdom	229	296	200	0.1
Germany	1,017	587	240	0.1	*United States*	*1,668*	*1,429*	*1,100*	*0.2*
Greece	756	842	270	(NA)	Venezuela	83	71	60	0.7
Hungary	-	944	10	0.1	Vietnam	10	10	80	1.9
India	678	265	140	0.5	Yemen (Sanaa)	5	20	230	8.7

- Represents or rounds to zero. NA Not available. [1] Includes countries not shown separately.

Source of tables 551 and 552: U.S. Arms Control and Disarmament Agency, *World Military Expenditures and Arms Transfers*, annual.

No. 553. Arms Transfers—Cumulative Value for Period 1984-94, by Major Supplier and Recipient Country

[In millions of dollars]

RECIPIENT	Total [1]	SUPPLIER						
		United States	United Kingdom	Russia	West Germany	France	China: Mainland	Canada
World, total [1]	78,615	39,460	12,460	6,550	3,695	3,125	2,795	2,180
Africa [1]	2,305	395	130	610	20	255	180	-
North Africa	600	235	5	150	10	60	50	-
Algeria	165	5	-	150	-	-	-	-
Libya	80	-	-	-	10	-	50	-
Morocco	275	160	5	-	-	60	-	-
Subsahara Africa	1,685	160	125	460	10	195	140	-
Angola	885	-	-	450	-	20	5	-
Nigeria	165	5	60	-	-	50	-	-
Rwanda	105	80	-	-	-	20	-	-
Zimbabwe	100	5	60	-	-	5	20	-
Americas:								
Central America & Carribbean	495	275	-	205	-	10	-	-
Cuba	200	-	-	200	-	-	-	-
El Salvador	120	120	-	-	-	-	-	-
North America (NAFTA)	5,080	530	1,420	40	375	210	120	600
Canada	775	390	20	-	5	40	-	(X)
Mexico	210	140	-	10	-	-	-	-
United States	4,095	(X)	1,400	30	370	170	120	600
South America	1,095	365	55	10	50	180	25	-
Brazil	240	110	10	-	-	90	-	-
Chile	170	20	5	-	-	10	-	-
Colombia	190	90	-	-	-	-	-	-
	0	-	-	-	-	-	-	-
Venezuela	200	60	-	-	40	60	-	-
Asia:								
Central Asia & Cauc.	185	-	-	95	-	-	-	-
Middle East	34,055	17,585	9,560	1,590	385	965	865	900
Egypt	4,060	3,800	10	30	5	-	-	-
Iran	1,765	-	-	1,000	40	-	525	-
Israel	2,970	2,600	-	-	310	-	60	-
Kuwait	2,040	1,800	-	-	-	100	-	-
Saudi Arabia	20,465	8,600	9,400	-	30	525	170	900
Syria	600	-	-	300	-	30	20	-
United Arab Emir.	995	360	-	260	-	110	-	-
Yemen	270	-	-	-	-	-	90	-
East Asia	12,210	6,580	800	1,855	1,315	155	580	-
Burma	370	-	-	-	-	-	300	-
China:								
Mainland	1,750	30	-	1,700	-	-	(X)	-
Taiwan	2,400	2,400	-	-	-	-	-	-
Indonesia	170	90	-	-	80	-	-	-
Japan	1,960	1,900	30	-	30	-	-	-
Korea, South	2,965	1,300	270	5	1,200	60	-	-
Malaysia	520	20	450	-	-	-	-	-
Singapore	640	240	10	-	-	90	-	-
Thailand	845	400	20	-	-	-	160	-
South Asia	2,520	50	65	940	80	150	1,015	-
India	1,075	20	-	925	80	-	-	-
Pakistan	1,225	20	60	-	-	150	875	-
Europe	14,885	8,175	400	1,205	1,470	1,180	-	650
Eastern Europe	1,535	25	-	1,025	90	-	-	10
Hungary	930	10	-	825	90	-	-	-
Western Europe	13,350	8,150	400	180	1,360	1,180	-	640
Belgium	460	200	-	-	-	-	-	-
Denmark	205	170	5	-	-	30	-	-
Finland	815	40	110	60	280	320	-	-
France	380	240	10	-	-	(X)	-	20
Germany	1,840	1,100	60	-	(X)	50	-	600
Greece	1,830	625	10	-	470	360	-	-
Italy	300	280	20	-	-	-	-	-
Netherlands	700	675	5	-	-	-	-	-
Norway	550	170	40	-	110	80	-	-
Portugal	560	430	60	-	10	50	-	-
Spain	1,090	825	5	-	40	-	-	20
Sweden	160	120	-	-	20	-	-	-
Switzerland	550	70	-	-	360	60	-	-
Turkey	3,070	2,500	70	120	90	220	-	-
United Kingdom	695	675	(X)	-	-	-	-	-
Oceania	1,195	915	20	-	-	-	-	10
Australia	975	875	10	-	-	-	-	10
New Zealand	160	40	10	-	-	-	-	-

- Represents $2.5 million or less. X Not applicable. [1] Includes countries not shown separately.

Source: U.S. Arms Control and Disarmament Agency, *World Military Expenditures and Arms Transfers*, annual.

No. 554. U.S. Military Sales and Assistance to Foreign Governments: 1987 to 1995

[In millions of dollars, except as indicated. For fiscal year ending in year shown; see text, section 9. Department of Defense (DOD) sales deliveries cover deliveries against DOD sales orders sales orders authorized under Arms Export Control Act, as well as earlier and applicable legislation. For details regarding individual programs, see source]

ITEM	1987	1988	1989	1990	1991	1992	1993	1994	1995
Military sales agreements	5,963	11,111	9,892	11,667	20,095	14,460	32,067	12,935	9,029
Military constr. sales agrmts	129	217	76	273	725	682	815	60	25
Military sales deliveries [1]	10,849	9,114	7,511	7,969	8,977	10,448	11,262	9,539	11,835
Military sales financing	4,053	4,049	4,273	4,758	4,693	4,274	4,124	3,917	3,712
Military assistance programs [2]	958	697	535	137	177	116	540	321	112
Military assist. program delivery [3]	83	56	53	27	150	87	51	5	9
IMET program/deliveries [4]	53	45	46	43	46	42	43	22	26

[1] Includes aircraft, ships, support vehicles, communications equipment, and other supplies. [2] Includes military construction sales deliveries. [3] Also includes Military Assistance Service Funded (MASF) program data, section 506(a) drawdown authority, and MAP Merger Funds. [4] Includes Military Assistance Service Funded (MASF) program data and section 506(a) drawdown authority.

No. 555. U.S. Military Sales Deliveries, by Country: 1987 to 1995

[In millions of dollars. For fiscal years ending in year shown; see text, section 9. Represents Department of Defense military sales]

COUNTRY	1987	1988	1989	1990	1991	1992	1993	1994	1995
Total [1]	**10,849**	**9,114**	**7,511**	**7,969**	**8,977**	**10,448**	**11,262**	**9,539**	**11,835**
Australia	588	850	583	381	205	156	233	350	303
Canada	127	212	144	103	164	107	122	154	117
China: Taiwan	366	484	353	460	556	708	694	736	1,161
Egypt	962	497	322	441	573	1,091	1,263	1,034	1,788
Germany	315	382	632	358	476	501	346	155	241
Greece	79	129	137	114	124	163	213	193	227
Israel	1,230	754	230	146	242	721	787	452	332
Italy	71	62	64	61	61	52	48	106	56
Japan	233	212	166	220	317	544	317	600	526
Kuwait	58	41	46	52	111	858	882	221	467
Netherlands	413	321	367	375	371	319	115	216	189
Portugal	24	15	32	72	40	89	83	228	91
Saudi Arabia	3,199	1,297	965	1,139	3,018	2,632	3,614	2,153	3,762
South Korea	344	326	316	328	230	309	306	374	431
Spain	822	637	656	403	155	138	203	390	115
Thailand	95	291	211	175	179	102	106	138	346
Turkey	277	699	619	720	600	703	749	885	362
United Kingdom	206	180	131	205	243	154	227	202	108

[1] Includes countries not shown.

Source of tables 554 and 555: U.S. Defense Security Assistance Agency, *Foreign Military Sales, Foreign Military Construction Sales*, and *Military Assistance Facts*, annual.

No. 556. Summary of Active and Reserve Military Personnel and Forces

ITEM	Cold War (1990)	1996	Force Target
Military personnel (1,000):			
Active	2,069	1,431	1,422
Guard and Reserve	1,128	892	889
Military Forces:			
Army divisions:			
Active	18	10	10
National Guard	10	[1]8	[1]8
Air Force:			
Fighter wing:			
Active	24	13	13
Reserve	12	7	7
Navy aircraft carriers:			
Active	15	11	11
Training	1	1	1
Navy air wings:			
Active	13	10	10
Reserve	2	1	1
Battle force ships [2]	546	346	330-346
Marine Corps:			
Divisions:			
Active	3	3	3
Reserve	1	1	1
Air wings:			
Active	3	3	3
Reserve	1	1	1
Strategic nuclear forces:			
Intercontinental Ballistic Missiles	1,000	550	500
Warheads	2,450	2,000	[3]500
Ballistic missile submarines	31	18	[3]14
Sea-launched ballistic missiles	568	432	336
Warheads	4,864	3,456	[3 4]1,750
Heavy bombers	324	[5]87	[5]92

[1] Plus 15 enhanced readiness brigades. [2] Includes active and reserve ships. [3] Upon entry-into-force of START II. [4] Not over 1,750. [5] Does not include 95 B-1 bombers dedicated to conventional missions.

Source: U.S. Office of Management and Budget, *Budget of the United States Government*, annual.

No. 557. Department of Defense Manpower: 1950 to 1995

[In thousands. As of end of fiscal year; see text, section 9. Includes National Guard, Reserve, and retired regular personnel on extended or continuous active duty. Excludes Coast Guard. Other officer candidates are included under enlisted personnel]

YEAR	Total [1] [2]	ARMY					NAVY [3]					MARINE CORPS					AIR FORCE				
		Total [2]	White	Black	Officers	Enlisted	Total [2]	White	Black	Officers	Enlisted	Total [2]	White	Black	Officers	Enlisted	Total [2]	White	Black	Officers	Enlisted
1950	1,459	593	(NA)	(NA)	73	519	381	(NA)	(NA)	45	333	74	(NA)	(NA)	7	67	411	(NA)	(NA)	57	354
1955	2,935	1,109	(NA)	(NA)	122	986	661	(NA)	(NA)	75	583	205	(NA)	(NA)	18	187	960	(NA)	(NA)	137	823
1960	2,475	873	(NA)	(NA)	101	770	617	(NA)	(NA)	70	545	171	(NA)	(NA)	16	154	815	(NA)	(NA)	130	683
1965	2,654	969	(NA)	(NA)	112	855	670	(NA)	(NA)	78	588	190	(NA)	(NA)	17	173	825	(NA)	(NA)	132	690
1966	3,092	1,200	(NA)	(NA)	118	1,080	743	(NA)	(NA)	80	659	262	(NA)	(NA)	21	241	887	(NA)	(NA)	131	753
1967	3,375	1,442	(NA)	(NA)	144	1,297	750	(NA)	(NA)	82	664	285	(NA)	(NA)	24	262	897	(NA)	(NA)	135	759
1968	3,546	1,570	(NA)	(NA)	166	1,402	764	(NA)	(NA)	85	674	307	(NA)	(NA)	25	283	905	(NA)	(NA)	140	762
1969	3,458	1,512	(NA)	(NA)	173	1,337	774	(NA)	(NA)	85	684	310	(NA)	(NA)	26	284	862	(NA)	(NA)	135	723
1970	3,065	1,323	(NA)	(NA)	167	1,153	691	(NA)	(NA)	81	606	260	(NA)	(NA)	25	235	791	(NA)	(NA)	130	657
1971	2,713	1,124	(NA)	(NA)	149	972	622	(NA)	(NA)	75	542	212	(NA)	(NA)	22	191	755	(NA)	(NA)	126	625
1972	2,322	811	(NA)	(NA)	121	687	587	(NA)	(NA)	73	511	198	(NA)	(NA)	20	178	726	(NA)	(NA)	122	600
1973	2,252	801	(NA)	(NA)	116	682	564	(NA)	(NA)	71	490	196	(NA)	(NA)	19	177	691	(NA)	(NA)	115	572
1974	2,162	783	(NA)	(NA)	106	674	546	(NA)	(NA)	67	475	189	(NA)	(NA)	19	170	644	(NA)	(NA)	110	529
1975	2,128	784	(NA)	(NA)	103	678	535	(NA)	(NA)	66	466	196	(NA)	(NA)	19	177	613	(NA)	(NA)	105	503
1976	2,082	779	(NA)	(NA)	99	678	525	(NA)	(NA)	64	458	192	(NA)	(NA)	19	174	585	(NA)	(NA)	100	481
1977	2,075	782	(NA)	(NA)	98	680	530	(NA)	(NA)	63	462	192	(NA)	(NA)	19	173	571	(NA)	(NA)	98	470
1978	2,062	772	(NA)	(NA)	98	670	530	(NA)	(NA)	63	463	191	(NA)	(NA)	18	172	570	(NA)	(NA)	95	470
1979	2,027	759	(NA)	(NA)	97	657	523	(NA)	(NA)	62	457	185	(NA)	(NA)	18	167	559	(NA)	(NA)	96	459
1980	2,051	777	503	229	99	674	527	436	55	63	460	188	142	39	18	170	558	460	80	98	456
1981	2,083	781	502	232	102	675	540	443	58	65	470	191	145	39	18	172	570	468	83	99	467
1982	2,109	780	504	230	103	673	553	450	62	67	481	192	149	38	19	173	583	476	87	102	476
1983	2,123	780	512	220	106	669	558	462	66	66	485	194	152	37	20	174	592	483	88	105	483
1984	2,138	780	520	215	108	668	565	455	67	69	491	196	153	36	20	176	597	486	89	106	486
1985	2,151	781	523	211	110	667	571	459	70	71	495	198	152	37	20	178	602	488	90	108	489
1986	2,169	781	524	210	110	667	581	464	75	72	504	199	151	38	20	179	608	491	92	109	495
1987	2,174	781	519	212	108	668	587	467	81	72	510	200	150	38	20	179	607	489	92	107	495
1988	2,138	772	507	213	107	660	593	466	85	72	516	197	147	38	20	177	576	462	88	105	467
1989	2,130	770	497	218	107	658	593	461	91	72	516	197	146	38	20	177	571	458	87	104	463
1990	2,044	732	466	213	104	624	579	446	93	72	503	197	145	38	20	177	535	428	82	100	431
1991	1,986	711	452	204	104	603	570	439	92	71	495	194	144	38	20	174	510	409	77	97	409
1992	1,807	610	388	173	95	511	542	415	88	69	468	185	138	32	19	165	470	377	70	90	378
1993	1,705	572	365	158	88	480	510	390	84	66	439	178	134	30	18	160	444	357	65	84	358
1994	1,610	541	344	147	85	452	469	356	78	62	403	174	131	28	18	156	426	341	62	81	341
1995	1,518	509	322	137	83	422	435	328	75	59	372	175	130	28	18	157	400	318	58	78	318

NA Not available. [1] Beginning 1980, excludes Navy Reserve personnel on active duty for Training and Administration of Reserves (TARS). From 1989, the full-time Guard and Reserve. [2] Includes Cadets and other not shown separately. [3] Prior to 1980, includes Navy Reserve personnel on active duty for Training and Administration of Reserves (TARS).

Source: U.S. Dept. of Defense, *Selected Manpower Statistics*, annual.

No. 558. Military Installations in the United States: 1995

[Represents bases with active-duty populations of 300 or more. Excludes the Coast Guard]

STATE AND BRANCH	Active duty personnel	Family members	Civilians
United States	1,275,896	1,568,828	624,294
Alabama	20,219	14,969	28,633
Army	11,297	11,895	20,633
Navy	4,461	1,537	4,000
Air Force	4,461	1,537	4,000
Alaska	16,688	24,453	4,409
Army	6,700	9,600	2,580
Navy	475	-	46
Air Force	9,513	14,853	1,783
Arizona	23,061	45,897	7,463
Army	5,750	11,700	4,000
Marine Corps	5,311	7,197	1,064
Air Force	12,000	27,000	2,399
Arkansas	13,678	14,910	2,714
Army	6839	7455	1357
Air Force	6,839	7,455	1,357
California	188,871	159,236	73,398
Army	7,698	9,384	5,351
Navy	100,884	41,044	29,333
Marine Corps	56,589	68,847	9,755
Air Force	23,700	39,963	28,959
Colorado	34,815	49,671	8,962
Army	15,000	32,000	3,300
Air Force	19,815	17,671	5,682
Connecticut	9,000	22,000	1,800
Navy	9,000	22,000	1,800
Delaware	4,040	6,000	1,128
Air Force	4,040	6,000	1,128
District of Columbia	9,115	4,190	9,200
Army	3,555	4,150	3,540
Navy	2,920	-	4,620
Marine Corps	1,168	40	-
Air Force	1,472	-	1,040
Florida	65,936	108,699	27,378
Navy	39,151	54,312	14,346
Air Force	26,785	54,387	13,032
Georgia	68,839	100,181	40,309
Army	53,696	70,376	20,005
Navy	5,907	19,950	4,308
Marine Corps	900	1,700	3,175
Air Force	8,336	8,155	12,821
Hawaii	50,984	42,140	19,744
Army	15,787	12,895	3,223
Navy	23,128	22,962	12,554
Marine Corps	8,671	6,283	2,674
Air Force	3,398	-	1,293
Idaho	4,274	3,400	430
Navy	(1)	(1)	-
Air Force	4,274	3,400	430
Illinois	25,635	22,877	13,347
Army	2,120	3,560	8,390
Navy	16,719	10,000	2,418
Air Force	6,796	9,317	2,539
Indiana	(1)	(1)	(1)
Army	(1)	(1)	(1)
Iowa	-	-	-
Kansas	18,621	27,350	5,755
Army	15,641	20,600	5,330
Air Force	2,980	6,750	425
Kentucky	29,906	46,373	11,491
Army	29,906	46,373	11,491
Louisiana	18,506	15,362	7,559
Army	8,851	13,782	2,363
Navy	3,636	1,580	3,352
Air Force	6,017	-	1,844
Maine	3,474	3,550	891
Navy	3,474	3,550	891
Air Force	-	-	-
Maryland	30,691	24,988	45,829
Army	14,255	14,304	35,755
Navy	10,446	2,684	7,981
Air Force	5,990	8,000	2,093
Massachusetts	2,622	1,755	1,872
Army	(2)	(2)	(2)
Navy	(2)	-	(2)
Air Force	2,622	1,755	1,872
Michigan	1,026	-	1,335
Air Force	1,026	-	1,335
Minnesota	-	-	-
Mississippi	19,394	18,301	7,841
Navy	7,088	1,655	2,436
Air Force	12,306	16,646	5,405
Missouri	7,828	12,200	4,635
Army	4,800	6,000	4,000
Air Force	3,028	6,200	635
Montana	3,871	5,159	441
Air Force	3,871	5,159	441
Nebraska	9,780	15,500	2,920
Air Force	9,780	15,500	2,920
Nevada	7,863	12,133	2,900
Navy	1,100	2,000	1,400
Air Force	6,763	10,133	1,500
New Hampshire	401	967	3,630
Navy	401	967	3,630
New Jersey	9,748	11,725	15,725
Army	2,048	2,220	9,968
Navy	2,199	1,100	2,795
Air Force	5,501	8,405	2,962
New Mexico	15,194	25,356	21,876
Army	786	1,637	6,927
Air Force	14,408	23,719	14,949
New York	14,395	22,187	6,069
Army	11,895	19,187	6,069
Navy	2,500	3,000	-
Air Force	-	-	-
North Carolina	112,424	173,762	17,380
Army	49,000	78,000	4,783
Marine Corps	54,003	88,535	11,083
Air Force	9,421	7,227	1,514
North Dakota	9,940	13,546	1,712
Air Force	9,940	13,546	1,712
Ohio	8,900	12,750	16,650
Air Force	8,900	12,750	16,650
Oklahoma	26,966	44,682	21,762
Army	14,585	38,982	5,668
Air Force	12,381	5,700	16,094
Oregon	-	-	-
Pennsylvania	2,284	4,616	1,729
Army	713	1,866	951
Navy	1,571	2,750	778
Rhode Island	3,652	3,000	3,976
Navy	3,677	3,000	3,897
South Carolina	25,661	33,326	5,852
Army	8,679	7,762	931
Navy	1,072	-	669
Marine Corps	5,750	9,164	1,477
Air Force	10,160	16,400	2,775
South Dakota	3,500	5,050	500
Air Force	3,500	5,050	500
Tennessee	2,272	2,192	1,707
Navy	2,272	2,192	1,707
Texas	120,456	150,118	59,368
Army	67,934	109,854	18,854
Navy	7,996	8,378	8,016
Air Force	44,526	31,866	32,498
Utah	4,700	-	9,800
Air Force	4,700	-	9,800
Vermont	-	-	-
Virginia	161,678	167,722	77,403
Army	23,526	19,472	24,314
Navy	130,152	144,750	50,289
Marine Corps	8,000	3,500	2,800
Air Force	8,985	13,000	2,256
Washington	60,884	91,517	23,892
Army	20,000	22,100	5,400
Navy	31,837	56,704	15,325
Air Force	9,047	12,713	3,167
West Virginia	-	-	-
Wisconsin	304	816	2,259
Army	304	816	2,259
Wyoming	3,500	4,200	600
Air Force	3,500	4,200	600

- Represents or rounds to zero. [1] Closed or scheduled to close.

Source: Army Times Publishing Co. Springfield, VA 22159, *Guide to Military Installations in the U. S.*, annual.

No. 559. Military Personnel on Active Duty, by Location: 1980 to 1996

[In thousands. As of end of fiscal year; see text, section 9]

ITEM	1980	1985	1988	1989	1990	1991	1992	1993	1994	1995	1996
Total	**2,051**	**2,151**	**2,138**	**2,130**	**2,044**	**1,986**	**1,807**	**1,705**	**1,611**	**1,518**	**1,472**
Shore-based [1]	1,840	1,920	1,891	1,884	1,794	1,743	1,589	1,505	1,431	1,361	1,317
Afloat [2]	211	231	248	246	252	243	218	200	180	167	155
United States [3]	1,562	1,636	1,596	1,620	1,437	1,539	1,463	1,397	1,324	1,280	1,231
Foreign countries	488	516	541	510	609	448	344	308	287	238	240

[1] Includes Navy personnel temporarily on shore. [2] Includes Marine Corps. [3] Includes outlying areas.

Source: U.S. Dept. of Defense, *Selected Manpower Statistics*, annual.

No. 560. Military Personnel on Active Duty in Foreign Countries: 1996

[As of end of fiscal year]

COUNTRY	1996	COUNTRY	1996	COUNTRY	1996
In foreign countries [1]	240,421	Estonia	2	Nicaragua	15
Ashore	213,467	Ethiopia	10	Niger	6
Afloat	26,954	Fiji	2	Nigeria	16
Albania	3	Finland	17	Norway	104
Algeria	8	France	73	Oman	30
Angola	3	Georgia	2	Pakistan	26
Antarctica	19	Germany	48,878	Panama	6,435
Antigua	2	Ghana	7	Paraguay	10
Argentina	25	Gibraltar	4	Peru	26
Armenia	1	Greece	507	Philippines	136
Australia	328	Greenland	141	Poland	20
Austria	37	Guatemala	17	Portugal	1,075
Azerbaijan	1	Guinea	6	Qatar	43
Bahamas, The	53	Haiti	277	Rep. of Korea	36,539
Bahrain	596	Honduras	865	Romania	12
Bangladesh	10	Hong Kong	29	Russia	74
Barbados	11	Hungary	6,523	Saudi Arabia	1,587
Belarus	2	Iceland	1,893	Senegal	11
Belgium	1,646	India	24	Serbia	8
Belize	2	Indonesia	43	Sierra Leone	6
Bolivia	24	Ireland	8	Singapore	158
Bosnia and Herzegovina	15,003	Israel	44	Slovakia	4
Botswana	7	Italy	12,401	South Africa	23
Brazil	47	Jamaica	10	Spain	2,746
Bulgaria	14	Japan	42,962	Sri Lanka	7
Burma	11	Jordan	24	St. Helena	3
Burundi	5	Kazakhstan	7	Suriname	2
Cambodia	5	Kenya	29	Sweden	13
Cameroon	9	Korea, Republic of	36,539	Switzerland	24
Canada	208	Kuwait	5,531	Syria	11
Chad	9	Kyrgyzstan	1	Tanzania, U. Rep. of	5
Chile	24	Laos	3	Thailand	242
China	32	Latvia	1	Togo	6
Colombia	34	Lebanon	2	Trinidad and Tabago	32
Congo	5	Liberia	9	Tunisia	19
Costa Rica	9	Lithuania	2	Turkey	2,922
Cote D'Ivoire	19	Luxembourg	9	Turkmenistan	1
Croatia	4,007	Macedonia	501	Uganda	9
Cuba (Guantanamo)	1,886	Madagascar	6	Ukraine	8
Cyprus	50	Malaysia	19	United Arab Emirates	23
Czech Republic	10	Mali	6	United Kingdom	11,662
Denmark	38	Malta	8	Uruguay	9
Diego Garcia	876	Mexico	36	Uzbekistan	1
Djibouti	7	Moldova	1	Venezuela	30
Dominican Republic	10	Morocco	17	Vietnam	6
Ecuador	70	Mozambique	5	Yemen	11
Egypt	1,066	Nepal	6	Zaire	9
El Salvador	26	Netherlands	747	Zambabwe	8
Eritrea	1	New Zealand	32	Zambia	6

[1] Includes areas not shown separately.

Source: U.S. Department of Defense, *Selected Manpower Statistics*, annual.

No. 561. Coast Guard Personnel on Active Duty: 1970 to 1995

[As of end of fiscal year; see text, section 9]

YEAR	Total	Officers	Cadets	Enlisted	YEAR	Total	Officers	Cadets	Enlisted
1970	37,689	5,512	653	31,524	1991	38,377	7,192	900	30,285
1975	36,788	5,630	1,177	29,981	1992	39,388	7,507	919	30,962
1980	39,381	6,463	877	32,041	1993	39,234	7,628	907	30,699
1985	38,595	6,775	733	31,087	1994	37,802	7,656	881	29,265
1990	36,939	6,876	927	29,136	1995	36,731	7,462	841	28,401

Source: U.S. Dept. of Transportation, *Annual Report of the Secretary of Transportation*.

No. 562. Armed Forces Personnel—Summary of Major Conflicts

[For Revolutionary War, number of personnel serving not known, but estimates range from 184,000 to 250,000; for War of 1812, 286,730 served; for Mexican War, 78,718 served. Dates of the major conflicts may differ from those specified in various laws providing benefits for veterans]

ITEM	Unit	Civil War[1]	Spanish-American War	World War I	World War II	Korean conflict	Vietnam conflict
Personnel serving[2]	1,000	2,213	307	4,735	[3]16,113	[4]5,720	[5]8,744
Average duration of service	Months	20	8	12	33	19	23
Service abroad: Personnel serving	Percent	(NA)	[6]29	53	73	[7]56	(NA)
Average duration[8]	Months	(NA)	1.5	6	16	13	(NA)
Casualties:[9] Battle deaths[2]	1,000	140	(Z)	53	292	34	[10]47
Wounds not mortal[2]	1,000	282	2	204	671	103	[10]153
Draftees: Classified	1,000	777	(X)	24,234	36,677	9,123	[5]75,717
Examined	1,000	522	(X)	3,764	17,955	3,685	[5]8,611
Rejected	1,000	160	(X)	803	6,420	1,189	[5]3,880
Inducted	1,000	46	(X)	2,820	10,022	1,560	[5]1,759

NA Not available. X Not applicable. Z Fewer than 500. [1] Union forces only. Estimates of the number serving in Confederate forces range from 600,000 to 1.5 million. [2] Source: U.S. Department of Defense, *Selected Manpower Statistics*, annual. [3] Covers Dec. 1, 1941, to Dec. 31, 1946. [4] Covers June 25, 1950, to July 27, 1953. [5] Covers Aug. 4, 1964, to Jan. 27, 1973. [6] Army and Marines only. [7] Excludes Navy. Covers July 1950 through Jan. 1955. Far East area only. [8] During hostilities only. [9] For periods covered, see footnotes 3, 4, and 5. [10] Covers Jan. 1, 1961, to Jan. 27, 1973. Includes known military service personnel who have died from combat related wounds.

Source: Except as noted, the President's Commission on Veterans' Pensions, Veterans' *Benefits in the United States*, vol. I, 1956; and U.S. Dept. of Defense, unpublished data.

No. 563. Enlisted Military Personnel Accessions: 1990 to 1996

[In thousands. For years ending Sept. 30]

BRANCH OF SERVICE	1990	1994	1995	1996	BRANCH OF SERVICE	1990	1994	1995	1996
Total	461.1	373.1	357.3	367.6	First enlistments	62.1	37.6	36.4	39.2
First enlistments	216.4	160.5	160.0	174.6	Reenlistments	58.6	45.0	41.4	40.6
Reenlistments	237.0	188.5	180.8	181.0	Marine Corps	47.7	44.6	46.7	48.7
Reserves to active duty	15.6	24.0	16.6	12.0	First enlistments	32.9	32.2	34.4	34.5
					Reenlistments	14.4	11.7	11.9	0.4
Army	181.7	138.0	135.9	146.0					
First enlistments	84.8	60.3	57.7	69.7	Air Force	104.4	84.5	81.3	81.6
Reenlistments	96.5	77.6	77.7	76.2	First enlistments	36.6	30.5	31.4	31.2
Navy	135.3	105.9	93.4	91.3	Reenlistments	67.5	54.0	49.7	50.3

Source: U.S. Dept. of Defense, *Selected Manpower Statistics* annual.

No. 564. Military Personnel on Active Duty: 1990 to 1996

[As of Sept. 30]

RANK/GRADE	1990	1991	1992	1993	1994	1995	1996
Total[1]	2,043.7	1,985.6	1,807.2	1,705.1	1,610.5	1,518.2	1,471.7
Recruit—E-1	97.6	74.6	83.2	75.4	73.3	63.4	69.3
Private—E-2	140.3	125.8	110.9	114.1	108.2	99.7	99.0
Pvt. 1st class—E-3	280.1	275.6	233.5	214.6	206.4	197.1	200.4
Corporal—E-4	427.8	426.1	383.5	352.2	322.2	317.2	283.8
Sergeant—E-5	361.5	355.5	305.1	295.6	281.0	261.4	254.8
Staff Sgt.—E-6	239.1	238.9	227.4	214.6	198.1	180.5	172.6
Sgt. 1st class—E-7	134.1	134.2	130.5	124.7	119.7	109.3	107.7
Master Sgt.—E-8	38.0	36.1	33.2	31.6	29.9	28.8	28.8
Sgt. Major—E-9	15.3	14.8	13.5	12.8	12.1	11.1	10.7
Warrant Officer—W-1	3.2	2.8	2.2	2.4	2.4	2.0	2.1
Chief Warrant—W-4	3.0	3.0	2.7	2.4	2.4	2.2	2.0
2d Lt.—0-1	31.9	27.3	25.8	25.0	24.8	25.6	25.2
1st Lt.—0-2	37.9	37.6	33.5	29.7	27.3	26.1	25.8
Captain—0-3	106.6	106.1	100.2	93.0	89.2	84.3	81.0
Major—0-4	53.2	53.1	50.4	48.0	44.8	43.9	43.9
Lt. Colonel—0-5	32.3	32.2	30.9	29.5	29.0	28.7	28.2
Colonel—0-6	14.0	13.7	13.2	12.5	12.2	11.7	11.6
Brig. General—0-7	0.5	0.5	0.5	0.4	0.5	0.4	0.4
Major General—0-8	0.4	0.3	0.3	0.3	0.3	0.3	0.3
Lt. General—0-9	0.1	0.1	0.1	0.1	0.1	0.1	0.1
General—0-10	(Z)	(Z)	(Z)	(Z)	(Z)	(Z)	(Z)

Z Fewer than 50. [1] Includes cadets and midshipmen and warrant officers, W-2 and W-3.

Source: U.S. Dept. of Defense, *Selected Manpower Statistics*, annual, and Office of the Comptroller, unpublished data.

No. 565. Military Reserve Personnel: 1980 to 1996

[In thousands. As of end of fiscal year; see text, section 9. Excludes U.S. Coast Guard Reserve. The ready reserve includes selected reservists who are intended to assist active forces in a war and the individual ready reserve who, in a major war, would be used to fill out active and reserve units and later would be a source of combat replacements; a portion of the ready reserve serves in an active status. The standby reserve cannot be called to active duty unless the Congress gives its explicit approval. The retired reserve represents a low potential for mobilization]

RESERVE STATUS AND BRANCH OF SERVICE	1980	1985	1986	1987	1988	1989	1990	1991	1992	1993	1994	1995	1996
Total reserves	1,349	1,610	1,653	1,657	1,677	1,661	1,671	1,786	1,883	1,867	1,805	1,659	1,580
Ready reserve	1,263	1,566	1,612	1,620	1,642	1,631	1,641	1,758	1,858	1,841	1,779	1,633	1,523
Standby reserve	86	44	41	38	34	29	29	28	25	26	26	26	28
Retired reserve	338	372	390	412	469	477	462	474	442	461	482	506	530
Army	804	1,045	1,067	1,064	1,070	1,082	1,050	1,124	1,156	1,132	1,077	1,001	921
Navy	207	214	228	238	244	248	252	271	297	302	317	280	262
Marine Corp	94	92	93	88	87	82	83	96	107	112	109	104	102
Air Force	243	259	266	268	275	270	286	295	323	321	302	274	265

Source: U.S. Dept. of Defense, *Official Guard and Reserve Manpower Strengths and Statistics*, quarterly.

No. 566. Ready Reserve Personnel Profile—Race, and Sex: 1990 to 1996

ITEM	RACE					PERCENT DISTRIBUTION			
	Total	White	Black	Asian	American Indian	White	Black	Asian	American Indian
1990	1,641,475	1,289,367	271,470	14,816	7,695	78.5	16.5	0.9	0.5
1993	1,840,650	1,425,255	309,699	21,089	9,068	77.4	16.8	1.1	0.5
1994	1,779,436	1,366,367	297,519	22,190	8,870	76.8	16.7	1.2	0.5
1995	1,633,497	1,254,592	273,847	21,792	8,591	76.8	16.8	1.3	0.5
1996, total [1]	1,522,518	1,166,681	249,120	21,241	8,390	76.6	16.4	1.4	0.6
Male	1,293,133	1,016,025	187,425	18,239	6,896	78.6	14.5	1.4	0.5
Officers	195,469	168,394	13,080	2,386	457	86.1	6.7	1.2	0.2
Enlisted	1,097,644	847,631	174,345	15,853	6,439	77.2	15.9	1.4	0.6
Female	229,365	150,656	61,695	3,002	1,494	65.7	26.9	1.3	0.7
Officers	43,462	33,019	6,748	529	92	76.0	15.5	1.2	0.2
Enlisted	185,923	117,637	54,947	2,473	1,402	63.3	29.6	1.3	0.8

[1] Includes unknown sex.

Source: U.S. Dept. of Defense, *Official Guard and Reserve Manpower Strengths and Statistics*, annual.

No. 567. Military Reserve Costs: 1980 to 1995

[In millions of dollars. As of end of fiscal year; see text, section 9. Army and Air Force data include National Guard]

TYPE OF COST	1980	1985	1989	1990	1991	1992	1993	1994	1995
Total	7,969	19,414	19,797	21,528	21,811	21,807	22,828	20,269	20,424
Operations and maintenance	3,526	5,734	6,694	6,687	7,398	7,714	8,095	8,173	8,632
Personnel	2,456	7,703	8,637	8,621	8,543	9,272	9,062	9,564	9,258
Procurement	1,459	5,009	3,520	4,914	4,460	3,533	4,396	1,168	1,102
Active-duty support	408	566	611	638	700	731	682	632	658
Construction	120	402	605	666	690	617	588	732	574

Source: U.S. Dept. of Defense, unpublished data.

No. 568. National Guard—Summary: 1980 to 1995

[As of end of fiscal year; see text, section 9. Includes Puerto Rico]

ITEM	Unit	1980	1985	1989	1990	1991	1992	1993	1994	1995
Army National Guard: Units	Number	3,379	4,353	5,715	4,055	6,470	6,727	6,339	6,000	5,872
Personnel [1]	1,000	368	438	457	444	446	427	410	397	375
Funds obligated [2]	Bil. dol.	1.8	4.4	5.4	5.2	5.4	6.3	6.3	6.0	6.0
Value of equipment	Bil. dol.	7.6	18.8	30.1	29.0	29.0	29.0	31.0	31.0	33.0
Air National Guard: Units	Number	1,054	1,184	1,339	1,339	1,450	1,425	1,330	1,665	1,604
Personnel [1]	1,000	96	109	116	118	115	119	117	114	110
Funds obligated [2]	Bil. dol.	1.7	2.8	3.2	3.2	1.2	1.9	2.6	3.1	4.2
Value of equipment (est.) [3]	Bil. dol.	5.2	21.4	27.5	26.4	27.1	38.3	41.7	40.2	38.3

[1] Officers and enlisted personnel. [2] Federal funds; includes personnel, operations, maintenance, and military construction. [3] Beginning 1985, increase due to repricing of aircraft to current year dollars to reflect true replacement value. Beginning 1993 includes value of aircraft and support equipment.

Source: National Guard Bureau, *Annual Review of the Chief, National Guard Bureau;* and unpublished data.

No. 569. Veterans—States: 1995

[In thousands. **As of end of fiscal year**; see text, section 9. Data were estimated starting with veteran's place of residence as of April 1, 1980, based on 1980 Census of Population data, extended to later years on the basis of estimates of veteran interstate migration, separations from the Armed Forces, and mortality; not directly comparable with earlier estimates previously published by the VA. Excludes 423,000 veterans whose only active-duty military service occurred since September 8, 1980, and who failed to satisfy the minimum service requirement. Also excludes a small indeterminate number of National Guard personnel or reservists who incurred service-connected disabilities while on an initial tour of active duty for training only]

STATE	Total veterans [1]	War veterans [1]	World War I	World War II	Korean conflict	Vietnam era [2]	Persian Gulf War
United States	26,067	20,072	13	7,410	4,465	8,237	1,442
Alabama	427	334	-	118	80	136	36
Alaska	65	45	-	8	8	30	3
Arizona	459	353	-	139	83	146	22
Arkansas	258	204	-	78	46	79	21
California	2,818	2,122	1	759	495	944	119
Colorado	385	295	-	89	66	146	22
Connecticut	339	260	-	104	58	99	12
Delaware	78	59	-	22	13	24	5
District of Columbia	50	39	-	15	10	14	4
Florida	1,709	1,343	1	613	316	484	82
Georgia	685	507	-	150	109	247	49
Hawaii	116	85	-	27	20	42	6
Idaho	112	87	-	31	18	36	8
Illinois	1,074	839	1	315	180	320	57
Indiana	593	453	-	160	97	181	34
Iowa	291	233	-	86	52	87	18
Kansas	263	207	-	76	45	86	14
Kentucky	367	288	-	103	62	117	24
Louisiana	378	300	-	108	63	118	34
Maine	153	117	-	40	25	51	9
Maryland	530	389	-	133	87	174	27
Massachusetts	594	459	-	191	104	166	21
Michigan	949	730	-	259	148	293	56
Minnesota	462	355	-	119	77	150	22
Mississippi	233	184	-	69	43	66	23
Missouri	586	456	-	166	104	183	34
Montana	95	76	-	27	16	31	7
Nebraska	168	132	-	47	31	52	10
Nevada	186	139	-	48	36	64	8
New Hampshire	136	101	-	34	22	46	6
New Jersey	741	577	-	242	133	201	27
New Mexico	172	132	-	46	29	60	11
New York	1,538	1,189	1	478	260	416	79
North Carolina	711	539	-	187	120	232	46
North Dakota	59	47	-	15	11	19	4
Ohio	1,188	923	1	345	192	356	69
Oklahoma	350	278	-	102	64	118	20
Oregon	371	289	-	106	59	124	19
Pennsylvania	1,363	1,070	1	446	230	376	67
Rhode Island	109	85	-	37	19	31	5
South Carolina	380	288	-	97	64	130	29
South Dakota	74	58	-	20	14	21	6
Tennessee	516	398	-	137	87	170	33
Texas	1,647	1,265	1	425	278	582	108
Utah	138	110	-	41	24	44	9
Vermont	62	46	-	16	10	20	3
Virginia	705	522	-	167	122	260	40
Washington	631	475	-	154	105	232	32
West Virginia	199	161	-	63	36	59	13
Wisconsin	507	389	-	140	83	152	28
Wyoming	48	38	-	12	8	17	3

- Represents zero. [1] Veterans who served in more than one wartime period are counted only once. "All Veterans" includes Vietnam era (no prior wartime service), Korean conflict (no prior wartime service), World War II, post Vietnam era, Persian Gulf War era, and other. [2] Excludes reservists.

Source: U.S. Dept. of Veterans Affairs, Management Sciences Service (008B2), *Annual Report of the Secretary of Veterans Affairs.*

No. 570. Veterans Living in the United States and Puerto Rico, by Age and by Service: 1995

[In thousands, except as indicated. As of July, 1. Estimated. Excludes 500,000 veterans whose only active duty military service of less than two years occurred since Sept. 30, 1980. See headnote, table 569]

AGE	Total veterans	WARTIME VETERANS						Peace-time veterans
		Total [1]	Persian Gulf	Vietnam era	Korean conflict	World War II	World War I	
All ages	26,198	20,169	1,450	8,273	4,499	7,433	13	6,029
Under 30 years old	1,133	735	735	-	-	-	-	398
30-34 years old	1,277	259	259	-	-	-	-	1,018
35-39 years old	1,587	426	146	298	-	-	-	1,161
40-44 years old	1,969	1,636	153	1,591	-	-	-	333
45-49 years old	3,535	3,422	105	3,402	-	-	-	113
50-54 years old	2,646	1,889	37	1,878	-	-	-	757
55-59 years old	2,362	644	11	526	361	-	-	1,518
60-64 years old	2,899	2,331	3	265	2,226	35	-	569
65 years old and over	8,791	8,626	-	312	1,912	7,398	13	165

- Represents zero. [1] Veterans who served in more than one wartime period are counted only once.

Source: U.S. Dept. of Veterans Affairs, Office of Information Management and Statistics, *Veteran Population*, annual.

No. 571. Disabled Veterans Receiving Compensation: 1980 to 1995

[In thousands, except as indicated. As of end of fiscal year; see text, section 9. Represents veterans receiving compensation for service-connected disabilities. Totally disabled refers to veterans with any disability, mental or physical, deemed to be total and permanent which prevents the individual from maintaining a livelihood and are rated for disability at 100 percent]

MILITARY SERVICE	1980	1985	1988	1989	1990	1991	1992	1993	1994	1995
Disabled, all periods [1]	2,274	2,240	2,199	2,192	2,184	2,179	2,181	2,198	2,218	2,236
Peace-time	262	352	398	421	444	468	500	471	492	514
World War I [1]	30	12	8	5	3	3	2	1	1	1
World War II	1,193	1,049	947	912	876	841	805	769	731	692
Korea	236	223	215	212	209	205	202	198	195	191
Vietnam	553	604	633	643	652	662	671	682	694	705
Persian Gulf	(X)	(X)	(X)	(X)	(X)	(X)	(X)	76	106	134
Totally disabled, all periods [1]	121	136	131	131	131	131	132	135	138	143
Peace-time	20	26	26	26	27	27	28	28	29	30
World War I [1]	3	1	1	(Z)	(Z)	(Z)	(Z)	(Z)	(Z)	-
World War II	51	54	47	45	43	41	39	37	36	34
Korea	16	17	16	16	16	16	15	15	15	15
Vietnam	31	38	41	43	44	46	49	52	56	61
Persian Gulf	(X)	(X)	(X)	(X)	(X)	(X)	(X)	2	2	3
Compensation (mil. dol.)	8,104	8,270	8,722	8,937	9,284	9,612	10,031	10,545	10,977	11,644

X Not applicable. Z Less than 500. [1] Includes Spanish-American War and Mexican Border service, not shown seperately.

Source: U.S. Dept. of Veterans Affairs, *Annual Report of the Secretary of Veterans Affairs;* and unpublis

No. 572. Veterans Benefits—Expenditures, by Program: 1980 to 1995

[In millions of dollars. For fiscal years ending in year shown; see text, section 9. Beginning with fiscal year 1989, data are for outlays]

PROGRAM	1980	1985	1989	1990	1991	1992	1993	1994	1995
Total	23,187	29,359	30,041	28,998	31,214	33,900	36,450	37,401	37,775
Medical programs	6,042	9,227	10,745	11,582	12,472	13,815	14,603	15,430	16,255
Construction	300	557	703	661	608	639	622	695	641
General operating expenses	605	765	766	811	884	920	904	908	954
Compensation and pension	11,044	14,037	15,009	14,674	16,080	16,282	16,882	17,188	17,765
Vocational rehabilitation and education	2,350	1,164	589	452	541	695	863	1,119	1,127
All other [1]	2,846	3,609	2,228	818	629	1,549	1,588	2,062	1,034

[1] Includes insurance and indemnities, and miscellaneous funds and expenditures. (Excludes expenditures from personal funds of patients.)

Source: U.S. Dept. of Veterans Affairs, *Trend Data, annual.*

No. 573. Veterans Compensation and Pension Benefits—Number on Rolls and Average Payment, by Period of Service and Status: 1980 to 1993

[As of Sept. 30. Living refers to veterans receiving compensation for disability incurred or aggravated while on active duty and war veterans receiving pension and benefits for nonservice connected disabilities. Deceased refers to deceased veterans whose dependents were receiving pensions and compensation benefits]

PERIOD OF SERVICE AND VETERAN STATUS	VETERANS ON ROLLS (1,000)					AVERAGE PAYMENT (annual basis)[1] (dol.)				
	1980	1990	1991	1992	1993	1980	1985	1990	1991	1993
Total	4,646	3,584	3,509	3,428	3,374	2,370	3,505	4,335	4,552	4,712
Living veterans	3,195	2,746	2,709	2,674	2,660	2,600	3,666	4,320	4,491	4,611
Service connected	2,273	2,184	2,179	2,181	2,198	2,669	3,692	4,250	4,406	4,593
Nonservice connected	922	562	530	493	462	2,428	3,581	4,591	4,637	4,689
Deceased veterans	1,451	838	800	754	714	1,863	3,066	4,382	4,761	5,071
Service connected	358	320	318	314	310	3,801	5,836	7,349	7,815	8,244
Nonservice connected	1,093	518	482	440	404	1,228	1,809	2,548	2,748	2,810
Prior to World War I	14	4	4	3	3	1,432	1,855	2,616	2,921	3,073
Living	(Z)	(Z)	(Z)	(Z)	(Z)	2,634	4,436	10,502	10,441	8,176
World War I	692	198	172	146	124	1,683	2,461	3,435	3,674	3,754
Living	198	18	13	9	6	2,669	4,439	6,922	7,239	6,476
World War II	2,520	1,723	1,636	1,543	1,453	2,307	3,317	4,052	4,238	4,334
Living	1,849	1,294	1,226	1,153	1,063	2,462	3,460	4,123	4,278	4,333
Korean conflict[2]	446	390	386	387	377	2,691	4,114	5,105	5,330	5,462
Living	317	305	304	300	296	2,977	4,260	5,103	5,288	5,390
Peacetime	312	495	518	550	518	3,080	3,973	4,132	4,216	4,292
Living	262	444	468	500	471	2,828	3,589	3,709	3,789	3,866
Vietnam era[3]	662	774	789	804	821	2,795	4,021	4,945	5,242	5,551
Living	569	685	698	711	727	2,709	3,849	4,671	4,936	5,234
Persian Gulf War[4]	(X)	(X)	(X)	(Z)	78	(X)	(X)	(X)	(X)	1,673
Living	(X)	(X)	(X)	(Z)	76	(X)	(X)	(X)	(X)	1,386

X Not applicable. Z Fewer than 500. [1] Averages calculated by multiplying average monthly payment by 12. [2] Service during period June 27, 1950, to Jan. 31, 1955. [3] Service from Aug. 5, 1964, to May 7, 1975. [4] Service from August 2, 1990 to the present.

Source: U.S. Dept. of Veterans Affairs, *Annual Report of the Secretary of Veterans Affairs;* and unpublished data.

No. 574. Veterans Administration Health Care Summary: 1980 to 1995

[For years ending Sept. 30]

ITEM	Unit	1980	1990	1995	ITEM	Unit	1980	1990	1995
Facilities operating:					Obligations[2]	Mil. dol.	6,215	11,827	16,546
Hospitals	Number	172	172	173	Prescriptions dispensed	Millions	36.7	58.6	66.1
Domiciliaries	Number	16	32	39	Laboratory	Millions	215	188	(NA)
Outpatient clinics	Number	226	339	391	Inpatients treated[3]	1,000	1,359	1,113	1,035
Nursing home units	Number	92	126	131	Average daily	1,000	105	88	81
Employment[1]	1,000	194	199	205	Outpatient visits	Millions	18.0	22.6	27.6

NA Not available. [1] Net full-time equivalent. [2] 1980, cost basis; thereafter, obligation basis. [3] Based on the number of discharges and deaths during the fiscal year, plus the number on the rolls (bed occupants and patients on authorized leave of absence) at the end of the fiscal year. Excludes interhospital transfers.

Source: U.S. Dept. of Veterans Affairs, *Annual Report of the Secretary of Veterans Affairs; Directory of VA Facilities,* biennial; and unpublished data.

No. 575. Veterans Assistance—Education and Training: 1980 to 1995

[In thousands, except where indicated. For fiscal years ending in year shown; see text, section 9. Represents persons in training during year]

PROGRAM	1980	1985	1990	1991	1992	1993	1994	1995
Veteran Education Assistance[1]	1,107	402	102	143	195	246	284	292
Institutions of higher education	842	326	94	132	177	223	258	264
Resident schools other than college	149	54	6	9	14	18	19	19
Correspondence schools	42	7	1	1	3	3	4	(NA)
On-the-job training	74	15	1	1	2	2	3	4
Children's Educational Assistance	82.6	55.3	37.5	37.3	37.2	36.4	35.7	34.8
Institutions of higher education	75.5	50.0	35.3	35.2	35.1	34.3	33.7	33.1
Schools other than college	6.5	5.2	2.1	2.1	2.1	2.0	1.9	1.7
Special restorative training	0.1	(Z)	(Z)	(Z)	(Z)	(Z)	(Z)	(Z)
On-the-job training	0.5	0.2	0.1	(Z)	(Z)	(Z)	(Z)	(Z)
Spouses, Widows/Widowers Educational Assistance Program	13.0	6.6	4.5	4.4	4.5	4.4	4.6	4.6
Institutions of higher education	10.8	5.7	4.1	4.0	4.0	4.0	4.1	4.2
Schools other than college	2.2	1.0	0.4	0.4	0.4	0.4	0.4	0.4
Disabled Veterans Vocational Rehab.	25.5	26.9	27.8	35.9	36.8	40.7	44.2	47.9
Guaranteed and insured loans, (1,000)	297.4	178.9	196.6	181.2	266.0	383.3	602.2	263.1
Guaranteed and insured loans, (mil. dol.)	14,815	11,452	15,779	15,454	22,960	34,635	55,141	25,341
Guaranty and insurance (mil. dol.)	6,370	4,363	5,561	5,299	7,819	11,601	18,332	8,383

NA Not available. Z Fewer than 50. [1] Data for 1980-85 are for Post-Korean Conflict GI Bill (Title 38 USC Chapter 34). Data for 1990-94 are for the Active Duty Montgomery GI Bill (Title 38 USC Chapter 30).

Source: U.S. Dept. of Veterans Affairs, *Annual Report of the Secretary of Veterans Affairs;* and unpublished data.

Figure 12.1
Social Security Trust Funds: 1980 to 1995

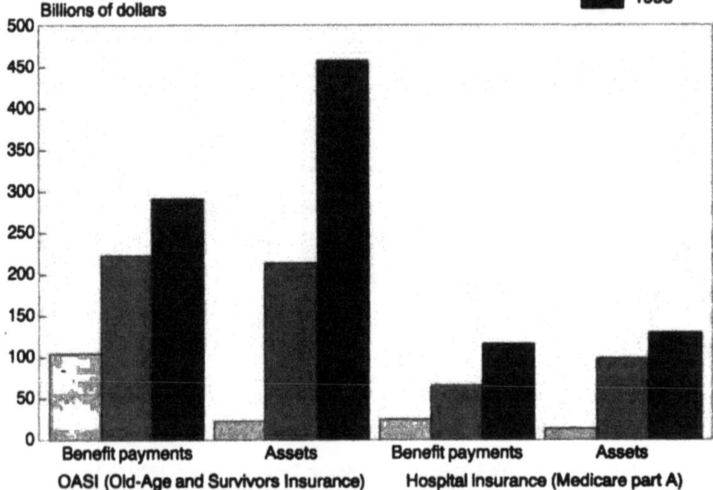

Source: Charts prepared by U.S. Bureau of the Census. For data, see table 586.

Figure12.2.
Percent of Households Contributing to Charity by Annual Dollar Amount: 1995

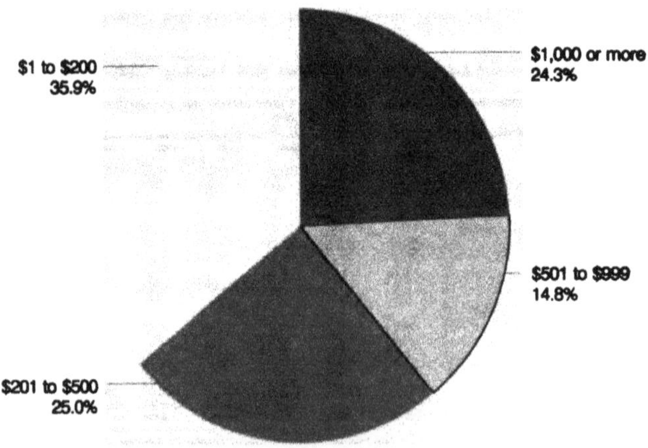

Source: Chart prepared by U.S. Bureau of the Census. For data, see table 615.

Social Insurance and Human Services

This section presents data related to governmental expenditures for social welfare; governmental programs for old-age, survivors, disability, and health insurance (OASDHI); governmental employee retirement; private pension plans; government unemployment and temporary disability insurance; Federal supplemental security income payments and aid to the needy; child and other welfare services; and Federal food programs. Also included here are selected data on workers' compensation, vocational rehabilitation; child support; child care; charity contributions; and philanthropic trusts and foundations.

The principal sources for these data are the Social Security Administration's quarterly *Social Security Bulletin* and the *Annual Statistical Supplement to the Social Security Bulletin* which present current data on many of the programs. Current data on employment security are published annually in the Department of Labor's *Unemployment Insurance, Financial Data.* Statistics on aid to families with dependent children (AFDC) are presented in the U.S. Administration for Children and Families' annual publication, *Quarterly Public Assistance Statistics.*

Social Insurance under the Social Security Act—Programs established by the Social Security Act provide protection against wage loss resulting from retirement, prolonged disability, death, or unemployment, and protection against the cost of medical care during old age and disability. The Federal OASDI program provides monthly benefits to retired or disabled insured workers and their dependents and to survivors of insured workers. To be eligible, a worker must have had a specified period of employment in which OASDI taxes were paid. A worker becomes eligible for full benefits at age 65, although reduced benefits may be obtained up to 3 years earlier; the worker's spouse is under the same limitations. Survivor benefits are payable to dependents of deceased insured workers. Disability benefits are payable to an insured worker under age 65 with a prolonged disability and to the disabled worker's dependents on the same basis as dependents of retired workers. Disability benefits are provided at age 50 to the disabled widow or widower of a deceased worker who was fully insured at the time of death. Disabled children, aged 18 or older, of retired, disabled, or deceased workers are also eligible for benefits. A lump-sum benefit is generally payable on the death of an insured worker to a spouse or minor children. For information on the Medicare (HI) program, see section 3.

In Brief

In 1995 percent of families receiving:

Social Security	*24%*
Other retirement income	*14%*
Unemployment compensation	*7%*

Social Security beneficiaries, 1995:

Total	*43 million*
Retired workers	*27 million*

Retirement, survivors, disability, and hospital insurance benefits are funded by a payroll tax on annual earnings (up to a maximum of earnings set by law) of workers, employers, and the self-employed. The maximum taxable earnings are adjusted annually to reflect increasing wage levels (see table 585). Effective January 1994, there is no dollar limit on wages and self-employment income subject to hospital insurance tax. Tax receipts and benefit payments are administered through Federal trust funds. Special benefits for uninsured persons; hospital benefits for persons 65 and over with specified amounts of Social Security coverage less than that required for cash benefit eligibility; and that part of the cost of supplementary medical insurance not financed by contributions from participants are financed from Federal general revenues.

Unemployment insurance is presently administered by the U.S. Employment and Training Administration and each State's employment security agency. By agreement with the U.S. Secretary of Labor, State agencies also administer unemployment compensation for eligible ex-service members and Federal employees, unemployment assistance under the Disaster Relief Act of 1970, and workers assistance and relocation allowances under the Trade Act. Under State unemployment insurance laws, benefits related to the individual's past earnings are paid to unemployed eligible workers. State laws vary concerning the length of time benefits are paid and their amount. In most States, benefits are payable for 26 weeks and, during periods of high unemployment, extended benefits are payable under a Federal-State program to those who have exhausted their regular State benefits. The basic benefit can vary among States by over 100 percent. Some States also supplement the basic benefit with allowances for dependents.

Unemployment insurance is funded by a Federal unemployment tax levied on the taxable payrolls of most employers. Taxable payroll under the Federal Act and 12 State laws is the first $7,000 in wages paid each worker during a year. Forty-one States have taxable payrolls above $7,000. Employers are allowed a percentage credit of taxable payroll for contributions paid to States under State unemployment insurance laws. The remaining percent of the Federal tax finances administrative costs, the Federal share of extended benefits, and advances to States. About 93 percent of wage and salary workers are covered by unemployment insurance.

Retirement Programs for Government Employees—The Civil Service Retirement System (CSRS) and the Federal Employees' Retirement System (FERS) are the two major programs providing age and service, disability, and survivor annuities for Federal civilian employees. In general, employees hired after December 31, 1983, are covered under FERS and the social security program (OASDHI), and employees on staff prior to that date are members of CSRS and transferring to FERS during 1987. There are separate retirement systems for the uniformed services (supplementing OASDHI) and for certain special groups of Federal employees. State and local government employees are covered for the most part by State and local retirement systems similar to the Federal civil service retirement system. In many jurisdictions these benefits supplement OASDHI coverage.

Workers' compensation—All States provide protection against work-connected injuries and deaths, although some States exclude certain workers (e.g., domestic help). Federal laws cover Federal employees, private employees in the District of Columbia, and longshoremen and harbor workers. In addition, the Social Security Administration and the Department of Labor administer "Black Lung" benefits programs for coal miners disabled by pneumoconiosis and for specified dependents and survivors. Specified occupational diseases are compensable to some extent. In most States, benefits are related to the worker's salary. The benefits may or may not be augmented by dependents' allowances or automatically adjusted to prevailing wage levels.

Public aid—State-administered public assistance programs (Aid to Families with Dependent Children (AFDC), emergency assistance and general assistance) and the Federal Supplemental Security Income (SSI) program administered by the Social Security Administration provide benefits to persons who qualify. AFDC and emergency assistance are in part federally funded while the costs of general assistance are met entirely with State and local funds. The SSI program replaced Federal grants for aid to the aged, blind, and disabled in the 50 States and the District of Columbia in 1974. Residents of the Northern Mariana Islands became eligible in 1978. Federal grants continue for aid to the aged, blind, and disabled in Guam, Puerto Rico, and the Virgin Islands. The SSI program provides a minimum income for the aged, blind, and disabled and establishes uniform national basic eligibility requirements and payment standards. Most

Federal Food Stamp program—Under the Food Stamp program, single persons and those living in households meeting nationwide standards for income and assets may receive coupons redeemable for food at most retail food stores. The monthly amount of coupons a unit receives is determined by household size and income. Households without income receive the determined monthly cost of a nutritionally adequate diet for their household size. This amount is updated to account for food price increases. Households with income receive the difference between the amount of a nutritionally adequate diet and 30 percent of their income, after certain allowable deductions.

To qualify for the program, a household must have less than $2,000 in disposable assets ($3,000 if one member is aged 60 or older), gross income below 130 percent of the official poverty guidelines, and net income below 100 percent of the poverty guidelines. Households with a person aged 60 or older or a disabled person receiving SSI, Social Security, or veterans' disability benefits may have gross income exceeding 130 percent of the poverty guidelines. All households must meet these requirements, even those receiving other Federal assistance payments. Households are certified for varying lengths of time, depending on their income sources and individual circumstances.

Health and welfare services—Programs providing health and welfare services are aided through Federal grants to States for child welfare services, vocational rehabilitation, activities for the aged, maternal and child health services, maternity and infant care projects, comprehensive health services, and a variety of public health activities. For information about the Medicaid program, see section 3.

Noncash benefits—The Bureau of the Census annually collects data on the characteristics of recipients of noncash (in-kind) benefits to supplement the collection of annual money income data in the Current Population Survey (see text, section 1, and section 15). Noncash benefits are those benefits received in a form other than money which serve to enhance or improve the economic well-being of the recipient. As for money income, the data for noncash benefits are for the calendar year prior to the date of the interview. The major categories of noncash benefits covered are public transfers (e.g. food stamps, school lunch, public housing, and Medicaid) and employer or union-provided benefits to employees.

Statistical reliability—For discussion of statistical collection, estimation, and sampling procedures and measures of statistical reliability applicable to HHS and Census Bureau data, see Appendix III.

No. 576. Social Welfare Expenditures Under Public Programs: 1980 to 1993

[In billions of dollars, except percent. See headnote, table 578]

YEAR	Total	Social insurance	Public aid	Health and medical programs [1]	Veterans programs	Education	Housing	Other social welfare	All health and medical care [2]
Total:									
1980	493	230	73	27	21	121	7	14	100
1985	732	370	98	39	27	172	13	14	171
1989	957	468	129	57	30	239	18	17	240
1990	1,049	513	147	61	31	258	19	18	274
1991	1,159	561	181	66	33	277	22	20	313
1992	1,264	617	208	70	35	292	21	22	354
1993	1,364	657	221	75	37	332	20	23	381
Federal:									
1980	303	191	49	13	21	13	6	9	69
1985	451	310	63	18	27	14	11	8	122
1989	565	387	82	24	30	19	15	8	165
1990	617	422	93	27	30	18	17	9	190
1991	676	454	113	30	32	19	19	10	213
1992	750	496	139	32	34	20	18	11	250
1993	805	534	152	33	36	20	18	11	275
State and local:									
1980	190	39	23	14	(Z)	108	1	5	31
1985	281	59	35	21	(Z)	158	2	6	49
1989	392	81	47	32	(Z)	220	3	8	75
1990	432	92	54	34	(Z)	240	3	9	84
1991	483	108	66	36	1	258	3	10	99
1992	515	121	69	38	1	272	3	11	105
1993	559	123	69	41	1	311	2	12	105
Percent Federal:									
1980	62	83	68	47	99	11	91	65	69
1985	62	84	64	46	99	8	88	56	71
1990	59	82	64	44	98	7	85	50	69
1991	58	81	62	44	98	7	87	50	68
1992	59	80	67	46	98	7	87	50	71
1993	59	81	69	45	98	6	91	48	72
Per capita (current dollars): [3]									
1980	2,126	990	314	118	92	523	30	59	434
1985	3,009	1,516	405	161	111	708	52	56	705
1990	4,123	2,017	579	242	120	1,018	77	71	1,079
1991	4,520	2,185	708	256	126	1,083	84	77	1,223
1992	4,861	2,371	801	270	130	1,126	79	83	1,357
1993	5,226	2,515	849	286	138	1,274	76	87	1,461
Per capita (constant (1993) dollars): [3] [4]									
1980	3,612	1,682	534	200	156	889	51	100	728
1985	3,939	1,984	530	212	145	927	68	73	920
1990	4,520	2,211	634	266	131	1,116	84	77	1,183
1991	4,766	2,304	747	270	133	1,142	89	81	1,290
1992	4,967	2,432	822	277	133	1,155	81	86	1,393
1993	5,226	2,515	849	286	138	1,274	76	87	1,461

Z Less than $500 million. [1] Excludes program parts of social insurance, public aid, veterans, and other social welfare. [2] Combines "Health and medical programs" with medical services included in social insurance, public aid, veterans, vocational rehabilitation, and antipoverty programs. [3] Excludes payments within foreign countries for education, veterans, OASDHI, and civil service retirement. [4] Constant dollar figures are based on implicit price deflators for personal consumption expenditures published by U.S. Bureau of Economic Analysis in *Survey of Current Business*.

No. 577. Social Welfare Expenditures Under Public Programs as Percent of GDP and Total Government Outlays: 1980 to 1993

[See headnote, table 578]

YEAR	TOTAL EXPENDITURES				FEDERAL				STATE AND LOCAL GOVERNMENT			
	Total (bil. dol.)	Percent change [1]	Percent of— Total GDP [2]	Percent of— Total govt. outlays	Total (bil. dol.)	Percent change [1]	Percent of— Total GDP [2]	Percent of— Total Federal outlays	Total (bil. dol.)	Percent change [1]	Percent of— Total GDP [2]	Percent of— Total State and local outlays
1980	493	14.7	18.6	57.2	303	15.2	11.4	54.4	190	13.8	7.2	62.9
1985	732	8.0	18.4	52.2	451	7.1	11.3	48.7	281	9.3	7.1	59.9
1989	957	7.9	18.5	55.2	565	7.2	10.9	49.5	392	8.8	7.6	68.0
1990	1,049	9.6	18.5	58.1	617	9.1	10.9	51.4	432	10.3	7.6	73.5
1991	1,159	10.6	19.8	60.3	676	9.7	11.5	52.8	483	11.8	8.2	77.3
1992	1,264	9.0	20.6	63.7	750	10.8	12.2	57.3	515	6.7	8.4	77.5
1993	1,364	7.9	21.1	66.7	805	7.4	12.4	60.0	559	8.6	8.6	81.0

[1] Percent change from immediate prior year. [2] Gross domestic product.

Source of tables 576 and 577: U.S. Social Security Administration, *Social Security Bulletin*, fall 1996; and unpublished data.

No. 578. Social Welfare Expenditures, by Source of Funds and Public Program: 1980 to 1993

[In millions of dollars. For fiscal years ending in year shown; see text, section 9. Represents outlays from trust funds (mostly social insurance funds built up by earmarked contributions from insured persons, their employers, or both) and budgetary outlays from general revenues. Includes administrative expenditures, capital outlay, and some expenditures and payments outside the United States]

PROGRAM	FEDERAL				STATE AND LOCAL			
	1980	1990	1992	1993	1980	1990	1992	1993
Total	303,167	616,639	749,556	804,702	189,060	432,167	514,871	568,182
Social insurance	191,162	422,257	496,061	534,310	38,592	91,565	121,266	123,018
Old-age, survivors, disability, health	152,110	355,264	416,564	449,277	(X)	(X)	(X)	(X)
Health insurance (Medicare)	34,992	109,709	132,246	148,094	(X)	(X)	(X)	(X)
Public employee retirement [1]	26,983	53,541	58,601	61,704	12,507	36,851	45,099	50,928
Railroad employee retirement	4,769	7,230	7,737	7,921	(X)	(X)	(X)	(X)
Unemployment insurance and employment services [2]	4,408	3,096	9,928	12,124	13,919	16,878	31,236	26,597
Other railroad employee insurance [3]	224	105	95	86	(X)	(X)	(X)	(X)
State temporary disability insurance [4]	(X)	(X)	(X)	(X)	1,377	3,224	4,009	3,316
Workers' compensation [5]	2,668	3,021	3,157	3,199	10,789	34,613	40,919	40,177
Hospital and medical benefits	130	457	571	597	3,596	13,849	17,344	17,116
Public aid	49,394	92,858	138,704	151,850	23,309	53,953	69,241	69,214
Public assistance [6]	23,542	54,747	86,747	95,340	21,522	50,347	65,264	65,355
Medical assistance payments [7]	14,550	40,690	69,766	77,367	13,020	35,485	47,848	47,771
Social services	1,757	2,065	2,031	2,785	586	688	677	928
Supplemental Security Income	6,440	13,625	19,446	22,642	1,787	3,605	3,978	3,859
Food stamps	9,083	16,254	23,233	24,497	(X)	(X)	(X)	(X)
Other [8]	10,329	8,232	9,279	9,372	(X)	(X)	(X)	(X)
Health and medical programs	12,840	27,204	31,873	33,209	13,936	34,282	38,276	41,294
Hospital and medical care	6,636	14,816	17,781	18,844	5,667	11,155	11,108	11,664
Civilian programs	2,438	3,654	5,012	5,435	5,667	11,155	11,108	11,664
Defense Department [9]	4,198	11,162	12,769	13,409	(X)	(X)	(X)	(X)
Maternal and child health programs	351	492	580	595	519	1,374	1,519	1,577
Medical research	4,428	9,172	10,641	10,690	496	1,676	1,958	2,090
Medical facilities construction	210	413	-93	-73	1,409	1,922	2,388	2,731
Other	1,215	2,311	2,963	3,153	5,844	18,155	21,303	23,232
Veterans programs	21,255	30,428	34,212	36,034	212	488	555	572
Pensions and compensation	11,306	15,793	16,539	17,205	(X)	(X)	(X)	(X)
Health and medical programs	6,204	12,004	14,567	15,641	(X)	(X)	(X)	(X)
Hospital and medical care	5,750	11,321	13,452	14,382	(X)	(X)	(X)	(X)
Hospital construction	323	445	845	980	(X)	(X)	(X)	(X)
Medical and prosthetic research	131	238	270	279	(X)	(X)	(X)	(X)
Education	2,401	523	772	938	(X)	(X)	(X)	(X)
Life insurance [10]	665	1,038	1,114	905	(X)	(X)	(X)	(X)
Welfare and other	679	1,070	1,220	1,345	212	488	555	572
Education [11]	13,452	18,374	20,060	20,455	107,597	240,011	272,011	311,466
Elementary and secondary [12]	7,430	9,944	12,891	13,238	79,720	189,333	214,015	239,182
Construction [13]	41	23	43	5	6,483	10,613	14,636	22,283
Higher	4,468	6,747	5,264	5,285	21,708	50,678	57,996	72,273
Construction	42	-	30	35	1,486	3,953	4,839	8,955
Vocational and adult [13]	1,207	1,293	1,452	1,495	6,169	([12])	([12])	([12])
Housing	6,278	16,612	17,950	18,006	601	2,856	2,866	1,796
Other social welfare	8,786	8,906	10,677	10,836	4,813	9,012	10,855	11,832
Vocational rehabilitation	1,006	1,661	1,912	1,830	245	466	534	549
Medical services and research	237	415	478	458	56	116	134	137
Institutional care [14]	74	143	144	143	406	486	541	579
Child nutrition [15]	4,209	5,470	6,722	7,139	643	1,696	2,054	2,253
Child welfare [16]	57	253	274	295	743	(NA)	(NA)	(NA)
Special CSA and ACTION programs [17]	2,303	169	194	208	(X)	(X)	(X)	(X)
Welfare, not elsewhere classified [18]	1,137	1,209	1,431	1,223	2,774	6,365	7,726	8,451

- Represents zero. NA Not available. X Not applicable. [1] Excludes refunds to those leaving service. Federal data include military retirement. [2] Includes compensation for Federal employees and ex-servicemen, trade adjustment and cash training allowance, and payments under extended, emergency, disaster, and special unemployment insurance programs. [3] Unemployment and temporary disability insurance. [4] Cash and medical benefits in five areas. Includes private plans where applicable. [5] Benefits paid by private insurance carriers, State funds, and self-insurers. Federal includes black lung benefit programs. [6] Includes payments under State general assistance programs and work incentive activities, not shown separately. [7] Medicaid payments and State and local general assistance medical payments. [8] Refugee assistance, surplus food for the needy, and work-experience training programs under the Comprehensive Employment and Training Act. Beginning 1990, includes low-income energy assistance program. [9] Includes medical care for military dependent families. [10] Excludes servicemen's group life insurance. [11] Federal expenditures include administrative costs (Department of Education) and research, not shown separately. [12] Beginning 1990, all State and local vocational education costs included with elementary-secondary. [13] Construction costs of vocational and adult education programs included under elementary-secondary expenditures. [14] Federal expenditures represent primarily surplus foods for nonprofit institutions. [15] Surplus food for schools and programs under National School Lunch and Child Nutrition Acts. [16] Represents primarily child welfare services under Title V of the Social Security Act. [17] Includes domestic volunteer programs under ACTION and community action and migrant workers programs under Community Services Administration. Beginning 1990, represents ACTION funds only. [18] Federal expenditures include administrative expenses of the Secretary of Health and Human Services; Indian welfare and guidance; and aging and juvenile delinquency activities. State and local include antipoverty and manpower programs, child care and adoption services, legal assistance, and other unspecified welfare services.

Source: U.S. Social Security Administration, *Social Security Bulletin*, fall 1996; and unpublished data.

No. 579. Private Expenditures for Social Welfare, by Type: 1980 to 1994

[In millions of dollars, except percent]

TYPE	1980	1985	1989	1990	1991	1992	1993	1994
Total expenditures	251,507	464,643	671,722	723,154	766,892	833,552	877,604	924,994
Percent of gross domestic product	9.0	11.1	12.4	12.6	13.0	13.3	13.4	13.3
Health	142,500	253,900	369,800	413,100	441,000	477,000	505,100	528,600
Income maintenance	53,564	118,871	167,260	164,772	170,754	187,461	192,340	204,736
Private pension plan payments [1] [2]	37,605	98,570	141,286	138,114	143,314	158,857	163,158	174,452
Short-term sickness and disability [2]	8,630	10,570	13,616	13,680	13,844	14,684	15,132	15,901
Long-term disability [2]	1,282	1,937	2,892	2,926	3,172	3,143	2,900	2,895
Life insurance and death	5,075	7,489	9,063	9,278	9,472	10,184	10,693	11,229
Supplemental unemployment	972	305	403	774	952	593	457	259
Education	32,667	52,873	75,350	80,699	86,140	93,069	99,265	105,361
Welfare and other services	22,776	38,999	59,312	64,583	68,998	76,022	80,899	86,297

[1] Covers benefits paid for solely by employers and all benefits of employment-related pension plans to which employee contributions are made. Excludes individual savings plans such as IRA's and Keogh plans. Pension plan benefits include monthly benefits and lump-sum distributions to retired and disabled employees and their dependents and to survivors of deceased employees. Also includes preretirement lump-sum distributions. [2] Covers wage and salary workers in private industry.

Source: U.S. Social Security Administration, *Annual Statistical Supplement* to the *Social Security Bulletin*, annual.

No. 580. Public Income-Maintenance Programs—Cash Benefit Payments: 1980 to 1995

[In billions of dollars. Includes payments outside the United States and benefits to dependents, where applicable]

PROGRAM	1980	1985	1987	1988	1989	1990	1991	1992	1993	1994	1995
Total [1]	228.1	335.2	372.0	393.8	421.9	455.8	503.3	541.9	547.2	(NA)	(NA)
Percent of personal income [2]	10.1	9.9	9.8	9.7	9.6	9.8	10.4	10.5	10.2	(NA)	(NA)
OASDI [3]	120.3	186.1	204.7	216.4	229.6	245.6	265.6	284.3	296.3	311.6	327.9
Public employee retirement [4]	40.6	63.0	72.1	78.0	83.8	90.4	97.3	103.7	112.6	(NA)	(NA)
Railroad retirement	4.9	6.3	6.5	6.7	6.9	7.2	7.5	7.3	7.9	8.0	8.1
Veterans' pensions, compensation	11.4	14.1	14.3	14.7	15.3	15.8	16.3	16.5	16.9	18.7	18.0
Unemployment benefits [5]	18.9	14.4	14.4	13.2	16.4	20.0	31.3	37.3	21.5	21.6	22.0
Temporary disability benefits	1.4	1.8	2.5	2.8	2.9	3.2	3.9	4.0	3.3	(NA)	(NA)
Workers' compensation [6]	9.7	22.3	27.1	30.3	33.8	37.6	41.7	44.1	43.4	(NA)	(NA)
Public assistance	12.1	15.3	16.5	17.0	17.4	19.3	20.1	22.4	21.0	23.3	22.8
Supplemental Security Income	7.9	11.1	13.6	14.7	14.9	15.2	18.5	22.3	24.7	26.1	27.9

NA Not available. [1] Includes lump sum death benefits, not shown separately. Lump sum death benefits for State and local government employee retirement systems are not available beginning 1987. [2] For base data, see table 703. [3] Old-age, survivors, and disability insurance under Federal Social Security Act; see text, section 12. [4] Excludes refunds of contributions to employees who leave service. [5] Beginning 1985, covers State unemployment insurance, Ex-Servicemen's Compensation Act and railroad unemployment insurance only. [6] Includes black lung benefits.

Source: U.S. Social Security Administration, *Social Security Bulletin*, quarterly; and unpublished data.

No. 581. Number of Families Receiving Specified Sources of Income, by Characteristic of Householder and Family Income: 1995

[In thousands. Families as of March 1996. Based on Current Population Survey; see text, sections 1 and 14, and Appendix III]

SOURCE OF INCOME	Total families [1]	Under 65 years old	65 years old and over	White	Black	Hispanic origin [2]	Under $15,000	$15,000 to $24,999	$25,000 to $34,999
Total	69,597	58,292	11,306	58,872	8,055	6,287	9,723	10,040	9,828
Earnings	59,055	54,301	4,753	50,186	6,555	5,406	5,358	7,367	8,279
Wages and salary	57,324	52,965	4,359	48,589	6,480	5,276	4,991	7,050	7,937
Social Security, railroad retirement	16,356	5,862	10,494	14,370	1,592	915	2,716	3,886	3,116
Supplemental Security Income (SSI)	2,421	1,921	500	1,592	669	360	1,026	591	323
Public assistance	3,616	3,530	86	2,153	1,262	767	2,493	594	251
Veterans payments	1,735	1,054	681	1,507	172	56	163	247	278
Unemployment compensation	5,022	4,807	215	4,336	514	503	521	732	860
Workers compensation	1,571	1,456	114	1,337	165	137	122	210	285
Retirement income	10,001	4,208	5,792	9,106	697	339	473	1,786	2,019
Private pensions	6,328	2,259	4,069	5,810	410	211	337	1,314	1,425
Military retirement	956	673	283	851	79	29	8	83	131
Federal employee pensions	1,182	445	737	1,030	125	27	47	150	226
State or local employee pensions	1,911	785	1,126	1,746	127	57	70	260	361
Other income	10,322	9,896	427	8,496	1,393	776	1,761	1,509	1,472
Alimony	248	237	11	210	33	12	38	31	46
Child support	4,421	4,378	43	3,645	664	307	1,054	801	774
Education assistance	4,784	4,648	137	3,895	642	371	603	598	591

[1] Includes other items not shown separately. [2] Persons of Hispanic origin may be of any race.

Source: U.S. Bureau of the Census, "Current Population Survey, Annual Demographic Survey, March Supplement"; published 18 November 1996; <http://ferret.bls.census.gov/macro/031996/faminc/09000.htm>.

No. 582. Cash and Noncash Benefits for Persons With Limited Income: 1990 and 1994

[For years ending September 30, except as noted. Programs covered provide cash, goods, or services to persons who make no payment and render no service in return. In case of job and training programs and some educational benefits, recipients must work or study for wages, training allowances, stipends, grants, or loans. Most of the programs base eligibility on individual, household, or family income, but some use group or area income tests; and a few offer help on the basis of presumed need]

PROGRAM	AVERAGE MONTHLY RECIPIENTS (1,000)		EXPENDITURES (mil. dol.)					
			Total		Federal		State and local	
	1990	1994	1990	1994	1990	1994	1990	1994
Total [1]	(X)	(X)	210,817	344,861	151,478	246,240	59,339	98,621
Medical care [2]	(X)	(X)	86,785	161,139	50,190	93,892	36,595	67,247
Medicaid [3 4]	25,253	34,047	72,492	143,593	41,103	82,147	31,389	61,446
Veterans [5 6 7]	565	1,537	6,624	8,162	6,624	8,162	-	-
General assistance [7]	(NA)	(NA)	4,853	5,370	-	-	4,853	5,370
Indian Health Services [3 4]	1,100	1,333	1,176	1,943	1,176	1,943	-	-
Maternal and child health services	(NA)	11,600	907	1,118	554	687	353	431
Cash aid [2]	(X)	(X)	54,255	83,749	36,445	61,477	17,810	22,272
Supplemental Security Income [4 8]	4,938	6,429	17,233	27,310	13,607	23,544	3,626	3,766
A.F.D.C. [4 9]	11,465	14,229	21,200	25,920	11,507	14,141	9,693	11,779
Earned income tax credit (refunded portion) [10]	37,836	54,177	5,303	16,549	5,303	16,549	-	-
Foster care	168	246	2,741	5,159	1,473	2,748	1,268	2,411
General assistance [10]	1,205	1,113	2,924	3,250	-	-	2,924	3,250
Pensions for needy veterans [11 12]	1,106	836	3,954	3,159	3,954	3,159	-	-
Food benefits [2]	(X)	(X)	25,106	38,100	23,871	36,233	1,235	1,867
Food stamps [4 13]	21,500	28,900	17,686	27,396	16,512	25,599	1,174	1,797
School lunch program [14 15]	11,600	14,000	3,154	4,438	3,154	4,438	(NA)	(NA)
Women, infants and children [4 16]	4,500	6,500	2,126	3,309	2,126	3,309	-	-
School breakfast [14]	3,600	5,200	548	936	548	936	-	-
Child and adult care food program [17]	842	1,116	447	774	447	774	-	-
Nutrition program for elderly [18]	3,540	(NA)	575	689	514	619	61	70
Housing benefits [2]	(X)	(X)	17,548	26,130	17,548	25,738	-	392
Low-income housing asst. (Sec. 8) [19]	2,500	2,926	10,577	14,576	10,577	14,576	-	-
Low-rent public housing [19 20]	1,405	1,409	3,918	6,609	3,918	6,609	(NA)	(NA)
Rural housing loans [21 22]	26	39	1,311	2,384	1,311	2,384	-	-
Interest reduction payments [19]	531	504	630	659	630	659	-	-
Home investment partnerships [4 22 23]	(NA)	68	3	595	3	219	-	376
Education aid [2]	(X)	(X)	14,390	15,707	13,761	14,804	629	903
Pell grants [24 25]	3,214	3,819	4,484	6,459	4,484	6,459	-	-
Head Start	541	740	1,940	4,156	1,552	3,325	388	831
Stafford loans [24]	4,496	3,854	5,648	2,757	5,648	2,757	-	-
Services [2]	(X)	(X)	6,460	11,982	3,781	6,737	2,679	5,245
Social services (Title 20) [26]	(NA)	(NA)	5,346	8,322	2,762	[27] 3,800	2,584	4,522
Child care for AFDC recipients and ex-recipients [28]	(NA)	519	211	1,199	116	700	95	499
Child care and development block grant	(X)	(NA)	(X)	893	(X)	893	(X)	-
Jobs and training [2]	(X)	(X)	4,242	5,531	3,975	4,870	267	661
Training for disadvantaged adults and youth [29]	630	759	1,745	1,597	1,745	1,597	-	-
JOBS (for AFDC recipients) [30]	444	579	452	1,417	265	850	187	567
Job Corps	61	100	803	1,040	803	1,040	-	-
Summer youth employment program [31]	585	569	709	877	709	877	-	-
Energy assistance [2]	(X)	(X)	1,728	1,871	1,604	1,837	124	34
Low-income energy assistance [4 32 33]	5,800	6,100	1,567	1,731	1,443	1,697	124	34

- Represents zero. NA Not available. X Not applicable. [1] Includes State Legalization Impact Assistance Grants to offset State and local costs of welfare, health care, and education provided to legalized aliens. [2] Includes other programs not shown separately. [3] Recipient data represent unduplicated annual number. [4] Expenditures include administrative expenses. [5] Medical care for veterans with a nonservice-connected disability. [6] Recipients are estimated number of inpatients. [7] Estimated expenditures. [8] Includes State-administered SSI supplements. [9] Aid to Families with Dependent Children program. Excludes data for foster care program and child support operations (cost and collections). [10] Estimated recipients. [11] Estimated recipients as of September. [12] Includes dependents and survivors. [13] Includes Puerto Rico's nutritional assistance program. [14] Free and reduced-price segments. [15] Includes estimate of commodity assistance. [16] Special supplemental food program for women, infants and children. [17] Recipient data are numbers of children receiving free or reduced price meals and snacks in child care centers and estimates of children in family day care homes with incomes below 185 percent of poverty. Adult participants and funding are not included. [18] No income test required but preference given to those with greatest need. [19] Recipient data represent units eligible for payment at end of year. [20] Includes operating subsidies and HUD-administered Indian housing. [21] Recipient data represent total families or dwelling units during year. [22] Expenditure data represent amounts obligated. [23] Recipient data are housing units provided or rehabilitated. [24] Recipient data are total numbers for the school year ending in year shown. [25] Expenditure data are appropriations available for school year ending the fiscal year named. [26] Non-Federal expenditure data are rough estimates. [27] Includes one-time authorization of $1 billion for enterprise communities and empowerment zones. [28] Recipient data are estimated number of children served. [29] Recipient data are total number of participants. [30] Job opportunities and basic skills training program (JOBS). [31] Total participants (June-August). [32] Households served during the year with heating and winter crisis aid. [33] Federal funds include amounts transferred to other programs serving the needy.

Source: Library of Congress, Congressional Research Service, "Cash and Noncash Benefits for Persons With Limited Income: Eligibility Rules, Recipient, and Expenditure Data, FY's 1992-94," Report 96-159 EPW, and earlier reports.

No. 583. Households Receiving Means-Tested Noncash Benefits: 1980 to 1995

[In thousands, except percent. Households as of March of following year. Covers civilian noninstitutional population, including persons in the Armed Forces living off post or with their families on post. A means-tested benefit program requires that the household's income and/or assets fall below specified guidelines in order to qualify for benefits. The means-tested noncash benefits covered are food stamps, free or reduced-price school lunches, public or subsidized housing, and Medicaid. There are general trends toward underestimation of noncash beneficiaries. Households are classified according to poverty status of family or nonfamily householder; for explanation of poverty level, see text, section 14. Data for 1980-90 based on 1980 census population controls; beginning 1994, based on 1990 census population controls. Based on Current Population Survey; see text, section 1, and Appendix III]

TYPE OF BENEFIT RECEIVED	1980	1985	1990	1994	1995			
					Total	Below poverty level		Above poverty level
						Number	Percent distribution	
Total households	82,368	88,458	94,312	98,990	99,627	12,928	100	86,701
Receiving at least one noncash benefit	14,266	14,466	16,098	21,267	21,148	8,298	64	12,850
Not receiving cash public assistance	7,860	7,860	8,819	13,269	13,335	3,874	30	9,461
Receiving cash public assistance [1]	6,407	6,607	7,279	7,998	7,813	4,425	34	3,388
Total households receiving—								
Food stamps	6,769	6,779	7,163	8,925	8,368	5,389	42	2,989
School lunch	5,532	5,752	6,252	8,534	8,607	3,749	29	4,858
Public housing	2,777	3,799	4,339	4,946	4,846	2,548	20	2,300
Medicaid	8,287	8,178	10,321	14,119	14,111	6,309	49	7,802

[1] Households receiving money from Aid to Families with Dependent Children program, Supplemental Security Income program or other public assistance programs.

Source: U.S. Bureau of the Census, *Current Population Reports*, P60-155, and earlier reports; and unpublished data.

No. 584. Persons Participating in Selected Means-Tested Government Assistance Programs, by Selected Characteristics: 1991 and 1992

[Average monthly participation. Covers noninstitutionalized population. Persons are considered participants in Aid to Families with Dependent Children (AFDC), General Assistance, and the Food Stamp Program if they are the primary recipient or if they are covered under another persons's allotment. Persons receiving Supplemental Security Income (SSI) payments are considered to be participants in an assistance program as are persons covered by Medicaid or living in public or subsidized rental housing. Based on the Survey of Income and Program Participation; for details on sample survey, see source]

YEAR AND SELECTED CHARACTERISTIC	NUMBER OF PARTICIPANTS (1,000)					PERCENT OF POPULATION PARTICIPATING				
	Major means-tested assistance programs [1]	AFDC or General Assistance	Food stamps	Medicaid	Housing assistance	Major means-tested assistance programs [1]	AFDC or General Assistance	Food stamps	Medicaid	Housing assistance
1991	31,695	11,869	19,383	(NA)	(NA)	12.7	4.7	7.8	(NA)	(NA)
1992, total	**33,954**	**11,862**	**20,700**	**23,924**	**10,878**	**13.4**	**4.7**	**8.2**	**9.4**	**4.3**
Under 18 years old	15,222	7,292	10,780	11,918	4,344	22.5	10.8	15.9	17.6	6.4
18 to 64 years old	14,751	4,492	8,716	9,376	4,789	9.5	2.9	5.6	6.0	3.1
65 years old and over	3,982	78	1,204	2,630	1,745	13.0	0.3	3.9	8.6	5.7
White	21,690	6,379	12,583	14,921	6,178	10.3	3.0	6.0	7.1	2.9
Black	10,507	4,723	7,072	7,683	4,094	33.0	14.8	22.2	24.2	12.9
Hispanic origin [2]	6,410	2,439	4,222	4,636	1,687	26.9	10.2	17.7	19.4	7.1
Poverty status: [3]										
Below the poverty level	20,031	9,288	15,926	15,320	6,050	56.5	26.2	44.9	43.2	17.1
At or above the poverty level	13,923	2,574	4,774	8,604	4,828	6.4	1.2	2.2	3.9	2.2
Family status:										
In married-couple families	12,895	3,012	7,313	8,298	2,964	7.5	1.7	4.2	4.8	1.7
With related children under 18 years old	10,870	2,929	6,654	7,033	2,473	10.0	2.7	6.1	6.5	2.3
In families with female householder, no spouse present	15,068	8,287	10,968	12,012	5,146	40.7	22.4	29.7	32.5	13.9
With related children under 18 years old	13,630	8,116	10,377	10,958	4,765	49.0	29.2	37.3	39.4	17.1
Unrelated individuals	4,891	272	1,853	2,844	2,597	13.5	0.8	5.1	7.9	7.2

NA Not available. [1] Covers AFDC, General Assistance, SSI, food stamps, Medicaid, and housing assistance. [2] Persons of Hispanic origin may be of any race. [3] For explanation of poverty level, see text, section 14.

Source: U.S. Bureau of the Census, *Current Population Reports*, P70-46 and unpublished data.

No. 585. Social Security—Covered Employment, Earnings, and Contribution Rates: 1980 to 1995

[Includes Puerto Rico, Virgin Islands, American Samoa, and Guam. Represents all reported employment. Data are estimated. OASDHI=Old-age, survivors, disability, and health insurance; SMI=Supplementary medical insurance]

ITEM	Unit	1980	1985	1988	1989	1990	1991	1992	1993	1994	1995
Workers with insured status [1]	Million	137.4	148.3	155.4	158.3	161.3	164.0	165.9	167.4	168.8	170.6
Male	Million	75.4	79.6	82.6	83.8	85.2	86.4	87.2	87.8	88.3	89.1
Female	Million	62.0	68.6	72.8	74.5	76.1	77.5	78.7	79.6	80.5	81.5
Under 25 years old	Million	25.5	22.4	21.3	21.3	21.4	21.3	20.8	20.1	19.3	19.0
25 to 34 years old	Million	34.9	39.4	41.0	41.3	41.5	41.6	41.3	40.8	40.2	39.8
35 to 44 years old	Million	22.4	28.6	32.3	33.5	34.9	36.4	37.2	38.0	38.9	39.8
45 to 54 years old	Million	18.6	19.0	20.5	21.4	22.1	22.8	24.1	25.5	26.8	28.1
55 to 59 years old	Million	9.2	9.1	8.8	8.7	8.7	8.7	8.8	9.0	9.2	9.5
60 to 64 years old	Million	7.9	8.7	8.7	8.7	8.7	8.8	8.7	8.5	8.4	8.4
65 to 69 years old	Million	6.7	7.3	7.7	7.9	8.1	8.2	8.1	8.2	8.2	8.1
70 years old and over	Million	12.1	13.9	15.0	15.4	15.8	16.3	16.8	17.3	17.7	18.0
Workers reported with—											
Taxable earnings [2]	Million	113	120	130	132	134	133	134	136	139	143
Maximum earnings [2]	Million	10	8	8	8	6	8	8	8	8	8
Earnings in covered employment [2]	Bil. dol.	1,329	1,942	2,432	2,573	2,704	2,761	2,916	3,033	3,171	3,369
Reported taxable [2]	Bil. dol.	1,178	1,725	2,092	2,238	2,358	2,422	2,533	2,644	2,784	2,924
Percent of total	Percent	88.6	88.8	86.0	87.0	87.2	87.7	86.9	87.2	87.8	86.8
Annual maximum taxable earnings [3]	Dollars	25,900	39,600	45,000	48,000	51,300	53,400	55,500	57,600	60,600	61,200
Contribution rates for OASDHI: [4]											
Each employer and employee	Percent	6.13	7.05	7.51	7.51	7.65	7.65	7.65	7.65	7.65	7.65
Self-employed [5]	Percent	8.10	14.10	15.02	15.02	15.30	15.30	15.30	15.30	15.30	15.30
SMI, monthly premium [6]	Dollars	9.60	15.50	24.80	31.90	28.60	29.90	31.80	36.60	41.10	46.10

[1] Fully insured for retirement and/or survivor benefits as of beginning of year. [2] Includes self-employment. [3] The maximum taxable earnings for HI was $125,000 in 1991; $130,200 in 1992, and 135,000 in 1993. Beginning 1994 upper limit on earnings subject to HI taxes was repealed. [4] As of January 1, 1996, and 1997, each employee and employer pays 7.65 percent and the self-employed pay 15.3 percent. [5] Self-employed pays 11.8 percent in 1985 and 13.02 percent in 1988 and 1989. The additional amount is supplied from general revenues. Beginning 1990, self-employed pays 15.3 percent, and half of the tax is deductible for income tax purposes and for computing self-employment income subject to social security tax. [6] 1980, as of July 1; beginning 1985, as of January 1. As of January 1, 1996, the monthly premium is $42.50; as of January 1, 1997, $43.80.

Source: U.S. Social Security Administration, *Annual Statistical Supplement* to the *Social Security Bulletin;* and unpublished data.

No. 586. Social Security Trust Funds: 1980 to 1995

[In billions of dollars]

TYPE OF TRUST FUND	1980	1985	1989	1990	1991	1992	1993	1994	1995
Old-age and survivors insurance (OASI):									
Net contribution income [1]	103.5	180.2	252.6	272.4	278.4	286.8	296.2	298.3	310.1
Interest received [2]	1.8	1.9	12.0	16.4	20.8	24.3	27.0	29.9	32.8
Benefit payments [3]	105.1	167.2	208.0	223.0	240.5	[4]254.9	[4]267.8	279.1	291.6
Assets, end of year	22.8	[5]35.8	155.1	214.2	267.8	319.2	369.3	413.5	458.5
Disability insurance (DI):									
Net contribution income [1]	13.3	17.4	24.1	28.7	29.3	30.4	31.5	51.7	54.7
Interest received [2]	0.5	0.9	0.7	0.9	1.1	1.1	0.8	1.2	2.2
Benefit payments [3]	15.5	18.8	22.9	24.8	27.7	[4]31.1	[4]34.6	37.7	40.9
Assets, end of year	3.6	[6]6.3	7.9	11.1	12.9	12.3	9.0	22.9	37.6
Hospital insurance (HI):									
Net contribution income [1 7]	23.9	47.7	68.5	71.1	78.4	82.4	84.9	97.9	103.3
Interest received [2]	1.1	3.4	7.3	8.5	9.5	10.5	12.5	10.7	10.6
Benefit payments	25.1	47.5	60.0	66.2	71.5	83.9	93.5	103.3	116.4
Assets, end of year	13.7	[8]20.5	85.6	98.9	115.2	124.0	127.8	132.8	130.3
Supplementary medical insurance (SMI):									
Net premium income	3.0	5.6	10.8	11.3	11.9	14.1	14.2	17.4	19.7
Transfers from general revenue	7.5	18.3	30.9	33.0	37.6	41.4	41.5	36.2	39.0
Interest received	0.4	1.2	1.1	1.6	1.7	1.8	2.0	2.0	1.6
Benefit payments	10.6	22.9	38.4	42.5	47.3	49.3	55.8	58.6	65.0
Assets, end of year	4.5	10.9	12.2	15.5	17.8	24.2	24.1	19.4	13.1

[1] Includes deposits by States and deductions for refund of estimated employee-tax overpayment. Beginning in 1985, includes government contributions on deemed wage credits for military service in 1957 and later. Includes tax credits on net earnings from self-employment in 1985-89. Includes taxation of benefits beginning in 1985 for OASI and DI and in 1994 for HI. [2] In 1985-90, includes interest on advance tax transfers. Beginning 1985, includes interest on reimbursement for unnegotiated checks. Data for 1985 reflect interest on interfund borrowing. [3] Includes payments for vocational rehabilitation services furnished to disabled persons receiving benefits because of their disabilities. Beginning in 1985, amounts reflect deductions for unnegotiated benefit checks. [4] Data adjusted to reflect 12 months of benefit payments. [5] Includes $13.2 billion borrowed from the DI and HI Trust Funds. [6] Excludes $2.5 billion lent to the OASI Trust Fund. [7] Includes premiums from aged ineligibles enrolled in HI. [8] Excludes $10.6 billion lent to the OASI Trust Fund.

Source: U.S. Social Security Administration, *Annual Report of Board of Trustees, OASI, DI, HI, and SMI Trust Funds.* Also published in *Social Security Bulletin*, quarterly.

No. 587. Social Security (OASDI)—Benefits, by Type of Beneficiary: 1980 to 1995

[A person eligible to receive more than one type of benefit is generally classified or counted only once as a retired-worker beneficiary. OASDI=Old-age, survivors, and disability insurance. See also headnote, table 585 and Appendix III]

TYPE OF BENEFICIARY	1980	1985	1988	1989	1990	1991	1992	1993	1994	1995
	BENEFITS IN CURRENT-PAYMENT STATUS [1] (end of year)									
Number of benefits (1,000)	35,585	37,058	38,627	39,151	39,832	40,592	41,507	42,246	42,883	43,387
Retired workers [2] (1,000)	19,562	22,432	23,858	24,327	24,838	25,289	25,758	26,104	26,408	26,673
Disabled workers [3] (1,000)	2,859	2,657	2,830	2,895	3,011	3,195	3,468	3,726	3,963	4,185
Wives and husbands [2,4] (1,000)	3,477	3,375	3,367	3,365	3,367	3,370	3,382	3,367	3,337	3,290
Children (1,000)	4,607	3,319	3,204	3,165	3,187	3,268	3,391	3,527	3,654	3,734
Under age 18	3,423	2,699	2,534	2,488	2,497	2,558	2,664	2,777	2,887	2,956
Disabled children [5]	450	526	574	586	600	616	637	656	673	686
Students [6]	733	94	96	91	89	95	90	94	94	92
Of retired workers	639	457	432	423	422	426	432	436	440	442
Of deceased workers	2,610	1,917	1,809	1,780	1,776	1,791	1,806	1,836	1,864	1,884
Of disabled workers	1,358	945	963	962	989	1,052	1,151	1,255	1,350	1,409
Widowed mothers [7] (1,000)	562	372	318	312	304	301	294	289	283	275
Widows and widowers [2,8] (1,000)	4,411	4,863	5,029	5,071	5,111	5,158	5,206	5,224	5,232	5,226
Parents [2] (1,000)	15	10	7	6	6	5	5	5	4	4
Special benefits [9] (1,000)	93	32	14	10	7	5	4	2	2	1
Average monthly benefit, current dollars										
Retired workers [2]	341	479	537	567	603	629	653	674	697	720
Retired worker and wife [2]	567	814	914	966	1,027	1,072	1,111	1,145	1,184	1,221
Disabled workers [3]	371	484	530	556	587	609	626	642	661	682
Wives and husbands [2,4]	164	236	265	281	298	311	322	332	343	354
Children of retired workers	140	196	228	242	259	273	285	297	309	322
Children of deceased workers	240	330	368	385	406	420	432	443	456	469
Children of disabled workers	110	142	151	157	164	168	170	173	178	183
Widowed mothers [7]	246	332	368	388	409	424	436	446	464	478
Widows and widowers, nondisabled [2]	311	433	493	522	557	584	608	630	655	680
Parents [2]	276	378	428	454	482	506	526	547	570	591
Special benefits [9]	105	136	151	158	167	173	178	183	187	192
Average monthly benefit, constant (1995) dollars [10]										
Retired workers [2]	607	673	684	690	692	700	706	710	715	720
Retired worker and wife [2]	1,009	1,143	1,164	1,176	1,178	1,193	1,202	1,205	1,214	1,221
Disabled workers [3]	660	680	675	677	673	678	677	676	678	682
Wives and husbands [2,4]	292	331	338	342	342	346	348	350	352	354
Children of deceased workers	427	465	469	469	466	466	467	466	468	469
Widowed mothers [7]	438	468	469	472	469	472	474	472	476	478
Widows and widowers, nondisabled [2]	553	608	628	635	638	649	658	663	672	680
	BENEFITS AWARDED DURING YEAR (1,000)									
Number of benefits	4,215	3,796	3,681	3,646	3,717	3,865	4,051	4,001	3,940	3,882
Retired workers [2]	1,620	1,690	1,654	1,657	1,665	1,695	1,708	1,661	1,625	1,609
Disabled workers [3]	389	377	409	426	468	536	637	635	632	646
Wives and husbands [2,4]	469	440	391	380	379	380	383	365	345	322
Children	1,174	714	708	675	695	727	795	816	824	809
Widowed mothers [7]	106	72	63	60	58	58	56	56	55	52
Widows and widowers [2,8]	452	502	458	449	452	469	472	466	459	445
Parents [2]	1	(Z)	(Z)	(Z)	(Z)	(Z)	(Z)	(Z)	(Z)	(Z)
Special benefits [9]	1	1	(Z)	(Z)	(Z)	(Z)	(Z)	(Z)	(Z)	(Z)
	BENEFIT PAYMENTS DURING YEAR (bil. dol.)									
Total amount [11]	120.5	186.2	217.2	230.9	247.8	268.1	286.0	302.4	316.8	332.6
Monthly benefits [12]	120.1	186.0	217.0	230.6	247.6	267.9	285.8	302.2	316.6	332.4
Retired workers [2]	70.4	116.8	137.0	146.0	156.8	169.1	179.4	188.4	196.4	205.3
Disabled workers [3]	12.8	16.5	19.2	20.3	22.1	24.7	27.9	30.9	33.7	36.6
Wives and husbands [2,4]	7.0	11.1	12.8	13.6	14.5	15.5	16.4	16.9	17.4	17.9
Children	10.5	10.7	11.3	11.5	12.0	12.8	13.6	14.6	15.4	16.1
Under age 18	7.4	8.5	8.7	8.7	9.0	9.5	10.1	10.8	11.4	11.9
Disabled children [5]	1.0	1.8	2.2	2.3	2.5	2.8	3.0	3.3	3.4	3.6
Students [6]	2.1	0.4	0.5	0.5	0.5	0.5	0.5	0.5	0.6	0.6
Of retired workers	1.1	1.1	1.2	1.2	1.3	1.4	1.5	1.6	1.6	1.7
Of deceased workers	7.4	7.8	8.1	8.3	8.6	9.0	9.4	9.9	10.3	10.7
Of disabled workers	2.0	1.8	2.0	2.0	2.2	2.4	2.7	3.1	3.4	3.7
Widowed mothers [7]	1.6	1.5	1.4	1.4	1.4	1.5	1.5	1.5	1.6	1.6
Widows and widowers [2,8]	17.6	29.3	35.2	37.7	40.7	44.1	47.1	49.7	52.1	54.8
Parents [2]	0.1	0.1	(Z)	(Z)	(Z)	(Z)	(Z)	(Z)	(Z)	(Z)
Special benefits [9]	0.1	0.1	(Z)	(Z)	(Z)	(Z)	(Z)	(Z)	(Z)	(Z)
Lump sum	0.4	0.2	0.2	0.2	0.2	0.2	0.2	0.2	0.2	0.2

Z Fewer than 500 or less than $50 million. [1] Benefit payment actually being made at a specified time with no deductions or with deductions amounting to less than a month's benefits; i.e., the benefits actually being received. [2] 62 years and over. [3] Disabled workers under age 65. [4] Includes wife beneficiaries with entitled children in their care and entitled divorced wives. [5] 18 years old and over. Disability began before age 18 and, beginning 1973, before age 22. [6] Full-time students aged 18-21 through 1984 and aged 18 and 19 beginning 1985. [7] Includes surviving divorced mothers with entitled children in their care and widowed fathers with entitled children in their care. [8] Includes widows aged 60-61, surviving divorced wives aged 60 and over, disabled widows and widowers aged 50 and over; and widowers aged 60-61. [9] Benefits for persons aged 72 and over not insured under regular or transitional provisions of Social Security Act. [10] Constant dollar figures are based on the consumer price index for December as published by the U.S. Bureau of Labor Statistics. [11] Represents total disbursements of benefit checks by the U.S. Dept. of the Treasury during the years specified. [12] Distribution by type estimated.

Source: U.S. Social Security Administration, *Annual Statistical Supplement* to the *Social Security Bulletin;* and unpublished data.

No. 586. Social Security—Beneficiaries, Annual Payments, and Average Monthly Benefit, 1980 to 1995, and by State and Other Areas, 1995

[Number of beneficiaries in current-payment status and average monthly benefit as of December. Data for number of beneficiaries based on 10-percent sample of administrative records. See also headnote, table 587 and Appendix III]

YEAR, DIVISION, STATE, AND OTHER AREA	NUMBER OF BENEFICIARIES (1,000)				ANNUAL PAYMENTS (mil. dol.)				AVERAGE MONTHLY BENEFIT (dol.)		
	Total	Retired workers and dependents [1]	Survivors	Disabled workers and dependents	Total	Retired workers and dependents [1]	Survivors [2]	Disabled workers and dependents	Retired workers [3]	Disabled workers	Widows and widowers [4]
1980	35,585	23,309	7,598	4,678	120,472	78,025	27,010	15,437	341	371	311
1990	39,832	28,369	7,197	4,266	247,796	172,042	50,951	24,803	603	587	557
1993	42,238	29,633	7,341	5,264	302,402	206,365	61,440	34,598	674	642	630
1994	42,878	29,913	7,371	5,592	316,835	214,895	64,223	37,717	697	661	655
1995, total [5]	43,380	30,139	7,379	5,862	332,581	224,381	67,302	40,898	720	682	680
United States	42,372	29,529	7,159	5,684	327,510	221,807	65,960	39,947	(NA)	(NA)	(NA)
New England	2,327	1,681	336	310	18,396	12,985	3,252	2,160	(NA)	(NA)	(NA)
Maine	237	163	36	38	1,683	1,127	319	238	664	620	640
New Hampshire	186	135	26	25	1,450	1,029	250	171	724	683	710
Vermont	98	68	15	16	738	500	136	102	707	659	680
Massachusetts	1,049	748	153	148	8,230	5,692	1,493	1,045	723	674	712
Rhode Island	190	140	26	25	1,478	1,067	244	167	718	654	711
Connecticut	566	427	80	59	4,817	3,570	810	437	790	696	757
Middle Atlantic	6,614	4,772	1,075	767	54,408	38,121	10,534	5,752	(NA)	(NA)	(NA)
New York	2,972	2,112	467	393	24,446	16,991	4,502	2,953	768	721	726
New Jersey	1,310	966	203	141	11,167	8,050	2,035	1,061	791	719	750
Pennsylvania	2,332	1,694	405	234	18,795	13,080	3,997	1,718	740	703	717
East North Central	7,182	5,013	1,255	914	58,065	39,115	12,288	6,661	(NA)	(NA)	(NA)
Ohio	1,913	1,308	356	249	15,153	9,902	3,463	1,787	736	702	711
Indiana	962	672	162	129	7,748	5,247	1,587	914	750	693	720
Illinois	1,829	1,295	318	216	14,976	10,274	3,106	1,596	760	709	733
Michigan	1,594	1,096	281	217	13,173	8,752	2,786	1,635	770	740	731
Wisconsin	884	643	138	103	7,015	4,940	1,346	729	737	685	714
West North Central	3,187	2,274	537	376	24,274	16,690	5,012	2,573	(NA)	(NA)	(NA)
Minnesota	713	521	117	75	5,431	3,807	1,094	530	708	663	680
Iowa	540	393	90	57	4,177	2,914	868	395	719	671	696
Missouri	968	664	165	139	7,317	4,867	1,500	951	705	669	674
North Dakota	116	82	22	12	834	558	199	77	676	648	650
South Dakota	136	95	25	15	959	648	214	97	664	618	636
Nebraska	282	206	46	30	2,138	1,500	441	196	709	654	701
Kansas	434	313	72	48	3,418	2,396	696	327	739	659	713
South Atlantic	8,064	5,600	1,336	1,128	60,436	40,849	11,727	7,860	(NA)	(NA)	(NA)
Delaware	122	88	19	15	973	681	184	109	747	703	722
Maryland	679	481	122	76	5,300	3,618	1,121	561	721	706	691
District of Columbia	78	54	15	9	528	351	112	65	609	627	565
Virginia	949	642	167	140	6,992	4,569	1,457	966	689	673	636
West Virginia	384	231	82	72	2,903	1,658	734	511	712	726	649
North Carolina	1,232	819	206	206	8,934	5,842	1,694	1,398	682	651	606
South Carolina	625	404	109	112	4,506	2,876	866	764	682	662	597
Georgia	1,010	636	189	184	7,269	4,485	1,557	1,227	679	656	616
Florida	2,984	2,244	426	314	23,031	16,769	4,002	2,259	718	692	701
East South Central	2,908	1,779	566	563	20,462	12,193	4,621	3,648	(NA)	(NA)	(NA)
Kentucky	712	420	139	153	5,026	2,853	1,160	1,013	669	683	610
Tennessee	926	588	172	166	6,672	4,136	1,440	1,096	680	647	620
Alabama	776	481	157	137	5,496	3,315	1,290	891	671	655	605
Mississippi	495	290	98	106	3,268	1,889	731	648	634	632	556
West South Central	4,249	2,776	851	622	30,790	19,411	7,297	4,086	(NA)	(NA)	(NA)
Arkansas	503	318	92	93	3,490	2,142	738	611	655	651	589
Louisiana	702	412	160	129	4,923	2,771	1,329	824	668	689	621
Oklahoma	575	393	105	76	4,226	2,786	927	514	687	662	653
Texas	2,470	1,652	494	323	18,151	11,712	4,303	2,137	696	672	659
Mountain	2,310	1,630	356	324	17,397	11,912	3,232	2,252	(NA)	(NA)	(NA)
Montana	152	104	25	23	1,127	746	225	156	696	684	683
Idaho	178	128	28	23	1,326	918	255	153	699	679	695
Wyoming	71	50	11	10	545	375	103	67	722	691	693
Colorado	495	340	79	77	3,694	2,439	724	531	700	678	682
New Mexico	258	170	46	42	1,793	1,157	373	262	675	666	638
Arizona	703	509	102	91	5,435	3,823	946	666	728	706	707
Utah	224	160	35	30	1,692	1,183	321	188	726	660	713
Nevada	229	169	30	30	1,785	1,271	285	229	726	720	711
Pacific	5,532	4,004	848	679	43,282	30,331	7,987	4,965	(NA)	(NA)	(NA)
Washington	793	578	117	98	6,334	4,478	1,145	711	748	689	725
Oregon	544	403	79	63	4,266	3,057	761	449	732	680	716
California	3,984	2,866	621	497	31,116	21,644	5,826	3,646	733	691	711
Alaska	45	28	9	8	323	203	70	51	706	678	629
Hawaii	166	130	22	14	1,243	949	195	98	709	691	650
Puerto Rico	613	333	122	158	3,016	1,500	681	835	465	570	420
Guam	8	4	2	1	37	21	12	4	514	608	487
American Samoa	5	2	2	1	19	6	8	5	422	497	376
Virgin Islands	12	8	2	1	72	47	15	10	598	649	503
Abroad	368	261	90	16	1,930	1,200	629	101	472	595	494

NA Not available. [1] Includes special benefits; see footnote 9, table 587. [2] Includes lump-sum payments to survivors of deceased workers. [3] Excludes persons with special benefits. [4] Nondisabled only. [5] Number of beneficiaries includes those with State or area unknown.

Source: U.S. Social Security Administration, *Social Security Bulletin*, quarterly.

No. 589. Public Employee Retirement Systems—Participants and Finances: 1980 to 1995

[For fiscal year of retirement system, except data for the Thrift Savings Plan are for calendar year]

RETIREMENT PLAN	Unit	1980	1985	1989	1990	1991	1992	1993	1994	1995
TOTAL PARTICIPANTS [1]										
Federal retirement systems:										
Defined benefit:										
Civil Service Retirement System	1,000	4,629	4,919	4,332	4,167	4,068	4,014	3,808	3,808	3,731
Federal Employees Retirement System [2]	1,000	(X)	(X)	1,068	1,180	1,325	1,367	1,764	1,764	1,512
Military Service Retirement System [3]	1,000	3,380	3,672	3,790	3,763	3,732	3,579	3,511	3,451	3,367
Thrift Savings Plan [4]	1,000	(X)	(X)	1,454	1,625	1,776	1,900	2,036	2,119	2,195
State and local retirement systems [5,6]	1,000	(NA)	15,234	16,684	16,858	17,502	18,310	(NA)	(NA)	(NA)
ACTIVE PARTICIPANTS										
Federal retirement systems:										
Defined benefit:										
Civil Service Retirement System	1,000	2,700	2,800	1,918	1,828	1,728	1,654	1,525	1,443	1,525
Federal Employees Retirement System [2]	1,000	(X)	(X)	1,052	1,136	1,260	1,276	1,318	1,376	1,318
Military Service Retirement System [3]	1,000	2,050	2,192	2,168	2,130	2,064	1,868	1,763	1,666	1,572
Thrift Savings Plan [4]	1,000	(X)	(X)	1,290	1,419	1,593	1,300	1,812	1,876	1,930
State and local retirement systems [5,6]	1,000	(NA)	10,364	11,357	11,345	11,696	(NA)	(NA)	(NA)	(NA)
ASSETS										
Total	Bil. dol.	258	529	922	1,047	1,150	1,276	1,384	1,519	(NA)
Federal retirement systems	Bil. dol.	73	154	289	326	367	411	455	494	537
Defined benefit	Bil. dol.	73	154	284	318	355	394	434	466	502
Civil Service Retirement System	Bil. dol.	73	142	204	220	237	256	277	294	311
Federal Employees Retirement System [2]	Bil. dol.	(X)	(X)	12	18	24	32	41	50	60
Military Service Retirement System [3]	Bil. dol.	(7)	12	68	80	94	106	116	124	131
Thrift Savings Plan [4]	Bil. dol.	(X)	(X)	5	8	12	16	21	28	35
State and local retirement systems [5]	Bil. dol.	185	374	633	721	783	866	929	1,025	(NA)
CONTRIBUTIONS										
Total	Bil. dol.	83	106	104	103	111	107	120	121	(NA)
Federal retirement systems	Bil. dol.	19	54	60	61	65	68	68	67	67
Defined benefit	Bil. dol.	19	54	58	59	62	64	63	62	61
Civil Service Retirement System	Bil. dol.	19	27	28	28	29	30	31	31	31
Federal Employees Retirement System [2]	Bil. dol.	(X)	(X)	4	4	5	6	6	6	6
Military Service Retirement System [3]	Bil. dol.	(7)	27	28	27	28	28	26	25	24
Thrift Savings Plan [4]	Bil. dol.	(X)	(X)	2	2	3	4	5	5	6
State and local retirement systems [5]	Bil. dol.	64	52	44	42	46	39	52	54	(NA)
BENEFITS										
Total	Bil. dol.	39	62	83	89	96	101	117	124	(NA)
Federal retirement systems	Bil. dol.	27	40	50	53	56	58	63	65	66
Defined benefit	Bil. dol.	27	40	50	53	56	58	62	64	65
Civil Service Retirement System	Bil. dol.	15	23	30	31	33	33	35	36	37
Federal Employees Retirement System [2]	Bil. dol.	(X)	(X)	(Z)	(Z)	(Z)	(Z)	(Z)	(Z)	1
Military Service Retirement System [3]	Bil. dol.	12	17	20	22	23	25	27	28	28
Thrift Savings Plan [4]	Bil. dol.	(X)	(X)	(Z)	(Z)	(Z)	(Z)	1	1	1
State and local retirement systems [5]	Bil. dol.	12	22	33	36	39	44	54	59	(NA)

NA Not available. X Not applicable. Z Less than $500 million. [1] Includes active, separated vested, retired employees, and survivors. [2] The Federal Employees Retirement system was established June 6, 1986. [3] Includes nondisability and disability retirees, surviving families, and all active personnel with the exception of active reserves. [4] The Thrift Savings Plan (a defined contribution plan) was established April 1, 1987. [5] Excludes State and local plans that are fully supported by employee contributions. [6] Not adjusted for double counting of individuals participating in more than one plan. [7] The Military Retirement System was unfunded until October 1, 1984.

Source: Employee Benefit Research Institute, Washington, DC, *EBRI Databook on Employee Benefits, Fifth Edition* (copyright).

No. 590. Federal Civil Service Retirement: 1980 to 1996

[As of Sept. 30 or for year ending Sept. 30. Covers both Civil Service Retirement System and Federal Employees Retirement System]

ITEM	Unit	1980	1985	1990	1991	1992	1993	1994	1995	1996
Employees covered [1]	1,000	2,720	2,750	2,945	2,885	2,933	2,843	2,778	2,668	2,629
Annuitants, total	1,006	1,675	1,955	2,143	2,184	2,185	2,242	2,263	2,311	2,333
Age and service	1,000	905	1,122	1,288	1,325	1,322	1,378	1,396	1,441	1,459
Disability	1,000	343	332	297	289	282	274	268	263	260
Survivors	1,000	427	501	558	570	581	589	597	607	614
Receipts, total [2]	Mil. dol	24,389	40,798	52,689	56,815	59,737	62,878	63,390	65,684	67,536
Employee contributions	Mil. dol	3,686	4,679	4,501	4,563	4,713	4,703	4,610	4,498	4,398
Federal government contributions	Mil. dol	15,562	22,301	27,368	29,509	30,785	32,668	32,434	33,130	33,991
Disbursements, total [3]	Mil. dol	14,977	23,203	31,416	33,209	33,187	35,123	36,532	38,436	39,711
Age and service annuitants [4]	Mil. dol	12,639	19,414	26,495	27,997	27,684	29,288	30,440	32,070	32,970
Survivors	Mil. dol	1,912	3,158	4,366	4,716	5,093	5,377	5,607	5,864	6,221
Average monthly benefit:										
Age and service	Dollars	992	1,189	1,369	1,439	1,493	1,537	1,587	1,643	1,698
Disability	Dollars	723	881	1,008	1,059	1,094	1,120	1,141	1,164	1,184
Survivors	Dollars	392	528	653	698	731	760	789	819	849
Cash and security holdings	Bil. dol.	73.7	142.3	238.0	261.6	289.6	317.4	344.3	366.2	394.1

[1] Excludes employees in Leave Without Pay status. [2] Includes interest on investments. [3] Includes refunds, death claims, and administration. [4] Includes disability annuitants.

Source: U.S. Office of Personnel Management, *Civil Service Retirement and Disability Trust Fund Annual Report.*

No. 591. State and Local Government Retirement Systems—Beneficiaries and Finances: 1980 to 1994

[In billions of dollars, except as indicated. For fiscal years closed during the 12 months ending June 30]

YEAR AND LEVEL OF GOVERNMENT	Number of beneficiaries (1,000)	RECEIPTS					BENEFITS AND WITHDRAWALS			Cash and security holdings
		Total	Employee contributions	Government contributions		Earnings on investments	Total	Benefits	Withdrawals	
				State	Local					
1980: All systems	(NA)	37.3	6.5	7.6	10.0	13.3	14.0	12.2	1.8	185
State-administered	(NA)	28.6	5.3	7.4	5.6	10.3	10.3	8.8	1.4	145
Locally administered	(NA)	8.7	1.2	0.2	4.3	3.0	3.8	3.4	0.4	41
1990: All systems	4,026	111.3	13.9	14.0	18.6	64.9	38.4	36.0	2.4	721
State-administered	3,232	89.2	11.6	14.0	11.5	52.0	29.6	27.6	2.0	575
Locally administered	794	22.2	2.2	(Z)	7.0	12.9	8.8	8.4	0.4	145
1993: All systems	4,562	135.4	16.5	15.2	20.4	83.3	51.6	49.1	2.5	929
State-administered	3,643	109.4	13.8	15.2	12.9	67.6	40.0	37.9	2.1	750
Locally administered	919	26.0	2.7	(Z)	7.5	15.8	11.6	11.2	0.4	180
1994: All systems	4,889	138.7	17.3	15.5	21.2	84.6	56.4	53.4	3.0	1,025
State-administered	3,979	113.2	14.7	15.5	13.6	69.4	43.8	41.2	2.6	826
Locally administered	910	25.5	2.6	(Z)	7.7	15.2	12.6	12.2	0.5	199

NA Not available. Z Less than $50 million.

Source: U.S. Bureau of the Census, *Finances of Employee-Retirement Systems of State and Local Governments*, series GF, No. 2, annual.

No. 592. Private Pension Plans—Summary, by Type of Plan: 1980 to 1993

["Pension plan" is defined by the Employee Retirement Income Security Act (ERISA) as "any plan, fund, or program which was heretofore or is hereafter established or maintained by an employer or an employee organization, or by both, to the extent that such plan (a) provides retirement income to employees, or (b) results in a deferral of income by employees for periods extending to the termination of covered employment or beyond, regardless of the method of calculating the contributions made to the plan, the method of calculating the benefits under the plan, or the method of distributing benefits from the plan." A defined benefit plan provides a definite benefit formula for calculating benefit amounts - such as a flat amount per year of service or a percentage of salary times years of service. A defined contribution plan is a pension plan in which the contributions are made to an individual account for each employee. The retirement benefit is dependent upon the account balance at retirement. The balance depends upon amounts contributed, investment experience, and, in the case of profit sharing plans, amounts which may be allocated to the account due to forfeitures by terminating employees. Employee Stock Ownership Plans (ESOP) and 401(k) plans (see table 594) are included among defined contribution plans. Data are based on Form 5500 series reports filed with the Internal Revenue Service]

ITEM	Unit	TOTAL				DEFINED CONTRIBUTION PLAN				DEFINED BENEFIT PLAN			
		1980	1985	1990	1993	1980	1985	1990	1993	1980	1985	1990	1993
Number of plans [1]	1,000	488.9	632.1	712.3	702.1	340.8	462.0	599.2	618.5	148.1	170.2	113.1	83.6
Total participants [2,3]	Million	57.9	74.7	76.9	83.9	19.9	35.0	38.1	43.6	38.0	39.7	38.8	40.3
Active participants [2,4]	Million	49.0	62.3	61.8	64.7	18.9	33.2	35.5	39.6	30.1	29.0	26.3	25.1
Contributions [5]	Bil. dol.	66.2	95.1	98.8	153.6	23.5	53.1	75.8	101.5	42.6	42.0	23.0	52.1
Benefits [6]	Bil. dol.	35.3	101.9	129.4	156.3	13.1	47.4	63.0	77.2	22.1	54.5	66.4	79.1

[1] Excludes all plans covering only one participant. [2] Includes double counting of workers in more than one plan. [3] Total participants include active participants, vested separated workers, and retirees. [4] Any workers currently in employment covered by a plan and who are earning or retaining credited service under a plan. Includes any nonvested former employees who have not yet incurred breaks in service. [5] Includes both employer and employee contributions. [6] Benefits paid directly from trust and premium payments made from plan to insurance carriers. Excludes benefits paid directly by insurance carriers.

Source: U.S. Dept. of Labor, Pension and Welfare Benefits Administration, *Private Pension Plan Bulletin*, winter 1996.

No. 593. Pension Plan Coverage of Workers, by Selected Characteristics: 1995

[Covers workers as of March 1996 who had earnings in 1995. Based on Current Population Survey; see text, section 1, and Appendix III]

SEX AND AGE	NUMBER WITH COVERAGE (1,000)				PERCENT OF TOTAL WORKERS			
	Total [1]	White	Black	Hispanic [2]	Total [1]	White	Black	Hispanic [2]
Total	57,837	49,435	6,260	3,191	41.2	41.4	41.2	25.1
Male	32,310	28,050	3,059	1,831	43.3	43.6	42.2	24.5
Under 65 years old	31,633	27,458	2,997	1,807	44.0	44.5	42.3	24.5
15 to 24 years old	1,633	1,368	179	138	13.3	13.1	13.8	8.7
25 to 44 years old	18,217	15,661	1,845	1,189	47.3	47.8	46.1	26.7
45 to 64 years old	11,784	10,430	973	480	55.9	56.4	54.5	36.5
65 years old and over	677	592	62	25	23.7	22.7	35.3	21.0
Female	25,527	21,385	3,202	1,360	38.9	38.9	40.3	26.0
Under 65 years old	25,057	20,967	3,157	1,344	39.4	39.5	40.5	26.1
15 to 24 years old	1,092	903	145	95	9.6	9.6	10.4	8.5
25 to 44 years old	14,672	12,099	2,004	869	43.7	43.8	45.1	29.6
45 to 64 years old	9,293	7,965	1,009	380	49.8	49.8	51.7	34.7
65 years old and over	470	418	44	16	22.3	22.0	27.0	24.5

[1] Includes other races, not shown separately. [2] Hispanic persons may be of any race.

Source: U.S. Bureau of the Census, unpublished data.

No. 594. 401(k) Plans—Summary: 1985 to 1993

[A 401(k) plan is a qualified retirement plan that allows participants to have a portion of their compensation (otherwise payable in cash) contributed pretax to a retirement account on their behalf]

ITEM	1985	1988	1989	1990	1991	1992	1993
Number of plans [1]	29,869	68,121	83,301	97,614	111,314	139,704	154,527
Active participants [2] (1,000)	10,339	15,203	17,337	19,548	19,126	22,404	23,136
Assets (mil. dol.)	143,939	276,995	357,015	384,854	440,259	552,959	616,316
Contributions (mil. dol.)	24,322	39,412	46,081	48,998	51,533	64,345	69,322
Benefits (mil. dol.)	16,399	25,235	30,875	32,026	32,734	43,166	44,206
Percentage of all private defined contribution plans:							
Assets	34	47	52	54	53	58	58
Contributions	46	61	63	65	64	69	68
Benefits	35	43	47	51	51	58	57

[1] Excludes single-participant plans. [2] May include some employees who are eligible to participate in the plan but have not elected to join. 401(k) participants may participate in one or more additional plans.

Source: Employee Benefit Research Institute, Washington, DC, *EBRI Databook on Employee Benefits, Fifth Edition* (copyright).

No. 595. State Unemployment Insurance—Summary: 1980 to 1995

[Includes unemployment compensation for State and local government employees where covered by State law]

ITEM	Unit	1980	1985	1988	1989	1990	1991	1992	1993	1994	1995
Insured unemployment, avg. weekly	1,000	3,356	2,617	2,081	2,158	2,522	3,342	3,245	2,751	2,670	2,575
Percent of covered employment [1]	Percent	3.9	2.9	2.0	2.1	2.4	3.1	3.1	2.6	2.5	2.3
Percent of civilian unemployed	Percent	43.9	31.5	31.1	33.1	36.7	39.7	34.6	31.5	33.4	34.8
Unemployment benefits, avg. weekly	Dollars	100	128	145	152	162	170	174	180	182	187
Percent of weekly wage	Percent	36.6	35.3	34.9	35.4	36.0	36.4	35.4	36.0	35.7	35.5
Weeks compensated	Million	149.0	119.3	94.2	97.6	116.0	155.1	150.2	125.6	123.4	118.3
Beneficiaries, first payments	1,000	9,992	8,372	6,861	7,369	8,629	10,075	9,243	7,884	7,959	8,036
Average duration of benefits [2]	Weeks	14.9	14.2	13.7	13.2	13.4	15.4	16.2	15.9	15.5	14.7
Claimants exhausting benefits	1,000	3,072	2,575	1,979	1,940	2,323	3,472	3,838	3,204	2,977	2,662
Percent of first payment [3]	Percent	33.2	31.2	28.5	28.0	29.4	34.8	39.9	39.2	36.3	34.3
Contributions collected [4]	Bil. dol.	11.4	19.3	17.7	16.5	15.2	14.5	17.0	19.8	21.8	22.0
Benefits paid	Bil. dol.	13.8	14.1	12.8	13.6	17.3	24.6	24.0	20.7	20.4	20.1
Funds available for benefits [5]	Bil. dol.	11.6	16.2	31.9	37.5	38.4	31.5	27.1	28.2	31.3	35.4
Average employer contribution rate [6]	Percent	2.4	3.1	2.5	2.2	2.0	2.0	2.2	2.5	2.6	2.4

[1] Insured unemployment as percent of average covered employment in preceding year. [2] Weeks compensated divided by first payment. [3] Based on first payments for 12-month period ending June 30. [4] Contributions from employers; also employees in States which tax workers. [5] End of year. Sum of balances in State clearing accounts, benefit-payment accounts, and State accounts in Federal unemployment trust funds. [6] As percent of taxable wages.

No. 596. State Unemployment Insurance, by State and Other Areas: 1995

[See headnote, table 595. For State data on insured unemployment, see table 658]

STATE OR OTHER AREA	Beneficiaries, first payments (1,000)	Benefits paid (mil. dol.)	Avg. weekly unemployment benefits (dol.)	STATE OR OTHER AREA	Beneficiaries, first payments (1,000)	Benefits paid (mil. dol.)	Avg. weekly unemployment benefits (dol.)	STATE OR OTHER AREA	Beneficiaries, first payments (1,000)	Benefits paid (mil. dol.)	Avg. weekly unemployment benefits (dol.)
Total	8,036	20,122	187	KY	123	211	167	OH	259	648	197
AL	149	178	139	LA	82	138	121	OK	48	100	173
AK	47	114	173	ME	50	102	166	OR	138	340	184
AZ	74	150	149	MD	117	331	186	PA	479	1,476	219
AR	89	156	166	MA	203	732	244	RI	57	182	228
CA	1,224	2,964	154	MI	365	843	221	SC	109	171	162
CO	71	179	202	MN	116	328	228	SD	8	13	145
CT	142	435	214	MS	74	112	134	TN	168	256	150
DE	24	60	195	MO	146	272	152	TX	366	931	187
DC	24	94	232	MT	26	53	160	UT	30	59	192
FL	271	635	172	NE	27	44	157	VT	23	47	166
GA	192	270	162	NV	55	143	190	VA	120	201	170
HI	48	180	270	NH	22	35	148	WA	237	794	205
ID	48	92	175	NJ	307	1,254	253	WV	61	133	172
IL	338	1,076	208	NM	26	65	153	WI	213	417	199
IN	121	224	179	NY	583	1,988	208	WY	13	29	180
IA	78	153	194	NC	233	316	190	PR	126	221	92
KS	59	137	196	ND	15	30	166	VI	6	11	163

Source of tables 595 and 596: U.S. Employment and Training Administration, *Unemployment Insurance Financial Handbook*, annual.

No. 597. Workers' Compensation Payments: 1980 to 1995

[In billions of dollars, except as indicated. See headnote, table 596]

ITEM	1980	1985	1987	1988	1989	1990	1991	1992	1993	1994	1995
Workers covered [1] (mil.)	79	84	88	91	104	106	104	104	106	109	113
Premium amounts paid [2]	**22.3**	**29.2**	**38.1**	**43.3**	**48.0**	**53.1**	**55.2**	**57.4**	**60.8**	**60.4**	**57.0**
Private carriers [2]	15.7	19.5	25.4	28.5	31.9	35.1	35.7	34.5	35.6	34.0	31.6
State funds	3.0	3.5	5.3	6.7	7.2	8.0	8.7	9.6	10.9	11.1	10.4
Federal programs [3]	1.1	1.7	1.8	1.9	2.0	2.2	2.1	2.5	2.5	2.5	2.6
Self-insurers	2.4	4.5	5.5	6.2	6.9	7.9	8.7	10.8	11.8	12.8	12.4
Annual benefits paid [2]	**13.6**	**22.2**	**27.3**	**30.7**	**34.3**	**38.2**	**42.2**	**45.7**	**45.3**	**44.7**	**43.5**
By private carriers [2]	7.0	12.3	15.5	17.5	19.9	22.2	24.5	25.3	24.1	22.6	21.4
From State funds [4]	4.3	5.7	6.8	7.5	8.0	8.7	9.7	10.7	10.6	10.6	10.9
Employers' self-insurance [5]	2.3	4.1	5.1	5.7	6.4	7.4	7.9	9.7	10.6	11.5	11.2
Type of benefit:											
Medical/hospitalization	3.9	7.5	9.9	11.5	13.4	15.2	16.8	17.6	17.5	17.2	16.7
Compensation payments	9.7	14.7	17.4	19.2	20.9	23.1	25.3	28.1	27.8	27.5	26.7
Disability	8.4	13.1	15.8	17.6	19.2	21.2	23.3	26.0	25.4	25.5	24.8
Survivor	1.3	1.7	1.6	1.6	1.7	1.8	2.0	2.1	2.4	2.0	2.0
Percent of covered payroll: [1]											
Workers' compensation costs [6] [7]	1.96	1.82	2.07	2.16	2.04	2.13	2.16	2.13	2.17	2.04	1.82
Benefits [7]	1.07	1.30	1.43	1.49	1.42	1.53	1.62	1.66	1.59	1.49	1.37

[1] Data for period 1980 to 1988 not comparable with later years. [2] Premium and benefit amounts include estimated benefit payments under insurance policy deductible provisions. Deductible benefits are allocated to private carriers and state funds. [3] Includes Federal employer compensation program and that portion of Federal black lung benefits program financed from employer contributions. [4] Net cash and medical benefits paid by competitive and exclusive State funds and by Federal workers' compensation programs, including black lung benefit program. [5] Cash and medical benefits paid by self-insurers, plus value of medical benefits paid by employers carrying workers' compensation policies that exclude standard medical coverage. [6] Premiums written by private carriers and State funds, and benefits paid by self-insurers increased by 5-10 percent prior to 1992 and by 11 percent for 1992-95 for administrative costs. Also includes benefits paid and administrative costs of Federal system for government employees. [7] Excludes programs financed from general revenue—black lung benefits and supplemental pensions in some States.

Source: 1980-1993, U.S. Social Security Administration, *Annual Statistical Supplement* to the *Social Security Bulletin*. Beginning 1994, Jack Schmulowitz, Baltimore, MD, unpublished estimates.

No. 598. Workers' Compensation Payments, by State: 1990 to 1995

[**In millions of dollars.** Calendar-year data, except fiscal-year data for Federal civilian and other programs and for some States with State funds. Payments represent compensation and medical benefits and include insurance losses paid by private insurance carriers (compiled from state workers' compensation agencies and A.M. Best Co); disbursements of state funds (compiled from the A.M. Best Co., state workers' compensation agencies and U.S. Bureau of the Census); and self-insurance payments, estimated from available state data. Includes benefit payments under Longshore and Harbor Workers' Compensation Act for States in which such payments are made]

STATE	1990	1992	1993	1994	1995
Total [1]	**38,238**	**45,668**	**45,330**	**44,697**	**43,512**
Alabama	444	481	[2]479	[2]480	516
Alaska	113	127	122	112	106
Arizona	371	399	402	406	386
Arkansas	229	244	224	209	159
California	6,065	7,907	7,625	7,390	[2]7,177
Colorado	595	722	683	612	584
Connecticut	694	783	[2]848	[2]773	[2]733
Delaware	75	89	[2]88	[2]103	[2]103
District of Columbia	86	126	122	115	113
Florida	1,976	1,861	2,296	2,720	2,518
Georgia	735	1,004	911	812	699
Hawaii	216	288	324	343	326
Idaho	105	123	125	147	148
Illinois	1,607	1,750	1,668	1,582	1,438
Indiana	350	375	364	378	361
Iowa	231	259	240	233	233
Kansas	266	297	307	[2] 302	[2] 280
Kentucky	383	475	595	585	498
Louisiana	575	586	531	531	516
Maine	380	429	341	282	286
Maryland	505	565	548	558	522
Massachusetts	1,235	1,206	[2]1,017	[2]917	[2]773
Michigan	1,205	1,428	[2]1,549	[2]1,589	[2]1,585
Minnesota	582	822	809	[2]783	[2]733
Mississippi	196	247	214	[2]213	[2]218
Missouri	496	698	656	785	733
Montana	150	165	167	154	151
Nebraska	137	157	160	156	141
Nevada	339	529	553	432	365
New Hampshire	169	206	194	178	169
New Jersey	844	956	968	[2]957	[2]972
New Mexico	228	216	182	162	145
New York	1,752	2,317	2,370	[2]2,725	[2]2,780
North Carolina	480	705	671	565	495
North Dakota	60	71	60	75	71
Ohio	1,960	2,364	2,353	2,149	2,303
Oklahoma	369	476	493	550	580
Oregon	573	476	468	468	463
Pennsylvania	2,019	2,531	[2]2,774	[2]2,582	[2]2,663
Rhode Island	219	266	185	160	138
South Carolina	277	350	[2]344	[2]339	[2]353
South Dakota	56	69	72	78	63
Tennessee	463	522	487	449	400
Texas	2,896	[2]3,082	[2]2,694	[2]2,232	[2]2,006
Utah	187	160	165	152	140
Vermont	61	73	73	67	65
Virginia	507	542	539	591	557
Washington	883	1,018	1,068	1,087	1,129
West Virginia	389	456	476	510	529
Wisconsin	561	598	608	609	608
Wyoming	49	66	76	77	75
Federal programs:					
Civilian employees	1,448	1,751	1,822	1,859	1,880
Black lung benefits [3]	1,435	1,396	1,356	1,306	1,222
Other [4]	11	11	11	(NA)	(NA)

NA Not available. [1] Beginning 1992 total includes an amount for benefits under deductible provisions not distributed by state. [2] Includes benefits under deductible provisions. [3] Includes payments by Social Security Administration and by Department of Labor. [4] Primarily payments made to dependents of reservists who died while on active duty in the Armed Forces.

Source: U.S. Social Security Administration, *Social Security Bulletin*, summer 1995, and selected prior issues. Beginning 1994, Jack Schmulowitz, Baltimore, MD, unpublished estimates.

No. 599. Persons With Work Disability, by Selected Characteristics: 1995

[In thousands, except percent. As of March. Covers civilian noninstitutional population and members of Armed Forces living off post or with their families on post. Persons are classified as having a work disability if they (1) have a health problem or disability which prevents them from working or which limits the kind or amount of work they can do; (2) have a service-connected disability or ever retired or left a job for health reasons; (3) did not work in survey reference week or previous year because of long-term illness or disability; or (4) are under age 65, and are covered by Medicare or receive Supplemental Security Income. Based on Current Population Survey; see text, section 1, and Appendix III]

AGE AND PARTICIPATION STATUS IN ASSISTANCE PROGRAMS	Total [1]	Male	Female	White	Black	Hispanic [2]
Persons with work disability	**16,846**	**8,444**	**8,402**	**12,993**	**3,191**	**1,650**
16 to 24 years old	1,357	661	696	957	336	166
25 to 34 years old	2,654	1,272	1,382	1,959	576	271
35 to 44 years old	3,993	2,089	1,904	3,025	835	366
45 to 54 years old	4,089	2,094	1,996	3,206	703	395
55 to 64 years old	4,752	2,327	2,425	3,846	741	451
Percent work disabled of total population	10.1	10.3	9.9	9.4	15.5	9.7
16 to 24 years old	4.2	4.1	4.3	3.7	7.0	3.9
25 to 34 years old	6.5	6.3	6.7	5.9	10.8	5.2
35 to 44 years old	9.5	10.1	8.9	8.7	16.3	9.5
45 to 54 years old	13.4	14.0	12.7	12.3	22.0	17.4
55 to 64 years old	22.9	23.6	22.3	21.3	35.8	32.4
Percent of work disabled—						
Receiving Social Security income	28.1	30.6	25.6	28.4	26.9	26.1
Receiving food stamps	24.4	19.8	29.1	19.8	41.0	32.6
Covered by Medicaid	31.7	27.2	36.2	26.9	48.9	42.7
Residing in public housing	5.6	4.4	6.8	3.2	15.0	8.0
Residing in subsidized housing	3.6	2.7	4.6	3.0	5.9	5.0

[1] Includes other races not shown separately. [2] Hispanic persons may be of any race.

Source: U.S. Bureau of the Census, unpublished data.

No. 600. Vocational Rehabilitation—Summary: 1980 to 1995

[For fiscal years ending in year shown; see text, section 9. Includes Puerto Rico, Guam, Virgin Islands, American Samoa, Northern Mariana Islands, and the Republic of Palau. State agencies, using matching State and Federal funds, provide vocational rehabilitation services to eligible individuals with disabilities to enable them to prepare for and engage in gainful employment. Services may include counseling, guidance and work related placement services, physical and mental restoration, training and rehabilitation technology]

ITEM	Unit	1980	1985	1989	1990	1991	1992	1993	1994	1995
Federal and State expenditures [1]	Mil. dol.	1,076	1,452	1,867	1,910	2,092	2,240	2,241	2,517	2,714
Federal expenditures	Mil. dol.	817	1,100	1,446	1,525	1,622	1,731	1,691	1,891	2,054
Applicants processed for program eligibility	1,000	717	594	623	625	619	713	713	675	625
Percent accepted into program	Percent	58	60	58	57	57	57	61	72	76
Total persons rehabilitated [2]	1,000	277	228	220	216	203	192	194	203	210
Rehabilitation rate [3]	Percent	64	64	63	62	60	58	56	49	46
Severely disabled persons rehabilitated [2 4]	1,000	143	135	147	146	140	134	139	149	159
Rehabilitation rate [3]	Percent	61	62	62	62	59	57	55	49	46
Percent of total persons rehabilitated	Percent	51	59	67	68	69	70	72	74	76
Persons served, total [5]	1,000	1,095	932	929	938	942	949	1,049	1,194	1,250
Persons served, severely disabled [4 5]	1,000	608	581	625	640	654	658	762	882	940
Percent of total persons served	Percent	55	62	67	68	69	70	73	74	75

[1] Includes expenditures only under the basic support provisions of the Rehabilitation Act. [2] Persons successfully placed into gainful employment. [3] Persons rehabilitated as a percent of all active case closures (whether rehabilitated or not). [4] An individual with a severe disability is an individual whose severe physical or mental impairment seriously limits one or more functional capacities in terms of an employment outcome, and whose vocational rehabilitation can be expected to require multiple vocational rehabilitation services over an extended period of time. [5] Includes active cases accepted for rehabilitation services during year plus active cases on hand at beginning of year.

Source: U.S. Dept. of Education, Rehabilitation Services Administration, *Caseload Statistics of State Vocational Rehabilitation Agencies in Fiscal Years*, and *State Vocational Rehabilitation Agency Program Data in Fiscal Years*, both annual.

No. 601. Protection Against Short-Term Sickness Income Loss: 1980 to 1994

[In millions of dollars, except percent. "Short-term sickness" refers to short-term or temporary nonwork-connected disability (lasting not more than 6 months) and the first 6 months of long-term disability]

ITEM	1980	1985	1988	1989	1990	1991	1992	1993	1994
Short-term sickness: Income loss	33,746	48,484	60,185	63,862	68,296	69,542	73,783	76,816	81,101
Total protection provided [1]	**17,480**	**22,918**	**27,922**	**30,006**	**31,683**	**32,991**	**35,464**	**35,869**	**36,874**
Protection as percent of loss	51.8	47.3	46.4	47.0	46.4	47.4	48.1	46.7	45.5
Benefits provided by protection:									
Individual insurance	1,280	1,796	2,057	2,451	2,701	2,588	3,497	3,560	3,263
Group benefits to workers in private employment	9,984	12,440	15,392	16,364	16,835	17,555	18,456	18,310	19,039
Private cash insurance [2]	3,271	2,601	2,903	2,732	2,711	2,605	2,703	2,608	2,558
Publicly operated cash sickness funds [3]	770	1,179	1,779	1,907	2,269	2,817	2,975	2,349	2,370
Sick leave	5,943	8,660	10,710	11,725	11,855	12,133	12,778	13,353	14,111
Sick leave for government employees	6,041	8,487	10,266	10,967	11,673	12,537	13,115	13,616	14,160

[1] Provided by individual insurance, group benefits to workers in private employment, and sick leave for government employees. Includes benefits for the sixth month of disability payable under old-age, survivors, disability, and health insurance program, not shown separately. [2] Group accident and sickness insurance and self-insurance privately written either on a voluntary basis or in compliance with State temporary disability insurance laws in CA, HI, NJ, and NY. Includes a small but undetermined amount of group disability insurance benefits paid to government workers and to self-employed persons through farm, trade, or professional associations. [3] Includes State-operated plans in RI, CA, and NJ; State Insurance Fund and special fund for disabled unemployed in New York; and provisions of Railroad Unemployment Insurance Act.

Source: U.S. Social Security Administration, *Social Security Bulletin*, fall 1994 and unpublished data.

No. 602. Public Aid—Recipients and Average Monthly Cash Payments Under Supplemental Security Income (SSI) and Public Assistance: 1980 to 1995

[As of December, except as noted. Public assistance data for all years include Puerto Rico, Guam, and Virgin Islands; SSI data are for federally administered payments only. See text, section 12. Excludes payments made directly to suppliers of medical care. See also Appendix III]

PROGRAM	RECIPIENTS (1,000)					AVG. MONTHLY PAYMENTS (dol.)				
	1980	1990	1993	1994	1995	1980	1990	1993	1994	1995
SSI, total	4,142	4,817	5,984	6,296	6,514	168	299	345	351	358
Aged	1,808	1,454	1,475	1,466	1,446	128	213	237	243	251
Blind	78	84	85	85	84	213	342	359	364	370
Disabled	2,256	3,279	4,424	4,745	4,984	198	337	361	384	389
Old-age assistance [1]	19	17	16	16	(NA)	39	45	45	37	(NA)
Aid to the blind [1]	(Z)	(Z)	(Z)	(Z)	(NA)	36	42	40	38	(NA)
Aid to permanently, totally disabled [1]	21	28	28	27	(NA)	35	40	41	40	(NA)
AFDC: [2] Families	3,843	4,218	5,050	4,981	(NA)	288	392	377	378	(NA)
Recipients [3]	11,101	12,159	14,257	13,974	(NA)	100	136	133	136	(NA)
Children	7,599	8,208	9,598	9,469	(NA)	(NA)	(NA)	(NA)	(NA)	(NA)
General assistance cases	796	1,060	971	909	(NA)	161	(NA)	(NA)	(NA)	(NA)

NA Not available. Z Fewer than 500. [1] Average monthly recipients and payments for the year. [2] Aid to Families with Dependent Children program. [3] Includes the children and one or both parents, or one caretaker relative other than a parent, in families where the needs of such adults were considered in determining the amount of assistance.

No. 603. Public Aid Payments: 1980 to 1995

[In millions of dollars. See headnote, table 602. Supplemental Security Income data cover federally- and State-administered payments. See also Appendix III]

PROGRAM	1980	1985	1988	1989	1990	1991	1992	1993	1994	1995
Payments, total	[1]21,994	26,431	30,910	32,752	36,047	39,788	44,661	47,659	49,701	(NA)
Supplemental Security Income [2]	7,941	11,060	13,786	14,980	16,599	18,524	22,233	24,557	25,677	27,628
Aged	2,734	3,035	3,299	3,476	3,736	3,890	4,140	4,248	4,367	4,467
Blind	190	264	302	316	334	347	371	375	372	375
Disabled	5,014	7,755	10,177	11,180	12,521	14,288	17,711	19,928	21,131	22,782
Public assistance	[1]14,048	15,371	17,124	17,782	19,446	21,264	22,428	23,102	23,824	(NA)
Old-age assistance	9	8	7	7	7	11	8	9	8	(NA)
Blind	(Z)	(Z)	(Z)	(Z)	(Z)	(Z)	(Z)	(Z)	(Z)	(NA)
Permanently, totally disabled	9	10	11	12	12	19	14	14	14	(NA)
Families with dependent children	12,475	15,196	16,827	17,466	19,078	20,931	22,106	22,688	22,667	(NA)
Emergency assistance	113	157	279	297	349	303	301	391	937	(NA)

NA Not available. Z Less than $500,000. [1] Includes general assistance payments. [2] Includes data not available by reason for eligibility.

Source of tables 602 and 603: U.S. Social Security Administration, *Social Security Bulletin*, quarterly and *Annual Statistical Supplement* to the *Social Security Bulletin*, and U.S. Administration for Children and Families, *Quarterly Public Assistance Statistics*, annual.

No. 604. Public Aid Recipients as Percent of Population, by State: 1996 and 1994

[Total recipients as of June of Aid to Families with Dependent Children and of Federal Supplemental Security Income as percent of resident population. Based on resident population as of April 1 for 1990 and as of July 1 for 1994]

DIVISION AND STATE	1990	1994	DIVISION AND STATE	1990	1994	DIVISION AND STATE	1990	1994	DIVISION AND STATE	1990	1994
U.S.	**6.5**	**7.7**	IL	7.1	8.3	WV	8.9	9.6	**Mountain**	**4.2**	**5.3**
			MI	8.6	9.1	NC	5.6	7.2	MT	4.9	5.6
N.E.	**5.6**	**6.9**	WI	6.6	6.5	SC	5.8	6.7	ID	2.7	3.4
ME	6.6	7.4	**W.N.C.**	**4.8**	**5.6**	GA	7.1	8.2	WY	3.8	4.5
NH	2.2	3.5	MN	4.9	5.4	FL	4.6	6.8	CO	4.3	4.7
VT	5.7	7.0	IA	4.7	5.4	**E.S.C.**	**7.9**	**8.8**	NM	5.8	8.7
MA	6.4	7.5	MO	5.8	7.1	KY	7.9	9.3	AZ	4.7	6.5
RI	6.4	8.6	ND	3.6	3.9	TN	7.2	9.0	UT	3.3	3.6
CT	4.7	6.4	SD	4.2	4.4	AL	6.5	6.8	NV	2.9	3.8
M.A.	**6.7**	**8.3**	NE	3.7	4.0	MS	11.4	10.9	**Pacific**	**8.4**	**10.4**
NY	7.7	10.0	KS	4.1	4.7				WA	6.0	7.1
NJ	5.3	6.0	**S.A.**	**5.4**	**6.9**	**W.S.C.**	**6.2**	**6.9**	OR	4.3	5.1
PA	6.0	7.2	DE	4.4	5.2	AR	6.3	6.6	CA	9.4	11.7
E.N.C.	**7.0**	**7.8**	MD	5.1	5.9	LA	9.8	9.7	AK	4.6	7.5
OH	7.3	8.1	DC	10.9	16.6	OK	5.6	6.2	HI	5.2	6.9
IN	3.9	5.2	VA	3.9	4.8	TX	5.4	6.3			

Source: Compiled by U.S. Bureau of the Census. Data from U.S. Social Security Administration, *Social Security Bulletin*, quarterly, and U.S. Administration for Children and Families, *Quarterly Public Assistance Statistics*, annual.

No. 605. Aid to Families With Dependent Children (AFDC) and Supplemental Security Income (SSI)—Recipients and Payments, by State and Other Areas: 1990 to 1995

[Recipients as of December. Data for SSI cover Federal SSI payments and/or federally-administered State supplementation except as noted. For explanation of methodology, see Appendix III]

DIVISION AND STATE OR OTHER AREA	AFDC						SSI					
	Recipients [1] (1,000)		Payments for year (mil. dol.)		Average monthly payment per family		Recipients (1,000)			Payments for year (mil. dol.)		
	1990	1994	1990	1994	1990	1994	1990	1994	1995	1990	1994	1995
Total	12,159	13,974	19,078	22,867	$392	$378	[2]4,817	[2]6,296	[2]6,514	16,133	25,291	27,037
U.S.	11,958	13,790	18,996	22,777	396	382	4,817	6,295	6,513	16,133	25,289	27,036
New England	577	639	1,250	1,497	536	527	209	274	287	652	1,061	1,168
ME	62	61	104	107	422	393	24	30	31	56	87	98
NH	21	29	36	62	431	451	[3]7	[3]10	[3]11	[3]19	[3]33	[3]39
VT	25	27	51	65	527	549	10	13	13	31	46	50
MA	282	288	647	730	556	553	119	157	164	397	643	700
RI	52	63	104	136	499	499	17	23	24	53	89	100
CT	135	171	309	397	571	553	[3]32	[3]43	[3]45	[3]96	[3]162	[3]181
Middle Atlantic	1,903	2,208	3,623	4,444	472	468	711	957	997	2,533	4,164	4,477
NY	1,031	1,273	2,337	2,993	556	543	415	564	589	1,557	2,542	2,724
NJ	323	324	459	524	352	358	105	140	144	340	562	594
PA	549	611	827	927	382	367	191	252	265	635	1,060	1,159
East North Central	2,397	2,383	3,611	3,659	379	356	622	898	925	2,021	3,740	3,934
OH	657	634	896	940	328	318	156	236	248	483	972	1,044
IN	164	203	174	229	263	263	[3]60	[3]86	[3]89	[3]174	[3]324	[3]348
IL	656	713	868	932	342	322	[3]177	[3]260	[3]267	[3]593	[3]1,107	[3]1,160
MI	684	619	1,232	1,136	464	430	143	207	210	483	870	896
WI	236	214	441	423	464	462	86	110	112	288	467	487
West North Central	647	690	956	1,072	366	356	216	288	299	584	1,022	1,107
MN	177	169	355	379	512	513	[3]40	[3]60	[3]62	[3]110	[3]215	[3]235
IA	96	105	164	169	371	356	33	41	42	86	139	148
MO	218	260	237	287	274	260	[3]85	[3]110	[3]114	[3]237	[3]400	[3]431
ND	16	15	24	26	359	381	[3]7	[3]9	[3]9	[3]18	[3]27	[3]29
SD	19	18	22	25	272	307	10	13	14	26	44	47
NE	44	42	60	62	336	330	[3]16	[3]21	[3]21	[3]42	[3]70	[3]76
KS	77	82	103	124	332	347	25	36	38	65	127	141
South Atlantic	1,664	2,116	1,844	2,587	272	269	847	1,100	1,151	2,370	3,867	4,218
DE	22	26	30	40	292	293	8	10	11	22	36	40
MD	198	227	304	313	370	324	60	[4]79	[4]82	185	[4]308	[4]332
DC	54	75	87	127	380	389	16	20	20	54	79	83
VA	158	190	181	253	265	282	[3]95	[3]125	[3]130	[3]257	[3]431	[3]471
WV	109	109	112	126	249	260	[5]47	[5]64	[5]68	[5]146	[5]255	[5]276
NC	255	322	257	356	237	227	[3]149	[3]182	[3]191	[3]403	[3]592	[3]639
SC	118	133	97	115	203	186	[3]90	[3]106	[4]111	[3]234	[3]360	[4]384
GA	320	390	333	430	265	254	159	194	199	415	646	692
FL	420	645	443	826	263	282	222	[4]317	[4]338	653	[4]1,160	[4]1,300
East South Central	742	747	510	589	168	167	501	632	651	1,371	2,218	2,387
KY	204	195	185	199	224	210	[3]115	[3]156	[3]165	[3]337	[3]578	[3]636
TN	230	261	176	216	186	164	140	175	180	384	602	648
AL	132	124	63	92	115	155	[3]133	[3]162	[3]165	[3]351	[3]558	[3]600
MS	176	147	86	82	120	123	114	140	141	300	480	504
West South Central	1,154	1,248	811	937	180	176	564	735	765	1,478	2,521	2,700
AR	73	66	57	58	190	188	76	94	94	167	310	326
LA	279	260	188	169	167	165	133	179	182	378	679	717
OK	129	127	135	166	279	296	[3]60	[3]72	[3]74	[3]158	[3]246	[3]266
TX	673	794	431	544	165	159	[5]295	[5]390	[5]404	[5]755	[5]1,286	[5]1,391
Mountain	464	579	523	796	297	323	162	239	252	476	882	966
MT	29	34	40	49	344	344	10	13	14	29	48	53
ID	17	24	20	30	266	285	[3]10	[3]16	[3]17	[3]29	[3]57	[3]63
WY	16	15	20	21	313	310	[3]3	[3]6	[3]6	[3]9	[3]19	[3]21
CO	109	115	138	158	320	321	[3]38	[3]55	[3]57	[3]110	[3]203	[3]217
NM	67	105	66	144	273	352	[3]32	[3]43	[3]45	[3]90	[3]152	[3]166
AZ	144	198	146	268	268	311	[3]45	[3]69	[3]73	[3]139	[3]259	[3]288
UT	47	48	65	77	347	364	13	20	20	38	75	80
NV	25	41	28	48	278	275	11	19	21	33	69	79
Pacific	2,427	3,179	5,866	7,197	606	548	984	1,172	1,196	4,646	5,811	6,081
WA	237	289	447	612	452	494	62	88	92	208	368	398
OR	99	107	150	197	374	395	[3]32	[3]45	[3]47	[3]95	[3]168	[3]183
CA	2,023	2,682	5,107	6,113	637	556	873	1,014	1,032	4,278	5,174	5,391
AK	24	37	62	113	651	740	[3]5	[3]6	[3]7	[3]14	[3]24	[3]27
HI	44	65	100	163	581	652	14	18	19	51	76	82
PR	193	173	74	74	103	106	(X)	(X)	(X)	(X)	(X)	(X)
GU	4	7	6	12	418	509	(X)	(X)	(X)	(X)	(X)	(X)
VI	3	4	3	3	279	220	(X)	(X)	(X)	(X)	(X)	(X)
N. Mariana	(X)	(X)	(X)	(X)	(X)	(X)	[5]1	[5]1	[5]1	[5]2	[5]2	[5]2

X Not applicable. [1] See footnote 3, table 602. [2] Includes data for those recipients whose residence was "unknown." [3] Data for persons with Federal SSI payments only; State has State-administered supplementation. [4] Data for Federal SSI payments and federally-administered State supplementation only; State also has State-administered supplementation. [5] Data for persons with Federal SSI payments only; State supplementary payments not made.

Source: U.S. Social Security Administration, *Social Security Bulletin*, quarterly, and *Annual Statistical Supplement* to the *Social Security Bulletin*; and U.S. Administration for Children and Families, *Quarterly Public Assistance Statistics*, annual.

No. 606. Mothers Who Receive AFDC and/or Food Stamp Benefits—Socioeconomic Characteristics: 1993

[As of summer. Covers mothers 15 to 44 years old. AFDC=Aid to Families with Dependent Children program. Based on Survey of Income and Program Participation; see text, section 14]

CHARACTERISTIC	AFDC MOTHERS		FOOD STAMP MOTHERS		CHARACTERISTIC	AFDC MOTHERS		FOOD STAMP MOTHERS	
	Number (1,000)	Percent distribution	Number (1,000)	Percent distribution		Number (1,000)	Percent distribution	Number (1,000)	Percent distribution
Total	3,754	100	5,303	100	Married, husband absent [2]	648	17	906	17
Age:					Widowed or divorced	851	23	1,244	23
15 to 19 years old	191	5	204	4	Never married	1,783	48	2,065	39
20 to 24 years old	866	23	1,162	22	Educational attainment:				
25 to 29 years old	865	23	1,150	22	Not a high school graduate	1,633	44	2,169	41
30 to 34 years old	921	25	1,335	25	High school, 4 years	1,422	38	2,141	40
35 to 39 years old	604	16	922	17	College: 1 or more years	696	19	992	19
40 to 44 years old	307	8	530	10	Labor force status:				
Race:					Worked all or some weeks	474	13	1,159	22
White	2,074	55	3,178	60	No job last month	3,280	87	4,144	78
Black	1,471	39	1,903	36	Monthly family income: [3]				
Hispanic origin:					Less than $500	1,351	36	1,635	31
Hispanic [1]	784	21	1,060	20	$500 to $999	1,360	36	1,797	34
Not Hispanic	2,970	79	4,242	80	$1,000 to $1,499	479	13	924	17
Marital status:					$1,500 and over	552	15	861	16
Married, husband present	472	13	1,087	20					

[1] Persons of Hispanic origin may be of any race. [2] Includes separated women. [3] Excludes those who did not report income.

Source: U.S. Bureau of the Census, *Statistical Brief*, Nos. SB/95-2 and SB/95-22.

No. 607. Federal Food Programs: 1980 to 1996

[For fiscal years ending in year shown; see text, section 9. Program data include Puerto Rico, Virgin Islands, Guam, American Samoa, Northern Marianas, and the former Trust Territory when a Federal food program was operated in these areas. Participation data are average monthly figures except as noted. Participants are not reported for the nutrition program for the elderly and the commodity distribution programs. Cost data are direct Federal benefits to recipients; they exclude Federal administrative payments and applicable State and local contributions. Federal costs for commodities and cash-in-lieu of commodities are shown separately from direct cash benefits for those programs receiving both]

PROGRAM	Unit	1980	1985	1990	1992	1993	1994	1995	1996
Food Stamp:									
Participants	Million	21.1	19.9	20.1	25.4	27.0	27.5	26.6	25.5
Federal cost	Mil. dol	8,721	10,744	14,187	20,906	22,006	22,749	22,765	22,456
Monthly average coupon value per recipient	Dollars	34.47	44.99	58.92	68.57	67.96	69.01	71.27	73.28
Nutrition assistance program for Puerto Rico: [1]									
Federal cost	Mil. dol	(X)	825	937	1,002	1,040	1,079	1,131	1,143
National school lunch program (NSLP): [2]									
Free lunches served	Million	1,671	1,657	1,662	1,891	1,981	2,049	2,090	2,122
Reduced-price lunches served	Million	308	255	273	285	287	298	309	326
Children participating [3]	Million	26.6	23.6	24.1	24.6	24.9	25.3	25.7	25.9
Federal cost	Mil. dol	2,279	2,578	3,214	3,856	4,081	4,291	4,467	4,649
School breakfast (SB):									
Children participating [3]	Million	3.6	3.4	4.1	4.9	5.4	5.8	6.3	6.6
Federal cost	Mil. dol	288	379	596	787	869	959	1,048	1,115
Special supplemental food program (WIC): [4]									
Participants	Million	1.9	3.1	4.5	5.4	5.9	6.5	6.9	7.2
Federal cost	Mil. dol	584	1,193	1,637	1,959	2,115	2,325	2,516	2,693
Commodity supplemental food program: [5]									
Participants	Million	0.1	0.2	0.3	0.3	0.4	0.4	0.4	0.4
Federal cost	Mil. dol	19	42	71	87	94	87	79	80
Child and adult care (CC): [6]									
Participants [7]	Million	0.7	1.0	1.5	1.8	2.0	2.2	2.4	2.4
Federal cost	Mil. dol	207	390	720	966	1,082	1,196	1,296	1,356
Summer feeding (SF): [8]									
Children participating [9]	Million	1.9	1.5	1.7	1.9	2.1	2.2	2.1	2.2
Federal cost	Mil. dol	104	103	145	182	195	205	212	225
Nutrition program for the elderly:									
Meals served	Million	166	225	246	245	244	247	251	246
Federal cost	Mil. dol	75	134	142	151	153	153	151	143
Federal cost of commodities donated to— [10]									
Child nutrition (NSLP, CC, SF, and SB)	Mil. dol	930	840	646	740	706	764	733	720

X Not applicable. [1] Puerto Rico was included in the food stamp program until June 30, 1982. [2] See headnote, table 606. [3] Nine month (September through May) average daily meals (lunches or breakfasts) served divided by the ratio of average daily attendance to enrollment. [4] WIC serves women, infants, and children. [5] Program provides commodities to women, infants, children, and the elderly. [6] Program provides year-round subsidies to feed preschool children in child care centers and family day care homes. Certain care centers serving disabled or elderly adults also receive meal subsidies. [7] Quarterly average daily attendance at participating institutions. [8] Program provides free meals to children in poor areas during summer months. [9] Peak month (July) average daily attendance at participating institutions. [10] Includes the Federal cost of commodity entitlements, cash-in-lieu of commodities, and bonus foods.

Source: U.S. Dept. of Agriculture, Food and Consumer Service. In "Annual Historical Review of FNS Programs" and unpublished data.

No. 608. Federal Food Stamp and National School Lunch Programs, by State: 1990 to 1996

[Cost data for years ending Sept. 30. Data on food stamp households and persons are average monthly number participating in year ending Sept. 30. Data on pupils participating in National School Lunch Program are for month in which the highest number of children participated nationwide. For National School Lunch Program, covers public and private elementary and secondary schools and residential child care institutions. Food Stamp costs are for benefits only and exclude administrative expenditures. National School Lunch Program costs include Federal cash reimbursements at rates set by law for each meal served but do not include the value of USDA donated commodities utilized in this program]

REGION, DIVISION, AND STATE	FOOD STAMP PROGRAM								NATIONAL SCHOOL LUNCH PROGRAM					
	Households participating (1,000)		Persons (1,000)			Cost (mil. dol.)			Persons (1,000)			Cost (mil. dol.)		
	1995	1996	1990	1995	1996	1990	1995	1996	1990	1995	1996	1990	1995	1996
Total [1]	10,879	10,553	20,067	26,619	25,534	14,187	22,765	22,456	24,589	26,242	26,438	3,214	4,467	4,649
U.S.	10,867	10,537	20,036	26,579	25,486	14,153	22,714	22,387	24,019	25,690	25,929	3,098	4,343	4,529
Northeast	2,206	2,122	3,589	4,886	4,690	2,462	4,347	4,294	4,033	4,259	4,317	489	711	744
N.E.	430	412	707	979	927	426	769	747	991	1,018	1,035	96	145	154
ME	60	61	94	132	131	63	112	113	108	105	104	11	16	16
NH	25	23	31	58	53	20	44	42	91	90	92	6	10	10
VT	27	26	38	59	56	22	46	44	47	50	52	4	7	7
MA	178	163	347	410	374	207	315	295	454	476	487	44	67	72
RI	40	39	64	93	91	42	82	78	60	62	60	7	12	13
CT	100	100	133	226	223	72	169	175	231	235	240	23	34	36
M.A.	1,776	1,710	2,882	3,907	3,763	2,036	3,578	3,547	3,042	3,241	3,281	393	566	590
NY	1,027	984	1,548	2,183	2,099	1,086	2,065	2,054	1,546	1,704	1,713	232	332	344
NJ	233	233	382	551	541	289	506	511	507	534	549	60	91	97
PA	516	493	952	1,173	1,124	661	1,006	983	990	1,002	1,019	102	143	150
Midwest	2,311	2,181	4,806	5,516	5,147	3,566	4,644	4,398	5,806	6,113	6,140	619	821	843
E.N.C.	1,713	1,598	3,616	4,067	3,759	2,765	3,482	3,270	3,687	3,876	3,891	421	556	573
OH	506	459	1,069	1,155	1,045	861	1,017	935	919	1,010	1,006	109	136	139
IN	183	166	311	470	390	226	382	330	635	605	604	54	70	72
IL	488	470	1,013	1,151	1,105	835	1,056	1,034	932	985	997	131	175	183
MI	418	409	917	971	935	663	806	773	733	770	772	82	113	117
WI	119	105	286	320	283	180	220	198	488	506	512	45	60	62
W.N.C	598	583	1,190	1,449	1,388	801	1,162	1,128	2,119	2,237	2,249	197	266	270
MN	131	128	263	306	295	166	240	221	489	536	542	42	58	59
IA	75	74	170	184	177	109	141	141	392	397	395	31	40	41
MO	237	233	431	576	554	312	488	480	547	581	583	56	79	80
ND	17	16	39	41	40	25	32	32	94	90	89	8	9	10
SD	19	18	50	50	49	35	40	41	102	109	108	12	14	15
NE	43	42	95	105	102	59	77	78	191	209	212	18	24	24
KS	75	72	142	184	172	96	144	135	302	316	319	29	40	41
South	4,240	4,142	8,040	10,696	10,268	5,928	9,201	9,096	9,890	10,487	10,581	1,334	1,836	1,909
S.A.	1,905	1,902	2,993	4,593	4,516	2,223	4,008	4,056	4,454	4,784	4,810	558	816	849
DE	21	21	33	57	58	25	47	47	59	68	68	6	9	10
MD	169	165	255	399	375	203	365	362	347	372	378	40	60	62
DC	43	42	62	94	93	43	93	95	47	50	50	10	14	14
VA	235	235	346	546	538	247	450	451	586	623	634	60	87	89
WV	123	121	262	309	300	192	253	252	198	241	206	29	33	33
NC	258	265	419	614	631	282	495	551	749	769	777	91	123	127
SC	140	140	299	364	358	240	297	299	451	463	463	60	82	83
GA	329	323	536	816	793	382	700	703	906	997	1,021	106	159	167
FL	588	590	781	1,395	1,371	609	1,307	1,296	1,110	1,200	1,213	158	249	263
E.S.C.	863	843	1,938	2,187	2,083	1,386	1,791	1,771	2,086	2,124	2,120	281	349	359
KY	187	186	458	520	478	334	413	414	498	519	517	61	79	82
TN	281	274	527	662	638	372	554	542	590	617	623	68	90	93
AL	209	204	454	525	509	328	441	440	570	568	563	77	93	95
MS	185	179	499	480	457	352	383	376	428	419	417	76	87	89
W.S.C	1,472	1,397	3,109	3,916	3,670	2,319	3,402	3,269	3,361	3,580	3,631	495	671	700
AR	107	109	235	272	274	155	212	224	292	318	320	41	53	55
LA	267	256	727	711	670	549	629	597	694	669	663	104	126	128
OK	153	147	267	375	354	186	315	308	362	379	376	46	64	66
TX	946	885	1,880	2,558	2,372	1,429	2,246	2,140	2,003	2,194	2,252	304	429	452
West	2,110	2,092	3,601	5,482	5,381	2,197	4,522	4,599	4,289	4,830	4,911	657	975	1,033
Mountain	529	507	985	1,373	1,297	726	1,152	1,108	1,362	1,558	1,548	170	248	261
MT	28	29	57	71	71	41	57	58	84	88	87	10	13	13
ID	30	30	59	80	80	40	59	61	131	142	142	14	19	20
WY	13	13	28	34	33	21	28	28	57	58	58	5	7	7
CO	103	101	221	252	244	156	217	210	282	309	315	31	43	45
NM	87	87	157	239	235	117	196	199	179	191	194	30	40	42
AZ	178	159	317	480	427	239	414	372	331	422	404	47	77	82
UT	44	42	99	119	110	71	90	87	233	251	251	24	33	33
NV	46	46	50	99	97	41	91	91	67	97	98	8	16	16
Pacific	1,581	1,585	2,613	4,109	4,084	1,471	3,371	3,492	2,927	3,272	3,363	487	727	772
WA	204	206	340	476	476	229	417	426	361	434	441	43	69	73
OR	132	135	216	289	288	168	254	259	234	257	254	26	39	40
CA	1,176	1,169	1,965	3,175	3,143	968	2,473	2,556	2,147	2,392	2,471	396	587	624
AK	15	16	25	45	46	25	50	54	39	48	48	8	13	13
HI	55	59	77	125	130	81	177	196	145	142	147	14	20	22

[1] Includes Puerto Rico (for NSLP), other outlying areas and Dept. of Defense overseas.

Source: U.S. Dept. of Agriculture, Food and Consumer Service. In "Annual Historical Review of FNS Programs" and unpublished data.

lo. 609. Child Support—Award and Recipiency Status of Custodial Parent: 1991

sands except as noted. Custodial parents 15 years and older with own children under 21 years of age present from absent as of spring 1992. Covers civilian noninstitutional population. Based on Current Population Survey; see text, section 1, and ix III. For definition of mean, see Guide to Tabular Presentation]

AWARD AND RECIPIENCY STATUS	ALL CUSTODIAL PARENTS				CUSTODIAL PARENTS BELOW THE POVERTY LEVEL			
	Total		Mothers	Fathers	Total		Mothers	Fathers
	Number	Percent distribution			Number	Percent distribution		
al	11,502	(X)	9,918	1,584	3,720	(X)	3,513	207
ld support agreement or award	6,190	(X)	5,542	648	1,438	(X)	1,368	71
osed to receive payments in 1991	5,326	100.0	4,883	443	1,257	100.0	1,200	57
ually received payments in 1991	4,006	75.2	3,728	278	859	68.3	845	14
Received full amount	2,742	51.5	2,552	189	499	39.7	497	2
Received partial payments	1,265	23.8	1,176	89	360	28.6	348	12
l not receive payments in 1991	1,320	24.8	1,156	164	398	31.7	355	43
pport not awarded	5,312	(X)	4,376	936	2,282	(X)	2,145	136
I INCOME AND CHILD SUPPORT								
d child support payments in 1991:								
total money income (dol.)	19,217	(X)	18,144	33,579	5,734	(X)	5,687	(B)
child support received (dol.)	2,961	(X)	3,011	2,292	1,910	(X)	1,922	(B)
ceived the full amount due:								
Mean total money income (dol.)	20,050	(X)	19,310	30,012	5,960	(X)	6,004	(B)
Mean child support received (dol.)	3,543	(X)	3,618	2,536	2,670	(X)	2,660	(B)
ceived partial payments:								
Mean total money income (dol.)	17,411	(X)	15,611	41,163	5,392	(X)	5,235	(B)
Mean child support received (dol.)	1,699	(X)	1,694	1,773	857	(X)	871	(B)
d no payments in 1991:								
total money income (dol.)	15,919	(X)	14,602	25,184	5,399	(X)	5,525	(B)
child support agreement or award:								
total money income (dol.)	13,283	(X)	10,226	27,578	4,979	(X)	4,942	5,560

ase too small to meet statistical standards for reliability. X Not applicable.
rce: U.S. Bureau of the Census, *Current Population Reports*, P60-187.

No. 610. Child Support—Selected Characteristics of Custodial Parents: 1991

[In thousands, except percent. See headnote, table 609]

CHARACTERISTIC	ALL CUSTODIAL PARENTS				CUSTODIAL PARENTS BELOW THE POVERTY LEVEL			
	Total		Mothers	Fathers	Total		Mothers	Fathers
	Number	Percent distribution			Number	Percent distribution		
al [1]	11,502	100.0	9,918	1,584	3,720	100.0	3,513	207
17 years old	92	0.8	88	5	61	1.6	58	3
29 years old	3,197	27.8	3,022	175	1,529	41.1	1,472	57
39 years old	5,058	44.0	4,379	679	1,555	41.8	1,455	100
ars old and over	3,154	27.4	2,429	725	575	15.5	528	47
d Hispanic origin:								
	8,319	72.3	6,966	1,352	2,134	57.4	1,979	154
ite, non-Hispanic	7,227	62.8	5,993	1,235	1,582	42.5	1,455	126
	2,886	25.1	2,698	188	1,478	39.7	1,433	45
nic origin [2]	1,160	10.1	1,043	118	591	15.9	563	28
marital status:								
d	3,428	29.8	2,707	721	410	11.0	338	73
t marriage	955	8.3	740	214	193	5.2	168	25
orced, remarried	2,474	21.5	1,967	507	217	5.8	170	47
ced	3,599	31.3	3,052	546	935	25.1	877	58
rated	1,705	14.8	1,514	191	874	23.5	836	38
wed [3]	85	0.7	80	5	14	0.4	14	-
married	2,685	23.3	2,565	120	1,487	40.0	1,449	38
onal attainment:								
than high school diploma	2,559	22.2	2,272	286	1,549	41.6	1,452	96
school graduate	4,695	40.8	4,092	603	1,489	40.0	1,419	70
college, no degree	2,250	19.6	1,931	319	468	12.6	449	19
iate degree	729	6.3	649	80	117	3.1	109	8
lor's degree or more	1,269	11.0	974	295	97	2.6	84	13
of own children present from an parent:								
	6,036	52.5	5,090	946	1,422	38.2	1,308	113
	3,565	31.0	3,085	480	1,152	31.0	1,097	55
	1,290	11.2	1,166	123	701	18.8	679	22
or more	612	5.3	577	35	445	12.0	429	17

presents zero. [1] Includes other items, not shown separately. [2] Hispanic persons may be of any race. [3] Includes l persons whose previous marriage ended in divorce.
rce: U.S. Bureau of the Census, *Current Population Reports*, P60-187.

No. 611. Child Support Enforcement Program—Caseload and Collections: 1980 to 1995

[For years ending Sept. 30. Includes Puerto Rico, Guam, and the Virgin Islands. The Child Support Enforcement program locates absent parents, establishes paternity of children born out-of-wedlock, and establishes and enforces support orders. By law, these services are available to all families that need them. The program is operated at the State and local government level but 66 percent of administrative costs are paid by the Federal government. Child support collected for families not receiving Aid to Families with Dependent Children (AFDC) goes to the family to help it remain self-sufficient. Most of the child support collected on behalf of AFDC families goes to Federal and State governments to offset AFDC payments. Based on data reported by State agencies. Minus sign (-) indicates net outlay]

ITEM	Unit	1980	1985	1990	1991	1992	1993	1994	1995
Total cases	1,000	5,432	8,401	12,796	13,423	15,158	17,125	18,610	19,162
AFDC and AFDC arrears only caseload	1,000	(NA)	(NA)	7,953	8,034	8,717	9,638	10,420	10,379
AFDC cases	1,000	4,583	6,242	5,872	6,166	6,752	7,472	7,986	7,880
AFDC arrears only cases [1]	1,000	(NA)	(NA)	2,082	1,868	1,965	2,166	2,434	2,499
Non-AFDC cases	1,000	849	2,159	4,843	5,389	6,441	7,487	8,190	8,783
Cases for which a collection was made:									
AFDC cases	1,000	503	684	701	755	837	879	926	978
AFDC arrears only cases [1]	1,000	(NA)	(NA)	224	278	255	289	308	342
Non-AFDC cases	1,000	243	654	1,363	1,555	1,749	1,958	2,169	2,408
Percentage of cases with collections:									
AFDC cases	Percent	11.0	11.0	11.9	12.2	12.4	11.8	11.6	12.4
AFDC arrears only cases [1]	Percent	(NA)	(NA)	10.8	14.9	13.0	13.4	12.7	13.7
Non-AFDC cases	Percent	28.7	30.3	28.1	28.9	27.2	26.1	26.5	27.4
Absent parents located, total	1,000	643	878	2,062	2,387	3,152	3,777	4,204	4,950
Paternities established, total	1,000	144	232	393	472	512	554	592	659
Support orders established, total [2]	1,000	374	669	1,022	821	879	1,026	1,025	1,051
FINANCES									
Collections, total	Mil. dol	1,478	2,694	6,010	6,885	7,964	8,907	9,850	10,828
AFDC collections [3]	Mil. dol	603	1,090	1,750	1,984	2,259	2,416	2,550	2,690
State share	Mil. dol	274	415	620	700	787	847	891	939
Incentive payments to States	Mil. dol	72	145	264	278	299	339	407	400
Federal share	Mil. dol	246	341	533	626	736	777	782	822
Payments to AFDC families [4]	Mil. dol	10	189	334	381	435	446	457	474
Non-AFDC collections	Mil. dol	874	1,604	4,260	4,902	5,705	6,491	7,300	8,138
Administrative expenditures, total	Mil. dol	466	814	1,606	1,804	1,995	2,241	2,556	3,012
State share	Mil. dol	117	243	545	593	652	724	816	917
Federal share	Mil. dol	349	571	1,061	1,212	1,343	1,517	1,741	2,095
Program savings, total	Mil. dol	127	86	-190	-201	-170	-278	-496	-852
State share	Mil. dol	230	317	338	385	434	462	482	422
Federal share	Mil. dol	-103	-231	-528	-586	-605	-740	-978	-1,273
Total fees and costs recovered for non-AFDC cases	Mil. dol	5	3	22	34	29	31	33	33
Percentage of AFDC payments recovered	Percent	5.2	7.3	10.3	10.7	11.4	12.0	12.5	13.6

NA Not available. [1] Reflects cases that are no longer receiving AFDC but still have outstanding child support due. [2] Through 1990 includes modifications to orders. [3] Beginning 1993 includes medical support payments not shown separately. [4] Beginning 1985, States were required to pass along to the family the first $50 of any current child support collected each month.

Source: U.S. Department of Health and Human Services, Office of Child Support Enforcement, *Annual Report to Congress.*

No. 612. Regular Child Care Arrangements for Children Under 6 Years Old, by Type of Arrangement: 1995

[In percent, except as indicated. Estimates are based on children under 6 years old who have yet to enter kindergarten. Based on 14,064 interviews from a sample survey of the civilian, noninstitutional population in households with telephones; see source for details]

CHARACTERISTIC	CHILDREN		TYPE OF NONPARENTAL ARRANGEMENT				No nonparental arrangement
	Number (1,000)	Percent distribution	Total [1]	In relative care	In nonrelative care	In center-based program [2]	
Total	21,421	100	60	21	18	31	40
Race-ethnicity:							
White, non-Hispanic	13,998	65	62	18	21	33	38
Black, non-Hispanic	3,344	16	66	31	12	33	34
Hispanic	2,838	13	46	23	12	17	54
Other	1,243	6	58	25	13	28	42
Mother's employment status: [3]							
35 or more hours per week	7,101	34	88	33	32	39	12
Less than 35 hours per week	4,034	19	75	30	26	35	25
Looking for work	1,835	8	42	16	4	25	58
Not in labor force	8,354	40	32	7	6	22	68
Household income:							
Less than $10,001	4,502	21	50	22	10	25	50
$10,001 to $20,000	2,909	14	54	27	12	24	46
$20,001 to $30,000	3,385	16	53	22	14	25	47
$30,001 to $40,000	3,047	14	60	23	20	27	40
$40,001 to $50,000	2,304	11	63	19	22	32	37
$50,001 to $75,000	3,063	14	74	20	26	40	26
$75,001 or more	2,211	10	77	14	30	49	23

[1] Columns do not add to total because some children participated in more than one type of nonparental arrangement. [2] Center-based programs include day care centers, head start programs, preschool, prekindergartens, and other early childhood programs. [3] Children without mothers are not included.

Source: U.S. National Center for Education Statistics, *Statistics in Brief*, October 1995 (NCES 95-824).

No. 613. Percent of Adult Population Doing Volunteer Work: 1995

[Covers persons 18 years and over. Volunteers are persons who worked in some way to help others for no monetary pay during the previous year. Based on a sample survey conducted during the spring of the following year and subject to sampling variability; see source]

AGE, SEX, RACE, AND HISPANIC ORIGIN	Percent of population volunteering	Average hours volunteered per week	EDUCATIONAL ATTAINMENT AND HOUSEHOLD INCOME	Percent of population volunteering	Average hours volunteered per week	TYPE OF ACTIVITY	Percent of population involved in activity
Total	48.8	4.2	Elementary school	18.7	(B)	Arts, culture, humanities	6.2
			Some high school	26.1	3.3	Education	17.5
18-24 years old	38.4	2.8	High school graduate	43.1	4.0	Environment	7.1
25-34 years old	50.8	4.3	Technical, trade, or			Health	13.2
35-44 years old	55.0	4.3	business school	51.2	4.4	Human services	12.7
45-54 years old	55.3	4.5	Some college	56.3	3.9		
55-64 years old	47.9	4.8	College graduate	70.7	4.8	Informal	20.3
65-74 years old	44.7	4.1				International, foreign	1.6
75 years old and over	33.7	4.4	Under $10,000	34.7	3.6	Political organizations	3.8
			$10,000-$19,999	34.3	3.2	Private, community	
Male	45.1	4.2	$20,000-$29,999	41.2	3.7	foundations	2.7
Female	52.2	4.2	$30,000-$39,999	46.0	3.7		
			$40,000-$49,999	52.7	5.8	Public and societal benefit	6.7
White	51.9	4.2	$50,000-$59,999	64.1	5.9	Recreation - adults	7.3
Black	35.3	4.5	$60,000-$74,999	56.4	4.4	Religion	25.8
			$75,000-$99,999	64.8	4.0	Work-related organizations	7.9
Hispanic [1]	40.4	4.3	$100,000 or more	69.4	4.4	Youth development	15.4

B Base figure too small to meet statistical standards for reliability. [1] Hispanic persons may be of any race.

No. 614. Charity Contributions—Average Dollar Amount and Percent of Household Income, 1991 to 1995, and by Age of Respondent and Household Income, 1995

[Estimates cover households' contribution activity for the year and are based on respondents' replies as to contribution and volunteer activity of household. See headnote, table 613]

YEAR AND AGE	ALL CONTRIBUTING HOUSEHOLDS: Average amount (dol.)	ALL CONTRIBUTING HOUSEHOLDS: Percent of household income	CONTRIBUTORS AND VOLUNTEERS: Average amount (dol.)	CONTRIBUTORS AND VOLUNTEERS: Percent of household income	HOUSEHOLD INCOME	ALL CONTRIBUTING HOUSEHOLDS: Average amount (dol.)	ALL CONTRIBUTING HOUSEHOLDS: Percent of household income	CONTRIBUTORS AND VOLUNTEERS: Average amount (dol.)	CONTRIBUTORS AND VOLUNTEERS: Percent of household income
1991	899	2.2	1,155	2.6	**1995—**				
1993	880	2.1	1,193	2.6	Under $10,000	295	4.3	(B)	(B)
1995, total	**1,017**	**2.2**	**1,279**	**2.6**	$10,000-$19,999	425	2.8	444	2.9
18-24 years	287	0.7	344	0.7	$20,000-$29,999	578	2.3	656	2.6
25-34 years	743	1.6	922	4.5	$30,000-$39,999	722	2.1	928	2.7
35-44 years	1,342	2.6	1,653	3.0	$40,000-$49,999	576	1.3	677	1.5
45-54 years	955	1.8	1,142	2.1	$50,000-$59,999	1,001	1.8	1,142	2.1
55-64 years	1,791	3.6	2,473	4.5	$60,000-$74,999	1,301	1.9	1,443	2.1
65-74 years	980	2.8	1,125	3.0	$75,000-$99,999	1,582	1.8	1,682	2.0
75 years and over	839	3.7	1,078	5.0	$100,000 and over	3,379	3.4	4,195	4.2

B Base too small to meet statistical standards for reliability.

No. 615. Charity Contributions—Percent of Households Contributing, by Dollar Amount, 1991 to 1995, and Type of Charity, 1995

[In percent, except as noted. See headnote, tables 613 and 614]

ANNUAL AMOUNT OF HOUSEHOLD CONTRIBUTIONS	ALL HOUSEHOLDS: 1991	ALL HOUSEHOLDS: 1993	ALL HOUSEHOLDS: 1995	GIVERS: 1991	GIVERS: 1993	GIVERS: 1995	TYPE OF CHARITY	1995: Percentage of households	1995: Average contribution [1] (dol.)
None	27.8	26.6	31.5	(X)	(X)	(X)	Arts, culture, humanities	9.4	216
Givers	72.2	73.4	68.5	100.0	100.0	100.0	Education	20.3	318
$1 to $100	14.9	20.9	15.2	24.9	32.3	24.3	Environment	11.5	106
$101 to $200	8.1	9.8	7.2	13.5	15.2	11.6	Health	27.3	214
$201 to $300	7.3	5.6	5.7	12.2	8.6	9.2	Human services	25.1	271
$301 to $400	3.3	3.7	4.7	5.6	5.8	7.5	International	6.1	283
$401 to $500	3.2	4.0	5.2	5.4	6.2	8.3	Private, community		
$501 to $600	2.6	3.0	3.0	4.4	4.6	4.7	foundations	6.1	181
$601 to $700	2.5	2.0	2.6	4.2	3.1	4.1	Public, societal benefit	10.3	122
$701 to $999	3.4	2.9	3.7	5.7	4.6	6.0	Recreation - adults	7.0	161
$1,000 or more	14.5	12.8	15.2	24.2	19.7	24.3	Religion	48.0	868
Not reported	12.4	8.6	5.9	(X)	(X)	(X)	Youth development	20.9	137

X Not applicable. [1] Average contribution per contributing household.

Source of tables 613-615: Hodgkinson, Virginia, Murray Weitzman, and the Gallup Organization, Inc., *Giving and Volunteering in the United States: 1996 Edition*. (Copyright and published by INDEPENDENT SECTOR, Washington, DC, fall 1996.)

No. 616. Private Philanthropy Funds, by Source and Allocation: 1980 to 1995

[In billions of dollars. Estimates for sources of funds based on U.S. Internal Revenue Service reports of individual charitable deductions, household surveys of giving by Independent Sector, and, for years prior to 1986, an econometric model. For corporate giving, data are those prepared by the Council for Aid to Education. Data about foundation donations are based upon surveys of foundations and data provided by the Foundation Center. Estimates of the allocation of funds were derived from surveys of nonprofits conducted by source and other groups]

SOURCE AND ALLOCATION	1980	1985	1986	1987	1988	1989	1990	1991	1992	1993	1994	1995
Total funds	48.6	73.0	83.8	90.0	98.1	106.7	111.5	117.2	121.1	126.5	128.9	143.9
Individuals	40.7	58.7	67.6	72.3	80.1	87.8	91.2	96.1	98.4	102.1	104.5	116.2
Foundations	2.8	4.9	5.4	5.9	6.2	6.6	7.2	7.7	8.6	9.5	9.7	10.4
Corporations	2.2	4.6	5.0	5.2	5.3	5.5	5.5	5.6	5.9	6.3	6.9	7.4
Charitable bequests	2.9	4.8	5.7	6.6	6.6	7.0	7.6	7.8	8.2	8.5	8.8	9.8
Allocation:												
Religion	22.2	38.2	41.7	43.5	45.2	47.8	49.8	53.9	54.9	56.3	60.2	63.5
Health	5.3	7.7	8.4	9.2	9.6	9.9	9.9	9.7	10.2	10.8	11.5	12.6
Education	5.0	8.2	9.4	9.8	10.2	11.0	12.4	13.5	14.3	15.4	16.6	17.9
Human service	4.9	8.5	9.1	9.8	10.5	11.4	11.8	11.1	11.6	12.5	11.7	11.7
Arts, culture and humanities	3.2	5.1	5.8	6.3	6.8	7.5	7.9	8.8	9.3	9.6	9.7	10.0
Public/societal benefit	1.5	2.2	2.5	2.9	3.2	3.8	4.9	4.9	5.1	5.4	6.1	7.1
Environment/wildlife	(1)	(1)	(1)	2.1	2.4	2.0	2.6	2.9	3.1	3.2	3.5	4.0
International	(1)	(1)	(1)	0.9	1.0	1.2	1.5	1.8	1.7	1.9	2.2	2.1
Unclassified	6.5	3.1	6.9	5.4	9.3	12.2	10.6	10.7	10.9	11.4	8.3	15.1

[1] Included in "Unclassified."

Source: AAFRC Trust for Philanthropy, New York, NY, *Giving USA*, annual, (copyright).

No. 617. Foundations—Number and Finances, by Asset Size: 1995

[Figures are for latest year reported by foundations. Covers nongovernmental nonprofit organizations with funds and programs managed by their own trustees or directors, whose goals were to maintain or aid social, educational, religious, or other activities deemed to serve the common good. Excludes organizations that make general appeals to the public for funds, act as trade associations for industrial or other special groups, or do not currently award grants]

ASSET SIZE	Number	Assets (mil. dol.)	Gifts received (mil. dol.)	Expenditures (mil. dol.)	Grants (mil. dol.)	PERCENT DISTRIBUTION				
						Number	Assets	Gifts received	Expenditures	Grants
Total	40,140	226,736	10,261	15,115	12,262	100.0	100.0	100.0	100.0	100.0
Under $50,000	8,296	148	251	331	303	20.7	0.1	2.4	2.2	2.5
$50,000-$99,999	3,554	260	90	119	103	8.9	0.1	0.9	0.8	0.8
$100,000-$249,999	6,539	1,072	201	235	203	16.3	0.5	2.0	1.6	1.7
$250,000-$499,999	5,256	1,895	262	290	243	13.1	0.8	2.6	1.9	2.0
$500,000-$999,999	4,896	3,484	362	405	342	12.2	1.5	3.5	2.7	2.8
$1,000,000-$4,999,999	7,560	16,878	1,561	1,711	1,434	18.8	7.4	15.2	11.3	11.7
$5,000,000-$9,999,999	1,686	11,873	918	1,028	851	4.2	5.2	8.9	6.8	6.9
$10,000,000-$49,999,999	1,791	37,562	2,539	3,018	2,443	4.5	16.6	24.7	20.0	19.9
$50,000,000-$99,999,999	269	18,776	886	1,363	1,102	0.7	8.3	8.6	9.0	9.0
$100,000,000-$249,999,999	169	25,889	1,339	1,628	1,302	0.4	11.4	13.1	10.8	10.6
$250,000,000 or more	118	108,896	1,852	4,988	3,936	0.3	48.0	18.1	33.0	32.1

Source: The Foundation Center, New York, NY, *Guide to U.S. Foundations, Their Trustees, Officers, and Donors*, vol. 1, 1996.

No. 618. Foundations—Grants Reported, by Subject Field and Recipient Organization: 1995

[Covers grants of $10,000 or more in size. Based on reports of 1,012 foundations. Grant sample totaling $6.3 billion represented over half of all grant dollars awarded by private, corporate, and community foundations. For definition of foundations, see headnote, table 617]

SUBJECT FIELD	NUMBER OF GRANTS: Number	NUMBER OF GRANTS: Percent distribution	DOLLAR VALUE: Amount (mil. dol.)	DOLLAR VALUE: Percent distribution	RECIPIENT ORGANIZATION [1]	NUMBER OF GRANTS: Number	NUMBER OF GRANTS: Percent distribution	DOLLAR VALUE: Amount (mil. dol.)	DOLLAR VALUE: Percent distribution
Total	73,763	100.0	6,318	100.0	Community improvement				
Arts and culture	10,730	14.5	759	12.0	organizations	3,536	4.8	253	4.0
Education	15,340	20.8	1,584	25.1	Educational institutions	20,499	27.8	2,359	37.3
Environment & animals	4,068	5.5	314	5.0	Colleges & universities	10,599	14.4	1,431	22.7
Health	9,393	12.7	1,098	17.3	Educational support				
Human services	17,146	23.2	1,040	16.5	agencies	4,341	5.9	407	6.4
International affairs,					Schools	3,765	5.1	308	4.9
development & peace	2,197	3.0	220	3.5	Federated funds	2,374	3.2	218	3.5
Public/societal benefit	8,984	12.2	732	11.6	Hospitals/medical care				
Science and technology	2,214	3.0	301	4.8	facilities	3,343	4.5	369	5.8
Social sciences	1,336	1.8	138	2.2	Human service agencies	13,596	18.4	738	11.7
Religion	2,228	3.0	126	2.0	Museums/historical societies	3,008	4.1	267	4.2
Other	127	0.2	10	0.2	Performing arts groups	3,518	4.8	184	2.9

[1] Grants may be awarded to multiple types of recipient organizations and would thereby be double-counted.

Source: The Foundation Center, New York, NY, *The Foundation Grants Index, 1997*, 25th Edition, 1996.

Section 13

Labor Force, Employment, and Earnings

:tion presents statistics on the labor ; distribution by occupation and ' affiliation; and the supply of, l for, and conditions of labor. The urce of these data is the Current ion Survey conducted by the U.S. of the Census. Comprehensive ıl data are published by the Bureau r Statistics (BLS) in *Labor Force s Derived From the Current Popu-urvey, 1948-87, BLS Bulletin 2307.* lata are supplemented on a current / the BLS monthly publications *Em-nt and Earnings* and the *Monthly Review.* Detailed data on the labor e also available from the Census 's decennial census of population.

f data—Most statistics in this are obtained by two methods: old interviews or questionnaires, orts of establishment payroll . Each method provides data which r cannot suitably supply. Popula-iracteristics, for example, are readi-iable only from the household sur-le detailed industrial classifications readily derived only from establish-cords.

iold data are obtained from a ' sample survey of the population. rrent Population Survey (CPS) is gather data for the calendar week g the 12th of the month and pro-urrent comprehensive data on the rce (see text, section 1). The CPS s information on the work status of ulation without duplication since erson is classified as employed, oyed, or not in the labor force. ed persons holding more than one counted only once, according to at which they worked the most uring the survey week.

' data from the CPS are published Bureau of Labor Statistics in *ment and Earnings* and the related mentioned above. Data presented national totals of the number of ; in the civilian labor force by sex, ispanic origin, and age; the number ed; hours of work; industry and

In Brief

Labor force participation rate of married women with children under 6 years old:

1960	*18.6%*
1970	*30.3%*
1980	*45.1%*
1996	*62.7%*

Fastest growing occupations, 1994-2005:

Personal and home care aides	*+119%*
Home health aides	*+102%*
Systems analysts	*92%*
Computer engineers	*+91%*

occupational groups; and the number unemployed, reasons for, and duration of unemployment. Monthly data from the CPS also are presented for census regions and divisions. Annual data shown in this section are averages of monthly figures for each calendar year, unless otherwise specified.

The CPS also produces annual estimates of employment and unemployment for each State, 50 large metropolitan statistical areas, and selected cities. These estimates are published by BLS in its annual *Geographic Profile of Employment and Unemployment.* More detailed geographic data (e.g., for counties and cities) are provided by the decennial population censuses.

Data based on establishment records are compiled by BLS and cooperating State agencies as part of an ongoing Current Employment Statistics Program. Data, gathered from a sample of employers who voluntarily complete mail questionnaires monthly, are supplemented by data from other government agencies and adjusted at intervals to data from government social insurance program reports. The estimates exclude proprietors of unincorporated firms, self-employed persons, private household workers, unpaid family workers, agricultural workers, and the Armed Forces. In March 1996, reporting establishments employed 9 million manufacturing workers (49 percent of the total manufacturing employment at the time), 20 million workers in nonmanufacturing industries (25 percent of the total in nonmanufacturing), and 15 million Federal, State, and local government employees (78 percent of total government).

The establishment survey counts workers each time they appear on a payroll during the reference week (as with the CPS, the week including the 12th of the month). Thus, unlike the CPS, a person with two jobs is counted twice. The establishment survey is designed to provide detailed industry information for the Nation, States, and metropolitan areas on nonfarm wage and salary employment, average weekly hours, and average hourly and weekly earnings. Establishment survey data are published in *Employment and Earnings* and the *Monthly Labor Review,* cited above. Historical national data are available on the Internet site: <http://stats.bls.gov>.

Labor force—According to the CPS definitions, the civilian labor force comprises all civilians in the noninstitutional population 16 years and over classified as "employed" or "unemployed" according to the following criteria: Employed civilians comprise (a) all civilians, who, during the reference week, did any work for pay or profit (minimum of an hour's work) or worked 15 hours or more as unpaid workers in a family enterprise, and (b) all civilians who were not working but who had jobs or businesses from which they were temporarily absent for noneconomic reasons (illness, weather conditions, vacation, labor-management dispute, etc.) whether they were paid for the time off or were seeking other jobs. Unemployed persons comprise all civilians who had no employment during the reference week, who made specific efforts to find a job within the previous 4 weeks (such as applying directly to an employer, or to a public employment service, or checking with friends), and who were available for work during that week, except for temporary illness. Persons on layoff from a job and expecting recall are also classified as unemployed. All other civilian persons,

Beginning in 1982, changes in the estimation procedures and the introduction of 1980 census data caused substantial increases in the population and estimates of persons in all labor force categories. Rates on labor force characteristics, however, were essentially unchanged. In order to avoid major breaks in series, some 30,000 labor force series were adjusted back to 1970. The effect of the 1982 revisions on various data series and an explanation of the adjustment procedure used are described in "Revisions in the Current Population Survey in January 1982," in the February 1982 issue of *Employment and Earnings.* The revisions did not, however, smooth out the breaks in series occurring between 1972 and 1979, and data users should make allowances for them in making certain data comparisons.

Beginning in January 1985, and again in January 1986, the CPS estimation procedures were revised due to the implementation of a new sample design (for the 1985 revision) and to reflect an explicit estimate of the number of undocumented immigrants (for the 1986 revision). The greatest impact of these revisions was on estimates of persons of Hispanic origin. Where possible, these estimates were revised back to January 1980. A description of the changes and an indication of their effect on the national estimates of labor force characteristics appear in the February 1985 and February 1986 issues of *Employment and Earnings* respectively.

Beginning in January 1994, several changes were introduced into the CPS that effect all data comparisons with prior years. These changes include the results of a major redesign of the survey questionnaire and collection methodology, revisions to some of the labor force concepts and definitions, and the introduction of 1990 census population controls, adjusted for the estimated undercount. An explanation of the changes and their effects on the labor force data appears in "Revisions in the Current Population Survey Effective January 1994" in the February 1994 issue of *Employment and Earnings.*

Beginning in 1996, 1990 census population controls, adjusted for the estimated undercount were extended back to

ata appears in "Revisions in ιold Survey Data Effective Febru-)6" in the March 1996 issue of *ment and Earnings.*

ınd earnings—Average hourly ıs, based on establishment data, ss earnings (i.e., earnings before deductions) and include overtime ns; they exclude irregular bonuses ue of payments-in-kind. Hours are ır which pay was received. Wages aries from the CPS consist of total received for work performed by an ee during the income year. It in-wages, salaries, commissions, tips, ate payments, and cash bonuses before deductions were made for onds, union dues, etc. Persons ırked 35 hours or more are classi-working full time.

ial and occupational groups—ıhments responding to the estab-t survey are classified into indus-the basis of their principal product ity (determined by annual sales vol-ı accordance with the *Standard In-Classification (SIC) Manual,* Office agement and Budget. The SIC is a ation structure for the entire nation-omy. The structure provides data ision and industry code basis, ac-to the level of industrial detail. For e, manufacturing is a major indus-ision; food and kindred products 0) is one of its major groups. One ays this group is further divided is at products (code 201) and meat plants (code 2011). Periodically, is revised to reflect changes in the al composition of the economy. The *IC Manual* has been issued; the s was the *1972 SIC Manual.* Tables in this *Abstract* indicate which *SIC* the data shown are based on.

y data derived from the CPS for 1 utilize the 1980 census indus-ssification developed from the IC. CPS data from 1971 to 1982 ased on the 1970 census classifi-system which was developed from 37 SIC. Most of the industry cate-were not affected by the change ification.

cupational classification system Standard Occupational Classification (SOC) system, first introduced in 1977. Occupational categories used in the 1980 census classification system are so radically different from the 1970 census system used in the CPS through 1982, that their implementation represented a break in historical data series. In cases where data have not yet been converted to the 1980 classifications and still reflect the 1970 classifications (e.g., table 673), comparisons between the two systems should not be made. To help users bridge the data gap, a limited set of estimates was developed for the 1972-82 period based on the new classifications. The estimates were developed by means of applying conversion factors created by double coding a 20-percent sample of CPS occupational records for 6 months during 1981-82. For further details, contact BLS.

Beginning in January 1992, the occupational and industrial classification systems used in the 1990 census were introduced into the CPS. (These systems were largely based on the 1980 Standard Occupational Classification and the 1987 Standard Industrial Classification.) There were a few breaks in comparability between the 1980 and 1990 census-based systems, particularly within the "technical, sales, and administrative support" categories. The most notable changes in industry classification were the shift of several industries from "business services" to "professional services" and the splitting of some industries into smaller, more detailed categories. A number of industry titles were changed as well, with no change in content.

Productivity—BLS publishes data on productivity as measured by output per hour (labor productivity), output per combined unit of labor and capital input (multifactor productivity), and, for manufacturing industries, output per combined unit of capital, labor, energy, materials, and purchased service inputs. Labor productivity and related indexes are published for the business sector as a whole and its major subsectors: nonfarm business, manufacturing, nonfinancial corporations, 178 specific industries, and various functional areas of the Federal Government. Multifactor productivity and related measures are published for the private business sector in-labor, energy, materials, and service inputs are published for the 20 major 2-digit industry groups which comprise the manufacturing sector and for the following industries: cotton and synthetic broadwoven fabrics, household furniture, tire and inner tubes, footwear, steel, metal stampings, farm and garden machinery, refrigeration and heating equipment, motor vehicles, and railroad transportation industries. The major sector data are published in the BLS quarterly news release, *Productivity and Costs* and in the annual *Multifactor Productivity Measures* release. The specific industry productivity measures are published annually in the BLS Bulletin, *Productivity Measures for Selected Industries and Government Services.* Detailed information on methods, limitations, and data sources appears in the *BLS Handbook of Methods,* BLS Bulletin 2490 (1997), chapters 10 and 11.

Unions—As defined here, unions include traditional labor unions and employee associations similar to labor unions. Data on union membership status provided by BLS are for employed wage and salary workers and relate to their principal job. Earnings by union membership status are usual weekly earnings of full-time wage and salary workers. The information is collected through the Current Population Survey. For a full description of the method of collection and comparability with earlier data, see "New Data on Union Members and Their Earnings" in the January 1985 issue of *Employment and Earnings,* and "Changing Employment Patterns of Organized Workers" in the February 1985 issue of the *Monthly Labor Review.* Collective bargaining settlements data had been collected for bargaining situations involving 1,000 or more workers in private industry and State and local government. These data series were discontinued with 1995 data.

Work stoppages—Work stoppages include all strikes and lockouts known to BLS which last for at least 1 full day or shift and involve 1,000 or more workers. All stoppages, whether or not authorized by a union, legal or illegal, are counted. Excluded are work slowdowns and instances where employees report to work late, or leave early, to attend mass meetings or mass rallies.

Seasonal adjustment—Many economic statistics reflect a regularly recurring seasonal movement which can be estimated on the basis of past experience. By eliminating that part of the change which can be ascribed to usual seasonal variation (e.g., climate or school openings and closings), it is possible to observe the cyclical and other nonseasonal movements in the series. However, in evaluating deviations from the seasonal pattern—that is, changes in a seasonally adjusted series—it is important to note that seasonal adjustment is merely an approximation based on past experience. Seasonally adjusted estimates have a broader margin of possible error than the original data on which they are based, since they are subject not only to sampling and other errors, but also are affected by the uncertainties of the adjustment process itself.

Statistical reliability—For discussion of statistical collection, estimation, sampling procedures, and measures of statistical reliability applicable to Census Bureau and BLS data, see Appendix III.

No. 619. Employment Status of the Civilian Population: 1950 to 1996

ands, except as indicated. Annual averages of monthly figures. For the civilian noninstitutional population 16 years old and over. Based on Current Population Survey; see text, section 1, and Appendix III]

R	Civilian noninstitutional population	CIVILIAN LABOR FORCE						NOT IN LABOR FORCE	
		Total	Percent of population	Employed	Employment/population ratio [1]	Unemployed			
						Number	Percent of labor force	Number	Percent of population
.....	104,995	62,208	59.2	58,918	56.1	3,288	5.3	42,787	40.8
.....	117,245	69,628	59.4	65,778	56.1	3,852	5.5	47,617	40.6
.....	137,085	82,771	60.4	78,678	57.4	4,093	4.9	54,315	39.6
.....	167,745	106,940	63.8	99,303	59.2	7,637	7.1	60,806	36.2
.....	170,130	108,670	63.9	100,397	59.0	8,273	7.6	61,460	36.1
.....	172,271	110,204	64.0	99,526	57.8	10,678	9.7	62,067	36.0
.....	174,215	111,550	64.0	100,834	57.9	10,717	9.6	62,665	36.0
.....	176,383	113,544	64.4	105,005	59.5	8,539	7.5	62,839	35.6
.....	178,206	115,461	64.8	107,150	60.1	8,312	7.2	62,744	35.2
.....	180,587	117,834	65.3	109,597	60.7	8,237	7.0	62,752	34.7
.....	182,753	119,865	65.6	112,440	61.5	7,425	6.2	62,888	34.4
.....	184,613	121,669	65.9	114,968	62.3	6,701	5.5	62,944	34.1
.....	186,393	123,869	66.5	117,342	63.0	6,528	5.3	62,523	33.5
.....	189,164	125,840	66.5	118,793	62.8	7,047	5.6	63,324	33.5
.....	190,925	126,346	66.2	117,718	61.7	8,628	6.8	64,578	33.8
.....	192,805	128,105	66.4	118,492	61.5	9,613	7.5	64,700	33.6
.....	194,838	129,200	66.3	120,259	61.7	8,940	6.9	65,638	33.7
.....	196,814	131,056	66.6	123,060	62.5	7,996	6.1	65,758	33.4
.....	198,584	132,304	66.6	124,900	62.9	7,404	5.6	66,280	33.4
.....	200,591	133,943	66.8	126,708	63.2	7,236	5.4	66,647	33.2

lan employed as a percent of the civilian noninstitutional population. [2] Data beginning in 1990 and again in 1994, not nparable with data for earlier years, See text, section 13, and February 1994 and March 1996 issues of *Employment and*

e: U.S. Bureau of Labor Statistics, Bulletin 2307; and *Employment and Earnings*, monthly.

20. Civilian Labor Force and Participation Rates, With Projections: 1980 to 2005

n noninstitutional population 16 years old and over. Annual averages of monthly figures. Rates are based on annual vilian noninstitutional population of each specified group and represent proportion of each specified group in the civilian . Based on Current Population Survey; see text, section 1, and Appendix III]

EX, AND AGE	CIVILIAN LABOR FORCE (millions)						PARTICIPATION RATE (percent)					
	1980	1990 [1]	1995	1996	2000, proj.	2005, proj.	1980	1990 [1]	1995	1996	2000, proj.	2005, proj.
[2]	106.9	125.8	132.3	133.9	140.0	147.1	63.8	66.5	66.6	66.8	67.1	67.1
....	93.6	107.4	112.0	113.1	117.7	122.9	64.1	66.9	67.1	67.2	67.8	68.1
....	54.5	59.6	61.1	61.8	63.1	64.9	78.2	77.1	75.7	75.8	74.9	73.9
....	39.1	47.8	50.8	51.3	54.6	58.0	51.2	57.4	59.0	59.1	61.6	62.6
....	10.9	13.7	14.8	15.1	15.7	16.6	61.0	64.0	63.7	64.1	62.7	61.9
....	5.6	6.8	7.2	7.3	7.5	7.9	70.3	71.0	69.0	68.7	67.4	65.8
....	5.3	6.9	7.6	7.9	8.1	8.7	53.1	58.3	59.5	60.4	59.0	58.8
....	6.1	10.7	12.3	12.8	14.3	16.3	64.0	67.4	65.8	66.5	65.4	64.7
....	3.8	6.5	7.4	7.6	8.4	9.5	81.4	81.4	79.1	79.6	77.6	76.1
....	2.3	4.2	4.9	5.1	5.8	6.8	47.4	53.1	52.6	53.4	53.3	53.6
....	61.5	69.0	71.4	72.1	74.2	76.8	77.4	76.4	75.0	74.9	74.0	72.9
years.....	5.0	4.1	4.0	4.0	4.3	4.4	60.5	55.7	54.8	53.2	53.1	52.0
years.....	8.6	7.9	7.3	7.1	7.5	8.2	85.9	84.4	83.1	82.5	82.1	81.9
years.....	17.0	19.9	18.7	18.4	16.8	16.3	95.2	94.1	93.0	93.2	91.9	91.5
years.....	11.8	17.5	19.2	19.6	20.1	18.8	95.5	94.3	92.3	92.4	92.0	91.4
years.....	9.9	11.1	13.4	14.0	15.8	17.6	91.2	90.7	88.8	89.1	88.4	87.7
years.....	7.2	6.6	6.5	6.7	7.4	9.2	72.1	67.8	66.0	67.0	66.0	65.6
and over ..	1.9	2.0	2.2	2.2	2.2	2.4	19.0	16.3	16.8	16.9	16.5	16.5
....	45.5	56.8	60.9	61.9	65.8	70.3	51.5	57.5	58.9	59.3	60.6	61.7
years.....	4.4	3.7	3.7	3.8	4.0	4.2	52.9	51.6	52.2	51.3	51.2	50.7
years.....	7.3	6.8	6.3	6.3	6.5	7.1	68.9	71.3	70.3	71.3	70.5	70.7
years.....	12.3	16.1	15.5	15.4	14.3	14.2	65.5	73.5	74.9	75.2	75.3	76.4
years.....	8.6	14.7	16.6	17.0	17.8	17.1	65.5	76.4	77.2	77.5	78.7	80.0
years.....	7.0	9.1	11.8	12.4	14.8	17.1	59.9	71.2	74.4	75.4	78.2	80.7
years.....	4.7	4.9	5.4	5.5	6.6	8.6	41.3	45.2	49.2	49.6	53.4	56.6
and over ..	1.2	1.5	1.6	1.6	1.8	2.0	8.1	8.6	8.8	8.6	9.5	10.2

footnote 2, table 619. [2] Includes other races, not shown separately. [3] Persons of Hispanic origin may be of any race.

: U.S. Bureau of Labor Statistics, Bulletin 2307; *Employment and Earnings*, monthly, January issues; *Monthly Labor* ovember 1995; and unpublished data.

No. 621. Employment Status of the Civilian Population: 1970 to 1996

[In thousands, except as indicated. Annual averages of monthly figures. For the civilian noninstitutional population 16 years old and over. Based on Current Population Survey; see text, section 1, and Appendix III]

YEAR, SEX, RACE, AND HISPANIC ORIGIN	Civilian noninstitutional population	Civilian labor force: Total	Civilian labor force: Percent of population	Civilian labor force: Employed	Civilian labor force: Employment/population ratio [1]	Civilian labor force: Unemployed: Number	Civilian labor force: Unemployed: Percent of labor force	Not in labor force: Number	Not in labor force: Percent of population
Total: [2]									
1970	137,085	82,771	60.4	78,678	57.4	4,093	4.9	54,315	39.6
1980	167,745	106,940	63.8	99,303	59.2	7,637	7.1	60,806	36.2
1985	178,206	115,461	64.8	107,150	60.1	8,312	7.2	62,744	35.2
1990 [3]	189,164	125,840	66.5	118,793	62.8	7,047	5.6	63,324	33.5
1992	192,805	128,105	66.4	118,492	61.5	9,613	7.5	64,700	33.6
1993	194,838	129,200	66.3	120,259	61.7	8,940	6.9	65,638	33.7
1994 [3]	196,814	131,056	66.6	123,060	62.5	7,996	6.1	65,758	33.4
1995	198,584	132,304	66.6	124,900	62.9	7,404	5.6	66,280	33.4
1996	200,591	133,943	66.8	126,708	63.2	7,236	5.4	66,647	33.2
Male:									
1970	64,304	51,228	79.7	48,990	76.2	2,238	4.4	13,076	20.3
1980	79,398	61,453	77.4	57,186	72.0	4,267	6.9	17,945	22.6
1985	84,469	64,411	76.3	59,891	70.9	4,521	7.0	20,058	23.7
1990 [3]	90,377	69,011	76.4	65,104	72.0	3,906	5.7	21,367	23.6
1992	92,270	69,964	75.8	64,440	69.8	5,523	7.9	22,306	24.2
1993	93,332	70,404	75.4	65,349	70.0	5,055	7.2	22,927	24.6
1994 [3]	94,355	70,817	75.1	66,450	70.4	4,367	6.2	23,538	24.9
1995	95,178	71,360	75.0	67,377	70.8	3,983	5.6	23,818	25.0
1996	96,206	72,087	74.9	68,207	70.9	3,880	5.4	24,119	25.1
Female:									
1970	72,782	31,543	43.3	29,688	40.8	1,855	5.9	41,239	56.7
1980	88,348	45,487	51.5	42,117	47.7	3,370	7.4	42,861	48.5
1985	93,736	51,050	54.5	47,259	50.4	3,791	7.4	42,686	45.5
1990 [3]	98,787	56,829	57.5	53,689	54.3	3,140	5.5	41,957	42.5
1992	100,535	58,141	57.8	54,052	53.8	4,090	7.0	42,394	42.2
1993	101,506	58,795	57.9	54,910	54.1	3,885	6.6	42,711	42.1
1994 [3]	102,460	60,239	58.8	56,610	55.3	3,629	6.0	42,221	41.2
1995	103,406	60,944	58.9	57,523	55.6	3,421	5.6	42,462	41.1
1996	104,385	61,857	59.3	58,501	56.0	3,356	5.4	42,528	40.7
White:									
1970	122,174	73,556	60.2	70,217	57.5	3,339	4.5	48,618	39.8
1980	146,122	93,600	64.1	87,715	60.0	5,884	6.3	52,523	35.9
1985	153,679	99,926	65.0	93,736	61.0	6,191	6.2	53,753	35.0
1990 [3]	160,625	107,447	66.9	102,261	63.7	5,186	4.8	53,178	33.1
1992	162,972	108,837	66.8	101,669	62.4	7,169	6.6	54,135	33.2
1993	164,289	109,700	66.8	103,045	62.7	6,655	6.1	54,589	33.2
1994 [3]	165,555	111,082	67.1	105,190	63.5	5,892	5.3	54,473	32.9
1995	166,914	111,950	67.1	106,490	63.8	5,459	4.9	54,965	32.9
1996	168,317	113,108	67.2	107,808	64.1	5,300	4.7	55,209	32.8
Black:									
1973	14,917	8,976	60.2	8,128	54.5	846	9.4	5,941	39.8
1980	17,824	10,865	61.0	9,313	52.2	1,553	14.3	6,959	39.0
1985	19,664	12,364	62.9	10,501	53.4	1,864	15.1	7,299	37.1
1990 [3]	21,477	13,740	64.0	12,175	56.7	1,565	11.4	7,737	36.0
1993	22,521	14,225	63.2	12,382	55.0	1,844	13.0	8,296	36.8
1994 [3]	22,879	14,502	63.4	12,835	56.1	1,666	11.5	8,377	36.6
1995	23,246	14,817	63.7	13,279	57.1	1,538	10.4	8,429	36.3
1996	23,604	15,134	64.1	13,542	57.4	1,592	10.5	8,470	35.9
Hispanic: [4]									
1980	9,598	6,146	64.0	5,527	57.6	620	10.1	3,451	36.0
1985	11,915	7,698	64.6	6,888	57.8	811	10.5	4,217	35.4
1990 [3]	15,904	10,720	67.4	9,845	61.9	876	8.2	5,184	32.6
1993	17,532	11,610	66.2	10,361	59.1	1,248	10.8	5,922	33.8
1994 [3]	18,117	11,975	66.1	10,788	59.5	1,187	9.9	6,142	33.9
1995	18,629	12,267	65.8	11,127	59.7	1,140	9.3	6,362	34.2
1996	19,213	12,774	66.5	11,642	60.6	1,132	8.9	6,439	33.5
Mexican:									
1986	7,377	4,941	67.0	4,387	59.5	555	11.2	2,436	33.0
1990 [3]	9,752	6,707	68.8	6,146	63.0	561	8.4	3,045	31.2
1993	10,795	7,281	67.4	6,499	60.2	782	10.7	3,514	32.6
1994 [3]	11,174	7,567	67.7	6,800	60.9	766	10.1	3,608	32.3
1995	11,609	7,765	66.9	7,016	60.4	750	9.7	3,844	33.1
1996	11,762	7,943	67.5	7,209	61.3	734	9.2	3,819	32.5
Puerto Rican:									
1986	1,494	804	53.8	691	46.3	113	14.0	690	46.2
1990 [3]	1,718	960	55.9	870	50.6	91	9.5	758	44.1
1994 [3]	1,854	1,026	55.4	907	48.9	119	11.6	828	44.6
1995	1,896	1,098	57.9	974	51.4	123	11.2	798	42.1
1996	2,017	1,170	58.0	1,057	52.4	112	9.6	848	42.0
Cuban:									
1986	842	570	67.7	533	63.3	36	6.4	272	32.3
1990 [3]	918	603	65.7	559	60.9	44	7.2	315	34.3
1994 [3]	1,002	604	60.3	555	55.4	49	8.1	398	39.7
1995	1,019	613	60.2	568	55.7	45	7.4	406	39.8
1996	991	637	64.3	591	59.7	46	7.2	354	35.7

[1] Civilian employed as a percent of the civilian noninstitutional population. [2] Includes other races, not shown separately. [3] See footnote 2, table 619. [4] Persons of Hispanic origin may be of any race. Includes persons of other Hispanic origin, not shown separately.

Source: U.S. Bureau of Labor Statistics, Bulletin 2307; and *Employment and Earnings,* monthly, January issues.

22. Civilian Labor Force and Participation Rates, by Educational Attainment, Sex, and Race: 1970 to 1990

ch. For civilian noninstitutional population 25 to 64 years of age. Beginning 1992, the method of computing attainment changed. See table 623 for later data. Based on Current Population Survey; see text, section 1, and Appendix III]

ITEM	CIVILIAN LABOR FORCE					PARTICIPATION RATE [1]				
	Total (1,000)	Percent distribution				Total	Less than high school	High school graduate	College	
		Less than high school	High school graduate	College 1-3 years	College 4 years or more				1-3 years	4 years or more
70	61,765	36.1	38.1	11.8	14.1	70.3	65.5	70.2	73.8	82.3
....	78,010	20.6	39.8	17.6	22.0	73.9	60.7	74.2	79.5	86.1
....	99,175	13.4	39.5	20.7	26.4	78.6	60.7	78.2	83.3	88.4
0	39,303	37.5	34.5	12.2	15.7	93.5	89.3	96.3	95.8	96.1
....	45,417	22.2	35.7	17.7	24.3	89.4	78.8	91.9	92.4	95.3
....	54,476	15.1	37.2	19.7	28.0	88.8	75.1	89.9	91.5	94.5
970	22,462	33.5	44.3	10.9	11.2	49.0	43.0	51.3	50.9	60.9
....	32,593	18.4	45.4	17.4	18.7	59.5	43.7	61.2	66.4	73.4
....	44,699	11.3	42.4	21.9	24.5	68.9	46.2	68.7	75.9	61.1
70	55,044	33.7	39.3	12.2	14.8	70.1	65.2	69.7	73.3	81.9
....	68,509	19.1	40.2	17.7	22.9	74.2	61.4	73.7	79.2	86.0
....	85,238	12.6	39.6	20.6	27.1	79.2	62.5	78.4	83.3	88.3
70	6,721	55.5	28.2	8.0	8.3	72.0	67.1	76.8	81.0	87.4
....	7,731	34.7	38.1	16.3	11.0	71.5	58.1	79.2	82.0	90.1
....	10,537	19.9	42.5	22.1	15.5	74.6	54.5	78.2	84.2	92.0

cent of the civilian population in each group in the civilian labor force. [2] Includes other races, not shown separately. White and Black races only.
e: U.S. Bureau of Labor Statistics, Bulletin 2307; and unpublished data.

23. Civilian Labor Force and Participation Rates, by Educational Attainment, Sex, Race, and Hispanic Origin: 1992 to 1996

arch. For the civilian noninstitutional population 25 to 64 years of age. See table 657 for unemployment data. Based on Current Population Survey; see text, section 1, and Appendix III]

EX, CE	CIVILIAN LABOR FORCE (1,000)					PARTICIPATION RATE [1]				
	Total	Percent distribution				Total	Less than high school diploma	High school graduates, no degree	Less than a bachelor's degree	College graduate
		Less than high school diploma	High school graduate, no degree	Less than a bachelor's degree	College graduate					
....	102,387	12.2	36.2	25.2	26.4	79.0	60.3	78.3	83.5	88.4
....	103,504	11.5	35.2	26.3	27.0	78.9	59.6	77.7	82.9	88.3
....	104,868	11.0	34.0	27.6	27.3	78.9	58.3	77.8	83.2	88.2
....	106,519	10.8	33.1	27.8	28.3	79.3	59.8	77.3	83.2	88.7
....	108,037	10.9	32.9	27.7	28.5	79.4	60.2	77.9	83.7	87.8
...	55,917	13.9	34.7	23.8	27.5	88.6	75.1	89.0	91.8	93.7
s ...	56,544	13.2	33.9	24.7	28.1	88.1	74.9	88.1	90.8	93.7
..	56,633	12.7	32.9	25.8	28.6	87.0	71.5	86.8	90.3	93.2
...	57,454	12.2	32.3	25.7	29.7	87.4	72.0	86.9	90.1	93.8
...	58,121	12.7	32.2	26.0	29.1	87.5	74.3	86.9	90.0	92.9
:										
...	46,469	10.2	37.9	26.9	25.0	70.0	45.6	69.1	76.2	82.2
s ...	46,961	9.3	36.7	28.2	25.8	70.0	44.2	68.8	76.1	82.2
..	48,235	9.1	35.3	29.8	25.8	71.1	44.7	70.0	77.0	82.5
...	49,065	9.1	34.1	30.2	26.6	71.5	47.2	68.9	77.3	82.8
...	49,916	8.8	33.7	29.7	27.8	71.8	45.7	69.8	78.1	82.3
...	87,656	11.3	36.1	25.5	27.1	79.8	61.5	78.7	83.8	88.7
s ...	88,457	10.7	35.0	26.4	27.9	79.7	61.1	78.2	83.1	88.8
..	89,009	10.5	33.7	27.7	28.1	79.8	60.3	78.3	83.5	88.5
...	90,192	10.0	32.8	27.8	29.3	80.1	61.6	77.9	83.4	88.8
...	91,506	10.4	32.8	27.5	29.3	80.4	62.5	78.6	83.9	88.2
...	10,936	19.2	40.3	24.9	15.6	74.4	55.4	76.9	83.4	89.1
s ...	11,051	16.8	39.5	27.6	16.1	73.8	53.4	74.7	83.0	89.6
..	11,368	14.5	39.3	29.2	17.0	73.5	49.4	75.2	82.5	89.5
...	11,695	14.1	38.6	29.6	17.7	74.2	51.0	74.5	82.8	90.9
...	11,891	14.2	37.2	31.2	17.4	73.7	50.1	74.3	83.0	87.9
c: [4]										
...	7,702	39.1	30.2	19.3	11.4	73.8	64.6	77.5	84.2	87.1
s ...	8,010	38.7	29.4	21.0	10.9	73.9	64.9	76.8	84.0	87.3
..	8,984	38.6	28.7	21.5	11.1	73.2	63.9	77.5	81.9	86.3
...	9,298	38.9	28.2	21.3	11.6	73.2	64.7	75.9	81.9	87.9
...	9,683	38.9	28.5	21.2	11.3	74.2	65.0	78.2	83.7	87.2

footnote 1, table 622. [2] Includes other races, not shown separately. [3] See footnote 3, table 631. [4] Persons of origin may be of any race.
e: U.S. Bureau of Labor Statistics, unpublished data.

No. 624. Civilian Labor Force—Percent Distribution, by Sex and Age: 1960 to 1996

[For civilian noninstitutional population 16 years old and over. Annual averages of monthly figures. Based on Current Population Survey; see text, section 1, and Appendix III]

YEAR AND SEX	Civilian labor force (1,000)	PERCENT DISTRIBUTION						
		16 to 19 years	20 to 24 years	25 to 34 years	35 to 44 years	45 to 54 years	55 to 64 years	65 yrs. and over
Total: 1960	69,628	7.0	9.6	20.7	23.4	21.3	13.5	4.6
1970	82,771	8.8	12.8	20.6	19.9	20.5	13.6	3.9
1980	106,940	8.8	14.9	27.3	19.1	15.8	11.2	2.9
1985	115,461	6.8	13.6	29.1	22.6	15.0	10.4	2.5
1990 [1]	125,840	6.2	11.7	28.6	25.5	16.1	9.2	2.7
1992	128,105	5.5	11.3	27.6	26.5	17.3	9.0	2.7
1993	129,200	5.5	11.1	26.9	26.8	18.0	9.0	2.7
1994 [1]	131,056	5.7	10.8	26.2	26.9	18.6	8.9	2.9
1995	132,304	5.9	10.3	25.8	27.0	19.1	9.0	2.9
1996	133,943	5.8	10.0	25.3	27.3	19.7	9.1	2.9
Male: 1960	46,388	6.0	8.9	22.1	23.6	20.6	13.8	4.9
1970	51,228	7.8	11.2	22.1	20.4	20.3	13.9	4.2
1980	61,453	8.1	14.0	27.6	19.3	16.1	11.8	3.1
1985	64,411	6.4	12.9	29.2	22.5	15.3	11.0	2.7
1990 [1]	69,011	5.9	11.4	28.8	25.3	16.1	9.6	2.9
1992	69,964	5.4	11.1	27.9	26.2	17.2	9.4	2.9
1993	70,404	5.3	10.9	27.3	26.6	17.8	9.2	2.8
1994 [1]	70,817	5.5	10.6	26.6	26.8	18.3	9.1	3.1
1995	71,360	5.7	10.3	26.2	26.9	18.8	9.1	3.1
1996	72,087	5.6	9.9	25.6	27.2	19.4	9.3	3.1
Female: 1960	23,240	8.8	11.1	17.8	22.8	22.7	12.8	3.9
1970	31,543	10.3	15.5	18.1	18.9	20.7	13.2	3.3
1980	45,487	9.6	16.1	26.9	19.0	15.4	10.4	2.6
1985	51,050	7.4	14.6	28.9	22.7	14.6	9.7	2.3
1990 [1]	56,829	6.5	12.0	28.3	25.8	16.1	8.7	2.6
1992	58,141	5.8	11.6	27.3	26.7	17.4	8.7	2.5
1993	58,795	5.8	11.4	26.5	27.0	18.3	8.7	2.5
1994 [1]	60,239	6.0	10.9	25.7	27.0	18.9	8.8	2.8
1995	60,944	6.1	10.4	25.5	27.2	19.4	8.8	2.7
1996	61,857	6.1	10.1	24.9	27.4	20.1	8.8	2.6

[1] See footnote 2, table 619.

Source: U.S. Bureau of Labor Statistics, Bulletin 2307, and *Employment Earnings*, monthly, January issues.

No. 625. Civilian Labor Force, by Selected Metropolitan Area: 1996

[For the civilian noninstitutional population 16 years old and over. Annual averages of monthly figures. Data are derived from the Local Area Unemployment Statistics Program. For composition of metropolitan areas, see Appendix II]

METROPOLITAN AREAS RANKED BY LABOR FORCE SIZE, 1996	Civilian labor force (1,000)	Unemployment rate [1]
U.S. total	133,943	5.4
Los Angeles-Long Beach, CA PMSA	4,415	8.2
Chicago, IL PMSA	4,051	5.0
New York, NY PMSA	3,923	8.0
Washington, DC-MD-VA-WV PMSA	2,545	3.9
Philadelphia, PA-NJ PMSA	2,463	5.3
Detroit, MI PMSA	2,156	4.5
Houston, TX PMSA	2,017	5.2
Atlanta, GA MSA	1,973	3.8
Boston, MA-NH PMSA	1,767	3.7
Dallas, TX PMSA	1,758	4.0
Minneapolis-St. Paul, MN-WI MSA	1,616	3.1
Phoenix-Mesa, AZ MSA	1,460	3.7
Nassau-Suffolk, NY PMSA	1,365	4.2
St. Louis, MO-IL MSA	1,363	4.5
Orange County, CA PMSA	1,344	4.1
Riverside-San Bernardino, CA PMSA	1,313	7.7
Baltimore, MD PMSA	1,303	5.4
Seattle-Bellevue-Everett, WA PMSA	1,278	5.0
San Diego, CA MSA	1,236	5.3
Pittsburgh, PA MSA	1,147	5.0
Oakland, CA PMSA	1,143	5.0
Cleveland-Lorain-Elyria, OH PMSA	1,104	5.2
Tampa-St. Petersburg-Clearwater, FL MSA	1,101	3.9
Denver, CO PMSA	1,055	3.8
Miami, FL PMSA	1,030	7.3
Portland-Vancouver, OR-WA PMSA	1,004	4.5
Newark, NJ PMSA	1,003	6.2
Kansas City, MO-KS MSA	940	4.1
San Francisco, CA PMSA	911	4.0
San Jose, CA PMSA	897	3.6
Fort Worth-Arlington, TX PMSA	839	3.9
Cincinnati, OH-KY-IN PMSA	820	4.2
Indianapolis, IN MSA	815	3.2
Milwaukee-Waukesha, WI PMSA	802	3.4
Columbus, OH MSA	794	3.1
Orlando, FL MSA	776	3.8
Charlotte-Gastonia-Rock Hill, NC-SC MSA	735	3.7
Fort Lauderdale, FL PMSA	733	5.1
San Antonio, TX MSA	732	4.3
Sacramento, CA PMSA	725	6.0
Norfolk-Virginia Beach-Newport News, VA-NC MSA	716	4.8
Bergen-Passaic, NJ PMSA	690	6.2
Salt Lake City-Ogden, UT MSA	642	3.2
Las Vegas, NV-AZ MSA	635	5.5
Austin-San Marcos, TX MSA	634	3.0
Greensboro-Winston-Salem-High Point, NC MSA	632	3.3
Nashville, TN MSA	620	3.3
New Orleans, LA MSA	613	6.5
Middlesex-Somerset-Hunterdon, NJ PMSA	610	4.6
Hartford, CT MSA	591	6.1
Raleigh-Durham-Chapel Hill, NC MSA	580	2.3
Buffalo-Niagara Falls, NY MSA	572	5.1
Rochester, NY MSA	570	4.0
Providence-Fall River-Warwick, RI-MA MSA	570	5.6
Grand Rapids-Muskegon-Holland, MI MSA	556	4.1
Memphis, TN-AR-MS MSA	536	4.4
Louisville, KY-IN MSA	529	4.4
Oklahoma City, OK MSA	518	3.4
Jacksonville, FL MSA	512	3.6
Monmouth-Ocean, NJ PMSA	510	5.6

[1] Percent unemployed of the civilian labor force.

Source: U.S. Bureau of Labor Statistics, Local Area Unemployment Statistics program.

No. 626. Characteristics of the Civilian Labor Force, by State: 1996

sands, except ratio and rate. Preliminary. For civilian noninstitutional population, 16 years old and over. Annual averages / figures. Because of separate processing and weighting procedures, the totals for the United States may differ from results by aggregating totals for States)

ATE	TOTAL: Number	TOTAL: Female	EMPLOYED: Total	EMPLOYED: Female	Employed/ population ratio [1]	UNEMPLOYED: Total: Number	UNEMPLOYED: Total: Female	UNEMPLOYED: Rate [2]: Total	UNEMPLOYED: Rate [2]: Male	UNEMPLOYED: Rate [2]: Female	PARTICIPATION RATE [3]: Male	PARTICIPATION RATE [3]: Female
States	133,943	61,857	126,708	58,501	63.2	7,236	3,356	5.4	5.4	5.4	74.9	59.3
	2,088	989	1,981	936	60.3	107	53	5.1	4.9	5.4	71.9	56.3
	316	147	291	137	68.4	25	9	7.8	9.1	6.3	80.3	68.2
	2,249	1,017	2,125	958	62.8	124	59	5.5	5.3	5.8	75.3	58.2
	1,234	582	1,168	550	61.2	67	31	5.4	5.4	5.4	71.7	58.4
	15,596	6,846	14,470	6,351	60.8	1,126	495	7.2	7.2	7.2	75.0	56.4
	2,102	958	2,013	917	69.3	89	39	4.2	4.4	4.0	79.0	65.7
ut	1,720	826	1,621	779	64.3	99	47	5.7	5.7	5.7	74.5	62.5
	382	188	363	180	65.0	20	9	5.2	5.8	4.5	73.9	63.7
Columbia	272	141	249	129	58.2	23	12	8.5	8.7	8.4	67.8	60.1
	6,936	3,227	6,586	3,053	58.8	352	175	5.1	4.8	5.4	69.9	54.8
	3,753	1,767	3,580	1,673	64.7	173	94	4.6	4.0	5.3	76.4	60.2
	591	286	553	270	64.0	38	17	6.4	6.9	5.8	75.7	61.9
	619	275	587	260	66.7	32	15	5.2	5.1	5.4	77.7	62.9
	6,100	2,809	5,778	2,663	64.9	322	146	5.3	5.3	5.2	77.1	60.7
	3,072	1,412	2,945	1,351	66.3	127	62	4.1	3.9	4.4	76.9	61.9
	1,599	769	1,539	738	70.8	60	31	3.8	3.5	4.1	79.4	66.1
	1,340	622	1,279	591	66.9	60	31	4.5	4.1	5.0	77.4	63.2
	1,867	878	1,762	827	59.0	105	52	5.6	5.4	5.9	69.6	56.1
	1,997	947	1,863	872	57.9	135	75	6.7	5.6	8.0	70.0	55.2
	669	317	635	302	65.5	34	15	5.1	5.4	4.8	74.8	63.5
	2,786	1,341	2,650	1,275	66.5	136	66	4.9	4.9	4.9	77.6	66.8
setts	3,189	1,512	3,052	1,456	64.6	137	56	4.3	4.9	3.7	74.0	61.5
	4,807	2,220	4,572	2,118	63.1	234	102	4.9	5.1	4.6	74.8	58.6
a	2,609	1,216	2,505	1,179	71.7	104	37	4.0	4.8	3.1	80.9	68.7
i.	1,262	588	1,185	545	58.5	77	42	6.1	5.2	7.2	70.9	54.7
	2,898	1,407	2,765	1,347	68.5	132	60	4.6	4.9	4.3	77.9	66.3
	447	208	423	199	63.0	24	10	5.3	5.9	4.6	72.9	60.6
	913	431	886	417	72.0	27	14	2.9	2.7	3.2	81.1	67.7
	844	373	798	350	65.4	46	23	5.4	4.8	6.2	77.5	60.8
pshire	624	291	598	278	67.3	26	13	4.2	3.9	4.5	78.2	62.9
sy	4,124	1,908	3,869	1,786	63.1	255	122	6.2	6.0	6.4	75.6	59.5
ico.	800	363	735	335	57.9	64	28	8.1	8.4	7.6	71.3	55.2
	8,639	4,018	8,100	3,780	57.8	540	238	6.2	6.5	5.9	70.5	53.9
rolina	3,796	1,771	3,631	1,692	65.5	165	79	4.3	4.3	4.5	76.1	61.5
kota	343	163	333	158	69.8	11	5	3.1	3.1	3.0	78.0	66.4
	5,643	2,605	5,365	2,479	63.0	278	126	4.9	5.0	4.8	74.6	58.6
a	1,577	730	1,513	696	61.3	64	34	4.1	3.6	4.6	72.9	55.8
	1,721	786	1,619	741	65.2	102	46	5.9	6.0	5.8	76.6	62.2
nia	5,903	2,727	5,590	2,602	60.2	313	125	5.3	5.9	4.6	72.4	55.6
and	496	237	470	224	62.3	25	13	5.1	4.9	5.4	73.3	58.9
rolina	1,848	861	1,737	807	61.5	111	54	6.0	5.8	6.2	73.3	58.2
kota	390	183	377	177	70.0	13	6	3.2	3.2	3.2	78.0	66.7
e.	2,751	1,301	2,609	1,230	63.5	142	71	5.2	4.9	5.4	73.8	60.8
	9,748	4,345	9,200	4,080	65.2	549	265	5.6	5.3	6.1	79.0	59.7
	998	441	964	425	68.8	35	16	3.5	3.3	3.7	81.4	61.6
	324	158	310	150	68.3	15	7	4.6	4.5	4.6	77.5	66.3
	3,389	1,621	3,240	1,546	64.3	149	74	4.4	4.2	4.6	74.5	60.8
on	2,887	1,319	2,699	1,224	64.4	188	94	6.5	5.9	7.2	77.1	61.1
inia	808	370	747	346	51.4	61	24	7.5	8.3	6.6	64.6	47.7
)	2,918	1,378	2,815	1,333	72.1	103	44	3.5	3.8	3.2	79.9	69.6
	258	119	245	113	67.4	13	6	5.0	5.1	5.0	78.9	63.5

lian employment as a percent of civilian noninstitutional population. [2] Percent unemployed of the civilian labor force. of civilian noninstitutional population of each specified group in the civilian labor force.

e: U.S. Bureau of Labor Statistics, *Employment and Earnings*, monthly, May 1997; and unpublished data

No. 627. Hispanic Persons—Civilian Labor Force Participation: 1995 and 1996

[For civilian noninstitutional population, 16 years old and over. Annual averages of monthly figures. Based on Current Population Survey; see text, section 1, and Appendix III]

ITEM	1995					1996				
	Total	Mexican	Puerto Rican	Cuban	Other Hispanic origin [1]	Total	Mexican	Puerto Rican	Cuban	Other Hispanic origin [1]
Total (1,000)	**18,629**	**11,609**	**1,896**	**1,019**	**4,105**	**19,213**	**11,782**	**2,017**	**991**	**4,443**
Percent in labor force:										
Male	79.1	80.9	70.6	69.9	79.5	79.6	81.4	69.2	74.8	80.2
Female	52.6	51.8	47.4	50.8	57.5	53.4	52.8	48.5	53.3	57.1
Employed (1,000)	11,127	7,016	974	568	2,569	11,642	7,209	1,057	591	2,785
Percent by occupation	100.0	100.0	100.0	100.0	100.0	100.0	100.0	100.0	100.0	100.0
Managerial and professional	13.9	11.7	19.6	22.0	16.0	14.2	12.1	19.0	21.7	16.3
Tech., sales, and admin. support	24.4	21.7	29.8	37.5	26.9	24.5	21.9	32.1	32.7	26.5
Services	19.7	19.5	17.4	14.1	22.6	20.2	19.3	19.8	14.6	23.9
Precision production, craft, and repair	12.9	13.5	10.8	10.4	12.5	12.9	14.0	9.4	12.7	11.3
Operators, fabricators and laborers	23.2	25.4	21.0	14.3	19.9	22.4	24.5	18.6	17.4	19.5
Farming, forestry, and fishing	5.9	8.3	1.4	1.8	2.1	5.9	8.4	1.2	1.2	2.3
Percent of labor force unemployed:										
Male	8.8	9.0	11.4	7.6	7.6	7.9	8.2	8.6	6.4	7.4
Female	10.0	10.8	11.0	7.0	8.3	10.2	11.0	10.8	8.3	8.7

[1] Includes Central or South American and other Hispanic origin.

Source: U.S. Bureau of Labor Statistics, *Employment and Earnings*, monthly, January issues; and unpublished data.

No. 628. School Enrollment and Labor Force Status: 1980 and 1996

[In thousands, except percent. As of October. For the civilian noninstitutional population 16 to 24 years old. Based on Current Population Survey; see text, section 1, and Appendix III]

CHARACTERISTIC	POPULATION		CIVILIAN LABOR FORCE		EMPLOYED		UNEMPLOYED		
	1980	1996 [1]	1980	1996 [1]	1980	1996 [1]	1980, total	1996 [1]	
								Total	Rate [2]
Total, 16 to 24 years [3]	**37,103**	**32,379**	**24,918**	**20,794**	**21,454**	**18,318**	**3,464**	**2,476**	**11.9**
Enrolled in school [3]	15,713	16,842	7,454	8,301	6,433	7,346	1,021	954	11.5
16 to 19 years	11,126	11,272	4,836	4,931	4,029	4,169	807	762	15.5
20 to 24 years	4,587	5,570	2,618	3,370	2,404	3,178	214	192	5.7
Sex:									
Male	7,997	8,504	3,825	4,062	3,259	3,555	566	506	12.5
Female	7,716	8,337	3,629	4,239	3,174	3,791	455	448	10.6
College level	7,664	8,697	3,996	4,996	3,632	4,639	364	357	7.1
Full-time	6,396	7,211	2,854	3,713	2,554	3,406	300	307	8.3
Race:									
White	13,242	13,379	6,687	7,030	5,889	6,322	798	708	10.1
Below college	6,566	6,251	3,095	2,793	2,579	2,357	516	435	15.6
College level	6,678	7,128	3,592	4,237	3,310	3,965	282	272	6.4
Black	2,028	2,431	595	862	406	667	189	195	22.6
Below college	1,282	1,418	294	376	174	248	120	128	34.0
College level	747	1,013	300	486	230	419	70	67	13.9
Not enrolled [3]	21,390	15,537	17,464	12,493	15,021	10,972	2,443	1,521	12.2
White	18,103	12,338	15,121	10,131	13,318	9,087	1,803	1,043	10.3
Black	2,864	2,408	2,055	1,745	1,451	1,349	604	396	22.7

[1] See footnote 3, table 631. [2] Percent of civilian labor force in each category. [3] Includes other races, not shown separately.

Source: U.S. Bureau of Labor Statistics, Bulletin 2307; *News*, USDL 96-152, April 25, 1996; and unpublished data.

.abor Force Participation Rates, by Marital Status, Sex, and Age: 1960 to 1996

ages of monthly figures. See table 626 for definition of participation rate. Based on Current Population Survey; see text, section 1, and Appendix III]

	MALE PARTICIPATION RATE							FEMALE PARTICIPATION RATE						
	otal	16-19 years	20-24 years	25-34 years	35-44 years	45-64 years	65 and over	Total	16-19 years	20-24 years	25-34 years	35-44 years	45-64 years	65 and over
	99.8	42.6	80.3	91.5	88.6	80.1	31.2	58.6	30.2	77.2	83.4	82.9	79.8	24.3
	55.5	54.6	73.8	87.9	86.2	75.7	25.2	56.8	44.7	73.0	81.4	78.6	73.0	19.7
	58.7	57.9	77.9	86.7	83.2	69.9	21.0	59.8	49.6	72.5	80.8	78.6	68.3	15.8
	72.6	59.9	81.3	89.2	82.2	66.9	16.8	64.4	53.6	75.2	83.3	76.9	65.6	13.9
	73.8	56.3	81.5	89.4	84.6	65.5	15.6	66.6	52.3	76.3	82.4	80.8	67.9	9.8
	74.8	55.1	81.6	89.9	84.5	67.3	15.7	66.7	51.7	74.5	80.9	80.8	66.2	12.1
	74.6	52.9	80.8	89.7	84.7	67.7	16.3	66.2	49.1	73.4	80.2	80.4	66.2	11.2
	74.2	52.6	80.5	89.2	84.3	68.4	15.0	66.2	49.6	73.8	78.9	78.9	68.8	12.4
	73.9	53.6	80.5	88.4	83.1	67.8	17.8	66.7	51.4	73.6	78.9	78.7	68.8	12.7
	73.7	54.4	80.3	88.7	81.4	67.0	17.9	66.8	52.2	72.9	80.2	79.5	67.3	11.6
	73.3	52.8	79.8	89.1	82.1	67.4	18.2	67.1	51.5	73.3	80.9	79.4	68.5	12.2
	89.2	91.5	97.1	98.8	98.6	93.7	36.6	31.9	27.2	31.7	28.8	37.2	36.0	6.7
	86.1	92.3	94.7	98.0	98.1	91.2	29.9	40.5	37.8	47.9	38.8	46.8	44.0	7.3
	83.0	92.9	95.3	97.4	97.1	86.8	23.3	44.3	46.2	57.0	48.4	52.0	43.8	7.0
	80.9	91.3	96.9	97.5	97.2	84.3	20.5	49.8	49.3	61.4	58.8	61.8	46.9	7.3
	78.7	91.0	95.6	97.4	96.8	81.7	16.8	53.8	49.6	65.7	65.8	68.1	49.4	6.6
	78.6	92.1	95.6	96.9	96.7	82.6	17.5	58.4	49.5	66.1	69.6	74.0	56.5	8.5
	78.0	90.2	94.7	96.5	96.1	82.7	17.1	59.3	48.8	65.8	70.8	74.7	58.6	7.8
	77.8	91.3	95.0	96.5	96.0	82.5	16.5	59.4	49.8	65.1	70.6	74.7	59.9	7.6
	77.4	88.7	94.2	95.9	95.6	81.9	18.1	60.7	48.9	65.8	71.6	75.8	61.9	9.4
	77.5	89.2	94.9	96.3	95.4	82.4	18.0	61.0	51.6	64.7	72.0	75.7	62.7	9.1
	77.8	84.4	94.5	96.4	95.4	83.2	18.3	61.2	48.6	66.0	71.7	75.8	63.7	9.0
	63.1	(B)	96.9	95.2	94.4	83.2	22.7	41.6	43.5	58.0	63.1	70.0	60.0	11.4
	60.7	(B)	90.4	93.7	91.1	78.5	19.3	40.3	48.6	60.3	64.6	68.8	61.9	10.0
	63.4	(B)	88.8	92.4	89.4	73.4	15.4	40.1	47.6	65.3	68.6	69.2	59.0	8.3
	57.5	(B)	92.6	94.1	91.9	73.3	13.7	43.6	50.0	68.4	76.5	77.1	60.2	8.2
	58.7	(B)	95.1	93.7	91.8	72.8	11.4	45.1	51.9	66.2	76.9	81.6	61.0	7.5
	58.9	(B)	93.1	93.0	90.7	74.9	12.0	47.2	53.9	65.4	77.0	82.1	65.0	8.4
	58.6	(B)	92.0	93.5	90.2	75.0	12.1	47.1	47.3	66.7	75.5	81.4	66.4	8.3
	57.9	(B)	91.9	91.9	89.5	74.5	12.0	47.2	53.0	64.8	75.0	81.4	66.9	8.2
	58.8	65.1	91.0	90.3	88.6	72.6	11.9	47.5	46.2	66.6	74.3	80.4	67.6	8.7
	58.2	43.8	92.7	90.9	88.2	72.4	12.1	47.4	55.8	67.2	77.1	80.7	67.2	8.4
	58.4	54.0	90.6	92.0	88.8	73.1	11.5	48.1	42.6	70.7	78.5	82.1	67.7	8.0

), percentage not shown where base is less than 50,000; beginning 1970, 35,000. [1] See footnote 2, table 619.
nt. [3] Widowed, divorced, and married (spouse absent).

S. Bureau of Labor Statistics, Bulletins 2217 and 2340; and unpublished data.

630. Marital Status of Women in the Civilian Labor Force: 1960 to 1996

verages of monthly figures. For civilian noninstitutional population 16 years old and over. Based on Current Population Survey; see text, section 1, and Appendix III]

	FEMALE LABOR FORCE (1,000)				FEMALE PARTICIPATION RATE [3]			
	Total	Single	Married [1]	Other [2]	Total	Single	Married [1]	Other [2]
.....	23,240	5,410	12,893	4,937	37.7	58.6	31.9	41.6
.....	26,200	5,976	14,829	5,396	39.3	54.5	34.9	40.7
.....	31,543	7,265	18,475	5,804	43.3	56.8	40.5	40.3
.....	37,475	9,125	21,484	6,866	46.3	59.8	44.3	40.1
.....	45,487	11,865	24,980	8,643	51.5	64.4	49.9	43.6
.....	46,696	12,124	25,428	9,144	52.1	64.5	50.5	44.6
.....	47,755	12,460	25,971	9,324	52.6	65.1	51.1	44.8
.....	48,503	12,659	26,468	9,376	52.9	65.0	51.8	44.4
.....	49,709	12,867	27,199	9,644	53.6	65.6	52.8	44.7
.....	51,050	13,163	27,894	9,993	54.5	66.6	53.8	45.1
.....	52,413	13,512	28,623	10,277	55.3	67.2	54.9	45.6
.....	53,658	13,885	29,381	10,393	56.0	67.4	55.9	45.7
.....	54,742	14,194	29,921	10,627	56.6	67.7	56.7	46.2
.....	56,030	14,377	30,548	11,104	57.4	68.0	57.8	47.0
.....	56,829	14,612	30,901	11,315	57.5	66.7	58.4	47.2
.....	57,178	14,681	31,112	11,385	57.4	66.2	58.5	46.8
.....	58,141	14,872	31,700	11,570	57.8	66.2	59.3	47.1
.....	58,795	15,031	31,980	11,784	57.9	66.2	59.4	47.2
.....	60,239	15,333	32,888	12,018	58.8	66.7	60.7	47.5
.....	60,944	15,467	33,359	12,118	58.9	66.8	61.0	47.4
.....	61,857	15,842	33,618	12,397	59.3	67.1	61.2	48.1

present. [2] Widowed, divorced, or separated. [3] See table 626 for definition of participation rate. [4] See 619.

S. Bureau of Labor Statistics, Bulletin 2307; and unpublished data.

No. 631. Employment Status of Women, by Marital Status and Presence and Age of Children: 1960 to 1996

[As of March. For 1960, civilian noninstitutional persons 14 years and over, thereafter 16 years old and over. Based on Current Population Survey; see text, section 1, and Appendix III]

ITEM	TOTAL			WITH ANY CHILDREN								
				Total			Children 6 to 17 only			Children under 6		
	Single	Married [1]	Other [2]	Single	Married [1]	Other [2]	Single	Married [1]	Other [2]	Single	Married [1]	Other [2]
IN LABOR FORCE (mil.)												
1960	5.4	12.3	4.9	(NA)	6.6	1.5	(NA)	4.1	1.0	(NA)	2.5	0.4
1970	7.0	18.4	5.9	(NA)	10.2	1.9	(NA)	6.3	1.3	(NA)	3.9	0.6
1980	11.2	24.9	8.8	0.6	13.7	3.6	0.2	8.4	2.6	0.3	5.2	1.0
1985	12.9	27.7	10.3	1.1	14.9	4.0	0.4	8.5	2.9	0.7	6.4	1.1
1990	14.0	31.0	11.2	1.5	16.5	4.2	0.6	9.3	3.0	0.9	7.2	1.2
1993	14.1	32.2	11.3	1.9	16.9	4.2	0.7	9.7	3.0	1.1	7.3	1.2
1994 [3]	14.9	32.9	11.9	2.2	17.6	4.4	0.8	9.9	3.2	1.4	7.7	1.2
1995	15.0	33.6	12.0	2.1	18.0	4.6	0.8	10.2	3.3	1.3	7.8	1.3
1996	15.4	33.4	12.4	2.2	17.8	4.7	0.9	10.2	3.4	1.4	7.6	1.3
PARTICIPATION RATE [4]												
1960	44.1	30.5	40.0	(NA)	27.6	56.0	(NA)	39.0	65.9	(NA)	18.6	40.5
1970	53.0	40.8	39.1	(NA)	39.7	60.7	(NA)	49.2	66.9	(NA)	30.3	52.2
1980	61.5	50.1	44.0	52.0	54.1	69.4	67.6	61.7	74.6	44.1	45.1	60.3
1985	65.2	54.2	45.6	51.6	60.8	71.9	64.1	67.8	77.8	46.5	53.4	59.7
1990	66.4	58.2	46.8	55.2	66.3	74.2	69.7	73.6	79.7	48.7	58.9	63.6
1993	64.5	59.4	45.9	54.4	67.5	72.1	70.2	74.9	78.3	47.4	59.6	60.0
1994 [3]	65.1	60.6	47.3	56.9	69.0	73.1	67.5	76.0	78.4	52.2	61.7	62.2
1995	65.5	61.1	47.3	57.5	70.2	75.3	67.0	76.2	79.5	53.0	63.5	66.3
1996	65.2	61.1	48.2	60.5	70.0	77.0	71.8	76.7	80.6	55.1	62.7	69.2
EMPLOYMENT (mil.)												
1960	5.1	11.6	4.6	(NA)	6.2	1.3	(NA)	3.9	0.9	(NA)	2.3	0.4
1970	6.5	17.5	5.6	(NA)	9.6	1.8	(NA)	6.0	1.2	(NA)	3.6	0.6
1980	10.1	23.6	8.2	0.4	12.8	3.3	0.2	8.1	2.4	0.2	4.8	0.9
1985	11.6	26.1	9.4	0.9	13.9	3.5	0.3	8.1	2.6	0.5	5.9	0.9
1990	12.9	29.9	10.5	1.2	15.8	3.8	0.5	8.9	2.7	0.7	6.9	1.1
1993	12.7	30.8	10.5	1.5	16.1	3.9	0.6	9.3	2.8	0.9	6.8	1.1
1994 [3]	13.4	31.4	11.0	1.7	16.8	4.0	0.7	9.5	2.9	1.1	7.3	1.0
1995	13.7	32.3	11.3	1.8	17.2	4.2	0.7	9.8	3.1	1.1	7.3	1.2
1996	14.1	32.3	11.7	1.8	17.1	4.4	0.7	9.8	3.2	1.1	7.3	1.2
UNEMPLOYMENT RATE [5]												
1960	6.0	5.4	6.2	(NA)	6.0	8.4	(NA)	4.9	6.8	(NA)	7.8	12.5
1970	7.1	4.8	4.8	(NA)	6.0	7.2	(NA)	4.8	5.9	(NA)	7.9	9.8
1980	10.3	5.3	6.4	23.2	5.9	9.2	15.6	4.4	7.9	29.2	8.3	12.8
1985	10.2	5.7	8.5	23.8	6.6	12.1	15.4	5.5	10.6	26.5	8.0	16.1
1990	8.2	3.5	5.7	18.4	4.2	8.5	14.5	3.8	7.7	20.8	4.8	10.2
1993	9.8	4.4	6.9	19.2	4.8	8.5	13.7	3.8	7.0	22.8	6.2	12.5
1994 [3]	10.0	4.5	7.4	19.5	5.0	9.8	13.2	4.5	7.7	23.0	5.6	15.1
1995	8.7	3.9	5.8	16.6	4.3	8.1	11.8	3.6	7.1	19.5	5.3	10.8
1996	8.6	3.4	5.5	18.5	3.5	6.4	15.7	3.2	5.1	20.3	3.9	9.7

NA Not available. [1] Husband present. [2] Widowed, divorced, or separated. [3] Data beginning 1994 not strictly comparable with data for earlier years. See text, section 13, and February 1994 and March 1996 issues of *Employment and Earnings*. [4] Percent of women in each specific category in the labor force. [5] Unemployed as a percent of civilian labor force in specified group.

Source: U.S. Bureau of Labor Statistics, Bulletin 2307; and unpublished data.

No. 632. Labor Force Participation Rates for Wives, Husband Present, by Age of Own Youngest Child: 1975 to 1996

[As of March. For civilian noninstitutional population, 16 years old and over. For definition of participation rate, see table 631. Based on Current Population Survey; see text, section 1, and Appendix III]

PRESENCE AND AGE OF CHILD	TOTAL			WHITE			BLACK		
	1975	1995	1996 [1]	1975	1995	1996 [1]	1975	1995	1996 [1]
Wives, total	44.4	54.2	61.1	43.6	53.3	60.6	54.1	63.8	67.3
No children under 18	43.8	48.2	53.4	43.6	47.5	53.1	47.6	55.2	54.9
With children under 18	44.9	60.8	70.0	43.6	59.9	69.6	58.4	71.7	79.2
Under 6, total	36.7	53.4	62.7	34.7	52.1	62.2	54.9	69.6	76.1
Under 3	32.7	50.5	60.5	30.7	49.4	60.2	50.1	66.2	70.7
1 year or under	30.8	49.4	59.3	29.2	48.6	59.1	50.0	63.7	70.2
2 years	37.1	54.0	64.1	35.1	52.7	64.0	56.4	69.9	72.6
3 to 5 years	42.2	58.4	66.0	40.1	56.6	65.1	61.2	73.8	83.8
3 years	41.2	55.1	61.9	39.0	52.7	61.2	62.7	72.3	80.0
4 years	41.2	59.7	69.1	38.7	58.4	67.5	64.9	70.6	82.6
5 years	44.4	62.1	68.2	43.8	59.9	67.8	56.3	79.1	83.5
6 to 13 years	51.8	68.2	76.0	50.7	67.7	75.8	65.7	73.3	81.6
14 to 17 years	53.5	67.0	78.4	53.4	66.6	78.2	52.3	74.4	82.3

[1] See footnote 3, table 631.

Source: U.S. Bureau of Labor Statistics, Bulletin 2340; and unpublished data.

No. 633. Civilian Labor Force—Employment Status, by Sex, Race, and Age: 1996

[For civilian noninstitutional population 16 years old and over. Annual averages of monthly figures. Based on Current Population Survey; see text, section 1, and Appendix III]

AGE AND RACE	TOTAL (1,000)	MALE (1,000)			FEMALE (1,000)			PERCENT OF LABOR FORCE			
								Employed		Unemployed	
		Total	Employed	Unemployed	Total	Employed	Unemployed	Male	Female	Male	Female
All workers [1]	133,943	72,087	68,207	3,880	61,857	58,501	3,356	94.6	94.6	5.4	5.4
16 to 19 years	7,806	4,043	3,310	733	3,763	3,190	573	81.9	84.8	18.1	15.2
20 to 24 years	13,377	7,104	6,429	675	6,273	5,709	564	90.5	91.0	9.5	9.0
25 to 34 years	33,833	18,430	17,527	903	15,403	14,549	854	95.1	94.5	4.9	5.5
35 to 44 years	36,556	19,602	18,816	786	16,954	16,235	720	96.0	95.8	4.0	4.2
45 to 54 years	26,397	13,967	13,483	484	12,430	12,031	399	96.5	96.8	3.5	3.2
55 to 64 years	12,146	6,693	6,470	223	5,452	5,269	183	96.7	96.6	3.3	3.4
65 years and over	3,828	2,247	2,172	76	1,581	1,518	63	96.6	96.0	3.4	4.0
White	113,108	61,783	58,888	2,896	51,325	48,920	2,404	95.3	95.3	4.7	4.7
16 to 19 years	6,607	3,444	2,911	532	3,163	2,756	407	84.5	87.1	15.5	12.9
20 to 24 years	11,003	5,922	5,444	478	5,081	4,705	376	91.9	92.6	8.1	7.4
25 to 34 years	27,901	15,475	14,820	655	12,426	11,858	568	95.8	95.4	4.2	4.6
35 to 44 years	30,683	16,728	16,136	592	13,955	13,430	525	96.5	96.2	3.5	3.8
45 to 54 years	22,781	12,217	11,834	383	10,563	10,237	326	96.9	96.9	3.1	3.1
55 to 64 years	10,648	5,943	5,755	188	4,706	4,558	148	96.8	96.9	3.2	3.1
65 years and over	3,486	2,054	1,987	67	1,431	1,376	55	96.7	96.2	3.2	3.8
Black	15,134	7,264	6,456	808	7,869	7,086	784	88.9	90.0	11.1	10.0
16 to 19 years	923	458	289	169	464	324	141	63.1	69.7	36.9	30.3
20 to 24 years	1,738	848	685	163	890	726	164	80.8	81.6	19.2	18.4
25 to 34 years	4,305	2,077	1,867	210	2,228	1,984	244	89.9	89.0	10.1	11.0
35 to 44 years	4,287	2,036	1,878	158	2,251	2,096	155	92.2	93.1	7.8	6.9
45 to 54 years	2,553	1,204	1,129	75	1,349	1,297	52	93.8	96.1	6.3	3.8
55 to 64 years	1,073	509	482	26	565	543	21	94.9	96.3	5.1	3.8
65 years and over	255	132	126	7	122	115	7	94.7	94.3	5.0	5.6
Hispanic [2]	12,774	7,646	7,039	607	5,128	4,602	525	92.1	89.8	7.9	10.2
16 to 19 years	845	496	384	112	349	261	88	77.4	74.8	22.5	25.1
20 to 24 years	1,845	1,132	1,015	117	713	612	100	89.7	86.0	10.3	14.1
25 to 34 years	4,054	2,510	2,345	165	1,544	1,412	131	93.4	91.5	6.6	8.5
35 to 44 years	3,361	1,966	1,842	124	1,395	1,273	122	93.7	91.3	6.3	8.7
45 to 54 years	1,697	967	918	49	729	677	52	94.9	92.9	5.1	7.2
55 to 64 years	806	469	438	31	338	310	27	93.4	92.0	6.7	8.0
65 years and over	166	105	96	9	61	56	5	91.4	91.8	8.3	8.0

[1] Includes other races not shown separately. [2] Persons of Hispanic origin may be of any race.

Source: U.S. Bureau of Labor Statistics, *Employment and Earnings*, monthly, January 1997.

No. 634. Employed Civilians and Weekly Hours: 1970 to 1996

[In thousands, except as indicated. For civilian noninstitutional population 16 years old and over. Annual averages of monthly figures. Based on Current Population Survey; see text, section 1, and Appendix III]

ITEM	1970	1980	1990 [1]	1992	1993	1994 [1]	1995	1996
Total employed	78,678	99,303	118,793	118,492	120,259	123,060	124,900	126,708
Age:								
16 to 19 years old	6,144	7,710	6,581	5,669	5,805	6,161	6,419	6,500
20 to 24 years old	9,731	14,087	13,401	12,872	12,840	12,758	12,443	12,138
25 to 34 years old	16,318	27,204	33,935	32,667	32,385	32,286	32,356	32,077
35 to 44 years old	15,922	19,523	30,817	31,923	32,666	33,599	34,202	35,051
45 to 54 years old	16,473	16,234	19,525	21,022	22,175	23,348	24,378	25,514
55 to 64 years old	10,974	11,586	11,189	10,998	11,058	11,228	11,435	11,739
65 years old and over	3,118	2,960	3,346	3,341	3,331	3,681	3,666	3,690
Class of worker:								
Nonagriculture	75,215	95,938	115,570	115,245	117,144	119,651	121,460	123,264
Wage and salary worker	69,491	88,525	106,598	106,437	107,966	110,517	112,448	114,171
Self-employed	5,221	7,000	8,719	8,575	8,959	9,003	8,902	8,971
Unpaid family workers	502	413	253	233	218	131	110	122
Agriculture	3,463	3,364	3,223	3,247	3,115	3,409	3,440	3,443
Wage and salary worker	1,154	1,425	1,740	1,750	1,689	1,715	1,814	1,869
Self-employed	1,810	1,642	1,378	1,385	1,320	1,645	1,580	1,518
Unpaid family workers	499	297	105	112	106	49	45	56
Weekly hours:								
Nonagriculture:								
Wage and salary workers	38.3	38.1	39.2	38.7	39.2	39.1	39.2	39.2
Self-employed	45.0	41.2	40.8	40.1	40.6	39.5	39.4	39.6
Unpaid family workers	37.9	34.7	34.0	34.6	34.2	33.7	33.5	34.1
Agriculture:								
Wage and salary workers	40.0	41.6	41.2	40.5	40.7	41.0	41.1	41.5
Self-employed	51.0	49.3	46.8	47.0	46.4	43.0	43.5	43.1
Unpaid family workers	40.0	38.6	38.5	40.4	36.9	39.0	42.0	38.0

[1] See footnote 2, table 619.

Source: U.S. Bureau of Labor Statistics, *Employment and Earnings*, monthly, January issues; and unpublished data.

No. 635. Persons At Work, by Hours Worked: 1996

[For civilian noninstitutional population 16 years old and over. Annual averages of monthly figures. Based on Current Population Survey; see text, section 1, and Appendix III]

HOURS OF WORK	PERSONS AT WORK (1,000)			PERCENT DISTRIBUTION		
	Total	Agriculture industries	Non-agriculture industries	Total	Agriculture industries	Non-agriculture industries
Total	**120,940**	**3,262**	**117,678**	**100.0**	**100.0**	**100.0**
1 to 34 hours	31,024	1,020	30,004	25.7	31.3	25.5
1 to 4 hours	1,295	78	1,216	1.1	2.4	1.0
5 to 14 hours	4,998	241	4,757	4.1	7.4	4.0
15 to 29 hours	15,423	483	14,940	12.8	14.8	12.7
30 to 34 hours	9,309	218	9,090	7.7	6.7	7.7
35 hours and over	89,916	2,242	87,674	74.3	68.7	74.5
35 to 39 hours	8,672	175	8,497	7.2	5.4	7.2
40 hours	42,992	692	42,299	35.5	21.2	35.9
41 hours and over	38,252	1,374	36,878	31.6	42.1	31.3
41 to 48 hours	14,059	256	13,803	11.6	7.8	11.7
49 to 58 hours	13,907	376	13,530	11.5	11.5	11.5
60 hours and over	10,286	742	9,544	8.5	22.8	8.1
Average weekly hours:						
Total at work	39.3	42.2	39.2	(X)	(X)	(X)
Persons usually working full time	43.3	49.3	43.2	(X)	(X)	(X)

X Not applicable.

Source: U.S. Bureau of Labor Statistics, *Employment and Earnings*, monthly, January, 1997 issue.

No. 636. Self-Employed Workers, by Industry and Occupation: 1970 to 1996

[In thousands. For civilian noninstitutional population 16 years old and over. Annual averages of monthly figures. Data from 1992 forward are not fully comparable with data for prior years because of the introduction of the occupational and industrial classification used in the 1990 census. Based on the Current Population Survey; see text, section 1, and Appendix III]

ITEM	1970	1980	1980 [1]	1992	1993	1994 [1]	1995	1996
Total self-employed	**7,031**	**8,642**	**10,097**	**9,960**	**10,280**	**10,648**	**10,482**	**10,490**
Industry: Agriculture	1,810	1,642	1,378	1,385	1,320	1,645	1,580	1,518
Nonagriculture	5,221	7,000	8,719	8,575	8,960	9,003	8,902	8,971
Mining	14	28	24	22	17	13	16	15
Construction	687	1,173	1,457	1,460	1,549	1,506	1,460	1,496
Manufacturing	264	358	427	390	439	426	433	406
Transportation and public utilities	196	282	301	337	372	385	396	432
Trade	1,687	1,899	1,851	1,770	1,886	1,906	1,772	1,760
Finance, insurance, and real estate	254	458	630	622	655	625	660	674
Services	2,140	2,804	4,030	3,975	4,041	4,142	4,166	4,189
Occupation:								
Managerial and professional specialty	(NA)	(NA)	3,050	2,895	3,078	3,106	3,147	3,288
Technical, sales, and administrative support	(NA)	(NA)	2,240	2,176	2,319	2,380	2,341	2,304
Service occupations	(NA)	(NA)	1,207	1,079	1,044	1,178	1,190	1,198
Precision production, craft, and repair	(NA)	(NA)	1,675	1,799	1,888	1,740	1,618	1,595
Operators, fabricators, and laborers	(NA)	(NA)	567	625	631	639	631	634
Farming, forestry, and fishing	(NA)	(NA)	1,358	1,377	1,320	1,605	1,556	1,471

NA Not available. [1] See footnote 2, table 619.

Source: U.S. Bureau of Labor Statistics, Bulletin 2307; *Employment and Earnings*, monthly, January issues; and unpublished data.

No. 637. Persons With a Job But Not at Work: 1970 to 1996

[In thousands, except percent. For civilian noninstitutional population 16 years old and over. Annual averages of monthly figures. Based on Current Population Survey; see text, section 1, and Appendix III]

REASON FOR NOT WORKING	1970	1975	1980	1985	1990 [1]	1991	1992	1993	1994 [1]	1995	1996
All industries, number	**4,645**	**5,221**	**5,881**	**5,789**	**6,160**	**5,914**	**6,068**	**6,041**	**5,619**	**5,582**	**5,768**
Percent of employed	**5.9**	**6.1**	**5.9**	**5.4**	**5.2**	**5.0**	**5.1**	**5.0**	**4.6**	**4.5**	**4.6**
Reason for not working:											
Vacation	2,341	2,815	3,320	3,338	3,529	3,291	3,409	3,328	2,877	2,962	3,065
Illness	1,324	1,343	1,426	1,308	1,341	1,305	1,259	1,295	1,184	1,084	1,090
Bad weather	128	139	155	141	90	119	128	153	165	122	256
Industrial dispute	156	95	105	42	24	17	19	24	15	21	11
All other	696	829	876	960	1,177	1,182	1,272	1,241	1,378	1,373	1,325

[1] See footnote 2, table 619.

Source: U.S. Bureau of Labor Statistics, *Employment and Earnings*, monthly, January issues; and unpublished data.

No. 638. Part-Time Workers, by Reason: 1996

[In thousands, except hours. For persons working 1 to 34 hours per week. For civilian noninstitutional population 16 years old and over. Annual average of monthly figures. Based on the Current Population Survey and subject to sampling error; see text, section 1, and Appendix III]

REASON	ALL INDUSTRIES			NONAGRICULTURAL INDUSTRIES		
	Total	Usually work—		Total	Usually work—	
		Full time	Part time		Full time	Part time
Total working fewer than 35 hours	**31,024**	**10,381**	**20,643**	**30,004**	**10,083**	**19,922**
Economic reasons	4,315	1,442	2,874	4,123	1,352	2,772
Slack work or business conditions	2,388	1,162	1,226	2,263	1,098	1,165
Could find only part-time work	1,605	-	1,605	1,576	-	1,576
Seasonal work	123	81	42	91	60	31
Job started or ended during the week	199	199	-	194	194	-
Noneconomic reasons	26,709	8,939	17,770	25,881	8,731	17,150
Child-care problems	810	65	745	797	65	732
Other family or personal obligations	5,469	706	4,763	5,296	689	4,607
Health or medical limitations	677	-	677	646	-	646
In school or training	6,026	88	5,938	5,874	83	5,792
Retired or Social Security limit on earnings	1,856	-	1,856	1,717	-	1,717
Vacation or personal day	3,319	3,319	-	3,260	3,260	-
Holiday, legal, or religious	664	664	-	654	654	-
Weather related curtailment	1,267	1,267	-	1,215	1,215	-
Other	6,621	2,830	3,791	6,422	2,766	3,656
Average hours per week:						
Economic reasons	22.7	23.8	22.2	22.8	23.9	22.3
Noneconomic reasons	21.4	25.3	19.4	21.5	25.4	19.5

- Represents or rounds to zero.

Source: U.S. Bureau of Labor Statistics, *Employment and Earnings*, monthly, January 1997 issue.

639. Multiple Jobholders: 1996

[Annual average of monthly figures. For the civilian noninstitutional population 16 years old and over. Multiple jobholders are employed persons who, either 1) had jobs as wage or salary workers with two employers or more; 2) were self-employed and also held a wage and salary job; or 3) were unpaid family workers on their primary jobs but also held wage and salary job. Based on the Current Population Survey; see text, section 1, and Appendix III]

CHARACTERISTIC	TOTAL		MALE		FEMALE	
	Number (1,000)	Percent of employed	Number (1,000)	Percent of employed	Number (1,000)	Percent of employed
Total [1]	**7,832**	**6.2**	**4,192**	**6.1**	**3,640**	**6.2**
Age:						
16 to 19 years old	336	5.2	146	4.4	190	5.9
20 to 24 years old	813	6.7	392	6.1	421	7.4
25 to 54 years old	6,001	6.5	3,249	6.5	2,752	6.4
55 to 64 years old	556	4.7	321	5.0	235	4.5
65 years old and over	126	3.4	84	3.9	42	2.7
Race and Hispanic origin:						
White	6,867	6.4	3,686	6.3	3,181	6.5
Black	705	5.2	376	5.8	329	4.6
Hispanic origin [2]	442	3.8	254	3.6	188	4.1
Marital status:						
Married, spouse present	4,471	6.0	2,696	6.4	1,775	5.5
Widowed, divorced, or separated	1,281	6.6	456	5.9	825	7.1
Single, never married	2,080	6.4	1,040	5.8	1,040	7.2
Full- or part-time status:						
Primary job full-time, secondary job part time	4,380	(X)	2,608	(X)	1,772	(X)
Both jobs part time	1,714	(X)	531	(X)	1,183	(X)
Both jobs full time	244	(X)	175	(X)	69	(X)
Hours vary on primary or secondary job	1,457	(X)	857	(X)	600	(X)

X Not applicable. [1] Includes a small number of persons who work part time on their primary job and full time on their secondary job(s), not shown separately. Includes other races, not shown separately. [2] Persons of Hispanic origin may be of any race.

Source: U.S. Bureau of Labor Statistics, *Employment and Earnings*, monthly, January 1996 issue.

No. 640. Employed Persons in Alternative and Traditional Work Arrangements, by Selected Characteristic: 1995

[As of February. For all employed persons, except unpaid family members, 16 years old and over. See source for definitions of working arrangements. Based on the Current Population Survey and subject to sampling error; see source and Appendix III]

CHARACTERISTIC	WORKERS IN ALTERNATIVE ARRANGEMENTS				Workers in traditional arrange-ments
	Independent contractors	On-call workers	Temporary help agency workers	Workers provided by contract firms	
Total (1,000)	**8,309**	**1,996**	**1,181**	**652**	**111,052**
AGE AND SEX					
Total (percent)	100.0	100.0	100.0	100.0	100.0
16 to 19 years old	1.5	7.8	5.2	2.5	4.7
20 to 24 years old	2.4	11.5	19.7	12.7	10.5
25 to 34 years old	19.7	25.4	34.1	39.0	26.4
35 to 44 years old	30.8	23.2	21.3	23.3	27.6
45 to 54 years old	25.3	15.9	12.1	11.8	19.2
55 to 64 years old	13.6	9.6	5.8	6.7	8.9
65 years and over	6.7	6.7	1.8	4.1	2.5
Male	67.3	48.4	47.2	71.5	52.8
16 to 19 years old	0.9	3.9	3.0	1.4	2.4
20 to 24 years old	1.6	6.7	11.4	6.4	5.6
25 to 34 years old	12.6	13.1	16.8	29.8	14.3
35 to 44 years old	21.0	10.8	7.7	19.0	14.5
45 to 54 years old	16.7	6.7	4.4	5.7	10.0
55 to 64 years old	9.6	3.7	2.8	5.2	4.7
65 years and over	4.9	3.6	1.1	4.1	1.4
Female	32.7	51.6	52.8	28.5	47.2
16 to 19 years old	0.6	3.9	2.3	1.1	2.4
20 to 24 years old	0.8	4.8	8.3	6.1	4.9
25 to 34 years old	7.1	12.3	17.4	9.2	12.1
35 to 44 years old	9.8	12.4	13.5	4.3	13.1
45 to 54 years old	8.5	9.1	7.7	6.3	9.2
55 to 64 years old	4.0	5.8	2.9	1.5	4.2
65 years and over	1.8	3.2	0.8	(Z)	1.1

Z Less than 0.05 percent.

Source: U.S. Bureau of Labor Statistics, *Monthly Labor Review*, October 1996.

No. 641. Distribution of Workers, by Tenure with Current Employer, by Selected Characteristic: 1996

[As of February. For employed wage and salary workers 16 years old and over. Based on the Current Population Survey and subject to sampling error; see source and Appendix III]

CHARACTERISTIC	Number em-ployed (1,000)	PERCENT DISTRIBUTION BY TENURE WITH CURRENT EMPLOYER								Median years[1]
		12 months or less	13 to 23 months	2 years	3 to 4 years	5 to 9 years	10 to 14 years	15 to 19 years	20 years or more	
Total	**110,281**	**26.0**	**8.5**	**4.8**	**15.2**	**19.6**	**10.0**	**6.8**	**9.0**	**3.8**
AGE AND SEX										
16 to 19 years old	5,749	77.6	11.8	5.5	5.0	0.2	-	-	-	0.7
20 years old and over	104,531	23.1	8.3	4.6	15.8	20.8	10.5	7.1	9.5	4.2
20 to 24 years old	11,468	52.2	14.1	8.9	18.3	6.3	0.1	-	-	1.2
25 to 34 years old	29,474	29.5	10.6	5.7	20.3	24.7	7.8	1.2	(Z)	2.8
35 to 44 years old	30,316	17.9	7.4	4.3	14.9	24.2	14.3	11.3	5.8	5.3
45 to 54 years old	21,330	13.0	5.1	3.0	12.1	20.0	13.5	11.1	22.3	8.3
55 to 64 years old	9,396	10.6	4.6	2.7	11.0	18.0	12.2	12.0	28.9	10.2
65 years old and over	2,545	13.0	5.1	3.4	11.8	19.3	13.1	7.4	26.9	8.4
Male	57,291	25.1	8.0	4.7	15.1	19.1	10.0	6.9	11.0	4.0
16 to 19 years old	2,932	77.3	9.9	6.8	5.8	0.2	-	-	-	0.7
20 years old and over	54,359	22.3	7.9	4.6	15.6	20.2	10.6	7.3	11.6	4.4
20 to 24 years old	5,979	52.7	13.2	8.2	19.1	6.6	0.2	-	-	1.2
25 to 34 years old	15,779	28.2	10.0	5.6	20.8	25.3	8.3	1.5	(Z)	3.0
35 to 44 years old	15,756	16.3	7.0	3.8	14.0	23.1	15.7	13.0	7.1	6.1
45 to 54 years old	10,712	11.9	4.6	2.6	10.7	17.7	12.3	11.0	29.3	10.1
55 to 64 years old	4,846	10.3	5.3	3.0	10.6	17.0	10.0	9.4	34.4	10.5
65 years old and over	1,287	12.2	5.8	3.1	14.6	16.7	12.4	5.7	29.5	8.3
Female	52,989	27.0	9.0	4.9	15.4	20.5	9.9	6.6	6.8	3.5
16 to 19 years old	2,817	77.9	13.7	4.0	4.2	0.2	-	-	-	0.7
20 years old and over	50,172	24.1	8.7	5.0	16.0	21.6	10.4	7.0	7.2	3.9
20 to 24 years old	5,489	51.7	15.0	9.8	17.4	6.0	0.1	-	-	1.2
25 to 34 years old	13,695	30.9	11.6	5.7	19.7	24.0	7.2	0.9	-	2.7
35 to 44 years old	14,561	19.6	7.8	4.7	15.9	25.5	12.7	9.5	4.4	4.8
45 to 54 years old	10,617	14.1	5.5	3.3	13.5	22.3	14.8	11.3	15.2	7.0
55 to 64 years old	4,551	11.0	3.9	2.4	11.4	19.1	14.5	14.8	23.1	10.0
65 years old and over	1,258	13.9	4.3	3.8	8.9	22.0	13.8	9.2	24.2	8.4

- Represents zero. Z Less than 0.05 percent. [1] For definition of median, see Guide to Tabular Presentation.

Source: U. S. Bureau of Labor Statistics, "Employee Tenure in the Mid-1990s", USDL 97-25, and unpublished data.

No. 642. Displaced Workers, by Selected Characteristics: 1996

[In percent, except total. As of February. For persons 20 years old and over with tenure of 3 years or more who lost or left a job between January 1993 and December 1995 because of plant closings or moves, slack work, or the abolishment of their positions. Data revised since originally published. Based on Current Population Survey and subject to sampling error; see source and and Appendix III]

CHARACTERISTIC	Total (1,000)	EMPLOYMENT STATUS			REASON FOR JOB LOSS		
		Employed	Unem- ployed	Not in the labor force	Plant or company closed down or moved	Slack work	Position or shift abolished
Total [1]	4,171	73.6	12.5	13.9	44.0	24.2	31.6
20 to 24 years old	149	71.3	17.9	10.7	52.9	30.0	17.1
25 to 54 years old	3,397	78.5	12.0	9.5	43.1	25.3	31.6
55 to 64 years old	487	52.1	16.6	31.3	45.3	15.1	39.7
65 years old and over	139	31.6	4.1	64.3	50.4	22.5	27.1
Males	2,358	77.8	13.1	9.1	42.8	27.3	29.9
20 to 24 years old	82	77.4	17.1	5.4	53.5	34.9	11.6
25 to 54 years old	1,929	82.0	13.2	4.8	42.4	28.6	28.9
55 to 64 years old	276	60.7	12.6	26.7	41.5	14.8	43.7
65 years old and over	71	(2)	(2)	(2)	(2)	(2)	(2)
Females	1,813	68.2	11.8	20.0	45.5	20.2	34.4
20 to 24 years old	67	63.9	18.9	17.2	52.3	23.9	23.8
25 to 54 years old	1,468	73.9	10.6	15.6	44.0	21.0	35.1
55 to 64 years old	211	40.8	21.9	37.3	50.1	15.5	34.4
65 years old and over	67	(2)	(2)	(2)	(2)	(2)	(2)
White	3,632	74.1	12.0	13.9	43.0	24.7	32.4
Black	420	67.4	17.1	15.5	51.8	20.0	28.2
Hispanic origin [3]	383	66.5	22.8	10.7	49.5	37.0	13.4

[1] Includes other races, not shown separately. [2] Data not shown where base is less than 75,000. [3] Persons of Hispanic origin may be of any race.

Source: U.S. Bureau of Labor Statistics, *News*, USDL 96-446.

No. 643. Percent Distribution of Employed Persons by Disability Status: 1991 to 1994

[Data from the Survey of Income and Program Participation]

DISABILITY STATUS	1991	1993	1994
All employed persons (1,000)	119,432	122,614	125,591
Total of employed persons	100.0	100.0	100.0
With no disability	86.6	86.2	86.2
With a disability	13.4	13.8	13.8
Severe	2.8	3.2	3.4
Not severe	10.6	10.6	10.4
With a functional limitation	8.4	8.9	7.9
Severe	1.7	2.0	2.1
With difficulty:			
Seeing words and letters	2.0	2.2	1.6
Hearing normal conversation	3.2	3.5	2.7

DISABILITY STATUS	1991	1993	1994
Lifting and carrying	2.3	2.6	2.5
Climbing stairs	2.3	2.6	2.6
Walking 3 city blocks	2.4	2.6	2.7
With an ADL [1] limitation	0.8	1.0	0.9
With an IADL [2] limitation	1.1	1.3	1.4
Needs personal assistance and an ADL or IADL	0.7	0.9	0.9
Uses a wheelchair	0.1	0.1	0.1
Does not use a wheelchair, but uses a cane, crutches, or a walker	0.4	0.5	0.4

[1] ADL's are activities of daily living and include getting around inside the home, getting in or out of a bed or chair, taking a bath or shower, dressing, eating, and using the toilet. [2] IADL's are instrumental activities of daily living and include going outside the home, keeping track of money and bills, preparing meals, doing light housework, and using the telephone.

Source: U.S. Census Bureau, Internet site <http://www.census.gov/hhes/www/disable/dissipp.html> (Accessed 18 June 1997)

No. 644. Persons Not in the Labor Force: 1996

[In thousands. Annual average of monthly figures. For the civilian noninstitutional population 16 years old and over. Based on the Current Population Survey; see text, section 1, and Appendix III]

STATUS AND REASON	Total	AGE			SEX	
		16 to 24 years old	25 to 54 years old	55 years old and over	Male	Female
Total not in the labor force	66,647	11,160	18,720	36,768	24,119	42,528
Do not want a job now [1]	61,197	9,110	16,205	35,882	21,929	39,267
Want a job now	5,451	2,050	2,514	886	2,190	3,261
In the previous year—						
Did not search for a job	3,161	1,100	1,407	654	1,185	1,976
Did search for a job [2]	2,290	950	1,108	232	1,005	1,285
Not available for work now	732	365	328	40	277	455
Available for work now, not looking for work	1,558	585	780	192	728	830
Reason for not currently looking:						
Discouraged over job prospects [3]	397	115	225	58	233	164
Family responsibilities	177	35	125	17	31	146
In school or training	257	211	43	3	138	119
Ill health or disability	121	22	73	27	49	72
Other [4]	605	203	314	88	277	328

[1] Includes some persons who are not asked if they want a job. [2] Persons who had a job in the prior 12 months must have searched since the end of that job. [3] Includes such things as believes no work available, could not find work, lacks necessary schooling or training, employer thinks too young or old, and other types of discrimination. [4] Includes such things as child care and transportation problems.

Source: U.S. Bureau of Labor Statistics, *Employment and Earnings*, monthly, January 1997 issue.

No. 645. Employed Civilians, by Occupation, Sex, Race, and Hispanic Origin: 1983 and 1996

[For civilian noninstitutional population 16 years old and over. Annual average of monthly figures. Based on Current Population Survey; see text, section 1, and Appendix III. Persons of Hispanic origin may be of any race. See headnote, table 636]

OCCUPATION	1983				1996[1]			
	Total employed (1,000)	Percent of total			Total employed (1,000)	Percent of total		
		Female	Black	Hispanic		Female	Black	Hispanic
Total	100,834	43.7	9.3	5.3	126,708	46.2	10.7	9.2
Managerial and professional specialty	23,592	40.9	5.6	2.6	36,497	48.6	7.4	4.5
Executive, administrative, and managerial[2]	10,772	32.4	4.7	2.8	17,746	43.8	6.9	4.8
Officials and administrators, public	417	38.5	8.3	3.8	636	47.7	12.9	4.9
Financial managers	357	38.6	3.5	3.1	621	54.0	6.5	5.1
Personnel and labor relations managers	106	43.9	4.9	2.6	122	51.6	12.9	4.3
Purchasing managers	82	23.6	5.1	1.4	121	45.7	4.6	6.5
Managers, marketing, advertising and public relations	396	21.8	2.7	1.7	655	37.8	2.9	2.8
Administrators, education and related fields	415	41.4	11.3	2.4	668	56.9	10.2	5.6
Managers, medicine and health	91	57.0	5.0	2.0	713	75.3	8.5	4.1
Managers, properties and real estate	305	42.8	5.5	5.2	530	48.0	7.7	8.1
Management-related occupations[2]	2,966	40.3	5.8	3.5	4,374	56.7	9.2	5.1
Accountants and auditors	1,105	38.7	5.5	3.3	1,538	56.0	8.8	4.8
Professional specialty[2]	12,820	48.1	6.4	2.5	18,752	53.3	7.9	4.3
Architects	103	12.7	1.6	1.5	160	16.7	2.7	4.3
Engineers[2]	1,572	5.8	2.7	2.2	1,960	8.5	4.2	3.8
Aerospace engineers	80	6.9	1.5	2.1	80	4.8	2.7	3.5
Chemical engineers	67	6.1	3.0	1.4	95	15.2	8.7	2.4
Civil engineers	211	4.0	1.9	3.2	243	7.2	4.7	4.3
Electrical and electronic	450	6.1	3.4	3.1	601	8.0	4.4	3.9
Industrial engineers	210	11.0	3.3	2.4	257	13.2	2.8	5.9
Mechanical	259	2.8	3.2	1.1	350	6.9	3.9	2.4
Mathematical and computer scientists[2]	463	29.6	5.4	2.6	1,345	30.6	7.2	2.6
Computer systems analysts, scientists	276	27.8	6.2	2.7	1,093	28.1	7.2	2.5
Operations and systems researchers and analysts	142	31.3	4.9	2.2	209	42.8	8.0	3.4
Natural scientists[2]	357	20.5	2.6	2.1	536	29.3	3.3	1.9
Chemists, except biochemists	98	23.3	4.3	1.2	149	28.6	3.7	2.1
Biological and life scientists	55	40.8	2.4	1.8	116	39.0	4.7	3.0
Medical scientists	([3])	([3])	([3])	([3])	73	48.5	4.8	3.5
Health diagnosing occupations[2]	735	13.3	2.7	3.3	960	25.5	3.7	4.3
Physicians	519	15.8	3.2	4.5	667	26.4	4.5	5.1
Dentists	126	6.7	2.4	1.0	137	13.7	1.2	0.9
Health assessment and treating occupations	1,900	85.8	7.1	2.2	2,812	85.7	8.7	3.1
Registered nurses	1,372	95.8	6.7	1.8	1,966	93.3	8.6	2.6
Pharmacists	158	26.7	3.8	2.6	184	42.6	6.8	1.3
Dietitians	71	90.8	21.0	3.7	105	90.2	29.3	7.4
Therapists[2]	247	76.3	7.6	2.7	474	73.3	6.8	4.4
Respiratory therapists	69	69.4	6.5	3.7	96	58.4	8.5	6.8
Physical therapists	55	77.0	9.7	1.5	118	61.9	3.8	4.3
Speech therapists	51	90.5	1.5	-	97	93.3	2.2	2.9
Physicians' assistants	51	36.3	7.7	4.4	63	55.9	1.8	5.2
Teachers, college and university	606	36.3	4.4	1.8	869	43.5	6.5	4.1
Teachers, except college and university[2]	3,365	70.9	9.1	2.7	4,724	74.4	9.8	4.8
Prekindergarten and kindergarten	299	98.2	11.8	3.4	543	98.1	13.6	5.8
Elementary school	1,350	83.3	11.1	3.1	1,846	83.3	9.9	4.8
Secondary school	1,209	51.8	7.2	2.3	1,228	55.9	7.9	5.0
Special education	81	82.2	10.2	2.3	340	84.8	12.5	2.1
Counselors, educational and vocational	184	53.1	13.9	3.2	275	69.8	15.0	5.9
Librarians, archivists, and curators	213	84.4	7.8	1.6	202	79.8	8.0	2.9
Librarians	193	87.3	7.9	1.8	180	82.7	7.9	3.2
Social scientists and urban planners[2]	261	46.8	7.1	2.1	438	56.9	9.0	3.7
Economists	98	37.9	6.3	2.7	148	54.4	3.9	5.4
Psychologists	135	57.1	8.6	1.1	245	61.4	12.2	3.1
Social, recreation, and religious workers[2]	831	43.1	12.1	3.8	1,332	53.8	17.1	6.4
Social workers	407	64.3	18.2	6.3	745	68.5	22.6	7.7
Recreation workers	65	71.9	15.7	2.0	106	74.0	13.8	5.0
Clergy	293	5.6	4.9	1.4	354	12.3	11.2	4.9
Lawyers and judges	651	15.8	2.7	1.0	911	29.0	3.4	2.9
Lawyers	612	15.3	2.6	0.9	880	29.5	3.5	2.8
Writers, artists, entertainers, and athletes[2]	1,544	42.7	4.8	2.9	2,188	49.4	6.0	6.0
Authors	62	46.7	2.1	0.9	114	54.1	5.4	0.9
Technical writers	([3])	([3])	([3])	([3])	63	40.2	7.4	2.6
Designers	393	52.7	3.1	2.7	603	57.5	2.1	5.9
Musicians and composers	155	28.0	7.9	4.4	175	34.2	12.8	10.4
Actors and directors	60	30.8	6.6	3.4	136	41.3	10.2	7.8
Painters, sculptors, craft-artists, and artist printmakers	186	47.4	2.1	2.3	235	50.4	1.7	5.2
Photographers	113	20.7	4.0	3.4	141	28.6	6.8	5.5
Editors and reporters	204	48.4	2.9	2.1	280	55.7	6.5	3.3
Public relations specialists	157	50.1	6.2	1.9	150	62.0	13.0	4.6
Announcers	([3])	([3])	([3])	([3])	62	17.4	13.1	5.6
Athletes	58	17.6	9.4	1.7	85	30.9	5.6	5.7

See footnotes at end of table.

No. 645. Employed Civilians, by Occupation, Sex, Race, and Hispanic Origin: 1983 and 1996—Continued

[See headnote, page 410]

OCCUPATION	1983				1996 [1]			
	Total employed (1,000)	Percent of total			Total employed (1,000)	Percent of total		
		Female	Black	Hispanic		Female	Black	Hispanic
Technical, sales, and administrative support	31,265	64.6	7.6	4.3	37,683	64.2	10.3	7.6
Technicians and related support	3,053	48.2	8.2	3.1	3,926	52.5	9.4	6.3
Health technologists and technicians [2]	1,111	84.3	12.7	3.1	1,605	80.6	12.2	6.7
Clinical laboratory technologists and technicians	255	76.2	10.5	2.9	376	73.3	16.1	8.7
Dental hygienists	66	98.6	1.6	-	94	98.2	-	2.9
Radiologic technicians	101	71.7	8.6	4.5	135	69.6	8.7	3.8
Licensed practical nurses	443	97.0	17.7	3.1	395	95.3	14.0	3.8
Engineering and related technologists and technicians [2]	822	18.4	6.1	3.5	919	19.9	8.5	6.1
Electrical and electronic technicians	260	12.5	8.2	4.6	361	12.7	8.2	6.5
Drafting occupations	273	17.5	5.5	2.3	233	20.9	5.6	4.5
Surveying and mapping technicians	(3)	(3)	(3)	(3)	73	12.6	10.8	4.4
Science technicians [2]	202	29.1	6.6	2.8	245	37.4	10.6	6.2
Biological technicians	52	37.7	2.9	2.0	79	57.6	9.3	4.0
Chemical technicians	82	26.9	9.5	3.5	78	26.7	14.5	7.3
Technicians, except health, engineering, and science [2]	917	35.3	5.0	2.7	1,157	42.6	5.8	6.0
Airplane pilots and navigators	69	2.1	-	1.6	114	1.4	1.4	3.5
Computer programmers	443	32.5	4.4	2.1	561	30.8	5.3	4.7
Legal assistants	128	74.0	4.3	3.6	307	82.9	7.5	8.3
Sales occupations	11,818	47.5	4.7	3.7	15,404	49.5	7.9	7.0
Supervisors and proprietors	2,958	28.4	3.6	3.4	4,501	37.5	5.4	5.9
Sales representatives, finance and business services [2]	1,853	37.2	2.7	2.2	2,529	42.9	6.1	4.8
Insurance sales	551	25.1	3.8	2.5	625	40.4	7.2	5.5
Real estate sales	570	48.9	1.3	1.5	737	49.2	3.3	4.5
Securities and financial services sales	212	23.6	3.1	1.1	406	30.4	4.5	3.5
Advertising and related sales	124	47.9	4.5	3.3	158	61.1	9.8	4.3
Sales representatives, commodities, except retail	1,442	15.1	2.1	2.2	1,559	25.0	3.1	5.0
Sales workers, retail and personal services	5,511	69.7	6.7	4.8	6,728	65.3	11.4	9.2
Cashiers	2,009	84.4	10.1	5.4	2,856	78.1	15.6	10.6
Sales-related occupations	54	58.7	2.8	1.3	87	75.8	5.3	4.8
Administrative support, including clerical	16,395	79.9	9.6	5.0	18,353	79.1	12.5	8.3
Supervisors	676	53.4	9.3	5.0	670	60.2	13.6	8.3
Computer equipment operators	605	63.9	12.5	6.0	402	60.5	13.8	7.8
Computer operators	597	63.7	12.1	6.0	398	60.2	13.3	7.9
Secretaries, stenographers, and typists [2]	4,861	98.2	7.3	4.5	3,868	97.8	10.3	6.4
Secretaries	3,891	99.0	5.8	4.0	3,164	98.6	9.3	6.2
Typists	906	95.6	13.8	6.4	595	94.8	16.9	8.1
Information clerks	1,174	88.9	8.5	5.5	1,927	89.0	10.2	8.7
Receptionists	602	96.8	7.5	6.6	960	96.9	9.8	8.3
Records processing occupations, except financial [2]	866	82.4	13.9	4.8	911	77.8	16.0	9.1
Order clerks	188	78.1	10.6	4.4	220	73.7	18.7	12.5
Personnel clerks, except payroll and time keeping	64	91.1	14.9	4.6	66	83.2	12.4	4.5
Library clerks	147	81.9	15.4	2.5	145	74.6	11.6	3.5
File clerks	287	83.5	16.7	6.1	309	77.6	18.3	11.3
Records clerks	157	82.8	11.6	5.6	163	85.2	13.7	7.5
Financial records processing [2]	2,457	89.4	4.6	3.7	2,272	91.1	6.8	6.1
Bookkeepers, accounting, and auditing clerks	1,970	91.0	4.3	3.3	1,774	91.9	5.6	5.6
Payroll and time keeping clerks	192	82.2	5.9	5.0	167	90.7	13.5	8.3
Billing clerks	146	88.4	6.2	3.9	169	88.5	12.1	8.0
Cost and rate clerks	96	75.6	5.9	5.3	57	78.7	6.1	4.4
Billing, posting, and calculating machine operators	(3)	(3)	(3)	(3)	104	89.6	7.5	9.2
Duplicating, mail and other office machine operators	68	62.6	16.0	6.1	75	63.6	13.2	13.1
Communications equipment operators	256	89.1	17.0	4.4	177	88.8	21.8	8.0
Telephone operators	244	90.4	17.0	4.3	164	90.5	21.4	7.2
Mail and message distributing occupations	799	31.6	18.1	4.5	998	37.2	21.3	9.1
Postal clerks, except mail carriers	248	36.7	26.2	5.2	310	46.8	28.3	7.9
Mail carrier, postal service	259	17.1	12.5	2.7	325	28.3	14.1	8.1
Mail clerks, except postal service	170	50.0	15.8	5.9	188	49.3	29.8	11.1
Messengers	122	26.2	16.7	5.2	176	23.7	13.1	11.1
Material recording, scheduling, and distributing [2]	1,562	37.5	10.9	6.6	1,922	44.6	14.7	9.5
Dispatchers	157	45.7	11.4	4.3	249	50.6	12.2	5.7
Production coordinators	182	44.0	6.1	2.2	214	53.3	8.6	5.0
Traffic, shipping, and receiving clerks	421	22.6	9.1	11.1	616	30.4	16.1	13.4
Stock and inventory clerks	532	38.7	13.3	5.5	497	44.2	16.4	10.5
Weighers, measurers, and checkers	79	47.2	16.9	5.8	55	54.0	18.1	9.5
Expediters	112	57.5	8.4	4.3	220	69.2	13.6	5.1
Adjusters and investigators	675	69.9	11.1	5.1	1,598	74.3	13.4	8.6
Insurance adjusters, examiners, and investigators	199	65.0	11.5	3.3	410	66.7	11.8	7.5
Investigators and adjusters, except insurance	301	70.1	11.3	4.8	907	76.3	13.5	8.1
Eligibility clerks, social welfare	69	88.7	12.9	9.4	114	87.2	12.7	16.0
Bill and account collectors	106	66.4	8.5	6.5	166	66.7	17.4	8.6
Miscellaneous administrative support [2]	2,397	85.2	12.5	5.9	3,533	84.0	13.8	10.1
General office clerks	648	80.6	12.7	5.2	762	80.8	12.1	9.9
Bank tellers	480	91.0	7.5	4.3	431	90.1	9.7	10.0
Data entry keyers	311	93.6	18.6	5.6	693	84.5	17.0	10.8
Statistical clerks	96	75.7	7.5	3.4	96	90.3	20.2	5.8
Teachers' aides	348	93.7	17.8	12.6	623	92.1	15.9	14.4

See footnotes at end of table.

No. 645. Employed Civilians, by Occupation, Sex, Race, and Hispanic Origin: 1983 and 1996—Continued

[See headnote, page 410]

OCCUPATION	1983				1996 [1]			
	Total employed (1,000)	Percent of total			Total employed (1,000)	Percent of total		
		Female	Black	Hispanic		Female	Black	Hispanic
Service occupations	13,857	60.1	16.6	6.8	17,177	59.4	17.2	13.7
Private household [2]	980	96.1	27.8	8.5	804	94.9	17.2	26.2
Child care workers	408	96.9	7.9	3.6	276	97.1	13.1	15.2
Cleaners and servants	512	95.8	42.4	11.8	504	93.6	18.5	32.4
Protective service	1,672	12.8	13.6	4.6	2,187	17.2	17.8	8.0
Supervisors, protective service	127	4.7	7.7	3.1	184	10.5	13.1	6.0
Supervisors, police and detectives	58	4.2	9.3	1.2	97	13.6	9.2	7.2
Firefighting and fire prevention	189	1.0	6.7	4.1	231	2.1	13.5	5.6
Firefighting occupations	170	1.0	7.3	3.8	217	1.8	13.8	5.0
Police and detectives	645	9.4	13.1	4.0	960	15.8	16.0	8.2
Police and detectives, public service	412	5.7	9.5	4.4	566	12.9	12.6	8.2
Sheriffs, bailiffs, and other law enforcement officers	87	13.2	11.5	4.0	126	15.8	18.7	7.9
Correctional institution officers	146	17.8	24.0	2.8	267	21.7	22.1	8.4
Guards	711	20.6	17.0	5.6	811	24.6	22.1	8.9
Guards and police, except public service	602	13.0	18.9	6.2	686	17.3	24.1	9.2
Service except private household and protective	11,205	64.0	16.0	6.9	14,186	63.9	17.2	13.8
Food preparation and service occupations [2]	4,860	63.3	10.5	6.8	5,906	56.6	11.4	15.1
Bartenders	338	48.4	2.7	4.4	314	53.8	2.4	7.0
Waiters and waitresses	1,357	87.8	4.1	3.6	1,375	77.9	4.8	9.6
Cooks	1,452	50.0	15.8	6.5	2,061	42.2	16.4	18.5
Food counter, fountain, and related occupations	326	76.0	9.1	6.7	311	67.2	12.8	10.4
Kitchen workers, food preparation	138	77.0	13.7	8.1	257	71.3	11.0	13.0
Waiters' and waitresses' assistants	364	38.8	12.6	14.2	523	46.9	10.6	19.8
Health service occupations	1,739	89.2	23.5	4.8	2,398	88.2	29.4	8.2
Dental assistants	154	98.1	6.1	5.7	212	99.1	6.2	11.2
Health aides, except nursing	316	86.8	16.5	4.8	336	79.8	23.3	6.8
Nursing aides, orderlies, and attendants	1,269	88.7	27.3	4.7	1,850	88.4	33.2	8.1
Cleaning and building service occupations [2]	2,736	38.8	24.4	9.2	3,125	44.4	22.8	19.6
Maids and housemen	531	81.2	32.3	10.1	683	81.8	29.6	21.1
Janitors and cleaners	2,031	28.6	22.6	8.9	2,205	34.9	21.1	19.7
Personal service occupations [2]	1,870	79.2	11.1	6.0	2,756	80.7	12.4	9.5
Barbers	92	12.9	8.4	12.1	65	25.2	30.3	8.0
Hairdressers and cosmetologists	622	88.7	7.0	5.7	737	91.1	10.2	8.2
Attendants, amusement and recreation facilities	131	40.2	7.1	4.3	197	38.4	6.3	7.6
Public transportation attendants	63	74.3	11.3	5.9	95	81.2	10.3	6.7
Welfare service aides	77	92.5	24.2	10.5	96	87.3	28.4	14.0
Family child care providers	(NA)	(NA)	(NA)	(NA)	479	98.5	8.8	10.2
Early childhood teachers' assistants	(NA)	(NA)	(NA)	(NA)	387	95.4	15.3	10.3
Precision production, craft, and repair	12,328	8.1	6.8	6.2	13,587	9.0	7.9	11.0
Mechanics and repairers	4,158	3.0	6.8	5.3	4,521	4.1	7.4	9.6
Mechanics and repairers, except supervisors [2]	3,906	2.8	7.0	5.5	4,296	3.9	7.6	9.8
Vehicle and mobile equipment mechanics/repairers [2]	1,683	0.8	6.9	6.0	1,831	1.0	7.9	11.2
Automobile mechanics	800	0.5	7.8	6.0	889	1.2	7.6	13.9
Aircraft engine mechanics	95	2.5	4.0	7.6	137	1.1	11.3	6.0
Electrical and electronic equipment repairers [2]	674	7.4	7.3	4.5	662	11.0	9.7	8.7
Data processing equipment repairers	98	9.3	6.1	4.5	188	18.3	9.9	7.9
Telephone installers and repairers	247	9.9	7.8	3.7	176	13.9	11.9	5.2
Construction trades	4,289	1.8	6.6	6.0	5,108	2.5	7.5	11.7
Construction trades, except supervisors	3,784	1.9	7.1	6.1	4,443	2.5	7.9	12.2
Carpenters	1,160	1.4	5.0	5.0	1,220	1.3	6.2	9.9
Extractive occupations	196	2.3	3.3	6.0	130	2.5	6.0	7.8
Precision production occupations	3,685	21.5	7.3	7.4	3,828	23.6	9.0	11.9
Operators, fabricators, and laborers	16,091	26.6	14.0	8.3	18,197	24.4	15.3	14.3
Machine operators, assemblers, and inspectors [2]	7,744	42.1	14.0	9.4	7,874	37.7	15.2	16.4
Textile, apparel, and furnishings machine operators [2]	1,414	82.1	18.7	12.5	1,071	74.1	19.7	24.4
Textile sewing machine operators	806	94.0	15.5	14.5	595	83.3	16.7	28.1
Pressing machine operators	141	66.4	27.1	14.2	100	76.3	22.7	38.4
Fabricators, assemblers, and hand working occupations	1,715	33.7	11.3	8.7	2,071	32.4	14.3	13.6
Production inspectors, testers, samplers, and weighers	794	53.8	13.0	7.7	771	50.7	12.6	17.3
Transportation and material moving occupations	4,201	7.8	13.0	5.9	5,302	9.5	14.6	10.3
Motor vehicle operators	2,978	9.2	13.5	6.0	4,025	11.2	14.8	10.4
Trucks drivers	2,195	3.1	12.3	5.7	3,019	5.3	12.4	10.3
Transportation occupations, except motor vehicles	212	2.4	6.7	3.0	184	2.0	11.4	4.5
Material moving equipment operators	1,011	4.8	12.9	6.3	1,093	4.6	14.4	11.1
Industrial truck and tractor operators	369	5.6	19.6	8.2	512	6.2	18.5	16.1
Handlers, equipment cleaners, helpers, and laborers [2]	4,147	16.8	15.1	8.6	5,021	19.3	16.4	15.2
Freight, stock, and material handlers	1,486	15.4	15.3	7.1	1,929	23.0	16.4	12.6
Laborers, except construction	1,024	19.4	16.0	8.6	1,334	20.2	17.8	13.5
Farming, forestry, and fishing [2]	3,700	16.0	7.5	8.2	3,566	19.0	3.9	19.2
Farm operators and managers	1,450	12.1	1.3	0.7	1,314	23.1	0.5	2.7
Other agricultural and related occupations	2,072	19.9	11.7	14.0	2,096	17.5	6.0	30.5
Farm workers	1,149	24.8	11.6	15.9	840	18.8	3.4	37.3
Forestry and logging occupations	126	1.4	12.8	2.1	108	3.5	5.2	6.9

- Represents or rounds to zero. NA Not available. [1] See footnote 2, table 614. [2] Includes other occupations, not shown separately. [3] Level of total employment below 50,000. [4] Includes clerks.

Source: U.S. Bureau of Labor Statistics, *Employment and Earnings*, monthly, January issues; and unpublished data.

No. 646. Civilian Employment in Occupations With the Largest Job Growth: 1994 to 2005

[Occupations are in descending order of absolute employment change 1994-2005 (moderate growth). Includes wage and salary jobs, self-employed, and unpaid family members. Estimates based on the Current Employment Statistics estimates and the Occupational Employment Statistics estimates. See source for methodological assumptions]

OCCUPATION	EMPLOYMENT (1,000)				PERCENT CHANGE 1994-2005		
	1994	2005 [1]			Low	Mod-erate	High
		Low	Mod-erate	High			
Total, all occupations [2]	127,014	140,261	144,708	150,212	10.4	13.9	18.3
Cashiers	3,005	3,493	3,567	3,645	16.2	18.7	21.3
Janitors and cleaners [3]	3,043	3,483	3,602	3,745	14.5	18.4	23.1
Salespersons, retail	3,842	4,244	4,374	4,506	10.5	13.8	17.3
Waiters and waitresses	1,847	2,361	2,326	2,291	27.8	25.9	24.0
Registered nurses	1,906	2,318	2,379	2,481	21.6	24.8	30.2
General managers and top executives	3,046	3,403	3,512	3,641	11.7	15.3	19.5
Systems analysts	483	893	928	972	84.9	92.1	101.3
Home health aides	420	832	848	863	98.3	102.0	105.7
Guards	867	1,248	1,282	1,322	44.0	47.9	52.5
Nursing aides, orderlies, and attendants	1,265	1,624	1,652	1,709	28.4	30.6	35.1
Teachers, secondary school	1,340	1,585	1,726	1,885	18.3	28.8	40.7
Marketing and sales worker supervisors	2,293	2,628	2,673	2,728	14.6	16.6	18.9
Teacher aides and educational assistants	932	1,211	1,296	1,393	29.9	39.0	49.5
Receptionists and information clerks	1,019	1,311	1,337	1,367	28.7	31.2	34.2
Truck drivers light and heavy	2,565	2,744	2,837	2,944	7.0	10.6	14.7
Secretaries, except legal and medical	2,842	2,983	3,109	3,258	5.0	9.4	14.6
Clerical supervisors and managers	1,340	1,550	1,600	1,658	15.7	19.5	23.8
Child care workers	757	1,009	1,005	1,006	33.2	32.8	33.0
Maintenance repairers, general utility	1,273	1,431	1,505	1,597	12.4	18.2	25.4
Teachers, elementary	1,419	1,509	1,639	1,787	6.3	15.5	25.9
Personal and home care aides	179	382	391	397	114.0	118.7	122.3
Teachers, special education	388	545	593	648	40.6	53.0	67.2
Licensed practical nurses	702	882	899	927	25.7	28.0	32.1
Food service and lodging managers	579	776	771	769	34.0	33.2	32.9
Food preparation workers	1,190	1,368	1,378	1,393	14.9	15.7	17.0
Social workers	557	712	744	778	27.9	33.5	39.8
Lawyers	656	824	839	856	25.6	27.9	30.6
Financial managers	768	919	950	988	19.7	23.6	28.5
Computer engineers	195	355	372	394	81.8	90.4	101.9
Hand packers and packagers	942	1,070	1,102	1,137	13.6	17.0	20.7
Correction officers	310	430	468	513	38.5	50.9	65.2
College and university faculty	823	893	972	1,062	8.6	18.2	29.1
Adjustment clerks	373	505	521	540	35.1	39.6	44.6
Teachers, preschool and kindergarten	462	588	602	620	27.2	30.3	34.2
Amusement and recreation attendants	267	398	406	414	49.2	52.0	55.2
Automotive mechanics	736	840	862	882	14.2	17.1	19.9
Residential counselors	165	284	290	295	72.7	76.5	79.5
General office clerks	2,946	2,959	3,071	3,204	0.5	4.3	8.8
Human services workers	168	284	293	303	68.8	74.5	80.0
Cooks, restaurant	704	839	827	815	19.3	17.5	15.8
Medical assistants	206	329	327	324	59.9	59.0	57.9
Accountants and auditors	962	1,056	1,083	1,119	9.7	12.6	16.3
Physicians	539	659	659	661	22.3	22.3	22.7
Marketing, advertising, and public relations managers	461	558	575	595	21.1	24.8	29.2
Police patrol officers	400	469	511	560	17.3	27.9	40.2
Counter and rental clerks	341	438	451	464	28.3	32.0	36.0
Cooks, short order and fast food	760	884	869	855	16.2	14.3	12.4
Instructors and coaches, sports and physical training	282	365	381	399	29.2	34.8	41.1
Engineering, mathematical, and natural science managers	337	415	432	453	23.3	28.1	34.5
Bill and account collectors	250	334	342	351	33.3	36.5	40.1
Securities and financial services sales workers	246	328	335	343	33.6	36.6	39.5
Instructors, adult (nonvocational) education	290	366	376	387	26.1	29.4	33.4
Hairdressers, hairstylists, and cosmetologists	595	675	677	680	13.4	13.8	14.3
Carpenters	992	1,044	1,074	1,122	5.2	8.3	13.2
Management analysts	231	308	312	319	33.4	35.4	38.2
Teachers and instructors, vocational ed. and training	299	356	381	409	19.0	27.2	36.6
Physical therapists	102	182	183	185	78.9	80.0	81.9
Dental assistants	190	271	269	266	43.1	41.9	40.0
Designers, except interior designers	238	308	314	322	29.3	31.9	35.1
Painters and paperhangers, construction and maintenance	439	497	509	529	13.3	16.0	20.6
Electrical and electronics engineers	349	402	417	439	15.3	19.7	25.9
Legal secretaries	281	341	350	358	21.3	24.3	27.3
Helpers, construction trades	513	549	581	630	6.9	13.2	22.8
Personnel, training, and labor relations specialists	307	360	374	391	17.2	21.9	27.4
Heat, air conditioning, and refrigeration mechanics [4]	233	286	299	319	22.9	28.5	36.8
Education administrators	393	431	459	491	9.8	16.9	25.0
Bus drivers, school	404	439	470	503	8.7	16.4	24.6
Computer programmers	537	577	601	631	7.4	12.0	17.6

[1] Based on low, moderate, or high trend assumptions. [2] Includes other occupations, not shown separately. [3] Includes maids and housekeepers. [4] Includes installers.

Source: U.S. Bureau of Labor Statistics, *Monthly Labor Review*, November 1995.

No. 647. Civilian Employment in the Fastest Growing and Fastest Declining Occupations: 1994 to 2005

[Occupations are in order of employment percent change 1994-2005 (moderate growth). Includes wage and salary jobs, self-employed, and unpaid family members. Estimates based on the Current Employment Statistics estimates and the Occupational Employment Statistics estimates. See source for methodological assumptions. Minus sign (-) indicates decrease]

OCCUPATION	EMPLOYMENT (1,000)				PERCENT CHANGE 1994-2005		
	1994	2005 [1]			Low	Mod-erate	High
		Low	Mod-erate	High			
Total, all occupations [2]	127,014	140,261	144,708	150,212	10.4	13.9	18.3
FASTEST GROWING							
Personal and home care aides	179	382	391	397	114.0	118.7	122.3
Home health aides	420	832	848	863	98.3	102.0	105.7
Systems analysts	483	893	928	972	84.9	92.1	101.3
Computer engineers	195	355	372	394	81.8	90.4	101.9
Physical and corrective therapy assistants and aides	78	141	142	143	82.3	83.1	84.5
Electronic pagination systems workers	18	32	33	34	77.2	82.8	88.2
Occupational therapy assistants and aides	16	28	29	29	80.0	82.1	86.5
Physical therapists	102	182	183	185	78.9	80.0	81.9
Residential counselors	165	284	290	295	72.7	76.5	79.5
Human services workers	168	284	293	303	68.8	74.5	80.0
Occupational therapists	54	91	93	95	68.7	72.2	77.3
Manicurists	38	63	64	64	68.7	69.5	69.9
Medical assistants	206	329	327	324	59.9	59.0	57.9
Paralegals	110	170	175	179	54.3	58.3	62.4
Medical records technicians	81	125	126	130	53.5	55.8	59.8
Teachers, special education	388	545	593	648	40.6	53.0	67.2
Amusement and recreation attendants	267	398	406	414	49.2	52.0	55.2
Correction officers	310	430	468	513	38.5	50.9	65.2
Operations research analysts	44	65	67	69	45.5	50.0	55.8
Guards	867	1,248	1,282	1,322	44.0	47.9	52.5
Speech-language pathologists and audiologists	85	120	125	130	40.3	46.0	52.8
Detectives, except public	55	77	79	80	41.7	44.3	47.2
Surgical technologists	46	64	65	68	39.3	42.5	48.6
Dental hygienists	127	182	180	178	43.3	42.1	40.1
Dental assistants	190	271	269	266	43.1	41.9	40.0
Adjustment clerks	373	505	521	540	35.1	39.6	44.6
Teacher aides and educational assistants	932	1,211	1,296	1,393	29.9	39.0	49.5
Data processing equipment repairers	75	100	104	108	33.3	38.2	44.1
Nursery and greenhouse managers	19	26	26	26	38.3	37.5	37.3
Securities and financial services sales workers	246	328	335	343	33.6	36.6	39.5
Bill and account collectors	250	334	342	351	33.3	36.5	40.1
Respiratory therapists	73	96	99	104	32.3	36.4	43.8
Pest controllers and assistants	56	75	76	78	33.2	35.6	38.6
Emergency medical technicians	138	178	187	197	29.0	35.6	42.6
FASTEST DECLINING							
Letterpress operators	14	4	4	4	-72.2	-71.3	-70.5
Typesetting and composing machine operators [3]	20	6	6	6	-72.0	-71.1	-70.2
Directory assistance operators	33	10	10	10	-71.5	-70.4	-69.4
Station installers and repairers, telephone	37	10	11	11	-71.5	-70.4	-69.4
Central office operators	48	14	14	15	-71.4	-70.3	-69.2
Billing, posting, and calculating machine operators	96	32	32	33	-67.2	-66.7	-66.1
Data entry keyers, composing	19	6	6	7	-67.7	-66.6	-65.5
Shoe sewing machine operators and tenders	14	4	5	7	-70.9	-63.6	-53.8
Roustabouts	28	13	13	16	-54.2	-55.0	-43.5
Peripheral EDP equipment operators	30	13	13	14	-56.9	-54.8	-52.3
Cooks, private household	9	5	5	4	-48.1	-49.2	-50.5
Motion picture projectionists	8	4	4	4	-46.4	-47.3	-48.0
Rail yard engineers, dinkey operators, and hostlers	6	3	4	4	-44.3	-40.4	-36.5
Central office and PBX installers and repairers	84	50	51	53	-41.0	-39.1	-37.1
Computer operators, except peripheral equipment	259	157	162	168	-39.6	-37.7	-35.3
Statement clerks	25	15	16	16	-39.8	-37.7	-35.5
Housekeepers and butlers	20	13	12	12	-36.1	-37.5	-39.1
Drilling/boring machine tool setters and set-up operators [4]	45	28	30	32	-38.1	-34.9	-29.6
Fitters, structural metal, precision	14	9	9	10	-38.3	-34.6	-29.4
Mining, quarrying, and tunneling occupations	18	11	12	13	-39.5	-33.9	-27.8
Typists and word processors	646	418	434	452	-35.2	-32.8	-30.0
Photoengraving and lithographic machine operators [3]	5	3	3	3	-33.7	-32.1	-30.5
Boiler operators and tenders, low pressure	18	12	12	13	-34.5	-31.9	-29.1
Railroad brake, signal, and switch operators	19	12	13	14	-35.8	-30.8	-26.1
Lathe and turning machine tool setters and set-up operators [4]	71	47	50	54	-34.2	-30.6	-24.9
Cement and gluing machine operators and tenders	36	24	25	27	-34.0	-30.1	-25.3
EKG technicians	16	11	11	12	-31.5	-29.7	-26.6
Machine tool cutting operators and tenders, metal and plastic	119	80	85	92	-32.8	-28.9	-22.8
Paste-up workers	22	16	16	17	-30.1	-27.8	-25.7
Shoe and leather workers and repairers, precision	24	16	17	19	-33.8	-27.6	-19.4
Bank tellers	559	391	407	423	-30.1	-27.3	-24.4

[1] Based on low, moderate, or high trend assumptions. [2] Includes other occupations, not shown separately. [3] Includes tenders. [4] Includes metal and plastic.

Source: U.S. Bureau of Labor Statistics, *Monthly Labor Review*, November 1995.

No. 648. Occupations of the Employed, by Selected Characteristics: 1996

[In thousands. Annual averages of monthly figures. For civilian noninstitutional population 25 to 64 years old. Based on Current Population Survey; see text, section 1, and Appendix III]

SEX, RACE, AND EDUCATIONAL ATTAINMENT	Total employed	Managerial/professional	Tech./sales/administrative	Service [1]	Precision production [2]	Operators/fabricators [3]	Farming, forestry, fishing
Male, total [4]	56,297	17,155	10,845	4,719	10,881	10,640	2,057
Less than a high school diploma	6,580	347	476	881	1,762	2,442	671
High school graduates, no college	18,036	1,963	2,932	1,782	5,179	5,359	800
Less than a bachelor's degree	14,755	3,576	3,774	1,479	3,255	2,300	372
College graduates	16,925	11,249	3,664	577	684	539	213
White	48,545	15,299	9,407	3,594	9,689	8,650	1,907
Less than a high school diploma	5,504	305	400	645	1,518	2,018	617
High school graduates, no college	15,444	1,792	2,535	1,307	4,684	4,393	734
Less than a bachelor's degree	12,662	3,195	3,241	1,166	2,898	1,812	351
College graduates	14,935	10,007	3,231	476	588	426	206
Black	5,357	996	896	883	835	1,644	103
Less than a high school diploma	610	24	50	176	172	345	43
High school graduates, no college	2,066	137	285	390	376	832	45
Less than a bachelor's degree	1,542	262	373	254	241	399	12
College graduates	940	572	188	64	46	68	2
Female, total [4]	48,064	16,210	19,135	7,382	1,076	3,751	530
Less than a high school diploma	3,953	230	789	1,574	203	1,035	121
High school graduates, no college	16,065	2,305	7,693	3,465	501	1,920	202
Less than a bachelor's degree	14,433	4,073	7,443	1,854	268	657	136
College graduates	13,614	9,602	3,211	487	103	140	72
White	40,063	14,060	16,236	5,582	857	2,836	509
Less than a high school diploma	3,069	186	670	1,163	154	802	115
High school graduates, no college	13,503	2,050	6,787	2,806	405	1,459	193
Less than a bachelor's degree	11,905	3,512	6,134	1,430	219	476	133
College graduates	11,585	8,311	2,644	382	80	101	69
Black	5,920	1,485	2,144	1,470	133	679	9
Less than a high school diploma	621	30	87	334	22	145	3
High school graduates, no college	2,064	203	706	719	63	369	5
Less than a bachelor's degree	2,027	448	1,041	358	37	142	-
College graduates	1,208	806	310	60	11	22	-

- Represents or rounds to zero. [1] Includes private household workers. [2] Includes craft and repair. [3] Includes laborers. [4] Includes other races, not shown separately.

Source: U.S. Bureau of Labor Statistics, unpublished data.

No. 649. Employment, by Industry: 1970 to 1996

[In thousands, except percent. See headnote, table 627. Data from 1985 to 1990, and also beginning 1995, not strictly comparable with other years due to changes in industrial classification]

INDUSTRY	1970	1980	1990 [1]	1995 [1]	1996			
					Total	Percent		
						Female	Black	Hispanic [2]
Total employed	78,678	99,303	118,793	124,900	126,708	46.2	10.7	9.2
Agriculture	3,463	3,364	3,223	3,440	3,443	25.3	2.9	17.7
Mining	516	979	724	627	569	13.2	4.6	6.6
Construction	4,818	6,215	7,764	7,668	7,943	10.0	6.6	10.4
Manufacturing	20,746	21,942	21,346	20,493	20,518	32.0	10.5	10.1
Transportation, communication, and other public utilities	5,320	6,525	8,168	8,709	8,817	28.6	14.6	8.2
Wholesale and retail trade	15,008	20,191	24,622	26,071	26,497	47.2	8.8	10.1
Wholesale trade	2,672	3,920	4,669	4,986	4,956	29.8	6.8	9.8
Retail trade	12,336	16,270	19,953	21,086	21,541	51.2	9.3	10.2
Finance, insurance, real estate	3,945	5,993	8,051	7,983	8,076	58.4	9.1	7.0
Services [3]	20,385	28,752	39,267	43,953	45,043	61.9	12.1	8.3
Business and repair services [3]	1,403	3,848	7,485	7,526	8,087	36.8	11.0	10.8
Advertising	147	191	277	267	276	55.1	4.1	6.1
Services to dwellings and buildings	(NA)	370	827	829	871	47.9	17.6	21.3
Personnel supply services	(NA)	235	710	853	866	58.4	19.6	11.1
Computer and data processing	(NA)	221	805	1,136	1,340	33.0	7.6	4.2
Detective/protective services	(NA)	213	378	506	540	22.7	22.6	8.2
Automobile services	600	952	1,457	1,459	1,630	14.5	9.3	15.3
Personal services [3]	4,276	3,839	4,733	4,375	4,358	68.7	14.3	16.0
Private households	1,782	1,257	1,036	971	936	89.1	17.8	25.2
Hotels and lodging places	979	1,149	1,818	1,495	1,504	54.4	15.5	17.0
Entertainment and recreation	717	1,047	1,526	2,238	2,386	44.0	8.7	9.8
Professional and related services [3]	12,904	19,853	25,351	29,661	30,085	69.2	12.3	6.5
Hospitals	2,843	4,036	4,700	4,961	5,041	76.1	16.5	6.7
Health services, except hospitals	1,628	3,345	4,673	5,967	6,158	79.2	13.8	6.4
Elementary, secondary schools	6,126	5,550	5,994	6,653	6,711	74.9	11.8	7.5
Colleges and universities	(⁴)	2,108	2,637	2,766	2,787	52.2	10.7	6.0
Social services	828	1,590	2,239	2,979	3,102	80.7	17.3	8.6
Legal services	429	776	1,215	1,335	1,303	56.0	4.9	4.9
Public administration [5]	4,476	5,342	5,627	5,957	5,802	44.4	16.5	6.6

NA Not available. [1] See footnote 2, table 619. [2] Persons of Hispanic origin may be of any race. [3] Includes industries not shown separately. [4] Included with elementary/secondary schools. [5] Includes workers involved in uniquely governmental activities, e.g., judicial and legislative.

Source: U.S. Bureau of Labor Statistics, *Employment and Earnings*, monthly, January issues; and unpublished data.

No. 650. Employment by Selected Industry, With Projections: 1983 to 2005

[Figures may differ from those in other tables since these data exclude establishments not elsewhere classified (SIC 99); in addition, agriculture services (SIC 074, 5, 8) are included in agriculture, not services. See source for details. Minus sign (-) indicates decrease]

INDUSTRY	1987 SIC [1] code	EMPLOYMENT (1,000)			ANNUAL GROWTH RATE	
		1983	1994	2005, proj. [2]	1983-1994	1994-2005, proj. [2]
Total	(X)	102,404	127,014	144,708	2.0	1.2
Nonfarm wage and salary	(X)	89,734	113,340	130,185	2.1	1.3
Goods-producing (excluding agriculture)	(X)	23,328	23,914	22,930	0.2	-0.4
Mining	10-14	952	601	439	-4.1	-2.8
Construction	15,16,17	3,946	5,010	5,500	2.2	0.9
Manufacturing	20-39	18,430	18,304	16,991	-0.1	-0.7
Durable manufacturing	24,25,32-39	10,707	10,431	9,290	-0.2	-1.0
Lumber and wood products	24	670	752	685	1.1	-0.9
Furniture and fixtures	25	448	502	515	1.0	0.2
Stone, clay and glass products	32	541	533	434	-0.1	-1.8
Primary metal industries	33	832	699	532	-1.6	-2.5
Blast furnaces/basic steel products	331	341	239	155	-3.2	-3.9
Fabricated metal products	34	1,368	1,387	1,181	0.1	-1.5
Industrial machinery and equipment	35	2,052	1,985	1,769	-0.3	-1.0
Computer equipment	357	474	351	263	-2.7	-2.8
Electronic and other electric equipment [3]	36	1,704	1,571	1,408	-0.7	-1.0
Communications equipment	366	279	244	210	-1.2	-1.3
Electronic components	367	563	544	553	-0.3	0.1
Transportation equipment	37	1,731	1,749	1,567	0.1	-1.0
Motor vehicles and equipment	371	754	899	775	1.6	-1.3
Instruments and related products [3]	38	990	863	798	-1.2	-0.7
Measuring/controlling devices	382	300	284	248	-0.5	-1.2
Medical instruments and supplies	384	198	265	306	2.7	1.3
Miscellaneous manufacturing industries	39	370	391	404	0.5	0.3
Nondurable manufacturing	20-23,26-31	7,723	7,673	7,700	0.2	-0.2
Food and kindred products	20	1,612	1,680	1,696	0.4	0.1
Tobacco manufactures	21	68	42	26	-4.2	-4.2
Textile mill products	22	742	673	568	-0.9	-1.5
Apparel and other textile products	23	1,163	969	772	-1.6	-2.1
Paper and allied products	26	654	691	708	0.5	0.2
Printing and publishing	27	1,298	1,542	1,627	1.6	0.5
Chemicals and allied products	28	1,043	1,061	1,067	0.2	0.1
Petroleum and coal products	29	196	149	140	-2.4	-0.5
Rubber/misc. plastics products	30	743	952	1,030	2.3	0.7
Leather and leather products	31	205	114	65	-5.2	-4.9
Service producing	(X)	66,407	89,425	107,256	2.7	1.7
Transportation, communications, utilities	40-42,44-49	4,958	6,006	6,431	1.8	0.6
Transportation	40-42,44-47	2,748	3,775	4,251	2.9	1.1
Communications	48	1,324	1,305	1,235	-0.1	-0.5
Electric, gas, and sanitary services	49	887	927	945	0.4	0.2
Wholesale trade	50,51	5,283	6,140	6,559	1.4	0.6
Retail trade	52-59	15,587	20,438	23,094	2.5	1.1
Eating and drinking places	58	5,038	7,069	8,089	3.1	1.2
Finance, insurance, and real estate	60-67	5,466	6,933	7,373	2.2	0.6
Services	70-87,89	19,242	30,792	42,810	4.4	3.0
Hotels and other lodging places	70	1,172	1,618	1,899	3.0	1.5
Personal services	72	869	1,139	1,374	2.5	1.7
Business services [3]	73	2,948	6,239	10,032	7.1	4.4
Advertising	731	171	224	250	2.5	1.0
Services to buildings	734	559	855	1,350	3.9	4.2
Personnel supply services	736	619	2,254	3,564	12.5	4.3
Computer and data processing services	737	416	950	1,611	7.8	4.9
Auto repair, services, and garages	75	619	971	1,345	4.2	3.0
Miscellaneous repair shops	76	287	334	400	1.4	1.7
Motion pictures	78	268	471	591	5.3	2.1
Video tape rental	784	54	138	165	8.9	1.7
Amusement and recreation services	79	853	1,344	1,844	4.2	2.9
Health services	80	5,986	9,001	12,075	3.8	2.7
Offices of health practitioners	801,2,3,4	1,503	2,546	3,525	4.9	3.0
Nursing and personal care facilities	805	1,106	1,649	2,400	3.7	3.5
Hospitals, private	806	3,037	3,774	4,250	2.0	1.1
Health services, n.e.c. [4]	807,8,9	341	1,032	1,900	10.6	5.7
Legal services	81	602	927	1,270	4.0	2.9
Educational services	82	1,225	1,822	2,400	3.7	2.5
Social services	83	1,188	2,181	3,639	5.7	4.8
Museums, botanical, zoological gardens	84	43	79	112	5.8	3.2
Membership organizations	86	1,510	2,059	2,336	2.9	1.2
Engineering, management, and services	87,89	1,673	2,607	3,494	4.1	2.7
Government	(X)	15,870	19,117	20,990	1.7	0.9
Federal government	(X)	2,774	2,870	2,635	0.3	-0.8
State and local government	(X)	13,096	16,247	18,355	2.0	1.1
Agriculture	01,02,07,08,09	3,508	3,623	3,399	0.3	-0.6
Private households	88	1,247	966	800	-2.3	-1.7
Nonagriculture self-employed and unpaid family	(X)	7,914	9,085	10,324	1.3	1.2

X Not applicable. [1] 1987 Standard Industrial Classification; see text, section 13. [2] Based on assumptions of moderate growth; see source. [3] Includes other industries, not shown separately. [4] N.e.c. means not elsewhere classified.

Source: U.S. Bureau of Labor Statistics, *Monthly Labor Review*, November 1995.

No. 651. High Technology Industries—Summary: 1995

[For workers on private industry payrolls and excludes the self-employed. Based on surveys of the Occupational Employment Statistics Program and subject to sampling error; for details see source]

INDUSTRY	1987 SIC [1] code	Establishments (1,000)	EMPLOYMENT		Average annual pay (dol.)
			Total (1,000)	Percent distribution	
All high technology industries [2]	(X)	**402.8**	**9,800**	**100.0**	**$45,186**
Level I industries [3]	(X)	365.8	8,474	86.5	46,754
Crude petroleum and natural gas operations	131	8.8	151	1.5	60,971
Cigarettes	211	(Z)	28	0.3	62,945
Industrial inorganic chemicals	281	1.6	119	1.2	50,295
Plastics materials and synthetics	282	1.1	157	1.6	49,527
Drugs	283	1.9	259	2.6	53,781
Soap, cleaners, and toilet goods	284	2.6	152	1.5	43,109
Paints and allied products	285	1.5	56	0.6	39,047
Industrial organic chemicals	286	1.1	145	1.5	57,487
Agricultural chemicals	287	1.2	53	0.5	45,201
Miscellaneous chemical products	289	2.7	92	0.9	43,629
Petroleum refining	291	0.7	104	1.1	58,968
Miscellaneous petroleum and coal products	299	0.5	14	0.1	41,270
Nonferrous rolling and drawing	335	1.3	167	1.7	38,294
Computer and office equipment	357	2.7	350	3.6	53,907
Electrical industrial apparatus	362	2.0	157	1.6	33,212
Communications equipment	366	2.4	264	2.7	45,991
Electronic components and accessories	367	6.8	581	5.9	40,209
Motor vehicles and equipment	371	6.3	968	9.9	46,663
Aircraft and parts	372	2.8	449	4.6	48,593
Guided missiles, space vehicles, parts	376	0.3	96	1.0	55,371
Search and navigation equipment	381	0.8	159	1.6	52,142
Measuring and controlling devices	382	5.5	286	2.9	41,790
Medical instruments and supplies	384	4.6	264	2.7	39,315
Photographic equipment and supplies	386	0.9	85	0.9	51,666
Computer and data-processing services	737	83.6	1,085	11.1	50,996
Engineering and architectural services	871	70.9	811	8.3	44,197
Research and testing services	873	25.8	567	5.8	41,490
Management and public relations	874	115.1	806	8.2	45,690
Services, n.e.c. [4]	899	10.2	45	0.5	51,574
Level II industries [5]	(X)	37.0	1,327	13.5	35,184
Miscellaneous textile goods	229	0.9	53	0.5	30,183
Pulp mills	261	0.1	13	0.1	49,219
Miscellaneous converted paper products	267	3.2	244	2.5	34,553
Ordinance and accessories, n.e.c. [4]	348	0.4	51	0.5	37,623
Engines and turbines	351	0.5	88	0.9	45,868
General industry machinery	356	4.8	251	2.6	36,613
Industrial machines, n.e.c. [4]	359	22.9	335	3.4	32,006
Household audio and video equipment	365	1.2	83	0.8	36,718
Miscellaneous electrical equipment and supplies	369	1.8	156	1.6	35,666
Miscellaneous transportation equipment	379	1.2	53	0.5	29,090

X Not applicable. Z Fewer than 50. [1] 1987 Standard Industrial Classification; see text, section 13. [2] Those industries whose proportion of R&D employment is at least equal to the average proportion of all industries surveyed. [3] Industries whose proportion of R&D employment is at least 50 percent higher than the average of all industries surveyed. [4] N.e.c. means not elsewhere classified. [5] Industries whose proportion of R&D employment is at least equal to the average of all industries surveyed, but less than 50 percent higher than the average.

Source: U.S. Bureau of Labor Statistics, *Employment and Wages, Annual Averages 1995*, BLS Bulletin 2483.

No. 652. Unemployed Workers—Summary: 1980 to 1996

[In thousands, except as indicated. For civilian noninstitutional population 16 years old and over. Annual averages of monthly figures. For data on unemployment insurance, see table 595]

AGE, SEX, RACE, HISPANIC ORIGIN	1980	1985	1990 [1]	1992	1993	1994 [1]	1995	1996
UNEMPLOYED								
Total [2]	7,637	8,312	7,047	9,613	8,940	7,996	7,404	7,236
16 to 19 years old	1,669	1,468	1,212	1,427	1,365	1,320	1,346	1,306
20 to 24 years old	1,835	1,738	1,299	1,649	1,514	1,373	1,244	1,239
25 to 44 years old	2,964	3,681	3,323	4,678	4,291	3,694	3,390	3,262
45 to 64 years old	1,075	1,331	1,109	1,727	1,662	1,456	1,269	1,289
65 years and over	94	93	105	132	108	153	153	139
Male	4,267	4,521	3,906	5,523	5,055	4,367	3,983	3,880
16 to 19 years old	913	806	667	806	768	740	744	733
20 to 24 years old	1,076	944	715	951	865	768	673	675
25 to 44 years old	1,619	1,950	1,803	2,647	2,387	1,968	1,776	1,689
45 to 64 years old	600	766	662	1,053	972	803	697	707
65 years and over	58	55	59	67	64	88	94	76
Female	3,370	3,791	3,140	4,090	3,885	3,629	3,421	3,356
16 to 19 years old	755	661	544	621	597	580	602	573
20 to 24 years old	760	794	584	698	648	605	571	564
25 to 44 years old	1,345	1,732	1,519	2,031	1,905	1,726	1,615	1,574
45 to 64 years old	473	566	447	673	690	653	574	582
65 years and over	36	39	46	66	45	66	60	63
White [3]	5,884	6,191	5,186	7,169	6,655	5,892	5,459	5,300
16 to 19 years old	1,291	1,074	903	1,037	992	960	952	939
20 to 24 years old	1,364	1,235	899	1,156	1,057	952	866	854
Black [3]	1,553	1,864	1,565	2,011	1,844	1,666	1,538	1,592
16 to 19 years old	343	357	268	324	313	300	325	310
20 to 24 years old	426	455	349	421	387	351	311	327
Hispanic [3] [4]	620	811	876	1,311	1,248	1,187	1,140	1,132
16 to 19 years old	145	141	161	219	201	198	205	199
20 to 24 years old	138	171	167	240	237	220	209	217
Full-time workers	6,269	6,793	5,677	7,923	7,305	6,513	5,909	5,803
Part-time workers	1,369	1,519	1,369	1,690	1,635	1,483	1,495	1,433
UNEMPLOYMENT RATE (percent) [5]								
Total [2]	7.1	7.2	5.6	7.5	6.9	6.1	5.6	5.4
16 to 19 years old	17.8	18.6	15.5	20.1	19.0	17.6	17.3	16.7
20 to 24 years old	11.5	11.1	8.8	11.4	10.5	9.7	9.1	9.3
25 to 44 years old	6.0	6.2	4.9	6.8	6.2	5.3	4.8	4.6
45 to 64 years old	3.7	4.5	3.5	5.1	4.8	4.0	3.4	3.3
65 years and over	3.1	3.2	3.0	3.8	3.2	4.0	4.0	3.6
Male	6.9	7.0	5.7	7.9	7.2	6.2	5.6	5.4
16 to 19 years old	18.3	19.5	16.3	21.5	20.4	19.0	18.4	18.1
20 to 24 years old	12.5	11.4	9.1	12.2	11.3	10.2	9.2	9.5
25 to 44 years old	5.6	5.9	4.8	7.0	6.3	5.2	4.7	4.4
45 to 64 years old	3.5	4.5	3.7	5.7	5.1	4.1	3.5	3.4
65 years and over	3.1	3.1	3.0	3.3	3.2	4.0	4.3	3.4
Female	7.4	7.4	5.5	7.0	6.6	6.0	5.6	5.4
16 to 19 years old	17.2	17.6	14.7	18.6	17.5	16.2	16.1	15.2
20 to 24 years old	10.4	10.7	8.5	10.3	9.7	9.2	9.0	9.0
25 to 44 years old	6.4	6.6	4.9	6.5	6.1	5.4	5.0	4.9
45 to 64 years old	4.0	4.6	3.2	4.4	4.4	3.9	3.3	3.3
65 years and over	3.1	3.3	3.1	4.5	3.1	4.0	3.7	4.0
White [3]	6.3	6.2	4.8	6.6	6.1	5.3	4.9	4.7
16 to 19 years old	15.5	15.7	13.5	17.2	16.2	15.1	14.5	14.2
20 to 24 years old	9.9	9.2	7.3	9.5	8.8	8.1	7.7	7.8
Black [3]	14.3	15.1	11.4	14.2	13.0	11.5	10.4	10.5
16 to 19 years old	38.5	40.2	30.9	39.7	38.8	35.2	35.7	33.6
20 to 24 years old	23.6	24.5	19.9	23.8	21.9	19.5	17.7	18.8
Hispanic [3] [4]	10.1	10.5	8.2	11.6	10.8	9.9	9.3	8.9
16 to 19 years old	22.5	24.3	19.5	27.5	26.1	24.5	24.1	23.6
20 to 24 years old	12.1	12.6	9.1	13.2	13.1	11.8	11.5	11.8
Experienced workers [6]	6.9	6.8	5.3	7.2	6.6	5.9	5.4	5.2
Women maintaining families [2]	9.2	10.4	8.3	10.0	9.7	8.9	8.0	8.2
White	7.3	8.1	6.3	7.9	7.8	(NA)	(NA)	(NA)
Black	14.0	16.4	13.2	14.8	13.9	(NA)	(NA)	(NA)
Married men, wife present [2]	4.2	4.3	3.4	5.1	4.4	3.7	3.3	3.0
White	3.9	4.0	3.1	4.7	4.1	3.4	3.0	2.8
Black	7.4	8.0	6.2	8.3	7.2	6.0	5.0	4.9
Percent without work for—								
Fewer than 5 weeks	43.2	42.1	46.3	35.1	36.5	34.1	36.5	36.4
5 to 10 weeks	23.4	22.2	23.5	20.9	20.6	20.6	22.0	21.8
11 to 14 weeks	9.0	8.0	8.5	8.5	8.3	9.5	9.6	9.8
15 to 26 weeks	13.8	12.3	11.7	15.1	14.5	15.5	14.6	14.6
27 weeks and over	10.7	15.4	10.0	20.3	20.1	20.3	17.3	17.4
Unemployment duration, average (weeks)	11.9	15.6	12.0	17.7	18.0	18.8	16.6	16.7

NA Not available. [1] See footnote 2, table 619. [2] Includes other races, not shown separately. [3] Includes other ages, not shown separately. [4] Persons of Hispanic origin may be of any race. [5] Unemployed as percent of civilian labor force in specified group. [6] Wage and salary workers.

Source: U.S. Bureau of Labor Statistics, *Employment and Earnings*, monthly, January issues; and unpublished data.

No. 653. Unemployed Persons, by Sex and Reason: 1970 to 1996

[In thousands. For civilian noninstitutional population 16 years old and over. Annual averages of monthly figures. Based on Current Population Survey; see text, section 1, and Appendix III]

SEX AND REASON	1970	1980	1985	1988	1989	1990 [1]	1991	1992	1993	1994 [1]	1995	1996
Male, total	**2,238**	**4,267**	**4,521**	**3,655**	**3,525**	**3,906**	**4,946**	**5,523**	**5,055**	**4,367**	**3,983**	**3,880**
Job losers [2]	1,199	2,649	2,749	2,078	1,975	2,257	3,172	3,593	3,150	2,416	2,190	2,158
Job leavers	282	438	409	503	495	528	507	495	507	408	407	372
Reentrants	533	776	876	697	726	806	891	978	939	1,265	1,113	1,076
New entrants	224	405	487	376	328	315	375	457	459	278	273	273
Female, total	**1,855**	**3,370**	**3,791**	**3,046**	**3,003**	**3,140**	**3,683**	**4,090**	**3,885**	**3,629**	**3,421**	**3,356**
Job losers [2]	614	1,297	1,390	1,014	1,008	1,130	1,522	1,796	1,699	1,399	1,286	1,212
Job leavers	267	453	468	480	529	513	497	507	469	383	417	402
Reentrants	696	1,152	1,380	1,112	1,117	1,124	1,247	1,307	1,259	1,521	1,412	1,435
New entrants	279	468	552	440	349	373	416	480	459	326	306	307

[1] See footnote 2, table 619. [2] Beginning 1994, persons who completed temporary jobs are identified separately and are included as job losers.

Source: U.S. Bureau of Labor Statistics, *Employment and Earnings*, monthly, January issues; Bulletin 2307; and unpublished data.

No. 654. Unemployment Rates, by Industry, 1975 to 1996, and by Sex, 1980 and 1996

[In percent. For civilian noninstitutional population 16 years old and over. Annual averages of monthly figures. Rate represents unemployment as a percent of labor force in each specified group. Data for 1985-90 not strictly comparable with other years due to changes in industrial classification]

INDUSTRY	1975	1980	1985	1990 [1]	1995 [1]	1996 [1]	MALE		FEMALE	
							1980	1996 [1]	1980	1995 [1]
All unemployed [2]	**8.5**	**7.1**	**7.2**	**5.6**	**5.6**	**5.4**	**6.9**	**5.4**	**7.4**	**5.4**
Industry: [3]										
Agriculture	10.4	11.0	13.2	9.8	11.1	10.2	9.7	10.2	15.1	10.3
Mining	4.1	6.4	9.5	4.8	5.2	5.1	6.7	5.2	4.5	4.2
Construction	18.0	14.1	13.1	11.1	11.5	10.1	14.6	10.5	8.9	6.3
Manufacturing	10.9	8.5	7.7	5.8	4.9	4.8	7.4	4.2	10.8	6.2
Transportation and public utilities	5.6	4.9	5.1	3.9	4.5	4.1	5.1	4.1	4.4	4.2
Wholesale and retail trade	8.7	7.4	7.6	6.4	6.5	6.4	6.6	5.7	8.3	7.1
Finance, insurance, and real estate	4.9	3.4	3.5	3.0	3.3	2.7	3.2	2.9	3.5	2.6
Services	7.1	5.9	6.2	5.0	5.4	5.4	6.3	5.6	5.8	5.2
Government	4.1	4.1	3.9	2.7	2.9	2.9	3.9	2.9	4.3	2.9

[1] See footnote 2, table 619. [2] Includes the self-employed, unpaid family workers, and persons with no previous work experience, not shown separately. [3] Covers unemployed wage and salary workers.

Source: U.S. Bureau of Labor Statistics, *Employment and Earnings*, monthly, January issues.

No. 655. Unemployment by Occupation, 1990 to 1996, and by Sex, 1996

[For civilian noninstitutional population 16 years old and over. Annual averages of monthly data. Rate represents unemployment as a percent of the labor force for each specified group. Based on Current Population Survey; see text, section 1, and Appendix III. See also headnote, table 636]

OCCUPATION	NUMBER (1,000)			UNEMPLOYMENT RATE				
	1990 [1]	1995 [1]	1996	1990 [1]	1995 [1]	1996		
						Total	Male	Female
Total [2]	**7,047**	**7,404**	**7,236**	**5.6**	**5.6**	**5.4**	**5.4**	**5.4**
Managerial and professional specialty	666	880	869	2.1	2.4	2.3	2.2	2.4
Executive, administrative, and managerial	350	420	431	2.3	2.4	2.4	2.3	2.5
Professional specialty	316	460	438	2.0	2.5	2.3	2.2	2.3
Technical sales, and administrative support	1,641	1,744	1,766	4.3	4.5	4.5	3.8	4.8
Technicians and related support	116	113	114	2.9	2.8	2.8	2.7	2.9
Sales occupations	720	795	843	4.8	5.0	5.2	3.7	6.7
Administrative support, including clerical	804	836	810	4.1	4.3	4.2	4.6	4.1
Service occupations	1,139	1,378	1,334	6.6	7.5	7.2	7.3	7.2
Private household	47	99	79	5.6	10.7	9.0	14.1	8.7
Protective service	74	86	84	3.6	3.7	3.7	3.4	5.2
Service except private household and protective	1,018	1,193	1,170	7.1	7.9	7.6	8.5	7.1
Precision production, craft, and repair	861	860	795	5.9	6.0	5.5	5.5	5.3
Mechanics and repairers	175	182	174	3.8	4.0	3.7	3.7	3.1
Construction trades	483	501	456	8.5	9.0	8.2	8.2	8.5
Other precision production, craft, and repair	202	177	165	4.7	4.2	4.0	3.6	5.3
Operators, fabricators, and laborers	1,714	1,618	1,570	8.7	8.2	7.9	7.5	9.3
Machine operators, assemblers, inspectors	727	629	654	8.1	7.4	7.7	6.5	9.5
Transportation and material moving occupations	329	329	292	6.3	6.0	5.2	5.2	5.7
Handlers, equipment cleaners, helpers, laborers	657	660	625	11.6	11.7	11.1	11.2	10.6
Construction laborers	177	179	158	18.1	18.7	16.3	16.3	16.1
Farming, forestry, and fishing	237	311	293	6.4	7.9	7.6	7.4	8.5

[1] See footnote 2, table 619. [2] Includes persons with no previous work experience and those whose last job was in the Armed Forces.

Source: U.S. Bureau of Labor Statistics, *Employment and Earnings*, monthly, January issues.

No. 656. Unemployment Rates, by Educational Attainment, Sex, and Race: 1970 to 1991

[In percent. As of March. For the civilian noninstitutional population 25 to 64 years of age. Due to a change in the method of reporting educational attainment, 1992 are not comparable with data for earlier years. See table 657 for data beginning 1992. Based on the Current Population Survey; see text, section 1, and Appendix III]

ITEM	1970	1975	1980	1984	1985	1986	1987	1988	1989	1990	1991
Total	3.3	6.9	5.0	6.6	6.1	6.1	5.7	4.7	4.4	4.5	6.1
Less than 4 years of high school [1]	4.6	10.7	8.4	12.1	11.4	11.6	11.1	9.4	8.9	9.6	12.3
4 years of high school, only	2.9	6.9	5.1	7.2	6.9	6.9	6.3	5.4	4.8	4.9	6.7
College: 1-3 years	2.9	5.5	4.3	5.3	4.7	4.7	4.5	3.7	3.4	3.7	5.0
4 years or more	1.3	2.5	1.9	2.7	2.4	2.3	2.3	1.7	2.2	1.9	2.9
Male: Total	2.9	6.7	4.9	6.9	6.1	6.2	6.0	5.1	4.7	4.8	6.8
Less than 4 years of high school [1]	4.0	10.5	8.2	12.3	11.2	11.7	11.2	10.0	9.4	9.6	13.4
4 years of high school, only	2.4	6.7	5.3	8.1	7.2	7.4	6.7	6.2	5.4	5.3	7.7
College: 1-3 years	2.7	5.1	4.4	5.2	4.5	4.7	5.0	3.9	3.2	3.9	5.2
4 years or more	1.1	2.2	1.7	2.7	2.4	2.3	2.5	1.6	2.3	2.1	3.2
Female: Total	4.0	7.4	5.0	6.1	6.0	5.8	5.2	4.2	4.0	4.2	5.2
Less than 4 years of high school [1]	5.7	10.5	8.9	11.7	11.7	11.4	10.9	8.5	8.1	9.5	10.7
4 years of high school, only	3.6	7.1	5.0	6.3	6.5	6.3	5.8	4.6	4.2	4.6	5.5
College: 1-3 years	3.1	6.3	4.1	5.3	4.8	4.8	4.0	3.4	3.7	3.5	4.8
4 years or more	1.9	3.4	2.2	2.7	2.5	2.4	2.1	1.9	2.0	1.7	2.5
White: Total	3.1	6.5	4.4	5.7	5.3	5.5	5.0	4.0	3.8	4.0	5.6
Less than 4 years of high school [1]	4.5	10.1	7.8	10.9	10.6	10.9	10.2	8.3	7.7	8.3	11.6
4 years of high school, only	2.7	6.5	4.6	6.4	6.1	6.2	5.5	4.6	4.2	4.4	6.2
College: 1-3 years	2.8	5.1	3.9	4.6	3.9	4.2	4.1	3.2	3.0	3.3	4.6
4 years or more	1.3	2.4	1.8	2.4	2.1	2.2	2.2	1.5	2.0	1.8	2.7
Black: Total [2]	4.7	10.9	9.6	13.3	12.0	10.7	10.6	10.0	9.2	8.6	10.1
Less than 4 years of high school [1]	5.2	13.5	11.7	17.4	15.3	15.3	14.8	14.6	14.6	15.9	15.9
4 years of high school, only	5.2	10.7	9.5	14.5	13.0	11.7	11.7	11.2	9.2	8.6	10.3
College: 1-3 years	3.5	9.8	9.0	9.7	10.6	8.7	7.6	7.4	6.9	6.5	8.0
4 years or more	0.9	3.9	4.0	6.2	5.4	3.2	4.2	3.3	4.7	1.9	5.2

[1] Includes persons reporting no school years completed. [2] For 1970 and 1975, data refer to Black and other workers.

Source: U.S. Bureau of Labor Statistics, Bulletin 2307; and unpublished data.

No. 657. Unemployed and Unemployment Rates, by Educational Attainment, Sex, Race, and Hispanic Origin: 1992 to 1996

[As of March. For the civilian noninstitutional population 25 to 64 years old. See table 623 for civilian labor force and participation rate data. Based on Current Population Survey; see text, section 1, and Appendix III]

YEAR, SEX, AND RACE	UNEMPLOYED (1,000)					UNEMPLOYMENT RATE [1]				
	Total	Less than high school diploma	High school gradu-ates, no degree	Less than a bachelor's degree	College graduate	Total	Less than high school diploma	High school graduate, no degree	Less than a bachelor's degree	College graduate
Total: [2]										
1992	6,846	1,693	2,851	1,521	782	6.7	13.5	7.7	5.9	2.9
1994 [3]	6,126	1,463	2,388	1,453	823	5.8	12.6	6.7	5.0	2.9
1995	5,065	1,150	1,833	1,329	753	4.8	10.0	5.2	4.5	2.5
1996	5,147	1,285	1,947	1,239	675	4.8	10.9	5.5	4.1	2.2
Male:										
1992	4,207	1,151	1,709	854	493	7.5	14.8	8.8	6.4	3.2
1994 [3]	3,498	920	1,333	779	468	6.2	12.8	7.2	5.3	2.9
1995	2,925	765	1,064	656	440	5.1	10.9	5.7	4.4	2.6
1996	3,088	815	1,205	682	385	5.3	11.0	6.4	4.5	2.3
Female:										
1992	2,639	542	1,142	666	289	5.7	11.4	6.5	5.3	2.5
1994 [3]	2,628	543	1,055	674	357	5.4	12.4	6.2	4.7	2.9
1995	2,140	385	770	673	313	4.4	8.6	4.6	4.5	2.4
1996	2,059	471	742	556	289	4.1	10.7	4.4	3.8	2.1
White:										
1992	5,247	1,285	2,146	1,176	641	6.0	12.9	6.8	5.3	2.7
1993	5,129	1,175	2,025	1,166	763	5.8	12.4	6.5	5.0	3.1
1994 [3]	4,598	1,092	1,738	1,109	659	5.2	11.7	5.8	4.5	2.6
1996	3,865	969	1,386	934	575	4.2	10.2	4.6	3.7	2.1
Black:										
1992	1,353	361	619	291	81	12.4	17.2	14.1	10.7	4.8
1994 [3]	1,202	286	546	277	94	10.6	17.4	12.2	8.3	4.9
1995	905	225	377	218	86	7.7	13.7	8.4	6.3	4.1
1996	1,061	258	479	255	69	8.9	15.3	10.8	6.9	3.3
Hispanic: [4]										
1992	757	408	224	88	36	9.8	13.6	9.6	5.9	4.2
1994 [3]	871	465	215	139	52	9.7	13.4	8.3	7.2	5.2
1995	746	393	211	102	40	8.0	10.9	8.1	6.2	3.7
1996	826	462	202	118	44	8.5	12.3	7.3	5.7	4.0

[1] Percent unemployed of the civilian labor force. [2] Includes other races, not shown separately. [3] See footnote 3, table 631. [4] Persons of Hispanic origin may be of any race.

Source: U.S. Bureau of Labor Statistics, unpublished data.

No. 658. Total Unemployed and Insured Unemployed—States: 1980 to 1995

[For civilian noninstitutional population 16 years old and over. Annual averages of monthly figures. Total unemployment estimates based on the Current Population Survey (CPS); see text, section 1, and Appendix III. U.S. totals derived by independent population controls; therefore State data may not add to U.S. totals]

STATE	TOTAL UNEMPLOYED								INSURED UNEMPLOYED [3]			
	Number (1,000)				Percent [1]				Number (1,000)		Percent [4]	
	1980	1985	1990 [2]	1995 [2]	1980	1985	1990 [2]	1995 [2]	1994	1995	1994	1995
United States	7,637	8,312	7,047	7,236	7.1	7.2	5.6	5.4	[5]2,670	[5]2,575	[5]2.5	[5]2.3
Alabama	147	160	130	107	8.8	8.9	6.9	5.1	31.0	30.7	1.9	1.9
Alaska	18	24	19	25	9.7	9.7	7.0	7.8	13.6	12.9	6.0	5.5
Arizona	83	96	99	124	6.7	6.5	5.5	5.5	27.4	25.2	1.8	1.5
Arkansas	76	91	78	67	7.6	8.7	7.0	5.4	24.9	26.5	2.6	2.7
California	790	934	874	1,126	6.8	7.2	5.8	7.2	485.9	450.2	4.0	3.7
Colorado	88	101	89	89	5.9	5.9	5.0	4.2	23.4	21.9	1.5	1.3
Connecticut	94	83	95	99	5.9	4.9	5.2	5.7	47.8	44.4	3.2	3.0
Delaware	22	17	19	20	7.7	5.3	5.2	5.2	6.5	6.4	1.9	1.9
District of Columbia	24	27	22	23	7.3	8.4	6.6	8.5	8.9	8.8	2.1	2.1
Florida	251	320	390	352	5.9	6.0	6.0	5.1	99.5	90.7	1.8	1.6
Georgia	163	188	182	173	6.4	6.5	5.5	4.6	40.0	39.1	1.3	1.3
Hawaii	21	27	16	38	4.9	5.6	2.9	6.4	14.8	15.3	2.9	3.0
Idaho	34	37	29	32	7.9	7.9	5.9	5.2	13.2	14.5	3.1	3.2
Illinois	459	513	369	322	8.3	9.0	6.2	5.3	119.4	119.8	2.3	2.3
Indiana	252	215	149	127	9.6	7.9	5.3	4.1	30.0	30.9	1.2	1.2
Iowa	82	112	62	60	5.8	8.0	4.3	3.8	18.6	18.8	1.5	1.5
Kansas	53	62	57	60	4.5	5.0	4.5	4.5	18.6	16.5	1.7	1.5
Kentucky	133	161	104	105	8.0	9.5	5.9	5.6	31.6	29.0	2.2	1.9
Louisiana	121	229	117	135	6.7	11.5	6.3	6.7	29.4	27.3	1.9	1.7
Maine	39	30	33	34	7.8	5.4	5.2	5.1	15.5	15.1	3.1	3.0
Maryland	140	104	122	136	6.5	4.6	4.7	4.9	45.8	44.1	2.4	2.2
Massachusetts	162	120	195	137	5.6	3.9	6.0	4.3	80.1	73.4	2.9	2.6
Michigan	534	433	350	234	12.4	9.9	7.6	4.9	92.0	88.3	2.4	2.2
Minnesota	125	133	117	104	5.9	6.0	4.9	4.0	37.1	35.6	1.7	1.6
Mississippi	79	116	90	77	7.5	10.3	7.6	6.1	19.1	21.5	2.0	2.1
Missouri	167	158	151	132	7.2	6.4	5.8	4.6	47.5	42.9	2.1	1.8
Montana	23	31	24	24	6.1	7.7	6.0	5.3	9.7	9.5	3.2	3.0
Nebraska	31	44	18	27	4.1	5.5	2.2	2.9	7.2	7.1	1.0	0.9
Nevada	27	41	33	46	6.2	8.0	4.9	5.4	16.0	16.5	2.4	2.3
New Hampshire	22	21	36	26	4.7	3.9	5.7	4.2	6.8	5.7	1.4	1.1
New Jersey	260	217	206	255	7.2	5.7	5.1	6.2	106.8	106.8	3.2	3.2
New Mexico	42	57	46	64	7.5	8.8	6.5	8.1	11.5	11.1	2.0	1.8
New York	597	544	467	540	7.5	6.5	5.3	6.2	227.6	227.7	3.0	3.0
North Carolina	187	168	144	165	6.6	5.4	4.2	4.3	44.3	47.6	1.4	1.5
North Dakota	15	20	13	11	5.0	5.9	4.0	3.1	3.9	4.0	1.5	1.5
Ohio	426	455	310	278	8.4	8.9	5.7	4.9	87.3	80.8	1.8	1.7
Oklahoma	66	112	86	64	4.8	7.1	5.7	4.1	16.7	15.5	1.4	1.3
Oregon	107	116	83	102	8.3	8.8	5.6	5.9	45.4	47.2	3.6	3.6
Pennsylvania	425	443	315	313	7.8	8.0	5.4	5.3	169.4	165.9	3.5	3.4
Rhode Island	34	25	35	25	7.2	4.9	6.8	5.1	18.9	19.1	4.6	4.6
South Carolina	96	107	83	111	6.9	6.8	4.8	6.0	29.3	27.6	2.0	1.8
South Dakota	16	18	13	13	4.9	5.1	3.9	3.2	2.1	2.3	0.7	0.7
Tennessee	152	180	126	142	7.3	8.0	5.3	5.2	41.4	41.1	1.9	1.8
Texas	352	565	544	549	5.2	7.0	6.3	5.6	128.7	123.7	1.8	1.7
Utah	40	43	35	35	6.3	5.9	4.3	3.5	8.4	7.9	1.1	1.0
Vermont	16	13	15	15	6.4	4.8	5.0	4.6	7.7	7.3	3.1	2.9
Virginia	128	160	141	149	5.0	5.6	4.3	4.4	31.0	29.5	1.2	1.1
Washington	156	170	125	188	7.9	8.1	4.9	6.5	94.4	90.2	4.3	4.0
West Virginia	74	100	64	61	9.4	13.0	8.4	7.5	18.2	18.6	3.0	3.0
Wisconsin	167	171	114	103	7.2	7.2	4.4	3.5	49.8	51.7	2.2	2.2
Wyoming	9	18	13	13	4.0	7.1	5.5	5.0	3.7	3.9	1.9	2.0

[1] Total unemployment as percent of civilian labor force. [2] See footnote 2, table 619. [3] Source: U.S. Employment and Training Administration, *Unemployment Insurance, Financial Handbook*, annual updates. [4] Insured unemployment as percent of average covered employment in the previous year. [5] Includes 62,100 in Puerto Rico and the Virgin Islands in 1994 and 56,500 in 1995.

Source: Except as noted, U.S. Bureau of Labor Statistics, *Geographic Profile of Employment and Unemployment*, annual.

No. 659. Job Openings and Placements and Help-Wanted Advertising: 1970 to 1995

[Openings 1970 and 1980, for years ending Sept. 30; beginning 1985, for years ending June 30]

ITEM	1970	1980	1985	1990	1991	1992	1993	1994	1995
Job openings: [1] Received (1,000)	6,130	8,122	7,529	5,651	5,635	5,752	6,343	6,619	5,917
Average per month	511	677	627	471	470	479	529	552	493
Nonagricultural placements [1] (1,000)	4,604	5,610	3,270	3,714	3,507	3,396	3,375	3,360	3,216
Index of help-wanted advertising in newspapers [2] (1967=100)	60	84	91	84	62	62	69	83	85

[1] As reported by State employment agencies. Beginning 1985, all placements. Placements include duplication for individuals placed more than once. [2] Source: U.S. Bureau of Economic Analysis, *Survey of Current Business*, monthly (series published through January/February 1996 issue). Based on data from the Conference Board, New York, NY. Index based on the number of advertisements in classified sections of 51 newspapers, each in a major employment area.

Source: Except as noted, U.S. Employment and Training Administration, unpublished data.

No. 660. Nonfarm Establishments—Employees, Hours, and Earnings, by Industry: 1960 to 1996

[Based on data from establishment reports. Includes all full- and part-time employees who worked during, or received pay for, any part of the pay period reported. Excludes proprietors, the self-employed, farm workers, unpaid family workers, private household workers, and Armed Forces. Establishment data shown here conform to industry definitions in the 1987 Standard Industrial Classification and are adjusted to March 1995 employment benchmarks, and reflect historical corrections to previously published data. Based on the Current Employment Statistics Program; see Appendix III]

ITEM AND YEAR	Total	GOODS-PRODUCING				SERVICE-PRODUCING						
		Total	Mining	Construction	Manufacturing	Total	Transportation and public utilities	Wholesale trade	Retail trade	Finance, insurance, and real estate	Services	Government
EMPLOYEES (1,000)												
1960	54,189	20,434	712	2,926	16,796	33,755	4,004	3,153	8,238	2,628	7,378	8,353
1970	70,880	23,578	623	3,588	19,367	47,302	4,515	4,006	11,034	3,645	11,548	12,554
1980	90,406	25,658	1,027	4,346	20,285	64,748	5,146	5,292	15,018	5,160	17,890	16,241
1985	97,387	24,842	927	4,668	19,248	72,544	5,233	5,727	17,315	5,948	21,927	16,394
1990	109,419	24,905	709	5,120	19,076	84,514	5,793	6,173	19,601	6,709	27,934	18,304
1991	108,256	23,745	689	4,650	18,406	84,511	5,762	6,081	19,284	6,646	28,336	18,402
1992	108,604	23,231	635	4,492	18,104	85,373	5,721	5,997	19,356	6,602	29,052	18,645
1993	110,730	23,352	610	4,668	18,075	87,378	5,829	5,981	19,773	6,757	30,197	18,841
1994	114,172	23,908	601	4,986	18,321	90,264	5,993	6,162	20,507	6,896	31,579	19,128
1995	117,203	24,206	580	5,158	18,468	92,997	6,165	6,412	21,173	6,830	33,107	19,310
1996	119,554	24,259	570	5,407	18,282	95,296	6,316	6,587	21,597	6,977	34,359	19,461
PERCENT DISTRIBUTION												
1960	100.0	37.7	1.3	5.4	31.0	62.3	7.4	5.8	15.2	4.8	13.6	15.4
1970	100.0	33.3	0.9	5.1	27.3	66.7	6.4	5.7	15.6	5.1	16.3	17.7
1980	100.0	28.4	1.1	4.8	22.4	71.6	5.7	5.9	16.6	5.7	19.8	18.0
1985	100.0	25.5	1.0	4.8	19.8	74.5	5.4	5.9	17.8	6.1	22.5	16.8
1990	100.0	22.8	0.6	4.7	17.4	77.2	5.3	5.6	17.9	6.1	25.5	16.7
1991	100.0	21.9	0.6	4.3	17.0	78.1	5.3	5.6	17.8	6.1	26.2	17.0
1992	100.0	21.4	0.6	4.1	16.7	78.6	5.3	5.5	17.8	6.1	26.8	17.2
1993	100.0	21.1	0.6	4.2	16.3	78.9	5.3	5.4	17.9	6.1	27.3	17.0
1994	100.0	20.9	0.5	4.4	16.0	79.1	5.2	5.4	18.0	6.0	27.7	16.8
1996	100.0	20.3	0.5	4.5	15.3	79.7	5.3	5.5	18.1	5.8	28.7	16.3
WEEKLY HOURS [1]												
1960	38.6	(NA)	40.4	36.7	39.7	(NA)	(NA)	40.5	38.0	37.2	(NA)	(NA)
1970	37.1	(NA)	42.7	37.3	39.8	(NA)	40.5	39.9	33.8	36.7	34.4	(NA)
1980	35.3	(NA)	43.3	37.0	39.7	(NA)	39.6	38.4	30.2	36.2	32.6	(NA)
1985	34.9	(NA)	43.4	37.7	40.5	(NA)	39.5	38.4	29.4	36.4	32.5	(NA)
1990	34.5	(NA)	44.1	38.2	40.8	(NA)	38.9	38.1	28.8	35.8	32.5	(NA)
1991	34.3	(NA)	44.4	38.1	40.7	(NA)	38.7	38.1	28.6	35.7	32.4	(NA)
1992	34.4	(NA)	43.9	38.0	41.0	(NA)	38.9	38.2	28.8	35.8	32.5	(NA)
1993	34.5	(NA)	44.3	38.5	41.4	(NA)	39.6	38.2	28.8	35.8	32.5	(NA)
1994	34.7	(NA)	44.8	38.9	42.0	(NA)	39.9	38.4	28.9	35.8	32.5	(NA)
1995	34.5	(NA)	44.7	38.8	41.6	(NA)	39.5	38.3	28.8	35.9	32.4	(NA)
1996	34.4	(NA)	45.3	38.9	41.6	(NA)	39.7	38.3	28.8	35.9	32.4	(NA)
HOURLY EARNINGS [1]												
1960	$2.09	(NA)	$2.60	$3.07	$2.26	(NA)	(NA)	$2.24	$1.52	$2.02	(NA)	(NA)
1970	3.23	(NA)	3.85	5.24	3.35	(NA)	3.85	3.43	2.44	3.07	2.81	(NA)
1980	6.66	(NA)	9.17	9.94	7.27	(NA)	8.87	6.95	4.88	5.79	5.85	(NA)
1985	8.57	(NA)	11.98	12.32	9.54	(NA)	11.40	9.15	5.94	7.94	7.90	(NA)
1990	10.01	(NA)	13.68	13.77	10.83	(NA)	12.97	10.79	6.75	9.97	9.83	(NA)
1991	10.32	(NA)	14.19	14.00	11.18	(NA)	13.22	11.15	6.94	10.39	10.23	(NA)
1992	10.57	(NA)	14.54	14.15	11.46	(NA)	13.45	11.39	7.12	10.82	10.54	(NA)
1993	10.83	(NA)	14.60	14.38	11.74	(NA)	13.62	11.74	7.29	11.35	10.78	(NA)
1994	11.12	(NA)	14.88	14.73	12.07	(NA)	13.86	12.06	7.49	11.83	11.04	(NA)
1995	11.44	(NA)	15.30	15.08	12.37	(NA)	14.23	12.43	7.69	12.33	11.39	(NA)
1996	11.82	(NA)	15.60	15.43	12.78	(NA)	14.52	12.84	7.98	12.80	11.80	(NA)
WEEKLY EARNINGS [1]												
1960	$81	(NA)	$105	$113	$90	(NA)	(NA)	$91	$58	$75	(NA)	(NA)
1970	120	(NA)	164	195	133	(NA)	156	137	82	113	97	(NA)
1980	235	(NA)	397	368	289	(NA)	351	267	147	210	191	(NA)
1985	299	(NA)	520	464	386	(NA)	450	351	175	289	257	(NA)
1990	345	(NA)	603	526	442	(NA)	505	411	194	357	319	(NA)
1991	354	(NA)	630	533	455	(NA)	512	425	198	371	331	(NA)
1992	364	(NA)	638	538	470	(NA)	523	435	205	387	343	(NA)
1993	374	(NA)	647	554	486	(NA)	539	448	210	406	350	(NA)
1994	386	(NA)	667	573	507	(NA)	553	463	216	424	359	(NA)
1995	395	(NA)	684	585	515	(NA)	562	476	221	443	369	(NA)
1996	407	(NA)	707	600	532	(NA)	576	492	230	460	382	(NA)

NA Not available. [1] Average hours and earnings. Private production and related workers in mining, manufacturing, and construction; nonsupervisory employees in other industries.

Source: U.S. Bureau of Labor Statistics, Bulletins 2445 and 2481, and *Employment and Earnings*, monthly, March and June issues.

No. 661. Employees in Nonfarm Establishments—States: 1980 to 1996

[In thousands. For coverage, see headnote, table 660. National totals differ from the sum of the State figures because of differing benchmarks among States and differing industrial and geographic stratification. Based on 1987 *Standard Industrial Classification Manual*, see text, section 13]

STATE	1980	1995	1996: Total [1]	1996: Construction	1996: Manufacturing	1996: Transportation and public utilities	1996: Wholesale and retail trade	1996: Finance, insurance, and real estate	1996: Services	1996: Government
United States	90,406	117,203	119,554	5,407	18,282	6,316	28,184	6,977	34,359	19,461
Alabama	1,356	1,804	1,825	94	383	90	419	82	406	342
Alaska	169	262	263	13	16	23	55	12	62	73
Arizona	1,014	1,796	1,896	127	200	92	468	115	561	321
Arkansas	742	1,069	1,086	47	254	65	247	43	247	179
California	9,849	12,422	12,775	511	1,853	642	2,973	733	3,917	2,117
Colorado	1,251	1,834	1,897	111	196	120	465	118	565	309
Connecticut	1,427	1,562	1,583	52	275	73	347	131	481	224
Delaware	259	366	377	21	58	16	84	44	102	53
District of Columbia	616	643	623	9	13	19	50	28	263	241
Florida	3,576	5,996	6,183	324	490	314	1,607	394	2,118	929
Georgia	2,159	3,402	3,526	165	585	222	897	180	903	569
Hawaii	405	533	529	[2]24	17	41	135	37	166	110
Idaho	330	477	492	30	73	23	125	25	115	98
Illinois	4,850	5,593	5,676	221	972	331	1,304	386	1,640	810
Indiana	2,130	2,787	2,813	132	674	139	680	135	653	394
Iowa	1,110	1,358	1,380	59	247	63	341	78	359	232
Kansas	945	1,198	1,228	57	196	70	303	59	301	235
Kentucky	1,210	1,643	1,671	77	312	93	401	68	406	290
Louisiana	1,579	1,772	1,811	113	188	106	423	83	486	361
Maine	418	536	540	23	88	22	136	27	150	93
Maryland	1,712	2,183	2,206	130	174	107	529	128	715	422
Massachusetts	2,652	2,976	3,036	94	444	129	697	209	1,063	400
Michigan	3,443	4,274	4,345	168	967	168	1,025	201	1,165	643
Minnesota	1,770	2,379	2,432	89	428	120	593	143	672	380
Mississippi	829	1,075	1,090	49	246	53	233	41	247	218
Missouri	1,970	2,521	2,564	116	414	160	613	150	708	400
Montana	280	351	359	17	24	21	96	16	102	77
Nebraska	628	816	834	37	114	50	208	53	220	152
Nevada	400	786	843	75	39	42	170	38	364	101
New Hampshire	385	540	560	21	105	20	145	28	162	79
New Jersey	3,060	3,601	3,640	123	485	254	855	232	1,122	567
New Mexico	465	682	694	43	46	31	164	32	192	171
New York	7,207	7,872	7,917	254	922	402	1,621	721	2,610	1,382
North Carolina	2,380	3,460	3,555	189	847	168	811	154	822	561
North Dakota	245	302	309	15	22	18	80	14	85	71
Ohio	4,367	5,221	5,296	213	1,094	232	1,300	277	1,415	752
Oklahoma	1,138	1,316	1,354	50	174	77	319	67	364	272
Oregon	1,045	1,418	1,475	78	235	73	365	91	385	246
Pennsylvania	4,753	5,253	5,306	202	929	272	1,205	309	1,651	721
Rhode Island	398	440	442	14	82	15	98	25	146	61
South Carolina	1,189	1,846	1,676	94	365	73	398	72	373	299
South Dakota	238	344	349	15	48	16	88	20	90	70
Tennessee	1,747	2,499	2,534	113	522	143	596	117	656	383
Texas	5,851	8,023	8,242	436	1,054	488	1,968	444	2,221	1,454
Utah	551	908	955	60	129	54	231	50	256	167
Vermont	200	270	275	13	46	12	65	12	82	45
Virginia	2,157	3,070	3,130	175	399	162	714	162	911	597
Washington	1,608	2,347	2,412	127	344	123	591	124	649	450
West Virginia	646	688	698	34	82	39	160	27	191	139
Wisconsin	1,938	2,559	2,602	105	601	121	595	138	655	383
Wyoming	210	219	221	14	11	14	52	8	48	59

[1] Includes mining, not shown separately. [2] Hawaii includes mining with construction.

Source: U.S. Bureau of Labor Statistics, *Employment and Earnings*, monthly, May issues. Compiled from data supplied by cooperating State agencies.

No. 662. Nonfarm Industries—Employees and Earnings: 1980 to 1996

[Annual averages of monthly figures. Covers all full- and part-time employees who worked during, or received pay for, any part of the pay period including the 12th of the month. For mining and manufacturing, data refer to production and related workers; for construction, to employees engaged in actual construction work; and for other industries, to nonsupervisory employees and working supervisors. See also headnote table 660]

INDUSTRY	1987 SIC [1] code	ALL EMPLOYEES TOTAL (1,000)			PRODUCTION WORKERS					
					Total (1,000)			Average hourly earnings (dollars)		
		1980	1990	1996	1980	1990	1996	1980	1990	1996
Total	(X)	90,406	109,419	119,554	(NA)	(NA)	(NA)	(NA)	(NA)	(NA)
Private sector [2]	(X)	74,166	91,115	100,094	60,331	73,800	81,998	6.66	10.01	11.82
Mining	(B)	1,027	709	570	762	509	424	9.17	13.68	15.60
Metal mining	10	98	58	52	74	46	41	10.26	14.05	17.37
Coal mining	12	246	147	100	204	119	82	10.86	16.71	18.72
Oil and gas extraction	13	560	395	311	389	261	220	8.59	12.94	14.79
Nonmetallic minerals, except fuels	14	123	110	108	96	83	82	7.52	11.58	13.84
Construction	(C)	4,346	5,120	5,407	3,421	3,974	4,192	9.94	13.77	15.43
General building contractors	15	1,173	1,298	1,230	900	938	869	9.22	13.01	14.66
Heavy construction, except building	16	895	770	764	720	643	639	9.20	13.34	15.08
Special trade contractors	17	2,278	3,051	3,412	1,802	2,393	2,684	10.63	14.20	15.76
Manufacturing	(D)	20,285	19,076	18,282	14,214	12,947	12,626	7.27	10.83	12.78
Durable goods	(X)	12,159	11,109	10,676	8,416	7,363	7,310	7.75	11.35	13.34
Lumber and wood products [3]	24	704	733	764	587	603	626	6.57	9.08	10.44
Logging	241	88	85	78	71	70	63	8.64	11.22	11.80
Sawmills and planing mills	242	215	198	182	190	172	158	6.70	9.22	10.59
Millwork, plywood, and structural members	243	206	262	283	170	210	227	6.44	9.04	10.49
Wood containers	244	43	45	50	37	38	43	4.95	6.64	8.02
Mobile homes	2451	46	41	64	36	33	54	6.08	8.67	10.81
Furniture and fixtures [3]	25	466	506	501	376	400	396	5.49	8.52	10.15
Household furniture	251	301	289	278	253	241	233	5.12	7.87	9.61
Office furniture	252	51	68	61	40	51	45	5.91	9.64	10.99
Partitions and fixtures	254	63	78	64	47	57	61	6.88	9.77	11.08
Stone, clay, and glass products [3]	32	629	556	536	486	432	417	7.50	11.12	12.81
Flat glass	321	18	17	15	14	13	12	9.65	15.15	18.46
Glass and glassware, pressed and blown	322	124	83	70	105	72	59	7.97	12.40	14.45
Products of purchased glass	323	45	60	61	32	46	47	6.50	9.75	11.38
Cement, hydraulic	324	31	18	18	25	14	13	10.55	13.90	16.88
Structural clay products	325	46	36	33	34	28	26	6.14	9.56	11.36
Pottery and related products	326	47	39	39	39	31	31	6.25	9.62	11.00
Concrete, gypsum, and plaster	327	204	206	210	157	157	161	7.45	10.76	12.29
Primary metal industries [3]	33	1,142	756	705	878	574	549	9.77	12.92	14.99
Blast furnaces and basic steel products	331	512	276	238	396	212	183	11.39	14.82	17.84
Iron and steel foundries	332	209	132	127	167	105	104	8.20	11.55	13.57
Primary nonferrous metals	333	71	46	41	53	34	31	10.63	14.36	16.19
Nonferrous rolling and drawing	335	211	172	167	151	124	127	8.81	12.29	14.06
Nonferrous foundries (castings)	336	90	84	89	72	66	73	7.30	10.21	11.82
Fabricated metal products [3]	34	1,609	1,419	1,451	1,194	1,045	1,090	7.45	10.83	12.48
Metal cans and shipping containers	341	75	50	40	63	43	34	9.84	14.27	16.09
Cutlery, handtools, and hardware	342	164	131	127	125	96	96	7.02	10.76	12.39
Plumbing and heating, exc. electric	343	71	60	57	52	43	41	6.59	9.75	11.29
Fabricated structural metal products	344	506	427	439	351	303	321	7.27	10.16	11.72
Screw machine products	345	109	96	99	84	73	77	6.96	10.70	12.44
Metal forgings and stampings	346	260	225	255	205	178	204	8.56	12.70	14.82
Industrial machinery and equipment [3]	35	2,517	2,095	2,087	1,614	1,260	1,302	8.00	11.77	13.59
Engines and turbines	351	135	89	85	87	58	53	9.73	14.55	16.35
Farm and garden machinery	352	169	106	97	116	78	70	8.78	10.99	13.47
Construction and related machinery	353	369	229	226	255	141	147	8.60	11.92	13.09
Metalworking machinery	354	398	330	344	290	236	244	8.13	12.27	14.40
Special industry machinery	355	194	159	175	125	94	98	7.53	11.90	14.06
General industrial machinery	356	300	247	254	196	158	163	7.95	11.32	13.34
Computer and office equipment	357	420	438	359	181	137	125	6.75	11.51	13.89
Refrigeration and service machinery	358	175	177	206	120	125	149	7.23	10.93	12.30
Electronic and other elec. equip. [3]	36	1,771	1,673	1,650	(4)	1,055	1,060	(4)	10.30	12.17
Electric distribution equipment	361	117	97	83	82	67	56	6.98	10.15	11.94
Electrical industrial apparatus	362	232	169	156	163	119	111	(4)	10.00	11.51
Household appliances	363	162	124	121	128	99	97	6.96	10.26	12.01
Electric lighting and wiring equip	364	211	189	175	157	136	125	6.43	10.12	12.31
Household audio and video equip	365	109	85	83	79	59	56	6.42	9.66	10.46
Communications equipment	366	(4)	264	263	(4)	133	127	(4)	11.03	12.86
Electronic components and accessories	367	539	582	613	325	329	366	6.05	10.00	12.03
Transportation equipment [3]	37	1,881	1,989	1,765	1,220	1,224	1,193	9.35	14.08	17.24
Motor vehicles and equipment	371	789	812	954	575	617	753	9.85	14.56	17.83
Aircraft and parts	372	633	712	454	344	345	215	9.28	14.79	18.56
Ship and boat building and repairing	373	221	188	154	176	141	118	8.22	10.94	12.80
Railroad equipment	374	71	33	35	53	25	26	9.93	13.41	16.32
Guided missiles, space vehicles, and parts	376	111	185	93	35	57	25	9.22	14.39	18.56

See footnotes at end of table.

No. 662. Nonfarm Industries—Employees and Earnings: 1980 to 1996—Continued

[See headnote, p. 424]

INDUSTRY	1987 SIC[1] code	ALL EMPLOYEES TOTAL (1,000)			PRODUCTION WORKERS Total (1,000)			PRODUCTION WORKERS Average hourly earnings (dollars)		
		1980	1990	1996	1980	1990	1996	1980	1990	1996
Durable goods—Continued	(X)									
Instruments and related products	38	1,022	1,006	832	(4)	499	413	(4)	11.29	13.14
Search and navigation equipment	381	(4)	284	152	(4)	94	44	(4)	14.62	16.73
Measuring and controlling devices	382	(4)	323	287	(4)	180	146	(4)	10.68	13.07
Medical instruments and supplies	384	(4)	246	267	(4)	144	155	(4)	9.85	12.07
Ophthalmic goods	385	44	43	35	31	30	23	5.30	8.18	9.79
Photographic equipment and supplies	386	135	100	84	67	43	39	8.83	14.08	15.81
Watches, clocks, watchcases, and parts	387	22	11	7	17	8	6	5.24	7.70	9.54
Misc. manufacturing industries[3]	39	418	375	386	313	272	272	5.46	8.61	10.40
Jewelry, silverware, and plated ware	391	56	52	49	40	37	34	5.76	9.23	10.70
Toys and sporting goods	394	117	104	115	88	76	81	5.01	7.94	9.85
Pens, pencils, office and art supplies	395	37	34	32	27	24	22	5.58	8.89	10.89
Costume jewelry and notions	396	(4)	34	25	(4)	25	18	(4)	7.40	9.06
Nondurable goods	(X)	8,127	7,968	7,808	5,798	5,684	5,316	6.56	10.12	11.97
Food and kindred products[3]	20	1,708	1,661	1,654	1,175	1,194	1,222	6.85	9.62	11.22
Meat products	201	358	422	465	298	359	396	6.99	7.94	9.13
Dairy products	202	175	155	146	96	95	96	6.86	10.56	12.80
Preserved fruits and vegetables	203	246	247	227	202	208	189	5.94	8.95	10.72
Grain mill products	204	144	128	126	99	89	90	7.67	11.52	13.93
Bakery products	205	230	213	203	139	133	137	7.14	10.85	12.17
Sugar and confectionery products	206	108	99	100	81	78	79	6.56	10.28	12.21
Fats and oils	207	44	31	31	32	22	22	7.03	10.10	12.02
Beverages	208	234	184	176	105	78	83	8.12	13.51	15.72
Tobacco products	21	69	49	41	54	36	31	7.74	16.23	19.54
Cigarettes	211	46	35	28	35	28	21	9.23	19.57	24.64
Textile mill products[3]	22	848	691	636	737	593	538	5.07	8.02	9.68
Broadwoven fabric mills, cotton	221	150	91	74	135	82	66	5.25	8.31	10.07
Broadwoven fabric mills, synthetics	222	116	77	67	104	68	56	5.30	8.63	10.64
Broadwoven fabric mills, wool	223	19	17	16	16	14	14	5.21	8.61	10.04
Narrow fabric mills	224	23	24	21	20	20	17	4.63	7.39	9.05
Knitting mills	225	224	206	184	194	179	158	4.77	7.37	8.85
Textile finishing, except wool	226	74	62	70	62	50	57	5.39	8.45	9.88
Carpets and rugs	227	54	61	61	44	50	50	5.20	8.25	9.76
Yarn and thread mills	228	125	103	92	113	92	81	4.76	7.68	9.45
Apparel and other textile products[3]	23	1,264	1,036	847	1,079	869	695	4.56	6.57	7.95
Men's and boys' suits and coats	231	77	50	33	67	42	26	5.34	7.34	8.22
Men's and boys' furnishings	232	362	274	224	310	235	189	4.23	6.06	7.41
Women's and misses outerwear	233	417	328	248	360	274	202	4.61	6.26	7.52
Women's and children's undergarments	234	90	62	41	76	51	33	4.15	6.18	7.55
Girls' and children's outerwear	236	64	56	37	55	47	31	4.20	5.95	7.10
Paper and allied products[3]	26	685	697	677	519	522	514	7.84	12.31	14.68
Papermills	262	178	180	160	133	136	124	9.05	15.10	18.46
Paperboard mills	263	65	52	51	51	40	39	9.28	15.26	18.55
Paperboard containers and boxes	265	205	209	218	157	162	169	6.94	10.39	12.40
Misc. converted paper products	267	220	241	237	163	174	173	6.89	10.79	12.83
Printing and publishing[3]	27	1,252	1,569	1,528	699	871	834	7.53	11.24	12.64
Newspapers	271	420	474	441	164	166	150	7.72	11.17	12.49
Periodicals	272	90	129	130	16	47	42	7.16	11.95	13.81
Books	273	101	121	122	52	66	65	6.76	10.10	11.96
Commercial printing	275	410	552	560	304	401	401	7.85	11.52	12.85
Blankbooks and bookbinding	278	62	72	67	51	56	52	5.78	8.83	9.92
Chemicals and allied products[3]	28	1,107	1,086	1,021	626	600	567	8.30	13.54	16.20
Industrial inorganic chemicals	281	161	138	116	88	70	53	9.07	14.66	17.92
Plastics materials and synthetics	282	205	180	154	137	116	102	8.21	13.97	16.94
Drugs	283	196	237	255	97	105	121	7.69	12.90	15.85
Soap, cleaners, and toilet goods	284	141	159	150	86	98	92	7.67	11.71	13.01
Paints and allied products	285	65	61	57	33	31	30	7.39	11.99	13.56
Industrial organic chemicals	286	174	155	146	88	86	83	9.67	15.97	19.61
Agricultural chemicals	287	72	56	52	45	34	31	8.12	13.73	16.13
Petroleum and coal products[3]	29	196	157	139	125	103	90	10.10	16.24	19.30
Petroleum refining	291	155	118	96	93	75	62	10.94	17.58	21.43
Asphalt paving and roofing materials	295	31	27	27	24	21	20	7.69	12.87	14.69
Rubber and misc. plastics products[3]	30	764	888	968	586	687	750	6.58	9.76	11.24
Tires and inner tubes	301	115	84	78	81	62	57	9.74	15.42	17.96
Rubber and plastics footwear	302	22	11	6	20	9	5	4.43	6.66	9.13
Leather and leather products[3]	31	233	133	98	197	109	74	4.58	6.91	8.57
Leather tanning and finishing	311	19	15	13	16	12	11	6.10	9.04	11.51
Footwear, except rubber	314	144	74	46	123	63	37	4.42	6.61	8.06
Luggage	316	16	11	11	12	8	8	4.90	6.91	8.50
Handbags and personal leather goods	317	30	15	11	25	12	7	4.33	6.06	7.61

See footnotes at end of table.

No. 662. Nonfarm Industries—Employees and Earnings: 1980 to 1996—Continued

[See headnote, p. 424]

INDUSTRY	1987 SIC [1] code	ALL EMPLOYEES TOTAL (1,000)			PRODUCTION WORKERS					
					Total (1,000)			Average hourly earnings (dollars)		
		1980	1990	1996	1980	1990	1996	1980	1990	1996
Transp. and public utilities [3]	(E)	5,146	5,793	6,316	4,293	4,807	5,310	8.87	12.97	14.52
Railroad transportation	40	532	279	232	(4)	(4)	(4)	(4)	(4)	(4)
Class I railroads, plus Amtrak [5]	4011	482	241	206	(4)	(4)	(4)	[6]9.92	[6]16.08	[6]17.71
Local and interurban passenger transit	41	265	338	451	244	308	413	6.34	9.23	10.73
Trucking and warehousing	42	1,260	1,625	1,878	1,121	1,416	1,634	9.13	11.71	13.09
Water transportation	44	211	177	172	(4)	(4)	(4)	(4)	(4)	(4)
Transportation by air	45	453	745	847	(4)	(4)	(4)	(4)	(4)	(4)
Pipelines, except natural gas	46	21	19	14	15	14	11	10.50	17.04	20.42
Transportation services	47	198	345	440	159	278	354	6.94	10.43	12.84
Communication [3]	48	1,357	1,309	1,387	1,014	978	1,068	8.50	13.51	16.04
Telephone communication	481	1,072	913	948	779	658	724	8.72	14.13	16.68
Radio and television broadcasting	483	192	234	244	154	193	204	7.44	12.71	15.92
Cable and other pay television services	484	(4)	126	175	(4)	105	148	(4)	10.50	12.66
Electric, gas, and sanitary services [3]	49	829	957	895	678	759	708	8.90	15.23	18.21
Electric services	491	391	454	386	316	351	305	9.12	15.80	19.28
Gas production and distribution	492	168	165	148	138	129	115	8.27	14.25	17.64
Combination utility services	493	197	193	163	162	156	126	9.64	17.58	21.91
Sanitary services	495	50	115	165	44	99	137	7.16	11.55	13.55
Wholesale trade	(F)	5,292	6,173	6,587	4,328	4,959	5,325	6.95	10.79	12.84
Retail trade [2]	(G)	15,018	19,601	21,597	13,484	17,358	18,991	4.88	6.75	7.99
General merchandise stores	53	2,245	2,540	2,723	2,090	2,380	2,537	4.77	6.83	7.87
Food stores	54	2,384	3,215	3,429	2,202	2,953	3,108	6.24	7.31	8.36
Automotive dealers and service stations	55	1,689	2,063	2,274	1,430	1,718	1,899	5.66	8.92	10.86
Apparel and accessory stores	56	957	1,183	1,102	820	991	906	4.30	6.25	7.73
Furniture and home furnishings stores	57	806	820	978	502	670	796	5.53	8.53	10.57
Eating and drinking places	58	4,626	6,509	7,485	4,256	5,905	6,741	3.69	4.97	5.79
Finance, insurance, real estate	(H)	5,160	6,709	6,977	3,907	4,860	5,091	5.79	9.97	12.80
Depository institutions	60	(4)	2,251	2,028	(4)	1,632	1,460	(4)	8.43	9.93
Nondepository institutions	61	(4)	373	513	(4)	270	370	(4)	10.40	12.90
Security and commodity brokers	62	227	424	541	(4)	(4)	(4)	(4)	(4)	(4)
Insurance carriers	63	1,224	1,462	1,550	854	982	1,107	6.29	11.18	15.31
Insurance, agents, brokers, service	64	464	663	709	(4)	(4)	(4)	(4)	(4)	(4)
Real estate	65	989	1,315	1,394	(4)	(4)	(4)	(4)	(4)	(4)
Holding and other investment offices	67	115	221	242	(4)	(4)	(4)	(4)	(4)	(4)
Services [3]	(I)	17,890	27,934	34,359	15,921	24,387	30,039	5.85	9.83	11.80
Hotels and other lodging places	70	1,076	1,631	1,682	(4)	(4)	(4)	(4)	(4)	(4)
Hotels and motels	701	1,038	1,578	1,620	954	1,398	1,424	4.45	6.95	8.15
Personal services [3]	72	818	1,104	1,178	(4)	(4)	(4)	(4)	(4)	(4)
Laundry, cleaning, garment services	721	356	426	436	318	379	384	4.47	6.82	7.75
Beauty shops	723	284	372	396	264	333	353	4.28	7.10	8.84
Business services [3]	73	2,564	5,139	7,174	(4)	4,522	6,362	(4)	9.48	11.20
Advertising	731	153	235	253	116	169	185	8.07	13.51	16.41
Personnel supply services	736	543	1,535	2,634	(4)	(4)	(4)	(4)	(4)	(4)
Employment agencies	7361	(4)	246	302	(4)	(4)	(4)	(4)	(4)	(4)
Help supply services	7363	(4)	1,288	2,332	(4)	1,245	2,266	(4)	8.09	9.20
Computer and data processing services	737	304	772	1,200	254	603	959	7.16	15.11	18.65
Prepackaged software	7372	(4)	113	206	(4)	(4)	(4)	(4)	(4)	(4)
Data processing and preparation	7374	(4)	197	243	(4)	(4)	(4)	(4)	(4)	(4)
Auto repair, services, and parking	75	571	914	1,091	488	756	899	6.10	8.77	10.21
Automotive repair shops	753	350	524	610	297	429	492	6.52	9.67	11.43
Motion pictures	78	(4)	408	526	(4)	344	440	(4)	10.95	14.00
Motion picture theaters	783	124	112	117	(4)	(4)	(4)	(4)	(4)	(4)
Amusement and recreation services	79	(4)	1,076	1,518	(4)	944	1,327	(4)	8.11	8.86
Health services [3]	80	5,278	7,814	9,566	4,712	6,948	8,477	5.68	10.41	12.84
Offices and clinics of medical doctors	801	802	1,338	1,672	(4)	1,105	1,369	(4)	10.58	13.10
Nursing and personal care facilities	805	997	1,415	1,742	896	1,279	1,568	4.17	7.24	8.96
Hospitals	806	2,750	3,549	3,852	2,522	3,248	3,526	6.06	11.79	14.69
Home health care services	808	(4)	291	658	(4)	269	606	(4)	8.72	11.18
Legal services	81	498	908	932	427	748	744	7.35	14.16	16.65
Educational services	82	1,138	1,661	2,002	(4)	(4)	(4)	(4)	(4)	(4)
Social services	83	1,134	1,734	2,394	(4)	1,494	2,078	(4)	7.11	8.55
Membership organizations	86	1,539	1,946	2,145	(4)	(4)	(4)	(4)	(4)	(4)
Engineering and management services	87	(4)	2,478	2,895	(4)	1,886	2,219	(4)	13.56	16.33
Government	(J)	16,241	18,304	19,461	(NA)	(NA)	(NA)	(NA)	(NA)	(NA)
Federal government	(X)	2,866	3,085	2,757	(NA)	(NA)	(NA)	(NA)	(NA)	(NA)
State government	(X)	3,610	4,305	4,645	(NA)	(NA)	(NA)	(NA)	(NA)	(NA)
Local government	(X)	9,765	10,914	12,059	(NA)	(NA)	(NA)	(NA)	(NA)	(NA)

NA Not available. X Not applicable. [1] 1987 Standard Industrial Classification, see text, section 13. [2] Excludes government. [3] Includes industries not shown separately. [4] Included in totals; not available separately. [5] For changes in "Class I" classification, see text, section 21. [6] Includes all employees except executives, officials, and staff assistants who received pay during the month.

Source: U.S. Bureau of Labor Statistics, Bulletins 2445 and 2481, and *Employment and Earnings*, March and June issues.

No. 663. Indexes of Output per Hour—Selected Industries: 1975 to 1996

[See text, section 13. Minus sign (-) indicates decrease]

INDUSTRY	1987 SIC code [1]	INDEXES (1987=100)						Average annual percent change [2], 1975-96
		1975	1980	1985	1990	1994	1996, prel.	
Mining:	(B)							
Coal mining	12	57.7	61.7	85.1	118.3	147.3	153.9	5.0
Crude petroleum and natural gas	131	142.8	97.2	83.0	96.9	112.4	120.5	-0.8
Nonmetallic minerals, except fuels	14	81.0	86.9	95.1	101.4	104.4	103.0	1.2
Manufacturing:	(D)							
Red meat products	2011,13	71.3	89.7	102.2	96.3	100.8	102.5	1.8
Poultry dressing and processing	2015	67.8	81.6	100.5	108.6	119.4	122.5	3.0
Dairy products	202	66.5	76.7	92.8	105.4	112.5	115.6	2.8
Preserved fruits and vegetables	203	77.2	82.9	94.3	96.2	108.0	111.5	1.9
Grain mill products	204	57.3	70.9	92.5	106.0	110.5	118.7	3.6
Bakery products	2051,52	82.0	82.4	95.6	93.2	91.1	92.2	0.6
Bottled and canned soft drinks	2086	55.7	66.5	85.2	126.7	150.4	160.0	5.4
Cotton and synthetic broadwoven fabrics	221,2	66.1	78.4	94.8	108.1	134.1	142.8	3.9
Yarn spinning mills	2281	67.4	65.5	89.6	106.0	125.5	133.2	3.5
Sawmills and planing mills, general	2421	68.2	71.5	93.5	99.9	103.2	110.3	2.4
Millwork	2431	98.8	97.6	97.4	97.8	88.5	86.0	-0.7
Wood kitchen cabinets	2434	82.3	94.1	87.1	93.6	101.3	102.8	1.1
Household furniture	251	82.1	93.2	93.5	104.3	112.2	117.0	1.8
Pulp, paper, and paperboard mills	261,2,3	63.5	77.1	87.6	102.6	112.4	116.2	3.1
Corrugated and solid fiber boxes	2653	78.6	90.5	99.6	100.9	110.0	107.8	1.6
Industrial inorganic chemicals	281	66.8	75.7	84.0	104.9	109.2	115.1	2.8
Synthetic fibers	2823,24	46.9	71.2	79.3	98.7	119.4	125.7	5.1
Cosmetics and other toiletries	2844	92.2	83.8	90.3	101.1	111.6	115.2	1.1
Industrial organic chemicals, n.e.c. [3]	2869	69.8	81.3	87.8	99.0	96.2	93.3	1.5
Petroleum refining	291	80.0	81.7	84.7	109.2	123.8	133.0	2.6
Tires and inner tubes	301	54.1	60.7	89.3	103.0	124.1	131.4	4.5
Miscellaneous plastics products, n.e.c. [3]	308	66.7	75.1	88.2	105.3	119.8	120.2	3.0
Concrete products	3271,72	91.5	89.2	99.5	103.8	108.6	114.3	1.1
Ready-mixed concrete	3273	93.3	90.0	93.6	100.2	93.0	95.8	0.1
Steel	331	59.3	65.4	85.8	110.5	144.6	145.4	4.6
Gray and ductile iron foundries	3321	90.3	86.3	96.9	107.9	115.5	112.4	1.1
Fabricated structural metal	3441	82.0	86.0	99.0	101.2	109.8	110.1	1.5
Metal doors, sash, and trim	3442	88.3	90.5	104.8	103.1	103.3	96.8	0.5
Fabricated plate work	3443	(NA)	(NA)	87.5	94.1	109.3	109.4	[4]2.3
Metal stampings	3465,66,69	80.6	84.2	91.9	93.0	117.6	120.4	2.0
Valves and pipe fittings	3491,92,94	84.0	93.5	94.4	102.1	109.7	109.7	1.3
Farm and garden machinery	352	94.2	91.3	92.7	116.6	125.2	135.9	1.8
Construction machinery	3531	87.7	88.5	92.2	109.6	123.2	132.9	2.1
Pumps and compressors	3561,63,94	79.9	87.2	92.1	104.9	113.7	114.8	1.8
Refrigeration and heating equipment	3585	85.3	90.7	96.1	106.3	115.1	115.0	1.5
Motors and generators	3621	82.7	87.9	94.9	100.9	124.4	139.1	2.6
Major household appliances	3631,32,33,39	70.9	79.3	93.9	101.6	131.2	125.7	2.9
Lighting fixtures and equipment	3645,46,47,48	80.5	84.4	96.7	96.0	110.0	107.5	1.5
Motor vehicles and equipment	371	70.2	71.6	95.3	102.4	107.3	104.4	2.0
Aircraft	3721	80.9	97.9	94.2	112.9	131.8	132.5	2.5
Instruments to measure electricity	3825	67.2	76.2	95.4	106.2	144.7	163.6	4.5
Photographic equipment and supplies	386	60.9	72.9	86.1	107.8	132.7	129.4	3.8
Service producing:	(E,G,H,I)							
United States postal service [5]	43	86.1	94.8	96.4	104.0	106.6	106.5	1.1
Air transportation [6]	4512,13,22 (pts)	55.6	70.8	92.0	92.9	105.8	108.4	3.4
Telephone communications	481	49.3	67.6	88.9	113.3	141.6	144.6	5.5
Gas and electric utilities	491,2,3	107.0	107.2	96.0	106.2	120.5	127.7	0.9
Scrap and waste materials	5093	(NA)	79.2	93.4	98.6	107.7	108.9	[7]2.1
Hardware stores	525	82.4	94.9	95.6	110.4	114.5	106.4	1.3
Department stores	531	63.7	73.6	92.6	94.2	107.1	107.6	2.7
Variety stores	533	151.6	128.6	129.2	151.3	160.5	159.3	0.2
Food stores	54	106.1	107.6	104.1	96.0	93.0	91.4	-0.7
New and used car dealers	551	83.9	87.9	99.8	106.1	106.3	107.1	1.2
Auto and home supply stores	553	70.3	82.8	94.5	102.8	103.0	106.8	2.1
Gasoline service stations	554	58.5	72.1	93.5	102.6	115.0	119.2	3.6
Apparel and accessory stores	56	74.0	82.4	101.3	101.7	113.8	121.8	2.5
Home furniture, furnishings, & equipment stores	57	64.7	75.1	92.9	106.3	133.3	143.1	4.0
Eating and drinking places	58	107.9	106.8	96.2	104.0	101.4	102.2	-0.3
Drug stores and proprietary stores	591	90.0	104.5	102.5	103.6	103.7	102.8	0.7
Liquor stores	592	90.4	95.7	101.9	105.2	96.7	104.4	0.7
Miscellaneous shopping goods stores	594	(NA)	88.4	94.1	101.5	108.2	114.0	[7]1.7
Commercial banks	602	76.3	78.5	94.3	104.6	119.5	124.4	2.5
Hotels and motels	701	99.9	103.9	101.2	96.0	111.0	113.2	0.6
Laundry, cleaning, and garment services	721	109.8	103.2	103.3	101.0	101.9	105.1	-0.2
Beauty and barber shops	723,4	80.2	85.7	94.6	97.4	103.4	107.1	1.5
Automotive repair shops	753	106.7	100.4	99.4	106.9	110.4	116.4	0.4

NA Not available. [1] 1987 Standard Industrial Classification; see text, section 13. [2] Average annual percent change based on compound rate formula. [3] N.e.c. means not elsewhere classified. [4] Change from 1985-95. [5] Refers to output per full-time equivalent employee years on fiscal basis. [6] Refers to output per employee. [7] Change from 1980-95.

Source: U.S. Bureau of Labor Statistics, Internet site <http://stats.bls.gov:80/iprhome.htm> (accessed 20 June 1997).

No. 664. Productivity and Related Measures: 1970 to 1996

[See text, section 13. Minus sign (-) indicates decrease]

ITEM	1970	1980	1985	1990	1992	1993	1994	1995	1996
INDEXES (1992=100)									
Output per hour, business sector	70.4	84.3	92.0	96.1	100.0	100.2	100.7	100.8	101.8
Nonfarm business	72.7	86.1	92.5	96.2	100.0	100.2	100.7	100.9	101.6
Manufacturing	55.0	71.2	83.7	94.2	100.0	102.1	105.2	108.9	113.1
Output, [1] business sector	51.8	72.9	85.9	98.7	100.0	102.7	107.0	109.6	112.9
Nonfarm business	52.2	73.5	85.8	98.8	100.0	102.9	107.0	109.9	113.0
Manufacturing	57.5	76.6	87.6	96.8	100.0	103.5	109.3	113.1	116.2
Hours, [2] business sector	73.6	86.5	93.4	102.6	100.0	102.5	106.2	108.8	110.9
Nonfarm business	71.7	85.3	92.8	102.7	100.0	102.8	106.3	108.9	111.2
Manufacturing	104.5	107.6	104.7	104.9	100.0	101.4	103.8	103.9	102.8
Compensation per hour, [3] business sector	23.6	54.5	73.2	90.7	100.0	102.5	104.5	107.8	111.8
Nonfarm business	23.8	54.9	73.5	90.6	100.0	102.3	104.3	107.7	111.6
Manufacturing	23.8	55.8	75.3	90.9	100.0	102.4	105.1	109.0	112.8
Real hourly compensation, [3] business sector	85.4	92.8	95.4	97.4	100.0	99.5	99.0	99.2	100.0
Nonfarm business	86.2	93.5	95.9	97.3	100.0	99.3	98.8	99.1	99.8
Manufacturing	86.1	95.0	96.1	97.6	100.0	99.4	99.5	100.4	100.9
Unit labor costs, [4] business sector	33.6	64.7	79.6	94.4	100.0	102.3	103.8	106.9	109.9
Nonfarm business	32.8	63.8	79.5	94.2	100.0	102.1	103.7	106.7	109.8
Manufacturing	43.3	78.4	90.0	96.5	100.0	100.3	99.9	100.2	99.8
ANNUAL PERCENT CHANGE [5]									
Output per hour, business sector	1.8	-0.2	1.8	0.8	3.4	0.2	0.5	0.1	1.0
Nonfarm business	1.4	-0.4	1.0	0.5	3.2	0.2	0.5	0.3	0.7
Manufacturing	3.0	0.7	3.7	1.8	3.6	2.1	3.1	3.4	3.9
Output, [1] business sector	-0.3	-1.1	4.1	0.9	3.2	2.7	4.2	2.5	3.0
Nonfarm business	-0.2	-1.2	3.6	0.7	3.0	2.9	4.0	2.7	2.9
Manufacturing	-3.0	-3.9	3.0	-0.4	3.0	3.5	5.6	3.5	2.8
Hours, [2] business sector	-2.0	-0.9	2.2	0.1	-0.2	2.5	3.7	2.4	2.0
Nonfarm business	-1.6	-0.8	2.5	0.2	-0.2	2.8	3.5	2.4	2.2
Manufacturing	-5.9	-4.6	-0.7	-2.2	-0.6	1.4	2.4	0.1	-1.0
Compensation per hour, [3] business sector	7.8	10.8	4.9	5.7	5.2	2.5	1.9	3.1	3.8
Nonfarm business	7.2	10.8	4.6	5.5	5.2	2.3	2.1	3.2	3.6
Manufacturing	7.1	11.9	5.4	4.8	4.5	2.4	2.7	3.7	3.5
Real hourly compensation, [3] business sector	1.9	-2.4	1.3	0.3	2.1	-0.5	-0.6	0.3	0.8
Nonfarm business	1.4	-2.4	1.0	0.1	2.1	-0.7	-0.5	0.3	0.7
Manufacturing	1.3	-1.4	1.8	-0.5	1.5	-0.6	0.1	0.9	0.5
Unit labor costs, [4] business sector	5.9	11.0	3.0	4.9	1.7	2.3	1.4	3.0	2.8
Nonfarm business	5.7	11.2	3.6	5.0	1.9	2.1	1.5	2.9	2.9
Manufacturing	4.0	11.2	1.6	3.0	0.9	0.3	-0.4	0.3	-0.3

[1] Refers to gross sectoral product, annual weighted. [2] Hours at work of all persons engaged in the business and nonfarm business sectors (employees, proprietors, and unpaid family workers); employees' and proprietors' hours in manufacturing. [3] Wages and salaries of employees plus employers' contributions for social insurance and private benefit plans. Also includes an estimate of same for self-employed. Real compensation deflated by the consumer price index for all urban consumers, see text, section 15. [4] Hourly compensation divided by output per hour. [5] All changes are from the immediate prior year.

Source: U.S. Bureau of Labor Statistics, News USDL 97-75, *Productivity and Costs.*

No. 665. Drug Testing in the Workplace: 1992-93

[In percent, except as indicated. For private industry establishments with 50 or more workers. Based on sample survey; see source for details]

CHARACTERISTIC	WORKSITES						EMPLOYEES		
	Total (1,000)	Worksites that test for drugs					Total (1,000)	In worksites that—	
		Total	Tests current employees [1]	Tests only applicants	Tests only transportation regulated employees	Tests for alcohol use		Test for drugs	Tests for alcohol use
All worksites	162.8	48.4	23.6	14.0	3.6	23.0	41,127	62.3	32.7
EMPLOYEE SIZE									
50 TO 99 employees	61.6	40.2	19.9	10.4	5.3	16.5	4,319	40.7	16.7
100 TO 249 employees	66.0	48.2	24.6	14.5	2.4	22.9	9,612	48.9	23.2
250 to 999 employees	29.0	61.4	28.3	19.2	2.8	32.7	12,520	62.8	33.5
1,000 employees or more	6.2	70.9	27.2	19.1	3.2	42.1	14,675	77.1	43.0
INDUSTRY									
Wholesale and retail trade	32.2	53.7	26.6	14.7	5.7	22.1	4,901	57.3	27.7
Communications, utilities, and transportation	13.5	72.4	27.4	13.0	13.4	34.9	4,202	85.8	43.9
Finance, insurance and real estate	14.2	22.6	7.0	12.3	(B)	7.8	4,369	50.2	12.2
Mining and construction	5.6	69.6	49.0	6.9	4.0	28.6	801	77.7	32.2
Services	43.3	27.9	16.5	6.0	1.2	17.4	12,796	47.5	32.7

[1] Many of these worksites also test applicants.

Source: U.S. Bureau of Labor Statistics, *Monthly Labor Review*, November 1996.

No. 666. Annual Total Compensation and Wages and Salary Accruals Per Full-Time Equivalent Employee, by Industry: 1990 to 1994

[In dollars. Wage and salary accruals include executives' compensation, bonuses, tips, and payments-in-kind; total compensation includes in addition to wages and salaries, employer contributions for social insurance, employer contributions to private and welfare funds, director's fees, jury and witness fees, etc. Based on the 1987 Standard Industrial Classification Code (SIC); See text, section 13]

INDUSTRY	ANNUAL TOTAL COMPENSATION				ANNUAL WAGES AND SALARIES			
	1990	1992	1993	1994	1990	1992	1993	1994
Domestic industries	32,093	35,173	36,123	36,834	26,396	28,667	29,351	29,922
Agriculture, forestry, and fisheries	16,638	19,438	20,320	21,435	16,014	16,746	17,365	18,404
Mining	46,053	52,046	54,015	55,491	38,081	42,242	43,598	44,161
Construction	33,701	36,025	36,338	36,718	27,832	29,347	29,417	29,560
Manufacturing	37,046	40,938	42,427	43,777	30,148	32,813	33,747	34,715
Transportation	36,636	39,956	40,394	39,853	29,019	31,514	31,675	31,325
Communication	46,481	50,865	54,535	53,308	36,930	42,212	45,123	44,027
Electric, gas, and sanitary services	48,057	53,360	56,324	58,653	39,538	43,160	45,346	47,069
Wholesale trade	37,394	40,815	42,258	43,528	31,810	34,352	35,367	36,504
Retail trade	18,678	20,409	20,613	21,071	16,065	17,430	17,598	18,044
Finance, insurance, and real estate	37,905	43,529	46,360	47,252	32,071	36,403	38,776	39,547
Services	29,141	31,650	32,404	32,924	24,996	26,943	27,464	27,839
Government	37,142	41,021	42,150	43,190	28,195	30,976	31,850	32,704

Source: U.S. Bureau of Economic Analysis, *National Income and Product Accounts of the United States, 1929-94*, forthcoming; and *Survey of Current Business*, May 1997.

No. 667. Average Hourly and Weekly Earnings, by Private Industry Group: 1980 to 1996

[Average earnings include overtime. Data are for production and related workers in mining, manufacturing, and construction, and nonsupervisory employees in other industries. Excludes agriculture. See headnote, table 660]

PRIVATE INDUSTRY GROUP	CURRENT DOLLARS					CONSTANT (1982) DOLLARS[1]				
	1980	1985	1990	1995	1996	1980	1989	1990	1995	1996
TOTAL AVERAGE HOURLY EARNINGS										
Total	6.66	8.57	10.01	11.44	11.82	7.78	7.77	7.52	7.40	7.43
Mining	9.17	11.98	13.68	15.30	15.60	10.71	10.86	10.28	9.90	9.81
Construction	9.94	12.32	13.77	15.08	15.43	11.61	11.17	10.35	9.75	9.70
Manufacturing	7.27	9.54	10.83	12.37	12.78	8.49	8.65	8.14	8.00	8.04
Transportation, public utilities	8.87	11.40	12.97	14.23	14.52	10.36	10.34	9.74	9.20	9.13
Wholesale trade	6.95	9.15	10.79	12.43	12.84	8.12	8.30	8.11	8.04	8.08
Retail trade	4.88	5.94	6.75	7.69	7.98	5.70	5.39	5.07	4.97	5.02
Finance, insurance, real estate	5.79	7.94	9.97	12.33	12.80	6.76	7.20	7.49	7.98	8.05
Services	5.85	7.90	9.83	11.39	11.80	6.83	7.16	7.39	7.37	7.42
TOTAL AVERAGE WEEKLY EARNINGS										
Total	235	299	345	395	407	275	271	259	255	256
Mining	397	520	603	684	707	464	471	453	442	444
Construction	368	464	526	585	600	430	421	395	378	378
Manufacturing	289	386	442	515	532	337	350	332	333	334
Transportation, public utilities	351	450	505	562	576	410	408	379	364	363
Wholesale trade	267	351	411	476	492	312	319	309	308	309
Retail trade	147	175	194	221	230	172	158	146	143	145
Finance, insurance, real estate	210	289	357	443	460	245	262	268	286	289
Services	191	257	319	369	382	223	233	240	239	240

[1] Earnings in current dollars divided by the Consumer Price Index (CPI-W) on a 1982 base; see text, section 15.

Source: U.S. Bureau of Labor Statistics, Bulletins 2445 and 2481, and *Employment and Earnings*, monthly, March and June issues.

No. 668. Annual Percent Changes in Earnings and Compensation: 1980 to 1996

[Annual percent change from immediate prior year. Minus sign (-) indicates decrease]

ITEM	1980	1985	1990	1991	1992	1993	1994	1995	1996
Current dollars:									
Hourly earnings, total[1]	8.1	3.0	3.6	3.1	2.4	2.5	2.7	2.9	3.3
Hourly earnings, manufacturing[2]	8.5	3.8	3.3	3.2	2.5	2.4	2.8	2.5	3.3
Compensation per employee-hour[3]	10.7	4.6	5.5	4.9	5.2	2.2	2.0	3.2	3.7
Constant (1982) dollars:									
Hourly earnings, total[1]	-4.8	-0.4	-1.6	-0.9	-0.5	-0.3	0.1	-	0.4
Hourly earnings, manufacturing[2]	-4.5	0.3	-1.7	-0.9	-0.4	-0.4	0.2	-0.4	0.5
Compensation per employee-hour[3]	-2.5	1.0	0.1	0.7	2.1	-0.7	-0.5	0.3	0.7
Consumer Price Index (CPI-U)[4]	13.5	3.6	5.4	4.2	3.0	3.0	2.6	2.8	3.0

- Represents zero. [1] Production or nonsupervisory workers on private nonfarm payrolls. [2] Production and related workers. [3] Nonfarm business sector. [4] See text, section 15.

Source: U.S. Bureau of Labor Statistics, News USDL 97-75, *Productivity and Costs*.

No. 669. Average Annual Pay, by State: 1994 and 1995

[In dollars, except percent change. For workers covered by State unemployment insurance laws and for Federal civilian workers covered by unemployment compensation for Federal employees, approximately 97 percent of wage and salary civilian employment in 1995. Excludes most agricultural workers on small farms, all Armed Forces, elected officials in most States, railroad employees, most domestic workers, most student workers at school, employees of certain nonprofit organizations, and most self-employed individuals. Pay includes bonuses, cash value of meals and lodging, and tips and other gratuities]

STATE	AVERAGE ANNUAL PAY		Percent change, 1994-95 [1]	STATE	AVERAGE ANNUAL PAY		Percent change, 1994-95 [1]
	1994	1995 [1]			1994	1995 [1]	
United States	26,939	27,845	3.4	Missouri	24,628	25,669	4.2
Alabama	23,616	24,396	3.3	Montana	20,218	20,516	1.5
Alaska	32,657	32,685	0.1	Nebraska	21,500	22,366	4.0
Arizona	24,276	25,324	4.3	Nevada	25,700	26,647	3.7
Arkansas	20,898	21,590	3.3	New Hampshire	25,555	26,602	4.1
California	29,878	30,716	2.8	New Jersey	33,439	34,534	3.3
Colorado	26,155	27,122	3.7	New Mexico	22,351	22,960	2.7
Connecticut	33,811	35,127	3.9	New York	33,439	34,938	4.5
Delaware	27,952	29,120	4.2	North Carolina	23,460	24,402	4.0
District of Columbia	40,919	42,453	3.7	North Dakota	19,893	20,492	3.0
Florida	23,918	24,710	3.3	Ohio	26,134	26,867	2.8
Georgia	25,313	26,303	3.9	Oklahoma	22,293	22,671	1.7
Hawaii	26,746	26,977	0.9	Oregon	24,780	25,833	4.2
Idaho	21,938	22,839	4.1	Pennsylvania	26,950	27,904	3.5
Illinois	29,107	30,099	3.4	Rhode Island	25,454	26,375	3.6
Indiana	24,908	25,571	2.7	South Carolina	22,477	23,292	3.6
Iowa	22,189	22,875	3.1	South Dakota	19,255	19,931	3.5
Kansas	22,907	23,709	3.5	Tennessee	24,106	25,046	3.9
Kentucky	22,747	23,490	3.3	Texas	25,959	26,900	3.6
Louisiana	23,178	23,894	3.1	Utah	22,811	23,626	3.6
Maine	22,389	23,117	3.3	Vermont	22,964	23,583	2.7
Maryland	28,416	29,133	2.5	Virginia	26,035	26,894	3.3
Massachusetts	31,024	32,352	4.3	Washington	26,362	27,453	4.1
Michigan	29,541	30,543	3.4	West Virginia	22,959	23,489	2.3
Minnesota	26,422	27,383	3.6	Wisconsin	24,324	25,099	3.2
Mississippi	20,382	21,120	3.6	Wyoming	22,054	22,351	1.3

[1] Preliminary.

Source: U.S. Bureau of Labor Statistics, USDL News 96-393, *Average Annual Pay by State and Industry.*

No. 670. Average Annual Pay, by Selected Metropolitan Areas: 1994 and 1995

[In dollars. Metropolitan areas ranked by average pay 1995. Includes data for Metropolitan Statistical Areas and Primary Metropolitan Statistical Areas defined as of July 5, 1994. In the New England areas, the New England County Metropolitan Area (NECMA) definitions were used. See source for details. See also headnote table 669]

METROPOLITAN AREA	1994	1995 [1]	METROPOLITAN AREA	1994	1995 [1]
Metropolitan areas	28,125	29,105	Dutchess County, NY	28,860	29,707
San Jose, CA	39,123	42,409	Rochester, NY	28,299	29,302
New York, NY	39,933	42,272	Sacramento, CA	28,125	29,289
San Francisco, CA	36,510	37,975	Rochester, MN	28,262	29,155
Middlesex-Somerset-Hunterdon, NJ	36,690	37,925	Monmouth-Ocean, NJ	28,338	29,033
New Haven-Bridgeport-Stamford-Danbury-			Bloomington-Normal, IL	27,769	29,020
Waterbury, CT	35,535	37,546	Baltimore, MD	27,955	28,745
Newark, NJ	35,910	37,224	Cleveland-Lorain-Elyria, OH	27,927	28,742
Trenton, NJ	35,345	36,614	Yolo, CA	27,825	28,616
Bergen-Passaic, NJ	34,675	35,746	Springfield, IL	27,963	28,614
Washington, DC-MD-VA-WV	33,947	34,891	St Louis, MO-IL	27,392	28,599
Detroit, MI	33,201	34,706	Boulder-Longmont, CO	26,948	28,441
Jersey City, NJ	33,012	34,621	Portland-Vancouver, OR-WA	27,065	28,357
Kokomo, IN	33,231	33,967	Lansing-East Lansing, MI	28,026	28,151
Hartford, CT	33,172	33,948	Indianapolis, IN	27,437	28,061
Anchorage, AK	34,098	33,650	Cincinnati, OH-KY-IN	27,106	28,057
Flint, MI	33,219	33,389	Pittsburgh, PA	27,121	28,051
Oakland, CA	32,157	33,180	Honolulu, HI	27,736	27,936
Boston-Worcester-Lawrence-Lowell-			Milwaukee-Waukesha, WI	26,958	27,926
Brockton, MA-NH	31,403	32,791	Raleigh-Durham-Chapel Hill, NC	26,703	27,925
Chicago, IL	31,340	32,524	West Palm Beach-Boca Raton, FL	26,617	27,911
Los Angeles-Long Beach, CA	31,831	32,445	Charlotte-Gastonia-Rock Hill, NC-SC	26,520	27,859
Philadelphia, PA-NJ	30,519	31,695	San Diego, CA	27,261	27,842
Nassau-Suffolk, NY	30,765	31,635	Allentown-Bethlehem-Easton, PA	26,602	27,804
Seattle-Bellevue-Everett, WA	30,181	31,550	Albany-Schenectady-Troy, NY	27,231	27,694
Dallas, TX	30,105	31,502	Dayton-Springfield, OH	26,721	27,673
Wilmington-Newark, DE-MD	30,175	31,439	Kansas City, MO-KS	26,601	27,597
Houston, TX	30,349	31,390	Richmond-Petersburg, VA	26,483	27,596
Huntsville, AL	30,389	31,233	Richland-Kennewick-Pasco, WA	26,835	27,570
New London-Norwich, CT	30,015	30,892	Peoria-Pekin, IL	27,010	27,548
Orange County, CA	30,315	30,889	Gary, IN	26,671	27,498
Minneapolis-St Paul, MN-WI	29,102	30,185	Fort Worth-Arlington, TX	26,463	27,454
Denver, CO	28,965	30,059	Miami, FL	26,488	27,452
Ann Arbor, MI	29,258	30,013	Reading, PA	26,705	27,442
Atlanta, GA	28,688	29,952	Nashville, TN	26,200	27,345
Brazoria, TX	28,941	29,892	Decatur, IL	27,071	27,339
Saginaw-Bay City-Midland, MI	29,080	29,863	Birmingham, AL	26,252	27,337

[1] Preliminary.

Source: U.S. Bureau of Labor Statistics, USDL News 96-463, *Average Annual Pay Levels in Metropolitan Areas, 1995.*

No. 671. Full-Time Wage and Salary Workers—Number and Earnings: 1985 to 1996

[In current dollars of usual weekly earnings. Data represent annual averages of quarterly data. See text, section 13, and headnote table 636, for a discussion of occupational data. Based on Current Population Survey; see text, section 1, and Appendix III. For definition of median, see Guide to Tabular Presentation]

CHARACTERISTIC	NUMBER OF WORKERS (1,000)				MEDIAN WEEKLY EARNINGS (dol.)			
	1985	1990 [1]	1995 [1]	1996 [1]	1985	1990 [1]	1995 [1]	1996 [1]
All workers [2]	77,002	85,804	89,282	90,918	343	412	479	490
Male	45,589	49,564	51,222	51,895	406	481	538	557
16 to 24 years old	6,956	6,824	6,118	5,976	240	282	303	307
25 years old and over	38,632	42,740	45,104	45,919	442	512	586	599
Female	31,414	36,239	38,060	39,023	277	346	406	418
16 to 24 years old	5,621	5,227	4,366	4,307	210	254	275	284
25 years old and over	25,793	31,012	33,695	34,715	296	369	428	444
White	66,481	72,811	74,874	76,151	355	424	494	506
Male	40,030	42,797	43,747	44,428	417	494	566	580
Female	26,452	30,014	31,127	31,724	281	353	415	428
Black	8,393	9,820	10,596	10,871	277	329	383	387
Male	4,367	4,983	5,279	5,316	304	361	411	412
Female	4,026	4,837	5,317	5,555	252	308	355	362
Hispanic origin [3]	(NA)	7,812	8,719	9,082	(NA)	304	329	339
Male	(NA)	5,000	5,597	5,831	(NA)	318	350	356
Female	(NA)	2,812	3,122	3,251	(NA)	278	305	316
Family relationship:								
Husbands	30,260	(NA)	(NA)	(NA)	455	(NA)	(NA)	(NA)
Wives	16,270	(NA)	(NA)	(NA)	285	(NA)	(NA)	(NA)
Women who maintain families	4,333	(NA)	(NA)	(NA)	278	(NA)	(NA)	(NA)
Men who maintain families	1,313	(NA)	(NA)	(NA)	396	(NA)	(NA)	(NA)
Other persons in families:								
Men	6,173	(NA)	(NA)	(NA)	238	(NA)	(NA)	(NA)
Women	4,309	(NA)	(NA)	(NA)	213	(NA)	(NA)	(NA)
All other men [4]	7,841	(NA)	(NA)	(NA)	380	(NA)	(NA)	(NA)
All other women [4]	6,503	(NA)	(NA)	(NA)	305	(NA)	(NA)	(NA)
Occupation, male:								
Managerial and professional	11,078	12,255	13,684	13,934	583	729	829	852
Exec., admin., managerial	5,835	6,389	7,172	7,187	593	740	833	846
Professional specialty	5,243	5,866	6,512	6,747	571	719	827	857
Technical, sales, and administrative support	8,803	9,677	9,894	9,988	420	493	556	567
Tech. and related support	1,563	1,762	1,688	1,662	472	567	641	650
Sales	4,227	4,692	5,000	5,114	431	502	579	589
Admin. support, incl. clerical	3,013	3,224	3,206	3,212	391	436	489	489
Service	3,947	4,602	4,779	4,958	272	317	357	357
Private household	13	12	15	19	(B)	(B)	(B)	(B)
Protective	1,327	1,531	1,691	1,627	391	477	552	562
Other service	2,607	3,059	3,073	3,312	230	271	300	304
Precision production [5]	10,026	10,259	10,046	10,076	408	486	534	560
Mechanics and repairers	3,752	3,687	3,658	3,672	400	475	538	571
Construction trades	3,308	3,650	3,541	3,585	394	478	507	518
Other	2,966	2,922	2,847	2,819	433	506	574	588
Operators, fabricators and laborers	10,585	11,464	11,529	11,613	325	375	413	422
Machine operators, assemblers, and inspectors	4,403	4,594	4,576	4,527	341	387	421	437
Transportation and material moving	3,459	3,752	3,870	3,982	369	416	482	486
Handlers, equipment cleaners, helpers, and laborers	2,724	3,118	3,083	3,105	261	306	328	343
Farming, forestry, and fishing	1,150	1,306	1,290	1,326	216	261	294	300
Occupation, female:								
Managerial and professional	8,302	10,575	12,609	13,288	399	510	605	616
Exec., admin., managerial	3,492	4,758	5,803	6,113	383	484	570	585
Professional specialty	4,810	5,816	6,806	7,175	408	534	632	647
Technical, sales, and administrative support	14,622	16,290	16,004	16,128	269	331	383	394
Tech. and related support	1,200	1,476	1,506	1,553	331	417	480	498
Sales	2,929	3,554	3,862	3,927	226	290	330	353
Admin. support, incl. clerical	10,494	11,260	10,636	10,648	270	332	384	391
Service	3,963	4,577	4,838	5,000	185	230	264	273
Private household	330	305	324	346	130	171	193	213
Protective	156	217	266	275	278	405	438	439
Other service	3,477	4,055	4,249	4,379	186	230	264	272
Precision production [5]	906	900	957	944	268	316	371	373
Mechanics and repairers	144	139	150	162	392	458	550	510
Construction trades	53	50	66	68	265	393	400	389
Other	709	711	741	714	253	299	346	357
Operators, fabricators, and laborers	3,482	3,722	3,462	3,487	216	261	297	307
Machine operators, assemblers, and inspectors	2,778	2,878	2,559	2,573	216	259	296	307
Transportation and material moving	189	227	261	272	252	314	354	350
Handlers, equipment cleaners, helpers and laborers	514	616	642	642	209	249	264	295
Farming, forestry, and fishing	138	175	190	176	185	216	249	255

B Data not shown where base is less than 50,000. NA Not available. [1] See footnote 2, table 619. [2] Includes other races, not shown separately. [3] Persons of Hispanic origin may be of any race. [4] The majority of these persons are living alone or with nonrelatives. Also included are persons in families where the husband, wife or other person maintaining the family is in the Armed Forces, and persons in unrelated subfamilies. [5] Includes craft and repair.

Source: U.S. Bureau of Labor Statistics, Bulletin 2307, and *Employment and Earnings*, monthly, January issues; and unpublished data.

No. 672. Workers With Earnings, by Occupation of Longest Held Job and Sex: 1995

[Covers persons 15 years old and over as of March 1996. Based on Current Population Survey; see text, section 1, and Appendix III. For definition of median, see Guide to Tabular Presentation]

MAJOR OCCUPATION OF LONGEST JOB HELD	ALL WORKERS				YEAR ROUND FULL-TIME			
	Women		Men		Women		Men	
	Number (1,000)	Median earnings	Number (1,000)	Median earnings	Number (1,000)	Median earnings	Number (1,000)	Median earnings
Total [1]	**65,567**	**15,322**	**74,819**	**25,016**	**35,482**	**22,497**	**52,667**	**31,496**
Executive, administrators, and managerial	8,013	26,787	10,156	42,304	6,022	30,635	8,718	46,534
Professional specialty	10,487	27,234	8,799	41,639	6,107	33,301	6,837	47,339
Technical and related support	2,515	21,968	1,835	31,619	1,534	26,806	1,463	36,035
Sales	9,056	9,571	8,479	26,047	3,815	20,279	6,073	35,064
Admin. support, incl. clerical	15,813	16,292	4,366	21,960	9,452	21,141	3,076	27,423
Precision production, craft and repair	1,288	16,792	13,180	26,074	806	21,343	9,602	30,421
Machine operators, assemblers, and inspectors	3,573	12,361	5,375	21,222	2,105	16,473	4,065	24,262
Transportation and material moving	549	12,787	5,124	22,151	245	19,063	3,630	26,607
Handlers, equipment cleaners, helpers, and laborers	1,123	9,686	4,948	11,796	496	14,864	2,358	18,858
Service workers	12,294	7,483	8,147	12,345	4,584	14,477	4,397	21,331
Private household	1,007	4,062	67	2,006	241	10,435	10	(B)
Service, except private household	11,288	7,925	8,079	12,432	4,343	14,718	4,386	21,359
Farming, forestry, and fishing	789	5,015	3,462	10,756	283	11,883	1,790	17,349

B Base less than 75,000. [1] Includes persons whose longest job was in the Armed Forces.

Source: U.S. Bureau of the Census, Internet site <http://www.census.gov/prod/2/pop/p60/p60-193.pdf> (accessed 23 June 1997).

No. 673. Employment Cost Index (ECI), by Industry and Occupation: 1982 to 1996

[As of December. The ECI is a measure of the rate of change in employee compensation (wages, salaries, and employer costs for employee benefits). Data are not seasonally adjusted: 1982-1985 based on fixed employment counts from 1970 Census of Population; 1986-94 based on fixed employment counts from the 1980 Census of Population; 1995 based primarily on 1990 Occupational Employment Survey]

ITEM	INDEXES (June 1989=100)						PERCENT CHANGE FOR 12 MONTHS ENDING DEC.—				
	1982	1985	1990	1994	1995	1996	1985	1990	1994	1995	1996
Civilian workers [1]	**74.8**	**86.8**	**107.6**	**123.8**	**127.2**	**130.9**	**4.3**	**4.9**	**3.0**	**2.7**	**2.9**
Workers, by occupational group:											
White-collar occupations	72.9	85.8	108.3	124.4	128.0	131.9	4.9	5.2	3.2	2.9	3.0
Blue-collar occupations	78.2	88.4	106.5	122.7	125.8	129.1	3.3	4.4	2.8	2.5	2.6
Service occupations	74.3	87.2	108.0	124.3	127.4	131.0	3.9	5.1	3.2	2.5	2.8
Workers, by industry division:											
Manufacturing	76.9	87.8	107.2	125.1	128.3	132.1	3.3	5.1	3.1	2.6	3.0
Nonmanufacturing	73.9	86.4	107.8	123.4	126.8	130.5	4.7	4.9	3.0	2.8	2.9
Service industries	70.5	84.1	110.2	126.4	129.4	133.2	4.7	6.3	2.8	2.4	2.9
Public administration [2]	71.9	85.4	108.7	124.2	128.3	131.8	4.9	5.3	3.5	3.3	2.7
Private industry workers [3]	**75.8**	**87.3**	**107.0**	**123.5**	**126.7**	**130.6**	**3.9**	**4.6**	**3.1**	**2.6**	**3.1**
Workers, by occupational group:											
White-collar occupations	73.7	86.4	107.4	124.1	127.6	131.7	4.9	4.9	3.2	2.8	3.2
Blue-collar occupations	78.4	88.5	106.4	122.6	125.6	129.0	3.1	4.4	2.8	2.4	2.7
Service occupations	76.3	88.4	107.3	122.9	125.2	128.9	3.0	4.7	2.8	1.9	3.0
Workers, by industry division:											
Manufacturing	76.9	87.8	107.2	125.1	128.3	132.1	3.3	5.1	3.1	2.6	3.0
Nonmanufacturing	75.1	87.0	106.9	122.6	125.9	129.8	4.3	4.5	3.0	2.7	3.1
Service industries	(NA)	84.1	109.3	126.6	129.4	133.4	(NA)	6.2	2.8	2.2	3.1
Business services	(NA)	(NA)	107.4	123.0	126.3	131.8	(NA)	6.0	3.7	2.7	4.4
Health services	(NA)	83.7	110.8	128.7	132.2	134.5	(NA)	6.8	2.1	2.7	1.7
Hospitals	(NA)	(NA)	110.7	128.6	131.3	133.7	(NA)	7.0	2.4	2.1	1.8
Workers by bargaining status:											
Union	79.6	90.1	106.2	124.2	127.7	130.8	2.6	4.3	2.7	2.8	2.4
Nonunion	74.3	86.3	107.3	123.2	126.5	130.4	4.6	4.8	3.1	2.7	3.1
State and local government	**70.8**	**84.6**	**110.4**	**125.6**	**129.3**	**132.7**	**5.6**	**5.8**	**3.0**	**2.9**	**2.6**
Workers, by occupational group:											
White-collar occupations	70.4	84.2	110.9	125.5	129.1	132.5	5.8	6.0	3.0	2.9	2.6
Blue-collar workers	73.9	86.7	108.7	124.7	128.0	131.2	5.3	4.8	2.7	2.6	2.5
Workers, by industry division:											
Service industries	70.0	84.0	111.3	126.1	129.6	133.1	5.9	6.3	2.9	2.8	2.7
Schools	69.0	83.6	111.6	126.3	129.8	133.4	6.2	6.0	2.8	2.8	2.8
Elementary and secondary	68.6	83.6	112.1	126.5	130.1	133.1	6.4	6.3	2.3	2.8	2.3
Colleges and universities	(NA)	(NA)	110.2	125.5	128.7	134.0	(NA)	5.3	4.0	2.5	4.1
Services, excluding schools [4]	73.1	85.2	110.2	125.6	129.4	132.0	4.7	6.8	3.0	3.0	2.0
Public administration [2]	71.9	85.4	108.7	124.2	128.3	131.8	4.9	5.3	3.5	3.3	2.7

NA Not available. [1] Includes private industry and State and local government workers and excludes farm, household, and Federal government workers. [2] Consists of legislative, judicial, administrative, and regulatory activities. [3] Excludes farm and household workers. [4] Includes library, social, and health services. Formerly called hospitals and other services.

Source: U.S. Bureau of Labor Statistics, *News, Employment Cost Index*, quarterly; and Internet site <http://stats.bls.gov/ecthome.htm>

No. 674. Federal Minimum Wage Rates: 1956 to 1995

YEAR	VALUE OF THE MINIMUM WAGE[1]		YEAR	VALUE OF THE MINIMUM WAGE[1]	
	Current dollars	Constant (1995) dollars[2]		Current dollars	Constant (1995) dollars[2]
1956	1.00	5.60	1976	2.30	6.16
1957	1.00	5.42	1977	2.30	5.78
1958	1.00	5.27	1978	2.65	6.19
1959	1.00	5.24	1979	2.90	6.09
1960	1.00	5.15	1980	3.10	5.73
1961	1.15	5.86	1981	3.35	5.62
1962	1.15	5.80	1982	3.35	5.29
1963	1.25	6.23	1983	3.35	5.13
1964	1.25	6.15	1984	3.35	4.91
1965	1.25	6.05	1985	3.35	4.74
1966	1.25	5.88	1986	3.35	4.66
1967	1.40	6.39	1987	3.35	4.49
1968	1.60	7.01	1988	3.35	4.32
1969	1.60	6.64	1989	3.35	4.12
1970	1.60	6.28	1990	3.80	4.43
1971	1.60	6.02	1991	4.25	4.76
1972	1.60	5.83	1992	4.25	4.62
1973	1.60	5.49	1993	4.25	4.48
1974	2.00	6.18	1994	4.25	4.37
1975	2.10	5.95	1995	4.25	4.25

[1] Effective October 1, 1996 the minimum wage rose to $4.75; on September 1, 1997 it will rise to $5.15. [2] Adjusted for inflation using the CPI-U; see text, section 15.

Source:U.S. Bureau of Labor Statistics, Internet site <http://www.dol.gov/esa/public/minwage> (accessed 25 June 1997).

No. 675. Workers Paid Hourly Rates, by Selected Characteristics: 1996

[Data are for the fourth quarter of 1996, not seasonally adjusted. For employed wage and salary workers. Based on Current Population Survey; see text, section 1, and Appendix III]

CHARACTERISTIC	NUMBER OF WORKERS[1] (1,000)				PERCENT OF ALL WORKERS PAID HOURLY RATES			Median hourly earnings of workers paid hourly rates[2]
	Total paid hourly rates	At or below $4.75			At or below $4.75			
		Total	At $4.75	Below $4.75	Total	At $4.75	Below $4.75	
Total, 16 years and over[3]	70,431	5,018	1,976	3,042	7.1	2.8	4.3	$8.63
16 to 24 years	15,477	2,587	1,032	1,555	16.7	6.7	10.0	6.01
16 to 19 years	5,918	1,578	702	876	26.7	11.9	14.8	5.22
25 years and over	54,955	2,431	944	1,487	4.4	1.7	2.7	9.77
Male, 16 years and over	35,147	1,795	724	1,071	5.1	2.1	3.0	9.81
16 to 24 years	7,936	1,069	472	597	13.5	5.9	7.5	6.27
16 to 19 years	2,905	640	332	308	22.0	11.4	10.6	5.37
25 years and over	27,211	727	252	475	2.7	0.9	1.7	10.98
Women, 16 years and over	35,285	3,223	1,252	1,971	9.1	3.5	5.6	7.81
16 to 24 years	7,541	1,518	560	958	20.1	7.4	12.7	5.75
16 to 19 years	3,013	938	370	568	31.1	12.3	18.9	5.15
25 years and over	27,744	1,705	692	1,013	6.1	2.5	3.7	8.52
White	58,250	4,047	1,582	2,465	6.9	2.7	4.2	8.79
Black	9,353	799	317	482	8.5	3.4	5.2	7.79
Hispanic origin[4]	8,238	795	359	436	9.7	4.4	5.3	7.24
Full-time workers	52,548	1,818	647	1,171	3.5	1.2	2.2	9.62
Part-time workers[5]	17,735	3,186	1,327	1,859	18.0	7.5	10.5	6.08
Private sector industries	61,685	4,626	1,773	2,853	7.5	2.9	4.6	8.35
Goods-producing[6]	18,911	483	169	314	2.6	0.9	1.7	10.05
Service-producing[7]	42,774	4,143	1,604	2,539	9.7	3.7	5.9	7.67
Public sector	8,746	392	203	189	4.5	2.3	2.2	10.45

[1] Excludes the incorporated self-employed. [2] For definition of median, see Guide to Tabular Presentation. [3] Includes races not shown separately. Also includes a small number of multiple jobholders whose full- part- time status can not be determined for their principal job. [4] Persons of Hispanic origin may be of any race. [5] Working fewer than 35 hours per week. [6] Includes agriculture, mining, construction, and manufacturing. [7] Includes transportation and public utilities; wholesale trade; finance, insurance, and real estate; private households; and other service industries.

Source: U.S. Bureau of Labor Statistics, unpublished data.

No. 676. Employer Costs for Employee Compensation per Hour Worked: 1996

[In dollars. As of March, for private industry workers. Based on a sample of establishments; see source for details]

COMPENSATION COMPONENT	Total	Goods producing [1]	Service producing [2]	Manufacturing	Non-manufacturing	Union members	Non-union members	Full-time workers	Part-time workers
Total compensation	17.49	21.27	16.28	20.99	16.69	23.31	16.61	20.01	9.19
Wages and salaries	12.58	14.38	12.01	14.13	12.23	14.93	12.23	14.16	7.38
Total benefits	4.91	6.89	4.27	6.86	4.46	8.38	4.39	5.85	1.82
Paid leave	1.12	1.43	1.02	1.60	1.00	1.63	1.04	1.38	0.25
Vacation	0.55	0.76	0.49	0.83	0.49	0.89	0.50	(NA)	(NA)
Holiday	0.38	0.51	0.34	0.58	0.33	0.49	0.36	(NA)	(NA)
Sick	0.14	0.11	0.15	0.12	0.14	0.17	0.13	(NA)	(NA)
Other	0.05	0.05	0.05	0.06	0.05	0.07	0.05	(NA)	(NA)
Supplemental pay	0.49	0.85	0.38	0.88	0.40	0.84	0.44	0.60	0.15
Premium pay	0.20	0.42	0.13	0.42	0.15	0.54	0.15	(NA)	(NA)
Nonproduction bonuses	0.24	0.36	0.20	0.37	0.21	0.17	0.25	(NA)	(NA)
Shift pay	0.06	0.07	0.05	0.09	0.05	0.13	0.04	(NA)	(NA)
Insurance	1.14	1.67	0.97	1.72	1.00	2.24	0.97	1.40	0.27
Health insurance	1.04	1.52	0.88	1.56	0.92	2.05	0.88	(NA)	(NA)
Retirement and savings	0.55	0.80	0.47	0.71	0.51	1.32	0.43	0.67	0.13
Defined benefit	0.30	0.48	0.24	0.42	0.27	1.06	0.18	(NA)	(NA)
Defined contributions	0.25	0.32	0.23	0.29	0.24	0.27	0.25	(NA)	(NA)
Legally required [3]	1.59	2.08	1.44	1.86	1.53	2.28	1.49	1.76	1.03
Social Security	1.05	1.22	0.99	1.22	1.01	1.28	1.01	(NA)	(NA)
Federal unemployment	0.03	0.03	0.03	0.03	0.03	0.03	0.03	(NA)	(NA)
State unemployment	0.12	0.16	0.11	0.13	0.11	0.16	0.11	(NA)	(NA)
Workers compensation	0.40	0.67	0.31	0.48	0.38	0.81	0.33	(NA)	(NA)
Other benefits [4]	0.03	0.07	-	0.08	-	0.07	0.02	0.03	-

- Represents or rounds to zero. NA Not available. [1] Mining, construction, and manufacturing. [2] Transportation, communications, public utilities, wholesale trade, retail trade, finance, insurance, real estate, and services. [3] Includes railroad retirement, railroad unemployment, railroad supplemental unemployment, and other legally required benefits, not shown separately. [4] Includes severance pay, and supplemental unemployment benefits.

Source: U.S. Bureau of Labor Statistics, *News, Employer Costs for Employee Compensation*, USDL, 96-424.

No. 677. Employees With Employer- or Union-Provided Pension Plans or Group Health Plans: 1995

[For wage and salary workers 15 years old and over as of March 1996. Based on Current Population Survey; see text, section 1, and Appendix III. Data based on 1990 population controls]

OCCUPATION	Total (1,000)	PERCENT— Included in pension plan	PERCENT— With group health plan
Total	140,337	41.2	53.0
Executive, admin., managerial	18,171	54.2	68.2
Professional specialty	19,289	59.5	67.5
Technical/related support	4,355	55.9	65.7
Sales workers	17,564	28.5	43.3
Admin. support, inc. clerical	20,227	46.4	56.1
Precision prod., craft/repair	14,488	42.9	56.7
Mach. operators, assemblers [1]	8,951	43.3	60.1
Transportation/material moving	5,673	41.5	56.6
Handlers, equipment cleaners [2]	6,080	27.4	40.5
Service workers	20,441	22.5	32.4
Private households	1,074	2.1	5.6
Other	19,367	23.6	33.8
Farming, forestry and fishing	4,294	9.6	22.8
Armed Forces	806	71.5	28.7

CHARACTERISTIC	Total (1,000)	PERCENT— Included in pension plan	PERCENT— With group health plan
AGE			
Total	140,337	41.2	53.0
15 to 24 years	23,572	11.6	22.8
25 to 44 years old	72,066	45.6	57.6
45 to 64 years	39,723	53.1	63.9
65 years and over	4,976	23.1	40.7
WORK EXPERIENCE			
Worked	140,337	41.2	53.0
Full time	110,120	49.0	62.3
50 weeks or more	88,177	54.5	68.2
27 to 49 weeks	12,973	34.3	48.2
26 weeks or fewer	8,970	16.4	24.5
Part time	30,218	12.8	19.0
50 weeks or more	12,794	18.3	25.4
27 to 49 weeks	6,883	13.9	20.0
26 weeks or fewer	10,540	5.4	10.7
EMPLOYER SIZE			
Under 25 persons	42,833	12.4	28.1
25 to 99 persons	17,777	36.3	53.4
100 to 499 persons	19,061	50.0	63.3
500 to 999 persons	8,091	55.3	64.9
Over 1,000 persons	52,575	61.3	67.5

[1] Includes' inspectors. [2] Includes helpers and laborers.

Source: U.S. Bureau of the Census, unpublished data.

No. 678. Employee Benefits in Private Establishments: 1993 and 1994

[Covers full-time employees in private industry. Medium and large establishments exclude establishments with fewer than 100 workers, executive and traveling operating employees, and Alaska and Hawaii. Small establishments include those with fewer than 100 employees. Covers only benefits for which the employer pays part or all of the premium or expenses involved, except unpaid parental leave and long-term care insurance. Based on a sample survey of establishments; for details, see sources. For data on employee benefits in State and local governments, see table 510]

MEDIUM AND LARGE PRIVATE ESTABLISHMENTS, 1993	All employees	Professional, technical and related	Clerical and sales	Production and service
Percent of employees participating in—				
Paid: Vacations	97	97	98	96
Holidays	91	89	93	92
Jury duty leave	90	95	92	85
Funeral leave	83	86	85	80
Rest time	68	54	66	76
Military leave	53	66	54	44
Sick leave	65	85	80	45
Personal leave	21	27	31	13
Lunch time	9	5	5	13
Maternity leave	3	4	3	1
Paternity leave	1	2	1	(Z)
Unpaid: Maternity leave	60	63	60	59
Paternity leave	53	55	51	52
Insurance plans:				
Medical care	82	84	79	82
Noncontributory	37	31	32	44
Hospital/room and board	82	84	79	82
Inpatient surgery	82	84	79	82
Mental health care:				
Inpatient care	80	83	77	80
Outpatient care	80	82	77	79
Dental	62	68	63	58
Extended care facility	67	71	68	66
Home health care	71	74	70	68
Hospice care	53	56	54	52
Vision	26	27	26	27
In HMO's	19	24	21	15
Alcohol abuse treatment:				
Inpatient detoxification	80	82	77	80
Inpatient rehabilitation	66	66	63	58
Outpatient	67	69	65	68
Drug abuse treatment:				
Inpatient detoxification	80	82	77	80
Inpatient rehabilitation	64	65	60	66
Outpatient	66	68	64	65
Life	91	95	92	89
Noncontributory	87	84	87	89
Accident/sickness	44	28	37	57
Noncontributory	75	65	67	81
Long-term disability	41	64	50	23
Noncontributory	73	69	71	80
Retirement and savings plans [1]	78	83	78	76
Defined benefit pension	56	57	54	56
Earnings-based formula [2]	40	50	45	32
Defined contribution	49	60	54	40
Savings and thrift	29	38	34	21
Employee stock ownership	3	3	4	2
Deferred profit sharing	13	12	16	12
Money purchase pension	8	13	7	6
Additional benefits:				
Parking [3]	88	86	85	92
Educational assistance	72	85	72	65
Travel accident insurance	44	59	52	32
Severance pay	42	56	48	31
Relocation allowance [3]	31	50	30	21
Recreation facilities [3]	26	34	25	23
Nonproduction bonuses, cash	38	37	38	38
Child care	7	12	6	4
Flexible benefits plans	12	21	13	6
Reimbursement accounts [4]	52	68	62	37
Eldercare	31	33	32	29
Long-term care insurance	6	8	8	3
Wellness programs	37	51	38	29
Employee assistance programs	62	74	64	53

SMALL PRIVATE ESTABLISHMENTS, 1994	All employees	Professional, technical and related	Clerical and sales	Blue collar and service
Percent of employees participating in—				
Paid time off: Holidays	82	91	89	75
Vacations	88	92	93	83
Personal leave	13	21	17	7
Funeral leave	50	58	55	45
Jury duty leave	58	74	66	48
Military leave	17	23	19	13
Family leave	2	5	2	1
Unpaid family leave	47	53	50	43
Disability benefits:				
Short-term disability	61	75	69	50
Paid sick leave	50	69	61	36
Sickness and accident insurance	26	27	27	25
Long-term disability	20	36	27	10
Survivor benefits:				
Life insurance	61	73	68	52
Accidental death and dismemberment	48	60	52	40
Health care benefits:				
Medical care	66	80	70	57
Dental care	28	40	31	22
Vision care	10	11	11	10
Outpatient prescription drug coverage	60	75	64	51
Retirement income benefits:				
All retirement [1]	42	53	47	35
Defined benefit	15	16	16	15
Defined contribution	34	45	39	26
Savings and thrift	17	23	20	13
Deferred profit sharing	13	16	17	10
Employee stock ownership	1	2	1	1
Money purchase pension	5	9	5	4
Cash or deferred arrangements:				
With employer contributions	20	26	23	15
No employer contributions	3	5	3	2
Income continuation plans:				
Severance pay	15	24	22	8
Supplemental unemployment benefits	(Z)	(Z)	(Z)	(Z)
Family benefits:				
Employer assistance for child care	1	2	1	1
Employer provided funds	1	1	1	(Z)
On-site child care	1	1	(Z)	1
Off-site child care	(Z)	-	(Z)	(Z)
Eldercare	33	38	35	29
Long-term care insurance	1	1	1	(Z)
Health promotion programs:				
Wellness programs	6	8	8	3
Employee assistance	15	19	18	11
Miscellaneous benefits:				
Employer-subsidized recreation facilities	5	7	5	4
Job-related travel accident insurance	13	18	14	10
Nonproduction bonuses	47	48	49	46
Financial counseling	2	3	2	2
Subsidized commuting	1	2	(Z)	(Z)
Sabbatical leave	1	3	1	1
Education assistance:				
Job-related	37	49	46	27
Not job-related	6	7	8	4
Flexible benefit plans	3	2	5	2
Reimbursement accounts [4]	19	26	23	13

- Represents zero. Z Less than .5 percent. [1] Employees may participate in both defined benefit and contribution plans. [2] Earnings-based formulas pay a percent of employee's annual earnings (usually earnings in the final years of employment) per year of service. [3] 1991 data. [4] Account which is used throughout the year to pay for plan premiums or to reimburse the employee for benefit related expenses. Account may be financed by employer, employee, or both.

Source: U.S. Bureau of Labor Statistics, *Employee Benefits in Medium and Large Private Establishments, 1993*, Bulletin 2456; and *Employee Benefits in Small Private Establishments, 1994*, Bulletin 2475.

No. 679. Major Collective Bargaining Agreements—Average Percent Wage Rate Changes Under All Agreements: 1970 to 1995

[In percent, except as indicated. Data represent all wage rate changes implemented under the terms of private nonfarm industry agreements affecting 1,000 workers or more. Series covers production and related workers in manufacturing and nonsupervisory workers in nonmanufacturing industries. Data measure all wage rate changes effective in the year stemming from settlements reached in the year, deferred from prior year settlements, and cost-of-living adjustment (COLA) clauses]

ITEM	1970	1975	1980	1985	1990	1991	1992	1993	1994	1995
Average wage rate change (prorated over all workers)	8.8	8.7	9.9	3.3	3.5	3.6	3.1	3.0	2.7	2.4
Source:										
Current settlements	5.1	2.8	3.6	0.7	1.3	1.1	0.8	0.9	0.6	0.7
Prior settlements	3.1	3.7	3.5	1.8	1.5	1.9	1.9	1.9	1.9	1.5
COLA provisions	0.6	2.2	2.8	0.7	0.7	0.5	0.4	0.2	0.2	0.2
Industry:										
Manufacturing	7.1	8.5	10.2	2.8	4.4	3.7	3.1	3.3	2.4	2.3
Nonmanufacturing	10.5	8.9	9.7	3.6	3.0	3.5	3.1	2.8	2.9	2.4
Construction	(NA)	8.1	9.9	3.0	3.4	3.4	3.4	2.7	2.7	2.8
Transportation and public utilities	(NA)	9.7	10.8	3.6	2.2	3.3	2.7	3.0	2.8	2.2
Wholesale and retail trade	(NA)	9.2	7.6	3.3	3.6	3.5	3.5	2.3	2.9	2.3
Services	(NA)	6.4	8.1	5.1	4.3	4.9	3.7	3.4	3.3	2.2
Nonmanufacturing, excluding construction	(NA)	9.3	9.6	3.7	2.9	3.6	3.0	2.8	2.9	2.3
Average wage rate increase for workers receiving an increase	9.4	9.0	10.1	4.2	4.2	4.0	3.7	3.5	3.3	3.1
Source:										
Current settlements	11.9	10.2	9.4	4.1	4.1	4.2	3.6	3.2	3.2	3.2
Prior settlements	5.8	5.2	5.6	3.7	3.3	3.7	3.8	3.4	3.4	3.1
COLA provisions	3.7	4.8	7.7	2.2	2.7	2.0	2.0	1.3	1.7	1.7
Total number of workers receiving a wage rate increase (mil.)	10.2	9.7	8.9	5.5	4.9	5.1	4.7	4.8	4.6	4.2
Source (mil.):										
Current settlements	4.7	2.7	3.5	1.4	1.9	1.5	1.3	1.7	1.1	1.1
Prior settlements	5.7	7.3	5.6	3.4	2.7	3.0	2.8	3.0	3.0	2.6
COLA provisions	1.8	4.7	3.4	2.3	1.4	1.3	1.0	0.9	0.8	0.7
Number of workers not receiving a wage rate increase (mil.)	0.6	0.4	0.2	1.5	1.0	0.5	0.9	0.7	0.8	1.2

NA Not available.

Source: U.S. Bureau of Labor Statistics, *Compensation and Working Conditions*, monthly through 1995. Data series discontinued. Publication quarterly beginning 1996.

No. 680. Major Collective Bargaining Settlements—Average Percent Changes in Wage and Compensation Rates Negotiated: 1970 to 1995

[In percent, except as indicated. Data represent private nonfarm industry settlements affecting production and related workers in manufacturing and nonsupervisory workers in nonmanufacturing industries. Wage data cover units with 1,000 workers or more. Compensation data relate to units of 5,000 or more. Data relate to contracts negotiated in each calendar year but exclude possible changes in wage rates under cost-of-living adjustment (COLA) clauses, except increases guaranteed by the contract. Includes all settlements, whether wage and benefit rates were changed or not. Minus sign (-) indicates decrease]

ITEM	1970	1975	1980	1985	1990	1991	1992	1993	1994	1995
Compensation rates:										
First year	13.1	11.4	10.4	2.6	4.6	4.1	3.0	3.0	2.3	2.6
Over life of contract [1]	9.1	8.1	7.1	2.7	3.2	3.4	3.1	2.4	2.4	2.5
Wage rates:										
All industries:										
First year	11.9	10.2	9.5	2.3	4.0	3.6	2.7	2.3	2.0	2.3
Contracts with COLA	(NA)	12.2	8.0	1.6	3.4	3.4	2.7	2.8	2.7	1.6
Contracts without COLA	(NA)	9.1	11.7	2.7	4.4	3.7	2.7	2.1	1.8	2.4
Over life of contract [1]	8.9	7.8	7.1	2.7	3.2	3.2	3.0	2.1	2.3	2.5
Contracts with COLA	(NA)	7.1	5.0	2.5	1.9	3.0	2.5	1.4	2.5	1.5
Contracts without COLA	(NA)	8.3	10.3	2.8	4.0	3.3	3.1	2.5	2.3	2.6
Manufacturing:										
First year	8.1	9.8	7.4	0.8	3.7	3.9	2.6	2.7	2.4	2.0
Over life of contract [1]	6.0	8.0	5.4	1.8	2.1	3.1	2.6	1.5	2.3	2.1
Nonmanufacturing:										
First year	15.2	10.4	10.9	3.3	4.3	3.4	2.7	2.1	1.8	2.4
Over life of contract [1]	11.5	7.8	8.3	3.3	4.0	3.3	3.0	2.5	2.3	2.6
Number of workers affected (mil.)	4.7	2.9	3.8	2.2	2.0	1.8	1.6	2.1	1.6	1.5
Manufacturing (mil.)	2.2	0.8	1.6	0.9	0.9	0.6	0.3	0.8	0.4	0.3
Nonmanufacturing (mil.)	2.5	2.1	2.2	1.3	1.1	1.2	1.3	1.3	1.1	1.2

NA Not available. [1] Average annual rate of change.

Source: U.S. Bureau of Labor Statistics, *Compensation and Working Conditions*, monthly through 1995. Data series discontinued. Publication quarterly beginning 1996.

No. 681. Workers Killed or Disabled on the Job: 1960 to 1995

[Data for 1995 are preliminary estimates. Excludes homicides and suicides. Estimates based on data from the U.S. National Center for Health Statistics, State vital statistics departments, State industrial commissions and beginning 1992, Bureau of Labor Statistics, Census of Occupational Fatalities. Numbers of workers based on data from the U.S. Bureau of Labor Statistics]

YEAR	DEATHS						Disabling injuries [2] (mil.)
	Total		Manufacturing		Nonmanufacturing		
	Number (1,000)	Rate [1]	Number (1,000)	Rate [1]	Number (1,000)	Rate [1]	
1960 ...	13.8	21	1.7	10	12.1	25	2.0
1965 ...	14.1	20	1.8	10	12.3	24	2.1
1970 ...	13.8	18	1.7	9	12.1	21	2.2
1975 ...	13.0	15	1.6	9	11.4	17	2.2
1980 ...	13.2	13	1.7	8	11.5	15	2.2
1985 ...	11.5	11	1.2	6	10.3	12	2.0
1986 ...	11.1	10	1.0	5	10.1	11	1.8
1987 ...	11.3	10	1.0	5	10.3	11	1.8
1988 ...	11.0	10	1.1	6	9.9	10	1.8
1989 ...	10.9	9	1.1	6	9.8	10	1.7
1990 ...	10.1	9	1.0	5	9.1	9	3.9
1991 ...	9.8	8	0.8	4	9.0	9	3.5
1992 ...	5.0	4	0.7	4	4.3	4	3.3
1993 ...	5.0	4	0.7	4	4.3	4	3.2
1994 ...	5.3	4	0.7	4	4.3	4	3.5
1995 ...	5.3	4	0.7	4	4.3	4	3.6

YEAR AND INDUSTRY GROUP	DEATHS		Disabling injuries [2] (1,000)
	Number	Rate [1]	
Total [3]	5,300	4	3,600
Agriculture [4]	800	24	140
Mining and quarrying [5]	180	30	20
Construction	1,040	16	350
Manufacturing	730	4	800
Transportation and utilities	850	13	300
Trade [6]	490	2	840
Services [7]	680	2	800
Government	530	3	550

[1] Per 100,000 workers. [2] Disabling injury defined as one which results in death, some degree of physical impairment, or renders the person unable to perform regular activities for a full day beyond the day of the injury. Due to change in methodology, data beginning 1990 not comparable with prior years. [3] Includes deaths where industry is not known. [4] Includes forestry and fishing. [5] Includes oil and gas extraction. [6] Includes wholesale and retail trade. [7] Includes finance, insurance, and real estate.

Source: National Safety Council, Itasca, IL, *Accident Facts*, annual (copyright).

No. 682. Worker Deaths and Injuries and Production Time Lost: 1993 to 1995

ITEM	DEATHS (1,000)			DISABLING INJURIES [1] (mil.)			PRODUCTION TIME LOST (mil. days)					
							In the current year			In future years [2]		
	1993	1994	1995	1993	1994	1995	1993	1994	1995	1993	1994	1995
All accidents	38.3	41.1	45.7	8.4	9.1	9.9	195	215	225	430	410	455
On the job	5.0	5.0	5.3	3.2	3.5	3.6	75	75	75	120	60	65
Off the job	33.3	36.1	40.4	5.2	5.6	6.3	120	140	150	310	350	390
Motor vehicle	19.8	19.6	22.9	1.0	0.9	1.2	(NA)	(NA)	(NA)	(NA)	(NA)	(NA)
Public nonmotor vehicle	7.0	7.6	7.5	2.3	2.4	2.3	(NA)	(NA)	(NA)	(NA)	(NA)	(NA)
Home	6.5	8.9	10.0	1.9	2.3	2.8	(NA)	(NA)	(NA)	(NA)	(NA)	(NA)

NA Not available. [1] See footnote 2, table 681 for a definition of disabling injuries. [2] Based on an average of 5,850 days lost in future years per fatality and 565 days lost in future years per permanent injury.

Source: National Safety Council, Itasca, IL, *Accident Facts*, annual (copyright).

No. 683. Industries With the Highest Total Case Incidence Rates for Nonfatal Injuries and Illnesses: 1994 and 1995

[Rates per 100 full-time employees. Industries shown are those with highest rates in 1995. See headnote, table 684]

INDUSTRY	1987 SIC [1] code	1994	1995
Private industry	(X)	8.4	8.1
Meat packing plants	2011	36.4	36.6
Ship building and repairing	3731	31.8	32.7
Motor vehicles and car bodies	3711	33.2	31.5
Truck trailers	3715	27.5	31.2
Gray and ductile iron foundries	3321	30.2	29.2
Steel foundries, n.e.c. [2]	3325	23.3	26.4
Secondary nonferrous metals	334	16.4	26.1
Malleable iron foundries	3322	21.4	26.0
Mobile homes	2451	29.3	24.3
Automotive stampings	3465	25.9	23.8
Aluminum die-castings	3363	23.3	23.1
Travel trailers and campers	3792	21.9	22.7
Truck and bus bodies	3713	22.2	22.5
Aluminum foundries	3365	-	22.1
Hoists, cranes, and monorails	3536	14.4	21.4
Prefabricated wood buildings	2452	20.8	21.4
Metal sanitary ware	3431	28.3	21.0
Structural wood members, n.e.c. [2]	2439	20.7	21.0
Flat glass	321	21.3	20.9
Sausages and other prepared meats	2013	20.4	20.4
Household laundry equipment	3633	17.7	20.0
Iron and steel forgings	3462	22.9	19.7
Prefabricated metal buildings	3448	13.0	19.6
Public building and related furniture	253	23.2	19.4
Fabricated structural metal	3441	17.7	19.1
Bottled and canned soft drinks	2086	17.0	19.1
Motorcycles, bicycles, and parts	375	24.2	18.6
Leather tanning and finishing	311	19.1	18.5

- Represents or rounds to zero. X Not applicable. [1] 1987 Standard Industrial Classification; see text, section 13. [2] N.e.c. means not elsewhere classified.

Source: U.S. Bureau of Labor Statistics, *Occupational Injuries and Illnesses in the United States by Industry*, annual.

No. 684. Nonfatal Occupational Injury and Illness Incidence Rates: 1994 and 1995

[Rates per 100 full-time employees. For nonfarm employment data, see table 662. Rates refer to any occupational injury or illness resulting in (1) lost workday cases, or (2) nonfatal cases without lost workdays. Incidence rates were calculated as: Number of injuries and illnesses divided by total hours worked by all employees during year multiplied by 200,000 as base for 100 full-time equivalent workers (working 40 hours per week, 50 weeks a year)]

INDUSTRY	1987 SIC [1] code	1994	1995
Private sector [2]	(X)	8.4	8.1
Agriculture, forestry, fishing [2]	A	10.0	9.7
Mining [3]	B	6.3	6.2
Metal mining [3]	10	5.6	5.2
Coal mining [3]	12	9.9	9.1
Oil and gas extraction	13	5.4	5.9
Nonmetallic minerals, exc. fuels	14	5.9	5.4
Construction	C	11.8	10.6
General building contractors	15	10.9	9.8
Heavy construction, except building	16	10.2	9.9
Special trade contractors	17	12.5	11.1
Manufacturing	D	12.2	11.6
Durable goods	(X)	13.5	12.8
Lumber and wood products	24	15.7	14.9
Furniture and fixtures	25	15.0	13.9
Stone, clay, and glass products	32	13.2	12.3
Primary metal industries	33	16.8	16.5
Fabricated metal products	34	16.4	15.8
Industrial machinery and equip	35	11.6	11.2
Electronic/other electric equip	36	8.3	7.6
Transportation equipment	37	19.6	18.6
Instruments/related products	38	5.9	5.3
Miscellaneous manufacturing industries	39	9.9	9.1
Nondurable goods	(X)	10.5	9.9
Food and kindred products	20	17.1	16.3
Tobacco products	21	5.3	5.6
Textile mill products	22	8.7	8.2
Apparel and other textile products	23	8.9	8.2
Paper and allied products	26	9.6	8.5
Printing and publishing	27	6.7	6.4
Chemicals and allied products	28	5.7	5.5
Petroleum and coal products	29	4.7	4.8
Rubber and misc. plastics products	30	14.0	12.9
Leather and leather products	31	12.0	11.4
Transportation/public utilities [3]	E	9.3	9.1
Railroad transportation [3]	40	5.1	4.2
Local passenger transit	41	9.6	10.3
Trucking and warehousing	42	14.8	13.8
Water transportation	44	9.5	9.0
Transportation by air	45	13.3	13.7
Pipelines, except natural gas	46	2.4	1.6
Transportation services	47	4.2	4.5
Communications	48	3.3	3.3
Electric, gas, sanitary services	49	7.3	7.5
Wholesale and retail trade	F, G	7.9	7.5
Wholesale trade	F	7.7	7.5
Retail trade	G	7.9	7.5
Finance, insurance, real estate	H	2.7	2.6
Depository institutions	60	2.1	2.2
Nondepository institutions	61	1.5	1.3
Security and commodity brokers	62	0.7	0.8
Insurance carriers	63	2.6	2.3
Insurance agents, brokers, and service	64	1.4	1.2
Real estate	65	5.7	5.7
Holding and other investment offices	67	1.9	2.6
Services [4]	I	6.5	6.4
Hotels and other lodging places	70	10.1	9.7
Personal services	72	4.1	4.1
Business services	73	4.9	4.6
Auto repair, services, and parking	75	6.9	6.7
Miscellaneous repair services	76	7.7	8.1
Motion pictures	78	3.0	3.3
Amusement and recreation services	79	9.0	9.5
Health services	80	9.4	9.2
Legal services	81	1.1	1.0
Educational services	82	4.2	3.9
Social services	83	7.5	7.6
Museums, botanical, zoological gardens	84	7.1	7.2
Engineering and management services	87	2.6	2.3
Services, n.e.c. [5]	89	(NA)	2.4

NA Not available. X Not applicable. [1] 1987 Standard Industrial Classification; see text, section 13. [2] Excludes farms with fewer than 11 employees. [3] Data conforming to OSHA definitions for employers in the railroad industry and for mining operators in coal, metal, and nonmetal mining. Independent mining contractors are excluded from the coal, metal, and nonmetal mining industries. [4] Includes categories not shown separately. [5] N.e.c means not elsewhere classified.

Source: U.S. Bureau of Labor Statistics, *Occupational Injuries and Illnesses in the United States by Industry*, annual.

No. 685. Fatal Work Injuries, by Cause: 1995

[For the 50 States and DC. Based on the 1995 Census of Fatal Occupational Injuries. Due to methodological differences, data differ from those in table 681. For details, see source]

CAUSE	Number of fatalities	Percent distribution
Total	6,210	100
Transportation accidents [1]	2,560	41
Highway accidents [1]	1,329	21
Collision between vehicles, mobile equipment	634	10
Noncollision accidents	350	6
Nonhighway accident (farm, industrial premises)	388	6
Aircraft accidents	278	4
Workers struck by a vehicle	385	6
Water vehicle accidents	84	1
Railway accidents	82	1
Assaults and violent acts [1]	1,262	20
Homicides [1]	1,024	16
Shooting	754	12
Stabbing	67	1
Self-inflicted injury	215	3
Contacts with objects and equipment [1]	915	15
Struck by object [1]	546	9
Struck by falling objects	340	5
Struck by flying object	63	1
Caught in or compressed by—		
Equipment or objects	255	4
Collapsing materials	99	2
Falls	643	10
Exposure to harmful substances or environments [1]	598	10
Contact with electric current	347	6
Exposure to caustic, noxious or allergenic substances	101	2
Oxygen deficiency	94	2
Drowning, submersion	74	1
Fires and explosions	206	3
Other events and exposures	24	(Z)

Z Less than 0.5 percent. [1] Includes other causes, not shown separately.

Source: U.S. Bureau of Labor Statistics, *USDL News*, Bulletin 96-315, August 8, 1996.

No. 686. Fatal Occupational Injuries, by Industry and Event: 1995

[See headnote, table 685]

INDUSTRY	1987 SIC [1] code	Fatalities [2]	EVENT OR EXPOSURE—PERCENT DISTRIBUTION					Rate [5]
			Transportation incidents	Assaults/violent acts	Contact with objects [3]	Falls	Exposure [4]	
Total	(X)	6,210	41	20	16	10	10	5
Private industry	(X)	5,438	40	19	16	11	10	5
Agriculture, forestry, fishing	A	793	53	6	22	8	10	22
Mining [6]	B	156	35	33	6	14	10	25
Coal mining	12	43	30	-	47	-	14	38
Oil and gas extraction	13	77	31	-	33	8	12	23
Construction	C	1,048	25	3	18	32	20	15
General building contractors	15	175	15	5	18	45	15	-
Heavy construction, except building	16	245	45	-	29	8	16	-
Special trade contractors	17	613	20	3	14	38	23	-
Manufacturing [6]	D	702	30	10	36	9	8	3
Food and kindred products	20	74	39	18	23	12	-	4
Lumber and wood products	24	182	30	-	60	4	4	22
Transportation and public utilities [6]	E	880	69	13	7	3	6	12
Local passenger transit	41	116	31	65	-	-	-	22
Trucking and warehousing	42	462	84	5	7	2	2	20
Transportation by air	45	75	87	-	-	-	-	9
Electric, gas, sanitary services	49	91	34	7	15	7	32	8
Wholesale trade	F	254	49	13	17	6	7	5
Retail trade [6]	G	675	22	66	3	4	4	3
Food stores	54	188	8	86	2	2	-	5
Automotive dealer and service stations	55	122	36	43	6	5	3	6
Eating and drinking places	58	164	14	77	-	6	3	3
Finance, insurance, real estate	H	124	32	49	6	6	5	2
Services [6]	I	737	39	27	9	10	10	2
Business services	73	211	43	23	9	15	10	4
Auto repair, services, and parking	75	114	28	35	21	4	6	8
Government	J	772	48	32	5	3	7	4

- No data reported or data do not meet publication standards. X Not applicable. [1] 1987 Standard Industrial Classification code, see text section 13. [2] Includes 69 fatalities, not available by type of industry. Includes fatalities caused by fires and explosions, not shown separately. [3] Includes equipment. [4] Exposure to harmful substances or environments. [5] Rate per 100,000 employed civilians 16 years old and over. [6] Includes other industries, not shown separately.

Source: U.S. Bureau of Labor Statistics, *USDL News*, 96-315, August 8, 1996; and unpublished data.

No. 687. Work Stoppages: 1960 to 1996

[Excludes work stoppages involving fewer than 1,000 workers and lasting less than 1 day. Information is based on reports of labor disputes appearing in daily newspapers, trade journals, and other public sources. The parties to the disputes are contacted by telephone, when necessary, to clarify details of the stoppages]

YEAR	Number of work stoppages [1]	Workers involved [2] (1,000)	DAYS IDLE: Number [3] (1,000)	DAYS IDLE: Percent estimated working time [4]	YEAR	Number of work stoppages [1]	Workers involved [2] (1,000)	DAYS IDLE: Number [3] (1,000)	DAYS IDLE: Percent estimated working time [4]
1960	222	896	13,260	0.09	1982	96	656	9,061	0.04
1965	268	999	15,140	0.10	1983	81	909	17,461	0.08
1969	412	1,576	29,397	0.16	1984	62	376	8,499	0.04
1970	381	2,468	52,761	0.29	1985	54	324	7,079	0.03
1971	298	2,516	35,538	0.19					
					1986	69	533	11,861	0.05
1972	250	975	16,764	0.09	1987	46	174	[5]4,481	0.02
1973	317	1,400	16,260	0.08	1988	40	118	[5]4,381	0.02
1974	424	1,796	31,809	0.16	1989	51	452	16,996	0.07
1975	235	965	17,563	0.09	1990	44	185	5,926	0.02
1976	231	1,519	23,962	0.12					
					1991	40	392	4,584	0.02
1977	298	1,212	21,258	0.10	1992	35	364	3,989	0.01
1978	219	1,006	23,774	0.11	1993	35	182	3,981	0.01
1979	235	1,021	20,409	0.09	1994	45	322	5,020	0.02
1980	187	795	20,844	0.09	1995	31	192	5,771	0.02
1981	145	729	16,908	0.07	1996	37	273	4,887	0.02

[1] Beginning in year indicated. [2] Workers counted more than once if involved in more than one stoppage during the year. [3] Resulting from all stoppages in effect in a year, including those that began in an earlier year. [4] Agricultural and government employees are included in the total working time; private household and forestry and fishery employees are excluded. [5] Revised since originally published.

Source: U.S. Bureau of Labor Statistics, *Compensation and Conditions*, monthly through 1995, thereafter quarterly.

No. 688. Labor Union Membership, by Sector: 1983 to 1996

[See headnote, table 690]

SECTOR	1983	1985	1990	1991	1992	1993	1994	1995	1996
TOTAL (1,000)									
Wage and salary workers:									
Union members	17,717.4	16,996.1	16,739.8	16,568.4	16,390.3	16,598.1	16,740.3	16,359.6	16,269.4
Covered by unions	20,532.1	19,358.1	19,057.8	18,733.8	18,540.1	18,646.4	18,842.5	18,346.3	18,158.1
Public sector workers:									
Union members	5,737.2	5,743.1	6,485.0	6,632.0	6,653.1	7,017.8	7,091.0	6,927.4	6,854.4
Covered by unions	7,112.2	6,920.6	7,691.4	7,796.0	7,840.6	8,162.4	8,191.8	7,986.6	7,829.7
Private sector workers:									
Union members	11,980.2	11,253.0	10,254.8	9,936.5	9,737.2	9,580.3	9,649.4	9,432.1	9,415.0
Covered by unions	13,419.9	12,437.5	11,366.4	10,937.8	10,699.5	10,484.0	10,650.6	10,359.8	10,328.4
PERCENT									
Wage and salary workers:									
Union members	20.1	18.0	16.1	16.1	15.8	15.8	15.5	14.9	14.5
Covered by unions	23.3	20.5	18.3	18.2	17.9	17.7	17.4	16.7	16.2
Public sector workers:									
Union members	36.7	35.7	36.5	36.9	36.6	37.7	38.7	37.7	37.6
Covered by unions	45.5	43.1	43.3	43.3	43.2	43.6	44.7	43.5	43.0
Private sector workers:									
Union members	16.5	14.3	11.9	11.7	11.4	11.1	10.8	10.3	10.0
Covered by unions	18.5	15.9	13.2	12.9	12.5	12.1	11.9	11.3	11.0

Source: The Bureau of National Affairs, Inc., Washington, DC, *Union Membership and Earnings Data Book: Compilations from the Current Population Survey (1997 edition)*, (copyright by BNA PLUS); authored by Barry Hirsch and David Macpherson of Florida State University. Internet site <http://www.bna.com/bnaplus>

No. 689. U.S. Membership in AFL-CIO Affiliated Unions, by Selected Union: 1975 to 1995

[In thousands. Figures represent the labor organizations as constituted in 1995 and reflect past merger activity. Membership figures based on average per capita paid membership to the AFL-CIO for the 2-year period ending in June of the year shown and reflect only actively-employed members. Labor unions shown had a membership of 50,000 or more in 1995]

LABOR ORGANIZATION	1975	1985	1995
Total [1]	11,199	13,287	13,014
Actors and Artists	76	100	80
Automobile, Aerospace and Agriculture (UAW)	(X)	974	751
Bakery, Confectionery and Tobacco	(X)	115	96
Bricklayers	143	95	84
Carpenters	700	609	378
Clothing and Textile Workers (ACTWU)	(X)	228	129
Communication Workers (CWA)	476	524	478
Electrical Workers (IBEW)	856	791	679
Electronic, Electrical and Salaried [2]	(X)	(X)	135
Operating Engineers	300	330	296
Fire Fighters	123	142	151
Food and Commercial Workers (UFCW)	(X)	989	983
Garment Workers (ILGWU)	363	210	123
Glass, Molders, Pottery, and Plastics	(X)	72	69
Government, American Federation (AFGE)	255	199	153
Graphic Communications	(X)	141	94
Hotel Employees and Restaurant Employees	421	327	241
Iron Workers	160	140	82
Laborers (UNA)	475	383	352
Letter Carriers (NALC)	151	186	210
Longshoreman's Association	60	65	61
Machinists and Aerospace (IAM)	780	520	448
Mine Workers	(X)	(X)	75
Office and Professional Employees	74	90	86
Oil, Chemical, Atomic Workers (OCAW)	145	108	83
Painters	160	133	95
Paperworkers International	275	232	233
Plumbing and Pipefitting of the US and Canada	228	226	220
Postal Workers	249	232	261
Retail, Wholesale Department Stores	118	106	76
Rubber, Cork, Linoleum, Plastic	173	106	79
Seafarers	80	80	80
Service Employees (SEIU)	480	688	1,027
Sheet Metal Workers	120	108	106
Stage Employees and Moving Picture Machine Operators of the US and Canada	50	50	51
State, County, Municipal (AFSCME)	647	997	1,183
Steelworkers	1,062	572	403
Teachers (AFT)	396	470	613
Teamsters [3]	(X)	(X)	1,285
Transit Union	90	94	95
Transport Workers	95	85	75
Transportation-Communications	(X)	(X)	58
Transportation Union, United	134	88	58

X Not applicable. [1] Includes other AFL-CIO, not shown separately. [2] Includes Machine and Furniture Workers. [3] Includes Chauffeurs, Warehousemen and Helpers.

Source: American Federation of Labor and Congress of Industrial Organizations, Washington, DC, *Report of the AFL-CIO Executive Council*, biennial.

No. 690. Labor Union Membership, by State: 1983 and 1996

[Annual averages of monthly figures. For wage and salary workers in agriculture and non-agriculture. Data represent union members by place of residence. Based on the Current Population Survey and subject to sampling error. For methodological details, see source]

STATE	UNION MEMBERS (1,000)		WORKERS COVERED BY UNIONS (1,000)		PERCENT OF WORKERS— Union members		PERCENT OF WORKERS— Covered by unions		PERCENT OF WORKERS— Private manufacturing sector union members	
	1983	1996	1983	1996	1983	1996	1983	1996	1983	1996
United States	17,717.4	16,269.4	20,532.1	18,158.1	20.1	14.5	23.3	16.2	27.8	17.2
Alabama [1]	228.2	200.7	268.2	226.2	16.9	11.4	19.8	12.8	25.9	16.5
Alaska	41.7	54.7	49.2	60.5	24.9	22.5	29.3	24.9	23.3	7.2
Arizona [1]	125.0	106.8	156.4	135.9	11.4	5.9	14.3	7.5	7.8	3.9
Arkansas [1]	82.2	74.4	103.2	86.4	11.0	7.1	13.8	8.4	18.7	12.5
California	2,118.9	2,080.6	2,505.2	2,339.9	21.9	16.5	25.9	18.8	21.0	9.2
Colorado	177.9	167.1	209.6	185.2	13.6	9.7	16.0	10.8	13.1	9.4
Connecticut	314.0	239.5	345.1	250.5	22.7	16.5	25.0	17.2	28.1	10.8
Delaware	49.2	40.0	54.1	45.2	20.1	12.4	22.1	14.0	27.3	16.2
District of Columbia	52.4	39.5	69.4	44.5	19.5	17.2	25.9	19.4	17.6	14.9
Florida [1]	393.7	429.8	532.9	568.4	10.2	7.5	13.8	9.9	11.3	8.0
Georgia [1]	267.0	242.1	345.1	285.5	11.9	7.7	15.3	9.1	16.9	8.7
Hawaii	112.6	111.9	124.9	118.3	29.2	23.2	32.4	24.5	35.6	18.8
Idaho [1]	41.3	42.5	53.7	52.1	12.5	8.7	16.2	10.7	19.0	11.2
Illinois	1,063.8	1,043.1	1,205.1	1,124.8	24.2	20.0	27.4	21.5	32.4	23.6
Indiana	503.3	395.2	544.5	427.8	24.9	14.9	27.0	16.1	48.7	29.6
Iowa [1]	185.9	168.7	231.3	203.0	17.2	13.0	21.5	15.7	40.3	21.5
Kansas [1]	125.2	105.6	170.4	134.7	13.7	9.6	18.7	12.3	25.5	20.0
Kentucky	223.7	198.8	259.8	220.5	17.9	12.7	20.8	14.1	37.4	22.6
Louisiana [1]	204.2	133.4	267.8	164.7	13.8	8.1	18.1	10.0	24.9	19.0
Maine	88.0	77.4	100.4	87.8	21.0	14.5	24.0	16.4	24.8	23.6
Maryland	346.5	353.5	423.1	415.4	18.5	14.8	22.6	17.4	29.2	22.0
Massachusetts	603.2	415.0	661.4	455.0	23.7	15.4	26.0	16.8	26.7	10.2
Michigan	1,005.4	983.3	1,084.6	1,042.2	30.4	24.0	32.8	25.4	46.2	34.9
Minnesota	393.9	437.4	439.4	457.9	23.2	20.3	25.9	21.2	22.3	17.0
Mississippi [1]	79.4	62.0	99.7	86.4	9.9	5.8	12.5	8.1	18.9	10.7
Missouri	374.4	375.2	416.7	408.9	20.8	15.4	23.2	16.8	36.6	26.2
Montana	49.5	52.0	55.5	56.6	18.3	15.6	20.5	16.9	33.0	13.9
Nebraska [1]	80.6	62.9	94.8	90.4	13.6	8.6	16.0	12.4	19.1	10.6
Nevada [1]	90.0	147.3	106.7	175.7	22.4	20.4	26.6	24.3	10.8	9.6
New Hampshire	48.5	57.4	60.8	64.8	11.5	11.2	14.4	12.6	10.6	4.9
New Jersey	822.1	768.0	918.2	832.4	26.9	21.8	30.0	23.7	31.4	20.6
New Mexico	52.6	52.6	70.6	67.3	11.8	8.4	15.8	10.8	11.9	8.9
New York	2,155.6	1,942.0	2,385.9	2,041.9	32.5	26.8	36.0	28.2	31.0	19.6
North Carolina [1]	178.7	134.0	238.1	161.3	7.6	4.1	10.2	5.0	6.9	2.5
North Dakota [1]	28.4	24.4	35.1	28.1	13.2	9.1	16.3	10.5	27.4	17.8
Ohio	1,011.0	933.2	1,125.0	997.6	25.1	19.5	27.9	20.8	40.9	31.3
Oklahoma	131.5	135.5	168.2	161.6	11.5	10.4	14.7	12.4	25.2	16.4
Oregon	222.9	246.2	261.9	266.8	22.3	18.0	26.2	19.5	28.7	19.7
Pennsylvania	1,195.7	885.8	1,350.0	978.3	27.5	17.7	31.1	19.5	42.3	22.9
Rhode Island	85.8	81.0	93.7	85.3	21.5	19.1	23.5	20.1	16.9	11.0
South Carolina [1]	69.6	58.2	100.6	78.7	5.9	3.7	8.6	5.0	5.5	4.3
South Dakota [1]	26.8	23.0	34.8	28.6	11.5	7.4	14.9	9.2	19.0	9.7
Tennessee [1]	252.4	219.2	300.9	254.2	15.1	9.6	18.0	11.1	21.4	14.8
Texas [1]	583.7	527.7	712.8	645.8	9.7	6.6	11.9	8.0	16.1	8.5
Utah [1]	81.6	71.1	100.9	94.2	15.2	8.4	18.9	11.1	14.9	5.4
Vermont	25.9	24.9	31.5	29.0	12.6	9.7	15.3	11.3	13.5	8.2
Virginia [1]	268.3	200.8	346.1	236.5	11.7	6.8	15.1	8.0	21.2	11.8
Washington	419.9	484.2	499.7	511.3	27.1	19.8	32.3	21.8	35.5	29.0
West Virginia	142.7	109.7	160.6	124.7	25.3	15.7	28.5	17.9	41.3	29.2
Wisconsin	465.5	469.7	526.7	493.2	23.8	18.8	26.9	19.8	36.0	23.9
Wyoming [1]	27.1	20.1	31.8	23.9	13.9	9.7	16.2	11.6	14.6	12.0

[1] Right to work State.

Source: The Bureau of National Affairs, Inc., Washington, DC, *Union Membership and Earnings Data Book: Compilations from the Current Population Survey, (1997 edition)* (copyright by BNA PLUS); authored by Barry Hirsch and David Macpherson of Florida State University. Internet site <http://www.bna.com/bnaplus>

No. 691. Union Members, by Selected Characteristics: 1983 and 1996

[Annual averages of monthly data. Covers employed wage and salary workers 16 years old and over. Excludes self-employed workers whose businesses are incorporated although they technically qualify as wage and salary workers. See headnote table 636 regarding data by occupation and industry. Based on Current Population Survey, see text, section 1, and Appendix III]

CHARACTERISTIC	EMPLOYED WAGE AND SALARY WORKERS: Total (1,000)		Percent union members [2]		Percent represented by unions [3]		MEDIAN USUAL WEEKLY EARNINGS[4] (dol.): Total		Union members [2]		Represented by unions [3]		Not represented by unions	
	1983	1996 [1]	1983	1996 [1]	1983	1996 [1]	1983	1996 [1]	1983	1996 [1]	1983	1996 [1]	1983	1996 [1]
Total [5]	88,290	111,960	20.1	14.5	23.3	16.2	313	490	388	615	383	610	288	462
16 to 24 years old	19,305	18,106	9.1	5.5	11.1	6.3	210	298	281	371	275	362	203	294
25 to 34 years old	25,978	29,564	19.6	12.0	23.1	13.5	321	463	382	554	376	548	304	447
35 to 44 years old	18,722	30,619	24.8	16.8	28.6	18.7	369	559	411	636	407	632	339	530
45 to 54 years old	13,150	21,641	27.0	21.4	30.5	23.6	366	594	404	687	402	686	335	552
55 to 64 years old	9,201	9,527	26.9	18.8	30.3	20.8	346	535	392	620	390	616	316	505
65 years and over	1,934	2,503	10.1	7.5	12.1	8.4	260	384	338	510	330	510	238	367
Men	47,856	58,473	24.7	16.9	27.7	18.4	378	557	416	653	414	651	349	520
Women	40,433	53,488	14.6	12.0	18.0	13.8	252	418	309	549	307	543	237	398
White	77,046	94,306	19.3	14.0	22.3	15.7	319	506	396	635	391	630	295	480
Men	42,168	49,961	24.0	16.4	26.9	17.9	387	580	423	675	421	673	362	544
Women	34,877	44,345	13.5	11.3	16.7	13.1	254	428	314	572	313	564	240	408
Black	8,979	12,909	27.2	18.9	31.7	21.2	261	387	331	507	324	502	222	358
Men	4,477	6,031	31.7	21.6	36.1	23.7	293	412	366	526	360	522	244	380
Women	4,502	6,878	22.7	16.5	27.4	19.0	231	362	292	485	287	480	209	336
Hispanic [6]	(NA)	10,800	(NA)	12.9	(NA)	14.6	(NA)	339	(NA)	484	(NA)	482	(NA)	319
Men	(NA)	6,455	(NA)	13.7	(NA)	15.0	(NA)	358	(NA)	511	(NA)	511	(NA)	330
Women	(NA)	4,345	(NA)	11.8	(NA)	13.9	(NA)	316	(NA)	436	(NA)	433	(NA)	305
Full-time workers	70,976	90,918	22.9	16.2	26.4	18.1	313	490	388	615	383	610	288	462
Part-time workers	17,314	20,810	8.4	7.1	10.3	8.2	(X)	(X)	(X)	(X)	(X)	(X)	(X)	(X)
Managerial and professional specialty	19,657	30,942	17.1	13.6	21.9	16.1	437	718	423	758	421	749	446	706
Technical sales, and admin. support	28,024	34,187	12.1	9.5	15.0	10.9	281	441	350	532	341	524	270	427
Service occupations	12,875	15,897	15.3	13.2	17.9	14.7	205	305	305	490	299	484	182	282
Precision, production, craft, and repair	10,542	11,615	32.9	22.8	35.7	24.1	377	540	456	703	450	698	322	494
Operators, fabricators, and laborers	15,416	17,428	35.4	23.0	37.9	24.1	275	391	366	528	361	522	226	353
Farming, forestry, and fishing	1,775	1,892	5.5	4.9	6.9	5.5	196	294	292	439	287	423	189	288
Agricultural wage and salary workers	1,446	1,710	3.4	1.9	3.8	2.2	198	308	(B)	(B)	(B)	(B)	195	305
Private nonagri. wage and salary workers	71,225	92,059	16.8	10.2	18.8	11.2	307	475	369	584	385	579	286	458
Mining	869	538	20.7	14.1	23.1	15.0	481	693	470	698	470	699	488	690
Construction	4,109	5,387	27.5	18.5	29.4	19.2	348	504	518	748	510	742	296	464
Manufacturing	19,066	19,653	27.8	17.2	30.5	18.3	335	507	370	560	368	558	315	494
Transportation and public utilities	5,142	6,623	42.4	28.5	46.2	28.3	417	596	449	680	445	676	386	555
Wholesale and retail trade, total	18,081	23,638	8.7	5.6	9.8	6.2	252	380	353	450	348	444	242	375
Finance, insurance, and real estate	5,559	6,863	2.9	2.4	4.1	3.1	296	521	284	534	285	533	297	520
Services	18,400	29,357	7.7	5.7	9.6	6.9	272	456	303	501	303	498	268	451
Government	15,618	18,191	36.7	37.7	45.5	43.0	351	592	386	657	381	651	316	519

B Data not shown where base is less than 50,000. NA Not available. X Not applicable. [1] See footnote 2, table 619. [2] Members of a labor union or an employee association similar to a labor union. [3] Members of a labor union or an employee association similar to a union as well as workers who report no union affiliation but whose jobs are covered by a union or an employee association contract. [4] For full-time employed wage and salary workers; 1983 revised since originally published. [5] Includes races not shown separately. 1996 includes a small number of multiple jobholders whose full- part- time status can not be determined for their principal job. [6] Persons of Hispanic origin may be of any race.

Source: U.S. Bureau of Labor Statistics, *Employment and Earnings*, monthly, January issues.

Income, Expenditures, and Wealth

This section presents data on gross domestic product (GDP), gross national product (GNP), national and personal income, saving and investment, money income, poverty, and national and personal wealth. The data on income and expenditures measure two aspects of the U.S. economy. One aspect relates to the national income and product accounts (NIPA's), a summation reflecting the entire complex of the Nation's economic income and output and the interaction of its major components; the other relates to the distribution of money income to families and individuals, or consumer income.

The primary source for data on GDP, GNP, national and personal income, gross saving and investment, and fixed reproducible tangible wealth is the *Survey of Current Business*, published monthly by the Bureau of Economic Analysis (BEA). A comprehensive revision to the NIPA's was completed in January 1996. Discussions of the revision appeared in the July, September, and October 1995 the January/February 1996, and the May 1997 issues of the *Survey of Current Business*. Summary historical estimates appeared in the May 1997 issue of the *Survey of Current Business*. Detailed historical data will appear in the *National Income and Product Accounts of the United States, 1929-94*.

Sources of income distribution data are the decennial censuses of population and the Current Population Survey (CPS), both products of the Bureau of the Census (see text, section 1). Annual data on income of families, individuals, and households are presented in *Current Population Reports-Consumer Income*, P60 series.

Data on individuals' saving and assets are published by the Board of Governors of the Federal Reserve System in the quarterly *Flow of Funds Accounts;* and detailed information on personal wealth is published periodically by the Internal Revenue Service (IRS) in *SOI Bulletin*.

In Brief

Real Gross Domestic Product (GDP) rose in 1996 at an annual rate of 2.4% marking the fifth consecutive annual increase. Real GDP per capita also increased in 1996 to $26,016.

Consumer spending rose to $32,264 per consumer unit in 1995, a 1.7% increase over 1994. The change in expenditures in 1995 was less than the rates for 1993 and 1994 of about 3% each.

The number of persons in poverty fell 1.6 million between 1994 and 1995 to 36.4 million.

The median net worth of families was $56,400 in 1995, up slightly from 1992 in real terms, but unchanged from 1989.

National income and product—*Gross domestic product* is the total output of goods and services produced by labor and property located in the United States, valued at market prices. GDP can be viewed in terms of the expenditure categories that comprise its major components—purchases of goods and services by consumers and government, gross private domestic investment, and net exports of goods and services. The goods and services included are largely those bought for final use (excluding illegal transactions) in the market economy. A number of inclusions, however, represent imputed values, the most important of which is rental value of owner-occupied housing. GDP, in this broad context, measures the output attributable to the factors of production located in the United States. *Gross State product* (GSP) is the gross market value of the goods and services attributable to labor and property located in a State. It is the State counterpart of the Nation's gross domestic product.

As part of the comprehensive revision released in January 1996, BEA replaced its fixed-weighted (1987 dollars) index as the featured measure of real GDP with an index based on chain-type annual weights. Changes in the new featured measures of real output and prices are calculated as the average of changes based on weights for the current and preceding years. (Components of real output are weighted by price and components of prices are weighted by output.) These annual changes are "chained" (multiplied) together to form a time series that allows for the effects of changes in relative prices and changes in the composition of output over time. Quarterly and monthly changes are also based on annual weights. The new output indexes are expressed as 1992 = 100, and for recent years, in 1992 dollars; the new price indexes are based to 1992 = 100.

Chained (1992) dollar estimates of most components of GDP are not published for periods prior to 1982, because during periods far from the base period, the levels of the components may provide misleading information about their contributions to an aggregate. Values are published in index form (1992 = 100) for 1929 to the present to allow users to calculate the percent changes all components, changes which are accurate for all periods. In addition, the Bureau of Economic Analysis publishes estimates of the contribution of major components to the percent change in GDP for all periods.

Gross national product measures the output attributable to all labor and property supplied by United States residents. GNP differs from "national income" mainly in that GNP includes allowances for depreciation and for indirect business taxes (sales and property taxes); see table 691.

In December 1991, the Bureau of Economic Analysis began featuring gross domestic product rather than gross national product as the primary measure of U.S. production. GDP is now the standard measure of growth because it is the appropriate measure for much of the short-term monitoring and analysis of the economy. In addition, the use of GDP facilitates comparisons of economic activity in the United States with that in other countries.

National income is the aggregate of labor and property earnings which arises in the current production of goods and services. It is the sum of employee compensation, proprietors' income, rental *income of persons*, corporate profits, produced by the economy. Income is measured before deduction of taxes.

Capital consumption adjustment for corporations and for nonfarm sole proprietorships and partnerships is the difference between capital consumption based on income tax returns and capital consumption measured using empirical evidence on prices of used equipment and structures in resale markets, which have shown that depreciation for most types of assets approximates a geometric pattern. The tax return data are valued at historical costs and reflect changes over time in service lives and depreciation patterns as permitted by tax regulations. *Inventory valuation adjustment* represents the difference between the book value of inventories used up in production and the cost of replacing them.

Personal income is the current income received by persons from all sources minus their personal contributions for social insurance. Classified as "persons" are individuals (including owners of unincorporated firms), nonprofit institutions that primarily serve individuals, private trust funds, and private noninsured welfare funds. Personal income includes transfers (payments not resulting from current production) from government and business such as Social Security benefits, public assistance, etc., but excludes transfers among persons. Also included are certain nonmonetary types of income—chiefly estimated net rental value to owner-occupants of their homes and the value of services furnished without payment by financial intermediaries. Capital gains (net losses) are excluded.

Disposable personal income is personal income less personal tax and nontax payments. It is the income available to persons for spending or saving. Personal tax and nontax payments are tax payments (net of refunds) by persons (except personal contributions for social insurance) that are not chargeable to business expense, and certain personal payments to general government that are treated like taxes. Personal taxes include income, estate and gift, and personal property taxes and motor vehicle licenses. Nontax payments include passport fees, fines and forfeitures, and donations.

was begun in late 1979. The principal objective of the survey is to collect current consumer expenditure data which provide a continuous flow of data on the buying habits of American consumers. The data are necessary for future revisions of the Consumer Price Index.

The survey conducted by the Bureau of the Census for the Bureau of Labor Statistics, consists of two components: (1) An interview panel survey in which the expenditures of consumer units are obtained in five interviews conducted every 3 months; and (2) a diary or recordkeeping survey completed by participating households for two consecutive 1-week periods.

Each component of the survey queries an independent sample of consumer units representative of the U.S. total population. Over 52 weeks of the year, 5,000 consumer units are sampled for the diary survey. Each consumer unit keeps a diary for two 1-week periods yielding approximately 10,000 diaries a year. The interview sample is selected on a rotating panel basis, targeted at 5,000 consumer units per quarter. Data are collected in 88 urban and 16 rural areas of the country that are representative of the U.S. total population. The survey includes students in student housing. Data from the two surveys are combined; integration is necessary to permit analysis of total family expenditures because neither the diary nor quarterly interview survey was designed to collect a complete account of consumer spending.

The Diary survey is designed to obtain expenditures on small, frequently purchased items which are normally difficult for respondents to recall. Detailed records of expenses are kept for food and beverages, both at home and in eating places, tobacco, housekeeping supplies, nonprescription drugs, and personal care products and services.

The Interview survey is designed to obtain data on the types of expenditures which respondents can be expected to recall for a period of 3 months or longer. In general, these include relatively large expenditures, such as those for property, automobiles, and major appliances, or expenditures which occur on a fairly regular basis, such as rent, utilities, or insurance premiums. Including "global estimates" for food, it is estimated that *about 95 percent of expenditures are covered in the interview.* Excluded are nonprescription drugs, household supplies, and personal care items. The interview survey also provides data on expenditures incurred while on trips. Both surveys exclude all business related expenditures for which the family is reimbursed.

Distribution of money income to families and individuals—Money income statistics are based on data collected in various field surveys of income conducted since 1936. Since 1947, the Bureau of the Census has collected the data on an annual basis and published them in *Current Population Reports,* P60 series. In each of the surveys, field representatives interview samples of the population with respect to income received during the previous year. Money income as defined by the Bureau of the Census differs from the BEA concept of "personal income."

Data on consumer income collected in the CPS by the Bureau of the Census cover money income received (exclusive of certain money receipts such as capital gains) before payments for personal income taxes, Social Security, union dues, Medicare deductions, etc. Therefore, money income does not reflect the fact that some families receive part of their income in the form of noncash benefits (see section 12) such as food stamps, health benefits, and subsidized housing; that some farm families receive noncash benefits in the form of rent-free housing and goods produced and consumed on the farm; or that noncash benefits are also received by some nonfarm residents which often take the form of the use of business transportation and facilities, full or partial payments by business for retirement programs, medical and educational expenses, etc. These elements should be considered when comparing income levels. For data on noncash benefits, see section 12. None of the aggregate income concepts (GDP, national income, or personal income) is exactly comparable with money income, although personal income is the closest.

Several changes were made in the collection and processing of the March 1994 CPS data. These changes included (1) a change in the data collection method from paper and pencil to computer-assisted interviewing, (2) revisions allowing for the coding of different income amounts on selected questionnaire items (limits either increased or decreased in the following categories: earnings increased to $999,999, Social Security increased to $49,999, Supplemental Security Income and Public Assistance increased to $24,999, Veterans' Benefits increased to $99,999, Child Support and Alimony decreased to $49,999), and (3) the introduction of 1990 census population controls. A detailed description of these changes and their effects on estimates can be found in *Current Population Reports*, Series P60-189.

In October 1983, the Census Bureau began to collect data under the new Survey of Income and Program Participation (SIPP). The information supplied by this survey is expected to provide better measures of the status and changes in income distribution and poverty of households and persons in the United States. The data collected in SIPP will be used to study Federal and State aid programs (such as food stamps, welfare, Medicaid, and subsidized housing), to estimate program costs and coverage, and to assess the effects of proposed changes in program eligibility rules or benefit levels. The core questions are repeated at each interview and cover labor force activity, the types and amounts of income received, and participation status in various programs. The core also contains questions covering attendance in postsecondary schools and private health insurance coverage. Various supplements or topical modules covering areas such as educational attainment, assets and liabilities, and pension plan coverage are periodically included.

Poverty—Families and unrelated individuals are classified as being above or below the poverty level using the poverty index originated at the Social Security Administration in 1964 and revised by Federal Interagency Committees in 1969 and 1980. The poverty index is based solely on money income and does not reflect the fact that many low-income persons receive noncash benefits such as food stamps, Medicaid, and public housing. The index is based on the Department of Agriculture's 1961 Economy Food Plan and reflects the different consumption requirements of families based on their size and composition. The poverty thresholds are updated every year to reflect changes in the Consumer Price Index. The following technical changes to the thresholds were made in 1981: (1) distinctions based on sex of householder have been eliminated; (2) separate thresholds for farm families have been dropped; and (3) the matrix has been expanded to families of nine or more persons from the old cutoff of seven or more persons. These changes have been incorporated in the calculation of poverty data beginning with 1981.

In the recent past, the Bureau of the Census has published a number of technical papers that presented experimental poverty estimates based on income definitions that counted the value of selected government noncash benefits. The Census Bureau has also published annual reports on after-tax income. The *Current Population Reports*, series P60-186RD brings together the benefit and tax data that previously appeared in the separate reports. This report shows the distribution of income among households and the prevalence of poverty under the official definition of money income and under definitions that add or subtract income components.

The poverty statistics presented by the Bureau of the Census and Congressional Budget Office reflect alternative adjustments for inflation. The study used a variation of the Consumer Price Index to adjust poverty thresholds for the effects of changing prices since 1967. The alternative measure of inflation uses estimates of the cost of renting equivalent housing to assess homeownership costs; this methodology has been used in the official Consumer Price Index since 1983. See text, section 15, and source for more details.

Statistical reliability—For a discussion of statistical collection and estimation, sampling procedures, and measures of statistical reliability pertaining to Census Bureau data, see Appendix III.

No. 692. GDP in Current and Real (1992) Dollars: 1960 to 1996

[In billions of dollars. For explanation of gross domestic product and chained dollars, see text, section 14]

ITEM	1960	1970	1980	1982	1983	1984	1985	1986	1987
CURRENT DOLLARS									
Gross domestic product (GDP)	**526.6**	**1,035.6**	**2,784.2**	**3,242.1**	**3,514.5**	**3,902.4**	**4,180.7**	**4,422.2**	**4,692.3**
Personal consumption expenditures	332.2	648.1	1,760.4	2,076.8	2,283.4	2,492.3	2,704.8	2,892.7	3,094.5
Durable goods	43.3	85.0	213.5	239.3	279.8	325.1	361.1	398.7	416.7
Nondurable goods	152.9	272.0	695.5	786.8	830.3	883.6	927.6	957.2	1,014.0
Services	136.0	291.1	851.4	1,050.7	1,173.3	1,283.6	1,416.1	1,536.8	1,663.8
Gross private domestic investment	78.8	150.2	465.9	501.1	547.1	715.6	715.1	722.5	747.2
Fixed investment	75.5	148.1	473.5	515.6	552.0	648.1	688.9	712.9	722.9
Nonresidential	49.2	106.7	350.3	409.9	399.4	468.3	502.0	494.8	495.4
Residential	26.3	41.4	123.2	105.7	152.5	179.8	186.9	218.1	227.6
Change in business inventories	3.2	2.2	-7.6	-14.5	-4.9	67.5	26.2	9.6	24.2
Net exports of goods and services	2.4	1.2	-14.9	-20.5	-51.7	-102.0	-114.2	-131.5	-142.1
Exports	25.3	57.0	278.9	282.6	277.0	303.1	303.0	320.7	365.7
Imports	22.8	55.8	293.8	303.2	328.6	405.1	417.2	452.2	507.9
Government consumption expenditures and gross investment	113.2	236.1	572.8	684.8	735.7	796.6	875.0	938.5	992.8
Federal	65.6	115.9	248.4	313.2	344.5	372.6	410.1	435.2	455.7
National defense	54.9	90.6	174.2	230.9	255.0	282.7	312.4	332.4	350.4
State and local	47.6	120.2	324.4	371.6	391.2	424.0	464.9	503.3	537.2
CHAINED (1992) DOLLARS									
Gross domestic product (GDP)	**2,262.9**	**3,397.6**	**4,615.0**	**4,620.3**	**4,803.7**	**5,140.1**	**5,323.5**	**5,487.7**	**5,649.5**
Personal consumption expenditures	1,432.6	2,197.8	3,009.7	3,081.5	3,240.6	3,407.6	3,566.5	3,708.7	3,822.3
Gross private domestic investment	270.5	426.1	628.3	587.2	642.1	833.4	823.8	811.8	821.5
Net exports of goods and services	-21.3	-65.0	10.1	-14.1	-63.3	-127.3	-147.9	-163.9	-156.2
Exports	86.8	158.1	331.4	311.4	303.3	328.4	337.3	362.2	402.0
Imports	108.1	223.1	321.3	325.5	366.6	455.7	485.2	526.1	558.2
Government consumption expenditures and gross investment	617.2	866.8	941.4	960.1	987.3	1,018.4	1,080.1	1,135.0	1,165.9

ITEM	1988	1989	1990	1991	1992	1993	1994	1995	1996
CURRENT DOLLARS									
Gross domestic product (GDP)	**5,049.6**	**5,438.7**	**5,743.8**	**5,916.7**	**6,244.4**	**6,553.0**	**6,935.7**	**7,253.8**	**7,576.1**
Personal consumption expenditures	3,349.7	3,594.8	3,839.3	3,975.1	4,219.8	4,454.1	4,700.9	4924.9	5,151.4
Durable goods	451.0	472.8	476.5	455.2	488.5	530.7	580.9	606.4	632.1
Nondurable goods	1,081.1	1,163.8	1,245.3	1,277.6	1,321.8	1,368.9	1,429.7	1,485.9	1,545.1
Services	1,817.6	1,958.1	2,117.5	2,242.3	2,409.4	2,554.6	2,690.3	2,832.6	2,974.3
Gross private domestic investment	773.9	829.2	799.7	736.2	790.4	871.1	1,014.4	1,065.3	1,117.0
Fixed investment	763.1	797.5	791.6	738.5	783.4	850.5	954.9	1,028.2	1,101.5
Nonresidential	530.6	566.2	575.9	547.3	557.9	598.8	667.2	738.5	791.1
Residential	232.5	231.3	215.7	191.2	225.6	251.7	287.7	289.8	310.5
Change in business inventories	10.9	31.7	8.0	-2.3	7.0	20.6	59.5	37.0	15.4
Net exports of goods and services	-106.1	-80.4	-71.3	-20.5	-29.5	-62.7	-94.4	-94.7	-98.7
Exports	447.2	509.3	557.3	601.8	639.4	657.8	719.1	807.4	855.2
Imports	553.2	589.7	628.6	622.3	669.0	720.5	813.5	902.0	953.9
Government consumption expenditures and gross investment	1,032.0	1,095.1	1,176.1	1,225.9	1,263.8	1,290.4	1,314.7	1,358.3	1,406.4
Federal	457.3	477.2	503.6	522.6	528.0	522.6	516.4	516.6	523.1
National defense	354.0	360.6	373.1	383.5	375.8	362.2	352.0	345.7	(NA)
State and local	574.7	617.9	672.6	703.4	735.8	767.8	798.4	841.7	883.3
CHAINED (1992) DOLLARS									
Gross domestic product (GDP)	**5,865.2**	**6,062.0**	**6,136.3**	**6,079.4**	**6,244.4**	**6,386.1**	**6,608.4**	**6,742.2**	**6,906.8**
Personal consumption expenditures	3,972.7	4,064.6	4,132.2	4,105.8	4,219.8	4,339.5	4,473.2	4,577.8	4,690.7
Gross private domestic investment	828.2	863.5	815.0	738.1	790.4	857.0	979.3	1,009.4	1,056.6
Net exports of goods and services	-114.4	-82.7	-61.9	-22.3	-29.5	-74.4	-108.1	-114.2	-113.6
Exports	465.8	520.2	564.4	599.9	639.4	658.2	712.0	775.4	825.9
Imports	580.2	603.0	626.3	622.2	669.0	730.2	817.6	883.0	939.5
Government consumption expenditures and gross investment	1,180.9	1,213.9	1,250.4	1,258.0	1,263.8	1,261.0	1,260.0	1,260.2	1,270.6

NA Not available.

Source: U.S. Bureau of Economic Analysis, *National Income and Product Accounts of the United States, 1929-94*, forthcoming; and *Survey of Current Business*, May 1997.

No. 693. Gross Domestic Product in Current and Real (1992) Dollars, by Industry: 1990 to 994

[In billions of dollars. 1980 data are based on the 1972 Standard Industrial Classification (SIC), and 1990-94 are based on the 1987 SIC. Data include nonfactor charges (capital consumption allowances, indirect business taxes, etc.) as well as factor charges against gross product; corporate profits and capital consumption allowances have been shifted from a company to an establishment basis]

INDUSTRY	CURRENT DOLLARS				CHAINED (1992) DOLLARS			
	1990	1992	1993	1994	1990	1992	1993	1994
Gross domestic product	5,743.8	6,244.4	6,550.2	6,931.4	6,138.7	6,244.4	6,383.8	6,604.2
Private industries	4,951.4	5,370.8	5,650.0	6,000.0	5,271.5	5,370.8	5,508.7	5,728.7
Agriculture, forestry, and fishing	108.7	112.4	106.3	117.8	101.5	112.4	103.3	115.7
Farms	79.6	80.5	72.0	82.2	72.8	80.5	70.9	83.9
Agricultural services	29.1	31.9	33.3	35.7	28.6	31.9	32.3	32.1
Mining [1]	112.3	92.2	89.0	90.1	96.9	92.2	90.7	96.7
Construction	245.2	229.7	243.6	269.2	247.5	229.7	236.1	253.1
Manufacturing	1,031.4	1,063.6	1,116.5	1,197.1	1,090.1	1,063.6	1,095.3	1,168.0
Durable goods	572.8	573.4	612.3	673.1	600.7	573.4	601.2	657.9
Lumber and wood products	31.8	32.0	35.3	41.0	37.0	32.0	28.7	31.5
Furniture and fixtures	15.4	16.2	17.6	19.0	15.8	16.2	17.8	18.4
Stone, clay, and glass products	24.8	25.1	25.7	27.9	25.5	25.1	25.0	26.2
Primary metal industries	42.6	39.0	40.8	44.2	39.0	39.0	41.9	42.9
Fabricated metal products	69.4	70.1	74.5	82.5	72.6	70.1	74.2	82.9
Industrial machinery	114.8	106.6	111.9	119.3	113.4	106.6	115.8	127.6
Electronic & other electric equipment	94.9	96.6	111.8	130.0	92.6	96.6	113.6	138.4
Motor vehicles and equipment	46.1	52.8	66.2	84.1	56.8	52.8	60.6	72.8
Other transportation equipment	60.5	56.5	53.2	47.6	69.1	56.5	51.6	45.1
Instruments and related products	52.2	54.2	53.6	54.5	56.6	54.2	51.3	50.9
Misc. manufacturing industries	20.2	20.1	21.8	23.1	22.2	20.1	21.1	22.4
Nondurable goods	458.5	490.2	504.3	524.0	489.3	490.2	494.1	510.2
Food and kindred products	94.2	102.1	103.7	108.1	103.1	102.1	102.2	104.8
Tobacco manufactures	16.4	18.4	16.5	16.6	24.9	18.4	17.5	22.0
Textile mill products	21.7	25.4	25.5	25.6	22.6	25.4	25.9	27.3
Apparel and other textile products	25.2	27.2	27.3	27.8	26.5	27.2	26.9	27.8
Paper and allied products	45.3	45.8	47.6	49.0	44.1	45.8	49.9	49.7
Printing and publishing	73.9	79.7	81.7	85.7	84.5	79.7	77.3	78.2
Chemicals and allied products	110.3	120.5	126.5	132.4	117.3	120.5	122.1	125.1
Petroleum and coal products	33.0	28.2	29.8	29.7	28.4	28.2	27.1	26.8
Rubber and misc. plastic products	34.0	38.1	41.1	45.0	34.4	38.1	40.9	45.7
Leather and leather products	4.6	4.8	4.6	4.1	4.8	4.8	4.6	3.9
Transportation and public utilities	482.3	528.8	566.2	606.4	494.7	528.8	555.8	585.3
Transportation	176.4	192.8	207.6	222.8	176.7	192.8	205.1	215.5
Railroad transportation	19.6	22.1	23.0	24.3	18.7	22.1	24.0	26.2
Local & interurban passenger transit	9.0	10.9	11.3	11.7	10.3	10.9	10.9	11.1
Trucking and warehousing	75.8	82.2	88.4	95.1	73.7	82.2	88.3	89.6
Water transportation	9.7	10.3	10.3	10.6	10.7	10.3	10.4	10.9
Transportation by air	39.4	43.0	46.6	51.1	39.5	43.0	45.2	49.9
Pipelines, except natural gas	5.0	4.9	5.2	5.7	4.8	4.9	5.7	6.0
Transportation services	17.8	19.6	20.8	24.3	19.2	19.6	20.8	21.9
Communications	146.6	161.0	173.4	188.3	149.3	161.0	170.1	182.1
Telephone and telegraph	119.0	129.5	137.4	148.6	120.7	129.5	136.3	143.7
Radio and television broadcasting	27.6	31.5	35.9	39.7	28.6	31.5	33.7	38.1
Electric, gas, and sanitary services	159.3	175.0	185.2	195.3	168.7	175.0	180.6	188.0
Wholesale trade	367.3	406.5	423.1	461.9	360.6	406.5	418.6	450.0
Retail trade	503.5	544.3	571.1	609.9	546.4	544.3	563.2	595.4
Finance, insurance, and real estate [2]	1,025.2	1,148.8	1,214.0	1,273.7	1,109.9	1,148.8	1,159.8	1,192.8
Depository institutions	169.2	200.1	202.0	212.1	214.9	200.1	196.9	197.2
Nondepository institutions	21.5	28.3	35.3	31.0	25.6	28.3	32.0	34.0
Security and commodity brokers	39.7	49.5	62.9	69.5	41.2	49.5	65.1	74.4
Insurance carriers	69.3	83.4	99.6	104.1	70.2	83.4	74.0	76.3
Real estate	673.0	735.8	762.4	802.3	706.8	735.8	740.4	758.4
Services [3]	1,059.4	1,200.8	1,266.1	1,342.7	1,181.7	1,200.8	1,222.1	1,249.6
Hotels and other lodging places	46.1	51.0	54.6	56.1	49.2	51.0	52.5	52.6
Personal services	38.2	41.0	44.5	46.5	41.7	41.0	42.8	43.1
Business services	199.0	218.9	233.4	253.5	216.5	218.9	234.3	247.0
Auto repair, services, and garages	48.9	51.1	54.0	57.4	54.0	51.1	51.0	51.6
Motion pictures	20.4	20.0	22.1	24.8	22.1	20.0	21.9	23.6
Amusement and recreation services	39.1	47.9	48.7	52.2	42.8	47.9	47.0	48.4
Health services	307.9	369.1	384.8	408.3	356.9	369.1	363.1	368.3
Legal services	80.7	90.1	92.3	94.4	91.5	90.1	87.9	86.7
Social services & membership organizations	29.6	36.9	40.1	43.4	32.5	36.9	39.3	41.2
Government	792.5	873.6	900.2	931.3	867.0	873.6	875.1	875.8
Federal	293.5	321.4	322.5	327.1	327.7	321.4	314.7	305.0
State and local	499.0	552.2	577.7	604.3	539.4	552.2	560.3	570.8

[1] For additional mining industries, see table 1131. [2] For additional finance, real estate, and insurance industries, see table 772. [3] For additional service industries, see table 1261.

Source: U.S. Bureau of Economic Analysis, *Survey of Current Business*, August 1996.

No. 694. Gross Domestic Product in Current and Real (1992) Dollars, by Type of Product and Sector: 1990 to 1996

[In billions of dollars. For explanation of chained dollars, see text, section 14]

ITEM	1990	1991	1992	1993	1994	1995	1996
CURRENT DOLLARS							
Gross domestic product	**5,743.8**	**5,916.7**	**6,244.4**	**6,553.0**	**6,935.7**	**7,253.8**	**7,576.1**
PRODUCT							
Goods	2,203.8	2,234.0	2,321.0	2,422.0	2,593.9	2,699.2	2,799.8
Durable goods	938.2	910.0	955.0	1,030.0	1,118.0	1,182.1	1,232.3
Nondurable goods	1,265.7	1,323.9	1,366.0	1,392.0	1,475.9	1,517.1	1,567.5
Services	3,016.9	3,201.3	3,411.1	3,584.0	3,746.5	3,926.9	4,105.2
Structures	523.1	481.4	512.3	547.0	595.3	627.6	671.1
SECTOR							
Business	4,796.9	4,908.5	5,184.4	5,451.6	5,798.4	6,078.2	6,360.6
Nonfarm	4,717.3	4,835.6	5,103.8	5,379.5	5,716.1	5,999.6	6,262.3
Farm	79.6	72.9	80.6	72.1	82.3	78.6	98.3
Households and institutions	237.9	257.4	279.1	294.9	310.3	323.0	340.9
General government	709.0	750.7	781.0	806.5	827.0	852.6	874.7
Federal	252.7	268.1	274.4	276.6	275.7	278.2	277.0
State and local	456.3	482.6	506.6	529.9	551.4	574.4	597.7
CHAINED (1992) DOLLARS							
Gross domestic product	**6,136.3**	**6,079.4**	**6,244.4**	**6,386.1**	**6,608.4**	**6,742.2**	**6,906.8**
PRODUCT							
Goods	2,304.8	2,262.7	2,321.0	2,389.7	2,524.0	2,586.5	2,662.0
Durable goods	966.5	917.2	955.0	1,023.1	1,099.3	1,157.4	1,212.0
Nondurable goods	1,337.9	1,345.6	1,366.0	1,366.8	1,425.1	1,432.3	1,451.9
Services	3,295.4	3,332.3	3,411.1	3,467.1	3,526.1	3,583.9	3,649.2
Structures	533.3	484.5	512.3	529.4	559.8	571.8	596.3
SECTOR							
Business	5,097.0	5,026.4	5,184.4	5,315.4	5,530.0	5,662.7	5,824.0
Nonfarm	5,026.5	4,954.9	5,103.8	5,244.7	5,446.6	5,587.2	5,740.7
Farm	70.8	71.6	80.6	70.7	83.7	75.3	83.8
Households and institutions	264.1	272.1	279.1	287.9	296.2	302.5	309.2
General government	774.7	781.1	781.0	782.9	782.4	777.5	774.6
Federal	280.3	281.0	274.4	267.3	256.8	246.4	238.5
State and local	494.5	500.1	506.6	515.6	525.8	531.7	536.9

Source: U.S. Bureau of Economic Analysis, *National Income and Product Accounts of the United States, 1929-94*, forthcoming; and *Survey of Current Business*, May 1997.

No. 695. GDP Components—Annual Percent Change: 1987 to 1996

[Change from previous year; for 1987, change from 1986. For explanation of chained dollars, see text, section 14. Minus sign (-) indicates decrease]

ITEM	1987	1988	1989	1990	1991	1992	1993	1994	1995	1996
CURRENT DOLLARS										
Gross	**6.1**	**7.8**	**7.7**	**5.6**	**3.0**	**5.5**	**4.9**	**5.8**	**4.6**	**4.4**
Personal consumption expenditures	7.0	8.2	7.3	6.8	3.5	6.2	5.6	5.5	4.8	4.6
Durable goods	4.5	8.2	4.8	0.8	-4.5	7.3	8.6	9.5	4.4	4.2
Nondurable goods	5.9	6.6	7.7	7.0	2.6	3.5	3.6	4.4	3.9	4.0
Services	8.3	9.2	7.7	8.1	5.9	7.5	6.0	5.3	5.3	5.0
Gross private domestic investment	3.4	3.6	7.1	-3.6	-7.9	7.4	10.2	16.5	5.0	4.9
Fixed investment	1.4	5.5	4.5	-0.7	-6.7	6.1	8.6	12.3	7.7	7.1
Nonresidential	0.1	7.1	6.7	1.7	-5.0	1.9	7.3	11.4	10.7	7.1
Residential	4.3	2.2	-0.5	-6.7	-11.4	16.0	11.6	14.3	0.7	7.1
Exports	14.0	22.3	13.9	9.4	8.0	6.3	2.9	9.3	12.3	5.9
Imports	12.3	8.9	6.6	6.6	-1.0	7.5	7.7	12.9	10.9	5.7
Govt. consumption expenditures and gross investment	5.6	3.9	6.1	7.4	4.2	3.1	2.1	1.9	3.3	3.5
Federal	4.7	0.4	4.4	5.5	3.8	1.0	-1.0	-1.2	-	1.3
National defense	5.4	1.0	1.9	3.5	2.8	-2.0	-3.5	-2.9	-1.8	0.4
State and local	6.7	7.0	7.5	8.9	4.6	4.6	4.4	4.0	5.4	4.9
CHAINED (1992) DOLLARS										
Gross	**2.9**	**3.8**	**3.4**	**1.2**	**-0.9**	**2.7**	**2.3**	**3.5**	**2.0**	**2.4**
Personal consumption expenditures	2.0	2.6	1.5	1.1	-0.4	1.9	1.9	2.1	1.6	1.7
Durable goods	0.1	0.6	0.2	-0.1	-0.5	0.4	0.6	0.6	0.3	0.5
Nondurable goods	0.4	0.6	0.5	0.2	-0.2	0.3	0.4	0.6	0.5	0.3
Services	1.5	1.4	0.8	0.9	0.3	1.1	0.9	0.9	0.9	0.9
Gross private domestic investment	0.2	0.1	0.6	-0.8	-1.3	0.8	1.1	1.9	0.4	0.7
Fixed investment	-0.1	0.4	0.3	-0.5	-1.1	0.7	0.8	1.3	0.8	1.0
Nonresidential	-0.1	0.5	0.4	-0.1	-0.6	0.1	0.6	0.9	0.9	0.8
Residential	-	-0.1	-0.2	-0.4	-0.5	0.5	0.3	0.4	-0.1	0.2
Exports	0.8	1.2	1.0	0.8	0.6	0.6	0.3	0.8	0.9	0.7
Imports	-0.6	-0.4	-0.4	-0.4	0.1	-0.7	-1.0	-1.3	-0.9	-0.8
Govt. consumption expenditures and gross investment	0.6	0.3	0.6	0.6	0.1	0.1	-	-	-	0.2
Federal	0.3	-0.2	0.1	0.2	0.0	-0.2	-0.3	-0.3	-0.3	-0.1
National defense	0.3	-0.1	-0.1	-	-0.1	-0.4	-0.3	-0.3	-0.3	-0.1
State and local	0.3	0.4	0.4	0.4	0.2	0.3	0.3	0.3	0.3	0.2

\- Represents or rounds to zero.

Source: U.S. Bureau of Economic Analysis, *National Income and Product Accounts of the United States, 1929-94*, forthcoming; and *Survey of Current Business*, May 1997.

No. 696. Gross State Product in Current and Real (1992) Dollars: 1990 to 1994

[In billions of dollars. For definition of gross State product or chained dollars, see text, section 14]

REGION, DIVISION, AND STATE	CURRENT DOLLARS					CHAINED (1992) DOLLARS				
	1990	1991	1992	1993	1994	1990	1991	1992	1993	1994
United States	5,662.0	5,837.4	6,136.0	6,430.5	6,835.6	6,023.9	5,969.2	6,136.0	6,256.5	6,518.5
Northeast	1,295.4	1,318.7	1,379.6	1,439.1	1,509.6	1,384.8	1,353.7	1,379.6	1,398.3	1,436.5
New England	337.7	341.1	353.2	369.4	389.3	360.6	349.7	353.2	358.2	369.7
Maine	23.2	23.2	24.0	25.1	26.1	24.8	23.9	24.0	24.3	24.6
New Hampshire	23.8	24.8	26.1	27.2	29.4	25.3	25.4	26.1	26.5	28.1
Vermont	11.5	11.4	12.2	12.7	13.3	12.2	11.7	12.2	12.4	12.6
Massachusetts	159.3	160.3	165.8	174.8	186.2	170.2	164.5	165.8	169.9	177.3
Rhode Island	21.5	21.6	22.4	23.3	23.9	23.1	22.2	22.4	22.6	22.7
Connecticut	98.4	99.7	102.7	106.3	110.4	105.1	101.9	102.7	102.5	104.3
Middle Atlantic	957.8	977.8	1,026.4	1,069.6	1,120.4	1,024.2	1,004.1	1,026.4	1,040.1	1,066.8
New York	497.5	501.4	525.6	542.8	571.0	534.5	516.1	525.6	528.2	544.7
New Jersey	214.8	220.2	231.5	244.8	254.9	228.3	225.6	231.5	237.8	242.2
Pennsylvania	245.4	256.0	269.4	282.0	294.4	261.3	262.4	269.4	274.0	279.9
Midwest	1,264.0	1,302.4	1,382.8	1,451.4	1,566.6	1,344.1	1,334.6	1,382.8	1,411.1	1,491.4
East North Central	896.7	920.3	976.8	1,030.9	1,111.6	955.0	943.5	976.8	1,002.2	1,057.5
Ohio	226.9	232.4	245.0	256.1	274.8	241.4	238.2	245.0	249.1	261.6
Indiana	108.8	112.5	120.3	127.4	138.2	115.3	115.1	120.3	124.0	131.6
Illinois	273.4	281.9	298.4	312.6	332.9	290.7	288.6	298.4	303.9	317.2
Michigan	188.4	190.5	202.6	217.1	240.4	202.6	196.3	202.6	210.4	227.4
Wisconsin	99.3	103.0	110.4	117.8	125.3	105.0	106.3	110.4	114.8	119.7
West North Central	367.3	382.0	406.0	420.5	455.0	389.1	391.0	406.0	408.9	433.9
Minnesota	99.6	102.9	110.7	115.2	124.6	105.3	105.2	110.7	111.9	118.7
Iowa	54.9	56.4	59.9	61.6	66.3	57.9	57.6	59.9	59.9	65.3
Missouri	104.1	109.0	114.7	118.6	128.2	111.2	111.9	114.7	115.2	121.8
North Dakota	11.4	11.5	12.6	12.7	13.5	11.9	11.7	12.6	12.4	13.0
South Dakota	12.8	13.8	14.9	16.1	17.3	13.7	14.2	14.9	15.7	16.5
Nebraska	33.2	35.0	37.2	38.2	41.4	34.9	35.7	37.2	37.2	39.6
Kansas	51.2	53.3	56.1	58.1	61.8	54.3	54.6	56.1	56.6	59.0
South	1,803.1	1,875.4	1,990.5	2,088.8	2,232.0	1,914.3	1,924.5	1,990.5	2,035.1	2,137.4
South Atlantic	955.9	994.3	1,060.1	1,111.0	1,182.1	1,027.5	1,024.7	1,060.1	1,082.4	1,130.3
Delaware	20.9	22.2	23.4	24.3	26.7	23.0	23.1	23.4	23.5	25.2
Maryland	113.9	116.2	119.1	124.6	132.7	122.3	119.6	119.1	121.0	125.6
District of Columbia	40.8	42.7	45.2	47.3	48.0	45.1	44.5	45.2	45.7	44.7
Virginia	148.0	152.9	160.6	169.4	177.7	160.1	158.3	160.6	165.4	170.6
West Virginia	28.2	29.1	30.6	32.1	34.7	29.4	29.6	30.6	31.6	33.5
North Carolina	143.5	150.1	161.4	169.6	181.5	156.0	155.6	161.4	166.3	177.2
South Carolina	65.4	67.9	71.1	75.1	79.9	69.5	69.6	71.1	73.3	76.7
Georgia	140.1	147.2	158.8	170.1	183.0	149.3	151.2	158.8	165.7	175.0
Florida	255.0	265.9	279.8	298.5	317.8	272.7	273.3	279.8	289.9	301.8
East South Central	270.7	285.2	308.2	324.4	352.3	287.9	292.6	308.2	316.2	336.7
Kentucky	67.4	69.8	76.1	80.4	86.5	71.9	71.7	76.1	78.6	83.2
Tennessee	94.2	100.3	109.1	115.3	126.5	100.4	103.0	109.1	112.3	120.7
Alabama	71.1	75.0	79.7	82.6	88.7	75.4	76.9	79.7	80.5	84.6
Mississippi	38.0	40.1	43.3	46.1	50.6	40.2	41.1	43.3	44.7	48.2
West South Central	576.5	595.9	622.2	653.3	697.6	598.8	607.2	622.2	636.6	670.5
Arkansas	37.9	40.6	44.2	46.7	50.6	40.0	41.5	44.2	45.5	48.3
Louisiana	91.4	91.9	90.8	94.3	101.1	93.9	93.5	90.8	91.7	97.0
Oklahoma	57.0	59.0	61.4	63.9	66.2	59.6	60.2	61.4	62.3	63.5
Texas	390.2	404.5	425.8	448.4	479.8	405.3	412.0	425.8	437.2	461.5
West	1,299.5	1,340.9	1,392.2	1,451.3	1,527.4	1,380.6	1,375.8	1,392.2	1,411.7	1,454.5
Mountain	275.9	292.7	316.3	342.5	374.0	291.0	299.7	316.3	333.8	357.1
Montana	13.3	14.0	15.1	16.1	16.9	13.9	14.3	15.1	15.7	16.0
Idaho	17.5	18.3	20.1	22.2	24.2	18.5	18.8	20.1	21.6	23.0
Wyoming	13.5	13.8	14.1	14.8	15.7	13.4	13.8	14.1	14.7	15.6
Colorado	74.3	79.0	85.4	93.2	99.8	78.8	81.0	85.4	90.8	95.3
New Mexico	26.7	30.2	31.8	34.4	37.8	27.8	30.9	31.8	33.6	36.5
Arizona	68.4	71.0	78.4	84.5	94.1	72.8	72.8	78.4	82.2	89.5
Utah	31.1	33.4	35.3	38.0	41.7	32.9	34.2	35.3	37.0	39.7
Nevada	31.1	33.2	36.0	39.3	44.0	33.0	34.0	36.0	38.2	41.5
Pacific	1,023.6	1,048.2	1,075.9	1,108.7	1,153.4	1,089.6	1,076.1	1,075.9	1,077.9	1,097.4
Washington	114.2	121.2	128.8	136.5	143.9	122.2	124.7	128.8	132.5	136.3
Oregon	57.0	59.8	63.3	68.9	74.4	60.8	61.5	63.3	66.5	70.1
California	794.4	810.3	826.5	842.1	875.7	846.6	831.7	826.5	819.2	833.9
Alaska	25.5	23.0	22.2	25.0	22.7	25.2	23.3	22.2	24.6	22.3
Hawaii	32.5	33.9	35.0	36.3	36.7	34.9	34.9	35.0	35.2	34.7

Source: U.S. Bureau of Economic Analysis, *Survey of Current Business*, June 1997.

No. 697. Gross State Product in Chained (1992) Dollars, by Industry: 1994

[In billions of dollars. For definition of gross state product or chained dollars, see text, section 14. Industries based on 1987 Standard Industrial Classification]

DIVISION AND STATE	Total [1]	Farms, forestry, fisheries [2]	Construction	Manufacturing	Transportation, public utilities	Wholesale trade	Retail trade	Finance, insurance, real estate	Services	Government [3]
United States	**6,518.5**	**115.7**	**263.1**	**1,168.0**	**585.3**	**450.0**	**595.4**	**1,192.8**	**1,249.6**	**815.6**
Northeast	**1,436.5**	**9.7**	**47.9**	**226.3**	**122.7**	**100.4**	**116.0**	**345.8**	**311.4**	**153.9**
New England	**369.7**	**2.9**	**12.4**	**65.4**	**26.7**	**25.3**	**32.4**	**85.3**	**82.4**	**36.7**
Maine	24.6	0.5	1.1	4.4	1.8	1.5	3.1	4.4	4.4	3.5
New Hampshire	28.1	0.2	1.0	6.1	2.2	1.7	2.8	6.0	5.3	2.7
Vermont	12.6	0.3	0.5	2.2	1.2	0.9	1.3	2.1	2.5	1.5
Massachusetts	177.3	1.0	5.6	30.2	12.4	12.9	14.4	40.2	44.0	16.6
Rhode Island	22.7	0.2	0.8	4.1	1.7	1.2	2.2	5.1	4.8	2.7
Connecticut	104.3	0.7	3.4	18.3	7.4	7.1	8.6	27.5	21.3	9.8
Middle Atlantic	**1,066.8**	**6.7**	**35.5**	**160.9**	**96.0**	**75.1**	**83.6**	**260.5**	**229.0**	**117.2**
New York	544.7	2.5	15.7	68.9	44.9	34.8	39.1	156.8	120.6	61.2
New Jersey	242.2	1.3	8.7	35.7	24.8	22.8	18.6	53.5	50.5	26.2
Pennsylvania	279.9	2.9	11.1	56.4	26.3	17.6	25.9	50.2	57.8	29.8
Midwest	**1,491.4**	**35.5**	**60.5**	**360.7**	**129.8**	**109.0**	**135.9**	**230.7**	**258.7**	**164.0**
East North Central	**1,057.5**	**15.4**	**42.4**	**274.8**	**87.7**	**75.7**	**95.0**	**166.6**	**184.6**	**110.8**
Ohio	261.6	3.1	9.9	71.4	21.8	18.1	25.3	38.6	44.4	27.8
Indiana	131.6	2.4	6.1	40.4	11.0	8.2	12.4	17.1	19.7	13.5
Illinois	317.2	4.8	13.2	61.2	30.8	26.0	26.9	58.8	62.4	31.9
Michigan	227.4	2.3	8.1	67.4	15.5	16.0	19.5	34.0	39.3	24.4
Wisconsin	119.7	2.9	5.1	34.4	8.5	7.5	10.9	18.2	18.8	13.1
West North Central	**433.9**	**20.0**	**18.0**	**85.8**	**42.1**	**33.3**	**41.0**	**64.2**	**74.1**	**53.1**
Minnesota	118.7	3.3	5.0	24.3	9.2	9.8	10.9	20.4	22.2	13.1
Iowa	65.3	4.8	2.5	16.5	5.2	4.6	5.8	8.8	9.3	7.7
Missouri	121.8	2.3	5.5	25.9	13.0	9.2	12.2	17.5	22.4	13.5
North Dakota	13.0	1.4	0.6	1.0	1.5	1.2	1.3	1.6	2.1	2.1
South Dakota	16.5	1.8	0.6	1.9	1.3	1.0	1.6	3.3	2.5	2.2
Nebraska	39.6	3.5	1.6	5.9	4.5	3.1	3.4	5.4	6.2	5.8
Kansas	59.0	2.9	2.3	10.3	7.3	4.4	5.8	7.3	9.3	8.7
South	**2,137.4**	**38.6**	**85.2**	**381.7**	**211.9**	**143.3**	**203.1**	**327.0**	**379.7**	**305.4**
South Atlantic	**1,130.3**	**18.0**	**45.9**	**186.2**	**103.9**	**74.4**	**106.8**	**198.0**	**214.4**	**175.9**
Delaware	25.2	0.3	0.8	5.1	1.3	1.0	1.5	9.7	3.2	2.2
Maryland	125.6	1.2	6.1	11.1	10.7	8.0	11.5	27.3	27.6	21.9
Dist. of Columbia	44.7	-	0.4	1.2	2.5	0.6	1.3	6.5	14.6	17.6
Virginia	170.6	1.8	7.0	27.9	14.9	9.4	14.5	28.9	31.5	33.5
West Virginia	33.5	0.3	1.6	5.6	4.4	1.8	3.0	3.6	5.0	4.4
North Carolina	177.2	4.2	6.7	55.7	13.8	11.4	15.9	21.9	24.5	23.0
South Carolina	76.7	1.1	3.3	21.6	6.2	4.3	7.9	9.6	10.8	12.0
Georgia	175.0	3.2	6.3	32.2	21.1	15.9	16.3	26.6	29.8	22.9
Florida	301.8	5.9	13.7	25.9	28.9	22.1	34.9	63.9	67.5	38.4
East South Central	**336.7**	**7.5**	**12.6**	**82.5**	**32.9**	**21.8**	**34.6**	**39.4**	**53.5**	**46.5**
Kentucky	83.2	2.3	3.2	22.7	8.0	4.6	7.5	8.9	11.5	11.2
Tennessee	120.7	1.7	4.4	29.7	10.3	9.0	13.6	15.2	22.0	14.6
Alabama	84.6	2.0	3.3	18.8	8.5	5.4	8.7	10.1	13.0	13.6
Mississippi	48.2	1.5	1.7	11.4	6.0	2.8	4.9	5.3	7.0	7.2
West South Central	**670.5**	**13.1**	**26.7**	**112.9**	**75.2**	**47.0**	**61.7**	**89.6**	**111.8**	**83.0**
Arkansas	48.3	2.4	1.7	12.1	6.0	3.0	5.1	5.3	6.7	5.7
Louisiana	97.0	1.2	4.2	16.4	10.8	5.6	8.5	12.4	15.5	11.7
Oklahoma	63.5	1.9	1.9	10.8	7.0	3.9	6.5	7.6	10.0	10.3
Texas	461.5	7.6	18.8	73.6	51.4	34.5	41.6	64.2	79.6	55.3
West	**1,454.5**	**32.1**	**59.5**	**199.2**	**121.1**	**97.3**	**140.3**	**289.1**	**299.8**	**192.3**
Mountain	**357.1**	**7.6**	**19.0**	**44.6**	**36.3**	**20.6**	**36.3**	**56.2**	**71.7**	**50.2**
Montana	16.0	1.0	0.7	1.2	2.1	1.0	1.7	2.1	2.8	2.6
Idaho	23.0	1.5	1.4	4.3	2.1	1.4	2.4	2.9	3.5	3.1
Wyoming	15.6	0.4	0.6	0.6	2.6	0.5	1.0	1.6	1.4	1.9
Colorado	95.3	1.7	4.9	12.1	10.6	6.2	9.8	15.8	19.3	13.2
New Mexico	36.5	0.7	1.7	5.1	3.6	1.6	3.5	4.8	6.2	6.5
Arizona	89.5	1.4	4.8	13.7	8.1	5.5	9.8	15.9	16.9	12.3
Utah	39.7	0.5	2.0	5.7	3.9	2.5	4.2	5.5	7.7	6.2
Nevada	41.5	0.3	2.9	1.9	3.3	1.9	4.0	7.6	14.0	4.4
Pacific	**1,097.4**	**24.5**	**40.4**	**154.6**	**84.8**	**76.7**	**104.0**	**232.9**	**228.1**	**142.0**
Washington	136.3	3.7	6.7	19.2	11.2	10.6	14.1	24.2	25.8	20.5
Oregon	70.1	2.2	3.2	13.7	5.7	5.7	6.6	11.6	12.3	8.9
California	833.9	17.9	27.5	119.5	60.7	58.3	77.8	186.7	180.4	100.7
Alaska	22.3	0.3	1.0	1.0	3.8	0.7	1.5	2.3	2.5	4.5
Hawaii	34.7	0.5	2.0	1.1	3.4	1.4	4.0	6.0	7.1	7.4

- Represents zero. [1] Includes mining not shown separately. [2] Includes agricultural services. [3] Includes Federal civilian and military and State and local government.

Source: U.S. Bureau of Economic Analysis, *Survey of Current Business*, June 1997.

No. 698. Relation of GDP, GNP, Net National Product, National Income, Personal Income, Disposable Personal Income, and Personal Saving: 1990 to 1996

[In billions of dollars. For definitions, see text, section 14]

ITEM	1990	1991	1992	1993	1994	1995	1996
Gross domestic product	5,743.8	5,916.7	6,244.4	6,553.0	6,935.7	7,253.8	7,576.1
Plus: Receipts of factor income from the rest of the world [1]	177.5	156.2	137.9	140.7	163.4	208.3	228.4
Less: Payments of factor income to the rest of the world [2]	156.4	140.5	126.8	130.1	167.2	215.3	237.3
Equals: Gross national product	5,764.9	5,932.4	6,255.5	6,563.5	6,931.9	7,246.7	7,567.1
Less: Consumption of fixed capital	651.5	679.9	713.5	729.7	784.8	811.1	845.5
Equals: Net national product [3]	5,113.4	5,252.5	5,542.0	5,833.8	6,147.2	6,435.7	6,721.6
Less: Indirect business tax and nontax liability	442.6	478.1	505.6	540.0	572.5	595.5	617.9
Plus: Subsidies [4]	25.3	23.6	27.1	31.7	25.1	18.2	17.5
Equals: National income [3]	4,652.1	4,761.6	4,990.4	5,238.5	5,535.2	5,828.9	6,164.2
Less: Corporate profits [5]	397.1	411.3	428.0	492.1	554.1	604.8	670.2
Net interest	467.3	448.0	414.3	398.9	394.9	403.6	403.3
Contributions for social insurance	518.5	543.5	571.4	592.9	628.3	660.0	689.7
Wage accruals less disbursements	0.1	-0.1	-15.8	4.6	15.5	2.7	-
Plus: Personal interest income	704.4	699.2	667.2	648.1	663.7	717.1	736.2
Personal dividend income	142.9	153.6	159.4	186.8	199.6	214.8	230.6
Government transfer payments to persons	666.5	749.1	835.7	888.6	933.8	1,000.0	1,056.7
Business transfer payments to persons	21.3	20.8	22.5	22.1	22.6	22.8	23.0
Equals: Personal income	4,804.2	4,981.6	5,277.2	5,495.6	5,762.0	6,112.4	6,449.5
Less: Personal tax and nontax payments	624.8	624.8	650.5	689.9	731.4	794.3	863.8
Equals: Disposable personal income	4,179.4	4,356.8	4,626.7	4,805.7	5,030.6	5,318.1	5,585.7
Less: Personal outlays	3,958.1	4,097.4	4,341.0	4,575.8	4,832.3	5,071.5	5,314.0
Equals: Personal saving	221.3	259.5	285.6	229.9	198.3	246.6	271.8

- Represents or rounds to zero. [1] Consists largely of receipts by U.S. residents of interest and dividends and reinvested earnings of foreign affiliates of U.S. corporations. [2] Consists largely of payments to foreign residents of interest and dividends and reinvested earnings of U.S. affiliates of foreign corporations. [3] Includes items not shown separately. [4] Less current surplus of government enterprises. [5] With inventory valuation and capital consumption adjustments.

Source: U.S. Bureau of Economic Analysis, *National Income and Product Accounts of the United States, 1929-94*, forthcoming; and *Survey of Current Business*, May 1997.

No. 699. Selected Per Capita Income and Product Items in Current and Real (1992) Dollars: 1960 to 1996

[In dollars. Based on Bureau of the Census estimated population including Armed Forces abroad; based on quarterly averages. For explanation of chained dollars, see text, section 14]

YEAR	CURRENT DOLLARS					CHAINED (1992) DOLLARS			
	Gross domestic product	Gross national product	Personal income	Disposable personal income	Personal consumption expenditures	Gross domestic product	Gross national product	Disposable personal income	Personal consumption expenditures
1960	2,913	2,931	2,277	2,006	1,838	12,512	12,585	8,660	7,926
1965	3,700	3,728	2,860	2,541	2,286	14,792	14,897	10,292	9,257
1970	5,050	5,081	4,077	3,545	3,160	16,520	16,616	12,022	10,717
1971	5,419	5,456	4,328	3,805	3,383	16,853	16,959	12,345	10,975
1972	5,894	5,935	4,703	4,074	3,671	17,579	17,694	12,770	11,508
1973	6,524	6,584	5,217	4,553	4,018	18,412	18,572	13,539	11,950
1974	6,996	7,071	5,672	4,928	4,353	18,178	18,360	13,310	11,756
1975	7,550	7,611	6,091	5,367	4,765	17,896	18,032	13,404	11,899
1976	8,341	8,419	6,673	5,837	5,268	18,713	18,878	13,793	12,446
1977	9,201	9,295	7,315	6,362	5,797	19,426	19,611	14,095	12,846
1978	10,292	10,392	8,176	7,097	6,418	20,185	20,367	14,662	13,258
1979	11,361	11,507	9,105	7,861	7,079	20,541	20,794	14,899	13,417
1980	12,226	12,381	10,037	8,665	7,730	20,252	20,497	14,813	13,216
1981	13,547	13,696	11,132	9,566	8,440	20,542	20,756	15,009	13,245
1982	13,961	14,095	11,744	10,145	8,943	19,896	20,076	15,053	13,270
1983	14,998	15,135	12,379	10,803	9,744	20,499	20,675	15,332	13,829
1984	16,508	16,640	13,602	11,929	10,543	21,744	21,904	16,309	14,415
1985	17,529	17,614	14,464	12,629	11,341	22,320	22,418	16,654	14,954
1986	18,374	18,427	15,200	13,289	12,019	22,801	22,857	17,039	15,409
1987	19,323	19,359	16,013	13,896	12,743	23,264	23,300	17,164	15,740
1988	20,605	20,659	17,076	14,905	13,669	23,934	23,988	17,678	16,211
1989	21,984	22,042	18,194	15,790	14,531	24,504	24,559	17,854	16,430
1990	22,979	23,064	19,220	16,721	15,360	24,549	24,632	17,996	16,532
1991	23,416	23,478	19,715	17,242	15,732	24,060	24,121	17,809	16,249
1992	24,447	24,490	20,660	18,113	16,520	24,447	24,490	18,113	16,520
1993	25,383	25,424	21,288	18,615	17,253	24,737	24,779	18,136	16,809
1994	26,606	26,592	22,104	19,298	18,033	25,351	25,340	18,362	17,159
1995	27,571	27,545	23,233	20,214	18,719	25,627	25,605	18,789	17,400
1996	28,537	28,503	24,294	21,040	19,404	26,016	25,989	19,158	17,669

Source: U.S. Bureau of Economic Analysis, *National Income and Product Accounts of the United States, 1929-94*, forthcoming; and *Survey of Current Business*, May 1997.

No. 700. National Income, by Type of Income: 1990 to 1996

[In billions of dollars]

INCOME	1990	1991	1992	1993	1994	1995	1996
National income	**4,652.1**	**4,761.6**	**4,990.4**	**5,238.5**	**5,535.2**	**5,828.9**	**6,164.2**
Compensation of employees	3,352.8	3,457.9	3,644.9	3,809.5	4,009.8	4,222.7	4,448.5
Wages and salaries	2,757.5	2,827.6	2,970.6	3,095.3	3,257.3	3,433.2	3,630.1
Government	517.2	546.0	567.8	584.2	602.5	621.7	641.2
Other	2,240.3	2,281.5	2,402.9	2,511.1	2,654.8	2,811.5	2,988.9
Supplements to wages and salaries	595.2	630.4	674.3	714.2	752.4	789.5	818.4
Employer contributions for social insurance	294.6	307.7	323.0	333.3	350.2	365.5	382.2
Other labor income	300.6	322.7	351.3	380.9	402.2	424.0	436.0
Proprietors' income [1] [2]	374.0	376.5	423.8	435.9	464.4	486.1	527.3
Farm	35.4	29.3	37.1	31.1	34.3	27.9	44.7
Nonfarm	338.6	347.2	386.7	404.8	430.0	458.2	482.6
Rental income of persons [1]	61.0	67.9	79.4	102.2	112.1	111.7	115.0
Corporate profits [1] [2]	397.1	411.3	428.0	492.1	554.1	604.8	670.2
Corporate profits [2]	358.2	378.2	398.9	457.7	517.9	570.8	631.0
Profits before tax	371.7	374.2	406.4	464.3	531.2	598.9	639.9
Profits tax liability	140.5	133.4	143.0	163.8	195.3	218.7	233.0
Profits after tax	231.2	240.8	263.4	300.5	335.9	380.2	406.8
Dividends	151.9	163.1	169.5	197.3	211.0	227.4	244.2
Undistributed profits	79.4	77.7	93.9	103.2	124.8	152.8	162.6
Inventory valuation adjustment	-13.5	4.0	-7.5	-6.6	-13.3	-28.1	-8.9
Capital consumption adjustment	38.9	33.1	29.1	34.4	36.2	34.0	39.2
Net interest	467.3	448.0	414.3	398.9	394.9	403.6	403.3
Addenda:							
Corporate profits after tax [1] [2]	256.6	277.9	285.0	328.3	358.8	386.1	437.1
Net cash flow [1] [2]	455.0	479.3	491.9	520.3	564.2	594.6	650.8
Undistributed profits [1] [2]	104.7	114.8	115.5	131.0	147.8	158.7	192.9
Consumption of fixed capital	350.3	364.5	376.4	389.3	416.4	435.9	457.9
Less: Inventory valuation adjustment	-13.5	4.0	-7.5	-6.6	-13.3	-28.1	-8.9
Equals: Net cash flow	468.5	475.3	499.4	526.9	577.4	622.7	659.7

[1] With capital consumption adjustment. [2] With inventory valuation adjustment. For corporate profits by industry, see section 17.

Source: U.S. Bureau of Economic Analysis, *National Income and Product Accounts of the United States, 1929-94,* forthcoming; and *Survey of Current Business,* May 1997.

No. 701. National Income, by Sector: 1990 to 1995

[In billions of dollars]

SECTOR	1990	1991	1992	1993	1994	1995
National income	**4,652.1**	**4,761.6**	**4,990.4**	**5,238.5**	**5,535.2**	**5,828.9**
Domestic business	3,785.0	3,844.2	4,029.4	4,241.2	4,521.1	4,785.7
Corporate business	2,704.8	2,745.4	2,865.9	3,040.3	3,257.4	3,454.1
Compensation of employees	2,222.0	2,264.6	2,387.7	2,502.5	2,652.1	2,804.5
Corporate profits [1]	331.3	342.6	363.1	422.5	489.9	528.1
Net interest	151.4	138.2	115.1	115.2	115.5	121.5
Sole proprietorships and partnerships	660.8	660.1	708.8	732.3	772.9	820.6
Compensation of employees	198.6	201.9	212.6	224.6	236.8	258.9
Proprietors' income [1]	371.8	374.1	421.1	433.1	461.3	482.8
Net interest	90.4	84.1	75.1	74.6	74.9	78.8
Other private business [2]	346.2	362.1	373.7	387.3	402.7	418.0
Compensation of employees	13.1	13.3	13.7	14.4	15.0	16.1
Proprietors' income [1]	2.2	2.4	2.6	2.8	3.1	3.2
Rental income of persons [3]	61.0	67.9	79.4	102.2	112.1	111.7
Net interest	269.9	278.6	277.9	267.9	272.6	286.9
Government enterprises [4]	73.3	76.5	81.0	81.3	88.1	93.0
Households and institutions [5]	237.9	257.4	279.1	294.9	310.3	323.0
General government [4]	608.1	644.3	670.8	691.8	707.6	727.3
Rest of the world	21.1	15.7	11.1	10.6	-3.8	-7.0

[1] With inventory valuation and capital consumption adjustments. [2] Consists of all business activities reported on the individual income tax return in Schedule E—Supplemental Income Schedule; tax-exempt cooperatives; and owner-occupied nonfarm housing and buildings and equipment owned and used by nonprofit institutions servicing individuals, which are considered to be business activities selling their current services to their owners. [3] With capital consumption adjustment. [4] Compensation of employees. [5] Compensation of employees in private households; nonprofit social and athletic clubs; labor organizations; nonprofit schools and hospitals; religious, charitable, and welfare organizations; and all other nonprofit organizations serving individuals.

Source: U.S. Bureau of Economic Analysis, *National Income and Product Accounts of the United States, 1929-94,* forthcoming, and *Survey of Current Business,* May 1997.

No. 702. Personal Consumption Expenditures in Current and Real (1992) Dollars, by Type: 1990 to 1995

[In billions of dollars. For definition of "chained" dollars, see text, section 14]

EXPENDITURE	CURRENT DOLLARS				CHAINED (1992) DOLLARS			
	1990	1993	1994	1995	1990	1993	1994	1995
Total expenditures [1]	3,839.3	4,484.1	4,700.9	4,924.9	4,132.2	4,339.5	4,473.2	4,577.5
Food and tobacco [1]	672.5	732.7	763.3	794.4	713.5	719.4	736.7	748.1
Food purchased for off-premise consumption	404.8	434.9	449.1	468.8	423.3	428.2	432.2	437.9
Purchased meals and beverages [2]	218.0	242.9	258.4	271.9	231.6	238.2	249.0	256.1
Tobacco products	42.0	47.0	47.7	47.2	50.9	45.2	47.6	46.0
Clothing, accessories, and jewelry [1]	262.7	296.6	310.5	320.2	279.4	292.7	306.4	318.4
Shoes	31.9	34.4	35.5	36.2	34	34.1	35.3	36.0
Clothing	173.8	201.2	212.3	218.1	183.7	199.1	211.9	221.1
Jewelry and watches	31.2	35.6	36.7	38.8	34	34.7	34.8	36.2
Personal care	57.3	65.1	67.7	70.0	60.6	63.3	64.1	65.6
Housing [1]	586.3	673.2	706.6	743.7	627.2	655.0	666.2	681.7
Owner-occupied nonfarm dwellings-space rent	410.7	481.1	502.6	528.5	437.6	468.2	475.4	483.7
Tenant-occupied nonfarm dwellings-space rent	150.1	162.3	172.5	181.6	160	158.3	163.7	168.3
Household operation [1]	436.2	503.5	528.1	554.3	457	494.0	507.9	525.6
Furniture [3]	39.0	42.6	45.4	47.7	40.6	41.6	42.7	43.9
Semidurable house furnishings [4]	21.2	24.9	26.9	28.8	22	24.6	25.4	26.8
Cleaning and polishing preparations	41.9	48.5	50.6	52.2	43.7	48.3	50.1	49.9
Household utilities	138.3	160.2	162.2	166.2	146.7	155.0	154.8	157.3
Electricity	71.9	83.0	84.1	87.1	76.1	81.4	82.4	83.5
Gas	26.8	32.9	31.6	30.9	27.7	31.0	29.2	30.2
Water and other sanitary services	27.5	33.7	36.5	38.2	31.9	31.9	32.9	33.3
Fuel oil and coal	12.0	10.6	10.1	10.0	11.2	10.7	10.3	10.3
Telephone and telegraph	60.4	74.1	79.8	85.6	61.3	73.4	76.8	82.2
Medical care [1]	615.6	787.1	833.7	883.1	691.1	745.6	757.9	775.6
Drug preparations and sundries [5]	65.1	77.9	81.7	85.7	74.5	75.2	76.8	79.2
Physicians	140.8	172.9	179.8	189.8	158.5	163.8	163.1	165.8
Dentists	32.9	40.9	43.8	46.6	37.7	38.8	39.7	40.3
Hospitals and nursing homes [6]	265.7	344.4	363.8	383.6	299	329.7	337.6	343.3
Health insurance	37.4	51.7	57.0	61.3	41.3	41.9	40.8	41.4
Medical care [7]	31.3	41.9	44.5	47.1	35.3	37.1	37.4	38.2
Personal business [1]	290.1	354.0	361.9	373.4	331.3	347.6	347.6	351.2
Expense of handling life insurance [8]	56.4	68.2	71.0	74.0	61.2	65.5	66.4	67.3
Legal services	41.8	47.9	48.6	50.3	46.4	45.9	45.1	45.2
Funeral and burial expenses	9.0	10.8	11.1	11.7	10.1	10.3	10.1	10.0
Transportation	463.3	503.8	536.6	554.8	491.3	490.3	510.0	511.2
User-operated transportation [1]	426.9	465.4	498.0	514.2	454.2	454.0	472.2	472.2
New autos	92.4	86.5	91.3	84.6	98.1	84.4	86.2	78.3
Net purchases of used autos	31.6	40.8	46.1	52.7	35	37.2	38.9	39.3
Tires, tubes, accessories, etc.	29.4	31.6	34.4	36.6	30	32.1	35.0	37.0
Repair, greasing, washing, parking, storage, rental, and leasing	84.1	102.0	113.0	121.2	94.7	98.3	105.3	109.9
Gasoline and oil	96.6	108.1	109.9	114.6	106.1	109.1	110.4	113.3
Purchased local transportation	7.8	8.3	8.6	8.8	8.6	8.1	8.2	8.2
Mass transit systems	5.2	5.5	5.6	5.8	5.7	5.4	5.4	5.3
Taxicab	2.6	2.8	2.9	3.0	2.9	2.7	2.8	2.9
Purchased intercity transportation [1]	28.5	30.1	30.0	31.8	28.6	28.3	29.6	30.9
Railway (commutation)	0.8	0.8	0.7	0.7	0.8	0.8	0.7	0.7
Bus	1.0	0.9	0.8	0.9	1.1	0.9	0.8	0.9
Airline	23.9	25.5	25.3	26.9	23.7	24.0	25.3	26.4
Recreation [1,9]	281.6	339.0	374.8	401.7	291.8	337.2	369.9	395.5
Magazines, newspapers, and sheet music	21.5	22.6	24.0	25.6	23.8	21.8	22.5	23.0
Nondurable toys and sport supplies	31.6	36.5	40.1	42.7	32.6	36.2	39.3	41.8
Video and audio products, computing equipment, musical instruments	53.8	68.6	80.0	88.3	47.9	73.4	89.0	106.0
Education and research	80.7	99.3	105.4	110.7	89.3	95.1	97.0	97.3
Higher education	44.0	55.9	59.7	63.5	50.2	52.7	53.6	54.2
Religious and welfare activities	100.4	121.3	131.2	137.4	106.6	118.7	125.3	128.4
Foreign travel and other, net	-7.4	-21.4	-18.9	-19.0	-8.2	-19.2	-16.5	-16.2
Foreign travel by U.S. residents	41.2	46.0	49.6	52.8	46.1	46.3	48.7	50.3
Less: Expenditures in the United States by nonresidents	51.6	68.7	69.9	73.1	57.7	66.9	66.5	67.5

[1] Includes other expenditures not shown separately. [2] Consists of purchases (including tips) of meals and beverages from retail, service, and amusement establishments; hotels; dining and buffet cars; schools; school fraternities; institutions; clubs; and industrial lunch rooms. Includes meals and beverages consumed both on and off-premise. [3] Includes mattresses and bedsprings. [4] Consists largely of textile house furnishings including piece goods allocated to house furnishing use. Also includes lamp shades, brooms, and brushes. [5] Excludes drug preparations and related products dispensed by physicians, hospitals, and other medical services. [6] Consists of (1) current expenditures (including consumption of fixed capital) of nonprofit hospitals and nursing homes and (2)payments by patients to proprietary and government hospitals and nursing homes. [7] Consists of (1) premiums, less benefits and dividends, for health hospitalization and accidental death and dismemberment insurance provided by commercial insurance carriers and (2)administrative expenses (including consumption of fixed capital) of Blue Cross and Blue Shield plans and of other independent prepaid and self-insured health plans. [8] Consists of (1) operating expenses of life insurance carriers and private noninsured pension plans and (2) premiums less benefits and dividends of fraternal benefit societies. Excludes expenses allocated by commercial carriers to accident and health insurance. [9] For additional details, see table 406.

Source: U.S. Bureau of Economic Analysis, *National Income and Product Accounts of the United States, 1929-94*, forthcoming; and *Survey of Current Business*, January 1997.

No. 703. Personal Income and Its Disposition: 1990 to 1996

[In billions of dollars, except as indicated. For definition of personal income and chained dollars, see text, section 14]

ITEM	1990	1991	1992	1993	1994	1995	1996
Personal income	**4,804.2**	**4,981.6**	**5,277.2**	**5,486.8**	**5,782.0**	**6,112.4**	**6,449.5**
Wage and salary disbursements	2,757.5	2,827.6	2,966.4	3,090.7	3,241.8	3,430.6	3,630.1
Commodity-producing industries [1]	754.2	746.3	765.7	781.3	824.9	863.5	902.7
Manufacturing	561.2	562.5	583.5	593.1	621.1	648.4	672.5
Distributive industries [2]	634.1	646.6	680.3	698.4	739.2	783.7	827.9
Service industries [3]	852.1	888.7	972.6	1,026.7	1,075.2	1,161.6	1,258.3
Government	517.2	546.1	567.8	584.3	602.5	621.7	641.2
Other labor income	300.6	322.7	351.3	380.9	402.2	424.0	436.2
Proprietors' income [4]	374.0	376.5	423.8	435.9	464.4	486.1	527.3
Rental income of persons [5]	61.0	67.9	79.4	102.2	112.1	111.7	115.0
Personal dividend income	142.9	153.6	159.4	186.8	199.6	214.8	230.6
Personal interest income	704.4	699.3	667.2	648.1	663.7	717.1	738.2
Transfer payments to persons	687.8	769.9	858.2	910.7	956.3	1,022.6	1,079.7
Less: Personal contributions for social insurance	*223.9*	*235.8*	*248.4*	*259.6*	*278.1*	*294.5*	*307.5*
Less: Personal tax and nontax payments	*624.8*	*624.8*	*650.6*	*689.9*	*731.4*	*794.3*	*863.8*
Equals: Disposable person	**4,179.4**	**4,356.8**	**4,626.7**	**4,806.6**	**5,030.6**	**5,318.1**	**5,585.7**
Less: Personal outlays	*3,958.1*	*4,097.4*	*4,341.0*	*4,575.8*	*4,832.3*	*5,071.5*	*5,314.0*
Personal consumption expenditures	3,839.3	3,975.1	4,219.8	4,454.1	4,700.9	4,924.9	5,151.4
Interest paid by persons	108.9	111.9	111.7	108.9	117.1	131.7	146.3
Personal transfer payments to the rest of the world (net)	9.9	10.4	9.6	12.8	14.2	14.9	16.3
Equals: Personal saving	**221.3**	**259.5**	**285.7**	**229.9**	**198.3**	**246.6**	**271.6**
Addenda:							
Disposable personal income:							
Total, billions of chained (1992) dollars	4,498.2	4,500.0	4,626.7	4,682.1	4,786.8	4,943.3	5,066.0
Per capita (dollars):							
Current dollars	16,720	17,242	18,112	18,615	19,297	20,214	21,040
Chained (1992) dollars	17,996	17,809	18,113	18,136	18,362	18,789	19,158
Personal saving as percentage of disposable personal income	5.3	6.0	6.2	4.8	3.9	4.6	4.9

1 Comprises agriculture, forestry, fishing, mining, construction, and manufacturing. [2] Comprises transportation, communication, public utilities, and trade. [3] Comprises finance, insurance, real estate, services, and rest of world. [4] With capital consumption and inventory valuation adjustments. [5] With capital consumption adjustment.

Source: U.S. Bureau of Economic Analysis, *National Income and Product Accounts of the United States, 1929-94*, forthcoming; and *Survey of Current Business*, May 1997.

No. 704. Gross Saving and Investment: 1990 to 1996

[In billions of dollars]

ITEM	1990	1991	1992	1993	1994	1995	1996
Gross saving	**903.1**	**934.0**	**994.3**	**934.6**	**1,055.9**	**1,152.3**	**1,275.9**
Gross private saving	860.3	930.6	970.7	961.6	1,006.3	1,072.3	1,161.0
Personal saving	221.3	259.5	285.6	229.9	198.3	246.6	271.6
Undistributed corporate profits [1]	104.7	114.8	115.5	131.0	147.8	158.7	192.9
Undistributed profits	79.4	77.7	93.9	103.2	124.8	152.8	162.6
Inventory valuation adjustment	-13.5	4.0	-7.5	-6.6	-13.3	-28.1	-8.9
Capital consumption adjustment	38.9	33.1	29.1	34.4	36.2	34.0	39.2
Corporate consumption of fixed capital	350.3	364.5	376.4	389.3	416.4	435.9	457.9
Noncorporate consumption of fixed capital	184.0	191.9	209.0	206.7	228.3	228.5	238.6
Wage accruals less disbursements	-	-	-15.8	4.6	15.5	2.7	-
Gross government saving	42.7	3.3	-66.5	-26.9	49.6	80.0	115.0
Federal	-94.0	-132.2	-215.0	-187.4	-119.6	-87.8	-54.6
State and local	136.7	135.5	148.6	160.5	169.2	167.9	169.6
Capital grants received by the U.S. (net)	-	-	-	-	-	-	-
Gross investment	**920.5**	**944.0**	**949.1**	**993.5**	**1,090.4**	**1,150.9**	**1,200.8**
Gross private domestic investment	799.7	736.2	790.4	871.1	1,014.4	1,065.3	1,117.0
Gross government investment	199.4	200.5	209.1	210.6	212.3	221.9	233.3
Net foreign investment	-78.6	7.3	-50.5	-88.2	-136.4	-136.3	-149.5
Statistical discrepancy	**17.4**	**10.1**	**44.6**	**58.6**	**34.5**	**-1.5**	**-75.1**

- Represents or rounds to zero. [1] With inventory valuation and capital consumption adjustments.

Source: U.S. Bureau of Economic Analysis, *National Income and Product Accounts of the United States, 1929-94*, forthcoming; and *Survey of Current Business*, May 1997.

No. 705. Personal Income in Current and Constant (1992) Dollars, by State: 1980 to 1996

[In billions of dollars, except percent. 1996 preliminary. Represents a measure of income received from all sources during the calendar year by residents of each State. Data exclude Federal employees overseas and U.S. residents employed by private U.S. firms on temporary foreign assignment. Totals may differ from those in tables 696, 699, and 703. For definition of average annual percent change, see Guide to Tabular Presentation]

REGION, DIVISION, AND STATE	CURRENT DOLLARS				CONSTANT (1992) DOLLARS							
									Average annual percent change		Percent distribution	
	1980	1990	1995	1996	1980	1990	1995	1996	1980-1990	1995-1996	1980	1996
United States	**2,279.2**	**4,774.0**	**6,098.0**	**6,428.1**	**3,896.0**	**5,138.3**	**5,669.9**	**5,852.3**	**2.5**	**3.2**	**100.0**	**100.0**
Northeast	**530.0**	**1,140.0**	**1,368.1**	**1,451.1**	**905.9**	**1,227.0**	**1,290.7**	**1,321.1**	**2.4**	**2.4**	**23.3**	**22.6**
New England	**131.8**	**300.3**	**364.8**	**382.3**	**225.3**	**323.2**	**339.0**	**348.0**	**2.8**	**2.7**	**5.8**	**5.9**
Maine	9.3	21.1	25.0	25.9	15.9	22.8	23.2	23.6	2.6	1.7	0.4	0.4
New Hampshire	9.1	23.0	29.4	30.8	15.6	24.7	27.3	28.1	3.8	2.9	0.4	0.5
Vermont	4.4	10.0	12.4	13.0	7.5	10.7	11.5	11.9	2.9	3.5	0.2	0.2
Massachusetts	61.7	139.6	170.2	179.4	105.5	150.3	158.2	163.3	2.7	3.2	2.7	2.8
Rhode Island	9.2	19.8	23.6	24.5	15.6	21.3	21.9	22.3	2.3	1.8	0.4	0.4
Connecticut	38.1	86.7	104.1	108.7	65.1	93.4	96.8	98.9	2.7	2.2	1.7	1.7
Middle Atlantic	**398.2**	**839.7**	**1,023.5**	**1,068.9**	**680.7**	**903.8**	**951.7**	**973.1**	**2.3**	**2.2**	**17.5**	**16.6**
New York	193.3	416.4	502.0	523.4	330.4	448.2	468.7	476.5	2.3	2.1	8.5	8.1
New Jersey	86.3	192.9	237.2	248.1	147.6	207.6	220.5	225.8	2.7	2.4	3.8	3.9
Pennsylvania	118.6	230.4	284.4	297.4	202.7	247.9	264.4	270.8	1.8	2.4	5.2	4.6
Midwest	**588.5**	**1,103.7**	**1,419.8**	**1,500.3**	**1,006.0**	**1,187.9**	**1,320.1**	**1,366.9**	**1.8**	**3.5**	**25.8**	**23.3**
East North Central	**425.1**	**788.0**	**1,016.2**	**1,067.2**	**726.7**	**848.1**	**944.9**	**971.6**	**1.8**	**2.8**	**18.7**	**16.6**
Ohio	106.6	196.9	251.0	263.0	182.3	211.9	233.4	239.4	1.7	2.6	4.7	4.1
Indiana	51.1	95.4	124.4	131.1	87.4	102.7	115.7	119.3	1.9	3.1	2.2	2.0
Illinois	125.7	234.6	296.4	315.1	214.9	252.5	277.5	286.9	1.7	3.4	5.5	4.9
Michigan	95.1	174.2	228.4	238.0	162.5	187.5	212.3	216.7	1.8	2.1	4.2	3.7
Wisconsin	46.5	86.9	114.0	120.1	79.6	93.5	106.0	109.3	1.9	3.1	2.0	1.9
West North Central	**163.4**	**315.7**	**403.5**	**433.0**	**279.4**	**339.8**	**376.2**	**394.3**	**2.0**	**6.1**	**7.2**	**6.7**
Minnesota	41.5	85.0	110.5	119.1	70.9	91.5	102.7	108.5	2.5	5.6	1.8	1.9
Iowa	27.7	47.1	59.5	64.3	47.4	50.7	55.3	58.6	1.0	6.0	1.2	1.0
Missouri	46.0	90.5	116.2	122.5	78.6	97.4	106.0	111.5	2.1	3.2	2.0	1.9
North Dakota	5.1	9.8	11.9	13.3	8.8	10.5	11.1	12.1	1.6	9.0	0.2	0.2
South Dakota	5.4	10.8	14.3	15.8	9.3	11.6	13.3	14.3	2.4	7.5	0.2	0.2
Nebraska	14.3	27.9	35.2	38.1	24.5	30.0	32.7	34.7	1.9	6.1	0.6	0.6
Kansas	23.4	44.6	56.0	59.9	40.0	48.0	52.1	54.5	1.8	4.6	1.0	0.9
South	**683.9**	**1,461.8**	**1,961.3**	**2,070.1**	**1,169.0**	**1,594.9**	**1,823.6**	**1,884.7**	**3.0**	**3.4**	**30.0**	**32.2**
South Atlantic	**344.2**	**814.2**	**1,066.0**	**1,125.4**	**588.3**	**876.3**	**991.2**	**1,024.6**	**3.5**	**3.4**	**15.1**	**17.5**
Delaware	6.3	14.5	18.8	20.0	10.8	15.6	17.5	18.2	3.3	4.0	0.3	0.3
Maryland	46.0	107.9	132.8	138.1	78.7	116.1	123.5	125.7	3.0	1.8	2.0	2.1
Dist. of Columbia	8.0	15.5	18.5	19.0	13.6	16.6	17.2	17.3	1.6	0.6	0.3	0.3
Virginia	53.2	124.3	158.7	166.4	91.0	133.7	147.5	151.5	3.3	2.7	2.3	2.6
West Virginia	15.7	25.4	32.3	33.7	26.8	27.3	30.1	30.7	0.8	2.0	0.7	0.5
North Carolina	47.6	110.9	151.8	161.2	81.3	119.4	141.2	146.7	3.7	3.9	2.1	2.5
South Carolina	23.9	54.0	69.8	73.1	40.9	58.1	64.9	66.5	3.1	2.5	1.0	1.1
Georgia	46.1	113.1	156.6	167.0	78.7	121.7	145.6	152.0	4.2	4.4	2.0	2.6
Florida	97.4	248.7	326.7	347.1	166.4	267.7	303.7	316.0	4.1	4.1	4.3	5.4
East South Central	**114.6**	**229.8**	**309.9**	**325.4**	**195.9**	**247.3**	**288.2**	**296.2**	**2.6**	**2.8**	**5.0**	**5.1**
Kentucky	29.6	55.7	72.8	76.5	50.6	60.0	67.7	69.6	2.0	2.8	1.3	1.2
Tennessee	37.4	79.7	110.6	115.8	63.9	85.8	102.8	105.4	3.2	2.5	1.6	1.8
Alabama	30.1	61.6	81.6	85.7	51.5	66.3	75.9	78.0	2.6	2.8	1.3	1.3
Mississippi	17.5	32.8	45.0	47.5	29.9	35.3	41.8	43.2	2.3	3.3	0.8	0.7
West South Central	**225.1**	**437.8**	**586.3**	**619.3**	**384.8**	**471.2**	**544.3**	**563.8**	**2.3**	**3.6**	**9.9**	**9.6**
Arkansas	17.1	33.0	45.0	47.5	29.2	35.6	41.8	43.3	2.4	3.6	0.7	0.7
Louisiana	37.0	62.3	82.4	86.2	63.3	67.0	76.6	78.5	1.3	2.5	1.6	1.3
Oklahoma	28.7	49.0	60.9	63.9	49.1	52.8	56.6	58.2	1.0	2.8	1.3	1.0
Texas	142.3	293.5	397.1	421.7	243.2	315.9	369.2	383.9	2.8	4.0	6.2	6.6
West	**476.8**	**1,048.5**	**1,328.8**	**1,406.6**	**815.0**	**1,128.5**	**1,235.6**	**1,280.6**	**2.8**	**3.6**	**20.9**	**21.9**
Mountain	**109.1**	**230.7**	**327.7**	**350.3**	**186.5**	**248.3**	**304.7**	**318.9**	**3.3**	**4.7**	**4.8**	**5.4**
Montana	7.0	12.0	16.1	16.7	11.9	12.9	14.9	15.2	1.5	2.0	0.3	0.3
Idaho	8.1	15.5	22.0	23.2	13.9	16.7	20.4	21.2	2.6	3.9	0.4	0.4
Wyoming	5.4	7.7	9.9	10.2	9.3	8.3	9.2	9.3	-0.1	1.1	0.2	0.2
Colorado	31.2	63.5	89.8	95.9	53.3	68.4	83.5	87.3	3.0	4.6	1.4	1.5
New Mexico	10.8	21.9	30.7	32.2	18.4	23.6	28.5	29.3	3.0	2.8	0.5	0.5
Arizona	25.5	60.9	86.4	92.9	43.6	65.5	80.4	84.6	4.2	5.2	1.1	1.4
Utah	11.8	24.6	35.6	38.3	20.1	26.4	33.1	34.9	3.4	5.4	0.5	0.6
Nevada	9.4	24.5	37.3	40.8	16.0	26.4	34.7	37.1	5.3	6.9	0.4	0.6
Pacific	**367.7**	**817.8**	**1,001.1**	**1,066.3**	**628.5**	**880.2**	**930.8**	**961.6**	**2.7**	**3.3**	**16.1**	**16.4**
Washington	44.7	96.0	129.1	137.4	76.4	103.3	120.1	125.1	3.1	4.2	2.0	2.1
Oregon	26.3	49.8	67.9	72.6	44.9	53.6	63.1	66.1	2.3	4.8	1.2	1.1
California	280.6	636.6	760.4	801.5	479.7	685.2	707.0	729.7	2.6	3.2	12.3	12.5
Alaska	5.6	11.6	14.5	14.9	9.6	12.5	13.5	13.6	2.3	0.7	0.2	0.2
Hawaii	10.5	23.7	29.2	29.8	18.0	25.6	27.1	27.1	2.8	-	0.5	0.5

- Represents or rounds to zero.

Source: U.S. Bureau of Economic Analysis, *Survey of Current Business*, May 1996 and 1997 issues.

No. 706. Personal Income Per Capita in Current and Constant (1992) Dollars, by State: 1980 to 996

[In dollars, except ranks. 1996 data preliminary. See headnote, table 705]

REGION, DIVISION, AND STATE	CURRENT DOLLARS				CONSTANT (1992) DOLLARS					
	1980	1990	1995	1996	1980	1990	1995	1996	Income rank 1980	Income rank 1996
United States	10,029	19,142	23,196	24,231	17,144	20,603	21,568	22,060	(X)	(X)
Northeast	10,776	22,415	26,951	28,134	18,420	24,126	25,059	25,614	(X)	(X)
New England	10,655	22,715	27,403	28,633	18,214	24,448	25,479	26,068	(X)	(X)
Maine	8,259	17,167	20,150	20,826	14,118	18,477	18,735	18,960	38	37
New Hampshire	9,854	20,672	25,587	26,520	16,844	22,249	23,791	24,144	23	8
Vermont	8,583	17,692	21,231	22,124	14,672	19,042	19,741	20,142	35	30
Massachusetts	10,745	23,203	28,032	29,439	18,368	24,974	26,064	26,802	12	3
Rhode Island	9,646	19,690	23,798	24,765	16,489	21,193	22,127	22,546	26	17
Connecticut	12,246	26,376	31,814	33,189	20,933	28,389	29,581	30,216	2	1
Middle Atlantic	10,816	22,310	26,793	27,959	18,489	24,012	24,912	25,454	(X)	(X)
New York	11,003	23,131	27,595	28,782	18,809	24,896	25,658	26,204	7	4
New Jersey	11,703	24,927	29,833	31,053	20,005	26,829	27,739	28,271	4	2
Pennsylvania	9,989	19,365	23,580	24,668	17,075	20,843	21,925	22,456	17	18
Midwest	9,989	18,467	22,999	24,166	17,075	19,877	21,384	22,001	(X)	(X)
East North Central	10,193	18,727	23,426	24,470	17,424	20,156	21,781	22,278	(X)	(X)
Ohio	9,872	18,126	22,547	23,537	16,875	19,509	20,964	21,428	25	21
Indiana	9,307	17,174	21,457	22,440	15,909	18,485	19,951	20,430	31	29
Illinois	10,986	20,496	25,310	26,598	18,779	22,060	23,533	24,215	8	7
Michigan	10,273	18,711	23,943	24,810	17,561	20,139	22,262	22,587	15	16
Wisconsin	9,874	17,720	22,265	23,269	16,879	19,072	20,702	21,184	24	23
West North Central	9,495	17,849	21,989	23,448	16,231	19,211	20,445	21,347	(X)	(X)
Minnesota	10,149	19,374	23,944	25,580	17,349	20,852	22,263	23,288	16	9
Iowa	9,505	16,959	20,911	22,560	16,248	18,253	19,443	20,539	27	28
Missouri	9,341	17,656	21,836	22,864	15,968	19,003	20,303	20,816	30	25
North Dakota	7,825	15,324	18,621	20,710	13,376	16,493	17,314	18,855	47	38
South Dakota	7,866	15,537	19,564	21,516	13,446	16,723	18,191	19,588	45	34
Nebraska	9,096	17,624	21,450	23,047	15,549	18,969	19,944	20,982	32	24
Kansas	9,877	17,986	21,855	23,281	16,884	19,361	20,321	21,195	22	22
South	9,030	17,285	21,328	22,236	15,435	18,604	19,831	20,244	(X)	(X)
South Atlantic	9,266	18,607	22,675	23,636	15,839	20,027	21,083	21,519	(X)	(X)
Delaware	10,614	21,695	26,279	27,622	18,144	23,351	24,434	25,147	14	5
Maryland	10,889	22,464	26,352	27,221	18,614	24,200	24,502	24,782	9	6
District of Columbia	12,487	25,620	33,435	34,932	21,345	27,575	31,088	31,803	(X)	(X)
Virginia	9,918	19,997	23,985	24,925	16,954	21,523	22,301	22,692	19	14
West Virginia	8,041	14,177	17,714	18,444	13,745	15,259	16,470	16,792	43	49
North Carolina	8,067	16,663	21,082	22,010	13,790	17,935	19,602	20,038	42	32
South Carolina	7,624	15,420	19,031	19,755	13,032	16,597	17,695	17,985	48	41
Georgia	8,395	17,377	21,718	22,709	14,350	18,703	20,193	20,675	37	26
Florida	9,894	19,107	23,030	24,104	16,913	20,565	21,413	21,945	21	20
East South Central	7,797	15,109	19,314	20,096	13,328	16,262	17,958	18,296	(X)	(X)
Kentucky	8,079	15,087	18,866	19,687	13,810	16,238	17,542	17,923	40	42
Tennessee	8,123	16,294	21,076	21,764	13,885	17,537	19,596	19,814	41	33
Alabama	7,720	15,225	19,212	20,055	13,197	16,387	17,863	18,258	46	39
Mississippi	6,915	12,710	16,690	17,471	11,821	13,680	15,518	15,906	50	50
West South Central	9,420	16,358	20,255	21,144	16,103	17,606	18,833	19,250	(X)	(X)
Arkansas	7,457	14,032	18,093	18,928	12,747	15,103	16,823	17,232	49	47
Louisiana	8,761	14,761	19,000	19,824	14,976	15,887	17,666	18,048	34	40
Oklahoma	9,444	15,583	18,596	19,350	16,144	16,772	17,291	17,617	28	44
Texas	9,922	17,218	21,119	22,045	16,961	18,532	19,636	20,070	20	31
West	10,982	19,766	23,033	24,036	18,772	21,274	21,416	21,882	(X)	(X)
Mountain	9,530	16,817	20,810	21,736	16,291	18,100	19,349	19,788	(X)	(X)
Montana	8,825	15,042	18,443	19,047	15,085	16,190	17,148	17,341	33	46
Idaho	8,569	15,316	18,860	19,539	14,648	16,485	17,536	17,789	36	43
Wyoming	11,414	17,062	20,727	21,245	19,511	18,364	19,272	19,342	6	35
Colorado	10,710	19,224	23,954	25,084	18,308	20,691	22,272	22,837	13	13
New Mexico	8,222	14,440	18,158	18,770	14,055	15,542	16,883	17,088	39	48
Arizona	9,328	16,539	20,074	20,989	15,945	17,801	18,665	19,109	29	36
Utah	8,003	14,204	18,167	19,156	13,680	15,288	16,892	17,440	44	45
Nevada	11,577	20,123	24,336	25,451	19,790	21,659	22,628	23,171	5	10
Pacific	11,602	20,795	23,867	24,909	19,862	22,382	22,192	22,678	(X)	(X)
Washington	10,755	19,583	23,701	24,838	18,385	21,077	22,037	22,613	11	15
Oregon	9,938	17,435	21,554	22,668	16,988	18,765	20,041	20,637	18	27
California	11,792	21,290	24,091	25,144	20,157	22,915	22,400	22,891	3	12
Alaska	13,863	21,048	24,045	24,558	23,697	22,654	22,357	22,358	1	19
Hawaii	10,860	21,337	24,749	25,159	18,564	22,965	23,012	22,905	10	11

X Not applicable.

Source: U.S. Bureau of Economic Analysis, *Survey of Current Business*, May 1996 and 1997 issues.

No. 707. Disposable Personal Income Per Capita in Current and Constant (1992) Dollars, by State: 1990 and 1996

[In dollars. 1996 data preliminary]

REGION, DIVISION, AND STATE	CURRENT DOLLARS 1990	CURRENT DOLLARS 1996	CONSTANT (1992) DOLLARS 1990	CONSTANT (1992) DOLLARS 1996
United States	16,642	20,979	17,912	19,100
Northeast	19,254	23,995	20,723	21,845
New England	19,592	24,263	21,087	22,099
Maine	15,067	18,219	16,217	16,587
New Hampshire	18,398	23,329	19,802	21,239
Vermont	15,448	19,381	16,627	17,645
Massachusetts	19,806	24,720	21,317	22,505
Rhode Island	17,277	21,659	18,595	19,719
Connecticut	22,715	27,706	24,448	25,224
Middle Atlantic	19,135	23,901	20,595	21,760
New York	19,592	24,380	21,087	22,196
New Jersey	21,536	26,570	23,179	24,190
Pennsylvania	16,880	21,410	18,168	19,492
Midwest	16,040	20,827	17,264	18,962
East North Central	16,251	21,052	17,491	19,166
Ohio	15,795	20,340	17,000	18,518
Indiana	14,970	19,433	16,112	17,692
Illinois	17,690	22,778	19,040	20,737
Michigan	16,277	21,376	17,519	19,461
Wisconsin	15,304	19,858	16,472	18,079
West North Central	15,537	20,298	16,723	18,480
Minnesota	16,567	21,597	17,831	19,662
Iowa	14,756	19,723	15,882	17,956
Missouri	15,461	19,906	16,641	18,123
North Dakota	13,640	18,351	14,681	16,707
South Dakota	13,979	19,381	15,046	17,645
Nebraska	15,490	20,180	16,672	18,372
Kansas	15,700	20,225	16,898	18,413
South	15,229	19,531	16,391	17,782
South Atlantic	16,250	20,541	17,490	18,701
Delaware	18,591	23,654	20,010	21,535
Maryland	19,151	23,158	20,612	21,083
District of Columbia	21,727	29,567	23,385	26,918
Virginia	17,305	21,434	18,626	19,514
West Virginia	12,653	16,494	13,619	15,016
North Carolina	14,568	19,110	15,680	17,398
South Carolina	13,644	17,467	14,685	15,902
Georgia	15,206	19,664	16,366	17,902
Florida	16,881	21,185	18,169	19,287
East South Central	13,505	17,873	14,536	16,272
Kentucky	13,229	17,192	14,239	15,652
Tennessee	14,678	19,441	15,798	17,699
Alabama	13,566	17,785	14,601	16,192
Mississippi	11,578	15,911	12,462	14,486
West South Central	14,538	18,808	15,647	17,123
Arkansas	12,549	16,783	13,507	15,279
Louisiana	13,259	17,786	14,271	16,193
Oklahoma	13,571	16,980	14,607	15,459
Texas	15,307	19,621	16,475	17,863
West	17,103	20,785	18,408	18,923
Mountain	14,724	18,753	15,848	17,073
Montana	13,140	16,656	14,143	15,164
Idaho	13,441	16,722	14,467	15,224
Wyoming	15,056	18,614	16,205	16,946
Colorado	16,692	21,265	17,966	19,360
New Mexico	12,898	16,674	13,882	15,180
Arizona	14,562	18,308	15,673	16,668
Utah	12,395	16,436	13,341	14,964
Nevada	17,442	21,805	18,773	19,852
Pacific	17,933	21,557	19,301	19,628
Washington	17,179	21,740	18,490	19,792
Oregon	15,111	19,189	16,264	17,470
California	18,315	21,760	19,713	19,811
Alaska	18,100	21,277	19,481	19,371
Hawaii	18,148	21,776	19,533	19,825

Source: U.S. Bureau of Economic Analysis, *Survey of Current Business*, May 1996 and 1997 issues.

No. 708. Personal Income, by Metropolitan Area: 1992 to 1994

[As defined June 30, 1994. CMSA=Consolidated Metropolitan Statistical Area; MSA=Metropolitan Statistical Area. See Appendix II]

METROPOLITAN AREA RANKED BY 1990 POPULATION	PERSONAL INCOME				PER CAPITA PERSONAL INCOME			
	1992 (mil. dol.)	1993 (mil. dol.)	1994 (mil. dol.)	Annual percent change, 1993-94	1992 (dol.)	1993 (dol.)	1994 (dol.)	Percent of national average, 1994
United States [1]	5,136,091	5,365,006	5,648,263	5.3	$20,147	$20,812	$21,696	100.0
New York-Northern New Jersey-Long Island, NY-NJ-CT-PA CMSA	534,539	552,201	571,868	3.6	27,324	28,105	29,021	133.8
Los Angeles-Riverside-Orange County, CA CMSA	321,067	324,296	329,646	1.6	21,316	21,321	21,542	99.3
Chicago-Gary-Kenosha, IL-IN-WI CMSA	196,420	205,074	215,361	5.0	23,384	24,223	25,257	116.4
Washington-Baltimore, DC-MD-VA-WV CMSA	173,493	181,186	189,819	4.8	25,115	25,957	26,919	124.1
San Francisco-Oakland-San Jose, CA CMSA	171,152	177,172	184,469	4.1	26,699	27,386	28,322	130.5
Philadelphia-Wilmington-Atlantic City, PA-NJ-DE-MD CMSA	138,314	143,257	149,311	4.2	23,333	24,108	25,056	115.5
Boston-Brockton-Nashua, MA-NH NECMA	136,289	141,685	149,517	5.5	24,020	24,858	26,093	120.3
Detroit-Ann Arbor-Flint, MI CMSA	113,216	118,481	128,545	8.5	21,622	22,585	24,456	112.7
Dallas-Fort Worth, TX CMSA	91,499	96,436	102,300	6.1	21,751	22,536	23,450	108.1
Houston-Galveston-Brazoria, TX CMSA	84,527	88,264	92,840	5.2	21,397	21,913	22,651	104.4
Miami-Fort Lauderdale, FL CMSA	63,663	70,760	74,698	5.6	19,193	21,098	21,918	101.0
Seattle-Tacoma-Bremerton, WA CMSA	73,606	76,373	79,941	4.7	23,498	23,949	24,784	114.2
Atlanta, GA MSA	68,433	73,325	78,720	7.4	21,828	22,711	23,633	108.9
Cleveland-Akron, OH CMSA	60,022	62,709	66,444	6.0	20,790	21,669	22,921	105.6
Minneapolis-St. Paul, MN-WI MSA	60,964	63,873	67,831	6.2	23,296	24,061	25,231	116.3
San Diego, CA MSA	53,829	55,046	56,923	3.4	20,689	21,075	21,627	99.7
St. Louis, MO-IL MSA	54,898	56,775	60,066	5.8	21,819	22,457	23,685	109.2
Pittsburgh, PA MSA	50,679	52,431	54,647	4.2	21,075	21,763	22,751	104.9
Phoenix-Mesa, AZ MSA	44,562	47,638	51,938	9.0	19,103	19,914	20,999	96.8
Tampa-St. Petersburg-Clearwater, FL MSA	40,584	43,231	46,059	6.5	19,172	20,232	21,358	98.4
Denver-Boulder-Greeley, CO CMSA	46,969	50,477	53,390	5.8	22,498	23,517	24,379	112.4
Cincinnati-Hamilton, OH-KY-IN CMSA	37,549	39,188	41,447	5.8	20,166	20,830	21,883	100.9
Portland-Salem, OR-WA CMSA	38,422	41,066	43,949	7.0	20,230	21,131	22,172	102.2
Milwaukee-Racine, WI CMSA	35,316	36,884	38,849	5.3	21,681	22,569	23,728	109.4

[1] Includes other areas not listed separately.

Source: U.S. Bureau of Economic Analysis, *Survey of Current Business*, June 1996 issue. Data for 1995 will appear in the August 1997 issue.

No. 709. Projections of Personal Income, Earnings, and Gross State Product in Constant (1987) Dollars, by State: 1992 to 2010

[In billions of dollars. For information on methodology, see source. Gross state product estimates are not available for 1993; therefore, 1992 shown for comparison]

STATE	PERSONAL INCOME			EARNINGS			GROSS STATE PRODUCT		
	1993	2000	2010	1993	2000	2010	1992	2000	2010
United States	**4,183.9**	**4,894.5**	**5,917.2**	**3,017.6**	**3,532.7**	**4,207.5**	**5,001.4**	**6,025.6**	**7,219.4**
Alabama	55.9	64.6	77.5	40.0	46.3	54.7	66.0	79.6	95.2
Alaska	10.6	12.6	15.3	9.0	10.4	12.4	23.0	26.8	30.9
Arizona	55.7	70.4	91.0	38.5	48.7	61.6	62.3	83.3	105.8
Arkansas	30.3	35.2	42.0	21.6	25.3	29.6	37.3	45.6	54.5
California	533.3	638.3	796.5	390.6	488.0	577.1	652.3	783.0	969.0
Colorado	59.8	73.3	92.5	45.0	55.2	68.7	69.0	88.8	110.5
Connecticut	71.5	81.8	97.5	50.8	58.3	68.7	82.5	97.0	115.1
Delaware	11.9	14.0	17.0	9.4	11.0	13.1	18.4	22.7	27.3
District of Columbia	13.5	14.3	15.5	25.1	27.6	30.9	32.0	34.2	37.7
Florida	221.2	276.7	367.2	136.2	170.1	215.3	222.6	286.4	364.2
Georgia	103.7	126.2	157.9	79.0	96.1	118.3	128.6	164.2	203.7
Hawaii	21.4	25.4	31.0	16.4	19.4	23.3	27.2	32.0	38.4
Idaho	15.0	18.2	22.4	11.2	13.5	16.4	17.7	22.9	28.4
Illinois	206.8	234.7	277.7	151.4	173.1	202.1	246.8	292.7	345.1
Indiana	85.5	98.4	116.8	62.4	71.9	83.8	103.3	126.8	150.5
Iowa	40.3	46.3	54.1	27.8	32.3	37.0	50.5	58.9	68.6
Kansas	39.3	45.9	54.8	27.5	32.2	37.8	47.1	56.6	67.2
Kentucky	50.1	57.8	68.6	35.6	41.0	47.9	63.7	76.9	90.9
Louisiana	55.6	63.8	75.8	39.0	44.9	52.4	79.9	92.5	106.8
Maine	18.2	20.9	25.2	12.3	14.2	16.8	20.1	23.8	28.3
Maryland	92.7	108.3	130.4	59.7	69.3	82.0	95.4	111.4	131.7
Massachusetts	114.9	130.8	154.8	84.8	97.6	114.3	135.1	160.0	187.6
Michigan	152.0	170.6	197.5	109.8	123.2	140.1	171.7	201.1	231.4
Minnesota	74.1	86.8	103.6	56.2	65.8	77.5	92.9	112.2	133.8
Mississippi	30.3	35.0	41.6	20.7	24.1	28.1	37.2	45.7	54.3
Missouri	79.9	92.5	110.4	57.6	66.5	77.9	93.6	111.3	131.8
Montana	11.4	13.6	16.6	7.6	9.0	10.8	13.0	16.2	19.6
Nebraska	24.8	28.9	34.4	18.3	21.2	24.8	31.6	37.9	45.2
Nevada	24.7	32.1	42.6	18.5	24.0	31.2	31.4	43.2	56.2
New Hampshire	19.5	23.1	28.0	12.7	15.2	18.2	21.6	26.8	32.4
New Jersey	164.4	189.0	223.1	111.3	128.4	150.1	184.1	215.9	253.4
New Mexico	20.6	25.0	31.4	14.6	17.7	21.9	27.3	35.4	43.7
New York	351.9	387.6	439.6	256.5	285.1	321.6	413.1	464.6	526.9
North Carolina	101.3	122.6	151.4	76.7	92.3	111.2	130.5	164.3	200.1
North Dakota	8.5	9.8	11.4	6.0	7.0	8.0	11.1	12.7	14.9
Ohio	169.9	192.6	225.0	123.1	140.0	161.3	203.2	240.4	279.7
Oklahoma	43.0	49.6	58.9	29.7	34.1	39.7	50.7	60.2	70.4
Oregon	46.0	55.3	68.1	33.2	39.9	48.3	52.5	65.2	79.3
Pennsylvania	199.8	223.9	260.5	137.3	154.6	177.3	222.1	255.7	294.5
Rhode Island	16.6	18.8	22.2	10.8	12.4	14.5	17.8	20.9	24.5
South Carolina	47.8	57.1	70.7	34.7	41.6	50.7	58.9	74.1	91.6
South Dakota	10.0	11.9	14.4	7.2	8.5	10.1	12.7	15.8	19.2
Tennessee	73.3	87.8	107.4	55.5	66.5	79.9	91.3	114.9	139.3
Texas	269.3	323.9	398.5	205.3	245.7	297.4	350.0	433.6	525.2
Utah	23.4	29.9	39.3	18.2	23.2	30.2	30.0	40.6	52.6
Vermont	8.6	10.2	12.4	6.1	7.3	8.7	10.0	12.2	14.6
Virginia	109.2	127.0	154.3	77.0	89.5	107.3	125.1	148.9	179.2
Washington	89.3	107.3	134.7	64.5	77.1	95.3	105.8	128.8	159.7
West Virginia	22.9	25.6	29.6	14.5	16.1	18.3	26.8	30.9	35.6
Wisconsin	78.0	90.8	108.8	55.5	64.5	75.8	92.8	113.2	135.1
Wyoming	7.2	8.5	10.2	5.1	5.9	6.9	12.0	14.7	17.6

Source: U.S. Bureau of Economic Analysis, *BEA Regional Projections to 2045: Volume 1, States.*

No. 710. Flow of Funds Accounts—Composition of Individuals' Savings: 1980 to 1996

[In billions of dollars. Combined statement for households, farm business, and nonfarm noncorporate business. Minus sign (-) indicates decrease]

COMPOSITION OF SAVINGS	1980	1985	1990	1991	1992	1993	1994	1995	1996
Increase in financial assets	323.2	622.5	590.8	418.1	529.6	512.4	542.8	482.7	541.5
Checkable deposits and currency	9.2	41.8	-19.0	43.2	98.9	54.5	-8.9	-38.2	-47.7
Time and savings deposits	125.5	119.7	48.7	-54.2	-76.5	-106.9	-5.8	152.6	144.4
Money market fund shares	23.9	2.3	26.9	9.1	-41.3	5.9	13.7	95.5	90.8
Securities	3.1	81.6	198.1	127.4	252.3	194.3	205.7	-56.5	-35.7
Open market paper	-5.0	-7.0	6.2	-29.9	-3.3	15.6	-10.5	0.3	11.4
U.S. savings bonds	-7.3	5.3	8.5	11.9	19.1	14.7	8.0	5.1	2.0
Other Treasury securities	19.6	3.7	61.3	-22.0	59.6	11.8	153.2	5.0	-82.1
Agency securities	4.8	12.2	41.5	12.3	36.8	-31.4	149.4	-31.9	54.8
Municipal securities	8.3	94.9	27.7	40.2	-27.2	-27.2	-51.9	-50.7	-21.4
Corporate and foreign bonds	-14.6	2.6	45.1	29.6	-8.5	37.3	2.1	51.4	27.7
Corporate equities	-4.3	-111.2	-28.8	-23.6	33.1	-57.7	-138.1	-176.1	-245.5
Mutual fund shares	1.8	81.2	36.6	109.0	142.8	231.3	93.7	140.4	197.4
Private life insurance reserves	9.7	10.4	25.3	25.6	27.7	35.7	34.3	44.8	36.2
Private insured pension reserves	22.3	55.6	95.9	46.4	76.7	86.3	71.2	66.7	69.2
Private noninsured pension reserves	60.2	126.6	64.1	72.5	81.8	82.7	87.1	98.3	86.2
Govt insurance and pension reserves	35.8	69.0	85.7	83.0	83.7	81.8	93.7	75.4	97.4
Investment in tangible assets	4.1	11.2	32.9	17.5	-7.1	0.9	17.8	-49.7	-25.0
Miscellaneous assets	29.2	103.5	30.8	46.4	32.4	76.9	30.8	101.9	123.5
Gross investment in tangible assets	407.5	661.1	815.8	758.3	823.0	897.9	1,021.5	1,050.9	1,137.4
Consumption of fixed capital	296.0	409.8	577.9	612.4	633.9	674.2	716.3	724.6	786.2
Net investment in tangible assets	111.4	251.3	237.9	145.8	189.1	223.7	305.2	326.4	351.2
Residential structures	58.8	105.2	113.3	92.0	114.5	142.3	164.7	164.0	178.9
Other fixed assets[1]	31.5	35.4	23.3	4.1	-10.1	4.8	22.2	53.8	60.5
Consumer durables	27.3	103.9	98.4	50.9	79.6	81.5	104.3	109.1	112.8
Inventories[1]	-6.2	6.8	2.9	-1.1	5.1	-4.8	13.9	-0.5	-1.0
Net increase in liabilities	196.6	435.5	267.3	217.4	204.0	297.1	401.6	441.9	478.0
Mortgage debt on nonfarm homes	94.1	174.7	226.2	177.7	188.9	186.6	203.4	195.7	277.4
Other mortgage debt[1]	50.9	98.1	16.9	5.3	-28.8	-17.8	3.7	21.5	45.7
Consumer credit	2.3	73.9	16.1	-13.7	5.0	61.5	126.3	141.6	94.4
Policy loans	6.7	-0.1	4.1	4.8	5.7	5.6	7.8	10.5	7.1
Security credit	7.3	18.9	-3.7	16.3	-1.6	22.6	-1.1	3.5	14.5
Other liabilities[1]	35.3	70.1	7.7	27.1	34.8	38.5	61.5	69.1	38.8
Personal saving (Flow of Funds measure)[2]	238.0	436.3	561.4	346.5	514.9	439.0	446.4	377.2	414.7
Personal saving as a percentage of of disposable personal income	12.1	14.6	13.5	8.0	11.2	9.2	8.9	7.1	7.4

[1] Includes corporate farms. [2] Net acquisition of financial assets plus net investment in tangible assets minus net increase in liabilities.

Source: Board of Governors of the Federal Reserve System, *Flow of Funds Accounts*, quarterly.

No. 711. Annual Expenditure Per Child by Husband-Wife Families, by Family Income and Expenditure Type: 1995

[In dollars. Expenditures based on data from the 1990-92 Consumer Expenditure Survey updated to 1995 dollars using the Consumer Price Index. For more on the methodology, see report cited below]

AGE OF CHILD	Total	EXPENDITURE TYPE						
		Housing	Food	Transportation	Clothing	Health care	Child care and education	Miscellaneous[1]
INCOME: LESS THAN $33,700								
Less than 2 yrs. old	5,490	2,100	780	700	370	370	630	540
3 to 5 yrs. old	5,610	2,080	870	680	360	360	710	550
6 to 8 yrs. old	5,740	2,010	1,120	790	410	410	420	580
9 to 11 yrs. old	5,770	1,810	1,340	860	450	450	250	610
12 to 14 yrs. old	6,560	2,020	1,410	970	760	450	180	770
15 to 17 yrs. old	6,480	1,630	1,520	1,300	670	480	300	580
INCOME: $33,700-$56,700								
Less than 2 yrs. old	7,610	2,840	930	1,050	440	490	1,030	830
3 to 5 yrs. old	7,810	2,820	1,080	1,020	430	470	1,140	850
6 to 8 yrs. old	7,870	2,750	1,370	1,130	470	540	730	880
9 to 11 yrs. old	7,860	2,550	1,620	1,200	520	580	480	910
12 to 14 yrs. old	8,580	2,760	1,630	1,310	880	590	350	1,080
15 to 17 yrs. old	8,710	2,370	1,810	1,660	790	620	600	860
INCOME: MORE THAN $56,700								
Less than 2 yrs. old	11,320	4,520	1,240	1,470	580	560	1,550	1,400
3 to 5 yrs. old	11,540	4,490	1,400	1,440	570	540	1,690	1,410
6 to 8 yrs. old	11,500	4,420	1,690	1,550	620	620	1,160	1,440
9 to 11 yrs. old	11,430	4,230	1,960	1,620	670	670	810	1,470
12 to 14 yrs. old	12,270	4,440	2,060	1,730	1,120	670	620	1,630
15 to 17 yrs. old	12,550	4,050	2,170	2,100	1,010	710	1,090	1,420

[1] Expenses include personal care items, entertainment, and reading materials.

Source: Dept. of Agriculture, Center for Nutrition Policy and Promotion, *Expenditures on Children by Families, 1995 Annual Report*.

No. 712. Average Annual Expenditures of All Consumer Units, by Race and Age of Householder: 1995

[In dollars. Preliminary. Based on Consumer Expenditure Survey. Data are averages for the noninstitutional population. Expenditures reported here are out-of-pocket]

ITEM	All consumer units	White and other	Black	AGE: Under 25 yrs.	AGE: 25 to 34 yrs.	AGE: 35 to 44 yrs.	AGE: 45 to 54 yrs.	AGE: 55 to 64 yrs.	AGE: 65 yrs. and over
Expenditures, total	$32,277	$33,386	$23,750	$18,429	$31,488	$38,425	$42,181	$32,604	$22,285
Food	4,505	4,650	3,446	2,690	4,470	5,367	5,469	4,539	3,386
Food at home	2,803	2,853	2,442	1,407	2,759	3,345	3,223	2,832	2,367
Cereals and bakery products	441	451	371	227	422	539	501	425	385
Cereals and cereal products	165	166	163	95	172	208	183	151	130
Bakery products	276	285	208	133	251	331	318	274	255
Meats, poultry, fish, and eggs	752	737	866	331	724	900	899	807	610
Beef	228	228	221	108	217	273	274	253	175
Pork	156	149	207	61	159	181	184	169	127
Other meats	104	103	107	52	99	129	114	111	86
Poultry	138	133	172	66	132	170	169	127	113
Fish and seafood	97	94	120	27	90	111	125	114	81
Eggs	30	29	39	16	28	36	32	33	28
Dairy products	297	309	209	155	301	352	338	293	248
Fresh milk and cream	123	127	92	66	135	147	134	121	98
Other dairy products	174	181	117	89	167	206	204	171	150
Fruits and vegetables	457	466	386	213	433	509	513	496	437
Fresh fruits	144	146	117	61	137	157	157	153	151
Fresh vegetables	137	141	106	57	122	148	166	157	132
Processed fruits	96	98	94	55	96	110	100	102	87
Processed vegetables	80	81	69	40	78	94	90	84	67
Other food at home	856	890	609	482	878	1,044	973	811	687
Nonalcoholic beverages	240	248	184	155	246	289	283	230	182
Food away from home	1,702	1,798	1,004	1,283	1,711	2,022	2,246	1,707	1,021
Alcoholic beverages	277	294	157	277	299	314	348	253	171
Housing	10,465	10,768	8,144	5,908	10,541	12,631	12,894	10,291	7,590
Shelter	5,932	6,114	4,502	3,625	6,162	7,552	7,560	5,358	3,866
Owned dwellings	3,754	3,988	1,922	485	3,104	5,066	5,576	3,799	2,401
Mortgage interest and charges	2,107	2,236	1,097	306	2,211	3,385	3,201	1,719	511
Property taxes	932	996	425	86	546	986	1,414	1,117	973
Maintenance, repair, insurance, other	716	756	400	93	347	695	961	963	917
Rented dwellings	1,786	1,703	2,433	2,985	2,873	2,102	1,334	986	931
Other lodging	392	423	147	155	185	384	650	572	335
Utilities, fuels, and public services	2,193	2,191	2,206	1,159	1,989	2,368	2,828	2,442	1,982
Natural gas	268	262	315	95	222	279	314	322	284
Electricity	870	873	840	436	762	962	1,034	984	801
Fuel oil and other fuels	87	92	48	17	49	86	92	106	129
Telephone	708	699	781	541	745	778	859	723	517
Water and other public services	260	264	222	69	211	264	329	306	251
Household operations	508	533	318	199	701	604	445	374	466
Personal services	258	262	226	155	559	378	115	65	127
Other household expenses	250	271	92	44	141	226	330	309	339
Housekeeping supplies	430	454	255	135	360	490	501	514	423
Household furnishings and equipment	1,403	1,476	862	790	1,329	1,567	1,760	1,603	1,051
Household textiles	100	106	46	24	83	112	158	126	67
Furniture	327	329	319	271	391	434	397	279	143
Floor coverings	177	197	34	38	85	142	165	167	366
Major appliances	155	153	170	93	137	171	189	176	132
Small appliances, misc. housewares	85	91	41	63	71	85	101	143	58
Miscellaneous household equipment	557	598	252	301	561	653	750	712	284
Apparel and services	1,704	1,695	1,765	1,206	1,904	2,079	2,090	1,833	876
Men and boys	425	434	366	279	511	536	519	431	191
Women and girls	660	662	656	383	611	774	868	830	407
Children under 2 years old	81	79	92	95	154	106	59	45	18
Footwear	278	261	405	230	334	380	311	207	145
Other apparel products and services	259	260	247	219	294	284	333	320	115
Transportation	6,016	6,209	4,515	4,033	6,188	7,488	8,017	5,726	3,377
Vehicle purchases (net outlay)	2,639	2,711	2,077	1,913	2,846	3,643	3,516	2,108	1,166
Cars and trucks, new	1,194	1,228	927	555	1,273	1,730	1,332	1,118	680
Cars and trucks, used	1,411	1,449	1,111	1,322	1,531	1,873	2,129	953	486
Gasoline and motor oil	1,006	1,044	713	701	1,014	1,182	1,324	1,063	604
Other vehicle expenses	2,016	2,089	1,453	1,236	2,029	2,289	2,725	2,142	1,286
Vehicle finance charges	261	263	245	179	347	322	361	223	78
Maintenance and repair	653	672	507	379	579	720	923	709	474
Vehicle insurance	713	740	503	455	668	781	930	792	531
Rent, lease, licenses, other	390	414	198	222	435	465	510	419	201
Public transportation	355	365	273	184	299	374	452	413	323
Health care [1]	1,732	1,819	1,059	465	1,096	1,609	1,850	1,909	2,647
Entertainment [2]	1,612	1,701	925	1,061	1,682	1,951	2,138	1,577	929
Personal care products and services	403	408	370	243	387	450	517	407	326
Reading	163	174	75	71	134	173	199	188	161
Education	471	499	256	667	335	436	1,028	366	155
Tobacco products and smoking supplies	269	281	176	245	270	310	347	314	139
Miscellaneous	766	806	456	347	687	815	1,018	948	603
Cash contributions	925	972	564	114	455	908	1,463	1,043	1,101
Personal insurance and pensions	2,967	3,111	1,842	1,081	3,040	3,894	4,803	3,211	802
Life and other personal insurance	374	378	345	69	251	440	563	555	245
Pensions and Social Security	2,593	2,733	1,498	1,012	2,788	3,453	4,240	2,656	558
Personal taxes	3,056	3,244	1,484	1,076	3,296	3,794	4,916	3,126	1,083

[1] For additional health care expenditures, see table 170. [2] For additional recreation expenditures, see table 407.

Source: U.S. Bureau of Labor Statistics, *Consumer Expenditures in 1995;* and unpublished data.

No. 713. Average Annual Expenditures of All Consumer Units, by Region and Size of Unit: 1994

[See headnote, page 461]

ITEM	REGION				SIZE OF CONSUMER UNIT				
	Northeast	Midwest	South	West	One person	Two persons	Three persons	Four persons	Five or more
Expenditures, total	$33,014	$31,837	$30,289	$35,222	$19,390	$33,095	$37,866	$42,800	$41,803
Food	4,870	4,348	4,272	4,726	2,500	4,366	5,228	6,280	6,805
Food at home	3,122	2,626	2,626	2,998	1,401	2,587	3,276	4,085	4,761
Cereals and bakery products	528	411	404	454	221	402	504	667	747
Cereals and cereal products	195	152	153	171	76	146	190	251	310
Bakery products	333	259	251	282	145	256	314	416	437
Meats, poultry, fish, and eggs	866	669	746	754	343	678	900	1,118	1,359
Beef	232	221	233	223	97	200	280	360	401
Pork	156	137	172	153	67	143	179	240	286
Other meats	131	101	93	97	49	89	129	157	182
Poultry	182	116	131	132	64	121	171	191	263
Fish and seafood	129	70	88	116	50	97	110	131	162
Eggs	36	24	29	34	15	27	32	39	65
Dairy products	328	279	270	331	148	271	339	436	520
Fresh milk and cream	132	118	116	132	60	104	140	184	242
Other dairy products	196	161	154	199	88	166	199	253	278
Fruits and vegetables	552	412	419	480	250	451	518	607	736
Fresh fruits	175	136	126	154	84	146	157	182	232
Fresh vegetables	176	114	127	145	76	141	156	172	215
Processed fruits	120	87	83	104	50	86	113	142	154
Processed vegetables	81	75	84	77	40	77	92	111	135
Other food at home	847	855	787	979	439	786	1,015	1,258	1,400
Nonalcoholic beverages	250	244	226	250	127	219	290	348	386
Food away from home	1,748	1,722	1,646	1,728	1,098	1,778	1,951	2,195	2,043
Alcoholic beverages	327	261	242	307	248	309	265	296	253
Housing	11,485	9,754	9,287	12,265	7,036	10,581	11,768	13,577	13,085
Shelter	6,993	5,198	4,859	7,550	4,359	5,760	6,563	7,717	7,258
Owned dwellings	4,311	3,521	3,026	4,691	1,850	3,901	4,376	5,613	4,935
Mortgage interest and charges	2,212	1,903	1,634	3,026	823	1,857	2,726	3,639	3,253
Property taxes	1,439	955	693	807	496	1,172	954	1,209	971
Maintenance, repair, insurance, other	659	663	700	859	531	872	696	764	711
Rented dwellings	2,164	1,316	1,524	2,416	2,283	1,360	1,770	1,613	1,982
Other lodging	518	361	309	443	226	499	416	492	339
Utilities, fuels, and public services	2,297	2,184	2,266	1,962	1,423	2,265	2,505	2,734	2,839
Natural gas	332	395	159	234	170	286	291	337	352
Electricity	810	783	1,065	713	532	895	1,017	1,119	1,141
Fuel oil and other fuels	223	77	47	33	65	99	88	96	95
Telephone	718	706	715	692	507	714	816	839	894
Water and other public services	214	224	281	311	149	272	293	344	357
Household operations	482	451	544	545	250	429	646	1,006	525
Personal services	238	270	261	258	61	129	414	673	351
Other household expenses	244	180	283	286	189	301	232	334	173
Housekeeping supplies	467	418	393	467	235	476	490	530	586
Household furnishings and equipment	1,245	1,504	1,225	1,721	768	1,651	1,565	1,589	1,879
Household textiles	122	109	100	70	58	130	106	103	111
Furniture	304	313	327	368	167	320	460	438	428
Floor coverings	54	221	50	450	96	332	79	119	165
Major appliances	132	167	166	145	79	168	174	179	263
Small appliances, misc. housewares	84	91	82	85	58	98	85	100	99
Miscellaneous household equipment	548	603	501	604	311	602	656	650	814
Apparel and services	1,751	1,721	1,667	1,697	991	1,524	2,097	2,479	2,499
Men and boys	421	418	414	457	235	353	512	648	720
Women and girls	695	713	622	628	391	642	820	910	863
Children under 2 years old	87	75	81	80	16	43	142	151	178
Footwear	278	277	289	262	176	201	322	483	437
Other apparel products and services	270	237	261	271	173	285	301	288	311
Transportation	5,468	6,378	6,039	6,069	2,916	6,158	7,852	8,156	8,222
Vehicle purchases (net outlay)	2,145	2,954	2,856	2,380	1,036	2,563	3,718	3,789	3,975
Cars and trucks, new	1,111	1,212	1,327	1,036	551	1,293	1,613	1,533	1,530
Cars and trucks, used	975	1,696	1,505	1,332	461	1,226	2,071	2,206	2,434
Gasoline and motor oil	877	1,043	1,031	1,045	531	1,016	1,248	1,376	1,382
Other vehicle expenses	1,960	2,078	1,881	2,214	1,111	2,146	2,552	2,567	2,493
Vehicle finance charges	182	278	305	244	92	277	342	377	382
Maintenance and repair	584	643	632	764	393	702	833	791	742
Vehicle insurance	767	689	682	739	411	752	886	908	878
Rent, lease, licenses, other	427	468	262	467	214	415	492	491	491
Public transportation	486	302	271	429	239	433	334	423	372
Health care [1]	1,757	1,759	1,790	1,584	1,109	2,126	1,775	1,969	1,866
Entertainment [2]	1,544	1,602	1,459	1,939	992	1,667	1,834	2,187	1,986
Personal care products and services	438	373	386	435	236	433	470	533	488
Reading	186	170	135	177	120	187	176	169	146
Education	576	492	436	403	293	360	616	759	695
Tobacco products and smoking supplies	260	299	283	217	172	272	325	323	382
Miscellaneous	708	794	722	860	654	822	766	843	797
Cash contributions	724	962	902	1,113	621	1,213	933	926	883
Personal insurance and pensions	2,920	3,022	2,670	3,432	1,502	3,079	3,751	4,281	3,556
Life and other personal insurance	353	403	392	330	140	422	434	565	508
Pensions and Social Security	2,567	2,619	2,277	3,102	1,363	2,657	3,317	3,716	3,048
Personal taxes	3,215	2,837	2,438	4,101	2,016	3,214	3,610	4,033	3,278

[1] For additional health care expenditures, see table 170. [2] For additional recreation expenditures, see table 407.

Source: U.S. Bureau of Labor Statistics, *Consumer Expenditures in 1995*; and unpublished data.

No. 714. Average Annual Expenditures of All Consumer Units, by Type of Household Unit: 1995

[See headnote, page 461]

ITEM	Husband and wife only	HUSBAND AND WIFE WITH CHILDREN: Total	HUSBAND AND WIFE WITH CHILDREN: Oldest child under 6	HUSBAND AND WIFE WITH CHILDREN: Oldest child 6 to 17	HUSBAND AND WIFE WITH CHILDREN: Oldest child 18 and over	One parent, at least one child under 18	Single person and other consumer units
Expenditures, total	36,062	44,969	40,559	45,020	48,294	22,626	22,351
Food	4,722	6,366	5,129	6,592	6,944	3,586	3,017
Food at home	2,772	4,041	3,455	4,181	4,264	2,529	1,830
Cereals and bakery products	430	649	533	688	670	406	284
Cereals and cereal products	151	249	199	273	243	172	105
Bakery products	279	400	334	415	427	234	180
Meats, poultry, fish, and eggs	717	1,078	849	1,115	1,207	752	490
Beef	214	322	248	337	357	241	145
Pork	146	218	179	221	248	164	106
Other meats	93	159	115	165	187	105	66
Poultry	126	201	156	212	222	134	91
Fish and seafood	109	136	119	135	150	79	61
Eggs	28	42	33	45	44	29	21
Dairy products	286	437	378	454	455	273	193
Fresh milk and cream	107	185	164	194	186	128	80
Other dairy products	179	252	214	260	270	146	112
Fruits and vegetables	490	621	549	635	655	372	307
Fresh fruits	161	189	164	194	200	115	98
Fresh vegetables	153	179	153	179	201	90	96
Processed fruits	93	142	140	143	141	90	62
Processed vegetables	82	112	92	119	113	77	51
Other food at home	849	1,256	1,145	1,290	1,276	726	555
Nonalcoholic beverages	230	343	264	362	375	202	166
Food away from home	1,950	2,327	1,675	2,411	2,680	1,057	1,187
Alcoholic beverages	336	303	250	304	350	95	251
Housing	11,512	13,997	14,527	14,318	13,002	8,171	7,643
Shelter	6,176	7,863	8,030	8,201	7,101	4,710	4,577
Owned dwellings	4,637	5,963	5,806	6,199	5,629	1,788	2,022
Mortgage interest and charges	2,190	3,857	4,133	4,179	3,047	1,176	941
Property taxes	1,419	1,263	1,016	1,234	1,495	404	537
Maintenance, repair, insurance, other	1,029	843	657	786	1,087	208	545
Rented dwellings	909	1,376	1,963	1,484	747	2,808	2,341
Other lodging	630	524	262	518	725	114	215
Utilities, fuels, and public services	2,396	2,751	2,346	2,709	3,121	1,880	1,685
Natural gas	304	328	259	320	395	238	208
Electricity	956	1,128	941	1,139	1,241	761	637
Fuel oil and other fuels	112	99	88	89	127	42	70
Telephone	723	845	777	808	965	658	592
Water and other public services	301	351	281	354	395	180	178
Household operations	451	888	1,919	767	376	589	276
Personal services	93	586	1,632	464	66	468	94
Other household expenses	358	302	287	303	311	121	182
Housekeeping supplies	548	584	541	587	615	270	266
Household furnishings and equipment	1,941	1,911	1,691	2,054	1,788	722	839
Household textiles	144	115	112	110	129	54	70
Furniture	367	520	599	531	442	236	183
Floor coverings	437	145	51	199	107	24	91
Major appliances	194	207	179	198	244	92	99
Small appliances, misc. housewares	109	106	63	100	157	51	63
Miscellaneous household equipment	689	818	687	916	709	265	333
Apparel and services	1,586	2,477	2,471	2,453	2,534	1,655	1,188
Men and boys	380	647	536	678	671	441	282
Women and girls	666	914	699	953	1,029	624	471
Children under 2 years old	41	159	470	86	50	120	33
Footwear	199	431	465	428	404	286	202
Other apparel products and services	301	326	301	308	380	184	199
Transportation	6,535	8,936	7,707	8,435	10,798	3,919	3,687
Vehicle purchases (net outlay)	2,584	4,169	3,584	4,060	4,798	1,913	1,635
Cars and trucks, new	1,417	1,776	1,281	1,947	1,808	617	742
Cars and trucks, used	1,128	2,343	2,266	2,078	2,901	1,274	867
Gasoline and motor oil	1,096	1,463	1,221	1,397	1,764	642	669
Other vehicle expenses	2,337	2,899	2,587	2,572	3,771	1,151	1,337
Vehicle finance charges	286	408	414	400	418	167	148
Maintenance and repair	759	888	693	769	1,282	406	461
Vehicle insurance	797	1,002	756	896	1,379	450	496
Rent, lease, licenses, other	494	601	724	507	692	128	232
Public transportation	518	404	315	406	465	213	246
Health care [1]	2,438	2,102	1,746	2,026	2,509	803	1,225
Entertainment [2]	1,830	2,319	1,980	2,501	2,222	1,082	1,099
Personal care products and services	451	530	401	561	573	305	294
Reading	211	206	182	199	235	77	122
Education	391	647	192	773	1,457	264	299
Tobacco products and smoking supplies	242	312	248	316	352	234	239
Miscellaneous	798	822	800	804	874	514	741
Cash contributions	1,457	1,033	500	1,091	1,306	550	646
Personal insurance and pensions	3,541	4,738	4,425	4,646	5,137	1,372	1,699
Life and other personal insurance	505	598	444	628	652	194	176
Pensions and Social Security	3,035	4,140	3,980	4,018	4,486	1,177	1,523
Personal taxes	3,717	4,635	4,287	4,577	5,006	830	2,039

[1] For additional health care expenditures, see table 170. [2] For additional recreation expenditures, see table 407.

Source: U.S. Bureau of Labor Statistics, *Consumer Expenditures in 1995;* and unpublished data.

No. 715. Average Annual Expenditures of All Consumer Units, by Type of Expenditure: 1989 to 1995

[In dollars. See headnote, table 712]

TYPE	1989	1990	1991	1992	1993	1994	1995
Number of consumer units (1,000)	95,818	96,968	97,918	100,019	100,049	102,210	103,024
Total expenditures	$27,810	$28,381	$29,614	$29,846	$30,692	$31,731	$32,277
Food	4,152	4,296	4,271	4,273	4,399	4,411	4,505
Food at home	2,390	2,485	2,651	2,643	2,735	2,712	2,803
Cereal and bakery products	359	368	404	411	434	429	441
Meats, poultry, fish, and eggs	611	668	709	687	734	732	752
Dairy products	304	295	294	302	295	289	297
Fruits and vegetables	408	408	429	426	444	437	457
Other food at home	708	746	815	814	827	825	856
Food away from home	1,762	1,811	1,620	1,631	1,664	1,698	1,702
Alcoholic beverages	284	293	297	301	268	278	277
Housing	8,434	8,703	9,252	9,477	9,636	10,106	10,465
Shelter	4,660	4,836	5,191	5,411	5,415	5,686	5,932
Fuels, utilities, public services	1,835	1,890	1,990	1,984	2,112	2,189	2,193
Household operations, furnishings	1,546	1,571	1,648	1,649	1,699	1,838	1,911
Housekeeping supplies	394	406	424	433	410	393	430
Apparel and services	1,582	1,618	1,735	1,710	1,676	1,644	1,704
Transportation	5,187	5,120	5,151	5,228	5,453	6,044	6,016
Vehicle purchase	2,291	2,129	2,111	2,189	2,319	2,725	2,639
Gasoline and motor oil	985	1,047	995	973	977	986	1,006
Other transportation	1,911	1,944	2,045	2,066	2,157	2,334	2,371
Health care	1,407	1,480	1,554	1,634	1,776	1,755	1,732
Tobacco products, smoking supplies	261	274	276	275	268	259	269
Life and other personal insurance	346	345	356	353	399	398	374
Pensions and Social Security	2,125	2,248	2,431	2,397	2,509	2,540	2,593
Other expenditures	4,030	4,003	4,291	4,198	4,308	4,297	4,340

No. 716. Average Annual Expenditures of All Consumer Units, by Metropolitan Area: 1994-95

[In dollars. Metropolitan areas defined June 30, 1983, CMSA=Consolidated Metropolitan Statistical Area; MSA=Metropolitan Statistical Area; PMSA=Primary Metropolitan Statistical Area. See text, section 1, and Appendix II. See headnote, table 712]

METROPOLITAN AREA	Total expenditures [1]	Food	HOUSING		Apparel and services	TRANSPORTATION			Health care
			Total [1]	Shelter		Total [1]	Vehicle purchases	Gasoline and motor oil	
Anchorage, AK MSA	$42,662	5,928	13,474	8,537	2,139	6,710	2,257	1,055	1,944
Atlanta, GA MSA	$40,214	4,721	12,315	7,181	2,441	8,284	4,180	991	2,226
Baltimore, MD MSA	$35,025	4,483	12,271	7,716	1,459	5,660	2,396	917	1,822
Boston-Lawrence-Salem, MA-NH CMSA	$35,529	4,577	12,807	7,846	1,995	5,765	2,284	864	1,878
Buffalo-Niagara Falls, NY CMSA	$24,828	4,298	9,174	5,007	1,503	3,619	1,233	781	1,299
Chicago-Gary-Lake County, IL-IN-WI CMSA	$37,946	5,099	13,067	7,984	2,525	6,899	3,240	992	1,820
Cincinnati-Hamilton, OH-KY-IN CMSA	$32,817	4,344	10,462	5,810	1,492	6,758	3,174	1,088	1,810
Cleveland-Akron-Lorain, OH CMSA	$28,199	4,182	9,477	5,175	1,341	5,198	2,061	853	1,466
Dallas-Fort Worth, TX CMSA	$38,895	5,300	11,606	6,267	2,152	7,875	3,530	1,272	1,840
Detroit-Ann Arbor, MI CMSA	$34,114	4,538	11,025	6,419	1,754	7,520	3,205	1,072	1,400
Honolulu, HI MSA	$40,996	5,920	14,161	9,718	1,481	6,349	2,231	911	1,861
Houston-Galveston-Brazoria, TX CMSA	$38,347	5,709	10,670	5,588	2,416	8,170	4,152	1,165	2,036
Kansas City, MO-Kansas City, KS CMSA	$34,254	4,526	10,016	5,292	1,815	6,579	2,847	1,060	2,090
Los Angeles-Long Beach, CA PMSA	$36,324	4,652	13,671	8,978	2,015	6,141	2,296	1,079	1,307
Miami-Fort Lauderdale, FL CMSA	$31,764	4,701	10,868	6,250	1,564	6,128	2,423	962	1,369
Milwaukee, WI PMSA	$34,907	4,032	11,191	6,868	1,637	7,308	3,828	1,055	1,506
Minneapolis-St. Paul, MN-WI MSA	$39,516	4,894	12,283	7,287	1,782	6,884	2,588	1,186	1,727
New York-Northern New Jersey-Long Island, NY-NJ-CT CMSA	$36,491	5,442	14,027	8,948	2,323	4,994	1,251	764	1,824
Philadelphia-Wilmington-Trenton, PA-NJ-DE-MD CMSA	$31,756	4,647	10,275	6,220	1,667	5,413	2,147	793	1,450
Pittsburgh-Beaver Valley, PA CMSA	$27,664	3,888	8,819	4,471	1,543	4,790	2,092	765	1,651
Portland-Vancouver, OR-WA CMSA	$34,853	4,414	11,707	7,318	1,777	6,088	2,736	972	1,559
San Diego, CA MSA	$34,027	4,077	12,208	8,346	1,490	6,396	2,314	1,114	1,455
San Francisco-Oakland-San Jose, CA CMSA	$41,960	5,221	15,989	9,902	2,049	6,465	2,125	1,082	1,582
Seattle-Tacoma, WA CMSA	$36,389	4,496	11,938	7,689	1,466	6,789	2,860	996	1,522
St. Louis-East St. Louis-Alton, MO-IL CMSA	$31,337	4,208	9,432	4,795	1,566	6,956	3,678	987	1,637
Washington, DC-MD-VA MSA	$41,838	4,950	14,447	9,261	2,088	6,775	2,801	1,006	1,783

[1] Includes expenditures not shown separately.

Sources of tables 715 and 716: U.S. Bureau of Labor Statistics, *Consumer Expenditures in 1994-95.*

17. Money Income of Households—Percent Distribution, by Income Level, Race, and Hispanic Origin, in Constant (1995) Dollars: 1970 to 1995

nt dollars based on CPI-U-X1 deflator. Households as of March of following year. Based on Current Population ey; see text, sections 1 and 14, and Appendix III. For definition of median, see Guide to Tabular Presentation]

YEAR	Number of house-holds (1,000)	PERCENT DISTRIBUTION							Median income (dollars)
		Under $10,000	$10,000-$14,999	$15,000-$24,999	$25,000-$34,999	$35,000-$49,999	$50,000-$74,999	$75,000 and over	
JSEHOLDS [1]									
....	64,778	14.3	8.0	15.8	16.9	21.3	16.3	7.5	32,229
....	82,368	13.3	8.7	16.5	14.6	19.3	17.4	10.3	32,795
....	94,312	12.5	8.1	15.5	14.4	17.7	17.6	14.2	34,914
....	98,990	13.2	8.9	16.3	14.1	16.3	16.7	14.6	33,178
....	99,627	12.3	8.7	15.9	14.2	16.9	17.1	14.8	34,076
WHITE									
....	57,575	13.0	7.5	15.2	17.0	22.1	17.1	8.1	33,569
....	71,872	11.7	8.1	16.1	14.8	19.9	18.3	11.1	34,596
....	80,968	10.6	7.7	15.3	14.5	18.2	18.5	15.1	36,416
....	83,737	11.3	8.6	16.1	14.2	16.7	17.5	15.6	34,992
....	84,511	10.6	8.4	15.6	14.4	17.3	17.9	15.9	35,766
LACK									—
....	6,180	25.8	12.7	21.4	15.2	14.2	8.3	2.4	20,432
....	8,847	26.7	13.2	20.3	12.9	13.9	9.8	3.4	19,932
....	10,671	26.8	11.2	17.4	13.5	14.1	10.7	6.2	21,777
....	11,655	26.1	11.2	18.5	13.0	13.5	10.9	6.8	21,623
....	11,577	24.0	11.5	18.8	13.6	14.6	11.2	6.2	22,393
PANIC [2]									
....	3,906	17.0	11.6	21.1	16.2	16.9	12.3	5.0	25,278
....	6,220	17.4	12.0	18.8	16.2	16.5	12.1	7.0	26,037
....	7,735	20.1	12.0	19.9	14.9	14.6	11.5	7.0	24,085
....	7,939	19.9	12.2	21.5	15.4	13.3	11.6	6.1	22,860

des other races not shown separately. [2] Persons of Hispanic origin may be of any race. Income data for Hispanic seholds are not available prior to 1972.

. Money Income of Households—Median Income, by Race and Hispanic Origin, in Current and Constant (1995) Dollars: 1970 to 1995

[See headnote, table 717]

R	MEDIAN INCOME IN CURRENT DOLLARS					MEDIAN INCOME IN CONSTANT (1995) DOLLARS				
	All house-holds [1]	White	Black	Asian, Pacific Islander	His-panic [2]	All house-holds [1]	White	Black	Asian, Pacific Islanders	His-panic [2]
.....	8,734	9,097	5,537	(NA)	(NA)	32,229	33,569	20,432	(NA)	(NA)
.....	17,710	18,684	10,764	(NA)	13,651	32,795	34,596	19,932	(NA)	25,278
.....	19,074	20,153	11,309	(NA)	15,300	32,263	34,088	19,129	(NA)	25,879
.....	20,171	21,117	11,968	(NA)	15,178	32,155	33,663	19,079	(NA)	24,196
.....	20,885	21,902	12,429	(NA)	15,906	31,957	33,513	19,018	(NA)	24,338
.....	22,415	23,647	13,471	(NA)	16,992	32,878	34,685	19,759	(NA)	24,924
.....	23,618	24,908	14,819	(NA)	17,465	33,452	35,279	20,989	(NA)	24,737
.....	24,897	26,175	15,080	(NA)	18,352	34,620	36,397	20,969	(NA)	25,519
.....	26,061	27,458	15,672	(NA)	19,336	34,962	36,836	21,025	(NA)	25,940
.....	27,225	28,781	16,407	32,267	20,359	35,073	37,077	21,136	41,568	26,227
.....	28,906	30,406	18,083	36,102	21,921	35,526	37,370	22,225	44,371	26,942
.....	29,943	31,231	18,676	38,450	22,330	34,914	36,416	21,777	44,834	26,037
.....	30,126	31,569	18,807	36,449	22,691	33,709	35,324	21,044	40,784	25,390
.....	30,636	32,209	18,755	37,801	22,597	33,278	34,987	20,373	41,061	24,546
.....	31,241	32,960	19,533	38,347	22,886	32,949	34,762	20,601	40,443	24,137
.....	32,264	34,028	21,027	40,482	23,421	33,178	34,992	21,623	41,629	24,085
.....	34,076	35,766	22,393	40,614	22,860	34,076	35,766	22,393	40,614	22,860

t available. [1] Includes other races not shown separately. [2] Persons of Hispanic origin may be of any race. g 1983, data based on revised Hispanic population controls and not directly comparable with prior years. [4] Beginning based on revised processing procedures and not directly comparable with prior years. [5] Based on 1990 census controls.

e of tables 717 and 718: U.S. Bureau of the Census, *Current Population Reports*, P60-193; and unpublished data.

No. 719. Money Income of Households—Percent Distribution, by Income Level and Selected Characteristics: 1995

[See headnote, table 717. For composition of regions, see table 27]

CHARACTERISTIC	Number of households (1,000)	PERCENT DISTRIBUTION: Under $10,000	$10,000-$14,999	$15,000-$24,999	$25,000-$34,999	$35,000-$49,999	$50,000-$74,999	$75,000 and over	Median income (dollars)
Total [1]	99,627	12,189	8,716	15,848	14,167	16,876	17,038	14,792	34,076
Age of householder:									
15 to 24 years	5,282	1,157	707	1,245	947	699	416	114	20,979
25 to 34 years	19,225	1,937	1,385	3,071	3,299	4,065	3,457	2,007	34,701
35 to 44 years	23,226	1,632	1,275	2,883	3,154	4,504	5,454	4,326	43,465
45 to 54 years	18,008	1,367	807	1,913	2,106	3,184	3,942	4,689	48,058
55 to 64 years	12,401	1,463	663	1,748	1,602	2,099	2,189	2,435	38,077
65 years and over	21,486	4,634	3,679	4,988	3,059	2,326	1,577	1,221	19,096
White	84,511	8,939	7,083	13,192	12,148	14,584	15,093	13,472	35,766
Black	11,577	2,783	1,336	2,178	1,568	1,695	1,299	719	22,393
Hispanic [2]	7,939	1,578	971	1,707	1,222	1,058	918	485	22,860
Northeast	19,695	2,527	1,666	2,700	2,656	3,196	3,580	3,370	38,111
Midwest	23,707	2,429	2,028	3,707	3,415	4,212	4,446	3,471	35,839
South	35,143	4,917	3,288	6,024	5,296	5,922	5,329	4,364	30,942
West	21,082	2,317	1,735	3,418	2,796	3,544	3,683	3,587	35,979
Size of household:									
One person	24,900	7,000	4,030	5,234	3,469	2,776	1,549	844	17,083
Two persons	32,526	2,384	2,562	5,680	5,280	6,103	5,622	4,890	35,700
Three persons	16,724	1,312	943	2,165	2,270	3,147	3,652	3,229	42,244
Four persons	15,118	816	600	1,507	1,778	2,940	3,836	3,640	49,531
Five persons	6,631	448	330	759	829	1,242	1,528	1,497	45,710
Six persons	2,357	139	151	301	319	385	586	475	44,283
Seven or more persons	1,372	90	100	201	222	282	268	209	39,013
Type of Household:									
Family households	69,594	4,841	4,378	9,870	9,824	13,077	14,432	13,173	41,224
Married-couple	53,567	1,736	2,398	6,615	7,292	10,445	12,752	12,326	47,129
Male householder, wife absent	3,513	291	293	669	570	738	576	375	33,534
Female householder, husband absent	12,514	2,812	1,686	2,586	1,962	1,892	1,105	472	21,348
Nonfamily households	30,033	7,349	4,339	5,978	4,343	3,801	2,606	1,618	19,929
Male householder	13,348	2,266	1,495	2,634	2,195	2,117	1,545	1,094	26,023
Female householder	16,685	5,084	2,844	3,345	2,147	1,683	1,062	524	15,892
Educational attainment of householder: [3]									
Total	94,346	11,033	8,010	14,603	13,220	16,178	16,623	14,678	35,235
Less than 9th grade	8,062	2,569	1,452	1,771	966	688	449	166	15,043
9th to 12th grade (no diploma)	9,683	2,363	1,551	2,259	1,285	1,175	731	320	18,298
High school graduate	29,507	3,363	2,682	5,379	4,976	5,572	4,975	2,559	31,376
Some college, no degree	16,951	1,525	1,271	2,516	2,591	3,339	3,374	2,335	37,158
Associate degree	6,719	435	326	914	978	1,376	1,647	1,041	42,118
Bachelor's degree or more	23,424	778	726	1,764	2,424	4,030	5,446	8,256	58,052
Bachelor's degree	14,871	567	549	1,315	1,759	2,730	3,556	4,394	52,857
Master's degree	5,706	152	115	322	458	947	1,386	2,325	64,980
Professional degree	1,641	32	36	86	137	190	264	896	82,010
Doctorate degree	1,206	27	26	39	69	161	240	640	80,005
Tenure:									
Owner occupied	65,143	4,944	4,351	8,751	8,720	11,837	13,627	12,911	41,832
Renter occupied	32,768	6,816	4,139	6,714	5,187	4,821	3,285	1,805	22,583
Occupier paid no cash rent	1,716	429	225	383	258	219	127	74	19,910

[1] Includes other races not shown separately. [2] Persons of Hispanic origin may be of any race. [3] 25 years old and over

Source: U.S. Bureau of the Census, *Current Population Reports*, P60-193; and Internet site, <http://ferret.bls.census.gov/cgi-bin/ferret> (accessed: 23 April 1997).

No. 720. Money Income of Households—Median Income and Income Level, by Household Type: 1995

[See headnote, table 717]

ITEM	All households	FAMILY HOUSEHOLDS				NONFAMILY HOUSEHOLDS		
		Total	Married couple	Male householder, wife absent	Female householder, husband absent	Total [1]	Single-person household: Male householder	Single-person household: Female householder
MEDIAN INCOME (dollars)								
All households	**34,076**	**41,224**	**47,129**	**33,534**	**21,348**	**19,929**	26,023	**15,892**
White	35,766	43,265	47,608	35,129	24,431	20,585	26,898	16,325
Black	22,393	26,838	41,362	27,071	15,589	15,007	19,172	11,872
Hispanic [2]	22,860	25,491	30,195	25,053	14,755	13,780	17,339	10,196
NUMBER (1,000)								
All households	**99,627**	**69,594**	**53,567**	**3,513**	**12,514**	**30,033**	13,348	**16,685**
Under $5,000	3,651	1,708	566	95	1,046	1,943	787	1,156
$5,000 to $9,999	8,538	3,133	1,170	196	1,766	5,406	1,479	3,928
$10,000 to $14,999	8,716	4,378	2,396	293	1,686	4,339	1,495	2,844
$15,000 to $19,999	8,294	4,923	3,187	321	1,415	3,370	1,357	2,014
$20,000 to $24,999	7,554	4,947	3,428	348	1,171	2,608	1,277	1,331
$25,000 to $34,999	14,167	9,824	7,292	570	1,962	4,343	2,195	2,147
$35,000 to $49,999	16,876	13,077	10,445	738	1,892	3,801	2,117	1,683
$50,000 to $74,999	17,038	14,432	12,752	576	1,105	2,606	1,545	1,062
$75,000 to $99,999	7,678	6,803	6,293	221	289	874	577	297
$100,000 and over	7,114	6,370	6,033	154	183	744	517	227

[1] Includes other nonfamily households not shown separately. [2] Persons of Hispanic origin may be of any race.

Source: U.S. Bureau of the Census, *Current Population Reports*, P60-193; and Internet site, <http://ferret.bls.census.gov/cgi-bin/ferret> (accessed: 23 April 1997).

No. 721. Money Income of Households—Percent Distribution, by Income Quintile and Top 5 Percent: 1995

[See headnote, table 717. For composition of regions, see table 27]

CHARACTERISTIC	Number (1,000)	PERCENT DISTRIBUTION: Total	Lowest fifth	Second fifth	Third fifth	Fourth fifth	Highest fifth	Top 5 percent
Total	**99,627**	**100.0**	**20.0**	**20.0**	**20.0**	**20.0**	**20.0**	**5.0**
Age of householder:								
15 to 24 years old	5,282	100.0	33.6	29.0	21.8	11.8	3.8	0.3
25 to 34 years old	19,225	100.0	16.7	20.3	24.4	23.4	15.2	2.7
35 to 44 years old	23,226	100.0	11.8	16.1	20.3	26.2	25.6	5.9
45 to 54 years old	18,008	100.0	11.7	13.3	18.3	22.9	33.8	9.4
55 to 64 years old	12,401	100.0	18.2	17.3	19.3	20.0	25.2	7.3
65 years old and over	21,488	100.0	36.5	28.9	17.0	9.9	7.6	2.2
White	84,511	100.0	18.0	19.8	20.2	20.8	21.3	5.4
Black	11,577	100.0	34.3	22.7	19.0	14.2	9.8	1.4
Hispanic origin [1]	7,939	100.0	30.9	26.2	19.7	14.3	9.0	1.6
Northeast	19,695	100.0	20.5	17.1	19.5	20.4	22.5	6.4
Midwest	23,707	100.0	17.8	19.6	20.3	22.0	20.3	4.5
South	35,143	100.0	22.2	21.7	20.9	18.3	16.9	4.3
West	21,082	100.0	18.2	20.4	18.7	20.2	22.4	5.5
Family households	69,594	100.0	12.5	17.8	20.8	23.5	25.4	6.4
Married-couple families	53,567	100.0	7.2	15.6	20.5	26.2	30.5	7.9
Male householder	3,513	100.0	15.4	23.9	24.0	20.9	15.8	2.8
Female householder	12,514	100.0	34.6	25.2	21.5	12.7	6.1	0.9
Nonfamily households	30,033	100.0	37.3	25.2	18.1	11.8	7.6	1.8
Male householder	13,348	100.0	26.9	25.3	21.3	15.2	11.3	2.8
Living alone	10,288	100.0	31.4	27.3	20.8	12.9	7.6	2.2
Female householder	16,685	100.0	45.7	25.1	15.5	9.1	4.6	0.9
Living alone	14,612	100.0	50.4	25.8	14.1	7.0	2.7	0.5
Worked	71,070	100.0	10.2	17.6	22.0	24.5	25.7	6.4
Worked at full-time jobs	61,729	100.0	7.6	16.8	22.5	25.7	27.4	6.7
Worked at part-time jobs	9,341	100.0	27.6	23.4	18.5	16.4	14.2	4.2
Did not work	28,557	100.0	44.3	25.9	15.0	8.9	5.9	1.6

[1] Persons of Hispanic origin may be of any race.

Source: U.S. Bureau of the Census, Current Population Survey, March 1996, and unpublished data.

No. 723. Money Income of Families—Percent Distribution, by Income Level, Race, and Hispanic Origin, in Constant (1995) Dollars: 1970 to 1995

[Constant dollars based on CPI-U-X1 deflator. Families as of March of following year. Beginning with 1980, based on householder concept and restricted to primary families. Based on Current Population Survey; see text, sections 1 and 14, and Appendix III. For definition of median, see Guide to Tabular Presentation]

YEAR	Number of families (1,000)	PERCENT DISTRIBUTION							Median income (dollars)
		Under $10,000	$10,000-$14,999	$15,000-$24,999	$25,000-$34,999	$35,000-$49,999	$50,000-$74,999	$75,000 and over	
ALL FAMILIES [1]									
1970	52,227	7.7	6.7	15.4	18.0	24.5	19.0	8.8	36,410
1980	60,309	7.3	6.7	15.2	14.9	21.9	21.3	12.8	38,930
1985	63,558	8.3	6.4	14.7	14.8	19.8	20.8	15.5	39,283
1990	66,322	7.7	6.1	13.7	14.2	19.4	21.0	18.0	41,223
1992	68,216	8.8	6.5	14.4	14.3	18.5	20.8	16.8	39,727
1993	68,506	9.1	6.7	14.6	14.5	17.6	20.0	17.4	38,980
1994	69,313	8.5	6.7	14.6	14.1	17.9	20.0	18.3	39,881
1995	69,597	7.5	6.5	14.4	14.1	18.5	20.4	18.6	40,611
WHITE									
1970	46,535	6.5	6.1	14.6	18.1	25.4	20.0	9.4	37,772
1980	52,710	5.8	5.9	14.5	15.1	22.7	22.4	13.8	40,561
1990	56,803	5.7	5.4	13.2	14.3	19.9	22.2	19.1	43,044
1994	58,444	6.6	6.0	14.2	14.2	18.4	21.0	19.6	42,043
1995	58,872	5.8	5.8	13.9	14.2	18.8	21.4	20.0	42,646
BLACK									
1970	4,928	18.6	12.6	23.0	16.9	16.5	9.8	2.6	23,170
1980	6,317	19.1	13.4	21.2	14.0	15.8	12.3	4.3	23,469
1990	7,471	21.4	11.2	17.5	13.7	15.6	12.8	7.8	24,980
1994	8,093	20.7	10.9	17.9	13.8	14.8	13.4	8.5	25,398
1995	8,055	19.4	10.9	18.3	14.3	15.9	13.3	8.0	25,970
HISPANIC ORIGIN [2]									
1980	3,235	13.2	11.5	21.2	17.1	18.4	13.4	5.3	27,251
1990	4,981	14.6	12.0	19.3	16.0	17.3	13.0	7.8	27,321
1994	6,202	17.2	12.4	20.5	14.9	15.1	12.2	7.6	25,007
1995	6,287	16.2	11.8	22.8	16.2	13.8	12.7	6.6	24,570

[1] Includes other races not shown separately. [2] Persons of Hispanic origin may be of any race.

No. 724. Money Income of Families—Median Income, by Race and Hispanic Origin, in Current and Constant (1995) Dollars: 1970 to 1995

[See headnote, table 723]

YEAR	MEDIAN INCOME IN CURRENT DOLLARS					MEDIAN INCOME IN CONSTANT (1995) DOLLARS				
	All families [1]	White	Black	Asian, Pacific Islander	Hispanic [2]	All families [1]	White	Black	Asian, Pacific Islander	Hispanic [2]
1970	9,867	10,236	6,279	(NA)	(NA)	36,410	37,772	23,170	(NA)	(NA)
1980	21,023	21,904	12,674	(NA)	14,716	38,930	40,561	23,469	(NA)	27,251
1981	22,388	23,517	13,266	(NA)	16,401	37,868	39,778	22,439	(NA)	27,742
1982	23,433	24,603	13,598	(NA)	16,227	37,356	39,221	21,677	(NA)	25,868
1983	24,580	25,757	14,506	(NA)	16,956	37,610	39,411	22,196	(NA)	25,945
1984 [3]	26,433	27,686	15,431	(NA)	18,832	38,772	40,610	22,634	(NA)	27,623
1985	27,735	29,152	16,786	(NA)	19,027	39,283	41,290	23,775	(NA)	26,949
1986	29,458	30,809	17,604	(NA)	19,995	40,962	42,840	24,479	(NA)	27,803
1987 [4]	30,970	32,385	18,406	(NA)	20,300	41,548	43,446	24,693	(NA)	27,233
1988	32,191	33,915	19,329	36,560	21,769	41,470	43,691	24,901	47,098	28,044
1989	34,213	35,975	20,209	40,351	23,446	42,049	44,214	24,838	49,593	28,816
1990	35,353	36,915	21,423	42,246	23,431	41,223	43,044	24,980	49,260	27,321
1991	35,939	37,783	21,548	40,974	23,895	40,214	42,277	24,111	45,848	26,737
1992 [5]	36,573	38,670	21,103	42,255	23,555	39,727	42,005	22,923	45,899	25,586
1993	36,959	39,300	21,542	44,456	23,654	38,980	41,449	22,720	46,886	24,947
1994	38,782	40,884	24,698	46,122	24,318	39,881	42,043	25,398	47,429	25,007
1995	40,611	42,646	25,970	46,356	24,570	40,611	42,646	25,970	46,356	24,570

NA Not available. [1] Includes other races not shown separately. [2] Persons of Hispanic origin may be of any race. [3] Beginning 1984, data based on revised Hispanic population controls and not directly comparable with prior years. [4] Beginning 1987, data based on revised processing procedures and not directly comparable with prior years. [5] Based on 1990 census population controls.

Source of tables 723 and 724: U.S. Bureau of the Census, *Current Population Reports*, P60-193; and Internet site, (accessed 24 April 1997).

No. 725. Share of Aggregate Income Received by Each Fifth and Top 5 Percent of Families, by Race and Hispanic Origin of Householder: 1970 to 1995

[Families as of March of the following year. Income in constant 1995 CPI-U-X1 adjusted dollars]

YEAR	Number (1,000)	INCOME AT SELECTED POSITIONS (dollars)					PERCENT DISTRIBUTION OF AGGREGATE INCOME					
		Upper limit of each fifth				Top 5 percent	Lowest 5th	Second 5th	Third 5th	Fourth 5th	Highest 5th	Top 5 percent
		Lowest	Second	Third	Fourth							
1970	52,227	18,819	30,701	41,694	57,311	89,484	5.4	12.2	17.6	23.8	40.9	15.6
1975	56,245	18,947	31,199	43,388	60,073	94,098	5.6	11.9	17.7	24.2	40.7	14.9
1980	60,309	19,258	32,424	45,924	64,441	101,847	5.3	11.6	17.6	24.4	41.1	14.6
1981	61,019	18,631	31,715	45,260	63,937	101,474	5.3	11.4	17.5	24.6	41.2	14.4
1982	61,393	18,172	31,121	44,556	63,928	104,118	5.0	11.3	17.2	24.4	42.2	15.3
1983 [1]	62,015	18,109	31,017	45,100	64,490	106,134	4.9	11.2	17.2	24.5	42.4	15.3
1984	62,706	18,445	32,065	46,474	66,832	109,423	4.8	11.1	17.1	24.5	42.5	15.4
1985	63,558	18,816	32,415	46,955	68,309	111,843	4.8	11.0	16.9	24.3	43.1	16.1
1986	64,491	19,467	33,511	48,635	70,318	115,969	4.7	10.9	16.9	24.1	43.4	16.5
1987 [2]	65,204	19,584	33,783	49,370	71,545	116,646	4.6	10.7	16.8	24.0	43.8	17.2
1988	65,837	19,455	33,729	49,596	72,021	118,520	4.6	10.7	16.7	24.0	44.0	17.2
1989	66,090	19,668	34,413	50,145	73,189	121,629	4.6	10.6	16.5	23.7	44.6	17.9
1990	66,322	19,643	33,866	49,020	71,699	119,352	4.6	10.8	16.6	23.8	44.3	17.4
1991	67,173	19,022	32,574	48,115	70,463	115,054	4.5	10.7	16.6	24.1	44.2	17.1
1992 [3]	68,216	18,154	32,233	47,795	69,574	115,155	4.3	10.5	16.5	24.0	44.7	17.6
1993	68,506	17,898	31,640	47,492	70,446	119,370	4.1	9.9	15.7	23.3	47.0	20.3
1994	69,313	18,448	32,187	48,332	71,982	123,445	4.2	10.0	15.7	23.3	46.9	20.1
1995	69,597	19,070	32,985	48,985	72,260	123,656	4.4	10.1	15.8	23.2	46.5	20.0
White	58,872	20,916	35,046	51,000	75,000	127,196	4.8	10.4	16.0	23.0	45.8	19.5
Black	8,055	10,200	20,000	32,296	51,016	84,744	3.3	8.7	15.2	24.1	48.7	20.0
Hispanic origin [4]	6,287	11,479	19,677	30,022	48,492	82,380	4.1	9.5	15.1	23.2	48.1	19.9

[1] Beginning 1983, data based on revised Hispanic population controls and not directly comparable with prior years. [2] Beginning 1987, data based on revised processing procedures and not directly comparable with prior years. [3] Based on 1990 census population controls. [4] Persons of Hispanic origin may be of any race.

Source: U.S. Bureau of the Census, *Current Population Reports*, P60-193; and Internet site, <http://www.census.gov/hhes/income/histinc/index.html> (accessed 24 April 1997).

No. 726. Money Income of Families—Percent Distribution, by Income Quintile and Top 5 Percent: 1995

[See headnote, table 723]

CHARACTERISTIC	Number (1,000)	PERCENT DISTRIBUTION						
		Total	Lowest fifth	Second fifth	Third fifth	Fourth fifth	Highest fifth	Top 5 percent
All families	69,597	100.0	20.0	20.0	20.0	20.0	20.0	5.0
Age of householder:								
15 to 24 years old	3,019	100.0	50.4	26.2	15.1	6.5	1.9	0.2
25 to 34 years old	13,727	100.0	24.3	21.3	22.8	19.3	12.2	2.1
35 to 44 years old	18,504	100.0	15.8	16.8	20.4	24.7	22.3	5.3
45 to 54 years old	13,908	100.0	10.9	13.5	18.8	24.1	32.6	8.6
55 to 64 years old	9,134	100.0	16.5	17.8	19.7	20.0	26.0	7.1
65 years old and over	11,306	100.0	27.5	31.6	19.0	11.6	10.2	3.1
White	58,872	100.0	17.3	19.8	20.4	21.0	21.5	5.4
Black	8,055	100.0	38.0	22.7	17.4	13.2	8.7	1.4
Hispanic origin [1]	6,287	100.0	38.8	25.2	16.1	12.5	7.3	1.3
Type of family:								
Married-couple families	53,570	100.0	12.7	18.5	21.0	23.2	24.5	6.3
Male householder, wife absent	3,513	100.0	28.5	26.3	20.5	14.6	10.0	1.6
Female householder, husband absent	12,514	100.0	48.8	24.5	15.5	7.7	3.4	0.5
Presence of related children under 18 years old:								
No related children	32,878	100.0	17.2	21.4	20.6	19.6	21.3	5.5
One or more related children	36,719	100.0	22.5	18.8	19.5	20.4	18.8	4.6
One child	15,046	100.0	22.8	19.5	18.9	19.5	19.3	4.3
Two children or more	21,674	100.0	22.3	18.3	19.9	20.9	18.6	4.8
Education attainment of householder: [2]								
Total	66,578	100.0	18.6	19.7	20.2	20.6	20.8	5.2
Less than 9th grade	5,063	100.0	46.1	28.6	14.5	7.7	3.0	0.5
9th to 12th grade (no diploma)	6,477	100.0	39.9	27.1	17.6	10.5	5.0	0.9
High school graduate (includes equivalency)	21,468	100.0	19.5	24.3	23.7	20.6	11.9	1.8
Some college, no degree	12,166	100.0	15.6	19.4	23.0	23.4	18.5	3.6
Associate degree	4,786	100.0	11.0	16.1	23.1	28.4	21.4	3.8
Bachelor's degree or more	16,618	100.0	5.2	9.4	15.6	24.3	45.5	14.3
Bachelor's degree	10,421	100.0	6.1	11.3	17.4	26.0	39.2	10.2
Master's degree	4,091	100.0	4.2	6.5	13.4	24.0	51.9	15.7
Professional degree	1,193	100.0	3.6	6.8	9.7	13.6	66.3	38.4
Doctorate degree	913	100.0	2.2	5.1	11.8	19.7	61.2	26.7

[1] Persons of Hispanic origin may be of any race. [2] 25 years old and over.

Source: U.S. Bureau of the Census, Current Population Survey, unpublished data.

No. 727. Money Income of Families—Median Income, by Race and Hispanic Origin: 1994

[See headnote, table 723. For composition of regions, see table 27]

CHARACTERISTIC	NUMBER (1,000)				MEDIAN INCOME (dollars)			
	All families [1]	White	Black	Hispanic [2]	All families [1]	White	Black	Hispanic [2]
All families	**69,313**	**58,444**	**8,093**	**6,202**	**38,782**	**40,884**	**24,698**	**24,318**
Region:								
Northeast	13,468	11,636	1,384	974	42,943	45,169	26,414	21,478
Midwest	16,264	14,438	1,509	389	39,760	41,453	21,844	31,188
South	24,873	19,755	4,538	2,087	35,388	37,790	24,332	23,961
West	14,687	12,616	662	2,752	40,298	40,883	31,104	24,462
Type of family:								
Married-couple families	53,865	47,905	3,842	4,236	44,959	45,474	40,432	29,621
Wife in paid labor force	32,902	29,045	2,626	2,279	53,309	53,977	47,235	38,559
Wife not in paid labor force	20,962	18,860	1,215	1,957	31,176	31,747	25,396	20,676
Male householder, wife absent	3,228	2,506	536	480	27,751	29,460	20,977	21,787
Female householder, husband absent	12,220	8,031	3,716	1,486	18,236	20,795	13,943	12,117
With related children, under 18	36,782	29,548	5,439	4,377	37,925	41,184	21,412	23,045
Married couple	26,367	22,839	2,147	2,923	47,244	48,272	42,085	29,435
Male householder, wife absent	1,750	1,319	341	272	24,092	26,043	19,109	17,351
Female householder, husband absent	8,665	5,390	2,951	1,182	14,902	16,734	11,914	11,133
Number of earners:								
No earners	10,308	8,467	1,500	873	16,445	18,575	7,375	8,235
One earner	19,455	15,681	2,988	2,148	27,145	29,484	17,842	16,954
Two earners	30,865	26,845	2,831	2,359	48,970	50,112	40,654	34,411
Three earners	6,558	5,642	640	601	61,017	62,412	49,938	44,213
Four or more earners	2,109	1,809	154	221	75,609	76,272	70,677	52,893

[1] Includes other races not shown separately. [2] Persons of Hispanic origin may be of any race.

No. 728. Money Income of Families—Selected Characteristics, by Income Level: 1995

[See headnote, table 723. For composition of regions, see table 27]

CHARACTERISTIC	Number of families (1,000)	INCOME LEVEL (1,000)							Median income (dollars)
		Under $10,000	$10,000 to $14,999	$15,000 to $24,999	$25,000 to $34,999	$35,000 to $49,999	$50,000 to $74,999	$75,000 and over	
All families	**69,597**	**5,216**	**4,507**	**10,040**	**9,828**	**12,841**	**14,204**	**12,961**	**40,611**
Age of householder:									
15 to 24 years old	3,019	807	408	667	495	409	197	39	18,756
25 to 34 years old	13,727	1,501	999	2,007	2,148	2,876	2,643	1,552	36,020
35 to 44 years old	16,504	1,113	925	2,146	2,270	3,578	4,658	3,813	46,527
45 to 54 years old	13,908	595	452	1,187	1,482	2,434	3,491	4,267	55,029
55 to 64 years old	9,134	549	495	1,117	1,179	1,681	1,901	2,212	45,264
65 years old and over	11,306	650	1,230	2,916	2,254	1,864	1,315	1,077	28,301
White	58,872	3,390	3,425	8,204	8,372	11,096	12,591	11,793	42,646
Black	8,055	1,559	860	1,478	1,149	1,279	1,070	640	25,970
Hispanic origin [1]	6,287	1,015	743	1,433	1,016	867	798	414	24,570
Northeast	13,508	1,009	750	1,697	1,809	2,386	2,939	2,918	43,909
Midwest	16,353	936	924	2,160	2,325	3,165	3,710	3,133	43,470
South	25,101	2,198	1,911	4,064	3,762	4,720	4,578	3,867	36,628
West	14,636	1,073	922	2,118	1,932	2,570	2,977	3,042	41,967
Type of family:									
Married-couple families	53,570	1,750	2,406	6,644	7,298	10,447	12,749	12,276	47,062
Male householder, wife absent	3,513	373	325	712	596	679	518	309	30,358
Female householder, husband absent	12,514	3,092	1,776	2,684	1,933	1,715	937	377	19,691
Unrelated subfamilies	588	231	94	126	58	57	14	7	12,927
Education attainment of householder: [2]									
Total	66,578	4,409	4,101	9,372	9,334	12,433	14,007	12,923	41,771
Less than 9th grade	5,063	838	823	1,404	848	617	398	135	20,550
9th to 12th grade (no diploma)	6,477	1,027	829	1,596	1,037	1,026	668	295	23,331
High school graduate (includes equiva lency)	21,468	1,436	1,364	3,496	3,801	4,619	4,436	2,316	36,751
Some college, no degree	12,166	652	631	1,557	1,747	2,616	2,881	2,081	43,448
Associate degree	4,786	160	169	484	636	1,029	1,371	936	48,700
Bachelor's degree or more	16,618	294	285	835	1,264	2,526	4,255	7,159	67,529
Bachelor's degree	10,421	201	215	618	953	1,765	2,821	3,848	61,780
Master's degree	4,091	58	57	151	212	546	1,074	1,993	73,926
Professional degree	1,193	22	9	44	61	108	177	772	96,935
Doctorate degree	913	13	3	23	38	107	182	546	90,463

[1] Persons of Hispanic origin may be of any race. [2] Persons 25 years old and over.

Source of tables 727 and 728: U.S. Bureau of the Census, *Current Population Reports*, P60-189 and P60-193; and Internet site, <http://ferret.bls.census.gov/cgi-bin/ferret> (accessed: 23 April 1997).

No. 729. Money Income of Families—Work Experience, by Income Level: 1995

[See headnote, table 723. For composition of regions, see table 27]

CHARACTERISTIC	Number of families (1,000)	INCOME LEVEL (1,000) Under $10,000	$10,000 to $14,999	$15,000 to $24,999	$25,000 to $34,999	$35,000 to $49,999	$50,000 to $74,999	$75,000 and over	Median income (dollars)
All families	**69,597**	**5,216**	**4,507**	**10,040**	**9,828**	**12,841**	**14,204**	**12,961**	**40,611**
Number of earners:									
No earners	10,180	2,634	1,660	2,621	1,491	947	513	312	17,713
1 earner	19,894	2,104	2,112	4,338	3,621	3,443	2,370	1,906	28,423
2 earners or more	39,524	479	735	3,081	4,716	8,451	11,321	10,743	54,006
2 earners	31,041	444	661	2,750	4,094	7,068	8,637	7,387	50,989
3 earners	6,249	28	65	297	522	1,107	2,001	2,229	63,924
4 earners or more	2,234	6	8	34	100	276	683	1,126	75,386
Work experience of householder:									
Total	69,597	5,216	4,507	10,040	9,828	12,841	14,204	12,961	40,611
Worked	52,701	2,165	2,326	6,109	7,068	10,543	12,586	11,884	46,983
Worked at full-time jobs	46,285	1,267	1,772	5,032	6,154	9,446	11,606	11,009	49,031
50 weeks or more	39,506	497	1,121	3,913	5,171	8,204	10,419	10,181	51,409
27 to 49 weeks	4,576	277	390	728	716	897	907	660	37,639
26 weeks or less	2,203	493	261	391	267	345	280	167	24,011
Worked at part-time	6,416	896	554	1,077	934	1,097	980	875	31,832
50 weeks or more	3,036	256	278	533	404	577	533	456	36,006
27 to 49 weeks	1,487	181	103	233	262	257	213	238	32,891
26 weeks or less	1,893	462	174	311	269	263	234	180	24,986

No. 730. Median Income of Families, by Type of Family in Current and Constant (1995) Dollars: 1970 to 1995

[See headnote, table 723]

YEAR	CURRENT DOLLARS Total	Married-couple families Total	Wife in paid labor force	Wife not in paid labor force	Male householder, no wife present	Female householder, no husband present	CONSTANT (1995) DOLLARS Total	Married-couple families Total	Wife in paid labor force	Wife not in paid labor force	Male householder, no wife present	Female householder, no husband present
1970	9,867	10,516	12,276	9,304	9,012	5,093	36,410	38,805	45,299	34,332	33,255	18,794
1980	21,023	23,141	26,879	18,972	17,519	10,408	38,930	42,852	49,774	35,132	32,441	19,273
1985	27,735	31,100	36,431	24,556	22,622	13,660	39,283	44,049	51,599	34,780	32,041	19,347
1986	29,458	32,805	38,346	25,803	24,962	13,647	40,962	45,616	53,321	35,879	34,710	18,976
1987[1]	30,970	34,879	40,751	26,640	25,208	14,683	41,548	46,792	54,669	35,739	33,818	19,698
1988	32,191	36,389	42,709	27,220	26,827	15,346	41,470	46,878	55,020	35,066	34,560	19,769
1989	34,213	38,547	45,266	28,747	27,847	16,442	42,049	47,375	55,633	35,331	34,225	20,208
1990	35,353	39,895	46,777	30,265	29,046	16,932	41,223	46,519	54,543	35,290	33,868	19,743
1991	35,939	40,995	48,169	30,075	28,351	16,692	40,214	45,871	53,898	33,652	31,723	18,677
1992[2]	36,573	41,890	49,775	30,174	27,576	17,025	39,727	45,503	54,068	32,776	29,954	18,493
1993	36,959	43,005	51,204	30,218	26,467	17,443	38,960	45,356	54,003	31,870	27,914	18,397
1994	38,782	44,959	53,309	31,176	27,751	18,236	39,881	46,233	54,820	32,060	28,537	18,753
1995	40,611	47,062	55,823	32,375	30,358	19,691	40,611	47,062	55,823	32,375	30,358	19,691

[1] Beginning 1987, data based on revised processing procedures and not directly comparable with prior years. [2] Based on 1990 census population controls.

No. 731. Median Income of Persons with Income in Constant (1995) Dollars, by Sex, Race, and Hispanic Origin: 1980 to 1995

[Age as of March of following year. Persons 15 years old and over beginning March 1980. Constant dollars based on CPI-U-X1 deflator]

ITEM	FEMALE 1980	1990	1993[1]	1994[2]	1995	MALE 1980	1990	1993[1]	1994[2]	1995
NUMBER WITH INCOME (1,000)										
All races	80,826	92,245	94,417	95,147	96,007	78,661	88,220	90,194	91,254	92,086
White	70,573	78,566	79,484	80,045	80,608	69,420	76,480	77,650	78,220	79,022
Black	8,596	10,687	11,267	11,450	11,607	7,387	8,820	8,947	9,199	9,339
Hispanic[3]	3,617	5,903	7,053	7,298	7,478	3,996	6,767	8,208	8,375	8,577
White, not Hispanic origin	67,084	72,939	73,128	73,665	73,506	65,564	69,967	70,179	70,919	70,754
MEDIAN INCOME (dol.)										
All races	9,111	11,742	11,650	11,791	12,130	23,203	23,662	22,256	22,336	22,562
White	9,161	12,030	11,882	11,960	12,316	24,680	24,685	23,183	23,311	23,895
Black	8,481	9,711	10,028	10,843	10,961	14,831	15,004	15,403	15,407	16,006
Hispanic[3]	8,157	8,783	8,543	8,857	8,928	17,886	15,706	14,437	14,911	14,840
White, not Hispanic origin	9,222	12,338	12,233	12,284	12,807	25,334	25,604	24,438	24,806	25,481

[1] Data collection method changed and questionaire was revised to allow for coding of different income amounts. See text, section 14 [2] Introduction of new 1990 census sample design. [3] Persons of Hispanic origin may be of any race.

Source of tables 729-731: U.S. Bureau of the Census, *Current Population Reports*, P60-193; and Internet site, <http://www.census.gov/hhes/income/histinc/index.html> (accessed 24 April 1997).

No. 732. Money Income of Persons—Selected Characteristics, by Income Level: 1995

[Constant dollars based on CPI-U-X1 deflator. As of March of following year. Covers persons 15 years old and over. For definition of median, see Guide to Tabular Presentation. For composition of regions, see table 27]

ITEM	All persons (mil.)	PERSONS WITH INCOME: Total (mil.)	Number (1,000): Under $5,000[1]	$5,000 to $9,999	$10,000 to $14,999	$15,000 to $24,999	$25,000 to $34,999	$35,000 to $49,999	$50,000 to $74,999	$75,000 and over	Median income (dollars)
MALE											
Total	98,893	92,066	9,548	10,224	10,793	19,018	14,135	13,153	9,383	5,811	22,562
15 to 24 years old	18,254	13,802	5,615	2,828	2,027	2,279	677	257	82	36	6,913
25 to 34 years old	20,390	19,617	1,185	1,710	2,406	5,091	4,102	3,070	1,464	586	23,609
35 to 44 years old	21,273	20,773	1,144	1,258	1,552	3,940	3,653	4,276	3,160	1,792	31,420
45 to 54 years old	15,324	14,920	604	963	1,006	2,264	2,458	3,130	2,662	1,830	35,586
55 to 64 years old	10,092	9,863	492	924	963	1,846	1,632	1,598	1,337	1,050	28,980
65 yr. old and over	13,260	13,092	506	2,542	2,815	3,596	1,614	822	680	515	16,484
Northeast	19,326	17,943	1,760	1,902	1,968	3,451	2,841	2,680	2,046	1,292	24,610
Midwest	22,964	21,839	2,101	2,108	2,343	4,622	3,539	3,428	2,367	1,331	24,298
South	34,228	31,785	3,392	3,912	3,993	6,928	4,830	4,161	2,797	1,775	21,162
West	22,077	20,498	2,295	2,302	2,490	4,018	2,928	2,886	2,169	1,411	22,314
White	83,463	79,022	7,474	8,220	9,084	16,112	12,351	11,760	8,619	5,401	23,895
Black	10,922	9,339	1,547	1,590	1,246	2,204	1,203	926	437	186	16,006
Hispanic[2]	9,826	8,577	1,194	1,564	1,572	2,084	1,015	660	350	135	14,840
Education attainment of householder:[3]											
Total	80,339	78,264	3,933	7,397	8,766	16,739	13,458	12,696	9,301	5,776	26,346
Less than 9th grade	6,604	6,277	634	1,916	1,405	1,515	446	235	96	27	11,723
9th to 12th grade[4]	7,931	7,490	683	1,416	1,428	2,100	1,040	540	193	90	15,791
High school graduate[5]	25,649	24,909	1,256	2,201	3,097	6,722	5,023	3,954	2,063	590	23,365
Some college, no degree	13,998	13,715	595	899	1,431	2,936	2,802	2,789	1,593	667	28,004
Associate degree	5,303	5,230	183	270	322	1,174	1,074	1,209	758	242	31,027
Bachelor's degree or more	20,855	20,644	580	695	1,063	2,291	3,071	4,168	4,599	4,159	43,322
Bachelor's degree	13,219	13,065	443	502	801	1,739	2,225	2,724	2,742	1,891	39,040
Master's degree	4,812	4,774	85	145	184	363	584	1,073	1,215	1,124	49,076
Professional degree	1,671	1,657	26	30	61	109	160	194	331	743	66,257
Doctorate degree	1,152	1,149	27	18	38	80	105	177	310	398	57,356
FEMALE											
Total	106,031	96,007	21,135	19,986	13,964	18,775	10,858	7,131	3,136	1,262	12,130
15 to 24 years old	18,047	13,550	6,544	3,051	1,805	1,571	432	81	43	22	5,310
25 to 34 years old	20,528	18,856	3,543	2,888	2,654	4,773	2,869	1,440	527	162	15,557
35 to 44 years old	21,805	20,458	3,642	2,831	2,576	4,427	3,043	2,446	1,075	421	17,397
45 to 54 years old	16,260	15,139	2,530	1,958	1,904	3,381	2,245	1,927	859	340	17,723
55 to 64 years old	10,992	10,014	2,269	2,042	1,409	1,875	1,094	750	378	197	12,381
65 yr. old and over	18,398	17,990	2,607	7,197	3,607	2,749	976	489	256	109	9,355
Northeast	21,185	19,248	4,071	3,960	2,656	3,554	2,368	1,561	765	314	12,482
Midwest	24,872	23,336	4,993	4,818	3,514	4,797	2,565	1,705	690	254	12,380
South	37,578	33,621	7,828	7,126	5,048	6,744	3,450	2,215	880	329	11,589
West	22,396	19,801	4,243	4,063	2,736	3,679	2,276	1,648	802	355	12,457
White	88,134	80,608	17,689	16,334	11,673	15,880	9,043	6,095	2,740	1,152	12,316
Black	13,292	11,607	2,493	2,930	1,765	2,241	1,180	717	240	41	10,961
Hispanic[2]	9,754	7,478	2,090	1,991	1,137	1,296	547	284	101	31	8,926
Education attainment of householder:[3]											
Total	87,984	82,457	14,591	16,915	12,148	17,204	10,226	7,050	3,093	1,231	13,821
Less than 9th grade	7,019	6,020	1,563	2,684	1,065	556	84	33	25	11	7,096
9th to 12th grade[4]	9,171	8,122	2,048	2,872	1,555	1,184	281	132	35	16	8,057
High school graduate[5]	30,911	28,785	5,436	6,617	5,000	6,944	2,853	1,357	426	153	12,046
Some college, no degree	15,203	14,619	2,372	2,439	2,265	3,670	2,168	1,172	394	141	15,552
Associate degree	6,868	6,642	896	853	817	1,651	1,224	822	303	77	19,450
Bachelor's degree or more	18,813	18,269	2,277	1,451	1,448	3,199	3,618	3,535	1,910	833	26,843
Bachelor's degree	13,321	12,875	1,814	1,146	1,157	2,544	2,623	2,144	1,053	393	24,065
Master's degree	4,288	4,205	396	210	219	552	832	1,117	648	236	33,509
Professional degree	745	732	45	69	45	74	89	145	120	146	38,588
Doctorate degree	459	457	22	27	27	30	74	129	90	60	39,821

[1] Includes persons with income deficit. [2] Persons of Hispanic origin may be of any race. [3] Persons 25 years old and over. [4] No diploma attained. [5] Includes high school equivalency.

Source: U.S. Bureau of the Census, *Current Population Reports*, P60-193; and Internet site, <http://ferret.bls.census.gov/cgi-bin/ferret> (accessed: 23 April 1997).

No. 733. Median Income of Married-Couple Families, by Work Experience of Husbands and Wives and Presence of Children: 1995

[As of March 1996. Based on Current Population Survey; see text, sections 1 and 14, and Appendix III. F.T.=full-time]

WORK EXPERIENCE OF HUSBAND OR WIFE	NUMBER (1,000)					MEDIAN INCOME (dollars)				
	All married-couple families	No related children	One or more related children under 18 years old			All married-couple families	No related children	One or more related children under 18 years old		
			Total	One child	Two children or more			Total	One child	Two children or more
All married-couple families	53,570	27,537	26,034	9,859	16,175	47,062	44,316	49,969	51,105	49,103
Husband worked	42,736	18,143	24,593	9,201	15,392	52,839	55,843	51,118	52,710	50,295
Wife worked	32,118	13,698	18,420	7,309	11,111	17,943	8,559	9,384	4,225	5,159
Wife year-round, f.t. worker	17,943	8,559	9,384	4,225	5,159	62,205	65,166	60,373	61,629	59,300
Wife did not work	10,618	4,445	6,173	1,892	4,281	39,700	41,777	37,518	36,105	38,126
Husband year-round, full-time worker	34,698	13,735	20,962	7,808	13,154	56,256	60,580	53,764	55,763	52,497
Wife worked	26,672	10,892	15,780	6,243	9,537	59,878	63,759	57,259	59,136	56,274
Wife year-round, f.t. worker	15,359	7,212	8,148	3,656	4,491	64,283	67,418	61,857	63,526	60,872
Wife did not work	8,025	2,843	5,182	1,565	3,617	43,128	46,704	41,146	40,044	41,671
Husband did not work	10,834	9,393	1,441	658	783	25,732	26,030	23,069	24,056	21,714
Wife worked	2,780	1,971	809	358	451	34,658	36,362	30,523	31,205	30,108
Wife year-round, f.t. worker	1,459	965	493	222	272	40,486	42,908	34,743	36,277	33,950
Wife did not work	8,054	7,422	632	300	332	23,205	23,851	15,466	17,158	14,065

No. 734. Average Earnings of Year-Round, Full-Time Workers, by Educational Attainment: 1995

[In dollars. For persons 18 years old and over as of March 1996]

AGE AND SEX	All workers	Less than 9th grade	HIGH SCHOOL		COLLEGE		
			9th to 12th grade (no diploma)	High school graduate (includes equivalency)	Some college, no degree	Associate degree	Bachelor's degree or more
Male, total	40,367	19,706	23,994	31,063	36,546	37,828	60,966
18 to 24 years old	18,389	15,137	15,186	17,816	18,586	20,450	25,674
25 to 34 years old	32,319	16,268	20,968	27,440	29,441	31,097	44,851
35 to 44 years old	44,523	19,824	26,229	32,689	39,268	41,433	68,326
45 to 54 years old	49,566	21,003	26,934	36,886	47,374	43,287	68,403
55 to 64 years old	45,848	23,149	31,128	36,546	45,092	45,203	67,874
65 years old and over	45,018	20,925	22,776	51,797	33,630	(B)	61,767
Female, total	26,547	14,546	16,686	21,298	23,750	28,510	37,269
18 to 24 years old	16,261	(B)	12,573	14,169	15,820	18,496	22,808
25 to 34 years old	25,145	13,538	14,665	20,091	21,589	25,870	33,332
35 to 44 years old	28,761	14,504	17,379	22,257	25,687	31,025	40,607
45 to 54 years old	28,801	14,810	17,904	22,982	28,018	29,765	40,176
55 to 64 years old	26,964	15,948	19,413	22,703	25,031	32,605	40,630
65 years old and over	23,295	(B)	(B)	22,117	22,264	(B)	36,395

B Base figure too small to meet statistical standards for reliability of derived figure.

No. 735. Per Capita Money Income in Current and Constant (1995) Dollars, by Race and Hispanic Origin: 1970 to 1995

[In dollars. Constant dollars based on CPI-U-X1 deflator. As of March of following year]

YEAR	CURRENT DOLLARS					CONSTANT (1995) DOLLARS				
	All races [1]	White	Black	Asian, Pacific Islander	Hispanic [2]	All races [1]	White	Black	Asian, Pacific Islander	Hispanic [2]
1970	3,177	3,354	1,869	(NA)	(NA)	11,723	12,377	6,897	(NA)	(NA)
1980	7,787	8,233	4,804	(NA)	4,865	14,420	15,246	8,896	(NA)	9,009
1985 [3]	11,013	11,671	6,840	(NA)	6,613	15,598	16,530	9,688	(NA)	9,366
1986	11,670	12,352	7,207	(NA)	7,000	16,227	17,176	10,021	(NA)	9,734
1987 [4]	12,391	13,143	7,645	(NA)	7,653	16,623	17,632	10,256	(NA)	10,267
1988	13,123	13,896	8,271	(NA)	7,956	16,906	17,902	10,655	(NA)	10,249
1989	14,056	14,896	8,747	(NA)	8,390	17,275	18,308	10,750	(NA)	10,312
1990	14,387	15,265	9,017	(NA)	8,424	16,776	17,799	10,514	(NA)	9,823
1991	14,617	15,510	9,170	(NA)	8,662	16,356	17,355	10,261	(NA)	9,692
1992 [5]	14,847	15,785	9,239	(NA)	8,591	16,127	17,146	10,036	(NA)	9,332
1993	15,777	16,800	9,863	15,691	8,830	16,640	17,718	10,402	16,549	9,313
1994	16,555	17,611	10,650	16,902	9,435	17,024	18,110	10,952	17,381	9,702
1995	$17,227	$18,304	$10,982	$16,567	$9,300	$17,227	$18,304	$10,982	$16,567	$9,300

NA Not available. [1] Includes other races not shown separately. [2] Persons of Hispanic origin may be of any race. [3] Beginning 1985, data based on revised Hispanic population controls [4] Beginning 1987, data based on revised processing procedures and not directly comparable with prior years. [5] Based on 1990 population controls.

Source of tables 733-735: U.S. Bureau of the Census, *Current Population Reports*, P60-193; and Internet site, (accessed 24 April 1997).

No. 736. Persons Below Poverty Level and Below 125 Percent of Poverty Level: 1960 to 1995

[Persons as of March of the following year. Based on Current Population Survey; see text, sections 1 and 14, and Appendix III]

YEAR	NUMBER BELOW POVERTY LEVEL (1,000)				PERCENT BELOW POVERTY LEVEL				BELOW 125 PERCENT OF POVERTY LEVEL		AVERAGE INCOME CUTOFFS FOR NONFARM FAMILY OF FOUR [3]	
	All races [1]	White	Black	Hispanic [2]	All races [1]	White	Black	Hispanic [2]	Number (1,000)	Percent of total population	At poverty level	At 125 percent of poverty level
1960	39,851	28,309	(NA)	(NA)	22.2	17.8	(NA)	(NA)	54,560	30.4	3,022	3,778
1970	25,420	17,484	7,548	(NA)	12.6	9.9	33.5	(NA)	35,624	17.6	3,968	4,960
1975	25,877	17,770	7,545	2,991	12.3	9.7	31.3	23.0	37,182	17.6	5,500	6,875
1976	24,975	16,713	7,595	2,783	11.8	9.1	31.1	26.9	35,509	16.7	5,815	7,269
1977	24,720	16,416	7,726	2,700	11.6	8.9	31.3	24.7	35,659	16.7	6,191	7,739
1978	24,497	16,259	7,625	2,607	11.4	8.7	30.6	22.4	34,155	15.8	6,662	8,328
1979 [4]	26,072	17,214	8,050	2,921	11.7	9.0	31.0	21.6	36,616	16.4	7,412	9,265
1980	29,272	19,699	8,579	3,491	13.0	10.2	32.5	21.8	40,658	18.1	8,414	10,518
1981	31,822	21,553	9,173	3,713	14.0	11.1	34.2	25.7	43,748	19.3	9,287	11,609
1982	34,398	23,517	9,697	4,301	15.0	12.0	35.6	26.5	46,520	20.3	9,862	12,328
1983 [5]	35,303	23,984	9,882	4,633	15.2	12.1	35.7	29.9	47,150	20.3	10,178	12,723
1984	33,700	22,955	9,490	4,806	14.4	11.5	33.8	28.0	45,288	19.4	10,609	13,261
1985	33,064	22,860	8,926	5,236	14.0	11.4	31.3	28.4	44,166	18.7	10,989	13,736
1986	32,370	22,183	8,983	5,117	13.6	11.0	31.1	29.0	43,486	18.2	11,203	14,004
1987 [6]	32,221	21,195	9,520	5,422	13.4	10.4	32.4	27.3	43,032	17.9	11,611	14,514
1988	31,745	20,715	9,356	5,357	13.0	10.1	31.3	28.0	42,551	17.5	12,092	15,115
1989	31,528	20,785	9,302	5,430	12.8	10.0	30.7	26.7	42,653	17.3	12,674	15,843
1990	33,585	22,326	9,837	6,006	13.5	10.7	31.9	28.2	44,837	18.0	13,359	16,699
1991	35,708	23,747	10,242	6,339	14.2	11.3	32.7	28.1	47,527	18.9	13,924	17,405
1992 [7]	38,014	25,259	10,827	7,592	14.8	11.9	33.4	29.6	50,592	19.7	14,335	17,919
1993	39,265	26,226	10,877	8,126	15.1	12.2	33.1	30.6	51,801	20.0	14,763	(NA)
1994	38,059	25,379	10,196	8,416	14.5	11.7	30.6	30.7	50,401	19.3	15,141	18,926
1995	36,425	24,423	9,872	8,574	13.8	11.2	29.3	30.3	48,761	18.5	15,569	19,461

NA Not available. [1] Includes other races not shown separately. [2] Persons of Hispanic origin may be of any race. [3] Beginning 1981, income cutoffs for nonfarm families are applied to all families, both farm and nonfarm. [4] Population controls based on 1980 census; see text, sections 1 and 14. [5] Beginning 1983, data based on revised Hispanic population controls and not directly comparable with prior years. [6] Beginning 1987, data based on revised processing procedures and not directly comparable with prior years. [7] Beginning 1992, based on 1990 population controls.

Source: U.S. Bureau of the Census, *Current Population Reports*, P60-194.

No. 737. Children Below Poverty Level, by Race and Hispanic Origin: 1970 to 1995

[Persons as of March of the following year. Covers only related children in families under 18 years old. Based on Current Population Survey; see text, sections 1 and 14, and Appendix III]

YEAR	NUMBER BELOW POVERTY LEVEL (1,000)				PERCENT BELOW POVERTY LEVEL			
	All races [1]	White	Black	Hispanic [2]	All races [1]	White	Black	Hispanic [2]
1970	10,235	6,138	3,922	(NA)	14.9	10.5	41.5	(NA)
1980	11,114	6,817	3,906	1,718	17.9	13.4	42.1	33.0
1981	12,068	7,429	4,170	1,874	19.5	14.7	44.9	35.4
1982	13,139	8,282	4,388	2,117	21.3	16.5	47.3	38.9
1983 [3]	13,427	8,534	4,273	2,251	21.8	17.0	46.2	37.7
1984	12,929	8,086	4,320	2,317	21.0	16.1	46.2	38.7
1985	12,483	7,838	4,057	2,512	20.1	15.6	43.1	39.6
1986	12,257	7,714	4,037	2,413	19.8	15.3	42.7	37.1
1987 [4]	12,275	7,398	4,234	2,606	19.7	14.7	44.4	38.9
1988	11,935	7,095	4,148	2,576	19.0	14.0	42.8	37.3
1989	12,001	7,164	4,257	2,496	19.0	14.1	43.2	35.5
1990	12,715	7,696	4,412	2,750	19.9	15.1	44.2	37.7
1991	13,658	8,316	4,637	2,977	21.1	16.1	45.6	39.8
1992 [5]	14,521	8,752	5,015	3,440	21.6	16.5	46.3	39.0
1993	14,961	9,123	5,030	3,666	22.0	17.0	45.9	39.9
1994	14,610	8,826	4,787	3,956	21.2	16.3	43.3	41.1
1995	13,999	8,474	4,644	3,938	20.0	15.5	41.5	39.3

NA Not available. [1] Includes other races not shown separately. [2] Persons of Hispanic origin may be of any race. [3] Beginning 1983, data based on revised Hispanic population controls and not directly comparable with prior years. [4] Beginning 1987, data based on revised processing procedures and not directly comparable with prior years. [5] Beginning 1992, based on 1990 population controls.

Source: U.S. Bureau of the Census, *Current Population Reports*, P60-194.

No. 738. Weighted Average Poverty Thresholds: 1980 to 1995

[Official poverty thresholds; see text, section 14]

SIZE OF UNIT	1980[1]	1988	1989	1990	1991	1992	1993	1994	1995
One person (unrelated individual)	$4,190	$6,022	$6,310	$6,652	$6,932	$7,143	$7,363	$7,547	$7,763
Under 65 years	4,290	6,155	6,451	6,800	7,086	7,299	$7,518	7,710	7,929
65 years and over	3,949	5,674	5,947	6,268	6,532	6,729	6,930	7,108	7,309
Two persons	5,363	7,704	8,076	8,509	8,865	9,137	9,414	9,661	9,933
Householder under 65 years	5,537	7,958	8,343	8,794	9,165	9,443	9,728	9,976	10,259
Householder 65 years and over	4,983	7,157	7,501	7,905	8,241	8,487	8,740	8,967	9,219
Three persons	6,565	9,435	9,885	10,419	10,860	11,186	11,522	11,821	12,158
Four persons	8,414	12,092	12,674	13,359	13,924	14,335	14,763	15,141	15,569
Five persons	9,966	14,304	14,990	15,792	16,456	16,952	17,449	17,900	18,408
Six persons	11,269	16,146	16,921	17,839	18,587	19,137	19,718	20,235	20,804
Seven persons	12,761	18,232	19,162	20,241	21,058	21,594	22,383	22,923	23,552
Eight persons	14,199	20,253	21,328	22,582	23,605	24,053	24,838	25,427	26,237
Nine or more persons	16,896	24,129	25,480	26,848	27,942	28,745	29,529	30,300	31,280

[1] Poverty levels for nonfarm families.

Source: U.S. Bureau of the Census, *Current Population Reports*, P60-194; and earlier reports.

No. 739. Persons Below Poverty Level, by Selected Characteristics: 1995

[Persons as of March 1996. Based on Current Population Survey; see text, sections 1 and 14, and Appendix III. For composition of regions, see table 27]

AGE AND REGION	NUMBER BELOW POVERTY LEVEL (1,000)				PERCENT BELOW POVERTY LEVEL			
	All races [1]	White	Black	Hispanic [2]	All races [1]	White	Black	Hispanic [2]
Total	**36,425**	**24,423**	**9,872**	**8,574**	**13.8**	**11.2**	**29.3**	**30.3**
Under 18 years old	14,665	8,981	4,761	4,080	20.8	16.2	41.9	40.0
18 to 24 years old	4,553	3,156	1,117	1,097	18.3	15.9	30.5	30.6
25 to 34 years old	5,196	3,601	1,304	1,325	12.7	10.8	24.4	24.7
35 to 44 years old	4,064	2,812	995	942	9.4	7.9	18.8	23.2
45 to 54 years old	2,470	1,683	630	429	7.8	6.3	18.2	19.7
55 to 59 years old	1,163	840	246	186	10.3	8.7	21.4	23.0
60 to 64 years old	996	777	191	174	10.2	9.2	19.5	26.4
65 years old and over	3,318	2,572	629	342	10.5	9.0	25.4	23.5
65 to 74 years old	1,573	1,196	301	213	8.6	7.3	20.3	21.7
75 years old and over	1,745	1,375	328	129	13.0	11.3	32.9	27.1
Northeast	6,445	4,289	1,878	1,586	12.5	9.9	30.8	36.5
Midwest	6,785	4,665	1,873	403	11.0	8.6	30.7	21.3
South	14,458	8,712	5,283	2,831	15.7	12.2	28.5	30.4
West	8,736	6,757	837	3,755	14.9	13.8	28.0	29.4

[1] Includes other races not shown separately. [2] Persons of Hispanic origin may be of any race.

Source: U.S. Bureau of the Census, *Current Population Reports*, P60-194; and unpublished data.

No. 740. Persons 65 Years Old and Over Below Poverty Level: 1970 to 1995

[Persons as of March of following year]

CHARACTERISTIC	NUMBER BELOW POVERTY LEVEL (1,000)					PERCENT BELOW POVERTY LEVEL				
	1970	1979 [1]	1990 [2]	1994	1995	1970	1970 [1]	1990 [2]	1994	1995
Total [3]	**4,793**	**3,682**	**3,658**	**3,663**	**3,318**	**24.6**	**15.2**	**12.2**	11.7	**10.5**
White	4,011	2,911	2,707	2,846	2,572	22.6	13.3	10.1	10.2	9.0
Black	683	740	860	700	629	48.0	36.2	33.8	27.4	25.4
Hispanic [4]	(NA)	154	245	323	342	(NA)	26.8	22.5	22.6	23.5
In families	2,013	1,380	1,172	1,254	1,058	14.8	8.4	5.8	6.0	5.0
Unrelated individuals	2,779	2,299	2,479	2,409	2,260	47.2	29.4	24.7	23.1	21.4

NA Not available. [1] Population controls based on 1980 census; see text, section 14. [2] Beginning 1987, data based on revised processing procedures and not directly comparable with prior years. [3] Beginning 1979, includes members of unrelated subfamilies not shown separately. For earlier years, unrelated subfamily members are included in the "in families" category. [4] Persons of Hispanic origin may be of any race.

Source: U.S. Bureau of the Census, *Current Population Reports*, P60-194; and earlier reports.

No. 741. Persons Below Poverty Level, by State: 1980 to 1995

on the Current Population Survey; see text, sections 1 and 14, and Appendix III. The CPS is designed to collect reliable income primarily at the national level and secondarily at the regional level. When the income data are tabulated by State, imates are considered less reliable and, therefore, particular caution should be used when trying to interpret the results; for nal detail, see source]

STATE	NUMBER BELOW POVERTY LEVEL (1,000)					PERCENT BELOW POVERTY LEVEL				
	1980	1990 [1]	1993	1994	1995	1980	1990 [1]	1993	1994	1995
ed States	**29,272**	**33,585**	**39,265**	**38,059**	**36,425**	**13.0**	**13.5**	**15.1**	**14.5**	**13.8**
na.	810	779	725	704	882	21.2	19.2	17.4	16.4	20.1
	36	57	52	61	45	9.6	11.4	9.1	10.2	7.1
a.	354	484	615	673	700	12.8	13.7	15.4	15.9	16.1
as	484	472	484	369	376	21.5	19.6	20.0	15.3	14.9
nia	2,619	4,128	5,803	5,658	5,342	11.0	13.9	18.2	17.9	16.7
do.	247	461	354	335	336	8.6	13.7	9.9	9.0	8.8
cticut.	255	196	277	344	318	8.3	6.0	8.5	10.8	9.7
are	68	48	73	57	74	11.8	6.9	10.2	8.3	10.3
of Columbia	131	120	158	129	122	20.9	21.1	26.4	21.2	22.2
	1,692	1,896	2,507	2,128	2,321	16.7	14.4	17.8	14.9	16.2
a	727	1,001	919	1,012	878	13.9	15.8	13.5	14.0	12.1
	81	121	91	97	122	8.5	11.0	8.0	8.7	10.3
	138	157	150	137	167	14.7	14.9	13.1	12.0	14.5
	1,386	1,606	1,600	1,464	1,459	12.3	13.7	13.6	12.4	12.4
1.	645	714	704	816	545	11.8	13.0	12.2	13.7	9.6
	311	289	290	302	352	10.8	10.4	10.3	10.7	12.2
s.	215	259	327	375	273	9.4	10.3	13.1	14.9	10.8
ky	701	626	763	710	572	19.3	17.3	20.4	18.5	14.7
na	868	952	1,119	1,117	849	20.3	23.6	26.4	25.7	19.7
	156	162	196	113	136	14.6	13.1	15.4	9.4	11.2
nd	389	468	479	541	520	9.5	9.9	9.7	10.7	10.1
chusetts.	542	626	641	585	665	9.5	10.7	10.7	9.7	11.0
an.	1,194	1,315	1,475	1,347	1,174	12.9	14.3	15.4	14.1	12.2
sota.	342	524	506	523	427	8.7	12.0	11.6	11.7	9.2
ippi	591	684	639	515	630	24.3	25.7	24.7	19.9	23.5
ri	625	700	832	797	484	13.0	13.4	16.1	15.6	9.4
na.	102	134	127	97	133	13.2	16.3	14.9	11.5	15.3
ska	199	167	169	146	159	13.0	10.3	10.3	8.8	9.6
a	70	119	141	166	173	8.3	9.8	9.8	11.1	11.1
ampshire	63	68	112	87	60	7.0	6.3	9.9	7.7	5.3
ersey	659	711	866	730	617	9.0	9.2	10.9	9.2	7.8
lexico	268	319	282	356	457	20.6	20.9	17.4	21.1	25.3
ork	2,391	2,571	2,981	3,097	3,020	13.8	14.3	16.4	17.0	16.5
Carolina	877	829	966	980	877	15.0	13.0	14.4	14.2	12.6
Dakota	99	87	70	65	76	15.5	13.7	11.2	10.4	12.0
	1,046	1,256	1,461	1,571	1,285	9.8	11.5	13.0	14.1	11.5
ma.	406	481	662	540	548	13.9	15.6	19.9	16.7	17.1
n.	309	267	363	373	360	11.5	9.2	11.8	11.8	11.2
ylvania.	1,142	1,328	1,598	1,496	1,464	9.8	11.0	13.2	12.5	12.2
Island.	97	71	108	99	102	10.7	7.5	11.2	10.3	10.6
Carolina.	534	548	678	501	744	16.8	16.2	18.7	13.8	19.9
Dakota	127	93	102	107	103	18.8	13.3	14.2	14.5	14.5
ssee	884	833	998	779	846	19.6	16.9	19.6	14.6	15.5
	2,247	2,684	3,177	3,603	3,270	15.7	15.9	17.4	19.1	17.4
	146	143	203	154	168	10.0	8.2	10.7	8.0	8.4
nt	62	61	59	45	61	12.0	10.9	10.0	7.6	10.3
a.	647	705	627	710	648	12.4	11.1	9.7	10.7	10.2
ngton.	536	434	634	614	677	12.7	8.9	12.1	11.7	12.5
irginia.	297	328	400	336	300	15.2	18.1	22.2	18.6	16.7
sin.	403	448	636	453	449	8.5	9.3	12.6	9.0	8.5
ng	49	51	64	45	59	10.4	11.0	13.3	9.3	12.2

[1] Beginning 1990, data based on revised processing procedures and not directly comparable with prior years.

Source: U.S. Bureau of the Census, *Current Population Reports*, P60-194.

No. 742. Persons Below Poverty Level, by Race and Family Status: 1979 to 1995

[Persons as of March of following year. Based on Current Population Survey; see text, sections 1 and 14, and Appendix III]

RACE AND FAMILY STATUS	NUMBER BELOW POVERTY LEVEL (mil.)					PERCENT BELOW POVERTY LEVEL				
	1979 [1]	1990 [2]	1993 [3]	1994	1995	1979 [1]	1990 [2]	1993 [3]	1994	1995
All persons [4]	**26.1**	**33.6**	**39.3**	**38.1**	**36.4**	**11.7**	**13.5**	**15.1**	**14.5**	**13.8**
In families	20.0	25.2	30.0	29.0	27.5	10.2	12.0	13.6	13.1	12.3
Householder	5.5	7.1	8.4	8.1	7.5	9.2	10.7	12.3	11.6	10.8
Related children under 18 years	10.0	12.7	15.0	14.6	14.0	16.0	19.9	22.0	21.2	20.2
Unrelated individuals	5.7	7.4	8.4	8.3	8.2	21.9	20.7	22.1	21.5	20.9
Male	2.0	2.9	3.3	3.3	3.4	16.9	16.9	18.1	17.8	18.0
Female	3.8	4.6	5.1	5.0	4.9	26.0	24.0	25.7	24.9	23.5
White [4]	**17.2**	**22.3**	**26.2**	**25.4**	**24.4**	**9.0**	**10.7**	**12.2**	**11.7**	**11.2**
In families	12.5	15.9	19.0	18.5	17.6	7.4	9.0	10.5	10.1	9.6
Householder	3.6	4.6	5.5	5.3	5.0	6.9	8.1	9.4	9.1	8.5
Related children under 18 years	5.9	7.7	9.1	8.8	8.5	11.4	15.1	17.0	16.3	15.5
Unrelated individuals	4.5	5.7	6.4	6.3	6.3	19.7	18.6	20.1	19.3	19.0
Black [4]	**8.1**	**9.8**	**10.9**	**10.2**	**9.9**	**31.0**	**31.9**	**33.1**	**30.6**	**29.3**
In families	6.8	8.2	9.2	8.4	8.2	30.0	31.0	32.9	29.6	28.5
Householder	1.7	2.2	2.5	2.2	2.1	27.8	29.3	31.3	27.3	26.4
Related children under 18 years	3.7	4.4	5.0	4.8	4.6	40.8	44.2	45.9	43.3	41.5
Unrelated individuals	1.2	1.5	1.5	1.6	1.6	37.3	35.1	33.4	34.8	32.6
In families with female householder, no spouse present	9.4	12.6	14.6	14.4	14.2	34.9	37.2	38.7	38.6	36.5
Householder	2.6	3.8	4.4	4.2	4.1	30.4	33.4	35.6	34.6	32.4
Related children under 18 years	5.6	7.4	8.5	8.4	8.4	48.6	53.4	53.7	52.9	50.3

[1] Population controls based on 1980 census; see text, section 14. [2] Beginning 1990, data based on revised processing procedures and not directly comparable with prior years. [3] Population controls based on 1990 census. [4] Includes other races and members of unrelated subfamilies not shown separately.

Source: U.S. Bureau of the Census, *Current Population Reports*, P60-194; and earlier reports.

No. 743. Monthly Measures of Poverty Status, by Selected Characteristics: 1992-93 Period

[Covers two-year calendar period. Based on Survey of Income and Program Participation, see text, section 14]

CHARACTERISTIC	PERSONS POOR IN AN AVERAGE MONTH OF 1992		PERSONS POOR 2 OR MORE MONTHS OF 1992		PERSONS POOR ALL 24 MONTHS OF 1992-93		Median duration of poverty spells (months)
	Number (1,000)	Percent	Number (1,000)	Percent	Number (1,000)	Percent	
Total [1]	**37,597**	**14.8**	**52,725**	**20.8**	**11,887**	**4.8**	**4.9**
Under 18 years old	15,464	22.3	20,782	30.3	5,659	8.3	5.2
18 to 64 years old	18,999	12.0	28,066	18.1	4,907	3.2	4.7
65 years old and over	3,134	10.2	3,877	13.3	1,321	4.9	7.2
White	25,474	11.8	37,195	17.6	6,480	3.1	4.6
Black	10,346	31.7	13,199	41.1	4,682	15.1	6.2
Hispanic origin [2]	7,553	29.0	10,022	40.0	2,383	10.3	5.8
Region: [3]							
Northeast	6,845	13.3	9,320	18.4	2,560	5.2	5.3
Midwest	8,718	13.3	12,656	19.4	2,668	4.2	5.2
South	14,346	16.4	19,909	23.0	4,939	5.8	5.2
West	7,688	14.5	10,840	21.4	1,720	3.5	4.0
Educational attainment: [4]							
Less than 4 years of high school	9,224	23.9	12,122	32.4	3,424	9.5	6.5
High school graduate, no college	7,977	11.3	11,853	17.2	2,056	3.0	4.7
One or more years of college	4,931	6.2	7,968	10.2	749	1.0	3.8
Disability status: [5]							
With a work disability	5,919	21.6	7,984	31.4	2,072	8.2	6.2
With no work disability	15,787	10.5	23,874	15.9	3,595	2.5	4.3

[1] Includes other characteristics not shown separately. [2] Persons of Hispanic origin may be of any race. [3] For composition of regions, see table 27. [4] Persons 18 years old and over. [5] Persons 15 to 69 years old.

Source: U.S. Bureau of the Census, *Current Population Reports*, P70-45.

No. 744. Families Below Poverty Level and Below 125 Percent of Poverty Level: 1960 to 1995

'amilies as of March of the following year. Based on Current Population Survey, see text, sections 1 and 14, and Appendix III]

'EAR	NUMBER BELOW POVERTY LEVEL (1,000)				PERCENT BELOW POVERTY LEVEL				BELOW 125 PERCENT OF POVERTY LEVEL	
	All races [1]	White	Black	Hispanic [2]	All races [1]	White	Black	Hispanic [2]	Number (1,000)	Percent
....	8,243	6,115	(NA)	(NA)	18.1	14.9	(NA)	(NA)	11,525	25.4
....	5,260	3,708	1,481	(NA)	10.1	8.0	29.5	(NA)	7,516	14.4
....	5,303	3,751	1,484	(NA)	10.0	7.9	28.8	(NA)	(NA)	(NA)
....	5,075	3,441	1,529	477	9.3	7.1	29.0	20.6	7,347	13.5
....	4,828	3,219	1,527	468	8.8	6.6	28.1	19.8	7,044	12.8
....	4,922	3,352	1,479	526	8.8	6.8	26.9	21.2	7,195	12.9
....	5,450	3,838	1,513	627	9.7	7.7	27.1	25.1	7,974	14.2
....	5,311	3,560	1,617	598	9.4	7.1	27.9	23.1	7,647	13.5
....	5,311	3,540	1,637	591	9.3	7.0	28.2	21.4	7,713	13.5
....	5,280	3,523	1,622	559	9.1	6.9	27.5	20.4	7,417	12.8
....	5,461	3,581	1,722	614	9.2	6.9	27.8	20.3	7,784	13.1
....	6,217	4,195	1,826	751	10.3	8.0	28.9	23.2	8,784	14.5
....	6,851	4,670	1,972	792	11.2	8.8	30.8	24.0	9,568	15.7
....	7,512	5,118	2,158	916	12.2	9.6	33.0	27.2	10,279	16.7
....	7,647	5,220	2,161	981	12.3	9.7	32.3	25.9	10,358	16.7
....	7,277	4,925	2,094	991	11.6	9.1	30.9	25.2	9,901	15.8
....	7,223	4,983	1,983	1,074	11.4	9.1	28.7	25.5	9,753	15.3
....	7,023	4,811	1,987	1,085	10.9	8.6	28.0	24.7	9,476	14.7
....	7,005	4,567	2,117	1,168	10.7	8.1	29.4	25.5	9,338	14.3
....	6,874	4,471	2,089	1,141	10.4	7.9	28.2	23.7	9,284	14.1
....	6,784	4,409	2,077	1,133	10.3	7.8	27.8	23.4	9,267	14.0
....	7,098	4,622	2,193	1,244	10.7	8.1	29.3	25.0	9,564	14.4
....	7,712	5,022	2,343	1,372	11.5	8.8	30.4	26.5	10,244	15.3
....	8,144	5,255	2,484	1,529	11.9	9.1	31.1	26.7	10,959	16.1
....	8,393	5,452	2,499	1,625	12.3	9.4	31.3	27.3	11,203	16.4
....	8,053	5,312	2,212	1,724	11.6	9.1	27.3	27.8	10,771	15.5
....	7,532	4,994	2,127	1,695	10.8	8.5	26.4	27.0	10,223	14.7

\ Not available. [1] Includes other races not shown separately. [2] Persons of Hispanic origin may be of any race. lation controls based on 1980 census; see text, section 14. [4] Beginning 1983, data based on revised Hispanic population s and not directly comparable with prior years. [5] Beginning 1987, data based on revised processing procedures and not ' comparable with prior years. [6] Beginning 1992, based on 1990 population controls.

ource: U.S. Bureau of the Census, *Current Population Reports*, P60-194.

No. 745. Families Below Poverty Level, by Selected Characteristics: 1995

[Families as of March 1996. Based on Current Population Survey; see text, sections 1 and 14, and Appendix III]

CHARACTERISTIC	NUMBER BELOW POVERTY LEVEL (1,000)				PERCENT BELOW POVERTY LEVEL			
	All races [1]	White	Black	Hispanic [2]	All races [1]	White	Black	Hispanic [2]
Total	**7,532**	**4,994**	**2,127**	**1,695**	**10.8**	**8.5**	**26.4**	**27.0**
householder:								
o 24 years old	993	653	294	255	33.6	28.4	55.6	44.9
o 34 years old	2,286	1,457	719	571	16.7	13.0	36.9	30.9
o 44 years old	1,959	1,301	536	473	10.6	8.4	23.5	26.5
o 54 years old	947	606	271	183	6.8	5.1	18.3	19.2
o 64 years old	706	521	152	114	7.7	6.6	16.8	19.1
ears old and over	618	443	151	92	5.5	4.4	17.0	17.8
ion of householder: [3]								
igh school diploma	2,776	1,867	752	967	24.1	20.3	39.5	35.7
school diploma, no college	2,113	1,371	641	297	9.8	7.5	24.3	20.6
e college, less than Bachelor's degree	1,222	780	383	144	7.2	5.4	18.9	13.8
helor's degree or more	403	309	53	27	2.4	2.1	5.6	5.3
xperience of householder:								
otal [4]	6,909	4,548	1,976	1,604	11.9	9.3	27.6	27.8
ked during year	3,768	2,658	934	901	7.5	6.2	16.9	19.4
ear-round, full-time	1,392	1,003	322	406	3.6	3.0	8.1	12.2
ot year-round, full-time	2,375	1,656	612	495	20.5	17.3	39.4	38.0
not work	3,141	1,890	1,042	703	39.2	31.6	63.9	62.0

ncludes other races not shown separately. [2] Hispanic persons may be of any race. [3] Householder 25 years old and [4] Persons 16 years old and over.

ource: U.S. Bureau of the Census, *Current Population Reports*, P60-194; and unpublished data.

No. 746. Persons Below Poverty Level, by Definition of Income: 1995

[Persons as of March 1996. For explanation of income definitions, see text, section 14]

Definition number	DEFINITION	NUMBER BELOW POVERTY LEVEL (1,000)				PERCENT BELOW POVERTY LEVEL			
		All races [1]	White	Black	Hispanic [2]	All races [1]	White	Black	Hispanic [2]
	All persons	263,733	218,028	33,740	28,344	(X)	(X)	(X)	(X)
	INCOME BEFORE TAXES								
1	Money income excluding capital gains [3]	36,425	24,423	9,872	8,574	13.8	11.2	29.3	30.3
2	Definition 1 less government money transfers	57,643	42,285	12,563	10,380	21.9	19.4	37.2	36.6
3	Definition 2 plus capital gains	57,515	42,149	12,567	10,385	21.8	19.3	37.2	36.6
4	Definition 3 plus health insurance supplements to wage or salary income [4]	55,558	40,743	12,117	9,960	21.1	18.7	35.9	36.1
	INCOME AFTER TAXES								
5	Definition 4 less Social Security payroll taxes	57,930	42,605	12,555	10,453	22.0	19.5	37.2	36.9
6	Definition 5 less Federal income taxes (excluding EITC) [5]	58,388	42,936	12,643	10,540	22.1	19.7	37.5	37.2
7	Definition 6 plus EITC [5]	55,061	40,449	11,980	9,764	20.9	18.6	35.5	34.4
8	Definition 7 less State income taxes	55,505	40,788	12,059	9,807	21.0	18.7	35.7	34.6
9	Definition 8 plus nonmeans-tested government cash transfers [6]	37,176	24,685	10,262	8,564	14.1	11.3	30.4	30.2
10	Definition 9 plus value of Medicare	36,193	23,998	9,979	8,423	13.7	11.0	29.6	29.7
11	Definition 10 plus value of regular-price school lunches	36,177	23,992	9,970	8,423	13.7	11.0	29.5	29.7
12	Definition 11 plus means-tested government cash transfers [7]	33,062	22,160	8,945	7,818	12.5	10.2	26.5	27.6
13	Definition 12 plus value of Medicaid	30,871	20,725	8,324	7,198	11.7	9.5	24.7	25.4
14	Definition 13 plus means-tested government noncash transfers [8]	27,190	18,492	7,048	6,307	10.3	8.5	20.9	22.3
15	Definition 14 plus net imputed return on equity in own home [9]	24,823	16,647	6,600	6,009	9.4	7.6	19.6	21.2

X Not applicable. [1] Includes other races not shown separately. [2] Persons of Hispanic origin may be of any race. [3] Official definition based on income before taxes and includes government cash transfers. [4] Employer contributions to the health insurance plans of employees. [5] Earned Income Tax Credit. [6] Includes Social Security and Railroad Retirement, veterans payments, unemployment and workers' compensation, Black Lung payments, Pell Grants, and other government educational assistance. [7] Includes AFDC and other public assistance or welfare payments, Supplemental Security Income, and veterans payments. Households must meet certain eligibility requirements in order to qualify for these benefits. [8] Includes Medicaid, food stamps, subsidies from free or reduced-price school lunches, and rent subsidies. [9] Estimated amount of income a household would receive if it chose to shift amount held as home equity into an interest bearing account.

Source: U.S. Bureau of the Census, *Current Population Reports*, P60-194.

No. 747. Family Net Worth—Mean and Median Net Worth in Constant (1995) Dollars, by Selected Family Characteristics: 1989 to 1995

[Net worth in thousands of constant (1995) dollars. Constant dollar figures are based on consumer price index for all urban consumers published by U.S. Bureau of Labor Statistics. Families include one-person units and as used in this table are comparable to the Bureau of Census household concept. Based on Survey of Consumer Finance; see Appendix III. For definition of median, see Guide to Tabular Presentation]

FAMILY CHARACTERISTIC	1989			1992			1995		
	Percent of families	Net worth Mean	Net worth Median	Percent of families	Net worth Mean	Net worth Median	Percent of families	Net worth Mean	Net worth Median
All families	**100.0**	**216.7**	**56.5**	**100.0**	**200.5**	**52.8**	**100.0**	**205.9**	**56.4**
Age of family head:									
Under 35 years old	27.2	66.3	9.2	25.8	50.3	10.1	24.8	47.2	11.4
35 to 44 years old	23.4	171.3	69.2	22.8	144.3	46.0	23.2	144.5	48.5
45 to 54 years old	14.4	338.9	114.0	16.2	287.8	83.4	17.8	277.8	90.5
55 to 64 years old	13.9	334.4	110.5	13.2	358.6	122.5	12.5	356.2	110.8
65 to 74 years old	12.0	336.8	88.4	12.6	308.3	105.8	11.9	331.6	104.1
75 years old and over	9.0	250.8	83.2	9.4	231.0	92.8	9.8	276.0	95.0
Family income in constant (1995) dollars:[1]									
Less than $10,000	15.4	26.1	1.6	15.5	30.9	3.3	16.0	45.6	4.8
$10,000 to $24,999	24.3	77.9	25.6	27.8	71.2	28.2	26.5	74.6	30.0
$25,000 to $49,999	30.3	121.8	56.0	29.5	124.4	54.8	31.1	119.3	54.9
$50,000 to $99,999	22.3	229.5	128.1	20.0	240.8	121.2	20.2	256.0	121.1
$100,000 and more	7.7	1,372.9	474.7	7.1	1,283.6	506.1	6.1	1,465.2	485.9
Education of householder:									
No high school diploma	24.3	92.1	28.5	20.4	75.8	21.6	19.0	87.2	26.3
High school diploma	32.1	134.4	43.4	29.9	120.6	41.4	31.6	138.2	50.0
Some college	15.1	213.8	56.4	17.7	185.4	62.6	19.0	186.6	43.2
College degree	28.5	416.9	132.1	31.9	363.3	103.1	30.5	361.8	104.1
Tenure:									
Owner occupied	63.8	311.7	119.9	63.9	289.6	106.1	64.7	295.4	102.3
Renter occupied or other	36.2	49.4	2.4	36.1	42.7	3.6	35.3	42.2	4.5

[1] Income for year preceding the survey.

Source: Board of Governors of the Federal Reserve System, *Federal Reserve Bulletin*, January 1997.

No. 748. Nonfinancial Assets Held by Families, by Type of Asset: 1995

lue in thousands of dollars. Constant dollar figures are based on consumer price index for all urban consumers pub-
S. Bureau of Labor Statistics. Families include one-person units and, as used in this table, are comparable to the Bureau
ousehold concept. for definition of family, see text, section 1. Based on Survey of Consumer Finance; see Appendix
on financial assets, see table 778. For definition of median, see Guide to Tabular Presentation]

OF FAMILY HEAD FAMILY INCOME	Any nonfinancial asset	Vehicles	Primary residence	Investment real estate	Business	Other nonfinancial
CENT OF FAMILIES WNING ASSET						
total	91.1	84.2	64.7	17.8	11.0	9.0
ly head:						
years old	87.6	83.9	37.9	7.2	9.3	7.6
years old	90.9	85.1	64.6	14.4	13.9	10.2
years old	93.7	88.2	75.4	23.9	14.8	10.7
years old	94.0	88.7	82.1	26.9	11.7	9.8
years old	92.5	82.0	79.0	26.5	7.9	8.9
old and over	90.2	72.8	73.0	16.6	3.8	5.4
me:						
n $10,000	69.8	57.7	37.6	6.9	4.8	3.8
to $24,999	89.4	82.7	55.4	11.5	6.2	6.2
to $49,999	96.6	92.2	68.4	16.5	9.8	9.6
to $99,999	99.1	93.3	84.4	24.9	17.5	11.5
and more	99.4	90.2	91.1	52.3	32.1	22.6
rk status of householder:						
nal, managerial	96.7	90.8	71.1	24.6	11.8	14.5
l, sales, clerical	92.9	88.0	63.4	10.5	6.4	10.6
production	97.2	93.4	66.9	16.2	7.3	9.0
operators and laborers	93.8	91.9	61.2	14.0	5.1	6.5
occupations	86.9	83.8	50.5	8.6	3.5	2.0
loyed	96.1	85.7	73.9	32.1	58.0	16.1
	88.3	76.6	70.3	18.6	2.9	5.6
t working	67.9	60.6	34.8	8.0	3.7	5.9
ccupied	100.0	90.8	100.0	22.3	13.4	10.3
ccupied or other	74.8	72.2	0.0	8.7	6.4	6.5
EDIAN VALUE [1]						
total	83.0	10.0	90.0	50.0	41.0	10.0
ly head:						
years old	21.5	9.0	80.0	33.5	20.0	5.0
years old	95.6	10.7	95.0	45.0	35.0	9.0
years old	111.7	12.4	100.0	55.0	60.0	12.0
years old	107.0	11.9	85.0	82.5	75.0	10.0
years old	93.5	8.0	80.0	55.0	100.0	16.0
old and over	79.0	5.3	80.0	20.0	30.0	15.0
me:						
n $10,000	13.1	3.6	40.0	16.2	50.6	2.5
$24,999	44.5	6.1	65.0	30.0	30.0	8.0
$49,999	81.5	11.1	80.0	40.0	26.3	6.0
$99,999	145.2	16.2	120.0	57.3	30.0	14.0
nd more	319.3	22.8	200.0	130.0	300.0	20.0
rk status of householder:						
nal, managerial	133.5	12.4	130.0	57.3	15.0	10.0
l, sales, clerical	83.1	10.4	90.0	40.0	17.5	10.0
production	72.9	12.2	78.0	37.5	30.0	5.0
operators and laborers	57.9	10.8	68.0	36.0	24.0	8.0
occupations	35.8	7.2	69.0	17.5	80.2	10.0
loyed	175.6	12.0	120.0	100.0	71.0	8.0
	78.0	7.3	76.0	45.0	90.0	10.0
t working	17.4	6.2	80.0	59.0	12.0	7.0
ccupied	115.4	11.9	90.0	53.0	50.0	10.0
ccupied or other	7.5	6.4	(B)	35.0	26.0	5.0

an value of financial asset for families holding such assets.

: Board of Governors of the Federal Reserve System, *Federal Reserve Bulletin*, January 1997.

No. 749. Household and Nonprofit Organization Sector Balance Sheet: 1980 to 1993

[In billions of dollars. As of December 31. For details of financial assets and liabilities, see table 777]

ITEM	1980	1985	1986	1987	1988	1989	1990	1991	1992	1993
Assets	11,109	16,271	17,781	19,036	20,448	22,510	22,797	24,820	26,022	27,511
Tangible assets	4,703	6,603	7,100	7,656	8,103	8,709	8,775	9,286	9,557	9,973
Reproducible assets	3,339	4,392	4,758	5,157	5,409	5,774	6,107	6,358	6,662	7,067
Residential structures	2,109	2,693	2,903	3,148	3,223	3,440	3,633	3,777	3,975	4,239
Owner-occupied housing	2,062	2,634	2,841	3,082	3,157	3,370	3,560	3,704	3,902	4,164
Nonprofit institutions	47	58	62	66	67	70	73	73	73	75
Nonprofit plant & equipment	216	306	328	350	377	404	427	443	464	493
Consumer durable goods	1,014	1,391	1,527	1,660	1,808	1,930	2,047	2,139	2,222	2,336
Land	1,364	2,211	2,343	2,499	2,694	2,935	2,668	2,928	2,895	2,906
Owner-occupied [1]	1,227	2,016	2,138	2,287	2,463	2,688	2,456	2,780	2,807	2,836
Nonprofit institutions	137	195	205	211	231	247	212	148	88	70
Financial assets	6,406	9,668	10,680	11,380	12,346	13,802	14,023	15,534	16,465	17,538
Liabilities	1,443	2,333	2,602	2,859	3,174	3,496	3,738	3,920	4,143	4,464
Home mortgages	905	1,379	1,574	1,795	2,023	2,253	2,455	2,614	2,768	2,970
Net worth	9,666	13,938	15,178	16,177	17,274	19,014	19,059	20,900	21,879	23,047
Addendum:										
Owner-occupied real estate [2]	3,289	4,650	4,978	5,369	5,620	6,059	6,016	6,484	6,709	7,000
Home mortgages as percent of owner-occupied real estate	28	30	32	33	36	37	41	40	42	42

[1] Includes vacant land. [2] Owner-occupied housing plus owner-occupied land.

Source: Board of Governors of the Federal Reserve System, *Balance Sheets for the U.S. Economy.*

No. 750. Stock of Fixed Reproducible Tangible Wealth: 1980 to 1995

[In billions of dollars. As of December 31]

ITEM	1980	1985	1988	1989	1990	1991	1992	1993	1994	1995
CURRENT DOLLARS										
Net stock	10,323	13,737	16,501	17,447	18,284	18,718	19,480	20,484	21,603	22,906
Private	7,154	9,583	11,500	12,149	12,707	12,955	13,484	14,194	14,980	15,686
Nonresidential equipment	1,375	1,850	2,196	2,322	24,582	2,520	2,590	2,701	2,863	3,061
Information processing and related equipment	(NA)	414	526	558	586	603	629	662	705	757
Industrial equipment	(NA)	647	770	823	877	898	917	945	991	1,052
Transportation equipment	(NA)	395	443	456	473	491	510	542	586	626
Other equipment	(NA)	396	456	485	516	527	534	552	581	616
Nonresidential structures	2,266	3,155	3,702	3,916	4,107	4,177	4,303	4,504	4,704	4,903
Nonresidential buildings, excluding farm	(NA)	1,787	2,216	2,372	2,518	2,594	2,686	2,815	2,971	3,110
Utilities	(NA)	853	951	997	1,017	1,032	1,062	1,115	1,152	1,201
Residential	3,513	4,578	5,603	5,911	6,147	6,259	6,591	6,989	7,413	7,733
Housing units	(NA)	3,730	4,566	4,808	4,984	5,057	5,327	5,674	6,022	6,255
Government	2,251	2,889	3,360	3,535	3,711	3,827	3,991	4,180	4,389	4,584
Equipment	(NA)	425	479	511	552	577	600	629	665	665
Structures	(NA)	2,464	2,881	3,024	3,159	3,250	3,391	3,552	3,724	3,919
Federal	698	889	994	1,042	1,090	1,127	1,169	1,232	1,284	1,298
Defense	(NA)	613	681	712	744	768	798	844	879	873
State and local	1,554	2,000	2,366	2,493	2,621	2,701	2,822	2,948	3,105	3,286
Consumer durable goods	918	1,265	1,641	1,763	1,866	1,935	2,005	2,110	2,234	2,339
Motor vehicles	(NA)	392	527	564	591	593	608	636	669	669
Furniture and household equipment	(NA)	605	753	804	846	885	926	983	1,043	1,100
Other	(NA)	268	362	396	429	457	471	491	522	550
CHAINED (1992) DOLLARS										
Net stock	14,269	16,178	17,692	18,160	18,586	18,883	19,212	19,610	20,099	20,595
Private	9,950	11,347	12,318	12,617	12,890	13,078	13,278	13,533	13,833	14,171
Nonresidential equipment	5,033	5,876	6,348	6,502	6,650	6,743	6,830	6,947	7,095	7,280
Nonresidential structures	3,177	3,696	3,968	4,051	4,142	4,205	4,251	4,298	4,340	4,399
Residential	4,921	5,471	5,969	6,115	6,240	6,335	6,448	6,587	6,738	6,891
Government	3,124	3,378	3,617	3,693	3,778	3,856	3,936	4,010	4,076	4,147
Federal	969	1,022	1,093	1,109	1,126	1,139	1,149	1,150	1,144	1,137
State and local	2,156	2,357	2,524	2,584	2,652	2,717	2,787	2,861	2,934	3,014
Consumer durable goods	1,198	1,455	1,757	1,850	1,919	1,950	1,998	2,067	2,152	2,241

NA Not available.

Source: U.S. Bureau of Economic Analysis, *Survey of Current Business*, May 1997.

Section 15

Prices

This section presents indexes of producer and consumer prices, actual prices for selected commodities, and energy prices. The primary sources of these data are monthly publications of the Department of Labor, Bureau of Labor Statistics (BLS), which include *Monthly Labor Review, Consumer Price Index, Detailed Report; Producer Price Indexes;* and *U.S. Import and Export Price Indexes.* The Department of Commerce, Bureau of Economic Analysis, is the source for gross domestic product measures.

Producer price index (PPI)—This index, dating from 1890, is the oldest continuous statistical series published by BLS. It is designed to measure average changes in prices received by producers of all commodities, at all stages of processing, produced in the United States.

The index has undergone several revisions (see *Monthly Labor Review,* February 1962, April 1978, and August 1988). It is now based on approximately 3,200 commodity price series and 80,000 quotations per month. Indexes for the net output of manufacturing and mining industries have been added in recent years. Prices used in constructing the index are collected from sellers and generally apply to the first significant large volume commercial transaction for each commodity—i.e., the manufacturer's or other producer's selling price or the selling price on an organized exchange or at a central market.

The weights used in the index represent the total net selling value of commodities produced or processed in this country. Values are f.o.b. (free-on-board) production point and are exclusive of excise taxes. Effective with the release of data for January 1988, many important producer price indexes were changed to a new reference base year, 1982=100, from 1967=100. The reference year of the PPI shipment weights has been taken primarily from the 1987 Census of Manufactures. For further detail regarding the PPI, see the *BLS Handbook of Methods, Bulletin 2414,* Chapter 16.

Consumer price indexes (CPI)—The CPI is a measure of the average change in prices over time in a fixed "market basket" of goods and services purchased either by urban wage earners and clerical workers or by all urban consumers.

In Brief

Consumer price changes: 1995-96:

- *All items index up 3.0 percent*
- *Medical care index up 3.5 percent*
- *Fuel oil index up 14.4 percent*

In 1919, BLS began to publish complete indexes at semiannual intervals, using a weighting structure based on data collected in the expenditure survey of wage-earner and clerical-worker families in 1917-19 (BLS Bulletin 357, 1924). The first major revision of the CPI occurred in 1940, with subsequent revisions in 1953, 1964, 1978, and 1987.

Beginning with the release of data for January 1988 in February 1988, most Consumer Price Indexes shifted to a new reference base year. All indexes previously expressed on a base of 1967=100, or any other base through December 1981, have been rebased to 1982-84=100. Selection of the 1982-84 period was made to coincide with the updated expenditure weights, which are based upon data tabulated from the Consumer Expenditure Surveys for 1982, 1983, and 1984.

BLS publishes CPI's for two population groups: (1) a CPI for All Urban Consumers (CPI-U) which covers approximately 80 percent of the total population; and (2) a CPI for Urban Wage Earners and Clerical Workers (CPI-W) which covers 32 percent of the total population. The CPI-U includes, in addition to wage earners and clerical workers, groups which historically have been excluded from CPI coverage, such as professional, managerial, and technical workers, the self-employed, short-term workers, the unemployed, and retirees and others not in the labor force.

The current CPI is based on prices of food, clothing, shelter, fuels, transportation fares, charges for doctors' and dentists' services, drugs, etc., purchased for day-to-day living. Prices are collected in 85 areas across the country from over

57,000 housing units and 19,000 establishments. Area selection was based on the 1980 census. All taxes directly associated with the purchase and use of items are included in the index. Prices of food, fuels, and a few other items are obtained every month in all 85 locations. Prices of most other commodities and services are collected monthly in the five largest geographic areas and every other month in other areas.

In calculating the index, each item is assigned a weight to account for its relative importance in consumers' budgets. Price changes for the various items in each location are then averaged. Local data are then combined to obtain a U.S. city average. Separate indexes are also published for regions, area size-classes, cross-classifications of regions and size-classes, and for 29 local areas, usually consisting of the Metropolitan Statistical Area (MSA); see Appendix II. Area definitions are those established by the Office of Management and Budget in 1983. Definitions do not include revisions made since 1983. Area indexes do not measure differences in the level of prices among cities; they only measure the average change in prices for each area since the base period. For further detail regarding the CPI, see the BLS *Handbook of Methods*, Bulletin 2414, Chapter 19; the Consumer Price Index, and Report 736, the CPI: 1987 Revision. In January 1983, the method of measuring homeownership costs in the CPI-U was changed to a rental equivalence approach. This treatment calculates homeowner costs of shelter based on the implicit rent owners would pay to rent the homes they own. The rental equivalence approach was introduced into the CPI-W in 1985. The CPI-U was used to prepare the consumer prices tables in this section.

International price indexes—The BLS International Price Program produces export and import price indexes for nonmilitary goods traded between the United States and the rest of the world. The export price index provides a measure of price change for all products sold by U.S. residents to foreign buyers. The import price index provides a measure of price change for goods purchased from other *countries by U.S. residents*. The reference *period for the indexes* is 1990=100, *unless otherwise indicated*.

The product universe for both the import and export indexes includes raw materials, agricultural products, semifinished manufactures, and finished manufactures, including both capital and consumer goods. Price data for these items are collected primarily by mail questionnaire. In nearly all cases, the data are collected directly from the exporter or importer, although in a few cases, prices are obtained from other sources.

To the extent possible, the data gathered refer to prices at the U.S. border for exports and at either the foreign border or the U.S. border for imports. For nearly all products, the prices refer to transactions completed during the first week of the month. Survey respondents are asked to indicate all discounts, allowances, and rebates applicable to the reported prices, so that the price used in the calculation of the indexes is the actual price for which the product was bought or sold.

In addition to general indexes for U.S. exports and imports, indexes are also published for detailed product categories of exports and imports. These categories are defined according to the five-digit level of detail for the Bureau of Economic Analysis End-Use Classification, the three-digit level of detail for the Standard International Trade Classification (SITC), and the four-digit level of detail for the Harmonized System. Aggregate import indexes by country or region of origin are also available.

Other price indexes—Chain-weighted price indexes are weighted averages of the detailed price indexes used in the deflation of goods and services that make up the gross domestic product (GDP). The weights used for the most recent year reflect the composition of goods and services in the preceding year; for all other years, the weights reflect the composition of goods and services in the preceding year and the current year. Chain-weighted price indexes provide the most reliable comparisons of rates of price of goods and services produced in the United States; another index, the gross domestic purchases chained price index, measures the average price of goods and services purchased in the United States. The difference between these two measures is due to net exports. Both price indexes are expressed in terms of the base year value 1992=100.

Measures of inflation—Inflation is defined as a time of generally rising prices for goods and factors of production. The Bureau of Labor Statistics samples prices of items in a representative market basket and publishes the results as the CPI. The media invariably announce the inflation rate as the percent change in the CPI from month to month. A much more meaningful indicator of inflation is the percent change from the same month of the prior year.

The Producer Price Index (PPI) measures prices at the producer/manufacturing level only. The PPI shows the same general pattern of inflation as does the CPI, but is more volatile. The PPI can be roughly viewed as a leading indicator. It often tends to foreshadow trends that later occur in the CPI.

Other measures of inflation include the gross domestic purchases chain-weighted price index, index of industrial materials prices; the Dow Jones Commodity Spot Price Index; Futures Price Index, the Employment Cost Index, the Hourly Compensation Index, or the Unit Labor Cost Index as a measure of the change in cost of the labor factor of production, and changes in long-term interest rates that are often used to measure changes in the cost of the capital factor of production.

Statistical reliability—For a discussion of statistical collection and estimation, sampling procedures, and measures of statistical reliability pertaining to the producer price index and the CPI, see Appendix III.

No. 751. Purchasing Power of the Dollar: 1950 to 1996

[Indexes: PPI, 1982=$1.00; CPI, 1982-84=$1.00. Producer prices prior to 1961, and consumer prices prior to 1964, exclude Alaska and Hawaii. Producer prices based on finished goods index. Obtained by dividing the average price index for the 1982=100, PPI; 1982-84=100, CPI base periods (100.0) by the price index for a given period and expressing the result in dollars and cents. Annual figures are based on average of monthly data]

YEAR	ANNUAL AVERAGE AS MEASURED BY—		YEAR	ANNUAL AVERAGE AS MEASURED BY—		YEAR	ANNUAL AVERAGE AS MEASURED BY—	
	Producer prices	Consumer prices		Producer prices	Consumer prices		Producer prices	Consumer prices
1950	$3.546	$4.151	1966	2.841	3.080	1982	1.000	1.035
1951	3.247	3.846	1967	2.809	2.993	1983	0.984	1.003
1952	3.268	3.765	1968	2.732	2.873	1984	0.964	0.961
1953	3.300	3.735	1969	2.632	2.726	1985	0.955	0.928
1954	3.289	3.717	1970	2.545	2.574	1986	0.969	0.913
1955	3.279	3.732	1971	2.469	2.466	1987	0.949	0.880
1956	3.195	3.678	1972	2.392	2.391	1988	0.926	0.846
1957	3.077	3.549	1973	2.193	2.251	1989	0.880	0.807
1958	3.012	3.457	1974	1.901	2.029	1990	0.839	0.766
1959	3.021	3.427	1975	1.718	1.859	1991	0.822	0.734
1960	2.994	3.373	1976	1.645	1.757	1992	0.812	0.713
1961	2.994	3.340	1977	1.546	1.649	1993	0.802	0.692
1962	2.985	3.304	1978	1.433	1.532	1994	0.797	0.675
1963	2.994	3.265	1979	1.289	1.380	1995	0.782	0.656
1964	2.985	3.220	1980	1.136	1.215	1996	0.762	0.638
1965	2.933	3.166	1981	1.041	1.098			

Source: U.S. Bureau of Labor Statistics. Monthly data in U.S. Bureau of Economic Analysis, *Survey of Current Business*.

Figure 15.1
Annual Percent Change in Producer Price Indexes by Stage of Processing: 1970 to 1996

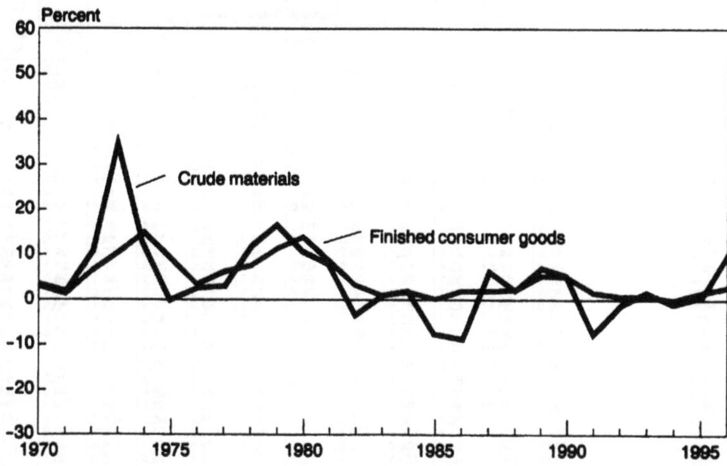

Source: Chart prepared by U.S. Bureau of the Census. For data, see table 757.

Figure 15.2
Annual Percent Change in Consumer Price Indexes: 1970 to 1996

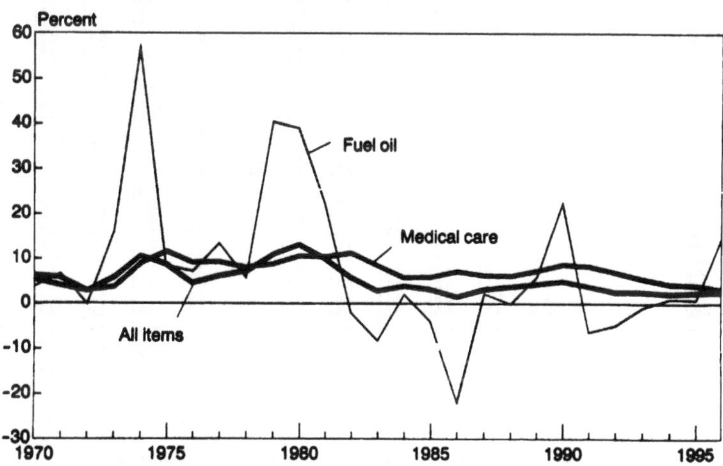

Source: Chart prepared by U.S. Bureau of the Census. For data, see table 752.

No. 752. Consumer Price Indexes (CPI-U), by Major Groups: 1939 to 1996

[1982-84=100. Represents annual averages of monthly figures. Reflects buying patterns of all urban consumers. Minus sign (-) indicates decrease. See text, section 15]

YEAR	All items	Commodities	Energy	Food	Shelter	Apparel and upkeep	Transportation	Medical care	Fuel oil	Electricity	Utility (piped) gas	Telephone services
1939	13.9	14.8	(NA)	11.8	(NA)	21.6	14.3	10.3	5.8	28.9	12.9	36.1
1940	14.0	14.9	(NA)	12.0	(NA)	21.8	14.2	10.4	6.1	28.6	12.8	36.1
1945	18.0	20.7	(NA)	17.3	(NA)	31.4	15.9	11.9	7.5	28.0	12.3	41.3
1950	24.1	29.0	(NA)	25.4	(NA)	40.3	22.7	15.1	11.0	27.2	13.2	49.5
1955	26.8	31.3	(NA)	27.8	22.7	42.9	25.8	18.2	13.0	28.5	14.6	52.9
1960	29.6	33.6	22.4	30.0	25.2	45.7	29.8	22.3	13.5	29.9	17.6	58.3
1965	31.5	36.2	22.9	32.2	27.0	47.8	31.9	25.2	14.3	29.7	18.0	57.7
1966	32.4	36.1	23.3	33.8	27.8	49.0	32.3	26.3	14.7	29.7	18.1	56.5
1967	33.4	36.8	23.8	34.1	28.8	51.0	33.3	28.2	15.1	29.9	18.1	57.3
1968	34.8	38.1	24.2	35.3	30.1	53.7	34.3	29.9	15.6	30.2	18.2	57.3
1969	36.7	39.9	24.8	37.1	32.6	56.8	35.7	31.9	15.9	30.8	18.6	58.0
1970	38.8	41.7	25.5	39.2	35.5	59.2	37.5	34.0	16.5	31.8	19.6	58.7
1971	40.5	43.2	26.5	40.4	37.0	61.1	39.5	36.1	17.6	33.9	21.0	61.6
1972	41.8	44.5	27.2	42.1	38.7	62.3	39.9	37.3	17.6	35.6	22.1	65.0
1973	44.4	47.8	29.4	48.2	40.5	64.6	41.2	38.8	20.4	37.4	23.1	66.7
1974	49.3	53.5	38.1	55.1	44.4	69.4	45.8	42.4	32.2	44.1	26.0	69.5
1975	53.8	58.2	42.1	59.8	48.8	72.5	50.1	47.5	34.9	50.0	31.1	71.7
1976	56.9	60.7	45.1	61.6	51.5	75.2	55.1	52.0	37.4	53.1	36.3	74.3
1977	60.6	64.2	49.4	65.5	54.9	78.6	59.0	57.0	42.4	56.6	43.2	75.2
1978	65.2	68.8	52.5	72.0	60.5	81.4	61.7	61.8	44.9	60.9	47.5	76.0
1979	72.6	76.6	65.7	79.9	68.9	84.9	70.5	67.5	63.1	65.6	55.1	75.8
1980	82.4	86.0	86.0	86.8	81.0	90.9	83.1	74.9	87.7	75.8	65.7	77.7
1981	90.9	93.2	97.7	93.6	90.5	95.3	93.2	82.9	107.3	87.2	74.9	84.6
1982	96.5	97.0	99.2	97.4	96.9	97.8	97.0	92.5	105.0	95.8	89.8	93.2
1983	99.6	99.8	99.9	99.4	99.1	100.2	99.3	100.6	96.5	98.9	104.7	99.2
1984	103.9	103.2	100.9	103.2	104.0	102.1	103.7	106.8	98.5	105.3	105.5	107.5
1985	107.6	105.4	101.6	105.6	109.8	105.0	106.4	113.5	94.6	108.9	104.8	111.7
1986	109.6	104.4	88.2	109.0	115.8	105.9	102.3	122.0	74.1	110.4	99.7	117.2
1987	113.6	107.7	88.6	113.5	121.3	110.6	105.4	130.1	75.8	110.0	95.1	116.5
1988	118.3	111.5	89.3	118.2	127.1	115.4	108.7	138.6	75.8	111.5	94.5	116.0
1989	124.0	116.7	94.3	125.1	132.8	118.6	114.1	149.3	80.3	114.7	97.1	117.2
1990	130.7	122.8	102.1	132.4	140.0	124.1	120.5	162.8	98.6	117.4	97.3	117.7
1991	136.2	126.6	102.5	136.3	146.3	128.7	123.8	177.0	92.4	121.8	98.5	119.7
1992	140.3	129.1	103.0	137.9	151.2	131.9	126.5	190.1	88.0	124.2	100.3	120.4
1993	144.5	131.5	104.2	140.9	155.7	133.7	130.4	201.4	87.2	126.7	106.5	121.2
1994	148.2	133.8	104.6	144.3	160.5	133.4	134.3	211.0	85.6	126.7	108.5	123.1
1995	152.4	136.4	105.2	148.4	165.7	132.0	139.1	220.5	84.8	129.6	102.9	124.0
1996	156.9	139.9	110.1	153.3	171.0	131.7	143.0	228.2	97.0	131.8	107.2	125.9
PERCENT CHANGE												
1940	0.7	0.7	(NA)	1.7	(NA)	0.9	-0.7	1.0	5.2	-1.0	-0.8	-
1945	2.3	3.0	(NA)	2.4	(NA)	5.4	-	2.6	-5.1	-0.7	-0.8	1.5
1950	1.3	0.7	(NA)	1.6	(NA)	-1.2	2.7	2.0	0.9	0.4	0.8	7.6
1955	-0.4	-0.9	(NA)	-1.4	0.9	-0.5	-1.1	2.2	3.2	1.4	3.5	-0.9
1960	1.7	0.9	2.3	1.0	2.0	1.6	-	3.7	-1.5	1.4	6.7	1.6
1965	1.6	1.1	1.8	2.2	1.9	1.1	1.6	2.4	2.1	-0.3	0.6	-1.5
1970	5.7	4.5	2.8	5.7	8.9	4.2	5.0	6.6	3.8	3.2	5.4	1.2
1971	4.4	3.6	3.9	3.1	4.2	3.2	5.3	6.2	6.7	6.6	7.1	4.9
1972	3.2	3.0	2.6	4.2	4.6	2.0	1.0	3.3	-	5.0	5.2	5.5
1973	6.2	7.4	8.1	14.5	4.7	3.7	3.3	4.0	15.9	5.1	4.5	2.6
1974	11.0	11.9	29.6	14.3	9.6	7.4	11.2	9.3	57.8	17.9	12.6	4.2
1975	9.1	8.8	10.5	8.5	9.9	4.5	9.4	12.0	8.4	13.4	19.6	3.2
1976	5.8	4.3	7.1	3.0	5.5	3.7	10.0	9.5	7.2	6.2	16.7	3.6
1977	6.5	5.8	9.5	6.3	6.6	4.5	7.1	9.6	13.4	6.6	19.0	1.2
1978	7.6	7.2	6.3	9.9	10.2	3.6	4.6	8.4	5.9	7.6	10.0	1.1
1979	11.3	11.3	25.1	11.0	13.9	4.3	14.3	9.2	40.5	7.7	16.0	-0.3
1980	13.5	12.3	30.9	8.6	17.6	7.1	17.9	11.0	39.0	15.5	19.2	2.5
1981	10.3	8.4	13.6	7.8	11.7	4.8	12.2	10.7	22.3	15.0	14.0	8.9
1982	6.2	4.1	1.5	4.1	7.1	2.6	4.1	11.6	-2.1	9.9	19.9	10.2
1983	3.2	2.9	0.7	2.1	2.3	2.5	2.4	8.8	-8.1	3.2	16.6	6.4
1984	4.3	3.4	1.0	3.8	4.9	1.9	4.4	6.2	2.1	6.5	0.8	8.4
1985	3.6	2.1	0.7	2.3	5.6	2.8	2.6	6.3	-4.0	3.4	-0.7	3.9
1986	1.9	-0.9	-13.2	3.2	5.5	0.9	-3.9	7.5	-21.7	1.4	-4.9	4.9
1987	3.6	3.2	0.5	4.1	4.7	4.4	3.0	6.6	2.3	-0.4	-4.6	-0.6
1988	4.1	3.5	0.8	4.1	4.8	4.3	3.1	6.5	-	1.4	-0.6	-0.4
1989	4.8	4.7	5.6	5.8	4.5	2.8	5.0	7.7	5.9	2.9	2.8	1.0
1990	5.4	5.2	8.3	5.8	5.4	4.6	5.6	9.0	22.8	2.4	0.2	0.4
1991	4.2	3.1	0.4	2.9	4.5	3.7	2.7	8.7	-6.3	3.7	1.2	1.7
1992	3.0	2.0	0.5	1.2	3.3	2.5	2.2	7.4	-4.8	2.0	1.8	0.6
1993	3.0	1.9	1.2	2.2	3.0	1.4	3.1	5.9	-0.9	2.0	6.2	0.7
1994	2.6	1.7	0.4	2.4	3.1	-0.2	3.0	4.8	-1.9	-	1.9	1.6
1995	2.8	1.9	0.6	2.8	3.2	-1.0	3.6	4.5	-0.9	2.3	-5.2	0.7
1996	3.0	2.6	4.7	3.3	3.2	-0.2	2.8	3.5	14.4	1.7	4.2	1.5

- Represents zero. NA Not available.

Source: Bureau of Labor Statistics, *Monthly Labor Review and Handbook of Labor Statistics*, periodic.

No. 753. Consumer Price Indexes for All Urban Consumers (CPI-U) for Selected Items and Groups: 1985 to 1996

[1982-84=100. Annual averages of monthly figures. See headnote, table 752]

ITEM	1985	1989	1990	1991	1992	1993	1994	1995	1996
All items	107.6	124.0	130.7	136.2	140.3	144.5	148.2	152.4	156.9
Food and beverages	105.6	124.9	132.1	136.8	138.7	141.6	144.9	148.9	153.7
Food	105.6	125.1	132.4	136.3	137.9	140.9	144.3	148.4	153.3
Food at home	104.3	124.2	132.3	135.8	136.8	140.1	144.1	148.8	154.3
Cereals and bakery products	107.9	132.4	140.0	145.8	151.5	156.6	163.0	167.5	174.0
Cereals and cereal products	107.2	133.8	141.1	147.5	153.3	157.9	164.8	167.1	168.9
Cereals	111.3	147.9	158.6	168.1	175.4	183.3	190.6	192.5	190.0
Rice, pasta, and cornmeal	102.1	120.0	122.0	126.5	128.3	129.7	139.7	140.2	144.2
Bakery products	108.2	131.5	139.2	144.7	150.4	155.7	161.9	167.4	176.1
White bread	105.8	129.4	136.4	139.3	146.2	152.2	159.0	165.5	177.5
Cookies, cakes, and cupcakes	110.2	134.5	142.7	151.1	155.6	159.3	165.1	169.1	174.1
Meats, poultry, fish and eggs	100.1	121.3	130.0	132.6	130.9	135.5	137.2	138.8	144.8
Meats	98.9	116.7	128.5	132.5	130.7	134.6	135.4	135.5	140.2
Beef and veal	98.2	119.3	128.8	132.4	132.3	137.1	136.0	134.9	134.5
Ground beef excl. canned	95.9	108.6	118.1	119.9	118.9	121.7	119.7	116.1	114.3
Chuck roast	95.6	116.8	130.3	135.8	137.1	141.9	140.3	138.7	140.0
Round steak	97.0	116.6	125.1	129.5	129.9	134.4	133.0	130.4	129.3
Sirloin steak	99.7	126.0	130.6	133.5	132.4	138.5	137.5	138.7	137.6
Pork	99.1	113.2	129.8	134.1	127.8	131.7	133.9	134.8	148.2
Bacon	101.3	95.8	113.4	119.8	104.6	110.8	118.1	120.0	148.9
Chops	98.7	122.7	140.2	141.7	136.9	144.6	144.2	144.2	153.0
Ham	99.8	117.3	132.4	139.9	135.6	137.9	139.3	139.6	149.2
Poultry	106.2	132.7	132.5	131.5	131.4	136.9	141.5	143.5	152.4
Fresh whole chicken	104.5	137.1	134.9	131.7	131.9	138.0	140.1	142.2	152.6
Fresh, frozen chicken parts	104.6	135.7	135.9	134.7	134.4	140.1	145.6	146.0	155.0
Fish and seafood	107.5	143.6	146.7	148.3	151.7	156.6	163.7	171.6	173.1
Canned fish and seafood	97.8	124.3	119.5	119.0	118.7	121.5	123.8	125.5	125.9
Fresh, frozen fish, seafood	112.9	155.2	161.4	163.8	166.7	174.5	183.6	194.1	196.0
Eggs	91.0	118.5	124.1	121.2	108.3	117.1	114.3	120.5	142.1
Dairy products	103.2	115.6	126.5	125.1	128.5	129.4	131.7	132.8	142.1
Fruits and vegetables	106.4	138.0	149.0	155.8	155.4	159.0	165.0	177.7	183.9
Fresh fruits and vegetables	(NA)	(NA)	(NA)	(NA)	(NA)	(NA)	186.7	206.0	211.8
Fresh fruits	116.3	152.4	170.9	193.9	184.2	188.8	201.2	219.0	234.4
Apples	113.1	140.5	147.5	172.8	179.5	169.0	174.0	183.5	202.3
Bananas	99.9	131.3	138.2	145.0	139.9	135.5	143.6	153.8	159.0
Oranges, tangerines	119.7	147.0	160.6	249.4	176.2	190.1	189.9	224.5	239.3
Fresh vegetables	103.5	143.1	151.1	154.4	157.9	168.7	172.3	193.1	189.2
Potatoes	101.6	153.5	162.6	144.6	141.5	154.6	174.3	174.7	180.6
Lettuce	106.1	151.5	150.3	159.8	156.7	178.2	170.3	221.2	185.7
Tomatoes	103.6	136.2	160.8	153.1	171.8	168.0	173.5	188.3	198.2
Processed fruits and vegetables	(NA)	(NA)	(NA)	(NA)	(NA)	(NA)	134.5	137.5	144.4
Processed fruits	109.5	125.9	136.9	131.8	137.7	132.3	133.1	137.2	146.2
Processed vegetables	104.4	124.2	127.5	128.5	126.8	130.8	136.6	138.3	143.9
Coffee	105.5	120.4	117.5	115.3	110.7	109.8	140.4	163.1	149.2
Food away from home	(NA)	(NA)	(NA)	(NA)	(NA)	(NA)	145.7	149.0	152.7
Lunch	107.8	127.6	133.9	138.4	141.3	144.0	146.4	149.6	153.3
Dinner	108.8	126.9	132.3	136.3	138.9	141.3	143.8	147.1	150.7
Alcoholic beverages	106.4	123.5	129.3	142.8	147.3	149.6	151.5	153.9	158.5
Alcoholic beverages at home	105.2	117.9	123.0	137.8	141.6	142.2	142.5	143.1	146.8
Beer and ale	106.7	118.2	123.6	138.4	143.5	143.2	143.4	143.9	147.4
Distilled spirits	105.3	119.9	125.7	139.2	141.5	143.2	144.3	145.7	147.5
Wine	100.2	110.9	114.4	129.9	132.6	134.0	133.3	133.6	139.3
Alcoholic beverages away from home	111.1	137.4	144.4	156.9	162.5	167.4	171.6	176.5	182.7
Housing	107.7	123.0	128.5	133.6	137.5	141.2	144.8	148.5	152.8
Shelter	109.8	132.8	140.0	146.3	151.2	155.7	160.5	165.7	171.0
Renters' cost	115.4	138.9	146.7	155.6	160.9	165.0	169.4	174.3	180.2
Rent, residential	111.8	132.8	138.4	143.3	146.9	150.3	154.0	157.8	162.0
Tenants' insurance	109.4	128.3	130.6	133.2	136.5	140.8	145.8	150.9	154.7
Homeowners' costs	113.1	137.3	144.6	150.2	155.3	160.2	165.5	171.0	176.5
Owners' equivalent rent	113.2	137.4	144.8	150.4	155.5	160.5	165.8	171.3	176.8
Household insurance	112.4	132.6	135.3	138.4	142.2	146.9	152.3	157.4	161.0
Maintenance and repair	106.5	118.0	122.2	126.3	128.6	130.6	130.8	135.0	139.0
Fuels and other utilities	106.5	107.8	111.6	115.3	117.8	121.3	122.8	123.7	127.5
Fuels	104.5	100.9	104.5	106.7	108.1	111.2	111.7	111.5	115.2
Fuel oil and other	95.9	81.7	99.3	94.6	90.7	90.3	88.8	88.1	99.2
Fuel oil	94.6	80.3	98.6	92.4	88.0	87.2	85.6	84.8	97.0
Gas (piped) and electricity	107.1	107.5	109.3	112.6	114.8	118.5	119.2	119.2	122.1
Electricity	108.9	114.7	117.4	121.8	124.2	126.7	126.7	129.6	131.8
Utility (piped) gas	104.8	97.1	97.3	98.5	100.3	106.5	106.5	102.9	107.2
Telephone services	111.7	117.2	117.7	119.7	120.4	121.2	123.1	124.0	125.9
Local charges	120.4	146.5	149.3	153.9	155.7	156.4	156.9	160.4	160.8
Interstate toll charges	94.9	70.0	68.2	67.6	68.0	69.6	75.2	74.9	77.9
Intrastate toll charges	106.8	97.0	95.1	93.1	91.4	90.7	90.2	86.0	89.4
Water and sewerage maintenance	113.4	140.8	150.2	161.1	172.1	181.4	190.6	196.5	204.5
Cable television	110.6	144.0	158.4	175.7	186.2	198.9	197.4	200.7	212.6
Refuse collection	109.9	155.6	171.2	189.2	207.3	220.5	231.4	241.2	246.0

See footnotes at end of table.

No. 753. Consumer Price Indexes for All Urban Consumers (CPI-U) for Selected Items and Groups: 1985 to 1996—Continued

[1982-84=100. Annual averages of monthly figures. See headnote, table 752]

ITEM	1985	1989	1990	1991	1992	1993	1994	1995	1996
Household furnishings and operations	103.8	111.2	113.3	116.0	118.0	119.3	121.0	123.0	124.7
Housefurnishings	101.7	105.5	106.7	107.5	109.0	109.5	111.0	111.2	111.3
Furniture and bedding	104.9	113.9	115.7	116.6	120.6	123.5	128.2	130.9	134.1
Bedroom furniture	107.4	117.6	118.5	120.1	126.8	132.5	135.1	136.4	139.3
Sofas	103.0	117.0	118.4	118.3	119.4	120.1	125.2	132.8	141.5
Living room chairs and tables	103.2	112.5	116.7	118.4	121.9	125.0	132.7	136.6	136.9
Appliances and electronic equip.	95.2	89.1	87.8	86.0	84.6	83.4	82.3	80.0	77.8
Video and audio equipment	91.9	82.2	80.8	79.4	78.4	77.1	76.0	73.9	71.3
Television	88.7	76.1	74.6	72.9	72.4	70.7	69.9	68.1	64.5
Video products other than TV	(NA)	96.8	91.5	84.6	81.0	78.5	73.8	70.3	66.3
Audio products	94.4	92.8	93.2	94.6	94.4	93.9	93.8	92.1	90.7
Housekeeping supplies	106.2	120.9	125.2	128.9	129.6	130.7	132.3	137.1	141.1
Housekeeping services	106.1	117.3	120.1	127.5	132.1	136.8	138.5	143.7	148.0
Postage	108.8	125.1	125.1	143.6	145.3	145.3	145.3	160.3	160.3
Apparel and upkeep	105.0	118.6	124.1	128.7	131.9	133.7	133.4	132.0	131.7
Apparel commodities	104.0	116.7	122.0	126.4	129.4	131.0	130.4	128.7	128.2
Apparel commodities less footwear	104.3	117.1	122.8	127.4	130.2	131.9	131.2	129.3	128.5
Men's and boy's apparel	106.0	117.0	120.4	124.2	126.5	127.5	126.4	126.2	127.7
Women's and girl's apparel	104.9	116.4	122.6	127.6	130.4	132.6	130.9	126.9	124.7
Infants' and toddlers'	107.2	119.1	125.8	128.9	129.3	127.1	128.1	127.2	129.7
Footwear	102.3	114.4	117.4	120.9	125.0	125.9	126.0	125.4	126.6
Transportation	106.4	114.1	120.5	123.8	126.5	130.4	134.3	139.1	143.0
Private transportation	106.2	112.9	118.8	121.9	124.6	127.5	131.4	136.3	140.0
New vehicles	106.1	119.2	121.4	126.0	129.2	132.7	137.6	141.0	143.7
New cars	106.1	119.2	121.0	125.3	128.4	131.5	136.0	139.0	141.4
New trucks	105.5	117.0	121.6	127.0	130.9	135.7	141.7	145.9	149.5
Used cars	113.7	120.4	117.6	118.1	123.2	133.9	141.7	156.5	157.0
Motor fuel	98.7	88.5	101.2	99.4	99.0	98.0	98.5	100.0	106.3
Automobile maintenance and repair	106.8	124.9	130.1	136.0	141.3	145.9	150.2	154.0	158.4
Automobile insurance	119.2	166.6	177.9	191.5	205.5	216.7	224.8	234.3	243.9
Automobile finance charges	94.5	100.5	99.6	98.0	86.1	78.6	83.8	99.0	94.4
Vehicle rental, registration, other	111.7	135.0	148.1	154.8	162.3	169.6	174.2	177.9	181.1
Public transportation	110.5	129.5	142.6	148.9	151.4	167.0	172.0	175.9	181.9
Airline fares	112.5	131.6	148.4	155.2	155.2	178.7	185.5	189.7	192.5
Other intercity transportation	114.7	138.5	143.3	149.0	152.5	150.9	152.8	153.3	156.0
Intracity transportation	107.7	125.2	133.5	138.9	146.9	150.7	152.7	157.5	173.2
Medical care	113.5	149.3	162.8	177.0	190.1	201.4	211.0	220.5	228.2
Medical care commodities	115.2	150.8	163.4	176.8	188.1	195.0	200.7	204.5	210.4
Prescription drugs	120.1	165.2	181.7	199.7	214.7	223.0	230.6	235.0	242.9
Nonprescription drugs, medical sup.	(NA)	114.6	120.6	126.3	131.2	135.5	138.1	140.5	143.1
Medical care services	113.2	148.9	162.7	177.1	190.5	202.9	213.4	224.2	232.4
Professional medical services	113.5	146.4	156.1	165.7	175.8	184.7	192.5	201.0	208.3
Physicians' services	113.3	150.1	160.8	170.5	181.2	191.3	199.8	208.8	216.4
Dental services	114.2	146.1	155.8	167.4	178.7	188.1	197.1	206.8	216.5
Eye care	(NA)	112.4	117.3	121.9	127.0	130.4	133.0	137.0	139.3
Hospital and related services	116.1	160.5	178.0	196.1	214.0	231.9	245.6	257.8	269.5
Hospital rooms	115.4	158.1	175.4	191.9	208.7	226.4	239.2	251.2	261.0
Entertainment	107.9	126.5	132.4	138.4	142.3	145.8	150.1	153.9	159.1
Entertainment commodities	105.8	119.8	124.0	128.6	131.3	133.4	136.1	138.7	143.0
Reading materials	110.7	129.5	136.2	144.7	150.9	156.2	161.3	168.1	176.4
Newspapers	109.3	129.2	134.6	146.5	154.8	161.1	168.2	178.7	188.9
Magazines, periodicals, and books	112.1	130.0	137.9	143.3	147.4	151.8	155.1	158.4	165.0
Sporting goods, equipment	104.6	111.1	114.9	118.5	120.2	120.1	122.2	123.5	123.4
Sport vehicles, including bicycles	106.3	112.3	115.3	117.5	119.7	120.6	122.3	125.3	125.7
Toys, hobbies; other entertainment	103.3	118.5	121.5	123.9	124.7	126.0	127.4	127.8	131.9
Pet supplies and expenses	106.4	120.7	124.6	129.1	128.1	128.8	130.9	132.3	139.0
Entertainment services	110.9	135.4	143.2	150.6	155.9	160.8	166.8	172.0	178.1
Club membership	(NA)	112.6	117.0	122.5	125.2	128.4	130.7	132.8	133.3
Admissions	112.8	141.4	151.2	159.3	164.5	167.3	175.2	182.3	192.1
Tobacco and smoking products	116.7	164.4	181.5	202.7	219.8	228.4	220.0	225.7	232.8
Personal care	108.3	125.0	130.4	134.9	138.3	141.5	144.6	147.1	150.1
Personal care services	108.9	126.8	132.8	137.0	140.0	144.0	147.9	151.5	156.6
Beauty parlor services for women	108.8	126.5	133.0	137.2	139.8	143.6	147.7	150.9	155.9
Haircuts, etc. for men	109.0	127.3	131.5	135.9	140.3	144.6	147.9	153.4	158.9
Personal and educational expenses	119.1	158.1	170.2	183.7	197.4	210.7	223.2	235.5	247.5
School books and supplies	118.2	158.0	171.3	180.3	190.3	197.6	205.5	214.4	226.9
Personal and educational services	119.2	158.3	170.4	184.2	198.1	211.9	224.8	237.3	249.3
Tuition and other school fees	119.7	162.7	175.7	191.4	208.5	225.3	239.8	253.8	267.1
College tuition	119.9	161.9	175.0	192.8	213.5	233.5	249.8	264.8	279.8
Elementary and high school tuition	119.0	166.0	182.8	196.0	213.7	228.9	242.6	259.2	272.8
Day care and nursery school	(NA)	(NA)	(NA)	103.2	108.3	113.6	119.6	124.5	129.4
All commodities	105.4	116.7	122.8	126.6	129.1	131.5	133.8	136.4	139.9
All commodities less food	105.2	112.0	117.4	121.3	124.2	126.3	127.9	129.8	132.6
Energy	101.6	94.3	102.1	102.5	103.0	104.2	104.6	105.2	110.1

NA Not available.

Source: U.S. Bureau of Labor Statistics, *Monthly Labor Review* and *CPI Detailed Report*, January issues.

No. 754. Consumer Price Indexes (CPI-U)—Selected Areas: 1985 to 1996

[1982-84=100, except as indicated. Represents annual averages of monthly figures. Local area CPI indexes are byproducts of the national CPI program. Each local index has a smaller sample size than the national index and is therefore, subject to substantially more sampling and other measurement error. As a result, local area indexes show greater volatility than the national index, although their long- term trends are similar. Area definitions are those established by the Office of Management and Budget in 1983. For further detail see the U.S. Bureau of Labor Statistics Handbook of Methods, Bulletin 2285, Chapter 19, the Consumer Price Index, and Report 736, the CPI: 1987 Revision. See also text, section 15]

AREA	1985	1990	1992	1993	1994	1995	1996								
							All items	Food and beverages	Food	Housing	Apparel and upkeep	Transportation	Medical care	Entertainment	Fuel and other utilities
U.S. city average	107.6	130.7	140.3	144.5	148.2	152.4	156.9	153.7	153.3	152.8	131.7	143.0	228.2	159.1	127.5
Anchorage, AK MSA	105.8	118.6	128.2	132.2	135.0	138.5	142.7	143.4	143.6	127.9	128.7	147.2	231.1	177.1	141.2
Atlanta, GA MSA	108.9	131.7	138.5	143.4	146.7	148.7	156.0	153.4	156.9	151.8	145.4	134.7	240.7	180.3	134.5
Baltimore, MD MSA	108.2	130.8	140.1	143.1	146.9	149.7	154.2	158.8	159.5	143.7	132.8	140.3	237.4	167.2	119.0
Boston-Lawrence-Salem, MA-NH CMSA	109.4	138.9	148.6	152.9	154.9	157.4	163.3	157.7	157.5	157.2	142.9	139.5	280.8	169.7	123.0
Buffalo-Niagara Falls, NY CMSA	108.6	127.7	137.9	142.7	146.8	146.3	157.1	153.0	152.1	165.5	119.0	132.4	187.3	197.1	133.4
Chicago-Gary-Lake County, IL-IN-WI CMSA	107.7	131.7	141.1	145.4	148.6	148.4	157.4	156.1	154.9	155.1	120.6	139.9	229.4	167.2	120.8
Cincinnati-Hamilton, OH-KY-IN CMSA	108.6	128.5	134.1	137.8	142.4	143.4	149.6	141.5	139.7	142.1	131.8	138.5	225.8	156.5	118.4
Cleveland-Akron-Lorain, OH CMSA	107.8	129.0	136.8	140.3	144.4	140.2	152.0	154.2	155.1	148.6	128.8	138.5	209.4	155.8	124.2
Dallas-Fort Worth, TX CMSA	108.2	125.1	133.9	137.3	141.2	144.6	148.8	152.8	150.4	135.5	141.9	142.1	224.6	162.8	128.4
Denver-Boulder, CO CMSA	107.1	120.9	130.3	135.8	141.8	144.0	153.1	142.2	144.4	142.6	103.6	162.7	250.8	152.1	120.5
Detroit-Ann Arbor, MI CMSA	106.8	128.6	135.9	139.6	144.0	143.9	152.5	147.9	147.3	145.5	131.7	148.0	213.7	154.8	121.2
Honolulu, HI MSA	106.8	138.1	155.1	160.1	164.5	168.4	170.7	158.6	156.6	176.8	118.5	167.0	215.0	147.8	133.8
Houston-Galveston-Brazoria, TX CMSA	104.9	120.6	127.1	133.4	137.9	139.4	142.7	142.9	142.6	123.9	137.7	140.4	222.6	160.4	105.4
Kansas City, MO-KS CMSA	107.7	126.0	134.3	138.1	141.3	141.7	151.6	154.1	154.8	142.4	129.6	137.6	212.2	169.1	132.5
Los Angeles-Anaheim-Riverside, CA CMSA	108.4	135.9	146.5	150.3	152.3	149.4	157.5	157.8	156.0	154.1	126.0	144.3	228.9	145.8	149.1
Miami-Fort Lauderdale, FL CMSA	106.5	128.0	134.5	139.1	143.6	146.9	153.7	161.4	161.4	145.1	146.0	144.3	214.4	146.1	118.2
Milwaukee, WI PMSA	107.0	126.2	137.1	142.1	147.0	153.5	154.7	151.9	152.7	154.4	123.2	141.6	220.1	130.7	104.4
Minneapolis-St. Paul, MN-WI MSA	107.0	127.0	135.0	139.2	143.6	144.8	151.9	158.8	156.4	138.0	143.1	141.9	215.5	165.1	119.5
New Orleans, LA MSA [1]	(NA)	111.5	120.2	124.7	129.0	132.9	138.4	136.5	136.4	122.8	202.7	131.0	175.1	145.9	129.0
New York-Northern New Jersey-Long Island, NY-NJ-CT CMSA	108.7	138.5	150.0	154.5	158.2	158.3	166.9	159.7	159.3	167.7	127.7	152.4	236.4	163.5	117.4
Philadelphia-Wilmington-Trenton, PA-NJ-DE-MD CMSA	108.8	135.8	146.6	150.2	154.6	158.3	162.8	152.2	151.1	162.4	103.8	151.5	242.2	178.2	127.8
Pittsburgh-Beaver Valley, PA CMSA	106.9	126.2	136.0	139.9	144.6	142.9	153.2	148.9	148.1	153.1	134.6	129.2	225.4	163.2	139.2
Portland-Vancouver, OR-WA CMSA	106.7	127.4	139.8	144.7	148.9	149.9	158.6	143.1	143.2	158.3	124.5	147.0	211.8	168.8	130.8
San Diego, CA MSA	110.4	138.4	147.4	150.6	154.5	147.0	160.9	157.0	155.7	159.9	129.8	150.8	231.6	163.2	119.7
San Francisco-Oakland-San Jose, CA CMSA	108.4	132.1	142.5	146.3	148.7	149.3	155.1	155.3	155.7	157.4	116.9	133.5	214.5	166.8	142.8
Seattle-Tacoma, WA CMSA	105.6	126.8	139.0	142.9	147.8	149.3	157.5	155.5	155.8	156.9	125.7	144.0	217.4	149.8	118.6
St. Louis-East St. Louis, MO-IL CMSA	107.1	128.1	134.7	137.5	141.3	144.7	149.6	151.2	150.1	142.6	122.2	141.8	218.4	160.8	123.0
Tampa-St. Petersburg-Clearwater, FL MSA [1]	(NA)	111.7	119.2	124.0	126.5	128.0	131.6	129.1	128.3	126.6	115.1	127.3	186.7	121.9	118.2
Washington, DC-MD-VA MSA	109.0	135.6	144.7	149.3	152.2	152.7	159.6	152.5	153.0	156.0	140.4	144.5	220.9	169.1	127.2

NA Not available. [1] 1987=100.

Source: U.S. Bureau of Labor Statistics, *Monthly Labor Review* and *CPI Detailed Report*, January issues.

No. 755. Cost of Living Index—Selected Metropolitan Areas: Third Quarter 1996

[Measures relative price levels for consumer goods and services in participating areas for a midmanagement standard of living. The nationwide average equals 100, and each index is read as a percent of the national average. The index does not measure inflation, but compares prices at a single point in time. Excludes taxes. Metropolitan areas as defined by the Office of Management and Budget. For definitions and components of MSA's, see source for details]

METROPOLITAN AREAS (MA)	Composite index (100%)	Grocery items (16%)	Housing (28%)	Utilities (8%)	Transportation (10%)	Health care (5%)
Abilene, TX MSA	92.4	88.9	92.2	102.6	100.0	97.0
Albany, GA MSA	92.8	98.1	105.7	96.8	88.4	101.1
Albuquerque, NM MSA	101.9	100.0	101.6	96.2	107.0	101.1
Alexandria, LA MSA	92.0	87.8	93.3	93.7	76.9	99.0
Allentown-Bethlehem-Easton, PA MSA	103.4	107.2	118.5	96.2	94.4	102.1
Altoona, PA MSA	96.1	101.2	118.8	87.0	88.8	92.5
Amarillo, TX MSA	90.0	92.9	62.8	102.3	86.8	95.0
Anchorage, AK MSA	124.8	121.9	84.0	109.7	173.5	123.6
Anniston, AL MSA	90.9	97.6	103.9	89.4	86.8	94.2
Appleton-Oshkosh-Neenah, WI MSA	98.2	94.9	93.7	97.9	96.9	97.8
Asheville, NC MSA	104.8	96.4	116.6	106.1	85.9	106.8
Atlanta, GA MSA	99.5	101.9	94.4	104.9	109.7	96.8
Augusta-Aiken, GA-SC MSA	94.0	96.9	110.5	97.3	94.9	99.1
Austin-San Marcos, TX MSA	101.3	87.6	89.2	100.0	105.5	106.9
Bakersfield, CA MSA	104.0	109.2	115.1	115.5	112.1	103.8
Baltimore, MD PMSA	100.4	101.9	112.5	105.6	95.9	96.9
Baton Rouge, LA MSA	100.0	101.8	107.5	103.8	92.5	99.3
Beaumont-Port Arthur, TX MSA	94.6	88.2	91.7	96.9	96.7	101.0
Bellingham, WA MSA	104.8	103.0	81.8	97.4	125.7	102.5
Benton Harbor, MI MSA	106.7	107.4	98.8	100.4	100.2	106.0
Billings, MT MSA	100.9	103.7	73.9	103.8	102.5	102.5
Biloxi-Gulfport-Pascagoula, MS MSA	94.8	97.0	109.9	90.5	97.0	97.9
Binghamton, NY MSA	103.8	105.8	130.7	102.8	87.8	105.1
Birmingham, AL MSA	98.4	97.3	96.6	96.3	99.5	99.3
Bismarck, ND MSA	99.4	106.5	87.8	94.7	103.1	102.1
Bloomington, IN MSA	97.2	103.2	86.5	95.6	94.8	97.3
Boise City, ID MSA	103.1	101.4	67.5	100.0	116.6	106.3
Boulder-Longmont, CO PMSA	109.5	98.9	77.5	104.4	121.3	97.9
Bremerton, WA PMSA	111.1	102.9	109.8	107.6	134.3	107.3
Brownsville-Harlingen-San Benito, TX MSA	88.2	83.5	96.4	104.0	93.3	92.8
Bryan-College Station, TX MSA	90.5	91.5	105.9	88.2	99.7	90.5
Buffalo-Niagara Falls, NY MSA	96.6	109.8	126.8	105.9	96.3	89.9
Canton-Massillon, OH MSA	97.1	100.9	83.5	96.6	91.2	97.3
Cedar Rapids, IA MSA	96.9	95.0	100.4	100.2	94.2	97.5
Champaign-Urbana, IL MSA	102.8	103.5	110.6	94.9	109.2	96.9
Charleston-North Charleston, SC MSA	97.1	97.5	123.5	93.9	97.9	100.8
Charleston, WV MSA	100.4	106.2	109.8	101.0	91.6	96.9
Charlotte-Gastonia-Rock Hill, NC-SC MSA	99.0	96.5	103.6	96.6	102.6	99.8
Chattanooga, TN-GA MSA	93.0	96.9	88.8	88.5	88.0	99.9
Cheyenne, WY MSA	97.5	106.7	89.2	96.5	95.0	100.6
Cincinnati, OH-KY-IN PMSA	90.4	95.9	88.0	92.1	96.5	91.8
Clarksville-Hopkinsville, TN-KY MSA	94.5	93.2	92.4	96.7	89.9	95.3
Cleveland-Lorain-Elyria, OH PMSA	104.4	103.5	115.2	106.7	111.4	100.8
Colorado Springs, CO MSA	103.4	96.6	71.2	96.5	123.8	94.6
Columbia, MO MSA	94.5	102.1	81.2	99.2	102.2	100.5
Columbia, SC MSA	94.0	97.5	111.5	96.5	88.6	95.3
Columbus, OH MSA	105.1	106.5	109.8	103.2	96.6	104.1
Cumberland, MD-WV MSA	101.0	96.8	114.5	96.1	91.3	96.8
Dallas, TX PMSA	96.9	96.7	99.9	105.0	107.9	99.8
Davenport-Moline-Rock Island, IA-IL MSA	96.9	103.7	101.7	96.5	93.7	97.3
Dayton-Springfield, OH MSA	105.9	98.0	114.6	102.7	101.3	101.3
Daytona Beach, FL MSA	95.9	99.2	101.1	95.8	97.2	96.7
Decatur, AL MSA	93.6	96.5	89.8	99.9	91.4	96.2
Decatur, IL MSA	93.9	99.6	109.9	98.7	90.1	96.2
Denver, CO PMSA	103.4	97.6	77.5	107.5	120.7	96.5

See footnotes at end of table.

No. 755. Cost of Living Index—Selected Metropolitan Areas: Third Quarter 1996—Continued

[See headnote, page 491]

METROPOLITAN AREAS (MA)	Composite index (100%)	Grocery items (16%)	Housing (28%)	Utilities (8%)	Transportation (10%)	He ca (5
Des Moines, IA MSA	97.7	96.6	87.6	95.2	102.9	
Detroit, MI PMSA	113.4	110.6	86.2	102.2	118.8	
Dothan, AL MSA	93.1	99.0	99.5	92.9	81.8	
Dover, DE MSA	102.8	110.7	112.2	98.0	105.0	
Dubuque, IA MSA	107.6	100.0	90.8	99.3	94.2	
Eau Claire, WI MSA	98.8	100.5	98.9	94.8	107.4	
Elkhart-Goshen, IN MSA	92.3	95.1	89.4	95.4	90.9	
Elmira, NY MSA	112.3	106.4	141.6	106.4	92.9	
Eugene-Springfield, OR MSA	106.3	93.4	73.6	105.0	115.7	
Evansville-Henderson, IN-KY MSA	93.1	102.1	86.4	94.4	89.5	
Fargo-Moorhead, ND-MN MSA	98.8	101.2	90.7	91.6	103.3	
Fayetteville, NC MSA	97.2	98.6	116.7	94.7	89.8	
Fayetteville-Springdale-Rogers, AR MSA	93.1	99.5	86.8	90.3	85.9	
Flagstaff, AZ-UT MSA	111.4	105.0	96.8	112.7	110.7	
Florence, AL MSA	94.1	96.1	98.5	97.5	95.3	
Fort Collins-Loveland, CO MSA	105.8	105.9	68.4	97.2	116.0	
Fort Myers-Cape Coral, FL MSA	98.4	98.7	102.4	106.2	103.8	
Fort Smith, AR-OK MSA	88.8	98.8	100.5	84.4	78.5	
Fort Walton Beach, FL MSA	98.5	98.0	98.4	97.6	107.8	
Fort Wayne, IN MSA	91.3	97.6	90.0	96.1	88.7	
Fort Worth-Arlington, TX PMSA	92.2	86.4	119.0	100.3	95.1	
Fresno, CA MSA	107.1	106.6	112.3	119.9	113.0	
Gadsden, AL MSA	92.1	98.8	100.4	92.7	90.9	
Gainesville, FL MSA	100.4	101.5	117.5	101.3	105.7	
Glens Falls, NY MSA	99.8	101.9	130.7	104.1	100.0	
Grand Forks, ND-MN MSA	101.2	103.9	98.5	104.4	93.7	
Grand Junction, CO MSA	101.4	102.3	77.7	104.3	96.9	
Grand Rapids-Muskegon-Holland, MI MSA	103.7	109.3	81.9	102.8	88.4	
Great Falls, MT MSA	107.0	105.2	70.4	100.9	103.2	
Greeley, CO PMSA	90.2	96.9	73.0	96.9	105.4	
Green Bay, WI MSA	98.7	96.1	88.4	100.6	102.4	
Greensboro—Winston-Salem—High Point, NC MS	100.9	94.9	110.1	100.3	87.7	
Greenville, NC MSA	97.6	96.1	132.7	92.1	94.4	
Greenville-Spartanburg-Anderson, SC MSA	94.2	97.8	103.8	91.0	87.9	
Hagerstown, MD PMSA	99.0	92.5	102.0	100.3	96.5	
Harrisburg-Lebanon-Carlisle, PA MSA	101.7	96.6	118.4	111.2	102.4	
Hattiesburg, MS MSA	92.4	95.9	102.7	102.4	90.7	
Houston, TX PMSA	93.8	92.2	98.7	106.3	104.0	
Huntington-Ashland, WV-KY-OH MSA	99.0	104.5	118.7	100.8	98.9	
Huntsville, AL MSA	95.7	95.5	90.3	98.4	104.0	
Indianapolis, IN MSA	94.7	99.2	87.9	95.9	93.0	
Jackson, MS MSA	95.5	98.7	102.9	98.3	82.2	
Jackson, TN MSA	94.8	97.5	94.1	100.5	84.3	
Jacksonville, FL MSA	96.0	100.2	107.7	97.2	93.0	
Johnson City-Kingsport-Bristol, TN-VA MSA	95.3	92.3	84.8	88.5	86.4	
Jonesboro, AR MSA	87.4	96.2	78.2	82.0	88.3	
Joplin, MO MSA	89.9	94.4	83.5	86.1	96.7	
Kansas City, MO-KS MSA	97.5	96.3	94.8	97.8	107.7	
Killeen-Temple, TX MSA	92.2	88.0	98.9	91.1	104.5	
Knoxville, TN MSA	97.5	94.9	93.2	90.8	97.4	
Lafayette, LA MSA	96.7	96.1	107.4	101.7	89.5	
Lake Charles, LA MSA	97.5	98.0	114.8	95.8	86.4	
Lancaster, PA MSA	103.2	96.7	106.8	109.6	90.7	
Lansing-East Lansing, MI MSA	107.2	109.6	77.7	99.0	107.5	
Las Cruces, NM MSA	98.0	97.4	90.4	96.9	96.2	

See footnotes at end of table.

No. 755. Cost of Living Index—Selected Metropolitan Areas: Third Quarter 1996—Continued

[See headnote, page 491]

METROPOLITAN AREAS (MA)	Composite index (100%)	Grocery items (16%)	Housing (28%)	Utilities (8%)	Transportation (10%)	Health care (5%)
Las Vegas, NV-AZ MSA	104.70	110.90	75.70	116.90	119.20	101.10
Lawrence, KS MSA	99.50	90.50	78.60	92.00	92.90	104.90
Lawton, OK MSA	92.90	95.70	87.10	94.20	92.90	98.60
Lexington, KY MSA	97.40	97.30	82.20	96.60	100.00	103.10
Lincoln, NE MSA	89.10	93.00	83.30	101.20	84.00	97.70
Little Rock-North Little Rock, AR MSA	86.90	96.20	101.10	93.30	72.00	85.10
Los Angeles-Long Beach, CA PMSA	119.70	117.10	116.00	116.20	137.50	109.10
Louisville, KY-IN MSA	94.00	95.00	94.90	102.10	96.00	95.70
Lubbock, TX MSA	90.50	93.00	72.20	95.90	92.90	96.80
Lynchburg, VA MSA	95.00	100.70	89.50	89.30	92.90	98.40
Macon, GA MSA	95.70	100.40	102.60	94.80	87.40	99.20
Madison, WI MSA	112.20	98.80	92.10	105.10	110.80	111.70
Mansfield, OH MSA	100.10	101.70	139.40	95.80	89.00	98.00
McAllen-Edinburg-Mission, TX MSA	94.50	91.10	102.50	91.50	85.80	103.40
Memphis, TN-AR-MS MSA	95.40	102.70	78.60	99.30	92.00	95.30
Miami, FL PMSA	107.70	103.60	107.10	114.10	123.40	101.90
Milwaukee-Waukesha, WI PMSA	105.40	102.10	82.50	104.30	102.10	100.30
Minneapolis-St. Paul, MN-WI MSA	101.40	97.40	100.90	113.90	126.90	99.10
Mobile, AL MSA	93.90	99.10	101.40	104.70	93.90	100.90
Monroe, LA MSA	96.70	93.60	131.20	94.50	89.00	103.10
Montgomery, AL MSA	94.30	95.30	95.70	107.00	97.10	97.90
Muncie, IN MSA	96.50	98.70	79.30	100.70	91.20	95.50
Myrtle Beach, SC MSA	99.90	99.20	101.30	95.20	93.90	102.40
Nashville, TN MSA	94.20	97.10	91.10	96.80	95.10	95.10
New Orleans, LA MSA	94.90	97.60	132.90	100.00	79.20	96.00
New York, NY PMSA	234.50	144.60	173.40	123.60	206.90	132.20
Norfolk-Virginia Beach-Newport News, VA-NC MSA	96.50	96.00	129.20	104.10	101.50	97.00
Odessa-Midland, TX MSA	93.00	93.00	96.00	101.10	91.20	100.90
Oklahoma City, OK MSA	90.00	89.60	92.70	92.40	94.50	96.90
Omaha, NE-IA MSA	92.00	92.90	86.70	102.70	88.90	90.60
Orlando, FL MSA	99.40	99.60	102.60	98.80	110.20	101.70
Owensboro, KY MSA	92.20	100.00	69.60	94.00	91.00	98.30
Panama City, FL MSA	94.70	98.70	98.10	95.60	90.40	99.20
Pensacola, FL MSA	96.20	102.20	95.30	97.30	99.70	100.40
Peoria-Pekin, IL MSA	101.10	104.30	94.80	101.00	96.20	100.40
Philadelphia, PA-NJ PMSA	125.50	112.70	199.90	117.40	99.30	108.30
Phoenix-Mesa, AZ MSA	103.30	104.60	106.60	118.30	117.70	99.70
Pittsburgh, PA MSA	109.50	103.10	133.60	106.40	111.40	108.70
Portland-Vancouver, OR-WA PMSA	109.10	99.70	89.20	112.80	124.00	104.10
Provo-Orem, UT MSA	103.90	97.30	81.90	107.40	118.60	98.90
Pueblo, CO MSA	90.00	102.00	81.50	95.00	116.70	87.10
Raleigh-Durham-Chapel Hill, NC MSA	103.00	100.90	112.30	93.70	104.70	99.50
Rapid City, SD MSA	96.70	100.50	103.80	98.50	92.30	96.40
Reno, NV MSA	112.40	106.40	90.90	117.70	110.90	105.30
Richland-Kennewick-Pasco, WA MSA	99.50	101.50	83.70	96.30	131.60	101.30
Richmond-Petersburg, VA MSA	103.00	99.40	117.70	106.40	108.30	99.70
Riverside-San Bernardino, CA PMSA	106.70	107.30	98.70	114.70	130.30	106.30
Roanoke, VA MSA	92.50	94.40	85.20	91.80	93.60	94.40
Rochester, MN MSA	97.70	97.00	96.10	108.60	98.60	101.10
Rochester, NY MSA	102.20	117.00	127.90	118.90	89.20	99.50
Rockford, IL MSA	105.30	101.30	110.30	108.40	101.90	103.80
St. Cloud, MN MSA	96.70	100.50	96.20	107.70	98.30	98.90
St. Joseph, MO MSA	94.10	88.20	82.50	95.10	95.20	97.40
St. Louis, MO-IL MSA	96.70	107.00	93.10	96.90	109.80	95.60
Salem, OR PMSA	106.00	95.10	103.60	108.40	124.80	101.80

See footnotes at end of table.

No. 755. Cost of Living Index—Selected Metropolitan Areas: Third Quarter 1996—Continued

[See headnote, page 491]

METROPOLITAN AREAS (MA)	Composite index (100%)	Grocery items (16%)	Housing (28%)	Utilities (8%)	Transportation (10%)	Health care (5%)
Salinas, CA MSA	143.6	112.8	100.4	128.6	160.6	111.5
Salt Lake City-Ogden, UT MSA	96.5	102.2	76.4	96.5	105.6	96.7
San Angelo, TX MSA	93.0	90.3	87.4	96.8	87.0	106.3
San Antonio, TX MSA	92.2	95.2	96.0	93.0	96.3	94.5
San Diego, CA MSA	121.9	113.4	100.9	131.0	120.0	103.4
Santa Barbara-Santa Maria-Lompoc, CA MSA	113.2	106.9	107.4	112.0	114.5	100.1
Santa Fe, NM MSA	107.4	99.5	86.8	104.3	111.8	100.7
Sarasota-Bradenton, FL MSA	102.0	94.8	107.0	92.9	106.1	100.1
Scranton—Wilkes-Barre—Hazleton, PA MSA	97.5	104.2	100.4	93.1	90.5	96.0
Seattle-Bellevue-Everett, WA PMSA	115.0	110.6	78.4	112.8	147.1	112.6
Sheboygan, WI MSA	101.2	103.9	81.8	100.1	90.4	95.8
Shreveport-Bossier City, LA MSA	93.7	88.4	95.9	96.4	86.9	94.9
Sioux Falls, SD MSA	95.1	97.0	92.4	95.8	102.3	95.2
South Bend, IN MSA	92.1	91.8	97.2	92.9	96.6	92.4
Spokane, WA MSA	107.7	102.4	61.2	101.0	119.8	106.3
Springfield, IL MSA	95.6	103.8	80.8	93.0	107.8	106.2
Springfield, MO MSA	91.4	93.5	72.5	96.0	95.7	94.4
Sumter, SC MSA	94.7	97.4	115.3	93.8	94.2	101.5
Syracuse, NY MSA	103.2	112.4	133.6	109.1	106.8	97.9
Tacoma, WA PMSA	104.6	110.6	76.2	111.5	136.4	101.8
Tallahassee, FL MSA	102.3	97.5	116.6	99.2	96.1	101.3
Tampa-St. Petersburg-Clearwater, FL MSA	94.3	101.7	106.3	96.0	96.4	93.0
Texarkana, TX-Texarkana, AR MSA	88.6	90.8	91.1	97.6	95.8	93.9
Toledo, OH MSA	100.6	102.5	137.0	106.2	95.8	97.7
Tucson, AZ MSA	99.8	104.5	110.9	102.1	113.8	95.6
Tulsa, OK MSA	93.0	93.6	100.1	91.7	95.9	99.2
Tuscaloosa, AL MSA	101.4	97.3	104.9	97.8	94.9	107.5
Tyler, TX MSA	91.2	88.8	96.9	101.3	89.2	96.8
Utica-Rome, NY MSA	104.3	101.7	136.7	107.3	96.2	102.7
Victoria, TX MSA	90.8	85.0	95.4	93.1	92.2	93.9
Visalia-Tulare-Porterville, CA MSA	106.6	99.6	124.2	116.4	124.8	106.0
Waco, TX MSA	91.2	86.2	117.1	101.2	86.4	96.1
Washington, DC-MD-VA-WV PMSA	125.4	109.0	94.2	125.3	120.9	113.5
Wausau, WI MSA	105.5	99.6	88.5	94.6	109.2	99.8
West Palm Beach-Boca Raton, FL MSA	107.7	101.9	117.6	105.6	110.0	107.4
Wichita Falls, TX MSA	89.7	93.8	97.8	96.7	92.2	95.8
Williamsport, PA MSA	101.9	99.3	137.8	97.1	95.7	98.1
Wilmington-Newark, DE-MD PMSA	110.1	115.8	124.1	99.2	118.2	104.8
Wilmington, NC MSA	102.6	96.1	113.8	89.3	99.8	100.0
Yakima, WA MSA	106.8	102.0	91.3	100.1	127.1	97.8
York, PA MSA	96.8	94.4	109.4	106.2	93.0	99.2
Youngstown-Warren, OH MSA	96.3	96.8	107.0	89.0	91.9	94.7
Yuma, AZ MSA	98.9	103.6	152.6	113.7	103.2	94.5

Source: ACCRA, Louisville KY 40206-6749, *ACCRA Cost of Living Index*, Third Quarter 1996 (copyright).

No. 756. Annual Percent Changes in Consumer Prices, United States and OECD Countries: 1990 to 1996

[Covers member countries of Organization for Economic Cooperation (OECD). For consumer price indexes for OECD countries, see section 30]

COUNTRY	1990	1991	1992	1993	1994	1995	1996
United States	5.4	4.2	3.0	3.0	2.6	2.8	2.9
OECD	5.6	5.2	4.0	3.6	4.3	5.5	4.9
Australia	7.3	3.2	1.0	1.8	1.9	4.6	2.6
Canada	4.8	5.6	1.5	1.8	0.2	2.2	1.6
Japan	3.1	3.3	1.7	1.3	0.7	-0.1	0.1
New Zealand	6.1	2.6	1.0	1.3	1.8	3.8	2.3
Austria	3.3	3.3	4.0	3.6	3.0	2.2	1.9
Belgium	3.4	3.2	2.4	2.8	2.4	1.5	2.1
Denmark	2.7	2.4	2.1	1.3	2.0	2.1	2.1
Finland	6.1	4.3	2.9	2.2	1.1	1.0	0.6
France	3.4	3.2	2.4	2.1	1.7	1.7	2.0
Greece	20.4	19.5	15.9	14.4	10.9	8.9	8.2
Ireland	3.3	3.2	3.1	1.4	2.3	2.5	1.7
Italy [1]	6.1	6.5	5.3	4.2	3.9	5.4	3.8
Luxembourg	3.7	3.1	3.2	3.6	2.2	1.9	1.4
Netherlands	2.5	3.9	3.2	2.6	2.8	1.9	2.1
Norway	4.1	3.4	2.3	2.3	1.4	2.5	1.3
Portugal [2]	13.4	11.4	8.9	6.5	5.2	4.1	3.1
Spain	6.7	5.9	5.9	4.6	4.7	4.7	3.6
Sweden	10.5	9.3	2.3	4.6	2.4	2.9	0.8
Switzerland	5.4	5.8	4.0	3.3	0.9	1.8	0.8
Turkey [2]	60.3	66.0	70.1	66.1	105.1	89.1	80.4
United Kingdom	9.5	5.9	3.7	1.6	2.5	3.4	2.4
Germany	2.7	3.5	4.0	3.6	2.7	1.8	1.5

[1] Households of wage and salary earners. [2] Excludes rent.

Source: Organization for Economic Cooperation and Development, Paris, France, *Main Economic Indicators*, monthly.

No. 757. Producer Price Indexes, by Stage of Processing: 1960 to 1996

[1982=100. Minus sign (-) indicates decline. See text, section 15]

YEAR	CRUDE MATERIALS				Intermediate materials, supplies, and components	FINISHED GOODS		CONSUMER FOODS		Finished consumer goods excl. food
	Total	Foodstuffs and feedstuffs	Fuel	Crude nonfood materials except fuel		Consumer goods	Capital equipment	Crude	Processed	
1960	30.4	38.4	10.5	26.9	30.8	33.6	32.8	39.8	35.2	33.5
1961	30.2	37.9	10.5	27.2	30.6	33.6	32.9	38.0	35.3	33.4
1962	30.5	38.6	10.4	27.1	30.6	33.7	33.0	38.4	35.6	33.4
1963	29.9	37.5	10.5	26.7	30.7	33.5	33.1	37.8	35.2	33.4
1964	29.6	36.6	10.5	27.2	30.8	33.6	33.4	38.9	35.2	33.3
1965	31.1	39.2	10.6	27.7	31.2	34.2	33.8	39.0	36.8	33.6
1966	33.1	42.7	10.9	28.3	32.0	35.4	34.6	41.5	39.2	34.1
1967	31.3	40.3	11.3	26.5	32.2	35.6	35.8	39.6	38.8	34.7
1968	31.8	40.9	11.5	27.1	33.0	36.5	37.0	42.5	40.0	35.5
1969	33.9	44.1	12.0	28.4	34.1	37.9	38.3	45.9	42.3	36.3
1970	35.2	45.2	13.8	29.1	35.4	39.1	40.1	46.0	43.9	37.4
1971	36.0	46.1	15.7	29.4	36.8	40.2	41.7	45.8	44.7	38.7
1972	39.9	51.5	16.8	32.3	38.2	41.5	42.8	48.0	47.2	39.4
1973	54.5	72.6	18.6	42.9	42.4	46.0	44.2	63.6	55.8	41.2
1974	61.4	76.4	24.8	54.5	52.5	53.1	50.5	71.6	63.9	48.2
1975	61.6	77.4	30.6	50.0	58.0	58.2	58.2	71.7	70.3	53.2
1976	63.4	76.8	34.5	54.9	60.9	60.4	62.1	76.7	69.0	56.5
1977	65.5	77.5	42.0	56.3	64.9	64.3	66.1	79.5	72.7	60.6
1978	73.4	87.3	48.2	61.9	69.5	69.4	71.3	85.8	79.4	64.9
1979	85.9	100.0	57.3	75.5	78.4	77.5	77.5	92.3	86.8	73.5
1980	95.3	104.6	69.4	91.8	90.3	88.6	85.8	93.9	92.3	87.1
1981	103.0	103.9	84.8	109.8	98.6	96.6	94.6	104.4	97.2	96.1
1982	100.0	100.0	100.0	100.0	100.0	100.0	100.0	100.0	100.0	100.0
1983	101.3	101.8	105.1	98.8	100.6	101.3	102.8	102.4	100.9	101.2
1984	103.5	104.7	105.1	101.0	103.1	103.3	105.2	111.4	104.9	102.2
1985	95.8	94.8	102.7	94.3	102.7	103.8	107.5	102.9	104.8	103.3
1986	87.7	93.2	92.2	76.0	99.1	101.4	109.7	105.6	107.4	98.5
1987	93.7	96.2	84.1	88.5	101.5	103.6	111.7	107.1	109.6	100.7
1988	96.0	106.1	82.1	85.9	107.1	106.2	114.3	109.8	112.7	103.1
1989	103.1	111.2	85.3	95.8	112.0	112.1	118.8	119.6	118.6	108.9
1990	108.9	113.1	84.8	107.3	114.5	118.2	122.9	123.0	124.4	115.3
1991	101.2	105.5	82.9	97.5	114.4	120.5	126.7	119.3	124.4	118.7
1992	100.4	105.1	84.0	94.2	114.7	121.7	129.1	107.6	124.4	120.8
1993	102.4	108.4	87.1	94.1	116.2	123.0	131.4	114.4	126.5	121.7
1994	101.8	106.5	82.4	97.0	118.5	123.3	134.1	111.3	127.9	121.6
1995	102.7	105.8	72.1	105.8	124.9	125.6	136.7	118.8	129.8	124.0
1996 prel	113.5	121.5	91.3	105.7	125.7	129.5	138.3	128.9	133.8	127.6
PERCENT CHANGE										
1960	-2.3	-1.0	1.0	3.7	-	0.9	0.3	6.7	1.4	0.6
1961	-0.7	-1.3	-	-4.3	-0.6	-	0.3	-4.5	0.3	-0.3
1962	1.0	1.8	-1.0	1.1	-	0.3	0.3	1.1	0.8	-
1963	-2.0	-2.8	1.0	-0.4	0.3	-0.6	0.3	-1.6	-1.1	-
1964	-1.0	-2.4	-	-1.5	0.3	0.3	0.9	2.9	-	-0.3
1965	5.1	7.1	1.0	1.9	1.3	1.8	1.2	0.3	4.5	0.9
1966	6.4	8.9	2.8	1.8	2.6	3.5	2.4	6.4	6.5	1.5
1967	-5.4	-5.6	3.7	2.2	0.6	0.6	3.5	-4.6	-1.0	1.8
1968	1.6	1.5	1.8	-6.4	2.5	2.5	3.4	7.3	3.1	2.3
1969	6.6	7.8	4.3	2.3	3.3	3.8	3.5	8.0	5.7	2.3
1970	3.8	2.5	15.0	4.8	3.8	3.2	4.7	0.2	3.8	3.0
1971	2.3	2.0	13.8	2.5	4.0	2.8	4.0	-0.4	1.8	3.5
1972	10.8	11.7	7.0	1.0	3.8	3.2	2.6	4.8	5.6	1.8
1973	36.6	41.0	10.7	9.9	11.0	10.8	3.3	32.5	18.2	4.6
1974	12.7	5.2	33.3	32.8	23.8	15.4	14.3	12.6	14.5	17.0
1975	0.3	1.3	23.4	27.0	10.5	9.6	15.2	0.1	10.0	10.4
1976	2.9	-0.8	12.7	-8.3	5.0	3.8	6.7	7.0	-1.8	6.2
1977	3.3	0.9	21.7	9.8	6.6	6.5	6.4	3.7	5.4	7.3
1978	12.1	12.6	14.8	2.6	7.1	7.9	7.9	7.9	9.2	7.1
1979	17.0	14.5	18.9	9.9	12.8	11.7	8.7	7.6	9.3	13.3
1980	10.9	4.6	21.1	22.0	15.2	14.3	10.7	1.7	6.3	18.5
1981	8.1	-0.7	22.2	21.6	9.2	9.0	10.3	11.2	5.3	10.3
1982	-2.9	-3.8	17.9	19.6	1.4	3.5	5.7	-4.2	2.9	4.1
1983	1.3	1.8	5.1	-8.9	0.6	1.3	2.8	2.4	0.9	1.2
1984	2.2	2.8	-	-1.2	2.5	2.0	2.3	8.8	4.0	1.0
1985	-7.4	-9.5	-2.3	2.2	-0.4	0.5	2.2	-7.6	-0.1	1.1
1986	-8.5	-1.7	-10.2	-6.6	-3.5	-2.3	2.0	2.6	2.5	-4.6
1987	6.8	3.2	-8.8	-19.4	2.4	2.2	1.8	1.4	2.0	2.2
1988	2.5	10.3	-2.4	16.4	5.5	2.5	2.3	2.5	2.8	2.4
1989	7.4	4.8	3.9	-2.9	4.6	5.6	3.9	8.9	5.2	5.6
1990	5.6	1.7	-0.6	11.5	2.2	5.4	3.5	2.8	4.9	5.9
1991	-7.1	-6.7	-2.2	12.0	-0.1	1.9	3.1	-3.0	-	2.9
1992	-0.8	-0.4	1.3	-9.1	0.3	1.0	1.9	-9.8	-	1.8
1993	2.0	3.1	3.7	-3.4	1.3	1.1	1.8	6.3	1.7	0.7
1994	-0.6	-1.8	-5.4	-0.1	2.0	0.2	2.1	-2.7	1.1	-0.1
1995	0.9	-0.7	-12.5	3.1	5.4	1.9	1.9	6.7	1.5	2.0
1996 prel	10.5	14.8	26.6	-0.1	0.6	3.1	1.2	8.5	3.1	2.9

- Represents or rounds to zero.

Source: U.S. Bureau of Labor Statistics, *Producer Price Indexes*, monthly and annual.

No. 758. Producer Price Indexes for Selected Commodity Groupings: 1980 to 1996

[1982=100, except as indicated]

COMMODITY	1980	1990	1991	1992	1993	1994	1995	1996
All commodities	89.8	116.3	116.5	117.2	118.9	120.4	124.7	127.8
Farm products	102.9	112.2	105.7	103.6	107.1	106.3	107.4	122.3
Fruits & melons, fresh/dry vegs. & nuts	94.1	117.5	114.7	96.9	106.9	104.6	106.5	122.1
Fresh fruits and melons	100.3	118.1	129.9	84.0	84.5	82.7	85.8	100.0
Fresh and dry vegetables	88.9	118.1	103.8	115.0	135.2	129.0	144.4	136.0
Wheat	108.3	87.6	79.4	98.5	98.4	104.8	118.6	136.6
Slaughter livestock	98.0	115.6	107.9	104.7	107.0	96.4	92.8	95.2
Wool	108.2	89.6	69.4	81.6	56.5	80.5	99.6	78.1
Fluid milk	96.0	100.8	89.5	96.1	94.1	95.7	93.6	107.8
Chicken eggs	95.7	117.6	110.7	94.1	105.9	97.8	104.1	130.7
Oilseeds	116.1	112.1	106.4	107.5	115.9	117.4	112.6	139.4
Processed foods and feeds	95.9	121.9	121.9	122.1	124.0	125.5	127.0	133.4
Cereal and bakery products	93.0	134.2	137.9	144.2	147.6	151.1	154.7	159.9
Bakery products	90.0	141.0	146.6	152.5	156.6	160.0	164.3	169.7
Flour and flour base mixes and doughs	98.3	107.9	103.8	111.5	112.0	113.8	120.8	130.7
Milled rice	131.5	102.5	109.9	108.8	101.3	118.3	113.1	129.3
Meats, poultry, and fish	94.4	119.6	116.6	112.2	115.5	112.2	111.8	116.4
Pork	78.4	119.8	113.4	98.9	105.7	101.4	101.5	(NA)
Processed poultry	108.2	113.6	109.9	109.0	111.7	114.7	114.2	119.8
Young chicken	106.8	111.0	105.1	104.9	109.5	113.3	113.5	(NA)
Turkeys	109.2	107.6	107.3	102.3	101.0	106.5	104.9	(NA)
Dairy products	92.7	117.2	114.6	117.9	118.1	119.4	119.7	130.9
Butter	93.2	71.3	69.5	59.3	54.4	50.4	55.4	71.2
Ice cream and frozen desserts	90.1	123.1	123.1	124.9	127.2	127.4	128.2	132.6
Processed fruits and vegetables	83.3	124.7	119.6	120.8	118.2	121.1	122.4	127.7
Frozen fruits, juices and ades	79.9	139.0	116.3	125.9	110.7	111.9	115.9	124.4
Frozen vegetables	79.4	118.4	117.6	116.4	120.9	125.9	124.2	125.4
Sugar and confectionery	119.6	123.1	128.4	127.7	127.9	132.5	134.0	137.5
Beverages and beverage materials	90.7	120.8	124.1	124.4	124.8	127.7	133.8	134.6
Alcoholic beverages	88.9	117.2	123.7	126.1	126.0	124.8	128.5	132.8
Coffee (whole bean, ground, & instant)	110.4	113.0	107.8	100.5	100.5	128.2	146.5	
Fats and oils	105.4	119.4	112.0	106.8	116.9	135.8	136.5	130.8
Textile products and apparel	89.7	115.0	116.3	117.8	118.0	118.3	120.8	122.4
Apparel	88.7	117.5	119.6	122.2	123.2	123.5	124.2	125.1
Textile housefurnishings	86.8	109.5	111.8	113.7	115.8	117.3	119.5	122.3
Footwear	95.2	125.6	128.6	132.0	134.4	135.5	139.2	141.7
Fuels and related products and power	82.8	82.3	81.2	80.4	80.0	77.8	78.0	85.8
Coal	87.4	97.5	97.2	95.0	96.1	96.7	95.0	94.9
Natural gas (to pipelines)	63.3	80.4	79.1	80.6	84.7	78.8	66.6	89.6
Electric power	79.1	117.6	124.3	126.3	128.6	128.7	130.9	131.6
Petroleum products, refined	88.6	74.8	67.2	64.7	62.0	59.1	60.8	70.2
Gasoline	93.3	78.7	69.9	68.1	63.9	61.7	63.7	72.8
Chemicals and allied products	89.0	123.6	125.6	125.9	128.2	132.1	142.5	142.1
Industrial chemicals	91.9	113.2	111.8	109.3	110.4	114.3	128.4	128.9
Drugs and pharmaceuticals	83.0	170.8	182.6	192.2	200.9	206.0	210.9	214.7
Lumber and wood products	101.5	129.7	132.1	146.6	174.0	180.0	178.1	176.1
Lumber	104.9	124.6	124.9	144.7	183.4	188.4	173.4	179.9
Wastepaper	172.2	138.9	121.4	117.5	117.4	209.5	371.1	141.7
Paper	89.7	128.8	126.9	123.2	123.8	126.0	159.0	149.2
Paperboard	92.0	135.7	130.2	134.3	130.0	140.5	183.1	155.8
Building paper & building board mill prods.	86.1	112.2	111.8	119.6	132.7	144.1	144.9	137.2
Hardboard, particleboard & fiberboard prods.	86.9	107.5	106.5	114.9	128.1	139.0	139.6	131.6
Metals and metal products	95.0	122.9	120.2	119.2	119.2	124.8	134.5	131.0
Iron and steel	90.0	117.2	114.1	111.5	116.0	122.0	128.8	125.9
Iron ore	87.8	83.3	83.6	83.7	82.7	82.7	91.8	96.7
Iron and steel scrap	140.9	166.0	147.6	139.2	172.5	192.9	202.7	190.8

See footnotes at end of table.

. 758. Producer Price Indexes for Selected Commodity Groupings: 1980 to 1996—Continued

[1982=100, except as indicated]

COMMODITY	1980	1990	1991	1992	1993	1994	1995	1996
ctric furnace products	97.1	120.1	116.9	115.5	115.7	117.0	126.0	157.0
ducts	86.6	112.1	109.5	106.4	108.2	113.4	120.1	115.7
netals	115.7	133.8	123.4	120.9	114.4	126.6	149.6	136.5
errous metals	132.7	133.4	114.0	108.1	98.1	115.7	146.8	128.2
crap	154.4	170.5	149.2	144.4	127.5	157.7	193.9	167.1
onferrous metals	123.0	125.6	106.7	108.1	99.3	118.8	135.9	122.3
ill shapes	97.1	130.7	124.8	124.5	120.0	127.8	155.5	143.4
wire and cable	107.5	142.6	139.2	136.7	133.1	139.8	151.5	147.5
ners	90.9	114.0	115.5	113.9	109.7	108.1	117.2	110.1
ns, and pails	87.4	115.9	117.2	116.6	117.9	126.4	139.7	139.9
	85.8	125.9	130.2	132.7	135.2	137.5	141.1	143.8
ge tools	81.2	134.8	141.6	146.1	149.1	152.6	157.5	160.9
tures and brass fittings	88.5	144.3	149.7	153.1	155.9	159.6	166.0	171.1
a fixtures	88.6	125.6	127.0	127.6	127.0	128.9	131.9	131.8
	88.2	155.8	162.5	167.7	172.3	177.3	185.1	192.0
pment	87.0	131.6	134.1	137.3	140.4	142.5	147.5	151.2
ot water equipment	89.1	132.6	135.2	138.0	138.9	138.6	141.6	144.8
naces	84.2	129.6	131.5	134.8	137.3	138.0	141.2	142.9
urners and parts	84.9	134.4	138.5	142.3	147.1	150.1	154.8	157.9
s, domestic	89.0	124.3	124.5	127.9	133.4	137.9	146.2	152.9
tructural metal products	88.8	121.8	122.4	122.1	123.2	127.3	135.1	137.8
sash, and trim	87.8	131.4	134.6	135.0	136.6	142.0	156.5	159.3
	89.3	113.8	114.9	115.0	113.9	114.2	118.6	120.8
products	91.3	129.2	129.0	128.0	128.9	131.7	138.9	139.6
pre-eng. metal products	88.5	117.0	115.7	114.7	115.8	120.7	127.7	131.7
s metal products	88.5	119.4	120.4	121.4	122.3	123.6	125.9	126.9
crews, rivets, and washers	91.3	116.3	118.3	118.7	119.8	120.9	123.0	125.3
res	81.8	127.5	129.8	131.0	131.2	132.2	135.9	137.5
and equipment	86.0	120.7	123.0	123.4	124.0	125.1	126.6	126.5
achinery and equipment	83.3	121.7	125.7	129.5	133.6	137.0	142.9	146.4
rden tractors	81.8	123.2	128.1	133.4	135.3	138.3	141.5	143.6
nachinery excl. tractors	83.9	121.5	125.4	128.2	131.8	136.1	142.5	146.4
quipment	86.5	119.2	121.3	124.0	129.9	132.1	140.5	143.3
machinery and equipment	84.2	121.6	125.2	126.7	132.0	133.7	136.7	139.8
s, excavators, and equipment	86.6	129.7	133.8	141.3	147.4	148.9	151.9	156.0
equipment for mounting	84.2	119.9	121.3	121.8	125.0	126.1	130.1	133.5
onstruction machinery	82.6	124.3	129.1	128.4	129.6	135.5	138.2	140.6
ompressors	97.7	117.3	117.7	120.4	121.2	120.7	123.1	123.5
rs, spreaders, etc	87.6	113.2	118.5	118.0	121.8	124.0	126.8	129.4
er than farm	83.0	124.0	128.2	132.7	137.0	140.3	143.1	146.5
machinery and equipment	85.5	123.0	127.6	130.9	133.5	136.5	139.8	143.1
hand tools	86.4	121.1	124.5	127.2	129.5	132.9	135.1	137.2
hines and equipment	88.2	127.5	132.8	137.7	142.5	147.8	153.0	157.4
and accessories	86.0	118.5	121.5	123.9	125.8	128.1	131.9	135.0
ducts	85.1	122.3	126.6	130.5	132.4	135.1	138.2	141.1
machine tools	85.1	129.8	134.6	138.9	141.1	143.1	148.0	152.6
machine tools	85.7	128.7	133.5	135.9	138.4	141.9	145.7	149.6
pressors, and equipment	82.8	119.2	124.6	129.1	132.8	135.2	139.4	143.4
calators, and other lifts	87.3	110.1	108.7	109.4	110.7	112.4	113.0	113.7
terial handling equipment	88.4	115.0	117.4	118.4	120.2	122.4	125.3	127.3
ts machinery	84.9	133.4	139.3	143.8	147.3	152.6	157.5	161.1
inery and equipment	87.2	128.8	135.0	138.9	143.7	144.9	146.7	148.5
machinery and equipment	86.0	122.1	124.5	128.4	132.8	133.4	137.1	141.9
s machinery and equipment	89.7	124.9	126.5	126.8	129.5	130.9	133.6	136.9
mponents and accessories	88.8	118.4	118.6	117.5	117.7	116.6	113.6	109.0
inery and equipment	85.2	121.0	125.2	127.4	129.5	131.1	135.6	138.9
ore machines and equipment	93.1	109.5	109.8	111.0	111.0	111.3	111.5	112.0
bustion engines	81.7	120.2	126.0	128.4	130.2	132.9	135.6	138.8
nd household durables	90.7	119.2	121.2	122.2	123.7	126.1	128.2	130.3
rniture	89.1	125.1	128.0	130.0	133.4	138.0	141.8	144.5
furniture	85.7	133.4	136.2	138.1	140.5	144.7	148.2	151.6
ppliances	87.5	110.8	111.3	111.4	112.9	112.8	112.4	112.7
nces	86.4	108.7	108.3	108.2	109.6	109.5	108.9	109.3
ewares and fans	90.9	109.7	111.8	112.6	113.4	112.0	110.8	111.0
s	81.9	133.0	133.5	134.1	138.6	140.4	142.7	144.1
nic equipment	103.8	82.7	83.2	82.0	80.2	80.3	78.9	79.0
ceivers	103.4	78.9	78.9	77.1	74.5	74.3	72.2	72.0
lassware	84.7	132.5	136.0	141.6	142.9	147.4	153.2	157.3
tware	148.0	122.1	119.5	125.2	130.7	133.9	138.3	138.3
equip. excl. garden tractors	87.5	123.0	124.7	125.3	126.2	128.4	130.4	132.2
rs and razor blades	82.5	129.8	140.9	142.3	146.1	150.0	154.1	158.4
c mineral products	88.4	114.7	117.2	117.3	120.0	124.2	129.0	131.0
	88.7	107.5	105.9	106.5	107.3	110.5	113.2	110.0
redients and related products	88.4	115.3	118.4	119.4	123.4	128.7	134.7	138.7
sand/gravel/crushed stone	85.3	125.4	128.6	130.6	134.0	137.9	142.3	145.5
ducts	92.0	113.5	116.6	117.2	120.2	124.6	129.4	133.3
r and wall tile	87.5	132.5	131.1	132.6	133.5	135.5	138.0	138.3
ducts	100.1	105.2	99.3	99.9	108.3	136.1	154.5	154.2
ners	82.3	120.4	125.4	125.1	125.8	127.5	130.5	129.6
terials	80.7	108.4	110.8	102.3	105.8	111.9	118.8	119.0
tion equipment	82.9	121.5	126.4	130.4	133.7	137.2	139.7	141.7
s and equipment	83.1	118.2	122.1	124.9	128.0	131.4	133.0	134.1
s	87.1	120.4	125.9	129.9	134.2	139.1	140.3	141.6

vailable.
U.S. Bureau of Labor Statistics, *Producer Price Indexes*, monthly and annual.

No. 759. Producer Price Indexes for the Net Output of Selected Industries: 1985 to 1995

[Indexes are based on selling prices reported by establishments of all sizes by probability sampling. Industries selected by value added. N.e.c.= not elsewhere classified. See text, section 27]

ITEM	SIC code [1]	Index base	1985	1990	1993	1994	1995
Meat packing plants	2011	12/80	90.9	119.8	113.6	108.0	105.9
Sausage and other prepared meats	2013	12/82	95.7	112.7	110.4	108.9	108.5
Fluid milk	2026	12/82	102.6	121.4	121.2	123.7	123.3
Canned fruits/vegetables/preserves/jams/jellies	2033	06/81	112.7	129.9	127.3	130.1	131.8
Frozen specialties	2038	12/82	110.8	127.3	130.7	132.2	133.2
Bread/other bakery prod., except cookies/crackers	2051	06/80	127.1	159.4	179.0	182.6	189.4
Cookies and crackers	2052	06/83	112.0	141.9	152.3	154.5	156.5
Malt beverages	2082	06/82	110.0	115.2	122.3	119.9	124.0
Bottled and canned soft drinks	2086	06/81	112.5	127.2	132.5	134.1	140.2
Coffee	2095	06/81	111.5	120.0	109.8	134.7	152.6
Cigarettes	2111	12/82	110.7	197.6	235.2	198.9	204.3
Women's, misses', and juniors' dresses	2335	12/80	108.0	125.6	130.1	127.0	124.9
Logging camps and logging contractors	2411	12/81	94.8	135.6	186.4	192.6	194.3
Sawmills and planing mills	2421	12/80	97.3	109.9	159.2	162.0	150.8
Millwork	2431	06/83	103.2	120.4	148.7	152.8	152.1
Wood household furniture, except upholstered	2511	12/79	133.3	158.9	173.3	180.3	186.3
Paper mills	2621	06/81	109.5	134.0	126.6	128.6	164.8
Paperboard mills	2631	12/82	112.0	146.0	138.3	152.6	203.2
Corrugated and solid fiber boxes	2653	03/80	119.7	139.6	135.8	146.2	188.5
Newspaper publishing	2711	12/79	164.0	220.4	259.5	269.5	288.7
Periodical publishing	2721	12/79	157.9	205.7	233.3	239.1	246.3
Book Publishing	2731	12/80	134.1	175.2	194.9	202.8	214.3
Commercial printing, lithographic	2752	06/82	111.0	127.9	135.0	138.5	145.0
Industrial inorganic chemicals, n.e.c.	2819	12/82	100.4	117.9	117.3	115.7	125.2
Plastic materials and resins	2821	12/80	113.6	139.5	132.3	137.7	159.0
Noncellulosic manmade fibers	2824	06/81	97.6	102.7	101.7	103.0	107.9
Pharmaceutical preparations	2834	06/81	141.3	203.5	240.7	244.6	249.9
Soap and other detergents	2841	06/83	104.2	115.2	119.9	119.5	121.7
Specialty cleaning, polish./sanitation preps.	2842	06/83	103.9	118.6	124.7	126.4	129.2
Toilet preparations	2844	03/80	135.4	153.2	166.7	166.5	167.1
Paints and Allied Products	2851	06/83	104.9	125.0	133.5	136.0	143.1
Cyclic crudes/intermed., organic dyes/pigments	2865	12/82	96.9	114.1	116.2	117.5	125.0
Nitrogenous fertilizers	2873	12/79	122.4	119.9	122.9	136.6	157.5
Phosphatic fertilizers	2874	12/79	105.4	115.7	97.5	118.6	139.1
Fertilizers, mixing only	2875	12/79	117.1	124.9	122.8	131.0	140.8
Adhesives and sealants	2891	12/83	103.5	123.4	132.7	136.8	145.1
Explosives	2892	12/80	121.6	174.9	206.7	220.8	218.2
Printing ink	2893	06/84	101.1	120.3	128.8	129.4	135.7
Carbon black	2895	12/83	96.7	84.5	97.8	102.6	115.3
Petroleum Refining	2911	06/85	98.3	90.1	75.2	72.2	74.5
Tires and inner tubes	3011	06/81	96.8	103.0	106.2	108.4	108.5
Ready-mixed concrete	3272	12/79	108.6	114.3	121.0	125.8	131.3
Blast furnaces and steel mills	3312	06/82	104.9	110.8	107.4	112.4	118.5
Gray iron foundries	3321	12/80	115.6	123.4	128.3	131.7	137.7
Nonferrous wire drawing and insulating	3357	12/82	100.5	148.7	138.1	144.7	157.4
Metal cans	3411	06/81	110.4	116.6	113.3	110.8	118.7
Plumbing fixture fittings and brass goods	3432	06/83	105.2	143.2	157.8	162.1	169.0
Nonelectric heating equipment	3433	06/80	126.0	152.5	163.0	165.4	175.1
Fabricated structural metal	3441	06/82	103.0	118.6	118.1	121.7	128.2
Fabricated plate work (boiler shops)	3443	03/80	120.8	142.3	146.5	149.7	155.6
Sheet metal work	3444	12/82	107.2	129.4	127.1	129.9	137.8
Automotive stampings	3465	12/82	110.4	112.6	111.4	111.9	111.7
Internal combustion engines, n.e.c.	3519	12/82	103.4	115.7	125.5	128.0	131.2
Farm machinery and equipment	3523	12/82	105.3	116.8	126.7	129.6	133.2
Construction machinery	3531	12/80	119.5	137.6	151.2	153.8	157.2
Elevators and moving stairways	3534	06/81	109.4	122.4	122.8	124.8	128.0
Conveyors and conveying equipment	3535	06/84	101.2	116.0	120.2	123.4	125.8
Hoists, cranes and monorails	3536	12/84	101.9	111.0	120.0	124.5	129.3
Industrial trucks and tractors	3537	12/79	119.8	134.9	145.5	147.1	150.2
Machine tools, metal cutting types	3541	06/83	105.0	126.3	137.3	139.5	143.9
Metal forming machine tools	3542	06/81	115.2	136.6	146.2	150.2	154.5
Industrial patterns	3543	12/84	101.2	111.0	119.8	119.7	123.0
Special tools/dies/jigs/fixtures & indus. molds	3544	06/81	113.5	124.5	134.3	137.7	140.1
Machine tool accessories	3545	06/83	103.6	115.7	123.3	125.3	128.9
Power driven hand tools	3546	12/80	122.6	139.2	147.5	154.7	162.0
Rolling mill machinery	3547	12/81	110.5	135.1	150.7	150.4	153.0
Gas and electric welding and soldering equip.	3548	12/84	100.7	120.4	134.7	139.3	143.9
Textile machinery	3552	12/80	127.0	151.6	169.1	170.3	172.0
Woodworking machinery	3553	12/80	108.8	128.7	137.3	141.7	145.8
Paper industries machinery	3554	06/82	109.7	136.3	148.1	150.9	155.8
Printing trades machinery	3555	12/82	108.8	126.2	130.6	132.0	133.9
Food products machinery	3556	12/83	107.4	128.5	141.2	145.9	150.2
Electric motors and generators	3621	06/83	108.2	127.5	133.5	134.2	137.5
Telephone & telegraph apparatus	3661	12/85	(NA)	112.0	114.9	116.9	118.2
Semiconductors and related devices	3674	06/81	106.6	105.0	98.3	97.1	91.3
Electronic components, n.e.c.	3679	06/82	108.6	115.1	119.4	118.9	117.8
Motor vehicles and passenger car bodies	3711	06/82	107.2	119.9	133.2	138.0	139.1
Motor vehicle parts and accessories	3714	12/82	100.6	108.9	111.7	112.0	113.5
Photographic equipment and supplies	3861	12/83	101.5	112.2	112.1	111.7	113.8

NA Not available. [1] Standard Industrial Classification code.

Source: U.S. Bureau of Labor Statistics, *Producer Price Indexes*, monthly.

[1992=100]

ITEM	1960	1965	1970	1975	1980	1985	1987	1988	1989	1990	1991	1993	1994	1995	1996
Personal consumption expenditures	23.2	24.7	29.5	40.0	58.5	75.8	81.0	84.3	88.4	92.9	96.8	102.6	105.1	107.6	110.0
Motor vehicles and parts	34.6	35.6	38.9	48.4	68.3	83.2	89.3	90.5	93.1	93.8	97.1	103.4	107.5	112.1	113.6
Furniture and household equipment	57.4	55.9	61.0	73.7	92.0	100.9	100.3	101.2	101.4	101.5	100.9	98.6	98.6	96.3	93.8
Nondurable goods	24.8	26.3	31.7	44.8	65.3	78.7	81.8	84.8	89.3	94.6	98.1	101.5	102.8	104.5	107.2
Food	23.0	24.7	30.1	44.4	63.6	77.5	82.8	86.9	90.5	95.1	98.5	101.7	103.9	106.4	109.7
Clothing and shoes	38.9	40.4	50.4	61.2	72.5	81.6	84.9	88.5	90.6	94.5	97.9	101.0	100.3	98.9	98.6
Gasoline and oil	24.7	25.4	28.3	45.7	97.8	99.4	81.1	81.8	89.4	101.8	100.5	98.1	99.6	101.1	107.0
Fuel oil and coal	15.0	16.0	18.6	39.7	93.7	104.6	85.9	86.1	90.1	107.8	104.0	99.6	98.0	97.3	108.7
Services	19.0	20.7	25.2	34.0	51.0	71.6	78.2	82.2	86.6	91.2	95.8	103.6	106.7	109.9	112.8
Housing	23.4	24.9	28.5	35.8	52.4	73.9	81.7	85.4	89.1	93.5	97.1	102.8	105.7	109.1	112.5
Household operation	24.3	25.5	29.0	41.2	60.3	87.7	88.8	90.2	92.5	94.2	97.6	102.8	104.9	106.3	109.0
Electricity and gas	21.4	21.5	23.2	36.7	62.1	92.4	90.3	91.0	93.6	95.2	98.1	103.1	103.7	103.9	106.3
Other household operation	27.3	29.5	34.9	45.9	59.1	83.6	87.7	89.5	91.6	93.5	97.3	102.6	105.7	108.0	111.0
Transportation	19.7	21.2	26.6	34.7	56.0	71.1	78.3	82.1	85.7	89.9	95.4	104.3	105.9	106.7	110.8
Medical care	12.9	14.8	20.1	27.7	43.6	65.6	70.9	76.4	82.9	89.2	94.4	105.9	110.5	114.6	116.8
Other	17.5	19.8	24.8	35.1	51.8	69.3	77.6	81.5	85.6	90.2	95.3	102.3	104.9	108.0	111.2
Addenda:															
Price indexes for personal consumption expenditures:															
Food	23.0	24.7	30.1	44.4	63.6	77.5	82.8	85.9	90.5	95.1	98.5	101.7	103.9	106.4	109.7
Energy	21.7	22.2	24.6	40.7	80.8	98.5	85.6	86.3	91.3	98.9	99.5	101.0	101.5	102.3	106.7
Personal consumption expenditures less food and energy	23.7	25.2	30.1	39.2	55.7	74.0	80.3	83.9	87.8	92.1	96.3	102.9	105.6	108.2	110.2

Source: U.S. Bureau of Economic Analysis, *The National Income and Product Accounts of the United States, 1929-94*, forthcoming, and *Survey of Current Business*, May 1997.

No. 761. Chain-Type Price Indexes: 1990 to 1996

[1992=100]

ITEM	1990	1991	1993	1994	1995	1996
Gross domestic product	93.6	97.3	102.6	105.0	107.6	109.9
Personal consumption expenditures	92.9	96.8	102.6	105.1	107.6	110.0
Durable goods	96.6	98.5	101.3	103.4	104.6	104.1
Nondurable goods	94.6	98.1	101.5	102.8	104.5	107.2
Services	91.2	95.8	103.6	106.7	110.0	112.8
Gross private domestic investment	98.4	99.7	101.7	103.6	105.6	(NA)
Fixed investment	98.2	99.6	101.7	103.7	105.4	106.3
Nonresidential	98.4	99.9	100.9	102.3	103.4	104.0
Structures	98.8	100.1	103.3	106.7	110.2	112.8
Residential	97.8	98.9	103.7	107.0	110.3	112.2
Exports of goods and services	98.7	100.3	99.9	101.0	104.1	104.3
Imports of goods and services	100.4	100.0	98.7	99.5	102.2	102.0
Government consumption expend [1]	94.1	97.5	102.3	104.3	107.8	110.7
Federal	92.9	96.9	102.6	105.4	109.4	112.0
National defense	92.9	96.5	102.1	104.5	108.3	(NA)
Nondefense	92.8	98.0	104.0	107.7	112.4	(NA)
State and local	94.9	97.9	102.1	103.6	106.7	109.8

NA Not available. [1] And gross investment.

Source: U.S. Bureau of Economic Analysis, *The National Income and Product Accounts of the United States, 1929-94*, forthcoming; and *Survey of Current Business*, May 1997.

No. 762. Chain-Type Price Indexes—Annual Percent Change: 1990 to 1995

[1992=100]

ITEM	1990	1991	1992	1993	1994	1995
Gross domestic product	4.4	3.9	2.8	2.6	2.3	2.5
Personal consumption expenditures	5.1	4.2	3.3	2.6	2.4	2.4
Durable goods	1.4	2.0	1.5	1.3	2.1	1.2
Nondurable goods	6.0	3.6	2.0	1.5	1.3	1.6
Services	5.4	5.0	4.4	3.6	3.0	3.0
Gross private domestic investment	2.4	1.4	0.3	1.7	1.9	1.7
Fixed investment	2.5	1.4	0.4	1.7	1.9	1.6
Nonresidential	2.4	1.5	0.1	0.9	1.4	1.0
Structures	3.3	1.3	-0.1	3.3	3.3	3.3
Producers' durable equipment	1.8	1.6	0.2	-0.1	0.7	0.2
Residential	2.9	1.1	1.2	3.7	3.1	3.1
Exports of goods and services	0.8	1.6	-0.3	-0.1	1.1	3.1
Exports of goods	-1.0	-0.1	-1.7	-1.1	0.6	3.2
Exports of services	5.8	5.8	3.1	2.4	2.2	2.7
Imports of goods and services	2.6	-0.3	0.0	-1.3	0.8	2.7
Imports of goods	1.8	-1.4	-0.7	-1.6	0.6	2.7
Imports of services	6.5	4.1	3.1	0.0	1.9	2.5
Gov't consumption expends and gross invest't	4.3	3.6	2.8	2.3	2.0	3.3
Federal	3.5	4.3	3.2	2.6	2.7	3.8
National defense	3.5	3.8	3.7	2.1	2.3	3.5
Nondefense	3.5	5.5	2.1	4.0	3.5	4.3
State and local	4.9	3.1	2.2	2.1	1.5	3.0

Source: U.S. Bureau of Economic Analysis, *National Income and Product Accounts of the Unites States, 1929-94, forthcoming; and Survey of Current Business*, May 1997.

No. 763. Commodity Research Bureau Futures Price Index: 1980 to 1996

[1967=100. Index computed daily. Represents unweighted geometric average of commodity futures prices (through 9 months forward) of 21 major commodity futures markets. Represents end of year index]

ITEM	1980	1985	1986	1987	1988	1989	1990	1991	1992	1993	1994	1995	1996
All commodities	308.5	229.2	209.1	232.5	251.8	229.9	222.6	208.0	205.9	212.4	229.7	237.1	247.9
Imported	426.0	398.2	321.2	356.1	365.2	271.7	276.0	264.4	232.4	246.9	352.3	364.4	322.2
Industrial	324.6	211.7	210.4	252.5	248.2	249.6	245.5	217.2	224.7	235.0	263.6	272.5	266.3
Grains	312.1	196.5	164.6	186.1	261.9	205.7	171.2	196.1	196.9	193.8	191.2	218.6	264.7
Oilseeds	314.6	245.4	189.8	223.6	309.6	254.2	223.6	195.4	218.8	239.8	259.9	277.5	307.9
Livestock and meats	217.4	206.9	200.2	189.9	199.1	206.5	226.2	174.0	179.8	201.4	192.3	192.4	241.7
Metals (precious)	531.4	256.6	296.6	346.4	316.7	296.9	257.8	226.0	228.5	242.2	273.9	276.0	271.3

Source: Commodity Research Bureau (CRB), New York City, NY, *CRB Commodity Index Report*, weekly (copyright).

No. 764. Indexes of Spot Primary Market Prices: 1980 to 1996

[1967=100. Computed weekly for 1980; daily thereafter. Represents unweighted geometric average of price quotations of 23 commodities; much more sensitive to changes in market conditions than is a monthly producer price index]

ITEMS AND NUMBER OF COMMODITIES	1980 (6-24)	1985 (5-21)	1987 (5-26)	1988 (5-27)	1989 (5-26)	1990 (5-25)	1991 (5-28)	1992 (5-26)	1993 (5-23)	1994 (5-24)	1995 (5-23)	1996 (5-21)
All commodities (23)	**265.1**	**251.4**	**250.0**	**270.3**	**281.3**	**279.2**	**235.3**	**242.3**	**237.7**	**261.5**	**290.6**	**297.7**
Foodstuffs (10)	260.9	248.1	215.2	230.1	222.5	231.5	197.7	201.3	208.3	215.5	229.1	251.3
Raw industrials (13)	268.0	253.6	277.3	302.0	329.0	317.0	265.2	275.5	260.4	299.2	348.2	334.9
Livestock and products (5)	250.5	284.5	303.3	316.1	285.2	306.9	286.6	276.4	291.3	296.9	314.6	338.4
Metals (5)	257.9	220.2	239.5	276.7	347.1	313.9	348.8	262.7	236.2	262.1	306.7	296.7
Textiles and fibers (4)	234.7	220.8	247.1	247.3	253.5	259.4	201.8	218.6	205.3	252.6	286.0	274.6
Fats and oils (4)	229.5	273.1	201.2	230.4	208.1	193.3	185.0	180.7	190.1	209.8	228.3	245.7

Source: Commodity Research Bureau, a Knight-Ridder Business Information Service, New York, NY, *CRB Commodity Index Report*, weekly (copyright).

No. 765. Average Prices of Selected Fuels and Electricity: 1980 to 1996

[In dollars per unit, except electricity, in cents per kWh. Represents price to end-users, except as noted]

ITEM	Unit [1]	1980	1985	1986	1990	1991	1992	1993	1994	1995	1996
Crude oil, composite [2]	Barrel	28.07	26.75	14.67	17.97	22.22	19.06	18.43	16.41	15.59	17.23
Motor gasoline: [3]											
Unleaded regular	Gallon	1.25	1.20	0.95	1.02	1.16	1.14	1.13	1.11	1.11	1.15
Unleaded premium	Gallon	(NA)	1.34	1.11	1.20	1.35	1.32	1.32	1.30	1.31	1.34
No. 2 heating oil	Gallon	0.79	0.85	0.54	0.59	0.73	0.67	0.63	0.60	0.57	0.56
No. 2 diesel fuel	Gallon	0.82	0.79	0.50	0.59	0.73	0.65	0.62	0.60	0.55	0.56
Residual fuel oil	Gallon	0.61	0.61	0.33	0.41	0.47	0.36	0.35	0.34	0.35	(NA)
Natural gas, residential	1,000 cu/ft.	3.68	6.12	5.47	5.64	5.80	5.82	5.89	6.16	6.41	6.06
Electricity, residential	kWh	5.4	7.8	7.5	7.6	7.9	8.1	8.2	8.3	8.4	8.4

NA Not available. [1] See headnote. [2] Refiner acquisition cost. [3] Average, all service.

Source: U.S. Energy Information Administration, *Monthly Energy Review*.

No. 766. Weekly Food Cost: 1990 and 1996

[In dollars. Assumes that food for all meals and snacks is purchased at the store and prepared at home. See source for details on estimation procedures]

FAMILY TYPE	DECEMBER 1990				JANUARY 1996			
	Thrifty plan	Low-cost plan	Moderate-cost plan	Liberal plan	Thrifty plan	Low-cost plan	Moderate-cost plan	Liberal plan
FAMILIES								
Family of 2:								
20-50 years	48.10	60.60	74.70	92.70	54.70	69.10	85.20	106.30
51 years and over	45.60	58.30	71.80	85.80	51.50	66.40	82.20	98.60
Family of 4:								
Couple, 20-50 years and children—								
1-2 and 3-5 years	70.10	87.30	106.60	131.00	79.50	99.60	121.60	150.00
6-8 and 9-11 years	80.10	102.60	128.30	154.40	91.30	117.10	146.20	176.30
INDIVIDUALS [1]								
Child:								
1-2 years	12.70	15.40	18.00	21.80	14.30	17.60	20.60	25.00
3-5 years	13.70	16.80	20.70	24.90	15.50	19.20	23.70	28.40
6-8 years	16.60	22.20	27.90	32.50	19.00	25.40	31.70	36.90
9-11 years	19.80	25.30	32.50	37.60	22.60	28.90	37.00	42.80
Male:								
12-14 years	20.60	28.60	35.70	42.00	23.40	32.60	40.50	47.60
15-19 years	21.40	29.60	36.80	42.60	24.20	33.60	41.80	48.40
20-50 years	22.90	29.30	36.60	44.30	26.10	33.40	41.80	50.70
51 years and over	20.90	27.90	34.30	41.10	23.60	31.90	39.30	47.20
Female:								
12-19 years	20.80	24.80	30.10	36.30	23.50	28.20	34.20	41.30
20-50 years	20.80	25.80	31.30	40.00	23.60	29.40	35.70	45.90
51 years and over	20.60	25.10	31.00	36.90	23.20	28.50	35.40	42.40

[1] The costs given are for individuals in 4-person families. For individuals in other size families, the following adjustments are suggested: 1-person, add 20 percent; 2-person, add 10 percent; 3-person, add 5 percent; 5- or 6-person, subtract 5 percent; 7- (or more) person, subtract 10 percent.

Source: U.S. Dept. of Agriculture, *Agricultural Research Service*, monthly.

No. 767. Food—Retail Prices of Selected Items: 1990 to 1996

[In dollars per pound, except as indicated. As of December]

FOOD	1990	1991	1992	1993	1994	1995	1996
Cereals and bakery products:							
Flour, white, all purpose	0.24	0.22	0.23	0.22	0.23	0.24	0.30
Rice, white, lg. grain, raw	0.49	0.51	0.53	0.50	0.53	0.55	0.55
Spaghetti and macaroni	0.85	0.86	0.86	0.84	0.87	0.88	0.84
Bread, white, pan	0.70	0.72	0.74	0.76	0.75	0.84	0.87
Meats, poultry, fish and eggs:							
Ground chuck, 100% beef	2.02	1.93	1.91	1.91	1.84	1.85	1.85
Rib roast, USDA Choice	4.54	4.59	4.69	4.73	4.88	4.81	5.09
Round steak, USDA Choice	3.42	3.38	3.34	3.32	3.24	3.20	3.22
Sirloin steak, bone-in	3.65	3.78	3.75	3.69	(NA)	(NA)	(NA)
T-bone steak	5.45	5.21	5.39	5.77	5.86	5.92	5.87
Pork:							
Bacon, sliced	2.28	1.99	1.86	2.02	1.89	2.17	2.64
Chops, center cut, bone-in	3.32	3.12	3.15	3.24	3.03	3.29	3.44
Shoulder picnic, bone-in, smoked	1.41	1.30	1.18	1.19	1.13	1.17	1.31
Sausage	2.42	2.24	2.14	1.99	1.85	1.92	2.15
Poultry:							
Chicken, fresh, whole	0.86	0.86	0.88	0.91	0.90	0.94	1.00
Chicken breast, bone-in	2.00	2.02	2.08	2.17	1.91	1.95	2.09
Chicken legs, bone-in	1.17	1.14	1.14	1.13	1.12	1.20	1.26
Turkey, frozen, whole	0.96	0.91	0.93	0.95	0.98	0.99	1.02
Eggs, Grade A, large, (dozen)	1.00	1.01	0.93	0.87	0.87	1.16	1.31
Dairy products:							
Milk, fresh, whole, fortified (1/2 gal.)	1.39	1.40	1.39	1.43	1.44	1.48	1.65
Butter, salted, grade AA, stick	1.92	1.94	1.64	1.61	1.54	1.73	2.17
Ice cream, prepack., bulk,reg.(1/2 gal.)	2.54	2.63	2.49	2.59	2.62	2.68	2.94
Fresh fruits and vegetables:							
Apples, red delicious	0.77	0.86	0.76	0.78	0.72	0.83	0.89
Bananas	0.43	0.42	0.40	0.41	0.46	0.45	0.48
Oranges, navel	0.56	0.65	0.52	0.56	0.55	0.64	0.59
Grapefruit	0.56	0.53	0.52	0.50	0.47	0.49	0.55
Lemons	0.97	1.21	0.90	1.05	1.04	1.12	1.14
Pears, anjou	0.79	0.88	0.80	0.89	(NA)	(NA)	1.06
Potatoes, white	0.32	0.28	0.31	0.36	0.34	0.38	0.33
Lettuce, iceberg	0.58	0.69	0.66	0.53	0.91	0.61	0.62
Tomatoes, field grown	0.86	0.79	1.23	1.31	1.43	1.51	1.21
Cabbage	0.39	0.46	0.38	0.37	0.45	0.41	0.40
Carrots, short trimmed and topped	0.44	0.51	0.44	0.41	0.48	0.53	0.54
Celery	0.49	0.45	0.48	0.49	0.52	0.54	0.44
Cucumbers	0.56	0.55	0.51	0.93	0.69	0.53	0.60
Processed fruits and vegetables:							
Orange juice, frozen concentrate, 12 oz. can, per 16 oz.	2.02	1.74	1.70	1.67	1.55	1.57	1.73
Potatoes, frozen, french fried	0.85	0.92	0.86	0.87	0.84	0.86	0.90

NA Not available.

Source: U.S. Bureau of Labor Statistics, *CPI Detailed Report*, *CPI Detailed Report*, January issues.

No. 768. Average Price of Energy in Selected Metropolitan Areas: 1996

[In dollars per unit shown. As of January. One therm contains approximately 100 cubic feet of natural gas. See Appendix II]

CITY/MSA	Utility (piped) gas (100 therms)	Electricity (500 kWh)	Fuel oil No. 2 (gallon)	GASOLINE		
				All types [1]	Unleaded regular	Unleaded premium
U.S. city average	68.82	49.23	1.12	1.32	1.26	1.44
Baltimore, MD MSA	67.97	47.87	1.28	1.34	1.29	1.43
Boston-Lawrence-Salem, MA-NH CMSA	98.29	63.44	1.17	1.35	1.30	1.47
Chicago-Gary-Lake County, IL-IN-WI CMSA	61.02	58.57	(NA)	1.44	1.39	1.57
Cleveland-Akron-Lorain, OH CMSA	62.03	60.56	(NA)	1.32	1.27	1.47
Dallas-Fort Worth, TX CMSA	57.92	45.39	(NA)	1.23	1.17	1.35
Detroit-Ann Arbor, MI CMSA	51.88	46.63	(NA)	1.34	1.30	1.47
Houston-Galveston-Brazoria, TX CMSA	49.67	39.91	(NA)	1.25	1.19	1.35
Los Angeles-Anaheim-Riverside, CA CMSA	67.69	63.96	(NA)	1.26	1.20	1.38
Miami-Fort Lauderdale, FL CMSA	102.74	45.79	(NA)	1.38	1.31	1.49
New York-N. NJ-Long Island, NY-NJ-CT CMSA	90.62	73.14	1.22	1.42	1.35	1.54
Philadelphia-Wilmington-Trenton, PA-NJ-DE-MD CMSA	82.99	62.60	1.08	1.36	1.24	1.43
Pittsburgh-Beaver Valley, PA CMSA	78.35	52.89	0.98	1.33	1.29	1.45
St. Louis-East St. Louis, MO-IL CMSA	66.60	37.39	(NA)	1.29	1.24	1.42
San Francisco-Oakland-San Jose, CA CMSA	62.16	61.08	(NA)	1.29	1.22	1.45
Washington, DC-MD-VA MSA	93.89	40.82	1.23	1.34	1.28	1.47

NA Not available. [1] Includes types of gasoline not shown separately.

Source: U.S. Bureau of Labor Statistics, *CPI Detailed Report*, January issues.

No. 769. Import Price Indexes—Selected Commodities: 1985 to 1996

[1990=100. Indexes are weighted by the 1990 Tariff Schedule of the United States Annotated, a scheme for describing and reporting product composition and value of U.S. imports. Import prices are based on U.S. dollar prices paid by importer. F.o.b. = Free on board; c.i.f. = Cost, insurance, and freight; n.e.s.=Not elsewhere specified]

COMMODITY	1985	1990 [1]	1991	1992	1993	1994	1995	1996
All commodities	80.2	96.1	96.8	100.3	100.5	101.9	107.3	106.5
Food and live animals	87.2	98.6	102.4	97.9	101.1	109.0	116.3	110.0
Meat	68.8	100.0	105.6	94.9	99.3	91.0	85.2	77.7
Meat of bovine animals	77.1	98.5	100.8	91.1	100.8	86.5	71.9	66.3
Fish	75.5	96.7	107.6	107.9	107.9	121.2	126.1	121.1
Crustaceans; fresh, chilled, frozen, salted or dried	85.0	97.4	107.3	105.4	106.4	129.8	137.4	126.3
Cereals and cereal preparations	63.2	96.7	96.4	99.3	102.9	102.0	101.4	119.1
Sugar [2]	87.4	99.7	96.7	95.3	95.1	98.2	103.9	101.2
Coffee, tea and cocoa	145.1	99.4	93.2	77.3	81.2	137.1	166.2	135.5
Beverages and tobacco	77.1	99.2	110.8	113.4	112.6	113.2	114.9	119.4
Beverages	75.9	99.3	110.3	112.5	112.9	112.8	114.8	116.5
Crude materials	77.8	101.9	95.9	96.8	96.3	106.7	123.5	116.6
Crude rubber	96.3	101.2	96.4	100.8	102.9	106.3	156.8	140.5
Cork and wood	93.4	102.4	107.7	116.8	130.3	159.9	131.0	160.5
Pulp and waste paper	56.9	102.8	79.2	74.4	63.7	70.1	116.0	69.9
Metalliferous ores and metal scrap	59.9	100.8	93.6	91.1	88.3	89.6	106.4	106.2
Mineral fuels and related products	114.5	73.1	83.2	86.7	79.9	76.3	82.7	87.0
Crude petroleum and petroleum products	112.1	72.0	82.8	86.7	79.2	75.7	82.7	87.2
Crude petroleum	123.8	66.8	81.4	87.8	76.6	73.6	79.0	84.1
Natural gas	(NA)	89.4	88.1	83.7	90.3	83.7	80.3	85.8
Chemicals and related products	83.7	96.5	100.7	101.7	102.8	102.6	112.3	110.2
Intermediate manufactured products	73.1	99.5	99.2	99.4	99.3	101.0	111.8	111.0
Rubber manufactures	85.9	99.8	100.6	102.0	103.8	102.4	105.0	105.1
Cork and wood manufactures	69.0	100.4	98.6	108.1	120.6	126.5	119.3	121.3
Paper and paperboard products	82.7	100.4	101.0	94.1	96.7	95.6	125.1	126.7
Textiles	77.6	98.7	103.0	106.0	108.1	108.9	114.8	113.9
Nonmetallic mineral manufactures	60.1	99.8	103.3	105.5	108.0	108.5	111.4	113.1
Iron and steel	79.3	99.7	99.3	97.6	96.2	99.1	106.5	106.4
Nonferrous metals	69.0	98.7	89.0	88.6	76.6	85.2	103.8	96.7
Silver, platinum and other platinum group metals	71.2	93.6	90.2	75.5	69.1	74.8	78.0	71.8
Copper	57.6	96.6	88.7	88.5	75.9	89.3	110.5	106.1
Nickel	62.4	95.5	97.6	87.5	72.9	75.3	91.0	97.8
Aluminum	(NA)	96.7	85.8	86.4	79.1	89.6	116.8	105.8
Zinc	56.7	113.4	77.2	89.3	67.7	65.8	72.4	70.3
Manufactures of metals, n.e.s.	72.9	96.9	101.2	103.0	104.5	104.6	110.8	110.7
Machinery and transport equipment	75.1	98.7	101.6	103.5	105.0	106.8	110.1	107.9
Machinery specialized for particular industries	59.1	97.3	101.7	105.4	107.5	109.7	117.0	117.0
Metalworking machinery	64.8	98.7	100.6	103.9	107.7	110.1	122.4	121.5
General industrial machinery, parts, n.e.s.	62.6	97.7	101.5	104.9	107.0	109.0	116.6	116.4
Computer equipment and office machines	85.0	99.8	97.3	95.7	91.9	87.1	84.1	76.8
Computer equipment	112.8	100.3	96.9	92.4	85.5	76.5	69.9	65.2
Telecommunications [3]	90.1	100.2	97.8	97.1	96.0	97.4	96.7	95.5
Electrical machinery and equipment	77.4	98.7	100.6	102.1	103.9	106.1	109.0	102.5
Electronic valves, diodes, transistors & integr. cir.	96.7	98.2	99.5	99.4	104.3	106.0	106.2	93.9
Road vehicles	75.1	96.4	103.5	105.6	108.4	112.7	116.7	117.3
Miscellaneous manufactured articles	74.3	98.9	100.6	103.7	105.2	105.4	107.8	108.1
Plumbing, heating & lighting fixtures	68.9	96.4	98.0	101.5	102.0	99.6	103.7	102.8
Furniture and parts	74.0	99.1	101.2	103.4	104.1	103.9	106.5	106.6
Articles of apparel and clothing	81.7	100.5	98.8	101.8	102.1	102.2	103.1	104.5
Footwear	70.6	99.0	100.9	102.6	101.2	100.2	101.9	103.2
Prof., scientific & contrlng instr & appratus, n.e.s.	64.4	97.5	102.1	104.4	110.5	113.0	117.2	115.9
Photographic apparatus [4]	73.5	96.0	100.1	102.9	106.9	109.1	115.3	115.2
Miscellaneous manufactured articles, n.e.s.	71.1	97.9	101.8	106.0	108.3	106.5	110.7	111.3

NA Not available. [1] June 1990 may not equal 100 because indexes were reweighted to an "average" trade value in 1990. [2] Includes sugar preparations and honey. [3] Includes sound recording and reproducing equipment. [4] Includes photographic supplies, optical goods, watches, and clocks.

Source: U.S. Bureau of Labor Statistics, *News*, quarterly.

No. 770. Export Price Indexes—Selected Commodities: 1985 to 1996

[1990=100. Indexes are weighted by 1980 export values according to the Schedule B classification system of the U.S. Bureau of the Census. Prices used in these indexes were collected from a sample of U.S. manufacturers of exports and are factory transaction prices, except as noted. F.a.s. = free alongside ship. N.e.s. = not elsewhere specified. F.o.b. = free on board]

COMMODITY	1985	1990 [1]	1991	1992	1993	1994	1995	1996
All commodities	88.4	99.5	100.6	101.0	101.4	103.2	109.4	110.4
Food and live animals	96.3	104.3	100.7	102.8	97.8	103.9	114.1	142.9
Meat	78.6	98.5	101.9	106.1	111.6	107.3	115.8	117.8
Fish	78.5	96.4	94.7	96.1	96.5	98.0	121.5	105.3
Cereals and cereal preparations	109.3	108.6	96.8	104.8	90.9	101.8	114.4	174.6
Wheat	115.5	112.1	91.2	108.4	94.1	91.2	127.2	180.4
Maize	107.8	108.6	97.8	102.2	87.7	105.6	109.1	184.0
Fruits and vegetables	88.6	102.0	121.5	100.0	103.0	109.6	117.4	128.9
Feeding stuff for animals	74.9	97.6	100.0	102.2	100.7	106.2	102.9	128.2
Miscellaneous food products	90.6	99.9	100.5	100.2	100.3	97.8	100.9	102.7
Beverages and tobacco	79.9	99.3	105.7	109.8	113.1	113.5	114.9	115.6
Tobacco and tobacco manufactures	79.6	99.4	105.7	109.6	112.8	113.1	114.8	115.4
Crude materials	74.4	100.5	95.4	93.4	99.6	108.1	130.3	112.9
Raw hides and skins	63.3	105.2	81.5	80.8	79.2	94.4	103.5	95.8
Oil seeds and oleaginous fruits	92.8	97.1	99.4	98.4	97.9	112.9	96.7	127.2
Crude rubber, f.a.s.	85.6	99.1	103.2	101.0	99.2	96.1	118.0	108.4
Cork and wood	56.2	102.1	97.9	110.1	161.4	149.4	156.8	145.4
Pulp and waste paper	57.6	100.2	86.6	82.6	70.2	94.6	172.7	87.9
Textile fibers	85.3	102.6	107.0	86.0	83.5	105.0	134.0	114.3
Cotton textile fibers	87.4	103.7	107.9	79.7	77.5	101.3	134.2	112.3
Crude fertilizers and minerals	100.8	100.1	101.1	99.7	95.0	95.6	97.7	95.1
Metalliferous ores and metal scrap	70.7	99.9	89.1	85.1	83.9	91.2	124.7	106.9
Ferrous waste and scrap	73.0	99.8	93.4	82.2	99.0	95.6	116.7	104.3
Nonferrous base metal waste and scrap	56.5	99.4	84.2	86.0	72.2	92.7	116.7	101.1
Mineral fuels and related materials	104.6	91.1	89.9	86.5	88.0	87.4	92.9	99.4
Coal, coke and briquettes	103.1	100.1	96.6	96.9	93.9	93.9	97.3	100.1
Crude petroleum and petroleum products	(NA)	83.9	80.1	77.2	80.7	80.3	87.0	95.5
Animal and vegetable oils, fats and waxes	123.5	103.0	93.8	94.9	96.4	110.0	114.8	113.5
Chemicals and related products	84.5	97.4	99.7	97.4	96.1	99.0	116.6	110.6
Organic chemicals	80.5	94.9	94.6	91.5	90.5	92.7	124.1	102.0
Hydrocarbons, n.e.s. and derivatives, f.a.s.	73.9	93.3	76.2	77.8	80.1	92.4	130.2	102.2
Alcohols, phenols, phenol-alcohols, & deriv., f.a.s.	78.6	96.3	101.8	93.1	93.2	89.3	131.7	109.4
Chemical materials and products, n.e.s.	86.7	98.7	103.4	102.9	105.7	108.7	115.0	117.2
Intermediate manufactured products	81.3	99.8	100.1	100.6	100.7	104.4	115.8	112.4
Rubber manufactures	86.6	96.9	105.0	105.6	108.5	109.2	116.3	119.8
Paper and paperboard products	76.7	99.5	99.5	96.4	93.9	96.2	126.8	107.1
Textiles	84.3	99.6	104.1	105.6	106.8	106.7	112.3	115.3
Nonmetallic mineral manufactures	(NA)	99.6	101.2	103.5	105.4	107.3	109.4	110.7
Nonferrous metals	77.1	100.2	88.1	87.9	81.3	92.5	113.0	105.8
Manufactures of metals, n.e.s.	84.9	99.8	102.7	103.6	105.1	107.3	113.5	115.1
Machinery and transport equipment [2]	90.7	99.8	102.9	104.4	104.5	104.1	104.8	106.7
Power generating machinery [3]	85.2	99.8	104.7	109.6	110.7	112.8	114.8	120.5
Rotating electric plant and parts thereof, n.e.s.	76.8	99.7	101.9	104.7	106.1	107.4	112.2	114.4
Machinery specialized for particular industries	87.7	99.3	103.3	105.5	108.0	109.8	112.8	115.8
Agricultural machinery and parts [4]	89.4	100.0	102.1	104.9	107.3	109.4	111.1	113.0
Civil engineering and contractors, plant and equip.	90.7	98.8	103.9	102.0	105.5	109.6	113.0	114.5
Metalworking machinery	82.1	99.6	106.5	109.1	111.0	110.7	112.0	114.6
General industrial machines, parts, n.e.s.	84.4	99.7	103.7	106.1	108.3	110.1	111.2	114.6
Computer equipment and office machines	105.9	100.3	98.4	94.7	87.7	81.0	76.6	71.3
Computer equipment	113.0	100.3	97.8	94.0	83.5	75.2	68.7	61.0
Telecommunications [5]	89.6	100.1	106.4	108.3	109.4	107.3	106.7	107.6
Electrical machinery and equipment	93.8	99.9	100.6	103.6	103.5	103.2	104.0	102.3
Electronic valves, diodes, transistors & integr. cir.	106.5	100.6	98.5	103.7	102.3	100.0	100.7	98.9
Road vehicles	89.8	99.6	102.4	104.0	105.2	106.3	107.9	109.2
Miscellaneous manufactured articles	85.4	99.1	104.2	106.2	106.9	107.1	108.0	108.9

NA Not available. [1] June 1990 may not equal 100 because indexes were reweighted to an "average" trade value in 1990. [2] Excludes military and commercial aircraft. [3] Includes equipment. [4] Excludes tractors. [5] Includes sound recording and reproducing equipment.

Source: U.S. Bureau of Labor Statistics, *News*, quarterly.

No. 771. Refiner/Reseller Sales Price of Gasoline, by State: 1994 to 1996

[...ts per gallon. As of March. Represents all refinery and gas plant operators' sales through company-operated retail outlets. Gasoline prices exclude excise taxes]

STATE	Gasoline excise taxes 1997	AVERAGE, ALL GRADES			UNLEADED REGULAR			PREMIUM		
		1994	1995	1996	1994	1995	1996	1994	1995	1996
nited States.	(NA)	67.2	73.2	74.5	71.3	77.1	78.6	80.3	86.1	87.2
ic										
gland:										
....	19	73.4	78.6	81.0	78.4	83.9	87.0	85.6	91.9	94.3
lampshire...	20	72.2	78.9	79.5	77.3	84.8	85.3	85.9	93.2	92.6
nt........	16	76.2	80.0	82.9	81.3	85.4	88.0	89.2	94.0	96.8
chusetts....	21	69.2	78.2	80.3	74.4	83.2	84.9	83.3	92.4	93.6
Island.....	29	71.1	73.6	77.2	74.7	78.2	81.1	82.5	85.4	88.9
cticut......	39	72.3	76.8	80.1	77.4	81.7	86.2	87.2	91.7	94.2
Atlantic:										
York.......	22	68.7	75.1	77.4	73.2	80.3	82.3	82.8	89.5	91.2
ersey......	11	74.9	81.4	81.9	81.0	86.2	86.5	88.6	94.6	94.7
ylvania.....	22	65.7	73.5	74.9	69.7	77.3	78.8	78.4	86.6	87.0
rth Central:										
....	22	66.3	69.6	74.1	70.6	74.8	79.5	77.6	78.5	86.8
a.........	16	65.1	70.4	71.5	69.1	74.1	75.7	75.0	77.6	82.7
....	20	64.0	72.0	76.9	68.1	73.6	79.2	75.7	79.3	89.7
an........	16	63.7	69.1	71.7	68.1	73.5	77.0	75.1	75.4	83.7
nsin.......	27	64.4	70.5	75.5	70.1	75.2	81.1	76.0	79.3	86.5
orth Central:										
sota.......	20	72.4	76.2	77.3	75.4	80.9	83.0	84.8	88.0	89.0
....	20	62.2	67.5	71.3	67.2	71.0	74.2	71.8	76.7	80.6
uri........	17	61.5	67.9	70.5	67.1	72.5	76.2	75.0	80.2	84.9
Dakota......	20	74.4	76.3	81.7	80.3	84.4	83.2	81.0	82.3	88.7
Dakota....	20	70.9	74.6	75.2	74.7	84.0	81.5	86.4	86.1	86.7
ska.......	26	69.3	71.1	70.4	72.9	76.4	73.8	77.4	80.5	80.0
s.........	18	62.5	68.4	68.7	68.2	74.1	73.4	73.2	80.3	80.2
tlantic:										
are.......	23	65.2	75.5	75.3	70.5	80.5	80.4	79.1	89.9	89.2
nd.......	24	66.0	76.2	77.6	70.8	80.2	81.1	77.1	86.8	88.1
t of Columbia.	20	(D)	(D)	(D)	(D)	(D)	(D)	(D)	(D)	(D)
a.........	18	67.7	74.5	73.7	72.2	79.0	78.0	81.3	87.4	85.8
Virginia......	21	71.9	76.2	75.6	77.2	81.1	79.6	83.6	87.4	88.0
Carolina....	23	63.9	69.4	69.7	67.5	72.9	73.3	77.4	82.7	83.1
Carolina....	17	63.2	67.4	69.0	68.4	71.6	73.4	78.3	82.3	83.7
ia.......	8	63.5	68.7	68.9	67.6	73.0	73.1	77.0	82.5	82.9
a.........	13	68.2	73.2	72.8	73.4	78.2	76.9	82.0	86.4	85.0
uth Central:										
cky.......	16	68.9	73.1	75.3	72.9	77.5	81.2	81.4	85.7	86.9
ssee......	21	64.3	69.7	71.4	68.1	74.6	76.2	77.6	82.0	85.1
na........	18	68.3	73.3	74.0	71.3	76.9	77.5	80.6	85.6	87.0
sippi......	18	66.1	74.1	75.1	70.1	78.5	79.7	76.6	87.5	86.6
outh Central:										
sas.......	19	63.6	69.1	68.7	69.7	74.3	74.1	76.1	81.6	81.9
ana.......	20	66.6	71.9	70.9	71.4	76.7	75.8	80.1	84.7	84.4
oma.......	17	59.9	66.0	67.0	64.4	70.1	70.5	70.3	76.8	76.6
....	20	65.0	74.5	73.1	70.0	79.1	77.4	78.0	87.8	85.8
in:										
na........	28	71.5	74.8	76.3	67.6	74.6	78.5	79.2	82.0	83.6
....	26	64.5	72.0	72.4	65.5	76.1	78.0	74.0	81.5	82.4
ing.......	9	72.8	79.7	79.5	76.0	83.0	83.6	82.7	89.7	88.9
do........	22	75.4	80.8	79.5	82.0	86.4	88.6	90.7	95.4	92.8
lexico.....	19	69.5	75.6	78.2	73.3	81.9	83.6	80.9	87.6	91.1
a.........	18	80.9	79.8	82.7	87.5	87.1	85.5	96.3	94.2	97.2
....	19	63.1	73.1	74.5	65.5	76.6	77.9	73.0	83.3	85.3
a........	24	80.2	82.9	90.3	84.3	80.2	91.3	96.3	96.1	101.8
ngton......	23	70.8	76.3	83.1	70.8	82.0	85.2	85.8	93.5	96.8
n.........	24	76.0	77.4	82.1	75.9	75.6	86.0	91.2	91.5	94.9
nia.......	19	70.1	77.5	76.0	76.6	79.2	78.5	85.7	91.6	89.4
....	8	107.7	112.4	111.8	(NA)	102.9	103.4	107.9	114.5	117.3
....	16	110.1	105.0	104.9	107.1	106.2	105.9	123.5	117.7	117.2

...ithheld to avoid disclosure of individual company data. NA Not available.

...ce: Except as noted, U.S. Energy Information Administration, *Petroleum Marketing Monthly.*

Figure 16.1
Insured Commercial Banks—Return on Assets and Percent of Banks Losing Money: 1980 to 1996

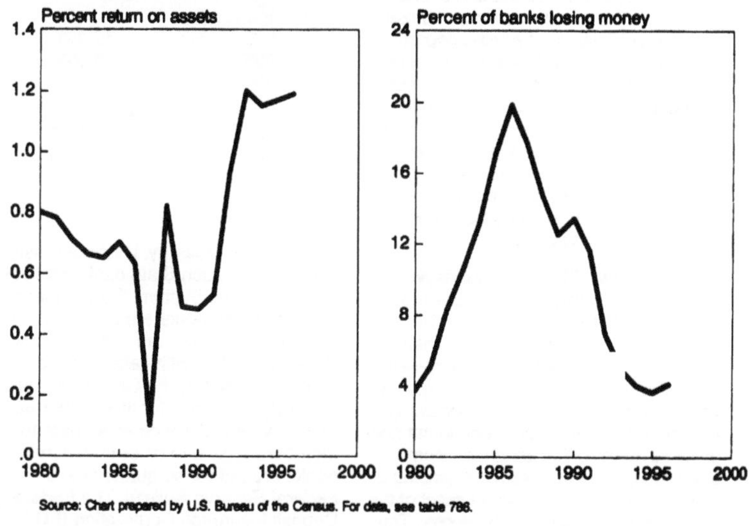

Source: Chart prepared by U.S. Bureau of the Census. For data, see table 786.

Figure 16.2.
Mutual Fund Shares Holdings: 1996

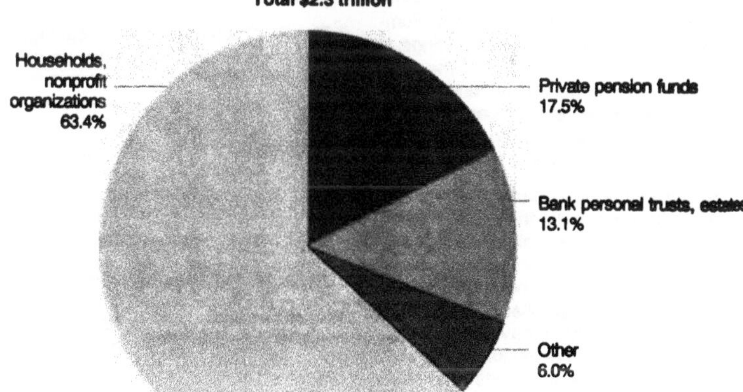

Source: Chart prepared by U.S. Bureau of the Census. For data, see table 821.

Banking, Finance, and Insurance

This section presents data on the Nation's finances, various types of financial institutions, money and credit, securities, and insurance. The primary sources of these data are publications of several departments of the Federal Government, especially the Treasury Department, and independent agencies such as the Federal Deposit Insurance Corporation, the Federal Reserve System, and the Securities and Exchange Commission. National data on insurance are available primarily from private organizations, such as the American Council of Life Insurance.

In Brief

Conventional new-home mortgage rates:

1990	*10.08%*
1995	*8.05%*
1996	*8.03%*

Dow-Jones industrial average:

1990	*2,678.7*
1995	*4,493.8*
1996	*5,742.9*

Flow of funds—The flow of funds accounts of the Federal Reserve System (see tables 774 to 777) bring together statistics on all of the major forms of financial instruments to present an economy-wide view of asset and liability relationships. In flow form, the accounts relate borrowing and lending to one another and to the nonfinancial activities that generate income and production. Each claim outstanding is included simultaneously as an asset of the lender and as a liability of the debtor. The accounts also indicate the balance between asset totals and liability totals over the economy as a whole. Several publications of the Board of Governors of the Federal Reserve System contain information on the flow of funds accounts: Summary data on flows and outstandings, in the *Federal Reserve Bulletin, Flow of Funds Accounts* (quarterly), and *Annual Statistical Digest;* and concepts and organization of the accounts, in *Guide to the Flow of Funds Accounts* (1993).

Banking system—Banks in this country are organized under the laws of both the States and the Federal Government and are regulated by several bank supervisory agencies. National banks are supervised by the Comptroller of the Currency. *Reports of Condition* have been collected from national banks since 1863. Summaries of these reports are published in the Comptroller's *Annual Report,* which also presents data on the structure of the national banking system.

The Federal Reserve System was established in 1913 to exercise central banking functions, some of which are shared with the U.S. Treasury. It includes national banks and such State banks that voluntarily join the System. Statements of State bank members are consolidated by the Board of Governors of the Federal Reserve System with data for national banks collected by the Comptroller of the Currency into totals for all member banks of the System. Balance sheet data for member banks and other commercial banks are published quarterly in the *Federal Reserve Bulletin*. The Federal Deposit Insurance Corporation (FDIC), established in 1933, insures each depositor up to $100,000. Major item balance sheet and income data for all commercial banks are published in the *FDIC Quarterly Banking Profile.*

The FDIC is the primary federal regulator of State-chartered banks that are not members of the Federal Reserve System and of most savings banks insured by the Bank Insurance Fund (BIF). The agency also has certain back-up supervisory authority, for safety and soundness purposes, over State-chartered banks that are members of the Federal Reserve System, national banks, and savings associations.

Savings institutions—Savings institutions are primarily involved in credit extension in the form of mortgage loans. Statistics on savings institutions are collected by the U.S. Office of Thrift Supervision and the FDIC. The Financial Institutions Reform, Recovery, and Enforcement Act of 1989 (FIRREA) authorized the establishment of the Resolution Trust Corporation (RTC) which was responsible for the disposal of assets from failed savings institutions. FIRREA gave the FDIC the job of managing the federal deposit insurance fund for savings institutions (SAIF=Savings Association Insurance Fund). Major balance sheet and income data for all insured savings institutions are published in the *FDIC Quarterly Banking Profile*.

Credit Unions—Federally chartered credit unions are under the supervision of the National Credit Union Administration, established in 1970. State-chartered credit unions are supervised by the respective State supervisory authorities. The Administration publishes comprehensive program and statistical information on all Federal and federally insured state credit unions in the *Annual Report of the National Credit Union Administration.* Deposit insurance (up to $100,000 per account) is provided to members of all Federal and those state credit unions that are federally-insured by the National Credit Union Share Insurance Fund which was established in 1970. Deposit insurance for state chartered credit unions is also available in some states under private or state-administered insurance programs.

Other credit agencies—Insurance companies, finance companies dealing primarily in installment sales financing, and personal loan companies represent important sources of funds for the credit market. Statistics on loans, investments, cash, etc., of life insurance companies are published principally by the American Council of Life Insurance in its *Life Insurance Fact Book* and in the *Federal Reserve Bulletin.* Consumer credit data are published currently in the *Federal Reserve Bulletin*.

Government corporations and credit agencies make available credit of specified types or to specified groups of private borrowers, either by lending directly or by insuring or guaranteeing loans made by private lending institutions. Data on operations of Government credit agencies, along with other Government corporations, are available in reports of individual agencies; data on their debt outstanding are published in the *Federal Reserve Bulletin.*

Currency—Currency, including coin and paper money, represents about 37 percent of all media of exchange in the United States, with most payments made by check. All currency is now issued by the Federal Reserve Banks.

Securities—The Securities and Exchange Commission (SEC) was established in 1934 to protect the interests of the public and investors against malpractices in the securities and financial markets and to provide the fullest possible disclosure of information regarding securities to the investing public. Statistical data are published in the *SEC Annual Report.*

Insurance—Insuring companies, which are regulated by the various States or the District of Columbia, are classified as either life or property. Companies that underwrite accident and health insurance only and those that underwrite accident and health insurance in addition to one or more property lines are included with property insurance. Insuring companies, other than those classified as life, are permitted to underwrite one or more property lines provided they are so licensed and have the necessary capital or surplus.

There are a number of published sources for statistics on the various classes of insurance—life, health, fire, marine, and casualty. Individual States collect data on all insurers operating within their respective jurisdictions, and many of the States publish an annual insurance report giving individual company data and aggregates of certain items for the companies operating within the State. Organizations representing certain classes of insurers publish reports for these classes. Among them are the annual commercial publishers, such as The National Underwriter Company whose *Argus Health Chart* (annual) contains financial and operating data for individual health and accident insurance companies, including Blue Cross and Blue Shield Plans. The American Council of Life Insurance publishes statistics on life insurance purchases, ownership, benefit payments, and assets in its biennial *Life Insurance Fact Book.*

No. 772. Gross Domestic Product in Finance, Insurance, and Real Estate, in Current and Real (1992) Dollars: 1990 to 1994

[In billions of dollars, except percent. For definition of gross domestic product, see text, section 14. Based on 1987 Standard Industrial Classification]

INDUSTRY	CURRENT DOLLARS				CHAINED (1992) DOLLARS [1]			
	1990	1992	1993	1994	1990	1992	1993	1994
Finance, insurance, real estate, total	1,026.2	1,148.8	1,214.0	1,273.7	1,109.9	1,148.8	1,169.8	1,192.8
Percent of gross domestic product	17.8	18.4	18.5	18.4	18.1	18.4	18.2	18.1
Depository institutions	169.2	200.1	202.0	212.1	214.9	200.1	196.9	197.2
Nondepository institutions	21.5	28.3	35.3	31.0	25.6	28.3	32.0	34.0
Security and commodity brokers	39.7	49.5	62.9	69.5	41.2	49.5	65.1	74.4
Insurance carriers	69.3	83.4	99.6	104.1	70.2	83.4	74.0	76.3
Insurance agents, brokers, and services	37.1	39.5	42.0	45.3	40.8	39.5	40.2	41.9
Real estate	673.0	735.8	762.4	802.3	706.8	735.8	740.4	758.4
Nonfarm housing services	492.3	553.5	568.7	605.2	525.6	553.5	552.9	571.9
Other real estate	180.7	182.3	193.7	197.1	180.7	182.3	187.6	186.4
Holding and other investment offices	15.5	12.3	9.8	9.3	12.3	12.3	12.8	12.9

[1] See text, section 14.

Source: U.S. Bureau of Economic Analysis, *Survey of Current Business*, August 1996.

No. 773. Finance, Insurance, and Real Estate—Establishments, Employees, and Payroll: 1990 and 1994

[Covers establishments with payroll. Employees are for the week including March 12. Most government employees are excluded. For statement on methodology, see Appendix III]

KIND OF BUSINESS	1987 SIC code [1]	ESTABLISHMENTS (1,000)		EMPLOYEES (1,000)		PAYROLL (bil. dol.)	
		1990	1994	1990	1994	1990	1994
Finance, insurance, real estate	(H)	544.7	617.4	6,967	7,002	197.4	239.0
Depository institutions [2 3]	60	81.2	104.6	2,033	2,091	48.4	59.7
Central reserve depositories	601	0.1	0.1	31	25	0.9	1.0
Commercial banks	602	52.3	65.8	1,472	1,521	35.6	43.2
Savings institutions	603	21.7	17.9	417	300	8.8	7.9
Credit unions	606	3.6	15.1	51	152	1.0	3.3
Functions closely related to banking	609	2.8	5.1	44	58	1.4	1.9
Nondepository institutions [2 3]	61	42.0	44.2	506	526	14.0	17.7
Federal and fed.-sponsored credit	611	0.6	1.3	14	23	0.4	1.0
Personal credit institutions	614	25.0	16.8	236	153	5.5	4.7
Business credit institutions	615	3.7	4.7	88	90	3.1	3.9
Mortgage bankers and brokers	616	10.9	20.1	153	258	4.6	8.0
Security and commodity brokers [2]	62	25.2	38.6	411	507	26.6	39.8
Security brokers and dealers	621	15.9	23.0	308	372	20.8	30.0
Commodity contracts brokers, dealers	622	1.2	1.5	15	13	0.7	0.7
Security and commodity exchanges	623	0.2	0.1	9	7	0.5	0.4
Security and commodity services	628	7.1	13.9	76	115	4.5	8.7
Insurance carriers [2]	63	43.3	40.9	1,407	1,538	41.5	53.9
Life insurance	631	14.1	12.0	572	574	16.3	19.4
Medical service and health insurance [2]	632	2.1	2.9	188	260	5.1	8.5
Accident and health insurance	6321	1.1	1.1	48	52	1.3	1.5
Hospital and medical service plans	6324	1.0	1.8	139	208	3.8	7.0
Fire, marine, and casualty insurance	633	18.3	19.9	533	610	17.0	23.0
Surety insurance	635	0.6	0.6	15	11	0.5	0.5
Title insurance	636	3.2	2.4	57	47	1.6	1.4
Pension, health and welfare funds	637	3.8	2.8	25	33	0.6	0.9
Insurance agents, brokers, and service	64	110.8	124.0	712	662	20.3	21.2
Real estate [2]	65	217.0	241.3	1,374	1,370	28.5	31.3
Real estate operators and lessors	651	95.7	99.9	509	483	8.7	9.1
Real estate agents and managers	653	72.2	114.9	585	733	13.3	18.1
Title abstract offices	654	3.1	4.9	24	43	0.5	1.0
Subdividers and developers [2]	655	19.6	16.9	140	106	3.4	2.8
Subdividers and developers, n.e.c. [4]	6552	10.8	10.0	88	62	2.3	1.9
Cemetery subdividers and developers	6553	4.4	6.3	35	44	0.6	0.9
Holding and other investment offices [2]	67	22.6	22.3	263	235	10.0	11.8
Holding offices	671	6.2	8.0	124	128	5.4	7.0
Investment offices	672	1.0	0.8	16	20	1.0	1.3
Trusts	673	7.8	4.9	65	31	1.4	0.8
Educational, religious, etc. trusts	6732	3.6	2.2	42	17	0.9	0.5
Miscellaneous investing	679	5.0	8.0	44	51	1.5	2.5
Patent owners and lessors	6794	0.9	1.6	15	19	0.4	0.8
Administrative and auxiliary	(X)	2.6	1.5	251	73	8.2	3.6

X Not applicable. [1] Standard Industrial Classification; see text, section 13. [2] Includes industries not shown separately. [3] Includes government employees. [4] N.e.c.=Not elsewhere classified.

Source: U.S. Bureau of the Census, *County Business Patterns*, annual.

No. 774. Flow of Funds Accounts—Financial Assets of Financial and Nonfinancial Institutions, by Holder Sector: 1980 to 1996

[In billions of dollars. As of Dec. 31]

SECTOR	1980	1985	1989	1990	1991	1992	1993	1994	1995	1996
All sectors	13,816	23,696	34,733	36,121	39,182	41,572	45,043	47,130	52,779	58,287
Households [1]	6,296	9,709	13,851	14,207	15,779	16,615	17,733	18,275	20,711	22,768
Nonfinancial business	1,624	2,964	4,062	4,168	4,293	4,478	4,860	5,157	5,520	5,961
Farm business	24	33	45	47	50	53	57	60	65	70
Nonfarm noncorporate	145	435	498	486	479	492	514	529	546	564
Nonfinancial corporations	1,455	2,496	3,519	3,634	3,764	3,932	4,289	4,567	4,910	5,327
State and local government	301	645	916	963	1,020	1,034	1,083	1,026	936	874
U.S. Government	229	372	371	443	501	477	491	442	424	415
U.S. Govt.-sponsored enterprises	193	323	451	474	494	549	627	776	890	981
Federally related mortgage pools	114	369	870	1,020	1,156	1,272	1,357	1,472	1,570	1,711
Monetary authority	174	243	315	342	365	382	424	452	472	495
Commercial banking [2]	1,482	2,376	3,231	3,337	3,442	3,655	3,892	4,160	4,494	4,710
U.S.-chartered commercial banks	1,266	1,990	2,545	2,644	2,677	2,775	2,932	3,123	3,322	3,446
Foreign banking offices in U.S.	98	144	359	367	438	509	542	590	666	713
Nonbank finance	2,884	5,720	8,777	9,155	9,967	10,769	11,876	12,459	14,308	16,253
Funding corporations	16	135	233	250	261	308	305	357	387	468
Savings institutions	792	1,275	1,513	1,358	1,172	1,079	1,029	1,013	1,016	1,036
Credit unions	68	135	202	217	240	265	282	294	311	327
Life insurance	464	796	1,260	1,367	1,505	1,614	1,785	1,889	2,091	2,239
Other insurance	182	299	503	533	576	596	642	676	737	804
Private pension funds	504	1,232	1,621	1,611	1,816	1,985	2,175	2,264	2,829	3,031
State and local govt. retirement funds	197	399	767	920	1,032	1,168	1,255	1,301	1,527	1,736
Finance companies	205	365	571	611	634	639	654	734	825	897
Mortgage companies	16	25	49	49	60	60	60	36	33	48
Real estate investment trusts	3	8	15	13	14	14	17	22	26	31
Mutual funds	62	246	590	608	769	993	1,375	1,477	1,853	2,349
Closed-end investment funds	8	8	52	53	71	91	110	111	129	143
Money market funds	76	242	425	493	535	539	560	603	745	891
Security brokers, dealers	45	156	237	262	333	362	479	455	568	629
Asset-backed securities issuers	-	39	225	285	339	404	487	556	669	819
Bank personal trusts	245	358	515	522	606	630	661	670	740	808
Rest of the world	520	976	1,888	2,012	2,165	2,342	2,700	2,911	3,455	4,100

- Represents zero. [1] Includes nonprofit organizations. [2] Includes other sectors not shown separately.

No. 775. Flow of Funds Accounts—Credit Market Debt Outstanding: 1980 to 1996

[In billions of dollars. As of Dec. 31. N.e.c.=Not elsewhere classified]

ITEM	1980	1985	1989	1990	1991	1992	1993	1994	1995	1996
Credit market debt	4,734	8,586	12,837	13,774	14,423	15,241	16,252	17,337	18,576	19,821
U.S. government	735	1,590	2,251	2,498	2,776	3,080	3,336	3,492	3,637	3,782
Nonfederal domestic nonfinancial	3,223	5,500	7,924	8,376	8,576	8,820	9,206	9,680	10,255	10,858
Households [1]	1,391	2,260	3,347	3,640	3,828	4,028	4,288	4,680	5,041	5,436
Corporations	894	1,545	2,347	2,457	2,401	2,437	2,497	2,621	2,819	2,966
Nonfarm noncorporate business	431	844	1,149	1,150	1,137	1,123	1,127	1,139	1,174	1,217
Farm business	161	173	134	135	135	136	138	141	143	146
State and local government	344	678	947	993	1,075	1,096	1,156	1,118	1,079	1,092
Rest of the world	197	237	262	286	301	315	386	370	440	507
Financial sectors	579	1,258	2,399	2,614	2,769	3,025	3,322	3,795	4,244	4,775
Commercial banking	91	188	225	198	185	195	208	228	251	262
Thrift institutions [2]	55	111	171	140	95	88	100	113	115	142
Life insurance companies	-	-	-	-	-	-	-	1	1	2
Government-sponsored enterprises [3]	163	264	378	399	408	448	528	701	807	897
Federally-related mortgage pools	114	369	870	1,020	1,156	1,272	1,357	1,472	1,570	1,711
Asset-backed securities issuers	-	39	225	285	339	404	487	556	669	819
Finance companies	127	224	350	374	392	390	391	441	492	540
Mortgage companies	12	17	25	25	22	30	30	19	19	36
Real estate investment trusts	5	5	12	12	14	14	17	31	37	43
Security brokers, dealers	-	1	14	15	19	22	34	34	29	27
Funding corporations	13	39	130	146	139	162	170	199	234	296
CORPORATE CREDIT MARKET DEBT OUTSTANDING, BY TYPE OF INSTRUMENT										
Total	894	1,545	2,347	2,457	2,401	2,437	2,497	2,621	2,819	2,966
Commercial paper	28	72	107	117	98	107	118	139	157	156
Municipal securities [4]	46	127	115	115	114	114	114	109	97	79
Corporate bonds	366	578	961	1,008	1,087	1,155	1,230	1,253	1,326	1,399
Bank loans, n.e.c.	230	424	543	545	508	488	478	525	590	636
Other loans and advances	111	256	436	498	441	447	432	481	523	556
Savings institutions	1	15	24	17	10	6	5	5	6	8
Finance companies	80	143	243	264	266	271	265	304	338	359
U.S. government	8	14	10	9	8	8	8	9	9	10
Acceptance liabilities to banks	17	28	36	29	23	20	17	15	14	13
Rest of the world	5	56	122	172	125	130	114	122	122	125
Asset-backed securities issuers	-	-	2	6	9	12	22	26	33	41
Mortgages	114	87	184	173	153	125	126	115	125	137

- Represents or rounds to zero. [1] Includes nonprofit organizations. [2] Covers savings institutions and credit unions. [3] U.S. Government. [4] Industrial revenue bonds. Issued by State and local governments to finance private investment and secured in interest and principal by the industrial user of the funds.

Source of tables 774 and 775: Board of Governors of the Federal Reserve System, *Flow of Funds Accounts*, March 1997 diskettes. Data are also published in the quarterly Z.1 release.

No. 776. Flow of Funds Accounts—Financial Assets and Liabilities of Financial and Nonfinancial Institutions, by Sector and Type of Instrument: 1996

[In billions of dollars. As of Dec. 31. Preliminary. A=Assets; L=Liabilities. SDR=Special drawing rights. IMF=International Monetary Fund. RP's=Repurchase Agreements. "N.e.c."=Not elsewhere classified]

TYPE OF INSTRUMENT	ALL SECTORS, TOTAL		PRIVATE DOMESTIC NONFINANCIAL INSTITUTIONS								U.S. GOVERNMENT		FINANCIAL INSTITUTIONS								FOREIGN SECTOR	
			Total		Households [1]		Business		State and local govts.				Total [2]		Commercial banking		Life insurance		Federally sponsored credit agencies and mortgage pools			
	A	L	A	L	A	L	A	L	A	L	A	L	A	L	A	L	A	L	A	L	A	L
Total	58,267	44,461	29,603	14,664	22,768	5,665	5,961	7,873	874	1,128	415	4,354	24,150	23,347	4,710	4,546	2,239	2,096	2,662	2,675	4,100	2,096
Gold stock and SDR's	21	-	-	-	-	-	-	-	-	-	10	-	11	-	-	-	-	-	-	-	-	-
IMF position	15	15	-	-	-	-	-	-	-	-	16	-	-	-	-	-	-	-	-	-	-	15
Official foreign exchange	38	38	-	-	-	-	-	-	-	-	19	-	19	-	-	-	-	-	-	-	-	38
Treasury currency, SDR certificates	35	28	-	-	-	-	-	-	-	-	-	28	35	-	-	-	-	-	-	-	-	-
Checkable deposits, currency	1,220	1,248	868	-	450	-	385	-	33	-	38	-	68	1,248	1	677	7	-	1	-	247	-
Time and savings deposits	2,962	2,962	2,752	-	2,520	-	160	-	72	-	2	-	151	2,962	-	2,108	-	-	-	-	58	-
Fed. funds and security RP's	576	698	75	-	-	-	5	-	70	-	-	-	433	698	-	462	-	-	102	-	69	-
Money market fund shares	891	891	645	-	538	-	107	-	-	-	-	-	246	891	-	-	39	-	-	-	-	-
Foreign deposits	62	409	39	-	23	-	16	-	-	-	-	-	23	-	-	-	-	-	-	-	-	409
Life insurance reserves	585	585	585	-	585	-	-	-	-	-	-	14	-	572	-	-	-	572	-	-	-	-
Pension fund reserves	6,319	6,319	6,319	-	6,319	-	-	-	-	-	-	419	-	5,899	-	-	-	1,109	-	-	-	-
Interbank claims	249	238	-	-	-	-	-	-	-	-	-	-	74	238	68	169	-	-	-	-	175	-
Mutual fund shares [3]	2,349	2,349	1,593	-	1,491	-	65	-	37	-	-	-	756	2,349	3	-	31	-	-	-	-	-
Other corporate equities [4]	10,090	-	4,793	-	4,780	-	-	-	14	-	-	-	4,671	-	7	-	424	-	-	-	626	-
Credit market instruments [5]	19,922	19,922	2,938	10,858	1,961	5,436	379	4,329	599	1,092	163	3,782	14,854	4,775	3,706	262	1,641	2	2,555	2,608	1,967	507
U.S. Treasury securities [6]	3,755	3,755	847	-	586	-	95	-	166	-	-	3,755	1,783	-	262	-	102	-	57	-	1,125	-
Federal agency securities [7]	2,635	2,635	568	-	289	-	37	-	242	-	-	27	1,850	2,608	496	-	245	-	243	2,608	217	-
Municipal securities	1,306	1,306	490	1,306	432	139	50	79	8	1,087	-	-	816	-	94	-	12	-	4	-	-	-
Corporate and foreign bonds	3,049	3,049	427	1,399	390	-	-	1,399	37	-	-	-	2,176	1,312	113	169	917	-	23	-	445	337
Mortgages	5,054	5,054	426	5,025	217	3,889	92	1,135	117	-	47	-	4,582	30	1,146	-	212	-	1,971	-	-	-
Consumer credit	1,226	1,226	80	1,226	-	1,226	80	-	-	-	-	-	1,147	-	528	-	-	-	-	-	-	-
Bank loans, n.e.c	1,040	1,040	-	914	-	37	-	877	-	-	-	-	1,040	82	1,040	-	-	-	-	-	-	44
Open-market paper	803	803	101	156	47	-	25	156	29	-	-	-	648	581	7	56	50	-	33	-	55	66
Security credit	352	352	158	93	158	93	-	-	-	-	-	-	194	259	101	-	-	-	-	-	-	-
Trade credit [8]	1,618	1,335	1,386	1,177	-	116	1,386	1,027	-	34	33	105	142	14	-	-	-	-	-	-	57	40
Taxes payable	47	92	26	82	-	-	-	82	26	-	21	-	-	10	-	4	-	1	-	-	-	-
Proprietors' equity	2,734	-	2,734	-	2,734	-	-	-	-	-	-	-	-	-	-	-	-	-	-	-	-	-
Investment in bank personal trusts	834	834	834	-	834	-	-	-	-	-	-	-	-	834	-	-	-	-	-	-	-	-
Miscellaneous claims	7,349	6,147	3,859	2,456	376	19	3,459	2,436	25	-	112	7	2,474	2,598	823	866	97	413	35	67	904	1,086

- Represents or rounds to zero. [1] Includes nonprofit organizations. [2] Includes other financial institutions, not shown separately. [3] Nonbank finance liability is redemption value of shares of open-end investment companies. [4] Assets shown at market value. No specific liability attributed to issuers of stocks other than open-end investment companies for amounts outstanding. [5] Includes "Other loans," not shown separately. [6] Includes savings bonds and other nonmarketable debt held by public. [7] Issues by agencies in the budget and by Government-sponsored enterprises in financial sectors, issues backed by federally-related mortgage pools, and loan participation certificates. [8] Asset is corporate only; noncorporate credit deducted in liability total to conform to quarterly flow tables.

Source: Board of Governors of the Federal Reserve System, *Flow of Funds Accounts*, quarterly.

777. Flow of Funds Accounts—Assets of Households: 1980 to 1996

[As of December 31. Includes nonprofit organizations]

NSTRUMENT	TOTAL (bil. dol.)							PERCENT DISTRIBUTION		
	1980	1985	1990	1993	1994	1995	1996	1980	1990	1996
al assets	6,298	9,709	14,207	17,733	18,275	20,711	22,768	100.0	100.0	100.0
	1,490	2,460	3,239	3,152	3,144	3,348	3,531	23.7	22.8	15.5
s	-	8	13	16	17	19	23	-	0.1	0.1
eits and currency	224	318	383	562	547	503	450	3.6	2.7	2.0
js deposits	1,203	1,941	2,478	2,236	2,228	2,378	2,520	19.1	17.4	11.1
und shares	62	193	365	338	352	448	538	1.0	2.6	2.4
uments	423	799	1,494	1,691	1,961	1,932	1,961	6.7	10.5	8.6
per	38	35	63	46	35	35	47	0.6	0.4	0.2
nt securities	165	267	514	594	938	881	875	2.6	3.6	3.8
es	160	239	390	477	669	646	586	2.5	2.7	2.6
nds	73	80	126	172	180	185	187	1.2	0.9	0.8
sury	88	159	264	305	489	461	399	1.4	1.9	1.8
s	5	28	124	117	269	235	289	0.1	0.9	1.3
ities	104	346	574	557	505	454	432	1.7	4.0	1.9
oreign bonds	31	75	195	312	311	382	390	0.5	1.4	1.7
	84	76	147	183	193	200	217	1.3	1.0	1.0
[1]	903	1,110	1,753	3,250	3,100	4,167	4,780	14.3	12.3	21.0
s	46	198	467	977	1,027	1,227	1,491	0.7	3.3	6.5
	16	35	62	102	109	128	158	0.3	0.4	0.7
erves	216	257	381	471	505	550	585	3.4	2.7	2.6
rves [2]	960	2,082	3,408	4,639	4,847	5,568	6,319	15.2	24.0	27.8
personal trusts	265	384	552	691	699	767	834	4.2	3.9	3.7
rate business	1,903	2,273	2,629	2,496	2,587	2,700	2,734	30.2	18.5	12.0
ets	74	133	224	264	275	325	376	1.2	1.6	1.7

zero. [1] Only those directly held and those in closed-end funds. Other equities are included in mutual funds, pension reserves, and bank personal trusts. [2] See also table 825.

l of Governors of the Federal Reserve System, *Flow of Funds Accounts*, March 1997 diskettes. Data are also uarterly Z.1 release.

8. Financial Assets Held by Families, by Type of Asset: 1992 and 1995

housands of constant 1995 dollars. Constant dollar figures are based on consumer price index data published Labor Statistics. Families include one-person units; for definition of family, see text, section 1. Based on Survey nce; see Appendix III. For definition of median, see Guide to Tabular Presentation]

ILY HEAD INCOME	Any financial asset [1]	Transaction accounts [2]	Certificates of deposit	Savings bonds	Stocks [3]	Mutual funds [4]	Retirement accounts [5]	Life insurance (cash value)	Other managed [6]
FAMILIES ASSET									
	90.3	87.0	16.7	22.3	16.9	10.4	37.9	34.8	4.0
	90.8	87.1	14.1	22.9	15.3	12.0	43.0	31.4	3.8
d	87.0	80.8	7.1	21.1	11.1	8.8	39.2	22.3	1.8
	92.0	87.4	8.2	31.0	14.5	10.5	51.5	28.9	3.4
	92.4	88.9	12.5	25.1	17.5	16.0	54.3	37.5	2.9
	90.5	88.2	16.2	19.6	14.9	15.2	47.2	37.5	7.1
	92.0	91.1	23.9	17.0	18.0	13.7	35.0	37.0	5.6
ver	93.8	93.0	34.1	15.3	21.3	10.4	16.5	35.1	5.7
	68.1	61.1	7.2	5.9	2.5	1.8	5.9	15.8	(B)
9	87.6	82.3	16.0	11.8	9.2	4.9	24.2	25.2	3.2
9	97.8	94.7	13.7	27.4	14.3	12.4	52.6	33.1	4.2
9	99.5	98.6	15.6	39.9	26.0	20.9	69.8	42.5	5.3
e	100.0	100.0	21.1	36.3	45.2	38.0	84.6	54.1	8.0
ALUE [7]									
	12.0	2.5	11.2	0.7	8.7	17.4	15.2	3.3	21.7
	13.0	2.1	10.0	1.0	8.0	19.0	15.6	5.0	30.0
d	5.3	1.2	6.0	0.5	3.7	5.0	5.2	3.4	3.8
	11.6	2.0	6.0	1.0	4.0	10.0	12.0	5.0	10.8
	24.8	2.7	12.0	1.0	10.0	17.5	25.0	6.5	43.0
	32.3	3.0	14.0	1.1	17.0	55.0	32.8	6.0	42.0
	19.1	3.0	17.0	1.5	15.0	50.0	28.5	5.0	26.0
ver	20.9	5.0	11.0	4.0	25.0	50.0	17.5	5.0	100.0
	1.2	0.7	7.0	0.4	2.0	25.0	3.5	1.5	(B)
9	5.4	1.4	10.0	0.8	5.7	8.0	6.0	3.0	19.7
9	12.1	2.0	10.0	0.7	6.9	12.5	10.0	5.0	25.0
9	40.7	4.5	13.0	1.2	5.7	15.0	23.0	7.0	35.0
e	214.5	15.8	15.6	1.5	30.0	48.0	85.0	12.0	62.5

too small. [1] Includes other types of financial assets, not shown separately. [2] Checking, savings, and money [3] Covers only those stocks that are directly held by families outside mutual funds, IRA's, Keogh or pension ludes money market mutual funds, individual retirement accounts (IRA's), Keogh accounts, and any type of sted in mutual funds. [5] Covers IRA's, Keogh accounts, and employer-provided pension plans from which s made, such as 401(k) plans. [6] Includes trusts, annuities, managed investment accounts, and other such n value of financial asset for families holding such assets.

l of Governors of the Federal Reserve System, *Federal Reserve Bulletin*, January 1997.

o. 779. Flow of Funds Accounts—Liabilities of Households: 1980 to 1996

[As of December 31. Includes nonprofit organizations]

OF INSTRUMENT	TOTAL (bil. dol.)							PERCENT DISTRIBUTION		
	1980	1985	1990	1993	1994	1995	1996	1980	1990	1996
abilities	1,443	2,380	3,785	4,471	4,880	5,245	5,665	100.0	100.0	100.0
t instruments	1,391	2,280	3,640	4,288	4,680	5,041	5,436	96.4	96.7	96.0
rtgages	905	1,410	2,491	2,980	3,178	3,376	3,654	62.7	66.2	64.5
credit	355	595	811	864	990	1,132	1,226	24.6	21.5	21.6
securities	17	81	86	115	129	135	139	1.2	2.3	2.5
s, n.e.c.[1]	28	32	12	18	29	42	37	1.9	0.3	0.7
s	55	79	101	127	135	145	144	3.8	2.7	2.5
al mortgages	31	63	139	165	199	212	235	2.2	3.7	4.1
it	25	51	39	76	75	79	93	1.7	1.0	1.6
les	14	24	69	90	97	107	116	1.0	1.8	2.1
surance premiums[2]	13	15	16	17	18	18	19	0.9	0.4	0.3

ewhere classified. [2] Includes deferred premiums.

Board of Governors of the Federal Reserve System, *Flow of Funds Accounts*, March 1997 diskettes.

o. 780. Financial Debt Held by Families, by Type of Debt: 1992 and 1995

[Median debt in thousands of constant 1995 dollars. See headnote, table 778]

FAMILY HEAD AMILY INCOME	Any debt	Mortgage, home equity	Installment	Other lines of credit	Credit card	Investment real estate	Other debt[1]
T OF FAMILIES DING DEBTS							
	73.6	39.1	46.1	2.4	43.8	7.8	8.8
l	75.2	41.1	46.5	1.9	47.8	6.3	9.0
ars old	83.8	32.9	62.2	2.6	55.4	2.6	7.8
rs old	87.2	54.1	60.7	2.2	55.8	6.5	11.1
rs old	86.5	61.9	54.0	2.3	57.3	10.4	14.1
rs old	75.2	45.8	36.0	1.4	43.4	12.5	7.5
rs old	54.5	24.8	16.7	1.3	31.3	5.0	5.5
and over	30.1	7.1	9.6	(B)	18.3	1.5	3.6
0,000	48.5	8.9	25.9	(B)	25.4	1.6	6.6
24,999	67.3	24.8	41.3	1.4	41.9	2.5	8.7
49,999	83.9	47.3	54.3	2.0	56.7	5.8	8.5
99,999	89.9	68.7	60.7	3.2	62.8	9.5	10.0
d more	86.4	73.6	37.0	4.0	37.0	27.9	15.8
IAN DEBT[2]							
	19.5	47.4	5.0	2.2	1.1	26.0	2.7
l	22.5	51.0	6.1	3.5	1.5	28.0	2.0
ars old	15.2	63.0	7.0	1.4	1.4	22.8	1.5
rs old	37.6	60.0	5.6	2.0	1.8	30.0	1.7
rs old	41.0	48.0	7.0	5.7	2.0	28.1	2.5
rs old	25.8	36.0	5.9	3.5	1.3	26.0	4.0
rs old	7.7	19.0	4.9	3.8	0.8	36.0	2.0
and over	2.0	15.9	3.9	(B)	0.4	8.0	3.0
0,000	2.6	14.0	2.9	(B)	0.6	15.0	2.0
24,999	9.2	26.0	3.9	3.0	1.2	18.3	1.2
49,999	23.4	46.0	6.6	3.0	1.4	25.0	1.5
99,999	65.0	68.0	9.0	2.2	2.2	34.0	2.5
d more	112.2	103.4	8.5	19.5	3.0	36.8	7.0

figure too small. [1] Includes loans on insurance policies, loans against pension accounts, and other unclassified edian amount of financial debt for families holding such debts.

'81. Percent Distribution of Amount of Debt Held by Families: 1992 and 1995

[See headnote, table 782]

DEBT	1992	1995	PURPOSE OF DEBT	1992	1995	TYPE OF LENDING INSTITUTION	1992	1993
	100.0	100.0	Total	100.0	100.0	Total	100.0	100.0
age and			Home purchase	59.9	65.2	Commercial bank	33.2	35.1
y lines of			Home improvement	2.3	1.9	Savings and loan	16.6	11.3
	64.2	68.2	Investment, excluding			Credit union	4.0	4.2
oans	10.3	11.2	real estate	1.6	0.9	Finance or loan company	13.5	21.0
alances	2.8	3.7	Vehicles	6.2	7.1	Brokerage	3.3	1.9
f credit	0.7	0.4	Goods and services	5.0	5.2	Real estate lender	14.2	12.9
eal estate			Investment real estate	20.5	15.3	Individual lender	4.5	4.4
	19.8	14.4	Education	2.5	2.5	Other nonfinancial	1.5	0.7
	2.2	2.2	Other loans	2.2	2.0	Government	1.9	1.7
						Credit and store cards	3.0	3.7
						Other loans	4.4	3.1

f tables 780 and 781: Board of Governors of the Federal Reserve System, *Federal Reserve Bulletin*, January 1997.

No. 782. Ratios of Debt Payments to Family Income: 1989 to 1995

[In percent. Constant dollar figures are based on consumer price index data published by U.S. Bureau of Labor Statistics. Families include one-person units; for definition of family, see text, section 1. Based on Survey of Consumer Finance; see Appendix III. For definition of median, see Guide to Tabular Presentation]

AGE OF FAMILY HEAD AND FAMILY INCOME (constant (1995) dollars)	RATIO OF DEBT PAYMENTS TO FAMILY INCOME						PERCENT OF DEBTORS WITH—					
	Aggregate			Median			Ratios above 40 percent			Any payment 60 days or more past due		
	1989	1992	1995	1989	1992	1995	1989	1992	1995	1989	1992	1995
All families	15.6	15.8	15.4	16.0	15.7	16.7	10.9	11.6	11.1	7.0	6.0	6.9
Under 35 years old	18.4	16.9	17.7	16.5	15.5	16.9	13.1	10.6	11.1	10.8	8.2	8.8
35 to 44 years old	18.8	18.4	17.6	18.4	18.5	18.2	9.2	12.2	9.8	5.9	7.0	7.4
45 to 54 years old	16.2	17.5	17.0	16.8	16.2	17.0	11.7	11.6	11.0	4.6	5.4	7.8
55 to 64 years old	14.6	14.4	14.9	13.5	15.2	15.2	10.0	15.6	15.3	7.5	4.6	2.5
65 to 74 years old	6.8	10.3	9.4	12.3	10.1	13.3	8.5	8.6	9.9	3.3	1.1	5.0
75 years old and over	2.6	4.6	3.8	8.8	3.1	3.8	11.2	9.6	9.5	1.1	2.1	4.2
Less than $10,000	16.2	17.1	21.1	19.3	13.2	15.1	25.6	28.9	26.9	21.4	11.1	8.0
$10,000 to $24,999	12.7	16.5	16.1	17.2	14.7	17.8	13.9	16.0	16.9	11.8	9.2	11.4
$25,000 to $49,999	16.7	17.0	17.2	16.0	16.0	16.9	10.6	9.7	8.5	4.2	6.2	7.8
$50,000 to $99,999	17.4	16.0	16.7	16.1	16.9	16.8	5.7	4.7	4.3	4.0	2.1	2.4
$100,000 and more	14.0	14.2	11.9	13.9	14.6	11.4	6.7	4.5	4.1	2.2	0.5	1.4

Source: Board of Governors of the Federal Reserve System, *Federal Reserve Bulletin*, January 1997.

No. 783. Selected Financial Institutions—Number and Assets, by Asset Size: 1996

[As of December. FDIC=Federal Deposit Insurance Corporation]

ASSET SIZE	NUMBER OF INSTITUTIONS			ASSETS (bil. dol.)		
	F.D.I.C.-insured		Credit unions [1]	F.D.I.C.-insured		Credit unions [1]
	Commercial banks	Savings institutions		Commercial banks [2]	Savings institutions	
Total	9,528	1,924	11,392	4,578.3	1,028.2	326.9
Less than $5.0 million	52	7	5,520	0.2	(Z)	10.0
$5.0 million to $9.9 million	188	31	1,774	1.5	0.3	12.6
$10.0 million to $24.9 million	1,340	120	1,848	24.2	2.2	29.8
$25.0 million to $49.9 million	2,207	268	966	81.0	10.3	34.0
$50.0 million to $99.9 million	2,416	418	619	173.0	31.0	43.0
$100.0 million to $499.9 million	2,650	789	591	523.4	180.8	119.7
$500.0 million to $999.9 million	277	130	51	190.1	89.3	33.5
$1.0 billion to $2.9 billion	207	98	21	342.6	156.8	31.0
$3.0 billion or more	191	63	2	3,242.2	557.5	13.2
	PERCENT DISTRIBUTION					
Total	100.0	100.0	100.0	100.0	100.0	100.0
Less than $5.0 million	0.5	0.4	48.5	(Z)	(Z)	3.1
$5.0 million to $9.9 million	2.0	1.6	15.6	(Z)	(Z)	3.9
$10.0 million to $24.9 million	14.1	6.2	16.2	0.5	0.2	9.1
$25.0 million to $49.9 million	23.2	13.9	8.5	1.8	1.0	10.4
$50.0 million to $99.9 million	25.4	21.7	5.4	3.8	3.0	13.2
$100.0 million to $499.9 million	27.8	41.0	5.2	11.4	17.6	36.6
$500.0 million to $999.9 million	2.9	6.8	0.4	4.2	8.7	10.2
$1.0 billion to $2.9 billion	2.2	5.1	0.2	7.5	15.3	9.5
$3.0 billion or more	2.0	3.3	(Z)	70.8	54.2	4.0

Z Less than $50 million or 0.05 percent. [1] Source: National Credit Union Administration, *National Credit Union Administration Yearend Statistics 1996*. Excludes nonfederally insured State chartered credit unions and federally insured corporate credit unions. [2] Includes foreign branches of U.S. banks.

Source: Except as noted, U.S. Federal Deposit Insurance Corporation, *Statistics on Banking, 1996*.

No. 784. Banking Offices, by Type of Bank: 1980 to 1996

[As of December 31. Includes Puerto Rico and outlying areas. Covers all FDIC-insured commercial banks and savings institutions. Data for 1980 include automatic teller machines which were reported by many banks as branches]

ITEM	1980	1985	1990	1991	1992	1993	1994	1995	1996
All banking offices	(NA)	85,083	84,672	84,098	82,002	81,745	82,673	81,893	82,476
Number of banks	(NA)	18,043	15,162	14,488	13,856	13,322	12,602	11,970	11,452
Number of branches	(NA)	67,040	69,510	69,610	68,146	68,423	70,071	69,923	71,024
Commercial banks	53,172	57,710	62,753	63,896	63,401	63,828	65,594	66,454	67,316
Number of banks	14,434	14,417	12,347	11,927	11,466	10,960	10,450	9,941	9,528
Number of branches	38,738	43,293	50,406	51,969	51,935	52,868	55,144	56,513	57,788
Savings institutions	(NA)	27,373	21,919	20,202	18,601	17,917	17,079	15,439	15,160
Number of banks	(NA)	3,626	2,815	2,561	2,390	2,362	2,152	2,029	1,924
Number of branches	(NA)	23,747	19,104	17,641	16,211	15,555	14,927	13,410	13,236

NA Not available.

Source: U.S. Federal Deposit Insurance Corporation, *Historical Statistics on Banking, 1934-1995*, 1996 and *Statistics on Banking*, annual.

No. 785. Insured Commercial Banks—Assets and Liabilities: 1980 to 1996

[In billions of dollars, except as indicated. As of Dec. 31. Includes outlying areas. Except as noted, includes foreign branches of U.S. banks]

ITEM	1980	1985	1990	1991	1992	1993	1994	1995	1996 [1]
Number of banks reporting	14,435	14,417	12,343	11,921	11,462	10,958	10,450	9,940	9,528
Assets, total	1,856	2,731	3,389	3,431	3,506	3,706	4,011	4,313	4,578
Net loans and leases	1,006	1,608	2,055	1,998	1,977	2,097	2,306	2,550	2,757
Real estate loans	269	438	830	851	868	923	998	1,080	1,140
Home equity lines of credit [2]	(NA)	(NA)	61	70	73	73	76	79	85
Commercial and industrial loans	391	578	615	559	536	539	589	661	710
Loans to individuals	187	309	404	392	385	419	487	535	561
Farm loans	32	36	33	35	35	37	39	40	41
Other loans and leases	158	288	242	227	218	239	251	292	364
Less: Reserve for losses	10	23	56	55	54	53	52	53	54
Less: Unearned income	21	18	14	11	9	7	6	6	5
Investment securities	325	439	605	691	773	837	823	811	801
Other	524	684	730	742	755	773	882	952	1,020
Domestic office assets	1,533	2,326	2,999	3,033	3,110	3,258	3,484	3,728	3,906
Foreign office assets	323	408	390	398	396	448	527	585	672
Liabilities and capital, total	1,856	2,731	3,389	3,431	3,506	3,706	4,011	4,313	4,578
Noninterest-bearing deposits [3]	432	471	489	480	541	572	572	612	664
Interest-bearing deposits [4]	1,049	1,646	2,162	2,207	2,158	2,182	2,302	2,416	2,533
Subordinated debt	7	15	24	25	34	37	41	44	51
Other liabilities	260	429	496	486	510	618	783	892	955
Equity capital	108	169	219	232	263	297	312	350	375
Domestic office deposits	1,187	1,796	2,357	2,383	2,412	2,424	2,442	2,573	2,724
Foreign office deposits	294	322	293	305	287	330	432	454	474

NA Not available. [1] Preliminary. [2] For one- to four-family residential properties. [3] Prior to 1985, demand deposits. [4] Prior to 1985, time and savings deposits.

Source: U.S. Federal Deposit Insurance Corporation, *The FDIC Quarterly Banking Profile, Annual Report*, and *Statistics on Banking*, annual.

No. 786. Insured Commercial Banks—Income and Selected Measures of Financial Condition: 1980 to 1996

[In billions of dollars, except as indicated. Includes outlying areas. Includes foreign branches of U.S. banks]

ITEM	1980	1985	1990	1991	1992	1993	1994	1995	1996 [1]
Interest income	177.4	248.2	320.4	289.2	255.2	245.1	257.8	302.4	312.8
Interest expense	120.1	157.3	204.9	167.3	121.8	105.7	111.3	148.2	150.0
Net interest income	57.3	90.9	115.5	121.9	133.4	139.3	146.6	154.2	162.8
Provisions for loan losses	4.5	17.8	32.1	34.3	26.0	16.8	10.9	12.6	16.2
Noninterest income	13.3	31.1	54.9	59.7	65.6	75.0	76.3	82.4	93.6
Noninterest expense	46.7	82.4	115.7	124.8	130.9	139.7	144.2	149.7	160.7
Income taxes	5.0	5.6	7.7	8.3	14.5	19.8	22.4	26.1	28.2
Securities gain/loss, net	-0.5	1.6	0.5	3.0	4.0	3.1	-0.6	0.5	1.1
Extraordinary gains, net	-	0.2	0.6	0.7	0.4	2.1	-	-	0.1
Net income	14.0	18.0	16.0	17.9	32.0	43.1	44.6	48.8	52.4
RATIOS OF CONDITION									
Return on assets [2] (percent)	0.80	0.70	0.48	0.53	0.93	1.20	1.15	1.17	1.19
Return on equity [3] (percent)	13.66	11.31	7.45	7.94	12.98	15.34	14.61	14.66	14.46
Equity capital to assets (percent)	5.80	6.20	6.45	6.75	7.51	8.00	7.78	8.11	8.20
Noncurrent assets plus other real estate owned to assets [4] (percent)	(NA)	1.87	2.94	3.02	2.54	1.61	1.01	0.85	0.75
Net charge-offs [5]	3.6	13.6	29.7	32.9	25.6	17.5	11.2	12.2	15.5
Net charge-offs to loans and leases (percent)	0.36	0.84	1.43	1.59	1.27	0.85	0.50	0.49	0.58
Net interest margin [6] (percent)	3.66	4.09	3.94	4.11	4.41	4.40	4.36	4.29	4.27
Percentage of banks losing money	3.7	17.1	13.4	11.6	6.9	4.9	4.0	3.6	4.1

- Represents or rounds to zero. NA Not available. [1] Preliminary. [2] Net income (including securities transactions and nonrecurring items) as a percentage of average total assets. [3] Net income as a percentage of average total equity capital. [4] The sum of loans, leases, debt securities and other assets that are 90 days or more past due, or in nonaccrual status plus foreclosed property. [5] Total loans and leases charged off (removed from balance sheet because of uncollectibility), less amounts recovered on loans and leases previously charged off. [6] Interest income less interest expense as a percentage of average earning assets (i.e. the profit margin a bank earns on its loans and investments).

Source: U.S. Federal Deposit Insurance Corporation, *Annual Report; Statistics on Banking*, annual; and *FDIC Quarterly Banking Profile*.

No. 787. Insured Commercial Banks—Selected Measures of Financial Condition, by Asset Size and Region: 1996

[In percent, except as indicated. Preliminary. See headnote, table 786]

ASSET SIZE AND REGION	Number of banks	Return on assets	Return on equity	Equity capital to assets	Noncurrent assets plus other real estate owned to total assets	Net charge-offs to loans and leases	Percentage of banks losing money
Total	**9,528**	**1.19**	**14.46**	**8.20**	**0.75**	**0.58**	**4.1**
Less than $100 million	6,205	1.17	11.02	10.56	0.77	0.26	5.3
$100 million to $1 billion	2,925	1.28	13.56	9.44	0.73	0.42	1.9
$1 billion to $10 billion	325	1.31	14.88	8.77	0.88	0.89	2.5
$10 billion or more	73	1.12	15.12	7.38	0.71	0.52	(NA)
Northeast [1]	743	1.10	14.72	7.36	0.84	0.63	4.8
Southeast [2]	1,577	1.22	14.52	8.48	0.72	0.45	4.9
Central [3]	2,110	1.21	14.30	8.43	0.57	0.44	3.7
Midwest [4]	2,401	1.43	16.18	8.74	0.65	0.70	2.6
Southwest [5]	1,683	1.22	13.98	8.74	0.61	0.34	2.9
West [6]	1,014	1.24	13.53	9.23	0.87	0.79	8.9

NA Not available. [1] CT, DE, DC, ME, MD, MA, NH, NJ, NY, PA, PR, RI, and VT. [2] AL, FL, GA, MS, NC, SC, TN, VA, and WV. [3] IL, IN, KY, MI, OH, and WI. [4] IA, KS, MN, MO, NE, ND, and SD. [5] AR, LA, NM, OK, and TX. [6] AK, AZ, CA, CO, HI, ID, MT, NV, OR, Pacific Islands, UT, WA, and WY.

Source: U.S. Federal Deposit Insurance Corporation, *The FDIC Quarterly Banking Profile*, Fourth Quarter 1996.

No. 788. Insured Commercial Banks, by State and Other Area: 1996

[In billions of dollars, except number of banks. As of December 31. Includes foreign branches of U.S. banks]

STATE	Number	Assets	Deposits
Total	**9,527**	**4,578.2**	**3,197.1**
United States	**9,507**	**4,547.4**	**3,174.9**
Northeast	**590**	**1,543.2**	**996.9**
New England	**148**	**197.3**	**140.9**
Maine	20	9.0	6.5
New Hampshire	20	10.7	9.0
Vermont	22	6.2	5.2
Massachusetts	50	154.0	106.6
Rhode Island	8	6.5	5.0
Connecticut	28	10.9	8.6
Middle Atlantic	**442**	**1,345.9**	**846.1**
New York	159	1,032.2	602.5
New Jersey	66	70.0	59.3
Pennsylvania	217	243.7	184.3
Midwest	**4,236**	**961.4**	**713.4**
East North Central	**1,835**	**664.2**	**485.7**
Ohio	257	172.7	117.0
Indiana	204	66.5	52.1
Illinois	833	247.0	181.3
Michigan	176	112.2	84.2
Wisconsin	365	65.7	51.1
West North Central	**2,401**	**297.2**	**227.7**
Minnesota	519	72.1	53.9
Iowa	467	42.5	35.0
Missouri	430	88.3	70.6
North Dakota	123	8.5	7.3
South Dakota	117	29.3	13.2
Nebraska	329	27.8	23.3
Kansas	416	28.6	24.5
South	**3,602**	**1,334.4**	**959.3**
South Atlantic	**1,182**	**795.2**	**530.5**
Delaware	39	115.2	40.1
Maryland	90	38.9	30.2
District of Columbia	8	3.4	2.6
Virginia	154	89.9	64.9
West Virginia	113	22.3	18.0
North Carolina	56	191.4	121.4
South Carolina	79	26.4	21.3
Georgia	354	147.1	101.6
Florida	269	160.7	130.5
East South Central	**807**	**220.4**	**166.8**
Kentucky	275	52.7	39.8
Tennessee	238	75.9	57.2
Alabama	183	63.2	46.5
Mississippi	111	28.5	23.4
West South Central	**1,613**	**318.8**	**262.9**
Arkansas	234	30.7	26.5
Louisiana	172	47.0	38.3
Oklahoma	332	36.1	30.1
Texas	875	205.0	168.1
West	**1,079**	**708.4**	**518.3**
Mountain	**570**	**196.4**	**122.8**
Montana	100	8.7	7.3
Idaho	15	6.6	5.3
Wyoming	54	8.2	7.0
Colorado	223	41.0	34.3
New Mexico	69	15.5	12.0
Arizona	35	48.1	26.2
Utah	48	36.0	18.9
Nevada	26	32.4	9.7
Pacific	**509**	**512.0**	**392.5**
Washington	84	44.7	35.5
Oregon	43	22.2	16.1
California	360	417.2	321.5
Alaska	8	5.8	4.2
Hawaii	14	22.1	15.2
American Samoa	1	0.1	(Z)
Puerto Rico	14	29.9	21.4
Guam	2	0.8	0.7
Pacific Islands	1	(Z)	(Z)
Virgin Islands	2	0.1	0.1

Z Less than $50 million.

Source: U.S. Federal Deposit Insurance Corporation, *Statistics on Banking*, annual.

No. 789. U.S. Banking Offices of Foreign Banks—Summary: 1980 to 1995

[In billions of dollars, except as indicated. As of December. Covers agencies, branches, subsidiary commercial banks, and New York State investment companies]

ITEM	1980	1985	1990	1992	1993	1994	1995	SHARE [1]			
								1980	1985	1990	1995
Assets	200.6	440.8	791.1	869.0	855.6	943.7	982.9	11.9	16.1	21.4	21.7
Loans, total	121.4	247.4	397.9	407.5	383.3	418.9	461.4	13.4	15.4	18.0	17.3
Business	59.6	108.8	193.3	208.7	196.5	216.2	249.4	18.2	22.5	30.8	35.1
Deposits	80.4	236.7	383.9	464.3	468.7	522.7	523.0	6.6	12.1	14.5	17.6

[1] Percent of "domestically owned" commercial banks plus U.S. offices of foreign banks

Source: Board of Governors of the Federal Reserve System, unpublished data.

No. 790. Foreign Lending by U.S. Banks, by Type of Borrower and Country: 1996

[In millions of dollars. As of December. Covers 123 U.S. banking organizations which do nearly all of the foreign lending in the country. Data represent claims on foreign residents and institutions held at all domestic and foreign offices of covered banks. Data cover only cross-border and nonlocal currency lending. These result from a U.S. bank's office in one country lending to residents of another country or lending in a currency other than that of the borrower's country. Excludes local currency loans and other claims and local currency liabilities held by banks' foreign offices on residents of the country in which the office was located (e.g. Deutsche mark loans to German residents booked at the German branch of the reporting U.S. bank). Criteria for country selection is $4 billion or more]

COUNTRY	Total	Bank	Public	Private non-bank	COUNTRY	Total	Bank	Public	Private non-bank
Total [1]	314,360	102,448	78,965	132,947	Hong Kong	8,857	3,126	99	5,632
					Indonesia	5,446	2,376	513	2,557
Argentina	13,346	1,605	3,584	8,157	Italy	9,194	1,891	6,002	1,301
Australia	4,830	1,307	619	2,903	Japan	15,736	6,406	3,346	5,982
Bahamas, The	4,177	3,073	17	1,087	Korea, South	10,028	6,542	173	3,314
Belgium-Luxembourg	7,805	3,190	1,806	2,809	Mexico	18,086	2,018	9,041	7,028
Brazil	18,949	3,677	7,790	7,483	Netherlands	6,468	1,879	1,029	3,560
Canada	10,346	2,009	3,242	5,096	Russia	5,348	247	4,580	521
Cayman Islands	13,104	7,639	13	5,452	Singapore	5,917	2,151	127	3,639
Chile	4,363	963	1,001	2,399	Spain	6,256	2,269	2,953	1,035
Colombia	4,230	978	989	2,263	Switzerland	5,945	2,098	281	3,567
France	10,902	5,279	2,606	3,017	Thailand	5,339	1,832	65	3,442
Germany	13,285	3,120	8,269	1,896	United Kingdom	42,832	17,584	1,673	23,575

[1] Includes other countries, not shown separately.

Source: Board of Governors of the Federal Reserve System, Federal Financial Institutions Examination Council, statistical release.

No. 791. Federal and State-Chartered Credit Unions—Summary: 1980 to 1996

[Except as noted, as of December 31. Federal data include District of Columbia, Puerto Rico, Canal Zone, Guam, and Virgin Islands. Excludes State-insured, privately-insured, and noninsured State-chartered credit unions and corporate central credit unions which have mainly other credit unions as members]

YEAR	OPERATING CREDIT UNIONS		Number of failed institutions [1]	MEMBERS (1,000)		ASSETS (mil. dol.)		LOANS OUTSTANDING (mil. dol.)		SAVINGS (mil. dol.)	
	Federal	State		Federal	State	Federal	State	Federal	State	Federal	State
1980	12,440	4,910	239	24,519	12,338	40,092	20,870	26,350	14,582	36,263	18,469
1985	10,125	4,920	94	29,579	15,689	78,188	41,525	48,241	26,168	71,616	37,917
1990	8,511	4,349	164	36,241	19,454	130,073	68,133	83,029	44,102	117,892	62,082
1992	7,906	4,686	114	38,124	23,238	162,066	96,312	87,350	52,192	145,637	87,371
1993	7,696	4,621	37	39,756	23,997	172,854	104,316	94,640	57,695	153,506	93,482
1994	7,498	4,493	33	40,837	24,295	182,529	106,937	110,090	65,769	160,226	94,797
1995	7,329	4,358	26	42,163	24,927	193,781	112,860	120,514	71,606	170,300	99,838
1996	7,152	4,240	19	43,544	25,666	206,685	120,176	134,117	79,651	180,960	105,728

[1] For year ending September 30, except 1995 reflects 15-month period from October 1994 through December 1995 and 1996 reflects calendar year. A failed institution is defined as a credit union which has ceased operation because it was involuntarily liquidated or merged with assistance from the National Credit Union Share Insurance Fund. Assisted mergers were not identified until 1981.

Source: National Credit Union Administration, *Annual Report of the National Credit Union Administration*, and unpublished data.

No. 792. Insured Savings Institutions—Financial Summary: 1987 to 1996

[In billions of dollars, except number of institutions. As of December 31. Includes Puerto Rico, Guam, and Virgin Islands. Covers SAIF (Savings Association Insurance Fund)- and BIF (Bank Insurance Fund)-insured savings institutions. Excludes institutions in RTC conservatorship and, beginning 1992, excludes one self-liquidating institution. Minus sign (-) indicates loss]

ITEM	1987	1988	1989	1990	1991	1992	1993	1994	1995	1996, prel.
Number of institutions	3,621	3,438	3,088	2,816	2,561	2,390	2,262	2,152	2,030	1,924
Assets, total	1,502	1,629	1,437	1,267	1,119	1,030	1,001	1,009	1,026	1,028
Loans and leases, net	912	1,001	920	816	727	648	626	635	648	681
Liabilities, total	1,448	1,563	1,368	1,200	1,051	956	923	929	940	942
Deposits	1,138	1,195	1,082	987	907	828	774	737	742	728
Equity capital	54	66	69	68	69	74	78	80	86	86
Interest and fee income	120	127	135	117	98	78	66	63	71	72
Interest expense	94	101	111	91	70	46	35	33	43	42
Net interest income	26	26	24	26	28	32	32	30	28	30
Net income	-5	-5	-6	-5	1	7	7	6	8	7

Source: U.S. Federal Deposit Insurance Corporation, *Statistics on Banking*, annual and *FDIC Quarterly Banking Profile*.

No. 793. Volume of Long-Term Mortgage Loans Originated, by Type of Property, 1980 to 1995, and by Lender, 1995

[In billions of dollars. Covers credit extended in primary mortgage markets for financing real estate acquisitions]

TYPE OF PROPERTY	1980	1985	1990	1991	1992	1993	1994	1995, BY LENDER				
								Total [1]	Commercial banks	Mortgage companies	Savings and loan	Life insurance companies
Loans, total	197.2	430.0	710.5	793.3	1,124.0	1,241.7	1,019.2	930.0	374.5	364.8	103.6	36.5
1-4 unit family home	133.8	289.8	458.4	562.1	893.7	1,019.9	768.7	639.4	155.4	358.7	95.6	0.7
New units	49.1	59.0	110.7	120.0	132.4	117.3	114.6	110.7	49.3	47.2	12.2	0.2
Existing units	84.6	230.8	347.7	442.1	761.3	902.5	654.2	528.7	106.1	311.5	83.4	0.5
Multifamily residential	12.5	31.9	32.6	25.5	25.7	31.7	32.7	39.2	23.1	6.1	3.9	1.6
New units	8.6	10.6	6.5	6.1	4.9	4.4	4.5	5.4	2.0	1.4	0.2	0.7
Existing units	3.9	21.3	26.0	19.4	20.9	27.3	28.2	33.8	21.1	4.7	3.7	0.9
Nonresidential	35.9	99.4	209.5	194.6	184.4	172.5	190.0	220.8	173.6	-	4.2	33.4
Farm properties	15.0	9.0	10.0	11.1	20.2	17.6	27.8	30.6	22.2	-	-	0.8

- Represents zero. [1] Includes other lenders not shown separately.

Source: U.S. Dept. of Housing and Urban Development, monthly and quarterly press releases based on the Survey of Mortgage Lending Activity.

No. 794. Mortgage Debt Outstanding, by Type of Property and Holder: 1980 to 1996

[In billions of dollars. As of Dec. 31. Includes Puerto Rico and Guam]

TYPE OF PROPERTY AND HOLDER	1980	1985	1988	1989	1990	1991	1992	1993	1994	1995	1996
Mortgage debt, total	1,463	2,334	3,280	3,582	3,804	3,967	4,160	4,275	4,481	4,714	5,054
Residential nonfarm	1,110	1,741	2,495	2,748	2,966	3,139	3,319	3,505	3,713	3,922	4,221
One- to four-family homes	969	1,536	2,217	2,459	2,677	2,855	3,044	3,234	3,436	3,634	3,912
Savings institutions	487	554	672	669	600	536	490	470	478	482	514
Mortgage pools or trusts [1]	125	407	758	887	1,046	1,227	1,395	1,514	1,653	1,766	1,925
Government National Mortgage Assoc.	92	207	331	358	392	416	411	405	441	461	494
Federal Home Loan Mortgage Corp.	13	100	220	266	308	352	402	443	488	512	552
Commercial banks	160	213	334	390	456	484	508	557	611	664	696
Individuals and others [2]	117	239	316	370	408	431	448	456	461	486	542
Federal and related agencies	61	110	126	131	153	163	192	228	228	229	227
Federal National Mortgage Assoc	52	92	88	91	94	100	124	151	162	168	170
Life insurance companies	18	12	11	12	13	12	11	9	8	7	7
Five or more units	141	205	278	288	290	284	274	271	276	288	309
Commercial	255	487	702	754	759	748	701	689	685	710	745
Farm	97	106	83	80	79	79	81	81	83	84	88
TYPE OF HOLDER											
Savings institutions	603	760	925	910	802	705	628	598	596	597	629
Commercial banks	263	429	674	767	845	876	895	941	1,004	1,080	1,136
Life insurance companies	131	172	233	254	268	265	247	229	215	212	212
Individuals and others [2]	206	367	474	535	570	591	604	609	619	650	713
Mortgage pools or trusts [1]	146	439	783	918	1,081	1,263	1,441	1,571	1,727	1,862	2,066
Government National Mortgage Assoc.	94	212	341	368	404	425	420	414	451	472	506
Federal Home Loan Mortgage Corp	17	100	226	273	316	359	408	447	491	515	554
Federal National Mortgage Association	(X)	55	178	228	300	372	445	496	530	583	651
Farmers Home Administration [3]	32	48	(Z)	(Z)	(Z)	(Z)	(Z)	(Z)	(Z)	(Z)	(Z)
Federal and related agencies	115	167	192	198	239	266	286	327	319	314	309
Federal National Mortgage Association	57	98	95	99	105	112	138	167	178	184	184
Farmers Home Administration [3]	3	1	42	41	41	42	42	41	42	42	42
Federal Land Banks	38	47	32	30	29	29	29	28	29	28	30
Federal Home Loan Mortgage Corp	5	14	17	22	22	27	34	47	42	44	45
Federal Housing and Veterans Admin	4	4	5	5	7	9	11	11	10	9	6
Government National Mortgage Assoc.	5	1	(Z)	(Z)	(Z)	(Z)	(Z)	(Z)	(Z)	(Z)	(Z)
Federal Deposit Insurance Corp.	(X)	(X)	(X)	(X)	(X)	(X)	(X)	14	8	4	(Z)
Resolution Trust Corporation	(X)	(X)	(X)	(X)	33	46	32	17	10	2	(X)

X Not applicable. Z Less than $500 million. [1] Outstanding principal balances of mortgage pools backing securities insured or guaranteed by the agency indicated. Includes other pools not shown separately. [2] Includes mortgage companies, real estate investment trusts, State and local retirement funds, noninsured pension funds, State and local credit agencies, credit unions, and finance companies. [3] FmHA-guaranteed securities sold to the Federal Financing Bank were reallocated from FmHA mortgage pools to FmHA mortgage holdings in 1986 because of accounting changes by the Farmers Home Administration.

Source: Board of Governors of the Federal Reserve System, *Federal Reserve Bulletin*, monthly.

No. 795. Characteristics of Conventional First Mortgage Loans for Purchase of Single-Family Homes: 1990 to 1996

[In percent, except as indicated. Annual averages. Covers fully amortized conventional mortgage loans used to purchase single-family nonfarm homes. Excludes refinancing loans, nonamortized and balloon loans, loans insured by the Federal Housing Administration, and loans guaranteed by the Veterans Administration. Based on a sample of mortgage lenders, including savings and loans associations, savings banks, commercial banks, and mortgage companies]

LOAN CHARACTERISTICS	NEW HOMES						PREVIOUSLY OCCUPIED HOMES					
	1990	1992	1993	1994	1995	1996	1990	1992	1993	1994	1995	1996
Contract interest rate,[1] all loans	9.7	8.0	7.0	7.3	7.7	7.6	9.8	7.8	6.9	7.3	7.7	7.6
Fixed-rate loans	10.1	8.3	7.3	7.9	8.0	7.8	10.1	8.2	7.3	8.0	8.0	7.8
Adjustable-rate loans[2]	8.9	6.6	5.8	6.5	7.2	7.0	8.9	6.3	5.5	6.2	7.0	6.9
Initial fees, charges[3]	1.96	1.59	1.29	1.29	1.20	1.21	1.74	1.58	1.19	1.07	0.93	0.93
Effective interest rate,[4] all loans	10.1	8.2	7.2	7.5	7.9	7.8	10.1	8.1	7.1	7.5	7.8	7.7
Fixed-rate loans	10.4	8.5	7.5	8.1	8.2	8.0	10.4	8.5	7.5	8.2	8.2	8.0
Adjustable-rate loans[2]	9.2	6.9	5.9	6.6	7.4	7.2	9.2	6.5	5.7	6.4	7.1	7.1
Term to maturity (years)	27.3	25.6	26.1	27.5	27.7	27.1	27.0	25.4	25.4	27.1	27.4	26.8
Purchase price ($1,000)	154.1	158.1	163.7	170.7	175.4	182.6	140.3	144.1	139.6	136.4	137.3	150.2
Loan to price ratio	74.9	76.6	78.0	78.7	78.6	78.1	74.9	76.5	77.1	80.1	80.1	79.1
Percent of number of loans with adjustable rates	31	17	18	41	37	26	27	21	20	39	31	27

[1] Initial interest rate paid by the borrower as specified in the loan contract. [2] Loans with a contractual provision for periodic adjustments in the contract interest rate. [3] Includes all fees, commissions, discounts and "points" paid by the borrower, or seller, in order to obtain the loan. Excludes those charges for mortgage, credit, life or property insurance; for property transfer; and for title search and insurance. [4] Contract interest rate plus fees and charges amortized over a 10-year period.

Source: U.S. Federal Housing Finance Board, *Rates & Terms on Conventional Home Mortgages, Annual Summary.*

No. 796. Mortgage Delinquency and Foreclosure Rates: 1980 to 1996

[In percent, except as indicated. Covers one- to four-family residential nonfarm mortgage loans]

ITEM	1980	1985	1990	1991	1992	1993	1994	1995	1996
Number of mortgage loans outstanding (1,000)	30,033	34,004	40,636	41,586	42,562	45,336	48,625	50,670	51,625
Delinquency rates:[1]									
Total	5.0	5.8	4.7	5.0	4.6	4.2	4.1	4.3	4.3
Conventional loans	3.1	4.0	3.0	3.3	2.9	2.7	2.6	2.8	2.8
VA loans	5.3	6.6	6.4	6.8	6.5	6.3	6.3	6.4	6.7
FHA loans	6.6	7.5	6.7	7.3	7.1	7.1	7.3	7.6	8.1
Foreclosure rates:[2]									
Total	0.5	1.0	0.9	1.0	1.0	1.0	0.9	0.9	1.0
Conventional loans	0.2	0.7	0.7	0.8	0.8	0.8	0.7	0.7	0.7
VA loans	0.6	1.1	1.2	1.3	1.3	1.3	1.3	1.3	1.6
FHA loans	0.7	1.3	1.3	1.4	1.4	1.5	1.5	1.4	1.6

[1] Number of loans delinquent 30 days or more as percentage of mortgage loans serviced in survey. Annual average of quarterly figures. [2] Percentage of loans in the foreclosure process at yearend, not seasonally adjusted.

Source: Mortgage Bankers Association of America, Washington, DC, *National Delinquency Survey,* quarterly.

No. 797. Delinquency Rates on Bank Installment Loans, by Type of Loan: 1980 to 1995

[In percent, except as indicated. As of end of year; seasonally adjusted, except as noted. Number of loans having an installment past due for 30 days or more as a percentage of total installment loans outstanding]

TYPE OF CREDIT	1980	1985	1987	1988	1989	1990	1991	1992	1993	1994	1995
DELINQUENCY RATES											
Closed-end installment loans, total	2.82	2.32	2.47	2.49	2.64	2.57	2.58	2.43	1.77	1.72	2.12
Personal loans[1]	3.53	3.63	3.66	3.34	3.52	3.37	2.95	3.18	2.30	2.36	2.81
Automobile, direct loans[2]	1.81	1.64	1.59	1.92	2.03	2.22	2.14	2.08	1.58	1.46	1.87
Automobile, indirect loans[3]	2.29	2.02	2.20	2.46	2.61	2.59	2.66	2.33	1.65	1.65	2.17
Property improvement[4]	1.93	1.91	1.88	2.06	2.25	2.30	2.38	2.18	1.61	1.66	1.77
Home equity and second mortgage loans[5]	(NA)	2.06	2.01	1.66	1.65	1.45	2.06	1.89	1.66	1.38	1.41
Mobile home loans	3.14	2.39	2.57	3.12	2.51	3.03	2.86	4.02	3.70	3.68	4.02
Recreational vehicle loans	1.94	1.64	1.99	2.07	2.24	2.63	2.25	2.27	1.26	1.23	1.62
Marine financing[5]	(NA)	(NA)	(NA)	(NA)	(NA)	(NA)	(NA)	2.52	1.72	1.51	2.22
Bank card loans	2.72	2.95	2.33	2.19	2.24	2.86	3.29	2.93	2.49	2.93	3.34
Revolving credit loans	2.70	1.96	2.33	2.87	2.92	3.00	2.75	2.63	2.90	2.38	3.14
Home equity lines of credit loans (open-end)[5]	(NA)	(NA)	0.74	0.68	0.78	0.85	0.88	0.85	0.70	0.63	0.90
REPOSSESSIONS PER 1,000 LOANS OUTSTANDING											
Mobile home	1.57	1.21	1.58	1.77	1.63	1.19	1.62	1.30	1.21	1.18	0.86
Automobile, direct loans[2]	1.10	1.11	0.86	1.03	1.03	1.75	1.17	0.92	0.83	0.53	0.96
Automobile, indirect loans[3]	2.75	2.08	2.04	1.86	1.70	1.61	2.07	1.47	0.97	1.17	1.36
Marine financing[5]	(NA)	(NA)	(NA)	(NA)	(NA)	(NA)	(NA)	1.21	1.03	0.82	0.81

NA Not available. [1] Beginning 1985, includes home appliance loans. [2] Made directly by bank's lending function. [3] Made by automobile dealerships; loans in bank's portfolio. [4] Beginning 1985, own plan and FHA Title I loans. [5] Not seasonally adjusted.

Source: American Bankers Association, Washington, DC, *Consumer Credit Delinquency Bulletin,* quarterly.

No. 798. Consumer Installment Credit Outstanding and Finance Rates: 1980 to 1996

[In billions of dollars, except percent. Estimated amounts of seasonally adjusted credit outstanding as of end of year; finance rates, annual averages]

TYPE OF CREDIT	1980	1985	1987	1988	1989	1990	1991	1992	1993	1994	1995	1996
Installment credit outstanding	**350.1**	**584.7**	**671.7**	**729.9**	**781.9**	**796.4**	**781.1**	**784.9**	**844.1**	**966.5**	**1,103.3**	**1,194.5**
Automobile	112.0	210.9	266.1	285.5	291.0	282.4	259.3	257.1	279.8	317.2	350.8	377.3
Revolving [1]	55.1	122.1	153.3	174.5	198.6	223.3	245.8	257.8	287.0	339.3	413.9	462.4
Other	183.0	251.7	252.4	269.9	292.3	290.7	276.1	269.9	277.3	309.9	338.6	354.8
FINANCE RATES (percent)												
Commercial banks:												
New automobiles (48 months) [2]	14.32	12.91	10.45	10.86	12.08	11.78	11.13	9.28	8.08	8.13	9.57	9.05
Other consumer goods (24 months)	15.48	15.94	14.23	14.69	15.44	15.46	15.17	14.04	13.46	13.20	13.94	13.53
Credit-card plans	17.31	18.69	17.93	17.79	18.02	18.17	18.23	17.77	16.81	15.69	16.02	15.63
Finance companies:												
New automobiles	14.82	11.98	10.74	12.60	12.62	12.54	12.41	9.93	9.47	9.80	11.19	9.89
Used automobiles	19.10	17.58	14.61	15.12	16.18	15.99	15.59	13.80	12.78	13.51	14.47	13.54

[1] Consists mainly of outstanding balances on credit card accounts, but also includes borrowing under check credit and overdraft plans, and unsecured personal lines of credit. [2] For 1980, maturities were 36 months for new car loans.

Source: Board of Governors of the Federal Reserve System, *Federal Reserve Bulletin*, monthly; and *Annual Statistical Digest*.

No. 799. Credit Cards—Holders, Numbers, Spending, and Debt, 1990 and 1995, and Projections, 2000

TYPE OF CREDIT CARD	CARDHOLDERS (mil.)			NUMBER OF CARDS (mil.)			CREDIT CARD SPENDING (bil. dol.)			CREDIT CARD DEBT (bil. dol.)		
	1990	1995	2000, proj.	1990	1995	2000, proj.	1990	1995	2000, proj.	1990	1995	2000, proj.
Total [1]	**113**	**119**	**128**	**1,026**	**1,382**	**1,650**	**466**	**991**	**1,540**	**236.4**	**510.0**	**783.3**
Bank [2]	79	96	105	217	383	523	243	614	1,001	154.1	366.3	595.2
Oil company	85	84	82	123	111	105	27	42	59	3.3	4.1	5.0
Phone	97	113	126	141	171	183	14	19	24	1.7	2.4	3.0
Retail store	96	106	114	469	622	744	75	114	153	51.0	82.2	103.8
Travel and entertainment [3]	23	24	27	28	31	34	85	140	213	13.8	22.9	34.8
Other [4]	11	8	9	48	64	60	22	62	89	12.5	32.1	41.6

[1] Cardholders may hold more than one type of card. [2] Visa and MasterCard credit cards. Excludes debit cards. [3] Includes American Express and Diners Club. [4] Includes Air Travel Card, automobile rental, Discover (except for cardholders), and miscellaneous cards.

Source: HSN Consultants Inc., Oxnard, CA, *The Nilson Report*, bimonthly. (Copyright used by permission.)

No. 800. Usage of General Purpose Credit Cards by Families: 1989 to 1995

[General purpose credit cards include Mastercard, Visa, Optima, and Discover cards. All dollar figures are given in constant 1995 dollars based on consumer price index data as published by U.S. Bureau of Labor Statistics. Families include one-person units; for definition of family, see text, section 1. Based on Survey of Consumer Finance; see Appendix III. For definition of median, see Guide to Tabular Presentation]

AGE OF FAMILY HEAD AND FAMILY INCOME	Percent having a general purpose credit card	Median number of cards	Median new charges on last month's bills	Percent having a balance after last month's bills	Median balance [1]	PERCENT OF CARDHOLDING FAMILIES WHO— Almost always pay off the balance	Sometimes pay off the balance	Hardly ever pay off the balance
1989, total	55.8	2	$100	52.0	$1,200	53.1	21.5	25.4
1992, total	62.2	2	100	52.8	1,100	52.8	19.6	27.6
1995, total	**66.4**	**2**	**200**	**56.3**	**1,500**	**51.9**	**20.4**	**27.7**
Under 35 years old	59.0	2	100	69.2	1,500	40.2	23.5	36.3
35 to 44 years old	68.5	2	200	68.1	1,900	40.7	26.9	32.4
45 to 54 years old	75.4	2	200	64.8	1,800	47.1	22.5	30.4
55 to 64 years old	71.9	2	200	48.0	1,800	59.3	18.4	22.3
65 to 74 years old	68.3	2	200	30.8	800	72.0	12.9	15.1
75 years old and over	54.6	1	100	18.2	700	85.8	2.5	11.7
Less than $10,000	26.3	1	100	55.8	1,000	56.4	12.4	31.2
$10,000 to $24,999	53.3	2	100	57.0	1,500	50.9	17.2	31.9
$25,000 to $49,999	75.0	2	100	59.2	1,500	47.6	20.9	31.5
$50,000 to $99,999	93.1	2	200	59.4	2,000	49.7	25.3	25.1
$100,000 and more	97.1	3	800	35.4	2,100	73.7	17.2	9.1

[1] Among families having a balance.

Source: Board of Governors of the Federal Reserve System, unpublished data.

[In billions of dollars. As of December. Seasonally adjusted averages of daily figures]

ITEM	1980	1981	1982	1983	1984	1985	1986	1987	1988	1989	1990	1991	1992	1993	1994	1995	1996
M1, total	**409**	**437**	**475**	**521**	**552**	**620**	**724**	**750**	**787**	**794**	**826**	**897**	**1,025**	**1,130**	**1,151**	**1,129**	**1,081**
Currency [1]	115	123	133	146	156	168	181	197	212	223	247	267	293	322	354	373	395
Travelers checks [2]	4	4	4	5	5	6	6	7	7	7	8	8	8	8	8	9	9
Demand deposits [3]	261	231	234	238	244	267	302	287	287	279	277	290	340	385	384	391	403
Other checkable deposits [4]	28	79	104	132	147	180	236	260	281	285	294	333	384	414	404	356	275
M2, total	**1,601**	**1,756**	**1,911**	**2,128**	**2,312**	**2,498**	**2,734**	**2,833**	**2,996**	**3,161**	**3,279**	**3,380**	**3,434**	**3,487**	**3,502**	**3,655**	**3,833**
M1	409	437	475	521	552	620	724	750	787	794	826	897	1,025	1,130	1,151	1,129	1,081
Non-M1 components in M2	1,192	1,319	1,436	1,607	1,760	1,878	2,010	2,083	2,209	2,367	2,454	2,482	2,409	2,357	2,351	2,526	2,752
Money market funds, retail	63	152	185	138	167	177	210	225	246	322	357	372	354	355	384	455	537
Savings deposits (including MMDA's [5])	400	344	400	685	705	815	941	937	926	894	924	1,045	1,187	1,219	1,150	1,137	1,271
Commercial banks	186	159	190	363	389	457	534	535	542	541	582	665	754	785	752	776	904
Thrift institutions	215	185	210	322	315	359	407	403	384	353	342	380	433	434	397	361	367
Small time deposits [6]	729	823	851	784	889	886	858	921	1,037	1,151	1,173	1,065	866	783	817	934	945
Commercial banks	286	348	380	351	388	386	369	392	451	534	610	602	506	468	503	576	592
Thrift institutions	442	475	471	433	501	499	489	529	586	616	562	463	360	314	314	358	353
M3, total	**1,992**	**2,241**	**2,442**	**2,685**	**2,980**	**3,198**	**3,486**	**3,673**	**3,913**	**4,066**	**4,126**	**4,180**	**4,190**	**4,254**	**4,329**	**4,595**	**4,936**
M2	1,601	1,756	1,911	2,128	2,312	2,498	2,734	2,833	2,996	3,161	3,279	3,380	3,434	3,487	3,502	3,655	3,833
Non-M2 components in M3	391	485	531	557	668	701	752	840	917	905	846	801	756	768	827	940	1,104
Large time deposits [7]	260	304	325	316	403	422	420	467	518	541	481	416	353	333	363	420	500
Commercial banks [8]	215	250	261	220	256	271	270	304	344	380	360	333	286	272	298	345	420
Thrift institutions	45	54	64	97	147	152	150	163	175	161	121	83	67	61	65	75	79
Repurchase agreements [9]	57	65	67	95	105	120	143	173	189	158	139	119	129	159	183	182	195
Eurodollars [9]	58	77	90	105	97	94	104	108	117	95	89	79	67	66	82	91	110
Money market funds, institution only	16	39	49	41	62	64	85	92	92	110	138	186	208	209	199	247	299
L, total	**2,328**	**2,599**	**2,843**	**3,147**	**3,516**	**3,825**	**4,123**	**4,341**	**4,666**	**4,893**	**4,978**	**5,006**	**5,079**	**5,169**	**5,312**	**5,704**	**6,073**
M3	1,992	2,241	2,442	2,685	2,980	3,198	3,486	3,673	3,913	4,066	4,126	4,180	4,190	4,254	4,329	4,595	4,936
Savings bonds	72	68	68	71	74	79	92	101	109	116	126	138	157	172	180	185	187
Short-term Treasury securities [10]	134	149	183	213	262	298	276	249	267	324	334	329	346	343	367	476	446
Bankers acceptances	32	40	44	45	45	42	37	45	40	41	36	24	21	15	14	12	12
Commercial paper [11]	98	101	106	133	155	208	232	274	337	346	355	335	365	388	402	437	492

[1] Currency outside U.S. Treasury, Federal Reserve Banks and the vaults of depository institutions. [2] Outstanding amount of nonbank issuers. [3] At commercial banks and foreign-related institutions. [4] Consists of negotiable order of withdrawal (NOW) and automatic transfer service (ATS) accounts at all depository institutions, credit union share draft balances, and demand deposits at thrift institutions. [5] Money market deposit accounts (MMDA). [6] Issued in amounts of less than $100,000. Includes retail repurchase agreements. Excludes individual retirement accounts (IRA's) and Keogh accounts. [7] Issued in amounts of $100,000 or more. Excludes those booked at international banking facilities. [8] Excludes those held by money market mutual funds, depository institutions, U.S. Government, foreign banks and official institutions. [9] Excludes those held by depository institutions and money market mutual funds. [10] U.S. Treasury bills and coupons with remaining maturities of less than 12 months held by other than depository institutions, Federal Reserve banks, money market mutual funds, and foreign entities. [11] Excludes commercial paper held by money market mutual funds.

Source: Board of Governors of the Federal Reserve System, *Federal Reserve Bulletin*, monthly, and *Money Stock, Liquid Assets, and Debt Measures, Federal Reserve Statistical Release H.6*, weekly.

No. 802. Electronic Funds Transfer Volume: 1980 to 1996

[Electronic funds transfer cover automated teller machine (ATM) transactions and transactions at point-of-sale (POS) terminals. Point-of-sale terminals are electronic terminals in retail stores that allow a customer to pay for goods through a direct debit to a customer's account at the bank]

ITEM	Unit	1980	1985	1990	1991	1992	1993	1994	1995	1996
Total number of transactions	Million	(NA)	**3,579**	**5,942**	**6,642**	**7,537**	**8,136**	**8,958**	**10,464**	**11,830**
ATM transactions	Million	(NA)	3,565	5,751	6,418	7,206	7,706	8,334	9,689	10,684
POS transactions	Million	(NA)	14	191	223	289	430	624	775	1,146
ATM terminals, total [1]	1,000	**18.5**	**60.0**	**80.2**	**83.5**	**87.3**	**94.8**	**109.1**	**122.7**	**139.1**
Monthly transactions per terminal	Number	5,405	4,951	5,980	6,403	6,876	6,772	6,459	6,580	6,399
Shared terminals	1,000	(NA)	35.5	75.3	79.6	84.7	92.6	108.1	122.6	139.0
Proprietary terminals	1,000	(NA)	24.5	4.9	4.0	2.6	2.3	1.0	0.1	0.1
POS terminals, total [2]	1,000	**(NA)**	**(NA)**	**53.1**	**78.1**	**95.2**	**155.0**	**340.5**	**528.6**	**875.4**

NA Not available. [1] As of September. [2] As of June.

Source: Faulkner & Gray, Chicago, IL, *Bank Network News*, November 11, 1996, (copyright).

No. 803. Selected Time Deposits and Other Accounts at Insured Commercial Banks—Deposits and Interest Rates: 1990 to 1996

[As of December. Estimates based on data collected from a sample of about 400 banks]

TYPE OF DEPOSIT	AMOUNT OUTSTANDING (bil. dol.)						ANNUAL EFFECTIVE YIELD (percent)					
	1990	1992	1993	1994	1995	1996	1990	1992	1993	1994	1995	1996
Interest-bearing time deposits: [1]												
7-91 day	50.2	38.5	29.4	32.3	32.2	32.9	6.94	2.90	2.65	3.79	4.10	4.03
92-182 day	168.0	127.8	109.0	96.7	93.9	92.3	7.19	3.16	2.91	4.44	4.66	4.63
183 day-1 year	221.0	163.1	145.4	163.1	183.8	201.4	7.33	3.37	3.13	5.12	5.02	5.00
1-2½ years	150.2	153.0	139.8	164.4	208.6	213.2	7.42	3.88	3.55	5.74	5.17	5.22
2½ years or more	139.4	169.7	180.5	192.7	199.0	199.9	7.53	4.77	4.28	6.30	5.40	5.46
All IRA and Keogh Plan deposits	131.0	147.4	144.0	144.1	150.1	151.4	(NA)	(NA)	(NA)	(NA)	(NA)	(NA)

NA Not available. [1] All interest-bearing time deposits and open account time deposits with balances of less than $100,000, including those held in IRA's and Keogh Plan deposits.

Source: Board of Governors of the Federal Reserve System, *Money Stock, Liquid Assets, and Debt Measures, Federal Reserve Statistical Release H.6*, Special Supplementary Table, Monthly Survey of Selected Deposits, monthly.

No. 804. Commercial Paper Outstanding, by Type of Company: 1980 to 1996

[In billions of dollars. As of December 31. Seasonally adjusted. Commercial paper is an unsecured promissory note having a fixed maturity of no more than 270 days]

TYPE OF COMPANY	1980	1985	1988	1989	1990	1991	1992	1993	1994	1995	1996
All issuers	**124.4**	**298.8**	**458.5**	**525.8**	**562.7**	**528.8**	**545.8**	**555.1**	**595.4**	**674.9**	**773.7**
Financial companies [1]	87.7	213.8	354.7	394.6	414.7	395.5	398.1	399.3	430.7	486.6	590.6
Dealer-placed paper [2]	19.9	78.4	159.8	183.6	214.7	213.0	226.5	218.9	223.0	275.8	360.9
Directly-placed paper [3]	67.8	135.3	194.9	210.9	200.0	182.5	171.6	180.4	207.7	210.8	229.7
Nonfinancial companies [4]	36.7	85.0	103.8	131.3	147.9	133.4	147.6	155.7	164.6	188.3	183.2

[1] Institutions engaged primarily in activities such as, but not limited to, commercial, savings, and mortgage banking; sales, personal, and mortgage financing; factoring, finance leasing, and other business lending; insurance underwriting; and other investment activities. [2] Includes all financial company paper sold by dealers in the open market. [3] As reported by financial companies that place their paper directly with investors. [4] Includes public utilities and firms engaged primarily in such activities as communications, construction, manufacturing, mining, wholesale and retail trade, transportation, and services.

Source: Board of Governors of the Federal Reserve System, *Federal Reserve Bulletin*, monthly.

No. 805. Federal Reserve Bank of New York—Discount Rates: 1980 to 1997

[Percent per year. Rates for short-term adjustment credit. For rates applicable to other types of discount window credit, see source]

EFFECTIVE DATE	Rate	EFFECTIVE DATE	Rate	EFFECTIVE DATE	Rate	EFFECTIVE DATE	Rate
1980: [1] Nov. 17	12	Nov. 22	9	**1987:** Sept. 4	6	**1994:** May 17	3 1/2
Dec. 5	13	Dec. 15	8 1/2	**1988:** Aug. 9	6 1/2	Aug. 16	4
1981: [1] May 5	14	**1984:** April 9	9	**1989:** Feb. 24	7	Nov. 15	4 3/4
Nov. 2	13	Nov. 21	8 1/2	**1990:** Dec. 19	6 1/2	**1995:** Feb. 1	5 1/4
Dec. 4	12	Dec. 24	8	**1991:** Feb. 1	6	**1996:** Jan. 31	5
1982: July 20	11 1/2	**1985:** May 20	7 1/2	April 30	5 1/2	In effect, July 4, 1997	5
Aug. 2	11	**1986:** March 7	7	Sept. 13	5		
Aug. 16	10 1/2	April 21	6 1/2	Nov. 6	4 1/2		
Aug. 27	10	July 11	6	Dec. 20	3 1/2		
Oct. 12	9 1/2	Aug. 21	5 1/2	**1992:** July 2	3		

[1] The discount rates for 1980 and 1981 do not include the surcharge applied to frequent borrowings by large institutions. The surcharge reached 3 percent in 1980 and 4 percent in 1981. Surcharge was eliminated in Nov. 1981.

Source: Board of Governors of the Federal Reserve System, *Federal Reserve Bulletin*, monthly, and *Annual Statistical Digest*.

[Percent per year. Annual averages of monthly data, except as indicated]

TYPE	1980	1985	1986	1987	1988	1989	1990	1991	1992	1993	1994	1995	1996
Federal funds, effective rate	13.35	8.10	6.80	6.66	7.57	9.21	8.10	5.69	3.52	3.02	4.21	5.83	5.30
Commercial paper, 3-month [1,2]	12.61	7.95	6.49	6.82	7.66	8.99	8.06	5.87	3.75	3.22	4.66	5.93	5.41
Commercial paper, 6-month [1,2]	12.24	8.00	6.39	6.85	7.68	8.80	7.95	5.85	3.80	3.30	4.93	5.93	5.42
Prime rate charged by banks	15.26	9.93	8.33	8.21	9.32	10.87	10.01	8.46	6.25	6.00	7.15	8.83	8.27
Eurodollar deposits, 3-month	14.00	8.27	6.70	7.07	7.85	9.16	8.16	5.86	3.70	3.18	4.63	5.93	5.38
Finance paper, 3-month [2,3]	11.45	7.77	6.38	6.54	7.38	8.72	7.87	5.71	3.65	3.16	4.53	5.78	5.29
Finance paper, 6-month [2,3]	11.25	7.74	6.31	6.37	7.14	8.16	7.53	5.60	3.63	3.15	4.56	5.68	5.21
Bankers acceptances, 3-month [2,4]	12.67	7.91	6.38	6.75	7.56	8.87	7.93	5.70	3.62	3.13	4.56	5.81	5.31
Bankers acceptances, 6-month [2,4]	12.20	7.95	6.28	6.78	7.60	8.67	7.80	5.67	3.67	3.21	4.83	5.80	5.31
Large negotiable CD's, 3-month, secondary market	13.07	8.05	6.52	6.86	7.73	9.09	8.15	5.83	3.68	3.17	4.63	5.92	5.39
Taxable money market funds [5]	12.68	7.71	6.26	6.12	7.11	8.87	7.82	5.71	3.36	2.70	3.75	5.48	4.95
Tax-exempt money market funds [5]	(NA)	4.90	4.31	4.14	4.79	5.90	5.45	4.13	2.58	1.97	2.38	3.39	2.99
Certificates of deposit (CD's): [6]													
6-month	(NA)	7.83	6.51	6.47	7.18	8.34	7.35	5.67	3.46	2.84	3.37	4.92	4.68
1-year	(NA)	8.29	6.75	6.77	7.47	8.41	7.42	5.88	3.72	3.12	3.94	5.39	4.95
2½-year	(NA)	9.00	7.13	7.16	7.77	8.33	7.52	6.29	4.47	3.73	4.49	5.69	5.14
5-year	(NA)	9.66	7.60	7.66	8.11	8.30	7.71	6.83	5.62	4.88	5.30	6.00	5.46
U.S. Government securities:													
Secondary market: [7]													
3-month Treasury bill	11.39	7.47	5.97	5.78	6.67	8.11	7.50	5.38	3.43	3.00	4.25	5.49	5.01
6-month Treasury bill	11.32	7.65	6.02	6.03	6.91	8.03	7.46	5.44	3.54	3.12	4.64	5.56	5.08
1-year Treasury bill	10.85	7.81	6.07	6.33	7.13	7.92	7.35	5.52	3.71	3.29	5.02	5.60	5.22
Auction average: [8]													
3-month Treasury bill	11.51	7.47	5.98	5.82	6.68	8.12	7.51	5.42	3.45	3.02	4.29	5.51	5.02
6-month Treasury bill	11.37	7.64	6.03	6.05	6.92	8.04	7.47	5.49	3.57	3.14	4.66	5.59	5.09
1-year Treasury bill	10.75	7.76	6.07	6.33	7.17	7.91	7.36	5.54	3.75	3.33	4.98	5.69	5.23
Home mortgages:													
HUD series: [9]													
FHA insured, secondary market [10]	13.44	12.24	9.91	10.16	10.49	10.24	10.17	9.25	8.46	7.46	8.68	8.18	8.19
Conventional, new-home [11,12]	13.95	12.28	10.07	10.17	10.30	10.21	10.08	9.20	8.43	7.37	8.58	8.05	8.03
Conventional, existing-home [11]	13.95	12.29	10.09	10.17	10.31	10.22	10.08	9.20	8.43	7.37	8.59	8.05	8.03
Conventional, 15 yr. fixed [6]	(NA)	11.53	10.05	10.04	10.14	10.05	9.67	8.76	7.80	6.65	7.77	7.39	7.28
Conventional, 30 yr. fixed [6]	(NA)	11.90	10.39	10.40	10.38	10.26	10.01	9.09	8.27	7.17	8.28	7.86	7.76

NA Not available. [1] Based on daily offering rates of dealers. [2] Yields are quoted on a bank-discount basis, rather than an investment yield basis (which would give a higher figure). [3] Placed directly; averages of daily offering rates quoted by finance companies. [4] Based on representative closing yields. From Jan. 1, 1981, rates of top-rated banks only. [5] 12 month return for period ending December 31. Source: IBC Financial Data, Inc., Ashland, MA, *IBC's Money Market Insight*, monthly (copyright). [6] Annual averages. Source: Financial Rates, Inc., North Palm Beach, FL, *Bank Rate Monitor*, weekly (copyright). [7] Averages based on daily closing bid yields in secondary market, bank discount basis. [8] Averages computed on an issue-date basis; bank discount basis. [9] HUD–Housing and Urban Development. [10] Averages based on quotations for 1 day each month as compiled by FHA. [11] Primary market. [12] Average contract rates on new commitments.

Source: Except as noted, Board of Governors of the Federal Reserve System, *Federal Reserve Bulletin*, monthly, and *Annual Statistical Digest*.

No. 807. Bond Yields: 1980 to 1996

[Percent per year. Annual averages of daily figures, except as indicated]

TYPE	1980	1985	1988	1989	1990	1991	1992	1993	1994	1995	1996
U.S. Treasury, constant maturities: [1] [2]											
3-year	11.51	9.64	8.26	8.55	8.26	6.82	5.30	4.44	6.27	6.25	5.99
5-year	11.45	10.12	8.47	8.50	8.37	7.37	6.19	5.14	6.69	6.38	6.18
7-year	11.40	10.50	8.71	8.52	8.52	7.68	6.63	5.54	6.91	6.50	6.34
10-year	11.43	10.62	8.85	8.49	8.55	7.86	7.01	5.87	7.69	6.57	6.44
20-year	(NA)	(NA)	(NA)	(NA)	(NA)	(NA)	(NA)	6.29	7.47	6.95	6.83
30-year	11.27	10.79	8.96	8.45	8.61	8.14	7.67	6.59	7.37	6.88	6.71
U.S. Govt., long-term bonds [2] [3]	10.81	10.75	8.98	8.58	8.74	8.16	7.52	6.45	7.41	6.93	6.80
State and local govt. bonds, Aaa [4]	7.86	8.60	7.36	7.00	6.96	6.56	6.09	5.38	5.78	5.79	5.55
State and local govt. bonds, Baa [4]	9.02	9.58	7.84	7.40	7.29	6.99	6.48	5.82	6.18	6.05	5.79
Municipal (Bond Buyer, 20 bonds)	8.59	9.11	7.68	7.23	7.27	6.92	6.44	5.60	6.18	5.95	5.76
Corporate Aaa seasoned [4]	11.94	11.37	9.71	9.26	9.32	8.77	8.14	7.22	7.97	7.59	7.37
Corporate Baa seasoned [4]	13.67	12.72	10.83	10.18	10.36	9.80	8.98	7.93	8.63	8.20	8.05
Corporate (Moody's) [4] [5]	12.75	12.05	10.18	9.66	9.77	9.23	8.55	7.54	8.26	7.83	7.66
Industrials (49 bonds) [6]	12.35	11.80	9.91	9.66	9.77	9.25	8.52	7.51	8.21	7.76	7.58
Public utilities (51 bonds) [7]	13.15	12.29	10.45	9.66	9.76	9.21	8.57	7.56	8.30	7.90	7.74

NA Not available. [1] Yields on the more actively traded issues adjusted to constant maturities by the U.S. Treasury. [2] Yields are based on closing bid prices quoted by at least five dealers. [3] Averages (to maturity or call) for all outstanding bonds neither due nor callable in less than 10 years, including several very low yielding "flower" bonds. [4] Source: Moody's Investors Service, New York, NY. [5] For 1980-88 includes railroad bonds which were discontinued as part of composite in 1989. [6] Covers 40 bonds for 1980, 38 bonds for 1985, and 37 bonds for 1988. [7] Covers 40 bonds for period 1980-88.

Source: Except as noted, Board of Governors of the Federal Reserve System, *Federal Reserve Bulletin*, monthly.

No. 808. Equities, Corporate Bonds, and Municipal Securities—Holdings and Net Purchases, by Type of Investor: 1990 to 1996

[In billions of dollars. Holdings as of Dec. 31. Minus sign (-) indicates net sales]

TYPE OF INVESTOR	HOLDINGS					NET PURCHASES				
	1990	1993	1994	1995	1996	1990	1993	1994	1995	1996
EQUITIES [1]										
Total [2]	3,525	6,280	6,263	8,390	10,090	-37.7	129.9	23.3	-19.0	-21.6
Household sector [3]	1,753	3,250	3,100	4,167	4,780	-28.8	-57.7	-138.1	-178.1	-245.5
Rest of the world [4]	244	374	369	509	626	-16.0	20.9	0.9	16.4	11.5
Bank personal trusts and estates	190	181	165	200	228	0.5	-55.2	-9.3	-17.7	-16.1
Life insurance companies	98	228	274	358	424	-5.7	31.8	63.3	26.0	29.1
Other insurance companies	80	103	112	134	161	-7.0	0.8	1.1	-1.5	-1.1
Private pension funds	593	925	922	1,150	1,345	-1.5	9.2	-14.6	-0.1	-39.8
State and local retirement funds	293	534	535	744	948	13.2	50.9	19.1	40.6	47.4
Mutual funds	233	607	710	1,025	1,460	14.4	115.3	100.8	87.4	193.5
CORPORATE & FOREIGN BONDS										
Total [2]	1,703	2,317	2,469	2,778	3,049	122.5	277.3	153.9	307.3	272.5
Household sector [3]	195	312	311	362	390	45.1	37.3	2.1	51.4	27.7
Rest of the world [4]	217	273	311	369	445	5.3	30.4	36.0	57.2	76.5
Commercial banking	89	98	102	111	113	4.6	3.5	4.3	8.4	1.8
Savings institutions	76	89	87	79	69	-19.3	9.1	-2.4	-8.2	-9.9
Life insurance companies	567	719	779	870	917	56.5	58.3	59.9	90.7	46.9
Other insurance companies	89	103	110	123	137	10.4	3.3	7.2	12.7	13.9
Private pension funds	149	211	233	267	300	15.2	22.7	22.3	33.6	33.0
State and local retirement funds	172	159	165	162	168	5.2	10.4	5.6	-2.7	5.9
Mutual funds	59	169	172	196	230	4.7	50.6	3.2	23.3	33.5
Brokers and dealers	29	73	64	76	91	-4.0	22.2	-8.7	12.0	14.4
Funding corporations	-	4	14	24	52	-	4.0	10.0	9.8	27.8
MUNICIPAL SECURITIES [5]										
Total [2]	1,184	1,378	1,348	1,304	1,308	49.3	74.8	-29.3	-44.2	1.9
Household sector [3]	574	557	505	454	432	27.7	-27.2	-51.9	-50.7	-21.4
Nonfinancial corporate business	25	55	59	55	50	-7.7	8.9	4.7	-4.7	-4.7
Commercial banking	117	99	98	93	94	-16.4	1.7	-1.6	-4.2	0.9
Bank personal trusts and estates	81	109	114	103	97	7.7	12.9	5.3	-11.1	-6.0
Other insurance companies	137	146	154	161	169	1.8	10.4	7.4	7.0	8.4
Money market mutual funds	84	106	113	128	144	13.9	9.6	7.8	14.3	16.8
Mutual funds	113	211	207	210	216	13.9	42.9	-4.3	3.2	5.7
Closed-end funds	14	46	55	60	65	2.0	7.9	7.4	5.0	4.9

- Represents or rounds to zero. [1] Excludes mutual fund shares. [2] Includes other types not shown separately. [3] Includes nonprofit organizations. [4] Holdings of U.S. issues by foreign residents. [5] Includes loans.

Source: Board of Governors of the Federal Reserve System, *Flow of Funds Accounts*, March 1997 quarterly diskettes. Data are also published in the quarterly Z.1 release.

). 809. United States Purchases and Sales of Foreign Bonds and Stocks, 1980 to 1996, and by Selected Country, 1996

billions of dollars. See headnote, table 810. Minus sign (-) indicates net sales by U.S. investors or a net inflow of capital into the United States]

YEAR AND COUNTRY	NET PURCHASES			TOTAL TRANSACTIONS [1]			BONDS		STOCKS	
	Total	Bonds	Stocks	Total	Bonds	Stocks	Purchases	Sales	Purchases	Sales
0	3.1	1.0	2.1	53.1	35.2	17.9	18.1	17.1	10.0	7.9
5	7.9	4.0	3.9	212.1	166.4	45.7	85.2	81.2	24.8	20.9
0	31.2	21.9	9.2	906.7	652.2	254.5	337.1	315.1	131.9	122.6
1	46.8	14.8	32.0	948.6	675.5	273.2	345.1	330.3	152.6	120.6
2	47.9	15.6	32.3	1,375.1	1,042.8	332.4	529.2	513.6	182.3	150.1
3	143.1	80.4	62.7	2,126.0	1,572.3	553.7	626.3	746.0	308.2	245.5
4	57.3	9.2	48.1	2,526.2	1,706.0	820.3	857.6	848.4	434.2	386.1
5	98.7	48.4	50.3	2,568.9	1,827.5	741.4	937.9	889.5	395.8	345.5
996, total [2]	103.1	45.2	57.9	3,258.0	2,281.5	976.5	1,163.4	1,118.1	517.2	459.3
ted Kingdom	36.5	20.7	15.8	1,528.8	1,155.9	373.0	588.3	567.6	194.4	178.6
nada	5.7	2.4	3.3	315.7	251.8	63.9	127.1	124.7	33.6	30.3
an	5.9	-3.7	9.6	189.3	65.3	124.0	30.8	34.5	66.8	57.2
muda	5.9	3.6	2.4	168.0	148.4	19.7	76.0	72.4	11.0	8.7
sh West Indies	0.0	0.3	-0.3	112.6	88.3	24.3	44.3	44.0	12.0	12.3
zil	1.4	-1.1	2.5	106.6	90.1	16.4	44.5	45.6	9.5	7.0
g Kong	7.6	3.1	4.6	79.2	27.3	51.9	15.2	12.1	28.2	23.7
herlands Antilles	-3.5	-1.1	-2.3	73.6	38.0	35.7	18.4	19.5	16.7	19.0
entina	0.4	-0.1	0.5	73.1	67.5	5.6	33.7	33.8	3.0	2.5
nce	5.4	0.6	4.8	61.4	35.0	26.4	17.8	17.2	15.6	10.8

[1] Total purchases plus total sales. [2] Includes other countries, not shown separately.

Source: U.S. Dept. of Treasury, *Treasury Bulletin*, quarterly.

No. 810. Foreign Purchases and Sales of U.S. Securities, by Type of Security, 1980 to 1996, and by Selected Country, 1996

billions of dollars. Covers transactions in all types of long-term domestic securities by foreigners as reported by banks, ers, and other entities in the United States (except nonmarketable U.S. Treasury notes, foreign series; and nonmarketable . Treasury bonds and notes, foreign currency series). Data cover new issues of securities, transactions in outstanding issues, redemptions of securities. Includes transactions executed in the United States for the account of foreigners, and transactions cuted abroad for the account of reporting institutions and their domestic customers. Data by country show the country of icile of the foreign buyers and sellers of the securities; in the case of outstanding issues, this may differ from the country of original issuer. The term "foreigner" covers all institutions and individuals domiciled outside the United States, including U.S. ens domiciled abroad, and the foreign branches, subsidiaries and other affiliates abroad of U.S. banks and businesses; the ral governments, central banks, and other official institutions of foreign countries; and international and regional organizations. reigner" also includes persons in the United States to the extent that they are known by reporting institutions to be acting on alf of foreigners. Minus sign (-) indicates net sales by foreigners or a net outflow of capital from the United States]

EAR AND COUNTRY	NET PURCHASES					TOTAL TRANSACTIONS [4]				
	Total	Treasury bonds and notes [1]	U.S. Govt. corporations [2] bonds	Corporate bonds [3]	Corporate stocks	Total	Treasury bonds and notes [1]	U.S. Govt. corporations [2] bonds	Corporate bonds [3]	Corporate stocks
0	15.8	4.9	2.6	2.9	5.4	198	97	17	9	75
5	78.3	29.2	4.3	39.8	4.9	1,256	968	46	84	159
0	18.7	17.9	6.3	9.7	-15.1	4,204	3,620	104	117	362
1	58.1	19.9	10.2	16.9	11.1	4,706	4,016	124	155	411
2	73.2	39.3	18.3	20.8	-5.1	5,282	4,444	204	187	448
3	111.1	23.6	35.4	30.6	21.6	6,314	5,195	263	239	618
4	140.4	78.8	21.7	38.0	1.9	6,562	5,343	297	222	699
5	231.9	134.1	28.7	57.9	11.2	7,243	5,828	222	278	915
996, total [5]	384.1	244.2	49.3	77.4	13.2	9,172	7,217	283	434	1,238
ted Kingdom	122.9	64.4	11.0	43.6	3.9	3,709	3,099	66	224	320
an	54.4	41.5	7.6	5.6	-0.3	970	854	30	14	72
nada	9.2	2.7	0.2	4.1	2.3	774	639	6	18	110
sh West Indies	23.1	8.5	8.7	3.0	3.0	416	210	60	32	114
herlands Antilles	17.6	12.4	0.3	0.9	4.1	391	260	4	21	107
muda	7.6	2.6	3.3	2.0	-0.3	324	144	46	25	109
gapore	12.3	7.7	1.4	1.1	2.2	270	237	4	5	24
nce	5.4	2.6	0.2	5.0	-2.3	227	173	2	12	41
many	24.3	18.1	1.6	3.5	1.1	219	173	3	14	29

[1] Marketable bonds and notes. [2] Includes federally-sponsored agencies. [3] Includes transactions in directly placed issues ued by U.S. corporations and issues of States and municipalities. [4] Total purchases plus total sales. [5] Includes other ntries, not shown separately.

Source: U.S. Dept. of Treasury, *Treasury Bulletin*, quarterly.

No. 811. New Security Issues of Corporations, by Type of Offering and Industry Group: 1990 to 1995

[In billions of dollars. Represents gross proceeds of issues maturing in more than one year. Figures are the principal amount or the number of units multiplied by the offering price. Excludes secondary offerings, employee stock plans, investment companies other than closed-end, intracorporate transactions, equities sold abroad, and Yankee bonds. Stock data include ownership securities issued by limited partnerships]

TYPE OF OFFERING AND INDUSTRY GROUP	1990	1992	1993	1994	1995	TYPE OF OFFERING AND INDUSTRY GROUP	1990	1992	1993	1994	1995
Total	339.1	559.8	769.1	583.2	674.1	Stocks, total	40.2	88.3	122.5	85.2	100.9
Bonds, total	296.9	471.5	646.6	498.0	573.2	Preferred	4.0	21.3	18.9	12.5	11.0
Public, domestic	188.8	378.1	487.0	365.2	408.8	Common	19.4	57.1	82.7	47.8	57.8
Private placement, domestic	87.0	65.9	121.2	76.1	87.5	Private placement	16.7	9.9	20.9	24.8	32.1
Sold abroad	23.1	27.6	38.4	56.8	76.9						
Manufacturing	51.8	82.1	88.2	43.4	61.1	Manufacturing	5.6	22.7	22.3	17.8	21.8
Commercial and miscellaneous	40.7	43.1	58.6	40.7	50.7	Commercial and miscellaneous	10.2	20.2	25.8	15.7	27.8
Transportation	12.8	10.0	10.8	6.9	8.4	Transportation	0.4	2.6	2.2	2.2	0.8
Public utility	17.6	48.1	56.3	13.3	13.8	Public utility	0.4	6.5	7.1	2.2	1.9
Communication	6.7	15.4	31.9	13.3	23.0	Communication	3.8	2.4	3.4	0.5	1.1
Real estate and financial	169.3	272.9	400.8	380.4	416.3	Real estate and financial	19.7	33.9	61.0	46.7	47.4

Source: Board of Governors of the Federal Reserve System, *Federal Reserve Bulletin*, monthly, and *Annual Statistical Digest*.

No. 812. Volume of Debt Markets by Type of Security: 1990 to 1996

[In billions of dollars. Covers debt markets as represented by the source]

TYPE OF SECURITY	1990	1991	1992	1993	1994	1995	1996
NEW ISSUE VOLUME							
Total	2,780	3,272	3,985	4,829	5,268	6,745	8,189
U.S. Treasury securities [1]	1,531	1,700	1,991	2,066	2,112	2,331	2,485
Federal agency debt	637	797	913	1,380	2,228	3,506	4,500
Municipal	163	217	278	340	205	196	226
Mortgage-backed securities [2]	235	268	455	568	359	269	371
Asset-backed securities [3]	42	50	51	59	75	108	153
Corporate debt [4]	173	240	310	416	289	333	427
DAILY TRADING VOLUME							
Total	111.2	146.0	175.2	204.6	237.7	246.3	274.8
U.S. Treasury securities [1,5]	111.2	127.5	152.1	173.6	191.3	193.2	203.7
Federal agency debt [5]	(NA)	5.7	6.1	8.9	16.0	23.7	31.1
Municipal	(NA)	(NA)	(NA)	(NA)	(NA)	(NA)	1.1
Mortgage-backed securities [2]	(NA)	12.8	17.0	22.1	30.4	29.4	38.1
VOLUME OF SECURITIES OUTSTANDING							
Total	7,431	7,971	8,504	9,093	9,633	10,404	11,221
U.S. Treasury securities [1]	2,196	2,472	2,754	2,990	3,126	3,307	3,459
Federal agency debt	435	443	484	571	739	845	925
Municipal	1,184	1,272	1,303	1,378	1,348	1,304	1,306
Mortgage-backed securities [2]	1,024	1,161	1,274	1,350	1,442	1,570	1,715
Asset-backed securities [3]	102	134	159	182	209	303	392
Money market instruments [6]	1,157	1,054	994	972	1,035	1,177	1,393
Corporate debt	1,334	1,435	1,536	1,653	1,734	1,897	2,039

NA Not available. [1] Marketable public debt. [2] Includes only Government National Mortgage Association (GNMA), Federal National Mortgage Association (FNMA), and Federal Home Loan Mortgage Corporation (FHLMC) mortgage-backed securities. [3] Excludes mortgage-related assets. [4] Non-convertible corporate debt. [5] Primary dealer transactions. [6] Commercial paper, bankers acceptances, and large time deposits.

Source: PSA, The Bond Market Trade Association, New York, NY. Based on data supplied by Board of Governors of the Federal Reserve System, U.S. Dept. of Treasury, Securities Data Company, FHLMC, FNMA, GNMA, Federal Home Loan Banks, Student Loan Marketing Association, Federal Farm Credit Banks, and the Tennessee Valley Authority.

No. 813. Stock Prices and Yields: 1990 to 1996

[Annual averages of daily figures, except as noted]

INDEX	1990	1991	1992	1993	1994	1995	1996
STOCK PRICES							
oor's composite index (500 stocks)							
) [1]	335.0	376.2	415.7	451.6	460.4	541.7	670.5
. . . . .	391.4	445.8	489.8	517.4	540.6	641.3	792.0
change common stock index							
65=50):							
. . . . .	183.7	206.4	229.0	249.7	254.2	291.2	358.0
high [2]	201.1	229.4	242.1	260.7	267.7	331.2	398.9
low [2]	162.2	171.0	217.9	236.2	243.1	250.7	321.4
l	226.1	258.2	284.3	300.1	315.3	367.4	453.6
tation	158.8	174.0	201.0	242.7	247.2	270.1	327.3
. . . . .	90.7	92.6	99.5	114.6	105.0	114.6	126.4
. . . . .	133.2	150.8	179.3	216.6	209.8	238.5	303.9
ck Exchange Market Value Index							
73=50)	338.3	360.3	391.3	438.8	449.5	498.1	570.9
posite index [3]	373.9	586.3	677.0	776.8	752.0	1,052.1	1,291.0
. . . . .	406.1	669.0	724.9	805.8	753.8	984.7	1,109.6
. . . . .	451.8	601.1	803.9	920.6	925.9	1,292.6	1,465.4
. . . . .	254.9	350.6	532.9	689.4	697.1	1,009.4	1,273.5
dustrial average (30 stocks) [4]	2,678.9	2,929.3	3,284.3	3,522.1	3,793.8	4,493.8	5,742.9
equity index							
80=1404.596) [5]	3,187.3	3,604.6	4,041.1	4,468.0	4,571.3	5,337.1	6,575.2
MON STOCK YIELDS (percent)							
oor's composite index (500 stocks):							
ice ratio [6]	3.61	3.24	2.99	2.78	2.82	2.56	2.19
ice ratio [4 7]	6.47	4.79	4.22	4.46	5.83	6.09	5.24

dex includes 400 industrial stocks, 20 transportation, 40 public utility, and 40 financial stocks. w York Stock Exchange, Inc., New York, NY, *Fact Book*, annual (copyright). [3] Source: National Association of alers, Washington, DC, *Fact Book*, annual. December monthly closing values. [4] Source: U.S. Council of Economic nomic *Report of the President*, annual. [5] Represents return on the market value of all common equity securities pricing is available. Source: Wilshire Associates, Santa Monica, CA, releases. [6] Aggregate cash dividends (based n annual rate) divided by by aggregate market value based on Wednesday closing prices. Averages of monthly erages of quarterly ratios which are ratio of earnings (after taxes) for 4 quarters ending with particular quarter to price day of that quarter.

Except as noted, Board of Governors of the Federal Reserve System, *Federal Reserve Bulletin*, monthly; *Annual est*; and unpublished data.

814. Sales of Stocks and Options on Registered Exchanges: 1980 to 1995

[Excludes over-the-counter trading]

CHANGE	Unit	1980	1985	1988	1989	1990	1991	1992	1993	1994	1995
ue of all sales,											
nges [1 2]	Bil. dol	522	1,260	1,702	2,010	1,752	1,903	2,149	2,734	2,966	3,690
. . . . .	Bil. dol	398	1,024	1,380	1,581	1,394	1,534	1,759	2,278	2,483	3,078
. . . . .	Bil. dol	47	36	59	80	65	67	69	83	83	105
. . . . .	Bil. dol	21	79	87	101	74	77	87	107	98	114
. . . . .	Bil. dol	28	38	64	88	81	74	63	65	87	107
. . . . .	Bil. dol	13	40	49	64	53	63	65	70	70	94
. . . . .	Bil. dol	11	23	34	50	41	39	49	55	51	59
OCKS [5]											
all exchanges [2]	Million.	15,488	37,046	52,533	54,239	53,338	58,025	65,463	82,808	90,482	106,393
. . . . .	Million.	12,390	30,222	44,018	44,140	43,829	47,674	53,344	68,732	76,665	90,062
. . . . .	Million.	1,659	2,115	2,576	3,248	3,125	3,103	3,631	4,470	4,300	4,843
. . . . .	Million.	598	2,274	2,771	2,960	2,511	2,715	3,035	3,792	3,526	3,925
. . . . .	Million.	435	1,352	1,576	1,791	1,682	2,068	2,087	2,330	2,147	2,738
all exchanges [2]	Bil. dol	476	1,200	1,587	1,845	1,612	1,776	2,032	2,610	2,817	3,507
. . . . .	Bil. dol	398	1,023	1,378	1,577	1,390	1,532	1,758	2,276	2,482	3,078
. . . . .	Bil. dol	35	26	31	43	36	40	42	54	56	73
. . . . .	Bil. dol	21	79	87	101	74	77	87	107	98	114
. . . . .	Bil. dol	11	37	41	52	45	63	58	62	59	79
TIONS [6]											
ed, all exchanges [2]	Million.	97	233	196	227	210	199	202	233	281	287
. . . . .	Million.	53	149	112	127	130	122	122	141	184	179
. . . . .	Million.	29	49	45	50	41	39	42	48	48	52
of contracts traded,											
s [2]	Bil. dol	45.8	59.1	62.6	76.8	79.0	76.1	72.2	75.2	94.5	118.9
. . . . .	Bil. dol	27.9	38.4	39.7	47.3	55.4	50.7	44.5	45.5	67.2	82.5
. . . . .	Bil. dol	12.5	11.6	12.4	15.1	12.8	14.0	14.1	14.9	13.2	17.3
ised:											
contracts	Million.	4.9	10.5	11.4	15.6	12.1	10.8	9.9	11.5	13.0	15.1
. . . . .	Bil. dol	20.4	49.2	51.5	65.2	55.8	49.2	43.9	48.4	53.8	62.9

s market value of stocks, rights, warrants, and options trading beginning 1988. [2] Includes other registered t shown separately. [3] The Chicago Stock Exchange, Inc. was formerly the Midwest Stock Exchange. [4] Chicago Exchange, Inc. [5] Includes voting trust certificates, American Depository Receipts, and certificate of deposit for ata for 1980 exclude nonequity options.

J.S. Securities and Exchange Commission, *SEC Monthly Statistical Review* (discontinued Feb. 1989); and ata.

No. 815. Dow-Jones U.S. Equity Market Index, by Industry: 1990 to 1996

[As of end of year]

INDUSTRY	1990	1991	1992	1993	1994	1995	1996
U.S. Equity Market Index, total	**305.59**	**391.90**	**413.29**	**442.19**	**433.07**	**581.43**	**700.86**
Basic materials	299.67	372.44	401.09	443.38	456.55	540.47	614.63
Consumer, cyclical	325.98	446.65	527.62	596.43	532.55	635.01	711.02
Consumer, noncyclical	543.87	784.85	734.03	684.89	740.25	1,052.90	1,287.32
Conglomerates	354.20	471.90	530.30	655.57	638.07	891.54	1,228.43
Energy	262.85	265.79	264.73	290.55	286.70	358.74	442.09
Financial services	233.04	338.52	410.85	436.98	408.25	611.76	809.78
Industrial	288.12	364.55	390.48	432.52	399.79	499.93	581.94
Technology	242.10	302.07	320.10	361.45	408.48	570.55	730.45
Utilities	248.91	278.77	286.74	316.02	272.82	362.66	359.67

Source: Dow Jones & Company, Inc., New York, NY, *Wall Street Journal*, selected issues, (copyright).

No. 816. Volume of Trading on New York Stock Exchange: 1980 to 1995

[Round lot: A unit of trading or a multiple thereof. On the NYSE the unit of trading is generally 100 shares in stocks. For some inactive stocks, the unit of trading is 10 shares. Odd lot: An amount of stock less than the established 100-share unit or 10-share unit of trading]

ITEM	Unit	1980	1985	1988	1989	1990	1991	1992	1993	1994	1995
Shares traded	**Million**	**11,562**	**27,774**	**41,118**	**42,022**	**39,946**	**45,599**	**51,826**	**67,461**	**74,003**	**87,873**
Round lots	Million	11,352	27,511	40,850	41,699	39,665	45,266	51,376	66,923	73,420	87,218
Average daily shares	Million	44.9	109.2	161.5	165.5	156.8	178.9	202.3	264.5	291.4	346.1
High day	Million	84.3	181.0	343.9	416.4	292.4	317.4	389.0	379.5	482.8	652.8
Low day	Million	16.1	62.1	72.1	68.9	56.9	69.6	95.1	89.9	113.8	117.7
Odd lots	Million	209	263	268	324	282	333	450	538	583	656
Value of shares traded	**Bil. dol**	**382**	**981**	**1,366**	**1,556**	**1,336**	**1,534**	**1,765**	**2,305**	**2,477**	**3,110**
Round lots	Bil. dol.	375	970	1,356	1,543	1,325	1,520	1,745	2,283	2,454	3,083
Odd lots	Bil. dol.	8	10	10	13	11	[1] 13	19	22	22	27
Bond volume [2]	**Mil. dol**	**5,190**	**9,047**	**7,702**	**8,836**	**10,893**	**12,698**	**11,629**	**9,743**	**7,197**	**6,979**
Daily average	Mil. dol	20.5	35.9	30.4	35.1	43.1	50.2	45.8	38.5	28.6	27.7

[1] Excludes odd lot statistics for February which were not available. [2] Par value.

Source: New York Stock Exchange, Inc., New York, NY, *Fact Book*, annual (copyright).

No. 817. Securities Listed on New York Stock Exchange: 1980 to 1995

[As of December 31, except cash dividends are for calendar year]

ITEM	Unit	1980	1985	1987	1988	1989	1990	1991	1992	1993	1994	1995
BONDS												
Number of issuers	Number	1,045	1,010	885	846	794	743	705	636	574	583	584
Number of issues	Number	3,057	3,856	3,346	3,106	2,961	2,912	2,727	2,354	2,103	2,141	2,097
Face value	Bil. dol	602	1,327	1,651	1,610	1,435	1,689	2,219	2,009	2,342	2,526	2,773
Market value	Bil. dol.	508	1,339	1,621	1,561	1,412	1,610	2,227	2,044	2,528	2,367	2,748
Average price	Percent	84.41	100.90	98.20	96.94	98.42	95.31	100.34	101.77	107.96	93.73	99.09
STOCKS												
Companies	Number	1,570	1,541	1,647	1,681	1,720	1,774	1,885	2,088	2,361	2,570	2,675
Number of issues	Number	2,228	2,298	2,244	2,234	2,246	2,284	2,426	2,658	2,904	3,060	3,126
Shares listed	Billion	33.7	52.4	71.8	76.2	83.0	90.7	99.6	115.8	131.1	142.3	154.7
Market value	Bil. dol	1,243	1,950	2,216	2,457	3,030	2,820	3,713	4,035	4,541	4,448	6,013
Average price	Dollars	36.87	37.20	30.87	32.26	36.51	31.08	37.27	34.83	34.65	31.26	38.86
Cash dividends on common stock	Bil. dol	53.1	74.2	84.4	102.2	101.8	103.2	123.4	109.7	120.2	130.0	147.0

Source: New York Stock Exchange, Inc., New York, NY, *Fact Book*, annual (copyright).

No. 818. NASDAQ—Securities Listed and Volume of Trading: 1980 to 1996

ITEM	Unit	1980	1985	1989	1990	1991	1992	1993	1994	1995	1996
Member firms	Number	2,932	6,307	6,141	5,827	5,386	5,254	5,296	5,426	5,451	5,553
Branch offices	Number	7,555	15,375	29,996	24,457	29,158	33,484	44,181	57,105	58,119	60,151
Companies listed	Number	2,894	4,136	4,293	4,132	4,094	4,113	4,611	4,902	5,112	5,556
Issues	Number	3,050	4,784	4,963	4,706	4,684	4,768	5,393	5,761	5,955	6,384
Shares traded	Million	6,692	20,699	33,530	33,380	41,311	48,455	66,541	74,353	101,158	138,112
Average daily volume	Million	26.5	82.1	133.1	131.9	163.3	190.8	263.0	295.1	401.4	543.7
Value of shares traded	Bil. dol.	69	234	431	452	694	891	1,350	1,449	2,398	2,302

Source: National Association of Securities Dealers, Washington, DC, *Fact Book*, annual.

No. 819. Commodity Futures Trading on U.S. Exchanges—Volume of Trading: 1980 to 1996

[In millions. For year ending Sept. 30]

COMMODITY	1980	1985	1988	1989	1990	1991	1992	1993	1994	1995	1996
Number of contracts traded	92.7	182.6	241.8	267.7	272.2	261.4	298.5	325.5	411.1	409.4	394.2
Grain	18.3	10.7	15.9	15.9	17.0	16.6	17.6	16.0	20.0	21.1	30.2
Oilseeds/products	15.7	14.9	22.5	21.1	20.4	19.8	18.6	20.7	21.0	20.7	25.6
Livestock/products	11.8	7.9	9.6	8.2	8.0	6.9	6.4	5.8	6.1	6.2	7.0
Other agriculturals	7.8	5.1	9.8	10.7	11.0	9.5	9.4	10.8	12.3	12.7	12.0
Energy products	1.1	7.0	26.3	31.3	35.2	31.8	38.4	42.8	50.5	47.9	46.9
Metals	14.1	18.4	18.9	17.9	17.8	13.9	12.2	15.2	18.2	17.4	16.9
Financial instruments	10.2	72.1	117.6	136.7	135.7	134.1	148.2	185.4	252.6	259.0	234.3
Currencies	3.7	16.4	21.2	25.7	27.2	28.8	36.7	28.8	30.4	24.3	21.2

Source: U.S. Commodity Futures Trading Commission, *Annual Report*.

No. 820. Stock Ownership, by Age of Head of Family and Family Income: 1989 to 1995

[Median value in thousands of constant 1995 dollars. Constant dollar figures are based on consumer price index data published by U.S. Bureau of Labor Statistics. Families include one-person units; for definition of family, see text, section 1. Based on Survey of Consumer Finance; see Appendix III. For definition of median, see Guide to Tabular Presentation]

AGE OF FAMILY HEAD AND FAMILY INCOME (constant (1995) dollars)	FAMILIES HAVING DIRECT OR INDIRECT STOCK HOLDINGS (percent)			MEDIAN VALUE AMONG FAMILIES WITH HOLDINGS			STOCK HOLDINGS' SHARE OF GROUP'S FINANCIAL ASSETS (percent)		
	1989	1992	1995	1989	1992	1995	1989	1992	1995
All families	31.7	37.2	41.1	10.4	11.5	13.5	26.3	34.4	40.4
Under 35 years old	23.3	28.3	36.5	3.7	3.8	5.4	25.4	25.6	32.4
35 to 44 years old	40.5	42.2	46.7	6.3	8.1	9.0	25.6	30.8	41.4
45 to 54 years old	40.2	47.3	49.3	12.3	14.4	24.0	29.9	39.4	44.2
55 to 64 years old	34.2	44.8	41.4	18.6	25.3	20.0	28.4	37.3	45.3
65 to 74 years old	26.1	31.9	34.0	25.8	21.7	25.0	26.2	34.4	34.3
75 years old and over	24.7	28.1	28.1	28.2	27.1	28.1	20.7	28.6	39.5
Less than $10,000	2.3	6.9	6.0	35.0	5.9	4.0	10.0	15.2	21.1
$10,000 to $24,999	13.1	19.4	25.3	9.2	4.3	6.0	10.3	18.6	21.6
$25,000 to $49,999	33.1	41.6	47.7	5.5	7.6	8.0	20.3	25.4	33.0
$50,000 to $99,999	54.0	64.1	66.7	10.4	14.6	21.3	25.6	35.1	39.9
$100,000 and more	79.7	79.1	83.9	47.9	74.6	90.8	31.4	40.2	47.6

Source: Board of Governors of the Federal Reserve System, *Federal Reserve Bulletin*, January 1997.

No. 821. Mutual Fund Shares—Holdings and Net Purchases, by Type of Investor: 1990 to 1996

[In billions of dollars. Holdings as of Dec. 31. Minus sign (-) indicates net sales]

TYPE OF INVESTOR	HOLDINGS					NET PURCHASES				
	1990	1993	1994	1995	1996	1990	1993	1994	1995	1996
Total	608.4	1,375.4	1,477.4	1,852.8	2,348.8	62.9	323.7	128.9	173.9	275.2
Households, nonprofit organizations	467.1	977.1	1,027.2	1,226.8	1,491.1	36.6	231.3	93.7	140.4	197.4
Nonfinancial corporate business	9.7	29.8	31.1	47.8	64.7	-1.0	6.8	2.1	4.2	6.5
State and local governments	4.8	21.4	29.1	35.0	37.0	3.3	6.5	7.8	5.9	2.0
Commercial banking	1.9	3.9	2.0	2.3	2.6	-0.3	0.5	-1.9	0.3	0.3
Credit unions	1.4	4.2	2.6	2.8	3.0	0.2	0.1	-1.6	0.2	0.2
Bank personal trusts and estates	62.7	183.5	202.4	256.0	308.6	9.7	44.9	22.3	-11.3	4.9
Life insurance companies	30.7	23.9	7.4	14.1	30.6	12.6	10.9	-16.5	6.1	12.8
Private pension funds	30.0	131.8	175.6	267.9	411.1	1.7	22.7	22.9	28.1	51.2

Source: Board of Governors of the Federal Reserve System, *Flow of Funds Accounts*, March 1997 quarterly diskettes. Data are also published in the quarterly Z.1 release.

No. 1014. Transportation to Work: 1990

[In thousands, except as indicated. Based on workers 16 years old or older]

REGION, DIVISION, AND STATE	MEANS OF TRANSPORTATION TO WORK: Car, truck, van: Drove alone	MEANS OF TRANSPORTATION TO WORK: Car, truck, van: Car-pooled	MEANS OF TRANSPORTATION TO WORK: Percent using public transportation	Worked at home	Average travel time to work [1] (minutes)	HOUSEHOLDS WITH VEHICLES AVAILABLE: None	HOUSEHOLDS WITH VEHICLES AVAILABLE: One vehicle	HOUSEHOLDS WITH VEHICLES AVAILABLE: Two or more vehicles
United States	84,215	15,378	5.3	3,406	22.4	10,602	31,039	60,306
Northeast	15,902	2,771	12.8	630	24.5	3,603	6,408	8,862
New England	4,892	749	5.1	191	21.5	568	1,699	2,676
Maine	424	80	0.9	24	19.0	40	159	266
New Hampshire	443	70	0.7	20	21.9	26	132	254
Vermont	200	36	0.7	17	18.0	17	72	122
Massachusetts	2,148	318	8.3	75	22.7	321	819	1,107
Rhode Island	376	58	2.5	10	19.2	40	132	206
Connecticut	1,301	187	3.9	45	21.1	124	386	721
Middle Atlantic	11,010	2,023	15.7	438	25.7	3,036	4,709	6,186
New York	4,461	861	24.8	213	28.6	1,994	2,153	2,492
New Jersey	2,731	472	8.8	80	25.3	360	966	1,468
Pennsylvania	3,818	690	6.4	145	21.6	681	1,589	2,226
Midwest	21,091	3,207	3.5	987	20.7	2,236	7,365	12,714
East North Central	14,749	2,206	4.3	551	21.7	1,693	5,230	8,674
Ohio	3,889	521	2.5	119	20.7	416	1,351	2,320
Indiana	2,040	332	1.3	73	20.4	175	670	1,221
Illinois	3,742	653	10.1	144	25.1	588	1,476	2,138
Michigan	3,328	429	1.6	100	21.2	344	1,133	1,943
Wisconsin	1,751	270	2.5	114	18.3	170	600	1,052
West North Central	6,342	1,002	1.9	436	18.4	545	2,135	4,040
Minnesota	1,593	247	3.6	116	19.1	142	517	988
Iowa	971	157	1.2	89	16.2	75	332	657
Missouri	1,816	312	2.0	84	21.6	191	652	1,118
North Dakota	210	31	0.6	24	13.0	16	73	152
South Dakota	233	33	0.3	31	13.8	17	76	166
Nebraska	590	87	1.2	44	15.8	43	182	377
Kansas	929	136	0.6	49	17.2	60	302	583
South	29,495	5,886	2.6	936	22.0	3,208	10,987	17,627
South Atlantic	15,481	3,156	3.4	501	22.5	1,725	5,725	9,053
Delaware	258	43	2.4	8	20.0	20	80	147
Maryland	1,733	376	8.1	65	27.0	216	554	979
District of Columbia	107	37	36.6	9	27.1	93	103	53
Virginia	2,281	500	4.0	103	24.0	205	717	1,370
West Virginia	493	107	1.1	16	21.0	94	247	347
North Carolina	2,528	530	1.0	71	19.8	242	786	1,489
South Carolina	1,235	277	1.1	31	20.5	137	402	720
Georgia	2,379	468	2.8	65	22.7	244	730	1,393
Florida	4,468	819	2.0	132	21.8	474	2,106	2,555
East South Central	5,110	1,005	1.2	149	21.1	607	1,814	3,231
Kentucky	1,195	229	1.6	47	20.7	169	447	773
Tennessee	1,763	324	1.3	52	21.5	181	593	1,079
Alabama	1,374	267	0.8	31	21.2	156	466	885
Mississippi	777	184	0.8	19	20.6	111	307	494
West South Central	8,904	1,725	2.0	286	21.6	876	3,448	5,343
Arkansas	765	153	0.5	28	19.0	88	303	501
Louisiana	1,239	247	3.0	31	22.3	209	542	749
Oklahoma	1,079	191	0.6	41	19.3	91	414	701
Texas	5,821	1,134	2.2	185	22.2	489	2,190	3,392
West	17,727	3,513	4.1	854	22.7	1,553	6,279	11,103
Mountain	4,586	873	2.1	229	19.7	343	1,697	2,993
Montana	250	41	0.6	22	14.8	20	91	194
Idaho	330	53	1.9	21	17.3	17	101	243
Wyoming	154	28	1.4	9	15.4	8	48	113
Colorado	1,217	210	2.9	67	20.7	89	412	761
New Mexico	472	96	1.0	24	19.1	38	165	320
Arizona	1,178	239	2.1	48	21.6	107	532	730
Utah	541	111	2.3	26	18.9	29	153	355
Nevada	444	94	2.7	12	19.8	36	174	256
Pacific	13,141	2,640	4.8	625	23.8	1,210	4,582	8,111
Washington	1,701	282	4.5	86	22.0	141	582	1,149
Oregon	949	165	3.4	56	19.6	88	355	660
California	9,982	2,036	4.9	453	24.6	923	3,452	6,008
Alaska	165	40	2.4	11	16.7	23	64	102
Hawaii	344	116	7.4	19	23.8	35	129	193

[1] Excludes persons who worked at home.

Source: U.S. Bureau of the Census, *Census of Population and Housing, 1990*.

No. 1015. National Personal Transportation Survey (NPTS)— Summary of Travel Trends: 1969 to 1990

[Data obtained by collecting information on all trips taken by the respondent on a specific day (known as travel day), combined with longer trips taken over a 2-week period (known as travel period). Contains data from previous NPTS surveys. For compatibility with previous survey data, all data are based only on trips taken during travel day. Be aware that terminology changes from survey to survey. See source for details]

CHARACTERISTICS	Unit	1969	1977	1983	1990	Percent change, 1969-90	Annual percent change, 1969-90
Households, total	1,000	62,504	75,412	85,371	93,347	49.0	1.9
1 person	1,000	10,980	16,214	19,354	22,999	109.0	3.6
2 persons	1,000	18,448	22,925	27,169	30,114	63.0	2.4
3 persons	1,000	10,746	13,046	14,756	16,128	50.0	2.0
4 persons or more	1,000	22,330	23,227	24,092	24,106	8.0	0.4
Persons, total	1,000	197,213	213,141	229,453	[1]239,416	21.0	0.9
Under 16 yrs. old	1,000	60,100	54,958	53,682	54,303	-10.0	-0.5
16-19 yrs. old	1,000	14,598	16,552	15,268	13,851	-5.0	-0.2
20-34 yrs. old	1,000	40,060	52,252	60,788	59,517	49.0	1.9
35-64 yrs. old	1,000	62,982	66,968	75,353	82,480	31.0	1.3
65 yrs. old and over	1,000	19,473	22,391	24,362	26,955	38.0	1.6
5 yrs. old and over	1,000	(NA)	198,434	212,932	222,101	12.0	0.9
Males, total	1,000	94,465	102,521	111,514	114,441	21.0	0.8
16 yrs. old and over	1,000	66,652	74,542	83,645	86,432	30.0	1.1
Females	1,000	102,748	110,620	117,939	124,975	22.0	0.8
16 yrs. old and over	1,000	73,526	83,721	92,080	96,371	31.0	1.1
Licensed drivers	1,000	102,986	127,552	147,015	163,025	58.0	2.2
Male	1,000	57,981	66,199	75,639	80,289	38.0	1.6
Female	1,000	45,005	61,353	71,376	82,707	84.0	2.9
Workers	1,000	75,758	93,019	103,244	118,343	56.0	2.1
Male	1,000	48,487	55,625	58,849	63,996	32.0	1.3
Female	1,000	27,271	37,394	44,395	54,334	99.0	3.3
Households with—							
No vehicle	1,000	12,876	11,538	11,548	8,573	-33.0	-1.9
One vehicle	1,000	30,252	26,092	28,780	30,654	1.0	0.1
Two vehicles	1,000	16,501	25,942	28,632	35,872	117.0	3.8
Three or more Vehicles	1,000	2,875	11,840	16,411	18,248	535.0	9.2
All vehicles available	1,000	72,500	120,098	143,714	165,221	128.0	4.0
Vehicle trips	Millions	87,284	108,826	126,874	158,927	82.0	2.9
Vehicle miles of travel (VMT)	Millions	775,940	907,603	1,002,139	1,409,600	82.0	2.9
Person trips	Millions	145,146	211,778	224,385	249,562	72.0	2.6
Person miles of travel	Millions	1,404,137	1,879,215	1,946,662	2,315,300	65.0	2.4
Ratios:							
Persons per household	Number	[2]3.16	2.83	2.69	2.56	(NA)	(NA)
Vehicles per household	Number	[2]1.16	1.59	1.68	1.77	(NA)	(NA)
Licensed drivers per household	Number	[2]1.65	1.69	1.72	1.75	(NA)	(NA)
Vehicles per licensed driver	Number	[2]0.70	0.94	0.98	1.01	(NA)	(NA)
Workers per household	Number	[2]1.21	1.23	1.21	1.27	(NA)	(NA)
Vehicles per worker	Number	[2]0.96	1.29	1.39	1.40	(NA)	(NA)
Daily vehicle trips per household	Number	[2]3.83	3.95	4.07	4.66	(NA)	(NA)
Daily VMT per household	Number	[2]34.01	32.97	32.16	41.37	(NA)	(NA)
Average vehicle trip length (miles)	Number	[2]8.89	8.34	7.90	8.87	(NA)	(NA)
Average annual VMT	Miles	12,423	12,036	11,739	15,100	22.0	(NA)
Home to work	Miles	4,183	3,815	3,538	4,853	16.0	(NA)
Shopping	Miles	929	1,336	1,567	1,743	88.0	(NA)
Other family or personal business	Miles	1,270	1,444	1,816	3,014	137.0	(NA)
Social and recreational	Miles	4,094	3,286	3,534	4,060	-1.0	(NA)
Average annual vehicle trips	Number	1,396	1,442	1,486	1,702	22.0	(NA)
Home to work	Number	445	423	414	448	0.7	(NA)
Shopping	Number	213	268	297	345	62.0	(NA)
Other family or personal business	Number	195	215	272	411	111.0	(NA)
Social and recreational	Number	312	320	335	349	12.0	(NA)
Average vehicle trip length	Miles	8.9	8.4	7.9	9.0	1.0	(NA)
Home to work	Miles	9.4	9.1	8.5	11.0	17.0	(NA)
Shopping	Miles	4.4	5.0	5.3	5.1	16.0	(NA)
Other family or personal business	Miles	6.5	6.8	6.7	7.4	14.0	(NA)
Social and recreational	Miles	13.1	10.3	10.5	11.8	-10.0	(NA)
Average vehicle occupancy [3]	Persons	(NA)	1.9	1.7	1.6	[4]-1.3	(NA)
Home to work	Persons	(NA)	1.3	1.3	1.1	[4]-1.3	(NA)
Shopping	Persons	(NA)	2.1	1.8	1.7	[4]-1.6	(NA)
Other family or personal business	Persons	(NA)	2.0	1.8	1.8	[4]-0.8	(NA)
Social and recreational	Persons	(NA)	2.4	2.1	2.1	[4]-1.0	(NA)
Journey-to-work trip mode	Percent	100.0	100.0	100.0	100.0	(NS)	(NS)
Auto	Percent	82.7	80.5	77.6	91.4	(NS)	(NS)
Truck [5]	Percent	8.1	12.5	14.8	(NA)	(NS)	(NS)
Public transit	Percent	8.4	4.7	5.8	5.5	(NS)	(NS)
Other	Percent	0.8	2.3	1.8	3.1	(NS)	(NS)

NA Not available. NS Percent change irrelevant. [1] Includes "don't know" and "refusals". [2] Excludes pickups and other light-trucks as household vehicles. [3] Includes other purposes not shown separately. [4] Change from 1977. [5] Household based trucks, primarily pickups.

Source: Federal Highway Administration, *National Personal Transportation Survey, Summary of Travel Trends, 1969, 1977, 1983, and 1990.*

No. 1016. Roadway Congestion: 1993

[Various Federal, State, and local information sources were used to develop the data base with the primary source being the Federal Highway Administration's Highway Performance Monitoring System]

URBANIZED AREAS	DAILY VEHICLE MILES OF TRAVEL		VEHICLE HOURS OF DELAY		ANNUAL CONGESTION COST		
	Total miles (1,000)	Per lane-mile of freeway	Total hours	Per 1,000 persons	Per driver (dol.)	Per capita (dol.)	Delay and fuel cost (mil. dol.)
Total, average	17,240	13,020	226,390	80	470	370	1,010
Northeastern cities	27,300	12,960	475,040	100	530	430	2,110
Baltimore MD	18,000	13,140	163,850	80	440	350	730
Boston MA	21,500	14,240	349,340	120	630	520	1,560
Hartford CT	7,030	11,520	45,040	70	430	330	200
New York NY	86,000	13,980	1,702,690	100	560	450	7,600
Philadelphia PA	20,200	11,950	304,300	60	320	250	1,320
Pittsburgh PA	9,350	8,130	128,880	70	360	290	560
Washington DC	29,000	17,790	631,170	190	980	820	2,790
Midwestern cities	16,170	12,510	150,490	60	320	250	660
Chicago IL	40,970	15,850	630,790	80	470	370	2,790
Cincinnati OH	12,870	13,330	62,150	50	290	220	280
Cleveland OH	14,970	12,580	71,490	40	240	180	320
Columbus OH	9,750	11,820	54,590	60	310	250	240
Detroit MI	29,500	16,160	538,020	130	790	590	2,340
Indianapolis IN	8,900	11,410	28,450	30	170	130	130
Kansas City MO	15,000	9,740	48,120	40	210	160	210
Louisville KY	7,000	11,380	33,490	40	220	180	140
Milwaukee WI	7,840	12,960	49,690	40	240	180	220
Minn-St. Paul MN	20,000	13,030	115,090	50	300	240	510
Oklahoma City OK	7,700	10,480	28,260	40	200	150	120
St. Louis MO	19,500	11,340	145,750	70	410	320	640
Southern cities	8,310	12,310	95,900	80	420	340	420
Atlanta GA	30,000	15,000	310,210	130	740	590	1,360
Charlotte NC	3,500	11,110	37,310	70	400	320	160
Ft. Lauderdale FL	8,500	12,500	83,940	60	350	290	370
Jacksonville FL	6,000	12,500	66,700	90	500	380	300
Memphis TN	5,150	11,320	28,420	30	180	140	120
Miami FL	9,890	15,450	249,230	130	710	560	1,090
Nashville TN	7,000	11,110	36,570	60	340	270	160
New Orleans LA	5,200	13,510	68,030	60	360	270	300
Norfolk VA	5,980	10,390	71,790	70	410	330	320
Orlando FL	6,230	10,120	52,460	60	310	250	230
Tampa FL	3,950	12,340	50,290	70	370	290	220
Southwestern cities	11,330	12,170	127,540	80	460	350	570
Albuquerque NM	2,740	11,420	28,090	50	300	230	120
Austin TX	6,420	12,110	59,490	100	590	470	270
Corpus Christi TX	1,950	9,290	4,930	20	110	80	20
Dallas TX	24,900	13,990	276,410	130	760	600	1,250
Denver CO	13,250	13,380	168,700	100	580	460	750
El Paso TX	3,700	10,000	14,560	30	160	120	70
Fort Worth TX	13,100	12,240	117,380	100	580	440	530
Houston TX	32,000	14,880	429,990	150	860	660	1,920
Phoenix AZ	9,800	13,600	198,790	100	580	420	870
Salt Lake City UT	6,060	11,330	25,670	30	170	130	110
San Antonio TX	10,700	11,380	78,930	70	400	290	350
Western cities	29,020	15,660	414,500	120	710	560	1,850
Honolulu HI	5,500	13,920	68,450	100	540	450	310
Los Angeles CA	113,950	20,810	1,921,250	160	920	710	8,540
Portland OR	8,350	13,920	93,830	90	480	390	420
Sacramento CA	10,280	12,770	84,680	70	410	310	380
San Bernardino-Riverside, CA	15,220	16,280	233,640	180	1,090	790	1,040
San Diego CA	27,750	15,900	168,020	70	380	300	770
San Fran-Oak CA	42,750	17,560	662,420	170	950	780	2,960
San Jose CA	16,650	13,650	196,300	130	750	580	880
Seattle-Everett WA	20,700	16,110	301,900	160	840	720	1,350

Source: Texas Transportation Institute, College Station, Texas; *Roadway Congestion in Major Urban Areas*, annual (copyright).

No. 1017. Motor Vehicle Accidents—Number and Deaths: 1972 to 1995

ITEM	Unit	1972 [1]	1980	1985	1990	1991	1992	1993	1994	1995
Motor vehicle accidents [2]	Million	17.0	17.9	19.3	11.5	11.3	(NA)	11.9	11.2	10.7
Cars	Million	24.5	22.8	25.6	14.3	13.7	(NA)	14.1	13.5	12.3
Trucks	Million	3.5	5.5	6.1	4.4	4.7	(NA)	5.9	5.2	4.5
Motorcycles	1,000	343	560	480	180	239	(NA)	187	178	152
Motor vehicle deaths within 1 yr. [3]	1,000	56.3	53.2	45.9	46.8	43.5	41.0	41.9	42.7	43.9
Noncollision accidents	1,000	15.8	14.7	12.6	4.9	4.7	4.1	4.2	4.3	4.4
Collision accidents:										
With other motor vehicles	1,000	23.9	23.0	19.9	19.9	18.2	17.6	18.3	19.3	19.4
With pedestrians	1,000	10.3	9.7	8.5	7.3	6.6	6.3	6.4	5.9	6.3
With fixed objects	1,000	3.9	3.7	3.2	13.1	12.6	11.7	11.5	11.8	12.3
Deaths within 30 days [4]	1,000	54.6	51.1	43.8	44.6	41.5	39.3	40.2	40.7	41.8
Vehicle occupants	1,000	41.4	36.8	31.5	33.9	31.9	30.5	31.1	32.0	33.1
Pedestrians	1,000	9.2	8.1	6.8	6.5	5.8	5.5	5.6	5.5	5.8
Motorcyclists [5]	1,000	3.0	5.1	4.6	3.2	2.8	2.4	2.4	2.3	2.2
Bicyclists	1,000	1.0	1.0	0.9	0.9	0.8	0.7	0.8	0.8	0.8
Traffic death rates: [4 6]										
Per 100,000 resident population	Rate	26.2	22.5	18.4	17.9	16.5	15.4	15.6	15.6	15.9
Per 100,000 registered vehicles	Rate	44.5	34.8	24.8	23.1	22.3	21.2	21.3	21.2	21.3
Per 100 million vehicle miles	Rate	4.3	3.3	2.5	2.1	1.9	1.7	1.7	1.7	1.7
Per 100,000 licensed drivers	Rate	46.1	35.2	27.9	26.7	24.6	22.7	23.2	23.2	23.6
Motor vehicle accidents [7]	Million	24.9	24.1	32.5	33.4	31.3	31.8	32.8	33.9	34.5
Injuries [7]	1,000	5,190	5,230	5,044	5,560	5,285	5,445	5,675	5,866	6,025
Economic loss [7 8]	Bil. dol.	28.7	57.1	76.0	95.9	93.8	96.1	104.1	110.5	115.6

NA Not available. [1] Represents peak year for deaths from motor vehicle accidents. [2] Covers only accidents occurring on the road. [3] Deaths that occur within 1 year of accident. Includes collision categories not shown separately. [4] Within 30 days of accident. Source: U.S. National Highway Traffic Safety Administration, unpublished data from Fatal Accident Reporting System. [5] Includes motor scooters and motorized bicycles (mopeds). [6] Based on 30-day definition of traffic deaths. [7] Source: Insurance Information Institute, New York, NY, *Insurance Facts*. Estimates based on official reports from a representative cross-section of States. Includes all motor vehicle accidents on and off the road and all injuries regardless of length of disability. [8] Wage loss; legal, medical, hospital, and funeral expenses; insurance administrative costs; and property damage.

Source: Except as noted, National Safety Council, Itasca, IL, *Accident Facts*, annual (copyright).

No. 1018. Motor Vehicle Deaths, by State: 1990 to 1995

[Includes both traffic and nontraffic motor vehicle deaths. See source for definitions]

REGION DIVISION STATE	1990	1993	1994	1995	MILEAGE RATE [1]	
					1990	1995
U.S.	47,151	42,200	42,700	43,900	2.2	1.8
Northeast	6,810	5,391	5,057	5,172	(NA)	(NA)
N.E.	1,817	1,310	1,197	1,248	(NA)	(NA)
ME	215	186	188	189	1.8	1.5
NH	154	122	119	118	1.6	1.1
VT	94	112	77	106	1.6	1.7
MA	655	474	440	448	1.4	0.9
RI	104	74	63	69	1.5	1.0
CT	395	342	310	318	1.5	1.1
M.A	4,993	4,081	3,860	3,924	(NA)	(NA)
NY	2,318	1,764	1,658	1,668	2.2	1.4
NJ	908	787	761	776	1.5	1.3
PA	1,767	1,530	1,441	1,480	2.1	1.6
Midwest	10,248	8,719	9,201	9,340	(NA)	(NA)
E.N.C	6,913	5,884	6,035	6,182	(NA)	(NA)
OH	1,708	1,484	1,371	1,357	2.0	1.4
IN	1,097	891	979	960	2.0	1.5
IL	1,650	1,392	1,554	1,589	2.0	1.7
MI	1,633	1,414	1,419	1,537	2.0	1.8
WI	825	703	712	739	1.9	1.4
W.N.C	3,335	2,835	3,166	3,158	(NA)	(NA)
MN	644	538	644	597	1.7	1.4
IA	481	437	478	527	2.1	2.0
MO	1,174	949	1,089	1,110	2.3	1.9
ND	128	89	88	74	2.2	1.1
SD	166	140	154	158	2.4	2.0
NE	289	254	271	254	2.1	1.6
KS	453	428	442	438	2.0	1.7
South	19,732	17,478	17,671	18,139	(NA)	(NA)
S.A.	9,760	8,424	8,506	8,707	(NA)	(NA)
DE	151	113	112	123	2.3	1.7
MD	741	672	656	682	1.8	1.5
DC	91	(NA)	-	-	2.7	(NA)
VA	1,091	875	930	900	1.8	1.3
WV	502	435	356	376	3.3	2.2
NC	1,489	1,384	1,431	1,438	2.4	2.0
SC	987	845	847	882	2.9	2.3
GA	1,659	1,407	1,438	1,494	2.3	1.8
FL	3,049	2,693	2,735	2,812	2.8	2.3
E.S.C	4,259	3,879	3,880	4,075	(NA)	(NA)
KY	850	875	791	856	2.5	2.1
TN	1,312	1,175	1,214	1,240	2.8	2.2
AL	1,234	1,016	1,083	1,111	2.9	2.2
MS	863	813	792	868	3.5	3.0
W.S.C	5,713	5,175	5,286	5,357	(NA)	(NA)
AR	625	583	611	631	3.0	2.5
LA	1,023	883	838	880	2.7	2.3
OK	684	672	695	674	2.1	1.8
TX	3,381	3,037	3,142	3,172	2.1	1.7
West	10,561	8,245	8,744	9,055	(NA)	(NA)
Mt	3,379	2,908	3,179	3,451	(NA)	(NA)
MT	225	194	202	215	2.7	2.3
ID	259	233	249	263	2.6	2.2
WY	130	120	144	170	2.2	2.5
CO	583	561	585	645	2.1	1.9
NM	534	433	447	485	3.3	2.3
AZ	947	801	915	1,040	2.7	2.6
UT	296	303	343	321	2.0	1.7
NV	405	263	294	312	4.0	2.4
Pac	7,182	5,337	5,565	5,604	(NA)	(NA)
WA	875	661	641	654	2.0	1.4
OR	608	522	491	572	2.3	1.9
CA	5,411	3,903	4,226	4,165	2.1	1.5
AK	102	117	85	86	2.6	2.0
HI	186	134	122	127	2.3	1.6

- Represents zero. NA Not available. [1] Deaths per 100 million vehicle miles.

Source: National Safety Council, Itasca, IL, *Accident Facts*, annual (copyright).

No. 1019. Fatal Motor Vehicle Accidents—National Summary: 1980 to 1995

[Based on data from the Fatal Accident Reporting System (FARS). FARS gathers data on accidents that result in loss of human life. FARS is operated and maintained by National Highway Traffic Safety Administration's (NHTSA) National Center for Statistics and Analysis (NCSA). FARS data are gathered on motor vehicle accidents that occurred on a roadway customarily open to the public, resulting in the death of a person within 30 days of the accident. Collection of these data depend on the use of police, hospital, medical examiner/coroner, and Emergency Medical Services reports; State vehicle registration, driver licensing, and highway department files; and vital statistics documents and death certificates. See source for further detail]

ITEM	1980	1985	1990	1991	1992	1993	1994	1995
Fatal accidents, total	45,284	39,196	39,836	36,937	34,942	35,780	36,254	37,221
One vehicle involved	28,306	22,875	23,445	21,910	20,388	20,569	20,526	21,245
Two or more vehicles involved	16,978	16,321	16,391	15,027	14,554	15,211	15,728	15,976
Persons killed in fatal accidents	51,091	43,825	44,599	41,508	39,250	40,150	40,716	41,798
Occupants [1]	41,927	36,043	37,134	34,740	32,880	33,574	34,318	35,274
Drivers	28,816	25,337	25,750	23,930	22,584	23,142	23,691	24,398
Passengers	12,972	10,619	11,276	10,888	10,211	10,361	10,518	10,759
Nonmotorists [1]	9,164	7,782	7,465	6,768	6,370	6,576	6,398	6,524
Pedestrians	8,070	6,808	6,482	5,801	5,549	5,649	5,489	5,585
Pedalcyclists	965	890	859	843	723	816	802	830
Occupant fatalities by type of vehicle, total	41,927	36,043	37,134	34,740	32,880	33,574	34,318	35,274
Passenger cars [1]	27,449	23,212	24,092	22,385	21,387	21,566	21,997	22,358
Mini-compact	3,141	3,571	3,556	3,039	2,714	2,635	2,339	2,163
Subcompact	4,158	4,422	4,753	4,655	4,314	4,333	4,721	4,488
Compact	927	2,635	5,310	5,338	5,354	5,707	6,322	6,767
Intermediate	3,878	4,391	4,849	4,681	4,418	4,483	4,407	4,583
Full size	4,831	2,974	2,386	2,073	2,120	2,067	2,074	2,074
Largest size	6,746	3,612	2,249	1,967	1,676	1,808	1,486	1,270
Motorcycles	4,961	4,417	3,129	2,703	2,291	2,336	2,190	2,108
Other motorized cycles	183	147	115	103	104	113	130	113
Multipurpose vehicles	895	855	1,214	1,478	1,335	1,521	1,757	1,931
Light trucks	6,591	5,834	7,387	6,915	6,763	6,990	7,147	7,606
Pickup	5,483	4,640	5,979	5,671	5,385	5,538	5,574	5,928
Van	1,000	791	1,154	1,154	1,292	1,365	1,508	1,625
Medium trucks	285	157	134	115	99	90	109	97
Heavy trucks	977	820	571	546	466	515	561	547
Buses	46	57	32	31	28	18	18	32
Persons involved in fatal accidents	113,289	104,045	107,777	99,369	95,691	97,589	98,945	101,931
Occupants [1]	103,049	95,482	99,297	91,707	88,367	90,150	91,644	94,465
Drivers	62,957	57,883	58,893	54,391	51,901	53,401	54,549	56,155
Passengers	39,892	37,477	40,229	37,108	36,330	36,599	36,898	38,104
Nonoccupants	10,240	8,563	8,480	7,662	7,324	7,439	7,301	7,466
Vehicle miles traveled (VMT) (100 million)	15,273	17,742	21,444	21,721	22,471	22,967	23,576	24,228
Licensed drivers (1,000)	145,295	156,868	167,015	168,995	173,125	173,149	175,403	177,432
Registered vehicles (1,000)	161,490	177,098	192,915	192,314	194,427	198,041	201,802	205,297
Fatalities by road type [1]	(NA)	(NA)	44,599	41,508	39,250	(NA)	(NA)	(NA)
Interstate	4,427	4,148	4,993	4,574	4,350	(NA)	(NA)	(NA)
Federal-aid primary	(NA)	14,526	14,203	13,158	12,052	(NA)	(NA)	(NA)
Federal-aid secondary	(NA)	6,429	6,892	6,249	5,849	(NA)	(NA)	(NA)
Federal-aid urban	(NA)	8,116	8,432	7,511	6,582	(NA)	(NA)	(NA)
Non-Federal-aid	(NA)	10,408	10,039	9,924	8,826	(NA)	(NA)	(NA)
Fatal accidents by the highest blood alcohol concentration (BAC) in accident:								
0.00 percent	(NA)	48.5	50.6	52.1	54.5	56.5	59.3	58.7
0.01 to 0.09 percent	(NA)	10.3	9.7	9.4	9.1	8.5	8.5	8.9
0.10 percent and over	(NA)	41.2	39.7	38.5	36.4	35.0	32.2	32.5
Rates:								
Fatality rate by age group:								
Under 5 years old	6.9	5.2	4.9	4.6	4.5	4.5	4.8	4.3
5 years to 15 years old	8.7	7.4	6.4	6.1	5.9	5.8	6.0	5.9
16 years to 24 years old	46.0	37.1	35.2	33.0	29.5	30.2	30.8	30.9
25 years to 44 years old	24.6	19.6	19.7	17.7	16.6	16.9	16.3	17.2
45 years to 64 years old	17.2	14.5	14.9	13.5	13.1	13.0	13.3	13.6
65 years to 79 years old	19.6	18.0	18.8	18.0	17.9	17.9	18.7	18.5
80 years old and over	25.3	25.1	26.8	26.9	26.0	28.0	28.2	28.2
Fatalities per 100 million VMT	3.3	2.5	2.1	1.9	1.8	1.7	1.7	1.7
Fatalities per 100,000 licensed drivers	35.2	27.9	26.7	24.6	22.7	23.2	23.2	23.7
Licensed driver per person	0.6	0.7	0.7	0.7	0.7	0.7	0.7	0.7
VMT per registered vehicle	9,458	10,018	11,107	11,294	11,558	12,189	11,683	11,801
Fatalities per 100,000 registered vehicles	31.6	24.8	23.1	21.6	20.2	21.3	20.2	21.3
Fatal crashes per 100 million VMT	2.9	2.2	1.9	1.7	1.6	1.6	1.5	1.5
Involved vehicles per fatal crash	1.4	1.5	1.5	1.5	1.5	1.5	1.5	1.5
Fatalities per fatal crash	1.2	1.1	1.1	1.1	1.1	1.1	1.1	1.1
Average occupants per fatal crash	2.3	2.4	2.5	2.5	2.5	2.5	2.5	2.5
Fatalities per 100,000 population	22.5	18.4	17.9	16.5	15.4	15.6	15.6	15.9

NA Not available. [1] Includes items not shown separately.

Source: National Highway Traffic Safety Administration, *Fatal Accident Reporting System*, annual.

No. 1020. Motor Vehicle Occupants and Non-Occupants Killed and Injured: 1985 to 1995

[Vehicle occupants accounted for almost 84 percent of traffic fatalities in 1995. The remaining 16 percent were pedestrians, pedalcyclists, and other non-occupants]

YEAR	Total	OCCUPANTS						NON-OCCUPANTS			
		Total	Passenger cars	Light trucks	Motorcycles	Buses	Other/ unknown	Total	Pedestrian	Pedalcyclist	Other
KILLED											
1985	43,825	36,043	23,212	6,689	4,564	57	544	7,782	6,808	890	84
1986	46,087	38,234	24,944	7,317	4,566	39	442	7,853	6,779	941	133
1987	46,390	38,565	25,132	8,058	4,036	51	436	7,825	6,745	948	132
1988	47,087	39,170	25,808	8,306	3,662	54	429	7,917	6,870	911	136
1989	45,582	38,087	25,063	8,551	3,141	50	424	7,495	6,556	832	107
1990	44,599	37,134	24,092	8,601	3,244	32	460	7,465	6,482	859	124
1991	41,508	34,740	22,385	8,391	2,806	31	466	6,768	5,801	843	124
1992	39,250	32,880	21,387	8,098	2,395	28	387	6,370	5,549	723	98
1993	40,150	33,574	21,566	8,511	2,449	18	425	6,576	5,649	816	111
1994	40,716	34,318	21,997	8,904	2,320	18	409	6,398	5,489	802	107
1995	41,798	35,274	22,358	9,539	2,221	32	480	6,524	5,585	830	109
INJURED											
1988	3,416,000	3,224,000	2,585,000	478,000	105,000	15,000	4,000	192,000	110,000	75,000	8,000
1989	3,284,000	3,088,000	2,431,000	511,000	83,000	15,000	5,000	196,000	112,000	73,000	11,000
1990	3,231,000	3,044,000	2,376,000	505,000	84,000	33,000	4,000	187,000	105,000	75,000	7,000
1991	3,097,000	2,931,000	2,235,000	563,000	80,000	21,000	4,000	166,000	88,000	67,000	11,000
1992	3,070,000	2,908,000	2,232,000	545,000	65,000	20,000	12,000	162,000	89,000	63,000	10,000
1993	3,125,000	2,958,000	2,257,000	590,000	58,000	17,000	4,000	166,000	93,000	65,000	9,000
1994	3,215,000	3,056,000	2,332,000	619,000	56,000	15,000	3,000	159,000	90,000	60,000	9,000
1995	3,386,000	3,232,000	2,416,000	709,000	55,000	18,000	4,000	154,000	84,000	61,000	9,000

U.S. National Highway Traffic Safety Administration, *Traffic Safety Facts 1995, Overview.*

No. 1021. Traffic Fatalities in Crashes Involving a Medium/Heavy Truck, by State: 1994

[Medium/heavy trucks represents trucks over 10,000 pounds GVW, including single unit trucks]

STATE	Total	Occupant fatalities med/ heavy trucks	Occupant fatalities other vehicles	Non-occupant fatalities	STATE	Total	Occupant fatalities med/ heavy trucks	Occupant fatalities other vehicles	Non-occupant fatalities
United States	5,112	663	3,988	461	Montana	20	5	14	1
Alabama	170	24	139	7	Nebraska	52	7	41	4
Alaska	5	-	3	2	Nevada	28	1	20	7
Arizona	93	9	71	13	New Hampshire	8	2	5	1
Arkansas	91	10	79	2					
California	386	69	275	42	New Jersey	81	7	68	6
Colorado	61	9	49	3	New Mexico	44	7	27	10
Connecticut	27	4	15	8	New York	205	18	137	50
Delaware	11	1	10	-	North Carolina	206	19	168	19
District of Columbia	2	1	-	1	North Dakota	9	1	8	-
Florida	307	33	236	38	Ohio	220	28	178	14
					Oklahoma	84	17	65	2
Georgia	214	24	178	12	Oregon	64	15	43	6
Hawaii	5	-	5	-	Pennsylvania	221	26	172	23
Idaho	38	8	30	-	Rhode Island	6	1	3	2
Illinois	178	14	146	18					
Indiana	147	24	110	13	South Carolina	104	12	84	8
Iowa	77	3	69	5	South Dakota	17	3	12	2
Kansas	60	13	46	1	Tennessee	145	18	118	9
Kentucky	109	8	97	4	Texas	411	66	311	34
Louisiana	117	13	95	9	Utah	32	6	23	3
Maine	27	-	25	2	Vermont	10	1	8	1
					Virginia	131	21	96	14
Maryland	76	10	60	6	Washington	54	10	36	8
Massachusetts	45	9	30	6	West Virginia	61	8	48	5
Michigan	186	18	151	17	Wisconsin	111	11	93	7
Minnesota	88	5	78	5	Wyoming	22	6	15	1
Mississippi	98	19	76	3					
Missouri	148	19	122	7					

- Represents zero

U.S. National Highway Traffic Safety Administration, *Traffic Safety Facts 1994.*

No. 1022. Speeding-Related Traffic Fatalities and Costs by Road Type and Speed Limit: 1995

[Includes fatalities that occurred on roads for which the speed limit was unknown. Includes costs for crashes that occurred on unknown road types. Totals may not equal sum of components due to independent rounding]

STATE	Traffic fatalities, total	SPEEDING-RELATED FATALITIES BY ROAD TYPE AND SPEED							
		Interstate		Non-Interstate					
		Over 55 mph	55 mph	55 mph	50 mph	45 mph	40 mph	35 mph	Under 35 mph
United States	41,798	855	684	5,614	518	1,369	729	1,405	1,430
Alabama	1,113	25	5	206	12	39	34	36	20
Alaska	87	-	12	5	3	5	2	3	-
Arizona	1,031	39	14	62	24	59	42	46	39
Arkansas	631	6	5	110	3	24	13	10	16
California	4,192	115	147	678	76	120	109	211	150
Colorado	645	33	11	75	17	21	22	38	41
Connecticut	317	-	14	4	7	8	16	12	36
Delaware	121	-	1	7	10	2	-	4	4
District of Columbia	58	-	-	-	-	-	-	-	20
Florida	2,805	46	15	177	16	141	52	75	90
Georgia	1,488	13	15	161	7	74	11	44	31
Hawaii	130	-	1	4	-	5	2	28	16
Idaho	262	8	1	39	13	5	2	16	5
Illinois	1,586	24	41	255	2	22	8	8	120
Indiana	960	20	8	10	3	-	-	1	2
Iowa	527	2	-	33	10	2	-	6	11
Kansas	442	7	5	63	2	9	3	10	20
Kentucky	849	24	8	139	1	14	1	17	4
Louisiana	883	10	11	92	4	29	10	43	12
Maine	187	1	-	10	13	18	3	7	3
Maryland	671	1	5	16	15	7	19	12	35
Massachusetts	444	1	18	5	4	3	10	23	38
Michigan	1,530	23	23	225	11	31	7	34	56
Minnesota	597	3	7	94	4	4	4	4	31
Mississippi	868	15	1	55	11	15	6	11	5
Missouri	1,109	21	22	272	5	21	16	36	28
Montana	215	7	-	55	3	-	1	1	1
Nebraska	254	3	-	18	20	3	1	2	9
Nevada	313	27	5	40	7	15	5	27	20
New Hampshire	118	1	3	2	5	2	2	3	9
New Jersey	773	-	4	2	18	8	8	3	16
New Mexico	485	32	5	38	6	21	12	24	25
New York	1,674	7	21	196	19	31	35	22	118
North Carolina	1,448	28	11	344	3	107	3	67	10
North Dakota	74	1	-	16	-	-	1	-	1
Ohio	1,366	13	14	184	9	26	13	48	28
Oklahoma	669	19	20	200	10	26	20	16	15
Oregon	572	10	7	113	1	13	7	16	11
Pennsylvania	1,480	14	37	177	13	101	58	109	47
Rhode Island	69	-	2	1	2	1	3	5	10
South Carolina	881	27	7	194	8	97	13	41	20
South Dakota	158	5	3	39	4	2	1	1	5
Tennessee	1,259	19	10	117	18	73	39	39	39
Texas	3,181	105	100	645	27	81	75	111	115
Utah	326	18	14	1	1	5	5	3	8
Vermont	106	4	-	-	21	1	3	5	6
Virginia	900	21	14	153	3	33	6	24	17
Washington	653	17	12	59	46	15	9	59	30
West Virginia	376	12	-	57	1	11	7	19	13
Wisconsin	745	5	5	114	2	14	6	24	16
Wyoming	170	25	-	50	-	5	4	1	8

- Represents or rounds to zero.

U.S. National Highway Traffic Safety Administration, *Traffic Safety Facts 1995, Speeding.*

No. 1023. Highway Mileage, Vehicle Miles of Travel, Accidents, and Fatalities, 1980 to 1994, and by Type of Highway System, 1994

YEAR AND TYPE OF SYSTEM	Highway mileage (1,000)	Vehicle miles of travel (bil.)	Daily vehicle miles per mile	FATAL ACCIDENTS		NONFATAL INJURY ACCIDENTS		FATALITIES [2]	
				Number	Rate [1]	Number (1,000)	Rate [1]	Number	Rate [1]
1980	3,857	1,527	1,082	45,284	2.96	2,006	131	51,091	3.35
1985	3,862	1,774	1,259	39,168	2.21	2,219	125	43,825	2.47
1986	3,880	1,835	1,298	41,062	2.23	2,254	123	46,087	2.51
1987	3,874	1,921	1,361	41,434	2.15	2,294	119	46,390	2.41
1988	3,871	2,026	1,430	42,119	2.08	2,302	114	47,087	2.32
1989	3,877	2,096	1,469	40,718	1.93	2,384	113	45,582	2.16
1990	3,880	2,148	1,516	39,779	1.85	2,501	116	44,529	2.07
1991	3,889	2,172	1,530	36,895	1.70	2,210	102	41,462	(NA)
1992	3,902	2,240	1,568	34,928	1.56	2,216	99	39,235	1.75
1993	3,905	2,297	1,611	35,750	1.56	(NA)	(NA)	40,115	1.75
1994, total	**3,967**	**2,360**	**1,655**	**36,223**	**1.53**	**(NA)**	**(NA)**	**40,676**	**1.72**
Urban	814	1,451	4,864	15,627	1.08	(NA)	(NA)	16,983	1.17
Rural	3,092	909	805	20,596	2.26	(NA)	(NA)	23,693	2.61
Interstate	45	547	33,303	4,047	0.74	(NA)	(NA)	4,641	0.85
Urban	14	331	64,775	1,907	0.58	(NA)	(NA)	2,107	0.64
Rural	32	216	18,493	2,140	0.99	(NA)	(NA)	2,534	1.17
Noninterstate	3,860	1,813	1,287	32,176	1.80	(NA)	(NA)	36,035	1.99
Urban	800	1,120	3,836	13,720	1.72	(NA)	(NA)	14,876	1.33
Rural	3,060	693	620	18,456	2.66	(NA)	(NA)	21,159	3.05

NA Not available. [1] Rate per 100 million vehicle miles of travel. [2] Represents fatalities occurring within 30 days of accident. Excludes nontraffic accidents which, for example, occur outside the rights-of-way or other boundaries of roads that are open for public use.

Source: U.S. Federal Highway Administration, *Fatal and Injury Accident Rates on Public Roads in the United States*, annual.

No. 1024. Motor Vehicle Safety Defect Recalls, by Domestic and Foreign Manufacturers: 1980 to 1996

[Covers manufacturers reporting to U.S. National Highway Traffic Administration under section 151 of National Traffic and Motor Vehicle Safety Act of 1966, as amended]

MANUFACTURER	Unit	1980	1985	1989	1990	1991	1992	1993	1994	1995	1996
Motor vehicles:											
Total recall campaigns [1]	Number	**167**	**173**	**237**	**208**	**220**	**187**	**221**	**244**	**266**	**265**
Domestic	Number	129	137	182	159	168	142	178	178	190	197
Foreign	Number	38	36	55	49	52	45	43	66	76	68
Total vehicles recalled	1,000	**4,868**	**5,629**	**7,137**	**5,985**	**8,279**	**10,122**	**10,922**	**6,063**	**18,295**	**17,084**
Domestic	1,000	3,943	4,995	6,173	4,070	6,646	6,545	7,655	4,280	9,041	15,104
Foreign	1,000	925	634	964	1,915	1,633	3,577	3,267	1,784	9,259	1,980
Motor vehicle tires:											
Recall campaigns [1]	Number	24	19	11	13	12	7	5	5	3	1
Tires recalled	1,000	7,070	28	115	172	153	8	6	93	10	6

[1] A recall campaign is the notification to the Secretary of the U.S. Dept. of Transportation and to owners, purchasers, and dealers of motor vehicles and motor vehicle equipment.

Source: U.S. National Highway Traffic Safety Administration, *Motor Vehicles Recall Campaigns*, annual.

No. 1025. Cost of Owning and Operating an Automobile: 1980 to 1996

ITEM	Unit	1980	1985	1990	1992	1993	1994	1995	1996
Cost per mile [1]	Cents	27.95	27.20	40.96	45.77	45.14	46.65	48.91	51.43
Cost per 10,000 miles [1]	Dollars	2,795	2,720	4,096	4,577	4,514	4,665	4,891	5,143
Variable cost	Cents/mile	7.62	8.04	8.40	9.10	9.30	9.20	10.00	10.10
Gas and oil	Cents/mile	5.86	6.16	5.40	6.00	6.00	5.60	6.00	5.90
Maintenance	Cents/mile	1.12	1.23	2.10	2.20	2.40	2.50	2.60	2.80
Tires	Cents/mile	0.64	0.65	0.90	0.90	0.90	1.10	1.40	1.40
Fixed cost	Dollars	2,033	2,441	3,877	4,538	4,486	4,584	4,755	4,997
Insurance	Dollars	490	503	675	747	724	697	716	782
License and registration	Dollars	82	115	165	179	183	204	211	229
Depreciation	Dollars	1,038	1,253	2,357	2,780	2,883	2,988	3,099	3,208
Finance charge	Dollars	423	570	680	832	696	695	729	778

[1] Beginning 1985, not comparable to previous data.

Source: American Automobile Manufacturers Association Inc., Detroit, MI, *Motor Vehicle Facts and Figures*, annual (copyright).

No. 1026. State Legislation—Alcohol and Road Safety Laws: Various Years

STATE	ALCOHOL LEGISLATION				MANDATORY BELT USE LAW		Motor-cycle helmet law [5]	Work zone speed law	1995/96 Speed limit changes: Road types affected [6]
	Adminis-trative license revocation since [1]	BAC limit [2]	Zero tolerance limit for minors [3]	Alcohol ignition interlock device [4]	Enforce-ment	Seating positions			
Alabama	No	.10	No	No	Secondary	Front	Yes	Yes	1, 2
Alaska	5/83	.10	(NA)	Yes	Secondary	All	18	No	No change
Arizona	1992	.10	.00	No	Secondary	Front	18	No	3
Arkansas	3/95	.10	.02	Yes	Secondary	Front	Yes	(NA)	No change
California	1989	.08	.01	Yes	Primary	All	Yes	Yes	4
Colorado	Yes	.10	No	Yes	Secondary	Front	No	Yes	(NA)
Connecticut	1/90	.10	.02	No	Primary	[7]Front	18	[8]No	No change
Delaware	Yes	.10	.02	Yes	Secondary	Front	[9 10]19	Yes	1
District of Columbia	Yes	.10	.00	No	Secondary	[11]Front	Yes	Yes	No change
Florida	Yes	.08	No	Yes	Secondary	Front	Yes	Yes	5
Georgia	(NA)	.10	.04	Yes	Secondary	Front	Yes	Yes	1
Hawaii	8/90	.08	No	No	Primary	Front	18	No	No change
Idaho	7/94	.10	.02	Yes	Secondary	Front	18	No	1
Illinois	1/86	.10	.00	Yes	Secondary	Front	No	Yes	6
Indiana	Yes	.10	.02	Yes	Secondary	Front	18	Yes	No change
Iowa	(NA)	.10	.02	Yes	Primary	Front	No	[8]No	No change
Kansas	1988	.08	No	Yes	Secondary	Front	18	Yes	7
Kentucky	No	.10	.02	No	Secondary	All	Yes	No	No change
Louisiana	1/84	.10	[12].04	Yes	Primary	Front	Yes	No	No change
Maine [13]	(NA)	.08	(NA)	No	(NA)	(NA)	[9 14]15	(NA)	No change
Maryland	5/89	[15].10	.01	Yes	Secondary	[7 11]Front	Yes	No	No change
Massachusetts [13]	(NA)	.10	(NA)	No	Secondary	All	Yes	(NA)	No change
Michigan	No	.10	.02	Yes	Secondary	[7]Front	Yes	Yes	No change
Minnesota	1976	.10	.01	No	Secondary	[7]Front	[9]18	Yes	No change
Mississippi	No	.10	.08	No	Secondary	Front	Yes	Yes	1, 2
Missouri	1987	.10	No	No	Secondary	Front	Yes	Yes	2, 10
Montana	No	.10	.02	No	Secondary	All	18	Yes	All
Nebraska	1/93	.10	.02	Yes	Secondary	Front	Yes	No	1
Nevada	1983	.10	No	Yes	Secondary	All	Yes	No	1
New Hampshire	1/94	.08	.01	No	(NA)	(NA)	18	Yes	1
New Jersey	(NA)	.10	.01	No	Secondary	Front	Yes	[8]No	No change
New Mexico [13]	(NA)	.08	.02	No	Primary	Front	18	(NA)	(NA)
New York	11/94	[15].10	(NA)	[17]Yes	Primary	[7]Front	Yes	(NA)	1
North Carolina	1983	.08	No	Yes	Primary	Front	Yes	Yes	8
North Dakota	1983	.10	No	No	Secondary	Front	18	Yes	No change
Ohio	9/93	.10	.02	Yes	Secondary	Front	[14]18	[8]No	No change
Oklahoma	(NA)	.10	.00	Yes	Secondary	Front	18	Yes	9
Oregon	1983	.08	.00	Yes	Primary	All	Yes	No	No change
Pennsylvania	No	.10	No	No	Secondary	Front	Yes	Yes	10
Rhode Island	No	.10	.04	[17]Yes	Secondary	All	([18])	No	1
South Carolina	No	.10	No	No	Secondary	[19]Front	21	Yes	No change
South Dakota	No	.10	No	No	Secondary	Front	18	Yes	1
Tennessee	No	.10	.02	Yes	Secondary	[7]Front	Yes	Yes	2, 8
Texas	1995	.10	.07	[17]Yes	Primary	Front	Yes	Yes	1
Utah	1983	.08	.00	Yes	Secondary	Front	18	(NA)	1
Vermont	[16]Yes	.08	[12].02	No	Secondary	[7]All	Yes	No	No change
Virginia	1/95	.08	.02	Yes	Secondary	Front	Yes	No	No change
Washington	[20]6/94	.10	.02	Yes	Secondary	All	Yes	Yes	1
West Virginia	(NA)	.10	.02	Yes	Secondary	[7]Front	Yes	Yes	No change
Wisconsin	1/88	[21].10	[22].00	[17]Yes	Secondary	[19]Front	[9]18	Yes	1, 4
Wyoming	1973	.10	No	No	Secondary	Front	18	No	1, 4

NA Not available. [1]Year original law became effective, not when grandfather clauses expired. [2]Blood alcohol concentration that constitutes the threshold of legal intoxication. [3]Blood alcohol concentration that constitutes "zero tolerance" threshold for minors less than 21 years old unless noted. [4]Legislation for instruments designed to prevent drivers from starting their cars when breath alcohol content is at or above a set point. [5]Presence of law or age below which riders are required to wear helmet. [6]"1" means rural interstates; "2" means four-lane highways; "3" means rural highways; "4" means inter/intra state freeways; "5" means rural interstates/turnpikes; "6" means county and township roads with no posted speed limit; "7" means separate multilane highways designated/posted by secretary of transportation; "8" means interstates within municipal city limits; "9" means turnpikes; "10" means interstates outside urban areas of population 50,000 or more plus others where posted. [7]Required for certain ages at all seating positions. [8]No work zone speed law per se, but double fine for violation. [9]Plus instruction permit holders. [10]Helmet possession required by all. [11]Excluding front center seat. [12]Blood alcohol concentration that constitutes "zero tolerance" threshold for minors less than 18 years of age. [13]Data from 1994/1995. [14]Plus novice license holders. [15]BAC of .07 is prima facie evidence of DUI (MD); BAC of .05-.10 constitutes driving while ability impaired (NY). [16]Revocation by judicial action (NY) or Dept. of Motor Vehicles (VT). [17]For repeat offenders. [18]Operators under 21 for first offense; passengers. [19]Belt use required in rear seat if lap/shoulder belt is available. [20]Applies only to second DUI offense. [21]Different legal limit for repeat offenders. [22]Blood alcohol concentration that constitutes "zero tolerance" threshold for minors less than 19 years of age.

Source: National Safety Council, Itasca, IL, *Accident Facts* (copyright).

No. 1027. Estimated Arrests for Driving Under the Influence, by Age: 1980 and 1989

[Total drivers and arrests in thousands. Represents licensed drivers and arrests for those 16 years old and over]

AGE	1980			1989			Percent change in rate, 1980-89
	Drivers	Arrests	Arrests per 100,000 drivers	Drivers	Arrests	Arrests per 100,000 drivers	
Total	145,207	1,425	981	165,518	1,736	1,048	6.9
Percent distribution	100.0	100.0	(X)	100.0	100.0	(X)	(X)
16 to 17 years old	3.2	2.2	668	2.3	1.1	503	-24.7
18 to 24 years old	7.2	12.9	1,757	5.4	8.3	1,607	-8.5
25 to 29 years old	13.0	17.9	1,347	12.4	22.2	1,869	38.8
30 to 34 years old	12.0	13.1	1,076	12.4	17.6	1,488	38.1
35 to 39 years old	9.4	9.6	996	11.2	12.0	1,123	12.8
40 to 44 years old	7.7	7.4	944	9.7	8.1	872	-7.6
45 to 49 years old	6.9	5.9	837	7.6	5.3	725	-13.4
50 to 54 years old	6.9	4.9	668	6.2	3.3	558	-16.7
55 to 59 years old	6.7	3.5	509	5.7	2.2	400	-21.4
60 to 64 years old	5.7	1.9	335	5.6	1.4	262	-21.8
65 years old and over	10.7	1.5	140	13.0	1.2	100	-28.6

X Not applicable.

Source: U.S. Bureau of Justice Statistics, *Drunk Driving, Special Report.*

No. 1028. Police-Reported Traffic Accidents, by Age Group: 1995

[Based on probability sample of police-reported accidents. See source for details]

ITEM	Total	15 yrs. and under	16 to 20 yrs.	21 to 24 yrs.	25 to 34 yrs.	35 to 44 yrs.	45 to 54 yrs.	55 to 64 yrs.	65 yrs. and older
Crash-involved	11,782,000	75,000	2,000,000	1,296,000	2,920,000	2,328,000	1,546,000	762,000	856,000
Percent male	61	68	62	60	61	60	62	65	62
Percent female	39	32	38	40	39	40	38	35	38
Percent alcohol-involved	4	5	4	5	5	4	4	2	1
Passengers injured or killed	3,269,000	339,000	569,000	353,000	699,000	544,000	345,000	190,000	230,000
Percent male	48	47	48	52	50	47	46	45	43
Percent female	52	53	52	48	50	53	54	55	57
Pedestrians injured or killed	90,000	30,000	7,000	6,000	17,000	13,000	6,000	3,000	8,000
Percent during day	60	69	56	49	49	48	56	62	81
Percent at night	40	31	44	51	51	52	44	38	19
Pedalcyclists injured or killed	63,000	29,000	8,000	6,000	7,000	7,000	3,000	1,000	2,000

Source: U.S. National Highway Traffic Safety Administration, *General Estimates System*, annual; and unpublished data.

No. 1029. Domestic Motor Fuel Consumption, by Type of Vehicle: 1970 to 1994

[Comprises all fuel types used for propulsion of vehicles under State motor fuels laws. Excludes Federal purchases for military use. Minus sign (-) indicates decrease]

YEAR	FUEL CONSUMPTION					AVG. FUEL CONSUMPTION PER VEHICLE (gal.)			AVG. MILES PER GALLON		
	All vehicles (bil. gal.)	Avg. annual percent change [1]	Cars [2] (bil. gal.)	Buses [3] (bil. gal.)	Trucks [4] (bil. gal.)	Cars [2]	Buses [3]	Trucks [4]	Cars [2]	Buses [3]	Trucks [4]
1970	92.3	5.4	67.8	0.8	23.6	760	2,172	1,257	13.5	5.5	7.9
1975	109.0	2.5	76.4	1.1	31.4	716	2,279	1,217	13.5	5.8	9.0
1980	115.0	-5.9	71.9	1.0	41.9	591	1,926	1,243	15.5	6.0	9.5
1981	114.5	-0.4	71.0	1.1	42.2	576	1,938	1,219	15.9	5.9	9.6
1982	113.4	-0.9	70.1	1.0	42.1	566	1,756	1,191	16.7	5.9	9.8
1983	116.1	2.4	69.9	0.9	45.1	553	1,507	1,229	17.1	5.9	9.8
1984	118.7	2.3	68.7	0.8	49.0	536	1,359	1,308	17.8	5.9	9.8
1985	121.3	2.2	69.3	0.8	51.0	525	1,407	1,302	18.2	5.8	9.8
1986	125.2	3.2	71.4	0.9	52.9	526	1,463	1,320	18.3	5.8	9.8
1987	127.5	1.8	70.6	0.9	55.8	514	1,500	1,357	19.2	5.9	9.9
1988	130.1	2.0	71.9	0.9	57.2	509	1,496	1,345	20.0	5.9	10.2
1989	131.8	1.3	72.7	0.9	57.9	509	1,518	1,328	20.4	6.0	10.4
1990	130.8	-0.8	72.0	0.9	57.7	502	1,428	1,290	21.0	6.4	10.7
1991	128.6	-1.7	70.7	0.9	56.8	496	1,369	1,264	21.7	6.7	11.0
1992	132.9	3.2	73.9	0.9	58.0	512	1,360	1,275	21.7	6.6	10.9
1993	[3]137.2	3.1	73.6	0.9	26.0	559	1,447	4,249	21.0	6.5	6.2
1994	[3]140.1	2.1	73.8	1.0	27.6	551	1,454	4,375	21.5	6.6	6.2

[1] From prior year, except 1970, change from 1965. [2] Includes taxicabs. The format used to report some vehicle types was changed. In previous years, some other 2-axle 4-tire vehicles were included in the passenger car category. Other 2-axle 4-tire vehicles are now separate from the truck category. [3] Includes school buses. [4] Includes combinations.

Source: U.S. Federal Highway Administration, *Highway Statistics Summary to 1985*, and *Highway Statistics, annual.*

No. 1030. Motor Vehicle Travel, by Type of Vehicle and by Speed: 1970 to 1994

[Travel in billions of vehicle-miles, except as indicated. Travel estimates based on automatic traffic recorder data. Speed trend data for 1970 were collected by several State highway agencies, normally during summer months; beginning Oct. 1975 all States have monitored speeds at locations on several highway systems Monitoring Program. Through 1992, the truck category included "other 2-axle, 4-tire vehicles" (vans, pickups and sport/utility vehicles); thereafter, these vehicles excluded from the truck category]

YEAR	VEHICLE-MILES OF TRAVEL (bil.)				AVG. MILES PER VEHICLE (1,000)			MOTOR VEHICLE SPEED ON RURAL INTERSTATE				
	Total	Cars [1]	Buses	Trucks	Passenger vehicles: Cars [1]	Passenger vehicles: Buses	Trucks	Citations recorded (1,000) [2]	Avg. speed (miles per hour)	Percent of vehicles exceeding— 55 mph	60 mph	65 mph
1970	1,110	917	4.5	186	10.3	12.0	9.9	200	63.8	87	69	44
1980	1,527	1,111	6.1	399	9.1	11.5	11.9	667	57.5	66	25	7
1985	1,774	1,261	4.9	500	9.6	6.2	12.7	8,449	59.5	75	44	17
1986	1,835	1,301	5.1	519	9.6	6.5	13.0	8,549	59.7	76	46	18
1987	1,921	1,355	5.3	551	9.9	6.8	13.4	7,992	59.7	74	46	19
1988	2,026	1,430	5.5	581	10.1	6.9	13.7	7,566	59.5	74	46	19
1989	2,096	1,478	5.7	603	10.3	9.0	13.8	7,488	60.1	77	49	22
1990	2,144	1,513	5.7	616	10.5	9.1	13.8	7,511	60.4	78	50	23
1991	2,172	1,543	5.7	624	10.8	9.1	13.9	7,594	59.9	76	48	21
1992	2,247	1,601	5.8	631	11.1	8.9	13.9	7,004	61.2	81	56	28
1993	2,297	1,547	6.1	160	11.8	9.4	26.1	6,433	60.8	78	51	24
1994	2,360	1,586	6.4	170	11.8	9.6	27.0	(NA)	(NA)	(NA)	(NA)	(NA)

NA Not available. [1] Includes motorcycles. [2] Citations issued for 55 mph violations.

Source: U.S. Federal Highway Administration, *Highway Statistics Summary, annual.*

No. 1031. Passenger Transit Industry—Summary: 1985 to 1995

[Includes Puerto Rico. Includes aggregate information for all transit systems in the United States. Excludes nontransit services such as taxicab, school bus, unregulated jitney, sightseeing bus, intercity bus, and special application mass transportation systems (e.g., amusement parks, airports, island, and urban park ferries) Includes active vehicles only]

ITEM	Unit	1985	1990	1991	1992	1993	1994	1995
Operating systems	Number	4,972	5,078	5,084	5,086	5,088	5,973	5,973
Motor bus systems	Number	2,631	2,688	2,689	2,693	1,934	2,250	2,250
Passenger vehicles owned [1]	Number	94,368	92,961	96,399	102,251	107,316	115,943	114,624
Motor bus	Number	64,258	58,714	60,377	63,080	64,850	68,123	67,086
Trolley bus	Number	676	832	752	907	851	877	885
Heavy rail	Number	9,326	10,419	10,331	10,245	10,261	10,138	10,157
Light rail	Number	717	913	1,095	1,058	1,025	1,054	999
Commuter rail	Number	4,035	4,415	4,370	4,413	4,494	4,517	4,565
Demand response	Number	14,490	16,471	17,879	20,695	23,527	28,729	28,233
Operating funding, total	Mil. dol	12,195	16,053	16,533	16,915	17,276	17,968	17,630
Passenger funding	Mil. dol	4,575	5,891	6,037	6,152	6,351	6,756	6,850
Other operating funding [2]	Mil. dol	702	895	767	646	764	2,271	2,362
Operating assistance	Mil. dol	6,918	9,267	9,729	10,117	10,161	8,941	8,418
Federal	Mil. dol	940	970	956	969	966	916	735
Local	Mil. dol	[3]5,979	5,327	5,573	5,268	5,491	4,171	3,871
State	Mil. dol	(3)	2,970	3,200	3,898	3,704	3,854	3,812
Total expense	Mil. dol	14,077	17,979	19,332	20,034	20,679	21,653	21,785
Operating expense	Mil. dol	12,381	15,742	16,541	16,781	17,350	17,920	18,052
Vehicle operations	Mil. dol	5,655	6,654	6,727	7,660	7,941	8,212	8,505
Maintenance	Mil. dol	3,672	4,631	4,597	4,831	4,894	5,004	5,166
General administration	Mil. dol	2,505	3,450	3,585	2,674	2,714	2,752	2,716
Purchased transportation	Mil. dol	549	1,008	1,633	1,616	1,800	1,952	1,666
Reconciling expense	Mil. dol	1,696	2,237	2,791	3,253	3,329	3,733	3,733
Capital expenditure, Federal	Mil. dol	2,510	2,380	2,396	2,613	3,465	3,577	5,461
Vehicle-miles operated [1]	Mil. dol	2,791	3,242	3,306	3,355	3,435	3,467	3,532
Motor bus	Million	1,863	2,130	2,167	2,178	2,210	2,162	2,178
Trolley bus	Million	16	14	14	14	13	14	14
Heavy rail	Million	451	537	527	525	522	532	537
Light rail	Million	17	24	28	29	28	34	35
Commuter rail	Million	183	213	215	219	224	231	238
Demand response	Million	247	306	335	364	406	464	495
Passengers carried [1]	Million	8,636	8,799	8,575	8,501	8,217	7,949	7,869
Motor bus	Million	5,675	5,677	5,624	5,517	5,381	4,871	4,968
Trolley bus	Million	142	126	125	126	121	118	119
Heavy rail	Million	2,290	2,346	2,172	2,207	2,046	2,169	2,033
Light rail	Million	132	175	184	188	188	284	251
Commuter rail	Million	275	328	318	314	322	339	344
Demand response	Million	59	68	71	72	81	88	79
Avg. funding per passenger	Cents	53.0	66.9	70.4	72.4	77.3	85.0	87.1
Employees, number (avg.) [4]	1,000	270	273	276	279	299	304	306
Payroll, employee	Mil. dol	5,843	7,226	7,395	7,671	7,932	8,224	8,414
Fringe benefits, employee	Mil. dol	2,868	3,986	3,998	4,319	4,400	4,452	4,630

[1] Includes other not shown separately. [2] Includes other operating revenue, nonoperating revenue, and auxiliary income. [3] For 1985, State and local combined. [4] Thru 1992, represents employee equivalents of 2,080 hours = one employee; beginning 1993, equals actual employees.

Source: American Public Transit Association, Washington, DC, *Transit Fact Book,* annual.

No. 1032. Class I Intercity Motor Carriers of Passengers: 1980 to 1995

[Carriers subject to ICC regulations. See text, section 21. Minus sign (-) indicates deficit]

ITEM	Unit	1980	1985	1987	1988	1989	1990	1991	1992	1993	1994	1995
Carriers reporting [1]	Number.	48	43	32	21	20	21	21	21	21	20	20
Number of employees, average	1,000	31	24	(NA)	(NA)	(NA)	(NA)	(NA)	(NA)	(NA)	(NA)	(NA)
Compensation of employees	Mil. dol	599	518	(NA)	(NA)	(NA)	(NA)	(NA)	(NA)	(NA)	(NA)	(NA)
Operating revenue	Mil. dol	1,397	1,233	1,079	1,122	1,205	943	980	938	928	870	917
Passenger revenue [2]	Mil. dol	947	836	751	825	890	738	793	755	751	721	770
Special bus revenue and other	Mil. dol	215	184	165	155	165	90	187	183	177	149	147
Operating expenses	*Mil. dol*	*1,318*	*1,168*	*1,081*	*1,059*	*1,133*	*1,015*	*967*	*874*	*880*	*919*	*899*
Net operating revenue	Mil. dol	79	65	-2	63	72	(72)	13	64	48	-49	18
Ordinary income:												
Before income taxes	Mil. dol	107	65	-11	(NA)	(NA)	(NA)	(NA)	(NA)	(NA)	(NA)	(NA)
After income taxes	Mil. dol	90	53	-21	(NA)	12	-180	162	21	14	-67	9
Passenger vehicles in service [2]	1,000	8.6	8.4	(NA)	(NA)	(NA)	(NA)	(NA)	(NA)	(NA)	(NA)	(NA)
Vehicle-miles, passenger	Million	781	567	(NA)	(NA)	(NA)	(NA)	(NA)	(NA)	(NA)	(NA)	(NA)
Revenue passengers carried	Million	134	86	82	55	54	43	42	41	40	41	43
Expense per vehicle-mile	Dollar	1.69	2.06	(NA)	(NA)	(NA)	(NA)	(NA)	(NA)	(NA)	(NA)	(NA)

NA Not available. [1] Excludes carriers preponderantly in local or suburban service and carriers engaged in transportation of both property and passengers. [2] Regular route, intercity, and local.

Source: Through 1993,U.S. Interstate Commerce Commission, *Transport Statistics in the United States*, part 2, annual, thereafter, Bureau of Transportation Statistics, *National Transportation Statistics*, annual.

No. 1033. Passenger Transportation Arrangement: 1993 to 1995

[In millions of dollars, except percent. Represents SIC 4722]

SOURCE OF RECEIPTS	1993	1994	1995	OPERATING EXPENSES	1993	1994	1995
Receipts, total [1]	**11,073**	**11,798**	**12,891**	**Expenses, total** [1]	**10,136**	**10,889**	**11,855**
Air carriers	6,138	6,375	6,846	Payroll, annual	4,031	4,526	4,818
Water carriers	528	564	663	Employer contributions [2]	558	628	663
Hotels and motels	758	808	867	Lease and rental payments	908	908	1,021
Motor coaches	388	397	413	Advertising and promotion	713	746	753
Railroads	125	126	145	Taxes and licenses	144	163	181
Rental cars	189	204	242	Utilities	386	388	412
Package tours	2,158	2,425	2,634	Depreciation	339	361	381
Other	789	876	1,081	Office Supplies	294	325	352
				Repair Services	134	152	168
				Other	2,629	2,692	2,806

[1] Receipts for firms primarily engaged in arranging passenger transportation. These estimates exclude receipts of transportation companies (airlines, railroads, etc.). [2] Includes contributions to Social Security and other supplemental benefits.

Source: U.S. Bureau of the Census, *Service Annual Survey.*

No. 1034. Motor Freight Transportation and Warehousing Services—Revenues, Expenses, and Payroll Expenses, and Payoll: 1994 and 1995

[In millions of dollars]

KIND OF BUSINESS	SIC [1] code	OPERATING REVENUE		OPERATING EXPENSES		ANNUAL PAYROLL	
		1994	1995	1994	1995	1994	1995
Motor frgt. transport. and warehousing services [2]	42	167,865	176,259	156,227	165,089	46,137	49,347
Trucking and courier services, except by air [3]	421	157,910	165,271	147,911	155,920	43,580	46,535
Local trucking without storage	4212	39,400	41,393	36,444	38,677	9,193	9,853
Trucking, except local	4213	91,971	95,814	87,078	91,883	24,658	26,590
Local trucking with storage	4214	4,282	4,410	4,131	4,172	1,362	1,380
Courier services, except by air	4215	22,257	23,654	20,258	21,188	8,367	8,732
Public warehousing and storage	422	9,911	10,941	8,271	9,120	2,540	2,794
Farm product warehousing and storage	4221	773	781	652	667	152	160
Refrigerated warehousing and storage	4222	1,970	2,271	1,667	1,879	522	599
General warehousing and storage	4225	4,652	5,060	3,803	4,183	1,170	1,278
Special warehousing and storage [4]	4226	2,516	2,829	2,149	2,391	696	757

[1] Standard Industrial Classification. [2] Includes terminal and joint terminal maintenance facilities for motor carrier transportation (SIC 4231) not shown separately. [3] Excludes private motor carriers that operate as auxiliary establishments to nontransportation companies and independent owner-operators with no paid employees. [4] Includes household goods warehousing.

Source: U.S. Bureau of the Census, *Current Business Reports, 1995 Motor Freight Transportation and Warehousing Survey*

No. 1035. Bus Profile: 1980 to 1995

ITEM	Unit	1980	1990	1993	1994	1995
FINANCIAL						
Expenditures, school bus	Mil. dol.	3,833	7,605	7,618	7,847	9,082
Operating revenues, intercity buc, Class I	Mil. dol.	1,397	943	926	956	1,195
Operating expenses, intercity bus, Class I	Mil. dol.	1,318	1,026	880	996	1,257
INVENTORY						
Operating companies, intercity bus, Class I	Number	61	31	30	27	28
Vehicles:						
Commercial & Federal bus	Number	110,576	118,726	119,560	122,705	125,057
School & other bus	Number	418,225	508,261	534,872	547,718	560,447
PERFORMANCE						
Vehicle-miles, all buses:						
Rural & urban highway	Millions	6,059	5,719	6,126	6,409	6,383
School bus	Millions	3,000	3,800	4,300	4,400	5,000
Revenue:—						
Passenger miles, intercity bus	Millions	27,400	23,000	24,700	28,200	29,000
Passengers, intercity bus	1,000	370,000	334,000	339,900	343,200	358,900
Avg. miles traveled per vehicle, all buses	Miles	11,458	9,121	9,361	9,560	9,311
Avg. annual fuel consumption, all buses	Gallon	1,926	1,426	1,447	1,462	1,406
Avg. miles per gallon, all buses	Mpg	6.0	6.4	6.5	6.5	6.6
Average revenue per passenger mile	Cents	7.3	11.6	12.0	11.6	11.6
SAFETY						
Fatalities:						
School bus related	Number	150	115	141	105	121
School bus occupants	Number	9	11	13	3	13
Other vehicle occupants	Number	88	64	86	64	71
Non-occupants	Number	53	40	42	38	37
Fatalities in vehicular accidents, all buses	Number	390	340	286	286	306
Occupant fatality rate:						
Per 100 million vehicle-miles, all buses	Rate	0.8	0.6	0.3	0.3	0.5
Per 10,000 registered vehicles, all buses	Rate	0.9	0.5	0.3	0.3	0.5

Source: U.S. Bureau of Transportation Statistics, *National Transportation Statistics, 1996.*

No. 1036. Truck Profile: 1980 to 1995

ITEM	Unit	1980	1990	1993	1994	1995
FINANCIAL						
Revenues:						
Local						
Intercity	Mil. dol	(NA)	127,314	143,601	157,910	(NA)
Class I intercity motor carriers of property:						
Operating revenue, total	Mil. dol	1,290	46,710	55,303	(NA)	
Operating expenses, total	Mil. dol	29,012	118,968	136,144	147,911	(NA)
INVENTORY						
Truck registrations, total	1,000	33,667	44,718	61,828	63,445	64,778
PERFORMANCE						
Vehicle miles, total	Millions	399,426	615,902	733,302	839,537	865,137
Average miles traveled per vehicle:						
All trucks, total	Avg. miles	11,864	13,773	11,880	13,232	13,355
Ton-miles, intercity	Millions	555,000	735,000	861,000	908,000	921,000
Average fuel consumption per vehicle	Gallons	1,243	1,290	1,010	1,137	1,139
Highway-user taxes, total	Mil. dol	9,888	19,356	22,255	23,836	(NA)
SAFETY						
Occupant fatalities	Number	8,748	9,306	9,116	9,574	10,183
Vehicle involvement, total (per 100 million vehicle-miles)	Rate	4.5	2.9	2.4	2.4	(NA)

NA Not available.

Source: U.S. Bureau of Transportation Statistics, *National Transportation Statistics, 1996.*

No. 1037. Trucking and Courier Services—Operating Revenue, Operating Expenses, and Equipment, by Type of Carrier: 1993 to 1995

[In millions of dollars, except as indicated. Data cover SIC group 421. Excludes private motor carriers that operate as auxiliary establishments to nontransportation companies and independent owner-operators with no paid employees. Estimates for years 1992 and 1993 reflect a benchmarking to the results of the 1992 Census of Transportation, Communications, and Utilities

ITEM	ALL CARRIERS			SPECIALTY CARRIERS			GENERAL CARRIERS		
	1993	1994	1995	1993	1994	1995	1993	1994	1995
Operating revenues:									
Total [1]	143,601	157,910	165,271	38,335	41,205	42,944	105,266	116,705	122,327
Motor carrier	135,383	149,160	155,971	34,279	37,015	38,411	101,104	112,145	117,560
Local trucking	34,086	38,157	40,062	17,442	19,231	20,353	16,644	18,926	19,709
Long-distance trucking	101,297	111,003	115,909	16,837	17,784	18,058	84,460	93,219	97,851
Operating expenses:									
Total	135,144	147,911	155,920	35,902	38,403	40,325	99,242	109,508	115,595
Annual payroll	39,889	43,580	46,535	8,735	9,349	9,961	31,154	34,231	36,574
Employer contrib. to Soc. Sec. and other benefits	10,745	11,502	11,857	2,042	2,283	2,317	8,703	9,219	9,540
Purchased fuels	12,119	13,287	14,018	2,314	2,498	2,566	9,805	10,789	11,452
Purchased transportation	26,678	29,329	30,379	7,586	7,906	7,977	19,092	21,423	22,402
Lease and rental	2,545	2,732	2,894	719	765	792	1,826	1,967	2,102
Insurance	5,097	5,489	5,617	1,473	1,577	1,565	3,624	3,912	4,052
Maintenance and repair	8,542	9,442	9,636	2,367	2,645	2,818	6,175	6,797	6,818
Depreciation	7,450	8,218	8,948	1,950	2,016	2,197	5,500	6,202	6,751
Taxes and licenses	3,351	3,676	3,931	688	746	803	2,663	2,930	3,128
Drug and alcohol testing and rehabilitation programs	64	82	98	18	23	25	46	59	73
Other operating expenses	18,664	20,574	22,007	8,010	8,595	9,304	10,654	11,979	12,703
Equipment (1,000 units): [2]									
Trucks	260	287	295	131	147	154	129	140	141
Truck-tractors	622	681	758	129	133	150	493	548	608
Trailers (full and semi)	1,337	1,456	1,583	200	212	222	1,137	1,244	1,361

[1] Includes other revenue not shown separately. [2] Represents revenue generating equipment as of December 31, 1994. Includes owned and leased equipment.

Source: U.S. Bureau of the Census, *Current Business Reports, 1994 Motor Freight Transportation and Warehousing Survey.*

No. 1038. Class I Intercity Motor Carriers of Property, by Carrier: 1980 to 1993

[See headnote, table 1055. Common carriers are carriers offering regular scheduled service. Contract carriers provide service at request of user. Minus sign (-) indicates loss]

ITEM	Unit	1980	1985	1987	1988	1989	1990	1991	1992	1993
Common carriers, gen. freight reporting	Number	298	237	200	209	192	191	201	208	220
Number of employees, average	1,000	413	378	405	430	461	465	474	490	511
Compensation of employees	Mil. dol.	9,803	10,217	11,208	12,074	12,854	13,556	14,032	14,967	15,967
Operating revenues	Mil. dol.	19,725	22,314	23,087	25,234	27,405	29,682	31,619	34,594	37,600
Operating expenses	Mil. dol.	18,870	21,037	22,326	24,000	26,242	28,340	30,269	32,977	35,729
Ordinary income before taxes	Mil. dol.	701	1,198	647	1,135	988	1,146	1,180	1,453	1,641
Net income	Mil. dol.	-72	658	406	804	659	746	749	878	985
Intercity vehicle-miles	Million	6,547	5,760	5,524	5,913	6,557	6,804	7,615	8,674	9,770
Intercity revenue freight carried	Mil. ton	178	136	129	124	145	157	169	196	225
Common carriers, other reporting [1]	Number	441	397	339	360	337	322	295	330	304
Number of employees, average	1,000	101	78	83	82	84	87	74	88	83
Compensation of employees	Mil. dol.	1,931	1,783	1,961	2,010	2,105	2,236	1,920	2,358	2,333
Operating revenues	Mil. dol.	8,792	7,962	8,047	8,344	8,321	9,042	7,761	9,367	9,315
Operating expenses	Mil. dol.	8,426	7,752	7,835	8,018	8,081	8,702	7,509	8,942	8,875
Ordinary income before taxes	Mil. dol.	230	123	129	248	117	198	122	309	354
Net income	Mil. dol.	14	94	97	194	88	153	85	221	250
Intercity vehicle-miles	Million	6,889	5,714	5,761	6,263	6,320	6,566	5,372	6,696	6,295
Intercity revenue freight carried	Mil. ton	324	303	295	299	278	302	253	298	296
Contract carrier, other [1]	Number	69	64	64	74	77	87	83	113	115
Number of employees, average	1,000	14	22	20	30	29	34	34	42	40
Compensation of employees	Mil. dol.	336	630	561	925	893	1,082	989	1,325	1,321
Operating revenues	Mil. dol.	1,272	1,942	1,922	3,026	2,946	3,486	3,644	4,501	4,561
Operating expenses	Mil. dol.	1,207	1,807	1,833	2,923	2,888	3,422	3,547	4,333	4,367
Ordinary income before taxes	Mil. dol.	48	103	59	55	15	3	53	127	181
Net income	Mil. dol.	28	69	38	38	3	-13	20	80	123
Intercity vehicle-miles	Million	934	1,227	1,304	1,682	1,826	2,044	2,339	2,933	2,913
Intercity revenue freight carried	Mil. ton	37	41	41	69	80	80	76	110	99
Carriers of household goods reporting	Number	28	40	37	36	36	36	36	32	31
Number of employees, average	1,000	10	11	11	11	12	13	12	12	10
Compensation of employees	Mil. dol.	157	240	247	254	276	296	298	291	252
Operating revenues	Mil. dol.	1,824	2,664	2,931	3,038	3,114	3,152	3,026	3,180	3,274
Intercity freight	Mil. dol.	1,676	2,388	2,591	2,336	2,703	2,702	2,318	2,787	2,834
Operating expenses	Mil. dol.	1,781	2,635	2,862	2,971	3,059	3,129	2,973	3,159	3,196
Ordinary income before taxes	Mil. dol.	74	79	74	33	41	12	27	-1	48
Net income	Mil. dol.	42	54	57	25	28	8	17	8	62
Power units, intercity service	1,000	25	35	35	(NA)	(NA)	(NA)	(NA)	(NA)	(NA)
Intercity vehicle-miles	Million	969	1,171	1,234	1,289	1,229	1,366	1,086	1,136	949
Intercity revenue freight carried	Mil. ton	5	7	8	8	7	8	7	9	5

NA Not available. [1] Other than general freight. $del

Source: Through 1992, U.S. Interstate Commerce Commission, Transport Statistics in the United States, part 2, annual; *thereafter, Bureau of* Transportation Statistics, *National Transportation Statistics*, annual.

No. 1039. Railroads, Class I—Summary: 1980 to 1995

[As of Dec. 31, or calendar year data, except as noted. Compiled from annual reports of class I railroads only except where noted. Beginning 1985, financial data are not comparable with earlier years due to change in method of accounting for track and related structures. Minus sign (-) indicates deficit]

ITEM	Unit	1980	1985	1989	1990	1991	1992	1993	1994	1995
Class I line-hauling companies [1]	Number.	40	23	15	14	14	13	13	13	11
Employees [2]	1,000	458	302	228	216	206	197	193	190	188
Compensation	Mil. dol	11,318	10,563	9,043	8,654	8,695	8,753	8,732	8,874	9,070
Average per hour	Dollars	10.2	14.3	15.8	15.8	16.8	17.8	17.9	18.5	19.0
Average per year	Dollars	24,695	34,991	39,742	39,987	42,131	44,336	45,354	46,714	48,188
Mileage:										
Railroad line owned [3]	1,000	178	162	149	146	143	139	137	132	(NA)
Railroad track owned [4]	1,000	292	269	250	244	241	234	231	222	(NA)
Equipment:										
Locomotives in service	Number.	28,094	22,548	19,015	18,835	18,344	18,004	18,161	18,505	18,812
Average horsepower	1,000 lb	2,302	2,469	2,624	2,665	2,714	2,750	2,777	2,832	2,927
Cars in service:										
Passenger train	Number.	4,347	2,502	(NA)	(NA)	(NA)	(NA)	(NA)	(NA)	(NA)
Freight train [5]	1,000	1,711	1,422	1,224	1,212	1,190	1,173	1,173	1,192	1,219
Freight cars [6]	1,000	1,168	867	682	659	633	605	587	591	583
Income and expenses:										
Operating revenues	Mil. dol	28,258	27,586	27,956	28,370	27,845	28,349	28,825	30,809	32,279
Operating expenses	Mil. dol	26,355	25,225	25,038	24,652	28,061	25,325	24,517	25,511	27,897
Net revenue from operations	*Mil. dol*	*1,902*	*2,361*	*2,918*	*3,718*	*-216*	*3,024*	*4,308*	*5,298*	*4,383*
Income before fixed charges	Mil. dol	2,897	3,393	4,162	4,627	928	4,127	4,990	6,184	5,016
Provision for taxes [7]	Mil. dol	592	660	1,040	1,088	-156	1,092	1,810	1,935	1,556
Ordinary income	Mil. dol	1,129	1,788	2,009	1,961	-91	2,055	2,258	3,315	2,439
Net income	Mil. dol	1,129	1,882	2,203	1,977	-281	1,800	2,240	3,298	2,324
Net railway operating income	Mil. dol	1,339	1,746	1,894	2,648	-37	1,955	2,517	3,392	2,858
Total taxes [8]	Mil. dol	2,585	3,169	3,742	3,780	2,649	3,732	4,343	4,512	4,075
Indus. return on net investment	Percent.	4.2	4.6	6.3	8.1	1.3	6.3	7.1	9.4	7.0
Gross capital expenditures	Mil. dol	3,238	4,485	3,865	3,591	3,439	3,680	4,504	5,035	5,720
Balance sheet:										
Total property investment	Mil. dol	43,923	64,241	67,661	70,348	71,822	72,677	75,217	78,384	86,186
Accrued depreciation and amortization	Mil. dol	10,706	19,756	21,481	22,222	23,057	23,378	23,892	24,200	23,439
Net investment	Mil. dol	33,419	46,237	47,370	48,126	48,565	49,299	51,325	54,184	62,746
Shareholder's equity	Mil. dol	19,860	27,605	25,753	23,662	22,603	23,115	24,658	27,389	31,419
Net working capital	Mil. dol	922	1,084	-2119	-3505	-3988	-4372	-3295	-3059	-2634
Cash dividends	Mil. dol	610	1,444	1,910	2,074	915	830	1,054	1,398	1,518
AMTRAK passenger traffic:										
Passenger revenue	Mil. dol	(NA)	604.9	893.0	941.9	962.3	933.2	777.6	717.9	734.1
Revenue passengers carried	1,000	21,303	20,945	21,394	22,382	21,693	21,678	21,511	21,239	20,349
Revenue passenger miles	Million	4,645	4,977	5,912	6,125	6,249	6,181	6,068	5,869	5,401
Averages:										
Revenue per passenger	Dollars	(NA)	28.9	41.8	42.1	44.4	43.0	36.1	33.8	36.1
Revenue per passenger mile	Cents	(NA)	12.2	15.1	15.4	15.4	15.1	12.8	12.2	13.6
Trip per passenger	Miles	218.1	237.6	276.3	273.7	288.0	285.1	277.7	(NA)	(NA)
Freight service:										
Freight revenue	Mil. dol	26,200	26,688	27,059	24,471	26,949	27,508	27,991	29,931	31,356
Per ton-mile	Cents	2.8	3.0	2.7	2.7	2.6	2.6	2.5	2.5	2.4
Per ton originated	Dollar	17.7	20.2	19.3	19.3	19.5	19.7	20.0	20.4	20.2
Revenue-tons originated	Million	1,492	1,320	1,402	1,425	1,383	1,399	1,397	1,470	1,550
Revenue-tons carried	Million	2,434	1,985	1,988	2,024	1,967	2,022	2,047	2,185	2,322
Tons carried one mile	Billion	919	877	1,014	1,034	1,039	1,067	1,109	1,201	1,306
Average miles of road operated	1,000	179	161	138	133	130	126	124	123	125
Revenue ton-miles per mile of road	1,000	5,133	5,446	7,373	7,763	8,001	8,451	8,985	9,735	10,439
Revenue per ton-mile	Cents	3	3	3	3	3	3	3	2	2
Train miles	Million	428	347	383	380	375	390	405	441	458
Net ton-miles per train-mile [9]	Number.	2,175	2,574	2,683	2,755	2,796	2,759	2,759	2,746	2,870
Net ton-miles per loaded car-mile [9]	Number.	63.5	62.7	67.0	69.1	71.6	70.9	71.6	72.2	73.6
Train-miles per train-hour	Miles	18.2	21.9	23.0	23.7	23.7	23.7	23.1	22.4	21.8
Haul per ton, U.S. as a system	Miles	616	664	723	726	751	763	794	817	843
Accident: [10]										
All railroads	Number.	63,663	35,340	28,039	26,440	24,862	22,553	20,400	18,038	15,586
Persons killed	Number.	1,417	1,036	1,324	1,297	1,194	1,170	1,279	1,226	1,146
Persons injured	Number.	62,246	34,304	26,715	25,143	23,468	21,383	19,121	16,812	14,440
	Number	57,755	29,388	21,809	20,450	18,728	17,055	15,058	12,428	10,565
Persons killed	Number.	1,344	955	1,195	1,166	1,069	1,047	1,124	1,060	994
Persons injured	Number.	56,411	28,433	20,614	19,284	17,659	16,008	13,934	11,348	9,571

NA Not available. [1] See text, section 21, for definition of Class I. [2] Average midmonth count. [3] Represents the aggregate length of roadway of all line-haul railroads. Excludes yard tracks, sidings, and parallel lines. (Includes estimate for class II and III railroads). [4] Includes multiple main tracks, yard tracks, and sidings owned by both line-haul and switching and terminal. (Includes estimate for class II and III railroads). [5] Includes cars owned by all railroads, private car companies, and shippers. [6] Class I railroads only. [7] Includes State income taxes. [8] Includes payroll, income, and other taxes. [9] Revenue and nonrevenue freight. [10] Source: Federal Railroad Admin., *Accident Bulletin*, annual. Includes highway grade crossing casualties.

Source: Except as noted, Association of American Railroads, Washington, DC, *Railroad Facts*, *Statistics of Railroads of Class I*, annual, and *Analysis of Class I Railroads*, annual.

No. 1040. Railroads, Class I-Cars of Revenue Freight Loaded, 1970 to 1995, and by Commodity Group, 19954 and 19965

[In thousands. Figures are 52-week totals. N.e.c.= Not elsewhere classified]

YEAR	CARLOADS		COMMODITY GROUP	CARLOADS		COMMODITY GROUP	CARLOADS	
	Total	Piggy-back		1995	1996		1995	1996
1970	27,160	1,450	Coal	6,545	6,695	Metals and products	564	584
1975	23,217	1,308	Metallic ores	462	442	Stone, clay, and glass products	493	480
1980	22,598	1,661	Chemicals, allied products	1,551	1,551	Crushed stone, gravel, sand	667	678
1985	19,574	2,863	Grain	1,362	1,226	Nonmetallic minerals, n.e.c	461	461
1990	16,177	(NA)	Motor vehicles and equipment	971	1,010	Waste and scrap materials	491	493
1993	15,911	(NA)	Pulp, paper, allied products	541	530	Lumber, wood products, n.e.c. [1]	261	270
1994	16,763	(NA)	Primary forest products	391	354	Coke	282	263
1995	16,706	(NA)	Food and kindred prod., n.e.c.	451	416	Petroleum product	272	261
1996	16,618	(NA)	Grain mill products	518	490	All other carloads	405	374

NA Not available. [1] Excludes furniture.

Source: Association of American Railroads, Washington, DC, *Weekly Railroad Traffic*, annual.

No. 1041. Railroads, Class I Line-Haul-Revenue Freight Originated, by Commodity Group: 1980 to 1995

COMMODITY GROUP	1980	1985	1989	1990	1991	1992	1993	1994	1995
Carloads (1,000) [1]	22,223	19,501	21,226	21,401	20,868	21,205	21,683	23,179	23,726
Coal	5,789	5,684	5,672	5,912	5,683	5,572	5,310	5,681	6,095
Farm products	1,866	1,494	1,781	1,689	1,605	1,646	1,636	1,459	1,692
Chemicals, allied products	1,322	1,296	1,486	1,531	1,556	1,568	1,606	1,695	1,642
Food and kindred products	1,767	1,224	1,284	1,307	1,316	1,352	1,380	1,381	1,377
Nonmetallic minerals [2]	1,474	1,196	1,254	1,202	1,075	1,029	1,044	1,136	1,159
Transportation equipment	1,004	1,202	1,141	1,091	1,068	1,181	1,355	1,448	1,473
Lumber and wood products [3]	1,384	948	843	780	716	726	710	771	719
Pulp, paper, allied products	954	703	615	611	616	618	620	651	626
Petroleum and coal products	596	491	561	573	533	583	584	602	596
Stone, clay, and glass products	776	551	565	539	479	483	487	512	516
Metallic ores	1,258	511	523	506	499	489	443	440	463
Primary metal products	756	449	452	477	469	481	526	579	575
Waste and scrap materials	632	429	444	439	433	487	558	604	623
Machinery, exc. electrical	77	35	38	39	39	39	37	40	41
Fabricated metal products [4]	72	31	27	31	34	32	37	37	32
Tons (mil.) [1]	1,492	1,320	1,403	1,425	1,383	1,399	1,397	1,470	1,550
Coal	522	538	551	579	560	554	534	574	627
Farm products	156	127	154	147	144	149	147	131	154
Chemicals, allied products	108	106	123	126	127	130	134	142	136
Nonmetallic minerals [2]	125	108	111	109	99	94	96	106	110
Food and kindred products	92	74	79	81	83	86	88	86	91
Lumber and wood products [3]	86	63	57	53	48	50	49	54	51
Metallic ores	105	47	47	47	45	45	41	40	44
Stone, clay, and glass products	54	44	47	44	39	40	40	42	43
Petroleum and coal products	38	33	39	40	37	41	41	43	43
Primary metal products	53	34	36	38	37	39	43	47	47
Pulp, paper, allied products	42	36	34	33	33	34	34	37	36
Waste and scrap materials	34	26	28	28	27	30	35	37	36
Transportation equipment	24	27	24	23	22	25	29	30	30
Machinery, exc. electrical	2	1	1	1	1	1	1	1	1
Fabricated metal products [4]	2	1	1	1	1	1	1	1	1
Gross revenue (mil. dol.) [1]	26,938	28,225	29,326	29,775	29,319	29,777	30,376	32,424	33,782
Coal	4,956	6,556	6,581	6,954	6,903	6,717	6,481	7,021	7,356
Chemicals, allied products	2,946	3,342	3,788	3,933	4,043	4,123	4,277	4,520	4,553
Transportation equipment	1,917	3,110	3,269	3,100	2,633	2,753	3,021	3,257	3,269
Farm products	2,801	1,977	2,444	2,422	2,332	2,454	2,528	2,407	3,020
Food and kindred products	2,837	2,256	2,126	2,188	2,254	2,308	2,336	2,427	2,464
Pulp, paper, allied products	1,652	1,641	1,514	1,486	1,502	1,508	1,511	1,510	1,543
Lumber and wood products [3]	1,543	1,525	1,500	1,390	1,282	1,342	1,324	1,421	1,385
Primary metal products	1,332	872	972	979	977	970	1,021	1,114	1,199
Stone, clay, and glass products	1,025	960	960	931	878	911	944	1,009	1,044
Petroleum and coal products	865	861	917	918	888	943	929	967	997
Nonmetallic minerals [2]	948	949	868	885	824	812	818	862	875
Waste and scrap materials	513	446	492	504	515	558	613	655	685
Metallic ores	597	403	397	406	400	409	385	378	394
Machinery, exc. electrical	176	72	66	67	62	61	59	65	69
Fabricated metal products [4]	110	48	38	42	48	45	50	50	44

[1] Includes commodity groups and small packaged freight shipments, not shown separately. [2] Except fuels. [3] Except furniture. [4] Except ordnance, machinery, and transport.

Source: Association of American Railroads, Washington, DC, *Freight Commodity Statistics*, annual.

No. 1042. Railroad Freight—Producer Price Indexes: 1980 to 1996

[Dec. 1984=100. Reflects prices for shipping a fixed set of commodities under specified and unchanging conditions]

COMMODITY	1980	1985	1989	1990	1991	1992	1993	1994	1995	1996
Total railroad freight	75.9	99.9	106.4	107.5	109.3	109.9	110.9	111.8	111.7	111.5
Coal	75.8	100.0	105.3	104.2	105.2	105.9	106.6	107.5	107.3	106.7
Farm products	75.6	99.0	108.5	110.4	111.4	111.1	113.7	114.5	115.6	115.8
Food products	75.2	100.0	103.9	105.4	108.1	108.7	109.0	111.0	111.2	108.8
Metallic ores	74.5	100.2	105.8	106.5	106.7	106.6	106.7	104.6	101.9	103.5
Chemicals or allied products	75.6	100.1	110.0	111.7	113.5	115.6	116.2	117.6	120.0	119.2
Nonmetallic minerals	72.2	100.1	108.3	111.7	115.9	117.6	119.3	119.7	119.5	119.6
Wood or lumber products	72.7	100.0	105.9	107.5	106.6	106.8	109.7	110.0	110.0	112.8
Transportation equipment	81.7	100.0	106.4	107.5	109.7	110.8	113.1	115.3	112.8	114.0
Pulp, paper, or allied products	76.7	100.0	105.1	108.0	111.5	111.8	112.6	111.1	106.7	(NA)
Primary metal products	77.8	99.7	112.3	113.1	116.1	117.5	116.3	115.6	115.6	115.6
Clay, concrete, glass, or stone products	74.2	100.0	110.5	114.1	117.1	116.5	117.9	120.1	121.4	121.3

NA Not available.

Source: U.S. Bureau of Labor Statistics, *Producer Price Indexes*, monthly and annual.

No. 1043. Petroleum Pipeline Companies—Characteristics: 1980 to 1995

[Covers pipeline companies operating in interstate commerce and subject to jurisdiction of Federal Energy Regulatory Commission]

ITEM	Unit	1980	1985	1989	1990	1991	1992	1993	1994	1995
Miles of pipeline, total	1,000	173	171	169	168	172	164	164	159	177
Gathering lines	1,000	36	35	33	32	31	29	29	30	35
Trunk lines	1,000	136	136	135	136	141	136	135	128	142
Total deliveries	Mil. bbl.	10,600	10,745	11,281	11,378	11,496	11,447	12,219	12,159	12,862
Crude oil	Mil. bbl.	6,405	6,239	6,435	6,563	6,685	6,541	6,708	6,785	6,952
Products	Mil. bbl.	4,195	4,506	4,847	4,816	4,811	4,906	5,511	5,373	5,910
Total trunk line traffic	Bil. bbl-miles	3,405	3,342	3,505	3,500	3,470	3,428	3,051	3,566	3,619
Crude oil	Bil. bbl-miles	1,948	1,842	1,918	1,891	1,899	1,853	1,382	1,823	1,899
Products	Bil. bbl-miles	1,458	1,500	1,587	1,609	1,571	1,575	1,669	1,743	1,720
Carrier property value	Mil. dol.	19,752	21,605	24,638	25,828	26,943	27,106	31,625	26,363	27,460
Operating revenues	Mil. dol.	6,356	7,461	6,512	7,149	6,796	7,154	6,931	7,281	7,711
Net income	Mil. dol.	1,912	2,431	2,227	2,340	1,788	2,061	1,763	2,148	2,670

Source: PennWell Publishing Co., Tulsa, OK, *Oil & Gas Journal*, annual (copyright).

No. 1044. Major Interstate Natural Gas Pipeline Companies—Summary: 1985 to 1991

[The classification of A and B interstate natural gas pipeline companies changed to major companies and nonmajor companies. Major natural gas pipleline companies are those whose combined sales for resale and natural gas transported or stored for a fee exceed 50 billion cubic feet. They account for more than 85 percent of all interstate natural gas]

ITEM	Unit	1985	1986	1987	1988	1989	1990	1991
Sales	Tril. cu. ft.	11.3	7.8	6.5	6.4	5.6	4.5	3.9
Residential	Tril. cu. ft.	0.3	0.2	0.2	0.3	0.1	0.2	0.2
Commercial, industrial	Tril. cu. ft.	1.1	0.5	0.4	0.5	0.5	0.4	0.3
For resale	Tril. cu. ft.	9.9	7.1	5.8	5.6	4.9	3.9	3.3
Operating revenues	Mil. dol	49,106	33,859	27,565	27,501	25,695	22,574	21,420
From sales [1]	Mil. dol	44,996	29,506	22,942	22,512	19,786	15,981	14,135
From transportation of gas of others	Mil. dol	2,272	3,027	3,622	4,059	4,959	5,505	6,117
Other	Mil. dol	1,838	1,325	1,002	929	950	1,088	1,167
Operation, maintenance expenses	Mil. dol	42,528	27,460	21,794	22,742	20,829	17,446	17,335
Production	Mil. dol	36,739	22,208	16,955	17,625	15,257	12,124	11,663
Storage	Mil. dol	418	420	409	436	458	417	460
Transmission	Mil. dol	3,409	2,964	2,598	2,589	2,589	2,720	2,880
Distribution	Mil. dol	132	80	80	127	94	112	133
Administrative, general, and other	Mil. dol	1,830	1,768	1,752	1,966	2,430	2,074	2,048
Pipeline mileage	1,000	230.2	217.3	249.5	246.9	253.2	230.2	249.5
Transmission lines	1,000	189.7	184.6	181.2	191.6	194.1	195.5	146.8
Field lines	1,000	69.6	64.5	62.9	55.5	55.1	54.0	50.7
Storage	1,000	4.8	4.6	4.3	4.8	4.8	5.0	4.7

[1] Includes other ultimate customers not shown separately.

Source: U.S. Energy Information Administration, *Statistics of Interstate Natural Gas Pipeline Companies*, annual.

Figure 22.1
**Revenue Passengers Enplaned—
Top 10 Airports: 1995**

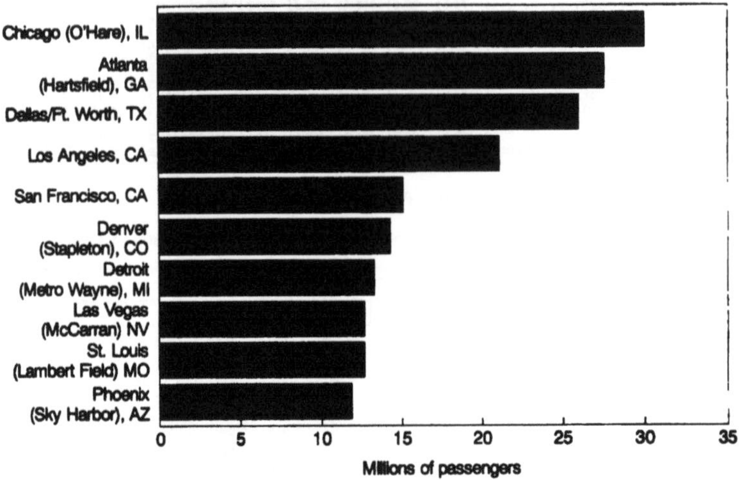

Source: Chart prepared by U.S. Bureau of the Census. For data, see table 1048.

Figure 22.2
**Consumer Complaints Against
U.S. Airlines: 1988 to 1996**

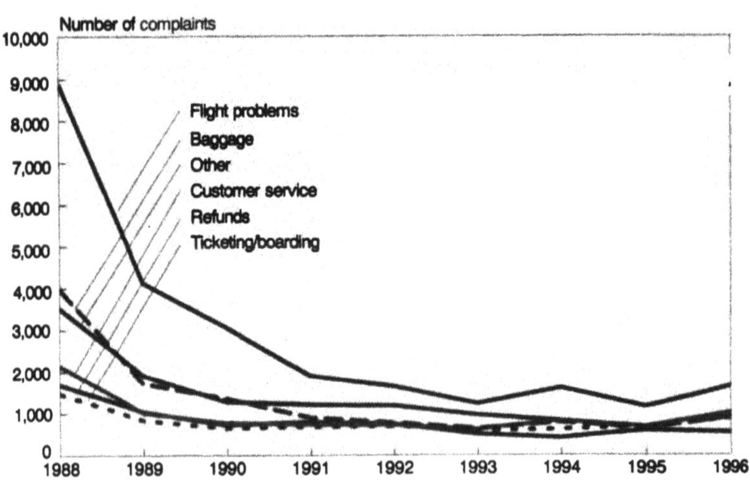

Source: Chart prepared by U.S. Bureau of the Census. For data, see table 1054

Section 22

Transportation—Air and Water

This section presents data on civil air transportation, both passenger and cargo, and on water transportation, including inland waterways, oceanborne commerce, the merchant marine, cargo and vessel tonnages, and shipbuilding. Comparative data on various types of transportation carriers are presented in section 21.

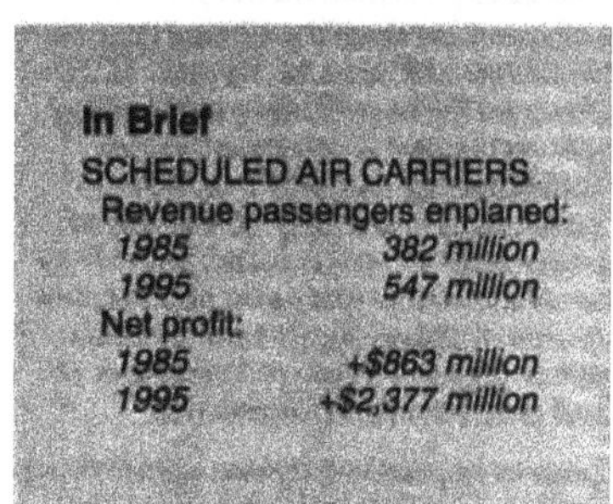

In Brief

SCHEDULED AIR CARRIERS

Revenue passengers enplaned:	
1985	*382 million*
1995	*547 million*
Net profit:	
1985	*+$863 million*
1995	*+$2,377 million*

Principal sources of these data are the annual *FAA Statistical Handbook of Aviation* issued by the Federal Aviation Administration (FAA); the annual *Waterborne Commerce of the United States* issued by the Corps of Engineers of the Department of the Army; the monthly and annual issues of *U.S. Waterborne Exports and General Imports,* and the annual *Vessel Entrances and Clearances,* and the monthly *Highlights of U.S. Export and Import Trade,* issued by the Bureau of the Census. In addition, the Bureau of the Census in its commodity transportation survey (part of the census of transportation, taken every 5 years, for years ending in "2" and "7") provides data on the type, weight, and value of commodities shipped by manufacturing establishments in the United States, by means of transportation, origin, and destination.

Air transportation data are also presented annually by the Air Transport Association of America, Washington, DC, in *Air Transport Facts and Figures.* Additional sources of data on water transportation include *Merchant Fleets of the World* issued periodically by the U.S. Maritime Administration; *The Bulletin,* issued monthly by the American Bureau of Shipping, New York, NY; and *World Fleet Statistics* and the *Register Book,* published by Lloyd's Register of Shipping, London, England.

Civil aviation—Federal promotion and regulation of civil aviation have been carried out by the FAA and the Civil Aeronautics Board (CAB). The CAB promoted and regulated the civil air transportation industry within the United States and between the United States and foreign countries. The Board granted licenses to provide air transportation service, approved or disapproved proposed rates and fares, and approved or disapproved proposed agreements and corporate relationships involving air carriers. In December 1984, the CAB ceased to exist as an agency. Some of its functions were transferred to the Department of Transportation (DOT), as outlined below. The responsibility for investigation of aviation accidents resides with the National Transportation Safety Board.

The Office of the Secretary, DOT aviation activities include the following: negotiation of international air transportation rights, selection of U.S. air carriers to serve capacity controlled international markets, oversight of international rates and fares, maintenance of essential air service to small communities, and consumer affairs. DOT's Bureau of Transportation Statistics (BTS) handles aviation information functions formerly assigned to CAB. Prior to BTS, the Research and Special Programs Administration handled these functions.

The principal activities of the FAA include the promotion of air safety, controlling the use of navigable airspace, prescribing regulations dealing with the competency of airmen, airworthiness of aircraft, and air traffic control, operation of air route traffic control centers, airport traffic control towers, and flight service stations, the design, construction, maintenance, and inspection of navigation, traffic control, and communications equipment, and the development of general aviation.

The CAB published monthly and quarterly financial and traffic statistical data for the certificated route air carriers. BTS continues these publications, including both certificated and noncertificated (commuter) air carriers. The FAA publishes data annually on the use of airway facilities; data related to the location of airmen, aircraft, and airports; the volume of activity in the field of nonair carrier (general aviation) flying; and aircraft production and registration.

General aviation comprises all civil flying (including such commercial operations as small demand air taxis, agriculture application, powerline patrol, etc.) but excludes certificated route air carriers, supplemental operators, large-aircraft commercial operators and commuter airlines.

Air carriers and service—The CAB previously issued "certificates of public convenience and necessity" under Section 401 of the Federal Aviation Act of 1958 for scheduled and nonscheduled (charter) passenger services and cargo services. It also issued certificates under Section 418 of the Act to cargo air carriers for domestic all-cargo service only. The DOT Office of the Secretary now issues the certificates under a "fit, willing, and able" test of air carrier operations. Carriers operating only 60 seat or less aircraft are given exemption authority to carry passengers, cargo, and mail in scheduled and nonscheduled service under Part 298 of the DOT (formerly CAB) regulations. Exemption authority carriers who offer scheduled passenger service to an essential air service point must meet the "fit, willing, and able" test.

Vessel shipments, entrances, and clearances—Shipments by dry cargo vessels comprise shipments on all types of watercraft, except tanker vessels; shipments by tanker vessels comprise all types of cargo, liquid and dry, carried by tanker vessels.

A vessel is reported as entered only at the first port which it enters in the United States, whether or not cargo is unloaded at that port. A vessel is reported as cleared only at the last port at which clearance is made to a foreign port, whether or not it takes on cargo. Army and Navy vessels entering or clearing without commercial cargo are not included in the figures.

Units of measurement—Cargo (or freight) tonnage and shipping weight both represent the gross weight of the cargo including the weight of containers, wrappings, crates, etc. However, shipping weight excludes lift and cargo vans and similar substantial outer containers. Other tonnage figures generally refer to stowing capacity of vessels, 100 cubic feet being called 1 ton. Gross tonnage comprises the space within the frames and the ceiling of the hull, together with those closed-in spaces above deck available for cargo, stores, passengers, or crew, with certain minor exceptions. Net or registered tonnage is the gross tonnage less the spaces occupied by the propelling machinery, fuel, crew quarters, master's cabin, and navigation spaces. Substantially, it represents space available for cargo and passengers. The net tonnage capacity of a ship may bear little relation to weight of cargo. Deadweight tonnage is the weight in long tons required to depress a vessel from light water line (that is, with only the machinery and equipment on board) to load line. It is, therefore, the weight of the cargo, fuel, etc., which a vessel is designed to carry with safety.

No. 1045. Air and Water Transportation Industries—Summary: 1992

[For establishments with payroll]

INDUSTRY	1987 SIC [1] Code	Establish-ments	Revenue (mil. dol.)	Annual payroll (mil. dol.)	Paid employees [2] (1,000)
Air transportation [3]	45	(NA)	82,670	24,530	707
Air transportation, including air courier services [3]	451,2	(NA)	76,503	22,734	627
Scheduled and air courier services [3]	451	(NA)	73,070	22,026	604
Scheduled [3]	4512	(NA)	62,057	19,090	505
Air courier services	4513	2,639	11,013	2,935	99
Nonscheduled	452	1,791	3,433	708	23
Airport terminal services	458	3,252	6,168	1,796	80
Water transportation	44	8,147	29,207	6,170	171
Water transportation of freight	441,2,3,4	836	14,704	1,523	37
Deep sea foreign and domestic freight	441, 2	615	11,948	1,148	27
Deep sea foreign freight	4412	334	8,490	629	13
Deep sea domestic freight	4424	281	3,458	519	13
Other water transportation of freight	443,4	221	2,756	375	10
Great Lakes-St. Lawrence Seaway freight	4432	26	559	81	1
Water transportation of freight, n.e.c. [4]	4449	195	2,197	293	9
Water transportation of passengers	448	1,033	4,133	508	23
Ferries	4482	118	155	51	2
Water transportation of passengers, except by ferry	4481,9	915	3,978	457	22
Deep sea transportation, except by ferry	4481	72	3,268	275	13
Water transportation of passengers, n.e.c. [4]	4489	843	710	182	9
Services incidental to water transportation	449	6,278	10,370	3,140	111
Marinas	4493	3,348	1,651	346	18
Other services incidental to water transportation	4491,2,9	2,930	8,719	2,794	93
Marine cargo handling	4491	871	5,066	1,841	59
Towing and tugboat services	4492	941	2,682	689	25
Water transportation services, n.e.c. [4]	4499	1,118	971	263	9

NA Not available. [1] 1987 Standard Industrial Classification code; see text, section 13. [2] For the pay period including March 12. [3] Revenue for scheduled air transportation includes revenues for large certificated passenger carriers that was reported to the Office of Airline Statistics, U.S. Dept. of Transportation, as published in *Air Carrier Financial Statistics Quarterly*. [4] N.e.c. means not elsewhere classified.

Source: U.S. Bureau of the Census, *Census of Transportation, Communications, and Utilities: 1992*, UC92-A-1.

No. 1046. U. S. Scheduled Airline Industry—Summary: 1985 to 1995

[For calendar years or Dec. 31. For domestic and international operations. Covers carriers certificated under Section 401 of the Federal Aviation Act. Minus sign (-) indicates loss]

ITEM	Unit	1985	1990	1990	1991	1992	1993	1994	1995
SCHEDULED SERVICE									
Revenue passengers enplaned	Mil.	382.0	453.7	465.6	452.3	475.1	488.5	528.8	547.4
Revenue passenger miles	Bil.	336.4	432.7	457.9	448.0	478.6	489.7	519.4	540.4
Available seat miles	Bil.	547.8	684.4	733.4	715.2	752.8	771.6	784.3	806.6
Revenue passenger load factor	Percent	61.4	63.2	62.4	62.6	63.6	63.5	66.2	67.0
Mean passenger trip length [1]	Miles	881	954	984	990	1,007	1,002	982	987
Freight and express ton miles	Mil.	6,030.5	10,275.0	10,546.3	10,225.2	11,129.7	11,943.6	13,792.2	14,568.4
Aircraft departures	1,000	5,835.5	6,622.1	6,923.6	6,782.8	7,050.6	7,245.4	7,531.0	8,053.6
FINANCES									
Total operating revenue [2]	Mil. dol.	46,664	69,316	76,142	75,159	78,140	84,559	88,313	94,325
Passenger revenue	Mil. dol.	39,236	53,802	58,453	57,092	59,829	63,945	65,422	69,485
Freight and express revenue	Mil. dol.	2,681	6,893	5,432	5,509	5,916	6,662	7,284	8,480
Mail revenue	Mil. dol.	890	955	970	957	1,184	1,212	1,183	1,266
Charter revenue	Mil. dol.	1,280	2,052	2,877	3,717	2,801	3,082	3,548	3,327
Total operating expense	Mil. dol.	45,238	67,505	78,054	76,943	80,585	83,121	85,600	88,433
Operating profit	Mil. dol.	1,426	1,811	-1,912	-1,785	-2,445	1,438	2,713	5,892
Interest expense	Mil. dol.	1,566	1,944	1,978	1,177	1,743	2,027	2,347	2,415
Net profit	Mil. dol.	863	128	-3,921	-1,940	-4,791	-2,136	-344	2,377
Revenue per passenger mile	Cents	11.7	12.4	12.8	12.7	12.5	13.1	12.6	12.9
Rate of return on investment	Percent	9.6	6.3	-6.0	-0.5	-9.3	-0.4	5.2	12.0
Operating profit margin	Percent	3.1	2.6	-2.5	-2.3	-3.1	1.7	3.1	6.2
Net profit margin	Percent	1.8	0.2	-5.1	-2.6	-6.1	-2.5	-0.4	2.5
EMPLOYEES									
Total	1,000	355	507	546	534	540	537	540	547
Pilots, copilots, and other flight personnel	1,000	40	52	56	56	59	60	61	64
Flight attendants	1,000	63	78	83	82	86	85	87	87
Mechanics	1,000	43	57	61	59	59	58	56	50
Aircraft and traffic servicing personnel	1,000	101	225	252	237	243	243	247	251
Other	1,000	106	95	94	98	93	92	90	95

[1] For definition of mean, see Guide to Tabular Presentation. [2] Includes other types of revenues, not shown separately.

Source: Air Transport Association of America, Washington, DC, *Air Transport*, annual, and *Air Transport, Facts and Figures*, annual.

No. 1047. Airline Cost Indexes: 1980 to 1995

[Covers U.S. major and national service carriers. Major carriers have operating revenues of $1 billion or more; nationals have operating revenues from $75 million to $1 billion. Minus sign (-) indicates decrease]

ITEM	INDEX (1982=100)								PERCENT DISTRIBUTION OF CASH OPERATING EXPENSES [1]			
	1980	1985	1990	1991	1992	1993	1994	1995	1985	1990	1994	1995
INDEX												
Composite	86.3	103.1	117.0	119.8	122.0	124.0	123.4	125.4	100.0	100.0	100.0	100.0
Labor	84.8	111.1	121.1	127.6	134.4	140.7	148.6	157.6	35.1	34.9	32.6	36.3
Interest [2]	86.7	105.5	107.3	88.3	84.8	89.1	88.0	102.1	2.9	3.5	2.5	3.2
Fuel	91.6	81.4	78.7	68.9	64.1	60.8	55.6	56.1	29.7	22.3	17.6	11.6
Passenger food	94.3	102.0	132.6	141.4	144.1	131.6	123.7	114.4	2.9	3.2	3.6	3.4
Advertising and promotion	69.5	99.8	107.6	97.9	89.8	80.3	77.6	71.4	1.7	2.3	2.1	1.5
Landing fees	90.0	101.2	148.1	161.9	179.5	183.1	185.4	187.4	1.7	1.7	1.9	2.2
Passenger traffic commissions	77.3	117.6	176.8	193.5	192.2	200.9	170.3	144.6	4.8	7.4	9.8	8.7
All other	85.6	112.7	134.7	140.6	144.6	147.5	149.7	153.4	21.3	24.6	29.9	33.0
PERCENT CHANGE [3]												
Composite	23.3	0.3	7.3	2.4	1.8	1.6	-0.8	1.6	(X)	(X)	(X)	(X)
Labor	10.0	2.9	2.3	5.4	5.3	4.7	5.6	6.1	(X)	(X)	(X)	(X)
Interest [2]	16.9	-3.2	-3.8	-17.7	-4.0	5.1	-1.2	16.0	(X)	(X)	(X)	(X)
Fuel	55.8	-5.7	28.6	-12.5	-7.0	-5.1	-8.6	0.9	(X)	(X)	(X)	(X)
Passenger food	11.9	-4.2	8.0	6.6	1.9	-8.7	-6.0	-7.5	(X)	(X)	(X)	(X)
Advertising and promotion	24.3	-0.2	2.5	-9.0	-8.3	-10.6	-3.4	-8.0	(X)	(X)	(X)	(X)
Landing fees	9.6	-0.2	8.0	9.3	10.8	2.0	1.3	1.1	(X)	(X)	(X)	(X)
Passenger traffic commissions	40.0	0.8	8.2	9.4	-0.7	4.5	-15.2	-15.1	(X)	(X)	(X)	(X)
All other	9.3	3.7	4.1	4.4	2.9	2.2	1.5	2.5	(X)	(X)	(X)	(X)

X Not applicable. [1] Total operating expenses plus interest on long term debt, less depreciation and amortization. [2] Interest on debt. [3] Change from immediate prior year.

Source: Air Transport Association of America, Washington, DC, *Air Transport*, annual; and unpublished data.

No. 1048. Top 10 Airports—Traffic Summary: 1995

[In thousands, except percent change. For calendar year. Airports ranked by revenue passengers enplaned. For scheduled carriers only; excludes charter-only carriers]

AIRPORT	Rank	AIRCRAFT DEPARTURES		REVENUE PASSENGERS ENPLANED		ENPLANED REVENUE TONS		
		Total [1]	Completed scheduled	Total	Percent change, 1980-1995	Total	Freight	U.S. mail
All airports [2]	(X)	7,928	7,630	518,952	86.0	9,207	7,056	2,151
Atlanta, Hartsfield International	2	348	341	27,557	37.8	337	206	131
Chicago, O'Hare	1	381	375	29,886	55.4	509	372	137
Dallas/Ft. Worth International	3	382	372	25,964	148.9	286	184	102
Denver International	6	179	173	14,328	49.0	153	89	64
Detroit, Metro Wayne	7	165	150	13,294	164.6	133	79	54
Las Vegas McCarran	9	131	124	12,657	173.4	32	18	14
Los Angeles International	4	234	230	21,072	48.8	527	438	89
Phoenix, Sky Harbor International	10	177	172	11,900	252.1	103	64	39
St. Louis, Lambert Field	8	227	224	12,736	139.4	115	58	57
San Francisco International	5	143	141	15,013	59.7	257	182	75

X Not applicable. [1] Includes completed scheduled and unscheduled. [2] Includes other airports, not shown separately.

Source: U.S. Federal Aviation Administration and Research and Special Programs Administration, *Airport Activity Statistics*, annual.

No. 1049. Domestic Airline Markets: 1995

[For calendar year. Data are for the 30 top markets and include all commercial airports in each metro area. Data do not include connecting passengers]

MARKET	Passengers	MARKET	Passengers
New York to—from Los Angeles	2,991,060	New York to—from San Juan	1,539,840
New York to—from Chicago	2,981,610	Chicago to—from Detroit	1,522,870
Honolulu to—from Kahului, Maui	2,761,470	New York to—from West Palm Beach	1,386,730
New York to—from Miami	2,675,590	Los Angeles to—from Honolulu	1,374,070
New York to—from Boston	2,491,390	Los Angeles to—from Phoenix	1,353,290
Dallas/Ft. Worth to—from Houston	2,208,430	Honolulu to—from Kona, Hawaii	1,341,890
New York to—from San Francisco	2,185,760	Chicago to—from Los Angeles	1,265,030
New York to—from Washington	2,118,170	Honolulu to—from Hilo, Hawaii	1,243,640
New York to—from Orlando	2,005,130	Chicago to—from Atlanta	1,163,540
Los Angeles to—from Las Vegas	1,956,390	Boston to—from Washington	1,140,750
Los Angeles to—from San Francisco	1,933,450	Chicago to—from Minneapolis	1,121,280
New York to—from Atlanta	1,782,330	San Francisco to—from San Diego	1,104,990
Honolulu to—from Lihue, Kauai	1,775,350	Chicago to—from St. Louis	1,100,600
New York to—from Ft. Lauderdale	1,669,160	New York to—from Dallas/Ft. Worth	1,061,340
Los Angeles to—from Oakland	1,615,040	Los Angeles to—from Seattle/Tacoma	1,050,240

Source: Air Transport Association of America, Washington, DC, *Air Transport 1996*.

No. 1050. Worldwide Airline Fatalities: 1970 to 1996

[For scheduled air transport operations]

YEAR	Fatal accidents	Passenger deaths	Death rate [1]	Death rate [2]	YEAR	Fatal accidents	Passenger deaths	Death rate [1]	Death rate [2]
1970	29	700	0.29	0.18	1989 [3]	27	817	0.07	0.05
1975	20	467	0.13	0.08	1990 [3]	25	495	0.04	0.03
1980	22	814	0.14	0.09	1991 [3]	30	653	0.06	0.04
1984	16	223	0.03	0.02	1992 [3]	29	1,097	0.09	0.06
1985	22	1,066	0.15	0.09	1993 [3]	34	936	0.08	0.05
1986 [3]	22	546	0.06	0.04	1994 [3]	28	941	0.07	0.05
1987 [3]	26	901	0.09	0.06	1995 [3]	26	710	0.04	0.03
1988 [3]	28	729	0.07	0.04	1996 [3,4]	23	1,135	0.06	0.05

[1] Rate per 100 million passenger miles flown. [2] Rate per 100 million passenger kilometers flown. [3] Includes the Commonwealth of Independent States which began reporting in 1986. [4] Preliminary.

Source: International Civil Aviation Organization, Montreal, Canada, *Civil Aviation Statistics of the World*, annual.

No. 1051. Airline Passenger Screening Results: 1980 to 1995

[Calendar year data]

YEAR	Passengers screened (mil.)	WEAPONS DETECTED				PERSONS ARRESTED	
		Firearms		Other [1]	Explosive/ incendiary devices	Carrying firearms/ explosives	Giving false information
		Handguns	Long guns				
1980	585	1,878	36	108	8	1,031	32
1985	993	2,823	90	74	12	1,310	42
1987	1,096	3,012	99	141	14	1,581	81
1988	1,055	2,591	74	106	11	1,493	222
1989	1,113	2,397	92	390	26	1,436	83
1990	1,145	2,490	59	304	15	1,336	18
1991	1,015	1,597	47	275	94	893	28
1992	1,111	2,503	105	2,341	167	1,282	13
1993	1,150	2,707	91	3,867	251	1,354	31
1994	1,261	2,860	134	6,051	505	1,433	35
1995	1,263	2,230	160	4,414	631	1,194	68

[1] Through 1991, includes other firearms; beginning 1992, includes stunning guns, chemical agents, martial arts equipment, knives, bludgeons, and other designated items.

Source: U.S. Federal Aviation Administration, *Annual Report to Congress on Civil Aviation Security*.

No. 1052. Aircraft Accidents and Hijackings: 1975 to 1995

[For years ending December 31]

ITEM	Unit	1975	1980	1985	1990	1993	1994	1995
Aircraft accidents: [1] General aviation [2]	Number	3,995	3,590	2,739	2,215	2,039	1,990	2,066
Fatal	Number	633	618	498	442	396	402	406
Rate per 100,000 aircraft hours flown	Rate	2.20	1.69	1.75	1.55	2	1.83	2.04
Fatalities	Number	1,252	1,239	955	766	736	723	732
Air carrier, all services [3]	Number	(NA)	19	21	24	23	23	36
Fatal	Number	(NA)	1	7	6	1	4	3
Rate per 1,000,000 aircraft miles flown	Rate	(NA)	(Z)	0.002	0.001	(Z)	0.001	0.001
Fatalities	Number	(NA)	1	526	39	1	239	168
Air carrier, scheduled services	Number	29	15	17	22	22	19	33
Fatal	Number	2	-	4	6	1	4	2
Rate per 1,000,000 aircraft miles flown	Rate	0.001	-	0.001	0.001	(Z)	0.001	(Z)
Fatalities	Number	122	-	197	39	1	239	166
Commuter air carriers [4]	Number	48	38	21	16	16	10	12
Fatal	Number	12	8	7	4	4	3	2
Rate per 1,000,000 aircraft miles flown	Rate	0.07	0.04	0.02	0.01	0.01	0.01	(Z)
Fatalities	Number	28	37	37	7	24	25	9
Air taxis [5]	Number	152	171	154	106	69	85	76
Fatal	Number	24	46	35	28	19	26	24
Rate per 100,000 aircraft hours flown	Rate	0.95	1.27	1.36	1.24	1.05	1.35	1.20
Fatalities	Number	69	105	76	50	42	63	52
Hijacking incidents, worldwide	Number	19	39	26	40	31	23	9
U.S. registered aircraft	Number	6	21	4	1	-	-	-
Foreign-registered aircraft	Number	13	18	22	39	31	23	9
Bomb threats:								
U.S. airports	Number	449	268	256	448	304	250	346
Explosions	Number	4	1	-	-	-	-	-
U.S. worldwide and foreign aircraft in U.S.	Number	1,853	1,179	372	338	248	218	327
Explosions	Number	2	1	1	-	-	-	-

- Represents zero. NA Not available. Z rounds to zero. [1] Data from National Transportation Safety Board. [2] See text, section 22. [3] U.S. air carriers operating under 14 CFR 121. [4] All scheduled service of U.S. air carriers operating under 14 CFR 135. [5] All nonscheduled service of U.S. air carriers operating under 14 CFR 135.

Source: U.S. Federal Aviation Administration, *FAA Statistical Handbook of Aviation*, annual, last published in 1993. Includes data from U.S. Department of Transportation, Bureau of Transportation Statistics. Internet site <http://api.hq.faa.gov/apohome.htm> and unpublished data.

No. 1053. On-Time Flight Arrivals and Departures at Major U.S. Airports: 1996

[In percent. Quarterly, based on gate arrival and departure times for domestic scheduled operations in the 48 contiguous States of major U.S. airlines, per DOT reporting rule effective September 1987. All U.S. airlines with 1 percent or more of total U.S. domestic scheduled airline passenger revenues are required to report on-time data. A flight is considered on time if it operated less than 15 minutes after the scheduled time shown in the carrier's computerized reservation system. Cancelled and diverted flights are considered late. Excludes flight operations delayed/cancelled due to aircraft mechanical problems reported on FAA maintenance records (4-5 percent of the reporting airlines' scheduled operations). See source for data on individual airlines]

AIRPORT	ON-TIME ARRIVALS				ON-TIME DEPARTURES			
	1st. qtr.	2d. qtr.	3d. qtr.	4th. qtr.	1st. qtr.	2d. qtr.	3d. qtr.	4th. qtr.
Total, all airports	70.2	77.9	76.2	73.9	74.9	82.5	81.3	78.8
Total major airports	69.0	77.2	75.5	73.6	72.3	80.6	79.2	77.4
Atlanta, Hartsfield International	59.0	77.2	74.6	74.2	62.1	80.9	80.3	79.4
Boston, Logan International	61.3	73.9	71.2	73.2	68.0	82.2	81.0	81.4
Charlotte Douglas	71.0	82.4	80.1	81.4	68.4	78.5	80.4	82.5
Chicago, O'Hare	68.9	71.9	77.9	78.0	69.7	73.2	77.4	77.8
Cincinnati International	68.6	78.0	78.6	74.8	69.1	80.3	81.5	81.3
Dallas/Ft. Worth Regional	76.0	81.3	74.1	77.3	74.7	81.4	74.2	77.3
Denver International	76.9	82.5	79.6	78.3	77.5	83.8	80.1	78.3
Detroit, Metro Wayne	76.0	81.1	80.0	77.0	73.7	76.4	76.9	75.0
Houston Intercontinental	81.5	84.0	80.5	82.5	86.2	86.9	84.8	86.0
Las Vegas, McCarran International	73.0	81.3	78.2	70.7	76.5	83.8	80.5	74.7
Los Angeles International	63.9	76.5	72.2	62.6	72.5	81.9	78.5	70.2
Miami International	68.9	73.2	70.9	74.4	77.7	81.7	77.9	83.9
Minneapolis/St. Paul International	75.5	78.2	80.6	73.3	76.5	80.1	81.2	74.7
Newark International	63.0	66.4	61.9	69.5	70.0	76.7	72.1	77.3
New York, Kennedy International	60.3	65.0	59.6	69.8	66.8	75.4	68.1	75.2
New York, LaGuardia	67.0	75.4	74.2	77.1	72.6	84.4	83.1	83.4
Orlando International	65.1	77.6	76.6	76.1	76.2	84.8	84.9	84.1
Philadelphia International	68.1	76.3	75.3	74.3	71.0	79.7	79.9	79.7
Phoenix, Sky Harbor International	73.4	81.2	78.5	71.4	77.6	82.1	79.8	73.2
Pittsburgh, Greater International	69.7	78.9	79.7	80.0	71.1	80.6	82.9	83.3
St. Louis, Lambert	67.1	74.7	74.8	72.3	67.8	75.4	75.8	72.5
Salt Lake City International	64.7	80.8	76.7	66.5	65.8	82.7	78.1	70.4
San Diego International, Lindbergh	70.6	81.0	79.3	70.0	77.8	87.2	86.5	76.1
San Francisco International	60.2	72.8	72.3	60.5	69.1	80.3	77.3	66.8
Seattle-Tacoma International	68.7	72.5	67.7	62.1	79.0	83.2	78.6	72.2
Tampa International	65.5	75.9	74.5	73.0	73.8	83.7	85.5	82.8
Washington National	67.9	77.1	75.5	78.8	73.5	84.7	84.4	86.0

Source: U.S. Department of Transportation, Office of Consumer Affairs, *Air Travel Consumer Report*, monthly.

No. 1054. Consumer Complaints Against U.S. Airlines: 1988 to 1996

[Calendar year data. See source for data on individual airlines]

COMPLAINT CATEGORY	1988	1989	1990	1991	1992	1993	1994	1995	1996
Total	21,493	10,553	7,703	6,106	5,639	4,438	5,179	4,629	5,778
Flight problems [1]	8,831	4,111	3,034	1,877	1,624	1,211	1,586	1,133	1,626
Customer service [2]	2,120	1,002	758	714	695	599	805	667	1,000
Baggage	3,938	1,702	1,329	883	752	627	761	628	881
Ticketing/boarding [3]	1,445	821	624	659	680	577	598	666	857
Refunds	1,667	1,023	701	783	721	482	393	576	521
Oversales [4]	1,353	607	399	301	265	257	301	263	353
Fares [5]	455	341	312	388	573	398	267	185	180
Advertising	141	89	96	96	54	51	94	66	61
Tours	37	22	29	23	12	16	127	18	16
Smoking	546	232	74	30	25	30	20	15	13
Credit	35	19	5	10	10	4	2	4	3
Other	925	584	342	342	228	186	225	408	267

[1] Cancellations, delays, etc. from schedule. [2] Unhelpful employees, inadequate meals or cabin service, treatment of delayed passengers. [3] Errors in reservations and ticketing; problems in making reservations and obtaining tickets. [4] All bumping problems, whether or not airline complied with DOT regulations. [5] Incorrect or incomplete information about fares, discount fare conditions, and availability, etc.

Source: U.S. Dept. of Transportation, Office of Consumer Affairs, *Air Travel Consumer Report*, monthly.

No. 1055. Commuter/Regional Airline Operations—Summary: 1980 to 1996

[Calendar year data. Commuter/regional airlines operate primarily aircraft of predominately 75 passengers or less and 18,000 pounds of payload capacity serving short haul and small community markets. Represents operations within all North America by U.S. Regional Carriers. Averages are means. For definition of mean, see Guide to Tabular Presentation]

ITEM	Unit	1980	1985	1990	1992	1993	1994	1995	1996
Passenger carriers operating	Number	214	179	150	127	130	125	124	109
Passengers enplaned	Millions	14.8	[1]26.0	42.1	46.9	52.7	57.1	57.2	61.8
Average passengers enplaned per carrier	1,000	69.2	[1]52.4	277.5	365.0	405.2	457.0	461.4	566.3
Revenue passenger miles (RPM)	Billions	1.92	[1]4.41	7.61	9.46	10.61	12.02	12.75	14.3
Average RPM's per carrier	Millions	8.97	[1]24.64	50.75	74.50	81.59	96.15	102.80	131.24
Airports served	Number	732	854	811	802	829	806	780	782
Average trip length	Miles	129	173	183	194	201	210	223	232
Passenger aircraft operated	Number	1,339	1,745	1,917	2,103	2,208	2,172	2,138	2,127
Average seating capacity (seats)	Number	13.9	19.2	22.1	23.4	23.0	23.7	24.6	25.1
Fleet flying hours [2]	1,000	1,740	2,854	3,447	4,259	4,490	4,565	4,659	4,668
Average annual utilization per aircraft	Hours	1,299	1,635	1,798	2,025	2,033	2,102	2,179	2,148

[1] Adjusted to exclude a merger in 1986. [2] Prior to 1992, utilization results reflected airborne rather than block hours. Data inclusive of carriers which may have operated during only part of calendar year 1996.

Source: Regional Airline Association, Washington, DC, Annual Report of the Regional Airline Industry (copyright).

No. 1056. Civil Flying—Summary: 1970 to 1995

[As of Dec. 31 or for years ending Dec. 31, except as noted]

ITEM	Unit	1970	1980	1985	1990	1993	1994	1995
Airports in operation [1]	Number	11,261	15,161	16,318	17,490	18,317	18,343	18,224
Heliports	Number	790	2,336	3,120	4,085	4,569	4,617	4,559
Public	Number	4,260	4,814	5,861	5,078	5,157	5,137	5,132
Private	Number	7,001	10,347	10,457	12,412	13,160	13,206	13,092
Airports with runway lights	Number	3,554	4,738	4,941	4,822	4,842	4,830	4,838
Airports with paved runways	Number	3,805	5,833	6,721	7,694	8,186	8,230	10,029
Airport Improvement Program [2]	Mil. dol.	50.5	639.0	842.1	1,244.7	1,830.0	1,628.0	1,418.1
Total civil aircraft	1,000	154.5	259.4	274.9	275.9	279.0	281.0	(NA)
Active aircraft [3]	1,000	134.5	214.8	215.4	218.9	183.3	178.0	188.7
Air carriers, total [4]	1,000	2.8	3.8	4.7	6.7	7.3	7.4	7.4
General aviation aircraft [5]	1,000	131.7	211.0	210.7	212.2	176.0	170.6	181.3
Fixed-wing aircraft: Multi-engine	1,000	18.4	31.7	33.6	32.7	24.6	23.8	25
Single-engine	1,000	109.5	168.4	164.4	165.1	130.7	123.3	129.5
Rotorcraft [6]	1,000	2.2	6.0	6.4	7.4	4.5	4.4	5.1
Balloons, blimps, gliders, etc	1,000	1.6	5.0	6.3	7.0	5.2	6.2	5.3
Airman certificates held	1,000	1,002	1,195	1,105	1,195	1,225	1,225	1,290
Pilot [7]	1,000	733	827	710	703	665	654	639
Held by women	Percent	4.0	6.4	6.1	5.8	5.9	5.9	6.0
Airline transport	1,000	34	70	83	108	117	117	124
Commercial	1,000	187	183	152	149	143	139	134
Private	1,000	304	357	311	299	284	284	261
Student	1,000	196	200	147	128	104	96	101
Nonpilot [8]	1,000	269	368	395	492	560	571	651
Ground technicians [9]	1,000	241	321	341	421	485	496	574
FAA employees: Total	Number	53,125	55,340	47,245	51,269	52,680	48,932	48,324
Air traffic control specialists [10]	Number	(NA)	27,190	23,580	24,339	24,630	23,628	23,430
Full performance [11]	Number	(NA)	16,317	11,672	12,985	14,931	14,997	14,845
Developmental [11]	Number	(NA)	4,387	4,304	5,042	3,040	2,548	2,272
Assistants [11]	Number	(X)	(X)	1,465	1,153	632	507	355
Traffic management coordinators [12]	Number	(X)	(X)	(X)	370	482	544	561
Electronic technicians/ATSS [13]	Number	(NA)	8,871	6,856	6,458	6,262	6,531	6,749
Aviation safety inspectors	Number	(NA)	2,038	1,897	2,964	2,920	2,813	2,991
Engineers	Number	(NA)	2,436	2,457	2,745	3,198	2,891	2,810
Other	Number	(NA)	14,805	12,455	14,743	15,670	13,069	12,344
General aviation: [5]								
Hours flown	Million	26.0	41.0	34.1	34.8	24.3	23.9	25.4
Fuel consumed: [14]								
Gasoline	Mil. gal.	362	520	420	353	268	264	276
Jet fuel [15]	Mil. gal.	415	766	691	663	454	471	544

NA Not available. X Not applicable. [1] Existing airports, heliports, seaplane bases, etc. recorded with FAA. Includes military airports with joint civil and military use. Includes U.S. outlying areas. Airport-type definitions: Public—publicly owned and under control of a public agency; private—owned by a private individual or corporation. May or may not be open for public use. [2] Fiscal year data. Does not include System Planning Grants. Includes U.S. outlying areas. 1970-1980 data are obligated Federal funds for the Airport Development Aid Program. Thereafter, data are appropriated Federal funds under the Airport and Airway Improvement Act of 1982. [3] Registered aircraft that flew 1 or more hours during the year. [4] Includes helicopters. [5] See text, section 22. Beginning 1993, excludes commuters and includes experimental aircraft, not shown separately. Prior to 1993, experimental aircraft were included in the appropriate type. [6] Includes autogyros; excludes air carrier helicopters. [7] Includes all active pilots. An active pilot is one with a pilot certificate and a valid medical certificate. Also includes pilots who hold only a helicopter, glider, or lighter than air certificate, not shown separately. [8] Includes dispatchers, flight navigators and engineers, and ground technicians—mechanics, parachute riggers, and ground instructors. [9] No medical examinations are required, therefore, data represent all certificates on record and include retired or otherwise inactive technicians. [10] Includes all air traffic control specialists (staff positions, managers, supervisors, and for 1970-1985 traffic management coordinators, not shown separately) and air traffic assistants. [11] Serving in-flight service stations, towers, and centers. [12] Prior to 1990, included in total air traffic control specialists. [13] Airway Transportation Systems Specialists [14] Source: 1970, U.S. Bureau of Mines; thereafter, FAA General Aviation Activity and Avionics Survey. [15] Includes kerosene-type and naphtha-type jet fuels.

Source: Except as noted, U.S. Federal Aviation Administration, *FAA Statistical Handbook of Aviation*, annual, last published in 1993. Includes data from U.S. Department of Transportation, Research and Special Programs Administration. Internet site <http://api.hq.faa.gov/apohome.htm> and unpublished data.

No. 1057. Net Orders for U.S. Civil Jet Transport Aircraft: 1985 to 1996

[Value in millions of dollars. 1985-1992 are net new firm orders; beginning 1993, net announced orders. Minus sign (-) indicates net cancellations]

TYPE OF AIRCRAFT AND CUSTOMER	1985	1990	1991	1992	1993	1994	1995	1996
Total number [1]	468	670	280	231	31	79	421	595
U.S. customers	242	259	36	82	44	12	138	408
Foreign customers	226	411	244	149	-13	67	283	187
Boeing 737, total	253	189	75	91	-34	49	189	349
U.S. customers	146	38	-8	43	-29	9	85	284
Foreign customers	107	151	83	48	-5	40	104	65
Boeing 747, total	37	153	48	41	-25	-5	35	66
U.S. customers	13	24	-5	-	-25	-1	2	22
Foreign customers	24	129	53	41	-	-4	33	44
Boeing 757, total	51	66	80	7	20	5	-7	44
U.S. customers	39	33	42	29	46	-1	-6	35
Foreign customers	12	33	38	-22	-26	6	-1	9
Boeing 767, total	10	60	58	20	43	27	26	10
U.S. customers	4	23	28	10	41	11	4	11
Foreign customers	6	37	30	10	2	16	22	-1
Boeing 777, total	-	34	52	36	29	-	83	88
U.S. customers	-	34	-	-	5	-	-	37
Foreign customers	-	-	52	36	24	-	83	51
McDonnell Douglas MD-11, total	-	52	-31	1	-1	2	-6	9
U.S. customers	-	16	-26	4	-	2	3	1
Foreign customers	-	36	-5	-3	-1	-	-9	8
McDonnell Douglas MD-80/90, total	114	116	-2	35	-1	1	51	29
U.S. customers	37	91	5	-4	6	-8	-	18
Foreign customers	77	25	-7	39	-7	9	51	11
McDonnell Douglas MD-95, total	-	-	-	-	-	-	50	-
U.S. customers	-	-	-	-	-	-	50	-
Foreign customers	-	-	-	-	-	-	-	-
Total value	14,811	45,485	23,351	16,640	(NA)	(NA)	(NA)	(NA)
U.S. customers	7,869	14,828	2,144	3,200	(NA)	(NA)	(NA)	(NA)
Foreign customers	6,942	30,657	21,207	13,440	(NA)	(NA)	(NA)	(NA)

- Represents zero. NA Not available [1] Includes types of aircraft not shown separately.

Source: Aerospace Industries Association of America, Washington, DC, Research Center, Statistical Series 23.

No. 1058. U.S. Aircraft Shipments With Projections: 1970 to 1995

[Value in millions of dollars]

YEAR	TOTAL		CIVIL						MILITARY	
			Large transports		General Aviation [1]		Helicopters			
	Units	Value	Units	Value	Units	Value	Units	Value	Units	Value
1970	11,632	7,511	311	3,158	7,292	337	495	49	3,534	3,987
1975	16,958	9,355	285	4,006	14,056	1,033	838	266	1,779	4,050
1980	14,660	18,845	383	9,793	11,877	2,486	1,353	674	1,047	5,892
1985	3,597	29,312	273	9,375	2,029	1,431	376	505	919	18,001
1989	3,675	34,229	398	15,074	1,535	1,804	515	251	1,227	17,100
1990	3,321	39,207	521	22,215	1,144	2,008	603	254	1,053	14,730
1991	3,092	40,776	589	26,856	1,021	1,968	571	211	911	11,741
1992	2,628	41,632	610	30,268	941	1,840	324	142	753	9,582
1993	2,585	40,430	408	26,456	964	2,144	258	113	955	11,717
1994	2,301	30,262	310	19,800	928	2,357	308	185	755	7,920
1995, est.	2,275	28,390	256	17,824	1,077	2,842	292	194	650	7,530

[1] Excludes off-the-shelf military aircraft.

Source: U.S. Department of Commerce, International Trade Administration, Internet site <http://www.ita.doc.gov/industry/tai/green/acah7196.txt> (accessed 8 July 1997).

No. 1059. Employment and Earnings in Aircraft Industries: 1985 to 1996

[Annual averages of monthly figures. See headnote, table 660]

ITEM	1987 SIC [1] code	Unit	1985	1990	1994	1995	1996
Employment: Total	(X)	1,000	794	898	589	549	547
Aircraft	3721	1,000	326	381	271	244	243
Aircraft engines and engine parts	3724	1,000	148	152	95	93	95
Aircraft equipment, n.e.c. [2]	3728	1,000	143	180	115	113	116
Guided missiles, space vehicles, and parts	376	1,000	177	185	108	99	93
Average weekly earnings: [3]	(X)						
Aircraft	3721	Dollars	(NA)	(NA)	(NA)	(NA)	(NA)
Aircraft engines and parts	3724	Dollars	542	637	763	770	813
Guided missiles, space vehicles, and parts	376	Dollars	515	612	738	765	793
Average hourly earnings: [3]	(X)						
Aircraft [4]	3721	Dollars	13.18	15.66	19.50	19.97	20.49
Aircraft engines and parts	3724	Dollars	12.85	14.84	17.31	17.34	18.22
Guided missiles, space vehicles, and parts	376	Dollars	12.14	14.39	17.48	17.75	18.56

NA Not available. X Not applicable. [1] 1987 Standard Industrial Classification; see text, section 13. [2] N.e.c. means not elsewhere classified. [3] For production workers. [4] Excludes lump-sum payments. Earnings which include proration of lump-sum payments were: $13.40 in 1985; $16.32 in 1990; $19.57 in 1994; $20.02 in 1995, and $20.79 in 1996.

Source: U.S. Bureau of Labor Statistics, Bulletins 2445 and 2481; and *Employment and Earnings*, monthly, March and June issues.

No. 1060. Aerospace—Sales, New Orders, and Backlog: 1989 to 1995

[In billions of dollars, except as indicated. Reported by establishments in which the principal business is the development and/or production of aerospace products]

ITEM	1989	1990	1991	1992	1993	1994	1995
Net sales	122.1	136.6	123.9	118.7	109.9	104.3	101.2
Percent U.S. Government	58.0	54.0	48.9	50.0	49.9	54.8	49.6
Complete aircraft and parts [1]	38.4	49.9	52.9	54.0	48.9	43.3	41.5
Aircraft engines and parts	15.4	16.4	15.6	13.7	12.2	11.3	12.0
Missiles and space vehicles, parts	22.6	22.0	23.3	21.3	18.1	18.4	15.8
Other products, services	45.7	48.3	32.0	29.7	30.7	31.3	31.8
Net, new orders	173.6	146.0	122.5	100.3	79.7	88.7	104.7
Backlog, Dec. 31	252.4	250.1	245.2	236.1	211.8	192.6	194.6

[1] Except engines sold separately.

Source: U.S. Bureau of the Census, *Current Industrial Reports*, series MA-37D. Internet site <http://www.census.gov/econ/www/manumenu.htm> (accessed 8 July 1997).

No. 1061. Aerospace Industry Sales, by Product Group and Customer: 1985 to 1997

[In billions of dollars. Due to reporting practices and tabulating methods, figures may differ from those in table 1060]

ITEM	CURRENT DOLLARS					CONSTANT (1987) DOLLARS [3]				
	1985	1990	1995	1996 [1]	1997 [2]	1985	1990	1995	1996 [1]	1997 [2]
Total sales	**96.6**	**134.4**	**106.3**	**112.4**	**125.0**	**97.8**	**121.6**	**84.3**	**87.9**	**95.3**
PRODUCT GROUP										
Aircraft, total	50.5	71.4	55.1	60.5	72.0	51.1	64.6	43.7	47.3	54.9
Civil [4]	13.7	31.3	24.0	27.7	40.6	13.9	28.3	19.0	21.7	31.0
Military	36.8	40.1	31.1	32.8	31.4	37.2	36.3	24.7	25.6	23.9
Missiles	11.4	14.2	6.3	5.6	5.2	11.6	12.8	5.0	4.4	4.0
Space	18.6	26.4	27.3	27.6	26.9	18.8	23.9	21.8	21.6	20.5
Related products and services [5]	16.1	22.4	17.7	18.7	20.8	16.3	20.3	14.1	14.7	15.9
CUSTOMER GROUP										
Aerospace, total	80.5	112.0	88.6	93.7	104.2	81.5	101.3	70.3	73.3	79.4
DOD [6]	53.2	60.5	41.3	38.3	36.1	53.9	54.8	32.8	30.0	27.5
NASA [7] and other agencies	6.3	11.1	11.3	12.3	11.5	6.3	10.0	8.9	9.6	8.8
Other customers [8]	21.0	40.4	36.0	43.0	56.5	21.3	36.5	28.6	33.7	43.1
Related products and services [5]	16.1	22.4	17.7	18.7	20.8	16.3	20.3	14.1	14.7	15.9

[1] Preliminary. [2] Estimate. [3] Based on AIA's aerospace composite price deflator. [4] All civil sales of aircraft (domestic and export sales of jet transports, commuters, business, and personal aircraft and helicopters). [5] Electronics, software, and ground support equipment, plus sales of non-aerospace products which are produced by aerospace-manufacturing use technology, processes, and materials derived from aerospace products. [6] Department of Defense. [7] National Aeronautics and Space Administration. [8] Includes civil aircraft sales (see footnote 4), commercial space sales, all exports of military aircraft and missiles and related propulsion and parts.

Source: Aerospace Industries Association of America, Inc., Washington, DC, *1996 Year-end Review and Forecast.*

No. 1062. Aerospace Industry—Net Profits After Taxes: 1980 to 1996

[For calendar year. Minus sign (-) indicates loss]

YEAR	AEROSPACE INDUSTRY PROFITS				ALL MANUFACTURING CORPORATIONS PROFITS AS A PERCENT OF—		
	Total (mil. dol.)	As percent of— Sales	Assets	Equity	Sales	Assets	Equity
1980	2,588	4.3	5.2	16.0	4.8	6.9	13.9
1982	2,193	3.3	3.7	12.0	3.5	4.5	9.2
1983	2,829	3.5	4.1	12.1	4.1	5.1	10.5
1984	3,639	4.1	4.7	14.1	4.6	6.0	12.5
1985	3,274	3.1	3.6	11.1	3.8	4.6	10.1
1986	3,093	2.8	3.1	9.4	3.7	4.2	9.5
1987	4,582	4.1	4.4	14.6	4.9	5.6	12.8
1988	4,883	4.3	4.4	14.9	6.0	6.9	16.2
1989	3,866	3.3	3.3	10.7	5.0	5.6	13.7
1990	4,487	3.4	3.4	11.5	4.0	4.3	10.7
1991	[1]2,484	1.8	1.9	6.1	2.5	2.6	6.4
1992	[1]-1,836	-1.4	-1.2	-5.2	1.0	1.0	2.6
1993	4,621	3.6	3.5	13.2	2.8	2.9	8.1
1994	5,655	4.7	4.3	14.8	5.4	5.8	15.6
1995	4,635	3.8	3.5	11.1	5.7	6.2	16.3
1996	7,326	5.7	5.2	16.9	6.2	6.7	17.2

[1] Reflects unusually large nonoperating expenses totalling $3.4 billion in 1991 and $8.7 billion in 1992 due to the initial implementation of a change in accounting for future retirement benefit costs and defense-downsizing restructuring charges. Many large aerospace corporations chose to write off against first quarter earnings amounts required to comply with FASB 106.

Source: Aerospace Industries Association of America, Washington, DC, *1996 Year-end Review and Forecast.*

No. 1063. U.S. Exports of Aerospace Vehicles and Equipment: 1990 to 1995

ITEM	NUMBER OF UNITS				VALUE (mil. dol.)			
	1990	1993	1994	1995	1990	1993	1994	1995
Aerospace vehicles and equipment	(NA)	(NA)	(NA)	(NA)	39,083	39,426	37,390	33,070
Civilian aircraft, (powered only)	3,779	1,583	1,899	1,946	18,150	19,846	18,399	12,876
Under 4,536 kg. unladen weight, new	1,134	555	446	516	318	230	258	286
4,536-15,000 kg. unladen weight, new	79	58	69	60	245	324	347	321
Over 15,000 kg. unladen weight, new	306	276	222	137	16,691	18,146	15,931	10,606
Rotocraft, new	349	175	154	210	161	120	82	170
Nonpowered aircraft, new	(NA)	(NA)	(NA)	(NA)	15	9	7	15
Used or rebuilt	1,911	694	639	613	712	1,012	1,111	876
Military aircraft, (powered only)	445	632	437	775	1,481	1,460	1,504	1,330
Aircraft engines and parts	(NA)	(NA)	(NA)	(NA)	6,883	6,278	6,494	6,169
Piston engines and parts	(NA)	(NA)	(NA)	(NA)	421	294	332	361
Complete engines, new and used	6,411	7,613	6,798	7,893	110	123	157	148
Engine parts	(NA)	(NA)	(NA)	(NA)	311	172	175	213
Turbine engines and parts	(NA)	(NA)	(NA)	(NA)	6,462	5,984	6,162	5,808
Complete engines, new and used	24,687	17,088	5,028	7,032	1,856	2,409	2,497	1,811
Engine parts	(NA)	(NA)	(NA)	(NA)	4,606	3,575	3,665	3,997
Propellers, rotors, and parts	(NA)	(NA)	(NA)	(NA)	343	308	307	333
Landing gear and parts	(NA)	(NA)	(NA)	(NA)	276	338	317	387
Aircraft parts and accessories, n.e.c. [1]	(NA)	(NA)	(NA)	(NA)	8,962	8,574	8,944	9,465
Avionics	(NA)	(NA)	(NA)	(NA)	747	646	681	674
Flight simulators	(NA)	(NA)	(NA)	(NA)	255	197	232	122
Guided missiles and parts	(NA)	(NA)	(NA)	(NA)	1,306	1,231	1,010	1,501
Space vehicles and parts	(NA)	(NA)	(NA)	(NA)	660	548	574	812

NA Not available. [1] N.e.c.=Not elsewhere classified.

Source: U.S. Dept. of Commerce, International Trade Administration, Internet site <http://www.ita.doc.gov/industry/tai/green/aerox895.txt> (accessed 10 July 1997).

No. 1064. International Transportation Transactions of the United States: 1980 to 1996

[In millions of dollars. Data are international transportation transactions recorded for balance of payment purposes (see table 1292). Receipts include freight on exports carried by U.S.-operated carriers and foreign carrier expenditures in U.S. ports. Payments include freight on imports carried by foreign carriers and U.S. carrier port expenditures abroad. Freight on exports carried by foreign carriers is excluded since such payments are directly or indirectly for foreign account. Similarly, freight on U.S. imports carried by U.S. carriers is a domestic rather than an international transaction. Minus sign (-) indicates excess of payments over receipts]

ITEM	1980	1985	1990	1991	1992	1993	1994	1995	1996 [1]
Total receipts	14,209	19,085	38,043	39,185	39,234	39,862	42,024	46,537	47,773
Ocean passenger fares	(Z)	60	154	156	176	237	287	285	329
Other ocean transportation	7,757	8,846	12,141	12,252	11,328	11,533	12,404	13,580	12,494
Freight	3,229	3,440	4,104	4,011	3,980	3,952	4,450	5,213	4,646
Port expenditures	4,435	5,274	7,815	8,041	7,192	7,477	7,898	8,299	7,791
Charter hire	93	132	222	200	156	104	56	68	57
Air passenger fares [2]	2,591	4,351	15,144	15,698	16,442	16,374	16,796	18,840	20,228
Other air transportation	3,355	5,347	8,878	9,256	9,206	9,378	10,211	10,968	11,693
Freight	742	706	2,432	2,722	2,589	2,814	3,175	3,654	3,821
Port expenditures	2,613	4,641	5,742	5,834	5,785	5,753	6,136	6,362	6,740
Aircraft leasing	(NA)	(NA)	704	700	832	811	900	952	1,132
Miscellaneous receipts	506	481	1,726	1,823	2,082	2,140	2,326	2,864	3,029
Total payments	15,397	22,067	35,699	35,216	35,450	37,069	40,140	42,682	44,229
Ocean passenger fares	268	154	248	279	301	341	353	353	453
Other ocean transportation	8,179	10,698	13,078	12,276	11,861	12,568	13,803	14,173	13,595
Import freight	5,809	8,114	10,290	9,593	9,269	10,028	10,965	11,133	10,930
Port expenditures	1,905	2,048	2,174	2,093	2,029	2,011	2,325	2,554	2,233
Charter hire	465	536	614	590	563	529	513	486	432
Air passenger fares [2]	3,339	6,290	10,283	9,733	10,255	10,972	12,532	14,080	15,323
Other air transportation	3,366	4,719	10,083	10,742	10,725	10,758	10,818	11,363	11,910
Import freight	562	1,666	2,207	2,257	2,376	2,580	2,914	3,113	3,201
Port expenditures	2,804	3,053	7,674	8,256	8,092	7,917	7,611	7,948	8,477
Aircraft leasing	(NA)	(NA)	202	229	257	261	293	302	232
Miscellaneous payments	245	226	2,007	2,186	2,308	2,420	2,634	2,713	2,948
Balance	-1,188	-3,002	2,345	3,969	3,784	2,803	1,884	3,856	3,544

NA Not available. Z Less than $500,000. [1] Preliminary. [2] Beginning 1990, includes interairline settlements.

Source: U.S. Bureau of Economic Analysis, *Survey of Current Business*, June issues; and unpublished data.

No. 1065. Exports and Imports, by Method of Transport: 1980 to 1996

[Exports are free alongside ship (f.a.s.) value (see text, section 28) for all years; imports are f.a.s. value for 1980 and customs value for other years. Export data include both domestic and foreign; import data for general imports only. For details, see source]

ITEM	Unit	EXPORTS					IMPORTS				
		1980	1990	1994	1995	1996	1980	1990	1994	1995	1996
All methods [1]	Bil. dol.	220.7	393.0	512.4	583.0	622.8	240.8	495.3	663.4	743.5	791.3
Vessel	Bil. dol.	120.9	150.8	177.6	215.9	221.3	165.1	283.4	339.4	356.6	369.9
Air	Bil. dol.	46.1	110.5	150.3	181.1	196.2	28.0	90.9	143.0	174.2	185.9
Shipping weight: Vessel	Bil. kg	363.7	372.4	334.5	401.1	384.5	443.1	496.3	586.9	562.5	580.8
Air	Bil. kg	1.0	1.5	2	2.3	2.4	0.6	1.7	2.2	2.3	2.5

[1] Includes types other than vessel and air and revisions that are not distributed by method of transport.

Source: U.S. Bureau of the Census, *Highlights of U.S. Export and Import Trade*, 1980, FT 990, monthly; thereafter, *U.S. Merchandise Trade: Selected Highlights*, FT-920, monthly.

No. 1066. Federal Expenditures for Civil Functions of the Corps of Engineers, United States Army: 1970 to 1995

[In millions of dollars. For fiscal years ending in year shown, see text, section 9. These expenditures represent the work of the Corps of Engineers to plan, design, construct, operate, and maintain civil works projects and activities, particularly in the management and improvement of rivers, harbors, and waterways for navigation, flood control, and multiple purposes. The amounts listed below do not include the expenditure of funds contributed, advanced, or reimbursed by other government agencies or local interests. Includes Puerto Rico and outlying areas]

FISCAL YEAR	Total program [1]	Navigation	Flood control	Multiple purpose	FISCAL YEAR	Total program [1]	Navigation	Flood control	Multiple purpose
1970	1,128	398	379	331	1988	3,066	1,271	1,271	423
1980	3,061	1,225	1,228	551	1989	3,252	1,395	1,253	462
1982	2,940	1,331	1,083	453	1990	3,297	1,391	1,397	375
1983	2,959	1,290	1,088	482	1991	3,511	1,473	1,447	443
1984	3,085	1,383	1,154	445	1992	3,675	1,562	1,469	469
1985	2,956	1,234	1,187	419	1993	3,335	1,461	1,243	464
1986	3,163	1,345	1,300	402	1994	3,727	1,607	1,436	521
1987	2,937	1,135	1,272	411	1995	3,796	1,620	1,399	598

[1] Includes expenditures which are not associated with a specific purpose (e.g., headquarters staff supervision, management, and administration activities, and some research and development activities).

Source: U.S. Army Corps of Engineers, *Report of Civil Works Expenditures by State and Fiscal Year*, annual.

No. 1067. Freight Carried on Major U.S. Waterways: 1975 to 1995

[In millions of tons]

ITEM	1975	1980	1985	1990	1991	1992	1993	1994	1995
Atlantic intracoastal waterway	3.2	4.0	3.1	4.2	4.7	3.7	3.8	3.7	3.5
Great Lakes	193.8	183.5	148.1	167.1	151.2	160.0	159.6	175.3	177.7
Gulf intracoastal waterway	97.0	94.5	102.5	115.5	111.0	112.2	114.9	117.6	117.9
Mississippi River system [1]	453.4	584.2	527.8	659.6	645.9	674.4	660.4	693.3	710.1
Mississippi River mainstem	311.2	441.5	384.0	475.6	471.6	490.7	475.1	496.8	520.2
Ohio River system [2]	171.4	179.3	203.9	260.0	251.4	261.2	257.2	270.5	267.6
Columbia River	38.1	49.2	42.4	51.4	50.4	49.6	51.2	50.9	57.1
Snake River	2.0	5.1	3.5	4.8	5.1	4.7	5.3	5.9	6.8

[1] Main channels and all tributaries of the Mississippi, Illinois, Missouri and Ohio Rivers. [2] Main channels and all navigable tributaries and embayments of the Ohio, Tennessee, and Cumberland Rivers.

Source: U.S. Army Corps of Engineers, *Waterborne Commerce of the United States*, annual.

No. 1068. Waterborne Commerce, by Type of Commodity: 1990 to 1995

[In millions of short tons. Domestic trade includes all commercial movements between United States ports and on inland rivers, Great Lakes, canals, and connecting channels of the United States, Puerto Rico, and Virgin Islands]

COMMODITY	1990	1993	1994	1995			
				Total	Domestic	Foreign imports	Foreign exports
Total [1]	2,163.9	2,128.2	2,214.8	2,240.4	1,093.0	672.7	474.7
Coal	339.9	300.4	314.1	324.5	223.5	10.2	90.7
Petroleum and petroleum products	923.2	930.6	961.3	907.1	403.6	449.6	53.9
Crude petroleum	485.7	505.7	531.5	504.6	133.2	371.4	(Z)
Petroleum products [1]	437.5	424.9	429.9	402.5	270.3	78.2	53.9
Gasoline	116.9	112.3	119.1	114.4	99.8	10.8	3.8
Distillate fuel oil	77.4	83.3	81.4	76.7	57.2	12.9	6.6
Residual fuel oil	145.2	123.2	123.4	111.9	75.8	25.9	10.1
Chemicals and related products	123.8	131.6	146.9	153.7	79.4	24.3	50.0
Crude material, inedible [1]	374.7	360.6	369.3	381.7	226.4	82.7	72.7
Forest products, wood and chips	55.7	48.1	47.0	47.2	20.7	3.9	22.7
Pulp and waste paper	11.8	11.3	12.3	14.9	0.5	1.0	13.5
Soil, sand, gravel, rock, and stone	144.2	147.5	147.8	152.5	119.2	23.0	10.3
Primary manufactured goods [1]	76.0	76.8	105.0	106.3	36.8	51.7	17.7
Papers products	10.7	11.6	12.4	13.1	1.5	3.8	7.8
Lime, cement and glass	28.3	24.2	30.9	33.9	16.2	15.9	1.8
Primary iron and steel products	25.1	27.4	46.4	44.1	13.9	25.2	4.9
Food and farm products [1]	267.5	269.3	255.8	303.2	103.4	23.2	176.7
Fish	3.2	3.3	2.7	3.6	1.9	0.9	0.8
Grain [1]	157.3	146.2	133.1	167.9	57.6	2.2	108.2
Corn	96.1	78.9	69.4	105.0	40.8	(Z)	64.2
Wheat	44.5	52.6	47.4	48.5	12.8	0.4	35.3
Oilseeds	36.0	41.3	38.7	46.1	21.6	0.1	24.4
Soybeans	32.2	37.7	35.7	42.0	18.4	(Z)	23.6
Vegetables products	6.7	7.3	8.4	9.0	2.1	2.2	4.7
Processed grain and animal feed	28.2	32.4	29.7	33.0	10.6	0.8	21.7

Z Rounds to zero. [1] Includes categories not shown separately.

Source: U.S. Army Corps of Engineers, *Waterborne Commerce of the United States*, annual.

No. 1069. Waterborne Imports and Exports, by Coastal District: 1980 to 1995

[Exports are free alongside ship (f.a.s.) value for all years; imports are f.a.s. value for 1980 and customs value for other years, see text, section 28. Includes commodities classified for security reasons as "Special Category" (exports only) and exports by Dept. of Defense (grant-aid shipments), and merchandise shipped in transit through the United States. See Appendix III]

DISTRICT	CARGO TONNAGE (mil. tons) [1]						VALUE (bil. dol.)					
	1980	1985	1990	1993	1994	1995	1980	1985	1990	1993	1994	1995
Imports:												
Atlantic	183	190	207	197	219	203	71.5	94.4	110.8	117.7	134.4	145.5
Gulf	243	141	225	267	294	285	56.4	32.8	41.0	38.7	44.0	46.5
Pacific	56	51	55	58	64	65	45.0	90.4	143.3	168.8	190.6	196.9
Great Lakes	16	17	16	16	21	17	1.9	2.8	7.6	10.3	7.4	2.6
Exports:												
Atlantic	117	93	101	83	78	96	51.0	35.2	62.4	75.4	78.7	91.7
Gulf	163	144	148	155	141	173	41.5	31.8	41.2	39.9	40.8	53.1
Pacific	78	81	100	98	97	111	25.2	25.8	53.7	59.9	68.2	80.8
Great Lakes	45	34	26	21	24	28	4.6	2.4	1.7	1.5	1.6	2.5

[1] 1980 and 1985, short tons; beginning 1990, metric tons.

Source: U.S. Bureau of the Census, *U.S. Waterborne Exports and General Imports*, 1980 and 1985, FT 985, annual; 1990, TM 985, monthly; thereafter TA 985, annual.

No. 1070. Vessels Entered and Cleared in Foreign Trade, Net Registered Tonnage: 1966 to 1995

[In millions of net registered tons, except as indicated. Includes Puerto Rico and Virgin Islands. Seaports comprise all ports except Great Lakes ports]

YEARLY AVERAGE OR YEAR	ALL PORTS				SEAPORTS					
	Number of vessels	Tonnage, all vessels			Tonnage, all vessels			Tonnage, with cargo		
		Total	U.S.	Foreign	Total	U.S.	Foreign	Total	U.S.	Foreign
Entered:										
1966-70	53,459	232	29	203	206	27	180	157	18	139
1971-75	53,760	319	30	290	292	28	264	220	24	196
1976-80	53,700	458	40	418	425	38	387	316	30	286
1981-85	50,124	452	57	395	424	55	369	277	36	241
1986-90	61,978	548	46	502	521	45	476	346	30	315
1991-95	55,347	522	36	487	499	34	465	328	27	302
1970	53,293	254	28	226	227	24	202	171	19	152
1975	51,443	355	32	323	326	30	297	240	26	215
1980	53,645	492	52	440	460	50	410	310	34	276
1985	53,531	451	53	398	426	52	374	283	34	249
1990	66,424	589	41	548	564	40	524	367	30	337
1992	55,056	515	37	478	493	36	457	312	28	284
1993	54,834	515	35	480	493	33	460	329	26	303
1994	54,408	527	35	492	503	33	469	349	27	322
1995	55,184	539	32	507	514	30	484	341	25	316
Cleared:										
1966-70	52,415	232	30	202	206	27	179	122	23	99
1971-75	53,039	324	31	293	296	29	267	149	21	127
1976-80	52,931	453	41	412	420	38	382	203	26	177
1981-85	50,291	460	57	403	432	55	377	251	34	217
1986-90	60,249	551	47	504	524	46	478	284	31	253
1991-95	53,734	526	37	490	503	35	468	274	27	247
1970	52,195	253	27	226	226	25	201	132	20	112
1975	51,017	363	34	329	334	31	303	168	23	144
1980	52,928	487	54	433	456	51	405	246	33	213
1985	53,095	461	55	406	435	53	382	253	36	217
1990	63,648	592	43	550	566	41	525	304	29	275
1992	54,127	519	38	481	498	37	460	276	28	248
1993	53,637	519	36	483	497	35	462	262	28	234
1994	53,036	532	36	496	508	34	473	265	27	238
1995	52,772	540	33	508	517	31	485	285	24	261

Source: U.S. Bureau of the Census, *Vessel Entrances and Clearances*, through 1985, FT 975, annual; thereafter TA 987, annual.

No. 1071. Domestic Merchant Vessels Completed by U.S. Shipyards: 1970 to 1995

[Vessels of 1,000 gross tons and over]

TYPE	Unit	1970	1980	1985	1986	1987	1988	1992	1993	1994	1995
Merchant vessels	Number	13	10	8	5	4	4	3	-	1	-
Gross tons	1,000	342	375	172	215	153	153	44	-	17	-
Cargo	Number	6	6	4	2	3	3	1	-	-	-
Gross tons	1,000	120	105	113	66	58	58	32	-	-	-
Deadweight tons	1,000	134	114	97	53	63	63	29	-	-	-
Tankers	Number	7	4	4	3	1	1	2	-	1	-
Gross tons	1,000	222	270	59	149	95	95	12	-	17	-
Deadweight tons	1,000	427	354	92	271	209	209	16	-	22	-

- Represents zero.

Source: U.S. Maritime Administration, *New Ship Construction*, annual.

No. 1072. United States Flag Merchant Vessels: 1996

[As of January. Covers ocean-going vessels of 1,000 gross tons and over engaged in foreign and domestic trade, and inactive vessels. Excludes vessels operating exclusively on Great Lakes, inland waterways, and those owned by the United States Army and Navy, and special types such as cable ships, tugs, etc.]

VESSEL TYPE	NUMBER						DEADWEIGHT TONS (1,000)					
	Total	Passenger [1]	Cargo [2]	Intercoastal	Bulk carrier [3]	Tanker [4]	Total	Passenger [1]	Cargo [2]	Intercoastal	Bulk carrier [3]	Tanker [4]
Total	509	13	125	170	20	181	18,585	115	1,803	4,714	925	11,028
Active vessels	303	8	19	124	17	137	13,543	55	309	3,628	846	8,705
Privately owned	292	1	15	123	17	136	13,425	7	259	3,625	846	8,688
U.S. foreign trade	97	-	5	62	12	18	3,714	-	56	2,130	673	855
Foreign-to-foreign	26	-	-	8	2	16	1,583	-	-	248	93	1,242
Domestic trade	127	1	5	26	3	92	7,017	7	85	559	80	6,286
Coastal	67	-	3	2	3	59	2,429	-	45	53	80	2,251
Noncontiguous	60	1	2	24	-	33	4,588	7	40	506	-	4,035
Military Sea Lift Command	42	-	5	27	-	10	1,111	-	118	688	-	305
Government owned	11	5	4	1	-	1	118	48	50	3	-	17
Ready reserve force	2	1	1	-	-	-	24	9	15	-	-	-
Other Custody	3	-	2	-	-	1	39	-	22	-	-	17
Other Reserve	6	4	1	1	-	-	55	39	13	3	-	-
Inactive vessels	206	7	106	46	3	44	5,042	60	1,494	1,086	79	2,323
Privately owned	27	1	5	1	3	17	1,627	7	68	19	79	1,454
Temporarily inactive	2	-	-	-	1	1	105	-	-	-	33	72
Lay-up	23	1	5	1	2	14	1,454	7	68	19	46	1,314
Lay-up (MARAD Custody) [5]	2	-	-	-	-	2	68	-	-	-	-	68
Government owned (MARAD Custody) [5]												
National defense reserve fleet	179	6	101	45	-	27	3,415	53	1,426	1,067	-	869
Ready reserve fleet	90	-	42	38	-	10	1,852	-	608	940	-	304
Other reserve	45	-	29	7	-	9	941	-	472	127	-	342
Nonretention [6]	44	6	30	-	-	8	622	53	346	-	-	223

- Represents zero. [1] Includes combination passenger and cargo vessels. [2] General cargo. [3] Includes tug barges. [4] Includes tanker barges and liquified natural gas vessels. [5] In the custody of the Maritime Administration. [6] Vessels not actively maintained.

Source: U.S. Maritime Administration, *Employment Report of the United States Flag Merchant Fleet Ocean-Going Vessels 1,000 Gross Tons and Over*, annual.

No. 1073. Private Shipyards—Summary: 1980 to 1993

[For calendar year, unless noted]

ITEM	Unit	1980	1985	1987	1988	1989	1990	1991	1992	1993
Employment [1]	1,000	177.3	130.3	120.4	121.0	123.4	121.8	127.2	123.5	111.0
Production workers	1,000	141.8	99.0	90.8	90.9	88.6	86.4	95.5	93.3	84.3
Value of work done	Mil. dol.	9,269	9,358	8,531	(NA)	(NA)	(NA)	(NA)	(NA)	(NA)
On ships only	Mil. dol.	8,889	9,463	8,377	(NA)	(NA)	(NA)	(NA)	(NA)	(NA)
Value added	Mil. dol.	5,336	5,740	5,227	(NA)	(NA)	(NA)	(NA)	(NA)	(NA)
Building activity:										
Merchant vessels: [2]										
Under construction [3]	Number	69	10	6	-	-	-	3	3	1
Ordered	Number	7	-	-	-	-	3	-	1	-
Delivered	Number	23	3	4	-	-	-	-	3	-
Cancelled	Number	4	-	-	-	-	-	-	-	-
Under contract [4]	Number	49	7	-	-	-	3	3	1	1
Naval vessels: [2]										
Under construction [3]	Number	99	100	79	83	105	96	91	90	82
Ordered	Number	11	11	20	32	16	8	13	10	12
Delivered	Number	19	26	16	10	23	15	14	18	19
Under contract [4,5]	Number	91	85	83	105	98	91	90	82	73
Repairs/conversions:										
Commercial ships	Mil. dol.	1,335	852	806	202	279	373	380	226	292
Naval ships	Mil. dol.	1,134	2,311	1,930	1,238	1,091	1,119	993	526	573
Unfinished work: [3]										
Commercial ships	Mil. dol.	2,070	450	53	-	-	-	99	32	42
Naval ships	Mil. dol.	7,107	12,091	8,265	10,500	16,010	15,450	14,151	12,286	(NA)

- Represents zero. NA Not available. [1] Annual average of monthly data. [2] Vessels of 1,000 tons or larger. [3] As of Jan. 1. [4] As of Dec. 31. [5] Two ships were cancelled in August 1993.

Source: Shipbuilders Council of America, Arlington, VA., *Annual Report*, for 1980; thereafter, unpublished data.

No. 1074. Employees in Government and Private Shipyards: 1960 to 1996

[In thousands. Annual average employment in establishments primarily engaged in building and repairing all types of ships, barges, canal boats, and lighters of 5 gross tons and over, whether propelled by sail or motor power or towed by other craft. Includes all full- and part-time employees]

YEAR	Total	Private yards	Navy yards	YEAR	Total	Private yards	Navy yards	YEAR	Total	Private yards	Navy yards
1960	208	112	96	1987	200	124	75	1992	183	124	59
1970	216	134	83	1988	197	124	73	1993	163	113	50
1975	217	154	65	1989	196	126	71	1994	148	107	41
1980	250	178	72	1990	198	130	68	1995	139	105	34
1985	219	138	80	1991	193	131	62	1996	124	98	26

Source: U.S. Bureau of Labor Statistics, Bulletins 2445 and 2481; *Employment and Earnings*, monthly, March and June issues; and unpublished data.

No. 1075. Employment on U.S. Flag Merchant Vessels and Basic Monthly Wage Scale for Able-Bodied Seamen, 1970 to 1996

[Employment in thousands]

YEAR	Employment [1]	YEAR	Employment [1]	YEAR	East coast wage rate [2]	West coast wage rate [2]	YEAR	East coast wage rate [2]	West coast wage rate [2]
1975	20.5	1991	11.7	1975	612	900	1991	1,518	2,329
1980	19.6	1992	9.2	1980	967	1,414	1992	1,655	2,436
1985	13.1	1993	9.3	1985	1,419	2,029	1993	1,721	2,436
1988	10.7	1994	9.1	1988	1,419	2,175	1994	1,790	2,536
1989	9.9	1995	7.9	1989	1,448	2,218	1995	1,918	2,637
1990	11.1	1996	7.5	1990	1,505	2,218	1996	2,014	2,769

[1] As of June 30, except beginning 1980, as of Sept. 30. Estimates of personnel employed on merchant ships, 1,000 gross tons and over. Excludes vessels on inland waterways, Great Lakes, and those owned by, or operated for, U.S. Army and Navy, and special types such as cable ships, tugs, etc. [2] As of January. Basic monthly wage, over and above subsistence (board and room); excludes overtime and fringe pay benefits. West coast incorporates extra pay for Saturdays and Sundays at sea into base wages but east coast does not.

Source: U.S. Maritime Administration, *U.S. Merchant Marine Data Sheet*, monthly; and unpublished data.

No. 1076. Worldwide Tanker Casualties: 1975 to 1996

[Data for 1975 and 1980 covers tankers, ore/oil carriers and bulk/oil vessels of 6,000 deadweight tons and over; beginning 1985, 10,000 deadweight tons and over; excludes liquid gas carriers. Incident is counted in the year it is reported. Based on data from "Lloyd's List" published by Lloyd's of London. "Casualties" include weather damage, strandings, collisions and other contact, fires and explosions, machinery damage, and other mishaps]

ITEM	Unit	1975	1980	1985	1990	1991	1992	1993	1994	1995	1996
Casualties	Number	906	(NA)	340	541	507	396	314	270	280	234
Total losses [1]	Number	22	15	12	10	10	11	9	11	6	2
Deaths	Number	90	132	53	119	205	86	26	88	8	15
Oil spills	Number	45	32	9	31	26	17	24	29	18	24
Amount	1,000 tons	188	136	80	61	439	152	120	110	4	72
Amount	Mil. gallons	58	42	25	19	136	47	37	33	1	22

NA Not available. [1] Excludes losses due to hostilities.

Source: Tanker Advisory Center, Inc., New York, NY, "Worldwide Tanker Casualty Returns," quarterly.

No. 1077. Merchant Vessels—World and United States: 1960 to 1993

[Through 1992, as of mid-year; thereafter for year-end. For propelled sea-going merchant ships of not less than 100 gross tonnage]

YEAR	WORLD: COMPLETED		WORLD: OWNED		U.S.: COMPLETED		U.S.: REGISTERED	
	Number	Gross tonnage (1,000)	Number	Gross tonnage (1,000)	Number	Gross tonnage (1,000)	Number	Gross tonnage (1,000)
1960	2,005	8,382	36,311	129,770	49	379	4,059	24,837
1970	2,814	20,980	52,444	227,490	156	375	2,983	18,463
1980	2,412	13,101	73,832	419,911	205	555	5,579	18,464
1985	1,964	18,157	76,395	416,269	66	180	6,447	19,518
1989	1,593	13,236	76,100	410,481	10	4	6,375	20,588
1990	1,672	15,885	78,336	423,627	16	15	6,348	21,328
1991	1,574	16,095	80,030	436,027	17	9	6,222	20,291
1992	1,506	18,633	79,845	444,305	27	54	5,737	18,228
1993	1,505	20,025	80,655	457,915	30	14	5,646	14,087

Source: Through 1992, Lloyd's Register of Shipping, London, England, *Statistical Tables*, annual; and *Annual Summary of Merchant Ships Completed in the World*; thereafter, *World Fleet Statistics*, annual.

No. 1078. Merchant Vessels—Ships and Tonnage Lost Worldwide: 1980 to 1993

[For merchant vessels of 100 gross tonnage and above. Excludes ships which have been declared constructive losses but have undergone repair during the year. Loss counted in the year the casualty occurred, providing that information was available at time of relevant publication]

TYPE OF SHIP	SHIPS LOST					GROSS TONNAGE LOST (1,000)				
	1980	1985	1990	1992	1993	1980	1985	1990	1992	1993
Total[1]	387	307	188	213	219	1,804	1,651	1,128	1,223	778
Tankers	24	19	8	7	12	707	776	138	332	198
Ore/bulk carriers[2]	21	22	15	13	7	458	405	687	576	160
General cargo	211	155	87	81	96	478	383	202	174	310
Container ships	2	5	-	4	1	6	41	-	40	5
Passenger[3]	9	-	-	1	1	112	-	-	13	4
Fishing	96	66	50	77	74	30	26	20	31	39

- Represents zero. [1] Includes types not shown separately. [2] Includes ore/bulk/oil carriers. [3] Includes passenger cargo ships.

Source: Lloyd's Register of Shipping, London, England, *Casualty Return*, annual.

No. 1079. Merchant Fleets of the World: 1996

[Vessels of 1,000 gross tons and over. As of Jan. 1. Specified countries have 100 or more ships]

YEAR AND COUNTRY OF REGISTRY, 1996	TOTAL		CONTAINER-SHIPS		BULK CARRIERS[1]		TANKERS		OTHERS	
	Number	Average age (yr.)	Number	Average age (yr.)	Number	Average age (yr.)	Number	Average age (yr.)	Number	Average age (yr.)
World total	25,608	18	1,734	12	5,474	16	6,080	17	12,320	19
United States	509	24	81	17	20	15	181	23	227	35
Privately-owned	319	20	77	18	20	15	153	21	69	35
Government-owned	190	33	4	28	-	-	28	27	158	42
Foreign	25,099	18	1,653	13	5,454	16	5,899	17	12,093	19
Antigua and Barbuda	357	12	63	7	8	15	11	17	275	13
Bahamas	930	14	39	17	140	15	243	13	508	15
Brazil	198	16	11	16	60	14	83	16	44	18
Bulgaria	108	19	5	12	33	18	16	13	54	23
China: Mainland	1,454	18	87	13	337	17	216	15	814	19
Cyprus	1,473	16	101	10	566	17	161	14	645	15
Denmark (DIS)[2]	333	9	60	8	12	6	82	8	179	11
Germany	404	7	145	6	8	11	38	7	213	9
Greece	952	18	34	21	461	16	275	17	182	21
Honduras	237	27	4	31	11	25	23	29	199	27
Hong Kong	239	10	40	11	131	8	21	12	47	13
India	299	13	6	10	134	13	87	12	72	15
Indonesia	432	18	5	19	17	14	112	17	298	19
Iran	119	18	1	26	47	14	27	22	44	19
Italy	389	16	14	6	37	12	220	17	118	17
Japan	762	8	38	9	189	10	305	7	230	8
Korea (South)	417	14	53	11	124	14	87	13	153	16
Liberia	1,584	12	142	10	464	13	648	11	330	13
Malaysia	254	14	24	13	39	8	83	10	108	31
Malta	1,006	19	23	16	315	18	244	19	424	19
Netherlands	406	9	31	10	6	13	66	10	303	9
Norway (NIS)[2]	630	14	5	13	115	12	285	13	225	18
Panama	3,692	13	289	12	924	12	826	12	1,653	15
Philippines	516	14	14	16	224	8	60	21	218	18
Poland	131	16	-	-	69	15	5	21	57	18
Romania	220	16	2	8	39	18	10	15	169	15
Russia	1,426	18	33	18	83	17	190	16	1,120	18
Saint Vincent	640	21	18	17	113	20	89	24	420	21
Singapore	655	13	90	14	111	10	280	13	174	17
Spain	106	16	15	17	5	21	26	15	60	17
Sweden	184	16	-	-	9	18	64	16	111	16
Taiwan	202	11	85	12	53	8	19	8	45	18
Thailand	251	22	7	21	28	17	67	23	149	22
Turkey	475	17	1	4	160	18	68	20	246	16
Ukraine	428	20	12	14	39	18	31	15	346	21
United Kingdom	148	16	24	17	7	13	63	17	54	15
U.A.R.(Egypt)	119	19	-	-	19	10	14	20	86	21
Vanuatu	112	13	3	14	39	12	15	18	55	12
All others	2,811	19	129	30	278	17	739	18	1,665	19

- Represents zero. [1] Includes bulk/oil, ore/oil, and ore/bulk/oil carriers. [2] International Shipping Registry which is an open registry under which the ship flies the flag of the specified nation but is exempt from certain taxation and other regulations.

Source: U.S. Maritime Administration, *Merchant Fleets of the World*, summary report, annual; and unpublished data.

Figure 23.1
Consumer Expenditures for Farm Foods: 1980, 1990, and 1995

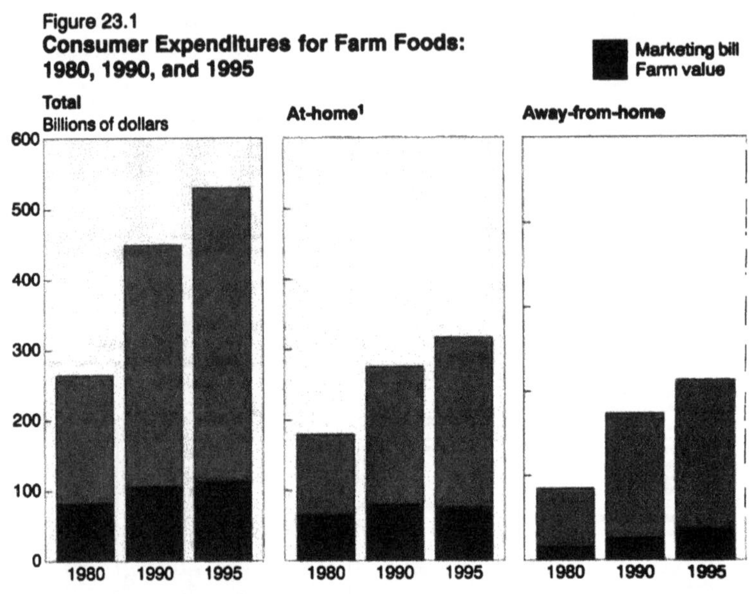

[1]Food purchased from retail food stores for use at home.
Source: Chart prepared by U.S. Bureau of the Census. For data, see table 1100.

Figure 23.2
Corn, Soybeans, and Wheat— U.S. Production and Exports: 1996

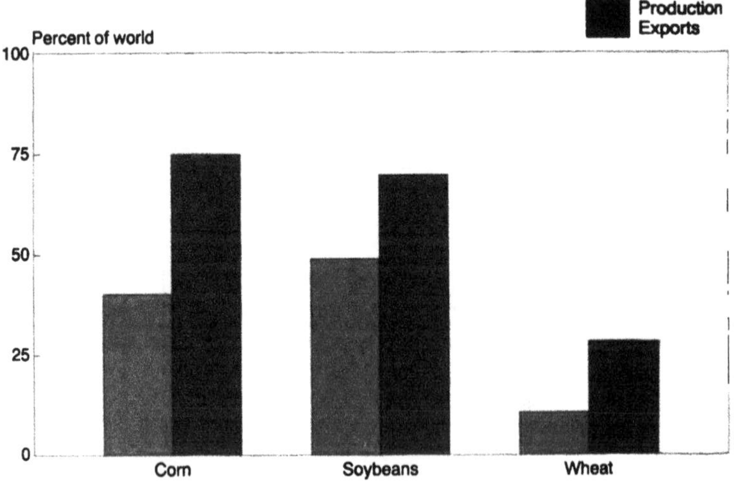

¹: Chart prepared by U.S. Bureau of the Census For data, see table 1107

Agriculture

This section presents statistics on farms and farm operators; land use and irrigation; farm income, expenditures, and debt; farm output, productivity, and marketings; foreign trade in agricultural products; specific crops; and livestock, poultry, and their products.

The principal sources are the reports issued by the U.S. Bureau of the Census and by the National Agricultural Statistics Service (NASS) and the Economic Research Service (ERS) of the U.S. Department of Agriculture. The 1992 Census of Agriculture is the 24th taken by the Bureau of the Census. The information is available in printed form in the volume 1, Geographic Area Series, and in electronic format on CD-ROM. The Department of Agriculture publishes annually *Agricultural Statistics*, a general reference book on agricultural production, supplies, consumption, facilities, costs, and returns. The Economic Research Service publishes data on farm assets, debt, and income in the annual *Farm Business Economic Report*. Sources of current data on agricultural exports and imports include *Foreign Agricultural Trade of the United States*, published by the ERS, and the reports of the Bureau of the Census, particularly *U.S. Imports for Consumption and General Imports—HTSUSA Commodity by Country of Origin* (FT247), *U.S. Exports, Harmonized Schedule B, Commodity by Country* (FT447) and *U.S. Merchandise Trade: Exports, General Imports, and Imports for Consumption* (FT925).

The 45 field offices of the NASS collect data on crops, livestock and products, agricultural prices, farm employment, and other related subjects mainly through sample surveys. Information is obtained on some 75 crops and 50 livestock items as well as scores of items pertaining to agricultural production and marketing. State estimates and supporting information are sent to the Agricultural Statistics Board of NASS which reviews the estimates and issues reports containing State and national data. Among these reports are annual summaries such as *Crop Production, Crop Values, Agricultural Prices*, and *Livestock Production, Disposition and Income*. For more information about concepts and methods underlying USDA's statistical series, see *Major Statistical Series of the U.S. Department of Agriculture* (Agricultural Handbook No. 671), a 12-volume set of publications.

In Brief

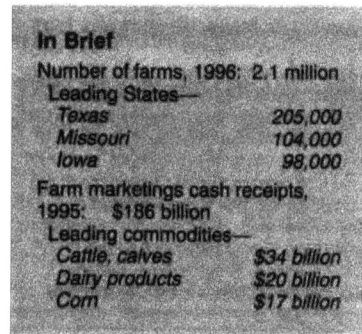

Number of farms, 1996: 2.1 million
Leading States—

Texas	*205,000*
Missouri	*104,000*
Iowa	*98,000*

Farm marketings cash receipts, 1995: $186 billion
Leading commodities—

Cattle, calves	*$34 billion*
Dairy products	*$20 billion*
Corn	*$17 billion*

Farms and farmland—The Bureau of the Census has used varying definitions of a farm. Since 1850, when minimum criteria defining a farm for census purposes first were established, the farm definition has been changed nine times. The current definition, first used for the 1974 census, is any place from which $1,000 or more of agricultural products were produced and sold, or normally would have been sold, during the census year.

Acreage designated as "land in farms" consists primarily of agricultural land used for crops, pasture, or grazing. It also includes woodland and wasteland not actually under cultivation or used for pasture or grazing, provided it was part of the farm operator's total operation. Land in farms includes acres set aside under annual commodity acreage programs as well as acres in the Conservation Reserve and Wetlands Reserve Programs for places meeting the farm definition. Land in farms is an operating unit concept and includes land owned and operated as well as land rented from others. All grazing land, except land used under government permits on a per-head basis, was included as "land in farms" provided it was part of a farm or ranch.

Coverage estimates for 1987 and 1992 indicate about 7.2 and 11.1 percent of all farms, respectively, were not included in census totals. Farms undercounted in these censuses were usually small and accounted for approximately 1 percent of the total value of agricultural products sold and approximately 2 percent of the land in farms. For more explanation about mail list compilation and census coverage, see appendixes A and C, *1992 Census of Agriculture*, volume 1 reports and *Coverage Evaluation*, volume 2, part 2.

Farm income—Gross farm income comprises cash receipts from farm marketings of crops and livestock, Federal government payments made directly to farmers for farm-related activities, rental value of farm homes, value of farm products consumed in farm homes, and other farm-related income such as machine hire and custom work. Farm marketings represent quantities of agricultural products sold by farmers multiplied by prices received per unit of production at the local market. Information on prices received for farm products is generally obtained by the NASS Agricultural Statistics Board from surveys of firms (such as grain elevators, packers, and processors) purchasing agricultural commodities directly from producers. In some cases, the price information is obtained directly from the producers.

Crops—Estimates of crop acreage and production by the NASS are based on current sample survey data obtained from individual producers and objective yield counts, reports of carlot shipments, market records, personal field observations by field statisticians, and reports from other sources. Prices received by farmers are marketing year averages. These averages are based on U.S. monthly prices weighted by monthly marketings during specific periods. U.S. monthly prices are State average prices weighted by marketings during the month. Marketing year average prices do not include allowances for outstanding loans, government purchases, deficiency payments or disaster payments.

All State prices are based on individual State marketing years, while U.S. marketing year averages are based on standard marketing years for each crop. For a listing of the crop marketing years and the participating States in the monthly program, see *Crop Values*, January 1992. Value of production is computed by multiplying State prices by each State's production. The U.S. value of production is the sum of State values for all States. Value of production figures shown in tables 1112-1115, 1119 and 1120 should not be confused with cash receipts from farm marketings which relate to sales during a calendar year, irrespective of the year of production.

Livestock—Annual inventory numbers of livestock and estimates of livestock, dairy, and poultry production prepared by the Department of Agriculture are based on information from farmers and ranchers obtained by probability survey sampling methods.

Statistical reliability—For a discussion of statistical collection and estimation, sampling procedures, and measures of statistical reliability pertaining to Census Bureau and Department of Agriculture data, see Appendix III.

No. 1080. Farms—Number and Acreage, by Size of Farm: 1982 to 1992

SIZE OF FARM	NUMBER OF FARMS (1,000)			LAND IN FARMS (mil. acres)			CROPLAND HARVESTED (mil. acres)			PERCENT DISTRIBUTION, 1992		
	1982	1987	1992	1982	1987	1992	1982	1987	1992	Number of farms	All land in farms	Cropland harvested
Total	2,241	2,088	1,925	986.8	964.5	945.5	326.3	282.2	295.9	100.0	100.0	100.0
Under 10 acres	188	183	166	0.7	0.7	0.7	0.3	0.2	0.2	8.6	0.1	0.1
10 to 49 acres	449	412	388	12.1	11.1	10.3	4.5	3.9	3.5	20.1	1.1	1.2
50 to 99 acres	344	311	283	24.8	22.5	20.4	9.5	7.9	7.2	14.7	2.2	2.4
100 to 179 acres	368	334	301	49.9	45.3	40.7	21.2	17.1	15.4	15.6	4.3	5.2
180 to 259 acres	211	192	172	45.7	41.5	37.2	21.7	17.2	15.5	8.9	3.9	5.2
260 to 499 acres	315	286	255	113.0	103.0	91.7	60.5	47.3	43.6	13.3	9.7	14.7
500 to 999 acres	204	200	186	140.5	138.5	129.3	77.6	67.4	68.6	9.7	13.7	23.2
1,000 to 1,999 acres	97	102	102	132.4	138.8	139.0	64.5	61.1	69.3	5.3	14.7	23.4
2,000 acres and over	65	67	71	467.5	463.2	476.3	66.6	60.2	72.5	3.7	50.4	24.5

No. 1081. Farms—Number and Acreage, by Tenure of Operator: 1982 to 1992

[*Full owners* own all the land they operate. *Part owners* own a part and rent from others the rest of the land they operate]

ITEM AND YEAR	Unit	Total	Full owner	Part owner	Tenant	PERCENT DISTRIBUTION			
						Total	Full owner	Part owner	Tenant
NUMBER OF FARMS									
1982	1,000	2,241	1,326	656	259	100.0	59.2	29.3	11.5
1987	1,000	2,088	1,239	609	240	100.0	59.3	29.2	11.5
1992	1,000	1,925	1,112	597	217	100.0	57.7	31.0	11.3
Under 50 acres	1,000	554	444	58	52	100.0	80.1	10.5	9.4
50 to 179 acres	1,000	584	395	130	59	100.0	67.6	22.3	10.1
180 to 499 acres	1,000	428	190	183	55	100.0	44.4	42.8	12.8
500 to 999 acres	1,000	186	48	111	27	100.0	25.8	59.7	14.5
1,000 acres or more	1,000	173	35	114	24	100.0	20.2	65.9	13.9
LAND IN FARMS									
1982	Mil. acres	987	342	531	114	100.0	34.7	53.8	11.6
1987	Mil. acres	964	318	520	127	100.0	32.9	53.9	13.2
1992	Mil. acres	946	296	527	123	100.0	31.3	55.7	13.0

No. 1082. Farm Operators—Tenure and Characteristics: 1987 and 1992

[In thousands, except as indicated]

CHARACTERISTIC	ALL FARMS		FARMS WITH SALES OF $10,000 AND OVER	
	1987	1992	1987	1992
Total operators	2,088	1,925	1,060	1,019
White	2,043	1,882	1,046	1,003
Black	23	19	4	5
American Indian, Eskimo, and Aleut	7	8	2	3
Asian or Pacific Islander	8	8	5	5
Other	7	8	2	3
Operators of Hispanic origin [1]	17	21	6	8
Female	132	145	42	50
Under 25 years old	36	28	21	17
25 to 34 years old	243	179	147	112
35 to 44 years old	411	382	212	217
45 to 54 years old	455	429	228	223
55 to 64 years old	496	430	263	229
65 years old and over	447	478	188	220
Average age (years)	52.0	53.3	50.6	51.9
Full owner	1,239	1,112	445	422
Part owner	609	597	454	448
Tenant	240	217	161	148
Principal occupation:				
Farming	1,138	1,053	811	754
Other	950	872	248	265
Place of residence: [2]				
On farm operated	1,488	1,379	776	736
Not on farm operated	443	409	215	215
Years on present farm: [2]				
2 years or less	114	95	49	41
3 to 4 years	135	133	56	58
5 to 9 years	304	259	138	121
10 years or more	1,163	1,113	653	648
Days worked off farm: [2]				
None	844	802	561	536
Less than 100 days	200	165	124	104
100 to 199 days	178	162	80	76
200 days or more	737	666	219	226

[1] Operators of Hispanic origin may be of any race. [2] Excludes not reported.

Source of tables 1080-1082: U.S. Bureau of the Census, *Census of Agriculture: 1987*, vol. 1; and *1992*, vol. 1.

No. 1083. Farms—Number, Acreage, and Value, by Type of Organization: 1987 and 1992

ITEM	Unit	Total [1]	Individual or family	Partnership	Corporation	PERCENT DISTRIBUTION: Total [1]	Individual or family	Partnership	Corporation
ALL FARMS									
Number of farms: 1987	1,000	2,088	1,809	200	67	100.0	86.7	9.6	3.2
1992	1,000	1,925	1,653	187	73	100.0	85.9	9.7	3.8
Land in farms: 1987	Mil. acres	964	628	153	119	100.0	65.1	15.9	12.4
1992	Mil. acres	946	604	153	123	100.0	63.9	16.2	13.0
Value of land and buildings: [2] 1987	Bil. dol.	604	424	95	69	100.0	70.1	15.7	11.4
1992	Bil. dol.	687	474	109	85	100.0	69.0	15.8	12.4
Value of farm products sold: 1987	Bil. dol.	136	77	23	35	100.0	56.3	17.1	25.6
1992	Bil. dol.	163	88	29	44	100.0	54.1	18.0	27.2
FARMS WITH SALES OF $10,000 AND OVER									
Number of farms: 1987	1,000	1,060	861	136	56	100.0	81.3	12.8	5.3
1992	1,000	1,019	820	131	61	100.0	80.5	12.8	6.0
Land in farms: 1987	Mil. acres	829	525	143	116	100.0	63.3	17.3	14.0
1992	Mil. acres	822	512	143	119	100.0	62.2	17.4	14.4

[1] Includes other types, not shown separately. [2] Based on a sample of farms.

No. 1084. Corporate Farms—Characteristics, by Type: 1992

ITEM	Unit	All corporations	FAMILY HELD CORPORATIONS: Total	1-10 stockholders	11 or more stockholders	OTHER CORPORATIONS: Total	1-10 stockholders	11 or more stockholders
Farms	Number	72,567	64,528	62,755	1,773	8,039	6,914	1,125
Percent distribution	Percent	100.0	88.9	86.5	2.4	11.1	9.5	1.6
Land in farms	Mil. acres	122.8	110.8	100.9	9.9	11.9	8.0	4.0
Average per farm	Acres	1,692	1,718	1,608	5,597	1,484	1,152	3,524
Value of—								
Land and buildings [1]	Bil. dol.	85.1	72.5	66.5	6.0	12.5	8.1	4.4
Average per farm	$1,000	1,172	1,131	1,068	3,385	1,484	1,105	3,950
Farm products sold	Bil. dol.	44.2	34.4	29.7	4.7	9.8	6.5	3.3
Average per farm	$1,000	609	533	474	2,626	1,218	941	2,915

[1] Based on a sample of farms.

No. 1085. Farms—Number, Acreage, and Value of Sales, by Size of Sales: 1992

VALUE OF PRODUCTS SOLD	Farms (1,000)	ACREAGE: Total (mil.)	Average per farm	VALUE OF SALES: Total (mil. dol.)	Average per farm (dol.)	PERCENT DISTRIBUTION: Farms	Acreage	Value of sales
Total	**1,925**	**945.5**	**491**	**162,608**	**84,459**	**100.0**	**100.0**	**100.0**
Less than $10,000	907	123.5	136	3,043	3,357	47.1	13.1	1.9
Less than $2,500	423	55.7	132	411	972	22.0	5.9	0.3
$2,500-$4,999	232	26.9	116	836	3,605	12.1	2.8	0.5
$5,000-$9,999	252	40.9	162	1,797	7,132	13.1	4.3	1.1
$10,000 or more	1,019	822.0	807	159,565	156,623	52.9	86.9	98.1
$10,000-$24,999	302	81.8	271	4,841	16,039	15.7	8.7	3.0
$25,000-$49,999	195	91.4	477	6,967	35,662	10.1	9.7	4.3
$50,000-$99,999	188	133.9	713	13,517	71,990	9.8	14.2	8.3
$100,000-$249,999	208	228.0	1,094	32,711	156,958	10.8	24.1	20.1
$250,000-$499,999	79	130.9	1,666	26,914	342,653	4.1	13.8	16.6
$500,000-$999,999	31	80.6	2,598	20,953	675,368	1.6	8.5	12.9
$1,000,000 or more	16	75.5	4,751	53,663	3,377,175	0.8	8.0	33.0

Source of tables 1083-1085: U.S. Bureau of the Census, *1992 Census of Agriculture*, vol. 1.

No. 1086. Farms—Number, Acreage, and Value, by State: 1987 and 1992

REGION, DIVISION, AND STATE	ALL FARMS: Number of farms (1,000)		Land in farms (mil. acres)		Average size of farm (acres)		Total value [1] (mil. dol.)		FARMS WITH SALES OF $10,000 OR MORE, 1992: Number of farms (1,000)	Land in farms (mil. acres)	Average size of farm (acres)	Total value [1] (mil. dol.)
	1987	1992	1987	1992	1987	1992	1987	1992				
U.S.	2,088	1,925	964.5	945.5	462	491	604,168	687,432	1,019	822.0	807	555,056
Northeast	123	109	21.4	19.4	174	177	32,045	38,306	56	14.7	261	27,504
N.E.	25	23	4.2	3.9	169	168	7,866	8,834	10	2.7	257	5,449
ME	6	6	1.3	1.3	214	218	1,321	1,396	3	0.9	340	842
NH	2	2	0.4	0.4	169	158	900	836	1	0.2	257	418
VT	6	5	1.4	1.3	240	235	1,521	1,730	3	1.0	328	1,219
MA	6	5	0.6	0.5	99	100	2,154	2,421	2	0.3	145	1,478
RI	1	1	0.1	0.1	84	76	295	313	(Z)	(Z)	118	194
CT	4	3	0.4	0.4	111	105	1,674	2,138	1	0.2	173	1,299
M.A	98	86	17.2	15.5	175	180	24,179	29,472	46	12.0	261	22,055
NY	38	32	8.4	7.5	223	231	8,263	9,130	18	6.0	332	7,012
NJ	9	9	0.9	0.8	99	93	3,579	5,590	4	0.6	179	3,734
PA	51	45	7.9	7.2	153	160	12,337	14,752	24	5.4	221	11,309
Midwest	862	777	350.5	343.6	407	442	228,073	263,320	514	310.8	605	235,102
E.N.C	365	326	86.6	82.7	237	254	96,291	110,003	200	73.7	368	96,755
OH	79	71	15.0	14.2	189	201	18,023	20,626	38	11.9	314	16,799
IN	70	63	16.2	15.6	229	249	18,716	21,732	37	14.1	384	19,151
IL	89	78	28.5	27.3	321	351	35,779	41,844	56	26.0	464	39,607
MI	51	47	10.3	10.1	202	217	10,034	11,517	24	8.3	352	8,999
WI	75	68	16.6	15.5	221	228	13,740	14,285	46	13.4	290	12,199
W.N.C	497	451	263.8	260.9	531	578	131,782	153,317	313	237.2	757	138,347
MN	85	75	26.6	25.7	312	342	18,616	23,319	53	23.2	438	21,005
IA	105	97	31.6	31.3	301	325	29,830	38,063	77	29.9	388	36,345
MO	106	98	29.2	28.5	275	291	18,634	22,070	47	22.5	477	16,771
ND	35	31	40.3	39.4	1,143	1,267	12,934	13,163	25	36.8	1,449	12,194
SD	36	34	44.2	44.8	1,214	1,316	11,871	12,264	27	39.0	1,452	10,955
NE	60	53	45.3	44.4	749	839	20,828	22,713	42	42.6	1,007	21,640
KS	69	63	46.6	46.7	680	738	19,068	21,725	41	43.2	1,041	19,438
South	824	775	281.2	277.0	341	357	207,777	222,294	315	222.2	706	158,473
S.A.	240	223	51.2	48.6	214	218	64,886	76,544	93	36.5	393	54,961
DE	3	3	0.6	0.6	205	224	1,098	1,351	2	0.5	309	1,184
MD	15	13	2.4	2.2	162	171	5,419	6,570	7	1.8	282	4,862
VA	45	42	8.7	8.3	194	197	10,409	13,534	17	6.0	355	9,100
WV	17	17	3.4	3.3	196	192	2,255	2,810	4	1.5	394	1,229
NC	59	52	9.4	8.9	159	172	11,845	13,950	25	7.0	281	10,118
SC	20	20	4.8	4.5	232	221	4,127	5,093	7	3.0	452	2,986
GA	44	41	10.7	10.0	247	246	9,852	11,437	17	7.5	431	7,547
FL	37	35	11.2	10.8	306	306	19,884	21,801	15	9.2	614	17,924
E.S.C	250	236	45.6	43.5	183	185	38,811	45,055	90	30.4	337	29,328
KY	92	90	14.0	13.7	152	151	12,545	14,775	41	10.0	248	10,603
TN	80	75	11.7	11.2	147	149	11,648	13,977	24	7.3	298	8,007
AL	43	38	9.1	8.5	211	223	7,264	8,350	14	5.7	410	5,152
MS	34	32	10.7	10.2	315	318	7,333	7,952	12	7.5	640	5,566
W.S.C	335	317	184.4	186.0	551	583	104,079	100,695	131	155.2	1,181	74,195
AR	48	44	14.4	14.1	298	322	10,884	12,407	21	11.3	536	9,668
LA	27	26	8.0	7.8	293	306	7,348	7,474	11	6.4	604	5,645
OK	70	67	31.5	32.1	449	480	15,102	15,754	30	26.3	889	11,851
TX	189	181	130.5	130.9	691	725	70,746	65,060	70	111.2	1,586	47,031
West	278	264	311.3	305.6	1,118	1,158	136,274	163,513	134	274.3	2,046	133,977
Mountain	124	118	244.1	240.7	1,965	2,035	62,906	69,720	65	217.3	3,362	58,517
MT	25	23	60.2	59.6	2,451	2,613	12,418	13,578	15	53.6	3,612	11,658
ID	24	22	13.9	13.5	577	609	8,126	9,077	13	11.6	909	7,829
WY	9	9	33.6	32.9	3,650	3,772	4,909	5,242	6	29.7	5,376	4,516
CO	27	27	34.0	34.0	1,248	1,252	12,519	14,568	15	30.7	2,029	11,932
NM	14	14	46.0	46.8	3,230	3,281	8,291	9,220	6	42.4	7,273	7,298
AZ	8	7	36.3	35.0	4,732	5,173	10,111	10,984	3	32.7	10,260	9,837
UT	14	14	10.0	9.6	710	712	4,259	4,704	6	8.2	1,372	3,546
NV	3	3	10.0	9.3	3,300	3,205	2,272	2,347	1	8.3	6,081	1,902
Pacific	154	146	67.3	64.8	466	445	73,367	93,793	69	57.0	821	75,461
WA	34	30	16.1	15.7	460	520	11,948	14,178	15	13.5	915	11,060
OR	32	32	17.8	17.6	556	552	9,597	11,824	12	15.6	1,289	8,534
CA	83	78	30.6	29.0	368	373	48,567	63,689	40	25.8	639	52,685
AK	1	1	1.0	0.9	1,789	1,803	317	249	(Z)	0.6	3,788	138
HI	5	5	1.7	1.6	353	298	2,938	3,854	2	1.5	729	3,044

Z Less than 500 farms or 50,000 acres. [1] Value of land and buildings. Based on reports for a sample of farms.

Source: U.S. Bureau of the Census, *1992 Census of Agriculture*, vol. 1.

No. 1087. Irrigated Farms and Acreage, by State: 1987 and 1992

STATE	IRRIGATED FARMS				LAND IN IRRIGATED FARMS				IRRIGATED LAND			
	Number (1,000)		Percent of all farms		Acreage (1,000)		Percent of all land in farms		Acreage (1,000)		Percent of all land in farms	
	1987	1992	1987	1992	1987	1992	1987	1992	1987	1992	1987	1992
U.S. [1]	291.6	279.4	13.9	14.5	241,069	231,853	24.9	24.5	46,386	49,404	4.8	5.2
California	58.9	56.5	70.7	72.8	17,567	16,444	57.4	54.9	7,596	7,571	24.8	26.1
Colorado	14.9	15.2	54.6	56.0	16,729	16,648	49.1	49.0	3,014	3,170	8.9	9.3
Florida	12.0	13.5	32.7	38.3	4,670	4,937	41.7	45.9	1,623	1,783	14.5	16.6
Idaho	16.6	15.5	68.8	70.0	9,053	8,579	64.9	63.7	3,219	3,260	23.1	24.2
Kansas	7.4	6.5	10.7	10.3	10,654	10,519	22.8	22.5	2,463	2,680	5.3	5.7
Montana	9.5	8.9	38.7	38.9	23,259	22,024	38.6	36.9	1,997	1,978	3.3	3.3
Nebraska	22.6	19.3	37.3	36.5	22,499	22,027	49.6	49.6	5,682	6,312	12.5	14.2
Oregon	14.4	15.0	45.0	47.0	11,340	10,419	63.6	59.2	1,648	1,622	9.3	9.2
Texas	19.8	18.8	10.4	10.4	20,270	19,353	15.5	14.8	4,271	4,912	3.3	3.8
Washington	15.4	14.1	45.9	46.5	5,468	5,101	33.9	32.4	1,519	1,641	9.4	10.4
Wyoming	5.2	5.1	56.7	58.2	18,207	17,955	54.1	54.6	1,518	1,465	4.5	4.5

[1] Includes other States not shown separately.

Source: U.S. Bureau of the Census, *1992 Census of Agriculture*, vol. 1.

No. 1088. Farms—Number and Acreage: 1980 to 1996

[As of June 1. Based on 1974 census definition; for definition of farms and farmland, see text, section 23. Data for census years (indicated by italics) have been adjusted for underenumeration and are used as reference points along with data from acreage and livestock surveys in estimating data for other years. Minus sign (-) indicates decrease]

YEAR	FARMS		LAND IN FARMS		YEAR	FARMS		LAND IN FARMS	
	Number (1,000)	Annual change [1] (1,000)	Total (mil. acres)	Average per farm (acres)		Number (1,000)	Annual change [1] (1,000)	Total (mil. acres)	Average per farm (acres)
1980	2,440	3	1,039	426	1991	2,117	-29	982	464
1985	2,293	-41	1,012	441	*1992*	*2,108*	*-9*	*979*	*464*
1987	*2,213*	*-37*	*999*	*451*	1993	2,083	-25	976	469
1988	2,201	-12	994	452	1994	2,065	-18	973	471
1989	2,175	-26	991	456	1995	2,072	7	972	469
1990	2,146	-29	987	460	1996	2,063	-9	968	469

[1] Annual change from immediate preceding year.

No. 1089. Farms—Number and Acreage, by State: 1990 and 1996

[See headnote, table 1088]

STATE	FARMS (1,000)		ACREAGE (mil.)		ACREAGE PER FARM		STATE	FARMS (1,000)		ACREAGE (mil.)		ACREAGE PER FARM	
	1990	1996	1990	1996	1990	1996		1990	1996	1990	1996	1990	1996
U.S.	**2,146**	**2,063**	**987**	**968**	**450**	**469**	Missouri	108	104	30	30	281	288
							Montana	25	22	61	60	2,449	2,714
Alabama	47	45	10	10	215	218	Nebraska	57	56	47	47	826	839
Alaska	1	1	1	1	1,707	1,804	Nevada	3	3	9	9	3,560	3,520
Arizona	8	8	36	35	4,641	4,720	New Hampshire	3	2	(Z)	(Z)	183	179
Arkansas	47	43	16	15	330	349	New Jersey	8	9	1	1	107	91
California	85	82	31	30	362	366	New Mexico	14	14	45	44	3,296	3,237
Colorado	27	25	33	33	1,249	1,327	New York	39	36	8	8	218	214
Connecticut	4	4	(Z)	(Z)	108	100	North Carolina	62	58	10	9	156	159
Delaware	3	3	1	1	207	226	North Dakota	34	31	41	40	1,209	1,300
Florida	41	40	11	10	266	258	Ohio	83	72	16	15	188	210
Georgia	48	43	13	12	260	274	Oklahoma	70	72	33	34	471	472
Hawaii	5	5	2	2	357	346	Oregon	37	39	18	18	488	455
Idaho	22	22	14	14	628	614	Pennsylvania	53	50	8	8	153	154
Illinois	83	76	28	28	342	370	Rhode Island	1	1	(Z)	(Z)	95	90
Indiana	68	60	16	16	240	265	South Carolina	25	22	5	5	208	233
Iowa	104	98	34	33	322	339	South Dakota	35	33	44	44	1,266	1,354
Kansas	69	66	48	48	694	724	Tennessee	87	80	12	12	139	148
Kentucky	93	88	14	14	152	159	Texas	196	205	132	127	673	620
Louisiana	32	27	9	9	278	322	Utah	13	13	11	11	856	821
Maine	7	7	1	1	201	181	Vermont	7	6	1	1	222	225
Maryland	15	14	2	2	148	153	Virginia	46	48	9	9	193	179
Massachusetts	6	6	1	1	100	92	Washington	37	36	16	16	432	436
Michigan	54	53	11	11	200	200	West Virginia	21	20	4	4	180	185
Minnesota	89	87	30	30	337	343	Wisconsin	80	79	18	17	220	213
Mississippi	40	44	13	13	325	286	Wyoming	9	9	35	35	3,899	3,802

Z Less than 500,000 acres.

Source of tables 1088 and 1089: U.S. Dept. of Agriculture, National Agricultural Statistics Service, *Farm Numbers, 1975-80; Farms and Land in Farms, Final Estimates by States, 1979-1987; Farms and Land in Farms, Final Estimates, 1988-1992*; and *Farms and Land in Farms*, July releases.

No. 1090. Farm Real Estate—Summary: 1980 to 1996

[1980 and 1985 and 1986, value data as of Feb. 1; 1988, as of April 1; 1990-96, as of January 1. Excludes Alaska and Hawaii. Total value of land and buildings is estimated by multiplying the number of acres of farmland by the average value per acre of land and buildings. Per acre values are based on data from the census of agriculture. For intercensal years, estimates are based on surveys conducted by the U.S. Dept. of Agriculture]

ITEM	Unit	1980	1985	1986	1988	1990	1991	1992	1993	1994	1995	1996
Total value	Bil. dol	783.3	719.4	626.8	660.0	671.4	688.0	695.5	717.1	759.2	807.0	859.7
Average value per acre	Dollars	737	713	632	668	683	703	713	736	782	832	890
Average value, operating unit	$1,000	313.5	314.5	285.5	304.3	313.7	325.9	330.8	345.1	368.7	390.6	417.8

No. 1091. Farm Real Estate—Value of Land and Buildings, by State: 1990 to 1995

[See headnote, table 1090]

STATE	VALUE OF LAND AND BUILDINGS (mil. dol.)			AVERAGE VALUE OF LAND AND BUILDINGS, PER ACRE			STATE	VALUE OF LAND AND BUILDINGS (mil. dol.)			AVERAGE VALUE OF LAND AND BUILDINGS, PER ACRE		
	1990	1995	1996	1990	1995	1996		1990	1995	1996	1990	1995	1996
U.S.	671,419	807,017	859,711	$683	$832	$890	MT	13,431	16,529	17,273	222	277	289
							NE	24,680	28,074	29,695	524	596	632
AL	8,989	12,875	13,594	890	1,262	1,367	NV	1,842	2,543	2,925	207	289	332
AZ	9,665	12,282	14,125	267	347	399	NH	998	1,094	1,109	2,269	2,486	2,578
AR	12,338	14,747	14,836	796	983	989	NJ	4,780	6,844	6,865	5,494	8,052	8,172
CA	58,027	66,456	72,105	1,884	2,215	2,404	NM	8,233	9,883	11,287	185	225	258
CO	12,379	17,020	18,150	374	520	558	NY	8,518	10,628	10,266	1,014	1,360	1,333
CT	2,114	2,495	2,588	5,033	6,567	6,810	NC	13,144	16,092	18,120	1,355	1,749	1,970
DE	1,328	1,533	1,643	2,214	2,689	2,907	ND	13,001	15,041	15,417	321	373	383
FL	22,563	22,860	23,752	2,070	2,219	2,306	OH	19,859	27,359	30,033	1,273	1,800	1,969
GA	13,488	15,076	16,025	1,079	1,256	1,358	OK	16,203	18,609	18,609	491	547	547
ID	9,015	11,286	12,223	658	836	905	OR	10,199	14,776	16,239	573	844	928
IL	39,902	52,346	58,000	1,405	1,863	2,064	PA	15,625	18,013	19,292	1,929	2,339	2,505
IN	20,440	26,302	28,642	1,254	1,654	1,801	RI	389	438	454	5,584	6,947	7,204
IA	36,515	44,786	47,876	1,090	1,349	1,442	SC	5,257	6,749	6,816	1,011	1,337	1,363
KS	21,555	25,573	26,417	450	535	553	SD	12,891	13,306	14,038	291	302	319
KY	13,790	17,498	19,283	978	1,250	1,377	TN	12,911	16,035	18,006	1,067	1,336	1,526
LA	8,233	9,199	10,234	925	1,082	1,176	TX	66,924	70,968	71,894	507	550	566
ME	1,556	1,681	1,730	1,073	1,245	1,291	UT	4,497	6,731	7,671	396	606	697
MD	5,767	8,155	8,034	2,563	3,707	3,826	VT	1,817	2,026	2,070	1,262	1,479	1,534
MA	2,705	3,077	3,190	4,227	5,398	5,597	VA	14,819	15,232	16,557	1,665	1,771	1,925
MI	10,854	14,219	15,579	1,005	1,329	1,470	WA	13,136	16,825	17,538	821	1,065	1,117
MN	24,300	27,907	29,079	810	936	976	WV	2,457	3,368	3,570	664	910	965
MS	9,568	11,432	11,557	736	886	917	WI	14,098	18,004	19,741	801	1,065	1,175
MO	21,310	26,411	28,445	701	880	948	WY	5,309	6,633	7,118	153	192	206

Source of tables 1090 and 1091: U.S. Dept. of Agriculture, Economic Research Service, 1980, *Farm Real Estate Market Developments*, annual; 1985-88, *Agricultural Resources, Agricultural Land Values and Markets, Situation and Outlook Report*, annual; 1989-95, *AREI Updates, Number 17: Agricultural Land Values*, annual.

No. 1092. Balance Sheet of the Farming Sector: 1980 to 1995

[In billions of dollars, except as indicated. As of December 31]

ITEM	1980	1985	1987	1988	1989	1990	1991	1992	1993	1994	1995
Assets	981.5	771.0	754.7	786.3	812.4	839.9	843.5	868.9	904.6	938.1	978.0
Real estate	782.8	586.2	563.5	582.7	600.8	620.0	625.5	642.8	674.0	706.9	755.7
Livestock and poultry	60.6	46.3	58.0	62.2	66.2	70.9	68.1	71.0	72.8	67.9	58.1
Machinery, motor vehicles	80.3	82.9	78.7	81.0	84.1	86.3	85.9	85.5	86.7	87.9	86.9
Crops stored	31.1	21.2	16.2	21.6	21.9	21.5	20.7	22.7	20.4	22.5	25.1
Purchased inputs	(NA)	1.2	3.2	3.5	2.6	2.8	2.7	3.9	4.2	5.0	3.4
Financial assets	26.7	33.3	35.1	35.4	36.8	38.3	40.5	43.0	46.5	47.9	48.8
Investment in cooperatives	19.3	24.3	25.3	25.1	26.3	27.5	28.7	29.4	31.3	32.4	33.9
Other financial assets	7.4	9.0	9.9	10.4	10.5	10.9	11.8	13.6	15.3	15.5	14.9
Claims	981.5	771.0	754.7	786.3	812.4	839.9	843.5	868.9	904.6	938.1	978.0
Debt	166.8	177.6	144.4	139.6	137.9	138.0	139.2	139.1	142.0	146.8	150.8
Real estate debt	89.7	100.1	82.4	77.8	76.0	74.7	74.9	75.4	76.0	77.7	79.3
Nonreal estate debt	77.1	77.5	62.0	61.7	61.9	63.2	64.3	63.6	65.9	69.1	71.5
Equity	814.7	593.4	610.3	646.7	674.5	701.9	704.3	729.9	762.6	791.3	827.2
Farm debt/asset ratio (percent)	17.0	23.0	19.1	17.8	17.0	16.4	16.5	16.0	15.7	15.6	15.4

NA Not available.

Source: U.S. Dept. of Agriculture, Economic Research Service, *Farm Business Economic Report, 1995* (ECI-1996).

No. 1093. Gross Farm Product—Summary: 1980 to 1994

[In billions of dollars. For definition of gross product, see text, section 14. Minus sign (-) indicates decrease]

ITEM	1980	1985	1986	1987	1988	1989	1990	1991	1992	1993	1994
CURRENT DOLLARS											
Farm output, total	142.9	152.7	144.0	152.0	158.5	177.2	185.6	180.3	187.7	186.0	201.6
Cash receipts from farm marketings	140.3	136.3	135.3	147.8	159.6	166.7	172.3	170.4	172.2	181.3	179.2
Farm housing	5.1	5.0	4.9	4.9	4.8	5.0	5.1	5.2	5.3	5.5	5.7
Farm products consumed on farms	1.2	0.9	0.9	0.7	0.7	0.7	0.7	0.6	0.6	0.5	0.5
Other farm income	2.4	4.6	4.4	5.0	5.2	4.9	4.8	5.1	4.6	4.8	4.7
Change in farm inventories	-6.1	5.8	-1.5	-6.4	-11.9	-	2.6	-1.1	5.0	-6.2	11.5
Less: Intermediate goods and services purchased [1]	86.8	85.6	81.1	86.9	94.7	101.0	106.0	107.3	107.1	113.9	119.3
Equals: **Gross farm product**	56.1	67.1	63.0	65.1	63.8	76.2	79.6	72.9	80.6	72.1	82.3
Less: Consumption of fixed capital	18.7	20.7	20.5	20.3	20.5	21.1	21.8	22.4	23.2	23.4	23.9
Indirect business tax [2]	3.0	3.3	3.3	3.6	3.7	3.9	4.4	4.4	4.5	4.6	5.0
Plus: Subsidies to operators	1.0	6.3	9.5	13.5	11.7	9.3	7.5	6.8	7.7	11.3	6.6
Equals: **Farm national income**	35.5	49.4	48.7	54.7	51.4	60.5	61.0	52.9	60.5	55.4	60.0
CHAINED (1992) DOLLARS [3]											
Farm output, total	(NA)	163.6	160.5	166.7	160.1	169.7	177.0	178.7	187.7	181.9	197.6
Cash receipts from farm marketings	(NA)	149.3	153.3	165.3	161.4	159.7	164.0	168.9	172.2	177.6	176.7
Farm housing	(NA)	6.2	6.0	5.8	5.8	5.6	5.6	5.5	5.3	5.1	4.9
Farm products consumed on farms	(NA)	1.1	1.1	0.8	0.8	0.7	0.6	0.6	0.6	0.5	0.5
Other farm income	(NA)	4.7	4.9	5.3	5.0	4.5	4.7	5.0	4.6	4.8	4.3
Change in farm inventories	(NA)	6.9	-1.6	-8.8	-12.6	-	2.5	-1.7	5.0	-7.3	12.3
Less: Intermediate goods and services purchased [1]	(NA)	96.6	96.3	101.7	103.0	104.1	106.2	107.1	107.1	111.2	114.3
Equals: **Gross farm product**	(NA)	66.9	64.2	65.3	58.2	65.9	70.8	71.6	80.6	70.7	83.7

- Represents zero. NA Not available. [1] Includes rent paid to nonoperator landlords. [2] Includes nontax liability. [3] See text, section 14.

Source: U.S. Bureau of Economic Analysis, *National Income and Product Accounts of the United States 1929-94*, and *Survey of Current Business*, January/February 1996.

No. 1094. Value Added to Economy by Agricultural Sector: 1980 to 1995

[In billions of dollars. Data are consistent with the net farm income accounts and include income and expenses related to the farm operator dwellings. The concept presented is consistent with that employed by the Organization for Economic Co-operation and Development]

ITEM	1980	1985	1987	1988	1989	1990	1991	1992	1993	1994	1995
Final agricultural sector output	148.0	153.5	151.7	163.4	181.0	188.9	183.7	191.4	190.8	208.0	203.1
Final crop output (sales) [1]	64.4	74.1	64.5	69.2	81.5	83.3	81.0	89.0	81.9	99.8	95.1
Final animal output (sales) [1]	70.3	68.7	75.7	78.6	83.8	90.2	87.3	87.1	91.7	89.7	87.7
Services and forestry	13.3	10.7	11.5	15.6	15.8	15.4	15.4	15.3	17.2	18.5	20.3
Machine hire and customwork	0.7	1.5	1.5	1.5	1.7	1.8	1.7	1.5	2.0	2.3	2.2
Forest products sold	1.0	1.4	1.7	1.8	2.0	1.9	1.8	2.2	2.6	2.7	2.7
Other farm income	0.6	3.2	3.2	4.5	4.9	4.5	4.7	4.4	4.6	4.1	6.0
Gross imputed rental value of farm dwellings	11.0	4.7	5.0	7.7	7.2	7.2	7.2	7.1	8.0	9.3	9.4
Less: Intermediate consumption outlays	77.0	73.5	76.7	84.3	88.7	92.9	94.5	93.4	100.4	104.7	111.2
Farm origin	34.9	29.3	32.6	37.3	38.1	39.5	38.6	38.6	41.2	41.3	42.5
Manufactured inputs	20.9	18.3	15.9	16.6	18.0	19.4	20.6	20.1	20.5	21.7	23.4
Other intermediate expenses	21.2	26.0	28.2	30.4	32.7	34.0	35.4	34.7	38.8	41.8	45.2
Repair and maintenance of capital items	7.1	6.4	6.8	7.7	8.4	8.6	8.6	8.5	9.2	9.2	9.4
Machine hire and customwork	1.8	2.4	2.5	3.1	3.4	3.6	3.5	3.8	4.4	4.8	4.8
Marketing, storage, and transportation expenses	3.1	4.1	4.1	3.5	4.2	4.2	4.7	4.5	5.6	6.7	7.2
Contract labor	1.0	1.5	1.3	1.1	1.3	1.6	1.6	1.7	1.8	1.8	2.0
Miscellaneous expenses	8.2	11.6	13.6	14.9	15.3	16.1	16.9	16.2	17.8	19.3	21.8
Plus: Net government transactions [2]	-2.8	2.9	11.5	9.0	5.1	2.9	1.9	2.6	6.7	0.8	-0.1
Direct Government payments	1.3	7.7	16.7	14.5	10.9	9.3	8.2	9.2	13.4	7.9	7.3
Motor vehicle registration and licensing fees	0.2	0.3	0.3	0.3	0.3	0.4	0.3	0.4	0.4	0.4	0.5
Property taxes	3.9	4.5	5.0	5.2	5.5	6.0	5.9	6.2	6.3	6.7	6.9
Equals: **Gross value added**	68.2	82.9	86.5	88.1	97.4	98.9	91.1	100.6	97.1	104.0	91.9
Less: Capital consumption	21.5	19.4	17.2	17.6	18.1	18.1	18.2	18.3	18.4	18.8	19.1
Equals: Net value added	46.7	63.5	69.3	70.5	79.3	80.8	72.9	82.3	78.7	85.2	72.8
Less: Employee compensation	8.3	8.5	8.7	9.8	10.7	12.5	12.3	12.3	13.2	13.5	14.3
Less: Net rent received by nonoperator landlords	6.1	7.7	8.2	8.4	9.4	10.1	9.9	10.8	10.9	11.5	10.9
Less: Real estate and nonreal estate interest	16.3	18.6	15.0	14.3	13.9	13.4	12.1	11.2	10.8	11.8	12.8
Equals: **Net farm income**	16.1	28.6	37.4	38.0	45.3	44.8	38.5	48.0	43.6	48.4	34.8

[1] Includes home consumption and value of inventory adjustment. [2] Direct Government payments minus motor vehicle registration and licensing fees and property taxes.

Source: U.S. Dept. of Agriculture, Economic Research Service, *Farm Business Economic Report, 1995* (ECI-1996).

No. 1095. Farm Income and Expenses: 1980 to 1995

[In billions of dollars]

ITEM	1980	1985	1987	1988	1989	1990	1991	1992	1993	1994	1995
ross farm income	**149.3**	**161.2**	**168.4**	**177.9**	**191.9**	**198.2**	**191.9**	**200.6**	**204.2**	**215.8**	**210.4**
Cash income	143.3	157.9	165.0	173.6	180.3	187.1	184.3	188.7	200.1	197.8	203.9
Farm marketings	139.7	144.1	141.8	151.2	160.8	169.5	167.9	171.3	177.6	180.8	185.8
Crops	71.7	74.3	65.8	71.6	76.9	80.3	82.1	85.7	87.5	92.6	98.9
Livestock and products	68.0	69.8	76.0	79.6	83.9	89.2	85.8	85.6	90.2	88.1	86.8
Government payments	1.3	7.7	16.7	14.5	10.9	9.3	8.2	9.2	13.4	7.9	7.3
Other farm income [1]	2.3	6.0	6.4	7.9	8.6	8.2	8.2	8.2	9.1	9.2	10.9
Value of home consumption	1.2	0.9	0.7	0.7	0.7	0.7	0.6	0.6	0.5	0.5	0.5
Rental value of dwellings [2]	11.0	4.7	5.0	7.7	7.2	7.2	7.2	7.1	8.0	9.3	9.4
Value of inventory adjustment [3]	-6.3	-2.3	-2.3	-4.1	3.8	3.3	-0.2	4.2	-4.5	8.2	-3.4
xpenses of farm production	**133.1**	**132.6**	**131.0**	**139.9**	**146.7**	**153.4**	**153.3**	**152.5**	**160.5**	**167.4**	**175.6**
Intermediate products	76.1	72.3	75.7	83.5	87.6	91.7	93.3	92.1	99.0	103.4	109.7
Farm origin	34.9	29.3	32.6	37.3	38.1	39.5	38.6	38.6	41.2	41.3	42.5
Feed purchased	21.0	16.9	17.5	20.2	20.7	20.4	19.3	20.1	21.4	22.6	24.5
Livestock, poultry purchased	10.7	9.2	11.8	13.0	12.9	14.6	14.1	13.6	14.6	13.2	12.6
Seed purchased [4]	3.2	3.1	3.3	4.1	4.4	4.5	5.1	4.9	5.2	5.4	5.5
Manufactured inputs	20.9	18.3	15.9	16.6	18.0	19.4	20.6	20.1	20.5	21.7	23.4
Fertilizer and lime	9.5	7.5	6.5	7.7	8.2	8.2	8.7	8.3	8.4	9.2	10.0
Pesticides	3.5	4.3	4.5	4.1	5.0	5.4	6.3	6.5	6.7	7.2	7.7
Fuel and oil	7.9	6.4	5.0	4.8	4.8	5.8	5.6	5.3	5.3	5.3	5.7
Repairs and maintenance [5]	7.1	6.4	6.8	7.7	8.4	8.6	8.6	8.5	9.2	9.2	9.4
Other [6]	13.3	18.4	20.4	21.9	23.2	24.2	25.5	24.9	28.2	31.2	34.3
Interest	16.3	18.6	15.0	14.3	13.9	13.4	12.1	11.2	10.8	11.8	12.8
Real estate	7.5	9.9	8.2	7.6	7.2	6.7	6.0	5.8	5.5	5.9	6.1
Nonreal estate	8.7	8.7	6.8	6.7	6.7	6.7	6.1	5.4	5.3	6.0	6.7
Contract, hired labor expenses [7]	9.3	10.0	10.0	10.9	12.0	14.1	13.9	14.0	15.0	15.3	16.3
Net rent to nonoperator landlords [8]	6.1	7.7	8.2	8.4	9.4	10.1	9.9	10.8	10.9	11.5	10.9
Capital consumption [9]	21.5	19.4	17.2	17.6	18.1	18.1	18.2	18.3	18.4	18.8	19.1
Property taxes	3.9	4.5	5.0	5.2	5.5	6.0	5.9	6.2	6.3	6.7	6.9
et farm income	**16.1**	**28.6**	**37.4**	**38.0**	**45.3**	**44.8**	**38.5**	**48.0**	**43.6**	**48.4**	**34.8**

[1] Includes forest product sales. [2] Data for 1980 are not comparable with later data. [3] Minus sign (-) indicates decrease in inventories. [4] Includes bulbs, plants, and trees. [5] Expenditures for repairs and maintenance of farm buildings, motor vehicles, and machinery. [6] Includes machine hire and customwork expenses; marketing, storage, and transportation expenses and miscellaneous expenses. Significant differences in the items included exist between 1987 and prior years. [7] Includes Social Security payments and perquisites. [8] Data for 1980 are based on different sources from those for 1985 and later, creating potential inconsistencies in estimates among these periods. Forest product sales by nonoperators are included beginning in 1987. Includes landlord capital consumption. [9] Capital replacement and accidental damage.

No. 1096. Farm Income—Cash Receipts From Farm Marketings: 1990 to 1995

[In millions of dollars. Represents gross receipts from commercial market sales as well as net Commodity Credit Corporation loans. The source estimates and publishes individual cash receipt values only for major commodities and major producing states. The U.S. receipts for individual commodities, computed as the sum of the reported states, may understate the value of sales for some commodities. The degree of underestimation in some of the minor commodities can be substantial]

COMMODITY	1990	1993	1994	1995	COMMODITY	1990	1993	1994	1995
Total	**169,517**	**177,817**	**180,775**	**185,750**	Carrots	261	296	342	449
					Cauliflower	188	201	196	217
Livestock and products [1]	89,220	90,166	88,129	86,844	Celery	215	319	238	269
Cattle and calves	39,302	39,362	36,395	33,983	Corn, sweet	476	532	635	644
Hogs	11,525	10,911	9,883	10,074	Cucumbers	215	296	290	297
Sheep and lambs	414	552	507	559	Lettuce	844	1,469	1,276	1,915
Dairy products	20,153	19,243	19,935	19,924	Onions	486	937	621	651
Broilers	8,365	10,415	11,370	11,761	Peppers, green	150	437	456	410
Chicken eggs	4,010	3,779	3,780	3,959	Tomatoes	1,627	1,712	1,723	1,577
Turkeys	2,393	2,509	2,644	2,774	Cantaloupe	195	297	301	383
Horses/mules	490	441	489	559	Watermelons	124	262	272	358
Aquaculture	541	642	639	712	Fruits/nuts [1]	9,416	10,281	10,176	10,775
					Grapefruit	358	316	301	285
Crops [1]	80,297	87,451	92,646	98,906	Lemons	305	283	239	235
Rice	1,052	699	1,665	1,281	Oranges	1,719	1,522	1,600	1,605
Wheat	6,412	7,464	7,859	8,769	Apples	1,078	1,361	1,353	1,602
Barley	823	655	703	772	Avocados	245	140	261	241
Corn	13,348	14,607	14,675	17,401	Cherries	156	225	249	212
Hay	3,271	3,521	3,646	3,617	Grapes	1,677	2,001	1,890	2,022
Sorghum grain	1,002	1,225	1,128	1,222	Peaches	374	399	315	407
Cotton	5,488	5,250	6,738	7,567	Pears	261	247	227	240
Tobacco	2,733	2,948	2,645	2,594	Plums and prunes	295	262	257	324
Peanuts	1,258	1,032	1,230	1,014	Strawberries	590	671	837	753
Soybeans	10,756	11,781	12,827	13,203	Almonds	596	931	900	858
Sunflower	217	298	465	476	Pecans	248	214	207	272
Vegetables [1]	11,464	13,466	13,740	14,773	Walnuts	236	361	232	314
Beans, dry	687	523	624	619	Sugarbeets	1,182	1,024	1,234	1,084
Potatoes	2,502	2,374	2,493	2,594	Cane for sugar	820	868	899	887
Beans, snap	198	271	292	285	Christmas trees	110	412	432	459
Broccoli	268	278	336	367	Greenhouse/nursery	8,677	9,592	10,021	10,408
Cabbage	124	287	241	283	Mushrooms	667	700	735	758

[1] Includes other commodities not shown separately.

Source of tables 1095 and 1096: U.S. Dept. of Agriculture, Economic Research Service, *Farm Business Economic Report, 1995* (ECI-1996).

No. 1097. Farm Assets, Debt, and Income, by State: 1994 and 1995

[Assets and debt, as of December 31. Farm income data are after inventory adjustment and include income and expenses related to the farm operator's dwelling]

DIVISION AND STATE	ASSETS (mil. dol.)		DEBT (mil. dol.)		DEBT/ASSET RATIO (percent)		GROSS FARM INCOME (mil. dol.)		NET FARM INCOME (mil. dol.)	
	1994	1995	1994	1995	1994	1995	1994	1995	1994	1995
United States	938,141	977,986	146,800	150,769	15.6	15.4	215,840	210,399	48,396	34,819
New England:										
Maine	2,025	2,061	324	337	16.0	16.3	546	567	86	80
New Hampshire	1,051	1,053	75	75	7.1	7.1	180	181	47	43
Vermont	2,424	2,447	344	347	14.2	14.2	533	540	112	100
Massachusetts	3,041	3,124	289	238	9.5	7.6	529	507	154	124
Rhode Island	412	426	39	61	9.4	14.3	90	91	43	43
Connecticut	2,359	2,403	199	199	8.4	8.3	537	548	170	166
Middle Atlantic:										
New York	13,045	12,513	2,150	2,171	16.5	17.4	3,160	3,251	420	364
New Jersey	6,596	6,608	416	417	6.3	6.3	904	927	259	250
Pennsylvania	20,057	20,906	2,458	2,486	12.3	11.9	4,232	4,265	711	543
East North Central:										
Ohio	29,771	31,749	3,329	3,431	11.2	10.8	5,512	5,404	1,179	950
Indiana	29,606	31,817	4,661	4,744	15.7	14.9	5,707	5,297	781	298
Illinois	58,816	64,464	7,797	8,079	13.3	12.5	9,790	8,034	2,017	445
Michigan	16,676	17,838	2,633	2,712	15.8	15.2	3,877	4,059	217	449
Wisconsin	25,013	26,160	4,969	5,176	19.9	19.8	6,532	6,181	540	284
West North Central:										
Minnesota	35,942	37,705	7,306	7,691	20.3	20.4	8,971	8,364	1,545	973
Iowa	56,163	59,313	10,725	10,933	19.1	18.4	13,166	11,992	2,976	1,766
Missouri	31,172	32,616	4,848	5,199	15.6	15.9	5,482	5,071	872	322
North Dakota	21,006	21,240	3,608	3,719	17.2	17.5	3,981	3,572	859	398
South Dakota	18,824	19,152	3,670	3,711	19.5	19.4	4,250	3,724	1,276	673
Nebraska	36,132	37,376	7,486	7,697	20.7	20.6	9,966	9,650	2,193	1,572
Kansas	31,877	31,988	5,929	6,017	18.6	18.8	9,052	8,574	1,706	889
South Atlantic:										
Delaware	1,592	1,689	306	313	19.2	18.5	733	766	163	132
Maryland	8,116	7,967	1,014	964	12.5	12.1	1,601	1,658	302	242
Virginia	16,614	17,302	1,879	1,836	11.3	10.6	2,603	2,599	632	531
West Virginia	3,525	3,570	402	390	11.4	10.9	507	479	77	36
North Carolina	18,241	20,065	2,970	3,273	16.3	16.3	7,804	7,996	3,076	2,860
South Carolina	7,420	7,449	847	842	11.4	11.3	1,673	1,645	528	369
Georgia	16,993	17,694	2,852	3,143	16.8	17.8	5,680	5,986	2,139	2,016
Florida	25,429	25,977	4,058	3,945	16.0	15.2	6,306	6,143	2,219	1,705
East South Central:										
Kentucky	19,826	20,945	2,758	2,861	13.9	13.7	3,906	3,729	1,210	953
Tennessee	17,919	19,078	1,993	2,070	11.1	10.9	2,749	2,628	676	464
Alabama	13,567	13,970	1,466	1,553	10.8	11.1	3,726	3,622	1,268	946
Mississippi	12,964	13,091	2,414	2,496	18.6	19.1	3,688	3,574	728	593
West South Central:										
Arkansas	17,482	17,496	3,396	3,609	19.4	20.6	6,047	5,843	1,480	1,363
Louisiana	8,413	9,224	1,604	1,609	19.1	17.4	2,490	2,435	506	521
Oklahoma	22,253	21,497	3,886	3,845	17.5	17.9	4,793	4,333	1,066	498
Texas	81,649	80,434	9,909	10,149	12.1	12.6	15,347	15,706	3,737	2,419
Mountain:										
Montana	19,490	19,907	2,613	2,565	13.4	12.9	2,424	2,407	467	392
Idaho	13,262	14,187	2,589	2,599	19.5	18.3	3,451	3,555	712	606
Wyoming	7,748	8,078	899	918	11.6	11.4	915	914	115	89
Colorado	19,682	20,455	3,055	3,281	15.5	16.0	4,657	4,707	625	444
New Mexico	11,240	12,380	1,123	1,181	10.0	9.5	1,778	1,585	362	255
Arizona	12,832	14,513	1,241	1,209	9.7	8.3	2,026	2,390	466	715
Utah	6,946	7,894	669	688	9.6	8.7	1,029	993	248	181
Nevada	2,712	2,978	235	235	8.7	7.9	364	342	61	39
Pacific:										
Washington	18,663	19,141	3,031	3,052	16.2	15.9	5,606	5,962	1,060	915
Oregon	15,731	16,861	2,157	2,182	13.7	12.9	3,587	3,583	619	381
California	71,002	76,083	13,927	14,307	19.6	18.8	22,741	23,462	5,575	4,347
Alaska	593	578	16	12	2.7	2.0	36	37	11	12
Hawaii	4,223	4,516	259	203	6.1	4.5	552	517	45	22

Source: U.S. Dept. of Agriculture, Economic Research Service, *Farm Business Economic Report, 1995* (ECI-1996).

No. 1096. Farm Income—Farm Marketings, 1994 and 1995, Government Payments, 1995, and Principal Commodities, 995, by State

[In millions of dollars. Cattle include calves; sheep include lambs; and greenhouse includes nursery]

DIVISION AND STATE	1994			1995				
	Farm marketings			Farm marketings			Government payments	State rank for total farm marketings and four principal commodities in order of marketing receipts
	Total	Crops	Livestock and products	Total	Crops	Livestock and products		
U.S.	180,775	92,646	88,129	185,750	98,906	86,844	7,252	Cattle, dairy products, corn, soybeans
N.E.	2,105	998	1,107	2,099	1,003	1,096	25	(X)
ME	458	188	270	479	198	281	14	43-Chicken eggs, potatoes, dairy products, aquaculture
NH	151	87	64	152	88	64	1	48-Dairy products, greenhouse, apples, Christmas trees
VT	479	89	390	472	92	380	4	44-Dairy products, cattle, greenhouse, hay
MA	460	342	117	430	327	103	2	45-Greenhouse, cranberries, dairy products, Christmas trees
RI	80	68	12	80	70	10	(Z)	49-Greenhouse, dairy products, chicken eggs, sweet corn
CT	478	224	254	484	226	257	2	41-Greenhouse, chicken eggs, dairy products, aquaculture
M.A	7,407	2,733	4,674	7,389	2,771	4,618	90	(X)
NY	2,868	979	1,888	2,877	1,012	1,865	43	27-Dairy products, greenhouse, cattle, apples
NJ	770	589	181	773	573	200	5	38-Greenhouse, dairy products, eggs, fresh tomatoes
PA	3,769	1,164	2,605	3,738	1,186	2,552	41	18-Dairy products, cattle, greenhouse, mushrooms
E.N.C	25,808	15,111	10,697	26,548	16,257	10,291	1,292	(X)
OH	4,438	2,875	1,564	4,576	2,987	1,589	167	15-Soybeans, corn, dairy products, greenhouse
IN	4,664	2,930	1,734	4,981	3,240	1,741	246	14-Corn, soybeans, hogs, dairy products
IL	7,946	5,897	2,049	7,887	6,177	1,710	544	5-Corn, soybeans, hogs, cattle
MI	3,381	1,992	1,389	3,521	2,197	1,324	151	20-Dairy products, greenhouse, corn, soybeans
WI	5,379	1,417	3,962	5,582	1,656	3,926	184	10-Dairy products, corn, cattle, soybeans
W.N.C	43,483	19,853	23,630	45,109	22,203	22,906	2,980	(X)
MN	6,408	2,960	3,448	7,002	3,551	3,451	466	7-Corn, dairy products, soybeans, hogs
IA	9,999	4,769	5,230	10,959	5,891	5,068	785	3-Corn, hogs, soybeans, dairy products
MO	4,562	2,098	2,463	4,399	2,134	2,265	256	16-Soybeans, cattle, hogs, corn
ND	3,028	2,403	625	3,154	2,588	566	296	23-Wheat, cattle, barley, sunflower
SD	3,336	1,634	1,702	3,384	1,707	1,676	245	21-Cattle, corn, soybeans, wheat
NE	8,525	3,120	5,405	8,690	3,503	5,187	507	4-Cattle, corn, hogs, soybeans
KS	7,626	2,868	4,758	7,521	2,829	4,693	423	6-Cattle, wheat, corn, sorghum
S.A.	23,087	12,235	10,852	24,155	12,838	11,318	246	(X)
DE	658	152	505	676	159	516	3	40-Broilers, soybeans, greenhouse, corn
MD	1,339	541	799	1,402	572	830	15	36-Broilers, greenhouse, dairy products, soybeans
VA	2,194	785	1,409	2,248	855	1,393	25	30-Broilers, dairy products, cattle, turkeys
WV	400	69	331	386	74	312	5	46-Broilers, cattle, turkeys, dairy products
NC	6,439	3,110	3,329	6,987	3,251	3,735	40	8-Hogs, broilers, tobacco, greenhouse
SC	1,383	768	615	1,441	830	611	34	34-Broilers, tobacco, greenhouse, cotton
GA	4,689	2,018	2,671	5,166	2,377	2,789	66	14-Broilers, cotton, peanuts, eggs
FL	5,984	4,792	1,192	5,849	4,719	1,130	56	9-Oranges, greenhouse, sugar, tomatoes
E.S.C	11,214	4,754	6,461	11,221	4,884	6,336	297	(X)
KY	3,220	1,571	1,649	3,059	1,444	1,616	67	25-Tobacco, horses/mules, cattle, corn
TN	2,172	1,200	972	2,127	1,258	868	47	31-Cattle, cotton, dairy products, tobacco
AL	2,951	802	2,150	2,908	741	2,166	53	26-Broilers, cattle, chicken eggs, cotton
MS	2,871	1,181	1,690	3,126	1,441	1,685	129	24-Broilers, cotton, soybeans, aquaculture
W.S.C	24,251	9,595	14,656	24,083	9,405	14,678	1,348	(X)
AR	5,395	2,250	3,145	5,065	2,042	3,023	383	13-Broilers, cotton, soybeans, rice
LA	2,029	1,329	700	2,025	1,395	630	157	32-Cotton, sugar cane, rice, soybeans
OK	3,898	1,199	2,699	3,705	1,133	2,571	165	19-Cattle, wheat, broilers, greenhouse
TX	12,930	4,817	8,112	13,288	4,834	8,454	643	2-Cattle, cotton, greenhouse, dairy products
Mountain	14,182	6,046	8,135	14,495	6,778	7,716	567	(X)
MT	1,885	1,029	856	1,845	1,047	798	185	33-Wheat, cattle, barley, hay
ID	2,955	1,756	1,199	3,166	1,945	1,221	90	22-Potatoes, cattle, dairy products, wheat
WY	783	160	623	726	182	544	31	39-Cattle, hay, sugar beets, sheep
CO	4,051	1,287	2,764	3,985	1,361	2,624	167	17-Cattle, wheat, corn, dairy products
NM	1,528	426	1,102	1,415	452	963	55	35-Cattle, dairy products, hay, pecans
AZ	1,854	1,049	804	2,256	1,446	810	10	29-Lettuce, cattle, cotton, dairy products
UT	827	230	597	815	223	592	25	37-Cattle, dairy products, hay, greenhouse
NV	299	110	190	286	122	164	4	47-Cattle, hay, dairy products, potatoes
Pacific	29,237	21,319	7,918	30,653	22,767	7,886	408	(X)
WA	4,769	3,143	1,626	5,158	3,564	1,594	116	12-Apples, dairy products, cattle, wheat
OR	2,651	1,930	721	2,720	2,055	665	52	28-Greenhouse, cattle, wheat, hay
CA	21,282	15,793	5,489	22,261	16,713	5,549	238	1-Dairy products, greenhouse, grapes, cotton
AK	28	22	6	30	24	6	2	50-Greenhouse, potatoes, hay, dairy products
HI	508	431	77	483	412	72	1	42-Sugar, pineapples, greenhouse, nuts

X Not applicable. Z Less than $500,000.

Source: U.S. Dept. of Agriculture, Economic Research Service, *Farm Business Economic Report, 1995* (ECI-1996).

No. 1099. Indexes of Prices Received and Paid by Farmers: 1990 to 1995

[1990-92=100, except as noted]

ITEM	1990	1993	1994	1995, prel.	ITEM	1990	1993	1994	1995, prel.
Prices received,					Prices paid, total [3]	99	102	106	109
all products	104	101	100	102	Production	99	103	107	109
					Feed	103	99	107	104
Crops [1]	103	102	105	112	Livestock & poultry	102	104	95	82
Food grains	100	105	119	134	Seed	102	105	109	110
Feed grains and hay	105	99	106	112	Fertilizer	97	97	105	121
Cotton	107	89	109	128	Agricultural chemicals	95	107	110	115
Tobacco	97	101	101	103	Fuels	100	92	89	91
Oil-bearing crops	105	108	110	104	Supplies & repairs	96	107	109	112
Fruits	97	91	89	97	Autos and trucks	97	109	114	121
Commercial vegetables [2]	102	116	109	119	Farm machinery	96	106	113	121
Potatoes & dry beans	133	107	110	106	Building materials	99	105	109	114
					Farm services	96	105	111	117
Livestock and products	105	100	95	92	Interest	107	88	92	103
Meat animals	105	100	90	85	Taxes	95	107	112	117
Dairy products	105	98	99	98	Wage rates	96	108	111	113
Poultry and eggs	105	105	106	107	Parity ratio (1910-14=100) [4]	51	47	45	45

[1] Includes other items not shown separately. [2] Excludes potatoes and dry beans. [3] Includes production items, interest, taxes, wage rates, and a family living component. The family living component is the Consumer Price Index for all urban consumers from the Bureau of Labor Statistics. See text, section 15, and table 752. [4] Ratio of prices received by farmers to prices paid.

Source: U.S. Dept. of Agriculture, National Agricultural Statistics Service, *Agricultural Prices: Annual Summary.*

No. 1100. Civilian Consumer Expenditures for Farm Foods—Farm Value and Marketing Bill: 1980 to 1995

[In billions of dollars, except percent. Excludes imported and nonfarm foods, such as coffee and seafood, as well as food consumed by the military, or exported]

ITEM	1980	1985	1987	1988	1989	1990	1991	1992	1993	1994	1995
Consumer expenditures, total	264.4	345.4	375.5	398.8	419.4	449.8	465.1	474.5	489.2	512.2	530.8
Farm value, total	81.7	86.4	90.4	96.8	103.8	106.2	101.6	105.1	109.6	109.6	114.1
Marketing bill, total [1]	182.7	259.0	285.1	301.9	315.6	343.6	363.5	369.4	379.6	402.6	416.7
Percent of total consumer expenditures	69.1	75.0	75.9	75.7	75.3	76.4	78.2	77.9	77.6	78.6	78.5
At-home expenditures [2]	180.1	220.8	230.2	242.1	255.5	276.2	286.1	289.6	294.9	308.7	317.4
Farm value	65.9	66.6	67.5	72.5	77.9	80.2	76.7	76.9	76.4	75.3	76.2
Marketing bill [1]	114.2	154.2	162.7	169.6	177.6	196.0	209.4	212.7	218.5	233.4	241.2
Away-from-home expenditures	84.3	124.6	145.3	156.7	163.9	173.6	179.0	184.9	194.3	203.5	213.4
Farm value	15.8	19.8	22.9	24.3	25.9	26.0	24.9	28.2	33.2	34.3	37.9
Marketing bill [1]	68.5	104.8	122.4	132.4	138.0	147.6	154.1	156.7	161.1	169.2	175.5
Marketing bill cost components:											
Labor cost [3]	81.5	115.6	130.0	137.9	145.1	154.0	160.9	168.4	178.0	186.1	195.7
Packaging materials	21.0	26.9	29.9	32.6	35.2	36.5	38.1	40.1	40.9	43.3	49.0
Rail and truck transport [4]	13.0	16.5	17.2	17.8	18.6	19.8	20.4	20.6	21.2	21.8	22.3
Corporate profits before taxes	9.9	10.4	11.1	12.0	12.9	13.2	15.2	15.7	18.1	20.5	22.0
Fuels and electricity	9.0	13.1	13.6	14.1	14.8	15.2	16.3	16.7	17.2	17.9	18.5
Advertising	7.3	12.5	13.8	14.1	15.7	17.1	17.5	18.0	18.5	19.1	19.9
Depreciation	7.8	15.4	15.8	16.2	16.4	16.3	15.8	16.2	17.2	17.9	18.5
Net interest	3.4	6.1	8.1	9.7	12.3	13.5	12.2	10.9	10.1	10.4	10.9
Net rent	6.8	9.3	10.9	11.7	12.7	13.9	15.9	17.2	17.9	18.7	19.4
Repairs	3.6	4.8	5.1	5.2	5.7	6.2	6.4	6.6	7.2	7.5	7.8
Taxes	8.3	11.7	12.6	13.7	14.6	15.7	16.5	17.5	18.2	19.0	19.7
Other	11.0	16.7	17.1	16.8	11.5	22.2	28.3	21.5	15.2	20.4	13.0

[1] The difference between expenditures for domestic farm-originated food products and the farm value or payment farmers received for the equivalent farm products. [2] Food primarily purchased from retail food stores for use at home. [3] Covers employee wages and salaries, and their health and welfare benefits. Also includes imputed earnings of proprietors, partners, and family workers not receiving stated remuneration. [4] Excludes local hauling.

Source: U.S. Dept. of Agriculture, Economic Research Service, *Food Cost Review*, annual; *FoodReview*, periodic; and *Agricultural Statistics*, annual.

No. 1101. Selected Indexes of Farm Inputs: 1980 to 1994

[1992=100. Inputs based on physical quantities of resources used in production]

INPUT	1980	1985	1986	1987	1988	1989	1990	1991	1992	1993	1994
Total	120	106	103	101	100	99	100	102	100	100	101
Farm labor	124	109	102	102	109	103	103	105	100	95	96
Farm real estate	112	107	104	100	100	102	101	100	100	98	99
Durable equipment	166	139	130	120	113	108	105	103	100	97	94
Energy	121	98	91	102	102	101	100	101	100	100	103
Agricultural chemicals [1]	127	96	106	96	89	92	95	99	100	105	106
Other purchased inputs [2]	114	97	86	93	96	99	101	102	100	108	113

[1] Includes fertilizer, lime, and pesticides. [2] Includes purchased services and miscellaneous inputs.

Source: U.S. Dept. of Agriculture, Economic Research Service, *Agricultural Outlook*, monthly.

No. 1102. Farm Machinery and Equipment: 1980 to 1995

ITEM	Unit	1980	1985	1986	1987	1988	1989	1990	1991	1992	1993	1994	1995
Value of farm implements and machinery [1]	Bil. dol.	80.3	82.9	81.5	80.0	81.2	85.1	85.4	85.8	85.6	86.7	87.9	86.9
Farmers' expenditures:													
Motor vehicles [2]	Mil. dol.	5,813	3,699	3,227	4,275	4,912	5,484	5,750	4,993	5,126	5,189	5,453	5,711
Tractors	Mil. dol.	3,683	1,937	1,513	2,104	2,540	2,903	3,119	2,593	2,826	2,689	2,893	2,911
Machinery, equipment	Mil. dol.	6,956	3,232	3,094	4,297	4,222	5,087	5,589	5,410	5,132	5,488	5,182	5,051
Repair and maintenance	Mil. dol.	5,205	4,834	4,825	5,017	5,869	6,607	6,311	6,414	5,966	6,474	6,370	6,741
Tractors, machinery and equipment	Mil. dol.	3,746	3,442	3,428	3,540	4,050	4,571	4,437	4,547	4,210	4,463	4,352	4,560
Autos and trucks	Mil. dol.	1,459	1,392	1,397	1,477	1,821	2,039	1,876	1,870	1,758	2,011	2,019	2,181
Retail sales: [3]													
Tractors, total [4]	1,000	119.3	58.5	47.1	48.3	52.0	59.7	66.3	58.1	52.8	57.8	63.2	64.3
Two-wheel drive	1,000	108.4	55.5	45.1	46.6	49.3	55.5	61.2	54.0	50.1	54.5	59.5	60.3
Four-wheel drive	1,000	10.9	3.0	2.0	1.7	2.7	4.2	5.1	4.1	2.7	3.3	3.7	4.4
Combines	1,000	25.7	8.4	7.7	7.2	6.0	9.1	10.4	8.7	7.7	7.9	8.5	9.2

[1] Farm inventory valuations as of December 31. [2] For farm business use. [3] Source: Equipment Manufacturers Institute, Chicago, IL, unpublished data. [4] Covers tractors over 40 hp. only.

Source: Except as noted, U.S. Dept. of Agriculture, Economic Research Service, *Farm Business Economic Report, 1995* ECI-1996). Also in *Agricultural Statistics*, annual.

No. 1103. Farm Output Indexes: 1980 to 1994

[1992=100]

ITEM	1980	1985	1986	1987	1988	1989	1990	1991	1992	1993	1994
Farm output [1]	79	88	87	88	82	89	94	94	100	94	106
Per unit of total input	66	84	84	87	82	90	93	93	100	94	104
Gross production:											
Livestock and products [2]	85	89	90	91	94	94	95	98	100	101	105
Meat animals	98	93	94	95	97	97	97	99	100	100	103
Dairy products	85	94	95	94	96	95	98	98	100	99	101
Poultry and eggs	64	71	74	81	83	86	92	96	100	104	110
Crops [3]	75	89	84	85	75	86	92	91	100	89	106
Feed crops	76	100	95	84	62	85	88	86	100	76	102
Food grains	94	95	83	84	76	83	107	82	100	96	96
Oil crops	81	96	89	88	72	88	87	94	100	85	115
Cotton and cottonseed	68	82	60	92	96	75	96	109	100	100	123
Tobacco	108	96	74	69	77	85	95	97	100	101	89
Vegetables and melons	69	81	82	89	81	84	92	97	100	94	106
Fruits and nuts	90	86	83	95	102	98	97	96	100	107	110
Other crops	57	69	75	82	86	89	94	96	100	99	105

[1] Annual production available for eventual human use. [2] Includes livestock products not shown separately. [3] Includes crops not shown separately.

Source: U.S. Dept. of Agriculture, Economic Research Service, *Agricultural Outlook*, monthly. Also published in the U.S. Council of Economic Advisors, *Economic Report of the President*, annual.

No. 1104. Agricultural Exports and Imports—Volume, by Principal Commodities: 1990 to 1995

[In thousands of metric tons]

EXPORTS	1990	1993	1994	1995	IMPORTS	1990	1993	1994	1995
Animal products [1]	2,737	3,824	4,529	5,626	Fruits, nuts, vegetables	4,573	5,113	5,379	6,019
Wheat and products [2]	28,282	36,691	31,680	33,458	Bananas	3,094	3,513	3,694	3,664
Feed grains and products	61,397	48,282	43,579	67,403	Green coffee	1,174	1,081	995	953
Rice	2,509	2,775	2,983	3,275	Cocoa and products	765	801	672	643
Feeds and fodders	10,979	11,724	11,638	13,338	Meat and products [5]	1,165	1,153	1,150	1,045
Protein meal	5,138	6,352	5,372	6,404					
Oilseeds and products [3]	15,778	20,020	18,834	23,599	Vegetable oils	1,183	1,419	1,588	1,570
Vegetable oils	1,204	1,708	1,891	2,510	Rubber, crude natural	840	1,000	992	1,044
Fruits, nuts, vegetables [4]	5,552	6,172	6,839	6,908	Sugar	1,856	1,617	1,545	1,599
Cotton and linters	1,733	1,184	1,829	2,118	Spices	129	144	164	155
Tobacco, unmanufactured	223	208	197	209	Tobacco, unmanufactured	187	461	244	190

[1] Includes meat and products, poultry meats, dairy products, and fats, oils and greases. Excludes live animals, hides, skins, and eggs. [2] Includes flour and bulgur. [3] Includes soybeans, sunflowerseeds, peanuts, cottonseed, safflowerseed, flaxseed, and nondefatted soybean flour. [4] Excludes fruit juices. [5] Excludes poultry.

Source: U.S. Dept. of Agriculture, Economic Research Service, *Foreign Agricultural Trade of the United States*, Jan./Feb. 1996, and calendar year supplements.

No. 1105. Agricultural Exports and Imports—Value: 1980 to 1996

[In billions of dollars, except percent. Includes Puerto Rico. Excludes forest products and distilled liquors; includes crude rubber and similar gums (now mainly plantation products). Includes shipments under foreign aid programs]

YEAR	Trade balance	Exports, domestic products	Percent of all exports	Imports for consumption	Percent of all imports	YEAR	Trade balance	Exports, domestic products	Percent of all exports	Imports for consumption	Percent of all imports
1980	23.9	41.2	18	17.4	7	1991	16.5	39.2	10	22.7	5
1985	9.1	29.0	13	20.0	6	1992	18.3	42.9	10	24.6	5
1987	8.3	28.7	12	20.4	5	1993	17.6	42.6	10	25.0	4
1988	16.1	37.1	12	21.0	5	1994	18.9	45.7	9	26.8	4
1989	18.2	39.9	11	21.7	5	1995	25.8	55.8	10	30.0	4
1990	16.6	39.4	10	22.8	5	1996	28.0	60.4	10	32.4	4

Source: U.S. Dept. of Agriculture, Economic Research Service, *Foreign Agricultural Trade of the United States*, Jan.-Feb. issues, and calendar year supplements. Also in *Agricultural Statistics*, annual.

No. 1106. Agricultural Imports—Value, by Selected Commodity, 1980 to 1995, and by Leading Countries of Origin, 1995

[In millions of dollars]

COMMODITY	1980	1985	1990	1992	1993	1994	1995	Leading countries of origin, 1995
Total	17,366	19,986	22,770	24,624	24,981	26,818	29,993	Canada, Mexico, Indonesia
Competitive products	10,374	13,067	17,202	18,946	19,362	20,067	21,586	Canada, Mexico, Italy
Cattle, live	237	307	978	1,245	1,341	1,152	1,413	Canada, Mexico, Japan
Beef and veal	1,780	1,276	1,872	1,891	1,938	1,798	1,447	Australia, New Zealand, Canada
Pork	486	861	938	620	694	706	686	Canada, Denmark, Poland
Dairy products	486	765	867	857	873	963	1,089	New Zealand, Ireland, Italy
Fruits and preparations	564	1,738	2,219	2,216	2,037	2,154	2,261	Mexico, Chile, Thailand
Vegetables and preparations	864	1,385	2,286	2,184	2,450	2,731	3,103	Mexico, Canada, Spain
Wine	692	996	917	1,087	976	1,035	1,153	France, Italy, Spain
Malt beverages	367	633	923	864	941	1,050	1,166	Netherlands, Mexico, Canada
Grains and feeds	371	623	1,189	1,586	1,813	2,339	2,362	Canada, Italy, Thailand
Sugar and related products	2,205	1,190	1,172	1,139	1,065	1,129	1,255	Canada, Brazil, Dominican Republic
Oilseeds and products	599	756	949	1,219	1,193	1,563	1,815	Canada, Philippines, Italy
Noncompetitive products	6,992	6,902	5,568	5,678	5,618	6,731	8,406	Indonesia, Mexico, Colombia
Coffee and products	4,186	3,322	1,915	1,706	1,522	2,485	3,263	Mexico, Colombia, Brazil
Rubber, crude natural	817	654	707	770	852	965	1,629	Indonesia, Thailand, Malaysia
Cocoa and products	920	1,351	1,094	1,080	1,062	1,034	1,134	Canada, Cote d'Ivoire, Indonesia
Bananas and plantains	430	763	939	1,097	1,071	1,072	1,140	Costa Rica, Ecuador, Colombia

Source: U.S. Dept. of Agriculture, Economic Research Service, *Foreign Agricultural Trade of the United States*, calendar year supplement.

No. 1107. Selected Farm Products—United States and World Production and Exports: 1994 to 1996

[In metric tons, except as indicated. Metric ton=1.102 short tons or .984 long tons]

ITEM	AMOUNT							UNITED STATES AS PERCENT OF WORLD		
	Unit	United States			World			1994	1995	1996
		1994	1995	1996	1994	1995	1996			
PRODUCTION [1]										
Wheat	Million	63	59	62	525	533	582	12.0	11.0	10.7
Corn for grain	Million	257	187	236	561	516	585	45.8	36.2	40.3
Soybeans	Million	68	59	65	138	125	133	49.8	47.6	48.9
Rice, milled	Million	6.6	5.6	5.6	358	366	371	1.8	1.7	1.5
Cotton [2]	Million bales [3]	16.1	19.7	17.9	76.7	85.5	92.2	21.0	23.0	19.4
EXPORTS [4]										
Wheat [5]	Million	32.2	33.6	26.5	97.4	93.3	93.8	33.1	36.0	28.3
Corn	Million	58.6	52.7	46.5	71.2	65.9	62.0	82.3	80.0	75.0
Soybeans	Million	22.8	23.2	24.4	32.1	32.0	34.9	71.0	72.5	69.8
Rice, milled basis	Million	3.1	2.6	2.4	21.0	19.3	17.7	14.8	13.5	13.6
Cotton [2]	Million bales [3]	6.9	9.4	7.7	26.7	28.5	27.4	25.7	33.0	28.1

[1] Production years vary by commodity. In most cases, includes harvests from July 1 of the year shown through June 30 of the following year. [2] For production and trade years ending in year shown. [3] Bales of 480 lb. net weight. [4] Trade years may vary by commodity. [5] Includes wheat flour on a grain equivalent.

Source: U.S. Department of Agriculture, Foreign Agricultural Service, *Foreign Agricultural Commodity Circular Series*, periodic.

No. 1108. Agricultural Exports—Value, by Principal Commodities: 1980 to 1996

[See headnote, table 1105]

COMMODITY	VALUE (mil. dol.)								PERCENT		
	1980	1985	1990	1992	1993	1994	1995	1996	1980	1990	1996
Total agricultural exports [1]	41,234	29,041	39,363	42,930	42,608	45,704	55,814	60,431	100.0	100.0	100.0
Grains and feeds [1]	19,128	11,882	14,378	14,174	13,979	13,515	18,537	20,864	46.4	36.5	34.5
Feed grains and products	9,852	6,112	7,151	5,881	5,174	4,912	8,341	9,575	23.9	18.2	15.8
Corn	8,492	5,206	6,027	4,708	4,220	3,936	7,304	(NA)	20.6	15.3	(NA)
Wheat and products	6,660	3,898	4,033	4,675	4,909	4,316	5,734	(NA)	16.2	10.2	(NA)
Rice	1,289	665	800	725	770	1,008	996	1,029	3.2	2.0	1.7
Oilseeds and products [1]	9,394	5,794	5,710	7,197	7,270	7,207	8,925	10,792	22.8	14.5	17.9
Soybeans	5,880	3,732	3,551	4,387	4,599	4,330	5,400	7,324	14.3	9.0	12.1
Soybean oilcake and meal	1,666	870	992	1,242	1,074	907	986	(NA)	4.1	2.5	(NA)
Vegetable oils and waxes	1,216	870	808	1,018	1,056	1,376	1,820	1,375	3.0	2.1	2.3
Animals and animal products [1]	3,768	4,150	6,712	7,925	7,931	9,149	10,933	(NA)	9.2	17.1	(NA)
Hides and skins, incl. furskins	1,046	1,295	1,747	1,346	1,285	1,523	1,748	1,675	2.6	4.4	2.8
Cattle hides	637	1,007	1,426	1,132	1,079	1,239	1,465	(NA)	1.6	3.6	(NA)
Meats and meat products	890	905	2,558	3,339	3,325	3,704	4,522	4,590	2.2	6.5	7.6
Beef and veal	249	467	1,579	2,043	1,995	2,304	2,647	(NA)	0.6	4.0	(NA)
Fats, oils, and greases	769	619	424	525	504	594	827	614	1.9	1.1	1.0
Poultry and poultry products	603	384	954	1,211	1,376	1,880	2,345	(NA)	1.5	2.4	(NA)
Cotton, excluding linters	2,864	1,633	2,783	1,999	1,528	2,653	3,681	2,715	7.0	7.1	4.5
Tobacco, unmanufactured	1,334	1,521	1,441	1,651	1,306	1,303	1,400	1,390	3.3	3.7	2.3
Fruits and preparations	1,335	1,186	2,359	2,732	2,764	3,091	3,240	(NA)	3.3	6.0	(NA)
Fresh fruits	739	743	1,486	1,683	1,707	1,954	1,973	(NA)	1.8	3.8	(NA)
Vegetables and preparations	1,188	930	2,302	2,872	3,277	3,876	3,889	3,872	2.9	5.8	6.4
Nuts and preparations	757	683	976	1,139	1,182	1,285	1,410	(NA)	1.9	2.5	(NA)
Other	1,468	1,262	2,702	3,241	3,371	3,625	3,799	(NA)	3.6	6.9	(NA)

NA Not available. [1] Includes commodities not shown separately.

Source: U.S. Dept. of Agriculture, Economic Research Service, *Foreign Agricultural Trade of the United States*, Jan./Feb. 1997, and calendar year supplements. Also in *Agricultural Statistics*, annual.

No. 1109. Agricultural Exports—Value, by Selected Countries of Destination: 1980 to 1996

[See headnote, table 1105. Data for 1980 are not adjusted for transshipments]

COUNTRY	VALUE (mil. dol.)								PERCENT		
	1980	1985	1990	1992	1993	1994	1995	1996	1980	1990	1996
Total agricultural exports [1]	41,234	29,041	39,363	42,930	42,608	45,704	55,814	60,431	100.0	100.0	100.0
Asia [1]	15,046	11,191	17,640	17,924	18,074	20,430	27,939	28,556	36.5	44.8	47.3
Japan	6,133	5,409	8,104	8,437	8,739	9,268	10,957	11,702	14.9	20.6	19.4
Korea, South	1,797	1,413	2,644	2,222	1,932	2,330	3,751	3,871	4.4	6.7	6.4
Taiwan [2]	1,095	1,231	1,661	1,900	2,043	2,145	2,597	2,964	2.7	4.2	4.9
China [2]	2,277	157	814	545	376	1,060	2,633	2,092	5.6	2.1	3.5
Hong Kong	437	389	701	862	875	1,233	1,488	1,490	1.1	1.8	2.5
Western Europe [1] [3]	12,917	7,002	7,353	7,805	7,324	7,365	9,003	9,698	31.4	18.7	16.0
European Union [4]	12,177	6,542	6,851	7,291	6,839	6,775	8,646	9,319	29.6	17.4	15.4
Netherlands	3,476	1,869	1,581	1,853	1,702	1,708	2,128	2,218	8.5	4.0	3.7
Germany	2,373	1,009	1,158	1,163	1,071	1,052	1,230	1,489	5.8	2.9	2.5
Spain [5]	1,488	837	937	936	782	862	1,270	1,124	3.6	2.4	1.9
United Kingdom	996	604	829	910	945	946	1,056	1,232	2.5	2.1	2.0
Italy	1,203	669	710	670	600	549	719	796	3.0	1.8	1.3
France	765	403	528	595	593	450	529	523	1.9	1.3	0.9
Latin America [1]	6,154	4,224	5,092	6,868	6,793	8,035	7,926	10,481	15.0	13.0	17.3
Mexico	2,469	1,439	2,553	3,791	3,603	4,513	3,519	5,446	6.0	6.5	9.0
Venezuela	703	638	351	440	489	401	477	481	1.7	0.9	0.8
Canada	1,906	1,622	4,197	4,902	5,271	5,504	5,738	6,145	4.7	10.7	10.2
Soviet Union (former)	1,138	1,923	2,271	2,346	1,758	999	1,346	1,747	2.8	5.8	2.9
Eastern Europe	1,644	414	537	317	432	335	293	439	4.0	1.4	0.7
Africa [1]	2,237	2,488	1,935	2,570	2,485	2,494	3,070	2,876	5.5	4.9	4.8
Algeria	195	227	513	437	516	595	401	322	0.5	1.3	0.5
Egypt	774	891	693	766	661	872	1,447	1,319	1.9	1.8	2.2

[1] Includes areas not shown separately. [2] See text, section 30. [3] Includes Canary Islands and Madeira Islands. [4] Includes Belgium, Luxembourg, Denmark, Greece, Ireland, and Portugal. For 1995 and 1996, also includes Austria, Finland, and Sweden. As of Jan. 1, 1981, Greece became a member of the European Union. As of Jan. 1, 1986, Spain and Portugal became members of the European Union. For consistency, data for all years are shown on same basis. [5] As of Jan. 1, 1984, includes Canary Islands and Spanish Africa, not elsewhere classified.

Source: U.S. Dept. of Agriculture, Economic Research Service, *Foreign Agricultural Trade of the United States*, Jan./Feb. 1997, and calendar year supplements. Also in *Agricultural Statistics*, annual.

No. 1110. Cropland Used for Crops and Acreages of Crops Harvested: 1980 to 1996

[In millions of acres, except as indicated]

ITEM	1980	1985	1988	1990	1991	1992	1993	1994	1995	1996
Cropland used for crops	**382**	**372**	**341**	**341**	**337**	**337**	**330**	**339**	**332**	**346**
Index (1977=100)	101	98	90	90	89	89	87	90	88	92
Cropland harvested [1]	342	334	306	310	306	305	297	310	302	314
Crop failure	10	7	8	6	7	8	11	7	8	10
Cultivated summer fallow	30	31	27	25	24	24	22	22	22	22
Acres of crops harvested [2]	**352**	**342**	**318**	**322**	**318**	**317**	**308**	**321**	**314**	**326**

[1] Land supporting one or more harvested crops. [2] Area in principal crops harvested as reported by Crop Reporting Board plus acreages in fruits, vegetables for sale, tree nuts, and farm gardens.

Source: U.S. Dept. of Agriculture, Economic Research Service, *Economic Indicators of the Farm Sector: Production and Efficiency Statistics*, annual. Also in *Agricultural Statistics*, annual. Beginning 1991 *Agricultural Resources and Environmental Indicators*, periodical, and *AREI Updates: Cropland Use*, No. 12, annual.

No. 1111. Crops—Acreage and Value, by State: 1994 to 1996

STATE	ACREAGE PLANTED (1,000)			ACREAGE HARVESTED (1,000)			FARM VALUE (mil. dol.)			
	1994	1995	1996	1994	1995	1996	1994	1995	1996 Value	1996 Rank
U.S. [1]	**323,964**	**318,236**	**334,562**	**308,136**	**301,032**	**313,533**	**96,634**	**102,030**	**105,984**	(X)
AL	2,258	2,204	2,274	2,141	2,093	2,190	691	570	742	34
AZ	750	795	835	744	787	831	992	1,325	1,211	29
AR	8,360	8,435	8,680	8,160	8,198	8,535	2,185	2,239	2,709	13
CA	5,132	5,220	5,212	4,682	4,660	4,771	13,022	13,736	13,965	1
CO	6,093	6,104	6,456	5,622	5,748	5,511	1,349	1,576	1,428	25
CT	130	112	120	123	107	115	72	71	79	46
DE	510	507	501	494	499	493	139	151	179	42
FL	1,069	1,070	1,108	1,047	1,027	1,083	3,409	3,366	3,636	10
GA	4,269	4,237	4,346	3,876	3,864	3,999	1,987	2,099	2,176	17
HI	69	53	43	69	53	43	332	320	311	38
ID	4,402	4,483	4,502	4,244	4,306	4,378	1,980	2,308	2,057	19
IL	23,695	23,221	23,926	23,288	22,526	23,183	7,021	7,048	7,361	3
IN	12,137	11,942	12,648	11,970	11,785	12,395	3,539	3,815	3,657	9
IA	24,207	23,502	24,247	23,967	22,872	24,057	7,184	7,692	7,835	2
KS	22,590	22,428	24,171	21,764	21,363	20,899	3,453	3,474	4,076	7
KY	5,558	5,709	5,849	5,354	5,454	5,645	1,955	1,814	2,161	18
LA	3,895	3,857	4,035	3,809	3,786	3,994	1,380	1,423	1,681	22
ME	349	364	327	337	356	316	167	166	153	44
MD	1,569	1,548	1,574	1,506	1,463	1,520	401	434	512	35
MA	139	134	131	134	131	125	167	149	165	43
MI	7,008	6,790	7,023	6,811	6,647	6,774	2,061	2,458	1,941	20
MN	20,050	19,578	19,971	19,510	18,976	19,587	4,775	5,374	5,228	4
MS	4,790	4,850	4,880	4,722	4,739	4,790	1,471	1,339	1,632	23
MO	12,719	12,056	13,275	12,483	11,689	12,794	2,566	2,480	3,105	12
MT	9,355	9,697	10,764	8,966	9,245	10,332	1,137	1,542	1,289	28
NE	19,103	18,280	18,911	18,570	17,769	18,327	4,443	4,559	5,171	5
NV	497	516	525	491	512	522	160	181	180	41
NH	98	85	84	96	83	82	34	31	29	48
NJ	458	452	427	410	413	394	315	298	338	37
NM	1,243	1,282	1,319	965	869	936	400	440	442	36
NY	3,116	3,045	3,018	3,070	2,981	2,941	1,037	1,050	974	32
NC	4,729	4,639	4,752	4,488	4,351	4,521	2,307	2,149	2,505	16
ND	21,714	20,707	22,651	20,720	20,120	22,237	2,686	2,942	3,305	11
OH	10,406	10,025	10,163	10,275	9,883	10,011	2,840	3,097	2,675	15
OK	10,741	10,621	11,341	8,804	8,635	8,967	1,098	1,064	1,206	30
OR	2,317	2,389	2,456	2,239	2,260	2,362	1,239	1,377	1,341	26
PA	4,153	4,146	4,140	4,062	4,050	4,035	1,367	1,403	1,471	24
RI	12	11	11	12	11	11	8	6	8	49
SC	2,036	1,976	1,971	1,923	1,871	1,891	716	712	768	33
SD	16,371	14,334	16,911	15,679	13,947	16,236	2,191	2,219	2,684	14
TN	4,666	4,892	4,999	4,394	4,530	4,703	1,253	1,229	1,325	27
TX	21,822	22,600	24,361	17,536	17,870	18,079	4,475	4,721	4,913	6
UT	1,114	1,099	1,139	1,049	1,042	1,070	289	276	267	40
VT	418	387	345	409	379	326	73	67	67	47
VA	2,906	2,910	2,937	2,749	2,748	2,794	859	881	1,013	31
WA	4,057	4,130	4,461	3,922	3,997	4,378	2,863	3,666	3,669	8
WV	646	650	657	636	642	646	114	111	108	45
WI	8,432	8,194	8,161	8,069	7,792	7,849	2,130	2,242	1,936	21
WY	1,716	1,883	1,864	1,638	1,820	1,816	285	338	295	39

X Not applicable. [1] Excludes Alaska. Acreage data include sunflower and sugarbeet acreage unallocated by State.

Source: U.S. Dept. of Agriculture, National Agricultural Statistics Service, *Crop Production*, annual; and *Crop Values*, annual.

1112. Principal Crops—Production, Supply, and Disappearance: 1990 to 1996

g year beginning May 1 for hay, June 1 for wheat, August 1 for cotton and rice, September 1 for soybeans, corn, and sorghum. Acreage, production, and yield of all crops periodically revised on basis of census data]

AND R	ACREAGE (mil.)— Set aside [1]	Planted	Harvested	Yield per acre	Production	Farm price [2]	Farm value (mil. dol.)	Total supply [3]	DISAPPEARANCE Total [4]	Exports	Ending stocks
grain:				Bu.	Mil. bu.	$/bu.			Mil. bu.		
......	10.7	74.2	67.0	119	7,934	2.28	18,192	9,282	7,761	1,725	1,521
......	10.9	73.2	62.9	101	6,336	2.50	16,032	8,470	7,620	1,328	850
......	2.4	79.2	72.9	139	10,103	2.26	22,992	10,962	9,405	2,177	1,558
......	7.7	71.2	65.0	114	7,374	3.24	24,118	8,948	8,522	2,228	426
......	(NA)	79.5	73.1	127	9,293	2.70	24,853	9,729	8,820	1,825	909
s:				Bu.	Mil. bu.	$/bu.			Mil. bu.		
......	-	57.8	56.5	34.1	1,926	5.74	11,042	2,169	1,840	557	329
......	-	60.1	57.3	32.6	1,871	6.40	11,950	2,170	1,961	589	209
......	-	61.7	60.9	41.4	2,517	5.48	13,756	2,731	2,396	838	335
......	-	62.6	61.6	35.3	2,177	6.72	14,617	2,516	2,333	851	183
......	-	64.2	63.4	37.6	2,382	6.85	16,277	2,576	2,451	895	125
				Sh. tons	Mil. sh. tons	$/ton			Mil. sh. tons		
......	-	(NA)	61.0	2.40	147	[5 6]80.60	10,462	173	146	(NA)	27
......	-	(NA)	59.7	2.46	147	[5 6]84.70	10,957	168	146	(NA)	22
......	-	(NA)	58.7	2.55	150	[5 6]86.70	11,114	172	151	(NA)	21
......	-	(NA)	59.6	2.59	154	[5 6]82.20	11,042	175	154	(NA)	21
......	-	(NA)	61.0	2.45	149	[5 6]93.00	11,970	170	(NA)	(NA)	(NA)
				Bu.	Mil. bu.	$/bu.			Mil. bu.		
......	7.5	77.0	69.1	39.5	2,730	2.61	7,184	3,303	2,435	1,069	868
......	5.7	72.2	62.7	38.2	2,396	3.26	7,648	3,036	2,467	1,228	568
......	5.2	70.3	61.8	37.6	2,321	3.45	7,968	2,981	2,475	1,188	507
......	6.1	69.1	60.9	35.8	2,183	4.55	9,787	2,757	2,381	1,241	376
......	(NA)	75.6	62.9	36.3	2,282	4.30	9,764	2,748	2,283	985	465
				Lb.	Mil. bales [7]	cents/lb.			Mil. bales [7]		
......	2.0	12.3	11.7	634	[8]15.5	68.2	5,076	18.5	16.5	7.8	[9]2.3
......	1.4	13.4	12.8	606	[8]16.1	58.4	4,521	20.8	17.3	6.9	[9]3.5
......	1.7	13.7	13.3	708	[8]19.7	72.0	6,797	23.2	20.6	9.4	[9]2.7
......	0.3	16.9	16.0	536	[8]17.9	76.5	6,575	21.0	18.3	7.7	[9]2.6
......	(NA)	14.6	12.9	707	[8]19.0	71.7	6,524	22.0	17.9	7.0	[9]4.1
; ld				Lb.	Mil. lb.	$/lb.			Mil. lb.		
......	(NA)	(NA)	0.7	2,218	1,626	[6]1.74	2,827	4,026	1,794	631	[11]2,232
......	(NA)	(NA)	0.7	2,159	1,614	[6]1.75	2,831	4,026	1,436	538	[11]2,588
......	(NA)	(NA)	0.7	2,359	1,583	[6]1.76	2,779	4,171	1,604	523	[11]2,541
......	(NA)	(NA)	0.7	1,913	1,269	[6]1.82	2,305	3,666	1,491	533	[11]2,225
......	(NA)	(NA)	0.7	2,133	1,565	[6]1.88	2,938	3,712	(NA)	(NA)	(NA)
:				Cwt.	Mil. cwt.	$/cwt.			Mil. cwt.		
......	(NA)	1.4	1.4	293	402	6.08	2,431	582	[12]319	[13]14	(NA)
......	(NA)	1.4	1.3	326	429	6.17	2,637	642	[12]353	[13]19	(NA)
......	(NA)	1.4	1.4	339	467	5.58	2,590	692	[12]367	[13]24	(NA)
......	(NA)	1.4	1.4	323	444	6.77	2,992	687	[12]369	[13]30	(NA)
......	(NA)	1.5	1.4	349	497	5.11	2,515	(NA)	(NA)	(NA)	(NA)
for				Bu.	Mil. bu.	$/bu.			Mil. bu.		
......	3.3	10.5	9.1	63.1	573	2.12	1,221	793	651	232	143
......	2.3	9.9	8.9	59.9	534	2.31	1,235	709	662	202	48
......	1.6	9.8	8.9	72.8	649	2.13	1,324	697	625	223	72
......	1.7	9.5	8.3	55.6	460	3.19	1,395	532	514	198	18
......	(NA)	13.2	11.9	67.5	803	2.35	2,053	821	765	215	56
gh:				Lb.	Mil. cwt.	$/cwt.			Mil. cwt.		
......	1.0	2.9	2.8	5,529	156	6.68	1,047	187	163	71	25
......	0.7	2.9	2.8	5,510	156	7.98	1,247	203	177	75	26
......	0.3	3.4	3.3	5,964	198	6.78	1,337	231	199	99	31
......	0.5	3.1	3.1	5,621	174	9.15	1,587	213	188	83	25
......	(NA)	2.8	2.8	6,121	171	9.50	1,612	207	183	78	24

presents zero. NA Not available. [1] Acreage set aside under diversion, PIK (payment-in-kind) and acreage reduction . [2] Except as noted, marketing year average price. U.S. prices are computed by weighting U.S. monthly prices by monthly marketings and do not include an allowance for outstanding loans and government purchases and payments. ses production, imports, and beginning stocks. [4] Includes feed, residual, and other domestic uses not shown y. [5] Prices are for hay sold baled. [6] Season average prices received by farmers. U.S. prices are computed by State prices by estimated sales and include an allowance for outstanding loans and government purchases, if any, for ler government programs. [7] Bales of 480 pounds, net weight. [8] State production figures, which conform with U.S. the Census annual ginning enumeration with allowance for cross-State ginnings, rounded to thousands and added for s. [9] Stock estimates based on Census Bureau data which results in an unaccounted difference between supply and nates and changes in ending stocks. [10] Flue-cured and cigar wrapper, crop year July-June; all other types September. Farm-sales-weight basis. [11] Includes tobacco carried over on farms. [12] Covers potatoes used for table n and canned products, chips, and dehydration. [13] Covers fresh potatoes, chips, frozen and dehydrated products.

ce: Production—U.S. Dept. of Agriculture, National Agricultural Statistics Service. In *Crop Production*, annual; and *Crop* nual. Supply and disappearance—U.S. Dept. of Agriculture, Economic Research Service, *Feed Situation*, quarterly; *Fats Situation*, quarterly; *Wheat Situation*, quarterly; *Tobacco Situation*, quarterly; *Cotton and Wool Outlook Statistics*, periodic; *ultural Supply and Demand Estimates*, periodic. All data are also in *Agricultural Statistics*, annual; and *Agricultural* monthly.

No. 1113. Corn—Acreage, Production, and Value, by Leading States: 1994 to 1996

[One bushel of corn=56 pounds]

STATE	ACREAGE HARVESTED (1,000 acres)			YIELD PER ACRE (bu.)			PRODUCTION (mil. bu.)			PRICE ($/bu.)			FARM VALUE (mil. dol.)		
	1994	1995	1996	1994	1995	1996	1994	1995	1996	1994	1995	1996	1994	1995	1996
U.S. [1]	72,887	64,995	73,147	139	114	127	10,103	7,374	9,293	2.26	3.24	2.70	22,992	24,118	24,853
IA	12,700	11,400	12,450	152	123	138	1,930	1,402	1,718	2.22	3.20	2.60	4,285	4,487	4,467
IL	11,450	10,000	10,800	156	113	136	1,786	1,130	1,469	2.27	3.30	2.70	4,055	3,729	3,966
NE	8,300	7,700	8,300	139	111	143	1,154	855	1,187	2.33	3.22	2.60	2,688	2,752	3,086
MN	6,450	6,150	6,950	142	119	125	916	732	869	2.23	3.14	2.40	2,042	2,298	2,085
IN	5,960	5,300	5,450	144	113	123	858	599	670	2.25	3.38	2.65	1,931	2,024	1,776
SD	3,400	2,450	3,700	108	79	100	367	194	370	2.01	3.23	2.20	738	625	814
KS	2,130	1,970	2,350	143	124	152	305	244	357	2.32	3.24	2.85	707	791	1,018
MO	2,300	1,470	2,650	119	102	134	274	150	355	2.25	3.48	2.80	616	522	994
WI	3,100	3,050	3,000	141	114	111	437	348	333	2.25	3.11	2.55	983	1,081	849
OH	3,500	3,100	2,750	139	121	111	487	375	305	2.23	3.32	2.55	1,085	1,245	778
MI	2,230	2,170	2,300	117	115	94	261	250	216	2.23	3.20	2.40	582	799	519
TX	2,040	1,900	1,800	117	114	112	239	217	202	2.51	3.19	3.25	599	691	655
KY	1,220	1,140	1,200	128	108	124	156	123	149	2.38	3.27	2.95	372	403	439
CO	890	830	940	150	111	142	134	92	133	2.38	3.33	2.75	318	307	367
PA	1,030	980	1,070	120	96	119	124	94	127	2.68	3.86	2.65	331	363	337
NC	900	700	900	91	107	95	82	75	86	2.48	3.54	3.40	203	265	291
TN	570	540	680	116	118	116	66	64	79	2.25	3.50	3.05	149	223	241
NY	590	610	630	116	105	107	68	64	67	2.65	3.85	3.20	181	247	216
ND	540	510	720	100	79	91	54	40	66	2.06	3.16	2.65	111	127	174
LA	306	221	523	115	105	125	35	23	65	2.40	2.95	3.65	84	68	239
MD	390	400	400	118	105	139	46	42	65	2.45	3.65	2.70	113	153	175

[1] Includes other States, not shown separately.

Source: U.S. Dept. of Agriculture, National Agricultural Statistics Service, *Crop Production*, annual; and *Crop Values*, annual.

No. 1114. Soybeans—Acreage, Production, and Value, by Leading States: 1994 to 1996

[One bushel of soybeans=60 pounds]

STATE	ACREAGE HARVESTED (1,000 acres)			YIELD PER ACRE (bu.)			PRODUCTION (mil. bu.)			PRICE ($/bu.)			FARM VALUE (mil. dol.)		
	1994	1995	1996	1994	1995	1996	1994	1995	1996	1994	1995	1996	1994	1995	1996
U.S. [1]	60,859	61,624	63,409	41	35	38	2,517	2,177	2,382	5.48	6.72	6.85	13,756	14,617	16,277
IA	8,770	9,260	9,450	51	44	44	443	407	416	5.43	6.65	6.80	2,405	2,709	2,827
IL	9,430	9,700	9,850	46	39	41	429	378	399	5.61	6.88	6.95	2,407	2,603	2,773
MN	5,600	5,800	5,900	40	41	38	224	235	224	5.37	6.59	6.75	1,203	1,548	1,513
IN	4,580	4,980	5,360	47	40	38	215	197	204	5.53	6.73	6.85	1,190	1,324	1,395
OH	3,990	4,030	4,490	44	38	35	174	153	157	5.51	6.70	6.85	956	1,026	1,076
MO	4,560	4,500	4,050	38	30	37	173	133	150	5.43	6.84	6.70	941	908	1,004
NE	2,860	3,060	3,010	47	33	45	134	101	135	5.29	6.56	6.75	711	662	914
AR	3,400	3,400	3,500	34	26	32	116	88	112	5.69	6.85	7.10	658	606	795
SD	2,400	2,500	2,670	38	30	34	91	75	91	5.10	6.28	6.50	465	471	590
KS	2,100	2,050	2,000	35	25	37	74	51	74	5.32	6.69	6.65	391	343	492
MS	1,870	1,800	1,750	31	21	31	57	38	54	5.59	6.76	7.10	319	256	385
MI	1,540	1,490	1,640	37	40	29	57	60	47	5.43	6.52	6.70	309	389	313
KY	1,130	1,150	1,180	38	36	38	42	41	45	5.65	7.01	6.90	239	290	309
TN	1,050	1,080	1,150	37	32	35	38	35	40	5.62	6.88	7.00	215	238	282

[1] Includes other States, not shown separately.

Source: U.S. Dept. of Agriculture, National Agricultural Statistics Service, *Crop Production*, annual; and *Crop Values*, annual.

No. 1115. Wheat—Acreage, Production, and Value, by Leading States: 1994 to 1996

[One bushel of wheat= 60 pounds]

STATE	ACREAGE HARVESTED (1,000 acres)			YIELD PER ACRE (bu.)			PRODUCTION (mil. bu.)			PRICE ($/bu.)			FARM VALUE (mil. dol.)		
	1994	1995	1996	1994	1995	1996	1994	1995	1996	1994	1995	1996	1994	1995	1996
U.S. [1]	61,770	60,945	62,860	37.6	35.8	36.3	2,321	2,183	2,282	3.45	4.55	4.30	7,968	9,787	9,784
ND	11,238	11,114	12,515	31.7	27.0	31.6	356	300	395	3.70	5.05	4.10	1,308	1,495	1,643
KS	11,400	11,000	8,800	38.0	26.0	29.0	433	286	255	3.32	4.59	4.70	1,438	1,313	1,199
WA	2,545	2,595	2,745	52.7	59.3	66.5	134	154	183	3.92	4.83	4.20	526	743	740
MT	5,378	5,435	6,350	31.7	36.0	27.8	171	196	177	3.54	4.63	4.00	602	904	712
SD	3,353	2,752	3,854	28.4	33.0	36.1	95	91	139	3.50	4.68	3.95	335	420	547
ID	1,410	1,330	1,560	71.1	77.7	76.4	100	103	119	3.55	4.45	4.05	356	460	472
MN	2,548	2,245	2,442	28.0	32.0	41.9	71	72	102	3.33	4.71	4.20	238	339	440
OK	5,300	5,200	4,900	27.0	21.0	19.0	143	109	93	3.41	4.41	4.95	488	482	461

[1] Includes other States, not shown separately.

Source: U.S. Dept. of Agriculture, National Agricultural Statistics Service, *Crop Production*, annual; and *Crop Values*, annual

1116. Greenhouse and Nursery Crops—Summary, by Type of Product: 1990 to 1996

llions of dollars, except per capita. Based on a survey of 36 commercial floriculture States and estimates by source]

ITEM	Total	Cut flowers	Potted flowering plants	Foliage plants	Bedding plants	Cut cultivated greens	Other [1]
ic production: [2]							
)	8,677	529	701	693	1,032	121	5,601
l	10,078	501	844	714	1,593	135	6,291
5	10,229	462	865	724	1,648	127	6,401
3	10,600	475	892	737	1,711	130	6,654
:							
)	526	326	18	25	(NA)	14	143
l	697	420	28	43	(NA)	20	186
5	855	512	30	53	(NA)	24	236
3	1,000	580	32	62	(NA)	26	300
RETAIL CONSUMER EXPENDITURES [3]							
)	29,273	4,826	2,707	2,510	1,548	679	17,003
l	33,574	5,264	3,288	2,712	2,390	769	19,151
5	34,746	5,668	3,376	2,790	2,473	770	19,669
3	36,539	6,200	3,463	2,878	2,567	796	20,615
pita (dol.): [4]							
)	117	19	11	10	6	3	68
5	132	22	13	11	9	3	75
3	138	23	13	11	10	3	78

Not available. [1] Includes turfgrass (sod), bulbs, nursery stock, groundcovers, and other greenhouse and nursery is except the following: seeds, cut Christmas trees, and food crops grown under cover. [2] Equivalent wholesale values. udes services such as landscaping, installation, and maintenance. [4] Based on U.S. Bureau of the Census estimated t population as of July 1.

urce: U.S. Dept. of Agriculture, Economic Research Service, unpublished data.

No. 1117. Fresh Fruits and Vegetables—Supply and Use: 1990 to 1996

[In millions of pounds, except per capita in pounds]

YEAR	Utilized production [1]	Imports [2]	Supply, [1] total	CONSUMPTION		Exports [2]
				Total	Per capita	
FRUITS						
)	6,920	123	7,151	5,004	20.1	2,147
l	8,096	315	8,434	5,941	22.8	2,493
5	8,102	373	8,509	5,877	22.4	2,632
3, prel	8,528	368	8,935	6,324	23.9	2,611
rus: [3]						
)	10,568	7,516	18,067	16,190	65.1	1,771
l	11,918	8,968	20,754	18,100	69.8	2,675
5	11,316	9,111	20,274	17,953	68.6	2,339
ETABLES & MELONS						
)	34,629	3,265	38,774	34,577	138.4	2,685
l	38,763	3,818	43,382	37,997	145.8	3,720
5	37,843	4,698	43,621	38,408	146.0	3,525
3, prel	39,461	5,134	45,619	40,419	152.2	3,563
POTATOES						
)	11,077	684	11,761	11,434	45.7	327
l	12,689	643	13,332	12,677	48.6	655
5	13,244	685	13,929	13,345	50.7	584
3, prel	12,498	1,005	13,503	12,913	48.6	590

Crop-year basis for fruits. [2] Fiscal year for fruits; calendar year for vegetables and potatoes. [3] Includes bananas.

No. 1118. Nuts—Supply and Use: 1990 to 1995

[In millions of pounds (shelled)]

YEAR	Beginning stocks	Marketable production [1]	Imports	Supply, total	Consumption	Exports	Ending stocks
	326.2	961.5	196.4	1,486.1	609.6	522.6	354.0
	237.0	947.1	214.6	1,398.7	581.1	538.2	279.4
	279.4	1,061.4	218.9	1,559.8	591.7	634.1	334.0
	334.0	755.5	171.2	1,260.7	510.2	503.7	246.8

tilized production minus inedibles and noncommercial usage.

urce of tables 1117 and 1118: U.S. Dept. of Agriculture, Economic Research Service, *Fruit and Tree Nuts Situation and* *k Yearbook* and *Vegetables and Specialties Situation and Outlook Yearbook.*

No. 1119. Commercial Vegetable and Other Specified Crops—Area, Production, and Value, 1994 to 1996, and Leading Producing States, 1996

[Except as noted, relates to commercial production for fresh market and processing combined. Includes market garden areas but excludes minor producing acreage in minor producing States. Excludes production for home use in farm and nonfarm gardens. Value is for season or crop year and should not be confused with calendar-year income]

CROP	AREA [1] (1,000 acres)			PRODUCTION [2] (1,000 short tons)			VALUE [3] (mil. dol.)			Leading States in order of production, 1996
	1994	1995	1996	1994	1995	1996	1994	1995	1996	
Beans, snap	303	302	278	1,014	917	945	291	283	291	WI, OR, IL [4]
Beans, dry edible	1,835	1,899	1,718	1,451	1,540	1,367	632	836	680	ND, MI, NE
Broccoli	121	121	116	704	740	716	374	415	396	CA, AZ
Cantaloups	103	103	104	912	963	1,105	301	351	401	CA, AZ, TX
Carrots	99	109	118	1,687	1,759	1,918	338	440	387	CA, CO, MI [5]
Corn, sweet	742	703	695	4,831	4,393	4,432	635	640	636	(NA)
Fresh market	226	219	221	1,100	1,069	1,136	379	389	377	FL, CA, GA
Processed	516	484	474	3,731	3,324	3,296	256	251	259	MN, WI, WA
Cucumbers	175	177	162	1,110	1,113	1,068	292	302	330	MI, NC, FL [4]
Lettuce, head	213	197	203	3,370	3,117	3,292	896	1,463	976	CA, AZ, CO
Lettuce, leaf	38	39	41	424	446	466	233	309	254	CA, AZ, OH
Mushrooms [6]	136	140	135	375	390	389	686	731	728	(NA)
Onions	160	164	161	3,176	3,209	3,078	627	634	590	CA, OR, WA
Peppers, green	64	68	69	771	721	825	456	453	461	CA, FL, NJ
Potatoes	1,380	1,372	1,425	23,352	22,180	24,855	2,590	2,992	2,515	ID, WA, CO
Strawberries	49	48	48	825	801	814	837	812	770	CA, FL, OR
Tomatoes	476	477	458	13,421	13,012	12,951	1,744	1,605	1,603	(NA)
Fresh market	136	133	119	1,879	1,726	1,542	1,029	891	879	FL, CA, GA
Processed	340	344	339	11,542	11,286	11,409	717	714	724	CA, OH, IN
Watermelons	208	204	206	1,999	2,022	2,206	272	357	276	TX, GA, CA

NA Not available. [1] Area of crops for harvest for fresh market, including any partially harvested or not harvested because of low prices or other factors, plus area harvested for processing. [2] Excludes some quantities not marketed. [3] Fresh market vegetables valued at f.o.b. shipping point. Processing vegetables are equivalent returns at packinghouse door. [4] Processed only. [5] Fresh market only. [6] Area is shown in million square feet. All data are for marketing year ending June 30.

Source: U.S. Dept. of Agriculture, National Agricultural Statistics Service, *Vegetables*, annual summary. Also in *Agricultural Statistics*, annual.

No. 1120. Fruits and Nuts—Utilized Production and Value, 1994 to 1996, and Leading Producing States, 1996

FRUIT OR NUT	UTILIZED PRODUCTION [1]				FARM VALUE (mil. dol.)			Leading States in order of production, 1996
	Unit	1994	1995	1996	1994	1995	1996	
Apples (36 States) [2]	Mil. lb	11,331	10,390	10,392	1,467	1,766	1,840	WA, NY, CA
Apricots	1,000 tons	140	61	80	49	28	37	CA, WA, UT
Avocados	1,000 tons	175	190	(NA)	241	238	(NA)	CA, FL
Bananas	Mil. lb	14	13	13	5	5	5	HI
Cherries, sweet	1,000 tons	193	153	152	201	193	223	WA, OR, CA
Cherries, tart	Mil. lb	296	311	259	48	18	(NA)	MI, UT, NY
Cranberries	1,000 bbl. [3]	4,682	4,193	4,617	231	224	(NA)	WI, MA, NJ
Dates (CA)	1,000 tons	23	22	21	17	16	19	CA
Figs (fresh) (CA)	1,000 tons	57	51	43	24	16	13	CA
Grapefruit (4 States)	Mil. boxes [4]	65	71	66	342	329	310	FL, CA, TX
Grapes (13 States)	1,000 tons	5,869	5,913	5,529	1,883	2,046	2,242	CA, WA, NY
Kiwifruit (CA)	1,000 tons	38	32	27	18	15	(NA)	CA
Lemons (2 States)	Mil. boxes [5]	26	24	26	257	263	253	CA, AZ
Limes (FL)	Mil. boxes [6]	(Z)	(Z)	(Z)	4	3	4	FL
Nectarines (CA)	1,000 tons	242	176	243	68	94	115	CA
Olives (CA)	1,000 tons	84	78	166	39	49	105	CA
Oranges and tangerines (4 States)	Mil. boxes [7]	248	270	280	1,633	1,734	2,007	FL, CA, AZ
Papayas	Mil. lb	62	51	45	14	18	16	HI
Peaches (31 States)	Mil. lb	2,359	2,191	2,010	315	405	378	CA, NJ, PA
Pears	1,000 tons	1,045	948	778	233	258	297	WA, CA, OR
Pineapples	1,000 tons	365	345	347	79	87	96	HI
Plums and prunes (fresh)	1,000 tons	841	721	916	295	313	(NA)	CA, OR, WA
Tangelos (FL)	Mil. boxes [5]	3	3	2	18	17	16	FL
Temples (FL)	Mil. boxes [8]	2	3	2	13	15	15	FL
Almonds (shelled basis) (CA)	Mil. lb	735	370	520	965	881	1,048	CA
Hazelnuts (in the shell)	1,000 tons	21	39	19	18	36	16	OR, WA
Macadamia nuts	Mil. lb	53	51	55	36	38	42	HI
Pecans (in the shell) (11 States)	Mil. lb	199	268	227	207	272	151	GA, TX, NM
Pistachios	Mil. lb	129	148	106	119	161	120	CA
Walnuts, English (in the shell)	1,000 tons	232	234	205	239	328	(NA)	CA

NA Not available. Z Less than 500,000 boxes. [1] Excludes quantities not harvested or not marketed. [2] Production in commercial orchards with 100 or more bearing age trees. [3] Barrels of 100 pounds. [4] Approximate average, net weight, is 67 lb. in AZ and CA; 85 in FL; and 80 in TX. [5] About 76 lb. net. [6] Approximate net weight is 88 lb. [7] Net contents of box varies. In CA and AZ approximate average for oranges and tangerines is 75 lb.; FL oranges, 90 lb.; TX oranges, 85 lb.; and FL tangerines, 95 lb. [8] Approximate net weight is 90 lb.

Source: U.S. Dept. of Agriculture, National Agricultural Statistics Service, *Noncitrus Fruits and Nuts*, annual; and *Citrus Fruits*, annual.

No. 1121. Meat Supply and Use: 1980 to 1996

millions of pounds (carcass weight equivalent). Carcass weight equivalent is the weight of the animal minus , hide, and internal organs; includes fat and bone. Covers Federal and State inspected, and farm slaughter]

YPE OF MEAT	Production	Imports	Supply, total [1]	Consumption [2]	Exports	Ending stocks
ND POULTRY						
	53,151	2,668	57,036	54,695	1,124	1,217
	56,271	3,255	60,631	58,651	926	1,054
	62,255	3,295	66,673	62,937	2,472	1,263
	71,795	3,161	76,471	69,378	5,363	1,730
	74,070	2,837	78,637	69,929	6,939	1,769
	75,303	2,769	79,841	70,149	7,957	1,734
D MEATS						
	38,978	2,668	42,481	41,170	429	882
	39,409	3,255	43,505	42,311	461	733
	38,787	3,295	42,742	40,784	1,250	707
	42,683	3,161	46,744	43,589	2,151	1,004
	43,677	2,831	47,512	43,985	2,598	930
	43,291	2,764	46,985	43,392	2,834	759
	21,643	2,064	24,166	23,560	173	432
	23,728	2,071	26,271	25,523	328	420
	22,743	2,356	25,434	24,031	1,006	397
	24,386	2,369	27,284	25,125	1,611	548
	25,222	2,103	27,873	25,533	1,821	519
	25,526	2,073	28,116	25,863	1,877	377
	16,617	550	17,521	16,838	252	431
	14,807	1,128	16,283	15,865	128	289
	15,354	898	16,565	16,031	238	296
	17,696	743	18,798	17,829	531	438
	17,849	664	18,951	17,784	771	396
	17,117	618	18,132	16,815	951	366
	400	21	432	420	2	9
	515	20	549	533	4	11
	327	(NA)	331	325	(NA)	6
	293	(NA)	297	290	(NA)	7
	319	(NA)	326	319	(NA)	7
	379	(NA)	386	379	(NA)	7
on:						
	318	33	362	351	1	9
	359	36	403	389	1	13
	363	41	412	397	6	8
	308	49	365	345	9	11
	287	64	362	348	6	8
	268	73	349	334	6	9
Y, TOTAL						
	14,173	-	14,555	13,525	695	334
	16,862	-	17,126	16,340	465	321
	23,468	-	23,931	22,153	1,222	556
	29,112	-	29,727	25,789	3,212	726
	30,393	6	31,125	25,944	4,342	839
	32,015	5	32,859	26,760	5,123	975
	11,252	-	11,364	10,682	567	115
	13,520	-	13,646	13,072	417	158
	18,430	-	18,651	17,266	1,143	242
	23,666	-	24,024	20,690	2,876	458
	24,827	1	25,287	20,832	3,694	560
	26,124	4	26,686	21,626	4,420	641
	551	-	581	507	53	21
	525	-	537	503	21	13
	523	-	530	496	25	9
	509	-	517	413	90	14
	496	3	513	406	99	7
	491	-	498	228	265	6
	2,370	-	2,610	2,337	75	198
	2,817	-	2,943	2,765	27	150
	4,514	-	4,750	4,390	54	306
	4,937	-	5,186	4,686	246	254
	5,069	2	5,326	4,706	348	271
	5,401	1	5,673	4,906	438	328

zero. NA Not available. [1] Total supply equals production plus imports plus ending stocks of previous year. nts to territories.

Department of Agriculture, Economic Research Service, *Food Consumption, Prices, and Expenditures, 1997: 70-1995*; and *Agricultural Outlook*, monthly.

No. 1122. Livestock Inventory and Production: 1980 to 1997

[Production in live weight; includes animals for slaughter market, younger animals shipped to other States for feeding or breeding purposes, farm slaughter and custom slaughter consumed on farms where produced, minus livestock shipped into States for feeding or breeding with an adjustment for changes in inventory]

TYPE OF LIVESTOCK	Unit	1980	1985	1989	1990	1991	1992	1993	1994	1995	1996	1997
ALL CATTLE [1]												
Inventory: [2] Number on farms	Mil	111.2	109.6	96.7	95.8	96.4	97.6	99.2	101.0	102.8	103.5	101.2
Total value	Bil. dol.	55.8	44.0	56.2	59.0	63.1	61.5	64.4	66.5	63.2	52.0	53.1
Value per head	Dol	502	402	581	616	655	630	649	659	615	503	525
Production: Quantity	Bil. lb	40.3	40.1	38.9	39.2	39.8	40.3	40.9	42.1	42.7	41.3	(NA)
Beef, price per 100 lb	Dol	62.40	53.70	69.50	74.60	72.70	71.30	72.60	66.70	61.80	58.70	(NA)
Calves, price per 100 lb	Dol	76.80	62.10	90.80	95.60	98.00	89.00	91.20	87.20	73.10	58.40	(NA)
Value of production	Bil. dol.	25.5	21.2	27.1	29.3	29.4	28.6	30.3	26.9	24.8	22.3	(NA)
HOGS AND PIGS												
Inventory: [3] Number on farms	Mil	67.3	54.1	55.5	53.8	54.4	57.6	58.2	57.9	60.0	58.3	58.2
Total value	Bil. dol.	3.8	4.1	3.7	4.3	4.6	4.0	4.1	4.3	3.2	4.1	5.3
Value per head	Dol	56.00	75.00	66.30	79.10	85.40	68.80	71.20	74.90	53.20	70.70	94.00
Production: Quantity	Bil. lb	23.4	20.2	21.9	21.3	22.7	23.9	23.7	24.4	24.4	23.3	(NA)
Price per 100 lb	Dol	38.00	44.00	42.50	53.70	49.10	41.60	45.20	39.90	40.50	51.90	(NA)
Value of production	Bil. dol.	8.9	8.9	9.3	11.3	11.1	9.9	10.6	9.7	9.8	12.0	(NA)
SHEEP AND LAMBS												
Inventory: [2] Number on farms	Mil	12.7	10.7	10.9	11.4	11.2	10.8	10.2	9.7	8.9	8.5	7.9
Total value	Mil. dol	993	654	894	901	733	661	714	681	663	732	762
Value per head	Dol	78.20	61.10	82.40	79.30	65.60	61.20	70.60	69.90	74.70	86.50	96.00
Production: Quantity	Mil. lb	746	704	811	781	796	746	689	630	599	560	(NA)
Sheep, price per 100 lb	Dol	21.30	23.90	24.40	23.20	19.70	25.80	28.60	30.90	28.00	29.90	(NA)
Lambs, price per 100 lb	Dol	63.60	67.70	66.10	55.50	52.20	59.50	64.40	65.60	78.20	82.20	(NA)
Value of production	Mil. dol	403	434	468	374	357	394	394	360	410	431	(NA)

NA Not available. [1] Includes milk cows. [2] As of Jan. 1. [3] As of Dec. 1 of preceding year.

Source: U.S. Dept. of Agriculture, National Agricultural Statistics Service, *Meat Animals—Production, Disposition, and Income*, annual; and annual livestock summaries. Also in *Agricultural Statistics*, annual.

No. 1123. Cattle and Calves—Number, Production, and Value, by State: 1994 to 1997

[Includes milk cows. See headnote, table 1122]

STATE	NUMBER ON FARMS [1] (1,000)			QUANTITY PRODUCED (mil. lb.)			VALUE OF PRODUCTION (mil. dol.)			COMMERCIAL SLAUGHTER [2] (mil. lb.)	
	1995	1996	1997	1994	1995	1996	1994	1995	1996	1994	1995
U.S. [3]	102,755	103,487	101,209	42,096	42,714	41,305	26,861	24,830	22,259	40,654	42,704
CA	4,650	4,600	4,550	1,943	1,969	1,913	1,102	907	786	1,107	1,277
CO	2,950	3,100	3,150	1,912	2,011	2,007	1,100	1,184	1,223	2,964	3,099
ID	1,760	1,770	1,750	847	873	888	525	487	447	(4)	(4)
IA	4,050	3,950	3,900	1,992	1,910	1,788	1,100	1,160	1,040	2,111	2,137
KS	6,300	6,500	6,550	3,584	3,631	3,605	2,345	2,210	2,084	8,235	8,444
MN	2,800	2,900	2,750	1,192	1,225	1,219	667	671	665	1,326	1,356
MO	4,500	4,550	4,450	1,178	1,168	1,175	858	703	593	168	198
MT	2,700	2,750	2,700	1,050	1,091	1,082	764	659	587	27	24
NE	6,000	6,350	6,550	3,904	3,953	3,886	2,386	2,476	2,565	7,982	8,190
OK	5,600	5,500	5,400	1,981	1,957	1,883	1,452	1,233	1,004	45	43
SD	3,900	3,850	3,800	1,461	1,420	1,404	1,011	879	799	280	279
TX	15,100	15,000	14,100	7,101	7,892	7,120	4,721	4,803	4,143	6,866	7,182
WI	3,850	3,800	3,700	1,112	1,100	1,010	649	576	479	1,673	1,782

[1] As of January 1. [2] Data cover cattle only. Includes slaughter in federally inspected and other slaughter plants; excludes animals slaughtered on farms. [3] Includes other States not shown separately. [4] Included in U.S. total. Not printed to avoid disclosing individual operation.

Source: U.S. Dept. of Agriculture, National Agricultural Statistics Service, *Meat Animals-Production, Disposition and Income*, annual.

No. 1124. Hogs and Pigs—Number, Production, and Value, by State: 1994 to 1996

[See headnote, table 1122]

STATE	NUMBER ON FARMS [1] (1,000)			QUANTITY PRODUCED (mil. lb.)			VALUE OF PRODUCTION (mil. dol.)			COMMERCIAL SLAUGHTER [2] (mil. lb.)	
	1994	1995	1996	1994	1995	1996	1994	1995	1996	1994	1995
U.S. [3]	59,990	58,264	56,171	24,437	24,426	23,263	9,692	9,829	11,997	24,430	24,843
IL	5,350	4,800	4,400	2,390	2,202	1,954	926	849	985	2,375	2,417
IN	4,500	4,000	3,750	1,721	1,772	1,588	658	685	790	892	869
IA	14,500	13,400	12,200	6,109	5,637	5,223	2,426	2,262	2,686	8,026	7,771
MN	4,850	4,950	4,850	1,976	2,003	1,991	811	831	1,047	1,817	1,751
MO	3,500	3,550	3,500	1,310	1,461	1,250	514	580	624	(4)	(4)
NE	4,350	4,050	3,600	1,780	1,691	1,515	728	706	812	1,437	1,452
NC	7,000	8,200	9,300	2,601	3,157	3,399	1,054	1,322	1,804	1,648	1,933

[1] As of December 1. [2] Includes slaughter in federally inspected and other slaughter plants; excludes animals slaughtered on farms. [3] Includes other States not shown separately. [4] Included in U.S. total. Not printed to avoid disclosing individual operation.

Source: U.S. Dept. of Agriculture, National Agricultural Statistics Service, *Meat Animals-Production, Disposition and Income*,

No. 1125. Milk Production and Commercial Use: 1980 to 1996

[In billions of pounds milkfat basis]

YEAR	Production	Farm use	COMMERCIAL: Farm marketings	COMMERCIAL: Beginning stock	Imports	Commercial supply, total	CCC net removals [1]	COMMERCIAL: Ending stock	COMMERCIAL: Disappearance	Milk price per 100 lb.[2] (dol.)
1980	128.4	2.3	126.1	5.3	2.1	133.5	8.8	5.6	119.0	13.1
1985	143.0	2.5	140.6	4.8	2.8	148.2	13.2	4.5	130.5	12.8
1990	147.7	2.0	145.7	4.1	2.7	152.5	8.5	5.1	138.8	13.7
1994	153.7	1.7	152.0	4.6	2.9	159.4	4.8	4.3	150.3	13.0
1995	155.4	1.6	153.9	4.3	2.9	161.1	2.1	4.1	154.9	12.7
1996	154.3	1.4	152.8	4.1	2.9	159.9	0.1	4.7	155.1	14.7

[1] Removals from commercial supply by Commodity Credit Corporation. [2] Wholesale price received by farmers for all milk delivered to plants and dealers.

Source: U.S. Dept. of Agriculture, Economic Research Service, *Agricultural Outlook*, monthly.

No. 1126. Milk Cows—Number, Production, and Value, by State: 1994 to 1996

STATE	NUMBER ON FARMS [1] (1,000)			MILK PRODUCED ON FARMS (mil. lb.)			VALUE OF PRODUCTION [2] (mil. dol.)		
	1994	1995	1996	1994	1995	1996	1994	1995	1996
United States [3]	9,500	9,458	9,351	153,664	155,425	154,331	20,162	20,099	23,067
California	1,235	1,254	1,264	25,242	25,344	25,859	2,972	3,086	3,724
Idaho	208	232	256	3,754	4,210	4,735	462	514	658
Iowa	255	251	250	3,960	4,050	3,826	511	510	555
Michigan	328	326	320	5,545	5,565	5,430	746	725	816
Minnesota	609	599	598	9,342	9,409	9,440	1,208	1,197	1,378
New York	718	703	702	11,400	11,600	11,529	1,520	1,510	1,720
Ohio	294	289	285	4,515	4,600	4,370	600	603	656
Pennsylvania	639	642	644	10,230	10,600	10,640	1,460	1,471	1,677
Texas	402	401	398	6,225	6,113	6,120	834	796	924
Washington	261	266	264	5,203	5,302	5,279	681	688	792
Wisconsin	1,494	1,490	1,449	22,412	22,942	22,376	2,912	2,951	3,300

[1] Average number during year. Represents cows and heifers that have calved, kept for milk; excluding heifers not yet fresh. [2] Valued at average returns per 100 pounds of milk in combined marketings of milk and cream. Includes value of milk fed to calves. [3] Includes other States not shown separately.

Source: U.S. Dept. of Agriculture, National Agricultural Statistics Service, *Dairy Products*, annual; and *Milk: Production, Disposition, and Income*, annual.

No. 1127. Milk Production and Manufactured Dairy Products: 1980 to 1996

ITEM	Unit	1980	1985	1990	1991	1992	1993	1994	1995	1996
Number of farms with milk cows	1,000	334	269	193	181	171	159	149	140	(NA)
Cows and heifers that have calved, kept for milk	Mil. head	10.8	11.0	10.0	9.8	9.7	9.6	9.5	9.5	9.4
Milk produced on farms	Bil. lb	128	143	148	148	151	151	154	155	154
Production per cow	1,000 lb.	11.9	13.0	14.8	15.0	15.6	15.7	16.2	16.4	16.5
Whole milk sold from farms [1]	Bil. lb	126	141	146	146	149	149	152	154	153
Sales to plants and dealers	Bil. lb	125	139	145	145	148	148	151	153	152
Value of milk produced	Bil. dol.	16.9	18.4	20.4	18.3	20.0	19.5	20.2	20.1	23.1
Gross farm income, dairy products	Bil. dol.	16.7	18.1	20.2	18.1	19.8	19.3	20.0	19.9	22.9
Cash receipts from marketing of milk and cream [1]	Bil. dol.	16.6	18.1	20.1	18.0	19.7	19.2	19.9	19.9	22.8
Sales to plants and dealers	Bil. dol.	16.3	17.8	19.9	17.8	19.5	19.0	19.6	19.5	22.4
Number of dairy manufacturing plants	Number	2,257	2,061	1,723	1,680	1,603	1,534	1,532	1,495	1,420
Manufactured dairy products:										
Butter (incl. whey butter)	Mil. lb	1,145	1,248	1,302	1,336	1,365	1,315	1,296	1,264	1,174
Cheese, total [2]	Mil. lb	3,984	5,081	6,059	6,055	6,488	6,528	6,735	6,917	7,218
American (excl. full-skim American)	Mil. lb	2,376	2,855	2,894	2,769	2,937	2,957	2,974	3,131	3,281
Cream and Neufchatel	Mil. lb	229	294	431	447	517	540	573	544	575
All Italian varieties	Mil. lb	983	1,491	2,207	2,329	2,509	2,495	2,626	2,674	2,812
Cottage cheese: Creamed [3]	Mil. lb	825	716	832	819	787	748	731	711	690
Curd, pot, and bakers	Mil. lb	667	599	493	491	502	471	463	459	448
Condensed bulk milk	Mil. lb	952	1,232	1,426	1,530	1,624	1,605	1,593	1,372	1,270
Evaporated and condensed canned milk	Mil. lb	740	656	615	560	599	557	565	503	492
Nonfat dry milk [4]	Mil. lb	1,168	1,398	902	885	872	964	1,242	1,243	1,068
Dry whey [5]	Mil. lb	690	987	1,143	1,167	1,237	1,196	1,212	1,147	1,117
Yogurt, plain and fruit flavored	Mil. lb	(NA)	(NA)	(NA)	(NA)	(NA)	(NA)	1,393	1,646	1,588
Ice cream of all kinds	Mil. gal	830	901	824	863	875	866	876	862	879
Ice milk	Mil. gal	293	301	352	345	329	325	359	357	366
Frozen yogurt	Mil. gal	(NA)	(NA)	(NA)	(NA)	(NA)	(NA)	151	152	118

NA Not available. [1] Comprises sales to plants and dealers, and retail sales by farmers direct to consumers. [2] Includes varieties not shown separately. [3] Includes partially creamed (low fat). [4] Includes dry skim milk for animal feed. [5] Includes animal but excludes modified whey production.

Source: U.S. Dept. of Agriculture, National Agricultural Statistics Service, *Dairy Products*, annual; and *Milk: Production, Disposition, and Income*, annual.

No. 1128. Broiler, Turkey, and Egg Production: 1980 to 1996

[For year ending November 30]

ITEM	Unit	1980	1985	1988	1989	1990	1991	1992	1993	1994	1995	1996
Broilers:[1]												
Number	Million	3,963	4,470	5,238	5,517	5,864	6,137	6,402	6,694	7,018	7,326	7,598
Weight	Bil. lb.	15.5	18.9	22.5	24.0	25.6	27.2	28.8	30.6	32.5	34.2	36.5
Price per lb	Cents	27.7	30.1	33.1	36.6	32.6	30.8	31.8	34.0	35.0	34.4	38.1
Production value	Mil. dol.	4,303	5,668	7,435	8,778	8,366	8,383	9,174	10,417	11,372	11,762	13,906
Turkeys:												
Number	Million	165	185	242	261	282	285	289	288	287	293	301
Weight	Bil. lb.	3.1	3.7	5.1	5.5	6.0	6.1	6.3	6.4	6.5	6.8	7.2
Price per lb	Cents	41.3	49.1	38.6	40.9	39.4	38.0	37.7	39.0	40.4	41.0	43.3
Production value	Mil. dol.	1,272	1,820	1,951	2,235	2,393	2,353	2,396	2,509	2,644	2,776	3,102
Eggs:												
Number	Billion	69.7	68.4	69.7	67.2	67.9	69.0	70.5	71.9	73.9	74.6	76.4
Price per dozen	Cents	56.3	57.2	52.8	68.9	70.9	67.8	57.6	63.4	61.4	62.4	75.0
Production value	Mil. dol.	3,268	3,262	3,073	3,877	4,021	3,915	3,397	3,800	3,780	3,880	4,757

[1] Young chickens of the heavy breeds and other meat-type birds, to be marketed at 2-5 lbs. live weight and from which no pullets are kept for egg production.

Source: U.S. Dept. of Agriculture, National Agricultural Statistics Service, *Poultry—Production and Value*, annual; *Turkeys*, annual; and *Layers and Egg Production*, annual.

No. 1129. Egg Supply and Use: 1980 to 1996

[In million dozen]

ITEM	1980	1985	1989	1990	1991	1992	1993	1994	1995	1996
Supply, total [1]	5,830	5,734	5,661	5,707	5,815	5,922	6,024	6,192	6,235	6,375
Production	5,806	5,710	5,621	5,687	5,801	5,905	6,006	6,178	6,216	6,358
Imports	5	13	25	9	2	4	5	4	4	5
Use, total	5,811	5,723	5,651	5,695	5,802	5,909	6,013	6,177	6,223	6,366
Consumption [2]	5,169	5,104	4,917	4,916	4,939	5,020	5,085	5,184	5,167	5,249
Hatching use	499	548	642	679	709	732	770	805	847	865
Exports	143	71	92	101	155	157	159	188	209	253

[1] Includes beginning stocks, not shown separately. [2] Includes shipments to territories.

Source: U.S. Dept. of Agriculture, Economic Research Service, *Agricultural Outlook*, monthly.

No. 1130. Broiler and Turkey Production, by State: 1994 to 1996

[In millions of pounds, liveweight production]

STATE	BROILERS			TURKEYS			STATE	BROILERS			TURKEYS		
	1994	1995	1996	1994	1995	1996		1994	1995	1996	1994	1995	1996
U.S. [1]	**32,529**	**34,222**	**36,486**	**6,541**	**6,779**	**7,172**	MS	2,712	2,962	3,109	(NA)	(NA)	(NA)
AL	4,184	4,230	4,192	(NA)	(NA)	(NA)	MO	658	801	1,059	478	551	579
AR	4,854	4,963	5,660	510	536	526	NC	3,218	3,418	3,542	1,362	1,420	1,458
CA	1,131	1,179	1,171	449	462	493	OH	166	215	243	176	192	227
DE	1,369	1,394	1,417	(NA)	(NA)	(NA)	OK	799	853	877	(NA)	(NA)	(NA)
FL	571	615	591	(NA)	(NA)	(NA)	PA	597	607	654	202	230	246
GA	4,724	5,136	5,655	42	44	17	SC	589	680	786	173	185	256
IN	(NA)	(NA)	(NA)	336	335	351	TN	549	572	603	(NA)	(NA)	(NA)
IA	83	72	77	250	227	222	TX	1,670	1,747	1,886	(NA)	(NA)	(NA)
KY	237	258	331	(NA)	(NA)	(NA)	VA	1,188	1,197	1,244	409	442	475
MD	1,311	1,360	1,386	3	5	7	WA	200	198	196	(NA)	(NA)	(NA)
MN	249	250	252	847	855	948	WV	384	391	395	89	90	86

NA Not available. [1] Includes other States not shown separately.

Source: U.S. Dept. of Agriculture, National Agricultural Statistics Service, *Poultry—Production and Value*, annual; and *Turkeys*, annual.

Natural Resources

In Brief

The Real Gross Domestic Product for this sector reached $294 billion in 1994, or about 4.4% of the U.S. economy.

Production of paper and paperboard products reached a record 91.4 million tons in 1995.

Domestic catch of fishery products decreased in 1995 for the second year in a row to 9.9 million pounds, from the record catch of 10.5 million of 1993.

U.S. crude oil production continued a five-year decline in 1996 as 2.36 billion barrels were extracted compared to 2.70 billion in 1991. Crude oil imports again exceeded production in 1996 with 2.7 billion barrels coming ashore.

ection presents data on the area, ship, production, trade, reserves, sposition of natural resources. Nat- sources is defined here as includ- estry, fisheries, and mining and al products.

try—Presents data on the area, ship, and timber resource of com- al timberland; forestry statistics cov- the National Forests and Forest e cooperative programs; product or lumber, pulpwood, woodpulp, and paperboard, and similar data.

rincipal sources of data relating to s and forest products are *An Analysis Timber Situation in the United ; 1989-2040, 1990*; *Forest Re- s of the United States, 1992*; *U.S. r Production, Trade, Consumption, rice Statistics*; *Land Areas of the Na- Forest System*, issued annually by rest Service of the Department of lture; Agricultural Statistics issued by partment of Agriculture; and reports census of manufactures (taken ev- years) and the annual Current Indus- eports, issued by the Bureau of the s. Additional information is published monthly *Survey of Current Business* Bureau of Economic Analysis; and nual *Wood Pulp and Fiber Statistics he Statistics of Paper, Paperboard, Vood Pulp* of the American Forest aper Association, Washington, DC.

ompleteness and reliability of sta- on forests and forest products vary derably. The data for forest land and stand volumes are much more le for areas which have been re- surveyed than for those for which estimates are available. In general, data are available for lumber and manufactured products such as le board and softwood panels, etc., or the primary forest products such les and piling and fuelwood.

ries—The principal source of elating to fisheries is *Fisheries of nited States*, issued annually by the nal Marine Fisheries Service (NMFS), National Oceanic and Atmospheric Administration (NOAA).

The NMFS collects and disseminates data on commercial landings of fish and shellfish. Annual reports include quantity and value of commercial landings of fish and shellfish disposition of landings, and number and kinds of fishing vessels and fishing gear. Reports for the fish-processing industry include annual output for the wholesaling and fish processing establishments, annual and seasonal employment. The Magnuson Fishery Conservation and Management Act of 1976 (Magnuson Act), Public Law 94-265 as amended, provides for the conservation and management of all fishery resources within the U.S. Exclusive Economic Zone (EEZ), and gives the Federal Government exclusive authority over domestic and foreign fisheries within 200 nautical miles of U.S. shores and over certain living marine resources beyond the EEZ. Within the EEZ, the total allowable level of foreign fishing, if any, is that portion of the "optimum yield" not harvested by U.S. vessels. Adjustments in the "optimum yield" level may occur periodically.

For details, see Fisheries of the United States, 1995.

Mining and mineral products—Presents data relating to mineral industries and their products, general summary measures of production and employment, and more detailed data on production, prices, imports and exports, consumption, and distribution for specific industries and products. Data on mining and mineral products may also be found in sections 26 and 30 of this *Abstract*; data on mining employment may be found in section 13.

Mining comprises the extraction of minerals occurring naturally (coal, ores, crude petroleum, natural gas) and quarrying, well operation, milling, refining and processing and other preparation customarily done at the mine or well site or as a part of extraction activity. (Mineral preparation plants are usually operated together with mines or quarries.) Exploration for minerals is included as is the development of mineral properties.

The principal governmental sources of these data are the *Minerals Yearbook*, published by the U.S. Geological Survey, Department of the Interior, and various monthly and annual publications of the Energy Information Administration, Department of Energy. See text, section 19, for list of Department of Energy publications. In addition, the Bureau of the Census conducts a census of mineral industries every 5 years. Nongovernment sources include the *Annual Statistical Report* of the American Iron and Steel Institute, Washington, DC; *Metals Week* and the monthly *Engineering and Mining Journal*, issued by the McGraw-Hill Publishing Co., New York, NY; *The Iron Age*, issued weekly by the Chilton Co., Philadelphia, PA; and the *Joint Association Survey* of the U.S. Oil and Gas Industry, conducted jointly by the American Petroleum Institute, Independent Petroleum Association of America, and Mid-Continent Oil and Gas Association.

Mineral statistics, with principal emphasis on commodity detail, have been collected by the U.S. Geological Survey since 1880. Current data in U.S. Geological Survey publications include quantity and value of nonfuel minerals produced, sold or used by producers, or shipped; quantity of minerals stocked; crude materials treated and prepared minerals recovered; and consumption of mineral raw materials.

Censuses of mineral industries have been conducted by the Bureau of the Census at various intervals since 1840. Beginning with the 1967 census, legislation provides for a census to be conducted every 5 years for years ending in "2" and "7." The censuses provide, for the various types of mineral establishments, information on operating costs, capital expenditures, labor, equipment, and energy requirements in relation to their value of shipments and other receipts. Commodity statistics on many manufactured mineral products are also collected by the Bureau at monthly, quarterly, or annual intervals and issued in its *Current Industrial Reports* series.

In general, figures shown in the individual commodity tables include data for outlying areas and may therefore not agree with summary tables. Except for crude petroleum and refined products, the export and import figures include foreign trade passing through the customs districts of United States and Puerto Rico, but exclude shipments between U.S. territories and the customs districts.

No. 1131. Gross Domestic Product of Agriculture, Forestry, Fishing, Mining, and Timber-Related Industries in Current and Real (1992) Dollars, by Industry: 1990 to 1994

[In billions of dollars, except as indicated. 1990-94 are based on the 1987 Standard Industrial Classification (SIC). Data include nonfactor charges (capital consumption allowances, indirect business taxes, etc.) as well as factor charges against gross product; corporate profits and capital consumption allowances have been shifted from a company to an establishment basis]

INDUSTRY	CURRENT DOLLARS				CHAINED (1992) DOLLARS			
	1990	1992	1993	1994	1990	1992	1993	1994
All industries, total [1]	5,743.8	6,244.4	6,550.2	6,931.4	6,138.7	6,244.4	6,383.8	6,604.2
Industries covered	298.1	282.5	277.2	297.9	279.5	282.5	272.6	293.8
Percent of all industries	5.2	4.5	4.2	4.3	4.6	4.5	4.3	4.4
Agriculture, forestry, and fishing	108.7	112.4	105.3	117.8	101.5	112.4	103.3	115.7
Farms	79.6	80.5	72.0	82.2	72.8	80.5	70.9	83.9
Agricultural services	29.1	31.9	33.3	35.7	28.6	31.9	32.3	32.1
Mining [1]	112.3	92.2	89.0	90.1	96.9	92.2	90.7	96.7
Metal mining	4.8	5.5	4.9	5.0	3.7	5.5	5.2	4.5
Coal mining	13.2	13.6	12.5	13.8	12.0	13.6	13.9	16.2
Oil and gas extraction	86.4	65.0	63.6	62.8	73.5	65.0	63.3	67.7
Nonmetallic minerals, except fuels	7.8	8.2	8.1	8.5	7.7	8.2	8.3	8.6
Timber-related manufacturing	77.1	77.8	82.9	90.0	81.1	77.8	78.6	81.2
Lumber and wood products	31.8	32.0	35.3	41.0	37.0	32.0	28.7	31.5
Paper and allied products	45.3	45.8	47.6	49.0	44.1	45.8	49.9	49.7

[1] For additional industries, see table 693.

Source: U.S. Bureau of Economic Analysis, *Survey of Current Business*, August 1996.

No. 1132. National Forest System—Summary: 1980 to 1994

[For fiscal years ending in year shown; see text, section 9. Includes Puerto Rico, except as noted]

ITEM	Unit	1980	1985	1988	1989	1990	1991	1992	1993	1994
Timber cut, total value	Mil. dol.	737	725	1,243	1,313	1,191	1,012	938	918	797
Commercial and cost sales: [1]										
Volume	Mil. bd. ft.	9,178	10,941	12,649	11,951	10,500	8,475	7,290	5,917	4,815
Value	Mil. dol.	730	721	1,240	1,310	1,188	1,009	935	915	783
Free use:										
Volume	Mil. bd. ft.	2,070	399	223	214	151	121	80	80	80
Value [2]	Mil. dol.	5.7	2.2	1.2	1.2	1.0	1.0	0.8	0.8	0.8
Misc. forest products:										
Value	Mil. dol.	1.1	1.7	2.0	2.2	2.6	2.7	2.7	2.8	3.1
Livestock grazing: [3]										
Cattle and horses [4]	1,000	1,521	1,565	1,313	1,526	1,236	1,265	1,408	1,318	1,229
Sheep and goats	1,000	1,328	1,183	1,067	972	958	1,029	1,183	1,111	941
Roads and trails:										
Road construction [5]	Miles	925	1,903	1,352	866	857	910	853	816	520
Trail construction [5,6]	Miles	2,419	967	1,834	1,944	1,635	1,921	1,976	1,976	2,113
Receipts, total	Mil. dol.	703	636	980	1,051	971	772	614	504	516
Timber use	Mil. dol.	625	515	888	910	849	667	520	425	431
Grazing use	Mil. dol.	16	9	9	11	10	11	11	11	11
Special land use, etc	Mil. dol.	62	112	83	130	112	93	84	88	72
Payments to local govt. [7]	Mil. dol.	240	229	325	368	368	335	322	323	320
Allotments to Forest Service [8]	Mil. dol.	73	60	104	111	106	88	(NA)	(NA)	(NA)

NA Not available. [1] Includes land exchanges. [2] Includes some free use timber not reducible to board feet. [3] Covers number actually grazed. Excludes Puerto Rico. [4] Excludes animals under 6 months of age. Includes burros. [5] Includes reconstruction. [6] Includes work accomplished by Human Resource Programs and volunteers. [7] Payments made in following year. [8] For use in following year.

Source: U.S. Forest Service, *Timber Demand and Technolgy Assessment*, RWU-4861. Also in *Agricultural Statistics*, annual.

No. 1133. National Forest System Land—States and Other Areas: 1992

[In thousands of acres. As of Sept. 30]

STATE	GROSS AREA WITHIN UNIT BOUNDARIES [1]	NATIONAL FOREST SYSTEM LAND [2]	OTHER LANDS WITHIN UNIT BOUNDARIES
United States	**231,502**	**191,453**	**40,049**
Alabama	1,288	659	629
Alaska	24,345	22,193	2,152
Arizona	11,887	11,247	641
Arkansas	3,490	2,529	961
California	24,401	20,616	3,785
Colorado	16,037	14,467	1,570
Connecticut	(Z)	(Z)	-
Delaware	-	-	-
Florida	1,254	1,135	119
Georgia	1,846	860	986
Hawaii	(Z)	(Z)	-
Idaho	21,674	20,441	1,233
Illinois	840	268	572
Indiana	644	189	455
Iowa	-	-	-
Kansas	116	108	8
Kentucky	2,102	673	1,428
Louisiana	1,022	601	421
Maine	93	53	40
Maryland	-	-	-
Massachusetts	-	-	-
Michigan	4,895	2,849	2,046
Minnesota	5,467	2,815	2,652
Mississippi	2,310	1,153	1,157
Missouri	3,082	1,478	1,603
Montana	19,102	16,806	2,296
Nebraska	442	352	90
Nevada	6,275	5,801	474
New Hampshire	825	721	104
New Jersey	-	-	-
New Mexico	10,367	9,321	1,045
New York	13	13	-
North Carolina	3,165	1,234	1,932
North Dakota	1,106	1,106	(Z)
Ohio	833	212	622
Oklahoma	465	301	164
Oregon	17,504	15,655	1,849
Pennsylvania	744	513	231
Rhode Island	-	-	-
South Carolina	1,376	609	767
South Dakota	2,352	2,013	339
Tennessee	1,212	628	585
Texas	1,994	755	1,240
Utah	9,186	8,099	1,087
Vermont	816	345	471
Virginia	3,223	1,648	1,575
Washington	10,061	9,160	901
West Virginia	1,863	1,025	838
Wisconsin	2,023	1,518	505
Wyoming	9,704	9,255	449
Puerto Rico	56	28	28
Virgin Islands	(Z)	(Z)	-

- Represents zero. Z Less than half the unit of measure. [1] Comprises all publicly and privately owned land within authorized boundaries of national forests, purchase units, national grasslands, Land utilization projects, research and experimental areas, and other areas. [2] Federally owned land within the "gross area within unit boundaries."

Source: U.S. Forest Service, *Land Areas of the National Forest System*, annual.

No. 1134. Forest and Timberland Area, Sawtimber and Stock: 1970 to 1992

[As of Jan. 1]

YEAR AND REGION	Total forest land (mil. acres)	TIMBERLAND, OWNERSHIP [1]				SAWTIMBER, NET VOLUME [3]		GROWING STOCK, NET VOLUME [4]	
		All ownerships (mil. acres)	Federally owned or managed [2] (mil. acres)	State, county, and municipal (mil. acres)	Private (mil. acres)	Total (bil. cu. ft.)	Softwood (bil. cu. ft.)	Total (bil. cu. ft.)	Softwood (bil. cu. ft.)
United States, 1970	**754**	**504**	**116**	**29**	**360**	**2,587**	**2,035**	**694**	**458**
North	(NA)	154	11	18	126	295	81	146	39
South	(NA)	203	15	3	185	569	302	191	87
Rocky Mountains	(NA)	65	42	2	20	398	384	101	95
Pacific Coast	(NA)	82	47	5	29	1,325	1,268	257	238
United States, 1987	**731**	**485**	**97**	**34**	**354**	**2,853**	**2,040**	**766**	**453**
North	165	154	11	19	124	459	126	190	48
South	203	197	16	4	177	781	388	245	106
Rocky Mountains	142	61	39	3	20	411	394	108	100
Pacific Coast	220	72	31	8	32	1,202	1,132	223	199
United States, 1992	**737**	**490**	**97**	**35**	**358**	**2,992**	**2,047**	**786**	**450**
North	168	158	11	19	127	540	137	207	51
South	212	199	16	4	179	842	389	251	103
Rocky Mountains	140	63	40	3	20	415	397	110	101
Pacific Coast	217	70	30	8	32	1,196	1,124	218	195

NA Not available. [1] Timberland is forest land that is producing or is capable of crops of industrial wood and not withdrawn from timber utilization by statute or administrative regulation. Areas qualifying as timberland have the capability of producing in excess of 20 cubic feet per acre per year of industrial wood in natural stands. Currently inaccessible and inoperable areas are included. [2] Includes Indian lands. [3] Sawtimber is timber suitable for sawing into lumber. Live trees of commercial species containing at least one 12-foot sawlog or two noncontiguous 8-foot logs, and meeting regional specifications for freedom from defect. Softwood trees must be at least 9.0-inches diameter, and hardwood trees must be at least 11.0-inches diameter at 4 1/2 feet above ground. International 1/4-inch rule. [4] Live trees of commercial species meeting specified standards of quality or vigor. Cull trees are excluded. Includes only trees 5.0-inches diameter or larger at 4 1/2 feet above ground.

Source: U.S. Forest Service, *Forest Resources of the United States, 1992*.

No. 1135. Timber-Based Industries—Summary of Manufactures: 1992 and 1995

[Data based on *1987 Standard Industrial Classification Manual*, published by the Office of Management and Budget, see text, section 26. N.e.c. = Not elsewhere classified]

INDUSTRY	SIC [1] code	1992			1995		
		All employees		Value of shipments (bil. dol.)	All employees		Value of shipments (bil. dol.)
		Number (1,000)	Payroll (mil. dol.)		Number (1,000)	Payroll (mil. dol.)	
Logging and sawmills	241/242	221.7	4,739	31.3	266.6	6,008	45.6
Logging	2411	83.6	1,693	13.8	86.8	1,891	16.6
Sawmills/planing mills, general	2421	138.1	3,046	21.1	142.7	3,432	25.8
Hardwood dimension and flooring mills	2426	28.5	502	2.0	35.3	654	1.5
Special product sawmills, n.e.c.	2429	1.8	31	0.1	1.7	31	0.1
Millwork and veneer [2]	243	224.8	5,029	24.8	255.5	5,957	31.3
Millwork	2431	86.3	1,984	9.6	93.9	2,220	11.1
Wood kitchen cabinets	2434	62.8	1,308	4.9	72.9	1,572	6.4
Hardwood veneer and plywood	2435	20.1	395	2.2	22.1	459	2.6
Softwood veneer and plywood	2436	31.3	827	5.4	32.3	934	6.9
Structural wood members, n.e.c.	2439	24.3	515	2.5	34.3	773	4.2
Wood containers	244	39.9	640	2.9	49.6	846	4.0
Wood buildings, mobile homes	245	56.1	1,227	6.6	75.2	1,799	10.7
Miscellaneous wood products	249	84.6	1,737	10.4	94.3	2,013	13.3
Pulp mills	261	15.9	689	5.5	13.4	631	6.9
Paper mills	262	130.6	5,421	32.8	118.7	5,548	45.1
Paperboard mills	263	51.5	2,136	16.1	56.9	2,563	24.5
Paperboard containers and boxes	265	198.8	5,706	32.6	206.5	6,437	41.7
Setup paperboard boxes	2652	6.6	129	0.4	(S)	(S)	(S)
Corrugated and solid fiber boxes	2653	111.7	3,264	19.8	124.2	3,863	27.5
Fiber cans, tubes, drums, and similar products	2655	12.4	337	1.9	11.9	349	2.1
Sanitary food containers, except folding	2656	15.4	386	2.5	14.0	377	2.6
Folding paperboard boxes, including sanitary	2657	52.7	1,590	7.9	53.5	1,716	8.8
Converted paper and paperboard products [3]	267	229.1	6,525	46.1	232.0	7,058	54.4

S Figure does not meet publication standards. [1] Standard Industrial Classification code; see text, section 13. [2] Includes plywood and structural members. [3] Except containers and boxes.

Source: U.S. Bureau of the Census, *Census of Manufactures, 1992 Final Industry Series, and Annual Survey of Manufactures.*

No. 1136. Timber Products—Production, Foreign Trade, and Consumption, by Type of Product: 1980 to 1994

[In millions of cubic feet, roundwood equivalent]

ITEM	Unit	1980	1985	1990	1991	1992	1993	1994, prel.
Industrial roundwood:								
Domestic production	Mil. cu. ft.	12,123	13,411	15,413	14,780	14,994	14,632	14,904
Imports	Mil. cu. ft.	2,570	3,430	3,000	2,873	3,104	3,464	3,649
Exports	Mil. cu. ft.	1,857	1,533	2,426	2,398	2,469	2,280	2,266
Consumption	Mil. cu. ft.	12,835	15,307	15,986	15,153	15,628	15,816	16,287
Lumber:								
Domestic production	Mil. cu. ft.	5,305	6,210	7,213	6,677	6,864	6,660	6,880
Imports	Mil. cu. ft.	1,545	2,251	1,786	1,726	1,970	2,246	2,420
Exports	Mil. cu. ft.	395	295	570	565	540	504	482
Consumption	Mil. cu. ft.	6,455	8,166	8,429	7,838	8,294	8,402	8,818
Plywood and veneer:								
Domestic production	Mil. cu. ft.	1,175	1,426	1,368	1,226	1,265	1,257	1,268
Imports	Mil. cu. ft.	120	196	96	83	100	101	95
Exports	Mil. cu. ft.	45	25	110	95	107	101	88
Consumption	Mil. cu. ft.	1,250	1,596	1,354	1,214	1,258	1,257	1,275
Pulp products:								
Domestic production	Mil. cu. ft.	4,390	4,561	5,353	5,434	5,463	5,391	5,417
Imports	Mil. cu. ft.	880	968	1,114	1,062	1,027	1,102	1,116
Exports	Mil. cu. ft.	579	454	784	806	946	889	913
Consumption	Mil. cu. ft.	4,691	5,075	5,683	5,588	5,544	5,604	5,620
Logs:								
Imports	Mil. cu. ft.	25	16	4	2	7	15	18
Pulpwood chips, exports	Mil. cu. ft.	278	144	288	331	351	326	354
Fuelwood consumption	Mil. cu. ft.	3,105	3,450	3,019	3,028	3,044	3,084	3,134

Source: U.S. Forest Service, *Timber Demand and Technolgy Assessment*, RWU-4861. Also in *Agricultural Statistics*, annual.

No. 1137. Selected Timber Products—Imports and Exports: 1980 to 1994

ITEM	Unit	1980	1985	1988	1989	1990	1991	1992	1993	1994, prel.
IMPORTS [1]										
Lumber, total [2]	Mil. bd. ft.	9,866	14,996	14,226	15,277	12,159	11,756	13,474	15,625	16,786
From Canada	Percent	97.5	97.6	97.5	91.3	96.5	96.3	96.3	97.6	96.1
Logs, total	Mil. bd. ft. [3]	128	99	68	42	28	15	46	94	110
From Canada	Percent	97.4	81.8	91.9	61.5	67.5	74.5	88.9	77.7	69.2
Paper and board [4]	1,000 tons	8,780	11,522	13,110	13,100	13,148	12,167	12,543	13,971	9,321
Woodpulp	1,000 tons	4,051	4,466	4,938	5,105	4,893	4,997	5,029	5,413	5,650
Plywood	Mil. sq. ft. [5]	1,235	1,817	1,696	1,955	1,687	1,457	1,776	1,796	1,692
EXPORTS										
Lumber, total [2]	Mil. bd. ft.	2,494	1,945	4,527	4,243	3,802	3,997	3,603	3,385	3,334
To: Canada	Percent	25.3	23.7	17.6	15.6	18.1	15.1	17.3	17.4	18.9
Japan	Percent	26.0	32.1	34.5	38.1	33.5	30.5	30.9	36.3	44.2
Europe	Percent	23.8	15.1	20.5	16.6	19.1	19.6	21.2	15.9	16.2
Logs, total	Mil. bd. ft. [3]	3,261	3,843	4,796	4,745	4,262	3,816	3,316	2,877	2,684
To: Canada	Percent	9.7	11.6	7.9	5.8	9.3	11.2	12.6	13.6	36.7
Japan	Percent	78.0	49.4	50.3	63.5	62.5	56.7	62.1	65.4	49.7
China: Mainland	Percent	2.7	27.8	23.4	9.6	8.5	9.7	7.1	4.6	5.3
Paper and board [4]	1,000 tons	5,214	4,071	5,691	6,300	6,796	8,331	8,971	9,126	4,302
Woodpulp	1,000 tons	3,806	3,796	5,528	6,231	5,906	6,337	7,222	6,499	6,728
Plywood	Mil. sq. ft. [5]	413	358	1,093	1,562	1,767	1,552	1,759	1,646	1,455

[1] Customs value of imports; see text, section 28. [2] Includes railroad ties. [3] Log scale. [4] Includes paper and board products. Excludes hardboard. [5] 3/8 inch basis.

Source: U.S. Forest Service, *Timber Demand and Technolgy Assessment*, RWU-4861. Also in *Agricultural Statistics*, annual.

No. 1138. Lumber Consumption, by Species Group and End Use: 1970 to 1994

[In million board feet, except per capita in board feet. Per capita consumption based on estimated resident population as of July 1]

ITEM	1970	1976	1986	1991	1994	END-USE	1970	1976	1986	1991
Total	39.9	44.7	57.0	54.8	60.4	New housing	13.3	17.0	19.3	15.0
Per capita	194	205	237	217	232	Residential upkeep and improvements	4.7	5.7	10.1	11.6
Species group:						New nonresidential construction [1]	4.7	4.5	5.3	5.4
Softwoods	32.0	36.6	48.0	44.0	48.2	Manufacturing	4.7	4.9	4.8	5.6
Hardwoods	7.9	8.0	9.0	10.8	12.2	Shipping	5.7	5.9	6.8	8.2
						Other [2]	6.8	6.7	10.9	8.8

[1] In addition to new construction, includes railroad ties laid as replacements in existing track and lumber used by railroads for railcar repair. [2] Includes upkeep and improvement of nonresidential buildings and structures; made-at-home projects, such as furniture, boats, and picnic tables; made-on-the-job items such as advertising and display structures; and miscellaneous products and uses.

Source: U.S. Forest Service, *Timber Demand and Technolgy Assessment*, RWU-4861. Also in *Agricultural Statistics*, annual.

No. 1139. Selected Timber Products—Producer Price Indexes: 1990 to 1996

[1982=100]

PRODUCT	1990	1991	1992	1993	1994	1995	1996
Lumber and wood products	129.7	132.1	146.6	174.0	180.0	178.1	176.1
Lumber	124.6	124.9	144.7	183.4	188.4	173.4	179.9
Softwood lumber	123.8	125.7	148.6	193.0	196.1	178.5	189.7
Hardwood lumber	131.0	128.5	140.7	163.3	168.3	167.0	164.0
Millwork	130.4	135.5	143.3	156.6	162.4	163.8	166.6
General millwork	132.0	138.1	146.3	158.5	163.6	165.4	167.9
Prefabricated structural members	122.3	122.4	132.7	159.7	169.3	163.5	167.5
Plywood	114.2	114.3	133.3	152.8	158.6	165.3	156.6
Softwood plywood	119.6	120.8	147.2	169.7	176.8	188.1	(NA)
Hardwood plywood and related products	102.7	102.8	106.9	115.4	122.3	122.2	125.0
Other wood products	114.7	118.6	124.5	135.3	137.7	143.7	127.3
Boxes	119.1	123.6	127.5	138.2	141.3	145.0	147.1
Pulp, paper, and allied products	141.2	142.9	145.2	147.3	152.5	172.2	166.6
Pulp, paper, and prod, ex bldg paper	132.9	129.8	129.2	127.6	133.1	163.4	149.7
Woodpulp	151.3	119.2	118.9	104.2	115.9	183.2	133.2
Wastepaper	138.9	121.4	117.5	117.4	209.5	371.1	141.7
Paper	128.8	126.9	123.2	123.8	126.0	159.0	149.2
Writing and printing papers	129.1	124.8	120.2	120.5	121.7	158.4	(NA)
Newsprint	119.6	120.9	109.8	112.1	116.7	161.8	(NA)
Paperboard	135.7	130.2	134.3	130.0	140.5	183.1	155.6
Converted paper and paperboard products	135.2	134.8	134.8	133.7	136.7	157.0	153.4
Office supplies and accessories	121.4	119.5	116.4	115.3	116.9	134.9	(NA)
Building paper & building board mill prods	112.2	111.8	119.6	132.7	144.1	144.9	137.2

NA Not available.

Source: U.S. Bureau of Labor Statistics, *Producer Price Indexes*, monthly.

No. 1140. Selected Species—Stumpage Prices in Current and Constant (1982) Dollars: 1990 to 1994

[In dollars per 1,000 board feet. Stumpage prices are based on sales of sawtimber from National Forests]

SPECIES	CURRENT DOLLARS					CONSTANT (1982) DOLLARS[1]				
	1990	1991	1992	1993	1994	1990	1991	1992	1993	1994
Softwoods:										
Douglas fir [2]	466	395	477	318	352	401	339	407	270	542
Southern pine [3]	127	166	198	217	253	109	143	169	184	218
Sugar pine [4]	285	241	492	598	617	245	207	419	508	512
Ponderosa pine [4 5]	252	238	292	535	318	217	204	249	455	264
Western hemlock [6]	203	164	165	364	336	175	141	140	309	278
Hardwoods:										
All eastern hardwoods [7]	146	160	167	264	192	126	137	142	224	128
Oak, white, red, and black [7]	188	164	211	195	278	162	140	180	166	231
Maple, sugar [8]	135	121	145	220	313	116	104	123	187	260

[1] Deflated by the producer price index, all commodities. [2] Western Washington and western Oregon. [3] Southern region. [4] Pacific Southwest region (formerly California region). [5] Includes Jeffrey pine. [6] Pacific Northwest region. [7] Eastern and Southern regions. [8] Eastern region.

Source: U.S. Forest Service, *Timber Demand and Technolgy Assessment*, RWU-4861. Also in *Agricultural Statistics*, annual.

No. 1141. Paper and Paperboard—Production and New Supply: 1980 to 1995

[In thousands of short tons]

ITEM	1980	1985	1988	1989	1990	1991	1992	1993	1994	1995
Total Production	63,600	68,683	78,299	78,573	80,445	81,234	84,701	86,693	90,897	91,339
Total paper	30,116	34,061	36,353	36,266	39,361	39,084	40,973	41,745	43,356	42,881
Total paperboard	30,926	32,922	38,234	38,519	39,318	40,343	41,895	43,113	45,724	46,640
Unbleached kraft	15,295	16,368	19,140	19,490	20,357	20,960	21,658	21,447	22,469	22,698
Semichemical	4,724	5,068	5,664	5,656	5,640	5,552	5,762	5,672	5,943	5,662
Bleached kraft	3,836	3,911	4,511	4,521	4,399	4,572	4,503	4,583	5,029	5,304
Recycled	7,071	7,555	8,919	8,852	8,921	9,259	9,973	11,410	12,283	12,977
Wet machine board E	138	130	100	99	96	96	93	95	96	96
Building paper E	1,369	680	732	706	723	782	795	797	787	787
Insulating board E	1,051	890	880	962	946	929	945	943	934	934
New supply, all grades, excl. products	67,783	76,199	86,427	86,123	87,683	86,014	89,631	93,146	97,447	98,142
Total paper	37,126	43,557	49,065	48,376	49,485	47,380	49,232	51,247	53,076	52,747
Newsprint	11,377	12,758	13,555	13,209	13,412	12,462	12,658	12,750	12,889	12,753
Printing/writing papers	16,124	20,658	25,006	24,449	25,456	24,651	26,013	27,846	29,442	29,551
Packaging and ind. conv. papers	5,243	5,163	5,030	4,982	4,718	4,596	4,783	4,628	4,640	4,227
Tissue	4,382	4,978	5,494	5,737	5,899	5,672	5,778	6,022	6,105	6,215
Paperboard, total	27,689	30,595	35,438	35,806	36,301	36,753	38,453	39,950	42,436	43,448
Construction and other	2,968	2,048	1,903	1,941	1,897	1,881	1,946	1,949	1,935	1,947

Source: American Forest and Paper Association, Washington, DC, *Monthly Statistical Summary of Paper, Paperboard and Woodpulp*.

No. 1142. Newsprint—Production, Stocks, Consumption, and Price Index: 1980 to 1995

[In thousands of metric tons, except price index]

COUNTRY AND ITEM	1980	1985	1989	1990	1991	1992	1993	1994	1995
Canada: Production	8,625	8,890	9,640	9,068	8,855	8,753	9,130	9,321	9,250
Shipments from mills	8,622	8,899	9,606	9,074	8,728	9,143	(NA)	(NA)	(NA)
Stocks at mills, end of year	165	288	321	315	564	351	(NA)	(NA)	(NA)
United States:									
Consumption, estimate	10,088	11,507	12,241	12,125	11,381	11,634	(NA)	(NA)	(NA)
Production	4,239	4,924	5,523	5,997	6,206	6,424	6,412	6,336	6,352
Shipments from mills	4,234	4,927	5,515	6,007	6,152	6,464	(NA)	(NA)	(NA)
Stocks, end of year: At mills	21	57	56	46	98	59	(NA)	(NA)	(NA)
At and in transit to publishers	732	910	749	801	932	938	(NA)	(NA)	(NA)
Producer price index (1982=100)	[1]88.5	105.3	122.5	119.6	120.9	109.8	112.1	116.7	161.8

NA Not available. [1] Average for 11 months.

Source: 1980-1993, U.S. Bureau of Economic Analysis, *Survey of Current Business*, monthly; beginning 1994, American Forest and Paper Association, Washington, DC, and Canadian Pulp & Paper Association.

No. 1143. Fishery Products—Domestic Catch, Imports, and Disposition: 1980 to 1995

[Live weight, in millions of pounds, except percent. For data on commercial catch for selected countries, see table 1375, section 30]

ITEM	1980	1985	1987	1988	1989	1990	1991	1992	1993	1994	1995
Total	11,357	15,150	15,744	14,628	15,486	16,349	16,364	16,106	20,334	19,309	16,600
For human food	8,006	9,337	10,561	10,505	12,268	12,662	13,020	13,242	13,821	13,714	13,700
For industrial use	3,351	5,813	5,183	4,123	3,217	3,687	3,344	2,864	6,513	5,595	2,900
Domestic catch	6,482	6,258	6,896	7,192	8,463	9,404	9,484	9,637	10,467	10,461	9,904
For human food	3,654	3,294	3,946	4,588	6,204	7,041	7,031	7,618	8,214	7,936	7,783
For industrial use	2,828	2,964	2,950	2,604	2,259	2,363	2,453	2,019	2,253	2,525	2,121
Imports [1]	4,875	8,892	8,848	7,436	7,022	6,945	6,879	6,469	9,867	8,848	6,696
For human food	4,352	6,043	6,615	5,917	6,064	5,621	5,989	5,624	5,607	5,778	5,917
For industrial use [2]	523	2,849	2,233	1,519	958	1,324	890	845	4,260	3,070	779
Disposition of domestic catch	6,482	6,258	6,896	7,192	8,463	9,404	9,484	9,637	10,467	10,461	9,904
Fresh and frozen	2,621	2,242	3,157	3,813	5,585	6,501	6,541	7,288	7,744	7,475	7,215
Canned	1,161	1,232	1,009	1,017	798	751	674	543	649	622	769
Cured	96	70	89	86	128	126	119	100	115	95	90
Reduced to meal, oil, etc	2,604	2,714	2,641	2,276	1,952	2,026	2,150	1,696	1,959	2,269	1,830

[1] Excludes imports of edible fishery products consumed in Puerto Rico; includes landings of tuna caught by foreign vessels in American Samoa. [2] Fish meal and sea herring.

No. 1144. Fisheries—Quantity and Value of Domestic Catch: 1980 to 1995

YEAR	QUANTITY (mil. lb. [1]) Total	For human food	For industrial products [2]	Value (mil. dol.)	Average price per lb. (cents)	YEAR	QUANTITY (mil. lb. [1]) Total	For human food	For industrial products [2]	Value (mil. dol.)	Average price per lb. (cents)
1980	6,482	3,654	2,828	2,237	34.5	1988	7,192	4,588	2,604	3,520	48.9
1981	5,977	3,547	2,430	2,388	40.0	1989	8,463	6,204	2,259	3,238	38.3
1982	6,367	3,285	3,082	2,390	37.5	1990	9,404	7,041	2,363	3,522	37.5
1983	6,439	3,238	3,201	2,355	36.6	1991	9,484	7,031	2,453	3,308	34.9
1984	6,438	3,320	3,118	2,350	36.5	1992	9,637	7,618	2,019	3,678	38.2
1985	6,258	3,294	2,964	2,326	37.2	1993	[3]10,467	8,214	2,253	3,471	33.2
1986	6,031	3,393	2,638	2,763	45.8	1994	10,461	7,936	2,525	3,807	36.8
1987	6,896	3,946	2,950	3,115	45.2	1995	9,904	7,783	2,121	3,770	38.2

[1] Live weight. [2] Meal, oil, fish solubles, homogenized condensed fish, shell products, bait, and animal food. [3] Represents record year.

No. 1145. Domestic Fish and Shellfish Catch and Value, by Species: 1990 to 1995

SPECIES	QUANTITY (1,000 lb.) 1990	1993	1994	1995	VALUE ($1,000) 1990	1993	1994	1995
Total	9,403,571	10,466,895	10,461,388	9,904,199	3,521,995	3,471,460	3,806,700	3,770,320
Fish, total [1]	8,091,068	8,999,142	9,132,276	8,636,731	1,900,097	1,884,121	1,984,376	1,950,347
Cod: Atlantic	95,881	50,503	38,653	29,631	61,329	44,956	36,160	28,184
Pacific	526,396	482,799	460,287	591,399	91,384	116,172	95,836	109,680
Flounder	254,519	599,180	426,855	423,443	112,921	135,598	126,580	150,239
Halibut	70,454	63,053	57,900	44,796	96,700	62,391	84,898	66,781
Menhaden	1,962,160	1,983,319	2,323,537	1,846,959	93,896	103,258	128,364	99,131
Pollock, Alaska	3,108,031	3,257,990	3,124,531	2,852,618	268,344	358,378	375,926	259,814
Sablefish	89,802	77,467	71,339	65,904	58,865	83,861	84,827	123,694
Salmon	733,146	888,134	901,088	1,137,410	612,367	423,530	456,407	520,812
Tuna	62,393	55,392	71,795	63,864	105,040	91,430	108,661	102,636
Shellfish, total [1]	1,312,503	1,467,753	1,329,112	1,267,468	1,621,898	1,587,339	1,822,324	1,819,973
Clams	139,198	147,752	131,427	134,224	130,194	138,030	122,362	140,414
Crabs	499,416	604,437	446,942	363,639	483,837	510,494	532,987	511,987
Lobsters: American	61,017	56,513	66,416	66,406	154,677	151,746	196,175	214,838
Oysters	29,193	33,575	38,086	40,380	93,718	86,698	93,737	101,574
Scallops: Calico	(NA)	(NA)	7,162	957	(NA)	(NA)	6,944	1,219
Sea	39,917	18,116	18,228	18,316	153,696	105,603	91,793	92,828
Shrimp	346,494	292,887	2,822,626	306,869	491,433	412,896	564,168	570,034

NA Not available. [1] Includes other types of fish and shellfish, not shown separately.

Source of tables 1143-1145: U.S. National Oceanic and Atmospheric Administration, National Marine Fisheries Service. *Fisheries of the United States*, annual.

No. 1146. U.S. Private Aquaculture—Trout and Catfish Production and Value: 1990 to 1996

[Periods are from Sept. 1 of the previous year to Aug. 31 of stated year. Data for for food-size fish, those over 12 inches long]

ITEM	Unit	1990	1991	1992	1993	1994	1995	1996
TROUT FOOD SIZE								
Number sold	Millions	67.8	67.7	64.5	60.9	58.3	60.2	56.5
Total weight	Mil. lb	56.8	58.9	55.2	54.6	52.1	55.6	53.6
Total value of sales	Mil. dol	64.6	58.3	51.0	54.3	52.7	60.8	56.9
Average price received	Dol./lb	1.14	0.99	0.92	0.99	1.01	1.09	1.06
Percent sold to processors	Percent	58	72	71	63	66	68	67
CATFISH FOOD SIZE								
Number sold	Millions	272.9	332.7	373.2	379.1	347.6	321.8	369.4
Total weight	Mil. lb	392.4	409.5	497.3	495.8	479.4	481.5	517.5
Total value of sales	Mil. dol	305.1	264.0	302.4	352.9	373.6	378.1	396.9
Average price received	Dol./lb	0.78	0.64	0.61	0.71	0.78	0.79	0.77
Fish sold to processors	Mil. lb	360.4	390.9	457.4	459.0	439.3	448.9	472.1
Avg. price paid by processors	Cents/lb.	75.8	63.1	59.8	70.9	78.4	78.6	77.3
Processor sales	Mil. lb	183.1	199.8	231.3	233.5	216.5	227.0	237.2
Avg. price received by processors	Cents/lb.	224.1	209.0	200.5	218.6	238.5	240.3	236.9
Inventory (Jan. 1)	Mil. lb	9.4	9.6	11.6	9.5	11.6	10.9	11.9

Catfish Production and *Catfish Processing*, February releases Annual.

Source: U.S. Dept. of Agriculture, National Agricultural Statistics Service, USDA.

No. 1147. Supply of Selected Fishery Items: 1980 to 1995

[In millions of pounds. Totals available for U.S. consumption are supply minus exports plus imports. Round weight is the complete or full weight as caught]

ITEM	Unit	1980	1985	1988	1989	1990	1991	1992	1993	1994	1995
Tuna, canned	Canned weight	666	759	843	1,028	856	933	922	835	850	875
Shrimp	Heads-off weight	425	633	767	743	734	744	820	808	847	832
Clams	Meat weight	102	164	145	150	152	144	155	156	144	144
Salmon, canned	Canned weight	126	113	59	159	148	131	73	114	117	149
American lobster	Round weight	69	108	121	85	95	107	95	92	101	94
Spiny lobster	Round weight	127	154	139	89	89	85	81	76	76	89
Scallops	Meat weight	51	72	74	79	74	82	69	66	76	82
Sardines, canned	Canned weight	69	76	63	61	61	52	41	41	46	44
Oysters	Meat weight	71	90	78	66	56	47	50	48	50	52
Crab meat, canned	Canned weight	9	8	8	8	9	11	9	9	9	12
Snow crab	Round weight	54	45	30	58	37	60	88	66	40	42
King crab	Round weight	133	11	10	18	19	20	15	8	12	21

Source: U.S. National Oceanic and Atmospheric Administration, National Marine Fisheries Service, *Fisheries of the United States*, annual.

No. 1148. Canned, Fresh, and Frozen Fishery Products: 1980 to 1995

[Fresh fishery products exclude Alaska and Hawaii. Canned fishery products data are for natural pack only]

PRODUCT	PRODUCTION (mil. lb.)						VALUE (mil. dol.)					
	1980	1985	1990	1993	1994	1995	1980	1985	1990	1993	1994	1995
Canned, [1]	1,516	1,161	1,178	1,709	1,768	1,927	1,928	1,360	1,562	1,688	1,796	1,667
Tuna	602	545	581	619	610	667	1,144	821	902	904	963	939
Salmon	200	159	196	198	207	244	376	228	366	307	329	419
Clam products	77	117	110	117	122	129	66	109	76	92	106	111
Mackerel [2]	38	15	23	(NA)	(NA)	(NA)	12	7	11	(NA)	(NA)	(NA)
Sardines, Maine	20	20	13	14	16	14	32	38	17	25	28	24
Shrimp	16	4	1	1	(Z)	(Z)	80	19	3	4	4	7
Crabs	5	1	1	(Z)	(Z)	(Z)	19	2	4	1	(Z)	(Z)
Oysters [3]	(Z)	2	1	(Z)	(Z)	(Z)	(Z)	2	1	(Z)	(Z)	(Z)
Fish fillets and steaks [4]	202	246	441	420	426	385	261	440	843	847	836	841
Cod	31	57	65	50	58	65	43	89	132	121	135	152
Flounder	49	69	54	35	35	35	87	157	154	100	89	86
Haddock	17	8	7	4	3	3	29	19	24	16	12	11
Ocean perch, Atlantic	7	2	1	1	(Z)	(Z)	9	3	1	2	1	1
Rockfish	14	18	33	18	23	25	13	25	53	30	33	38
Pollock, Atlantic	9	15	12	8	7	4	9	17	21	17	16	10
Pollock, Alaska	(NA)	11	164	161	141	135	(NA)	24	174	185	144	184
Other	74	66	105	143	158	118	71	106	284	376	406	359

NA Not available. Z Less than 500,000 pounds or $500,000. [1] Includes other products, not shown separately. [2] Includes Jack and a small amount of Pacific mackerel. [3] Includes oyster specialties. [4] Fresh and frozen.

Source: U.S. National Oceanic and Atmospheric Administration, National Marine Fisheries Service, *Fisheries of the United States*, annual.

No. 1149. Summary of Mineral Operations: 1963 to 1992

[Represents mineral operations only. Beginning 1967, excludes single unit establishments without paid employees]

ITEM	Unit	1963	1967	1972	1977	1982	1987	1992
Establishments	Number	38,651	28,579	25,269	31,359	42,241	33,617	30,787
With 20 or more employees	Number	5,499	5,682	5,312	6,632	(NA)	6,299	5,600
Including all operations in manufactures	Number	40,532	29,688	26,178	31,967	42,585	34,041	31,261
Excluding oil and gas extraction	Number	19,290	13,330	11,680	13,520	12,267	10,707	9,896
Employees, total	1,000	616	567	595	799	1,114	698	638
Production workers [1]	1,000	482	433	443	593	762	451	415
All other	1,000	134	134	152	206	352	247	223
Worker-hours, production workers [1]	Million	973	892	909	1,183	1,578	942	876
Worker-hours per production workers	1,000	2.0	2.1	2.1	2.0	2.1	2.1	2.1
Payroll, total	Mil. dol.	3,743	4,187	6,226	13,167	28,637	21,739	24,199
Wages, production workers [1]	Mil. dol.	2,680	2,888	4,250	9,082	18,030	12,443	13,833
Salaries, all other employees	Mil. dol.	1,063	1,299	1,976	4,085	10,607	9,296	10,366
Cost of supplies, etc. [2]	Mil. dol.	8,974	10,576	14,884	46,079	109,697	62,423	65,653
Value added in mining	Mil. dol.	15,910	19,330	26,471	68,013	188,055	110,959	113,621
Metal mining	Mil. dol.	1,418	1,557	2,382	3,504	3,215	4,610	6,724
Coal mining	Mil. dol.	1,727	2,091	3,754	11,266	18,631	17,068	17,252
Oil and gas extraction	Mil. dol.	11,020	13,394	17,612	48,587	159,937	80,049	80,016
Nonmetallic minerals mining	Mil. dol.	1,745	2,288	2,723	4,656	6,273	9,233	9,629
Value of shipments and receipts [3]	Mil. dol.	16,804	22,784	36,319	96,375	250,000	157,964	162,095
Capital expenditures	Mil. dol.	3,264	4,058	5,036	17,718	47,753	15,418	17,179

NA Not available. [1] Represents employees up through the working foreman level in manual work. Includes development and exploration workers. [2] Includes purchased machinery installed. [3] See footnote 5, table 1152.

Source: U.S. Bureau of the Census, *Census of Mineral Industries, 1972, 1977, 1982, 1987,* and *1992.*

No. 1150. Mining and Primary Metal Production Indexes: 1980 to 1996

[Index 1982=100]

INDUSTRY GROUP	1980	1985	1989	1990	1991	1992	1993	1994	1995	1996
Mining	110.8	110.3	101.5	103.7	101.6	100.0	98.9	101.5	100.9	103.6
Coal	83.4	89.1	98.9	103.7	100.1	100.0	95.1	104.1	104.3	105.9
Oil and gas extraction	123.4	122.0	103.6	104.7	103.3	100.0	99.4	100.2	98.4	100.4
Crude oil and natural gas	115.1	111.4	102.5	101.6	101.9	100.0	98.0	98.1	96.5	96.6
Oil and gas drilling	226.3	248.4	116.9	136.1	116.2	100.0	107.8	113.7	109.0	120.5
Metal mining	65.2	56.6	85.6	93.1	93.3	100.0	98.7	100.2	101.9	101.9
Iron ore	128.5	90.2	105.4	101.4	101.7	100.0	100.0	104.3	112.3	111.3
Nonferrous ores	52.8	50.8	83.0	91.9	92.1	100.0	98.6	99.6	100.5	100.6
Copper ore	65.6	61.2	84.6	89.4	92.4	100.0	102.0	104.7	104.8	107.6
Primary metals, manufacturing	106.0	98.4	104.9	104.0	96.7	100.0	105.5	113.0	115.7	117.1
Nonferrous metals	92.4	98.2	103.2	100.9	97.7	100.0	103.5	112.6	115.0	117.6
Copper	75.9	79.7	79.0	81.6	88.3	100.0	109.5	111.3	106.7	109.6
Aluminum	115.1	86.9	100.0	100.4	102.2	100.0	91.7	81.8	83.7	88.5
Iron and steel	119.0	98.8	106.2	106.4	96.0	100.0	107.1	113.2	116.3	116.5

Source: Board of Governors of the Federal Reserve System, *Federal Reserve Bulletin,* monthly; and *Industrial Production and Capacity Utilization,* Statistical Release G.17, monthly.

No. 1151. Mineral Industries—Employment, Hours, and Earnings: 1990 to 1996

ITEM	Unit	1990	1995	1996
All mining:				
All employees	1,000	709	580	570
Production workers	1,000	509	424	424
Avg. weekly hours	Number	44.1	44.7	45.3
Avg. weekly earnings	Dol	603	684	707
Coal mining:				
All employees	1,000	147	106	100
Production workers	1,000	119	85	82
Avg. weekly hours	Number	44.0	44.9	45.8
Avg. weekly earnings	Dol	735	828	857
Oil and gas extraction:				
All employees	1,000	395	318	311
Production workers	1,000	261	217	220
Avg. weekly hours	Number	43.9	44.2	44.7
Avg. weekly earnings	Dol	568	641	661
Metal mining:				
All employees	1,000	58	51	52
Production workers	1,000	46	41	41
Avg. weekly hours	Number	42.8	43.8	44.0
Avg. weekly earnings	Dol	601	735	764
Nonmetallic minerals, except fuels:				
All employees	1,000	110	106	106
Production workers	1,000	83	80	82
Avg. weekly hours	Number	45.3	46.5	47.0
Avg. weekly earnings	Dol	525	624	650

Source: U.S. Bureau of Labor Statistics, *Bulletin 2370* and *Employment and Earnings,* March and June issues.

No. 1152. Mineral Industries—Summary: 1987 and 1992

["N.e.c." means not elsewhere classified]

MINERAL INDUSTRY	1987						1992										
	All employees		Production workers [3]		Value added in mining [4] (mil. dol.)	Value of shipments and receipts [5] (mil. dol.)	Establishments		All employees		Production workers			Value added in mining [4] (mil. dol.)	Value of shipments and receipts [5] (mil. dol.)	Capital expenditures (mil. dol.)
	Number [1] (1,000)	Payroll [2] (mil. dol.)	Number [1] (1,000)	Wages (mil. dol.)			Total	With 20 or more employees	Number [1] (1,000)	Payroll [2] (mil. dol.)	Number [1] (1,000)	Hours [6] (millions)	Wages (mil. dol.)			
All industries	**698**	**21,739**	**451**	**12,443**	**110,959**	**157,964**	**30,787**	**5,600**	**638**	**24,199**	**415**	**876**	**13,833**	**113,621**	**162,095**	**17,179**
Metal mining	**44**	**1,354**	**34**	**952**	**4,610**	**6,852**	**1,023**	**273**	**53**	**2,111**	**42**	**88**	**1,540**	**6,724**	**9,864**	**1,580**
Iron ores	7	224	6	166	768	1,362	40	18	9	348	7	15	274	985	1,715	53
Copper ores	14	405	11	283	1,301	2,150	62	35	15	550	12	25	405	2,169	3,375	516
Lead and zinc ores	2	58	1	40	176	268	44	24	3	113	2	5	86	287	472	22
Gold and silver ores	13	423	10	306	1,814	2,261	426	116	19	825	16	33	601	2,746	3,555	(D)
Ferroalloy ores, except vanadium	1	46	1	24	61	110	(NA)	(NA)	(NA)	(NA)	(NA)	(NA)	(NA)	(NA)	(NA)	(NA)
Metal mining services	3	81	2	60	176	251	266	37	3	117	3	6	90	259	350	(D)
Miscellaneous metal ores	5	162	4	99	374	559	185	43	4	157	3	5	84	277	398	61
Coal mining	**163**	**5,567**	**129**	**4,251**	**17,068**	**25,955**	**3,069**	**1,238**	**135**	**5,461**	**108**	**227**	**4,205**	**17,262**	**27,134**	**1,943**
Bituminous coal and lignite mining	158	5,410	124	4,125	16,679	25,347	2,635	1,155	129	5,282	103	217	4,062	16,777	26,435	1,912
Anthracite mining	2	41	2	32	109	206	76	18	1	39	1	2	30	97	160	4
Coal mining services	4	116	3	94	280	402	358	65	5	141	4	8	113	378	536	26
Oil and gas extraction	**378**	**11,961**	**206**	**5,283**	**80,049**	**112,363**	**20,891**	**2,703**	**345**	**13,397**	**188**	**395**	**5,939**	**80,016**	**111,523**	**12,519**
Crude petroleum and natural gas	199	7,510	69	2,154	67,955	76,518	9,391	1,015	175	8,422	64	131	2,597	66,575	72,245	10,953
Natural gas liquids	13	433	10	320	4,025	24,750	591	198	12	518	9	19	364	4,242	27,214	615
Oil and gas field services	167	4,018	127	2,810	8,069	11,095	10,909	1,490	158	4,457	115	245	2,978	9,200	12,064	951
Drilling oil and gas wells	55	1,318	46	1,012	2,549	3,626	2,125	450	48	1,371	39	81	994	2,516	3,584	289
Oil, gas exploration services	17	452	13	311	771	1,096	1,490	84	14	460	8	19	238	725	965	172
Oil, gas field services, n.e.c	95	2,248	69	1,486	4,748	6,373	7,294	956	96	2,626	68	145	1,747	5,958	7,515	491
Nonmetallic mining	**113**	**2,858**	**83**	**1,958**	**9,233**	**12,795**	**5,804**	**1,386**	**106**	**3,230**	**77**	**166**	**2,148**	**9,629**	**13,574**	**1,137**
Dimension stone [7]	1	25	1	18	65	86	166	17	1	31	1	2	21	77	99	5
Crushed and broken stone [8]	44	1,082	33	754	3,465	4,768	2,142	662	42	1,207	31	67	827	3,621	5,002	424
Sand and gravel [8]	33	772	24	551	2,320	3,139	2,677	439	30	888	21	47	593	2,318	3,161	259
Clay and related minerals [8]	10	272	7	165	827	1,249	200	100	10	318	8	17	211	936	1,400	84
Chemical and fertilizer minerals	16	501	12	336	1,999	2,772	160	80	15	579	11	22	359	2,122	3,127	309
Nonmetallic minerals, services	2	45	1	32	119	165	178	16	2	52	2	3	39	136	189	15
Miscellaneous [8]	7	162	5	101	438	616	281	72	6	156	4	8	97	419	596	42

D Withheld to avoid disclosure. NA Not available. [1] Excludes proprietors and firm members of unincorporated concerns. [2] Gross earnings paid to all employees on payroll. [3] Represents employees up through the working foreman level engaged in manual work. Includes development and exploration workers. [4] Computed by subtracting cost of supplies, minerals received for preparation, purchased fuel and electric energy, contract work, and purchased machinery from the value of shipments and capital expenditures. [5] Represents value of shipments of primary and secondary products of the industry and amount received for services performed for other establishments on a contract, fee, or other basis. [6] Excludes paid vacations, holidays, and sick leave; includes actual overtime hours (not straight-time equivalent). [7] Excludes data for dimension stone quarries operated in conjunction with dressing plants. [8] Excludes data for mining included in establishments classified in manufacturing industries.

Source: U.S. Bureau of the Census, *Census of Mineral Industries: 1987, and 1992*, final industry series reports.

No. 1153. Mineral Production: 1990 to 1996

[Data represent production as measured by mine shipments, mine sales or marketable production]

MINERAL	Unit	1990	1994	1995	1996
FUEL MINERALS					
Coal, total	Mil. sh. tons	1,029.1	1,033.5	1,033.0	1,056.7
Bituminous	Mil. sh. tons	693.2	640.3	613.8	(NA)
Subbituminous	Mil. sh. tons	244.3	300.5	328.0	(NA)
Lignite	Mil. sh. tons	88.1	88.1	86.5	(NA)
Anthracite	Mil. sh. tons	3.5	4.6	4.7	(NA)
Natural gas (marketed production)	Tril. cu. ft.	18.59	19.64	19.62	19.96
Petroleum (crude)	Mil. bbl. [1]	2,686	2,420	2,394	2,362
Uranium (recoverable content)	Mil. lb.	8.9	3.4	6.0	(NA)
NONFUEL MINERALS					
Abrasive stone [2]	Metric tons	3,709	(Z)	(Z)	(Z)
Asbestos (sales)	1,000 metric tons	(D)	10.0	(D)	9
Asphalt and related bitumens (native) [3]	Mil. metric tons	25	(3)	(3)	(3)
Barite, primary, sold/used by producers	1,000 metric tons	430	583	543	650
Boron minerals, sold or used by producers	1,000 metric tons	1,094	1110	798	622
Bromine, sold or used by producers	1,000 metric tons	177	195	218	227
Calcium chloride (natural)	1,000 sh. tons	(D)	-	-	-
Cement:					
Portland	Mil. sh. tons	75.6	74.3	73.3	75.0
Masonry	Mil. sh. tons	3.3	4.0	4	4
Clays	1,000 metric tons	42,904	42,200	43,100	44,000
Diatomite	1,000 metric tons	631	613	687	700
Feldspar [4]	1,000 metric tons	630	765	882	900
Fluorspar, finished shipments	1,000 metric tons	64	50	(D)	(D)
Garnet (abrasive)	1,000 metric tons	47.0	51.0	53.0	54.0
Gypsum, crude	Mil. metric tons	16.4	17.2	17.0	17.0
Helium [5]	Mil. cu. meters	87	100	99	101
Lime, sold or used by producers	Mil. sh. tons	17.5	17.4	18.5	18.9
Mica, scrap & flake, sold/used by producers	1,000 metric tons	109	110	108	109
Peat, sales by producers	1,000 sh. tons	795	552	660	667
Perlite, processed, sold or used	1,000 metric tons	576	644	700	701
Phosphate rock (marketable)	Mil. metric tons	46.3	41.0	44	43
Potash (K_2O equivalent) sales	1,000 metric tons	1,713	2,970	2,880	2,810
Pumice & pumicite, producer sales	1,000 metric tons	443	490	529	465
Pyrites	1,000 metric tons	(D)	(D)	(NA)	(NA)
Salt, common, sold/used by producers	Mil. metric tons	36.9	39.7	41	40
Sand & gravel, sold/used by producer	Mil. metric tons	852	918	938	992
Construction	Mil. metric tons	829	891	910	963
Industrial	Mil. metric tons	26	27	28	29
Sodium carbonate (natural) (soda ash)	1,000 metric tons	9,156	9,320	10,100	10,100
Sodium sulfate (natural)	1,000 metric tons	349	298	327	325
Stone [6]	Mil. metric tons	1,110	1,230	1,260	1,300
Crushed and broken	Mil. metric tons	1,109	1,230	1,260	1,300
Dimension	1,000 metric tons	1,118	(D)	(D)	(D)
Sulfur: Frasch mines (shipments)	1,000 metric tons	3,676	3,010	3,070	(D)
Talc, and pyrophyllite, crude	1,000 metric tons	1,267	(D)	(D)	(D)
Tripoli	1,000 metric tons	94	82	80	(D)
Vermiculite concentrate	1,000 metric tons	209	177	171	(D)
METALS					
Antimony ore and concentrate	Metric tons	(D)	(D)	(D)	(D)
Bauxite (dried)	1,000 metric tons	(D)	(D)	(D)	(D)
Copper (recoverable content)	1,000 metric tons	1,590	1,810	1,850	1,900
Gold (recoverable content)	Metric tons	294	327	320	325
Iron ore (gross weight) [7]	Mil. metric tons	57.0	57.6	61	61
Lead (recoverable content)	1,000 metric tons	497	363	366	430
Magnesium metal	1,000 metric tons	139	128	142	143
Manganiferous ore (gross weight) [8]	1,000 metric ton	(D)	(D)	(D)	(D)
Mercury [9]	Metric tons	562	(D)	(D)	(D)
Molybdenum (concentrate)	1,000 metric tons	62	46	(D)	(D)
Nickel	1,000 metric tons	0.3	(NA)	1.6	(NA)
Palladium metal	Kilograms	5,930	6,440	5,260	5,000
Platinum metal	Kilograms	1,810	1,960	1,590	1,600
Silver (recoverable content)	Metric tons	2,121	1,490	1,640	1,800
Titanium concentrate: Ilmenite (gross weight)	1,000 metric tons	(D)	(D)	(D)	(D)
Tungsten ore and concentrate [10]	Metric tons	(D)	(D)	(D)	(D)
Zinc (recoverable content)	1,000 metric tons	515	570	614	620

- Represents zero. D Withheld to avoid disclosing individual company data. NA Not available. Z Less than half the unit of measure. [1] 42 gal. bbl. [2] Includes grindstones, oilstones, whetstones, and deburring media. Excludes grinding pebbles, and tubemill liners. [3] Contains bituminous limestone and sandstone, and gilsonite. Includes road oil, 1990-93. Discontinued. [4] Includes aplite, 1992-93. [5] Refined only. [6] Excludes abrasive stone, bituminous limestone and sandstone, and ground soapstone, all included elsewhere in table; 1993 excludes dimension stone. Includes calcareous marl and slate. [7] Represents shipments; includes byproduct ores. [8] 5 to 35 percent manganiferous ore. [9] Mercury produced as a byproduct of gold ores only. [10] Content of ore and concentrate.

Source: Nonfuels, through 1994, U.S. Bureau of Mines, thereafter, U.S. Geological Survey, *Minerals Yearbook*, annual, and *Mineral Commodities Summaries*, annual; fuels, U.S. Energy Information Administration, *Annual Energy Review*.

No. 1154. Mineral Production Value: 1990 to 1995

[In millions of dollars. Value derived by multiplying production times price at source of production]

MINERAL	1990	1992	1993	1994	1995
Mineral production, total	141,597	127,486	125,266	122,015	118,614
Mineral fuels, total	108,133	95,453	93,265	86,815	80,114
Coal, total [1]	22,404	20,976	18,766	20,076	19,709
Bituminous	22,266	20,856	18,624	19,906	19,537
Anthracite	138	120	141	168	172
Natural gas (wellhead)	31,789	32,555	38,834	34,819	28,828
Petroleum (crude)	53,801	41,846	35,625	31,920	31,577
Uranium U_3O_8	140	76	40	(NA)	(NA)
Industrial minerals, total	21,022	20,496	21,200	23,100	24,400
Abrasive stone [2]	(Z)	(Z)	(Z)	(NA)	(NA)
Asbestos (sales)	(4)	6	6	5	(D)
Asphalt, related bitumens (native) [3]	3,480	2,794	(NA)	(NA)	(NA)
Barite, primary, sold/used by producers	16	20	19	22	17
Boron minerals, sold/used by producers	436	339	373	443	372
Bromine, sold/used by producers	173	170	123	155	186
Calcium chloride (natural)	(4)	(4)	(X)	(X)	(X)
Cement:					
Portland	3,683	3,500	3,920	4,460	4,920
Masonry	225	195	229	286	307
Clays	1,620	1,482	1,480	1,600	1,730
Diatomite	138	141	150	152	171
Feldspar [5]	28	29	31	31	37
Fluorspar, finished shipments	(4)	(4)	(4)	(4)	(4)
Garnet (abrasive)	7	5	(D)	15	10
Gemstones (estimate)	53	66	58	51	74
Gypsum, crude	100	101	107	115	121
Helium [6]	113	187	189	199	196
Lime, sold/used by producers	902	950	965	1,020	1,100
Mica, scrap and flake, sold/used by producers	6	5	4	6	6
Peat (sales by producers)	19	17	17	15	17
Perlite, processed, sold/used by producers	17	16	17	19	22
Phosphate rock (marketable)	1,075	1,058	759	839	945
Potash (K_2O equivalent)	303	334	266	285	284
Pumice and pumicite (sales by producers)	11	15	12	12	13
Salt (common), sold/used by producers	827	803	893	990	1,000
Sand and gravel, sold/used by producers	3,686	3,766	3,980	4,230	4,410
Sodium carbonate (natural) (soda ash)	836	836	734	724	829
Sodium sulfate (natural)	34	26	(D)	24	29
Stone: [7]	5,822	5,775	6,030	6,620	6,750
Crushed and broken	5,591	5,594	6,030	6,820	6,750
Dimension	231	181	216	(D)	(D)
Sulfur: Frasch mines (shipments)	335	159	101	162	207
Talc and pyrophyllite, crude [8]	31	31	(D)	32	(4)
Tripoli	3	3	4	11	11
Vermiculite concentrate	19	15	15	14	(D)
Industrial minerals, undistributed	504	478	417	531	622
Metals, total	12,442	11,537	10,800	12,100	14,100
Antimony ore and concentrate [9]	(10)	(10)	(10)	(10)	(10)
Bauxite (dried equivalent)	(10)	(10)	(10)	(10)	(10)
Copper (recoverable content)	4,311	4,179	3,640	4,430	5,640
Gold (recoverable content)	3,650	3,662	3,840	4,050	3,990
Iron ore (gross weight) [11]	1,741	1,732	1,640	1,580	1,710
Lead (recoverable content)	491	306	249	298	359
Magnesium metal [12]	433	360	377	389	476
Manganiferous ore (gross weight) [13]	(10)	(10)	(10)	(10)	(10)
Mercury [14]	(10)	0.4	(D)	(D)	(10)
Molybdenum (concentrate)	348	209	165	264	(D)
Palladium metal	22	18	25	29	22
Platinum metal	27	21	21	25	21
Silver (recoverable content)	329	229	227	253	271
Titanium concentrate: ilmenite (gross weight)	(10)	(10)	(10)	(10)	(10)
Tungsten ore and concentrate	(10)	(10)	(10)	(10)	(10)
Vanadium (recoverable content)	(10)	(10)	(10)	(10)	(10)
Zinc mine production (recoverable content)	847	674	497	619	756
Metals, undistributed	242	156	132	147	812

D Withheld to avoid disclosing individual company data. NA Not available. X Not applicable. Z Less than $500,000. [1] Includes subbituminous and lignite. [2] Includes grindstones, oilstones, whetstones, and deburring media. [3] 1990-92, excluded from industrial minerals. [4] Included in "Industrial minerals, undistributed." [5] 1992-93, includes aplite. [6] Refined only. [7] Excludes abrasive stone, bituminous limestone and sandstone, and ground soapstone; 1993 excludes dimension stone. State ranks based on publishable data. Includes calcareous marl and slate. [8] 1990-92, talc only. [9] Antimony content. [10] Included with "Metals, undistributed". [11] Represents shipments; includes byproduct ores. [12] Canvass for magnesium chloride for magnesium metal discontinued in 1986. [13] 5 to 35 percent manganiferous ore. [14] Mercury produced as a byproduct of gold ores only.

Source: Nonfuels, through 1994, U.S. Bureau of Mines, thereafter, U.S. Geological Survey, *Minerals Yearbook* and *Mineral Commodities Summaries*, annual; fuels, U.S. Energy Information Administration, *Annual Energy Review*.

No. 1155. Nonfuel Mineral Commodities—Summary: 1996

[Preliminary estimates. Average price in dollars per metric tons except as noted]

MINERAL	MINERAL DISPOSITION					Average price per unit (dollars)	Employment (number)
	Unit	Production	Exports	Net import reliance [1] (percent)	Consumption, apparent		
Aluminum	1,000 metric tons	5,000	1,500	21	6,300	[2]0.70	21,600
Antimony (contained)	Metric tons	[3]22,700	5,400	(NA)	(NA)	[2]152	100
Arsenic	Metric tons	(NA)	20	100	22,000	[2]0.53	(NA)
Asbestos	1,000 metric tons	9	16	30	23	(D)	30
Barite	1,000 metric tons	650	18	66	1,930	[4]50	350
Bauxite and alumina	1,000 metric tons	(D)	1,090	100	4,370	15-18	20
Beryllium (contained)	Metric tons	217	50	([5])	220	[2,6]327	425
Bismuth (contained)	Metric tons	(D)	120	(D)	(NA)	[2]3.60	30
Boron (B_2O_3 content)	1,000 metric tons	622	590	([5])	234	[4,8]375	900
Bromine (contained)	1,000 metric tons	227	14	([5])	315	[9]86.1	1,700
Cadmium (contained)	Metric tons	[3]1,450	40	33	2,200	[2,10]1.25	145
Cement	1,000 short tons	78,600	750	12	89,400	70.00	17,900
Chromium	1,000 metric tons	[11]104	63	79	497	[4,12]230	(NA)
Clays	1,000 metric tons	44,000	4,800	([5])	39,200	(NA)	13,900
Cobalt (contained)	Metric tons	[11]1,500	1,500	83	8,900	[2]26.00	(NA)
Columbium (contained)	Metric tons	(NA)	300	100	3,800	[2,13]3.00	(NA)
Copper (Mine, contained)	1,000 metric tons	1,900	840	13	2,760	[2]108	14
Diamond (industrial)	Million carats	158	107	(NA)	263	[14]0.45	(NA)
Diatomite	1,000 metric tons	700	137	([5])	563	[4]249	1,000
Feldspar	1,000 metric tons	900	15	([5])	895	[4]42.44	400
Fluorspar	1,000 metric tons	102	30	99	692	(NA)	5
Gallium (contained)	Kilograms	(NA)	(NA)	(NA)	[7]21,000	425	20
Garnet (industrial)	Metric tons	54,000	9,000	([5])	32,200	90-1600	200
Gemstones	Million dollars	88	2,660	98	4,570	(NA)	850
Germanium (contained)	Kilograms	[3]18,000	(NA)	(NA)	(NA)	[15]2,000	120
Gold (contained)	Metric tons	325	600	([5])	(NA)	[16]390.00	15,200
Graphite (crude)	1,000 metric tons	(NA)	25	100	35	[4,17]675.00	(NA)
Gypsum (crude)	1,000 short tons	17,000	100	30	26,500	[4]7.50	[18]6,700
Indium	Metric tons	(NA)	(NA)	(NA)	45	[19]300.00	(NA)
Iodine	Metric tons	1,200	2,000	62	4,000	[20]13.50	40
Iron ore (usable)	Million metric tons	60	5	17	72.6	[21]72.5-74.0	7,400
Iron and steel scrap (metal)	Million metric tons	66	9.1	([5])	70	[4,22]130.00	37,000
Iron and steel slag (metal)	1,000 metric tons	21,400	4	1	21,700	[4]6.90	2,500
Lead (contained)	1,000 metric tons	430	25	17	1,560	[23]48.8	1,800
Lime	1,000 short tons	19,000	55	1	19,200	[4]57.00	5,800
Magnesium compounds	1,000 metric tons	450	60	30	640	(NA)	600
Magnesium metal	1,000 metric tons	208	41	([5])	171	[24]1.75	1,400
Manganese (gross weight)	1,000 metric tons	(NA)	41	100	[25]716	[26]2.55	(NA)
Mercury	Metric tons	[27]550	100	(D)	(D)	[28]260.00	(NA)
Mica, scrap and flake	1,000 metric tons	109	8	8	119	[4]61.00	(NA)
Molybdenum (contained)	Metric tons	57,000	47,500	([5])	14,500	[29]7.50	700
Nickel (contained)	Metric tons	14,600	12,800	63	158,000	[30]7,515	1
Nitrogen (fixed)-ammonia	1,000 metric tons	13,800	500	18	16,900	[4,31]215	2,500
Nonrenewable organics	Million metric tons	(NA)	(NA)	(NA)	(NA)	(NA)	(NA)
Peat	1,000 short tons	535	18	58	1,260	[4]25.34	1,000
Perlite	1,000 metric tons	701	40	6	746	[4]29.16	125
Phosphate rock	1,000 metric tons	42,500	2,800	([5])	40,900	[4]20.50	5,500
Platinum-group metals	Kilograms	6,600	38,000	(NA)	(NA)	[32]410.00	500
Potash (K_2O equivalent)	1,000 metric tons	1,380	400	76	5,840	[4,33]133	1,690
Pumice and pumicite	1,000 metric tons	465	15	28	650	[4]22.96	60
Salt	1,000 metric tons	40,100	950	18	48,700	[4,34]111.00	4,150
Silicon (contained)	1,000 metric tons	414	44	31	597	[35]64.00	(NA)
Silver (contained)	Metric tons	1,800	2,600	(NA)	(NA)	[16]5.30	1,400
Sodium carbonate (soda ash)	1,000 metric tons	10,100	3,650	([5])	6,550	[4,36]105.00	2,800
Sodium sulfate	1,000 metric tons	325	100	13	595	[37]114.00	240
Stone (crushed)	Million short tons	1,300	6	-	1,304	[4]5.43	77,500
Sulfur (all forms)	1,000 metric tons	11,800	1,000	11	13,400	[4,38]38.00	3,100
Talc	1,000 metric tons	976	179	([5])	939	[4]7-525	750
Thallium (contained)	Kilograms	(NA)	(NA)	100	300	1,200	-
Tin (contained)	Metric tons	[11]12,000	3,600	83	48,400	[2]291	-
Titanium dioxide	1,000 metric tons	1,230	275	([5])	1,140	[2,39]1.09	4,600
Tungsten (contained)	Metric tons	(D)	32	82	15,100	[40]67	20
Vermiculite	1,000 metric tons	(D)	5	(D)	(D)	(D)	230
Zinc (contained)	1,000 metric tons	620	430	33	[41]1,470	[23]51.0	2,700
Zirconium (Z,02) content	Metric tons	(D)	24,200	(D)	(D)	[42]400	(NA)

- Represents or rounds to zero. D Withheld to avoid disclosure. NA Not available. [1] Calculated as a percent of apparent consumption. [2] Price per pound. [3] Refinery production. [4] Price per metric ton. [5] Net exporter. [6] Metal, vacuum-cast ingot. [7] Estimated consumption. [8] Granulated pentahydrate borax in bulk, f.o.b mine. [9] Cents per kilogram, bulk, purified bromine. [10] 1- to 5-short ton lots. [11] Secondary production. [12] Turkish, chromite price. [13] Columbite price. [14] Value of imports per carat. [15] Zone refined, first reduction quality. [16] Price per troy ounce. [17] Price of flake imports. [18] Includes employment at calcining plants. [19] 99.97% indium, per kilogram. [20] C.i.f. value, crude, per kilogram. [21] Lake Superior pellets. Cents per long ton unit of iron. [22] Delivered, No. 1 Heavy Melting composite price. [23] Cents per pound. [24] Year-end price, per pound. [25] Estimated manganese content. [26] 46%-48% Mn metallurgical ore, per unit contained Mn, c.i.f. U.S. ports. [27] Secondary industrial production. [28] Price per 76-pound flask. [29] Price per kilogram. [30] London Metal Exchange cash price. [31] F.o.b. gulf coast. [32] Dealer price of platinum. Per troy ounce. [33] Price of K20, muriate. [34] Vacuum and open pan, bulk, pellets and packaged, f.o.b. mine and plant. [35] Ferrosilicon, 50% Si. [36] Quoted year-end price, dense, bulk, f.o.b Green River, WY. [37] Quoted price, bulk, f.o.b. works, East, per short ton. [38] Elemental sulfur, f.o.b. mine and/or plant. [39] Rutile, list, year-end. [40] Price per unit W03 (7.93 kilograms of contained tungsten per unit). [41] All forms. [42] Price for imported zircon, f.o.b. U.S. east coast.

Source: U.S. Geological Survey, *Mineral Commodity Summaries*, annual.

No. 1156. Selected Mineral Products—Average Prices: 1980 to 1996

[Excludes Alaska and Hawaii, except as noted]

YEAR	Copper, electrolytic [1] (cents per lb.)	Platinum [2] (dol./troy oz.)	Gold (dol./fine oz.)	Silver (dol./fine oz.)	Lead [3] (cents per lb.)	Tin (New York) [4] (cents per lb.)	Zinc [5] (cents per lb.)	Sulfur, crude [6] (dol./metric ton)	Bituminous coal [7] (dol./short ton)	Crude petroleum [7] (dol./bbl.)	Natural gas [7] (dol./1,000 cu. ft.)
1980	101	677	613	20.63	43	846	37	89.06	24.52	21.59	1.59
1981	84	446	460	10.52	37	733	45	111.48	26.29	31.77	1.98
1982	73	327	376	7.95	26	654	39	108.27	27.14	28.52	2.46
1983	77	424	424	11.44	22	655	41	87.24	25.85	26.19	2.59
1984	67	357	361	8.14	26	624	49	94.31	25.51	25.88	2.66
1985	67	291	318	6.14	19	596	40	106.46	25.10	24.09	2.51
1986	66	461	368	5.47	22	383	38	105.22	23.70	12.51	1.94
1987	83	553	478	7.01	36	419	42	89.78	23.00	15.40	1.67
1988	121	523	438	6.53	37	441	60	85.95	22.00	12.58	1.69
1989	131	507	383	5.50	39	520	82	86.62	21.76	15.86	1.69
1990	123	467	385	4.82	46	386	75	80.14	21.71	20.03	1.71
1991	109	371	363	4.04	34	363	53	71.45	21.45	16.54	1.64
1992	107	360	345	3.94	35	402	58	48.14	20.98	15.99	1.74
1993	92	374	361	4.30	32	350	46	31.86	19.79	14.25	2.04
1994	111	411	385	5.29	37	369	49	28.60	19.35	13.19	1.85
1995	138	425	386	5.15	42	416	56	43.74	19.00	14.62	1.55
1996	108	410	390	5.3	49	449	51	38.00	(NA)	18.46	2.25

NA Not available. [1] Domestic market prices for wirebar, 1970, 1975-77; prices for cathode thereafter. [2] Average annual dealer prices. [3] 1970, New York prices; beginning 1975, nationwide delivered basis. [4] Straits tin through 1975; thereafter, composite price. [5] Prime western. Beginning 1975, delivered price. [6] F.o.b. works. [7] Average value at the point of production. Source: U.S. Energy Information Administration, *Annual Energy Review.*

Source: Nonfuels, through 1994, U.S. Bureau of Mines,thereafter, U.S. Geological Survey, *Minerals Yearbook* and *Mineral Commodities Summaries*, annual; fuels, U.S. Energy Information Administration, *Annual Energy Review.*

No. 1157. Value of Domestic Nonfuel Mineral Production: 1990 to 1996

[In millions of dollars. Data may not add due to rounding]

AREA	1990	1994	1995	1996
U.S. [1]	**33,445**	**36,050**	**37,400**	**38,020**
Northeast	**2,479**	**2,620**	**2,677**	**2,860**
N.E.	446	444	467	510
ME	55	61	59	73
NH	36	44	39	[1]44
VT	87	53	53	[1]67
MA	128	178	206	191
RI	18	26	30	[1]32
CT	122	82	81	103
M.A	2,033	2,180	2,210	2,150
NY	773	893	863	891
NJ	229	289	289	[1]222
PA	1,031	997	1,050	[1]1,040
Midwest	**7,163**	**7,890**	**8,050**	**8,830**
E.N.C	3,483	4,000	4,030	4,240
OH	733	880	871	934
IN	428	555	561	617
IL	667	823	820	777
MI	1,440	1,460	1,460	1,510
WI	215	284	295	399
W.N.C	3,680	3,870	4,050	4,590
MN	1,482	1,340	1,490	1,800
IA	310	451	484	490
MO	1,105	1,090	1,110	1,250
ND	25	25	25	30
SD	319	323	315	353
NE	90	146	142	147
KS	349	497	492	524
South	**9,291**	**9,520**	**10,000**	**10,560**
S.A	5,132	5,090	5,290	5,540
DE [2]	10	[1]9	9	[1]11
MD	368	340	341	[1]324
VA	507	502	517	529
WV	133	181	193	191
NC	586	710	743	731
SC	450	433	426	495
GA	1,504	1,550	1,670	1,720
FL	1,574	1,370	1,390	1,540
E.S.C	1,692	1,790	1,860	1,980
KY	359	428	401	452
TN	663	602	660	648
AL	559	626	678	735
MS	111	135	125	140
W.S.C	2,467	2,630	2,850	3,030
AR	381	405	479	453
LA	368	350	362	428
OK	259	356	388	372
TX	1,459	1,520	1,620	1,780
West	**14,512**	**15,030**	**16,650**	**15,990**
Mt	10,380	11,000	12,400	11,630
MT	573	543	581	523
ID	375	346	399	411
WY	911	880	976	918
CO	377	410	448	528
NM	1,103	930	1,080	963
AZ	3,085	3,280	4,150	3,530
UT	1,335	1,520	1,810	1,560
NV	2,621	3,070	2,920	3,200
Pac.	4,132	4,030	4,250	4,350
WA	483	570	613	626
OR	205	243	261	251
CA	2,771	2,580	2,680	2,840
AK	577	519	594	[1]523
HI	106	[1]116	[1]106	[1]112

[1] Partial data only. [2] Includes District of Columbia.

Source: Through 1994, U.S. Bureau of Mines, thereafter, U.S. Geological Survey,*Annual Reports, and Mineral Commodities Summary*, annual.

No. 1158. Principal Fuels, Nonmetals, and Metals—World Production and the U.S. Share: 1980 to 1995

MINERAL	WORLD PRODUCTION					PERCENT U.S. OF WORLD			
	Unit	1980	1990	1994	1995	1980	1990	1994	1995
Fuels: [1]									
Coal	Bil. sh. ton	4.2	5.4	5.0	5.1	20	19	21	20
Petroleum (crude)	Bil. bbl	21.7	22.1	22.3	22.8	14	12	11	11
Natural gas (dry, marketable)	Tril. cu. ft	53.1	73.6	76.7	78.3	37	24	24	24
Natural gas plant liquids	Bil. bbl	1.4	1.7	1.9	2.0	43	34	33	32
Nonmetals:									
Asbestos	1,000 metric tons	4,699	4,003	2,460	2,400	2	(D)	(Z)	(NA)
Barite	1,000 metric tons	7,495	5,633	4,210	4,410	27	8	14	12
Feldspar	1,000 metric tons	3,202	5,456	5,970	6,110	20	12	13	14
Fluorspar	1,000 metric tons	5,006	5,131	3,810	3,940	2	1	1	1
Gypsum	Mil. metric tons	78	100	100	98	14	15	17	17
Mica (incl. scrap)	1,000 metric tons	228	215	238	245	46	51	46	44
Nitrogen, (fixed) - ammonia	Mil. metric tons	74	97	91	92	20	13	15	15
Phosphate rock, gross wt.	Mil. metric tons	144	162	128	131	38	29	32	33
Potash (K_2O equivalent)	Mil. metric tons	28	28	23	25	8	6	6	6
Sulfur, elemental	Mil. metric tons	55	58	54	54	22	20	21	22
Metals, mine basis:									
Bauxite	Mil. metric tons	89	109	107	109	2	(D)	(NA)	(NA)
Columbian concentrates (Nb content)	1,000 metric tons	15	15	37	43	(NA)	(NA)	-	-
Copper	1,000 metric tons	7,405	9,017	9,500	10,000	16	18	14	13
Gold	Metric tons	1,219	2,133	2,260	2,250	2	14	15	14
Iron ore	Mil. metric tons	891	962	968	1,030	8	6	6	6
Lead [2]	1,000 metric tons	3,470	3,353	2,810	2,710	17	15	13	15
Mercury	Metric tons	6,806	4,523	1,800	2,820	16	12	(NA)	(NA)
Molybdenum	1,000 metric tons	111	128	105	124	62	48	45	49
Nickel [2]	1,000 metric tons	779	965	924	1,040	2	(Z)	(NA)	(Z)
Silver	1,000 metric tons	11	16	14	15	9	13	11	11
Tantalum concentrates	Metric tons	544	400	(NA)	(NA)	(NA)	(NA)	(NA)	(NA)
Titanium concentrates:									
Ilmenite	1,000 metric tons	3,728	4,072	3,570	3,810	14	(D)	(NA)	(NA)
Rutile	1,000 metric tons	436	481	469	312	(D)	(D)	(NA)	(NA)
Tungsten [2]	1,000 metric tons	52	43	35	31	5	14	(NA)	(NA)
Vanadium [2]	1,000 metric tons	37	31	35	35	12	(D)	8	6
Zinc [2]	1,000 metric tons	5,954	7,184	7,020	7,120	6	8	9	9
Metals, smelter basis:									
Aluminum	1,000 metric tons	15,383	19,292	19,200	19,400	30	21	17	17
Cadmium	1,000 metric tons	18	20	18	19	9	8	6	7
Copper	1,000 metric tons	7,649	9,472	11,200	11,700	14	15	20	19
Iron, pig	Mil. metric tons	514	532	514	525	12	9	10	10
Lead [3]	1,000 metric tons	5,430	5,763	5,380	5,400	23	23	24	25
Magnesium [4]	1,000 metric tons	316	354	284	339	49	39	45	42
Raw Steel	Mil. metric tons	717	771	730	752	14	12	13	13
Tin [5]	1,000 metric tons	251	223	207	209	1	-	(NA)	(NA)
Zinc	1,000 metric tons	6,049	7,060	7,370	7,480	6	5	5	5

- Represents or rounds to zero. D Withheld to avoid disclosing company data. NA Not available. Z Less than half the unit of measure. [1] Source: Energy Information Administration, *International Energy Annual*. [2] Content of ore and concentrate. [3] Refinery production. [4] Primary production; no smelter processing necessary. [5] Production from primary sources only.

Source: Nonfuels, through 1994, U.S. Bureau of Mines, thereafter, U.S. Geological Survey, *Minerals Yearbook*, annual, and *Mineral Commodities Summaries*, annual; fuels, U.S. Energy Information Administration, *Annual Energy Review*.

No. 1159. Federal Strategic and Critical Materials Inventory: 1980 to 1994

[As of Dec. 31. Covers strategic and critical materials essential to military and industrial requirements in time of national emergency]

MINERAL	QUANTITY [1]					VALUE (mil. dol.) [2]			
	Unit	1980	1985	1990	1994	1980	1985	1990	1994
Tin	1,000 metric ton	200	185	169	145	3,158	2,324	962	684
Silver	1,000 troy oz	139,500	136,006	92,151	59,507	2,288	801	374	158
Cobalt	Mil. lb.	41	53	53	52	1,020	590	443	561
Bauxite [3]	1,000 lg. ton	14,333	17,957	18,033	16,549	583	871	888	191
Manganese [4]	1,000 sh. ton	5,130	4,470	4,017	2,792	599	520	962	468
Tungsten [5]	Mil. lb.	97	87	82	82	817	369	253	178
Zinc	1,000 sh. ton	380	378	379	360	317	268	483	307
Titanium	1,000 sh. ton	43	48	37	37	432	405	402	221
Platinum	1,000 troy oz	466	466	453	453	215	154	186	131
Chromium [6]	1,000 sh. ton	804	854	1,074	1,149	773	836	917	837
Diamonds: Stones	Carat 1,000	19,224	12,549	7,777	6,457	349	336	267	533
Industrial, bort	Carat 1,000	23,693	22,001	17,353	4,012	73	39	16	3

[1] Consists of stockpile and nonstockpile grades and reflects uncommitted balances. [2] Market values are estimated trade values of similar materials and not necessarily amounts that would be realized at time of sale. [3] Consists of abrasive grade, metallic grade Jamaica, metallic grade Suriname, and refractory. [4] Consists of chemical grade, dioxide battery natural, dioxide battery synthetic, electrolytic, ferro-high carbon, ferro-med. carbon, ferro-silicon, and metal. [5] Consists of carbide powder, ferro, metal powder, and ores and concentrates. [6] Consists of ferro-high carbon, ferro-low carbon, ferro-silicon, and metal.

Source: U.S. Defense Logistics Agency, *Statistical Supplement, Stockpile Report to the Congress* (AP-3).

No. 1160. Net U.S. Imports of Selected Minerals and Metals as Percent of Apparent Consumption, 1980 to 1995

[Percent, based on net imports which equal the difference between imports and exports plus or minus Government stockpile and industry stock changes]

MINERAL	1980	1985	1990	1991	1992	1993	1994	1995
Columbium	100	100	100	100	100	100	100	100
Manganese	98	100	100	100	100	100	100	100
Mica (sheet)	100	100	100	100	100	100	100	100
Strontium	100	100	100	100	100	100	100	100
Bauxite [1]	94	96	98	100	100	100	99	99
Tin	79	72	71	74	80	84	83	84
Tungsten	53	68	81	91	86	82	81	84
Cobalt	93	94	84	80	76	79	79	82
Chromium	91	75	71	72	73	81	75	80
Tantalum	90	89	86	86	85	80	81	80
Potash	65	76	68	69	68	72	76	75
Barite	44	74	71	66	52	72	64	65
Nickel	76	71	64	61	59	63	64	59
Selenium	59	(D)	46	50	48	39	31	38
Zinc [2]	60	70	41	24	33	36	35	35
Gypsum	35	38	36	31	31	31	31	32
Aluminum	([3])	16	([3])	(NA)	1	19	30	23
Iron and steel	13	22	13	12	13	15	22	21
Sulfur	14	3	15	19	20	12	12	21
Iron ore	25	21	21	11	12	14	18	14
Copper	16	28	3	(NA)	2	7	13	7
Platinum group	87	92	88	90	87	89	91	(NA)
Silver	7	(NA)	(NA)	(NA)	(NA)	(NA)	(NA)	(NA)
Mercury	27	(NA)	(D)	(D)	(NA)	(D)	(D)	(D)
Vanadium	35	(D)	(D)	(D)	(D)	(D)	(D)	(D)
Cadmium	55	57	46	50	50	64	1	21

D Withheld to avoid disclosure. NA Not available. [1] Includes alumina. [2] Beginning 1990, effect of sharp rise in exports of concentrates. If calculated on a refined zinc-only basis, reliance would be about the same as pre-1990 level; 1990, 64%; 1991, 61%, 1992, 64%, and 1993, 67%. [3] Net exports.

Source: Except as noted, through 1994, U.S. Bureau of Mines; thereafter, U.S. Geological Survey, *Mineral Commodity Summaries;* import and export data from U.S. Bureau of the Census.

No. 1161. Federal Offshore Leasing, Exploration, Production, and Revenue: 1980 to 1995

[See source for explanation of terms and for reliability statement]

ITEM	Unit	1980	1985	1989	1990	1991	1992	1993	1994	1995
Tracts offered	Number	483	15,754	11,013	10,459	16,600	9,618	10,164	10,861	10,995
Tracts leased	Number	218	681	1,049	825	676	204	336	560	835
Acres offered	1,000	2,563	87,029	60,098	56,789	90,288	52,380	55,070	58,895	59,700
Acres leased	1,000	1,134	3,574	5,581	4,263	3,414	1,021	1,714	2,775	4,342
Bonus paid for leased tracts	Bil. dol.	4.2	1.6	0.6	0.6	0.3	0.1	0.1	0.3	0.4
New wells being drilled:										
Active	Number	191	195	123	120	64	104	129	120	124
Suspended	Number	739	348	361	266	249	180	193	222	247
Wells completed	Number	9,638	12,285	12,938	13,167	13,184	13,209	13,181	13,342	13,475
Wells plugged and abandoned	Number	8,057	10,487	13,846	14,677	15,430	16,348	16,709	17,427	18,006
Revenue, total [1]	Bil. dol.	6.4	5.3	2.9	3.4	2.8	2.6	2.9	2.6	2.6
Bonuses	Bil. dol.	4.2	1.6	0.6	0.6	0.3	0.1	0.1	0.3	0.4
Oil and gas royalties [1]	Bil. dol.	2.1	3.6	2.1	2.6	2.3	2.3	2.5	2.3	2.1
Rentals	Bil. dol.	(Z)	0.1	0.1	0.1	0.1	0.1	(Z)	(Z)	0.9
Sales value [2]	Bil. dol.	13.1	22.2	13.4	17.0	14.9	15.1	16.4	15.0	13.8
Crude oil	Bil. dol.	4.8	9.6	4.4	5.9	5.2	5.3	4.9	4.4	5.4
Condensate	Bil. dol.	0.4	1.0	0.8	1.1	1.1	1.0	0.9	0.7	0.9
Natural gas	Bil. dol.	7.9	11.4	7.8	9.5	7.9	8.2	9.9	9.8	7.5
Sales volume:										
Crude oil	Mil. bbls.	259	351	260	274	263	302	307	319	357
Condensate	Mil. bbls.	19	38	45	51	52	52	55	51	52
Natural gas	Bil. cu. ft	4,641	4,001	4,200	5,093	4,516	4,686	4,533	4,700	4,692

Z Less than $50 million. [1] Includes condensate royalties. [2] Production value is value at time of production, not current value.

Source: U.S. Dept. of the Interior, Minerals Management Service, *Federal Offshore Statistics*, annual. .

No. 1162. Petroleum Industry—Summary: 1980 to 1996

[Includes all costs incurred for drilling and equipping wells to point of completion as productive wells or abandonment after drilling becomes unproductive. Based on sample of operators of different size drilling establishments]

ITEM	Unit	1980	1985	1990	1991	1992	1993	1994	1995	1996
Completed wells drilled, total	1,000	56.9	57.9	26.3	24.8	20.2	21.8	17.5	14.6	(NA)
Crude oil	1,000	30.5	33.1	11.5	11.3	8.5	8.3	6.2	5.9	(NA)
Gas	1,000	15.1	13.0	10.1	8.9	7.7	9.4	8.2	6.4	(NA)
Dry	1,000	11.3	11.8	4.8	4.5	4.0	4.2	3.1	2.3	(NA)
Average depth per well [1]	Feet	4,188	4,225	4,662	4,805	5,194	5,422	6,079	5,866	(NA)
Average cost per well [1]	$1,000	368	349	384	422	383	427	483	513	(NA)
Offshore	$1,000	3,024	4,073	3,112	3,550	3,223	3,250	3,412	3,686	(NA)
Average cost per foot [1]	Dollars	77.02	75.35	76.07	82.64	70.27	75.30	79.49	87	(NA)
Crude oil production, total	Mil. bbl.	3,138	3,274	2,685	2,707	2,617	2,499	2,432	2,394	2,362
Value at wells	Bil. dol.	67.7	78.9	53.8	44.8	41.9	35.6	32.1	35.0	43.6
Average price per barrel	Dollars	21.59	24.09	20.03	16.54	15.99	14.25	13.19	14.62	18.46
Lower 48 states	Mil. bbl.	2,548	2,608	2,037	2,051	1,992	1,921	1,863	1,842	1,852
Alaska	Mil. bbl.	590	666	647	656	626	577	569	542	510
Onshore	Mil. bbl.	2,760	2,819	2,290	2,279	2,173	2,046	1,931	1,891	(NA)
Offshore	Mil. bbl.	377	456	395	428	445	453	500	493	(NA)
Imports: Crude oil	Mil. bbl.	1,920	1,168	2,150	2,110	2,219	2,478	2,577	2,639	2,731
Refined petroleum products	Mil. bbl.	602	683	774	672	657	668	706	586	700
Proved reserves	Bil. bbl.	29.8	28.4	26.5	26.3	24.7	23.7	23.0	22.5	(NA)
Operable refineries	Number	319	223	205	202	199	187	179	175	(NA)
Capacity (Jan. 1)	Mil. bbl.	6,566	5,716	5,683	5,723	5,731	5,519	5,486	5,632	(NA)
Refinery input, total	Mil. bbl.	5,117	4,814	5,325	5,307	5,340	5,482	5,482	5,541	(NA)
Crude oil	Mil. bbl.	4,920	4,380	4,895	4,855	4,895	4,968	5,063	5,099	(NA)
Natural gas plant liquids	Mil. bbl.	168	186	172	172	172	179	172	172	(NA)
Other liquids	Mil. bbl.	29	248	259	281	274	336	252	270	(NA)
Refinery output, total	Mil. bbl.	5,336	5,019	5,574	5,570	5,621	5,763	5,763	5,822	(NA)
Motor gasoline	Mil. bbl.	2,369	2,343	2,540	2,548	2,577	2,665	2,621	2,712	(NA)
Jet fuel	Mil. bbl.	365	434	544	526	511	518	529	515	(NA)
Distillate fuel oil	Mil. bbl.	971	962	1,066	1,080	1,084	1,142	1,168	1,150	(NA)
Residual fuel oil	Mil. bbl.	577	321	347	339	325	307	303	286	(NA)
Liquefied petroleum gases	Mil. bbl.	120	142	183	197	223	215	223	237	(NA)
Other products	Mil. bbl.	934	796	894	880	902	913	920	916	(NA)
Utilization rate	Percent	75.4	77.6	87.1	86.0	87.9	91.5	92.6	91.9	(NA)

NA Not available. [1] Source: American Petroleum Institute, *Joint Association Survey on Drilling Costs*, annual.

Source: Except as noted, U.S. Energy Information Administration, *Annual Energy Review*, *Petroleum Supply Annual*; *U.S. Crude Oil, Natural Gas, and Natural Gas Liquids Reserves*; and *Monthly Energy Review*, May 1997 issue.

No. 1163. U.S. Petroleum Balance: 1980 to 1995

[In millions of barrels]

ITEM	1980	1985	1990	1991	1992	1993	1994	1995
Petroleum products supplied for domestic use	6,242	5,740	6,201	6,101	6,234	6,291	6,467	6,469
Production of products	5,765	5,363	5,934	5,933	6,050	6,182	6,244	6,323
Crude input to refineries	4,934	4,381	4,894	4,855	4,909	4,969	5,061	5,100
Oil, field production	3,138	3,274	2,685	2,707	2,617	2,499	2,431	2,394
Alaska	592	666	647	656	627	577	569	542
Lower 48 States	2,555	2,608	2,037	2,050	1,997	1,922	1,863	1,853
Net imports	1,821	1,094	2,112	2,068	2,194	2,441	2,542	2,604
Imports (gross excluding SPR) [1]	1,910	1,125	2,142	2,111	2,223	2,472	2,574	2,639
SPR [1] imports	16	43	10	-	4	5	4	-
Exports	-105	75	40	42	32	36	36	35
Other sources	33	12	98	80	90	28	88	102
Natural gas liquids (NGL), supply	577	604	574	613	628	664	694	706
Other liquids	253	378	465	466	513	550	489	514
Net imports of refined products	484	313	326	177	156	134	217	101
Imports	578	523	598	500	471	461	518	407
Exports	94	210	272	323	315	327	302	307
Stock withdrawal, refined products	-7	64	-59	-	28	-	6	46
TYPE OF PRODUCT SUPPLIED								
Total products supplied for domestic use	6,242	5,740	6,201	6,101	6,234	6,291	6,467	6,469
Finished motor gasoline	2,407	2,493	2,641	2,623	2,660	2,729	2,774	2,843
Distillate fuel oil	1,049	1,047	1,103	1,066	1,090	1,110	1,154	1,170
Residual fuel oil	918	439	449	423	401	394	373	311
Liquified petroleum gases [2]	414	584	568	616	642	633	686	693
Other	1,454	1,177	1,440	1,373	1,441	1,425	1,460	1,452
ENDING STOCKS								
Ending stocks, all oils	1,392	1,519	1,621	1,617	1,592	1,647	1,653	1,563
Crude oil and lease condensate	358	321	323	325	318	335	337	303
Strategic Petroleum Reserve (SPR) [1]	108	493	586	569	575	587	592	592
Other	926	705	712	723	699	725	724	668

- Represents zero. [1] SPR=Strategic petroleum reserve. See table 940. [2] Includes ethane.

Source: U.S. Energy Information Administration, *Petroleum Supply Annual*

No. 1164. Crude Petroleum and Natural Gas—Production and Value, by Major Producing States: 1990 to 1995

STATE	CRUDE PETROLEUM						NATURAL GAS MARKETED PRODUCTION [1]					
	Quantity (mil. bbl.)			Value (mil. dol.)			Quantity (bil. cu. ft.)			Value (mil. dol.)		
	1990	1994	1995	1990	1994	1995	1990	1994	1995	1990	1994	1995
Total [2]	2,685	2,431	2,394	53,772	32,071	35,004	18,594	19,835	19,506	31,658	36,536	30,235
AL	16	18	19	387	275	306	135	515	520	373	1,119	946
AK	658	569	557	10,086	5,559	6,514	403	453	470	554	578	770
AR	10	10	9	222	131	132	175	188	187	360	497	565
CA	322	286	279	5,732	3,467	3,906	363	309	280	857	940	484
CO	31	29	28	722	442	486	243	453	523	377	629	497
FL	6	6	6	(NA)	(NA)	(NA)	6	7	6	15	10	8
IL	20	17	16	467	270	274	1	(Z)	(Z)	1	1	(NA)
IN	3	2	3	73	39	47	(Z)	(Z)	(Z)	1	(Z)	(NA)
KS	59	47	44	1,359	687	709	574	713	721	893	1,139	961
KY	5	4	3	124	62	57	75	73	75	169	164	123
LA	148	126	123	3,409	1,973	2,096	5,242	5,170	5,106	9,587	10,728	8,071
MI	20	12	11	456	188	189	140	223	238	420	436	396
MS	30	20	20	630	271	294	95	63	96	167	95	118
MT	20	17	17	429	222	247	50	50	50	90	73	68
NE	5	4	4	119	57	58	1	3	2	2	5	3
NM	66	66	65	1,472	1,009	1,080	965	1,558	1,626	1,629	2,463	2,049
NY	(Z)	(Z)	(Z)	9	(NA)	(NA)	25	20	18	55	48	42
ND	39	28	29	849	388	457	52	58	49	93	(NA)	(NA)
OH	8	9	8	196	140	138	155	132	126	393	321	294
OK	117	91	87	2,690	1,395	1,459	2,258	1,935	1,812	3,546	3,290	2,609
PA	2	3	2	54	41	33	178	150	111	417	414	315
TX	674	591	560	15,060	8,849	9,167	6,343	6,354	6,330	9,939	11,965	10,191
UT	23	21	20	524	336	354	146	271	241	249	417	277
WV	2	2	2	43	30	32	178	182	186	568	460	413
WY	103	80	79	2,169	1,067	1,223	736	696	674	656	1,429	1,199

NA Not available. Z Less than 500 million cubic feet or less than $500,000. [1] Excludes nonhydrocarbon gases. [2] Includes other States not shown separately. State production does not include State offshore production.

Source: U.S. Energy Information Administration, *Energy Data Reports, Petroleum Supply Annual, Natural Gas Annual,* and *Natural Gas Monthly.*

No. 1165. Crude Oil, Natural Gas, and Natural Gas Liquids—Reserves by State: 1990 and 1995

[As of December 31. Proved reserves are estimated quantities of the mineral, which geological and engineering data demonstrate with reasonable certainty, to be recoverable in future years from known reservoirs under existing economic and operating conditions. Indicated reserves of crude oil are quantities other than proved reserves, which may become economically recoverable from existing productive reservoirs through the application of improved recovery techniques using current technology. Based on a sample of operators of oil and gas wells]

STATE	1990				1995			
	Crude oil		Natural gas (bil. cu. ft.)	Natural gas liquids (mil. bbl.)	Crude oil		Natural gas (bil. cu. ft.)	Natural gas liquids (mil. bbl.)
	Proved (mil. bbl.)	Indicated			Proved (mil. bbl.)	Indicated		
United States	26,254	3,483	169,346	7,586	22,351	2,669	165,146	7,399
Alabama	44	(1) [1]	4,125	170	43	-	4,668	120
Alaska	6,524	969	9,300	340	5,580	582	9,497	306
Arkansas	60	1	1,731	9	48	-	1,563	6
California	[2]4,658	[2]1,425	[2]3,185	[2]105	[2]3,462	[2]823	[2]2,243	[2]92
Colorado	305	8	4,555	169	252	24	7,256	273
Florida	42	-	46	8	71	-	92	17
Illinois	131	-	(NA)	(NA)	119	-	(NA)	(NA)
Indiana	12	-	(NA)	(NA)	13	-	(NA)	(NA)
Kansas	321	(1)	9,614	313	275	(1)	8,571	369
Kentucky	33	-	1,016	25	24	-	1,044	43
Louisiana	[2]705	[2]22	[2]11,728	[2]538	[2]637	[2]475	[2]9,274	[2]601
Michigan	124	3	1,243	81	76	1	1,294	45
Mississippi	227	8	1,126	11	140	6	663	8
Montana	221	-	899	15	178	-	782	8
Nebraska	26	-	(NA)	(NA)	25	-	(NA)	(NA)
New Mexico	687	256	17,260	990	732	185	17,491	943
New York	(NA)	(NA)	354	(NA)	(NA)	(NA)	197	(NA)
North Dakota	285	-	586	60	233	6	463	53
Ohio	65	-	1,214	(NA)	53	-	1,054	(NA)
Oklahoma	734	37	16,151	657	676	48	13,438	674
Pennsylvania	22	-	1,720	(NA)	11	-	1,482	(NA)
Texas	[2]7,106	618	[2]38,192	[2]2,575	[2]5,743	[2]395	[2]38,542	[2]2,524
Utah	249	44	1,510	(³)	216	50	1,580	(³)
Virginia	(NA)	(NA)	138	(NA)	(NA)	(NA)	1,836	(NA)
West Virginia	31	-	2,207	86	28	-	2,499	62
Wyoming	794	42	9,944	[4]812	605	12	12,166	[4]593
Federal offshore	2,805	49	31,433	619	3,069	62	29,182	655

- Represents or rounds to zero. NA Not available. [1] Includes state offshore. [2] Excludes Federal offshore. [3] Included with Wyoming. [4] Includes Utah.

Source: Energy Information Administration, *U.S. Crude Oil, Natural Gas, and Natural Gas Liquids Reserves, Annual Report 1995.*

No. 1166. World Crude Oil Production, by Major Producing Country: 1980 to 1996

[In thousands of barrels per day]

COUNTRY	1980	1985	1989	1990	1991	1992	1993	1994	1995
World, total [1]	**59,599**	**53,981**	**59,863**	**60,566**	60,207	60,216	**60,847**	**61,003**	**62,446**
Saudi Arabia	9,900	3,388	5,064	6,410	8,115	8,332	8,198	8,120	8,231
United States	8,597	8,971	7,613	7,355	7,417	7,171	6,847	6,662	6,560
Russia	(X)	(X)	(X)	(X)	(X)	7,632	6,730	6,135	5,995
Iran	1,662	2,250	2,810	3,088	3,312	3,429	3,540	3,618	3,643
China	2,114	2,505	2,757	2,774	2,835	2,845	2,890	2,939	2,990
Norway	(NA)	(NA)	1,554	1,704	1,890	2,230	2,350	2,521	2,768
Venezuela	2,168	1,677	1,907	2,137	2,375	2,371	2,450	2,588	2,750
Mexico	1,936	2,745	2,520	2,553	2,680	2,669	2,673	2,685	2,618
United Kingdom	1,622	2,530	1,802	1,820	1,797	1,825	1,915	2,375	2,489
United Arab Emirates	1,709	1,193	1,860	2,117	2,386	2,266	2,159	2,193	2,279
Kuwait	1,656	1,023	1,783	1,175	190	1,058	1,852	2,025	2,057
Nigeria	2,055	1,495	1,716	1,810	1,892	1,943	1,960	1,931	1,993
Canada	1,435	1,471	1,560	1,553	1,548	1,605	1,679	1,746	1,805
Indonesia	1,577	1,325	1,409	1,462	1,592	1,504	1,511	1,510	1,503
Libya	1,787	1,059	1,150	1,375	1,483	1,433	1,361	1,378	1,390
Algeria	1,106	1,037	1,095	1,175	1,230	1,214	1,162	1,180	1,202

NA Not available. X Not applicable. [1] Includes countries not shown separately.

Source: U. S. Energy Information Administration, *International Energy Annual, 1995.*

No. 1167. World Natural Gas Production, by Major Producing Country: 1980 to 1996

[In quadrillion Btu's]

COUNTRY	1980	1985	1989	1990	1991	1992	1993	1994	1995
World, total [1]	**52.58**	**61.42**	**71.49**	**72.53**	**73.29**	**73.70**	**75.17**	**75.81**	**77.42**
United States	19.91	16.96	17.85	18.36	18.23	18.38	18.58	19.27	19.23
Russia	(X)	(X)	(X)	(X)	(X)	20.60	19.87	19.41	19.01
Canada	2.80	3.08	3.85	3.90	4.12	4.60	4.99	5.45	5.80
United Kingdom	1.37	1.57	1.64	1.92	2.01	2.01	2.40	2.57	2.77
Netherlands	3.04	2.69	2.39	2.41	2.72	2.73	2.78	2.63	2.86
Indonesia	0.66	1.29	1.57	1.53	1.72	1.79	1.97	2.21	2.23
Algeria	0.44	1.44	1.81	1.90	2.05	2.09	2.02	1.92	2.18
Saudi Arabia	0.39	0.75	1.10	1.13	1.18	1.26	1.33	1.39	1.49
Iran	0.26	0.63	0.83	0.88	0.97	0.93	1.01	1.19	1.31
Norway	0.99	1.02	1.18	1.06	1.05	1.14	1.06	1.16	1.20
Mexico	0.97	0.92	0.94	0.96	1.14	1.13	1.10	1.11	1.15
Australia	0.34	0.49	0.59	0.76	0.79	0.87	0.92	0.98	1.13
Venezuela	0.56	0.70	0.88	0.91	0.95	0.91	0.97	1.04	1.11
United Arab Emirates	0.21	0.51	0.85	0.82	0.96	1.07	0.98	0.95	1.11
Malaysia	0.04	0.45	0.63	0.68	0.78	0.83	0.92	0.96	1.10

X Not applicable. [1] Includes other countries not shown separately.

Source: U. S. Energy Information Administration, *International Energy Annual, 1995.*

No. 1168. Liquefied Petroleum Gases—Summary: 1980 to 1995

[In millions of 42-gallon barrels. Includes ethane]

ITEM	1980	1985	1989	1990	1991	1992	1993	1994	1995
Production	561	622	654	638	683	720	850	734	760
At natural gas plants	441	479	452	456	488	500	634	511	521
At refineries	121	143	202	182	196	222	216	223	234
Imports	79	68	66	68	54	57	70	67	53
Refinery input	85	111	115	107	111	172	179	108	105
Exports	9	23	13	14	15	18	16	14	21
Stocks, Dec. 31	116	74	80	98	92	98	117	99	93

Source: U.S. Energy Information Administration, *Petroleum Supply Annual*

No. 1169. Natural Gas Plant Liquids—Production and Value: 1980 to 1995

[Barrels of 42 gallons]

ITEM	Unit	1980	1985	1989	1990	1991	1992	1993	1994	1995
Field production [1]	Mil. bbl	576	587	564	566	606	621	634	630	643
Pentanes plus	Mil. bbl	126	103	113	112	118	121	122	119	122
Liquefied petroleum gases	Mil. bbl	441	479	451	454	488	500	512	511	521
Natural gas processed	Tril. cu. ft.	15	13	13	15	16	16	16	(NA)	17

NA Not available. [1] Includes other finished petroleum products, not shown separately.

Source: U.S. Energy Information Administration, *Energy Data Reports, Petroleum Statement Annual, Petroleum Supply Annual,* and *Natural Gas Annual.*

No. 1170. Natural Gas—Supply, Consumption, Reserves, and Marketed Production: 1980 to 1996

ITEM	Unit	1980	1985	1989	1990	1991	1992	1993	1994	1995	1996
Producing wells (year-end)	1,000	182	243	262	269	276	276	282	292	299	(NA)
Production value at wells	Bil. dol.	32.1	43.4	30.6	31.8	30.3	32.6	38.8	36.5	30.3	44.9
Avg. per 1,000 cu. ft.	Dollars	1.59	2.51	1.69	1.71	1.64	1.74	2.04	1.85	1.55	2.25
Proved reserves [1]	Tril. cu. ft.	199	193	167	169	167	165	162	164	165	(NA)
Marketed production [2]	Tril. cu. ft.	20.2	17.3	18.1	18.6	18.5	18.7	19.1	19.7	19.5	20.0
Minus: Extraction losses [3]	Tril. cu. ft.	0.8	0.8	0.8	0.8	0.8	0.9	0.9	0.9	0.9	0.9
Equals: Dry production	Tril. cu. ft.	19.4	16.5	17.3	17.8	17.7	17.8	18.1	18.8	18.6	19.0
Plus: Withdrawals from storage	Tril. cu. ft.	2.0	2.4	2.9	2.0	2.8	2.8	2.8	2.6	3.0	(NA)
Plus: Imports [4]	Tril. cu. ft.	1.0	0.9	1.4	1.5	1.8	2.1	2.4	2.6	2.8	(NA)
Plus: Balancing item	Tril. cu. ft.	-0.6	-0.4	-0.2	-0.2	-0.5	-0.5	-0.1	-0.4	-0.2	(NA)
Equals: Total supply	Tril. cu. ft.	21.9	19.5	21.4	21.3	21.8	22.4	23.3	23.7	24.3	(NA)
Minus: Exports	Tril. cu. ft.	0.5	0.6	0.1	0.9	0.1	0.2	0.1	0.2	0.2	(NA)
Minus: Additions to storage [5]	Tril. cu. ft.	1.9	2.2	2.5	2.5	2.7	2.6	2.8	2.9	2.6	(NA)
Equals:											
Consumption, total	Tril. cu. ft.	19.9	17.3	18.8	18.7	19.0	19.5	20.3	20.7	21.6	21.9
Lease and plant fuel	Tril. cu. ft.	1.0	1.0	1.1	1.2	1.1	1.2	1.2	1.1	1.2	1.2
Pipeline fuel	Tril. cu. ft.	0.6	0.5	0.6	0.7	0.6	0.6	0.6	0.7	0.7	0.7
Residential	Tril. cu. ft.	4.8	4.4	4.8	4.4	4.6	4.7	5.0	4.8	4.9	5.2
Commercial [6]	Tril. cu. ft.	2.6	2.4	2.7	2.6	2.7	2.8	2.9	2.9	3.0	3.2
Industrial	Tril. cu. ft.	7.2	5.9	6.8	7.0	7.2	7.5	8.0	8.2	8.6	8.8
Vehicle fuel	Tril. cu. ft.	(NA)	(NA)	(NA)	(Z)	(Z)	(Z)	(Z)	(Z)	(Z)	(NA)
Electric utilities	Tril. cu. ft.	3.7	3.0	2.8	2.8	2.8	2.8	2.7	3.0	3.2	2.7
World production (dry)	Tril. cu. ft.	53.1	62.0	71.5	72.5	73.3	73.7	75.2	75.8	77.4	(NA)
U.S. production (dry)	Tril. cu. ft.	19.4	16.5	17.6	18.4	18.2	18.4	18.6	19.3	19.3	(NA)
Percent U.S. of world	Percent	36.5	26.4	24.6	25.3	24.9	24.9	24.7	25.4	25.0	(NA)

NA Not available. Z Less than .05 trillion cubic feet. [1] Estimated, end of year. Source: U.S. Energy Information Administration, *U.S. Crude Oil, Natural Gas, and Natural Gas Liquids Reserves, annual.* [2] Marketed production includes gross withdrawals from reservoirs less quantities used for reservoir repressuring and quantities vented or flared. For 1980 and thereafter, it excludes the nonhydrocarbon gases subsequently removed. [3] Volumetric reduction in natural gas resulting from the extraction of natural gas constituents at natural gas processing plants. [4] Includes imports of liquefied natural gas. [5] Includes liquefied natural gas (LNG) storage in above ground tanks. [6] Includes deliveries to municipalities and public authorities for institutional heating and other purposes.

Source: Except as noted, U.S. Energy Information Administration, *Annual Energy Review, International Energy Annual, Natural Gas Annual*, Volume I and II and *Monthly Energy Review.*

No. 1171. Natural Gas—Financial Performance Measure: 1985 to 1994

[LT = Long term. S&P = Standard & Poor's]

ITEM	1985	1987	1988	1989	1990	1991	1992	1993	1994
Producer segment, majors:									
Average adjusted stock price	28.24	37.01	41.64	51.79	49.20	50.01	48.50	57.50	(NA)
S&P bond rating	AA-	A	AA-	AA	AA	AA	AA	BBB-	BB+
LT debt as a percent of invested capital	32.06	28.33	30.54	30.35	27.76	29.19	30.10	42.15	40.40
Times interest earned ratio	5.09	3.76	4.42	4.32	5.07	4.04	3.93	2.25	2.55
Rate of return on common equity (percent)	14.30	10.64	17.67	18.56	17.78	12.54	9.05	7.30	6.72
Price/earnings ratio	7.35	11.69	9.11	10.65	9.98	15.15	15.14	23.53	33.63
Market/book value ratio	1.18	1.69	1.65	1.99	1.92	2.01	2.07	2.61	2.51
Producer segment, independents:									
Average adjusted stock price	14.66	12.33	12.84	17.34	15.14	12.01	11.93	14.53	(NA)
S&P bond rating	A-	BBB	BBB-	BBB-	BBB-	BBB-	BB+	BB+	BB+
LT debt as a percent of invested capital	47.39	61.13	73.47	68.00	63.00	55.87	53.93	45.01	45.64
Times interest earned ratio	0.36	0.52	0.91	1.59	1.46	1.21	1.46	1.83	1.04
Rate of return on common equity (percent)	-10.39	-7.85	-1.69	6.51	1.93	-1.17	1.99	5.14	0.61
Price/earnings ratio	6.78	15.70	17.96	16.45	23.75	31.28	21.50	26.46	35.71
Market/book value ratio	1.23	1.96	1.84	2.32	2.63	2.05	1.85	2.30	2.35
Pipeline segment, w/Columbia:									
Average adjusted stock price	19.68	17.96	20.52	27.84	23.76	20.10	23.49	26.26	(NA)
S&P bond rating	BBB-	BBB-	BBB	BBB	BBB	BBB-	BB+	BBB-	BBB
LT debt as a percent of invested capital	53.35	52.92	52.29	52.99	53.24	55.91	54.61	50.24	47.30
Times interest earned ratio	1.89	1.75	1.44	1.79	1.65	1.00	1.74	2.33	2.72
Rate of return on common equity (percent)	6.32	7.97	6.18	8.63	7.47	1.01	6.23	10.88	12.25
Price/earnings ratio	10.94	12.04	13.42	14.66	16.00	17.36	13.18	16.68	14.42
Market/book value ratio	1.11	1.31	1.28	1.51	1.55	1.52	1.53	1.86	1.77
Average adjusted stock price	17.69	18.84	18.66	23.29	21.21	20.53	22.78	26.06	(NA)
S&P bond rating	BBB+	A	A	A	A	A	A	A	A
LT debt as a percent of invested capital	44.21	44.27	47.30	46.31	47.28	48.62	48.83	46.62	47.93
Times interest earned ratio	2.81	3.01	2.51	2.49	2.04	1.95	2.42	2.88	2.92
Rate of return on common equity (percent)	8.55	12.19	10.35	12.35	9.17	7.17	4.09	10.95	11.45
Price/earnings ratio	8.42	11.96	10.16	12.01	12.69	15.15	14.38	14.83	13.02
Market/book value ratio	1.29	1.48	1.36	1.49	1.51	1.47	1.56	1.77	1.56

NA Not available.

Source: U.S. Energy Information Administration, *Natural Gas 1995: Issues and Trends.*

No. 1172. Coal and Coke—Summary: 1980 to 1996

[Includes coal consumed at mines. Demonstrated coal reserve base for United States on Jan. 1, 1992, was an estimated 476 billion tons. Recoverability varies between 40 and 90 percent for individual deposits; 50 percent or more of overall U.S. coal reserve base is believed to be recoverable]

ITEM	Unit	1980	1985	1990	1992	1993	1994	1995	1996, prel.
COAL									
Coal production, total [1]	Mil. sh. tons	830	884	1,029	996	945	1,034	1,033	1,057
Value	Mil. dol.	20,453	22,277	22,404	20,976	18,624	20,076	19,709	(NA)
Anthracite production	Mil. sh. tons	6.1	4.7	3.5	3.4	4.3	4.6	4.7	(NA)
Bituminous coal and lignite:									
Production	Mil. sh. tons	824	879	1,026	996	945	1,034	1,033	(NA)
Underground	Mil. sh. tons	337	350	425	407	351	399	396	(NA)
Surface	Mil. sh. tons	487	529	605	590	594	634	637	(NA)
Exports	Mil. sh. tons	92	93	106	103	75	71	89	90
Imports	Mil. sh. tons	1.2	2.0	2.7	3.8	7.3	7.6	7.2	7.1
Consumption [2]	Mil. sh. tons	703	818	896	892	926	930	941	963
Electric power utilities	Mil. sh. tons	569	694	774	800	814	817	829	(NA)
Industrial	Mil. sh. tons	126	116	76	74	75	75	73	(NA)
Number of mines	Number	5,598	4,547	3,243	2,134	2,326	2,209	1,905	(NA)
Daily employment	1,000	225	169	131	110	101	98	90	(NA)
Production, by State:									
Alabama	Mil. sh. tons	26	28	29	26	25	23	25	24
Illinois	Mil. sh. tons	63	59	60	60	41	53	48	46
Indiana	Mil. sh. tons	31	33	36	31	29	31	26	30
Kentucky	Mil. sh. tons	150	152	173	161	156	162	154	150
Montana	Mil. sh. tons	30	33	38	39	36	42	39	38
Ohio	Mil. sh. tons	39	36	35	30	29	30	26	29
Pennsylvania	Mil. sh. tons	93	71	71	69	60	62	62	68
Virginia	Mil. sh. tons	41	41	47	43	39	37	34	36
West Virginia	Mil. sh. tons	122	128	169	162	131	162	163	166
Wyoming	Mil. sh. tons	95	141	184	190	210	237	264	278
Other States	Mil. sh. tons	140	162	187	188	189	195	192	192
World production	Mil. sh. tons	4,103	4,779	5,356	5,030	4,958	5,041	5,091	(NA)
COKE									
Coke production [3]	Mil. sh. tons	46.10	28.40	27.60	23.40	22.20	22.69	23.75	23.08
Imports	Mil. sh. tons	0.66	0.58	0.77	1.74	1.53	1.61	1.82	1.11
Exports	Mil. sh. tons	2.07	1.12	0.57	0.64	0.84	0.86	0.75	1.12
Consumption	Mil. sh. tons	41.28	29.06	27.81	24.73	24.30	24.16	24.45	(NA)

NA Not available. [1] Includes bituminous coal, lignite, and anthracite. [2] Includes some categories not shown separately. [3] Includes beehive coke.

Source: U.S. Energy Information Administration, *Coal Industry*, annual; *Annual Energy Review*, and *Quarterly Coal Report*, and unpublished data.

No. 1173. World Coal Production, by Major Producing Country: 1986 to 1995

[In millions of short tons]

COUNTRY	1986	1987	1988	1989	1990	1991	1992	1993	1994	1995
World, total	**5,022.3**	**5,131.3**	**5,235.4**	**5,324.2**	**5,356.3**	**5,033.3**	**5,030.4**	**4,958.2**	**5,040.5**	**5,090.9**
Canada	63.7	67.5	77.9	77.7	75.4	78.4	72.3	76.1	80.3	82.6
United States	**890.3**	**918.8**	**950.3**	**980.7**	**1,029.1**	**996.0**	**997.5**	**945.4**	**1,033.5**	**1,033.0**
Germany	(X)	(X)	(X)	(X)	(X)	388.4	346.1	315.2	291.8	274.2
Greece	42.0	49.2	53.3	57.2	57.2	58.1	60.7	60.4	62.5	64.1
Spain	52.4	47.3	45.1	48.4	39.6	37.0	36.9	34.8	32.7	31.5
Turkey	51.0	51.6	43.2	57.6	52.3	50.8	56.7	53.5	59.9	59.7
United Kingdom	119.2	115.1	114.8	111.4	106.0	106.6	94.9	76.3	54.0	52.4
Serbia and Montenegro	(X)	(X)	(X)	(X)	(X)	(X)	46.9	40.9	40.6	44.4
Czech Republic	(X)	(X)	(X)	(X)	(X)	(X)	(X)	77.2	82.1	78.6
Poland	285.9	293.4	293.8	275.0	237.3	231.2	218.8	218.9	220.9	217.7
Romania	52.4	56.8	64.8	68.5	42.1	35.7	42.2	42.8	45.3	43.9
Kazakstan	(X)	(X)	(X)	(X)	(X)	(X)	139.4	123.5	115.1	91.7
Russia	(X)	(X)	(X)	(X)	(X)	(X)	405.9	364.0	320.3	310.0
Ukraine	(X)	(X)	(X)	(X)	(X)	(X)	147.3	127.6	104.2	91.4
South Africa	194.8	194.6	199.9	194.5	193.2	196.4	191.9	203.0	215.8	227.3
Australia	186.8	208.9	196.4	216.1	225.8	235.9	249.0	247.6	249.2	268.0
China	985.5	1,022.9	1,060.1	1,161.9	1,190.4	1,198.7	1,230.6	1,330.5	1,410.4	1,478.1
India	207.4	208.6	214.5	221.4	233.4	252.7	262.6	290.1	295.6	311.1
Indonesia	3.1	3.6	4.6	9.2	11.9	15.1	23.3	30.4	32.5	41.5
Korea, North	60.6	62.3	66.1	69.1	71.3	72.8	73.9	77.7	77.7	78.1

X Not applicable.

Source: U.S. Energy Information Administration, *International Energy Annual*.

No. 1174. Demonstrated Coal Reserves, by Type of Coal and Major Producing State: 1995

[In millions of short tons. As of January 1. The demonstrated reserve base represents the sum of coal in both measured and indicated resource categories of reliability. Measured resources of coal are estimates that have a high degree of geologic assurance from sample analyses and measurements from closely spaced and geological well known sample sites. Indicated resources are estimates based partly from sample and analyses and measurements and partly from reasonable geologic projections. For more information on the classification of coal resources and related terminology, see report cited below]

STATE	Total reserves	TYPE OF COAL				METHOD OF MINING	
		Anthracite	Bituminous	Subbituminous	Lignite	Underground	Surface
United States	**495,665**	**7,483**	**257,780**	**185,950**	**44,453**	**328,552**	**167,113**
Alabama	4,635	-	3,552	-	1,083	1,362	3,273
Alaska	6,130	-	698	5,418	14	5,423	707
Colorado	16,844	26	8,777	3,852	4,190	12,049	4,795
Illinois	89,956	-	89,956	-	-	73,781	16,175
Indiana	9,991	-	9,991	-	-	8,873	1,118
Iowa	2,190	-	2,190	-	-	1,733	457
Kentucky	32,565	-	32,565	-	-	18,885	13,680
Kentucky, Eastern	12,485	-	12,485	-	-	2,525	9,960
Kentucky, Western	20,080	-	20,080	-	-	16,360	3,720
Missouri	5,996	-	5,996	-	-	1,479	4,517
Montana	119,773	-	1,385	102,627	15,761	70,959	48,815
New Mexico	12,547	2	3,741	8,804	-	6,205	6,341
North Dakota	9,470	-	-	-	9,470	-	9,470
Ohio	23,754	-	23,754	-	-	17,847	5,907
Oklahoma	1,580	-	1,580	-	-	1,237	342
Pennsylvania	28,868	7,225	21,643	-	-	24,408	4,460
Anthracite	7,225	7,225	-	-	-	3,850	3,375
Bituminous	21,643	-	21,643	-	-	20,558	1,085
Texas	13,065	-	-	-	13,065	-	13,065
Utah	5,956	-	5,955	1	-	5,688	268
Virginia	2,327	126	2,202	-	-	1,630	697
Washington	1,401	-	304	1,089	8	1,332	69
West Virginia	35,983	-	35,983	-	-	31,420	4,564
Wyoming	68,496	-	4,354	64,141	-	42,525	25,971
East of the MS River	229,779	7,351	221,346	-	1,083	179,529	50,250
West of the MS River	265,886	132	36,434	185,950	43,370	149,023	116,863

- Represents or rounds to zero.

Source: U.S. Energy Information Administration, *U.S. Coal Reserves: A Review and Update*, August 1996.

No. 1175. Uranium Concentrate (U_3O_8) Industry—Summary: 1980 to 1995

[Middle demand case. See table 951]

ITEM	Unit	1980	1985	1988	1990	1991	1992	1993	1994	1995
Production	1,000 sh. tons	21.9	5.7	6.9	4.4	4.0	2.8	1.5	1.7	3.0
Net imports (U_3O_8)	1,000 sh. tons	-1.1	3.2	5.5	10.9	6.4	10.3	9.0	9.5	15.8
Utility and Suppliers inventories (U_3O_8 equivalent)	1,000 sh. tons	(NA)	[1]88.5	[1]69.1	[1]64.6	[1]59.4	[1]58.7	[1]52.9	[1]43.4	[1]35.1
Price (1992 dol./lb. U_3O_8):										
Long-term contract price	Dollars	48.62	28.88	(NA)	(NA)	(NA)	(NA)	(NA)	11.55	11.69
Spot market price	Dollars	52.63	19.90	11.15	10.43	8.94	7.95	9.73	[2]8.87	[2]10.66
Delivered price	Dollars	46.61	[3]40.09	[3]21.81	16.77	14.04	13.45	12.81	9.81	10.47
Capital expenditures (1992 dollars)	Mil. dol.	1306	50	87	86	68	52	(NA)	(NA)	(NA)
Employment	1,000 person years	19.9	2.4	1.6	1.3	1.0	0.7	0.9	[4]1.0	[4]1.1

NA Not available. [1] Includes natural U_3O_8 (uranium oxide), natural UF_6 (uranium hexafluoride), natural UF_6 under usage agreement, UF_6 at enrichment suppliers, enriched UF_6 and fabricated fuel. [2] Tradetech's restricted exchange value. [3] Average U.S. contract prices and market price settlements. [4] Includes reclamation activities (491 person years in 1993, 528 person years in 1994, and 573 person years in 1995).

Source: U.S. Department of Energy, *Domestic Uranium Mining and Milling Industry*, annual, and *Uranium Industry*, annual.

Figure 25.1
Single-Family Houses Sold and Sales Price: 1970 to 1996

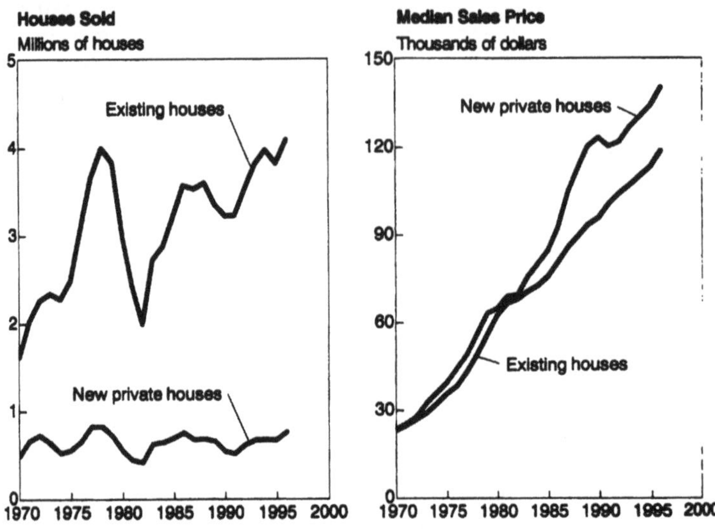

Source: Chart prepared by U.S. Bureau of the Census. For data, see tables 1188, 1189, and 1191.

Figure 25.2
Commercial Office Space—Ten Highest Vacancy Rates for Market Areas: 1996

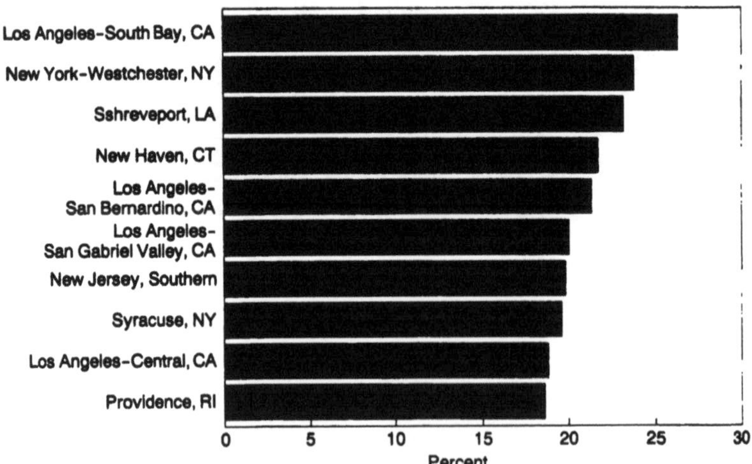

Source: Chart prepared by U.S. Bureau of the Census. For data, see table 1213.

Section 25

Construction and Housing

ı presents data on the ı industry and on various indi- activity and costs; on housing eir characteristics and occu- ɔn the characteristics and es for commercial buildings. ew data from the 1995 Ameri- ɟ Survey and the Property ł Managers Survey.

ıl source of these data is the ı of the Census, which issues a ırrent publications. Construction mpiled by the Bureau appear in *Current Construction Reports* /arious quarterly or annual s; *Housing Starts* and *Housing* ; present data by type of struc- four major census regions; *amily Houses Sold and For* rovides statistics annually on ɟ financial characteristics for sing by the four major census *ɔe Index of New One-Family d* presents quarterly figures regional data; and *Housing rized by Building Permits* cov- nately 19,000 permit-issuing in the United States (prior ,000 places). Statistics on ex- ɔy owners of residential proper- ıed quarterly and annually in *s for Residential Upkeep and ıts. Value of New Construction* ı presents data on all types of ı and includes monthly com- indexes. Reports of the cen- nstruction industries (see also issued on various topics.

us Bureau publications include *Housing Reports* series, which he quarterly *Housing Vacan-* arterly *Market Absorption of* , the American Housing Survey ınual Housing Survey) and re- censuses of housing and of ı industries. *Construction Re-* hed quarterly by the Interna- ı Administration, U.S. Depart- mmerce, contains many of the es and other construction sta- ; from the Federal Government agencies.

In Brief

Value of new construction in constant (1992) dollars reached $496 billion in 1996, its highest level since 1988.

Sales of existing one-family homes increased 7.2% between 1995 and 1996 to just under 4.1 million units.

In 1995, there were 63.5 million owner-occupied housing units. Of these, 61.2% were mortgaged.

Other sources include the monthly *Dodge Construction Potentials* of F. W. Dodge Division, McGraw-Hill Information Systems Company, New York, NY, which presents national and State data on construction contracts; the National Association of Home Builders with-State-level data on housing starts; the NATIONAL ASSOCIATION OF REAL-TORS, which presents data on existing home sales; the Society of Industrial and Office Realtors and Oncor International on commercial 2nd industrial office space; and the U.S. Energy Information Administration, which provides data on commercial buildings through its periodic sample surveys.

Censuses and surveys—Censuses of the construction industry were first conducted by the Bureau of the Census for 1929, 1935, and 1939; beginning in 1967, a census has been taken every five years (for years ending in "2" and "7"). The latest reports are for 1992.

The 1992 Census of Construction Industries, in accordance with the 1987 *Standard Industrial Classification Manual* (see text, section 13), covers all employer establishments primarily engaged in (1) building construction by general contractors or operative builders; (2) heavy (nonbuilding) construction by general contractors; and (3) construction by special trade contractors.

From 1850 through 1930, the Bureau of the Census collected some housing data as part of its censuses of population and agriculture. Beginning in 1940, separate censuses of housing have been taken at 10-year intervals. For the 1970 and 1980 censuses, data on year-round housing units were collected and issued on occupancy and structural characteristics, plumbing facilities, value, and rent; for 1990 such characteristics were presented for all housing units.

The American Housing Survey (*Current Housing Reports* series H-150 and H-170), which began in 1973, provided an annual and ongoing series of data on selected housing and demographic characteristics until 1983. In 1984 the name of the survey was changed from the Annual Housing Survey. It is currently based on a biennial national sample and on 11 annual MSA samples. All samples represent a cross section of the housing stock in their respective areas. Estimates are subject to both sampling and nonsampling errors; caution should therefore, be used in making comparisons with 1970 and 1980 census data.

Data on residential mortgages were collected continuously from 1890 to 1970, except 1930, as part of the decennial census by the Bureau of the Census. Since 1973, mortgage status data, limited to single family homes on less than ten acres with no business on the property, have been presented in the American Housing Survey. Data on mortgage activity are covered in section 16.

Housing units—In general, a housing unit is a group of rooms or a single room occupied or intended for occupancy as separate living quarters; that is, the occupants do not live and eat with any other persons in the structure and there is direct access from the outside or through a common hall. Transient accommodations, barracks for workers, and institutional-type quarters are not counted as housing units.

Statistical reliability—For a discussion of statistical collection and estimation, sampling procedures, and measures of statistical reliability applicable to Census Bureau data, see Appendix III.

No. 1176. Construction Industries—Summary, by Industry: 1992

[Based on a probability sample of about 167,000 construction establishments with payroll in 1992; see Appendix III. N.e.c.= Not elsewhere classified]

INDUSTRY	1987 SIC[1] code	Establishments with payroll (1,000)	EMPLOYEES (1,000)		PAYROLL (mil. dol.)		VALUE OF CONSTRUCTION WORK (mil. dol.)		Value added[3] (mil. dol.)
			Total	Construction workers	Total	Construction workers	Total	Net[2]	
All industries, total	(X)	572.9	4,656	3,596	117,730	83,048	528,106	391,190	234,616
General building contractors	15	168.4	1,097	759	27,078	16,125	215,629	114,722	63,117
Single-family houses	1521	107.5	404	296	7,278	4,869	48,633	33,660	17,183
Other residential buildings	1522	6.5	49	35	1,161	718	7,835	4,338	2,454
Operative builders	1531	17.0	114	50	3,359	1,045	44,586	26,843	15,289
Industrial buildings and warehouses	1541	7.7	123	92	3,476	2,310	20,586	10,967	6,438
Nonresidential buildings, n.e.c	1542	29.7	407	286	11,804	7,183	93,967	38,913	21,754
Heavy construction contractors	16	37.2	799	647	23,728	17,622	96,571	77,526	49,165
Highway and street construction	1611	10.1	257	211	7,358	5,457	35,332	27,863	15,711
Bridge, tunnel, and elevated highway	1622	1.0	44	36	1,485	1,125	7,198	5,316	3,078
Water, sewer, and utility lines	1623	10.2	194	160	5,624	4,252	20,205	17,587	11,734
Heavy construction, n.e.c	1629	15.8	304	240	9,261	6,788	32,837	26,760	18,642
Special trade contractors	17	367.3	2,772	2,190	66,924	49,302	216,905	198,942	122,336
Plumbing, heating, air-conditioning	1711	75.4	613	455	16,613	11,781	56,902	50,756	29,432
Painting and paperhanging	1721	32.0	163	136	3,164	2,470	8,690	8,095	5,855
Electrical work	1731	54.0	487	379	13,624	10,039	40,259	38,541	23,548
Masonry and other stonework	1741	22.6	148	130	2,883	2,366	8,458	7,956	5,146
Plastering, drywall, insulation	1742	18.6	207	173	4,910	3,826	14,056	12,824	8,143
Terrazzo, tile, marble, and mosaic work	1743	6.5	34	27	775	568	2,439	2,323	1,358
Carpentry	1751	38.2	178	145	3,489	2,683	12,852	11,334	6,760
Floorlaying and other floor work	1752	10.2	49	36	1,065	724	4,428	4,032	2,166
Roofing, siding, and sheet metal work	1761	27.6	216	169	4,623	3,230	16,788	15,590	8,906
Concrete work	1771	26.1	193	161	4,038	3,093	14,423	13,179	7,703
Water well drilling	1781	3.6	19	15	444	323	1,727	1,676	995
Structural steel erection	1791	3.8	58	47	1,629	1,227	4,952	4,487	3,021
Glass and glazing work	1793	4.6	32	21	796	495	2,724	2,634	1,424
Excavation work	1794	13.9	77	62	1,817	1,401	6,870	6,129	4,340
Wrecking and demolition work	1795	1.0	13	10	296	215	1,059	928	775
Installing building equipment, n.e.c	1796	3.9	83	64	2,324	1,742	6,611	6,132	4,494
Special trade contractors, n.e.c.	1799	25.3	204	157	4,435	3,120	13,667	12,325	8,270

X Not applicable. [1] Based on the 1987 Standard Industrial Classification code; see text, section. 13. [2] Value of construction work less payments for construction work subcontracted to others, not shown separately. [3] Dollar value of business done less (a) payments for materials, components, and supplies, and (b) payments for construction work subcontracted to others.

Source: U.S. Bureau of the Census, *Census of Construction Industries, 1992*, series CC92-I-1(P) through CC92-I-27(P).

No. 1177. Construction Materials—Producer Price Indexes: 1980 to 1996

[1982=100, except as noted. For discussion of producer price index, see text, section 15. This index, more formally known as the special commodity grouping index for construction materials, covers materials incorporated as integral part of a building or normally installed during construction and not readily removable. Excludes consumer durables such as kitchen ranges, refrigerators, etc. This index is not the same as as the stage-of-processing index of intermediate materials and components for construction]

COMMODITY	1980	1985	1989	1990	1991	1992	1993	1994	1995	1996[1]
Construction materials	**92.5**	**107.6**	**119.5**	**119.6**	**120.4**	**122.5**	**128.6**	**133.8**	**138.8**	**139.6**
Interior solvent based paint	91.3	107.3	128.8	133.0	140.2	141.7	142.9	148.1	164.5	175.6
Plastic construction products	103.9	108.6	120.1	117.2	115.1	112.7	116.6	122.9	133.8	130.7
Douglas fir, dressed	132.6	126.5	151.6	138.4	139.6	169.5	237.6	236.2	198.8	229.3
Southern pine, dressed	104.0	105.2	108.0	111.2	111.0	130.6	168.8	182.6	166.9	177.7
Millwork	93.2	111.7	127.3	130.4	135.5	143.3	156.6	162.4	163.8	166.6
Softwood plywood	109.5	107.4	124.2	119.6	120.8	147.2	169.7	176.8	188.1	174.0
Hardwood plywood and related products	97.5	89.9	99.8	102.7	102.8	106.9	115.4	122.3	122.2	125.0
Softwood plywood veneer, ex. reinforced/backed	126.0	100.1	142.1	142.3	138.5	168.3	216.0	207.8	203.5	189.5
Building paper and building board mill products	86.1	107.4	115.6	112.2	111.8	119.6	132.9	144.1	144.9	137.2
Builders hardware	84.9	113.5	127.8	133.0	138.1	141.4	144.9	148.0	153.2	156.5
Plumbing fixtures and brass fittings	88.5	111.9	137.7	144.3	149.7	153.1	155.9	159.6	166.0	171.1
Heating equipment	87.0	109.5	125.1	131.6	134.1	137.3	140.4	142.5	147.5	151.2
Metal doors, sash, and trim	87.8	107.3	130.0	131.4	134.6	135.0	136.6	142.0	156.5	159.3
Siding, aluminum[2]	(NA)	110.1	(NA)	(NA)	(NA)	116.7	117.2	119.3	132.4	(NA)
Incandescent outdoor lighting fixtures	82.7	109.2	128.0	137.3	136.5	139.1	138.5	141.5	151.8	152.9
Bright nails	90.9	100.2	110.4	(NA)	(NA)	115.1	115.9	118.0	119.8	119.5
Welded steel wire fabric for concrete reinforcing	98.9	101.3	108.6	109.7	100.0	101.3	104.5	108.7	109.0	108.8
Elevators, escalators, and other lifts	87.3	97.7	107.1	110.1	108.7	109.4	110.7	112.4	113.0	113.7
Stamped metal outlet box	82.7	119.7	171.7	179.4	179.7	187.2	195.7	179.1	183.5	186.3
Concrete ingredients and related products	88.4	108.5	113.2	115.3	118.4	119.4	123.4	128.7	134.7	138.7
Concrete products	92.0	107.5	111.2	113.5	116.6	117.2	120.2	124.6	129.4	133.3
Clay construction products exc. refractories	88.8	113.5	127.0	129.9	130.2	132.0	135.1	138.3	141.3	142.4
Prep. asphalt and tar roofing and siding products	105.5	100.5	95.6	95.8	96.2	94.3	94.9	92.9	97.8	97.5
Gypsum products	100.1	132.3	110.0	105.2	99.3	99.9	108.3	136.1	154.5	154.2
Insulation materials	80.7	105.2	106.7	108.4	110.8	102.3	105.8	111.9	118.8	119.0
Paving mixtures and blocks	83.7	111.6	101.0	101.2	103.2	100.2	102.0	103.2	105.8	107.6

NA Not available. [1] Preliminary. [2] December 1982=100.

Source: U.S. Bureau of Labor Statistics, *Producer Price Indexes*, monthly and annual.

No. 1178. Price and Cost Indexes for Construction: 1980 to 1996

[1992=100. Excludes Alaska and Hawaii. Indexes of certain of these sources are published on bases different from those shown here]

NAME OF INDEX	1980	1985	1990	1991	1992	1993	1994	1995	1996
Bureau of the Census:									
Composite fixed-weighted [1]	68.6	82.9	98.5	99.3	100.0	103.7	108.0	112.4	114.4
Implicit price deflator [2]	67.8	81.8	97.8	98.7	100.0	103.8	108.1	112.4	114.6
Bureau of the Census houses under construction: [3]									
Fixed-weighted	67.6	81.4	98.6	98.9	100.0	104.9	109.7	114.3	115.5
Price deflator	66.4	79.6	97.2	98.0	100.0	104.8	109.5	114.0	115.5
Federal Highway Administration, composite [4]	92.5	97.1	103.2	102.3	100.0	103.0	109.5	116.2	116.0
Bureau of Reclamation composite [5]	70	84	96	99	100	103	108	110	112
Turner Construction Co.: Building construction [6]	61	83	98	100	100	102	105	109	112
E. H. Boeckh, building cost index: [7]									
Residences	(NA)	82.4	94.2	96.8	100.0	103.9	107.4	111.0	112.9
Apartments, hotels, and office buildings	(NA)	83.8	94.9	97.5	100.0	102.8	105.6	109.0	111.1
Commercial and factory buildings	(NA)	82.3	94.4	97.3	100.0	102.6	105.7	108.3	110.7
Engineering News-Record: [8]									
Buildings	68.5	85.7	95.4	97.1	100.0	105.7	109.8	109.8	112.9
Construction	64.9	84.2	94.9	97.0	100.0	104.5	108.5	109.8	112.7
Handy-Whitman public utility: [9]									
Buildings	78	90	101	98	100	105	112	115	118
Electric [10]	68	83	97	99	100	103	107	111	112
Gas	67	85	96	98	100	103	109	111	112
Water [11]	73	88	98	98	100	104	109	112	114
C. A. Turner Telephone Plant [12]	90	89	99	100	100	102	103	109	114

NA Not available. [1] Weighted average of the various indexes used to deflate the Construction Put in Place series. In calculating the index, the weights (i.e., the composition of current dollar estimates in 1992 by category) are held constant. [2] Derived ratio of total current to constant dollar Construction Put in Place (multiplied by 100). [3] Excludes value of site. [4] Based on average contract unit bid prices for composite mile (involving specific average amounts of excavation, paving, reinforcing steel, structural steel, and structural concrete). [5] Derived from the four quarterly indexes which are weighted averages of costs of labor, materials, and equipment for the construction of dams and reclamation projects. [6] Based on firm's cost experience with respect to labor rates, materials prices, competitive conditions, efficiency of plant and management, and productivity. [7] Average of 20 cities for types shown. Weights based on surveys of building costs. Wage rates used for both common and skilled labor. [8] Building construction index computed on the basis of a hypothetical unit of construction requiring 6 bbl. of portland cement, 1,088 M bd. ft. of 2" x 4" lumber, 2,500 lb. of structural steel, and 68.38 hours of skilled labor. General construction index based on same materials components combined with 200 hours of common labor. [9] Based on data covering public utility construction costs in six geographic regions. Covers skilled and common labor. [10] As derived by U.S. Bureau of the Census. Covers steam generation plants only. [11] As derived by U.S. Bureau of the Census. Reflects costs for structures and improvements at water pumping and treatment plants. [12] Computed by the Census Bureau by averaging the weighted component indexes published for six geographic regions.

Source: U.S. Bureau of the Census. In U.S. Department of Commerce, International Trade Administration, *Construction Review*, quarterly.

No. 1179. Value of New Construction Put in Place: 1964 to 1996

[In millions of dollars. Represents value of construction put in place during year; differs from building permit and construction contract data in timing and coverage. Includes installed cost of normal building service equipment and selected types of industrial production equipment (largely site fabricated). Excludes cost of shipbuilding, land, and most types of machinery and equipment. For methodology, see Appendix III]

YEAR	CURRENT DOLLARS					CURRENT (1992) DOLLARS				
	Total	Private			Public	Total	Private			Public
		Total [1]	Residential buildings	Nonresidential buildings			Total [1]	Residential buildings	Nonresidential buildings	
1964	75,097	54,893	30,526	17,385	20,203	351,300	259,680	145,486	84,232	91,620
1970	105,890	77,982	35,863	28,171	27,908	372,274	279,212	133,133	100,780	93,062
1975	152,635	109,342	51,581	35,409	43,293	351,973	259,048	128,254	84,282	92,925
1976	172,132	128,153	68,273	34,628	43,980	378,691	288,446	159,545	79,058	90,245
1977	200,501	157,418	92,004	38,245	43,083	408,528	324,777	193,479	81,170	83,751
1978	239,867	189,721	109,838	48,824	50,146	439,075	350,182	203,568	93,436	88,893
1979	272,873	216,228	116,444	64,765	56,646	446,503	357,949	192,873	111,235	88,554
1980	273,936	210,290	100,381	72,480	63,646	403,900	315,821	150,943	112,874	88,079
1981	289,070	224,378	99,241	85,569	64,691	396,267	313,358	139,656	122,748	82,910
1982	279,332	216,268	84,676	92,690	63,064	369,135	290,057	115,525	126,705	79,077
1983	311,576	248,126	125,521	87,069	63,450	403,929	324,785	166,981	114,716	79,144
1984	369,025	298,787	153,849	107,680	70,238	463,057	377,445	197,126	135,650	85,612
1985	401,370	323,555	158,474	127,466	77,815	490,943	399,530	199,105	156,349	91,413
1986	429,924	345,342	187,148	120,917	84,582	507,275	411,174	224,557	143,070	96,101
1987	441,647	350,999	194,656	123,247	90,648	502,468	401,642	223,516	140,110	100,826
1988	455,618	360,883	198,101	130,854	94,735	499,621	397,693	218,972	143,467	101,928
1989	469,797	371,623	196,551	139,953	98,174	495,387	393,262	206,748	147,825	102,124
1990	468,532	361,054	182,856	143,506	107,478	479,016	370,102	188,045	146,661	108,914
1991	424,176	314,067	157,836	116,570	110,109	429,592	319,248	160,989	118,266	110,345
1992	452,086	336,239	187,819	105,646	115,847	451,998	336,126	187,687	105,615	115,872
1993	482,737	362,587	210,455	110,635	120,150	464,985	347,754	200,502	106,729	117,231
1994	527,063	400,008	238,874	120,285	127,055	487,644	367,898	217,996	111,416	119,747
1995	547,079	410,196	236,597	133,949	136,883	486,666	363,086	207,392	119,835	123,579
1996, prel.	568,908	427,776	246,899	140,692	141,132	496,299	372,453	213,619	123,361	123,846

[1] Includes other types of private construction, not shown separately.

Source: U.S. Bureau of the Census, *Current Construction Reports*, series C30, *Value of New Construction*, monthly.

No. 1180. Value of New Construction Put in Place: 1990 to 1996

[In millions of dollars. Represents value of construction put in place during year; differs from building permit and construction contract data in timing and coverage. Includes installed cost of normal building service equipment and selected types of industrial production equipment (largely site fabricated). Excludes cost of shipbuilding, land, and most types of machinery and equipment. For methodology, see Appendix III]

TYPE OF CONSTRUCTION	CURRENT DOLLARS					CONSTANT (1992) DOLLARS				
	1990	1993	1994	1995	1996, prel.[1]	1990	1993	1994	1995	1996, prel.[1]
Total new construction	468,532	482,737	527,063	547,079	568,908	479,016	464,985	487,644	486,658	496,299
Private construction	361,054	362,587	400,008	410,196	427,776	370,102	347,754	367,896	363,086	372,453
Residential buildings	182,856	210,455	238,874	238,597	246,899	188,045	200,502	217,996	207,392	213,619
New housing units	127,987	144,071	167,919	162,898	176,378	131,632	137,243	153,250	142,790	152,606
1 unit	108,737	133,282	153,838	145,009	156,510	111,832	126,960	140,416	127,108	135,411
2 or more units	19,250	10,788	14,081	17,889	19,868	19,800	10,283	12,833	15,682	17,196
Improvements	54,869	66,384	70,955	73,699	(NA)	56,414	63,259	64,746	64,601	(NA)
Nonresidential buildings	143,506	110,635	120,285	133,949	140,692	146,661	106,729	111,416	119,835	123,361
Industrial	33,636	26,482	28,947	32,301	30,068	34,373	25,554	26,803	28,902	26,372
Office	35,055	20,920	22,178	25,254	25,191	35,838	20,197	20,553	22,603	22,063
Hotels, motels	10,679	4,565	4,648	7,201	11,147	10,917	4,405	4,308	6,438	9,775
Other commercial	40,047	32,453	37,551	42,272	44,966	40,922	31,292	34,756	37,809	39,423
Religious	3,566	3,887	3,869	4,318	4,490	3,642	3,748	3,584	3,862	3,936
Educational	4,616	4,649	4,822	5,493	6,211	4,715	4,484	4,471	4,915	5,442
Hospital and institutional	10,868	12,492	12,268	11,173	11,346	11,103	12,050	11,377	9,996	9,949
Miscellaneous [2]	5,040	5,188	6,002	5,937	7,273	5,151	5,000	5,565	5,309	6,379
Farm nonresidential	2,801	3,291	3,246	3,473	(NA)	2,862	3,174	3,007	3,107	(NA)
Public utilities	28,933	34,925	34,713	33,348	(NA)	29,537	34,120	32,717	30,169	(NA)
Telecommunications	9,803	9,619	10,157	10,747	11,162	9,891	9,468	9,875	9,796	9,781
Other public utilities	19,130	25,306	24,556	22,601	(NA)	19,646	24,652	22,842	20,372	(NA)
Railroads	2,600	3,108	3,340	3,341	(NA)	2,633	3,056	3,188	3,046	(NA)
Electric light and power	11,299	15,567	14,918	13,126	(NA)	11,572	15,096	13,877	11,825	(NA)
Gas	4,820	5,645	5,300	5,205	(NA)	5,013	5,536	4,861	4,667	(NA)
Petroleum pipelines	411	986	998	929	(NA)	428	965	918	834	(NA)
All other private [3]	2,957	3,281	2,890	2,829	2,458	2,997	3,229	2,763	2,583	2,170
Public construction	107,478	120,150	127,055	136,883	141,132	108,914	117,231	119,747	123,579	123,846
Buildings	43,615	52,071	53,930	59,783	63,418	44,583	50,167	49,882	53,373	55,841
Housing and redevelopment	3,808	4,855	5,247	6,156	5,417	3,914	4,629	4,788	5,397	4,688
Industrial	1,434	1,718	1,465	1,510	1,414	1,465	1,658	1,358	1,351	1,241
Educational	16,055	22,103	23,457	25,608	28,185	16,398	21,314	21,731	22,905	24,709
Hospital	2,860	3,666	3,940	4,345	4,674	2,924	3,537	3,652	3,888	4,100
Other [4]	19,458	19,730	19,821	22,164	23,729	19,882	19,029	18,353	19,832	20,803
Highways and streets	32,105	34,341	37,671	38,159	39,408	31,777	34,205	36,463	34,931	34,480
Military facilities	2,665	2,453	2,318	3,002	2,878	2,683	2,405	2,196	2,721	2,529
Conservation and development	4,686	5,909	6,370	6,389	5,753	4,870	5,745	6,002	5,798	5,109
Sewer systems	10,276	9,354	10,061	10,869	11,256	10,670	9,095	9,499	9,859	9,993
Water supply facilities	4,909	5,373	5,388	6,065	6,421	4,987	5,143	4,911	5,407	5,602
Miscellaneous public [5]	9,223	10,649	11,298	12,597	12,000	9,344	10,470	10,793	11,491	10,592

NA Not available. [1] Includes estimates for types of construction indicated as (NA). [2] Includes amusement and recreational buildings, bus and airline terminals, animal hospitals and shelters, etc. [3] Includes privately owned streets and bridges, parking areas, sewer and water facilities, parks and playgrounds, golf courses, airfields, etc. [4] Includes federal administrative buildings, prisons, police and fire stations, courthouses, civic centers, passenger terminals, space facilities, postal facilities, etc. [5] Includes open amusement and recreational facilities, power generating facilities, transit systems, airfields, open parking facilities, etc.

Source: U.S. Bureau of the Census, *Current Construction Reports*, series C30, *Value of New Construction*, monthly.

No. 1181. Value of Privately Owned Nonresidential Building Projects, by Construction Status, 1987 to 1995, and by Type of Project, 1995

[In billions of dollars. Series discontinued]

CONSTRUCTION STATUS	1987	1988	1989	1990	1991	1992	1993	1994	1995				
									Total	Industrial	Office building	Other commercial	Other [1]
Value of projects—													
Started	95.7	107.7	109.9	89.5	72.9	81.3	81.3	98.7	113.2	19.5	19.8	40.0	33.9
Completed	91.4	101.6	107.7	114.0	109.5	100.1	94.8	104.7	102.5	23.4	18.1	32.7	28.4

[1] Privately owned hotels and motels, religious, educational, hospital and institutional, and miscellaneous nonresidential building projects.

Source: U.S. Bureau of the Census, *Current Construction Reports*, series C30, *Value of New Construction*, monthly.

No. 1182. Construction Contracts—Value of Construction and Floor Space of Buildings, by Class of Construction: 1980 to 1996

[Building construction includes new structures and additions; nonbuilding construction; and major alterations to existing structures which affect only valuation, since no additional floor area is created by "alteration"]

YEAR	Total	Residential buildings	NONRESIDENTIAL BUILDINGS: Total	Commercial [1]	Manufacturing	Educational [2]	Hospital	Public buildings	Religious	Social and recreational	Miscellaneous	Nonbuilding construction
VALUE (bil. dol.)												
1980	151.8	60.4	56.9	27.7	9.2	7.4	5.4	1.6	1.2	2.7	1.7	34.5
1985	235.6	102.1	92.1	54.6	8.1	10.0	7.8	3.1	2.0	4.0	2.5	41.4
1986	249.3	115.6	91.6	52.4	7.3	11.7	7.9	3.2	2.1	4.2	2.8	42.1
1987	259.0	114.1	98.8	53.7	8.6	13.2	9.0	4.7	2.1	4.3	3.2	46.1
1988	262.2	116.2	97.9	51.6	9.5	14.1	8.2	4.4	2.2	4.7	3.2	48.1
1989	271.3	116.2	106.1	53.6	12.7	15.9	8.8	5.2	2.0	5.0	2.9	49.0
1990	246.0	100.9	95.4	44.8	8.4	16.6	9.2	5.7	2.2	5.3	3.1	49.7
1991	230.8	94.4	86.2	32.7	8.3	19.0	9.6	6.2	2.4	5.1	3.0	50.2
1992	252.2	110.6	87.0	32.8	8.9	17.6	10.9	5.8	2.5	5.5	3.1	54.6
1993	271.5	123.9	88.8	34.2	9.0	19.3	10.5	3.9	2.4	6.8	2.6	58.9
1994	296.2	133.6	101.0	40.9	10.7	21.0	10.5	6.1	2.5	6.5	3.0	61.6
1995	305.5	127.9	113.6	46.6	13.3	23.0	10.8	6.1	2.8	7.1	3.8	64.0
1996	330.1	146.2	119.1	51.3	12.8	22.8	10.9	6.3	2.9	8.1	4.0	64.8
FLOOR SPACE (mil. sq. ft.)												
1980	3,102	1,839	1,263	738	220	103	55	18	28	49	52	(X)
1985	3,853	2,324	1,529	1,039	165	111	73	28	32	44	36	(X)
1986	3,935	2,461	1,454	960	148	129	73	30	32	44	39	(X)
1987	3,756	2,288	1,469	933	160	139	78	42	32	46	38	(X)
1988	3,594	2,181	1,413	883	162	142	71	38	32	49	37	(X)
1989	3,516	2,115	1,400	867	156	151	72	41	27	48	35	(X)
1990	3,020	1,817	1,203	694	128	152	69	47	29	51	32	(X)
1991	2,634	1,653	981	476	100	177	72	50	29	45	33	(X)
1992	2,799	1,864	936	462	95	156	77	41	30	42	32	(X)
1993	3,062	2,091	971	481	110	165	75	30	30	51	29	(X)
1994	3,410	2,266	1,144	601	142	172	72	45	30	51	31	(X)
1995	3,452	2,172	1,280	700	163	186	70	39	33	56	33	(X)
1996	3,757	2,474	1,283	715	152	176	76	41	32	60	32	(X)

X Not applicable. [1] Includes nonindustrial warehouses. [2] Includes science.

Source: F.W. Dodge, a Division of the McGraw-Hill Companies, New York, NY (copyright).

No. 1183. Construction Contracts—Value, by State: 1990 to 1996

[In millions of dollars. Represents value of construction in States in which work was actually done. See headnote, table 1182]

STATE	1990	1996	1996: Total [1]	1996: Residential	1996: Nonresidential	STATE	1990	1996	1996: Total [1]	1996: Residential	1996: Nonresidential
U.S.	246,022	305,464	330,073	146,212	119,078	MO	3,633	6,440	6,050	2,653	2,229
AL	2,939	4,311	4,794	2,092	1,768	MT	332	865	916	372	247
AK	1,919	1,660	983	392	239	NE	1,318	1,694	1,870	709	643
AZ	4,553	8,787	9,795	5,902	2,561	NV	3,334	5,555	7,026	2,700	3,424
AR	1,438	2,903	2,795	1,347	873	NH	1,021	1,039	1,211	532	461
CA	37,318	28,919	31,758	13,211	11,360	NJ	6,141	6,457	7,134	2,324	2,963
CO	3,235	6,476	7,973	4,601	2,540	NM	1,124	2,108	2,227	813	796
CT	3,058	3,124	3,414	1,078	1,678	NY	14,137	13,456	13,891	3,574	6,549
DE	787	871	800	386	297	NC	6,614	10,574	12,448	6,518	3,944
DC	795	656	1,162	44	836	ND	506	791	656	202	213
FL	16,975	21,534	22,323	12,248	6,617	OH	9,865	12,407	14,021	5,827	5,487
GA	7,120	12,161	12,320	6,850	3,771	OK	2,164	2,967	3,184	1,466	868
HI	2,831	2,273	1,805	758	680	OR	3,101	4,965	5,411	2,643	1,836
ID	986	1,864	1,879	1,068	530	PA	10,117	9,326	9,406	3,429	3,819
IL	10,796	11,736	12,614	5,316	4,496	RI	594	465	658	288	166
IN	6,350	7,896	8,927	4,293	3,296	SC	3,664	4,580	5,457	2,559	2,037
IA	2,034	2,883	2,795	1,036	971	SD	468	706	814	258	249
KS	2,193	3,264	3,770	1,591	1,074	TN	4,388	7,167	8,273	4,124	2,955
KY	3,174	4,457	4,702	2,100	1,555	TX	13,197	22,968	25,017	11,799	8,707
LA	3,191	4,354	4,874	1,532	2,151	UT	1,884	3,725	3,756	1,952	1,313
ME	897	1,076	983	450	318	VT	515	484	586	236	236
MD	6,056	6,299	6,480	2,537	2,473	VA	7,180	8,794	9,213	4,096	3,583
MA	5,135	7,411	7,679	2,424	3,033	WA	6,185	7,330	8,539	3,836	3,130
MI	7,646	9,946	10,796	5,224	3,856	WV	1,253	1,215	1,258	230	481
MN	4,953	5,607	5,429	2,724	1,729	WI	4,654	5,649	5,994	2,732	2,079
MS	1,569	2,718	3,563	924	1,817	WY	462	532	642	210	139

[1] Includes nonbuilding construction, not shown separately.

Source: F.W. Dodge, a Division of the McGraw-Hill Companies, New York, NY (copyright).

lo. 1184. New Privately-Owned Housing Units Authorized, by State: 1995 and 1996

[Based on about 19,000 places in United States having building permit systems]

TE	HOUSING UNITS (1,000)			VALUATION (mil. dol.)			STATE	HOUSING UNITS (1,000)			VALUATION (mil. dol.)		
	1995	1996		1995	1996			1995	1996		1995	1996	
		Total	1 unit		Total	1 unit			Total	1 unit		Total	1 unit
S .	1,332.5	1,425.6	1,069.5	120,811	134,176	116,535	MO . . .	24.3	26.3	20.1	2,033	2,276	2,006
							MT . . .	3.1	2.7	1.5	224	209	150
. .	20.1	19.9	14.6	1,429	1,509	1,301	NE . . .	8.2	10.1	5.7	570	681	541
. .	2.2	2.6	1.8	257	316	249	NV . . .	32.8	37.2	23.8	2,738	2,854	2,259
. . .	52.7	53.7	41.3	5,133	5,449	4,760	NH . . .	4.4	4.9	4.2	464	517	474
. . .	11.7	11.1	7.7	766	777	674	NJ. . . .	21.5	24.2	20.9	1,947	2,134	1,966
. . .	83.9	92.1	73.5	10,836	12,472	11,131	NM . . .	11.0	10.2	8.8	899	1,084	1,029
. . .	38.6	41.1	30.4	3,859	4,275	3,622	NY . . .	28.1	34.9	20.2	2,616	3,110	2,381
. . .	8.6	8.5	7.6	956	987	941	NC . . .	60.9	67.0	51.8	5,275	6,043	5,418
. . .	4.6	4.4	4.2	332	352	343	ND . . .	3.2	2.3	1.5	201	181	148
. . .	(Z)	-	-	5	-	-	OH . . .	44.8	49.3	35.7	4,375	5,001	4,431
. . .	122.9	125.0	91.0	10,827	11,472	9,361	OK . . .	10.1	10.6	8.8	878	981	907
. . .	72.2	74.9	59.4	5,581	6,075	5,429	OR . . .	28.2	27.8	17.2	2,492	2,760	2,226
. . .	6.6	3.9	2.7	752	486	374	PA . . .	36.3	37.9	32.4	3,318	3,550	3,299
. . .	10.7	10.8	9.2	944	1,059	983	RI. . . .	2.3	2.5	2.1	214	220	202
. . .	47.5	49.6	35.9	4,844	5,199	4,423	SC . . .	24.0	29.4	22.5	1,984	2,464	2,146
. . .	35.7	37.2	29.9	3,378	3,719	3,429	SD . . .	3.8	3.6	2.4	258	279	220
. . .	11.3	12.0	7.9	976	1,051	863	TN . . .	35.1	40.5	28.2	2,838	3,334	2,739
. . .	12.7	14.7	10.1	1,175	1,322	1,124	TX . . .	105.1	118.8	83.1	8,324	9,935	8,481
. . -	17.6	18.8	14.1	1,276	1,484	1,314	UT . . .	20.9	23.5	16.7	1,870	2,111	1,749
. . .	14.7	18.0	14.4	1,141	1,436	1,308	VT . . .	2.3	2.1	1.9	205	201	191
. . .	4.4	4.7	4.5	391	436	426	VA . . .	43.1	45.9	35.2	3,658	3,947	3,534
. . .	26.6	25.1	22.6	2,293	2,284	2,171	WA . . .	38.2	39.6	27.0	3,578	3,773	3,020
. . .	16.4	17.3	15.1	1,895	2,055	1,928	WV . . .	3.7	3.6	2.9	261	276	247
. .	47.2	52.4	43.4	4,411	5,179	4,734	WI. . . .	32.4	33.3	21.8	2,727	3,047	2,472
. .	25.5	27.0	22.1	2,590	2,903	2,582	WY . . .	1.7	2.2	1.6	168	201	175
. .	10.8	10.4	8.1	651	710	634							

Represents zero. Z Less than 50 units.

ource: U.S. Bureau of the Census, *Construction Reports*, series C40, *Building Permits*, monthly.

No. 1185. New Privately-Owned Housing Units Started—Selected Characteristics: 1970 to 1996

[In thousands. For composition of regions, see table 26]

YEAR	Total units	STRUCTURES WITH—			REGION				CONDOMINIUM UNITS [1]		
		One unit	2 to 4 units	5 or more units	North-east	Mid-west	South	West	Total	Single-family	Multi-family
. . . .	1,434	813	85	536	218	294	612	311	(NA)	(NA)	(NA)
. . . .	2,052	1,151	120	781	264	434	869	486	(NA)	(NA)	(NA)
. . . .	2,357	1,309	141	906	330	443	1,057	527	(NA)	(NA)	(NA)
. . . .	2,045	1,132	118	795	277	440	899	429	241	69	172
. . . .	1,338	888	68	382	183	317	553	285	175	46	130
. . . .	1,160	892	64	204	149	294	442	275	65	20	45
. . . .	1,538	1,162	86	289	169	400	569	400	95	30	64
. . . .	1,987	1,451	122	414	202	465	783	538	118	41	77
. . . .	2,020	1,433	125	462	200	451	824	545	156	42	114
. . . .	1,745	1,194	122	429	178	349	748	470	198	43	156
. . . .	1,292	852	110	331	125	218	643	306	186	35	150
. . . .	1,084	705	91	288	117	165	562	240	181	36	145
. . . .	1,062	663	80	320	117	149	591	205	170	40	130
. . . .	1,703	1,068	113	522	168	218	935	382	276	77	199
. . . .	1,750	1,084	121	544	204	243	866	436	291	96	194
. . . .	1,742	1,072	93	576	252	240	782	468	225	79	146
. . . .	1,805	1,179	84	542	294	296	733	483	214	80	134
. . . .	1,621	1,146	65	409	269	298	634	420	196	73	123
. . . .	1,488	1,081	59	348	235	274	575	404	148	53	95
. . . .	1,376	1,003	55	318	179	266	536	396	118	37	82
. . . .	1,193	895	37	260	131	253	479	329	75	22	53
. . . .	1,014	840	36	138	113	233	414	254	60	21	39
. . . .	1,200	1,030	31	139	127	288	497	288	74	35	40
. . . .	1,288	1,126	29	133	126	296	562	302	86	45	41
. . . .	1,457	1,198	35	224	138	329	639	351	96	48	48
. . . .	1,354	1,076	34	244	118	290	615	331	93	47	47
. . . .	1,477	1,161	45	271	132	322	662	361	(NA)	(NA)	(NA)

A Not available. [1] Type of ownership under which the owners of the individual housing units are also joint owners of the on areas of the building or community. Includes a small number of cooperatively-owned units.

ource: U.S. Bureau of the Census, *Current Construction Reports*, series C20, *Housing Starts*, monthly.

No. 1186. New Privately-Owned Housing Units Started, by State: 1993 to 1996

[In thousands of units]

REGION, DIVISION, AND STATE	1993	1994	1995	1996, est. Total units	1996, est. Single-family units
U.S.	1,199.0	1,457.0	1,354.0	1,451.0	1,147.0
Northeast	125.0	138.0	118.0	127.0	107.0
N.E.	38.9	42.6	38.2	40.2	37.3
ME	4.4	4.9	4.2	4.6	4.4
NH	4.2	4.6	4.3	4.5	3.7
VT	2.5	2.5	2.0	2.1	1.9
MA	16.7	18.3	16.3	16.6	15.6
RI	2.5	2.6	2.5	2.6	2.4
CT	8.5	9.7	9.1	9.8	9.3
M.A.	86.1	95.4	79.8	86.6	69.8
NY	24.9	29.1	23.4	28.6	17.9
NJ	22.5	25.5	25.3	25.8	23.3
PA	38.7	40.7	31.1	32.2	28.5
Midwest	297.9	329.0	290.0	318.0	255.0
E.N.C	205.2	225.6	203.9	222.7	181.5
OH	48.8	50.4	43.6	49.0	39.7
IN	35.7	38.1	36.8	40.3	35.1
IL	45.9	53.7	48.8	49.9	40.8
MI	41.6	49.2	47.6	53.7	45.2
WI	33.1	34.1	27.1	29.7	20.7
W.N.C	92.7	103.4	86.1	94.9	73.2
MN	26.6	27.6	25.0	24.7	21.6
IA	12.2	13.3	9.4	11.0	7.7
MO	24.9	30.9	25.6	28.6	24.0
ND	3.3	3.8	3.2	2.0	1.6
SD	4.3	4.7	3.9	4.3	2.8
NE	8.8	8.5	8.0	9.7	5.9
KS	12.5	14.6	11.0	14.6	9.7
South	562.8	639.0	615.0	648.0	512.0
S.A.	345.5	382.3	375.4	386.4	306.8
DE	5.8	5.7	5.3	4.9	4.7
MD	31.3	30.8	28.9	27.7	24.9
DC	0.3	0.2	0.1	0.0	0.0
VA	46.9	47.4	45.2	48.7	37.6
WV	4.4	5.3	4.8	4.6	4.1
NC	60.8	66.9	64.4	67.6	54.9
SC	23.4	25.6	26.1	30.3	23.3
GA	57.3	69.4	77.2	79.8	65.8
FL	115.1	131.0	123.4	122.8	91.2
E.S.C	87.2	93.9	88.6	95.9	75.5
KY	20.7	21.5	18.9	20.2	16.8
TN	33.6	35.5	36.4	40.3	31.0
AL	21.9	23.7	21.2	21.9	17.7
MS	11.1	13.2	12.2	13.6	10.0
W.S.C	130.1	162.8	151.0	166.3	130.3
AR	13.0	15.1	12.2	13.2	10.2
LA	14.3	16.4	14.4	16.5	14.1
OK	12.9	12.7	11.8	13.4	10.9
TX	89.9	118.6	112.5	122.2	95.1
West	301.8	351.0	331.0	358.0	273.0
Mountain	140.7	176.4	171.8	186.8	139.0
MT	3.7	3.9	3.1	2.8	1.8
ID	13.1	13.3	9.5	9.4	8.2
WY	2.1	2.8	1.9	2.5	2.0
CO	32.4	41.6	39.7	41.7	32.0
NM	7.8	9.3	9.7	9.2	7.3
AZ	38.7	52.9	53.5	57.7	45.3
UT	19.3	21.6	20.7	21.6	15.7
NV	23.6	31.1	33.8	41.0	26.8
Pacific	161.1	174.8	159.2	172.1	133.8
WA	41.1	43.7	37.9	43.4	31.7
OR	21.6	24.6	25.0	26.9	18.5
CA	90.3	97.6	86.9	95.3	78.9
AK	2.1	2.2	2.5	2.7	1.8
HI	6.0	6.6	6.9	3.9	2.6

Source: National Association of Home Builders, Economics Division, Washington, DC. Data provided by the Econometric Forecasting Service.

No. 1187. Characteristics of New Privately Owned One-Family Houses Completed: 1970 to 1995

[Percent distribution, except as indicated. Data beginning 1980 show percent distribution of characteristics for all houses completed (includes new houses completed, houses built for sale completed, contractor-built and owner-built houses completed, and houses completed for rent). Data for 1970 cover contractor-built, owner-built, and houses for rent for rent for year construction started and houses sold for year of sale. Percents exclude houses for which characteristics specified were not reported]

CHARACTERISTIC	1970	1980	1990	1995	1996
Total houses (1,000)	793	957	966	1,066	1,129
Financing	100	100	100	100	100
Mortgage	84	82	82	88	87
FHA-insured	30	16	14	8	8
VA-guaranteed	7	8	4	5	5
Conventional	47	55	62	74	74
Rural Housing Service [1]	(2)	3	2	1	1
Cash or equivalent	16	18	18	12	11
Floor area	100	100	100	100	100
Under 1,200 sq. ft	36	21	11	10	9
1,200 to 1,599 sq. ft	28	29	22	22	21
1,600 to 1,999 sq. ft	16	22	22	23	23
2,000 to 2,399 sq. ft	21	13	17	17	18
2,400 sq. ft. and over	(3)	15	29	28	30
Average (sq. ft.)	1,500	1,740	2,080	2,095	2,120
Median (sq. ft.)	1,385	1,595	1,905	1,920	1,950
Number of stories	100	100	100	100	100
1	74	60	46	49	49
2 or more	17	31	49	48	47
Split level	10	8	4	3	3
Foundation	100	100	100	100	100
Full or partial basement	37	36	38	39	37
Slab	36	45	40	42	44
Crawl space	27	19	21	19	19
Bedrooms	100	100	100	100	100
2 or less	13	17	15	13	13
3	63	63	57	57	56
4 or more	24	20	29	30	31
Bathrooms	100	100	100	100	100
1 1/2 or less	52	27	13	11	9
2	32	48	42	41	41
2 1/2 or more	16	25	45	48	49
Heating fuel	100	100	100	100	100
Electricity	28	50	33	28	26
Gas	62	41	59	67	69
Oil	8	3	5	3	3
Other	1	5	3	1	1
Heating system	100	100	100	100	100
Warm air furnace	71	57	65	67	70
Electric heat pump	(NA)	24	23	25	23
Other	29	19	12	9	7
Central air-conditioning	100	100	100	100	100
With	34	63	76	80	81
Without	66	37	24	20	19
Fireplaces	100	100	100	100	100
No fireplace	65	43	34	37	38
1 or more	35	56	66	63	62
Parking facilities	100	100	100	100	100
Garage	58	69	82	84	86
Carport	17	7	2	2	1
No garage or carport	25	24	16	14	13

NA Not available. [1] Prior to 1996, Farmers Home Administration. [2] Included with "Conventional" financing. [3] Included with floor area of 2,000 to 2,399 square feet.

Source: U.S. Bureau of the Census and U.S. Dept. of Housing and Urban Development, *Current Construction Reports*, series C25, *New One-Family Houses Sold*, monthly, and *Characteristics of New Housing*, annual

No. 1188. New Privately Owned One-Family Houses Sold, by Region and Type of Financing, 1980 to 1996, and by Sales-Price Group, 1996

[In thousands. Based on a national probability sample of monthly interviews with builders or owners of 1-family houses for which building permits have been issued or, for nonpermit areas, on which construction has started. For details, see source. For composition of regions, see table 26]

YEAR AND SALES-PRICE GROUP	Total sales	REGION				FINANCING TYPE			
		Northeast	Midwest	South	West	Conventional	FHA and VA	Rural Housing Service[1]	Cash
1980	545	50	81	267	145	302	196	14	32
1985	688	112	82	323	170	403	208	11	64
1986	750	136	96	322	196	411	268	12	59
1987	671	117	97	271	186	408	190	8	64
1988	676	101	97	276	202	437	171	6	62
1989	650	86	102	260	202	416	162	14	58
1990	534	71	89	225	149	337	138	10	50
1991	509	57	93	215	144	329	128	9	43
1992	610	65	116	259	170	428	134	7	41
1993	666	60	123	295	188	476	147	6	37
1994	670	61	123	295	191	490	130	9	41
1995	667	55	125	300	187	490	129	9	39
1996	757	74	137	337	209	570	140	9	38
Under $70,000	26	(B)	(B)	21	(B)	11	11	3	(B)
$70,000 to $79,999	33	(B)	4	24	4	15	16	(B)	(B)
$80,000 to $99,999	104	5	21	63	16	56	42	(B)	4
$100,000 to $119,999	101	5	20	45	30	65	29	(B)	6
$120,000 to $149,999	159	11	32	69	47	121	27	(B)	10
$150,000 to $199,999	160	18	29	61	51	137	14	(B)	8
$200,000 to $249,999	79	14	14	27	23	74	(B)	(B)	4
$250,000 to $299,999	40	5	6	13	15	38	(B)	(B)	(B)
$300,000 and over	56	13	8	14	21	54	(B)	(B)	3

B Withheld because estimate did not meet publication standards on the basis of sample size. [1] Formerly, the Farmers Home Administration.

Source: U.S. Bureau of the Census and U.S. Dept. of Housing and Urban Development, *Current Construction Reports*, series C25, *Characteristics of New Housing*, annual; and *New One-Family Houses Sold*, monthly.

No. 1189. Median Sales Price of New Privately Owned One-Family Houses Sold, by Region: 1980 to 1996

[In dollars. For definition of median, see Guide to Tabular Presentation. For composition of regions, see table 26]

YEAR	U.S.	Northeast	Midwest	South	West	YEAR	U.S.	Northeast	Midwest	South	West
1980	64,600	69,500	63,400	59,600	72,300	1989	120,000	159,600	108,800	96,400	139,000
1982	69,300	78,200	68,900	66,100	75,000	1990	122,900	159,000	107,900	99,000	147,500
1983	75,300	82,200	79,500	70,900	80,100	1991	120,000	155,900	110,000	100,000	141,100
1984	79,900	88,600	85,400	72,000	87,300	1992	121,500	169,000	115,600	105,500	130,400
1985	84,300	103,300	80,300	75,000	92,600	1993	126,500	162,600	125,000	115,000	135,000
1986	92,000	125,000	88,300	80,200	95,700	1994	130,000	169,000	132,900	116,900	140,400
1987	104,500	140,000	95,000	88,000	111,000	1995	133,900	180,000	134,000	124,500	141,400
1988	112,500	149,000	101,600	92,000	126,500	1996	140,000	186,000	138,000	126,200	153,900

Source: U.S. Bureau of the Census and U.S. Dept. of Housing and Urban Development, *Current Construction Reports*, series C25, *Characteristics of New Housing*, annual; and *New One-Family Houses Sold*, monthly.

No. 1190. New Mobile Homes Placed for Residential Use and Average Sales Price, by Region: 1980 to 1996

[A mobile home is a moveable dwelling, 10 feet or more wide and 35 feet or more long, designed to be towed on its own chassis and without need of permanent foundation. Excluded are travel trailers, motor homes, and modular housing. Data are based on a probability sample and subject to sampling variability; see source. For composition of regions, see table 26]

YEAR	UNITS PLACED (1,000)					AVERAGE SALES PRICE (dol.)				
	Total	Northeast	Midwest	South	West	U.S.	Northeast	Midwest	South	West
1980	233.7	12.3	32.3	140.3	48.7	19,800	18,500	18,600	18,200	25,400
1985	283.4	20.2	38.6	187.6	36.9	21,800	22,700	21,500	20,400	28,700
1986	256.1	21.2	37.2	162.3	35.4	22,400	24,400	21,800	20,700	29,900
1987	239.2	23.6	40.0	145.5	30.1	23,700	25,600	23,700	21,900	31,000
1988	224.3	22.7	39.1	130.7	31.8	25,100	27,000	24,600	22,700	33,900
1989	202.8	20.2	39.1	112.8	30.6	27,200	30,200	26,700	24,100	37,600
1990	195.4	18.8	37.7	108.4	30.6	27,800	30,000	27,000	24,500	39,300
1991	174.3	14.3	35.4	97.6	27.0	27,700	30,400	27,600	24,500	38,800
1992	212.0	15.0	42.2	124.4	30.4	28,400	30,900	28,600	25,400	39,000
1993	242.5	15.4	44.5	146.7	35.9	30,500	32,000	31,400	27,700	40,500
1994	286.1	16.2	53.0	174.4	42.5	33,500	33,900	34,600	30,500	44,600
1995	310.7	14.6	56.0	198.3	41.8	36,300	36,600	36,600	34,000	46,800
1996	319.7	15.4	56.6	205.1	42.6	38,400	40,200	39,600	36,100	47,700

Source: U.S. Bureau of the Census, *Current Construction Reports*, series C20, *Housing Starts*, monthly.

No. 1191. Existing One-Family Houses Sold and Price, by Region: 1970 to 1996

[Based on data (adjusted and aggregated to regional and national totals) reported by participating real estate multiple listing services. For definition of median, see Guide to Tabular Presentation. For composition of regions, see table 26]

YEAR	HOUSES SOLD (1,000)					MEDIAN SALES PRICE (dol.)				
	Total	Northeast	Midwest	South	West	Total	Northeast	Midwest	South	West
1970	1,612	251	501	568	292	23,000	25,200	20,100	22,200	24,300
1971	2,018	311	583	735	389	24,800	27,100	22,100	24,300	26,500
1972	2,252	361	630	788	473	26,700	29,800	23,900	26,400	28,400
1973	2,334	367	674	847	446	28,900	32,800	25,300	29,000	31,000
1974	2,272	354	645	839	434	32,000	35,800	27,700	32,300	34,800
1975	2,476	370	701	862	543	35,300	39,300	30,100	34,800	39,600
1976	3,064	439	881	1,033	712	38,100	41,800	32,900	36,500	46,100
1977	3,650	515	1,101	1,231	803	42,900	44,400	36,700	39,800	57,300
1978	3,986	516	1,144	1,416	911	48,700	47,900	42,200	45,100	66,700
1979	3,827	526	1,061	1,353	887	55,700	53,800	47,800	51,300	77,400
1980	2,973	403	806	1,092	672	62,200	60,800	51,900	58,300	89,300
1981	2,419	353	632	917	516	66,400	63,700	54,300	64,400	96,200
1982	1,990	354	490	780	366	67,800	63,500	55,100	67,100	98,900
1983	2,697	477	692	1,004	524	70,300	72,200	56,600	69,200	94,900
1984	2,829	478	720	1,006	624	72,400	78,700	57,100	71,300	95,800
1985	3,134	561	806	1,063	704	75,500	88,900	58,900	75,200	95,400
1986	3,474	635	922	1,145	773	80,300	104,800	63,500	78,200	100,900
1987	3,436	618	892	1,163	763	85,600	133,300	66,000	80,400	113,200
1988	3,513	606	865	1,224	817	89,300	143,000	68,400	82,200	124,900
1989	3,346	531	855	1,185	775	93,100	145,200	71,300	84,500	139,900
1990	3,211	469	831	1,202	709	95,500	141,200	74,000	85,900	139,600
1991	3,220	479	840	1,199	702	100,300	141,900	77,800	88,900	147,200
1992	3,520	534	939	1,292	755	103,700	140,000	81,700	92,100	143,800
1993	3,802	571	1,007	1,416	808	106,800	139,500	85,200	95,000	142,600
1994	3,967	595	1,038	1,469	865	109,900	139,100	87,900	96,000	147,000
1995	3,812	577	992	1,431	813	113,100	136,900	93,600	97,800	148,300
1996	4,087	611	1,048	1,516	912	118,200	140,900	99,600	102,800	152,900

Source: NATIONAL ASSOCIATION OF REALTORS, Washington, DC, prior to 1990, *Home Sales*, monthly, and *Home Sales Yearbook: 1990;* (copyright); thereafter, *Real Estate Outlook; Market Trends & Insights*, monthly, (copyright).

No. 1192. Median Sales Price of Existing One-Family Homes, by Selected Metropolitan Area: 1993 to 1996

[In thousands of dollars. For the top 60 areas in sales price in 1996. Areas are metropolitan statistical areas (MSA's) except as indicated; for definitions and components, see Appendix II]

METROPOLITAN AREA	1993	1994	1995	1996
U.S., all areas	106.8	109.9	113.1	118.2
Akron, OH	83.2	84.9	92.1	96.8
Albany-Schenectady-Troy, NY	112.3	112.0	105.9	106.9
Albuquerque, NM	100.4	110.0	117.0	122.3
Anaheim-Santa Ana, CA MSA	217.2	211.0	208.4	213.9
Atlanta, GA	91.8	93.6	97.5	100.7
Atlantic City, NJ	106.7	107.6	107.0	108.0
Aurora-Elgin, IL	121.7	124.4	131.6	137.0
Austin-San Marcos, TX	91.3	96.2	101.4	108.1
Baltimore, MD	115.7	115.4	111.3	113.0
Birmingham, AL	96.5	100.2	103.6	114.1
Boise City, ID	91.4	99.0	98.9	101.2
Boston, MA PMSA	173.2	179.3	179.0	189.3
Charlotte-Gastonia-Rock Hill, NC-SC	106.1	106.5	107.8	116.8
Chicago, IL PMSA	142.0	144.1	147.9	153.2
Cincinnati, OH-KY-IN PMSA	91.4	96.5	100.4	104.8
Cleveland, OH PMSA	95.0	98.5	104.7	111.9
Colorado Springs, CO	93.7	104.2	114.7	126.6
Columbus, OH	91.8	94.8	99.1	108.2
Dallas, TX PMSA	94.5	95.0	96.4	103.5
Denver, CO PMSA	104.7	116.8	127.3	133.4
Detroit, MI PMSA	86.0	87.0	98.2	111.4
Eugene-Springfield, OR	84.4	96.2	104.9	116.2
Ft. Lauderdale-Hollywood-Pompano Beach, FL PMSA	103.1	103.1	105.9	112.3
Greensboro-Winston-Salem-High Point, NC	94.7	98.8	102.5	112.7
Greenville-Spartanburg, SC	84.9	87.4	92.4	105.5
Hartford, CT PMSA	135.3	133.4	133.4	139.2
Honolulu, HI	358.5	360.0	349.0	335.0
Kansas City, MO-KS	83.6	87.1	91.7	96.8
Lake County, IL	130.1	130.8	136.2	144.7
Las Vegas, NV	108.2	110.5	113.5	118.5
Los Angeles-Long Beach, CA PMSA	195.4	189.1	179.9	172.9
Madison, WI	104.6	116.0	124.5	122.2
Miami-Hialeah, FL PMSA	98.8	103.2	107.1	113.2
Milwaukee, WI PMSA	104.1	109.0	114.7	119.4
Minneapolis-St. Paul, MN-WI	98.2	101.5	106.8	113.9
Nashville, TN	90.4	96.5	107.3	112.7
New Haven-Meriden, CT	142.5	139.6	135.1	133.3
New York-Northern New Jersey-Long Island, NY-NJ-CT CMSA	173.2	173.2	169.7	174.5
Norfolk-Virginia Beach-Newport News, VA	98.2	103.8	104.4	110.2
Phoenix, AZ	89.1	91.4	96.8	105.3
Portland, OR PMSA	106.0	116.9	128.4	141.5
Providence, RI PMSA	116.3	116.4	115.6	118.1
Reno, NV	126.3	133.6	137.1	140.0
Richland-Kennewick-Pasco, WA	101.9	111.3	100.9	101.3
Richmond-Petersburg VA	94.1	95.4	103.1	108.7
Riverside/San Bernardino, CA PMSA	134.4	129.1	120.9	115.2
Sacramento, CA	129.2	124.5	119.5	115.2
Salt Lake City-Ogden, UT	84.9	98.0	113.7	122.7
San Diego, CA	176.9	176.0	171.6	174.5
San Francisco, CA PMSA	254.4	255.6	254.4	266.4
Sarasota-Bradenton, FL	94.1	97.0	104.5	107.7
Seattle-Tacoma, WA CMSA	150.2	155.9	159.0	164.6
Spokane, WA	85.5	94.6	98.4	101.2
Springfield, MA	112.4	107.7	106.1	105.7
Tacoma, WA	113.5	118.9	121.4	125.4
Tallahassee, FL	92.5	97.8	99.8	109.8
Trenton, NJ	133.4	131.3	129.0	136.4
Tucson, AZ	88.2	95.4	100.5	105.5
Washington, DC-MD-VA	158.3	157.9	156.5	160.7
West Palm Beach-Boca Raton-Delray Beach, FL	114.6	117.6	121.3	126.6
Worcester, MA MSA	129.0	130.6	130.1	131.2

Source: National Association of REALTORS, Washington, DC, *Real Estate Outlook: Market Trends & Insights*, monthly, (copyright).

No. 1193. Existing Home Sales, by State: 1990 to 1996

[In thousands]

STATE	1990	1993	1994	1995	1996
United States [1]	3,211	4,203	4,404	4,240	4,559
Alabama	61.1	77.9	77.4	74.6	78.5
Alaska	(NA)	(NA)	(NA)	(NA)	(NA)
Arizona	86.3	107.9	123.8	122.0	133.1
Arkansas	44.8	52.8	52.3	55.3	58.5
California [2]	452.1	435.0	482.5	425.4	505.2
Colorado	54.2	82.1	80.6	76.9	84.3
Connecticut	34.3	45.9	49.8	51.4	49.2
Delaware	9.7	9.4	10.4	10.3	(NA)
District of Columbia	13.1	12.3	12.3	11.7	11.1
Florida	183.3	208.9	229.7	220.8	229.7
Georgia	73.2	(NA)	(NA)	(NA)	(NA)
Hawaii	19.2	12.5	13.1	10.0	10.1
Idaho	18.1	23.4	23.1	22.8	23.4
Illinois	160.9	193.9	188.4	181.2	189.8
Indiana	80.1	100.8	103.3	100.3	103.0
Iowa	51.9	53.5	54.3	51.3	55.3
Kansas	38.8	53.7	55.7	54.2	57.9
Kentucky	66.4	83.3	81.1	78.2	80.2
Louisiana	41.6	49.3	51.4	50.1	51.9
Maine	(NA)	11.6	13.0	(NA)	(NA)
Maryland	67.1	73.4	69.5	59.2	61.6
Massachusetts	44.0	66.0	66.7	68.1	82.2
Michigan	145.0	170.6	184.2	176.3	182.5
Minnesota	64.8	81.8	82.1	78.5	88.4
Mississippi	34.7	43.6	43.5	43.8	45.0
Missouri	84.1	106.4	110.2	108.3	114.0
Montana	12.7	16.2	15.6	14.8	15.8
Nebraska	19.3	23.2	23.3	21.0	20.1
Nevada	26.2	30.5	32.9	31.9	35.4
New Hampshire	7.9	13.6	16.2	(NA)	17.7
New Jersey	114.8	139.0	145.4	138.3	147.9
New Mexico	23.6	31.0	30.4	28.9	27.4
New York	125.5	143.0	156.3	150.4	165.8
North Carolina	135.9	185.0	204.1	200.1	219.7
North Dakota	10.4	11.8	10.9	10.6	12.0
Ohio	151.6	179.1	186.4	181.4	190.9
Oklahoma	53.4	61.5	59.7	58.1	62.0
Oregon	56.6	58.8	58.1	57.7	60.6
Pennsylvania	182.7	216.1	216.4	217.2	222.8
Rhode Island	7.8	11.0	11.6	11.9	13.2
South Carolina	57.8	62.2	67.3	69.1	76.2
South Dakota	11.6	13.7	13.2	13.2	14.5
Tennessee	92.7	120.5	129.8	133.2	145.3
Texas	240.0	258.8	266.9	260.2	284.4
Utah	22.1	31.2	32.4	33.8	37.1
Vermont	6.1	11.0	10.9	9.0	8.5
Virginia	96.9	104.2	99.5	94.0	95.8
Washington	87.7	97.0	101.2	95.5	101.7
West Virginia	42.0	45.7	45.8	44.5	44.5
Wisconsin	71.7	94.6	94.3	93.2	97.4
Wyoming	7.4	10.9	11.0	10.5	10.5

NA Not available. [1] U.S. totals are derived independently and therefore are not equal to the sum of the States. [2] Provided by the California Association of Realtors.

Source: National Association of REALTORS, Washington, DC, *Real Estate Outlook: Market Trends & Insights*, monthly, (copyright).

No. 1194. New Apartments Completed and Rented in 3 Months, by Region: 1980 to 1995

[Structures with five or more units, privately financed, nonsubsidized, unfurnished rental apartments. Based on sample and subject to sampling variability; see source for details. For composition of regions, see table 26]

YEAR AND RENT	NUMBER (1,000)					PERCENT RENTED IN 3 MONTHS				
	U.S.	Northeast	Midwest	South	West	U.S.	Northeast	Midwest	South	West
1980	196.1	14.2	43.8	91.5	46.6	75	77	77	74	75
1981	135.3	4.9	36.9	68.4	25.1	80	85	86	78	75
1982	117.0	4.6	21.9	66.8	23.7	72	74	79	70	72
1983	191.5	3.5	41.1	115.1	31.8	69	73	86	63	69
1984	313.2	3.8	41.2	194.4	73.9	67	64	79	63	70
1985	365.2	8.1	54.0	166.1	137.0	65	69	72	59	68
1986	407.6	16.9	64.5	171.7	154.5	66	70	70	62	67
1987	345.6	11.3	66.0	124.5	143.9	63	73	65	59	64
1988	284.5	8.7	60.4	91.7	123.8	66	52	73	58	69
1989	247.8	13.4	45.8	86.3	102.3	70	74	74	68	69
1990 [1]	214.3	12.7	44.3	77.2	80.0	67	66	75	64	65
1991	165.3	6.8	37.9	63.6	57.0	70	83	78	65	68
1992	110.2	10.9	34.0	37.4	28.0	74	75	80	72	70
1993	77.2	3.7	25.3	27.7	20.5	75	37	81	76	73
1994	104.0	3.7	32.2	44.5	23.6	80	96	78	78	85
1995	155.0	7.1	31.7	78.5	37.7	73	74	75	72	73
Less than $350	9.3	(Z)	0.7	7.4	1.2	71	(Z)	88	68	79
$350-$549	38.7	0.4	16.4	15.9	6.2	71	91	70	76	62
$350-$449	12.0	0.2	5.4	4.9	1.6	68	100	70	71	47
$450-$549	26.7	0.2	11.0	11.0	4.6	73	84	70	78	68
$550-$749	55.6	1.6	11.4	27.1	15.4	75	92	84	72	73
$550-$649	28.0	0.8	6.3	13.4	7.5	73	94	83	68	69
$650-$749	27.6	0.8	5.1	13.7	7.9	78	90	85	75	77
$750 or more	51.4	5.1	3.2	28.2	14.9	73	68	67	72	78
Median monthly asking rent	$654	$750	$538	$669	$700	(X)	(X)	(X)	(X)	(X)

X Not applicable. Z Fewer than 50 units and less than .5 percent. [1] Due to revised estimation procedures, data beginning 1990 not strictly comparable with prior years.

Source: U.S. Bureau of the Census, *Current Housing Reports*, series H130, *Market Absorption of Apartments*, and unpublished data.

No. 1195. Total Housing Inventory for the United States: 1970 to 1996

[In thousands. Based on the Current Population Survey and the Housing Vacancy Survey and subject to sampling error; see source for details]

ITEM	1970	1975	1980	1985	1990	1991	1992	1993	1994	1995	1996
All housing units	**69,778**	**78,821**	**87,739**	**97,333**	**106,283**	**107,276**	**108,316**	**109,611**	**110,952**	**112,655**	**114,139**
Vacant	6,137	6,896	8,101	9,448	12,059	12,023	11,926	11,894	12,257	12,669	13,155
Year-round vacant	4,391	5,202	5,996	7,400	9,128	9,137	8,932	8,937	9,229	9,570	9,945
For rent	1,299	1,647	1,575	2,221	2,662	2,780	2,769	2,809	2,858	2,946	3,008
For sale only	427	591	734	1,006	1,084	1,070	970	894	953	1,022	1,082
Rented or sold	427	536	623	664	660	602	628	625	772	810	834
Held off market	2,238	2,429	3,064	3,510	4,742	4,686	4,564	4,609	4,646	4,793	5,022
Occasional use	615	649	814	977	1,485	1,494	1,443	1,508	1,612	1,667	1,709
Usual residence elsewhere	429	470	568	659	1,068	1,084	1,011	994	815	801	852
Other	1,195	1,309	1,683	1,875	2,189	2,107	2,111	2,108	2,219	2,325	2,461
Seasonal [1]	1,746	1,694	2,106	2,048	2,931	2,886	2,994	2,957	3,028	3,099	3,209
Total occupied	63,640	71,925	79,638	87,887	94,224	95,253	96,391	97,717	98,695	99,985	100,984
Owner	40,834	46,463	52,223	56,152	60,248	61,010	61,823	62,533	63,136	64,739	66,041
Renter	22,806	25,462	27,415	31,736	33,976	34,242	34,568	35,184	35,558	35,246	34,943
Percent distribution:											
All housing units	100.0	100.0	100.0	100.0	100.0	100.0	100.0	100.0	100.0	100.0	100.0
Vacant	8.8	8.7	9.2	9.7	11.3	11.2	11.0	10.9	11.0	11.2	11.5
Total occupied	91.2	91.3	90.8	90.3	88.7	88.8	89.0	89.1	89.0	88.8	88.5
Owner	58.5	58.9	59.5	57.7	56.7	56.9	57.1	57.0	56.9	57.5	57.9
Renter	32.7	32.3	31.2	32.6	32.0	31.9	31.9	32.1	32.0	31.3	30.6

[1] Beginning 1990 includes vacant seasonal mobile homes. For years shown, seasonal vacant housing units were underreported prior to 1990.

Source: U.S. Bureau of the Census, Internet site <http://www.census.gov/hhes/www/housing/hvs/historic/index.html> (accessed 23 April 1997).

No. 1196. Housing Units—Current Trends for Selected Characteristics: 1991 to 1995

[As of a of Oct. 1. Based on the American Housing Survey and subject to sampling error. See Appendix III]

CHARACTERISTIC	NUMBER OF UNITS (1,000)			PERCENT DISTRIBUTION		
	1991	1993	1995	1991	1993	1995
UNITS IN STRUCTURE						
All housing units	**104,592**	**106,611**	**109,457**	**100.0**	**100.0**	**100.0**
1 detached	62,646	64,283	66,169	59.9	60.3	60.5
1 attached	6,156	6,079	6,213	5.9	5.7	5.7
3 or 4	10,890	10,732	10,700	10.4	10.1	9.8
5 or more	17,918	18,444	18,727	17.1	17.3	17.1
5 to 9	5,368	5,521	5,594	5.1	5.2	5.1
10 to 49	8,477	8,851	8,993	8.1	8.3	8.2
50 or more	4,073	4,072	4,140	3.9	3.8	3.8
Mobile home or trailer	6,983	7,072	7,647	6.7	6.6	7.0
PLUMBING FACILITIES						
All housing units	**104,592**	**106,611**	**109,457**	**100.0**	**100.0**	**100.0**
Complete plumbing facilities	101,197	104,302	106,942	96.8	97.8	97.7
Lacking complete plumbing facilities	3,394	2,309	2,515	3.2	2.2	2.3
VEHICLES KEPT AT HOME						
Occupied housing units	93,147	94,724	97,693	100.0	100.0	100.0
None	10,148	9,793	9,583	10.9	10.3	9.8
1	31,280	31,662	32,731	33.6	33.4	33.5
2	35,290	36,673	38,173	37.9	38.7	39.1
3 or more	16,428	16,596	17,206	17.6	17.5	17.6
TELEPHONE AVAILABLE						
Occupied housing units	**93,147**	**94,724**	**97,693**	**100.0**	**100.0**	**100.0**
With telephone	87,291	88,442	91,544	93.7	93.4	93.7
No telephone	5,856	6,282	6,149	6.3	6.6	6.3

Source: U.S. Bureau of the Census, *Current Housing Reports*, series H150/91, H150/93, and H150/95 *American Housing Survey in the United States.*

No. 1197. Housing Units—Characteristics, by Tenure and Region: 1995

[In thousands of units, except as indicated. As of Oct. 1. Based on the American Housing Survey; see Appendix III. For composition of regions, see table 26]

CHARACTERISTIC	Total housing units	Seasonal	YEAR-ROUND UNITS							
			Occupied							Vacant
			Total	Owner	Renter	Northeast	Midwest	South	West	
Total units	109,457	3,054	97,693	63,544	34,150	19,200	23,662	34,236	20,596	8,710
Percent distribution	100.0	2.8	89.3	58.1	31.2	17.5	21.6	31.3	18.8	8.0
Units in structure:										
Single family detached	66,169	1,804	60,826	52,257	8,569	9,818	16,175	22,406	12,427	3,539
Single family attached	6,213	41	5,545	2,936	2,609	1,571	1,053	1,867	1,055	627
2 to 4 units	10,700	124	9,299	1,734	7,565	3,126	2,168	2,083	1,922	1,277
5 to 9 units	5,594	102	4,803	520	4,283	970	1,023	1,592	1,218	690
10 to 19 units	5,092	93	4,342	368	3,974	791	880	1,575	1,096	657
20 to 49 units	3,901	74	3,244	342	2,903	896	559	656	933	583
50 or more units	4,140	55	3,470	550	2,920	1,470	668	641	691	615
Mobile home or trailer	7,647	761	6,164	4,837	1,328	557	1,136	3,216	1,254	722
Stories in structure: [1]										
One story	3,065	35	2,678	279	2,399	158	374	1,204	942	352
2 stories	10,828	149	9,318	1,055	8,263	1,065	1,321	3,594	3,338	1,361
3 stories	8,268	152	7,056	1,179	5,877	2,363	2,451	1,249	992	1,060
4 to 6 stories	4,652	79	3,904	591	3,312	2,287	793	395	429	670
7 or more stories	2,627	32	2,213	415	1,799	1,382	359	312	160	381
Foundation: [2]										
Full or partial basement	32,423	367	30,636	27,080	3,554	9,859	13,077	4,894	2,803	1,420
Crawlspace	18,891	762	16,727	13,155	3,572	573	2,413	9,007	4,735	1,402
Concrete slab	19,255	358	17,722	13,988	3,734	855	1,556	9,610	5,702	1,175
Other	1,813	358	1,287	970	317	101	181	762	243	168
Year structure built:										
1939 and earlier	22,116	544	19,308	11,068	8,239	7,162	6,228	3,574	2,345	2,263
1940 to 1949	8,400	228	7,487	4,671	2,817	1,680	1,750	2,500	1,558	685
1950 to 1959	13,569	371	12,398	8,798	3,600	2,546	3,245	3,936	2,670	800
1960 to 1969	15,806	472	14,267	9,349	4,918	2,415	3,266	5,286	3,300	1,068
1970 to 1979	23,717	784	21,033	13,347	7,685	2,716	4,872	8,358	5,086	1,899
1980 or later	25,849	654	23,201	16,311	6,890	2,679	4,301	10,582	5,639	1,994
Median year	1967	1968	1967	1968	1965	1953	1962	1972	1971	1966
Main heating equipment:										
Warm-air furnace	57,840	836	53,165	38,301	14,863	6,881	17,711	17,212	11,361	3,837
Electric heat pump	10,614	311	9,406	7,027	2,379	433	692	7,003	1,278	897
Steam or hot water system	14,895	87	13,669	7,323	6,345	9,503	2,587	834	745	1,139
Floor, wall, or pipeless furnace	5,674	128	4,963	2,148	2,815	234	389	1,534	2,806	583
Built-in electric units	8,344	422	7,036	2,870	4,166	1,303	1,342	2,286	2,104	887
Room heaters with flue	2,083	178	1,620	869	752	187	245	864	324	285
Room heaters without flue	1,886	49	1,642	964	678	43	31	1,500	69	194
Stoves	2,877	339	2,320	1,735	585	360	379	962	619	218
Fireplaces	1,066	141	850	661	187	37	81	385	347	75
None	1,795	359	1,044	463	581	38	31	457	518	393
Portable electric heaters	950	78	809	413	395	19	18	576	195	63
Other	1,432	124	1,171	768	403	162	156	623	231	137
Kitchen equipment:										
Lacking complete facilities	3,629	391	1,075	461	614	241	281	302	252	2,163
With complete facilities	105,827	2,662	96,618	63,083	33,536	18,959	23,382	33,934	20,344	6,546
Kitchen sink	108,395	2,903	97,034	63,231	33,803	19,033	23,484	34,085	20,452	8,458
Refrigerator	106,872	2,739	97,433	63,469	33,964	19,133	23,597	34,180	20,523	6,701
Burners and oven	107,394	2,795	97,207	63,443	33,764	19,093	23,528	34,113	20,473	7,392
Burners only	151	21	105	31	74	28	17	40	20	25
Oven only	119	4	99	32	68	14	44	19	22	16
Dishwasher	56,635	818	52,508	40,236	12,272	9,064	11,160	19,210	13,054	3,309
Washing machine	79,403	1,129	75,745	60,034	15,711	13,526	18,804	28,015	15,399	2,530
Clothes dryer	74,165	1,062	70,756	57,184	13,571	12,150	18,341	25,694	14,571	2,347
Disposal in kitchen sink	46,353	717	42,451	28,793	13,659	4,159	10,301	14,086	13,906	3,185
Air conditioning: Central	50,824	780	46,577	34,161	12,415	3,656	11,694	23,772	7,255	3,467
Percent of total units	46.4	25.5	47.7	53.8	36.4	20.1	49.4	69.4	35.2	39.8
One or more room units	29,141	530	27,181	16,126	11,054	8,732	7,107	8,361	2,982	1,431
Source of water:										
Public system or private company	94,108	1,767	84,818	52,643	32,175	16,307	19,749	29,445	19,316	7,523
Percent of total units	86.0	57.9	86.8	82.8	94.2	84.9	83.5	86.0	93.8	86.4
Well serving 1 to 5 units	14,265	955	12,270	10,463	1,807	2,783	3,778	4,496	1,211	1,041
Other	1,083	332	606	438	167	110	136	293	67	146
Means of sewage disposal:										
Public sewer	83,308	1,222	75,282	44,527	30,755	14,859	18,618	24,111	17,694	6,804
Percent of total units	76.1	40.0	77.1	70.1	90.1	77.4	78.7	70.4	85.9	78.1
Septic tank, cesspool, chemical toilet	25,635	1,521	22,296	18,937	3,359	4,335	5,029	10,041	2,891	1,819
Other	513	311	116	80	36	6	15	83	11	87

[1] Limited to multiunit structures. [2] Limited to single-family units.

Source: U.S. Bureau of the Census, *Current Housing Reports*, series H-150-95, *American Housing Survey in the United States*.

No. 1198. Housing Units—Size of Units and Lot: 1995

[In thousands, except as indicated. As of Oct. 1. Based on the American Housing Survey; see Appendix III]

ITEM	Total housing units	Seasonal	YEAR-ROUND UNITS							
			Occupied							Vacant
			Total	Owner	Renter	Northeast	Midwest	South	West	
Total units	109,457	3,064	97,693	63,544	34,150	19,200	23,662	34,236	20,596	8,710
Rooms:										
1 room	862	104	550	22	528	246	109	72	123	208
2 rooms	1,422	215	958	60	898	279	139	235	305	249
3 rooms	10,166	484	8,311	859	7,452	2,299	1,691	2,240	2,081	1,371
4 rooms	20,789	1,070	17,062	6,069	10,993	3,124	3,858	6,135	3,945	2,656
5 rooms	24,328	660	21,600	13,895	7,705	3,749	5,292	8,380	4,178	2,068
6 rooms	22,151	327	20,700	16,686	4,014	3,797	5,122	7,725	4,055	1,125
7 rooms	14,183	88	13,560	12,007	1,554	2,606	3,467	4,781	2,706	536
8 rooms or more	15,555	106	14,952	13,946	1,006	3,100	3,985	4,667	3,202	496
Median number of rooms	5.4	4.2	5.5	6.2	4.2	5.5	5.6	5.5	5.4	4.5
Complete bathrooms:										
No bathrooms	1,201	468	465	195	270	133	116	159	57	268
1 bathroom	50,700	1,703	43,777	19,069	24,709	10,472	11,456	13,627	8,221	5,219
1 and one-half bathrooms	15,887	237	14,780	11,319	3,461	3,610	4,889	4,006	2,273	870
2 or more bathrooms	41,669	645	38,671	32,961	5,710	4,964	7,201	16,442	10,044	2,353
Square footage of unit:										
Single detached and mobile homes [1]	73,816	2,564	66,990	57,094	9,897	10,375	17,312	25,622	13,682	4,261
Less than 500	1,242	360	667	379	288	59	107	295	206	216
500 to 749	3,293	483	2,356	1,386	969	244	521	1,166	424	455
750 to 999	6,676	393	5,697	4,126	1,571	521	1,400	2,675	1,101	586
1,000 to 1,499	16,741	406	15,450	12,697	2,753	1,408	3,327	7,147	3,568	885
1,500 to 1,999	14,576	202	13,785	12,218	1,567	1,839	3,288	5,343	3,314	589
2,000 to 2,499	10,344	69	9,943	9,211	732	1,913	2,960	3,124	1,947	333
2,500 to 2,999	5,739	39	5,486	5,147	339	1,265	1,689	1,590	942	214
3,000 to 3,999	5,178	55	4,956	4,737	219	1,214	1,532	1,449	761	167
4,000 or more	2,938	31	2,785	2,597	189	739	814	879	353	121
Other [2]	7,089	527	5,867	4,596	1,271	1,174	1,673	1,953	1,066	695
Median square footage	1,686	862	1,732	1,814	1,270	2,139	1,875	1,552	1,652	1,297
Lot size:										
Single detached and attached units and mobile homes	(NA)	(NA)	72,522	60,020	12,500	11,943	18,364	27,480	14,736	(NA)
Less than one-eighth acre	(NA)	(NA)	6,292	5,367	924	1,324	1,528	1,710	1,730	(NA)
One-eighth to one-quarter acre	(NA)	(NA)	12,184	11,077	1,107	1,777	3,212	3,725	3,470	(NA)
One-quarter to one-half acre	(NA)	(NA)	10,077	9,303	774	1,707	2,643	3,741	1,986	(NA)
One-half up to one acre	(NA)	(NA)	7,394	6,656	738	1,537	1,635	3,275	947	(NA)
1 to 4 acres	(NA)	(NA)	10,450	9,396	1,051	2,138	2,188	4,990	1,134	(NA)
5 to 9 acres	(NA)	(NA)	1,713	1,574	139	225	477	768	244	(NA)
10 acres or more	(NA)	(NA)	3,670	3,185	485	452	1,258	1,529	431	(NA)
Other [2]	(NA)	(NA)	20,742	13,460	7,282	2,783	5,423	7,742	4,793	(NA)
Median acreage	(NA)	(NA)	0.43	0.43	0.44	0.47	0.41	0.61	0.24	(NA)

NA Not available. [1] Does not include selected vacant units. [2] Represents units not reported or size unknown.

Source: U.S. Bureau of the Census, *Current Housing Reports*, series H150/95, *American Housing Survey in the United States.*

No. 1199. Occupied Housing Units—Tenure, by Race of Householder: 1991 to 1995

[In thousands, except percent. As of fall. Based on the American Housing Survey; see Appendix III]

RACE OF HOUSEHOLDER AND TENURE	1991	1993	1995
ALL RACES			
Occupied units, total	93,147	94,724	97,693
Owner occupied	59,796	61,252	63,544
Percent of occupied	64.2	64.7	65.0
Renter occupied	33,351	33,472	34,150
WHITE			
Occupied units, total	79,140	80,029	81,611
Owner occupied	53,749	54,878	56,507
Percent of occupied	67.9	68.6	69.2
Renter occupied	25,391	25,151	25,104
BLACK			
Occupied units, total	10,832	11,128	11,773
Owner occupied	4,635	4,788	5,137
Percent of occupied	42.8	43.0	43.6
Renter occupied	6,197	6,340	6,637
HISPANIC ORIGIN [1]			
Occupied units, total	6,239	6,614	7,757
Owner occupied	2,423	2,788	3,245
Percent of occupied	38.8	42.2	41.8
Renter occupied	3,816	3,826	4,512

[1] Persons of Hispanic origin may be of any race.

Source: U.S. Bureau of the Census, *Current Housing Reports*, series H150/91, H150/93, and H150/95, *American Housing* ~~vey in the United States.~~

No. 1200. Homeownership Rates, by Age of Householder: 1985 to 1995

[In percent. Represents the proportion of owner households to the total number of occupied households. Based on the Current Population Survey/Housing Vacancy Survey; see source for details]

AGE OF HOUSEHOLDER	1985	1987	1988	1989	1990	1991	1992	1993 [1]	1994	1995	1996
United States	63.9	64.0	63.8	63.9	63.9	64.1	64.1	64.0	64.0	64.7	65.4
Less than 35 years old	39.9	39.5	39.3	39.1	38.5	37.8	37.6	37.3	37.3	38.6	39.1
Less than 25 years old	17.2	16.0	15.8	16.6	15.7	15.3	14.9	14.8	14.9	15.9	18.0
25 to 29 years old	37.7	36.4	35.9	35.3	35.2	33.8	33.6	33.6	34.1	34.4	34.7
30 to 34 years old	54.0	53.5	53.2	53.2	51.8	51.2	50.5	50.8	50.6	53.1	53.0
35 to 44 years old	68.1	67.2	66.9	66.6	66.3	65.8	65.1	65.1	64.5	65.2	65.5
35 to 39 years old	65.4	64.1	63.6	63.4	63.0	62.2	61.4	61.8	61.2	62.1	62.1
40 to 44 years old	71.4	70.8	70.7	70.2	69.8	69.5	69.1	68.6	68.2	68.6	69.0
45 to 54 years old	75.9	76.1	75.6	75.5	75.2	74.8	75.1	75.3	75.2	75.2	75.6
45 to 49 years old	74.3	74.6	74.4	74.1	73.9	73.7	74.2	73.7	73.8	73.7	74.4
50 to 54 years old	77.5	77.8	77.1	77.2	76.8	76.1	76.2	77.2	76.8	77.0	77.2
55 to 64 years old	79.5	80.2	79.5	79.6	79.3	80.0	80.2	79.9	79.3	79.5	80.0
55 to 59 years old	79.2	80.0	79.3	79.1	78.8	79.5	79.3	78.9	78.4	78.8	79.4
60 to 64 years old	79.9	80.4	79.8	80.1	79.8	80.5	81.2	80.9	80.1	80.3	80.7
65 years and over	74.8	75.5	75.6	75.8	76.3	77.2	77.1	77.3	77.4	78.1	78.9
65 to 69 years old	79.5	79.5	80.0	80.0	80.0	81.4	80.8	80.7	80.6	81.0	82.4
70 to 74 years old	76.8	77.7	77.7	77.8	78.4	78.8	79.0	79.9	80.1	80.9	81.4
75 years old and over	69.8	70.8	70.8	71.2	72.3	73.1	73.3	73.4	73.5	74.6	75.3

[1] Based on 1990 census controls.

Source: Bureau of the Census, Internet site <http://www.census.gov/ftp/pub/hhes/www/hvs.html> (accessed 29 July 1997)

No. 1201. Homeownership Rates, by State: 1985 to 1996

[In percent. See headnote, table 1200]

STATE	1985	1990	1993 [1]	1994	1995	1996
United States	63.9	63.9	64.0	64.0	64.7	65.4
Alabama	70.4	68.4	70.2	68.5	70.1	71.0
Alaska	61.2	58.4	55.4	58.8	60.9	62.9
Arizona	64.7	64.5	69.1	67.7	62.9	62.0
Arkansas	66.6	67.8	70.5	68.1	67.2	66.6
California	54.2	53.8	56.0	55.5	55.4	55.0
Colorado	63.6	59.0	61.8	62.9	64.6	64.5
Connecticut	69.0	67.9	64.5	63.8	68.2	69.0
Delaware	70.3	67.7	74.1	70.5	71.7	71.5
Dist of Columbia	37.4	36.4	35.7	37.8	39.2	40.4
Florida	67.2	65.1	65.5	65.7	66.6	67.1
Georgia	62.7	64.3	66.5	63.4	66.6	69.3
Hawaii	51.0	55.5	52.8	52.3	50.2	50.6
Idaho	71.0	69.4	72.1	70.7	72.0	71.4
Illinois	60.6	63.0	61.8	64.2	66.4	68.2
Indiana	67.6	67.0	68.7	68.4	71.0	74.2
Iowa	69.9	70.7	68.2	70.1	71.4	72.8
Kansas	68.3	69.0	68.9	69.0	67.5	67.5
Kentucky	68.5	65.8	68.8	70.6	71.2	73.2
Louisiana	70.2	67.8	65.4	65.8	65.3	64.9
Maine	73.7	74.2	71.9	72.6	76.7	76.5
Maryland	65.6	64.9	65.5	64.1	65.8	66.9
Massachusetts	60.5	58.6	60.7	60.6	60.2	61.7
Michigan	70.7	72.3	72.3	72.0	72.2	73.3
Minnesota	70.0	68.0	65.8	68.9	73.3	75.4
Mississippi	69.6	69.4	69.7	69.2	71.1	73.0
Missouri	69.2	64.0	66.4	68.4	69.4	70.2
Montana	66.5	69.1	69.7	68.8	68.7	68.6
Nebraska	68.5	67.3	67.7	68.0	67.1	66.8
Nevada	57.0	55.8	55.8	55.8	58.6	61.1
New Hampshire	65.5	65.0	65.4	65.1	66.0	65.0
New Jersey	62.3	65.0	64.5	64.1	64.9	64.6
New Mexico	68.2	68.6	69.1	66.8	67.0	67.1
New York	50.3	53.3	52.8	52.5	52.7	52.7
North Carolina	68.0	69.0	68.8	68.7	70.1	70.4
North Dakota	69.9	67.2	62.7	63.3	67.3	68.2
Ohio	67.9	68.7	68.5	67.4	67.9	69.2
Oklahoma	70.5	70.3	70.3	68.5	69.6	68.4
Oregon	61.5	64.4	63.8	63.9	63.2	63.1
Pennsylvania	71.6	73.8	72.0	71.8	71.5	71.7
Rhode Island	61.4	58.5	57.6	56.5	57.9	56.6
South Carolina	72.0	71.4	71.1	72.0	71.3	72.9
South Dakota	67.6	66.2	65.6	66.4	67.5	67.8
Tennessee	67.6	68.3	64.1	65.2	67.0	68.8
Texas	60.5	59.7	58.7	59.7	61.4	61.8
Utah	71.5	70.1	68.9	69.3	71.5	72.7
Vermont	69.5	72.6	68.5	69.4	70.4	70.3
Virginia	68.5	69.8	68.5	69.3	68.1	68.5
Washington	66.8	61.8	63.1	62.4	61.6	63.1
West Virginia	75.9	72.0	73.3	73.7	73.1	74.3
Wisconsin	63.8	68.3	65.7	64.2	67.5	68.2
Wyoming	73.2	68.9	67.1	65.8	69.0	68.0

[1] Based on 1990 population controls.

Source: U.S. Bureau of the Census, Internet site <http://www.census.gov/ftp/pub/hhes/www/hvs.html> (accessed 29 July 1997).

No. 1202. Occupied Housing Units—Costs and Value, by Region: 1995

[As of fall. Specified owner-occupied units are limited to one-unit structures on less than 10 acres and no business on property. Specified renter-occupied units exclude one-unit structures on 10 acres or more. See headnote table 1203 for an explanation of housing costs. Based on the American Housing Survey; see Appendix III]

CATEGORY	NUMBER (1,000)					PERCENT DISTRIBUTION				
	Total units	Northeast	Midwest	South	West	Total units	Northeast	Midwest	South	West
OWNER OCCUPIED UNITS										
Total	**63,544**	**11,861**	16,567	**22,959**	**12,157**	100.0	**100.0**	**100.0**	**100.0**	**100.0**
Monthly housing costs:										
Less than $300	17,027	1,694	4,633	8,008	2,692	26.8	14.3	27.9	34.9	22.1
$300 to $399	6,360	1,341	1,838	2,144	1,036	10.0	11.3	11.1	9.4	8.5
$400 to $499	5,268	1,143	1,594	1,801	730	8.3	9.6	9.6	7.8	6.0
$500 to $599	4,921	914	1,452	1,811	744	7.7	7.7	8.8	7.9	6.1
$600 to $699	4,356	838	1,267	1,572	679	6.9	7.1	7.6	6.8	5.6
$700 to $799	4,142	751	1,180	1,459	753	6.5	6.3	7.1	6.4	6.2
$800 to $999	6,684	1,373	1,717	2,337	1,257	10.5	11.6	10.4	10.2	10.3
$1,000 to $1,249	5,477	1,253	1,293	1,650	1,280	8.6	10.6	7.8	7.2	10.5
$1,250 to $1,499	3,518	939	685	848	1,047	5.5	7.9	4.1	3.7	8.6
$1,500 or more	5,791	1,616	908	1,328	1,939	9.1	13.6	5.5	5.8	15.9
Median (dol.) [1]	563	700	515	474	726	(X)	(X)	(X)	(X)	(X)
RENTER OCCUPIED UNITS										
Total	**34,150**	**7,338**	7,096	**11,277**	**8,439**	100.0	**100.0**	**100.0**	**100.0**	**100.0**
Less than $300	4,815	1,003	1,318	1,766	729	14.1	13.7	18.6	15.7	8.6
$300 to $399	4,285	669	1,265	1,722	629	12.5	9.1	17.8	15.3	7.5
$400 to $499	5,645	956	1,455	2,029	1,206	16.5	13.0	20.5	18.0	14.3
$500 to $599	5,076	1,106	1,070	1,609	1,292	14.9	15.1	15.1	14.3	15.3
$600 to $699	4,188	1,024	730	1,199	1,235	12.3	14.0	10.3	10.6	14.6
$700 to $799	2,910	726	372	846	966	8.5	9.9	5.2	7.5	11.4
$800 to $999	2,856	788	292	694	1,081	8.4	10.7	4.1	6.2	12.8
$1,000 to $1,249	1,244	380	97	239	528	3.6	5.2	1.4	2.1	6.3
$1,250 to $1,499	420	122	25	88	185	1.2	1.7	0.4	0.8	2.2
$1,500 or more	365	114	30	68	152	1.1	1.6	0.4	0.6	1.8
No cash rent	2,344	451	442	1,017	435	6.9	6.1	6.2	9.0	5.2
Median (dol.) [1]	523	574	451	479	612	(X)	(X)	(X)	(X)	(X)

X Not applicable. [1] For explanation of median, see Guide to Tabular Presentation.

No. 1203. Occupied Housing Units—Financial Summary, by Selected Characteristics of the Householder: 1995

[In thousands of units, except as indicated. As of fall. Housing costs include real estate taxes, property insurance, utilities, fuel, water, garbage collection, and mortgage. Based on the American Housing Survey; see Appendix III]

CHARACTERISTIC	Total occupied units	TENURE		BLACK		HISPANIC ORIGIN [1]		ELDERLY [2]		HOUSEHOLDS BELOW POVERTY LEVEL	
		Owner	Renter	Owner	Renter	Owner	Renter	Owner	Renter	Owner	Renter
Total units [3]	**97,693**	**63,544**	**34,150**	**5,137**	**6,637**	**3,245**	**4,512**	**16,299**	**4,542**	**6,034**	**8,661**
Monthly housing costs:											
Less than $300	21,844	17,027	4,815	1,721	1,423	883	549	8,833	1,364	3,015	2,682
$300-$399	10,644	6,360	4,285	555	1,004	287	529	2,560	558	710	1,305
$400-$499	10,913	5,268	5,645	444	1,182	249	762	1,479	583	510	1,345
$500-$599	9,997	4,921	5,076	430	928	227	797	947	485	389	904
$600-$699	8,544	4,356	4,188	381	698	219	652	585	389	258	621
$700-$799	7,052	4,142	2,910	323	409	209	388	455	240	227	420
$800-$999	9,540	6,684	2,856	496	417	296	369	582	245	282	309
$1,000 or more	16,815	14,786	2,029	786	167	877	201	855	196	644	166
Median amount (dol.) [4]	543	563	523	465	459	590	535	282	418	300	391
Monthly housing costs as percent of income: [5]											
Less than 5 percent	3,036	2,845	191	174	16	104	19	669	14	17	15
5 to 9 percent	10,508	9,570	938	677	121	455	88	2,749	67	88	55
10 to 14 percent	14,002	11,260	2,741	827	446	444	216	3,222	129	223	116
15 to 19 percent	14,673	10,637	4,035	755	727	470	424	2,382	192	296	194
20 to 24 percent	12,318	8,174	4,144	668	796	397	482	1,724	381	348	297
25 to 29 percent	9,519	5,523	3,996	405	758	293	517	1,196	556	319	578
30 to 34 percent	6,514	3,586	2,928	298	540	205	410	866	485	338	472
35 to 39 percent	4,703	2,402	2,301	227	421	164	370	662	325	262	418
40 percent or more	18,234	8,377	9,857	964	2,219	649	1,639	2,515	1,826	3,007	4,999
Median amount (percent) [4]	22	19	29	20	31	21	34	18	38	52	62
Median monthly costs (dol.): [4]											
Electricity	63	69	48	71	52	64	44	59	40	62	46
Piped gas	38	42	29	46	35	29	25	41	26	38	30
Fuel oil	59	61	52	57	54	60	43	61	54	53	52

[1] Persons of Hispanic origin may be of any race. [2] Householders 65 years old and over. [3] Includes units with mortgage payment not reported and no cash rent not shown separately. [4] For explanation of median, see Guide to Tabular Presentation [5] Money income before taxes.

Source of tables 1202 and 1203: U.S. Bureau of the Census, *Current Housing Reports*, series H-150/95RV, *American Housing Survey in the United States (Revised)*. Internet site <http://www.census gov/prod/2/constr/h150/h15095rv.pdf> (accessed 25 August 1997).

No. 1204. Owner Occupied Housing Units—Mortgage Characteristics, by Region: 1995

[As of fall. Based on the American Housing Survey; see Appendix III]

CHARACTERISTIC	NUMBER (1,000)					PERCENT DISTRIBUTION				
	Total units	North-east	Mid-west	South	West	Total units	North-east	Mid-west	South	West
ALL OWNERS										
Total units	**63,544**	**11,881**	**16,567**	**22,969**	**12,157**	**100.0**	**100.0**	**100.0**	**100.0**	**100.0**
Mortgages currently on property:										
None, owned free and clear	24,518	4,607	6,479	9,666	3,765	38.6	38.8	39.1	42.1	31.0
Mortgaged	39,026	7,254	10,088	13,292	8,392	61.4	61.2	60.9	57.9	69.0
One mortgage or land contract	34,730	6,326	8,913	12,183	7,307	54.7	53.3	53.8	53.1	60.1
Two mortgages	4,244	914	1,167	1,102	1,062	6.7	7.7	7.0	4.8	8.7
Three mortgages or more	52	14	7	7	23	0.1	0.1	0.0	0.0	0.2
OWNERS WITH MORTGAGES										
Total units	**39,026**	**7,254**	**10,089**	**13,292**	**8,392**	**100.0**	**100.0**	**100.0**	**100.0**	**100.0**
Type of primary mortgage:										
FHA	5,172	514	1,182	2,252	1,225	13.3	7.1	11.7	16.9	14.6
VA	2,356	170	467	1,086	632	6.0	2.3	4.6	8.2	7.5
Farmers Home Administration [1]	381	47	114	158	62	1.0	0.6	1.1	1.2	0.7
Other types	27,906	5,732	7,793	8,583	5,798	71.5	79.0	77.3	64.6	69.1
Don't know	1,336	265	202	585	284	3.4	3.7	2.0	4.4	3.4
Not reported	1,875	527	330	628	390	4.8	7.3	3.3	4.7	4.6
Payment plan of primary mortgage:										
Fixed payment, self amortizing	30,002	5,392	7,925	10,519	6,166	76.9	74.3	78.6	79.1	73.5
Adjustable rate mortgage	4,473	900	1,116	1,233	1,224	11.5	12.4	11.1	9.3	14.6
Graduated payment mortgage	370	67	79	114	109	0.9	0.9	0.8	0.9	1.3
Balloon	586	53	244	178	112	1.5	0.7	2.4	1.3	1.3
Other	567	102	144	200	121	1.5	1.4	1.4	1.5	1.4
Combination	336	71	93	103	69	0.9	1.0	0.9	0.8	0.8
Not reported	2,691	669	486	946	590	6.9	9.2	4.8	7.1	7.0
Home equity loan:										
With a home equity loan	8,474	1,771	2,271	2,384	2,048	21.7	24.4	22.5	17.9	24.4
No home equity loan	27,696	4,906	7,243	9,776	5,770	71.0	67.6	71.8	73.5	68.8
Not reported	2,857	576	574	1,132	574	7.3	7.9	5.7	8.5	6.8

[1] Due to a reorganization, now the Rural Housing Service handles these mortgage functions.

Source: U.S. Bureau of the Census, *Current Housing Reports*, series H-150/95, *American Housing Survey in the United States*.

No. 1205. Heating Equipment and Fuels for Occupied Units: 1991 to 1995

[As of fall. Based on American Housing Survey. See Appendix III]

TYPE OF EQUIPMENT OR FUEL	NUMBER (1,000)			PERCENT DISTRIBUTION		
	1991	1993	1995	1991	1993	1995
Occupied units, total	**93,147**	**94,724**	**97,692**	**100.0**	**100.0**	**100.0**
Heating equipment:						
Warm air furnace	49,423	51,248	53,165	53.1	54.1	54.4
Heat pumps	7,638	8,422	9,406	8.2	8.9	9.6
Steam or hot water	13,929	13,657	13,669	15.0	14.4	14.0
Floor, wall, or pipeless furnace	4,291	4,746	4,963	4.6	5.0	5.1
Built-in electric units	6,755	6,722	7,035	7.3	7.1	7.2
Room heaters with flue	2,549	1,766	1,620	2.7	1.9	1.7
Room heaters without flue	2,111	1,597	1,642	2.3	1.7	1.7
Fireplaces, stoves, portable heaters or other	5,590	5,654	5,150	6.0	6.0	5.3
None	861	911	1,044	0.9	1.0	1.1
House main heating fuel:						
Utility gas	47,018	47,669	49,203	50.5	50.3	50.4
Fuel oil, kerosene, etc	12,462	12,189	12,029	13.4	12.9	12.3
Electricity	23,714	25,107	26,771	25.5	26.5	27.4
Bottled, tank, or LP gas	3,882	3,922	4,251	4.2	4.1	4.4
Coal or coke	319	297	210	0.3	0.3	0.2
Wood and other fuel	4,890	4,630	4,166	5.2	4.9	4.3
None	862	910	1,043	0.9	1.0	1.1
Cooking fuel:						
Electricity	54,232	55,887	57,621	58.2	59.0	59.0
Gas [1]	38,119	37,996	39,218	40.9	40.1	40.1
Other fuel	424	479	566	0.5	0.5	0.6
None	372	362	287	0.4	0.4	0.3

[1] Includes utility, bottled, tank, and LP gas.

Source: U.S. Bureau of the Census, *Current Housing Reports*, series H150/91, H150/93, and H150/95, *American Housing Survey in the United States*.

No. 1206. Occupied Housing Units—Housing Indicators, by Selected Characteristics of the Householder: 1995

[In thousands of units. As of fall. Based on the American Housing Survey. See Appendix III]

CHARACTERISTIC	Total occupied units	TENURE		BLACK		HISPANIC ORIGIN [1]		ELDERLY [2]		HOUSEHOLDS BELOW POVERTY LEVEL	
		Owner	Renter	Owner	Renter	Owner	Renter	Owner	Renter	Owner	Renter
Total units	**97,693**	**63,544**	**34,150**	**5,137**	**6,637**	**3,245**	**4,612**	**16,299**	**4,542**	**6,034**	**8,661**
Amenities:											
Porch, deck, balcony or patio	75,657	54,319	21,338	4,052	3,873	2,597	2,406	13,572	2,492	4,804	4,841
Usable fireplace	31,734	27,280	4,454	1,438	554	992	430	5,611	354	1,661	596
Separate dining room	46,657	36,374	10,283	2,934	2,074	1,652	1,155	8,293	1,028	2,600	2,140
With 2 or more living rooms or recreation rooms	28,941	26,179	2,762	1,659	355	925	197	5,680	277	1,578	428
Garage or carport with home	57,352	46,906	10,446	2,804	1,171	2,326	1,363	12,268	1,190	3,598	1,860
Cars and trucks available:											
No cars, trucks, or vans	9,583	2,491	7,092	538	2,375	125	1,202	1,745	2,100	881	3,565
Other households without cars	7,006	4,669	2,337	201	165	347	355	758	108	549	444
1 car with or without trucks or vans	48,263	30,648	17,615	2,399	3,176	1,464	2,100	9,870	2,074	3,180	3,869
2 cars	26,149	19,986	6,163	1,544	819	996	721	3,397	228	1,147	678
3 or more cars	6,692	5,750	942	455	102	314	133	529	33	276	106
With cars, no trucks or vans	52,068	32,256	19,812	3,093	3,702	1,557	2,282	9,950	2,153	3,036	4,092
1 truck or van with or without cars	28,423	22,304	6,119	1,276	523	1,168	875	3,648	269	1,650	880
2 or more trucks or vans	7,619	6,493	1,126	230	37	396	153	756	20	467	125
Internal deficiencies:											
Signs of rats in last 3 months	2,708	1,219	1,489	230	555	193	463	263	132	236	637
Holes in floors	1,074	503	571	106	177	71	125	84	36	126	222
Open cracks or holes	4,527	1,943	2,584	356	750	168	426	347	176	346	921
Broken plaster or peeling paint (interior of unit)	3,673	1,672	2,002	273	584	145	333	375	167	304	729
No electrical wiring	26	22	4	-	-	-	-	3	2	15	-
Exposed wiring	1,760	873	887	88	240	80	175	260	105	104	306
Rooms without electric outlet	1,816	891	925	130	269	44	147	276	98	167	353
Water leakage [3]	11,411	6,325	5,086	641	1,197	354	662	1,067	443	616	1,434

- Represents zero. [1] Persons of Hispanic origin may be of any race. [2] Householders 65 years old and over. [3] During the 12 months prior to the survey.

Source: U.S. Bureau of the Census, *Current Housing Reports*, series H150/95, *American Housing Survey in the United States.*

No. 1207. Appliances Used by Households, by Region and Family Income: 1993

[In millions, except percent. Represents appliances possessed and generally used by the household. Based on Residential Energy Consumption Survey; see source. For composition of regions, see table 26]

TYPE OF APPLIANCE	HOUSEHOLDS USING APPLIANCE		REGION				FAMILY INCOME IN 1993			
	Number	Percent of total	Northeast	Midwest	South	West	Under $25,000	$25,000-$34,999	$35,000-$49,999	$50,000 and over
Total households	**96.6**	**100.0**	**19.5**	**23.3**	**33.5**	**20.4**	**35.4**	**22.8**	**10.8**	**27.8**
Air conditioners	66.1	68.4	11.3	17.1	29.9	7.8	21.7	15.7	7.9	20.8
Room	25.7	26.6	7.6	6.6	9.0	2.6	11.4	5.8	3.0	5.5
Central system [1]	42.1	43.5	3.9	10.8	21.8	5.5	10.6	10.5	5.1	15.9
Clothes washer	74.5	77.1	14.4	18.4	27.0	14.7	21.9	18.4	9.3	24.9
Clothes dryer	68.8	71.2	12.5	18.0	24.6	13.6	18.2	17.5	8.9	24.2
Dehumidifier	9.1	9.4	2.5	5.1	1.2	0.2	1.7	1.8	1.4	4.1
Dishwasher	43.7	45.2	8.1	9.4	15.7	10.5	7.7	10.2	6.5	19.4
Freezer	33.4	34.5	5.0	10.2	12.5	5.7	9.9	8.2	4.2	11.0
Microwave oven [2]	81.3	84.1	15.1	20.8	27.8	17.5	25.6	20.3	9.8	25.5
Office equipment	23.3	24.2	4.8	5.5	7.2	5.8	3.2	4.7	3.8	11.7
Facsimile machine	2.9	3.0	0.6	0.4	1.0	0.8	(B)	0.5	0.5	1.6
Laser printer	5.3	5.5	0.9	1.0	1.8	1.6	0.5	0.9	0.7	3.0
Personal computer	22.6	23.3	4.7	5.3	6.9	5.7	3.2	4.4	3.6	11.4
Outdoor gas grill	27.5	28.5	7.0	7.4	8.5	4.7	4.0	6.9	4.3	12.4
Oven: Electric	59.4	61.5	9.2	13.5	23.8	12.9	19.0	14.5	7.2	18.9
Gas	30.7	31.8	8.6	8.4	6.9	6.7	13.0	6.6	3.2	7.9
Range: Electric	59.3	61.4	9.3	13.6	23.9	12.6	19.1	14.5	7.2	18.6
Gas	32.2	33.3	9.0	8.7	7.2	7.2	13.7	6.8	3.3	8.4
Refrigerator: Frost-free	81.8	84.6	16.1	19.3	29.4	17.0	26.4	19.9	9.8	25.6
Nonfrost-free [3]	14.7	15.2	3.4	4.0	4.0	3.4	6.9	2.8	1.0	2.0
Television set: Color	94.4	97.7	19.1	22.8	32.7	19.9	33.7	22.6	10.7	27.4
Black and white	19.0	19.6	3.9	5.5	6.5	3.1	6.7	4.3	2.0	6.0
Toaster oven	27.5	28.5	7.2	4.5	10.1	5.7	9.2	5.8	3.5	9.0
Water heater: [4] Gas	51.2	53.0	10.1	15.3	12.6	13.2	18.4	11.0	5.8	16.0
Electric	37.1	38.4	4.5	6.9	19.2	6.5	14.1	9.8	4.1	9.3
Ceiling fan	51.8	53.6	8.6	13.2	22.1	8.0	15.2	12.6	7.0	17.1

B Base figure too small to meet statistical standards for reliability. [1] Includes the households with both central air conditioning and window or wall air conditioning units. [2] Microwave is first or second most used oven. [3] Includes refrigerators without freezer compartments. [4] Excludes water heaters that serve more than one household.

Source: U.S. Energy Information Administration, *Housing Characteristics: 1993.*

No. 1208. Expenditures by Residential Property Owners for Improvements and Maintenance and Repairs, by Type of Property and Activity: 1980 to 1995

[In millions of dollars]

YEAR AND TYPE OF EXPENDITURE	Total	1-unit properties with owner occupant	Other properties	ADDITIONS AND ALTERATIONS				Major replacements	Maintenance and repairs
				Total	To structures		To property outside of structures		
					Additions	Alterations			
1980	46,338	31,481	14,857	21,336	4,183	11,193	5,960	9,816	15,187
1981	46,351	30,201	16,150	20,414	3,164	11,947	5,303	9,915	16,022
1982	45,291	29,779	15,512	18,774	2,641	10,711	5,423	9,707	16,810
1983	49,295	32,524	16,771	20,271	4,739	11,673	3,859	10,895	18,128
1984	69,784	43,781	26,003	27,822	6,007	14,486	7,329	13,067	28,894
1985	80,267	47,742	32,525	28,775	3,966	17,599	7,211	16,134	35,358
1986	91,274	54,298	36,976	38,608	7,377	21,192	10,040	16,695	35,971
1987	94,082	54,791	39,291	39,978	9,557	21,641	8,779	15,875	38,229
1988	101,117	60,822	40,295	43,339	11,333	22,703	9,303	16,893	40,885
1989	100,891	59,858	41,033	39,786	6,828	23,129	9,828	18,415	42,689
1990	106,773	59,683	47,090	37,253	8,561	21,920	6,771	18,215	51,305
1991	97,528	58,083	39,445	30,944	7,914	16,076	6,954	16,744	49,840
1992	103,734	67,316	36,418	40,186	6,783	22,700	10,704	18,393	45,154
1993	108,305	70,746	37,559	45,797	12,757	24,781	8,259	20,809	41,699
1994, total [1]	**115,030**	**77,270**	**37,760**	**48,828**	**9,647**	**28,672**	**10,509**	**23,248**	**42,953**
Heating and air conditioning [2]	8,581	5,712	2,869	2,060	(NA)	2,060	(NA)	3,904	2,617
Plumbing	8,941	5,222	3,719	1,677	(NA)	1,677	(NA)	2,836	4,428
Roofing	11,406	6,371	5,034	(NA)	(NA)	(NA)	(NA)	7,008	4,398
Painting	11,446	6,439	5,007	(NA)	(NA)	(NA)	(NA)	(NA)	11,446
1995, total [1]	**111,683**	**75,362**	**36,321**	**44,726**	**7,936**	**26,893**	**9,897**	**24,910**	**42,047**
Heating and air conditioning [2]	10,151	7,480	2,671	1,872	(NA)	1,872	(NA)	5,639	2,640
Plumbing	9,489	5,145	4,344	2,354	(NA)	2,354	(NA)	3,053	4,082
Roofing	10,415	6,972	3,443	(NA)	(NA)	(NA)	(NA)	6,280	4,135
Painting	10,910	6,169	4,741	(NA)	(NA)	(NA)	(NA)	(NA)	10,910

NA Not available. [1] Includes types of expenditures not separately specified. [2] Central air-conditioning.

Source: U.S. Bureau of the Census, *Current Construction Reports*, series C50, *Expenditures for Residential Improvements*, quarterly.

No. 1209. Characteristics of Property Owners and Managers: 1995

[In thousands. For privately owned rental units. Based on survey and subject to sampling error; see source for details]

CHARACTERISTIC	SINGLE FAMILY PROPERTIES		MULTI FAMILY PROPERTIES						
	Total	Detached	Total	2 units	3 to 4 units	5 to 9 units	10 to 19 units	20 to 49 units	50 units or more
All owners [1]	**8,773**	**6,438**	**20,585**	**3,085**	**2,471**	**1,894**	**1,468**	**2,224**	**9,443**
Individual or partnership owners [2]	7,746	5,752	16,915	2,953	2,347	1,713	1,236	1,858	6,806
Under 25 years old	-	-	14	5	3	-	3	-	3
25 to 34 years old	218	118	490	155	130	68	24	44	69
35 to 44 years old	1,146	823	1,514	475	281	232	114	122	289
45 to 54 years old	1,663	1,237	2,808	670	496	372	184	341	744
55 to 64 years old	1,747	1,336	2,698	561	494	337	218	373	716
65 to 74 years old	1,425	1,093	1,995	428	349	232	167	201	618
75 years or older	891	713	958	270	200	94	109	65	221
Male	5,130	3,814	9,584	1,866	1,540	1,103	768	1,181	3,125
Female	2,316	1,744	2,261	836	545	347	150	174	208
White	6,307	4,654	10,400	2,264	1,731	1,270	825	1,234	3,077
Black	595	499	599	241	197	79	17	14	51
American Indian or Alaskan Native	41	30	22	4	8	3	-	-	7
Asian or Pacific Islander	254	192	442	90	79	53	50	63	107
Other	174	127	217	56	49	32	7	30	43
Hispanic	436	322	479	135	126	80	27	59	52
Non-Hispanic	6,719	5,017	11,104	2,492	1,925	1,334	884	1,276	3,213
Percent of rental income spent on maintenance:									
None	1,261	1,020	283	185	27	27	7	-	36
1 to 4 percent	1,426	1,022	1,530	407	280	141	105	122	475
5 to 9 percent	1,429	1,057	2,844	513	385	275	230	338	1,103
10 to 19 percent	1,741	1,303	4,446	784	658	400	380	431	1,793
20 to 29 percent	764	516	2,287	317	283	256	145	263	1,023
30 to 39 percent	316	211	1,270	158	118	103	58	162	671
40 to 49 percent	182	114	751	78	35	95	83	89	370
50 to 74 percent	231	174	935	73	128	73	65	130	466
75 percent or more	300	219	639	132	123	78	26	91	190

- Represents zero. [1] Includes other owners not shown separately. [2] Includes those not reporting.

Source: U.S. Bureau of the Census, Internet site <http://www.census.gov/hhes/www/poma.html> (accessed 23 April 1997).

No. 1210. Net Stock of Residential Capital: 1985 to 1995

[In billions of dollars. End of year estimates]

ITEM	1985	1986	1987	1988	1989	1990	1991	1992	1993	1994	1995
Total residential capital [1]	4,683.3	5,043.1	5,386.5	5,737.1	6,054.7	6,295.7	6,407.8	6,749.5	7,156.9	7,591.2	7,917.7
By type of owner and legal form of organization:											
Private	4,578.2	4,934.1	5,267.7	5,602.7	5,911.1	6,147.3	6,258.5	6,591.4	6,989.0	7,412.6	7,732.8
Corporate	55.6	59.3	62.6	65.3	67.1	68.6	69.4	72.3	74.6	75.7	77.7
Noncorporate	4,522.6	4,874.7	5,205.0	5,537.4	5,844.0	6,078.7	6,189.1	6,519.1	6,914.4	7,336.9	7,655.2
Government	105.1	109.0	118.9	134.4	143.6	148.4	149.3	158.2	167.9	178.7	184.9
Federal	32.0	30.4	35.4	46.2	50.3	51.4	50.1	52.9	55.3	58.4	59.5
State and local	73.1	78.6	83.4	88.3	93.3	97.0	99.2	105.3	112.7	120.3	125.4
By tenure group:											
Owner-occupied	3,254.0	3,520.0	3,774.7	4,043.9	4,298.3	4,494.3	4,597.9	4,870.7	5,208.7	5,589.7	5,869.9
Farm	128.6	133.6	138.4	142.5	146.9	151.2	152.0	156.8	162.1	168.4	172.1
Nonfarm	3,125.3	3,386.4	3,636.3	3,901.4	4,151.4	4,343.1	4,445.9	4,713.9	5,046.6	5,421.4	5,697.8
Tenant-occupied	1,302.3	1,391.1	1,469.1	1,534.0	1,587.1	1,626.7	1,634.7	1,694.1	1,752.6	1,794.2	1,834.5
Farm	5.6	5.9	6.1	6.3	6.4	6.7	6.7	6.9	7.3	7.6	7.8
Nonfarm	1,296.7	1,385.2	1,463.0	1,527.7	1,580.7	1,620.1	1,628.0	1,687.2	1,745.4	1,786.6	1,826.7

[1] Includes stocks of other nonfarm residential capital, which consists of dormitories, fraternity and sorority houses, and nurses' homes.

Source: U.S. Bureau of Economic Analysis, *Survey of Current Business*, monthly, May 1997 issue.

No. 1211. Vacancy Rates for Housing Units—Characteristics: 1990 to 1996

[In percent. Rate is relationship between vacant housing for rent or for sale and the total rental and homeowner supply, which comprises occupied units, units rented or sold and awaiting occupancy, and vacant units available for rent or sale. For composition of regions, see table 26. Based on the Current Population Survey/Housing Vacancy Survey; see source for details]

CHARACTERISTIC	RENTAL UNITS					HOMEOWNER UNITS				
	1990	1993 [1]	1994	1995	1996	1990	1993 [1]	1994	1995	1996
Total units	7.2	7.3	7.4	7.6	7.8	1.7	1.4	1.5	1.5	1.6
Inside MSA's	7.1	7.5	7.3	7.6	7.7	1.7	1.4	1.5	1.5	1.6
Outside MSA's	7.6	6.5	7.7	7.9	8.7	1.8	1.5	1.5	1.6	1.7
Northeast	6.1	7.0	7.1	7.2	7.4	1.6	1.3	1.5	1.5	1.6
Midwest	6.4	6.6	6.8	7.2	7.9	1.3	1.1	1.1	1.3	1.3
South	8.8	7.9	8.0	8.3	8.6	2.1	1.7	1.7	1.7	1.8
West	6.6	7.4	7.1	7.5	7.2	1.8	1.4	1.6	1.7	1.7
Units in structure:										
1 unit	4.0	3.7	4.5	5.4	5.5	1.4	1.2	1.3	1.4	1.4
2 units or more	9.0	9.4	9.1	9.0	9.2	7.1	5.3	4.9	4.8	5.1
5 units or more	9.6	10.2	9.8	9.5	9.6	8.4	6.8	5.6	5.1	6.0
Units with—										
3 rooms or less	10.3	10.7	11.1	11.4	11.4	10.2	6.9	9.7	9.2	9.9
4 rooms	8.0	8.1	7.9	8.2	8.8	3.2	2.5	3.0	2.8	3.0
5 rooms	5.7	5.7	5.7	5.8	5.9	2.0	1.7	1.8	1.8	1.9
6 rooms or more	3.0	3.2	3.4	3.8	3.8	1.1	1.0	0.9	1.1	1.1

[1] Beginning 1993, based on 1990 population census controls.

Source: Bureau of the Census, Internet site <http://www.census.gov/ftp/pub/hhes/www/hvs.html> (accessed 29 July 1997)

No. 1212. Recent Home Buyers—General Characteristics: 1976 to 1996

[As of October. Based on a sample survey; subject to sampling variability]

ITEM	Unit	1976	1980	1985	1990	1992	1993	1994	1995	1996
Median purchase price	Dollars	43,340	68,714	90,400	131,200	141,000	141,900	145,400	147,700	153,200
First-time buyers	Dollars	37,670	61,450	75,100	106,000	122,400	121,100	125,000	128,300	130,100
Repeat buyers [1]	Dollars	50,090	75,750	106,200	149,400	158,000	159,600	163,500	164,300	170,700
Average monthly mortgage payment	Dollars	329	599	896	1,127	1,064	1,015	1,028	1,062	1,067
Percent of income	Percent	24.0	32.4	30.0	33.8	33.2	31.5	31.4	32.6	32.6
Percent buying—										
New houses	Percent	15.1	22.4	23.8	21.2	20.5	22.3	22.0	21.5	22.7
Existing houses	Percent	84.9	77.6	76.2	78.8	79.5	77.7	78.0	78.5	77.3
Single-family houses	Percent	88.8	82.4	87.0	83.8	85.0	84.2	83.9	83.1	82.6
Condominiums [2]	Percent	11.2	17.6	10.6	13.1	13.1	12.8	12.1	14.0	14.2
For the first time	Percent	44.8	32.9	36.6	41.9	47.7	46.0	47.1	46.2	44.7
Average age:										
First-time buyers	Years	28.1	28.3	28.4	30.5	31.0	31.6	31.6	32.1	32.4
Repeat buyers [1]	Years	35.9	36.4	38.4	39.1	40.8	41.0	41.7	40.7	41.1
Downpayment/sales price	Percent	25.2	28.0	24.8	23.3	21.4	20.2	20.2	20.4	19.5
First-time buyers	Percent	18.0	20.5	11.4	15.7	14.3	14.0	13.7	13.3	12.4
Repeat buyers [1]	Percent	30.8	32.7	32.7	28.9	28.0	25.4	26.1	26.8	25.3

[1] Buyers who previously owned a home. [2] Includes multiple-family houses.

Source: Chicago Title Insurance Company, Chicago, IL, *The Guarantor*, quarterly (copyright).

No. 1213. Commercial Office Space—Overview for Selected Metropolitan Areas: 1996

[As of mid-October. For the 75 market areas with the highest vacancy rates in 1996. Data based on responses from individuals knowledgeable in the local markets]

MARKET AREA	Inventory (1,000 sq. ft.)	Vacant space (1,000 sq. ft.)	Vacancy rate (percent)	Construction (1,000 sq. ft.)	Net absorption [1] (1,000 sq. ft.)
United States, all 123 market areas [2]	3,237,856	375,349	11.6	28,535	83,115
Albuquerque, NM	9,615	1,038	10.8	419	-133
Allentown, PA	5,750	549	9.5	(NA)	1,053
Baltimore, MD	43,966	5,599	12.7	810	310
Bridgeport, CT	7,378	1,044	14.2	-	78
Buffalo, NY	7,607	1,111	14.6	72	13
Charleston, SC	3,444	396	11.5	136	210
Chicago, IL	203,869	19,440	9.5	300	1,297
Cleveland, OH	35,720	5,136	14.4	263	327
Columbia, SC	9,915	1,243	12.5	122	272
Dallas, TX	116,326	19,822	17.0	435	4,543
Dayton, OH	11,652	1,571	13.5	-	-47
Denver, CO	60,621	6,947	11.5	800	1,163
Detroit, MI	13,706	1,803	13.2	-	-148
El Paso, TX	6,487	810	12.5	-	930
Fort Lauderdale, FL	15,151	1,665	11.0	277	437
Fort Wayne, IN	5,401	585	10.8	-	75
Fort Worth, TX	17,978	2,095	11.7	79	880
Fresno, CA	12,633	1,362	10.8	78	394
Greensboro, NC	12,994	1,651	12.7	245	-190
Greenville, SC	4,064	468	11.5	125	189
Hartford, CT	21,400	3,200	15.0	-	200
Honolulu, HI	14,642	2,168	14.8	637	-30
Houston, TX	133,268	20,047	15.0	-	5,188
Indianapolis, IN	19,500	2,313	11.9	125	1,144
Knoxville, TN	9,715	1,085	11.2	-	70
Lansing, MI	6,047	572	9.5	220	473
Los Angeles-Central, CA	19,962	3,766	18.8	(NA)	(NA)
Los Angeles-Orange County, CA	54,234	7,864	14.5	-	825
Los Angeles-San Bernardino, CA	3,660	781	21.3	-	42
Los Angeles-San Fernando Valley, CA	31,040	4,036	13.0	120	52
Los Angeles-San Gabriel Valley, CA	11,541	2,308	20.0	-	1,226
Los Angeles-South Bay, CA	29,463	7,762	26.3	-	-885
Louisville, KY	13,876	1,985	14.3	160	215
Marin County, CA	5,403	558	10.3	(NA)	135
Miami, FL	27,113	3,137	11.6	730	328
Milwaukee, WI	25,000	3,056	12.2	(NA)	(NA)
Mobile, AL	3,000	428	14.3	100	-
Nashua, NH	1,818	218	12.0	30	59
New Haven, CT	11,200	2,430	21.7	-	220
New Jersey-Central	52,123	6,751	13.0	80	3,365
New Jersey-Northern	83,406	14,471	17.3	(NA)	2,889
New Jersey-Southern	14,430	2,861	19.8	150	165
New Orleans, LA	17,962	3,302	18.4	-	593
New York-Brooklyn/Queens, NY	64,822	7,001	10.8	-	995
New York-Long Island, NY	37,593	6,117	16.3	65	613
New York-Manhattan, NY	337,439	46,744	13.9	-	1,710
New York-Westchester, NY	25,313	6,034	23.8	-	-742
Oakland, CA	15,912	2,320	14.6	-	1,094
Oklahoma City, OK	14,240	2,297	16.1	-	1,009
Philadelphia, PA	68,532	10,407	15.2	570	330
Pittsburgh, PA	34,674	4,743	13.7	271	1,748
Providence, RI	8,634	1,602	18.6	-	86
Roanoke, VA	2,638	424	16.1	-	-23
Sacramento, CA	26,206	2,613	10.0	833	606
Saint Louis, MO	33,396	4,155	12.4	150	1,492
San Antonio, TX	16,029	1,981	12.4	-	680
San Diego, CA	59,310	6,733	11.4	210	3,118
Santa Rosa, CA	6,463	832	12.9	-	-16
Savannah, GA	699	101	14.5	(NA)	(NA)
Seattle, WA	29,092	2,904	10.0	95	-135
Shreveport, LA	3,653	848	23.2	-	80
Sioux Falls, SD	1,690	196	11.6	79	20
Springfield, MA	3,400	335	9.9	-	265
Stamford, CT	25,851	3,759	14.5	790	403
Stockton, CA	5,537	706	12.8	(NA)	(NA)
Syracuse, NY	9,229	1,805	19.6	-	220
Tampa, FL	20,717	2,401	11.6	90	240
Toledo, OH	5,815	850	14.6	-	-33
Tucson, AZ	6,203	593	9.6	10	56
Tulsa, OK	13,470	1,665	12.4	-	917
Washington, DC-Suburban MD	62,322	6,977	11.2	190	1,108
West Palm Beach, FL	6,917	781	11.3	165	140
Wichita, KS	5,436	868	16.0	-	72
Wilmington, DE	10,253	1,010	9.8	52	1,003
Youngstown, OH	2,500	370	14.8	25	-15

- Represents zero. NA Not available. [1] Net change in occupied stock. [2] Includes other market areas, not shown separately.

Source: Society of Industrial and Office REALTORS, Washington DC, *1997 Comparative Statistics of Industrial and Office Real Estate Markets.*

No. 1214. Commercial Buildings—Selected Characteristics, by Square Footage of Floorspace: 1995

[Preliminary. Excludes buildings 1,000 square feet or smaller. Building type based on predominant activity in which the occupants were engaged. Based on a sample survey of building representatives conducted between August and December 1995; therefore, subject to sampling variability. For composition of regions, see table 26]

CHARACTERISTIC	Number of buildings (1,000)	FLOORSPACE (mil. sq. ft.)							Mean sq. ft. per building (1,000)	Median sq. ft. per building (1,000)
		Total	Within buildings having square footage of—							
			5,000 or less	5,001 to 10,000	10,001 to 25,000	25,001 to 50,000	50,001 to 100,000	100,001 and over		
All buildings	4,579	58,772	6,338	7,530	11,617	7,676	7,968	17,643	12.8	5.0
Region:										
Northeast	725	11,883	995	1,223	2,118	1,380	1,371	4,795	16.4	5.0
Midwest	1,139	14,322	1,772	1,678	2,701	1,726	1,920	4,526	12.6	4.5
South	1,750	20,830	2,428	2,786	4,481	2,664	2,980	5,491	11.9	4.8
West	964	11,736	1,144	1,842	2,317	1,906	1,697	2,831	12.2	5.5
Year constructed:										
1919 or before	353	3,673	442	756	957	407	386	[3]340	10.4	5.5
1920 to 1945	562	6,710	855	961	1,241	595	750	2,288	11.9	4.8
1946 to 1959	867	9,298	1,180	1,710	1,942	1,260	1,293	1,913	10.7	4.3
1960 to 1969	718	10,858	889	1,132	2,163	1,650	1,453	3,572	15.1	5.5
1970 to 1979	813	11,333	1,245	1,186	2,071	1,337	1,453	4,040	13.9	5.0
1980 to 1989	846	12,252	1,067	1,102	2,809	1,701	1,816	3,737	14.5	5.0
1990 to 1992	218	2,590	316	368	251	378	410	867	11.9	3.5
1993 to 1995	202	2,059	324	296	184	349	407	[4]264	10.2	3.5
Principal activity within building:										
Education	309	7,740	250	404	1,045	1,825	1,752	[1]2,216	25.1	8.5
Food sales	137	642	234	(S)	(S)	(S)	(S)	(NA)	4.7	2.5
Food service	285	1,353	550	390	(S)	(S)	(S)	(NA)	4.8	3.0
Health care	105	2,333	152	(S)	243	175	(S)	1,483	22.2	4.5
Lodging	158	3,618	150	269	748	512	613	[1]1,105	22.8	9.0
Mercantile/services	1,289	12,728	1,841	2,202	2,939	1,180	1,274	3,292	9.9	4.0
Office	705	10,478	1,084	915	1,580	1,293	1,542	4,064	14.9	4.0
Public assembly	326	3,948	312	786	940	485	499	[1]655	12.1	6.0
Public order and safety	87	1,271	(S)	(S)	368	(S)	(S)	(NA)	14.6	5.0
Religious worship	269	2,792	301	662	1,120	392	(S)	(NA)	10.4	8.0
Warehouse	580	8,481	807	991	1,530	1,165	1,147	2,841	14.6	5.5
Other	67	1,004	(S)	(S)	(S)	(S)	(S)	(NA)	14.9	5.0
Vacant	261	2,384	399	497	503	148	225	(NA)	9.1	4.0
Government owned	553	12,076	630	924	1,546	2,023	2,211	4,741	21.8	7.0
Nongovernment owned	4,025	46,696	5,709	6,606	10,071	5,653	5,757	9,209	11.6	4.8
Fuels used alone or in combination:										
Electricity	4,358	57,275	6,008	7,064	11,310	7,641	7,925	17,326	13.1	5.0
Natural gas	2,522	38,838	3,020	4,542	7,654	5,309	5,658	12,655	15.4	5.5
Fuel oil	634	14,670	987	713	1,445	1,164	1,992	8,368	23.1	4.8
Propane	589	5,344	997	881	1,342	562	637	[1]772	9.1	4.0
District heat	115	5,941	(S)	(S)	407	673	792	3,848	51.6	12.5
District chilled water	53	2,521	(S)	(S)	239	275	348	1,576	47.7	12.5
Any other	213	2,336	278	414	413	223	419	[2]252	16.2	4.0
Workers:										
Fewer than 5	2,505	13,885	4,184	3,636	3,806	770	518	[3]415	5.5	3.0
5 to 9	798	6,291	1,202	1,606	2,090	529	567	(NA)	7.9	4.8
10 to 19	625	7,102	695	1,637	2,399	1,099	557	[3]480	11.4	7.5
20 to 49	400	9,132	225	615	2,513	2,620	2,087	[1]940	22.8	16.3
50 to 99	138	6,931	(S)	(S)	567	1,644	2,108	[1]2,325	50.3	37.5
100 to 249	71	5,988	(S)	(S)	155	913	1,472	3,431	84.4	55.0
250 or more	43	9,443	(S)	(S)	(S)	(S)	658	8,596	220.1	120.0
Weekly operating hours:										
39 or less	899	6,143	1,544	1,619	1,354	576	426	(NA)	6.8	4.0
40 to 48	1,257	13,233	1,701	2,033	3,382	1,981	1,776	[1]2,144	10.5	4.8
49 to 60	969	12,242	1,264	1,707	2,562	2,103	1,897	2,709	12.6	5.5
61 to 84	567	10,052	653	1,020	1,873	1,182	1,354	3,970	17.7	6.0
85 to 167	420	6,202	618	503	1,024	749	988	2,319	14.8	4.3
168 (open continuously)	466	10,908	559	647	1,422	1,065	1,527	5,670	23.4	6.0

NA Not available. S Figure does not meet publication standards. [1] 100,001 to 500,000 square feet. [2] 200,001 to 500,000 square feet. [3] 100,001 to 200,000 square feet. [4] 200,001 square feet and over.

Source: U.S. Energy Information Administration, *Commercial Buildings Energy Consumption Survey, 1995*, Internet site <http://www.eia.doe.gov/emeu/cbecs/contents.html> (accessed 17 June 1997).

No. 1215. Commercial Buildings—Number and Size, by Principal Activity: 1995

[See headnote, table 1214. For composition of regions, see table 26]

BUILDING CHARACTERISTICS	All buildings[1]	Education	Food sales	Food service	Health care	Lodging	Mercantile/services	Offices	Public assembly	Religious worship	Warehouse
NUMBER (1,000)											
All buildings	**4,579**	**309**	**137**	**285**	**105**	**158**	**1,289**	**705**	**326**	**269**	**580**
Region: Northeast	725	39	(S)	41	14	10	241	112	46	41	88
Midwest	1,139	42	(S)	69	19	38	390	157	89	57	163
South	1,750	111	73	109	51	51	457	298	134	97	223
West	964	117	32	66	21	59	201	138	57	74	105
Year constructed:											
1919 or before	353	18	(S)	(S)	(S)	(S)	112	57	37	20	31
1920 to 1945	562	42	(S)	(S)	(S)	7	154	74	72	(S)	59
1946 to 1959	867	72	(S)	(S)	19	33	278	128	38	65	79
1960 to 1969	718	66	(S)	25	7	53	229	75	63	50	68
1970 to 1979	813	45	42	66	34	24	207	158	60	53	73
1980 to 1986	846	36	(S)	74	(S)	25	212	151	33	58	161
1990 to 1992	218	17	(S)	(S)	(S)	(S)	47	38	20	(S)	38
1993 to 1995	202	13	(S)	(S)	(S)	(S)	49	23	(S)	(S)	71
FLOORSPACE (mil. sq. ft.)											
All buildings	**58,772**	**7,740**	**642**	**1,353**	**2,333**	**3,618**	**12,728**	**10,478**	**3,948**	**2,792**	**8,481**
Region: Northeast	11,883	1,930	(S)	166	406	350	2,838	2,154	694	442	1,480
Midwest	14,322	1,997	(S)	474	466	909	3,203	2,338	957	633	2,044
South	20,830	2,315	287	443	916	1,313	4,864	3,483	1,367	1,006	3,436
West	11,736	1,498	209	271	543	1,047	1,822	2,503	930	711	1,522
Year constructed:											
1919 or before	3,673	521	(S)	(S)	(S)	(S)	816	599	381	266	192
1920 to 1945	6,710	1,080	(S)	(S)	(S)	170	1,118	1,155	706	(S)	1,076
1946 to 1959	9,298	1,921	(S)	(S)	356	607	1,895	1,262	498	637	1,236
1960 to 1969	10,858	1,841	(S)	192	428	972	2,342	1,206	821	535	1,530
1970 to 1979	11,333	1,232	165	285	748	576	2,749	2,095	736	510	1,616
1980 to 1986	12,252	614	(S)	305	425	829	2,727	3,377	399	598	2,104
1990 to 1992	2,590	236	(S)	(S)	(S)	(S)	632	568	221	(S)	318
1993 to 1995	2,059	293	(S)	(S)	(S)	(S)	449	217	(S)	(S)	409

S Figure does not meet publication standards. [1] Includes other commercial buildings, not shown separately.

Source: U.S. Energy Information Administration, *Commercial Buildings Energy Consumption Survey, 1995*, Internet site <http://www.eia.doe.gov/emeu/cbecs/contents.html> (accessed 17 June 1997).

No. 1216. Office Buildings—Vacancy Rates for Major Cities: 1980 to 1996

[As of end of year. Excludes government owned and and occupied, owner-occupied, and medical office buildings]

CITY	1980	1985	1988	1989	1990	1991	1992	1993	1994	1995	1996
Total[1]	**4.6**	**16.9**	**18.6**	**19.5**	**20.0**	**20.2**	**20.5**	**19.4**	**16.2**	**14.3**	**12.4**
Atlanta, GA	10.0	21.0	18.3	19.9	19.1	19.5	19.4	16.8	13.0	10.4	9.2
Baltimore, MD	7.2	11.5	13.4	16.4	20.0	21.0	20.6	17.3	15.5	17.0	14.3
Boston, MA	3.8	13.1	14.1	15.3	19.6	19.1	17.5	17.7	13.3	10.4	6.2
Charlotte, NC	(NA)	16.7	16.5	14.3	16.5	19.4	(NA)	(NA)	10.0	8.9	8.2
Chicago, IL	7.0	16.5	15.9	17.0	18.6	20.0	22.1	21.4	18.7	15.5	15.5
Cincinnati, OH	(NA)	(NA)	13.9	16.6	(NA)	(NA)	19.4	(NA)	15.3	(NA)	13.1
Dallas, TX	8.6	23.0	29.7	26.9	25.8	26.0	31.3	29.5	21.7	18.7	16.2
Denver, CO	6.6	24.7	27.6	26.1	24.8	23.0	21.5	15.9	12.8	12.1	10.8
Detroit, MI	(NA)	(NA)	(NA)	(NA)	(NA)	(NA)	(NA)	21.4	19.7	16.9	11.1
Fort Lauderdale, FL	(NA)	(NA)	19.5	26.3	23.0	24.9	22.9	(NA)	10.8	(NA)	10.5
Hartford, CT	(NA)	(NA)	12.9	17.0	20.0	21.3	23.1	(NA)	21.7	(NA)	22.6
Houston, TX	4.0	27.6	29.2	27.5	24.9	27.3	27.0	25.1	24.7	21.9	17.5
Las Vegas, NV	(NA)	(NA)	(NA)	(NA)	(NA)	(NA)	(NA)	(NA)	8.7	(NA)	10.5
Los Angeles, CA	0.9	15.3	15.8	19.7	16.8	20.2	21.2	21.0	19.6	23.2	22.1
Memphis, TN	(NA)	(NA)	(NA)	(NA)	(NA)	(NA)	(NA)	(NA)	(NA)	(NA)	13.6
Miami, FL	2.4	20.9	24.0	22.0	23.4	22.6	18.5	19.0	15.4	13.8	12.4
Minneapolis, MN	(NA)	(NA)	18.5	20.2	(NA)	18.9	19.9	(NA)	8.2	(NA)	6.5
Nashville, TN	(NA)	(NA)	(NA)	(NA)	25.1	18.4	(NA)	(NA)	7.5	(NA)	6.9
New York, NY[2]	3.1	7.9	11.5	15.1	16.0	18.8	18.3	17.9	16.3	17.0	16.0
Orlando, FL	(NA)	(NA)	(NA)	(NA)	(NA)	(NA)	(NA)	(NA)	12.1	(NA)	6.5
Philadelphia, PA	6.3	14.5	15.8	16.3	18.2	17.3	19.0	17.8	16.3	16.2	13.7
Phoenix, AZ	(NA)	(NA)	(NA)	(NA)	27.6	24.8	24.4	(NA)	11.8	(NA)	11.5
Portland, OR	(NA)	(NA)	(NA)	(NA)	(NA)	(NA)	14.5	(NA)	9.4	(NA)	5.8
Richmond, VA	(NA)	(NA)	(NA)	(NA)	(NA)	(NA)	(NA)	(NA)	11.9	(NA)	9.7
Sacramento, CA	(NA)	(NA)	(NA)	(NA)	(NA)	(NA)	(NA)	(NA)	14.1	(NA)	12.4
San Diego, CA	(NA)	24.7	20.1	17.6	19.5	23.7	23.8	22.1	18.8	17.4	14.1
San Francisco, CA	0.4	13.7	15.5	15.7	14.7	13.3	12.5	13.7	11.7	10.2	5.4
Seattle, WA	(NA)	(NA)	13.2	12.4	12.3	12.8	15.9	17.6	14.7	7.1	5.3
Silicon Valley, CA	(NA)	(NA)	(NA)	(NA)	(NA)	(NA)	(NA)	(NA)	12.7	(NA)	8.7
St Louis, MO	(NA)	(NA)	18.4	22.6	21.0	20.5	21.8	19.1	18.1	12.7	13.4
St Paul, MN	(NA)	(NA)	(NA)	(NA)	(NA)	19.7	18.5	(NA)	15.2	(NA)	12.5
Stamford, CT	(NA)	(NA)	28.4	29.7	27.8	26.4	24.8	(NA)	15.4	(NA)	13.0
Tampa/St. Petersburg	(NA)	(NA)	(NA)	(NA)	(NA)	(NA)	(NA)	(NA)	(NA)	(NA)	13.0
Washington, DC	2.5	9.0	13.2	14.4	19.0	17.6	15.4	14.1	13.4	10.8	9.3
West Palm Beach, CA	(NA)	(NA)	(NA)	(NA)	(NA)	(NA)	(NA)	(NA)	16.8	(NA)	12.0
White Plains, NY	(NA)	(NA)	18.6	20.1	18.6	20.3	22.7	(NA)	18.7	(NA)	19.7
Wilmington, DE	(NA)	(NA)	15.5	12.4	20.3	21.0	19.8	(NA)	16.7	(NA)	9.5
Winston-Salem/Greensboro	(NA)	(NA)	(NA)	(NA)	(NA)	(NA)	(NA)	(NA)	13.2	(NA)	14.1

NA Not available. [1] Includes other cities not shown separately. In 1996, 44 cities were covered. [2] Refers to Manhattan.

Source: ONCOR International, Houston, TX, 1980 and 1985, *National Office Market Report*, semi-annual; 1988-1990, *International Office Market Report*, semi-annual; thereafter, *Year-End (year) Market Data Book, annual* (copyright).

Figure 26.1
Value of Manufacturers' Shipments and New Orders: 1992 to 1996

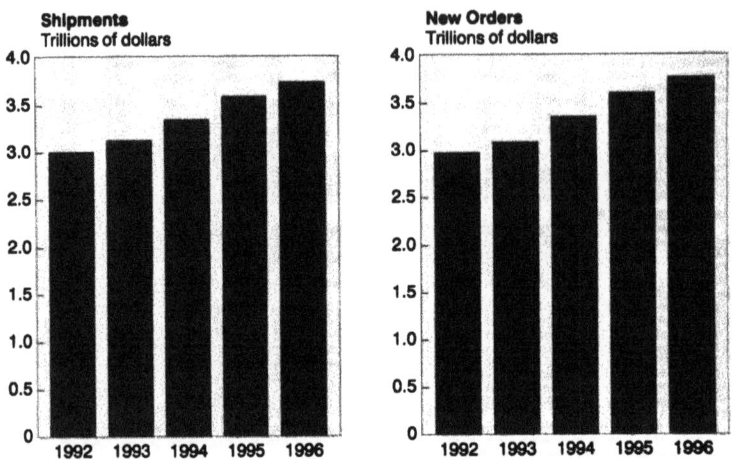

Source: Chart prepared by U.S. Bureau of the Census. For data, see table 1225.

Figure 26.2
Personal Computer Shipments and Revenue: 1992 to 1995

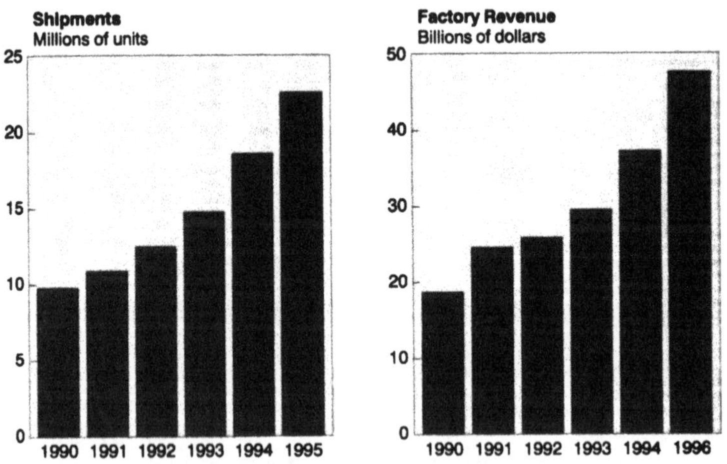

Source: Chart prepared by U.S. Bureau of the Census. For data, see table 1251.

Manufactures

section presents summary data anufacturing as a whole and more ed information for major industry is and selected products. The types asures shown at the different levels le data for establishments; employ- and wages; plant and equipment ex- tures; value and quantity of produc- nd shipments; value added by facture; inventories; and various itors of financial status.

principal sources of these data are au of the Census reports of the cen- s of manufactures conducted every ırs; the *Annual Survey of Manufac-* ; and *Manufacturing Profiles*, an al compilation of the formerly d series of *Current Industrial Re-* . Indexes of industrial production resented monthly in the Federal Re- Board's *Federal Reserve Bulletin.* e numbers were changed to a new base year (1992 = 100) as of early . Reports on current activities of in- ies, or current movements of indi- l commodities, are compiled by government agencies as the Bu- of Labor Statistics; the Economic arch Service of the Department of ulture; the International Trade Ad- tration; and by private research or associations such as The Confer- Board, Inc., the American Iron and Institute, the Electronic Industries ciation, and Dataquest, Inc.

on financial aspects of manufacturing tries are collected by the Bureau of omic Analysis (BEA) and the Bureau Census. Industry aggregates in the of balance sheets, profit and loss nents, analyses of sales and ex- es, lists of subsidiaries, and types and nts of security issues are published ading manufacturing corporations reg- d with the Securities and Exchange nission. The BEA issues data on l in manufacturing industries and ca- utilization rates in manufacturing. also section 17, Business Enterprise.

uses and annual surveys—The ensus of manufactures covered the 1809. Between 1809 and 1963, a is was conducted at periodic inter- vals. Since 1967 it has been taken every 5 years (for years ending in "2" and "7"). Census data, either direct reports or estimates from administrative records, are obtained for every manufacturing plant with one paid employee or more.

In Brief

The Gross Domestic Product for this sector was almost $7 trillion in 1994.

The manufacturing sector employed almost 19 million workers in 1995. The leading states were California, Ohio, Texas, Illinois, and Michigan.

Manufacturing shipments reached a new high in 1996 at $3.7 trillion. Information technology industry and health care equipment sectors also reached new record levels in shipments with $241 and $125 billion, respectively.

The *Annual Survey of Manufactures (ASM)*, conducted for the first time in 1949, collects data for the years between censuses for the more general measures of manufacturing activity covered in detail by the censuses. The annual survey data are estimates derived from a scientifically selected sample of establishments. The 1995 annual survey is based on a sample of about 58,000 establishments of an approximate total of 230,000. These establishments represent all manufacturing establishments of multiunit companies and all single-establishment manufacturing companies mailed schedules in the 1992 Census of Manufactures. The 1994 through 1998 ASM sample is similar to the previous sample. For the current panel, all establishments of companies with 1992 shipments in manufacturing in excess of $500 million were included in the survey with certainty. For the remaining portion of the mail survey, the establishment was defined as the sampling unit. For this portion, all establishments with 250 employees or more and establishments with a very large value of shipments also were included. Therefore, of the 58,000 establishments included in the ASM panel, approximately 33,000 are selected with certainty. These establishments account for approximately 80 percent of total value of shipments in the 1992 census. Smaller establishments in the remaining portion of the mail survey were selected by sample.

Establishments and classification—The censuses of manufactures for 1947 through 1992 cover operating manufacturing establishments as defined in the *Standard Industrial Classification Manual (SIC)*, issued by the U.S. Office of Management and Budget (see text, section 13). The *Manual* is also used for classifying establishments in the annual surveys. The comparability of manufactures data over time is affected by changes in the official definitions of industries as presented in the *Manual*. It is important to note, therefore, that the 1987 edition of the *Manual* was used for the 1987 and 1992 censuses; and the 1972 edition of the *Manual* and the *1977 Supplement* were used for the 1972 through 1982 censuses. For the censuses from 1947 to 1963, reports were required from all establishments employing one or more persons at any time during the census year. Beginning with the 1967 census, an effort was made to relieve the very small establishments from the necessity of filing a census report. Approximately 150,000 small single-unit manufacturing firms identified as having less than 20 employees (cutoff varied by industry) benefited from this procedure. Data for these single-unit companies were estimated on the basis of government administrative records and industry averages. Each of the establishments tabulated was classified in 1 of the approximately 459 manufacturing industries as defined by the *SIC Manual* in 1987. The *Manual* defines an industry as a number of establishments producing a single product or a closely related group of products. In the main, an establishment is classified in a particular industry if its production of a product or product group exceeds in value added its production of any other product group. While some establishments produce only the products of the industry in which they are classified, few within an industry specialize to that extent. The statistics on employment, payrolls, value added, inventories, and expenditures, therefore, reflect both the primary and secondary activities of the establishments in that industry. For this reason, care should be exercised in relating such statistics to the total shipments figures of products primary to the industry.

The censuses for 1947 through 1992 were conducted on an establishment basis. The term "establishment" signifies a single physical plant site or factory. It is not necessarily identical to the business unit or company, which may consist of one or more establishments. A company operating establishments at more than one location is required to submit a separate report for each location. An establishment engaged in distinctly different lines of activity and maintaining separate payroll and inventory records is also required to submit separate reports.

Durable goods—Items with a normal life expectancy of 3 years or more. Automobiles, furniture, household appliances, and mobile homes are common examples.

Nondurable goods—Items which generally last for only a short time (3 years or less). Food, beverages, clothing, shoes, and gasoline are common examples.

Statistical reliability—For a discussion of statistical collection and estimation, sampling procedures and measures of statistical reliability applicable to Census Bureau data, see Appendix III.

No. 1217. Gross Domestic Product in Manufacturing in Current and Real (1992) Dollars, by Industry: 1987 to 1994

[In millions of dollars. Data are based on the 1987 Standard Industrial Classification (SIC). Data include nonfactor charges (capital consumption allowances, indirect business taxes, etc.) as well as factor charges against gross product; corporate profits and capital consumption allowances have been shifted from a company to an establishment basis]

INDUSTRY	1987	1988	1989	1990	1991	1992	1993	1994
CURRENT DOLLARS								
Gross domestic product, total [1]	4,692,340	5,049,586	5,438,676	5,743,837	5,916,668	6,244,445	6,550,241	6,931,357
Manufacturing	889,047	971,297	1,013,422	1,031,359	1,028,065	1,063,575	1,116,536	1,197,098
Percent of all industries	18.9	19.2	18.6	18.0	17.4	17.0	17.0	17.3
Durable goods	513,310	556,617	574,877	572,836	558,312	573,373	612,284	673,139
Lumber and wood products	31,884	32,665	33,579	31,799	29,972	32,016	35,283	40,952
Furniture and fixtures	14,602	15,019	15,710	15,404	15,056	16,206	17,644	18,952
Stone, clay, and glass products	23,687	23,961	24,891	24,836	22,932	25,076	25,660	27,925
Primary metal industries	35,214	43,504	45,056	42,636	39,571	38,999	40,783	44,166
Fabricated metal products	61,577	66,193	68,264	69,383	67,590	70,055	74,474	82,465
Industrial machinery	94,595	106,379	113,826	114,831	105,739	108,640	111,871	119,341
Electronic & other electric equipment	83,281	88,412	96,707	94,926	98,191	98,601	111,774	129,990
Motor vehicles and equipment	57,920	59,634	53,003	46,102	42,328	52,848	66,160	84,064
Other transportation equipment	55,649	55,644	57,715	60,470	62,029	56,535	53,235	47,630
Instruments and related products	39,061	47,096	46,632	52,212	54,625	54,246	53,638	54,507
Misc. manufacturing industries	15,840	18,110	19,494	20,237	20,279	20,149	21,762	23,147
Nondurable goods	375,737	414,680	438,545	458,521	469,753	490,202	504,252	523,959
Food and kindred products	78,020	81,726	87,662	94,160	99,148	102,094	103,673	108,076
Tobacco manufactures	13,129	14,279	14,894	16,380	17,790	18,365	16,517	16,550
Textile mill products	20,127	20,487	20,916	21,742	22,279	25,434	25,519	25,585
Apparel and other textile products	22,844	23,939	25,221	25,151	25,890	27,190	27,268	27,823
Paper and allied products	38,073	44,036	45,818	45,323	44,849	45,828	47,610	49,048
Printing and publishing	62,438	66,822	72,243	73,875	75,870	79,743	81,684	85,711
Chemicals and allied products	85,112	96,982	104,922	110,348	114,148	120,457	126,492	132,375
Petroleum and coal products	22,719	31,940	28,826	32,965	29,702	28,225	29,771	29,706
Rubber and misc. plastic products	29,369	30,192	33,498	33,963	35,650	38,095	41,076	44,952
Leather and leather products	3,906	4,277	4,545	4,594	4,427	4,771	4,642	4,131
CHAINED (1992) DOLLARS								
Gross domestic product, total [1]	5,648,410	5,862,907	6,060,356	6,138,661	6,078,964	6,244,445	6,383,756	6,604,247
Manufacturing	1,041,619	1,110,891	1,106,018	1,090,112	1,050,388	1,063,575	1,095,312	1,168,029
Percent of all industries	18.4	18.9	18.3	17.8	17.3	17.0	17.2	17.7
Durable goods	565,131	616,085	613,119	600,678	568,132	573,373	601,179	657,864
Lumber and wood products	40,047	39,928	38,736	36,972	34,127	32,016	28,729	31,546
Furniture and fixtures	16,912	16,858	16,900	15,842	14,947	16,206	17,845	18,448
Stone, clay, and glass products	23,504	24,556	25,643	25,513	22,916	25,076	24,992	26,213
Primary metal industries	38,572	41,106	39,397	38,963	38,638	38,999	41,908	42,853
Fabricated metal products	72,262	77,134	75,211	72,567	68,210	70,055	74,231	82,911
Industrial machinery	91,340	106,174	112,367	113,363	103,653	108,640	115,781	127,573
Electronic & other electric equipment	78,115	85,331	92,821	92,559	95,963	98,601	113,638	138,430
Motor vehicles and equipment	69,940	74,239	64,220	56,840	46,784	52,848	60,573	72,763
Other transportation equipment	74,398	76,601	72,465	69,059	63,957	56,536	51,649	45,148
Instruments and related products	46,804	59,551	56,239	58,822	58,065	54,246	51,346	50,867
Misc. manufacturing industries	18,737	21,367	22,178	22,154	21,068	20,149	21,123	22,372
Nondurable goods	477,759	494,520	492,826	489,287	482,249	490,202	494,123	510,171
Food and kindred products	95,884	104,566	102,534	103,082	102,264	102,094	102,204	104,849
Tobacco manufactures	31,806	30,730	27,176	24,851	21,527	18,365	17,452	22,005
Textile mill products	21,795	21,466	21,875	22,573	23,068	25,434	25,858	27,251
Apparel and other textile products	25,320	26,567	27,194	26,487	26,378	27,190	26,940	27,787
Paper and allied products	42,996	45,066	43,763	44,146	44,622	45,828	49,914	49,658
Printing and publishing	84,136	86,846	87,893	84,496	80,822	79,743	77,329	78,183
Chemicals and allied products	110,397	110,440	111,401	117,260	115,814	120,457	122,100	125,128
Petroleum and coal products	36,260	37,128	33,397	28,434	28,281	28,225	27,061	26,782
Rubber and misc. plastic products	29,280	30,944	34,523	34,436	35,337	38,095	40,872	45,746
Leather and leather products	4,675	4,708	4,896	4,767	4,527	4,771	4,567	3,899

For additional industry detail, see table 693.

Source: U.S. Bureau of Economic Analysis, *Survey of Current Business*, August 1996.

No. 1218. Manufactures—Summary: 1982 to 1995

[For establishment coverage, see text, section 26. For compostion of regions, see table 26]

ITEM	Unit	1982	1987	1992	1993 [1]	1994 [1]	1995 [1]
ALL ESTABLISHMENTS							
Number of establishments [2]	1,000	358	369	382	(NA)	(NA)	(NA)
With 20 or more employees	1,000	123	126	125	(NA)	(NA)	(NA)
Employee size-class:							
Establishments [3]	1,000	348	359	371	(NA)	(NA)	(NA)
Under 20	1,000	230	238	252	(NA)	(NA)	(NA)
20 to 99	1,000	84	86	85	(NA)	(NA)	(NA)
100 to 249	1,000	21	22	22	(NA)	(NA)	(NA)
250 to 999	1,000	11	11	11	(NA)	(NA)	(NA)
1,000 and over	1,000	2	2	2	(NA)	(NA)	(NA)
Form of organization:							
Corporate	1,000	283.2	287.4	304.0	(NA)	(NA)	(NA)
Noncorporate [4]	1,000	74.0	81.5	77.7	(NA)	(NA)	(NA)
Individual proprietorship	1,000	45.6	35.4	40.9	(NA)	(NA)	(NA)
Partnership	1,000	15.0	13.2	10.3	(NA)	(NA)	(NA)
All employees: [5]							
Annual average [6]	Million	19.1	18.9	18.2	18.2	18.3	18.7
Payroll	Bil. dol.	380	476	559	573	594	624
Payroll per employee	$1,000	19.9	25.2	30.7	31.5	32.4	33.3
Production workers:							
Annual average	Million	12.4	12.2	11.6	11.7	11.9	12.3
Percent of all employees	Percent	64.9	64.6	63.8	64.3	65.1	65.4
Hours	Billion	23.5	24.3	23.6	23.8	24.5	25.1
Hours per worker	1,000	1.9	2.0	2.0	2.0	2.1	2.0
Wages	Bil. dol.	205	251	282	290	304	317
Percent of payroll for all employees	Percent	53.9	52.8	50.4	50.6	51.2	50.9
Wages per worker	$1,000	16.5	20.6	24.2	24.8	25.5	25.9
Wages per worker hour	Dollar	8.72	10.35	11.95	12.17	12.40	12.65
Value added by manufacture [7]	Bil. dol.	824	1,166	1,425	1,483	1,596	1,709
Per production worker	$1,000	66.5	95.5	122.6	126.5	133.9	139.5
Per production worker hour	Dollar	35.06	47.97	60.56	62.20	65.14	68.19
Per dollar of workers' wages	Dollar	4.02	4.64	5.07	5.11	5.25	5.39
Value added, percent distribution:							
Northeast	Percent	23.7	23.7	19.9	(NA)	(NA)	(NA)
Midwest	Percent	29.8	29.8	30.2	(NA)	(NA)	(NA)
South	Percent	29.5	29.5	32.1	(NA)	(NA)	(NA)
West	Percent	17.0	17.0	17.8	(NA)	(NA)	(NA)
Cost of materials	Bil. dol.	1,130	1,320	1,571	1,647	1,752	1,893
Value of shipments [8]	Bil. dol.	1,960	2,476	3,006	3,128	3,340	3,589
Per production worker	$1,000	158.1	203.0	258.0	266.7	279.7	292.9
End-of-year inventories	Bil. dol.	307	333	374	383	397	419
New capital expenditures [9]	Bil. dol.	75.0	78.6	104.0	103.0	112.0	128.2
Gross book value of depreciable assets	Bil. dol.	692	868	1,128	(NA)	(NA)	(NA)
Machinery and equipment	Bil. dol.	527	671	896	(NA)	(NA)	(NA)
Assets per employee	$1,000	36.2	48.6	66.6	(NA)	(NA)	(NA)
Operation ratios:							
Value added to shipments	Ratio	42.0	47.1	47.9	47.4	47.9	47.6
Inventories to shipments	Ratio	15.7	13.4	12.5	12.2	11.9	11.7
Payroll to value added	Ratio	46.1	40.8	34.7	38.7	37.2	36.5
MULTIUNIT COMPANIES							
Establishments	1,000	81.7	80.9	81.0	(NA)	(NA)	(NA)
Employees	Million	14.3	13.8	13.1	(NA)	(NA)	(NA)
Production workers	Million	8.8	8.5	8.0	(NA)	(NA)	(NA)
Payroll	Bil. dol.	307.5	377.3	436.0	(NA)	(NA)	(NA)
Wages, production workers	Bil. dol.	159.1	191.8	211.2	(NA)	(NA)	(NA)
Value added by manufacture	Bil. dol.	678.4	953.6	1,160	(NA)	(NA)	(NA)
New capital expenditures	Bil. dol.	65.2	66.5	87.8	(NA)	(NA)	(NA)
SINGLE UNIT COMPANIES							
Establishments	1,000	276.3	288.0	300.7	(NA)	(NA)	(NA)
Employees	Million	4.8	5.1	5.1	(NA)	(NA)	(NA)
Payroll	Bil. dol.	72.1	98.3	123.1	(NA)	(NA)	(NA)
Value added by manufacture	Bil. dol.	145.7	212.1	265.0	(NA)	(NA)	(NA)

NA Not available. [1] Estimated data based on *Annual Survey of Manufactures*; see text, section 26. [2] Includes administrative and auxiliary units. [3] Excludes administrative offices and auxiliary units. [4] Includes forms of organization not shown separately. [5] Includes data for employees of manufacturing establishments engaged in distribution and construction work. [6] Data are based on pay periods ending nearest 15th of March, May, August, and November. [7] Adjusted value added; takes into account (a) value added by merchandising operations (that is, difference between the sales value and cost of merchandise sold without further manufacture, processing, or assembly), plus (b) net change in finished goods and work-in-process inventories between beginning and end of year. [8] Includes extensive and unmeasurable duplication from shipments between establishments in the same industry classification. [9] Includes plants under construction and not yet in operation.

Source: Except as noted, U.S. Bureau of the Census, *Census of Manufactures*, 1982, 1987 and 1992, and *Annual Survey of Manufactures*.

No. 1219. Manufactures—Summary, by Industry: 1992 and 1995

[Data based on various editions of the *Standard Industrial Classification (SIC) Manual*, published by the Office of Management and Budget; see text, section 26. N.e.c.=Not elsewhere classified]

INDUSTRY	SIC code	1992: All employees: Number [1] (1,000)	1992: All employees: Payroll (mil. dol.)	1992: Production workers (1,000)	1992: Value added by manufacture (mil. dol.)	1992: Value of shipments (mil. dol.)	1995: All employees: Number [1] (1,000)	1995: All employees: Payroll: Total (mil. dol.)	1995: All employees: Payroll: Per employee (dol.)	1995: Production workers (1,000)	1995: Value added by manufacture: Total (mil. dol.)	1995: Value added by manufacture: Per production worker (dol.)	1995: Value of shipments (mil. dol.)
All manufacturing establishments	(X)	**16,949**	**494,109**	**11,641**	**1,424,700**	**3,004,723**	**18,740.6**	**623,418**	**33,266**	**12,253.8**	**1,709,180**	**139,482**	**3,589,157**
Food and kindred products	20	1,503	36,772	1,100	157,260	406,963	1,525.9	39,715	26,027	1,123.6	180,975	161,067	448,405
Meat products	201	400	7,564	343	19,141	94,072	428.8	8,750	20,405	369.9	24,698	66,770	100,260
Dairy products	202	135	3,720	85	15,258	52,720	133.7	3,954	29,572	83.6	15,698	187,772	55,466
Preserved fruits and vegetables	203	216	4,825	179	23,644	47,806	211.2	5,047	23,895	175.5	24,977	142,321	51,349
Grain mill products	204	107	3,375	74	21,000	49,957	106.0	3,485	32,878	74.1	26,980	364,107	58,555
Bakery products	205	215	5,599	133	17,905	28,494	219.3	6,047	27,574	137.9	20,313	147,305	32,585
Sugar and confectionery products	206	91	2,402	71	10,950	22,710	91.9	2,621	28,524	70.8	11,935	168,566	24,990
Fats and oils	207	28	778	19	3,770	18,724	25.9	799	30,865	17.9	4,417	246,749	21,538
Beverages	208	144	4,786	74	29,260	57,957	140.8	4,983	35,387	71.8	32,488	452,479	64,415
Miscellaneous foods and kindred products	209	166	3,723	121	16,333	34,523	168.2	4,029	23,955	122.1	19,468	159,445	39,248
Tobacco products	21	38	1,524	27	27,207	35,198	31.3	1,484	47,409	22.2	24,715	1,113,306	32,984
Cigarettes	211	25	1,205	19	24,802	29,746	20.1	1,182	58,791	14.4	22,264	1,546,118	27,609
Cigars	212	3	53	2	190	287	2.6	59	22,500	2.0	250	124,950	391
Chewing and smoking tobacco	213	3	92	2	1,213	1,608	2.9	100	34,379	1.8	1,600	888,889	1,975
Tobacco stemming and redrying	214	7	174	5	1,002	3,557	5.7	144	25,246	4.0	601	150,350	3,010
Textile mill products	22	616	12,398	529	30,060	70,753	606.8	13,454	22,172	518.1	32,705	63,124	79,742
Broadwoven fabric mills, cotton	221	56	1,147	50	2,504	5,811	55.5	1,264	22,766	50.1	2,508	50,054	6,675
Broadwoven fabric mills, manmade	222	87	1,850	77	4,008	8,767	80.3	1,907	23,753	69.7	4,333	62,159	9,836
Broadwoven fabric mills, wool	223	14	279	12	691	1,612	14.0	311	22,207	12.2	724	59,328	1,836
Narrow fabric mills	224	17	323	14	706	1,274	17.3	376	21,728	13.8	851	61,638	1,543
Knitting mills	225	195	3,400	170	8,052	16,985	179.9	3,474	19,309	156.9	8,921	56,860	19,216
Textile finishing, except wool	226	51	1,143	41	2,786	7,089	51.8	1,276	24,631	42.5	3,215	75,642	7,452
Carpets and rugs	227	49	1,088	39	3,480	9,828	55.6	1,336	24,023	43.6	4,016	92,115	10,732
Yarn and thread mills	228	92	1,744	84	4,059	11,274	88.6	1,840	20,770	80.5	4,068	50,538	12,776
Miscellaneous textile goods	229	55	1,423	42	3,775	8,113	63.9	1,671	26,142	48.8	4,069	83,367	9,675
Apparel and other textile products	23	985	15,325	824	36,423	71,658	950.1	15,753	16,580	793.8	39,519	49,784	78,097
Men's and boys' suits and coats	231	44	723	37	1,375	2,430	31.1	550	17,672	26.3	1,274	48,445	2,078
Men's and boys' furnishings	232	261	3,649	228	9,864	17,867	234.5	3,508	14,959	206.7	10,199	49,340	18,698
Women's and misses' outerwear	233	306	4,597	256	10,836	21,631	315.0	4,910	15,587	264.9	11,345	42,829	22,868
Women's and children's undergarments	234	54	798	46	2,193	3,943	45.9	771	16,793	38.0	2,218	58,363	4,577

See footnotes at end of table.

No. 1219. Manufactures—Summary, by Industry: 1992 and 1995—Continued

[See headnote, page 739]

INDUSTRY	SIC code	1992: All employees: Number[1] (1,000)	1992: All employees: Payroll (mil. dol.)	1992: Production workers (1,000)	1992: Value added by manufacture (mil. dol.)	1992: Value of shipments (mil. dol.)	1995: All employees: Number[1] (1,000)	1995: All employees: Payroll: Total (mil. dol.)	1995: All employees: Payroll: Per employee (dol.)	1995: Production workers (1,000)	1995: Value added by manufacture: Total (mil. dol.)	1995: Value added by manufacture: Per production worker (1,000)	1995: Value of shipments (mil. dol.)
Apparel, other textile products—Con.													
Hats, caps, and millinery	235	19	280	16	572	976	18	316	17,448	15	675	45,615	1,043
Girls' and children's outerwear	236	53	775	44	1,667	3,145	43	627	14,640	34	2,064	60,345	3,679
Fur goods	237	1	21	1	66	172	1	12	19,833	-	30	101,333	101
Miscellaneous apparel and accessories	238	37	566	30	1,260	2,378	33	553	16,616	27	1,427	53,427	2,687
Miscellaneous fabricated textile products	239	211	3,918	169	8,586	19,118	229	4,507	19,696	182	10,287	56,553	22,365
Lumber and wood products	24	656	13,882	540	33,154	81,565	741	16,622	22,429	614	40,937	66,684	104,923
Logging	241	83	1,689	69	5,017	13,592	87	1,891	21,763	71	6,133	86,383	16,776
Sawmills and planing mills	242	168	3,585	144	8,848	23,294	180	4,117	22,897	154	10,109	65,514	28,870
Millwork, plywood, and structural members	243	224	5,006	181	10,844	24,744	256	5,957	23,316	208	13,206	63,399	31,330
Wood containers	244	40	645	33	1,321	2,942	50	846	17,046	41	1,820	44,056	3,957
Wood buildings and mobile homes	245	56	1,234	44	2,531	6,645	75	1,799	23,924	61	4,054	66,235	10,689
Miscellaneous Wood Products	249	84	1,725	69	4,583	10,346	94	2,013	21,346	78	5,616	72,188	13,302
Furniture and fixtures[2]	25	471	10,227	372	22,840	43,826	514	11,907	23,157	415	26,238	63,195	53,571
Household furniture	251	253	4,804	213	10,492	20,508	272	5,536	20,343	232	12,011	51,816	24,613
Office Furniture	252	68	1,868	51	4,626	7,979	70	2,083	29,678	54	5,201	96,857	8,943
Public building and related furniture	253	30	732	23	1,736	4,483	37	930	25,073	29	2,006	70,372	6,608
Partitions and fixtures	254	75	1,818	55	3,633	6,580	81	2,164	26,686	61	4,293	70,039	8,084
Miscellaneous furniture and fixtures	259	45	1,005	31	2,353	4,276	54	1,215	22,333	40	2,727	68,351	5,323
Paper and allied products	26	626	20,492	479	60,174	133,201	630	22,237	35,325	486	79,836	164,306	172,636
Pulp mills	261	16	689	12	2,554	5,486	13	631	47,075	10	3,917	376,606	6,924
Paper mills	262	131	5,421	100	14,848	32,786	119	5,546	46,741	92	22,468	244,746	45,121
Paperboard mills	263	52	2,136	39	8,195	16,140	57	2,563	45,046	43	12,655	292,947	24,528
Paperboard containers and boxes	265	199	5,722	151	12,406	32,655	209	6,437	30,873	160	15,144	94,825	41,669
Miscellaneous converted paper products	267	229	6,524	176	22,171	46,154	232	7,058	30,424	181	25,653	141,866	54,365
Printing and publishing	27	1,492	41,136	785	112,446	166,153	1,534	44,747	29,174	809	125,936	155,726	186,439
Newspapers	271	414	10,437	134	26,920	33,782	415	11,096	26,748	135	29,254	217,175	37,732
Periodicals	272	115	4,077	20	15,880	22,104	123	4,572	37,137	18	17,365	964,700	23,906
Books	273	130	4,037	57	14,325	21,378	133	4,485	33,848	57	17,857	312,510	26,089
Miscellaneous publishing	274	65	1,720	24	8,473	10,908	67	1,910	28,343	26	9,349	366,616	11,992
Commercial printing	275	567	15,337	408	31,898	56,229	604	17,150	28,378	440	36,492	82,964	66,093
Manifold business forms	276	48	1,341	34	3,922	7,429	44	1,234	28,307	29	4,024	139,706	7,911
Greeting cards	277	23	584	12	3,389	4,190	23	642	27,922	13	3,707	296,576	4,726
Blankbooks and bookbinding	278	66	1,461	51	3,640	5,049	67	1,606	23,862	51	4,146	81,162	6,061
Printing trade services	279	65	2,142	46	3,999	5,086	58	2,061	35,476	42	3,941	94,513	5,000

See footnotes at end of table.

No. 1219. Manufactures—Summary, by Industry: 1992 and 1995—Continued

[See headnote, page 739]

INDUSTRY	SIC code	1992					1995						
		All employees		Production workers (1,000)	Value added by manufacture (mil. dol.)	Value of shipments (mil. dol.)	All employees			Production workers (1,000)	Value added by manufacture		Value of shipments (mil. dol.)
		Number [1] (1,000)	Payroll (mil. dol.)				Number [1] (1,000)	Payroll			Total (mil. dol.)	Per production worker (dol.)	
								Total (mil. dol.)	Per employee (dol.)				
Chemicals and allied products	28	849	32,502	479	164,346	305,420	839	35,424	42,207	487	196,906	404,324	362,126
Industrial inorganic chemicals	281	103	4,214	55	16,724	27,331	82	3,576	43,774	46	16,305	354,450	26,722
Plastics materials and synthetics	282	129	5,137	86	20,979	48,696	127	5,516	43,607	85	27,689	327,676	63,506
Drugs	283	194	7,840	93	48,602	67,792	218	9,720	44,628	113	56,718	503,282	80,884
Soap, cleaners, and toilet goods	284	123	3,927	75	26,182	42,875	123	4,149	33,813	74	30,701	416,563	50,158
Paints and allied products	285	51	1,710	26	7,154	14,973	52	1,961	37,807	26	8,411	303,657	17,943
Industrial organic chemicals	286	125	5,495	72	26,132	64,397	118	5,914	50,245	69	34,168	492,330	76,539
Agricultural chemicals	287	40	1,451	25	8,659	18,841	39	1,596	40,816	25	11,566	455,362	22,525
Miscellaneous chemical products	289	84	2,727	48	9,915	20,512	81	2,972	36,509	48	11,349	237,825	23,850
Petroleum and coal products	29	114	4,967	74	23,408	150,227	110	5,260	47,644	72	31,589	438,838	151,281
Petroleum refining	291	75	3,640	48	18,607	136,551	70	3,796	53,820	46	26,248	570,615	136,023
Asphalt paving and roofing materials	295	26	846	18	3,006	7,749	26	969	37,265	18	3,358	183,514	8,992
Miscellaneous petroleum and coal products	299	14	481	7	1,796	5,927	14	495	35,357	6	1,974	263,173	6,246
Rubber and misc. plastics products	30	907	23,156	698	58,652	113,593	1,018	27,301	26,810	801	73,023	91,210	145,426
Tires and inner tubes	301	65	2,499	53	6,504	11,814	66	2,717	41,361	54	7,397	136,472	14,074
Rubber and plastics footwear	302	14	216	11	464	868	10	179	18,604	8	435	54,388	910
Hose and belting and plastics and packing	305	52	1,411	38	3,290	3,290	61	1,779	29,397	45	4,320	95,564	7,814
Fabricated rubber products, n.e.c	306	105	2,617	79	6,024	11,474	119	2,949	24,757	94	7,557	80,566	14,074
Miscellaneous plastics products, n.e.c.	308	671	16,413	516	42,370	83,487	763	19,676	25,777	599	53,314	88,946	108,555
Leather and leather products	31	101	1,806	83	4,527	9,694	86	1,632	18,927	72	4,126	57,143	9,064
Leather tanning and finishing	311	17	420	13	891	2,905	15	393	25,673	13	1,015	81,208	3,119
Footwear cut stock	313	4	63	3	149	317	3	58	18,161	3	134	51,385	282
Footwear, except rubber	314	49	762	41	2,060	3,896	45	741	16,652	38	1,845	48,817	3,696
Leather gloves and mittens	315	3	35	2	69	140	3	41	15,577	2	61	26,391	114
Luggage	316	10	191	8	509	988	6	156	27,421	4	465	108,209	835
Handbags and personal leather goods	317	11	202	9	470	861	8	138	16,576	7	358	54,167	626
Leather goods, n.e.c	319	8	133	6	304	575	7	107	15,986	6	248	40,016	391

See footnotes at end of table.

No. 1219. Manufactures—Summary, by Industry: 1992 and 1995—Continued

[See headnote, page 739]

INDUSTRY	SIC code	1992: All employees: Number[1] (1,000)	1992: All employees: Payroll (mil. dol.)	1992: Production workers (1,000)	1992: Value added by manufacture (mil. dol.)	1992: Value of shipments (mil. dol.)	1995: All employees: Number[1] (1,000)	1995: All employees: Payroll: Total (mil. dol.)	1995: All employees: Payroll: Per employee (dol.)	1995: Production workers (1,000)	1995: Value added by manufacture: Total (mil. dol.)	1995: Value added by manufacture: Per production worker (dol.)	1995: Value of shipments (mil. dol.)
Stone, clay, and glass products	32	469	13,113	367	34,641	62,528	503	14,912	29,675	390	42,404	109,238	75,989
Flat glass	321	12	461	10	1,311	2,073	11	506	46,045	9	1,802	198,000	2,595
Glass and glassware, pressed or blown	322	66	2,075	56	5,900	9,033	61	2,040	33,496	52	6,269	121,860	9,817
Products of purchased glass	323	55	1,369	42	3,757	6,904	60	1,636	27,121	47	4,309	91,685	8,095
Cement, hydraulic	324	17	585	13	2,149	4,051	17	659	39,196	13	3,205	254,381	5,342
Structural clay products	325	31	734	24	1,695	2,857	32	817	25,656	25	2,064	82,227	3,330
Pottery and related products	326	37	863	29	1,995	2,817	44	1,076	24,517	36	2,518	70,716	3,532
Concrete, gypsum, and plaster products	327	174	4,741	126	11,008	23,024	195	5,567	28,507	146	14,028	96,277	29,590
Cut stone and stone products	328	12	282	9	604	1,007	13	319	24,729	10	661	64,765	1,096
Miscellaneous nonmetallic mineral products	329	66	2,004	49	6,222	10,756	70	2,294	33,004	52	7,549	146,596	12,592
Primary metal industries [2]	33	682	22,202	506	52,027	138,287	686	25,078	36,467	541	66,994	123,691	180,368
Steel furnace and basic steel products	331	239	9,179	182	22,173	58,449	224	9,924	44,246	175	29,142	166,147	74,547
Iron and steel foundries	332	122	3,739	99	6,873	11,880	130	4,304	33,028	107	8,881	82,771	15,237
Primary nonferrous metals	333	36	1,334	27	3,391	13,906	34	1,323	38,921	26	5,710	219,600	18,421
Secondary nonferrous metals	334	13	407	9	1,233	6,131	15	494	33,571	11	1,393	126,636	7,629
Nonferrous rolling and drawing	335	147	4,635	109	12,336	37,101	158	5,311	33,529	120	15,536	129,269	46,317
Nonferrous foundries (castings)	336	75	1,942	59	3,927	7,002	91	2,516	27,663	76	5,405	70,742	9,831
Fabricated metal products	34	1,362	38,962	994	85,761	166,532	1,466	44,577	30,436	1,100	102,672	93,372	204,819
Metal cans and shipping containers	341	40	1,465	33	3,736	13,263	36	1,366	38,069	30	3,867	128,277	13,634
Cutlery, handtools, and hardware	342	134	3,648	99	9,044	15,448	142	4,140	29,176	107	10,923	101,992	19,009
Plumbing and heating, except electric	343	42	1,152	29	3,106	5,826	44	1,303	29,340	31	3,938	128,666	7,026
Fabricated structural metal products	344	369	10,362	275	21,256	44,896	416	11,766	28,290	302	26,516	87,947	56,077
Screw machine products, bolts, etc.	345	91	2,824	68	6,269	9,026	101	3,106	30,800	79	6,772	86,154	11,524
Metal forgings and stampings	346	234	7,749	185	14,913	30,621	259	9,517	36,744	210	18,650	88,810	39,417
Metal services, n.e.c.	347	108	2,662	83	6,679	9,963	126	3,263	25,972	98	7,392	75,560	13,277
Ordnance and accessories, n.e.c.	348	62	2,124	35	4,536	6,855	43	1,532	35,706	26	3,836	146,366	5,574
Miscellaneous fabricated metal products	349	283	7,186	186	16,224	30,667	297	8,547	28,747	217	20,760	95,490	39,264
Industrial machinery and equipment	35	1,739	57,231	1,086	132,823	258,661	1,926	67,476	35,031	1,260	172,945	137,323	361,114
Engines and turbines	351	83	3,136	52	7,736	17,549	82	3,297	40,209	57	9,463	165,439	22,815
Farm and garden machinery	352	86	2,364	63	7,316	14,784	94	2,827	30,203	71	9,336	131,864	20,716
Construction and related machinery	353	176	5,664	108	12,469	27,193	200	6,666	33,348	130	16,997	130,279	38,457
Metalworking machinery	354	258	8,571	178	16,542	26,474	284	10,336	36,336	204	21,932	107,722	35,057
Special industry machinery	355	162	5,515	91	11,667	21,522	184	7,136	38,836	105	17,560	167,301	32,046
General industrial machinery	356	244	7,742	154	17,817	31,443	260	8,833	34,011	169	22,017	130,048	39,222
Computer and office equipment	357	261	10,143	89	29,229	66,709	250	10,496	41,963	92	35,966	389,259	90,240
Refrigeration and service machinery	358	179	6,264	128	13,597	27,544	198	6,232	31,552	144	16,469	114,062	36,574
Industrial machinery, n.e.c.	359	304	8,843	227	16,827	26,443	376	11,669	31,058	287	23,312	81,199	35,977

See footnotes at end of table.

No. 1219. Manufactures—Summary, by Industry: 1992 and 1995—Continued

[See headnote, page 739]

INDUSTRY	SIC code	1992 All employees Number[1] (1,000)	1992 All employees Payroll (mil. dol.)	1992 Production workers (1,000)	1992 Value added by manufacture (mil. dol.)	1992 Value of shipments (mil. dol.)	1995 All employees Number[1] (1,000)	1995 Payroll Total (mil. dol.)	1995 Payroll Per employee (dol.)	1995 Production workers (1,000)	1995 Value added by manufacture Total (mil. dol.)	1995 Value added Per production worker (dol.)	1995 Value of shipments (mil. dol.)
Electronics; other electric equipment	36	1,439	44,197	911	121,158	216,764	1,534	51,121	33,332	986	173,920	174,741	299,537
Electric distribution equipment	361	66	1,946	48	5,437	9,797	74	2,281	31,037	52	6,726	129,098	12,141
Electrical industrial apparatus	362	157	4,387	106	10,850	19,266	168	5,068	30,111	119	13,368	112,623	24,991
Household appliances	363	103	2,571	83	7,964	18,633	111	3,064	27,656	89	9,437	106,150	22,391
Electric lighting and wiring equipment	364	148	3,974	107	11,307	19,844	159	4,516	28,454	118	12,989	110,281	23,238
Household audio and video equipment	365	47	1,123	35	3,486	10,614	48	1,324	27,420	37	3,924	107,210	13,712
Communications equipment	366	239	9,111	114	26,522	42,955	240	9,864	41,061	112	36,990	329,682	58,815
Electronic components and accessories	367	530	16,752	317	44,306	73,642	587	20,297	34,559	366	77,561	211,857	119,268
Misc. electrical equipment and supplies	369	147	4,332	100	11,287	22,013	147	4,708	32,092	103	12,945	125,431	25,282
Transportation equipment	37	1,647	62,736	1,080	158,326	399,269	1,623	64,163	42,134	1,059	172,926	163,336	482,616
Motor vehicles and equipment	371	703	26,213	565	80,935	238,384	802	33,602	41,897	657	105,461	160,641	326,181
Aircraft and parts	372	548	22,647	281	47,661	104,858	394	18,661	47,364	192	41,889	217,729	83,865
Ship and boat building and repairing	373	163	4,634	122	8,560	15,249	143	4,320	30,232	109	8,175	74,930	15,226
Railroad equipment	374	26	900	21	2,015	4,714	32	1,085	34,339	23	2,305	98,491	7,317
Motorcycles, bicycles, and parts	375	13	343	10	891	2,134	16	503	31,217	12	1,311	109,233	2,833
Guided missiles, space vehicles, parts	376	146	6,780	50	15,246	26,506	89	4,792	53,725	31	10,566	338,641	18,667
Miscellaneous transportation equipment	379	46	1,218	33	3,018	7,423	47	1,190	25,486	34	3,241	94,751	8,526
Instruments and related products	38	907	33,067	460	88,394	134,940	809	31,588	39,408	418	92,534	221,373	140,916
Search and navigation equipment	381	253	10,962	103	24,299	35,039	185	9,070	48,971	69	20,369	295,926	29,435
Measuring and controlling devices	382	276	9,632	138	21,775	34,730	267	10,062	37,684	140	26,480	189,404	42,678
Medical instruments and supplies	384	264	8,522	154	26,062	39,535	261	9,124	34,959	152	28,350	186,143	43,220
Ophthalmic goods	385	29	714	20	1,938	2,675	27	716	26,212	17	2,254	130,312	3,213
Photographic equipment and supplies	386	77	3,061	39	14,862	22,119	61	2,720	44,522	35	14,707	416,640	21,584
Watches, clocks, watchcases and parts	387	8	177	6	438	843	7	174	25,203	5	394	82,021	781
Misc. manufacturing industries	39	368	8,417	255	21,975	39,408	387	9,885	24,425	280	25,672	91,588	46,891
Jewelry, silverware, and plated ware	391	46	1,068	32	2,501	5,731	43	1,053	24,767	29	2,660	92,997	6,222
Musical instruments	393	12	273	9	589	982	13	313	24,240	10	690	66,337	1,144
Toys and sporting goods	394	98	2,133	71	6,816	12,123	107	2,521	23,650	79	7,826	98,941	14,625
Pens, pencils, office, and art supplies	395	30	684	21	2,030	3,515	34	786	22,977	25	2,414	98,134	3,954
Costume jewelry and notions	396	27	557	19	1,368	2,316	27	578	21,502	20	1,465	75,118	2,523
Miscellaneous manufactures	399	153	3,702	103	8,674	14,832	174	4,434	25,542	118	10,617	89,898	18,423

- Represents zero. X Not applicable. [1] Represents the average of production workers plus all other employees for the payroll period ended nearest the 15th of March. [2] Includes other industries not shown separately.

Source: U.S. Bureau of the Census, *1992 Census of Manufactures* and *Annual Survey of Manufactures*.

No. 1220. Manufactures—Summary, by Selected Industry Based on Value Added: 1992 and 1995

[Data based on various editions of the *Standard Industrial Classification (SIC) Manual*, published by the Office of Management and Budget; see text, section 26. N.e.c.=Not elsewhere classified]

INDUSTRY	SIC code	1992: All employees: Number [1] (1,000)	1992: All employees: Payroll (mil. dol.)	1992: Production workers (1,000)	1992: Value added by manufacture (mil. dol.)	1992: Value of shipments (mil. dol.)	1995: All employees: Number [1] (1,000)	1995: All employees: Payroll: Total (mil. dol.)	1995: All employees: Payroll: Per employee (dol.)	1995: Production workers (1,000)	1995: Value added by manufacture: Total (mil. dol.)	1995: Value added by manufacture: Per production worker (dol.)	1995: Value of shipments (mil. dol.)
Meat packing plants	2011	121.2	2,441	105.0	6,958	50,167	125.7	2,898	23,055	108.1	8,282	76,614	50,888
Sausages and other prepared meats	2013	85.4	2,023	65.6	5,480	19,940	88.6	2,197	24,797	70.2	6,201	88,333	20,665
Poultry slaughtering and processing	2015	193.8	3,100	172.8	6,703	23,965	214.5	3,654	17,035	191.8	10,215	53,314	28,887
Fluid milk	2026	63.4	1,840	32.5	5,965	21,928	62.1	1,912	30,789	31.0	6,345	204,677	22,865
Canned fruits and vegetables	2033	63.6	1,465	53.2	6,976	15,071	60.0	1,461	24,350	50.3	6,435	127,932	14,712
Frozen specialties, n.e.c.	2038	46.7	972	38.3	4,076	7,886	43.9	976	22,232	36.4	4,982	136,868	9,263
Cereal breakfast foods	2043	16.1	745	13.1	7,259	9,737	16.7	762	45,629	13.8	10,038	727,391	12,808
Bread, cake, and related products	2051	154.9	4,059	88.1	11,453	18,130	155.2	4,277	27,558	87.0	12,381	142,310	19,640
Cookies and crackers	2052	47.0	1,247	35.0	5,513	8,668	49.2	1,372	27,886	38.7	6,610	170,801	10,500
Candy and other confectionery products	2064	51.5	1,261	41.0	6,347	10,202	53.8	1,425	26,487	41.7	6,894	165,324	11,341
Malt beverages	2082	34.5	1,567	25.1	10,189	17,340	32.6	1,535	47,086	23.6	10,307	436,737	17,151
Bottled and canned soft drinks	2086	77.1	2,163	30.5	9,582	25,423	73.8	2,247	30,447	28.5	11,853	415,895	30,203
Flavoring extracts and syrups, n.e.c.	2087	10.3	342	5.8	5,275	6,923	11.1	407	36,667	6.4	5,778	902,813	7,815
Food preparations, n.e.c.	2099	61.4	1,413	43.7	5,881	12,165	67.7	1,598	23,604	47.9	6,906	144,175	14,025
Cigarettes	2111	25.4	1,205	18.1	24,802	29,746	20.1	1,812	90,149	14.4	22,264	1,546,111	27,809
Logging	2411	83.2	1,689	69.2	5,017	13,592	86.8	1,891	21,786	71.0	6,133	86,380	16,776
Sawmills and planing mills, general	2421	137.6	3,040	117.7	7,755	21,061	142.7	3,432	24,050	121.5	8,649	71,185	25,796
Wood household furniture	2511	121.1	2,174	105.2	4,726	8,730	125.5	2,399	19,116	109.6	5,295	48,312	10,238
Paper mills	2621	130.6	5,421	100.4	14,848	32,786	118.7	5,548	46,740	91.8	22,468	244,749	45,121
Paperboard mills	2631	51.5	2,136	39.4	8,195	16,140	56.9	2,563	45,044	43.2	12,655	292,940	24,528
Corrugated and solid fiber boxes	2653	112.3	3,276	81.4	6,760	19,834	124.2	3,863	31,103	92.8	9,052	97,543	27,521
Sanitary paper products	2676	40.6	1,454	32.8	8,226	15,647	37.8	1,436	37,963	31.1	9,410	302,572	17,831
Newspapers	2711	413.9	10,437	133.8	26,920	33,782	414.8	11,095	26,748	134.7	29,254	217,179	37,732
Periodicals	2721	115.1	4,077	20.2	15,880	22,104	123.1	4,572	37,141	18.0	17,365	964,722	23,905
Book publishing	2731	79.0	2,876	18.2	11,494	16,698	83.6	3,022	36,148	18.5	14,557	786,865	20,804
Miscellaneous publishing	2741	65.1	1,720	23.5	8,473	10,908	67.4	1,910	28,338	25.5	9,349	366,627	11,992
Commercial printing, lithographic	2752	438.2	12,016	316.2	24,704	43,352	451.5	13,004	28,802	331.3	27,465	82,901	48,774
Commercial printing, n.e.c.	2759	107.4	2,588	74.2	5,484	9,265	130.0	3,395	26,115	89.1	7,132	80,045	12,329
Manifold business forms	2761	47.9	1,341	33.7	3,922	7,429	43.6	1,234	28,303	28.8	4,024	139,722	7,911
Industrial inorganic chemicals, n.e.c.	2819	78.9	3,268	39.7	11,212	18,129	58.9	2,624	44,550	31.9	10,415	326,489	17,174
Plastics materials and resins	2821	61.2	2,698	36.5	12,599	31,601	69.7	3,309	47,475	41.5	17,711	426,771	43,529
Organic fibers, noncellulosic	2824	44.4	1,545	33.9	5,661	11,113	38.6	1,438	37,254	30.1	6,533	217,043	12,813
Pharmaceutical preparations	2834	122.9	4,958	62.4	37,224	50,415	142.4	6,257	43,940	78.3	41,186	526,003	57,943
Soap and other detergents	2841	32.8	1,171	19.9	7,709	14,729	32.1	1,232	38,380	18.3	9,288	507,541	16,132
Polishes and sanitation goods	2842	22.0	682	13.4	4,219	6,659	23.0	702	30,522	14.0	5,482	391,571	8,700
Toilet preparations	2844	59.8	1,774	37.0	13,084	18,629	59.5	1,872	31,462	37.4	13,449	359,599	20,439
Paints and allied products	2851	51.1	1,710	25.7	7,154	14,973	52.4	1,981	37,805	27.7	8,411	303,646	17,943
Industrial organic chemicals, n.e.c.	2869	99.8	4,494	57.2	22,423	54,103	92.1	4,801	52,128	53.9	28,308	525,158	63,303
Agricultural chemicals, n.e.c.	2879	16.8	689	9.6	5,514	9,142	14.8	672	45,405	8.7	6,161	708,161	10,079
Chemical preparations, n.e.c.	2899	37.1	1,233	21.4	5,048	9,927	38.0	1,445	38,026	20.8	6,169	298,587	12,199

See footnotes at end of table.

INDUSTRY	SIC code	1992: All employees: Number [1] (1,000)	1992: All employees: Payroll (mil. dol.)	1992: Production workers (1,000)	1992: Value added by manufacture (mil. dol.)	1992: Value of shipments (mil. dol.)	1995: All employees: Number [1] (1,000)	1995: All employees: Payroll: Total (mil. dol.)	1995: All employees: Payroll: Per employee (dol.)	1995: Production workers (1,000)	1995: Value added by manufacture: Total (mil. dol.)	1995: Value added by manufacture: Per production worker (dol.)	1995: Value of shipments (mil. dol.)
Petroleum refining	2911	74.9	3,640	47.9	18,607	136,551	70	3,796	53,920	46	26,248	570,615	136,023
Tires and inner tubes	3011	64.6	2,499	52.8	6,504	11,814	66	2,717	41,361	54	7,397	136,472	14,074
Unsupported plastics film and sheet	3081	54.7	1,680	39.0	5,268	10,619	60	1,909	31,920	44	6,511	146,646	13,912
Plastics products, n.e.c.	3089	427.8	9,996	33.2	24,398	45,376	502	12,268	24,434	398	30,673	77,069	58,542
Ready-mixed concrete	3273	82.4	2,293	61.0	5,346	12,015	92	2,715	29,443	73	6,733	92,736	15,061
Blast furnaces and steel mills	3312	170.1	7,022	131.0	16,541	42,154	153	7,483	48,907	120	22,003	182,897	54,113
Nonferrous wiredrawing and insulating	3357	60.6	1,724	44.8	4,841	13,044	67	2,041	30,502	50	5,989	119,625	16,277
Hardware, n.e.c.	3429	75.4	2,063	56.3	4,824	8,806	78	2,284	29,360	60	5,576	93,402	10,622
Fabricated structural metal	3441	72.0	1,964	50.8	3,947	8,919	74	2,156	29,254	54	4,772	88,704	10,822
Fabricated plate work (boiler shops)	3443	78.4	2,312	55.4	4,789	8,975	84	2,561	30,564	61	5,826	95,046	10,912
Sheet metal work	3444	103.9	2,834	75.3	5,715	11,299	115	3,324	28,903	84	7,358	87,181	14,394
Automotive stampings	3465	105.1	4,094	87.0	7,231	15,803	119	5,140	43,046	100	9,091	90,914	20,639
Metal stampings, n.e.c.	3469	91.8	2,470	70.0	5,100	9,559	102	3,028	29,772	80	6,623	82,377	12,545
Internal combustion engines, n.e.c.	3519	55.5	2,029	37.0	4,786	11,707	58	2,246	38,863	42	6,762	159,491	16,671
Farm machinery and equipment	3523	61.5	1,786	42.6	5,167	9,620	66	2,142	32,559	48	6,831	141,140	13,745
Construction machinery	3531	74.6	2,458	47.8	5,683	13,139	86	2,866	33,446	59	8,376	142,688	19,979
Special dies, tools, jigs, and fixtures	3544	110.8	3,883	84.9	6,617	9,265	129	4,845	37,474	101	8,911	88,574	12,476
Special industry machinery, n.e.c.	3559	83.3	2,947	44.7	6,331	11,479	96	3,998	41,597	53	10,501	198,125	18,828
Electronic computers	3571	110.8	4,849	31.1	16,129	38,202	109	4,846	44,585	35	22,174	631,726	57,054
Refrigeration and heating equipment	3585	120.7	3,594	89.0	9,450	19,739	135	4,301	31,909	103	11,384	110,306	26,227
Industrial machinery, n.e.c.	3599	248.9	7,040	189.1	12,882	19,117	319	9,662	30,288	247	18,795	76,187	28,040
Motors and generators	3621	67.9	1,762	51.9	4,328	8,168	77	2,052	26,550	62	5,341	86,416	10,757
Relays and industrial controls	3625	62.5	1,864	36.0	4,686	7,741	63	2,173	34,270	37	5,617	150,992	9,841
Telephone and telegraph apparatus	3661	91.1	3,739	44.8	12,475	20,510	88	3,836	43,539	40	14,925	373,130	25,859
Radio and TV communications equip.	3663	124.9	4,721	58.6	12,279	19,521	128	5,266	41,044	60	19,862	329,934	29,360
Semiconductors and related devices	3674	172.0	6,884	84.8	22,343	32,191	193	8,803	45,518	99	51,272	517,899	65,623
Electronic components, n.e.c.	3679	180.2	5,119	107.8	11,818	23,670	204	6,172	30,209	126	13,193	104,377	31,071
Motor vehicles and car bodies	3711	227.8	10,434	192.8	45,963	151,682	237	12,956	54,782	207	55,696	269,061	200,939
Motor vehicle parts and accessories	3714	400.0	13,955	313.4	31,074	75,058	470	18,169	38,641	373	43,084	115,662	107,417
Aircraft	3721	264.6	11,493	122.0	23,107	62,940	201	9,894	49,124	86	20,904	241,948	49,504
Aircraft engines and engine parts	3724	120.4	4,966	66.5	11,726	22,408	76	3,618	47,423	42	9,081	216,260	17,519
Aircraft parts and equipment, n.e.c.	3728	163.1	6,187	92.0	12,827	19,511	116	5,149	44,276	64	11,904	185,992	16,841
Ship building and repairing	3731	118.2	3,631	87.0	6,538	10,601	95	3,222	33,771	71	5,720	81,129	9,586
Guided missiles and space vehicles	3761	97.7	4,637	30.1	10,939	19,423	61	3,401	55,942	20	7,770	388,510	14,315
Search and navigation equipment	3812	253.0	10,962	103.1	24,299	35,039	185	9,070	48,971	69	20,369	296,926	29,436
Instruments to measure electricity	3825	68.5	2,544	32.2	5,685	8,826	62	2,599	41,913	31	7,512	243,117	11,909
Surgical and medical instruments	3841	98.2	3,099	58.5	9,400	13,396	99	3,453	34,772	60	10,820	181,840	15,442
Surgical appliances and supplies	3842	96.4	2,846	61.6	8,901	13,801	93	2,919	31,247	59	9,637	163,342	14,850
Photographic equipment and supplies	3861	77.3	3,061	39.2	14,862	22,119	61	2,720	44,522	35	14,707	416,840	21,584

[1] Represents the average of production workers plus all other employees for the payroll period ended nearest the 15th of the month.

Source: U.S. Bureau of the Census, *1992 Census of Manufactures* and *Annual Survey of Manufactures*.

No. 1221. Manufactures Summary: 1995

[Sum of State totals may not add to U.S. total because U.S. and State figures were independently derived]

REGION, DIVISION, AND STATE	ALL EMPLOYEES [1]			PRODUCTION WORKERS [1]		VALUE ADDED BY MANUFACTURES [2]		Value of ship-ments [3] (mil. dol.)
	Number (1,000)	Payroll		Total (1,000)	Wages (mil. dol.)	Total (mil. dol.)	Per production worker (dol.)	
		Total (mil. dol.)	Per employee (dol.)					
U.S.	18,741	623,418	33,266	12,254	317,106	1,709,180	139,482	3,591,157
Northeast	3,556	128,904	36,247	2,103	55,549	314,215	149,366	588,435
N.E.	1,094	40,148	36,715	640	17,350	91,449	142,844	168,226
ME	91	2,622	28,969	67	1,706	7,030	105,087	14,477
NH	103	3,304	32,017	68	1,708	8,659	127,518	15,437
VT	46	1,389	30,065	31	702	3,445	111,128	8,886
MA	467	17,860	38,261	261	7,334	41,901	160,539	75,250
RI	85	2,511	29,611	56	1,271	5,426	96,895	10,074
CT	302	12,462	41,264	157	4,627	24,988	158,756	44,102
M.A.	2,463	88,757	36,039	1,463	38,199	222,766	152,267	420,207
NY	982	35,809	36,458	572	14,489	89,924	157,209	162,945
NJ	545	21,748	39,942	285	7,862	48,260	169,157	92,383
PA	936	31,199	33,329	606	15,847	84,582	139,643	164,879
Midwest	5,795	203,839	35,177	3,863	111,986	527,949	136,679	1,152,166
E.N.C.	4,333	157,402	36,328	2,902	87,766	396,854	136,761	860,527
OH	1,084	39,506	36,438	730	22,669	103,713	142,112	222,923
IN	666	22,371	33,595	480	13,998	60,992	127,093	130,899
IL	1,009	35,823	35,521	633	17,281	93,763	148,031	193,095
MI	970	40,534	41,783	637	22,687	87,398	137,310	204,018
WI	604	19,169	31,731	422	11,131	50,969	120,770	109,593
W.N.C.	1,462	46,437	31,766	961	24,221	131,095	136,429	291,639
MN	419	14,565	34,804	251	6,492	32,553	129,798	69,419
IA	254	7,740	30,495	182	4,728	26,215	144,357	59,003
MO	412	13,196	32,006	265	6,507	39,737	150,233	82,557
ND	22	547	24,959	15	323	1,559	101,253	4,382
SD	42	1,047	25,224	30	634	3,927	130,910	9,213
NE	111	3,010	27,237	81	1,907	9,361	115,420	24,425
KS	203	6,332	31,133	138	3,630	17,743	129,037	42,641
South	6,171	179,884	29,150	4,326	100,776	566,442	130,927	1,248,052
S.A.	3,084	90,126	29,224	2,127	48,846	267,071	125,562	549,734
DE	63	2,815	44,610	30	908	5,666	188,857	14,469
MD	191	6,834	35,800	112	3,227	17,148	152,969	34,478
DC	14	692	50,109	3	108	1,636	511,375	2,051
VA	401	12,057	30,066	284	6,894	40,134	141,515	75,782
WV	80	2,561	32,008	58	1,616	8,948	155,612	17,765
NC	889	23,828	26,815	653	13,892	73,919	113,252	152,709
SC	375	10,580	28,250	278	6,438	31,467	113,314	66,903
GA	592	16,916	28,565	416	9,455	50,220	120,604	112,023
FL	480	13,845	28,850	294	6,309	37,934	129,114	73,574
E.S.C.	1,486	39,911	26,853	1,122	25,366	123,279	109,823	282,640
KY	302	8,965	29,657	222	5,609	33,632	151,564	79,406
TN	552	14,965	27,092	414	9,302	43,126	104,294	98,206
AL	387	10,384	26,810	290	6,610	29,079	100,375	65,481
MS	244	5,597	22,911	196	3,844	17,443	88,811	39,547
W.S.C.	1,601	49,847	31,142	1,078	26,564	176,092	163,365	415,678
AR	244	5,760	23,617	194	4,018	18,640	96,180	42,929
LA	176	5,868	33,415	125	3,644	30,405	243,822	74,493
OK	163	4,536	27,896	115	2,770	14,622	127,483	33,165
TX	1,019	33,683	33,071	645	16,132	112,425	174,384	265,092
West	3,219	110,790	34,419	1,962	48,796	300,575	153,230	602,484
Mountain	693	21,950	31,683	434	10,504	71,442	164,537	134,885
MT	22	566	25,950	15	373	1,779	115,519	4,899
ID	71	2,162	30,358	50	1,232	7,932	159,917	16,484
WY	10	262	26,505	8	176	1,030	137,307	2,705
CO	192	6,434	33,528	116	3,042	18,943	164,009	37,536
NM	43	1,262	29,206	28	609	8,358	301,736	12,561
AZ	198	6,715	33,914	114	2,629	20,912	182,954	35,185
UT	119	3,498	29,391	79	1,873	9,496	120,222	20,069
NV	38	1,052	27,841	25	572	2,991	118,694	5,445
Pacific	2,526	88,840	35,169	1,527	38,292	229,133	150,015	467,600
WA	339	12,256	36,185	203	5,763	28,150	138,672	69,062
OR	227	7,312	32,266	156	4,056	19,677	126,298	42,338
CA	1,928	68,288	35,425	1,146	27,877	178,358	155,636	348,765
AK	16	475	30,082	12	335	1,459	122,571	3,994
HI	17	509	29,434	11	261	1,489	139,112	3,440

[1] Includes employment and payroll at administrative offices and auxiliary units. All employees represents the average of production workers plus all other employees for the payroll period ended nearest the 12th of March. Production workers represents the average of the employment for the payroll periods ended nearest the 12th of March, May, August, and November. [2] Adjusted value added; takes into account (a) value added by merchandising operations (that is, difference between the sales value and cost of merchandise sold without further manufacture, processing, or assembly), plus (b) net change in finished goods and work-inprocess inventories between beginning and end of year. [3] Includes extensive and unmeasurable duplication from shipments between establishments in the same industry classification.

Source: U.S. Bureau of the Census, *Annual Survey of Manufactures, Geographic Area Statistics*, series M95(AS)-3.

No. 1222. Average Hourly Earnings of Production Workers in Manufacturing Industries, by State: 1980 to 1996

[In dollars]

STATE	1980	1990	1994	1995	1996	STATE	1980	1990	1994	1995	1996
United States	7.27	10.83	12.07	12.37	12.78	Missouri	7.26	10.74	11.77	12.16	12.54
Alabama	6.49	9.39	10.75	11.14	11.53	Montana	8.78	11.51	12.49	12.94	13.00
Alaska	10.22	12.46	10.96	11.00	11.14	Nebraska	7.38	9.66	10.94	11.19	11.51
Arizona	7.29	10.21	11.17	11.16	11.49	Nevada	7.72	11.05	11.83	12.62	13.59
Arkansas	5.71	8.51	9.65	10.05	10.41	New Hampshire	5.87	10.83	11.74	11.94	12.24
California	7.70	11.48	12.44	12.55	12.83	New Jersey	7.31	11.76	13.36	13.56	13.86
Colorado	7.63	10.94	12.26	12.51	12.82	New Mexico	5.79	9.04	10.13	10.68	10.97
Connecticut	7.08	11.53	13.53	13.71	14.01	New York	7.18	11.11	12.19	12.50	12.78
Delaware	7.58	12.39	13.92	14.20	14.00	North Carolina	5.37	8.79	10.19	10.56	10.96
District of Columbia	8.46	12.51	13.46	13.66	13.68	North Dakota	6.56	9.27	10.19	10.75	10.94
Florida	5.98	8.98	9.97	10.18	10.54	Ohio	8.57	12.64	14.40	14.42	14.69
Georgia	5.77	9.17	10.34	10.71	11.17	Oklahoma	7.36	10.73	11.42	11.52	11.77
Hawaii	6.83	10.99	12.22	12.82	12.79	Oregon	8.65	11.15	12.31	12.75	13.01
Idaho	7.55	10.60	11.88	11.46	12.15	Pennsylvania	7.59	11.04	12.49	12.81	13.39
Illinois	8.02	11.44	12.25	12.64	13.03	Rhode Island	5.59	9.45	10.35	10.62	10.94
Indiana	8.49	12.03	13.55	13.91	14.33	South Carolina	5.59	8.84	10.00	10.16	10.26
Iowa	8.67	11.27	12.45	12.73	13.13	South Dakota	6.50	8.48	9.19	9.36	9.59
Kansas	7.37	10.94	12.15	12.39	12.88	Tennessee	6.08	9.55	10.50	10.78	11.28
Kentucky	7.34	10.70	11.81	12.22	12.70	Texas	7.15	10.47	11.13	11.47	11.82
Louisiana	7.74	11.61	13.11	13.43	13.66	Utah	7.02	10.32	11.28	11.62	12.22
Maine	6.00	10.59	11.91	12.39	12.71	Vermont	6.14	10.52	11.96	12.21	12.42
Maryland	7.61	11.57	13.15	13.49	13.71	Virginia	6.22	10.07	11.24	11.72	12.19
Massachusetts	6.51	11.39	12.59	12.79	13.04	Washington	(NA)	12.61	14.86	14.73	14.70
Michigan	9.52	13.86	16.13	16.31	16.67	West Virginia	8.06	11.53	12.60	12.64	12.96
Minnesota	7.61	11.23	12.58	12.79	13.18	Wisconsin	8.03	11.11	12.41	12.76	13.14
Mississippi	5.44	8.37	9.41	9.76	10.19	Wyoming	7.01	10.83	11.79	11.96	13.16

NA Not available.

Source: U.S. Bureau of Labor Statistics, *Employment and Earnings*, monthly.

No. 1223. Manufacturers' Shipments, Inventories, and Orders: 1950 to 1996

[In billions of dollars, except ratio]

YEAR	Shipments	Inventories (Dec. 31) [1]	Ratio of inventories to shipments [2]	New orders	Unfilled orders (Dec. 31)	YEAR	Shipments	Inventories (Dec. 31) [1]	Ratio of inventories to shipments [2]	New orders	Unfilled orders (Dec. 31)
1950	224	32	1.41	242	41	1974	1,018	158	1.86	1,047	187
1951	261	39	1.78	287	67	1975	1,039	160	1.77	1,023	171
1952	270	42	1.71	279	76	1976	1,186	175	1.66	1,194	180
1953	298	44	1.90	283	60	1977	1,358	188	1.58	1,381	202
1954	280	42	1.71	268	48	1978	1,523	209	1.55	1,580	259
1955	318	45	1.63	330	60	1979	1,727	239	1.61	1,771	303
1956	333	51	1.74	340	68	1980	1,853	262	1.61	1,876	326
1957	345	52	1.90	331	53	1981	2,018	280	1.74	2,015	323
1958	327	50	1.75	324	47	1982	1,960	307	1.97	1,946	309
1959	363	53	1.68	369	52	1983	2,071	308	1.67	2,105	343
1960	371	54	1.79	363	45	1984	2,288	334	1.75	2,315	370
1961	371	55	1.67	373	47	1985	2,334	330	1.72	2,348	384
1962	400	58	1.76	401	48	1986	2,336	318	1.63	2,342	390
1963	421	60	1.66	426	53	1987	2,476	333	1.58	2,513	427
1964	448	63	1.62	460	65	1988	2,695	363	1.56	2,739	471
1965	492	68	1.58	505	79	1989	2,840	385	1.65	2,875	506
1966	538	78	1.70	557	97	1990	2,912	398	1.70	2,934	527
1967	558	84	1.71	565	104	1991	2,878	384	1.65	2,866	515
1968	603	90	1.76	608	110	1992	3,005	375	1.47	2,979	489
1969	642	98	1.81	647	115	1993	3,128	376	1.44	3,092	453
1970	634	101	1.91	625	106	1994	3,348	396	1.38	3,357	462
1971	671	102	1.78	672	107	1995	3,589	419	1.41	3,804	477
1972	756	108	1.58	770	120	1996	3,735	425	1.37	3,770	512
1973	875	124	1.63	913	158						

[1] Beginning in 1982, inventories are stated at current cost and are not comparable to the book value estimates for prior years. [2] Ratio based on December seasonally adjusted data.

Source: U.S. Bureau of the Census, Current Industrial Reports, *Manufacturers' Shipments, Inventories, and Orders: 1987-1996*, series M3; and monthly press releases.

No. 1224. Value of Manufactures Shipments, Inventories, and New Orders, by Industry: 1992 to 1996

[In millions of dollars. Based on 1987 Standard Industrial Classification (SIC). Based on a sample survey of most manufacturing companies with $500 million or more in annual shipments]

INDUSTRY	SIC code	SHIPMENTS					INVENTORIES (Dec. 31)					NEW ORDERS				
		1992	1993	1994	1995	1996	1992	1993	1994	1995	1996	1992	1993	1994	1995	1996
All manufacturing industries	(X)	3,004,727	3,127,825	3,348,019	3,589,395	3,735,183	374,906	375,982	395,974	419,188	424,462	2,978,548	3,082,381	3,356,797	3,604,239	3,770,398
Durable goods	(X)	1,541,866	1,630,635	1,789,576	1,921,210	2,005,997	232,318	233,306	247,001	258,699	263,937	1,515,694	1,596,974	1,794,508	1,937,624	2,039,558
Stone, clay, and glass prods.	32	62,521	65,610	71,230	75,991	83,365	7,846	7,443	7,688	8,378	8,385	61,921	65,945	71,562	76,149	83,133
Primary metals	33	138,287	142,885	161,188	180,303	173,619	19,967	20,093	22,555	24,066	24,801	136,849	144,018	167,685	178,681	174,865
Fabricated metal products	34	166,532	175,118	190,544	204,820	215,427	23,372	23,402	25,127	26,927	26,940	165,793	172,121	191,099	205,894	217,468
Industrial machinery and equipment	35	258,662	278,063	313,047	351,113	378,366	45,688	47,092	51,189	57,033	56,104	258,608	277,416	325,788	356,282	379,817
Computer and office equipment	357	66,709	69,249	78,230	90,249	101,207	10,352	10,473	10,640	12,668	10,875	65,066	68,497	81,595	89,836	101,542
Electronic and other	36	216,764	233,622	266,405	299,838	323,001	29,709	30,765	34,571	37,855	38,025	217,966	233,991	266,386	305,738	321,390
Electronic components	367	73,642	81,236	97,131	119,288	128,942	9,759	10,311	11,391	12,766	12,755	75,215	79,822	97,910	124,689	127,371
Transportation equipment [1]	37	399,270	414,694	450,809	462,849	471,661	61,533	59,140	59,364	56,350	60,504	377,147	386,643	440,817	472,332	502,861
Motor vehicles and parts	371	238,384	267,365	314,637	326,415	334,633	12,920	13,865	15,341	15,780	16,151	(NA)	(NA)	(NA)	(NA)	(NA)
Aircraft, missiles, and parts	372, 6	131,366	116,345	103,316	102,531	103,753	44,234	40,905	39,521	36,031	39,834	110,830	88,070	90,217	114,099	134,097
Instruments and related products	38	134,941	137,387	138,400	140,911	146,199	23,925	22,492	22,273	22,643	23,623	132,314	133,249	133,232	137,593	145,455
All other durable goods	39	164,889	183,456	197,953	205,385	214,359	20,278	22,879	24,234	25,447	25,555	165,096	183,591	197,939	204,957	214,569
Nondurable goods [1]	(X)	1,462,861	1,496,990	1,558,443	1,668,185	1,729,186	142,588	142,676	148,973	160,489	160,525	1,462,854	1,495,407	1,562,289	1,666,615	1,730,810
Food and kindred products [1]	20	406,964	422,220	430,963	448,408	471,633	31,376	31,529	32,652	34,752	34,966	(NA)	(NA)	(NA)	(NA)	(NA)
Beverages	208	57,957	58,562	61,347	64,415	68,786	5,708	5,721	5,902	6,477	6,496	(NA)	(NA)	(NA)	(NA)	(NA)
Tobacco products	21	35,198	28,383	30,021	32,984	34,492	6,871	6,575	6,063	6,110	6,661	(NA)	(NA)	(NA)	(NA)	(NA)
Textile mill products	22	70,753	73,955	78,027	79,743	78,505	8,297	8,821	9,346	9,807	9,591	(NA)	(NA)	(NA)	(NA)	(NA)
Paper and allied products	26	133,201	133,263	143,649	172,637	161,968	13,843	13,795	14,290	17,165	16,026	(NA)	(NA)	(NA)	(NA)	(NA)
Chemicals and allied products [1]	28	305,420	314,907	333,905	362,127	372,848	35,476	35,505	36,737	39,606	41,033	(NA)	(NA)	(NA)	(NA)	(NA)
Industrial chemicals	281,2,6,8	157,619	158,771	169,909	187,404	182,458	17,548	17,142	17,710	19,131	19,565	(NA)	(NA)	(NA)	(NA)	(NA)
Drugs, soaps, toiletries	283-4	110,667	117,888	122,352	131,042	144,458	13,473	13,964	14,425	15,641	16,322	(NA)	(NA)	(NA)	(NA)	(NA)
Petroleum and coal products	29	150,227	144,834	143,328	151,261	180,122	10,975	9,865	10,661	10,957	11,844	(NA)	(NA)	(NA)	(NA)	(NA)
Rubber and plastics products	30	113,593	122,777	135,145	145,426	143,888	12,517	12,770	14,145	15,137	15,549	(NA)	(NA)	(NA)	(NA)	(NA)

NA Not available. X Not applicable. [1] Includes industries not shown separately.

Source: U.S. Bureau of the Census, Current Industrial Reports, series M3-1(96), *Manufactures' Shipments, Inventories, and Orders: 1987-1996*, and monthly press releases.

No. 1225. Value of Manufactured Shipments, Inventories, and New Orders, by Market Grouping: 1992 to 1996

[In millions of dollars. Based on 1987 Standard Industrial Classification (SIC). For definition of individual market groupings, see publication cited below. Based on a sample survey of most manufacturing companies with $500 million or more in annual shipments]

MARKET GROUPING	SHIPMENTS					INVENTORIES (Dec. 31)					NEW ORDERS				
	1992	1993	1994	1995	1996	1992	1993	1994	1995	1996	1992	1993	1994	1995	1996
All manufacturing industries	**3,004,727**	**3,127,625**	**3,348,019**	**3,589,395**	**3,735,183**	**374,906**	**375,962**	**386,975**	**419,188**	**424,462**	**2,978,548**	**3,092,381**	**3,358,797**	**3,604,239**	**3,770,398**
Market categories:															
Automotive equipment	120,632	134,229	155,405	160,464	166,342	6,588	6,776	7,284	7,545	7,757	120,525	134,526	155,704	160,532	166,309
Home goods and apparel	185,588	195,574	205,984	210,752	219,057	25,717	27,423	29,409	30,367	30,017	185,713	194,976	205,506	211,076	219,082
Consumer staples	678,502	691,290	706,035	743,516	802,092	60,459	59,946	61,776	65,825	67,145	678,613	691,347	706,180	743,712	802,369
Machinery and equipment	500,554	524,481	569,332	611,996	653,894	86,871	86,613	92,596	98,204	102,411	491,195	505,543	567,922	625,988	674,135
Business supplies	241,855	248,469	258,551	276,979	293,499	22,130	21,886	23,155	25,397	25,008	241,903	248,204	258,914	277,220	293,768
Construction materials and supplies	184,498	199,228	217,556	228,364	235,093	22,283	23,488	24,939	26,489	26,260	184,385	198,463	219,305	228,339	235,777
Defense products	92,889	86,034	80,792	77,559	76,791	23,630	21,858	19,230	16,108	15,441	78,493	73,528	76,283	76,063	84,210
Other material, supplies and intermediate products	1,000,209	1,048,320	1,154,364	1,279,763	1,288,415	127,228	127,992	137,585	149,255	150,423	997,721	1,045,794	1,166,983	1,281,309	1,294,738
Durable goods industries:															
Nondefense capital goods	389,448	400,884	429,273	473,290	503,781	81,647	80,561	86,884	92,823	96,822	378,293	380,331	428,365	486,726	526,951
Excluding aircraft and parts	308,487	330,245	368,195	410,354	439,096	55,008	55,906	60,949	67,559	66,583	309,575	331,278	380,162	414,026	439,222
Defense capital goods	91,809	84,083	77,095	72,895	72,622	24,809	22,557	19,665	16,291	15,641	76,155	71,902	71,682	70,317	79,998
Durables excluding capital goods	1,060,609	1,145,668	1,283,208	1,375,025	1,429,594	125,862	130,188	140,452	149,585	151,474	1,061,246	1,144,741	1,294,461	1,380,581	1,432,609
Miscellaneous series:															
Producers' durable equipment	966,194	1,032,476	1,143,390	1,221,177	1,287,317	141,976	144,239	155,298	164,346	168,322	954,302	1,016,531	1,151,556	1,239,053	1,305,998
Household durable goods	82,276	88,522	95,167	99,063	108,875	12,008	12,499	13,834	14,839	15,182	82,175	88,914	95,500	98,950	108,715
Information technology industries	173,501	179,581	199,494	220,273	241,414	26,852	28,506	29,923	33,276	32,202	172,526	178,434	202,338	220,072	239,996
Health care equipment and products	99,690	106,335	108,895	114,553	125,293	14,089	14,233	14,422	15,485	16,337	101,002	105,737	107,265	114,012	125,407

Source: U.S. Bureau of the Census, Current Industrial Reports, series M3-1(96), *Manufactures' Shipments, Inventories, and Orders: 1987-1996*, and monthly press releases.

No. 1226. Ratios of Manufacturers' Inventories to Shipments and Unfilled Orders to Shipments, by Industry Group: 1992 to 1996

[Based on seasonally adjusted data. NA = Not available]

INDUSTRY	INVENTORY/SHIPMENTS RATIO					UNFILLED ORDERS/SHIPMENTS RATIO				
	1992	1993	1994	1995	1996	1992	1993	1994	1995	1996
All manufacturing industries	1.47	1.44	1.38	1.41	1.37	3.51	3.15	2.93	2.84	2.96
Durable goods industries	1.77	1.67	1.62	1.62	1.60	4.30	3.80	3.51	3.43	3.54
Stone, clay, and glass products	1.54	1.32	1.24	1.29	1.24	1.31	1.23	1.17	1.13	1.04
Primary metals	1.74	1.62	1.46	1.65	1.68	1.88	1.86	1.92	1.92	1.98
Fabricated metal products	1.63	1.55	1.56	1.57	1.52	1.75	1.46	1.40	1.38	1.45
Industrial machinery and equipment	2.10	1.95	1.93	1.93	1.80	2.53	2.27	2.55	2.45	2.37
Electronic, other electrical equipment	1.62	1.57	1.55	1.49	1.42	2.34	2.21	1.95	1.95	1.79
Transportation equipment	1.77	1.68	1.56	1.50	1.60	12.40	11.51	10.63	10.90	12.48
Instruments and related products	2.13	1.99	1.96	1.94	1.97	5.07	4.70	4.23	3.84	3.68
Nondurable goods industries	1.15	1.17	1.11	1.16	1.11	0.75	0.70	0.75	0.67	0.71
Food and kindred products	0.91	0.88	0.85	0.89	0.88	(NA)	(NA)	(NA)	(NA)	(NA)
Tobacco products	1.91	2.58	2.25	2.10	2.10	(NA)	(NA)	(NA)	(NA)	(NA)
Textile mill products	1.42	1.50	1.44	1.59	1.49	(NA)	(NA)	(NA)	(NA)	(NA)
Paper and allied products	1.24	1.25	1.11	1.23	1.22	(NA)	(NA)	(NA)	(NA)	(NA)
Chemicals and allied products	1.36	1.36	1.25	1.31	1.29	(NA)	(NA)	(NA)	(NA)	(NA)
Petroleum and coal products	0.90	0.95	0.89	0.89	0.77	(NA)	(NA)	(NA)	(NA)	(NA)
Rubber and plastics products	1.27	1.21	1.16	1.28	1.31	(NA)	(NA)	(NA)	(NA)	(NA)

Source: U.S. Bureau of the Census, Current Industrial Reports, Series, M3-1(96), *Manufacturers' Shipments, Inventories, and Orders: 1987-1996.*

No. 1227. Industrial Production Indexes, by Industry: 1980 to 1996

[1992=100. Beginning 1990, data based on 1987 Standard Industrial Classification (SIC), earlier years based on 1977 SIC; see text, section 26]

INDUSTRY	SIC code	1980	1985	1989	1990	1991	1992	1993	1994	1995	1996
Total index	(X)	79.7	88.0	99.0	98.9	96.9	100.0	103.4	108.6	112.1	115.2
Manufacturing	(X)	75.5	85.7	99.0	98.5	96.2	100.0	103.7	109.4	113.2	116.4
Durable goods	(X)	73.4	85.6	100.5	99.0	95.5	100.0	105.5	113.4	119.7	125.8
Lumber and products	24	80.4	92.0	104.3	101.6	94.5	100.0	100.9	105.9	106.2	109.8
Furniture and fixtures	25	79.1	88.9	102.4	100.9	94.8	100.0	104.7	107.9	108.6	108.9
Stone, clay, and glass products	32	96.5	98.0	107.4	105.0	97.2	100.0	102.1	107.9	109.1	111.0
Primary metals	33	108.0	98.4	104.9	104.0	96.7	100.0	105.5	113.0	115.7	117.1
Fabricated metal products	34	94.4	96.5	104.8	101.2	96.2	100.0	104.4	112.0	115.7	118.6
Industrial, commercial machinery [1]	35	70.5	81.2	103.0	100.1	95.4	100.0	109.9	125.3	141.4	156.4
Computer and office equipment	357	13.9	50.3	83.0	81.4	82.3	100.0	121.5	152.1	213.6	297.0
Electrical machinery	36	48.6	68.4	85.8	87.7	89.6	100.0	110.0	126.3	148.2	163.3
Transportation equipment	37	70.3	88.8	105.1	102.3	96.5	100.0	103.7	107.4	105.0	106.2
Motor vehicles and parts	371	65.8	95.0	101.2	95.3	88.5	100.0	113.7	129.7	128.5	127.1
Instruments	38	73.6	89.3	98.2	98.4	99.8	100.0	100.6	99.9	100.4	102.8
Nondurable goods	(X)	78.3	86.0	97.3	97.9	97.0	100.0	101.7	105.0	106.2	106.3
Foods	20	79.7	88.9	95.9	97.0	96.4	100.0	102.1	103.7	105.7	106.4
Tobacco products	21	108.5	101.8	105.4	105.4	98.9	100.0	84.0	103.7	106.2	105.6
Textile mill products	22	89.0	86.5	96.5	93.2	92.7	100.0	105.5	110.8	109.9	106.7
Paper and products	26	75.2	83.8	95.4	96.0	96.8	100.0	104.0	108.4	109.9	106.0
Printing and publishing	27	72.4	90.2	103.5	103.1	99.1	100.0	100.8	100.5	99.8	98.5
Chemicals and products	28	75.9	79.4	95.1	97.3	96.4	100.0	101.0	104.1	106.5	108.8
Petroleum products	29	95.9	89.5	99.3	100.3	99.1	100.0	102.9	103.0	104.5	106.5
Rubber and plastics products	30	53.3	73.8	91.2	92.2	90.7	100.0	106.8	116.1	118.9	120.6
Leather and products	31	181.6	126.1	111.9	107.8	96.4	100.0	101.0	93.6	85.7	80.0

X Not applicable. [1] Includes computer equipment.

Source: Board of Governors of the Federal Reserve System, *Federal Reserve Bulletin*, monthly; and *Industrial Production and Capacity Utilization*, Statistical Release G.17, monthly.

No. 1228. Index of Manufacturing Capacity: 1980 to 1996

[1992 output=100. Annual figures are averages of quarterly data. Capacity represents estimated quantity of output relative to output in 1992 which the *current* stock of plant and equipment in manufacturing industries was capable of producing. Primary processing industries comprise textiles, lumber, paper and pulp, petroleum, rubber, stone, clay, glass, primary metals, fabricated metals, and a portion of chemicals. Advanced processing industries comprise chemical products, food, beverages, tobacco, apparel, furniture, printing and publishing, leather, machinery, transportation equipment, instruments, ordnance, and miscellaneous industry groups]

YEAR	Index of capacity	RELATION OF OUTPUT TO CAPACITY (percent)			YEAR	Index of capacity	RELATION OF OUTPUT TO CAPACITY (percent)		
		All manufacturing	Primary processing	Advanced processing			All manufacturing	Primary processing	Advanced processing
1980	95	79	77	81	1991	123	78	80	77
1985	109	79	79	79	1992	126	80	82	78
1986	112	79	80	78	1993	128	81	84	79
1987	114	81	84	80	1994	132	83	87	81
1988	116	84	87	82	1995	136	83	87	81
1989	118	84	86	82	1996	142	82	86	80
1990	121	81	84	80					

Source: Board of Governors of the Federal Reserve System, *Capacity Utilization in Manufacturing, Mining, Utilities, and Industrial Materials*, G.3., monthly.

No. 1229. Finances and Profits of Manufacturing Corporations: 1980 to 1996

lons of dollars. Beginning 1989, data exclude estimates for corporations with less than $250,000 in assets at time of sample lection. Prior years include estimates for corporations in this size category. See table 880 for individual industry data]

ITEM	1980	1985	1989	1990	1991	1992	1993	1994	1995	1996
les	1,897	2,331	2,745	2,811	2,761	2,890	3,015	3,261	3,519	3,753
perating profit	129	138	182	173	133	151	180	241	268	278
ofit:										
ore taxes	145	137	189	160	100	33	119	244	277	313
r taxes	92	88	136	112	68	23	84	175	200	231
dividends	36	46	65	62	60	63	67	70	81	95
come retained in business	58	42	71	49	7	-40	17	105	120	137

ource: 1980, U.S. Federal Trade Commission; thereafter, U.S. Bureau of the Census, *Quarterly Financial Report for facturing, Mining, and Trade Corporations.*

. 1230. Manufacturing Establishments—Export-Related Shipments and Employment: 1977 to 1991

xport-related employment data do not include the jobs involved in the export of nonmanufactured goods and various services foreign buyers. Thus, jobs in the manufacturing sector that relate to the export of nonmanufactured goods are excluded from timates. In addition, all of the indirect exports being reported are domestically produced; that is, they exclude imports. See for further details on methodology]

INDUSTRY	MANUFACTURER'S SHIPMENT VALUE				MANUFACTURING EMPLOYMENT			
	Total [1] (bil. dol.)	Export related		Export related as percent of shipments	Total (1,000)	Export related		Export related as percent of total employment
		Total (bil. dol.)	Direct exports[2] (bil. dol.)			Total (1,000)	Direct exports [3] (1,000)	
	1,358.4	142.4	85.8	10.4	19,590	1,990	1,106	10.2
	1,852.7	249.8	151.2	13.5	20,647	2,639	1,486	12.8
	2,017.5	271.7	164.3	13.4	20,264	2,604	1,486	12.9
	2,055.3	246.4	141.6	12.0	18,737	2,173	1,118	11.6
	2,253.8	268.3	151.0	11.9	19,141	2,179	1,083	11.4
	2,278.9	286.7	156.9	12.6	18,788	2,295	1,083	12.2
	2,260.3	294.3	159.4	13.0	18,371	2,318	1,061	12.6
	2,475.9	378.8	193.6	15.3	18,900	2,771	1,185	14.7
	2,684.7	395.3	242.9	14.7	19,147	2,638	1,412	13.8
	2,793.0	460.5	287.4	16.5	19,042	2,948	1,610	15.5
	2,873.5	515.0	293.7	17.9	18,840	3,214	1,614	17.1
	2,826.2	546.9	314.1	19.4	18,062	3,363	1,697	18.6

Not applicable. [1] Includes total domestic and export shipments for all manufacturing establishments. [2] Includes only the of manufactured products exported by the producing plants. [3] Employment is limited to paid employees in manufacturing producing the export product. The number of employees related to export shipments was calculated for each establishment, gated by industry and by States, and inflated to a level comparable to the plant value of exports reported in the official foreign statistics at port value.

ource: U.S. Bureau of the Census, *Annual Survey of Manufactures, 1987* and *1992 Census of Manufactures*; and *Exports Manufacturing Establishments*, series AR91-1.

No. 1231. U.S. Exports of Manufactures, Origin of World Exports of Manufacture: 1981 to 1995

[In billions of dollars, except percents]

ITEM	1981-85, average	1986-90, average	1991	1992	1993	1994	1995
nanufactures export value	143	212	305	327	339	381	429
chinery & transport equipment	93	135	190	203	211	233	257
micals	21	31	40	44	45	52	61
er	29	46	75	80	83	97	111
of world exports of manu. (percent):							
ted States [1]	12.7	10.7	12.0	11.8	12.1	11.8	11.5
Machinery & transport equip	17.1	14.2	15.1	14.9	15.2	14.4	13.5
Chemicals	15.0	12.9	13.3	13.1	13.6	13.2	13
Other	8.5	5.9	7.6	7.4	7.8	7.9	8.2
many [2]	13.4	14.6	14.2	13.9	12.0	11.7	12.2
an	13.4	12.4	11.9	11.8	12.5	11.8	11.4
er G-7 countries [3]	21.7	21.5	21.6	21.0	19.9	19.7	20.4
t Asian NICs [4]	6.4	7.8	8.2	8.1	8.9	8.8	9.4

U.S. exports are domestic exports only. [2] Prior to 1991, data for are for former West Germany only. r Group of Seven (G-7) Countries: Canada, France, Italy, United Kingdom. [4] East Asian newly industrialized countries : Hong Kong, S. Korea, Singapore, Taiwan.

ource: U.S. Dept. of Commerce, International Trade Administration, Office of Trade and Economic Analysis. Based on United Commodity Trade Statistics, *Statistical Yearbook of the Republic of China (Taiwan)*, and unpublished data.

No. 1232. Alcoholic Beverages—Summary: 1980 to 1995

[For 1980-1985, stocks on hand for years ending June 30; later data for years ending September 30. All other items for fiscal years ending in year shown; see text, section 9. Includes Puerto Rico. Excludes imports]

ITEM	Unit	1980	1985	1990	1991	1992	1993	1994	1995
Beer: Breweries operated	Number	86	103	286	333	392	480	619	879
Production [1]	Mil. bbl. [2]	193	194	202	204	202	202	203	200
Value of shipments [3]	Mil. dol.	9,382	12,216	15,186	15,925	17,302	16,629	16,714	(NA)
Tax-paid withdrawals	Mil. bbl. [2]	172	175	182	183	182	180	180	177
Stocks on hand	Mil. bbl. [2]	15	14	14	14	13.4	13.7	13.4	13.5
Distilled spirits:									
Production facilities operated	Number	143	117	143	145	143	132	150	153
Production [1] [4]	Mil. tax gal. [5]	236	117	122	129	110	111	99	104
Tax-paid withdrawals [6]	Mil. tax gal. [5]	330	306	251	242	246	240	229	235
Stocks on hand [4]	Mil. tax gal. [5]	896	588	451	459	365	420	410	452
Whiskey: Production [1]	Mil. tax gal. [5]	87	65	77	75	62	59	59	69
Stocks on hand	Mil. tax gal. [5]	566	467	365	368	309	361	354	358
Still wines: Production [1]	Mil. wine gal. [7]	982	622	577	478	484	417	436	412
Tax-paid withdrawals [8]	Mil. wine gal. [7]	340	414	468	387	387	354	356	366
Stocks on hand [9]	Mil. wine gal. [7]	486	602	562	539	525	520	477	398
Effervescent wines [10]: Prod. [1]	Mil. wine gal. [7]	26.8	32.0	26.9	22.8	24.7	27.7	23.7	24.3
Tax-paid withdrawals	Mil. wine gal. [7]	24.1	30.9	26.2	24.6	24.1	24.4	23.7	22.8
Stocks on hand	Mil. wine gal. [7]	11.9	21.3	22.1	20.4	16.8	19.5	16.5	16.8

NA Not available. [1] Production represents total amount removed from fermenters, including distilling material, and includes increase after fermentation (by amelioration, sweetening, and addition of wine spirits). [2] Barrels of 31 wine gallons. [3] Source: U.S. Bureau of the Census, *Census of Manufactures*, and *Annual Survey of Manufactures*. [4] Excludes alcohol produced for industrial use. Also excludes vodka and gin production. [5] For spirits of 100 proof or over, a tax gallon is equivalent to the proof gallon; for spirits of less than 100 proof, the tax gallon is equivalent to the wine gallon. A proof gallon is the alcoholic equivalent of a U.S. gallon at 60 degrees F, containing 50 percent of ethyl alcohol by volume. [6] Includes ethyl alcohol. [7] A wine gallon is the U.S. gallon equivalent to the volume of 231 cubic inches. [8] Includes special natural wines. [9] Excludes distilling materials. [10] Includes champagne, other effervescent wines, and artificially carbonated wines.

Source: Except as noted, U.S. Bureau of Alcohol, Tobacco, and Firearms, *Alcohol and Tobacco Summary Statistics*, annual; beginning 1985, *Monthly Statistical Release, Distilled Spirits*, Report Symbol 76; and *Wines*, Report Symbol, ATF A:I 5120-3.

No. 1233. Tobacco Products—Production, Consumption, and Expenditures: 1980 to 1995

[Production data are for calendar years. Excludes cigars produced in customs bonded manufacturing warehouses]

ITEM	Unit	1980	1985	1986	1989	1990	1991	1992	1993	1994	1995
PRODUCTION											
Cigarettes	Billions	714	665	695	677	710	695	719	661	726	747
Cigars	Billions	4	3	2	2	2	2	2	2	2	2
Tobacco [1]	Mil. lb.	163	158	142	141	142	142	141	133	132	131
Consumption per person	Lb. [3]	7.9	6.8	6.1	5.7	5.5	5.4	5.4	5.0	5.0	5.0
Cigarettes	1,000	4	3	3	3	3	3	3	3	3	3
Cigars [4]	Number	24	18	14	14	13	12	12	11	12	13
Consumer expenditures	Bil. dol.	21.0	32.2	37.8	40.9	43.8	47.4	48.4	49.0	47.7	48.6
Cigarettes	Bil. dol.	19.4	30.3	35.9	38.3	41.6	45.2	45.8	46.2	44.5	45.1
Cigars	Bil. dol.	0.7	0.7	0.6	0.7	0.7	0.7	0.6	0.7	0.9	1.0
Other	Bil. dol.	0.9	1.2	1.4	1.4	1.5	1.8	2.0	2.1	2.3	2.5

[1] Smoking and chewing tobaccos and snuff output. [2] Based on estimated population 18 years old and over, as of July 1, including Armed Forces abroad. [3] Unstemmed processing weight equivalent. [4] Weighing over 3 pounds per 1,000.

Source: U.S. Dept. of Agriculture, Economic Research Service, *Tobacco Situation and Outlook*, quarterly.

No. 1234. Textiles and Apparel Products—U.S. Exports and Imports: 1993 to 1995

[In millions of dollars. Excludes glass fibers, rubber and leather apparel, and clothing donated for charity. Minus sign (-) indicates deficit]

PRODUCT	EXPORTS			GENERAL IMPORTS			MERCHANDISE TRADE BALANCE		
	1993	1994	1995	1993	1994	1995	1993	1994	1995
Total	**10,977**	**12,208**	**14,023**	**42,225**	**45,952**	**49,348**	**-31,248**	**-33,744**	**-35,325**
Textile yarn fabrics	6,025	6,592	7,372	8,438	9,208	9,910	-2,413	-2,616	-2,538
Textile yarn	1,045	1,213	1,530	1,146	1,335	1,407	-101	-122	123
Cotton fabric, woven	641	725	834	1,552	1,498	1,613	-911	-773	-779
Woven fabric of manmade textiles	883	925	952	1,261	1,291	1,224	-378	-366	-272
Woven fabric of textile material	210	236	258	662	695	690	-452	-459	-432
Special yarns	1,418	1,588	1,748	878	977	1,040	540	611	708
Other	1,828	1,905	2,050	2,939	3,412	3,936	-1,111	-1,507	-1,886
Apparel	4,952	5,616	6,651	33,787	36,744	39,438	-28,835	-31,128	-32,787

Source: U.S Bureau of the Census, *U.S. Merchandise Trade: Exports, General Imports, and Imports for Consumption*, Report FT925, monthly.

No. 1235. Cotton, Wool, and Manufactured Fibers—Consumption, by End-Use: 1995

[Represents products manufactured by U.S. mills. Excludes glass fiber]

YEAR	Total (mil. lb.)	COTTON		WOOL		MANUFACTURED FIBERS					
								Artificial [1]		Synthetic [2]	
		Total (mil. lb.)	Percent of end-use	Total (mil. lb.)	Percent of end-use	Total (mil. lb.)	Percent of end-use	Total (mil. lb.)	Percent of end-use	Total (mil. lb.)	Percent of end-use
Total	16,696	5,456	32.7	205	1.2	11,036	66.1	498	3.0	10,538	63.1
Apparel	6,727	3,599	53.5	146	2.2	2,983	44.3	265	3.9	2,718	40.4
Home textiles	2,522	1,484	58.8	14	0.6	1,024	40.6	89	3.5	936	37.1
Floor coverings	3,727	26	0.7	29	0.8	3,672	98.5	-	0.0	3,672	98.5
Industrial [3]	3,720	347	9.3	15	0.4	3,357	90.3	144	3.9	3,213	86.4

- Represents or rounds to zero. [1] Rayon and acetate. [2] Nylon, polyester, acrylic, and olefin. [3] Includes consumer-type products.

Source: Fiber Economics Bureau, Inc., Roseland, NJ, *Textile Organon*, monthly (copyright).

No. 1236. Broadwoven and Knit Fabrics—Shipments, Foreign Trade, and Apparent Consumption: 1995

[Fabric blends as shown in the CIR report, MQ22T are reported based on the chief weight of the fiber; whereas, fabrics blends as shown for imports are based on the chief value of the fiber. Apparent consumption represents new domestic supply and is derived by subtracting exports for the total manufacturers' shipments plus imports]

PRODUCT DESCRIPTION	Manufacturers' shipments (quantity)	IMPORTS FOR CONSUMPTION		Percent imports to manufacturers' shipments	EXPORTS OF DOMESTIC MERCHANDISE		Percent exports to manufacturers' shipments	Apparent consumption (quantity)
		Quantity	Value ($1,000)		Quantity	Value ($1,000)		
BROADWOVEN FABRICS (quantity 1,000 sq. meters)								
Cotton fabrics [1]	3,752,553	1,486,065	1,763,361	39.6	277,748	613,980	7.4	4,960,870
Manmade fiber fabrics	9,858,192	838,609	1,208,233	8.5	335,120	819,615	3.4	10,361,681
Silk fabrics	461	28,820	295,476	6,255.7	2,086	15,895	452.8	27,195
Wool fabrics	135,616	27,055	268,456	19.9	9,296	56,539	6.9	153,375
KNIT FABRICS (quantity in 1,000 kilograms)								
Total	1,026,905	66,692	389,696	6.5	51,137	368,308	5.0	1,042,460
Pile fabrics	74,997	37,739	81,585	50.3	20,310	141,100	27.1	92,426
Elastic fabric	(D)	10,602	139,475	(D)	10,816	75,765	(D)	(D)
Other warp knit fabrics	126,728	4,310	39,814	3.4	3,650	41,545	2.9	127,388
Other narrow knit fabrics	(D)	424	5,878	(D)	1,738	16,026	(D)	(D)
Other knit fabrics	783,919	13,617	122,944	1.7	14,623	93,872	1.9	782,913

D Data withheld to avoid disclosing figures for individual companies. [1] Includes all cotton and chiefly cotton mixed with manmade fiber.

Source: U.S. Bureau of the Census, *Manufacturing Profiles*, series MP/95.

No. 1237. Selected Apparel—Shipments, Foreign Trade, and Apparent Consumption: 1996

[Quantity in thousands of units, value in millions of dollars]

PRODUCT DESCRIPTION	MANUFACTURERS' SHIPMENTS		EXPORTS OF DOMESTIC MERCHANDISE		IMPORTS FOR CONSUMPTION		APPARENT CONSUMPTION	
	Quantity	Value	Quantity	Value	Quantity	Value	Quantity	Value
Men's and boys' apparel:								
Sweaters	14,869	214.4	22,488	100.6	35,568	466.7	27,949	580.5
Tops, except sweaters	(D)	(D)	371,352	1,020.3	1,352,496	6,722.8	(D)	(D)
Bottoms	625,097	7,963.3	256,728	1,032.4	610,488	3,926.8	978,857	10,857.7
Coats:								
Suit type, dress and sport	11,266	711.7	6,816	57.0	11,472	414.4	15,924	1,069.1
Other coats	53,205	1,491.0	20,376	99.1	117,528	1,840.4	150,357	3,232.3
Suits	(D)	(D)	5,184	54.0	79,584	532.1	(D)	(D)
Swimwear	2,269	21.7	1,320	6.3	42,456	149.2	43,405	164.6
Women's and girls' apparel:								
Sweaters	46,996	611.5	3,972	22.7	152,088	1,601.2	195,112	2,190.0
Dresses	182,780	4,373.5	21,432	114.1	189,564	1,928.0	350,912	6,187.4
Tops, except sweaters	596,810	4,156.1	176,748	434.6	1,013,892	5,433.2	1,433,954	9,154.7
Skirts	83,820	1,206.7	10,248	43.8	137,760	1,063.2	211,332	2,228.1
Coats and jackets	48,320	1,816.9	16,632	124.7	127,560	2,847.6	159,248	4,539.8
Bottoms, except skirts	481,963	4,971.8	139,896	480.3	597,072	3,800.5	939,139	8,292.0
Suits	(D)	(D)	7,032	62.4	105,288	361.1	(D)	(D)
Swimwear	51,153	741.7	7,332	37.6	30,780	189.3	74,601	893.4
Foundation garments	350,962	1,881.6	294,288	372.3	352,524	867.1	409,218	2,376.4
Infants' apparel	151,677	785.8	104,952	135.7	424,260	1,039.9	470,985	1,690.0

D Data withheld to avoid disclosing figures for individual companies.

Source: U.S. Bureau of the Census, *Manufacturing Profiles*, series MP/95.

No. 1238. Footwear—Production, Foreign Trade, and Apparent Consumption: 1995

[Quantity in thousands of pairs, value in thousands of dollars]

PRODUCT DESCRIPTION	Manufacturers' shipments (quantity)	EXPORTS OF DOMESTIC MERCHANDISE		Percent exports to domestic production	IMPORTS FOR CONSUMPTION		Apparent consumption (quantity)	Percent imports to apparent consumption
		Quantity	Value		Quantity	Value		
Total	**227,108**	**27,679**	**387,886**	**12.2**	**1,390,814**	**13,395,237**	**1,590,043**	**87.5**
Rubber or plastic uppers and rubber or plastic soles	30,312	4,938	50,927	16.3	458,744	2,950,431	484,118	94.8
Waterproof	13,216	434	5,662	3.3	3,110	21,427	15,892	19.6
Not waterproof	17,096	4,504	45,265	26.3	455,634	2,929,004	468,226	97.3
Leather uppers	83,720	9,515	242,353	11.4	579,078	8,512,081	653,283	88.6
Athletic	6,499	4,426	155,767	68.1	405,706	5,193,728	407,779	99.5
Leather soles	27,492	3,454	44,907	12.6	51,374	1,255,710	75,412	68.1
Made with steel safety toes	1,579	233	12,147	(D)	6,068	126,875	(D)	(D)
Boots, except with steel safety toes	7,718	552	16,380	(D)	5,213	123,236	(D)	(D)
Shoes, except with steel safety toes	18,195	2,669	16,380	14.7	40,093	1,005,599	55,619	72.1
Other soles	49,729	1,635	41,679	3.3	121,998	2,082,643	170,092	71.7
Made with steel safety toes	2,659	-	-	(NA)	-	-	2,659	(NA)
Boots, except with steel safety toes	7,890	1,635	41,679	20.7	121,998	2,082,643	128,253	95.1
Shoes, except with steel safety toes	39,180	-	-	(NA)	-	-	39,180	(NA)
Fabric uppers	112,203	13,226	94,405	11.8	352,792	1,902,725	451,769	78.1
Rubber or plastic soles	72,983	11,894	83,987	16.3	300,445	1,630,495	361,534	83.1
Athletic	20,791	6,757	68,289	32.5	83,382	813,208	97,416	85.6
All other	52,192	5,137	15,698	9.8	217,063	817,287	264,118	82.2
With all other soles	39,220	1,332	10,418	3.4	52,347	272,230	90,235	58.0

- Represents zero. D Data withheld to avoid disclosure. NA Not available.

Source: U.S. Bureau of the Census, *Manufacturing Profiles*, series MP/95, annual.

No. 1239. Inorganic Chemicals and Pharmaceutical Preparations—Value of Shipments: 1990 to 1995

PRODUCT	Product code	Unit	1990	1992	1993	1994	1995
INORGANIC CHEMICAL SHIPMENTS							
Alkalies and chlorine	2812	Mil. dol	3,187	2,761	2,278	2,281	3,144
Inorganic color pigments	2816	Mil. dol	2,261	2,428	2,391	2,471	2,284
Inorganic chemicals n.e.c.	2819	Mil. dol	13,612	12,838	11,860	12,442	14,252
Household bleaching compounds	28422 00	Mil. dol	724	920	915	950	929
PHARMACEUTICAL PREP. SHIPMENTS							
Affecting neoplasms, endocrine systems, and metabolic disease	28341	Mil. dol	2,743	3,318	3,820	4,132	4,020
Acting on the central nervous system and sense organs	28341	Mil. dol	7,219	8,319	8,927	9,066	10,064
Acting on the cardiovascular system	28343	Mil. dol	4,815	4,909	5,234	5,547	6,172
Acting on the respiratory system	28344	Mil. dol	3,724	5,277	5,510	5,675	5,190
Acting on the digestive system	28345	Mil. dol	4,840	7,111	7,996	8,827	8,571
Acting on the skin	28346	Mil. dol	1,558	1,760	1,960	2,219	2,193
Vitamin, nutrient, and hematinic preps.	28347	Mil. dol	2,588	2,924	3,560	4,408	4,523
Affecting parasitic and infective disease	28348	Mil. dol	5,411	7,018	7,234	8,189	7,197
Pharmaceutical preps. for veterinary use	28349	Mil. dol	1,057	1,327	1,353	1,315	1,585

Source: U.S. Bureau of the Census, through 1992, *Current Industrial Reports*, MA28A, and MA28G, annual; thereafter, *Manufacturing Profiles*, series MP, annual.

No. 1240. Fiber, Rugs, Carpeting, and Sheets—Shipments: 1990 to 1995

PRODUCT	Unit	1990	1991	1992	1993	1994	1995
All fibers [1]	Mil. lbs.	812	837	926	1,008	1,036	953
Raw wool [2,3]	Mil. lbs.	133	152	151	157	153	142
Noils, and fiber [4]	Mil. lbs.	20	21	21	23	19	20
Other fibers	Mil. lbs.	659	664	754	829	864	792
Knit fabric production	Mil. lbs.	1,901	1,983	2,179	2,188	2,230	2,173
Rugs, carpet and carpeting	Mil. dol.	8,527	7,980	8,749	9,283	9,895	9,538
Sheets	1,000 doz.	15,408	14,001	15,198	16,331	16,190	15,210
Pillow cases	1,000 doz.	12,665	11,301	12,523	14,484	14,622	14,199
Terry towels	1,000 doz.	42,376	43,158	48,789	47,161	48,348	47,933

[1] Includes man-made fiber top converted from tow without combing. A number of companies were added for 1990 based on information in the 1987 Census of Manufactures. Data were received from these companies for 1990; therefore, the information shown for years prior to 1990 may not be directly comparable. These changes represent approximately 20 percent of the total fibers consumed on the woolen system and worsted combing. [2] Data are shown on a scoured basis for greasy wool. [3] Shorn and pulled wool of sheep excludes raw wool consumed in cotton system spinning to avoid disclosing figures for individual companies. [4] Includes reprocessed and reused wool, mohair, alpaca, vicuna, and other specialty fibers as well as tops and noils consumed in woolen spinning and mohair consumed in worsted combing. Does not include wool tops consumed in cotton system spinning.

Source: U.S. Bureau of the Census, 1990-1992, *Current Industrial Reports*, MA22K, MA22Q, and MQ23X, annual; thereafter, *Manufacturing Profiles*, series MP, annual.

No. 1241. Glass Containers, Clay Construction Products, and Refractories—Shipments: 1990 to 1995

[In millions of dollars]

PRODUCT	1990	1991	1992	1993	1994	1995
Glass container shipments	285	279	283	290	285	269
Brick shipments [1]	1,014	883	920	1,008	1,103	1,054
Clay tile shipments [2]	687	639	646	701	723	719
Clay pipe and fittings shipments	60	51	38	32	33	36
Refractory shipments	2,003	1,947	1,956	1,930	1,997	2,218
Clay	771	784	786	773	851	929
Nonclay	1,232	1,163	1,170	1,157	1,146	1,289

[1] Building or common and face bricks. [2] Floor and wall tile including quarry tile.

Source: U.S. Bureau of the Census, 1990-1992, *Current Industrial Reports*, M32G, MQ32D, and MA32C, annual; thereafter, *Manufacturing Profiles*, series MP, annual.

No. 1242. Aluminum Mill Products—Value of Shipments, by Product: 1994 and 1995

[In thousands of pounds]

PRODUCT DESCRIPTION	1994			1995		
	Gross shipments	Total receipts	Net shipments [1]	Gross shipments	Total receipts	Net shipments [1]
Aluminum mill products	**16,258,871**	**1,512,739**	**14,746,132**	**15,723,667**	**1,316,423**	**14,407,244**
Sheet, plate, and foil	11,418,043	806,452	10,611,591	10,807,903	801,942	10,005,961
Sheet and plate	10,362,372	806,452	9,555,920	9,745,709	801,942	8,943,767
Sheet	10,058,901	806,452	9,252,449	9,407,190	801,942	8,605,248
Plate	303,471	-	303,471	338,519	-	338,519
Foil	1,055,671	-	1,055,671	1,062,194	-	1,062,194
Rod, wire, and cable	1,101,483	448,648	652,835	1,159,235	382,325	776,910
Rod and bare wire	486,812	448,648	38,164	552,322	382,325	169,997
Cable and insulated wire	614,671	(²)	614,671	606,913	(²)	606,913
Rod, bar, pipe, tube and shapes	3,378,637	257,639	3,120,998	3,396,583	132,156	3,264,427
Rod and bar(rolled and extruded)	346,469	257,639	88,830	431,121	132,156	298,965
Pipe and tube (extruded and drawn)	300,326	(³)	300,326	317,646	(³)	317,646
Extruded shapes	2,731,842	-	2,731,842	2,647,814	-	2,647,814
All other	360,706	-	360,706	359,946	-	359,946

- Represents zero. [1] Net shipments are derived by subtracting domestic receipts from gross shipments. [2] Included in "Rod and bare wire." [3] Included in "Rod and bar."

Source: U.S. Bureau of the Census, *Manufacturing Profiles, 1995*, series MP/95.

No. 1243. Iron and Steel Industry—Summary: 1980 to 1996

[For financial data, the universe in 1992 consists of the companies that produced 68 percent of the total reported raw steel production. The financial data represent the operations of the steel segment of the companies. Minus sign (-) indicates net loss]

ITEM	Unit	1980	1985	1990	1991	1992	1993	1994	1995	1996
Steel mill products, apparent supply	Mil. tons [1]	95.2	96.4	97.8	88.3	95.0	104.6	121.3	114.8	125.0
Net shipments	Mil. tons [1]	83.9	73.0	85.0	78.8	82.2	89.0	95.1	97.5	100.9
Exports	Mil. tons [1]	4.1	1.0	4.3	6.3	4.3	4.0	3.8	7.1	5.0
Imports	Mil. tons [1]	15.5	24.3	17.2	15.8	17.1	19.5	30.1	24.4	29.2
Scrap consumed	Mil. tons [1]	66.6	53.2	50.1	50.5	51.9	56.5	60.0	62.0	62.0
Scrap inventory	Mil. tons [1]	6.9	4.0	3.6	3.7	3.3	3.6	4.0	4.1	5.3
Iron and steel products: Exports	Mil. tons [1]	5.1	1.6	5.3	7.4	5.3	4.7	4.9	8.2	6.2
Imports	Mil. tons [1]	17.9	27.6	21.9	20.2	21.9	21.8	32.7	27.3	32.1
Capacity by steelmaking process	Mil. net tons	153.7	133.6	116.7	117.6	113.1	109.9	108.2	112.4	116.1
Revenue	Bil. dol.	37.7	28.4	30.9	27.1	26.9	29.5	33.5	35.1	35.0
Net income	Bil. dol.	0.7	-1.8	0.1	-2.0	-4.1	1.9	1.3	1.5	0.4
Stockholders' equity	Bil. dol.	14.5	6.9	4.3	2.8	-0.6	3.7	7.1	8.6	9.2
Total assets	Bil. dol.	30.8	24.0	28.3	27.4	28.8	30.6	32.0	35.3	35.1
Capital expenditures	Bil. dol.	2.7	1.6	2.6	2.3	1.8	1.5	2.2	2.5	2.1
Working capital ratio [2]	Ratio	1.6	1.3	1.6	1.4	1.4	1.3	1.6	1.5	1.7
Inventories	Bil. dol.	4.7	3.5	4.7	4.4	4.5	4.6	4.9	0.3	0.3
Average employment	1,000	399	208	164	146	140	127	126	123	119
Hours worked	Million	758	419	350	304	293	274	273	269	259
Producer price indexes: [3]										
Iron and steel, total	1982=100	90.0	104.8	117.2	114.1	111.5	116.0	122.0	128.8	125.9
Steel mill products	1982=100	86.6	104.7	112.1	109.5	106.4	108.2	113.4	120.1	115.7
Blast and electric furnace products	1982=100	97.1	95.6	120.1	116.9	115.5	115.7	117.0	126.0	157.0
Iron ore	1982=100	87.8	97.5	83.3	83.6	83.7	82.7	82.7	91.8	96.7
Scrap, iron and steel	1982=100	140.9	112.6	166.0	147.6	139.2	172.5	192.9	202.7	190.8
Foundry and forge shop products	1982=100	89.7	105.2	117.2	119.0	120.1	121.3	123.9	129.3	132.6

NA Not available. [1] In millions of short tons. [2] Current assets to current liabilities. [3] Source: U.S. Bureau of Labor Statistics, *Producer Price Indexes*, monthly and annual.

Source: American Iron and Steel Institute, Washington, DC, *Annual Statistical Report* (copyright).

No. 1244. Raw Steel, Pig Iron, and Ferroalloys Production: 1980 to 1996

[In millions, except percent]

ITEM	1980	1985	1990	1991	1992	1993	1994	1995	1996
Raw steel (net tons):									
World production	790.4	792.9	848.8	811.1	810.2	814.6	800.1	833.8	824.9
U.S. production	111.8	88.3	98.9	87.9	92.9	97.9	100.6	104.9	105.3
Percent of world	14	11	12	11	12	12	13	13	13
Furnace:									
Basic oxygen process	67.6	51.9	58.5	52.7	57.6	59.3	61.0	62.5	60.4
Electric	31.2	29.9	36.9	33.8	35.3	38.5	39.6	42.4	44.9
Open hearth	13.0	6.4	3.5	1.4	-	-	-	-	-
Grade:									
Carbon	94.7	76.7	86.6	77.9	82.5	86.9	89.5	92.7	93.6
Alloy and stainless	17.1	11.6	12.3	10.0	10.4	11.0	11.1	12.3	11.7
Pig iron and ferroalloys, production (sh. tons)	68.7	50.4	54.8	48.6	52.2	53.1	54.4	56.1	54.5

- Represents or rounds to zero.

Source: American Iron and Steel Institute, Washington, DC, *Annual Statistical Report* (copyright).

No. 1245. Steel Products—Net Shipments, by Market Classes: 1980 to 1996

[In thousands of short tons. Comprises carbon, alloy, and stainless steel]

MARKET CLASS	1980	1985	1990	1991	1992	1993	1994	1995	1996
Total [1]	83,853	73,043	84,981	78,846	82,241	89,022	95,084	97,494	100,878
Automotive	12,124	12,950	11,100	10,015	11,092	12,719	14,753	14,622	14,665
Steel service centers, distributors	16,172	18,439	21,111	19,464	21,328	23,714	24,153	23,751	27,124
Construction, incl. maintenance [2]	8,742	7,900	9,245	9,161	9,536	13,429	10,935	14,892	15,561
Containers, packaging, shipping	5,551	4,089	4,474	4,278	3,974	4,355	4,495	4,139	4,101
Machinery, industrial equipment, tools	4,543	2,271	2,388	1,982	1,951	2,191	2,427	2,310	2,410
Steel for converting and processing	4,117	5,484	9,441	8,265	9,226	9,451	10,502	10,440	10,245
Rail transportation	3,155	1,061	1,080	999	1,052	1,223	1,246	1,373	1,400
Contractors' products	3,146	3,330	2,870	2,306	2,694	2,913	3,348	(2)	(2)
Oil and gas industries	5,371	2,044	1,892	1,425	1,454	1,526	1,703	2,643	3,254
Electrical equipment	2,441	1,869	2,453	2,102	2,136	2,213	2,299	2,397	2,401
Appliances, utensils, and cutlery	1,725	1,466	1,540	1,388	1,503	1,592	1,736	1,589	1,713

[1] Includes nonclassified shipments and other classes not shown separately. [2] Beginning 1994, contractors' products included with construction.

Source: American Iron and Steel Institute, Washington, DC, *Annual Statistical Report* (copyright).

No. 1246. Machine Tools—New Orders and Shipments: 1970 to 1996

[In millions of dollars. Data represents total industry volume based on reports from over 200 manufacturers]

YEAR	METAL CUTTING TOOLS					METAL FORMING TOOLS				
	New orders (net)		Shipments		Order backlog, end of period	New orders (net)		Shipments		Order backlog, end of period
	Total	Domestic	Total	Domestic		Total	Domestic	Total	Domestic	
1970	651	507	993	827	471	261	227	450	412	235
1971	609	524	672	554	408	252	223	328	286	162
1972	1,009	877	714	627	702	403	368	304	267	260
1973	1,825	1,550	1,074	935	1,454	787	717	427	388	621
1974	2,017	1,716	1,445	1,241	2,025	566	470	585	522	600
1975	916	781	1,879	1,548	1,062	361	284	573	485	388
1976	1,662	1,477	1,482	1,270	1,243	541	485	578	474	351
1977	2,202	1,961	1,651	1,470	1,794	793	729	630	580	515
1978	3,373	3,043	2,189	1,960	2,961	973	901	825	729	663
1979	4,495	3,866	2,930	2,606	4,546	1,126	991	947	860	843
1980	3,885	3,496	3,681	3,206	4,750	870	744	1,011	879	701
1981	2,228	1,946	4,105	3,552	2,873	717	617	991	824	427
1982	1,064	890	2,895	2,599	1,043	433	372	710	600	151
1983	1,152	1,069	1,372	1,200	823	545	489	474	430	222
1984	1,916	1,700	1,807	1,484	1,132	1,000	932	679	609	542
1985	1,853	1,652	1,742	1,549	1,243	675	610	803	743	414
1986	1,544	1,377	1,890	1,685	897	581	507	688	621	307
1987	1,451	1,294	1,677	1,499	672	667	536	647	538	327
1988	2,708	2,316	1,575	1,400	1,806	883	749	825	702	386
1989	1,977	1,723	2,359	2,059	1,423	832	719	837	704	380
1990	2,070	1,772	2,330	2,004	1,164	894	761	970	851	304
1991	1,894	1,549	1,872	1,595	1,186	748	546	802	625	251
1992	1,756	1,532	1,918	1,605	1,025	726	609	678	547	299
1993	2,322	2,177	2,160	1,955	1,187	971	825	1,044	881	225
1994	2,969	2,833	2,640	2,424	1,535	1,698	1,519	1,370	1,196	554
1995	3,105	2,770	3,195	2,923	1,445	1,748	1,398	1,671	1,347	630
1996, est.	3,489	3,180	3,050	2,708	1,665	1,752	1,173	1,973	1,583	520

Source: The Association For Manufacturing Technology, McLean, VA, *The Economic Handbook of The Machine Tool Industry*, annual, (copyright).

No. 1247. Metalworking Machinery—Shipments: 1990 to 1996

[In thousands of dollars]

PRODUCT	Product code	1990	1991	1992	1993	1994	1995	1996
Metalworking machinery	(X)	3,426,081	3,171,746	3,073,862	3,222,456	3,760,074	4,547,133	4,607,757
Metal cutting type	(X)	2,371,266	2,138,713	1,999,668	2,064,864	2,463,001	3,036,592	3,141,128
Boring machines	3541D	(1)	77,655	97,975	84,667	129,835	172,417	88,929
Drilling machines [1]	3541D	184,116	37,374	37,472	37,076	51,967	78,936	99,453
Gear cutting machines	35413	102,678	115,226	79,600	87,662	100,612	137,121	164,256
Grinding and polishing machines	35414	433,574	378,946	335,121	360,894	443,262	549,580	541,277
Lathes	35415	355,632	317,087	258,885	305,488	390,843	478,003	451,115
Milling machines	35416	214,254	201,137	210,403	180,174	138,852	194,757	199,667
Machining centers [2]	3541A	436,999	361,799	377,941	485,375	552,358	698,780	779,433
Station type machines	3541B	502,066	450,366	434,705	374,772	455,138	477,021	498,592
Other metal cutting machine tools [3]	3541C	141,945	195,654	166,535	166,248	200,114	246,237	315,977
Metal forming type	(X)	1,064,815	1,033,035	1,074,194	1,139,581	1,277,187	1,510,541	1,466,629
Punching and shearing machines	35421 pt.	200,050	180,756	172,872	213,402	294,441	326,318	331,382
Bending and forming machines	35421 pt.	229,271	204,357	270,044	255,299	253,219	256,882	283,020
Presses, except forging	35422	319,436	297,889	288,248	345,653	376,398	379,203	401,990
Forging machines	35423 pt.	73,947	(4)	(4)	(4)	(4)	(4)	(4)
Other metal forming	35423 pt.	274,965	350,033	342,830	325,227	393,015	548,138	450,237

X Not applicable. [1] Prior to 1991, boring machines are included with drilling machines. [2] Multi-function numerically controlled machines. [3] Excludes those designed primarily for home workshops, labs, etc. [4] Forging machines included in other metal forming to prevent disclosure of individual company data.

Source: U.S. Bureau of the Census, through 1992, *Current Industrial Reports*, MQ35W, annual; thereafter, *Manufacturing Profiles*, series MP95, annual.

No. 1248. Selected Types of Construction Machinery—Value of Shipments: 1990 to 1995

[In millions of dollars]

PRODUCT DESCRIPTION	Product code	1990	1991	1992	1993	1994	1995
Contractors' off-highway wheel tractors	3531A	360.5	244.2	324.0	355.6	492.4	548.3
Crawler (or tracklaying) tractors	3531B	1,092.6	998.7	775.6	(D)	(D)	(D)
Tractor shovel loaders	3531C	2,235.9	1,855.5	1,833.1	2,354.4	2,632.6	3,041.8
Power cranes, draglines, and shovels	3531E	1,511.8	1,239.1	1,582.3	1,719.4	2,252.5	2,555.2
Mixers, pavers, and related equipment	3531F	609.6	509.6	635.8	677.1	1,079.8	1,164.1
Scrapers; graders; compactors; rollers; off-highway trucks, trailers, and wagons; and rough terrain forklifts	3531G	2,023.7	1,631.6	1,560.7	(D)	2,164.2	2,645.3
Equipment for mounting on tractors	3531N	258.6	214.6	256.1	249.8	286.6	310.1
Self-propelled continuous ditchers and trenchers	3531P 20	129.7	112.2	124.1	143.6	174.0	194.0
Aerial work platforms	3531P 90	814.9	568.9	590.3	637.4	844.9	1,128.0

D Data withheld to avoid disclosing figures for individual companies.

Source: U.S. Bureau of the Census, through 1992, *Current Industrial Reports*, series MA35D; thereafter, *Manufacturing Profiles*, series MP, annual.

No. 1249. Mining and Mineral Processing Equipment—Shipments: 1995 and 1996

PRODUCT	Product code	Number of companies 1996	QUANTITY (units)		VALUE (mil. dol.)	
			1995	1996	1995	1996
Mining and mineral processing equipment	(X)	(X)	(X)	(X)	1,629	1,751
Portable crushing, screening, washing, and combination plants	3531K	17	649	676	96	97
Underground mining machinery [1]	35325	34	4,396	6,838	463	434
Crushing/pulverizing/screening machinery [2]	35327	46	3,871	4,026	295	332
Drills and other mining machinery, n.e.c. [1 3]	35328	30	13,473,018	13,473,018	382	446
Portable drilling rigs and parts	3533A	30	2,155,275	2,267,380	393	443

X Not applicable. [1] Excludes parts. [2] Excludes portables and parts. [3] N.e.c. = Not elsewhere classified.

Source: U.S. Bureau of the Census, *Manufacturing Profiles, 1995* series MP95, annual.

No. 1250. Engines, Refrigeration and Heating Equipment, and Pumps and Compressors—Shipments: 1993 to 1995

PRODUCT	Product code	Unit	1993	1994	1995
Internal combustion engines produced	(X)	1,000	21,342	24,178	23,248
Gasoline (except outboard, aircraft, and auto)	35191	1,000	20,561	23,287	22,263
Nonautomotive diesel (except aircraft)	35193	1,000	197	220	242
Automotive diesel	35194	1,000	608	661	734
Natural gas and LPG	35196	1,000	6	9	9
Air-conditioning, heating equipment shipments:					
Heat transfer equipment	35851	Mil. dol	4,951	5,509	6,171
Unitary air-conditioners	35852	Mil. dol	3,937	4,339	4,797
Commercial refrigeration equipment	35853 pt	Mil. dol	183	220	203
Compressors and compressor units	35854	Mil. dol	3,101	3,717	4,307
Condensing units, refrigeration (complete)	35855	Mil. dol	240	277	286
Room air-conditioners and dehumidifiers	35856	Mil. dol	824	1,106	1,267
Nonelectric warm air furnaces and humidifiers	3585C pt	Mil. dol	1,334	1,426	1,522
Pumps and compressors [1]	(X)	Mil. dol	6,216	6,563	7,198
Industrial pumps	35612	Mil. dol	2,571	2,638	2,672
Domestic water systems	35613	Mil. dol	330	339	329
Oil well, oilfield, and other pumps (including laboratory pumps)	35615	Mil. dol	916	907	(NA)
Compressors and vacuum pumps	35631	Mil. dol	2,400	2,680	(NA)

NA Not available. X Not applicable. [1] Excludes hand pumps, automotive circulating pumps, compressors for icemaking and refrigeration equipment, air conditioning units, and replacements and repair parts for pumps and compressors.

Source: U.S. Bureau of the Census, *Manufacturing Profiles*, series MP95, annual.

No. 1251. Computer Shipments and Revenues: 1990 to 1995

[Revenue is in if-sold, end-user dollars]

ITEM	FACTORY REVENUE (mil. dol.)			SHIPMENTS (units)		
	1990	1994	1995	1990	1994	1995
United States:						
Supercomputer	789	856	631	531	821	735
Mainframe	12,538	5,120	3,753	3,952	2,862	2,095
Midrange	9,816	7,752	8,623	208,102	141,147	206,008
Workstation	3,147	4,976	5,715	161,488	316,083	357,765
Personal computer	18,661	37,313	47,708	9,646,593	18,605,000	22,582,900
Canada:						
Supercomputer	30	40	34	19	45	46
Mainframe	892	187	220	257	125	157
Midrange	744	459	711	17,832	9,596	20,145
Workstation	226	256	292	12,077	18,627	19,949
Personal computer	1,448	3,586	4,292	857,706	1,732,564	2,043,436
Western Europe:						
Supercomputer	506	493	480	291	341	647
Mainframe	10,862	5,339	4,894	4,307	2,031	2,111
Midrange	10,062	5,831	5,890	243,340	152,665	162,726
Workstation	2,396	2,862	3,752	121,577	202,048	235,171
Personal computer	14,810	22,861	29,483	7,954,834	11,760,736	14,672,340
Japan:						
Supercomputer	470	755	729	116	297	380
Mainframe	5,698	4,933	4,551	6,222	3,962	3,401
Midrange	5,392	4,781	5,494	231,571	175,716	187,124
Workstation	1,512	2,276	2,435	96,267	146,232	156,196
Personal computer	4,746	8,753	13,943	2,243,500	3,344,710	5,695,389
Asia/Pacific:						
Supercomputer	(NA)	74	133	(NA)	64	136
Mainframe	(NA)	360	346	(NA)	238	321
Midrange	(NA)	670	1,023	(NA)	21,862	33,128
Workstation	(NA)	343	739	(NA)	25,475	46,673
Personal computer	(NA)	9,323	12,305	(NA)	5,421,495	6,822,135
Rest of World:						
Supercomputer	(NA)	39	44	(NA)	39	49
Mainframe	(NA)	368	319	(NA)	519	230
Midrange	(NA)	724	836	(NA)	22,176	25,455
Workstation	(NA)	355	365	(NA)	26,412	25,594
Personal computer	(NA)	13,621	15,871	(NA)	7,029,806	8,354,798

NA Not available.

No. 1252. Microcontrollers and Chip Shipments: 1990 to 1993

ITEM	REVENUE (mil. dol.)				SHIPMENTS (millions of units)			
	1990	1991	1992	1993	1990	1991	1992	1993
Microcontrollers, worldwide	3,667	4,519	4,613	5,813	1,365	1,562	1,895	2,155
8-bit	2,079	2,618	(NA)	3,612	567	729	844	1,096
4-bit	1,394	1,596	(NA)	1,705	781	801	1,003	999
16-bit	194	303	(NA)	496	17	32	48	60
32-bit processors	1,402	2,456	4,363	8,427	26	44	61	77
RISC [1]	175	270	305	642	1	1	3	7
CISC [2]	1,227	2,186	4,057	7,785	25	42	27	70
256K DRAM [3] chips	1,322	622	270	162	620	299	193	105
1-Megabit DRAM chips	4,229	3,776	2,644	2,031	665	835	821	601

NA Not available. [1] RISC=Reduced Instruction Set Computer. [2] CISC=Complex Instruction Set Computer. [3] DRAM=Dynamic Random Access Memory.

Source of tables 1251 and 1252: Dataquest, Inc., San Jose, CA, Consolidate Data Base, January 1994, and unpublished data.

No. 1253. Computers and Industrial Electronics—Factory Shipments: 1990 to 1995

[In millions of dollars]

ITEM	1990	1991	1992	1993	1994	1995
Computer and peripheral equipment, total	**50,793**	**50,121**	**51,932**	**54,821**	**59,254**	**76,603**
Computers	25,973	26,691	29,036	30,002	38,261	50,301
Peripheral equipment	24,820	23,430	22,896	24,819	20,993	26,302
Industrial electronics, total	**26,183**	**26,126**	**26,778**	**27,250**	**29,916**	**32,568**
Controlling, processing equipment	12,728	12,633	12,881	13,961	15,014	16,164
Testing, measuring equipment	6,859	7,492	7,484	7,332	8,416	9,564
Nuclear electronic equipment	567	571	533	519	466	461
Robots, accessories, and components	275	294	(NA)	(NA)	(NA)	(NA)
Other electronic equipment	5,754	5,137	5,880	5,438	6,020	6,380

NA Not available.

Source: Electronic Industries Association, Washington, DC, *Electronic Market Data Book*, annual (copyright).

No. 1254. Computers and Office and Accounting Machines—Shipments: 1994 and 1995

PRODUCT	Product code	Number of companies, 1995	QUANTITY (number)		VALUE (mil. dol.)	
			1994	1995	1994	1995
Electronic computers (automatic data processors)	3571	207	16,697	20,525	38,261	50,301
Large-scale processing equipment [1]	35713	32	49	58	4,459	4,985
Medium- and small-scale processing equipment [2]	35714	40	253	213	2,816	2,136
Personal computers and workstations	35715	89	13,206	15,686	24,298	36,225
Portable computers	35716	35	2,812	4,104	5,028	5,789
Computer storage devices and equipment	35721	92	(X)	(X)	5,556	8,072
Parts for computer storage devices and subassemblies	35722	17	(X)	(X)	1,952	2,208
Computer terminals	35751	57	(X)	(X)	1,244	1,086
Parts for computer terminals	35752	15	(X)	(X)	(³)	(D)
Computer peripheral equipment, n.e.c. [4]	35771	259	(X)	(X)	11,944	12,624
Calculating and accounting machines	35784	45	(X)	(X)	1,262	1,234
Automatic typing and word processing machines	35792	3	(NA)	(D)	(D)	(D)
Mailing, letter handling, addressing machines	35795	30	(NA)	(X)	967	1,106
Other office machines, n.e.c. [4]	35799	45	(X)	(X)	664	824
Printed circuit assemblies	36798	647	(X)	(X)	17,515	19,454
Magnetic and optical recording media	36950	61	(X)	(X)	4,777	5,369

D Data withheld to avoid disclosure of company data. NA Not available. X Not applicable. [1] 64 megabytes in MINIMUM main memory configuration. [2] Up to 64 megabytes in MINIMUM main memory configuration. [3] Data not shown because it is not comparable to prior years. [4] N.e.c. = Not elsewhere classified.

Source: U.S. Bureau of the Census, *Manufacturing Profiles, 1995*,series MP/95.

No. 1255. Consumer Electronics and Electronic Components—Factory Sales, by Product Category: 1985 to 1996

[In millions of dollars. Factory sales include imports]

PRODUCT CATEGORY	1985	1988	1990	1991	1992	1993	1994	1995	1996
Total	**22,940**	**33,373**	**43,033**	**42,668**	**47,408**	**52,469**	**58,230**	**62,541**	**66,027**
Video products:									
Direct-view color TV	5,514	6,490	6,197	5,979	6,591	7,316	7,225	6,798	6,492
LCD color TV	7	40	50	56	51	45	42	44	39
Projection TV	488	478	626	683	714	841	1,117	1,417	1,426
TV/VCR combinations	(NA)	(NA)	178	265	375	599	710	723	697
Monochrome TV	306	116	99	61	47	40	38	34	29
LCD Monochrome TV	(NA)	40	33	31	32	33	32	31	32
VCR decks	4,173	2,625	2,439	2,454	2,947	2,851	2,869	2,767	2,621
Camcorders	793	2,007	2,260	2,013	1,841	1,958	1,985	2,135	2,084
Laserdisc players	23	50	72	81	93	123	122	108	66
Home satellite earth stations	(NA)	365	421	370	379	408	900	1,265	1,493
Videocassette players	(NA)	63	65	71	49	61	64	59	43
Home and portable products:									
Audio systems	1,372	1,217	1,270	1,264	1,370	1,464	1,703	1,677	1,672
Separate audio components	1,132	1,871	1,935	1,805	1,586	1,635	1,686	1,911	1,911
Home radios	379	379	360	310	324	307	306	284	284
Portable audio equipment	1,140	1,595	1,645	1,780	2,096	2,187	2,495	2,506	2,506
Mobile electronics:									
Aftermarket autosound equipment	961	1,125	1,192	1,232	1,467	1,804	1,898	1,931	1,814
Factory installed autosound	1,800	3,000	3,100	2,875	2,990	3,199	3,225	3,100	2,512
Cellular telephones	115	653	1,133	962	1,146	1,257	1,275	1,431	1,656
Pagers	(NA)	(NA)	118	139	168	198	230	300	370
Vehicle security	(NA)	(NA)	190	210	240	294	401	464	478
Home office products:									
Cordless telephones	280	830	842	1,125	1,091	1,046	1,106	1,141	1,176
Corded telephones	630	532	638	605	575	617	610	557	553
Telephone answering devices	325	838	827	1,000	934	1,026	1,153	1,077	1,004
Home computers	2,175	3,711	4,187	4,287	6,825	8,190	10,088	12,600	15,040
Computer peripherals	(NA)	(NA)	1,980	2,060	2,220	2,450	3,100	3,850	4,500
Computer software (inc. CDROM)	(NA)	(NA)	971	1,045	1,250	1,600	2,050	2,500	3,000
Personal wordprocessors	(NA)	688	656	600	555	558	504	451	404
Home fax machines	(NA)	(NA)	920	869	826	888	964	919	839
Home security systems	(NA)	1,000	1,440	1,030	830	940	1,110	1,130	1,360
Electronic gaming:									
Electronic gaming hardware	(NA)	(NA)	975	1,275	1,575	1,650	1,575	1,500	1,600
Electronic gaming software	(NA)	(NA)	2,400	2,325	2,400	2,625	2,925	3,000	3,500
Blank media:									
Blank audio cassettes	270	367	376	373	376	362	353	334	314
Blank videocassettes	1,055	923	948	980	872	779	730	708	725
Blank floppy diskettes	(NA)	297	314	308	320	345	353	373	300
Accessories and batteries:									
Electronic accessories	(NA)	829	793	721	715	759	874	816	821
Total primary batteries	(NA)	1,244	1,383	1,424	1,538	2,215	2,412	2,600	2,876
U.S. electronic component shipments	**44,064**	**59,120**	**61,303**	**61,698**	**65,295**	**71,480**	**95,704**	**118,816**	**(NA)**
Electron tubes	2,068	2,586	2,646	2,586	2,655	3,038	3,647	3,605	(NA)
Solid State products	14,651	22,246	23,543	26,238	27,292	31,534	46,379	63,601	(NA)
Passive and other components	27,345	34,288	35,114	32,874	35,349	36,909	45,677	51,409	(NA)

NA Not available.

Source: Electronic Industries Association, Washington, DC, Electronic Market Data Book, annual (copyright).

No. 1256. Semiconductors, Printed Circuit Boards, and Other Electronic Components—Value of Shipments, by Class of Product: 1990 to 1995

[In millions of dollars. N.e.c.=not elsewhere classified]

CLASS OF PRODUCT	Product code	1990	1991	1992	1993	1994	1995
Transmittal, industrial, and special-purpose electron tubes (except x-ray)	36713	1,096.5	1,072.5	868.4	677.8	1,120.5	940.2
Electron tubes, receiving type	36714	24.2	21.8	24.6	27.1	(1)	(1)
Cathode ray picture tubes, including rebuilt	36714	1,344.1	1,903.5	2,022.8	2,231.5	[1]2,627.1	[1]2,868.6
Electron tube parts	36715	142.6	120.3	129.5	160.1	114.9	120.2
Printed circuit boards	36720	7,174.5	6,275.3	5,721.7	6,273.0	6,812.3	8,310.4
Integrated microcircuits (semiconductor networks)	36741	16,623.3	19,150.9	20,065.4	23,636.1	36,020.4	51,551.0
Transistors	36742	682.3	736.9	674.8	704.5	834.6	942.3
Diodes and rectifiers	36743	668.2	653.5	652.2	640.7	829.5	1,065.8
Other semiconductor devices	36749	5,741.0	5,760.8	5,899.2	6,908.2	9,915.4	12,936.3
Capacitors for electronic applications	36750	1,391.5	1,224.0	1,288.0	1,294.3	1,512.3	1,794.4
Resistors	36760	799.8	721.5	708.3	716.5	869.5	1,058.7
Coils, transformers, reactors, and chokes for electronic applications	36770	975.6	1,006.6	1,095.3	1,121.4	1,250.7	1,386.6
Coaxial connectors	36781	420.0	384.4	424.5	419.0	642.4	692.1
Cylindrical connectors	36782	513.6	483.4	503.9	482.8	511.3	547.8
Rack and panel connectors	36783	500.0	484.9	461.9	427.6	545.6	563.9
Printed circuit connectors	36784	804.9	843.8	855.2	859.4	923.4	1,023.7
Other connectors including parts	36785	1,085.0	1,068.9	1,123.3	1,152.8	1,377.2	1,419.4
Filters (except microwave) and piezoelectric devices	36791	457.4	451.5	448.8	534.3	674.1	691.3
Microwave components and devices	36793	1,368.7	1,178.5	1,258.4	1,136.3	1,227.2	1,269.1
Transducers, electrical/electronic input or output	36795	741.1	799.5	810.3	832.5	970.5	1,093.9
Switches, mechanical types for electronic circuitry	36796	579.4	545.1	541.7	572.6	621.5	654.6
Printed circuit assemblies	36798	8,269.3	12,590.4	13,745.8	15,087.1	17,514.8	20,555.7
All other electronic components n.e.c	36799	4,896.3	5,997.3	5,260.3	5,257.6	6,149.7	6,470.4

[1] Product codes combined to avoid disclosing figures for individual companies.

Source: U.S Bureau of the Census, *Manufacturing Profiles*, 1995 series MP/95.

No. 1257. Selected Instruments and Related Products—Shipments: 1990 to 1995

[In millions of dollars]

PRODUCT	Product code	1990	1991	1992	1993	1994	1995
Automatic regulating and control valves	34918	1,418	1,537	1,579	1,648	1,807	1,846
Solenoid-operated valves (except nuclear and fluid power transfer)	34919	346	360	405	408	452	452
Aeronautical, nautical, and navigational instruments	38121	2,518	2,672	2,517	2,121	1,859	1,997
Search & detection, navigation & guidance systems and equipment	38122	32,420	31,774	31,311	28,604	25,567	24,887
Laboratory apparatus and laboratory furniture [1]	38210	1,675	1,612	1,715	1,598	1,811	1,828
Controls for monitoring residential and commercial environments and appliance	38220	1,982	1,982	2,197	2,310	2,521	2,537
Process control instruments	38230	5,224	5,230	5,731	5,935	6,240	6,299
Integrating and totalizing meters for gas and liquids	38242	725	698	727	777	859	917
Counting devices	38243	210	228	273	285	354	370
Motor vehicle instruments [2]	38244	1,457	1,330	1,576	1,768	2,092	2,194
Integrating instruments, electrical	38251	398	390	439	461	440	447
Test equipment for testing electrical, radio and communication circuits, and motors	38252	6,156	6,525	6,493	6,572	7,582	8,838
Instruments to measure electricity	38253	586	584	558	526	554	557
Analytical, scientific instruments (except optical)	38260	4,412	4,519	4,886	4,766	5,534	5,690
Sighting, tracking, and fire-control equipment, optical type	38271	581	547	771	769	652	659
Optical instruments and lenses [3]	38274	1,252	1,292	1,322	1,456	1,597	1,749
Aircraft engine instruments (except flight)	38291	579	682	590	552	430	427
Physical properties and kinematic testing equip.	38292	1,012	1,024	1,149	1,175	1,199	1,382
Nuclear radiation detection and monitoring instruments	38294	567	570	533	519	489	492
Commercial, geophysical, meteorological, and general purpose instruments	38295	1,140	1,335	1,361	1,271	1,344	1,348
Surveying and drafting instruments	38296	274	235	255	301	324	348

[1] Includes laboratory furniture. Prior to 1990, laboratory furniture was included in product class 38298. [2] Includes some data previously classified in product class 37149, "Other motor vehicle parts and accessories, new, n.e.c." [3] Beginning 1992, product classes 38272, "Binoculars and astronomical instruments," and 38273, "Other optical instruments and lenses" were combined into product class 38274; prior years have been restated to reflect revision.

Source: U.S. Bureau of the Census, through 1992, *Current Industrial Reports*, MA38B; thereafter *Manufacturing Profiles*, series MP, annual.

No. 1258. Fluid Power Products—Shipments: 1990 to 1995

[In millions of dollars. Includes aerospace]

PRODUCT	Product code	1990	1991	1992	1993	1994	1995
Fluid power products, incl. aerospace	(X)	7,207	6,475	6,330	6,742	7,738	8,790
Hydraulic valves, nonaerospace type	34921	663	606	583	649	765	(NA)
Pneumatic valves, nonaerospace type	34922	458	434	458	418	525	(NA)
Aerospace type hydraulic & pneumatic valves	34923	498	527	443	356	284	(NA)
Fittings for metal and plastic tubing [1]	34924	500	471	516	518	604	(NA)
Hydraulic and pneumatic fittings and couplings for hose (nonaerospace)	34925	620	552	630	489	652	(NA)
Hydraulic and pneumatic hose or tube end fitting and assemblies (aerospace)	(X)	394	386	354	304	323	(NA)
Parts for hydraulic & pneumatic valves	34927	209	161	151	151	188	(NA)
Filters for hydraulic and pneumatic fluid power systems	35692	385	409	395	381	391	(NA)
Hydraulic and pneumatic cylinders etc.:							
Nonaerospace	35931	941	800	864	1,075	1,254	(NA)
Aerospace	35932	636	510	479	464	388	361
Parts for hydraulic and pneumatic cylinders [2]	35933	264	269	171	197	202	(NA)
Hydraulic fluid power pumps and motors	35941	1,240	997	974	1,014	(NA)	(NA)
Parts for pumps and motors	35942	399	354	312	321	347	(NA)

NA Not available. X Not applicable. [1] Used in fluid and power transfer systems (nonaerospace). [2] Includes parts for actuators, accumulators, cushions, and nonvehicular shock absorbers.

Source: U.S. Bureau of the Census, through 1992, *Current Industrial Reports*, MA35N, annual; thereafter, *Manufacturing Profiles*, series MP/95, annual.

No. 1259. Switchgear, Switchboard Apparatus, Relays, and Industrial Controls—Shipments: 1990 to 1995

[In millions of dollars]

PRODUCT	Product code	Companies, 1995 (number)	1990	1991	1992	1993	1994	1995
Power circuit breakers	36132	30	388	368	481	516	531	427
Low volt panelboards & dist. boards [1]	36133	128	1,722	1,643	1,531	1,681	1,744	1,996
Fuses and fuse equipment [2]	36134	22	419	409	413	320	332	423
Molded case circuit breakers, 1,000 volts and under	36135	33	959	917	955	1,010	1,107	1,175
Duct [3]	36136	27	194	184	189	200	228	239
Switchgear, except ducts	36139	132	1,324	1,398	1,615	1,581	1,636	1,726
General purpose and other relays	36251	116	805	772	782	751	676	742
Specific purpose industrial controls	36252	246	2,020	1,993	1,916	2,322	2,732	3,178
General purpose industrial controls	36253	271	2,912	2,879	2,778	3,326	3,699	4,195
Motor controller accessories [4]	36254	124	452	434	448	476	502	496

[1] Includes other switching and interruption devices, 1,000 volts and below. [2] Under 2,300 volts, except power distribution cutouts. [3] Includes plug-in units and accessories, 1,000 volts and under, consisting of enclosed sectionalized prefabricated bus bars rated 20 amperes or more, associated structures and fittings. [4] Includes parts for industrial controls.

Source: U.S. Bureau of the Census, through 1992, *Current Industrial Reports*, MA36A, annual; thereafter, *Manufacturing Profiles*, series MP95, annual.

No. 1260. Selected Industrial Air Pollution Control Equipment—Shipments: 1995

[Quantity in number of units, value in millions of dollars]

PRODUCT	Product code	Number of companies	NEW ORDERS		SHIPMENTS		BACKLOG (Dec. 31)	
			Quantity	Value	Quantity	Value	Quantity	Value
Selected indus. air pollution control equip.	35646	106	(S)	664,176	(S)	752,833	(S)	292,177
Particulate emissions collectors	(X)	67	(S)	476,226	(S)	489,761	(S)	203,114
Electrostatic precipitators	35646 51	17	(S)	134,797	(S)	152,055	(S)	88,549
Fabric filters	35646 54	55	53,992	239,347	51,955	227,912	7,627	60,194
Mechanical collectors	35646 55	35	6,116	65,885	6,030	61,624	700	26,519
Wet scrubbers	35646 56	30	1,263	36,197	1,245	48,170	256	27,852
Gaseous emissions control devices	(X)	39	1,089	199,753	1,204	220,227	234	76,027
Catalytic oxidation systems	35646 70	12	207	27,648	249	34,832	43	12,774
Thermal and direct oxidation systems	35646 72	15	302	68,697	311	71,402	38	9,273
Scrubbers (gas absorber)	35646 73	12	519	25,290	571	25,403	115	3,815
Gas absorbers	35646 76	5	35	7,147	38	3,067	23	5,477
Other	35646 79	18	10,048	38,197	9,948	42,845	366	13,036

S Figure does not meet publication standards. X Not applicable.

Source: U.S. Bureau of the Census, *Manufacturing Profiles*, series MP95, annual.

Domestic Trade and Services

This section presents statistics relating to the distributive trades and service industries. Data shown for the trades, classified by kind of business, and for the various categories of services (e.g., personal, business, repair, hotel) cover sales or receipts, establishments, employees, payrolls, and other items. The principal sources of these data are census reports and survey reports of the Bureau of the Census. Data on gross product in trade and service industries usually appear in the *Survey of Current Business*, issued by the U.S. Bureau of Economic Analysis. Financial data for firms engaged in retail, wholesale, or service activities appear in the annual *Statistics of Income*, published by the Internal Revenue Service.

In Brief

Retail sales, 1996:

Total	*$2.4 trillion*
Automotive dealers	*$.6 trillion*
Food stores	*$.4 trillion*

Annual receipts of taxable service firms ($ billions):

	1990	1995
Business services	*281*	*424*
Health services	*271*	*383*

Censuses—Censuses of retail trade and wholesale trade have been taken at various intervals since 1929. Limited coverage of the service industries started in 1933. Beginning with the 1967 census, legislation provides for a census of each area to be conducted every 5 years (for years ending in "2" and "7"). The industries covered in the censuses and surveys of business are those classified in three divisions defined in the *Standard Industrial Classification Manual* (see text, section 13). *Retail trade* refers to places of business primarily engaged in selling merchandise for personal or household consumption; *wholesale trade,* to establishments primarily engaged in selling goods to dealers and distributors for resale or to purchasers who buy for business and farm uses; and *services,* to establishments primarily engaged in providing a wide range of services for individuals and for businesses.

Beginning with the 1954 Censuses of Retail Trade and Service Industries, data for nonemployer establishments are included and published separately. The census of wholesale trade excludes establishments with no paid employees. Beginning in 1977, sales taxes and finance charges are excluded from sales (or receipt) figures of the three censuses. *In 1982 and prior censuses,* the count of establishments represented the number in business at the end of the year. Beginning 1987, the count of establishments represents those in business at any time during the year.

For the 1987 and 1992 Censuses of Service Industries, hospitals operated by governmental organizations are included. Government-operated facilities in other service kind-of-business classifications are excluded from the census. In 1987 and 1992, data were not collected for elementary and secondary schools, colleges and universities, labor unions and similar organizations, and political organizations.

The census of retail trade beginning in 1977, excludes nonemployer direct sellers. Beginning 1982, the census treated each leased department in a store as a separate establishment and classified it according to the kind of business it conducted. In prior years, data for leased departments were consolidated with the data for stores in which they were located.

Current surveys—Current sample surveys conducted by the Bureau of the Census cover various aspects of the retail and wholesale trade and selected service industries. Its *Monthly Retail Trade Report* contains monthly estimates of sales, inventories, and inventory/sales ratios for the United States, by kind of business. Annual figures on sales, year-end inventories, sales/inventory ratios, by kind of busi appear in the *Annual Benchmark Report for Retail Trade*.

Statistics from the Bureau's monthly wholesale trade survey include national estimates of merchant wholesalers' sales, inventories, and stock-sales ratios by major summary groups—durable and nondurable—and selected kinds of business. Merchant wholesalers are those wholesalers who take title to the goods they sell (e.g., jobbers, exporters, importers, major distributors). These data, based on reports submitted by a sample of firms, appear in the *Monthly Wholesale Trade Report*. Annual figures on sales, sales-inventory ratios, and year-end inventories appear in the *Annual Benchmark Report for Wholesale Trade*. The *Service Annual Survey* provides annual estimates of receipts for selected service kinds of business for the United States as a whole.

For the current sample survey programs retail trade coverage is the same as for the census; wholesale trade coverage is limited to merchant wholesalers; and selected services coverage is less inclusive than the census.

Estimates obtained from annual and monthly surveys are based on sample data and are not expected to agree exactly with results that would be obtained from a complete census of all establishments. Data include estimates for sampling units not reporting.

Statistical reliability—For a discussion of statistical collection and estimation, sampling procedures, and measures of statistical reliability applicable to Census Bureau data, see Appendix III.

Figure 27.1

U.S. Mail Order Sales, by Kind of Business: [illegible]

[illegible] Mail Order Sales: [illegible]

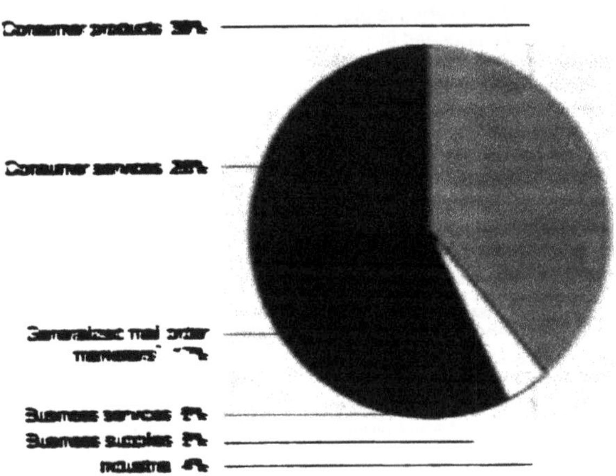

[illegible]

Source: [illegible]

No. 1261. Gross Domestic Product in Domestic Trade and Service Industries in Current and Real (1992) Dollars: 1990 to 1994

[In billions of dollars, except percent. For definition of gross domestic product, see text, section 14. Based on 1987 Standard Industrial Classification]

INDUSTRY	CURRENT DOLLARS				CHAINED (1992) DOLLARS[1]			
	1990	1992	1993	1994	1990	1992	1993	1994
Wholesale and retail trade	870.8	950.8	994.2	1,071.8	907.0	950.8	981.8	1,045.3
Percent of gross domestic product	15.2	15.2	15.2	15.5	14.8	15.2	15.4	15.8
Wholesale trade	367.3	406.5	423.1	461.9	360.6	406.5	418.6	450.0
Retail trade	503.5	544.3	571.1	609.9	546.4	544.3	563.2	595.4
Services	1,059.4	1,200.8	1,266.1	1,342.7	1,181.7	1,200.8	1,222.1	1,249.6
Percent of gross domestic product	18.4	19.2	19.3	19.4	19.3	19.2	19.1	18.9
Hotels and other lodging places	46.1	51.0	54.6	56.1	49.2	51.0	52.5	52.6
Personal services	38.2	41.0	44.5	46.5	41.7	41.0	42.8	43.1
Business services	199.0	218.9	233.4	253.5	216.5	218.9	234.3	247.0
Auto repair, services, and garages	48.9	51.1	54.0	57.4	54.0	51.1	51.0	51.6
Miscellaneous repair services	17.7	17.5	19.2	19.4	21.5	17.5	17.2	16.9
Motion pictures	20.4	20.0	22.1	24.8	22.1	20.0	21.9	23.6
Amusement and recreation services	39.1	47.9	48.7	52.2	42.8	47.9	47.0	48.4
Health services	307.9	369.1	384.8	406.3	356.9	369.1	363.1	368.3
Legal services	80.7	90.1	92.3	94.4	91.5	90.1	87.9	86.7
Educational services	39.8	46.3	48.5	51.4	44.3	46.3	46.6	47.6
Social services	29.6	36.9	40.1	43.4	32.5	36.9	39.3	41.2
Membership organizations	35.0	38.9	42.1	44.5	38.3	38.9	40.8	42.8
Other services	147.8	162.2	171.2	180.0	160.4	162.2	167.5	170.6
Private households	9.4	10.1	10.7	10.8	10.2	10.1	10.3	10.2

[1] See text, section 14.

Source: U.S. Bureau of Economic Analysis, *Survey of Current Business*, August 1996.

No. 1262. Retail Trade—Summary: 1972 to 1992

[1972 through 1982 based on 1972 Standard Industrial Classification (SIC) code; beginning 1987 based on 1987 SIC code. Comparability of data over time is affected by changes in the SIC code]

ITEM	Unit	1972	1977	1982	1987	1992
Firms, total [1]	1,000	1,665	1,567	1,573	1,992	2,212
Multiunit establishments [1,2]	1,000	301	343	415	496	528
Establishments, total [1]	1,000	1,780	1,855	1,923	2,420	2,672
With payroll	1,000	1,265	1,304	1,324	1,504	1,526
With sales of $1,000,000 or more [3]	1,000	74	119	193	259	326
Consumer Price Index: [4]						
All items	1982-84=100	41.8	60.6	96.5	113.6	140.3
All commodities	1982-84=100	44.5	64.2	97.0	107.7	129.1
Sales	Bil. dol.	457	723	1,066	1,540	1,949
By establishments with payroll	Bil. dol.	440	700	1,039	1,493	1,895
By multiunit establishments [2]	Bil. dol.	202	341	567	844	1,137
Percent of total sales	Percent	44.0	47.1	53.2	54.8	58.3
Percent of multiunit sales by 100-or-more establishment multiunits [2,5]	Percent	55.8	55.8	54.5	54.6	57.0
In 1987 dollars [6]	Bil. dol.	1,042	1,170	1,175	1,540	1,669
Percent of sales by corporations	Percent	76.4	79.8	84.6	88.9	89.9
Per capita sales: [7]						
Current dollars	Dollars	2,186	3,291	4,601	6,357	7,643
Constant (1987) dollars [6]	Dollars	4,978	5,325	5,073	6,357	6,544
Sales as percent of personal income	Percent	46.6	45.2	39.6	40.5	37.9
Payroll, entire year	Bil. dol.	55.4	85.9	123.6	177.5	222.9
Percent of sales [8]	Percent	12.6	12.3	11.9	11.9	11.8
Paid employees, March 12 pay period	1,000	11,211	13,040	14,468	17,780	18,407

[1] Through 1982, represents the number of establishments and firms in business at the end of year. Beginning 1987, represents the number of establishments and firms in business at any time during year. [2] Establishments of firms that operate at two or more locations. [3] Through 1982, represents establishments with and without payroll. Beginning 1987, represents only establishments with payroll. [4] Source: U.S. Bureau of Labor Statistics, *Monthly Labor Review*. Beginning 1982, CPI-U annual averages, see text, section 15. [5] Prior to 1982, data provided for percent of multiunit sales by 101-or-more establishment units. [6] Based on implicit price deflators for retail sales supplied by U.S. Bureau of Economic Analysis. [7] Based on estimated resident population as of July 1. [8] Covers only establishments with payroll.

Source: Except as noted, U.S. Bureau of the Census, *Census of Retail Trade, 1972*, RC72-S-1; *1977*, RC77-52; *1982*, RC82-A-52 and RC82-I-1; *1987*, RC87-A-52, RC87-N-1, and RC87-S-1; and *1992*, RC92-A-52, RC92-N-1, and RC92-S-1.

No. 1263. Retail Trade—Establishments, Employees, and Payroll: 1990 and 1994

[Covers establishments with payroll. Employees are for the week including March 12. Most government employees are excluded. For statement on methodology, see Appendix III]

KIND OF BUSINESS	1987 SIC code [1]	ESTABLISHMENTS (1,000)		EMPLOYEES (1,000)		PAYROLL (bil. dol.)	
		1990	1994	1990	1994	1990	1994
Retail trade, total	(G)	1,529.7	1,564.2	19,815	20,320	241.7	282.3
Building materials and garden supplies [2]	52	71.9	69.9	703	728	11.9	14.1
Lumber and other building materials	521	27.5	26.1	403	439	7.5	9.1
Paint, glass, and wallpaper stores	523	10.2	10.1	54	48	0.9	1.0
Hardware stores	525	19.0	18.2	143	140	1.9	2.0
Retail nurseries and garden stores	526	10.1	11.0	76	73	1.0	1.2
Mobile home dealers	527	4.2	4.3	23	29	0.4	0.8
General merchandise stores [2]	53	36.6	36.7	2,135	2,196	22.9	27.0
Department stores	531	10.1	10.8	1,710	1,786	18.3	21.7
Variety stores	533	10.0	13.2	109	107	1.0	1.0
Misc. general merchandise stores	539	15.0	12.4	310	302	3.6	4.2
Food stores [2]	54	186.1	182.5	3,124	3,095	35.8	39.8
Grocery stores	541	132.5	131.7	2,757	2,785	32.4	36.3
Meat and fish markets	542	9.3	8.5	54	45	0.6	0.6
Fruit and vegetable markets	543	2.9	3.1	19	17	0.2	0.2
Candy, nut, confectionery stores	544	5.4	4.9	29	28	0.2	0.2
Retail bakeries	546	19.9	21.3	176	162	1.5	1.7
Automotive dealers and service stations [2]	55	207.3	198.4	2,104	2,097	40.0	48.0
New and used car dealers	551	26.1	24.1	917	949	23.9	30.7
Used car dealers	552	14.3	19.6	56	73	1.0	1.5
Auto and home supply stores	553	43.4	41.3	305	295	5.1	5.5
Gasoline service stations	554	104.8	99.3	701	692	7.5	8.3
Boat dealers	555	4.6	4.8	34	29	0.6	0.7
Recreational vehicle dealers	556	2.7	2.9	24	26	0.5	0.7
Motorcycle dealers	557	3.4	3.6	22	25	0.4	0.5
Apparel and accessory stores [2]	56	150.2	142.4	1,193	1,184	12.2	13.3
Men's and boys' clothing stores	561	14.7	14.6	108	107	1.5	1.4
Women's clothing stores	562	50.2	47.7	439	420	4.0	4.1
Women's accessory and specialty stores	563	7.7	8.3	46	45	0.5	0.5
Children's and infants' wear stores	564	5.6	5.3	36	38	0.3	0.4
Family clothing stores	565	17.8	19.5	283	338	3.0	3.9
Shoe stores	566	37.4	34.8	206	185	2.2	2.2
Misc. apparel and accessory stores	569	9.1	9.5	47	47	0.5	0.6
Furniture and homefurnishings stores [2]	57	106.1	114.5	749	790	12.3	14.3
Furniture and homefurnishings stores [2]	571	61.1	66.8	430	451	7.2	8.3
Furniture stores	5712	30.8	32.8	245	252	4.3	5.0
Floor covering stores	5713	13.2	14.2	77	73	1.5	1.6
Drapery and upholstery stores	5714	3.4	2.7	16	11	0.2	0.2
Misc. homefurnishings stores	5719	13.3	16.8	92	115	1.1	1.6
Household appliance stores	572	10.0	9.6	63	61	1.1	1.1
Radio, television, and computer stores [2]	573	34.2	37.5	245	277	3.9	4.8
Radio, TV, and electronic stores	5731	16.5	16.9	120	135	2.1	2.6
Computer and software stores	5734	5.1	7.5	33	48	0.8	1.0
Record and prerecorded tape stores	5735	7.1	8.7	60	69	0.6	0.7
Eating and drinking places [2]	58	402.6	449.1	6,461	6,928	49.6	60.7
Eating places	5812	286.8	367.2	5,700	6,477	43.8	56.7
Drinking places	5813	43.6	52.9	267	310	2.0	2.5
Miscellaneous retail [2]	59	349.0	354.8	2,487	2,477	33.2	37.8
Drug stores and proprietary stores	591	50.0	45.7	593	583	8.3	9.7
Liquor stores [3]	592	30.8	29.5	141	129	1.6	1.6
Used merchandise stores	593	15.0	21.6	79	112	0.9	1.4
Sporting goods and bicycle shops	5941	21.4	24.5	139	157	1.6	2.2
Book stores	5942	11.7	13.5	86	102	0.8	1.1
Stationery stores	5943	4.8	4.2	34	23	0.4	0.3
Jewelry stores	5944	26.6	27.0	161	142	2.3	2.4
Hobby, toy, and game shops	5945	9.4	10.4	83	94	0.8	1.1
Camera, photo supply stores	5946	3.6	3.0	22	18	0.4	0.3
Gift, novelty, and souvenir shops	5947	29.5	34.4	164	179	1.4	1.7
Sewing, needlework, and piece goods	5949	8.2	7.5	68	59	0.5	0.5
Catalog and mail-order houses	5961	7.2	6.4	141	160	2.6	3.4
Merchandising machine operators	5962	5.1	6.0	76	71	1.3	1.3
Direct selling establishments	5963	8.8	13.2	107	120	1.7	2.2
Fuel dealers	598	12.0	11.1	100	89	2.2	2.2
Florists	5992	25.8	26.8	131	120	1.2	1.3
Optical goods stores	5995	13.2	14.3	66	73	1.1	1.3
Administrative and auxiliary	(X)	16.0	15.9	860	825	23.7	27.4

X Not applicable. [1] Based on 1987 Standard Industrial Classification; see text, section 13. [2] Includes kinds of business not shown separately. [3] Includes government employees.

Source: U.S Bureau of the Census, *County Business Patterns*, annual

No. 1264. Retail Trade Establishments—Number, Sales, Payroll, and Employees, by Kind of Business: 1987 and 1992

[Each kind-of-business classification includes leased departments classified in that kind of business as if they were separate establishments]

KIND OF BUSINESS	1987 SIC code [1]	ALL ESTABLISHMENTS				ESTABLISHMENTS WITH PAYROLL		
		Number [2] (1,000)		Sales (mil. dol.)		Annual payroll, 1992 (mil. dol.)	Paid employees [3] (1,000)	
		1987	1992	1987	1992		1987	1992
Retail trade, total [4]		2,420	2,872	1,540,263	1,949,193	222,868	17,780	18,407
Building materials & garden supplies	52	107	105	83,454	100,837	11,790	668	666
Building materials, supply stores	521, 3	51	51	61,302	75,358	8,423	432	435
Lumber and other building materials	521	36	36	55,868	68,930	7,519	380	386
Paint, glass, and wallpaper stores	523	15	15	5,434	6,428	903	52	49
Hardware stores	525	27	25	11,036	12,729	1,871	138	136
Retail nurseries and garden stores	526	21	22	5,809	6,773	1,018	71	71
Mobile home dealers	527	8	7	5,307	5,978	478	27	23
General merchandise stores	53	57	63	181,971	246,420	24,503	2,003	2,079
Department stores (incl. leased depts.) [5]	531	10	11	153,679	190,785	(NA)	(NA)	(NA)
Department stores (excl. leased depts.) [5]	531	10	11	144,017	186,423	20,136	1,651	1,719
Variety stores	533	21	23	7,134	9,516	1,088	121	116
Misc. general merchandise stores	539	26	29	30,819	50,481	3,279	231	243
Food stores [6]	54	290	278	309,460	377,098	37,228	2,855	2,969
Grocery stores	541	197	186	290,979	358,148	34,425	2,502	2,682
Meat and fish markets	542	[7]11	[7]9	[7]5,616	[7]5,041	556	59	45
Retail bakeries	546	31	31	5,194	5,732	1,407	185	157
Automotive dealers [6]	55 ex. 554	194	207	342,896	406,936	31,807	1,373	1,268
New and used car dealers	551	28	24	280,529	333,801	24,421	940	860
Used car dealers	552	75	92	18,295	25,511	1,132	55	63
Auto and home supply stores	553	67	63	26,622	29,817	4,683	286	269
Boat dealers	555	[7]5	[7]5	[7]6,824	[7]5,537	558	35	27
Recreational vehicle dealers	556	[7]3	[7]3	[7]5,538	[7]6,314	514	25	22
Motorcycle dealers	557	[7]4	[7]4	[7]3,475	[7]4,163	427	27	22
Gasoline service stations	554	137	120	104,769	136,950	7,569	702	675
Apparel and accessory stores [6]	56	197	221	79,322	104,211	12,039	1,121	1,145
Men's and boys' clothing stores	561	19	19	9,017	10,197	1,440	115	105
Women's clothing, specialty stores	562, 3	77	87	29,208	35,749	4,170	455	467
Women's clothing stores	562	64	65	26,366	31,828	3,690	419	423
Family clothing stores	565	27	33	21,472	33,222	3,469	268	310
Shoe stores	566	43	42	14,594	18,122	2,185	205	184
Furniture and homefurnishings stores	57	180	189	78,072	96,947	11,869	703	702
Furniture stores	5712	46	48	26,740	31,216	4,355	247	233
Homefurnishings stores	5713, 4, 9	63	64	17,737	21,132	2,835	176	181
Floor covering stores	5713	[7]14	[7]14	[7]9,226	[7]9,616	1,382	75	69
Household appliance stores	572	17	16	8,642	8,407	965	65	54
Radio, television, computer stores [6]	573	54	61	24,953	36,192	3,714	215	235
Radio, TV, and electronic stores	5731	31	28	15,679	20,275	2,112	123	121
Computer and software stores	5734	8	15	2,799	7,120	607	22	30
Record and prerecorded tape stores	5735	[7]6	[7]8	[7]3,930	[7]5,860	593	44	60
Eating and drinking places	58	490	558	153,462	200,163	52,570	6,100	6,548
Eating places [6]	5812	402	474	142,627	187,758	50,307	5,787	6,244
Restaurants	5812 pt.	[7]155	[7]170	[7]66,364	[7]85,178	25,369	2,822	2,989
Refreshment places	5812 pt.	[7]138	[7]164	[7]56,870	[7]77,686	18,808	2,352	2,652
Cafeterias	5812 pt.	[7]7	[7]6	[7]3,778	[7]3,619	1,037	138	109
Drinking places	5813	88	84	10,834	12,406	2,263	313	304
Drug stores and proprietary stores	591	56	51	54,142	77,788	9,060	574	588
Miscellaneous retail stores [4] [6]	59 ex. 591	710	881	152,716	201,842	24,434	1,682	1,769
Liquor stores	592	45	40	19,826	21,698	1,523	157	133
Used merchandise stores	593	89	124	5,217	8,219	1,124	69	93
Misc. shopping goods stores [6]	594	263	311	53,777	71,650	8,563	706	750
Sporting goods, bicycle shops	5941	50	55	11,256	15,617	1,733	121	137
Book stores	5942	19	23	5,338	8,329	928	72	92
Jewelry stores	5944	50	55	12,925	15,259	2,224	163	148
Hobby, toy, and game shops	5945	28	38	7,451	11,298	992	76	95
Gift, novelty, souvenir shops	5947	79	104	8,446	12,036	1,467	151	164
Nonstore retailers [4]	596	66	116	34,878	52,790	6,280	318	339
Catalog and mail-order houses	5961	31	66	20,765	35,538	3,079	123	150
Merchandising machine operators	5962	24	36	6,258	7,082	1,232	74	70
Direct selling establishments [4]	5963	11	14	7,855	10,170	1,969	121	119
Fuel dealers	598	17	15	14,503	14,202	1,928	99	82
Florists	5992	50	55	5,441	6,433	1,207	125	122
Optical goods stores	5995	15	16	3,480	4,917	1,114	54	65

NA Not available. [1] Based on 1987 Standard Industrial Classification; see text, section 13. [2] Represents the number of establishments in business at any time during year. [3] For pay period including March 12. [4] Excludes nonemployer direct sellers, SIC 5963. [5] Includes sales from catalog order desks. Data for leased departments not included in broader kind-of-business totals. [6] Includes other kinds of businesses, not shown separately. [7] Covers only establishments with payroll.

Source: U.S. Bureau of the Census, *1987* and *1992 Census of Retail Trade*, RC87-N-1, RC92-A-52, and RC92-N-1.

No. 1265. Retail Trade—Sales, by Broad Merchandise Lines: 1987 and 1992

[For establishments with payroll]

MERCHANDISE LINES	1987			1992			
	Establishments (1,000)	Sales of specified merchandise lines		Establishments (1,000)	Sales of specified merchandise lines		
		Total (mil. dol.)	Percent distribution		Total (mil. dol.)	Percent distribution	Percent of total sales of establishments handling line
Retail trade, total [1]	[2]1,504	1,493,309	100.0	[2]1,526	1,894,880	100.0	(X)
Groceries and other food	369	247,410	16.6	371	308,488	16.3	41.4
Meals and snacks	478	137,954	9.2	548	183,957	9.7	34.4
Alcoholic drinks	170	18,721	1.3	187	22,318	1.2	24.5
Packaged alcoholic beverages	179	29,651	2.0	179	35,569	1.9	9.3
Cigars, cigarettes, and tobacco	275	23,231	1.6	284	31,328	1.7	4.5
Drugs, health and beauty aids	219	69,040	4.6	224	107,336	5.7	14.9
Soaps, detergents, and household cleaners	116	9,902	0.7	140	14,979	0.8	3.1
Paper and related products	119	9,232	0.6	152	14,159	0.8	2.8
Men's wear	117	41,647	2.8	118	48,519	2.6	13.4
Women's, junior's and misses' wear	175	85,617	5.7	162	91,972	4.9	24.2
Children's wear	(NA)	(NA)	(NA)	75	21,862	1.2	7.4
Footwear	111	22,732	1.5	110	29,198	1.5	9.3
Sewing, knitting, and needlework goods	37	4,155	0.3	35	5,127	0.3	3.5
Curtains, draperies, and dry goods	68	13,037	0.9	66	15,763	0.8	5.1
Major household appliances	68	17,571	1.2	56	17,866	0.9	7.2
Small electric appliances	80	6,245	0.4	76	6,404	0.3	2.1
TV's, video equipment, videotapes	66	13,360	0.9	66	18,567	1.0	6.8
Audio equipment, musical instruments and supplies	86	16,944	1.1	86	21,710	1.2	8.2
Furniture and sleep equipment	79	29,843	2.0	73	34,359	1.8	12.0
Floor coverings	59	11,385	0.8	47	11,902	0.6	5.6
Computer hardware, software, and supplies	30	5,828	0.4	25	11,437	0.6	8.9
Kitchenware and home furnishings	167	21,512	1.4	162	24,885	1.3	5.1
Jewelry	118	20,691	1.4	131	25,872	1.4	6.6
Books	(NA)	(NA)	(NA)	69	10,475	0.6	5.3
Photographic equipment and supplies	64	5,381	0.4	55	5,524	0.3	2.1
Toys, hobby goods, and games	108	12,917	0.9	105	18,059	1.0	5.1
Optical goods	29	3,717	0.2	35	5,300	0.3	4.3
Sporting goods	73	21,190	1.4	81	25,361	1.3	9.0
Recreational vehicles, parts, and accessories	9	6,092	0.4	7	6,449	0.3	13.6
Hardware, tools, plumbing, and electrical supplies	107	20,784	1.4	106	28,581	1.5	7.8
Lawn and garden equipment	119	16,847	1.1	111	20,952	1.1	4.9
Lumber, millwork, building materials	65	45,491	3.0	57	50,103	2.6	28.8
Paint and related preservatives and supplies	57	7,103	0.5	53	10,399	0.6	5.0
Mobile homes	5	4,866	0.3	4	5,607	0.3	89.0
Cars, vans, trucks, and other powered vehicles	51	251,243	16.8	50	299,852	15.8	83.9
Automotive fuels	151	87,432	5.9	141	114,754	6.1	57.6
Automotive lubricants	154	3,021	0.2	146	3,503	0.2	0.8
Automobile tires, batteries, accessories	158	37,734	2.5	131	45,158	2.4	7.0
Household fuels	26	12,450	0.8	24	12,121	0.6	27.4
Pets, pet food, and supplies	82	5,009	0.3	87	8,197	0.4	2.5
All other merchandise	261	37,211	2.5	301	48,118	2.5	7.2
Unclassified merchandise	161	6,708	0.4	133	9,930	0.5	3.4
Nonmerchandise receipts	342	52,381	3.5	316	62,841	3.3	7.5

NA Not available. X Not applicable. [1] Includes other merchandise lines not shown separately. [2] Detail will not add to total because establishments may carry more than one merchandise line.

Source: U.S. Bureau of the Census, *Census of Retail Trade 1987*, and *1992, Merchandise Line Sales*, RC87-S-3 and RC92-S-3RV.

No. 1266. Retail Trade Sales—Summary: 1980 to 1996

[Sales and inventories for leased departments and concessions are tabulated in the kind-of-business category of the leased department or concession. Based on Current Business Survey, see Appendix III]

YEAR	SALES: Total (bil. dol.)	Annual percent change [1]	Per capita [2] (dol.)	Index of sales (1982=100)	Durable goods (bil. dol.)	Nondurable goods (bil. dol.): Total	Nondurable goods (bil. dol.): Dept. stores [3]	Inventories at cost [4] (bil. dol.)	Inventory/sales ratios [4, 5]
1980	957	6.7	4,213	89.5	299	658	86	121	(NA)
1985	1,375	6.8	5,779	128.6	498	877	126	182	1.55
1987	1,541	6.3	6,361	144.2	576	965	144	208	1.57
1988	1,656	7.5	6,774	154.9	629	1,027	152	219	1.53
1989	1,759	6.2	7,127	164.5	657	1,102	161	237	1.59
1990	1,845	4.9	7,396	172.5	669	1,176	166	240	1.57
1991	1,856	0.6	7,362	173.6	650	1,206	173	243	1.57
1992	1,952	5.2	7,653	182.5	704	1,248	186	252	1.50
1993	2,073	6.2	8,040	193.8	776	1,297	200	268	1.49
1994	2,227	7.5	8,554	208.3	873	1,354	219	290	1.52
1995	2,324	4.3	8,840	217.3	925	1,399	233	304	1.53
1996	2,445	5.2	9,218	228.7	993	1,452	244	314	1.52

NA Not available. [1] Change from immediate prior year. [2] Based on Bureau of the Census estimates of resident population as of July 1. [3] Excludes leased departments. [4] As of Dec. 31. Includes warehouses. Adjusted for seasonal variations. [5] Sales data also adjusted for holiday and trading-day differences.

No. 1267. Retail Trade—Sales, by Kind of Business: 1980 to 1996

[In billions of dollars. See headnote, table 1266. Based on Current Business Survey, see Appendix III]

KIND OF BUSINESS	1987 SIC code [1]	1980	1985	1990	1992	1993	1994	1995	1996
Retail trade, total		957.4	1,375.0	1,844.6	1,951.6	2,072.8	2,227.3	2,324.0	2,445.3
Durable goods stores, total [2]		299.2	498.1	668.8	703.6	776.1	873.4	925.0	993.3
Building materials and garden supplies [2]	52	50.8	71.2	94.6	100.8	109.4	122.3	125.8	134.5
Building materials, supply stores	521,3	35.0	50.8	70.3	75.4	82.4	92.9	95.5	102.0
Hardware stores	525	8.3	10.5	12.5	12.7	13.2	14.2	14.3	15.2
Automotive dealers	55 exc. 554	164.1	303.2	387.6	406.9	456.3	518.5	551.3	592.9
Motor vehicle, misc. automotive dealers	551,2,5,6,7,9	146.2	278.0	356.8	377.1	425.5	485.5	517.2	556.9
Motor vehicle dealers	551,2	137.7	263.1	338.7	359.3	405.2	462.7	492.0	529.8
New and used car dealers	551	130.5	251.6	316.0	333.8	377.2	430.3	455.7	490.6
Auto and home supply stores	553	18.0	25.2	30.8	29.8	30.8	33.0	34.1	36.0
Furniture and homefurnishings stores [2]	57	44.2	68.3	91.5	97.0	105.4	118.6	127.3	133.5
Furniture, homefurnishings stores [2]	571	26.3	38.3	50.5	52.3	55.6	61.0	63.8	66.7
Furniture stores	5712	(NA)	23.9	30.8	31.2	33.4	36.0	37.5	38.8
Floor covering stores	5713	(NA)	7.9	10.7	10.4	10.6	11.4	11.5	12.2
Household appliance, radio, TV, and computer stores	5722,31,34	14.0	25.1	33.0	35.8	40.5	47.7	53.0	56.1
Household appliance stores	5722	(NA)	8.4	8.8	8.4	9.0	8.7	9.5	9.5
Radio, TV, and computer stores	5731,34	(NA)	16.7	24.3	27.4	31.6	39.0	43.5	46.6
Sporting goods and bicycle shops	5941	(NA)	8.7	15.0	15.6	16.9	19.1	20.3	22.1
Book stores	5942	(NA)	4.5	7.4	8.3	9.0	9.9	10.9	11.5
Jewelry stores	5944	(NA)	11.2	15.2	15.1	16.5	17.7	18.6	20.1
Nondurable goods stores, total [2]		658.1	876.9	1,175.8	1,248.0	1,296.6	1,354.0	1,399.0	1,452.0
General merchandise stores	53	109.0	158.6	215.5	246.4	264.6	283.2	299.2	312.8
Department stores [3]	531	85.5	126.4	165.8	186.4	200.5	218.6	232.7	244.4
Variety stores	533	7.8	8.5	8.3	9.5	9.0	8.1	7.7	8.3
Misc. general merchandise stores	539	15.7	23.8	41.4	50.5	55.1	56.5	58.7	60.1
Food stores	54	220.2	285.1	368.3	377.1	385.0	399.0	409.6	423.3
Grocery stores	541	205.6	269.5	348.2	358.1	365.4	378.4	388.0	400.5
Gasoline service stations	554	94.1	113.3	138.5	137.0	138.2	141.7	146.1	155.0
Apparel and accessory stores [2]	56	49.3	70.2	95.8	104.2	107.2	109.9	110.4	113.7
Men's and boys' clothing stores	561	7.7	8.5	10.5	10.2	10.3	10.7	10.2	10.2
Women's clothing specialty stores	562,3	17.6	26.1	32.8	35.8	36.8	35.9	35.0	33.3
Women's clothing stores	562	15.9	23.6	29.8	31.8	33.0	31.9	30.7	28.6
Family clothing stores	565	10.8	17.8	28.4	33.2	34.9	37.1	38.4	42.4
Shoe stores	566	10.5	13.1	18.0	18.1	18.2	18.7	18.8	19.2
Eating and drinking places	58	90.1	127.9	190.1	200.2	213.5	223.5	232.1	236.5
Eating places [2]	5812	80.4	117.6	178.7	187.8	201.3	211.8	219.7	223.7
Restaurants, lunchrooms, cafeterias	5812 pt	(NA)	68.2	99.9	103.6	110.4	118.1	121.9	123.2
Refreshment places	5812 pt	(NA)	48.1	75.7	81.5	87.9	90.5	94.1	95.2
Drinking places	5813	(NA)	10.3	11.5	12.4	12.2	11.7	12.3	12.9
Drug stores and proprietary stores	591	31.0	47.0	70.6	77.8	79.6	81.8	85.6	90.7
Liquor stores	592	16.9	19.5	21.7	21.7	21.5	22.0	22.0	22.8
Nonstore retailers	596	22.8	28.3	45.6	55.2	58.5	64.2	65.8	66.2
Catalog and mail-order houses	5961	(NA)	15.8	26.6	35.5	39.3	43.6	46.2	48.0
Fuel dealers	598	(NA)	16.8	15.6	14.2	14.0	13.7	13.6	15.3

NA Not available. [1] Based on 1987 Standard Industrial Classification code; see text, section 13. [2] Includes kinds of business, not shown separately. [3] Excludes leased departments.

Source of tables 1266 and 1267: U.S. Bureau of the Census, *Current Business Reports, Annual Benchmark Report for Retail Trade, January 1987 Through December 1996*, (BR/96-RV) and prior issues.

No. 1268. Retail Trade—Merchandise Inventories and Inventory/Sales Ratios, by Kind of Business: 1990 to 1996

[As of Dec. 31. Includes warehouses. Adjusted for seasonal variations. Sales data also adjusted for holiday and trading-day differences. See headnote, table 1266]

KIND OF BUSINESS	1987 SIC code [1]	INVENTORIES AT COST [2] (bil. dol.)				INVENTORY/SALES RATIOS			
		1990	1994	1995	1996	1990	1994	1995	1996
Total		239.8	290.1	303.8	314.2	1.57	1.52	1.53	1.52
Excluding automotive group		*176.7*	*211.3*	*218.0*	*226.1*	*1.45*	*1.45*	*1.45*	*1.44*
Durable goods stores [3]		121.1	149.8	159.8	166.0	2.27	1.97	2.00	1.96
Building materials and garden supplies	52	17.0	20.3	21.1	22.5	2.28	1.94	1.96	1.99
Automotive dealers	55 exc. 554	63.1	78.9	85.8	88.1	2.05	1.74	1.80	1.76
Furniture and homefurnishings stores	57	17.4	22.2	23.1	22.4	2.36	2.12	2.11	2.01
Nondurable goods stores [3]		118.7	140.3	144.0	148.2	1.19	1.22	1.22	1.20
General merchandise stores	53	42.4	55.1	58.1	58.8	2.34	2.28	2.30	2.21
Department stores	531	33.4	43.6	46.3	47.7	2.40	2.33	2.35	2.26
Food stores	54	25.0	26.7	27.4	28.7	0.81	0.79	0.79	0.80
Apparel and accessory stores	56	19.7	24.1	23.9	23.9	2.50	2.60	2.57	2.54

[1] Based on 1987 Standard Industrial Classification code; see text, section 13. [2] Excludes supplies and equipment used in store and warehouse operations that are not for resale. [3] Includes kinds of business not shown separately.

Source: U.S. Bureau of the Census, *Current Business Reports, Annual Benchmark Report for Retail Trade, January 1987 Through December 1996* (BR/96-RV).

No. 1269. Franchised New Car Dealerships—Summary: 1980 to 1996

ITEM	Unit	1980	1985	1989	1990	1991	1992	1993	1994	1995	1996
Dealerships [1]	Number	27,900	24,725	25,000	24,825	24,200	23,500	22,950	22,850	22,800	22,750
Sales	Bil. dol.	130.5	251.6	311.6	316.0	301.3	333.8	377.2	434.1	459.0	495.0
New cars sold [2]	1,000	8,979	10,983	9,770	9,296	8,176	8,211	8,519	8,991	8,636	8,527
Used vehicles sold	1,000	9,717	13,300	14,610	14,180	14,270	15,140	16,300	17,760	18,480	18,582
Employment	1,000	745	857	956	926	886	876	907	964	996	1,040
Annual payroll	Bil. dol.	11.0	20.1	24.4	24.1	23.5	25.1	26.7	29.8	31.6	34.0
Advertising expenses	Bil. dol.	1.2	2.8	3.9	3.7	3.5	3.8	4.1	4.3	4.7	5.1
Dealer pretax profits as a percentage of sales	Percent	0.6	2.2	1.0	1.0	1.0	1.4	1.6	1.8	1.4	1.5
Inventory: [3]											
Domestic: [4]											
Total	1,000	1,506	1,510	1,677	1,436	1,296	1,260	1,347	1,397	1,686	1,474
Days' supply	Days	71	58	72	66	66	63	62	60	72	64
Imported: [4]											
Total	1,000	458	271	648	597	584	504	450	381	358	246
Days' supply	Days	55	30	70	74	86	81	78	69	73	60

[1] At beginning of year. [2] Data provided by Ward's Automotive Reports. [3] Annual average. [4] Classification based on where automobiles are produced (i.e., automobiles manufactured by foreign companies but produced in the United States are classified as domestic).

Source: National Automobile Dealers Association, McLean, VA, *NADA Data*, annual.

No. 1270. Motor Vehicle Factory Sales and Retail Sales: 1980 to 1996

[In thousands]

YEAR	1980	1985	1988	1989	1990	1991	1992	1993	1994	1995	1996
Factory sales, total	8,067	11,359	11,226	10,869	9,769	8,783	9,747	10,857	12,189	12,023	11,916
Passenger cars	6,400	8,002	7,105	6,807	6,050	5,407	5,685	5,962	6,549	6,310	6,140
Trucks and buses	1,667	3,357	4,121	4,062	3,719	3,375	4,062	4,895	5,640	5,713	5,776
Retail sales, total	11,466	15,724	15,679	14,713	14,146	12,539	13,116	14,199	15,411	15,116	15,456
Passenger cars (new), total	8,979	11,042	10,530	9,772	9,300	8,175	8,213	8,518	8,991	8,635	8,527
Domestic	6,581	8,205	7,526	7,073	6,897	6,137	6,277	6,742	7,255	7,129	7,254
Imports	2,398	2,838	3,004	2,699	2,403	2,038	1,937	1,776	1,735	1,506	1,273
Trucks (new), total	2,487	4,682	5,149	4,941	4,846	4,365	4,903	5,681	6,421	6,481	6,930
Domestic	2,001	3,902	4,508	4,403	4,215	3,813	4,481	5,287	5,995	6,064	6,478
Imports	486	780	641	538	631	551	422	394	426	417	452

Source: American Automobile Manufacturers Association, Detroit, MI, *Motor Vehicle Facts and Figures*, annual (copyright).

No. 1271. Retail Foodstores—Number and Sales, by Type: 1990 to 1995

TYPE OF FOODSTORE	NUMBER [1] (1,000)					SALES [2] (bil. dol.)					PERCENT DISTRIBUTION			
											Number		Sales	
	1990	1992	1993	1994	1995	1990	1992	1993	1994	1995	1990	1995	1990	1995
Total	254.4	250.4	249.3	248.3	247.3	368.3	377.1	385.4	399.3	410.5	100.0	100.0	100.0	100.0
Grocery stores	172.9	168.3	166.9	165.6	164.3	348.2	358.1	365.7	378.6	389.1	67.7	66.4	94.5	94.8
Supermarkets [3]	25.0	25.1	25.6	24.8	23.8	260.1	275.9	281.0	289.0	293.3	9.9	9.6	70.6	71.4
Conventional	13.7	13.0	13.3	12.0	10.9	90.7	84.7	78.6	81.5	69.0	5.7	4.4	24.6	16.8
Superstore [4]	5.8	6.0	6.3	6.5	6.8	87.6	93.3	100.6	107.6	116.7	2.2	2.7	23.8	28.4
Warehouse [5]	3.4	3.4	3.1	2.9	2.7	33.1	33.1	31.9	27.7	26.0	1.3	1.1	9.0	6.3
Combination food and drug [6]	1.6	2.1	2.2	2.4	2.7	34.8	42.3	45.8	51.7	59.3	0.5	1.1	9.4	14.4
Superwarehouse [7]	0.3	0.5	0.5	0.5	0.6	12.6	13.9	15.3	16.2	17.8	0.2	0.2	3.4	4.3
Hypermarket [8]	0.1	0.1	0.2	0.2	0.2	1.3	7.0	8.8	4.3	4.5	(Z)	0.1	0.4	1.1
Convenience stores [9]	59.2	60.3	60.9	61.5	62.1	37.0	39.1	39.8	40.3	40.9	19.1	25.1	10.0	10.0
Superette [10]	88.7	82.9	80.4	79.6	78.4	51.1	43.1	44.9	49.2	54.9	38.6	31.7	13.9	13.4
Specialized food stores [11]	81.5	82.1	82.4	82.7	83.0	20.1	19.0	19.7	20.7	21.4	32.3	33.6	5.5	5.2

Z Less than 0.05 percent. [1] Estimated. [2] Includes nonfood items. [3] A grocery store, primarily self-service in operation, providing a full range of departments, and having at least $2.5 million in annual sales in 1985 dollars. [4] Contains greater variety of products than conventional supermarkets, including specialty and service departments, and considerable nonfood (general merchandise) products. [5] Contains limited product variety and fewer services provided, incorporating case lot stocking and shelving practices. [6] Contains a pharmacy, a nonprescription drug department, and a greater variety of health and beauty aids than that carried by conventional supermarkets. [7] A larger warehouse store that offers expanded product variety and often service meat, deli, or seafood departments. [8] A very large store offering a greater variety of general merchandise—like clothes, hardware, and seasonal goods—and personal care products than other grocery stores. [9] A small grocery store selling a limited variety of food and nonfood products, typically open extended hours. [10] A grocery store, primarily self-service in operation, selling a wide variety of food and nonfood products with annual sales below $2.5 million (1985 dollars). [11] Primarily engaged in the retail sale of a single food category such as meat and seafood stores and retail bakeries.

Source: U.S. Dept. of Agriculture, Economic Research Service, *Food Marketing Review*, annual.

No. 1272. Percent of Supermarkets Offering Selected Services and Product Lines: 1990 to 1996

[In percent. Based on a sample survey of chain and independent supermarkets and subject to sampling variability; for details, see source]

SERVICE OR PRODUCT LINE OFFERED	1990	1993	1996	SERVICE OR PRODUCT LINE OFFERED	1990	1993	1996
Service delicatessen	73	79	80	Carryout services	82	82	(NA)
Service bakery	60	62	69	Scanning checkouts	71	85	(NA)
Service meat	42	47	74	Automated teller machines (ATM's)	20	38	60
Service fish	33	37	46	Accept credit cards	19	51	(NA)
Separate cheese department	33	34	31	Pharmacy	15	20	26
Salad bar	18	19	27				

NA Not available.

Source: Maclean Hunter Media Inc., Stamford, CT, *Progressive Grocer Annual Report*, April 1997 and previous issues (copyright).

No. 1273. Food and Alcoholic Beverage Sales, by Sales Outlet: 1985 to 1994

[In billions of dollars]

SALES OUTLET	1985	1986	1987	1988	1989	1990	1991	1992	1993	1994
Food sales, total [1]	400.2	422.5	449.3	480.6	515.0	554.8	574.4	585.3	607.5	639.7
Off-premise use	228.7	237.2	246.0	258.9	277.4	302.1	314.6	316.0	321.6	336.5
Food stores	204.9	210.4	217.7	227.4	242.0	262.3	271.6	270.5	273.8	286.4
Other stores	16.4	19.3	19.7	21.8	24.7	28.2	30.8	32.4	34.2	36.4
Home-delivered, mail order	2.8	2.9	3.4	4.0	4.6	5.3	5.8	6.4	6.8	6.9
Farmers, manufacturers, wholesalers	4.6	4.7	5.3	5.6	6.0	6.3	6.5	6.6	6.8	6.7
Food service [2]	171.5	185.3	203.3	221.7	236.2	252.7	259.8	269.3	285.9	303.2
Alcoholic beverage sales, total	64.0	67.6	69.5	71.7	74.8	80.2	81.7	81.6	82.3	85.5
Packaged alcoholic beverages	38.2	40.0	40.5	41.1	43.3	46.7	47.6	46.5	46.3	47.6
Liquor stores	17.1	17.4	17.3	17.1	17.5	18.9	19.5	18.8	18.7	18.9
Food stores	17.0	17.6	18.2	18.7	19.8	21.2	21.2	20.8	20.7	21.7
All other	4.2	5.0	5.0	5.3	6.0	6.7	6.9	6.8	6.9	7.1
Alcoholic drinks	25.8	27.6	29.0	30.6	31.5	33.5	34.1	35.0	36.1	37.9
Eating and drinking places [3]	20.7	22.3	23.2	24.3	24.8	26.5	26.9	27.3	27.9	29.3
Hotels and motels [3]	3.4	3.4	3.7	4.0	4.2	4.5	4.6	4.9	5.2	5.5
All other	1.8	1.9	2.1	2.3	2.5	2.6	2.7	2.8	3.0	3.1

[1] Includes taxes and tips. Excludes home food production. [2] Includes food furnished and donations. [3] Includes tips.

Source: U.S. Dept. of Agriculture, Economic Research Service, *Food Marketing Review, 1994-95* (Agricultural Economic Report No. 743).

No. 1274. Commercial and Institutional Groups—Food and Drink Sales: 1980 to 1996

[Excludes military. Data refer to sales to consumers of food and alcoholic beverages. Sales are estimated. For details, see source]

TYPE OF GROUP	Number, 1993	SALES (mil. dol.)							
		1980	1985	1990	1992	1993	1994 [1]	1995 [1]	1996 [1]
Total	771,857	119,004	172,787	237,700	257,561	268,828	275,647	297,012	311,772
Commercial foodservice [2 3]	595,203	101,529	151,762	211,083	229,704	240,419	246,114	267,482	281,424
Eating places [2]	367,531	72,276	111,657	154,227	168,675	177,469	182,488	198,589	209,529
Full-service restaurants	173,416	39,307	57,939	76,072	83,561	87,011	85,290	95,702	100,008
Limited-service restaurants [4]	169,601	28,699	47,477	69,458	76,975	82,061	87,082	93,864	100,153
Bars and taverns [5]	36,435	7,785	8,338	9,212	10,203	10,162	9,106	10,864	11,201
Food contractors [2]	19,117	6,818	9,460	14,149	15,400	15,951	16,358	17,656	18,491
Manufacturing and industrial plants	(NA)	2,121	2,721	3,856	4,040	4,153	4,275	4,513	4,716
Colleges and universities	(NA)	1,140	1,738	2,788	3,238	3,455	3,505	3,893	4,157
Lodging places [2]	27,251	6,768	10,557	14,272	15,053	15,565	16,219	17,095	17,847
Hotel restaurants	17,369	4,964	8,986	12,907	13,733	14,253	14,917	15,714	16,437
Motel restaurants	8,281	1,151	975	820	788	783	775	818	833
Retail hosts [2 6]	123,937	3,264	5,254	9,888	10,689	11,220	11,779	12,407	13,015
Department store restaurants	4,721	857	865	950	906	941	(NA)	(NA)	(NA)
Grocery store restaurants [6]	54,369	830	2,074	5,733	5,808	6,017	(NA)	(NA)	(NA)
Gasoline service stations	38,695	492	1,052	1,681	2,055	2,199	(NA)	(NA)	(NA)
Recreation and sports [2]	14,627	1,452	1,972	2,916	3,085	3,185	3,291	3,453	3,617
Institutional foodservice [2]	176,654	17,475	21,025	26,617	27,857	28,409	29,533	29,529	30,348
Employee foodservice	7,370	1,635	1,971	1,985	1,835	1,728	1,753	1,731	1,730
Industrial, commercial organizations	2,776	1,377	1,682	1,603	1,457	1,344	(NA)	(NA)	(NA)
Educational foodservice	97,106	4,610	5,978	7,671	8,548	8,697	9,077	9,139	9,391
Elementary and secondary schools	94,254	2,312	2,919	3,700	4,012	4,183	4,239	4,528	4,739
Hospitals	6,439	6,668	7,104	8,968	8,988	9,208	9,582	9,557	9,702
Miscellaneous [2]	31,568	1,521	2,077	2,845	3,053	3,231	3,376	3,645	3,883
Clubs	10,310	1,056	1,537	1,993	2,010	2,090	2,339	(NA)	(NA)

NA Not available. [1] Projection. [2] Includes other types of groups, not shown separately. [3] Data for establishments with payroll. [4] Fast-food restaurants. [5] For establishments serving food. [6] Beginning 1990, a portion of delicatessen sales in grocery stores are considered foodservice.

Source: National Restaurant Association, Washington, DC, *Foodservice Numbers: A Statistical Digest for the Foodservice Industry*, 1992; *Foodservice Industry in Review*, annual; and *National Restaurant Association Foodservice Industry Forecast*, December 1995, (copyright).

No. 1275. U.S. Mail Order Sales, by Kind of Business: 1990 to 1994

[In millions of dollars. Mail order sales represent orders placed by mail, phone, or electronically without the person ordering coming to the point of sale to place the order, or the seller coming to the office or home of the orderer to take the order or using an agent to collect the order. Excludes orders placed at catalog desks or elsewhere in stores even in response to a catalog but does include products or services delivered in the store as long as the order was placed by mail, phone, or electronically. Statistics are generated independently each year and are not adjusted for any discontinuities of available data]

KIND OF BUSINESS	1990	1991	1992	1993	1994
Total mail order sales	151,640	162,050	168,050	186,700	200,760
Consumer, total	96,190	107,970	110,740	118,970	129,740
Products	57,500	64,940	65,210	71,960	78,460
Specialty [1]	44,520	50,010	50,560	57,720	64,810
Apparel	4,250	4,410	4,820	5,230	6,160
Books	2,760	2,770	3,120	3,100	3,200
Collectibles	1,690	1,810	2,000	2,360	2,200
Computer software & hardware	1,000	1,330	2,160	3,350	4,430
Health products	2,480	2,770	2,940	4,010	5,080
Magazines	6,020	6,580	6,340	6,280	6,600
Multi-products	7,410	8,440	6,860	10,190	10,760
Newspapers	3,020	3,020	3,020	3,020	3,080
Sporting goods	3,460	3,910	3,650	4,030	4,610
General merchandising	12,980	14,930	14,650	14,240	13,650
Services	40,690	43,030	45,530	47,010	51,280
Nonfinancial	21,660	25,740	26,620	26,980	28,400
Financial	19,030	17,290	18,910	20,030	22,880
Business products and services	53,450	54,080	57,310	67,730	71,020
Business supplies [1]	7,160	9,180	10,060	14,060	16,420
Data processing-oriented supplies	1,520	2,060	2,320	1,840	770
Computer hardware	700	1,800	2,400	6,000	8,000
Business services [1]	8,900	8,940	10,410	13,300	12,640
Communications	4,240	4,140	5,580	8,050	7,900
Information	2,500	2,500	2,500	2,850	2,310
Industrial	5,390	5,560	6,440	8,150	8,160
Generalized mail order marketers [2]	32,000	30,400	30,400	32,200	33,800

[1] Includes other kinds of business not shown separately. [2] Mail order as part of the overall selling channel mix of multichannel industrial marketers not specializing in mail order selling.

Source: Fishman, Arnold L., data are extracted from *Annual Guides to Mail Order Sales, 1990-1995*, Marketing Logistics, Inc., Highland Park, IL, 60035 (copyright). For 1990-92, *Portable Mail Order Industry Statistics, 1993 Edition*, Richard D. Irwin, Inc., Burr Ridge, IL, 1994 (copyright).

No. 1276. Retail Trade—Summary of Establishments, by State: 1994

[Covers establishments with payroll. Employees are for the week including March 12. Most government employees are excluded. Kind-of-business classification based on 1987 Standard Industrial Classification (SIC) code; see text, section 13. For statement on methodology, see Appendix III]

DIVISION AND STATE	ESTABLISHMENTS (1,000)				PAID EMPLOYEES (1,000)				ANNUAL PAYROLL (mil. dol.)			
	Total [1]	Food stores (SIC 54)	Automotive dealers and service stations (SIC 55)	Eating and drinking places (SIC 58)	Total [1]	Food stores (SIC 54)	Automotive dealers and service stations (SIC 55)	Eating and drinking places (SIC 58)	Total [1]	Food stores (SIC 54)	Automotive dealers and service stations (SIC 55)	Eating and drinking places (SIC 58)
U.S.	**1,564.2**	**182.5**	**196.4**	**449.1**	**20,320**	**3,096**	**2,097**	**6,928**	**282,293**	**39,757**	**48,006**	**60,662**
N.E.	**90.1**	**10.9**	**10.3**	**26.1**	**1,101**	**197**	**101**	**343**	**16,649**	**2,502**	**2,439**	**3,396**
ME	9.5	1.4	1.3	2.5	100	18	12	29	1,404	217	228	273
NH	8.7	1.1	1.0	2.2	106	19	11	30	1,537	233	274	283
VT	5.3	0.8	0.6	1.3	50	9	6	17	660	111	116	145
MA	39.0	4.5	4.2	12.0	510	90	41	166	7,733	1,110	984	1,695
RI	6.6	0.8	0.8	2.2	74	13	7	26	1,028	157	138	242
CT	21.1	2.3	2.5	6.0	261	47	25	75	4,287	675	699	759
M.A.	**232.3**	**31.6**	**24.0**	**67.7**	**2,632**	**458**	**236**	**791**	**40,139**	**6,155**	**5,749**	**7,933**
NY	110.9	16.9	9.7	32.9	1,146	203	87	356	18,133	2,723	2,161	3,902
NJ	49.7	6.6	5.5	13.8	567	100	54	153	9,675	1,574	1,509	1,679
PA	71.8	8.1	8.8	21.1	919	155	94	281	12,330	1,858	2,078	2,353
E.N.C.	**253.2**	**26.9**	**32.8**	**78.6**	**3,580**	**491**	**372**	**1,250**	**47,066**	**5,843**	**8,223**	**10,034**
OH	64.7	7.3	8.5	20.2	952	136	97	330	12,325	1,606	2,017	2,616
IN	34.5	3.0	5.1	10.2	495	68	56	180	6,063	771	1,108	1,391
IL	66.4	6.9	7.7	21.0	927	125	89	317	13,093	1,591	2,135	2,754
MI	55.3	7.0	7.1	16.1	773	100	80	269	10,345	1,195	1,997	2,146
WI	32.3	2.8	4.4	11.1	433	62	49	153	5,259	679	966	1,127
W.N.C.	**120.4**	**11.6**	**18.2**	**34.6**	**1,568**	**220**	**181**	**544**	**19,638**	**2,506**	**3,579**	**4,139**
MN	28.5	2.7	3.9	7.8	417	53	46	138	5,546	620	891	1,111
IA	19.9	1.9	3.1	6.0	244	42	30	81	2,832	442	552	564
MO	32.9	3.3	5.2	9.3	433	57	50	156	5,722	708	1,059	1,266
ND	4.9	0.5	0.7	1.5	55	8	7	20	604	73	140	132
SD	5.8	0.6	0.9	1.7	64	10	8	22	706	99	154	155
NE	11.6	1.2	1.8	3.5	144	22	16	52	1,603	227	296	364
KS	16.8	1.5	2.6	4.9	211	29	24	76	2,626	338	487	547
S.A.	**289.6**	**33.5**	**38.5**	**76.2**	**3,848**	**609**	**403**	**1,312**	**51,863**	**7,138**	**9,394**	**11,512**
DE	4.9	0.5	0.5	1.3	63	9	7	21	880	140	161	201
MD	28.2	3.2	3.0	7.8	394	58	43	127	5,917	966	1,053	1,182
DC	3.8	0.4	0.2	1.5	49	5	2	26	814	92	31	356
VA	38.5	4.9	5.1	9.9	531	83	59	170	7,242	1,033	1,380	1,501
WV	10.8	1.5	1.8	2.8	120	21	15	37	1,420	236	277	295
NC	45.6	5.3	6.9	11.2	577	87	61	196	7,465	902	1,361	1,609
SC	23.6	2.7	3.5	5.9	292	49	32	101	3,582	485	658	835
GA	42.9	4.9	6.2	11.1	594	94	61	209	7,785	990	1,392	1,765
FL	91.3	9.9	11.4	23.8	1,226	203	124	424	16,746	2,296	3,080	3,770
E.S.C.	**95.1**	**12.7**	**15.4**	**21.8**	**1,196**	**195**	**139**	**391**	**14,936**	**2,004**	**2,861**	**3,120**
KY	22.5	2.9	3.7	5.4	296	47	36	102	3,545	481	640	803
TN	31.8	4.1	4.8	7.5	421	64	47	142	5,667	692	1,083	1,211
AL	25.2	3.2	4.4	5.7	309	52	36	97	3,725	514	728	742
MS	15.6	2.5	2.5	3.1	170	31	20	51	1,999	317	399	363
W.S.C.	**162.3**	**21.2**	**23.2**	**44.0**	**2,157**	**351**	**235**	**736**	**28,343**	**3,820**	**5,207**	**6,257**
AR	15.7	1.9	2.6	3.7	179	26	21	55	2,329	281	404	399
LA	23.6	3.8	3.2	6.0	317	59	36	106	3,726	560	706	869
OK	20.1	2.5	3.0	5.7	236	35	28	86	2,833	390	573	660
TX	103.0	13.0	14.4	28.6	1,426	232	150	489	19,454	2,589	3,524	4,329
Mountain	**94.4**	**8.3**	**12.0**	**29.0**	**1,266**	**176**	**141**	**474**	**17,172**	**2,665**	**3,214**	**3,913**
MT	7.3	0.7	0.9	2.4	71	10	9	27	848	129	166	208
ID	7.6	0.7	1.2	2.2	88	12	12	31	1,142	165	248	219
WY	4.0	0.3	0.7	1.2	41	5	6	16	491	72	112	124
CO	24.8	1.9	2.8	7.6	334	49	32	130	4,701	791	782	1,137
NM	10.0	0.9	1.4	2.9	128	16	15	50	1,634	239	312	401
AZ	22.7	2.2	2.6	7.2	336	47	37	127	4,606	714	902	1,023
UT	10.0	0.9	1.5	2.9	155	21	17	53	1,951	279	351	398
NV	8.1	0.8	0.9	2.6	113	15	13	40	1,799	275	341	405
Pacific	**226.7**	**25.8**	**24.0**	**72.2**	**2,973**	**397**	**289**	**1,068**	**46,478**	**7,124**	**7,350**	**10,358**
WA	33.1	3.7	3.7	10.6	425	60	43	155	6,473	969	1,091	1,438
OR	20.5	2.3	2.3	6.6	258	34	30	93	3,752	488	693	815
CA	161.1	18.5	16.9	51.2	2,138	282	204	781	33,700	5,269	5,229	7,352
AK	4.0	0.4	0.4	1.2	43	7	4	14	809	141	129	199
HI	8.0	0.9	0.6	2.6	109	14	9	45	1,743	237	208	555

[1] Includes other kinds of business not shown separately.

Source: U.S. Bureau of the Census, *County Business Patterns*, annual.

No. 1277. Retail Sales, by Type of Store and State: 1994 and 1995

[In millions of dollars, except as indicated. Kind-of-business classification based on 1987 Standard Industrial Classification (SIC) code; see text, section 13. Data are estimates]

REGION, DIVISION, AND STATE	ALL STORES[1]				FOOD STORES				GENERAL MERCHANDISE STORES			
	1994, total	1995			Total (SIC 54)		Grocery stores (SIC 541)		Total (SIC 53)		Department stores (SIC 531)	
		Total	Sales per household[2]: Amount (dol.)	Sales per household[2]: Percent change, 1994-95	1994	1995	1994	1995	1994	1995	1994	1995
U.S.	2,241,319	2,355,242	24,120	3.9	406,018	409,318	385,202	387,499	285,351	297,878	219,239	231,899
Northeast	429,674	439,450	(NA)	(NA)	82,731	80,966	76,536	74,653	45,382	46,169	34,995	36,035
N.E.	121,796	122,784	24,611	0.1	25,356	25,191	23,678	23,472	13,133	13,074	9,391	9,433
ME	11,681	11,598	24,348	-1.6	2,689	2,812	2,575	2,496	1,225	1,199	747	740
NH	12,761	12,967	30,239	0.4	2,818	2,807	2,702	2,688	1,754	1,754	1,163	1,182
VT	5,125	5,144	23,129	-1.1	1,241	1,214	1,199	1,170	357	358	261	282
MA	52,466	53,873	23,652	1.7	10,564	10,714	9,695	9,816	5,483	5,566	3,904	3,995
RI	7,536	7,359	19,766	-2.0	1,610	1,551	1,467	1,409	813	782	591	573
CT	32,224	31,844	25,947	-1.5	6,433	6,293	6,040	5,893	3,501	3,414	2,726	2,661
M.A.	307,878	316,667	22,469	2.7	57,375	55,774	52,859	51,181	32,248	33,095	25,604	26,602
NY	134,422	137,771	20,759	2.5	25,391	24,651	22,943	22,168	13,467	13,792	10,432	10,839
NJ	72,315	74,425	25,979	2.4	13,654	13,283	12,713	12,315	7,412	7,567	5,807	5,986
PA	101,141	104,471	22,749	3.1	18,329	17,841	17,203	16,698	11,370	11,736	9,365	9,777
Midwest	549,225	579,536	(NA)	(NA)	89,528	90,127	84,812	85,369	73,708	77,659	60,748	64,352
E.N.C.	381,998	403,481	24,892	4.7	59,780	59,519	56,318	56,041	51,577	54,401	42,670	45,242
OH	98,330	104,900	24,837	6.0	16,808	16,896	15,921	16,003	13,086	13,938	10,684	11,447
IN	49,462	53,056	24,264	5.9	7,624	7,696	7,260	7,334	6,720	7,182	5,435	5,836
IL	99,964	104,528	24,093	3.8	15,534	15,348	14,569	14,377	11,963	12,536	9,819	10,357
MI	87,884	91,524	25,867	3.3	12,396	12,127	11,538	11,266	13,997	14,541	12,193	12,744
WI	46,358	49,473	25,736	5.8	7,419	7,451	7,030	7,060	5,811	6,204	4,536	4,859
W.N.C.	167,227	176,055	25,064	4.4	29,748	30,608	28,494	29,328	22,131	23,258	18,079	19,110
MN	42,137	44,277	25,371	4.1	6,995	7,179	6,588	6,759	5,140	5,390	4,184	4,397
IA	25,536	26,988	24,536	4.7	5,036	5,219	4,796	4,977	3,300	3,490	2,712	2,884
MO	48,783	52,511	25,589	6.7	8,636	9,080	8,347	8,776	6,875	7,392	5,876	6,361
ND	6,182	6,361	25,898	2.2	1,001	1,009	967	974	924	946	753	769
SD	6,853	7,244	26,603	4.8	1,178	1,211	1,144	1,177	849	892	663	698
NE	15,227	15,731	25,073	2.4	2,760	2,773	2,627	2,641	1,899	1,945	1,485	1,542
KS	22,506	22,943	23,371	1.6	4,141	4,137	4,024	4,024	3,144	3,203	2,406	2,460
South	780,018	832,767	(NA)	(NA)	141,266	145,080	135,791	138,977	104,057	109,602	80,429	85,388
S.A.	418,512	445,368	24,755	4.9	75,662	78,262	72,458	74,763	51,349	54,174	39,081	41,527
DE	6,578	7,545	28,050	12.7	1,109	1,235	1,036	1,154	1,000	1,140	773	892
MD	44,184	45,644	24,552	2.1	8,518	8,556	8,063	8,089	5,249	5,375	3,952	4,081
DC	3,762	3,760	16,406	1.3	641	631	565	556	224	224	193	195
VA	62,293	66,648	26,932	5.7	12,105	12,560	11,642	12,061	7,616	8,098	5,543	5,842
WV	13,056	13,616	19,193	3.5	2,809	2,826	2,754	2,760	1,903	1,975	1,488	1,561
NC	60,196	65,781	23,898	7.1	11,199	11,888	10,773	11,369	7,182	7,804	5,703	6,264
SC	29,754	31,320	23,205	4.4	5,871	5,981	5,732	5,818	3,613	3,762	2,917	3,068
GA	60,877	65,369	24,643	5.4	10,710	11,162	10,277	10,676	8,125	8,641	6,466	6,926
FL	137,812	145,665	25,686	4.0	22,700	23,421	21,617	22,259	16,437	17,155	12,047	12,697
E.S.C.	128,070	137,207	22,685	5.7	23,392	23,309	22,657	22,432	18,917	20,170	15,000	16,125
KY	30,966	33,020	22,663	5.4	5,800	5,760	5,651	5,561	4,531	4,847	3,771	4,053
TN	45,897	49,132	24,299	5.3	7,705	7,695	7,520	7,472	6,565	6,977	5,156	5,529
AL	33,586	35,946	22,430	6.0	6,200	6,138	5,976	5,877	4,881	5,180	3,838	4,122
MS	17,619	19,109	19,763	7.0	3,687	3,716	3,510	3,503	2,939	3,166	2,234	2,421
W.S.C.	233,436	250,191	23,902	6.7	42,211	43,510	40,676	41,783	33,792	35,258	26,348	27,736
AR	19,091	20,999	22,099	8.5	3,275	3,432	3,199	3,336	3,127	3,370	2,511	2,716
LA	35,422	37,668	24,271	5.3	7,117	7,268	6,852	6,963	5,362	5,584	4,166	4,383
OK	25,620	25,998	20,727	1.1	4,457	4,318	4,279	4,130	3,780	3,740	3,018	3,007
TX	153,303	165,526	24,665	6.2	27,363	28,491	26,346	27,354	21,503	22,564	16,652	17,630
West	482,403	503,488	(NA)	(NA)	92,493	93,145	88,062	88,499	62,204	64,447	43,066	45,124
Mountain	137,910	145,871	24,833	3.0	27,964	28,270	27,150	27,449	17,169	18,132	12,998	13,874
MT	7,592	7,831	23,181	1.5	1,535	1,507	1,489	1,461	866	887	613	636
ID	10,489	10,766	25,309	-	2,211	2,160	2,161	2,110	1,178	1,214	869	900
WY	4,385	4,501	24,785	1.6	830	813	816	799	556	569	400	412
CO	35,670	36,808	24,823	1.1	6,894	6,783	6,682	6,579	4,394	4,521	3,358	3,481
NM	14,092	14,634	24,021	2.2	2,741	2,706	2,653	2,619	1,804	1,864	1,432	1,497
AZ	36,517	39,322	24,544	4.4	7,604	7,862	7,375	7,625	4,665	5,023	3,456	3,779
UT	14,268	15,331	24,920	4.6	3,110	3,196	3,030	3,115	1,834	1,969	1,379	1,494
NV	14,898	16,678	26,900	5.8	3,039	3,243	2,942	3,141	1,872	2,085	1,493	1,675
Pacific	344,492	357,617	23,953	2.6	64,529	64,875	60,913	61,050	45,036	46,316	30,068	31,250
WA	48,468	49,561	23,562	0.2	9,065	9,004	8,733	8,664	6,345	6,457	4,525	4,633
OR	29,609	31,193	25,416	3.6	4,978	5,049	4,795	4,854	4,738	4,952	3,289	3,445
CA	247,689	257,662	23,427	3.0	46,882	47,256	43,976	44,162	30,960	31,892	20,786	21,645
AK	6,041	6,405	30,199	5.2	1,333	1,357	1,295	1,320	850	900	606	638
HI	12,685	12,806	32,911	0.2	2,272	2,209	2,114	2,052	2,142	2,115	862	888

See footnotes at end of table.

No. 1277. Retail Sales, by Type of Store and State: 1994 and 1995—Continued

[See headnote, page 774]

REGION, DIVISION, AND STATE	AUTOMOTIVE DEALERS (SIC 55 exc. 554)		EATING AND DRINKING PLACES (SIC 58)		GASOLINE SERVICE STATIONS (SIC 554)		BUILDING MATERIALS AND GARDEN SUPPLIES (SIC 52)		APPAREL AND ACCESSORY STORES (SIC 56)		FURNITURE AND HOME FURNISHINGS STORES (SIC 57)	
	1994	1995	1994	1995	1994	1995	1994	1995	1994	1995	1994	1995
U.S	521,583	569,571	229,542	241,780	142,342	153,262	116,109	119,570	107,916	110,166	125,302	128,362
Northeast	88,514	94,111	42,320	41,709	23,130	25,221	20,597	21,595	27,184	27,278	21,725	22,096
N.E.	21,381	22,883	13,244	11,537	7,033	8,027	6,395	6,567	6,934	6,951	5,369	5,364
ME	1,982	2,092	1,069	899	673	750	759	768	586	578	368	364
NH	2,349	2,526	1,105	960	616	704	794	821	621	623	585	592
VT	950	1,013	514	443	329	374	390	401	219	219	170	170
MA	9,160	9,988	6,476	5,779	2,933	3,422	2,425	2,531	3,333	3,410	2,419	2,464
RI	1,193	1,249	945	794	511	567	325	327	363	353	309	297
CT	5,747	6,015	3,135	2,663	1,972	2,210	1,702	1,720	1,811	1,769	1,518	1,477
M.A	67,134	71,228	29,076	30,172	16,097	17,194	14,203	15,028	20,250	20,327	16,356	16,731
NY	25,411	26,921	13,856	14,415	6,515	6,941	6,274	6,631	10,166	10,205	7,585	7,764
NJ	17,432	18,433	6,140	6,378	3,903	4,175	3,090	3,269	5,137	5,143	4,325	4,415
PA	24,290	25,873	9,080	9,379	5,679	6,078	4,839	5,128	4,947	4,979	4,445	4,552
Midwest	136,512	148,032	57,306	61,226	36,298	40,108	30,066	28,034	21,920	22,384	29,979	31,732
E.N.C	94,116	102,603	41,077	43,602	23,576	26,165	20,385	19,226	15,869	16,412	22,506	23,500
OH	23,645	26,058	11,039	11,827	6,235	6,987	5,006	4,778	3,641	3,804	5,440	5,733
IN	11,962	13,224	5,294	5,706	3,453	3,874	2,790	2,671	1,670	1,761	2,609	2,765
IL	24,157	26,068	11,111	11,703	5,517	6,052	4,690	4,381	5,139	5,280	6,616	6,862
MI	23,010	24,771	8,852	9,284	5,282	5,784	4,858	4,498	3,874	3,947	5,157	5,314
WI	11,343	12,481	4,781	5,082	3,089	3,467	3,042	2,898	1,545	1,619	2,685	2,826
W.N.C	42,396	45,429	16,229	17,624	12,722	13,943	9,680	8,808	6,050	5,972	7,473	8,232
MN	10,121	10,847	3,941	4,270	3,073	3,382	2,801	2,537	1,631	1,613	1,975	2,183
IA	6,525	7,030	2,347	2,539	2,053	2,251	1,627	1,484	838	834	1,067	1,166
MO	12,697	13,840	5,030	5,606	3,819	4,255	2,577	2,401	1,779	1,788	2,062	2,324
ND	1,695	1,780	559	593	499	548	395	351	200	193	219	237
SD	1,831	1,969	647	697	595	654	401	368	238	235	276	306
NE	3,633	3,844	1,533	1,627	1,123	1,205	750	668	575	556	823	889
KS	5,895	6,119	2,172	2,293	1,560	1,648	1,129	1,000	788	754	1,051	1,127
South	192,032	217,547	78,886	81,978	52,644	55,216	40,172	42,144	36,079	37,655	41,964	43,343
S.A	100,456	113,197	43,329	44,566	25,257	26,870	22,399	23,277	20,515	21,582	25,994	26,531
DE	1,363	1,650	641	714	362	425	379	441	278	318	454	489
MD	9,698	10,844	4,623	4,640	2,596	2,702	2,087	2,098	2,408	2,464	2,870	2,843
DC	146	162	1,080	1,065	185	189	52	51	348	349	294	283
VA	13,584	15,386	6,017	6,294	3,926	4,196	3,160	3,302	3,209	3,414	4,277	4,393
WV	2,997	3,307	1,116	1,136	976	1,002	865	882	432	451	571	573
NC	14,030	16,423	6,448	6,462	3,792	4,131	4,169	4,463	2,647	2,887	3,636	3,807
SC	6,795	7,550	3,158	3,233	2,118	2,223	1,982	2,032	1,486	1,549	1,647	1,660
GA	14,460	16,396	6,433	6,760	4,065	4,350	3,350	3,502	2,873	3,067	3,600	3,735
FL	37,383	41,680	13,812	14,261	7,237	7,652	6,355	6,506	6,834	7,083	8,645	8,747
E.S.C	30,267	35,075	12,341	12,893	10,649	10,902	7,560	7,969	4,944	5,278	5,624	5,869
KY	6,538	7,584	3,152	3,314	2,885	2,958	1,948	2,059	1,039	1,095	1,304	1,362
TN	11,587	13,377	4,689	4,861	3,681	3,768	2,623	2,768	1,821	1,948	2,135	2,222
AL	8,102	9,377	3,033	3,168	2,757	2,791	1,992	2,081	1,469	1,572	1,502	1,568
MS	4,041	4,737	1,467	1,549	1,326	1,386	997	1,061	615	663	682	717
W.S.C	61,308	69,275	23,215	24,518	16,739	17,443	10,213	10,898	10,620	10,795	10,336	10,943
AR	5,193	5,990	1,537	1,672	1,671	1,754	1,118	1,247	640	674	675	731
LA	8,462	9,523	3,501	3,661	2,655	2,743	1,715	1,818	1,503	1,517	1,444	1,514
OK	7,237	7,699	2,577	2,564	1,950	1,894	1,078	1,084	1,020	983	1,022	1,038
TX	40,416	46,063	15,600	16,621	10,463	11,053	6,303	6,749	7,458	7,620	7,195	7,660
West	104,525	109,881	51,030	56,867	30,270	32,716	25,274	27,797	22,734	22,847	31,644	31,192
Mountain	29,780	31,473	17,376	19,604	8,511	9,349	7,265	7,979	5,073	5,306	8,406	8,593
MT	1,680	1,731	1,027	1,123	501	546	525	564	236	241	427	424
ID	2,644	2,692	1,129	1,227	697	756	749	799	336	346	624	608
WY	925	944	559	615	495	523	189	205	141	141	176	171
CO	7,568	7,805	4,672	5,145	1,936	2,085	1,854	1,978	1,296	1,310	2,434	2,417
NM	2,915	3,012	1,871	2,053	1,057	1,102	725	786	514	526	773	784
AZ	7,934	8,572	4,629	5,342	2,140	2,408	1,662	1,870	1,371	1,455	2,095	2,190
UT	3,173	3,428	1,590	1,838	906	1,016	776	866	575	614	1,001	1,038
NV	2,941	3,288	1,899	2,262	780	912	785	911	604	673	876	962
Pacific	74,745	78,408	33,654	37,263	21,758	23,367	18,009	19,818	17,661	17,541	23,239	22,598
WA	10,822	11,117	4,461	4,873	3,091	3,279	3,089	3,360	2,169	2,125	3,006	2,880
OR	7,232	7,655	2,589	2,899	1,842	1,994	1,822	2,041	1,233	1,238	1,699	1,668
CA	53,675	56,523	24,113	26,812	15,841	17,058	12,346	13,575	12,957	12,919	17,638	17,200
AK	1,082	1,162	674	728	355	384	366	413	278	281	252	249
HI	1,934	1,951	1,817	1,951	629	652	387	429	1,023	979	642	601

- Represents or rounds to zero. NA Not available. [1] Includes other types of stores, not shown separately. [2] Based on number of households as of July 1 as estimated by source. Minus sign (-) indicates decrease.

Source: Market Statistics, New York, NY, *The Survey of Buying Power Data Service*, annual (copyright).

No. 1278. Shopping Centers—Number, Gross Leasable Area, and Retail Sales, by Gross Leasable Area: 1990 to 1996

[As of December 31. A shopping center is a group of architecturally unified commercial establishments built on a site that is planned, developed, owned, and managed as an operating unit related in its location, size, and type of shops to the trade area that the unit serves. The unit provides on-site parking in definite relationship to the types and total size of the stores. The data base attempts to include all centers with three or more stores. Estimates are based on a sample of data available on shopping center properties; for details, contact source]

YEAR	Total	GROSS LEASABLE AREA (sq. ft.)					
		Less than 100,001	100,001-200,000	200,001-400,000	400,001-800,000	800,001-1,000,000	More than 1 million
NUMBER							
1990	36,515	23,231	8,756	2,781	1,102	288	357
1994	40,368	25,450	9,784	3,251	1,210	297	376
1995	41,235	26,001	9,974	3,345	1,234	301	380
1996	42,130	26,497	10,186	3,477	1,276	309	385
Percent distribution	100.0	62.9	24.2	8.3	3.0	0.7	0.9
Percent change, 1995-96	2.2	1.9	2.1	3.9	3.4	2.7	1.3
GROSS LEASABLE AREA							
1990 (mil. sq. ft.)	4,390	1,125	1,197	734	618	259	457
1994 (mil. sq. ft.)	4,861	1,239	1,339	859	675	267	482
1995 (mil. sq. ft.)	4,967	1,267	1,368	886	689	271	486
1996 (mil. sq. ft.)	5,101	1,293	1,399	926	711	278	493
Percent distribution	100.0	25.3	27.4	18.1	13.9	5.5	9.7
Percent change, 1995-96	2.7	2.1	2.3	4.5	3.2	2.7	1.4
RETAIL SALES							
1990 (bil. dol.)	706.4	205.1	179.5	108.0	91.7	45.1	77.0
1994 (bil. dol.)	851.3	247.3	216.3	129.9	110.3	54.3	93.1
1995 (bil. dol.)	893.8	259.6	227.1	136.4	115.8	57.0	97.8
1996 (bil. dol.)	933.9	271.2	237.3	142.6	121.0	60.0	102.2
Percent distribution	100.0	29.0	25.4	15.3	13.0	6.4	10.9
Percent change, 1995-96	4.5	4.5	4.5	4.5	4.4	5.2	4.5

No. 1279. Shopping Centers—Number, Gross Leasable Area, and Retail Sales, by State: 1996

[See headnote, table 1278]

DIVISION AND STATE	Number	Gross leasable area (mil. sq. ft.)	Retail sales (bil. dol.)	PERCENT CHANGE, 1995-96		
				Number	Gross leasable area	Retail sales per sq. ft.
U.S.	**42,130**	**5,101**	**933.9**	**2.2**	**2.7**	**1.8**
N.E.	**2,443**	**264**	**49.7**	**1.7**	**2.4**	**2.8**
ME	200	17	3.6	-	-	5.7
NH	214	22	3.7	1.4	1.0	5.5
VT	111	8	1.6	3.7	9.9	-4.1
MA	964	109	20.9	1.3	2.5	2.4
RI	197	18	3.4	1.5	0.8	3.7
CT	757	90	16.4	2.6	2.9	2.5
M.A.	**4,380**	**609**	**102.0**	**2.6**	**2.6**	**1.9**
NY	1,660	229	40.4	1.6	1.7	2.6
NJ	1,143	155	25.2	5.4	4.9	0.2
PA	1,577	225	36.3	1.8	2.1	2.4
E.N.C.	**6,136**	**802**	**131.1**	**1.8**	**2.5**	**1.9**
OH	1,647	236	37.9	2.5	3.4	0.7
IN	879	116	19.6	2.0	2.1	2.0
IL	2,018	246	37.6	1.5	2.2	2.5
MI	982	130	22.9	1.0	2.0	2.3
WI	610	74	13.2	2.2	1.7	2.9
W.N.C.	**2,481**	**314**	**59.0**	**1.8**	**2.2**	**2.0**
MN	457	64	12.6	2.5	2.8	1.6
IA	295	38	6.8	3.1	2.4	1.7
MO	861	108	20.6	1.2	2.1	2.1
ND	87	9	1.9	-	-	4.4
SD	54	7	1.2	5.9	0.2	3.9
NE	253	33	5.2	1.2	0.3	3.9
KS	474	54	10.6	1.5	3.4	0.8
S.A.	**9,425**	**1,127**	**212.5**	**2.0**	**2.3**	**2.3**
DE	133	20	3.8	3.1	6.0	-0.6
MD	860	118	22.5	1.2	1.6	2.8
DC	79	9	1.6	3.9	0.5	3.9
VA	1,214	158	28.4	2.6	3.6	1.1
WV	159	22	3.5	2.6	2.6	0.8
NC	1,524	161	26.3	3.3	3.4	0.8
SC	779	75	14.3	0.8	0.8	3.2
GA	1,497	161	28.7	2.5	2.6	1.6
FL	3,180	403	83.3	1.3	1.5	3.5
E.S.C.	**2,826**	**304**	**55.4**	**1.3**	**1.3**	**2.7**
KY	608	65	12.7	0.8	0.5	3.5
TN	1,174	128	20.8	1.5	1.6	2.7
AL	618	71	14.2	1.8	2.0	1.8
MS	426	40	7.7	0.7	0.5	2.7
W.S.C.	**4,513**	**520**	**115.5**	**1.5**	**2.4**	**1.7**
AR	354	34	6.9	2.3	4.1	-0.6
LA	690	81	17.0	1.0	1.2	3.0
OK	563	59	12.2	0.5	1.3	2.0
TX	2,906	345	79.4	1.6	2.6	1.6
Mountain	**2,825**	**340**	**66.5**	**2.8**	**4.0**	**0.5**
MT	91	9	1.8	-	-	4.4
ID	150	18	3.0	3.4	7.0	-3.1
WY	53	6	1.2	-	-	3.9
CO	700	92	20.5	2.2	4.1	0.9
NM	299	29	5.8	2.7	6.0	-1.9
AZ	991	116	22.1	2.8	2.1	2.5
UT	225	31	6.0	3.7	3.2	0.5
NV	316	39	6.0	4.3	9.7	-4.4
Pacific	**7,101**	**820**	**142.3**	**3.3**	**4.0**	**0.5**
WA	722	94	15.9	4.2	3.8	0.8
OR	473	54	8.4	3.5	4.4	0.4
CA	5,665	647	112.6	3.2	4.0	0.4
AK	66	8	1.8	4.8	0.3	5.3
HI	175	18	3.6	1.7	2.5	4.0

- Represents zero.

Source of tables 1278 and 1279: National Research Bureau, Chicago, IL. Data for 1990 published by Monitor Publishing, Clearwater, FL, in *Monitor Magazine*, November/December 1991, (copyright). Data for 1994-96 published by International Council of Shopping Centers in *Shopping Centers Today*, April issues, (copyright—Interactive Market Systems, Inc.).

No. 1280. Wholesale Trade—Summary: 1972 to 1992

[Comparability of data over time is affected by changes in the Standard Industrial Classification (SIC) code; for details, see source]

ITEM	Unit	1972 [1]	1977 [1]	1982 [1]	1987 [1]	1987 [2]	1992 [2]
Firms, total [3]	1,000	276	289	335	(NA)	364	387
Establishments, total [3]	1,000	370	383	435	467	470	495
With sales of $1,000,000 or more	1,000	103	152	(NA)	(NA)	222	250
Sales, all establishments	Bil. dol	695	1,258	1,998	2,524	[4]2,508	[4]3,239
Merchant wholesalers	Bil. dol	354	676	1,159	1,477	[4]1,462	[4]1,847
Inventories, end of year	Bil. dol	45.7	82.3	130.7	(NA)	165.1	213.4
Payroll, entire year	Bil. dol	36.9	58.3	95.2	133.2	133.4	173.3
Paid employees, Mar. 12 workweek	1,000	4,026	4,397	4,985	5,594	5,596	[4]5,791

NA Not available. [1] Based on 1972 SIC code. [2] Based on 1987 SIC code. [3] Through 1977 number of firms and establishments in business at end of year; beginning 1982 number of firms and establishments in business at any time during year. [4] Revised since publication of report.

Source: U.S. Bureau of the Census, *Census of Wholesale Trade: 1972*, vol. I; *1977*, WC77-A-52; *1982*, WC82-A-52; *1987*, WC87-A-52 and *1992*, WC92-A-52.

No. 1281. Wholesale Trade, by Type of Operation and Kind of Business: 1987 and 1992

[Based on 1987 Standard Industrial Classification (SIC) code; see text, section 13]

TYPE OF OPERATION AND KIND OF BUSINESS	ESTABLISHMENTS [1] (1,000)		SALES (mil. dol.)		ANNUAL PAYROLL (mil. dol.)		PAID EMPLOYEES [2] (1,000)	
	1987	1992	1987	1992	1987	1992	1987	1992
Wholesale trade	469.5	495.5	2,508,258	3,238,520	133,357	173,272	5,596	5,791
Merchant wholesalers	391.0	414.8	1,461,700	1,847,274	100,413	127,987	4,476	4,588
Other operating types	78.6	80.6	1,046,558	1,391,247	32,944	45,285	1,120	1,203
Durable goods	297.3	313.5	1,262,302	1,593,874	82,767	105,155	3,332	3,349
Motor vehicles, parts, and supplies	45.8	47.3	326,625	394,104	9,872	12,065	483	489
Furniture and home furnishings	14.5	16.5	46,123	58,927	3,652	4,612	153	161
Lumber and construction materials	19.1	19.5	79,946	89,764	5,476	6,080	231	211
Professional & commercial equipment	44.2	46.8	175,149	262,974	19,728	26,380	698	685
Metals and minerals, except petroleum	11.1	11.2	114,528	118,322	4,038	4,884	143	138
Electrical goods	36.3	39.3	179,727	227,784	12,104	15,070	441	436
Hardware, plumbing, heating equipment	23.1	24.7	57,126	76,088	5,610	7,106	235	241
Machinery, equipment, supplies	71.7	73.9	178,892	230,004	16,731	21,267	682	690
Miscellaneous durable goods	32.3	34.3	102,185	135,906	5,556	7,912	266	299
Nondurable goods	172.2	182.0	1,245,956	1,644,647	50,589	68,117	2,264	2,442
Paper and paper products	16.8	19.7	83,173	106,580	5,202	6,939	228	269
Drugs, proprietaries, and sundries	4.9	6.1	64,280	129,306	2,968	5,368	120	156
Apparel, piece goods, and notions	16.9	19.6	81,476	109,203	4,661	6,522	181	196
Groceries and related products	42.1	42.9	380,945	504,567	16,729	21,723	763	812
Farm-product raw materials	12.6	11.6	117,606	136,869	1,847	2,100	117	109
Chemicals and allied products	12.7	14.2	94,620	132,471	3,847	5,596	131	147
Petroleum and petroleum products	16.7	16.1	234,874	281,585	3,658	4,447	175	169
Beer, wine, and distilled beverages	5.8	5.3	49,433	59,487	3,849	4,670	146	142
Misc. nondurable goods	43.7	46.8	139,550	184,577	7,828	10,754	404	441

[1] Number of establishments in business at any time during the year. [2] For pay period including March 12.

Source: U.S. Bureau of the Census, *Census of Wholesale Trade: 1987*, WC87-A-52 and *1992*, WC92-A-52.

No. 1282. Merchant Wholesalers—Summary: 1990 to 1996

[Inventories and stock/sales ratios, as of December, seasonally adjusted. Data reflect latest revision. Based on Current Business Survey; see Appendix III]

KIND OF BUSINESS	1987 SIC code [1]	1990	1992	1993	1994	1995	1996
SALES (bil. dol.)							
Merchant wholesalers		**1,793.8**	**1,843.7**	**1,940.6**	**2,075.7**	**2,265.7**	**2,420.7**
Durable goods	50	**881.2**	**906.0**	**987.1**	**1,082.3**	**1,179.2**	**1,245.8**
Motor vehicles, parts, and supplies	501	173.9	170.3	179.5	197.2	202.6	211.1
Furniture and homefurnishings	502	33.9	33.1	34.9	36.7	40.9	43.6
Lumber and construction materials	503	63.6	63.7	71.7	78.1	77.1	85.8
Professional and commercial equipment	504	114.3	139.2	159.1	165.7	194.6	231.4
Metals and minerals, except petroleum	505	77.8	76.6	80.3	92.4	100.5	98.4
Electrical goods	506	116.5	115.0	131.7	150.2	169.8	173.8
Hardware, plumbing and heating equipment	507	52.7	52.9	55.4	63.7	67.6	70.5
Machinery, equipment and supplies	508	157.0	148.8	160.7	169.8	182.7	187.3
Miscellaneous durable goods	509	91.4	106.3	113.7	128.3	143.3	143.9
Nondurable goods	51	**912.6**	**937.7**	**953.5**	**993.4**	**1,086.5**	**1,174.9**
Paper and paper products	511	51.6	54.6	59.2	67.6	82.0	82.7
Drugs, proprietaries, and sundries	512	51.5	66.8	72.2	83.2	95.0	102.9
Apparel, piece goods, and notions	513	64.9	67.7	70.2	72.5	70.6	75.5
Groceries and related products	514	272.5	278.3	285.7	288.6	304.7	315.4
Farm-product raw materials	515	107.6	105.9	96.0	95.4	113.7	130.2
Chemicals and allied products	516	35.7	39.0	39.2	41.8	47.8	53.5
Petroleum and petroleum products	517	148.5	142.1	139.5	143.0	150.6	177.8
Beer, wine, and distilled beverages	518	49.3	50.2	51.1	53.0	54.1	56.4
Miscellaneous nondurable goods	519	131.0	133.1	140.4	148.2	168.2	180.7
INVENTORIES (bil. dol.)							
Merchant wholesalers		**195.6**	**207.7**	**215.9**	**234.9**	**253.1**	**255.8**
Durable goods	50	**126.2**	**131.1**	**135.6**	**149.0**	**160.3**	**161.5**
Motor vehicles, parts, and supplies	501	23.5	24.1	24.4	25.5	27.0	26.4
Furniture and homefurnishings	502	4.6	4.8	4.8	4.9	5.1	5.3
Lumber and construction materials	503	6.0	6.3	6.7	7.4	7.4	7.7
Professional and commercial equipment	504	15.8	17.0	17.9	20.5	22.8	22.3
Metals and minerals, except petroleum	505	10.7	10.0	11.1	12.8	12.8	12.7
Electrical goods	506	15.9	17.2	17.5	20.2	23.5	23.0
Hardware, plumbing and heating equipment	507	8.5	8.8	9.3	10.8	11.0	12.1
Machinery, equipment and supplies	508	31.5	30.0	29.2	31.6	34.7	35.9
Miscellaneous durable goods	509	9.8	12.8	14.6	15.2	15.8	16.0
Nondurable goods	51	**69.4**	**76.6**	**80.2**	**85.9**	**92.8**	**94.3**
Paper and paper products	511	4.9	5.6	6.3	7.0	8.3	8.7
Drugs, proprietaries, and sundries	512	6.5	9.0	10.4	11.6	12.0	13.7
Apparel, piece goods, and notions	513	9.8	10.6	11.4	12.2	11.9	11.7
Groceries and related products	514	14.7	16.0	15.7	16.1	16.7	17.7
Farm-product raw materials	515	8.8	9.0	10.0	10.4	12.3	9.4
Chemicals and allied products	516	3.1	3.2	3.7	4.1	4.6	4.7
Petroleum and petroleum products	517	4.4	4.4	4.0	4.9	4.9	5.8
Beer, wine, and distilled beverages	518	4.4	4.3	4.5	4.6	4.8	5.0
Miscellaneous nondurable goods	519	12.7	14.4	14.2	14.9	17.3	17.8
STOCK/SALES RATIO							
Merchant wholesalers		**1.31**	**1.33**	**1.33**	**1.28**	**1.28**	**1.24**
Durable goods	50	**1.75**	**1.67**	**1.61**	**1.58**	**1.56**	**1.54**
Motor vehicles, parts, and supplies	501	1.66	1.64	1.63	1.50	1.54	1.46
Furniture and homefurnishings	502	1.71	1.62	1.69	1.45	1.48	1.42
Lumber and construction materials	503	1.33	1.12	1.01	1.03	1.13	1.06
Professional and commercial equipment	504	1.58	1.39	1.35	1.37	1.29	1.12
Metals and minerals, except petroleum	505	1.60	1.55	1.62	1.54	1.54	1.50
Electrical goods	506	1.71	1.72	1.50	1.51	1.58	1.69
Hardware, plumbing and heating equipment	507	1.90	2.01	1.94	1.90	1.89	2.03
Machinery, equipment and supplies	508	2.49	2.34	2.16	2.11	2.10	2.26
Miscellaneous durable goods	509	1.27	1.37	1.52	1.35	1.31	1.32
Nondurable goods	51	**0.90**	**0.98**	**1.03**	**0.99**	**0.99**	**0.94**
Paper and paper products	511	1.16	1.20	1.21	1.11	1.20	1.22
Drugs, proprietaries, and sundries	512	1.49	1.51	1.65	1.59	1.44	1.51
Apparel, piece goods, and notions	513	1.77	1.80	2.12	2.07	2.00	1.70
Groceries and related products	514	0.66	0.68	0.67	0.64	0.63	0.68
Farm-product raw materials	515	1.04	1.01	1.20	1.19	1.25	0.87
Chemicals and allied products	516	0.97	0.97	1.14	1.09	1.06	1.06
Petroleum and petroleum products	517	0.33	0.39	0.39	0.40	0.37	0.35
Beer, wine, and distilled beverages	518	0.95	1.06	1.06	1.02	1.03	1.07
Miscellaneous nondurable goods	519	1.17	1.41	1.22	1.13	1.18	1.19

[1] Based on 1987 Standard Industrial Classification code; see text, section 13.

Source: U.S. Bureau of the Census, *Current Business Reports, Annual Benchmark Report for Wholesale Trade, January 1987 Through February 1997*, (BW/96-RV).

No. 1283. Services—Establishments, Employees, and Payroll: 1990 and 1994

[Covers establishments with payroll. Employees are for the week including March 12. Most government employees are excluded. For statement on methodology, see Appendix III]

KIND OF BUSINESS	1987 SIC code [1]	ESTABLISHMENTS (1,000)		EMPLOYEES (1,000)		PAYROLL (bil. dol.)	
		1990	1994	1990	1994	1990	1994
Services, total [2]	(I)	2,059.3	2,342.3	28,800	33,253	588.4	794.0
Hotels and other lodging places	70	50.6	53.5	1,529	1,535	19.1	22.5
Hotels and motels	701	39.2	42.9	1,463	1,484	18.3	21.7
Personal services [2]	72	186.1	201.8	1,196	1,246	13.5	15.8
Laundry, cleaning, and garment services	721	50.4	56.5	418	434	5.2	6.1
Drycleaning plants, except rug	7216	17.6	22.0	148	166	1.6	1.9
Beauty shops	723	76.1	82.5	371	389	3.9	4.6
Barber shops	724	5.1	4.6	16	14	0.2	0.2
Funeral service and crematories	726	14.9	15.9	85	94	1.7	2.1
Business services [2]	73	292.3	340.3	5,119	6,240	96.1	136.6
Advertising	731	19.1	19.8	204	209	7.3	8.1
Advertising agencies	7311	11.1	13.7	137	136	5.4	6.2
Credit reporting and collection	732	6.6	7.4	94	106	2.0	2.5
Mailing, reproduction, stenographic [2]	733	26.2	33.0	233	256	5.1	6.4
Direct mail advertising services	7331	3.5	4.1	84	82	1.7	2.0
Commercial art and graphic design	7336	9.0	12.4	52	53	1.5	1.8
Services to buildings	734	48.5	61.5	802	876	8.3	10.5
Misc. equipment rental and leasing	735	22.6	25.1	209	216	4.9	5.9
Personnel supply services [2]	736	27.0	33.1	1,518	2,298	20.6	36.7
Employment agencies	7361	12.8	12.5	247	200	4.3	4.1
Help supply services	7363	13.3	20.5	1,210	2,098	15.6	32.6
Computer and data processing services [2]	737	40.5	66.8	773	984	28.5	43.4
Computer programming services	7371	12.4	24.0	217	272	8.9	13.4
Prepackaged software	7372	3.8	6.9	76	150	3.5	8.3
Computer integrated systems design	7373	3.3	5.4	82	103	3.5	4.6
Data processing and preparation	7374	6.8	7.1	229	237	6.4	7.8
Computer maintenance and repair	7378	3.3	4.8	53	56	1.9	2.1
Miscellaneous business services	738	62.7	84.0	1,093	1,281	17.2	22.6
Detective and armored car services	7381	9.4	12.0	467	500	5.2	6.5
Automotive repair, services, and parking [2]	75	156.6	178.4	877	936	15.2	18.2
Automotive rentals, no drivers [2]	751	10.5	10.6	147	133	2.9	3.0
Truck rental and leasing, no drivers	7513	4.0	4.6	51	37	1.2	1.0
Passenger car rental	7514	4.5	4.6	78	86	1.3	1.7
Automotive repair shops [2]	753	112.7	133.3	507	558	9.6	12.1
Top and body repair and paint shops	7532	30.5	35.0	164	178	3.2	4.1
General automotive repair shops	7538	54.8	68.4	214	250	3.8	5.2
Automotive services, except repair	754	18.1	24.3	145	184	1.5	2.2
Miscellaneous repair services	76	67.4	72.8	403	442	6.7	11.0
Electrical repair shops	762	17.2	20.7	115	156	2.6	4.0
Motion pictures [2]	78	35.4	42.7	430	479	8.6	10.1
Motion picture production and services	781	9.2	12.5	189	200	5.9	7.1
Motion picture distribution and services	782	1.0	1.5	24	22	0.9	1.1
Motion picture theaters	783	7.0	6.6	107	112	0.8	0.8
Video tape rental	784	16.4	21.6	103	145	0.8	1.1
Amusement and recreation services [2]	79	75.2	90.8	1,032	1,246	16.1	22.5
Producers, orchestras, entertainers	792	9.7	14.1	126	152	3.3	4.4
Commercial sports	794	3.3	4.1	79	93	3.0	4.6
Amusement parks	7996	0.7	0.9	69	90	1.1	1.4
Membership sports and recreation clubs	7997	13.1	14.6	242	268	3.4	4.4
Health services [2]	80	436.7	476.2	8,811	10,624	213.6	295.8
Offices and clinics of medical doctors	801	193.6	198.5	1,387	1,621	63.0	80.1
Offices and clinics of dentists	802	104.7	110.6	533	594	11.6	15.0
Offices of other health practitioners	804	62.5	79.0	250	315	5.0	7.1
Offices and clinics of chiropractors	8041	22.9	28.8	73	89	1.3	1.7
Nursing and personal care facilities	805	19.1	21.6	1,461	1,707	18.6	26.2
Hospitals [3]	806	6.3	7.4	4,325	5,130	99.2	140.6
Medical and dental laboratories	807	14.4	16.3	158	190	3.8	5.3
Medical laboratories	8071	7.1	8.8	118	151	3.0	4.4
Home health care services	808	7.7	12.9	351	680	4.8	11.2
Legal services	81	142.4	161.6	932	963	36.0	41.7
Elementary and secondary schools	821	14.3	16.9	451	563	6.6	9.4
Colleges and universities	822	3.0	3.5	1,082	1,235	19.2	25.7
Social services [2]	83	115.6	151.1	1,750	2,138	20.9	29.5
Child day care services	835	39.0	51.2	405	526	3.4	5.2
Residential care	836	21.0	28.9	417	518	5.4	7.6
Museums, botanical, zoological gardens	84	3.2	3.7	64	74	1.1	1.4
Business associations	861	12.7	14.6	99	107	2.7	3.5
Civic and social associations	864	40.0	41.9	366	375	3.7	4.2
Engineering and management services [2]	87	201.1	259.1	2,473	2,693	79.8	99.1
Engineering services	8711	33.1	42.6	652	663	24.9	28.6
Architectural services	8712	15.7	18.3	140	126	4.8	5.0
Accounting, auditing, and bookkeeping	872	67.9	83.0	524	548	13.8	16.5
Research and testing services	873	14.9	18.8	393	446	12.3	16.1
Management services	8741	15.3	23.8	286	386	7.7	11.8
Management consulting services	8742	24.5	37.5	226	295	8.6	13.5
Facilities support services	8744	0.7	0.9	70	66	2.2	2.0

[1] Based on 1987 Standard Industrial Classification; see text, section 13. [2] Includes kinds of business not shown separately. [3] Includes government employees.

Source: U.S. Bureau of the Census, *County Business Patterns*, annual.

No. 1284. Selected Service Industries—Summary: 1987 and 1992

[For establishments with payroll]

KIND OF BUSINESS	1987 SIC code [1]	ESTABLISHMENTS [2] (1,000)		RECEIPTS OR EXPENSES [3] (mil. dol.)		PAID EMPLOYEES [4] (1,000)	
		1987	1992	1987	1992	1987	1992
Firms subject to Federal income tax [5]	(X)	1,626	1,826	772,194	1,202,613	16,066	19,280
Hotels and other lodging places [6]	70 ex. 704	47	49	51,665	69,204	1,411	1,489
Personal services	72	185	197	31,491	43,280	1,106	1,218
Business services	73	252	307	166,322	274,892	4,414	5,542
Automotive repair, services, and parking	75	151	172	51,423	70,033	785	864
Miscellaneous repair services	76	66	72	20,838	30,732	346	428
Amusement and recreation services and museums [7]	78, 79, 84	99	115	57,638	92,915	1,094	1,382
Health services	80	407	442	182,289	299,067	3,592	4,453
Legal services	81	136	152	66,998	101,114	806	924
Social services	83	43	59	7,330	13,349	357	506
Engineering and management services [8]	87 ex. 8733	205	233	127,344	192,819	1,969	2,271
Firms exempt from Federal income tax [5]	(X)	176	209	263,284	423,900	6,737	8,109
Selected health services	8011 pt.; 8021 pt.; 805, 6, 8, 9	19	24	184,920	312,050	4,848	5,565
Social services	83	63	82	26,884	47,170	1,110	1,407
Selected membership organizations	861, 2, 4, 9	68	72	22,028	33,795	539	603
Research, testing, and consulting services [9]	873, 4 ex. 8744	4	6	8,837	14,314	121	147

X Not applicable. [1] Based on 1987 Standard Industrial Classification; see text, section 13. [2] Number of establishments in business at any time during the year. [3] Receipts refer to establishments subject to Federal income tax. Expenses refer to establishments exempt from Federal income tax. [4] For pay period including March 12. [5] Includes other kinds of business, not shown separately. [6] Excludes membership lodging. [7] Includes motion pictures. [8] Except noncommercial research organizations. [9] Excludes facilities support management services.

Source: U.S. Bureau of the Census, *1992 Census of Service Industries*, Geographic Area Series, SC92-A-52.

No. 1285. Exported Services, by Selected Kinds of Business: 1992

[For establishments with payroll]

KIND OF BUSINESS	1987 SIC code [1]	Establishments	Receipts (mil. dol.)	ESTABLISHMENTS WITH RECEIPTS FROM EXPORTED SERVICES		
				Number	Receipts (mil. dol.)	Receipts from exported services (mil. dol.)
Business services	73	306,551	274,892	12,326	38,254	6,961
Advertising	731	19,023	19,456	1,406	1,640	91
Credit reporting and collection	732	7,472	6,151	106	105	6
Mailing, reproduction, stenographic	733	32,066	18,339	939	1,041	107
Services to dwellings and other buildings	734	57,649	19,003	196	95	6
Miscellaneous equipment rental and leasing	735	24,816	21,778	329	1,265	192
Personnel supply services	736	31,166	38,163	588	721	205
Computer and data processing services	737	59,052	101,073	6,770	30,024	5,802
Miscellaneous business services	738	75,287	50,929	1,968	3,363	551
Legal services	81	151,737	101,114	5,365	20,524	1,482
Engineering and architectural services	871	68,127	78,770	3,832	18,729	2,739
Accounting, auditing, and bookkeeping	872	79,097	34,036	1,131	3,575	91
Research and testing services	873 ex. 8733	13,531	22,690	1,771	5,012	1,006
Management and public relations	874	72,130	57,321	5,655	7,212	2,002

[1] Based on 1987 Standard Industrial Classification; see text, section 13.

Source: U.S. Bureau of the Census, *1992 Census of Service Industries*, Subject Series, SC92-S-5.

No. 1286. National Nonprofit Associations—Number, by Type: 1980 to 1997

[Data compiled during last few months of year previous to year shown and the beginning months of year shown]

TYPE	1980	1990	1995	1997	TYPE	1980	1990	1995	1997
Total	14,726	22,289	22,663	22,901	Fraternal, foreign interest, nationality, ethnic	435	573	562	541
Trade, business, commercial	3,118	3,918	3,757	3,755	Religious	797	1,172	1,230	1,230
Agriculture	677	940	1,122	1,124	Veteran, hereditary, patriotic	208	462	686	745
Legal, governmental, public admin., military	529	792	776	780	Hobby, avocational	910	1,475	1,549	1,548
Scientific, engineering, tech	1,039	1,417	1,355	1,381	Athletic sports	504	840	836	836
Educational	[1] 2,376	1,291	1,290	1,310	Labor unions	235	253	245	245
Cultural	(1)	1,886	1,918	1,918	Chambers of Commerce [2]	105	168	168	162
Social welfare	994	1,705	1,885	1,934	Greek and non-Greek letter societies	318	340	336	335
Health, medical	1,413	2,227	2,348	2,453	Fan clubs	(NA)	581	460	491
Public affairs	1,068	2,249	2,148	2,113					

NA Not available. [1] Data for cultural associations included with educational associations. [2] National and binational.

Source: Gale Research Inc., Detroit, MI. Compiled from *Encyclopedia of Associations*, annual (copyright).

No. 1287. Service Industries—Summary of Taxable Firms: 1992

KIND OF BUSINESS	1987 SIC code [1]	ALL ESTABLISHMENTS		ESTABLISHMENTS WITH PAYROLL			
		Establishments [2] (1,000)	Receipts (mil. dol.)	Establishments [2] (1,000)	Receipts (mil. dol.)	Annual payroll (mil. dol.)	Paid employees [3] (1,000)
Firms subject to Federal income tax [4]	(X)	8,593.5	1,345,146	1,826.4	1,202,613	452,697	19,290
Hotels and other lodging places [4] [5]	70 ex. 704	92.9	71,038	48.6	69,204	19,633	1,489
Hotels and motels	701	89.1	68,508	41.7	67,193	19,187	1,456
Personal services [4]	72	1,320.9	59,598	197.1	43,280	14,379	1,218
Laundry, cleaning, and garment services	721	124.4	18,805	55.8	17,140	5,588	426
Photographic studios, portrait	722	64.3	4,280	11.4	3,191	853	67
Beauty and barber shops	723, 4	471.6	15,951	87.7	10,347	4,428	402
Funeral service and crematories	726	25.2	7,588	15.6	7,145	1,856	88
Business services [4]	73	2,056.2	309,439	306.6	274,892	109,299	5,542
Advertising [4]	731	91.6	22,673	19.0	19,456	7,223	196
Advertising agencies	7311	(NA)	(NA)	13.9	13,608	5,649	132
Credit reporting and collection	732	14.6	6,377	7.5	6,151	2,163	98
Mailing, reproduction, stenographic [4]	733	154.5	20,990	32.1	18,339	5,522	235
Direct mail advertising services	7331	(NA)	(NA)	3.9	6,434	1,777	79
Services to dwellings and other buildings	734	460.5	23,586	57.6	19,003	9,164	818
Miscellaneous equipment rental and leasing	735	52.4	22,782	24.8	21,778	4,905	200
Personnel supply services [4]	736	54.1	38,709	31.2	38,163	26,436	1,975
Help supply services	7363	(NA)	(NA)	19.0	33,587	24,075	1,842
Computer and data processing services [4]	737	223.6	104,650	59.1	101,073	35,598	886
Computer programming services	7371	(NA)	(NA)	23.3	23,548	10,890	243
Prepackaged software	7372	(NA)	(NA)	7.1	20,802	6,614	131
Computer integrated systems design	7373	(NA)	(NA)	5.0	14,805	4,151	98
Data processing and preparation	7374	(NA)	(NA)	7.3	20,200	6,796	230
Computer maintenance and repair	7378	(NA)	(NA)	5.0	7,353	2,300	63
Detective and armored car services	7381	(NA)	(NA)	11.6	9,193	5,794	482
Auto repair, services, and parking [4]	75	454.3	78,512	172.0	70,033	15,550	864
Automotive rentals, no drivers [4]	751	22.2	20,906	10.6	20,574	2,757	132
Truck rental and leasing, no drivers	7513	(NA)	(NA)	4.3	7,445	1,029	42
Passenger car rental	7514	(NA)	(NA)	4.9	10,280	1,475	81
Automotive repair shops [4]	753	334.5	46,200	128.7	39,746	10,337	520
Top and body repair and paint shops	7532	(NA)	(NA)	35.0	12,262	3,445	166
General automotive repair shops	7538	(NA)	(NA)	64.8	17,773	4,406	230
Automotive services, except repair	754	85.8	7,661	22.5	6,047	1,776	160
Miscellaneous repair services [4]	76	269.8	35,237	71.6	30,732	9,695	428
Electrical repair shops	762	71.6	11,875	21.2	10,667	3,707	162
Amusement and recreation services [4] [6]	78, 79, 84	691.7	103,556	114.8	92,915	25,357	1,362
Motion picture prod., distribution, services	781, 2	54.1	34,289	13.0	33,062	8,084	249
Motion picture theaters	783	8.1	5,879	6.9	5,817	788	105
Video tape rental	784	33.7	5,495	22.0	5,075	944	124
Producers, orchestras, entertainers [7]	792	288.6	13,054	10.1	8,625	2,895	69
Commercial sports	794	71.6	9,010	3.8	7,594	4,022	90
Physical fitness facilities	7991	29.6	4,135	9.2	3,824	1,043	130
Health services [4]	80	1,005.5	321,650	441.7	299,067	129,093	4,453
Offices and clinics of doctors of medicine	801	328.9	151,824	197.7	141,429	68,732	1,357
Offices and clinics of dentists	802	138.5	36,939	108.8	35,523	13,039	555
Offices, clinics of doctors of osteopathy	803	14.2	4,008	8.7	3,638	1,650	47
Offices, clinics of other health practitioners [4]	804	243.0	23,892	74.7	18,926	6,150	283
Offices and clinics of chiropractors	8041	41.4	6,555	27.3	5,918	1,652	85
Offices and clinics of optometrists	8042	26.0	5,333	17.1	4,940	1,301	69
Nursing and personal care facilities	805	51.8	34,742	15.0	33,990	15,954	1,135
Hospitals [4]	806	(NA)	(NA)	1.4	31,083	10,556	428
General medical and surgical hospitals	8062	(NA)	(NA)	0.7	24,162	8,013	323
Medical and dental laboratories [4]	807	29.4	15,172	16.0	14,460	4,804	178
Medical laboratories	8071	(NA)	(NA)	8.4	12,511	3,980	139
Home health care services	808	(NA)	(NA)	8.0	10,414	4,853	342
Legal services	81	326.9	108,443	151.7	101,114	39,328	924
Selected educational services	823, 4, 9	240.7	9,158	14.7	7,242	2,457	133
Social services [4]	83	617.4	18,201	59.1	13,349	5,466	505
Child day care services	835	524.4	8,708	35.3	5,270	2,388	283
Engineering and architectural services [4]	871	225.4	83,033	68.1	78,770	32,745	825
Engineering services	8711	131.3	67,716	41.8	65,245	27,247	658
Architectural services	8712	71.6	12,682	17.9	11,244	4,408	122
Accounting, auditing, and bookkeeping	872	325.5	37,191	79.1	34,038	14,001	521
Research and testing services [8]	873 ex. 8733	30.4	22,910	13.5	22,690	9,227	282
Management and public relations [4]	874	735.8	72,490	72.1	57,321	23,371	644
Management services	8741	111.0	23,774	19.7	21,728	8,516	278
Management consulting services	8742	(NA)	(NA)	33.8	22,629	9,620	212

NA Not available. [1] Based on 1987 Standard Industrial Classification; see text, section 13. [2] Represents the number of establishments in business at any time during year. [3] For pay period including March 12. [4] Includes other kinds of business, not shown separately. [5] Excludes membership lodging. [6] Includes motion pictures and museums. [7] Excludes motion picture producers. [8] Excludes noncommercial research organizations.

Source: U.S. Bureau of the Census, *1992 Census of Service Industries*, SC92-A-52 and SC92-N-1.

No. 1288. Service Industries—Annual Receipts of Taxable Firms: 1985 to 1995

[In billions of dollars. Covers employer and nonemployer firms except as noted. Estimated]

KIND OF BUSINESS	1987 SIC code [1]	1985	1990	1991	1992	1993	1994	1995
Hotels and other lodging places [2]	70 ex. 704	45.4	64.2	65.3	71.0	74.8	80.8	86.3
Hotels and motels	701	43.5	62.0	63.1	68.5	72.0	77.8	82.9
Personal services [3]	72	36.7	54.7	54.6	59.6	62.4	65.6	69.9
Laundry, cleaning, and garment services	721	12.8	17.3	17.6	18.8	19.2	19.9	21.0
Drycleaning plants, except rug cleaning	7216	3.8	4.4	4.5	5.5	5.5	5.7	6.0
Beauty shops	7231	9.0	12.8	13.1	14.4	14.7	15.4	16.7
Barber shops	7241	1.2	1.4	1.5	1.5	1.5	1.6	1.7
Funeral service and crematories	726	5.2	6.8	7.1	7.6	8.1	8.4	9.2
Business services [3]	73	155.9	280.7	287.2	309.4	336.5	374.9	424.3
Advertising	731	14.9	22.0	21.3	22.7	23.8	25.0	28.6
Advertising agencies	7311	11.1	16.1	15.2	16.0	16.8	17.5	20.0
Credit reporting and collection	732	3.7	5.8	6.0	6.4	6.9	7.0	7.7
Mailing, reproduction, stenographic [3]	733	14.5	20.8	20.4	21.0	22.2	22.9	25.4
Direct mail advertising services	7331	3.8	7.0	6.5	6.8	7.6	7.9	8.5
Commercial art and graphic design	7336	(NA)	6.1	6.1	6.2	6.1	6.4	6.9
Services to dwellings and other buildings	734	13.3	22.3	22.4	23.6	23.8	26.4	28.8
Miscellaneous equipment rental and leasing	735	(NA)	23.1	22.6	22.8	24.6	26.5	29.6
Personnel supply services	736	14.7	32.5	33.4	36.7	42.9	49.7	62.5
Employment agencies	7361	3.7	6.2	5.2	5.0	5.5	6.2	7.3
Help supply services	7363	(NA)	26.4	28.3	33.7	37.4	43.5	55.2
Computer and data processing services [3]	737	45.1	88.3	94.4	104.7	116.8	133.1	152.2
Computer programming services	7371	(NA)	21.3	23.4	25.0	28.0	32.4	37.4
Prepackaged software	7372	(NA)	16.5	18.3	21.2	24.6	27.6	31.1
Computer integrated systems design	7373	(NA)	12.9	13.8	15.2	17.1	19.0	20.6
Data processing and preparation	7374	(NA)	17.8	18.8	20.4	22.6	26.6	31.1
Computer maintenance and repair	7378	(NA)	7.0	6.9	7.7	7.6	7.8	8.2
Miscellaneous business services	738	(NA)	65.8	66.6	69.7	75.4	84.2	89.5
Detective and armored car services	7381	(NA)	9.0	9.6	9.7	10.2	10.6	11.8
Automotive repair, services, and parking [3]	75	51.7	73.7	71.5	78.5	84.1	91.3	98.3
Automotive rentals, no drivers [3]	751	14.6	20.8	20.3	20.9	22.3	23.4	24.9
Truck rental and leasing, without drivers	7513	5.5	8.5	7.9	7.6	7.7	8.1	8.7
Passenger car rental	7514	(NA)	9.0	9.5	10.4	11.4	12.1	12.8
Automotive repair shops [3]	753	30.5	43.5	41.2	46.2	49.4	54.0	57.5
Top & body repair & paint shops	7532	(NA)	13.5	12.8	13.9	14.8	15.9	16.9
General automotive repair shops	7538	(NA)	19.6	17.7	21.3	22.8	25.4	27.7
Automotive services, except repair	754	(NA)	6.5	6.7	7.7	8.4	9.7	11.0
Miscellaneous repair services	76	20.7	32.8	32.4	35.2	36.0	39.1	42.7
Electrical repair shops	762	(NA)	11.3	11.3	11.9	12.2	12.8	14.2
Motion pictures	78	21.5	40.0	42.8	45.7	50.2	54.3	58.1
Motion picture produc., distribution, allied services	781,2	15.0	28.9	31.6	34.3	38.1	41.2	44.4
Motion picture theaters	783	3.8	6.1	6.2	5.9	6.1	6.6	7.0
Video tape rental	784	(NA)	5.0	5.0	5.5	6.0	6.6	6.7
Amusement and recreation services [3]	79	31.2	50.1	51.7	57.7	63.6	68.2	77.4
Producers, orchestras, entertainers	792	6.4	10.7	11.7	13.1	15.4	16.0	17.5
Commercial sports	794	5.0	8.6	8.6	9.0	9.1	9.4	10.2
Amusement parks	7996	2.6	4.9	4.8	5.4	5.7	5.9	6.4
Membership sports and recreation clubs	7997	3.5	4.8	5.2	5.4	6.0	6.4	6.8
Health services [3]	80	147.4	271.2	293.9	321.7	337.2	355.2	382.6
Offices and clinics of doctors of medicine	801	72.1	128.9	138.6	151.8	154.8	160.8	170.3
Offices and clinics of dentists	802	20.6	31.5	33.3	36.9	39.1	42.1	45.6
Offices of other health practitioners	804	7.9	20.1	21.4	23.9	25.2	25.5	28.6
Offices and clinics of chiropractors	8041	2.7	5.5	5.6	6.6	7.1	7.2	7.3
Nursing and personal care facilities	805	17.5	30.2	32.9	34.7	37.4	39.6	44.2
Hospitals [4]	806	15.7	26.5	28.8	31.1	32.9	34.1	36.7
Medical and dental laboratories	807	5.4	12.0	13.6	15.2	16.2	17.8	19.2
Medical laboratories	8071	3.9	10.0	11.5	12.9	13.9	15.4	16.7
Home health care services	808	(NA)	7.6	9.1	11.2	13.0	15.0	17.5
Legal services	81	52.8	97.6	100.0	106.4	111.7	113.8	114.4
Social services	83	(NA)	15.5	16.4	18.2	19.7	21.5	23.4
Child day care services	8351	2.6	7.1	7.4	8.7	9.5	10.3	11.4
Residential care	8361	(NA)	4.6	4.9	4.9	5.3	5.6	6.0
Museums, botanical, zoological gardens	84	(NA)	0.1	0.2	0.2	0.2	0.2	0.2
Engineering and management services [3]	87	(NA)	198.4	202.7	215.6	224.7	238.9	269.7
Engineering services	8711	(NA)	64.8	65.8	67.7	67.9	69.8	76.6
Architectural services	8712	(NA)	13.0	12.3	12.7	13.5	14.8	16.4
Accounting, auditing, & bookkeeping	8721	21.2	32.6	33.7	37.2	40.0	43.1	49.7
Research and testing services [5]	873, ex. 87	(NA)	20.4	20.9	22.9	25.1	26.6	28.2
Management services	8741	(NA)	20.6	21.8	23.8	24.6	26.8	32.0
Management consulting services	8742	(NA)	28.9	29.8	31.9	33.7	36.7	43.3
Facilities support services	8744	(NA)	5.3	5.6	5.6	5.5	6.3	6.4
Arrangement of passenger transportation	472	6.3	12.3	11.4	11.9	12.4	13.2	14.4
Real estate agents and managers	653	31.3	63.0	63.2	73.1	80.6	83.9	88.1

NA Not available. [1] Standard Industrial Classification; see text, section 13. [2] Excludes those on membership basis. [3] Includes other kinds of businesses, not shown separately. [4] Covers employer firms only. [5] Excludes noncommercial research organizations.

Source: U.S. Bureau of the Census, *Current Business Reports, Service Annual Survey: 1995* (BS/95); and unpublished data.

No. 1289. Lodging Industry Summary: 1990 to 1995

YEAR	Average occupancy rate (percent)	Average room rate (dol.)	ROOM SIZE OF PROPERTY	1995 Establishments	1995 Rooms (mil.)	ITEM	1995 Business traveler	1995 Leisure traveler
1990	63.3	58.40	Total	46,000	3.5	Typical night:		
1991	60.9	58.91				Made reservations	91%	80%
1992	61.7	59.87	Percent:			Amount paid	$70.40	$64.80
1993	63.6	61.04	Under 75 rooms	66.8	25.2			
1994	65.2	63.63	75-149 rooms	21.5	30.8	Length of stay:		
1995	65.5	67.34	150-299 rooms	8.6	22.6	One night	38%	47%
			300 or more	3.1	21.4	Two nights	24%	26%
						Three or more	37%	27%

Source: American Hotel & Motel Association, Washington, DC, *Lodging Industry Profile* (copyright).

No. 1290. Service Industries—Summary of Tax-Exempt Firms: 1992

[Covers establishments with payroll]

KIND OF BUSINESS	1987 SIC code [1]	Establishments [2] (1,000)	Revenues (mil. dol.)	Annual payroll (mil. dol.)	Paid employees [3] (1,000)
Firms exempt from Federal income tax [4]	(X)	**206.9**	**446,256**	**186,672**	**8,109**
Nursing and personal care facilities	805	5.9	15,220	7,591	496
Hospitals	806	5.7	279,735	126,202	4,566
Hospitals, excluding government	806	3.6	203,360	87,062	3,252
Social services [4]	83	81.7	53,672	19,331	1,407
Individual and family social services	832	28.9	16,046	6,381	434
Residential care	836	15.0	10,615	4,830	319
Business associations	861	14.3	11,068	3,157	102
Civic, social, and fraternal associations	864	41.8	13,176	3,657	355
Research and testing services	873	3.8	12,535	4,511	126

X Not applicable. [1] Based on 1987 Standard Industrial Classification; see text, section 13. [2] Represents the number of establishments in business at any time during year. [3] For pay period including March 12. [4] Includes other kinds of business, not shown separately.

Source: U.S. Bureau of the Census, *1992 Census of Service Industries*, SC92-A-52 and SC92-N-1.

No. 1291. Selected Service Industries—Revenue and Expenses for Tax-Exempt Firms: 1990 to 1995

[In billions of dollars. Estimated from a sample of employer firms only]

KIND OF BUSINESS	1987 SIC code [1]	REVENUE 1990	REVENUE 1994	REVENUE 1995	EXPENSES 1990	EXPENSES 1994	EXPENSES 1995
Selected amusement and recreation services [2]	792, 7991, 7997, 7999	7.9	10.5	11.1	(NA)	10.6	10.9
Offices and clinics of doctors of medicine	801	12.9	20.7	22.8	12.5	20.1	22.0
Nursing and personal care facilities	805	12.1	18.0	19.8	(NA)	17.7	19.3
Hospitals	806	233.6	304.8	319.7	225.6	301.4	313.1
Home health care services	808	3.9	7.9	8.8	3.6	7.6	8.5
Health and allied services, n.e.c.	809	5.3	9.0	9.7	5.2	8.7	9.4
Social services	83	45.3	62.8	69.1	39.4	55.4	61.4
Individual and family social services	8322	13.0	19.4	21.6	12.6	18.8	21.0
Job training and related services	8331	4.9	6.7	7.1	4.5	6.5	6.9
Child day care services	8351	2.9	4.5	5.0	3.0	4.4	4.8
Residential care	8361	8.8	12.8	14.1	8.6	12.2	13.4
Selected membership organizations [3]	86 (pt)	31.5	39.4	41.8	28.6	36.4	39.0
Research and testing services	873	11.0	14.0	14.5	10.0	13.4	14.1

NA Not available. [1] Standard Industrial Classification; see text, section 13. [2] Covers theatrical producers, bands, orchestras, and entertainers (SIC 792); physical fitness facilities (SIC 7991); membership sports and recreation clubs (SIC 7997); and amusement and recreation services, not elsewhere classified (SIC 7999). [3] Includes business associations (SIC 861); professional membership organizations (SIC 862); civic, social, and fraternal organizations (SIC 864); and other membership organizations, except labor unions and political and religious organizations (SIC 869).

Source: U.S. Bureau of the Census, *Current Business Reports, Service Annual Survey: 1995* (BS/95).

Figure 28.1
U.S. International Transaction Balances: 1960 to 1996

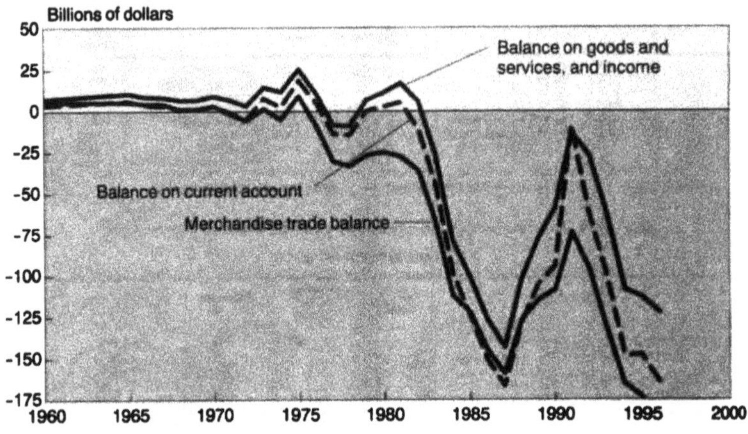

Source: Chart prepared by U.S. Bureau of the Census. For data, see table 1292.

Figure 28.2
Top Purchasers of U.S. Exports and Suppliers of U.S. General Imports: 1995

Total U.S. Exports $585 billion

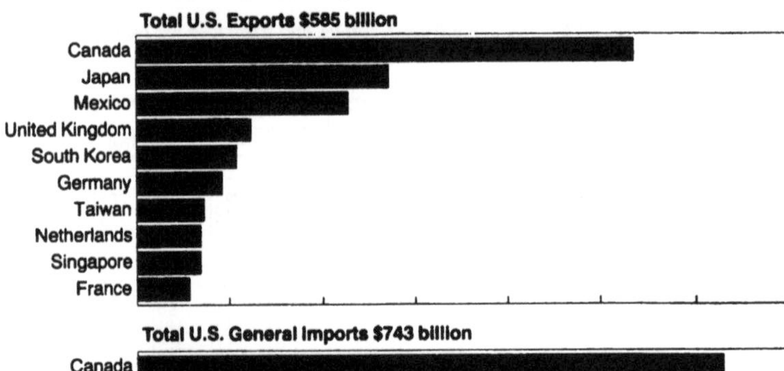

Total U.S. General Imports $743 billion

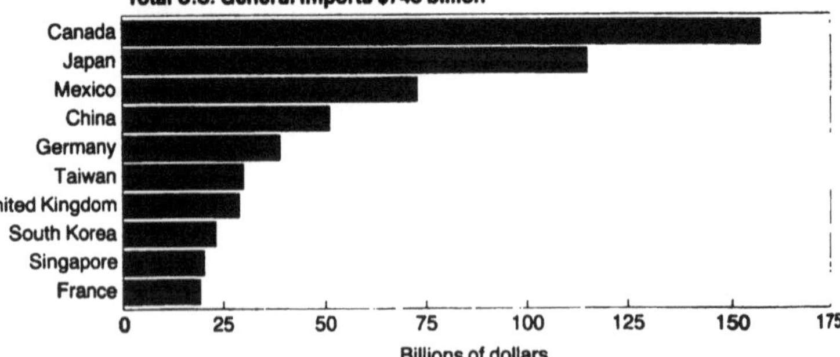

Chart prepared by U.S. Bureau of the Census. For data, see table 1313.

Section 28

Foreign Commerce and Aid

ion presents data on the flow services, and capital between d States and other countries; in official reserve assets of the ates; international investments; sistance programs; and ties.

au of Economic Analysis current figures on U.S. interna- isactions and the U.S. interna- estment position in its monthly *f Current Business.* Statistics for n aid programs are presented ency for International Develop- D) in its annual *U.S. Overseas d Grants and Assistance from nal Organizations;* and by the nt of Agriculture in its *Foreign al Trade of the United States.*

ipal source of merchandise d export data is the Bureau of us. Current data are presented n *U.S. Merchandise Trade*, (be- 994, retitled *U.S. International Goods and Services*) report 900' and *U.S. Merchandise ports, General Imports, and r Consumption*, report series iscontinued after 1996). The *f the Census Catalog* and the *Foreign Trade Statistics* lists the monthly and annual reports in In addition, the International ministration and the Bureau of : Analysis present summary as lected commodity and country J.S. foreign trade in the *Over- iness Reports* and the *Survey t Business,* respectively. The lise trade data in the latter clude balance of payments ad- to the Census data. The Trea- artment's *Monthly Treasury t of Receipts and Outlays of the ates Government* contains in- on import duties.

onal accounts—The interna- isactions tables (Nos. 1292 to ow, for given time periods, the f goods, services, grants, and assets and liabilities between d States and the rest of the e major revisions to this series were incorporated this year due to the first benchmark survey of the stock of U.S. portfolio investment abroad in over 50 years. The international investment position table (No. 1295) presents, for specific dates, the value of U.S. invest- ments abroad and of foreign investments in the United States. The movement of foreign and U.S. capital as presented in the balance of payments is not the only factor affecting the total value of foreign investments. Among the other factors are changes in the valuation of assets or liabilities, including changes in prices of securities, defaults, expropriations, and write-offs.

Direct investment abroad means the ownership or control, directly or indirectly, by one person of 10 percent or more of the voting securities of an incorporated business enterprise or an equivalent in- terest in an unincorporated business en- terprise. Direct investment position is the value of U.S. parents' claims on the equi- ty of, and receivables due from, foreign affiliates, less foreign affiliates' receiv- ables due from their U.S. parents. In- come consists of parents' shares in the earnings of their affiliates plus net inter- est received by parents on intercompany accounts, less withholding taxes on divi- dends and interest.

Foreign aid—Foreign assistance is di- vided into three major categories—grants (military supplies and services and other grants), credits, and other assistance

In Brief

The U.S. current account deficit increased to $165 billion in 1996 from $148 billion the year before.

Employment of U.S. affiliates of foreign companies was almost 4.9 million workers in 1994 or about 5% of the labor force.

The U.S. merchandise trade deficit for all goods was $167 billion in 1996. However, advance technology goods and agricultural products ran surpluses of $25 billion and $27 billion, respectively.

(through net accumulation of foreign currency claims from the sale of agricultural commodities). *Grants* are transfers for which no payment is expected (other than a limited percentage of the foreign currency "counterpart" funds generated by the grant), or which at most involve an obligation on the part of the receiver to extend aid to the United States or other countries to achieve a common objective. *Credits* are loan disbursements or transfers under other agreements which give rise to specific obligations to repay, over a period of years, usually with interest. All known returns to the U.S. Government stemming from grants and credits (reverse grants, returns of grants, and payments of principal) are taken into account in net grants and net credits, but no allowance is made for interest or commissions. *Other assistance* represents the transfer of U.S. farm products in exchange for foreign currencies (plus, since enactment of Public Law 87-128, currency claims from principal and interest collected on credits extended under the farm products program), *less* the Government's disbursements of the currencies as grants, credits, or for purchases. The net acquisition of currencies represents net transfers of resources to foreign countries under the agricultural programs, in addition to those classified as grants or credits.

The basic instrument for extending military aid to friendly nations has been the Mutual Defense Assistance Program authorized by the Congress in 1949. Prior to 1952, economic and technical aid was authorized in the Foreign Assistance Act of 1948, the 1950 Act for International Development, and other legislation which set up programs for specific countries. In 1952, these economic, technical, and military aid programs were combined under the Mutual Security Act, which in turn was followed by the Foreign Assistance Act passed in 1961. Appropriations to provide military assistance were also made in the Department of Defense Appropriation Act (rather than the Foreign Assistance Appropriation Act) beginning in 1966 for certain countries in Southeast Asia and in other legislation concerning program for specific as reported in the *Foreign Grants and Credits* series differ from data published by AID or its immediate predecessors, due largely to differences in reporting, timing, and treatment of particular items.

Exports—The Bureau of the Census compiles export data primarily from Shipper's Export Declarations required to be filed with customs officials for shipments leaving the United States. They include U.S. exports under mutual security programs and exclude shipments to U.S. Armed Forces for their own use.

The value reported in the export statistics is generally equivalent to a free alongside ship (f.a.s.) value at the U.S. port of export, based on the transaction price, including inland freight, insurance, and other charges incurred in placing the merchandise alongside the carrier at the U.S. port of exportation. This value, as defined, excludes the cost of loading merchandise aboard the exporting carrier and also excludes freight, insurance, and any other charges or transportation and other costs beyond the U.S. port of exportation. The country of destination is defined as the country of ultimate destination or country where the merchandise is to be consumed, further processed, or manufactured, as known to the shipper at the time of exportation. When ultimate destination is not known, the shipment is statistically credited to the last country to which the shipper knows the merchandise will be shipped in the same form as exported.

For certain "low-valued" shipments, the export statistics include estimates based upon selected samples of such shipments. The dollar value of the "low-valued" shipments has varied. For instance, effective January 1987 through September 1989, data are estimated for shipments valued under $1,501; from October 1989 through December 1989, data are estimated for shipments valued under $2,501 to all countries.

Effective January 1990, the United States began substituting Canadian import statistics for U.S. exports to Canada. As a result of the data exchange between the United States and Canada, the United States has adopted the Cana-

Data are estimated for shipments valued under $2,501 to all countries, except Canada, using factors based on the ratios of low-valued shipments to individual country totals. These shipments represent slightly less than 2.5 percent of the monthly value of U.S. exports to those countries. Data are estimated for shipments reported on Canadian import documents which total less than $900 (Canadian). Such shipments represent 2 percent of the monthly value of U.S. exports to Canada.

Prior to 1989, exports were based on Schedule B, Statistical Classification of Domestic and Foreign Commodities Exported from the United States. These statistics were retabulated and published using Schedule E, Standard International Trade Classification, Revision 2. Beginning in 1989, Schedule B classifications were based on the Harmonized System and made to coincide with the Standard International Trade Classification, Revision 3. This revision will affect the comparability of most export series beginning with the 1989 data for commodities.

Imports—The Bureau of the Census compiles import data from various customs forms required to be filed with customs officials. Data on import values are presented on two bases in this section: the c.i.f. (cost, insurance, and freight) and the customs import value (as appraised by the U.S. Customs Service in accordance with legal requirements of the Tariff Act of 1930, as amended). This latter valuation, primarily used for collection of import duties, frequently does not reflect the actual transaction value. Country of origin is defined as country where the merchandise was grown, mined, or manufactured. If country of origin is unknown, country of shipment is reported.

Imports are classified either as "General imports" or "Imports for consumption." *General imports* are a combination of entries for immediate consumption, entries into customs bonded warehouses, and entries into U.S. Foreign Trade Zones, thus generally reflecting total arrivals of merchandise. *Imports for consumption* are a combination of entries for immediate consumption, withdrawals from warehouses for consumption, and entries of merchandise into U.S. customs territory from U.S. Foreign Trade Zones, thus generally reflecting the total of the commodities entered into U.S. consumption channels.

Since July 1953, the import statistics include estimates, not classified by commodity, for certain low-valued shipments. For instance, from January 1985 through September 1989, import statistics include estimates for shipments valued under $1,001. Effective October 1989, import statistics are fully compiled on shipments valued over $1,250 or, under certain textile programs, for any article which must be reported on a formal entry. Value data for shipments valued under $1,251 and not required to be reported on formal entries are estimated for individual countries using factors based on the ratios of low-valued shipments to individual country totals for past periods. The estimated low-valued shipments generally amount to slightly less than 4 percent of the import total.

Prior to 1989, imports were based on the Tariff Schedule of the United States Annotated. The statistics were retabulated and published using Schedule A, Standard International Trade Classification, Revision 2. Beginning in 1989, the statistics are based on the Harmonized Tariff Schedule of the United States, which coincides with the Standard International Trade Classification, Revision 3. This revision will affect the comparability of most import commodity series beginning with the 1989 data.

Area coverage—Except as noted, the geographic area covered by the export and import trade statistics is the United States Customs area (includes the 50 States, the District of Columbia and Puerto Rico), the U.S. Virgin Islands (effective January 1981), and U.S. Foreign Trade Zones (effective July 1982). Data for selected tables and total values for 1980, have been revised to reflect the U.S. Virgin Islands' trade with foreign countries, where possible.

No. 1292. U.S. International Transactions, by Type of Transaction: 1980 to 1996

[In millions of dollars. Minus sign (-) indicates debits]

TYPE OF TRANSACTION	1980	1985	1988	1989	1990	1991	1992	1993	1994	1995	1996
Exports of goods and services [1]	344,440	382,747	580,233	641,659	697,083	717,728	736,704	762,861	840,006	968,189	1,032,478
Merchandise, excl. military [2 3]	224,250	215,915	320,230	362,120	389,307	416,913	440,352	456,832	502,463	575,940	611,869
Foods, feeds, and beverages	36,278	24,566	33,770	37,475	35,172	35,829	40,336	40,692	42,017	50,533	55,493
Industrial supplies and materials	72,066	61,159	90,019	99,826	105,503	109,826	109,592	111,870	121,552	146,375	147,860
Capital goods, except automotive	76,283	79,322	119,103	138,908	152,543	166,453	176,070	182,096	205,247	233,776	252,918
Automotive vehicles and parts [4]	17,443	24,945	33,397	34,866	36,465	40,008	47,027	52,534	57,777	61,827	64,460
Consumer goods (nonfood) [5]	17,751	14,593	26,961	37,317	43,719	46,858	51,424	54,655	59,981	64,425	70,160
Services	47,584	73,155	110,833	127,022	147,477	163,810	177,305	186,119	195,839	210,590	223,907
Transfers under U.S. military agency sales contracts	9,029	8,718	9,284	8,564	9,932	11,135	12,387	13,082	12,255	13,405	13,802
Travel	10,588	17,762	29,434	36,205	43,007	48,385	54,742	57,875	58,417	61,137	64,499
Passenger fares	2,591	4,411	8,976	10,657	15,298	15,854	16,618	16,611	17,083	18,534	19,579
Other transportation	11,618	14,674	19,811	21,106	22,745	23,331	23,691	23,894	25,861	28,063	29,115
Royalties and license fees	7,085	6,678	12,146	13,818	16,634	17,819	19,715	20,323	22,272	26,953	28,829
Other private services	6,276	20,035	[6]30,618	36,064	39,193	46,598	49,291	53,436	59,071	61,724	67,268
U.S. Government misc. services	398	878	664	587	668	690	861	899	880	775	815
Income on U.S. assets abroad	72,606	93,677	129,070	152,517	160,300	137,003	119,046	119,900	141,704	182,659	196,902
Direct investment	37,146	30,547	52,092	55,368	58,740	52,198	51,912	61,460	68,659	88,882	98,260
Other private receipts	32,898	57,631	70,275	91,496	91,048	76,781	60,020	53,332	68,946	89,064	94,078
U.S. Government receipts	2,562	5,499	6,703	5,653	10,512	8,023	7,114	5,108	4,099	4,713	4,564
Imports of goods, services and income	-333,774	-484,037	-662,403	-719,539	-756,522	-731,763	-763,773	-825,147	-948,544	-1,082,268	-1,155,101
Merchandise, excl. military [2 3]	-249,750	-338,088	-447,189	-477,365	-498,337	-490,981	-536,458	-589,441	-668,584	-749,364	-799,343
Foods, feeds, and beverages	-18,564	-21,850	-24,928	-24,898	-26,407	-26,205	-27,610	-27,866	-30,957	-33,176	-35,704
Industrial supplies and materials	-132,472	-114,008	-122,684	-135,363	-145,168	-132,983	-140,591	-152,437	-164,862	-183,818	-204,383
Capital goods, except automotive	-31,576	-61,287	-102,202	-112,156	-116,061	-120,802	-134,252	-152,305	-184,366	-221,431	-228,959
Automotive vehicles and parts [4]	-28,257	-64,905	-87,947	-87,356	-88,480	-85,696	-91,787	-102,420	-118,268	-124,773	-130,085
Consumer goods (nonfood) [5]	-34,268	-66,336	-96,425	-103,621	-105,053	-107,777	-122,656	-134,076	-146,358	-160,010	-171,118
Services	-41,491	-72,862	-99,491	-103,535	-118,783	-119,614	-119,464	-125,549	-134,097	-142,230	-150,440
Direct defense expenditures	-10,851	-13,108	-15,604	-15,313	-17,531	-16,409	-13,835	-12,202	-10,292	-9,820	-10,993
Travel	-10,397	-24,558	-32,114	-33,416	-37,349	-35,322	-38,552	-40,713	-43,782	-45,855	-48,712
Passenger Fares	-3,607	-6,444	-7,729	-8,249	-10,531	-10,012	-10,556	-11,313	-12,885	-14,313	-14,287
Other transportation	-11,790	-15,643	-20,969	-22,260	-25,168	-25,204	-25,459	-26,326	-27,983	-29,205	-29,100
Royalties and license fees	-724	-1,170	-2,601	-2,528	-3,135	-4,035	-5,074	-4,765	-5,518	-6,312	-7,036
Other private services	-2,909	-10,203	[6]-18,554	-19,896	-23,150	-26,516	-23,687	-27,897	-30,960	-33,970	-37,626
U.S. Government miscellaneous services	-1,214	-1,735	-1,921	-1,871	-1,919	-2,116	-2,301	-2,331	-2,657	-2,755	-2,886
Income on foreign assets in the United States	-42,532	-73,087	-115,722	-138,639	-139,402	-121,159	-107,851	-110,158	-145,863	-190,674	-205,318
Direct investment	-8,635	-7,213	-11,693	-6,507	-2,871	3,433	-317	-5,556	-21,230	-31,418	-33,817
Other private payments	-21,214	-42,745	-72,314	-93,768	-95,489	-83,063	-67,054	-63,041	-77,614	-97,977	-100,159
U.S. Government payments	-12,684	-23,129	-31,715	-38,364	-41,042	-41,529	-40,480	-41,561	-47,019	-61,279	-71,342
Unilateral transfers (excl. military grants, net	-8,349	-22,954	-26,266	-27,696	-35,219	4,510	-35,514	-37,640	-39,866	-35,075	-42,472
U.S. Government grants	-5,486	-11,268	-10,537	-10,911	-17,433	24,160	-15,799	-16,823	-15,816	-10,959	-14,634
U.S. Government pensions	-1,818	-2,138	-2,709	-2,744	-3,184	-3,730	-4,018	-4,061	-4,544	-3,420	-4,233
Private remittances and other transfers	-1,044	-9,549	-13,020	-14,041	-14,602	-15,920	-15,896	-16,736	-19,506	-20,696	-23,605

TYPE OF TRANSACTION	1980	1985	1988	1989	1990	1991	1992	1993	1994	1995	1996
U.S. assets abroad, net (increase/capital outflow (-))	**-86,967**	**-39,889**	**-100,087**	**-168,744**	**-74,011**	**-57,881**	**-68,622**	**-194,609**	**-150,695**	**-307,856**	**-306,830**
U.S. official reserve assets, net	-8,155	-3,858	-3,912	-25,293	-2,158	5,763	3,901	-1,379	5,346	-9,742	6,668
Special drawing rights	-16	-897	127	-535	-192	-177	2,316	-537	-441	-808	370
Reserve position in the International Monetary Fund	-1,667	908	1,025	471	731	-367	-2,692	-44	494	-2,466	-1,280
Foreign currencies	-6,472	-3,869	-5,064	-25,229	-2,697	6,307	4,277	-797	5,293	-6,468	7,578
U.S. Govt. assets, other than official reserve assets, net	-5,162	-2,821	2,967	1,259	2,307	2,911	-1,657	-342	-341	-280	-665
U.S. credits and other long-term assets	-9,860	-7,657	-7,680	-5,590	-8,430	-12,874	-7,398	-6,299	-5,208	-4,640	-4,909
Repayments on U.S. credits and other long-term assets [7]	4,456	4,719	10,370	6,723	10,867	16,776	5,807	6,270	5,052	4,258	4,155
U.S. foreign currency holdings and U.S. short-term assets, net	242	117	277	125	-130	-992	-66	-313	-185	102	89
U.S. private assets, net	-73,651	-33,211	-99,141	-144,710	-74,160	-66,555	-70,866	-192,889	-155,700	-297,834	-312,833
Direct investments abroad	-19,222	-14,065	-16,175	-36,834	-29,950	-31,369	-42,640	-78,164	-54,465	-95,509	-88,304
Foreign securities	-3,568	-7,481	-7,846	-22,070	-28,765	-45,673	-49,166	-146,253	-60,270	-98,960	-104,533
U.S. claims on unaffiliated foreigners reported by U.S. nonbanking concerns	-4,023	-10,342	-21,193	-27,646	-27,824	11,097	45	1,581	-32,804	-34,219	-31,777
U.S. claims reported by U.S. banks, n.i.e. [8]	-46,838	-1,323	-53,927	-58,160	12,379	-610	20,895	29,947	-8,161	-69,146	-88,219
Foreign assets in the U.S., net (increase/capital inflow (+))	**58,112**	**141,183**	**240,265**	**218,490**	**122,192**	**94,241**	**154,285**	**250,996**	**285,376**	**424,462**	**525,046**
Foreign official assets in the U.S., net	15,497	-1,119	39,758	8,503	33,910	17,389	40,477	72,153	40,253	109,757	122,778
U.S. Government securities	11,895	-1,139	43,050	1,532	30,243	16,147	22,403	53,014	36,822	72,547	115,482
U.S. Treasury securities	9,708	-838	41,741	149	29,576	14,846	18,454	48,952	30,745	68,813	111,151
Other	2,187	-301	1,309	1,383	667	1,301	3,949	4,062	6,077	3,734	4,331
Other U.S. Government liabilities	615	844	-467	160	1,868	1,367	2,191	1,713	2,344	1,082	1,404
U.S. liabilities reported by U.S. banks, n.i.e. [8]	-159	645	-319	4,976	3,385	-1,484	16,571	14,841	3,560	32,862	4,614
Other foreign official assets	3,145	-1,469	-2,506	1,835	-1,586	1,359	-688	2,585	-2,473	3,266	1,278
Other foreign assets in the United States, net	42,615	142,301	200,507	209,987	88,282	76,853	113,808	178,843	245,123	314,705	402,268
Direct investments in the United States	16,918	20,010	57,278	67,736	47,915	22,004	17,600	43,022	49,760	60,236	83,950
U.S. Treasury securities	2,645	20,433	20,239	29,618	-2,534	18,826	37,131	24,381	34,225	99,340	153,784
U.S. securities other than U.S. Treasury securities	5,457	50,962	26,353	38,767	1,592	35,144	30,043	80,092	57,006	95,268	131,682
U.S. liabilities to unaffiliated foreigners reported by U.S. nonbanking concerns	6,852	9,851	32,893	22,086	45,133	-3,115	13,573	10,489	-7,710	34,578	34,410
U.S. liabilities reported by U.S. banks, n.i.e. [8]	10,743	41,045	63,744	51,780	-3,824	3,994	15,461	20,859	111,842	25,283	-1,558
Allocations of special drawing rights	1,152	(X)	(X)	(X)	(X)	(X)	(X)	(X)	(X)	(X)	(X)
Statistical discrepancy	25,386	22,950	-11,743	55,830	46,476	-26,843	-23,080	43,550	13,724	31,548	-53,122
Balance on merchandise trade	-25,500	-122,173	-126,959	-115,245	-109,030	-74,068	-96,106	-132,609	-166,121	-173,424	-187,674
Balance on services	6,093	294	11,442	23,487	28,694	44,196	57,842	60,570	61,742	68,360	73,467
Balance on investment income	30,073	20,590	13,348	13,878	20,897	15,844	11,195	9,742	-4,159	-8,016	-8,416
Balance on goods, services, and income	10,666	-101,290	-102,170	-77,880	-59,439	-14,028	-27,069	-62,297	-108,539	-113,079	-122,623
Unilateral transfers, net	-8,349	-22,954	-26,266	-27,696	-35,219	4,510	-35,514	-37,640	-39,886	-35,075	-42,472
Balance on current account	2,317	-124,243	-128,436	-105,575	-94,657	-9,518	-62,583	-99,936	-148,405	-148,154	-165,095

- Represents zero. NA Not available. X Not applicable. [1] Excludes transfers of goods and services under U.S. military grant programs. [2] Excludes exports of goods under U.S. military agency sales contracts identified in Bureau of the Census export documents, excludes imports of goods under direct defense expenditures identified in Census import documents, and reflects various other adjustments (for valuation, coverage, and timing) of Census statistics to a balance of payments basis. [3] Includes other end-use items, not shown separately. [4] Includes engines. [5] Excludes automotive. [6] Break in series due to inclusion of new data. See Technical Note in *Survey of Current Business*, June 1979. [7] Includes sales of foreign obligations to foreigners. [8] Not included elsewhere.

Source: U.S. Bureau of Economic Analysis, *Survey of Current Business*, July 1996 and April 1997 issues. Major revisions to these data appear in the July 1997 issue of the *Survey of Current Business*.

No. 1293. U.S. Balances on International Transactions, by Area and Selected Country: 1994 to 1996

[In millions of dollars. Minus sign (-) indicates debits]

AREA OR COUNTRY	1994, BALANCE ON—			1995, BALANCE ON—			1996, BALANCE ON—		
	Merchandise trade[1]	Goods, services, and income	Current account	Merchandise trade[1]	Goods, services, and income	Current account	Merchandise trade[1]	Goods, services, and income	Current account
All areas	-166,121	-108,539	-148,405	-173,424	-113,079	-148,154	-187,674	-122,623	-165,095
Western Europe	-17,562	-21,979	-21,615	-15,206	-18,730	-18,051	-24,061	-27,766	-27,291
European Economic	-11,958	-18,548	-17,440	-12,711	-17,376	-15,993	-21,269	-26,559	-25,298
United Kingdom	1,112	-14,873	-13,641	1,291	-22,618	-21,394	1,485	-19,903	-18,697
Other Western Europe	-13,844	-7,501	-6,828	-11,537	1,090	1,991	-17,390	-6,478	-5,679
Eastern Europe	-481	-481	-4,181	-1,290	-989	-3,935	376	733	-2,364
Canada	-16,289	-5,610	-5,970	-20,502	-8,078	-8,443	-25,222	-12,014	-12,356
Latin America, other Western Hemisphere	3,506	18,050	8,528	-8,783	1,891	-8,072	-13,836	-1,615	-12,261
Australia	6,385	11,873	11,790	7,099	12,755	12,662	7,816	14,400	14,306
Japan[2]	-67,319	-64,500	-64,640	-60,351	-60,206	-60,334	-49,214	-49,163	-49,295
Other Asia and Africa	-74,450	-57,349	-73,467	-74,389	-52,790	-64,788	-83,535	-62,071	-79,189
International and unallocated	89	11,458	1,151	-	13,069	2,806	2	14,874	3,356

- Represents or rounds to zero. [1] Adjusted to balance of payments basis; excludes exports under U.S. military sales contracts and imports under direct defense expenditures. [2] Includes Ryukyu Islands.

Source: U.S. Bureau of Economic Analysis, *Survey of Current Business*, July 1996 and April 1997 issues. Major revisions to these data appear in the July 1997 issue of the *Survey of Current Business*.

No. 1294. Private Services Transaction, by Type of Service and Country: 1990 to 1995

[In millions of dollars]

TYPE OF SERVICE AND COUNTRY	EXPORTS				IMPORTS			
	1990	1993	1994	1995	1990	1993	1994	1995
Total private services	136,877	172,139	182,704	196,411	99,333	111,016	121,148	129,655
Travel	43,007	57,875	58,417	61,137	37,349	40,713	43,782	45,855
Overseas	30,806	45,298	47,299	52,073	28,929	31,859	34,534	36,220
Canada	7,093	7,458	6,252	6,207	3,541	3,692	3,914	4,319
Mexico	5,108	5,119	4,866	2,857	4,879	5,162	5,334	5,316
Passenger fares	15,298	16,611	17,083	18,534	10,531	11,313	12,885	14,313
Other transportation	22,745	23,894	25,861	28,063	25,168	26,328	27,983	29,205
Freight	8,063	8,668	9,698	10,780	14,353	14,846	16,444	17,089
Port services	13,662	14,222	15,101	16,091	9,920	10,587	10,621	11,215
Other	1,020	1,005	1,066	1,193	895	895	919	902
Royalties and license fees	16,634	20,323	22,272	26,953	3,135	4,765	5,518	6,312
Other private services	39,193	53,436	59,071	61,724	23,150	27,897	30,980	33,970
Affiliated services	13,622	16,740	18,162	19,458	9,118	10,618	11,755	13,723
Unaffiliated services	25,571	36,696	40,910	42,265	14,033	17,279	19,225	20,247
Education	5,126	6,738	7,175	7,517	658	767	816	877
Financial services	4,417	4,999	5,626	6,109	2,475	1,371	1,611	1,707
Insurance, net	230	1,020	1,506	1,395	1,910	3,095	3,781	4,481
Telecommunications	2,735	2,785	2,871	2,848	5,583	6,365	6,924	6,773
Business, professional, and technical services	6,951	13,296	15,728	16,264	1,891	4,012	4,262	4,502
Advertising	130	338	489	510	243	646	725	686
Computer and data processing services	1,031	2,308	2,724	2,823	44	304	244	462
Management, consulting, and public relations services	354	826	1,138	1,228	135	287	318	351
Legal services	451	1,442	1,614	1,568	111	321	388	406
Construction, engineering, architectural, & mining services	867	2,407	2,461	2,623	170	319	308	305
Other services	947	1,573	1,655	1,832	135	806	1,009	953
Canada	16,011	17,657	17,363	17,949	9,282	10,443	11,521	12,378
Europe	48,644	63,085	65,808	71,268	39,849	44,734	48,862	52,187
Belgium-Luxembourg	1,795	2,230	2,509	2,610	1,023	938	1,119	1,363
France	5,565	6,870	6,563	7,548	4,168	4,841	5,559	5,804
Germany	7,478	11,400	11,472	12,675	6,824	6,888	7,296	7,764
Italy	3,319	4,099	4,164	4,401	3,474	3,491	3,791	3,794
Netherlands	3,278	4,149	4,900	5,757	1,937	2,056	2,396	2,928
United Kingdom	13,027	17,265	17,092	17,958	11,567	13,839	14,585	16,163
Other	(NA)	8,613	10,040	10,660	(NA)	7,215	8,391	9,045
Eastern Europe	1,003	1,791	2,201	2,478	799	1,520	1,944	2,029
Latin America and other Western Hemisphere	21,226	27,786	30,499	30,294	19,401	21,443	23,406	24,155
Mexico	7,387	8,427	8,814	6,205	7,386	8,183	8,525	8,586
Venezuela	1,284	2,449	2,129	2,441	669	727	750	688
Other	(NA)	6,996	7,580	8,348	(NA)	3,952	4,379	4,467
Other countries	45,674	58,847	64,341	71,622	28,095	32,511	35,719	38,638
Int'l organizations and unallocated	5,325	4,764	4,688	5,277	2,706	1,887	1,637	2,296

NA Not available.

Source: U.S. Bureau of Economic Analysis, *Survey of Current Business, November 1996.*

No. 1295. International Investment Position: 1980 to 1995

[In millions of dollars. Estimates for end of year; subject to considerable error due to nature of basic data]

TYPE OF INVESTMENT	1980	1985	1990	1991	1992	1993	1994	1995
U.S. net international investment position:								
Current cost	**392,547**	**132,845**	**-251,112**	**-355,064**	**-512,784**	**-503,541**	**-580,095**	**-813,976**
Market value	(NA)	135,767	-211,670	-349,019	-568,398	-412,544	-492,482	-773,653
U.S. assets abroad:								
Current cost	**936,275**	**1,303,965**	**2,066,353**	**2,131,731**	**2,146,389**	**2,437,613**	**2,546,189**	**2,931,904**
Market value	(NA)	1,295,557	2,178,114	2,314,961	2,285,593	2,750,318	2,825,830	3,352,911
U.S. official reserve assets	171,412	117,930	174,664	159,223	147,435	164,945	163,394	176,061
Gold	155,816	85,834	102,406	92,561	87,168	102,556	100,110	101,279
Special drawing rights	2,610	7,293	10,989	11,240	8,503	9,039	10,039	11,037
Reserve position in IMF	2,852	11,947	9,076	9,488	11,759	11,818	12,030	14,649
Foreign currencies	10,134	12,856	52,193	45,934	40,005	41,532	41,215	49,096
U.S. Government assets, other	63,865	87,752	81,993	79,079	80,656	80,945	81,269	81,548
U.S. loans and other long-term assets	62,023	85,814	81,365	77,433	79,021	79,032	79,188	79,570
U.S. foreign currency holdings and short-term assets	1,842	1,938	628	1,646	1,635	1,913	2,081	1,978
U.S. private assets:								
Current cost	700,998	1,098,283	1,809,726	1,893,429	1,918,298	2,191,723	2,301,526	2,674,295
Market value	(NA)	1,089,875	1,921,457	2,076,659	2,057,502	2,504,428	2,581,167	3,095,302
Direct investments abroad:								
Current cost	396,249	394,760	620,031	644,307	659,426	714,842	779,300	880,123
Market value	(NA)	386,352	731,762	827,537	798,630	1,027,547	1,058,941	1,301,130
Foreign securities	62,454	114,288	228,693	302,425	336,546	550,633	556,241	721,749
U.S. claims on unaffiliated foreigners [1]	38,429	141,872	265,315	256,295	254,303	242,022	273,686	311,140
U.S. claims reported by U.S. banks [2]	203,866	447,363	695,687	690,402	668,023	684,226	692,299	761,283
Foreign assets in the U.S.:								
Current cost	**543,728**	**1,171,120**	**2,317,465**	**2,486,785**	**2,659,173**	**2,941,154**	**3,126,284**	**3,745,880**
Market value	(NA)	1,159,790	2,389,784	2,663,980	2,853,991	3,162,862	3,318,312	4,126,564
Foreign official assets in the U.S.	176,062	202,482	375,339	401,678	442,753	516,603	546,015	677,910
U.S. Government securities	118,189	145,063	295,005	315,932	335,695	388,312	415,005	496,900
Other U.S. Government liabilities	13,367	15,803	17,243	18,610	20,801	22,514	24,858	25,941
U.S. liabilities reported by U.S. banks [2]	30,381	26,734	39,880	38,396	54,967	69,721	73,281	108,143
Other foreign official assets	14,125	14,882	23,211	28,740	31,290	36,056	32,871	46,926
Other foreign assets in the U.S:								
Current cost	367,666	968,638	1,942,156	2,085,107	2,216,420	2,424,551	2,580,269	3,067,970
Market value	(NA)	957,306	2,014,445	2,262,302	2,411,238	2,646,259	2,772,297	3,448,654
Direct investments:								
Current cost	125,944	231,326	467,312	491,942	499,394	539,151	579,826	638,519
Market value	(NA)	219,996	539,601	669,137	694,212	760,859	771,854	1,019,203
U.S. securities other than U.S. Treasury securities	74,114	207,868	467,437	559,180	620,219	730,569	752,792	998,596
U.S. liabilities to unaffiliated foreigners [1]	30,426	86,993	213,406	208,908	220,666	229,038	197,325	232,891
U.S. liabilities reported by U.S. banks [2]	121,069	354,497	631,597	635,571	651,031	671,890	783,732	809,015
U.S. Treasury securities	16,113	87,954	162,404	189,506	225,110	253,903	266,594	388,949

NA Not available. [1] Reported by U.S. nonbanking concerns. [2] Not included elsewhere.

Source: U.S. Bureau of Economic Analysis, *Survey of Current Business*, July 1996. Major revisions to these data appear in the July 1997 issue of the *Survey of Current Business*.

No. 1296. U.S. Reserve Assets: 1980 to 1996

[In billions of dollars. As of end of year, except as indicated]

TYPE	1980	1985	1989	1990	1991	1992	1993	1994	1995	1996
Total	**26.8**	**43.2**	**74.6**	**83.3**	**77.7**	**71.3**	**73.4**	**74.3**	**85.8**	**75.1**
Gold stock [1]	11.2	11.1	11.1	11.1	11.1	11.1	11.1	11.1	11.1	11.0
Special drawing rights	2.6	7.3	10.0	11.0	11.2	8.5	9.0	10.0	11.0	10.2
Foreign currencies	10.1	12.9	44.6	52.2	45.9	40.0	41.5	41.2	49.1	38.3
Reserve position in IMF [2]	2.9	11.9	9.0	9.1	9.5	11.8	11.8	12.0	14.6	15.4

[1] Includes gold in Exchange Stabilization Fund; excludes gold held under earmark at Federal Reserve banks for foreign and international accounts. Beginning 1975, gold assets were valued at $42.22 pursuant to the amending of Section 2 of the Par Value Modification Act, PL-93-110, approved September 21, 1973. [2] International Monetary Fund.

Source: Board of Governors of the Federal Reserve System, *Federal Reserve Bulletin*, monthly; and Department of the Treasury, *Treasury Bulletin*, monthly.

No. 1297. Foreign Direct Investment Position in the U.S. on a Historical Cost Basis—Value, by Area and Industry: 1980 to 1994

[In millions of dollars. Book value at year end. Covers U.S. firms, including real estate investments in which foreign interest or ownership was 10 percent or more. Minus sign (-) indicates a negative position]

AREA AND INDUSTRY	1980	1985	1988	1989	1990	1991	1992	1993	1994, prel.
All areas [1]	**83,046**	**184,615**	**314,754**	**368,924**	**394,911**	**419,108**	**427,566**	**464,110**	**504,401**
Petroleum	12,200	28,270	36,006	40,345	42,882	40,051	37,555	31,740	34,048
Manufacturing	32,993	59,584	122,582	150,949	152,805	157,115	158,873	166,397	184,484
Finance and insurance	12,027	27,429	44,010	59,597	35,482	44,748	48,780	74,733	78,048
Trade, wholesale and retail	15,210	35,873	53,590	54,005	60,152	65,334	67,866	72,808	79,542
Canada	**12,162**	**17,131**	**26,566**	**30,370**	**29,544**	**36,834**	**37,843**	**40,143**	**43,223**
Petroleum	1,817	1,589	1,181	1,141	1,373	2,468	2,443	2,455	2,585
Manufacturing	5,227	4,607	9,730	9,766	9,201	15,716	15,598	15,306	16,911
Finance and insurance	1,612	4,006	5,769	7,356	6,033	7,354	7,235	8,168	8,496
Europe	**54,688**	**121,413**	**208,942**	**239,190**	**247,320**	**256,053**	**255,570**	**287,084**	**312,876**
Petroleum	10,137	25,636	33,499	32,649	34,284	31,436	29,167	24,396	25,818
Manufacturing	21,953	45,841	95,641	118,129	115,831	114,248	115,215	124,454	138,804
Finance and insurance	8,873	17,022	27,121	33,157	21,310	27,715	28,550	46,895	45,194
United Kingdom	14,105	43,555	95,698	103,458	98,676	100,085	90,931	102,351	113,504
Petroleum	-257	12,155	19,522	16,666	15,900	14,068	11,060	9,963	10,906
Manufacturing	6,159	11,687	41,708	50,166	42,365	41,924	40,818	42,783	48,190
Finance and insurance	3,350	6,483	11,256	12,790	11,609	13,391	12,436	19,927	16,343
Netherlands	19,140	37,056	48,128	56,734	64,671	63,113	69,191	72,172	70,645
Petroleum	9,265	11,481	9,045	10,061	13,267	12,444	11,590	12,067	12,770
Manufacturing	4,777	13,351	17,843	23,090	24,734	19,540	22,793	23,286	19,881
Switzerland	5,070	10,568	14,372	18,746	17,674	18,482	19,048	22,161	25,330
Manufacturing	3,116	6,881	7,613	11,798	10,651	10,222	10,280	11,337	13,111
Finance and insurance	1,033	5,425	3,506	4,492	4,833	4,806	4,460	5,497	6,923
Germany [2]	7,596	14,816	25,250	28,386	28,232	29,335	29,768	34,849	39,550
Manufacturing	3,875	6,015	13,980	15,560	15,716	15,659	15,765	17,903	21,321
Finance and insurance	1,248	(D)	2,683	3,139	1,652	1,413	2,073	4,893	5,506
Other Europe [3]	8,777	15,417	25,494	31,866	38,067	45,038	46,632	55,551	63,847
Petroleum	991	(D)	4,580	4,786	4,835	4,653	5,768	1,959	1,604
Manufacturing	4,026	7,907	14,497	17,515	22,363	26,903	25,559	29,145	34,301
Finance and insurance	1,193	(D)	406	2,519	-1,817	-589	-298	5,433	5,398
Japan	**4,723**	**19,313**	**51,126**	**67,268**	**83,091**	**95,142**	**96,626**	**99,208**	**103,120**
Other areas	**11,472**	**26,758**	**28,120**	**32,096**	**34,956**	**31,079**	**34,525**	**37,675**	**45,182**

D Withheld to avoid disclosure of data of individual companies. [1] Area totals include industries not shown separately. [2] For 1980 to 1989, includes only the Federal Republic of Germany. For 1990 to 1994, also includes the former German Democratic Republic (GDR). This change has no effect on the data because, prior to 1990, there were no U.S. affiliates of the former GDR. [3] Direct investments in 1994 (in millions of dollars): Belgium and Luxembourg, 5,673; France, 33,496; Italy, 2,437; and Sweden, 8,077. France, 33,496; Italy, 2,437; and Sweden, 9,112.

Source: U.S. Bureau of Economic Analysis, *Survey of Current Business*, August 1995, and earlier issues.

No. 1298. U.S. Affiliates of Foreign Companies—Assets, Sales, Employment, Land, Exports, and Imports: 1994

[A U.S. affiliate is a U.S. business enterprise in which one foreign owner (individual, branch, partnership, association, trust, corporation, or government) has a direct or indirect voting interest of 10 percent or more. Universe estimates based on a sample survey of nonbank affiliates with assets, sales, or net income of $10 million or more]

INDUSTRY	Total assets (mil. dol.)	Sales (mil. dol.) [1]	Employment (1,000) [2]	Employee compensation (mil. dol.)	GROSS BOOK VALUE (mil. dol.)		Merchandise exports [4] (mil. dol.)	Merchandise imports [4] (mil. dol.)
					Plant and equipment [3]	Land		
Total	2,208,329	**1,447,626**	**4,866.6**	**200,841**	**687,264**	**63,841**	**113,774**	**219,172**
Petroleum	99,416	109,210	110.2	6,115	104,257	2,643	3,973	16,815
Manufacturing	546,422	518,517	2,251.6	105,703	285,946	17,075	48,365	66,961
Chemicals and allied products	190,512	144,256	508.5	28,187	112,935	9,644	14,198	13,870
Wholesale trade [5]	219,325	452,615	485.6	21,888	67,099	3,126	57,106	131,290
Motor vehicles and auto parts and supplies	74,288	120,172	79.9	4,155	34,670	877	8,552	42,487
Farm-product raw materials	9,158	42,655	20.6	719	2,527	123	15,466	2,317
Retail trade	46,588	94,183	764.6	14,004	24,442	2,852	1,466	3,154
Finance, except banking	523,641	33,527	46.7	5,493	6,822	791	12	6
Insurance	443,147	78,250	151.6	7,877	24,022	1,331	-	-
Real estate	104,823	14,968	30.4	1,166	69,026	23,348	13	2
Services	121,337	61,741	595.5	18,659	45,993	7,570	698	367
Other	103,630	84,618	430.3	19,896	59,658	5,105	2,136	537

- Represents zero. [1] Excludes returns, discounts, allowances, and sales and excise taxes. [2] Average number of full-time and part-time employees. [3] Includes mineral rights and minor amounts of property other than land. [4] F.a.s. value at port of exportation. [5] Includes industries not shown separately.

Source: U.S. Bureau of Economic Analysis, *Survey of Current Business*, July 1996; and *Foreign Direct Investment in the United States, Operations of U.S. Affiliates of Foreign Companies*, Revised 1993 Estimates and Preliminary 1994 Estimates.

No. 1299. Foreign Direct Investment in the United States—Gross Book Value and Employment of U.S. Affiliates of Foreign Companies, by State: 1981 to 1994

[A U.S. affiliate is a U.S. business enterprise in which one foreign owner (individual, branch, partnership, association, trust corporation, or government) has a direct or indirect voting interest of 10 percent or more. Universe estimates based on a sample survey of nonbank affiliates with assets, sales, or net income of $10 million or more]

DIVISION, STATE, AND OTHER AREA	GROSS BOOK VALUE OF PROPERTY, PLANT, AND EQUIPMENT (mil. dol.)				TOTAL EMPLOYMENT				
								1994	
	1981	1990	1993	1994	1981 (1,000)	1990 (1,000)	1993 (1,000)	Total (1,000)	Percent of all businesses
Total	187,956	578,355	705,685	751,105	2,416.6	4,734.5	4,765.6	4,886.6	(X)
United States	178,003	552,902	687,065	716,032	2,402.3	4,704.4	4,722.5	4,828.2	4.9
New England	5,686	19,524	25,464	27,861	143.9	280.8	273.6	285.0	(NA)
Maine	1,637	2,080	2,511	2,692	17.7	26.6	24.2	24.8	5.5
New Hampshire	409	1,446	2,045	2,136	13.9	25.9	30.7	29.6	6.4
Vermont	315	631	861	907	6.0	7.7	7.1	7.8	3.5
Massachusetts	1,712	8,890	10,928	11,878	55.6	131.2	119.6	129.8	5.0
Rhode Island	359	1,120	2,032	2,131	9.9	13.3	14.1	16.5	4.3
Connecticut	1,254	5,357	7,077	8,137	40.8	75.9	77.9	76.5	5.6
Middle Atlantic	20,216	71,619	93,901	98,601	480.2	796.1	800.1	800.3	(NA)
New York	7,892	36,424	47,936	49,588	210.3	347.5	351.1	356.0	5.4
New Jersey	6,552	18,608	23,865	25,757	134.9	227.0	212.6	211.2	6.9
Pennsylvania	5,772	16,587	22,101	23,256	135.0	221.6	236.4	233.1	5.1
East North Central	19,215	74,495	94,782	100,809	388.5	812.8	796.6	801.7	(NA)
Ohio	5,178	20,549	25,166	27,249	99.9	219.1	206.9	209.4	4.7
Indiana	1,883	13,426	15,880	17,032	47.0	126.9	124.6	129.0	5.4
Illinois	5,646	23,420	30,374	31,994	113.6	245.8	236.2	229.0	4.8
Michigan	4,188	12,012	16,459	17,224	65.9	139.6	150.1	159.4	4.4
Wisconsin	2,320	5,068	6,903	7,110	62.2	81.4	78.8	74.9	3.4
West North Central	8,400	28,155	24,391	26,773	112.2	248.4	247.4	258.6	(NA)
Minnesota	2,902	11,972	8,229	8,506	33.0	89.8	84.6	82.9	4.1
Iowa	1,032	2,712	3,831	4,329	21.6	32.8	31.4	35.4	3.1
Missouri	1,894	5,757	6,804	7,922	32.6	73.7	76.7	80.4	3.7
North Dakota	1,155	1,251	1,192	1,210	3.5	3.1	4.5	3.8	1.6
South Dakota	299	553	644	671	1.3	4.5	4.6	5.4	2.0
Nebraska	241	776	1,065	1,183	5.6	14.9	16.3	17.2	2.6
Kansas	877	5,134	2,626	2,952	14.6	29.6	29.3	31.5	3.2
South Atlantic	33,271	94,795	119,855	126,296	476.0	934.7	971.5	996.0	(NA)
Delaware	1,869	5,818	6,505	6,679	36.0	43.1	33.2	33.7	10.7
Maryland	2,103	5,713	6,503	7,342	45.1	79.6	74.9	78.9	4.4
District of Columbia	547	3,869	4,766	4,968	3.2	11.4	10.8	11.1	2.7
Virginia	3,046	10,702	14,246	16,635	49.8	113.3	128.9	131.6	5.3
West Virginia	3,992	7,975	9,015	9,230	35.4	34.9	35.1	34.6	6.4
North Carolina	5,543	15,234	21,189	22,718	89.0	161.0	211.4	221.8	7.6
South Carolina	5,318	10,067	13,348	13,966	65.1	104.7	105.8	112.4	8.3
Georgia	4,558	16,729	20,401	21,272	78.5	161.0	167.6	173.7	6.2
Florida	6,295	18,659	23,682	23,488	73.9	205.7	203.8	196.2	3.9
East South Central	9,802	29,766	42,055	45,382	121.7	261.9	290.2	294.7	(NA)
Kentucky	1,848	9,229	13,543	14,993	26.0	65.7	75.7	78.7	5.6
Tennessee	3,747	10,280	15,392	16,373	57.4	116.9	129.7	131.4	6.2
Alabama	2,776	7,300	9,574	10,058	27.0	55.7	61.6	60.6	4.2
Mississippi	1,431	2,969	3,546	3,958	11.3	23.6	23.2	24.0	2.8
West South Central	34,651	82,904	94,294	101,479	268.5	433.7	434.5	449.0	(NA)
Arkansas	636	2,344	3,078	3,554	17.5	29.2	30.4	31.6	3.6
Louisiana	7,872	17,432	21,945	23,475	47.0	61.4	60.4	59.4	4.2
Oklahoma	2,760	6,049	5,623	5,849	25.0	43.6	39.0	37.9	3.6
Texas	23,383	57,079	63,648	68,601	179.0	299.5	304.7	320.1	4.9
Mountain	12,353	33,197	36,461	39,498	97.9	197.1	198.1	208.9	(NA)
Montana	1,235	2,181	2,523	2,434	3.0	5.1	5.3	5.0	1.8
Idaho	312	776	838	937	3.8	11.7	11.3	11.8	3.1
Wyoming	2,144	2,782	3,048	3,544	4.2	5.8	5.8	5.8	3.5
Colorado	2,369	6,544	7,158	8,250	24.7	56.3	60.0	65.3	4.3
New Mexico	997	4,312	4,565	4,717	7.9	17.4	16.2	18.4	3.6
Arizona	2,949	7,234	6,695	5,681	30.6	57.1	52.4	50.1	3.4
Utah	1,791	3,918	4,636	5,620	16.8	21.0	25.0	27.7	3.8
Nevada	556	5,450	6,998	8,315	6.9	22.7	22.1	22.8	3.4
Pacific	34,409	118,445	143,063	149,514	313.3	739.7	710.6	737.7	(NA)
Washington	2,430	7,965	10,294	10,817	26.0	77.5	77.6	78.5	4.0
Oregon	845	3,427	4,734	5,449	13.1	39.1	42.5	47.0	4.0
California	20,404	75,768	87,300	92,367	248.4	555.9	528.6	552.4	5.2
Alaska	(D)	19,435	24,705	24,399	8.8	13.2	9.5	8.8	4.6
Hawaii	(D)	11,830	16,030	16,482	17.0	53.0	52.4	51.0	11.5
Puerto Rico	413	1,499	2,240	2,290	9.5	16.1	26.9	21.6	(NA)
Other territories and offshore	7,496	18,484	17,547	17,596	3.1	9.0	11.3	11.4	(NA)
Foreign	2,044	5,470	18,823	15,188	1.6	5.0	2.9	5.4	(NA)

D Withheld to avoid disclosure of data of individual companies. NA Not available. X Not applicable.

Source: U.S. Bureau of Economic Analysis, *Survey of Current Business*, May 1995, and *Foreign Direct Investment in the United States, Operations of U.S. Affiliates of Foreign Companies*, annual; and *Foreign Direct Investment in the United States, 1992 Benchmark Survey*.

No. 1300. U.S. Businesses Acquired or Established by Foreign Direct Investors—Investment Outlays, by Industry of U.S. Business Enterprise and Country of Ultimate Beneficial Owner: 1990 to 1995

[In millions of dollars. Foreign direct investment is the ownership or control, directly or indirectly, by one foreign individual branch, partnership, association, trust, corporation, or government of 10 percent or more of the voting securities of a U.S. business enterprise or an equivalent interest in an unincorporated one. Data represent number and full cost of acquisitions of existing U.S. business enterprises, including business segments or operating units of existing U.S. business enterprises and establishments of new enterprises. Investments may be made by the foreign direct investor itself, or indirectly by an existing U.S. affiliate of the foreign direct investor. Covers investments in U.S. business enterprises with assets of over $1 million, or ownership of 200 acres of U.S. land]

INDUSTRY AND COUNTRY	1990	1991	1992	1993	1994	1995, prel.
Total	**65,932**	**25,538**	**15,333**	**26,229**	**45,626**	**54,368**
INDUSTRY						
Petroleum	1,141	702	463	882	469	1,731
Manufacturing	23,898	11,461	6,014	11,090	21,218	28,493
Wholesale trade	1,676	623	696	837	2,156	(D)
Retail trade	1,250	1,605	256	1,495	1,542	2,957
Banking [1]	897	482	529	958	2,026	2,592
Finance, except banking [1]	2,121	2,199	797	1,599	2,195	5,751
Insurance	2,093	2,102	291	1,105	150	(D)
Real estate	7,771	3,823	2,161	1,883	2,647	2,679
Services	19,369	2,256	2,023	4,162	7,163	4,142
Other [2]	5,716	284	2,101	2,218	5,760	3,963
COUNTRY						
Canada	3,430	3,454	1,351	3,797	4,128	6,481
Europe	36,011	13,994	8,344	16,845	31,920	36,654
France	10,217	4,976	406	1,249	1,404	1,217
Germany [3]	2,363	1,922	1,964	2,841	3,328	14,155
Netherlands	2,247	1,661	1,331	2,074	1,537	885
Switzerland	3,905	1,327	1,259	804	5,044	4,198
United Kingdom	13,096	2,169	2,255	8,238	17,261	9,676
Other Europe	4,183	1,939	1,129	1,639	3,346	6,523
Latin America and other Western Hemisphere	796	375	1,436	874	1,352	1,329
South and Central America	399	108	1,152	527	(D)	(D)
Other Western Hemisphere	397	267	286	347	(D)	(D)
Africa	(D)	(D)	(D)	(D)	(D)	(D)
Middle East	472	1,006	238	1,306	(D)	500
Asia and Pacific	23,170	6,560	3,716	3,004	5,263	9,169
Australia	1,412	251	164	129	1,522	2,486
Japan	19,933	5,357	2,921	2,065	2,715	3,758
Other Asia and Pacific	1,825	952	631	810	1,026	2,923

D Suppressed to avoid disclosure of data of individual companies. [1] Prior to 1992, "banking" excludes, and "finance, except banking" includes, savings institutions and credit unions. Beginning with 1992, savings institutions and credit unions have been reclassified from "finance, except banking" to "banking". [2] For investments in which more than one investor participated, each investor and each investor's outlays are classified by country of each ultimate beneficial owner. [3] Prior to 1990, this line includes data only for the Federal Republic of Germany. Beginning in 1990, this line also includes the former German Democratic Republic (GDR). This change has no effect on the data because, prior to 1991, there were no U.S. affiliates of the former GDR.

Source: U.S. Bureau of Economic Analysis, *Survey of Current Business*, July 1996.

No. 1301. U.S. Businesses Acquired by Foreign Direct Investors—Assets, Sales, and Employment, by Industry of U.S. Business Enterprise: 1994 and 1995

[See headnote, table 1300. Minus sign (-) indicates loss]

INDUSTRY	1994					1995, prel.				
	Total assets (mil. dol.)	Sales (mil. dol.)	Net income (mil. dol.)	Employment (1,000)	Acres of land owned (1,000)	Total assets (mil. dol.)	Sales (mil. dol.)	Net income (mil. dol.)	Employment (1,000)	Acres of land owned (1,000)
Total	**77,829**	**56,261**	**1,229**	**289**	**1,208.2**	**98,390**	**53,849**	**1,886**	**386**	**1,006.7**
Petroleum	1,217	(D)	1	1	(D)	4,460	(D)	(D)	(D)	(D)
Manufacturing	25,251	19,593	114	101	(D)	40,196	28,190	(D)	130	40.9
Wholesale trade	3,259	6,582	(D)	10	1.6	(D)	5,410	-1	9	(D)
Retail trade	2,894	(D)	-109	(D)	(D)	4,139	8,069	72	130	1.5
Depository institutions	12,619	(D)	(D)	(D)	(D)	16,325	(D)	(D)	(D)	(D)
Finance, except banking	4,903	569	79	(D)	-	12,277	812	(D)	3	-
Insurance	1,870	519	8	(D)	(D)	(D)	(D)	(D)	(D)	-
Real estate	4,064	(D)	-4	(D)	14.8	2,915	288	40	(Z)	9.5
Services	5,348	3,292	-68	32	10.9	5,888	3,393	45	48	(D)
Other [1]	16,413	15,093	648	66	(D)	7,933	2,820	(D)	(D)	(D)

- Represents or rounds to zero. D Withheld to avoid disclosure of data of individual companies. [1] Includes agriculture, forestry, and fishing; mining; construction; transportation; and communication and public utilities.

Source: U.S. Bureau of Economic Analysis, *Survey of Current Business*, July 1996; and unpublished data.

No. 1302. U.S. Direct Investment Position Abroad on a Historical-Cost Basis, by Country: 1990 to 1995

[In millions of dollars. U.S. investment abroad is the ownership or control by one U.S. person of 10% or more of the voting securities of an incorporated foreign business enterprise or an equivalent interest in a unincorporated foreign business enterprise. Negative position can occur when a U.S. parent company's liabilities to the foreign affiliate are greater than its equity in, and loans to the foreign affiliate]

COUNTRY	1990	1991	1992	1993	1994	1995
All countries	430,521	467,844	502,063	564,283	621,044	711,621
Canada	69,508	70,711	68,690	69,922	74,987	81,387
Europe	214,739	235,163	248,744	285,735	310,031	363,527
Austria	1,113	1,268	1,371	1,312	1,577	2,094
Belgium	9,464	10,611	11,381	11,697	14,213	17,786
Denmark	1,726	1,940	1,876	1,735	1,963	2,251
Finland	544	386	343	414	621	830
France	19,164	21,569	25,157	24,312	27,860	32,645
Germany	27,609	32,411	33,003	36,811	39,622	43,001
Greece	282	306	372	410	447	437
Ireland	5,894	6,471	7,607	9,019	10,159	10,970
Italy	14,063	15,085	13,015	12,748	14,578	16,718
Luxembourg	1,697	1,734	2,031	5,611	6,112	7,661
Netherlands	19,120	20,293	20,700	20,911	25,127	37,421
Norway	4,209	4,318	3,825	3,757	4,282	4,904
Portugal	897	1,034	1,290	1,264	1,465	1,712
Spain	7,868	8,088	6,757	6,689	6,316	9,689
Sweden	1,787	2,323	1,881	2,374	2,675	12,226
Switzerland	25,099	25,682	28,696	33,056	34,351	36,342
Turkey	522	545	732	995	1,079	1,167
United Kingdom	72,707	79,819	85,176	109,208	111,255	119,938
Other	974	1,282	1,729	3,411	4,307	5,735
Latin America	71,413	77,677	91,308	100,482	112,226	122,765
South America	22,933	24,607	28,760	31,210	37,841	46,970
Argentina	2,531	2,831	3,327	4,442	5,945	7,962
Brazil	14,384	14,997	16,313	16,772	18,796	23,590
Chile	1,896	2,069	2,544	2,749	4,384	5,510
Colombia	1,677	1,876	3,053	2,930	3,282	3,414
Ecuador	280	321	295	555	736	830
Peru	599	492	620	622	819	1,213
Venezuela	1,087	1,427	1,972	2,362	2,991	3,372
Other	479	594	636	778	686	1,078
Central America	20,415	23,939	25,579	28,092	30,408	31,408
Costa Rica	251	417	274	296	566	790
Guatemala	130	107	115	139	134	155
Honduras	262	255	239	159	186	236
Mexico	10,313	12,501	13,730	15,221	15,714	14,037
Panama	9,289	10,484	11,038	12,043	13,538	15,908
Other	169	175	182	233	269	282
Other Western Hemisphere	28,065	29,131	36,969	41,180	43,978	44,387
Bahamas	4,004	3,864	4,167	3,138	2,736	1,566
Barbados	252	291	340	471	551	792
Bermuda	20,169	22,262	26,736	28,686	27,561	27,807
Dominican Republic	529	661	779	1,039	1,191	1,274
Jamaica	625	763	892	1,049	1,259	1,400
Netherlands Antilles	-4,501	-5,072	-1,989	-62	1,823	2,473
Trinidad and Tobago	485	510	565	691	771	813
U.K. Islands, Caribbean	5,929	5,397	5,401	5,544	7,327	7,615
Other	574	455	75	645	759	648
Africa	3,650	4,427	4,469	5,469	5,530	6,516
Egypt	1,231	1,246	1,334	1,510	1,412	1,409
Nigeria	-401	529	301	478	322	595
South Africa	775	868	879	900	1,013	1,269
Other	2,045	1,784	1,955	2,581	2,783	3,244
Middle East	3,959	4,963	5,759	6,571	6,794	7,982
Israel	746	826	1,335	1,604	1,357	1,574
Saudi Arabia	1,899	2,303	2,351	2,587	2,655	3,371
United Arab Emirates	409	416	429	524	531	675
Other	905	1,419	1,644	1,856	2,250	2,362
Asia and Pacific	64,716	72,218	79,963	92,671	108,075	125,968
Australia	15,110	16,072	16,928	19,047	19,900	24,713
China	354	426	563	916	1,856	1,997
Hong Kong	6,055	6,656	8,693	10,063	13,018	13,780
India	372	415	484	599	783	836
Indonesia	3,207	3,826	4,384	4,864	4,885	7,050
Japan	22,599	25,403	26,591	31,095	36,677	39,198
Korea, Republic of	2,695	2,900	2,912	3,427	4,061	5,322
Malaysia	1,466	1,774	1,596	1,975	2,343	3,653
New Zealand	3,156	2,949	3,314	3,084	3,622	4,530
Philippines	1,355	1,395	1,666	1,953	2,324	2,648
Singapore	3,975	5,363	6,715	8,875	10,310	12,570
Taiwan	2,226	2,666	2,827	3,113	3,878	4,391
Thailand	1,790	2,025	2,594	2,943	3,741	4,596
Other	356	348	696	737	857	685
International	2,535	2,684	3,131	3,433	3,401	3,476
Addenda:						
Eastern Europe	(D)	307	731	2,356	3,159	4,490
European Communities(12)	180,491	199,361	210,164	240,414	261,138	315,378
OPEC [1]	7,145	9,729	10,692	11,737	12,605	16,537

[1] OPEC=Organization of Petroleum Exporting Countries. Includes Algeria, Ecuador, Gabon, Indonesia, Iran, Iraq, Kuwait, Libya, Nigeria, Qatar, Saudi Arabia, United Arab Emirates, and Venezuela. Prior to 1993, Ecuador was also a member and was included in this line.

Source: U.S. Bureau of Economic Analysis, *Survey of Current Business*, September 1996, and earlier issues.

No. 1303. U.S. Government Foreign Grants and Credits, by Type and Country: 1966 to 1996

[In millions of dollars. See text, section 28. Negative figures (-) occur when the total of grant returns, principal repayments, and/or foreign currencies disbursed by the U.S. Government exceeds new grants and new credits utilized and/or acquisitions of foreign currencies through new sales of farm products]

TYPE AND COUNTRY	1966-1975, total	1976-1985, total	1990	1991	1992	1993	1994	1995	1996
Total, net	70,356	104,190	14,253	-32,040	17,718	17,110	15,836	12,090	15,937
Western Europe	1,004	1,618	-103	-6,040	325	300	128	155	271
Austria	-19	34	-10	-19	-1	-1	-1	-1	-1
Belgium and Luxembourg	17	-46	-9	-3	-	-	-	-	-
Bosnia and Hercegovina	-	-	-	-	40	30	50	59	186
Croatia	-	-	-	-	62	37	50	9	-14
Denmark	64	-58	-	-	-	-	-	-	-
Finland	-19	21	-8	-5	-5	-26	-1	-1	-1
France	-93	-222	-15	-8	-2	-2	-1	-	-
Germany	-117	-117	-338	-6,117	-	-1	-	(Z)	(Z)
Iceland	-8	-12	(Z)	-	-	-	-	-	-
Ireland	-51	7	2	-6	-6	-8	25	21	24
Italy	85	133	-30	-14	-	(Z)	-	(Z)	-
Macedonia	-	-	-	-	67	1	3	1	2
Netherlands	116	-180	-	-	-	-	-	-	-
Norway	379	-257	-	-1	-15	4	-	-	-
Portugal	34	1,003	56	44	159	113	115	-18	-9
Slovenia	-	-	-	-	118	-6	-18	-24	-27
Spain	607	965	-122	-76	-54	31	-55	-59	-48
Sweden	17	-1	-	-	-	-	-	-	-
United Kingdom	-546	-964	-111	-113	-115	-118	-120	-123	-125
Yugoslavia	84	174	-39	-58	-308	1	-1	(Z)	-1
Other [1] and unspecified	455	1,139	520	335	386	246	82	290	285
Eastern Europe	228	1,029	948	779	731	2,862	2,713	1,757	1,863
Albania	-	-	-	9	59	29	10	9	53
Armenia	-	-	-	-	19	62	78	60	73
Azerbaijan	-	-	-	-	(Z)	-	14	11	8
Belarus	-	-	-	-	27	74	37	47	30
Bulgaria	-	-	-	17	1	20	5	6	11
Czechoslovakia	-	-5	(Z)	1	1	15	1	-2	3
Czech Republic	-	-	-	-	-	2	2	3	9
Estonia	-	-	-	-	21	1	(Z)	1	3
Georgia	-	-	-	-	5	65	53	53	49
Hungary	-5	6	1	3	2	3	4	5	13
Kazakhstan	-	-	-	-	17	9	12	16	57
Kyrgyzstan	-	-	-	-	1	63	22	18	25
Latvia	-	-	-	-	21	1	3	2	6
Lithuania	-	-	-	-	21	24	15	27	14
Moldova	-	-	-	-	9	25	22	15	13
Poland	-75	1,017	902	646	77	21	5	5	40
Romania	92	55	64	39	10	14	9	8	28
Russia	-	-	-	-	149	1,896	1,134	427	400
Slovakia	-	-	-	-	-	1	1	2	11
Soviet Union	214	-44	-30	3	-	5	-	-	-
Tajikistan	-	-	-	-	10	17	19	18	20
Turkmenistan	-	-	-	-	7	24	13	16	19
Ukraine	-	-	-	-	8	50	103	165	257
Uzbekistan	-	-	-	-	(Z)	1	4	1	5
Other [2] and unspecified	-	-	11	60	265	442	1,148	842	706
Near East and South Asia	17,196	60,777	8,606	-24,670	8,121	7,933	7,023	2,946	7,322
Afghanistan	185	56	57	59	70	49	8	8	10
Bangladesh	701	1,670	175	168	154	109	178	73	22
Cyprus	20	138	16	18	10	14	16	6	10
Egypt	271	13,600	4,976	2,508	2,537	2,760	2,240	1,637	1,548
Greece	905	362	282	-179	665	315	266	243	-12
India	3,810	1,021	-8	100	78	54	32	39	39
Iran	914	-847	-	-23	(Z)	-	-	-	-21
Iraq [3]	-5	5	-7	365	119	115	135	128	112
Israel	3,760	25,417	4,379	2,002	4,691	3,276	3,134	420	5,301
Jordan	618	1,320	139	67	112	127	95	128	163
Kuwait	-	-	-2,506	-13,550	-2	-	-	-	-
Lebanon	90	233	8	5	11	7	5	4	11
Nepal	105	177	20	16	19	20	20	19	17
Oman	(Z)	79	4	3	13	24	1	4	11
Pakistan	2,048	1,971	526	346	123	-39	-162	-190	-167
Saudi Arabia	23	-20	-1,614	-13,913	-1,328	-	-	-	-
Sri Lanka	153	512	72	109	53	72	35	25	3
Syria	15	262	(Z)	-	-	2	-	-	-
Turkey	2,703	3,760	367	798	673	623	241	150	-61
United Arab Emirates	-	-	-361	-3,709	-	-	-	-	-
Yemen (Sanaa)	24	216	14	-	-	-	-	-	-
Yemen	-	-	28	19	14	21	1	3	4
UNRWA [4]	298	596	7	76	69	140	7	103	72
West Bank-Gaza	11	13	1	5	11	19	64	57	27
Other and unspecified	548	236	29	40	31	26	705	91	233

See footnotes at end of table.

No. 1303. U.S. Government Foreign Grants and Credits, by Type and Country: 1966 to 1996—Continued

[In millions of dollars. See headnote, p. 796]

COUNTRY	1966-1975, total	1976-1985 total	1990	1991	1992	1993	1994	1995	1996
Africa	3,610	11,066	1,863	1,484	1,624	1,779	1,802	1,868	1,431
Algeria	263	345	59	-42	-14	-11	28	759	365
Angola	6	115	-15	-4	-20	8	39	25	28
Benin	12	44	5	10	17	12	16	12	7
Botswana	35	169	17	11	8	15	14	15	6
Burkina	40	287	15	32	17	20	13	16	9
Burundi	5	62	18	6	16	19	36	23	2
Cameroon	50	150	42	57	42	23	13	4	3
Cape Verde	1	68	6	7	9	5	6	8	8
Chad	20	145	24	26	26	22	9	13	5
Eritrea	-	-	-	-	-	4	19	5	11
Ethiopia	297	310	54	123	88	137	126	91	76
Ghana	203	152	14	32	36	48	54	57	30
Guinea	68	74	15	22	21	34	33	28	24
Cote d'Ivoire	57	57	25	58	46	21	38	17	22
Kenya	76	549	110	87	90	79	41	34	-6
Lesotho	27	197	15	11	16	7	6	12	3
Liberia	86	459	31	64	40	29	42	40	35
Madagascar	13	86	33	31	20	26	22	26	33
Malawi	30	56	34	48	47	41	33	58	32
Mali	58	199	31	44	31	37	30	31	5
Mauritania	20	161	11	6	3	7	2	2	2
Morocco	413	948	95	100	26	21	26	-53	-24
Mozambique	1	175	80	89	72	75	68	100	46
Niger	64	223	33	44	34	29	16	31	12
Nigeria	264	267	156	34	31	18	52	1	-5
Rwanda	13	91	13	27	10	32	200	70	47
Senegal	48	361	60	39	47	54	32	24	36
Sierra Leone	36	86	2	10	16	8	7	8	17
Somalia	47	582	77	11	338	506	24	17	7
South Africa	-11	2	20	28	44	66	71	112	76
Sudan	52	1,358	145	113	32	36	44	8	10
Swaziland	8	58	14	13	13	14	10	12	10
Tanzania	123	259	51	42	27	28	24	17	13
Togo	18	60	10	19	12	8	7	3	1
Tunisia	376	563	38	5	16	-4	1	-5	-25
Uganda	33	40	43	39	26	58	51	51	30
Zaire	342	938	241	48	33	9	1	1	(Z)
Zambia	35	331	63	50	76	52	21	25	18
Zimbabwe	(Z)	271	10	27	67	28	34	29	17
Other and unspecified	361	769	156	113	165	160	491	240	444
Far East and Pacific	34,767	9,651	38	-8,966	801	13	747	751	747
Australia	276	-12	-34	-26	-18	-2	-1	-	-
Burma	43	31	1	-3	(Z)	-2	-2	-2	-2
Cambodia	1,760	87	5	6	14	29	16	37	29
China: Mainland	-	49	71	55	31	14	6	136	113
Taiwan	1,523	648	-7	-6	-7	-9	-6	-5	-3
Hong Kong	41	11	-8	-	-	1	1	73	133
Indonesia	1,390	1,661	46	23	82	-64	23	25	39
Japan and Ryukyu Islands	-345	-210	-635	-9,377	-30	-2	-1	(Z)	(Z)
Laos	1,868	8	(Z)	(Z)	1	(Z)	(Z)	3	3
Malaysia	66	39	-1	-2	-	-	1	-	1
Mongolia	-	-	-	17	2	36	17	11	6
New Zealand	95	-66	-2	-2	-1	-	-	-	-
Pacific Islands,	-	-	-	-	-	-	-	-	-
Trust Territory of the [5]	488	1,260	220	179	204	152	317	209	215
Philippines	729	1,466	556	391	543	129	-53	54	48
Singapore	78	110	(Z)	(Z)	(Z)	(Z)	(Z)	1	(Z)
South Korea	5,426	3,518	-192	-331	-133	-431	-55	-50	-62
Thailand	996	733	-19	49	44	84	245	207	195
Vietnam	19,720	18	-	-	-	-	-	-	-
Other and unspecified	595	302	39	64	71	75	242	51	32
Western Hemisphere	6,816	9,848	2,002	2,020	2,462	678	796	441	328
Argentina	34	21	64	87	90	80	26	-30	-53
Bolivia	270	413	112	197	186	129	115	92	86
Brazil	1,518	399	260	-22	410	-188	-60	-204	-192
Canada	272	317	-41	-50	-38	-41	-120	-	-
Chile	724	-565	-32	-40	-55	-39	-36	-27	-6
Colombia	846	298	-30	7	-78	-235	-4	-8	9
Costa Rica	103	687	108	63	24	15	-1	-30	-50
Dominican Republic	360	550	27	25	3	163	9	-21	-14
Ecuador	144	153	61	26	30	17	19	5	3
El Salvador	93	1,681	303	306	278	212	87	114	65
Guatemala	160	270	96	82	109	74	52	37	-1
Guyana	71	36	42	11	9	6	9	9	11
Haiti	42	370	53	69	54	59	122	199	70
Honduras	113	801	223	193	126	92	49	72	27
Jamaica	120	643	108	109	84	34	99	27	-18

See footnotes at end of table.

No. 1303. U.S. Government Foreign Grants and Credits, by Type and Country: 1946 to 1996—Continued

[In millions of dollars. See headnote, p. 796]

COUNTRY	1946-1975, total	1976-1989, total	1990	1991	1992	1993	1994	1995	1996
Western Hemisphere—Continued:									
Mexico	305	1,162	140	38	-109	-160	-23	[illegible]	-3
Nicaragua	150	197	100	396	207	37	41	27	28
Panama	210	205	102	153	193	49	6	8	-8
Paraguay	86	22	(Z)	1	(Z)	1	2	1	2
Peru	274	757	87	139	672	113	44	38	[illegible]
Trinidad and Tobago	21	151	5	5	-10	-11	-9	-4	-5
Uruguay	116	-9	-4	-5	2	-1	2	(Z)	-
Venezuela	115	-35	-16	-14	-2	1	(Z)	-3	-
Other [5] and unspecified	671	1,325	236	242	280	271	575	250	[illegible]
Other international organizations and unspecified areas	4,016	9,768	1,816	1,864	2,236	2,413	1,289	2,574	2,170

Z Less than $500,000. [1] Includes European Atomic Energy Community, European Coal and Steel Community, European Payments Union, European Productivity Agency, North Atlantic Treaty Organization, and Organization for European Economic Cooperation. [2] Foreign assistance in 1989-94 to the countries of Eastern Europe and to the Newly Independent States of the former Soviet Union was reported primarily on a regional basis. [3] Foreign assistance to Iraq in 1991-94 was direct humanitarian assistance to ethnic minorities of Northern Iraq after the conflict in the Persian Gulf. [4] United Nations Relief and Works Agency for Palestine refugees. [5] Excludes transactions with Commonwealth of the Northern Mariana Islands after October 1986. Includes transactions with Federated States of Micronesia, Republic of the Marshall Islands, and Republic of Palau. [6] Includes Andean Development Corporation, Caribbean Development Bank, Central American Bank for Economic Integration, Eastern Caribbean Central Bank, Inter-American Institute of Agricultural Science, Organizations of American States, and Pan American Health Organization.

Source: U.S. Bureau of Economic Analysis, press releases, and unpublished data.

No. 1304. U.S. Foreign Economic and Military Aid Programs: 1970 to 1995

[In millions of dollars. For years ending June 30 except, beginning 1977, ending Sept. 30. Economic aid shown here represents U.S. economic aid—not just aid under the Foreign Assistance Act. Major components in recent years include AID, Food for Peace, Peace Corps, and paid-in subscriptions to international financial institutions, such as IBRD, and IDB. Annual figures are gross unadjusted program figures]

YEAR	Total economic and military aid	ECONOMIC AID			MILITARY AID		
		Total	Loans	Grants	Total	Loans	Grants
1970	6,568	3,676	1,389	2,288	2,892	70	2,822
1975	6,916	4,908	1,679	3,229	2,009	750	1,259
1976	6,412	3,878	1,759	2,119	2,535	1,442	1,093
1976, TQ [1]	2,603	1,931	840	1,091	672	494	178
1977	7,784	5,594	2,083	3,511	2,190	1,411	779
1978	9,014	6,661	2,530	4,131	2,353	1,601	752
1979	13,845	7,120	1,900	5,220	6,725	5,173	1,552
1980	9,695	7,573	1,993	5,580	2,122	1,450	672
1981	10,550	7,305	1,460	5,845	3,245	2,546	699
1982	12,324	8,129	1,454	6,675	4,195	3,084	1,111
1983	14,202	8,603	1,619	6,984	5,599	3,932	1,667
1984	15,524	9,038	1,621	7,417	6,486	4,401	2,085
1985	18,128	12,327	1,579	10,748	5,801	2,365	3,436
1986	16,739	10,900	1,330	9,570	5,839	1,980	3,859
1987	14,488	9,386	1,138	8,248	5,102	953	4,149
1988	13,792	8,961	852	8,109	4,831	763	4,068
1989	14,688	9,860	694	9,166	4,828	410	4,418
1990	15,727	10,834	756	10,078	4,893	404	4,489
1991	16,663	11,904	354	11,550	4,760	428	4,332
1992	15,589	11,242	494	10,748	4,347	345	4,002
1993	28,196	24,054	462	23,592	4,143	855	3,288
1994	15,870	11,940	(NA)	(NA)	3,931	(NA)	(NA)
1995	15,107	11,295	(NA)	(NA)	3,813	(NA)	(NA)

- Represents zero. NA Not available. [1] Transition quarter, July-Sept.

Source: U.S. Agency for International Development, *U.S. Overseas Loans and Grants and Assistance from International Organizations*, annual.

No. 1305. U.S. Foreign Military Aid, by Region and Selected Countries: 1994 and 1995

[For years ending Sept. 30. Military aid data include Military Assistance Program (MAP) grants, foreign military credit sales, International Military Education and Training, and excess defense articles. N.I.S.=New Independent States]

REGION AND COUNTRY	1994 ($1,000)	1995 Total ($1,000)	1995 Percent of total assistance	1995 Percent change, 1994-95
Total	**3,930,672**	**3,812,746**	**26.2**	**-3.0**
Near East [1]	3,112,098	3,111,501	57.4	-
Egypt	1,300,800	1,301,000	57.1	-
Israel	1,800,000	1,800,000	60.0	-
Jordan	9,800	8,303	38.1	-15.3
Morocco	528	724	4.6	37.1
Tunisia	500	800	27.0	60.0
Sub-Saharan Africa [1]	4,506	4,955	0.4	10.0
Ghana	514	222	0.6	-56.8
Kenya	288	283	1.1	-1.7
Senegal	450	598	2.4	32.9
Latin America [1]	17,301	21,881	3.0	26.5
Bolivia	3,406	3,597	5.2	5.6
Colombia	8,600	10,588	38.0	23.1
Dominican Rep	608	213	1.3	-65.0
Ecuador	509	293	2.0	-42.4
El Salvador	400	404	0.6	1.0
Honduras	524	325	1.1	-38.0
Jamaica	501	174	0.7	-65.3
Mexico	201	400	3.9	99.0
Panama	-	425	8.0	(X)
Asia [1]	2,847	3,804	0.7	33.6
Malaysia	318	504	100.0	58.5
Philippines	876	-	-	-100.0
Thailand	895	96	0.7	-89.3
Viet Nam	-	999	16.3	(X)
Europe [1]	774,776	566,928	45.2	-26.8
Bulgaria	300	400	1.0	33.3
Czech Republic	500	500	2.5	-
Greece	283,600	229,683	100.0	-19.0
Hungary	700	796	3.0	13.7
Latvia	195	903	12.5	363.1
Poland	700	1,747	2.0	149.6
Portugal	81,500	500	100.0	-99.4
Turkey	406,008	329,152	66.5	-18.9
N.I.S [1]	1,481	1,722	0.2	16.3
Russia	471	413	0.1	-12.3
Ukraine	600	707	0.4	17.8
Oceania and other	88	376	5.3	327.3
Nonregional	**17,575**	**101,579**	**2.0**	**478.0**

- Represents zero or rounds to zero. [1] Includes countries not shown separately.

Source: U.S. Agency for International Development, *U.S. Overseas Loans and Grants and Assistance from International Organizations*, annual.

No. 1306 U.S. Foreign Aid—Economic Assistance, by Region and Selected Countries: 1994 and 1995

[For years ending Sept. 30. N.I.S.=New Independent States]

REGION AND COUNTRY	1994 ($1,000)	1995 Total ($1,000)	1995 Percent of total assistance	1995 Percent change, 1994-95
Total	**11,939,559**	**11,294,639**	**74.8**	**-5.4**
Near East [1]	1,972,814	2,310,372	42.6	17.1
Egypt	606,486	975,825	42.9	60.9
Israel	1,200,000	1,200,000	40.0	0.0
Morocco	42,947	15,035	95.4	-65.0
West Bank/Gaza	58,480	80,909	100.0	38.4
Sub-Saharan Africa [1]	1,457,752	1,306,061	99.6	-10.4
Angola	66,656	44,760	100.0	-32.8
Benin	25,251	20,337	99.2	-19.5
Eritrea	40,546	10,452	98.1	-74.2
Ethiopa	145,179	119,494	99.8	-17.7
Ghana	55,004	39,172	99.4	-28.8
Guinea	31,394	19,671	99.2	-37.3
Kenya	48,533	26,450	98.9	-45.5
Liberia	60,107	51,643	100.0	-14.1
Madagascar	33,318	30,015	100.0	-9.9
Malawi	54,554	67,820	99.8	24.3
Mali	41,458	34,758	99.5	-16.2
Mozambique	74,745	66,709	99.8	-10.8
Namibia	18,367	16,815	99.3	-8.4
Niger	26,696	18,895	99.0	-29.2
Rwanda	54,171	166,021	100.0	206.5
Senegal	35,524	24,386	97.6	-31.4
Somalia	24,815	14,778	100.0	-40.4
South Africa	133,674	100,120	99.7	-25.1
Sudan	66,331	30,067	100.0	-54.7
Tanzania	25,955	31,469	99.7	21.2
Uganda	47,370	57,826	99.8	22.1
Zambia	35,190	29,555	99.7	-16.0
Zimbabwe	40,246	21,584	98.9	-46.4
Latin America [1]	941,698	717,121	97.0	-23.8
Bolivia	106,059	65,570	94.8	-38.2
Colombia	21,593	17,306	62.0	-19.9
Dominican Rep	90,731	15,692	98.7	-82.7
Ecuador	19,392	14,286	98.0	-26.3
El Salvador	56,807	63,214	99.4	11.3
Guatemala	67,878	39,199	100.0	-42.3
Haiti	106,024	157,592	98.1	48.6
Honduras	47,229	29,685	98.9	-37.1
Jamaica	32,095	23,967	99.3	-25.3
Mexico	11,426	9,931	96.1	-13.1
Nicaragua	93,053	31,373	100.0	-66.3
Peru	156,044	131,576	99.8	-15.7
Asia [1]	596,349	571,818	99.3	-4.1
Bangladesh	125,223	146,774	99.9	17.2
India	155,419	164,429	99.9	5.8
Indonesia	24,371	61,564	100.0	152.6
Kampuchea	29,694	42,115	99.4	41.8
Pakistan	49,608	16,993	99.4	-65.7
Philippines	77,565	17,121	100.0	-77.9
Thailand	12,113	13,255	99.3	9.4
Europe [1]	693,480	686,098	54.8	-1.1
Bosnia Hercegovina	86,271	71,900	99.4	-16.7
Bulgaria	7,817	38,525	99.0	392.8
Croatia	18,367	12,345	99.2	-32.8
Hungary	2,308	26,012	97.0	1027.0
Lithuania	15,015	22,252	96.1	48.2
Macedonia	12,000	13,512	99.1	12.6
Ireland, Rep. of	39,406	39,200	100.0	-0.5
N.I.S [1]	2,118,374	842,503	99.8	-60.2
Armenia	89,174	52,526	100.0	-41.1
Azerbaijan	21,274	9,848	100.0	-53.7
Belarus	50,718	11,067	99.2	-78.2
Georgia	36,816	39,273	99.8	6.7
Kazakhstan	104,623	40,191	99.8	-61.6
Kyrgyz Rep.	42,650	25,104	99.5	-41.1
Moldova	62,368	21,723	100.0	-65.2
Russia	1,410,594	353,196	99.9	-75.0
Tajikistan	46,233	8,401	100.0	-81.8
Turkemenistan	27,871	5,343	97.8	-80.8
Ukraine	160,771	178,779	99.6	11.2
Uzberistan	24,723	11,515	99.2	-53.4
Oceania and other	26,538	6,765	94.7	-74.5
Nonregional	**4,132,554**	**4,853,881**	**98.0**	**17.5**

[1] Includes countries and regional organizations not shown separately.

Source: U.S. Agency for International Development, *U.S. Overseas Loans and Grants and Assistance from International Organizations*, annual.

No. 1307. U.S. International Trade in Goods and Services: 1994 to 1996

[In millions of dollars. Data presented on a balance of payments basis and will not agree with the following merchandise trade tables 1308 to 1316]

CATEGORY	EXPORTS			IMPORTS			TRADE BALANCE		
	1994	1995	1996	1994	1995	1996	1994	1995	1996
Total	698,301	786,529	835,853	802,682	891,593	949,882	-104,381	-105,064	-114,229
Goods	502,462	575,939	611,721	668,585	749,363	799,338	-166,123	-173,424	-187,617
Services	195,839	210,590	223,932	134,097	142,230	150,544	61,742	68,360	73,388
Travel	58,417	61,137	64,516	43,782	45,855	48,826	14,635	15,282	15,690
Passenger fares	17,083	18,534	19,641	12,885	14,313	14,327	4,198	4,221	5,314
Other transportation	25,861	28,063	28,918	27,983	29,205	28,797	-2,122	-1,142	121
Royalties and license fees	22,272	26,953	28,688	5,518	6,312	7,283	16,754	20,641	21,405
Other private services	59,071	61,724	67,448	30,980	33,970	37,606	28,091	27,754	29,842
Direct defense expenditures	12,255	13,405	13,900	10,292	9,820	11,041	1,963	3,585	2,859
U.S. Government miscellaneous services	880	775	821	2,657	2,755	2,664	-1,777	-1,980	-1,843

Source: U.S. Bureau of the Census, *U.S. International Trade in Goods and Services*, series FT-900(96-12).

No. 1308. U.S. Exports and Imports of Merchandise: 1970 to 1996

[In billions of dollars, except percent. Includes silver ore and bullion; beginning 1974, includes shipments of nonmonetary gold. Data may differ from those shown in other tables due to revisions and inclusion of the Virgin Islands since 1974. For basis of dollar values, see text, section 28]

YEAR	Merchandise trade balance	EXPORTS [1]				GENERAL IMPORTS [4]			AVERAGE ANNUAL PERCENT CHANGE [5]	
		Total [2]	Domestic			Total [3]	Petroleum	Machinery	Domestic exports	General imports
			Total [3]	Agricultural	Machinery					
1970	2.7	42.7	42.0	7.2	11.4	40.0	2.8	5.3	14.1	10.8
1971	-2.0	43.5	42.9	7.7	11.6	45.6	3.3	6.0	1.9	14.0
1972	-6.4	49.2	48.4	9.4	13.2	55.6	4.3	7.8	13.1	21.9
1973	1.3	70.8	69.7	17.7	17.1	69.5	7.6	10.0	43.9	25.0
1974	-4.5	98.1	96.5	22.0	23.7	102.6	24.3	11.6	38.6	47.6
1975	9.1	107.7	106.1	21.9	28.5	98.5	24.8	12.0	9.8	-4.0
1976	-8.3	115.2	113.5	23.0	31.3	123.5	31.8	15.2	7.0	25.4
1977	-29.2	121.2	118.9	23.7	32.5	150.4	41.5	17.7	5.2	21.8
1978	-31.1	143.7	141.0	29.4	37.0	174.8	39.1	24.4	18.6	16.2
1979	-27.6	181.9	178.6	34.8	44.7	209.5	56.0	28.0	26.6	19.9
1980	-24.2	220.6	216.5	41.3	55.8	244.9	77.6	31.9	21.3	16.9
1981	-27.3	233.7	226.9	43.3	62.9	261.0	75.6	38.2	5.9	6.6
1982	-31.8	212.3	207.1	36.6	60.3	244.0	59.4	39.7	-9.2	-6.5
1983	-57.5	200.5	196.0	36.1	54.3	258.0	52.3	47.0	-5.6	5.7
1984	-107.9	217.9	212.1	37.8	60.3	325.7	55.9	68.4	8.7	26.2
1985	-132.1	213.1	206.9	29.2	59.5	345.3	49.6	75.3	-2.2	6.0
1986	-152.7	217.3	206.4	26.1	60.4	370.0	34.1	87.5	2.0	7.2
1987	-152.1	254.1	243.9	28.6	69.6	408.2	41.5	99.4	16.9	9.8
1988	-118.6	322.4	310.0	37.0	88.4	441.0	38.8	117.3	26.9	8.6
1989	-109.6	363.8	349.4	40.0	98.3	473.4	49.1	126.8	12.8	7.3
1990	-101.7	393.6	375.1	38.7	122.4	495.3	60.5	134.8	8.2	4.6
1991	-65.4	421.7	401.1	38.5	139.7	487.1	50.1	131.8	7.1	-1.7
1992	-84.5	448.2	425.7	42.2	126.6	532.7	50.4	148.3	6.3	9.4
1993	-115.6	465.1	439.3	41.9	136.4	580.7	49.7	168.7	3.8	9.0
1994	-151.1	512.7	472.3	45.0	156.7	663.8	49.6	204.6	10.2	14.3
1995	-158.7	584.7	548.1	54.9	182.7	743.4	52.8	241.7	14.1	12.0
1996	-166.6	624.8	584.1	59.3	(NA)	791.4	65.7	221.5	6.8	6.4

NA Not available. [1] Includes "Special Category" items and beginning 1974, includes trade of Virgin Islands with foreign countries. F.a.s. value basis. [2] Domestic and foreign exports excluding M.A.P. Grant-Aid shipments, through 1985; 1986 through 1988 include Grant-Aid shipments. [3] Includes commodity groups not shown separately. [4] 1970-73, 1982-91, customs value basis; 1974-81, f.a.s. value basis. Beginning 1974, includes trade of Virgin Islands with foreign countries. [5] 1970, change from 1965; thereafter, from previous year. For explanation of average annual percent change, see Guide to Tabular Presentation.

Source: U.S. Bureau of the Census, 1970-88, *Highlights of U.S. Export and Import Trade*, FT 990, monthly; beginning 1989, *U.S. Merchandise Trade: Export, General Imports, and Imports for Consumption*, series FT 925, monthly.

No. 1309. U.S. Exports and Imports for Consumption of Merchandise, by Major Customs District: 1980 to 1996

[In billions of dollars. Exports are f.a.s. (free alongside ship) value all years; imports are on customs value basis]

CUSTOMS DISTRICT	EXPORTS					IMPORTS FOR CONSUMPTION				
	1980	1990	1994	1995	1996	1980	1990	1994	1995	1996
Total [1]	225.8	393.0	512.6	583.0	622.8	244.0	490.6	657.3	739.6	790.5
Anchorage, AK	1.0	3.7	5.3	5.9	6.1	0.2	0.7	3.6	5.7	6.9
Baltimore, MD	9.0	6.7	8.2	9.0	8.2	6.0	11.2	13.4	14.4	14.0
Boston,	0.8	5.6	4.7	4.6	5.0	5.0	12.2	12.6	13.4	13.7
Buffalo, NY	6.3	15.8	21.3	30.5	32.1	7.4	19.2	27.0	29.3	29.7
Charleston, SC [2]	3.1	6.7	7.9	10.1	10.7	1.8	6.8	8.6	10.4	11.6
Chicago, IL	4.2	10.2	15.2	18.4	18.7	4.1	18.3	28.5	31.3	33.5
Cleveland, OH	1.8	4.0	5.3	7.8	10.3	1.5	11.3	18.2	21.7	23.7
Dallas/Fort Worth, TX	0.5	3.4	4.1	4.4	3.8	1.2	4.8	7.7	8.8	9.8
Detroit, MI	14.6	35.6	54.4	56.8	59.8	12.7	37.8	58.1	65.4	70.2
Duluth, MN	1.5	0.8	1.1	1.4	1.5	3.0	3.9	4.7	6.0	6.5
El Paso, TX	1.8	3.9	7.4	7.9	9.6	1.4	5.0	11.2	12.9	13.6
Great Falls, MT	1.8	2.4	3.2	3.0	3.2	3.2	4.7	7.1	6.9	7.9
Honolulu, HI.	0.2	0.5	1.0	1.1	1.3	1.8	2.1	2.5	2.7	2.7
Houston/Galveston, TX	15.7	17.6	21.2	27.4	27.0	20.1	21.6	21.9	23.4	28.2
Laredo, TX	8.3	15.2	28.3	24.3	29.7	2.7	10.0	17.5	24.7	31.9
Los Angeles, CA	14.8	42.1	55.8	67.0	68.9	20.0	64.1	89.4	96.3	99.9
Miami, FL	6.9	11.2	19.5	22.7	24.5	2.6	7.1	10.3	11.9	13.5
Milwaukee, WI	0.4	0.1	0.1	0.1	0.1	0.4	1.1	1.4	1.5	1.4
Minneapolis, MN	0.1	0.9	1.3	1.3	1.4	0.3	2.0	2.6	2.8	3.2
Mobile, AL [2]	2.6	1.9	2.7	3.4	3.4	3.0	3.4	3.8	3.9	4.9
New Orleans, LA	19.5	18.0	20.7	28.4	31.0	22.5	24.1	29.1	34.4	35.2
New York, NY	38.9	50.9	56.4	61.4	61.9	43.4	68.0	81.8	87.6	93.4
Nogales, AZ	0.8	2.1	4.1	4.0	4.2	1.2	4.2	7.5	7.7	7.2
Norfolk, VA [2]	8.0	11.7	12.4	14.4	15.1	4.7	7.4	7.9	8.6	9.4
Ogdensburg, NY	3.8	7.9	8.9	9.2	9.9	4.6	9.8	12.3	14.4	15.9
Pembina, ND	2.3	3.4	5.9	5.5	5.9	3.0	4.1	6.1	7.2	7.5
Philadelphia, PA	3.2	4.0	5.1	6.7	9.2	15.6	18.3	16.8	18.3	19.0
Port Arthur, TX	2.0	0.9	0.9	1.3	1.0	9.4	3.2	4.0	4.8	6.0
Portland, ME	4.3	1.7	2.0	2.1	2.1	1.6	4.3	4.3	4.4	5.2
Portland, OR	3.8	5.8	8.1	10.2	10.0	2.6	5.6	7.0	7.9	7.6
Providence, RI	2.7	(Z)	0.1	0.1	(Z)	1.5	1.3	0.9	0.9	1.4
San Diego, CA	1.4	3.4	5.6	6.1	7.5	1.0	4.3	7.4	8.9	11.0
San Francisco, CA	10.6	23.1	34.2	43.7	47.7	8.3	28.0	46.2	58.8	57.7
San Juan, PR	0.9	2.5	2.6	2.6	2.5	3.7	5.4	5.7	6.8	7.2
Savannah, GA	2.4	7.4	9.3	10.9	10.9	2.2	9.6	13.3	14.7	16.1
Seattle, WA	12.0	32.6	33.1	31.4	37.1	9.2	20.9	23.6	24.1	24.8
St. Albans, VT	0.7	4.0	4.1	4.4	4.1	1.6	5.2	6.2	7.4	7.9
St. Louis, MO	0.2	0.3	0.3	0.3	1.6	0.9	3.0	4.3	4.4	4.8
Tampa, FL	2.8	4.3	5.7	6.7	6.9	3.7	7.0	9.1	9.2	9.2
Virgin Islands of the U.S.	0.1	0.2	0.2	0.2	0.2	4.1	2.1	2.1	2.1	2.8
Washington, DC	0.3	1.1	2.0	2.3	2.1	0.4	0.8	0.9	1.2	1.3
Wilmington, NC	1.3	3.0	3.9	4.4	4.2	1.1	3.3	6.0	7.4	7.7

Z Less than $50 million. [1] Totals shown for exports reflect the value of estimated parcel post and Special Category shipments, and beginning 1990, adjustments for undocumented exports to Canada which are not distributed by customs district. Beginning 1990, the value of bituminous coal exported through Norfolk, VA; Charleston, SC; and Mobile, AL is reflected in the total but not distributed by district. [2] Beginning 1990, excludes exports of bituminous coal.

Source: U.S. Bureau of the Census, 1980, *Highlights of U.S. Export and Import Trade*, FT 990; 1990, *U.S. Merchandise Trade: Selected Highlights*, series FT 920, monthly; and beginning 1994, *U.S. Export History* and *U.S. Import History* on compact disc.

No. 1310. Export and Import Unit Value Indexes—Selected Countries: 1992 to 1996

[Indexes in U.S. dollars, 1990=100. A unit value is an implicit price derived from value and quantity data]

COUNTRY	EXPORT UNIT VALUE					IMPORT UNIT VALUE				
	1992	1993	1994	1995	1996	1992	1993	1994	1995	1996
United States	101.0	101.4	103.6	106.8	109.4	100.8	100.1	101.8	106.4	107.4
Australia	87.7	82.3	86.0	93.6	94.7	99.3	99.4	104.3	109.6	109.5
Austria	98.0	88.6	(NA)	(NA)	(NA)	102.2	93.4	(NA)	(NA)	(NA)
Belgium-Luxembourg	100.5	(NA)	(NA)	(NA)	(NA)	99.2	(NA)	(NA)	(NA)	(NA)
Canada	95.3	94.4	94.6	101.2	104.3	99.2	98.6	99.1	102.6	104.4
Denmark	101.6	91.4	94.1	106.8	106.2	99.7	89.2	92.0	106.8	104.1
France	99.6	90.1	98.3	111.1	108.2	97.9	87.0	92.4	104.5	102.6
Germany	102.1	92.0	92.9	107.6	(NA)	102.0	91.1	94.6	110.0	(NA)
Italy	100.8	87.9	88.9	96.2	(NA)	95.9	83.9	85.2	(NA)	(NA)
Japan	114.0	124.5	134.1	144.8	(NA)	96.3	97.0	97.2	105.3	(NA)
Netherlands	96.4	90.1	92.4	106.7	101.9	101.0	89.7	91.6	104.4	100.3
Norway	88.7	77.7	75.4	86.6	92.1	97.2	85.8	86.4	97.2	95.4
Sweden	98.9	81.2	78.1	(NA)	(NA)	98.4	80.9	75.8	(NA)	(NA)
United Kingdom	101.8	97.6	101.5	111.6	111.9	100.9	94.3	99.4	112.5	111.8

NA Not available.

Source: International Monetary Fund, Washington, DC, *International Financial Statistics*, monthly.

No. 1311. U.S. Exports, by State of Origin: 1990 to 1996

[In millions of dollars. Exports are on a f.a.s. value basis]

STATE AND OTHER AREAS	1990	1995	1996	
			Total	Rank
Total	394,045	583,865	624,767	(X)
United States	315,065	467,761	555,960	(X)
Alabama	2,834	4,764	5,170	26
Alaska	2,850	2,772	2,879	33
Arizona	3,729	7,327	10,503	17
Arkansas	920	1,994	2,003	37
California	44,520	77,529	93,418	1
Colorado	2,274	4,460	4,883	28
Connecticut	4,356	5,666	6,100	24
Delaware	1,344	1,402	1,594	39
District of Columbia	320	231	305	(X)
Florida	11,634	18,909	20,744	9
Georgia	5,763	10,291	10,982	16
Hawaii	179	241	284	50
Idaho	898	1,804	1,571	40
Illinois	12,965	22,163	24,176	6
Indiana	5,273	10,363	10,984	15
Iowa	2,189	3,842	4,400	29
Kansas	2,113	3,433	3,784	30
Kentucky	3,175	5,253	6,385	23
Louisiana	14,199	19,793	21,667	8
Maine	870	1,357	1,380	42
Maryland	2,592	5,223	5,019	27
Massachusetts	9,501	12,946	14,524	11
Michigan	18,474	25,275	27,553	4
Minnesota	5,091	7,747	8,992	19
Mississippi	1,605	2,592	2,823	34
Missouri	3,130	3,876	5,404	25
Montana	229	358	440	49
Nebraska	693	1,759	1,907	38
Nevada	394	665	1,266	43
New Hampshire	973	1,253	1,481	41
New Jersey	7,633	11,071	13,119	13
New Mexico	249	432	931	44
New York	22,072	28,095	34,230	3
North Carolina	8,010	14,313	15,734	10
North Dakota	360	526	707	46
Ohio	13,378	20,967	22,677	7
Oklahoma	1,648	2,079	2,365	35
Oregon	4,065	7,667	8,948	20
Pennsylvania	8,491	13,031	14,364	12
Rhode Island	596	897	919	45
South Carolina	3,116	6,423	6,698	22
South Dakota	205	388	443	48
Tennessee	3,746	7,778	8,094	21
Texas	32,931	59,116	66,862	2
Utah	1,596	3,282	3,296	32
Vermont	1,154	1,620	3,302	31
Virginia	9,333	11,512	12,215	14
Washington	24,432	21,879	26,482	5
West Virginia	1,550	2,040	2,169	36
Wisconsin	5,158	8,931	9,504	18
Wyoming	264	411	481	47
Puerto Rico	3,600	4,501	5,134	(X)
Virgin Islands	51	216	184	(X)
Other [1]	75,328	91,387	63,490	(X)

X Not applicable. [1] Includes unreported, not specified, special category, estimated shipments, foreign trade zone, re-exports, and any timing adjustments.

Source: U.S. Bureau of the Census, *U.S. Merchandise Trade*, series FT 900, December issues.

No. 1312. U.S. Trade in Advanced Technology Products: 1990 to 1996

[In billions of dollars. Exports are f.a.s. value basis and imports are on customs value basis]

PRODUCT CATEGORY	EXPORTS					GENERAL IMPORTS				
	1990	1993	1994	1995	1996	1990	1993	1994	1995	1996
Total	93.4	106.4	120.8	138.4	154.9	59.3	81.2	96.4	124.8	130.3
Advanced materials [1]	6.4	0.7	0.9	(NA)	1.7	1.0	0.5	0.6	(NA)	1.2
Aerospace	37.0	37.4	35.0	(NA)	38.2	10.7	11.6	11.4	(NA)	12.8
Biotechnology [2]	0.6	0.8	1.0	(NA)	1.2	(Z)	0.1	0.1	(NA)	0.5
Electronics	7.5	19.6	25.8	(NA)	36.4	11.0	19.4	25.9	(NA)	36.8
Flexible manufacturing [3]	3.1	4.0	5.2	(NA)	8.6	1.7	2.2	2.9	(NA)	5.7
Information and communications	31.4	36.7	42.9	(NA)	55.4	30.2	40.1	49.9	(NA)	61.9
Life science	4.9	6.1	6.8	(NA)	9.2	3.4	4.7	4.8	(NA)	7.3
Nuclear technology	1.3	1.4	1.6	(NA)	1.3	(Z)	(Z)	(Z)	(NA)	0.6
Opto-electronics [4]	0.5	0.7	0.9	(NA)	1.4	1.1	2.5	2.5	(NA)	3.2
Weapons	0.7	0.7	0.7	(NA)	1.5	0.1	0.2	0.1	(NA)	0.3

NA Not available. Z Less than $50 million. [1] Encompasses recent advances in the development of materials that allow for further development and application of other advanced technologies. Examples are semiconductor materials, optical fiber cable and video discs. [2] Biotechnology is the medical and industrial application of advanced scientific discoveries in genetics to the creation of new drugs, hormones and other therapeutic items for both agricultural and human use. [3] Encompasses advances in robotics, numerically—controlled machine tools, and similar products involving industrial automation that allow for greater flexibility to the manufacturing process and reduce the amount of human intervention. Includes robots, numerically controlled machine tools and semiconductor production and assembly machines. [4] Encompasses electronic products and components that involve the emitting and/or detection of light. Examples of products included are optical scanners, optical disc players, solar cells, photo-sensitive semiconductors and laser printers.

Source: U. S. Bureau of the Census, *U. S. Merchandise Trade*, series FT 900, December issues; and unpublished data.

No. 1313. U.S. Exports, Imports, and Merchandise Trade Balance, by Country: 1992 to 1996

[In millions of dollars. Includes silver ore and bullion. Country totals include exports of special category commodities, if any. Data include nonmonetary gold and includes trade of Virgin Islands with foreign countries, see footnote 2 for exception. Minus sign (-) denotes an excess of imports over exports]

COUNTRY	EXPORTS, DOMESTIC AND FOREIGN					GENERAL IMPORTS [1]					MERCHANDISE TRADE BALANCE				
	1992	1993	1994	1995	1996	1992	1993	1994	1995	1996	1992	1993	1994	1995	1996
Total [2]	448,164	464,767	512,670	584,742	624,767	532,665	580,511	663,768	743,445	791,364	-84,501	-115,744	-151,098	-158,703	-166,597
Afghanistan	4	10	5	4	17	2	3	6	5	16	2	7	-1	-1	1
Albania	36	34	16	14	12	5	8	6	10	10	31	27	10	4	2
Algeria	686	938	1,191	774	632	1,586	1,583	1,525	1,674	2,103	-898	-645	-334	-900	-1,471
Andorra	16	15	5	16	25	(Z)	(Z)	(Z)	(Z)	3	16	15	5	16	22
Angola	158	174	197	260	268	2,303	2,092	2,061	2,212	2,687	-2,145	-1,918	-1,864	-1,953	-2,419
Anguilla	11	14	13	15	13	(Z)	(Z)	(Z)	(Z)	1	11	14	13	15	12
Antigua	68	73	65	97	82	5	15	5	3	9	63	58	59	94	73
Argentina	3,223	3,776	4,466	4,189	4,516	1,256	1,206	1,725	1,761	2,278	1,967	2,570	2,741	2,428	2,237
Armenia	25	78	74	70	57	1	1	1	16	2	23	77	73	54	55
Aruba	288	266	274	247	226	212	457	462	421	558	76	-191	-188	-173	-333
Australia	8,876	8,277	9,781	10,789	11,992	3,688	3,297	3,200	3,323	3,855	5,188	4,979	6,581	7,466	8,137
Austria	1,256	1,326	1,373	2,017	2,009	1,306	1,411	1,749	1,963	2,199	-50	-85	-377	54	-190
Azerbaijan	(Z)	37	27	38	54	(Z)	(Z)	(Z)	1	5	(Z)	37	27	36	50
Bahamas, The	712	704	685	661	725	605	328	203	157	165	107	376	482	505	560
Bahrain	489	636	443	255	244	61	97	155	134	115	428	539	288	121	129
Bangladesh	188	255	234	325	210	831	887	1,080	1,257	1,343	-643	-632	-846	-932	-1,134
Barbados	128	146	161	186	222	31	34	35	38	41	97	111	127	148	181
Byelarus	25	92	47	48	53	25	34	53	45	52	(Z)	58	-7	3	1
Belgium	9,775	8,878	10,944	12,466	12,520	4,476	5,149	6,342	6,054	6,779	5,299	3,729	4,602	6,412	5,741
Belize	117	138	115	100	107	59	54	51	52	68	58	82	64	48	38
Benin	27	22	26	34	27	10	16	10	10	18	17	7	16	24	9
Bermuda	242	265	300	299	282	7	15	9	10	12	236	250	291	288	270
Bolivia	222	218	186	214	269	162	191	260	263	275	60	27	-74	-49	-6
Bosnia-Hercegovina [3]	5	25	39	28	59	10	7	5	3	10	-4	18	35	25	49
Botswana	47	25	23	36	29	12	8	14	21	27	34	17	9	15	2
Brazil	5,751	6,058	8,118	11,439	12,699	7,609	7,479	8,708	8,830	8,762	-1,858	-1,421	-590	2,610	3,938
British Virgin Islands	44	46	47	49	54	3	14	15	11	7	41	32	32	38	47
Brunei	453	473	376	190	375	30	30	46	38	49	424	442	330	152	327
Bulgaria	86	115	110	132	138	79	159	212	189	128	7	-44	-102	-57	11
Burkina	13	18	7	15	10	(Z)	(Z)	(Z)	(Z)	4	13	18	7	15	7
Cameroon	57	49	54	46	71	84	101	56	48	65	-27	-53	-2	-2	6
Canada	90,594	100,444	114,441	127,226	133,668	98,630	111,216	128,948	145,349	156,506	-8,036	-10,772	-14,506	-18,123	-22,838
Cayman Islands	282	164	202	180	208	10	35	53	18	17	272	130	150	162	191
Chad	5	8	8	11	3	(Z)	(Z)	2	3	7	5	8	6	8	-4
Chile	2,466	2,599	2,776	3,615	4,132	1,388	1,462	1,822	1,931	2,256	1,078	1,137	954	1,684	1,876
China	7,418	8,763	9,287	11,754	11,978	25,728	31,540	38,781	45,543	51,495	-18,309	-22,777	-29,494	-33,790	-39,517
Colombia	3,286	3,235	4,070	4,624	4,709	2,837	3,032	3,172	3,751	4,273	449	203	899	873	436
Congo (Brazzaville)	59	27	38	55	62	510	500	403	207	315	-451	-473	-365	-152	-253
Costa Rica	1,357	1,542	1,867	1,737	1,814	1,411	1,541	1,646	1,843	1,974	-54	1	220	-107	-160
Croatia [3]	91	103	147	140	106	43	106	115	94	71	48	-3	32	46	35
Cyprus	166	138	209	258	257	11	16	18	13	17	155	122	191	245	239
Czechoslovakia	413	(X)	(X)	(X)	(X)	242	(X)	(X)	(X)	(X)	171	(X)	(X)	(X)	(X)
Czech Republic	(X)	267	297	363	410	(X)	277	316	363	482	(X)	-10	-18	-1	-71
Denmark	1,473	1,092	1,215	1,518	1,730	1,667	1,664	2,122	1,945	2,137	-194	-572	-907	-427	-408

See footnotes at end of table.

No. 1313. U.S. Exports, Imports, and Merchandise Trade Balance, by Country: 1992 to 1996-Continued

[See headnote, page 803]

COUNTRY	EXPORTS, DOMESTIC AND FOREIGN					GENERAL IMPORTS [1]					MERCHANDISE TRADE BALANCE				
	1992	1993	1994	1995	1996	1992	1993	1994	1995	1996	1992	1993	1994	1995	1996
Djibouti	11	13	7	9	8	(X)	(Z)	-	(Z)	(Z)	11	13	7	9	8
Dominica	34	27	26	27	34	5	6	7	7	8	29	22	19	20	26
Dominican Republic	2,100	2,350	2,800	3,015	3,183	2,372	2,672	3,094	3,399	3,575	-273	-322	-294	-384	-392
Ecuador	999	1,100	1,196	1,538	1,257	1,343	1,399	1,727	1,929	1,916	-344	-299	-531	-391	-659
Egypt	3,088	2,768	2,844	2,985	3,146	435	613	548	606	665	2,654	2,155	2,295	2,379	2,481
El Salvador	742	873	932	1,111	1,072	384	486	609	812	1,074	358	386	323	298	-2
Equatorial Guinea	11	3	2	5	17	(Z)	(Z)	(Z)	31	76	(Z)	(Z)	(Z)	(Z)	-59
Estonia	59	54	33	139	83	13	20	29	62	60	46	34	4	77	23
Ethiopia	250	139	143	148	148	9	22	34	33	35	241	117	109	115	113
Federated States of Micronesia	32	25	25	23	25	13	14	13	13	11	19	11	11	10	13
Fiji	59	27	118	32	28	67	69	97	78	75	-8	-42	21	-46	-47
Finland	785	848	1,069	1,250	2,438	1,185	1,608	1,803	2,270	2,345	-400	-761	-734	-1,020	93
France	14,593	13,267	13,622	14,245	14,428	14,797	15,279	16,775	17,209	18,630	-205	-2,013	-3,152	-2,964	-4,202
French Guiana	82	323	196	442	301	3	3	3	5	5	78	321	193	436	296
French Polynesia	82	102	72	82	88	11	9	14	14	17	71	94	58	68	71
Gabon	55	48	40	54	56	921	961	1,155	1,449	1,949	-866	-913	-1,114	-1,395	-1,893
Gambia	10	10	4	6	9	(Z)	9	2	2	2	10	1	2	4	7
Georgia	16	48	79	95	83	7	21	1	11	8	9	27	77	85	75
Germany	21,249	18,932	19,237	22,394	23,474	28,820	28,562	31,749	36,844	38,943	-7,572	-9,630	-12,512	-14,450	-15,469
Ghana	124	215	125	167	295	96	216	199	196	171	27	-1	-74	-29	124
Gibraltar	11	8	23	18	12	2	4	4	5	7	9	5	19	14	5
Greece	901	880	830	1,519	820	370	348	455	397	496	531	533	375	1,122	324
Greenland	3	3	3	2	4	12	13	10	7	6	-8	-10	-6	-5	-2
Grenada	24	24	24	27	36	8	8	7	5	4	16	16	16	22	32
Guadeloupe	60	49	51	69	66	1	5	2	1	1	59	44	49	68	65
Guatemala	1,205	1,312	1,355	1,647	1,564	1,081	1,194	1,283	1,527	1,673	124	118	72	120	-109
Guinea	61	59	50	67	87	103	117	92	99	117	-42	-58	-42	-32	-29
Guyana	118	122	110	141	137	102	91	98	107	110	17	32	12	34	27
Haiti	209	229	211	550	474	107	154	59	130	144	102	74	152	420	330
Honduras	811	899	1,012	1,279	1,641	783	914	1,097	1,441	1,796	28	-15	-86	-162	-155
Hong Kong	9,077	9,874	11,445	14,231	13,956	9,793	9,554	9,698	10,291	9,868	-716	319	1,748	3,940	4,088
Hungary	295	435	309	295	331	347	401	470	547	677	-52	34	-161	-252	-346
Iceland	119	147	112	171	257	165	233	249	233	236	-46	-86	-137	-62	21
India	1,917	2,778	2,296	3,296	3,318	3,780	4,554	5,302	5,726	6,169	-1,863	-1,776	-3,006	-2,430	-2,851
Indonesia	2,780	2,770	2,811	3,360	3,965	4,530	5,435	6,523	7,435	8,213	-1,750	-2,665	-3,712	-4,076	-4,248
Iran	748	616	329	277	(Z)	1	(Z)	1	(Z)	(Z)	747	616	328	277	(Z)
Iraq	1	4	1	(Z)	3	-	-	-	-	(-)	1	4	1	(Z)	3
Ireland	2,862	2,728	3,416	4,109	3,660	2,262	2,519	2,890	4,079	4,798	600	209	525	30	-1,139
Israel	4,077	4,429	5,006	5,621	6,009	3,816	4,420	5,223	5,709	6,426	261	9	-217	-88	-417
Italy	8,721	6,464	7,193	8,862	8,785	12,314	13,216	14,711	16,348	18,222	-3,593	-6,752	-7,518	-7,487	-9,437
Ivory Coast	87	89	111	173	141	188	178	185	214	397	-100	-90	-74	-41	-256
Jamaica	939	1,116	1,066	1,420	1,491	599	720	747	847	839	340	397	320	573	652
Japan	47,813	47,892	53,481	64,343	67,536	97,414	107,246	119,149	123,479	115,218	-49,601	-59,355	-65,669	-59,137	-47,683
Jordan	258	361	288	335	345	18	19	29	29	25	240	342	259	307	320
Kazakhstan	15	68	131	81	138	21	41	60	123	114	-6	27	71	-42	24
Kenya	124	131	170	114	104	73	92	109	102	107	51	39	61	13	-2
Kiribati	35	31	23	2	4	(Z)	2	1	1	1	35	29	23	1	3

See footnotes at end of table.

COUNTRY	EXPORTS, DOMESTIC AND FOREIGN					GENERAL IMPORTS [1]					MERCHANDISE TRADE BALANCE				
	1992	1993	1994	1995	1996	1992	1993	1994	1995	1996	1992	1993	1994	1995	1996
Kuwait	1,337	999	1,175	1,437	1,979	281	1,819	1,445	1,336	1,640	1,055	-819	-270	102	340
Kyrgyzstan	2	18	6	25	47	1	2	8	8	5	1	16	-2	16	42
Latvia	55	90	101	90	165	11	22	51	82	99	44	67	51	8	66
Lebanon	311	377	443	592	627	28	27	25	35	42	283	351	418	557	586
Lesotho	3	7	3	2	3	53	56	63	62	65	-50	-48	-60	-60	-63
Liberia	31	39	46	42	50	12	3	4	10	27	18	36	43	32	23
Liechtenstein	12	11	14	15	9	36	100	96	126	91	-24	-89	-82	-111	-82
Lithuania	44	57	41	52	63	5	16	16	26	34	39	41	26	26	29
Luxembourg	272	560	228	374	242	227	253	288	234	204	45	307	-59	140	39
Macao	19	28	21	30	30	721	669	791	895	858	-702	-641	-770	-865	-828
Macedonia [3]	4	11	14	21	14	46	111	82	89	125	-42	-100	-68	-68	-111
Madagascar	6	11	48	10	12	54	43	57	57	46	-47	-32	-9	-47	-34
Malawi	14	26	19	18	13	60	58	57	41	73	-46	-32	-38	-23	-59
Malaysia	4,363	6,064	6,965	8,816	8,521	8,294	10,563	13,977	17,453	17,825	-3,931	-4,499	-7,012	-8,637	-9,304
Mali	11	33	19	23	18	2	1	4	4	6	10	32	15	20	13
Malta	58	172	88	107	125	91	104	96	132	208	-33	68	-8	-26	-84
Marshall Islands	34	36	33	32	29	8	12	8	11	5	26	24	25	21	24
Martinique	33	33	31	38	35	1	1	4	2	1	31	31	28	36	34
Mauritania	59	20	14	43	15	9	7	4	6	5	51	13	11	38	10
Mauritius	22	18	24	25	25	136	198	217	230	217	-113	-180	-193	-205	-192
Mexico	40,592	41,581	50,840	46,292	56,761	35,211	39,917	49,493	61,685	72,963	5,381	1,664	1,348	-15,393	-16,202
Moldova	9	31	23	10	22	(Z)	(Z)	3	25	30	9	31	20	-15	-8
Monaco	6	6	6	10	3	13	16	18	12	16	-6	-10	-12	-3	-13
Morocco	496	600	405	517	476	178	185	192	239	252	318	415	213	278	224
Mozambique	150	59	39	49	23	19	9	15	28	27	130	50	24	22	-4
Namibia	34	22	16	27	22	23	22	28	12	27	11	-1	-12	15	-5
Netherlands	13,752	12,839	13,591	16,558	16,615	5,300	5,443	6,015	6,405	6,617	8,452	7,395	7,576	10,153	9,997
Netherlands Antilles	478	519	520	504	528	644	397	425	288	663	-166	123	96	216	-135
New Caledonia	36	23	27	22	29	15	24	23	40	55	21	-2	5	-18	-26
New Zealand	1,307	1,249	1,508	1,691	1,727	1,219	1,208	1,421	1,452	1,464	88	41	88	240	263
Nicaragua	185	150	186	250	262	69	128	167	239	350	117	22	19	11	-88
Niger	13	16	12	40	27	3	3	2	2	1	10	13	10	38	26
Nigeria	1,001	895	509	603	816	5,103	5,301	4,430	4,801	5,849	-4,102	-4,407	-3,921	-4,198	-5,033
Norway	1,279	1,212	1,268	1,293	1,556	1,969	1,958	2,373	3,087	3,869	-690	-745	-1,105	-1,794	-2,312
Oman	257	251	219	222	215	186	277	459	295	411	71	-26	-240	-73	-196
Pakistan	881	811	719	941	1,277	865	897	1,012	1,197	1,266	16	-86	-293	-256	11
Panama	1,103	1,187	1,276	1,390	1,378	254	280	323	307	346	850	908	954	1,083	1,032
Papua New Guinea	72	50	65	51	69	64	98	108	50	86	8	-48	-43	1	-16
Paraguay	415	521	794	992	897	35	50	80	55	42	380	472	713	937	855
Peru	1,005	1,072	1,408	1,775	1,767	739	754	840	1,035	1,262	267	318	568	741	505
Philippines	2,759	3,529	3,888	5,295	6,125	4,355	4,894	5,720	7,007	8,162	-1,597	-1,364	-1,832	-1,712	-2,038
Poland	641	912	625	776	968	375	454	651	664	627	266	458	-26	112	341
Portugal	1,024	727	1,055	896	960	664	785	898	1,057	1,016	360	-59	156	-159	-56
Qatar	189	166	162	226	207	70	65	81	91	157	119	101	81	135	50
Romania	248	324	337	253	266	87	69	195	222	249	161	254	142	31	16

See footnotes at end of table.

No. 1313. U.S. Exports, Imports, and Merchandise Trade Balance, by Country: 1992 to 1996-Continued

[See headnote, page 803]

COUNTRY	EXPORTS, DOMESTIC AND FOREIGN					GENERAL IMPORTS [1]					MERCHANDISE TRADE BALANCE				
	1992	1993	1994	1995	1996	1992	1993	1994	1995	1996	1992	1993	1994	1995	1996
Russia	2,112	2,970	2,579	2,823	3,340	481	1,743	3,235	4,030	3,561	1,631	1,227	-656	-1,207	-221
Saudi Arabia	7,167	8,661	6,011	6,155	7,295	10,371	7,708	7,687	8,237	8,781	-3,204	-1,047	-1,676	-2,082	-1,486
Senegal	80	70	43	68	56	10	8	11	5	6	70	63	31	63	50
Singapore	9,626	11,678	13,022	15,333	16,686	11,313	12,798	15,361	18,561	20,340	-1,687	-1,120	-2,339	-3,227	-3,655
Slovakia	(X)	34	43	61	63	(X)	65	129	130	124	(X)	-31	-86	-69	-62
Somalia	21	46	30	8	4	2	(Z)	(Z)	(Z)	(Z)	18	46	30	8	4
South Africa	2,434	2,188	2,173	2,751	3,106	1,727	1,845	2,030	2,208	2,323	707	344	143	543	784
South Korea	14,639	14,782	18,028	25,380	26,583	16,682	17,118	19,658	24,184	22,667	-2,043	-2,336	-1,629	1,196	3,916
Spain	5,537	4,168	4,625	5,526	5,486	3,002	2,992	3,554	3,875	4,281	2,535	1,176	1,071	1,651	1,205
Sri Lanka	178	203	198	279	211	789	1,002	1,093	1,260	1,393	-612	-799	-895	-981	-1,181
Sudan	53	59	55	43	50	11	12	36	23	19	42	47	19	21	32
Suriname	142	114	122	190	223	46	58	43	100	97	96	56	79	90	126
Sweden	2,844	2,354	2,520	3,080	3,429	4,716	4,534	5,044	6,256	7,158	-1,872	-2,180	-2,524	-3,177	-3,730
Switzerland	4,540	6,807	5,614	6,228	8,371	5,645	5,973	6,376	7,594	7,793	-1,105	834	-762	-1,366	578
Syria	165	187	199	223	226	42	130	64	56	15	123	56	134	168	211
Taiwan	15,250	16,168	17,078	19,290	18,413	24,596	25,102	26,711	28,972	29,911	-9,346	-8,934	-9,633	-9,682	-11,498
Tajikistan	9	12	15	18	17	2	18	60	41	33	7	-6	-44	-23	-16
Tanzania	34	33	49	66	50	11	11	15	22	19	23	21	34	44	31
Thailand	3,989	3,766	4,861	6,665	7,211	7,529	8,542	10,307	11,348	11,336	-3,540	-4,775	-5,446	-4,683	-4,125
Togo	20	13	13	19	20	6	3	4	4	4	13	9	8	15	16
Trinidad and Tobago	447	529	541	689	665	848	803	1,109	968	1,017	-401	-274	-569	-279	-352
Tunisia	233	232	327	215	189	48	41	54	70	76	184	192	273	145	113
Turkey	2,735	3,429	2,754	2,768	2,886	1,110	1,198	1,575	1,798	1,777	1,625	2,231	1,178	970	1,109
Turkmenistan	35	46	137	34	201	1	2	2	1	1	34	44	136	33	200
Turks and Caicos Islands	38	22	29	34	44	6	4	4	5	5	32	18	25	29	38
Uganda	15	21	28	22	17	12	10	35	13	16	3	11	-7	9	1
Ukraine	307	310	181	223	394	89	166	327	406	507	218	145	-146	-182	-113
United Arab Emirates	1,553	1,811	1,593	2,007	2,527	812	727	449	453	496	741	1,084	1,144	1,553	2,031
United Kingdom	22,800	26,438	26,833	28,857	30,916	20,093	21,730	25,063	26,898	28,892	2,707	4,706	1,770	1,959	2,024
Uruguay	231	254	311	396	484	266	266	168	167	260	-35	-12	143	229	224
U.S.S.R. (former)	1,036	(X)	(X)	(X)	(X)	187	(X)	(X)	(X)	(X)	849	(X)	(X)	(X)	(X)
Uzbekistan	51	73	90	63	352	(Z)	7	3	19	157	51	66	87	45	195
Venezuela	5,444	4,590	4,042	4,640	4,741	8,181	8,140	8,378	9,721	12,903	-2,737	-3,550	-4,337	-5,080	-8,162
Vietnam	5	7	172	253	616	(Z)	-	51	199	319	5	7	122	54	297
Western Samoa	73	10	7	8	12	1	1	(Z)	1	1	72	9	7	7	11
Yemen, Republic of	321	322	178	186	256	41	98	183	42	27	281	224	-5	144	228
Yugoslavia (former) [3]	167	(X)	(X)	(X)	(X)	225	(X)	(X)	(X)	(X)	-58	(X)	(X)	(X)	(X)
Yugoslavia, Fed. Rep. of	6	2	1	2	46	39	(Z)	-	-	8	-33	2	1	2	38
Zaire	33	35	40	77	73	250	238	188	261	250	-218	-203	-148	-184	-177
Zambia	68	42	33	49	46	70	41	64	33	64	-2	2	-31	16	-19
Zimbabwe	144	84	93	122	91	106	110	102	98	133	38	-26	-10	24	-42

- Represents zero. Z Less than $500,000. X Not applicable. [1] Imports are on a customs value basis. Exports are f.a.s. value. [2] Includes revisions not carried to country values; therefore, country values will not add to total. [3] Beginning June 1992 trade data were reported for the following countries which were formerly part of Yugoslavia — Croatia, Slovenia, Bosnia-Hercegovina, and Macedonia. The Federal Republic of Yugoslavia, which now includes only Serbia and Montenegro, will continue to be shown as "Yugoslavia." Yugoslavia (former)" reflects data for the former country and includes data for the period of January through May 1992.

Source: U.S. Bureau of the Census, *U.S. Merchandise Trade*, series FT 900, monthly.

No. 1314. U.S. Exports and General Imports, by Selected SITC Commodity Groups: 1993 to 1996

[In millions of dollars. SITC=Standard International Trade Classification. N.e.s.=Not elsewhere specified]

COMMODITY GROUP	EXPORTS [1]				GENERAL IMPORTS [2]			
	1993	1994	1995	1996	1993	1994	1995	1996
Total	**465,091**	**512,626**	**584,742**	**624,767**	**580,659**	**663,256**	**743,445**	**791,364**
Agricultural commodities	**41,938**	**44,936**	**54,850**	**59,311**	**23,641**	**25,955**	**29,258**	**32,565**
Animal feeds	3,464	3,353	3,667	4,183	368	433	472	633
Bulbs	107	112	110	106	217	238	283	312
Cereal flour	1,099	1,159	1,163	1,170	802	970	1,082	1,213
Cocoa	39	34	39	111	739	696	722	962
Coffee	32	53	15	4	1,383	2,270	2,985	2,491
Corn	4,504	4,197	7,521	8,623	61	85	66	116
Cotton, raw and linters	1,575	2,641	3,711	2,740	12	21	29	300
Dairy products; eggs	820	717	776	713	544	583	620	717
Furskins, raw	98	131	127	181	59	78	59	74
Grains, unmilled	683	695	721	800	157	181	176	212
Hides and skins	1,187	1,391	1,621	1,515	119	126	140	133
Live animals	519	587	521	533	1,536	1,392	1,729	1,595
Meat and preparations	4,353	5,195	6,450	6,958	2,792	2,627	2,317	2,317
Oils/fats, animal	472	566	789	613	21	21	24	43
Oils/fats, vegetable	734	963	1,293	1,024	859	1,051	1,157	1,416
Plants	112	117	120	94	92	105	130	145
Rice	791	1,009	994	1,029	106	130	121	157
Seeds	294	315	321	355	154	152	172	200
Soybeans	4,580	4,355	5,422	7,447	22	46	32	31
Sugar	2	5	5	5	606	552	682	1,001
Tobacco, unmanufactured	1,299	1,304	1,397	1,390	942	697	555	1,053
Vegetables and fruit	6,008	6,757	7,098	7,313	5,665	6,075	6,581	7,514
Wheat	4,679	4,055	5,464	6,302	213	291	238	247
Other agricultural	4,489	5,225	5,504	6,102	6,172	7,134	8,887	9,683
Manufactured goods	**364,849**	**402,674**	**461,826**	**483,874**	**479,896**	**557,310**	**629,685**	**669,967**
ADP equipment, office machinery	27,177	30,867	36,410	39,666	43,193	52,058	62,703	66,499
Airplanes	21,270	18,803	13,836	18,962	3,805	3,719	3,651	3,943
Airplane parts	9,487	9,824	10,349	11,723	2,613	2,727	2,616	3,464
Aluminum	2,310	2,787	3,775	3,486	3,277	4,943	5,819	4,828
Artwork/antiques	951	1,184	1,071	887	2,673	2,432	2,666	2,791
Basketware, etc	1,644	1,816	1,996	2,239	2,392	2,588	2,942	3,014
Chemicals, cosmetics	3,047	3,537	3,835	4,323	1,808	1,998	2,307	2,443
Chemicals, dyeing	2,014	2,330	2,585	2,716	1,700	1,869	2,079	2,165
Chemicals, fertilizers	1,798	2,703	3,219	3,070	1,136	1,298	1,391	1,400
Chemicals, inorganic	3,810	4,067	4,541	4,657	3,284	4,067	4,658	4,954
Chemicals, medicinal	5,751	6,096	6,434	7,160	4,135	4,674	5,543	7,076
Chemicals, organic	11,076	12,789	16,106	14,744	9,279	10,806	13,334	14,820
Chemicals, plastics	10,743	12,485	14,958	15,467	4,848	5,941	7,155	7,443
Chemicals, n.e.s.	6,835	7,657	9,131	9,651	2,941	3,235	3,925	4,568
Clothing	4,815	5,461	6,482	7,285	33,780	36,748	39,523	41,559
Copper	1,200	1,266	1,728	1,553	1,733	2,295	2,983	2,953
Electrical machinery	36,817	44,454	53,139	56,637	46,735	57,750	75,051	75,525
Footwear	605	646	671	761	11,173	11,712	12,098	12,749
Furniture and parts	2,948	3,131	3,125	3,323	6,249	7,565	8,338	9,431
Gem diamonds	153	184	171	151	5,103	5,756	5,951	6,588
General industrial machinery	19,515	21,813	24,394	26,599	17,082	21,330	24,125	25,286
Glass	1,341	1,503	1,644	1,814	1,004	1,350	1,468	1,679
Glassware	502	560	630	680	1,031	1,158	1,333	1,413
Gold, nonmonetary	9,115	5,689	5,055	6,641	2,014	1,933	2,155	2,737
Iron and steel mill products	3,330	3,554	5,349	4,795	9,027	12,896	12,279	13,368
Lighting, plumbing	1,097	1,249	1,293	1,358	1,762	2,024	2,284	2,579
Metal manufactures, n.e.s.	5,975	7,034	8,080	9,234	7,647	8,847	10,010	10,843
Metalworking machinery	3,256	3,897	4,626	5,241	3,683	4,596	5,926	6,789
Motorcycles, bicycles	1,433	1,515	1,786	1,009	2,161	2,322	2,825	2,150
Nickel	199	210	284	307	686	735	1,197	1,137
Optical goods	797	965	1,113	1,378	1,683	1,817	2,148	2,327
Paper and paperboard	6,463	7,448	9,572	9,837	8,640	9,066	12,470	11,637
Photographic equipment	2,932	3,016	3,351	3,743	4,267	4,676	5,145	5,271
Plastic articles, n.e.s.	2,988	3,574	3,847	4,439	3,937	4,517	5,101	5,306
Platinum	339	306	318	248	1,255	1,325	1,694	1,716
Pottery	110	104	99	95	1,436	1,555	1,667	1,569
Power generating machinery	19,167	20,346	21,856	22,292	17,125	19,543	20,493	22,499
Printed materials	3,995	3,971	4,325	4,346	2,026	2,234	2,584	2,700
Records/magnetic media	5,317	5,864	6,263	6,555	3,443	3,612	3,896	4,078
Rubber articles, n.e.s.	679	795	888	972	1,014	1,253	1,415	1,465
Rubber tires and tubes	1,465	1,614	1,858	1,959	2,736	3,034	3,144	3,074

See footnotes at end of table.

No. 1314. U.S. Exports and General Imports, by Selected SITC Commodity Groups: 1993 to 1996—Continued

[In millions of dollars]

COMMODITY GROUP	EXPORTS [1]				GENERAL IMPORTS [2]			
	1993	1994	1995	1996	1993	1994	1995	1996
Manufactured goods—Continued								
Scientific instruments	15,223	16,475	18,616	20,599	8,457	9,963	11,581	12,385
Ships, boats	976	1,165	1,178	1,064	969	808	816	1,029
Silver and bullion	203	256	663	638	390	486	580	569
Spacecraft	393	444	655	636	-	219	169	232
Specialized industrial machinery	17,626	19,677	23,311	25,659	13,565	16,733	18,972	18,509
Telecommunications equipment	13,122	15,872	19,005	19,838	27,297	32,418	34,457	34,167
Textile yarn, fabric	5,895	6,445	7,192	7,814	8,438	9,207	9,980	10,248
Toys/games/sporting goods	2,707	3,079	3,560	3,693	11,637	11,824	13,074	14,734
Travel goods	199	233	253	306	2,653	3,085	3,408	3,581
Vehicles/new cars, Canada	6,350	7,465	7,187	7,899	17,654	21,687	24,623	25,351
Vehicles/new cars, Japan	962	1,787	2,642	2,327	21,581	24,020	21,441	20,134
Vehicles/new cars, Other	4,914	5,824	5,100	6,021	12,022	13,470	18,041	21,574
Vehicles/trucks	4,144	5,126	5,646	5,991	10,109	10,355	11,284	11,355
Vehicles/chassis/bodies	370	427	441	516	406	429	436	499
Vehicles/parts	19,307	21,314	23,354	24,628	17,653	19,609	20,132	20,859
Watches/clocks/parts	236	276	248	277	2,546	2,641	2,785	2,805
Wood manufactures	1,475	1,543	1,633	1,685	2,869	3,390	3,687	4,037
Other manufactured goods	26,260	28,152	30,971	32,281	36,133	42,941	46,127	49,963
Mineral fuel	9,786	8,911	10,368	12,067	55,900	56,391	59,109	73,026
Coal	3,197	2,966	3,714	3,849	514	646	703	606
Crude oil	20	49	6	460	38,469	38,479	42,814	50,582
Petroleum preparations	3,920	3,167	3,244	3,948	10,789	10,270	9,096	13,858
Liquified propane/butane	229	195	316	302	951	873	852	1,263
Natural gas	241	254	266	261	3,678	3,937	3,182	4,002
Electricity	102	31	57	69	662	973	858	402
Other mineral fuels	2,046	2,248	2,755	3,168	836	1,213	1,606	2,315
Selected commodities:								
Fish and preparations	2,991	3,036	3,177	2,930	5,820	6,590	6,739	6,657
Cork, wood, lumber	5,786	5,572	5,637	5,501	5,633	6,680	6,149	7,532
Pulp and waste paper	2,976	3,794	6,206	4,034	1,886	2,315	3,827	2,848
Metal ores; scrap	3,227	3,713	5,564	4,278	3,030	3,262	4,004	4,048
Crude fertilizers	1,346	1,446	1,525	1,526	936	1,026	1,164	1,176
Cigarettes	3,919	4,965	4,770	4,736	491	70	64	69
Alcoholic bev. distilled	343	355	390	385	1,737	1,826	1,844	2,048
Re-exports	25,244	29,961	36,581	40,690	(X)	(X)	(X)	(X)
Agricultural commodities	889	987	1,174	1,252	(X)	(X)	(X)	(X)
Manufactured goods	23,832	28,383	34,848	38,798	(X)	(X)	(X)	(X)
Mineral fuels	107	78	120	168	(X)	(X)	(X)	(X)
Other, re-exports	416	532	439	472	(X)	(X)	(X)	(X)

- Represents zero. X Not applicable. [1] F.A.S. basis. [2] Customs value basis.

Source: U.S. Bureau of the Census, *U.S. Merchandise Trade*, series FT 900, monthly.

No. 1315. Imports for Consumption—Values and Duties: 1980 to 1996

[Imports are on customs value basis. Includes trade of Virgin Islands with foreign countries. For basis of dollar values for area coverage, see text, section 28]

YEAR	VALUES				Duties calculated [1] (mil. dol.)	RATIO OF DUTIES TO VALUES		Duties per capita [2] (dollar)
	Total (mil. dol.)	Free (mil. dol.)	Dutiable (mil. dol.)	Percent free		Total imports (percent)	Dutiable imports (percent)	
1980	[3]244,007	106,992	132,951	45	7,535	3.1	5.7	33.09
1981	259,012	76,338	182,674	29	8,893	3.4	4.9	38.67
1982	242,340	75,856	166,484	31	8,688	3.6	5.2	37.40
1983	256,679	83,397	173,283	32	9,430	3.7	5.4	40.21
1984	322,989	102,977	220,012	32	12,042	3.7	5.5	50.90
1985	343,553	106,035	237,518	31	13,067	3.8	5.5	54.73
1986	368,657	121,742	246,915	33	13,312	3.6	5.4	55.10
1987	402,066	132,152	269,914	33	13,923	3.5	5.2	57.06
1988	437,140	151,693	285,447	35	15,054	3.4	5.3	61.12
1989	468,012	156,365	311,647	33	16,096	3.4	5.2	64.70
1990	490,554	161,108	329,446	33	16,339	3.3	5.0	65.38
1991	483,028	167,641	315,386	35	16,197	3.4	5.1	64.10
1992	525,091	194,583	330,508	37	17,164	3.3	5.2	67.12
1993	574,863	236,007	338,856	41	18,334	3.2	5.4	70.99
1994	657,885	292,257	365,628	44	19,846	3.0	5.6	73.64
1995	739,660	373,948	365,713	51	18,597	2.5	5.1	64.70
1996	790,470	406,640	383,829	51	18,005	2.3	4.7	67.87

[1] Customs duties (including import excise taxes) calculated on the basis of reports of quantity and value of imports merchandise entered directly for consumption or withdrawn from bonded customs warehouses. [2] Based on estimated population including Armed Forces abroad as of July 1. [3] Total includes revisions not carried to free and dutiable values.

Source: U.S. Bureau of the Census, 1970-1988, *Highlights of U.S. Export and Import Trade*, series FT 990, monthly; beginning 1989, *U.S. Merchandise Trade: Selected Highlights*, series FT 920; and unpublished data.

No. 1316. Domestic Exports and Imports for Consumption of Merchandise, by Selected SIC-Based Product Category: 1990 to 1996

[In millions of dollars. Includes nonmonetary gold]

SIC-BASED PRODUCT CATEGORY	SIC[1] code	1990	1991	1992	1993	1994	1995	1996
Domestic exports, total[2]	(X)	374,537	400,842	425,377	439,282	482,141	547,300	583,221
Agricultural, forestry and fishery products	(X)	26,225	25,052	26,785	25,324	26,102	33,418	36,234
Agricultural products	01	22,597	21,075	22,633	21,615	22,169	29,391	32,380
Livestock and livestock products	02	829	970	871	836	973	920	989
Forestry products	08	281	306	324	276	263	272	271
Fish, fresh or chilled; and other marine products[3]	09	2,518	2,701	2,959	2,596	2,677	2,836	2,594
Mineral commodities	(X)	7,336	7,442	7,210	5,584	5,850	7,159	7,284
Metallic ores and concentrates	10	1,137	1,014	1,084	799	1,018	1,562	1,091
Bituminous, lignite and anthracite coal	11,12	4,513	4,623	4,241	3,090	2,858	3,572	3,694
Crude petroleum and natural gas	13	638	675	737	588	576	729	1,197
Nonmetallic minerals, exc. fuels	14	1,047	1,130	1,148	1,107	1,199	1,296	1,302
Manufactured commodities	(X)	330,403	359,635	383,082	400,721	441,501	496,421	530,484
Food and kindred products	20	16,160	17,492	19,761	20,509	23,094	26,021	27,041
Tobacco manufactures	21	5,040	4,574	4,509	4,253	5,367	5,222	5,238
Textile mill products	22	3,635	4,108	4,473	4,667	5,151	5,696	6,177
Apparel and related products	23	2,848	3,679	4,599	5,433	6,145	7,190	8,104
Lumber and related products	24	6,523	6,477	6,802	7,361	7,252	7,424	7,401
Furniture and fixtures	25	1,569	2,086	2,518	2,818	3,030	2,953	3,101
Paper and allied products	26	8,631	9,214	9,969	9,457	11,000	14,943	14,002
Printing and publishing	27	3,150	3,590	3,808	4,057	4,070	4,471	4,534
Chemicals and allied products	28	37,806	41,483	41,953	42,742	48,950	57,897	58,503
Petroleum and coal products	29	6,794	7,026	6,403	6,163	5,510	6,014	7,158
Rubber and misc. plastics products	30	6,396	7,049	7,872	8,554	9,942	11,025	12,093
Leather and leather products	31	1,368	1,413	1,541	1,536	1,539	1,565	1,725
Stone, clay, and glass products	32	3,296	3,533	3,855	3,844	4,215	4,796	5,097
Primary metal products	33	13,116	15,243	15,105	18,669	16,327	20,191	21,279
Fabricated metal products	34	11,138	11,962	13,265	13,497	13,395	15,161	16,612
Machinery, except electrical	35	61,229	65,300	66,554	72,279	82,120	95,909	104,055
Electric and electronic machinery	36	39,807	42,330	45,992	52,947	63,839	76,235	79,533
Transportation equipment	37	68,113	76,172	82,862	80,196	85,068	82,699	92,887
Instruments and related products	38	19,524	21,699	22,815	24,699	26,560	29,581	32,842
Misc. manufactured commodities	39	4,296	4,621	5,446	5,288	5,813	7,383	6,763
Imports for consumption, total[2]	(X)	490,554	483,028	526,091	574,863	657,884	739,661	790,470
Agricultural, forestry and fishery products	(X)	12,750	13,148	14,216	15,866	17,427	19,799	20,661
Agricultural products	01	5,925	6,107	6,716	7,839	8,657	9,803	10,950
Livestock and livestock products	02	1,453	1,501	1,873	2,161	2,047	2,450	2,377
Forestry products	08	1,015	978	1,088	1,068	1,208	1,932	1,810
Fish, fresh or chilled; and other marine products[3]	09	4,357	4,562	4,540	4,798	5,515	5,614	5,525
Mineral commodities	(X)	51,391	44,581	44,823	45,965	47,300	51,050	57,144
Metallic ores and concentrates	10	1,500	1,244	1,167	1,108	1,283	1,413	1,407
Bituminous, lignite and anthracite coal	11,12	93	112	127	218	229	248	238
Crude petroleum and natural gas	13	48,917	42,415	42,796	43,871	44,949	48,495	54,463
Nonmetallic minerals, exc. fuels	14	881	810	734	767	839	894	1,035
Manufactured commodities	(X)	407,043	406,550	445,127	490,289	567,052	639,729	680,609
Food and kindred products	20	16,564	16,298	17,445	16,090	17,342	18,326	20,948
Tobacco manufactures	21	94	199	285	467	163	169	245
Textile mill products	22	6,807	7,132	7,806	6,161	6,534	6,965	7,169
Apparel and related products	23	24,644	25,497	30,533	35,475	38,561	41,206	43,075
Lumber and related products	24	5,446	5,229	6,700	8,901	10,528	10,406	12,194
Furniture and fixtures	25	5,235	5,130	5,601	6,242	7,522	8,303	9,320
Paper and allied products	26	11,669	10,431	10,382	10,891	11,772	16,757	14,784
Printing and publishing	27	1,849	1,878	2,046	2,211	2,422	2,902	2,996
Chemicals and allied products	28	21,611	22,999	25,849	27,259	31,697	38,079	42,826
Petroleum and coal products	29	14,472	11,097	10,410	9,906	9,504	8,971	18,768
Rubber and misc. plastics products	30	9,731	9,855	11,287	13,053	14,393	15,973	16,891
Leather and leather products	31	10,944	10,714	11,342	11,692	12,977	13,628	14,187
Stone, clay, and glass products	32	5,845	5,558	5,951	6,431	7,594	8,496	9,088
Primary metal products	33	23,232	22,262	22,891	22,772	30,106	33,519	34,583
Fabricated metal products	34	11,606	11,396	12,436	12,941	14,664	16,213	17,492
Machinery, except electrical	35	55,021	55,578	62,274	73,370	89,705	106,391	112,907
Electric and electronic machinery	36	55,736	58,610	65,596	76,869	94,332	114,912	114,066
Transportation equipment	37	89,599	88,004	92,930	102,259	115,998	122,344	129,235
Instruments and related products	38	16,846	18,668	20,338	22,060	24,410	27,473	28,747
Misc. manufactured commodities	39	20,090	20,015	23,025	25,219	26,830	28,694	31,088

X Not applicable. [1] Standard Industrial Classification. [2] Includes scrap and waste, used or secondhand merchandise, manufactured commodities not identified by kind, and timing adjustments. [3] Includes frozen and packaged fish.

Source: U.S. Bureau of the Census, 1985 and 1988, *Highlights of U.S. Export and Import Trade*, series FT 990; beginning 1990, *U.S. Merchandise Trade*, series FT 900, December issues.

Figure 29.1
Selected Outlying Areas of the United States

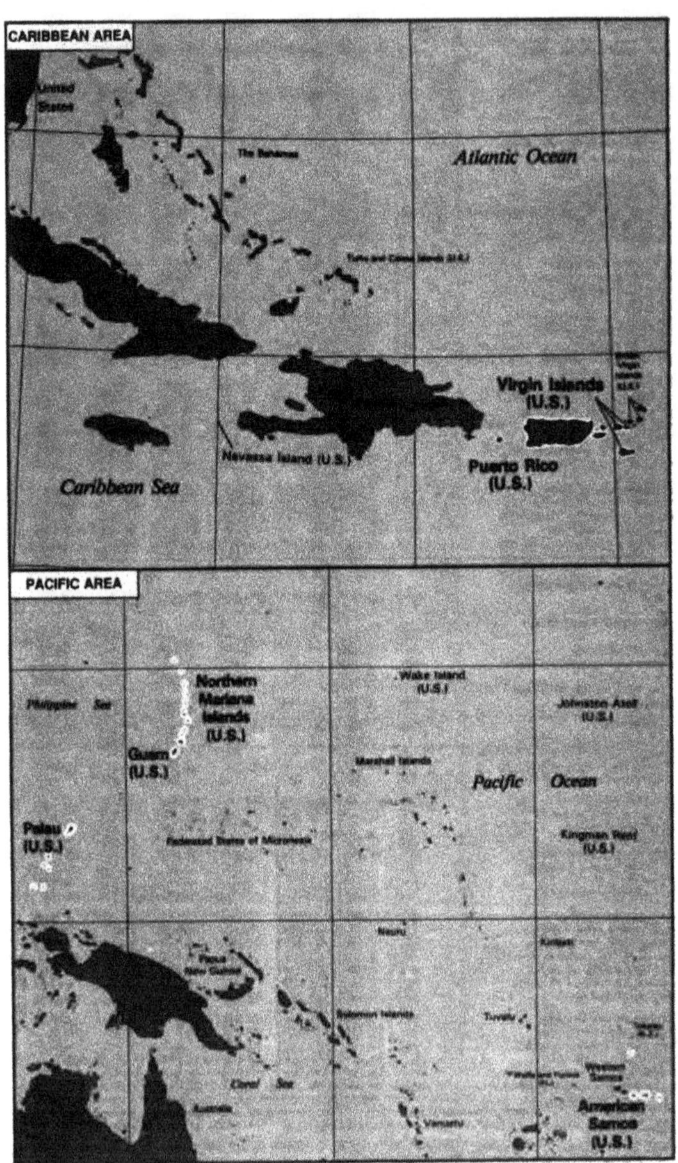

Section 29

Outlying Areas

This section presents summary economic and social statistics for Puerto Rico, Virgin Islands, Guam, American Samoa, and the Northern Mariana Islands.

Primary sources are the decennial censuses of population and housing, and the censuses of agriculture, business, manufactures, and construction (taken every 5 years) conducted by the Bureau of the Census; the annual *Vital Statistics of the United States,* issued by the National Center for Health Statistics; and the annual *Income and Product* of the Puerto Rico Planning Board, San Juan.

Jurisdiction—The United States gained jurisdiction over these areas as follows:

The islands of *Puerto Rico* and *Guam,* surrendered by Spain to the United States in October 1898, were ceded to the United States by the Treaty of Paris, ratified in 1899. Puerto Rico became a commonwealth on July 25, 1952, thereby achieving a high degree of local autonomy under its own constitution. The *Virgin Islands,* comprising 50 islands and cays, was purchased by the United States from Denmark in 1917. *American Samoa,* a group of seven islands, was acquired by the United States in accordance with a convention among the United States, Great Britain, and Germany, ratified in 1900 (Swains Island was annexed in 1925).

By an agreement approved by the Security Council and the United States, the Northern Mariana Islands, previously under Japanese mandate, was administered by the United States between 1947 and 1986 under the United Nations trusteeship system. The Northern Mariana Islands became a commonwealth in 1986.

Censuses—Because characteristics of the outlying areas differ, the presentation of census data for them is not uniform. The 1960 Census of Population covered all of the places listed above except the Northern Mariana Islands (their census was conducted in April 1958 by the Office of the High Commissioner), while the 1960 Census of Housing also excluded American Samoa. The 1970, 1980, and 1990 Censuses of Population and Housing covered all five areas. The 1959, 1969, and 1978 Censuses of Agriculture covered Puerto Rico, American Samoa, Guam, and the Virgin Islands; the 1964, 1974, and 1982 censuses covered the same areas except American Samoa; and the 1969, 1978, 1987, and 1992 censuses included the Northern Mariana Islands. Beginning in 1967, Congress authorized the economic censuses, to be taken at 5-year intervals, for years ending in "2" and "7." Prior economic censuses were conducted in Puerto Rico for 1949, 1954, 1958, and 1963 and in Guam and the Virgin Islands for 1958 and 1963. In 1967, the census of construction industries was added for the first time in Puerto Rico; in 1972, Virgin Islands and Guam were covered. For 1982, 1987, and 1992 the economic censuses covered the Northern Mariana Islands.

In Brief

Persons per household, 1990:

Puerto Rico	*3.3*
Virgin Islands	*3.1*
Guam	*4.0*
American Samoa	*7.0*
Northern Mariana Islands	*4.6*

Information in other sections—In addition to the statistics presented in this section, other data are included as integral parts of many tables showing distribution by States in various sections of the *Abstract.* See "Outlying areas of the United States" in the index. For definition and explanation of terms used, see section 1, Population; section 4, Education; section 23, Agriculture; section 25, Construction and Housing; section 26, Manufactures; and section 27, Domestic Trade and Services.

No. 1317. Estimated Resident Population With Projections: 1960 to 2020

[In thousands. Population data generally are de facto figures for the present territory. Population estimates were derived from information available as of early 1997. See text, section 30, for general comments regarding the data. For details of methodology, coverage, and reliability, see source]

AREA	1960	1970	1980	1990	1993	1996	1997	2000, proj.	2010, proj.	2020, proj.
Puerto Rico	2,358	2,722	3,210	3,537	3,743	3,783	3,818	3,908	4,152	4,332
American Samoa	20	27	32	47	57	60	62	69	85	86
Guam	67	86	107	134	153	157	161	171	202	230
Virgin Islands	33	63	98	101	97	97	97	99	107	111
Northern Mariana Islands	9	12	17	44	51	52	54	57	71	86

Source: U.S. Bureau of the Census, International Data Base.

No. 1318. Vital Statistics—Specified Areas: 1960 to 1994

[Births, deaths, and infant deaths by place of residence; marriages and divorces by place of occurrence. Rates for 1960, 1970, 1980, and 1990 based on population enumerated as of April 1; for other years, on population estimated as of July 1]

AREA AND YEAR	BIRTHS		DEATHS		INFANT DEATHS		MARRIAGES		DIVORCES [3]	
	Number	Rate [1]	Number	Rate [1]	Number	Rate [2]	Number	Rate [1]	Number	Rate [1]
Puerto Rico: 1960	76,314	32.5	15,791	6.7	3,307	43.3	[4]20,212	[4]8.6	5,218	2.2
1970	67,628	24.8	18,080	6.7	1,930	28.6	29,905	11.0	9,658	3.6
1980	72,986	22.8	20,413	6.4	1,351	18.5	33,167	10.4	15,276	4.8
1990	66,417	18.9	25,957	7.4	888	13.4	33,080	11.0	13,695	3.8
1993	65,121	(NA)	(NA)	(NA)	(NA)	(NA)	(NA)	(NA)	(NA)	(NA)
1994	64,213	(NA)	26,292	(NA)	727	11.3	(NA)	(NA)	(NA)	(NA)
Guam: 1965	2,523	32.8	336	4.4	82	32.5	471	6.2	53	0.7
1970	2,842	28.8	355	5.8	62	21.6	874	9.9	84	1.0
1980	2,945	27.8	393	3.7	43	14.6	(NA)	(NA)	(NA)	(NA)
1990	3,839	28.8	520	3.9	31	8.1	(NA)	(NA)	(NA)	(NA)
1993	4,404	(NA)	(NA)	(NA)	(NA)	(NA)	(NA)	(NA)	(NA)	(NA)
1994	4,410	(NA)	605	(NA)	41	9.3	(NA)	(NA)	(NA)	(NA)
Virgin Islands: 1960	1,180	36.8	332	10.3	42	35.6	369	11.1	135	4.2
1970	2,896	46.8	469	7.9	72	24.6	1,149	18.4	270	4.3
1980	2,504	25.9	504	5.2	61	24.4	1,112	11.5	478	4.9
1990	2,267	22.3	480	4.7	33	14.6	2,377	23.4	(NA)	(NA)
1993	2,484	(NA)	(NA)	(NA)	(NA)	(NA)	(NA)	(NA)	(NA)	(NA)
1994	2,396	(NA)	602	(NA)	33	13.8	(NA)	(NA)	(NA)	(NA)

NA Not available. [1] Per 1,000 population. [2] Per 1,000 live births. [3] Includes reported annulments. [4] Data are incomplete.

Source: U.S. National Center for Health Statistics, *Vital Statistics of the United States*, annual.

No. 1319. Land Area and Population Characteristics, by Area: 1990

[As of April 1. For definition of median, see Guide to Tabular Presentation]

ITEM	United States	Puerto Rico	Virgin Islands	Guam	American Samoa	Northern Mariana Islands
Land area (sq. miles)	3,536,338	3,427	134	210	77	179
Total resident population	248,709,873	3,522,037	101,809	133,152	46,773	43,345
Per square mile	70.3	1,027.9	760.9	634.1	607.4	242.2
Percent increase, 1980-90	9.8	10.2	5.4	25.6	44.8	158.3
Urban	187,053,487	2,508,346	37,885	50,801	15,599	12,151
Rural	61,656,386	1,013,691	63,924	82,351	31,174	31,194
Male	121,239,418	1,705,642	49,210	70,945	24,023	22,802
Female	127,470,455	1,816,395	52,599	62,207	22,750	20,543
Males per 100 females	95.1	93.9	93.6	114.0	105.6	111.0
Median age (years)	32.9	28.4	28.2	25.0	20.9	27.4
Male (years)	31.7	27.2	27.1	25.2	20.6	29.9
Female (years)	34.1	29.6	29.2	24.9	21.2	24.9
Marital status, persons 15 years and over	195,142,002	2,563,818	72,365	93,200	28,952	33,030
Never married	52,559,853	711,470	27,539	30,759	11,412	13,810
Married [1]	111,498,578	1,499,449	35,199	54,717	15,958	17,869
Widowed or divorced	31,053,571	352,899	9,627	7,724	1,582	1,351
Households and families:						
Households	91,947,410	1,054,924	32,020	31,373	6,607	6,873
Persons in households	242,012,129	3,487,667	100,488	124,596	46,267	31,866
Persons per household	2.63	3.31	3.14	3.97	7.00	4.63
Families	64,517,947	986,339	23,012	27,313	6,301	5,312
Husband-wife families	50,708,322	634,872	13,197	21,342	5,153	3,947
Children ever born per 1,000 females 15 to 44 years	1,223	1,512	1,662	1,523	1,757	1,226

[1] For Puerto Rico, includes consensually married couples and for all areas, includes separated couples.

Source: U.S. Bureau of the Census, *1990 Census of Population*, CP-1 and CP-2 parts 1, (United States), 53 (Puerto Rico). (Virgin Islands); *1990 Census of Population and Housing*, CPH-1, parts 53A and 55; CPH-6, parts G (Guam), AS (American Samoa) and CNMI (Commonwealth of the Northern Mariana Islands); and Summary Tape File, parts 3C, (United States), 3A (Puerto Rico), and 3 (Virgin Islands).

No. 1320. Selected Social and Economic Characteristics, by Area: 1990

[As of April 1]

CHARACTERISTIC	United States	Puerto Rico	Virgin Islands	Guam	American Samoa	Northern Mariana Islands
EDUCATIONAL ATTAINMENT						
Persons 25 years and over	158,868,436	1,952,297	55,639	66,700	19,570	24,633
Less than 9th grade	16,502,211	691,835	12,908	9,238	3,664	4,285
9th to 12th grade, no diploma	22,841,507	290,173	11,278	8,602	5,239	4,016
High school graduate	47,642,763	410,559	14,021	22,220	6,253	8,659
Some college or associate degree	39,571,702	281,248	9,011	14,984	3,062	3,818
Bachelor's degree or higher	32,310,253	278,482	8,421	11,656	1,352	3,855
EMPLOYMENT STATUS						
Total persons, 16 years old and over	191,829,271	2,497,078	70,323	90,990	27,991	32,522
In labor force	125,182,378	1,180,162	47,553	66,138	14,198	26,589
Percent of total	65.3	47.3	67.6	72.7	50.7	81.8
Armed forces	1,708,928	5,486	110	11,952	11	8
Civilian labor force	123,473,450	1,174,676	47,443	54,186	14,187	26,581
Employed	115,681,202	934,736	44,267	52,144	13,461	25,965
Unemployed	7,792,248	239,940	3,176	2,042	726	616
Percent of civilian labor force	6.3	20.4	6.7	3.8	5.1	2.3
Not in labor force	66,646,893	1,316,916	22,770	24,852	13,793	5,933
FAMILY INCOME IN 1989						
Families, census year	65,049,428	889,998	23,012	27,313	6,301	5,312
Percent distribution by income class	100.0	100.0	100.0	100.0	100.0	100.0
Less than $5,000	4.0	25.1	8.8	4.0	11.0	8.2
$5,000 to $9,999	5.6	24.9	9.5	4.7	19.2	13.9
$10,000 to $14,999	7.2	16.5	12.8	8.3	17.0	13.1
$15,000 to $24,999	16.4	17.5	20.6	21.1	23.6	21.6
$25,000 or more	66.9	16.0	48.3	61.9	29.1	43.2
Median income (dollars)	35,225	9,988	24,036	31,178	15,979	21,275
RESIDENCE IN 1985						
Persons 5 years and over	230,445,777	3,219,765	92,579	118,055	39,821	39,206
Same house	122,796,970	2,190,479	56,098	54,665	30,759	11,479
Different house in this area	102,540,097	879,691	25,003	24,763	2,763	6,870
Outside area	5,108,710	149,595	11,478	38,627	6,299	20,857
LANGUAGE SPOKEN AT HOME						
Persons 5 years and over	230,445,777	3,219,765	92,579	118,055	39,821	39,206
Speak only English at home	198,600,798	(NA)	70,442	44,048	1,203	1,878

NA Not available.

Source: U.S. Bureau of the Census, *1990 Census of Population and Housing*, Summary Tape File, parts 3C, (United States), 3A, and unpublished data, (Puerto Rico), and 3 (Virgin Islands); *1990 Census of Population*, CP-2 parts 1,(United States), 53 (Puerto Rico), 55 (Virgin Islands); CPH-L-98, *The Foreign Born Population in the United States: 1990; 1990 Census of Population and Housing*, CPH-6, parts G (Guam), AS (American Samoa), and CNMI (Commonwealth of the Northern Mariana Islands).

No. 1321. Federal Direct Payments for Individuals: 1995 and 1996

[In thousands of dollars. For fiscal years ending September 30]

PROGRAM PAYMENTS	1995				1996			
	Puerto Rico	Guam	Virgin Islands	American Samoa	Puerto Rico	Guam	Virgin Islands	American Samoa
Total	**5,142,735**	**139,287**	**160,136**	**29,584**	**5,626,618**	**177,398**	**109,079**	**26,348**
Pell Grants	289,526	1,369	1,142	2,139	257,919	1,306	1,141	820
Medicare: Hospital insurance	388,061	402	6,755	-	464,766	663	11,651	-
Supplemental medical insurance	421,016	828	5,288	-	567,130	347	6,231	-
Social Security:								
Disability insurance	872,817	5,368	10,272	4,611	907,106	5,884	7,680	5,266
Retirement insurance	1,459,956	29,914	46,853	5,954	1,546,002	32,789	37,038	6,344
Survivors insurance	643,835	15,920	15,582	6,024	682,418	16,351	11,943	6,287
Veterans:								
Pension and disability	357,528	5,435	1,949	2,383	363,330	5,736	1,955	2,564
Education assistance	5,157	497	106	362	14,662	509	110	365
Federal retirement and disability	198,542	65,926	14,786	1,874	210,076	72,024	15,452	3,039
Food Stamps	(1)	24,280	27,544	-	(1)	26,824	41,835	-
Housing assistance [2]	64,121	12,217	17,414	6,127	249,911	13,306	[3]-39,059	1,540
Other	[3]442,156	[3]-21,253	12,445	110	363,296	1,657	13,102	121

- Represents or rounds to zero. [1] Food stamp program in Puerto Rico was replaced by the Nutritional Assistance Grant Program. Figures shown represent grants to State and local governments, not included in totals. [2] Amounts shown for Housing assistance to nonpublic agencies reflects reductions to allow for offsetting amounts included for payments to public agencies. Also includes FEMA individual assistance payments under the Disaster Assistance Program; for disaster relief payments to government agencies. [3] Reflects deobligated funds awarded in an earlier period

Source: U.S. Bureau of the Census, *Federal Expenditures by State for Fiscal Year*, annual.

No. 1322. Public Elementary and Secondary Schools, by Areas: 1995

[For school year ending in year shown, unless otherwise indicated]

ITEM	Puerto Rico	Guam	Virgin Islands	American Samoa	ITEM	Puerto Rico	Guam	Virgin Islands	American Samoa
PUBLIC EL/SEC					School staff	47,517	2,550	2,157	885
					Teachers	39,933	1,826	1,528	698
Enrollment, fall	621,121	32,185	23,126	14,445	Other support services staff	20,292	2,019	636	353
Elementary (kindergarten-grade 8)	455,653	24,189	16,659	11,054	Current expenditures [1] ($1,000)	1,679,009	175,729	120,617	25,801
Secondary (grades 9-12 and post graduates)	166,468	7,996	6,467	3,391	HIGHER EDUCATION				
Staff, fall	66,866	4,730	3,193	1,340					
School district staff	1,059	161	401	102	Enrollment, fall	156,439	6,449	3,095	1,249

[1] Public elementary and secondary day schools.

Source: U.S. National Center for Education Statistics, unpublished data.

No. 1323. Puerto Rico—Summary: 1970 to 1996

ITEM	Unit	1970	1980	1985	1990	1993	1994	1995	1996
POPULATION									
Total [1]	1,000	2,722	3,184	3,378	3,527	3,622	3,686	3719	3733
Persons per family	Number	4.6	4.3	3.9	3.7	3.6	3.6	3.5	3.5
EDUCATION [2]									
Enrollment, total	1,000	922.6	1,090.9	1,107.9	(NA)	(NA)	(NA)	(NA)	(NA)
Public day school	1,000	672.3	716.1	692.9	651.2	637.0	631.4	621.4	627.6
Other public	1,000	103.9	149.5	152.0	(NA)	(NA)	(NA)	(NA)	(NA)
Private schools	1,000	89.1	95.2	107.3	145.8	117.4	140.0	145.9	148.0
College and university	1,000	57.3	130.1	155.7	155.9	160.7	161.7	167.1	171.6
Expenses	Mil. dol.	288.8	825.0	1,171.8	1,686.4	2,214.0	2,251.4	2,495.4	2,731.1
As percent of GNP	Percent	6.2	7.5	7.8	7.8	8.8	8.5	8.8	9.0
Public	Mil. dol.	254.6	612.2	810.2	1,054.2	1,456.8	1,467.9	1,695.0	1,912.3
Private	Mil. dol.	34.2	212.8	361.6	644.2	757.2	783.5	800.4	818.8
LABOR FORCE [3]									
Total [4]	1,000	765	907	985	1,124	1,201	1,203	1,219	1,266
Employed [5]	1,000	686	753	774	963	999	1,011	1,051	1,092
Agriculture [6]	1,000	68	38	39	36	34	34	34	32
Manufacturing	1,000	132	143	141	168	168	166	172	167
Trade	1,000	128	138	150	185	201	201	211	218
Government	1,000	106	184	183	222	217	224	232	246
Unemployed	1,000	79	154	211	161	202	192	168	175
Unemployment rate [7]	Rate	10	17	21	14	17	16	14	14
Compensation of employees	Mil. dol.	2,800	7,200	9,442	13,639	16,042	16,721	17,773	18,760
Avg. compensation	Dollar	4,082	9,563	12,456	14,854	16,058	16,539	16,911	17,179
Salary and wages	Mil. dol.	2,555	6,290	8,137	11,681	13,737	14,420	15,280	16,144
INCOME [8]									
Personal income:									
Current dollars	Mil. dol.	3,753	11,002	14,588	21,105	24,612	25,864	27,303	29,370
Constant (1954) dollars	Mil. dol.	2,654	3,985	4,274	5,551	6,056	6,243	6,518	6,907
Disposable personal income:									
Current dollars	Mil. dol.	3,565	10,403	13,760	19,914	23,195	24,248	15,516	27,432
Constant (1954) dollars	Mil. dol.	2,521	3,768	4,032	5,236	5,708	5,853	6,091	6,452
Average family income:									
Current dollars	Dollar	6,366	14,858	16,914	22,234	24,608	25,484	25,810	27,587
Constant (1954) dollars	Dollar	4,503	5,361	4,957	5,646	6,055	6,151	6,161	6,486
BANKING [9]									
Assets	Mil. dol.	3,322	10,223	21,209	27,902	31,636	32,778	40,309	39,671
TOURISM [8]									
Number of visitors	1,000	1,225.0	2,140.0	2,061.6	3,425.8	3,869.0	4,022.6	4,086.6	4,110.2
Visitor expenditures	Mil. dol.	235.4	618.7	757.7	1,366.4	1,628.1	1,728.3	1,827.6	1,898.3
Average per visitor	Dollar	192	289	368	399	421	430	447	462
Net income from tourism	Mil. dol.	89.8	202.2	223.1	383.3	441.3	469.2	502.8	529.7

NA Not available. [1] 1970, 1980, and 1990 enumerated as of April 1; all other years estimated as of July 1. [2] Enrollment for the first school month. Expenses for school year ending in year shown [3] Annual average of monthly figures. For fiscal years. [4] Beginning 1980, for population 16 years old and over; 1970, for population 14 years and over. [5] Includes other employment not shown separately. [6] Includes forestry and fisheries. [7] Percent unemployed of the labor force. [8] For fiscal years. [9] As of June 30. Includes domestic and governmental banks.

Source: Puerto Rico Planning Board, San Juan, PR, *Income and Product*, annual; and *Socioeconomics Statistics*, annual

No. 1324. Puerto Rico—Gross Product and Net Income: 1980 to 1996

[In millions of dollars. For fiscal years ending June 30. Data for 1996 are preliminary]

ITEM	1980	1985	1990	1992	1993	1994	1995	1996
Gross product	11,065	15,002	21,619	23,696	25,133	26,641	28,413	30,254
Agriculture	380	357	434	420	411	370	317	307
Manufacturing	5,306	7,909	12,126	14,183	15,428	16,748	17,863	18,861
Contract construction and mining [1]	369	334	720	798	874	928	955	1,003
Transportation [2]	1,279	1,709	2,468	2,830	3,009	3,134	3,284	3,487
Trade	2,273	3,160	4,728	4,990	5,303	5,635	5,959	6,224
Finance, insurance, real estate	1,486	2,547	3,896	4,596	4,897	5,246	5,596	5,878
Services	1,279	1,637	3,015	3,582	3,909	4,332	4,693	4,991
Government	1,897	2,346	3,337	3,672	3,881	3,987	4,440	4,871
Commonwealth	1,574	1,996	2,884	3,154	3,327	3,395	3,793	4,152
Municipalities	323	350	453	518	555	592	647	719
Rest of the world	-3,372	-5,287	-8,965	-10,934	-11,790	-13,050	-14,194	-15,251
Statistical discrepancy	166	91	-121	-439	-789	-689	-501	-117
Net income	9,007	12,182	17,941	19,631	21,185	22,041	23,448	24,491
Agriculture	435	410	486	476	469	420	447	413
Manufacturing	4,756	7,117	11,277	13,215	14,482	15,688	16,737	17,679
Mining	9	10	26	28	25	28	30	31
Contract construction	337	309	679	753	805	830	854	895
Transportation [2]	1,022	1,248	1,778	1,943	2,132	2,193	2,358	2,436
Trade	1,609	2,285	3,420	3,538	3,712	3,878	4,087	4,256
Finance, insurance, and real estate	1,200	2,141	3,280	3,814	4,073	4,294	4,612	4,800
Services	1,114	1,606	2,643	3,125	3,415	3,775	4,114	4,360
Commonwealth government [3]	1,897	2,346	3,337	3,672	3,881	3,987	4,440	4,871
Rest of the world	-3,372	-5,287	-8,965	-10,934	-11,790	-13,050	-14,194	-15,251

[1] Mining includes only quarries. [2] Includes other public utilities, and radio and television broadcasting. [3] Includes public enterprises not elsewhere classified.

Source: Puerto Rico Planning Board, San Juan, PR, *Economic Report of the Governor, 1995-96.*

No. 1325. Puerto Rico—Transfer Payments: 1985 to 1996

[In millions of dollars. Data represent transfer payments between Federal and State governments and other nonresidents. See headnote, table 1324]

ITEM	1985	1990	1992	1993	1994	1995	1996
Total receipts	3,531	4,871	5,108	5,478	5,957	6,348	6,951
Federal government	3,348	4,649	4,903	5,279	5,630	6,020	6,667
Transfers to individuals [1]	3,283	4,577	4,818	5,186	5,559	5,962	6,620
Veterans benefits	317	349	383	405	414	439	471
Medicare	220	388	487	517	570	861	1,061
Old age, disability, survivors	1,581	2,055	2,315	2,463	2,722	2,912	3,116
Nutritional assistance	780	880	957	975	995	1,063	1,077
Industry subsidies	65	72	86	93	96	84	73
U.S. State governments	17	18	29	33	23	21	17
Other nonresidents	166	205	175	166	304	307	268
Total payments	1,180	1,801	1,982	2,089	2,211	2,323	2,341
Federal government	1,145	1,756	1,912	2,021	2,055	2,153	2,260
Transfers from individuals	506	817	918	980	143	164	183
Contribution to Medicare	44	97	108	122	142	162	182
Employee contribution for Social Security	463	720	809	856	859	903	950
Transfers from industries	13	16	24	26	32	49	37
Unemployment insurance	169	247	209	208	211	184	191
Employer contribution for Social Security	435	675	761	807	810	853	899
Other nonresidents	35	45	69	69	149	165	76
Net balance	2,351	3,070	3,126	3,389	3,746	4,113	4,611
Federal government	2,203	2,893	2,991	3,258	3,575	3,804	4,407
U.S. State governments	14	16	25	27	16	16	12
Other nonresidents	134	162	110	104	155	293	193

[1] Includes other receipts and payments not shown separately.

Source: Puerto Rico Planning Board, San Juan, PR, *Economic Report of the Governor, 1995-96.*

No. 1326. Puerto Rico—Merchandise Imports and Exports: 1980 to 1994

[In millions of dollars. Imports are imports for consumption; see text, section 28]

ITEM	1980	1984	1985	1986	1987	1988	1989	1990	1991	1992	1993	1994
Imports	9,018	10,116	10,162	10,321	11,308	13,096	15,010	16,200	15,079	16,476	16,124	17,152
From U.S	5,345	5,738	6,130	6,467	7,307	8,788	10,193	10,792	10,306	11,463	11,179	11,455
From other	3,673	4,378	4,032	3,854	4,001	4,308	4,817	5,408	4,773	5,013	4,945	5,697
Exports	6,576	9,426	11,087	11,854	12,508	14,436	17,455	20,402	21,128	20,455	20,351	22,711
To U.S.	5,643	8,074	9,873	10,524	11,153	12,756	15,334	17,915	18,729	17,990	17,613	20,098
To other	933	1,352	1,214	1,330	1,355	1,680	2,121	2,487	2,399	2,465	2,738	2,613

Source: U.S. Bureau of the Census, *Foreign Commerce and Navigation of the United States*, annual; *U.S. Trade with Puerto Rico and U.S. Possessions, FT 895;* and, through 1988, *Highlights of U.S. Export and Import Trade, FT990*; thereafter, *FT920 Supplement.*

No. 1327. Puerto Rico—Economic Summary, by Industry: 1994

[Covers establishments with payroll. Employees are for the week including March 2. Most government employees are excluded. For statement on methodology, see Appendix III]

INDUSTRY	1987 SIC code [1]	Total establishments	EMPLOYMENT-SIZE CLASS OF ESTABLISHMENTS: 1 to 4	5 to 9	10 to 19	20 to 49	50 or more	Employees	Annual payroll (mil. dol.)
Total [2]	(X)	37,790	22,569	6,042	4,138	3,030	2,011	597,389	8,983.0
Agricultural services, forestry, and fishing	A	84	59	15	6	4	-	428	3.3
Mining	B	30	5	10	4	7	4	813	10.1
Nonmetallic minerals, except fuels	14	22	2	7	4	6	3	581	8.1
Construction [2]	C	1,406	584	234	206	204	177	37,782	447.4
General contractors and operative builders	15	539	208	89	80	85	77	16,221	192.2
Special trade contractors	17	716	337	121	110	85	63	14,203	169.3
Manufacturing [2]	D	2,036	583	221	327	374	531	151,233	2,860.3
Food and kindred products	20	293	89	42	51	52	59	18,493	348.5
Textile mill products	22	21	5	2	3	4	7	2,811	28.0
Apparel and other textile products	23	232	41	19	31	38	103	24,093	231.3
Furniture and fixtures	25	121	51	13	25	25	7	2,048	20.4
Paper and allied products	26	44	5	4	10	10	15	2,230	41.9
Printing and publishing	27	197	87	33	42	21	14	4,867	94.3
Chemicals and allied products	28	192	27	10	24	31	100	32,782	977.8
Petroleum and coal products	29	25	3	3	8	4	7	1,678	49.1
Rubber and misc. plastic products	30	82	15	9	15	23	20	3,870	63.3
Leather and leather products	31	25	3	3	1	2	16	7,932	88.5
Stone, clay, and glass products	32	159	47	16	38	46	12	4,271	80.7
Fabricated metal products	34	194	76	16	32	47	23	4,640	65.4
Industrial machinery and equip	35	70	30	10	6	7	17	3,802	76.0
Electronic and other electronic equip	36	95	8	6	7	14	60	17,040	305.1
Instruments and related products	38	63	6	6	4	7	40	12,210	246.9
Transportation and public utilities [2]	E	1,027	617	158	105	75	72	26,526	593.5
Trucking and warehousing	42	294	174	50	33	25	12	3,164	58.4
Water transportation	44	60	20	9	5	11	15	6,288	114.3
Air transportation	45	63	18	11	11	10	13	2,387	47.1
Transportation services	47	406	317	55	16	10	8	2,653	42.2
Communication	48	112	35	19	27	15	16	10,647	309.1
Electric, gas, and sanitary services	49	22	11	1	3	1	6	895	15.3
Wholesale trade [2]	F	2,419	1,056	510	411	290	152	35,156	699.4
Durable goods	50	1,258	534	286	228	158	52	15,243	295.1
Nondurable goods	51	1,143	521	217	181	126	98	19,511	391.3
Retail trade [2]	G	12,670	7,151	2,441	1,577	1,070	431	130,842	1,306.0
Building materials, garden supplies	52	908	582	166	91	58	11	6,040	70.2
General merchandise stores	53	440	178	55	59	65	83	18,885	189.8
Food stores	54	1,808	1,110	267	157	122	152	25,902	225.8
Automotive dealers and service stations	55	2,025	1,314	426	166	89	30	12,094	148.0
Apparel and accessory stores	56	1,853	783	513	369	163	25	16,120	142.3
Furniture and home furnishings	57	919	503	212	143	57	4	6,296	75.7
Eating and drinking places	58	2,438	1,323	328	332	376	79	27,428	221.1
Finance, insurance, and real estate [2]	H	1,805	832	349	299	224	101	38,182	787.0
Depository institutions	60	327	60	58	120	65	24	13,919	307.5
Nondepository institutions	61	377	84	100	85	82	26	9,270	154.8
Insurance carriers	63	80	24	11	10	20	15	3,918	97.2
Insurance agents, brokers, and service	64	227	123	42	26	21	15	3,544	86.6
Real estate	65	720	494	130	53	30	13	6,114	80.4
Services [2]	I	10,243	6,781	1,456	924	589	493	151,596	1,959.3
Personal services	72	780	555	128	64	29	4	3,900	38.3
Business services	73	1,268	626	202	174	120	146	41,204	475.2
Auto repair, services, and parking	75	899	657	134	72	26	10	4,759	59.4
Motion pictures	78	128	59	16	35	17	1	1,295	13.1
Amusement and recreation services	79	227	139	33	28	21	6	2,302	24.9
Health services	80	3,074	2,407	370	143	69	85	33,782	428.6
Legal services	81	1,072	899	82	63	22	6	3,976	74.6
Education services	82	448	103	62	66	104	113	22,960	288.8
Social services	83	283	122	69	43	20	29	5,290	58.4
Membership organizations	86	522	333	78	44	41	26	6,153	63.2
Engineering and management services	87	871	521	160	107	55	28	8,827	173.5

- Represents or rounds to zero. X Not applicable. [1] 1987 Standard Industrial Classification (SIC) code; see text, section 13. [2] Includes other establishments not shown separately.

Source: U.S. Bureau of the Census, *County Business Patterns, 1994*.

No. 1328. Puerto Rico—Agriculture: 1987 and 1992

[1 cuerda=.97 acre]

ITEM	1987	1992
Farms	20,245	22,350
Percent—		
Less than 10 cuerdas	48.7	46.6
10 to 19 cuerdas	19.5	20.0
20 to 49 cuerdas	16.7	17.7
50 to 99 cuerdas	6.7	7.7
100 to 174 cuerdas	3.7	3.7
175 or more cuerdas	4.7	4.3
Cuerdas in farms	886,646	826,893
Tenure of operator:		
Percent—		
Full-owners	79.8	79.5
Part-owners	13.1	9.9
Tenants	7.1	10.6
Avg. farm size—cuerdas:		
Full-owners	33.4	26.6
Part-owners	85.7	92.3
Tenants	84.0	63.4
SALES ($1,000)		
Sugarcane	26,643	24,739
Coffee	41,786	56,802
Pineapples	15,495	11,254
Plantains	(NA)	23,227
Bananas	(NA)	5,695
Grains	7,263	9,767
Fruits/nuts [1]	20,645	11,277
Vegetables and melons [2]	8,236	16,214
Horticulture specialities	14,489	28,364
Cattle and calves	30,206	51,616
Poultry	70,560	98,939
Dairy products	157,864	197,703
Hogs and pigs	9,525	11,633
Sheep and goats	437	522
Fish and aquaculture	(NA)	628

NA Not available. [1] 1987 data include plantains and bananas. [2] 1987 data exclude melons.

Source: U.S. Bureau of the Census, *1992 Census of Agriculture*, vol. 1, part 52.

No. 1329. Virgin Islands—Agriculture: 1987 and 1992

[1 cuerda=.97 acre]

ITEM	1987	1992
Farms	267	202
Percent—		
Less than 3 acres	30.0	35.1
3 to 9 acres	30.3	29.7
10 to 19 acres	12.0	13.9
20 or more acres	27.7	21.3
Acres in farms	17,785	13,666
Tenure of operator:		
Percent—		
Full-owners	77.9	60.9
Part-owners	13.5	23.8
Tenants	8.6	15.3
SALES ($1,000)		
Vegetables	355	429
Fruits and nuts	147	142
Horticulture specialities	241	1,093
Cattle and calves	613	501
Hogs and pigs	125	291
Livestock	839	844
Poultry	3	9
Chicken eggs	14	23
Milk	1,043	780

Source: U.S. Bureau of the Census, *1992 Census of Agriculture*, vol. 1, part 54.

No. 1330. Guam, Virgin Islands, and Northern Mariana Islands—Economic Summary: 1992

[Sales and payroll in millions of dollars]

ITEM	Guam	Virgin Islands	No. Mariana Islands
Total: Establishments	1,955	2,932	1,266
Sales	3,018	2,281	1,132
Annual payroll	567	338	161
Paid employees [1]	33,057	20,968	20,105
Unpaid family workers [2]	337	330	268
Construction: Establishments	240	147	103
Sales	709	169	88
Annual payroll	178	44	18
Paid employees [1]	9,131	2,224	3,036
Unpaid family workers [2]	17	3	20
Manufacturing:			
Establishments	48	78	73
Sales	110	134	264
Annual payroll	23	23	49
Paid employees [1]	1,130	1,196	6,267
Unpaid family workers [2]	8	3	4
Wholesale trade:			
Establishments	154	114	60
Sales	428	414	132
Annual payroll	32	21	6
Paid employees [1]	1,715	1,030	534
Unpaid family workers [2]	4	1	3
Retail trade:			
Establishments	886	1,339	616
Sales	1,114	881	384
Annual payroll	141	120	38
Paid employees [1]	9,565	8,859	4,715
Unpaid family workers [2]	237	239	157
Services: Establishments	627	1,254	414
Sales	656	682	264
Annual payroll	193	130	51
Paid employees [1]	11,516	7,659	5,553
Unpaid family workers [2]	71	84	84

[1] For pay period including March 12. [2] Includes those who worked 15 hours or more during the week including March 12.

Source: U.S. Bureau of the Census, *1992 Economic Census of Outlying Areas*, OA92-E-5 to OA92-E-7.

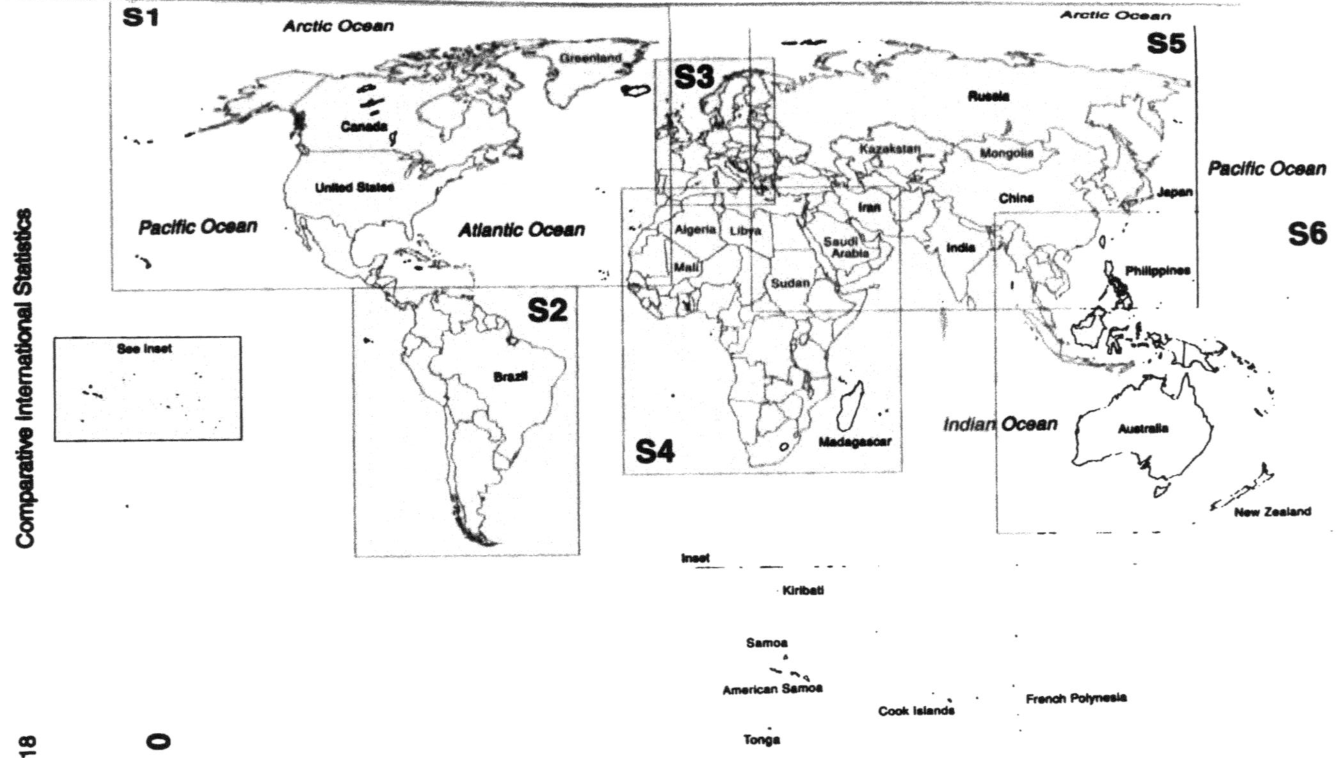
S1
Arctic Ocean
Greenland
Canada
United States
Pacific Ocean
Atlantic Ocean
S2
Brazil
See Inset
S3
S4
Algeria
Libya
Mali
Sudan
Saudi Arabia
Madagascar
Iran
Kazakstan
Russia
Mongolia
China
India
Japan
Arctic Ocean
S5
Pacific Ocean
S6
Philippines
Indian Ocean
Australia
New Zealand
Inset
Kiribati
Samoa
American Samoa
Cook Islands
French Polynesia
Tonga
0

Comparative International Statistics

This section presents statistics for the world as a whole and for many countries on a comparative basis with the United States. Data are shown for population, births and deaths, social and industrial indicators, finances, agriculture, communication, and military affairs.

Statistics of the individual nations may be found primarily in official national publications, generally in the form of yearbooks, issued by most of the nations at various intervals in their own national languages and expressed in their own or customary units of measure. (For a listing of selected publications, see Guide to Sources.) For handier reference, especially for international comparisons, the Statistical Office of the United Nations compiles data as submitted by member countries and issues a number of international summary publications, generally in English and French. Among these are the *Statistical Yearbook;* the *Demographic Yearbook*; the *Yearbook of International Trade Statistics*; the *Yearbook of National Accounts Statistics: Vol. II, International Tables; Population and Vital Statistics Reports* (quarterly); the *Monthly Bulletin of Statistics*; and the *Energy Statistics Yearbook*. Specialized agencies of the United Nations also issue international summary publications on agricultural, labor, health, and education statistics. Among these are the *Production Yearbook* and *Trade Yearbook* issued by the Food and Agriculture Organization, the *Yearbook of Labour Statistics* issued by the International Labour Office, *World Health Statistics* issued by World Health Organization, and the *Statistical Yearbook* issued by the Educational, Scientific, and Cultural Organization.

The Bureau of the Census presents estimates and projections of basic demographic measures for countries and regions of the world in the *World Population Profile* series. The *International Population Reports* (series P95) and *International Briefs* (series IB) also present population figures for many foreign countries. Detailed population statistics are also available from the Bureau of the Census' International Data Base.

In Brief

Ten most populous countries in 1997:

	(million persons)
China	*1,222*
India	*968*
United States	*268*
Indonesia	*210*
Brazil	*165*
Russia	*148*
Pakistan	*132*
Japan	*126*
Bangladesh	*125*
Nigeria	*107*

The U.S. Arms Control and Disarmament Agency and the International Monetary Fund (IMF) also compile data on international statistics. In its annual *World Military Expenditures and Arms Transfers*, the Arms Control and Disarmament Agency presents data on various economic indicators, as well as basic military data. Among the topics presented have been military expenditures, gross national product, imports and exports, and armed forces. The IMF publishes a series of reports relating to financial data. These include *International Financial Statistics*, *Direction of Trade,* and *Balance of Payments Yearbook*, published in English, French, and Spanish.

Statistical coverage, country names, and classifications— Problems of space and availability of data limit the number of countries and the extent of statistical coverage shown. The list of countries included and the spelling of country names are based almost entirely on the list of sovereign nations, dependencies, and areas of special sovereignty provided by the U.S. Department of State.

In recent years, several important changes took place in the status of the world's nations. In 1990, a unified Germany was formed from the Federal Republic of Germany (West) and the German Democratic Republic (East). The Republic of Yemen was formed by union of the Yemen Arab Republic and the People's Democratic Republic of Yemen. Also in 1990, Namibia, once a United Nations mandate, realized its independence from South Africa.

In 1991, the Soviet Union broke up into 15 independent countries: Armenia, Azerbaijan, Belarus, Estonia, Georgia, Kazakstan, Kyrgyzstan, Latvia, Lithuania, Moldova, Russia, Tajikistan, Turkmenistan, Ukraine, and Uzbekistan.

In 1992, the Socialist Federal Republic of Yugoslavia dissolved; none of the successor states has been recognized as its continuation. The United States recognizes Bosnia and Herzegovina, Croatia, Slovenia, and The Former Yugoslav Republic of Macedonia as independent countries. Serbia and Montenegro have asserted the formation of a joint independent state, but this entity has not been formally recognized as a state by the United States.

On January 1, 1993, Czechoslovakia was succeeded by two independent countries: the Czech Republic and Slovakia. Eritrea announced its independence from Ethiopia in April 1993, and was subsequently recognized as an independent nation by the United States.

The population estimates and projections used in tables 1334-1336 were prepared by the Census Bureau. For each country, the data on population, by age and sex, fertility, mortality, and international migration were evaluated and, where necessary, adjusted for inconsistencies and errors in the data. In most instances, comprehensive projections were made by the component method, resulting in distributions of the population by age and sex, and requiring an assessment of probable future trends of fertility, mortality, and international migration.

Economic associations—The Organization for European Economic Cooperation (OEEC), a regional grouping of Western European countries established in 1948 for the purpose of harmonizing national economic policies and conditions, was succeeded on September 30, 1961, by the Organization for Economic Cooperation and Development (OECD). The member nations of the OECD are Australia, Austria, Belgium, Canada, Czech Republic, Denmark, Finland, France, Germany, Greece, ngary, Iceland, Ireland, Italy, Japan, Lux- rg, Mexico, the Netherlands, New Norway, Poland, Portugal, South n, Sweden, Switzerland, Turkey, the United Kingdom, and the United States.

Quality and comparability of the data—The quality and comparability of the data presented here are affected by a number of factors:

(1) The year for which data are presented may not be the same for all subjects for a particular country, or for a given subject for different countries, though the data shown are the most recent available. All such variations have been noted. The data shown are for calendar years except as otherwise specified.

(2) The bases, methods of estimating, methods of data collection, extent of coverage, precision of definition, scope of territory, and margins of error may vary for different items within a particular country, and for like items for different countries.

Footnotes and headnotes to the tables give a few of the major time-period and coverage qualifications attached to the figures; considerably more detail is presented in the source publications. Many of the measures shown are, at best, merely rough indicators of magnitude.

(3) Figures shown in this section for the United States may not always agree with figures shown in the preceding sections. Disagreements may be attributable to the use of differing original sources, a difference in the definition of geographic limits (the 50 States, conterminous United States only, or the United States including certain outlying areas and possessions), or to possible adjustments made in the United States figures by the United Nations or other sources in order to make them more comparable with figures from other countries.

International comparisons of national accounts data—In order to compare national accounts data for different countries, it is necessary to convert each country's data into a common unit of currency, usually the U.S. dollar. The market exchange rates which are often used in converting national currencies do not necessarily reflect the relative purchasing power in the various countries. It is necessary that the goods and services produced in different countries be valued consistently if the differences observed are meant to reflect real differences in the volumes of goods and services produced. The use of purchasing power parities (see table 1348) instead of exchange rates is intended to achieve this objective.

The method used to present the data shown in table 1348 is to construct volume measures directly by revaluing the goods and services sold in different countries at a common set of international prices. By dividing the ratio of the gross domestic products of two countries expressed in their own national currencies by the corresponding ratio calculated at constant international prices, it is possible to derive the implied purchasing power parity (PPP) between the two currencies concerned. PPP's show how many units of currency are needed in one country to buy the same amount of goods and services which one unit of currency will buy in the other country. For further information, see *National Accounts, Main Aggregates*, volume I, issued annually by the Organization for Economic Cooperation and Development, Paris, France.

International Standard Industrial Classification—The original version of the International Standard Industrial Classification of All Economic Activities (ISIC) was adopted in 1948. Wide use has been made both nationally and internationally in classifying data according to kind of economic activity in the fields of production, employment, national income, and other economic statistics. A number of countries have utilized the ISIC as the basis for devising their industrial classification scheme. Substantial comparability has been attained between the industrial classifications of many other countries, including the United States, and the ISIC by ensuring, as far as practicable, that the categories at detailed levels of classification in national schemes fitted into only one category of the ISIC. For more detail, see Bureau of the Census, The *International Standard Industrial Classification and the U.S. Standard Industrial Classification*, Technical Paper No. 14 and text, section 27. The United Nations, the International Labour Organisation, the Food and Agriculture Organization, and other international bodies have utilized the ISIC in publishing and analyzing statistical data. Revisions of the ISIC were issued in 1958, 1968, and 1989.

International maps—A series of regional world maps is provided on pages 818 and 822-827. References are included in table 1334 for easy location of individual countries on the maps. The Robinson map projection is used for this series of maps. A map projection is used to portray all or part of the round Earth on a flat surface, but this cannot be done without some distortion. For the Robinson projection, distortion is very low along the Equator and within 45 degrees of the center but is greatest near the poles. For additional information on map projections and maps, please contact the Earth Science Information Center, U.S. Geological Survey, 507 National Center, Reston, VA 22092.

S1

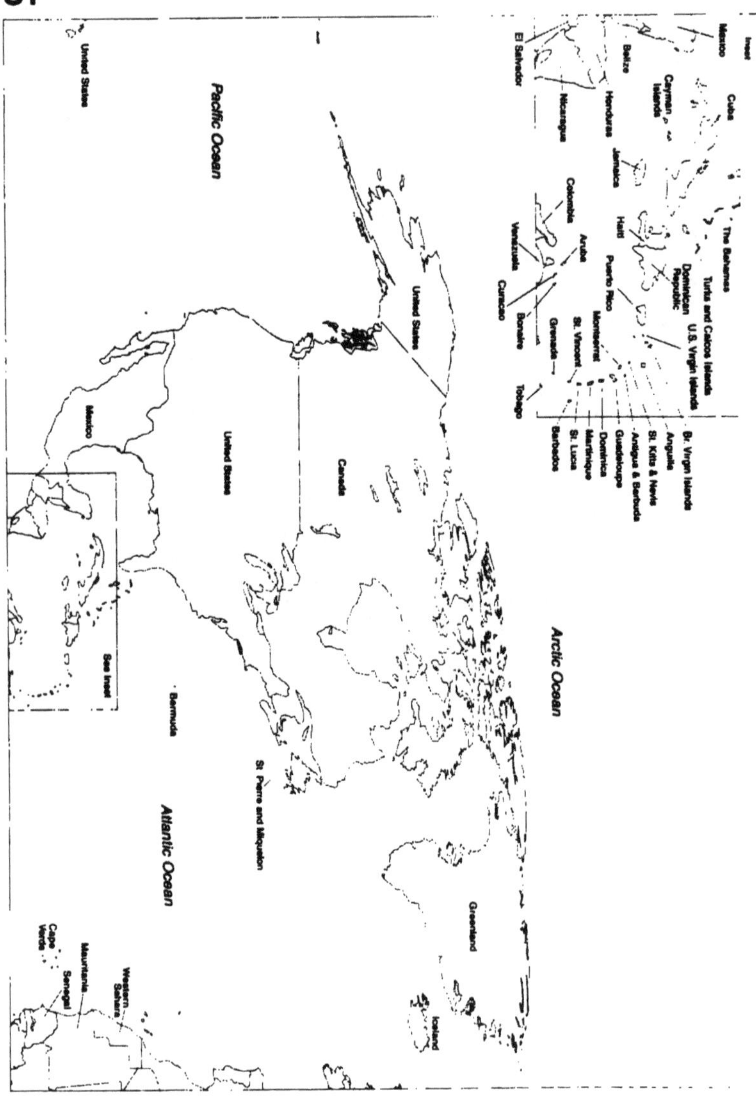
United States
Pacific Ocean
United States
Mexico
United States
Canada
Arctic Ocean
See inset
Bermuda
St. Pierre and Miquelon
Atlantic Ocean
Greenland
Iceland
Cape Verde
Senegal
Mauritania
Western Sahara
Inset
Mexico
Cuba
Cayman Islands
Belize
Honduras
Nicaragua
El Salvador
Jamaica
Colombia
Haiti
The Bahamas
Aruba
Venezuela
Dominican Republic
Puerto Rico
Curacao
Turks and Caicos Islands
U.S. Virgin Islands
Bonaire
Montserrat
St. Vincent
Grenada
Tobago
Br. Virgin Islands
Anguilla
St. Kitts & Nevis
Antigua & Barbuda
Guadeloupe
Dominica
Martinique
St. Lucia
Barbados

Aruba
Curacao
Bonaire
Barbados
Grenada
Isla de Margarita
Trinidad & Tobago
Nicaragua
Costa Rica
Panama
Venezuela
Guyana
Suriname
French Guiana
Colombia
Ecuador
Galapagos Islands
Peru
Brazil
Bolivia
Paraguay
Chile
Argentina
Uruguay
Pacific Ocean
Atlantic Ocean

S3

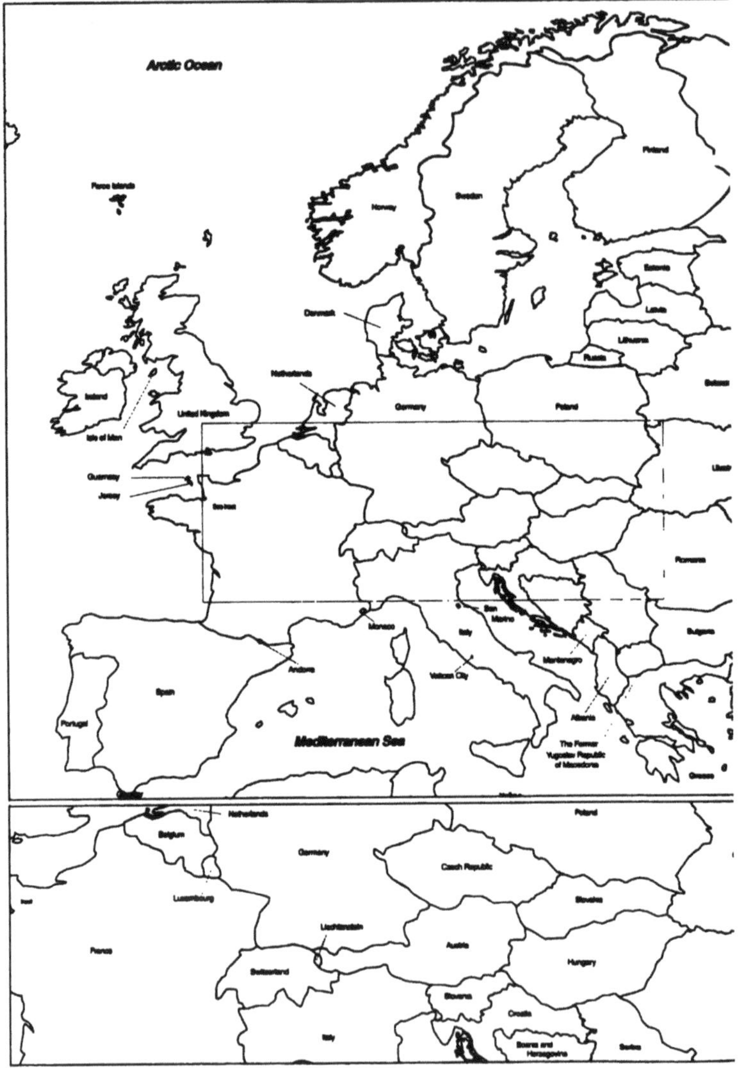
Arctic Ocean
Norway
Sweden
Finland
Estonia
Latvia
Lithuania
Russia
Denmark
Netherlands
Germany
Poland
Ireland
United Kingdom
Isle of Man
Guernsey
Jersey
Romania
Monaco
San Marino
Italy
Bulgaria
Montenegro
Andorra
Vatican City
Spain
Portugal
Albania
Mediterranean Sea
The Former Yugoslav Republic of Macedonia
Greece
Netherlands
Poland
Belgium
Germany
Czech Republic
Luxembourg
Slovakia
Liechtenstein
Austria
France
Hungary
Switzerland
Slovenia
Croatia
Italy
Bosnia and Herzegovina
Serbia

Spain
Morocco
Tunisia
Malta
Greece
Cyprus
Syria
Lebanon
West Bank
Gaza Strip
Israel
Iraq
Iran
Afghanistan
Western Sahara
Algeria
Libya
Egypt
Jordan
Kuwait
Bahrain
Qatar
Pakistan
United Arab Emirates
Saudi Arabia
Mauritania
Mali
Niger
Oman
Chad
Sudan
Yemen
Eritrea
Djibouti
Nigeria
Ethiopia
Central African Republic
See inset
Cameroon
Somalia
Sao Tome & Principe
Uganda
Kenya
Rwanda
Gabon
Indian Ocean
Congo (Kinshasa)
Equatorial Guinea
Burundi
Congo (Brazzaville)
Tanzania
Seychelles
Comoros
Mayotte
Angola
St. Helena
Zambia
Madagascar
Malawi
Zimbabwe
Mauritius
Mozambique
Namibia
Botswana
Reunion
Atlantic Ocean
Swaziland
South Africa
Lesotho

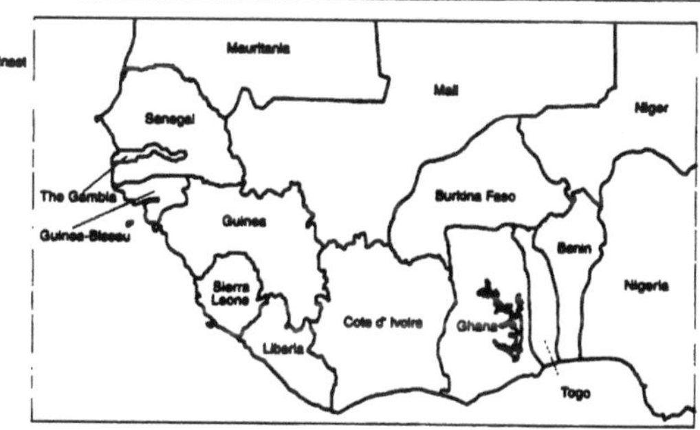
Inset
Mauritania
Mali
Niger
Senegal
The Gambia
Burkina Faso
Guinea-Bissau
Guinea
Benin
Sierra Leone
Nigeria
Cote d' Ivoire
Ghana
Liberia
Togo

S5

Gulf of Bothnia
Gulf of Finland
Mediterranean Sea
Black Sea
Caspian Sea
Red Sea
Indian Ocean
Pacific Ocean
Arctic Ocean

S6

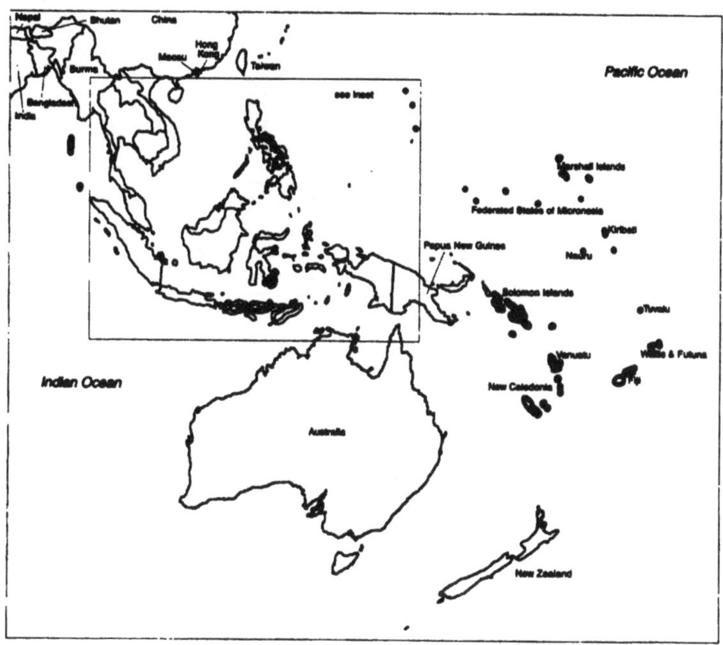
Nepal
Bhutan
China
Hong Kong
Macau
Taiwan
Burma
Bangladesh
India
see inset
Pacific Ocean
Marshall Islands
Federated States of Micronesia
Kiribati
Nauru
Papua New Guinea
Solomon Islands
Tuvalu
Vanuatu
Wallis & Futuna
Fiji
New Caledonia
Indian Ocean
Australia
New Zealand

Inset

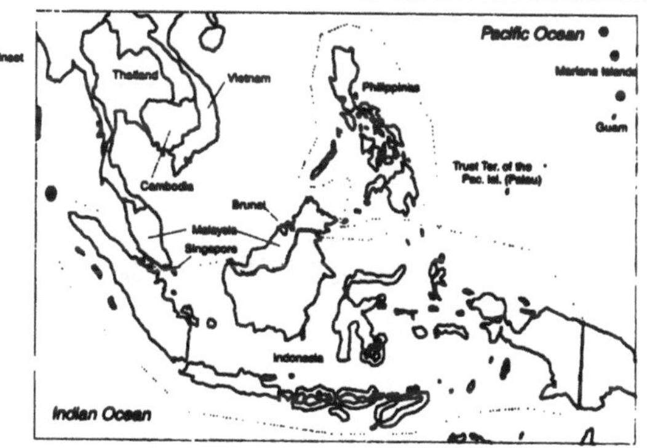
Pacific Ocean
Mariana Islands
Guam
Thailand
Vietnam
Philippines
Cambodia
Trust Ter. of the Pac. Isl. (Palau)
Brunei
Malaysia
Singapore
Indonesia
Indian Ocean

No. 1331. Total World Population: 1980 to 2050

[As of midyear]

YEAR	Population (mil.)	AVERAGE ANNUAL[1]		YEAR	Population (mil.)	AVERAGE ANNUAL[1]		YEAR	Population (mil.)	AVERAGE ANNUAL[1]	
		Growth rate (percent)	Population change (mil.)			Growth rate (percent)	Population change (mil.)			Growth rate (percent)	Population change (mil.)
1980	4,458	1.71	76.7	1996	5,771	1.38	80.2	2030	8,265	0.77	63.7
1985	4,855	1.69	82.5	2000	6,090	1.28	78.6	2040	8,865	0.61	54.6
1990	5,282	1.58	83.9	2010	6,858	1.09	75.5	2050	9,366	(NA)	(NA)
1995	5,691	1.41	80.5	2020	7,593	0.92	70.2				

NA Not available. [1] Represents change from year shown to immediate succeeding year.

Source: U.S. Bureau of the Census, "Total Midyear Population for the World: 1950-2050", published 25 March 1997; <http://www.census.gov/ipc/www/worldpop.html>.

No. 1332. World Summary: 1980 to 1995

[See text, section 30, for general comments concerning quality of the data]

ITEM	Unit	1980	1985	1989	1990	1991	1992	1993	1994	1995
Agriculture, forestry, fishing:[1]										
Coffee	Mil. metric tons	4.8	5.8	6.0	6.1	6.1	6.1	5.8	5.7	5.7
Cotton (lint)	Mil. metric tons	13.8	17.3	17.1	18.5	20.6	18.1	16.7	18.7	19.8
Tobacco	Mil. metric tons	5.3	7.0	7.0	7.0	7.5	8.3	6.4	6.5	6.4
Roundwood	Mil. cubic meters	2,932	3,169	3,472	3,506	3,397	3,405	3,415	3,440	(NA)
Fish catches	Mil. metric tons	72.0	86.3	100.1	97.4	97.4	98.8	101.4	(NA)	(NA)
Industrial production:										
Wine[1]	Mil. metric tons	35.3	29.5	28.8	28.6	25.8	29.2	26.2	25.0	24.2
Sugar[1]	Mil. metric tons	84.4	98.5	106.1	111.3	112.6	117.2	111.1	110.8	118.9
Wheat flour[1]	Mil. metric tons	237.2	267.6	295.9	293.1	308.6	315.1	306.9	300.5	(NA)
Electricity	Bil. kWh.	8,247	9,747	11,505	11,788	12,017	11,461	12,078	12,343	(NA)
Pig iron and ferroalloys	Mil. metric tons	542	507	570	529	501	500	502	523	(NA)
Sawnwood	Mil. cubic meters	451	468	507	505	370	377	420	413	(NA)
Woodpulp	Mil. metric tons	125.8	141.8	166.9	155.1	155.2	151.9	151.2	155.4	(NA)
Newsprint	Mil. metric tons	25.4	28.3	32.1	32.6	32.4	32.1	32.5	34.3	(NA)
Merchant vessels, launched	Mil. gross tons	13.9	17.3	12.7	14.7	16.7	20.5	18.7	16.3	(NA)
External trade:										
Imports, c.i.f	Bil. U.S. dollars	2,047	2,028	3,162	3,555	3,539	3,797	3,727	4,245	5,001
Exports, f.o.b	Bil. U.S. dollars	1,998	1,927	3,044	3,425	3,410	3,661	3,652	4,165	4,919

NA Not available. [1] Source: U.S. Department of Agriculture, Economic Research Service, *World Agriculture-Trends and Indicators*. See also table 1374.

Source: Except as noted, Statistical Division of the United Nations, New York, NY, *Monthly Bulletin of Statistics*, (copyright).

No. 1333. Religious Population of the World: 1996

[In thousands, except percent. Refers to adherents of all religions as defined and enumerated for each of the world's countries in *World Encyclopedia (1982)*, projected to mid-1996, adjusted for recent data]

RELIGION	Total	Percent distribution	Africa	Asia	Latin America	Northern America	Europe[1]	Oceania
Total population	5,804,120	100.0	748,130	3,513,218	490,444	295,677	727,678	28,973
Christians	1,955,229	33.7	360,874	303,127	455,819	255,542	555,614	24,253
Roman Catholics	981,465	16.9	125,376	94,250	408,968	75,398	269,021	8,452
Protestants	404,020	7.0	114,726	45,326	34,816	121,361	79,534	8,257
Orthodox	218,350	3.8	25,215	13,970	460	6,390	171,665	650
Anglicans	69,136	1.2	27,200	650	1,089	6,300	28,357	5,540
Other Christians	282,258	4.9	68,357	148,931	10,486	46,093	7,037	1,354
Muslims	1,126,325	19.4	308,660	778,362	1,356	5,530	32,032	385
Nonreligious[2]	886,929	15.3	3,567	752,759	16,053	21,315	90,390	2,845
Hindus	793,076	13.7	1,986	788,991	760	1,365	1,650	323
Buddhists	325,275	5.6	38	321,985	569	920	1,563	200
Atheists	222,195	3.8	440	175,450	3,010	1,650	40,845	600
Chinese folk-religionists[3]	220,971	3.8	13	220,653	68	100	120	17
New-religionists[4]	106,016	1.8	21	103,361	919	900	803	11
Ethnic religionists	102,945	1.8	70,250	30,350	1,042	45	1,150	108
Sikhs	19,506	0.3	37	18,465	9	496	494	7
Jews	13,866	0.2	165	4,257	1,084	5,836	2,432	92
Spiritists	10,293	0.2	5	1,120	8,834	315	18	1
Baha'is	6,404	0.1	1,923	3,230	722	357	95	77
Confucians	5,086	0.1	1	5,050	3	27	5	1
Jains	4,920	0.1	59	4,835	5	5	16	1
Shintoists	2,898	-	-	2,893	1	2	1	1
Other religionists	1,952	-	90	100	190	1,072	450	50
Parsees	191	-	2	185	1	1	1	1
Mandeans	45	-	-	45	-	-	-	-

- Represents or rounds to zero. [1] Includes Russia. [2] Persons professing no religion, nonbelievers, agnostics, freethinkers, and dereligionized secularists indifferent to all religion. [3] Followers of traditional Chinese religion. [4] Followers of Asiatic 20th-century New Religions, New Religious movements, radical new crisis religions, and non-Christian syncretistic mass religions.

Source: Encyclopaedia Britannica, Inc., Chicago, IL, *Britannica Book of the Year*. Reprinted with permission from *Britannica Book of the Year*, 1997 C 1997 Encyclopaedia Britannica, Inc.

No. 1334. Population, by Country: 1980 to 2000

[Population data generally are de facto figures for the present territory. Population estimates were derived from information available as of early 1997. See text, section 31, for general comments concerning the data. For details of methodology, coverage, and reliability, see source. Minus sign (-) indicates decrease]

COUNTRY OR AREA	Map reference	MIDYEAR POPULATION (1,000)				Population rank, 1997	Annual rate of growth,[1] 1990-2000 (percent)	Population per sq. mile, 1997	Area (sq. mile)
		1980	1990	1997	2000, proj.				
World	S0	4,457,653	5,281,551	5,851,569	6,089,800	(X)	1.4	116	50,627,993
Afghanistan	S5	14,985	14,767	23,738	26,668	41	5.9	95	250,000
Albania	S3	2,699	3,273	3,293	3,427	128	0.5	311	10,579
Algeria	S4	18,862	25,352	29,830	31,788	34	2.3	32	919,591
Andorra	S3	34	53	75	80	200	4.2	430	174
Angola	S4	6,794	8,430	10,624	11,513	68	3.1	22	481,351
Antigua and Barbuda	S1	69	64	66	68	203	0.7	390	170
Argentina	S2	28,237	32,634	35,798	37,218	31	1.3	34	1,056,637
Armenia	S5	3,115	3,366	3,466	3,481	125	0.3	301	11,506
Australia	S6	14,616	17,033	18,439	18,950	51	1.1	6	2,941,285
Austria	S3	7,549	7,718	8,054	8,124	86	0.5	252	31,942
Azerbaijan	S5	6,173	7,200	7,736	7,902	88	0.9	231	33,436
Bahamas, The	S1	210	241	262	269	177	1.1	67	3,888
Bahrain	S4	348	502	603	642	162	2.5	2,524	239
Bangladesh	S5	88,077	110,118	125,340	132,081	9	1.8	2,424	51,703
Barbados	S1	252	254	258	260	178	0.2	1,552	166
Belarus	S3	9,644	10,215	10,440	10,545	70	0.3	130	80,154
Belgium	S3	9,847	9,962	10,204	10,286	72	0.3	874	11,672
Belize	S1	144	190	225	242	181	2.4	26	8,803
Benin	S4	3,444	4,676	5,902	6,517	97	3.3	138	42,710
Bhutan	S5	1,281	1,585	1,865	1,996	144	2.3	103	18,147
Bolivia	S2	5,439	6,620	7,670	8,139	89	2.1	18	418,683
Bosnia and Herzegovina	S3	4,092	4,360	2,606	2,618	132	-5.1	132	19,741
Botswana	S4	903	1,304	1,501	1,557	146	1.8	7	226,012
Brazil	S2	122,830	150,062	164,511	169,545	5	1.2	50	3,265,061
Brunei	S6	185	254	308	331	174	2.6	151	2,035
Bulgaria	S3	8,844	8,966	8,653	8,769	84	-0.2	203	42,683
Burkina Faso	S4	6,939	9,033	10,891	11,684	67	2.6	103	105,714
Burma	S5	33,766	41,078	46,822	49,388	25	1.8	184	253,954
Burundi	S4	4,138	5,633	6,053	6,493	95	1.4	611	9,903
Cambodia	S5	6,499	8,731	11,164	12,098	65	3.3	164	68,154
Cameroon	S4	8,761	11,905	14,678	15,966	58	2.9	81	181,251
Canada	S1	24,070	26,620	29,123	29,989	36	1.2	8	3,560,219
Cape Verde	S1	296	349	394	411	172	1.6	253	1,556
Central African Republic	S4	2,244	2,806	3,342	3,539	127	2.3	14	240,533
Chad	S4	4,507	5,889	7,166	7,760	92	2.8	15	486,178
Chile	S2	11,094	13,121	14,508	14,996	59	1.3	50	289,112
China [2]	S5	984,736	1,133,710	1,221,592	1,253,438	1	1.0	339	3,600,930
Colombia	S2	26,560	32,983	37,418	39,172	30	1.7	93	401,042
Comoros	S4	334	460	590	656	163	3.5	704	838
Congo (Brazzaville) [3]	S4	1,620	2,204	2,583	2,750	134	2.2	20	131,853
Congo (Kinshasa) [3]	S4	27,954	37,831	47,440	51,374	24	3.1	54	875,521
Costa Rica	S2	2,307	3,022	3,534	3,744	124	2.1	181	19,560
Cote d'Ivoire	S4	8,276	11,896	14,986	16,031	57	3.0	122	122,780
Croatia	S3	4,593	4,754	5,027	5,044	108	0.6	230	21,829
Cuba	S1	9,653	10,545	10,999	11,131	66	0.5	257	42,803
Cyprus	S5	627	681	753	777	157	1.3	211	3,568
Czech Republic	S3	10,289	10,310	10,319	10,358	71	-	213	48,440
Denmark	S3	5,123	5,141	5,269	5,320	104	0.3	322	16,359
Djibouti	S4	279	370	434	454	167	2.0	51	8,486
Dominica	S1	75	81	83	84	197	0.4	287	290
Dominican Republic	S1	5,697	7,213	8,228	8,635	85	1.8	440	18,680
Ecuador	S2	8,315	10,116	11,691	12,360	62	2.0	109	106,888
Egypt	S4	42,441	56,106	64,792	68,437	16	2.0	169	384,344
El Salvador	S1	4,527	5,041	5,662	5,931	99	1.6	708	8,000
Equatorial Guinea	S4	256	369	443	478	166	2.6	41	10,830
Eritrea	S4	2,555	2,896	3,590	4,461	121	4.3	77	46,842
Estonia	S3	1,482	1,573	1,445	1,422	148	-1.0	83	17,413
Ethiopia	S4	36,413	48,242	58,733	63,514	19	2.8	136	432,310
Fiji	S6	635	738	792	823	156	1.1	112	7,054
Finland	S3	4,780	4,986	5,109	5,115	107	0.3	43	117,942
France	S3	53,870	56,735	58,470	59,079	21	0.4	278	210,668
Gabon	S4	806	1,078	1,190	1,244	151	1.4	12	99,486
Gambia, The	S4	676	964	1,248	1,381	150	3.6	323	3,861
Georgia	S5	5,048	5,457	5,175	5,132	105	-0.6	192	26,911
Germany	S3	78,298	79,357	84,068	85,684	12	0.8	622	135,236
Ghana	S4	10,880	15,190	18,101	19,272	53	2.4	204	88,811
Greece	S3	9,643	10,123	10,583	10,735	69	0.6	210	50,502
Grenada	S2	90	94	96	98	195	0.4	730	131
Guatemala	S1	7,232	9,633	11,558	12,406	63	2.5	276	41,865
Guinea	S4	4,320	5,936	7,405	7,611	90	2.5	78	94,927
Guinea-Bissau	S4	789	996	1,179	1,263	152	2.4	109	10,811
Guyana	S2	759	747	706	693	158	-0.7	9	76,004
Haiti	S1	5,056	6,031	6,611	6,901	93	1.3	621	10,641
Honduras	S1	3,625	4,741	5,751	6,192	98	2.7	133	43,201
Hungary	S3	10,711	10,352	9,936	9,795	76	-0.6	279	35,653
Iceland	S1	228	255	273	280	176	0.9	7	38,707
India	S5	692,394	855,591	967,613	1,012,909	2	1.7	843	1,147,950
Indonesia	S6	154,936	187,728	209,774	219,267	4	1.6	297	705,189
Iran	S5	39,274	56,946	67,540	71,879	15	2.3	107	631,660

See footnotes at end of table.

No. 1334. Population, by Country: 1980 to 2000—Continued

[See headnote, page 829]

COUNTRY OR AREA	Map reference	MIDYEAR POPULATION (1,000)				Population rank, 1997	Annual rate of growth,[1] 1990-2000 (percent)	Population per sq. mile, 1997	Area (sq. mile)
		1980	1990	1997	2000, proj.				
Iraq	S5	13,233	18,425	22,219	24,731	44	2.9	133	167,556
Ireland	S3	3,401	3,508	3,556	3,493	123	-	134	26,598
Israel	S4	3,737	4,512	5,535	5,852	102	2.6	705	7,849
Italy	S3	56,451	57,661	57,534	57,807	22	-	507	113,521
Jamaica	S1	2,229	2,466	2,616	2,669	131	0.8	626	4,181
Japan	S5	116,807	123,537	125,717	126,582	8	0.2	825	152,411
Jordan	S4	2,168	3,277	4,325	4,704	116	3.6	122	35,344
Kazakstan	S5	14,994	16,708	16,899	16,943	54	0.1	16	1,049,150
Kenya	S4	16,685	23,896	28,803	30,490	37	2.4	131	219,788
Kiribati	S6	58	72	82	87	198	1.9	298	277
Korea, North	S5	17,999	21,412	24,317	25,491	39	1.7	523	46,490
Korea, South	S5	38,124	42,869	45,949	47,351	26	1.0	1,212	37,911
Kuwait	S5	1,370	2,128	2,077	2,420	141	1.3	302	6,880
Kyrgyzstan	S5	3,623	4,390	4,540	4,664	111	0.6	59	76,641
Laos	S5	3,293	4,191	5,117	5,557	106	2.8	57	89,112
Latvia	S3	2,525	2,672	2,438	2,380	136	-1.2	98	24,903
Lebanon	S4	3,137	3,387	3,859	4,115	118	2.0	977	3,950
Lesotho	S4	1,346	1,735	2,008	2,114	142	2.0	171	11,718
Liberia	S4	1,900	2,265	2,602	3,090	133	3.1	70	37,189
Libya	S4	3,119	4,355	5,648	6,294	101	3.7	8	679,359
Liechtenstein	S3	25	29	31	33	214	1.3	506	62
Lithuania	S5	3,436	3,702	3,636	3,629	120	-0.2	144	25,174
Luxembourg	S3	364	382	422	442	169	1.5	423	998
Macedonia, The Former Yugoslav Republic of	S3	1,893	2,031	2,114	2,152	140	0.6	213	9,928
Madagascar	S4	8,678	11,525	14,062	15,295	60	2.8	63	224,533
Malawi	S4	6,129	9,136	9,609	10,011	78	0.9	265	36,324
Malaysia	S6	13,764	17,507	20,376	21,610	48	2.1	161	126,853
Maldives	S5	154	218	280	310	175	3.5	2,421	116
Mali	S4	6,728	8,234	9,945	10,911	74	2.8	21	471,042
Malta	S4	364	354	379	391	173	1.0	3,061	124
Marshall Islands	S6	31	46	61	68	207	3.9	868	70
Mauritania	S4	1,456	1,935	2,411	2,653	137	3.2	6	397,838
Mauritius	S4	964	1,074	1,154	1,196	153	1.1	1,617	714
Mexico	S1	68,686	85,121	97,563	102,912	11	1.9	131	742,486
Micronesia, Federated States of	S6	77	109	128	133	190	2.0	471	271
Moldova	S5	3,996	4,398	4,475	4,543	113	0.3	344	13,012
Monaco	S3	27	30	32	32	213	0.7	41,300	1
Mongolia	S5	1,662	2,216	2,538	2,655	135	1.8	4	604,247
Montenegro[4]	S3	579	616	638	647	161	0.5	120	5,333
Morocco	S4	20,457	26,164	30,391	32,229	33	2.1	176	172,317
Mozambique	S4	12,103	14,056	18,165	19,614	52	3.3	60	302,737
Namibia	S4	975	1,409	1,727	1,886	145	2.9	5	317,873
Nauru	S6	8	9	10	11	224	1.3	1,281	8
Nepal	S5	15,001	19,104	22,641	24,364	42	2.4	429	52,819
Netherlands	S3	14,144	14,952	15,653	15,893	56	0.6	1,195	13,104
New Zealand	S6	3,113	3,299	3,587	3,698	122	1.1	35	103,734
Nicaragua	S2	2,776	3,591	4,386	4,729	115	2.8	94	46,430
Niger	S4	5,629	7,644	9,389	10,260	80	2.9	19	489,073
Nigeria	S4	65,699	86,488	107,129	117,328	10	3.0	305	351,649
Norway	S3	4,086	4,242	4,404	4,461	114	0.5	37	118,865
Oman	S5	1,164	1,751	2,265	2,512	138	3.6	28	82,031
Pakistan	S5	85,219	113,914	132,185	141,145	7	2.1	440	300,664
Palau	S6	13	15	17	18	218	1.7	97	177
Panama	S2	1,956	2,388	2,693	2,821	130	1.7	92	29,340
Papua New Guinea	S6	2,991	3,823	4,496	4,812	112	2.3	26	174,405
Paraguay	S2	3,379	4,651	5,652	6,104	100	2.7	37	153,398
Peru	S2	17,295	21,841	24,950	26,198	38	1.8	50	494,208
Philippines	S6	51,092	65,037	76,104	80,961	13	2.2	661	115,124
Poland	S3	35,578	38,109	38,700	39,010	29	0.2	329	117,571
Portugal	S3	9,778	9,871	9,868	9,906	77	-	279	35,382
Qatar	S5	231	481	665	736	160	4.3	157	4,247
Romania	S5	22,109	22,775	21,399	20,996	46	-0.8	241	88,934
Russia	S5	139,045	148,081	147,987	147,938	6	-	22	6,592,817
Rwanda	S4	5,170	7,145	7,738	8,900	87	2.2	803	9,633
Saint Kitts and Nevis	S1	44	40	42	43	211	0.8	301	139
Saint Lucia	S1	122	146	160	165	187	1.2	677	236
Saint Vincent and the Grenadines	S1	98	113	119	121	191	0.7	910	131
San Marino	S3	21	23	25	25	216	0.9	1,087	23
Sao Tome and Principe	S4	94	123	148	159	189	2.6	399	371
Saudi Arabia	S4	9,949	15,871	20,088	22,246	49	3.4	24	829,996
Senegal	S4	5,640	7,408	9,404	10,390	79	3.4	127	74,131
Serbia[4]	S3	9,262	9,705	10,017	10,140	73	0.4	294	34,116
Seychelles	S4	66	73	78	80	199	0.8	444	176
Sierra Leone	S4	3,333	4,283	4,892	5,509	109	2.5	177	27,653
Singapore	S6	2,414	3,039	3,462	3,620	126	1.8	14,369	241
Slovakia	S3	4,966	5,263	5,393	5,472	103	0.4	111	48,440
Slovenia	S3	1,885	1,969	1,946	1,937	143	-0.2	249	7,819
Solomon Islands	S6	233	336	427	470	168	3.4	40	10,633
Somalia	S4	6,665	8,334	9,940	10,880	75	2.7	41	242,216

See footnotes at end of table.

No. 1334. Population, by Country: 1980 to 2000—Continued

[See headnote, page 829]

COUNTRY OR AREA	Map reference	MIDYEAR POPULATION (1,000) 1980	1990	1997	2000, proj.	Population rank, 1997	Annual rate of growth,[1] 1990-2000 (percent)	Population per sq. mile, 1997	Area (sq. mile)
South Africa	S4	29,252	37,191	42,327	44,018	27	1.7	90	471,444
Spain	S3	37,488	38,793	39,244	39,545	28	0.2	204	192,819
Sri Lanka	S5	14,900	17,227	18,762	19,377	50	1.2	751	24,996
Sudan	S4	19,064	26,628	32,594	35,530	32	2.9	36	917,375
Suriname	S2	355	398	443	465	165	1.6	7	62,344
Swaziland	S4	607	853	1,032	1,137	154	2.9	155	6,641
Sweden	S3	8,310	8,559	8,946	9,052	83	0.6	56	158,927
Switzerland	S3	6,385	6,779	7,249	7,374	91	0.8	472	15,355
Syria	S4	8,692	12,620	16,138	17,759	55	3.4	227	71,062
Tajikistan	S5	3,969	5,332	6,014	6,384	96	1.8	109	55,251
Tanzania	S4	18,689	24,826	29,461	31,045	35	2.2	86	342,100
Thailand	S5	47,026	55,052	59,451	61,164	18	1.1	301	197,595
Togo	S4	2,596	3,680	4,736	5,263	110	3.6	226	21,000
Tonga	S0	93	101	107	110	192	0.8	388	277
Trinidad and Tobago	S2	1,091	1,256	1,273	1,273	149	0.1	643	1,981
Tunisia	S4	6,443	8,048	9,183	9,671	82	1.8	153	59,985
Turkey	S5	45,121	56,123	63,528	66,618	17	1.7	213	297,591
Turkmenistan	S5	2,875	3,668	4,225	4,466	117	2.0	22	188,456
Tuvalu	S6	7	9	10	11	225	1.6	1,026	10
Uganda	S4	12,252	17,040	20,605	21,891	47	2.5	267	77,108
Ukraine	S5	50,047	51,592	50,685	50,380	23	-0.2	217	233,089
United Arab Emirates	S5	1,000	1,952	2,262	2,386	139	2.0	70	32,278
United Kingdom	S3	56,314	57,418	58,610	58,894	20	0.3	628	93,278
United States	S1	227,726	249,907	267,955	274,943	3	1.0	76	3,539,227
Uruguay	S2	2,920	3,106	3,262	3,333	129	0.7	49	67,035
Uzbekistan	S5	16,000	20,624	23,860	25,245	40	2.0	138	172,741
Vanuatu	S6	117	154	181	193	185	2.2	32	5,699
Venezuela	S2	14,768	19,325	22,396	23,596	43	2.0	66	340,560
Vietnam	S5	54,234	66,314	75,124	78,350	14	1.7	598	125,622
Western Samoa	S0	155	186	220	235	182	2.3	200	1,100
Yemen	S5	7,439	10,489	13,972	15,547	61	3.9	69	203,849
Zambia	S4	5,638	8,019	9,350	9,899	81	2.1	33	285,992
Zimbabwe	S4	7,298	10,121	11,423	11,777	64	1.5	77	149,293
Taiwan[2]	S5	17,848	20,279	21,656	22,214	45	0.9	1,739	12,456
AREAS OF SPECIAL SOVEREIGNTY AND DEPENDENCIES									
American Samoa	S0	32	47	62	69	206	3.8	805	77
Anguilla	S1	7	8	11	12	223	3.5	307	35
Aruba	S1	60	67	68	69	202	0.4	913	75
Bermuda	S1	55	59	63	64	205	0.8	3,307	19
Cayman Islands	S1	17	27	36	41	212	4.3	360	100
Cook Islands	S0	18	18	20	20	217	1.1	213	93
Faroe Islands	S3	43	47	43	41	210	-1.6	80	541
French Guiana	S2	68	116	157	173	188	4.0	5	34,421
French Polynesia	S0	151	201	233	246	179	2.0	165	1,413
Gaza Strip[5]	S4	453	635	988	1,163	155	6.0	6,715	147
Gibraltar	S3	29	31	29	29	215	-0.6	12,481	2
Greenland	S1	50	56	59	60	208	0.8	(Z)	131,931
Guadeloupe	S1	337	378	413	426	170	1.2	607	680
Guam	S6	107	134	161	171	186	2.4	769	209
Guernsey	S3	53	61	64	66	204	0.8	851	75
Hong Kong	S5	5,063	5,688	6,413	6,685	94	1.6	16,794	382
Jersey	S3	76	84	89	90	196	0.8	1,959	45
Macau	S6	318	456	502	516	164	1.2	81,314	6
Man, Isle of	S3	64	69	75	76	201	1.0	328	227
Martinique	S1	339	374	404	416	171	1.1	987	409
Mayotte	S4	52	80	105	117	193	3.8	721	145
Montserrat	S1	12	13	13	13	222	0.3	332	39
Netherlands Antilles	S2	173	195	211	217	183	1.1	569	371
New Caledonia	S6	139	168	191	200	184	1.7	26	7,243
Northern Mariana Islands	S6	17	44	54	57	209	2.6	291	184
Puerto Rico	S1	3,210	3,537	3,818	3,908	119	1.0	1,104	3,459
Reunion	S4	507	600	692	730	159	2.0	717	965
Saint Helena	S4	6	7	7	7	227	0.3	43	158
Saint Pierre and Miquelon	S1	6	6	7	7	226	0.8	74	93
Turks and Caicos Islands	S1	7	12	15	15	220	2.7	88	166
Virgin Islands	S1	98	101	97	99	194	-0.2	720	135
Virgin Islands, British	S1	11	12	13	14	221	1.3	231	58
Wallis and Futuna	S6	11	14	15	15	219	1.1	140	106
West Bank[5]	S4	833	1,080	1,496	1,662	147	4.3	687	2,178
Western Sahara	S4	126	191	228	245	180	2.5	2	102,703

- Represents or rounds to zero. X Not applicable. Z Less than one person per square mile. [1] Computed by the exponential method. For explanation of average annual percent change, see Guide to Tabular Presentation. [2] With the establishment of diplomatic relations with China on January 1, 1979, the U.S. government recognized the People's Republic of China as the sole legal government of China and acknowledged the Chinese position that there is only one China and that Taiwan is part of China. [3] "Congo" is the official short-form name for both the Republic of Congo and the Democratic Republic of the Congo. To distinguish one from the other the U.S. Dept. of State adds the capital in parentheses. This practice is unofficial and provisional. [4] The U.S. view is that the Socialist Federal Republic of Yugoslavia has dissolved and no successor state represents its continuation. Serbia and Montenegro have asserted the formation of a joint independent state, but this entity has not been recognized by the United States. [5] The Gaza Strip and West Bank are Israeli occupied with interim status subject to Israeli/Palestinian negotiations. The final status is to be determined.

Source: U.S. Bureau of the Census, unpublished data from the International Data Base.

No. 1335. Age Distribution, by Country: 1997 and 2000

[In percent. Covers countries with 10 million or more population in 1997]

COUNTRY OR AREA	1997		2000, proj.		COUNTRY OR AREA	1997		2000, proj.	
	Under 15 years old	65 years old and over	Under 15 years old	65 years old and over		Under 15 years old	65 years old and over	Under 15 years old	65 years old and over
World	30.8	6.6	29.9	6.8	Kenya	44.0	2.6	41.8	2.8
Afghanistan	43.0	2.7	42.7	2.8	Korea, North	29.6	4.3	29.4	4.7
Algeria	39.0	3.8	36.4	3.9	Korea, South	22.7	6.2	21.9	6.9
Angola	44.7	2.7	44.8	2.8	Madagascar	44.8	3.3	44.5	3.3
Argentina	27.7	10.0	27.3	10.2	Malaysia	35.6	3.9	34.3	4.1
Australia	21.4	12.3	20.8	12.6	Mexico	36.0	4.5	34.7	4.8
Bangladesh	36.1	3.2	36.1	3.3	Morocco	37.1	4.4	35.3	4.6
Belarus	21.1	12.8	20.2	13.0	Mozambique	44.9	2.3	44.7	2.3
Belgium	17.8	16.4	17.7	16.8	Nepal	42.0	2.9	41.3	3.0
Brazil	29.9	4.8	28.4	5.2	Netherlands	18.3	13.4	18.2	13.7
Burkina	48.1	3.1	48.0	3.0	Nigeria	44.9	2.9	44.8	3.0
Burma	36.6	4.1	35.9	4.2	Pakistan	42.2	4.0	40.9	4.1
Cambodia	45.4	3.1	44.9	3.0	Peru	34.3	4.6	32.4	4.9
Cameroon	45.9	3.3	45.7	3.3	Philippines	37.9	3.5	37.0	3.6
Canada	20.4	12.5	19.9	12.9	Poland	21.6	11.5	20.1	11.9
Chile	28.2	6.9	26.9	7.3	Romania	19.2	13.0	18.4	13.9
China [1]	25.9	6.4	25.0	6.9	Russia	20.5	12.2	19.3	12.1
Colombia	31.5	4.6	29.8	5.0	Saudi Arabia	43.0	2.4	42.9	2.6
Congo (Kinshasa) [2]	48.1	2.6	48.2	2.6	Serbia [3]	21.1	12.6	20.6	13.6
Cote d'Ivoire	46.9	2.2	46.4	2.2	South Africa	35.0	4.5	34.1	4.6
Cuba	22.2	9.4	21.4	9.7	Spain	15.7	16.0	15.3	16.9
Czech Republic	17.9	13.6	17.5	13.8	Sri Lanka	27.5	6.2	25.6	6.6
Ecuador	34.8	4.5	33.0	4.6	Sudan	45.6	2.2	44.8	2.3
Egypt	36.4	3.6	35.2	3.7	Syria	46.4	2.9	45.3	2.9
Ethiopia	45.9	2.7	46.1	2.7	Taiwan [1]	22.9	8.0	21.5	8.6
France	18.7	15.6	18.1	16.2	Tanzania	44.9	2.9	44.5	3.0
Germany	16.0	15.4	15.8	15.7	Thailand	24.9	5.8	23.5	6.5
Ghana	43.2	3.1	41.7	3.2	Turkey	31.5	5.6	29.9	6.0
Greece	16.1	16.4	15.5	17.5	Uganda	49.6	2.3	49.5	2.3
Guatemala	42.4	3.5	41.2	3.7	Ukraine	19.6	14.2	18.8	13.9
India	34.0	4.1	32.5	4.4	United Kingdom	19.5	15.7	19.4	15.6
Indonesia	31.3	3.8	30.1	4.3	United States	21.8	12.7	21.4	12.6
Iran	44.0	4.0	41.7	4.2	Uzbekistan	39.6	4.7	36.0	4.7
Iraq	47.4	3.0	46.9	2.9	Venezuela	34.3	4.4	32.8	4.6
Italy	14.8	17.0	14.9	17.8	Vietnam	35.5	5.2	32.7	5.4
Japan	15.5	15.4	15.0	16.9	Yemen	47.7	2.7	47.6	2.7
Kazakstan	29.5	7.1	28.0	7.2	Zimbabwe	43.6	2.8	42.0	2.9

[1] See footnote 2, table 1334. [2] See footnote 3, table 1334. [3] See footnote 4, table 1334.

Source: U.S. Bureau of the Census, unpublished data from the International Data Base.

No. 1336. Vital Statistics, by Country: 1997 and 2000

[Covers countries with 6 million or more population in 1997]

COUNTRY OR AREA	CRUDE BIRTH RATE [1]		CRUDE DEATH RATE [2]		EXPECTATION OF LIFE AT BIRTH (years)		INFANT MORTALITY RATE [3]		TOTAL FERTILITY RATE [4]	
	1997	2000, proj.	1997	2000, proj.	1997	2000, proj.	1997	2000, proj.	1997	2000, proj.
United States	14.6	14.2	8.8	8.8	76.0	76.3	6.6	6.2	2.06	2.07
Afghanistan	42.7	41.6	17.8	16.6	46.3	47.8	146.7	137.5	6.07	5.87
Algeria	28.0	26.5	5.8	5.4	68.6	69.6	47.1	42.2	3.48	3.16
Angola	44.1	42.6	17.2	15.9	47.3	48.9	135.7	125.9	6.27	6.05
Argentina	20.0	19.9	7.7	7.6	74.4	75.0	19.4	17.8	2.69	2.64
Australia	13.7	13.0	6.9	6.9	79.6	80.4	5.4	5.0	1.83	1.80
Austria	10.9	10.3	10.4	10.3	76.7	77.3	6.1	5.8	1.49	1.52
Azerbaijan	22.0	21.1	8.6	8.6	65.0	65.4	73.9	72.3	2.63	2.61
Bangladesh	29.8	27.4	10.9	10.1	56.3	57.5	100.0	93.0	3.45	3.08
Belarus	12.7	14.0	13.5	12.9	68.8	69.4	12.6	12.0	1.76	1.92
Belgium	12.0	11.2	10.3	10.4	77.2	77.7	6.3	6.1	1.72	1.69
Bolivia	32.1	30.0	10.2	9.3	60.3	62.0	65.7	60.2	4.18	3.81
Brazil	20.4	19.2	9.4	10.1	61.4	60.9	53.4	47.7	2.29	2.14
Bulgaria	8.4	12.5	13.5	13.6	71.1	71.6	15.4	14.8	1.17	1.74
Burkina Faso	46.4	44.9	20.3	21.4	42.3	39.8	116.6	112.8	6.72	6.48
Burma	29.5	28.1	11.4	10.7	56.6	58.1	78.5	71.8	3.76	3.57
Burundi	42.3	41.0	15.1	15.3	49.0	48.1	100.5	95.2	6.48	6.25
Cambodia	42.6	41.0	15.4	14.3	50.3	51.5	106.0	100.5	5.81	5.81
Cameroon	42.2	41.4	13.6	13.9	52.3	51.3	77.6	74.1	5.93	5.73
Canada	13.1	12.3	7.2	7.2	79.3	80.0	6.0	5.5	1.81	1.80
Chad	43.9	42.8	17.2	16.3	47.9	48.9	118.7	113.6	5.79	5.64
Chile	17.5	15.9	5.7	5.7	74.7	75.5	13.2	11.9	2.17	2.00
China [5]	16.5	15.0	6.9	6.8	70.0	71.1	37.9	32.6	1.81	1.81
Colombia	20.8	19.0	4.6	4.6	73.1	74.2	24.7	21.3	2.31	2.17

See footnotes at end of table.

No. 1336. Vital Statistics, by Country: 1997 and 2000—Continued

[See headnote, page 832]

COUNTRY OR AREA	CRUDE BIRTH RATE [1]		CRUDE DEATH RATE [2]		EXPECTATION OF LIFE AT BIRTH (years)		INFANT MORTALITY RATE [3]		TOTAL FERTILITY RATE [4]	
	1997	2000, proj.	1997	2000, proj.	1997	2000, proj.	1997	2000, proj.	1997	2000, proj.
Congo (Kinshasa) [5]	47.7	46.5	16.6	15.6	47.0	48.1	105.7	96.9	6.56	6.39
Cote d'Ivoire	42.4	41.3	17.1	17.6	44.8	43.7	99.7	94.9	6.06	5.80
Cuba	13.2	12.7	7.4	7.5	75.2	75.6	8.9	8.6	1.54	1.60
Czech Republic	10.5	13.3	10.9	11.0	73.9	74.2	8.3	8.0	1.38	1.74
Dominican Republic	22.9	21.1	5.6	5.4	69.4	70.4	46.0	40.8	2.60	2.42
Ecuador	24.6	23.0	5.4	5.1	71.4	72.5	33.4	29.3	2.82	2.59
Egypt	27.7	26.2	8.6	8.1	61.6	62.7	71.0	65.7	3.50	3.24
Ethiopia	45.6	44.3	17.6	17.6	46.6	46.0	121.5	117.7	6.94	6.75
France	10.8	12.1	9.0	9.0	78.6	79.1	6.0	5.6	1.49	1.73
Germany	9.5	10.5	11.1	10.8	76.1	76.7	5.9	5.7	1.30	1.56
Ghana	33.9	30.8	10.9	10.2	56.5	57.5	78.9	74.8	4.43	3.95
Greece	9.7	10.7	9.5	9.5	78.3	79.0	7.2	6.6	1.37	1.52
Guatemala	33.3	31.2	7.0	6.5	65.6	66.9	49.2	44.6	4.38	4.00
Guinea	42.0	40.0	18.2	16.9	45.5	47.0	131.5	123.7	5.66	5.46
Haiti	33.1	32.3	15.3	14.7	49.5	50.2	102.4	98.4	4.76	4.50
Hong Kong	10.4	10.2	5.3	5.6	82.4	82.8	5.0	4.5	1.33	1.42
Hungary	10.9	13.1	15.0	14.8	69.2	69.6	12.2	11.7	1.51	1.78
India	25.3	23.5	9.4	8.9	60.2	61.5	69.2	63.5	3.12	2.90
Indonesia	23.4	22.4	8.3	8.1	62.1	63.4	61.2	55.4	2.66	2.53
Iran	32.5	29.2	6.4	5.8	67.8	69.1	50.8	45.1	4.52	3.90
Iraq	42.5	40.8	6.3	5.6	67.4	68.7	57.5	50.1	6.26	5.81
Italy	9.8	11.4	9.9	10.1	78.2	78.6	6.8	6.4	1.27	1.55
Japan	10.4	10.7	7.9	8.4	79.7	80.0	4.4	4.3	1.47	1.50
Kazakstan	18.9	18.8	9.7	9.8	64.2	64.7	62.3	59.6	2.34	2.29
Kenya	32.4	29.5	10.8	12.6	54.4	51.1	55.2	54.9	4.26	3.69
Korea, North	22.3	19.9	5.4	5.4	70.6	71.5	26.0	22.2	2.29	2.21
Korea, South	16.2	15.8	5.7	5.7	73.6	74.7	8.0	7.4	1.78	1.80
Madagascar	42.3	41.2	14.1	13.3	52.5	53.6	92.0	87.6	5.83	5.64
Malawi	40.8	38.7	25.1	27.1	35.3	33.0	138.9	136.8	5.77	5.33
Malaysia	25.7	24.1	5.4	5.2	70.0	71.0	23.2	20.9	3.22	3.10
Mali	50.9	49.3	19.0	17.5	47.3	48.8	101.0	95.6	7.16	6.91
Mexico	25.8	24.3	4.5	4.4	74.0	75.0	23.9	20.7	2.97	2.79
Morocco	26.8	25.1	5.6	5.1	70.1	71.8	40.7	32.9	3.47	3.13
Mozambique	44.3	42.0	18.3	16.8	44.9	46.4	122.9	114.9	6.11	5.76
Nepal	36.7	35.6	12.2	11.2	54.2	55.9	76.8	70.1	4.96	4.66
Netherlands	11.8	11.5	8.7	8.7	77.9	78.2	4.8	4.7	1.49	1.53
Niger	53.7	51.6	24.0	22.2	41.1	42.4	116.0	111.2	7.37	7.17
Nigeria	42.6	41.5	12.5	11.7	54.7	55.6	70.2	63.7	6.17	5.95
Pakistan	35.3	32.6	11.0	10.2	58.8	59.7	95.1	90.3	5.06	4.56
Peru	23.8	21.8	6.0	5.8	69.6	70.8	50.2	44.4	2.95	2.66
Philippines	29.0	27.3	6.6	6.4	66.1	66.8	35.2	33.2	3.62	3.38
Poland	12.0	14.2	10.1	10.2	72.2	72.6	12.3	11.8	1.69	1.93
Portugal	10.6	11.9	10.2	10.3	75.5	76.1	7.5	7.1	1.36	1.53
Romania	9.9	14.3	12.4	12.7	69.6	70.0	22.9	21.7	1.25	1.83
Russia	10.9	14.5	15.7	14.8	63.8	65.4	24.3	21.6	1.51	1.95
Rwanda	38.7	36.5	21.1	23.5	39.1	36.5	118.8	118.8	5.93	5.73
Saudi Arabia	37.9	37.2	5.2	4.7	69.5	71.1	43.9	36.3	6.41	6.30
Senegal	44.9	43.4	11.4	10.4	56.9	58.3	62.6	58.4	6.24	6.04
Serbia [7]	14.0	14.8	10.3	10.5	72.1	72.5	22.5	21.3	2.00	2.10
Somalia	43.5	41.7	13.0	12.0	55.9	57.0	118.7	111.6	6.89	6.53
South Africa	26.9	25.3	11.9	14.4	56.3	51.9	53.2	55.4	3.22	3.02
Spain	10.1	12.0	8.9	9.1	78.5	79.1	6.1	5.7	1.26	1.51
Sri Lanka	17.6	16.9	5.8	5.9	72.6	73.2	20.3	18.7	2.03	1.95
Sudan	40.5	38.8	11.2	10.3	55.5	56.8	74.3	69.2	5.79	5.47
Sweden	10.8	10.5	11.3	11.1	78.2	78.5	4.5	4.4	1.61	1.60
Switzerland	11.2	11.2	9.6	9.5	77.8	78.1	5.4	5.2	1.47	1.59
Syria	36.7	36.1	5.7	5.3	67.4	68.4	38.8	35.2	5.73	5.19
Taiwan [6]	14.8	14.4	5.6	5.7	76.3	77.3	6.9	6.3	1.76	1.75
Tajikistan	34.0	34.5	8.4	8.3	64.6	66.1	110.9	104.1	4.40	4.47
Tanzania	40.9	39.8	19.8	20.9	41.7	40.0	104.8	101.4	5.58	5.31
Thailand	17.0	16.2	7.1	7.2	68.8	69.4	32.1	28.3	1.86	1.80
Tunisia	23.7	22.5	5.1	5.1	72.9	73.6	33.9	30.1	2.86	2.68
Turkey	21.8	20.4	5.4	5.2	72.4	73.8	40.7	33.3	2.52	2.35
Uganda	46.1	43.1	21.0	21.8	39.7	38.1	98.4	95.6	6.52	6.24
Ukraine	11.8	13.2	15.1	14.9	67.1	67.8	22.2	21.2	1.68	1.87
United Kingdom	12.8	12.1	11.2	10.9	76.6	77.1	6.3	6.0	1.81	1.79
Uzbekistan	29.5	28.9	7.9	7.7	64.8	65.2	79.1	77.5	3.65	3.56
Venezuela	23.7	21.5	5.0	4.9	72.4	73.3	28.5	25.5	2.78	2.53
Vietnam	22.3	20.0	6.8	6.5	67.4	68.5	37.2	33.7	2.60	2.31
Yemen	44.8	43.3	9.2	7.9	60.3	62.6	68.1	57.9	7.18	6.86
Zambia	44.4	43.8	24.2	25.8	35.6	33.7	96.5	97.6	6.46	6.28
Zimbabwe	31.7	29.3	19.0	21.6	40.8	38.2	72.6	72.2	3.94	3.50

[1] Number of births during 1 year per 1,000 persons (based on midyear population). [2] Number of deaths during 1 year per 1,000 persons (based on midyear population). [3] Number of deaths of children under 1 year of age per 1,000 live births in a calendar year. [4] Average number of children that would be born if all women lived to the end of their childbearing years and, at each year of age, they experienced the birth rates occurring in the specified year. [5] See footnote 2, table 1334. [6] See footnote 3, table 1334. [7] Serbia and Montenegro have asserted the formation of a joint independent state, but this entity has not been recognized by the United States. Data in this table are for Serbia alone.

Source: U.S. Bureau of the Census, unpublished data from the International Data Base.

No. 1337. Marriage and Divorce Rates, by Country: 1970 to 1994

COUNTRY	MARRIAGE RATE PER 1,000 POPULATION, 15 TO 64 YEARS OLD						DIVORCE RATE PER 1,000 MARRIED WOMEN					
	1970	1980	1990	1992	1993	1994	1970	1980	1990	1992	1993	1994
United States [1]	17	16	15	14	14	14	15	23	21	21	21	21
Canada	14	12	10	9	8	8	6	10	11	11	11	11
Denmark	12	8	9	9	9	10	8	11	13	13	13	13
France	12	10	8	7	7	7	3	6	8	(NA)	(NA)	(NA)
Germany [2]	12	9	9	8	9	8	5	6	8	7	7	(NA)
Italy	11	9	8	8	8	7	1	1	2	2	(NA)	(NA)
Japan	14	10	8	9	9	(NA)	4	5	5	6	6	(NA)
Netherlands	15	10	9	9	8	7	3	8	8	9	9	(NA)
Sweden	8	7	7	7	6	6	7	11	12	13	13	(NA)
United Kingdom	14	12	10	9	9	(NA)	[3] 5	[3] 12	13	13	13	(NA)

NA Not available. [1] Beginning 1980, includes unlicensed marriages registered in California. [2] Prior to 1991, data are for former West Germany. [3] England and Wales only.

No. 1338. Births to Unmarried Women, by Country: 1970 to 1994

[For U.S. figures, beginning 1990, marital status is inferred from a comparison of the child's and parents' surnames on the birth certificate for those States that do not report on marital status. No estimates are included for misstatements on birth records or failures to register births]

COUNTRY	1970		1980		1990		1994	
	Total live births (1,000)	Percent born to unmarried women	Total live births (1,000)	Percent born to unmarried women	Total live births (1,000)	Percent born to unmarried women	Total live births (1,000)	Percent born to unmarried women
United States	3,731	11	3,612	18	4,158	28	3,953	33
Canada [1]	372	10	360	13	398	24	385	25
Denmark	71	11	57	33	63	46	70	47
France	850	7	800	11	762	30	711	36
Germany [2]	811	6	621	8	906	11	770	15
Italy	902	2	640	4	554	6	527	8
Japan	1,932	1	1,616	1	1,222	1	1,238	1
Netherlands	239	2	181	4	198	11	196	14
Sweden	110	18	97	40	124	47	112	52
United Kingdom	904	8	754	12	799	28	751	32

[1] 1980 through 1990 excludes Newfoundland. After 1990, a significant number of births are not allocated according to marital status, resulting in an understatement of the proportion of births to unmarried women. [2] Prior to 1990, data are for former West Germany.

Source of tables 1337 and 1338: U.S. Bureau of Labor Statistics, *Monthly Labor Review*, March 1990 and unpublished data.

No. 1339. Death Rates, by Cause and Country

[Age-standardized death rate per 100,000 population. For explanation of age-adjustment, see text, section 2. The standard population for this table is the old European standard; see source for details. Deaths classified to ninth revision of *International Classification of Diseases*; see text, section 2]

COUNTRY	Year	Ischemic heart disease	Cerebro-vascular disease	CANCER OF — Lung, trachea, bronchus	CANCER OF — Stomach	CANCER OF — Female breast	Bronchitis,[1] emphysema, asthma	Chronic liver disease and cirrhosis	Motor vehicle traffic accidents	Suicide and self-inflicted injury
United States	1992	164.4	47.3	57.3	5.0	30.5	8.9	10.5	15.2	11.8
Australia	1993	162.1	63.9	37.1	7.0	29.2	11.0	6.3	10.6	11.4
Austria	1994	148.9	83.6	33.9	15.9	31.0	12.1	24.8	14.5	20.4
Bulgaria	1994	231.4	230.3	33.5	19.6	22.0	9.9	20.1	13.3	15.9
Canada	1993	146.2	48.7	53.8	6.7	31.1	6.9	8.2	11.6	12.8
Czech Republic	1993	276.6	168.0	53.1	17.4	31.2	19.6	16.5	13.6	18.1
Denmark	1992	190.3	72.0	51.1	7.8	40.6	36.5	13.5	10.2	20.4
Finland	1994	206.8	86.4	31.0	11.2	23.2	14.1	9.6	8.6	26.4
France	1993	58.0	49.7	35.3	8.0	28.4	9.5	15.6	14.4	19.8
Germany	1994	152.3	82.5	35.8	14.3	31.3	16.8	21.3	11.1	13.8
Hungary	1994	250.2	161.0	65.9	22.4	35.4	39.6	81.3	16.0	33.5
Italy	1992	90.4	86.6	42.8	17.2	28.4	21.4	20.8	15.2	7.1
Japan	1994	36.4	75.8	28.0	31.2	9.6	10.1	11.2	9.9	15.1
Netherlands	1993	121.6	66.3	52.0	11.4	38.4	16.4	4.6	7.4	9.6
New Zealand	1993	195.1	76.1	40.7	8.2	34.0	11.3	4.1	16.6	12.6
Norway	1993	161.9	80.0	30.0	9.8	27.7	12.6	4.5	5.9	13.0
Poland	1994	110.1	79.0	52.1	18.3	22.3	17.7	12.8	18.8	14.8
Portugal	1994	75.6	187.1	22.0	22.8	25.0	9.7	21.3	20.9	7.1
Russia	1994	409.0	297.0	44.7	34.2	22.1	40.7	(NA)	23.2	41.7
Spain	1992	73.0	81.9	34.1	14.1	24.4	7.3	17.7	16.0	6.6
Sweden	1993	172.0	65.8	23.3	8.2	24.7	10.6	5.6	6.3	14.7
Switzerland	1994	100.4	46.8	33.7	8.6	33.1	17.7	8.4	8.4	19.6
United Kingdom:										
England and Wales	1993	197.6	75.1	49.1	10.6	37.6	10.2	5.4	6.1	6.9
Scotland	1993	250.4	114.9	68.1	11.7	38.0	8.4	9.4	7.3	11.7

NA Not available. [1] Chronic and unspecified.

Source: World Health Organization, Geneva, Switzerland, *World Health Statistics Annual*.

1340. Foreign or Immigrant Population, 1982 and 1993, and Foreign Labor Force, 1991, by Country

[...lia, Canada, and the United States the data refer to people present in the country who are foreign born. In the European ... and Japan they generally refer to foreigners and represent the nationalities of residents; as a result, persons born in these ... may be counted among the foreign population, whereas others, who are foreign born, may have acquired the host-country ...y. Except as noted, data are from population registers. Data for foreign labor in European Union (EU) countries are taken ... EU labor force survey. For the other European countries data are based on population registers]

COUNTRY	FOREIGNERS				FOREIGN LABOR FORCE, 1991	
	Number (1,000)		Percent of total population		Number (1,000)	Percent of total labor force
	1982	1993	1982	1993		
...States [1]	[2]14,990	[3]19,767	[2]4.7	[3]7.9	[3]11,636	[3]9.3
...[4]	[5]3,004	[6]4,125	[5]20.6	[6]22.7	[6]2,164	[6]24.8
...	303	[7]562	4.0	[7]7.1	[7]296	[7]8.9
...[1]	891	[7]909	9.0	[7]9.0	297	7.4
...	[5]3,843	[6]4,343	[5]16.1	[6]15.6	2,681	18.5
...(	103	189	2.0	3.6	74	2.5
...	14	56	0.3	1.1	(NA)	(NA)
...	3,714	[3]3,597	6.8	[3]6.3	1,505	6.2
.../	4,667	[6]6,878	7.6	8.5	[9]2,703	8.9
...	359	987	0.6	1.7	(NA)	(NA)
...	802	1,321	0.7	1.1	[7]590	[7]0.9
...ourg	96	[7]120	26.2	[7]30.3	55	33.3
...nds	547	[6]757	3.8	[6]5.0	269	3.9
...	91	162	2.2	3.8	[7]47	[7]4.4
...	200	[7]393	0.5	[7]1.0	[11]59	0.4
...	406	[7]499	4.9	[7]5.7	[7]244	[7]5.5
...nd	926	1,260	14.4	18.1	[7]717	[7]20.1
...ngdom [4]	1,601	2,001	2.8	3.5	960	3.3

...Not available. [1] Census data. [2] 1980 data. [3] 1990 data. [4] Labor force survey. [5] 1981 data. [6] 1994 data. ...ata. [8] 1991 data. [9] Western Germany only. [10] Residence permits. [11] Excludes unemployed.

...rce: Organization for Economic Cooperation and Development, Paris, France, *The OECD Observer*, No. 192, .../March 1995, (copyright.)

No. 1341. Health Expenditures, by Country: 1980 to 1995

[...D.P.=gross domestic product; for explanation, see text, section 14. For explanation of purchasing power parities, see text, section 30]

...UNTRY	TOTAL HEALTH EXPENDITURES							PUBLIC HEALTH EXPENDITURES		
	Percent of gross domestic product					Per capita on basis of G.D.P. purchasing power parities		Percent of gross domestic product		
	1980	1985	1990	1994	1995	1985	1995	1980	1985	1995
...States	9.2	10.7	12.4	14.2	14.2	$1,733	$3,701	3.9	4.3	6.6
...	7.3	7.7	8.2	8.5	8.6	989	1,741	4.6	5.5	5.8
...	7.9	6.7	8.4	9.7	7.9	992	1,634	5.4	5.2	5.9
...	6.6	7.4	7.6	8.2	8.0	890	1,665	5.5	6.0	7.0
...	7.4	8.4	9.5	9.8	9.6	1,206	2,049	5.5	6.4	6.9
...epublic	(NA)	(NA)	(NA)	7.6	7.9	(NA)	749	(NA)	(NA)	(NA)
...(	6.8	6.3	6.3	6.6	6.4	816	1,368	5.8	5.3	5.3
...	6.5	7.3	8.0	8.3	7.7	852	1,373	5.1	5.7	5.8
...	7.6	8.5	8.9	9.7	9.8	1,088	1,956	6.0	6.5	7.7
.../ [1]	8.4	8.5	8.3	[2]8.6	10.4	1,274	2,134	6.3	6.6	8.2
...	(NA)	4.0	(NA)	[2]3.6	5.8	288	703	(NA)	3.3	4.4
...	(NA)	(NA)	(NA)	(NA)	7.1	(NA)	562	(NA)	(NA)	4.9
...	6.4	7.3	8.3	8.1	8.2	929	1,774	5.7	6.3	6.9
...	9.2	7.8	7.0	7.3	6.4	586	1,106	7.5	6.1	5.1
...	6.9	7.0	8.1	[2]8.6	7.7	830	1,507	5.6	5.4	5.4
...	6.6	6.7	6.7	[2]7.3	7.2	823	1,581	4.6	4.7	5.7
...outh	(NA)	3.9	(NA)	(NA)	5.3	171	866	(NA)	1.4	2.1
...ourg	(NA)	6.1	(NA)	3.1	7.0	895	2,206	(NA)	5.5	6.5
...	(NA)	(NA)	(NA)	(NA)	4.9	(NA)	386	(NA)	(NA)	2.8
...nds	8.0	7.9	8.2	8.8	8.8	932	1,728	6.0	5.9	6.8
...aland	7.2	5.3	7.3	[2]7.7	7.1	592	1,203	6.0	4.8	5.4
...	(NA)	6.6	(NA)	[2]5.5	8.0	910	1,821	(NA)	5.7	6.6
...	(NA)	(NA)	(NA)	4.4	(NA)	(NA)	[3]219	(NA)	(NA)	(NA)
...	5.9	6.3	6.7	[2]7.4	8.2	387	1,035	4.3	3.4	5.0
...	5.6	5.7	6.6	[2]7.3	7.6	455	1,075	4.5	4.6	6.0
...	9.4	9.0	8.6	7.7	7.2	1,174	1,360	8.7	8.1	5.9
...nd	7.3	8.1	7.8	9.6	9.8	1,297	2,412	4.9	5.3	7.1
...	4.0	2.2	4.0	5.2	(NA)	73	[3]272	1.1	1.1	[3]2.6
...ngdom	5.8	5.9	6.2	6.9	6.9	670	1,246	5.2	5.0	5.9

...Not available. [1] Data prior to 1991 are for former West Germany. [2] 1993 data. [3] 1994 data.

...rce: Organization for Economic Cooperation and Development, Paris, France, *OECD Health Data 97*; *OECD Health ...: Facts and Trends*, 1993; *OECD in Figures, 1997 Edition*, and unpublished data.

No. 1342. Educational Attainment, by Country: 1994

[Percent distribution. Persons 25 to 64 years old]

COUNTRY	Total	Early childhood, primary, and lower secondary education only	Upper secondary education only	Non-university tertiary education only	University education only
Australia	100	50	27	10	13
Austria	100	32	60	2	6
Belgium	100	51	27	12	10
Canada	100	26	28	29	17
Denmark	100	40	40	6	14
Finland	100	36	44	9	11
France	100	33	50	8	9
Germany	100	16	62	10	13
Greece	100	55	27	6	12
Ireland	100	55	27	10	9
Italy	100	67	26	([1])	[1]8
Netherlands	100	40	38	([1])	[1]21
New Zealand	100	43	34	14	9
Norway	100	19	53	11	16
Portugal	100	81	8	3	7
Spain	100	74	11	4	11
Sweden	100	28	46	14	12
Switzerland	100	18	61	13	8
Turkey	100	80	13	([1])	[1]7
United Kingdom	100	26	54	9	12
United States	100	15	53	8	24

[1] Non-university tertiary education included in University education only.

Source: Organization for Economic Cooperation and Development, Paris, France, *Education at a Glance*, annual, (copyright).

No. 1343. Participation in Job-Related Continuing Education and Training, by Country

[Percentage of the employed population 25 to 64 years old. Data refer to all job-related education and training organized, financed, or sponsored by authorities, provided by employers, or self-financed. Job-related continuing education and training refers to all organized, systematic education and training activities in which people take part in order to obtain knowledge and/or learn new skills for a current or a future job, to increase earnings, improve job and/or career opportunities in current or other fields, and generally to improve their opportunities for advancement and promotion]

COUNTRY	Year	Total	Male	Female	COUNTRY	Year	Total	Male	Female
United States [1] [2]	1995	34	31	36	Greece [4]	1994	1	1	1
Australia [1] [3]	1993	38	37	40	Ireland [4]	1994	4	3	6
Belgium [4] [5]	1994	3	3	2	Italy [4] [8]	1994	1	1	2
Canada [1]	1993	28	27	30	Spain [4]	1994	3	2	4
Denmark [4]	1994	15	13	18	Sweden [9]	1995	44	40	47
Finland [1] [6]	1993	41	38	44	Switzerland [1]	1993	38	42	34
France [1]	1994	40	38	43	United Kingdom [4]	1994	13	12	14
Germany [1] [7]	1994	33	35	31					

[1] During the 12-month period preceding the survey. [2] Excludes full-time students. [3] Excludes persons enrolled only in full-time programs at any time during the survey period and people pursuing only on-the-job training. [4] During the 4-week period preceding the survey. [5] Covers all forms of continuing education and training. [6] Includes only the training of employees which is sponsored by employers. [7] Excludes initial training of students over 25 years old in vocational schools and in the dual system and forms of continuing vocational training other than formal courses. [8] Excludes persons enrolled in ordinary school courses. [9] During the 6-month period preceding the survey. Includes only training supplied or sponsored by employers.

Source: Organization for Economic Cooperation and Development, Paris, France, *Education at a Glance*, annual (copyright)

No. 1344. Land Area, Forested Area, and Deforestation: 1991-93

COUNTRY	Land area (mil. hectares)	Forest and woodland area, percent of total, 1991-93	Deforestation,[1] percent change from 1981-83	COUNTRY	Land area (mil. hectares)	Forest and woodland area, percent of total, 1991-93	Deforestation,[1] percent change from 1981-83
Bangladesh	13.0	15	-12.2	Madagascar	58.2	40	-
Brazil	845.7	58	-4.8	Malawi	9.4	39	1.1
Burma	65.8	44	1.2	Malaysia	32.9	62	-1.8
Colombia	103.9	48	-5.8	Mexico	191.0	26	4.1
Cote d'Ivoire	31.8	22	-24.4	Nepal	13.7	42	4.4
Ecuador	27.7	56	0.6	Nicaragua	11.9	27	-24.3
Guatemala	10.8	49	17.4	Niger	126.7	2	0.8
Honduras	11.2	54	-	Nigeria	91.1	13	-20.3
India	297.3	23	1.4	Philippines	29.8	46	13.4
Indonesia	181.2	61	-3.7	Thailand	51.1	27	-13.8
Liberia	9.6	18	-13.2	Vietnam	32.5	30	-33.3

- Represents zero. [1] Deforestation refers only to clearing of land for agriculture or other land uses. It excludes logging.

No. 1345. Paper Production, Consumption, and Waste Paper Recovery: 1987-1989

[In thousands of metric tons, except percent]

COUNTRY	Production,[1] 1987-89	Consumption, 1988	Waste paper recovery, percent of consumption	COUNTRY	Production,[1] 1987-89	Consumption, 1988	Waste paper recovery, percent of consumption
Argentina	973	971	43	Japan	24,657	24,940	48
Australia	1,729	2,570	30	Netherlands	2,399	2,800	54
Austria	2,600	1,083	49	New Zealand	693	561	18
Brazil	4,734	3,710	39	Portugal	679	662	41
Canada	16,417	5,950	21	South Korea	3,613	3,300	39
Chile	445	370	54	Spain	3,368	3,897	37
China	14,159	13,200	22	Sweden	8,111	2,050	48
Denmark	326	1,085	31	Switzerland	1,207	1,005	61
Finland	8,472	1,115	34	Thailand	500	811	35
France	6,216	7,934	33	Turkey	413	979	24
Germany[2]	10,591	12,346	41	United Kingdom	4,318	9,286	30
Hungary	520	680	29	United States	68,878	77,057	30

[1] Annual average. [2] Data are for former West Germany.

Source of tables 1344 and 1345: U.S. Central Intelligence Agency, *Handbook of International Economic Statistics*, annual.

No. 1346. Municipal Waste Generation and Disposal: 1980 to 1992

[**In thousands of metric tons, except as indicated.** Municipal waste is that which is collected and treated by or for municipalities: household waste and bulky waste as well as comparable waste from small communities or industrial enterprises; and market and garden residue. The definition of municipal waste and the surveying methods used vary from country to country]

COUNTRY	AMOUNT GENERATED					AMOUNT DISPOSED				
	Total				Per capita, 1992 (kilograms)	Year	Total[1]	Method		
	1980	1985	1990	1992				Incineration	Landfill	Recycling
United States	137,350	149,144	177,539	187,790	730	1993	187,790	2,993	117,028	34,929
Austria[2]	(NA)	(NA)	3,283	(NA)	(NA)	1990	2,506	310	1,700	400
Canada	12,600	(NA)	18,000	18,800	660	1992	18,800	1,101	14,070	3,400
Denmark	2,046	2,430	(NA)	2,377	460	1993	2,377	1,500	468	203
Finland	(NA)	2,500	3,100	(NA)	(NA)	1990	3,100	50	2,400	600
France[2]	(NA)	(NA)	26,220	27,000	470	1992	20,500	7,600	9,500	740
Germany, West	21,417	19,387	21,615	(NA)	(NA)	1990	21,615	6,039	14,219	(NA)
Greece	2,500	3,023	3,000	3,200	310	1992	3,200	1	2,970	226
Italy	14,041	15,000	20,000	20,033	350	1991	26,600	2,100	22,800	1,700
Japan	43,950	41,530	50,441	50,767	410	1991	50,767	3,616	19,379	1,688
Mexico	(NA)	(NA)	[3]21,062	28,090	310	1993	28,089	(NA)	7,768	192
Netherlands	7,050	6,357	7,430	7,602	500	1991	7,602	2,500	3,610	578
Norway	1,700	1,900	2,000	2,220	510	1992	2,223	416	1,678	175
Portugal	1,980	2,350	3,000	3,270	330	1992	3,270	(NA)	2,826	(NA)
Spain	10,100	10,014	12,546	14,256	360	1993	14,256	635	12,061	(NA)
Sweden	2,510	2,650	3,200	(NA)	(NA)	1990	3,200	1,300	1,400	400
Switzerland	2,290	2,610	2,930	2,820	400	1992	[4]2,820	2,140	650	1,370
United Kingdom[2]	(NA)	(NA)	(NA)	(NA)	(NA)	1989	20,000	2,500	14,000	1,000

NA Not available. [1] Total waste generated. Includes other methods not shown separately. Total may be lower than the total of all disposals because residues of some treatments (e.g. incineration) are landfilled. [2] Disposal data refer to household waste only. [3] 1991 data. [4] Excludes recycled material.

Source: Organization for Economic Cooperation and Development, Paris, France, *OECD Environmental Data, Compendium 1995*, 1995 (copyright).

No. 1347. Gross National Product, by Country: 1985 to 1995

[In billions of dollars, except per capita. For most countries, data for GNP are based on local currencies which are deflated to constant 1995 local currency values before conversion to U.S. dollar equivalents. In general, rates used for conversion are the 1995 average par/market exchange rates as supplied by the International Bank for Reconstruction and Development]

COUNTRY	CURRENT DOLLARS				CONSTANT (1995) DOLLARS						
									Per capita (dollars)		
	1985	1990	1994	1995	1985	1990	1994	1995	1985	1990	1995
United States	4,201	5,765	6,932	7,247	5,758	6,625	7,106	7,247	24,140	26,510	27,550
Algeria	28	34	37	39	39	39	38	39	1,744	1,544	1,365
Argentina	147	181	278	271	201	209	285	271	6,627	6,437	7,909
Australia	185	250	324	342	254	288	332	342	16,070	16,900	18,920
Austria	132	183	221	231	182	210	226	231	24,010	27,630	28,860
Bangladesh	14	21	27	29	19	24	28	29	194	215	240
Belgium	158	219	262	269	217	252	268	269	21,970	25,300	26,550
Brazil	371	502	610	657	509	576	626	657	3,718	3,841	4,084
Bulgaria	41	45	37	38	56	52	38	38	6,316	5,805	4,394
Canada	319	436	517	542	437	501	530	542	17,370	18,810	19,000
Chile	20	36	53	59	28	41	55	59	2,322	3,109	4,173
China [1]	799	1,382	2,461	2,759	1,095	1,588	2,523	2,759	1,040	1,401	2,303
Colombia	35	52	71	76	48	60	73	76	1,627	1,818	2,107
Congo (Kinshasa) [2]	6	8	5	5	8	9	5	5	235	230	114
Croatia [1]	(X)	(X)	19	20	(X)	(X)	20	20	(X)	(X)	4,045
Cuba [1]	30	34	22	23	40	39	23	23	4,014	3,672	2,088
Czech Republic [1]	(X)	(X)	94	101	(X)	(X)	96	101	(X)	(X)	9,779
Denmark	110	141	173	170	151	162	178	170	29,570	31,540	32,540
Egypt	24	37	44	46	34	42	45	46	677	750	746
El Salvador	5	6	9	10	6	7	9	10	1,311	1,325	1,671
Ethiopia	3	4	5	5	4	5	5	5	92	102	96
Finland	86	121	121	119	118	139	124	119	24,150	27,820	23,410
France	895	1,251	1,452	1,521	1,226	1,438	1,488	1,521	22,330	25,460	26,290
Germany [3]	1,232	1,738	2,079	2,172	1,689	1,998	2,131	2,172	27,670	25,170	26,190
Ghana	3	4	6	6	4	5	6	6	306	330	357
Greece	56	72	87	91	76	82	89	91	7,656	8,144	8,696
Hungary [1]	53	63	64	66	72	72	65	66	6,767	6,949	6,519
India	142	229	299	326	195	263	307	326	252	307	348
Indonesia	67	113	172	189	92	130	177	189	532	694	931
Iran	111	134	158	158	152	154	162	158	3,200	2,702	2,449
Iraq [1]	31	23	(NA)	(NA)	42	26	(NA)	(NA)	2,683	1,435	(NA)
Israel	38	57	83	91	52	65	85	91	12,870	14,470	17,070
Italy	644	886	1,025	1,082	882	1,019	1,050	1,082	15,430	17,670	18,850
Japan	2,809	4,187	4,961	5,153	3,849	4,811	5,106	5,153	31,880	38,950	41,160
Kenya	4	6	7	8	5	7	7	8	262	286	274
Korea, North [1]	26	(NA)	21	21	36	(NA)	22	21	1,839	(NA)	894
Korea, South	130	259	380	425	179	297	390	425	4,380	6,935	9,437
Kuwait [1]	26	25	28	30	36	25	28	30	20,930	13,400	16,500
Malaysia	27	46	71	81	37	53	73	81	2,386	3,033	4,134
Mexico	157	204	254	237	215	235	261	237	2,806	2,756	2,521
Morocco	18	26	33	32	25	30	34	32	1,064	1,162	1,107
Netherlands	224	310	373	391	307	356	382	391	21,180	23,830	25,240
Nigeria	51	72	94	95	70	83	96	95	935	958	946
Norway	74	95	121	128	101	109	124	128	24,320	25,700	29,350
Pakistan	29	44	57	61	40	51	59	61	402	445	482
Peru	33	37	51	57	46	43	53	57	2,331	1,961	2,363
Philippines	37	57	71	77	51	66	73	77	877	1,011	1,052
Poland [1]	144	163	188	209	196	188	193	209	5,318	4,925	5,404
Portugal	53	84	98	103	73	97	100	103	7,292	9,826	10,430
Romania	99	105	91	99	136	121	93	99	6,059	5,294	4,513
Russia [1]	(X)	(X)	676	664	(X)	(X)	693	664	(X)	(X)	4,478
Saudi Arabia [1]	94	113	121	128	129	130	124	128	9,769	8,157	6,815
Serbia and Montenegro [1]	(X)	(X)	(NA)	21	(X)	(X)	(NA)	21	(X)	(X)	1,948
Slovakia [1]	(X)	(X)	18	19	(X)	(X)	19	19	(X)	(X)	3,619
Slovenia [1]	(X)	(X)	21	23	(X)	(X)	22	23	(X)	(X)	11,550
South Africa	83	107	124	131	113	123	127	131	3,394	3,317	3,185
Spain	303	451	525	554	415	519	538	554	10,810	13,370	14,160
Sri Lanka	6	9	12	13	8	10	12	13	521	572	699
Sweden	145	192	207	219	199	221	212	219	23,800	25,830	24,730
Switzerland	198	267	302	316	271	307	309	316	41,440	45,270	44,070
Syria	25	30	45	50	34	34	46	50	3,258	2,730	3,283
Taiwan	91	169	243	264	125	194	249	264	6,440	9,575	12,390
Tanzania	2	3	4	4	2	3	4	4	115	131	134
Thailand	49	96	147	163	67	111	151	163	1,310	2,012	2,806
Turkey	78	124	153	167	106	142	157	167	2,100	2,536	2,714
United Kingdom	653	903	1,058	1,110	895	1,037	1,084	1,110	15,800	18,070	19,020
Venezuela	41	56	71	75	56	65	73	75	3,298	3,339	3,457

NA Not available. X Not applicable. [1] Estimated. [2] See footnote 3, table 1334. [3] Prior to 1991, data are for former West Germany.

Source: U.S. Arms Control and Disarmament Agency, *World Military Expenditures and Arms Transfers*, annual. Data from International Bank for Reconstruction and Development and U.S. Central Intelligence Agency.

No. 1348. Gross Domestic Product, by Country: 1980 to 1996

COUNTRY	PURCHASING POWER PARITY BASIS [1]												CONSTANT (1990) PRICE LEVELS AND EXCHANGE RATES [2]								
	Amount (bil. dol.)						Per capita (dollars)						Amount (bil. dol.)							Annual growth rate [3] (percent)	
	1980	1985	1990	1993	1994	1995	1980	1985	1990	1993	1994	1995	1980	1985	1990	1993	1994	1995	1996	1995	1996
OECD, total	7,405	10,818	15,092	17,366	18,242	18,980	8,539	11,990	16,058	17,998	18,759	19,366	12,828	14,390	16,859	17,497	17,999	18,347	18,777	1.9	2.3
OECD Europe	3,089	4,369	6,108	6,923	7,238	7,556	7,525	10,400	14,139	15,705	16,332	16,964	5,718	6,201	7,231	7,362	7,558	7,748	7,881	2.5	1.7
European Union [4]	2,873	4,036	5,623	6,334	6,651	6,925	8,083	11,246	15,426	17,131	17,928	18,612	5,349	5,777	6,733	6,832	7,029	7,202	7,315	2.5	1.6
Australia	127	194	272	309	330	349	8,671	12,293	15,947	17,478	18,516	19,354	214	251	295	310	326	336	350	3.2	4.1
Austria	67	93	128	153	162	167	8,850	12,278	16,623	19,167	20,206	20,773	128	137	158	167	172	175	177	1.8	1.0
Belgium	87	118	164	196	206	211	8,851	11,976	16,467	19,451	20,316	20,792	160	166	194	197	202	206	209	1.9	1.3
Canada	246	370	509	559	594	623	10,020	14,262	18,304	19,310	20,298	21,031	427	493	568	575	598	612	622	2.3	1.5
Denmark	45	67	85	100	106	113	8,749	12,997	16,552	19,191	20,445	21,529	106	120	129	133	139	143	146	2.8	1.9
Finland	38	57	81	79	83	91	8,004	11,682	16,193	15,646	16,273	17,787	99	114	135	119	125	130	133	4.2	2.5
France	511	711	984	1,077	1,114	1,159	9,475	12,851	17,347	18,675	19,233	19,939	963	1,030	1,195	1,202	1,234	1,260	1,276	2.1	1.3
Germany	658	921	1,269	1,502	1,601	1,674	8,407	11,862	15,991	18,500	19,668	20,497	1,321	1,421	1,640	1,704	1,753	1,787	1,808	1.9	1.1
Greece	51	71	93	115	121	127	5,315	7,175	9,187	11,032	11,590	12,174	71	76	83	86	88	90	92	2.0	2.2
Iceland	2	3	4	5	5	6	9,492	13,100	17,271	18,696	19,324	21,938	5	5	6	6	6	7	7	2.0	5.8
Ireland	18	27	40	51	56	62	5,291	7,501	11,402	14,236	15,783	17,228	32	36	46	51	54	60	65	10.7	7.0
Italy	476	668	922	1,011	1,067	1,115	8,440	11,782	16,257	17,710	18,648	19,465	877	945	1,094	1,100	1,123	1,157	1,166	3.0	0.8
Japan	958	1,472	2,202	2,580	2,646	2,737	8,204	12,188	17,824	20,691	21,170	21,795	2,007	2,369	2,970	3,125	3,140	3,169	3,283	0.9	3.6
Luxembourg	4	5	9	11	12	13	9,970	14,566	22,809	28,176	30,116	31,303	7	8	10	12	13	13	14	3.8	2.3
Mexico	251	360	467	683	728	700	3,606	4,617	5,416	7,484	7,822	7,383	220	242	263	289	302	283	295	-6.2	4.1
Netherlands	124	172	239	272	288	306	8,750	11,839	15,958	17,817	18,724	19,782	229	243	284	298	308	315	323	2.1	2.6
New Zealand	24	37	45	53	57	60	7,731	11,218	13,332	15,263	16,189	16,851	38	42	43	46	48	50	50	3.1	1.3
Norway	37	57	74	92	95	99	9,124	13,775	17,497	21,380	21,954	22,672	90	106	115	128	133	137	144	3.3	5.1
Portugal	45	61	93	113	119	124	4,588	6,087	9,372	11,431	12,018	12,457	51	53	67	71	71	72	74	1.9	2.5
Spain	219	308	458	521	532	558	5,849	8,018	11,787	13,329	13,596	14,226	366	395	492	500	511	525	536	2.8	2.1
Sweden	77	109	146	147	154	165	9,250	13,057	17,004	16,870	17,582	18,673	188	205	230	219	226	234	238	3.6	1.7
Switzerland	75	104	143	161	168	176	11,720	15,969	21,020	23,014	23,859	24,809	184	197	226	223	226	226	225	0.1	-0.3
Turkey	102	169	264	331	319	351	2,299	3,351	4,691	5,562	5,271	5,691	91	115	151	174	165	176	190	7.2	7.5
United Kingdom	453	649	912	987	1,029	1,042	8,039	11,449	15,847	16,955	17,622	17,776	752	828	976	971	1,009	1,034	1,059	2.5	2.4
United States	2,708	4,017	5,490	6,260	6,650	6,955	11,892	16,844	21,966	24,252	25,512	26,438	4,205	4,793	5,490	5,791	6,027	6,150	6,297	2.0	2.4

[1] The goods and services produced in different countries should be valued consistently if the differences observed are meant to reflect real differences in the volumes of goods and services produced. The use of purchasing power parities (PPP) instead of exchange rates is intended to achieve this objective. PPP's show how many units of currency are needed in one country to buy the same amount of goods and services which one unit of currency will buy in the other country. See text, section 30. [2] Based on constant (1990) price data converted to U.S. dollars using 1990 exchange rates. [3] Percent change from immediate prior year. Minus sign (-) indicates decrease. [4] For countries, see text, section 30.

Source: Organization for Economic Cooperation and Development, Paris, France, *National Accounts, Main Aggregates*, vol. I, annual; and "OECD Statistics GDP;" published January 1997; <http://www.oecd.org/std/gdp.htm> (copyright).

No. 1349. International Economic Composite Indexes, by Country: 1980 to 1996

[Average annual percent change from previous year; derived from indexes with base 1980=100. The coincident index changes are for calendar years and the leading index changes are for years ending June 30 because they lead the coincident indexes by about 6 months, on average. The G-7 countries are United States, Canada, France, Germany, Italy, United Kingdom, and Japan. Minus sign (-) indicates decrease]

COUNTRY	1980	1985	1987	1988	1989	1990	1991	1992	1993	1994	1995	1996
LEADING INDEX												
Total, 11 countries	2.4	3.1	4.3	8.0	5.0	2.3	-0.8	0.8	1.2	4.9	5.9	2.6
10 countries, excluding U.S.	6.6	4.4	5.2	8.2	5.9	3.3	-0.8	-1.8	-1.6	3.5	5.6	3.0
G-7 countries	2.3	2.9	4.2	7.8	4.9	2.3	-0.8	0.6	1.0	4.8	5.9	2.6
North America	-2.8	1.3	3.2	7.3	3.5	0.7	-1.1	4.5	5.2	7.0	6.3	1.9
United States	-3.3	1.0	3.2	7.5	3.7	0.9	-0.8	4.8	5.1	6.9	6.3	2.0
Canada	3.2	4.3	2.7	6.1	1.0	-2.5	-4.7	1.7	5.5	8.3	6.5	0.6
Four European countries	2.8	2.3	3.6	3.1	4.2	1.5	1.0	1.0	0.3	4.0	4.4	0.7
France	4.5	2.6	6.1	5.1	6.0	0.5	0.8	2.6	0.2	4.7	5.8	-0.3
Germany [1]	2.4	2.0	1.6	3.4	5.2	4.7	3.8	0.4	-1.7	4.2	4.5	0.9
Italy	3.0	2.7	4.3	0.6	2.1	0.3	-0.7	0.7	2.4	3.9	3.1	1.2
United Kingdom	1.0	2.2	3.4	1.9	2.4	-0.9	-1.8	-	2.1	3.0	3.2	1.5
Five Pacific region countries	14.4	7.8	7.9	16.1	8.6	6.1	-2.5	-5.8	-5.0	1.9	7.4	6.7
Australia	5.2	6.5	3.2	7.6	5.2	-3.3	-3.9	3.6	5.3	6.2	2.5	-0.4
Taiwan	4.7	6.5	13.6	14.9	12.3	7.0	1.4	8.2	5.5	8.0	8.1	4.5
Japan	17.2	8.3	7.6	17.6	8.9	7.2	-3.0	-8.3	-7.6	-	7.7	8.1
Korea, South	-2.6	4.7	17.2	13.7	10.0	4.5	3.9	4.9	4.1	11.8	10.5	4.4
New Zealand	1.8	5.4	2.8	-1.5	0.8	1.2	-2.7	3.0	3.4	2.7	1.4	0.9
COINCIDENT INDEX												
Total, 11 countries	0.3	3.7	4.1	6.1	4.8	3.6	-	0.9	0.2	3.4	3.3	2.6
10 countries, excluding U.S.	2.5	4.0	4.5	6.9	6.4	5.8	2.3	0.8	-0.9	2.5	3.4	2.5
G-7 countries	0.2	3.6	4.0	6.0	4.6	3.6	-	0.9	0.1	3.1	3.1	2.5
North America	-2.4	3.6	3.8	4.8	2.4	-0.1	-3.9	1.0	2.3	5.1	3.3	2.6
United States	-2.8	3.4	3.7	4.7	2.3	-	-3.9	1.1	2.3	4.9	3.3	2.7
Canada	2.0	5.3	4.8	5.8	2.8	-	-4.3	0.1	2.2	4.4	2.6	1.4
Four European countries	1.4	2.9	3.8	6.1	6.0	5.6	1.2	0.1	-2.4	2.4	4.0	2.4
France	1.3	1.4	5.0	8.0	8.7	7.1	2.1	0.8	-1.9	4.0	6.4	3.3
Germany [1]	2.5	3.5	3.0	3.6	5.4	7.2	5.1	1.4	-1.9	1.2	2.0	1.0
Italy	5.2	2.5	1.5	5.3	2.0	4.7	0.3	-0.5	-7.5	-1.0	2.6	1.5
United Kingdom	-2.1	4.3	5.2	8.0	5.9	2.3	-4.8	-2.4	0.2	4.5	4.5	3.8
Five Pacific region countries	4.2	5.0	5.2	8.2	7.5	6.8	4.6	1.8	0.5	2.3	2.7	2.9
Australia	4.8	7.6	4.3	8.5	9.9	0.9	-7.7	-1.0	2.3	9.6	8.8	4.1
Taiwan	7.1	3.7	11.9	8.0	7.3	2.8	5.8	6.1	5.1	5.8	3.4	1.6
Japan	4.5	4.7	4.6	8.3	7.3	7.6	5.8	1.7	-0.2	0.9	1.5	2.5
Korea, South	-4.3	5.5	13.5	10.6	6.2	9.5	7.9	4.5	3.9	9.0	9.1	6.0
New Zealand	1.9	1.8	1.4	-0.8	-0.7	1.2	-0.7	1.4	3.6	5.5	4.7	4.4

- Represents or rounds to zero. [1] Former West Germany.

Source: Center for International Business Cycle Research, Columbia Business School, New York, NY, *International Economic Indicators*, monthly.

No. 1350. Selected International Economic Indicators, by Country: 1980 to 1996

[Data cover gross domestic product (GDP) at market prices. Gross fixed capital formation covers private and government sectors except military. Savings data are calculated by deducting outlays—such as personal consumption expenditures, interest paid, and transfer payments to foreigners—from disposable personal income]

YEAR	United States	France	Germany	Italy	Netherlands	United Kingdom	Japan	Canada
Ratio of gross fixed capital formation to GDP (current prices):								
1980	19.6	23.0	22.6	24.3	21.6	17.9	31.6	23.3
1985	18.8	19.3	19.5	20.7	19.7	17.0	27.5	19.7
1990	16.2	21.4	20.9	20.3	20.9	19.5	31.7	21.1
1992	15.0	20.1	23.1	19.2	20.0	15.6	30.5	18.7
1993	15.4	18.5	21.8	16.9	19.2	14.9	29.5	18.1
1994	16.2	18.5	22.0	16.6	18.7	14.9	28.6	18.5
1995	16.6	17.9	21.7	17.3	19.4	15.1	28.3	17.3
1996	17.0	17.5	21.0	17.0	19.9	15.0	29.6	17.5
Ratio of savings to disposable personal income:								
1980	8.5	17.6	14.2	21.6	11.0	13.4	17.9	13.3
1985	7.2	14.0	12.8	19.2	13.1	10.7	15.6	13.1
1990	5.3	12.5	14.7	18.5	15.5	8.1	12.1	9.5
1992	6.2	13.6	13.9	17.9	13.0	12.2	13.1	10.2
1993	4.8	14.1	12.9	15.8	11.9	11.3	13.4	9.4
1994	3.9	13.6	12.3	14.7	11.4	10.1	12.8	7.5
1995	4.9	14.3	12.3	14.4	12.8	11.0	13.0	6.9
1996	4.9	12.5	12.4	13.4	(NA)	11.6	13.2	4.6

NA Not available.

Source: U.S. Dept. of Commerce, International Trade Administration, Office of Trade and Economic Analysis, based on official statistics of listed countries.

No. 1351. Annual Percent Change in Consumer Prices, by Country: 1992 to 1996

[Change from previous year. See text, section 30, for general comments concerning the data. For additional qualifications of the data for individual countries, see source]

COUNTRY	1992	1993	1994	1995	1996	COUNTRY	1992	1993	1994	1995	1996
United States	3.0	3.0	2.6	2.8	2.9	Korea, South	6.2	4.8	6.3	4.5	5.0
Argentina	24.9	10.6	4.2	3.4	0.2	Malaysia	4.8	3.5	3.7	5.3	3.5
Australia	1.0	1.8	1.9	4.6	2.6	Mexico	15.5	9.8	7.0	35.0	34.4
Belgium	2.4	2.8	2.4	1.5	2.1	Netherlands	1.4	2.1	1.8	2.8	4.0
Brazil	1,009	2,148	2,669	84	18	Nigeria	44.6	57.2	57.0	72.8	29.3
Canada	1.5	1.8	0.2	2.2	1.6	Norway	2.3	2.3	1.4	2.5	1.3
Chile	15.4	12.7	11.4	8.2	7.4	Pakistan	9.5	10.0	12.4	12.3	10.4
Colombia	27.0	22.6	23.8	21.0	20.2	Philippines	8.9	7.6	9.1	8.1	8.4
France	2.4	2.1	1.7	1.8	2.0	Romania	211	255	137	32	(NA)
Germany	4.0	5.0	3.0	1.8	1.5	South Africa	13.9	9.7	9.0	8.7	7.4
India	11.8	6.4	10.2	10.2	9.0	Spain	5.9	4.6	4.7	4.7	3.6
Indonesia	7.5	9.7	8.5	9.4	7.9	Sweden	2.3	4.6	2.2	2.5	0.5
Iran	25.6	21.2	31.5	49.6	28.9	Switzerland	4.1	3.3	0.8	1.8	0.8
Israel	11.9	10.9	12.3	10.0	11.3	Turkey	70.1	66.1	106.3	88.1	80.3
Italy	5.1	4.5	4.0	5.2	4.0	United Kingdom	3.7	1.6	2.5	3.4	2.4
Japan	1.7	1.3	0.7	-0.1	0.1	Venezuela	31.4	38.1	60.8	59.9	99.9

NA Not available.

Source: International Monetary Fund, Washington, DC, *International Financial Statistics*, monthly (copyright).

No. 1352. At-Home Food and Beverage Expenditures, by Country: 1993

[Percent of total personal consumption expenditures. Expenditures spent on food and alcoholic beverages that were consumed at home]

COUNTRY	Food [1]	Alcoholic beverages	COUNTRY	Food [1]	Alcoholic beverages
United States	7.7	1.1	Netherlands	11.6	1.5
Australia	14.6	4.3	Pakistan [2]	39.3	(NA)
Bangladesh [2]	62.6	(NA)	Philippines	[3]54.6	(NA)
Canada	10.1	2.3	Singapore	14.8	1.6
France	15.2	2.0	South Africa	27.0	5.9
Germany	[3]17.7	(NA)	Spain	[4]21.0	(NA)
Greece	30.8	3.1	Sweden	14.5	2.7
India	51.4	0.6	Switzerland	17.9	(NA)
Israel	21.0	0.7	Turkey [2]	25.3	(NA)
Italy	17.6	1.0	United Kingdom	11.5	6.0
Japan	[4]17.8	(NA)	Venezuela	[3]37.3	(NA)
Mexico	[4]33.2	(NA)			

NA Not available. [1] Food expenditures include nonalcoholic beverages. [2] Calculated by using World Bank data on food as a share of gross domestic product. [3] Food expenditures include nonalcoholic and alcoholic beverages. [4] Food expenditures include all beverages and tobacco.

Source: U.S. Dept. of Agriculture, Economic Research Service, *Food Consumption, Prices, and Expenditures, 1997: Annual Data, 1970-95.*

No. 1353. Per Capita Consumption of Meat and Poultry: 1996

[Preliminary. In kilograms per capita. Beef, veal, and pork quantities are as of September and in carcass-weight equivalents; poultry quantities are as of July and are on ready-to-cook basis]

COUNTRY	PORK		COUNTRY	POULTRY		COUNTRY	BEEF AND VEAL	
	Quantity	Rank		Quantity	Rank		Quantity	Rank
Denmark	65.7	1	Hong Kong	48.7	1	Uruguay	61.7	1
Czech Republic	64.8	2	United States	46.0	2	Argentina	60.9	2
Hungary	60.3	3	Israel	43.9	3	United States	44.8	3
Austria	57.7	4	Singapore	33.3	4	Australia	35.2	4
Spain	54.1	5	Saudi Arabia	31.8	5	Canada	33.6	5
Belgium-Luxembourg	53.7	6	Canada	31.7	6	New Zealand	33.0	6
Germany	48.6	7	Taiwan	30.4	7	Czech Republic	30.7	7
Hong Kong	46.8	8	Australia	27.0	8	Brazil	29.2	8
Netherlands	44.1	9	Spain	25.4	9	Kazakstan	26.7	9
Taiwan	42.4	10	Portugal	25.3	10	France	24.9	10
United States	28.7	21						

Source: U.S. Department of Agriculture, Foreign Agricultural Service, *Livestock and Poultry: World Markets and Trade*, annual.

No. 1354. Telephones, Newspapers, Television, and Radio, by Country

[See text, section 30, for general comments about the data. For data qualifications for countries, see source]

COUNTRY	Telephone main lines per 100 people,[1] 1995	Cellular telephone subscribers per 100,000 people,[1] 1995	Daily newspaper circulation per 1,000 people,[2] 1994	Television receivers per 1,000 people,[3] 1995	Radio receivers per 1,000 people,[4] 1994
Algeria	4	17	46	[5]71	236
Argentina	16	965	138	347	673
Australia	51	12,767	258	482	1,291
Austria	47	4,762	472	497	619
Belgium	46	2,321	321	464	774
Brazil	7	795	45	278	393
Bulgaria	30	193	209	358	454
Canada	[5]59	8,647	189	[5]647	1,051
Chile	13	1,382	100	280	345
China	3	302	23	250	184
Colombia	10	707	64	188	178
Costa Rica	16	549	99	220	260
Cuba	3	18	120	200	347
Cyprus	47	6,065	110	143	300
Czech Republic	24	473	219	406	631
Denmark	61	15,728	365	536	1,036
Dominican Republic	[5]8	422	34	87	173
Ecuador	6	462	72	148	327
Egypt	5	13	64	126	307
Finland	55	19,922	473	519	1,003
France	56	2,375	237	579	891
Germany	49	4,275	317	550	935
Ghana	-	36	18	(NA)	229
Greece	49	2,608	156	442	418
Guatemala	3	282	23	54	68
Honduras	3	-	44	80	408
Hungary	19	2,594	228	441	625
Iceland	55	11,524	515	447	793
India	1	15	(NA)	61	81
Indonesia	2	112	20	[5]147	148
Iran	8	[5]14	(NA)	140	237
Iraq	3	-	27	(NA)	218
Ireland	37	4,406	170	382	636
Israel	42	5,349	281	[5]295	478
Italy	43	6,738	105	436	802
Jamaica	12	1,789	66	285	436
Japan	49	8,149	576	619	912
Korea, South	41	3,659	404	[5]323	1,017
Kuwait	23	7,068	401	379	445
Lebanon	8	2,996	172	268	889
Luxembourg	56	6,578	384	[5]591	636
Malaysia	17	4,337	142	[5]231	432
Mexico	10	699	113	192	256
Morocco	4	110	13	[5]145	219
Netherlands	53	3,318	334	495	909
New Zealand	48	10,801	297	[5]508	991
Norway	56	22,445	607	561	799
Pakistan	2	33	21	[5]22	88
Panama	11	-	62	169	227
Paraguay	[5]3	320	42	73	172
Peru	5	313	86	100	255
Philippines	2	730	65	[5]121	144
Poland	15	194	141	408	441
Portugal	36	3,434	41	332	233
Puerto Rico	33	4,756	184	322	713
Romania	13	40	297	[5]201	204
Russia	17	60	267	[5]379	339
Saudi Arabia	10	90	54	257	294
Singapore	48	9,773	364	362	645
South Africa	9	1,290	33	101	314
Spain	39	2,408	104	490	312
Sweden	68	22,936	483	476	879
Switzerland	61	6,352	409	461	841
Syria	6	-	18	89	257
Taiwan	43	3,616	(NA)	317	(NA)
Thailand	6	1,852	48	[5]221	190
Trinidad and Tobago	16	430	135	318	491
Tunisia	6	36	46	156	199
Turkey	21	699	44	240	162
United Kingdom	50	9,799	351	612	1,429
United States	63	12,840	228	776	2,122
Uruguay	20	1,258	237	305	605
Venezuela	11	1,801	215	180	443

- Represents or rounds to zero. NA Not available. [1] As of December 31. [2] Publications containing general news and appearing at least 4 times a week; may range in size from a single sheet to 50 or more pages. Circulation data refer to average circulation per issue or number of printed copies per issue and include copies sold outside the country. [3] Estimated number of sets in use. [4] Data cover estimated number of receivers in use and apply to all types of receivers for radio broadcasts to the public, including receivers connected to a radio "redistribution system" but excluding television sets. [5] For 1994.

Source: International Telecommunications Union, Geneva, Switzerland, *World Telecommunication Indicators*, (copyright); and United Nations Educational, Scientific, and Cultural Organization, Paris, France, *Statistical Yearbook*, (copyright).

No. 1355. Motor Vehicle Registrations, by Country: 1995

COUNTRY	ALL VEHICLES Number (mil.)	ALL VEHICLES Persons per vehicle	PASSENGER CARS Number (mil.)	PASSENGER CARS Persons per car	COUNTRY	ALL VEHICLES Number (mil.)	ALL VEHICLES Persons per vehicle	PASSENGER CARS Number (mil.)	PASSENGER CARS Persons per car
Argentina	5.9	6	4.7	7	Israel	1.4	4	1.1	5
Australia	11.2	2	9.0	2	Italy	32.8	2	30.0	2
Austria	4.4	2	3.6	2	Japan	66.9	2	44.7	3
Belgium	4.8	2	4.2	2	Kuwait	0.7	3	0.5	4
Bulgaria	1.8	5	1.6	5	Netherlands	6.3	2	5.6	3
Canada	16.7	2	13.2	2	New Zealand	2.0	2	1.7	2
Chile	1.4	11	0.9	16	Norway	2.1	2	1.7	3
Costa Rica	0.1	26	0.1	60	Panama	0.2	12	0.1	19
Denmark	2.0	3	1.7	3	Paraguay	0.1	44	0.1	73
Dominican Republic	0.2	40	0.1	67	Poland	3.9	10	3.5	11
Ecuador	0.5	24	0.2	57	Portugal	3.4	3	2.6	4
Finland	2.2	2	1.9	3	Puerto Rico	1.7	2	1.4	3
France	30.3	2	25.1	2	Singapore	0.5	7	0.3	10
Germany	43.6	2	40.5	2	Sweden	4.0	2	3.6	2
Greece	3.1	3	2.2	5	Switzerland	3.5	2	3.2	2
Hong Kong	0.5	13	0.3	21	Syria	0.3	56	0.1	130
Hungary	2.5	4	2.2	5	Thailand	5.0	12	1.4	44
Ireland	1.2	3	1.0	4	United States	200.4	1	136.0	2
					Uruguay	0.5	7	0.4	7

Source: American Automobile Manufactures Association, Inc., Detroit, MI, *AAMA Motor Vehicle Facts & Figures*, annual, (copyright).

No. 1356. Motor Vehicle Miles of Travel for Selected Countries

COUNTRY	Year	TOTAL VEHICLE MILES (billions) Auto-mobiles	Motor-cycles	Buses	Trucks	AVERAGE VEHICLE MILES PER— Auto-mobile	Motor-cycle	Bus	Truck
Canada	1990	138.2	0.7	1.3	48.3	10,251	2,184	19,809	6,785
France	1994	214.7	3.7	2.5	69.6	8,622	1,247	31,865	13,748
Germany	1993	306.9	7.9	2.9	33.9	7,688	3,720	33,407	20,400
Japan	1994	256.6	(NA)	4.3	163.9	6,013	(NA)	17,588	7,384
Mexico	1991	22.7	0.7	0.3	9.7	3,027	2,532	3,141	2,765
Sweden	1993	26.6	(NA)	(NA)	(NA)	7,456	(NA)	(NA)	(NA)
United Kingdom	1994	212.9	2.6	2.9	41.0	10,593	4,015	26,713	13,982
United States [1]	1994	2,172.9	10.3	6.4	170.4	11,372	2,759	9,570	27,036

NA Not available. [1] Automobiles cover passenger cars and other 2-axle, 4-tire vehicles; trucks cover single-unit 2-axle, 6-tire or more and combination trucks.

Source: U.S. Federal Highway Administration, *Highway Statistics, 1995.*

No. 1357. Employee-Employer Payroll Tax Rates for Social Security Programs, by Country: 1981 to 1996

[In percent. Covers old-age, disability and survivors insurance, sickness and maternity, work injury, unemployment and family allowances. In some cases, only certain groups, such as wage earners, are represented. When the contribution rate varies, either the average rate or the lowest rate in the range is used]

COUNTRY	ALL SOCIAL SECURITY PROGRAMS 1981	1991	1996 Total	1996 Employer	1996 Employee	OLD-AGE, DISABILITY, SURVIVORS INSURANCE 1981	1991	1996 Total	1996 Employer	1996 Employee
United States	17.60	20.50	21.00	13.35	7.65	10.70	12.40	12.40	6.20	6.20
Australia [1]	-	1.25	[2]1.25	[2]-	[2]1.25	-	-	[2]-	[2]-	[2]-
Austria	[3]40.30	[3]43.90	[3]44.90	27.70	17.20	21.10	22.80	22.80	12.55	10.25
Belgium	34.70	39.33	37.94	24.87	13.07	15.11	16.36	16.36	8.86	7.50
Canada	[4]7.92	[4]10.00	[2,4]14.10	[2]8.40	[2]5.70	3.60	4.60	[2]5.40	[2]2.70	[2]2.70
France	47.55	54.41	50.32	34.45	15.87	13.00	17.00	16.45	9.80	6.65
Germany	[5]34.80	36.16	[4]40.55	21.00	19.55	[5]18.50	17.70	19.20	9.60	9.60
Italy	54.30	55.72	54.32	44.33	9.89	24.46	27.42	28.27	19.38	8.89
Japan	21.41	24.86	[2]26.62	[2]14.38	[2]12.24	10.60	14.50	[2]16.50	[2]8.25	[2]8.25
Netherlands	54.85	51.73	[4]56.55	12.05	44.50	32.45	28.25	31.75	-	31.75
Norway	26.50	24.50	[4,6]21.90	14.10	7.80	26.50	24.50	[6]21.90	14.10	7.80
Spain	38.00	37.30	[7]38.30	32.00	6.30	33.10	28.80	[7]28.30	23.60	4.70
Sweden	32.65	34.11	[4]36.09	31.14	4.95	21.15	20.95	20.06	19.06	1.00
Switzerland	11.90	12.00	12.94	6.54	6.40	9.40	9.60	9.80	4.90	4.90
United Kingdom	[4,6,8]21.45	[4,6,8]21.45	[4,6,8]22.20	10.20	12.00	21.45	21.45	[6,8]22.20	10.20	12.00

- Represents zero. [1] The central government pays the entire cost of most programs through general revenues. [2] Data for 1995. [3] Sickness and maternity refers to wage earners. [4] The central government pays the whole cost of family allowances. [5] Data are for former West Germany. [6] Old-age, disability, survivors insurance contribution also covers sickness and maternity, work injury, and unemployment. [7] Old-age, disability, survivors insurance contribution also covers sickness and maternity and family allowances. [8] Old-age, disability, survivors insurance range according to earnings bracket; higher rate is shown, which applies to highest earnings class.

Source: U.S. Social Security Administration, Office of Research and Statistics, *Social Security Programs Throughout the World*, biannual.

No. 1358. Tax Revenues, by Country: 1980 to 1994

[Covers national and local taxes and Social Security contributions. Minus sign (-) indicates decrease]

COUNTRY	TAX REVENUES, 1994		PERCENT CHANGE IN TOTAL TAX REVENUE AS EXPRESSED IN NATIONAL CURRENCY[1]					TAX REVENUES AS PERCENT OF GROSS DOMESTIC PRODUCT				
	Total (bil. dol.)	Per capita (dol.)	1990	1991	1992	1993	1994	1980	1985	1990	1993	1994
Australia	100	5,569	3.0	-3.4	3.1	6.4	10.5	28.4	30.0	30.8	28.8	29.9
Austria	85	10,569	8.4	8.5	9.7	4.3	5.0	41.2	43.1	41.3	43.5	42.8
Belgium	106	10,500	7.3	5.0	5.4	4.1	7.3	44.4	47.7	44.8	45.6	46.6
Canada	201	6,858	5.5	2.5	1.2	2.0	6.1	31.6	33.1	36.5	35.8	36.1
Czech Republic	17	1,648	(X)	(X)	(X)	(X)	12.6	(X)	(X)	(X)	47.8	47.3
Denmark	75	14,460	0.2	3.6	4.1	4.6	8.8	45.5	49.0	48.7	50.3	51.6
Finland	46	9,051	10.7	-1.7	-2.9	-1.9	9.8	36.9	40.8	45.4	45.4	47.3
France	586	10,129	5.7	4.6	2.7	1.8	4.7	41.7	44.5	43.7	43.9	44.1
Germany[2]	803	12,197	4.5	22.4	10.0	2.9	5.7	38.2	38.1	36.7	39.1	39.3
Greece	33	3,169	30.1	27.0	20.4	14.1	16.2	29.4	35.1	37.5	41.2	42.5
Hungary	17	1,648	(NA)	(NA)	17.7	19.4	20.1	(NA)	(NA)	(NA)	42.0	41.0
Iceland	2	7,191	14.3	8.9	2.7	0.5	4.5	29.2	28.4	31.4	31.3	30.9
Ireland	19	5,451	6.3	5.6	7.3	7.9	11.1	33.8	36.4	35.2	36.4	37.5
Italy	424	7,416	13.6	10.4	11.7	7.2	0.7	30.2	34.5	39.1	43.8	41.7
Japan	1,304	10,434	9.6	3.6	-3.3	0.6	-2.5	25.4	27.6	31.3	29.1	27.8
Luxembourg	6	16,271	8.8	5.9	6.9	15.1	10.7	46.3	46.7	43.6	44.3	45.0
Mexico	71	784	35.3	27.8	21.2	12.2	8.0	17.4	18.3	18.6	19.7	18.8
Netherlands	154	9,983	5.9	11.2	3.4	4.3	1.2	45.0	44.1	44.6	47.7	45.9
New Zealand	19	5,434	-0.7	-3.8	4.2	8.3	8.3	32.9	33.3	37.6	35.6	37.0
Norway	51	11,706	7.0	5.7	0.8	2.9	8.4	47.1	47.6	41.8	40.2	41.2
Poland	40	1,040	(NA)	(NA)	46.0	50.5	37.6	(NA)	(NA)	(NA)	42.4	43.2
Portugal	29	2,902	18.5	19.4	20.5	0.1	11.3	25.2	27.8	31.0	31.4	33.0
Spain	173	4,410	10.7	10.6	11.5	0.1	8.6	24.1	28.8	34.4	35.0	35.8
Sweden	101	11,481	10.6	2.8	-5.4	-1.4	7.3	48.8	50.0	55.6	50.1	51.0
Switzerland	87	12,464	7.3	4.4	4.6	5.6	4.6	30.8	32.0	31.5	33.2	33.9
Turkey	29	480	85.4	68.0	85.4	83.2	91.5	17.9	15.4	20.0	22.7	22.2
United Kingdom	348	5,965	7.5	2.5	2.2	0.4	7.8	35.3	37.9	36.4	33.4	34.1
United States	1,886	7,234	4.9	3.5	4.3	6.5	8.0	26.9	26.0	26.7	27.0	27.6

NA Not available. X Not applicable. [1] Change from previous year. [2] Prior to 1991, data are for former West Germany.

No. 1359. Percent Distribution of Tax Receipts, by Country: 1980 to 1994

COUNTRY	Total[1]	INCOME AND PROFITS TAXES[2]			SOCIAL SECURITY CONTRIBUTIONS			TAXES ON GOODS AND SERVICES[5]		
		Total[3]	Individual	Corporate	Total[4]	Employees	Employers	Total[3]	General consumption taxes[6]	Taxes on specific goods, services[7]
United States: 1980	100.0	47.0	39.1	10.8	26.2	9.2	11.9	16.6	7.0	8.3
1990	100.0	43.2	37.7	7.7	29.5	11.0	13.4	16.5	8.0	7.1
1994	100.0	44.6	36.7	8.9	25.5	10.8	13.3	17.9	7.9	7.9
Canada: 1980	100.0	46.6	34.1	11.6	10.5	3.7	6.6	32.6	11.5	13.0
1990	100.0	48.8	41.0	7.0	14.4	4.4	9.7	26.0	14.4	9.5
1994	100.0	44.4	37.2	6.6	16.9	5.5	11.1	26.3	15.5	8.7
France: 1980	100.0	18.1	12.9	5.1	42.7	11.1	28.4	30.4	21.1	8.4
1990	100.0	17.2	11.8	5.3	44.1	13.2	27.2	28.4	18.8	8.7
1994	100.0	17.7	14.0	3.7	43.4	13.3	26.8	27.1	17.2	9.1
Germany[8]: 1980	100.0	35.1	29.6	5.5	34.3	15.3	18.4	27.1	16.6	9.3
1990	100.0	32.4	27.6	4.8	37.5	16.2	19.1	26.7	16.6	9.2
1994	100.0	29.4	26.5	2.9	39.1	17.1	19.9	28.7	18.1	9.5
Italy: 1980	100.0	31.1	23.1	7.8	38.0	6.9	28.4	26.5	15.6	9.7
1990	100.0	36.5	26.3	10.0	32.9	6.3	23.6	28.0	14.7	10.6
1994	100.0	34.7	25.4	8.9	31.2	6.6	20.8	26.3	15.4	10.6
Japan: 1980	100.0	46.1	24.3	21.8	29.1	10.2	14.8	16.3	-	14.1
1990	100.0	48.3	26.8	21.6	29.2	11.0	15.0	13.2	4.3	7.3
1994	100.0	37.7	22.8	14.8	35.1	13.5	18.0	15.5	5.3	8.2
Netherlands: 1980	100.0	32.8	26.3	6.6	38.1	15.7	17.8	25.2	15.8	7.3
1990	100.0	32.2	24.7	7.5	37.4	23.1	7.5	26.4	16.5	7.5
1994	100.0	27.5	20.3	7.3	42.1	27.3	6.5	25.8	14.7	8.6
Sweden: 1980	100.0	43.5	41.0	2.5	28.8	0.1	27.6	24.0	13.4	9.2
1990	100.0	41.6	38.5	3.1	27.2	0.1	26.0	25.0	14.9	9.2
1994	100.0	42.4	36.7	5.4	27.2	1.9	24.6	25.8	15.9	9.3
United Kingdom: 1980	100.0	38.2	29.8	8.3	16.6	6.7	9.5	29.2	14.4	13.1
1990	100.0	39.3	28.5	10.8	17.1	6.5	9.9	30.9	16.6	12.7
1994	100.0	35.7	27.6	8.0	18.0	7.3	10.0	35.3	19.8	13.8

- Represents zero. [1] Includes property taxes, employer payroll taxes other than Social Security contributions, and miscellaneous taxes, not shown separately. [2] Includes taxes on capital gains. [3] Includes other taxes not shown separately. [4] Includes contributions of self-employed not shown separately. [5] Taxes on the production, sales, transfer, leasing, and delivery of goods and services and rendering of services. [6] Primary value-added and sales taxes. [7] For example, excise taxes on alcohol, tobacco, and gasoline. [8] Prior to 1990, data are for former West Germany.

Source of tables 1358 and 1359: Organization for Economic Cooperation and Development, Paris, France, *Revenue Statistics of OECD Member Countries*, annual (copyright).

No. 1360. Civilian Labor Force, Employment, and Unemployment, by Country: 1980 to 1995

[Data based on U.S. labor force definitions (see source) except that minimum age for population base varies as follows: United States, France, Sweden, and United Kingdom, 16 years; Australia, Canada, Japan, Netherlands, Germany, and Italy (beginning 1993), 15 years; and Italy (prior to 1993) 14 years]

YEAR	United States	Australia	Canada	France	Germany [1]	Italy	Japan	Netherlands	Sweden	United Kingdom
Civilian labor force (mil.):										
1980	106.9	6.7	12.0	22.9	27.3	21.1	55.7	5.9	4.3	26.5
1985	115.5	7.3	13.1	23.6	28.0	21.8	58.8	6.2	4.4	27.2
1990	[2]125.8	8.4	14.3	24.3	29.4	22.7	63.0	6.7	[2]4.6	28.5
1993	129.2	8.6	14.7	24.6	[3]30.0	[2,3]22.8	65.5	7.1	4.4	28.3
1994	[2]131.1	8.8	14.8	24.8	[3]29.8	[3]22.6	65.8	7.2	4.4	[3]28.3
1995	132.3	9.0	14.9	24.8	[3]29.7	[3]22.7	66.0	7.3	4.5	[3]28.2
Labor force participation rate: [4]										
1980	63.8	62.1	64.6	57.5	54.7	48.2	62.6	55.4	66.9	62.5
1985	64.8	61.6	65.8	56.8	54.7	47.2	62.3	55.5	66.9	62.1
1990	[2]66.5	64.6	67.3	56.0	55.3	47.2	62.6	56.3	[2]67.4	63.7
1993	66.3	63.6	65.5	55.6	[3]54.2	[2,3]48.1	63.3	58.6	64.5	62.8
1994	[2]66.6	63.9	65.3	[3]55.5	[3]53.7	[3]47.5	63.1	58.9	63.8	[3]62.6
1995	66.6	64.6	64.8	[3]55.3	[3]53.1	[3]47.6	62.9	[3]59.7	[3]64.3	[3]62.2
Civilian employment (mil.):										
1980	99.3	6.3	11.1	21.4	26.5	20.2	54.6	5.5	4.2	24.7
1985	107.2	6.7	11.7	21.2	26.0	20.5	57.3	5.6	4.3	24.2
1990	[2]118.8	7.9	13.2	22.1	28.0	21.1	61.7	6.2	[2]4.5	26.6
1993	120.3	7.7	13.0	21.7	[3]28.2	[2,3]20.4	63.8	6.6	4.0	25.3
1994	[2]123.1	7.9	13.3	21.7	[3]27.9	[3]20.1	63.9	6.6	4.0	[3]25.6
1995	124.9	8.2	13.5	21.9	[3]27.7	[3]20.0	63.9	6.8	4.1	[3]25.7
Employment-population ratio: [5]										
1980	59.2	58.3	59.7	53.8	53.1	46.1	61.3	52.1	65.6	58.1
1985	60.1	56.5	58.9	50.9	50.7	44.4	60.6	50.1	65.0	55.1
1990	[2]62.8	60.1	61.9	50.9	52.6	43.9	61.3	52.8	[2]66.1	59.2
1993	61.7	56.6	58.2	49.0	[3]51.1	[2,3]43.1	61.7	54.8	58.5	56.2
1994	[2]62.5	57.7	58.5	48.7	[3]50.2	[3]42.1	61.3	54.6	57.6	[3]56.5
1995	62.9	59.1	58.6	[3]48.8	[3]49.7	[3]41.8	60.9	[3]55.4	[3]58.4	[3]56.7
Unemployment rate:										
1980	7.1	6.1	7.5	6.5	2.8	4.4	2.0	6.0	2.0	7.0
1985	7.2	8.3	10.5	10.5	7.2	6.0	2.6	9.6	2.8	11.2
1990	[2]5.6	6.9	8.1	9.1	5.0	7.0	2.1	6.2	[2]1.8	7.0
1993	6.9	10.9	11.2	11.8	[3]5.7	[2,3]10.2	2.5	6.6	9.3	10.5
1994	[2]6.1	9.7	10.4	12.3	[3]6.5	[3]11.3	2.9	7.2	9.6	[3]9.6
1995	5.6	8.5	9.5	11.7	[3]6.5	[3]12.0	3.2	7.3	9.1	[3]8.8
Under 25 years old	12.1	15.4	15.6	(NA)	(NA)	(NA)	6.2	(NA)	19.9	(NA)
Teenagers [6]	17.3	20.6	18.5	(NA)	(NA)	(NA)	8.4	(NA)	21.1	(NA)
20 to 24 years old	9.1	12.0	13.7	(NA)	(NA)	(NA)	5.7	(NA)	19.5	(NA)
25 years old and over	4.3	6.6	8.3	(NA)	(NA)	(NA)	2.7	(NA)	7.7	(NA)

NA Not available. [1] Former West Germany. [2] Break in series. Data not comparable with prior years. [3] Preliminary. [4] Civilian labor force as a percent of the civilian working age population. Germany and Japan include the institutionalized population as part of the working age population. [5] Civilian employment as a percent of the civilian working age population. Germany and Japan include the institutionalized population as part of the working age population. [6] 16 to 19 years old in the United States and Sweden, and 15 to 19 years old in Canada, Australia, and Japan.

Source: U.S. Bureau of Labor Statistics, *Comparative Labor Force Statistics for Ten Countries, 1959-1995*, June 1996, and *Monthly Labor Review*.

No. 1361. Unemployment Rates, by Country: 1994 to 1996

[Annual averages. The standardized unemployment rates shown here are calculated as the number of unemployed persons as a percentage of the civilian labor force. The unemployed are persons of working age who, in the reference period, are without work, available for work and have taken specific steps to find work]

COUNTRY	1994	1995	1996
OECD, total	7.9	7.5	7.6
European Union	11.1	10.8	10.9
United States	6.1	5.6	5.4
Australia	9.8	8.6	8.6
Austria	(NA)	3.9	4.4
Belgium	10.0	9.9	9.8
Canada	10.4	9.5	9.7
Denmark	8.2	7.1	6.0
Finland	17.9	16.6	15.7
France	12.3	11.7	12.4
Germany	8.4	8.2	9.0
Ireland	14.3	12.4	12.3
Italy	11.4	11.9	12.0
Japan	2.9	3.1	3.4
Luxembourg	3.2	2.9	3.1
Netherlands	7.1	6.9	6.3
New Zealand	8.1	6.3	6.1
Norway	5.5	5.0	(NA)
Portugal	7.0	7.3	7.3
Spain	24.1	22.9	22.2
Sweden	9.8	9.2	10.0
Switzerland	3.6	3.3	(NA)
United Kingdom	9.6	8.8	8.2

NA Not available.

Source: Organization for Economic Cooperation and Development, Paris, France, *OECD News Release, Standardized Unemployment Rates*, 15 April 1997

No. 1362. Civilian Employment-Population Ratio and Females as Percent of Total Civilian Employment, by Country: 1980 to 1995

[See headnote, table 1360]

COUNTRY	CIVILIAN EMPLOYMENT-POPULATION RATIO [1]								CIVILIAN EMPLOYMENT, PERCENT FEMALE			
	Women				Men							
	1980	1985	1990	1995	1980	1985	1990	1995	1980	1985	1990	1995
United States	47.7	50.4	[2]54.3	[2]55.6	72.0	70.9	[2]72.0	[2]70.8	42.4	44.1	[2]45.2	[2]46.1
Australia	41.9	42.9	49.3	50.3	75.1	70.4	71.2	68.1	36.4	38.4	41.5	43.1
Canada	46.7	49.2	54.0	52.1	73.1	69.0	70.1	65.5	39.6	42.4	44.4	45.2
France	40.3	40.5	41.6	[3]40.6	68.9	62.4	61.3	[3]58.0	39.5	42.0	43.0	[3]43.7
Germany [4]	38.9	[2]37.6	40.9	[3 5]41.2	69.9	[2]65.8	65.6	[3 5]60.0	39.2	[2]39.5	41.0	[3 5]42.8
Italy	27.9	27.8	29.2	[2 3]28.4	66.0	62.5	60.0	[2 3]56.5	31.7	32.8	34.7	[2 3]35.3
Japan	45.7	46.3	48.0	47.7	77.9	75.9	75.4	75.0	38.4	39.4	40.3	40.3
Sweden	58.0	59.7	[2]61.8	54.9	73.6	70.5	[2]70.6	62.2	45.2	47.2	[2]47.8	48.1
United Kingdom	44.8	44.3	49.6	[3 5]49.0	72.8	67.0	69.7	[3 5]64.7	40.4	42.0	43.5	[3 5]45.0

[1] Civilian employment as a percent of the civilian working age population. [2] Break in series. Data not comparable with prior years. [3] Preliminary. [4] Former West Germany. [5] 1994 data.

Source: U.S. Bureau of Labor Statistics, *Comparative Labor Force Statistics for Ten Countries, 1959-1995*, June 1996 and *Monthly Labor Review*.

No. 1363. Female Labor Force Participation Rates, by Country: 1984 and 1994

[In percent. Female labor force of all ages divided by female population 15-64 years old]

COUNTRY	1984	1994	COUNTRY	1984	1994
United States	62.8	70.5	Japan	57.2	62.1
Australia	52.8	63.4	Korea, South	43.8	52.7
Austria	51.5	62.1	Luxembourg	42.2	58.5
Belgium	[1]48.7	[2]55.1	Mexico	(NA)	40.0
Canada	63.5	67.8	Netherlands	40.7	57.4
Czech Republic	(NA)	65.6	New Zealand	46.0	65.0
Denmark	73.8	73.8	Norway	66.3	71.1
Finland	72.9	69.9	Poland	(NA)	62.0
France	54.7	59.6	Portugal	56.0	62.2
Germany	[3]52.3	61.8	Spain	33.2	44.1
Greece	40.9	44.6	Sweden	77.3	74.4
Hungary	(NA)	53.0	Switzerland	55.7	67.5
Iceland	82.7	80.0	Turkey	(NA)	33.7
Ireland	36.9	47.2	United Kingdom	59.1	66.2
Italy	40.7	42.9			

NA Not available. [1] 1983 data. [2] 1993 data. [3] Former West Germany.

Source: Organization for Economic Cooperation and Development, Paris, France, *OECD in Figures, Statistics on the Member Countries*, annual.

No. 1364. Civilian Employment, by Industry and Country: 1990 and 1995

[Data based on U.S. labor force definitions except that minimum age for population base varies as follows: United States, France, Sweden, and United Kingdom, 16 years; Australia, Canada, Germany, Italy (1995), Japan, 15 years; and Italy (1990), 14 years. For the United States and Italy the data are not comparable between 1990 and 1995. Industries based on International Standard Industrial Classification; see text, section 31]

INDUSTRY	United States	Australia	Canada	France	Germany	Italy	Japan	Sweden	United Kingdom
TOTAL EMPLOYMENT (1,000)									
1990, total	118,793	7,859	13,165	22,096	27,952	21,080	61,710	4,501	26,639
Agriculture, forestry, fishing	3,394	440	551	1,248	965	1,879	4,270	178	567
Industry [1]	29,834	1,865	3,117	6,425	10,875	[2]6,842	20,890	1,268	7,470
Manufacturing	21,346	1,170	2,105	4,706	8,839	4,755	15,010	943	5,358
Services	85,565	5,554	9,497	14,425	16,112	12,355	36,550	3,056	18,603
1995, total	124,900	8,235	13,506	21,998	[3]27,906	19,974	63,900	4,044	[3]25,163
Agriculture, forestry, fishing	3,592	412	555	1,015	[3]786	1,482	3,510	143	[3]565
Industry [1]	28,788	1,805	2,957	5,564	[3]9,719	[2]6,488	21,160	1,011	[3]6,391
Manufacturing	20,493	1,117	2,061	(NA)	(NA)	(NA)	14,520	770	(NA)
Services	92,520	6,018	9,994	15,419	[3]17,399	12,003	39,230	2,891	[3]18,206
PERCENT DISTRIBUTION									
1990, total	100	100	100	100	100	100	100	100	100
Agriculture, forestry, fishing	3	6	4	6	3	9	7	4	2
Industry [1]	25	24	24	29	39	[2]32	34	28	28
Manufacturing	18	15	16	21	32	23	24	21	20
Services	72	71	72	65	58	59	59	68	70
1995, total	100	100	100	100	[3]100	100	100	100	[3]100
Agriculture, forestry, fishing	3	5	4	5	[3]3	7	6	3	[3]2
Industry [1]	23	22	22	25	[3]35	[2]33	33	25	[3]25
Manufacturing	16	14	15	(NA)	(NA)	(NA)	23	19	(NA)
Services	74	73	74	70	[3]62	60	61	72	[3]72

NA Not available. [1] Includes mining and construction. [2] Public utilities included in industry. [3] 1994 data.

Source: U.S. Bureau of Labor Statistics, Office of Productivity and Technology, *Comparative Labor Force Statistics*, August

No. 1365. Index of Industrial Production, by Country: 1980 to 1996

[Industrial production index measures output in the manufacturing, mining, and electric and gas utilities industries. Minus sign (-) indicates decrease]

COUNTRY	INDEX (1990=100)								ANNUAL PERCENT CHANGE				
	1980	1985	1991	1992	1993	1994	1995	1996	1991-92	1992-93	1993-94	1994-95	1995-96
OECD, total	78.9	86.3	99.6	99.4	98.8	102.9	106.1	108.1	-0.2	-0.6	4.1	3.1	1.9
Australia	(NA)	(NA)	(NA)	97.8	100.4	105.8	105.5	108.8	(NA)	2.7	5.4	-0.3	3.1
Austria	76.1	82.5	101.9	100.5	99.0	102.4	107.9	(NA)	-1.4	-1.5	3.4	5.4	(NA)
Belgium	82.1	85.5	98.0	98.0	92.9	94.6	98.6	99.1	-	-5.2	1.8	4.2	0.5
Canada [1]	81.5	94.5	95.8	96.9	101.2	108.3	112.0	113.9	1.1	4.4	7.0	3.4	1.7
Finland	75.3	87.8	90.3	92.4	97.2	108.3	116.4	120.7	2.3	5.2	11.4	7.5	3.7
France	89.2	89.3	98.9	98.9	93.9	97.4	99.4	100.0	-	-5.1	3.7	2.1	0.6
Germany [2]	83.0	85.6	103.6	101.0	93.6	96.9	98.9	99.0	-2.5	-7.3	3.5	2.1	0.1
Greece	90.8	98.2	98.6	97.4	95.4	96.3	98.5	98.6	-1.2	-2.1	0.9	2.3	0.1
Ireland	54.2	69.5	103.3	112.7	119.0	133.2	158.3	170.9	9.1	5.6	11.9	18.8	8.0
Italy	87.5	84.8	99.1	97.8	95.7	101.7	107.9	104.8	-1.3	-2.1	6.3	6.1	-2.9
Japan	67.3	79.8	101.9	96.0	92.0	93.1	96.2	98.8	-5.8	-4.2	1.2	3.3	2.7
Luxembourg	69.7	84.7	100.1	99.3	95.2	100.9	102.3	100.6	-0.8	-4.1	6.0	1.4	-1.7
Mexico [3]	(NA)	(NA)	(NA)	106.5	108.2	113.4	104.6	115.5	(NA)	1.6	4.8	-7.8	10.4
Netherlands	86.8	91.7	101.7	101.6	100.3	104.6	106.7	110.2	-0.1	-1.3	4.3	2.0	3.3
Norway	58.3	79.0	102.1	108.6	112.1	120.0	127.2	134.1	6.4	3.2	7.0	6.0	5.4
Portugal	62.8	73.9	100.0	97.7	95.2	95.0	99.4	100.8	-2.3	-2.6	-0.2	4.6	1.4
Spain	83.3	86.1	99.3	96.5	92.0	98.7	103.3	102.6	-2.8	-4.7	7.3	4.7	-0.7
Sweden [4]	82.5	91.5	94.9	93.5	94.3	105.5	115.1	117.5	-1.5	0.9	11.9	9.1	2.1
Switzerland [5]	82.0	84.8	100.8	99.0	97.0	102.0	104.0	103.0	-1.8	-2.0	5.2	2.0	-1.0
United Kingdom	81.6	88.2	96.4	96.3	98.4	103.4	105.9	107.3	-0.1	2.2	5.1	2.4	1.3
United States	79.3	89.0	98.0	101.1	104.6	109.8	113.4	116.5	3.2	3.4	5.0	3.3	2.7

- Represents or rounds to zero. NA Not available. [1] Gross domestic product in industry at factor cost and 1986 prices. [2] 1980-90 former West Germany; later data use 1990 annual average data for West Germany as base year. [3] Includes construction. [4] Mining and manufacturing. [5] Excludes mining and quarrying.

Source: Organization for Economic Cooperation and Development, Paris, France, *Main Economic Indicators, Historical Statistics, 1969-1988*, 1990; and *Main Economic Indicators*, monthly (copyright).

No. 1366. Patents, by Country: 1994

[Includes only U.S. patents granted to residents of areas outside of the United States and its territories]

COUNTRY	Total [1]	Inventions	Designs	COUNTRY	Total [1]	Inventions	Designs
Total	**49,346**	**45,810**	**3,397**	Korea, South	1,008	943	65
				Netherlands	999	853	83
Japan	23,508	22,384	1,056	Sweden	800	706	93
Germany	6,990	6,732	208	Australia	564	467	91
France	2,984	2,779	182	Belgium	391	351	30
United Kingdom	2,468	2,234	186	Israel	388	350	24
Canada	2,379	2,008	360	Finland	341	312	29
Taiwan	1,814	1,443	368	Austria	316	289	25
Italy	1,360	1,215	142	Denmark	313	207	93
Switzerland	1,244	1,169	73	Other countries	1,479	1,168	289

[1] Includes patents for botanical plants and reissues, not shown separately.
Source: U.S. Patent and Trademark Office, Technology Assessment and Forecast Data Base.

No. 1367. World's 500 Largest Corporations, by Country: 1995

[For company's fiscal year ended on or before March 31, 1996. All companies on the list must publish financial data and report part or all of their figures to a government agency. Includes revenues from discontinued operations and consolidated subsidiaries; excludes excise taxes. Profits are shown after taxes, after extraordinary credits or charges, and after cumulative effects of accounting changes. Minus sign (-) indicates loss]

COUNTRY	Number of companies	Revenues (bil. dol.)	Profits (bil. dol.)	COUNTRY	Number of companies	Revenues (bil. dol.)	Profits (bil. dol.)	COUNTRY	Number of companies	Revenues (bil. dol.)	Profits (bil. dol.)
Total [1]	500	11,378	323	Switzerland	16	345	18	Spain	6	81	4
Japan	141	3,985	30	Korea, South	12	263	7	Canada	6	66	6
U.S.	153	3,221	158	Italy	12	255	7	Belgium	5	56	2
Germany	40	1,017	17	Netherlands	8	171	9	Sweden	3	54	2
France	42	880	3	Britain/				Brazil	4	54	-3
U.K.	32	516	38	Netherlands	2	160	9	Australia	4	45	4

[1] Includes other countries not shown separately.

Source: Time Warner, New York, NY, *Fortune*, August 5, 1996, (copyright).

No. 1368. Selected Indexes of Manufacturing Activity, by Country: 1980 to 1995

[1992=100. Data relate to employees (wage and salary earners) in Belgium, Italy, the Netherlands, and the United Kingdom, and to all employed persons (employees and self-employed workers) in the other countries. Minus sign (-) indicates decrease. For explanation of average annual percent change, see Guide to Tabular Presentation]

INDEX	United States	Canada	Japan	Belgium	France	Germany [1]	Italy	Netherlands	Norway	Sweden	United Kingdom
Output per hour:											
1980	71.9	78.5	63.9	64.5	70.5	77.0	64.0	70.0	75.2	74.0	54.9
1985	87.7	94.1	77.3	86.3	83.8	88.6	81.5	89.8	90.4	87.1	71.9
1990	97.7	95.8	95.4	96.9	99.1	98.2	92.8	98.6	96.8	95.0	90.1
1993	101.6	101.7	100.5	104.1	101.8	100.7	104.5	102.1	100.4	106.7	105.6
1994	105.8	106.2	101.2	110.0	110.4	107.3	106.9	112.1	102.2	116.1	108.7
1995	109.4	107.3	107.0	111.0	113.7	110.6	111.2	115.9	103.1	122.0	107.9
Average annual percent change:											
1979-85	3.3	2.4	3.5	6.1	3.0	2.1	4.9	4.4	2.9	3.0	4.4
1985-90	2.2	0.4	4.3	2.3	3.4	2.1	2.6	1.9	1.4	1.8	4.6
1990-95	2.3	2.3	2.3	2.8	2.8	2.4	3.7	3.3	1.3	5.1	3.7
Compensation per hour, national currency basis: [2]											
1980	55.8	50.2	58.6	52.5	41.4	53.7	27.9	64.8	38.5	37.4	33.9
1985	75.3	74.6	72.5	74.1	73.8	70.0	60.1	82.0	62.7	58.3	54.9
1990	90.9	91.3	90.7	89.6	91.8	89.0	84.0	90.8	92.3	87.6	83.5
1993	102.4	100.0	104.6	105.0	103.6	106.0	107.1	103.8	101.5	98.0	106.6
1994	105.1	102.2	106.8	108.4	106.2	111.1	106.4	107.1	104.8	101.0	109.9
1995	109.0	103.8	110.3	112.0	107.9	116.5	109.7	109.9	109.4	107.3	111.0
Average annual percent change:											
1979-85	7.1	8.7	4.7	7.8	12.7	5.9	16.7	4.9	10.0	9.6	11.8
1985-90	3.9	4.1	4.6	3.9	4.5	4.9	6.9	2.1	8.1	8.5	8.7
1990-95	3.7	2.6	4.0	4.6	3.3	5.5	5.5	3.9	3.4	4.1	5.9
Real hourly compensation: [2,3]											
1980	95.0	95.7	75.4	86.6	80.8	74.5	78.8	87.9	84.9	87.5	70.5
1985	98.1	99.4	81.4	87.1	91.0	80.5	88.9	90.7	89.8	87.1	80.5
1990	97.6	97.8	95.3	94.8	97.4	95.9	94.3	96.5	97.7	97.4	91.7
1993	99.4	98.2	103.2	102.2	101.6	102.1	102.8	101.3	99.2	95.4	105.0
1994	99.5	100.2	104.7	103.1	102.4	103.9	98.2	101.7	101.1	96.1	105.6
1995	100.4	99.6	106.2	105.0	102.3	106.9	96.1	102.5	103.0	97.9	103.1
Average annual percent change:											
1979-85	0.3	0.7	1.1	0.8	2.2	1.8	1.5	0.3	0.6	-0.5	2.6
1985-90	-0.1	-0.3	3.2	1.7	1.4	3.6	1.2	1.3	1.7	2.3	2.6
1990-95	0.6	0.4	2.6	2.0	1.0	2.2	0.4	1.2	1.0	0.1	2.4
Unit labor costs, national currency:											
1980	77.6	63.9	91.7	81.4	58.7	69.7	43.7	92.6	51.2	50.5	61.7
1985	85.8	79.3	93.8	85.9	88.1	79.0	73.8	91.3	69.4	67.0	76.4
1990	93.1	95.2	95.0	92.5	92.7	90.7	90.5	92.1	95.4	92.3	92.6
1993	100.8	98.3	104.1	100.9	101.8	105.3	102.5	101.7	101.1	91.8	101.0
1994	99.4	96.2	105.6	98.6	96.2	103.5	99.5	95.5	102.6	86.9	101.1
1995	99.6	96.8	103.1	100.9	94.9	105.3	98.6	94.9	106.1	87.9	102.9
Average annual percent change:											
1979-85	3.7	6.1	1.2	1.6	9.5	3.8	11.2	0.5	6.9	6.4	7.1
1985-90	1.6	3.7	0.3	1.5	1.0	2.8	4.2	0.2	6.6	6.6	3.9
1990-95	1.4	0.3	1.6	1.8	0.5	3.0	1.7	0.6	2.1	-1.0	2.1
Unit labor costs, U.S. dollar basis: [4]											
1980	77.6	66.1	51.5	89.6	73.7	60.0	62.9	82.0	64.5	69.6	81.3
1985	85.8	70.1	49.9	46.5	51.9	41.9	47.6	48.4	50.2	45.4	56.2
1990	93.1	98.6	83.1	88.9	90.1	87.6	93.0	88.9	94.8	90.8	93.5
1993	100.8	92.1	118.8	93.8	95.1	99.4	80.3	96.2	88.5	68.6	85.9
1994	99.4	85.1	131.0	94.8	91.8	99.7	76.1	92.4	90.4	65.6	87.7
1995	99.6	85.2	139.1	110.1	100.8	114.9	74.6	104.0	104.0	71.7	91.9
Average annual percent change:											
1979-85	3.7	3.4	-0.3	-9.7	-3.4	-4.1	-3.2	-7.6	-2.1	-5.2	-1.3
1985-90	1.6	7.1	10.8	13.8	11.6	15.9	14.3	12.9	13.6	14.9	10.7
1990-95	1.4	-2.9	10.9	4.4	2.3	5.6	-4.3	3.2	1.9	-4.6	-0.3
Employment:											
1980	111.6	110.5	87.4	120.9	124.7	102.2	126.4	107.0	135.6	130.9	159.0
1985	106.0	105.6	91.9	104.6	110.0	94.9	105.4	94.5	121.8	122.0	123.3
1990	105.5	111.6	95.8	102.5	105.1	100.3	106.8	101.1	105.4	117.2	116.2
1993	100.1	101.4	97.9	94.6	95.3	94.0	94.3	96.3	101.8	92.6	96.5
1994	101.3	103.5	95.9	91.1	92.7	89.3	94.1	92.2	105.0	94.2	97.0
1995	102.2	106.0	93.2	93.8	92.7	87.3	92.9	91.0	107.7	97.5	99.3
Average annual percent change:											
1979-85	-1.4	-0.8	1.2	-2.7	-2.3	-1.1	-2.9	-2.3	-1.8	-1.2	-4.9
1985-90	-0.1	1.1	0.8	-0.4	-0.9	1.1	0.3	1.4	-2.9	-0.8	-1.2
1990-95	-0.6	-1.0	-0.5	-1.8	-2.5	-2.8	-2.8	-2.1	0.4	-3.6	-3.1
Aggregate hours:											
1980	107.6	109.5	93.8	121.4	131.5	110.7	123.0	111.0	136.5	124.0	160.3
1985	104.7	104.8	98.4	103.0	108.9	99.6	101.4	95.8	121.5	119.4	125.1
1990	104.9	110.8	100.9	104.3	104.5	101.0	108.2	101.6	103.7	116.4	118.0
1993	101.4	103.0	95.6	93.2	94.5	90.9	92.4	96.3	102.1	94.9	96.0
1994	103.8	106.2	93.7	92.2	91.8	86.8	94.8	92.2	105.7	99.6	97.2
1995	103.9	109.1	91.7	94.1	91.9	84.4	96.4	91.3	107.8	104.1	100.1
Average annual percent change:											
1979-85	-1.2	-0.9	1.1	-3.3	-3.3	-1.8	-3.1	-2.5	-1.9	-0.8	-5.3
1985-90	-	1.1	0.5	0.2	-0.8	0.3	1.3	1.2	-3.1	-0.5	-1.2
1990-95	-0.2	-0.3	-1.9	-2.0	-2.5	-3.5	-2.3	-2.1	0.8	-2.2	-3.2

- Represents or rounds to zero. [1] Former West Germany. [2] Compensation includes, but real hourly compensation excludes, adjustments for payroll and employment taxes that are not compensation to employees, but are labor costs to employers. [3] Index of hourly compensation divided by the index of consumer prices to adjust for changes in purchasing power. [4] Indexes in national currency adjusted for changes in prevailing exchange rates.

Source: U.S. Bureau of Labor Statistics, unpublished data.

No. 1369. Indexes of Hourly Compensation Costs for Production Workers in Manufacturing, by Country: 1980 to 1996

[United States=100. Compensation costs include all pay made directly to the worker—pay for time worked and not worked (eg. leave, except sick leave), other direct pay, employer expenditures for legally required insurance programs and contractual and private benefit plans, and for some countries, other labor taxes. Data adjusted for exchange rates. Area averages are trade-weighted to account for difference in countries' relative importance to U.S. trade in manufactured goods. The trade weights used are the sum of U.S. imports of manufactured products for consumption (customs value) and U.S. domestic exports of manufactured products (f.a.s. value) in 1992; see source for detail]

AREA OR COUNTRY	1980	1985	1990	1994	1995	1996	AREA OR COUNTRY	1980	1985	1990	1994	1995	1996
United States	100	100	100	100	100	100	Austria [6]	90	58	119	128	148	141
Total [1]	67	52	83	89	95	91	Belgium	133	69	129	136	156	147
OECD [2]	74	57	90	96	103	98	Denmark	110	62	120	121	141	137
Europe	101	61	116	114	128	125	Finland [7]	83	63	141	113	144	136
Asian newly industrializing economies [3]	12	13	25	34	37	39	France	91	58	102	101	113	109
							Germany [8, 9]	125	74	147	159	185	180
Canada	88	84	106	94	93	94	Greece	38	28	45	45	52	(NA)
Mexico	22	12	11	15	9	8	Ireland	60	46	79	75	80	80
Australia [4]	86	63	88	83	88	93	Italy	83	59	119	95	96	102
Hong Kong [5]	15	13	21	27	28	29	Luxembourg	121	59	110	119	134	(NA)
Israel	38	31	57	54	61	62	Netherlands	122	67	123	124	141	132
Japan	56	49	86	125	138	119	Norway	117	80	144	124	142	141
Korea, South	10	9	25	38	43	46	Portugal	21	12	25	27	31	(NA)
New Zealand	54	34	56	53	59	62	Spain	60	36	76	68	74	75
Singapore	15	19	25	37	43	47	Sweden	127	74	140	112	128	136
Sri Lanka	2	2	2	3	3	(NA)	Switzerland	112	74	140	148	170	160
Taiwan	10	12	26	33	34	33	United Kingdom	77	48	85	76	80	80

NA Not available. [1] The 26 foreign economies shown below. [2] Organization for Economic Cooperation and Development; see text, section 30. [3] Hong Kong, South Korea, Singapore, and Taiwan. [4] Includes non-production workers, except in managerial, executive, professional, and higher supervisory positions. [5] Average of selected manufacturing industries. [6] Excludes workers in establishments considered handicraft manufactures (including all printing and publishing and miscellaneous manufacturing in Austria). [7] Includes workers in mining and electrical power plants. [8] Former West Germany.

Source: U.S. Bureau of Labor Statistics, *News Release* USDL 97-213, June 27, 1997.

No. 1370. Manufacturing Labor Productivity Levels in Major OECD Economies: 1993

[Value added per hour worked, leader country=100 (the productivity level of the leader country in each industry is indicated in bold). Data are updated from benchmark productivity comparisons for 1987 using output and employment series from OECD's STAN database. The trend in total hours worked at the sectoral level is assumed to be identical to the trend for total manufacturing. A mix of industry-of-origin and expenditure purchasing power parities (PPPs) (see text, section 30) for the conversion of value added to a common currency were used. Industry-of-origin price comparisons were used where possible and were applied in more than 65 percent of all cases. These price ratios are all based on price comparisons between the United States and one other country. Conversion factors from sector-specific private studies were used for Japan and Germany for those industries where these estimates were available. For the other cases expenditure PPPs, adjusted for net indirect tax rates and industry-specific distribution margins were applied. Estimates of productivity levels were derived from a combination of PPPs, hours worked, employment, and value added]

SECTOR	United States	Japan	Germany [1]	France	United Kingdom	Canada	Australia	Netherlands	Sweden
Total manufacturing	100.0	76.6	81.3	84.2	64.1	71.3	52.0	95.6	91.8
Food, beverages and tobacco	100.0	35.6	82.6	87.0	41.7	64.3	51.1	96.6	72.8
Textiles, clothing & footwear	78.3	41.9	70.3	67.1	51.5	46.3	32.3	100.0	66.5
Wood products & furniture	56.0	17.6	50.6	55.3	28.1	52.6	27.1	100.0	71.9
Paper products & printing	85.0	49.7	56.6	64.3	76.4	67.6	53.7	64.5	100.0
Chemical products	66.9	52.6	50.9	56.9	79.7	52.6	39.8	100.0	89.4
Non-metallic mineral products	81.8	62.9	73.9	99.4	70.6	78.4	77.4	100.0	81.0
Basic metal products	76.8	78.3	78.0	63.3	61.4	87.9	56.8	70.4	100.0
Metal products	66.9	67.6	67.2	46.4	42.5	54.8	35.9	54.0	100.0
Machinery & equipment	100.0	67.4	58.7	67.3	47.9	55.5	46.4	34.6	45.2
Electrical machinery	80.3	89.0	54.0	78.9	48.2	51.9	28.0	82.2	100.0
Transport equipment	86.4	100.0	62.6	85.0	47.8	71.9	45.5	41.8	49.5
Other manufacturing	100.0	41.4	39.6	31.4	43.5	33.5	22.1	27.0	47.4

[1] Productivity levels are for 1992.

Source: Pilat, Dirk, "Labour Productivity Levels in OECD Countries: Estimates for Manufacturing and Selected Service Sectors", *Economics Department Working Papers, No. 169*, Organisation for Economic Cooperation and Development, Paris, France, 1996 (copyright).

No. 1371. World Production of Major Mineral Commodities: 1990 to 1995

COUNTRY	Unit	1990	1993	1994	1995	Leading producers, 1994
MINERAL FUELS [1]						
Coal	Mil. short tons	5,356	4,956	5,041	5,091	China, United States, Russia
Dry natural gas	Tril. cu. ft.	73.6	76.3	76.7	78.3	Russia, United States, Canada
Natural gas plant liquids [2]	Mil. barrels [3]	1,691	1,867	1,926	1,996	United States, Saudi Arabia, Canada
Petroleum, crude	Mil. barrels [3]	22,107	21,990	22,266	22,793	Saudi Arabia, United States, Russia
Petroleum, refined	Mil. barrels [3]	23,791	(NA)	24,512	(NA)	United States, Japan, Russia
NONMETALLIC MINERALS						
Cement, hydraulic	Mil. metric tons	1,148	1,300	1,370	1,390	China, Japan, United States
Diamond, gem and industrial	1,000 carats	110,919	105,000	111,000	(NA)	Australia, Russia, Congo (Kinshasa)
Nitrogen in ammonia	Mil. metric tons	97.1	92.0	92.0	96.0	China, United States, India
Phosphate rock	Mil. metric tons	162	120	128	137	United States, China, Morocco
Potash, marketable	Mil. metric tons	27.8	21.0	22.5	26.2	Canada, Germany, Belarus
Salt	Mil. metric tons	184	190	180	185	United States, China, Germany
Sulfur, elemental basis	Mil. metric tons	58.1	52.0	51.0	52.0	United States, Canada, China
METALS						
Aluminum [4]	Mil. metric tons	19.3	20.0	19.1	19.3	United States, Russia, Canada
Bauxite, gross weight	Mil. metric tons	108.6	110.0	107.0	109.0	Australia, Guinea, Jamaica
Chromite, gross weight [2]	1,000 metric tons	12,966	10,001	9,570	10,600	South Africa, Kazakstan, India
Copper, metal content [5]	1,000 metric tons	9,017	9,400	9,430	9,800	Chile, United States, Canada
Gold, metal content	Metric tons	2,133	2,300	2,300	2,200	South Africa, United States, Australia
Iron ore, gross weight [6]	Mil. metric tons	962	1,000	1,000	1,000	China, Brazil, Russia
Lead, metal content [5]	1,000 metric tons	3,353	2,900	2,800	2,800	Australia, United States, China
Manganese ore, gross weight	Mil. metric tons	25.3	21.8	21.2	21.0	China, Ukraine, South Africa
Nickel, metal content [5]	1,000 metric tons	965	900	906	920	Russia, Canada, New Caledonia
Steel, crude	Mil. metric tons	771	730	726	760	European Union, Japan, China
Tin, metal content [5]	1,000 metric tons	222	180	184	180	China, Indonesia, Brazil
Zinc, metal content [5]	1,000 metric tons	7,184	6,900	6,810	7,070	Australia, Canada, China

NA Not available. [1] 1995 data preliminary. [2] Excludes China. [3] 42-gallon barrels. [4] Unalloyed ingot metal. [5] Mine output. [6] Includes iron ore concentrates and iron ore agglomerates.

Source: Mineral fuels, Energy Information Administration, *International Energy Annual*; nonmetallic minerals and metals, through 1994, U.S. Bureau of Mines, thereafter, U.S. Geological Survey, *Minerals Yearbook*; *Annual Reports*; and *Mineral Commodity Summaries, 1996.*

No. 1372. Selected Petroleum Product Prices, by Country: 1995

[Data are averages for the available time period (daily, monthly, quarterly, year) that is closest to January 1, 1996. Includes taxes]

COUNTRY	AUTOMOTIVE FUELS (U.S. dollars per gallon)		RESIDENTIAL (U.S. dollars per gallon)			INDUSTRIAL (U.S. dollars per barrel)	
	Premium gasoline	Diesel fuel	Light fuel oil	Kerosene	Liquified petroleum gases	Light fuel oil	Heavy fuel oil
United States	1.28	1.15	0.95	0.72	0.84	26.46	19.79
Argentina	3.04	1.00	0.55	1.09	1.74	(NA)	(NA)
Australia	2.07	1.95	(NA)	(NA)	(NA)	(NA)	(NA)
Belgium	4.26	3.20	0.99	(NA)	(NA)	34.33	20.93
Brazil	[1]2.15	1.41	0.75	1.49	0.78	(NA)	(NA)
Canada	1.80	1.43	1.03	(NA)	(NA)	27.53	15.90
Chile	2.02	1.35	0.58	1.08	1.35	(NA)	(NA)
France	4.41	3.10	1.59	(NA)	(NA)	46.73	28.07
Germany	4.32	3.02	1.19	(NA)	(NA)	43.55	22.94
Greece	3.15	2.41	1.63	(NA)	(NA)	58.01	31.88
India [2]	[1]2.25	0.92	(NA)	(NA)	(NA)	30.77	24.51
Ireland	3.58	3.37	1.53	(NA)	(NA)	46.47	27.45
Italy	4.24	3.40	3.24	(NA)	(NA)	114.41	27.76
Japan	[1]3.77	2.51	1.44	1.57	(NA)	42.57	24.25
Korea, South [2]	2.93	1.13	(NA)	(NA)	(NA)	(NA)	21.86
Mexico	1.25	0.92	0.41	0.92	0.39	35.58	11.17
Netherlands	5.31	3.67	1.39	(NA)	(NA)	(NA)	27.74
Norway	5.05	4.39	1.99	(NA)	(NA)	62.29	52.61
Peru	1.82	1.00	0.52	0.85	0.84	(NA)	(NA)
Philippines [2]	1.38	1.08	(NA)	1.08	0.81	(NA)	17.12
Russia [2]	[1]1.25	0.83	0.30	(NA)	(NA)	(NA)	(NA)
Saudi Arabia [2]	[1]0.60	0.37	0.13	0.44	(NA)	0.37	(NA)
Spain	3.32	2.66	1.28	(NA)	(NA)	46.29	28.83
Sweden	4.36	3.58	2.26	(NA)	(NA)	37.05	30.05
Switzerland	3.71	3.80	0.94	(NA)	(NA)	31.72	28.63
Turkey	2.39	1.63	1.84	(NA)	(NA)	(NA)	26.45
United Kingdom	3.47	3.26	0.92	(NA)	(NA)	31.39	22.23
Venezuela	0.08	0.04	0.03	0.03	0.04	3.85	3.81

NA Not available. [1] Regular gasoline. [2] Data for 1995.

Source: Energy Information Administration, *International Energy Annual.*

No. 1373. Energy Consumption and Production, by Country: 1990 and 1995

[See text, section 30, for general comments about the data. For data qualifications for countries, see source]

COUNTRY	PRIMARY ENERGY CONSUMED				DRY NATURAL GAS PRODUCTION (tril. cu. ft)		CRUDE PETROLEUM PRODUCTION (1,000 barrels per day)		COAL PRODUCTION (mil. short tons)	
	Total (quad. Btu)		Per capita (mil. Btu)							
	1990	1995	1990	1995	1990	1995	1990	1995	1990	1995
World	**343.0**	**362.2**	**66**	**63**	**73.61**	**78.30**	**60,566**	**62,446**	**5,356**	**5,091**
United States	**82.0**	**88.3**	**328**	**336**	**17.81**	**18.80**	**7,355**	**6,560**	**1,029**	**1,033**
Algeria	1.1	1.3	45	44	1.79	2.05	1,175	1,202	(Z)	(Z)
Argentina	1.8	2.5	56	71	0.63	0.89	483	715	(Z)	(Z)
Australia	4.0	4.4	233	245	0.72	1.05	575	562	226	268
Austria	1.2	1.3	150	147	0.05	0.05	22	23	3	1
Bahrain	0.3	0.3	532	536	0.21	0.23	42	41	(NA)	(NA)
Bangladesh	0.3	0.4	2	3	0.16	0.26	1	1	(NA)	(NA)
Belarus	(X)	1.0	(X)	96	(X)	0.01	(X)	38	(NA)	(NA)
Belgium	2.2	2.4	216	233	(Z)	(Z)	(NA)	(NA)	3	1
Brazil	5.7	6.8	39	43	0.10	0.16	631	695	5	5
Bulgaria	1.3	1.0	141	118	-	(Z)	4	1	35	31
Burma	(NA)	(NA)	(NA)	(NA)	0.04	0.06	13	16	(Z)	(Z)
Canada	11.0	11.7	413	396	3.85	5.60	1,553	1,805	75	83
Chile	0.6	0.7	43	51	0.07	0.07	20	11	2	2
China	27.0	35.7	24	29	0.51	0.60	2,774	2,990	1,190	1,478
Colombia	1.0	1.2	30	35	0.15	0.18	440	585	23	29
Congo (Kinshasa) [1]	(NA)	(NA)	(NA)	(NA)	(NA)	(NA)	29	30	(Z)	(Z)
Cuba	0.5	0.4	46	37	(Z)	(Z)	14	26	(NA)	(NA)
Czech Republic	(X)	2.2	(X)	210	(X)	0.01	(X)	3	(X)	79
Denmark	0.8	0.9	159	179	0.11	0.19	121	186	(NA)	(NA)
Ecuador	(NA)	(NA)	(NA)	(NA)	(Z)	(Z)	285	392	(NA)	(NA)
Egypt	1.4	1.6	27	26	0.29	0.44	873	920	(NA)	(NA)
Finland	1.2	1.1	233	219	(NA)	(NA)	(NA)	(NA)	(NA)	(NA)
France	8.9	9.4	157	162	0.10	0.11	61	50	15	10
Germany	(X)	13.7	(X)	168	(X)	0.72	(X)	59	(X)	274
Greece	1.0	1.2	103	111	0.01	(Z)	15	9	57	64
Hong Kong	0.5	0.6	86	96	(NA)	(NA)	(NA)	(NA)	(NA)	(NA)
Hungary	1.3	1.1	120	107	0.17	0.17	40	35	19	15
India	7.7	10.5	9	11	0.40	0.66	660	703	233	311
Indonesia	2.2	3.1	12	16	1.53	2.23	1,462	1,503	12	41
Iran	3.1	3.9	57	64	0.84	1.24	3,088	3,643	1	2
Iraq	0.9	1.3	51	61	0.15	0.11	2,040	560	(NA)	(NA)
Ireland	0.4	0.5	104	134	0.08	0.10	(NA)	(NA)	(Z)	(Z)
Israel	0.5	0.7	96	118	(Z)	(Z)	(Z)	(Z)	(NA)	(NA)
Italy	7.0	7.4	121	127	0.61	0.71	87	93	1	(Z)
Japan	18.0	21.4	146	171	0.07	0.08	11	11	11	7
Korea, North	2.1	2.1	96	87	(NA)	(NA)	(NA)	(NA)	71	78
Korea, South	3.7	6.3	87	140	(NA)	(NA)	(NA)	(NA)	19	6
Kuwait	0.5	0.6	206	323	0.19	0.21	1,175	2,057	(NA)	(NA)
Libya	0.5	0.5	123	103	0.22	0.22	1,375	1,390	(NA)	(NA)
Malaysia	1.0	1.6	55	77	0.65	1.05	619	682	(Z)	(Z)
Mexico	4.9	5.6	57	59	0.94	0.94	2,553	2,618	7	10
Morocco	0.3	0.4	13	15	(Z)	(Z)	(Z)	(Z)	1	1
Netherlands	3.4	3.8	228	244	2.69	2.96	70	66	(NA)	(NA)
New Zealand	0.7	0.9	218	240	0.17	0.17	40	32	3	3
Nigeria	0.7	0.8	6	6	0.13	0.16	1,810	1,993	(Z)	(Z)
Norway	1.6	1.7	373	390	0.96	1.07	1,704	2,768	(Z)	(Z)
Pakistan	1.2	1.5	11	12	0.48	0.64	62	57	3	3
Peru	(NA)	(NA)	(NA)	(NA)	0.02	0.03	129	130	(Z)	(Z)
Philippines	0.7	1.0	12	13	(NA)	(NA)	5	3	1	2
Poland	3.9	3.8	103	97	0.14	0.17	2	5	237	218
Portugal	0.8	0.9	77	79	(NA)	(NA)	(NA)	(NA)	(Z)	(Z)
Romania	2.9	2.0	124	87	1.00	0.66	163	135	42	44
Russia	(X)	26.8	(X)	181	(X)	21.01	(X)	5,995	(X)	310
Saudi Arabia	3.2	3.7	212	208	1.06	1.42	6,410	8,231	(NA)	(NA)
Serbia	(X)	0.6	(X)	58	(X)	0.03	(X)	22	(X)	44
South Africa	4.3	5.5	116	134	-	0.07	-	10	193	227
Spain	3.9	4.5	100	114	0.05	0.01	16	13	40	31
Sweden	2.2	2.2	251	244	(NA)	(NA)	(Z)	(Z)	(Z)	(Z)
Switzerland	1.2	1.2	174	165	(Z)	(Z)	(NA)	(NA)	(NA)	(NA)
Syria	0.6	0.7	50	52	0.10	0.17	388	610	(NA)	(NA)
Taiwan	2.0	2.7	100	126	0.08	0.03	3	1	1	(Z)
Tajikistan	(X)	(NA)	(X)	(NA)	(X)	(Z)	(X)	1	(X)	(Z)
Thailand	1.3	2.0	22	33	0.21	0.37	44	51	14	19
Trinidad and Tobago	(NA)	(NA)	(NA)	(NA)	0.18	0.27	150	131	(NA)	(NA)
Tunisia	(NA)	(NA)	(NA)	(NA)	0.01	0.01	93	89	(NA)	(NA)
Turkey	1.9	2.5	34	41	0.01	0.01	73	67	52	60
Ukraine	(X)	6.3	(X)	122	(X)	0.62	(X)	65	(X)	91
United Arab Emirates	1.2	1.6	735	817	0.78	1.06	2,117	2,279	(NA)	(NA)
United Kingdom	9.4	9.9	163	169	1.75	2.66	1,820	2,489	106	52
Venezuela	2.1	2.5	106	117	0.76	0.93	2,137	2,750	2	5
Vietnam	0.3	0.5	4	7	(Z)	0.05	50	173	5	7

- Represents zero. NA Not available. X Not applicable. Z Less than 5 bil. cu. ft, 500 barrels per day, or 500,000 short tons. [1] See footnote 3, table 1334.

Source: U.S. Energy Information Administration, *International Energy Annual*.

No. 1374. World Food Production, by Commodity: 1990 to 1996

[In millions of metric tons]

COMMODITY	1990	1991	1992	1993	1994	1995	1996, prel.
Grains, total	1,766.7	1,708.1	1,787.5	1,712.2	1,760.6	1,708.2	1,858.5
Wheat	588.0	542.2	561.8	559.3	524.6	537.9	583.0
Coarse grains	826.5	809.1	869.9	797.3	871.2	798.7	901.6
Corn	480.7	492.0	532.0	474.7	570.4	514.7	576.8
Rice, milled	352.2	354.8	355.8	355.5	364.9	371.5	381.2
Oils	58.1	60.6	61.1	63.1	69.4	72.4	73.4
Soybeans	108.4	103.3	114.2	115.1	136.2	125.8	130.3
Rapeseed	24.4	27.9	26.8	26.5	29.8	34.5	30.4
Pulses [1] [2]	58.1	53.2	50.8	55.7	57.0	56.0	56.6
Vegetables and melons [1]	471.5	472.3	491.6	520.4	545.7	565.6	557.3
Fruits [1]	355.1	354.4	382.6	368.0	392.2	403.8	414.2
Nuts [1]	4.6	4.7	5.0	4.7	4.9	4.7	5.0
Red meat	113.3	117.7	117.3	118.2	123.2	128.2	132.1
Poultry	33.8	39.6	38.0	40.0	43.2	47.0	49.9
Milk	395.0	385.2	379.9	380.7	381.9	384.7	384.7

[1] Data from Food and Agriculture Organization of the United Nations. [2] Edible seeds of peas, beans, lentils and similar crops.

Source: U.S. Department of Agriculture, Economic Research Service, *Agricultural Outlook*, monthly.

No. 1375. Fisheries—Commercial Catch, by Country: 1990 to 1994

[In thousands of metric tons, live weight. Catch of fish, crustaceans, mollusks (including weight of shells). Does not include marine mammals and aquatic plants. Countries shown had a commercial catch of one million metric tons or more in 1994]

COUNTRY	1990	1992	1993	1994	COUNTRY	1990	1992	1993	1994
World [1]	97,854	99,349	102,184	109,585	Korea, South	1,745	2,561	2,562	2,551
Canada	1,626	1,276	1,172	1,011	Mexico	1,401	1,248	1,201	1,260
Chile	5,195	6,502	6,037	7,841	Norway	1,745	2,561	2,562	2,551
China	12,095	15,007	17,568	20,719	Peru	6,875	6,871	8,452	11,587
Denmark	1,518	1,996	1,656	1,867	Philippines	2,210	2,272	2,264	2,276
Iceland	1,508	1,577	1,718	1,560	Russia	7,808	5,611	4,461	3,781
India	3,794	4,232	4,338	4,540	Spain	1,380	1,320	1,290	1,380
Indonesia	3,044	3,440	3,676	3,954	Thailand	2,786	3,240	3,331	3,432
Japan	10,354	8,502	8,128	7,363	United States	5,868	5,599	5,948	5,941
Korea, North (est.)	1,753	1,778	1,780	1,800	Vietnam	960	1,080	1,100	1,150

[1] Includes other countries, not shown separately.

Source: U.S. National Oceanic and Atmospheric Administration, National Marine Fisheries Service, *Fisheries of the United States*, annual. Data from Food and Agriculture Organization of the United Nations, Rome, Italy.

No. 1376. Meat Production, by Country: 1990 to 1996

[In thousands of metric tons, carcass weight. Covers beef and veal (incl. buffalo meat), pork (incl. bacon and ham), mutton and lamb (incl. goat meat), horsemeat, and poultry. Refers to meat from animals slaughtered within the national boundaries irrespective of origin of animals, and relates to commercial and farm slaughter. Excludes lard, tallow, and edible offals. See text, section 30, for general comments concerning the data]

COUNTRY	1990	1995	1996	COUNTRY	1990	1995	1996
World [1]	178,775	208,260	212,030	Italy	3,948	3,986	3,985
Argentina	3,290	3,459	3,396	Japan	3,503	3,242	3,481
Brazil	7,709	10,486	10,969	Mexico	2,601	3,797	3,600
China	30,073	54,266	56,572	Russia	(X)	5,896	5,607
France	5,744	6,312	6,326	Spain	3,467	3,992	3,800
Germany	7,259	5,748	5,846	United Kingdom	3,319	3,656	3,424
India	3,829	4,272	4,295	United States	28,610	33,882	34,808

X Not applicable. [1] Includes other countries, not shown separately.

Source: Food and Agriculture Organization of the United Nations, Rome, Italy, FAOSTAT database.

No. 1377. Wheat, Rice, and Corn Production, by Country: 1990 to 1995

[In thousands of metric tons. Rice data cover paddy. Data for each country pertain to the calendar year in which all or most of the crop was harvested. See text, section 30, for general comments concerning quality of the data]

COUNTRY	WHEAT			RICE			CORN		
	1990	1994	1995	1990	1994	1995	1990	1994	1995
World	**592,589**	**526,676**	**543,457**	**519,407**	**537,063**	**553,415**	477,090	**570,073**	**516,373**
Argentina	10,992	11,306	9,185	428	606	926	5,047	10,360	11,404
Australia	15,066	9,036	17,263	846	1,042	1,016	219	204	242
Bangladesh	890	1,131	1,274	26,778	25,248	27,128	3	3	3
Brazil	3,094	2,096	1,534	7,421	10,541	11,220	21,348	32,487	36,268
Burma	124	109	89	13,969	18,195	19,568	187	284	212
Canada	32,096	23,122	25,037	(X)	(X)	(X)	7,066	7,043	7,251
China	98,232	99,301	102,211	191,589	178,032	187,334	97,158	99,674	112,362
Egypt	4,268	4,786	5,722	3,167	4,583	4,789	4,799	5,112	5,178
France	33,346	30,549	30,879	121	124	126	9,401	12,943	12,784
Germany	15,242	16,481	17,816	(X)	(X)	(X)	1,552	2,446	2,395
Hungary	6,196	4,874	4,614	39	15	13	4,500	4,761	4,680
India	49,850	57,840	65,469	111,517	121,559	121,562	8,962	8,952	10,270
Indonesia	(X)	(X)	(X)	45,179	46,642	49,744	6,734	6,869	8,246
Iran	8,012	10,870	11,228	1,981	2,259	2,301	130	512	545
Italy	8,109	8,166	7,996	1,291	1,316	1,284	5,864	7,320	8,446
Japan	952	565	444	13,124	14,976	13,435	1	-	-
Kazakstan	16,197	9,052	6,490	579	283	184	442	234	136
Korea, South	1	2	10	7,722	6,882	6,343	120	89	74
Mexico	3,931	4,151	3,468	394	374	367	14,635	18,236	16,187
Nigeria	50	35	44	2,500	2,427	2,920	5,768	6,902	7,048
Pakistan	14,316	15,213	17,002	4,891	5,144	5,920	1,185	1,318	1,283
Philippines	-	-	-	9,885	10,538	10,541	4,854	4,519	4,129
Romania	7,289	6,135	7,667	67	15	24	6,810	9,343	9,923
Russia	49,596	32,129	30,118	896	523	462	2,451	892	1,739
South Africa	1,730	1,840	2,125	3	3	3	8,709	13,275	4,670
Thailand	-	1	1	17,193	21,111	21,130	3,722	3,965	4,155
Turkey	20,022	17,514	18,015	230	200	230	2,100	1,850	1,900
Ukraine	30,374	13,857	16,273	118	79	80	4,737	1,539	3,392
United Kingdom	14,033	13,314	14,310	(X)	(X)	(X)	-	-	-
United States	**74,473**	**63,168**	**59,400**	**7,080**	**8,971**	**7,887**	**201,534**	**256,621**	**187,305**

- Represents or rounds to zero. X Not applicable.

No. 1378. Wheat, Rice, and Corn—Exports and Imports of 10 Leading Countries: 1990 to 1995

[In thousands of metric tons. Countries listed are the ten leading exporters or importers in 1995]

LEADING EXPORTERS	EXPORTS			LEADING IMPORTERS	IMPORTS		
	1990	1994	1995		1990	1994	1995
WHEAT				WHEAT			
United States	**27,567**	**30,571**	**32,420**	China	13,375	8,281	12,602
Canada	17,955	21,378	16,960	Japan	5,474	6,352	5,965
France	17,165	12,650	16,310	Brazil	1,962	6,123	5,800
Australia	11,507	12,730	7,818	Italy	4,663	4,907	5,079
Argentina	5,837	5,172	6,913	Egypt	5,400	6,597	5,070
Germany	2,153	5,524	3,682	Indonesia	1,724	3,297	4,054
Hungary	1,120	759	2,765	Algeria	2,612	3,512	3,505
United Kingdom	4,460	3,494	2,669	Iran	3,382	2,324	3,100
Czechoslovakia, former	(X)	10	1,634	Soviet Union, former	(X)	4,425	2,775
Denmark	1,685	988	1,540	Spain	695	2,049	2,757
RICE				RICE			
Thailand	4,017	4,859	6,198	Indonesia	50	630	3,158
India	505	891	5,512	China	63	517	1,646
United States	**2,474**	**2,822**	**3,084**	Iran	620	482	1,300
Vietnam	1,624	1,970	2,308	Brazil	414	987	875
Pakistan	744	984	1,852	Bangladesh	380	66	813
Australia	424	585	542	Korea, North	27	60	654
Italy	577	620	524	Saudi Arabia	280	434	605
Uruguay	290	408	462	South Africa	306	431	511
Burma	214	934	392	Malaysia	330	341	428
Argentina	75	217	390	Senegal	392	348	420
CORN				CORN			
United States	**52,172**	**35,877**	**60,240**	Japan	16,008	15,930	16,580
France	7,195	8,010	6,474	China	5,440	5,601	11,702
Argentina	2,998	4,154	6,001	Korea, South	6,158	5,749	9,035
South Africa	2,001	3,760	1,340	Spain	1,810	2,339	2,912
Hungary	156	181	601	Mexico	4,104	2,747	2,687
Canada	122	381	444	Egypt	1,900	2,021	2,425
Belgium-Luxembourg	20	489	443	Malaysia	1,480	1,969	2,383
Zimbabwe	742	1,280	288	Belgium-Luxembourg	1,035	1,557	1,816
Germany	226	320	244	Netherlands	2,012	1,981	1,590
Paraguay	1	74	203	United Kingdom	1,627	1,626	1,502

X Not applicable.

Source of tables 1377 and 1378: Food and Agriculture Organization of the United Nations, Rome, Italy, FAOSTAT database.

No. 1379. United States and Foreign Stock Markets—Market Capitalization and Value of Shares Traded: 1985 to 1996

[In millions of U.S. dollars. Market capitalization is the total amount of the various securities (bonds, debentures, and stock) issued by corporations]

COUNTRY	MARKET CAPITALIZATION [1]				VALUE OF SHARES TRADED [2]			
	1985	1990	1995	1996	1985	1990	1995	1996
United States	**2,324,646**	**3,059,434**	**6,857,622**	**8,484,433**	**997,189**	**1,815,476**	**5,108,591**	**7,121,487**
Argentina	2,037	3,268	37,783	44,679	631	852	4,594	4,382
Australia	60,163	107,611	245,218	311,988	15,736	39,333	97,884	145,482
Austria	4,602	11,476	32,513	33,953	686	18,609	25,759	20,528
Belgium	20,871	65,449	104,960	119,831	1,876	6,425	15,249	26,120
Brazil	42,768	16,354	147,636	216,990	21,484	5,598	79,186	112,108
Canada	147,000	241,920	366,344	486,268	39,905	71,278	183,686	265,360
Chile	2,012	13,645	73,860	65,940	57	783	11,072	8,460
China	(NA)	(NA)	42,055	113,755	(NA)	(NA)	49,774	256,008
Colombia	416	1,416	17,893	17,137	30	71	1,254	1,360
Czech Republic	(NA)	(NA)	15,664	18,077	(NA)	(NA)	3,630	8,431
Denmark	15,096	39,063	56,223	71,688	1,274	11,105	25,942	34,667
Finland	5,855	22,721	44,138	63,078	502	3,933	19,006	22,422
France	79,000	314,384	522,053	591,123	14,672	116,893	364,550	277,100
Germany	183,765	355,073	577,365	670,997	71,572	501,805	573,549	768,745
Greece	765	15,228	17,060	24,178	17	3,924	6,091	8,283
Hong Kong	34,504	83,397	303,705	449,381	9,732	34,633	106,888	166,419
India	14,364	38,567	127,199	122,605	4,959	21,918	13,738	109,448
Indonesia	117	8,081	66,585	91,016	3	3,992	14,403	32,142
Italy	58,502	148,766	209,522	258,160	13,782	42,566	86,904	102,351
Japan	978,663	2,917,679	3,667,292	3,088,850	329,970	1,602,388	1,231,552	1,251,998
Korea, South	7,381	110,594	181,955	138,817	4,162	75,949	185,197	177,266
Luxembourg	12,658	10,456	30,443	32,692	36	87	205	534
Malaysia	16,229	48,611	222,729	307,179	2,335	10,871	76,822	173,568
Mexico	3,815	32,725	90,694	106,540	2,360	12,212	34,377	43,040
Netherlands	59,363	119,825	356,481	378,721	16,864	40,199	248,606	339,500
New Zealand	8,761	8,835	31,950	38,288	935	1,933	8,407	9,871
Norway	10,063	26,130	44,587	57,423	1,877	13,996	24,420	35,882
Pakistan	1,370	2,850	9,286	10,639	236	231	3,210	6,054
Peru	760	812	11,795	12,291	38	99	3,935	3,805
Philippines	669	5,927	58,859	80,649	111	1,216	14,727	25,519
Portugal	192	9,201	18,362	24,660	5	1,687	4,233	7,147
South Africa	55,439	137,540	280,526	241,571	2,836	8,158	17,048	27,202
Spain	19,000	111,404	197,788	242,779	3,382	40,967	59,791	249,128
Sweden	37,296	92,102	178,049	247,217	9,644	15,718	93,197	136,898
Switzerland	90,000	160,044	433,621	402,104	(NA)	(NA)	310,928	392,783
Taiwan	10,432	100,710	187,206	273,608	4,899	715,005	383,099	470,193
Thailand	1,856	23,896	141,507	99,828	568	22,894	57,000	44,365
Turkey	(NA)	19,065	20,772	30,020	(NA)	5,841	51,392	36,831
United Kingdom	328,000	848,866	1,407,737	1,740,246	68,417	278,740	510,131	578,471
Venezuela	1,128	8,361	3,655	10,055	31	2,232	510	1,275

NA Not available. [1] Year-end total market values of listed domestic companies. [2] Annual total turnover of listed company shares.

Source: International Finance Corporation, Washington, DC, *Emerging Stock Markets Factbook*, annual, (copyright).

No. 1380. Dow-Jones World Stock Index, by Country and Industry: 1993 to 1996

[Index figures shown are as of December 31. Indexes based on June 30, 1982=100 for United States; December 31, 1991=100 for World. Based on share prices denominated in U.S. dollars. Stocks in countries that impose significant restrictions on foreign ownership are included in the world index in the same proportion that shares are available to foreign investors]

INDUSTRY	1993	1994	1995	1996
World, total	**111.08**	**113.91**	**133.46**	**147.57**
Americas	112.18	108.53	143.61	173.40
United States	442.19	433.07	581.43	700.56
Canada	100.36	95.23	108.25	135.41
Mexico	182.88	107.06	77.96	94.31
Europe	116.08	115.70	136.54	162.41
Austria	104.82	104.36	101.29	110.00
Belgium	111.55	115.75	142.56	158.64
Denmark	95.73	98.16	112.42	137.26
Finland	138.66	205.90	202.88	280.72
France	117.78	109.17	120.03	142.38
Germany	118.94	122.57	138.24	161.41
Ireland	111.95	122.90	152.83	196.04
Italy	99.11	109.54	103.51	113.62
Netherlands	125.74	133.88	167.30	207.58
Norway	103.12	122.41	129.21	159.87
Spain	94.89	89.33	114.31	149.44
Sweden	104.06	119.43	163.14	213.88
Switzerland	158.28	162.99	232.62	236.03
United Kingdom	112.30	107.34	124.49	152.02
Asia/Pacific	106.76	119.39	119.80	108.93
Australia	113.29	114.89	127.90	148.78
Hong Kong	270.36	184.06	223.67	299.50
Indonesia	233.92	176.25	172.48	187.42
Japan	95.71	116.21	114.08	95.63
Malaysia	269.99	216.69	223.08	285.49
New Zealand	151.52	155.86	176.17	203.35
Singapore	179.22	178.06	195.91	199.84
Thailand	243.90	207.44	196.78	128.66
Basic materials	109.04	124.40	130.91	136.62
Conglomerate	129.80	127.47	146.57	171.32
Consumer, cyclical	123.24	124.27	135.13	148.64
Consumer, noncyclical	93.01	98.64	130.19	152.04
Energy	107.82	110.23	132.32	163.27
Financial services	114.97	112.75	134.62	142.84
Industrial	106.00	112.24	118.38	122.31
Technology	114.61	134.91	168.07	197.94
Utilities	114.42	101.12	118.44	123.90

Source: Dow Jones & Company, Inc., New York, NY, Wall Street Journal, selected issues (copyright).

No. 1381. Foreign Stock Market Activity—Morgan Stanley Capital International Indexes: 1990 to 1996

[Index figures shown are as of December 31. January 1, 1970=100, except as noted. Based on share prices denominated in U.S. dollars. EMG=Emerging Markets Global. GDP=Gross Domestic Product]

INDEX AND COUNTRY	INDEX			PERCENT CHANGE [1]	
	1990	1995	1996	1995	1996
All Country World index [2]	114.3	182.0	201.7	15.7	10.8
DEVELOPED MARKETS					
World index [3]	462	734	820	18.7	11.7
EAFE index [4]	789	1,136	1,186	9.4	4.4
Europe index	479	733	869	18.9	18.5
Pacific index	1,735	2,362	2,139	1.8	-9.4
Far East index	2,514	3,384	3,015	1.3	-10.9
GDP-weighted indexes: EAFE index [4]	817	1,205	1,278	9.5	6.1
United States	306.9	581.1	705.2	34.7	21.4
Canada	341.9	403.9	510.3	16.1	26.4
Australia	184.6	304.2	345.1	8.3	13.4
New Zealand [5]	53.0	114.2	129.6	17.3	13.5
Austria	1,052	890	919	-5.8	3.2
Belgium	568	897	976	21.8	8.8
Denmark	867	1,124	1,349	17.3	20.0
Finland [5]	66.3	128.8	169.7	3.4	31.7
France	461	672	802	12.2	19.4
Germany	551	818	917	14.8	12.1
Ireland [5]	138.4	215.7	277.8	19.4	28.8
Italy	205.2	208.6	231.3	-0.2	10.9
Netherlands	594	1,192	1,485	24.3	24.5
Norway	896	1,023	1,296	4.6	26.8
Spain	132.0	162.3	221.5	26.0	36.5
Sweden	915	1,796	2,431	31.7	35.4

INDEX AND COUNTRY	INDEX			PERCENT CHANGE [1]	
	1990	1995	1996	1995	1996
Switzerland	567	1,569	1,589	42.4	1.2
United Kingdom	514	716	883	17.2	23.3
Hong Kong	1,547	4,818	6,213	18.2	29.0
Japan	2,638	3,348	2,813	(Z)	-16.0
Singapore	1,166	2,735	2,515	5.0	-8.1
EMERGING MARKETS					
EMG Far East index	168.2	263.7	273.1	-10.5	3.6
India [6]	(NA)	98.8	95.1	-31.9	-3.8
Indonesia	610.8	508.2	637.2	7.5	25.4
Korea, South	139.4	173.8	107.1	-4.6	-38.4
Malaysia	170.4	347.0	432.1	4.0	24.5
Pakistan [6]	(NA)	91.5	73.8	-38.3	-19.4
Philippines	94.1	442.5	509.3	-15.4	15.1
Sri Lanka [6]	(NA)	105.6	88.4	-32.7	-16.3
Taiwan	177.7	227.9	316.6	-30.2	38.9
Thailand	205.0	523.3	324.7	-5.7	-38.0
EMG Latin America	237	782	928	-15.8	18.7
Argentina	318	1,239	1,447	8.7	16.9
Brazil	89	578	798	-21.3	38.0
Chile	214	903	754	-6.2	-16.4
Colombia [6]	(NA)	110	118	-27.8	6.6
Mexico	424	744	864	-23.2	16.1
Peru [6]	(NA)	221	215	22.1	-2.8
Greece [5]	321.9	238.2	241.6	10.2	1.4
Jordan	55.3	96.1	85.2	5.4	-11.4
Portugal [5]	66.8	68.4	90.5	-2.5	32.3
Turkey	195.2	103.1	136.0	-5.9	31.9

NA Not available. Z Less than 0.05 percent. [1] Percent change during calendar year (e.g. December 31, 1994, through December 31, 1995). Adjusted for foreign exchange fluctuations relative to U.S. dollar. [2] Comprises World index, all emerging markets, and Luxembourg. [3] Includes South African gold mines quoted in London. [4] Europe, Australasia, Far East Index. Comprises all European and Far East countries listed under developed markets plus Australia, Malaysia, and New Zealand. [5] January 1, 1988=100. [6] December 1992=100.

Source: Morgan Stanley Capital International, New York, NY, unpublished data (copyright). This information may not be reproduced or redisseminated in any form without prior written permission from Morgan Stanley Capital International. This information is provided on an "as is" basis. Neither Morgan Stanley or any other party makes any representation or warranty of any kind either express or implied, with respect to this information (or the results to be obtained by the use thereof) and Morgan Stanley expressly disclaims any and all warranties of originality, accuracy, completeness, merchantability, and fitness for any particular purpose. The user of this information assumes the entire risk of any use made of the information. In no event shall Morgan Stanley or any other part be liable to the user for any direct or indirect damages, including without limitation, any lost profits, lost savings, or other incidental or consequential damages arising out of use of this information.

No. 1382. Central Bank Discount Rates, Money Market Rates, and Government Bond Yields, by Country: 1990 to 1997

[In percent per annum. Central bank discount rates refer to the rate at which the monetary authority lends or discounts eligible paper for deposit money banks. Money market rates refer to the rate at which short-term borrowings are effected between financial institutions. Government bond yields refer to one or more series representing average yields to maturity of government bonds or other bonds that would be indicative of longer term rates]

NATIONAL INTEREST RATE AND YEAR	United States	Canada	Japan	France	Germany	Italy	Netherlands	Sweden	Switzerland	United Kingdom
Central bank discount rates: [1]										
1990	6.50	11.78	6.00	9.50	6.00	12.50	7.25	11.50	6.00	([2])
1995	5.25	5.79	0.50	(NA)	3.00	9.00	(NA)	[3] 7.00	1.50	([2])
1996	5.00	3.25	0.50	(NA)	2.50	7.50	(NA)	3.50	1.00	([2])
1997, March	5.00	3.25	0.50	(NA)	2.50	6.75	(NA)	2.50	1.00	([2])
Money market rates: [4]										
1990	8.10	11.62	7.24	9.85	7.92	12.38	8.29	13.45	8.33	14.64
1995	5.84	5.71	[3] 1.21	6.35	4.50	10.46	4.22	8.54	2.89	5.98
1996	5.30	3.01	0.47	3.73	3.27	8.82	2.89	6.28	1.78	5.89
1997, March	5.39	2.96	0.51	3.19	3.15	7.43	3.03	4.20	2.05	5.94
Government bond yields:										
1990	8.55	10.85	7.36	9.96	8.88	11.51	8.92	13.08	6.68	11.08
1995	6.58	8.28	2.53	7.59	6.50	[3] 12.21	7.20	(NA)	3.73	8.26
1996	6.44	7.50	2.23	6.39	5.63	9.40	6.49	(NA)	3.63	8.10
1997, March	6.69	6.97	1.85	5.73	5.10	7.71	5.87	(NA)	3.56	7.62

NA Not available. [1] End of period. [2] Minimum lending rate suspended as of August 20, 1981. [3] Beginning in year shown, data not comparable with 1990. [4] Period averages.

Source: International Monetary Fund, Washington, DC, *International Financial Statistics*, monthly, (copyright).

No. 1383. Reserve Assets and International Transaction Balances, by Country: 1990 to 1996

[In millions of U.S. dollars. Assets include holdings of convertible foreign currencies, special drawing rights, and reserve position in International Monetary Fund and exclude gold holdings. Minus sign (-) indicates debits]

COUNTRY	TOTAL RESERVE ASSETS				CURRENT ACCOUNT BALANCE			MERCHANDISE TRADE BALANCE		
	1990	1995	1996		1990	1995	1996	1990	1995	1996
			Total	Currency holdings[1]						
United States	72,260	74,780	64,040	38,290	-92,910	-148,230	-165,590	-109,030	-171,990	-186,280
Algeria	725	2,005	4,235	4,230	1,420	(NA)	(NA)	4,179	(NA)	(NA)
Argentina	4,592	14,288	18,104	17,705	4,552	-2,390	(NA)	8,628	2,237	(NA)
Australia	16,265	11,896	14,534	14,016	-16,088	-19,167	-15,371	358	-4,166	-726
Austria	9,376	18,730	22,865	21,861	1,166	-4,842	(NA)	-6,969	-5,103	(NA)
Bangladesh	629	2,340	1,835	1,725	-398	-824	(NA)	-1,587	-2,324	(NA)
Belgium	12,151	16,177	16,953	15,380	3,627	15,013	15,393	1,671	10,206	10,023
Brazil	7,441	49,708	58,323	58,322	-3,823	-18,136	(NA)	10,747	-3,157	(NA)
Burma	313	561	229	229	(NA)	(NA)	(NA)	(NA)	(NA)	(NA)
Cameroon	26	4	(NA)	(NA)	-478	(NA)	(NA)	778	(NA)	(NA)
Canada	17,845	15,049	20,422	18,028	-22,577	-8,693	-2,076	8,334	22,341	27,164
Chile	6,069	14,140	14,833	14,781	-536	157	(NA)	1,335	1,383	(NA)
China	29,586	75,377	(NA)	(NA)	11,878	1,618	(NA)	9,165	18,050	(NA)
Colombia	4,212	8,102	9,597	9,183	542	-4,116	(NA)	1,971	-2,546	(NA)
Congo (Kinshasa)[2]	219	147	83	83	-643	(NA)	(NA)	599	(NA)	(NA)
Cote d'Ivoire	4	529	622	620	-1,214	-447	-204	1,094	1,345	1,860
Denmark	10,591	11,016	14,140	13,366	1,372	1,607	1,920	4,875	6,820	7,313
Ecuador	839	1,628	1,859	1,831	-366	-735	296	1,003	354	1,402
Egypt	2,684	16,181	17,398	17,198	185	-254	(NA)	-6,379	-7,597	(NA)
Finland	9,644	10,038	6,916	6,205	-6,939	5,385	4,178	718	12,346	10,946
France	36,778	26,853	26,796	23,120	-9,946	16,443	21,216	-13,253	11,175	15,261
Germany[3]	67,902	85,005	83,178	75,803	48	-21	(NA)	69	66	(NA)
Ghana	219	696	829	802	-224	(NA)	(NA)	-314	(NA)	(NA)
Greece	3,412	14,780	17,501	17,337	-3,537	-2,864	(NA)	-10,106	-14,425	(NA)
Hungary	1,070	12,052	9,796	9,714	379	-2,535	-1,689	534	-2,433	-2,652
India	1,521	17,922	20,170	19,742	-6,836	(NA)	(NA)	-5,151	(NA)	(NA)
Indonesia	7,459	13,708	18,251	17,820	-2,988	-7,023	(NA)	5,352	5,710	(NA)
Ireland	5,223	8,630	8,205	7,715	-262	1,379	(NA)	3,969	13,125	(NA)
Israel	6,275	8,119	11,415	11,413	-66	-5,282	-6,296	-3,091	-7,694	-8,069
Italy	62,927	34,905	45,948	44,064	-17,586	25,706	(NA)	1,373	44,062	(NA)
Japan	78,501	183,250	216,648	207,335	35,870	111,040	65,880	63,580	131,790	83,560
Kenya	205	353	747	726	-527	-400	(NA)	-915	-738	(NA)
Korea, South	14,793	32,678	34,037	33,237	-1,745	-8,251	(NA)	-2,004	-4,746	(NA)
Kuwait	1,952	3,561	3,515	3,221	3,886	4,198	(NA)	3,179	5,478	(NA)
Libya	5,839	(NA)	(NA)	(NA)	2,201	(NA)	(NA)	3,777	(NA)	(NA)
Malaysia	9,754	23,774	27,009	26,156	-870	-7,362	(NA)	2,525	-100	(NA)
Mexico	9,863	16,847	19,433	19,176	-7,451	-654	(NA)	-881	7,089	(NA)
Morocco	2,066	3,601	3,794	3,743	-196	-1,521	(NA)	-2,108	-2,397	(NA)
Nepal	295	586	(NA)	(NA)	-289	-356	(NA)	-449	-961	(NA)
Netherlands	17,484	33,714	26,767	24,119	9,207	17,996	(NA)	12,058	20,979	(NA)
Nigeria	3,864	1,443	(NA)	(NA)	4,988	(NA)	(NA)	8,653	(NA)	(NA)
Norway	15,332	22,518	26,517	25,236	3,992	(NA)	(NA)	7,761	(NA)	(NA)
Pakistan	296	1,733	548	535	-1,654	(NA)	(NA)	-2,714	(NA)	(NA)
Peru	1,040	8,222	10,578	10,578	-678	-4,245	(NA)	394	-2,111	(NA)
Philippines	924	6,372	10,030	9,902	-2,695	-1,980	(NA)	-4,020	-8,944	(NA)
Poland	4,492	14,774	17,844	17,729	3,067	-4,245	(NA)	3,589	-3,224	(NA)
Portugal	14,485	15,850	15,918	15,359	-181	-229	(NA)	-6,684	-8,484	(NA)
Romania	524	1,579	2,103	2,099	-3,254	-1,342	(NA)	-3,344	-1,231	(NA)
Saudi Arabia	11,668	8,622	6,794	5,295	-4,152	-5,324	(NA)	22,889	24,390	(NA)
Singapore	27,748	68,695	76,847	76,491	3,181	15,093	(NA)	-1,549	1,625	(NA)
South Africa	1,008	2,820	942	940	2,065	-2,820	(NA)	6,783	1,610	(NA)
Spain	51,228	34,485	57,927	55,879	-18,010	1,158	1,756	-29,158	-17,661	-14,912
Sri Lanka	423	2,088	1,962	1,931	-298	-546	(NA)	-473	-880	(NA)
Sudan	11	163	(NA)	(NA)	-372	-500	(NA)	-322	-510	(NA)
Sweden	17,988	24,051	19,107	18,172	-6,338	4,634	5,723	3,402	15,973	18,211
Switzerland	29,223	36,413	38,433	36,775	6,941	21,622	(NA)	-7,174	3,237	(NA)
Syria	(NA)	(NA)	(NA)	(NA)	1,762	440	(NA)	2,094	-143	(NA)
Thailand	13,305	35,982	37,731	37,192	-7,281	-13,554	(NA)	-6,751	-7,968	(NA)
Trinidad and Tobago	492	358	544	544	459	294	(NA)	1,013	588	(NA)
Turkey	6,050	12,442	16,436	16,388	-2,625	-2,339	(NA)	-9,555	-13,212	(NA)
United Kingdom	35,850	42,020	39,900	37,120	-33,468	-6,230	(NA)	-32,742	-18,390	(NA)
Venezuela	8,321	6,283	11,788	11,124	8,279	2,255	(NA)	10,706	7,290	(NA)

NA Not available. [1] Holdings of convertible foreign currencies. [2] See footnote 3, table 1334. [3] Prior to July 1990, data for former West Germany.

Source: International Monetary Fund, Washington, DC, *International Financial Statistics*, monthly, (copyright).

No. 1384. Foreign Trade—Source of Imports and Destination of Exports, by Country: 1994

[In billions of dollars. All exports are f.o.b. (free on board) and all imports are c.i.f. (cost insurance freight) except for United States, Australian, and Canadian imports, which are f.o.b.]

COUNTRY	Total [1]	O.E.C.D. [2] Total	O.E.C.D. [2] E.U. [3]	C.E.E.C. [4]	China, Vietnam, North Korea	O.P.E.C. [5]	Other developing countries [6]	Africa	America [7]	Middle East [8]	Far East [9]
IMPORTS											
Value (bil. dol.):											
Australia	49.9	35.9	11.8	0.6	2.6	1.8	9.2	0.6	0.5	1.2	8.3
Austria	55.3	48.0	37.8	1.3	0.8	1.0	4.0	0.7	0.5	0.5	2.0
Belgium-Luxembourg	122.0	105.8	91.1	0.8	1.3	1.3	10.8	3.6	1.7	1.3	4.1
Canada	147.8	128.9	14.4	0.2	2.9	2.0	11.0	0.8	2.5	0.6	8.5
France	230.4	186.5	144.6	2.2	4.3	8.4	25.1	10.4	4.3	5.2	10.4
Germany	378.1	299.0	209.6	12.0	10.0	8.2	47.3	8.8	8.3	3.7	25.1
Italy	166.7	127.0	101.2	3.6	3.1	8.8	21.6	11.5	4.1	3.6	6.0
Japan	274.8	132.6	38.9	0.2	29.3	38.0	72.4	4.1	7.9	27.8	67.8
Netherlands	122.8	96.5	74.2	1.7	2.0	6.4	16.0	3.0	4.6	4.3	9.4
Spain	92.5	73.6	59.3	0.5	1.9	5.6	10.2	5.9	3.1	2.3	3.6
Sweden	51.7	44.4	32.5	1.1	1.1	0.8	4.2	0.4	0.8	0.6	2.3
Switzerland	67.7	61.7	53.8	0.2	0.8	0.8	4.0	0.1	0.7	0.7	2.3
United Kingdom	229.0	189.4	127.7	2.0	2.6	4.2	28.6	4.9	3.8	3.4	20.2
United States	663.8	433.2	119.5	1.6	38.9	33.4	149.5	14.2	38.5	15.8	117.5
Percent distribution:											
Australia	100.0	71.9	23.6	1.2	5.3	3.6	18.5	1.2	1.0	2.4	16.6
Austria	100.0	86.8	68.3	2.4	1.5	1.7	7.2	1.3	0.9	0.9	3.7
Belgium-Luxembourg	100.0	86.7	74.6	0.7	1.1	1.1	8.9	3.0	1.4	1.1	3.3
Canada	100.0	87.2	9.7	0.2	2.0	1.4	7.5	0.6	1.7	0.4	5.8
France	100.0	80.9	62.8	0.9	1.9	3.7	10.9	4.5	1.9	2.2	4.5
Germany	100.0	79.1	55.4	3.2	2.6	2.2	12.5	2.3	2.2	1.0	6.6
Italy	100.0	76.2	60.7	2.2	1.9	5.3	13.0	6.9	2.5	2.2	3.6
Japan	100.0	48.3	14.2	0.1	10.7	13.8	26.3	1.5	2.9	10.1	24.7
Netherlands	100.0	78.6	60.4	1.4	1.7	5.2	13.0	2.4	3.7	3.5	7.6
Spain	100.0	79.5	64.1	0.5	2.1	6.1	11.0	6.4	3.4	2.5	4.2
Sweden	100.0	85.9	62.9	2.1	2.1	1.6	8.1	0.7	1.6	1.2	4.4
Switzerland	100.0	91.1	79.4	0.4	1.2	1.2	5.9	0.2	1.1	1.1	3.4
United Kingdom	100.0	82.7	55.8	0.9	1.2	1.8	12.5	2.2	1.7	1.5	8.8
United States	100.0	65.3	18.0	0.2	5.9	5.0	22.5	2.1	5.8	2.4	17.7
EXPORTS											
Value (bil. dol.):											
Australia	47.4	24.6	5.3	0.1	2.2	2.5	16.4	0.7	0.5	1.2	15.4
Austria	45.0	38.3	29.2	1.9	0.4	1.0	3.4	0.7	0.4	0.7	1.3
Belgium-Luxembourg	134.3	115.4	100.3	1.1	1.0	2.2	13.6	2.9	1.2	4.4	6.5
Canada	165.8	154.4	9.0	0.1	1.7	2.0	7.3	0.8	2.5	1.1	4.9
France	234.2	186.1	148.6	2.3	2.5	8.0	34.2	14.3	7.3	6.4	11.9
Germany	424.1	339.0	244.8	12.4	6.5	11.0	51.5	9.0	7.7	10.4	26.3
Italy	188.5	142.9	108.6	5.0	2.4	7.2	29.5	6.8	6.1	7.6	10.9
Japan	395.6	205.1	61.3	0.2	19.4	16.4	150.8	6.8	13.4	9.8	138.4
Netherlands	134.9	116.8	102.7	1.9	0.6	2.6	11.4	2.5	1.9	2.5	5.4
Spain	73.3	60.4	51.7	0.6	0.8	2.4	8.9	3.0	3.2	1.7	2.5
Sweden	61.3	51.8	36.4	1.2	1.1	1.1	6.0	1.0	1.1	1.2	3.5
Switzerland	70.1	55.7	43.4	0.7	0.6	2.2	10.4	1.3	1.7	2.6	6.7
United Kingdom	206.5	165.4	118.1	1.7	1.4	7.2	27.8	6.4	3.4	8.2	16.7
United States	512.4	348.0	107.8	1.4	9.5	19.1	132.0	9.2	41.8	16.1	82.0
Percent distribution:											
Australia	100.0	51.9	11.1	0.3	4.6	5.3	34.7	1.5	1.0	2.5	32.4
Austria	100.0	85.1	64.8	4.3	0.8	2.1	7.5	1.6	0.8	1.6	2.9
Belgium-Luxembourg	100.0	86.0	74.7	0.8	0.7	1.6	10.1	2.1	0.9	3.3	4.8
Canada	100.0	93.1	5.4	0.1	1.0	1.2	4.4	0.5	1.5	0.7	3.0
France	100.0	79.5	63.4	1.0	1.1	3.4	14.6	6.1	3.1	2.7	5.1
Germany	100.0	79.9	57.7	2.9	1.5	2.6	12.1	2.1	1.8	2.5	6.2
Italy	100.0	75.8	57.6	2.7	1.3	3.8	15.7	3.6	3.3	4.0	5.8
Japan	100.0	51.8	15.5	0.1	4.9	4.2	38.1	1.7	3.4	2.5	35.0
Netherlands	100.0	86.6	76.2	1.4	0.4	2.0	8.5	1.9	1.4	1.9	4.0
Spain	100.0	82.3	70.5	0.8	1.2	3.3	12.1	4.1	4.4	2.3	3.4
Sweden	100.0	84.5	59.3	2.0	1.8	1.8	9.8	1.6	1.8	2.0	5.7
Switzerland	100.0	79.5	62.0	1.0	0.9	3.1	14.9	1.9	2.4	3.8	9.6
United Kingdom	100.0	80.1	57.2	0.8	0.7	3.5	13.5	3.1	1.6	4.0	8.1
United States	100.0	67.9	21.0	0.3	1.9	3.7	25.8	1.8	8.2	3.1	16.0

[1] Includes other areas not shown separately. [2] Organization for Economic Cooperation and Development. For member countries, see text, section 30. [3] European Union comprises Austria, Belgium-Luxembourg, Denmark, Finland, France, Germany, Greece, Ireland, Italy, Netherlands, Portugal, Spain, Sweden, and United Kingdom. [4] Central and Eastern European countries comprises Albania, the Baltic States (Estonia, Latvia, Lithuania), Bulgaria, Poland, Romania, Slovakia and Slovenia. [5] Organization of Petroleum Exporting Countries comprises Algeria, Ecuador, Gabon, Iran, Iraq, Kuwait, Libya, Nigeria, Qatar, Saudi Arabia, United Arab Emirates, and Venezuela. [6] Comprises trade with all countries other than China, North Korea, Vietnam, South Africa, Eastern Europe, and members of OPEC and OECD. [7] All countries comprising the continent except Canada, Mexico, and the United States. [8] Comprises Syria, Lebanon, Israel, Gaza Strip, Jordan, Iraq, Saudi Arabia, Yemen, Kuwait, Bahrain, United Arab Emirates, Qatar, Oman, and Iran. [9] All countries comprising the continent of Asia except Japan, China, North Korea, Vietnam, and those countries listed under Middle East.

Source: *Organization for Economic Cooperation and Development*, Paris, France. Data derived from Monthly Statistics *Foreign Trade, (copyright).*

No. 1385. Foreign Exchange Rates: 1996

[Foreign currency units per U.S. dollar; annual average. Rates shown include market, official, and principal rates, as published by the International Monetary Fund in *International Financial Statistics*]

COUNTRY	Currency	1996
Afghanistan	Afghanis	50.6
Albania	Leks	104.5
Algeria	Algerian Dinars	54.75
Antigua and Barbuda	E.Caribbean Dollar	2.70
Argentina	Pesos	1.000
Armenia	Dram	414.0
Aruba	Aruban Florins	1.79
Australia	Australian Dollar	1.278
Austria	Schillings	10.59
Bahamas, The	Bahamian Dollar	1.000
Bahrain	Dinars	0.376
Bangladesh	Taka	41.79
Barbados	Barbados Dollar	2.011
Belgium	Francs	30.96
Belize	Belize Dollar	2.000
Benin	Cfa Francs	511.6
Bhutan	Ngultrum	35.43
Botswana	Pula	3.324
Brazil	Reals	1.005
Bulgaria	Leva	177.9
Burkina Faso	Cfa Francs	511.6
Burma	Kyats	5.918
Cambodia	Riels	2,624
Cameroon	Cfa Francs	511.6
Canada	Canadian Dollar	1.363
Cape Verde	Escudos	82.59
Central African Republic	Cfa Francs	511.6
Chad	Cfa Francs	511.6
Chile	Pesos	412.27
China	Yuan	8.31
Comoros	Comorian Francs	383.7
Congo (Brazzaville)	Cfa Francs	511.6
Costa Rica	Colones	207.7
Cote d'Ivoire	Cfa Francs	511.6
Croatia	Kuna	5.43
Cyprus	Cyprus Pounds	0.466
Czech Republic	Koruny	27.14
Denmark	Kroner	5.799
Djibouti	Djibouti Francs	177.7
Dominica	E.Caribbean Dol	2.70
Dominican Republic	Pesos	13.78
Ecuador	Sucres	3,189
Egypt	Egyptian Pounds	3.391
El Salvador	Colones	8.755
Equatorial Guinea	Cfa Francs	511.6
Estonia	Krooni	12.03
Ethiopia	Birr	6.352
Fiji	Fiji Dollar	1.403
Finland	Markkaa	4.594
France	Francs	5.116
Gabon	Cfa Francs	511.6
Germany	Deutsche Mark	1.505
Greece	Drachmas	240.7
Grenada	E.Caribbean Dollar	2.70
Guatemala	Quetzales	6.05
Guyana	Guyana Dollar	140.4
Haiti	Gourdes	15.70
Honduras	Lempiras	11.71
Hong Kong	Hong Kong Dollar	7.734
Hungary	Forint	152.6
Iceland	Kronur	66.50
India	Rupees	35.43
Indonesia	Rupiah	2,342
Iran	Rials	1,751
Iraq	Dinars	0.311
Ireland	Irish Pounds	0.625
Israel	New Sheqalim	3.192
Italy	Lire	1,543
Jamaica	Jamaica Dollar	37.12
Japan	Yen	108.8
Jordan	Dinars	0.709
Kazakstan	Tenge	67.30
Kenya	Kenya Shilling	57.12
Kiribati	Australian Dollar	1.278
Korea, South	Won	804.5
Kuwait	Dinars	0.299
Laos	Kip	921.1
Latvia	Lats	0.551
Lebanon	Lebanese Pounds	1,571
Lesotho	Maloti	4.299
Liberia	Liberian Dollar	1.00
Libya	Libyan Dinars	0.362
Lithuania	Litai	4.00
Luxembourg	Francs	30.96
Macedonia, The Former Yugoslav Republic of	Denar	39.98
Madagascar	Malagasy Francs	4,061
Maldives	Rufiyaa	11.77
Mali	Cfa Francs	511.6
Malta	Maltese Liri	0.360
Mauritania	Ouguiyas	137.2
Mauritius	Rupees	17.95
Mexico	New Pesos	7.601
Micronesia, Federated States of	U.S. Dollar	1.00
Moldova	Lei	4.603
Mongolia	Tugriks	548.4
Morocco	Dirhams	8.716
Mozambique	Meticais	11,294
Namibia	Namibia Dollar	4.299
Nepal	Rupees	56.69
Netherlands	Guilders	1.686
Netherlands Antilles	Guilders	1.790
New Zealand	New Zealand Dollar	1.455
Nicaragua	Cordobas	8.436
Niger	Cfa Francs	511.6
Norway	Kroner	6.450
Oman	Rials Omani	0.385
Pakistan	Rupees	36.08
Panama	Balboas	1.00
Papua New Guinea	Kina	1.319
Paraguay	Guaranies	2,064
Philippines	Pesos	26.22
Poland	Zlotys	2.696
Portugal	Escudos	154.2
Qatar	Riyals	3.64
Russia	Rubles	5,121
Rwanda	Rwanda Francs	306.8
Saint Kitts and Nevis	E.Caribbean Dollar	2.70
Saint Lucia	E.Caribbean Dollar	2.70
Saint Vincent and the Grenadines	E.Caribbean Dollar	2.70
Saudi Arabia	Riyals	3.745
Senegal	Cfa Francs	511.6
Seychelles	Rupees	4.970
Sierra Leone	Leones	920.7
Singapore	Singapore Dollar	1.410
Slovakia	Koruny	30.65
Slovenia	Tolars	135.4
Solomon Islands	Solomon Isl Dollar	3.566
South Africa	Rand	4.299
Spain	Pesetas	126.7
Sri Lanka	Rupees	55.27
Suriname	Guilders	401.3
Swaziland	Emalangeni	4.299
Sweden	Kronor	6.706
Switzerland	Swiss Francs	1.236
Syria	Syrian Pounds	11.23
Tanzania	Tanzania Shilling	580.0
Thailand	Baht	25.34
Togo	Cfa Francs	511.6
Tonga	Pa'Anga	1.232
Trinidad and Tobago	Tt Dollar	6.005
Tunisia	Dinars	0.973
Turkey	Liras	81,405
Uganda	Uganda Shilling	1,046
Ukraine	Karbovanets	1.830
United Arab Emirates	Dirhams	3.671
United Kingdom	Pounds Sterling	0.641
Uruguay	Pesos	7.972
Vanuatu	Vatu	111.7
Western Samoa	Tala	2.459
Yemen	Rials	50.04
Zambia	Kwacha	1,204

Source: U.S. Dept. of Commerce, International Trade Administration, "Foreign Exchange Rates, 1991-96;" <http://www.ita.doc.gov/industry/otea/usfth/t37.prn>; (accessed: 12 August 1997).

No. 1386. International Tourism Receipts—Leading Countries: 1990 to 1996

[In millions of dollars, except as indicated]

COUNTRY	TOTAL RECEIPTS			Percent change, 1995-96	PERCENT OF WORLD TOTAL	
	1990	1995	1996		1990	1996
World, total	266,207	393,276	423,022	7.56	100.00	100.00
United States	43,007	61,137	64,373	5.29	16.16	15.22
Spain	18,593	25,343	28,428	12.17	6.98	6.72
France	20,185	27,527	28,241	2.59	7.58	6.68
Italy	20,016	27,451	27,349	-0.37	7.52	6.47
United Kingdom	14,940	19,133	20,415	6.70	5.61	4.83
Austria	13,410	14,618	15,095	3.26	5.04	3.57
Germany	11,471	12,810	13,168	2.79	4.31	3.11
Hong Kong	5,032	9,604	11,200	16.62	1.89	2.65
China	2,218	8,733	10,500	20.23	0.83	2.48
Switzerland	7,411	9,459	9,892	4.58	2.78	2.34
Singapore	4,596	8,212	9,410	14.59	1.73	2.22
Canada	6,339	8,012	8,727	8.92	2.38	2.06
Thailand	4,326	7,664	8,600	12.21	1.63	2.03
Australia	4,088	7,100	8,264	16.39	1.54	1.95
Poland	358	6,400	7,000	9.38	0.13	1.65
Mexico	5,467	6,164	6,898	11.91	2.05	1.63
Turkey	3,225	4,957	6,536	31.85	1.21	1.55
Korea, South	3,559	5,579	6,315	13.19	1.34	1.49
Belgium	3,721	5,719	5,893	3.04	1.40	1.39
Netherlands	3,636	5,762	5,877	2.00	1.37	1.39

Source: World Tourism Organization, Madrid, Spain, "World's Top Tourism Earners 1996;" published February 1997; <http://www.world-tourism.org/esta/highlights/topearn.htm>.

No. 1387. Net Flow of Financial Resources to Developing Countries: 1980 to 1995

[In billions of U.S. dollars. Net flow covers loans, grants, and grant-like flows minus amortization on loans. Military flows are excluded. Developing countries cover countries designated by Development Assistance Committee (DAC) as developing. Official development assistance covers all flows to developing countries and multilateral institutions provided by official agencies, including State and local governments, or by their executive agencies, which are administered with the promotion of economic development and welfare of developing countries as their main objective and whose financial terms are intended to be concessional in character with grant element of at least 25 percent. Other official flows cover export credits and portfolio investment from the official sector]

ORIGIN AND TYPE OF RESOURCE	1980	1985	1986	1990	1991	1992	1993	1994	1995
DAC countries [1]	75.4	45.2	84.3	76.4	94.7	115.8	136.1	165.9	166.7
Official development assistance	27.3	29.4	45.7	53.0	56.7	60.9	56.5	59.2	58.9
Other official flows	5.3	3.4	5.8	8.6	7.1	8.9	7.9	10.1	9.8
Private flows at market terms	40.4	9.4	28.8	9.8	25.5	40.1	66.0	90.7	92.0
Private voluntary agencies	2.4	2.9	4.0	5.1	5.4	6.0	5.7	6.0	6.0
Total net flow to developing countries, by DAC country [1]	75.4	45.2	87.1	76.4	94.7	115.8	136.1	165.9	166.7
United States	13.9	1.8	16.4	11.1	20.8	33.5	58.2	59.7	47.8
Official development assistance	7.1	9.4	7.7	11.4	11.3	11.7	10.1	9.9	7.4
Other official flows	1.1	0.2	-0.5	-0.4	-0.8	1.3	0.1	0.9	1.5
Private flows at market terms	4.3	-9.3	7.3	-2.4	7.6	17.7	45.4	46.3	36.5
Private voluntary agencies	1.3	1.5	1.9	2.5	2.7	2.8	2.6	2.6	2.5
Australia	0.9	1.2	1.5	1.5	-2.1	4.2	2.1	2.1	2.5
Austria	0.3	0.2	0.2	0.6	0.7	0.8	0.7	1.0	0.9
Belgium	2.9	1.3	1.5	0.1	1.5	2.2	0.7	2.2	-0.2
Canada	3.2	1.7	2.7	3.5	4.0	4.2	5.3	5.6	4.7
Denmark	0.8	0.4	0.9	1.1	1.1	1.6	1.4	1.3	1.8
Finland	0.2	0.3	0.9	1.0	1.0	0.8	0.3	0.6	0.6
France	11.6	8.9	5.3	5.7	6.5	10.8	10.9	12.7	12.8
Germany [2]	10.6	5.8	12.1	13.6	13.1	8.9	15.4	23.9	21.2
Ireland	(Z)	0.1	0.1	0.2	0.1	0.2	0.1	0.2	0.2
Italy	4.0	2.2	5.8	3.2	7.5	6.2	2.4	3.4	2.8
Japan	6.8	11.6	22.0	17.2	24.5	16.2	15.9	26.5	42.3
Luxembourg	(NA)	(NA)	(NA)	(NA)	(Z)	5.9	0.1	0.1	0.1
Netherlands	2.4	2.6	2.5	4.0	4.4	3.4	5.6	4.7	6.8
New Zealand	0.1	0.1	0.1	0.1	0.1	0.1	0.1	0.1	0.2
Norway	0.9	0.6	0.9	1.2	1.4	1.4	1.2	1.5	1.5
Portugal	(NA)	(NA)	0.1	0.3	0.2	0.4	0.2	0.2	0.3
Spain	(NA)	(NA)	0.4	1.0	1.3	1.6	1.4	3.5	1.6
Sweden	1.9	1.4	2.3	2.8	1.8	3.0	2.5	2.4	2.2
Switzerland	2.7	2.5	1.8	3.4	3.0	3.1	2.9	0.1	0.9
United Kingdom	12.2	2.5	9.5	6.5	5.6	9.3	8.8	12.0	15.5

NA Not available. Z Less than $50 million. [1] Includes flows to OPEC countries: Algeria, Ecuador, Gabon, Iran, Iraq, Kuwait, Libya, Nigeria, Qatar, Saudi Arabia, United Arab Emirates, and Venezuela. DAC countries listed below. Country totals may not add to DAC total because debt forgiveness of non-official development assistance claims is not included in DAC totals. [2] Former West Germany.

Source: Organization for Economic Cooperation and Development, Paris, France, *Annual Reports of the Development Assistance Committee.*

No. 1368. External Public Debt, by Country: 1980 to 1995

[External public debt is defined as debt repayable to external creditors in foreign currency, goods, or services, with an original or extended maturity of more than 1 year, which is a direct obligation of, or has repayment guaranteed by, a public body in the borrowing country. Excludes undisbursed debt (amounts not yet drawn by recipient) and unguaranteed private debt, which for some countries is substantial. Debt contracted for the purchase of military equipment is not usually reported. Debt service payments represent the sum of interest payments and repayments of principal on external public debt]

COUNTRY	TOTAL EXTERNAL PUBLIC DEBT (mil. dol.)						DEBT SERVICE PAYMENTS (mil. dol.)			DEBT SERVICE RATIO [3] (percent)		
	1980	1994	1995									
			Total [1]	Bilateral official	Multilateral organizations	Bonds [2]	1980	1994	1995	1980	1994	1995
Argentina	46,906	55,832	62,181	11,709	9,414	39,441	4,812	4,523	6,302	29	21	22
Bangladesh	12,289	15,356	15,543	5,533	9,766	-	529	537	658	19	13	12
Bolivia	3,690	4,117	4,452	1,802	2,577	17	275	286	291	28	23	23
Brazil	89,187	95,309	96,609	19,451	9,366	54,663	5,716	8,888	13,838	16	17	23
Bulgaria	9,834	9,844	9,574	1,710	1,829	5,412	1,316	581	936	19	11	14
Cameroon	4,709	7,230	8,060	5,467	1,674	-	320	296	348	14	13	13
Chile	10,426	8,989	7,178	713	2,871	-	1,612	1,217	2,921	15	8	15
China	45,515	82,391	94,675	19,960	16,302	10,684	5,853	10,161	13,693	10	8	9
Colombia	14,671	13,617	12,983	1,696	5,320	1,014	3,115	3,299	3,145	33	25	21
Congo (Brazzaville) [4]	4,208	4,774	4,956	3,332	703	-	475	533	142	32	52	11
Congo (Kinshasa) [4]	9,006	9,280	9,621	6,362	2,382	5	137	1	-	6	-	-
Costa Rica	3,063	3,223	3,132	1,144	1,347	572	432	388	531	21	11	13
Cote d'Ivoire	9,849	11,240	11,899	5,317	3,897	-	524	693	771	15	21	17
Croatia	(X)	1,544	1,693	975	528	-	(X)	161	158	(X)	2	2
Dominican Republic	3,442	3,543	3,550	1,877	1,022	520	139	482	346	6	14	10
Ecuador	9,867	10,523	12,032	2,260	2,991	5,999	874	870	1,286	27	19	24
Egypt	26,976	30,538	31,325	25,376	4,228	-	2,489	1,856	2,073	18	12	13
Ethiopia	3,634	4,754	4,958	2,193	2,386	-	201	107	153	24	13	13
Gabon	3,135	3,509	4,099	3,237	663	-	104	198	368	4	8	13
Ghana	2,757	4,148	4,568	1,159	2,884	-	194	241	218	20	17	14
Guatemala	2,241	2,461	2,493	1,114	943	285	164	232	286	10	9	9
Honduras	3,425	3,900	3,979	1,485	2,162	139	307	379	444	29	26	25
Hungary	18,006	22,157	23,572	900	3,282	15,756	3,751	4,592	4,791	30	40	27
India [5]	69,328	86,499	79,725	27,097	29,996	3,279	6,011	8,029	10,150	23	20	22
Indonesia	48,056	63,891	65,347	31,221	20,010	704	7,395	8,799	9,491	25	19	18
Jamaica	3,934	3,438	3,409	1,877	1,216	25	481	470	522	20	14	14
Jordan	7,050	6,781	6,904	3,792	1,187	801	550	484	549	19	12	11
Kenya	4,760	5,547	5,927	2,294	2,913	-	502	704	666	22	26	23
Macedonia, The Former Yugoslav Republic of	(X)	640	773	327	291	-	(X)	137	28	(X)	10	2
Madagascar	3,380	3,548	3,691	1,928	1,686	-	147	48	52	30	7	7
Malaysia	12,684	13,850	15,857	3,331	1,645	5,380	2,827	4,022	3,043	8	6	4
Mali	2,345	2,837	2,840	1,451	1,386	-	40	116	71	7	24	11
Mexico	75,981	79,284	94,027	19,790	18,642	45,195	7,843	11,782	12,139	14	15	12
Morocco	22,143	20,806	21,347	9,105	6,830	-	1,499	3,154	3,405	18	33	31
Nicaragua	8,245	9,013	7,937	5,479	1,469	524	10	184	260	2	38	36
Oman	2,400	2,608	2,563	413	178	-	714	525	465	12	9	7
Pakistan	16,503	22,669	23,711	10,440	12,204	150	1,366	2,915	2,254	17	30	19
Panama	3,988	3,923	3,906	646	612	3	141	303	233	2	3	2
Papua New Guinea	1,501	1,636	1,614	530	930	-	270	318	286	18	11	9
Peru	13,634	17,679	18,929	10,455	3,717	-	178	930	892	4	14	12
Philippines	24,076	30,271	29,908	13,804	8,466	5,099	2,896	3,622	4,259	22	15	13
Poland	39,059	39,503	41,073	30,165	2,067	8,110	636	2,484	2,274	4	11	7
Senegal	2,939	3,046	3,191	1,246	1,861	-	211	169	192	13	11	11
Slovenia	(X)	1,358	1,491	190	536	-	(X)	207	298	(X)	2	3
Sri Lanka	4,934	6,653	7,010	3,627	2,858	-	285	356	348	10	6	6
Sudan	9,155	9,399	9,779	5,787	2,133	-	23	3	17	3	-	(NA)
Syria	14,917	16,540	16,757	14,570	1,030	-	1,191	229	155	22	4	2
Tanzania	5,822	5,986	6,085	2,848	2,868	-	135	159	187	25	17	15
Thailand	12,570	17,120	17,231	7,820	3,208	1,586	3,272	2,630	2,820	10	4	4
Tunisia	6,662	8,008	8,814	3,505	3,695	535	1,220	1,346	1,377	21	18	16
Turkey	36,664	48,579	50,128	8,319	8,962	13,836	6,480	7,672	9,138	26	23	22
Uganda	2,236	2,867	3,054	768	2,202	4	65	122	104	35	35	16
Uruguay	3,045	3,745	3,823	338	1,259	1,963	711	448	764	29	13	21
Venezuela	24,509	28,042	28,494	1,463	3,300	20,885	4,168	2,125	3,456	19	11	15
Yemen	5,154	5,460	5,526	2,532	1,278	-	108	81	91	4	3	3
Yugoslavia, former [6]	12,986	8,511	8,725	3,277	1,311	-	2,719	-	-	(NA)	-	-
Zambia	4,852	4,897	5,077	2,731	2,186	-	173	309	369	13	26	29
Zimbabwe	2,464	3,296	3,360	1,170	1,616	120	370	441	485	16	19	(NA)

- Represents or rounds to zero. NA Not available. X Not applicable. [1] Includes other types of creditors not shown separately. [2] Covers publicly issued and privately placed bonds. [3] Debt service payments as percent of exports. [4] See footnote 3, table 1334. [5] Fiscal year basis. [6] The bulk of the debt of Yugoslavian enterprises is reported as nonguaranteed.

Source: The World Bank, Washington, DC, *World Debt Tables*, periodic.

No. 1389. Military Expenditures, by Country: 1985 to 1995

[In millions of dollars, except as indicated. See also table 553. For most countries, data for expenditures and for gross national product (GNP) were based on local currencies which were deflated to constant 1995 local currency values before conversion to U.S. dollar equivalents. In general, the rates used for conversion are the 1995 average par/market exchange rates as supplied by the International Bank for Reconstruction and Development]

COUNTRY	CURRENT DOLLARS				CONSTANT (1995) DOLLARS				
	1985	1990	1994	1995	1985	1990	1995		
							Total	Percent of GNP	Per capita (dollars)
United States	**258,200**	**306,200**	**288,100**	277,800	**353,800**	**351,900**	**277,800**	**3.8**	**1,056**
Algeria [1]	716	697	1,226	1,238	982	801	1,238	3.2	43
Angola [1]	(NA)	(NA)	453	225	(NA)	(NA)	225	3.0	22
Argentina	5,599	3,436	4,724	4,684	7,673	3,949	4,684	1.7	137
Australia	4,960	5,866	8,358	8,401	6,796	6,741	8,401	2.5	465
Bangladesh	245	317	475	502	336	365	502	1.7	4
Belgium	4,880	5,356	4,496	4,449	6,688	6,155	4,449	1.7	439
Brazil	3,044	6,555	7,185	10,900	4,172	9,832	10,900	1.7	68
Bulgaria [1]	5,808	3,887	962	1,073	7,960	4,467	1,073	2.8	125
Burma	877	1,093	1,696	1,833	1,202	1,256	1,833	3.9	41
Canada	7,169	9,187	9,408	9,077	9,825	10,560	9,077	1.7	318
Chile [2]	821	1,154	1,832	2,243	1,125	1,327	2,243	3.8	158
China [1]	39,010	48,440	57,040	63,510	53,470	55,660	63,510	2.3	53
Colombia	559	1,225	1,302	2,000	766	1,408	2,000	2.6	55
Congo (Kinshasa) [3]	68	(NA)	36	17	93	(NA)	17	0.3	-
Croatia [1]	(X)	(X)	1,827	2,114	(X)	(X)	2,114	10.5	425
Cuba	1,335	1,400	600	350	1,830	1,609	350	1.6	32
Czech Republic [1]	(X)	(X)	2,495	2,368	(X)	(X)	2,368	2.3	229
Egypt [1]	3,129	1,468	1,835	2,653	4,289	1,687	2,653	5.7	43
France	35,740	44,800	48,960	47,770	48,990	51,480	47,770	3.1	826
Germany [4]	39,400	48,540	41,020	41,160	54,000	55,790	41,160	1.9	496
Greece	3,898	4,182	4,811	5,056	5,343	4,806	5,056	5.5	482
Hungary [1]	3,782	1,277	1,203	961	5,183	1,468	961	1.5	95
India	5,022	6,635	8,294	7,831	6,883	7,626	7,831	2.4	8
Indonesia [2]	1,600	1,699	2,364	3,396	2,193	1,952	3,396	1.8	17
Iran [1]	8,523	8,098	5,449	4,191	11,680	9,307	4,191	2.6	65
Iraq [1]	12,650	14,110	(NA)	(NA)	17,340	16,210	(NA)	(NA)	(NA)
Israel	7,773	7,168	8,171	8,734	10,650	8,237	8,734	9.6	1,646
Italy	14,200	19,150	20,700	19,380	19,460	22,010	19,380	1.8	338
Japan	27,400	40,740	49,300	50,240	37,550	46,820	50,240	1.0	401
Jordan	620	397	437	481	849	456	481	7.7	117
Kazakstan [1]	(X)	(X)	450	426	(X)	(X)	426	0.9	25
Kenya	89	173	147	173	122	198	173	2.3	6
Korea, North [1]	5,260	5,940	5,500	6,000	7,209	6,827	6,000	28.6	255
Korea, South	6,507	10,760	13,930	14,410	8,919	12,390	14,410	3.4	320
Kuwait	1,501	13,170	3,069	3,488	2,057	15,130	3,488	11.6	1,919
Libya [2]	(NA)	(NA)	1,297	1,999	(NA)	(NA)	1,999	6.0	381
Malaysia	1,023	1,271	2,247	2,444	1,402	1,461	2,444	3.0	125
Mexico	1,063	1,058	1,992	2,321	1,457	1,215	2,321	1.0	25
Netherlands	6,792	8,129	8,034	8,012	9,309	9,343	8,012	2.1	518
New Zealand	702	897	702	740	962	1,030	740	1.3	211
Nigeria [2]	757	674	793	(NA)	1,036	775	(NA)	(NA)	(NA)
Pakistan	1,809	3,120	3,933	3,740	2,480	3,586	3,740	6.1	30
Peru	2,244	683	847	989	3,075	784	989	1.7	41
Philippines	506	1,232	1,368	1,151	693	1,416	1,151	1.5	16
Poland [1]	14,670	8,752	4,644	4,887	20,110	10,060	4,887	2.3	127
Romania [1]	6,840	3,869	2,178	2,520	9,374	4,446	2,520	2.5	115
Russia [1]	(X)	(X)	93,000	76,000	(X)	(X)	76,000	11.4	513
Saudi Arabia	21,340	23,160	17,200	17,210	29,240	26,620	17,210	13.5	919
Singapore	1,687	2,106	3,304	3,970	2,312	2,421	3,970	4.7	1,191
Slovakia [1]	(X)	(X)	440	577	(X)	(X)	577	3.0	108
Slovenia [1]	(X)	(X)	438	344	(X)	(X)	344	1.5	176
South Africa	3,124	4,545	3,015	2,895	4,282	5,223	2,895	2.2	71
Spain	7,338	8,382	8,156	8,652	10,060	9,633	8,652	1.6	221
Sri Lanka	174	411	541	585	238	472	585	4.6	32
Sweden	4,306	5,138	5,832	6,042	5,904	5,905	6,042	2.8	683
Syria [1,2]	5,432	4,391	(NA)	3,563	7,445	5,046	3,563	7.2	236
Taiwan	6,395	8,938	11,480	13,140	8,765	10,270	13,140	5.0	618
Tanzania	68	98	82	69	94	112	69	1.8	2
Thailand	2,066	2,372	3,970	4,014	2,832	2,726	4,014	2.5	69
Turkey	3,568	4,323	6,168	6,606	4,890	4,968	6,606	4.0	106
Ukraine [1]	(X)	(X)	4,378	3,588	(X)	(X)	3,588	2.9	70
United Kingdom	33,450	37,090	35,440	33,400	45,850	42,630	33,400	3.0	572
Vietnam [1]	(NA)	723	435	544	(NA)	831	544	2.6	7

- Represents or rounds to zero. NA Not available. X Not applicable. [1] Estimated. [2] Data probably omit a major share of total military expenditures, probably including most arms acquisitions. [3] See footnote 3, table 1334. [4] Prior to 1990, data for former West Germany.

Source: U.S. Arms Control and Disarmament Agency, *World Military Expenditures and Arms Transfers*, annual.

No. 1390. Armed Forces Personnel, by Country: 1985 to 1995

[Personnel data as of July. Armed Forces refer to active-duty military personnel, including paramilitary forces where those forces resemble regular units in their organization, equipment, training, or mission. Reserve forces are not included]

COUNTRY	ARMED FORCES PERSONNEL (1,000)					ARMED FORCES PER 1,000 POPULATION				
	1985	1990	1993	1994	1995	1985	1990	1993	1994	1995
United States	2,244	2,181	1,815	1,715	1,620	9.4	8.7	7.0	6.6	6.2
Algeria	170	126	139	126	120	7.7	5.0	5.1	4.5	4.2
Angola	66	115	128	120	82	8.7	13.6	13.4	12.2	8.1
Argentina	129	85	65	69	65	4.2	2.6	1.9	2.0	1.9
Australia	70	68	68	59	58	4.4	4.0	3.8	3.3	3.2
Bangladesh	91	103	107	113	115	0.9	0.9	0.9	1.0	1.0
Belgium	107	106	70	53	47	10.9	10.6	6.9	5.2	4.6
Brazil	496	295	296	296	285	3.6	2.0	1.9	1.9	1.8
Bulgaria	189	129	52	80	86	21.2	14.4	6.1	9.4	10.0
Burma	186	230	286	370	322	5.0	5.6	6.6	8.4	7.1
Canada	83	87	76	75	70	3.3	3.3	2.7	2.7	2.5
Chile	124	95	92	102	102	10.3	7.2	6.7	7.3	7.2
China	4,100	3,500	3,031	2,930	2,930	3.9	3.1	2.6	2.5	2.4
Colombia	66	110	139	146	146	2.2	3.3	4.0	4.1	4.0
Congo (Kinshasa) [1]	62	55	55	53	49	1.9	1.5	1.3	1.2	1.1
Croatia	(X)	(X)	(NA)	80	60	(X)	(X)	(NA)	16.2	12.1
Cuba	297	297	175	140	70	29.5	28.1	16.2	12.9	6.4
Czech Republic	(X)	(X)	107	90	68	(X)	(X)	10.3	8.7	6.6
Egypt	466	434	424	430	430	9.4	7.7	7.1	7.0	6.9
France	563	550	506	506	504	10.2	9.7	8.8	8.8	8.7
Germany [2]	495	545	398	362	352	8.1	6.9	4.9	4.4	4.2
Greece	201	201	213	206	213	20.2	19.9	20.5	19.7	20.3
Hungary	117	94	(NA)	60	71	11.0	9.1	(NA)	5.9	7.0
India	1,260	1,262	1,265	1,305	1,265	1.6	1.5	1.4	1.4	1.4
Indonesia	278	283	271	280	280	1.6	1.5	1.4	1.4	1.4
Iran	345	440	528	528	440	7.3	7.7	8.5	8.4	6.8
Iraq	788	1,390	407	425	390	50.2	75.4	21.2	21.4	18.9
Israel	195	190	181	185	185	47.9	42.1	35.8	35.7	34.9
Italy	504	493	450	436	435	8.8	8.5	7.9	7.6	7.6
Japan	241	250	242	233	240	2.0	2.0	1.9	1.9	1.9
Jordan	81	100	100	100	112	30.6	30.5	25.7	25.0	27.3
Kazakstan	(X)	(X)	44	18	28	(X)	(X)	2.6	1.1	1.7
Kenya	19	20	24	22	22	0.9	0.8	0.9	0.8	0.8
Korea, North	784	1,200	1,200	1,200	1,040	40.0	56.0	53.0	52.0	44.3
Korea, South	600	650	750	750	655	14.7	15.2	17.0	16.8	14.5
Kuwait	16	7	12	15	20	9.3	3.3	7.8	8.9	11.0
Libya	91	86	85	80	76	24.6	19.7	17.4	15.8	14.5
Malaysia	110	130	115	115	122	7.1	7.4	6.1	6.0	6.2
Mexico	140	175	175	175	175	1.8	2.1	1.9	1.9	1.9
Netherlands	103	104	86	77	67	7.1	7.0	5.6	5.0	4.3
New Zealand	13	11	11	10	10	4.0	3.3	3.2	2.9	2.9
Nigeria	134	94	76	80	89	1.8	1.1	0.8	0.8	0.9
Pakistan	483	550	580	540	587	4.9	4.8	4.8	4.4	4.6
Peru	128	125	112	112	115	6.5	5.7	4.8	4.7	4.8
Philippines	115	109	107	109	110	2.0	1.7	1.5	1.5	1.5
Poland	439	313	180	255	278	11.8	8.2	4.7	6.6	7.2
Romania	237	126	167	200	209	10.5	5.5	7.4	9.0	9.5
Russia	(X)	(X)	1,500	1,400	1,400	(X)	(X)	10.1	9.4	9.4
Saudi Arabia	80	146	172	164	175	6.1	9.2	9.9	9.1	9.3
Singapore	56	56	56	56	60	20.7	18.4	17.4	17.1	18.0
Slovakia	(X)	(X)	33	47	52	(X)	(X)	6.2	8.8	9.7
Slovenia	(X)	(X)	12	17	10	(X)	(X)	6.1	8.7	5.1
South Africa	95	85	72	102	100	2.8	2.3	1.8	2.5	2.4
Spain	314	263	204	213	210	8.2	6.8	5.2	5.5	5.4
Sri Lanka	22	22	110	110	110	1.4	1.3	6.1	6.1	6.0
Sweden	69	65	44	70	51	8.3	7.6	5.0	8.0	5.8
Syria	402	408	408	320	320	38.2	32.3	29.0	22.0	21.2
Taiwan	444	370	442	425	425	23.0	18.2	21.2	20.2	20.0
Tanzania	43	40	46	50	35	2.0	1.6	1.7	1.8	1.2
Thailand	235	283	295	290	288	4.6	5.1	5.2	5.0	4.9
Turkey	814	769	686	811	805	16.1	13.7	11.6	13.4	13.1
Ukraine	(X)	(X)	510	495	476	(X)	(X)	9.9	9.6	9.3
United Kingdom	334	308	271	257	233	5.9	5.4	4.7	4.4	4.0
Vietnam	1,027	1,052	550	550	550	16.9	15.9	7.8	7.7	7.6

NA Not available. X Not applicable. [1] See footnote 3, table 1334. [2] Prior to 1990, data for former West Germany.

Source: U.S. Arms Control and Disarmament Agency, *World Military Expenditures and Arms Transfers*, annual.

Industrial Outlook

This section presents industry statistics for selected manufacturing industries. The industry groupings correspond to those used in the *1994 U.S. Industrial Outlook*. The tables contain new and revised data from the *1995 Annual Survey of Manufactures* along with revised industry data for 1987 through 1992 from the *1992 Census of Manufactures: General Summary.*

To provide a more accurate picture of industry trends, the value of shipments shown in these tables are expressed both in "current dollars" and in inflation-adjusted or "constant dollars." Current dollars show the value of the goods in the year they are produced. Constant dollars (or "real" dollars) show the value of shipments as they would be valued if produced in the base year. This permits shipment levels from different years to be compared. The constant dollar shipments (base year 1992) were derived by deflating the product class shipments from the Bureau of the Census using the Bureau of Labor Statistics' producer price indexes.

The tables contain both "industry" and "product" shipments. The Bureau of the Census collects shipments data from individual factories (or establishments) rather than at the company level. Most factories make a variety of products, but for statistical purposes each factory is classified in the industry associated with its major product. For instance, the total output of a plant may consist of 80 percent tires and 20 percent hose and belting. In this case, the total output of the plant would be credited to the tire industry, and the shipments of all plants so classified would make up the "industry shipments" of the tire industry. The value of all tires shipped by all establishments is aggregated to derive "product shipments."

Trade data were tabulated following the Bureau of the Census's 1997 trade concordance (with a few exceptions) to approximate the Standard Industrial Classification (SIC) industry groupings. Exports are limited to domestic exports and are valued "free alongside ship" or f.a.s. Imports are restricted to goods imported for consumption and are on a customs value basis. Trade data should only be compared with product shipments data.

Researchers who once relied on the *U.S. Industrial Outlook* will be greatly assisted by the publication of the *U.S. Industry and Trade Outlook 1998* in the fall of 1997. This new publication is the result of an innovative public-private partnership between the International Trade Administration of the Department of Commerce and the McGraw-Hill companies. Authorship is shared by the Commerce Department, other government agencies, and McGraw-Hill. As in years past, the new *Outlook* is anchored by historical statistical data provided by the Bureau of the Census.

The *Outlook* is a basic resource for industry analysis and business development. The 1998 edition will contain 50 chapters covering important manufacturing and service sectors, along with industry snapshots, and hundreds of industry reviews, analyses, and forecasts. This new publication continues the legacy of the *U.S. Industrial Outlook*, the most widely read and respected single source industry-by-industry overview of the U.S. economy. Like its predecessor, the *Industry and Trade Outlook* is a single source reference for business planners, investors, researchers, and students who need to know where major sectors of the U.S. economy have been and where they are going in an increasingly global marketplace. For sales information contact the National Technical Information Service, 703/487-4650.

No. 1391. Recent Trends in Food and Kindred Products (SIC 20): 1990 to 1996

ITEM	Unit	1990	1991	1992	1993	1994	1995	1996
INDUSTRY DATA								
Value of shipments [1]	Mil. dol.	391,728	397,892	406,963	422,220	430,963	448,408	(NA)
Value of shipments (1992 dollars)	Mil. dol.	390,859	398,551	406,963	415,104	419,167	433,686	(NA)
Total employment	1,000	1,497	1,511	1,503	1,520	1,511	1,526	(NA)
Production workers	1,000	1,084	1,101	1,100	1,118	1,112	1,123	(NA)
Average hourly earnings	Dollar	9.87	10.15	10.41	10.58	10.74	10.97	(NA)
Capital expenditures	Mil. dol.	9,332	9,993	9,896	9,389	10,093	11,929	(NA)
PRODUCT DATA								
Value of shipments [2]	Mil. dol.	359,713	363,943	382,869	397,633	405,490	421,329	(NA)
Value of shipments (1992 dollars)	Mil. dol.	358,812	364,419	382,869	391,063	394,415	407,159	(NA)
TRADE DATA								
Value of imports	Mil. dol.	19,834	19,780	20,883	20,891	22,842	23,956	26,496
Value of exports	Mil. dol.	18,554	20,063	22,642	23,138	25,801	28,868	29,667

NA Not available. [1] Value of all products and services sold by establishments in the food and kindred products industry. [2] Value of products classified in the food and kindred products industry produced by all industries.

Source: U.S. Department of Commerce, Bureau of the Census, International Trade Administration (ITA).

No. 1392. Recent Trends in Higher Value Added Foods and Beverages and Lower Value Foods and Feeds: 1990 to 1996

ITEM	Unit	1990	1991	1992	1993	1994	1995	1996
HIGHER VALUE ADDED FOODS AND BEVERAGES [1]								
Industry data:								
Value of shipments [2]	Mil. dol.	188,822	196,594	202,519	209,326	216,694	226,948	(NA)
Value of shipments (1992 dollars)	Mil. dol.	195,511	199,523	202,519	208,666	210,061	215,924	(NA)
Total employment	1,000	828	830	830	836	826	833	(NA)
Production workers	1,000	565	570	574	578	572	577	(NA)
Average hourly earnings	Dollar	11.00	11.33	11.57	11.83	12.06	12.09	(NA)
Capital expenditures	Mil. dol.	5,716	6,312	6,405	5,935	6,247	7,216	(NA)
Product data:								
Value of shipments [3]	Mil. dol.	175,899	182,570	191,278	197,567	204,380	214,269	(NA)
Value of shipments (1992 dollars)	Mil. dol.	181,908	185,227	191,278	195,237	198,364	204,069	(NA)
Trade data:								
Value of imports	Mil. dol.	9,077	8,722	9,727	9,459	10,360	11,333	13,004
Value of exports	Mil. dol.	4,883	5,742	6,696	7,543	8,670	9,196	9,956
LOWER VALUE ADDED FOODS AND FEEDS [4]								
Industry data:								
Value of shipments [2]	Mil. dol.	202,903	201,297	204,444	212,894	214,269	221,457	(NA)
Value of shipments (1992 dollars)	Mil. dol.	195,348	199,028	204,444	206,438	209,106	217,742	(NA)
Total employment	1,000	667	679	673	684	685	693	(NA)
Production workers	1,000	516	528	527	540	540	547	(NA)
Average hourly earnings	Dollar	8.70	8.94	9.21	9.29	9.39	9.81	(NA)
Capital expenditures	Mil. dol.	3,613	3,680	3,494	3,454	3,846	4,714	(NA)
Product data:								
Value of shipments [3]	Mil. dol.	183,814	181,373	191,611	200,065	201,102	203,159	(NA)
Value of shipments (1992 dollars)	Mil. dol.	176,904	179,192	191,611	195,826	196,043	199,170	(NA)
Trade data:								
Value of imports	Mil. dol.	10,757	11,058	11,156	11,431	12,482	12,623	13,494
Value of exports	Mil. dol.	13,672	14,342	15,946	15,596	17,132	19,673	19,711

NA Not available. [1] SIC's 2023, 24, 32-38, 43, 45, 47, 51-53, 64-68, 82, 84-86, 95, 96, 98, and 99. This aggregation includes those industries defined as higher value added. [2] Value of all products and services sold by establishments in this industry. [3] Value of products classified in this industry produced by all industries. [4] SIC 20 excluding 2023, 24, 32-38, 43, 45, 47, 51-53, 64-68, 82, 84-86, 95, 96, 98, and 99. This aggregation includes those industries defined as lower value added.

Source: U.S. Department of Commerce, Bureau of the Census, International Trade Administration (ITA).

No. 1393. Recent Trends in Red Meat and Poultry Slaughtering and Processing: 1990 to 1996

ITEM	Unit	1990	1991	1992	1993	1994	1995	1996
RED MEAT (SIC 2011, 2013)								
Industry data:								
Value of shipments [1]	Mil. dol.	71,484	69,795	70,107	73,941	70,701	71,373	(NA)
Value of shipments (1992 dollars)	Mil. dol.	65,711	66,307	70,107	71,369	71,809	73,855	(NA)
Total employment	1,000	204	205	207	209	204	214	(NA)
Production workers	1,000	165	167	171	173	169	178	(NA)
Average hourly earnings	Dollar	8.64	8.74	8.99	9.06	9.43	9.83	(NA)
Capital expenditures	Mil. dol.	806	811	719	703	699	662	(NA)
Product data:								
Value of shipments [2]	Mil. dol.	64,079	62,676	64,351	68,216	64,839	65,300	(NA)
Value of shipments (1992 dollars)	Mil. dol.	58,874	59,535	64,351	65,856	65,679	67,581	(NA)
Trade data:								
Value of imports	Mil. dol.	3,165	3,141	2,926	3,070	2,984	2,662	2,636
Value of exports	Mil. dol.	4,364	4,348	4,807	4,696	5,273	6,303	6,226
POULTRY SLAUGHTERING AND PROCESSING (SIC 2015)								
Industry data:								
Value of shipments [1]	Mil. dol.	21,418	22,379	23,965	25,501	27,415	28,887	(NA)
Value of shipments (1992 dollars)	Mil. dol.	20,398	22,070	23,965	24,783	25,912	27,459	(NA)
Total employment	1,000	180	194	194	205	216	215	(NA)
Production workers	1,000	161	173	173	184	193	192	(NA)
Average hourly earnings	Dollar	6.67	7.02	7.39	7.4	7.49	8.09	(NA)
Capital expenditures	Mil. dol.	530	635	469	555	594	728	(NA)
Product data:								
Value of shipments [2]	Mil. dol.	20,353	21,246	23,592	24,983	27,027	28,463	(NA)
Value of shipments (1992 dollars)	Mil. dol.	19,383	20,953	23,592	24,279	25,546	27,056	(NA)
Trade data:								
Value of imports	Mil. dol.	29.7	35.7	25.8	29.9	25.3	30.5	44.7
Value of exports	Mil. dol.	717	879	990	1,157	1,633	2,097	2,585

NA Not available. [1] Value of all products and services sold by establishments in this industry. [2] Value of products classified in this industry produced by all industries.

Source: U.S. Department of Commerce, Bureau of the Census, International Trade Administration (ITA).

No. 1394. Recent Trends in Alcoholic Beverages (SIC 2082, 2084, 2085): 1990 to 1996

ITEM	Unit	1990	1991	1992	1993	1994	1995	1996
INDUSTRY DATA								
Value of shipments [1]	Mil. dol.	22,840	23,888	25,035	24,739	24,983	25,720	(NA)
2082 Malt beverages	Mil. dol.	15,542	16,421	17,340	16,656	16,795	17,151	(NA)
2084 Wines & brandy	Mil. dol.	3,743	3,697	4,301	4,514	4,301	4,743	(NA)
2085 Distilled liquor	Mil. dol.	3,555	3,770	3,394	3,569	3,888	3,827	(NA)
Value of shipments (1992 dollars)	Mil. dol.	24,547	24,337	25,035	24,734	25,315	25,277	(NA)
2082 Malt beverages	Mil. dol.	16,640	16,722	17,340	16,791	17,314	17,066	(NA)
2084 Wines & brandy	Mil. dol.	3,953	3,781	4,301	4,465	4,267	4,668	(NA)
2085 Distilled liquor	Mil. dol.	3,954	3,835	3,394	3,478	3,734	3,543	(NA)
Total employment	1,000	55.2	54.8	55.6	56.4	53.8	54.8	(NA)
2082 Malt beverages	1,000	33.1	33.1	34.5	35.3	33.5	32.6	(NA)
2084 Wines & brandy	1,000	14.6	14.2	14.0	14.1	13.7	15.3	(NA)
2085 Distilled liquor	1,000	7.5	7.5	7.1	7.0	6.6	6.9	(NA)
Production workers	1,000	36.4	36.3	36.7	37	34.9	36	(NA)
2082 Malt beverages	1,000	23.9	24.1	25.1	25.3	23.6	23.6	(NA)
2084 Wines & brandy	1,000	7.2	6.9	6.5	6.6	6.6	7.5	(NA)
2085 Distilled liquor	1,000	5.3	5.3	5.1	5.1	4.7	4.9	(NA)
Average hourly earnings	Dollar	18.47	19.26	19.83	19.81	20.15	20.37	(NA)
2082 Malt beverages	Dollar	21.48	22.49	22.89	22.71	23.01	23.89	(NA)
2084 Wines & brandy	Dollar	12.09	12.26	12.68	12.8	13.53	13.03	(NA)
2085 Distilled liquor	Dollar	13.89	14.44	15.05	15.49	15.43	15.59	(NA)
Capital expenditures	Mil. dol.	731	871	736	668	754	1,138	(NA)
2082 Malt beverages	Mil. dol.	578	702	565	479	564	861	(NA)
2084 Wines & brandy	Mil. dol.	115	105	115	146	151	209	(NA)
2085 Distilled liquor	Mil. dol.	38.7	63.9	56.3	42.1	39.7	67.3	(NA)
PRODUCT DATA								
Value of shipments [2]	Mil. dol.	21,864	22,758	24,607	24,324	24,370	25,169	(NA)
2082 Malt beverages	Mil. dol.	15,111	15,887	17,302	16,629	16,714	17,101	(NA)
2084 Wines & brandy	Mil. dol.	3,505	3,467	4,050	4,355	4,196	4,578	(NA)
2085 Distilled liquor	Mil. dol.	3,248	3,404	3,255	3,340	3,460	3,490	(NA)
Value of shipments (1992 dollars)	Mil. dol.	23,493	23,186	24,607	24,326	24,718	24,753	(NA)
2082 Malt beverages	Mil. dol.	16,179	16,178	17,302	16,763	17,231	17,016	(NA)
2084 Wines & brandy	Mil. dol.	3,701	3,545	4,050	4,308	4,163	4,506	(NA)
2085 Distilled liquor	Mil. dol.	3,613	3,463	3,255	3,255	3,324	3,231	(NA)
TRADE DATA								
Value of imports	Mil. dol.	3,374	3,065	3,527	3,387	3,668	3,980	4,619
2082 Malt beverages	Mil. dol.	939	840	881	961	1,073	1,192	1,341
2084 Wines & brandy	Mil. dol.	1,129	1,094	1,347	1,152	1,268	1,402	1,724
2085 Distilled liquor	Mil. dol.	1,306	1,131	1,299	1,274	1,328	1,386	1,554
Value of exports	Mil. dol.	585	661	751	777	983	1,250	1,342
2082 Malt beverages	Mil. dol.	178	207	221	234	391	526	453
2084 Wines & brandy	Mil. dol.	134	155	182	184	201	246	330
2085 Distilled liquor	Mil. dol.	273	300	347	359	391	479	559

NA Not available. [1] Value of all products and services sold by establishments in the alcoholic beverages industry. [2] Value of products classified in the alcoholic beverages industry industry produced by all industries.

Source: *U.S. Department of Commerce*, Bureau of the Census, International Trade Administration (ITA).

No. 1395. Recent Trends in Textile Mill Products (SIC 22): 1990 to 1996

ITEM	Unit	1990	1991	1992	1993	1994	1995	1996
INDUSTRY DATA								
Value of shipments [1]	Mil. dol.	65,532	65,439	70,753	73,955	78,027	79,742	(NA)
Value of shipments (1992 dollars)	Mil. dol.	66,645	65,979	70,753	74,409	78,451	77,780	(NA)
Total employment	1,000	630	594	617	610	624	607	(NA)
Production workers	1,000	544	510	528	524	534	518	(NA)
Average hourly earnings	Dollar	7.99	8.17	8.62	8.92	9.29	9.40	(NA)
PRODUCT DATA								
Value of shipments [2]	Mil. dol.	64,966	65,266	70,008	73,216	77,249	79,092	(NA)
Value of shipments (1992 dollars)	Mil. dol.	66,125	65,807	70,008	73,662	77,686	77,130	(NA)
TRADE DATA								
Value of imports	Mil. dol.	4,888	5,375	5,843	6,161	6,534	6,965	7,169
Value of exports	Mil. dol.	3,636	4,101	4,467	4,667	5,151	5,696	6,177

NA Not available. [1] Value of all products and services sold by establishments in the textile mill products industry. [2] Value of products classified in the textile mill products industry produced by all industries.

Source: U.S. Department of Commerce, Bureau of the Census, International Trade Administration (ITA).

No. 1396. Recent Trends in Cotton, Manmade, and Wool Broadwoven Fabric Mills: 1990 to 1990

ITEM	Unit	1990	1991	1992	1993	1994	1995	1996
COTTON BROADWOVEN FABRIC MILLS (SIC 221)								
Industry data:								
Value of shipments [1]	Mil. dol.	5,244	5,583	5,811	5,990	6,172	6,675	(NA)
Value of shipments (1992 dollars)	Mil. dol.	5,474	5,756	5,811	5,925	6,027	6,267	(NA)
Total employment	1,000	61.9	65.0	55.9	55.0	55.0	55.5	(NA)
Production workers	1,000	54.9	57.8	50.1	49.9	50.0	50.1	(NA)
Average hourly earnings	Dollar	8.25	8.43	8.92	9.38	9.82	9.95	(NA)
Product data:								
Value of shipments [2]	Mil. dol.	5,286	5,498	5,708	5,863	6,084	6,586	(NA)
Value of shipments (1992 dollars)	Mil. dol.	5,518	5,668	5,708	5,799	5,942	6,183	(NA)
Trade data:								
Value of imports	Mil. dol.	1,120	1,277	1,475	1,525	1,482	1,614	1,507
Value of exports	Mil. dol.	503	542	579	621	705	813	881
MANMADE BROADWOVEN FABRIC MILLS (SIC 222)								
Industry data:								
Value of shipments [1]	Mil. dol.	8,448	8,153	8,767	9,145	9,605	9,838	(NA)
Value of shipments (1992 dollars)	Mil. dol.	8,603	8,345	8,767	9,303	10,005	10,039	(NA)
Total employment	1,000	84.5	77.2	87.2	85.8	81.5	80.3	(NA)
Production workers	1,000	73.7	67.3	76.7	75.0	71.4	69.7	(NA)
Average hourly earnings	Dollar	8.61	8.77	9.21	9.46	9.91	10.22	(NA)
Product data:								
Value of shipments [2]	Mil. dol.	8,133	7,898	8,500	8,853	9,442	9,688	(NA)
Value of shipments (1992 dollars)	Mil. dol.	8,282	8,084	8,500	9,006	9,836	9,865	(NA)
Trade data:								
Value of imports	Mil. dol.	1,241	1,381	1,468	1,541	1,586	1,550	1,598
Value of exports	Mil. dol.	756	791	891	974	1,049	1,099	1,209
WOOL BROADWOVEN FABRIC MILLS (SIC 223)								
Industry data:								
Value of shipments [1]	Mil. dol.	1,738	1,725	1,612	1,681	1,861	1,838	(NA)
Value of shipments (1992 dollars)	Mil. dol.	1,667	1,669	1,612	1,683	1,861	1,772	(NA)
Total employment	1,000	15.1	14.6	13.7	13.8	14.6	14.0	(NA)
Production workers	1,000	13	12.5	11.8	11.9	12.6	12.2	(NA)
Average hourly earnings	Dollar	8.34	8.36	8.46	8.87	9.7	9.89	(NA)
Product data:								
Value of shipments [2]	Mil. dol.	1,443	1,492	1,388	1,502	1,518	1,480	(NA)
Value of shipments (1992 dollars)	Mil. dol.	1,383	1,444	1,388	1,504	1,518	1,428	(NA)
Trade data:								
Value of imports	Mil. dol.	241	247	240	230	242	252	267
Value of exports	Mil. dol.	49	62.4	99.3	84.6	87.2	114	116

NA Not available. [1] Value of all products and services sold by establishments in this industry. [2] Value of products classified in this industry produced by all industries.

Source: U.S. Department of Commerce, Bureau of the Census, International Trade Administration (ITA).

No. 1397. Recent Trends in Broadwoven Fabric Mills (SIC 221, 222, 223): 1990 to 1996

ITEM	Unit	1990	1991	1992	1993	1994	1995	1996
INDUSTRY DATA								
Value of shipments [1]	Mil. dol.	15,431	15,460	16,190	16,816	17,638	18,349	(NA)
Value of shipments (1992 dollars)	Mil. dol.	15,744	15,770	16,190	16,911	17,894	18,079	(NA)
Total employment	1,000	162	157	157	155	151	150	(NA)
Production workers	1,000	142	138	139	137	134	132	(NA)
Average hourly earnings	Dollar	8.45	8.59	9.04	9.38	9.86	10.09	(NA)
PRODUCT DATA								
Value of shipments [2]	Mil. dol.	14,862	14,888	15,597	16,218	17,045	17,753	(NA)
Value of shipments (1992 dollars)	Mil. dol.	15,184	15,196	15,597	16,309	17,295	17,497	(NA)
TRADE DATA								
Value of imports	Mil. dol.	2,602	2,905	3,183	3,295	3,310	3,417	3,372
Value of exports	Mil. dol.	1,306	1,395	1,569	1,680	1,840	2,027	2,206

NA Not available. [1] Value of all products and services sold by establishments in the food and kindred products industry. [2] Value of products classified in the food and kindred products industry produced by all industries.

Source: U.S. Department of Commerce, Bureau of the Census, International Trade Administration (ITA).

No. 1398. Recent Trends in Carpets and Rugs, Weft, Lace, and Knit, and Yarn Spinning Mills: 1990 to 1996

ITEM	Unit	1990	1991	1992	1993	1994	1995	1996
CARPETS AND RUGS (SIC 227)								
Industry data:								
Value of shipments [1]	Mil. dol.	10,081	9,045	9,828	10,234	10,600	10,732	(NA)
Value of shipments (1992 dollars)	Mil. dol.	10,101	9,006	9,828	10,286	10,537	10,532	(NA)
Total employment	1,000	51.6	48.3	49.4	50.6	55.1	56.6	(NA)
Production workers	1,000	41.0	37.8	38.9	39.6	42.9	43.6	(NA)
Average hourly earnings	Dollar	8.01	8.33	8.83	9.17	9.54	9.58	(NA)
Product data:								
Value of shipments [2]	Mil. dol.	9,611	8,555	9,518	9,953	10,141	10,313	(NA)
Value of shipments (1992 dollars)	Mil. dol.	9,630	8,521	9,518	10,003	10,061	10,121	(NA)
Trade data:								
Value of imports	Mil. dol.	590	584	700	660	736	843	820
Value of exports	Mil. dol.	535	683	705	698	687	632	702
WEFT, LACE, AND WARP KNIT FABRIC MILLS (SIC 2257, 2258)								
Industry data:								
Value of shipments [1]	Mil. dol.	5,798	6,274	7,270	7,526	8,110	7,836	(NA)
Value of shipments (1992 dollars)	Mil. dol.	5,822	6,289	7,270	7,644	8,279	7,828	(NA)
Total employment	1,000	52.4	52.5	63.9	60.6	61.2	57.8	(NA)
Production workers	1,000	44.1	43.9	53.9	50.6	51.5	48.5	(NA)
Average hourly earnings	Dollar	8.16	8.17	8.54	8.9	9.43	9.51	(NA)
Product data:								
Value of shipments [2]	Mil. dol.	5,923	6,542	7,436	7,478	8,102	7,802	(NA)
Value of shipments (1992 dollars)	Mil. dol.	5,949	6,558	7,436	7,589	8,269	7,792	(NA)
Trade data:								
Value of imports	Mil. dol.	164	200	233	302	354	356	542
Value of exports	Mil. dol.	253	334	377	375	400	495	547
YARN SPINNING MILLS (SIC 2281)								
Industry data:								
Value of shipments [1]	Mil. dol.	7,150	7,123	7,669	7,618	7,999	8,474	(NA)
Value of shipments (1992 dollars)	Mil. dol.	7,236	7,109	7,669	7,960	8,289	8,340	(NA)
Total employment	1,000	74.3	68.9	68.7	65.6	66.1	64.4	(NA)
Production workers	1,000	66	62.5	62.6	59.7	60.2	58.9	(NA)
Average hourly earnings	Dollar	8.06	8.36	8.48	8.62	8.95	9.13	(NA)
Product data:								
Value of shipments [2]	Mil. dol.	7,551	7,519	7,756	7,898	8,196	8,619	(NA)
Value of shipments (1992 dollars)	Mil. dol.	7,843	7,504	7,756	8,041	8,493	8,483	(NA)
Trade data:								
Value of imports	Mil. dol.	234	264	321	337	388	400	420
Value of exports	Mil. dol.	175	202	169	146	209	299	327

NA Not available. [1] Value of all products and services sold by establishments in this industry. [2] Value of products classified in this industry produced by all industries.

Source: U.S. Department of Commerce, Bureau of the Census, International Trade Administration (ITA).

No. 1399. Recent Trends in Apparel and Other Textile Products (SIC 23): 1990 to 1996

ITEM	Unit	1990	1991	1992	1993	1994	1995	1996
INDUSTRY DATA								
Value of shipments [1]	Mil. dol.	66,637	68,309	71,658	74,010	76,979	78,097	(NA)
Value of shipments (1992 dollars)	Mil. dol.	69,371	69,578	71,658	73,323	76,010	76,546	(NA)
Total employment	1,000	1,010	982	985	980	954	950	(NA)
Production workers	1,000	857	832	824	825	799	794	(NA)
Average hourly earnings	Dollar	6.69	6.93	7.12	7.34	7.44	7.55	(NA)
PRODUCT DATA								
Value of shipments [2]	Mil. dol.	61,962	62,649	68,844	70,986	73,258	73,547	(NA)
Value of shipments (1992 dollars)	Mil. dol.	64,468	63,780	68,844	70,329	72,330	72,077	(NA)
TRADE DATA								
Value of imports	Mil. dol.	26,747	27,377	32,644	35,475	38,561	41,208	43,075
Value of exports	Mil. dol.	2,867	3,746	4,659	5,433	6,145	7,190	8,104

NA Not available. [1] Value of all products and services sold by establishments in the apparel and other textile products industry. [2] Value of products classified in the apparel and other textile products industry produced by all industries.

Source: U.S. Department of Commerce, Bureau of the Census, International Trade Administration (ITA).

No. 1400. Recent Trends in Selected Men's and Boys' Apparel (SIC 231, 2321, -3, -5, -6): 1990 to 1996

ITEM	Unit	1990	1991	1992	1993	1994	1995	1996
INDUSTRY DATA								
Value of shipments [1]	Mil. dol.	14,983	16,083	16,991	16,819	17,088	17,302	(NA)
2311 Men/boys' suits/coats	Mil. dol.	2,713	2,579	2,430	2,463	2,362	2,078	(NA)
2321 Men's and boys' shirts	Mil. dol.	4,389	4,696	5,921	5,012	5,082	5,201	(NA)
2323 Men's and boys' neckwear	Mil. dol.	517	556	618	619	705	666	(NA)
2325 Men/boys' trousers	Mil. dol.	5,853	6,780	6,519	7,056	7,226	7,494	(NA)
2326 Men/boys' work clothing	Mil. dol.	1,512	1,491	1,503	1,670	1,714	1,863	(NA)
Value of shipments (1992 dollars)	Mil. dol.	15,911	16,640	16,991	16,526	16,671	16,714	(NA)
2311 Men/boys' suits/coats	Mil. dol.	2,850	2,639	2,430	2,456	2,340	2,042	(NA)
2321 Men's and boys' shirts	Mil. dol.	4,724	4,888	5,921	4,936	5,017	5,119	(NA)
2323 Men's and boys' neckwear	Mil. dol.	538	565	618	611	695	648	(NA)
2325 Men/boys' trousers	Mil. dol.	6,226	7,042	6,519	6,869	6,975	7,156	(NA)
2326 Men/boys' work clothing	Mil. dol.	1,573	1,506	1,503	1,629	1,644	1,748	(NA)
Total employment	1,000	243.0	236.0	245.0	229.0	225.0	216.0	(NA)
2311 Men/boys' suits/coats	1,000	49.2	44.6	44.0	41.2	34.0	31.1	(NA)
2321 Men's and boys' shirts	1,000	70.8	70.3	84.4	72.7	73.8	70.9	(NA)
2323 Men's and boys' neckwear	1,000	7.5	6.5	7.5	6.3	6.2	5.4	(NA)
2325 Men/boys' trousers	1,000	83.0	82.3	78.9	78.5	82.2	79.6	(NA)
2326 Men/boys' work clothing	1,000	32.0	31.5	30.4	30.0	28.5	28.6	(NA)
Production workers	1,000	211	204	214	199	197	190	(NA)
2311 Men/boys' suits/coats	1,000	41.8	37.2	37.4	34.7	28.7	26.3	(NA)
2321 Men's and boys' shirts	1,000	62.5	62.1	74.2	64.1	67.0	64.3	(NA)
2323 Men's and boys' neckwear	1,000	6.0	5.2	5.8	4.8	4.6	4.0	(NA)
2325 Men/boys' trousers	1,000	72.6	72.2	69.8	68.4	71.9	70.6	(NA)
2326 Men/boys' work clothing	1,000	28.2	27.7	26.4	26.5	24.4	24.8	(NA)
Average hourly earnings	Dollar	6.76	7.00	6.94	7.21	7.18	7.45	(NA)
2311 Men/boys' suits/coats	Dollar	8.02	8.39	7.96	8.32	8.36	8.13	(NA)
2321 Men's and boys' shirts	Dollar	6.60	7.08	6.85	6.90	6.96	7.20	(NA)
2323 Men's/boys' neckwear	Dollar	7.48	8.32	7.39	8.43	9.21	9.82	(NA)
2325 Men/boys' trousers	Dollar	6.57	6.55	6.81	7.15	7.03	7.39	(NA)
2326 Men/boys' work clothing	Dollar	5.59	5.86	6.06	6.47	6.49	7.19	(NA)
PRODUCT DATA								
Value of shipments [2]	Mil. dol.	13,771	14,143	15,810	15,405	16,129	16,145	(NA)
2311 Men/boys' suits/coats	Mil. dol.	2,633	2,450	2,387	2,257	2,417	2,004	(NA)
2321 Men's and boys' shirts	Mil. dol.	3,740	3,915	5,318	4,632	4,709	4,797	(NA)
2323 Men's and boys' neckwear	Mil. dol.	498	525	544	529	594	616	(NA)
2325 Men/boys' trousers	Mil. dol.	5,544	5,911	6,065	6,338	6,636	6,807	(NA)
2326 Men/boys' work clothing	Mil. dol.	1,355	1,341	1,495	1,650	1,773	1,921	(NA)
Value of shipments (1992 dollars)	Mil. dol.	14,618	14,628	15,810	15,136	15,736	15,593	(NA)
2311 Men/boys' suits/coats	Mil. dol.	2,766	2,506	2,387	2,252	2,395	1,969	(NA)
2321 Men's and boys' shirts	Mil. dol.	4,026	4,074	5,318	4,563	4,649	4,721	(NA)
2323 Men's and boys' neckwear	Mil. dol.	518	533	544	521	586	600	(NA)
2325 Men/boys' trousers	Mil. dol.	5,898	6,158	6,065	6,190	6,405	6,502	(NA)
2326 Men/boys' work clothing	Mil. dol.	1,410	1,365	1,495	1,609	1,700	1,802	(NA)
TRADE DATA								
Value of imports	Mil. dol.	5,716	6,168	7,624	8,281	9,178	10,873	11,426
2311 Men/boys' suits/coats	Mil. dol.	650	678	789	824	964	1,042	1,134
2321 Men's and boys' shirts	Mil. dol.	2,792	3,039	4,028	4,519	4,917	5,875	6,006
2323 Men's and boys' neckwear	Mil. dol.	110	140	151	158	156	167	174
2325 Men/boys' trousers	Mil. dol.	2,164	2,310	2,657	2,780	3,151	3,789	4,113
2326 Men/boys' work clothing	Mil. dol.	(NA)	(NA)	(NA)	(NA)	(NA)	(NA)	(NA)
Value of exports	Mil. dol.	907	1,140	1,478	1,796	2,036	2,158	2,374
2311 Men/boys' suits/coats	Mil. dol.	129	161	197	237	292	269	284
2321 Men's and boys' shirts	Mil. dol.	268	333	457	595	721	842	919
2323 Men's and boys' neckwear	Mil. dol.	9.8	14.5	15.5	21.1	17.9	18.4	21.1
2325 Men/boys' trousers	Mil. dol.	500	631	809	942	1,006	1,029	1,170
2326 Men/boys' work clothing	Mil. dol.	(NA)	(NA)	(NA)	(NA)	(NA)	(NA)	(NA)

...e. [1] Value of all products and services sold by establishments in the selected men's and boys' apparel in... [2] products classified in the selected men's and boys' apparel industry produced by all industries.

...rtment of Commerce, Bureau of the Census, International Trade Administration (ITA).

No. 1401. Recent Trends in Men's and Boys' Underwear and Nightwear (SIC 2322): 1990 to 1996

ITEM	Unit	1990	1991	1992	1993	1994	1995	1996
INDUSTRY DATA								
Value of shipments [1]	Mil. dol.	750	742	820	581	664	718	(NA)
Value of shipments (1992 dollars)	Mil. dol.	764	755	820	578	660	711	(NA)
Total employment	1,000	15.5	12.0	14.2	11.3	10.5	8.0	(NA)
Production workers	1,000	14.6	11.1	13.1	10.5	10.1	7.5	(NA)
Average hourly earnings	Dollar	6.22	7.66	6.67	6.48	7.03	7.10	(NA)
PRODUCT DATA								
Value of shipments [2]	Mil. dol.	738	744	808	689	743	674	(NA)
Value of shipments (1992 dollars)	Mil. dol.	752	757	808	685	738	668	(NA)
TRADE DATA								
Value of imports	Mil. dol.	251	289	396	528	652	963	1,229
Value of exports	Mil. dol.	95.4	157.0	219.0	314.0	331.0	431.0	531.0

NA Not available. [1] Value of all products and services sold by establishments in the men's and boys' underwear and nightwear industry. [2] Value of products classified in the men's and boys' underwear and nightwear industry produced by all industries.

Source: U.S. Department of Commerce, Bureau of the Census, International Trade Administration (ITA).

No. 1402. Recent Trends in Selected Women's Outerwear (SIC 2331, 2335, 2337): 1990 to 1996

ITEM	Unit	1990	1991	1992	1993	1994	1995	1996
INDUSTRY DATA								
Value of shipments [1]	Mil. dol.	14,287	14,415	13,733	14,123	14,598	14,458	(NA)
2331 Women's/misses' blouses	Mil. dol.	3,862	3,973	3,970	4,012	4,147	3,771	(NA)
2335 Women's/misses' dresses	Mil. dol.	6,119	5,922	5,366	5,602	6,396	6,983	(NA)
2337 Women's suits and coats	Mil. dol.	4,306	4,520	4,397	4,509	4,055	3,704	(NA)
Value of shipments (1992 dollars)	Mil. dol.	14,865	14,610	13,733	14,063	14,599	14,642	(NA)
2331 Women's/misses' blouses	Mil. dol.	4,100	4,096	3,970	3,976	4,053	3,672	(NA)
2335 Women's/misses' dresses	Mil. dol.	6,321	5,957	5,366	5,597	6,507	7,206	(NA)
2337 Women's suits and coats	Mil. dol.	4,444	4,556	4,397	4,491	4,039	3,764	(NA)
Total employment	1,000	220	214	188	190	182	186	(NA)
2331 Women's/misses' blouses	1,000	65.4	60.8	56.1	52.9	51.8	47.6	(NA)
2335 Women's/misses' dresses	1,000	108.0	105.0	83.2	87.1	87.5	99.4	(NA)
2337 Women's suits and coats	1,000	46.6	49.0	48.3	49.6	43.1	38.8	(NA)
Production workers	1,000	187	182	156	159	151	155	(NA)
2331 Women's/misses' blouses	1,000	55.0	50.3	47.1	44.7	42.2	39.3	(NA)
2335 Women's/misses' dresses	1,000	94.8	91.3	71.0	74.5	74.8	85.1	(NA)
2337 Women's suits and coats	1,000	37.1	40.0	37.8	40.0	34.1	31.0	(NA)
Average hourly earnings	Dollar	6.27	6.57	6.88	7.02	7.09	7.00	(NA)
2331 Women's/misses' blouses	Dollar	5.99	6.11	6.44	6.96	6.61	6.55	(NA)
2335 Women's/misses' dresses	Dollar	6.07	6.49	6.82	6.71	7.10	6.94	(NA)
2337 Women's suits and coats	Dollar	7.16	7.31	7.56	7.64	7.68	7.75	(NA)
PRODUCT DATA								
Value of shipments [2]	Mil. dol.	12,817	12,805	13,581	14,275	14,400	14,041	(NA)
2331 Women's/misses' blouses	Mil. dol.	3,660	3,618	4,195	4,580	4,425	3,998	(NA)
2335 Women's/misses' dresses	Mil. dol.	5,746	5,443	5,278	5,431	6,042	6,364	(NA)
2337 Women's suits and coats	Mil. dol.	3,410	3,745	4,108	4,264	3,933	3,679	(NA)
Value of shipments (1992 dollars)	Mil. dol.	13,341	12,980	13,581	14,211	14,389	14,199	(NA)
2331 Women's/misses' blouses	Mil. dol.	3,886	3,730	4,195	4,539	4,325	3,893	(NA)
2335 Women's/misses' dresses	Mil. dol.	5,936	5,475	5,278	5,426	6,146	6,567	(NA)
2337 Women's suits and coats	Mil. dol.	3,519	3,775	4,108	4,247	3,918	3,739	(NA)
TRADE DATA								
Value of imports	Mil. dol.	6,190	6,119	7,073	7,718	7,960	8,430	8,943
2331 Women's/misses' blouses	Mil. dol.	3,005	2,923	3,501	3,864	3,948	3,906	3,980
2335 Women's/misses' dresses	Mil. dol.	1,028	981	1,054	1,130	1,339	1,688	1,870
2337 Women's suits and coats	Mil. dol.	2,157	2,215	2,518	2,724	2,673	2,836	3,093
Value of exports	Mil. dol.	291	362	519	590	591	714	725
2331 Women's/misses' blouses	Mil. dol.	80.6	101.0	171.0	213.0	243.0	342.0	339.0
2335 Women's/misses' dresses	Mil. dol.	50.9	65.0	98.3	105.0	103.0	113.0	115.0
2337 Women's suits and coats	Mil. dol.	159	197	250	272	245	259	272

NA Not available. Value of all products and services sold by establishments in the selected women's outerwear industry. [2] Value of products classified in the selected women's outerwear industry produced by all industries.

Source: U.S. Department of Commerce, Bureau of the Census, International Trade Administration (ITA).

No. 1403. Recent Trends in Women's and Children's Undergarments (SIC 234): 1990 to 1996

ITEM	Unit	1990	1991	1992	1993	1994	1995	1996
INDUSTRY DATA								
Value of shipments [1]	Mil. dol.	3,542	3,850	3,943	3,943	4,245	4,577	(NA)
2341 Women/child's underwear	Mil. dol.	2,418	2,494	2,368	2,155	2,438	2,494	(NA)
2342 Bras and allied garments	Mil. dol.	1,124	1,356	1,575	1,789	1,807	2,083	(NA)
Value of shipments (1992 dollars)	Mil. dol.	3,686	3,947	3,943	3,884	4,129	4,417	(NA)
2341 Women/child's underwear	Mil. dol.	2,514	2,561	2,368	2,135	2,390	2,431	(NA)
2342 Bras and allied garments	Mil. dol.	1,172	1,386	1,575	1,748	1,739	1,986	(NA)
Total employment	1,000	61.2	58.7	53.7	52.1	47.1	45.9	(NA)
2341 Women/child's underwear	1,000	49.5	47.9	41.6	38.0	33.5	30.2	(NA)
2342 Bras and allied garments	1,000	11.7	10.8	12.1	14.1	13.6	15.7	(NA)
Production workers	1,000	51.5	49.4	45.4	43.7	39.4	38.0	(NA)
2341 Women/child's underwear	1,000	42.9	41.5	35.8	33.0	29.0	26.3	(NA)
2342 Bras and allied garments	1,000	8.6	7.9	9.6	10.7	10.4	11.7	(NA)
Average hourly earnings	Dollar	6.17	6.43	6.74	6.89	6.70	7.01	(NA)
2341 Women/child's underwear	Dollar	6.1	6.28	6.46	6.54	6.51	6.96	(NA)
2342 Bras + allied garments	Dollar	6.52	7.22	7.8	7.93	7.22	7.09	(NA)
PRODUCT DATA								
Value of shipments [2]	Mil. dol.	3,322	3,660	3,821	3,587	3,917	4,221	(NA)
2341 Women/child's underwear	Mil. dol.	2,119	2,260	2,237	1,928	2,128	2,179	(NA)
2342 Bras and allied garments	Mil. dol.	1,203	1,400	1,584	1,659	1,789	2,041	(NA)
Value of shipments (1992 dollars)	Mil. dol.	3,457	3,752	3,821	3,532	3,808	4,070	(NA)
2341 Women/child's underwear	Mil. dol.	2,202	2,320	2,237	1,911	2,086	2,124	(NA)
2342 Bras and allied garments	Mil. dol.	1,254	1,431	1,584	1,621	1,722	1,946	(NA)
TRADE DATA								
Value of imports	Mil. dol.	1,079	1,256	1,519	1,787	2,067	2,443	2,492
2341 Women/child's underwear	Mil. dol.	727	829	985	1,168	1,342	1,540	1,646
2342 Bras and allied garments	Mil. dol.	352	427	534	619	725	903	845
Value of exports	Mil. dol.	266	355	407	466	521	654	650
2341 Women/child's underwear	Mil. dol.	95.9	136	155	186	222	267	274
2342 Bras and allied garments	Mil. dol.	170	219	252	280	299	387	376

NA Not available. [1] Value of all products and services sold by establishments in the women's and children's undergarments industry. [2] Value of products classified in the women's and children's undergarments industry produced by all industries.

Source: U.S. Department of Commerce, Bureau of the Census, International Trade Administration (ITA).

No. 1404. Recent Trends in Girls' and Children's Outerwear (SIC 236): 1990 to 1996

ITEM	Unit	1990	1991	1992	1993	1994	1995	1996
INDUSTRY DATA								
Value of shipments [1]	Mil. dol.	3,825	3,741	3,145	3,221	3,926	3,679	(NA)
2361 Child's dresses/blouses	Mil. dol.	1,784	1,881	1,619	1,567	1,716	1,631	(NA)
2369 Children's outerwear n.e.c.	Mil. dol.	2,041	1,860	1,525	1,655	2,210	2,048	(NA)
Value of shipments (1992 dollars)	Mil. dol.	3,961	3,785	3,145	3,203	3,932	3,670	(NA)
2361 Child's dresses/blouses	Mil. dol.	1,851	1,912	1,619	1,570	1,728	1,572	(NA)
2369 Children's outerwear n.e.c.	Mil. dol.	2,111	1,873	1,525	1,633	2,203	2,098	(NA)
Total employment	1,000	61.8	60.0	53.3	49.2	48.0	42.8	(NA)
2361 Child's dresses/blouses	1,000	29.4	30.8	23.9	23.1	19.5	17.3	(NA)
2369 Children's outerwear n.e.c.	1,000	32.4	29.2	29.4	26.1	28.5	25.5	(NA)
Production workers	1,000	51.3	50.6	43.6	39.8	38.4	34.2	(NA)
2361 Child's dresses/blouses	1,000	24.5	26.1	19.1	18.6	15.2	13.1	(NA)
2369 Children's outerwear n.e.c.	1,000	26.8	24.5	24.5	21.2	23.2	21.1	(NA)
Average hourly earnings	Dollar	5.65	5.90	6.36	6.63	6.78	6.54	(NA)
2361 Child's dresses/blouses	Dollar	5.93	6.13	6.49	6.24	6.53	6.33	(NA)
2369 Children's outerwear n.e.c	Dollar	5.43	5.68	6.26	6.97	6.96	6.65	(NA)
PRODUCT DATA								
Value of shipments [2]	Mil. dol.	3,648	3,592	3,503	3,452	3,636	3,563	(NA)
2361 Child's dresses/blouses	Mil. dol.	1,812	1,812	1,719	1,626	1,680	1,614	(NA)
2369 Children's outerwear n.e.c.	Mil. dol.	1,836	1,780	1,784	1,826	1,957	1,949	(NA)
Value of shipments (1992 dollars)	Mil. dol.	3,778	3,634	3,503	3,432	3,642	3,552	(NA)
2361 Child's dresses/blouses	Mil. dol.	1,880	1,841	1,719	1,629	1,692	1,554	(NA)
2369 Children's outerwear n.e.c.	Mil. dol.	1,898	1,792	1,784	1,803	1,951	1,997	(NA)
TRADE DATA								
Value of imports	Mil. dol.	6,487	6,694	8,016	8,196	8,926	8,890	9,191
2361 Child's dresses/blouses	Mil. dol.	-	-	-	-	-	-	-
2369 Children's outerwear n.e.c.	Mil. dol.	6,487	6,694	8,016	8,196	8,926	8,890	9,191
Value of exports	Mil. dol.	341	458	625	703	920	1,273	1,723
2361 Child's dresses/blouses	Mil. dol.	-	-	-	-	-	-	-
2369 Children's outerwear n.e.c.	Mil. dol.	341	458	625	703	920	1,273	1,723

- Represents or rounds to zero. NA Not available. [1] Value of all products and services sold by establishments in the girls' and children's outerwear industry. [2] Value of products classified in the girls' and children's outerwear industry produced by all industries.

Source: U.S. Department of Commerce, Bureau of the Census, International Trade Administration (ITA).

No. 1405. Recent Trends in Misc. Fabricated Textile Products (SIC 239): 1990 to 1996

ITEM	Unit	1990	1991	1992	1993	1994	1995	1996
INDUSTRY DATA								
Value of shipments [1]	Mil. dol.	17,675	17,660	19,118	20,264	21,738	22,365	(NA)
239A Homefurnishings	Mil. dol.	6,591	6,777	6,886	7,154	7,411	7,626	(NA)
239B Misc. textile products	Mil. dol.	11,084	10,883	12,232	13,110	14,327	14,739	(NA)
Value of shipments (1992 dollars)	Mil. dol.	18,300	17,906	19,118	20,022	21,300	21,541	(NA)
239A Homefurnishings	Mil. dol.	6,876	6,870	6,886	7,011	7,206	7,273	(NA)
239B Misc. textile products	Mil. dol.	11,424	11,037	12,232	13,012	14,094	14,267	(NA)
Total employment	1,000	192	190	211	212	222	229	(NA)
239A Homefurnishings	1,000	69.2	68.6	73.7	72.1	71.3	74.9	(NA)
239B Misc. textile products	1,000	123	122	137	140	151	154	(NA)
Production workers	1,000	157	154	168	171	179	182	(NA)
239A Homefurnishings	1,000	56.9	56.3	61	59.5	59	60.4	(NA)
239B Misc. textile products	1,000	99.8	98	107	112	120	122	(NA)
Average hourly earnings	Dollar	8.26	8.45	8.34	8.61	8.78	8.85	(NA)
239A Homefurnishings	Dollar	6.58	6.85	7.24	7.79	7.90	7.97	(NA)
239B Misc. textile products	Dollar	9.26	9.42	8.98	9.06	9.21	9.28	(NA)
PRODUCT DATA								
Value of shipments [2]	Mil. dol.	16,397	16,207	18,220	19,555	20,738	21,067	(NA)
239A Homefurnishings	Mil. dol.	6,013	6,100	6,540	6,980	7,230	7,227	(NA)
239B Misc. textile products	Mil. dol.	10,385	10,106	11,681	12,575	13,508	13,840	(NA)
Value of shipments (1992 dollars)	Mil. dol.	16,956	16,423	18,220	19,320	20,322	20,289	(NA)
239A Homefurnishings	Mil. dol.	6,275	6,184	6,540	6,840	7,031	6,895	(NA)
239B Misc. textile products	Mil. dol.	10,682	10,240	11,681	12,480	13,291	13,395	(NA)
TRADE DATA								
Value of imports	Mil. dol.	2,138	2,316	2,698	3,116	3,428	3,556	3,614
239A Homefurnishings	Mil. dol.	976	1,000	1,178	1,334	1,553	1,736	1,734
239B Misc. textile products	Mil. dol.	1,162	1,315	1,520	1,782	1,875	1,820	1,880
Value of exports	Mil. dol.	622	780	862	972	1,079	1,151	1,286
239A Homefurnishings	Mil. dol.	245	317	338	349	362	350	371
239B Misc. textile products	Mil. dol.	377	463	524	623	718	801	916

NA Not available. [1] Value of all products and services sold by establishments in the misc. fabricated textile products industry. The designation 239A represents SIC's 2391 and 2392; 239B represents SIC 239 less SIC's 2391 and 2392. [2] Value of products classified in the misc. fabricated textile products industry produced by all industries.

Source: U.S. Department of Commerce, Bureau of the Census, International Trade Administration (ITA).

No. 1406. Recent Trends in Logging and Sawmills and Planing Mills, General: 1990 to 1996

ITEM	Unit	1990	1991	1992	1993	1994	1995	1996
LOGGING (SIC 2411)								
Industry data:								
Value of shipments [1]	Mil. dol.	12,219	11,422	13,592	15,976	16,488	16,776	(NA)
Value of shipments (1992 dollars)	Mil. dol.	13,699	12,635	13,592	13,085	13,107	13,240	(NA)
Total employment	1,000	82.7	77.2	83.2	86.2	87.0	86.8	(NA)
Production workers	1,000	68.1	64.3	69.2	71.6	71.7	71.0	(NA)
Average hourly earnings	Dollar	9.66	9.98	10.01	9.86	9.98	10.41	(NA)
Capital expenditures	Mil. dol.	432	322	374	366	472	592	(NA)
Product data:								
Value of shipments [2]	Mil. dol.	11,572	10,728	12,962	15,362	15,648	15,949	(NA)
Value of shipments (1992 dollars)	Mil. dol.	12,973	11,868	12,962	12,581	12,439	12,588	(NA)
Trade data:								
Value of imports	Mil. dol.	210	199	219	265	273	293	291
Value of exports	Mil. dol.	2,930	2,715	2,749	3,077	2,915	3,026	2,851
SAWMILLS AND PLANING MILLS, GENERAL (SIC 2421)								
Industry data:								
Value of shipments [1]	Mil. dol.	17,909	17,468	21,061	24,480	26,964	25,798	(NA)
Value of shipments (1992 dollars)	Mil. dol.	20,873	20,052	21,061	19,862	21,181	21,641	(NA)
Total employment	1,000	136	128	138	142	142	143	(NA)
Production workers	1,000	123	114	118	122	122	122	(NA)
Average hourly earnings	Dollar	9.34	9.49	9.65	9.83	9.97	10.22	(NA)
Capital expenditures	Mil. dol.	555	511	459	548	694	849	(NA)
Product data:								
Value of shipments [2]	Mil. dol.	17,862	17,515	20,347	23,641	26,001	24,927	(NA)
Value of shipments (1992 dollars)	Mil. dol.	20,818	20,109	20,347	19,004	20,425	20,912	(NA)
Trade data:								
Value of imports	Mil. dol.	2,659	2,638	3,472	5,022	6,039	5,505	6,813
Value of exports	Mil. dol.	2,128	2,203	2,323	2,450	2,428	2,412	2,393

NA Not available. [1] Value of all products and services sold by establishments in this industry. [2] Value of products classified in this industry produced by all industries.

Source: U.S. Department of Commerce, Bureau of the Census, International Trade Administration (ITA).

No. 1407. Recent Trends in Hardwood Veneer and Softwood Veneer: 1990 to 1996

ITEM	Unit	1990	1991	1992	1993	1994	1995	1996
HARDWOOD VENEER AND PLYWOOD (SIC 2435)								
Industry data:								
Value of shipments [1]	Mil. dol.	2,050	1,894	2,238	2,537	2,609	2,647	(NA)
Value of shipments (1992 dollars)	Mil. dol.	2,116	1,975	2,238	2,369	2,296	2,278	(NA)
Total employment	1,000	18.5	17.1	19.9	19.8	21.9	22.1	(NA)
Production workers	1,000	15.5	14.5	16.9	16.8	18.8	18.8	(NA)
Average hourly earnings	Dollar	7.94	8.18	8.12	8.55	8.21	8.72	(NA)
Capital expenditures	Mil. dol.	43.3	50.0	45.1	46.6	52.5	32.4	(NA)
Product data:								
Value of shipments [2]	Mil. dol.	1,879	1,743	2,023	2,305	2,444	2,518	(NA)
Value of shipments (1992 dollars)	Mil. dol.	1,939	1,817	2,023	2,152	2,151	2,167	(NA)
Trade data:								
Value of imports	Mil. dol.	888	588	729	857	890	924	997
Value of exports	Mil. dol.	230	248	278	297	348	376	369
SOFTWOOD VENEER AND PLYWOOD (SIC 2436)								
Industry data:								
Value of shipments [1]	Mil. dol.	5,026	4,587	5,350	6,035	6,544	6,867	(NA)
Value of shipments (1992 dollars)	Mil. dol.	5,440	5,013	5,350	5,721	5,822	5,866	(NA)
Total employment	1,000	35.3	31.3	30.9	30.7	30.3	32.3	(NA)
Production workers	1,000	31.8	28.1	27.7	27.7	27.2	29.0	(NA)
Average hourly earnings	Dollar	10.57	10.97	11.06	11.42	11.83	12.17	(NA)
Capital expenditures	Mil. dol.	110	95	95	118	150	185	(NA)
Product data:								
Value of shipments [2]	Mil. dol.	4,412	3,972	4,778	5,321	5,700	5,947	(NA)
Value of shipments (1992 dollars)	Mil. dol.	4,775	4,341	4,778	5,044	5,071	5,083	(NA)
Trade data:								
Value of imports	Mil. dol.	44.3	35.5	59.0	76.9	96.4	99.3	88.4
Value of exports	Mil. dol.	326	275	336	369	323	334	317

NA Not available. [1] Value of all products and services sold by establishments in this industry. [2] Value of products classified in this industry produced by all industries.

Source: U.S. Department of Commerce, Bureau of the Census, International Trade Administration (ITA).

No. 1408. Recent Trends in Reconstituted Wood Products (SIC 2493): 1990 to 1996

ITEM	Unit	1990	1991	1992	1993	1994	1995	1996
INDUSTRY DATA								
Value of shipments [1]	Mil. dol.	3,040	3,037	3,986	4,669	5,344	5,196	(NA)
Value of shipments (1992 dollars)	Mil. dol.	3,197	3,177	3,986	4,180	4,356	4,252	(NA)
Total employment	1,000	22.1	20.7	22.8	23.5	24.3	24.9	(NA)
Production workers	1,000	17.9	16.8	18.6	19.2	19.7	20.3	(NA)
Average hourly earnings	Dollar	10.56	10.91	11.49	11.72	11.85	11.88	(NA)
Capital expenditures	Mil. dol.	138	206	143	171	333	354	(NA)
PRODUCT DATA								
Value of shipments [2]	Mil. dol.	3,050	3,046	3,987	4,658	5,338	5,146	(NA)
Value of shipments (1992 dollars)	Mil. dol.	3,207	3,186	3,987	4,170	4,350	4,211	(NA)
TRADE DATA								
Value of imports	Mil. dol.	262	234	402	581	834	963	1,067
Value of exports	Mil. dol.	214	225	244	256	292	306	306

NA Not available. [1] Value of all products and services sold by establishments in the reconstituted wood products industry. [2] Value of products classified in the reconstituted wood products industry produced by all industries.

Source: U.S. Department of Commerce, Bureau of the Census, International Trade Administration (ITA).

No. 1409. Recent Trends in Household Furniture (SIC 251): 1990 to 1996

ITEM	Unit	1990	1991	1992	1993	1994	1995	1996
INDUSTRY DATA								
Value of shipments [1]	Mil. dol.	19,837	19,396	20,507	21,906	23,603	24,613	(NA)
2511 Wood furniture, house	Mil. dol.	8,271	7,938	8,730	9,267	9,921	10,236	(NA)
2512 Upholstered furniture, house	Mil. dol.	5,793	5,828	6,231	6,690	7,458	7,922	(NA)
2514 Metal furniture, house	Mil. dol.	2,176	2,079	1,955	2,141	2,126	2,007	(NA)
2515 Mattresses and bedsprings	Mil. dol.	2,894	2,907	2,821	3,001	3,255	3,477	(NA)
2517 Wood TV & radio cabinets	Mil. dol.	246	234	319	315	391	466	(NA)
2519 Other furniture	Mil. dol.	457	410	451	493	451	505	(NA)
Value of shipments (1992 dollars)	Mil. dol.	20,614	19,697	20,507	21,376	22,355	22,667	(NA)
2511 Wood furniture, house	Mil. dol.	8,725	8,141	8,730	8,911	9,136	9,107	(NA)
2512 Upholstered furniture, house	Mil. dol.	5,965	5,875	6,231	6,591	7,206	7,480	(NA)
2514 Metal furniture, house	Mil. dol.	2,259	2,117	1,955	2,118	2,070	1,901	(NA)
2515 Mattresses and bedsprings	Mil. dol.	2,929	2,919	2,821	2,953	3,115	3,277	(NA)
2517 Wood TV & radio cabinets	Mil. dol.	249	235	319	311	381	480	(NA)
2519 Other furniture	Mil. dol.	467	410	451	492	448	472	(NA)
Total employment	1,000	272	255	253	255	267	272	(NA)
Production workers	1,000	228	213	213	217	229	232	(NA)
Average hourly earnings	Dollar	7.63	8.04	8.36	8.77	8.83	8.93	(NA)
Capital expenditures	Mil. dol.	345	294	346	393	436	532	(NA)
2511 Wood furniture, house	Mil. dol.	184	166	197	238	257	272	(NA)
2512 Upholstered furniture, house	Mil. dol.	72.6	49.4	73.9	70.2	79.6	84.2	(NA)
2514 Metal furniture, house	Mil. dol.	35.5	33.8	29.2	27.1	49.8	115	(NA)
2515 Mattresses and bedsprings	Mil. dol.	28	36.1	30.9	38.6	29.5	36.4	(NA)
2517 Wood TV & radio cabinets	Mil. dol.	6.1	3.7	3.7	5.8	6.4	7.9	(NA)
2519 Other furniture	Mil. dol.	18.7	7.5	10.8	13.9	13.7	16.4	(NA)
PRODUCT DATA								
Value of shipments [2]	Mil. dol.	19,233	18,842	19,517	20,825	22,690	23,622	(NA)
2511 Wood furniture, house	Mil. dol.	7,847	7,592	7,976	8,396	9,251	9,281	(NA)
2512 Upholstered furniture, house	Mil. dol.	5,392	5,402	5,811	6,235	7,125	7,614	(NA)
2514 Metal furniture, house	Mil. dol.	2,054	1,962	1,792	1,967	1,882	1,916	(NA)
2515 Mattresses and bedsprings	Mil. dol.	3,185	3,182	3,079	3,282	3,528	3,794	(NA)
2517 Wood TV & radio cabinets	Mil. dol.	313	292	376	435	468	523	(NA)
2519 Other furniture	Mil. dol.	442	392	483	520	437	494	(NA)
Value of shipments (1992 dollars)	Mil. dol.	19,973	19,130	19,517	20,331	21,499	21,804	(NA)
2511 Wood furniture, house	Mil. dol.	8,278	7,787	7,976	8,075	8,518	8,257	(NA)
2512 Upholstered furniture, house	Mil. dol.	5,570	5,446	5,811	6,143	6,884	7,190	(NA)
2514 Metal furniture, house	Mil. dol.	2,133	2,019	1,792	1,936	1,833	1,815	(NA)
2515 Mattresses and bedsprings	Mil. dol.	3,224	3,195	3,079	3,230	3,376	3,576	(NA)
2517 Wood TV & radio cabinets	Mil. dol.	316	293	376	429	457	505	(NA)
2519 Other furniture	Mil. dol.	452	392	483	519	432	462	(NA)
TRADE DATA								
Value of imports	Mil. dol.	2,738	2,729	2,995	3,397	3,965	4,448	4,988
Value of exports	Mil. dol.	756	955	1,113	1,184	1,307	1,320	1,326

NA Not available. [1] Value of all products and services sold by establishments in the household furniture industry. [2] Value of products classified in the household furniture industry produced by all industries.

Source: U.S. Department of Commerce, Bureau of the Census, International Trade Administration (ITA).

No. 1410. Recent Trends in Office Furniture (SIC 252): 1990 to 1996

ITEM	Unit	1990	1991	1992	1993	1994	1995	1996
INDUSTRY DATA								
Value of shipments [1]	Mil. dol.	7,999	7,224	7,979	8,265	8,664	8,943	(NA)
Value of shipments (1992 dollars)	Mil. dol.	8,146	7,207	7,979	8,142	8,169	8,203	(NA)
Total employment	1,000	74.1	65.0	68.0	69.5	69.6	69.5	(NA)
Production workers	1,000	54.7	46.9	50.5	52.2	53.3	53.7	(NA)
Average hourly earnings	Dollar	10.77	11.03	10.85	11.19	11.07	11.70	(NA)
Capital expenditures	Mil. dol.	291	171	200	235	243	303	(NA)
PRODUCT DATA								
Value of shipments [2]	Mil. dol.	7,680	7,130	7,676	7,885	8,428	8,901	(NA)
Value of shipments (1992 dollars)	Mil. dol.	8,034	7,116	7,676	7,766	7,948	8,163	(NA)
TRADE DATA								
Value of imports	Mil. dol.	9.9	13.2	13.3	12.1	9.1	12.6	11.6
Value of exports	Mil. dol.	5.4	5.3	5.7	5.9	6.0	8.7	7.2

NA Not available. Value of all products and services sold by establishments in the office furniture industry. [2] Value of products classified in the office furniture industry produced by all industries.

Source: U.S. Department of Commerce, Bureau of the Census, International Trade Administration (ITA).

No. 1411. Recent Trends in Household Consumer Durables (SIC 251, 3524, 363, 3651): 1990 to 1996

ITEM	Unit	1990	1991	1992	1993	1994	1995	1996
INDUSTRY DATA								
Value of shipments [1]	Mil. dol.	49,944	49,379	53,098	57,329	63,369	65,254	(NA)
Value of shipments (1992 dollars)	Mil. dol.	51,009	49,694	53,098	56,702	61,832	63,208	(NA)
Total employment	1,000	435	412	412	416	434	441	(NA)
Production workers	1,000	358	335	339	345	363	366	(NA)
Average hourly earnings	Dollar	8.66	8.99	9.30	9.69	9.73	9.87	(NA)
Capital expenditures	Mil. dol.	1,082	1,175	1,280	1,178	1,301	1,560	(NA)
PRODUCT DATA								
Value of shipments [2]	Mil. dol.	47,167	46,363	48,314	51,650	56,958	57,999	(NA)
Value of shipments (1992 dollars)	Mil. dol.	48,137	46,640	48,314	51,086	55,514	56,077	(NA)
TRADE DATA								
Value of imports	Mil. dol.	17,340	17,904	20,413	21,627	25,298	27,308	28,952
Value of exports	Mil. dol.	5,181	5,923	6,544	7,100	7,788	8,098	8,431

NA Not available. [1] Value of all products and services sold by establishments in the househol consumer durables industry. [2] Value of products classified in the household consumer durables industry produced by all industries.

Source: U.S. Department of Commerce, Bureau of the Census, International Trade Administration (ITA).

No. 1412. Recent Trends in Paper and Allied Products (SIC 26): 1990 to 1996

ITEM	Unit	1990	1991	1992	1993	1994	1995	1996
INDUSTRY DATA								
Value of shipments [1]	Mil. dol.	132,424	130,131	133,201	133,262	143,649	172,636	(NA)
Value of shipments (1992 dollars)	Mil. dol.	129,041	129,289	133,201	135,076	141,329	141,416	(NA)
Total employment	1,000	631	625	627	626	622	630	(NA)
Production workers	1,000	480	477	479	479	480	486	(NA)
Average hourly earnings	Dollar	12.97	13.39	13.81	14.09	14.52	14.74	(NA)
Capital expenditures	Mil. dol.	10,957	9,206	7,963	7,370	7,731	8,219	(NA)
PRODUCT DATA								
Value of shipments [2]	Mil. dol.	127,526	124,658	128,941	128,695	138,540	166,827	(NA)
Value of shipments (1992 dollars)	Mil. dol.	124,086	123,906	128,941	130,568	136,386	136,292	(NA)
TRADE DATA								
Value of imports	Mil. dol.	11,737	10,512	10,461	10,891	11,772	16,757	14,784
Value of exports	Mil. dol.	8,671	9,263	10,042	9,456	11,000	14,943	14,002

NA Not available. [1] Value of all products and services sold by establishments in the paper and allied products industry. [2] Value of products classified in the paper and allied products produced by all industries.

Source: U.S. Department of Commerce, Bureau of the Census, International Trade Administration (ITA).

No. 1413. Recent Trends in Pulp Mills and Paper and Paperboard Mills: 1990 to 1996

ITEM	Unit	1990	1991	1992	1993	1994	1995	1996
PULP MILLS (SIC 2611)								
Industry data:								
Value of shipments [1]	Mil. dol.	6,265	5,363	5,466	4,282	4,827	6,924	(NA)
Value of shipments (1992 dollars)	Mil. dol.	4,812	5,243	5,466	4,899	5,141	4,561	(NA)
Total employment	1,000	16.3	17.1	15.9	14.2	13.3	13.4	(NA)
Production workers	1,000	12.4	13.0	12.1	10.8	10.2	10.4	(NA)
Average hourly earnings	Dollar	17.46	18.31	19.15	19.49	20.08	20.17	(NA)
Capital expenditures	Mil. dol.	1,049	985	772	426	315	462	(NA)
Product data:								
Value of shipments [2]	Mil. dol.	6,917	5,741	6,104	4,995	5,952	8,755	(NA)
Value of shipments (1992 dollars)	Mil. dol.	5,313	5,612	6,104	5,715	6,339	5,767	(NA)
Trade data:								
Value of imports	Mil. dol.	2,851	2,142	2,104	1,868	2,285	3,745	2,601
Value of exports	Mil. dol.	3,288	2,920	3,236	2,482	2,954	4,698	3,358
PAPER AND PAPERBOARD MILLS (SIC 262, 263)								
Industry data:								
Value of shipments [1]	Mil. dol.	51,296	48,427	48,926	48,267	53,381	69,649	(NA)
Value of shipments (1992 dollars)	Mil. dol.	48,998	47,612	48,926	48,625	52,187	53,505	(NA)
Total employment	1,000	183	181	182	180	177	176	(NA)
Production workers	1,000	139	138	140	138	136	135	(NA)
Average hourly earnings	Dollar	17.15	17.57	17.97	18.22	19.17	19.80	(NA)
Capital expenditures	Mil. dol.	7,325	5,883	4,952	4,507	4,960	4,837	(NA)
Product data:								
Value of shipments [2]	Mil. dol.	49,701	47,148	47,232	46,513	51,104	66,557	(NA)
Value of shipments (1992 dollars)	Mil. dol.	47,499	46,414	47,232	46,866	49,939	51,110	(NA)
Trade data:								
Value of imports	Mil. dol.	7,390	6,925	6,736	7,224	7,371	10,236	9,154
Value of exports	Mil. dol.	3,449	4,056	4,263	4,190	4,813	6,437	6,339

NA Not available. [1] Value of all products and services sold by establishments in this industry. [2] Value of products classified in this industry produced by all industries.

Source: U.S. Department of Commerce, Bureau of the Census, International Trade Administration (ITA).

No. 1414. Recent Trends in Printing and Publishing (SIC 27): 1990 to 1996

ITEM	Unit	1990	1991	1992	1993	1994	1995	1996
INDUSTRY DATA								
Value of shipments [1]	Mil. dol.	159,749	160,271	166,153	172,633	176,876	188,439	(NA)
2711 Newspapers	Mil. dol.	35,235	34,474	33,782	34,651	36,091	37,732	(NA)
2721 Periodicals	Mil. dol.	20,746	20,811	22,104	22,653	21,892	23,905	(NA)
2731 Book publishing	Mil. dol.	15,560	16,976	16,696	18,616	19,695	20,604	(NA)
2732 Book printing	Mil. dol.	4,203	4,235	4,681	4,810	4,745	5,425	(NA)
2741 Misc publishing	Mil. dol.	9,027	9,965	10,906	11,807	11,976	11,992	(NA)
275 Commercial printing	Mil. dol.	53,810	53,137	56,229	58,173	60,411	65,093	(NA)
2761 Manifold business forms	Mil. dol.	7,941	7,399	7,429	7,491	6,958	7,911	(NA)
2771 Greeting cards	Mil. dol.	3,764	3,897	4,190	4,275	4,546	4,726	(NA)
2782 Blankbooks and binders	Mil. dol.	3,241	3,317	3,758	3,771	4,276	4,539	(NA)
2789 Bookbinding	Mil. dol.	1,367	1,359	1,291	1,258	1,367	1,512	(NA)
279 Printing trade services	Mil. dol.	4,796	4,681	5,065	5,129	4,920	5,000	(NA)
Value of shipments (1992 dollars)	Mil. dol.	171,458	165,225	166,153	167,488	167,296	168,855	(NA)
2711 Newspapers	Mil. dol.	39,769	36,441	33,782	33,222	33,294	32,810	(NA)
2721 Periodicals	Mil. dol.	23,415	21,999	22,104	22,122	21,009	22,279	(NA)
2731 Book publishing	Mil. dol.	16,825	17,519	16,696	18,197	18,476	18,380	(NA)
2732 Book printing	Mil. dol.	4,629	4,586	4,681	4,753	4,625	5,047	(NA)
2741 Misc publishing	Mil. dol.	9,974	10,412	10,906	11,309	11,058	10,641	(NA)
275 Commercial printing	Mil. dol.	55,123	53,478	56,229	56,774	58,262	59,494	(NA)
2761 Manifold business forms	Mil. dol.	7,770	7,261	7,429	7,027	6,240	5,792	(NA)
2771 Greeting cards	Mil. dol.	4,118	4,030	4,190	4,040	4,016	3,969	(NA)
2782 Blankbooks and binders	Mil. dol.	3,507	3,392	3,758	3,697	4,096	4,074	(NA)
2789 Bookbinding	Mil. dol.	1,425	1,364	1,291	1,249	1,343	1,433	(NA)
279 Printing trade services	Mil. dol.	4,903	4,741	5,065	5,096	4,878	4,918	(NA)

NA Not available. Value of all products and services sold by establishments in the printing and publishing industry.

Source: U.S. Department of Commerce, Bureau of the Census, International Trade Administration (ITA).

No. 1415. Recent Trends in Periodicals, Book Publishing, and Commercial Printing: 1990 to 1996

ITEM	Unit	1990	1991	1992	1993	1994	1995	1996
PERIODICALS (SIC 2721)								
Industry data:								
Value of shipments [1]	Mil. dol.	20,746	20,811	22,104	22,653	21,892	23,905	(NA)
Value of shipments (1992 dollars)	Mil. dol.	23,415	21,999	22,104	22,122	21,009	22,279	(NA)
Total employment	1,000	117	113	115	117	117	123	(NA)
Production workers	1,000	21.9	21.1	20.2	19.7	18.2	18.0	(NA)
Average hourly earnings	Dollar	13.17	13.28	13.4	12.51	12.78	13.49	(NA)
Capital expenditures	Mil. dol.	289	241	235	290	306	332	(NA)
Product data:								
Value of shipments [2]	Mil. dol.	19,256	19,424	20,942	21,892	21,642	23,080	(NA)
Value of shipments (1992 dollars)	Mil. dol.	21,733	20,533	20,942	21,183	20,769	21,509	(NA)
Trade data:								
Value of imports	Mil. dol.	122	121	134	194	209	222	217
Value of exports	Mil. dol.	668	705	732	737	789	825	819
BOOK PUBLISHING (SIC 2731)								
Industry data:								
Value of shipments [1]	Mil. dol.	15,560	16,976	16,696	18,616	19,695	20,604	(NA)
Value of shipments (1992 dollars)	Mil. dol.	16,825	17,519	16,696	18,197	18,476	18,380	(NA)
Total employment	1,000	74.5	78.8	79	83.2	83.5	83.6	(NA)
Production workers	1,000	17.5	17.4	18.2	18.2	18.2	18.5	(NA)
Average hourly earnings	Dollar	11.74	12.78	12.51	12.90	13.56	13.61	(NA)
Capital expenditures	Mil. dol.	346	357	327	282	283	353	(NA)
Product data:								
Value of shipments [2]	Mil. dol.	14,267	15,215	14,761	16,596	17,229	18,413	(NA)
Value of shipments (1992 dollars)	Mil. dol.	15,407	15,701	14,761	16,223	16,162	16,425	(NA)
Trade data:								
Value of imports	Mil. dol.	855	868	953	966	1,023	1,185	1,240
Value of exports	Mil. dol.	1,415	1,505	1,637	1,664	1,703	1,780	1,776
COMMERCIAL PRINTING (SIC 275)								
Industry data:								
Value of shipments [1]	Mil. dol.	53,810	53,137	56,229	58,173	60,411	65,093	(NA)
Value of shipments (1992 dollars)	Mil. dol.	55,123	53,478	56,229	56,774	58,262	59,494	(NA)
Total employment	1,000	589	567	567	572	577	604	(NA)
Production workers	1,000	427	409	408	415	417	440	(NA)
Average hourly earnings	Dollar	10.51	10.8	11.5	11.69	11.75	11.71	(NA)
Capital expenditures	Mil. dol.	2,336	2,215	2,144	2,238	2,706	2,663	(NA)
Product data:								
Value of shipments [2]	Mil. dol.	52,572	51,761	54,902	56,960	58,902	63,666	(NA)
Value of shipments (1992 dollars)	Mil. dol.	53,862	52,096	54,902	55,587	56,802	58,164	(NA)
Trade data:								
Value of imports	Mil. dol.	393	420	442	505	585	756	748
Value of exports	Mil. dol.	772	1,026	1,056	1,201	1,061	1,197	1,195

NA Not available. [1] Value of all products and services sold by establishments in this industry. [2] Value of products classified in this industry produced by all industries.

Source: U.S. Department of Commerce, Bureau of the Census, International Trade Administration (ITA).

No. 1416. Recent Trends in Chemicals and Allied Products (SIC 28): 1990 to 1996

ITEM	Unit	1990	1991	1992	1993	1994	1995	1996
INDUSTRY DATA								
Value of shipments [1]	Mil. dol.	292,803	298,544	305,420	314,907	333,905	362,126	(NA)
Value of shipments (1992 dollars)	Mil. dol.	305,527	302,217	305,420	307,610	317,570	323,643	(NA)
Total employment	1,000	869	867	849	836	823	839	(NA)
Production workers	1,000	489	484	479	474	472	467	(NA)
Average hourly earnings	Dollar	14.37	14.94	15.27	15.62	16.25	16.57	(NA)
Capital expenditures	Mil. dol.	15,645	16,599	16,381	15,690	15,411	17,627	(NA)
PRODUCT DATA								
Value of shipments [2]	Mil. dol.	266,505	268,935	282,242	292,416	309,592	336,065	(NA)
Value of shipments (1992 dollars)	Mil. dol.	278,546	271,468	282,242	285,755	294,562	301,340	(NA)
TRADE DATA								
Value of imports	Mil. dol.	21,732	23,138	26,008	27,259	31,697	36,079	42,626
Value of exports	Mil. dol.	38,056	41,869	42,129	42,742	46,950	57,897	58,503

NA Not available. [1] Value of all products and services sold by establishments in the chemicals and allied products industry. [2] Value of products classified in the chemicals and allied products industry produced by all industries.

Source: U.S. Department of Commerce, Bureau of the Census, International Trade Administration (ITA).

No. 1417. Recent Trends in Industrial Inorganic Chemicals, Except Pigments (SIC 2812, 2813, 2819): 1990 to 1996

ITEM	Unit	1990	1991	1992	1993	1994	1995	1996
INDUSTRY DATA								
Value of shipments [1]	Mil. dol.	23,649	23,792	24,012	23,063	21,676	23,509	(NA)
Value of shipments (1992 dollars)	Mil. dol.	23,922	23,652	24,012	22,771	20,929	21,348	(NA)
Total employment	1,000	92.5	95.8	94.6	85	77.9	73.1	(NA)
Production workers	1,000	49.5	51.1	49.3	44.1	41.0	40.3	(NA)
Average hourly earnings	Dollar	15.78	16.17	16.65	16.90	17.82	19.09	(NA)
PRODUCT DATA								
Value of shipments [2]	Mil. dol.	19,448	19,063	18,607	18,425	17,783	20,665	(NA)
Value of shipments (1992 dollars)	Mil. dol.	19,836	18,944	18,607	18,202	17,133	18,441	(NA)
TRADE DATA								
Value of imports	Mil. dol.	4,324	4,284	4,166	4,039	4,707	5,607	6,250
Value of exports	Mil. dol.	4,662	4,990	5,130	4,822	5,215	6,178	6,373

NA Not available. [1] Value of all products and services sold by establishments in the industrial inorganic chemicals., except pigments industry. [2] Value of products classified in the industrial inorganic chemicals, except pigments industry produced by all industries.

Source: U.S. Department of Commerce, Bureau of the Census, International Trade Administration (ITA).

No. 1418. Recent Trends in Petrochemicals (SIC 2821, 2822, 2824, 2843, 2865, 2869, 2873): 1990 to 1996

ITEM	Unit	1990	1991	1992	1993	1994	1995	1996
INDUSTRY DATA								
Value of shipments [1]	Mil. dol.	119,813	116,681	117,277	119,225	132,458	148,111	(NA)
Value of shipments (1992 dollars)	Mil. dol.	120,783	115,894	117,277	115,945	124,852	126,109	(NA)
Total employment	1,000	264	263	257	255	252	252	(NA)
Production workers	1,000	165	162	159	158	156	157	(NA)
Average hourly earnings	Dollar	16.53	17.06	17.62	17.93	18.63	19.1	(NA)
Capital expenditures	Mil. dol.	9,161	9,255	7,837	7,554	7,319	8,559	(NA)
PRODUCT DATA								
Value of shipments [2]	Mil. dol.	115,972	112,464	113,476	115,269	126,971	143,069	(NA)
Value of shipments (1992 dollars)	Mil. dol.	116,269	111,539	113,476	112,236	119,801	121,666	(NA)
TRADE DATA								
Value of imports	Mil. dol.	9,667	9,941	11,084	12,098	14,599	17,671	18,745
Value of exports	Mil. dol.	21,173	23,103	22,150	22,047	26,555	32,763	31,583

NA Not available. [1] Value of all products and services sold by establishments in the petrochemicals industry. [2] Value of products classified in the petrochemicals industry produced by all industries.

Source: U.S. Department of Commerce, Bureau of the Census, International Trade Administration (ITA).

No. 1419. Recent Trends in Plastics Materials and Resins and Synthetic Rubber: 1990 to 1996

ITEM	Unit	1990	1991	1992	1993	1994	1995	1996
PLASTIC MATERIALS AND RESINS (SIC 2821)								
Industry data:								
Value of shipments [1]	Mil. dol.	31,543	29,842	31,601	31,546	37,305	43,529	(NA)
Value of shipments (1992 dollars)	Mil. dol.	29,701	28,945	31,601	31,172	35,327	35,161	(NA)
Total employment	1,000	62.5	60.6	61.2	62.2	68.9	69.7	(NA)
Production workers	1,000	37.9	36.7	36.5	36.6	40.4	41.5	(NA)
Average hourly earnings	Dollars	16.90	17.27	18.61	18.75	19.39	19.97	(NA)
Capital expenditures	Mil. dol.	2,466	2,289	1,712	1,926	2,536	2,337	(NA)
Product data:								
Value of shipments [2]	Mil. dol.	33,038	31,723	33,299	33,589	38,043	44,009	(NA)
Value of shipments (1992 dollars)	Mil. dol.	31,109	30,769	33,299	33,191	36,025	35,548	(NA)
Trade data:								
Value of imports	Mil. dol.	1,811	1,775	2,062	2,518	3,280	4,084	4,176
Value of exports	Mil. dol.	6,263	7,383	7,007	7,181	8,427	10,337	10,587
SYNTHETIC RUBBER (SIC 2822)								
Industry data:								
Value of shipments [1]	Mil. dol.	4,239	4,127	4,235	4,739	4,964	5,942	(NA)
Value of shipments (1992 dollars)	Mil. dol.	4,007	4,098	4,235	4,623	4,755	4,931	(NA)
Total employment	1,000	11.4	11.5	11.9	12.2	11.9	12.0	(NA)
Production workers	1,000	7.2	7.4	7.6	7.7	7.7	8.0	(NA)
Average hourly earnings	Dollar	17.97	17.85	18.73	19.27	19.52	20.61	(NA)
Capital expenditures	Mil. dol.	383	366	321	256	266	268	(NA)
Product data:								
Value of shipments [2]	Mil. dol.	4,219	3,939	4,318	4,643	4,963	5,934	(NA)
Value of shipments (1992 dollars)	Mil. dol.	3,968	3,912	4,318	4,530	4,773	4,924	(NA)
Trade data:								
Value of imports	Mil. dol.	514	466	530	555	624	691	681
Value of exports	Mil. dol.	865	900	1,010	947	1,061	1,264	1,344

NA Not available. [1] Value of all products and services sold by establishments in this industry. [2] Value of products classified in this industry produced by all industries.

Source: U.S. Department of Commerce, Bureau of the Census, International Trade Administration (ITA).

No. 1420. Recent Trends in Man-Made Fibers (SIC 2823, 2824): 1990 to 1996

ITEM	Unit	1990	1991	1992	1993	1994	1995	1996
INDUSTRY DATA								
Value of shipments [1]	Mil. dol.	12,973	12,698	12,861	13,293	13,366	14,035	(NA)
Value of shipments (1992 dollars)	Mil. dol.	13,262	12,713	12,861	13,198	13,112	13,586	(NA)
Total employment	1,000	57.9	57.5	55.4	51.6	46.9	44.7	(NA)
Production workers	1,000	43.3	42.7	41.7	39.8	36.6	35.0	(NA)
Average hourly earnings	Dollar	13.65	14.50	14.22	14.63	14.23	14.87	(NA)
PRODUCT DATA								
Value of shipments [2]	Mil. dol.	11,191	10,930	10,924	11,092	11,779	12,460	(NA)
Value of shipments (1992 dollars)	Mil. dol.	11,438	10,938	10,924	11,017	11,623	12,094	(NA)
TRADE DATA								
Value of imports	Mil. dol.	703	784	907	1,127	1,302	1,384	1,401
Value of exports	Mil. dol.	1,627	1,694	1,473	1,407	1,594	2,078	2,113

NA Not available. [1] Value of all products and services sold by establishments in the man-made fibers industry. [2] Value of products classified in the man-made fibers industry produced by all industries.

Source: U.S. Department of Commerce, Bureau of the Census, International Trade Administration (ITA).

No. 1421. Recent Trends in Drugs (SIC 283): 1990 to 1996

ITEM	Unit	1990	1991	1992	1993	1994	1995	1996
INDUSTRY DATA								
Value of shipments [1]	Mil. dol.	56,715	64,829	67,792	70,965	75,804	80,884	(NA)
2833 Medicinals and botanicals	Mil. dol.	5,194	6,722	6,526	5,926	6,093	7,036	(NA)
2834 Pharmaceutical preps.	Mil. dol.	46,646	50,486	50,415	53,281	56,123	57,943	(NA)
2835 Diagnostic substances	Mil. dol.	2,599	5,058	6,857	6,864	8,278	9,676	(NA)
2836 Bio. prod. exc. diagnostic	Mil. dol.	2,276	2,564	3,993	4,914	5,310	6,227	(NA)
Value of shipments (1992 dollars)	Mil. dol.	64,964	68,803	67,792	68,216	71,108	73,813	(NA)
2833 Medicinals and botanicals	Mil. dol.	5,658	6,866	6,526	5,523	5,460	6,179	(NA)
2834 Pharmaceutical preps.	Mil. dol.	54,176	54,111	50,415	51,084	52,159	52,107	(NA)
2835 Diagnostic substances	Mil. dol.	2,725	5,156	6,857	6,796	8,253	9,506	(NA)
2836 Bio. prod. exc. diagnostic	Mil. dol.	2,406	2,670	3,993	4,813	5,237	6,022	(NA)
Total employment	1,000	197	203	194	200	205	218	(NA)
2833 Medicinals and botanicals	1,000	11.7	13.7	13.1	13.0	12.9	14.3	(NA)
2834 Pharmaceutical preps.	1,000	155	142	123	128	133	142	(NA)
2835 Diagnostic substances	1,000	16.0	33.5	39.9	39.3	39.1	39.8	(NA)
2836 Bio. prod. exc. diagnostic	1,000	14.3	13.3	18.5	19.0	19.8	21.1	(NA)
Production workers	1,000	86.8	90.1	92.7	94.6	102.0	113.0	(NA)
2833 Medicinals and botanicals	1,000	6.9	7.8	7.5	7.7	7.5	7.7	(NA)
2834 Pharmaceutical preps.	1,000	65.7	64.6	62.4	62.8	68.0	78.3	(NA)
2835 Diagnostic substances	1,000	7.0	10.8	14.7	14.9	16.1	15.6	(NA)
2836 Bio prod ex diagnostic	1,000	7.2	6.9	8.1	9.2	9.9	11.0	(NA)
Average hourly earnings	Dollar	14.02	15.00	14.78	15.80	16.34	16.03	(NA)
2833 Medicinals and botanicals	Dollar	17.16	19.67	18.93	19.62	19.70	20.09	(NA)
2834 Pharmaceutical preps.	Dollar	14.48	14.41	14.71	15.81	16.11	15.40	(NA)
2835 Diagnostic substances	Dollar	11.68	17.80	14.09	15.64	17.23	18.31	(NA)
2836 Bio. prod. exc. diagnostic	Dollar	9.06	10.79	12.50	12.57	13.81	13.74	(NA)
Capital expenditures	Mil. dol.	2,557	3,038	3,867	4,047	4,034	4,526	(NA)
2833 Medicinals and botanicals	Mil. dol.	218	555	554	482	483	384	(NA)
2834 Pharmaceutical preps.	Mil. dol.	2,028	2,017	2,450	2,493	2,618	3,134	(NA)
2835 Diagnostic substances	Mil. dol.	165	344	588	667	573	556	(NA)
2836 Bio. prod. exc. diagnostic	Mil. dol.	146	123	295	405	361	453	(NA)
PRODUCT DATA								
Value of shipments [2]	Mil. dol.	47,831	51,880	60,793	63,970	67,751	71,416	(NA)
2833 Medicinals and botanicals	Mil. dol.	5,789	6,647	7,002	6,749	6,772	7,328	(NA)
2834 Pharmaceutical preps.	Mil. dol.	35,260	37,416	43,082	45,522	48,086	49,535	(NA)
2835 Diagnostic substances	Mil. dol.	4,234	4,973	6,196	6,453	7,179	8,271	(NA)
2836 Bio. prod. exc. diagnostic	Mil. dol.	2,529	2,844	4,512	5,246	5,715	6,282	(NA)
Value of shipments (1992 dollars)	Mil. dol.	54,393	54,924	60,793	61,462	63,550	65,180	(NA)
2833 Medicinals and botanicals	Mil. dol.	6,306	6,790	7,002	6,290	6,068	6,434	(NA)
2834 Pharmaceutical preps.	Mil. dol.	40,975	40,102	43,082	43,645	44,690	44,546	(NA)
2835 Diagnostic substances	Mil. dol.	4,438	5,070	6,196	6,389	7,157	8,125	(NA)
2836 Bio. prod. exc. diagnostic	Mil. dol.	2,673	2,963	4,512	5,138	5,636	6,075	(NA)
TRADE DATA								
Value of imports	Mil. dol.	3,884	4,812	5,958	6,094	6,966	8,583	11,161
2833 Medicinals and botanicals	Mil. dol.	2,303	2,854	3,277	3,101	3,366	4,632	6,121
2834 Pharmaceutical preps.	Mil. dol.	1,103	1,442	1,859	2,096	2,517	2,877	3,702
2835 Diagnostic substances	Mil. dol.	207	191	336	379	530	465	546
2836 Bio. prod. exc. diagnostic	Mil. dol.	271	325	486	518	553	608	792
Value of exports	Mil. dol.	5,050	5,731	6,774	7,222	7,565	7,996	8,889
2833 Medicinals and botanicals	Mil. dol.	1,909	2,064	2,444	2,401	2,281	2,445	2,511
2834 Pharmaceutical preps.	Mil. dol.	1,258	1,478	1,819	2,027	2,315	2,247	2,718
2835 Diagnostic substances	Mil. dol.	909	1,160	1,370	1,485	1,507	1,741	1,891
2836 Bio. prod. exc. diagnostic	Mil. dol.	974	1,028	1,142	1,309	1,462	1,563	1,769

NA Not available. [1] Value of all products and services sold by establishments in the drugs industry. [2] Value of products classified in the drugs industry produced by all industries.

Source: U.S. Department of Commerce, Bureau of the Census, International Trade Administration (ITA).

No. 1422. Recent Trends in Soap, Cleaners, and Toilet Goods (SIC 284): 1990 to 1996

ITEM	Unit	1990	1991	1992	1993	1994	1995	1996
INDUSTRY DATA								
Value of shipments [1]	Mil. dol.	41,725	42,245	42,875	46,903	46,548	50,158	(NA)
2841 Soap and other detergents	Mil. dol.	15,480	15,442	14,729	15,458	14,603	16,132	(NA)
2842 Polishes/sanitation goods	Mil. dol.	5,886	6,229	6,659	8,079	8,405	8,700	(NA)
2843 Surface active agents	Mil. dol.	3,190	3,330	2,859	3,661	3,721	4,887	(NA)
2844 Toilet preparations	Mil. dol.	17,166	17,245	18,629	19,706	19,820	20,439	(NA)
Value of shipments (1992 dollars)	Mil. dol.	43,279	43,103	42,875	46,174	45,873	48,789	(NA)
2841 Soap and other detergents	Mil. dol.	15,860	15,854	14,729	15,259	14,530	15,862	(NA)
2842 Polishes/sanitation goods	Mil. dol.	6,108	6,324	6,659	8,014	8,264	8,374	(NA)
2843 Surface active agents	Mil. dol.	3,316	3,346	2,859	3,599	3,609	4,554	(NA)
2844 Toilet preparations	Mil. dol.	17,994	17,579	18,629	19,301	19,469	19,999	(NA)
Total employment	1,000	126	123	123	124	119	123	(NA)
2841 Soap and other detergents	1,000	36.3	36.7	32.8	31.2	31.3	32.1	(NA)
2842 Polishes/sanitation goods	1,000	19.6	19.6	22.0	22.8	21.4	23.0	(NA)
2843 Surface active agents	1,000	9.1	9.3	8.2	8.6	8.1	8.0	(NA)
2844 Toilet preparations	1,000	61.2	57.5	59.8	61.7	58.1	59.5	(NA)
Production workers	1,000	77.8	75.7	74.5	74.6	71.1	73.7	(NA)
2841 Soap and other detergents	1,000	22.8	23.1	19.9	17.9	18.6	18.3	(NA)
2842 Polishes/sanitation goods	1,000	12.3	12.2	13.4	13.8	13.1	14.0	(NA)
2843 Surface active agents	1,000	4.6	4.8	4.2	4.3	3.9	4.0	(NA)
2844 Toilet preparations	1,000	38.1	35.6	37.0	38.6	35.5	37.4	(NA)
Average hourly earnings	Dollars	11.75	12.28	12.32	12.26	12.36	12.78	(NA)
2841 Soap and other detergents	Dollars	14.69	14.70	14.86	15.06	14.89	15.33	(NA)
2842 Polishes/sanitation goods	Dollars	10.66	11.13	11.84	11.94	11.12	11.49	(NA)
2843 Surface active agents	Dollars	13.75	14.33	15.09	15.95	16.80	16.35	(NA)
2844 Toilet preparations	Dollars	10.15	10.83	10.80	10.59	10.93	11.49	(NA)
Capital expenditures	Mil. dol.	1,029	1,245	1,290	1,320	1,334	1,051	(NA)
2841 Soap and other detergents	Mil. dol.	482	641	571	514	494	364	(NA)
2842 Polishes/sanitation goods	Mil. dol.	96	139	121	130	124	155	(NA)
2843 Surface active agents	Mil. dol.	167	160	92	203	225	122	(NA)
2844 Toilet preparations	Mil. dol.	284	304	506	473	491	410	(NA)
PRODUCT DATA								
Value of shipments [2]	Mil. dol.	38,634	38,695	39,999	43,293	42,622	45,670	(NA)
2841 Soap and other detergents	Mil. dol.	11,660	11,785	11,022	11,594	11,089	12,300	(NA)
2842 Polishes/sanitation goods	Mil. dol.	5,531	5,546	6,477	7,492	7,601	7,772	(NA)
2843 Surface active agents	Mil. dol.	3,877	3,975	3,776	4,032	3,648	4,686	(NA)
2844 Toilet preparations	Mil. dol.	17,366	17,390	18,724	20,175	20,284	20,911	(NA)
Value of shipments (1992 dollars)	Mil. dol.	40,123	39,450	39,999	42,603	41,971	44,404	(NA)
2841 Soap and other detergents	Mil. dol.	12,152	12,099	11,022	11,445	11,033	12,095	(NA)
2842 Polishes/sanitation goods	Mil. dol.	5,737	5,630	6,477	7,433	7,474	7,460	(NA)
2843 Surface active agents	Mil. dol.	4,030	3,995	3,776	3,965	3,538	4,369	(NA)
2844 Toilet preparations	Mil. dol.	18,203	17,726	18,724	19,760	19,926	20,460	(NA)
TRADE DATA								
Value of imports	Mil. dol.	995	1,076	1,308	1,463	1,689	1,936	2,100
2841 Soap and other detergents	Mil. dol.	191	179	213	254	335	421	486
2842 Polishes/sanitation goods	Mil. dol.	36.6	33.5	46.0	49.8	56.3	61.6	69.4
2843 Surface active agents	Mil. dol.	134	152	158	204	263	296	286
2844 Toilet preparations	Mil. dol.	634	712	892	956	1,035	1,157	1,257
Value of exports	Mil. dol.	1,633	2,236	2,529	2,853	3,368	3,710	4,132
2841 Soap and other detergents	Mil. dol.	370	511	583	644	716	828	899
2842 Polishes/sanitation goods	Mil. dol.	112	130	144	170	174	205	212
2843 Surface active agents	Mil. dol.	465	477	548	604	734	790	826
2844 Toilet preparations	Mil. dol.	686	1,118	1,254	1,437	1,733	1,867	2,195

NA Not available. [1] Value of all products and services sold by establishments in the soap, cleaners, and toilet goods industry. [2] Value of products classified in the soap, cleaners, and toilet goods industry produced by all industries.

Source: U.S. Department of Commerce, Bureau of the Census, International Trade Administration (ITA).

No. 1423. Recent Trends in Paints and Allied Products (SIC 2851): 1990 to 1996

ITEM	Unit	1990	1991	1992	1993	1994	1995	1996
INDUSTRY DATA								
Value of shipments [1]	Mil. dol.	14,337	14,388	14,973	16,030	17,404	17,943	(NA)
Value of shipments (1992 dollars)	Mil. dol.	15,172	14,607	14,973	15,825	16,897	16,522	(NA)
Total employment	1,000	54.0	51.2	51.1	50.3	50.0	52.4	(NA)
Production workers	1,000	27.2	25.2	25.7	25.9	27.0	27.7	(NA)
Average hourly earnings	Dollar	11.90	12.12	12.71	13.00	14.00	13.88	(NA)
Capital expenditures	Mil. dol.	275	260	273	256	280	417	(NA)
PRODUCT DATA								
Value of shipments [2]	Mil. dol.	13,681	13,722	14,283	15,356	16,426	16,742	(NA)
Value of shipments (1992 dollars)	Mil. dol.	14,477	13,931	14,283	15,159	15,947	15,416	(NA)
TRADE DATA								
Value of imports	Mil. dol.	137	141	184	197	261	343	393
Value of exports	Mil. dol.	570	686	754	811	936	1,009	1,091

NA Not available. [1] Value of all products and services sold by establishments in the paints and allied products industry. [2] Value of products classified in the paints and allied products industry produced by all industries.

Source: U.S. Department of Commerce, Bureau of the Census, International Trade Administration (ITA).

No. 1424. Recent Trends in Organic Chemicals, Except Gum and Wood (SIC 2865, 2869): 1990 to 1996

ITEM	Unit	1990	1991	1992	1993	1994	1995	1996
INDUSTRY DATA								
Value of shipments [1]	Mil. dol.	65,503	64,317	63,663	63,541	69,205	75,722	(NA)
Value of shipments (1992 dollars)	Mil. dol.	68,083	64,490	63,663	61,162	65,016	65,283	(NA)
Total employment	1,000	124	125	122	121	113	115	(NA)
Production workers	1,000	72.7	72.5	70.4	70.9	66.0	67.1	(NA)
Average hourly earnings	Dollar	17.75	18.32	18.72	18.88	20.23	20.60	(NA)
Capital expenditures	Mil. dol.	5,177	5,338	4,749	4,028	3,509	4,906	(NA)
PRODUCT DATA								
Value of shipments [2]	Mil. dol.	61,044	59,326	58,655	59,135	65,003	72,322	(NA)
Value of shipments (1992 dollars)	Mil. dol.	63,059	59,427	58,655	57,017	61,256	62,551	(NA)
TRADE DATA								
Value of imports	Mil. dol.	6,273	6,585	7,243	7,332	8,656	10,567	11,535
Value of exports	Mil. dol.	9,791	10,127	10,081	10,452	12,387	15,619	14,195

NA Not available. $del [1] Value of all products and services sold by establishments in the organic chemicals, except gum and wood industry. [2] Value of products classified in the organic chemicals, except gum and wood industry produced by all industries.

Source: U.S. Department of Commerce, Bureau of the Census, International Trade Administration (ITA).

No. 1425. Recent Trends in Nitrogenous Fertilizers and Phosphatic Fertilizers: 1990 to 1996

ITEM	Unit	1990	1991	1992	1993	1994	1995	1993
NITROGENOUS FERTILIZERS (SIC 2873)								
Industry data:								
Value of shipments [1]	Mil. dol.	3,135	3,268	3,177	3,467	4,246	4,446	(NA)
Value of shipments (1992 dollars)	Mil. dol.	3,192	3,146	3,177	3,340	3,614	3,267	(NA)
Total employment	1,000	7.5	7.3	7.0	7.0	8	7.3	(NA)
Production workers	1,000	4.8	4.7	4.7	4.7	5.4	5.1	(NA)
Average hourly earnings	Dollar	13.84	14.82	15.66	16.11	16.69	16.37	(NA)
Capital expenditures	Mil. dol.	101	224	209	186	175	176	(NA)
Product data:								
Value of shipments [2]	Mil. dol.	3,357	3,438	3,589	3,737	4,428	4,752	(NA)
Value of shipments (1992 dollars)	Mil. dol.	3,418	3,309	3,589	3,600	3,769	3,492	(NA)
PHOSPHATIC FERTILIZERS (SIC 2874)								
Industry data:								
Value of shipments [1]	Mil. dol.	4,668	5,030	4,318	3,648	4,597	5,358	(NA)
Value of shipments (1992 dollars)	Mil. dol.	4,206	4,401	4,318	4,155	4,152	4,059	(NA)
Total employment	1,000	10.5	10.3	9.5	9.4	8.5	8.6	(NA)
Production workers	1,000	7.5	7.3	6.7	6.6	6.2	6.5	(NA)
Average hourly earnings	Dollar	13.74	14.70	13.84	14.70	16.69	16.70	(NA)
Capital expenditures	Mil. dol.	139	200	307	150	159	195	(NA)
Product data:								
Value of shipments [2]	Mil. dol.	4,462	4,572	3,929	3,397	4,272	5,165	(NA)
Value of shipments (1992 dollars)	Mil. dol.	4,020	4,000	3,929	3,869	3,859	3,913	(NA)

NA Not available. [1] Value of all products and services sold by establishments in this industry. [2] Value of products classified in this industry produced by all industries.

Source. U.S. Department of Commerce, Bureau of the Census, International Trade Administration (ITA).

No. 1426. Recent Trends in Agricultural Chemicals, n.e.c. (SIC 2879): 1990 to 1996

ITEM	Unit	1990	1991	1992	1993	1994	1995	1996
INDUSTRY DATA								
Value of shipments [1]	Mil. dol.	8,596	8,424	9,142	9,554	9,636	10,079	(NA)
Value of shipments (1992 dollars)	Mil. dol.	9,236	8,639	9,142	9,142	8,800	8,967	(NA)
Total employment	1,000	17.7	16.4	16.8	16.3	15.3	14.8	(NA)
Production workers	1,000	10.2	9.1	9.8	9.2	8.8	8.7	(NA)
Average hourly earnings	Dollar	16.32	15.21	15.57	16.41	18.40	19.86	(NA)
Capital expenditures	Mil. dol.	566	489	428	356	299	318	(NA)
PRODUCT DATA								
Value of shipments [2]	Mil. dol.	7,280	7,448	8,226	8,737	8,848	9,616	(NA)
Value of shipments (1992 dollars)	Mil. dol.	7,820	7,639	8,225	8,361	8,060	8,565	(NA)

NA Not available. [1] Value of all products and services sold by establishments in the agricultural chemicals, n.e.c. industry. [2] Value of products classified in the agricultural chemicals, n.e.c. industry produced by all industries.

Source: U.S. Department of Commerce: Bureau of the Census, International Trade Administration (ITA).

No. 1427. Recent Trends in Adhesives and Sealants (SIC 2891): 1990 to 1996

ITEM	Unit	1990	1991	1992	1993	1994	1995	1996
INDUSTRY DATA								
Value of shipments [1]	Mil. dol.	5,523	5,615	5,667	5,859	5,869	5,935	(NA)
Value of shipments (1992 dollars)	Mil. dol.	5,789	5,655	5,667	5,711	5,537	5,285	(NA)
Total employment	1,000	21.4	20.9	21.1	20.9	19.2	18.8	(NA)
Production workers	1,000	11.9	11.7	11.7	11.5	11.3	11.2	(NA)
Average hourly earnings	Dollar	11.53	11.48	12.36	12.57	13.37	13.40	(NA)
Capital expenditures	Mil. dol.	129	142	168	183	204	197	(NA)
PRODUCT DATA								
Value of shipments [2]	Mil. dol.	5,403	5,382	5,415	5,607	5,427	5,592	(NA)
Value of shipments (1992 dollars)	Mil. dol.	5,663	5,420	5,415	5,660	5,129	4,960	(NA)
TRADE DATA								
Value of imports	Mil. dol.	89.8	94.1	112	119	135	140	145
Value of exports	Mil. dol.	159	169	202	241	283	316	369

NA Not available. [1] Value of all products and services sold by establishments in the adhesives and sealants industry. [2] Value of products classified in the adhesives and sealants industry produced by all industries.

Source: U.S. Department of Commerce, Bureau of the Census, International Trade Administration (ITA).

No. 1428. Recent Trends in Petroleum Refining (SIC 2911): 1990 to 1996

ITEM	Unit	1990	1991	1992	1993	1994	1995	1996
INDUSTRY DATA								
Value of shipments [1]	Mil. dol.	160,135	146,357	136,551	129,961	126,666	136,023	(NA)
Value of shipments (1992 dollars)	Mil. dol.	138,886	141,403	136,551	135,376	139,271	143,032	(NA)
Total employment	1,000	73.1	75.5	74.9	73.1	72.0	70.4	(NA)
Production workers	1,000	47.9	48.4	47.9	47.3	46.6	46.0	(NA)
Average hourly earnings	Dollar	18.49	19.35	19.76	21.04	21.16	21.81	(NA)
Capital expenditures	Mil. dol.	3,843	5,633	6,182	5,966	5,524	5,876	(NA)
PRODUCT DATA								
Value of shipments [2]	Mil. dol.	151,559	138,322	131,640	125,456	123,825	130,525	(NA)
Value of shipments (1992 dollars)	Mil. dol.	131,447	133,645	131,640	130,683	134,010	137,250	(NA)
TRADE DATA								
Value of imports	Mil. dol.	14,269	10,890	10,185	9,742	9,274	8,765	18,510
Value of exports	Mil. dol.	5,988	6,356	5,759	5,641	4,958	5,333	6,300

NA Not available. [1] Value of all products and services sold by establishments in the petroleum refining industry. [2] Value of products classified in the petroleum refining industry produced by all industries.

Source: U.S. Department of Commerce, Bureau of the Census, International Trade Administration (ITA).

No. 1429. Recent Trends in Tires and Inner Tubes (SIC 3011): 1990 to 1996

ITEM	Unit	1990	1991	1992	1993	1994	1995	1996
INDUSTRY DATA								
Value of shipments [1]	Mil. dol.	11,815	11,822	11,814	12,601	13,183	14,074	(NA)
Value of shipments (1992 dollars)	Mil. dol.	12,106	11,953	11,814	12,614	13,236	13,990	(NA)
Total employment	1,000	67.1	64.7	64.6	65.1	66.1	65.7	(NA)
Production workers	1,000	54.5	52.2	52.8	53.3	54.0	54.2	(NA)
Average hourly earnings	Dollar	16.8	17.64	18.54	18.63	19.00	18.86	(NA)
Capital expenditures	Mil. dol.	869	514	506	490	518	514	(NA)
PRODUCT DATA								
Value of shipments [2]	Mil. dol.	11,340	11,303	11,316	12,241	12,816	13,713	(NA)
Value of shipments (1992 dollars)	Mil. dol.	11,619	11,426	11,316	12,253	12,867	13,631	(NA)
TRADE DATA								
Value of imports	Mil. dol.	2,563	2,271	2,463	2,681	2,979	3,069	3,020
Value of exports	Mil. dol.	1,140	1,262	1,395	1,453	1,596	1,856	1,955

NA Not available. [1] Value of all products and services sold by establishments in the tires and inner tubes industry. [2] Value of products classified in the tires and inner tubes industry produced by all industries.

Source: U.S. Department of Commerce, Bureau of the Census, International Trade Administration (ITA).

No. 1430. Recent Trends in Fabricated Rubber Products, n.e.c. (SIC 3069): 1990 to 1996

ITEM	Unit	1990	1991	1992	1993	1994	1995	1996
INDUSTRY DATA								
Value of shipments [1]	Mil. dol.	6,773	6,842	6,933	7,606	7,748	8,332	(NA)
Value of shipments (1992 dollars)	Mil. dol.	7,026	6,883	6,933	7,474	7,442	7,630	(NA)
Total employment	1,000	58.1	57.9	56.5	58.4	57.9	57.5	(NA)
Production workers	1,000	44.1	43.2	42.0	43.4	43.1	43.5	(NA)
Average hourly earnings	Dollar	9.33	9.87	10.06	10.33	10.31	10.97	(NA)
Capital expenditures	Mil. dol.	192	175	205	222	215	225	(NA)
PRODUCT DATA								
Value of shipments [2]	Mil. dol.	6,462	6,490	6,600	7,179	7,364	7,711	(NA)
Value of shipments (1992 dollars)	Mil. dol.	6,704	6,530	6,600	7,052	7,093	7,062	(NA)
TRADE DATA								
Value of imports	Mil. dol.	744	847	1,090	1,303	1,528	1,779	1,982
Value of exports	Mil. dol.	660	716	735	786	930	993	1,070

NA Not available. [1] Value of all products and services sold by establishments in the fabricated rubber products, n.e.c industry. [2] Value of products classified in the fabricated rubber products, n.e.c., industry produced by all industries.

Source: U.S. Department of Commerce, Bureau of the Census, International Trade Administration (ITA).

No. 1431. Recent Trends in Miscellaneous Plastic Products Excluding Bottles and Plumbing (SIC 3081-4, -6, -7, -9): 1990 to 1996

ITEM	Unit	1990	1991	1992	1993	1994	1995	1996
INDUSTRY DATA								
Value of shipments [1]	Mil. dol.	71,368	71,938	77,891	84,160	93,893	100,805	(NA)
Value of shipments (1992 dollars)	Mil. dol.	71,390	71,681	77,891	83,479	91,624	92,896	(NA)
Total employment	1,000	623	612	627	650	682	717	(NA)
Production workers	1,000	476	465	480	504	533	561	(NA)
Average hourly earnings	Dollar	9.35	9.71	9.96	10.23	10.34	10.44	(NA)
Capital expenditures	Mil. dol.	3,143	3,353	3,449	3,465	4,033	4,826	(NA)
PRODUCT DATA								
Value of shipments [2]	Mil. dol.	67,410	66,669	75,532	81,512	90,633	97,187	(NA)
Value of shipments (1992 dollars)	Mil. dol.	67,473	66,453	75,532	80,851	88,450	89,506	(NA)
TRADE DATA								
Value of imports	Mil. dol.	3,682	3,760	4,338	4,899	5,306	6,094	6,501
Value of exports	Mil. dol.	3,462	3,806	4,400	4,941	5,822	6,375	7,018

NA Not available. [1] Value of all products and services sold by establishments in the miscellaneous plastic products excluding bottles and plumbing industry. [2] Value of products classified in the miscellaneous plastic products excluding bottles and plumbing industry produced by all industries.

Source: U.S. Department of Commerce, Bureau of the Census, International Trade Administration (ITA).

No. 1432. Recent Trends in Footwear, Except Rubber (SIC 314): 1990 to 1996

ITEM	Unit	1990	1991	1992	1993	1994	1995	1996
INDUSTRY DATA								
Value of shipments [1]	Mil. dol.	4,067	3,588	3,898	3,974	3,923	3,698	(NA)
3142 House slippers	Mil. dol.	267	264	285	302	204	113	(NA)
3143 Men's footwear	Mil. dol.	2,075	1,962	2,210	2,351	2,461	2,430	(NA)
3144 Women's footwear	Mil. dol.	1,345	1,097	1,095	1,010	950	758	(NA)
3149 Footwear n.e.c.	Mil. dol.	400	266	309	310	309	397	(NA)
Value of shipments (1992 dollars)	Mil. dol.	4,293	3,660	3,898	3,907	3,816	3,488	(NA)
3142 House slippers	Mil. dol.	258	258	285	310	205	110	(NA)
3143 Men's footwear	Mil. dol.	2,198	2,016	2,210	2,305	2,382	2,267	(NA)
3144 Women's footwear	Mil. dol.	1,419	1,135	1,095	987	927	730	(NA)
3149 Footwear n.e.c.	Mil. dol.	418	271	309	305	302	381	(NA)
Total employment	1,000	60.6	51.1	48.8	48.5	46.8	44.6	(NA)
Production workers	1,000	51.9	44.0	41.4	41.3	40.3	37.9	(NA)
Average hourly earnings	Dollar	6.70	7.14	7.33	7.43	7.44	7.86	(NA)
Capital expenditures	Mil. dol.	39.0	28.1	51.2	40.3	58.8	34.1	(NA)
3142 House slippers	Mil. dol.	3.0	2.1	2.1	2.5	4.8	1.5	(NA)
3143 Men's footwear	Mil. dol.	21.2	16.2	32.8	26.1	43.3	23.6	(NA)
3144 Women's footwear	Mil. dol.	12.4	8.1	10.5	6.8	7.6	4.3	(NA)
3149 Footwear n.e.c.	Mil. dol.	2.4	1.7	5.8	4.9	3.1	4.7	(NA)
PRODUCT DATA								
Value of shipments [2]	Mil. dol.	3,780	3,495	3,608	3,707	3,739	3,404	(NA)
3142 House slippers	Mil. dol.	257	256	259	258	208	119	(NA)
3143 Men's footwear	Mil. dol.	1,839	1,763	1,807	1,970	2,040	1,932	(NA)
3144 Women's footwear	Mil. dol.	1,311	1,186	1,229	1,186	1,190	960	(NA)
3149 Footwear n.e.c.	Mil. dol.	373	289	314	293	301	393	(NA)
Value of shipments (1992 dollars)	Mil. dol.	3,970	3,586	3,608	3,643	3,639	3,219	(NA)
3142 House slippers	Mil. dol.	249	251	259	263	209	115	(NA)
3143 Men's footwear	Mil. dol.	1,948	1,812	1,807	1,931	1,975	1,802	(NA)
3144 Women's footwear	Mil. dol.	1,382	1,228	1,229	1,160	1,161	925	(NA)
3149 Footwear n.e.c.	Mil. dol.	390	295	314	289	294	377	(NA)
TRADE DATA								
Value of imports	Mil. dol.	8,431	8,336	8,616	9,290	9,698	9,984	10,478
Value of exports	Mil. dol.	256	307	343	332	382	370	385

NA Not available. [1] Value of all products and services sold by establishments in the footwear, except rubber industry. [2] Value of products classified in the footwear, except rubber industry produced by all industries.

No. 1433. Recent Trends in Leather Tanning and Finishing (SIC 3111): 1990 to 1996

ITEM	Unit	1990	1991	1992	1993	1994	1995	1996
INDUSTRY DATA								
Value of shipments [1]	Mil. dol.	2,328	2,075	2,905	3,198	3,041	3,119	(NA)
Value of shipments (1992 dollars)	Mil. dol.	2,226	2,067	2,905	3,098	2,808	2,719	(NA)
Total employment	1,000	11.8	11.1	16.6	16.9	15.9	15.3	(NA)
Production workers	1,000	10.0	9.4	13.3	13.8	13.4	12.5	(NA)
Average hourly earnings	Dollar	9.88	11.10	10.56	10.65	10.62	10.54	(NA)
Capital expenditures	Mil. dol.	36.3	37.1	48.5	52.2	45.5	57.6	(NA)
PRODUCT DATA								
Value of shipments [2]	Mil. dol.	2,458	2,226	2,952	3,218	3,064	3,121	(NA)
Value of shipments (1992 dollars)	Mil. dol.	2,350	2,217	2,952	3,115	2,829	2,721	(NA)
TRADE DATA								
Value of imports	Mil. dol.	683	571	631	736	960	1,089	1,139
Value of exports	Mil. dol.	751	680	705	764	812	870	951

NA Not available. [1] Value of all products and services sold by establishments in the leather tanning and finishing industry. [2] Value of products classified in the leather tanning and finishing industry produced by all industries.

Source: U.S. Department of Commerce, Bureau of the Census, International Trade Administration (ITA).

No. 1434. Recent Trends in Luggage and Personal Leather Goods (SIC 2386, 315, 316, 317): 1990 to 1996

ITEM	Unit	1990	1991	1992	1993	1994	1995	1996
INDUSTRY DATA								
Value of shipments [1]	Mil. dol.	2,332	2,252	2,207	2,106	2,070	1,780	(NA)
2386 Leather and sheep-lined clothing	Mil. dol.	172	166	209	224	237	206	(NA)
3151 Leather gloves/mittens	Mil. dol.	149	134	140	169	145	114	(NA)
3161 Luggage	Mil. dol.	1,129	1,091	968	930	991	835	(NA)
3171 Women's handbags/purses	Mil. dol.	528	518	463	387	304	305	(NA)
3172 Personal leather goods	Mil. dol.	353	344	428	395	393	321	(NA)
Value of shipments (1992 dollars)	Mil. dol.	2,431	2,289	2,207	2,090	2,064	1,777	(NA)
2386 Leather and sheep-lined clothing	Mil. dol.	173	165	209	225	247	217	(NA)
3151 Leather gloves/mittens	Mil. dol.	152	136	140	168	137	104	(NA)
3161 Luggage	Mil. dol.	1,186	1,115	968	922	979	832	(NA)
3171 Women's handbags/purses	Mil. dol.	546	522	463	385	313	307	(NA)
3172 Personal leather goods	Mil. dol.	373	351	428	389	388	317	(NA)
Total employment	1,000	31.0	28.2	28.4	24.3	22.1	18.5	(NA)
Production workers	1,000	24.5	22.0	21.1	19.0	17.7	14.8	(NA)
Average hourly earnings	Dollar	7.45	7.69	7.43	7.41	7.55	7.85	(NA)
Capital expenditures	Mil. dol.	22.6	16.1	27.9	28.2	26.8	30.9	(NA)
2386 Leather and sheep-lined clothing	Mil. dol.	0.4	0.3	1.3	1.6	0.1	0.6	(NA)
3151 Leather gloves/mittens	Mil. dol.	0.4	0.1	0.5	0.3	12.2	18.4	(NA)
3161 Luggage	Mil. dol.	10.7	8.8	15.9	16.4	9.5	6.1	(NA)
3171 Women's handbags/purses	Mil. dol.	6.3	2.7	3.4	4.2	3.1	3.7	(NA)
3172 Personal leather goods	Mil. dol.	4.8	4.4	6.8	5.7	1.9	2.1	(NA)
PRODUCT DATA								
Value of shipments [2]	Mil. dol.	2,170	2,164	2,109	2,013	2,050	1,754	(NA)
2386 Leather and sheep-lined clothing	Mil. dol.	161	201	199	216	222	193	(NA)
3151 Leather gloves/mittens	Mil. dol.	113	127	114	115	115	102	(NA)
3161 Luggage	Mil. dol.	1,064	1,028	864	814	880	708	(NA)
3171 Women's handbags/purses	Mil. dol.	453	432	411	366	328	313	(NA)
3172 Personal leather goods	Mil. dol.	379	375	522	503	505	437	(NA)
Value of shipments (1992 dollars)	Mil. dol.	2,264	2,199	2,109	1,997	2,045	1,751	(NA)
2386 Leather and sheep-lined clothing	Mil. dol.	162	201	199	217	231	204	(NA)
3151 Leather gloves/mittens	Mil. dol.	115	129	114	114	109	93	(NA)
3161 Luggage	Mil. dol.	1,118	1,052	864	807	869	705	(NA)
3171 Women's handbags/purses	Mil. dol.	468	436	411	364	338	316	(NA)
3172 Personal leather goods	Mil. dol.	400	383	522	495	498	432	(NA)
TRADE DATA								
Value of imports	Mil. dol.	3,592	3,556	3,882	4,069	4,560	4,670	4,772
2386 Leather and sheep-lined clothing	Mil. dol.	1,209	1,079	1,229	1,221	1,238	969	910
3151 Leather gloves/mittens	Mil. dol.	181	158	171	214	261	291	295
3161 Luggage	Mil. dol.	1,081	1,129	1,273	1,403	1,700	1,985	2,042
3171 Women's handbags/purses	Mil. dol.	848	899	890	910	959	972	1,055
3172 Personal leather goods	Mil. dol.	274	292	319	321	402	454	470
Value of exports	Mil. dol.	200	230	271	283	311	355	384
2386 Leather and sheep-lined clothing	Mil. dol.	51.9	57.3	65.5	69.5	64.9	86.7	67.6
3151 Leather gloves/mittens	Mil. dol.	14.0	13.1	12.2	14.0	13.8	13.4	10.0
3161 Luggage	Mil. dol.	89.3	109.0	135.0	138.0	166.0	176.0	231.0
3171 Women's handbags/purses	Mil. dol.	26.6	29.2	35.1	41.3	42.4	49.6	46.0
3172 Personal leather goods	Mil. dol.	17.8	21.3	22.8	20.0	23.9	27.2	29.3

NA Not available. [1] Value of all products and services sold by establishments in the luggage and personal leather goods industry. [2] Value of products classified in the luggage and personal leather goods industry produced by all industries.

Source: U.S. Department of Commerce, Bureau of the Census, International Trade Administration (ITA).

No. 1435. Recent Trends in Flat Glass (SIC 3211): 1990 to 1996

ITEM	Unit	1990	1991	1992	1993	1994	1995	1996
INDUSTRY DATA								
Value of shipments [1]	Mil. dol.	2,249	2,065	2,073	2,263	2,600	2,595	(NA)
Value of shipments (1992 dollars)	Mil. dol.	2,167	2,056	2,073	2,234	2,346	2,222	(NA)
Total employment	1,000	14.4	12.9	11.8	11.3	11.2	11.2	(NA)
Production workers	1,000	11.7	10.5	9.7	9.2	9.2	9.1	(NA)
Average hourly earnings	Dollar	16.30	16.92	17.45	18.03	19.01	19.73	(NA)
Capital expenditures	Mil. dol.	165	163	148	159	137	170	(NA)
PRODUCT DATA								
Value of shipments [2]	Mil. dol.	2,241	2,089	1,994	2,151	2,474	2,474	(NA)
Value of shipments (1992 dollars)	Mil. dol.	2,159	2,081	1,994	2,105	2,233	2,118	(NA)
TRADE DATA								
Value of imports	Mil. dol.	280	283	278	342	416	399	463
Value of exports	Mil. dol.	458	497	499	583	620	687	793

NA Not available. [1] Value of all products and services sold by establishments in the flat glass industry. [2] Value of products classified in the flat glass industry produced by all industries.

Source: U.S. Department of Commerce, Bureau of the Census, International Trade Administration (ITA).

No. 1436. Recent Trends in Hydraulic Cement, Ceramic Tile, and Gypsum Products: 1990 to 1996

ITEM	Unit	1990	1991	1992	1993	1994	1995	1996
HYDRAULIC CEMENT (SIC 3241)								
Industry data:								
Value of shipments [1]	Mil. dol.	4,277	3,811	4,051	4,187	4,806	5,342	(NA)
Value of shipments (1992 dollars)	Mil. dol.	4,391	3,796	4,051	3,967	4,278	4,441	(NA)
Total employment	1,000	17.5	16.3	17.0	16.6	16.6	16.8	(NA)
Production workers	1,000	13.3	12.0	12.8	12.5	12.4	12.6	(NA)
Average hourly earnings	Dollar	15.38	15.17	15.15	15.48	15.80	16.40	(NA)
Capital expenditures	Mil. dol.	270	232	226	227	280	282	(NA)
Product data:								
Value of shipments [2]	Mil. dol.	4,113	3,701	3,929	4,051	4,699	5,167	(NA)
Value of shipments (1992 dollars)	Mil. dol.	4,223	3,686	3,929	3,858	4,180	4,295	(NA)
Trade data:								
Value of imports	Mil. dol.	446	335	251	285	444	542	596
Value of exports	Mil. dol.	39.7	47.2	50.3	49.3	46.8	56.0	59.1
CERAMIC WALL AND FLOOR TILE (SIC 3253)								
Industry data:								
Value of shipments [1]	Mil. dol.	850	757	731	811	847	938	(NA)
Value of shipments (1992 dollars)	Mil. dol.	851	766	731	806	829	902	(NA)
Total employment	1,000	9.7	9.4	8.9	8.7	8.6	9.4	(NA)
Production workers	1,000	8.0	7.6	7.3	7.3	7.1	7.8	(NA)
Average hourly earnings	Dollar	9.72	9.16	9.50	10.41	9.92	10.35	(NA)
Capital expenditures	Mil. dol.	70.0	22.7	48.9	68.0	73.1	61.5	(NA)
Product data:								
Value of shipments [2]	Mil. dol.	696	683	678	739	735	787	(NA)
Value of shipments (1992 dollars)	Mil. dol.	697	690	678	734	719	756	(NA)
Trade data:								
Value of imports	Mil. dol.	421	365	419	472	519	562	628
Value of exports	Mil. dol.	20.5	21.0	19.3	22.6	23.5	26.1	24.6
GYPSUM PRODUCTS (SIC 3275)								
Industry data:								
Value of shipments [1]	Mil. dol.	2,390	2,026	2,100	2,290	2,954	3,456	(NA)
Value of shipments (1992 dollars)	Mil. dol.	2,209	2,020	2,100	2,067	2,147	2,220	(NA)
Total employment	1,000	11.4	10.2	10.6	10.4	10.8	11.2	(NA)
Production workers	1,000	9.0	8.0	8.5	8.3	8.6	8.9	(NA)
Average hourly earnings	Dollar	12.50	13.11	12.70	13.06	13.42	14.35	(NA)
Capital expenditures	Mil. dol.	69.3	35.1	43.8	39.8	74.6	154.0	(NA)
Product data:								
Value of shipments [2]	Mil. dol.	2,258	1,899	1,948	2,133	2,729	3,215	(NA)
Value of shipments (1992 dollars)	Mil. dol.	2,087	1,893	1,948	1,925	1,963	2,065	(NA)
Trade data:								
Value of imports	Mil. dol.	25.8	12.8	13.2	24.5	50.6	75.2	101.0
Value of exports	Mil. dol.	67.0	65.6	71.2	55.3	50.5	52.9	60.3

NA Not available. [1] Value of all products and services sold by establishments in this industry. [2] Value of products classified in this industry produced by all industries.

Source: U.S. Department of Commerce: Bureau of the Census, International Trade Administration (ITA).

No. 1437. Recent Trends in Steel Mill Products (SIC 3312, 3315, 3316, 3317): 1990 to 1996

ITEM	Unit	1990	1991	1992	1993	1994	1995	1996
INDUSTRY DATA								
Value of shipments [1]	Mil. dol.	61,632	56,103	57,187	61,301	68,753	73,336	(NA)
Value of shipments (1992 dollars)	Mil. dol.	59,256	54,965	57,187	60,320	64,669	65,265	(NA)
Total employment	1,000	256	244	234	225	222	220	(NA)
Production workers	1,000	197	185	179	173	172	173	(NA)
Capital expenditures	Mil. dol.	3,057	3,399	2,568	2,166	3,130	3,254	(NA)
PRODUCT DATA								
Value of shipments [2]	Mil. dol.	60,065	53,968	56,132	60,199	67,681	72,045	(NA)
Value of shipments (1992 dollars)	Mil. dol.	57,727	52,866	56,132	59,247	63,669	64,130	(NA)
TRADE DATA								
Value of imports	Mil. dol.	8,918	8,344	8,508	9,300	13,445	12,908	13,853
Value of exports	Mil. dol.	2,958	3,868	3,191	2,988	3,205	4,893	4,346

NA Not available. [1] Value of all products and services sold by establishments in the steel mill products industry. [2] Value of products classified in the steel mill products industry produced by all industries.

Source: U S. Department of Commerce, Bureau of the Census, International Trade Administration (ITA).

No. 1438. Recent Trends in General Components (SIC 345, 3491, 3494, 3562): 1990 to 1996

[The code 349A in the table represents an aggregation of SIC's 3491 and 3494]

ITEM	Unit	1990	1991	1992	1993	1994	1995	1996
INDUSTRY DATA								
Value of shipments [1]	Mil. dol.	21,851	21,515	22,038	23,202	25,014	27,141	(NA)
3451 Screw machine products	Mil. dol.	3,059	3,007	3,831	4,170	4,686	5,131	(NA)
3452 Industrial fasteners	Mil. dol.	5,735	5,570	5,195	5,373	5,819	6,393	(NA)
349A Valves and pipe fittings	Mil. dol.	8,740	8,872	8,723	9,102	9,618	10,336	(NA)
3562 Ball and roller bearings	Mil. dol.	4,318	4,066	4,290	4,557	4,891	5,281	(NA)
Value of shipments (1992 dollars)	Mil. dol.	22,762	21,670	22,038	22,806	24,080	25,260	(NA)
3451 Screw machine products	Mil. dol.	3,121	3,023	3,831	4,137	4,599	4,929	(NA)
3452 Industrial fasteners	Mil. dol.	5,870	5,586	5,195	5,320	5,699	6,153	(NA)
349A Valves and pipe fittings	Mil. dol.	9,163	8,925	8,723	8,869	9,080	9,297	(NA)
3562 Ball and roller bearings	Mil. dol.	4,608	4,136	4,290	4,481	4,702	4,881	(NA)
Total employment	1,000	206	198	194	194	196	206	(NA)
3451 Screw machine products	1,000	42.5	40.7	46.4	47.1	51.9	54.7	(NA)
3452 Industrial fasteners	1,000	52.9	50.2	44.1	43.7	43.4	46.1	(NA)
349A Valves and pipe fittings	1,000	72.5	71.2	68.0	69.0	66.8	69.2	(NA)
3562 Ball and roller bearings	1,000	38.4	35.9	35.0	33.8	33.4	35.6	(NA)
Production workers	1,000	154	145	142	144	147	155	(NA)
3451 Screw machine products	1,000	34.3	32.3	36.5	38.5	41.9	44.4	(NA)
3452 Industrial fasteners	1,000	39.0	36.3	31.9	32.0	31.9	34.2	(NA)
349A Valves and pipe fittings	1,000	49.0	47.7	45.6	46.6	45.8	47.5	(NA)
3562 Ball and roller bearings	1,000	31.6	29.1	28.2	27.3	27.2	29.2	(NA)
Average hourly earnings	Dollar	11.56	11.95	12.57	12.70	12.90	13.27	(NA)
3451 Screw machine products	Dollar	10.17	10.28	11.29	11.36	11.25	11.6	(NA)
3452 Industrial fasteners	Dollar	11.42	11.88	12.80	12.74	12.76	13.58	(NA)
349A Valves and pipe fittings	Dollar	11.71	12.14	12.39	12.76	12.78	13.18	(NA)
3562 Ball and roller bearings	Dollar	13.13	13.83	14.35	14.48	15.97	15.65	(NA)
Capital expenditures	Mil. dol.	957	845	758	778	825	1,194	(NA)
3451 Screw machine products	Mil. dol.	131	108	135	152	226	254	(NA)
3452 Industrial fasteners	Mil. dol.	174	186	151	163	157	387	(NA)
349A Valves and pipe fittings	Mil. dol.	305	263	265	257	269	306	(NA)
3562 Ball and roller bearings	Mil. dol.	348	288	207	206	173	248	(NA)
PRODUCT DATA								
Value of shipments [2]	Mil. dol.	21,106	20,407	20,754	21,930	23,702	25,500	(NA)
3451 Screw machine products	Mil. dol.	3,034	2,926	3,660	3,986	4,642	5,108	(NA)
3452 Industrial fasteners	Mil. dol.	5,529	5,275	4,854	5,043	5,439	5,861	(NA)
349A Valves and pipe fittings	Mil. dol.	8,301	8,313	8,100	8,461	8,828	9,390	(NA)
3562 Ball and roller bearings	Mil. dol.	4,242	3,893	4,140	4,440	4,794	5,124	(NA)
Value of shipments (1992 dollars)	Mil. dol.	21,978	20,544	20,754	21,561	22,829	23,754	(NA)
3451 Screw machine products	Mil. dol.	3,096	2,941	3,660	3,954	4,555	4,905	(NA)
3452 Industrial fasteners	Mil. dol.	5,660	5,291	4,854	4,993	5,327	5,660	(NA)
349A Valves and pipe fittings	Mil. dol.	8,696	8,353	8,100	8,248	8,338	8,454	(NA)
3562 Ball and roller bearings	Mil. dol.	4,527	3,960	4,140	4,366	4,609	4,735	(NA)
TRADE DATA								
Value of imports	Mil. dol.	3,922	3,863	4,221	4,630	5,490	6,264	6,458
3451 Screw machine products	Mil. dol.	(NA)	(NA)	(NA)	(NA)	(NA)	(NA)	(NA)
3452 Industrial fasteners	Mil. dol.	1,213	1,121	1,231	1,386	1,666	1,894	1,847
349A Valves and pipe fittings	Mil. dol.	1,836	1,931	2,096	2,240	2,653	2,988	3,221
3562 Ball and roller bearings	Mil. dol.	873	812	895	1,004	1,171	1,381	1,389
Value of exports	Mil. dol.	2,796	2,974	3,154	3,332	3,849	4,570	5,167
3451 Screw machine products	Mil. dol.	(NA)	(NA)	(NA)	(NA)	(NA)	(NA)	(NA)
3452 Industrial fasteners	Mil. dol.	621	634	685	710	905	1,061	1,366
349A Valves and pipe fittings	Mil. dol.	1,488	1,666	1,810	1,965	2,211	2,620	2,890
3562 Ball and roller bearings	Mil. dol.	689	674	659	658	733	889	912

NA Not available. [1] Value of all products and services sold by establishments in the general components industry. [2] Value of products classified in the general components industry produced by all industries.

Source: U.S. Department of Commerce, Bureau of the Census, International Trade Administration (ITA).

No. 1439. Recent Trends in Automotive Parts and Accessories (SIC 3465, 3592, 3647, 3691, 3694, 3714): 1990 to 1996

ITEM	Unit	1990	1991	1992	1993	1994	1995	1996
INDUSTRY DATA								
Value of shipments [1]	Mil. dol.	93,379	91,215	105,841	119,678	138,982	146,195	(NA)
Value of shipments (1992 dollar)	Mil. dol.	94,468	91,624	105,841	119,264	137,833	143,522	(NA)
Total employment	1,000	614	580	609	633	679	700	(NA)
Production workers	1,000	488	457	482	506	548	560	(NA)
Average hourly earnings	Dollar	15.29	15.61	15.84	16.22	16.57	16.95	(NA)
Capital expenditures	Mil. dol.	4,986	4,690	4,585	5,308	6,010	7,585	(NA)
PRODUCT DATA								
Value of shipments [2]	Mil. dol.	89,444	88,768	104,109	118,293	134,468	141,800	(NA)
Value of shipments (1992 dollar)	Mil. dol.	90,472	89,150	104,109	117,882	133,369	139,223	(NA)
TRADE DATA								
Value of imports	Mil. dol.	20,000	18,438	21,055	23,461	27,267	28,800	30,837
Value of exports	Mil. dol.	18,607	18,987	22,437	26,064	27,927	29,323	30,285

NA Not available. [1] Value of all products and services sold by establishments in the automotive parts and accessories industry. [2] Value of products classified in the automotive parts and accessories industry produced by all industries.

Source: U.S. Department of Commerce, Bureau of the Census, International Trade Administration (ITA).

No. 1440. Recent Trends in Farm Machinery and Equipment (SIC 3523): 1990 to 1996

ITEM	Unit	1990	1991	1992	1993	1994	1995	1996
INDUSTRY DATA								
Value of shipments [1]	Mil. dol.	11,682	10,522	9,620	11,190	12,759	13,745	(NA)
Value of shipments (1992 dollars)	Mil. dol.	12,480	10,870	9,620	10,938	12,163	12,762	(NA)
Total employment	1,000	69.6	65.1	61.5	63.5	66.5	65.8	(NA)
Production workers	1,000	49.9	45.4	42.6	45.8	47.7	48.4	(NA)
Average hourly earnings	Dollar	12.41	12.80	13.18	13.18	13.60	14.35	(NA)
Capital expenditures	Mil. dol.	222	220	196	229	260	290	(NA)
PRODUCT DATA								
Value of shipments [2]	Mil. dol.	10,871	9,724	8,940	10,340	11,911	12,625	(NA)
Value of shipments (1992 dollars)	Mil. dol.	11,615	10,045	8,940	10,106	11,355	11,722	(NA)
TRADE DATA								
Value of imports	Mil. dol.	2,475	1,911	2,022	2,148	2,917	3,069	2,990
Value of exports	Mil. dol.	2,296	2,130	2,176	2,473	2,647	3,119	3,804

NA Not available. [1] Value of all products and services sold by establishments in the farm machinery and equipment industry. [2] Value of products classified in the farm machinery and equipment industry produced by all industries.

Source: U.S. Department of Commerce, Bureau of the Census, International Trade Administration (ITA).

No. 1441. Recent Trends in Lawn and Garden Equipment (SIC 3524): 1990 to 1996

ITEM	Unit	1990	1991	1992	1993	1994	1995	1996
INDUSTRY DATA								
Value of shipments [1]	Mil. dol.	4,968	4,901	5,164	5,828	6,836	6,971	(NA)
Value of shipments (1992 dollars)	Mil. dol.	5,121	4,946	5,164	5,782	6,650	6,684	(NA)
Total employment	1,000	24.5	24.4	24.9	25.7	28.0	27.7	(NA)
Production workers	1,000	18.3	18.9	19.9	20.5	22.4	22.3	(NA)
Average hourly earnings	Dollar	9.91	9.99	10.73	10.88	10.56	10.26	(NA)
Capital expenditures	Mil. dol.	86.9	98.2	125.0	92.1	129.0	126.0	(NA)
PRODUCT DATA								
Value of shipments [2]	Mil. dol.	4,343	4,267	4,344	4,884	5,730	6,029	(NA)
Value of shipments (1992 dollars)	Mil. dol.	4,477	4,306	4,344	4,845	5,574	5,780	(NA)
TRADE DATA								
Value of imports	Mil. dol.	177	118	135	162	175	172	225
Value of exports	Mil. dol.	495	562	612	686	740	765	721

NA Not available. [1] Value of all products and services sold by establishments in the lawn and garden equipment industry. [2] Value of products classified in the lawn and garden equipment industry produced by all industries.

Source: U.S. Department of Commerce, Bureau of the Census, International Trade Administration (ITA).

No. 1442. Recent Trends in Construction Machinery (SIC 3531): 1990 to 1996

ITEM	Unit	1990	1991	1992	1993	1994	1995	1996
INDUSTRY DATA								
Value of shipments [1]	Mil. dol.	16,149	13,710	13,139	15,444	17,697	19,979	(NA)
Value of shipments (1992 dollars)	Mil. dol.	17,052	14,076	13,139	15,053	17,065	18,812	(NA)
Total employment	1,000	88.6	81.0	74.6	74.7	77.9	85.7	(NA)
Production workers	1,000	60.6	53.6	47.8	49.1	52.9	58.7	(NA)
Average hourly earnings	Dollar	14.95	15.32	15.13	15.33	14.84	14.82	(NA)
Capital expenditures	Mil. dol.	648	485	395	346	359	444	(NA)
PRODUCT DATA								
Value of shipments [2]	Mil. dol.	14,888	12,297	12,001	14,122	16,123	18,290	(NA)
Value of shipments (1992 dollars)	Mil. dol.	15,721	12,626	12,001	13,764	15,547	17,222	(NA)
TRADE DATA								
Value of imports	Mil. dol.	3,079	2,106	2,574	3,396	4,269	4,443	4,422
Value of exports	Mil. dol.	4,561	4,383	4,250	4,340	5,192	5,445	5,769

NA Not available. [1] Value of all products and services sold by establishments in the construction machinery industry. [2] Value of products classified in the construction machinery industry produced by all industries.

Source: U.S. Department of Commerce, Bureau of the Census, International Trade Administration (ITA).

No. 1443. Recent Trends in Mining Machinery (SIC 3532): 1990 to 1996

ITEM	Unit	1990	1991	1992	1993	1994	1995	1996
INDUSTRY DATA								
Value of shipments [1]	Mil. dol.	1,875	1,655	1,548	1,881	1,715	2,114	(NA)
Value of shipments (1992 dollars)	Mil. dol.	1,969	1,682	1,548	1,844	1,659	1,972	(NA)
Total employment	1,000	15.2	14.2	12.6	12.6	12.6	14.1	(NA)
Production workers	1,000	9.6	8.4	7.4	7.7	8.0	9.2	(NA)
Average hourly earnings	Dollar	10.93	10.91	11.92	12.21	13.08	12.93	(NA)
Capital expenditures	Mil. dol.	38.7	33.3	33.0	58.9	29.5	28.9	(NA)
PRODUCT DATA								
Value of shipments [2]	Mil. dol.	1,754	1,584	1,417	1,745	1,639	1,999	(NA)
Value of shipments (1992 dollars)	Mil. dol.	1,843	1,610	1,417	1,711	1,585	1,865	(NA)
TRADE DATA								
Value of imports	Mil. dol.	347	317	268	307	379	466	515
Value of exports	Mil. dol.	720	764	811	846	967	1,111	1,235

NA Not available. [1] Value of all products and services sold by establishments in the mining machinery industry. [2] Value of products classified in the mining machinery industry produced by all industries.

Source: U.S. Department of Commerce, Bureau of the Census, International Trade Administration (ITA).

No. 1444. Recent Trends in Oil and Gas Field Machinery (SIC 3533): 1990 to 1996

ITEM	Unit	1990	1991	1992	1993	1994	1995	1996
INDUSTRY DATA								
Value of shipments [1]	Mil. dol.	3,653	4,102	3,921	3,740	3,758	3,791	(NA)
Value of shipments (1992 dollars)	Mil. dol.	3,781	4,030	3,921	3,762	3,677	3,610	(NA)
Total employment	1,000	26.8	28.1	26.3	24.5	25.5	24.3	(NA)
Production workers	1,000	15.2	15.9	15.4	13.8	14.7	15.1	(NA)
Average hourly earnings	Dollar	13.11	13.52	13.63	14.22	15.57	15.05	(NA)
Capital expenditures	Mil. dol.	73.3	102.0	105.0	79.8	77.7	123.0	(NA)
PRODUCT DATA								
Value of shipments [2]	Mil. dol.	3,013	3,400	2,981	2,939	2,976	2,968	(NA)
Value of shipments (1992 dollars)	Mil. dol.	3,119	3,339	2,981	2,956	2,912	2,826	(NA)
TRADE DATA								
Value of imports	Mil. dol.	50.5	64.0	36.2	47.1	67.5	93.2	145.0
Value of exports	Mil. dol.	2,691	3,938	3,986	3,746	3,546	4,168	5,236

NA Not available. [1] Value of all products and services sold by establishments in the oil and gas field machinery industry [2] Value of products classified in the oil and gas field machinery industry produced by all industries.

Source: U.S. Department of Commerce, Bureau of the Census, International Trade Administration (ITA).

No. 1445. Recent Trends in Machine Tools (SIC 3541, 3542): 1990 to 1996

ITEM	Unit	1990	1991	1992	1993	1994	1995	1996
INDUSTRY DATA								
Value of shipments[1]	Mil. dol.	5,126	4,702	5,102	5,231	5,366	6,036	(NA)
3541 Metal cutting machines	Mil. dol.	3,517	3,250	3,618	3,518	3,672	4,056	(NA)
3542 Metal forming machines	Mil. dol.	1,611	1,452	1,484	1,713	1,694	1,982	(NA)
Value of shipments (1992 dollars)	Mil. dol.	5,471	4,831	5,102	5,154	5,196	5,636	(NA)
3541 Metal cutting machines	Mil. dol.	3,769	3,351	3,618	3,476	3,579	3,801	(NA)
3542 Metal forming machines	Mil. dol.	1,701	1,450	1,484	1,677	1,617	1,837	(NA)
Total employment	1,000	43.6	39.8	39.9	38.0	37.1	40.3	(NA)
3541 Metal cutting machines	1,000	29.4	26.9	27.4	25.3	24.0	26.9	(NA)
3542 Metal forming machines	1,000	14.2	12.9	12.5	12.7	13.1	13.4	(NA)
Production workers	1,000	26.6	23.9	23.3	22.3	22.0	24.4	(NA)
3541 Metal cutting machines	1,000	17.6	15.8	15.4	14.5	13.7	15.9	(NA)
3542 Metal forming machines	1,000	9.0	8.1	7.9	7.8	8.3	8.5	(NA)
Average hourly earnings	Dollar	14.40	14.76	15.34	15.72	16.16	16.25	(NA)
3541 Metal cutting machines	Dollar	14.32	14.81	15.54	15.75	16.31	16.26	(NA)
3542 Metal forming machines	Dollar	14.56	14.67	14.93	15.68	15.91	16.22	(NA)
Capital expenditures	Mil. dol.	118	98	124	96	131	190	(NA)
3541 Metal cutting machines	Mil. dol.	84.2	66.4	82.8	63.0	106.0	134.0	(NA)
3542 Metal forming machines	Mil. dol.	33.3	31.6	40.7	32.7	25.4	56.1	(NA)
PRODUCT DATA								
Value of shipments[2]	Mil. dol.	4,806	4,291	4,521	4,524	5,098	5,711	(NA)
3541 Metal cutting machines	Mil. dol.	3,249	2,838	3,093	2,915	3,435	3,853	(NA)
3542 Metal forming machines	Mil. dol.	1,557	1,453	1,428	1,609	1,663	1,828	(NA)
Value of shipments (1992 dollars)	Mil. dol.	5,127	4,407	4,521	4,456	4,934	5,334	(NA)
3541 Metal cutting machines	Mil. dol.	3,483	2,926	3,093	2,881	3,347	3,639	(NA)
3542 Metal forming machines	Mil. dol.	1,644	1,481	1,428	1,576	1,587	1,694	(NA)
TRADE DATA								
Value of imports	Mil. dol.	2,795	2,587	2,311	2,596	3,369	4,380	4,770
3541 Metal cutting machines	Mil. dol.	2,056	1,926	1,681	1,882	2,365	3,101	3,415
3542 Metal forming machines	Mil. dol.	740	661	630	714	1,004	1,279	1,356
Value of exports	Mil. dol.	1,600	1,555	1,836	1,744	2,179	2,265	2,753
3541 Metal cutting machines	Mil. dol.	913	878	1,017	975	1,353	1,350	1,662
3542 Metal forming machines	Mil. dol.	687	678	819	769	826	914	1,090

NA Not available. [1] Value of all products and services sold by establishments in the machine tools industry. [2] Value of products classified in the machine tools industry produced by all industries.

Source: U.S. Department of Commerce, Bureau of the Census, International Trade Administration (ITA).

No. 1446. Recent Trends in Special Dies, Tools, Jigs and Fixtures (SIC 3544): 1990 to 1996

ITEM	Unit	1990	1991	1992	1993	1994	1995	1996
INDUSTRY DATA								
Value of shipments[1]	Mil. dol.	9,250	8,575	9,265	9,951	11,146	12,476	(NA)
Value of shipments (1992 dollars)	Mil. dol.	9,769	8,706	9,265	9,708	10,604	11,660	(NA)
Total employment	1,000	117	110	111	118	119	129	(NA)
Production workers	1,000	89.6	84.0	84.9	90.7	91.8	101.0	(NA)
Average hourly earnings	Dollar	13.75	13.87	14.58	14.70	15.03	15.32	(NA)
Capital expenditures	Mil. dol.	413	387	369	532	541	719	(NA)
PRODUCT DATA								
Value of shipments[2]	Mil. dol.	10,056	9,692	10,230	10,990	12,235	13,534	(NA)
Value of shipments (1992 dollars)	Mil. dol.	10,640	9,839	10,230	10,722	11,641	12,649	(NA)
TRADE DATA								
Value of imports	Mil. dol.	1,202	1,662	1,399	1,880	2,608	2,948	2,656
Value of exports	Mil. dol.	882	863	1,033	1,239	1,306	1,480	1,616

NA Not available. [1] Value of all products and services sold by establishments in the special dies, tools, jigs and fixtures industry. [2] Value of products classified in the special dies, tools, jigs and fixtures industry produced by all industries.

Source: U.S. Department of Commerce, Bureau of the Census, International Trade Administration (ITA).

No. 1447. Recent Trends in Power-Driven Handtools and Welding Apparatus: 1990 to 1996

ITEM	Unit	1990	1991	1992	1993	1994	1995	1996
POWER-DRIVEN HANDTOOLS (SIC 3546)								
Industry data:								
Value of shipments [1]	Mil. dol.	2,736	2,489	2,873	3,480	3,608	3,791	(NA)
Value of shipments (1992 dollars)	Mil. dol.	2,896	2,556	2,873	3,406	3,450	3,563	(NA)
Total employment	1,000	17.5	16.8	16.1	17.0	16.1	17.0	(NA)
Production workers	1,000	12.2	10.9	10.6	11.7	11.2	11.9	(NA)
Average hourly earnings	Dollar	10.32	11.06	11.08	10.96	11.27	12.13	(NA)
Capital expenditures	Mil. dol.	96.4	74.8	72.3	112.0	108.0	118.0	(NA)
Product data:								
Value of shipments [2]	Mil. dol.	2,365	2,239	2,415	3,074	3,281	3,366	(NA)
Value of shipments (1992 dollars)	Mil. dol.	2,503	2,296	2,415	3,006	3,137	3,163	(NA)
Trade data:								
Value of imports	Mil. dol.	716	690	766	824	953	1,086	1,209
Value of exports	Mil. dol.	521	550	568	600	699	736	720
WELDING APPARATUS (SIC 3548)								
Industry data:								
Value of shipments [1]	Mil. dol.	2,616	2,557	2,736	3,101	3,086	3,303	(NA)
Value of shipments (1992 dollars)	Mil. dol.	2,819	2,650	2,736	2,984	2,871	2,960	(NA)
Total employment	1,000	18.6	18.7	19.6	20.3	18.6	18.9	(NA)
Production workers	1,000	11.6	11.3	11.7	13.1	12.0	12.7	(NA)
Average hourly earnings	Dollar	13.34	13.39	13.87	14.76	15.28	15.92	(NA)
Capital expenditures	Mil. dol.	67.7	50.5	65.3	80.6	73.5	89.3	(NA)
Product data:								
Value of shipments [2]	Mil. dol.	2,475	2,434	2,391	2,717	3,043	3,301	(NA)
Value of shipments (1992 dollars)	Mil. dol.	2,667	2,523	2,391	2,615	2,630	2,958	(NA)
Trade data:								
Value of imports	Mil. dol.	367	480	382	535	530	659	751
Value of exports	Mil. dol.	566	599	624	655	685	770	851

NA Not available. [1] Value of all products and services sold by establishments in this industry. Value of products classified in this industry produced by all industries.

Source: U.S. Department of Commerce, Bureau of the Census, International Trade Administration (ITA).

No. 1448. Recent Trends in Textile Machinery and Paper Industries Machinery: 1990 to 1996

ITEM	Unit	1990	1991	1992	1993	1994	1995	1996
TEXTILE MACHINERY (SIC 3552)								
Industry data:								
Value of shipments [1]	Mil. dol.	1,545	1,446	1,571	1,853	1,906	1,996	(NA)
Value of shipments (1992 dollars)	Mil. dol.	1,672	1,492	1,571	1,792	1,837	1,903	(NA)
Total employment	1,000	16.3	15.3	15.0	16.5	16.7	16.9	(NA)
Production workers	1,000	11.0	10.1	9.6	10.1	10.6	10.6	(NA)
Average hourly earnings	Dollar	10.77	11.27	11.06	10.96	11.92	13.00	(NA)
Capital expenditures	Mil. dol.	49.6	36.1	39.5	46.9	71.4	66.3	(NA)
Product data:								
Value of shipments [2]	Mil. dol.	1,325	1,236	1,334	1,612	1,615	1,611	(NA)
Value of shipments (1992 dollars)	Mil. dol.	1,434	1,274	1,334	1,559	1,554	1,536	(NA)
Trade data:								
Value of imports	Mil. dol.	1,449	1,165	1,464	1,781	1,772	1,687	1,447
Value of exports	Mil. dol.	580	534	547	553	567	602	581
PAPER INDUSTRIES MACHINERY (SIC 3554)								
Industry data:								
Value of shipments [1]	Mil. dol.	2,843	2,286	2,524	2,529	2,828	3,424	(NA)
Value of shipments (1992 dollars)	Mil. dol.	2,977	2,328	2,524	2,506	2,759	3,289	(NA)
Total employment	1,000	20.7	18.3	18.2	18.1	17.5	19.4	(NA)
Production workers	1,000	12.2	9.6	10.2	9.8	9.8	10.9	(NA)
Average hourly earnings	Dollar	13.07	14.63	14.76	15.24	16.11	16.48	(NA)
Capital expenditures	Mil. dol.	76.7	68.8	65.4	55.9	49.7	90.7	(NA)
Product data:								
Value of shipments [2]	Mil. dol.	2,453	2,061	2,225	2,253	2,479	2,965	(NA)
Value of shipments (1992 dollars)	Mil. dol.	2,569	2,099	2,225	2,233	2,418	2,849	(NA)
Trade data:								
Value of imports	Mil. dol.	880	694	637	709	907	981	1,182
Value of exports	Mil. dol.	600	637	583	652	653	862	853

NA Not available. [1] Value of all products and services sold by establishments in this industry. [2] Value of products classified in this industry produced by all industries.

Source: U.S. Department of Commerce, Bureau of the Census, International Trade Administration (ITA).

No. 1449. Recent Trends in Printing Trades Machinery, Food Products Machinery, and Packaging Machinery: 1990 to 1996

ITEM	Unit	1990	1991	1992	1993	1994	1995	1996
PRINTING TRADES MACHINERY (SIC 3555)								
Industry data:								
Value of shipments [1]	Mil. dol.	3,631	3,665	2,636	2,727	3,079	3,496	(NA)
Value of shipments (1992 dollars)	Mil. dol.	3,724	3,688	2,635	2,663	2,969	3,310	(NA)
Total employment	1,000	25.5	24.6	19.2	18.9	21.4	21.6	(NA)
Production workers	1,000	12.9	12.1	10.7	10.3	11.7	12.1	(NA)
Average hourly earnings	Dollar	12.95	13.09	13.65	14.59	14.48	14.80	(NA)
Capital expenditures	Mil. dol.	95.4	82.1	62.7	52.9	74.0	101.0	(NA)
Product data:								
Value of shipments [2]	Mil. dol.	3,141	3,171	2,342	2,345	2,814	3,189	(NA)
Value of shipments (1992 dollars)	Mil. dol.	3,222	3,190	2,342	2,290	2,713	3,017	(NA)
Trade data:								
Value of imports	Mil. dol.	1,127	1,146	1,220	1,350	1,556	1,995	1,782
Value of exports	Mil. dol.	1,061	1,072	1,054	1,064	1,029	1,215	1,336
FOOD PRODUCTS MACHINERY (SIC 3556)								
Industry data:								
Value of shipments [1]	Mil. dol.	2,320	2,272	2,417	2,630	2,674	2,819	(NA)
Value of shipments (1992 dollars)	Mil. dol.	2,500	2,342	2,417	2,564	2,520	2,579	(NA)
Total employment	1,000	19.3	18.4	18.9	18.8	19.8	19.9	(NA)
Production workers	1,000	11.2	10.5	11.2	11.3	12.0	12.1	(NA)
Average hourly earnings	Dollar	11.93	12.53	13.06	13.23	13.05	13.46	(NA)
Capital expenditures	Mil. dol.	48.7	46.3	46.8	48.8	48.5	43.0	(NA)
Product data:								
Value of shipments [2]	Mil. dol.	1,954	1,970	2,102	2,311	2,266	2,329	(NA)
Value of shipments (1992 dollars)	Mil. dol.	2,105	2,030	2,102	2,252	2,136	2,131	(NA)
Trade data:								
Value of imports	Mil. dol.	452	427	474	439	481	591	545
Value of exports	Mil. dol.	551	621	687	696	734	792	821
PACKAGING MACHINERY (SIC 3565)								
Industry data:								
Value of shipments [1]	Mil. dol.	2,770	2,890	3,150	3,418	3,690	4,185	(NA)
Value of shipments (1992 dollars)	Mil. dol.	2,906	2,952	3,150	3,322	3,491	3,860	(NA)
Total employment	1,000	23.1	23.4	26.4	24.9	24.8	28.0	(NA)
Production workers	1,000	13.0	13.4	15.6	14.2	14.9	16.9	(NA)
Average hourly earnings	Dollar	13.60	13.97	13.86	14.29	14.52	14.69	(NA)
Capital expenditures	Mil. dol.	70.2	64.5	70.6	90.2	96.6	87.0	(NA)
Product data:								
Value of shipments [2]	Mil. dol.	2,680	2,767	2,861	3,096	3,257	3,630	(NA)
Value of shipments (1992 dollars)	Mil. dol.	2,812	2,826	2,861	3,011	3,061	3,349	(NA)
Trade data:								
Value of imports	Mil. dol.	621	643	699	719	842	932	1,042
Value of exports	Mil. dol.	579	611	606	672	792	639	841

NA Not available. [1] Value of all products and services sold by establishments in this industry. [2] Value of products classified in this industry produced by all industries.

Source: U.S. Department of Commerce, Bureau of the Census, International Trade Administration (ITA).

No. 1450. Recent Trends in Computers and Peripherals (SIC 3571,2,5,7): 1990 to 1996

[Census reclassified some parts for electronic computers (3571) to component industries (367) for 1989-1990]

ITEM	Unit	1990	1991	1992	1993	1994	1995	1996
INDUSTRY DATA								
Value of shipments [1]	Mil. dol.	60,118	56,236	61,969	64,374	73,345	84,997	(NA)
Total employment	1,000	252	232	221	211	201	214	(NA)
Production workers	1,000	89.2	75.8	74.2	73.9	75.8	79.9	(NA)
Average hourly earnings	Dollar	11.68	12.45	12.26	12.77	13.67	13.56	(NA)
Capital expenditures	Mil. dol.	1,997	1,817	2,137	2,045	1,907	1,936	(NA)
PRODUCT DATA								
Value of shipments [2]	Mil. dol.	52,628	49,144	54,722	57,928	65,635	81,015	(NA)
TRADE DATA								
Value of imports	Mil. dol.	22,064	25,216	30,710	36,978	45,124	55,185	60,245
Value of exports	Mil. dol.	22,941	23,900	24,867	25,263	26,966	34,304	37,629

NA Not available. [1] Value of all products and services sold by establishments in the computers and peripherals industry. [2] Value of products classified in the computers and peripherals industry produced by all industries.

Source: U.S. Department of Commerce, Bureau of the Census, International Trade Administration (ITA).

No. 1451. Recent Trends in Electrical Equipment (SIC 361, 3621, 3625): 1989 to 1995

ITEM	Unit	1989	1990	1991	1992	1993	1994	1995 [1]
INDUSTRY								
Value of shipments (1992 dollars)	Mil. dol.	26,780	26,234	24,555	25,237	27,337	29,036	30,940
3612 Transformers	Mil. dol.	4,252	4,216	3,875	4,096	4,028	4,783	5,680
3613 Switchgear and apparatus	Mil. dol.	5,942	5,776	5,361	5,528	5,723	5,859	5,996
3621 Motors and generators	Mil. dol.	8,534	7,869	7,759	8,040	9,064	9,199	9,336
3625 Relays and controls	Mil. dol.	8,052	8,373	7,560	7,573	8,522	9,197	9,926

[1] Estimate.

Source: U.S. Department of Commerce, Bureau of the Census, International Trade Administration (ITA). Estimates by ITA.

No. 1452. Recent Trends in Transformers, Except Electronic (SIC 3612): 1990 to 1996

ITEM	Unit	1990	1991	1992	1993	1994	1995	1996
INDUSTRY DATA								
Value of shipments [1]	Mil. dol.	4,143	3,952	4,118	3,940	4,706	5,344	(NA)
Value of shipments (1992 dollars)	Mil. dol.	4,181	3,833	4,118	4,026	4,819	5,291	(NA)
Total employment	1,000	33.0	30.8	29.0	27.9	30.7	32.4	(NA)
Production workers	1,000	25.0	23.5	22.0	21.1	21.7	23.4	(NA)
Average hourly earnings	Dollar	10.92	11.20	11.62	12.00	11.91	12.17	(NA)
Capital expenditures	Mil. dol.	114.0	122.0	65.3	77.8	166.0	133.0	(NA)
PRODUCT DATA								
Value of shipments [2]	Mil. dol.	4,032	3,966	4,086	3,906	4,485	4,770	(NA)
Value of shipments (1992 dollars)	Mil. dol.	4,069	3,837	4,086	3,994	4,591	4,723	(NA)
TRADE DATA								
Value of imports	Mil. dol.	360	435	500	606	592	815	826
Value of exports	Mil. dol.	261	301	336	359	384	469	518

NA Not available. [1] Value of all products and services sold by establishments in the transformers, except electronic industry. [2] Value of products classified in the transformers, except electronic industry produced by all industries.

Source: U.S. Department of Commerce, Bureau of the Census, International Trade Administration (ITA).

No. 1453. Recent Trends in Household Appliances (SIC 363): 1990 to 1996

ITEM	Unit	1990	1991	1992	1993	1994	1995	1996
INDUSTRY DATA								
Value of shipments [1]	Mil. dol.	17,661	17,175	18,633	20,435	22,829	22,391	(NA)
3631 Household cooking equipment	Mil. dol.	2,930	2,806	2,950	3,010	3,849	3,788	(NA)
3632 Household refrigerators	Mil. dol.	3,718	3,613	4,232	4,463	5,149	5,006	(NA)
3633 Household laundry equipment	Mil. dol.	3,165	3,112	3,329	3,871	4,612	3,969	(NA)
3634 Electric housewares and fans	Mil. dol.	2,990	3,021	2,897	3,106	3,053	3,164	(NA)
3635 Household vacuums	Mil. dol.	1,820	1,752	1,905	2,096	1,933	2,031	(NA)
3639 Home appliances, n.e.c.	Mil. dol.	3,056	2,872	3,320	3,889	4,233	4,433	(NA)
Value of shipments (1992 dollars)	Mil. dol.	17,860	17,246	18,633	20,199	22,520	22,077	(NA)
3631 Household cooking equipment	Mil. dol.	2,918	2,806	2,950	2,931	3,762	3,740	(NA)
3632 Household refrigerators	Mil. dol.	3,649	3,616	4,232	4,436	5,066	4,966	(NA)
3633 Household laundry equipment	Mil. dol.	3,131	3,075	3,329	3,887	4,666	4,029	(NA)
3634 Electric housewares and fans	Mil. dol.	3,086	3,061	2,897	3,087	3,065	3,193	(NA)
3635 Household vacuums	Mil. dol.	1,874	1,743	1,905	2,037	1,843	1,927	(NA)
3639 Home appliances, n.e.c.	Mil. dol.	3,202	2,945	3,320	3,820	4,114	4,222	(NA)
Total employment	1,000	108	101	103	105	111	111	(NA)
Production workers	1,000	86.4	81.1	83.2	85.0	90.6	88.9	(NA)
Average hourly earnings	Dollar	11.02	11.13	11.34	11.72	11.74	12.09	(NA)
Capital expenditures	Mil. dol.	383	487	556	481	517	632	(NA)
PRODUCT DATA								
Value of shipments [2]	Mil. dol.	16,500	16,089	16,789	18,027	19,841	19,430	(NA)
3631 Household cooking equipment	Mil. dol.	3,027	2,942	3,007	3,162	3,821	3,792	(NA)
3632 Household refrigerators	Mil. dol.	3,711	3,621	4,048	4,309	4,995	4,936	(NA)
3633 Household laundry equipment	Mil. dol.	2,906	2,860	2,995	3,299	3,671	3,360	(NA)
3634 Electric housewares and fans	Mil. dol.	2,684	2,608	2,653	2,710	2,651	2,746	(NA)
3635 Household vacuums	Mil. dol.	1,876	1,834	1,809	2,015	1,788	1,892	(NA)
3639 Home appliances, n.e.c.	Mil. dol.	2,296	2,224	2,279	2,531	2,916	2,665	(NA)
Value of shipments (1992 dollars)	Mil. dol.	16,637	16,141	16,789	17,813	19,566	19,194	(NA)
3631 Household cooking equipment	Mil. dol.	3,015	2,942	3,007	3,079	3,735	3,743	(NA)
3632 Household refrigerators	Mil. dol.	3,642	3,625	4,048	4,283	4,916	4,897	(NA)
3633 Household laundry equipment	Mil. dol.	2,874	2,825	2,995	3,312	3,715	3,432	(NA)
3634 Electric housewares and fans	Mil. dol.	2,769	2,642	2,653	2,694	2,662	2,771	(NA)
3635 Household vacuums	Mil. dol.	1,932	1,825	1,809	1,958	1,705	1,795	(NA)
3639 Home appliances, n.e.c.	Mil. dol.	2,405	2,281	2,279	2,486	2,634	2,557	(NA)
TRADE DATA								
Value of imports	Mil. dol.	3,400	3,675	4,322	4,535	4,915	5,131	5,444
Value of exports	Mil. dol.	1,828	2,120	2,353	2,540	2,624	2,679	2,869

NA Not available. [1] Value of all products and services sold by establishments in the household appliances industry. [2] Value of products classified in the household appliances industry produced by all industries.

Source: U.S. Department of Commerce, Bureau of the Census, International Trade Administration (ITA).

No. 1454. Recent Trends in Lighting Fixtures and Wiring Devices: 1990 to 1996

ITEM	Unit	1990	1991	1992	1993	1994	1995	1996
LIGHTING FIXTURES (SIC 3645, 3646, 3648)								
Industry data:								
Value of shipments [1]	Mil. dol.	6,646	6,247	6,727	7,075	8,050	8,102	(NA)
Value of shipments (1992 dollars)	Mil. dol.	6,830	6,303	6,727	7,041	7,945	7,750	(NA)
Total employment	1,000	55.0	51.8	51.6	52.4	54.1	56.3	(NA)
Production workers	1,000	38.0	35.5	35.9	36.5	38.5	40.4	(NA)
Average hourly earnings	Dollar	8.96	9.30	9.36	9.50	10.06	10.30	(NA)
Product data:								
Value of shipments [2]	Mil. dol.	6,621	6,194	6,720	7,150	7,806	8,006	(NA)
3645 Residential lighting fixtures	Mil. dol.	1,586	1,409	1,681	1,896	2,041	1,999	(NA)
3646 Commercial lighting fixtures	Mil. dol.	3,196	2,955	3,047	3,122	3,294	3,558	(NA)
3648 Lighting equipment, n.e.c.	Mil. dol.	1,838	1,830	1,993	2,132	2,472	2,448	(NA)
Value of shipments (1992 dollars)	Mil. dol.	6,803	6,249	6,720	7,111	7,699	7,657	(NA)
3645 Residential lighting fixtures	Mil. dol.	1,618	1,423	1,681	1,861	1,977	1,895	(NA)
3646 Commercial lighting fixtures	Mil. dol.	3,309	2,984	3,047	3,110	3,242	3,376	(NA)
3648 Lighting equipment, n.e.c.	Mil. dol.	1,876	1,841	1,993	2,141	2,480	2,386	(NA)
WIRING DEVICES (SIC 3643, 3644)								
Industry data:								
Value of shipments (1992 dollars)	Mil. dol.	7,958	7,175	7,892	7,896	8,206	8,528	(NA)
3643 Wiring devices, current	Mil. dol.	4,554	4,316	4,668	4,576	4,714	(NA)	(NA)
3644 Wiring goods, noncurrent	Mil. dol.	3,404	2,859	3,224	3,320	3,491	(NA)	(NA)

NA Not available. [1] Value of all products and services sold by establishments in this industry. [2] Value of products classified in this industry produced by all industries.

Source: U.S. Department of Commerce, Bureau of the Census, International Trade Administration (ITA).

No. 1455. Recent Trends in Household Audio and Video Equipment (SIC 3651): 1990 to 1996

ITEM	Unit	1990	1991	1992	1993	1994	1995	1996
INDUSTRY DATA								
Value of shipments [1]	Mil. dol.	7,459	7,907	8,794	9,159	10,102	11,278	(NA)
Value of shipments (1992 dollars)	Mil. dol.	7,414	7,805	8,794	9,346	10,306	11,760	(NA)
Total employment	1,000	31.0	31.4	31.3	31.2	28.5	30.5	(NA)
Production workers	1,000	22.7	22.0	22.4	22.6	21.7	22.5	(NA)
Average hourly earnings	Dollar	9.02	9.39	9.55	9.60	9.74	10.38	(NA)
Capital expenditures	Mil. dol.	268	295	253	212	219	270	(NA)
PRODUCT DATA								
Value of shipments [2]	Mil. dol.	7,092	7,154	7,664	7,915	8,697	8,918	(NA)
Value of shipments (1992 dollars)	Mil. dol.	7,050	7,062	7,664	8,076	8,874	9,299	(NA)
TRADE DATA								
Value of imports	Mil. dol.	11,026	11,381	12,961	13,533	16,243	17,555	16,295
Value of exports	Mil. dol.	2,102	2,286	2,466	2,691	3,116	3,334	3,516

NA Not available. [1] Value of all products and services sold by establishments in the household audio and video equipment industry. [2] Value of products classified in the household audio and video equipment industry produced by all industries.

Source: U.S. Department of Commerce, Bureau of the Census, International Trade Administration (ITA).

No. 1456. Recent Trends in Telecommunications Equipment (SIC 3661, 3663): 1990 to 1996

ITEM	Unit	1990	1991	1992	1993	1994	1995	1996
INDUSTRY DATA								
Value of shipments [1]	Mil. dol.	36,153	35,719	40,031	42,190	49,371	55,219	(NA)
Value of shipments (1992 dollars)	Mil. dol.	36,961	36,178	40,031	41,736	48,616	54,561	(NA)
Total employment	1,000	228	217	216	208	220	216	(NA)
Production workers	1,000	106	99	103	95	100	100	(NA)
Average hourly earnings	Dollar	13.06	13.52	14.28	14.35	14.25	15.38	(NA)
Capital expenditures	Mil. dol.	1,366	1,080	1,317	1,445	1,518	1,952	(NA)
PRODUCT DATA								
Value of shipments [2]	Mil. dol.	33,772	32,531	36,106	38,151	45,494	51,762	(NA)
Value of shipments (1992 dollars)	Mil. dol.	34,553	32,973	36,106	37,742	44,804	51,153	(NA)
TRADE DATA								
Value of imports	Mil. dol.	8,347	8,778	9,137	10,159	12,346	13,322	14,447
Value of exports	Mil. dol.	5,210	5,296	6,403	8,063	10,074	12,571	13,025

NA Not available. [1] Value of all products and services sold by establishments in the telecommunications equipment industry. [2] Value of products classified in the telecommunications equipment industry produced by all industries.

Source: U.S. Department of Commerce, Bureau of the Census, International Trade Administration (ITA).

No. 1457. Recent Trends in Telephone and Telegraph Apparatus, and Radio and TV Communications Equipment: 1990 to 1996

ITEM	Unit	1990	1991	1992	1993	1994	1995	1996
TELEPHONE AND TELEGRAPH APPARATUS (SIC 3661)								
Industry data:								
Value of shipments [1]	Mil. dol.	17,344	17,486	20,510	21,540	23,243	25,859	(NA)
Value of shipments (1992 dollars)	Mil. dol.	17,328	17,384	20,510	21,411	23,150	25,833	(NA)
Total employment	1,000	92.6	94.0	91.1	84.9	86.5	88.1	(NA)
Production workers	1,000	45.9	46.0	44.8	38.5	41.3	40.0	(NA)
Average hourly earnings	Dollar	14.58	14.61	14.90	15.34	15.35	16.79	(NA)
Capital expenditures	Mil. dol.	602	471	615	595	662	740	(NA)
Product data:								
Value of shipments [2]	Mil. dol.	16,037	15,284	18,328	19,589	21,861	24,606	(NA)
Value of shipments (1992 dollars)	Mil. dol.	16,021	15,193	18,328	19,472	21,575	24,584	(NA)
RADIO AND TV COMMUNICATIONS EQUIPMENT (SIC 3663)								
Industry data:								
Value of shipments [1]	Mil. dol.	18,810	18,231	19,521	20,650	26,128	29,360	(NA)
Value of shipments (1992 dollars)	Mil. dol.	19,655	18,795	19,521	20,325	25,466	28,728	(NA)
Total employment	1,000	135	123	125	123	133	128	(NA)
Production workers	1,000	61.6	52.7	58.6	56.0	59.0	60.2	(NA)
Average hourly earnings	Dollar	11.99	12.63	13.82	13.66	13.51	14.49	(NA)
Capital expenditures	Mil. dol.	764	609	702	851	856	1,212	(NA)
Product data:								
Value of shipments [2]	Mil. dol.	17,735	17,247	17,778	18,562	23,833	27,154	(NA)
Value of shipments (1992 dollars)	Mil. dol.	18,532	17,781	17,778	18,269	23,229	26,569	(NA)

NA Not available. [1] Value of all products and services sold by establishments in this industry. [2] Value of products classified in this industry produced by all industries.

Source: U.S. Department of Commerce, Bureau of the Census, International Trade Administration (ITA).

No. 1458. Recent Trends in Electronic Components and Accessories (SIC 367): 1990 to 1996

ITEM	Unit	1990	1991	1992	1993	1994	1995	1996
INDUSTRY DATA								
Value of shipments [1]	Mil. dol.	62,579	67,547	73,642	81,236	97,131	119,286	(NA)
Value of shipments (1992 dollars)	Mil. dol.	61,640	66,557	73,642	81,048	97,511	125,122	(NA)
Total employment	1,000	549	537	530	531	551	587	(NA)
Production workers	1,000	330	320	317	321	340	366	(NA)
Average hourly earnings	Dollar	10.22	10.33	10.83	10.98	11.14	11.38	(NA)
PRODUCT DATA								
Value of shipments [2]	Mil. dol.	59,307	62,766	71,372	77,840	92,718	113,949	(NA)
Value of shipments (1992 dollars)	Mil. dol.	58,549	61,920	71,372	77,661	93,019	119,254	(NA)
TRADE DATA								
Value of imports	Mil. dol.	20,530	21,729	24,259	29,238	37,586	53,111	50,824
Value of exports	Mil. dol.	16,973	17,086	17,670	20,513	26,636	34,038	35,749

NA Not available. [1] Value of all products and services sold by establishments in the electronic components and accessories industry. [2] Value of products classified in the electronic components and accessories industry produced by all industries.

Source: U.S. Department of Commerce, Bureau of the Census, International Trade Administration (ITA).

No. 1459. Recent Trends in Electron Tubes (SIC 3671): 1990 to 1996

ITEM	Unit	1990	1991	1992	1993	1994	1995	1996
INDUSTRY DATA								
Value of shipments [1]	Mil. dol.	2,644	2,659	3,145	3,052	3,148	3,448	(NA)
Value of shipments (1992 dollars)	Mil. dol.	2,641	2,618	3,145	3,065	3,126	3,380	(NA)
Total employment	1,000	23.9	22.8	22.2	20.2	20.4	21.5	(NA)
Production workers	1,000	17.7	16.6	16.8	15.3	15.8	16.6	(NA)
Average hourly earnings	Dollar	12.57	12.90	13.21	13.73	13.25	13.10	(NA)
Capital expenditures	Mil. dol.	175.0	81.0	61.7	85.5	132.0	142.0	(NA)
PRODUCT DATA								
Value of shipments [2]	Mil. dol.	2,650	2,659	3,357	3,330	3,561	3,846	(NA)
Value of shipments (1992 dollars)	Mil. dol.	2,647	2,617	3,357	3,367	3,536	3,771	(NA)
TRADE DATA								
Value of imports	Mil. dol.	782	817	928	990	1,218	1,390	1,239
Value of exports	Mil. dol.	641	759	771	929	1,232	1,541	1,720

NA Not available. [1] Value of all products and services sold by establishments in the electron tubes industry. [2] Value of products classified in the electron tubes industry produced by all industries.

Source: U.S. Department of Commerce, Bureau of the Census, International Trade Administration (ITA).

No. 1460. Recent Trends in Printed Circuit Boards and Semiconductors and Related Devices: 1990 to 1996

ITEM	Unit	1990	1991	1992	1993	1994	1995	1996
PRINTED CIRCUIT BOARDS (SIC 3672)								
Industry data:								
Value of shipments [1]	Mil. dol.	8,068	6,578	7,320	7,378	8,416	9,578	(NA)
Value of shipments (1992 dollars)	Mil. dol.	7,988	6,532	7,320	7,551	8,803	9,996	(NA)
Total employment	1,000	78.5	72.2	76.0	73.6	76.9	82.8	(NA)
Production workers	1,000	51.8	48.1	51.0	50.5	54.0	59.6	(NA)
Average hourly earnings	Dollar	9.67	9.92	10.16	10.56	10.49	10.32	(NA)
Capital expenditures	Mil. dol.	418	326	318	283	381	455	(NA)
Product data:								
Value of shipments [2]	Mil. dol.	7,617	5,899	6,293	6,930	7,555	8,762	(NA)
Value of shipments (1992 dollars)	Mil. dol.	7,541	5,858	6,293	7,093	7,902	9,146	(NA)
Trade data:								
Value of imports	Mil. dol.	2,601	2,712	2,097	2,141	2,364	2,741	2,509
Value of exports	Mil. dol.	1,818	1,374	1,092	973	1,377	1,651	1,694
SEMICONDUCTORS AND RELATED DEVICES (SIC 3674)								
Industry data:								
Value of shipments [1]	Mil. dol.	26,718	30,721	32,191	35,152	47,266	65,623	(NA)
Value of shipments (1992 dollars)	Mil. dol.	24,806	29,230	32,191	35,222	47,790	71,252	(NA)
Total employment	1,000	186	181	172	163	183	193	(NA)
Production workers	1,000	89.1	88.1	84.8	82.2	92.9	99.0	(NA)
Average hourly earnings	Dollar	12.58	12.68	13.55	14.08	14.46	14.86	(NA)
Product data:								
Value of shipments [2]	Mil. dol.	23,978	27,438	29,391	33,689	44,064	60,029	(NA)
Value of shipments (1992 dollars)	Mil. dol.	22,263	26,106	29,391	33,757	44,554	65,178	(NA)
Trade data:								
Value of imports	Mil. dol.	11,787	12,740	15,075	19,173	25,619	38,625	36,468
Value of exports	Mil. dol.	10,575	10,725	11,279	13,544	17,423	22,404	23,754

NA Not available. [1] Value of all products and services sold by establishments in this industry. [2] Value of products classified in this industry produced by all industries.

Source: U.S. Department of Commerce, Bureau of the Census, International Trade Administration (ITA).

No. 1461. Recent Trends in Passive Components (SIC 3675-9): 1990 to 1996

ITEM	Unit	1990	1991	1992	1993	1994	1995	1996
INDUSTRY DATA								
Value of shipments [1]	Mil. dol.	25,150	27,588	30,986	35,656	38,302	40,639	(NA)
Value of shipments (1992 dollars)	Mil. dol.	26,203	28,177	30,986	35,189	37,791	40,492	(NA)
Total employment	1,000	260	261	260	275	271	290	(NA)
Production workers	1,000	172	168	165	173	177	191	(NA)
Average hourly earnings	Dollar	8.94	8.99	9.45	9.48	9.53	9.83	(NA)
Capital expenditures	Mil. dol.	814	833	983	1,314	1,248	1,426	(NA)
PRODUCT DATA								
Value of shipments [2]	Mil. dol.	25,063	26,771	32,330	33,892	37,540	41,312	(NA)
Value of shipments (1992 dollars)	Mil. dol.	26,098	27,339	32,330	33,445	37,027	41,159	(NA)
TRADE DATA								
Value of imports	Mil. dol.	5,360	5,460	6,160	6,934	8,365	10,354	10,606
Value of exports	Mil. dol.	3,940	4,228	4,527	5,067	6,605	8,442	8,582

NA Not available. [1] Value of all products and services sold by establishments in the passive components industry. [2] Value of products classified in the passive components industry produced by all industries.

Source: U.S. Department of Commerce, Bureau of the Census, International Trade Administration (ITA).

No. 1462. Recent Trends in Motor Vehicles and Car Bodies (SIC 3711): 1990 to 1996

ITEM	Unit	1990	1991	1992	1993	1994	1995	1996
INDUSTRY DATA								
Value of shipments [1]	Mil. dol.	141,940	135,881	151,682	167,826	197,514	200,939	(NA)
Value of shipments (1992 dollars)	Mil. dol.	153,283	140,228	151,682	162,151	183,905	186,883	(NA)
Total employment	1,000	244	224	228	224	234	237	(NA)
Production workers	1,000	203	182	193	191	203	207	(NA)
Average hourly earnings	Dollar	20.14	21.07	21.96	22.61	23.39	24.48	(NA)
Capital expenditures	Mil. dol.	3,136	3,447	2,988	4,034	4,247	4,521	(NA)
PRODUCT DATA								
Value of shipments [2]	Mil. dol.	135,741	128,754	147,447	163,324	194,977	196,021	(NA)
Value of shipments (1992 dollars)	Mil. dol.	146,588	132,873	147,447	157,801	181,543	183,183	(NA)
TRADE DATA								
Value of imports	Mil. dol.	60,573	59,134	60,399	68,526	79,376	84,441	87,213
Value of exports	Mil. dol.	12,862	15,202	17,657	18,458	21,150	21,618	23,008

NA Not available. [1] Value of all products and services sold by establishments in the motor vehicles and car bodies industry. [2] Value of products classified in the motor vehicles and car bodies industry produced by all industries.

Source: U.S. Department of Commerce, Bureau of the Census, International Trade Administration (ITA).

No. 1463. Recent Trends in Aerospace (SIC 372, 376): 1990 to 1996

ITEM	Unit	1990	1991	1992	1993	1994	1995	1996
INDUSTRY DATA								
Value of shipments [1]	Mil. dol.	125,822	132,182	131,367	116,346	103,316	102,532	(NA)
Value of shipments (1992 dollars)	Mil. dol.	136,522	137,510	131,367	113,891	98,739	95,744	(NA)
Total employment	1,000	821	752	694	612	525	483	(NA)
Production workers	1,000	398	362	331	279	241	224	(NA)
Average hourly earnings	Dollar	16.37	16.75	18.74	19.05	20.00	20.39	(NA)
Capital expenditures	Mil. dol.	3,485	3,400	3,837	2,725	2,363	2,156	(NA)
PRODUCT DATA								
Value of shipments [2]	Mil. dol.	118,141	124,109	122,800	110,312	96,968	95,248	(NA)
Value of shipments (1992 dollars)	Mil. dol.	127,856	129,061	122,800	107,971	92,664	88,983	(NA)
TRADE DATA								
Value of imports	Mil. dol.	11,008	12,426	12,918	11,542	11,715	10,947	13,128
Value of exports	Mil. dol.	36,055	41,177	42,179	36,704	34,781	29,870	37,393

NA Not available. [1] Value of all products and services sold by establishments in the aerospace industry. [2] Value of products classified in the aerospace industry produced by all industries.

Source: U.S. Department of Commerce, Bureau of the Census, International Trade Administration (ITA).

No. 1464. Recent Trends in Aircraft and Aircraft Engines and Engine Parts: 1990 to 1996

ITEM	Unit	1990	1991	1992	1993	1994	1995	1996
AIRCRAFT (SIC 3721)								
Industry data:								
Value of shipments [1]	Mil. dol.	51,653	58,486	62,940	55,120	50,970	49,504	(NA)
Value of shipments (1992 dollars)	Mil. dol.	56,513	60,796	62,940	53,775	48,222	45,292	(NA)
Total employment	1,000	291	260	265	241	218	201	(NA)
Production workers	1,000	140	125	122	104	93	86	(NA)
Average hourly earnings	Dollar	17.05	17.86	20.00	19.90	20.75	22.14	(NA)
Capital expenditures	Mil. dol.	1,018	1,043	1,660	1,154	877	628	(NA)
Product data:								
Value of shipments [2]	Mil. dol.	46,886	52,514	56,569	51,006	46,814	44,434	(NA)
Value of shipments (1992 dollars)	Mil. dol.	51,297	54,588	56,569	49,762	44,289	40,653	(NA)
Trade data:								
Value of imports	Mil. dol.	2,838	3,438	3,921	3,738	3,809	3,557	3,948
Value of exports	Mil. dol.	19,631	24,173	26,419	21,306	18,831	13,614	18,970
AIRCRAFT ENGINES AND ENGINE PARTS (SIC 3724)								
Industry data:								
Value of shipments [1]	Mil. dol.	22,939	22,901	22,408	18,946	16,584	17,519	(NA)
Value of shipments (1992 dollars)	Mil. dol.	25,488	24,157	22,408	18,575	15,855	16,528	(NA)
Total employment	1,000	130	123	120	103	84	76	(NA)
Production workers	1,000	72.5	67.2	66.5	53.6	45.5	41.9	(NA)
Average hourly earnings	Dollar	15.71	15.60	17.25	17.15	18.79	18.17	(NA)
Capital expenditures	Mil. dol.	783	768	598	440	435	475	(NA)
Product data:								
Value of shipments [2]	Mil. dol.	21,580	21,315	20,933	17,995	15,218	15,701	(NA)
Value of shipments (1992 dollars)	Mil. dol.	23,978	22,484	20,933	17,642	14,549	14,812	(NA)
Trade data:								
Value of imports	Mil. dol.	4,843	5,100	5,864	5,366	5,430	4,875	5,829
Value of exports	Mil. dol.	6,859	7,025	6,674	6,243	6,451	6,130	6,798

NA Not available. [1] Value of all products and services sold by establishments in this industry. [2] Value of products classified in this industry produced by all industries.

Source: U.S. Department of Commerce, Bureau of the Census, International Trade Administration (ITA).

No. 1465. Recent Trends in Aircraft Parts and Equipment, n.e.c. (SIC 3728): 1990 to 1996

ITEM	Unit	1990	1991	1992	1993	1994	1995	1996
INDUSTRY DATA								
Value of shipments [1]	Mil. dol.	20,571	21,691	19,511	18,264	17,049	16,841	(NA)
Value of shipments (1992 dollars)	Mil. dol.	22,263	22,713	19,511	17,750	16,206	15,948	(NA)
Total employment	1,000	198	189	163	139	122	116	(NA)
Production workers	1,000	111.0	107.0	92.0	78.4	66.1	64.0	(NA)
Average hourly earnings	Dollar	14.92	15.09	16.71	18.37	19.20	19.73	(NA)
Capital expenditures	Mil. dol.	813	1,003	1,112	713	656	673	(NA)
PRODUCT DATA								
Value of shipments [2]	Mil. dol.	23,082	25,288	21,940	18,684	17,710	17,627	(NA)
Value of shipments (1992 dollars)	Mil. dol.	24,980	26,480	21,940	18,157	16,835	16,692	(NA)
TRADE DATA								
Value of imports	Mil. dol.	3,324	3,888	3,132	2,437	2,476	2,515	3.337
Value of exports	Mil. dol.	9,518	9,953	9,050	9,133	9,472	10,070	11,497

NA Not available. [1] Value of all products and services sold by establishments in the aircraft parts and equipment, n.e c [2] Value of products classified in the aircraft parts and equipment, n.e.c. industry produced by all industries.

U.S. Department of Commerce, Bureau of the Census, International Trade Administration (ITA).

No. 1466. Recent Trends in Ship Building and Repairing (SIC 3731): 1990 to 1996

ITEM	Unit	1990	1991	1992	1993	1994	1995	1996
INDUSTRY DATA								
Value of shipments [1]	Mil. dol.	10,915	10,936	10,601	9,964	9,865	9,586	(NA)
Value of shipments (1992 dollars)	Mil. dol.	11,311	11,068	10,601	9,454	9,017	8,794	(NA)
Total employment	1,000	122	122	118	112	102	95.4	(NA)
Production workers	1,000	91.5	90.9	87.0	81.9	76.0	70.5	(NA)
Average hourly earnings	Dollar	12.47	12.79	13.05	13.45	14.00	14.76	(NA)
Capital expenditures	Mil. dol.	232	180	128	156	166	232	(NA)
PRODUCT DATA								
Value of shipments [2]	Mil. dol.	10,741	10,700	10,361	9,801	9,877	9,544	(NA)
Value of shipments (1992 dollars)	Mil. dol.	11,131	10,830	10,361	9,299	9,028	8,756	(NA)
TRADE DATA								
Value of imports	Mil. dol.	14.8	14.4	50.9	517.0	12.4	29.4	54.0
Value of exports	Mil. dol.	434	321	652	379	595	483	346

NA Not available. [1] Value of all products and services sold by establishments in the ship building and repairing industry. [2] Value of products classified in the ship building and repairing industry produced by all industries.

Source: U.S. Department of Commerce, Bureau of the Census, International Trade Administration (ITA).

No. 1467. Recent Trends in Boat Building and Repairing (SIC 3732): 1990 to 1996

ITEM	Unit	1990	1991	1992	1993	1994	1995	1996
INDUSTRY DATA								
Value of shipments [1]	Mil. dol.	5,025	3,705	4,648	4,975	5,334	5,640	(NA)
Value of shipments (1992 dollars)	Mil. dol.	5,295	3,800	4,648	4,887	5,154	5,296	(NA)
Total employment	1,000	54.3	41.0	44.5	47.0	47.6	47.6	(NA)
Production workers	1,000	42.9	31.9	34.6	36.8	36.4	36.6	(NA)
Average hourly earnings	Dollar	8.59	9.04	9.58	9.57	9.70	10.45	(NA)
Capital expenditures	Mil. dol.	85.4	40.5	63.6	63.2	96.9	86.9	(NA)
PRODUCT DATA								
Value of shipments [2]	Mil. dol.	4,877	3,518	4,331	4,632	4,867	5,066	(NA)
Value of shipments (1992 dollars)	Mil. dol.	5,140	3,608	4,331	4,550	4,722	4,756	(NA)
TRADE DATA								
Value of imports	Mil. dol.	279	207	257	425	564	807	997
Value of exports	Mil. dol.	793	774	714	534	507	658	621

NA Not available. [1] Value of all products and services sold by establishments in the boat building and repairing industry. [2] Value of products classified in the boat building and repairing industry produced by all industries

Source: U.S. Department of Commerce, Bureau of the Census, International Trade Administration (ITA).

No. 1468. Recent Trends in Motorcycles, Bicycles, and Parts (SIC 3751): 1990 to 1996

ITEM	Unit	1990	1991	1992	1993	1994	1995	1996
INDUSTRY DATA								
Value of shipments [1]	Mil. dol.	1,274	1,582	2,134	2,566	2,632	2,833	(NA)
Value of shipments (1992 dollars)	Mil. dol.	1,328	1,615	2,134	2,513	2,546	2,673	(NA)
Total employment	1,000	8.5	9.5	12.8	14.1	15.7	16.1	(NA)
Production workers	1,000	6.8	7.3	9.9	10.5	11.7	12.0	(NA)
Average hourly earnings	Dollar	10.24	11.73	12.18	13.53	14.50	13.97	(NA)
Capital expenditures	Mil. dol.	22.0	56.6	62.0	50.6	92.3	118.0	(NA)
PRODUCT DATA								
Value of shipments [2]	Mil. dol.	1,799	2,112	2,153	2,640	2,549	2,619	(NA)
Value of shipments (1992 dollars)	Mil. dol.	1,876	2,155	2,153	2,585	2,465	2,471	(NA)
TRADE DATA								
Value of imports	Mil. dol.	1,199	1,329	1,537	1,717	1,763	2,130	2,015
Value of exports	Mil. dol.	420	615	671	703	711	850	906

NA Not available. [1] Value of all products and services sold by establishments in the motorcycles, bicycles, and parts industry. [2] Value of products classified in the motorcycles, bicycles, and parts industry produced by all industries.

Source: U.S. Department of Commerce, Bureau of the Census, International Trade Administration (ITA).

No. 1469. Recent Trends in Guided Missiles and Space Vehicles and Space Propulsion Units and Parts: 1990 to 1996

ITEM	Unit	1990	1991	1992	1993	1994	1995	1996
GUIDED MISSILES AND SPACE VEHICLES (SIC 3761)								
Industry data:								
Value of shipments [1]	Mil. dol.	25,169	23,513	19,423	15,800	13,954	14,315	(NA)
Value of shipments (1992 dollars)	Mil. dol.	26,634	24,165	19,423	15,659	13,761	13,791	(NA)
Total employment	1,000	158.0	138.0	97.7	86.6	66.5	60.8	(NA)
Production workers	1,000	54.3	45.1	30.1	27.6	23.8	20.0	(NA)
Average hourly earnings	Dollar	18.17	18.94	22.58	20.88	21.30	20.65	(NA)
Capital expenditures	Mil. dol.	660	452	313	308	297	294	(NA)
Product data:								
Value of shipments [2]	Mil. dol.	16,907	16,075	13,972	13,452	10,795	11,756	(NA)
Value of shipments (1992 dollars)	Mil. dol.	17,891	16,521	13,972	13,332	10,648	11,326	(NA)
Trade data:								
Value of imports	Mil. dol.	0.1	-	-	0.2	0.3	0.6	0.4
Value of exports	Mil. dol.	17.2	19.3	22.9	22.1	24.4	15.5	104.0
SPACE PROPULSION UNITS AND PARTS (SIC 3764)								
Industry data:								
Value of shipments [1]	Mil. dol.	3,769	3,676	5,121	6,201	3,374	2,954	(NA)
Value of shipments (1992 dollars)	Mil. dol.	3,988	3,778	5,121	6,146	3,327	2,854	(NA)
Total employment	1,000	29.9	26.0	32.0	29.2	22.8	19.6	(NA)
Production workers	1,000	10.6	9.5	13.2	8.9	7.8	6.7	(NA)
Average hourly earnings	Dollar	18.78	18.98	23.81	22.03	22.10	19.60	(NA)
Capital expenditures	Mil. dol.	182.0	103.0	121.0	85.4	68.9	48.8	(NA)
Product data:								
Value of shipments [2]	Mil. dol.	4,662	4,530	5,207	5,862	3,705	3,121	(NA)
Value of shipments (1992 dollars)	Mil. dol.	4,934	4,656	5,207	5,810	3,654	3,015	(NA)
Trade data:								
Value of imports	Mil. dol.	0.1	0.5	0.4	0.2	(NA)	0.1	14.8
Value of exports	Mil. dol.	30.7	6.7	12.6	1.1	1.6	40.1	22.3

- Represents or rounds to zero. NA Not available. [1] Value of all products and services sold by establishments in this industry. [2] Value of products classified in this industry produced by all industries.

Source: U.S. Department of Commerce, Bureau of the Census, International Trade Administration (ITA).

No. 1470. Recent Trends in Space Vehicle Equipment, n.e.c. (SIC 3769): 1990 to 1996

ITEM	Unit	1990	1991	1992	1993	1994	1995	1996
INDUSTRY DATA								
Value of shipments [1]	Mil. dol.	1,722	1,917	1,964	2,015	1,386	1,396	(NA)
Value of shipments (1992 dollars)	Mil. dol.	1,636	1,901	1,964	1,967	1,368	1,331	(NA)
Total employment	1,000	14.5	14.3	16.2	12.3	9.1	8.8	(NA)
Production workers	1,000	8.0	7.7	6.8	5.6	4.7	4.6	(NA)
Average hourly earnings	Dollar	16.63	18.27	18.04	19.95	20.29	21.49	(NA)
Capital expenditures	Mil. dol.	28.0	31.5	33.8	25.3	29.1	37.0	(NA)
PRODUCT DATA								
Value of shipments [2]	Mil. dol.	5,024	4,387	4,179	3,313	2,727	2,609	(NA)
Value of shipments (1992 dollars)	Mil. dol.	4,776	4,352	4,179	3,267	2,692	2,485	(NA)

NA Not available. [1] Value of all products and services sold by establishments in the space vehicle equipment, n.e.c industry. [2] Value of products classified in the space vehicle equipment, n.e.c., industry produced by all industries.

Source: U.S. Department of Commerce, Bureau of the Census, International Trade Administration (ITA).

No. 1471. Recent Trends in Search and Navigation Equipment (SIC 3812): 1990 to 1996

ITEM	Unit	1990	1991	1992	1993	1994	1995	1996
INDUSTRY DATA								
Value of shipments [1]	Mil. dol.	38,615	38,612	35,039	33,546	30,110	29,435	(NA)
Value of shipments (1992 dollars)	Mil. dol.	40,140	39,360	35,039	32,824	29,176	28,033	(NA)
Total employment	1,000	328	298	253	225	199	185	(NA)
Production workers	1,000	136.0	119.0	103.0	88.5	80.3	68.6	(NA)
Average hourly earnings	Dollar	15.96	16.74	17.28	18.79	18.84	19.79	(NA)
Capital expenditures	Mil. dol.	1,201	909	849	706	688	685	(NA)
PRODUCT DATA								
Value of shipments [2]	Mil. dol.	35,250	34,173	34,171	31,203	29,191	28,308	(NA)
Value of shipments (1992 dollars)	Mil. dol.	36,642	34,835	34,171	30,532	28,286	26,960	(NA)
TRADE DATA								
Value of imports	Mil. dol.	779	875	913	803	757	863	928
Value of exports	Mil. dol.	2,009	2,124	2,052	2,042	1,958	1,860	1,961

NA Not available. [1] Value of all products and services sold by establishments in the search and navigation equipment industry. [2] Value of products classified in the search and navigation equipment industry produced by all industries.

Source: U.S. Department of Commerce, Bureau of the Census, International Trade Administration (ITA).

No. 1472. Recent Trends in Laboratory Instruments (SIC 3821, 3826, 3827): 1990 to 1996

ITEM	Unit	1990	1991	1992	1993	1994	1995	1996
INDUSTRY DATA								
Value of shipments [1]	Mil. dol.	9,267	9,534	9,823	10,384	11,119	12,019	(NA)
3821 Lab apparatus and furniture	Mil. dol.	1,965	1,840	2,111	2,173	2,453	2,349	(NA)
3826 Analytical instruments	Mil. dol.	5,029	5,236	5,223	5,657	6,023	6,770	(NA)
3827 Optical instruments	Mil. dol.	2,273	2,458	2,489	2,554	2,643	2,900	(NA)
Value of shipments (1992 dollars)	Mil. dol.	9,930	9,787	9,823	10,221	10,849	11,546	(NA)
3821 Lab apparatus and furniture	Mil. dol.	2,099	1,929	2,111	2,081	2,309	2,153	(NA)
3826 Analytical instruments	Mil. dol.	5,266	5,342	5,223	5,596	5,888	6,516	(NA)
3827 Optical instruments	Mil. dol.	2,566	2,516	2,489	2,544	2,651	2,877	(NA)
Total employment	1,000	79.3	76.5	78.2	78.0	76.6	77.0	(NA)
3821 Lab apparatus and furniture	1,000	18.2	15.2	17.8	16.9	18.5	17.4	(NA)
3826 Analytical instruments	1,000	38.6	38.2	40.1	40.3	38.7	38.9	(NA)
3827 Optical instruments	1,000	22.5	23.1	20.3	20.8	19.4	20.7	(NA)
Production workers	1,000	37.5	33.6	34.3	34.0	35.2	35.3	(NA)
3821 Lab apparatus and furniture	1,000	9.3	7.1	9.0	8.2	9.2	8.9	(NA)
3826 Analytical instruments	1,000	15.4	15.1	15.3	15.5	15.2	14.7	(NA)
3827 Optical instruments	1,000	12.8	11.4	10.0	10.3	10.8	11.7	(NA)
Average hourly earnings	Dollar	11.69	12.42	12.74	13.06	13.47	14.11	(NA)
3821 Lab apparatus and furniture	Dollar	10.86	11.43	11.58	11.86	12.28	12.56	(NA)
3826 Analytical instruments	Dollar	11.81	12.33	13.35	13.51	14.14	14.81	(NA)
3827 Optical instruments	Dollar	12.74	13.15	12.90	13.35	13.53	14.40	(NA)
Capital expenditures	Mil. dol.	286	323	355	330	325	355	(NA)
3821 Lab apparatus and furniture	Mil. dol.	58.9	52.2	55.8	42.9	41.2	46.0	(NA)
3826 Analytical instruments	Mil. dol.	151	194	228	213	178	172	(NA)
3827 Optical instruments	Mil. dol.	76.5	76.8	71.4	74.5	106.0	136.0	(NA)
PRODUCT DATA								
Value of shipments [2]	Mil. dol.	8,251	8,464	9,481	9,654	10,014	10,684	(NA)
3821 Lab apparatus and furniture	Mil. dol.	1,779	1,673	1,846	1,833	1,941	1,966	(NA)
3826 Analytical instruments	Mil. dol.	4,461	4,763	5,126	5,267	5,647	6,028	(NA)
3827 Optical instruments	Mil. dol.	2,011	2,029	2,509	2,554	2,425	2,690	(NA)
Value of shipments (1992 dollars)	Mil. dol.	8,841	8,690	9,481	9,509	9,781	10,272	(NA)
3821 Lab apparatus and furniture	Mil. dol.	1,901	1,754	1,848	1,755	1,828	1,802	(NA)
3826 Analytical instruments	Mil. dol.	4,671	4,860	5,126	5,210	5,520	5,802	(NA)
3827 Optical instruments	Mil. dol.	2,269	2,077	2,509	2,544	2,432	2,669	(NA)
TRADE DATA								
Value of imports	Mil. dol.	1,534	1,650	1,819	1,861	2,116	2,467	2,805
3821 Lab apparatus and furniture	Mil. dol.	(NA)	(NA)	(NA)	(NA)	(NA)	(NA)	(NA)
3826 Analytical instruments	Mil. dol.	740	785	880	863	979	1,110	1,280
3827 Optical instruments	Mil. dol.	794	866	939	998	1,137	1,358	1,525
Value of exports	Mil. dol.	2,018	2,566	2,733	2,840	3,108	3,561	3,947
3821 Lab apparatus and furniture	Mil. dol.	(NA)	(NA)	(NA)	(NA)	(NA)	(NA)	(NA)
3826 Analytical instruments	Mil. dol.	1,355	1,779	1,924	2,090	2,223	2,523	2,679
3827 Optical instruments	Mil. dol.	662	789	809	750	885	1,038	1,269

NA Not available. [1] Value of all products and services sold by establishments in the laboratory instruments industry. [2] Value of products classified in the laboratory instruments industry produced by all industries.

Source: U.S. Department of Commerce, Bureau of the Census, International Trade Administration (ITA).

No. 1473. Recent Trends in Measuring and Controlling Instruments (SIC 3822, 3823, 3824, 3829): 1990 to 1996

ITEM	Unit	1990	1991	1992	1993	1994	1995	1996
INDUSTRY DATA								
Value of shipments [1]	Mil. dol.	14,378	15,270	16,081	16,279	[illegible]	18,751	(NA)
3822 Environmental controls	Mil. dol.	2,458	2,317	2,594	2,813	[illegible]	2,739	(NA)
3823 Process controls	Mil. dol.	6,072	6,095	6,470	6,356	7,036	[illegible]	(NA)
3824 Fluid meters and devices	Mil. dol.	1,708	2,320	2,601	2,824	3,300	3,258	(NA)
3829 Instruments, n.e.c.	Mil. dol.	4,141	4,538	4,416	4,287	4,495	4,891	(NA)
Value of shipments (1992 dollars)	Mil. dol.	15,129	15,617	16,081	15,876	16,950	17,882	(NA)
3822 Environmental controls	Mil. dol.	2,594	2,357	2,594	2,614	2,830	2,472	(NA)
3823 Process controls	Mil. dol.	6,365	6,239	6,470	6,219	6,600	7,577	(NA)
3824 Fluid meters and devices	Mil. dol.	1,844	2,372	2,601	2,815	3,204	3,140	(NA)
3829 Instruments, n.e.c.	Mil. dol.	4,335	4,650	4,416	4,227	4,347	4,694	(NA)
Total employment	1,000	130	128	129	126	128	128	(NA)
3822 Environmental controls	1,000	26.7	23.2	24.7	24.4	24.5	23.6	(NA)
3823 Process controls	1,000	55.9	52.0	50.5	50.0	50.6	52.3	(NA)
3824 Fluid meters and devices	1,000	10.6	13.2	16.2	15.8	16.6	16.5	(NA)
3829 Instruments, n.e.c.	1,000	37.1	39.9	37.6	35.7	34.5	35.6	(NA)
Production workers	1,000	70.4	68.3	71.3	69.4	71.3	73.5	(NA)
3822 Environmental controls	1,000	18.6	15.3	16.8	17.2	17.2	16.3	(NA)
3823 Process controls	1,000	26.6	24.4	24.1	23.6	24.4	25.9	(NA)
3824 Fluid meters and devices	1,000	6.7	8.5	11.3	10.7	11.8	12.0	(NA)
3829 Instruments, n.e.c.	1,000	18.5	20.1	19.1	17.9	17.9	19.3	(NA)
Average hourly earnings	Dollar	11.23	11.78	12.61	12.81	12.87	13.43	(NA)
3822 Environmental controls	Dollar	10.44	11.29	11.04	11.29	11.30	11.29	(NA)
3823 Process controls	Dollar	11.40	11.41	12.25	12.32	12.38	12.84	(NA)
3824 Fluid meters and devices	Dollar	10.79	13.20	15.29	15.55	16.70	18.18	(NA)
3829 Instruments, n.e.c.	Dollar	11.88	11.98	12.85	13.58	12.92	13.11	(NA)
Capital expenditures	Mil. dol.	382	610	501	420	488	538	(NA)
3822 Environmental controls	Mil. dol.	60.6	55.4	80.6	67.8	75.9	83.0	(NA)
3823 Process controls	Mil. dol.	149	344	165	133	227	224	(NA)
3824 Fluid meters and devices	Mil. dol.	58.5	81.0	74.1	76.1	82.3	93.7	(NA)
3829 Instruments, n.e.c.	Mil. dol.	128	130	181	129	102	125	(NA)
PRODUCT DATA								
Value of shipments [2]	Mil. dol.	14,221	14,121	15,448	16,071	17,185	17,779	(NA)
3822 Environmental controls	Mil. dol.	2,312	2,184	2,370	2,433	2,770	2,734	(NA)
3823 Process controls	Mil. dol.	5,515	5,304	5,997	6,213	6,586	[illegible]	(NA)
3824 Fluid meters and devices	Mil. dol.	2,470	2,300	2,731	3,086	3,509	3,512	(NA)
3829 Instruments, n.e.c.	Mil. dol.	3,924	4,353	4,350	4,359	4,318	4,617	(NA)
Value of shipments (1992 dollars)	Mil. dol.	14,980	14,442	15,448	[illegible]	[illegible]	[illegible]	(NA)
3822 Environmental controls	Mil. dol.	2,413	2,202	2,370	[illegible]	[illegible]	[illegible]	(NA)
3823 Process controls	Mil. dol.	[illegible]	5,425	5,997	[illegible]	[illegible]	[illegible]	(NA)
3824 Fluid meters and devices	Mil. dol.	[illegible]	2,352	2,731	3,056	3,407	[illegible]	(NA)
3829 Instruments, n.e.c.	Mil. dol.	[illegible]	4,460	4,350	[illegible]	4,212	[illegible]	(NA)
TRADE DATA								
Value of imports	Mil. dol.	[illegible]	[illegible]	[illegible]	[illegible]	[illegible]	[illegible]	[illegible]
3822 Environmental controls	Mil. dol.	163	[illegible]	238	264	[illegible]	[illegible]	[illegible]
3823 Process controls	Mil. dol.	[illegible]	[illegible]	[illegible]	[illegible]	[illegible]	2,304	[illegible]
3824 Fluid meters and devices	Mil. dol.	[illegible]	[illegible]	[illegible]	554	[illegible]	[illegible]	[illegible]
3829 Instruments, n.e.c.	Mil. dol.	[illegible]	426	[illegible]	[illegible]	[illegible]	[illegible]	[illegible]
Value of exports	Mil. dol.	[illegible]	[illegible]	[illegible]	[illegible]	[illegible]	[illegible]	[illegible]
3822 Environmental controls	Mil. dol.	[illegible]	[illegible]	[illegible]	[illegible]	[illegible]	[illegible]	[illegible]
3823 Process controls	Mil. dol.	[illegible]	[illegible]	[illegible]	2,423	[illegible]	[illegible]	[illegible]
3824 Fluid meters and devices	Mil. dol.	[illegible]	[illegible]	[illegible]	[illegible]	[illegible]	[illegible]	[illegible]
3829 Instruments, n.e.c.	Mil. dol.	[illegible]	[illegible]	[illegible]	[illegible]	[illegible]	[illegible]	[illegible]

NA Not available. [1] Value of all products and services sold by establishments in the measuring and controlling instruments industry. [2] Value of products classified in the measuring and controlling instruments industry produced by all industries.

Source: U.S. Department of Commerce, Bureau of the Census; International Trade Administration (ITA).

No. 1474. Recent Trends in Instruments to Measure Electricity (SIC 3825): 1990 to 1996

ITEM	Unit	1990	1991	1992	1993	1994	1995	1996
INDUSTRY DATA								
Value of shipments [1]	Mil. dol.	8,600	8,508	8,826	8,746	10,124	11,909	(NA)
Value of shipments (1992 dollars)	Mil. dol.	9,119	8,726	8,826	8,606	9,800	11,364	(NA)
Total employment	1,000	80.2	71.5	68.5	64.9	63.0	62.0	(NA)
Production workers	1,000	39.5	35.0	32.2	30.5	32.0	30.9	(NA)
Average hourly earnings	Dollar	12.89	12.49	14.20	14.56	14.84	15.09	(NA)
Capital expenditures	Mil. dol.	290	255	324	402	334	397	(NA)
PRODUCT DATA								
Value of shipments [2]	Mil. dol.	7,943	7,804	7,985	8,180	9,020	10,273	(NA)
Value of shipments (1992 dollars)	Mil. dol.	8,423	8,004	7,985	8,051	8,731	9,803	(NA)
TRADE DATA								
Value of imports	Mil. dol.	1,146	1,240	1,200	1,341	1,536	1,966	2,271
Value of exports	Mil. dol.	2,610	2,739	2,957	3,054	3,388	4,166	4,897

NA Not available. [1] Value of all products and services sold by establishments in the instruments to measure electricity industry. [2] Value of products classified in the instruments to measure electricity industry produced by all industries.

Source: U.S. Department of Commerce, Bureau of the Census, International Trade Administration (ITA).

No. 1475. Recent Trends in Surgical and Medical Instruments and Surgical Appliances and Supplies: 1990 to 1996

ITEM	Unit	1990	1991	1992	1993	1994	1995	1996
SURGICAL AND MEDICAL INSTRUMENTS (SIC 3841)								
Industry data:								
Value of shipments [1]	Mil. dol.	10,787	11,420	13,396	15,113	14,809	15,442	(NA)
Value of shipments (1992 dollars)	Mil. dol.	11,201	11,689	13,396	14,860	14,448	14,905	(NA)
Total employment	1,000	93.0	93.4	98.2	103.0	99.7	99.3	(NA)
Production workers	1,000	56.0	56.1	58.5	61.4	59.6	59.5	(NA)
Average hourly earnings	Dollar	9.85	10.63	10.88	11.32	11.53	11.69	(NA)
Capital expenditures	Mil. dol.	500	586	689	809	619	608	(NA)
Product data:								
Value of shipments [2]	Mil. dol.	9,867	10,474	13,276	14,759	14,264	14,701	(NA)
Value of shipments (1992 dollars)	Mil. dol.	10,236	10,720	13,276	14,512	13,916	14,190	(NA)
Trade data:								
Value of imports	Mil. dol.	846	1,060	1,182	1,378	1,471	1,674	1,863
Value of exports	Mil. dol.	1,842	2,145	2,427	2,519	2,467	2,784	3,423
SURGICAL APPLIANCES AND SUPPLIES (SIC 3842)								
Industry data:								
Value of shipments [1]	Mil. dol.	11,697	13,386	13,801	14,553	14,423	14,850	(NA)
Value of shipments (1992 dollars)	Mil. dol.	12,511	13,786	13,801	14,034	13,479	13,905	(NA)
Total employment	1,000	90.6	99.3	96.4	98.0	95.4	93.4	(NA)
Production workers	1,000	58.1	64.1	61.6	61.9	58.9	59.0	(NA)
Average hourly earnings	Dollar	9.64	10.16	10.84	10.93	11.14	11.59	(NA)
Capital expenditures	Mil. dol.	284	466	504	433	372	346	(NA)
Product data:								
Value of shipments [2]	Mil. dol.	10,355	11,514	12,438	13,285	13,118	13,277	(NA)
Value of shipments (1992 dollars)	Mil. dol.	11,075	11,858	12,438	12,811	12,259	12,432	(NA)
Trade data:								
Value of imports	Mil. dol.	504	587	818	823	875	1,068	1,157
Value of exports	Mil. dol.	1,200	1,425	1,662	1,805	1,993	2,218	2,393

NA Not available. [1] Value of all products and services sold by establishments in this industry. [2] Value of products classified in this industry produced by all industries.

Source: U.S. Department of Commerce, Bureau of the Census, International Trade Administration (ITA).

No. 1476. Recent Trends in Dental Equipment and Supplies (SIC 3843): 1990 to 1996

ITEM	Unit	1990	1991	1992	1993	1994	1995	1996
INDUSTRY DATA								
Value of shipments [1]	Mil. dol.	1,435	1,681	1,914	2,012	2,191	2,391	(NA)
Value of shipments (1992 dollars)	Mil. dol.	1,404	1,692	1,914	1,912	2,009	2,152	(NA)
Total employment	1,000	13.4	14.6	15.1	15.4	15.2	16.5	(NA)
Production workers	1,000	8.7	9.1	8.9	9.2	9.7	10.3	(NA)
Average hourly earnings	Dollar	11.43	11.30	11.50	11.89	11.49	11.66	(NA)
Capital expenditures	Mil. dol.	26.0	35.2	48.6	58.5	51.7	75.6	(NA)
PRODUCT DATA								
Value of shipments [2]	Mil. dol.	1,265	1,397	1,621	1,664	1,917	2,117	(NA)
Value of shipments (1992 dollars)	Mil. dol.	1,238	1,407	1,621	1,582	1,757	1,906	(NA)
TRADE DATA								
Value of imports	Mil. dol.	173	183	230	226	221	262	274
Value of exports	Mil. dol.	332	376	448	496	512	574	632

NA Not available. [1] Value of all products and services sold by establishments in the dental equipment and supplies industry. [2] Value of products classified in the dental equipment and supplies industry produced by all industries.

Source: U.S. Department of Commerce, Bureau of the Census, International Trade Administration (ITA).

No. 1477. Recent Trends in X-Ray Apparatus and Tubes and Electromedical Equipment: 1990 to 1996

ITEM	Unit	1990	1991	1992	1993	1994	1995	1996
X-RAY APPARATUS AND TUBES (SIC 3844)								
Industry data:								
Value of shipments [1]	Mil. dol.	2,708	3,211	3,235	3,372	3,373	3,423	(NA)
Value of shipments (1992 dollars)	Mil. dol.	2,845	3,240	3,235	3,352	3,330	3,356	(NA)
Total employment	1,000	13.1	13.8	14.3	14.2	14.0	13.5	(NA)
Production workers	1,000	7.0	6.9	7.1	6.9	6.6	6.4	(NA)
Average hourly earnings	Dollar	13.88	14.42	14.79	15.44	15.26	15.39	(NA)
Capital expenditures	Mil. dol.	97.7	71.4	63.6	85.6	84.8	93.5	(NA)
Product data:								
Value of shipments [2]	Mil. dol.	1,854	2,201	2,360	2,510	2,494	2,531	(NA)
Value of shipments (1992 dollars)	Mil. dol.	1,947	2,221	2,360	2,495	2,462	2,482	(NA)
Trade data:								
Value of imports	Mil. dol.	970	1,075	1,102	1,167	1,062	1,139	1,170
Value of exports	Mil. dol.	587	742	782	824	965	1,158	1,182
ELECTROMEDICAL EQUIPMENT (SIC 3845)								
Industry data:								
Value of shipments [1]	Mil. dol.	5,891	6,123	7,189	7,186	7,512	7,114	(NA)
Value of shipments (1992 dollars)	Mil. dol.	6,036	6,223	7,189	7,193	7,713	7,366	(NA)
Total employment	1,000	35.1	35.3	40.1	39.9	39.2	38.2	(NA)
Production workers	1,000	14.3	15.3	18.1	17.6	17.6	17.1	(NA)
Average hourly earnings	Dollar	11.55	11.82	11.94	12.12	12.60	12.90	(NA)
Capital expenditures	Mil. dol.	186	198	255	241	306	292	(NA)
Product data:								
Value of shipments [2]	Mil. dol.	4,608	5,194	6,306	6,515	6,894	6,852	(NA)
Value of shipments (1992 dollars)	Mil. dol.	4,926	5,278	6,306	6,521	7,078	7,116	(NA)
Trade data:								
Value of imports	Mil. dol.	1,139	1,273	1,263	1,281	1,289	1,399	1,480
Value of exports	Mil. dol.	1,796	2,043	2,256	2,396	2,820	3,092	3,552

NA Not available. [1] Value of all products and services sold by establishments in this industry. [2] Value of products classified in this industry produced by all industries.

Source: U.S. Department of Commerce, Bureau of the Census, International Trade Administration (ITA).

No. 1478. Recent Trends in Photographic Equipment and Supplies (SIC 3861): 1990 to 1996

ITEM	Unit	1990	1991	1992	1993	1994	1995	1996
INDUSTRY DATA								
Value of shipments [1]	Mil. dol.	21,035	21,420	22,119	22,368	23,261	21,584	(NA)
Value of shipments (1992 dollars)	Mil. dol.	19,351	21,208	22,119	23,276	24,825	22,912	(NA)
Total employment	1,000	80.1	79.0	77.3	75.7	63.9	61.1	(NA)
Production workers	1,000	41.6	40.5	39.2	38.0	34.7	35.3	(NA)
Average hourly earnings	Dollar	13.69	14.70	14.65	14.64	15.82	16.41	(NA)
Capital expenditures	Mil. dol.	1,019	1,102	805	775	753	746	(NA)
PRODUCT DATA								
Value of shipments [2]	Mil. dol.	17,854	18,518	18,861	19,686	20,227	19,143	(NA)
Value of shipments (1992 dollars)	Mil. dol.	16,425	18,334	18,861	20,485	21,586	20,321	(NA)
TRADE DATA								
Value of imports	Mil. dol.	5,476	5,893	6,466	7,126	7,951	8,736	8,725
Value of exports	Mil. dol.	3,457	3,787	3,761	3,635	3,705	4,062	4,459

NA Not available. [1] Value of all products and services sold by establishments in the photographic equipment and supplies industry. [2] Value of products classified in the photographic equipment and supplies industry produced by all industries.

Source: U.S. Department of Commerce, Bureau of the Census, International Trade Administration (ITA).

No. 1479. Recent Trends in Jewelry, Precious Metal (SIC 3911): 1990 to 1996

ITEM	Unit	1990	1991	1992	1993	1994	1995	1996
INDUSTRY DATA								
Value of shipments [1]	Mil. dol.	4,316	3,895	4,190	4,278	4,459	4,439	(NA)
Value of shipments (1992 dollars)	Mil. dol.	4,350	3,887	4,190	4,215	4,350	4,293	(NA)
Total employment	1,000	36.0	33.1	32.5	34.0	31.1	30.0	(NA)
Production workers	1,000	24.4	21.9	22.5	23.6	20.1	20.2	(NA)
Average hourly earnings	Dollar	8.96	9.01	9.41	9.53	9.78	9.59	(NA)
Capital expenditures	Mil. dol.	44.4	41.9	36.8	45.3	49.2	57.9	(NA)
PRODUCT DATA								
Value of shipments [2]	Mil. dol.	3,959	3,502	3,739	4,006	4,063	4,002	(NA)
Value of shipments (1992 dollars)	Mil. dol.	3,991	3,495	3,739	3,947	3,964	3,871	(NA)
TRADE DATA								
Value of imports	Mil. dol.	2,448	2,451	2,711	3,142	3,438	3,573	3,766
Value of exports	Mil. dol.	408	414	476	388	366	375	392

NA Not available. [1] Value of all products and services sold by establishments in the jewelry, precious metal industry. [2] Value of products classified in the jewelry, precious metal industry produced by all industries.

Source: U.S. Department of Commerce, Bureau of the Census, International Trade Administration (ITA).

No. 1480. Recent Trends in Dolls, Toys, and Games (SIC 3942, 3944): 1990 to 1996

ITEM	Unit	1990	1991	1992	1993	1994	1995	1996
INDUSTRY DATA								
Value of shipments [1]	Mil. dol.	4,133	4,494	4,542	4,968	4,550	5,037	(NA)
3942 Dolls and stuffed toys	Mil. dol.	393	438	251	273	239	227	(NA)
3944 Games and toys	Mil. dol.	3,740	4,056	4,291	4,696	4,311	4,810	(NA)
Value of shipments (1992 dollars)	Mil. dol.	4,251	4,570	4,542	4,968	4,523	4,931	(NA)
3942 Dolls and stuffed toys	Mil. dol.	411	445	251	268	234	220	(NA)
3944 Games and toys	Mil. dol.	3,840	4,126	4,291	4,700	4,289	4,711	(NA)
Total employment	1,000	33.1	32.4	35.5	39.0	35.3	38.4	(NA)
3942 Dolls and stuffed toys	1,000	4.9	5.0	3.6	4.2	3.2	2.9	(NA)
3944 Games and toys	1,000	28.2	27.4	31.9	34.8	32.1	35.5	(NA)
Production workers	1,000	23.4	22.9	26.8	28.8	27.5	29.8	(NA)
3942 Dolls and stuffed toys	1,000	3.7	3.7	2.8	3.1	2.5	2.2	(NA)
3944 Games and toys	1,000	19.7	19.2	24.0	25.7	25.0	27.6	(NA)
Average hourly earnings	Dollar	7.89	8.56	8.43	9.03	9.31	9.53	(NA)
3942 Dolls and stuffed toys	Dollar	6.49	9.09	6.88	6.73	7.66	7.45	(NA)
3944 Games and toys	Dollar	8.12	8.48	8.60	9.31	9.45	9.66	(NA)
Capital expenditures	Mil. dol.	93.0	107.0	146.0	142.0	140.0	135.0	(NA)
3942 Dolls and stuffed toys	Mil. dol.	12.1	11.8	3.0	2.7	1.7	1.8	(NA)
3944 Games and toys	Mil. dol.	80.9	95.4	143.0	139.0	139.0	134.0	(NA)
PRODUCT DATA								
Value of shipments [2]	Mil. dol.	3,666	3,840	3,983	4,248	4,170	4,474	(NA)
3942 Dolls and stuffed toys	Mil. dol.	395	399	291	294	290	217	(NA)
3944 Games and toys	Mil. dol.	3,271	3,440	3,693	3,955	3,880	4,257	(NA)
Value of shipments (1992 dollars)	Mil. dol.	3,771	3,905	3,983	4,247	4,144	4,379	(NA)
3942 Dolls and stuffed toys	Mil. dol.	413	405	291	289	283	210	(NA)
3944 Games and toys	Mil. dol.	3,358	3,500	3,693	3,959	3,861	4,170	(NA)
TRADE DATA								
Value of imports	Mil. dol.	6,201	5,752	7,111	7,897	7,445	8,041	9,523
3942 Dolls and stuffed toys	Mil. dol.	1,384	1,466	1,661	1,687	1,711	2,034	2,464
3944 Games and toys	Mil. dol.	4,817	4,286	5,450	6,210	5,734	6,006	7,059
Value of exports	Mil. dol.	540	568	720	744	867	916	898
3942 Dolls and stuffed toys	Mil. dol.	33.9	39.3	54.5	45.1	56.1	59.0	54.5
3944 Games and toys	Mil. dol.	506	529	665	698	811	857	844

NA Not available. [1] Value of all products and services sold by establishments in the dolls, toys, and games industry. [2] Value of products classified in the dolls, toys, and games industry produced by all industries.

Source: U.S. Department of Commerce, Bureau of the Census, International Trade Administration (ITA).

No. 1481. Recent Trends in Sporting and Athletic Goods, n.e.c. and Costume Jewelry: 1990 to 1996

ITEM	Unit	1990	1991	1992	1993	1994	1995	1995
SPORTING AND ATHLETIC GOODS, n.e.c. (SIC 3949)								
Industry data:								
Value of shipments [1]	Mil. dol.	7,288	7,340	7,581	8,459	8,943	9,586	(NA)
Value of shipments (1992 dollars)	Mil. dol.	7,700	7,552	7,581	8,359	8,599	9,080	(NA)
Total employment	1,000	66.5	62.2	62.0	64.4	68.2	68.2	(NA)
Production workers	1,000	49.1	44.9	44.2	46.8	49.7	49.3	(NA)
Average hourly earnings	Dollar	8.37	8.43	8.52	8.74	8.67	9.28	(NA)
Capital expenditures	Mil. dol.	174	143	178	218	192	226	(NA)
Product data:								
Value of shipments [2]	Mil. dol.	6,202	6,504	6,994	7,865	8,285	8,774	(NA)
Value of shipments (1992 dollars)	Mil. dol.	6,570	6,691	6,994	7,772	7,967	8,306	(NA)
Trade data:								
Value of imports	Mil. dol.	1,899	2,060	2,518	2,543	3,129	3,392	3,472
Value of exports	Mil. dol.	1,023	1,148	1,289	1,490	1,758	2,171	2,313
COSTUME JEWELRY (SIC 3961)								
Industry data:								
Value of shipments [1]	Mil. dol.	1,462	1,430	1,444	1,429	1,627	1,666	(NA)
Value of shipments (1992 dollars)	Mil. dol.	1,540	1,460	1,444	1,417	1,603	1,630	(NA)
Total employment	1,000	19.4	17.8	17.4	17.1	18.8	18.3	(NA)
Production workers	1,000	13.0	12.2	12.5	12.0	14.3	13.5	(NA)
Average hourly earnings	Dollar	6.80	7.15	7.25	7.50	8.06	8.24	(NA)
Capital expenditures	Mil. dol.	11.8	9.7	12.8	9.7	13.6	11.8	(NA)
Product data:								
Value of shipments [2]	Mil. dol.	1,417	1,399	1,532	1,556	1,679	1,771	(NA)
Value of shipments (1992 dollars)	Mil. dol.	1,493	1,426	1,532	1,542	1,654	1,733	(NA)
Trade data:								
Value of imports	Mil. dol.	483	514	550	561	586	514	484
Value of exports	Mil. dol.	115	128	121	135	149	150	152

NA Not available. [1] Value of all products and services sold by establishments in this industry. [2] Value of products classified in this industry produced by all industries.

Source: U.S. Department of Commerce, Bureau of the Census, International Trade Administration (ITA).

Appendix I

Guide to—Sources of Statistics, State Statistical Abstracts, and Foreign Statistical Abstracts

Alphabetically arranged by subject, this guide contains references to the important primary sources of statistical information for the United States published since 1990. Secondary sources have been included if the information contained in them is presented in a particularly convenient form or if primary sources are not readily available. Nonrecurrent publications presenting compilations or estimates for years later than 1990 or types of data not available in regular series are also included.

Much valuable information may also be found in State reports, foreign statistical abstracts, which are included at the end of this appendix and in reports for particular commodities, industries, or similar segments of our economic and social structures, many of which are not included here.

Publications listed under each subject are divided into two main groups: "U.S. Government" and "Other." The location of the publisher of each report is given except for Federal agencies located in Washington, DC. Most Federal publications may be purchased from the Superintendent of Documents, U.S. Government Printing Office, Washington, DC 20402, tel. 202-512-1800, or from Government Printing Office bookstores in certain major cities. In some cases, Federal publications may be obtained from the issuing agency.

Major reports, such as the Census of Population, which consist of many volumes, are listed by their general, all-inclusive titles.

Bureau of the Census Publications

In most cases, separate reports of the most recent censuses are available for each State, subject, industry, etc. Complete information on publications of all the censuses and current surveys conducted by the Bureau of the Census appears in the *Bureau of the Census Catalog,* published annually and available from the Superintendent of Documents.

Abortions—*see* Vital Statistics.

Accidents —*see also* Health; Insurance; and Vital Statistics

U.S. Government

Bureau of Labor Statistics

Evaluating Your Firm's Injury and Illness Record, Construction Industries, Report 776 (1990).

Heatburn Injuries, Bulletin 2358 (1990).

Occupational Injuries and Illnesses in the United States by Industry. Annual.

Department of Transportation

Transportation Safety Information Report. Quarterly.

Federal Railroad Administration

Accident/Incident Bulletin. Summary, statistics, and analysis of accidents on railroads in the United States. Annual.

Rail-Highway Crossing Accident/Incident and Inventory Bulletin. Annual.

Mine Safety and Health Administration

Accidents —Con.

U.S. Government —Con.

Informational Reports by Mining Industry: Coal; Metallic Minerals; Nonmetallic Minerals (except stone and coal); Stone, Sand, and Gravel. Annual.

Mine Injuries and Worktime. (Some preliminary data.) Quarterly.

National Center for Health Statistics

Vital Statistics of the United States. Annual.

Volume I, Natality

Volume II, Mortality

National Transportation Safety Board

Accidents; Air Carriers. Annual.

Accidents; General Aviation. Annual.

Other

Metropolitan Life Insurance Company, New York, NY

Health and Safety Education.

Accidents —Con.
Other—Con.
Statistical Bulletin. Quarterly.
National Fire Protection Association, Quincy, MA
NFPA Journal. Bimonthly.
National Safety Council, Itasca, IL
Accident Facts. Annual.

Agriculture —*see also* Food; Foreign Commerce; Labor; Money and Banking; *and* Population
U.S. Government
Bureau of the Census
Census of Agriculture. Quinquennial. (1992, most recent.)
U.S. Commodity Exports and Imports as Related to Output. Annual. (Series ES2.)
Bureau of Reclamation
Summary Statistics:
Vol. I, Water, Land, and Related Data.
Commodity Futures Trading Commission
Annual Report.
Commitments of Traders in Commodity Futures. Every two weeks.
Department of Agriculture
Agricultural Income and Finance. Situation and Outlook Report. Quarterly.
Agricultural Outlook. 11 issues per year.
Agricultural Price Reports. Reports on prices received for farm commodities, prices paid for farm supplies, indexes and parity ratios. Monthly and annual.
Agriculture and Trade Reports (five per year).
Western Europe
Pacific Rim
Developing Economies
China
USSR
Crop Production Reports. Acreage, yield, and production of various commodities. Monthly and annual.
Crop Values Report. Price and value of various commodities. Annual.
Economic Indicators of the Farm Sector. A series of five annual issues.
Farmline. 11 issues per year.
Financial Characteristics of U.S. Farms, January 1, 1989. (Agriculture Information Bulletin. No. 569.) Annual.
Food Consumption, Prices, and Expenditures, 1996. (Statistical Bulletin No. 928.) Revised annually.
Food Marketing Review, 1994-95. (Agricultural Economic Report No. 743). Revised annually.
Food Spending in American Households. (Statistical Bulletin No. 824.) Annual.
Foreign Agricultural Trade of the United States (FATUS) six issues with annual supplements on calendar year and fiscal year trade data.

Agriculture —Con.
U.S. Government —Con.
Fruit and Vegetable Reports. Acreage, yield, production, value, and utilization of various fruits and vegetables. Periodic.
Journal of Agricultural Economics Research. Quarterly.
Livestock and Meat Statistics, 1970-92. (Statistical Bulletin No. 874.) Annual.
Milk and Dairy Products Reports. Milk cows, milk production, and dairy products. Monthly and Annual.
Other Reports. Reports on varied items including cold storage, farm employment and wages, farm production expenditures, mink, mushrooms, and floriculture crops. Monthly and annual.
Poultry and Egg Reports. Reports covering eggs, chickens, turkeys, hatcheries, egg products, and poultry slaughter. Weekly, monthly, annual.
Rural Development Perspectives. Three issues per year.
Rural Conditions and Trends. Quarterly.
Situation and Outlook Reports. Issued for agricultural exports, cotton and wool, dairy, feed, fruit and tree nuts, agricultural resources, livestock and poultry, oil crops, rice, aquaculture, sugar and sweeteners, tobacco, vegetables, wheat, and world agriculture. Periodic.
Stock Reports. Stocks of grain, hops, peanuts, potatoes, rice, and soybeans. Quarterly, annual, periodic.
U.S. Egg and Poultry Statistical Series, 1960-92. (Statistical Bulletin No. 872.) Periodic.
U.S. Rice Distribution Patterns, 1988/89. (Statistical Bulletin No. 836.) Periodic.
Weekly Weather and Crop Bulletin. Report summarizing weather and its effect on crops the previous week. Weekly.
Farm Credit Administration. Annual Report.
Loans and Discounts of Farm Credit Banks and Associations. Annual.
National Oceanic and Atmospheric Administration
Weekly Weather and Crop Bulletin. National summary.
Soil Conservation Service
National Resources Inventory, 1982. Periodic.
Report of Administrator of Soil Conservation Service. Annual.

Air Force —*see* National Defense.
Air Pollution —*see* Environment.
Aliens —*see* Immigration.
American Samoa —*see* Outlying Areas.
Area —*see* Geography.
Army— *see* National Defense.
Aviation— *see* Transportation.
Banks and Banking— *see* Money.

Births— *see* Vital Statistics.

Broadcasting— *see* Communications.

Building Permits— *see* Construction.

Business —*see also* Economic Indexes; Investments; Manufactures; Retail and Wholesale Trade; Science Resources; *and* Service Establishments

U.S. Government

Administrative Office of the United States Courts

Judicial Business of the United States Courts.

Board of Governors of the Federal Reserve System

Annual Statistical Digest.

Federal Reserve Bulletin. Monthly.

Bureau of the Census

Census of Finance, Insurance, and Real Estate Industries. Quinquennial. (1992, most recent.)

Census of Retail Trade. Quinquennial. (1992, most recent.)

Census of Service Industries. Quinquennial. (1992, most recent.)

Census of Transportation, Communications, and Utilities. Quinquennial. (1992, most recent.)

Census of Wholesale Trade. Quinquennial. (1992, most recent.)

County Business Patterns. Annual.

Current Business Reports. Retail Trade, Sales, and Inventories, BR; and Wholesale Trade, Sales, and Inventories, BW.

Minority-Owned Businesses. Quinquennial. (1992, most recent.)

Quarterly Financial Report for Manufacturing, Mining, and Trade Corporations.

Bureau of Economic Analysis

Business Statistics, 1963-91. 1992. (Discontinued.)

Fixed Reproducible Tangible Wealth in the United States, 1925-94, 1997.

The National Income and Product Accounts of the United States, 1929-1994: Statistical Tables, 1997.

Benchmark Input-Output Accounts of the United States, 1987 (1994.)

Survey of Current Business. Monthly.

U.S. Direct Investment Abroad: 1994 Benchmark Survey, 1997.

U.S. Direct Investment Abroad: Operations of U.S. Parent Companies and their Foreign Affiliates, Revised 1993 Estimates, 1996.

Council of Economic Advisers

Economic Indicators. Monthly.

Economic Report of the President. Annual.

Internal Revenue Service

Statistics of Income Division.

Corporation Income Tax Returns. Annual.

Statistics of Income Bulletin. Quarterly.

Trade Administration

Business —Con.

U.S. Government —Con.

U.S. Industrial Outlook. Annual, (1994, most recent.)

Patent and Trademark Office

Commissioner of Patents and Trademarks Annual Report.

Technology Assessment and Forecast Report - "All Technologies." Annual.

"State Country." Annual.

"Patenting Trends in the United States." Annual.

Securities and Exchange Commission

Annual Report.

Small Business Administration

Annual Report.
Handbook of Small Business Data.

The State of Small Business.

Other

The Dun & Bradstreet Corporation, Murray Hill, NJ.

The Business Failure Record. Annual.

Monthly Business Failure Report.

Monthly New Business Incorporations Report.

Quarterly Survey of Business Expectations.

Fortune (Time Warner), New York, NY

The Fortune Directory of the 500 Largest Industrial Corporations.

The Fortune Directory of the 500 Global Industrial Corporations.

Child Welfare —*see* Education; *and* Social Insurance.

City Government —*see* State and Local Government.

Civil Service —*see* Federal Government; *and* State and Local Government.

Climate —*see also* Agriculture

U.S. Government

National Oceanic and Atmospheric Administration

Climatography of the United States, No. 20, Supplement No. 1, Freeze/Frost Data.

Climatography of the United States, No. 81: Monthly Normals of Temperature, Precipitation, and Heating and Cooling Degree Days 1961-90. 1992. Issued by State.

Climatological Data. Issued in sections for States and outlying areas. Monthly with annual summary.

Comparative Climatic Data Through 1992.

General Summary of Tornadoes. Annual.

Hourly Precipitation Data. Monthly with annual summary; for each State.

Local Climatological Data. Monthly with annual summary; for major cities.

Storm Data. Monthly.

[Cli]mate —Con.
U.S. Government —Con.
Weekly Weather and Crop Bulletin. National summary.

[Co]mmerce —*see* Foreign Commerce; Retail and [W]holesale Trade; *and* Transportation.

[Co]mmodity Prices —*see also* Economic Indexes
U.S. Government
Board of Governors of the Federal Reserve System
Annual Statistical Digest.
Federal Reserve Bulletin. Monthly.
Bureau of Labor Statistics
Consumer Prices: Energy and Food. Monthly.
CPI Detailed Report. Monthly.
Monthly Labor Review.
Producer Price Indexes. Monthly, with annual supplement.
Relative Importance of Components in the Consumer Price Indexes. Annual.
U.S. Import and Export Price Indexes. Monthly.
Department of Agriculture
Agricultural Price Reports. Monthly and annual.
Other
Commodity Research Bureau, a Bridge Information Systems Inc. Chicago, IL.
Commodity Year Book Statistical Abstract Service. (Three editions annually.)
CRB Commodity Index Report. Weekly.
CRB Commodity Year Book. Annual.
CRB Futures Perspective. Weekly.
CRB Infotech.
Electronic Futures Trend Analyzer. Daily.
Final Markets. End of day.
Futures Market Service. Weekly.
Futures Market Service Fundamental & Technical Commentary. Daily and weekly.
Bridge News Summaries. Daily
Price Service. Daily
The Blue Line. Daily
Wall Street Journal. (Dow Jones & Co., New York, NY.) Daily except Saturdays, Sundays, and holidays.

[Co]mmunications —*see also* Newspapers
U.S. Government
Bureau of the Census
Census of Transportation, Communications, and Utilities. Quinquennial. (1992, most recent.)
Federal Communications Commission
Annual Report.
Statistics of Communications Common Carriers. Annual.
Rural Electrification Administration
Annual Statistical Report—Rural Telephone Borrowers.

Communications —Con.
U.S. Government —Con.
U.S. Postal Service
Annual Report of the Postmaster General.
Cost and Revenue Analysis. Annual.
Other
John Blair & Company, New York, NY
Statistical Trends in Broadcasting. Annual.
Book Industry Study Group, Inc., New York, NY
Book Industry Trends. Annual.
Reed Publishing USA, Newton, MA
Broadcasting & Cable Market Place. Annual.
Broadcasting Magazine. Weekly.
Corporation for Public Broadcasting, Washington, DC
Average Revenue Profiles for Public Broadcasting Grantees. Annual.
Frequently asked Questions About Public Broadcasting Periodic.
Public Broadcasting Stations' Income from State Governments and State Colleges & Universities Ranked State-By-State. Annual.
Public Radio and Television Programming Content by Category. Biennial.
Editor & Publisher Co., New York, NY
International Year Book. Annual.
Market Guide. Annual.
Electronic Industries Association, Arlington, VA
Electronic Market Data Book. Annual.
Electronic Market Trends. Monthly.
Electronics Foreign Trade. Monthly.
Radio Advertising Bureau, New York, NY
Radio Facts. Annual.
United States Telephone Association, Washington, DC
Statistics of the Independent Telephone Industry. Annual.
Warren Publishing, Inc., Washington, DC
Cable Action Update. Weekly.
Cable and Station Coverage Atlas. Annual.
Television Action Update. Weekly.
Television and Cable Factbook. Annual.
TV Station & Cable Ownership Directory. Semi-annual.

Construction, Housing, and Real Estate —*see also* Money *and* Transportation
U.S. Government
Board of Governors of the Federal Reserve System
Annual Statistical Digest.
Federal Reserve Bulletin. Monthly.
Bureau of Census
Census of Construction Industries. Quinquennial. (1992, most recent.)

Construction, Housing, and Real Estate —Con.

U.S. Government —Con.

Census of Housing. Decennial. (1990, most recent.)

Current Construction Reports: Housing Starts, C20 (monthly); New Residential Construction in Selected Metropolitan Statistical Areas, C21 (quarterly); Housing Completions, C22 (monthly); New One-Family Houses Sold and for Sale, C25 (monthly with annual report, Characteristics of New Housing); Price Index of New One-Family Houses Sold, C27 (quarterly); Value of New Construction Put in Place, C30 (monthly with occasional historical supplement); Housing Units Authorized by Building Permits, C40 (monthly and annual); Residential Alterations and Repairs, C50 (quarterly and annual).

Current Housing Reports: Housing Vacancies, H-111 (quarterly and annual); Market Absorption of Apartments, H-130 (quarterly and annual); Characteristics of Apartments Completed, H-131 (annual); Annual Housing Survey, H-150 (series of six biennial reports); Annual Housing Survey—Housing Characteristics for Selected Metropolitan Areas, H-170.

Bureau of Economic Analysis

Business Statistics, 1963-91. 1992. (Discontinued).

Fixed Reproducible Tangible Wealth in the United States, 1925-89. 1993.

The National Income and Product Accounts of the United States, 1929-88: Volume I, 1993 and Volume II, 1992.

Survey of Current Business. Monthly.

Bureau of Labor Statistics

Compensation and Working Conditions. Quarterly.

Employment and Earnings. Monthly.

Employment, Hours, and Earnings, United States, 1909-94. 1994. (Bulletin 2445.)

Employment, Hours, and Earnings, United States, 1988-96. 1996. (Bulletin 2481.)

Evaluating Your Firm's Injury and Illness Record, Construction Industries Report 812, (1991).

Monthly Labor Review.

Occupational Employment in Mining, Construction, Finance, and Services. 1995. (Bulletin 2460.)

Occupational Injuries and Illnesses in the United States by Industry. Annual.

Department of Housing and Urban Development

Survey of Mortgage Lending Activity. Monthly and quarterly press releases.

Department of Veterans Affairs

Loan Guaranty Highlights. Quarterly.

Energy Information Administration

Residential Energy Consumption Survey: Housing Characteristics. Triennial.

Construction, Housing, and Real Estate —Con.

U.S. Government —Con.

International Trade Administration

Construction Review. Quarterly.

Office of Thrift Supervision

Annual Report.

Other

Dodge, F.W., National Information Services Division, McGraw-Hill Information Systems Co., New York, NY

Dodge Construction Potentials. Monthly.

NATIONAL ASSOCIATION OF REALTORS, Washington, DC

Real Estate Outlook: Market Trends & Insights. Monthly.

Consumer Income and Expenditures, and Personal Income —*see also* Agriculture; Economic Indexes; Investments; *and* National Income

U.S. Government

Board of Governors of the Federal Reserve System

Annual Statistical Digest.

Federal Reserve Bulletin. Monthly.

Bureau of the Census

Census of Population. Decennial. (1990, most recent.)

Current Population Reports. (Series on Consumer Income, P60.)

Current Population Reports. (Series on Household Economic Studies, P70.)

Special Studies Reports. (Series on Special Studies, P23.)

Bureau of Economic Analysis

Business Statistics, 1963-91. 1992. (Discontinued.)

Survey of Current Business. Monthly.

Bureau of Labor Statistics

Consumer Expenditure Survey, Integrated Diary and Interview Survey data.

Annual press releases and reports, biannual bulletins.

Consumer Expenditure Survey: 1988-89. 1991. (Bulletin 2383.)

Consumer Expenditure Interview Survey. Quarterly.

Congressional Budget Office

The Changing Distribution of Federal Taxes: 1975-1990. October 1987.

Internal Revenue Service

Statistics of Income Division.

Individual Income Tax Returns. Annual.

Statistics of Income Bulletin. Quarterly.

National Science Foundation

Characteristics of Recent Science/Engineering Graduates. Detailed Statistical Tables. Biennial.

Science Resources Studies. Data Brief. Frequent.

Other

American Financial Services Association, Washington, DC

Consumer Income and Expenditures, and Personal Income —Con.

Other—Con.

AFSA Annual Research Report and Second Mortgage Lending Report on Finance Companies. Annual.

AFSA Annual Research Report and Second Mortgage Lending Report Supplements. Annual.

Consumer Prices —*see* Commodity Prices.

Corporations —*see* Business; *and* Manufactures.

Correctional Institutions —*see* Law Enforcement.

Cost of Living —*see* Commodity Prices.

Courts —*see* Law Enforcement.

Crime —*see* Law Enforcement.

Crops —*see* Agriculture.

Deaths —*see* Vital Statistics.

Defense —*see* National Defense.

Divorce —*see* Vital Statistics.

Domestic Trade —*see* Retail and Wholesale Trade; *and* Service Establishments.

Economic Indexes —*see also* Agriculture; Business; Commodity Prices; Manufactures; *and* Science Resources

U.S. Government

Board of Governors of the Federal Reserve System

Annual Statistical Digest.

Federal Reserve Banks. Monthly review published by each Bank with special reference to its own Federal Reserve District.

Federal Reserve Bulletin. Monthly. (Also monthly releases on industrial production indexes.)

Bureau of Economic Analysis

Business Statistics, 1963-91. 1992. (Discontinued.)

The National Income and Product Accounts of the United States, 1929-94: Statistical Tables, 1997.

Survey of Current Business. Monthly.

Bureau of Labor Statistics

CPI Detailed Report. Monthly.

Employment Cost Indexes and Levels. Annual.

Producer Price Indexes. Monthly, with annual supplement.

Monthly Labor Review.

Council of Economic Advisers

Economic Indicators. Monthly.

Economic Report of the President. Annual.

Other

The Conference Board, New York, NY

The Conference Board Economic Times. Monthly.

Education —*see also* Science Resources; *and* Vocational Rehabilitation

U.S. Government

Bureau of the Census

Education —Con.

U.S. Government—Con.

Census of Population. Decennial. (1990, most recent.)

Current Population Reports. (Series on Population Characteristics, P20; Special Studies, P23; and Household Economic Studies, P70.)

Finances of Public School Systems. Annual. (GF No. 10.)

Bureau of Labor Statistics

Occupational Projections and Training Data. Biennial.

Department of Education

Annual Report.

Employment and Training Administration

Employment and Training Report of the President. Annual.

National Center for Education Statistics

Associate Degrees and Other Formal Awards Below the Baccalaureate. Annual.

College and University Library Survey. (1990, most recent.)

The Condition of Education. Annual.

Digest of Education Statistics. Annual.

Earned Degrees Conferred. Annual.

Faculty Salaries, Tenure, and Benefits. Annual.

Fall Enrollment in Colleges and Universities. Annual.

High School and Beyond. Reports issued on 1980 high school sophomores and seniors and their transition to further education and labor force participation.

National Longitudinal Study. Reports issued on high school seniors from class of 1972 and their transition to higher education and the labor force.

Participation in Adult Education. (1991, most recent.)

Projections of Education Statistics. Annual.

Residence and Migration of College Students. (1992, most recent.)

Revenues and Expenditures for Public Elementary and Secondary Education. Annual.

National Science Foundation

Academic Research Equipment and Equipment Needs in Selected Science/Engineering Fields: 1989-90.

Academic Science and Engineering: Graduate Enrollment and Support. Detailed Statistical Tables. Annual.

Academic Science/Engineering: R&D Expenditures. Detailed Statistical Tables. Annual.

Blacks in Undergraduate Science and Engineering Education, April 1992. Special Report (NSF (92-305.)

Characteristics of Doctoral Scientists and Engineers in the United States. Detail Statistical Tables. Biennial.

Education —Con.

U.S. Government —Con.

Characteristics of Recent Science/Engineering Graduates. Detailed Statistical Tables. Biennial.

Characteristics of Science/Engineering Equipment in Academic Settings: 1989-90. Report.

Federal Support to Universities, Colleges, and Nonprofit Institutions. A report to the President and Congress. Detailed Statistical Tables. Annual.

International Science and Technology Data Update. Report. Annual.

National Patterns of R&D Resources. Report. Annual.

Science and Engineering Degrees. A Source Book. Detailed Statistical Tables. Annual.

Science and Engineering Degrees, by Race/Ethnicity of Recipients: 1977-90. Detailed Statistical Tables. Biennial.

Science and Engineering Doctorates. Detailed Statistical Tables. Annual.

Science and Engineering Indicators. Report. Biennial.

Science and Engineering Personnel: A National Overview. Report. Biennial.

Science and Technology Pocket Data Book. Report. Annual.

Scientific and Engineering Research Facilities at Universities and Colleges. Report. Biennial.

Undergraduate Origins of Recent Science and Engineering Doctorate Recipients. Special Report (NSF 92-332.)

U.S. Universities and Colleges Report a 9-percent Net Increase in Research Space Since 1988, the Majority of it Within Doctorate-Granting Institutions (NSF 92-333.)

Women and Minorities in Science and Engineering. Report. Biennial.

Other

American Council on Education, Washington, DC

A Fact Book on Higher Education. Quarterly.

National Norms for Entering College Freshmen. Annual.

Bowker (R.R.) Company, New Providence, NJ

American Library Directory. Annual.

Bowker Annual Library and Book Trade Almanac.

Chronicle of Higher Education, Inc., Washington, DC

Almanac. Annual.

College Entrance Examination Board, New York, NY

National Report on College-Bound Seniors. Annual.

National Catholic Educational Association, Washington, DC

Education —Con.

Other —Con.

Catholic Schools in America. Annual.

United States Catholic Elementary and Secondary Schools. Staffing and Enrollment. Annual.

U.S. Catholic Elementary Schools and their Finances. Biennial.

U.S. Catholic Secondary Schools and their Finances. Biennial.

National Education Association, Washington, DC

Estimates of School Statistics. Annual.

Rankings of the States. Annual.

Status of the American Public School Teacher, 1995-96. Quinquennial.

Research Associates of Washington, Washington, DC

Inflation Measures for Schools, Colleges, and Libraries. Annual.

State Profiles: Financing Public Higher Education 1996 Rankings. Annual.

Wages and Cost of Living: 508 County Indexes. (1995, most recent.)

Elections

U.S. Government

Bureau of the Census

Congressional District Data:

1990 Census of Population and Housing, 1990 CPH-4, Congressional Districts of the 103rd Congress.

Current Population Reports. (Series P20, Voting and Registration in the Election of November 19—. Biennial survey; and P25, Projections of the Population of Voting Age for States: November 19—. Biennial projection.)

Congress. Clerk of the House

Statistics of the Presidential and Congressional Election Years. Biennial.

Congress. Joint Committee on Printing

Congressional Directory. Biennial.

Other

The Council of State Governments, Lexington, KY

The Book of the States. Biennial.

State Elective Officials and the Legislatures. Biennial.

State Legislative Leadership, Committees, and Staff. Biennial.

Congressional Quarterly Inc. Washington, DC

America Votes. A handbook of contemporary American election statistics, compiled and edited by Richard M. Scammon, Alice V. McGillivray and Rhodes Cook. Biennial.

Joint Center for Political and Economic Studies, Washington, DC

Black Elected Officials: A National Roster. Annual.

Elections —Con.
Other —Con.
Michigan, The University of, Center for Political Studies, Institute for Social Research, Ann Arbor, MI
National Election Studies Cumulative Datafile. Biennial.
National Association of Latino Elected and Appointed Officials, Washington, DC
National Roster of Hispanic Elected Officials. Annual.
Pharos Books/World Almanac, New York, NY
The World Almanac and Book of Facts. Annual.
World Almanac of U.S. Politics. 1989. 2nd edition, May 1991.

Electric Utilities —*see* Energy.

Emigration —*see* Immigration.

Employment —*see* Federal Government; Labor; *and* State and Local Government.

Energy —*see also* Communications; Manufactures; Minerals; *and* Transportation
U.S. Government
Bureau of the Census
Current Industrial Reports. Monthly, quarterly, and annual series on various industries.
Bureau of the Census and Bureau of Mines
Technology and Labor in Three Service Industries: Utilities, Retail Trade, and Lodging. (Bulletin 2367). 1990.
Bureau of Labor Statistics
CPI Detailed Report. Monthly.
Consumer Prices: Energy and Food. Monthly.
Monthly Labor Review.
Energy Information Administration
Annual Energy Outlook.
Annual Energy Review.
Coal Industry. Annual.
Cost and Quality of Fuels for Electric Utility Plants. Annual.
Electric Power Annual.
Electric Power Monthly.
Electric Sales and Revenue. Annual.
Financial Statistics of Selected Electric Utilities. Annual.
Inventory of Power Plants in the United States. Annual.
International Energy Annual.
Monthly Energy Review.
Natural Gas Annual.
Natural Gas Monthly.
Performance Profiles of Major Energy Producers. Annual.
Petroleum Marketing Monthly.
Petroleum Supply Annual.
Petroleum Supply Monthly.
Quarterly Coal Report.
Renewable Energy Annual.

Energy —Con.
U.S. Government —Con.
Residential Energy Consumption Survey: Consumption and Expenditures. Triennial.
Residential Transportation Energy Consumption Survey. Triennial.
Short-Term Energy Outlook. Quarterly.
State Energy Data Report. Annual.
State Energy Price and Expenditure Report. Annual.
Uranium Industry Annual.
U.S. Crude Oil, Natural Gas, and Natural Gas Liquids Reserves. Annual.
Weekly Coal Production.
National Science Foundation
Federal Funds for Research and Development. Detailed Statistical Tables. Annual.
Federal R&D Funding by Budget Function, Report. Annual.
Science and Engineering Indicators. Report. Biennial.
Rural Electrification Administration
Annual Statistical Report Rural Electrification Borrowers.
Other
American Gas Association, Arlington, VA
Gas Facts. Annual.
Gas Stats:
Monthly Gas Utility Statistical Report.
Quarterly Report of Gas Industry Operations.
American Petroleum Institute, Washington, DC
The Basic Petroleum Data Book. Annual.
Edison Electric Institute, Washington, DC
Statistical Yearbook of the Electric Utility Industry. Annual.
McGraw-Hill Publications Co., New York, NY
Electrical World Directory of Electric Utilities. Annual.
National Coal Association, Washington, DC
Steam-Electric Plant Factors. Annual.
Carl H. Pforzheimer & Co., New York, NY
Comparative Oil Company Statistics, 1991-1992.
U.S. Council for Energy Awareness, Washington, DC
Electricity from Nuclear Energy: The Economic Context. July 1990.
Electricity from Nuclear Energy. (Map booklet of U.S. Nuclear Power Plants.) 1990-91.
Key Data on Nuclear Energy. July 1990.
U.S. Public Opinion on Nuclear Energy. (Polling reports updated periodically.)

Environment
U.S. Government
Bureau of the Census

Environment —Con.

U.S. Government —Con.

Current Industrial Report, Survey of Pollution Abatement Costs and Expenditures, series MA-200.

Council on Environmental Quality

Environmental Quality. Annual.

Environmental Protection Agency

Air Quality Data. Annual.

Cost of Clean Water. Annual.

Federal Certification Test Results for Motor Vehicles. Annual.

Municipal Water Facilities Inventory. Quinquennial.

National Air Pollutant Emission Trends, 1900-92.

National Air Quality and Emissions Trends Report. 1993.

Needs Survey, Conveyance and Treatment of Municipal Wastewater Summaries of Technical Data. Biennial.

Pesticides Monitoring Journal. Quarterly.

Radiation Data and Reports. Monthly.

Sewage Facility Construction. Annual.

Summary of Water Enforcement Actions Pursued by EPA since December 3, 1970. (Updated continuously.)

Geological Survey

A Statistical Summary of Data from the U.S. Geological Survey's National Water Quality Networks. (Open-File Report 83-533.)

Other

American Petroleum Institute, Washington, DC

Petroleum Industry Environmental Report. Annual.

Executions —*see* Law Enforcement.

Exports —*see* Foreign Commerce.

Family Characteristics —*see* Population.

Farms and Farm Characteristics —*see* Agriculture.

Federal Government Finances and Employment —*see also* Elections; Science Resources; *and* State and Local Government

U.S. Government

Board of Governors of the Federal Reserve System

Annual Statistical Digest.

Federal Reserve Bulletin. Monthly.

Bureau of the Census

Federal Expenditures by State for Fiscal Year. Annual.

Bureau of Economic Analysis

Business Statistics, 1963-91. 1992. (Discontinued.)

Survey of Current Business. Monthly.

Council of Economic Advisers

Economic Indicators. Monthly.

Economic Report of the President. Annual.

Council on Environmental Quality

Environmental Quality. Annual.

Federal Government Finances and Employment —Con.

U.S. Government —Con.

Department of Labor

Annual Report of the Secretary.

Department of the Treasury

Consolidated Financial Statements of the United States Government. (Prototype.)

Daily Treasury Statement.

Monthly Statement of the Public Debt of the United States.

Monthly Treasury Statement of Receipts and Outlays of the United States Government.

Treasury Bulletin. Quarterly.

United States Government Annual Report and Appendix.

Internal Revenue Service

IRS Data Book.

Statistics of Income Division.

Corporation Income Tax Returns. Annual.

Statistics of Income Bulletin. Quarterly.

National Science Foundation

Federal Funds for Research and Development. Detailed Statistical Tables. Annual.

Federal R&D Funding by Budget Function. Report. Annual.

Federal Scientists and Engineers. Detailed Statistical Tables. Annual.

Federal Support to Universities, Colleges, and Nonprofit Institutions. Detailed Statistical Tables. Annual.

International Science and Technology Data Update. Report. Annual.

National Patterns of R&D Resources. Report. Annual.

Science and Engineering Indicators. Report. Biennial.

Science and Engineering Personnel: A National Overview. Report. Biennial.

Science and Technology Pocket Data Book. Report. Annual.

SRS (Science Resources Studies) Data Briefs.

Federal Academic R&D Support Increased by 6 Percent Between FYs 1989 and 1990. (NSF 92-328.)

Office of Management and Budget

The Budget of the United States Government. Annual.

Office of Personnel Management

Civil Service Retirement and Disability Fund. Report. Annual.

Demographic Profile of the Federal Workforce. Biennial. (Even years.)

Employment by Geographic Area. Biennial. (Even years.)

Employment and Trends. Bimonthly. (Odd months.)

Federal Government Finances and Employment —Con.

U.S. Government —Con.

Occupations of Federal White-Collar and Blue-Collar Workers. Biennial. (Odd years.)

Pay Structure of the Federal Civil Service. Annual.

Statistical Abstract for the Federal Employee Benefit Programs. Annual.

Work Years and Personnel Costs. Annual.

Other

Advisory Commission on Intergovernmental Relations, Washington, DC

Characteristics of Federal Grant-in-Aid Programs to State and Local Governments: Grants Funded FY 93. (Every 3 years.)

Changing Public Attitudes on Governments and Taxes. Annual.

Significant Features of Fiscal Federalism. Annual.

Moody's Investors Service, New York, NY

Moody's Municipal and Government Manual. Annual with weekly supplements.

Tax Foundation, Washington, DC

Facts and Figures on Government Finance. Annual.

Finance —*see* Federal Government; Investments; Money; *and* State and Local Government.

Fisheries

U.S. Government

Department of Agriculture

CATFISH. 12 issues of Catfish processing, plus 4 issues of catfish production and annual issue of Trout Production.

National Oceanic and Atmospheric Administration, National Marine Fisheries Service

Fisheries of the United States. Annual.

Food —*see also* Agriculture

U.S. Government

Bureau of Labor Statistics

Consumer Expenditure Survey, Integrated Diary and Interview Survey data. Annual press releases and reports, biannual bulletins.

Consumer Expenditure Survey, 1988-89. 1991. (Bulletin 2383.)

Consumer Expenditure Survey, 1987. (Bulletin 2354.) 1990.

Consumer Prices: Energy and Food. Monthly.

CPI Detailed Report. Monthly.

Monthly Labor Review.

Producer Price Indexes. Monthly, with annual supplement.

Department of Agriculture

Agricultural Outlook. 11 issues per year.

Food Consumption, Prices, and Expenditures, *1996 (SB-928)*. Revised annually.

Food —Con.

U.S. Government —Con.

Food Cost Review. 1995. (Agricultural Economic Report No. 729.) Revised annually.

Food Review. Quarterly.

Department of Agriculture, Food and Consumer Service

Annual Historical Review:

Food and Consumer Service Programs.

Department of Agriculture, Science and Education Administration.

Family Economics Review. Quarterly.

Other

American Frozen Food Institute, Burlingame, CA

Frozen Food Pack Statistics. Annual.

National Food Processors Association, Washington, DC

Canned Fruit and Vegetable Pack and Stock Situation Reports. Quarterly.

Foreign Commerce —*see also* Economic Indexes; *and* International Accounts and Aid

U.S. Government

Army, Corps of Engineers

Waterborne Commerce of the United States (in five parts). Annual.

Bureau of the Census

Summary of U.S. Export and Import Merchandise Trade. Monthly; includes cumulative data. (FT 900.)

Survey of the Origin of Exports of Manufacturing Establishments. Triennial. (Current Industrial Reports M76 (AS)-8.)

U.S. Airborne Exports and General Imports. Monthly and annual. (FT 986.)

U.S. Commodity Exports and Imports as Related to Output. Annual. (Series ES 2.)

U.S. Exports of Domestic Merchandise, SIC-Based Products by World Areas. Annual. (FT 610.)

U.S. Exports, Schedule B Commodity by Country. Annual. (FT 446.)

U.S. Exports, Schedule E Commodity by Country. Monthly; includes cumulative data. (FT 410.)

U.S. Exports, Schedule E Commodity Groupings by World Area and Country. Annual. (FT 450.)

U.S. Exports, World Area and Country by Schedule E Commodity Groupings. Annual. (FT 455.)

U.S. General Imports and Imports for Consumption, Schedule A Commodity by Country. Monthly; includes cumulative data. (FT 135.)

U.S. General Imports, Schedule A Commodity Groupings by World Area and Country. Annual. (FT 150.)

U.S. General Imports, World Area by Schedule A Commodity Groupings. Annual. (FT 155.)

Health and Medical Care —Con.
U.S. Government —Con.
Annual Report of The Secretary of Veterans Affairs.
Summary of Medical Programs. Semiannaul.
Drug Enforcement Administration
Drug Abuse and Law Enforcement Statistics. Irregular.
Health Care Financing Administration
Health Care Financing Program Statistics. Medicare and Medicaid data. Annual.
Health Care Financing Research Reports. Occasional.
Health Care Financing Review. Quarterly.
National Center for Health Statistics
Health: United States. Annual. (DHHS Pub. No. PHS *year*-1232.)
Vital and Health Statistics. (A series of statistical reports covering health-related topics.)
Series 10: Health Interview Survey Statistics. Irregular.
Current Estimates from the Health Interview Survey. Annual.
Series 11: Health and Nutrition Examination Survey Statistics. Irregular.
Series 13: Health Resources Utilization Statistics. Irregular.
National Hospital Discharge Survey: Annual Summary. Annual.
Series 14: Health Resources: Manpower and Facilities Statistics. Irregular.
National Institute on Drug Abuse
High School Senior Survey. 1975-1991.
Substance Abuse and Mental Health Services Administration
Drug Abuse Warning Network. Advance Reports, Annual Report, latest year available 1992.
National Drug and Alcoholism Treatment Unit Survey, latest year available 1992.
National Household Survey on Drug Abuse. Advance Reports, Main Findings, Population Estimates, latest year available 1993.
Social Security Administration
Social Security Bulletin. Quarterly with annual statistical supplement.
Other
American Dental Association, Chicago, IL
Dental Statistics Handbook. Triennial.
Dental Students' Register. Annual.
Distribution of Dentists in the United States by Region and State. Triennial.
Survey of Dental Practice. Annual.
American Hospital Association, Chicago, IL
Hospital Statistics. Annual.
American Medical Association, Chicago, IL

Health and Medical Care —Con.
Other —Con.
Physician Characteristics and Distribution in the U.S. Annual.
Socioeconomic Characteristics of Medical Practice. 1995.
Physicians' Visits, Hours, Earnings and Expenses.
U.S. Medical Licensure Statistics, and License Requirements. Annual.
American Osteopathic Association, Chicago, IL
Yearbook and Directory of Osteopathic Physicians. Annual.
Metropolitan Life Insurance Company, New York, NY
Health and Safety Education.
Statistical Bulletin. Quarterly.
Hospitals —*see* Health.
Hotels —*see* Service Establishments.
Household Appliances —*see* Construction, Housing, and Real Estate. Housing—*see* Construction.
Immigration and Naturalization
U.S. Government
Department of State, Bureau of Consular Affairs
Report of the Visa Office. Annual. (Dept. of State Pub. 8810.)
Department of Transportation
Report of Passenger Travel Between the United States and Foreign Countries. Annual, semiannual, quarterly, monthly.
Immigration and Naturalization Service
I&N Reporter. Quarterly.
Statistical Yearbook of the Immigration and Naturalization Service. Annual.
National Science Foundation
Immigrant Scientists and Engineers. Detailed Statistical Tables. Annual.
Science and Engineering Doctoral Awards Reached Record Highs in 1990. SRS Data Brief. (NSF 91-308.)
Survey of Direct U.S. Private Capital Investment in Research and Development Facilities in Japan. (NSF 91-312)
Science and Engineering Doctorates. Detailed Statistical Tables. Annual.
Imports —*see* Foreign Commerce.
Income —*see* Consumer Income; *and* National Income.
Industry —*see* Business; Economic Indexes; *and* Manufactures.
Institutions —*see* Education; Health; *and* Law Enforcement.
Insurance—*see also* Social Insurance
U.S. Government
Bureau of the Census
Census of Finance, Insurance, and Real Estate. Quinquennial. (1992, most recent)
Department of Veterans Affairs
Annual Report of The Secretary of Veterans Affairs.

Insurance—*see also* Social Insurance —Con.
U.S. Government —Con.
Government Life Insurance Programs for Veterans and Members of the Service. Annual.
Other
American Council of Life Insurance, Washington, DC
Life Insurance Fact Book. Biennial. (Odd years)
Health Insurance Association of America, Washington, DC
Source Book of Health Insurance Data. Annual.
Insurance Information Institute, New York, NY
Insurance Facts. Annual.
National Association of Insurance Commissioners, Washington DC
Auto Insurance Database Report. December 1993.
The National Underwriter Co., Cincinnati, OH
Statistical Compilation of Annual Statement Information for Life/Health Insurance Companies. 1992.
Statistical Compilation of Annual Statement Information for Property/Casualty Insurance Companies. 1992.
Argus Chart. Health insurance company financial data. Annual.
Argus F.C. & S. Chart. Property and liability insurance company financial data. Annual.
Life Rates and Data. Premiums, values, dividends, and contract analysis by company. Annual.
Life Reports. Life company financial data. Annual.
Timesaver. Health insurance costs and contract analysis by company. Annual.

International Accounts and Aid
U.S. Government
Agency for International Development
U.S. Overseas Loans and Grants and Assistance From International Organizations. Annual.
Board of Governors of the Federal Reserve System
Annual Statistical Digest.
Federal Reserve Bulletin. Monthly.
Bureau of Economic Analysis
Business Statistics, 1963-1991. 1992. (Discontinued.)
Survey of Current Business. Monthly. (March, June, September, and December issues contain data on U.S. international transactions. Articles on foreign direct investment in the United States, U.S. direct investment abroad, and [illegible] topics appear periodically in other

International Accounts and Aid —Con.
U.S. Government —Con.
U.S. Merchandise Trade: Exports and Imports by End-Use Category. Annually.
Department of Defense
Foreign Military Sales and Military Assistance Facts. Annual.
Department of State
United States Contribution to International Organizations. Issued in the House Documents series. Annual.
Department of the Treasury
Active Foreign Credits of the United States Government. Quarterly.
Treasury Bulletin. Quarterly.
Export-Import Bank of the United States
Annual Report.
Report to the U.S. Congress on Export Credit Competition and the Export-Import Bank of the United States. Annual.
National Advisory Council on International Monetary and Financial Policies
Annual Report to the President and to the Congress.
Office of Management and Budget
The Budget of the United States Government. Annual.
U.S. Arms Control and Disarmament Agency
World Military Expenditures and Arms Transfers. Annual.
Other
International Monetary Fund, Washington, DC
Annual Report.
Balance of Payments Statistics. Monthly with annual yearbook.
Direction of Trade Statistics. Monthly with annual yearbook.
Government Finance Statistics Yearbook.
International Financial Statistics. Monthly with annual yearbook.
The World Bank, Washington, DC
Annual Report.
Social Indicators of Development 1993-94.
World Bank Atlas. 1994.
World Debt Tables. 1994-95.
World Development Report. 1994.
World Tables: 1994.

International Statistics —*see also* International Accounts
U.S. Government
Bureau of the Census
Country Demographic Profiles. (Series ISP- 30.)
International Population Reports. Irregular. (Series P-91.)
World Population Profile: 1996 (most recent.)
Bureau of Labor Statistics

International Statistics —Con.

U.S. Government —Con.

Comparative Labor Force Statistics, Ten Countries. Annual.

International Comparisons of Hourly Compensation Costs for Production Workers in Manufacturing. Annual.

International Comparisons of Manufacturing Productivity and Unit Labor Cost Trends. Annual.

Monthly Labor Review.

Energy Information Administration

International Energy Annual.

Internal Revenue Service

Statistics of Income Bulletin. Quarterly. (Includes periodic reports on international income and taxes.)

National Science Foundation

International Science and Technology Data Update. Report. Annual.

National Patterns of R&D Resources. Report. Annual.

Science and Engineering Indicators. Report. Biennial.

Science and Technology Pocket Data Book. Report. Annual.

Survey of Direct U.S. Private Capital Investment in Research and Development Facilities in Japan. Report. (NSH 91-312.)

Other

American Automobile Manufacturers Association, Detroit MI.

Motor Vehicle Facts and Figures. Annual

World Motor Vehicle Data. Annual.

Euromonitor London, England

Consumer South Africa 1995.

Consumer Asia. Annual.

Consumer Canada 1996.

Consumer China. Annual.

Consumer Eastern Europe. Annual.

Consumer Europe. Annual.

Consumer International. Annual.

Consumer Japan 1993.

Consumer Latin America. Annual.

Consumer Mexico 1996.

Consumer Southern Europe 1993.

Consumer USA 1996

European Marketing Data and Statistics. Annual.

International Marketing Data and Statistics. Annual.

World Economic Factbook. Annual.

Food and Agriculture Organization of the United Nations, Rome, Italy

Production Yearbook.

Trade Yearbook.

Yearbook of Fishery Statistics.

Yearbook of Forest Products.

Inter-American Development Bank, Washington, DC

International Statistics —Con.

Other —Con.

Annual Report.

Economic and Social Progress in Latin America. Annual Survey.

The International Institute for Strategic Studies, London, England

The Military Balance. Annual.

International Labour Office, Geneva, Switzerland

Yearbook of Labour Statistics.

International Monetary Fund, Washington, DC

International Financial Statistics. Monthly with annual yearbook.

Jane's Information Group, Couledon, UK and Alexandria, VA

Jane's Air-Launched Weapons. (Binder-4 monthly update.)

Jane's All the World's Aircraft. Annual.

Jane's Armour and Artillery. Annual.

Jane's Avionics. Annual.

Jane's Fighting Ships. Annual.

Jane's Infantry Weapons. Annual.

Jane's Merchant Ships. Annual.

Jane's Military Communications. Annual.

Jane's Military Logistics. Annual.

Jane's Military Training Systems. Annual.

Jane's NATO Handbook. Annual.

Jane's Spaceflight Directory. Annual.

Organization for Economic Cooperation and Development, Paris, France

Annual Oil Market Report.

Coal Information. Annual.

Demographic Trends 1950-1990.

Energy Balances of OECD Countries. Annual.

Energy Prices and Taxes. Quarterly.

Energy Statistics. Annual.

Financial Market Trends. Triennial.

Food Consumption Statistics. Irregular.

Geographical Distribution of Financial Flows to Developing Countries.

Historical Statistics of Foreign Trade Series A. Annual.

Indicators of Industrial Activity. Quarterly.

Industrial Structure Statistics. Annual.

The Iron and Steel Industry. Annual.

Labour Force Statistics. Annual.

Latest Information on National Accounts of Developing Countries. Annual.

Main Economic Indicators. Monthly.

Main Science and Technology Indicators. Biennial.

Maritime Transport. Annual.

Meat Balances in OECD Countries. Annual.

Milk and Milk Products Balances in OECD Countries. Annual.

International Statistics —Con.

Other—Con.

National Accounts of OECD Countries. Annual.

Vol. I: Main Aggregates.

Vol. II: Detailed Tables.

OECD Economic Outlook. Bi-annual. Historical Statistics. Annual.

OECD Economic Studies. Annual for member countries.

OECD Employment Outlook. Annual.

OECD Financial Statistics. Annual (three vols.) and monthly supplements.

OECD Health Data (Diskette)

OECD Health Systems: Facts and Trends.

OECD Microtables on Foreign Trade by Commodities covering Series B (individual reporting countries) and Series C (total reporting countries). Annual from 1977.

Oil and Gas Information. Annual.

The Pulp and Paper Industry. Annual.

Quarterly Labor Force Statistics.

Quarterly National Accounts.

Quarterly Oil Statistics and Energy Balances.

Revenue Statistics of OECD Member Countries. Annual.

Review of Fisheries in OECD Member Countries. Annual.

Statistical Trends in Transport (ECMT.)

Statistics of Area Production and Field of Crop Products in OECD Member Countries.

Statistics of Foreign Trade:

Monthly Statistics of Foreign Trade. (Series A.)

Foreign Trade by Commodities. (Series C.) Annual.

Tourism Policy and International Tourism in OECD Member Countries. Annual.

Uranium Resources Production and Demand. Biennial.

World Energy Statistics and Balances.

Pan American Health Organization, Washington DC

Health Conditions in the Americas. 1990 Edition. Quadrennial.

Health Statistics from the Americas, 1991 Edition. PAHO Scientific Publication No. 537. 1991.

Health Statistics from the Americas, 1992 Edition. PAHO Scientific Publication No. 542. 1992.

United Nations Educational, Scientific and Cultural Organization, Paris, France

Statistical Yearbook.

United Nations Statistics Division, New York, NY

Compendium of Human Settlements Statistics. (Series N.)

International Statistics —Con.

Other—Con.

Demographic Yearbook. (Series R.)

Energy Balances and Electricity Profiles. (Series W.)

Energy Statistics Yearbook. (Series J.)

Industrial Statistics Yearbook: (Series P.)

Commodity Production Statistics.

International Trade Statistics Yearbook. (Series G.)

Monthly Bulletin of Statistics. (Series Q.)

National Accounts Statistics: (Series X, Annually.)

Main Aggregates and Detailed Tables.

Analysis of Main Aggregates.

Population and Vital Statistics Report. (Series A, Quarterly.)

Social Statistics and Indicators: (Series K, Occasional.)

The World's Women: Trends and Statistics.

Women's Indicators and Statistics Database (CD and diskette only.)

Statistical Yearbook. (Series; also available in CD-ROM, Series S/CD)

World Statistics Pocketbook. (Series V, Annually.)

World Health Organization, Geneva, Switzerland

World Health Statistics Annual.

International Trade —*see* Foreign Commerce; *and* International Statistics.

Investments and Securities —*see also* Business; Construction; Insurance; International Accounts; *and* Money

U.S. Government

Board of Governors of the Federal Reserve System

Annual Statistical Digest.

Federal Reserve Bulletin. Monthly.

Commodity Futures Trading Commission

Annual Report.

Commitments of Traders in Commodity Futures. (Every two weeks.)

Securities and Exchange Commission

Annual Report.

Other

William B. Dana Co., New York, NY

Commercial and Financial Chronicle. Semi-weekly.

Investment Company Institute, Washington, DC

Mutual Fund Fact Book. Annual.

Moody's Investors Service, New York, NY

Moody's Manuals. (Volumes on Industriales, OTC, Banks and Finance, International, Municipals and Governments, Transportation, and Public Utilities.) Annual with weekly supplements.

New York Stock Exchange, Inc., New York, NY

Investments and Securities—Con.
Other—Con.
Fact Book. Annual.
Securities Industry Association, New York, NY
Foreign Activity Report. Quarterly.
Securities Industry Trends. Periodic.
SIA Securities Industry Fact Book. Annual.
Standard and Poor's Corporation, New York, NY
Analyst's Handbook. Annual with monthly cumulative supplements.
Corporation Records. Six basic volumes; News Supplements, daily; Dividend Record, daily, and cumulative monthly and annual.
Daily Stock Price Records. Quarterly.
Security Owner's Stock Guide. Monthly.
Statistical Service. (Security Price Index Record; business and financial basic statistics with monthly supplement.)
Wall Street Journal. (Dow Jones & Co., New York, NY.) Daily except Saturdays, Sundays, and holidays.

Irrigation, Drainage, and Soil Conservation—*see* Agriculture

Juvenile Court—*see* Law Enforcement.

Labor—*see also* Accidents; Business; Economic Indexes; International Statistics; Science Resources; *and* Social Insurance
U.S. Government
Board of Governors of the Federal Reserve System
Annual Statistical Digest.
Federal Reserve Bulletin. Monthly.
Bureau of the Census
Census of Population. Decennial. (1990, most recent.)
County Business Patterns. Annual.
Current Governments Reports: Public Employment, GE No. 1 (annual); City Employment, GE No. 2 (annual); Local Government Employment in Selected Metropolitan Areas and Large Counties, GE No. 3 (annual); County Government Employment, GE No. 4 (annual).
Population Profile of the United States. (Biennial Series P23.)
Bureau of Justice Statistics and Bureau of the Census
Justice Expenditure and Employment in the U.S. Annual.
Bureau of Labor Statistics
Compensation and Working Conditions. Quarterly.
Employee Benefits in Medium and Large Firms. Biennial.
Employee Benefits in Small Private Establishments. Biennial.
Employee Benefits in State and Local Governments. Biennial.

Labor—Con.
U.S. Government—Con.
Employer Costs for Employee Compensation. Annual.
Employment and Earnings. Monthly.
Employment and Wages. Annual.
Employment Cost Index. Quarterly.
Employment, Hours, and Earnings, United States, 1909-94. 1994. (Bulletin 2445.)
Employment, Hours, and Earnings, United States, 1988-96. 1996. (Bulletin 2481.)
Employment Outlook: 1994-2005. Job Quality and Other Aspects of Projected Employment Growth. 1995. (Bulletin 2472.)
The Employment Situation. Monthly.
Geographic Profile of Employment and Unemployment. Annual.
Monthly Labor Review.
Occupational Employment in Manufacturing Industries. 1994. (Bulletin 2437.)
Occupational Employment in Mining, Construction, Finance, and Services. 1995. (Bulletin 2460.)
Occupational Employment Statistics. 1994.(Bulletin 2468.)
Occupational Injuries and Illnesses in the United States, by Industry. Annual.
Occupational Projections and Training Data. Biennial.
Productivity Measures for Selected Industries and Government Services. Annual.
Real Earnings. Monthly.
State and Metropolitan Area Employment and Unemployment. Monthly.
Usual Weekly Earnings of Wage and Salary Workers. Quarterly.
Work Experience of the Population. Annual.
Department of Agriculture
Farm Labor. Monthly.
Department of Labor
Annual Report of the Secretary.
Employment and Training Administration
Employment and Training Report of the President. Annual.
Unemployment Insurance Claims. Weekly.
Interstate Commerce Commission
Monthly Report of Class I Railroad Employees, by Group. (Statement No. 350.)
Wage Statistics of Class I Railroads in the United States. Annual. (Statement No. 300.)
Maritime Administration
Employment Report of United States Flag Merchant Fleet Ocean-going Vessels 1,000 Gross Tons and Over. Quarterly.
Seafaring Wage Rates. Biennial.

Labor—Con.

U.S. Government—Con.

National Science Foundation

Characteristics of Doctoral Scientists and Engineers in the United States. Detailed Statistical Tables. Biennial.

Characteristics of Recent Science and Engineering Graduates. Detailed Statistical Tables. Biennial.

Immigrant Scientists and Engineers. Detailed Statistical Tables. Annual.

U.S. Scientists and Engineers. Detailed Statistical Tables. Biennial.

Women and Minorities in Science and Engineering. Report. Biennial.

Office of Personnel Management

Demographic Profile of the Federal Workforce. Biennial. (Even years.)

Occupations of Federal White-Collar and Blue-Collar Workers. Biennial. (Odd years.)

Women's Bureau

Handbook on Women Workers. Periodic.

Other

Aerospace Industries Association of America, Washington, DC

Employment in the Aerospace Industry. Monthly.

Survey of Aerospace Employment. Annual.

The Bureau of National Affairs, Inc., Washington, DC

Basic Patterns in Union Contracts. Annual.

BNA's Employment Outlook. Quarterly.

BNA's Job Absence and Turnover. Quarterly.

Briefing Sessions on Employee Relations Workbook. Annual.

Calendar of Negotiations. Annual.

Directory of U.S. Labor Organizations. Annual.

National Labor Relations Board Election Statistics. Annual.

NLRB Representation and Decertification Elections Statistics. Quarterly.

101 Key Statistics on Work and Family for the 1990's. (The BNA Special Report Series on Work and Family Special Report No. 21. September 21 1989.)

PPF Survey (Personnel Policies Forum). Three times a year.

Law Enforcement, Courts, and Prisons

U.S. Government

Administrative Office of the United States Courts

Judicial Business of the United States Courts.

Calendar Year Reports on Authorized Wiretaps. (State and Federal.)

Law Enforcement, Courts, and Prisons—Con.

U.S. Government—Con.

Federal Court Management Statistics. Annual.

Federal Justice Case Statistics. Annual.

Statistical Tables for the Federal Judiciary. Semiannual.

Bureau of the Census

Census of Population. Decennial. (1990 most recent.)

Bureau of Justice Statistics

American Response to Crime: An Overview of Criminal Justice Systems. December 1983.

Black Victims. April 1990.

Capital Punishment 1991. October 1992.

Census of Local Jails, 1988. February 1990.

Census of State and Federal correctional facilities 1990. June 1992.

Compendium of Federal justice statistics 1989. May 1992.

Correctional Populations in the United States 1989. October 1991.

Correctional Populations in the United States 1990. July 1992.

Crime and the Nation's households 1990. July 1992.

Criminal Victimization. Annual.

Criminal Victimization in the United States. Annual.

Drug enforcement and treatment in prisons 1990. July 1992.

Drug enforcement by police and sheriffs departments 1990. May 1992.

Drugs and crime facts: 1991. September 1992.

Drugs and jail inmates. August 1991.

Drunk driving: 1989 Survey of Inmates of Local Jails. September 1992.

Elderly Victims. October 1992.

Expenditure and Employment Data for the Criminal Justice System. Annual.

Federal Criminal Cases, 1980-1990, with preliminary data for 1991. September 1991.

Felony Case Processing in State Courts, 1986. February 1990.

Female Victims of violent crime. January 1991.

Handgun crime victims. July 1990.

Hispanic Victims. January 1990.

Households Touched by Crime. Annual.

Jail Inmates. Annual.

Justice Expenditure and Employment 1990. September 1992.

Motor Vehicle Theft.

National Corrections Reporting Program: 1989. November 1992.

Parole in the United States. Annual.

Manufactures —Con.

U.S. Government —Con.

International Trade Commission

Synthetic Organic Chemicals, U.S. Production and Sales. Annual.

National Science Foundation

International Science and Technology Data Update. Report. Annual.

Planned R&D Expenditures of Major U.S. Firms. Special Report. (NSF 91-306.)

Research and Development in Industry. Detailed Statistical Tables. Annual.

Science and Engineering Indicators. Report. Biennial.

Science and Engineering Personnel: A National Overview, Report. Biennial.

Scientists, Engineers, and Technicians in Manufacturing Industries. Detailed Statistical Tables. Triennial.

Scientists, Engineers, and Technicians in Nonmanufacturing Industries. Detailed Statistical Tables. Triennial.

Scientists, Engineers, and Technicians in Trade and Regulated Industries. Detailed Statistical Tables. Triennial.

Other

Aerospace Industries Association of America, Washington, DC

Aerospace Facts and Figures. Annual.

Aerospace Industry Year-End Review and Forecast. Annual.

AIA Survey of Aerospace Employment. Annual.

Commercial Helicopter Shipments. Quarterly.

Manufacturing Production, Capacity, and Utilization in Aerospace and Aircraft and Parts. Quarterly.

Orders, Shipments, Backlog and Inventories for Aircraft, Missiles, & Parts. Quarterly.

American Automobile Manufacturers Association of the United States, Inc., Detroit MI

Motor Vehicle Facts and Figures. Annual.

American Frozen Food Institute, Burlingame, CA

Frozen Food Pack Statistics. Annual.

American Iron and Steel Institute, Washington, DC

Annual Statistical Report.

Commodity Research Bureau, New York, NY

Commodity Yearbook. Annual.

Dataquest Inc., San Jose, CA

Consolidated Data Base.

Dealerscope Merchandising, Philadelphia, PA

Merchandising. Annual.

Electronic Industries Association, Arlington, VA

Electronic Market Data Book. Annual.

Electronic Market Trends. Monthly.

Electronics Foreign Trade. Monthly.

Manufactures —Con.

Other —Con.

National Association of Hosiery Manufacturers, Charlotte, NC

Hosiery Statistics. Annual.

National Food Processors Association, Washington, DC

Canned Fruit and Vegetable Pack and Stock Situation Reports. Quarterly.

Marine Corps —*see* National Defense.

Marriage —*see* Vital Statistics.

Medical Care; Mental Health —*see* Health.

Merchant Vessels —*see* Transportation

Military Services —*see* National Defense.

Minerals and Metals —*see also* Economic Indexes; Energy; Foreign Commerce; *and* Manufactures

U.S. Government

Bureau of the Census

Census of Mineral Industries. Quinquennial.(1992, most recent.)

U.S. Geological Survey

Mineral Commodity Summaries. Annual.

Mineral Industry Surveys. (Monthly, quarterly, or annual report.)

Minerals Yearbook. (Monthly, quarterly, or annual report.)

Department of the Treasury

Treasury Bulletin. Quarterly.

Energy Information Administration

Annual Energy Review.

Coal Industry. Annual.

International Energy Annual.

Monthly Energy Review.

Natural Gas Annual.

Petroleum Supply Annual.

Quarterly Coal Report.

U.S. Crude Oil, Natural Gas, and Natural Gas Liquids Reserves. Annual.

Other

American Bureau of Metal Statistics, Inc., Secaucus, NJ

Non-Ferrous Metal Data.

American Gas Association, Arlington, VA

Gas Facts. Annual.

Year Book.

American Metal Market, New York, NY

Daily Newspapers.

Metal Statistics. Annual.

American Petroleum Institute, Washington, DC

Quarterly Well Completion Report.

American Petroleum Institute, Independent Petroleum Association of America, and Mid-Continent Oil and Gas Association

Joint Association Survey on Drilling Costs. Annual.

Knight-Ridder Commodity Research Bureau, Chicago, IL

Commodity Yearbook. Annual.

Minerals and Metals —Con.
Other—Con.
Independent Petroleum Association of America, Washington, DC
IPAA Weekly Oil Trends.
IPAA Wholesale Oil Prices. Monthly.
The Oil & Natural Gas Producing Industry in Your State. Annual.
U.S. Petroleum Statistics. Semiannual.
McGraw-Hill Publications Co., New York, NY
Engineering and Mining Journal. Monthly.
Keystone Coal Industry Manual. Annual.
National Coal Association, Washington, DC
Coal Data. Annual.
PennWell Publishing Co., Tulsa, OK
Offshore. Monthly.
Oil and Gas Journal. Weekly.
Carl H. Pforzheimer & Co., New York, NY
Comparative Oil Company Statistics, 1991-1990. Annual.

Money and Banking —*see also* Construction; Insurance; International Accounts; *and* Investments
U.S. Government
Board of Governors of the Federal Reserve System
Annual Statistical Digest.
Domestic Offices, Commercial Bank Assets and Liabilities Consolidated Report of Condition. Quarterly.
Federal Reserve Bulletin. Monthly.
Flow of Funds Accounts: Seasonally Adjusted and Unadjusted. Z.1(780). Quarterly.
Money Stock, Liquid Assets, and Debt Measures. H.6. Weekly.
Bureau of the Census
Census of Finance, Insurance, and Real Estate. Quinquennial. (1992, most recent.)
Bureau of the Mint
Annual Report of the Director.
Comptroller of the Currency
Quarterly Journal.
Department of the Treasury
Daily Treasury Statement.
Monthly Treasury Statement of Receipts and Outlays of the United States Government.
Statement of United States Currency and Coin. Monthly.
Treasury Bulletin. Quarterly.
Farm Credit Administration
Annual Report on the Work of the Cooperative Farm Credit System.
Production Credit Association: Summary of Operations. Annual.
Report to the Federal Land Bank Associations. Annual.
Federal Deposit Insurance Corporation
Annual Report.

Money and Banking —Con.
U.S. Government—Con.
Data Book-Operating Banks and Branches. Annual.
Quarterly Banking Profile.
Statistics on Banking. Annual and Historical 1934-94 Volume I.
Trust Assets of Insured Commercial Banks. Annual.
Quarterly Banking Review.
National Credit Union Administration
Annual Report.
Yearend Statistics.
Midyear Statistics.
Office of Thrift Supervision
Annual Report.
Other
Credit Union National Association, Inc., Madison, WI
Credit Union Services Profile. Annual.
The Credit Union Report. Annual.
Operating Ratios and Spreads. Semiannual.
William B. Dana Co., New York, NY
The Market Chronicle. Weekly.
Federal National Mortgage Association, Washington, DC
Annual Report.
Investment Company Institute, Washington, DC
Mutual Fund Fact Book. Annual.
National Council of Savings Institutions, Washington, DC
Fact Book of National Council of Savings Institutions. Annual.
United States League of Savings Institutions, Chicago, IL
Savings Institutions Sourcebook. Annual.

Mortgages —*see* Construction; *and* Money.

Motor Carriers and Vehicles —*see* Transportation

National Defense —*see also* Federal Government
U.S. Government
Bureau of the Census
Manufacturers' Shipments to Federal Government Agencies. (Current Industrial Reports MA-175.) Conducted for economic census years ending in 2 and 7.)
Department of Defense
Annual Fact Sheet of Department of Defense.
Annual Report of Secretary of Defense.
Atlas/Data Abstract for the United States and Selected Areas. Annual.
The Black in the Armed Forces. Statistical Fact Book. Annual.
Five Year Defense Plan. Annual.

National Defense —Con.
U.S. Government —Con.
Foreign Military Sales and Military Assistance Facts. Annual.
Military Manpower Statistics. Quarterly.
Military Posture Report. Annual.
Prime Contract Awards. Semiannual.
Prime Contract Awards by State. Semiannual.
Selected Defense Department Economic Indicators. Monthly.
Selected Manpower Statistics. Annual.
Department of Veterans Affairs
Annual Report of the Secretary of Veterans Affairs.
National Guard Bureau
Annual Review of the Chief.
Office of Civil Defense
Annual Statistical Report.
Office of Management and Budget
The Budget of the United States Government. Annual.
Selective Service System, National Headquarters
Semiannual Report of the Director of Selective Service
U.S. Arms Control and Disarmament Agency
World Military Expenditures and Arms Transfers. Annual.

National Income and Wealth —*see also* Consumer Income; *and* Money and Banking
U.S. Government
Bureau of Economic Analysis
Business Statistics, 1963-91. 1992. (Discontinued.)
Fixed Reproducible Tangible Wealth in the United States, 1925-89. 1993.
The National Income and Product Accounts of the United States, 1929-94: Statistical Tables, 1997.
Survey of Current Business. Monthly.
Council of Economic Advisers
Economic Indicators. Monthly.
Economic Report of the President. Annual.
Internal Revenue Service
Statistics of Income Bulletin. Quarterly.

Naturalization —*see* Immigration.

Navy —*see* National Defense.

Newspapers, Periodicals, and Books —*see also* Communications
U.S. Government
Bureau of the Census
Annual Survey of Manufactures. (1996, most recent.)
Census of Manufactures. Quinquennial. (1992, most recent.)
Library of Congress
Annual Report.
The National Library of Medicine (for clinical medical reports)

Newspapers, Periodicals, and Books —Con.
U.S. Government —Con.
Annual Report.
The National Agricultural Library (for technical agricultural publications)
Annual Report
Other
Book Industry Study Group, Inc., New York, NY
Book Industry Trends. Annual.
Cahners/Bowker (R.R.) New York, NY
Library Journal. Bimonthly.
Publishers Weekly.
School Library Journal. Monthly.
Editor & Publisher Co., New York, NY.
Editor & Publisher. Weekly
International Year Book. Annual.
Market Guide. Annual.
Gale Research Inc., Detroit, MI
Gale Directory of Publications and Broadcast Media. 1995.

Nutrition —*see* Food *and* Health.

Occupation —*see* Labor; Population; *and* Social Insurance.

Outlying Areas —*see also* Foreign Commerce
U.S. Government
Bureau of the Census
Census of Agriculture. (1992, most recent.)
Census of Housing. Decennial. (1990, most recent.)
Census of Population. Decennial. (1990, most recent.)
Current Population Reports. (Series on Population Estimates, P25.)
Economic Censuses of Outlying Areas. Quinquennial. (1992, most recent.)
Bureau of Mines
Minerals Yearbook. Annual.
National Center for Education Statistics
Digest of Education Statistics. Annual.
Statistics of Public Elementary and Secondary School Systems. Fall. Annual.
National Center for Health Statistics
Vital Statistics of the United States. Annual.
Volume I, Natality
Volume II, Mortality
Volume III, Marriage and Divorce
Other
Puerto Rico Planning Board, San Juan, PR
Balance of Payments—Puerto Rico. Annual.
Economic Activity Index. Monthly.
Economic Indicators. Monthly.
Economic Projections. Annual.
External Trade Statistics-Puerto Rico. Annual.
Input-Output—Puerto Rico. Every five years.

Recreation —Con.

U.S. Government —Con.

Federal Aid in Fish and Wildlife Restoration. Annual.

National Survey of Fishing, Hunting, and Wildlife-Associated Recreation. Quinquennial. (1991, most recent.)

National Park Service

Federal Recreation Fee Report. Annual.

National Park Statistical Abstract. Annual.

Other

Association of Racing Commissioners International, Inc., Lexington, KY

Statistical Reports on Greyhound Racing in the United States. Annual.

Statistical Reports on Horse Racing in the United States. Annual.

Statistical Reports on Jai Alai in the United States. Annual.

National Golf Foundation, Jupiter, FL

Americans' Attitudes Toward Golf in Their Community.

An Operational Profile of Canadian Golf Facilities.

Commercial Golf Ranges in the U.S.

Golf Consumer Spending and Facility Fees.

Golf Course Operations.

Golf Facilities in Canada.

Golf Facilities in the United States. 1994.

Golf Participation in Canada.

Golf Participation in the United States. 1994.

Golf Travel in the United States.

Trends in the Golf Industry 1989-1993.

Women in Golf.

National Marine Manufacturers Association, Chicago, IL

Boating. (A Statistical Report on America's Top Family Sport.) Annual.

State Boat Registration. Annual.

National Sporting Goods Association, Mt. Prospect, IL

The Sporting Goods Market in 1996. Annual.

Sports Participation in 1995. Annual.

Religious Bodies

Other

American Jewish Committee. New York, NY

American Jewish Year Book.

Glenmary Research Center, Atlanta, GA

Churches and Church Membership in the United States 1990 by M. Bradley; N.Green, Jr; D. Jones; M.Lynn; and L. McNeil. 1992.

National Council of the Churches of Christ in the U.S.A., New York, NY

Yearbook of American and Canadian Churches. Annual.

Research and Development —see Science Resources.

Retail and Wholesale Trade —*see also* Commodity Prices; Economic Indexes; *and* Service Establishments

U.S. Government

Bureau of the Census

Annual Benchmark Report for Retail Trade.

Annual Benchmark Report for Wholesale Trade.

Census of Retail Trade. Quinquennial. (1992, most recent.)

Census of Wholesale Trade. Quinquennial. (1992, most recent.)

County Business Patterns. Annual.

Merchant Wholesalers Measures of Value Produced, Capital Expenditures, Depreciable Assets, and Operating Expenses. (1992, most recent.)

Monthly Retail Trade Report. Sales and Inventories.

Monthly Wholesale Trade Report. Sales and Inventories.

Selected Characteristics of Retail Trade-Measures of Value Produced, Capital Expenditures, Depreciable Assets, and Operating Expenses. (1992, most recent.)

Bureau of Economic Analysis

Business Statistics, 1963-91. 1992. (Discontinued.)

Survey of Current Business. Monthly.

Bureau of Labor Statistics

Compensation and Working Conditions. Quarterly.

CPI Detailed Report. Monthly.

Employment and Earnings. Monthly.

Employment, Hours, and Earnings, United States, 1909-94. 1994. (Bulletin 2445.)

Employment, Hours, and Earnings, United States, 1988-96. 1996. (Bulletin 2481.)

Monthly Labor Review.

Occupational Employment Statistics, 1994. 1996. (Bulletin 2468.)

Occupational Injuries and Illnesses in the United States by Industry. Annual.

Producer Price Indexes. Monthly, with annual supplement.

Productivity Measures for Selected Industries and Government Services. Annual.

Technology and Labor in Three Service Industries: Utilities, Retail Trade, and Lodging. 1990. (Bulletin 2367.)

Other

Dealerscope Merchandising, Philadelphia, PA

Merchandising. Annual.

Lebhar-Friedman, Inc., New York, NY

Accounting Today. Biweekly.

Apparel Merchandising. Monthly.

Retail and Wholesale Trade —Con.

Other —Con.

Market Statistics, New York, NY

- The Survey of Buying Power Data Service. Annual.

National Restaurant Association, Washington, DC

- Foodservice Industry Forecast. Annual.
- Foodservice Industry in Review. Annual.
- Foodservice Market Measure. Monthly in Restaurants USA.
- Foodservice Numbers: A Statistical Digest for the Foodservice Industry. 1992.
- Restaurant Industry Operations Report. Annual.
- Restaurants USA. Monthly.
- Survey of Wage Rates for Hourly Employees. Biennial.
- Compensation for Salaried Personnel in Foodservice. Triennial.

Roads —*see* Transportation.

Sales —*see* Retail and Wholesale Trade.

Savings Institutions —*see* Money.

Science Resources

U.S. Government

Bureau of the Census

- Current Industrial Reports, MA37D. Annual.

Energy Research and Development Administration

- The Nuclear Industry. Annual.

National Aeronautics and Space Administration

- Annual Procurement Report.
- The Civil Service Work Force.
- Pocket Statistics. Annual.

National Science Foundation

- Academic Research Equipment and Equipment needs in Selected Science/Engineering Fields: 1989-90.
- Academic Research and Equipment Needs in the Physical Sciences: 1989.
- Academic Science and Engineering: Graduate Enrollment and Support. Detailed Statistical Tables. Annual.
- Academic Science and Engineering: R&D Expenditures. Detailed Statistical Tables. Annual.
- Blacks in Undergraduate Science and Engineering Education, April 1992. Special Report. (NSF 92-305.)
- Characteristics of Doctoral Scientists and Engineers in the United States. Detailed Statistical Tables. Biennial.
- Characteristics of Recent Grads.
- Characteristics of Recent Scientists and Engineers. Detailed Statistical Tables. Biennial.
- Characteristics of Science and Engineering Equipment in Academic Settings: *1989-90.*

Science Resources —Con.

U.S. Government —Con.

- Federal R&D Funding by Budget Function. Report. Annual.
- Federal Funds for Research and Development. Detailed Statistical Tables. Annual.
- Federal Academic R&D Support Increased by 6 Percent Between FYs 1989 and 1990. (NSF 92-328.)
- Federal Support to Universities, Colleges, and Nonprofit Institutions. Detailed Statistical Tables. Annual.
- Immigrant Scientists and Engineers. Detailed Statistical Tables. Annual.
- International Science and Technology Data Update. Report. Annual.
- National Patterns of R&D Resources. Report. Annual.
- Planned R&D Expenditures of Major U.S. firms: 1990-91. Special Report. (NSF 91-306.)
- Research and Development Expenditures of State Government Agencies: Fiscal Years 1987 and 1988. Special Report. (NSF 90-309.)
- Research and Development in Industry. Detailed Statistical Tables. Annual.
- Science and Engineering Degrees. Detailed Statistical Tables. Annual.
- Science and Engineering Degrees, by Race/Ethnicity of Recipients: 1977-90. Detailed Statistical Tables. Annual.
- Science and Engineering Doctorates. Detailed Statistical Tables. Annual.
- Science and Engineering Indicators. Report. Biennial.
- Science and Engineering Personnel: A National Overview. Report. Biennial.
- Science and Technology Pocket Data Book. Report. Annual.
- Scientific and Engineering Research Facilities at Universities and Colleges. Report. Biennial.
- Scientists, Engineers, and Technicians in Manufacturing are Concentrated in High Technology Industries. (NSF 91-321.)
- Scientists, Engineers, and Technicians in Manufacturing Industries. Detailed Statistical Tables. Triennial.
- Scientists, Engineers, and Technicians in Nonmanufacturing Industries. Detailed Statistical Tables. Triennial.
- Scientists, Engineers, and Technicians in Trade and Regulated Industries. Detailed Statistical Tables. Triennial.
- Superconductivity Research and Development Activities in U.S. Industry: 1987 and 1988. Special Report.
- Survey of Direct U.S. Private Capital Investment in Research and Development Facilities in Japan. Special Report. (NSF 91-12.)

Science Resources —Con.

U.S. Government —Con.

Undergraduate Origins of Recent Science and Engineering Doctorate Recipients. Special Report (NSF 92-332.)

U.S. Firms Report Real R&D Expenditures Declining in 1991 and 1992. (NSF 92-306.)

U.S. Scientists and Engineers. Detailed Statistical Tables. Biennial.

Women and Minorities in Science and Engineering: An Update. Report. Biennial.

Women Continue to Earn Increasing Percentage of Science and Engineering Baccalaureates. (NSF 92-313.)

Patent and Trademark Office

Commissioner of Patents and Trademarks Annual Report.

Technology Assessment and Forecast Reports "All Technologies." Annual.

State Country." Annual

Patenting Trends in the United States." Annual

Other

National Academy of Sciences, Washington, DC

Science, Engineering, and Humanities Doctorates in the United States. Biennial. Summary Report. Doctorate Recipients from United States Universities. Annual.

Securities —*see* Investments; *and* Money.

Service Establishments—*see also* Retail and Wholesale Trade

U.S. Government

Bureau of the Census

Annual Survey of Communication Services.

Census of Service Industries. Quinquennial. (1992, most recent.)

Transportation Annual Survey.

Selected Characteristics of Selected Service Industries—Capital Expenditures, Depreciable Assets, and Operating Expenses. (1992, most recent.)

Services Annual Survey Report.

Internal Revenue Service

Statistics of Income Division. (Annual report on Corporation Income Tax Returns. Periodic compendiums on Studies of International Income and Taxes.)

Statistics of Income Bulletin. Quarterly.

Other

Decker Communications, Inc., New York, NY

Marketing Communications. (Advertising.) Monthly.

Laventhol & Horwath, Philadelphia, PA

Service Establishments—Con.

Other —Con.

The Executive Conference Center: A Statistical and Financial Profile. Annual.

Gaming Industry Study. Annual.

Lifecare Industry. Annual. (Analysis of facilities by size and section of the country for selected financial data, resident census information, and medical costs.)

National Trends of Business in the Lodging Industry. Monthly. (Analysis of nationwide trends in sales, occupancy, and room rates of hotels, motor hotels, and economy lodging facilities.)

Separate reports on the segments of lodging industries. Annuals. (Reports covering economy, all-suite, and resort

U.S. Lodging Industry. Annual. (Report on hotel and motor hotel operations.)

Worldwide Lodging Industry. Annual. (Report on international hotel operations.)

Pannell Kerr Forster, Houston, TX

Clubs in Town and Country. Annual.

Trends in the Hotel Industry, International Edition. Annual.

Trends in the Hotel Industry, U.S.A. Edition. Annual.

Social Insurance and Human Services —*see also* Insurance *and* Labor

U.S. Government

Bureau of the Census

Census of Governments. Quinquennial. (1992, most recent.)

Consolidated Federal Funds Report. Annual.

Federal Expenditures by State

Volume I County Areas

Volume II Subcounty Areas

Current Population Reports (series P60, Consumer Income.)

Finances of Employee-Retirement Systems of State and Local Governments. Annual. (GF No. 2.)

Finances of Selected Public Employee Retirement Systems. Quarterly. (GR Nos. 1-4.)

Bureau of Labor Statistics

Employee Benefits in Medium and Large Firms. Biennial.

Employee Benefits in Small Private Establishments. Biennial.

Employee Benefits in State and Local Governments. Biennial.

Department of Health and Human Services

Annual Report.

Department of Labor

Annual Report of the Secretary.

Department of Veterans Affairs

Annual Report of The Secretary of Veterans Affairs.

Social Insurance and Human Services —Con.

U.S. Government —Con.

Government Life Insurance Programs for Veterans and Members of the Services. Annual.

Employment and Training Administration

Unemployment Insurance Claims. Weekly.

Administration for Children and Families

Quarterly Public Assistance Statistics. Annual.

Health Care Financing Administration

Health Care Financing Program Statistics. Medicare and Medicaid data. Annual.

Health Care Financing Review. Quarterly.

Office of Personnel Management

Civil Service Retirement and Disability Fund Annual Report. (P.L. 95-595.)

Employment and Trends. Bimonthly. (Odd Months.)

Statistical Abstract for the Federal Employee Benefit Programs. Annual.

Rehabilitation Services Administration. Annual Report.

Caseload Statistics of State Vocational Rehabilitation Agencies in Fiscal Year. Annual.

Railroad Retirement Board, Chicago, IL

Annual Report.

Monthly Benefit Statistics.

Statistical Supplement to the Annual Report.

Social Security Administration

Benefits and Beneficiaries Under Public Employee Retirement Systems, Fiscal Year 1991, Social Security Bulletin, Spring 1995.

Income of the Population 55 and over,1994. 1996.

Private Social Welfare Expenditures, 1972-91, Social Security Bulletin, Fall 1992. Social Security Bulletin, Spring 1994.

Public Social Welfare Expenditures, Fiscal Year 1993. Social Security Bulletin, Fall 1996.

Social Security Beneficiaries by State and County. Annual.

Social Security Bulletin. Quarterly with annual statistical supplement. (Data on Social Security Benefits, OASDI, Supplemental Security Income, Aid to Families with Dependent Children, Medicare, Medicaid, Low Income Home Energy Assistance, Food Stamps, Black Lung benefits, and other programs.)

Social Security Programs in the United States, Social Security Bulletin, Winter 1993.

SSA's 1982 New Beneficiary Survey: Compilation of Reports, 1993.

State Assistance Programs for SSI Recipients. Annual.

Statistical Notes from the New Beneficiary Data System, Social Security Bulletin, Spring 1994.

Supplemental Security Income, State and County Data. Annual.

Workers' Compensation Coverage, Benefits, and Costs, 1992-93, Social Security Bulletin, Summer 1995.

Other

AAFRC Trust For Philanthropy, New York, NY

Giving USA. Annual.

American Red Cross, Washington, DC

Annual Report.

The Foundation Center, New York, NY

The Foundation Grants Index, 1997. Edition 25. 1996.

Guide to U.S. Foundations, Their Trustees, Officers, and Donors, Vol. 1, 1996 Edition.

Girl Scouts of the U.S.A., New York, NY

Annual Report.

United Way of America, Alexandria, VA

Annual Directory.

Soil Conservation —*see* Agriculture.

Sports —*see* Recreation.

State and Local Government —*see also* Federal Government

U.S. Government

Bureau of the Census

Census of Governments. Quinquennial. (1992, most recent.)

City Employment. Annual. (GE No. 2.)

City Government Finances. Annual. (GF No. 4.)

County Government Employment. Annual. (GE No. 4.)

County Government Finances. Annual. (GF No. 8.)

Federal Expenditures by State. Annual.

Finances of Employee-Retirement Systems of State and Local Governments. Annual. (GF No. 2.)

Finances of Public School Systems. Annual. (GF No. 10.)

Finances of Selected Public Employee Retirement Systems. Quarterly. (GR Nos. 1-4.)

Government Finances. Annual. Covers Federal, State, and local governments. (GF No. 5.)

Local Government Employment in Major County Areas. Annual. (GE No. 3.)

Local Government Finances in Major County Areas. Annual. (GF No. 6.)

Public Employment. Annual. (GE No. 1.)

Quarterly Summary of Federal, State, and Local Tax Revenue. (GT Nos. 1-4.)

State Government Finances. Annual. (GF No. 3.)

State and Local Government —Con.
U.S. Government —Con.
State Government Tax Collections. Annual. (GF No. 1.)
Bureau of Labor Statistics
Employee Benefits in State and Local Governments. Biennial.
Employment and Earnings. Monthly.
Employment, Hours, and Earnings, United States, 1909-94. 1994. (Bulletin 2445.)
Employment, Hours, and Earnings, United States, 1988-96. 1996. (Bulletin 2481.)
Occupational Employment Statistics, 1994. 1996. (Bulletin 2468.)
Federal Highway Administration
Highway Statistics. Annual.
Office of Management and Budget
The Budget of the United States Government. Annual.
Social Security Administration
Benefits and Beneficiaries Under Public Employee Retirement Systems, Fiscal Year 1991, Social Security Bulletin, Spring 1995.
Other
Advisory Commission on Intergovernmental Relations,Washington, DC
1991: State Revenue Capacity and Effort.
Significant Features of Fiscal Federalism. Annual.
The Council of State Governments, Lexington, KY
The Book of the States. Biennial.
State Administrative Officials Classified by Function. Biennial.
International City Management Association, Washington, DC
Baseline Data Reports. Bimonthly.
Compensation: An Annual Report on Local Government Executive Salaries and Fringe Benefits.
Municipal Year Book. Annual.
Special Data Issues. Periodical.
National Governors' Association, Washington, DC
Directory of Governors of the American States, Commonwealths & Territories. Annual.
Governors' Staff Directory. Biannual.
National Governors' Association and National Association of State Budget Officers, Washington, DC
The Fiscal Survey of States. Biannual.
Tax Foundation, Washington, DC
Facts and Figures on Government Finance. Annual.
Stocks and Bonds —*see* Investments.
Stores —*see* Retail and Wholesale Trade *and* Service Establishments.
Tax Collections —*see* Federal Government; *and* State and Local Government.
Telephone and Telegraph Systems —*see* Communications.
Television —*see* Communications.
Trade —*see* Foreign Commerce; Retail and Wholesale Trade; *and* Service Establishments.
Transportation —*see also* Foreign Commerce.
U.S. Government
Army, Corps of Engineers
Waterborne Commerce of the United States (in five parts). Annual.
Bureau of the Census
Census of Transportation, Communications and Utilities. Quinquennial. (1992, most recent.)
Commodity Flow Survey. 1993.
Transportation Annual Survey.
Truck Inventory and Use Survey. Quinquennial. (1992, most recent.)
Vessel Entrances and Clearances. Annual. (FT 975.)
Bureau of Economic Analysis
Business Statistics, 1963-91. 1992. (Discontinued.)
Survey of Current Business. Monthly.
Bureau of Transportation Statistics
Coast Guard
Annual Report of the Secretary of Transportation.
Marine Casualty Statistics. Annual.
Polluting Incidents In And Around U.S. Waters. Annual.
Department of State, Bureau of Consular Affairs
Summary of Passport Statistics. Annual.
Department of Transportation
Airport Activity Statistics of Certified Route Air Carriers. Annual.
Transportation Safety Information Report. Quarterly.
U.S. International Air Travel Statistics. Annual.
Federal Highway Administration
Drivers Licenses. Annual.
Highway Statistics. Annual.
Highway Statistics, Summary to 1985. (Published every 10 years.)
Selected Highway Statistics and Charts. Annual.
Interstate Commerce Commission
Class I Freight Railroads Selected Earnings Data. Quarterly.
Quarterly Report.
Transport Statistics in the United States. Issued annually in two separate parts:
Part 1: Railroads
Part 2: Motor Carriers
Maritime Administration
Annual Report.

Transportation —Con.

U.S. Government —Con.

Employment Report of United States Flag Merchant Fleet Ocean-going Vessels 1,000 Gross Tons and Over. Quarterly.

Foreign Flag Merchant Ships Owned by U.S. Parent Companies. Annual.

Maritime Manpower Report. Quarterly.

Research and Special Programs Administration

Other

Aerospace Industries Association of America, Washington, DC

Aerospace Facts and Figures. Annual.

Commercial Helicopter Shipments. Quarterly.

Air Transport Association of America, Washington, DC

Air Transport Facts and Figures. Annual.

American Automobile Manufacturers Association, Detroit, MI.

Motor Vehicle Facts and Figures. Annual.

World Motor Vehicle Data. Annual.

American Bureau of Shipping, Paramus, NJ

The Record. Annual with one supplement.

American Public Transit Association, Washington, DC

Transit Fact Book. Annual.

Association of American Railroads, Washington, DC

Analysis of Class I Railroads. Annual.

Cars of Revenue Freight Loaded. Weekly with annual summary.

Freight Commodity Statistics, Class I Railroads in the United States. Annual.

Yearbook of Railroad Facts.

ENO Transportation Foundation, Leesburg, VA

Transportation in America. mid-year, annually with periodic supplements.

General Aviation Manufacturers Association, Washington, DC

Shipment Report. Quarterly and Annual.

Statistical Databook. Annual.

Lake Carriers' Association, Cleveland, OH

Annual Report.

Monthly Bulk Commodities Report.

Lloyd's Register of Shipping, London, England

Casualty Return. (Annual statistical summary of all merchant ships totally lost or reported broken up during year.)

Merchant Shipbuilding Returns. (Quarterly Statistical summary of world shipbuilding.)

World Fleet Statistics. (An end-year analysis of world merchant fleet.)

National Air Carrier Association, Washington, DC

Annual Report.

Transportation —Con.

Other —Con.

Regional Airline Association, Washington, DC

Statistical Reports.

Shipbuilders Council of America, Arlington, VA

Annual Report.

Tanker Advisory Center, Inc., New York, NY

Worldwide Tanker Casualty Returns. Annual.

Travel —*see* Recreation *and* Transportation.

Unemployment Insurance —*see* Labor; *and* Social Insurance.

Utilities, Public—*see* Communications; Energy; Public Utilities *and* Transportation.

Veterans —*see* National Defense; *and* Population.

Virgin Islands of the United States —*see* Outlying Areas.

Vital Statistics —*see also* Accidents; *and* Health

U.S. Government

Centers for Disease Control and Prevention, Atlanta, GA

Morbidity and Mortality Weekly Report. Annual summary also.

National Center for Health Statistics

Monthly Vital Statistics Report. Preliminary data births and deaths: United States, 1995.

Vital and Health Statistics. (A series of statistical reports covering health-related topics.)

Series 20: Mortality Data. Irregular.

Series 21: Natality, Marriage, and Divorce Data. Irregular.

Series 23: National Survey of Family Growth Statistics. Irregular.

Vital Statistics of the United States. Annual.

Other

The Alan Guttmacher Institute, New York, NY

Abortion Factbook, 1992 Edition: Readings, Trends, and State and Local Data to 1988. 1992.

Family Planning Perspectives. Monthly.

United Nations Statistics Division, New York, NY

Demographic Yearbook.

Population and Vital Statistics Report. (Series A.) Quarterly.

World Health Organization, Geneva, Switzerland

Annual Epidemiological and Vital Statistics.

Epidemiological and Vital Statistics Report. Monthly.

World Health Statistics. Quarterly and annual.

Vocational Rehabilitation and Education

U.S. Government

Department of Education

Guide to State Statistical Abstracts

This bibliography includes the most recent statistical abstracts for States published since 1986 plus those that will be issued in late 1997 or early 1998. For some States, a near equivalent has been listed in substitution for, or in addition to, a statistical abstract. All sources contain statistical tables on a variety of subjects for the State as a whole, its component parts, or both. The page counts given for publications are approximate. Internet sites also contain statistical data and were accessed in early September 1997.

Alabama

University of Alabama, Center for Business and Economic Research, Box 870221, Tuscaloosa 35487 205-348-6191. Internet site <http://www.cba.ua.edu/cber/>

Economic Abstract of Alabama. 1997. 488 pp.

Alaska

Department of Commerce and Economic Development, Division of Trade & Development, P.O. Box 110804, Juneau 99811-0804 907-465-2017. Internet site <http://www.state.ak.us/local/akpages/COMMERCE/tdpub/htm>

The Alaska Economy Performance Report. 1996

Arizona

University of Arizona, Economic and Business Research, College of Business and Public Administration, McClelland Hall 204 Tucson Arizona 85721-0001 520-621-2155 Fax 520-621-2150. Internet site <http://www.bpa.arizona.edu/newpage>

Arizona Statistical Abstract: A 1993 Data Handbook. 616 pp.

Arizona Economic Indicators. 52 pp. Biennial.

Arizona's Economy. 20 pp. (Quarterly newsletter and data.)

Arkansas

University of Arkansas at Little Rock, Institute for Economic Advancement, Economic Research, 2801 South University, Little Rock 72204 501-569-8550

Arkansas State and County Economic Data. 16 pp. (Revised annually.)

University of Arkansas at Little Rock, Institute for Economic Advancement, Census State Data Center, Little Rock 72204 501-569-8530

Arkansas Statistical Abstract, 1996. 688 pp. (Revised biennially.)

California

Department of Finance, 915 L Street, 8th Floor, Sacramento 95814 916-322-2263. Internet site <http://www.dof.ca.gov/>

California Statistical Abstract, 1996.

Pacific Data Resources, P.O. Box 1922, Santa Barbara, CA 93116-1922 800-422-2546

California Almanac, 6th ed. Biennial. 275 pp.

Colorado

University of Colorado, Business Research Division, Campus Box 420, Boulder 80309 303-492-8227. Internet site <http://www.colorado.edu/libraries/govpubs/online/htm>

Statistical Abstract of Colorado, 1987. 600 pp. (Latest and last edition).

Connecticut

Connecticut Department of Economic & Community Development, 505 Hudson St., Hartford 06106 1-800-392-2122. Internet site <http://www.state.ct.us/ecd/>

Connecticut Market Data. 1995, 140 pp. (Diskette also available.)

Connecticut Town Profiles, 1996-97. 340 pp.

Delaware

Delaware Economic Development Office, P.O. Box 1401, 99 Kings Highway, Dover 19903 302-739-4271. Internet site <http://www.state.de.us/govern/agencies/dedo/index.htm>

Delaware Statistical Overview, 1996.

University of Delaware, Bureau of Economic Research, College of Business and Economics, Newark 19716-2730 302-831-8401

Delaware Economic Report 1994-95. 200 pp. (Last edition. Bureau of Economic Research no longer exists.)

District of Columbia

Office of Planning, Data Management Division, Presidential Bldg., Suite 500, 415 12th St., N.W. Washington 20004 202-727-6533

1990 Census, Population and Housing for the District of Columbia 72 pp.

1990 Census: Social, Economic and Housing. (44 pp. for each of nine volumes).

Socio-Economic Indicators by Census Tract. 221 pp.

Socio-Economic Indicators of Change by Census Tract, 1980-1990. 146 pp.

Office of Policy and Evaluation, Executive Office of the Mayor, 1 Judiciary Square, Suite 1000, 441 4th St., N.W., Washington 20001 202-727-6979

Indices—A Statistical Index to DC Services, Dec. 1994-96. 331 pp.

Florida

University of Florida, Bureau of Economic and Business Research, Box 117145, Gainesville 32611-7145 352-392-0171. Internet site <http://www.cba.ufl.edu/bebr/>

Florida Statistical Abstract, 1996. 30th ed. 800 pp. Also available on diskette.

Florida County Perspectives, 1996. One profile for each county. Annual.

Florida County Rankings, 1996.

Florida and the Nation, 1997.

Georgia

University of Georgia, Selig Center for Economic Growth, Terry College of Business, Athens 30602-6269 706-542-4085. Internet site <http://www.selig.uga.edu/>

Georgia Statistical Abstract, 1996-97. 466 pp.

University of Georgia, College of Agricultural and Environmental Sciences, Cooperative Extension Service, Athens 30602-4356 706-542-8938 Fax 706-542-8934. Internet site <http://www.uga.edu/caes/>

The Georgia County Guide. 1997. 16th ed. Annual. 200 pp.

Office of Planning and Budget, 254 Washington St., S.W., Atlanta 30334-8501 404-656-0911

Georgia Descriptions in Data. 1990-91. 249 pp. (No longer being published.)

Hawaii

Hawaii State Department of Business, and Economic Development & Tourism, Research and Economic Analysis Division, Statistics Branch P.O. Box 2359, Honolulu 96804. Inquiries 808-586-2481; Copies 808-586-2424. Internet site <http://www.hawaii.gov/dbedt>

The State of Hawaii Data Book 1996: A Statistical Abstract. 29th ed. 649 pp.

Idaho

Department of Commerce, 700 West State St., Boise 83720-0093 208-334-2470. Internet site <http://www.idoc.state.id.us>

County Profiles of Idaho, 1996.

Idaho Community Profiles, 1997.

Idaho Facts, 1997.

Idaho Facts Data Book, 1995.

Profile of Rural Idaho 1993.
University of Idaho, Center for Business Development and Research, Moscow 83844-3229 208-885-6611

Idaho Statistical Abstract, 4th ed. 1996.

Illinois

University of Illinois, Bureau of Economic and Business Research, 428 Commerce West, 1206 South 6th Street, Champaign 61820 217-333-2332

Illinois Statistical Abstract. 1996. 875 pages

Indiana

Indiana University, Indiana Business Research Center, School of Business, 801 W. Michigan BS4015 Indianapolis 46202-5151 317-274-2204. Internet site <http://www.iupui.edu/it/ibrc/>

Indiana Factbook, 1994-95. 413 pages.

Iowa

Public Interest Institute at Iowa Wesleyan College, 600 N. Jackson Street, Mount Pleasant, IA 52641 319-385-3462

1996 Statistical Profile of Iowa.

Kansas

University of Kansas, Institute for Public Policy and Business Research, 607 Blake Hall, Lawrence 66045-2960 785-864-3701. Internet site <http://www.ukans.edu/cwis/units/IPPBR/IPPBRmain.html>

Kansas Statistical Abstract, 1996. 35th ed. 1997.

Kentucky

Kentucky Cabinet for Economic Development, Division of Research, 500 Mero Street, Capital Plaza Tower, Frankfort 40601 502-564-4886. Internet site <http://www.state.ky.us/edc/cabmain.htm>

Kentucky Deskbook of Economic Statistics. 33rd ed. 1997.

Louisiana

University of New Orleans, Division of Business and Economic Research, New Orleans 70148 504-286-6248. Internet site <http://leap.nlu.edu/STAAB.HTM>

Statistical Abstract of Louisiana. 9th ed. 1994.

Maine

Maine Department of Economic and Community Development, State House Station 59, Augusta 04333 207-287-2656

Maine: A Statistical Summary. (Updated periodically.)

Maryland

Regional Economic Studies Institute, Towson University, Towson 21252-7097 410-830-3778

Maryland Statistical Abstract. 1995-96. 349 pp.

Massachusetts

Massachusetts Institute for Social and Economic Research, Box 37515, University of Massachusetts at Amherst 01003-7515 413-545-3460 Fax 413-545-3686. Internet site <http://www.umass.edu/miser/>

Population Estimates for Massachusetts Cities and Towns. 1995.

Projection of the Population, Mass., Cities and Towns, Years 1990-2010.

Minnesota

Department of Trade and Economic Development, Business and Community Development Division, 500 Metro Square Building, St. Paul 55101 612-296-8283

Compare Minnesota: An Economic and Statistical Factbook, 1994-95. 165 pp.

*Economic Report to the Governor: State of Minnesota, 1992.*148 pp.

Office of State Demographer, Minnesota Planning, 300 Centennial Bldg., St. Paul 55155 612-296-2557

Minnesota Population and Household Estimates, 1996. . Available diskette in Lotus, dBase or ASCII formats.

Minnesota Population Projections, 1990.

Mississippi

Mississippi State University, College of Business and Industry, Division of Research, Mississippi State 39762. 601-325-3817

Mississippi Statistical Abstract. 1996. 554 pp.

Missouri

University of Missouri, Business and Public Administration Research Center, Columbia 65211. 573-882-4805. Internet site <http://tiger.bpa.missouri.edu/research/centers/bparc/>

Statistical Abstract for Missouri, 1995 Biennial. 256 pp.

Montana

Montana Department of Commerce, Census and Economic Information Center, 1424 9th Ave., Helena 59620 406-444-2896. Internet site <http://commerce.mt.gov/ceic/index.htm>

Statistical Reports from the Montana County Database. (Separate county and State reports; available by subject section as well as complete reports by county and State, updated periodically.)

Nebraska

Department of Economic Development, Division of Research, Box 94666, Lincoln 68509 402-471-3784 . Internet site <http://www.ded.state.ne.us/>

Nebraska Statistical Handbook. 1995-1996. 300 pp. (Available only on internet).

Nevada

Department of Administration, Budget and Planning Division, Capitol Complex, Carson City 89710 702-687-4065

Nevada Statistical Abstract. 1996. Biennial. 225 pp.

New Hampshire

Office of State Planning, 2 1/2 Beacon St., Concord 03301-4497 603-271-2155

Current Estimates and Trends in New Hampshire's Housing Supply. Update: 1996. 32 pp.

1996 Population Estimates for New Hampshire Cities and Towns

New Hampshire Population Projections for Counties by Age & Sex, Apr. 1997, 2000-2020.

New Jersey

New Jersey State Data Center, NJ Department of Labor, CN 388, Trenton 08625-0388 609-984-2595. Internet site <http://www.state.nj.us/labor/lra/njsdc.html>

New Jersey Source Book, 1993. 156 pp.

New Mexico

University of New Mexico, Bureau of Business and Economic Research, 1919 Lomas N.E. Albuquerque 87131-6021 505-277-6626 Fax 505-277-2773. Internet site <http://www.unm.edu/bber/>

County Profiles. *1997. 72 pp.*

Community Profiles for Selected New Mexico cities.

Population Projections for the State of New Mexico, 1997.

New York

Nelson A. Rockefeller Institute of Government, 411 State Street, Albany 12203-1003 518-443-5522

New York State Statistical Yearbook, 1996. 21st ed. 582 pp.

North Carolina

Office of Governor Office of State Planning, 116 West Jones Street, Raleigh 27603-8003 919-733-4131. Internet site <http://www.ospl.state.nc.us/Demographer>

Statistical Abstract of North Carolina Counties, 1991. 6th edition. (No longer being published.)

North Dakota

University of North Dakota, Box 8369, Bureau of Business and Economic Research, Grand Forks 58202. 701-777-2637

The Statistical Abstract of North Dakota. 1988. 700 pp.

North Dakota Department of Economic Development & Finance, 1833 E. Bismark Expressway, Bismark 58504-6708 701-328-5300

State of North Dakota Economic, Demographic, Public Services, and Fiscal Condition. Sept. 1995. 155 pp.

Ohio

Department of Development, Office of Strategic Research, P.O. Box 1001, Columbus 43216-1001 614-466-2115. Internet site <http://www.odod.ohio.gov/>

Research products and services. (Updated continuously.)

The Ohio State University, School of Public Policy and Management, 1775 College Road, Columbus 43210-1399 614-292-7731

Benchmark Ohio, 1993. Biennial. 300 pp.

Oklahoma

University of Oklahoma, Center for Economic and Management Research, 307 West Brooks Street, Room 4, Norman 73019 405-325-2931. Internet site <http://www.rt.cba.ou.edu/>

Statistical Abstract of Oklahoma, 1996. Annual. 441 pp.

Oregon

Secretary of State, P.O. Box 3370 Room 136, State Capitol, Salem 97310 503-986-2234. Internet site <http://sosinet.sos.state.or.us/>

Oregon Blue Book. 1997-1998. Biennial. 476 pp. $14.

Pennsylvania

Pennsylvania State Data Center, Institute of State and Regional Affairs, Penn State Harrisburg, 777 West Harrisburg Pike, Middletown Pennsylvania 17057-4898. 717-948-6336. Internet site <http://howard.hbg.psu.edu/psdc/psdchome1.1.html>

Pennsylvania Statistical Abstract, 1996. 301 pp.

Rhode Island

Rhode Island Economic Development Corporation, 1 West Exchange Street, Providence 02903 401-277-2601 Fax 401-277-2102. Internet site <http://www.riedc.com/>

Rhode Island 1990 Census of Population and Housing Summary. May 1994.

The Rhode Island Economy. May 1997.

South Carolina

Budget and Control Board, Office of Research and Statistical Services, R. C. Dennis Building, Room 425, Columbia 29201. 803-734-3781. Internet site <http://www.state.sc.us/drss/>

South Carolina Statistical Abstract: 1997. 440 pp.

South Dakota

University of South Dakota, State Data Center, Vermillion 57069 605-677-5287

Selected Social and Economic Characteristics. 550 pp.

1997 South Dakota Community Abstracts. 400 pp.

Tennessee

University of Tennessee, Center for Business and Economic Research, Knoxville 37996-4170 615-974-5441. Internet site <http://cber.bus.utk.edu/>

Tennessee Statistical Abstract, 1996-97. 16th ed. 807 pp. Biennial.

Texas

Dallas Morning News, Communications Center, P.O. Box 655237, Dallas 75265-5237 214-977-8261

Texas Almanac, 1998-99. 672 pp.

University of Texas, Bureau of Business Research, Austin 78713. 512-471-5180

Texas Fact Book, 1989. 6th ed. 250 pp. (No longer published.)

Utah

University of Utah, Bureau of Economic and Business Research, 401 Kendall D. Garff Building, Salt Lake City 84112. 801-581-6333. Internet site <http://www.business.utah.edu/BEBR/>

Statistical Abstract of Utah. 1996. (*Triennial.*)

Utah —Con.

Utah Foundation, 10 West 100 South, Suite 323, Salt Lake City 84101-1544 801-364-1837

*Statistical Review of Government in Utah.*1997.

Vermont

Labor Market Information, Department of Employment and Training, 5 Green Mountain Drive, P.O. Box 488, Montpelier 05601-0488 802-828-4202. Internet site <http://www.det.state.vt.us/>

Demographic and Economic Profiles. Annual. Regional county reports also available.

Virginia

University of Virginia, Weldon Cooper Center for Public Service, 918 Emmet Street, North Suite 300, Charlottesville 22903-4832 804-982-5585. Internet site <http://128.143.238.20/cpspubs/default.html>

Virginia Statistical Abstract, 1996-97. Biennial. 950 pp.

Washington

Washington State Office of Financial Management, Forecasting Division P.O. Box 43113 Olympia 98504-3113 360-902-0599. Internet site <http://www.wa.gov/ofm/>

*Washington State Data Book, 1995.*300 pp.

Population Trends for Washington State. Annual. 48 pages.

West Virginia

West Virginia University, College of Business and Economics, Bureau of Business and Economic Research, P.O. Box 6025, Morgantown 26506-6026 304-293-7835. Internet site <http://www.wvu.edu/colbe/research/bureau/home.htm>

West Virginia Statistical Abstract, 1995, Biennial. 400 pp.

County Data Profiles. Annual. 50 pp.

Census Data Profiles. Decennial. 30 pp.

West Virginia Economic Outlook. Annual. 50 pp.

West Virginia Research League, Inc., 405 Capitol Street, Suite 414, Charleston 25301-1721 304-346-9451

Economic Indicators. 1995. 215 pp.

The 1996 Statistical Handbook. 94 pp.

Wisconsin

Wisconsin Legislative Reference Bureau, P.O. Box 2037, Madison 53701-2037 608-266-7098

1997-1998 Wisconsin Blue Book. 950 pp. Biennial.

Wyoming

Department of Administration and Information, Division of Economic Analysis, 327 E. Emerson Building, Cheyenne 82002-0060 307-777-7504. Internet site <http://www.state.wy.us/ai/ai.html>

The Equality State Almanac 1996. 120 pp.

Socioeconomic *Statistics of Puerto Rico.* 1992.

Guide to Foreign Statistical Abstracts

This bibliography presents recent statistical abstracts for Mexico, Russia, and member nations of the Organization for Economic Cooperation and Development. All sources contain statistical tables on a variety of subjects for the individual countries. Many of the following publications provide text in English as well as in the national language(s). For further information on these publications, contact the named statistical agency which is responsible for editing the publication.

Austria

Osterreichisches Statistisches Zentralamt, P.O. Box 9000, A-1033 Vienna

Statistisches Jahrbuch for die Republik Osterreich. Annual. 1996 612 pp. (In German.)

Australia

Australian Bureau of Statistics, Canberra

Yearbook Australia. Annual. 1997 767 pp. (In English.)

Belgium

Institut National de Statistique, 44 rue de Louvain, 1000 Brussels

Annuaire statistique de la Belgique. Annual. 1994 822 pp. (In French and Dutch.)

Canada

Statistics Canada, Ottawa, Ontario, KIA OT6

Canada Yearbook: A review of economic, social and political developments in Canada. 1997 515 pp. Irregular. (In English and French.)

Croatia

Republika Hrvatska, Republicki Zavod Za Statistiku

Statisticki ljetopis 1995 644 pp. (In English and Serbo-Croatian.)

Czech Republic

Czech Statistical Office, Sokolovska 142, 186 04 Praha 8

Statisticka Rocenka Ceske Rpubliky 1996 707 pp. (In English and Czech.)

Denmark

Danmarks Statistik, Postboks 2550 Sejrogade 11, DK 2100, Copenhagen

Statistical Yearbook. 1995. Annual. 559 pp. (In Danish with English translations of table headings.)

Finland

Central Statistical Office of Finland, Box 504 SF-00101 Helsinki

Statistical Yearbook of Finland. Annual. 1996 661 pp. (In English, Finnish, and Swedish.)

France

Institut National de la Statistique et des Etudes Economiques, Paris 18, Bld. Adolphe Pinard, 75675 Paris (Cedex 14)

Annuaire Statistique de la France. Annual. 1997 *1002 pp. (In French.)*

Greece

National Statistical Office, 14-16 Lycourgou St., 101-66 Athens

Concise Statistical Yearbook 1995 254 pp. (In English.)

Statistical Yearbook of Greece. Annual. 1994-1995 528 pp. (plus 7 pages of diagrams). (In English and Greek.)

Iceland

Hagstofa Islands/Statistical Bureau, Hverfisgata 8-10, Reykjavik.

Statistical Abstract of Iceland. 1994. Irregular. 303 pp. (In English and Icelandic.)

Ireland

Central Statistics Office, Earlsfort Terrace, Dublin 2

Statistical Abstract. Annual. 1996 411 pp. (In English.)

Italy

ISTAT (Istituto Centrale di Statistica), Via Cesare Balbo 16, 00100 Rome

Annuario Statistico Italiano. Annual. 1996 679 pp. (In Italian.)

Japan

Statistics Bureau, Management & Coordination Agency, 19-1 Wakamatsucho, Shinjuku Tokyo 162

Japan Statistical Yearbook. Annual. 1997 914 pp. (In English and Japanese.)

Luxembourg

STATEC (Service Central de la Statistique et des Etudes), P.O. Box 304, L-2013, Luxembourg

Annuaire Statistique. Annual. 1996. (In French.)

Mexico

Instituto Nacional de Estadistica Geografia e Informatica, Avda. Insurgentes Sur No. 795-PH Col. Napoles, Del. Benito Juarez 03810 Mexico, D.F.

Anuario estadistico de los Estados Unidos Mexicanos. Annual. 1993 610 pp. Also on disc. (In Spanish.) *Agenda Estadistica 1994* 186 pp.

Netherlands

Centraal Bureau voor de Statistiek. 428 Prinses Beatrixlaan P.O. Box 959, 2270 AZ Voorburg

Statistisch Yearbook 1996. 599 pp. (In Dutch.)

New Zealand

Department of Statistics, Wellington

New Zealand Official Yearbook. Annual. 1996 592 pp. (In English.)

Norway

Central Bureau of Statistics, Skippergate 15, P.B. 8131 Dep. N-Oslo 1

Statistical Yearbook. Annual. 1996 445 pp. (In English and Norwegian.)

Portugal

INE (Instituto Nacional de Estatistica), Avenida Antonio Jose de Almeida, P-1078 Lisbon Codex

Anuario Estatistico: de Portugal. 1995 339 pp. (In Portugese.)

Russia

State Committee of Statistics of Russia, Moscow

Russian Federation in the Year 1993. Statistical Yearbook. 1993 383 pp. (In Russian.)

Slovakia

Statistical Office of the Slovak Republic, Mileticova 3, 824 67 Bratislava

Statisticka Rocenka Slovensak 1996. 681 pp. (In English and Slovak)

Slovenia

Statistical Office of the Republic of Slovenia, Vozarski Pot 12, 61000 Ljubljana

Statisticni Letopis Republike Slovenije 1996. 619 pp. (In Slovenian.)

Spain

INE (Instituto Nacional de Estadistica), Paseo de la Castellana, 183, Madrid 16

Anuario Estadistico de Espana. Annual. 1995 878 pp. (In Spanish.)

Anuario Estadistico. 1988. (Edicion Manual.) 976 pp.

Sweden

Statistics Sweden, S-11581 Stockholm

Statistical Yearbook of Sweden. Annual. 1997 586 pp. (In English and Swedish.)

Switzerland

Bundesamt fur Statistik, Hallwylstrasse 15, CH-3003, Bern

Statistisches Jahrbuch der Schweiz. Annual. 1997 464 pp. (In French and German.)

Turkey

State Institute of Statistics, Prime Ministry, 114 Necatibey Caddesi, Bakanliklar, Yenisehir, Ankara

Statistical Yearbook of Turkey. 1996 690 pp. (In English and Turkish.)

Turkey in Statistics 1994 150 pp. (In English and Turkish.)

United Kingdom

Central Statistical Office, Great George Street, London SW1P 3AQ

Annual Abstract of Statistics. Annual. 1991 349 pp. (In English.)

West Germany

Statistische Bundesamt, Postfach 5528, 6200 Wiesbaden

Statistisches Jahrbuch fur die Bundesrepublic Deutschland. Annual. 1996 755 pp. (In German.)

Statistisches Jahrbuch fur das Ausland. 1996. 399 pp.

Appendix II

Metropolitan Areas: Concepts, Components, and Population

Statistics for metropolitan areas (MA's) shown in the *Statistical Abstract* represent areas designated by the U.S. Office of Management and Budget (OMB) as metropolitan statistical areas (MSA's), consolidated metropolitan statistical areas (CMSA's), and primary metropolitan statistical areas (PMSA's).

The general concept of an MA is that of a core area containing a large population nucleus, together with adjacent communities having a high degree of economic and social integration with that core. Currently defined MA's are based on application of 1990 standards (which appeared in the *Federal Register* on March 30, 1990) to 1990 decennial census data. These MA definitions were announced by OMB effective June 30, 1996.

In this appendix, tables A, B, and C present historical summary information for MA's and nonmetropolitan areas as defined on certain dates. Table E presents geographic components and 1996 population estimates for each MSA, CMSA, and PMSA outside of New England. As of the June 1996 OMB announcement, there were 255 MSA's, and 18 CMSA's comprising 73 PMSA's in the United States. (In addition, there were three MSA's, one CMSA, and three PMSA's in Puerto Rico; MA's in Puerto Rico do not appear in these tables.) Table D presents definitions and data for New England county metropolitan areas (NECMA's), the county-based alternative metropolitan areas for the city- and town-based MSA's and CMSA's of the six New England States.

Standard definitions of metropolitan areas were first issued in 1949 by the then Bureau of the Budget (predecessor of OMB), under the designation "standard metropolitan area" (SMA). The term was changed to "standard metropolitan statistical area" (SMSA) in 1959, and to "metropolitan statistical area" (MSA) in 1983. The current collective term "metropolitan area" (MA) became effective in 1990. OMB has been responsible for the official metropolitan areas since they were first defined, except for the period 1977 to 1981, when they were the responsibility of the Office of Federal Statistical Policy and Standards, Department of Commerce.

The standards for defining metropolitan areas were modified in 1958, 1971, 1975, 1980, and 1990.

Defining MSA's, CMSA's, and PMSA's—The current standards provide that each MSA must include at least: (a) One city with 50,000 or more inhabitants, or (b) A Census Bureau-defined urbanized area (of at least 50,000 inhabitants) and a total metropolitan population of at least 100,000 (75,000 *in New England).*

Under the standards the county (or counties) that contains the largest city becomes the central county (counties), along with any adjacent counties that have at least 50 percent of their population in the urbanized area surrounding the largest city. Additional "outlying counties" are included in the MSA if they meet specified requirements of commuting to the central counties and other selected requirements of metropolitan character (such as population density and percent urban). In New England, the MSA's are defined in terms of cities and towns rather than counties.

An area that meets these requirements for recognition as an MSA and also has a population of one million or more may be recognized as a CMSA if: (1) separate component areas can be identified within the entire area by meeting statistical criteria specified in the standards, and (2) local opinion indicates there is support for the component areas. If recognized, the component areas are designated PMSA's, and the entire area becomes a CMSA. (PMSA's, like the CMSA's that contain them, are composed of individual or groups of counties outside New England, and cities and towns within New England.) If no PMSA's are recognized, the entire area is designated as an MSA.

The largest city in each MSA/CMSA is designated a "central city," and additional cities qualify if specified requirements are met concerning population size and commuting patterns. The title of each MSA consists of the names of up to three of its central cities and the name of each State into which the MSA extends. However, a central city with less than one-third the population of the area's largest city is not included in an MSA title unless local opinion desires its inclusion. Titles of PMSA's also typically are based on central city names but in certain cases consist of county names. Generally, titles of CMSA's are based on the names of their component PMSA's.

A 1990 census list, CPH-L-145, showing 1990 and 1980 populations for current MA's and their component counties or New England subcounty areas is available through the Statistical Information Office, Population Division, 301-457-2422. A 1990 census Supplementary Report, 1990 CPH-S-1-1, *Metropolitan Areas as Defined by the Office of Management and Budget, June 30, 1993,* contains extensive population and housing statistics for the then current MA's and is available from the U.S. Government Printing Office (GPO) (stock number 003-024-08738-3). Also available from the GPO is the Census Bureau's wall map for the 1994 MA's (stock number 003-024-08768-5).

Defining NECMA's—The OMB defines NECMA's as a county-based alternative for the city- and town-based New England MSA's and CMSA's. The NECMA for an MSA or CMSA includes: (1) the county containing the first-named city in that MSA/CMSA title (this county may include the first-named cities of other MSA's/CMSA's as well), and (2) each additional county having at least half its population in the MSA's/CMSA's whose first-named cities are in the previously identified county. NECMA's are not identified for individual PMSA's. There are twelve NECMA's, including one for the Boston-Worcester-Lawrence CMSA and one for the portion of the New York-Northern New Jersey-Long Island CMSA in Connecticut.

Central cities of a NECMA are those cities in the NECMA that qualify as central cities of an MSA or a CMSA. NECMA titles derive from names of central cities of MSA's/CMSA's.

Changes in MA definitions over time—Changes in the definitions of MA's since the 1950 census have consisted chiefly of (1) the recognition of new areas as they reached the minimum required city or area population; and (2) the addition of counties or New England cities and towns to existing areas as new census data showed them to qualify. Also, former separate MA's have been merged with other areas, and occasionally territory has been transferred from one MA to another or from an MA to nonmetropolitan territory. The large majority of changes have taken place on the basis of decennial census data, although the MA standards specify the bases for intercensal updates.

Because of these changes in definition, users must be cautious in comparing MA data from different dates. For some purposes, comparisons of data for MA's as defined at given dates may be appropriate. To facilitate constant-area comparisons, data for earlier dates have been revised in tables where possible to reflect the MA boundaries of the more recent date.

In tables A, B, and C below, data are given for MA's as defined for specific dates, thereby indicating the extent of change in population and land area resulting from revisions in definitions.

Table A. Number, Population, and Land Area of MA's as Defined at Specified Dates From 1960 to 1993

[The differences in population shown here for each year within each column of the table result entirely from net expansion of metropolitan territory through changes in the MA definitions. The differences in population over time shown for each MA definition (on the successive lines of the table) result entirely from population changes within that territory, unaffected by changes in MA definitions. The changes in 1990 land area result entirely from net change in MA territory. All data include Alaska and Hawaii and exclude Puerto Rico. Subtraction of any line of the table from the line below will show the net effect of change in population and land area undergone by the MA's as the result of changes in definitions between the specified dates. Such changes may have occurred throughout the period, not on any single date, and may have included reductions in, as well as additions to, MA territory. Census population data through 1980 include corrections made since publication. The area data for the 1960, 1970, and 1980 census definitions of MA's differ from the data published in those censuses because of subsequent remeasurement of land areas and changes in inland water area occurring for the 1990 census]

MA DEFINITION AS OF—	Number of MA's	POPULATION					Land area, 1990 (sq. mi.)
		1960 (April 1)	1970 (April 1)	1980 (April 1)	1990 (April 1)	1992 (July 1)	
1960 census (Nov. 1960)	212	[1]112,885,139	130,982,661	140,793,427	155,088,626	(NA)	308,742
1964 (Aug. 31)[2]	217	115,876,343	134,700,911	145,503,863	160,500,956	(NA)	348,400
1968 (Jan. 31)[3]	230	118,413,604	137,976,252	149,811,057	165,707,672	(NA)	377,042
1970 census (Feb. 28, 1971)	243	[4]119,593,498	[5]139,479,806	151,862,221	167,896,646	(NA)	385,241
1974 (Apr. 30)[6]	265	[7]126,613,710	148,198,993	162,753,335	181,125,276	(NA)	490,551
1977 (Dec. 31)[8]	277	127,674,818	149,482,664	164,383,496	182,969,860	(NA)	509,841
1980 census (June 30, 1981)[9]	318	131,318,714	153,693,767	169,430,623	188,759,597	(NA)	565,288
1983 (June 30)	[10]275	132,633,988	155,411,328	171,776,970	191,834,355	(NA)	559,752
1984 (June 30)	[10]277	132,707,748	155,519,340	171,955,900	191,903,497	(NA)	563,795
1985 (June 30)	[10]280	132,887,134	155,700,823	172,169,456	192,135,964	(NA)	569,816
1986 (June 30)	[10]281	132,977,580	155,805,452	172,304,016	192,314,367	(NA)	571,745
1987 (June 30)[11]	[10]281	133,003,445	155,832,688	172,334,547	192,345,395	(NA)	572,284
1988 (June 30)[12]	[10]282	133,088,400	155,937,275	172,454,948	192,476,951	(NA)	573,560
1989 (June 30)[12]	[10]283	133,233,777	156,084,580	172,601,873	192,618,846	(NA)	574,822
1990 census (June 30, 1990)[12]	[10]284	133,275,412	156,137,337	172,679,870	192,725,741	(NA)	580,136
1992 (Dec. 31)[12]	[10]268	(NA)	(NA)	176,662,797	197,466,567	202,903,519	669,927
1993 (June 30)[12 13]	[10]268	(NA)	(NA)	176,892,735	197,724,892	203,172,185	673,057

NA Not available. [1] Corresponds to total MA population for 1960 published in 1960 census (112,885,178), corrected by subtracting population (39) erroneously included in Franklin County, Ohio (Columbus metropolitan area). [2] MA's as defined for the 1963 economic censuses. [3] MA's as defined for the 1967 economic censuses. [4] Corresponds to total 1960 population for 1970 MA's published in 1970 census (119,594,754), corrected by subtracting 1,256 population from Lawrence-Haverhill metropolitan area; this represented an addition to the 1960 population of Andover town made subsequent to the original census tabulations, and therefore not reflected in State or national totals. [5] Corresponds to total MA population for 1970 published in 1970 census (139,418,811), plus net corrections made subsequent to publication. [6] MA's as defined for the 1972 economic censuses. [7] Includes 1960 population (82,833) of Anchorage Census Division, as defined in 1970. [8] MA's as defined for the 1977 economic censuses. [9] MA's as defined for the 1982 economic censuses. [10] MSA's and CMSA's. [11] MA's as defined for the 1987 economic censuses. [12] Data exclude the portion of Sullivan city in Crawford County, MO (1990 population 1,118) added to the St. Louis, MO-IL MSA by congressional action effective Dec. 22, 1987. [13] MA's as defined for the 1992 economic censuses.

Source: U.S. Bureau of the Census, 1960-70, *U.S. Census of Population*, vol. 1; *1980 Census of Population*, vol. 1, chapters A and B and *Supplementary Report, Metropolitan Statistical Areas* (PC80-S1-18); *1990 Census of Population and Housing Data Paper Listing* (CPH-L-10 and CPH-L-118); *1990 Census of Population and Housing, Supplementary Reports, Metropolitan Areas as Defined by the Office of Management and Budget, June 30, 1993*, (1990 CPH-S-1-1); and *Population Paper Listing* (PPL-2).

Table B. Nonmetropolitan Population and Land Area as Defined at Specified Dates From 1960 to 1993

[See headnote for table A. Nonmetropolitan population and land area are equivalent to that portion of the total national population and land area not included within MA's at the dates specified]

METROPOLITAN AREA DEFINITION AS OF—	POPULATION					Land area, 1990 (sq. mi.)
	1960 (April 1)	1970 (April 1)	1980 (April 1)	1990 (April 1)	1992 (July 1)	
1960 census (Nov. 1960)	66,438,036	72,319,370	85,752,378	93,621,247	(NA)	3,231,027
1964 (Aug. 31)	63,446,832	68,601,120	81,041,942	88,208,917	(NA)	3,191,368
1968 (Jan. 31)	60,909,571	65,325,779	76,734,748	83,002,201	(NA)	3,162,726
1970 census (Feb. 28, 1971)	59,729,677	63,822,225	74,883,584	80,813,227	(NA)	3,153,527
1974 (Apr. 30)	52,709,465	55,103,038	63,792,470	67,584,597	(NA)	3,049,218
1977 (Dec. 31)	51,648,357	53,819,367	62,162,309	65,720,013	(NA)	3,029,928
1980 census (June 30, 1981)	48,004,461	49,608,264	57,115,182	59,950,276	(NA)	2,974,481
1983 (June 30)	46,689,187	47,890,703	54,768,835	57,075,518	(NA)	2,980,016
1984 (June 30)	46,615,427	47,782,691	54,589,905	56,806,376	(NA)	2,975,972
1985 (June 30)	46,436,041	47,601,208	54,376,349	56,573,909	(NA)	2,969,952
1986 (June 30)	46,345,595	47,496,579	54,241,789	56,395,506	(NA)	2,968,023
1987 (June 30)	46,319,730	47,469,343	54,211,258	56,364,478	(NA)	2,967,484
1988 (June 30)	46,234,775	47,364,756	54,090,857	56,232,922	(NA)	2,966,206
1989 (June 30)	46,089,398	47,217,451	53,943,932	56,091,027	(NA)	2,965,146
1990 census (June 30, 1990)	46,047,763	47,164,694	53,865,935	55,984,132	(NA)	2,959,632
1992 (Dec. 31)	(NA)	(NA)	49,883,008	51,243,306	52,174,017	2,866,411
1993 (June 30)	(NA)	(NA)	49,649,464	50,984,981	51,905,351	2,863,281

NA Not available.

Table C. Percent of Total U.S. Population and Percent of Land Area Inside MA's As Defined at Specified Dates From 1960 to 1993

[See headnote for table A]

METROPOLITAN AREA DEFINITION AS OF—	PERCENT OF POPULATION					Percent of land area, 1990
	1960 (April 1)	1970 (April 1)	1980 (April 1)	1990 (April 1)	1992 (July 1)	
1960 census (Nov. 1960)	63.0	64.4	62.1	62.4	(NA)	8.7
1964 (Aug. 31)	64.6	66.3	64.2	64.5	(NA)	9.8
1968 (Jan. 31)	66.0	67.9	66.1	66.6	(NA)	10.7
1970 census (Feb. 28, 1971)	66.7	68.6	66.9	67.5	(NA)	10.9
1974 (Apr. 30)	70.6	72.9	71.8	72.8	(NA)	13.9
1977 (Dec. 31)	71.2	73.5	72.6	73.6	(NA)	14.4
1980 census (June 30, 1981)	73.2	75.6	74.8	75.9	(NA)	16.0
1983 (June 30)	74.0	76.4	75.8	77.1	(NA)	15.8
1984 (June 30)	74.0	76.5	75.9	77.2	(NA)	15.9
1985 (June 30)	74.1	76.6	76.0	77.3	(NA)	16.1
1986 (June 30)	74.2	76.6	76.1	77.3	(NA)	16.2
1987 (June 30)	74.2	76.7	76.1	77.3	(NA)	16.2
1988 (June 30)	74.2	76.7	76.1	77.4	(NA)	16.2
1989 (June 30)	74.3	76.8	76.2	77.4	(NA)	16.2
1990 census (June 30, 1990)	74.3	76.8	76.2	77.5	(NA)	16.4
1992 (Dec. 31)	(NA)	(NA)	78.0	79.4	79.5	18.9
1993 (June 30)	(NA)	(NA)	78.1	79.5	79.7	19.0

NA Not available.

Source: U.S. Bureau of the Census, 1960-70, *U.S. Census of Population*, vol. 1; *1980 Census of Population*, vol. 1, chapters A and B and *Supplementary Report, Metropolitan Statistical Areas* (PC80-S1-18); *1990 Census of Population and Housing Data Paper Listing* (CPH-L-10 and CPH-L-118); *1990 Census of Population and Housing, Supplementary Reports, Metropolitan Areas as Defined by the Office of Management and Budget, June 30, 1993*, (1990 CPH-S-1-1); and *Population Paper Listing* (PPL-2).

Table D. New England County Metropolitan Areas (NECMA's)

[In thousands. As of July 1]

NECMA	Population, 1990	NECMA	Population, 1996	NECMA	Population, 1996
Bangor, ME	**145**	**Burlington, VT**	**191**	**New London-Norwich, CT**	**251**
Penobscot County	145	Chittenden County	141	New London County	251
		Franklin County	43		
Barnstable-Yarmouth, MA	**202**	Grand Isle County	6	**Pittsfield, MA**	**135**
Barnstable County	202			Berkshire County	135
Boston-Worcester-Lawrence-Lowell-Brockton, MA-NH	**5,796**	**Hartford, CT**	**1,110**	**Portland, ME**	**251**
Bristol County, MA	514	Hartford County	832	Cumberland County	251
Essex County, MA	687	Middlesex County	148	**Providence-Warwick-Pawtucket, RI**	**907**
Middlesex County, MA	1,413	Tolland County	130	Bristol County	49
Norfolk County, MA	637	**Lewiston-Auburn, ME**	**102**	Kent County	162
Plymouth County, MA	457	Androscoggin County	102	Providence County	578
Suffolk County, MA	645	**New Haven-Bridgeport-Stamford-Waterbury-Danbury, CT**	**1,628**	Washington County	118
Worcester County, MA	720	Fairfield County	834	**Springfield, MA**	**592**
Hillsborough County, NH	354	New Haven County	795	Hampden County	442
Rockingham County, NH	263			Hampshire County	150
Strafford County, NH	107				

Source: U.S. Bureau of the Census, "County Population Estimates: 1996;" published 9 July 1997; <http://www.census.gov\population/www/estimates/co96.html>.

Table E. Metropolitan Areas Outside of New England and Their Components as of June 30, 1996

[Population estimated as of July 1, 1996. All metropolitan areas are arranged alphabetically. PMSA's are included under their respective CMSA's, see CMSA entry. This table presents data for MAs outside New England only]

	Population, 1996 (1,000)
Abilene, TX MSA	122
Taylor County	122
Albany, GA MSA	117
Dougherty County	97
Lee County	21
Albany-Schenectady-Troy, NY MSA	879
Albany County	296
Montgomery County	52
Rensselaer County	155
Saratoga County	195
Schenectady County	148
Schoharie County	33
Albuquerque, NM MSA	670
Bernalillo County	527
Sandoval County	83
Valencia County	60
Alexandria, LA MSA	126
Rapides Parish	126
Allentown-Bethlehem-Easton, PA MSA	614
Carbon County	59
Lehigh County	296
Northampton County	258
Altoona, PA MSA	131
Blair County	131
Amarillo, TX MSA	206
Potter County	109
Randall County	97
Anchorage, AK MSA	251
Anchorage Borough	251
Anniston, AL MSA	114
Calhoun County	114
Appleton-Oshkosh-Neenah, WI MSA	341
Calumet County	38
Outagamie County	153
Winnebago County	150
Asheville, NC MSA	210
Buncombe County	192
Madison County	18
Athens, GA MSA	137
Clarke County	91
Madison County	24
Oconee County	22
Atlanta, GA MSA	3,541
Barrow County	37
Bartow County	66
Carroll County	79
Cherokee County	121
Clayton County	202
Cobb County	539
Coweta County	76
DeKalb County	590
Douglas County	84
Fayette County	82
Forsyth County	69
Fulton County	718
Gwinnett County	478
Henry County	91
Newton County	53
Paulding County	64
Pickens County	18
Rockdale County	65
Spalding County	58
Walton County	49
Augusta-Aiken, GA-SC MSA	454
Columbia County, GA	86
McDuffie County, GA	21
Richmond County, GA	194
Aiken County, SC	133
Edgefield County, SC	19
Austin-San Marcos, TX MSA	1,041
Bastrop County	47
Caldwell County	31
Hays County	82
Travis County	684
Williamson County	196
Bakersfield, CA MSA	623
Kern County	623
Baton Rouge, LA MSA	567
Ascension Parish	68
East Baton Rouge Parish	396
Livingston Parish	83
West Baton Rouge Parish	21
Beaumont-Port Arthur, TX MSA	376
Hardin County	48
Jefferson County	244
Orange County	84
Bellingham, WA MSA	153
Whatcom County	153
Benton Harbor, MI MSA	161
Berrien County	161
Billings, MT MSA	126
Yellowstone County	126
Biloxi-Gulfport-Pascagoula, MS MSA	343
Hancock County	38
Harrison County	177
Jackson County	128
Binghamton, NY MSA	254
Broome County	202
Tioga County	53
Birmingham, AL MSA	895
Blount County	43
Jefferson County	662
St. Clair County	59
Shelby County	130
Bismarck, ND MSA	90
Burleigh County	66
Morton County	24
Bloomington, IN MSA	116
Monroe County	116
Bloomington-Normal, IL MSA	139
McLean County	139
Boise City, ID MSA	373
Ada County	260
Canyon County	113
Brownsville-Harlingen, TX MSA	315
Cameron County	315
Bryan-College Station, TX MSA	132
Brazos County	132
Buffalo-Niagara Falls, NY MSA	1,175
Erie County	954
Niagara County	221
Canton-Massillon, OH MSA	403
Carroll County	29
Stark County	374
Casper, WY MSA	64
Natrona County	64
Cedar Rapids, IA MSA	179
Linn County	179
Champaign-Urbana, IL MSA	167
Champaign County	167
Charleston-North Charleston, SC MSA	495
Berkeley County	133
Charleston County	276
Dorchester County	86
Charleston, WV MSA	255
Kanawha County	205
Putnam County	50
Charlotte-Gastonia-Rock Hill, NC-SC MSA	1,321
Cabarrus County, NC	113
Gaston County, NC	183
Lincoln County, NC	58
Mecklenburg County, NC	598
Rowan County, NC	122
Union County, NC	102
York County, SC	147
Charlottesville, VA MSA	146
Albemarle County	74
Fluvanna County	17
Greene County	13
Charlottesville city	41
Chattanooga, TN-GA MSA	446
Hamilton County, TN	295
Marion County, TN	27
Catoosa County, GA	49
Dade County, GA	14
Walker County, GA	61
Cheyenne, WY MSA	79
Laramie County	79
Chicago-Gary-Kenosha, IL-IN-WI CMSA	8,600
Chicago, IL PMSA	7,734
Cook County, IL	5,097
DeKalb County, IL	83
DuPage County, IL	859

	Population, 1996 (1,000)
Grundy County, IL	36
Kane County, IL	370
Kendall County, IL	46
Lake County, IL	563
McHenry County, IL	231
Will County, IL	428
Gary, IN PMSA	622
Lake County, IN	480
Porter County, IN	142
Kankakee, IL PMSA	102
Kankakee County, IL	102
Kenosha, WI PMSA	142
Kenosha County, WI	142
Chico-Paradise, CA MSA	193
Butte County	193
Cincinnati-Hamilton, OH-KY-IN CMSA	1,921
Cincinnati, OH-KY-IN PMSA	1,597
Brown County, OH	39
Clermont County, OH	170
Hamilton County, OH	858
Warren County, OH	135
Boone County, KY	73
Campbell County, KY	87
Gallatin County, KY	6
Grant County, KY	19
Kenton County, KY	146
Pendleton County, KY	14
Dearborn County, IN	46
Ohio County, IN	5
Hamilton-Middletown, OH PMSA	324
Butler County, OH	324
Clarksville-Hopkinsville, TN-KY MSA	186
Montgomery County, TN	121
Christian County, KY	65
Cleveland-Akron, OH CMSA	2,913
Akron, OH PMSA	680
Portage County	150
Summit County	531
Cleveland-Lorain-Elyria, OH PMSA	2,233
Ashtabula County	102
Cuyahoga County	1,402
Geauga County	86
Lake County	223
Lorain County	281
Medina County	139
Colorado Springs, CO MSA	473
El Paso County	473
Columbia, MO MSA	126
Boone County	126
Columbia, SC MSA	488
Lexington County	196
Richland County	293
Columbus, GA-AL MSA	272
Chattahoochee County, GA	16
Harris County, GA	21
Muscogee County, GA	183
Russell County, AL	51
Columbus, OH MSA	1,448
Delaware County	83
Fairfield County	119
Franklin County	1,014
Licking County	138
Madison County	41
Pickaway County	53
Corpus Christi, TX MSA	384
Nueces County	316
San Patricio County	68
Cumberland, MD-WV MSA	101
Allegany County, MD	73
Mineral County, WV	28
Dallas-Fort Worth, TX CMSA	4,575
Dallas, TX PMSA	3,048
Collin County	372
Dallas County	2,000
Denton County	348
Ellis County	97
Henderson County	66
Hunt County	68
Kaufman County	62
Rockwall County	34
Fort Worth-Arlington, TX PMSA	1,527
Hood County	35
Johnson County	110
Parker County	76
Tarrant County	1,305
Danville, VA MSA	109
Pittsylvania County	56
Danville city	53
Davenport-Moline-Rock Island, IA-IL MSA	358
Scott County, IA	157
Henry County, IL	52
Rock Island County, IL	149
Dayton-Springfield, OH MSA	951
Clark County	147
Greene County	140
Miami County	97
Montgomery County	566
Daytona Beach, FL MSA	456
Flagler County	42
Volusia County	414
Decatur, AL MSA	140
Lawrence County	33
Morgan County	107
Decatur, IL MSA	115
Macon County	115
Denver-Boulder-Greeley, CO CMSA	2,277
Boulder-Longmont, CO PMSA	258
Boulder County	258
Denver, CO PMSA	1,867
Adams County	310
Arapahoe County	455
Denver County	498
Douglas County	112
Jefferson County	493
Greeley, CO PMSA	152
Weld County	152
Des Moines, IA MSA	427
Dallas County	34
Polk County	354
Warren County	39
Detroit-Ann Arbor-Flint, MI CMSA	5,284
Ann Arbor, MI PMSA	530
Lenawee County	97
Livingston County	138
Washtenaw County	295
Detroit, MI PMSA	4,318
Lapeer County	85
Macomb County	735
Monroe County	140
Oakland County	1,162
St. Clair County	156
Wayne County	2,040
Flint, MI PMSA	436
Genesee County	436
Dothan, AL MSA	133
Dale County	49
Houston County	84
Dover, DE MSA	122
Kent County	122
Dubuque, IA MSA	88
Dubuque County	88
Duluth, MN-WI MSA	239
St. Louis County, MN	196
Douglas County, WI	43
Eau Claire, WI MSA	143
Chippewa County	54
Eau Claire County	89
El Paso, TX MSA	684
El Paso County	684
Elkhart-Goshen, IN MSA	169
Elkhart County	169
Elmira, NY MSA	93
Chemung County	93
Enid, OK MSA	57
Garfield County	57
Erie, PA MSA	281
Erie County	281
Eugene-Springfield, OR MSA	307
Lane County	307
Evansville-Henderson, IN-KY MSA	289
Posey County, IN	27
Vanderburgh County, IN	168
Warrick County, IN	50
Henderson County, KY	44
Fargo-Moorhead, ND-MN MSA	165
Cass County, ND	113
Clay County, MN	52
Fayetteville, NC MSA	285
Cumberland County	285
Fayetteville-Springdale-Rogers, AR MSA	261
Benton County	126
Washington County	135
Flagstaff, AZ-UT MSA	118
Coconino County, AZ	112
Kane County, UT	6
Florence, AL MSA	136
Colbert County	52
Lauderdale County	84
Florence, SC MSA	123
Florence County	123
Fort Collins-Loveland, CO MSA	222
Larimer County	222
Fort Myers-Cape Coral, FL MSA	380
Lee County	380
Fort Pierce-Port St. Lucie, FL MSA	287
Martin County	113
St. Lucie County	175
Fort Smith, AR-OK MSA	191
Crawford County, AR	49
Sebastian County, AR	106
Sequoyah County, OK	37
Fort Walton Beach, FL MSA	166
Okaloosa County	166
Fort Wayne, IN MSA	475
Adams County	33
Allen County	311
De Kalb County	38

	Population, 1996 (1,000)
Huntington County	37
Wells County	27
Whitley County	30
Fresno, CA MSA	862
Fresno County	751
Madera County	110
Gadsden, AL MSA	102
Etowah County	102
Gainesville, FL MSA	197
Alachua County	197
Glens Falls, NY MSA	122
Warren County	61
Washington County	61
Goldsboro, NC MSA	112
Wayne County	112
Grand Forks, ND-MN MSA	104
Grand Forks County, ND	71
Polk County, MN	32
Grand Junction, CO MSA	108
Mesa County	108
Grand Rapids-Muskegon-Holland, MI MSA	1,015
Allegan County	99
Kent County	536
Muskegon County	165
Ottawa County	215
Great Falls, MT MSA	81
Cascade County	81
Green Bay, WI MSA	213
Brown County	213
Greensboro—Winston-Salem—High Point, NC MSA	1,141
Alamance County	117
Davidson County	137
Davie County	30
Forsyth County	284
Guilford County	379
Randolph County	117
Stokes County	42
Yadkin County	34
Greenville, NC MSA	119
Pitt County	119
Greenville-Spartanburg-Anderson, SC MSA	897
Anderson County	157
Cherokee County	48
Greenville County	345
Pickens County	104
Spartanburg County	243
Harrisburg-Lebanon-Carlisle, PA MSA	615
Cumberland County	207
Dauphin County	247
Lebanon County	117
Perry County	44
Hattiesburg, MS MSA	108
Forrest County	73
Lamar County	35
Hickory-Morganton, NC MSA	315
Alexander County	30
Burke County	81
Caldwell County	75
Catawba County	129
Honolulu, HI MSA	872
Honolulu County	872

	Population, 1996 (1,000)
Houma, LA MSA	190
Lafourche Parish	88
Terrebonne Parish	102
Houston-Galveston-Brazoria, TX CMSA	4,253
Brazoria, TX PMSA	221
Brazoria County	221
Galveston-Texas City, TX PMSA	241
Galveston County	241
Houston, TX PMSA	3,792
Chambers County	23
Fort Bend County	307
Harris County	3,127
Liberty County	63
Montgomery County	246
Waller County	26
Huntington-Ashland, WV-KY-OH MSA	317
Cabell County, WV	96
Wayne County, WV	42
Boyd County, KY	50
Carter County, KY	26
Greenup County, KY	37
Lawrence County, OH	64
Huntsville, AL MSA	330
Limestone County	60
Madison County	270
Indianapolis, IN MSA	1,492
Boone County	42
Hamilton County	148
Hancock County	52
Hendricks County	89
Johnson County	104
Madison County	133
Marion County	818
Morgan County	63
Shelby County	43
Iowa City, IA MSA	102
Johnson County	102
Jackson, MI MSA	155
Jackson County	155
Jackson, MS MSA	421
Hinds County	250
Madison County	68
Rankin County	102
Jackson, TN MSA	98
Chester County	14
Madison County	84
Jacksonville, FL MSA	1,009
Clay County	129
Duval County	721
Nassau County	52
St. Johns County	107
Jacksonville, NC MSA	145
Onslow County	145
Jamestown, NY MSA	141
Chautauqua County	141
Janesville-Beloit, WI MSA	151
Rock County	151
Johnson City-Kingsport-Bristol, TN-VA MSA	458
Carter County, TN	53
Hawkins County, TN	48
Sullivan County, TN	150
Unicoi County, TN	17
Washington County, TN	100
Scott County, VA	23
Washington County, VA	48
Bristol city, VA	18

	Population, 1996 (1,000)
Johnstown, PA MSA	239
Cambria County	159
Somerset County	81
Jonesboro, AR MSA	76
Craighead County	76
Joplin, MO MSA	146
Jasper County	98
Newton County	48
Kalamazoo-Battle Creek, MI MSA	444
Calhoun County	140
Kalamazoo County	229
Van Buren County	75
Kansas City, MO-KS MSA	1,690
Cass County, MO	76
Clay County, MO	170
Clinton County, MO	18
Jackson County, MO	646
Lafayette County, MO	32
Platte County, MO	67
Ray County, MO	23
Johnson County, KS	408
Leavenworth County, KS	70
Miami County, KS	26
Wyandotte County, KS	153
Killeen-Temple, TX MSA	297
Bell County	222
Coryell County	74
Knoxville, TN MSA	649
Anderson County	72
Blount County	99
Knox County	365
Loudon County	37
Sevier County	61
Union County	16
Kokomo, IN MSA	101
Howard County	84
Tipton County	16
La Crosse, WI-MN MSA	122
La Crosse County, WI	102
Houston County, MN	19
Lafayette, LA MSA	369
Acadia Parish	58
Lafayette Parish	182
St. Landry Parish	83
St. Martin Parish	46
Lafayette, IN MSA	171
Clinton County	33
Tippecanoe County	138
Lake Charles, LA MSA	179
Calcasieu Parish	179
Lakeland-Winter Haven, FL MSA	441
Polk County	441
Lancaster, PA MSA	451
Lancaster County	451
Lansing-East Lansing, MI MSA	448
Clinton County	62
Eaton County	100
Ingham County	286
Laredo, TX MSA	177
Webb County	177
Las Cruces, NM MSA	164
Dona Ana County	164
Las Vegas, NV-AZ MSA	1,201
Clark County, NV	1,049

	Population, 1996 (1,000)
Nye County, NV	26
Mohave County, AZ	126
Lawrence, KS MSA	90
Douglas County	90
Lawton, OK MSA	111
Comanche County	111
Lexington, KY MSA	441
Bourbon County	19
Clark County	32
Fayette County	240
Jessamine County	35
Madison County	64
Scott County	29
Woodford County	22
Lima, OH MSA	155
Allen County	108
Auglaize County	47
Lincoln, NE MSA	232
Lancaster County	232
Little Rock-North Little Rock, AR MSA	548
Faulkner County	74
Lonoke County	48
Pulaski County	352
Saline County	75
Longview-Marshall, TX MSA	207
Gregg County	112
Harrison County	60
Upshur County	35
Los Angeles-Riverside-Orange County, CA CMSA	15,495
Los Angeles-Long Beach, CA PMSA	9,128
Los Angeles County	9,128
Orange County, CA PMSA	2,637
Orange County	2,637
Riverside-San Bernardino, CA PMSA	3,016
Riverside County	1,417
San Bernardino County	1,598
Ventura, CA PMSA	715
Ventura County	715
Louisville, KY-IN MSA	992
Bullitt County, KY	57
Jefferson County, KY	673
Oldham County, KY	42
Clark County, IN	93
Floyd County, IN	71
Harrison County, IN	33
Scott County, IN	23
Lubbock, TX MSA	232
Lubbock County	232
Lynchburg, VA MSA	206
Amherst County	30
Bedford County	53
Campbell County	49
Bedford city	7
Lynchburg city	67
Macon, GA MSA	313
Bibb County	156
Houston County	101
Jones County	22
Peach County	24
Twiggs County	10
Madison, WI MSA	395
Dane County	395
Mansfield, OH MSA	175
Crawford County	47
Richland County	128
McAllen-Edinburg-Mission, TX MSA	496
Hidalgo County	496
Medford-Ashland, OR MSA	169
Jackson County	169
Melbourne-Titusville-Palm Bay, FL MSA	454
Brevard County	454
Memphis, TN-AR-MS MSA	1,078
Fayette County, TN	28
Shelby County, TN	867
Tipton County, TN	45
Crittenden County, AR	50
DeSoto County, MS	88
Merced, CA MSA	192
Merced County	192
Miami-Fort Lauderdale, FL CMSA	3,514
Fort Lauderdale, FL PMSA	1,438
Broward County	1,438
Miami, FL PMSA	2,076
Dade County	2,076
Milwaukee-Racine, WI CMSA	1,643
Milwaukee-Waukesha, WI PMSA	1,458
Milwaukee County	922
Ozaukee County	80
Washington County	111
Waukesha County	344
Racine, WI PMSA	185
Racine County	185
Minneapolis-St. Paul, MN-WI MSA	2,765
Anoka County, MN	282
Carver County, MN	61
Chisago County, MN	38
Dakota County, MN	326
Hennepin County, MN	1,059
Isanti County, MN	29
Ramsey County, MN	484
Scott County, MN	73
Sherburne County, MN	55
Washington County, MN	185
Wright County, MN	81
Pierce County, WI	35
St. Croix County, WI	56
Mobile, AL MSA	519
Baldwin County	123
Mobile County	396
Modesto, CA MSA	416
Stanislaus County	416
Monroe, LA MSA	147
Ouachita Parish	147
Montgomery, AL MSA	315
Autauga County	40
Elmore County	58
Montgomery County	216
Muncie, IN MSA	119
Delaware County	119
Myrtle Beach, SC MSA	164
Horry County	164
Naples, FL MSA	188
Collier County	188
Nashville, TN MSA	1,117
Cheatham County	33
Davidson County	535
Dickson County	40
Robertson County	50
Rutherford County	154
Sumner County	120
Williamson County	106
Wilson County	80
New Orleans, LA MSA	1,313
Jefferson Parish	455
Orleans Parish	477
Plaquemines Parish	26
St. Bernard Parish	67
St. Charles Parish	47
St. James Parish	21
St. John the Baptist Parish	42
St. Tammany Parish	178
New York-Northern New Jersey-Long Island, NY-NJ-CT-PA CMSA (pt.) [1]	18,218
Bergen-Passaic, NJ PMSA	1,311
Bergen County, NJ	846
Passaic County, NJ	465
Dutchess County, NY PMSA	263
Dutchess County, NY	263
Jersey City, NJ PMSA	551
Hudson County, NJ	551
Middlesex-Somerset-Hunterdon, NJ PMSA	1,091
Hunterdon County, NJ	119
Middlesex County, NJ	702
Somerset County, NJ	270
Monmouth-Ocean, NJ PMSA	1,065
Monmouth County, NJ	591
Ocean County, NJ	474
Nassau-Suffolk, NY PMSA	2,660
Nassau County, NY	1,303
Suffolk County, NY	1,357
New York, NY PMSA	8,643
Bronx County, NY	1,194
Kings County, NY	2,274
New York County, NY	1,534
Putnam County, NY	91
Queens County, NY	1,961
Richmond County, NY	399
Rockland County, NY	278
Westchester County, NY	893
Newark, NJ PMSA	1,940
Essex County, NJ	755
Morris County, NJ	449
Sussex County, NJ	141
Union County, NJ	497
Warren County, NJ	98
Newburgh, NY-PA PMSA	363
Orange County, NY	324
Pike County, PA	38
Trenton, NJ PMSA	330
Mercer County, NJ	330
Norfolk-Virginia Beach-Newport News, VA-NC MSA	1,540
Gloucester County, VA	34
Isle of Wight County, VA	28
James City County, VA	41
Mathews County, VA	9
York County, VA	55
Chesapeake city, VA	192
Hampton city, VA	139
Newport News city, VA	176
Norfolk city, VA	233
Poquoson city, VA	12
Portsmouth city, VA	101
Suffolk city, VA	59
Virginia Beach city, VA	430
Williamsburg city, VA	13
Currituck County, NC	17
Ocala, FL MSA	230
Marion County	230
Odessa-Midland, TX MSA	239
Ector County	123
Midland County	116
Oklahoma City, OK MSA	1,027
Canadian County	83
Cleveland County	195
Logan County	31

	Population, 1996 (1,000)
McClain County	25
Oklahoma County	631
Pottawatomie County	62
Omaha, NE-IA MSA	682
Cass County, NE	23
Douglas County, NE	439
Sarpy County, NE	116
Washington County, NE	18
Pottawattamie County, IA	85
Orlando, FL MSA	1,417
Lake County	187
Orange County	759
Osceola County	136
Seminole County	336
Owensboro, KY MSA	91
Daviess County	91
Panama City, FL MSA	145
Bay County	145
Parkersburg-Marietta, WV-OH MSA	152
Wood County, WV	88
Washington County, OH	64
Pensacola, FL MSA	386
Escambia County	278
Santa Rosa County	108
Peoria-Pekin, IL MSA	347
Peoria County	183
Tazewell County	128
Woodford County	35
Philadelphia-Wilmington-Atlantic City, PA-NJ-DE-MD CMSA	5,973
Atlantic-Cape May, NJ PMSA	334
Atlantic County, NJ	235
Cape May County, NJ	98
Philadelphia, PA-NJ PMSA	4,953
Bucks County, PA	579
Chester County, PA	411
Delaware County, PA	548
Montgomery County, PA	709
Philadelphia County, PA	1,478
Burlington County, NJ	411
Camden County, NJ	506
Gloucester County, NJ	244
Salem County, NJ	68
Vineland-Millville-Bridgeton, NJ PMSA	136
Cumberland County, NJ	136
Wilmington-Newark, DE-MD PMSA	551
New Castle County, DE	471
Cecil County, MD	79
Phoenix-Mesa, AZ MSA	2,747
Maricopa County	2,611
Pinal County	135
Pine Bluff, AR MSA	83
Jefferson County	83
Pittsburgh, PA MSA	2,379
Allegheny County	1,296
Beaver County	187
Butler County	168
Fayette County	146
Washington County	207
Westmoreland County	376
Pocatello, ID MSA	74
Bannock County	74
Portland-Salem, OR-WA CMSA	2,078
Portland-Vancouver, OR-WA PMSA	1,759
Clackamas County, OR	324
Columbia County, OR	43
Multnomah County, OR	625
Washington County, OR	384
Yamhill County, OR	78
Clark County, WA	305
Salem, OR PMSA	319
Marion County, OR	261
Polk County, OR	59
Provo-Orem, UT MSA	320
Utah County	320
Pueblo, CO MSA	131
Pueblo County	131
Punta Gorda, FL MSA	130
Charlotte County	130
Raleigh-Durham-Chapel Hill, NC MSA	1,025
Chatham County	44
Durham County	197
Franklin County	43
Johnston County	98
Orange County	109
Wake County	534
Rapid City, SD MSA	87
Pennington County	87
Reading, PA MSA	352
Berks County	352
Redding, CA MSA	162
Shasta County	162
Reno, NV MSA	299
Washoe County	299
Richland-Kennewick-Pasco, WA MSA	180
Benton County	134
Franklin County	46
Richmond-Petersburg, VA MSA	935
Charles City County	7
Chesterfield County	243
Dinwiddie County	23
Goochland County	17
Hanover County	77
Henrico County	233
New Kent County	12
Powhatan County	20
Prince George County	28
Colonial Heights city	17
Hopewell city	23
Petersburg city	38
Richmond city	196
Roanoke, VA MSA	229
Botetourt County	28
Roanoke County	82
Roanoke city	96
Salem city	24
Rochester, MN MSA	113
Olmsted County	113
Rochester, NY MSA	1,088
Genesee County	61
Livingston County	66
Monroe County	722
Ontario County	100
Orleans County	45
Wayne County	94
Rockford, IL MSA	352
Boone County	37
Ogle County	50
Winnebago County	265
Rocky Mount, NC MSA	144
Edgecombe County	56
Nash County	88
Sacramento-Yolo, CA CMSA	1,632
Sacramento, CA PMSA	1,482
El Dorado County	152
Placer County	213
Sacramento County	1,117
Yolo, CA PMSA	150
Yolo County	150
Saginaw-Bay City-Midland, MI MSA	403
Bay County	111
Midland County	81
Saginaw County	212
St. Cloud, MN MSA	159
Benton County	33
Stearns County	127
St. Joseph, MO MSA	97
Andrew County	15
Buchanan County	82
St. Louis, MO-IL MSA	2,548
Franklin County, MO	89
Jefferson County, MO	188
Lincoln County, MO	34
St. Charles County, MO	255
St. Louis County, MO	1,004
Warren County, MO	23
St. Louis city, MO	352
Clinton County, IL	35
Jersey County, IL	21
Madison County, IL	258
Monroe County, IL	25
St. Clair County, IL	264
Salinas, CA MSA	339
Monterey County	339
Salt Lake City-Ogden, UT MSA	1,218
Davis County	215
Salt Lake County	828
Weber County	175
San Angelo, TX MSA	103
Tom Green County	103
San Antonio, TX MSA	1,490
Bexar County	1,318
Comal County	68
Guadalupe County	75
Wilson County	29
San Diego, CA MSA	2,655
San Diego County	2,655
San Francisco-Oakland-San Jose, CA CMSA	6,605
Oakland, CA PMSA	2,210
Alameda County	1,328
Contra Costa County	881
San Francisco, CA PMSA	1,655
Marin County	233
San Francisco County	735
San Mateo County	687
San Jose, CA PMSA	1,600
Santa Clara County	1,600
Santa Cruz-Watsonville, CA PMSA	236
Santa Cruz County	236
Santa Rosa, CA PMSA	421
Sonoma County	421
Vallejo-Fairfield-Napa, CA PMSA	482
Napa County	117
Solano County	366
San Luis Obispo-Atascadero-Paso Robles, CA MSA	229
San Luis Obispo County	229
Santa Barbara-Santa Maria-Lompoc, CA MSA	386
Santa Barbara County	386

	Population, 1996 (1,000)
Santa Fe, NM MSA	137
Los Alamos County	18
Santa Fe County	119
Sarasota-Bradenton, FL MSA	529
Manatee County	232
Sarasota County	297
Savannah, GA MSA	293
Bryan County	22
Chatham County	227
Effingham County	33
Scranton—Wilkes-Barre—Hazleton, PA MSA	628
Columbia County	64
Lackawanna County	213
Luzerne County	321
Wyoming County	29
Seattle-Tacoma-Bremerton, WA CMSA	3,321
Bremerton, WA PMSA	232
Kitsap County	232
Olympia, WA PMSA	197
Thurston County	197
Seattle-Bellevue-Everett, WA PMSA	2,235
Island County	69
King County	1,619
Snohomish County	546
Tacoma, WA PMSA	657
Pierce County	657
Sharon, PA MSA	122
Mercer County	122
Sheboygan, WI MSA	110
Sheboygan County	110
Sherman-Denison, TX MSA	101
Grayson County	101
Shreveport-Bossier City, LA MSA	380
Bossier Parish	92
Caddo Parish	245
Webster Parish	43
Sioux City, IA-NE MSA	121
Woodbury County, IA	103
Dakota County, NE	19
Sioux Falls, SD MSA	157
Lincoln County	18
Minnehaha County	138
South Bend, IN MSA	258
St. Joseph County	258
Spokane, WA MSA	405
Spokane County	405
Springfield, IL MSA	204
Menard County	12
Sangamon County	192
Springfield, MO MSA	296
Christian County	45
Greene County	224
Webster County	28
State College, PA MSA	131
Centre County	131
Steubenville-Weirton, OH-WV MSA	138
Jefferson County, OH	77
Brooke County, WV	27
Hancock County, WV	35
Stockton-Lodi, CA MSA	533
San Joaquin County	533
Sumter, SC MSA	107
Sumter County	107
Syracuse, NY MSA	746
Cayuga County	82
Madison County	72
Onondaga County	467
Oswego County	125
Tallahassee, FL MSA	259
Gadsden County	44
Leon County	216
Tampa-St. Petersburg-Clearwater, FL MSA	2,199
Hernando County	121
Hillsborough County	898
Pasco County	312
Pinellas County	869
Terre Haute, IN MSA	150
Clay County	26
Vermillion County	17
Vigo County	106
Texarkana, TX-Texarkana, AR MSA	124
Bowie County, TX	85
Miller County, AR	39
Toledo, OH MSA	611
Fulton County	41
Lucas County	453
Wood County	118
Topeka, KS MSA	165
Shawnee County	165
Tucson, AZ MSA	768
Pima County	768
Tulsa, OK MSA	756
Creek County	65
Osage County	43
Rogers County	64
Tulsa County	532
Wagoner County	53
Tuscaloosa, AL MSA	159
Tuscaloosa County	159
Tyler, TX MSA	165
Smith County	165
Utica-Rome, NY MSA	302
Herkimer County	66
Oneida County	236
Victoria, TX MSA	82
Victoria County	82
Visalia-Tulare-Porterville, CA MSA	350
Tulare County	350
Waco, TX MSA	202
McLennan County	202
Washington-Baltimore, DC-MD-VA-WV CMSA	7,165
Baltimore, MD PMSA	2,474
Anne Arundel County, MD	466
Baltimore County, MD	718
Carroll County, MD	144
Harford County, MD	209
Howard County, MD	224
Queen Anne's County, MD	38
Baltimore city, MD	675
Hagerstown, MD PMSA	127
Washington County, MD	127
Washington, DC-MD-VA-WV PMSA	4,563
District of Columbia, DC	543
Calvert County, MD	67
Charles County, MD	114
Frederick County, MD	179
Montgomery County, MD	817
Prince George's County, MD	774
Arlington County, VA	175
Clarke County, VA	13
Culpeper County, VA	32
Fairfax County, VA	902
Fauquier County, VA	52
King George County, VA	16
Loudoun County, VA	123
Prince William County, VA	249
Spotsylvania County, VA	74
Stafford County, VA	82
Warren County, VA	30
Alexandria city, VA	118
Fairfax city, VA	21
Falls Church city, VA	10
Fredericksburg city, VA	23
Manassas city, VA	33
Manassas Park city, VA	8
Berkeley County, WV	68
Jefferson County, WV	40
Waterloo-Cedar Falls, IA MSA	123
Black Hawk County	123
Wausau, WI MSA	122
Marathon County	122
West Palm Beach-Boca Raton, FL MSA	993
Palm Beach County	993
Wheeling, WV-OH MSA	156
Marshall County, WV	36
Ohio County, WV	50
Belmont County, OH	70
Wichita, KS MSA	513
Butler County	59
Harvey County	31
Sedgwick County	422
Wichita Falls, TX MSA	136
Archer County	8
Wichita County	128
Williamsport, PA MSA	119
Lycoming County	119
Wilmington, NC MSA	207
Brunswick County	63
New Hanover County	144
Yakima, WA MSA	216
Yakima County	216
York, PA MSA	368
York County	368
Youngstown-Warren, OH MSA	599
Columbiana County	111
Mahoning County	260
Trumbull County	227
Yuba City, CA MSA	137
Sutter County	76
Yuba County	61
Yuma, AZ MSA	125
Yuma County	125

Five PMSAs of the New York-Northern New Jersey-Long Island, NY-NJ-CTPA CMSA are in Connecticut and therefore do not appear in this table; also, the CMSA's population shown here reflects the absence of those PMSAs.

Source: U.S. Bureau of the Census, "County Population Estimates: 1996;" published 9 July 1997; <*http://www.census.population/www/estimates/co96.html*>.

Limitations of the Data

Introduction.—The data presented in this *Statistical Abstract* came from many sources. The sources include not only Federal statistical bureaus and other organizations that collect and issue statistics as their principal activity, but also governmental administrative and regulatory agencies, private research bodies, trade associations, insurance companies, health associations, and private organizations such as the National Education Association and philanthropic foundations. Consequently, the data vary considerably as to reference periods, definitions of terms and, for ongoing series, the number and frequency of time periods for which data are available.

The statistics presented were obtained and tabulated by various means. Some statistics are based on complete enumerations or censuses while others are based on samples. Some information is extracted from records kept for administrative or regulatory purposes (school enrollment, hospital records, securities registration, financial accounts, social security records, income tax returns, etc.), while other information is obtained explicitly for statistical purposes through interviews or by mail. The estimation procedures used vary from highly sophisticated scientific techniques, to crude "informed guesses."

Each set of data relates to a group of individuals or units of interest referred to as the *target universe* or *target population*, or simply as the *universe* or *population*. Prior to data collection the target universe should be clearly defined. For example, if data are to be collected for the universe of households in the United States, it is necessary to define a "household." The target universe may not be completely tractable. Cost and other considerations may restrict data collection to a *survey universe* based on some available list, such list may be inaccurate and out of date. This list is called a *survey frame* or *sampling frame*.

The data in many tables are based on data obtained for all population units, a *census*, or on data obtained for only a portion, or *sample*, of the population units. When the data presented are based on a sample, the sample is usually a scientifically selected *probability sample*. This is a sample selected from a list or sampling frame in such a way that every possible sample has a known chance of selection and usually each unit selected can be assigned a number, greater than zero and less than or equal to one, representing its likelihood or probability of selection.

For large-scale sample surveys, the probability sample of units is often selected as a multistage sample. The first stage of a multistage sample is the selection of a probability sample of large groups of population members, referred to as primary sampling units (PSU's). For example, in a national multistage household sample, PSU's are often counties or groups of counties. The second stage of a multistage sample is the selection, within each PSU selected at the first stage, of smaller groups of population units, referred to as secondary sampling units. In subsequent stages of selection, smaller and smaller nested groups are chosen until the ultimate sample of population units is obtained. To qualify a multistage sample as a probability sample, all stages of sampling must be carried out using probability sampling methods.

Prior to selection at each stage of a multistage (or a single stage) sample, a list of the sampling units or sampling frame for that stage must be obtained. For example, for the first stage of selection of a national household sample, a list of the counties and county groups that form the PSU's must be obtained. For the final stage of selection, lists of households, and sometimes persons within the households, have to be compiled in the field. For surveys of economic entities and for the economic censuses the Bureau generally uses a frame constructed from the Bureau's Standard Statistical Establishment List (SSEL). The SSEL contains all establishments with payroll in the United States including small single establishment firms as well as large multi-establishment firms.

Wherever the quantities in a table refer to an entire universe, but are constructed from data collected in a sample survey, the table quantities are referred to as *sample estimates*. In constructing a sample estimate, an attempt is made to come as close as is feasible to the corresponding universe quantity that would be obtained from a complete census of the universe. Estimates based on a sample will, however, generally differ from the hypothetical census figures. Two classifications of errors are associated with estimates based on sample surveys: (1) *sampling error*—the error arising from the use of a sample, rather than a census, to estimate population quantities and (2) *nonsampling error*—those errors arising from nonsampling sources. As discussed below, the magnitude of the sampling error for an estimate can usually be estimated from the sample data. However, the magnitude of the nonsampling error for an estimate can rarely be estimated. Consequently, actual error in an estimate exceeds the error that can be estimated.

The particular sample used in a survey is only one of a large number of possible samples of the same size which could have been selected using the same sampling procedure. Estimates derived from the different samples would, in general, differ from each other. The *standard error* (SE) is a measure of the variation among the estimates derived from all possible samples. The standard error is the most commonly used measure of the sampling error of an estimate. Valid estimates of the standard errors of survey estimates can usually be calculated from the data collected in a probability sample. For convenience, the standard error is sometimes expressed as a percent of the estimate and is called the relative standard error or *coefficient of variation* (CV). For example, an estimate of 200 units with an estimated standard error of 10 units has an estimated CV of 5 percent.

A sample estimate and an estimate of its standard error or CV can be used to construct interval estimates that have a prescribed confidence that the interval includes the average of the estimates derived from all possible samples with a known probability. To illustrate, if all possible samples were selected under essentially the same general conditions, and using the same sample design, and if an estimate and its estimated standard error were calculated from each sample, then: 1) Approximately 68 percent of the intervals from one standard error below the estimate to one standard error above the estimate would include the average estimate derived from all possible samples; 2) approximately 90 percent of the intervals from 1.6 standard errors below the estimate to 1.6 standard errors above the estimate would include the average estimate derived from all possible samples; and 3) approximately 95 percent of the intervals from two standard errors below the estimate to two standard errors above the estimate would include the average estimate derived from all possible samples.

Thus, for a particular sample, one can say with the appropriate level of confidence (e.g., 90 or 95 percent) that the average of all possible samples is included in the constructed interval. Example of a confidence interval: An estimate is 200 units with a standard error of 10 units. An approximately 90 percent confidence interval (plus or minus 1.6 standard errors) is from 184 to 216.

All surveys and censuses are subject to nonsampling errors. Nonsampling errors are of two kinds—*random* and *nonrandom*. Random nonsampling errors arise because of the varying interpretation of questions (by respondents or interviewers) and varying actions of coders, keyers, and other processors. Some randomness is also introduced when respondents must estimate values. These same errors usually have a nonrandom component. Nonrandom nonsampling errors result from total nonresponse (no usable data obtained for a sampled unit), partial or item nonresponse (only a portion of a response may be usable), inability or unwillingness on the part of respondents to provide correct information, difficulty interpreting questions, mistakes in recording or keying data, errors of collection or processing, and coverage problems (overcoverage and undercoverage of the target universe). Random nonresponse errors usually, but not always, result in an understatement of sampling errors and thus an overstatement of the precision of survey estimates. Estimating the magnitude of nonsampli errors would require special experiments or access to independent data and, consequently, the magnitudes are seldom available.

Nearly all types of nonsampling errors that affect surveys also occur in complete censuses. Since surveys can be conducted on a smaller scale than censuses, nonsampling errors can presumably be controlled more tightly. Relatively more funds and effort can perhaps be expended toward eliciting responses, detecting and correcting response error, and reducing processing errors. As a result, survey results can sometimes be more accurate than census results.

To compensate for suspected nonrandom errors, adjustments of the sample estimates are often made. For example, adjustments are frequently made for nonresponse, both total and partial. Adjustments made for either type of nonresponse are often referred to as *imputations.* Imputation for total nonresponse is usually made by substituting for the questionnaire responses of the nonrespondents the "average" questionnaire responses of the respondents. These imputations usually are made separately with in various groups of sample members, formed by attempting to place respondents and nonrespondents together that have "similar" design or ancillary characteristics. Imputation for item nonresponse is usually made by substituting for a missing item the response to that item of a respondent having characteristics that are "similar" to those of the nonrespondent.

For an estimate calculated from a sample survey, the *total error* in the estimate is composed of the sampling error, which can usually be estimated from the sample, and the nonsampling error, which usually cannot be estimated from the sample. The total error present in a population quantity obtained from a complete census is composed of only nonsampling errors. Ideally, estimates of the total error associated with data given in the *Statistical Abstract* tables should be given. However, due to the unavailability of estimates of nonsampling *errors,* only estimates of the levels of *sampling errors*, in terms of estimated *standard errors* or coefficients of variation, are available. To obtain estimates of the estimated standard errors from the sample of interest, obtain a copy of the referenced report which appears at the end of each table.

Principal data bases.—Beginning below are brief descriptions of 36 of the sample surveys and censuses that provide a substantial portion of the data contained in this *Abstract*.

SECTION 1. POPULATION

Source and Title: Bureau of the Census, *Census of Population*

Tables: See tables citing *Census of Population* in section 1 and also in sections 2, 4, 6, 8, 13, 14, 21, 25, and 29.

Universe, Frequency, and Types of Data: Complete count of U.S. population conducted every 10 years since 1790. Data obtained on number and characteristics of inhabitants.

Type of Data Collection Operation: In 1970, 1980, and 1990 complete census for some items—age, sex, race, marital status, and relationship to household head. In 1970, other items collected from a 5% and a 15% probability (systematic) sample of the population. In 1980, approximately 19% of the housing units were included in the sample; in 1990, approximately 17%.

Data Collection and Imputation Procedures: In 1970, extensive use of mail questionnaires in urban areas; personal interviews in most rural areas. In 1980 and 1990, mail questionnaires were used in even more areas than in 1970, with personal interviews in the remainder. Extensive telephone and personal followup for nonrespondents was done in the censuses. Imputations were made for missing characteristics.

Estimates of Sampling Error: Sampling errors for data are estimated for all items collected by sample and vary by characteristic and geographic area. The CV's for national and State estimates are generally very small.

Other (nonsampling) Errors: Since 1950, evaluation programs have been conducted to provide information on the magnitude of some sources of nonsampling errors such as response bias and undercoverage in each census. Results from the evaluation program for the 1990 census indicate that the net undercoverage amounted to about 1.5 to 2 percent of the total resident population.

Sources of Additional Material: U.S. Bureau of the Census, *The Coverage of* Population in the 1980 Census, PHC80-E4;

Content Reinterview Study: Accuracy of Data for Selected Population and Housing Characteristics as Measured by Reinterview, PHC80-E2; *1980 Census of Population*, vol. 1., (PC80-1), appendixes B, C, and D.

Source and Title: U.S. Bureau of the Census, *Current Population Survey (CPS)*

Tables: See tables citing *Current Population Reports* primarily in section 1, but also in sections 2, 3, 4, 6, 12, 13, 14, 18, 23, and 29. Many Bureau of Labor Statistics' (BLS) tables in section 13 are CPS based.

Universe, Frequency, and Types of Data: Nationwide monthly sample survey of civilian noninstitutional population, 15 years old or over, to obtain data on employment, unemployment, and a number of other characteristics.

Type of Data Collection Operation: Multistage probability sample of about 60,000 households in 729 PSU's in 1993. Oversampling in some States and the largest MSA's to improve reliability for those areas of employment data on annual average basis . A continual sample rotation system is used. Households are in sample 4 months, out for 8 months, and in for 4 more. Month-to-month overlap is 75%; year-to-year overlap is 50%.

Data Collection and Imputation Procedures: For first and fifth months that a household is in sample, personal interviews; other months, approximately, 85% of the data collected by phone. Imputation is done for both item and total nonresponse. Adjustment for total nonresponse is done by a predefined cluster of units, by MSA size and residence; for item nonresponse imputation varies by subject matter.

Estimates of Sampling Error: Estimated CV's on national annual averages for labor force, total employment, and nonagricultural employment, 0.2%; for total unemployment and agricultural employment, 1.0% to 2.5%. The estimated CV's for family income and poverty rate for all persons in 1986 are 0.5% and 1.5%, respectively. CV's for subnational areas, such as States, would be larger and would vary by area.

Other (nonsampling) Errors: Estimates of response bias on unemployment are not available, but estimates of unemployment are usually 5% to 9% lower than estimates from reinterviews. Four to 5.0% of sample households unavailable for interviews.

Sources of Additional Material: U.S. Bureau of the Census and Bureau of Labor Statistics, *Concepts and Methods Used in Labor Force Statistics from Current Population Survey* (Census series P-23, No. 62; BLS *Report No. 463)* and Bureau of the Census, *Current Population Survey* (Tech. Paper 40) and Bureau of Labor Statistics, *Employment and Earnings*, monthly, Explanatory Notes and Estimates of Error, tables 1-A through 1-H and *BLS Handbook of Methods*, Chapter 1 (Bulletin 2414.)

SECTION 2. VITAL STATISTICS

Source and Title: U.S. National Center for Health Statistics (NCHS), *Vital Registration System*

Tables: See tables citing *Vital Statistics of the United States;* 319 in section 5; and 1318 in section 29.

Universe, Frequency, and Types of Data: Annual data on births and deaths in the United States.

Type of Data Collection Operation: Mortality data based on complete file of death records, except 1972, based on 50% sample. Natality statistics 1951-71, based on 50% sample of birth certificates, except a 20% to 50% in 1967, received by NCHS. Beginning 1972, data from some States received through Vital Statistics Cooperative Program (VSCP) and complete file used; data from other States based on 50% sample. Beginning 1986, all reporting areas participated in the VSCP.

Data Collection and Imputation Procedures: Reports based on records from registration offices of all States, District of Columbia, New York City, Puerto Rico, Virgin Islands, and Guam.

Estimates of Sampling Error: For recent years, CV's for births are small due to large portion of total file in sample (except for very small estimated totals).

Other (nonsampling) Errors: Data on births and deaths believed to be at least 99% complete.

Sources of Additional Material: U.S. National Center for Health Statistics, *Vital Statistics of the United States*, vol. I and vol. II, annual, and *Monthly Vital Statistics Report*.

(See section 1 above for information pertaining to tables 102-107.)

SECTION 3. HEALTH AND NUTRITION

Source and Title: U.S. National Center for Health Statistics, *National Health Interview Survey (NHIS)*

Tables: 180, 183, 197, 206, 207, 212, 217, 218, 221, and 228.

Universe, Frequency, and Types of Data: Continuous data collection covering the civilian noninstitutional population to obtain information on personal and demographic characteristics, illnesses, injuries, impairments, and other health topics.

Type of Data Collection Operation: Multistage probability sample of 42,000 households (in 376 PSU's) selected in groups of about four adjacent households.

Data Collection and Imputation Procedures: Personal household interviews with extensive followup of nonrespondents. Data are adjusted for nonresponse by imputation procedure based on "average" characteristics of persons in interviewed households in the same geographic area.

Estimates of Sampling Error: Estimated CV's: For physician visits by males, 1.5%; for workdays lost by males, 3.5%; for persons injured at home, 4.7%.

Other (nonsampling) Errors: Response rate was 95.7% in 1985 for the NHIS.

Sources of Additional Material: U.S. National Center for Health Statistics, "Current Estimates from the National Health Interview Survey, U.S., 1983," Vital and Health Statistics, series 10.

(See section 13 for information pertaining to table 175, section 15 for table 169, and section 27 for table 174.)

SECTION 4. EDUCATION

Source and Title: U.S. Department of Education, National Center for Education Statistics, *Higher Education General Information Survey (HEGIS), Fall Enrollment in Institutions of Higher Education;* beginning 1986, *Integrated Postsecondary Education Data Survey (IPEDS), Fall Enrollment*

Tables: 283, 284, 287 and 288.

Universe, Frequency, and Types of Data: Annual survey of all institutions and branches listed in the *Directory* to obtain data on total enrollment by sex, level of enrollment, type of program, racial/ethnic characteristics (in alternate years) and attendance status of student, and on first-time students.

Type of Data Collection Operation: Complete census.

Data Collection and Imputation Procedures: Survey package is usually mailed in the spring with surveys due at varying dates in the summer and fall; mail and phone followup procedures for nonrespondents. Missing data are imputed by using data of similar institutions.

Estimates of Sampling Error: Not applicable.

Other (nonsampling) Errors: Approximately 87% response rate.

Sources of Additional Material: U.S. Department of Education, National Center for Education Statistics, *Fall Enrollment in Higher Education*, annual.

Source and Title: U.S. Department of Education, National Center for Education Statistics, *Higher Education General Information Survey (HEGIS), Financial Statistics of Institutions of Higher Education;* beginning 1986, *Integrated Postsecondary Education Data Survey (IPEDS), Financial Statistics of Institutions of Higher Education.*

Tables: 234, 237, 287, and 290.

Universe, Frequency, and Types of Data: Annual survey of all institutions and branches listed in the *Education Directory, Colleges and Universities* to obtain data on financial status and operations, including current funds revenues, current funds expenditures, and physical plant assets.

Type of Data Collection Operation: Complete census.

Data Collection and Imputation Procedures: Survey package is usually mailed in the spring with surveys due at varying dates in the summer and fall; mail and phone followup procedures for nonrespondents. Missing data are imputed by using data of similar institutions.

Estimates of Sampling Error: Not applicable.

Other (nonsampling) Errors: For 1990, a 87% response rate. Imputed expenditures amounted to about 2.8% of total expenditures.

Sources of Additional Material: U.S. Department of Education, National Center for Education Statistics, *Financial Statistics of Institutions of Higher Education*, annual.

Source and Title: U.S. Department of Education, National Center for Education Statistics, *Higher Education General Information Survey (HEGIS), Degrees and Other Formal Awards Conferred.* Beginning 1986, *Integrated Postsecondary Education Data Survey (IPEDS), Degrees and Other Formal Awards Conferred.*

Tables: 303-308.

Universe, Frequency, and Types of Data: Annual survey of all institutions and branches listed in the *Education Directory, Colleges and Universities* to obtain data on earned degrees and other formal awards, conferred by field of study, level of degree, sex, and by racial/ethnic characteristics (in alternate years).

Type of Data Collection Operation: Complete census.

Data Collection and Imputation Procedures: Survey package is usually mailed in the spring with surveys due at varying dates in the summer and fall; mail and phone followup procedures for nonrespondents. Missing data are imputed by using data of similar institutions.

Estimates of Sampling Error: Not applicable.

Other (nonsampling) Errors: For 1989-90, approximately 92.3% response rate.

Sources of Additional Material: U.S. Department of Education, National Center for Education Statistics, *Earned Degrees Conferred*, annual.

(See sections 1 and 9 for information pertaining to the Bureau of the Census.)

SECTION 5. LAW ENFORCEMENT, COURTS, AND PRISONS

Source and Title: U.S. Federal Bureau of Investigation, *Uniform Crime Reporting (UCR) Program*

Tables: 313-318, 320-323, 328-330, and 332.

Universe, Frequency, and Types of Data: Monthly reports on the number of criminal offenses that become known to law enforcement agencies. Data are collected on crimes cleared by arrest, by age, sex, and race of offender, and on assaults on law enforcement officers.

Type of Data Collection Operation: Crime statistics are based on reports of crime data submitted either directly to the FBI by contributing law enforcement agencies or through cooperating State UCR programs.

Data Collection and Imputation Procedures: States with UCR programs collect data directly from individual law enforcement agencies and forward reports, prepared in accordance with UCR standards, to FBI. Accuracy and consistency edits are performed by FBI.

Estimates of Sampling Error: Not applicable.

Other (nonsampling) Errors: Coverage of 96% of the population (97.4% in MSA's, 90.6% in "other cities," and 87.8% in rural areas) by UCR program, though varying number of agencies report. Some error may be present through incorrect reporting.

Sources of Additional Material: U.S. Federal Bureau of Investigation, *Crime in the United States*.

Source and Title: U.S. Bureau of Justice Statistics (BJS), *National Crime Victimization Survey*

Tables: 324-327.

Universe, Frequency, and Types of Data: Monthly survey of individuals and households in the United States to obtain data on criminal victimization of those units for compilation of annual estimates.

Type of Data Collection Operation: National probability sample survey of about 50,000 interviewed households in 376 *PSU's selected from a list of addresses* from the 1980 census, supplemented by new construction permits and an area sample where permits are not required.

Data Collection and Imputation Procedures: Interviews are conducted every 6 months for 3 years for each household in the sample; 8,000 households are interviewed monthly. Personal interviews are used in the first and fifth interviews; the intervening interviews are conducted by telephone whenever possible.

Estimates of Sampling Error: CV's in 1994: 2.7% for crimes of violence; 8.5% for estimate of rape/sexual assault counts; 5.5% for robbery counts; 2.8% for assault counts; 8.0% for personal theft counts; 1.9% for property crimes; 3.0% for burglary counts; 2.0% for theft; and 4.4% for motor vehicle theft counts.

Other (nonsampling) Errors: Respondent recall errors which may include reporting incidents for other than the reference period; interviewer coding and processing errors; and possible mistaken reporting or classifying of events. Adjustment is made for a household noninterview rate of about 4% and for a within-household noninterview rate of 7%.

Sources of Additional Material: U.S. Bureau of Justice Statistics, *Criminal Victimization in the United States*, annual.

(See section 2 for details on table 319.)

SECTION 7. PARKS AND RECREATION

(See section 27 for details on tables 408 and 431.)

SECTION 8. ELECTIONS

(See section 1 above for information pertaining to tables 462 and 463 and section 9 for information pertaining to tables 456.)

SECTION 9. STATE AND LOCAL GOVERNMENT FINANCES AND EMPLOYMENT

Source and Title: U.S. Bureau of the Census, *Census of Governments*

Tables: See tables in section 9 citing *Census of Governments and table 456 in section 8.*

Universe, Frequency, and Types of Data: Survey of all governmental units in the United States conducted every 5 years to obtain data on government revenue, expenditures, debt, assets, employment and employee retirement systems, property values, public school systems, and number, size, and structure of governments.

Type of Data Collection Operation: Complete census. List of units derived through classification of government units recently authorized in each State and identification, counting, and classification of existing local governments and public school systems.

Data Collection and Imputation Procedures: Data collected through field and office compilation of financial data from official records and reports for States and large local governments; mail canvass of selected data items, like State tax revenue and employee retirement systems; and collection of local government statistics through central collection arrangements with State governments.

Estimates of Sampling Error: Not applicable.

Other (nonsampling) Errors: Some nonsampling errors may arise due to possible inaccuracies in classification, response, and processing.

Sources of Additional Material: U.S. Bureau of the Census, *Census of Governments, 1992,* various reports, and *State Government Finances in 1992,* GF 90, No. 3.

Source and Title: U.S. Bureau of the Census, *Annual Surveys of State and Local Government*

Tables: See tables citing *Public Employment* and *Government Finances* in section 9 and table 261 in section 4; and table 591 in section 12.

Universe, Frequency, and Types of Data: Sample survey conducted annually to obtain data on revenue, expenditure, debt, and employment of State and local governments. Universe is all governmental units in the United States (about 83,000).

Type of Data Collection Operation: Sample of about 13,000 units includes all State governments and other governments meeting certain criteria; probability sample for remaining units.

Data Collection and Imputation Procedures: Field and office compilation of data from official records and reports for States and large local governments; central collection of local governmental financial data through cooperative agreements with a number of State governments; mail canvass of other units with mail and telephone followups of nonrespondents. Data for nonresponses are imputed from previous year data or obtained from secondary sources, if available.

Estimates of Sampling Error: CV's for estimates of major employment and financial items are generally less than 2% for most States and less than 1.2% for the majority of States.

Other (nonsampling) Errors: Nonresponse rate is less than 15% for number of units. Other possible errors may result from undetected inaccuracies in classification, response, and processing.

Sources of Additional Material: U.S. Bureau of the Census, *Public Employment in 1992,* GE 90, No. 1, *Governmental Finances in 1991-92,* GF 90, No. 5, and *Census of Governments, 1992,* various reports.

SECTION 10. FEDERAL GOVERNMENT

Source and Title: U.S. Internal Revenue Service, *Statistics of Income, Individual Income Tax Returns*

Tables: 529-533.

Universe, Frequency, and Types of Data: Annual study of unaudited individual income tax returns, forms 1040, 1040A, and 1040EZ, filed by U.S. citizens and residents. Data provided on various financial characteristics by size of adjusted gross income, marital status, and by taxable and nontaxable returns. Data by State, based on 100% file, also include returns from 1040NR, filed by nonresident aliens plus certain self-employment tax returns.

Type of Data Collection Operation: Annual stratified probability sample of approximately 125,000 returns broken into sample strata based on the larger of total income or total loss amounts as well as the size of business plus farm receipts. Sampling rates for sample strata varied from .025% to 100%.

Data Collection and Imputation Procedures: Computer selection of sample of tax return records. Data adjusted during editing for incorrect, missing, or inconsistent entries to ensure consistency with other entries on return.

Estimates of Sampling Error: Estimated CV's for tax year 1987: Adjusted gross income less deficit .13%; salaries and wages .20%; and tax-exempt interest received 4.51%. (State data not subject to sampling error.)

Other (nonsampling) Errors: Processing errors and errors arising from the use of tolerance checks for the data.

Sources of Additional Material: U.S. Internal Revenue Service, *Statistics of Income, Individual Income Tax Returns,* annual.

SECTION 12. SOCIAL INSURANCE AND HUMAN SERVICES

Source and Title: U.S. Social Security Administration, Benefit Data

Tables: 587 and 588.

Universe, Frequency, and Types of Data: All persons receiving monthly benefits under Title II of Social Security Act. Data on number and amount of benefits paid by type and State.

Type of Data Collection Operation: Data based on administrative records. Data based on 100% files, as well as 10% and 1% sample files.

Data Collection and Imputation Procedures: Records used consist of actions pursuant to applications dated by subsequent post-entitlement actions.

Estimates of Sampling Error: Varies by size of estimate and sample file size.

Other (nonsampling) Errors: Processing errors, which are believed to be small.

Sources of Additional Material: U.S. Social Security Administration, *Annual Statistical Supplement to the Social Security Bulletin.*

Source and Title: U.S. Social Security Administration, *Supplemental Security Income (SSI) Program*

Tables: 602-605.

Universe, Frequency, and Types of Data: All eligible aged, blind, or disabled persons receiving SSI benefit payments under SSI program. Data include number of persons receiving federally administered SSI, amounts paid, and State administered supplementation.

Type of Data Collection Operation: Data based on administrative records.

Data Collection and Imputation Procedures: Data adjusted to reflect returned checks and overpayment refunds. For federally administered payments, actual adjusted amounts are used.

Estimates of Sampling Error: Not applicable.

Other (nonsampling) Errors: Processing errors, which are believed to be small.

Sources of Additional Material: U.S. Social Security Administration, *Annual Statistical Supplement to the Social Security Bulletin.*

(See section 1 above for information pertaining to the Current Population Survey, section 3 for information pertaining to the National Center for Health Statistics, and section 9 for information pertaining to Annual Surveys of State and Local Government.)

SECTION 13. LABOR FORCE, EMPLOYMENT, AND EARNINGS

Source and Title: U.S. Bureau of Labor Statistics (BLS), *Current Employment Statistics (CES)* Program

Tables: 660-662, 667; in section 3, table 175; in section 21, table 991; and in section 22, table *1059.*

Universe, Frequency, and Types of Data: Monthly survey covering about 6 million nonagricultural establishments to obtain data on employment, hours, and earnings, by industry.

Type of Data Collection Operation: Sample survey of over 390,000 establishments in March 1993.

Data Collection and Imputation Procedures: Cooperating State agencies mail questionnaires to sample establishments to develop State and local estimates; information is forwarded to BLS where national estimates are prepared.

Estimates of Sampling Error: Estimated CV's for employment, 0.1%, for average weekly hours paid, 0.1% and for average hourly earnings, 0.2%.

Other (nonsampling) Errors: Estimates of employment adjusted annually to reflect complete universe. Average adjustment is 0.2%.

Sources of Additional Material: U.S. Bureau of Labor Statistics, *Employment and Earnings,* monthly, Explanatory Notes and Estimates of Error, tables 2-A through 2-G.

(See section 1 above for information pertaining to the Current Population Survey.)

SECTION 14. INCOME, EXPENDITURES, AND WEALTH

Source and Title: Board of Governors of the Federal Reserve System, *Survey of Consumer Finances*

Tables: 747 and 748, and in section 16, 778, 780, 782 and 800.

Universe, Frequency, and Types of Data: Periodic sample survey of families. In this survey a given household is divided into a primary economic unit and other economic units. The primary economic unity, which may be a single individual, is generally chosen as the unit that contains the person who either holds the title to the home or is the first person listed on the lease. The primary unit is used as the reference family. The survey collects detailed data on the composition of family balance sheets, the terms of loans, and relationships with financial institutions. It also gathered information on the employment history and pension rights of the survey respondent and the spouse or partner of the respondent.

Type of Data Collection Operation: The survey employs a two-part strategy for sampling families. Some families were selected by standard multistage area-probability sampling methods from the forty-eight contiguous states. The remaining families in survey were selected using tax data under the strict rules governing confidentiality and the rights of potential respondents to refuse participation.

Data Collection and Imputation Procedures: The Survey Research Center at the University of Michigan collected the 1989 survey data between August 1989 and March 1990. Adjustments for nonresponse errors are made through systematic imputation of unanswered questions and through weighting adjustments based on data used in the sample design for families that refused participation.

Estimates of Sampling Error: Because of the complex design of the survey, the estimation of potential sampling errors is not straightforward.

Other (nonsampling) Errors: The achieved sample of 3,143 families represents a response rate of about 69 percent in the area-probability sample and a rate of about 34 percent in the tax-data sample. Proper training of interviewers and careful design of questionnaires were used to control inaccurate survey responses.

Sources of Additional Material: Board of Governors of the Federal Reserve System, "Changes in Family Finances from 1983 to 1989: Evidence from the Survey of Consumer Finances", *Federal Reserve Bulletin*, January 1992.

(See section 1 above for information pertaining to the Bureau of the Census.)

SECTION 15. PRICES

Source and Title: U.S. Bureau of Labor Statistics (BLS), *Consumer Price Index (CPI)*

Tables: 751-754, 767, 768, and in section 3, table 169.

Universe, Frequency, and Types of Data: Monthly survey of price changes of all types of consumer goods and services purchased by urban wage earners and clerical workers prior to 1978, and urban consumers thereafter. Both indexes continue to be published.

Type of Data Collection Operation: Prior to 1978, sample of various consumer items in 56 urban areas; thereafter, in 85 PSU's, except from January 1987 through March 1988, when 91 areas were sampled.

Data Collection and Imputation Procedures: Prices of consumer items are obtained from about 57,000 housing units, and 19,000 other reporters in 85 areas. Prices of food, fuel, and a few other items are obtained monthly; prices of most other commodities and services are collected every month in the five largest geographic areas and every other month in others.

Estimates of Sampling Error: Estimates of standard errors are not available at present.

Other (nonsampling) Errors: Errors result from inaccurate reporting, difficulties in defining concepts and their operational implementation, and introduction of product quality changes and new products.

Sources of Additional Material: U.S. Bureau of Labor Statistics, *The Consumer Price Index: 1987 Revision*, Report 736, and *BLS Handbook of Methods*, Chapter 19, Bulletin 2414.

Source and Title: U.S. Bureau of Labor Statistics, *Producer Price Index (PPI)*

Tables: 751, 757-759, and in section 21, table 1042; in section 24, table 1139; and in section 25, table 1177.

Universe, Frequency, and Types of Data: Monthly survey of producing companies to determine price changes of all commodities produced in the United States for sale in commercial transactions. Data on agriculture, forestry, fishing, manufacturing, mining, gas, electricity, public utilities, and a few services.

Type of Data Collection Operation: Probability sample of approximately 3,100 about 75,000 quotations per month.

Data Collection and Imputation Procedures: Data are collected by mail. If transaction prices are not supplied, list prices are used. Some prices are obtained from trade publications, organized exchanges, and government agencies. To calculate index, price changes are multiplied by their relative weights based on total net selling value of all commodities in 1982.

Estimates of Sampling Error: Not applicable.

Other (nonsampling) Errors: Not available at present.

Sources of Additional Material: U.S. Bureau of Labor Statistics, *BLS Handbook of Methods*, Chapter 16, Bulletin 2414.

SECTION 16.

(See section 14 for information pertaining to tables 778, 780-782, and 800 and section 17 for information pertaining to table 773.)

SECTION 17. BUSINESS ENTERPRISE

Source and Title: U.S. Bureau of the Census, *County Business Patterns*

Tables: 844-847, and in section 16, table 773; in section 27 tables 1263 and 1283; and in section 29 table 1327.

Universe, Frequency, and Types of Data: Annual tabulation of basic data items extracted from the Standard Statistical Establishment List, a file of all known single and multiestablishment companies maintained and updated by the Bureau of the

Census. Data include number of establishments, number of employees, first-quarter and annual payrolls, and number of establishments by employment size class. Data are excluded for self-employed persons, domestic service workers, railroad employees, agricultural production workers, and most government employees.

Type of Data Collection Operation: The annual Company Organization Survey provides individual establishment data for multiestablishment companies. Data for single establishment companies are obtained from various Census Bureau programs, such as the Annual Survey of Manufactures and Current Business Surveys, as well as from administrative records of the Internal Revenue Service and the Social Security Administration.

Estimates of Sampling Error: Not Applicable.

Other (nonsampling) Error: Response rates of greater than 90% for the 1993 Company Organization Survey.

Sources of Additional Materials: U.S. Bureau of the Census, *General Explanation of County Business Patterns.*

Source and Title: U.S. Internal Revenue Service, *Statistics of Income, Sole Proprietorship Returns* and *Statistics of Income Bulletin*

Tables: 833-836.

Universe, Frequency, and Types of Data: Annual study of unaudited income tax returns of nonfarm sole proprietorships, form 1040 with business schedules. Data provided on various financial characteristics by industry.

Type of Data Collection Operation: Stratified probability sample of approximately 31,000 sole proprietorships for tax year 1990. The sample is classified based on presence or absence of certain business schedules; the larger of total income or loss; and size of business plus farm receipts. Sampling rates vary from .043% to 100%.

Data Collection and Imputation Procedures: Computer selection of sample of tax return records. Data adjusted during editing for incorrect, missing, or inconsistent entries to ensure consistency with other entries on return.

Estimates of Sampling Error: Estimated CV's for tax year 1990 are not available; for 1987 (the latest available): For sole proprietorships, business receipts, 1.66%; net income, (less loss), 1.33%; depreciation 2.17%; interest expense 2.80%; and *employee benefit programs 7.55%.*

Other (nonsampling) Errors: Processing errors and errors arising from the use of tolerance checks for the data.

Sources of Additional Material: U.S. Internal Revenue Service, *Statistics of Income, Sole Proprietorship Returns* (for years through 1980) and *Statistics of Income Bulletin,* vol. 10, No. 1 (summer 1990).

Source and Title: U.S. Internal Revenue Service, *Statistics of Income, Partnership Returns* and *Statistics of Income Bulletin*

Tables: 833-835, 837, and 838.

Universe, Frequency, and Types of Data: Annual study of unaudited income tax returns of partnerships, Form 1065. Data provided on various financial characteristics by industry.

Type of Data Collection Operation: Stratified probability sample of approximately 28,000 partnership returns from a population of 1,660,000 filed during calendar year 1990. The sample is classified based on combinations of gross receipts, net income or loss, and total assets, and on industry. Sampling rates vary from .04% to 100%.

Data Collection and Imputation Procedures: Computer selection of sample of tax return records. Data are adjusted during editing for incorrect, missing, or inconsistent entries to ensure consistency with other entries on return. Data not available due to regulations are not imputed.

Estimates of Sampling Error: Estimated CV's for tax year 1988 (latest available): For number of partnerships, .51%; business receipts, .78%; net income, 3.03%; net loss, 2.21% and total assets, 1.22%.

Other (nonsampling) Errors: Processing errors and errors arising from the use of tolerance checks for the data.

Sources of Additional Material: U.S. Internal Revenue Service, *Statistics of Income, Partnership Returns* and *Statistics of Income Bulletin,* vol. 10, No. 1 (summer 1990).

Source and Title: U.S. Internal Revenue Service, *Corporation Income Tax Returns*

Tables: 833-835 and 841-843.

Universe, Frequency, and Types of Data: Annual study of unaudited corporation income tax returns, Forms 1120 and 1120 (A, F, L, PC, REIT, RIC, and S), filed by corporations or businesses legally defined as corporations. Data provided on various financial characteristics by industry and size of total assets, and business receipts.

Type of Data Collection Operation: Stratified probability sample of approximately 85,000 returns for 1987, distributed by sample classes generally based on type of return, size of total assets, size of net income or deficit, and selected business activity. Sampling rates for sample strata varied from .25% to 100%.

Data Collection and Imputation Procedures: Computer selection of sample of tax return records. Data adjusted during editing for incorrect, missing, or inconsistent entries to ensure consistency with other entries on return and to achieve statistical definitions.

Estimates of Sampling Error: Estimated CV's for 1988: Number of returns in subgroups ranged from 1.4% with assets under $100,000, to 0% with assets over $100 mil.; for amount of net income and amount of income tax, .18%

Other (nonsampling) Errors: Processing errors and errors arising from the use of tolerance checks for the data.

Sources of Additional Material: U.S. Internal Revenue Service, *Statistics of Income, Corporation Income Tax Returns*, annual.

SECTION 18. COMMUNICATIONS

(See section 26 for information pertaining to table 905.)

SECTION 19. ENERGY

Source and Title: U.S. Energy Information Administration, *Residential Energy Consumption Survey*

Tables: 928, 929 and table 1207 in section 25.

Universe, Frequency, and Types of Data: Triennial survey of households and fuel suppliers. Data are obtained on energy-related household characteristics, housing unit characteristics, use of fuels, and energy consumption and expenditures by fuel type.

Type of Data Collection Operation: Probability sample of 7,183 eligible units in 129 PSU's. For responding units, fuel consumption and expenditure data obtained from fuel suppliers to those households.

Data Collection and Imputation Procedures: Personal interviews. Extensive followup of nonrespondents including mail questionnaires for some households. Adjustments for nonrespondents were made in weighting for respondents. Most item nonresponses were imputed.

Estimates of Sampling Error: Estimated CV's for household averages: For consumption, 1.3%; for expenditures, 1.0%; for various fuels, values ranged from 1.4% for electricity to 5.9% for LPG.

Other (nonsampling) Errors: Household response rate of 86.7%. Nonconsumption data were mostly imputed for mail respondents (5.2% of eligible units). Usable responses from fuel suppliers for various fuels ranged from 82.8% for electricity to 55.7% for fuel oil.

Sources of Additional Material: U.S. Energy Information Administration, *Household Energy Consumption and Expenditures, 1990* and *Housing Characteristics, 1990*.

SECTION 21. TRANSPORTATION—LAND

(See section 1 for information pertaining to table 1014, section 13 for table 991, and section 15 for table 1042 and section 27 for table 1033.)

SECTION 22. TRANSPORTATION—AIR AND WATER

Source and Title: U.S. Bureau of the Census, *Foreign Trade—Export Statistics*

Tables: See Bureau of the Census citations for export statistics in source notes in sections 22 and 28 and also table 1326 in section 29.

Universe, Frequency, and Types of Data: The export declarations collected by Customs are processed each month to obtain data on the movement of U.S. merchandise exports to foreign countries. Data obtained include value, quantity, and shipping weight of exports by commodity, country of destination, Customs district of exportation, and mode of transportation.

Type of Data Collection Operation: Shipper's Export Declarations are required to be filed for the exportation of merchandise valued over $1,500. Customs officials collect and transmit the documents to the Bureau of the Census on a flow basis for data compilation. Value data for shipments valued under $1,501 are estimated, based on established percentages of individual country totals.

Data Collection and Imputation Procedures: Statistical copies of Shipper's Export Declarations are received on a daily basis from Customs ports throughout the country and subjected to a monthly processing cycle. They are fully processed to the extent they reflect items valued over $1,500. Estimates for shipments valued at $1,500 or less are made, based on established percentages of individual country totals.

Estimates of Sampling Error: Not applicable.

Other (nonsampling) Errors: Clerical and complex computer checks intercept most processing errors and minimize otherwise significant reporting errors; other nonsampling errors are caused by undercounting of exports to Canada due to the nonreceipt of some Shipper's Export Declarations.

Sources of Additional Material: U.S. Bureau of the Census, *U.S. Merchandise Trade: Exports, General Imports, and Imports for Consumption, SITC, Commodity by Country,* FT 925.

Source and Title: U.S. Bureau of the Census, *Foreign Trade—Import Statistics*

Tables: See Bureau of the Census citations for import statistics in source notes in sections 22 and 28 and also table 1326 in section 29.

Universe, Frequency, and Types of Data: The import entry documents collected by Customs are processed each month to obtain data on the movement of merchandise imported into the United States. Data obtained include value, quantity, and shipping weight by commodity, country of origin, Customs district of entry, and mode of transportation.

Type of Data Collection Operation: Import entry documents are required to be filed for the importation of goods into the United States valued over $1,000 or for articles which must be reported on formal entries. Customs officials collect and transmit statistical copies of the documents to the Bureau of the Census on a flow basis for data compilation. Estimates for shipments valued under $1,001 and not reported on formal entries are based on established percentages of individual country totals.

Data Collection and Imputation Procedures: Statistical copies of import entry documents, received on a daily basis from Customs ports of entry throughout the country, are subjected to a monthly processing cycle. They are fully processed to the extent they reflect items valued at $1,001 and over or items which must be reported on formal entries.

Estimates of Sampling Error: Not applicable.

Other (nonsampling) Errors: Verification of statistical data reporting by Customs officials prior to transmittal and a subsequent program of clerical and computer checks are utilized to hold nonsampling errors arising from reporting and/or processing errors to a minimum.

Sources of Additional Material: U.S. Bureau of the Census, *U.S. Merchandise Trade: Exports, General Imports and Imports for Consumption, SITC, Commodity by Country,* FT 925.

(See section 13 for information pertaining to table 1059.)

SECTION 23. AGRICULTURE

Source and Title: U.S. Bureau of the Census, *Census of Agriculture.*

Tables: *1080-1087.*

Universe, Frequency, and Types of Data: Complete count of U.S. farms and ranches conducted once every five years with data at the national, state, and county level. Data published on farm numbers and related items/characteristics.

Type of Data Collection Operation: Complete census for— number of farms; land in farms; estimated market value of land and buildings, machinery and equipment, agriculture products sold; total cropland; irrigated land; total farm production expenses; farm operator characteristics; livestock and poultry inventory and sales; and selected crops harvested.

Data Collection and Imputation Procedures: Data collection is by mailing questionnaires to all farmers and ranchers. Nonrespondents are conducted by telephone and correspondence followups. Imputations were made for all nonresponse item/characteristics.

Estimates of Sampling Error: Variability in the estimates is due to the sample selection and estimation for items collected by sample and census nonresponse estimation procedures. The CV's for national and state estimates are generally very small . Approximately 85% response rate.

Other (nonsampling) Errors: Nonsampling errors are due to incompleteness of the census mailing list, duplications on the list, respondent reporting errors, errors in editing reported data, and in imputation for missing data. Evaluation studies are conducted to measure certain nonsampling errors such as list coverage and classification error. Results from the evaluation program for the 1987 census indicate the net under coverage amounted to about 7.2% of the nations total farms.

Sources of Additional Material: U.S. Bureau of the Census, *1992 Census of Agriculture,* Volume 2, Subject Series—Part 1, *Agriculture Atlas of the U.S.,* Part 2, *Coverage Evaluation,* Part 3, *Rankings of States and Counties,* Part 4, *History,* Part 5, *ZIP Code Tabulation of Selected Items,* ; and Volume 4 *Farm and Ranch Irrigation Survey.*

Source and Title: U.S. Department of Agriculture, National Agricultural Statistics Service (NASS), *Basic Area Frame Sample*

Tables: See tables citing NASS in source notes in section 23, which pertain to this or the following two surveys.

Universe, Frequency, and Types of Data: Two annual area sample surveys of U.S. farm operators: June agricultural survey collects data on planted acreage and livestock inventories; and a February Farm Costs and Returns survey that collects data on total farm production, expenses and specific commodity costs of production.

Type of Data Collection Operation: Stratified probability sample of about 16,000 land area units of about 1 sq. mile (range from 0.1 sq. mile in cities to several sq. miles in open grazing areas). Sample includes 60,000 parcels of agricultural land. About 20% of the sample replaced annually.

Data Collection and Imputation Procedures: Data collection is by personal enumeration. Imputation is based on enumerator observation or data reported by respondents having similar agricultural characteristics.

Estimates of Sampling Error: Estimated CV's range from 1% to 2% for regional estimates to 3% to 6% for State estimates of livestock inventories.

Other (nonsampling) Errors: Minimized through rigid quality controls on the collection process and careful review of all reported data.

Sources of Additional Material: U.S. Department of Agriculture, SRS, *Scope and Methods of the Statistical Reporting Service,* (name changed to National Agricultural Statistics Service), Miscellaneous Publication No. 1308, September 1983 (revised).

Source and Title: U.S. Department of Agriculture National Agricultural Statistics Service (NASS), *Multiple Frame Surveys*

Tables: See tables citing NASS in source notes in section 23, which pertain to this or the following survey.

Universe, Frequency, and Types of Data: Surveys of U.S. farm operators to obtain data on major livestock inventories, selected crop acreages and production, grain stocks, and farm labor characteristics; and to obtain farm economic data for price indexing.

Type of Data Collection Operation: Primary frame is obtained from general or special purpose lists, supplemented by a probability sample of land areas used to estimate for list incompleteness.

Data Collection and Imputation Procedures: Mail, telephone, or personal interviews used for initial data collection. Mail nonrespondent followup by phone and personal interviews. Imputation based on average of respondents.

Estimates of Sampling Error: Estimated CV for number of hired farm workers is about 3%. Estimated CV's range from 1% to 2% for regional estimates to 3% to 6% for State estimates of livestock inventories.

Other (nonsampling) Errors: In addition to above, replicated sampling procedures used to monitor effects of changes in survey procedures.

Sources of Additional Material: U.S. Department of Agriculture, SRS, *Scope and Methods of the Statistical Reporting Service,* (name changed to National Agricultural Statistics Service), Miscellaneous Publication No. 1308, September 1983 (revised).

Source and Title: U.S. Department of Agriculture, National Agricultural Statistics Service (NASS), *Objective Yield Surveys*

Tables: See tables citing NASS in source notes in section 23, which pertain to this or the preceding survey.

Universe, Frequency, and Types of Data: Surveys for data on corn, cotton, potatoes, soybeans, wheat, and rice to forecast and estimate yields.

Type of Data Collection Operation: Random location of plots in probability samples selected in June from Basic Area Frame Sample (see above).

Data Collection and Imputation Procedures: Enumerators count and measure plant characteristics in sample fields. Production measured from plots at harvest. Harvest loss measured from post harvest gleanings.

Estimates of Sampling Error: CV's for national estimates of production are about 2-3%.

Other (nonsampling) Errors: In addition to above, replicated sampling procedures used to monitor effects of changes in survey procedures.

Sources of Additional Material: U.S. Department of Agriculture, SRS, *Scope and Methods of the Statistical Reporting Service,* (name changed to National Agricultural Statistics Service), Miscellaneous Publication No. 1308, September 1983 (revised).

(See section 1 above for information pertaining to the Census of Population and Current Population Survey.)

SECTION 24. NATURAL RESOURCES

(See section 15 for table 1139.)

SECTION 25. CONSTRUCTION AND HOUSING

Source and Title: U.S. Bureau of the Census, *Monthly Survey of Construction*

Tables: 1185 and 1187-1189.

Universe, Frequency, and Types of Data: Survey conducted monthly of newly constructed housing units (excluding mobile homes). Data are collected on the start, completion, and sale of housing. (Annual figures are aggregates of monthly estimates.)

Type of Data Collection Operation: Probability sample of housing units obtained from building permits selected from 17,000 places. For nonpermit places, multistage probability sample of new housing units selected in 169 PSU's. In those areas, all roads are canvassed in selected enumeration districts.

Data Collection and Imputation Procedures: Data are obtained by telephone inquiry and field visit.

Estimates of Sampling Error: Estimated CV of 3% to 4% for estimates of national totals, but are as high as 20% for estimated totals of more detailed characteristics, such as housing units in multiunit structures.

Other (nonsampling) Errors: Response rate is over 90% for most items. Nonsampling errors are attributed to definitional problems, differences in interpretation of questions, incorrect reporting, inability to obtain information about all cases in the sample, and processing errors.

Sources of Additional Material: U.S. Bureau of the Census, *Construction Reports,* series C20, *Housing Starts;* C22, *Housing Completions; and* C25, *New One-Family Houses Sold and For Sale.*

Source and Title: U.S. Bureau of the Census, *Value of New Construction Put in Place*

Tables: 1179-1181.

Universe, Frequency, and Types of Data: Survey conducted monthly on total value of all construction put in place in the current month, both public and private projects. Construction values include costs of materials and labor, contractors' profits, overhead costs, cost of architectural and engineering work, and miscellaneous project costs. (Annual figures are aggregates of monthly estimates.)

Type of Data Collection Operation: Varies by type of activity: Total cost of private one-family houses started each month is distributed into value put in place using fixed patterns of monthly construction progress; using a multistage probability sample, data for private multifamily housing are obtained by mail from owners of multiunit projects. Data for residential additions and alterations are obtained in a quarterly survey measuring expenditures; monthly estimates are interpolated from quarterly data. Estimates of value of private nonresidential buildings, and State and local government construction are obtained by mail from owners (or agents) for a probability sample of projects. Estimates of farm nonresidential construction expenditures are based on U.S. Department of Agriculture annual estimates of *construction; public utility* estimates are obtained from reports submitted to Federal regulatory agencies and from private utility companies; estimates for all other I private construction (nonbuilding) are obtained by phasing F. W. Dodge contract award data; estimates of Federal construction are based on monthly data supplied by Federal agencies.

Data Collection and Imputation Procedures: See "Type of Data Collection Operation." Imputation accounts for approximately 20% of estimated value of construction each month.

Estimates of Sampling Error: CV estimates for private nonresidential building construction range from 3% for estimated value of industrial buildings to 9% for religious buildings. CV is approximately 2% for total new private nonresidential buildings.

Other (nonsampling) Errors: For directly measured data series based on samples, some nonsampling errors may arise from processing errors, imputations, and misunderstanding of questions. Indirect data series are dependent on the validity of the underlying assumptions and procedures.

Sources of Additional Material: U.S. Bureau of the Census, *Construction Reports,* series C30, *Value of New Construction Put in Place.*

Source and Title: U.S. Bureau of the Census, *Census of Housing*

Tables: See tables citing *Census of Housing* in source notes in section 25.

Universe, Frequency, and Types of Data: Census of all occupied and vacant housing, excluding group quarters, conducted every 10 years as part of the decennial census (see section 1 above) to determine characteristics of U.S. housing.

Type of Data Collection Operation: For 1970, 1980, and 1990, a complete count of some housing items (e.g. Owned or rented, and value). In 1970, other items collected from 5% and 15% probability samples selected from two sets of detailed questions on housing (these two sets having some common items). In 1980, approximately 19% of the housing units were included in the sample; in 1990, approximately 17%.

Data Collection and Imputation Procedures: In 1970, a self-enumeration census using a mail-out/mail-back procedure was used in most areas. In 1980 and 1990, mail questionnaires were used in even more areas than in 1970, with personal interviews in the remainder. Followup for nonrespondents and identification of vacant units done by phone and personal visit.

Estimates of Sampling Error: Sampling errors for data are estimated for all items collected by sample and vary by characteristic and geographic area.

Other (nonsampling) Errors: Evaluation studies for 1980 estimated the underenumeration of occupied housing units at 1.5%. The missed rate in 1980 for all units was 2.6% or approximately 2.3 million units, 1 million of which were vacant housing units.

Sources of Additional Material: U.S. Bureau of the Census, *1980 Census of Population and Housing, The Coverage of Housing in the 1980 Census*, PHC80-E1, July 1985.

Source and Title: U.S. Bureau of the Census, *American Housing Survey*

Tables: See tables citing *American Housing Survey* in source notes.

Universe, Frequency, and Types of Data: Conducted nationally in the fall in odd numbered years to obtain data on the approximately 103 million occupied or vacant housing units in the United States (group quarters are excluded). Data include characteristics of occupied housing units, vacant units, new housing and mobile home units, financial characteristics, recent mover households, housing and neighborhood quality indicators, and energy characteristics.

Type of Data Collection Operation: The national sample was a multistage probability sample with about 51,300 units eligible for interview in 1987. Sample units, selected within 394 PSU's, were surveyed over a 5-month period.

Data Collection and Imputation Procedures: For 1987, the survey was conducted by personal interviews. The interviewers obtained the information from the occupants or, if the unit was vacant, from informed persons such as landlords, rental agents, or knowledgeable neighbors.

Estimates of Sampling Error: For the national sample, illustrations of the S.E. of the estimates are provided in the appendix B of the 1987 report. As an example, the estimated CV is about 0.5% for the estimated percentage of owner occupied units with two persons.

Other (nonsampling) Errors: Response rate was about 97%. Nonsampling errors may result from incorrect or incomplete responses, errors in coding and recording, and processing errors. For the 1985 national sample, approximately 6% of the total housing inventory was not adequately represented by the AHS sample.

Sources of Additional Material: U.S. Bureau of the Census, *Current Housing Reports*, series H-150 and H-170, *American Housing Survey.*

(See section 1 above for information pertaining to the Census of Population, section 15 pertaining to table 1177, and section 19 for table 1207.)

Section 26. MANUFACTURES

Source and Title: U.S. Bureau of the Census, *Census of Manufactures*

Tables: See tables citing *Census of Manufactures* in source notes in section 26 and also table 905 in section 18 and table 1330 in section 29.

Universe, Frequency, and Types of Data: Conducted every 5 years to obtain information on labor, materials, capital input and output characteristics, plant location, and legal form of organization for all plants in the United States with one or more paid employees. Universe was 350,000 manufacturing establishments in 1987.

Type of Data Collection Operation: Complete enumeration of data items obtained from 200,000 firms. Administrative records from Internal Revenue Service and Social Security Administration are used for 150,000 smaller single-location firms, which were determined by various cutoffs based on size and industry.

Data Collection and Imputation Procedures: Five mail and telephone followups for larger nonrespondents. Data for small single-location firms (generally those with fewer than 10 employees) not mailed census questionnaires were estimated from administrative records of IRS and SSA. Data for nonrespondents were imputed from related responses or administrative records from IRS and SSA. Approximately 8% of total value of shipments was represented by fully imputed records in 1987.

Estimates of Sampling Error: Not applicable.

Other (nonsampling) Errors: Based on evaluation studies, estimates of nonsampling errors for 1972 were about 1.3% for estimated total payroll; 2% for total employment; and 1% for value of shipments. Estimates for later years are not available.

Sources of Additional Material: U.S. Bureau of the Census, *1987 Census of Manufactures, Industry Series, Geographic Area Series, and Subject Series.*

Source and Title: U.S. Bureau of the Census, *Annual Survey of Manufactures*

Tables: See tables citing *Annual Survey of Manufactures* in source notes.

Universe, Frequency, and Types of Data: Conducted annually to provide basic measures of manufacturing activity for intercensal years for all manufacturing establishments having one or more paid employees.

Type of Data Collection Operation: Sampling frame is 350,000 establishments in the 1987 Census of Manufactures (see above), supplemented by Social Security Administration lists of new manufacturers and new manufacturing establishments of multi-establishment companies identified annually by the Census Bureau's Company Organization Survey. A probability sample of about 55,000 establishments is selected. All establishments of companies with more than $500 million of manufacturing shipments in 1987 a re included with certainty. All establishments with 250+ employees are also included with certainty along with a probability sample of smaller establishments.

Data Collection and Imputation Procedures: Survey is conducted by mail with phone and mail followups of nonrespondents. Imputation (for all nonresponse items) is based on previous year reports, or for new establishments in survey, on industry averages.

Estimates of Sampling Error: Estimated standard errors for number of employees, new expenditure, and for value added totals are given in annual publications. For U.S. level industry statistics, most estimated standard errors are 2% or less , but vary considerably for detailed characteristics.

Other (nonsampling) Errors: Response rate is about 85%. Nonsampling errors include those due to collection, reporting, and transcription errors, many of which are corrected through computer and clerical checks.

Sources of Additional Material: U.S. Bureau of the Census, *Annual Survey of Manufactures*, and Technical Paper 24.

Section 27. DOMESTIC TRADE AND SERVICES

Source and Title: U.S. Bureau of the Census, *Census of Wholesale Trade, Census of Retail Trade, Census of Service Industries*

Tables: See tables citing the above censuses in source notes in section 27 and table 1330 in section 29.

Universe, Frequency, and Types of Data: Conducted every 5 years to obtain data on number of establishments, number of employees, total payroll size, total sales, and other industry-specific statistics. In 1987, the universe was all employer establishments primarily engaged in wholesale trade, and employer and nonemployer establishments in retail trade or service industries.

Type of Data Collection Operation: All wholesale firms with paid employees surveyed; all retail and service large employer firms surveyed (i.e. all employer firms above the payroll size cutoff established to separate large from small employers) plus a 10-percent sample of smaller employer firms. Firms with no employees were not required to file a census return.

Data Collection and Imputation Procedures: Mail questionnaire is utilized with both mail and telephone followups for nonrespondents. Data for nonrespondents and all employer firms in retail trade and service industries are obtained from administrative records of IRS and the Social Security Administration.

Estimates of Sampling Error: Not applicable.

Other (nonsampling) Errors: Response rate in 1987 of 80% for single establishment firms; 83% for multi-establishment firms. Item response ranged from 60% to 90% with higher rates for less detailed questions.

Sources of Additional Material: U.S. Bureau of the Census, Appendix A of *Census of Retail Trade; Census of Service Industries; Census of Wholesale Trade;* and *History of the 1987 Economic Censuses*, April 1992.

Source and Title: U.S. Bureau of the Census, *Current Business Surveys*

Tables: 1266-1268, 1282, 1288, 1291, and table 174 in section 3, tables 408 and 431 in section 7, and table 1033 in section 21.

Universe, Frequency, and Types of Data: Provides monthly estimates of retail sales by kind of business and geographic area, and end-of-month inventories of retail stores; wholesale sales and end-of-month inventories; and annual receipts of selected service industries.

Type of Data Collection Operation: Probability sample of all firms from a list frame and, additionally, for retail and service an area frame. The list frame is the Bureau's Standard Statistical Establishment List (SSEL) updated quarterly for recent birth Employer Identification (EI) Numbers issued by the Internal Revenue Service and assigned a kind-of-business code by the Social Security Administration. The largest firms are included monthly; a sample of others is included every three months on a rotating basis. The area frame covers businesses not subjected to sampling on the list frame.

Data Collection and Imputation Procedures: Data are collected by mail questionnaire with telephone followups for nonrespondents. Imputation made for each nonresponse item and each item failing edit checks.

Estimates of Sampling Error: For the 1989 monthly surveys, CV's are about 0.6% for estimated total retail sales, 1.7% for wholesale sales, 1.3% for wholesale inventories. For dollar volume of receipts, CV's from the *Service Annual Survey vary by kind of business and range between 1.5% to 15.0%. Sampling errors are shown in monthly publications.*

Other (nonsampling) Errors: Imputation rates are about 18% to 23% for monthly retail sales, 20% to 25% for wholesale sales, about 25% to 30% for monthly wholesale inventories and 14% for the *Service Annual Survey*.

Sources of Additional Material: U.S. Bureau of the Census, *Current Business Reports, Monthly Retail Trade, Monthly Wholesale Trade,* and *Service Annual Survey.*

(See section 17 for information pertaining to tables 1263 and 1283.)

Section 29. OUTLYING AREAS

(See section 1 for information pertaining to tables 1319 and 1320, section 2 for table 1318, section 17 for table 1327, section 22 for table 1326, sections 26 and 27 for table 1330.)

Appendix IV

Tables Deleted From the 1996 Edition of the Statistical Abstract

1996 table number	
	Sec. 14. **INCOME, EXPENDITURES, AND WEALTH**
712	Money Income of Households—Aggregate and Average Income, by Race and Hispanic Origin: 1993
715	Money Income of Households—Percent Distribution, by Income Level, Race, and Hispanic Origin: 1993
723	Money Income of Families—Distribution, by Type of Family and Income Level: 1994
725	Median Income of Year-Round Full-Time Workers With Income: 1980 to 1994
726	Money Income of Persons—Percent Distribution, by Income Level, in Constant (1993) Dollars: 1970 to 1993
727	Median Income of Married-Couple Families, by Work Experience of Husbands and Wives: 199
	Sec. 16. **BANKING, FINANCE, AND INSURANCE**
789	Home Equity Lending—Percentage of Homeowners With Credit, Sources of Credit, and Uses for Funds Borrowed: 1988 and 1993-94
790	Estimated Home Equity Debt Outstanding, by Type and Source of Credit: 1988 to 1994
797	Bank Debits and Deposit Turnover: 1980 to 1995
820	Households Owning Mutual Funds, by Age of Head of Household and Income: 1989 and 1992
	Sec. 17. **BUSINESS ENTERPRISE**
841	Black-Owned Firms by Major Industry Group: 1992
	Sec. 18. **COMMUNICATIONS AND INFORMATION TECHNOLOGY**
875	Communications Industry—Summary: 1992
883	Percent of Households With Telephone Service: 1984 to 1994
907	Advertising—Indexes of National Advertising Expenditures, by Medium: 1980 to 1994
	Sec. 19. **ENERGY**
923	Commercial Buildings—Energy Consumption and Expenditures, by Major Fuel Type Used: 1992
933	Strategic Petroleum Reserve: 1977 to 1994
935	Energy Producing Companies—Selected Financial and Investment Indicators: 1985 to 1994
	Sec. 21. **TRANSPORTATION—LAND**
988	Commodity Flow Survey (CFS) Shipment Characteristics: 1993
998	New Plant and Equipment Expenditures and Capacity Utilization: 1980 to 1995
1020	U.S. Vehicle, by Model Year and Vehicle Fuel Efficiency: 1991
1021	Household Vehicles—Annual Mileage, Fuel Consumption, and Fuel Expenditures: 1991
	Sec. 23. **AGRICULTURE**
1091	Commodity Credit Corporation—Net Outlays, by Commodity and Function: 1990 to 1995
1092	Average Income to Farm Operator Households: 1991 to 1995
	Sec. 24. **NATURAL RESOURCES**
1124	Public Lands—Disposal: 1980 to 1993
1139	Gross Domestic Product (GDP) in Mining: 1980 to 1993
1143	Mineral Industries—Gross Assets and Capital Expenditures: 1977 to 1992
1152	Selected Mineral and Metal Products—Quantity and Value of Imports and Exports: 1990 to 19
1153	Mineral Industries—Lost Workday Injuries and Fatalities: 1994
1160	Domestic Motor Gasoline Supply: 1980 to 1996
1166	World Coal Trade: 1980 to 1991

1996 table number	
	Sec. 25. **CONSTRUCTION AND HOUSING**
1181	Characteristics of New One-Family Houses Sold, by Metropolitan Area: 1992 to 1994
1189	Housing Units—Historical Trends for Selected Characteristics: 1950 to 1993
1190	Occupied Housing Units—Tenure, by Race of Householder: 1920 to 1993
1191	Occupied Housing Units—Tenure, by Race and Hispanic Origin of Householder: 1980 and 1990
1196	Heating Equipment and Fuels for Occupied Units: 1950 to 1993
1199	Gross Housing Product in Real (1992) Dollars: 1990 to 1994
1203	Low-Income Public Housing Units, by Progress Stage: 1970 to 1993
1208	Industrial Buildings—Floorspace and Vacancy Rates for Major Cities: 1995
	Sec. 26. **MANUFACTURES**
1215	Capital in Manufacturing Establishments: 1980 to 1994
1221	Manufacturing Technology—Percent of Establishments Using and Planning to Use: 1993
1222	Employment Related to Manufactured Exports, by Industry: 1985 to 1991
1224	Export-Related Shipments and Employment of Manufacturing Establishments, by State: 1991
1226	Foreign Direct Investment Position in the United States— Manufacturing: 1993 and 1994
1251	Robots—Shipments: 1987 to 1989
	Sec. 27. **DOMESTIC TRADE AND SERVICES**
1259	Retail Trade—Sales of Multiunit Organizations, by Kind of Business: 1980 to 1995
1268	Retail Trade—Sales, by Metropolitan Area: 1992
1282	Service Industries—Summary of Establishments, by State: 1992
	Sec. 28. **FOREIGN COMMERCE AND AID**
1304	U.S. Exports and General Imports of Major SITC Commodity Groups—Value, by Area: 1995
	Sec. 30. **COMPARATIVE INTERNATIONAL STATISTICS**
1339	Percent of Households Owning Selected Appliances, by Country: 1990-91
1372	External Debt of Eastern European Countries: 1990 to 1994
1375	Per Capita Public and Private Aid to Developing Countries: 1990 to 1993

Appendix V

New Tables

Index

NOTE: Index citations refer to table numbers, not page numbers.

NOTE: Index citations refer to table numbers, not page numbers.

NOTE: Index citations refer to table numbers, not page numbers.

Table

B

NOTE: Index citations refer to table numbers, not page numbers.

NOTE: Index citations refer to table numbers, not page numbers.

NOTE: Index citations refer to table numbers, not page numbers.

NOTE: Index citations refer to table numbers, not page numbers.

NOTE: Index citations refer to table numbers, not page numbers.

NOTE: Index citations refer to table numbers, not page numbers.

NOTE: Index citations refer to table numbers, not page numbers.

NOTE: Index citations refer to table numbers, not page numbers.

NOTE: Index citations refer to table numbers, not page numbers.

NOTE: Index citations refer to table numbers, not page numbers.

NOTE: Index citations refer to table numbers, not page numbers.

NOTE: Index citations refer to table numbers, not page numbers.

NOTE: Index citations refer to table numbers, not page numbers.

NOTE: Index citations refer to table numbers, not page numbers.

NOTE: *Index* citations refer to table numbers, not page numbers.

NOTE: Index citations *refer* to table numbers, not page numbers.

NOTE: *Index citations refer to table numbers, not page numbers.*

NOTE: Index citations refer to table numbers, not page numbers.

NOTE: Index citations refer to table numbers, not page numbers.

NOTE: Index citations *refer to* table numbers, not page numbers.

NOTE: Index citations refer to table numbers, not page numbers.

NOTE: Index citations *refer to* table numbers, not page numbers.

NOTE: Index citations refer to table numbers, not page numbers.

NOTE: Index citations refer to table numbers, not page numbers.

NOTE: *Index citations refer to table numbers, not page numbers.*

NOTE: Index citations *refer* to table numbers, not page numbers.

NOTE: *Index* citations refer to table numbers, not page numbers.

NOTE: *Index citations refer to table numbers, not page numbers.*

NOTE: Index citations refer to table numbers, not page numbers.

NOTE: Index citations refer to table numbers, not page numbers.

NOTE: Index citations refer to table numbers, not page numbers.

NOTE: Index citations refer to table numbers, not page numbers.

NOTE: Index citations refer to table numbers, not page numbers.

NOTE: Index citations refer to table numbers, not page numbers.

NOTE: *Index citations refer to table numbers, not page numbers.*

NOTE: Index citations refer to table numbers, not page numbers.

NOTE: Index citations refer to table numbers, not page numbers.

NOTE: Index citations refer to table numbers, not page numbers.

NOTE: Index citations refer to table numbers, not page numbers.

NOTE: Index citations refer to table numbers, not page numbers.

NOTE: Index citations refer to table numbers, not page numbers.

NOTE: Index citations refer to table numbers, not page numbers.

***NOTE:** Index citations refer to table numbers, not page numbers.*

NOTE: Index citations refer to table numbers, not page numbers.

NOTE: Index citations refer to table numbers, not page numbers.

NOTE: *Index citations refer* to table numbers, not page numbers.

NOTE: Index citations refer to table numbers, not page numbers.

NOTE: Index citations refer to table numbers, not page numbers.

NOTE: Index citations refer to table numbers, not page numbers.

NOTE: Index citations *refer to* table numbers, not page numbers.

ISBN 0-16-049280-7

Statistical Abstract and Supplements

Printed Products

Statistical Abstract of the United States, 1997. Since 1878, the authoritative summary of statistics on the social, political, and economic organization of the United States. Includes a representative selection of statistics widely used by public officials, business analysts, educators, librarians, research workers, and students.

State and Metropolitan Area Data Book, 1997–98. This volume, the fifth in a series, presents a vast array of demographic and economic data for the United States, the 50 States and the District of Columbia; metropolitan areas (MA's); and component counties of MA's. Includes State and metropolitan area ranking tables. Expected availability: early 1998.

County and City Data Book, 1994. The latest in a series of publications which contains 220 data items for all counties and 194 data items for all cities with population of 25,000 or more. It also includes 1990 census population and income data for places of 2,500 or more inhabitants. Among its features are rankings for counties and cities and a complete set of State maps showing all counties, places of 25,000 or more, and metropolitan areas. Price: $40 (clothbound). GPO stock number: 003-024-08753-7. NTIS stock number: PB94-140993. Next update scheduled for 1999.

GPO orders may be mailed to: Superintendent of Documents, Government Printing Office (GPO), P.O. Box 371954, Pittsburgh, PA 15250-7954. Payment must accompany order. Telephone: 202-512-1800. FAX: 202-512-2250. Publications also available in GPO bookstores located in major cities.

NTIS orders may be mailed to: National Technical Information Service (NTIS), U.S. Department of Commerce, 5285 Port Royal Road, Springfield, VA 22161. Payment must accompany order. Telephone: 703-487-4650. FAX: 703-321-8547; to verify receipt of FAX order, call 703-487-4679.

Electronic Products

Statistical Abstract 1997 on CD-ROM. Contains more than 1,400 tables found in the printed version, contains Adobe Acrobat software with hyperlinks to Lotus spreadsheets and to the Internet. Price: $50.

State and Metropolitan Area Data Book 1997–98 on CD-ROM. Contains tables covering state and metropolitan area data found in the printed version of this product in Lotus worksheet format. Also includes Adobe Acrobat software. Price: $50.

USA Counties 1998 on CD-ROM. Contains over 4,000 data items for the United States, States, and counties and equivalent areas from a variety of sources. Includes 1996 population estimates and over 500 items from the 1990 Census of Population and Housing, as well as data from the 1980 census and the 1992, 1987, 1982, and 1977 economic censuses. Major noncensus sources include the Bureau of Economic Analysis, Bureau of Labor Statistics, and Federal Bureau of Investigation. Now with Windows software. Price: $150. 1998 CD-ROM forthcoming in early 1998.

County and City Data Book 1994 on CD-ROM or diskettes. Provides data from major tables in this book for the United States, States, census regions and divisions, counties and equivalent areas, cities of 25,000 or more inhabitants, and places of 2,500 or more inhabitants. Price: $150 on CD-ROM; $55 on 3 1/2" high density diskettes.

If you order 10 or more of any one of the titles at the same time, you may take a 40-percent discount. We will offer a free copy of the *Statistical Abstract of the United States: 1997* on CD-ROM to purchasers of *State and Metropolitan Area Data Book, 1997–98 CD-ROM* and *USA Counties: 1998.* Purchased as a package, the total for all three CD-ROMs is $200.

Electronic product orders may be mailed to: U.S. Department of Commerce, Bureau of the Census, P.O. Box 277943, Atlanta, GA 30384-7943. Payment must accompany order. To order or obtain more information, call 301-457-4100. To fax orders, dial 301-457-3842; for FAX inquiries, call 301-457-4714.

Lightning Source UK Ltd.
Milton Keynes UK
UKHW010907060219
336748UK00007B/241/P